# *The Complete*

# BIBLICAL LIBRARY

# *The Complete* BIBLICAL LIBRARY

## THE NEW TESTAMENT STUDY BIBLE

# ACTS

# The Complete BIBLICAL LIBRARY

**The Complete Biblical Library**, part 1, a 16-volume study series on the New Testament. Volume 6: STUDY BIBLE, ACTS Revised Edition.  Printed in the United States of America 1991 by R.R. Donnelley and Sons Company, Chicago, Illinois 60606. Library of Congress Catalog Card Number 91-70856 International Standard Book Number 0-88243-366-0.

**THE NEW TESTAMENT**
Study Bible, Greek-English Dictionary, Harmony of the Gospels

**THE OLD TESTAMENT**
Study Bible, Hebrew-English Dictionary

**THE BIBLE ENCYCLOPEDIA**

---

## INTERNATIONAL EDITOR
THORALF GILBRANT

---

**Executive Editor:** Ralph W. Harris, M.A.
**Computer Systems:** Tor Inge Gilbrant

---

## NATIONAL EDITORS

**U.S.A.**
Stanley M. Horton, Th.D.

**NORWAY**
Erling Utnem, Bishop
Arthur Berg, B.D.

**DENMARK**
Jorgen Glenthoj, Th.M.

**SWEDEN**
Hugo Odeberg, Ph.D., D.D.
Bertil E. Gartner, D.D.
Thorsten Kjall, M.A.
Stig Wikstrom, D.Th.M.

**FINLAND**
Aapelii Saarisalo, Ph.D.
Valter Luoto, Pastor
Matti Liljequist, B.D.

**HOLLAND**
Herman ter Welle, Pastor
Henk Courtz, Drs.

**Project Coordinator:** William G. Eastlake

---

INTERNATIONAL AND
INTERDENOMINATIONAL
BIBLE STUDY SYSTEM

# THE NEW TESTAMENT STUDY BIBLE ACTS

**Executive Editor:** Ralph W. Harris, M.A.

**Editor:** Stanley M. Horton, Th.D.

**Managing Editor:** Gayle Garrity Seaver, J.D.

**THE COMPLETE BIBLICAL LIBRARY**
Springfield, Missouri, U.S.A.

# Table of Contents

## VERSE-BY-VERSE COMMENTARY
STANLEY M. HORTON, Th.D.

## VARIOUS VERSIONS
GERARD J. FLOKSTRA, JR., D.Min.

---

### BOARD OF REVIEW

Zenas Bicket, Ph.D.
Jesse Moon, D.Min.
Charles Harris, Ed.D.
Opal Reddin, D.Min.

### STAFF

**Editor of Greek-English Dictionary:** Denis W. Vinyard, M.Div.

**Associate Editor of Greek-English Dictionary:** Donald F. Williams, M.Div.

**Production Coordinator:** Cynthia Riemenschneider

**Senior Editors:** Gary Leggett, M.A.; Dorothy B. Morris

**Editorial Team:** Faye Faucett; Charlotte Gribben; Connie Leggett

**Art Director:** Terry Van Someren, B.F.A.

**Layout Artist:** Jim Misloski, B.A.

**Word Processing and Secretarial:** Sonja Jensen; Rochelle Holman; Rachel Wisehart Harvey, B.A.

# Introduction

This volume of the *Study Bible* is part of a 16-volume set titled *The Complete Biblical Library*. It is an ambitious plan to provide all the information one needs for a basic understanding of the New Testament—useful for scholars but also for students and lay people.

In addition to the Harmony, *The Complete Biblical Library* provides a 9-volume *Study Bible* and a 6-volume *Greek-English Dictionary*. They are closely linked. You will find information about the *Study Bible*'s features later in the Introduction. The *Greek-English Dictionary* lists all the Greek words of the New Testament in their alphabetic order, provides a concordance showing each place the words appear in the New Testament, and includes an article explaining the background, significance, and meaning of the words.

## FEATURES OF THE STUDY BIBLE

The *Study Bible* is a unique combination of study materials which will help both the scholar and the layman achieve a better understanding of the New Testament and the language in which it was written. All of these helps are available in various forms but bringing them together in combination will save many hours of research. Most scholars do not have in their personal libraries all the volumes necessary to provide the information so readily available here.

The editors of *The Complete Biblical Library* are attempting an unusual task: to help scholars in their research but also to make available to laymen the tools by which to acquire knowledge which up to this time has been available only to scholars.

Following are the major divisions of the *Study Bible*:

### Overview

Each volume contains an encyclopedic survey of the New Testament book. It provides a general outline, discusses matters about which there may be a difference of opinion, and provides background information regarding the history, culture, literature, and philosophy of the era covered by the book.

### Interlinear

Following the overall principle of providing help for both the scholar and the layman, we supply a unique *Interlinear*. Most interlinears, if not all, give merely the Greek text and the meanings of the words. Our *Interlinear* contains *five* parts:

1. *Greek Text*. Our Greek text is a comparative text which includes both the traditional text type and the text which is common in modern textual editions.

2. *Grammatical Forms*. These are shown above each Greek word, alongside its assigned number. This information is repeated, along with the Greek word, in the *Greek-English Dictionary* where more details may be found.

3. *Transliteration*. No other interlinears provide this. Its purpose is to familiarize laymen with the proper pronunciation of Greek words so they will feel comfortable when using them in teaching situations. Complete information on pronunciation is found on the page showing the Greek and Hebrew alphabets.

4. *Translation*. The basic meaning of each Greek word is found beneath it. Rather than merely accepting the work of past interlinears, we have assigned scholars to upgrade words to a more modern description. See a later section for the principles we have followed in translation of the Greek words in our *Interlinear*.

5. *Assigned Numbers*. The unique numbering system of *The Complete Biblical Library* makes cross-reference study between the *Study Bible* and the *Greek-English Dictionary* the ultimate in simplicity. Each Greek word has been assigned a number. *Alpha* is the first word in alphabetic order as well as the first letter of the Greek alphabet, so the number *1* has been assigned to it. The rest of the almost 5,000 words follow in numerical and alphabetic sequence.

The *Greek-English Dictionary* follows the same plan with each word listed in alphabetic sequence. If a student desires further study on a certain word, he can find its number above it and locate it in the dictionary. In moments he has access to all the valuable information he needs for a basic understanding of that word.

## Textual Apparatus

As said above, our Greek text is a comparative text. A text based only upon the *Textus Receptus* is not adequate for today's needs. Also, an eclectic text—using the "best" from various text types—will not be satisfactory, because such an approach may be quite subjective, with decisions influenced by the personal viewpoint of the scholar. Our text is a combination of both the main types of the Greek New Testament text. We have the *Textus Receptus*, a Stephanus text, based on the Byzantine text type. When there are important variants which differ from the *Textus Receptus*, they are included within brackets in the text. In the narrow column to the left of the *Interlinear*, the sources of the variants are listed. This will provide a fascinating study for a scholar and student, and will save him innumerable hours of research.

## Verse-by-Verse Commentary

Many Bible-loving scholars have combined their knowledge, study, and skills to provide this. It is not an exhaustive treatment (many other commentaries are available for that), but again it provides a basic understanding of every verse in the New Testament. It does not usually deal with textual criticism (that can be dealt with in another arena), but it opens up the nuances of the Greek New Testament as written by the inspired writers.

## Various Versions

This offers a greatly amplified New Testament. Each verse is broken down into its phrases; the King James Version is shown in boldface type; then from more than 60 other versions we show various ways the Greek of that phrase may be translated. The Greek of the First Century was such a rich language that to obtain the full meaning of words, several synonyms may be needed.

# TRANSLATION OF GREEK WORDS

No word-for-word translation can be fully "literal" in the sense of expressing all the nuances of the original language. Rather, our purpose is to help the student find the English word which most correctly expresses the original Greek word in that particular context. The Greek language is so rich in meaning that the same word may have a slightly different meaning in another context.

In any language idioms offer a special translation problem. According to the dictionary, this is an expression which has "a meaning which cannot be derived from the conjoined meanings of its elements." The Greek language abounds in such phrases which cannot be translated literally.

We have come to what we consider a splendid solution to the problem, whether the translation should be strictly literal or abound in a plethora of idiomatic expressions. From more than 60 translations, the *Various Versions* column presents the various ways phrases have been translated. Here the student will find the translations of the idioms. This enables us to make our English line in the *Interlinear* strictly literal. The student will have available both types of translation—and will have a fresh appreciation for the struggles through which translators go.

# HOW THE NEW TESTAMENT CAME TO US

Volume 1 of *The Complete Biblical Library*, the *Harmony of the Gospels*, contains information on how the four Gospels came into being. The preponderance of proof points to the fact that the rest of the New Testament was written before A.D. 100. Like the Gospels, it was written in Greek, the universal language of that era. It was qualified in a special way for this purpose. Probably no other language is so expressive and able to provide such fine nuances of meaning.

Yet the New Testament Greek is not the perfectly structured form of the language from the old classical period. It is the more simple Koine Greek from the later Hellenistic age. This had become the lingua franca of the Hellenistic and Roman world. The Egyptian papyri have shown that the language which the New Testament writers used was the common language of the people. It seems as though God accomodated himself to a form of communication which would make His Word most readily accepted and easily understood.

At the same time we should recognize that the language of the Greek New Testament also is a *religious language*, with a tradition going back a couple of centuries to the Septuagint, the Greek translation of the Old Testament.

## The Manuscripts

None of the original manuscripts (handwritten documents) still exist. Even in the First Century they must have often been copied so as to share their treasured truths with numerous congregations of believers. The original documents then soon became worn out through use. Evidently, only copies of the New Testament still exist.

Over 5,000 manuscripts of the New Testament have been discovered up to the present time. Most of them are small fragments of verses or chapters, a few books of the New Testament, some copies of the Gospels. Very few contain all or nearly all of the New Testament.

The manuscripts have come to us in various forms: (1) Egyptian papyri, (2) majuscules, (3) minuscules, (4) writings of the Early Church fathers, (5) lectionaries, and (6) early versions.

## The Egyptian Papyri

These are the oldest copies of parts of the Greek New Testament. The earliest are dated about A.D. 200, a few even earlier, and the youngest are from the Seventh Century. Most of them date back to the Third, Fourth and Fifth Centuries of the Christian Era.

They were found in the late 1800s in Egypt. The dry climatic conditions of that country enabled them to be preserved. The largest fragments contain only a few dozen pages, while the smallest are the size of a postage stamp.

The papyri are listed in the back of this volume under the heading "Manuscripts."

## The Majuscules

These are the second oldest kind of copies of New Testament manuscripts. They received this description because they were written in majuscules; that is, large letters (the uncials are a form of majuscules). Three major majuscules are the following:

1. Codex Aleph, also called Codex Sinaiticus, because it was discovered in the mid-1840s by the great scholar Tischendorf at St. Catharine's Monastery, located at the foot of Mount Sinai. Numbered 01, it contains all the New Testament and is dated in the Fourth Century.

2. Codex A, numbered 02, is named Alexandrinus, because it came from Alexandria in Egypt. In the Gospels, this manuscript is the foremost witness to the Byzantine text type.

3. Codex B, 03, is called Codex Vaticanus, because it is in the Vatican library. Along with the Sinaiticus, it is the main witness for the Egyptian text type. However, it is important to realize there are more than 3,000 differences between these 2 manuscripts in the Gospels alone (Hoskier).

See the list of majuscules in the back of this volume, under "Manuscripts."

## The Minuscules

This is a kind of manuscript written in small letters. They are only a few hundred years old, beginning with the Ninth Century. Most come from the 12th to the 14th Century A.D. They form, by far, the greatest group of the New Testament manuscripts, numbering almost 2,800.

The minuscules represent the unbroken text tradition in the Greek Orthodox Church, and about 90 percent of them belong to the Byzantine text group. They are numbered 1, 2, 3, etc.

## Lectionaries and Church Fathers

Lectionaries include manuscripts which were not Scripture themselves but contain Scripture quotations, used for the scheduled worship services of the annual church calendar. These are numbered consecutively and are identified by *lect.*

Practically all the New Testament could be retrieved from the writings of early Christian leaders, called church fathers. These lists are located in the back of this volume.

## Early Versions

Translations of the New Testament from Greek are also of value. They are listed under "Manuscripts" in the back of this volume. The best known is the Latin Vulgate by Jerome.

## Major Greek Texts

From the manuscripts which have just been described, various types of Greek texts have been formed:

The Western text can possibly be traced back to the Second Century. It was used mostly in Western Europe and North Africa. It tends to add to the text and makes long paraphrases of it. Today some scholars do not recognize it as a special text type.

The Caesarean text may have originated in Egypt and was brought, it is believed, to the city of Caesarea in Palestine. Later, it was carried to Jerusalem, then by Armenian missionaries into a province in the kingdom of Georgia, now a republic of the U.S.S.R. Some scholars consider it a mixture of other text types.

The two most prominent text types, however, are the Egyptian (also called the Alexandrian) and the Byzantine. These are the major ones considered in our *Interlinear* and *Textual Apparatus.* Except for the papyrus texts which are highly varied, these are the only text families which have any degree of support. References to numerous text groups which were so common a few decades ago must now probably be considered out of date. At any rate, out of practical considerations, we have kept the Byzantine and Egyptian (Alexandrian) as fixed text groups in our *Textual Apparatus.* Following is historical information about them.

## The Byzantine Text

Many titles have been applied to this text type. It has been called the *K* (Koine), Syrian, Antiochian, and Traditional. It is generally believed to have been produced at Antioch in Syria, then taken to Byzantium, later known as Constantinople. For about 1,000 years, while the Byzantine Empire ruled the Middle East, this was the text used by the Greek Orthodox Church. It also influenced Europe.

Because of this background it became the basis for the first printed text editions, among others the famous *Textus Receptus,* called "the acknowledged text."

The Byzantine text form is also called the Majority text, since 80 to 90 percent of all existing manuscripts are represented in this text, though most of them are quite recent and evidently copies of earlier manuscripts. Like the Egyptian text, the Byzantine text can be traced back to the Fourth Century. It also contains some readings which seem to be the same as some papyri which can be traced back to a much earlier time. Among the oldest majuscules the Byzantine is, among others, represented by Codex Alexandrinus (02, A), 07, 08, 09, 010, 011, 012, 013, 015, and others.

## The Egyptian Text

This text type originated in Egypt and is the one which gained the highest recognition and acceptance there in the Fourth Century. It was produced mainly by copyists in Alexandria, from which it received the name *Alexandrian.* This text form is represented mostly by two codices: Sinaiticus (01, Aleph) and Vaticanus (03, B) from the Fourth Century, also from Codex Ephraemi (04, C) from the Fifth Century. The use of this text type ceased about the year 450 but lived on in the Latin translation, the Vulgate version.

## Printed Greek Texts

The invention of printing about 1450 opened the door for wider distribution of the Scriptures. In 1516 Erasmus, a Dutch scholar, produced the first *printed* Greek New Testament. It was based on the Byzantine text type, with most of the New Testament coming from manuscripts dated at about the 12th Century. He did his work very hurriedly, finishing his task in just a few months. His second edition, produced in 1519 with some of the mistakes corrected, became the basis for translations into German by Luther and into English by Tyndale.

A printed Greek New Testament was produced by a French printer, Stephanus, in 1550. His edition and those produced by Theodore Beza, of Geneva, between 1565 and 1604, based on the Byzantine text, have been entitled the *Textus Receptus.* That description, however, originated with the text produced by Elzevir. He described his second edition of 1633 by the Latin phrase *Textus Receptus,* or the "Received Text"; that is, the one accepted generally as the correct one.

A list of the printed editions of the Greek text is found in the section describing the relationship of the *Interlinear* and the *Textual Apparatus.*

## Contribution of Westcott and Hort

Two British scholars, Westcott and Hort, have played a prominent role in deciding which text type should be used. They (especially Hort) called the Byzantine text "corrupt," because of the young age of its supporting manuscripts and proceeded to develop their own text (1881-86). It was really a restoration of the Egyptian text from the Fourth Century. It depended mainly on two codices, Sinaiticus and Vaticanus, but was also supported by numerous majuscules such as 02, 04, 019, 020, 025, 032, 033, 037, and 044.

Westcott and Hort opposed the *Textus Receptus* because it was based on the Byzantine text form. Most scholars agreed with their contention, and the *Textus Receptus* fell into disrepute. However, Westcott and Hort made their assumptions before the Greek papyri were discovered, and in recent years some scholars have come to the defense of the Byzantine text and the *Textus Receptus.* They have learned that some of the readings in the Byzantine text are the same as those found in the earliest papyri, dated about A.D. 200 and even earlier (p45, p46, p64 and p66, for example). This seems to take the Byzantine text back at least as far as the Egyptian.

Two important statements must be made: (1) We should always remember there are good men and scholars on both sides of the controversy, and their major concern is to obtain as pure a text as possible, to reassure Bible students that the New Testament we now possess conforms to that written in the First Century. (2) Since it was the original writings which were inspired by the Holy Spirit, it is important for us to ascertain as closely as possible how well our present-day text agrees with the original writings. It should alleviate the fears some may have as to whether we have the true gospel enunciated in the First Century to know that most of the differences in the Greek text (about 1 percent of the total) are minor in nature and do not affect the great Christian doctrines we hold dear. Significant differences may be found in only a very few cases.

We have consciously avoided polemics in the area of textual criticism. There is legitimacy for such discussion, but *The Complete Biblical Library* is not the arena for such a conflict. (1) Often the opposing views are conjectural. (2) There is insufficient space to treat subjects adequately and to raise questions without answering them fully leads to confusion.

## LITERARY AND BIBLICAL STANDARDS

Several hundred people, highly qualified scholars and specialists in particular fields have participated in producing *The Complete Biblical Library.* Great care has been taken to maintain high standards of scholarship and ethics. By involving scholars in Boards of Review for the *Study Bible* and the *Greek-English Dictionary,* we added an extra step to the editorial process. We have been particularly concerned about giving proper credit for citations from other works and have instructed our writers to show care in this regard. Any deviation from this principle has been inadvertent and not intentional.

Obviously, with writers coming from widely differing backgrounds, there are differences of opinion as to how to interpret certain passages.

We have tried to be just. When there are strong differences on the meaning of a particular passage, we have felt it best to present the contrasting viewpoints.

## STUDY HELPS

As you come to the Scripture section of this volume, you will find correlated pages for your study. The facing pages are designed to complement each other, so you will have a better understanding of the Word of God than ever before. Each two-page spread will deal with a group of verses.

On the left-hand page is the *Interlinear* with its fivefold helps: (1) the Greek text in which the New Testament was written; (2) the transliteration, showing how to pronounce each word; (3) the basic meaning of each word; (4) next to Greek words an assigned number (you will need this number to learn more about the word in the *Greek-English Dictionary*, companion to the *Study Bible*); and (5) the grammatical forms of each Greek word. The left-hand page also contains a column called the *Textual Apparatus*. This column is explained later.

The right-hand page contains two features. The *Verse-by-Verse Commentary* refers to each verse, except when occasionally it deals with some closely related verses. The *Various Versions* column provides an expanded understanding of the various ways Greek words or phrases can be translated. The phrase from the King James Version appears first in boldface print, then other meaningful ways the Greek language has been translated. This feature will bring to you the riches of the language in which the New Testament first appeared.

## General Abbreviations

In a work of this nature it is necessary to use some abbreviations in order to conserve space. In deference to the Scriptures it is our custom not to abbreviate the titles of the books of the Bible, but abbreviations are used elsewhere. Becoming familiar with them will enable you to pursue in-depth study more effectively.

The following are general abbreviations which you will find used throughout the book:

| | |
|---|---|
| cf. | compared to or see |
| ibid. | in the same place |
| id. | the same |
| idem | the same |
| i.e. | that is |
| e.g. | for example |
| f. ff. | and following page or pages |
| sic | intended as written |
| MS(S) | manuscript(s) |
| ET | editor's translation |

## Greek and Hebrew Alphabets with Pronunciation Guide

Some readers may want to become better acquainted with the Greek and Hebrew alphabets (the latter the language of the Old Testament). If so, the following lists will be of service to you.

**Greek**

| | | | | |
|---|---|---|---|---|
| Α | α | alpha | a | (father) |
| Β | β | beta | b | |
| Γ | γ | gamma | g | (got) |
| Δ | δ | delta | d | |
| Ε | ε | epsilon | e | (get) |
| Ζ | ζ | zeta | z | dz (leads) |
| Η | η | eta | e | (ate) |
| Θ | θ | theta | th | (thin) |
| Ι | ι | iota | i | (sin or machine) |
| Κ | κ | kappa | k | |
| Λ | λ | lambda | l | |
| Μ | μ | mu | m | |
| Ν | ν | nu | n | |
| Ξ | ξ | xi | x | |
| Ο | ο | omicron | o | (lot) |
| Π | π | pi | p | |
| Ρ | ρ | rho | r | |
| Σ | σ,ς[1] | sigma | s | |
| Τ | τ | tau | t | |
| Υ | υ | upsilon | u | German ü |
| Φ | φ | phi | ph | (philosophy) |
| Χ | χ | chi | ch | (chaos) |
| Ψ | ψ | psi | ps | (lips) |
| Ω | ω | omega | o | (ocean) |

**Hebrew**

| | | | |
|---|---|---|---|
| א | aleph | ’[2] | |
| ב | beth | b, bh | (v)[3] |
| ג | gimel | g, gh | |
| ד | daleth | d, dh | (they)[3] |
| ה | he | h | |
| ו | waw | w | |
| ז | zayin | z | |
| ח | heth | h | (kh) |
| ט | teth | t | |
| י | yod | y | |
| כ ך | kaph | k, kh | |
| ל | lamed | l | |
| מ ם | mem | m | |
| נ ן | nun | n | |
| ס | samekh | s | |
| ע | ayin | ‘ | |
| פ ף | pe | p, ph | |
| צ ץ | sadhe | s | (ts) |
| ק | qoph | q | |
| ר | resh | r | |
| שׂ | sin | s | |
| שׁ | shin | sh | |
| ת | taw | t, th | (thing)[3] |

**Greek Pronunciation Rules**

Before another *g*, or before a *k* or a *ch*, *g* is pronounced and spelled with an *n*, in the transliteration of the Greek word.

In the Greek, ς is written at the end of a word, elsewhere it appears as σ. The rough breathing mark ( ʽ ) indicates that an *h*-sound is to be pronounced before the initial vowel or diphthong. The smooth breathing mark ( ʼ ) indicates that no such *h*-sound is to be pronounced.

There are three accents, the acute (—́), the circumflex (—̂) and the grave (—̀). These stand over a vowel and indicate that stress in pronunciation is to be placed on the syllable having any one of the accents.

**Pronouncing Diphthongs**

*ai* is pronounced like *ai* in aisle
*ei* is pronounced like *ei* in eight
*oi* is pronounced like *oi* in oil
*au* is pronounced like *ow* in cow
*eu* is pronounced like *eu* in feud
*ou* is pronounced like *oo* in food
*ui* is pronounced like *ui* in suite (sweet)

1. Where two forms of a letter are given, the one at the right is used at the end of a word.
2. Not represented in transliteration when the initial letter.
3. Letters underscored represent pronunciation of the second form only.

## Old and New Testament Books and Apocrypha

As a service to you, we have listed the books of the Bible in their order. The Apocrypha is a series of books which were included in the Vulgate version (the Latin translation of the Bible endorsed by the Roman Catholic Church). Though not considered part of the canon by either the Jews or Protestants, they give interesting insights, on occasion, concerning the times with which they deal. They are not on the same level as the 66 books of our canon. These lists are located in the back of the book.

## Bibliographic Citations

*The Complete Biblical Library* has adopted a system of coordinated citations in the text and bibliography material which accommodates every type of reader. For the sake of simplicity and space, information given in the text to document a source is minimal, often including only the last name of the writer, or a shortened title and a page number.

Those who would like to research the subject more deeply can easily do so by looking in the Bibliography in the back of the book under the last name or shortened title. The Bibliography lists complete information necessary to locate the source in a library, supplemented by the page number given in the citation in the text.

## RELATIONSHIP OF THE INTERLINEAR AND THE TEXTUAL APPARATUS

The Greek text of the *Study Bible* provides a means of collating the traditional texts with modern text editions; that is, comparing them critically to discover their degree of similarity or divergence. The *Textual Apparatus* column provides information as to which manuscripts or groups of manuscripts support certain readings. Some scholarly works use an eclectic text, selecting from various sources the text they consider to be the best. In our view, our comparative text provides a better system for considering the relative merits of the major texts.

The *Textual Apparatus* refers to many different manuscripts but to just two text groups, the Byzantine and the Egyptian, also known as Alexandrian. Except for the papyri texts, which are highly varied, these two text families are the only ones which have a significant degree of support. Reference to many different text groups is now becoming passé. Using only the byz (Byzantine) and eg (Egyptian) text groups makes the work of the researcher less complicated and provides an adequate system of reference.

The *Interlinear* uses the Stephanus text as its basis but is not confined to it. Actually, most of the Greek text is the same in all the text types. For easy comparison variants are inserted in the text and are then considered in the *Textual Apparatus* column, which provides their background in the major and minor manuscripts.

## Abbreviations and Signs Used in the Textual Apparatus

Using the information which follows you will be able to identify the variants and their sources and to compare them with the basic text and other variants.

| | |
|---|---|
| Txt | The Greek text used, the TR |
| byz | Byzantine text form |
| eg | Egyptian text form |
| p 1, etc. | Papyrus manuscripts |
| 01, etc. | Majuscule manuscripts |
| 1, etc. | Minuscule manuscripts |
| lect | Lectionaries |
| org | Reading of original copier |
| corr 1, etc. | Change by another person |
| ( ) | Supports in principle |
| sa | Sahidic |
| bo | Bohairic |

## Printed Editions of the Greek Text (with abbreviations)

| | |
|---|---|
| Steph | Stephanus, 1550 |
| Beza | Beza, 1564-1604 |
| Elzev | Elzevir, 1624 |
| Gries | Griesbach, 1805 |
| Lach | Lachmann, 1842-50 |
| Treg | Tregelles, 1857-72 |
| Alf | Alford, 1862-71 |
| Tisc | Tischendorf, 1865-95 |
| Word | Wordsworth, 1870 |
| We/Ho | Westcott and Hort, 1881-86 |
| Wey | Weymouth, 1885 |
| Weis | Weiss, 1894-1900 |
| Sod | von Soden, 1902-10 |
| H/Far | Hodges and Farstad (Majority text) |
| ☆ | various modern text editions |
| UBS | United Bible Society |

## Understanding the Codes in the Greek Text and the Textual Apparatus

Definitions:

TR. The *Textus Receptus,* the basic text of this *Interlinear.*

Reading. A word or phrase from a Greek text.

Variant. A reading which differs from the TR.

The *Textual Apparatus* contains two divisions for analyzing the text when variants occur: *Txt,* meaning the TR (*Textus Receptus*); and *Var,* meaning variants, readings which differ from the TR. Under these two headings are listed the manuscripts which support either the TR or the variant.

Illustrations:

The following examples from Luke 10:19-21 show how to understand the relationship between the Greek text and the *Textual Apparatus.*

The half-parenthesis indicates that the next word begins a TR reading for which a variant is shown. See example A.

The variant itself is enclosed in brackets (note the example of this at the beginning of verse 19). The text (TR) reads, "I give . . . , " but the variant reads, "I have given . . . ." See example B.

The small *a* at the beginning of the bracket refers back to the *Textual Apparatus* column, showing it is the first variant in that particular verse. See example C. Only those variants identified by *a, b, c,* etc., are considered in the *Textual Apparatus.*

The star following the *a* means that the variant is used in some modern text editions, such as the UBS text. See example D.

Note that in variant *b* of verse 19 the star appears before the TR word. This means that in this case UBS and/or others do not follow the variant but read the same as the TR. See example E.

In verse 20, variant *a* appears between two half-parentheses, showing *mallon* ("rather") is not included in some texts. The TR reads, "Rejoice but rather that . . . ," while the variant (without *mallon*) reads, "Rejoice but that . . . ." See example F.

It is important to recognize that the star in the *Textual Apparatus* for verse 20 means that UBS and other modern texts support the variant reading. If the UBS supported the TR, the star would have appeared under the *Txt* heading. See example G.

Sometimes there is more than one variant reading, as in variant *b* of verse 20. In such cases they are numbered in order (see the *2* before the star in the second reading). This shows the difference and also provides an easy reference in the *Textual Apparatus.* See example H.

In verse 21, variant *a* presents a case where the word *en* ("in") is not a part of the TR but appears in other texts. The + sign indicates this. See example I.

# Understanding the Codes in the Greek Text and the Textual Apparatus

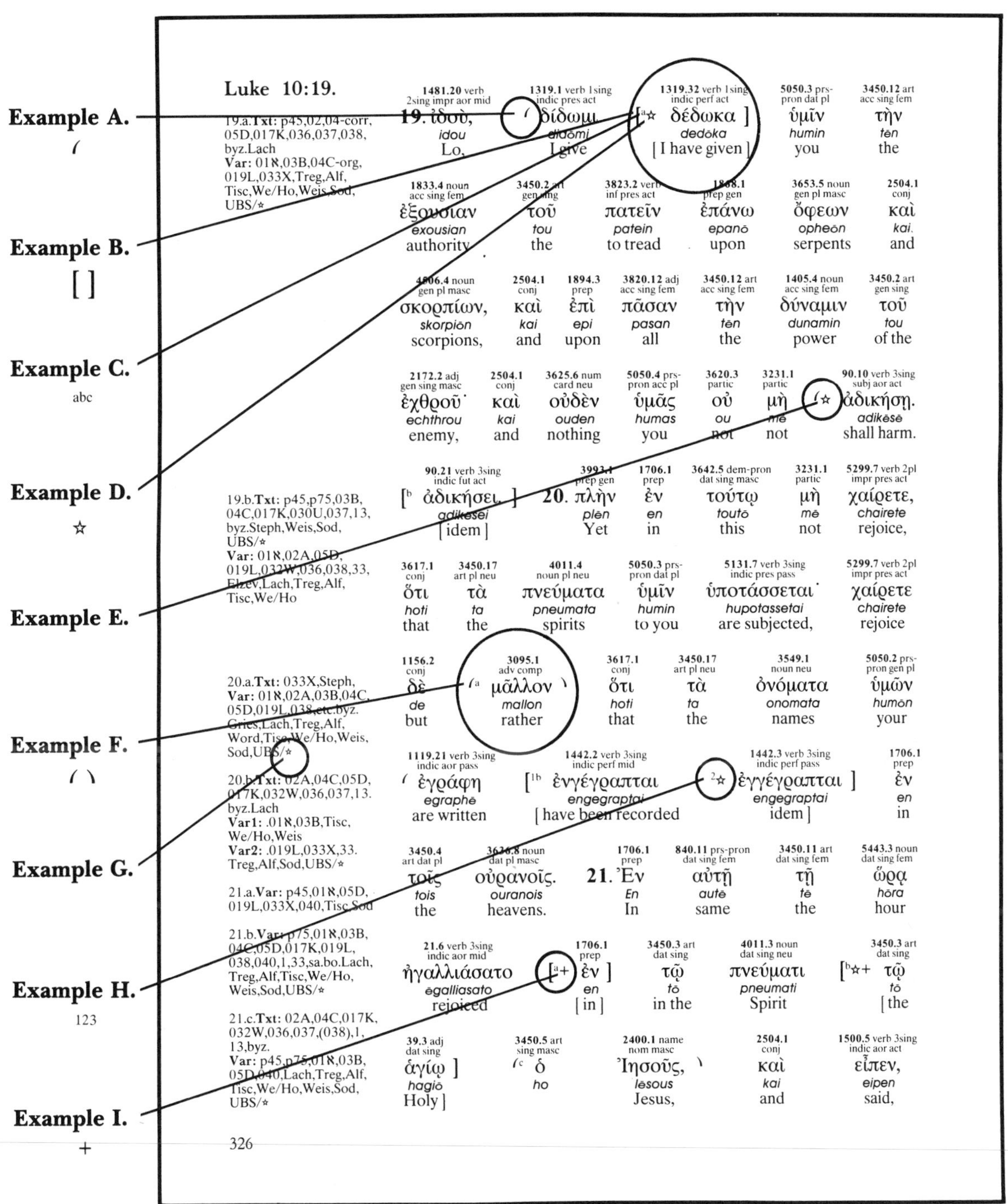


Luke 10:19.

19.a.Txt: p45,02,04-corr, 05D,017K,036,037,038, byz.Lach
Var: 01ℵ,03B,04C-org, 019L,033X,Treg,Alf, Tisc,We/Ho,Weis,Sod, UBS/☆

19.b.Txt: p45,p75,03B, 04C,017K,030U,037,13, byz.Steph,Weis,Sod, UBS/☆
Var: 01ℵ,02A,05D, 019L,032W,036,038,33, Elzev,Lach,Treg,Alf, Tisc,We/Ho

20.a.Txt: 033X,Steph,
Var: 01ℵ,02A,03B,04C, 05D,019L,038,etc.byz. Gries,Lach,Treg,Alf, Word,Tisc,We/Ho,Weis, Sod,UBS/☆

20.b.Txt: 02A,04C,05D, 017K,032W,036,037,13. byz.Lach
Var1: .01ℵ,03B,Tisc, We/Ho,Weis
Var2: .019L,033X,33. Treg,Alf,Sod,UBS/☆

21.a.Var: p45,01ℵ,05D, 019L,033X,040,Tisc,Sod

21.b.Var: p75,01ℵ,03B, 04C,05D,017K,019L, 038,040,1,33,sa.bo.Lach, Treg,Alf,Tisc,We/Ho, Weis,Sod,UBS/☆

21.c.Txt: 02A,04C,017K, 032W,036,037,(038),1, 13,byz.
Var: p45,p75,01ℵ,03B, 05D,040,Lach,Treg,Alf, Tisc,We/Ho,Weis,Sod, UBS/☆

| 1481.20 verb 2sing impr aor mid | 1319.1 verb 1sing indic pres act | 1319.32 verb 1sing indic perf act | 5050.3 prs-pron dat pl | 3450.12 art acc sing fem |
|---|---|---|---|---|
| 19. ἰδοὺ, | ( δίδωμι | [ᵃ☆ δέδωκα ] | ὑμῖν | τὴν |
| idou | didōmi | dedōka | humin | tēn |
| Lo, | I give | [ I have given ] | you | the |

| 1833.4 noun acc sing fem | 3450.2 art gen sing | 3823.2 verb inf pres act | 1868.1 prep gen | 3653.5 noun gen pl masc | 2504.1 conj |
|---|---|---|---|---|---|
| ἐξουσίαν | τοῦ | πατεῖν | ἐπάνω | ὄφεων | καὶ |
| exousian | tou | patein | epanō | opheōn | kai |
| authority | the | to tread | upon | serpents | and |

| 4806.4 noun gen pl masc | 2504.1 conj | 1894.3 prep | 3820.12 adj acc sing fem | 3450.12 art acc sing fem | 1405.4 noun acc sing fem | 3450.2 art gen sing |
|---|---|---|---|---|---|---|
| σκορπίων, | καὶ | ἐπὶ | πᾶσαν | τὴν | δύναμιν | τοῦ |
| skorpiōn | kai | epi | pasan | tēn | dunamin | tou |
| scorpions, | and | upon | all | the | power | of the |

| 2172.2 adj gen sing masc | 2504.1 conj | 3625.6 num card neu | 5050.4 prs-pron acc pl | 3620.3 partic | 3231.1 partic | 90.10 verb 3sing subj aor act |
|---|---|---|---|---|---|---|
| ἐχθροῦ˙ | καὶ | οὐδὲν | ὑμᾶς | οὐ | μὴ | (☆ ἀδικήσῃ. |
| echthrou | kai | ouden | humas | ou | mē | adikēsē |
| enemy, | and | nothing | you | not | not | shall harm. |

| 90.21 verb 3sing indic fut act | 3993.1 prep gen | 1706.1 prep | 3642.5 dem-pron dat sing masc | 3231.1 partic | 5299.7 verb 2pl impr pres act |
|---|---|---|---|---|---|
| [ᵇ ἀδικήσει. ] | 20. πλὴν | ἐν | τούτῳ | μὴ | χαίρετε, |
| adikēsei | plēn | en | toutō | mē | chairete |
| [ idem ] | Yet | in | this | not | rejoice, |

| 3617.1 conj | 3450.17 art pl neu | 4011.4 noun pl neu | 5050.3 prs-pron dat pl | 5131.7 verb 3sing indic pres pass | 5299.7 verb 2pl impr pres act |
|---|---|---|---|---|---|
| ὅτι | τὰ | πνεύματα | ὑμῖν | ὑποτάσσεται˙ | χαίρετε |
| hoti | ta | pneumata | humin | hupotassetai | chairete |
| that | the | spirits | to you | are subjected, | rejoice |

| 1156.2 conj | 3095.1 adv comp | 3617.1 conj | 3450.17 art pl neu | 3549.1 noun neu | 5050.2 prs-pron gen pl |
|---|---|---|---|---|---|
| δὲ | (ᵃ μᾶλλον \ | ὅτι | τὰ | ὀνόματα | ὑμῶν |
| de | mallon | hoti | ta | onomata | humōn |
| but | rather | that | the | names | your |

| 1119.21 verb 3sing indic aor pass | 1442.2 verb 3sing indic perf mid | 1442.3 verb 3sing indic perf pass | 1706.1 prep |
|---|---|---|---|
| ( ἐγράφη | [¹ᵇ ἐνγέγραπται | ²☆ ἐγγέγραπται ] | ἐν |
| egraphē | engegraptai | engegraptai | en |
| are written | [ have been recorded | idem ] | in |

| 3450.4 art dat pl | 3636.8 noun dat pl masc | 1706.1 prep | 840.11 prs-pron dat sing fem | 3450.11 art dat sing fem | 5443.3 noun dat sing fem |
|---|---|---|---|---|---|
| τοῖς | οὐρανοῖς. | 21. Ἐν | αὐτῇ | τῇ | ὥρᾳ |
| tois | ouranois | En | autē | tē | hōra |
| the | heavens. | In | same | the | hour |

| 21.6 verb 3sing indic aor mid | 1706.1 prep | 3450.3 art dat sing | 4011.3 noun dat sing neu | 3450.3 art dat sing |
|---|---|---|---|---|
| ἠγαλλιάσατο | [ᵃ+ ἐν ] | τῷ | πνεύματι | [ᵇ☆+ τῷ |
| ēgalliasato | en | tō | pneumati | tō |
| rejoiced | [ in ] | in the | Spirit | [ the |

| 39.3 adj dat sing | 3450.5 art sing masc | 2400.1 name nom masc | 2504.1 conj | 1500.5 verb 3sing indic aor act |
|---|---|---|---|---|
| ἁγίῳ ] | (ᶜ ὁ | Ἰησοῦς, \ | καὶ | εἶπεν, |
| hagiō | ho | Iēsous | kai | eipen |
| Holy ] | | Jesus, | and | said, |

326

# ACTS

*Expanded Interlinear*
*Textual Critical Apparatus*
*Verse-by-Verse Commentary*
*Various Versions*

| **4093.4** noun acc pl fem | **3450.1** art gen pl | **39.4** adj gen pl | **646.5** noun gen pl masc |
|---|---|---|---|
| Πράξεις | τῶν | ἁγίων | ἀποστόλων |
| *Praxeis* | *tōn* | *hagiōn* | *apostolōn* |
| Acts | of the | holy | apostles. |

## Textual Apparatus

1.a.**Txt:** 01ℵ,02A,08E byz.Tisc,Weis,Sod UBS/☆
**Var:** 03B,05D,Lach Treg,Alf,Word,We/Ho

| **3450.6** art acc sing masc | **3173.1** conj | **4272.2** num ord sing | **3030.4** noun acc sing masc | **4020.67** verb 1sing indic aor mid | **3875.1** prep |
|---|---|---|---|---|---|
| 1:1. Τὸν | μὲν | πρῶτον | λόγον | ἐποιησάμην | περὶ |
| *Ton* | *men* | *prōton* | *logon* | *epoiēsamēn* | *peri* |
| The | indeed | former | account | I made | concerning |

| **3820.4** adj gen pl | **5434.1** intrj | **2298.1** name voc masc | **3614.1** rel-pron gen pl | **751.5** verb 3sing indic aor mid | **3450.5** art nom sing masc |
|---|---|---|---|---|---|
| πάντων, | ὦ | Θεόφιλε, | ὧν | ἤρξατο | ⸂a ὁ ⸃ |
| *pantōn* | *ō* | *Theophile* | *hōn* | *ērxato* | *ho* |
| all things, | O | Theophilus, | which | began | |

| **2400.1** name nom masc | **4020.20** verb inf pres act | **4885.1** conj | **2504.1** conj | **1315.10** verb inf pres act | **884.2** conj | **3614.10** rel-pron gen sing fem |
|---|---|---|---|---|---|---|
| Ἰησοῦς | ποιεῖν | τε | καὶ | διδάσκειν, | 2. ἄχρι | ἧς |
| *Iēsous* | *poiein* | *te* | *kai* | *didaskein* | *achri* | *hēs* |
| Jesus | to do | both | and | to teach, | until | which |

| **2232.1** noun fem | **1765.4** verb nom sing masc part aor mid | **3450.4** art dat pl | **646.6** noun dat pl masc | **1217.2** prep |
|---|---|---|---|---|
| ἡμέρας | ἐντειλάμενος | τοῖς | ἀποστόλοις | διὰ |
| *hēmeras* | *enteilamenos* | *tois* | *apostolois* | *dia* |
| day, | having given command | to the | apostles | by |

| **4011.2** noun gen sing neu | **39.2** adj gen sing | **3614.8** rel-pron acc pl masc | **1573.3** verb 3sing indic aor mid | **351.6** verb 3sing indic aor pass |
|---|---|---|---|---|
| πνεύματος | ἁγίου | οὓς | ἐξελέξατο, | ⸀ ἀνελήφθη. |
| *pneumatos* | *hagiou* | *hous* | *exelexato* | *anelēphthē* |
| Spirit | Holy | whom | he chose, | he was taken up: |

| **351.8** verb 3sing indic aor pass | **3614.4** rel-pron dat pl | **2504.1** conj | **3798.4** verb 3sing indic aor act | **1431.6** prs-pron acc sing masc |
|---|---|---|---|---|
| [☆ ἀνελήμφθη· ] | 3. οἷς | καὶ | παρέστησεν | ἑαυτὸν |
| *anelēmphthē* | *hois* | *kai* | *parestēsen* | *heauton* |
| [ idem ] | to whom | also | he presented | himself |

| **2180.9** verb part pres act | **3196.3** prep | **3450.16** art sing neu | **3819.18** verb inf aor act | **840.6** prs-pron acc sing masc | **1706.1** prep |
|---|---|---|---|---|---|
| ζῶντα | μετὰ | τὸ | παθεῖν | αὐτὸν, | ἐν |
| *zōnta* | *meta* | *to* | *pathein* | *auton* | *en* |
| living | after | the | to suffer | he | with |

| **4044.4** adj dat pl | **4887.1** noun dat pl neu | **1217.1** prep | **2232.6** noun gen pl fem | **4910.2** num card |
|---|---|---|---|---|
| πολλοῖς | τεκμηρίοις, | δι' | ἡμερῶν | ⸀ τεσσαράκοντα |
| *pollois* | *tekmēriois* | *di'* | *hēmerōn* | *tessarakonta* |
| many | proofs, | during | days | forty |

| **4910.1** num card | **3563.1** verb nom sing masc part pres mid | **840.2** prs-pron dat pl | **2504.1** conj | **2978.15** verb nom sing masc part pres act |
|---|---|---|---|---|
| [ τεσσεράκοντα ] | ὀπτανόμενος | αὐτοῖς, | καὶ | λέγων |
| *tesserakonta* | *optanomenos* | *autois* | *kai* | *legōn* |
| [ idem ] | being seen | by them, | and | speaking |

# THE ACTS OF THE APOSTLES

**1:1.** Originally this book had no title. Since the middle of the Second Century A.D., however, it has been known as *The Acts of the Apostles*, probably because the apostles are named in 1:13. Yet the Holy Spirit is more prominent than the apostles. A better title would be "The Acts of the Risen Lord by the Holy Spirit in and Through the Church," since the "former treatise" (Luke's Gospel) recorded what Jesus "began" to do and teach, and Acts records what the risen, ascended Lord continued "to do and teach."

Theophilus ("lover of God; dear to God") was the first recipient of this book, as he was of Luke's Gospel. Most likely he was a personal friend. Luke could count on him to read the book and to have copies made and circulated.

The fact that Luke's Gospel was what Jesus "began to do and teach" shows two things. First, the Church had its beginning in the gospel. Luke's Gospel ends with a convinced group of believers. The Cross put the new covenant into effect (Hebrews 9:15). Jesus "opened . . . their understanding, that they might understand the Scriptures" (Luke 24:45). They were no longer an easily scattered group of disciples, but a commissioned, New Testament Body, united, worshiping, waiting to be endued with power from on high (Luke 24:46-53). They were already the Church.

Second, the work of Jesus did not end when He ascended. As has already been noted, the Holy Spirit continued the work of Jesus in and through the Church. During His life and ministry on earth Jesus practiced what He was teaching the apostles. The truth of His doctrines was confirmed by the miracles He performed and by the purity of His life-style.

**1:2,3.** Jesus did not ascend until after He gave instructions through the Holy Spirit to the apostles whom He had chosen to carry out His work. "Taken up" reminds us of Elijah's translation (2 Kings 2:9-11). It was the occasion of the beginning of Elisha's ministry, just as Christ's ascension was the beginning of the Church's ministry.

Acts here includes those to whom Jesus presented himself in definite ways at definite times after His suffering, giving many positive proofs (or sure signs) and unmistakable, convincing evidence that He is alive.

In these appearances He made it clear He was not a spirit or a ghost. They touched Him. He showed them His hands and feet, saying, "It is I myself" (Luke 24:28-43). During 40 days He came

## Various Versions

**1. The former treatise have I made, O Theophilus:** O God-lover, *Klingensmith* . . . In my earlier work I dealt with everything, *JB* . . . first account, *Concordant* . . . first historical narrative, *Wuest* . . . I wrote my first volume, *Williams* . . . composed the first discourse, *Darby* . . . In the former book, *Confraternity* . . . I made a continuous report, *AmpB.*

**of all that Jesus began both to do and teach:** . . . from the very first, *TCNT.*

**2. Until the day in which he was taken up:** . . . until the day of His ascension, *Berkeley* . . . Before he ascended, *Phillips.*

**after that he through the Holy Ghost had given commandments:** . . . through the intermediate agency, *Wuest* . . . when through the Holy Spirit He gave...their orders, *Williams* . . . their instructions, *Norlie* . . . charged the apostles, *Darby* . . . having equipped, *Fenton.*

**unto the apostles whom he had chosen:** . . . those legates, *Murdock.*

**3. To whom also he showed himself alive:** . . . gave ample proof, *NEB* . . . presented himself living, *Darby.*

**after his passion:** His death, *ET.*

**by many infallible proofs:** . . . in many convincing manifestations, *Montgomery* . . . sure tokens, *Rotherham* . . . clear and certain signs, *BB* . . . convincing demonstrations, *AmpB.*

**being seen of them forty days:** . . . at successive intervals, *Wuest* . . . He appeared to them from time to time, *TCNT* . . . over a period of forty days, *Adams* . . . appearing to them at intervals, *PNT* . . . appeared to them repeatedly, *Phillips.*

| **3450.17** art pl neu | **3875.1** prep | **3450.10** art gen sing fem | **926.1** noun fem | **3450.2** art gen sing | **2296.2** noun gen sing masc |
|---|---|---|---|---|---|
| τὰ | περὶ | τῆς | βασιλείας | τοῦ | θεοῦ. |
| *ta* | *peri* | *tēs* | *basileias* | *tou* | *theou* |
| the things | concerning | the | kingdom | of | God: |

| **2504.1** conj | **4722.1** verb nom sing masc part pres mid | **3715.7** verb 3sing indic aor act | **840.2** prs-pron dat pl | **570.3** prep |
|---|---|---|---|---|
| **4.** καὶ | συναλιζόμενος | παρήγγειλεν | αὐτοῖς | ἀπὸ |
| *kai* | *sunalizomenos* | *parēngeilen* | *autois* | *apo* |
| and | being assembled with | he commanded | them | from |

| **2389.2** name gen pl neu | **3231.1** partic | **5398.6** verb inf pres mid | **233.2** conj | **3900.1** verb inf pres act |
|---|---|---|---|---|
| Ἱεροσολύμων | μὴ | χωρίζεσθαι, | ἀλλὰ | περιμένειν |
| *Hierosolumōn* | *mē* | *chōrizesthai* | *alla* | *perimenein* |
| Jerusalem | not | to depart, | but | to wait for |

| **3450.12** art acc sing fem | **1845.4** noun acc sing fem | **3450.2** art gen sing | **3824.2** noun gen sing masc | **3614.12** rel-pron acc sing fem | **189.23** verb 2pl indic aor act |
|---|---|---|---|---|---|
| τὴν | ἐπαγγελίαν | τοῦ | πατρὸς, | ἣν | ἠκούσατέ |
| *tēn* | *epangelian* | *tou* | *patros* | *hēn* | *ēkousate* |
| the | promise | of the | Father, | which | you heard |

| **1466.2** prs-pron gen 1sing | **3617.1** conj | **2464.1** name nom masc | **3173.1** conj | **901.8** verb 3sing indic aor act | **5045.3** noun dat sing neu |
|---|---|---|---|---|---|
| μου· | **5.** ὅτι | Ἰωάννης | μὲν | ἐβάπτισεν | ὕδατι, |
| *mou* | *hoti* | *Iōannēs* | *men* | *ebaptisen* | *hudati* |
| from me. | For | John | indeed | baptized | with water, |

| **5050.1** prs-pron nom 2pl | **1156.2** conj | **901.27** verb 2pl indic fut pass | **1706.1** prep | **4011.3** noun dat sing neu |
|---|---|---|---|---|
| ὑμεῖς | δὲ | ʻ βαπτισθήσεσθε | ἐν | πνεύματι |
| *humeis* | *de* | *baptisthēsesthe* | *en* | *pneumati* |
| you | but | shall be baptized | with | Spirit |

| **1706.1** prep | **4011.3** noun dat sing neu | **901.27** verb 2pl indic fut pass | **39.3** adj dat sing | **3620.3** partic | **3196.3** prep |
|---|---|---|---|---|---|
| [☆ ἐν | πνεύματι | βαπτισθήσεσθε ] | ἁγίῳ | οὐ | μετὰ |
| *en* | *pneumati* | *baptisthēsesthe* | *hagiō* | *ou* | *meta* |
| [ with | Spirit | shall be baptized ] | Holy | not | after |

| **4044.15** adj acc pl fem | **3642.15** dem-pron acc pl fem | **2232.1** noun fem | **3450.7** art nom pl masc | **3173.1** conj | **3631.1** partic |
|---|---|---|---|---|---|
| πολλὰς | ταύτας | ἡμέρας. | **6.** Οἱ | μὲν | οὖν |
| *pollas* | *tautas* | *hēmeras* | *Hoi* | *men* | *oun* |
| many | these | days. | The | now | therefore |

6.a.**Txt:** 04C-corr,05D 08E,byz.
**Var:** 01ℵ,02A,03B 04C-org,Lach,Treg,Alf Tisc,We/Ho,Weis,Sod UBS/☆

| **4755.6** verb nom pl masc part aor act | **1890.13** verb 3pl indic imperf act | **2049.17** verb 3pl indic imperf act | **840.6** prs-pron acc sing masc |
|---|---|---|---|
| συνελθόντες | ʻ ἐπηρώτων | [a☆ ἠρώτων ] | αὐτὸν |
| *sunelthontes* | *epērōtōn* | *ērōtōn* | *auton* |
| having come together | were asking | [ idem ] | him |

| **2978.16** verb nom pl masc part pres act | **2935.5** noun voc sing masc | **1479.1** conj | **1706.1** prep | **3450.3** art dat sing | **5385.3** noun dat sing masc |
|---|---|---|---|---|---|
| λέγοντες, | Κύριε, | εἰ | ἐν | τῷ | χρόνῳ |
| *legontes* | *Kurie* | *ei* | *en* | *tō* | *chronō* |
| saying, | Lord, | | at | the | time |

| **3642.5** dem-pron dat sing masc | **595.1** verb 2sing indic pres act | **3450.12** art acc sing fem | **926.4** noun acc sing fem | **3450.3** art dat sing |
|---|---|---|---|---|
| τούτῳ | ἀποκαθιστάνεις | τὴν | βασιλείαν | τῷ |
| *toutō* | *apokathistaneis* | *tēn* | *basileian* | *tō* |
| this | you restore | the | kingdom | to |

to them again and again. These were not visions. They were objective, real, personal appearances. They knew Him, and He taught them truth concerning the Kingdom (or rule, royal power, and authority of God). Now they understood how the Cross and the Resurrection are both necessary for salvation. Both are revelations of God's mighty power and love.

During Moses' 40 days on Mount Sinai God gave him the Law. But during these 40 days Jesus gave His disciples a better "law." (The Hebrew word for law, *torah*, means "instruction.") He was preparing them to carry on after His departure.

**1:4.** Luke's Gospel condenses his account of the 40 days after the Resurrection and jumps to the final exhortation for the 120 to wait in Jerusalem until they had received the Promise of the Father (Luke 24:49). In Acts Luke goes again to the time immediately preceding the Ascension. Jesus repeated the command not to leave Jerusalem.

"The promise of the Father" relates the gift of the Spirit to Old Testament prophecies. The idea of promise is one of the bonds that unites the Old and New Testaments. The promise to Abraham spoke of personal blessings, and blessings to the nation, as well as to all the families of the earth (Genesis 12:3).

The story of God's dealings with His people is a step-by-step revelation. First was the promised defeat of that old serpent, the devil, through the seed of the woman (Genesis 3:15). Next, the promise was given to Abraham, to Isaac, and to Jacob. The chosen line was then narrowed down to Judah, then to David. This led to Jesus, David's greater Son. Now through Jesus would come the Promise of the Father, the gift of the Spirit.

**1:5.** Jesus had already promised this mighty outpouring of the Spirit to His followers (John 7:38,39 and chapters 14–16). So had John the Baptist. Jesus, as John promised, would baptize them in the Holy Spirit (Mark 1:8). Now Jesus further promised that it would be after "not many days."

**1:6.** Acts and the Epistles contain a great deal more about the Holy Spirit and the Church than about the kingdom of God. But the Kingdom was important in Jesus' teaching. Jesus told the disciples it was the Father's good pleasure to give them the Kingdom. *Kingdom* in the New Testament deals primarily with the King's power and rule. Righteousness, peace, and joy in the Holy Spirit show God is ruling in the lives of believers and they are in His kingdom (Romans 14:17).

The future rule of Christ was what the disciples had in mind here. They knew the prophecy of Ezekiel 36:24-27. They knew God's promise to Abraham included not only the seed, but the land. All through the Old Testament God's promise to Israel was connected with the promise of the land.



**and speaking of the things pertaining to the kingdom of God:** . . . discussing the interests, *Berkeley* . . . regarding the welfare, *Fenton* . . . God's empire, *Adams.*

**4. And, being assembled together with them:** While he was staying with them, *Noli* . . . and once when, *Montgomery* . . . On one occasion, while he was eating with them, *NIV.*

**commanded them that they should not depart from Jerusalem:** . . . charged them, *ASV* . . . ordered them, *Beck* . . . he emphasized, *Phillips* . . . Do not leave Jerusalem, *Noli* . . . told them not to leave, *NAB.*

**but wait for the promise of the Father:** You must wait, *NEB* . . . for the fulfillment of the promise made, *Norlie* . . . but to wait for the Father's promised gift, *Weymouth* . . . of my Father's promise, *NAB.*

**which, saith he, ye have heard of me:** You have heard me speak of it, *Williams.*

**5. For John truly baptized with water:** For John indeed immersed with water, *Rotherham* . . . baptized people in water, *Williams* . . . was with water, *BB.*

**but ye shall be baptized with the Holy Ghost:** . . . immersed, *HBIE.*

**not many days hence:** . . . within a few days, *Campbell* . . . after a little time, *BB.*

**6. When they therefore were come together:** On one occasion, when the Apostles had met together, *TCNT* . . . Those who were present then, *Norlie* . . . While they were with him, *NAB.*

**they asked of him, saying:** They...began to question him, *Rotherham* . . . they asked Jesus this question, *TCNT.*

**Lord, wilt thou at this time restore again the kingdom to Israel?:** . . . are you now going to make Israel an independent kingdom again, *Beck* . . . dost thou duly establish the kingdom, *Rotherham* . . . set up the kingdom again, *Williams* . . . the sovereignty of Israel? *NEB* . . . will you now bring back the kingdom to Israel? *Klingensmith* . . . to restore the rule to Israel now? *NAB.*

## Acts 1:7

7.a.**Txt:** 01ℵ,02A,byz.bo. Sod
**Var:** 03B-org,sa.Treg Tisc,We/Ho,Weis UBS/⋆

| 2447.1 name masc | 1500.5 verb 3sing indic aor act | 1156.2 conj | 4242.1 prep | 840.8 prs-pron acc pl masc | 3620.1 partic |
|---|---|---|---|---|---|
| Ἰσραήλ; | 7. Εἶπεν | ⸂a δὲ ⸃ | πρὸς | αὐτούς, | Οὐχ |
| *Israēl* | *Eipen* | *de* | *pros* | *autous* | *Ouch* |
| Israel? | He said | but | to | them, | Not |

| 5050.2 prs-pron gen 2pl | 1498.4 verb 3sing indic pres act | 1091.29 verb inf aor act | 5385.7 noun acc pl masc | 2211.1 conj | 2511.8 noun acc pl masc |
|---|---|---|---|---|---|
| ὑμῶν | ἐστιν | γνῶναι | χρόνους | ἢ | καιροὺς |
| *humōn* | *estin* | *gnōnai* | *chronous* | *ē* | *kairous* |
| yours | it is | to know | times | or | seasons |

| 3614.8 rel-pron acc pl masc | 3450.5 art nom sing masc | 3824.1 noun nom sing masc | 4935.30 verb 3sing indic aor mid | 1706.1 prep | 3450.11 art dat sing fem |
|---|---|---|---|---|---|
| οὓς | ὁ | πατὴρ | ἔθετο | ἐν | τῇ |
| *hous* | *ho* | *patēr* | *etheto* | *en* | *tē* |
| which | the | father | placed | in | the |

| 2375.10 adj dat sing fem | 1833.3 noun dat sing fem | 233.2 conj | 2956.41 verb 2pl indic fut mid | 2956.47 verb 2pl indic fut mid |
|---|---|---|---|---|
| ἰδίᾳ | ἐξουσίᾳ· | 8. ἀλλὰ | ⸀ λήψεσθε | [⋆ λήμψεσθε ] |
| *idia* | *exousia* | *alla* | *lēpsesthe* | *lēmpsesthe* |
| his own | authority; | but | you will receive | [ idem ] |

| 1405.4 noun acc sing fem | 1889.4 verb gen sing neu part aor act | 3450.2 art gen sing | 39.2 adj gen sing | 4011.2 noun gen sing neu | 1894.1 prep |
|---|---|---|---|---|---|
| δύναμιν, | ἐπελθόντος | τοῦ | ἁγίου | πνεύματος | ἐφ' |
| *dunamin* | *epelthontos* | *tou* | *hagiou* | *pneumatos* | *eph'* |
| power, | having come | the | Holy | Spirit | upon |

8.a.**Txt:** byz.
**Var:** 01ℵ,02A,03B,04C 05D,Lach,Treg,Alf Word,Tisc,We/Ho,Weis Sod,UBS/⋆

| 5050.4 prs-pron acc 2pl | 2504.1 conj | 1498.42 verb 2pl indic fut mid | 1466.4 prs-pron dat 1sing | 1466.2 prs-pron gen 1sing | 3116.4 noun nom pl masc |
|---|---|---|---|---|---|
| ὑμᾶς, | καὶ | ἔσεσθέ | ⸀ μοι | [a⋆ μου ] | μάρτυρες |
| *humas* | *kai* | *esesthe* | *moi* | *mou* | *martures* |
| you, | and | you shall be | to me | [ of me ] | witnesses |

8.b.**Txt:** p74,01ℵ,03B 04C-corr,08E,044,byz. Tisc,We/Ho,Weis,Sod UBS/⋆
**Var:** 02A,04C-org,05D Lach

| 1706.1 prep | 4885.1 conj | 2395.2 name fem | 2504.1 conj | 1706.1 prep | 3820.11 adj dat sing fem | 3450.11 art dat sing fem |
|---|---|---|---|---|---|---|
| ἔν | τε | Ἱερουσαλὴμ | καὶ | ⸂b ἐν ⸃ | πάσῃ | τῇ |
| *en* | *te* | *Ierousalēm* | *kai* | *en* | *pasē* | *tē* |
| in | both | Jerusalem | and | in | all | |

| 2424.3 name dat fem | 2504.1 conj | 4397.3 name dat fem | 2504.1 conj | 2175.1 conj | 2057.2 adj gen sing | 3450.10 art gen sing fem |
|---|---|---|---|---|---|---|
| Ἰουδαίᾳ | καὶ | Σαμαρείᾳ | καὶ | ἕως | ἐσχάτου | τῆς |
| *Ioudaia* | *kai* | *Samareia* | *kai* | *heōs* | *eschatou* | *tēs* |
| Judea | and | Samaria | and | to | end | of the |

| 1087.2 noun gen sing fem | 2504.1 conj | 3642.18 dem-pron pl neu | 1500.15 verb nom sing masc part aor act | 984.15 verb gen pl masc part pres act |
|---|---|---|---|---|
| γῆς. | 9. Καὶ | ταῦτα | εἰπὼν, | βλεπόντων |
| *gēs* | *Kai* | *tauta* | *eipōn* | *blepontōn* |
| earth. | And | these things | having said, | looking |

| 840.1 prs-pron gen pl | 1854.11 verb 3sing indic aor pass | 2504.1 conj | 3369.1 noun nom sing fem | 5112.3 verb 3sing indic aor act |
|---|---|---|---|---|
| αὐτῶν | ἐπήρθη, | καὶ | νεφέλη | ὑπέλαβεν |
| *autōn* | *epērthē* | *kai* | *nephelē* | *hupelaben* |
| they | he was taken up, | and | a cloud | received |

| 840.6 prs-pron acc sing masc | 570.3 prep | 3450.1 art gen pl | 3652.6 noun gen pl masc | 840.1 prs-pron gen pl | 2504.1 conj |
|---|---|---|---|---|---|
| αὐτὸν | ἀπὸ | τῶν | ὀφθαλμῶν | αὐτῶν. | 10. Καὶ |
| *auton* | *apo* | *tōn* | *ophthalmōn* | *autōn* | *Kai* |
| him | from | the | eyes | their. | And |

**1:7.** Jesus did not deny that it was still God's plan to restore the kingdom (the rule) of God (the theocracy) to Israel. But on earth they would never know the specific times and proper occasions of that restoration before Jesus returned.

In Old Testament times God did not reveal the timespan between the first and second comings of Christ. Sometimes the prophets jump from one to the other in almost the same breath. At Nazareth, Jesus stopped His reading from Isaiah 61 in the middle of verse 2 because the rest of the verse refers to the Second Coming. Again and again Jesus warned the disciples that no man knows the day or the hour of His return (Mark 13:32-35, for example). Jesus also warned that the kingdom of God would not immediately appear (Luke 19:11,12). The Father has placed the times and seasons under His own authority. He alone has the knowledge and wisdom to take all things into account. In His wisdom He has made the times and seasons His business; it is not the concern of the Church.

**1:8.** What is the believers' business? Verse 8 gives the answer. The disciples would receive power after the Holy Spirit came upon them. Through the Spirit's power their business would be to serve as Christ's witnesses (1 John 1:1) telling what they had seen, heard, and experienced. Beginning at Jerusalem they would carry their witness through Judea (probably including Galilee) and Samaria, and then to the uttermost parts of the earth. This method of procedure for witnessing gives a virtual table of contents for the Book of Acts.

Christians do not need to fail. The coming of the Spirit is an empowering experience. "Ye shall receive power" (Greek, *dunamis*, "mighty power, ability"). Jesus (Matthew 24) emphasized that His followers could not wait for ideal conditions before spreading the gospel to the nations. He told them this age, and especially the end times, would be characterized by wars, rumors of wars, famines, and earthquakes. Followers of Jesus must spread the gospel to all nations despite all these natural calamities and political upheavals. How would this be possible? Jesus promised they would receive power as a result of being filled with the Spirit. This would be the secret of success in the Church Age until its final consummation when Jesus returns.

**1:9.** Luke's Gospel is climaxed by Christ's ascension. Luke 24:50 indicates Jesus led His followers out to the Mount of Olives opposite Bethany. As He blessed them He was taken up into heaven (that is, taken gradually, not snatched away). Acts 1:10 adds that this happened "while they looked." They were not dreaming. They actually saw Him go. Then "a cloud," not an ordinary cloud but undoubtedly a glory cloud like the Old Testament Shekinah, took Him up. This could well mean the cloud swept under Him and He rode it up out of their sight. But not only did He leave the surface of the earth, He ascended to the right hand of the Father, and He is still bodily present in heaven. Stephen saw Him there (7:55).

**7. And he said unto them:** He answered, *Noli.*

**It is not for you to know the times or the seasons:** . . . your business to learn times and dates, *Williams* . . . your affair, *Berkeley* . . . to decide dates and times, *Everyday* . . . and occasions, *Montgomery* . . . or periods, *Fenton* . . . the chronological events, *Wuest* . . . moments, *Douay.*

**which the Father hath put in his own power:** . . . under His personal authority, *Berkeley* . . . has appointed by his own authority, *Sawyer* . . . has reserved at His own absolute disposal, *Fenton* . . . has decided, *JB* . . . set within his own control, *NEB* . . . is the only One who has the authority, *Everyday* . . . has a right to fix, *Williams* . . . has kept within his own providence, *Noli.*

**8. But ye shall receive power:** Instead, *Adams* . . . you shall be obtaining power, *Concordant* . . . receive energy, *Murdock* . . . you shall lay hold of power, *Klingensmith.*

**after that the Holy Ghost is come upon you:** . . . from the Holy Spirit coming upon, *Fenton* . . . descends upon, *Noli.*

**and ye shall be witnesses unto me:** . . . will testify of Me, *Beck* . . . my witnesses, *Darby.*

**both in Jerusalem, and in all Judaea, and in Samaria, and unto the uttermost part of the earth:** . . . even to the remotest parts, *Campbell* . . . the farthest ends, *Norlie* . . . to the utmost limit, *Worrell* . . . farthest parts, *Beck* . . . the very last part of, *Klingensmith* . . . the very ends of, *TCNT* . . . in every part of the world, *Everyday.*

**9. And when he had spoken these things, while they beheld, he was taken up:** Jesus had no sooner said this than he was caught up before their very eyes, *TCNT* . . . With these words, while they were looking, *Noli* . . . as they were looking on, he was lifted up, *RSV* . . . as they were watching, *Everyday.*

**and a cloud received him out of their sight:** . . . a cloud swept under Him and carried Him out, *Williams* . . . caught him away from their eyes, *Rotherham* . . . hid him, *Everyday* . . . a cloud took Him up from, *Adams.*

# Acts 1:11

10.a.**Txt:** 04C-corr,05D 08E,byz.Gries,Word **Var:** 01א,02A,03B 04C-org,sa.bo.Lach,Treg Tisc,We/Ho,Weis,Sod UBS/☆

11.a.**Txt:** 04C-corr,08E byz.Sod **Var:** 01א,02A,03B 04C-org,05D,Lach,Treg Alf,Tisc,We/Ho,Weis UBS/☆

11.b.**Txt:** p56,01א-corr 02A,04C,05D,044,byz. Sod **Var:** 01א-org,03B,08E 33,Treg,Tisc,We/Ho UBS/☆

| **5453.1** conj | **810.2** verb nom pl masc part pres act | **1498.37** verb 3pl indic imperf act | **1519.1** prep | **3450.6** art acc sing masc | **3636.4** noun acc sing masc |
|---|---|---|---|---|---|
| ὡς | ἀτενίζοντες | ἦσαν | εἰς | τὸν | οὐρανὸν |
| *hōs* | *atenizontes* | *ēsan* | *eis* | *ton* | *ouranon* |
| as | looking intently | they were | into | the | heaven |

| **4057.8** verb gen sing masc part pres mid | **840.3** prs-pron gen sing | **2504.1** conj | **1481.20** verb 2sing impr aor mid | **433.6** noun nom pl masc |
|---|---|---|---|---|
| πορευομένου | αὐτοῦ, | καὶ | ἰδοὺ | ἄνδρες |
| *poreuomenou* | *autou* | *kai* | *idou* | *andres* |
| going | he, | also | behold | men |

| **1411.3** num card | **3798.14** verb 3pl indic plperf act | **840.2** prs-pron dat pl | **1706.1** prep | **2051.1** noun dat sing fem | **2996.5** adj dat sing fem |
|---|---|---|---|---|---|
| δύο | παρειστήκεισαν | αὐτοῖς | ἐν | ʼ ἐσθῆτι | λευκῇ, |
| *duo* | *pareistēkeisan* | *autois* | *en* | *esthēti* | *leukē* |
| two | stood by | them | in | clothes | white, |

| **2050.2** noun dat pl fem | **2996.10** adj dat pl fem | **3614.7** rel-pron nom pl masc | **2504.1** conj | **1500.3** verb indic aor act |
|---|---|---|---|---|
| [a☆ ἐσθήσεσι | λευκαῖς, ] | **11.** οἳ | καὶ | ʼ εἶπον, |
| *esthēsesi* | *leukais* | *hoi* | *kai* | *eipon* |
| [ clothes | white, ] | who | also | said, |

| **1500.28** verb 3pl indic aor act | **433.6** noun nom pl masc | **1050.3** name-adj nom pl masc | **4949.9** intr-pron sing neu | **2449.20** verb 2pl indic perf act |
|---|---|---|---|---|
| [a☆ εἶπαν, ] | Ἄνδρες | Γαλιλαῖοι, | τί | ἑστήκατε |
| *eipan* | *Andres* | *Galilaioi* | *ti* | *hestēkate* |
| [ idem ] | Men | Galileans, | why | do you stand |

| **1676.1** verb nom pl masc part pres act | **984.14** verb nom pl masc part pres act | **1519.1** prep | **3450.6** art acc sing masc | **3636.4** noun acc sing masc |
|---|---|---|---|---|
| ʼ ἐμβλέποντες | [b☆ βλέποντες ] | εἰς | τὸν | οὐρανόν; |
| *emblepontes* | *blepontes* | *eis* | *ton* | *ouranon* |
| looking | [ idem ] | into | the | heaven? |

| **3642.4** dem-pron nom sing masc | **3450.5** art nom sing masc | **2400.1** name nom masc | **3450.5** art nom sing masc | **351.7** verb nom sing masc part aor pass |
|---|---|---|---|---|
| οὗτος | ὁ | Ἰησοῦς | ὁ | ʼ ἀναληφθεὶς |
| *houtos* | *ho* | *Iēsous* | *ho* | *analēphtheis* |
| This | | Jesus | the | having been taken up |

| **351.9** verb nom sing masc part aor pass | **570.1** prep | **5050.2** prs-pron gen 2pl | **1519.1** prep | **3450.6** art acc sing masc | **3636.4** noun acc sing masc |
|---|---|---|---|---|---|
| [☆ ἀναλημφθεὶς ] | ἀφ' | ὑμῶν | εἰς | τὸν | οὐρανὸν |
| *analēmphtheis* | *aph'* | *humōn* | *eis* | *ton* | *ouranon* |
| [ idem ] | from | you | into | the | heaven |

| **3643.1** adv | **2048.55** verb 3sing indic fut mid | **3614.6** rel-pron acc sing masc | **4999.3** noun acc sing masc | **2277.4** verb 2pl indic aor mid |
|---|---|---|---|---|
| οὕτως | ἐλεύσεται | ὃν | τρόπον | ἐθεάσασθε |
| *houtōs* | *eleusetai* | *hon* | *tropon* | *etheasasthe* |
| thus | will come | what | manner | you beheld |

| **840.6** prs-pron acc sing masc | **4057.6** verb sing part pres mid | **1519.1** prep | **3450.6** art acc sing masc | **3636.4** noun acc sing masc | **4966.1** adv |
|---|---|---|---|---|---|
| αὐτὸν | πορευόμενον | εἰς | τὸν | οὐρανόν. | **12.** Τότε |
| *auton* | *poreuomenon* | *eis* | *ton* | *ouranon* | *Tote* |
| him | going | into | the | heaven. | Then |

| **5128.7** verb 3pl indic aor act | **1519.1** prep | **2395.1** name fem | **570.3** prep | **3598.2** noun gen sing neu | **3450.2** art gen sing |
|---|---|---|---|---|---|
| ὑπέστρεψαν | εἰς | Ἱερουσαλὴμ | ἀπὸ | ὄρους | τοῦ |
| *hupestrepsan* | *eis* | *Hierousalēm* | *apo* | *orous* | *tou* |
| they returned | to | Jerusalem | from | mountain | the |

**1:10.** After Jesus disappeared, the disciples stood there in amazement with their gaze fixed on the heavens where He had gone. Suddenly, two men in white clothing stood beside them. The white speaks of purity. Though the Bible does not call them angels, it is generally assumed they were. Hebrews 1:14 states that angels are ministering *spirits*; however, on this occasion God enabled the disciples to see them. The white clothing is a reminder of the angels who appeared at the tomb the morning of the Resurrection. Luke calls them "men" (Luke 24:4), John says "angels" (John 20:12).

**1:11.** The angels asked why these disciples, men of Galilee (only Judas was of Judea), stood gazing into heaven. This implies they were straining their eyes as if they hoped to see into heaven where Jesus had gone. But Christ's first coming was fulfilled. His work of redemption was complete. It would be a long time before His return, but He would be with them as truly as He had been before (Matthew 28:20). Furthermore, He had left them a great commission, a work to do. He had given them instructions to wait in Jerusalem for the Promise of the Father and for power to be His witnesses. They must obey with the assurance He would come again.

The promise of His return is as emphatic as it could possibly be. Many have tried to interpret this return in some symbolic or spiritual way. Some say it was fulfilled by the outpouring of the Holy Spirit at Pentecost. But Paul makes it clear, long after Pentecost, that "the Lord *himself* shall descend from heaven with a shout, with the voice of the archangel (Michael), and with the trump of God: and the dead in Christ shall rise first," then living believers who remain will "be caught up (snatched up, raptured up) together with them in the clouds," for a meeting with the Lord in the air (1 Thessalonians 4:16,17).

Others have said the Second Coming is fulfilled when Christ comes for believers at death, but the passage just quoted shows the dead will rise to meet Him. Still others say some other person from some other place will arise or come into prominence and be the Christ, the Messiah. Any such claim reminds us of Jesus' warnings against false christs (Matthew 24:5,11). In fact, if anyone has time to say, "Here is Christ, or there" (Matthew 24:23), Christians will know he is false. When Jesus comes back, believers will be caught away and changed in the twinkling of an eye. No one will have to tell them Christ has come (1 Corinthians 15:23,51,52).

The Greek makes it perfectly clear. "*This same* Jesus . . . shall *so* come in like manner (in the *same* way) as ye have seen him go." He had already told them He would return in the clouds (Mark 13:26). At His trial He identified himself with the "Son of man," whom Daniel speaks of as coming with clouds (Daniel 7:13,14). No wonder the fact of His return continues to be one of the most important motivations for Christian living. (See 1 John 3:2,3.)

**1:12.** The Gospel of Luke describes the return of Jesus' followers to Jerusalem as being "with great joy" (Luke 24:52). It was only a

**10. And while they looked stedfastly toward heaven as he went up:** They were still looking intently up to heaven, watching His departure, *Norlie* . . . while they were in rapt attention toward heaven, *Swann* . . . gazing intently, *Worrell* . . . gazing up into the heavens, *NAB* . . . at His departure, *Fenton* . . . they were looking earnestly up, *Williams C.K.* . . . while He was departing, *Beck* . . . after him into the sky, *Goodspeed* . . . As he was going, *Everyday, Hanson* . . . going away from them, *MLNT.*

**behold, two men stood by them in white apparel:** . . . at that moment, *Kleist* . . . All at once two men dressed in white, *NLT* . . . suddenly there were two men in white garments standing by them, *Weymouth* . . . two angels, *SEB* . . . in white robes suddenly appeared, *Noli* . . . two men in white, *NAB* . . . in white clothes were standing right beside them, *Beck.*

**11. Which also said:** Who also said, *ASV.*

**Ye men of Galilee, why stand ye gazing up into heaven?:** Men! Galileans! *KJII* . . . of the country of, *NLT* . . . fixed on the sky? *TCNT* . . . looking up to heaven, *Moffatt* . . . into the sky? *Everyday* . . . up at the skies? *NAB.*

**this same Jesus, which is taken up from you into heaven:** This very Jesus, *Phillips* . . . This Jesus who has been taken from you, *NAB* . . . was caught away, *AmpB* . . . who ascended into, *Noli* . . . who had been caught up from you, *Goodspeed.*

**shall so come in like manner as ye have seen him go into heaven:** He will come back in the same way, *Everyday* . . . will come in just the way that you have seen him go up, *Goodspeed* . . . in the same manner in which, *MLNT* . . . will return in the same way as you have seen him going there, *TNT.*

**12. Then returned they unto Jerusalem from the mount called Olivet:** After that, *NAB* . . . The followers went back to, *NLT* . . . Then they went back to, *Everyday, MLNT* . . . the Olive-yard, *PNT* . . . the hill called 'The Olive-Orchard,' *Goodspeed, Moffatt.*

| 2535.28 verb gen sing part pres mid | 1625.1 name gen masc | 3614.16 rel-pron sing neu | 1498.4 verb 3sing indic pres act | 1445.1 adv |
|---|---|---|---|---|
| καλουμένου | ἐλαιῶνος, | ὅ | ἐστιν | ἐγγὺς |
| *kaloumenou* | *elaiōnos* | *ho* | *estin* | *engus* |
| being called | Olives, | which | is | near |

| 2395.1 name fem | 4378.2 noun gen sing neu | 2174.28 verb sing neu part pres act | 3461.4 noun acc sing fem | 2504.1 conj |
|---|---|---|---|---|
| Ἱερουσαλὴμ, | σαββάτου | ἔχον | ὁδόν. | **13.** Καὶ |
| *Hierousalēm* | *sabbatou* | *echon* | *hodon* | *Kai* |
| Jerusalem, | of a sabbath | having | a way. | And |

| 3616.1 conj | 1511.1 verb indic aor act | 303.14 verb 3pl indic aor act | 1519.1 prep | 3450.16 art sing neu | 5091.2 noun sing neu |
|---|---|---|---|---|---|
| ὅτε | εἰσῆλθον | ⸀ ἀνέβησαν | εἰς | τὸ | ὑπερῷον, |
| *hote* | *eisēlthon* | *anebēsan* | *eis* | *to* | *huperōon* |
| when | they had entered | they went up | to | the | upper room |

| 1519.1 prep | 3450.16 art sing neu | 5091.2 noun sing neu | 303.14 verb 3pl indic aor act | 3619.1 adv | 1498.37 verb 3pl indic imperf act |
|---|---|---|---|---|---|
| [☆ εἰς | τὸ | ὑπερῷον | ἀνέβησαν ] | οὗ | ἦσαν |
| *eis* | *to* | *huperōon* | *anebēsan* | *hou* | *ēsan* |
| [ to | the | upper room | they went up ] | where | were |

| 2620.1 verb nom pl masc part pres act | 3614.16 rel-pron sing neu | 4885.1 conj | 3935.1 name nom masc | 2504.1 conj | 2362.1 name nom masc |
|---|---|---|---|---|---|
| καταμένοντες, | ὅ | τε | Πέτρος | καὶ | ⸀ Ἰάκωβος |
| *katamenontes* | *ho* | *te* | *Petros* | *kai* | *Iakōbos* |
| staying | | both | Peter | and | James |

| 2504.1 conj | 2464.1 name nom masc | 2464.1 name nom masc | 2504.1 conj | 2362.1 name nom masc | 2504.1 conj |
|---|---|---|---|---|---|
| καὶ | Ἰωάννης | [☆ Ἰωάννης | καὶ | Ἰάκωβος ] | καὶ |
| *kai* | *Iōannēs* | *Iōannēs* | *kai* | *Iakōbos* | *kai* |
| and | John | [ John | and | James ] | and |

| 404.1 name nom masc | 5213.1 name nom masc | 2504.1 conj | 2358.1 name nom masc | 913.1 name nom masc | 2504.1 conj |
|---|---|---|---|---|---|
| Ἀνδρέας, | Φίλιππος | καὶ | Θωμᾶς, | Βαρθολομαῖος | καὶ |
| *Andreas* | *Philippos* | *kai* | *Thōmas* | *Bartholomaios* | *kai* |
| Andrew, | Philip | and | Thomas, | Bartholomew | and |

| 3128.1 name nom masc | 3128.3 name nom masc | 2362.1 name nom masc | 254.2 name gen masc | 2504.1 conj |
|---|---|---|---|---|
| ⸀ Ματθαῖος, | [☆ Μαθθαῖος, ] | Ἰάκωβος | Ἁλφαίου | καὶ |
| *Matthaios* | *Maththaios* | *Iakōbos* | *Halphaiou* | *kai* |
| Matthew, | [ idem ] | James | of Alpheus | and |

| 4468.1 name nom masc | 3450.5 art nom sing masc | 2191.1 name nom masc | 2504.1 conj | 2430.1 name nom masc | 2362.2 name gen masc |
|---|---|---|---|---|---|
| Σίμων | ὁ | ζηλωτὴς | καὶ | Ἰούδας | Ἰακώβου. |
| *Simōn* | *ho* | *zēlōtēs* | *kai* | *Ioudas* | *Iakōbou* |
| Simon | the | Zealot, | and | Jude | of James. |

| 3642.7 dem-pron nom pl masc | 3820.7 adj nom pl masc | 1498.37 verb 3pl indic imperf act | 4201.4 verb nom pl masc part pres act |
|---|---|---|---|
| **14.** οὗτοι | πάντες | ἦσαν | προσκαρτεροῦντες |
| *houtoi* | *pantes* | *ēsan* | *proskarterountes* |
| These | all | were | steadfastly continuing |

14.a.**Txt:** 04C-corr,byz.
**Var:** 01ℵ,02A,03B
04C-org,05D,08E,sa.bo.
Gries,Lach,Treg,Alf
Tisc,We/Ho,Weis,Sod
UBS/☆

| 3524.1 adv | 3450.11 art dat sing fem | 4194.3 noun dat sing fem | 2504.1 conj | 3450.11 art dat sing fem |
|---|---|---|---|---|
| ὁμοθυμαδὸν | τῇ | προσευχῇ | ⸀a καὶ | τῇ |
| *homothumadon* | *tē* | *proseuchē* | *kai* | *tē* |
| with one accord | in the | prayer | and | the |

Sabbath day's journey (about 1,000 yards) from the Mount of Olives back to the city. (Compare Exodus 16:29 and Numbers 35:5.)

**1:13.** The 11 apostles were staying in a large upper room. Judas the son of James is called Thaddeus in Matthew 10:3. Zealots were Jewish nationalists (cf. the Aramaic *Kan'ana*, "Canaanite" in Mark 3:18). The Upper Room may be the place of the Last Supper and the Resurrection appearances. Some believe it was at the home of Mary the mother of John Mark (12:12).

**1:14.** Five things are seen here: (1) The Eleven were in one accord, in contrast to the jealousy exhibited before the Cross where each wanted to be the greatest (Matthew 20:24). Jesus had dealt with them all after the Resurrection. Now all were restored and recommissioned. There was no more conflict, no more jealousy. All were with one mind, with one accord. "One accord" (Greek, *homothumadon*) is an important repeated word in Acts. Being in one accord is an important key to getting God's work done.

(2) They all continued steadfastly in prayer. This included faithfulness to the morning and evening hours of prayer at the temple as well as prayer in the Upper Room. Prayer and praise were the chief occupation during those days (Luke 24:49).

(3) The women joined them in prayer with the same steadfastness. Actually, the women were present all along. In those days, if one man was present, the masculine pronoun was used for the mixed group. Even when Peter calls them brethren (verse 16), the women were included. The Jews all understood this. But Luke wanted the Gentiles to know the women were present and praying, so he mentioned them specifically. They included Mary Magdalene, Salome, Joanna, Mary and Martha of Bethany, John Mark's mother, and others.

(4) Mary the mother of Jesus is given special mention. She was present because the apostle John was fulfilling Jesus' request to take care of her. She was not there as a leader but simply joined the others in prayer and in waiting for the Promise of the Father, the baptism in the Holy Spirit. This also indicates she had accepted Jesus as her Saviour from sin and as her Lord and Master. She was obeying His command to stay in Jerusalem. She, along with the others, felt her need of the power of the Spirit. Thus, it is certain she received the Spirit even though this is the last time she is mentioned in the Book of Acts. Some traditions say she died in Jerusalem and point to a tomb near St. Stephen's gate. Other writers of the Early Church said she went with the apostle John to Ephesus and died there.

(5) The brothers of Jesus were present, though before the Cross they did not believe on Him (John 7:5). Some say these were cousins of Jesus or children of Joseph by a previous marriage. However, Matthew 1:25 makes it clear that Joseph entered into a physical marriage relation with Mary after Jesus was born. Thus, there is every reason to believe these brothers were actual children of Mary



**which is from Jerusalem a sabbath day's journey:** . . . which is near Jerusalem, *RSV* . . . This was near Jerusalem, a little over a half mile away, *Norlie* . . . only half a mile away, *Williams* . . . a mere sabbath's journey away, *NAB*.

**13. And when they were come in:** When they got there, *TCNT* . . . When they reached the city, *Williams* . . . and when they had entered, *RSV* . . . On entering the city, *Williams C.K.*

**they went into an upper room:** . . . they ascended into the upper chamber, *Concordant* . . . to the second-floor room, *Beck* . . . upper-story, *Rotherham* . . . to the upstairs room, *Everyday*.

**where abode:** . . . which was now, *PNT* . . . their fixed place for meeting, *Weymouth* . . . where they usually met, *Berkeley* . . . where they were making their abode, *Noyes* . . . where they were accustomed to meet, *Montgomery* . . . where they were in the habit of meeting, *Klingensmith* . . . where they were indefinitely staying, *AmpB* . . . Among those present were, *Noli*.

**both Peter, and James, and John, and Andrew:**

**Philip, and Thomas, Bartholomew, and Matthew, James the son of Alphaeus, and Simon Zelotes:** Simon the Zealot, *ASV* . . . known as the Revolutionary, *SEB* . . . the Zealot party member, *NAB*.

**and Judas the brother of James:** Judas the son of James, *ASV*.

**14. These all continued with one accord in prayer and supplication:** Together they devoted themselves to constant prayer, *NAB* . . . all unanimously persevered, *Campbell* . . . They were all united, *Noli* . . . were persevering, *Concordant* . . . continued stedfastly in prayer, *ASV* . . . engaged constantly, *Berkeley* . . . All of these with one mind continued earnest in prayer, *Weymouth* . . . All these engaged constantly and with one mind in prayer, *Berkeley* . . . These all gave themselves to prayer together, *Williams C.K.* . . . persevering in prayer together, *Adams* . . . joined in continuous prayer, *JB* . . . all kept praying together, *Beck*.

14.b.**Txt:** 01ℵ,02A,04C 05D,byz.bo.Sod **Var:** 03B,08E,sa.Treg Tisc,We/Ho,Weis UBS/☆

| **1157.3** noun dat sing fem | **4713.1** prep | **1129.8** noun dat pl fem | **2504.1** conj | **3109.3** name dat fem | **3110.1** name fem |
|---|---|---|---|---|---|
| δεήσει ⸃ | σὺν | γυναιξὶν | καὶ | ⸀ Μαρίᾳ | [b☆ Μαριὰμ ] |
| *deēsei* | *sun* | *gunaixin* | *kai* | *Maria* | *Mariam* |
| entreaty, | with | women | and | Mary | [ idem ] |

14.c.**Txt:** 03B,04C-corr 08E,33,byz.We/Ho,Weis UBS/☆ **Var:** 01ℵ,02A,04C-org 05D,sa.bo.Lach,Alf Word,Tisc,Sod

| **3450.11** art dat sing fem | **3251.3** noun dat sing fem | **3450.2** art gen sing | **2400.2** name masc | **2504.1** conj | **4713.1** prep | **3450.4** art dat pl |
|---|---|---|---|---|---|---|
| τῇ | μητρὶ | τοῦ | Ἰησοῦ, | καὶ | ⸂c σὺν ⸃ | τοῖς |
| *tē* | *mētri* | *tou* | *Iēsou* | *kai* | *sun* | *tois* |
| the | mother | | of Jesus, | and | with | the |

| **79.8** noun dat pl masc | **840.3** prs-pron gen sing | **2504.1** conj | **1706.1** prep | **3450.14** art dat pl fem | **2232.7** noun dat pl fem |
|---|---|---|---|---|---|
| ἀδελφοῖς | αὐτοῦ. | **15.** Καὶ | ἐν | ταῖς | ἡμέραις |
| *adelphois* | *autou* | *Kai* | *en* | *tais* | *hēmerais* |
| brothers | his. | And | in | the | days |

| **3642.14** dem-pron dat pl fem | **448.9** verb nom sing masc part aor act | **3935.1** name nom masc | **1706.1** prep | **3189.1** adj dat sing | **3450.1** art gen pl |
|---|---|---|---|---|---|
| ταύταις | ἀναστὰς | Πέτρος | ἐν | μέσῳ | τῶν |
| *tautais* | *anastas* | *Petros* | *en* | *mesō* | *tōn* |
| those | having stood up | Peter | in | midst | of the |

15.a.**Txt:** 04C-corr,05D 08E,byz. **Var:** 01ℵ,02A,03B 04C-org,sa.bo.Lach,Treg Alf,Word,Tisc,We/Ho Weis,Sod,UBS/☆

| **3073.6** noun gen pl masc | **79.7** noun gen pl masc | **1500.5** verb 3sing indic aor act | **1498.34** verb sing indic imperf act | **4885.1** conj |
|---|---|---|---|---|
| ⸀ μαθητῶν | [a☆ ἀδελφῶν ] | εἶπεν· | ἦν | τε |
| *mathētōn* | *adelphōn* | *eipen* | *ēn* | *te* |
| disciples | [ brothers ] | said, | was | and |

| **3657.1** noun nom sing masc | **3549.5** noun gen pl neu | **1894.3** prep | **3450.16** art sing neu | **840.15** prs-pron sing neu | **5453.1** conj |
|---|---|---|---|---|---|
| ὄχλος | ὀνομάτων | ἐπὶ | τὸ | αὐτὸ | ⸀ ὡς |
| *ochlos* | *onomatōn* | *epi* | *to* | *auto* | *hōs* |
| crowd | of names | upon | the | same | as |

15.b.**Txt:** 03B,05D,08E byz.We/Ho **Var:** 01ℵ,02A,04C,044 Tisc,Weis,Sod,UBS/☆

| **5448.1** adv | **1526.1** num card | **1489.2** num card | **433.6** noun nom pl masc | **79.6** noun nom pl masc |
|---|---|---|---|---|
| [b ὡσεὶ ] | ἑκατὸν | εἴκοσι· | **16.** Ἄνδρες | ἀδελφοί, |
| *hōsei* | *hekaton* | *eikosi* | *Andres* | *adelphoi* |
| [ idem ] | a hundred | twenty, | Men | brothers, |

16.a.**Txt:** 04C-corr,05D 08E,byz. **Var:** 01ℵ,02A,03B 04C-org,sa.bo.Lach,Treg Word,Tisc,We/Ho,Weis Sod,UBS/☆

| **1158.6** verb 3sing indic imperf act | **3997.27** verb inf aor pass | **3450.12** art acc sing fem | **1118.4** noun acc sing fem | **3642.12** dem-pron acc sing fem |
|---|---|---|---|---|
| ἔδει | πληρωθῆναι | τὴν | γραφὴν | ⸂a ταύτην ⸃ |
| *edei* | *plērōthēnai* | *tēn* | *graphēn* | *tautēn* |
| it was necessary | to be fulfilled | the | scripture, | this |

| **3614.12** rel-pron acc sing fem | **4135.2** verb 3sing indic aor act | **3450.16** art sing neu | **4011.1** noun sing neu | **3450.16** art sing neu | **39.1** adj sing |
|---|---|---|---|---|---|
| ἣν | προεῖπεν | τὸ | πνεῦμα | τὸ | ἅγιον |
| *hēn* | *proeipen* | *to* | *pneuma* | *to* | *hagion* |
| which | spoke before | the | Spirit | the | Holy |

| **1217.2** prep | **4601.2** noun gen sing neu | **1132.1** name masc | **3875.1** prep | **2430.2** name masc | **3450.2** art gen sing |
|---|---|---|---|---|---|
| διὰ | στόματος | Δαβὶδ | περὶ | Ἰούδα | τοῦ |
| *dia* | *stomatos* | *Dabid* | *peri* | *Iouda* | *tou* |
| by | mouth | of David | concerning | Judas | the |

16.b.**Txt:** 04C-corr,05D 08E,byz.Sod **Var:** 01ℵ,02A,03B 04C-org,Lach,Treg,Alf Tisc,We/Ho,Weis UBS/☆

| **1090.50** verb gen sing part aor mid | **3458.1** noun gen sing masc | **3450.4** art dat pl | **4666.4** verb dat pl masc part aor act | **3450.6** art acc sing masc |
|---|---|---|---|---|
| γενομένου | ὁδηγοῦ | τοῖς | συλλαβοῦσιν | ⸂b τὸν ⸃ |
| *genomenou* | *hodēgou* | *tois* | *sullabousin* | *ton* |
| having become | guide | to the | having arrested | |

and Joseph. Their names were James (a form of Jacob), Joses (a form of Joseph), Judah, and Simon (Mark 6:3).

After His resurrection, Jesus made a special appearance to His eldest brother James (1 Corinthians 15:7). James later became the leader and chief elder, or bishop, of the Jerusalem church. Jude also became a leader in the church (Acts 12:17; 15:13; 21:18; Galatians 2:9; James 1:1; Jude 1). Now these brothers were in one accord with the apostles and the rest of the 120 as they all waited for the promised Holy Spirit.

**1:15.** Apparently not all the 500 or more who saw Jesus in Galilee (1 Corinthians 15:6) followed Him back to Jerusalem. But about 120 men and women returned after Christ's ascension and were united in this atmosphere of prayer and praise. But they did more than pray. They also gave attention to the Scriptures. What Peter saw in the Scriptures caused him to stand up and address the 120, who are here called disciples (students, learners, eager to learn more about the gospel and about God's will and plan).

Some ancient manuscripts, which form the critical text used by the NIV and NASB, read "brothers" (*adelphōn*) in place of "disciples" (*mathētōn*). If "brothers" is the original, the word still includes the women who were present (cf. verse 14). Luke, to a greater extent than all other New Testament writers, relates the important role women had in the ministry of Christ and in the Early Church (for example, the virgin Mary, Elisabeth, Anna, Martha and Mary, the women in the parables of the Lost Coin and the Unjust Judge, and others [in the Gospels]; Tabitha, Lydia, Priscilla, and the four daughters of Philip the Evangelist [in Acts]).

**1:16.** Peter drew attention to the fulfillment of David's prophecy, spoken by the Spirit, through David's mouth. Peter saw that Psalms 41:9 and 109:8 applied to Judas who acted as a guide to those who arrested Jesus in the Garden of Gethsemane. Peter recognized that the Holy Spirit is the real author of God's written Word, and that what David said about God's enemies in his day applied to the enemies of Jesus (since David is seen by some as a type pointing to Jesus, and God's covenant with David finds its complete and final fulfillment in Jesus).

The phrase "men and brethren" apparently was a style of formal address in the First Century. The phrase does not occur in the extant literature of the day (except Maccabees 8:19), but it is common in Acts, always in a context where there was a gathering of Jews. Peter (2:29; 15:7), Stephen (7:2), James (15:13), and Paul (13:26,38; 22:1; 23:1,6; 28:17) all use this same phrase.

The verb *edei* is related to *dei,* "it is necessary," a term Luke frequently used to indicate divine necessity. It speaks of the providence of God governing the events of history, especially in relation to His plan of redemption. As in this passage and in verse 21, the word is occasionally used specifically in connection with the fulfillment of Scripture (see Luke 22:37; 24:7,26,44,46; Acts 17:3).

**with the women:** . . . together with some women, *Weymouth* . . . along with their wives, *Klingensmith* . . . There were some women in their company, *NAB.*

**and Mary the mother of Jesus:**

**and with his brethren:** . . . his brothers, *NAB.*

**15. And in those days Peter stood up in the midst of the disciples, and said:** During this time there was a meeting of the believers, *Everyday, NCV* . . . At one point...Peter stood up in the center, *NAB* . . . About this time, at a gathering of the Brethren, Peter rose to speak, *TCNT* . . . stood up at a meeting of the brethren, *Williams C.K.* . . . in the midst of the brethren, *ASV* . . . among the brotherhood, *Berkeley* . . . in the congregation, *JB* . . . and addressed them, *Kleist.*

**(the number of names together were about an hundred and twenty,):** . . . they were a large group numbering, *TNT* . . . the number of names assembled, *Hanson* . . . the company of persons was in all, *RSV* . . . there were about a hundred and twenty persons present, *Goodspeed.*

**16. Men and brethren:** Brethren, *ASV* . . . Brothers, *TCNT.*

**this scripture must needs have been fulfilled:** . . . it was necessary that the Scripture should be fulfilled, *Weymouth* . . . that the passage of Scripture, *Kleist* . . . the prediction of the Scriptures, *Goodspeed* . . . what he wrote had to come true, *Beck* . . . was destined to be fulfilled, *NAB* . . . according to the prediction of, *Noli.*

**which the Holy Ghost by the mouth of David spake before concerning Judas:** . . . predicted, *Concordant* . . . long ago, *Beck* . . . foretold through the lips of David, *Berkeley* . . . uttered by the mouth of David, *Williams* . . . dictated through the mouth of David, *Fenton* . . . the fate of Judas, *JB.*

**which was guide to them that took Jesus:** . . . who acted as guide to those who arrested Jesus, *Weymouth* . . . who became leader, *Swann* . . . who was the leader, *Douay* . . . of those apprehending Jesus, *Concordant* . . . that Judas would lead men to arrest Jesus, *Everyday* . . . to the men that arrested Jesus, *TCNT.*

## Acts 1:17

| 2400.3 name acc masc | 3617.1 conj | 2644.1 verb nom sing masc part perf mid | 1498.34 verb sing indic imperf act | 4713.1 prep |
|---|---|---|---|---|
| Ἰησοῦν, | 17. ὅτι | κατηριθμημένος | ἦν | ʻ σὺν |
| *Iēsoun* | *hoti* | *katērithmēmenos* | *ēn* | *sun* |
| Jesus; | For | having been numbered | he was | with |

17.a.**Txt:** byz.
**Var:** 01ℵ,02A,03B,04C 05D,08E,sa.bo.Gries Lach,Treg,Alf,Word Tisc,We/Ho,Weis,Sod UBS/☆

| 1706.1 prep | 2231.3 prs-pron dat 1pl | 2504.1 conj | 2948.1 verb 3sing indic aor act | 3450.6 art acc sing masc | 2792.3 noun acc sing masc |
|---|---|---|---|---|---|
| [[a]☆ ἐν ] | ἡμῖν, | καὶ | ἔλαχεν | τὸν | κλῆρον |
| *en* | *hēmin* | *kai* | *elachen* | *ton* | *klēron* |
| [ among ] | us, | and | he obtained | the | part |

| 3450.10 art gen sing fem | 1242.2 noun gen sing fem | 3642.10 dem-pron gen sing fem | 3642.4 dem-pron nom sing masc | 3173.1 conj | 3631.1 partic |
|---|---|---|---|---|---|
| τῆς | διακονίας | ταύτης. | 18. Οὗτος | μὲν | οὖν |
| *tēs* | *diakonias* | *tautēs* | *Houtos* | *men* | *oun* |
| in the | ministry | this. | This | indeed | then |

18.a.**Txt:** Steph
**Var:** 01ℵ,02A,03B,04C 05D,08E,Gries,Lach Treg,Alf,Word,Tisc We/Ho,Weis,Sod UBS/☆

| 2904.4 verb 3sing indic aor mid | 5399.2 noun sing neu | 1523.2 prep gen | 3450.2 art gen sing | 3272.2 noun gen sing masc | 3450.10 art gen sing fem |
|---|---|---|---|---|---|
| ἐκτήσατο | χωρίον | ἐκ | ⸂[a] τοῦ ⸃ | μισθοῦ | τῆς |
| *ektēsato* | *chōrion* | *ek* | *tou* | *misthou* | *tēs* |
| bought | a field | out of | the | reward | of the |

| 92.2 noun gen sing fem | 2504.1 conj | 4107.1 adj nom sing masc | 1090.53 verb nom sing masc part aor mid | 2970.1 verb 3sing indic aor act |
|---|---|---|---|---|
| ἀδικίας, | καὶ | πρηνὴς | γενόμενος | ἐλάκησεν |
| *adikias* | *kai* | *prēnēs* | *genomenos* | *elakēsen* |
| unrighteousness, | and | headlong | having fallen | burst |

| 3189.2 adj nom sing masc | 2504.1 conj | 1619.2 verb 3sing indic aor pass | 3820.1 adj | 3450.17 art pl neu | 4551.1 noun pl neu |
|---|---|---|---|---|---|
| μέσος, | καὶ | ἐξεχύθη | πάντα | τὰ | σπλάγχνα |
| *mesos* | *kai* | *exechuthē* | *panta* | *ta* | *splanchna* |
| in midst, | and | were poured out | all | the | bowels |

19.a.**Var:** 01ℵ-org,05D Tisc

| 840.3 prs-pron gen sing | 3614.16 rel-pron sing neu | 2504.1 conj | 1104.4 adj sing neu | 1090.33 verb 3sing indic aor mid | 3820.5 adj dat pl |
|---|---|---|---|---|---|
| αὐτοῦ. | 19. [[a]+ ὃ ] | καὶ | γνωστὸν | ἐγένετο | πᾶσιν |
| *autou* | *ho* | *kai* | *gnōston* | *egeneto* | *pasin* |
| his. | [ Which ] | And | known | it became | to all |

| 3450.4 art dat pl | 2700.8 verb dat pl masc part pres act | 2395.1 name fem | 5452.1 conj | 2535.45 verb inf aor pass |
|---|---|---|---|---|
| τοῖς | κατοικοῦσιν | Ἱερουσαλήμ, | ὥστε | κληθῆναι |
| *tois* | *katoikousin* | *Hierousalēm* | *hōste* | *klēthēnai* |
| the | dwelling | in Jerusalem, | so that | to be called |

| 3450.16 art sing neu | 5399.2 noun sing neu | 1552.16 dem-pron sing neu | 3450.11 art dat sing fem | 2375.10 adj dat sing fem | 1252.1 noun dat sing fem |
|---|---|---|---|---|---|
| τὸ | χωρίον | ἐκεῖνο | τῇ | ἰδίᾳ | διαλέκτῳ |
| *to* | *chōrion* | *ekeino* | *tē* | *idia* | *dialektō* |
| the | field | that | in the | own | language |

19.b.**Txt:** 04C,byz.
**Var1:** 03B,05D,Lach,Alf We/Ho,Weis,Sod UBS/☆
**Var2:** 01ℵ,02A,Treg Tisc

| 840.1 prs-pron gen pl | 182.1 name | 182.2 name | 182.3 name |
|---|---|---|---|
| αὐτῶν | ʻ Ἀκελδαμά, | [[1b]☆ Ἀκελδαμάχ, | [2] Ἀχελδαμάχ ] |
| *autōn* | *Akeldama* | *Akeldamach* | *Acheldamach* |
| their | Aceldama; | [ idem | idem ] |

| 4969.1 verb | 3642.16 dem-pron sing neu | 1498.4 verb 3sing indic pres act | 5399.2 noun sing neu | 129.2 noun gen sing neu |
|---|---|---|---|---|
| ʻ τουτέστιν, | [☆ τοῦτ' | ἔστιν, ] | Χωρίον | Αἵματος. |
| *toutestin* | *tout'* | *estin* | *Chōrion* | *Haimatos* |
| that is, | [ idem] | | field | of blood. |

**1:17.** The tragedy was that Judas was numbered among the apostles as one of the Twelve, and yet he failed. Jesus included him when He called together a large group of disciples and out of them chose 12 to be with Him (Luke 6:12,13). Jesus did this knowing the character of Judas (John 6:70). Yet He also knew the Scripture must be fulfilled (John 13:18). Even though Jesus knew what Judas would do, He gave him an assigned portion in the ministry which He gave to all of the Twelve. Judas was sent out with the same commission and the same authority as the others.

Judas was present also when Jesus declared He was appointing a kingdom (a kingly rule and authority) for His 12 apostles like the one His Father had appointed for Him. They would have a special place in His kingdom. They would sit on 12 thrones judging (and therefore ruling) the 12 tribes of Israel (Luke 22:29,30).

Even at the Last Supper Jesus washed the feet of Judas along with the others. When Jesus took the sop (a broken piece of bread), dipped it, and offered it to Judas, it was a final offer of His love. But Judas turned his heart from Jesus. Then Satan entered Judas, and he went out to betray the Lord.

**1:18.** At this point Acts adds a parenthetic note about the death of Judas which adds some new details to the account in Matthew 27:3-5. Matthew says Judas, when he knew the Jewish leaders had condemned Jesus, changed his mind, brought the money back, and confessed he had sinned. When these leaders rejected him, he threw down the money, went out, and hanged himself. Acts says Judas purchased a field with the reward money, and falling headlong, he burst open, and all his internal organs gushed out.

Since Luke had searched out all that was written about Jesus, he knew the priests took the money, bought the potter's field where Judas hanged himself, and used it as a cemetery to bury foreigners in (Matthew 27:6,7). He also knew Judas hanged himself and added this further information about the event.

This incident can be understood better by recognizing that hanging by a rope was not common in ancient times. The two common methods of hanging were crucifixion and impalement through the middle of the body over a sharp stake. Judas, of course, could not nail himself to a cross. But he could set up a sharp stake and fall headlong over it with the result described here. There is evidence also that the Greek includes the idea that when he fell over the stake, his body first swelled up and thus burst open.

It is also true that since the priests took the money which they considered still belonging to Judas, they bought the potter's field in the name of Judas. They called the field *Aceldama* (verse 19, Aramaic for "the field of blood") because the 30 pieces of silver were the price of blood, that is, of Christ's death.

**1:19.** Judas' suicide soon became known to all the residents of Jerusalem. They also called the field Aceldama, but they had in mind the violent death of Judas which took place there.

**17. For he was numbered with us:** . . . one of our number, *Williams* . . . Judas was one of us twelve, *Beck* . . . he was enumerated with us, *Fenton.*

**and had obtained part of this ministry:** . . . and received his portion in, *ASV* . . . and having had his part allotted him in this work of ours, *TCNT* . . . obtained the inheritance of this service, *Sawyer* . . . was alloted his share, *Adams* . . . actually sharing, *JB* . . . his alloted share, *Montgomery.*

**18. Now this man purchased a field with the reward of iniquity:** . . . acquired a field, *HBIE* . . . bought a farm, *Fenton* . . . had bought a piece of land with the payment for his treachery, *TCNT* . . . the wages of crime, *Berkeley* . . . the price of his villainy, *NEB* . . . the wages of injustice, *Concordant* . . . wages of sin, *Murdock* . . . reward of unrighteousness, *Young* . . . which he took for his treachery, *Williams* . . . the money he got for his crime, *Beck* . . . his dishonest money, *SEB.*

**and falling headlong:** . . . and falling from a height, *TCNT* . . . having fallen down head first, *Norlie* . . . fell there face downward, *Williams* . . . having fallen prone (on his face), *PNT.*

**he burst asunder in the midst:** . . . his intestines, *Adams* . . . his body burst open, *TCNT* . . . he was ruptured in the middle, *Norlie* . . . brake asunder in-the-midst, *Rotherham* . . . his body broke in two, *Williams.*

**and all his bowels gushed out:** . . . his intestines gushed out, *Berkeley* . . . all his entrails were poured out, *Murdock* . . . his intestines poured out, *Beck* . . . all his entrails poured out, *JB* . . . he became disembowelled, *PNT.*

**19. And it was known unto all the dwellers at Jerusalem:** And it became known, *ASV* . . . Everybody living in Jerusalem heard about it, *Beck.*

**insomuch as that field is called in their proper tongue:** . . . and so the field got its name, in their language, *TCNT.*

**Aceldama, that is to say, The field of blood:** . . . a bloody piece of ground, *Wuest* . . . Blood-Farm, *Fenton* . . . the Bloody Acre, *JB.*

| 1119.22 verb 3sing indic perf mid | 1056.1 conj | 1706.1 prep | 969.3 noun dat sing fem | 5403.3 noun gen pl masc | 1090.45 verb 3sing impr aor pass |
|---|---|---|---|---|---|
| 20. Γέγραπται | γὰρ | ἐν | βίβλῳ | ψαλμῶν, | Γενηθήτω |
| *Gegraptai* | *gar* | *en* | *biblō* | *psalmōn* | *Genēthētō* |
| It has been written | for | in | book | of Psalms, | Let become |

| 3450.9 art nom sing fem | 1871.1 noun nom sing fem | 840.3 prs-pron gen sing | 2032.1 adj nom sing | 2504.1 conj | 3231.1 partic |
|---|---|---|---|---|---|
| ἡ | ἔπαυλις | αὐτοῦ | ἔρημος, | καὶ | μὴ |
| *hē* | *epaulis* | *autou* | *erēmos* | *kai* | *mē* |
| the | homestead | his | desolate, | and | not |

| 1498.17 verb 3sing impr pres act | 3450.5 art nom sing masc | 2700.4 verb nom sing masc part pres act | 1706.1 prep | 840.11 prs-pron dat sing fem | 2504.1 conj |
|---|---|---|---|---|---|
| ἔστω | ὁ | κατοικῶν | ἐν | αὐτῇ. | καί, |
| *estō* | *ho* | *katoikōn* | *en* | *autē* | *kai* |
| let there be | the | dwelling | in | it; | and, |

20.a.**Txt:** 08E,byz.
**Var:** 01א,02A,03B,04C
05D,Lach,Treg,Alf
Word,Tisc,We/Ho,Weis
Sod,UBS/☆

| 3450.12 art acc sing fem | 1968.2 noun acc sing fem | 840.3 prs-pron gen sing | 2956.22 verb 3sing opt aor act | 2956.44 verb 3sing impr aor act |
|---|---|---|---|---|
| Τὴν | ἐπισκοπὴν | αὐτοῦ | ‛ λαβοι | [a☆ λαβέτω ] |
| *Tēn* | *episkopēn* | *autou* | *laboi* | *labetō* |
| the | office | his | let take | [ idem ] |

| 2066.5 adj nom sing masc | 1158.1 verb 3sing indic pres act | 3631.1 partic | 3450.1 art gen pl | 4755.7 verb gen pl masc part aor act |
|---|---|---|---|---|
| ἕτερος. | 21. Δεῖ | οὖν | τῶν | συνελθόντων |
| *heteros* | *Dei* | *oun* | *tōn* | *sunelthontōn* |
| another. | It is necessary | therefore | the | having associated with |

21.a.**Txt:** 01א-corr
04C-corr,08E,byz.
**Var:** 01א-org,02A,03B
04C-org,05D-corr,Lach
Treg,Alf,Tisc,We/Ho
Weis,Sod,UBS/☆

| 2231.3 prs-pron dat 1pl | 433.7 noun gen pl masc | 1706.1 prep | 3820.3 adj dat sing | 5385.3 noun dat sing masc | 1706.1 prep | 3614.3 rel-pron dat sing |
|---|---|---|---|---|---|---|
| ἡμῖν | ἀνδρῶν | ἐν | παντὶ | χρόνῳ | ‛a ἐν ’ | ᾧ |
| *hēmin* | *andrōn* | *en* | *panti* | *chronō* | *en* | *hō* |
| us | men | during | all | time | in | which |

| 1511.3 verb 3sing indic aor act | 2504.1 conj | 1814.3 verb 3sing indic aor act | 1894.1 prep | 2231.4 prs-pron acc 1pl | 3450.5 art nom sing masc |
|---|---|---|---|---|---|
| εἰσῆλθεν | καὶ | ἐξῆλθεν | ἐφ’ | ἡμᾶς | ὁ |
| *eisēlthen* | *kai* | *exēlthen* | *eph’* | *hēmas* | *ho* |
| came in | and | went out | among | us | the |

| 2935.1 noun nom sing masc | 2400.1 name nom masc | 751.10 verb nom sing masc part aor mid | 570.3 prep | 3450.2 art gen sing |
|---|---|---|---|---|
| κύριος | Ἰησοῦς, | 22. ἀρξάμενος | ἀπὸ | τοῦ |
| *kurios* | *Iēsous* | *arxamenos* | *apo* | *tou* |
| Lord | Jesus, | having begun | from | the |

22.a.**Var:** 01א,02A,Tisc

| 902.2 noun gen sing neu | 2464.2 name gen masc | 2175.1 conj | 884.2 conj | 3450.10 art gen sing fem | 2232.1 noun fem |
|---|---|---|---|---|---|
| βαπτίσματος | Ἰωάννου | ‛ ἕως | [a ἄχρι ] | τῆς | ἡμέρας |
| *baptismatos* | *Iōannou* | *heōs* | *achri* | *tēs* | *hēmeras* |
| baptism | of John | until | [ idem ] | the | day |

| 3614.10 rel-pron gen sing fem | 351.6 verb 3sing indic aor pass | 351.8 verb 3sing indic aor pass | 570.1 prep | 2231.2 prs-pron gen 1pl |
|---|---|---|---|---|
| ἧς | ‛ ἀνελήφθη | [☆ ἀνελήμφθη ] | ἀφ’ | ἡμῶν, |
| *hēs* | *anelēphthē* | *anelēmphthē* | *aph’* | *hēmōn* |
| which | he was taken up | [ idem ] | from | us, |

| 3116.3 noun acc sing masc | 3450.10 art gen sing fem | 384.2 noun gen sing fem | 840.3 prs-pron gen sing | 1090.63 verb inf aor mid |
|---|---|---|---|---|
| μάρτυρα | τῆς | ἀναστάσεως | αὐτοῦ | ‛ γενέσθαι |
| *martura* | *tēs* | *anastaseōs* | *autou* | *genesthai* |
| a witness | of | resurrection | his | to become |

**1:20.** Peter's emphasis, however, was on the fulfillment of Psalms 69:25 and 109:8, with special attention to the latter: "His bishopric (overseership, rulership) let another take." The Twelve were chosen by Jesus himself as primary witnesses to His teaching. They had heard His words and sayings again and again as they followed Him from place to place and listened to Him teach. They had the promise also that the Holy Spirit would bring to their remembrance all Jesus said (John 14:26). They would have positions of authority, ruling the 12 tribes of Israel in the coming kingdom (Luke 22:29,30; Matthew 19:28).

It is important to notice also that it was only because Judas became a lost soul for all eternity that it was necessary to replace him. When the apostle James, the brother of the apostle John, was martyred by King Herod Agrippa I, no one was chosen to replace him (12:2). James would rise again at the second coming of Christ and would reign on 1 of the 12 thrones along with the rest of the Twelve in the coming kingdom.

**1:21,22.** Peter then proceeded to lay down the qualifications for the one who would replace Judas. Jesus had chosen the Twelve out of a large group of disciples. Many of these other disciples continued to follow Jesus. Among the 120 in the Upper Room there were some men who had accompanied the Twelve while Jesus went in and out among the people, traveling from place to place, from village to village.

This implies the one chosen would need to be a first-hand witness to the sayings and teachings of Jesus. Jesus did not give brand-new teachings in every one of the many villages He visited on His teaching tours in Galilee, Judea, the Decapolis, and Peraea. He undoubtedly introduced such teachings as are found in the Sermon on the Mount at the place indicated in Matthew's Gospel (chapters 5–7). But there is indication that He also taught these same truths in other places.

It is also evident in many cases that the Gospels condense or give key points of the teaching of Jesus. Often Jesus spent hours teaching, even all day. In line with Old Testament methodology, He undoubtedly used a great deal of repetition to bring emphasis. This methodology also would bring out the same truths by using different words. The audience of Jesus sometimes included Gentiles, especially in the Decapolis and Peraea. People often asked questions. Thus Jesus must have given much explanation. He did to His own disciples. This may help to explain why the wording of the Gospels sometimes differs a little from each other. The Holy Spirit inspired each of the Gospel writers to select out of the actual words of Jesus the terminology that would bring home the truth to the audience to which the particular Gospel was addressed.

It is worth noting also that the apostle Paul had to defend his apostleship, since he was not among this group who heard the sayings of Jesus and since he was not commissioned before the Ascension as a witness to the resurrection of Jesus.

**20. For it is written in the book of Psalms, Let his habitation be desolate:** Let his homestead, *Adams* . . . camp, *JB* . . . dwelling, *TCNT* . . . should not go near his property, *SEB* . . . Let his habitacion be voyde, *Geneva* . . . Let his house be a ruin, *Williams C.K.* . . . May his place be empty, *Everyday.*

**and let no man dwell therein:** And let no one live in it, *TCNT* . . . let no resident be in it, *Murdock* . . . let there be no one living there, *Norlie* . . . No one should live there! *SEB.*

**and his bishoprick let another take:** . . . and His office, *RSV* . . . his office of oversight, *Adams* . . . Let another man replace him as leader, *Everyday* . . . let another person of a different character take, *Wuest* . . . His work, *Weymouth* . . . His supervision, *Concordant* . . . let another take his service, *Murdock* . . . Let someone else take his position, *Goodspeed* . . . let a different one take, *Rotherham* . . . his overseership, *Darby.*

**21. Wherefore of these men which have companied with us:** It is necessary, therefore, that of the men who have been with us, *Weymouth* . . . This person must be one...who has been associated with our company, *Noli* . . . who have been associated, *Williams* . . . who have been in our society, *Williams C.K.*

**all the time that the Lord Jesus went in and out among us:** . . . the whole time...Jesus was traveling, *JB* . . . moved about among us, *TCNT* . . . who were part of our group, *Everyday.*

**22. Beginning from the baptism of John:** . . . during all the time the Lord Jesus was with us, *Everyday* . . . from his baptism by John, *TCNT.*

**unto that same day that he was taken up from us:** . . . down to the day on which he was taken up away from us, *TCNT* . . . to the day of his Ascension, *Noli* . . . unto His ascension, *ET.*

**must one be ordained to be a witness with us of his resurrection:** . . . must one become a witness, *ASV* . . . someone must be found to join us as a witness, *TCNT* . . . must be an eyewitness, *Phillips* . . . as a witness to, *Noli.*

## Acts 1:23

| 4713.1 prep | 2231.3 prs-pron dat 1pl | 4713.1 prep | 2231.3 prs-pron dat 1pl | 1090.63 verb inf aor mid | 1518.4 num card acc masc |
|---|---|---|---|---|---|
| σὺν | ἡμῖν | [☆ σὺν | ἡμῖν | γενέσθαι ] | ἕνα |
| *sun* | *hēmin* | *sun* | *hēmin* | *genesthai* | *hena* |
| with | us | [ with | us | to be ] | one |

| 3642.2 dem-pron gen pl | 2504.1 conj | 2449.5 verb 3pl indic aor act | 1411.3 num card | 2473.1 name masc | 3450.6 art acc sing masc |
|---|---|---|---|---|---|
| τούτων. | 23. Καὶ | ἔστησαν | δύο, | Ἰωσὴφ | τὸν |
| *toutōn* | *Kai* | *estēsan* | *duo* | *Iōsēph* | *ton* |
| of these. | And | they set forth | two, | Joseph | the |

| 2535.29 verb sing part pres mid | 917.1 name acc masc | 917.2 name acc masc | 3614.5 rel-pron nom sing masc |
|---|---|---|---|
| καλούμενον | ‘ Βαρσαβᾶν, | [☆ Βαρσαββᾶν, ] | ὃς |
| *kaloumenon* | *Barsaban* | *Barsabban* | *hos* |
| being called | Barsabas, | [ idem ] | who |

| 1926.11 verb 3sing indic aor pass | 2434.1 name nom masc | 2504.1 conj | 3131.1 name acc masc | 3131.2 name acc masc |
|---|---|---|---|---|
| ἐπεκλήθη | Ἰοῦστος, | καὶ | ‘ Ματθίαν. | [☆ Μαθθίαν. ] |
| *epeklēthē* | *Ioustos* | *kai* | *Matthian* | *Maththian* |
| was called | Justus, | and | Matthias. | [ idem ] |

24.a.**Txt:** 08E,byz.Sod
**Var:** 01ℵ,02A,03B,04C 05D,Lach,Treg,Alf Word,Tisc,We/Ho,Weis UBS/☆

| 2504.1 conj | 4195.25 verb nom pl masc part aor mid | 1500.3 verb indic aor act | 1500.28 verb 3pl indic aor act | 4622.1 prs-pron nom 2sing |
|---|---|---|---|---|
| 24. καὶ | προσευξάμενοι | ‘ εἶπον, | [a☆ εἶπαν, ] | Σὺ |
| *kai* | *proseuxamenoi* | *eipon* | *eipan* | *Su* |
| And | having prayed | they said, | [ idem ] | You |

| 2935.5 noun voc sing masc | 2560.2 noun voc sing masc | 3820.4 adj gen pl | 320.2 verb 2sing impr aor act | 1523.2 prep gen |
|---|---|---|---|---|
| κύριε, | καρδιογνῶστα | πάντων, | ἀνάδειξον | ‘ ἐκ |
| *kurie* | *kardiognōsta* | *pantōn* | *anadeixon* | *ek* |
| Lord, | knower of the hearts | of all, | show | of |

| 3642.2 dem-pron gen pl | 3450.1 art gen pl | 1411.3 num card | 1518.4 num card acc masc | 3614.6 rel-pron acc sing masc | 1573.2 verb 2sing indic aor mid |
|---|---|---|---|---|---|
| τούτων | τῶν | δύο | ἕνα | ὃν | ἐξελέξω |
| *toutōn* | *tōn* | *duo* | *hena* | *hon* | *exelexō* |
| these | the | two | one | which | you chose |

| 3614.6 rel-pron acc sing masc | 1573.2 verb 2sing indic aor mid | 1523.2 prep gen | 3642.2 dem-pron gen pl | 3450.1 art gen pl | 1411.3 num card |
|---|---|---|---|---|---|
| [☆ ὃν | ἐξελέξω | ἐκ | τούτων | τῶν | δύο |
| *hon* | *exelexō* | *ek* | *toutōn* | *tōn* | *duo* |
| [ which | you chose | of | these | the | two |

25.a.**Txt:** 01ℵ,04C-corr 08E,33,byz.
**Var:** p74,02A,03B 04C-org,05D,044,Lach Treg,Alf,Tisc,We/Ho Weis,Sod,UBS/☆

| 1518.4 num card acc masc | 2956.31 verb inf aor act | 3450.6 art acc sing masc | 2792.3 noun acc sing masc | 4964.4 noun acc sing masc |
|---|---|---|---|---|
| ἕνα ] | 25. λαβεῖν | τὸν | ‘ κλῆρον | [a☆ τόπον ] |
| *hena* | *labein* | *ton* | *klēron* | *topon* |
| one ] | to receive | the | part | [ place ] |

| 3450.10 art gen sing fem | 1242.2 noun gen sing fem | 3642.10 dem-pron gen sing fem | 2504.1 conj | 645.1 noun gen sing fem | 1523.1 prep gen |
|---|---|---|---|---|---|
| τῆς | διακονίας | ταύτης | καὶ | ἀποστολῆς, | ‘ ἐξ |
| *tēs* | *diakonias* | *tautēs* | *kai* | *apostolēs* | *ex* |
| of the | ministry | this | and | apostleship, | from |

25.b.**Txt:** 08E,byz.
**Var:** 01ℵ,02A,03B,04C 05D,33,Lach,Treg,Alf Word,Tisc,We/Ho,Weis Sod,UBS/☆

| 570.1 prep | 3614.10 rel-pron gen sing fem | 3707.4 verb 3sing indic aor act | 2430.1 name nom masc | 4057.29 verb inf aor pass |
|---|---|---|---|---|
| [b☆ ἀφ' ] | ἧς | παρέβη | Ἰούδας, | πορευθῆναι |
| *aph'* | *hēs* | *parebē* | *Ioudas* | *poreuthēnai* |
| [ idem ] | which | fell | Judas, | to go |

He defended his apostleship in three ways. First, in Galatians 1:11,12,16 he declared he did not receive his gospel from man but by revelation of Jesus Christ. Some believe this took place during Paul's 3 years in Arabia. Paul thus claimed to be a *firsthand* witness to the teachings and sayings of Jesus. In fact, he gave one saying of Jesus not recorded in the four Gospels (Acts 20:35). Second, Paul defended his apostleship by declaring he was a *firsthand* witness to the resurrection of Jesus, even though the appearance of Jesus to him was after the Ascension (1 Corinthians 15:8). He was personally commissioned by Jesus to be an apostle. Third, God wrought apostolic miracles through him (2 Corinthians 12:11,12).

It is probable also that the qualifications set down by Peter fitted best those who were among the 70 Jesus sent out (Luke 10:1-20). They were directly commissioned by Jesus to heal the sick and proclaim the Kingdom.

**1:23.** Peter laid down the conditions, but the people made the choice. Two men met the conditions best. One was Joseph named Barsabas ("son of the Sabbath," born on the Sabbath) who, like so many Jews, had a Roman name, Justus. The other was Matthias. Eusebius, the third-century church historian, says he was indeed one of the Seventy sent out in Luke 10:1.

**1:24.** To make the choice between Joseph Barsabas and Matthias, the apostles first prayed. They knew they needed divine guidance. They did not attempt to make the decision on the basis of their own reasoning or wisdom. In their prayer they addressed Jesus as Lord. This indicated their recognition of Jesus as the divine Lord, truly God as well as truly man. They recognized too that they could not make the decision on the basis of the outward appearance or apparent qualifications of these men. They needed the help of the One who knows the hearts of everyone. Some note that this verse lays down an important principle in understanding election: God's sovereign election takes into consideration the heart of the individual whom He chooses.

They wanted Jesus to make the choice also because He had chosen them. When Jesus told the Twelve, "Ye have not chosen me, but I have chosen you" (John 15:16), He was not talking of their salvation, but of their ministry as apostles. Actually, no Christian has the right to follow his own desires, inclinations, dreams, or fantasies in order to decide what kind of ministry he would like to pursue. Just as the Holy Spirit distributes gifts as He wills (1 Corinthians 12:11), so Jesus alone knows enough about each believer's heart, nature, and the future, to know where he can fit best into His purpose and plan.

**1:25.** So Jesus alone could know which of the two was His choice for this ministry, or service, and this apostleship (the office of apostle from which Judas fell).

**23. And they appointed two:** At that, *NAB* . . . And they put forward two, *RSV* . . . Then they nominated two men, *Williams* . . . they proposed two, *Goodspeed, Noli, Noyes* . . . Having nominated two candidates, *JB* . . . brought two men in front of them, *NLT* . . . They put the names of two men before the group, *NCV.*

**Joseph called Barsabas:** . . . also called Barsabbas Justus, *NLT.*

**who was surnamed Justus:** . . . was known as, *ET.*

**and Matthias:** The other was, *NCV.*

**24. And they prayed, and said:** Then the followers prayed, *NLT* . . . and they offered this prayer, *TCNT.*

**Thou, Lord, which knowest the hearts of all men:** . . . knower of all hearts, *Berkeley* . . . Heart-knower, *Adams* . . . you know the minds of everyone, *Everyday* . . . you read the hearts of men, *NAB.*

**shew whether of these two thou hast chosen:** . . . show of these two the one whom thou hast chosen, *ASV* . . . Make known to us which of these two you choose, *NAB* . . . make clear which one of these two, *Berkeley* . . . thou didst select, *Hanson* . . . manifest, *Murdock.*

**25. That he may take part of this ministry and apostleship:** . . . to take the place in this ministry, *RSV* . . . this apostolic ministry, *Kleist, NAB* . . . to take a share in this service as an apostle, *Williams* . . . to serve in this office of apostle, *Beck* . . . to succeed to this apostolic service, *TNT* . . . to take the place of this dispensation, *Concordant* . . . as servant and apostle, *Williams C.K.* . . . and be a missionary, *NLT.*

**from which Judas by transgression fell:** . . . replacing Judas, who deserted the cause, *NAB* . . . from which Judas broke away, *Murdock* . . . Judas went aside, *Rotherham* . . . Judas went astray, *Fenton* . . . Judas abandoned, *JB, TNT* . . . Judas forfeited, *Phillips* . . . Judas fell from, *Williams C.K.* . . . Judas turned away from it, *Everyday* . . . Judas has fallen away, *Noli* . . . Judas left, *Goodspeed* . . . Judas lost his place...because of sin, *NLT.*

## Acts 1:26

| **1519.1** prep | **3450.6** art acc sing masc | **4964.4** noun acc sing masc | **3450.6** art acc sing masc | **2375.4** adj sing | **2504.1** conj | **1319.17** verb 3pl indic aor act |
|---|---|---|---|---|---|---|
| εἰς | τὸν | τόπον | τὸν | ἴδιον. | **26.** Καὶ | ἔδωκαν |
| *eis* | *ton* | *topon* | *ton* | *idion* | *Kai* | *edōkan* |
| to | the | place | the | his own. | And | they gave |

26.a.**Txt:** 05D-org,08E 044,1241,byz.it.Gries Word
**Var:** 01ℵ,02A,03B,04C 05D-corr,33,sa.bo.Lach Treg,Alf,Tisc,We/Ho Weis,Sod,UBS/☆

| **2792.5** noun acc pl masc | **840.1** prs-pron gen pl | **840.2** prs-pron dat pl | **2504.1** conj | **3959.5** verb 3sing indic aor act |
|---|---|---|---|---|
| κλήρους | ʻ αὐτῶν, | [a☆ αὐτοῖς, ] | καὶ | ἔπεσεν |
| *klērous* | *autōn* | *autois* | *kai* | *epesen* |
| lots | their, | [ to them ] | and | fell |

| **3450.5** art nom sing masc | **2792.1** noun nom sing masc | **1894.3** prep | **3131.1** name acc masc | **3131.2** name acc masc | **2504.1** conj |
|---|---|---|---|---|---|
| ὁ | κλῆρος | ἐπὶ | ʻ Ματθίαν, | [☆ Μαθθίαν, ] | καὶ |
| *ho* | *klēros* | *epi* | *Matthian* | *Maththian* | *kai* |
| the | lot | on | Matthias, | [ idem ] | and |

| **4636.1** verb 3sing indic aor pass | **3196.3** prep | **3450.1** art gen pl | **1717.1** num card | **646.5** noun gen pl masc |
|---|---|---|---|---|
| συγκατεψηφίσθη | μετὰ | τῶν | ἕνδεκα | ἀποστόλων. |
| *sunkatepsēphisthē* | *meta* | *tōn* | *hendeka* | *apostolōn* |
| he was numbered | with | the | eleven | apostles. |

| **2504.1** conj | **1706.1** prep | **3450.3** art dat sing | **4696.1** verb inf pres mid | **3450.12** art acc sing fem | **2232.4** noun acc sing fem |
|---|---|---|---|---|---|
| **2:1.** Καὶ | ἐν | τῷ | συμπληροῦσθαι | τὴν | ἡμέραν |
| *Kai* | *en* | *tō* | *sumplērousthai* | *tēn* | *hēmeran* |
| And | during | the | to be completed | of the | day |

| **3450.10** art gen sing fem | **3868.1** noun gen sing fem | **1498.37** verb 3pl indic imperf act | **533.4** adj nom pl masc | **3524.1** adv |
|---|---|---|---|---|
| τῆς | πεντηκοστῆς | ἦσαν | ʻ ἅπαντες | ὁμοθυμαδὸν |
| *tēs* | *pentēkostēs* | *ēsan* | *hapantes* | *homothumadon* |
|  | of Pentecost | they were | all | with one accord |

1.a.**Txt:** byz.Gries,Word
**Var:** 01ℵ-corr,02A,03B 04C-org,Lach,Treg,Alf Tisc,We/Ho,Weis,Sod UBS/☆

| **3820.7** adj nom pl masc | **3537.1** adv | **1894.3** prep | **3450.16** art sing neu | **840.15** prs-pron sing neu | **2504.1** conj |
|---|---|---|---|---|---|
| [a☆ πάντες | ὁμοῦ ] | ἐπὶ | τὸ | αὐτό. | **2.** καὶ |
| *pantes* | *homou* | *epi* | *to* | *auto* | *kai* |
| [ all | together ] | in | the | same place. | And |

| **1090.33** verb 3sing indic aor mid | **862.1** adv | **1523.2** prep gen | **3450.2** art gen sing | **3636.2** noun gen sing masc | **2256.1** noun sing neu |
|---|---|---|---|---|---|
| ἐγένετο | ἄφνω | ἐκ | τοῦ | οὐρανοῦ | ἦχος |
| *egeneto* | *aphnō* | *ek* | *tou* | *ouranou* | *ēchos* |
| came | suddenly | out of | the | heaven | a sound |

| **5450.1** conj | **5179.25** verb gen sing fem part pres mid | **4017.1** noun gen sing fem | **965.1** adj gen sing fem | **2504.1** conj | **3997.3** verb 3sing indic aor act |
|---|---|---|---|---|---|
| ὥσπερ | φερομένης | πνοῆς | βιαίας, | καὶ | ἐπλήρωσεν |
| *hōsper* | *pheromenēs* | *pnoēs* | *biaias* | *kai* | *eplērōsen* |
| as | of rushing | a wind | violent, | and | filled |

| **3513.1** adj sing | **3450.6** art acc sing masc | **3486.4** noun acc sing masc | **3619.1** adv | **1498.37** verb 3pl indic imperf act | **2493.10** verb nom pl masc part pres mid |
|---|---|---|---|---|---|
| ὅλον | τὸν | οἶκον | οὗ | ἦσαν | ʻ καθήμενοι· |
| *holon* | *ton* | *oikon* | *hou* | *ēsan* | *kathēmenoi* |
| whole | the | house | where | they were | sitting |

2.a.**Var:** 04C,05D,Lach

| **2493.10** verb nom pl masc part pres mid | **2504.1** conj | **3571.22** verb 3pl indic aor pass | **840.2** prs-pron dat pl |
|---|---|---|---|
| [a☆ καθήμενοι· ] | **3.** καὶ | ὤφθησαν | αὐτοῖς |
| *kathēmenoi* | *kai* | *ōphthēsan* | *autois* |
| [ idem. ] | And | there appeared | to them |

They also recognized that Judas fell away by his own choice and by his deliberate, rebellious sinning. He went to his own place, that is, the place he had chosen, the place of punishment.

**1:26.** They used the Old Testament method of casting lots, probably following the precedent of Proverbs 16:33. They believed God would overrule the laws of chance and show His choice by this means. The Book of Acts never mentions the use of this method again, however. After Pentecost they relied on the Holy Spirit for guidance.

Some modern writers question whether Peter and the others were right in doing this and say Paul should have been chosen. But he was the apostle to the Gentiles. Though He was equal in calling and authority to the others, he never included himself with the Twelve (1 Corinthians 15:7,8).

Actually, the Bible states without adverse comment that Matthias was numbered with the 11 apostles. In 6:2 he is still included with the Twelve. Though he is not mentioned again by name, neither are most of the other apostles.

Because Judas became a lost soul, his replacement was necessary. He had been commissioned. He had the opportunity. But through his own choice he became "the son of perdition," a Hebraistic way of saying he was headed for eternal loss.

**2:1.** On the 50th day after the waving of the sheaf of firstfruits (Leviticus 23:15), the Jews waved two loaves for firstfruits (Leviticus 23:17). Thus this feast of harvest was called *Weeks* (because of the "week" of weeks between) or *Pentecost* ("fiftieth"). Pentecost was now being completed or fulfilled, a word indicating that the period of waiting was coming to an end, and Old Testament prophecies were about to be fulfilled. The Sadducees who controlled the temple took the "sabbath" of Leviticus 23:15 to be the weekly Sabbath after Passover. This made Pentecost occur on a Sunday.

The 120 were still in one accord in one place. The Bible does not name the place, but most believe it was the Upper Room. Others, in view of Peter's statement that it was the third hour of the day (9 a.m.), believe they were in the temple, probably in the Court of the Women. Believers were habitually in the temple at the hours of prayer. One of the roofed colonnades on the edge of the court would have provided a good place for them to gather. (The temple is called a "house" in 7:47.) This would help explain the crowd that gathered after the Spirit was outpoured. (Others believe the Upper Room was open to the street, or that the 120 left the Upper Room.)

**2:2,3.** Suddenly a sound came from heaven like that of a violent rushing wind or tornado. But it was the sound that filled the house and overwhelmed them, not an actual wind.

**that he might go to his own place:** . . . left to go where he belonged, *Beck* . . . to go to his own place, *Adams* . . . and gone to his own doom, *Noli.*

**26. And they gave forth their lots:** Then they drew lots between them, *TCNT* . . . Subsequently, they cast lots, *Noli.*

**and the lot fell upon Matthias:** . . . and so Matthias was chosen, *Beck.*

**and he was numbered with the eleven apostles:** . . . he was added to the number of, *TCNT* . . . elected to work, *Fenton* . . . as one of the twelve apostles, *JB* . . . the Eleven Missionaries, *Klingensmith* . . . was considered equally an apostle, *Phillips* . . . So he took his place, *Noli.*

**1. And when the day of Pentecost was fully come:** During the celebration, *Fenton* . . . In the course of the Harvest Thanksgiving-day, *TCNT* . . . when the actual day, *Phillips* . . . When the fyftith daye, *Tyndale* . . . When Pentecost day came round, *JB* . . . being fulfilled, *Young* . . . had arrived, *Adams* . . . was now accomplishing, *Darby* . . . were drawing to a close, *Confraternity.*

**they were all with one accord in one place:** . . . they were all together in one place, *RSV* . . . the disciples had all met together, *TCNT* . . . unitedly, *Berkeley* . . . assembled together, *Murdock* . . . harmoniously assembled, *Fenton* . . . at the same place, *Young* . . . for the same object, *Rotherham* . . . and of one mind, *Norlie.*

**2. And suddenly there came a sound from heaven:** . . . there came suddenly out of the heaven, *Young* . . . from the sky, *Fenton* . . . came from the heavens a noise, *TCNT* . . . a roaring, *Berkeley.*

**as of a rushing mighty wind:** . . . like that of a strong wind coming nearer and nearer, *TCNT* . . . as of a rushing violent wind, *Campbell* . . . as a violent carrying blast, *Concordant* . . . like a terrific blast of wind, *Williams* . . . violent tempest-blast, *Fenton* . . . like a roar, *Norlie* . . . a violent impetuous blowing, *Darby.*

**and it filled all the house where they were sitting:** . . . entire house, *JB* . . . was full of it, *BB.*

# Acts 2:4

| **1260.4** verb nom pl fem part pres mid | **1094.5** noun nom pl fem | **5448.1** adv | **4300.2** noun gen sing neu | **2495.3** verb 3sing indic aor act |
|---|---|---|---|---|
| διαμεριζόμεναι | γλῶσσαι | ὡσεὶ | πυρός, | ʻ ἐκάθισεν |
| *diamerizomenai* | *glōssai* | *hōsei* | *puros* | *ekathisen* |
| being distributed | tongues | as | of fire, | sat |

3.a.**Txt:** 02A,04C-corr 08E,byz.Sod
**Var:** 01ℵ,03B,Lach Treg,Tisc,We/Ho,Weis UBS/☆

| **4885.1** conj | **2504.1** conj | **2495.3** verb 3sing indic aor act | **1894.1** prep | **1518.4** num card acc masc | **1524.1** adj sing |
|---|---|---|---|---|---|
| τε | [a☆ καὶ | ἐκάθισεν ] | ἐφ’ | ἕνα | ἕκαστον |
| *te* | *kai* | *ekathisen* | *eph'* | *hena* | *hekaston* |
| and | [ and | sat ] | upon | one | each |

4.a.**Txt:** 03B-corr,04C byz.Sod
**Var:** 01ℵ,02A,03B-org 05D,08E,Lach,Treg Tisc,We/Ho,Weis UBS/☆

| **840.1** prs-pron gen pl | **2504.1** conj | **3990.5** verb 3pl indic aor pass | **533.4** adj nom pl masc | **3820.7** adj nom pl masc |
|---|---|---|---|---|
| αὐτῶν, | 4. καὶ | ἐπλήσθησαν | ʻ ἅπαντες | [a☆ πάντες ] |
| *autōn* | *kai* | *eplēsthēsan* | *hapantes* | *pantes* |
| of them. | And | they were filled | all | [ idem ] |

| **4011.2** noun gen sing neu | **39.2** adj gen sing | **2504.1** conj | **751.6** verb 3pl indic aor mid | **2953.24** verb inf pres act | **2066.14** adj dat pl fem |
|---|---|---|---|---|---|
| πνεύματος | ἁγίου, | καὶ | ἤρξαντο | λαλεῖν | ἑτέραις |
| *pneumatos* | *hagiou* | *kai* | *ērxanto* | *lalein* | *heterais* |
| with Spirit | Holy, | and | began | to speak | with other |

| **1094.7** noun dat pl fem | **2503.1** conj | **3450.16** art sing neu | **4011.1** noun sing neu | **1319.40** verb 3sing indic imperf act | **840.2** prs-pron dat pl |
|---|---|---|---|---|---|
| γλώσσαις | καθὼς | τὸ | πνεῦμα | ἐδίδου | ʻ αὐτοῖς |
| *glōssais* | *kathōs* | *to* | *pneuma* | *edidou* | *autois* |
| tongues, | as | the | Spirit | was giving | to them |

| **663.2** verb inf pres mid | **663.2** verb inf pres mid | **840.2** prs-pron dat pl | **1498.37** verb 3pl indic imperf act |
|---|---|---|---|
| ἀποφθέγγεσθαι. | [☆ ἀποφθέγγεσθαι | αὐτοῖς. ] | 5. Ἦσαν |
| *apophthengesthai* | *apophthengesthai* | *autois* | *Ēsan* |
| to speak out. | [ to speak out | to them. ] | Were |

5.a.**Txt:** 01ℵ-corr,03B 04C,05D,08E,byz. We/Ho,Sod
**Var:** 01ℵ-org,02A,Tisc Weis,UBS/☆

| **1156.2** conj | **1706.1** prep | **1519.1** prep | **2395.1** name fem | **2700.6** verb nom pl masc part pres act |
|---|---|---|---|---|
| δὲ | ʻ ἐν | [a εἰς ] | Ἱερουσαλὴμ | κατοικοῦντες |
| *de* | *en* | *eis* | *Hierousalēm* | *katoikountes* |
| now | in | [ idem ] | Jerusalem | dwelling |

| **2428.2** name-adj nom pl masc | **433.6** noun nom pl masc | **2107.2** adj nom pl masc | **570.3** prep | **3820.2** adj gen sing | **1477.2** noun gen sing neu |
|---|---|---|---|---|---|
| Ἰουδαῖοι, | ἄνδρες | εὐλαβεῖς | ἀπὸ | παντὸς | ἔθνους |
| *Ioudaioi* | *andres* | *eulabeis* | *apo* | *pantos* | *ethnous* |
| Jews, | men | devout | from | every | nation |

| **3450.1** art gen pl | **5097.3** prep | **3450.6** art acc sing masc | **3636.4** noun acc sing masc | **1090.57** verb gen sing fem part aor mid | **1156.2** conj |
|---|---|---|---|---|---|
| τῶν | ὑπὸ | τὸν | οὐρανόν. | 6. γενομένης | δὲ |
| *tōn* | *hupo* | *ton* | *ouranon* | *genomenēs* | *de* |
| of the | under | the | heaven. | Having arisen | but |

| **3450.10** art gen sing fem | **5292.2** noun gen sing fem | **3642.10** dem-pron gen sing fem | **4755.1** verb 3sing indic aor act | **3450.16** art sing neu | **3988.1** noun sing neu |
|---|---|---|---|---|---|
| τῆς | φωνῆς | ταύτης | συνῆλθεν | τὸ | πλῆθος |
| *tēs* | *phōnēs* | *tautēs* | *sunēlthen* | *to* | *plēthos* |
| the | rumor | of this, | came together | the | multitude |

| **2504.1** conj | **4648.3** verb 3sing indic aor pass | **3617.1** conj | **189.46** verb 3pl indic imperf act | **1518.3** num card nom masc |
|---|---|---|---|---|
| καὶ | συνεχύθη˙ | ὅτι | ἤκουον | εἷς |
| *kai* | *sunechuthē* | *hoti* | *ēkouon* | *heis* |
| and | were confounded, | because | were hearing | one |

The sound of wind would remind them of Old Testament divine manifestations (Exodus 14:21; Job 38:1; 40:6). Thus, the sound of the wind indicated God was about to manifest himself by His Spirit in a special way.

Just as suddenly, cloven tongues looking like flames of fire appeared. "Cloven" means "distributed." What looked like a mass of flames appeared and then broke up, and a single tongue of flame settled on the head of each person. Fire and light are common symbols of the divine presence (as in Exodus 3:2; 19:18).

The fire here signified God's acceptance of the Church body as the temple of the Holy Spirit (1 Corinthians 3:16; Ephesians 2:21,22). It also indicated the acceptance of individual believers as being temples of the Spirit.

Notice also that these signs *preceded* the filling with the Holy Spirit. They were not part of it, nor were they repeated on other occasions when the Spirit was outpoured.

**2:4.** Now that God had acknowledged the Church as the new temple, the next thing was to pour out the Holy Spirit on the members of the Body.

In 1:5 Jesus said, "Ye shall be *baptized* with the Holy Ghost." Here, Luke wrote that the 120 were "filled with the Holy Ghost," in fulfillment of Jesus' promise. In 11:16 Peter connected the outpouring of the Spirit in Caesarea to Jesus' promise that He would baptize in the Spirit. Actually, the Bible uses a variety of terms. It was also a pouring out of the Spirit as Joel prophesied, a receiving and an active taking of the Spirit as a gift (2:38), a falling upon (8:16; 10:44; 11:15), a pouring out of the gift (10:45), and a coming upon (19:6).

As soon as they were filled, the 120 began to speak with other tongues (languages). This speaking came as the Spirit proceeded to give them utterance (to speak out). They spoke, but the words did not come from their mind or thinking. Through the Spirit they spoke out boldly. This is the one sign of the baptism in the Spirit that was repeated (10:44-47; 19:1-7).

**2:5.** "Dwelling" usually implies permanent residence. Many Jews from the dispersion had settled in Jerusalem. But on the Feast of Pentecost many Jews from all over the known world would be there. Actually, more would be present than at Passover, since travel on the Mediterranean was safer at this season.

**2:6.** As the sound of the 120 speaking in tongues became heard, a crowd came from all directions. All were confounded for each kept hearing them speak in his own language. "Own" is emphatic, meaning his own language he used as a child. *Tongue* means a

**3. And there appeared unto them cloven tongues like as of fire:** . . . tongues parting asunder, *ASV* . . . like split tongues, *Adams* . . . tongues of what appeared to be flame, separating, *TCNT* . . . fiery tongues, *Fenton.*

**and it sat upon each of them:** . . . on the head of each person a tongue alighted, *Weymouth* . . . separating and resting on their heads, *Williams* . . . distributing themselves over the assembly, *PNT.*

**4. And they were all filled with the Holy Ghost:** . . . all were controlled by the Holy Spirit, *Wuest.*

**and began to speak with other tongues:** . . . different languages, *Concordant* . . . diverse languages, *Murdock* . . . strange tongues, *TCNT* . . . foreign languages, *Fenton.*

**as the Spirit gave them utterance:** . . . granted them expression, *Berkeley* . . . was giving them to declare, *Young* . . . was giving them to be sounding out, *Rotherham* . . . granted them to utter divine things, *Williams* . . . endowed them with clear expression, *Fenton* . . . gave them the gift of speech, *JB* . . . enabled them, *NIV* . . . gave them words to utter, *PNT* . . . prompted them to speak, *Confraternity* . . . gave them power to proclaim his message, *Phillips.*

**5. And there were dwelling at Jerusalem Jews:** . . . residing in, *PNT* . . . sojourning Jews, *Rotherham.*

**devout men:** God-fearing, *NIV* . . . religious men, *Klingensmith* . . . of deep faith, *Phillips.*

**out of every nation under heaven:** . . . from every part of the world, *Weymouth* . . . from many and distant lands, *Montgomery.*

**6. Now when this was noised abroad:** . . . this sound took place, *Alford* . . . this speaking was heard, *Norlie* . . . this report having been circulated, *Wilson.*

**the multitude came together:** . . . throng, *Rotherham* . . . they came crowding together, *Weymouth* . . . the crowd rushed together, *Williams* . . . they all assembled, *JB* . . . a crowd quickly collected, *Phillips.*

**and were confounded:** . . . confused, *Concordant* . . . thrown

## Acts 2:7

7.a.**Txt:** 01ℵ-corr,02A 04C,08E,byz.sa.bo.Tisc Sod
**Var:** 03B,05D,Lach,Alf We/Ho,Weis,UBS/☆

7.b.**Txt:** 04C-corr,05D 08E,1241,1739,byz.
**Var:** p74,01ℵ,02A,03B 04C-org,sa.bo.Lach,Treg Alf,Tisc,We/Ho,Weis Sod,UBS/☆

7.c.**Txt:** p74,02A,04C 044,byz.Gries,Word,Sod
**Var1:** 01ℵ,05D,08E 07E,Lach,Tisc
**Var2:** 03B,Treg,Alf We/Ho,Weis,UBS/☆

7.d.**Var:** 01ℵ,02A 03B-corr,04C,05D,Lach Alf,Tisc,Sod

| **1524.3** adj nom sing masc | **3450.11** art dat sing fem | **2375.10** adj dat sing fem | **1252.1** noun dat sing fem | **2953.17** verb gen pl masc part pres act | **840.1** prs-pron gen pl |
|---|---|---|---|---|---|
| ἕκαστος | τῇ | ἰδίᾳ | διαλέκτῳ | λαλούντων | αὐτῶν. |
| *hekastos* | *tē* | *idia* | *dialektō* | *lalountōn* | *autōn* |
| each | in the | his own | language | speaking | them. |

| **1822.8** verb 3pl indic imperf mid | **1156.2** conj | **3820.7** adj nom pl masc | **2504.1** conj | **2273.17** verb 3pl indic imperf act |
|---|---|---|---|---|
| 7. ἐξίσταντο | δὲ | ⸂a πάντες ⸃ | καὶ | ἐθαύμαζον, |
| *existanto* | *de* | *pantes* | *kai* | *ethaumazon* |
| Were amazed | and | all | and | were marveling, |

| **2978.16** verb nom pl masc part pres act | **4242.1** prep | **238.3** prs-pron acc pl masc | **3620.2** partic | **3620.1** partic |
|---|---|---|---|---|
| λέγοντες | ⸂b πρὸς | ἀλλήλους, ⸃ | ⸂ Οὐκ | [1c☆ Οὐχ |
| *legontes* | *pros* | *allēlous* | *Ouk* | *Ouch* |
| saying | to | one another, | Not | [ idem |

| **3644.1** adv | **1481.20** verb 2sing impr aor mid | **3820.7** adj nom pl masc | **533.4** adj nom pl masc | **3642.7** dem-pron nom pl masc |
|---|---|---|---|---|
| 2 οὐχὶ ] | ἰδοὺ | ⸂ πάντες | [d ἅπαντες ] | οὗτοί |
| *ouchi* | *idou* | *pantes* | *hapantes* | *houtoi* |
| idem ] | lo | all | [ idem ] | these |

| **1498.7** verb 3pl indic pres act | **3450.7** art nom pl masc | **2953.16** verb nom pl masc part pres act | **1050.3** name-adj nom pl masc | **2504.1** conj | **4316.1** adv |
|---|---|---|---|---|---|
| εἰσιν | οἱ | λαλοῦντες | Γαλιλαῖοι; | 8. καὶ | πῶς |
| *eisin* | *hoi* | *lalountes* | *Galilaioi* | *kai* | *pōs* |
| are | the | speaking | Galileans? | and | how |

| **2231.1** prs-pron nom 1pl | **189.6** verb 1pl indic pres act | **1524.3** adj nom sing masc | **3450.11** art dat sing fem | **2375.10** adj dat sing fem | **1252.1** noun dat sing fem |
|---|---|---|---|---|---|
| ἡμεῖς | ἀκούομεν | ἕκαστος | τῇ | ἰδίᾳ | διαλέκτῳ |
| *hēmeis* | *akouomen* | *hekastos* | *tē* | *idia* | *dialektō* |
| we | are hearing | each | in the | own | language |

| **2231.2** prs-pron gen 1pl | **1706.1** prep | **3614.11** rel-pron dat sing fem | **1074.14** verb 1pl indic aor pass | **3796.1** name nom pl masc |
|---|---|---|---|---|
| ἡμῶν | ἐν | ᾗ | ἐγεννήθημεν; | 9. Πάρθοι |
| *hēmōn* | *en* | *hē* | *egennēthēmen* | *Parthoi* |
| our | in | which | we were born, | Parthians |

| **2504.1** conj | **3238.1** name nom pl masc | **2504.1** conj | **1626.1** name nom pl masc | **2504.1** conj | **3450.7** art nom pl masc |
|---|---|---|---|---|---|
| καὶ | Μῆδοι | καὶ | Ἐλαμῖται, | καὶ | οἱ |
| *kai* | *Mēdoi* | *kai* | *Elamitai* | *kai* | *hoi* |
| and | Medes | and | Elamites, | and | the |

| **2700.6** verb nom pl masc part pres act | **3450.12** art acc sing fem | **3188.2** name acc fem | **2424.4** name acc fem | **4885.1** conj |
|---|---|---|---|---|
| κατοικοῦντες | τὴν | Μεσοποταμίαν, | Ἰουδαίαν | τε |
| *katoikountes* | *tēn* | *Mesopotamian* | *Ioudaian* | *te* |
| inhabiting | | Mesopotamia, | Judea | both |

| **2504.1** conj | **2558.2** name acc fem | **4054.2** name acc masc | **2504.1** conj | **3450.12** art acc sing fem | **767.4** name acc fem |
|---|---|---|---|---|---|
| καὶ | Καππαδοκίαν, | Πόντον | καὶ | τὴν | Ἀσίαν, |
| *kai* | *Kappadokian* | *Ponton* | *kai* | *tēn* | *Asian* |
| and | Cappadocia, | Pontus | and | | Asia, |

| **5271.2** name acc fem | **4885.1** conj | **2504.1** conj | **3690.2** name acc fem | **125.4** name acc fem | **2504.1** conj |
|---|---|---|---|---|---|
| 10. Φρυγίαν | τε | καὶ | Παμφυλίαν, | Αἴγυπτον | καὶ |
| *Phrugian* | *te* | *kai* | *Pamphulian* | *Aigupton* | *kai* |
| Phrygia | both | and | Pamphylia, | Egypt | and |

distinct language. They were not speaking merely in a variety of Galilean or Aramaic dialects but in a variety of different languages.

**2:7.** The result was total amazement. The listeners were astonished. They were filled with awestruck wonder, for they recognized, perhaps by their clothing, that the 120 were Galileans. They could not understand how this was happening.

**2:8.** Some suppose the 120 were all really speaking the same language and by a miracle of hearing the multitude were made to hear it in their mother tongue. But verses 6 and 7 are too specific for that. Each man heard them *speak* in his own dialect without any Galilean accent. There would have been no surprise if the 120 had spoken in Aramaic or Greek.

Others suppose the 120 really spoke in tongues but no one understood them. They propose that the Spirit interpreted unknown tongues in the ears of the hearers into their own language. But verses 6 and 7 rule that out too. The 120 spoke in real languages which were actually understood by a variety of people from a variety of places. This gave witness to the universality of the Gift and to the universality and unity of the Church.

**2:9.** The places named were in all directions, but they also follow a general order (with exceptions), beginning in the northeast. Parthia was east of the Roman Empire, between the Caspian Sea and the Persian Gulf, in the southern part of Persia. Mesopotamia was the ancient Babylonia, mostly outside the Roman Empire. Babylon had a large Jewish population in New Testament times and later became a center for orthodox Judaism (1 Peter 5:13). There is evidence that the listeners included members of all 12 tribes. (Some of the northern 10 tribes settled in Media and later joined the synagogues. Compare James 1:1; see also Acts 26:7.)

Judea is mentioned because Jews there still spoke Hebrew and would have been amazed at the lack of a Galilean accent. It is also possible that Luke included all of Syria with Judea, in fact, all the territory of David and Solomon from the Euphrates river to the River of Egypt (Genesis 15:18). Cappadocia was a large Roman province in northern Asia Minor on the Black Sea. Asia was the Roman province comprising the western third of Asia Minor.

**2:10.** Phrygia was an ethnic district, part of which was in the province of Asia and part in Galatia. Pamphylia was a Roman province on the south coast of Asia Minor. Egypt to the south had a large Jewish population. The Jewish philosopher Philo said in A.D. 38 that about a million Jews lived there, many in Alexandria. Cyrene was a district west of Egypt on the Mediterranean coast.

Others present in Jerusalem were strangers (sojourners, temporary residents) in Jerusalem, citizens of Rome, including Jews

into confusion, *Rotherham* . . . amazed, *Weymouth* . . . they were bewildered, *RSV* . . . agitated, *Murdock* . . . dumbfounded, *Beck* . . . in great excitement, *Williams.*

**because that every man heard them speak in his own language:** . . . because each of them heard the disciples speaking, *TCNT* . . . they were hearing words in their own language, *NLT* . . . his own vernacular, *Concordant* . . . proper dialect, *Young* . . . peculiar dialect, *Fenton* . . . native language, *MLNT.*

**7. And they were all amazed and marvelled:** They were beside themselves with wonder, *Weymouth* . . . The whole occurrence astonished them...in utter amazement, *NAB* . . . They were surprised and wondered about it, *NLT* . . . utterly amazed, *TCNT* . . . were delighted, *Fenton* . . . were perfectly amazed and...in their astonishment, *Goodspeed.*

**saying to one another:** . . . and kept saying in their astonishment, *TCNT* . . . They asked, *NAB.*

**Behold, are not all these which speak Galileans?:** Look! *Adams* . . . all these men who are speaking, *Goodspeed.*

**8. And how hear we every man in our own tongue, wherein we were born?:** How does it happen, *JB* . . . how can it be possible...our own private dialect, *Wuest* . . . how is it that each of us hears his own native tongue? *Goodspeed* . . . we each hear them in our...speech in which we were born? *MLNT* . . . our own language, *ASV.*

**9. Parthians, and Medes, and Elamites:** We are, *NAB, NLT* . . . Some of us are Parthians, some Medes, some Elamites, *TCNT.*

**and the dwellers in Mesopotamia, and in Judaea, and Cappadocia, in Pontus, and Asia:** . . . and some of us live in Mesopotamia, *TCNT* . . . and from the countries of, *NLT* . . . residents of, *Goodspeed* . . . inhabitants of Mesopotamia, *Weymouth* . . . the province of Asia, *NAB.*

**10. Phrygia, and Pamphylia, in Egypt, and in parts of Libya about Cyrene:** Egypt and the parts of Libya belonging to Cyrene,

| 3450.17 art pl neu | 3183.4 noun pl neu | 3450.10 art gen sing fem | 3007.1 name gen fem | 3450.10 art gen sing fem | 2567.3 prep | 2930.1 name acc fem |
|---|---|---|---|---|---|---|
| τὰ | μέρη | τῆς | Λιβύης | τῆς | κατὰ | Κυρήνην, |
| *ta* | *merē* | *tēs* | *Libuēs* | *tēs* | *kata* | *Kurēnēn* |
| the | parts | | of Libya | which is | about | Cyrene, |

| 2504.1 conj | 3450.7 art nom pl masc | 1912.1 verb nom pl masc part pres act | 4371.3 name-adj nom pl masc | 2428.2 name-adj nom pl masc | 4885.1 conj |
|---|---|---|---|---|---|
| καὶ | οἱ | ἐπιδημοῦντες | Ῥωμαῖοι, | Ἰουδαῖοί | τε |
| *kai* | *hoi* | *epidēmountes* | *Rhōmaioi* | *Ioudaioi* | *te* |
| and | the | sojourning | Romans, | Jews | both |

| 2504.1 conj | 4198.2 noun nom pl masc | | 2886.1 name nom pl masc | 2504.1 conj | 684.1 name nom pl masc | 189.6 verb 1pl indic pres act |
|---|---|---|---|---|---|---|
| καὶ | προσήλυτοι, | 11. | Κρῆτες | καὶ | Ἄραβες, | ἀκούομεν |
| *kai* | *prosēlutoi* | | *Krētes* | *kai* | *Arabes* | *akouomen* |
| and | proselytes, | | Cretans | and | Arabians, | we hear |

| 2953.17 verb gen pl masc part pres act | 840.1 prs-pron gen pl | 3450.14 art dat pl fem | 2233.8 adj dat 1pl fem | 1094.7 noun dat pl fem |
|---|---|---|---|---|
| λαλούντων | αὐτῶν | ταῖς | ἡμετέραις | γλώσσαις |
| *lalountōn* | *autōn* | *tais* | *hēmeterais* | *glōssais* |
| speaking | them | in the | our own | tongues |

| 3450.17 art pl neu | 3138.1 adj pl neu | 3450.2 art gen sing | 2296.2 noun gen sing masc | | 1822.8 verb 3pl indic imperf mid | 1156.2 conj |
|---|---|---|---|---|---|---|
| τὰ | μεγαλεῖα | τοῦ | θεοῦ; | 12. | Ἐξίσταντο | δὲ |
| *ta* | *megaleia* | *tou* | *theou* | | *Existanto* | *de* |
| the | great things | | of God? | | Were amazed | and |

12.a.**Txt:** 04C,05D,08E byz.Gries,Lach,Word Sod **Var:** 01ℵ,02A,03B,Treg Alf,Tisc,We/Ho,Weis UBS/☆

| 3820.7 adj nom pl masc | 2504.1 conj | 1274.2 verb 3pl indic imperf act | 1274.4 verb 3pl indic imperf mid | 241.4 adj nom sing masc |
|---|---|---|---|---|
| πάντες | καὶ | ‹ διηπόρουν, | [a διηπορούντο, ] | ἄλλος |
| *pantes* | *kai* | *diēporoun* | *diēporounto* | *allos* |
| all | and | were in perplexity | [ idem ] | other |

| 4242.1 prep | 241.5 adj acc sing masc | 2978.16 verb nom pl masc part pres act | 4949.9 intr-pron sing neu | 300.1 partic | 2286.11 verb 3sing opt pres act |
|---|---|---|---|---|---|
| πρὸς | ἄλλον | λέγοντες, | Τί | ‹ ἂν | θέλοι |
| *pros* | *allon* | *legontes* | *Ti* | *an* | *theloi* |
| to | another | saying, | What | | would |

12.b.**Txt:** 08E,byz. **Var:** 02A,03B,04C,05D Lach,Treg,Tisc,We/Ho Weis,Sod,UBS/☆

| 2286.3 verb 3sing indic pres act | 3642.17 dem-pron sing neu | 1498.32 verb inf pres act | | 2066.7 adj nom pl masc | 1156.2 conj |
|---|---|---|---|---|---|
| [b☆ θέλει ] | τοῦτο | εἶναι; | 13. | Ἕτεροι | δὲ |
| *thelei* | *touto* | *einai* | | *Heteroi* | *de* |
| [ wishes ] | this | to be? | | Others | but |

13.a.**Txt:** 08E,byz. **Var:** 01ℵ,02A,03B,04C 05D-corr,Gries,Lach Treg,Alf,Word,Tisc We/Ho,Weis,Sod UBS/☆

| 5348.1 verb nom pl masc part pres act | 1309.1 verb nom pl masc part pres act | 2978.25 verb indic imperf act | 3617.1 conj |
|---|---|---|---|
| ‹ χλευάζοντες | [a☆ διαχλευάζοντες ] | ἔλεγον, | Ὅτι |
| *chleuazontes* | *diachleuazontes* | *elegon* | *Hoti* |
| mocking | [ idem ] | were saying, | |

| 1092.1 noun gen sing neu | 3195.1 verb nom pl masc part perf mid | 1498.7 verb 3pl indic pres act | | 2449.43 verb nom sing masc part aor pass | 1156.2 conj |
|---|---|---|---|---|---|
| Γλεύκους | μεμεστωμένοι | εἰσίν. | 14. | Σταθεὶς | δὲ |
| *Gleukous* | *memestōmenoi* | *eisin* | | *Statheis* | *de* |
| Of new wine | having been filled | they are. | | Having stood up | but |

14.a.**Var:** 01ℵ,02A,03B 05D,Lach,Treg,Alf,Tisc We/Ho,Weis,Sod UBS/☆

| 3450.5 art nom sing masc | 3935.1 name nom masc | 4713.1 prep | 3450.4 art dat pl | 1717.1 num card | 1854.2 verb 3sing indic aor act | 3450.12 art acc sing fem |
|---|---|---|---|---|---|---|
| [a☆+ ὁ ] | Πέτρος | σὺν | τοῖς | ἕνδεκα | ἐπῆρεν | τὴν |
| *ho* | *Petros* | *sun* | *tois* | *hendeka* | *epēren* | *tēn* |
| | Peter | with | the | eleven | lifted up | the |

and proselytes (Gentile converts to Judaism). Full proselytes took circumcision, a self-baptism, and offered a sacrifice to declare their purpose to keep the Jewish law and live as Jews.

**2:11.** Still others were from the island of Crete and from Arabia, the district east and southeast of Palestine.

All these kept hearing in their own languages the wonderful works (the mighty, magnificent, sublime deeds) of God. This may have been in the form of ejaculations of praise to God. No discourse or preaching is implied. There is no record here or elsewhere, however, of the gift of tongues being used as a means of preaching the gospel.

**2:12.** Instead, the hearers were amazed (astounded) and in doubt (perplexed). "What meaneth this?" is literally, "What will this be?" It expresses their total confusion as well as their extreme amazement. They understood the meaning of the words, but not the purpose.

**2:13.** Others apparently did not understand any of the languages, and because they could not understand the meaning they jumped to the conclusion that it had no meaning. Therefore, they proceeded to mock, saying the people were "full of new wine" (sweet wine). "New wine" here is the Greek *gleukous* from which we get our word *glucose,* a name for grape sugar. It is not the ordinary word for new wine and probably represents an intoxicating wine made from a very sweet grape which would have a higher alcoholic content. It would be some time before the grape harvest began in August and real new wine or grape juice would again be available.

Some drinkers do become noisy and this may be what the mockers were thinking of, but one must not suppose there was any sign of the kind of frenzy that marked heathen drunken debauchery. The chief emotion of the 120 was still joy. They had been thanking and praising God in their own language (Luke 24:53), and now the Holy Spirit had given them new languages to praise God. Their hearts were still going out to God in praise, even though they did not understand what they were saying.

**2:14.** When Peter and the 11 other apostles (including Matthias) stood, the whole crowd gave their attention to Peter (the 120 probably stopped speaking in other tongues). Still anointed by the Spirit, he raised his voice and proceeded to "utter forth" (*apephthenxato*) or speak out to them. The word used for this speaking is from the same verb used of the utterance in tongues in 2:4. It suggests that Peter spoke in his own language (Aramaic) as the Spirit gave utterance. In other words, what follows is not a sermon in the ordinary sense of the word. Certainly, Peter did not sit down and

*RSV* . . . and the district of Africa, *Goodspeed* . . . the regions of Libya, *NAB* . . . near Cyrene, *NLT.*

**and strangers of Rome:** . . . some of us are visitors from Rome, *TCNT* . . . transient dwellers from Rome, *Williams.*

**Jews and proselytes:** . . . either Jews by birth or converts, *TCNT* . . . Jews and those who have accepted the Jewish religion, *Beck.*

**11. Cretes and Arabians, we do hear them speak in our tongues the wonderful works of God:** . . . about the majesty, *Weymouth* . . . the excellencies, *Berkeley* . . . the great things, *Concordant* . . . the wonders, *Murdock* . . . magnificent things, *Rotherham* . . . the great acts, *Adams* . . . the marvels, *JB* . . . mighty wonders, *Norlie* . . . the greatness, *Klingensmith* . . . of the triumphs, *Moffatt.*

**12. And they were all amazed, and were in doubt:** Nay, all were...quite at a loss, *Rotherham* . . . and upset, *Adams* . . . bewildered, *Concordant* . . . utterly amazed and bewildered, *TCNT* . . . astounded and bewildered, *Weymouth* . . . amazed and puzzled, *Beck* . . . in...perplexity, *Campbell* . . . wholly at a loss what to think, *Wuest* . . . they were all excited and did not know what to think, *Klingensmith.*

**saying one to another, What meaneth this?:** How will this turn out, *Berkeley* . . . From whom is this thing? *Murdock* . . . What can it all possibly mean? *Norlie.*

**13. Others mocking said:** But others said with a sneer, *TCNT* . . . taunting, *Concordant* . . . But others, scornfully jeering, *Weymouth* . . . laughed it off, *JB* . . . said contemptuously, *NEB* . . . in mockery, *Norlie* . . . made fun of them, *NIV.*

**These men are full of new wine:** They are brimfull of sweet wine, *Weymouth* . . . They are running over with new wine, *Williams* . . . They are simply drunk with new wine, *Norlie* . . . are intoxicated, *Murdock.*

**14. But Peter, standing up with the eleven:** Then arose Peter, representing the eleven, *Berkeley.*

| **5292.4** noun acc sing fem | **840.3** prs-pron gen sing | **2504.1** conj | **663.3** verb 3sing indic aor mid | **840.2** prs-pron dat pl | **433.6** noun nom pl masc |
|---|---|---|---|---|---|
| φωνὴν | αὐτοῦ | καὶ | ἀπεφθέγξατο | αὐτοῖς, | Ἄνδρες |
| *phōnēn* | *autou* | *kai* | *apephthenxato* | *autois* | *Andres* |
| voice | his | and | spoke forth | to them, | Men |

| **2428.2** name-adj nom pl masc | **2504.1** conj | **3450.7** art nom pl masc | **2700.6** verb nom pl masc part pres act | **2395.1** name fem |
|---|---|---|---|---|
| Ἰουδαῖοι | καὶ | οἱ | κατοικοῦντες | Ἱερουσαλὴμ |
| *Ioudaioi* | *kai* | *hoi* | *katoikountes* | *Hierousalēm* |
| Jews, | and | the | inhabiting | Jerusalem |

14.b.**Txt:** 08E,025P,byz.
**Var:** 01ℵ,02A,03B,04C
05D,Lach,Treg,Tisc
We/Ho,Weis,Sod
UBS/☆

| **533.4** adj nom pl masc | **3820.7** adj nom pl masc | **3642.17** dem-pron sing neu | **5050.3** prs-pron dat 2pl | **1104.4** adj sing neu |
|---|---|---|---|---|
| ʹ ἅπαντες, | [b☆ πάντες, ] | τοῦτο | ὑμῖν | γνωστὸν |
| *hapantes* | *pantes* | *touto* | *humin* | *gnōston* |
| all | [ idem ] | this | to you | known |

| **1498.17** verb 3sing impr pres act | **2504.1** conj | **1785.1** verb 2pl impr aor mid | **3450.17** art pl neu | **4343.4** noun pl neu | **1466.2** prs-pron gen 1sing |
|---|---|---|---|---|---|
| ἔστω, | καὶ | ἐνωτίσασθε | τὰ | ῥήματά | μου. |
| *estō* | *kai* | *enōtisasthe* | *ta* | *rhēmata* | *mou* |
| let be, | and | give heed to | the | words | my: |

| **3620.3** partic | **1056.1** conj | **5453.1** conj | **5050.1** prs-pron nom 2pl | **5112.2** verb 2pl indic pres act | **3642.7** dem-pron nom pl masc |
|---|---|---|---|---|---|
| **15.** οὐ | γὰρ | ὡς | ὑμεῖς | ὑπολαμβάνετε, | οὗτοι |
| *ou* | *gar* | *hōs* | *humeis* | *hupolambanete* | *houtoi* |
| not | for | as | you | take it, | these |

| **3155.2** verb 3pl indic pres act | **1498.4** verb 3sing indic pres act | **1056.1** conj | **5443.2** noun nom sing fem | **4995.4** num ord nom sing fem | **3450.10** art gen sing fem |
|---|---|---|---|---|---|
| μεθύουσιν· | ἔστιν | γὰρ | ὥρα | τρίτη | τῆς |
| *methuousin* | *estin* | *gar* | *hōra* | *tritē* | *tēs* |
| are drunken, | it is | for | hour | third | of the |

| **2232.1** noun fem | **233.2** conj | **3642.17** dem-pron sing neu | **1498.4** verb 3sing indic pres act | **3450.16** art sing neu |
|---|---|---|---|---|
| ἡμέρας· | **16.** ἀλλὰ | τοῦτό | ἐστιν | τὸ |
| *hēmeras* | *alla* | *touto* | *estin* | *to* |
| day; | but | this | is | the |

| **2029.16** verb sing neu part perf mid | **1217.2** prep | **3450.2** art gen sing | **4254.2** noun gen sing masc | **2466.1** name masc |
|---|---|---|---|---|
| εἰρημένον | διὰ | τοῦ | προφήτου | Ἰωήλ, |
| *eirēmenon* | *dia* | *tou* | *prophētou* | *Iōēl* |
| having been spoken | by | the | prophet | Joel, |

| **2504.1** conj | **1498.40** verb 3sing indic fut mid | **1706.1** prep | **3450.14** art dat pl fem | **2057.10** adj dat pl fem | **2232.7** noun dat pl fem |
|---|---|---|---|---|---|
| **17.** Καὶ | ἔσται | ἐν | ταῖς | ἐσχάταις | ἡμέραις, |
| *Kai* | *estai* | *en* | *tais* | *eschatais* | *hēmerais* |
| And | it shall be | in | the | last | days, |

| **2978.5** verb 3sing indic pres act | **3450.5** art nom sing masc | **2296.1** noun nom sing masc | **1618.5** verb 1sing indic fut act | **570.3** prep | **3450.2** art gen sing |
|---|---|---|---|---|---|
| λέγει | ὁ | θεός, | ἐκχεῶ | ἀπὸ | τοῦ |
| *legei* | *ho* | *theos* | *ekcheō* | *apo* | *tou* |
| says |  | God, | I will pour out | of | the |

| **4011.2** noun gen sing neu | **1466.2** prs-pron gen 1sing | **1894.3** prep | **3820.12** adj acc sing fem | **4418.4** noun acc sing fem | **2504.1** conj |
|---|---|---|---|---|---|
| πνεύματός | μου | ἐπὶ | πᾶσαν | σάρκα, | καὶ |
| *pneumatos* | *mou* | *epi* | *pasan* | *sarka* | *kai* |
| Spirit | my | upon | all | flesh; | and |

figure out three points. It seems likely this was a spontaneous manifestation of the gift of prophecy (1 Corinthians 12:10; 14:3).

Peter's address was directed to the Jewish men and the inhabitants of Jerusalem. This was a polite way to begin and followed their custom, but it does not rule out the women.

**2:15.** Apparently, as the 120 were speaking in tongues, the mocking increased until most were mocking. Even some of those who understood the languages may have joined them. Peter drew no attention to the fact that some did understand. He answered only those who mocked.

The 120 were not drunk as the crowd supposed. Actually, even the sweet wine was not very strong. In those days they had no way of distilling alcohol or fortifying drinks. Their strongest drinks were wine and beer, and they made it a practice to dilute wine with several parts of water. It would have taken a great deal to make them drunk that early in the morning. Also, they would not be drinking in a public place at that hour. Thus, the mockers were shown to be absurd.

**2:16.** Peter declared that what they had seen and heard was a fulfillment of Joel 2:28-32. The context in Joel goes on to deal with the coming judgment at the end of the age. But Joel, like the other Old Testament prophets, did not see the timespan between the first and second comings of Christ. Even Peter himself did not understand how long it would be. He did see, however, that the Messianic Age was coming and that the present fulfillment of Joel's prophecy would continue until then.

**2:17.** Peter made one apparent change in the prophecy. Under the inspiration of the Spirit he specified what the word "afterward" in Joel's prophecy means: *the outpouring* is "in the last days." Thus he recognized that the last days began with the ascension of Jesus (3:19-21). This evidences that the Holy Spirit recognizes the entire Church Age as the "last days."

The first part of the quotation from Joel had an obvious application to the 120. The many languages highlight God's purpose to pour out His Spirit on all flesh. In the Hebrew "all flesh" usually means "all mankind," as in Genesis 6:12.

The emphasis (verses 17,18) is on the pouring out of the Spirit so those filled would prophesy. In the Bible, to prophesy means to speak for God as His spokesman or "mouth." (Compare Exodus 4:15,16; 7:2.) It does not necessarily mean to foretell the future.

"All flesh" is then broken down to sons and daughters. Concerning this outpouring of the Spirit there would be no distinction



**lifted up his voice, and said unto them:** . . . spoke forth unto them, *ASV* . . . addressed them in a loud voice, *Weymouth* . . . raised his voice, *Wuest* . . . and declared to them, *Young* . . . and addressed them, *Phillips.*

**Ye men of Judaea, and all ye that dwell at Jerusalem:** . . . all you inhabitants of Jerusalem, *Weymouth* . . . Jewish men and Jerusalem residents, *Berkeley* . . . all men residing in Jerusalem, *Fenton.*

**be this known to you:** . . . let me tell you what this means, *TCNT* . . . understand this, *Beck.*

**and hearken to my words:** . . . pay attention, *Noli* . . . and give ear unto my words, *RSV* . . . and mark my words, *TCNT* . . . and attend to what I say, *Weymouth* . . . and give close attention to my words, *Williams* . . . give ear to my declarations, *Concordant* . . . mark my assertions, *Fenton* . . . I will explain this to you, *Adams* . . . take note of this, *Norlie* . . . I will tell you something you need to know, *SEB.*

**15. For these are not drunken, as ye suppose:** You are wrong in thinking that these men are drunk, *TCNT* . . . as you imagine, *Adams.*

**seeing it is but the third hour of the day:** . . . indeed it is only nine in the morning! *TCNT* . . . for it is still the middle of the forenoon, *Klingensmith.*

**16. But this is that which was spoken by the prophet Joel:** On the contrary, *Adams, Noli* . . . declared through, *Concordant* . . . spoken through, *Berkeley* . . . this is something that the Prophet Joel foretold, *Norlie* . . . Joel predicted, *Montgomery.*

**17. And it shall come to pass:** And it shall be in the last days, *ASV* . . . It will occur in the last days, *Williams* . . . In the days to come, *JB* . . . it shall come about, *Klingensmith.*

**in the last days, saith God:** This is what God says, *Norlie* . . . God declares, *Noli.*

**I will pour out of my Spirit upon all flesh:** . . . abundantly bestow my Spirit, *Wuest* . . . upon everyone a portion, *NEB* . . . all mankind, *Noli, TCNT* . . . all people, *Beck.*

| 4253.14 verb 3pl indic fut act | 3450.7 art nom pl masc | 5048.6 noun nom pl masc | 5050.2 prs-pron gen 2pl | 2504.1 conj | 3450.13 art nom pl fem |
|---|---|---|---|---|---|
| προφητεύσουσιν | οἱ | υἱοὶ | ὑμῶν | καὶ | αἱ |
| *prophēteusousin* | *hoi* | *huioi* | *humōn* | *kai* | *hai* |
| shall prophesy | the | sons | your | and | the |

| 2341.6 noun nom pl fem | 5050.2 prs-pron gen 2pl | 2504.1 conj | 3450.7 art nom pl masc | 3358.4 noun nom pl masc | 5050.2 prs-pron gen 2pl |
|---|---|---|---|---|---|
| θυγατέρες | ὑμῶν˙ | καὶ | οἱ | νεανίσκοι | ὑμῶν |
| *thugateres* | *humōn* | *kai* | *hoi* | *neaniskoi* | *humōn* |
| daughters | your; | and | the | young men | your |

| 3569.2 noun acc pl fem | 3571.34 verb 3pl indic fut mid | 2504.1 conj | 3450.7 art nom pl masc | 4104.5 adj comp nom pl masc | 5050.2 prs-pron gen 2pl |
|---|---|---|---|---|---|
| ὁράσεις | ὄψονται, | καὶ | οἱ | πρεσβύτεροι | ὑμῶν |
| *horaseis* | *opsontai* | *kai* | *hoi* | *presbuteroi* | *humōn* |
| visions | shall see, | and | the | elders | your |

17.a.**Txt:** 08E,025P,byz.
**Var:** 01ℵ,02A,03B,04C
05D,Gries,Lach,Treg
Alf,Word,Tisc,We/Ho
Weis,Sod,UBS/⋆

| 1782.1 noun pl neu | 1782.2 noun dat pl neu | 1781.2 verb 3pl indic fut pass | 2504.1 conj |
|---|---|---|---|
| ‹ ἐνύπνια | [a⋆ ἐνυπνίοις ] | ἐνυπνιασθήσονται˙ | **18.** καί |
| *enupnia* | *enupniois* | *enupniasthēsontai* | *kai* |
| dreams | [ in dreams ] | shall dream; | and |

| 1058.1 partic | 1894.3 prep | 3450.8 art acc pl masc | 1395.9 noun acc pl masc | 1466.2 prs-pron gen 1sing | 2504.1 conj | 1894.3 prep |
|---|---|---|---|---|---|---|
| γε | ἐπὶ | τοὺς | δούλους | μου | καὶ | ἐπὶ |
| *ge* | *epi* | *tous* | *doulous* | *mou* | *kai* | *epi* |
| even | upon | the | male servants | my | and | upon |

| 3450.15 art acc pl fem | 1393.3 noun acc pl fem | 1466.2 prs-pron gen 1sing | 1706.1 prep | 3450.14 art dat pl fem | 2232.7 noun dat pl fem |
|---|---|---|---|---|---|
| τὰς | δούλας | μου | ἐν | ταῖς | ἡμέραις |
| *tas* | *doulas* | *mou* | *en* | *tais* | *hēmerais* |
| the | female servants | my | in | the | days |

| 1552.14 dem-pron dat pl fem | 1618.5 verb 1sing indic fut act | 570.3 prep | 3450.2 art gen sing | 4011.2 noun gen sing neu | 1466.2 prs-pron gen 1sing |
|---|---|---|---|---|---|
| ἐκείναις | ἐκχεῶ | ἀπὸ | τοῦ | πνεύματός | μου, |
| *ekeinais* | *ekcheō* | *apo* | *tou* | *pneumatos* | *mou* |
| those | will I pour out | of | the | Spirit | my, |

| 2504.1 conj | 4253.14 verb 3pl indic fut act | 2504.1 conj | 1319.36 verb 1sing indic fut act | 4907.1 noun pl neu |
|---|---|---|---|---|
| καὶ | προφητεύσουσιν. | **19.** καὶ | δώσω | τέρατα |
| *kai* | *prophēteusousin* | *kai* | *dōsō* | *terata* |
| and | they shall prophesy; | and | I will give | wonders |

| 1706.1 prep | 3450.3 art dat sing | 3636.3 noun dat sing masc | 504.1 adv | 2504.1 conj | 4447.2 noun pl neu | 1894.3 prep |
|---|---|---|---|---|---|---|
| ἐν | τῷ | οὐρανῷ | ἄνω | καὶ | σημεῖα | ἐπὶ |
| *en* | *tō* | *ouranō* | *anō* | *kai* | *sēmeia* | *epi* |
| in | the | heaven | above | and | signs | on |

| 3450.10 art gen sing fem | 1087.2 noun gen sing fem | 2706.1 adv | 129.1 noun sing neu | 2504.1 conj | 4300.1 noun sing neu | 2504.1 conj |
|---|---|---|---|---|---|---|
| τῆς | γῆς | κάτω, | αἷμα | καὶ | πῦρ | καὶ |
| *tēs* | *gēs* | *katō* | *haima* | *kai* | *pur* | *kai* |
| the | earth | below, | blood | and | fire | and |

| 816.2 noun acc sing fem | 2557.2 noun gen sing masc | 3450.5 art nom sing masc | 2229.1 noun nom sing masc | 3214.3 verb 3sing indic fut pass |
|---|---|---|---|---|
| ἀτμίδα | καπνοῦ. | **20.** ὁ | ἥλιος | μεταστραφήσεται |
| *atmida* | *kapnou* | *ho* | *hēlios* | *metastraphēsetai* |
| cloud | of smoke. | The | sun | shall be turned |

with regard to sex. This is another indication that all 120 were baptized in the Spirit, including the women.

Young men would see visions and old men dream dreams. No division with respect to age would exist. Nor does there seem to be any real distinction here between dreams and visions. The Bible often uses the words interchangeably. Here, at least, they are parallel. (See 10:17; 16:9,10; and 18:9 for examples of visions.)

**2:18.** Even upon male and female slaves God would pour out His Spirit. Thus, the Spirit would pay no attention to social distinctions. Though there were probably no slaves among the 120, the Roman Empire had many areas where slaves comprised as high as 80 percent of the population. Fulfillment would come. The gospel has often reached the lower levels of society first.

**2:19.** Many interpret verses 18 and 19 symbolically. Others suppose they were somehow fulfilled during the 3 hours of darkness while Jesus hung on the cross. It seems rather that the mention of the signs indicates the outpouring and the prophesying would continue until these signs come at the end of the age. Peter also meant that these signs can just as confidently be expected.

The gift of the Spirit can also be seen as the firstfruits of the age to come (Romans 8:23). The unregenerate human heart and mind has no conception of what God has prepared for those who love Him, but God "hath revealed them unto us by his Spirit" (1 Corinthians 2:9,10). The believers' future inheritance is no mystery, for they have already experienced it, at least in a measure. As Hebrews 6:4,5 points out, all who have tasted (really experienced) the heavenly gift and are made partakers of the Holy Spirit have already experienced the good word (promise) of God and the mighty powers (miracles) of the age to come.

Some also see in the fire and smoke a reference to the signs of God's presence at Mount Sinai (Exodus 19:16-18; 20:18), and view Pentecost as the giving of a new law or the renewing of the new covenant. However, as Hebrews 9:15-18,26,28 indicates, the death of Christ inaugurated the new covenant, and there was no need for anything further.

**2:20.** The signs here also include blood and refer to the increasing bloodshed, wars, and smoke from wars that will cover the sun and make the moon appear red. These things will happen before "that great and notable (manifest) day of the Lord" comes. They are part of the present age.

The Day of the Lord in the Old Testament, in some contexts, spoke of God's judgment on Israel and Judah and of their being sent into exile to rid them of their idolatry. It also spoke of the

**and your sons and your daughters shall prophesy:** Then will, *Norlie* . . . shall become Prophets, *TCNT* . . . will speak God's Word, *Beck* . . . shall speak forth by divine inspiration, *Wuest* . . . preach, *Fenton.*

**and your young men shall see visions:** . . . your youths, *Concordant.*

**and your old men shall dream dreams:** . . . your elders, *Concordant* . . . will have special dreams, *NCV.*

**18. And on my servants and on my handmaidens:** And even upon my men-servants and upon my maid-servants, *Rotherham* . . . At that time I will give my Spirit even to, *Everyday* . . . Even on the servants—for they are mine—both men and women, *TCNT* . . . Even on your servants, men and women alike, *Norlie* . . . bondmen and...bondwomen, *Darby* . . . on my very slaves, *Moffatt* . . . and my slave-girls, *Williams C.K.*

**I will pour out in those days of my Spirit:** At that time I will pour out My Spirit, *Weymouth* . . . pour out a portion of, *NAB.*

**and they shall prophesy:** And they will become prophets, *Williams* . . . and they will prophesy also, *Noli.*

**19. And I will shew wonders in heaven above:** I will display marvels in the sky above, *Weymouth* . . . will work wonders, *NAB* . . . I will show miracles, *Everyday* . . . I will give you startling wonders in the sky above, *Beck* . . . strange things, *Klingensmith* . . . I will show amazing things, *NCV, SEB* . . . I will show portents, *Noli.*

**and signs in the earth beneath:** . . . marvelous signs, *Beck* . . . prodigies, *Murdock* . . . and tokens in the erth benethe, *Tyndale* . . . and miracles, *Noli* . . . on the earth below, *TCNT.*

**blood, and fire, and vapour of smoke:** . . . mist of smoke, *TCNT* . . . cloud of smoke, *Weymouth* . . . and thick smoke, *Everyday.*

**20. The sun shall be turned into darkness:** . . . shall be changed into darkness, *Moffat* . . . be transformed to, *Fenton* . . . converted into darkness, *Concordant* . . . turned dark, *Beck.*

20.a.**Txt:** 03B,025P,byz. Weis
**Var:** 01ℵ,02A,04C,05D 08E,Lach,Treg,Tisc We/Ho,Sod,UBS/⋆

20.b.**Txt:** 01ℵ-corr,02A 04C,08E,025P,Sod
**Var:** 01ℵ-org,03B,05D Lach,Treg,Alf,Tisc We/Ho,Weis,UBS/⋆

20.c.**Txt:** p74,02A,03B 04C,08E,025P,etc.byz. Treg,Alf,Word,We/Ho Weis,Sod,UBS/⋆
**Var:** 01ℵ,05D,Tisc

21.a.**Txt:** 01ℵ-corr,02A 04C,05D,025P,byz.Tisc Sod
**Var:** 03B,08E,Treg,Alf We/Ho,Weis,UBS/⋆

22.a.**Txt:** 04C-corr,025P byz.Gries,Word
**Var:** 01ℵ,02A,03B 04C-org,05D,08E,sa.bo. Lach,Treg,Alf,Tisc We/Ho,Weis,Sod UBS/⋆

| **1519.1** prep | **4510.1** noun sing | **2504.1** conj | **3450.9** art nom sing fem | **4437.1** noun nom sing fem | **1519.1** prep | **129.1** noun sing neu |
|---|---|---|---|---|---|---|
| εἰς | σκότος | καὶ | ἡ | σελήνη | εἰς | αἷμα, |
| *eis* | *skotos* | *kai* | *hē* | *selēnē* | *eis* | *haima* |
| into | darkness | and | the | moon | into | blood, |

| **4109.1** adv | **3614.9** rel-pron nom sing fem | **2048.23** verb inf aor act | **3450.12** art acc sing fem | **2232.4** noun acc sing fem | **2935.2** noun gen sing masc |
|---|---|---|---|---|---|
| πρὶν | (a ἣ ) | ἐλθεῖν | (b τὴν ) | ἡμέραν | κυρίου |
| *prin* | *hē* | *elthein* | *tēn* | *hēmeran* | *kuriou* |
| before | which | to come | the | day | of Lord |

| **3450.12** art acc sing fem | **3144.12** adj acc sing fem | **2504.1** conj | **2000.1** adj acc sing fem | | **2504.1** conj | **1498.40** verb 3sing indic fut mid |
|---|---|---|---|---|---|---|
| τὴν | μεγάλην | (c καὶ | ἐπιφανῆ. ) | 21. | καὶ | ἔσται, |
| *tēn* | *megalēn* | *kai* | *epiphanē* | | *kai* | *estai* |
| the | great | and | manifest. | | And | it shall be, |

| **3820.6** adj nom sing masc | **3614.5** rel-pron nom sing masc | **300.1** partic | **1430.1** partic | **1926.12** verb 3sing subj aor mid | **3450.16** art sing neu |
|---|---|---|---|---|---|
| πᾶς | ὃς | ( ἂν | [a⋆ ἐὰν] | ἐπικαλέσηται | τὸ |
| *pas* | *hos* | *an* | *ean* | *epikalesētai* | *to* |
| everyone | whoever | | | shall call upon | the |

| **3549.2** noun sing neu | **2935.2** noun gen sing masc | **4834.33** verb 3sing indic fut pass | | **433.6** noun nom pl masc | **2448.2** name nom pl masc |
|---|---|---|---|---|---|
| ὄνομα | κυρίου | σωθήσεται. | 22. | Ἄνδρες | Ἰσραηλῖται, |
| *onoma* | *kuriou* | *sōthēsetai* | | *Andres* | *Israēlitai* |
| name | of Lord | shall be saved. | | Men | Israelites, |

| **189.29** verb 2pl impr aor act | **3450.8** art acc pl masc | **3030.8** noun acc pl masc | **3642.8** dem-pron acc pl masc | **2400.3** name acc masc |
|---|---|---|---|---|
| ἀκούσατε | τοὺς | λόγους | τούτους· | Ἰησοῦν |
| *akousate* | *tous* | *logous* | *toutous* | *Iēsoun* |
| hear | the | words | these: | Jesus |

| **3450.6** art acc sing masc | **3343.3** name acc sing masc | **433.4** noun acc sing masc | **570.3** prep | **3450.2** art gen sing | **2296.2** noun gen sing masc |
|---|---|---|---|---|---|
| τὸν | Ναζωραῖον, | ἄνδρα | ( ἀπὸ | τοῦ | θεοῦ |
| *ton* | *Nazōraion* | *andra* | *apo* | *tou* | *theou* |
| the | Nazarene, | a man | from | | God |

| **579.4** verb acc sing masc part perf mid | **579.4** verb acc sing masc part perf mid | **570.3** prep | **3450.2** art gen sing |
|---|---|---|---|
| ἀποδεδειγμένον | [⋆ ἀποδεδειγμένον | ἀπὸ | τοῦ |
| *apodedeigmenon* | *apodedeigmenon* | *apo* | *tou* |
| having been attested | [ having been attested | from | |

| **2296.2** noun gen sing masc | **1519.1** prep | **5050.4** prs-pron acc 2pl | **1405.7** noun dat pl fem | **2504.1** conj | **4907.3** noun dat pl neu |
|---|---|---|---|---|---|
| θεοῦ ] | εἰς | ὑμᾶς | δυνάμεσιν· | καὶ | τέρασιν |
| *theou* | *eis* | *humas* | *dunamesin* | *kai* | *terasin* |
| God ] | to | you | by works of power | and | wonders |

| **2504.1** conj | **4447.4** noun dat pl neu | **3614.4** rel-pron dat pl | **4020.24** verb 3sing indic aor act | **1217.1** prep | **840.3** prs-pron gen sing |
|---|---|---|---|---|---|
| καὶ | σημείοις, | οἷς | ἐποίησεν | δι' | αὐτοῦ |
| *kai* | *sēmeiois* | *hois* | *epoiēsen* | *di'* | *autou* |
| and | signs, | which | did | by | him |

| **3450.5** art nom sing masc | **2296.1** noun nom sing masc | **1706.1** prep | **3189.1** adj dat sing | **5050.2** prs-pron gen 2pl | **2503.1** conj | **2504.1** conj |
|---|---|---|---|---|---|---|
| ὁ | θεὸς | ἐν | μέσῳ | ὑμῶν, | καθὼς | (a καὶ ) |
| *ho* | *theos* | *en* | *mesō* | *humōn* | *kathōs* | *kai* |
| | God | in | midst | your, | as | also |

judgment on nations God brought in due time, such as Assyria and Babylon. In other contexts the Day of the Lord spoke of end-time judgments on the nations of the world which the Book of Revelation places in the tribulation period. It also includes the restoration of Israel to the Promised Land and a spiritual restoration, as well as the establishment of the messianic kingdom.

**2:21.** This verse gives the purpose of the outpouring of the Holy Spirit. Through its empowering, the convicting work of the Spirit will be done in the world, not just in the end of the age but throughout the entire age right down to the great Day of the Lord. All during this period, whoever calls (for help for his need, that is, for salvation) on the name of the Lord will be saved. The Greek is strong, "all whoever." No matter what happens in the world or what forces oppose the Church, the door of salvation will remain open. Based upon this, believers can expect many to respond and be saved. There was a tremendous response in the First Century as the gospel was spread to all parts of the known world of that day. There have been periods of great revival from time to time since then. Now, as the end of the age approaches, even greater revival is evident in all parts of the world.

**2:22.** The main body of Peter's message centers around Jesus, not the Holy Spirit. The outpouring on the Day of Pentecost was intended to bear powerful witness to Jesus (Acts 1:8; John 15:26; 16:14).

Peter first drew attention to the fact that the inhabitants of Jerusalem knew the "man" of Nazareth, Jesus. (*Nazareth* in Hebrew is derived from the word *branch*, Hebrew *nētser*, used in Isaiah 11:1 of the greater Son of David, the Messiah. *Nazarene*, Hebrew *nētseri*, can mean either "the man of Nazareth" or "the man of the branch," and thus identifies Jesus as the Messiah. Jeremiah 23:5; 33:15; Zechariah 3:8; 6:12 and other passages use related words to describe the Messiah as the righteous Branch, the new shoot that will arise from the stump of what was left of David's line and bring in the coming Kingdom.)

Peter's audience knew how God had approved Jesus for their benefit by miracles (mighty works, mighty manifestations of power), wonders, and signs. These are the three words used in the Bible for supernatural works. They refer to the variety of miracles Jesus did, and Peter had in mind especially the miracles Jesus did in the temple at the feast times when many in this crowd had undoubtedly been present (John 2:23; 4:45; 11:47).

**2:23.** Peter next declared that the Jews in Jerusalem, by wicked hands (the hands of lawless men, men outside the Jewish law, that



**and the moon into blood:** . . . blood-red, *TCNT.*

**before that great and notable day of the Lord come:** Before the day of the Lord come, That great and notable day, *ASV* . . . the great and manifest day, *Kleist, Rotherham* . . . To usher in the day of the Lord—That great and illustrious day, *Weymouth* . . . the great advent day, *Concordant* . . . Before that great and conspicuous Day of the Lord arrives, *Berkeley* . . . splendid day, *Beck* . . . great and glorious, *NIV* . . . obvious day, *AmpB.*

**21. And it shall come to pass:** And it shall be, *RSV.*

**that whosoever shall call on the name of the Lord:** . . . every one who invokes, *TCNT* . . . trusts in the name of the Lord, *SEB.*

**shall be saved:** . . . shall live, *Murdock.*

**22. Ye men of Israel:** Men of Israel, *TCNT.*

**hear these words:** . . . listen to this, *TCNT* . . . listen to what I say, *Williams.*

**Jesus of Nazareth:**

**a man approved of God among you:** . . . a Man pointed out of God unto you, *Rotherham* . . . a man whose mission from God was proved, *TCNT* . . . a man accredited to you from God, *Weymouth* . . . a man attested to you by God, *RSV* . . . a Man divinely accredited, *Berkeley* . . . demonstrated to be from God, *Concordant* . . . made known to you, *Norlie* . . . God showed you who the Man is, *Beck* . . . a man chosen of God, *Klingensmith* . . . celebrated among you, *Wilson* . . . a very special man, *SEB* . . . God clearly showed this to you, *Everyday* . . . whom God has revealed to you, *Noli.*

**by miracles and wonders and signs, which God did by him in the midst of you:** . . . through him, *Rotherham* . . . was proved by miracles, *TCNT* . . . by means of, *Norlie* . . . by powers, marvels, and evidences, *Fenton* . . . right here among you, *Williams* . . . which God did among you through Him, *PNT.*

**as ye yourselves also know:** . . . as you personally know, *Berkeley* . . . you yourselves know positively, *Wuest.*

| 840.7 prs-pron nom pl masc | 3471.6 verb 2pl indic perf act | 3642.6 dem-pron acc sing masc | 3450.11 art dat sing fem | 3587.7 verb dat sing fem part perf mid |
|---|---|---|---|---|
| αὐτοὶ | οἴδατε, | 23. τοῦτον | τῇ | ὡρισμένῃ |
| *autoi* | *oidate* | *touton* | *tē* | *hōrismenē* |
| yourselves | know: | this one | by the | having been fixed |

23.a.**Txt:** 01ℵ-corr 04C-corr,05D,08E,025P byz.
**Var:** 01ℵ-org,02A,03B 04C-org,sa.bo.Lach,Treg Alf,Tisc,We/Ho,Weis Sod,UBS/☆

23.b.**Txt:** 04C-corr,08E 025P,byz.sa.bo.
**Var:** 01ℵ,02A,03B 04C-org,05D,Lach,Treg Alf,Tisc,We/Ho,Weis Sod,UBS/☆

23.c.**Txt:** byz.
**Var:** 01ℵ,02A,03B,04C 05D,08E,025P,Gries Lach,Treg,Alf,Word Tisc,We/Ho,Weis,Sod UBS/☆

| 1005.3 noun dat sing fem | 2504.1 conj | 4127.1 noun dat sing fem | 3450.2 art gen sing | 2296.2 noun gen sing masc | 1547.1 adj acc sing masc |
|---|---|---|---|---|---|
| βουλῇ | καὶ | προγνώσει | τοῦ | θεοῦ | ἔκδοτον |
| *boulē* | *kai* | *prognōsei* | *tou* | *theou* | *ekdoton* |
| purpose | and | foreknowledge | | of God | given up, |

| 2956.27 verb nom pl masc part aor act | 1217.2 prep | 5331.6 noun gen pl fem | 5331.2 noun gen sing fem | 456.3 adj gen pl masc |
|---|---|---|---|---|
| ⸂a λαβόντες ⸃ | διὰ | ⸀ χειρῶν | [b☆ χειρὸς ] | ἀνόμων |
| *labontes* | *dia* | *cheirōn* | *cheiros* | *anomōn* |
| having taken | by | hands | [ a hand ] | lawless, |

| 4220.1 verb nom pl masc part aor act | 335.6 verb 2pl indic aor act | 335.15 verb 2pl indic aor act | 3614.6 rel-pron acc sing masc |
|---|---|---|---|
| προσπήξαντες | ⸀ ἀνείλετε· | [c☆ ἀνείλατε, ] | 24. ὃν |
| *prospēxantes* | *aneilete* | *aneilate* | *hon* |
| having crucified | you put to death | [ idem ] | Whom |

| 3450.5 art nom sing masc | 2296.1 noun nom sing masc | 448.3 verb 3sing indic aor act | 3061.13 verb nom sing masc part aor act | 3450.15 art acc pl fem | 5438.3 noun acc pl fem |
|---|---|---|---|---|---|
| ὁ | θεὸς | ἀνέστησεν, | λύσας | τὰς | ὠδῖνας |
| *ho* | *theos* | *anestēsen* | *lusas* | *tas* | *ōdinas* |
| | God | raised up, | having loosed | the | bonds |

| 3450.2 art gen sing | 2265.2 noun gen sing masc | 2502.1 conj | 3620.2 partic | 1498.34 verb sing indic imperf act | 1409.3 adj sing neu |
|---|---|---|---|---|---|
| τοῦ | θανάτου, | καθότι | οὐκ | ἦν | δυνατὸν |
| *tou* | *thanatou* | *kathoti* | *ouk* | *ēn* | *dunaton* |
| of the | death, | inasmuch as | not | it was | possible |

| 2875.23 verb inf pres mid | 840.6 prs-pron acc sing masc | 5097.2 prep | 840.3 prs-pron gen sing | 1132.1 name masc | 1056.1 conj |
|---|---|---|---|---|---|
| κρατεῖσθαι | αὐτὸν | ὑπ' | αὐτοῦ. | 25. Δαβὶδ | γὰρ |
| *krateisthai* | *auton* | *hup'* | *autou* | *Dabid* | *gar* |
| to be held | him | by | it; | David | for |

| 2978.5 verb 3sing indic pres act | 1519.1 prep | 840.6 prs-pron acc sing masc | 4167.2 verb 1sing indic imperf mid | 4167.3 verb 1sing indic imperf mid |
|---|---|---|---|---|
| λέγει | εἰς | αὐτόν, | ⸀ Προωρώμην | [☆ Προορώμην ] |
| *legei* | *eis* | *auton* | *Proōrōmēn* | *Proorōmēn* |
| says | as to | him, | I was foreseeing | [ idem ] |

| 3450.6 art acc sing masc | 2935.4 noun acc sing masc | 1783.1 prep | 1466.2 prs-pron gen 1sing | 1217.2 prep | 3820.2 adj gen sing |
|---|---|---|---|---|---|
| τὸν | κύριον | ἐνώπιόν | μου | διὰ | παντός, |
| *ton* | *kurion* | *enōpion* | *mou* | *dia* | *pantos* |
| the | Lord | before | me | through | all, |

| 3617.1 conj | 1523.2 prep gen | 1182.7 adj gen pl neu | 1466.2 prs-pron gen 1sing | 1498.4 verb 3sing indic pres act | 2419.1 conj |
|---|---|---|---|---|---|
| ὅτι | ἐκ | δεξιῶν | μού | ἐστιν, | ἵνα |
| *hoti* | *ek* | *dexiōn* | *mou* | *estin* | *hina* |
| because | at | right hand | my | he is, | that |

| 3231.1 partic | 4388.8 verb 1sing subj aor pass | 1217.2 prep | 3642.17 dem-pron sing neu | 2146.6 verb 3sing indic aor pass |
|---|---|---|---|---|
| μὴ | σαλευθῶ. | 26. διὰ | τοῦτο | ⸀ εὐφράνθη |
| *mē* | *saleuthō* | *dia* | *touto* | *euphranthē* |
| not | I may be shaken. | Because of | this | rejoiced |

is, the Roman soldiers), crucified and slew (nailed up and slew) this Jesus. The Jerusalem Jews were responsible. But Peter also made it clear that Jesus was delivered up (given over) to them by the determinate counsel (the designated will) and foreknowledge of God. (Compare Luke 24:26,27,46.) If they had understood the prophets they would have known Messiah had to suffer. Peter did not intend, however, to lessen their guilt by saying this. Note that the Bible never puts this kind of responsibility on the Jews in general.

**2:24.** Peter quickly added that this Jesus is the One whom God raised up. The Resurrection took away the stigma of the cross, which was the Roman method of hanging criminals whom they considered enemies of society. It is hard for us to realize today how much shame there was in being crucified. As Hebrews 12:2 brings out, Jesus, as the Author (leader) and Finisher (perfecter) of our faith, for "the joy that was set before him, endured the cross," caring nothing for the shame, and He is now seated "at the right hand of the throne of God."

By the Resurrection also, God released Jesus from the pains (pangs) of death because it was not possible for Him to be held by it. *Pangs*, "pains," here usually means "birth pangs," so that the "death" here is perceived as labor. Just as labor pains are relieved by the birth of a child, so the Resurrection brought an end to the pangs of death.

Why was it not possible for Jesus to be held by death? Since the wages of sin is death (Romans 6:23), some say the reason death could not hold Him was because He had no sin of His own for death to claim Him. Hebrews 9:14 points out that Jesus, through His own eternal Spirit, offered himself without spot to God. He was in all points tempted (and tested) just as believers are, yet without sin (Hebrews 4:15). As the Lamb of God He was undefiled, without blemish and without spot (1 Peter 1:19; 2:22-24). Because He was righteous He was able to bear away our sins without being defiled himself (Romans 5:18; Hebrews 7:26). In 2 Corinthians 5:21, the Bible says God made Jesus to be sin for us, who knew no sin. But this does not mean He was made sinful or made a sinner. In fact, the Old Testament word for sin means both *sin* or a *sin offering*, depending on the context. The context in 2 Corinthians 5 is of reconciliation accomplished because He died for all and thus became a sin offering, literally, "instead of us." But He remained always the spotless Lamb of God.

**2:25.** Peter's reason for the fact that death could not hold Jesus, however, is that His resurrection was necessary in order to fulfill the prophetic Word of God. Under the inspiration of the Spirit Peter said David was speaking of Jesus in Psalm 16:8-11. Jewish tradition of the time also applied this to the Messiah. David foresaw the Lord before his face (present with him) and at his right hand to help, so that he would not be moved (so he would be established).

**23. Him, being delivered by the determinate counsel and foreknowledge of God:** . . . in accordance with, *Williams* . . . by the settled purpose, *Noyes* . . . by the settled counsel, *HBIE* . . . resolute decision, *Fenton* . . . in accordance with God's definite plan and with his previous knowledge, *TCNT* . . . deliberate intention, *JB* . . . God definitely planned and intended to have Him betrayed, *Beck* . . . it was part of His plan, *SEB* . . . by the predetermined plan, *Phillips* . . . in the predestined course of God's deliberate purpose, *Moffatt*.

**ye have taken, and by wicked hands:** Ye by the hand of lawless men, *ASV* . . . with the help of heathen men, *TCNT* . . . with lawless hands, *Concordant* . . . and you used for your purpose men without the Law! *Phillips*.

**have crucified and slain:** . . . assassinate, *Concordant* . . . nailed him to a cross and put him to death, *TCNT*.

**24. Whom God hath raised up:** But God has raised Him to life, *Weymouth* . . . resurrected Him, *Adams*.

**having loosed the pains of death:** . . . released him from the pangs, *TCNT* . . . by unfastening the cords, *Berkeley* . . . having liberated from the grip, *Fenton* . . . cords of the grave, *Murdock* . . . putting an end to the agony, *Beck*.

**because it was not possible that he should be holden of it:** . . . it being impossible for death to retain its hold upon him, *TCNT* . . . for him to be held fast by death, *Weymouth* . . . to be mastered by it, *Wuest* . . . to continue held fast under it, *Rotherham* . . . death could not possibly hold Him in its power, *Norlie*.

**25. For David speaketh concerning him:** . . . in reference to Him, *PNT*.

**I foresaw the Lord always before my face:** I beheld, *ASV* . . . I have ever fixed my eyes upon the Lord, *Weymouth* . . . I always kept my eyes upon the Lord, *Williams*.

**for he is on my right hand:**

**that I should not be moved:** . . . may not be shaken, *Rotherham* . . . not be disquieted, *TCNT* . . . need not be disturbed, *Norlie*.

26.a.**Txt:** byz.
**Var:** 01א,02A,03B,04C 05D,08E,025P,Lach Treg,Alf,Word,Tisc We/Ho,Weis,Sod UBS/☆

| **2146.15** verb 3sing indic aor pass | **3450.9** art nom sing fem | **2559.2** noun nom sing fem | **1466.2** prs-pron gen 1sing | **1466.2** prs-pron gen 1sing |
|---|---|---|---|---|
| [a☆ ηὐφράνθη ] | ʻ ἡ | καρδία | μου | [ μου |
| *euphranthē* | *hē* | *kardia* | *mou* | *mou* |
| [ idem ] | the | heart | my | [ my |

| **3450.9** art nom sing fem | **2559.2** noun nom sing fem | **2504.1** conj | **21.6** verb 3sing indic aor mid | **3450.9** art nom sing fem |
|---|---|---|---|---|
| ἡ | καρδία ] | καὶ | ἠγαλλιάσατο | ἡ |
| *hē* | *kardia* | *kai* | *ēgalliasato* | *hē* |
| the | heart ] | and | rejoiced | the |

| **1094.1** noun nom sing fem | **1466.2** prs-pron gen 1sing | **2068.1** adv | **1156.2** conj | **2504.1** conj | **3450.9** art nom sing fem | **4418.1** noun nom sing fem |
|---|---|---|---|---|---|---|
| γλῶσσά | μου· | ἔτι | δὲ | καὶ | ἡ | σάρξ |
| *glōssa* | *mou* | *eti* | *de* | *kai* | *hē* | *sarx* |
| tongue | my; | further | but | also | the | flesh |

| **1466.2** prs-pron gen 1sing | **2651.3** verb 3sing indic fut act | **1894.2** prep | **1667.3** noun dat sing fem | | **3617.1** conj | **3620.2** partic |
|---|---|---|---|---|---|---|
| μου | κατασκηνώσει | ἐπ' | ἐλπίδι· | **27.** | ὅτι | οὐκ |
| *mou* | *kataskēnōsei* | *ep'* | *elpidi* | | *hoti* | *ouk* |
| my | shall rest | in | hope, | | for | not |

| **1452.6** verb 2sing indic fut act | **3450.12** art acc sing fem | **5425.4** noun acc sing fem | **1466.2** prs-pron gen 1sing | **1519.1** prep | **85.2** noun gen sing masc |
|---|---|---|---|---|---|
| ἐγκαταλείψεις | τὴν | ψυχήν | μου | εἰς | ʻ ᾅδου, |
| *enkataleipseis* | *tēn* | *psuchēn* | *mou* | *eis* | *hadou* |
| you will leave | the | soul | my | in | hades |

27.a.**Txt:** 08E,025P,byz.
**Var:** 01א,02A,03B,04C 05D,Lach,Treg,Alf Word,Tisc,We/Ho,Weis Sod,UBS/☆

| **85.5** noun acc sing masc | **3624.1** conj | **1319.37** verb 2sing indic fut act | **3450.6** art acc sing masc | **3603.2** adj acc sing masc | **4622.2** prs-pron gen 2sing |
|---|---|---|---|---|---|
| [a☆ ᾅδην, ] | οὐδὲ | δώσεις | τὸν | ὅσιόν | σου |
| *hadēn* | *oude* | *dōseis* | *ton* | *hosion* | *sou* |
| [ idem ] | nor | will you give | the | holy one | your |

| **1481.19** verb inf aor act | **1306.1** noun acc sing fem | | **1101.4** verb 2sing indic aor act | **1466.4** prs-pron dat 1sing | **3461.8** noun acc pl fem |
|---|---|---|---|---|---|
| ἰδεῖν | διαφθοράν. | **28.** | ἐγνώρισάς | μοι | ὁδοὺς |
| *idein* | *diaphthoran* | | *egnōrisas* | *moi* | *hodous* |
| to see | corruption. | | You did make known | to me | paths |

| **2205.2** noun gen sing fem | **3997.13** verb 2sing indic fut act | **1466.6** prs-pron acc 1sing | **2148.1** noun gen sing fem | **3196.3** prep | **3450.2** art gen sing |
|---|---|---|---|---|---|
| ζωῆς· | πληρώσεις | με | εὐφροσύνης | μετὰ | τοῦ |
| *zōēs* | *plērōseis* | *me* | *euphrosunēs* | *meta* | *tou* |
| of life, | you will fill | me | with joy | with | the |

| **4241.2** noun gen sing neu | **4622.2** prs-pron gen 2sing | | **433.6** noun nom pl masc | **79.6** noun nom pl masc | **1815.2** verb sing neu part pres act |
|---|---|---|---|---|---|
| προσώπου | σου. | **29.** | Ἄνδρες | ἀδελφοί, | ἐξὸν |
| *prosōpou* | *sou* | | *Andres* | *adelphoi* | *exon* |
| countenance | your. | | Men | brothers, | it is permitted |

| **1500.21** verb inf aor act | **3196.3** prep | **3816.2** noun gen sing fem | **4242.1** prep | **5050.4** prs-pron acc 2pl | **3875.1** prep |
|---|---|---|---|---|---|
| εἰπεῖν | μετὰ | παῤῥησίας | πρὸς | ὑμᾶς | περὶ |
| *eipein* | *meta* | *parrhēsias* | *pros* | *humas* | *peri* |
| to speak | with | confidence | to | you | concerning |

| **3450.2** art gen sing | **3828.2** noun gen sing masc | **1132.1** name masc | **3617.1** conj | **2504.1** conj | **4901.5** verb 3sing indic aor act |
|---|---|---|---|---|---|
| τοῦ | πατριάρχου | Δαβίδ, | ὅτι | καὶ | ἐτελεύτησεν |
| *tou* | *patriarchou* | *Dabid* | *hoti* | *kai* | *eteleutēsen* |
| the | patriarch | David, | that | both | he died |

**2:26.** God's presence caused David's heart to rejoice and his tongue to express gladness. His flesh also made God-given hope his rest, his tabernacle, his place of encampment.

**2:27.** The central point of David's prophecy is the promise that God would not leave (abandon) His soul in hell (Greek, *hadēs*, the place of the afterlife, a translation of the Hebrew word *sh^e'ôl*), and that He would not permit His Holy One to see corruption (putrefaction).

Some contend that the Old Testament does not reflect a belief in a resurrection of the dead. This passage from Psalm 16 seems to indicate otherwise as do the following: Daniel 12:2—"And many of them that sleep in the dust of the earth shall awake, some to everlasting life, and some to shame and everlasting contempt"; Job 19:25-27—"I know that my Redeemer lives . . . Even after my skin is destroyed, Yet from my flesh I shall see God" (NASB); Psalm 17:15—"As for me, I will behold thy face in righteousness: I shall be satisfied, when I awake, with thy likeness." (See also Deuteronomy 32:39; 1 Samuel 2:6; Psalms 49:15; 73:24; and Isaiah 26:19 for passages that may point to an Old Testament teaching on resurrection.)

Everywhere else in the New Testament *Hades* refers to the place of punishment during the intermediate state between death and the final (Great White Throne) judgment. It, along with death, will be cast into the lake of fire (Revelation 20:14). That is, it will be fused with the lake of fire so that the lake of fire will then be the only place of death and punishment.

According to some scholars, the view that Hades was a place of punishment developed during the period between the Testaments. Until then the term *Hades* simply referred to the grave or to the underworld abode of the dead. This understanding, they say, is reflected in the Septuagint where *hadēs* is used to translate the Hebrew term *sh^e'ôl.* If this is the case, Sheol is the place everyone went after they died. However, others hold that in the Old Testament *sh^e'ôl* referred to the place where the wicked were punished after death. In this verse, the quotation taken from Psalm 16 does not seem to convey either theological conclusion; it simply says Death could not hold the Messiah.

**2:28.** "The ways of life" is best understood in terms of Proverbs 15:24 where the Hebrew reads: "The way of life is to the place above for the wise (the godly), that he may avoid Sheol beneath." For Christ they would speak of His resurrection and ascension to the right hand of the Father. There, the Father's countenance would be turned toward Him and make Him full of joy. (Compare Hebrews 12:2.)

**2:29.** Peter declared it was proper for him to say boldly (freely and openly) of the patriarch (chief father, ancestral ruler) David

**26. Therefore did my heart rejoice:** . . . my heart was glad, *RSV* . . . my heart was cheered, *TCNT.*

**and my tongue was glad:** . . . rejoiced, *ASV* . . . exulted, *Rotherham* . . . my tongue exults, *Concordant* . . . told its delight, *TCNT* . . . greatly rejoiced, *ABUV* . . . is jubilant, *Berkeley* . . . rejoiced exceedingly, *Wuest.*

**moreover also my flesh shall rest in my hope:** Yea further even my flesh shall encamp on hope, *Rotherham* . . . And my body still lives in hope, *Williams* . . . repose in hope, *Wilson* . . . shall dwell, *ASV.*

**27. Because thou wilt not leave my soul in hell:** For thou wilt not abandon my soul to the Place of Death, *TCNT* . . . to the underworld, *HBIE* . . . to the nether world, *NAB* . . . unto hades, *ASV.*

**neither wilt thou suffer thine Holy One to see corruption:** Nor give up Thy Holy One to undergo decay, *Weymouth* . . . Your Loved One experience decay, *Beck* . . . your faithful servant to suffer death, *Noli* . . . to undergo, *NAB* . . . to see utter-corruption, *Rotherham* . . . experience decay, *Williams.*

**28. Thou hast made known to me the ways of life:** Thou hast shown me the path of life, *TCNT.*

**thou shalt make me full of joy with thy countenance:** Thou wilt fill me with happiness in thy presence, *TCNT* . . . You will fill Me with joy by being with Me, *Beck* . . . fill me with gladness, *Weymouth* . . . with delight, *Moffat* . . . with good cheer, *Berkeley* . . . in your presence, *NAB.*

**29. Men and brethren:** Brethren, *ASV* . . . Brothers, *NAB.*

**let me freely speak unto you of the patriarch David:** I can speak to you confidently about, *TCNT* . . . I can tell you with confidence, *Adams* . . . say to you with boldness, *Concordant* . . . I can tell you frankly, *Beck* . . . As to the patriarch David, I need hardly remind you, *Weymouth* . . . our progenitor David, *Wuest.*

**that he is both dead and buried:** That he both died and was buried, *ASV* . . . that he is deceased also, *Concordant* . . . not only that he died, *Norlie.*

# Acts 2:30

| 2504.1 conj | 2267.4 verb 3sing indic aor pass | 2504.1 conj | 3450.16 art sing neu | 3282.1 noun sing neu | 840.3 prs-pron gen sing | 1498.4 verb 3sing indic pres act |
|---|---|---|---|---|---|---|
| καὶ | ἐτάφη, | καὶ | τὸ | μνῆμα | αὐτοῦ | ἔστιν |
| *kai* | *etaphē* | *kai* | *to* | *mnēma* | *autou* | *estin* |
| and | was buried, | and | the | tomb | his | is |

| 1706.1 prep | 2231.3 prs-pron dat 1pl | 884.2 conj | 3450.10 art gen sing fem | 2232.1 noun fem | 3642.10 dem-pron gen sing fem |
|---|---|---|---|---|---|
| ἐν | ἡμῖν | ἄχρι | τῆς | ἡμέρας | ταύτης. |
| *en* | *hēmin* | *achri* | *tēs* | *hēmeras* | *tautēs* |
| among | us | until | the | day | this. |

| 4254.1 noun nom sing masc | 3631.1 partic | 5062.6 verb nom sing masc part pres act | 2504.1 conj | 3471.18 verb nom sing masc part perf act |
|---|---|---|---|---|
| **30.** προφήτης | οὖν | ὑπάρχων, | καὶ | εἰδὼς |
| *prophētēs* | *oun* | *huparchōn* | *kai* | *eidōs* |
| A prophet | therefore | being, | and | having known |

| 3617.1 conj | 3590.3 noun dat sing masc | 3523.6 verb 3sing indic aor act | 840.4 prs-pron dat sing | 3450.5 art nom sing masc | 2296.1 noun nom sing masc |
|---|---|---|---|---|---|
| ὅτι | ὅρκῳ | ὤμοσεν | αὐτῷ | ὁ | θεὸς, |
| *hoti* | *horkō* | *ōmosen* | *autō* | *ho* | *theos* |
| that | with an oath | swore | to him | | God, |

| 1523.2 prep gen | 2561.2 noun gen sing masc | 3450.10 art gen sing fem | 3613.1 noun gen sing fem | 840.3 prs-pron gen sing | 3450.16 art sing neu |
|---|---|---|---|---|---|
| ἐκ | καρποῦ | τῆς | ὀσφύος | αὐτοῦ | ⸂[a] τὸ |
| *ek* | *karpou* | *tēs* | *osphuos* | *autou* | *to* |
| of | fruit | of the | loins | his | the |

| 2567.3 prep | 4418.4 noun acc sing fem | 448.16 verb inf fut act | 3450.6 art acc sing masc | 5382.4 name acc masc |
|---|---|---|---|---|
| κατὰ | σάρκα | ἀναστήσειν | τὸν | χριστόν, ⸃ |
| *kata* | *sarka* | *anastēsein* | *ton* | *christon* |
| according to | flesh | to raise up | the | Christ, |

| 2495.12 verb inf aor act | 1894.3 prep | 3450.2 art gen sing | 2339.2 noun gen sing masc | 3450.6 art acc sing masc | 2339.4 noun acc sing masc |
|---|---|---|---|---|---|
| καθίσαι | ἐπὶ | ⸂ τοῦ | θρόνου | [ [b]☆ τὸν | θρόνον ] |
| *kathisai* | *epi* | *tou* | *thronou* | *ton* | *thronon* |
| to sit | upon | the | throne | [ the | throne ] |

| 840.3 prs-pron gen sing | 4134.1 verb nom sing masc part aor act | 2953.27 verb 3sing indic aor act | 3875.1 prep | 3450.10 art gen sing fem |
|---|---|---|---|---|
| αὐτοῦ, | **31.** προϊδὼν | ἐλάλησεν | περὶ | τῆς |
| *autou* | *proidōn* | *elalēsen* | *peri* | *tēs* |
| his, | having foreseen | he spoke | concerning | the |

| 384.2 noun gen sing fem | 3450.2 art gen sing | 5382.2 name gen masc | 3617.1 conj | 3620.3 partic | 3641.1 conj |
|---|---|---|---|---|---|
| ἀναστάσεως | τοῦ | Χριστοῦ, | ὅτι | ⸂ οὐ | [ [a]☆ οὔτε ] |
| *anastaseōs* | *tou* | *Christou* | *hoti* | *ou* | *oute* |
| resurrection | of the | Christ, | that | not | [ neither ] |

| 2611.10 verb 3sing indic aor pass | 1452.8 verb 3sing indic aor pass | 3450.9 art nom sing fem | 5425.1 noun nom sing fem | 840.3 prs-pron gen sing |
|---|---|---|---|---|
| ⸂ κατελείφθη | [ [b]☆ ἐγκατελείφθη ] | ⸂[c] ἡ | ψυχὴ | αὐτοῦ ⸃ |
| *kateleiphthē* | *enkateleiphthē* | *hē* | *psuchē* | *autou* |
| was left | [ idem ] | the | soul | his |

| 1519.1 prep | 85.2 noun gen sing masc | 85.5 noun acc sing masc | 3624.1 conj | 3450.9 art nom sing fem | 3641.1 conj |
|---|---|---|---|---|---|
| εἰς | ⸂ ᾅδου, | [ [d]☆ ᾅδην ] | ⸂ οὐδὲ | ἡ | [ [e]☆ οὔτε ] |
| *eis* | *hadou* | *hadēn* | *oude* | *hē* | *oute* |
| in | hades | [ idem ] | nor | the | [ idem ] |

30.a.**Txt:** 05D-org,025P 1241,byz.Sod
**Var:** p74,01ℵ,02A,03B 04C,05D-corr,sa.bo. Gries,Lach,Treg,Alf Tisc,We/Ho,Weis UBS/☆

30.b.**Txt:** 08E,025P,byz.
**Var:** 01ℵ,02A,03B,04C 05D,Lach,Treg,Alf,Tisc We/Ho,Weis,Sod UBS/☆

31.a.**Txt:** 08E,025P,byz. sa.bo.
**Var:** 01ℵ,02A,03B,04C 05D,Lach,Treg,Alf Word,Tisc,We/Ho,Weis Sod,UBS/☆

31.b.**Txt:** 025P,byz.
**Var:** 02A,Lach,Treg,Alf Sod,UBS/☆

31.c.**Txt:** 04C-corr,08E 025P,byz.
**Var:** 01ℵ,02A,03B 04C-org,05D,sa.bo.Gries Lach,Treg,Alf,Tisc We/Ho,Weis,Sod UBS/☆

31.d.**Txt:** 02A,04C,05D 08E,025P,byz.
**Var:** 01ℵ,03B,1739,Tisc We/Ho,Weis,Sod UBS/☆

31.e.**Txt:** 03B,08E,025P byz.Weis
**Var:** 01ℵ,02A,04C,05D Lach,Treg,Alf,Word Tisc,We/Ho,Sod,UBS/☆

that the psalm could not possibly apply to him. He not only died and was buried, his tomb was still there in Jerusalem. Obviously David's flesh did see corruption. But Jesus' did not. This clearly implies Jesus' tomb was empty.

There have been several suggestions concerning the precise location of David's tomb. Some place it in the town of Bethlehem, the place of David's birth. Others believe it was somewhere in the vicinity of Gethsemane. More likely the tomb was actually near Siloam. This conclusion is based upon a statement made in Nehemiah 3:16 concerning the work which was done in repairing the walls of Jerusalem: "After him Nehemiah the son of Azbuk . . . made repairs as far as a point opposite the tombs of David, and as far as the artificial pool and the house of the mighty men" (NASB). The artificial pool referred to in this verse is apparently the pool of Siloam which served as a major source of water for the city of Jerusalem. The Jewish historian Josephus reports that during the siege of Jerusalem (ca. 135 B.C.). John Hyrcanus, the high priest during the period of the Maccabees, robbed the tomb of David. About 100 years later King Herod made a similar attempt but was thwarted, supposedly through God's intervention (see *Wars of the Jews* 1.2.5; *Antiquities* 8.8.4; 16.7.1; cf. Bruce, *New International Commentary, Acts,* p.66).

**2:30.** Because David was a prophet (a speaker for God), and because he knew God had sworn an oath that of the fruit of his loins One would sit on his throne, he foresaw and spoke of the resurrection of Christ (the Messiah, God's Anointed One). The reference here is to the Davidic covenant. In it God promised David there would always be a man from his seed for the throne. This was first given with respect to Solomon (2 Samuel 7:11-16). But it recognized that if David's descendants sinned they would have to be punished. God, however, would never turn His back on David's line and substitute another as He had done in the case of King Saul (Psalms 89:3,4; 132:11,12).

Because the kings of David's line did not follow the Lord, God finally had to bring an end to their kingdom and send the people to Babylon. His purpose was to rid Israel of idolatry. But the promise to David still stood. There would yet be One to sit on David's throne and make it eternal.

**2:31.** Peter did not give any details of Christ's descent into Hades. The notion that Jesus spent the 3 days following His crucifixion leading the righteous dead out of paradise and snatching the keys of Hades and Death from Satan is not supported by the Scriptures. Speculation about this goes beyond what the Scripture teaches. Instead, Peter declared that what David foresaw in the psalm was the resurrection of Christ (literally, the Christ, that is, the Messiah, God's Anointed Prophet, Priest, and King). In other words, Peter



**and his sepulchre is with us unto this day:** . . . his monument, *Darby* . . . His tomb is known to us, *Noli* . . . we still have his tomb among us, *Weymouth* . . . His grave is still here with us today, *Everyday* . . . is in our midst to this day, *NAB* . . . until the present time, *Fenton.*

**30. Therefore being a prophet:** Speaking, then, as a Prophet, *TCNT* . . . He was one who spoke for God, *NLT* . . . but he was a prophet, *Williams C.K.*

**and knowing that God had sworn with an oath to him:** . . . had solemnly sworn to him, *TCNT, TNT* . . . sworn to him with an oath, *Norlie.*

**that of the fruit of his loins, according to the flesh:** . . . that of the fruit of his loins, *ASV* . . . of his body, *Williams C.K.* . . . From his family, *NLT* . . . to set one of his descendants, *TCNT.*

**he would raise up Christ to sit on his throne:** Christ would come and take His place as King, *NLT* . . . he would set one upon his throne, *ASV* . . . place one of his descendants, *Adams* . . . set (one) upon his throne, *PNT.*

**31. He seeing this before:** . . . he foreseeing this, *ASV* . . . David looked into the future, *TCNT* . . . with prophetic foresight he spoke of, *Weymouth* . . . David saw what was ahead, *Beck* . . . knew this before it happened, *Everyday, NCV* . . . thus proclaiming beforehand, *NAB* . . . with a prevision, *Moffatt.*

**spake of the resurrection of Christ:** . . . and was referring to, *TCNT* . . . the resurrection of the Messiah, *NAB* . . . and said the promised Saviour would rise again, *Beck.*

**that his soul was not left in hell:** . . . that he had not been abandoned to the Place of Death, *TCNT* . . . abandoned in the unseen, *Concordant* . . . to the underworld, *Noyes* . . . to the effect that He was not left forsaken in the grave, *Weymouth* . . . He was not deserted when He was dead, *Beck* . . . abandoned to the realm of the dead, *Berkeley* . . . neither was He left...in the unseen world reserved for the human dead, *Wuest* . . . was not deserted in death, *Phillips* . . . was not abandoned to the nether world, *NAB.*

| 4418.1 noun nom sing fem | 840.3 prs-pron gen sing | 1481.3 verb 3sing indic aor act | 1306.1 noun acc sing fem | 3642.6 dem-pron acc sing masc |
|---|---|---|---|---|
| σὰρξ | αὐτοῦ | εἶδεν | διαφθοράν. | 32. τοῦτον |
| *sarx* | *autou* | *eiden* | *diaphthoran* | *touton* |
| flesh | his | saw | corruption. | This |

| 3450.6 art acc sing masc | 2400.3 name acc masc | 448.3 verb 3sing indic aor act | 3450.5 art nom sing masc | 2296.1 noun nom sing masc |
|---|---|---|---|---|
| τὸν | Ἰησοῦν | ἀνέστησεν | ὁ | θεός |
| *ton* | *Iēsoun* | *anestēsen* | *ho* | *theos* |
|  | Jesus | raised up |  | God |

| 3614.2 rel-pron gen sing | 3820.7 adj nom pl masc | 2231.1 prs-pron nom 1pl | 1498.5 verb 1pl indic pres act | 3116.4 noun nom pl masc | 3450.11 art dat sing fem |
|---|---|---|---|---|---|
| οὗ | πάντες | ἡμεῖς | ἐσμεν | μάρτυρες. | 33. τῇ |
| *hou* | *pantes* | *hēmeis* | *esmen* | *martures* | *tē* |
| of which | all | we | are | witnesses. | By the |

| 1182.5 adj dat sing fem | 3631.1 partic | 3450.2 art gen sing | 2296.2 noun gen sing masc | 5150.8 verb nom sing masc part aor pass |
|---|---|---|---|---|
| δεξιᾷ | οὖν | τοῦ | θεοῦ | ὑψωθεὶς, |
| *dexia* | *oun* | *tou* | *theou* | *hupsōtheis* |
| right hand | therefore |  | of God | having been exalted, |

| 3450.12 art acc sing fem | 4885.1 conj | 1845.4 noun acc sing fem | 3450.2 art gen sing | 39.2 adj gen sing | 4011.2 noun gen sing neu |
|---|---|---|---|---|---|
| τήν | τε | ἐπαγγελίαν | τοῦ | ⸀ ἁγίου | πνεύματος |
| *tēn* | *te* | *epangelian* | *tou* | *hagiou* | *pneumatos* |
| the | and | promise | of the | Holy | Spirit |

33.a.**Txt:** 05D,025P,byz. **Var:** 01ℵ,02A,03B,04C 08E,Lach,Treg,Alf,Tisc We/Ho,Weis,Sod UBS/☆

| 4011.2 noun gen sing neu | 3450.2 art gen sing | 39.2 adj gen sing | 2956.25 verb nom sing masc part aor act | 3706.2 prep |
|---|---|---|---|---|
| [a☆ πνεύματος | τοῦ | ἁγίου ] | λαβὼν | παρὰ |
| *pneumatos* | *tou* | *hagiou* | *labōn* | *para* |
| [ Spirit | of the | Holy ] | having received | from |

33.b.**Txt:** 04C-corr,08E 025P,byz. **Var:** 01ℵ,02A,03B 04C-org,05D-corr,sa.bo. Gries,Lach,Treg,Alf Tisc,We/Ho,Weis,Sod UBS/☆

| 3450.2 art gen sing | 3824.2 noun gen sing masc | 1618.1 verb 3sing indic aor act | 3642.17 dem-pron sing neu | 3614.16 rel-pron sing neu | 3431.1 adv |
|---|---|---|---|---|---|
| τοῦ | πατρὸς, | ἐξέχεεν | τοῦτο | ὃ | ⸂b νῦν ⸃ |
| *tou* | *patros* | *execheen* | *touto* | *ho* | *nun* |
| the | Father, | he poured out | this | which | now |

33.c.**Var:** 03B,05D,Alf Tisc,We/Ho,Weis,Sod UBS/☆

| 5050.1 prs-pron nom 2pl | 2504.1 conj | 984.1 verb 2pl pres act | 2504.1 conj | 189.2 verb 2pl pres act | 3620.3 partic | 1056.1 conj |
|---|---|---|---|---|---|---|
| ὑμεῖς | [c☆+ καὶ ] | βλέπετε | καὶ | ἀκούετε. | 34. οὐ | γὰρ |
| *humeis* | *kai* | *blepete* | *kai* | *akouete* | *ou* | *gar* |
| you | [ also ] | see | and | hear. | Not | for |

| 1132.1 name masc | 303.13 verb 3sing indic aor act | 1519.1 prep | 3450.8 art acc pl masc | 3636.9 noun acc pl masc | 2978.5 verb 3sing indic pres act |
|---|---|---|---|---|---|
| Δαβὶδ | ἀνέβη | εἰς | τοὺς | οὐρανούς, | λέγει |
| *Dabid* | *anebē* | *eis* | *tous* | *ouranous* | *legei* |
| David | ascended | into | the | heavens, | he says |

34.a.**Txt:** 01ℵ-corr,02A 03B-corr,04C,08E,025P etc.byz.Sod **Var:** 01ℵ-org,03B-org 05D,Treg,Alf,Tisc We/Ho,Weis,UBS/☆

| 1156.2 conj | 840.5 prs-pron nom sing masc | 1500.5 verb 3sing indic aor act | 3450.5 art nom sing masc | 2935.1 noun nom sing masc | 3450.3 art dat sing |
|---|---|---|---|---|---|
| δὲ | αὐτός, | Εἶπεν | ⸂a ὁ ⸃ | κύριος | τῷ |
| *de* | *autos* | *Eipen* | *ho* | *kurios* | *tō* |
| but | himself, | Said | the | Lord | to the |

| 2935.3 noun dat sing masc | 1466.2 prs-pron gen 1sing | 2493.4 verb 2sing impr pres mid | 1523.2 prep gen | 1182.7 adj gen pl neu | 1466.2 prs-pron gen 1sing |
|---|---|---|---|---|---|
| κυρίῳ | μου, | Κάθου | ἐκ | δεξιῶν | μου· |
| *kuriō* | *mou* | *Kathou* | *ek* | *dexiōn* | *mou* |
| Lord | my, | Sit | at | right hand | my, |

declared Jesus to be the messianic King. Because God raised Him up, He was not left in Hades, nor did His flesh see corruption.

**2:32.** Again Peter emphasized that God is the One who raised up Jesus from the dead. He and all of the 120 who were gathered in the Upper Room were witnesses to His resurrection. First Corinthians 15:6 states that having appeared to Peter and then to the Twelve, Jesus also was seen by more than 500 men and women. It is reasonable to surmise that some or all of those now gathered for prayer were among the 500 who had seen the resurrected Christ.

This was important. The elders of the Sanhedrin knew the tomb of Jesus was empty, and the soldiers who were set to watch it told them of the angel who rolled back the stone. But they spread the story that the disciples came by night and stole the body while the guard slept. Peter made no reference to this story, but the crowd had undoubtedly heard it. Actually, it was ridiculous to believe that a Roman guard or even temple guards would sleep on duty and that the Roman seal could have been broken by disciples who had fled when Jesus was arrested. Now the people were faced, not by a few fearful disciples, but by 120 who were firsthand witnesses to the fact of Christ's resurrection, and who were filled with power through the baptism in the Holy Spirit.

**2:33.** Christ's resurrection, however, was only part of a process whereby God, by His right hand of power, raised Jesus to an exalted position of power and authority at His right hand. (Both *by* and *at* His right hand are indicated in the Greek.) This is also the place of triumph and victory. By paying the full price, Jesus won the battle against sin and death. He remains at God's right hand. (See Mark 16:9; Romans 8:34; Ephesians 1:20,21; Colossians 3:1; Hebrews 1:3; 8:1; 10:12; 12:2; 1 Peter 3:22.)

In Christ, believers also are seated "in heavenly places" (Ephesians 2:6). Because this is their position in Christ, they do not need their own works of righteousness to claim His promise. There can be no higher position than they already have in Christ.

Next Peter used Christ's exalted position to explain what had just occurred. Now at the Father's right hand, He had received from the Father the Promise of the Spirit and poured out the Spirit, as the crowd had seen and heard as the 120 spoke in other tongues. The outpouring of the Spirit was *evidence* that Jesus was actually exalted at the Father's right hand.

Before His death Jesus told the Twelve that it was necessary for Him to go away in order for the Comforter to come (John 16:7). Though the baptism in the Spirit is the Promise of the Father, Jesus is the One who pours it forth. God is the Giver; Jesus, the Baptizer. There is clear distinction between the Persons of the Trinity here.

**2:34,35.** That none of this could apply to David is further evidenced by another quotation from Scripture. David did not ascend



**neither his flesh did see corruption:** . . . nor did His body undergo decay, *Weymouth* . . . did not experience decay, *Beck* . . . nor was His flesh acquainted with decay, *Concordant* . . . his body was never destroyed, *Phillips* . . . did not rot, *Everyday* . . . his flesh was not allowed to suffer death, *Noli.*

**32. This Jesus hath God raised up:** It was this Jesus, whom God raised to life, *TCNT* . . . Jesus is this one, *NLT.*

**whereof we all are witnesses:** . . . and of that fact we are ourselves all witnesses, *TCNT* . . . a fact to which all of us testify, *Weymouth* . . . and we have all seen Him, *NLT.*

**33. Therefore being by the right hand of God exalted:** So then, now that he has been exalted to the right hand of God, *TCNT* . . . when He was exalted, *Adams* . . . Being therefore lifted high by the right hand of God, *Weymouth* . . . Since he is by the mighty hand of God exalted, *Montgomery* . . . Lifted up to God's right side, *Beck.*

**and having received of the Father:** . . . and, as promised, *Norlie.*

**the promise of the Holy Ghost:** . . . the promised gift of the Holy Spirit, *TCNT* . . . that Spirit, *Everyday.*

**he hath shed forth this:** He hath poured forth this, *ASV* . . . He was pouring forth this, *Worrell* . . . flows from him, *NEB* . . . So now Jesus has poured out, *Everyday* . . . this Spirit, *Confraternity* . . . which he poured out as you see, *Noli.*

**which ye now see and hear:** This is what you, *Everyday* . . . you are observing, *Concordant* . . . as you now see and hear for yourselves, *TCNT.*

**34. For David is not ascended into the heavens:** For it was not David who went up into Heaven, *TCNT* . . . did not go up into heaven, *Williams C.K.*

**but he saith himself:** Indeed he says himself, *TCNT.*

**The LORD said unto my Lord:** The Lord said to my master, *TCNT.*

**Sit thou on my right hand:** Sit at my right hand, *Weymouth.*

| **2175.1** conj | **300.1** partic | **4935.12** verb 1sing subj aor act | **3450.8** art acc pl masc | **2172.7** adj acc pl masc | **4622.2** prs-pron gen 2sing |
|---|---|---|---|---|---|
| **35.** ἕως | ἂν | θῶ | τοὺς | ἐχθρούς | σου |
| *heōs* | *an* | *thō* | *tous* | *echthrous* | *sou* |
| until | | I place | the | enemies | your |

| **5124.1** noun sing neu | **3450.1** art gen pl | **4087.5** noun gen pl masc | **4622.2** prs-pron gen 2sing | **800.1** adv |
|---|---|---|---|---|
| ὑποπόδιον | τῶν | ποδῶν | σου. | **36.** Ἀσφαλῶς |
| *hupopodion* | *tōn* | *podōn* | *sou* | *Asphalōs* |
| a footstool | of the | feet | your. | Assuredly |

| **3631.1** partic | **1091.10** verb 3sing impr pres act | **3820.6** adj nom sing masc | **3486.1** noun nom sing masc | **2447.1** name masc | **3617.1** conj |
|---|---|---|---|---|---|
| οὖν | γινωσκέτω | πᾶς | οἶκος | Ἰσραήλ, | ὅτι |
| *oun* | *ginōsketō* | *pas* | *oikos* | *Israēl* | *hoti* |
| therefore | let know | all | house | of Israel, | that |

| **2504.1** conj | **2935.4** noun acc sing masc | **2504.1** conj | **5382.4** name acc masc | **840.6** prs-pron acc sing masc | **840.6** prs-pron acc sing masc | **2504.1** conj |
|---|---|---|---|---|---|---|
| καὶ | κύριον | ʿ καὶ | Χριστὸν | αὐτὸν | [☆ αὐτὸν | καὶ |
| *kai* | *kurion* | *kai* | *Christon* | *auton* | *auton* | *kai* |
| both | Lord | and | Christ | him | [ him | and |

| **5382.4** name acc masc | **3450.5** art nom sing masc | **2296.1** noun nom sing masc | **4020.24** verb 3sing indic aor act | **4020.24** verb 3sing indic aor act |
|---|---|---|---|---|
| Χριστὸν ] | ʿ ὁ | θεός | ἐποίησεν, | [☆ ἐποίησεν |
| *Christon* | *ho* | *theos* | *epoiēsen* | *epoiēsen* |
| Christ ] | | God | made | [ made |

| **3450.5** art nom sing masc | **2296.1** noun nom sing masc | **3642.6** dem-pron acc sing masc | **3450.6** art acc sing masc | **2400.3** name acc masc |
|---|---|---|---|---|
| ὁ | θεός, ] | τοῦτον | τὸν | Ἰησοῦν |
| *ho* | *theos* | *touton* | *ton* | *Iēsoun* |
| | God, ] | this | | Jesus |

| **3614.6** rel-pron acc sing masc | **5050.1** prs-pron nom 2pl | **4568.2** verb 2pl indic aor act | **189.32** verb nom pl masc part aor act |
|---|---|---|---|
| ὃν | ὑμεῖς | ἐσταυρώσατε. | **37.** Ἀκούσαντες |
| *hon* | *humeis* | *estaurōsate* | *Akousantes* |
| whom | you | crucified. | Having heard |

37.a.**Txt:** 05D,08E,025P byz.
**Var:** 01ℵ,02A,03B,04C Lach,Treg,Alf,Tisc We/Ho,Weis,Sod UBS/☆

| **1156.2** conj | **2630.1** verb 3pl indic aor pass | **3450.11** art dat sing fem | **2559.3** noun dat sing fem | **3450.12** art acc sing fem |
|---|---|---|---|---|
| δὲ | κατενύγησαν | ʿ τῇ | καρδίᾳ, | [a☆ τὴν |
| *de* | *katenugēsan* | *tē* | *kardia* | *tēn* |
| and | they were pricked | in the | heart | [ the |

| **2559.4** noun acc sing fem | **1500.3** verb indic aor act | **4885.1** conj | **4242.1** prep | **3450.6** art acc sing masc | **3935.4** name acc masc | **2504.1** conj |
|---|---|---|---|---|---|---|
| καρδίαν, ] | εἶπόν | τε | πρός | τὸν | Πέτρον | καὶ |
| *kardian* | *eipon* | *te* | *pros* | *ton* | *Petron* | *kai* |
| heart, ] | said | both | to | | Peter | and |

| **3450.8** art acc pl masc | **3036.4** adj acc pl masc | **646.7** noun acc pl masc | **4949.9** intr-pron sing neu | **4020.53** verb 1pl indic fut act |
|---|---|---|---|---|
| τοὺς | λοιποὺς | ἀποστόλους, | Τί | ʿ ποιήσομεν, |
| *tous* | *loipous* | *apostolous* | *Ti* | *poiēsomen* |
| the | remaining | apostles, | What | shall we do |

37.b.**Txt:** 05D,byz.
**Var:** 01ℵ,02A,03B,04C 08E,025P,Treg,Alf,Tisc We/Ho,Weis,Sod UBS/☆

| **4020.30** verb 1pl subj aor act | **433.6** noun nom pl masc | **79.6** noun nom pl masc | **3935.1** name nom masc | **1156.2** conj |
|---|---|---|---|---|
| [b☆ ποιήσωμεν, ] | ἄνδρες | ἀδελφοί; | **38.** Πέτρος | δὲ |
| *poiēsōmen* | *andres* | *adelphoi* | *Petros* | *de* |
| [ should we do, ] | men | brothers? | Peter | and |

into the heavens as Jesus did, but he prophesied that exaltation of Jesus in Psalm 110:1. Again, David could not be speaking of himself for he said, "The Lord said unto my Lord, Sit thou at my right hand, until I make thine enemies thy footstool." Making enemies a footstool signified complete and final defeat, a total triumph over them. (See Joshua 10:24 where Joshua had his generals put their feet on the necks of the conquered kings.) Jesus also referred to Psalm 110:1 in Luke 20:41-44 where He recognized that David called his greater Son "Lord." (See also Matthew 22:42-45; Mark 12:36,37.)

The resurrection and ascension of Jesus are inseparably linked. Though they were separated by 40 days, they are both important elements of the redemption act. (Hebrews 9:12,24 also emphasizes that Christ's entrance into heaven was necessary for the completion of the believer's redemption.) Jesus was not simply raised from the dead, He was raised to the right hand of the Father where He is now exalted. In John 17:5 Jesus prayed that the Father would glorify Him with His own self, with the glory which He had before the world was brought into being. This was accomplished when Jesus rose and ascended to the place of authority in heaven which is His by right of His eternal sonship.

**2:36.** The conclusion Peter drew is that all the house of Israel needed to know assuredly that God has made this Jesus, whom they (the Jerusalem residents) crucified, both Lord and Christ (Messiah, God's anointed Prophet, Priest, and King).

In fulfillment of Joel's prophecy, Jesus is the Lord on whom all must call for salvation. Paul also recognized that God has highly exalted Him and given Him a name that is above every other name (Philippians 2:9). *The Name* in the Old Testament Hebrew always means the name of God. (The Hebrew has other ways of referring to the name of a human being without using the word *the*, so whenever the Hebrew uses *the* with the word *name* it refers to the name of God.) *The Name* stands for the authority, person, and especially the character of God in His righteousness, holiness, faithfulness, goodness, love, and power. *Lord* was used in the New Testament for the name of God. Mercy, grace, and love are part of the holiness, the holy Name by which Jesus is recognized as "Lord," the full revelation of God to man.

**2:37.** The response to this manifestation of the gift of prophecy was immediate. The listeners were pierced to the heart. No longer were they saying, "What does this mean?" Peter's words from the Holy Spirit stung their consciences. They cried out to him and to the other apostles (who were evidently still standing with him), "Brothers, what shall we do?"

They did not feel completely cut off, however. Peter had called them brothers, and they responded by calling the apostles brothers. Their sin in rejecting and crucifying Christ was great, but their very cry shows they believed there was hope.

**35. Until I make thy foes thy footstool:** Till I put thy enemies as a footstool under thy feet, *TCNT* . . . for those who hate You will be a place to rest Your feet, *NLT* . . . put your enemies under your control, *Everyday, NCV* . . . the footstool of your feet, *Williams* . . . underneath thy feet, *Wilson.*

**36. Therefore let all the house of Israel know assuredly:** . . . the whole nation...must understand, *Goodspeed* . . . So let all Israel know beyond all doubt, *TCNT* . . . Without a shadow of doubt, then, let the whole house of Israel acknowledge, *Berkeley* . . . The whole Jewish nation must know for sure, *NLT* . . . certainly know, *Wilson* . . . should know this truly, *Everyday, NCV* . . . safely know, *Swann.*

**that God hath made that same Jesus, whom ye have crucified both Lord and Christ:** . . . that God has declared, *Goodspeed* . . . that God has made him both Master and Christ—this very Jesus whom you crucified, *TCNT* . . . and Messiah, *NAB* . . . He is the man you nailed to the cross! *Everyday.*

**37. Now when they heard this, they were pricked in their heart:** As they were listening, *MLNT* . . . heard this statement, they were deeply moved, *Noli* . . . it went straight to their hearts, *Moffatt* . . . stabbed to the heart, *Williams* . . . moved to the depths of their hearts, *Berkeley* . . . cut to the heart, *RSV, TNT* . . . they felt crushed, *Beck* . . . their heart was pricked with compunction, *Concordant* . . . they were deeply shaken, *NAB* . . . stung to the heart, *Goodspeed, Wuest* . . . their consciences pricked them, *TCNT* . . . their hearts were troubled, *NLT, Norlie* . . . pierced to the heart, *Confraternity, Hanson* . . . felt a sharp, cutting pain in their conscience, *SEB* . . . they were sick at heart, *Everyday.*

**and said unto Peter and to the rest of the apostles:** They asked Peter and the other apostles, *Beck* . . . and to the other missionaries, *NLT.*

**Men and brethren, what shall we do?:** What are we to do, Brothers, *TCNT* . . . Fellow Jews, what should we do, *Beck.*

## Acts 2:39

38.a.**Txt:** 08E,025P,044 byz.sa.bo.
**Var:** p74,01ℵ,02A,03B 04C,05D,Lach,Treg,Alf Tisc,We/Ho,Weis,Sod UBS/☆

38.b.**Var:** p74,01ℵ,02A 04C,05D,Tisc,Sod

38.c.**Var:** 03B,04C,05D 1739,Lach,Treg,We/Ho

| **5183.4** verb 3sing indic act | **4242.1** prep | **840.8** prs-pron acc pl masc | **3210.12** verb 2pl impr aor act | **5183.2** verb 3sing indic pres act |
|---|---|---|---|---|
| ⸀a ἔφη ⸌ | πρὸς | αὐτούς, | Μετανοήσατε, | [b+ φησίν, ] |
| *ephē* | *pros* | *autous* | *Metanoēsate* | *phēsin* |
| said | to | them, | Repent | [ says, ] |

| **2504.1** conj | **901.21** verb 3sing impr aor pass | **1524.3** adj nom sing masc | **5050.2** prs-pron gen 2pl | **1894.3** prep | **1706.1** prep |
|---|---|---|---|---|---|
| καὶ | βαπτισθήτω | ἕκαστος | ὑμῶν | ⸀ ἐπὶ | [c ἐν ] |
| *kai* | *baptisthētō* | *hekastos* | *humōn* | *epi* | *en* |
| and | let be baptized | each | of you | in | [ idem ] |

| **3450.3** art dat sing | **3549.4** noun dat sing neu | **2400.2** name masc | **5382.2** name gen masc | **1519.1** prep | **852.3** noun acc sing fem |
|---|---|---|---|---|---|
| τῷ | ὀνόματι | Ἰησοῦ | Χριστοῦ, | εἰς | ἄφεσιν |
| *tō* | *onomati* | *Iēsou* | *Christou* | *eis* | *aphesin* |
| the | name | of Jesus | Christ, | for | remission |

38.d.**Txt:** 05D,08E,025P byz.
**Var:** 01ℵ,02A,03B,04C sa.bo.Lach,Treg,Tisc We/Ho,Weis,Sod UBS/☆

| **264.6** noun gen pl fem | **3450.1** art gen pl | **264.6** noun gen pl fem | **5050.2** prs-pron gen 2pl | **2504.1** conj |
|---|---|---|---|---|
| ⸀ ἁμαρτιῶν, | [d☆ τῶν | ἁμαρτιῶν | ὑμῶν, ] | καὶ |
| *hamartiōn* | *tōn* | *hamartiōn* | *humōn* | *kai* |
| of sins | [ of the | sins | your, ] | and |

| **2956.41** verb 2pl indic fut mid | **2956.47** verb 2pl indic fut mid | **3450.12** art acc sing fem | **1424.4** noun acc sing fem | **3450.2** art gen sing |
|---|---|---|---|---|
| ⸀ λήψεσθε | [☆ λήμψεσθε ] | τὴν | δωρεὰν | τοῦ |
| *lēpsesthe* | *lēmpsesthe* | *tēn* | *dōrean* | *tou* |
| you will receive | [ idem ] | the | gift | of the |

| **39.2** adj gen sing | **4011.2** noun gen sing neu | | **5050.3** prs-pron dat 2pl | **1056.1** conj | **1498.4** verb 3sing indic pres act | **3450.9** art nom sing fem |
|---|---|---|---|---|---|---|
| ἁγίου | πνεύματος. | **39.** | ὑμῖν | γάρ | ἐστιν | ἡ |
| *hagiou* | *pneumatos* | | *humin* | *gar* | *estin* | *hē* |
| Holy | Spirit. | | To you | for | is | the |

| **1845.2** noun nom sing fem | **2504.1** conj | **3450.4** art dat pl | **4891.6** noun dat pl neu | **5050.2** prs-pron gen 2pl | **2504.1** conj | **3820.5** adj dat pl |
|---|---|---|---|---|---|---|
| ἐπαγγελία | καὶ | τοῖς | τέκνοις | ὑμῶν, | καὶ | πᾶσιν |
| *epangelia* | *kai* | *tois* | *teknois* | *humōn* | *kai* | *pasin* |
| promise | and | to the | children | your, | and | to all |

| **3450.4** art dat pl | **1519.1** prep | **3089.1** adj acc sing fem | **3607.4** rel-pron acc pl masc | **300.1** partic | **4200.2** verb 3sing subj aor mid |
|---|---|---|---|---|---|
| τοῖς | εἰς | μακρὰν, | ὅσους | ἂν | προσκαλέσηται |
| *tois* | *eis* | *makran* | *hosous* | *an* | *proskalesētai* |
| the | at | a distance, | as many as | | may call |

| **2935.1** noun nom sing masc | **3450.5** art nom sing masc | **2296.1** noun nom sing masc | **2231.2** prs-pron gen 1pl | | **2066.4** adj dat pl |
|---|---|---|---|---|---|
| κύριος | ὁ | θεὸς | ἡμῶν. | **40.** | Ἑτέροις |
| *kurios* | *ho* | *theos* | *hēmōn* | | *Heterois* |
| Lord | | God | our. | | With other |

40.a.**Txt:** 025P,byz.
**Var:** 01ℵ,02A,03B,04C 05D,08E,Lach,Treg,Alf Word,Tisc,We/Ho,Weis Sod,UBS/☆

40.b.**Var:** 01ℵ,02A,03B 04C,05D,sa.bo.Lach Treg,Alf,Word,Tisc We/Ho,Weis,Sod UBS/☆

| **4885.1** conj | **3030.7** noun dat pl masc | **3979.6** adj comp dat pl masc | **1257.10** verb 3sing indic imperf mid |
|---|---|---|---|
| τε | λόγοις | πλείοσιν | ⸀ διεμαρτύρετο, |
| *te* | *logois* | *pleiosin* | *diemartureto* |
| and | words | many | he was earnestly testifying |

| **1257.6** verb 3sing indic aor mid | **2504.1** conj | **3731.18** verb 3sing indic imperf act | **840.8** prs-pron acc pl masc |
|---|---|---|---|
| [a☆ διεμαρτύρατο, ] | καὶ | παρεκάλει | [b☆+ αὐτοὺς ] |
| *diemarturato* | *kai* | *parekalei* | *autous* |
| [ he earnestly testified ] | and | was exhorting | [ them ] |

**2:38.** Peter answered by calling them to repent, that is, to change their minds and fundamental attitudes by accepting the change required. This would produce a renewing of their minds as well as a change in attitude toward sin and self.

The repentant ones could show that change of mind and heart by being baptized in the name of Jesus. A survey of New Testament passages discussing water baptism for believers reveals it is described in various ways. In verse 38 the phrase "*in* the name of Jesus Christ" employs the preposition *epi* with the dative case. Matthew 28:19 reads "*in* the name of the Father, and of the Son, and of the Holy Ghost" and uses the preposition *eis* ("in, into") along with the Trinitarian confession. Acts 8:16 and 19:5 use the phrase "in (*eis*) the name of the Lord Jesus" while 10:48 shows "in (*en*) the name of the Lord" (KJV) or "in the name of Jesus Christ" (NIV), depending on the Greek manuscripts being followed. (Modern versions translate the Greek differently either in an attempt to clarify what is meant or because the manuscripts which serve as a basis for the translation show numerous variants at these passages.) The various Greek prepositions which are used do not greatly change the meaning of the phrase "in the name of Jesus." It may be understood to mean upon the authority of Jesus. (For similar uses of this phrase in Luke's writings see Luke 9:49; 10:17; Acts 3:6,16; 4:7; 9:27.)

This baptism would also be for (*eis*) the forgiveness of sins. *Eis* here means "because of" or "with a view toward" just as it does in Matthew 3:11 where John baptized "because of" repentance. John baptized no one to produce repentance. Rather, he demanded works demonstrating true repentance.

**2:39.** Peter identified the gift with the Promise (1:4). This promise, or "gift of the Holy Ghost," was not limited to the 120. It would continue to be available, not only to the 3,000 who responded, but to their children (including all their descendants), and to all who were far away, even to as many as the Lord should call to himself. In verse 38 Peter said that in order to receive the Promise of the Father a person must "repent, and be baptized . . . in the name of Jesus Christ."

The "calling" here may refer to Joel 2:32, but it cannot be limited to the Jews. In Isaiah 57:19 God speaks peace to the one far off. Ephesians 2:17 applies this to the Gentiles. Acts 1:8 speaks of the uttermost part of the earth. It is clear that the promise of the Spirit is for the Gentiles also.

**2:40.** Luke did not record the rest of Peter's witness and exhortation. But in this exhortation Peter was evidently exercising another of the gifts of the Spirit. (Romans 12:8 lists exhortation as a distinct gift of the Holy Spirit, though 1 Corinthians 14:3 includes it as part of the gift of prophecy. The Bible does not draw hard and fast lines between gifts.) Thus, Peter became the instrument or agent through whom the Holy Spirit carried out the work fore-

**38. Then Peter said unto them, Repent:** Each one of you must turn from sin, return to God, *Taylor* . . . change your minds, *Fenton* . . . Get a new mind, *Klingensmith* . . . Amend your lives, *Geneva*.

**and be baptized every one of you in the name of Jesus Christ:** . . . and, as an expression of it, let every one, *Williams* . . . and be immersed, *ABUV* . . . for the pardon of your sins, *Concordant* . . . on the basis of the name of Jesus Christ, *Adams* . . . in reliance on the name, *HBIE*.

**for the remission of sins:** . . . that you may have your sins forgiven, *Williams* . . . for a release, *Fenton* . . . for the forgiveness of your sins, *TCNT*.

**and ye shall receive the gift of the Holy Ghost:** . . . you will be given the Holy Spirit, *Beck* . . . the gratuity of, *Concordant* . . . the free-gift of the Holy Spirit, *Rotherham*.

**39. For the promise is unto you, and to your children:** For the promise is for you, *TCNT* . . . this great promise, *Phillips* . . . For to you belongs the promise, *Weymouth* . . . What is promised belongs to you, *Beck* . . . the promise is meant for you, *Moffatt*.

**and to all that are afar off:** . . . all who are far away, *Beck*.

**even as many as the Lord our God shall call:** . . . as many as the Lord our God invites and bids come to Himself, *AmpB* . . . shall call unto him, *ASV* . . . every one whom the Lord our God calls to him, *RSV* . . . with a divine summons call to himself, *Wuest* . . . our God may call unto him, *Rotherham* . . . shall call to himself! *Phillips* . . . those who may be marked out, *BB*.

**40. And with many other words did he testify and exhort, saying:** In many other ways Peter bore his testimony, and urged the people, *TCNT* . . . And with many different words bare he full witness, and went on exhorting them saying, *Rotherham* . . . more appeals he solemnly warned and entreated them, saying, *Weymouth* . . . With many more words he continued to testify and to plead with them, *Williams* . . . using many arguments, *JB* . . . with emphasis on the plea, *Norlie*.

## Acts 2:41

| 2978.15 verb nom sing masc part pres act | 4834.24 verb 2pl aor pass | 570.3 prep | 3450.10 art gen sing fem | 1067.1 noun fem | 3450.10 art gen sing fem |
|---|---|---|---|---|---|
| λέγων, | Σώθητε | ἀπὸ | τῆς | γενεᾶς | τῆς |
| *legōn* | *Sōthēte* | *apo* | *tēs* | *geneas* | *tēs* |
| saying, | Be saved | from | the | generation | the |

| 4501.2 adj gen sing fem | 3642.10 dem-pron gen sing fem | 3450.7 art nom pl masc | 3173.1 conj | 3631.1 partic |
|---|---|---|---|---|
| σκολιᾶς | ταύτης. | **41.** Οἱ | μὲν | οὖν |
| *skolias* | *tautēs* | *Hoi* | *men* | *oun* |
| crooked | this. | The | | therefore |

41.a.**Txt:** 08E,025P,byz.
**Var:** 01ℵ,02A,03B,04C 05D,sa.bo.Lach,Treg Alf,Tisc,We/Ho,Weis Sod,UBS/*

| 774.1 adv | 583.4 verb nom pl masc part aor mid | 3450.6 art acc sing masc | 3030.4 noun acc sing masc | 840.3 prs-pron gen sing |
|---|---|---|---|---|
| ⸂ᵃ ἀσμένως ⸃ | ἀποδεξάμενοι | τὸν | λόγον | αὐτοῦ |
| *asmenōs* | *apodexamenoi* | *ton* | *logon* | *autou* |
| gladly | having welcomed | the | word | his |

41.b.**Var:** 01ℵ,02A,03B 04C,05D,Lach,Treg,Alf Tisc,We/Ho,Weis,Sod UBS/*

| 901.17 verb 3pl indic aor pass | 2504.1 conj | 4227.8 verb 3pl indic aor pass | 1706.1 prep | 3450.11 art dat sing fem |
|---|---|---|---|---|
| ἐβαπτίσθησαν· | καὶ | προσετέθησαν | [ᵇ☆+ ἐν ] | τῇ |
| *ebaptisthēsan* | *kai* | *prosetethēsan* | *en* | *tē* |
| were baptized; | and | were added | [ in ] | the |

| 2232.3 noun dat sing fem | 1552.11 dem-pron dat sing fem | 5425.5 noun nom pl fem | 5448.1 adv | 4993.1 num card nom fem |
|---|---|---|---|---|
| ἡμέρᾳ | ἐκείνῃ | ψυχαὶ | ὡσεὶ | τρισχίλιαι. |
| *hēmera* | *ekeinē* | *psuchai* | *hōsei* | *trischiliai* |
| day | that | souls | about | three thousand. |

| 1498.37 verb 3pl indic imperf act | 1156.2 conj | 4201.4 verb nom pl masc part pres act | 3450.11 art dat sing fem | 1316.3 noun dat sing fem |
|---|---|---|---|---|
| **42.** Ἦσαν | δὲ | προσκαρτεροῦντες | τῇ | διδαχῇ |
| *Ēsan* | *de* | *proskarterountes* | *tē* | *didachē* |
| They were | and | steadfastly continuing | in the | teaching |

42.a.**Txt:** 01ℵ-corr 05D-corr,08E,025P,byz.
**Var:** 01ℵ-org,02A,03B 04C,05D-org,sa.bo.Lach Treg,Alf,Tisc,We/Ho Weis,Sod,UBS/*

| 3450.1 art gen pl | 646.5 noun gen pl masc | 2504.1 conj | 3450.11 art dat sing fem | 2815.3 noun dat sing fem | 2504.1 conj |
|---|---|---|---|---|---|
| τῶν | ἀποστόλων | καὶ | τῇ | κοινωνίᾳ, | ⸂ᵃ καὶ ⸃ |
| *tōn* | *apostolōn* | *kai* | *tē* | *koinōnia* | *kai* |
| of the | apostles | and | in the | fellowship | and |

| 3450.11 art dat sing fem | 2773.1 noun dat sing fem | 3450.2 art gen sing | 735.2 noun gen sing masc | 2504.1 conj | 3450.14 art dat pl fem |
|---|---|---|---|---|---|
| τῇ | κλάσει | τοῦ | ἄρτου | καὶ | ταῖς |
| *tē* | *klasei* | *tou* | *artou* | *kai* | *tais* |
| the | breaking | of the | bread | and | in the |

43.a.**Txt:** 08E,025P,byz.
**Var:** 01ℵ,02A,03B,04C 05D,Lach,Treg,Alf,Tisc We/Ho,Weis,Sod UBS/*

| 4194.7 noun dat pl fem | 1090.33 verb 3sing indic aor mid | 1090.72 verb 3sing indic imperf mid | 1156.2 conj |
|---|---|---|---|
| προσευχαῖς. | **43.** ⸀ Ἐγένετο | [ᵃ☆ Ἐγίνετο ] | δὲ |
| *proseuchais* | *Egeneto* | *Egineto* | *de* |
| prayers. | There came | [ There was coming ] | and |

43.b.**Txt:** 02A,04C 05D-corr,08E,025P,byz. Sod
**Var:** 01ℵ,03B,bo.Tisc We/Ho,Weis,UBS/*

| 3820.11 adj dat sing fem | 5425.3 noun dat sing fem | 5238.1 noun nom sing masc | 4044.17 adj pl neu | 4885.1 conj | 1156.2 conj |
|---|---|---|---|---|---|
| πάσῃ | ψυχῇ | φόβος, | πολλά | ⸀ τε | [ᵇ δὲ ] |
| *pasē* | *psuchē* | *phobos* | *polla* | *te* | *de* |
| upon every | soul | fear, | many | and | [ idem ] |

| 4907.1 noun pl neu | 2504.1 conj | 4447.2 noun pl neu | 1217.2 prep | 3450.1 art gen pl | 646.5 noun gen pl masc |
|---|---|---|---|---|---|
| τέρατα | καὶ | σημεῖα | διὰ | τῶν | ἀποστόλων |
| *terata* | *kai* | *sēmeia* | *dia* | *tōn* | *apostolōn* |
| wonders | and | signs | through | the | apostles |

told by Jesus in John 16:8, for there was indeed conviction with respect to sin, righteousness, and judgment to come.

The essence of Peter's exhortation was that they should save themselves (the Greek is better translated "be saved") from this "untoward" (perverse, crooked) generation. That is, they should turn away from the perversity and corruptness of those around them who were rejecting the truth about Jesus. (Compare Luke 9:41; 11:29; 17:25. In these passages Jesus is disturbed by the unbelief, perversity, and evil of that generation, and He knew He must endure many things from them and be rejected by them.)

**2:41.** Those who received (welcomed) Peter's message then testified to their faith by being baptized in water. The Bible shows baptism was an important element in the conversion experiences of the Early Church.

Though Luke did not mention it, it seems certain all the 3,000 who were added to the Church received the Promise of the Father, as Peter had said they would.

**2:42.** By the Spirit they also were baptized into the body of Christ (1 Corinthians 12:13). God never saves a person and then lets him wander off by himself. Thus, the 3,000 did not scatter but remained together, continuing steadfastly in the apostles' doctrine (teaching) and fellowship, and in the breaking of bread and prayers.

A further evidence of their faith was this persistent desire for teaching. Their acceptance of Christ and the gift of the Spirit opened up to them a whole new understanding of God's plan and purpose. With joy, they became hungry to learn more. This shows also that the apostles were obeying Jesus and teaching (making disciples) as He had commanded them (Matthew 28:19). It also shows that discipleship includes this kind of eager desire to learn more of Jesus and God's Word.

Fellowship was experienced in the teaching. It was more than just getting together. It was partnership in the ministry of the Church, sharing the message and the work. As in 1 John 1:3, the Word, as witnessed by the teaching of the apostles, brought this fellowship, one that was also with the Father and with the Son.

Some take the breaking of bread to be the Lord's Supper, but it also included table fellowship. They could not observe the Lord's Supper in the temple, so this was done in homes, at first in connection with a meal (since Jesus instituted it at the close of the Passover meal).

Their prayers also included daily gathering in the temple at the hours of prayer, which they still continued, plus prayer meetings in the homes.

**2:43.** The continuing witness of the apostles to the resurrection of Jesus brought a reverential fear on every soul (every person) who heard. Their "fear" included a sense of awe in the presence



**Save yourselves from this untoward generation:** Be saved from this perverse age, *TCNT* . . . this crooked generation, *ASV* . . . this pointless generation, *Klingensmith* . . . the punishment coming on this wicked people! *TEV.*

**41. Then they that gladly received his word were baptized:** Those therefore, who joyfully welcomed his word, *Weymouth* . . . Then those, who welcomed his message, *Berkeley* . . . They were convinced...and they accepted, *JB* . . . readily received his discourse, *Murdock.*

**and the same day there were added unto them about three thousand souls:** . . . and about three thousand joined the disciples on that day alone, *TCNT.*

**42. And they continued stedfastly:** And they went on to give constant attention, *Rotherham* . . . They were regularly present, *TCNT* . . . and they were constant in attendance, *Weymouth* . . . They were loyal, *Beck* . . . firmly adhering to, *Rotherham* . . . they persevered, *Adams* . . . constantly attending, *HBIE* . . . kept their attention fixed, *BB.*

**in the apostles' doctrine and fellowship:** . . . to the instruction, *Moffatt* . . . at the teaching of the Apostles and at the sharing of the offerings, *TCNT* . . . to the teaching of the apostles and to fellowship with one another, *Williams* . . . the teaching and companionship of the apostles, *Sawyer.*

**and in breaking of bread, and in prayers:** . . . eating the supper of the Lord, *SEB* . . . were associated together in prayer, *Murdock.*

**43. And fear came upon every soul:** A deep impression was made upon every one, *TCNT* . . . Awe came upon everyone, *Weymouth* . . . A sense of reverence seized everyone, *Williams* . . . a reverential fear, *Wuest* . . . a sense of awe came over everybody, *Adams.*

**and many wonders and signs were done by the apostles:** . . . and many wonders and signs through means of the apostles were coming to pass, *Rotherham* . . . and many marvels...were wrought by the Apostles, *Weymouth.*

## Acts 2:44

43.c.**Var:** p74,01ℵ,02A 04C,bo.Tisc,Sod

44.a.**Var:** p74,01ℵ,02A 04C,Tisc,Sod

44.b.**Txt:** 02A,04C,05D 08E,025P,byz. **Var:** 01ℵ,03B,Tisc We/Ho,Weis,Sod UBS/☆

44.c.**Txt:** p74,01ℵ,02A 04C,05D,08E,025P,044 etc.byz.Tisc,Sod **Var:** 03B,We/Ho,Weis UBS/☆

44.d.**Txt:** p74,01ℵ,02A 04C,05D,08E,025P,044 etc.byz.Tisc,Sod **Var:** 03B,We/Ho,Weis UBS/☆

| **1090.72** verb 3sing indic imperf mid | **1706.1** prep | **2395.1** name fem | **5238.1** noun nom sing masc | **4885.1** conj |
|---|---|---|---|---|
| ἐγίνετο. | [c+ ἐν | Ἱερουσαλήμ, | φόβος | τε |
| *egineto* | *en* | *Hierousalēm* | *phobos* | *te* |
| were taking place | [ in | Jerusalem, | Fear | and |

| **1498.34** verb sing indic imperf act | **3144.2** adj nom sing masc | **1894.3** prep | **3820.8** adj acc pl masc | **2504.1** conj |
|---|---|---|---|---|
| ἦν | μέγας | ἐπὶ | πάντας. ] | 44. [a+ καὶ ] |
| *ēn* | *megas* | *epi* | *pantas* | *kai* |
| was | great | upon | all. ] | [ and ] |

| **3820.7** adj nom pl masc | **1156.2** conj | **3450.7** art nom pl masc | **3961.13** verb nom pl masc part pres act | **3961.31** verb nom pl masc part aor act |
|---|---|---|---|---|
| πάντες | δὲ | οἱ | ‹ πιστεύοντες | [b☆ πιστεύσαντες ] |
| *pantes* | *de* | *hoi* | *pisteuontes* | *pisteusantes* |
| All | and | the | believing | [ having believed ] |

| **1498.37** verb 3pl indic imperf act | **1894.3** prep | **3450.16** art sing neu | **840.15** prs-pron sing neu | **2504.1** conj | **2174.42** verb indic imperf act |
|---|---|---|---|---|---|
| ‹c ἦσαν › | ἐπὶ | τὸ | αὐτὸ | ‹d καὶ › | εἶχον |
| *ēsan* | *epi* | *to* | *auto* | *kai* | *eichon* |
| were | on | the | same | and | were having |

| **533.1** adj | **2812.5** adj pl neu | **2504.1** conj | **3450.17** art pl neu | **2905.2** noun pl neu | **2504.1** conj |
|---|---|---|---|---|---|
| ἅπαντα | κοινά, | 45. καὶ | τὰ | κτήματα | καὶ |
| *hapanta* | *koina* | *kai* | *ta* | *ktēmata* | *kai* |
| all things | common, | and | the | possessions | and |

| **3450.15** art acc pl fem | **5061.2** noun acc pl fem | **3958.2** verb 3pl indic imperf act | **2504.1** conj | **1260.2** verb 3pl indic imperf act |
|---|---|---|---|---|
| τὰς | ὑπάρξεις | ἐπίπρασκον, | καὶ | διεμέριζον |
| *tas* | *huparxeis* | *epipraskon* | *kai* | *diemerizon* |
| the | goods | they were selling, | and | were dividing |

| **840.16** prs-pron pl neu | **3820.5** adj dat pl | **2502.1** conj | **300.1** partic | **4948.3** indef-pron nom sing | **5367.3** noun acc sing fem |
|---|---|---|---|---|---|
| αὐτὰ | πᾶσιν, | καθότι | ἄν | τις | χρείαν |
| *auta* | *pasin* | *kathoti* | *an* | *tis* | *chreian* |
| them | to all, | according as | | anyone | need |

| **2174.44** verb 3sing indic imperf act | **2567.2** prep | **2232.4** noun acc sing fem | **4885.1** conj | **4201.4** verb nom pl masc part pres act |
|---|---|---|---|---|
| εἶχεν. | 46. καθ' | ἡμέραν | τε | προσκαρτεροῦντες |
| *eichen* | *kath'* | *hēmeran* | *te* | *proskarterountes* |
| was having. | By | day | and | steadfastly continuing |

| **3524.1** adv | **1706.1** prep | **3450.3** art dat sing | **2387.2** adj dat sing neu | **2779.2** verb nom pl masc part pres act | **4885.1** conj |
|---|---|---|---|---|---|
| ὁμοθυμαδὸν | ἐν | τῷ | ἱερῷ, | κλῶντές | τε |
| *homothumadon* | *en* | *tō* | *hierō* | *klōntes* | *te* |
| with one accord | in | the | temple, | breaking | and |

| **2567.1** prep | **3486.4** noun acc sing masc | **735.4** noun acc sing masc | **3205.5** verb 3pl indic imperf act | **5001.2** noun gen sing fem | **1706.1** prep |
|---|---|---|---|---|---|
| κατ' | οἶκον | ἄρτον, | μετελάμβανον | τροφῆς | ἐν |
| *kat'* | *oikon* | *arton* | *metelambanon* | *trophēs* | *en* |
| by | house | bread, | they were partaking | of food | with |

| **20.3** noun dat sing fem | **2504.1** conj | **851.1** noun dat sing fem | **2559.1** noun fem | **134.4** verb nom pl masc part pres act |
|---|---|---|---|---|
| ἀγαλλιάσει | καὶ | ἀφελότητι | καρδίας, | 47. αἰνοῦντες |
| *agalliasei* | *kai* | *aphelotēti* | *kardias* | *ainountes* |
| gladness | and | simplicity | of heart, | praising |

of the supernatural. The word "soul" is used here in the Old Testament sense where it often means "person" (Genesis 46:26).

This reverential fear was further enhanced by the many wonders and signs done by the apostles, that is, done by God through the apostles. (The Greek *dia* here is used of secondary agency; hence, God really did the work.) The apostles were God's instruments, His agents. As Paul indicated in 1 Corinthians 3:6, Paul planted, and Apollos watered, but all the while Paul was planting and Apollos was watering, God was giving the increase.

Later God gave miracles through many others, including ordinary disciples who had no office. But here God was using the apostles to train all the believers so they could all do a work of ministry or service. (See Ephesians 4:8,11-16 where those taken captive by Christ were given to the Church to train the saints to do the work of ministry.)

The apostles were the primary witnesses to the teaching of Jesus, which they had received from Him personally. They had the background of His commission and His encouragement to their faith. These miracles were not for display, but rather were to confirm the Word, the teaching, as Jesus promised (Mark 16:20). The miracles also helped to establish the faith of the new believers.

**2:44,45.** The believers remained together and had things common; that is, they shared with one another what they had. From time to time many sold pieces of land they owned and personal property as well. The money was distributed (by the apostles) to those who had need. The words "as every man had need" is a key statement. They did not sell property until there was a need.

This was not communism in the modern sense. Neither was it communal living. It was just Christian sharing. They all realized the importance of becoming established in the apostles' teaching (which today is the written New Testament). Some of those from outside Jerusalem soon ran out of money, so those who were able simply sold what they could to make it possible for these Christians to remain nearby. Later Peter made it clear that no one was under any compulsion to sell anything or give anything (5:4). But the fellowship, joy, love, and the example and teachings of Jesus made it easy for the believers to share what they had.

**2:46.** The picture then is of a loving body of believers meeting daily in the temple with one accord, one mind, one purpose, and sharing table fellowship in their homes. ("From house to house" means by households.) Each home became a center of Christian fellowship and worship. Mark's mother's home was one such center. Probably the home of Mary and Martha in Bethany was another. Jerusalem was not able to hold such a multitude, and many certainly stayed in surrounding villages.

The table fellowship was very important. They took their food with rejoicing (delight and great joy) and with simplicity of heart. There was no jealousy, no criticism.

**44. And all that believed were together:** All who had become believers in Christ, *TCNT* . . . And all the believers kept together, *Weymouth* . . . The believers all met together, *Berkeley* . . . All the believers lived together, *Norlie.*

**and had all things common:** . . . had everything jointly, *Berkeley* . . . agreed in having everything in common, *TCNT* . . . formed an organized community, *Fenton* . . . and held all they had as common goods to be shared by one another, *Williams* . . . had a common treasury, *Klingensmith.*

**45. And sold their possessions and goods, and parted them to all men, as every man had need:** And so they continued to sell their property and goods and to distribute the money to all, *Williams* . . . sold their possessions and belongings, *Klingensmith* . . . shared them with all, *Adams* . . . to anyone as he needed it, *Beck* . . . as anyone might have need, *Darby.*

**46. And they, continuing daily with one accord in the temple:** Every day, too, they met regularly in the Temple Courts, *TCNT* . . . Daily they regularly frequented the temple with a united purpose, *Berkeley* . . . All were one at heart as they went to the temple regularly every day, *Beck* . . . regularly attended, *Williams* . . . in harmony, *Fenton* . . . in unity of spirit, *Adams.*

**and breaking bread from house to house:** . . . they practiced breaking their bread together in their homes, *Williams* . . . They had their meals in their homes, *Beck.*

**did eat their meat with gladness and singleness of heart:** . . . they were partaking of food with exultation, *Rotherham* . . . combined with humility, *Fenton* . . . partaking of their food in simple-hearted gladness, *TCNT* . . . they took their meals with great happiness and single-heartedness, *Weymouth* . . . with joy and simplicity of heart, *Campbell* . . . partook of nourishment with exultation and simplicity, *Concordant* . . . shared their food gladly and generously, *JB* . . . with happy and unruffled hearts, *Berkeley* . . . with joyful and generous hearts, *Klingensmith.*

| 3450.6 art acc sing masc | 2296.4 noun acc sing masc | 2504.1 conj | 2174.19 verb nom pl masc part pres act | 5322.4 noun acc sing fem | 4242.1 prep | 3513.1 adj sing |
|---|---|---|---|---|---|---|
| τὸν | θεὸν, | καὶ | ἔχοντες | χάριν | πρὸς | ὅλον |
| *ton* | *theon* | *kai* | *echontes* | *charin* | *pros* | *holon* |
| | God, | and | having | favor | with | whole |

| 3450.6 art acc sing masc | 2967.4 noun acc sing masc | 3450.5 art nom sing masc | 1156.2 conj | 2935.1 noun nom sing masc | 4227.5 verb 3sing indic imperf act |
|---|---|---|---|---|---|
| τὸν | λαόν. | ὁ | δὲ | κύριος | προσετίθει |
| *ton* | *laon* | *ho* | *de* | *kurios* | *prosetithei* |
| the | people; | the | and | Lord | was adding |

47.a.**Txt:** 08E,010F 025P,044,33,1241,byz. **Var:** p74,01ℵ,02A,03B 04C,095,81,1175,sa.bo. Lach,Treg,Alf,Tisc We/Ho,Weis,UBS/⋆

| 3450.8 art acc pl masc | 4834.20 verb acc pl masc part pres mid | 2567.2 prep | 2232.4 noun acc sing fem | 3450.11 art dat sing fem | 1564.3 noun dat sing fem |
|---|---|---|---|---|---|
| τοὺς | σῳζομένους | καθ' | ἡμέραν | ⸂ τῇ | ἐκκλησίᾳ. ⸃ |
| *tous* | *sōzomenous* | *kath'* | *hēmeran* | *tē* | *ekklēsia* |
| the | being saved | by | day | to the | assembly. |

1.a.**Txt:** p74,01ℵ,02A 03B,04C,095,81,1175 sa.bo.Lach,Treg,Alf,Tisc We/Ho,Weis,UBS/⋆ **Var:** 08E,010F,025P 044,33,1241,byz.

| 1894.3 prep | 3450.16 art sing neu | 840.15 prs-pron sing neu | | 1894.3 prep | 3450.16 art sing neu | 840.15 prs-pron sing neu |
|---|---|---|---|---|---|---|
| [a+ ἐπὶ | τὸ | αὐτό. ] | 3:1. ⸂a | Ἐπὶ | τὸ | αὐτὸ ⸃ |
| *epi* | *to* | *auto* | | *Epi* | *to* | *auto* |
| [ upon | the | same. ] | | Upon | the | same |

| 1156.2 conj | 3935.1 name nom masc | 3935.1 name nom masc | 1156.2 conj | 2504.1 conj | 2464.1 name nom masc |
|---|---|---|---|---|---|
| ⸂ δὲ | Πέτρος | [⋆ Πέτρος | δὲ ] | καὶ | Ἰωάννης |
| *de* | *Petros* | *Petros* | *de* | *kai* | *Iōannēs* |
| and | Peter | [ Peter | and ] | and | John |

| 303.24 verb 3pl indic imperf act | 1519.1 prep | 3450.16 art sing neu | 2387.3 adj sing neu | 1894.3 prep | 3450.12 art acc sing fem | 5443.4 noun acc sing fem |
|---|---|---|---|---|---|---|
| ἀνέβαινον | εἰς | τὸ | ἱερὸν | ἐπὶ | τὴν | ὥραν |
| *anebainon* | *eis* | *to* | *hieron* | *epi* | *tēn* | *hōran* |
| were going up | to | the | temple | at | the | hour |

| 3450.10 art gen sing fem | 4194.2 noun gen sing fem | 3450.12 art acc sing fem | 1750.4 num ord acc sing fem | 1712.3 num ord acc sing fem |
|---|---|---|---|---|
| τῆς | προσευχῆς | τὴν | ⸀ ἐννάτην. | [⋆ ἐνάτην. ] |
| *tēs* | *proseuchēs* | *tēn* | *ennatēn* | *enatēn* |
| of the | prayer, | the | ninth | [ idem ] |

| 2504.1 conj | 4948.3 indef-pron nom sing | 433.1 noun nom sing masc | 5395.2 adj nom sing masc | 1523.2 prep gen | 2809.2 noun gen sing fem |
|---|---|---|---|---|---|
| 2. καί | τις | ἀνὴρ | χωλὸς | ἐκ | κοιλίας |
| *kai* | *tis* | *anēr* | *chōlos* | *ek* | *koilias* |
| and | a certain | man | lame | from | womb |

| 3251.2 noun gen sing fem | 840.3 prs-pron gen sing | 5062.6 verb nom sing masc part pres act | 934.18 verb 3sing indic imperf pass | 3614.6 rel-pron acc sing masc |
|---|---|---|---|---|
| μητρὸς | αὐτοῦ | ὑπάρχων | ἐβαστάζετο· | ὃν |
| *mētros* | *autou* | *huparchōn* | *ebastazeto* | *hon* |
| mother | of his | being | was being carried, | whom |

| 4935.25 verb 3pl indic imperf act | 2567.2 prep | 2232.4 noun acc sing fem | 4242.1 prep | 3450.12 art acc sing fem | 2351.4 noun acc sing fem |
|---|---|---|---|---|---|
| ἐτίθουν | καθ' | ἡμέραν | πρὸς | τὴν | θύραν |
| *etithoun* | *kath'* | *hēmeran* | *pros* | *tēn* | *thuran* |
| they were placing | by | day | at | the | door |

| 3450.2 art gen sing | 2387.1 adj gen sing neu | 3450.12 art acc sing fem | 2978.35 verb acc sing fem part pres mid | 5444.3 adj acc sing fem | 3450.2 art gen sing |
|---|---|---|---|---|---|
| τοῦ | ἱεροῦ | τὴν | λεγομένην | Ὡραίαν, | τοῦ |
| *tou* | *hierou* | *tēn* | *legomenēn* | *Hōraian* | *tou* |
| of the | temple | the | being called | Beautiful, | the |

**2:47.** The joy in the hearts of believers kept them praising God. Their praise found expression also in psalms (the word includes musical accompaniment especially on stringed instruments), hymns, and spiritual songs coming from their hearts (Colossians 3:16).

The result was that they found favor with the whole of the people of Jerusalem. At this point there was no opposition, no persecution. The common people who had not yet accepted Christ saw the believers' worship, their good works, and their joy, and were attracted by what they saw. Thus the Lord kept adding (together, to the Church) day by day those who were being saved. Certainly, the Church accepted the new believers joyfully into their fellowship and brought them under the teaching of the apostles.

The phrase "were being saved" does not suggest that salvation is a progressive experience. Rather, the Greek is a simple statement that every day some were being saved and the saved ones were added to the Church. Notice too that no high pressure methods were used to persuade others to come and join. The people saw the joy and the power, and they opened their hearts to the truth about Jesus.

**3:1.** Luke often made a general statement and then gave a specific example. Acts 2:43 states that many wonders and signs were done through the apostles. Luke then proceeded to give one example to illustrate this.

On this occasion Peter and John were going up the temple hill into the temple to join the others for the hour of evening prayer, "the ninth hour" (about 3 p.m.). Sacrifice and incense were being offered by the priests at the same time.

Peter, James, and John constituted the inner circle of Jesus' disciples during much of His ministry. Yet James and John had asked Jesus for the chief places in His coming kingdom, and this had excited the jealousy of others, including Peter. But all that was in the past. In many ways Peter and John were opposites. But now they were going into the temple together. This was part of the new unity brought about by Christ's commission and by the Holy Spirit. Together, in one accord, they were going up to worship God and exalt the name of Jesus.

Between the Court of the Gentiles and the Court of the Women was a Corinthian-style, bronze gate with beautifully carved gold and silver inlays. It was worth more than if it had been made of solid gold. (The Court of the Gentiles was as far as Gentiles were allowed to go. The Court of the Women was as far as the women were allowed to go. Pharisees had long used the Court of the Women to gather both men and women for their teaching sessions. So it was the best place for the Church to gather also.)

**3:2.** At this Beautiful Gate, Peter and John were confronted by a man, lame from birth, who daily was carried and laid outside it to ask alms (gifts of charity). The man was over 40 years old (4:22).

**47. Praising God, and having favour with all the people:** They praised God, and all the people liked them, *Everyday* . . . continually praising God, and winning respect from all the people, *TCNT* . . . and enjoying the good will of all the people, *Berkeley* . . . stood in favor, *Norlie* . . . They praised God continually, *Phillips* . . . praised God constantly...won the favor of, *Noli* . . . and approved by all the people, *Williams C.K.*

**And the Lord added to the church daily such as should be saved:** . . . to them day by day those that were saved, *ASV* . . . Also day by day the Lord added to their number those whom He was saving, *Weymouth* . . . And every day the Lord continued to add to them the people who were being saved, *Williams* . . . while daily the group who were being saved, *Berkeley* . . . added daily to the assembly, *Murdock* . . . multiplied every day, *Noli* . . . to the congregation, *Wilson* . . . those who were in the path of Salvation, *TCNT* . . . who were getting saved, *Adams* . . . those who were saved, *Wesley.*

**1. Now Peter and John went up together into the temple:** One day Peter and John went to, *Everyday.*

**at the hour of prayer, being the ninth hour:** . . . during the time of the three o'clock Prayers, *TCNT* . . . at three in the afternoon, *Beck* . . . in the middle of the afternoon, *Klingensmith.*

**2. And a certain man lame from his mother's womb was carried:** . . . and, just then, some men were carrying there one who had been lame from his birth, *Weymouth* . . . whose lameness was due to prenatal causes, *Wuest* . . . who had been crippled all his life, *Everyday* . . . been a cripple from his birth, *Beck* . . . had had no power in his legs, *BB.*

**whom they laid daily at the gate of the temple which is called Beautiful:** . . . those accustomed to bring, *Murdock* . . . The man used to be set down every day...of the Temple called the Beautiful Gate, *TCNT* . . . placed daily at the entrance, *Noli* . . . at the door, *ASV.*

| 153.10 verb inf pres act | 1641.2 noun acc sing fem | 3706.2 prep | 3450.1 art gen pl | 1515.5 verb gen pl masc part pres mid | 1519.1 prep |
| --- | --- | --- | --- | --- | --- |
| αἰτεῖν | ἐλεημοσύνην | παρὰ | τῶν | εἰσπορευομένων | εἰς |
| *aitein* | *eleēmosunēn* | *para* | *tōn* | *eisporeuomenōn* | *eis* |
| to ask | alms | from | the | going | into |

| 3450.16 art sing neu | 2387.3 adj sing neu | 3614.5 rel-pron nom sing masc | 1481.16 verb nom sing masc part aor act | 3935.4 name acc masc | 2504.1 conj |
| --- | --- | --- | --- | --- | --- |
| τὸ | ἱερόν. | 3. ὃς | ἰδὼν | Πέτρον | καὶ |
| *to* | *hieron* | *hos* | *idōn* | *Petron* | *kai* |
| the | temple; | who | having seen | Peter | and |

| 2464.4 name acc masc | 3165.14 verb acc pl masc part pres act | 1510.2 verb inf pres act | 1519.1 prep | 3450.16 art sing neu | 2387.3 adj sing neu |
| --- | --- | --- | --- | --- | --- |
| Ἰωάννην | μέλλοντας | εἰσιέναι | εἰς | τὸ | ἱερὸν, |
| *Iōannēn* | *mellontas* | *eisienai* | *eis* | *to* | *hieron* |
| John | being about | to enter | into | the | temple, |

| 2049.16 verb 3sing indic imperf act | 1641.2 noun acc sing fem | 2956.31 verb inf aor act | 810.3 verb nom sing masc part aor act |
| --- | --- | --- | --- |
| ἠρώτα | ἐλεημοσύνην | λαβεῖν. | 4. ἀτενίσας |
| *ērōta* | *eleēmosunēn* | *labein* | *atenisas* |
| was asking | alms | to receive. | Having looked intently |

| 1156.2 conj | 3935.1 name nom masc | 1519.1 prep | 840.6 prs-pron acc sing masc | 4713.1 prep | 3450.3 art dat sing | 2464.3 name dat masc |
| --- | --- | --- | --- | --- | --- | --- |
| δὲ | Πέτρος | εἰς | αὐτὸν | σὺν | τῷ | Ἰωάννῃ |
| *de* | *Petros* | *eis* | *auton* | *sun* | *tō* | *Iōannē* |
| and | Peter | upon | him | with | | John |

| 1500.5 verb 3sing indic aor act | 984.19 verb 2sing impr aor act | 1519.1 prep | 2231.4 prs-pron acc 1pl | 3450.5 art nom sing masc | 1156.2 conj |
| --- | --- | --- | --- | --- | --- |
| εἶπεν, | Βλέψον | εἰς | ἡμᾶς. | 5. Ὁ | δὲ |
| *eipen* | *Blepson* | *eis* | *hēmas* | *Ho* | *de* |
| said, | Look | on | us. | The | and |

| 1892.5 verb 3sing indic imperf act | 840.2 prs-pron dat pl | 4186.3 verb nom sing masc part pres act | 4948.10 indef-pron sing neu | 3706.1 prep |
| --- | --- | --- | --- | --- |
| ἐπεῖχεν | αὐτοῖς, | προσδοκῶν | τι | παρ’ |
| *epeichen* | *autois* | *prosdokōn* | *ti* | *par’* |
| he was paying attention | to them, | expecting | something | from |

| 840.1 prs-pron gen pl | 2956.31 verb inf aor act | 1500.5 verb 3sing indic aor act | 1156.2 conj | 3935.1 name nom masc | 688.1 noun sing neu |
| --- | --- | --- | --- | --- | --- |
| αὐτῶν | λαβεῖν. | 6. εἶπεν | δὲ | Πέτρος, | Ἀργύριον |
| *autōn* | *labein* | *eipen* | *de* | *Petros* | *Argurion* |
| them | to receive. | Said | but | Peter, | Silver |

| 2504.1 conj | 5388.1 noun sing neu | 3620.1 partic | 5062.2 verb 3sing indic pres act | 1466.4 prs-pron dat 1sing | 3614.16 rel-pron sing neu | 1156.2 conj |
| --- | --- | --- | --- | --- | --- | --- |
| καὶ | χρυσίον | οὐχ | ὑπάρχει | μοι· | ὃ | δὲ |
| *kai* | *chrusion* | *ouch* | *huparchei* | *moi* | *ho* | *de* |
| and | gold | not | there is | to me, | what | but |

| 2174.1 verb 1sing pres act | 3642.17 dem-pron sing neu | 4622.3 prs-pron dat 2sing | 1319.1 verb 1sing indic pres act | 1706.1 prep | 3450.3 art dat sing |
| --- | --- | --- | --- | --- | --- |
| ἔχω, | τοῦτό | σοι | δίδωμι. | ἐν | τῷ |
| *echō* | *touto* | *soi* | *didōmi* | *en* | *tō* |
| I have, | this | to you | I give: | in | the |

| 3549.4 noun dat sing neu | 2400.2 name masc | 5382.2 name gen masc | 3450.2 art gen sing | 3343.2 name gen sing masc | 1446.28 verb 2sing impr aor mid |
| --- | --- | --- | --- | --- | --- |
| ὀνόματι | Ἰησοῦ | Χριστοῦ | τοῦ | Ναζωραίου | (a ἔγειραι |
| *onomati* | *Iēsou* | *Christou* | *tou* | *Nazōraiou* | *egeirai* |
| name | of Jesus | Christ | | of Nazareth | rise up |

6.a.**Txt:** 02A,04C,08E 025P,it.bo.byz.
**Var:** 01ℵ,03B,05D,sa. Tisc,We/Ho,Weis UBS/*

Jesus had passed this way many times, but apparently the man had never asked Him for healing. Possibly Jesus, in divine providence and timing, left this man so he could become a greater witness when he was healed later.

**3:3.** When this man who was born lame saw Peter and John about to enter the temple, he asked them for a gift of charity. Giving to the poor and disabled was encouraged by the Law and was considered by the Jews an important way to please God. This man did not seem to recognize Peter and John. After spending his days at the temple gate begging, he was then carried by friends or relatives back to some lonely room. If he had heard about what was going on in Jerusalem or of the miracles done through the apostles, he did not seem to have any idea that this could affect him.

**3:4.** When this man asked to receive a gift of money, Peter, together with John, fastened his eyes on him. What a tremendous contrast to the jealousy that once characterized the disciples (Matthew 20:24). Now they worked in complete unity of faith and purpose. As the spokesman Peter said, "Look on us."

It may seem strange that Peter and John called attention to themselves. But this man, like so many beggars, must have been lying there listlessly with a rather pitiable, hopeless expression on his face. Daily as the crowds passed by, he probably paid no attention to who they were or what they said to him. His only concern was the few coins that were dropped into his hand. Peter and John needed to get his attention. They needed to raise his expectation. Expectation is at least a step toward faith.

**3:5.** Peter's words did catch the man's attention, and he did in fact rivet his full attention on them. They also aroused an expectation that he would receive something. Probably he expected money. But money is not always the thing people really need. In fact, this man did not know what he really needed. Since he was born lame, he had never known what it was to walk. If his parents had taken him to physicians, both they and he had long ago given up any hope that he would ever walk.

**3:6.** Peter, however, did not do the expected. What money he possessed had probably already been given to needy believers. But he did have something better to give. His statement, "Silver and gold have I none; but such as I have give I thee," took faith on Peter's part. Then Peter gave the positive command, "In the name (and by the authority) of Jesus Christ of Nazareth rise up and walk."



**to ask alms of them that entered into the temple:** . . . to beg from the people as they went in, *Weymouth* . . . so he could beg the people for gifts as they went, *Beck* . . . to ask a kindness, *Young* . . . to beg for money, *Williams C.K.* . . . from those who entered the sanctuary, *Noli* . . . from the people on their way in, *Goodspeed.*

**3. Who seeing Peter and John about to go into the temple asked an alms:** . . . on their way into, *Noli* . . . on the point of going, *Goodspeed* . . . was requesting to receive an alms, *Rotherham* . . . asked them for money, *Everyday* . . . he kept asking them for alms, *Montgomery.*

**4. And Peter, fastening his eyes upon him with John:** But Peter directed his gaze at him, *RSV* . . . But Peter looking steadfastly at him, *Rotherham* . . . Peter fixing his eyes on him, as did John also, *Weymouth* . . . looked straight at him, *Everyday* . . . Peter looked him straight in the eye, and so did John, *Williams* . . . with a piercing gaze, *Wuest* . . . Peter, as well as John, looked intently at him, *Norlie.*

**said, Look on us:** Look at us, *Williams C.K., Goodspeed.*

**5. And he gave heed unto them:** The man gave them his attention, *TCNT* . . . He looked at them attentively, *Noli* . . . So he looked and waited, *Weymouth* . . . So he watched them closely, *Berkeley* . . . attended to them, *Concordant.*

**expecting to receive something of them:** . . . supposing that they were going to give him something, *Goodspeed* . . . he thought they were going to give him some money, *Everyday.*

**6. Then Peter said, Silver and gold have I none:** I do not possess, *Concordant* . . . I possess none, *Fenton* . . . I don't have any, *Everyday.*

**but such as I have give I thee:** I'll give you what I have, *Beck.*

**In the name of Jesus Christ of Nazareth rise up and walk:** By the power of Jesus Christ, *Everyday* . . . walk, *Concordant* . . . start walking and keep on walking, *Wuest* . . . be walking about, *Rotherham.*

# Acts 3:7

| 2504.1 conj | 3906.9 verb 2sing impr pres act | 2504.1 conj | 3945.5 verb nom sing masc part aor act | 840.6 prs-pron acc sing masc | 3450.10 art gen sing fem |
|---|---|---|---|---|---|
| καὶ ˋ | περιπάτει. | 7. καὶ | πιάσας | αὐτὸν | τῆς |
| *kai* | *peripatei* | *kai* | *piasas* | *auton* | *tēs* |
| and | walk. | And | having taken | him | by the |

7.a.**Var:** 01א,02A,03B 04C,sa.bo.Lach,Treg,Alf Tisc,We/Ho,Weis,Sod UBS/☆

| 1182.4 adj fem | 5331.2 noun gen sing fem | 1446.5 verb 3sing indic aor act | 840.6 prs-pron acc sing masc | 3777.1 adv |
|---|---|---|---|---|
| δεξιᾶς | χειρὸς | ἤγειρεν· | [a☆+ αὐτόν· ] | παραχρῆμα |
| *dexias* | *cheiros* | *ēgeiren* | *auton* | *parachrēma* |
| right | hand | he raised up | [ him ] | immediately |

| 1156.2 conj | 4583.2 verb 3pl indic aor pass | 840.3 prs-pron gen sing | 3450.13 art nom pl fem | 932.1 noun nom pl fem | 3450.13 art nom pl fem |
|---|---|---|---|---|---|
| δὲ | ἐστερεώθησαν | ʻ αὐτοῦ | αἱ | βάσεις | [☆ αἱ |
| *de* | *estereōthēsan* | *autou* | *hai* | *baseis* | *hai* |
| and | were strengthened | his | the | feet | [ the |

7.b.**Txt:** 01א-corr 03B-corr,04C-corr,05D 08E,025P,byz.Sod
**Var:** 01א-org,02A 03B-org,04C-org,Tisc We/Ho,Weis,UBS/☆

| 932.1 noun nom pl fem | 840.3 prs-pron gen sing | 2504.1 conj | 3450.17 art pl neu | 4826.1 noun pl neu | 4825.1 noun pl neu |
|---|---|---|---|---|---|
| βάσεις | αὐτοῦ ] | καὶ | τὰ | ʻ σφυρά· | [b☆ σφυδρά, ] |
| *baseis* | *autou* | *kai* | *ta* | *sphura* | *sphudra* |
| feet | his ] | and | the | ankles | [ idem ] |

| 2504.1 conj | 1798.1 verb nom sing masc part pres mid | 2449.3 verb 3sing indic aor act | 2504.1 conj | 3906.28 verb 3sing indic imperf act | 2504.1 conj |
|---|---|---|---|---|---|
| 8. καὶ | ἐξαλλόμενος | ἔστη | καὶ | περιεπάτει, | καὶ |
| *kai* | *exallomenos* | *estē* | *kai* | *periepatei* | *kai* |
| And | leaping up | he stood | and | was walking, | and |

| 1511.3 verb 3sing indic aor act | 4713.1 prep | 840.2 prs-pron dat pl | 1519.1 prep | 3450.16 art sing neu | 2387.3 adj sing neu | 3906.12 verb nom sing masc part pres act |
|---|---|---|---|---|---|---|
| εἰσῆλθεν | σὺν | αὐτοῖς | εἰς | τὸ | ἱερὸν, | περιπατῶν |
| *eisēlthen* | *sun* | *autois* | *eis* | *to* | *hieron* | *peripatōn* |
| entered | with | them | into | the | temple, | walking |

| 2504.1 conj | 240.1 verb nom sing masc part pres mid | 2504.1 conj | 134.2 verb nom sing masc part pres act | 3450.6 art acc sing masc | 2296.4 noun acc sing masc |
|---|---|---|---|---|---|
| καὶ | ἁλλόμενος | καὶ | αἰνῶν | τὸν | θεόν. |
| *kai* | *hallomenos* | *kai* | *ainōn* | *ton* | *theon* |
| and | leaping | and | praising | | God. |

| 2504.1 conj | 1481.3 verb 3sing indic aor act | 840.6 prs-pron acc sing masc | 3820.6 adj nom sing masc | 3450.5 art nom sing masc | 2967.1 noun nom sing masc |
|---|---|---|---|---|---|
| 9. καὶ | εἶδεν | ʻ αὐτὸν | πᾶς | ὁ | λαὸς |
| *kai* | *eiden* | *auton* | *pas* | *ho* | *laos* |
| And | saw | him | all | the | people |

| 3820.6 adj nom sing masc | 3450.5 art nom sing masc | 2967.1 noun nom sing masc | 840.6 prs-pron acc sing masc | 3906.11 verb part pres act |
|---|---|---|---|---|
| [☆ πᾶς | ὁ | λαὸς | αὐτὸν ] | περιπατοῦντα |
| *pas* | *ho* | *laos* | *auton* | *peripatounta* |
| [ all | the | people | him ] | walking |

10.a.**Txt:** 05D,08E,025P byz.
**Var:** 01א,02A,03B,04C bo.Lach,Treg,Alf,Tisc We/Ho,Weis,Sod UBS/☆

| 2504.1 conj | 134.3 verb acc sing masc part pres act | 3450.6 art acc sing masc | 2296.4 noun acc sing masc | 1906.17 verb 3pl indic imperf act |
|---|---|---|---|---|
| καὶ | αἰνοῦντα | τὸν | θεόν· | 10. ἐπεγίνωσκον |
| *kai* | *ainounta* | *ton* | *theon* | *epeginōskon* |
| and | praising | | God. | They were recognizing |

10.b.**Var:** 01א,02A,04C Lach,Tisc,Sod

| 4885.1 conj | 1156.2 conj | 840.6 prs-pron acc sing masc | 3617.1 conj | 3642.4 dem-pron nom sing masc | 840.5 prs-pron nom sing masc |
|---|---|---|---|---|---|
| ʻ τε | [a☆ δὲ ] | αὐτὸν | ὅτι | ʻ οὗτος | [b☆ αὐτὸς ] |
| *te* | *de* | *auton* | *hoti* | *houtos* | *autos* |
| and | [ idem ] | him | that | this | [ he ] |

**3:7.** As Peter spoke these words, he put his own faith into action by taking hold of the man's right hand and, with a firm grip, lifted him up. This must have encouraged the man to exercise faith as well. An atmosphere of faith does help encourage faith in others, and it is certain these apostles exuded an atmosphere of positive faith wherever they went. They had seen Jesus. They had experienced God's power. They knew what Jesus could do.

At the very moment Peter took hold of the man's hand, strength went into the man's feet and ankle bones, and the wobbly ankles were made firm. It is quite possible also that the man's faith was stirred by the mention of the Messiah, Jesus of Nazareth. It may be that some of the 3,000 saved at Pentecost had witnessed to him. He had heard perhaps of others healed by Jesus, and he may have wondered why Jesus passed him by. But now, even though up to this point he had felt hopeless, the positive faith and the positive action of Peter brought the healing power of God into his body.

**3:8.** As strength flowed into his feet and ankles, Peter no longer had to lift the man. He jumped to his feet, stood for a moment, and then began to walk for the first time in his entire life.

Now that the man was healed he could go into the temple. Since he had been laid outside the gate every day for all those years, it is probable that he had never been through the gate before. Now he went into the temple walking normally, not limping, not stumbling, but joyfully erect. Every few steps he would leap for pure joy and excitement. All the while he was shouting the praises of God.

As verse 11 indicates, the man still held on to Peter's hand and had taken a firm hold on John's hand as well. This was not to help hold himself up. It was rather in a joyful sense of fellowship with them. In his new, God-given strength he was taking the lead. What a scene this must have been as the man came walking and jumping in the temple court where crowds of the Jews were gathered for prayer.

**3:9.** As they were praying in the temple, the Jews may have been sitting, standing, kneeling, or prostrate. Many may have been crying out to God for help. But now they saw this man as he kept walking through the temple court, shouting God's praises.

**3:10.** The people could hardly believe their eyes. They all recognized that this was the man born lame who had always been sitting at the Beautiful Gate begging for alms. He was a very familiar sight to all of them, and there was no question about his identity.

His healing therefore filled them with wonder and amazement when they saw what had happened to him. The word "wonder" is not the ordinary word so translated, but another word related to awe. The people were overwhelmed with a sense that something great, something totally supernatural had taken place.

**7. And he took him by the right hand, and lifted him up:** And gripping him, *MLNT* . . . And laying hold of him by the right hand he raised him up, *Rotherham* . . . having seized him by the right hand, *Young* . . . Grasping the lame man...Peter lifted him up, *TCNT* . . . and pulled him up, *NAB.*

**and immediately his feet and ankle bones received strength:** . . . and instantly were his feet and ankles strengthened, *Rotherham* . . . his feet and the bones in his legs became strong, *NLT* . . . Instantly his feet and ankles grew firm, *Berkeley, MLNT* . . . insteps and ankles were given stability, *Concordant* . . . and ankles became strong, *Everyday* . . . and he positively jumped, *Phillips* . . . immediately became strong, *Goodspeed* . . . instantly grew strong, *Williams.*

**8. And he leaping up stood, and walked:** . . . he stood erect, *Kleist* . . . and leaping forward he stood, *Rotherham* . . . he staggered, *Fenton* . . . jumped up on his feet, *NLT* . . . and jumping up, he began to walk about, *TCNT* . . . He jumped up, stood on his feet, and began to walk, *Everyday* . . . springing, *Young* . . . at once he leaped to his feet, *Williams* . . . stood for a moment, then began to walk around, *NAB* . . . And he sprange, stode and also walked, *Tyndale.*

**and entered with them into the temple:** . . . and then went with them into the Temple Courts, *TCNT* . . . went into the house of God with them, *NLT.*

**walking, and leaping, and praising God:** . . . walking, jumping, and praising God, *TCNT* . . . jumping about, *NAB* . . . and laude God, *Tyndale* . . . He gave thanks to God as he walked, *NLT.*

**9. And all the people saw him walking and praising God:** . . . walking about, *TCNT* . . . walking around, *MLNT* . . . moving and giving praise, *NAB* . . . and giving thanks to God, *NLT* . . . recognized him, *Everyday.*

**10. And they know that it was he which sat for alms at the Beautiful gate of the temple:** And they began to recognize him, that

| **1498.34** verb sing indic imperf act | **3450.5** art nom sing masc | **4242.1** prep | **3450.12** art acc sing fem | **1641.2** noun acc sing fem |
|---|---|---|---|---|
| ἦν | ὁ | πρὸς | τὴν | ἐλεημοσύνην |
| *ēn* | *ho* | *pros* | *tēn* | *eleēmosunēn* |
| was | the | for | the | alms |

| **2493.6** verb nom sing masc part pres mid | **1894.3** prep | **3450.11** art dat sing fem | **5444.2** adj dat sing fem | **4297.3** noun dat sing fem | **3450.2** art gen sing | **2387.1** adj gen sing neu |
|---|---|---|---|---|---|---|
| καθήμενος | ἐπὶ | τῇ | Ὡραίᾳ | πύλῃ | τοῦ | ἱεροῦ· |
| *kathēmenos* | *epi* | *tē* | *Hōraia* | *pulē* | *tou* | *hierou* |
| sitting | at | the | Beautiful | gate | of the | temple, |

| **2504.1** conj | **3990.5** verb 3pl indic aor pass | **2262.2** noun gen sing neu | **2504.1** conj | **1598.2** noun gen sing fem | **1894.3** prep |
|---|---|---|---|---|---|
| καὶ | ἐπλήσθησαν | θάμβους | καὶ | ἐκστάσεως | ἐπὶ |
| *kai* | *eplēsthēsan* | *thambous* | *kai* | *ekstaseōs* | *epi* |
| and | they were filled | with wonder | and | amazement | at |

| **3450.3** art dat sing | **4670.6** verb dat sing neu part perf act | **840.4** prs-pron dat sing | **2875.8** verb gen sing masc part pres act | **1156.2** conj |
|---|---|---|---|---|
| τῷ | συμβεβηκότι | αὐτῷ. | **11.** Κρατοῦντος | δὲ |
| *tō* | *sumbebēkoti* | *autō* | *Kratountos* | *de* |
| the | having happened | to him. | Holding | and |

11.a.**Txt:** 025P,byz.
**Var:** 01ℵ,02A,03B,04C
05D,08E,sa.bo.Gries
Lach,Treg,Alf,Word
Tisc,We/Ho,Weis,Sod
UBS/☆

11.b.**Var:** 01ℵ,02A,03B
Lach,Treg,Tisc,We/Ho
Word,Elzev,Sod,UBS/☆

| **3450.2** art gen sing | **2367.12** verb gen sing masc part aor pass | **5395.3** adj gen sing masc | **840.3** prs-pron gen sing | **3450.6** art acc sing masc |
|---|---|---|---|---|
| ʻ τοῦ | ἰαθέντος | χωλοῦ | [a☆ αὐτοῦ ] | τὸν |
| *tou* | *iathentos* | *chōlou* | *autou* | *ton* |
| the | having been healed | lame | [ he ] | |

| **3935.4** name acc masc | **2504.1** conj | **3450.6** art acc sing masc | **2464.4** name acc masc | **4788.2** verb 3sing indic aor act | **4242.1** prep |
|---|---|---|---|---|---|
| Πέτρον | καὶ | [b☆+ τὸν ] | Ἰωάννην, | συνέδραμεν | ʻ πρὸς |
| *Petron* | *kai* | *ton* | *Iōannēn* | *sunedramen* | *pros* |
| Peter | and | | John, | ran together | to |

| **840.8** prs-pron acc pl masc | **3820.6** adj nom sing masc | **3450.5** art nom sing masc | **2967.1** noun nom sing masc | **3820.6** adj nom sing masc | **3450.5** art nom sing masc |
|---|---|---|---|---|---|
| αὐτοὺς | πᾶς | ὁ | λαὸς | [ πᾶς | ὁ |
| *autous* | *pas* | *ho* | *laos* | *pas* | *ho* |
| them | all | the | people | [ all | the |

| **2967.1** noun nom sing masc | **4242.1** prep | **840.8** prs-pron acc pl masc | **1894.3** prep | **3450.11** art dat sing fem | **4596.1** noun dat sing fem | **3450.11** art dat sing fem |
|---|---|---|---|---|---|---|
| λαὸς | πρὸς | αὐτοὺς ] | ἐπὶ | τῇ | στοᾷ | τῇ |
| *laos* | *pros* | *autous* | *epi* | *tē* | *stoa* | *tē* |
| people | to | them ] | on | the | porch | the |

| **2535.33** verb dat sing fem part pres mid | **4526.2** name gen masc | **1556.1** adj nom pl masc | **1481.16** verb nom sing masc part aor act |
|---|---|---|---|
| καλουμένῃ | Σολομῶντος, | ἔκθαμβοι. | **12.** ἰδὼν |
| *kaloumenē* | *Solomōntos* | *ekthamboi* | *idōn* |
| being called | Solomon's, | greatly amazed. | Having seen |

12.a.**Var:** 01ℵ,02A,03B
04C,05D,Lach,Treg,Alf
Tisc,We/Ho,Weis,Sod
UBS/☆

| **1156.2** conj | **3450.5** art nom sing masc | **3935.1** name nom masc | **552.7** verb 3sing indic aor mid | **4242.1** prep | **3450.6** art acc sing masc |
|---|---|---|---|---|---|
| δὲ | [a☆+ ὁ ] | Πέτρος | ἀπεκρίνατο | πρὸς | τὸν |
| *de* | *ho* | *Petros* | *apekrinato* | *pros* | *ton* |
| and | | Peter | answered | to | the |

| **2967.4** noun acc sing masc | **433.6** noun nom pl masc | **2448.2** name nom pl masc | **4949.9** intr-pron sing neu | **2273.1** verb 2pl pres act |
|---|---|---|---|---|
| λαόν, | Ἄνδρες | Ἰσραηλῖται, | τί | θαυμάζετε |
| *laon* | *Andres* | *Israēlitai* | *ti* | *thaumazete* |
| people, | Men | Israelites, | why | marvel you |

The word "amazement" also implies bewilderment, the kind of bewilderment that comes when a person is in a state of shock. Their minds were in a whirl trying to figure out how this could have happened. Yet it was obvious something had happened. Like most ancient beggars, this man's shriveled ankles and misshapen feet were undoubtedly displayed when he was placed at the Beautiful Gate. Attention was usually drawn to such things by beggars in order to excite pity and stir people to give. If the man had any shoes (and he probably did not), they would have been sandals. So as the man walked and jumped it was easy for them all to see the well-formed feet and strong, firm ankles that he now had. They were completely astonished.

**3:11.** The temple area was quite large. King Herod was a megalomaniac and wanted to make everything bigger than it had been before. When he rebuilt the temple he could not make it bigger because the dimensions were given in the Scriptures, so he made the courts twice as big as they had been in Solomon's time and in Zerubbabel's rebuilding. The so-called Wailing or Western Wall is just a retaining wall which was necessary to enlarge the top of the temple mount so he could make the courts larger. Thus, it took a few minutes for the man to walk across the court. By the time he reached Solomon's Porch, still holding the hands of Peter and John, the crowd began to gather.

God has often used miraculous healings to get people's attention. There was very little of the miraculous during the Intertestamental Period before Jesus came. His miracles and the miracles done by the 12 and the 70 helped to draw the crowds. But this crowd did not yet know the power of Christ's resurrection. They probably thought the day of miracles was past. They needed a visible manifestation of the supernatural to let them know God was still visiting His people. Miraculous healings in many parts of the world today are again bringing crowds.

**3:12.** This was Peter's opportunity, and he was quick to answer the unspoken questions on the perplexed and astonished faces. His message follows the same general pattern given by the Spirit through the gift of prophecy on the Day of Pentecost, but adapted to this new situation.

Peter addressed them as Israelite men. (This was the custom even though there were women in the crowd, and the message was for them too.) By referring to them as "Israel," instead of as Jews, he was using the more honorific title, the name given to Jacob as God's fighter and God's prince. It would remind them too of God's promises and of His good purpose for His people.

Peter asked the people why they marveled at this happening and why they fastened their eyes on him and John as if the man's ability to walk had its source in their own power or holiness. The word "power" here is mighty, supernatural power. No man has this on

the same was he who for the alms used to sit at the...Gate, *Rieu* . . . All the people recognized him, *NCV* . . . this was the very man, *Moffatt.*

**and they were filled with wonder and amazement at that which had happened unto him:** They were surprised he was walking, *NLT* . . . they were filled with awe and amazement, *Weymouth* . . . filled with amazement and transport, *Rotherham* . . . mingled with ecstacy, *Fenton* . . . They were struck with astonishment—utterly stupefied at what had happened to him, *NAB* . . . they were completely astounded and bewildered, *Williams* . . . filled with wonder and admiration at what had occurred, *Murdock* . . . unable to explain, *JB* . . . very much surprised, *Beck* . . . they were at a loss to know what had happened, *Klingensmith* . . . they were all overcome with wonder and sheer astonishment, *Phillips* . . . filled with excitement and wonder, *Williams C.K.* . . . at the miracle which healed him, *Noli.*

**11. And as the lame man which was healed held Peter and John:** While he was still clinging to, *Williams* . . . As he clung, *Adams* . . . while the man kept his hands on, *Williams C.K.*

**all the people ran together unto them:** . . . all the people quickly gathered round them, *TCNT* . . . the entire crowd, *Wuest* . . . all the people crowded awe-struck around them, *Montgomery.*

**in the porch that is called Solomon's:** . . . in the portico called Solomon's, *RSV* . . . in the Colonnade called after Solomon, *TCNT* . . . in what was known as Solomon's Portico, *Weymouth.*

**greatly wondering:** . . . greatly amazed, *Rotherham* . . . in the greatest astonishment, *TCNT* . . . awe-struck, *Weymouth* . . . in utter amazement, *Williams* . . . overawed, *Concordant* . . . completely flabbergasted, *Wuest* . . . stunned, *SEB* . . . full of astonishment, *Williams C.K.*

**12. And when Peter saw it, he answered unto the people:** On seeing this, Peter spoke to the people, *TCNT.*

**Ye men of Israel, why marvel ye at this?:** . . . why are you surprised at this? *Norlie.*

## Acts 3:13

| 1894.3 prep | 3642.5 dem-pron dat sing masc | 2211.1 conj | 2231.3 prs-pron dat 1pl | 4949.9 intr-pron sing neu | 810.1 verb 2pl indic pres act | 5453.1 conj |
|---|---|---|---|---|---|---|
| ἐπὶ | τούτῳ, | ἢ | ἡμῖν | τί | ἀτενίζετε | ὡς |
| *epi* | *toutō* | *ē* | *hēmin* | *ti* | *atenizete* | *hōs* |
| at | this? | or | on us | why | look intently | as if |

| 2375.10 adj dat sing fem | 1405.3 noun dat sing fem | 2211.1 conj | 2131.3 noun dat sing fem | 4020.50 verb dat pl masc part perf act | 3450.2 art gen sing |
|---|---|---|---|---|---|
| ἰδίᾳ | δυνάμει | ἢ | εὐσεβείᾳ | πεποιηκόσιν | τοῦ |
| *idia* | *dunamei* | *ē* | *eusebeia* | *pepoiēkosin* | *tou* |
| by our own | power | or | godliness | having made | the |

| 3906.17 verb inf pres act | 840.6 prs-pron acc sing masc | 3450.5 art nom sing masc | 2296.1 noun nom sing masc | 11.1 name masc | 2504.1 conj |
|---|---|---|---|---|---|
| περιπατεῖν | αὐτόν; | **13.** ὁ | θεὸς | Ἀβραὰμ | καὶ |
| *peripatein* | *auton* | *ho* | *theos* | *Abraam* | *kai* |
| to walk | him? | The | God | of Abraham | and |

13.a.**Var:** p74,01ℵ,02A 04C,05D,bo.Tisc,Sod

13.b.**Var:** p74,01ℵ,02A 04C,05D,bo.Tisc,Sod

| 3450.5 art nom sing masc | 2296.1 noun nom sing masc | 2439.1 name masc | 2504.1 conj | 2361.1 name masc | 3450.5 art nom sing masc |
|---|---|---|---|---|---|
| [a+ ὁ | θεὸς ] | Ἰσαὰκ | καὶ | Ἰακώβ, | [b+ ὁ |
| *ho* | *theos* | *Isaak* | *kai* | *Iakōb* | *ho* |
| [ the | God ] | Isaac | and | Jacob | [ the |

| 2296.1 noun nom sing masc | 3450.5 art nom sing masc | 2296.1 noun nom sing masc | 3450.1 art gen pl | 3824.7 noun gen pl masc | 2231.2 prs-pron gen 1pl |
|---|---|---|---|---|---|
| θεὸς ] | ὁ | θεὸς | τῶν | πατέρων | ἡμῶν, |
| *theos* | *ho* | *theos* | *tōn* | *paterōn* | *hēmōn* |
| God ] | the | God | of the | fathers | our, |

| 1386.9 verb 3sing indic aor act | 3450.6 art acc sing masc | 3679.1 noun acc sing | 840.3 prs-pron gen sing | 2400.3 name acc masc | 3614.6 rel-pron acc sing masc |
|---|---|---|---|---|---|
| ἐδόξασεν | τὸν | παῖδα | αὐτοῦ | Ἰησοῦν· | ὃν |
| *edoxasen* | *ton* | *paida* | *autou* | *Iēsoun* | *hon* |
| glorified | the | servant | his | Jesus, | whom |

13.c.**Var:** 01ℵ,02A,03B 04C,08E,025P,Gries Lach,Treg,Alf,Word Tisc,We/Ho,Weis,Sod UBS/⋆

| 5050.1 prs-pron nom 2pl | 3173.1 conj | 3722.12 verb 2pl indic aor act | 2504.1 conj | 714.8 verb 2pl indic aor mid |
|---|---|---|---|---|
| ὑμεῖς | [c⋆+ μὲν ] | παρεδώκατε, | καὶ | ἠρνήσασθε |
| *humeis* | *men* | *paredōkate* | *kai* | *ērnēsasthe* |
| you | | delivered up, | and | denied |

13.d.**Txt:** 05D,08E,025P byz.sa.
**Var:** 01ℵ,02A,03B,04C bo.Lach,Tisc,We/Ho Weis,Sod,UBS/⋆

| 840.6 prs-pron acc sing masc | 2567.3 prep | 4241.1 noun sing neu | 3952.2 name gen masc | 2892.17 verb gen sing masc part aor act |
|---|---|---|---|---|
| ⸀d αὐτὸν ⸌ | κατὰ | πρόσωπον | Πιλάτου, | κρίναντος |
| *auton* | *kata* | *prosōpon* | *Pilatou* | *krinantos* |
| him | in the | presence | of Pilate, | having judged |

| 1552.2 dem-pron gen sing | 624.4 verb inf pres act | 5050.1 prs-pron nom 2pl | 1156.2 conj | 3450.6 art acc sing masc | 39.1 adj sing |
|---|---|---|---|---|---|
| ἐκείνου | ἀπολύειν. | **14.** ὑμεῖς | δὲ | τὸν | ἅγιον |
| *ekeinou* | *apoluein* | *humeis* | *de* | *ton* | *hagion* |
| that one | to release. | You | but | the | holy |

| 2504.1 conj | 1337.1 adj sing | 714.8 verb 2pl indic aor mid | 2504.1 conj | 153.29 verb 2pl indic aor mid |
|---|---|---|---|---|
| καὶ | δίκαιον | ἠρνήσασθε, | καὶ | ᾐτήσασθε |
| *kai* | *dikaion* | *ērnēsasthe* | *kai* | *ētēsasthe* |
| and | righteous one | denied, | and | requested |

| 433.4 noun acc sing masc | 5243.2 noun acc sing masc | 5319.9 verb inf aor pass | 5050.3 prs-pron dat 2pl | 3450.6 art acc sing masc |
|---|---|---|---|---|
| ἄνδρα | φονέα | χαρισθῆναι | ὑμῖν, | **15.** τὸν |
| *andra* | *phonea* | *charisthēnai* | *humin* | *ton* |
| a man | a murderer | to be granted | to you, | the |

his own. It is God's power ministered through the gifts of the Holy Spirit. No one ever receives a reservoir of this power. Believers can only become channels through whom the Holy Spirit can work. If the connection is broken, if individuals lose touch with the divine Source, they have nothing.

The word "holiness" here is not the ordinary word used but one often translated "godliness." It implies a God-fearing attitude that gives respect and obedience to God because it is His right, His due. But this is only what God deserves. It does not give any person any special merit or make him the source of power, so he cannot take any credit to himself. God is always the believer's Source. True godly people do not call attention to themselves. Rather, they direct attention to the Lord.

**or why look ye so earnestly on us:** . . . or why fasten ye your eyes on us, *ASV* . . . Or upon us why are ye intently looking, *Rotherham* . . . and why do you stare so at us, *TCNT* . . . Or why gaze at us, *Weymouth.*

**as though by our own power or holiness we had made this man to walk?:** Do you think this happened because we are good? *Everyday* . . . power or godliness, *Rotherham* . . . or devoutness, *Concordant* . . . our own individual power, or active piety, *Fenton* . . . as though we, by any power or piety of our own, had enabled this man to walk, *TCNT.*

**3:13.** Peter continually bore witness to Jesus. Here he identified Jesus as the One glorified by the God the Bible describes as the God of Abraham, Isaac, and Jacob, the God of their fathers (Exodus 3:6,15). This God had exalted His Son Jesus on high.

The word "Son" here is not the ordinary word but one that may mean "child" or "servant." Another word is used when the Bible talks about the divine sonship of Jesus. Here Peter probably had in mind the identification of Jesus with the Suffering Servant of Isaiah 52:13. The servant of the Lord is the one who does the Lord's work. This healing was thus the result of the fulfillment of Isaiah's prophecy that spoke of the sufferings of Jesus on the sinner's behalf when He bore his griefs (literally, his "sicknesses") and carried away his sorrows (literally, his "pains") as in Isaiah 53:4.

Again Peter reminded the people that they were the ones who were responsible for arresting Jesus and denying Him before Pilate, even when Pilate had decided to release Him.

**13. The God of Abraham, and Isaac, and of Jacob:**

**the God of our fathers:** The God of our ancestors, *TCNT* . . . the God of our forefathers, *Weymouth.*

**hath glorified his Son Jesus:** . . . hath done honour, *TCNT* . . . has done it, *Norlie* . . . glorified his servant, *Noli.*

**whom ye delivered up:** . . . though you indeed surrendered him, *TCNT* . . . whom you yourselves betrayed, *Williams* . . . handed over and then disowned, *JB.*

**and denied him in the presence of Pilate:** . . . and disowned him even before Pilate, *TCNT* . . . denied him to Pilate's face, *Rotherham* . . . renounced him, *Wesley* . . . turning your backs on him, *BB.*

**when he was determined to let him go:** . . . when he had decided to release him, *RSV* . . . after he had made up his mind to set Him free, *Norlie* . . . that one's verdict to release Him, *Wuest* . . . resolved to release him, *Wilson.*

**3:14.** The One they denied was the Holy and Just (righteous) One. Again, this was a reference to the Suffering Servant in Isaiah 53:11. (Compare Zechariah 9:9.) These two terms would have been recognized by those who listened as prevalent messianic titles. This is reinforced further in Acts 7:52 which says, "Which one of the prophets did your fathers not persecute? And they killed those who had previously announced the coming of the Righteous One, whose betrayers and murderers you have now become" (NASB). (See also 1 John 2:1.) As in his Gospel, Luke placed full responsibility for the death of the Messiah on the Jews, not on Pilate who sought to have Jesus released (Luke 23:4,14-16,20-25). But the people had turned from Jesus so completely that they asked for a murderer to be released to them instead.

The murderer was, of course, Barabbas, whom the Bible also describes as one who caused a certain sedition (political upheaval and riot) in Jerusalem (Luke 23:19,25). Jesus not only died in his place, but also in the place of every individual.

**14. But ye denied the Holy One and the Just:** Righteous One, *ASV* . . . You disavowed the...man, *Noli* . . . Yes, you disowned the holy and righteous One, *Weymouth.*

**and desired a murderer to be granted unto you:** . . . and asked for yourselves the release of a murderer! *TCNT* . . . to be surrendered, *Concordant* . . . and asked as a favour, *Weymouth* . . . demanded the reprieve, *JB* . . . and asked a murderer to be pardoned as a favor to you, *Williams* . . . the man you requested, *Klingensmith.*

| 1156.2 conj | 742.1 noun acc sing masc | 3450.10 art gen sing fem | 2205.2 noun gen sing fem | 609.6 verb 2pl indic aor act | 3614.6 rel-pron acc sing masc |
|---|---|---|---|---|---|
| δὲ | ἀρχηγὸν | τῆς | ζωῆς | ἀπεκτείνατε· | ὃν |
| *de* | *archēgon* | *tēs* | *zōēs* | *apekteinate* | *hon* |
| but | Author | of the | life | you killed, | whom |

| 3450.5 art nom sing masc | 2296.1 noun nom sing masc | 1446.5 verb 3sing indic aor act | 1523.2 prep gen | 3361.2 adj gen pl | 3614.2 rel-pron gen sing |
|---|---|---|---|---|---|
| ὁ | θεὸς | ἤγειρεν | ἐκ | νεκρῶν, | οὗ |
| *ho* | *theos* | *ēgeiren* | *ek* | *nekrōn* | *hou* |
|  | God | raised up | from | dead, | of which |

| 2231.1 prs-pron nom 1pl | 3116.4 noun nom pl masc | 1498.5 verb 1pl indic pres act | 2504.1 conj | 1894.3 prep | 3450.11 art dat sing fem |
|---|---|---|---|---|---|
| ἡμεῖς | μάρτυρές | ἐσμεν. | **16.** καὶ | ἐπὶ | τῇ |
| *hēmeis* | *martures* | *esmen* | *kai* | *epi* | *tē* |
| we | witnesses | are: | and | upon | the |

| 3963.3 noun dat sing fem | 3450.2 art gen sing | 3549.3 noun gen sing neu | 840.3 prs-pron gen sing | 3642.6 dem-pron acc sing masc | 3614.6 rel-pron acc sing masc |
|---|---|---|---|---|---|
| πίστει | τοῦ | ὀνόματος | αὐτοῦ | τοῦτον | ὃν |
| *pistei* | *tou* | *onomatos* | *autou* | *touton* | *hon* |
| faith | in the | name | his | this | whom |

| 2311.1 verb 2pl pres act | 2504.1 conj | 3471.6 verb 2pl indic perf act | 4583.1 verb 3sing indic aor act | 3450.16 art sing neu | 3549.2 noun sing neu |
|---|---|---|---|---|---|
| θεωρεῖτε | καὶ | οἴδατε | ἐστερέωσεν | τὸ | ὄνομα |
| *theōreite* | *kai* | *oidate* | *estereōsen* | *to* | *onoma* |
| you see | and | know | made strong | the | name |

| 840.3 prs-pron gen sing | 2504.1 conj | 3450.9 art nom sing fem | 3963.1 noun nom sing fem | 3450.9 art nom sing fem | 1217.1 prep | 840.3 prs-pron gen sing |
|---|---|---|---|---|---|---|
| αὐτοῦ· | καὶ | ἡ | πίστις | ἡ | δι’ | αὐτοῦ |
| *autou* | *kai* | *hē* | *pistis* | *hē* | *di’* | *autou* |
| his; | and | the | faith | the | by | him |

| 1319.14 verb 3sing indic aor act | 840.4 prs-pron dat sing | 3450.12 art acc sing fem | 3510.1 noun acc sing fem | 3642.12 dem-pron acc sing fem |
|---|---|---|---|---|
| ἔδωκεν | αὐτῷ | τὴν | ὁλοκληρίαν | ταύτην |
| *edōken* | *autō* | *tēn* | *holoklērian* | *tautēn* |
| gave | to him | the | wholeness | this |

| 558.1 prep | 3820.4 adj gen pl | 5050.2 prs-pron gen 2pl | 2504.1 conj | 3431.1 adv | 79.6 noun nom pl masc |
|---|---|---|---|---|---|
| ἀπέναντι | πάντων | ὑμῶν. | **17.** καὶ | νῦν, | ἀδελφοί, |
| *apenanti* | *pantōn* | *humōn* | *kai* | *nun* | *adelphoi* |
| before | all | of you. | And | now, | brothers, |

| 3471.2 verb 1sing indic perf act | 3617.1 conj | 2567.3 prep | 51.3 noun acc sing fem | 4097.17 verb 2pl indic aor act | 5450.1 conj |
|---|---|---|---|---|---|
| οἶδα | ὅτι | κατὰ | ἄγνοιαν | ἐπράξατε, | ὥσπερ |
| *oida* | *hoti* | *kata* | *agnoian* | *epraxate* | *hōsper* |
| I know | that | according to | ignorance | you acted, | as |

| 2504.1 conj | 3450.7 art nom pl masc | 752.5 noun nom pl masc | 5050.2 prs-pron gen 2pl | 3450.5 art nom sing masc | 1156.2 conj | 2296.1 noun nom sing masc |
|---|---|---|---|---|---|---|
| καὶ | οἱ | ἄρχοντες | ὑμῶν· | **18.** ὁ | δὲ | θεὸς |
| *kai* | *hoi* | *archontes* | *humōn* | *ho* | *de* | *theos* |
| also | the | rulers | your; |  | but | God |

| 3614.17 rel-pron pl neu | 4152.1 verb 3sing indic aor act | 1217.2 prep | 4601.2 noun gen sing neu | 3820.4 adj gen pl | 3450.1 art gen pl |
|---|---|---|---|---|---|
| ἃ | προκατήγγειλεν | διὰ | στόματος | πάντων | τῶν |
| *ha* | *prokatēngeilen* | *dia* | *stomatos* | *pantōn* | *tōn* |
| what | before announced | by | mouth | of all | the |

**3:15.** Because of the determination of the Jerusalem Jews to have Jesus crucified, they became guilty of killing the "Prince of life." What a contrast! They gave death to the One who gave them life. "Prince" (Greek, *archēgon*) is a word that usually means originator, author, or founder. In Hebrews 2:10 it is translated "captain." In Hebrews 12:2 it is translated "author." It speaks of the part Jesus had in creation. As John 1:3 says of Jesus, the living, active Word, "All things were made through Him, and apart from Him was not anything made that was made" (literal translation). In other words, the preincarnate Jesus was the living Word who spoke the worlds into existence, and through Him God breathed life into the first man, Adam (Genesis 2:7). They had killed this Jesus, the very source of both physical and spiritual life, but God had raised Him from the dead. Peter and John were witnesses to this.

**3:16.** Notice the repetition of the Name in this verse. "And his name, through faith (on the grounds of faith, on the basis of faith) in his name, hath made this man strong, whom ye see and know." And the faith that is by (through) Him (Jesus) had given him this freedom from bodily defect "in the presence of you all."

The Name, of course, refers to the character and nature of Jesus as the Healer, the great Physician. The healing came on the ground of faith in Jesus for who He is. But it was not their faith as such that brought the healing. It was the Name, that is, the fact that Jesus is true to His name, His nature, His character. He is the Healer. Faith had a great part, of course, but it was the faith that came through Jesus. The faith Jesus himself had imparted (not only to Peter and John, but also to the man) gave complete freedom from defect to this lame man before their very eyes. ("Perfect soundness" reflects the terminology used in the Law for the freedom from defect necessary for animals used in Jewish sacrifices.) Jesus had healed the lame when He was on earth. He was still healing them through His disciples.

**3:17.** Peter added that he knew it was because of ignorance they and their rulers killed Jesus. (Paul later confessed that he persecuted the Church because of ignorance and unbelief [1 Timothy 1:13].) Peter's words imply they did not really know Jesus to be Messiah, nor did they know He is God's own Son. This ignorance did not lessen their guilt, yet even in the Old Testament there was always forgiveness for sins done in ignorance. On the cross Jesus cried out, "Father, forgive them; for they know not what they do" (Luke 23:34). Thankfully, the Bible says, "God hath not cast away his people which he foreknew" (Romans 11:2).

**3:18.** The sufferings and death of Jesus were also the fulfillment of prophecies God had revealed by the mouth of all His prophets, that is, by the body of prophets as a whole. Their message, taken as a whole, had for a focal point the death of the Messiah, the

**15. And killed the Prince of life:** The very Guide to Life you put to death, *TCNT* . . . You killed the Lord and Giver of, *Beck* . . . Inaugurator of, *Concordant* . . . Author of the life, *Wuest* . . . originator of, *Darby*.

**whom God hath raised from the dead:** Whom God raised from among the dead, *Rotherham*.

**whereof we are witnesses:** . . . and of that fact we are ourselves witnesses, *TCNT* . . . We saw this with our own eyes, *SEB*.

**16. And his name through faith in his name:** And it is by faith in the name of Jesus, *TCNT* . . . In virtue of faith in, *Weymouth* . . . It is His name, that is, on condition of faith in, *Williams*.

**hath made this man strong, whom ye see and know:** . . . has strengthened this man whom you behold and know, *Weymouth* . . . that has made strong again this man whom you see and recognize, *Williams* . . . gives stability to him whom you are beholding, *Concordant* . . . has entirely restored this man, *PNT*.

**yea, the faith which is by him:** Yes, it is the faith inspired by Jesus, *TCNT* . . . and the faith which He has bestowed, *Weymouth*.

**hath given him this perfect soundness in the presence of you all:** . . . unimpaired soundness, *Concordant* . . . that has made this complete cure of the man, before the eyes of you all, *TCNT* . . . has given this man the perfect health you all see, *Williams* . . . has completely restored this man, *Norlie*.

**17. And now, brethren, I wot that through ignorance ye did it, as did also your rulers:** . . . fellow Jews, *Beck* . . . you did not realize what you were doing, *Williams* . . . you had no idea what you were doing, *Phillips* . . . with your rulers also, *PNT*.

**18. But those things, which God before had shewed:** But the things which God foreshowed, *ASV* . . . But in this way God has fulfilled the declarations He made, *Weymouth* . . . God accomplished what He had foretold, *Norlie* . . . in this way God did what He predicted, *Beck* . . . he made it come true in this way, *TEV*.

18.a.**Txt:** 025P,byz.bo. **Var:** 01ℵ,03B,04C,05D 08E,Lach,Treg,Alf,Tisc We/Ho,Weis,Sod UBS/☆

| 4254.5 noun gen pl masc | 840.3 prs-pron gen sing | 3819.18 verb inf aor act | 3450.6 art acc sing masc | 5382.4 name acc masc |
|---|---|---|---|---|
| προφητῶν | ⸂a αὐτοῦ ⸃ | παθεῖν | τὸν | Χριστὸν, |
| *prophētōn* | *autou* | *pathein* | *ton* | *Christon* |
| prophets | his | to suffer | the | Christ, |

18.b.**Var:** 01ℵ,03B,04C 05D,08E,Lach,Treg,Alf Word,Tisc,We/Ho,Weis Sod,UBS/☆

| 840.3 prs-pron gen sing | 3997.3 verb 3sing indic aor act | 3643.1 adv | 3210.12 verb 2pl impr aor act |
|---|---|---|---|
| [b☆+ αὐτοῦ ] | ἐπλήρωσεν | οὕτως. | **19.** μετανοήσατε |
| *autou* | *eplērōsen* | *houtōs* | *metanoēsate* |
| [ his ] | he fulfilled | thus. | Repent |

19.a.**Txt:** 02A,04C,05D 08E,025P,etc.byz.Sod **Var:** 01ℵ,03B,Tisc We/Ho,Weis,UBS/☆

| 3631.1 partic | 2504.1 conj | 1978.10 verb 2pl impr aor act | 1519.1 prep | 4242.1 prep | 3450.16 art sing neu |
|---|---|---|---|---|---|
| οὖν | καὶ | ἐπιστρέψατε, | ⸂ εἰς | [a πρὸς ] | τὸ |
| *oun* | *kai* | *epistrepsate* | *eis* | *pros* | *to* |
| therefore | and | turn back, | for | [ to ] | the |

| 1797.4 verb inf aor pass | 5050.2 prs-pron gen 2pl | 3450.15 art acc pl fem | 264.1 noun fem | 3567.1 conj | 300.1 partic | 2048.9 verb 3pl subj aor act |
|---|---|---|---|---|---|---|
| ἐξαλειφθῆναι | ὑμῶν | τὰς | ἁμαρτίας, | ὅπως | ἂν | ἔλθωσιν |
| *exaleiphthēnai* | *humōn* | *tas* | *hamartias* | *hopōs* | *an* | *elthōsin* |
| to be blotted out | your | the | sins, | so that | | may come |

| 2511.5 noun nom pl masc | 401.1 noun gen sing fem | 570.3 prep | 4241.2 noun gen sing neu | 3450.2 art gen sing | 2935.2 noun gen sing masc |
|---|---|---|---|---|---|
| καιροὶ | ἀναψύξεως | ἀπὸ | προσώπου | τοῦ | κυρίου, |
| *kairoi* | *anapsuxeōs* | *apo* | *prosōpou* | *tou* | *kuriou* |
| times | of refreshing | from | face | of the | Lord, |

| 2504.1 conj | 643.10 verb 3sing subj aor act | 3450.6 art acc sing masc | 4155.2 verb acc sing masc part perf mid |
|---|---|---|---|
| **20.** καὶ | ἀποστείλῃ | τὸν | ⸂ προκεκηρυγμένον |
| *kai* | *aposteilē* | *ton* | *prokekērugmenon* |
| and | he may send | the | having been proclaimed before |

20.a.**Txt:** byz.bo. **Var:** 01ℵ,02A,03B,04C 05D,08E,025P,Gries Lach,Treg,Alf,Word Tisc,We/Ho,Weis,Sod UBS/☆

| 4258.3 verb sing part perf mid | 5050.3 prs-pron dat 2pl | 2400.3 name acc masc | 5382.4 name acc masc |
|---|---|---|---|
| [a☆ προκεχειρισμένον ] | ὑμῖν, | ⸂ Ἰησοῦν | Χριστόν, |
| *prokecheirismenon* | *humin* | *Iēsoun* | *Christon* |
| [ having been appointed before ] | to you, | Jesus | Christ |

| 5382.4 name acc masc | 2400.3 name acc masc | 3614.6 rel-pron acc sing masc | 1158.1 verb 3sing indic pres act | 3636.4 noun acc sing masc |
|---|---|---|---|---|
| [☆ Χριστόν, | Ἰησοῦν, ] | **21.** ὃν | δεῖ | οὐρανὸν |
| *Christon* | *Iēsoun* | *hon* | *dei* | *ouranon* |
| [ Christ | Jesus, ] | whom | must | heaven |

| 3173.1 conj | 1203.16 verb inf aor mid | 884.2 conj | 5385.5 noun gen pl masc | 600.1 noun gen sing fem |
|---|---|---|---|---|
| μὲν | δέξασθαι | ἄχρι | χρόνων | ἀποκαταστάσεως |
| *men* | *dexasthai* | *achri* | *chronōn* | *apokatastaseōs* |
| indeed | to receive | until | times | of restoration |

| 3820.4 adj gen pl | 3614.1 rel-pron gen pl | 2953.27 verb 3sing indic aor act | 3450.5 art nom sing masc | 2296.1 noun nom sing masc | 1217.2 prep |
|---|---|---|---|---|---|
| πάντων, | ὧν | ἐλάλησεν | ὁ | θεὸς | διὰ |
| *pantōn* | *hōn* | *elalēsen* | *ho* | *theos* | *dia* |
| of all things, | of which | spoke | | God | by |

21.a.**Txt:** byz. **Var:** 01ℵ,02A,03B,04C 05D,sa.bo.Gries,Lach Treg,Alf,Word,Tisc We/Ho,Weis,Sod UBS/☆

| 4601.2 noun gen sing neu | 3820.4 adj gen pl | 3450.1 art gen pl | 39.4 adj gen pl | 840.3 prs-pron gen sing | 4254.5 noun gen pl masc |
|---|---|---|---|---|---|
| στόματος | ⸂ πάντων | [a☆ τῶν ] | ἁγίων | ⸂ αὐτοῦ | προφητῶν |
| *stomatos* | *pantōn* | *tōn* | *hagiōn* | *autou* | *prophētōn* |
| mouth | of all | [ the ] | holy | his | prophets |

Christ. Even so, this did not lessen the guilt of the people of Jerusalem. God has never accepted ignorance as an excuse for sin. Sin always brings guilt.

**3:19.** As on the Day of Pentecost, Peter then called on the people to repent, to change their minds and attitudes about Jesus. Let them be converted (turn to God) he said, so that their sins (including the sin of rejecting and killing Jesus) might be blotted out (wiped away, obliterated) when (literally, in order that) times (seasons, occasions) of refreshing from the presence (face) of the Lord might come.

This can be taken as a general principle. Whenever a person changes his mind and attitude and turns to God, his sins will be obliterated, and he can have seasons of refreshing from the throne of God.

Too many put all their emphasis on the warnings of perilous times to come and on the statement that there will be a falling away (2 Timothy 3:1; 2 Thessalonians 2:3). These things will come. The falling away, of course, may mean spiritual falling away, though the Greek word ordinarily means revolt or revolution and war. Though the warnings are necessary, the Christian does not need to make them the focus of his attention. Repentance (a real change of mind and attitude) and a turning to God will still bring seasons of refreshing from the presence of the Lord.

**3:20.** To those who repent, God will send the appointed-for-you Messiah Jesus. Christians must keep their eyes on Jesus as the One who is to come. But it does not mean they have to wait until Jesus comes back before they can enjoy God-sent times of refreshing. It is clear in the Greek that they can have them now and continue to do so until the time Jesus comes again.

**3:21.** These times of refreshing can come even though Jesus is not personally present. The heavens must receive Him until the times of restoration (reestablishment) of all things which were spoken by God through the mouth of His holy prophets from the beginning of the age (or from of old). "Since the world began" is a paraphrase which could mean "from eternity" or "from the beginning of time." The sense is "all the prophets ever since there ever were prophets."

The times of reestablishment refer to the coming age. Then God will restore and renew the Kingdom, and Jesus will reign personally on the earth. The restoration includes a further outpouring of the Spirit. But care must be taken as to the interpretation of this. Only those things which God has spoken by the prophets will be restored.

The prophets also show the Kingdom must be brought in through judgment. Daniel 2:35,44,45 shows the Babylon image (represent-

**by the mouth of all his prophets, that Christ should suffer, he hath so fulfilled:** . . . by the lips of all the Prophets, *TCNT* . . . that His Christ would suffer, *Weymouth* . . . suffer many hard things, *NLT* . . . He fulfilled in this way, *Adams* . . . he thus fulfilled, *ASV*.

**19. Repent ye therefore, and be converted:** Change your minds, *Sawyer* . . . and turn again, *RSV* . . . you must be sorry for, *NLT* . . . You must, therefore, repent and turn, *Weymouth* . . . and turn around, *Adams* . . . you must turn to God, *Norlie*.

**that your sins may be blotted out:** . . . for your sins to be wiped away, *TCNT* . . . cancelled, *Weymouth* . . . for the erasure of your sins, *Concordant* . . . that your sins may be obliterated, *Wuest* . . . maye be done awaye, *Tyndale*.

**when the times of refreshing shall come from the presence of the Lord:** . . . so there may come seasons of refreshing, *ASV* . . . and then better and brighter days will come direct from the Lord himself, *TCNT* . . . that times of revival may come, *Williams* . . . a time of recovery, *NEB* . . . when the Lord refreshes you, *Beck* . . . your soul will receive new strength, *NLT*.

**20. And he shall send Jesus Christ, which before was preached unto you:** And he may send forth him who had been fore-appointed for you—Christ Jesus, *Rotherham* . . . the pre-appointed Messiah, *Fenton* . . . and he will send you, in Jesus, your long-appointed Christ, *TCNT* . . . your long-heralded Christ, *Phillips*.

**21. Whom the heaven must receive:** But Heaven must be his home, *TCNT* . . . Yet heaven must retain him, *Williams*.

**until the times of restitution of all things:** . . . of universal restoration, *TCNT* . . . of the reconstitution of all things, *Weymouth* . . . until the final recovery of all things from sin, *LivB* . . . times of spiritual rest, *SEB*.

**which God hath spoken by the mouth of all his holy prophets since the world began:** . . . of which God has spoken from the

# Acts 3:22

22.a.**Txt:** 025P,byz.
**Var:** 01ℵ,02A,03B,04C 05D,08E,sa.bo.Gries Lach,Treg,Alf,Word Tisc,We/Ho,Weis,Sod UBS/☆

22.b.**Txt:** 05D,08E,025P 044,1241,byz.
**Var:** 01ℵ,02A,03B,04C bo.Lach,Treg,Alf,Tisc We/Ho,Weis,Sod UBS/☆

| **570.2** prep | **163.1** noun gen sing masc | **570.2** prep | **163.1** noun gen sing masc | **840.3** prs-pron gen sing | **4254.5** noun gen pl masc |
|---|---|---|---|---|---|
| ἀπ' | αἰῶνος. | [☆ ἀπ' | αἰῶνος | αὐτοῦ | προφητῶν. ] |
| *ap'* | *aiōnos* | *ap'* | *aiōnos* | *autou* | *prophētōn* |
| from | of old | [from | of old | his | prophets.] |

| **3337.1** name nom masc | **3338.1** name nom masc | **3173.1** conj | **1056.1** conj | **4242.1** prep |
|---|---|---|---|---|
| **22.** ⸂ Μωσῆς | [☆ Μωϋσῆς ] | μὲν | ⸂a γὰρ ⸃ | ⸂b πρὸς |
| *Mōsēs* | *Mōusēs* | *men* | *gar* | *pros* |
| Moses | [idem] | indeed | for | to |

| **3450.8** art acc pl masc | **3824.9** noun acc pl masc | **1500.5** verb 3sing indic aor act | **3617.1** conj | **4254.3** noun acc sing masc | **5050.3** prs-pron dat 2pl |
|---|---|---|---|---|---|
| τοὺς | πατέρας ⸃ | εἶπεν, | Ὅτι | Προφήτην | ὑμῖν |
| *tous* | *pateras* | *eipen* | *Hoti* | *Prophētēn* | *humin* |
| the | fathers | said, | | A prophet | to you |

| **448.15** verb 3sing indic fut act | **2935.1** noun nom sing masc | **3450.5** art nom sing masc | **2296.1** noun nom sing masc | **5050.2** prs-pron gen 2pl | **1523.2** prep gen |
|---|---|---|---|---|---|
| ἀναστήσει | κύριος | ὁ | θεὸς | ⸂ ὑμῶν | ἐκ |
| *anastēsei* | *kurios* | *ho* | *theos* | *humōn* | *ek* |
| will raise up | Lord | | God | your | from |

22.c.**Txt:** 01ℵ-corr,02A 05D,Steph
**Var1:** 01ℵ-org,04C,08E 025P,33,1241,sa.Tisc Sod
**Var2:** p74,03B,bo. We/Ho,Weis,UBS/☆

| **2231.2** prs-pron gen 1pl | **1523.2** prep gen | **1523.2** prep gen | **3450.1** art gen pl | **79.7** noun gen pl masc | **5050.2** prs-pron gen 2pl |
|---|---|---|---|---|---|
| [1c ἡμῶν | ἐκ | 2 ἐκ ] | τῶν | ἀδελφῶν | ὑμῶν, |
| *hēmōn* | *ek* | *ek* | *tōn* | *adelphōn* | *humōn* |
| [our | from | from] | the | brothers | your, |

| **5453.1** conj | **1466.7** prs-pron acc 1sing | **840.3** prs-pron gen sing | **189.53** verb 2pl indic fut mid | **2567.3** prep | **3820.1** adj |
|---|---|---|---|---|---|
| ὡς | ἐμέ· | αὐτοῦ | ἀκούσεσθε | κατὰ | πάντα |
| *hōs* | *eme* | *autou* | *akousesthe* | *kata* | *panta* |
| like | me: | him | shall you hear | according to | all things |

| **3607.8** rel-pron pl neu | **300.1** partic | **2953.31** verb 3sing subj aor act | **4242.1** prep | **5050.4** prs-pron acc 2pl | **1498.40** verb 3sing indic fut mid |
|---|---|---|---|---|---|
| ὅσα | ἂν | λαλήσῃ | πρὸς | ὑμᾶς. | **23.** ἔσται |
| *hosa* | *an* | *lalēsē* | *pros* | *humas* | *estai* |
| whatever | | he should say | to | you. | It shall be |

23.a.**Txt:** 03B,04C,08E byz.Steph,We/Ho
**Var:** 01ℵ,02A,04C,025P Alf,Tisc,Weis,Sod UBS/☆

| **1156.2** conj | **3820.9** adj nom sing fem | **5425.1** noun nom sing fem | **3610.3** rel-pron nom sing fem | **300.1** partic | **1430.1** partic | **3231.1** partic |
|---|---|---|---|---|---|---|
| δὲ | πᾶσα | ψυχὴ | ἥτις | ⸂ ἂν | [a☆ ἐὰν ] | μὴ |
| *de* | *pasa* | *psuchē* | *hētis* | *an* | *ean* | *mē* |
| and | every | soul | which | | | not |

| **189.18** verb sing act | **3450.2** art gen sing | **4254.2** noun gen sing masc | **1552.2** dem-pron gen sing | **1826.2** verb 3sing indic fut pass |
|---|---|---|---|---|
| ἀκούσῃ | τοῦ | προφήτου | ἐκείνου | ⸂ ἐξολοθρευθήσεται |
| *akousē* | *tou* | *prophētou* | *ekeinou* | *exolothreuthēsetai* |
| may hear | the | prophet | that | shall be destroyed |

23.b.**Txt:** 01ℵ,03B-corr 08E,025P,etc.byz.Sod
**Var:** 02A,03B-org,04C 05D,Lach,Treg,Alf,Tisc We/Ho,Weis,UBS/☆

| **1826.1** verb 3sing indic fut pass | **1523.2** prep gen | **3450.2** art gen sing | **2967.2** noun gen sing masc | **2504.1** conj |
|---|---|---|---|---|
| [b☆ ἐξολεθρευθήσεται ] | ἐκ | τοῦ | λαοῦ. | **24.** Καὶ |
| *exolethreuthēsetai* | *ek* | *tou* | *laou* | *Kai* |
| [idem] | from among | the | people. | And |

| **3820.7** adj nom pl masc | **1156.2** conj | **3450.7** art nom pl masc | **4254.4** noun nom pl masc | **570.3** prep | **4402.1** name masc |
|---|---|---|---|---|---|
| πάντες | δὲ | οἱ | προφῆται | ἀπὸ | Σαμουὴλ |
| *pantes* | *de* | *hoi* | *prophētai* | *apo* | *Samouēl* |
| all | indeed | the | prophets | from | Samuel |

ing the entire world system) must be destroyed. Even the good in the present system must be ground to powder and blown away in order to make room for the better things of the Kingdom.

No one knows when that will be. But the important thing is that believers do not have to wait for the Kingdom to come before they experience God's blessings and power. The Holy Spirit even now brings believers an earnest, a first installment of things to come.

**3:22.** Peter next referred to Moses and quoted from Deuteronomy 18:18,19 where God promised to raise up a prophet like Moses. The people must listen to (and therefore obey) this Prophet. In fact, they must give heed to everything He says, whatever it might be. Moses did not know what this coming Prophet would say, but he was sure He would speak for God, and the people could have full confidence in Him and His words. (See also Leviticus 26:12; Deuteronomy 18:15; Acts 7:37.)

This was the promise the people had in mind also when they asked John the Baptist if he were "that prophet" (John 1:21,25). Now Peter was speaking of a specific Prophet foretold by Moses. Peter said Jesus was the complete and final fulfillment of God's promise of the Prophet like Moses.

In what sense was Jesus like Moses? God used Moses to bring in the old covenant; Jesus brought in the new covenant. Moses led the nation of Israel out of Egypt and brought them to Sinai where God brought them to himself, that is, into a covenant relation with himself. (See Exodus 19:4,5.)

Moses also gave Israel the command to sacrifice the Passover lamb; Jesus is the Lamb of God, our Passover. Moses was used by God to perform great miracles and signs; Jesus performed many miracles and signs, but most were signs of love rather than of judgment. Moses instituted the Day of Atonement where the blood was sprinkled on the mercy seat (the solid gold cover of the ark of the covenant); Jesus is the believer's "propitiation," literally, his "mercy seat" (Romans 3:25). By His blood He entered into heaven's Holy Place once for all, and by His blood He obtained eternal redemption for believers (Hebrews 9:12).

**3:23.** Moses warned the people they would be cut off if they did not receive and obey this Prophet. Thus, though God is good, there is a penalty for those who do not repent. Peter emphasized the meaning of Moses' warning. They would be destroyed from among the people. That is, God would not destroy His people Israel as a whole, but individuals could lose out.

**3:24.** Samuel was the next great prophet after Moses (1 Samuel 3:20). From that time on, all the prophets foretold of "these days," that is, the days of God's work through Christ. Since those who were listening to Peter's sermon were mainly Jews, his argument

earliest ages through the lips of His holy Prophets, *Weymouth* . . . from a remote age, *Rotherham.*

**22. For Moses truly said unto the fathers:** Moses indeed said, *ASV, KJII* . . . In fact Moses said, *MLNT.*

**A prophet shall the Lord your God raise up unto you of your brethren, like unto me:** The Lord your God will raise up from among your brothers a Prophet, as he did me, *TCNT* . . . will give you a prophet like me...He will come from, *NCV* . . . One Who speaks for God, *NLT* . . . as he raised me, *Goodspeed, Weymouth* . . . He will be one of your own people, *Everyday* . . . from among your own kinsmen, *NAB* . . . One like me, *KJII.*

**him shall ye hear in all things whatsoever he shall say unto you:** You must attentively listen to everything that he tells you, *Beck* . . . You must obey everything he tells you, *Everyday* . . . listen to whatever He tells you, *Adams* . . . listen to all the things that he shall say to you, *Williams C.K.* . . . To him you must hearken, *Kleist* . . . to everything He says, *NLT.*

**23. And it shall come to pass, that every soul, which will not hear that prophet:** And it shall be true, *KJII* . . . And every one who refuses to listen to the Prophet, *Weymouth* . . . Everyone among the people who will not listen, *NLT* . . . Anyone that will not listen, *Goodspeed* . . . that every life that shall not hear, *Hanson* . . . that refuses to obey, *Williams C.K.* . . . to hearken to, *Kleist.*

**shall be destroyed from among the people:** . . . shall be utterly destroyed, *ASV* . . . utterly exterminated, *Concordant* . . . will be cut off entirely, *Adams* . . . will be put to death, *NLT* . . . shall be ruthlessly cut off from, *NAB* . . . will be annihilated from among, *Goodspeed* . . . then he will die, *NCV* . . . separated from God's people, *Everyday.*

**24. Yea, and all the prophets from Samuel and those that follow after, as many as have spoken:** All the early preachers who have spoken from Samuel until now, *NLT* . . . all the prophets that

# Acts 3:25

| 2504.1 conj | 3450.1 art gen pl | 2489.1 adv | 3607.2 rel-pron nom pl masc | 2953.30 verb 3pl indic aor act | 2504.1 conj |
|---|---|---|---|---|---|
| καὶ | τῶν | καθεξῆς, | ὅσοι | ἐλάλησαν | καὶ |
| *kai* | *tōn* | *kathexēs* | *hosoi* | *elalēsan* | *kai* |
| and | the | subsequent, | as many as | spoke | also |

24.a.**Txt:** 04C-corr,byz. **Var:** 01א,02A,03B 04C-org,05D,08E,025P Gries,Lach,Treg,Alf Word,Tisc,We/Ho,Weis Sod,UBS/☆

| 4152.2 verb 3pl indic aor act | 2576.11 verb 3pl indic aor act | 3450.15 art acc pl fem | 2232.1 noun fem |
|---|---|---|---|
| ʽ προκατήγγειλαν | [a☆ κατήγγειλαν ] | τὰς | ἡμέρας |
| *prokatēngeilan* | *katēngeilan* | *tas* | *hēmeras* |
| before announced | [ announced ] | the | days |

25.a.**Var:** 01א,02A,03B 04C,08E,sa.bo.Gries Lach,Treg,Alf,Word Tisc,We/Ho,Weis,Sod UBS/☆

| 3642.15 dem-pron acc pl fem | 5050.1 prs-pron nom 2pl | 1498.6 verb 2pl indic pres act | 3450.7 art nom pl masc | 5048.6 noun nom pl masc | 3450.1 art gen pl |
|---|---|---|---|---|---|
| ταύτας. | **25.** ὑμεῖς | ἐστε | [a☆+ οἱ ] | υἱοὶ | τῶν |
| *tautas* | *humeis* | *este* | *hoi* | *huioi* | *tōn* |
| these. | You | are | [ the ] | sons | of the |

| 4254.5 noun gen pl masc | 2504.1 conj | 3450.10 art gen sing fem | 1236.2 noun gen sing fem | 3614.10 rel-pron gen sing fem | 1297.2 verb 3sing indic aor mid |
|---|---|---|---|---|---|
| προφητῶν | καὶ | τῆς | διαθήκης | ἧς | ʽ διέθετο |
| *prophētōn* | *kai* | *tēs* | *diathēkēs* | *hēs* | *dietheto* |
| prophets | and | of the | covenant | which | appointed |

| 3450.5 art nom sing masc | 2296.1 noun nom sing masc | 3450.5 art nom sing masc | 2296.1 noun nom sing masc | 1297.2 verb 3sing indic aor mid | 4242.1 prep |
|---|---|---|---|---|---|
| ὁ | θεὸς | [ ὁ | θεὸς | διέθετο ] | πρὸς |
| *ho* | *theos* | *ho* | *theos* | *dietheto* | *pros* |
| | God | | [ God | appointed ] | to |

25.b.**Txt:** 01א-org,04C 05D,025P,1241,byz.it.bo. Tisc **Var:** p74,01א-corr,02A 03B,08E,sa.Treg,Alf We/Ho,Weis,Sod UBS/☆

| 3450.8 art acc pl masc | 3824.9 noun acc pl masc | 2231.2 prs-pron gen 1pl | 5050.2 prs-pron gen 2pl | 2978.15 verb nom sing masc part pres act |
|---|---|---|---|---|
| τοὺς | πατέρας | ʽ ἡμῶν, | [b☆ ὑμῶν, ] | λέγων |
| *tous* | *pateras* | *hēmōn* | *humōn* | *legōn* |
| the | fathers | our, | [ your, ] | saying |

25.c.**Var:** 01א,02A,03B 04C,05D,08E,025P,sa. bo.Gries,Lach,Treg,Alf Word,Tisc,We/Ho,Weis Sod,UBS/☆

| 4242.1 prep | 11.1 name masc | 2504.1 conj | 1706.1 prep | 3450.3 art dat sing | 4543.3 noun dat sing neu |
|---|---|---|---|---|---|
| πρὸς | ᾿Αβραάμ, | Καὶ | [c☆+ ἐν ] | τῷ | σπέρματί |
| *pros* | *Abraam* | *Kai* | *en* | *tō* | *spermati* |
| to | Abraham, | And | [ in ] | the | seed |

| 4622.2 prs-pron gen 2sing | 1741.1 verb 3pl indic fut pass | 3820.13 adj nom pl fem | 3450.13 art nom pl fem | 3827.3 noun nom pl fem |
|---|---|---|---|---|
| σου | ἐνευλογηθήσονται | πᾶσαι | αἱ | πατριαὶ |
| *sou* | *eneulogēthēsontai* | *pasai* | *hai* | *patriai* |
| your | shall be blessed | all | the | families |

| 3450.10 art gen sing fem | 1087.2 noun gen sing fem | 5050.3 prs-pron dat 2pl | 4270.1 adv | 3450.5 art nom sing masc | 2296.1 noun nom sing masc |
|---|---|---|---|---|---|
| τῆς | γῆς. | **26.** ὑμῖν | πρῶτον | ʽ ὁ | θεὸς |
| *tēs* | *gēs* | *humin* | *prōton* | *ho* | *theos* |
| of the | earth. | To you | first | | God, |

| 448.10 verb nom sing masc part aor act | 448.10 verb nom sing masc part aor act | 3450.5 art nom sing masc | 2296.1 noun nom sing masc | 3450.6 art acc sing masc |
|---|---|---|---|---|
| ἀναστήσας | [☆ ἀναστήσας | ὁ | θεὸς ] | τὸν |
| *anastēsas* | *anastēsas* | *ho* | *theos* | *ton* |
| having raised up | [ having raised up | | God ] | the |

26.a.**Txt:** 02A,025P,byz. **Var:** 01א,03B,04C,05D 08E,sa.bo.Gries,Lach Treg,Alf,Tisc,We/Ho Weis,Sod,UBS/☆

| 3679.1 noun acc sing | 840.3 prs-pron gen sing | 2400.3 name acc masc | 643.8 verb 3sing indic aor act | 840.6 prs-pron acc sing masc |
|---|---|---|---|---|
| παῖδα | αὐτοῦ | ʽa ᾿Ιησοῦν, ʼ | ἀπέστειλεν | αὐτὸν |
| *paida* | *autou* | *Iēsoun* | *apesteilen* | *auton* |
| servant | his | Jesus, | sent | him, |

in these verses (22-26) appealed to those with whom the Jews would be most familiar and accept. In verses 22 and 23 the appeal is to Moses. Longenecker states that the implied emphasis of Peter's argument was twofold: "(1) True belief in Moses will lead to a belief in Jesus, and (2) belief in Jesus places one in true continuity with Moses" (*Expositor's Bible Commentary, Acts,* p.298). In verse 24 the continuity with their Jewish heritage is described in terms of the prophet Samuel who anointed David, the man chosen by God to establish an everlasting kingdom, as the ruler over His people (1 Samuel 13:14; 16:13). Through Jesus, the son of David, all prophecy either has been or will yet be fulfilled. Some may not have given specific prophecies, but all gave prophecies which led up to or prepared for "these days."

**3:25.** Peter next reminded these residents of Jerusalem and Judea that they were the literal descendants of the prophets, heirs also of the Abrahamic covenant with its promise that in Abraham's seed all the families of the earth would be blessed (Genesis 22:18). This promise is actually repeated five times in Genesis. Some modern versions of the Bible translate Genesis 22:18 (et al.) as follows: "In your seed shall all the nations of the earth *bless themselves.*" However, the Greek rendering of this same passage in verse 25 is ". . . all the kindreds of the earth (will) *be blessed.*" The verb for "be blessed" is a future tense, passive voice form, *eneulogēthēsontai;* if the verb was to have been translated "bless themselves," the future middle form could have been selected, *eneulogēsontai.* Although the original Hebrew could be rendered either way, the Septuagint version and Luke (inspired of God) used the passive form which maintains the prophetic nature of the Genesis passage.

Galatians 3:14,16 also shows that believers become heirs of this promise through faith in Jesus, for Jesus is the one "Seed" through whom the promise comes. Thus, by faith all can become children of Abraham, heirs of the same promise.

**3:26.** The blessing promised to all the families of the earth came first to the people of Israel. What a privilege! Yet this was not favoritism on God's part. It was their opportunity to receive the blessing by repenting and by turning from their "iniquities" (their sins, their evil or malicious acts).

Actually, someone had to be the first to carry the message of the gospel. (Compare Romans 1:16; 2:9,10; 3:1,2 which emphasize that the gospel came to the Jew first, and the responsibility to do God's work and to spread the gospel was put on them first.) Paul always went to the Jew first because they had the Scriptures and the background and knew about the Promise. But they could not carry the message and the blessing to others without first repenting and experiencing the blessing for themselves. God had prepared the Jews for this. The first evangelists (spreaders of the good news) were all Jews.

have spoken successively, *MLNT* . . . and all the other prophets who spoke for God after Samuel, *NCV* . . . Yes...Samuel onwards, and all of their successors who taught the people, *TCNT.*

**have likewise foretold of these days:** . . . have also predicted these days, *Weymouth* . . . these times of ours, *MLNT* . . . proclaimed, *TNT* . . . announced the events of, *NAB.*

**25. Ye are the children of the prophets:** You are yourselves the heirs of the Prophets, *TCNT* . . . the descendants of, *Goodspeed* . . . You are of the family of the early preachers, *NLT* . . . You have received what the prophets talked about, *Everyday.*

**and of the covenant which God made with our fathers:** . . . and the heirs of the covenant, *Noli* . . . God covenanted, *Rotherham* . . . which God instituted for your fathers, *Swann* . . . and of the promise that God made with our early fathers, *NLT* . . . You have received the agreement God made with your ancestors, *Everyday* . . . that God established with, *MLNT* . . . and of the bond which God made, *Williams C.K.* . . . and the heirs of the sacred compact, *Williams.*

**saying unto Abraham:** . . . when he said unto Abraham, *Goodspeed, TCNT.*

**And in thy seed shall all the kindreds of the earth be blessed:** In your descendants will all the nations, *TCNT* . . . And in your Descendant all the people, *Beck* . . . In thy children's children, *Williams C.K.* . . . through one of your children, *NCV* . . . all the races of the earth, *Norlie* . . . all the families, *Montgomery* . . . will receive God's favor through, *NLT* . . . are to be blessed through your posterity, *Williams* . . . in your offspring, *NAB.*

**26. Unto you first God:** It was for you first that God, *TCNT* . . . he sent him to you first, *NAB* . . . It is to you first that God, *Weymouth* . . . for you primarily, *Berkeley.*

**having raised up his Son Jesus:** . . . after raising His Servant from the grave, *Weymouth* . . . His special servant, *SEB* . . . after he had raised him from the dead, *Goodspeed.*

| **2108.4** verb acc sing masc part pres act | **5050.4** prs-pron acc 2pl | **1706.1** prep | **3450.3** art dat sing | **648.2** verb inf pres act | **1524.1** adj sing |
|---|---|---|---|---|---|
| εὐλογοῦντα | ὑμᾶς | ἐν | τῷ | ἀποστρέφειν | ἕκαστον |
| *eulogounta* | *humas* | *en* | *tō* | *apostrephein* | *hekaston* |
| blessing | you | in | the | to turn | each |

| **570.3** prep | **3450.1** art gen pl | **4049.5** noun gen pl fem | **5050.2** prs-pron gen 2pl | **2953.17** verb gen pl masc part pres act | **1156.2** conj |
|---|---|---|---|---|---|
| ἀπὸ | τῶν | πονηριῶν | ὑμῶν. | **4:1.** Λαλούντων | δὲ |
| *apo* | *tōn* | *ponēriōn* | *humōn* | *Lalountōn* | *de* |
| from | the | wicked ways | your. | Speaking | and |

| **840.1** prs-pron gen pl | **4242.1** prep | **3450.6** art acc sing masc | **2967.4** noun acc sing masc | **2168.2** verb 3pl indic aor act | **840.2** prs-pron dat pl |
|---|---|---|---|---|---|
| αὐτῶν | πρὸς | τὸν | λαὸν, | ἐπέστησαν | αὐτοῖς |
| *autōn* | *pros* | *ton* | *laon* | *epestēsan* | *autois* |
| they | to | the | people, | came upon | them |

| **3450.7** art nom pl masc | **2385.4** noun pl masc | **2504.1** conj | **3450.5** art nom sing masc | **4606.1** noun nom sing masc | **3450.2** art gen sing |
|---|---|---|---|---|---|
| οἱ | ἱερεῖς | καὶ | ὁ | στρατηγὸς | τοῦ |
| *hoi* | *hiereis* | *kai* | *ho* | *stratēgos* | *tou* |
| the | priests | and | the | captain | of the |

| **2387.1** adj gen sing neu | **2504.1** conj | **3450.7** art nom pl masc | **4380.1** name nom pl masc | **1272.1** verb nom pl masc part pres mid |
|---|---|---|---|---|
| ἱεροῦ | καὶ | οἱ | Σαδδουκαῖοι, | **2.** διαπονούμενοι |
| *hierou* | *kai* | *hoi* | *Saddoukaioi* | *diaponoumenoi* |
| temple | and | the | Sadducees, | being distressed |

| **1217.2** prep | **3450.16** art sing neu | **1315.10** verb inf pres act | **840.8** prs-pron acc pl masc | **3450.6** art acc sing masc | **2967.4** noun acc sing masc |
|---|---|---|---|---|---|
| διὰ | τὸ | διδάσκειν | αὐτοὺς | τὸν | λαὸν, |
| *dia* | *to* | *didaskein* | *autous* | *ton* | *laon* |
| because | the | to teach | them | the | people, |

| **2504.1** conj | **2576.6** verb inf pres act | **1706.1** prep | **3450.3** art dat sing | **2400.2** name masc | **3450.12** art acc sing fem |
|---|---|---|---|---|---|
| καὶ | καταγγέλλειν | ἐν | τῷ | Ἰησοῦ | τὴν |
| *kai* | *katangellein* | *en* | *tō* | *Iēsou* | *tēn* |
| and | to announce | in | | Jesus | the |

| **384.4** noun acc sing fem | **3450.12** art acc sing fem | **1523.2** prep gen | **3361.2** adj gen pl | **2504.1** conj | **1896.4** verb 3pl indic aor act |
|---|---|---|---|---|---|
| ἀνάστασιν | τὴν | ἐκ | νεκρῶν· | **3.** καὶ | ἐπέβαλον |
| *anastasin* | *tēn* | *ek* | *nekrōn* | *kai* | *epebalon* |
| resurrection | the | from | dead; | and | they laid on |

| **840.2** prs-pron dat pl | **3450.15** art acc pl fem | **5331.8** noun acc pl fem | **2504.1** conj | **4935.33** verb 3pl indic aor mid | **1519.1** prep | **4932.3** noun acc sing fem |
|---|---|---|---|---|---|---|
| αὐτοῖς | τὰς | χεῖρας | καὶ | ἔθεντο | εἰς | τήρησιν |
| *autois* | *tas* | *cheiras* | *kai* | *ethento* | *eis* | *tērēsin* |
| them | the | hands | and | put | in | hold |

| **1519.1** prep | **3450.12** art acc sing fem | **833.1** adv | **1498.34** verb sing indic imperf act | **1056.1** conj | **2055.1** noun nom sing fem | **2218.1** adv |
|---|---|---|---|---|---|---|
| εἰς | τὴν | αὔριον· | ἦν | γὰρ | ἑσπέρα | ἤδη. |
| *eis* | *tēn* | *aurion* | *ēn* | *gar* | *hespera* | *ēdē* |
| to | the | next day; | it was | for | evening | already. |

| **4044.7** adj nom pl masc | **1156.2** conj | **3450.1** art gen pl | **189.33** verb gen pl masc part aor act | **3450.6** art acc sing masc | **3030.4** noun acc sing masc |
|---|---|---|---|---|---|
| **4.** πολλοὶ | δὲ | τῶν | ἀκουσάντων | τὸν | λόγον |
| *polloi* | *de* | *tōn* | *akousantōn* | *ton* | *logon* |
| Many | but | of the | having heard | the | word |

**4:1.** Peter and John continued to speak to the crowd for a considerable time. As verse 3 indicates, it was now evening. Since the miracle took place about 3 p.m., Peter and John had continued to talk to the crowd about 3 hours. Suddenly, the priests (chief priests), the captain of the temple (the priest next in rank to the high priest who commanded the temple guard of chosen Levites), and a group of their Sadducean supporters came upon them.

The high priest was a Sadducee, as were many of the priests in Jerusalem. They did not accept the traditions of the Pharisees, denied the existence of angels and spirits, and said there was no resurrection (Acts 23:8; Matthew 22:23).

**4:2.** At first the high priest and these Sadducees were disturbed because of the great crowd around Peter and John, and they may have feared a possible riot. But when they understood what Peter and John were saying, they became "grieved" (deeply annoyed) because the apostles proclaimed through or in Jesus the resurrection from the dead. They thought Jesus would stay dead. That would be the end of His teaching and would cause His followers to scatter. But now here were two of the once frightened disciples speaking out boldly, with everyone in the temple court listening to them, just as had been the case when Jesus performed His miracles there.

The high priest and even the Pharisees who were members of the Sanhedrin never denied the reality of the miracles of Jesus. In fact, after Lazarus was raised from the dead the priests and the Pharisees, who were usually on opposite sides of the fence, consulted together and said, "What do we? for this man doeth many miracles. If we let him thus alone, all men will believe on him; and the Romans shall come and take away both our place and nation" (John 11:47,48). In other words, they were more concerned over their own status, position, and power than they were over the truth of God.

They knew Peter was preaching a resurrected Jesus. They understood he was presenting this as evidence for the truth of the resurrection of all believers. The Sadducees felt they could not tolerate this teaching.

**4:3.** These temple officials therefore arrested Peter and John and put them in jail overnight. It was evening, too late to call the Sanhedrin together.

**4:4.** It was too late also to stop the gospel from having its effect. Many who heard the Word believed; they were truly born again, saved by grace through faith. No doubt they were soon baptized in water, perhaps the next day in one of the several pools in and around Jerusalem. (Compare 2:41,42.)

**sent him to bless you:** Hath sent him forth, ready to bless you, *Rotherham* . . . and sent him with blessings for you, *TCNT.*

**in turning away every one of you from his iniquities:** . . . by turning each of you from his wicked ways, *TCNT* . . . by causing every one of you to turn from his wickedness, *Weymouth* . . . as each of you turns from his evil ways, *Berkeley.*

**1. And as they spake unto the people:** While Peter and John were still speaking to, *TCNT.*

**the priests:** . . . the Chief Priests, *TCNT.*

**and the captain of the temple, and the Sadducees:** . . . the Commander of the Temple Guard, *Weymouth* . . . the military commander of the temple, *Williams.*

**came upon them:** . . . came up to them, *TCNT* . . . surprised them, *Berkeley* . . . stepped up to them, *Beck* . . . burst suddenly upon them, *Wuest.*

**2. Being grieved that they taught the people:** . . . being indignant, *Noyes* . . . chagrined, *Berkeley* . . . much annoyed, *TCNT* . . . exasperated, *Concordant* . . . being tired out because, *Rotherham* . . . extremely annoyed, *JB* . . . angered, *Norlie* . . . being sore troubled, *ASV* . . . highly incensed at their teaching, *Weymouth.*

**and preached through Jesus the resurrection from the dead:** . . . and announcing in Jesus, *Rotherham* . . . preaching Jesus as an example, *BB* . . . and preaching that in Jesus the dead rise, *Beck.*

**3. And they laid hands on them:** They arrested the Apostles, *TCNT.*

**and put them in hold unto the next day:** . . . in ward unto the morrow, *ASV* . . . in custody for the morrow, *Rotherham* . . . in prison till, *TCNT.*

**for it was now eventide:** . . . for it was already evening, *RSV* . . . already dusk, *Concordant.*

**4. Howbeit many of them which heard the word believed:** Many, however, of those who had heard their Message believed it, *TCNT* . . . of those who had heard the sermon, *Norlie.*

4.a.**Txt:** 02A,08E,025P etc.byz.Gries,Word,Sod
**Var:** 01ℵ,03B,05D,Lach Alf,Tisc,We/Ho,Weis UBS/☆

| **3961.23** verb 3pl indic aor act | **2504.1** conj | **1090.32** verb 3sing indic aor pass | **3450.5** art nom sing masc | **700.1** noun nom sing masc | **3450.1** art gen pl |
|---|---|---|---|---|---|
| ἐπίστευσαν, | καὶ | ἐγενήθη | ⸂a ὁ ⸃ | ἀριθμὸς | τῶν |
| *episteusan* | *kai* | *egenēthē* | *ho* | *arithmos* | *tōn* |
| believed, | and | became | the | number | of the |

| **433.7** noun gen pl masc | **5448.1** adv | **5453.1** conj | **5342.1** noun nom pl fem | **3864.1** num card | **1090.33** verb 3sing indic aor mid |
|---|---|---|---|---|---|
| ἀνδρῶν | ⸀ ὡσεὶ | [☆ ὡς ] | χιλιάδες | πέντε. | 5. Ἐγένετο |
| *andrōn* | *hōsei* | *hōs* | *chiliades* | *pente* | *Egeneto* |
| men | about | [ idem ] | thousand | five. | It came to pass |

| **1156.2** conj | **1894.3** prep | **3450.12** art acc sing fem | **833.1** adv | **4714.23** verb inf aor pass | **840.1** prs-pron gen pl |
|---|---|---|---|---|---|
| δὲ | ἐπὶ | τὴν | αὔριον | συναχθῆναι | αὐτῶν |
| *de* | *epi* | *tēn* | *aurion* | *sunachthēnai* | *autōn* |
| and | on | the | next day | to be gathered together | their |

5.a.**Var:** 01ℵ,02A,03B Lach,Treg,Alf,Tisc We/Ho,Weis,Sod UBS/☆

5.b.**Var:** 01ℵ,02A,03B Lach,Treg,Alf,Tisc We/Ho,Weis,Sod UBS/☆

5.c.**Txt:** 01ℵ,025P,byz. Tisc
**Var:** 02A,03B,05D,08E Lach,Treg,Alf,Word We/Ho,Weis,Sod UBS/☆

| **3450.8** art acc pl masc | **752.8** noun acc pl masc | **2504.1** conj | **3450.8** art acc pl masc | **4104.2** adj comp acc pl masc | **2504.1** conj |
|---|---|---|---|---|---|
| τοὺς | ἄρχοντας | καὶ | [a☆+ τοὺς ] | πρεσβυτέρους | καὶ |
| *tous* | *archontas* | *kai* | *tous* | *presbuterous* | *kai* |
| the | rulers | and | [ the ] | elders | and |

| **3450.8** art acc pl masc | **1116.2** noun pl masc | **1519.1** prep | **1706.1** prep | **2395.2** name fem |
|---|---|---|---|---|
| [b☆+ τοὺς ] | γραμματεῖς | ⸀ εἰς | [c☆ ἐν ] | Ἰερουσαλήμ |
| *tous* | *grammateis* | *eis* | *en* | *Ierousalēm* |
| [ the ] | scribes | at | [ in ] | Jerusalem, |

| **2504.1** conj | **450.3** name acc masc | **3450.6** art acc sing masc | **744.4** noun acc sing masc | **2504.1** conj | **2505.3** name acc masc |
|---|---|---|---|---|---|
| 6. καὶ | ⸀ Ἄνναν | τὸν | ἀρχιερέα | καὶ | Καϊάφαν |
| *kai* | *Annan* | *ton* | *archierea* | *kai* | *Kaiaphan* |
| and | Annas | the | high priest | and | Caiaphas |

| **2504.1** conj | **2464.4** name acc masc | **2504.1** conj | **221.3** name acc masc | **450.4** name nom masc |
|---|---|---|---|---|
| καὶ | Ἰωάννην | καὶ | Ἀλέξανδρον, | [☆ Ἅννας |
| *kai* | *Iōannēn* | *kai* | *Alexandron* | *Hannas* |
| and | John | and | Alexander, | [ Annas |

| **3450.5** art nom sing masc | **744.1** noun nom sing masc | **2504.1** conj | **2505.1** name nom masc | **2504.1** conj | **2464.1** name nom masc |
|---|---|---|---|---|---|
| ὁ | ἀρχιερεὺς | καὶ | Καϊάφας | καὶ | Ἰωάννης |
| *ho* | *archiereus* | *kai* | *Kaiaphas* | *kai* | *Iōannēs* |
| the | high priest | and | Caiaphas | and | John |

| **2504.1** conj | **221.1** name nom masc | **2504.1** conj | **3607.2** rel-pron nom pl masc | **1498.37** verb 3pl indic imperf act | **1523.2** prep gen |
|---|---|---|---|---|---|
| καὶ | Ἀλέξανδρος ] | καὶ | ὅσοι | ἦσαν | ἐκ |
| *kai* | *Alexandros* | *kai* | *hosoi* | *ēsan* | *ek* |
| and | Alexander, ] | and | as many as | were | from |

| **1079.2** noun gen sing neu | **743.1** adj gen sing neu | **2504.1** conj | **2449.12** verb nom pl masc part aor act | **840.8** prs-pron acc pl masc |
|---|---|---|---|---|
| γένους | ἀρχιερατικοῦ | 7. καὶ | στήσαντες | αὐτοὺς |
| *genous* | *archieratikou* | *kai* | *stēsantes* | *autous* |
| family | high priestly. | And | having placed | them |

| **1706.1** prep | **3450.3** art dat sing | **3189.1** adj dat sing | **4299.7** verb 3pl indic imperf mid | **1706.1** prep | **4029.6** intr-pron dat sing fem |
|---|---|---|---|---|---|
| ἐν | τῷ | μέσῳ | ἐπυνθάνοντο, | Ἐν | ποίᾳ |
| *en* | *tō* | *mesō* | *epunthanonto* | *En* | *poia* |
| in | the | midst | they were inquiring, | In | what |

The number is given as about 5,000 men. The Greek may mean "became about 5,000 men," so some writers today understand this to mean the total number of believers was now up to 5,000. But the way it is stated here indicates the number was so large they counted only the men. There must have been a great number of women who believed also.

**4:5.** Luke presented a rather detailed description of the prestigious group that had assembled in Jerusalem. Among the 71 members of this Council were the *archontas* which consisted of the high priest and other senior priests. These men conducted worship and were in charge of the daily functioning of the temple. Others, such as temple wardens, treasurers, and perhaps former high priests, also made up this first group. The second were the *presbuterous*, composed primarily of the Sadducees. Lastly, the *grammateis* (scribes, experts in the Law, Pharisees) were also present (see Haenchen, p.215).

**4:6.** Among the Sanhedrin who came were Annas, Caiaphas, John, Alexander, and all the rest of the relatives of the high priest who happened to be in the city.

Annas is called the high priest. He was officially high priest from A.D. 6–15. Then his son Jonathan was appointed for about 3 years. Next Caiaphas, the son-in-law of Annas, was made high priest and remained in office until A.D. 36. But Annas remained the power behind the throne. The people did not accept his deposition by the Romans and still considered him to be the true high priest. In the Old Testament Aaron was made high priest for life. The Law made no provision for the secular governors or kings to change this. Consequently, Jesus was taken to Annas' house first (John 18:13), then to Caiaphas (who probably occupied a portion of the same building around the same courtyard). Annas and Caiaphas, along with some of the rest of the relatives of Annas, actually formed a closed corporation that ran the temple.

John may have been Jonathan the son of Annas. (Codex Bezae, manuscript D of the New Testament, has Jonathan here.) Alexander was probably one of the leading Sadducees.

**4:7.** They made Peter and John stand in the midst of the assembled court. This was the Sanhedrin, called the *Gerousia* (Council or Senate) as in 5:21, and the *Presbuterion* (Body of Elders) as in 22:5. According to Josephus, they met just west of the temple area. According to the Mishnah (a collection of oral laws and traditional Jewish doctrines compiled before A.D. 200), the Sanhedrin sat in a semicircle, apparently around the accused.

The inquiry began with two important questions. First, the Council wanted to know what sort of power effected this healing. They

**and the number of the men was about five thousand:** . . . and it raised the number of the people, *Klingensmith* . . . increased, *Norlie* . . . The group of followers was now about, *NLT* . . . came to be about, *ASV* . . . and the number of the men alone mounted up to some five thousand, *TCNT* . . . grew to about five thousand, *Beck* . . . There were now about 5,000 men, *NCV* . . . in the group of believers, *Everyday*.

**5. And it came to pass on the morrow:** The next day, *TCNT* . . . it chaunsed on the morowe, *Tyndale* . . . And it occurred on, *Hanson* . . . On the following day, *Noli*.

**that their rulers, and elders, and scribes:** . . . the Jewish leaders, the older Jewish leaders, and the teachers of the law, *Everyday* . . . the leading men, Councillors, and Rabbis, *TCNT* . . . the leaders of the court and the leaders of the people, *NLT*.

**6. And Annas the high priest, and Caiaphas, and John, and Alexander:** . . . the head religious leader, *NLT*.

**And as many as were of the kindred of the high priest:** . . . in fact, all the members of the high priestly family were there, *Norlie* . . . of high-priestly descent, *Rotherham* . . . and all the High Priest's relations, *TCNT* . . . all who were of, *TNT* . . . and the other members of the High Priest's family, *Weymouth* . . . and all who were in the family of the head religious leader, *NLT* . . . and whoever belonged to the high priest's clan, *Berkeley*.

**were gathered together at Jerusalem:** . . . assembled, *Concordant* . . . came together, *Swann*.

**7. And when they had set them in the midst:** They had Peter and John brought before them, *TCNT* . . . Then they made the men stand before them, *Montgomery* . . . and placing them in the center, *Berkeley* . . . put the missionaries in front of them, *NLT*.

**they asked:** . . . and repeatedly inquired of them, *Williams* . . . inquired to ascertain, *Concordant* . . . they interrogated them, *Murdock* . . . demanded to know, *Norlie* . . . repeatedly demanded, *AmpB*.

| 1405.3 noun dat sing fem | 2211.1 conj | 1706.1 prep | 4029.2 intr-pron dat sing | 3549.4 noun dat sing neu | 4020.26 verb 2pl indic aor act | 3642.17 dem-pron sing neu |
|---|---|---|---|---|---|---|
| δυνάμει | ἢ | ἐν | ποίῳ | ὀνόματι | ἐποιήσατε | τοῦτο |
| *dunamei* | *ē* | *en* | *poiō* | *onomati* | *epoiēsate* | *touto* |
| power | or | in | what | name | did | this |

| 5050.1 prs-pron nom 2pl | 4966.1 adv | 3935.1 name nom masc | 3990.7 verb nom sing masc part aor pass | 4011.2 noun gen sing neu |
|---|---|---|---|---|
| ὑμεῖς; | **8.** Τότε | Πέτρος | πλησθεὶς | πνεύματος |
| *humeis* | *Tote* | *Petros* | *plēstheis* | *pneumatos* |
| you? | Then | Peter, | having been filled | with Spirit |

| 39.2 adj gen sing | 1500.5 verb 3sing indic aor act | 4242.1 prep | 840.8 prs-pron acc pl masc | 752.5 noun nom pl masc | 3450.2 art gen sing |
|---|---|---|---|---|---|
| ἁγίου | εἶπεν | πρὸς | αὐτούς, | Ἄρχοντες | τοῦ |
| *hagiou* | *eipen* | *pros* | *autous* | *Archontes* | *tou* |
| Holy, | said | to | them, | Rulers | of the |

8.a.**Txt:** 05D,08E,025P 044,33,byz.it.Sod
**Var:** p74,01ℵ,02A,03B sa.bo.Lach,Treg,Tisc We/Ho,Weis,UBS/⋆

| 2967.2 noun gen sing masc | 2504.1 conj | 4104.5 adj comp nom pl masc | 3450.2 art gen sing | 2447.1 name masc | 1479.1 conj |
|---|---|---|---|---|---|
| λαοῦ | καὶ | πρεσβύτεροι | ⸂[a] τοῦ | Ἰσραήλ, ⸃ | **9.** εἰ |
| *laou* | *kai* | *presbuteroi* | *tou* | *Israēl* | *ei* |
| people | and | elders | | of Israel, | If |

| 2231.1 prs-pron nom 1pl | 4449.1 adv | 348.9 verb 1pl indic pres mid | 1894.3 prep | 2087.2 noun dat sing fem |
|---|---|---|---|---|
| ἡμεῖς | σήμερον | ἀνακρινόμεθα | ἐπὶ | εὐεργεσίᾳ |
| *hēmeis* | *sēmeron* | *anakrinometha* | *epi* | *euergesia* |
| we | this day | are being examined | as to | a good work |

| 442.2 noun gen sing masc | 766.3 adj gen sing masc | 1706.1 prep | 4949.2 intr-pron dat sing | 3642.4 dem-pron nom sing masc |
|---|---|---|---|---|
| ἀνθρώπου | ἀσθενοῦς, | ἐν | τίνι | οὗτος |
| *anthrōpou* | *asthenous* | *en* | *tini* | *houtos* |
| man | sick, | by | what | this one |

9.a.**Var:** 01ℵ,02A,Tisc

| 4834.29 verb 3sing indic perf mid | 4834.36 verb 3sing indic perf mid | 1104.4 adj sing neu | 1498.17 verb 3sing impr pres act |
|---|---|---|---|
| ⸂ σέσῳσται, | [[a] σέσωται, ] | **10.** γνωστὸν | ἔστω |
| *sesōstai* | *sesōtai* | *gnōston* | *estō* |
| has been healed, | [ idem ] | known | let it be |

| 3820.5 adj dat pl | 5050.3 prs-pron dat 2pl | 2504.1 conj | 3820.3 adj dat sing | 3450.3 art dat sing | 2967.3 noun dat sing masc | 2447.1 name masc |
|---|---|---|---|---|---|---|
| πᾶσιν | ὑμῖν | καὶ | παντὶ | τῷ | λαῷ | Ἰσραήλ, |
| *pasin* | *humin* | *kai* | *panti* | *tō* | *laō* | *Israēl* |
| to all | you | and | to all | the | people | of Israel, |

| 3617.1 conj | 1706.1 prep | 3450.3 art dat sing | 3549.4 noun dat sing neu | 2400.2 name masc | 5382.2 name gen masc | 3450.2 art gen sing |
|---|---|---|---|---|---|---|
| ὅτι | ἐν | τῷ | ὀνόματι | Ἰησοῦ | Χριστοῦ | τοῦ |
| *hoti* | *en* | *tō* | *onomati* | *Iēsou* | *Christou* | *tou* |
| that | in | the | name | of Jesus | Christ | |

| 3343.2 name gen sing masc | 3614.6 rel-pron acc sing masc | 5050.1 prs-pron nom 2pl | 4568.2 verb 2pl indic aor act | 3614.6 rel-pron acc sing masc |
|---|---|---|---|---|
| Ναζωραίου, | ὃν | ὑμεῖς | ἐσταυρώσατε, | ὃν |
| *Nazōraiou* | *hon* | *humeis* | *estaurōsate* | *hon* |
| of Nazareth, | whom | you | crucified, | whom |

| 3450.5 art nom sing masc | 2296.1 noun nom sing masc | 1446.5 verb 3sing indic aor act | 1523.2 prep gen | 3361.2 adj gen pl | 1706.1 prep |
|---|---|---|---|---|---|
| ὁ | θεὸς | ἤγειρεν | ἐκ | νεκρῶν, | ἐν |
| *ho* | *theos* | *ēgeiren* | *ek* | *nekrōn* | *en* |
| | God | raised | from | dead, | by |

apparently suspected idolatry or black magic was involved. Second, the Council asked "by what name" had they healed this man. Magical formulas discovered on papyri reveal that the ancients believed there was a potential power resident in the names of certain gods and demons. This power, it was thought, could be released or controlled by invoking the name (Bietenhard, "onoma," *Kittel,* 5:250f.). While the Council may not have believed such myths, the evidence which stood before them needed an explanation. The question raised by the Sanhedrin, therefore, was an attempt to discover the source of the power as well as the authority behind the men who performed the miraculous healing. The question they posed could be restated as "How were you able to do this?" or "Who gave you the ability to heal this man?"

**4:8.** Peter had once cringed before a girl in the courtyard of the high priest. Now there was a difference. As he began to speak, Peter was filled with the Holy Spirit. The form of the Greek verb indicates a new, fresh filling. This does not mean he had lost any of the power and presence of the Spirit he received on the Day of Pentecost. In view of the pressures of this critical situation, the Lord simply enlarged his capacity and gave him this fresh filling to meet this new need for power to witness.

There was also a practical application of Jesus' instructions given in Matthew 10:19,20 and Luke 21:12-15. They were to take no advance thought of what they should speak, for the Spirit of their Heavenly Father would speak in (and by) them. Thus, instead of trying to defend themselves, the Spirit would make their words a witness. Knowing this Peter and John probably slept well during the night in jail and awakened refreshed.

Filled anew with the Spirit, Peter did not let the Jewish leaders frighten him. Truly, God has not given believers a spirit of cowardly fear, but of power, of love, and of a sound mind; that is, a mind that shows self-discipline (2 Timothy 1:7). Politely, Peter addressed the Council as rulers and elders.

**4:9.** Then, in a dignified way, he told them that if they were making a judicial examination concerning the good deed done for a weak human being, if they wanted to know by what means the man had been and still was restored (saved, healed), then he had the answer.

**4:10.** What a contrast there is in this verse between what Jewish leaders did to Jesus and what God did to Him!

Peter proclaimed that in (by) the name of Jesus, whom they ("you" is plural) crucified, whom God raised from the dead, by Him (in Him—Jesus) this man stood before them whole (restored



**By what power, or by what name, have ye done this?:** In what power, or in what name, *ASV* . . . By what sort of power and authority, *Williams* . . . What power do you have or whose name did you use? *TEV* . . . have you done this healing? *Noli.*

**8. Then Peter, filled with the Holy Ghost:** . . . because he was filled, *Williams* . . . being controlled, *Wuest.*

**said unto them:** . . . spoke as follows, *TCNT.*

**Ye rulers of the people, and elders of Israel:** Princes of the people, *Fenton* . . . Leaders of the people, and Councillors, *TCNT* . . . Rulers and Elders of the people, *Weymouth.*

**9. If we this day be examined of the good deed done to the impotent man:** . . . are you questioning us about a good thing that was done, *Everyday* . . . if we are being cross-examined today, *Klingensmith* . . . we are under investigation today concerning a benefit done to, *Noli* . . . are to be examined for doing good to a sick man, *Rotherham* . . . since we are on trial to-day for a kind act done to a helpless man, *TCNT* . . . benevolent service to a cripple, *Berkeley* . . . benefit to a feeble man, *Fenton* . . . a benefit conferred upon a cripple, *Montgomery* . . . that we are today being tried, *Williams* . . . on a man helplessly lame, *PNT.*

**by what means he is made whole:** In whom this man hath been made well, *Rotherham* . . . as to how this man has been cured, *Weymouth* . . . by what means this man has been healed, *RSV* . . . Maybe you are questioning us as to how he was healed, *Norlie* . . . to learn how he was cured, *Williams* . . . restored, *Noyes.*

**10. Be it known unto you all, and to all the people of Israel:** So let me tell you all, *TCNT* . . . then you and all...should know, *Berkeley.*

**that by the name of Jesus Christ of Nazareth:** . . . that it is by the authority of, *TCNT* . . . that through the name of, *Weymouth.*

**whom ye crucified, whom God raised from the dead:** . . . whom God raised from among the dead, *Rotherham.*

| 3642.5 dem-pron dat sing masc | 3642.4 dem-pron nom sing masc | 3798.13 verb 3sing indic perf act | 1783.1 prep | 5050.2 prs-pron gen 2pl |
|---|---|---|---|---|
| τούτῳ | οὗτος | παρέστηκεν | ἐνώπιον | ὑμῶν |
| *toutō* | *houtos* | *parestēken* | *enōpion* | *humōn* |
| this one | this | stands | before | you |

| 5040.1 adj nom sing | 3642.4 dem-pron nom sing masc | 1498.4 verb 3sing indic pres act | 3450.5 art nom sing masc | 3012.1 noun nom sing masc |
|---|---|---|---|---|
| ὑγιής. | **11.** οὗτός | ἐστιν | ὁ | λίθος |
| *hugiēs* | *houtos* | *estin* | *ho* | *lithos* |
| healthy. | This | is | the | stone |

| 3450.5 art nom sing masc | 1832.8 verb nom sing masc part aor pass | 5097.1 prep | 5050.2 prs-pron gen 2pl |
|---|---|---|---|
| ὁ | ἐξουθενηθεὶς | ὑφ' | ὑμῶν |
| *ho* | *exouthenētheis* | *huph'* | *humōn* |
| the | having been treated with contempt | by | you |

11.a.**Txt:** 08E,025P,byz.
**Var:** 01ℵ,02A,03B,05D
Lach,Treg,Alf,Tisc
We/Ho,Weis,Sod
UBS/⋆

| 3450.1 art gen pl | 3481.17 verb gen pl part pres mid | 3482.1 noun gen pl masc | 3450.5 art nom sing masc |
|---|---|---|---|
| τῶν | ' οἰκοδομούντων, | [a⋆ οἰκοδόμων, ] | ὁ |
| *tōn* | *oikodomountōn* | *oikodomōn* | *ho* |
| the | building, | [ builders, ] | the |

| 1090.53 verb nom sing masc part aor mid | 1519.1 prep | 2747.4 noun acc sing fem | 1131.1 noun fem | 2504.1 conj | 3620.2 partic |
|---|---|---|---|---|---|
| γενόμενος | εἰς | κεφαλὴν | γωνίας. | **12.** καὶ | οὐκ |
| *genomenos* | *eis* | *kephalēn* | *gōnias* | *kai* | *ouk* |
| having become | to | head | of corner. | And | not |

| 1498.4 verb 3sing indic pres act | 1706.1 prep | 241.3 adj dat sing | 3625.7 num card dat neu | 3450.9 art nom sing fem | 4843.1 noun nom sing fem |
|---|---|---|---|---|---|
| ἔστιν | ἐν | ἄλλῳ | οὐδενὶ | ἡ | σωτηρία· |
| *estin* | *en* | *allō* | *oudeni* | *hē* | *sōtēria* |
| there is | in | other | no one | the | salvation, |

12.a.**Txt:** 08E,025P,byz.
**Var:** 01ℵ,02A,03B,sa.bo.
Lach,Treg,Word,Tisc
We/Ho,Weis,Sod
UBS/⋆

| 3641.1 conj | 3624.1 conj | 1056.1 conj | 3549.2 noun sing neu | 1498.4 verb 3sing indic pres act | 2066.1 adj sing |
|---|---|---|---|---|---|
| ' οὔτε | [a⋆ οὐδὲ ] | γάρ | ὄνομά | ἐστιν | ἕτερον |
| *oute* | *oude* | *gar* | *onoma* | *estin* | *heteron* |
| neither | [ nor ] | for | name | is there | another |

| 5097.3 prep | 3450.6 art acc sing masc | 3636.4 noun acc sing masc | 3450.16 art sing neu | 1319.56 verb sing neu part perf mid | 1706.1 prep |
|---|---|---|---|---|---|
| ὑπὸ | τὸν | οὐρανὸν | τὸ | δεδομένον | ἐν |
| *hupo* | *ton* | *ouranon* | *to* | *dedomenon* | *en* |
| under | the | heaven | the | having been given | among |

| 442.8 noun dat pl masc | 1706.1 prep | 3614.3 rel-pron dat sing | 1158.1 verb 3sing indic pres act | 4834.28 verb inf aor pass |
|---|---|---|---|---|
| ἀνθρώποις, | ἐν | ᾧ | δεῖ | σωθῆναι |
| *anthrōpois* | *en* | *hō* | *dei* | *sōthēnai* |
| men, | by | which | must | to be saved |

| 2231.4 prs-pron acc 1pl | 2311.11 verb nom pl masc part pres act | 1156.2 conj | 3450.12 art acc sing fem | 3450.2 art gen sing | 3935.2 name gen masc |
|---|---|---|---|---|---|
| ἡμᾶς. | **13.** Θεωροῦντες | δὲ | τὴν | τοῦ | Πέτρου |
| *hēmas* | *Theōrountes* | *de* | *tēn* | *tou* | *Petrou* |
| us. | Seeing | but | the | | of Peter |

| 3816.4 noun acc sing fem | 2504.1 conj | 2464.2 name gen masc | 2504.1 conj | 2608.10 verb nom pl masc part aor mid |
|---|---|---|---|---|
| παρρησίαν | καὶ | Ἰωάννου, | καὶ | καταλαβόμενοι |
| *parrhēsian* | *kai* | *Iōannou* | *kai* | *katalabomenoi* |
| confidence | and | of John, | and | having perceived |

to sound health). Again Peter recognized that the lame man was both saved and healed and was now "in Christ"; that is, he was in right relationship to Christ as a member of the body of Christ.

**4:11.** Peter quoted a passage these same chief priests and elders had heard from Jesus himself. On one occasion they had challenged Jesus' authority to teach. He gave them parables and then quoted Psalm 118:22. (See Matthew 21:23,42,45; 1 Peter 2:7.) Peter, however, made it personal. *This* One (emphatic) "is the stone which was set at nought (ignored, despised) of you (plural) builders," but this stone (Jesus) had "become the head of the corner." (That is, because He is now exalted to the Father's right hand.)

**4:12.** Next Peter explained what this means. There is no salvation in any other. The promised salvation which the Jews hoped would be brought by the Messiah is not in any other than Jesus. "For there is none other name under heaven given among men (human beings)" by which "we must be saved." (Some ancient Greek manuscripts have "you must be saved.") "Must" is an emphatic word. If a person does not find salvation through the name of Jesus, he will never find it. (Here, the "name" means the person of Jesus.)

The healing of the lame man thus witnessed to Jesus as the only Saviour. The Jewish leaders could see no value in Jesus, yet God had made Him of unique and supreme worth. In Him, as Isaiah chapter 53 also shows, is (the promised) salvation. There is only one salvation, only one way to God (Hebrews 10:12-22).

Many have claimed to be messiahs or saviors. Many have presented other ways of salvation. But they are all put in opposition to our Lord Jesus Christ. There is only one choice when an individual faces the claims of Christ: he can accept or reject. Other ways which may seem right lead to destruction (Proverbs 14:12; Matthew 7:13).

It is not popular to be so exclusive. Many unbelievers who are not atheists want to think there are many ways to find God. Some of the so-called world religions would be quite happy to include Jesus in their list of gods, or in their list of prophets or saviors. Some cults even try to combine what they suppose is the good in a variety of religions. But all this is in vain; God has rejected all other ways. Even in the Old Testament the prophets condemned idolatry, but they condemned the worship of the Lord *plus other gods* even more strongly. Such mixed worship has never been acceptable to God.

**4:13.** The priests and elders marveled (wondered) when they saw the boldness (freedom in speech) of Peter and John, especially since they perceived they were unlearned (uneducated in the sense of not having attended a rabbinic school or having sat under a great rabbi like Gamaliel) and ignorant men (unprofessional men, laymen). This does not mean they were totally unschooled. They had



**even by him doth this man stand here before you whole:** . . . in him does this man stand before you strong and well, *Montgomery* . . . it is, I say, by his authority that this man stands here before you cured, *TCNT* . . . in prime condition, *Berkeley* . . . stands healthy, *Beck* . . . doth this (man) stand here before you recovered, *Murdock* . . . is standing restored before you, *Noli.*

**11. This is the stone which was set at nought of you builders:** He is the stone, *ASV* . . . the Scriptural stone, *Noli* . . . scorned by you, the builders, *TCNT* . . . treated with contempt, *Weymouth* . . . cast aside, *Montgomery* . . . thrown away, *Williams* . . . the stone despised by you, *Berkeley* . . . by you builders, *Klingensmith.*

**which is become the head of the corner:** . . . which was made, *ASV* . . . but it has been made the Cornerstone, *Weymouth* . . . the keystone, *JB* . . . the capstone, *NIV.*

**12. Neither is there salvation in any other:** And Salvation comes through no one else, *TCNT* . . . No one else can save us, *Beck* . . . by anyone else, *Williams* . . . by nobody else, *Adams.*

**for there is none other name under heaven given among men:** . . . for there is no other Name in the whole world, given to men, *TCNT* . . . His name is the only means under heaven, *Noli* . . . for no one else in all the wide world has been appointed among men, *Williams* . . . this is the only one, *JB* . . . no second name, *PNT.*

**whereby we must be saved:** . . . to which we must look for our Salvation, *TCNT* . . . as our only medium by which to be saved, *Williams* . . . we must needs be saved, *Rotherham.*

**13. Now when they saw the boldness of Peter and John:** . . . beholding the openness, *Young* . . . Seeing how boldly Peter and John spoke, *TCNT* . . . As they looked on...so fearlessly outspoken, *Weymouth* . . . the glad fearlessness of Peter and John, *Montgomery* . . . when they saw the intrepidity of, *Noli* . . . the courage, *Williams* . . . the freedom of speech, *Berkeley.*

## Acts 4:14

| **3617.1** conj | **442.6** noun nom pl masc | **61.1** adj nom pl masc | **1498.7** verb 3pl indic pres act | **2504.1** conj | **2376.3** noun nom pl masc |
|---|---|---|---|---|---|
| ὅτι | ἄνθρωποι | ἀγράμματοί | εἰσιν | καὶ | ἰδιῶται, |
| *hoti* | *anthrōpoi* | *agrammatoi* | *eisin* | *kai* | *idiōtai* |
| that | men | unlettered | they are | and | laymen, |

| **2273.17** verb 3pl indic imperf act | **1906.17** verb 3pl indic imperf act | **4885.1** conj | **840.8** prs-pron acc pl masc |
|---|---|---|---|
| ἐθαύμαζον, | ἐπεγίνωσκόν | τε | αὐτοὺς |
| *ethaumazon* | *epeginōskon* | *te* | *autous* |
| they were wondering, | they were recognizing | and | them |

| **3617.1** conj | **4713.1** prep | **3450.3** art dat sing | **2400.2** name masc | **1498.37** verb 3pl indic imperf act | **3450.6** art acc sing masc | **1156.2** conj |
|---|---|---|---|---|---|---|
| ὅτι | σὺν | τῷ | Ἰησοῦ | ἦσαν· | **14.** τόν | ʽ δὲ |
| *hoti* | *sun* | *tō* | *Iēsou* | *ēsan* | *ton* | *de* |
| that | with | | Jesus | they were. | The | but |

14.a.**Txt:** 025P,byz.bo.
**Var:** 01ℵ,02A,03B,05D 08E,sa.Lach,Treg,Alf Tisc,We/Ho,Weis,Sod UBS/☆

| **4885.1** conj | **442.4** noun acc sing masc | **984.14** verb nom pl masc part pres act | **4713.1** prep | **840.2** prs-pron dat pl | **2449.25** verb part perf act |
|---|---|---|---|---|---|
| [a☆ τε ] | ἄνθρωπον | βλέποντες | σὺν | αὐτοῖς | ἑστῶτα |
| *te* | *anthrōpon* | *blepontes* | *sun* | *autois* | *hestōta* |
| [ and ] | man | seeing | with | them | standing |

| **3450.6** art acc sing masc | **2300.18** verb acc sing masc part perf mid | **3625.6** num card neu | **2174.42** verb indic imperf act | **468.1** verb inf aor act |
|---|---|---|---|---|
| τὸν | τεθεραπευμένον, | οὐδὲν | εἶχον | ἀντειπεῖν. |
| *ton* | *tetherapeumenon* | *ouden* | *eichon* | *anteipein* |
| the | having been healed, | nothing | they had | to say against. |

| **2724.7** verb nom pl masc part aor act | **1156.2** conj | **840.8** prs-pron acc pl masc | **1838.1** adv | **3450.2** art gen sing |
|---|---|---|---|---|
| **15.** κελεύσαντες | δὲ | αὐτοὺς | ἔξω | τοῦ |
| *keleusantes* | *de* | *autous* | *exō* | *tou* |
| Having commanded | but | them | outside | the |

15.a.**Txt:** 05D,byz.sa.
**Var:** 01ℵ,02A,03B,08E 025P,bo.Lach,Treg,Alf Tisc,We/Ho,Weis,Sod UBS/☆

| **4742.2** noun gen sing neu | **562.12** verb inf aor act | **4671.3** verb 3pl indic aor act | **4671.5** verb 3pl indic imperf act |
|---|---|---|---|
| συνεδρίου | ἀπελθεῖν | ʽ συνέβαλον | [a☆ συνέβαλλον ] |
| *sunedriou* | *apelthein* | *sunebalon* | *suneballon* |
| Sanhedrin | to go | they conferred | [ they were conferring ] |

| **4242.1** prep | **238.3** prs-pron acc pl masc | **2978.16** verb nom pl masc part pres act | **4949.9** intr-pron sing neu | **4020.53** verb 1pl indic fut act |
|---|---|---|---|---|
| πρὸς | ἀλλήλους | **16.** λέγοντες, | Τί | ʽ ποιήσομεν |
| *pros* | *allēlous* | *legontes* | *Ti* | *poiēsomen* |
| with | one another, | saying, | What | shall we do |

16.a.**Txt:** 05D,025P,byz. Gries,Lach,Word
**Var:** 01ℵ,02A,03B,08E Treg,Alf,Tisc,We/Ho Weis,Sod,UBS/☆

| **4020.30** verb 1pl subj aor act | **3450.4** art dat pl | **442.8** noun dat pl masc | **3642.3** dem-pron dat pl | **3617.1** conj | **3173.1** conj |
|---|---|---|---|---|---|
| [a☆ ποιήσωμεν ] | τοῖς | ἀνθρώποις | τούτοις; | ὅτι | μὲν |
| *poiēsōmen* | *tois* | *anthrōpois* | *toutois* | *hoti* | *men* |
| [ may we do ] | to the | men | these? | That | indeed |

| **1056.1** conj | **1104.4** adj sing neu | **4447.1** noun sing neu | **1090.3** verb 3sing indic perf act | **1217.1** prep | **840.1** prs-pron gen pl |
|---|---|---|---|---|---|
| γὰρ | γνωστὸν | σημεῖον | γέγονεν | δι' | αὐτῶν, |
| *gar* | *gnōston* | *sēmeion* | *gegonen* | *di'* | *autōn* |
| for | a known | sign | has come to pass | through | them, |

| **3820.5** adj dat pl | **3450.4** art dat pl | **2700.8** verb dat pl masc part pres act | **2395.1** name fem | **5156.1** adj sing | **2504.1** conj |
|---|---|---|---|---|---|
| πᾶσιν | τοῖς | κατοικοῦσιν | Ἱερουσαλὴμ | φανερόν, | καὶ |
| *pasin* | *tois* | *katoikousin* | *Hierousalēm* | *phaneron* | *kai* |
| to all | the | inhabiting | Jerusalem | manifest, | and |

gone to the synagogue schools in their hometowns, but they were not professional teachers or trained speakers like the rabbis, scribes, and lawyers. Ordinary laymen did not speak with such authority.

It must have been hard for Peter and John to face such snobbishness. But the key to their boldness and freedom in speaking was, of course, the new fresh filling with the Spirit. He gave them the words to say.

Then something else struck these Jewish leaders. The phrase "took knowledge of them" does not mean they inquired further of them. Rather, the Greek simply means the Jewish leaders gradually began to recognize that the disciples (apostles) had been with Jesus. Perhaps the words of Peter jogged their memory of what Jesus had said. As these men thought about their confrontation with Jesus, they remembered Peter and John were His disciples.

Jesus had spoken with authority. The leaders had believed they would be rid of Jesus by crucifying Him. But now the disciples, trained by Him, were speaking with the same authority. Jesus had done miracles as signs. Now the apostles were also working miracles.

**4:14.** The elders were confronted with something else. The man who was healed was standing there with Peter and John. (The man himself was not on trial.) Suddenly, the priests and elders had nothing else to say. What could they say against such an obvious miracle?

**4:15.** The leaders then commanded Peter and John to go outside the council, that is, out of the room where the Sanhedrin was meeting. The Sanhedrin then engaged in a discussion.

**4:16.** They did not know what to do with Peter and John. They could not deny that a notable miracle (a known supernatural sign) had been done through them, visible to all the inhabitants of Jerusalem.

This could imply they were aware of the resurrection of Jesus. What bothered them was the fact that the apostles were using it to teach a future resurrection for all believers. In order to avoid this problem earlier, they had bribed the soldiers to say the body of Jesus had been stolen (Matthew 28:12,13). Some even today contend the women and the disciples looked into the wrong tomb. But the women paid special attention to where Jesus was laid (Luke 23:55). Actually, these Jewish leaders were neither stupid nor unsophisticated. They knew how difficult it is to get rid of a body. If they had thought the body of Jesus was in some other tomb they would have made an intensive search for it. They did not, because they *knew* He had risen from the dead. But this knowledge did not help them. It takes more than a head belief or a mental acceptance of the truth of Christ's resurrection to be saved. (See Romans 10:9,10.)



**and perceived that they were unlearned and ignorant men:** . . . they took note, *NIV* . . . and having discovered that they were unlettered and obscure men, *Rotherham* . . . ordinary men, *Concordant* . . . illiterate persons, untrained in the schools, *Weymouth* . . . men without schooling or skill, *Berkeley* . . . in private stations in life, *Campbell* . . . uneducated laymen, *Adams* . . . had no education or training, *Beck* . . . uninstructed, *Darby* . . . unordained and unschooled, *Klingensmith* . . . ungifted, *Wilson*.

**they marvelled:** . . . they were surprised to note, *Norlie* . . . they were staggered, *Phillips*.

**and they took knowledge of them that they had been with Jesus:** . . . realized that they had been companions of Jesus, *TCNT* . . . now they recognized them as having been, *Weymouth*.

**14. And beholding the man which was healed standing with them:** But since they saw, *Montgomery* . . . even the (man) who had been cured, *Rotherham*.

**they could say nothing against it:** . . . they had nothing wherewith to contradict, *Rotherham* . . . they had nothing controversial to say, *Berkeley* . . . they could say nothing to confront them, *Murdock* . . . nothing to say in opposition, *Adams* . . . they had nothing to answer, *Montgomery* . . . no effective reply, *Phillips*.

**15. But when they had commanded them to go aside out of the council:** So they ordered them out of court, *TCNT* . . . So they ordered them to withdraw from the Sanhedrin, *Weymouth*.

**they conferred among themselves:** . . . and then began consulting together, *TCNT* . . . they parleyed with one another, *Concordant* . . . held a consultation, *Norlie* . . . talked the matter over among themselves, *Beck*.

**16. Saying, What shall we do to these men?:**

**for that indeed a notable miracle hath been done by them is manifest to all them that dwell in Jerusalem:** . . . a notorious sign, *Rotherham* . . . a remarkable sign, *TCNT* . . . an unmistakable wonder-work, *Williams* . . . a signal miracle, *Campbell*.

## Acts 4:17

16.b.**Txt:** 08E,025P,byz.
**Var:** 01ℵ,02A,03B,05D Lach,Treg,Alf,Tisc We/Ho,Weis,Sod UBS/☆

17.a.**Txt:** 08E,025P,byz. Weis
**Var:** 01ℵ,02A,03B,05D sa.bo.Lach,Treg,Tisc We/Ho,Sod,UBS/☆

18.a.**Txt:** 025P,byz.sa.bo.
**Var:** 01ℵ,02A,03B,05D 08E,Lach,Treg,Alf,Tisc We/Ho,Weis,Sod UBS/☆

18.b.**Txt:** 01ℵ-corr,02A 08E,025P,etc.byz.Sod
**Var:** 01ℵ-org,03B,Lach Tisc,We/Ho,Weis UBS/☆

| **3620.3** partic | **1404.5** verb 1pl indic pres mid | **714.13** verb inf aor mid | **714.19** verb inf pres mid | **233.1** conj |
|---|---|---|---|---|
| οὐ | δυνάμεθα | ʼ ἀρνήσασθαι˙ | [ᵇ☆ ἀρνεῖσθαι˙ ] | **17.** ἀλλ' |
| *ou* | *dunametha* | *arnēsasthai* | *arneisthai* | *all'* |
| not | we are able | to deny. | [ idem ] | But |

| **2419.1** conj | **3231.1** partic | **1894.3** prep | **3979.8** adj comp sing neu | **1262.1** verb 3sing subj aor pass | **1519.1** prep | **3450.6** art acc sing masc |
|---|---|---|---|---|---|---|
| ἵνα | μὴ | ἐπὶ | πλεῖον | διανεμηθῇ | εἰς | τὸν |
| *hina* | *mē* | *epi* | *pleion* | *dianemēthē* | *eis* | *ton* |
| that | not | on | further | it may spread | among | the |

| **2967.4** noun acc sing masc | **543.2** noun dat sing fem | **542.2** verb 1pl subj aor mid | **840.2** prs-pron dat pl | **3239.1** adv |
|---|---|---|---|---|
| λαόν, | ʼᵃ ἀπειλῇ ˎ | ἀπειλησώμεθα | αὐτοῖς | μηκέτι |
| *laon* | *apeilē* | *apeilēsōmetha* | *autois* | *mēketi* |
| people, | with a threat | let us threaten | them | no longer |

| **2953.24** verb inf pres act | **1894.3** prep | **3450.3** art dat sing | **3549.4** noun dat sing neu | **3642.5** dem-pron dat sing masc | **3235.2** num card dat |
|---|---|---|---|---|---|
| λαλεῖν | ἐπὶ | τῷ | ὀνόματι | τούτῳ | μηδενὶ |
| *lalein* | *epi* | *tō* | *onomati* | *toutō* | *mēdeni* |
| to speak | in | the | name | this | to no one |

| **442.7** noun gen pl masc | **2504.1** conj | **2535.17** verb nom pl masc part aor act | **840.8** prs-pron acc pl masc | **3715.9** verb 3pl indic aor act |
|---|---|---|---|---|
| ἀνθρώπων. | **18.** καὶ | καλέσαντες | αὐτοὺς | παρήγγειλαν |
| *anthrōpōn* | *kai* | *kalesantes* | *autous* | *parēngeilan* |
| of men. | And | having called | them | they charged |

| **840.2** prs-pron dat pl | **3450.16** art sing neu | **2499.1** adv | **3231.1** partic | **5187.2** verb inf pres mid | **3234.1** adv |
|---|---|---|---|---|---|
| ʼᵃ αὐτοῖς ˎ | ʼᵇ τὸ ˎ | καθόλου | μὴ | φθέγγεσθαι | μηδὲ |
| *autois* | *to* | *katholou* | *mē* | *phthengesthai* | *mēde* |
| them | the | at all | not | to speak | nor |

| **1315.10** verb inf pres act | **1894.3** prep | **3450.3** art dat sing | **3549.4** noun dat sing neu | **3450.2** art gen sing | **2400.2** name masc |
|---|---|---|---|---|---|
| διδάσκειν | ἐπὶ | τῷ | ὀνόματι | τοῦ | Ἰησοῦ. |
| *didaskein* | *epi* | *tō* | *onomati* | *tou* | *Iēsou* |
| to teach | in | the | name | | of Jesus. |

| **3450.5** art nom sing masc | **1156.2** conj | **3935.1** name nom masc | **2504.1** conj | **2464.1** name nom masc | **552.13** verb nom pl masc part aor pass |
|---|---|---|---|---|---|
| **19.** ὁ | δὲ | Πέτρος | καὶ | Ἰωάννης | ἀποκριθέντες |
| *ho* | *de* | *Petros* | *kai* | *Iōannēs* | *apokrithentes* |
| | But | Peter | and | John | answering |

| **4242.1** prep | **840.8** prs-pron acc pl masc | **1500.3** verb indic aor act | **1500.3** verb indic aor act | **4242.1** prep | **840.8** prs-pron acc pl masc |
|---|---|---|---|---|---|
| ʼ πρὸς | αὐτούς | εἶπον, | [☆ εἶπον | πρὸς | αὐτούς, ] |
| *pros* | *autous* | *eipon* | *eipon* | *pros* | *autous* |
| to | them | said | [ said | to | them, ] |

| **1479.1** conj | **1337.1** adj sing | **1498.4** verb 3sing indic pres act | **1783.1** prep | **3450.2** art gen sing | **2296.2** noun gen sing masc |
|---|---|---|---|---|---|
| Εἰ | δίκαιόν | ἐστιν | ἐνώπιον | τοῦ | θεοῦ |
| *Ei* | *dikaion* | *estin* | *enōpion* | *tou* | *theou* |
| Whether | right | it is | before | | God |

| **5050.2** prs-pron gen 2pl | **189.17** verb inf pres act | **3095.1** adv comp | **2211.1** conj | **3450.2** art gen sing | **2296.2** noun gen sing masc | **2892.16** verb 2pl impr aor act |
|---|---|---|---|---|---|---|
| ὑμῶν | ἀκούειν | μᾶλλον | ἢ | τοῦ | θεοῦ, | κρίνατε. |
| *humōn* | *akouein* | *mallon* | *ē* | *tou* | *theou* | *krinate* |
| to you | to listen | rather | than | | God, | judge you; |

**4:17.** Since the priests and elders had no logical reply to Peter and John, they decided the best course was to try to suppress their teaching about Jesus and the Resurrection. They would threaten the disciples to speak no longer in (on the ground of, on the authority of, or concerning) this Name.

Like so many in the later history of the Church, they had committed themselves to a religious structure, a religious hierarchy, and a religious system that was largely of human devising and human interpretation. They knew what was in the Scriptures, but they ignored or twisted those parts that did not fit their system. They were not open to searching the Scriptures to see whether these things were so.

Since Peter and John were outside the room, some wonder where Luke got his information. Some suggest that Saul, who became the apostle Paul, was in this session of the Sanhedrin and later told Luke what was said in that meeting.

**4:18.** When the elders called Peter and John back into the room, they commanded them not to speak (open their mouth, utter a word) at all or teach in the name of Jesus. They, of course, were the Supreme Court of the Jews. Except for the death penalty, the Roman government gave them full authority in matters pertaining to the temple and to the conduct of their religious rites and duties. They were used to giving imperious, dictatorial commands, and they were used to having them obeyed. In this case they must have sensed that men who were this bold, this free to speak, would need an extra authoritative command. So they spoke as emphatically as possible.

**4:19.** These threats did not intimidate the two apostles. Courteously, but very firmly, they put the responsibility back on the Jewish leaders to judge or decide whether it was right before God to listen to them rather than to Him.

Clearly, the apostles were not afraid of the threats of the Sanhedrin. They had already done their worst to Jesus. They could not do any more than that to the apostles, and because of the hope of the resurrection of the dead they were not afraid of death. Moreover, they had committed themselves to Jesus, not as to a human leader, but as to the divine Son of God.

From that day to this, followers of Jesus have faced the same question. The commands of human leaders, even religious leaders, have all too often been contrary to the commands of God and Christ. Paul warned Timothy the time would come when some church members would not put up with sound, healthy, Biblical teaching. Instead, following their own desires, they would heap to themselves teachers who would tell them what they wanted to hear. They would turn away their ears and refuse to listen to the truth. They would instead turn to (and believe) fables (idle tales, fanciful stories coming from the imaginations of these false teachers). (See 2 Timothy 4:3,4.)

**and we cannot deny it:** We cannot say it is not true, *Everyday, NCV.*

**17. But that it spread no further among the people:** But, that it may go no further with, *Williams C.K.* . . . this report must not be spread any further, *Noli* . . . But we must warn them not to talk to people anymore, *Everyday* . . . lest it may disseminate more, *Concordant* . . . to keep the news of it from spreading farther, *Norlie.*

**let us straitly threaten them:** . . . let us warn them, *TCNT* . . . let us stop them by threats, *Weymouth* . . . severely threaten, *Williams* . . . we must give them a stern warning, *NAB* . . . let us terrify them with threats, *Fenton* . . . forbid them, *Williams C.K.*

**that they speak henceforth to no man in this name:** . . . not to plead the Cause, *TCNT* . . . to say anything to anyone, *Williams C.K.* . . . never to mention that man's name to anyone again, *NAB* . . . to preach no more to anyone, *Noli.*

**18. And they called them:** So they recalled the Apostles, *Weymouth* . . . called them back, *NAB.*

**and commanded them not to speak at all nor teach in the name of Jesus:** . . . and charged them, *ASV* . . . and ordered them altogether to give up speaking or teaching, *Weymouth* . . . commanded them not to utter even a sound nor to teach, *Swann* . . . made it clear that under no circumstances were they to speak the name, *NAB* . . . imperatively forbade them, *Fenton* . . . ordered them bluntly...a single further word, *Phillips* . . . under no condition, *TEV* . . . to speak or teach a single sentence about the Name of Jesus, *Moffatt.*

**19. But Peter and John answered and said unto them:** . . . replied to them, *Berkeley.*

**Whether it be right in the sight of God to hearken unto you more than unto God, judge ye:** What do you think is right? What would God want? Should we obey you or God? *Everyday* . . . to listen to you rather than to him—you must decide, *TCNT* . . . Does God consider it right to listen to you, *Beck* . . . you must judge, *Williams C.K.* . . . Judge for yourselves, *Noli.*

| 3620.3 partic | 1404.5 verb 1pl indic pres mid | 1056.1 conj | 2231.1 prs-pron nom 1pl | 3614.17 rel-pron pl neu | 1481.5 verb 1pl indic aor act |
|---|---|---|---|---|---|
| 20. οὐ | δυνάμεθα | γὰρ | ἡμεῖς | ἃ | ⸀ εἴδομεν |
| *ou* | *dunametha* | *gar* | *hēmeis* | *ha* | *eidomen* |
| not | are able | for | we | what | we saw |

| 1481.23 verb 1pl indic aor act | 2504.1 conj | 189.22 verb 1pl indic aor act | 3231.1 partic | 2953.24 verb inf pres act | 3450.7 art nom pl masc |
|---|---|---|---|---|---|
| [a☆ εἴδαμεν ] | καὶ | ἠκούσαμεν | μὴ | λαλεῖν. | 21. Οἱ |
| *eidamen* | *kai* | *ēkousamen* | *mē* | *lalein* | *Hoi* |
| [ idem ] | and | heard | not | to speak. | The |

20.a.**Txt:** 03B-corr,08E 025P,byz.Sod
**Var:** 01ℵ,02A,03B,05D Lach,Treg,Alf,Tisc We/Ho,Weis,UBS/☆

| 1156.2 conj | 4182.1 verb nom pl masc part aor mid | 624.7 verb 3pl indic aor act | 840.8 prs-pron acc pl masc | 3235.6 num card neu |
|---|---|---|---|---|
| δὲ | προσαπειλησάμενοι | ἀπέλυσαν | αὐτούς, | μηδὲν |
| *de* | *prosapeilēsamenoi* | *apelusan* | *autous* | *mēden* |
| but | having further threatened | let go | them, | nothing |

| 2128.5 verb nom pl masc part pres act | 3450.16 art sing neu | 4316.1 adv | 2822.2 verb 3pl subj aor mid | 840.8 prs-pron acc pl masc |
|---|---|---|---|---|
| εὑρίσκοντες | τὸ | πῶς | κολάσωνται | αὐτούς |
| *heuriskontes* | *to* | *pōs* | *kolasōntai* | *autous* |
| finding | the | how | they might punish | them |

| 1217.2 prep | 3450.6 art acc sing masc | 2967.4 noun acc sing masc | 3617.1 conj | 3820.7 adj nom pl masc | 1386.18 verb 3pl indic imperf act |
|---|---|---|---|---|---|
| διὰ | τὸν | λαόν, | ὅτι | πάντες | ἐδόξαζον |
| *dia* | *ton* | *laon* | *hoti* | *pantes* | *edoxazon* |
| on account of | the | people, | because | all | were glorifying |

| 3450.6 art acc sing masc | 2296.4 noun acc sing masc | 1894.3 prep | 3450.3 art dat sing | 1090.12 verb dat sing neu part perf act |
|---|---|---|---|---|
| τὸν | θεὸν | ἐπὶ | τῷ | γεγονότι. |
| *ton* | *theon* | *epi* | *tō* | *gegonoti* |
|  | God | for | the | having taken place; |

| 2073.4 noun gen pl neu | 1056.1 conj | 1498.34 verb sing indic imperf act | 3979.2 adj comp gen pl | 4910.2 num card |
|---|---|---|---|---|
| 22. ἐτῶν | γὰρ | ἦν | πλειόνων | ⸀ τεσσαράκοντα |
| *etōn* | *gar* | *ēn* | *pleionōn* | *tessarakonta* |
| years | for | was | above | forty |

| 4910.1 num card | 3450.5 art nom sing masc | 442.1 noun nom sing masc | 1894.1 prep | 3614.6 rel-pron acc sing masc |
|---|---|---|---|---|
| [ τεσσεράκοντα ] | ὁ | ἄνθρωπος | ἐφ' | ὃν |
| *tesserakonta* | *ho* | *anthrōpos* | *eph'* | *hon* |
| [ idem ] | the | man | on | whom |

| 1090.65 verb 3sing indic plperf mid | 1090.74 verb 3sing indic perf act | 3450.16 art sing neu | 4447.1 noun sing neu | 3642.17 dem-pron sing neu |
|---|---|---|---|---|
| ⸀ ἐγεγόνει | [a☆ γεγόνει ] | τὸ | σημεῖον | τοῦτο |
| *egegonei* | *gegonei* | *to* | *sēmeion* | *touto* |
| had taken place | [ idem ] | the | sign | this |

22.a.**Txt:** 01ℵ,02A,08E 025P,etc.byz.Sod
**Var:** 03B,05D,Lach Treg,Alf,Tisc,We/Ho Weis,UBS/☆

| 3450.10 art gen sing fem | 2369.1 noun gen sing fem | 624.17 verb nom pl masc part aor pass | 1156.2 conj | 2048.1 verb indic aor act | 4242.1 prep |
|---|---|---|---|---|---|
| τῆς | ἰάσεως. | 23. Ἀπολυθέντες | δὲ | ἦλθον | πρὸς |
| *tēs* | *iaseōs* | *Apoluthentes* | *de* | *ēlthon* | *pros* |
| of the | healing. | Having been let go | and | they came | to |

| 3450.8 art acc pl masc | 2375.8 adj acc pl masc | 2504.1 conj | 514.8 verb 3pl indic aor act | 3607.8 rel-pron pl neu | 4242.1 prep |
|---|---|---|---|---|---|
| τοὺς | ἰδίους, | καὶ | ἀπήγγειλαν | ὅσα | πρὸς |
| *tous* | *idious* | *kai* | *apēngeilan* | *hosa* | *pros* |
| the | their own, | and | reported | whatever | to |

**4:20.** The apostles then boldly declared they were not able to stop telling what they had seen and heard. They had in mind, of course, the Great Commission. All four Gospels and the Book of Acts tell of this command of Jesus given not only to the apostles but to all His followers. Some have said the believer's chief purpose is to glorify God and enjoy Him forever. There is truth in this, but God is also glorified when believers serve Him, praise Him, and worship Him in Spirit and in truth. They glorify God also as they fulfill His purposes as expressed in the Great Commission.

**4:21.** After the high priest and elders added further threats to their warnings, they released Peter and John from custody. Though they searched their minds to try to find some way to punish the apostles, they could not think of any way to do it. At least they could not think of how to do it without antagonizing the people. The people were glorifying God because of what had taken place. The man who was healed had come into the temple glorifying and praising God. Peter and John had given God all the praise. For the Sanhedrin to punish the apostles at this point could have made the people think they were against God.

Actually, the very fact that the leaders let the apostles go must have made the crowd believe God was putting His approval on the gospel the apostles were proclaiming. It also let the people know God could deliver from the Sanhedrin. The crowd understood from this also that the Sanhedrin had no case against the apostles, nor did they have any way to refute their message.

**4:22.** This miracle of healing was especially outstanding because the man was over 40 years old. If normal muscles are not used even for a few weeks or months, one does not stand up and begin to walk and jump the way this man did. For a person whose muscles were shriveled and his ankles without strength suddenly to do so was beyond any human expectation.

The Greek word translated "miracle" here literally means a "sign," an outward, visible manifestation of the truth of the gospel the apostles were preaching. John's Gospel uses the same Greek word for the miracles of Jesus that were signs pointing to His authority and deity as the Son of God.

**4:23.** As soon as they were released, Peter and John went back to their own company, their own people. The Greek expression used here could mean to the people of their own nation or tribe, or it could mean to their own family. In this case it meant the body of believers who had become the true family of God. It corresponds to what Ephesians 2:19 calls the household of God, the family that belongs to God.

**20. For we cannot but speak:** . . . as for us, we cannot help speaking of, *TCNT* . . . keep from telling, *Williams* . . . refrain from telling, *Berkeley* . . . We can't stop telling, *Beck* . . . We cannot keep quiet, *Everyday.*

**the things which we have seen and heard:**

**21. So when they had further threatened them:** But after further threats, *Noli* . . . After they had spoken more sharp words to them, *NLT.*

**they let them go:** . . . the Council set them at liberty, *TCNT* . . . they turned them loose, *Williams* . . . and then freed them, *Berkeley* . . . they released them, *Noli.*

**finding nothing how they might punish them:** . . . not seeing any safe way of punishing them, *TCNT* . . . nothing to accuse them of, *Klingensmith* . . . could not find a way to punish, *Everyday.*

**because of the people:** . . . on account of the people, *Rotherham* . . . because all the people, *Everyday* . . . before the people, *Klingensmith.*

**for all men glorified God for that which was done:** . . . continued to praise God for what had taken place, *Williams* . . . everybody was praising God for what had happened, *Adams* . . . everybody was glorifying God, *Montgomery* . . . This miracle was a proof from God, *Everyday.*

**22. For the man was above forty years old:** . . . was more than forty years old, *TCNT.*

**on whom this miracle of healing was shewed:** . . . the more so as the man who was the subject of this miraculous cure, *TCNT* . . . this sign of healing, *Rotherham* . . . this act of power, *BB.*

**23. And being let go:** After they had been set at liberty, *TCNT* . . . After their release, *Weymouth* . . . were free again, *Beck* . . . On their release, *NIV* . . . after their dismissal, *Confraternity* . . . When the Apostles were released, *Noli.*

**they went to their own company:** . . . they came unto their own friends, *Rotherham* . . . the apostles went to their companions, *Williams* . . . their associates, *Wuest.*

## Acts 4:24

| **840.8** prs-pron acc pl masc | **3450.7** art nom pl masc | **744.5** noun pl masc | **2504.1** conj | **3450.7** art nom pl masc | **4104.5** adj comp nom pl masc |
|---|---|---|---|---|---|
| αὐτοὺς | οἱ | ἀρχιερεῖς | καὶ | οἱ | πρεσβύτεροι |
| *autous* | *hoi* | *archiereis* | *kai* | *hoi* | *presbuteroi* |
| them | the | chief priests | and | the | elders |

23.a.**Txt:** 02A,08E,025P byz.Sod
**Var:** 01ℵ,03B,05D,Lach Treg,Alf,Tisc,We/Ho Weis,UBS/☆

| **1500.3** verb indic aor act | **1500.28** verb 3pl indic aor act | **3450.7** art nom pl masc | **1156.2** conj | **189.32** verb nom pl masc part aor act |
|---|---|---|---|---|
| ⸂ εἶπον. | [a☆ εἶπαν. ] | **24.** οἱ | δὲ | ἀκούσαντες, |
| *eipon* | *eipan* | *hoi* | *de* | *akousantes* |
| said | [ idem ] | The | and | having heard, |

24.a.**Txt:** 08E,byz.Sod
**Var:** 01ℵ,02A,03B,05D 025P,Lach,Treg,Alf Tisc,We/Ho,Weis UBS/☆

| **3524.1** adv | **142.10** verb 3pl indic aor act | **5292.4** noun acc sing fem | **4242.1** prep | **3450.6** art acc sing masc | **2296.4** noun acc sing masc |
|---|---|---|---|---|---|
| ὁμοθυμαδὸν | ἦραν | φωνὴν | πρὸς | τὸν | θεόν, |
| *homothumadon* | *ēran* | *phōnēn* | *pros* | *ton* | *theon* |
| with one accord | lifted up | voice | to | | God, |

24.b.**Txt:** 05D,08E,025P 044,byz.sa.Sod
**Var:** p74,01ℵ,02A,03B bo.Lach,Treg,Tisc We/Ho,Weis,UBS/☆

| **2504.1** conj | **1500.3** verb indic aor act | **1500.28** verb 3pl indic aor act | **1197.4** noun voc sing masc | **4622.1** prs-pron nom 2sing | **3450.5** art nom sing masc |
|---|---|---|---|---|---|
| καὶ | ⸂ εἶπον, | [a☆ εἶπαν, ] | Δέσποτα, | σὺ | ⸂b ὁ |
| *kai* | *eipon* | *eipan* | *Despota* | *su* | *ho* |
| and | said | [ idem ] | O master, | you | the |

| **2296.1** noun nom sing masc | **3450.5** art nom sing masc | **4020.37** verb nom sing masc part aor act | **3450.6** art acc sing masc | **3636.4** noun acc sing masc | **2504.1** conj |
|---|---|---|---|---|---|
| Θεὸς ⸃ | ὁ | ποιήσας | τὸν | οὐρανὸν | καὶ |
| *Theos* | *ho* | *poiēsas* | *ton* | *ouranon* | *kai* |
| God | the | having made | the | heaven | and |

| **3450.12** art acc sing fem | **1087.4** noun acc sing fem | **2504.1** conj | **3450.12** art acc sing fem | **2258.4** noun acc sing fem | **2504.1** conj | **3820.1** adj |
|---|---|---|---|---|---|---|
| τὴν | γῆν | καὶ | τὴν | θάλασσαν | καὶ | πάντα |
| *tēn* | *gēn* | *kai* | *tēn* | *thalassan* | *kai* | *panta* |
| the | earth | and | the | sea | and | all |

25.a.**Var:** p74,01ℵ,02A 03B,08E,33,Lach,Treg Alf,Tisc,We/Ho,Sod UBS/☆

| **3450.17** art pl neu | **1706.1** prep | **840.2** prs-pron dat pl | **3450.5** art nom sing masc | **3450.2** art gen sing | **3824.2** noun gen sing masc |
|---|---|---|---|---|---|
| τὰ | ἐν | αὐτοῖς, | **25.** ὁ | [a☆+ τοῦ | πατρὸς |
| *ta* | *en* | *autois* | *ho* | *tou* | *patros* |
| the things | in | them, | the | [ of the | father |

25.b.**Var:** p74,01ℵ,02A 03B,08E,33,Lach,Treg Alf,Tisc,We/Ho,Sod UBS/☆

| **2231.2** prs-pron gen 1pl | **1217.2** prep | **4011.2** noun gen sing neu | **39.2** adj gen sing | **4601.2** noun gen sing neu |
|---|---|---|---|---|
| ἡμῶν ] | διὰ | [b☆+ πνεύματος | ἁγίου ] | στόματος |
| *hēmōn* | *dia* | *pneumatos* | *hagiou* | *stomatos* |
| our ] | by | [ Spirit | Holy ] | mouth |

25.c.**Txt:** byz.
**Var:** 01ℵ,02A,03B,05D 08E,025P,Gries,Lach Treg,Alf,Word,Tisc We/Ho,Weis,Sod UBS/☆

| **1132.1** name masc | **3450.2** art gen sing | **3679.4** noun gen sing fem | **4622.2** prs-pron gen 2sing | **1500.15** verb nom sing masc part aor act |
|---|---|---|---|---|
| Δαβὶδ | ⸂c τοῦ ⸃ | παιδός | σου | εἰπών, |
| *Dabid* | *tou* | *paidos* | *sou* | *eipōn* |
| of David | the | servant | your | having said, |

| **2420.1** adv | **5269.1** verb 3pl indic aor act | **1477.4** noun pl neu | **2504.1** conj | **2967.5** noun nom pl masc | **3161.3** verb 3pl indic aor act |
|---|---|---|---|---|---|
| Ἱνατί | ἐφρύαξαν | ἔθνη, | καὶ | λαοὶ | ἐμελέτησαν |
| *Hinati* | *ephruaxan* | *ethnē* | *kai* | *laoi* | *emeletēsan* |
| Why | were arrogant | nations, | and | peoples | did plan |

| **2727.8** adj pl neu | **3798.6** verb 3pl indic aor act | **3450.7** art nom pl masc | **928.6** noun pl masc | **3450.10** art gen sing fem |
|---|---|---|---|---|
| κενά; | **26.** παρέστησαν | οἱ | βασιλεῖς | τῆς |
| *kena* | *parestēsan* | *hoi* | *basileis* | *tēs* |
| futile things? | Stood up | the | kings | of the |

From what Luke records on other occasions, it seems certain these believers were gathered together to pray for Peter and John, and that they rejoiced and gave God praise for their release. Then the apostles reported all the high priest and elders had said to them, holding nothing back.

**and reported all that the chief priests and elders had said unto them:**

**24. And when they heard that they lifted up their voice to God with one accord:** When they heard their report, *Noli* . . . moved by a common impulse, they raised their voice to God in prayer, *TCNT* . . . one and all lifted up their voices to God, *Weymouth* . . . they prayed to God with one purpose, *Everyday* . . . with one consent, *Sawyer.*

**and said, Lord, thou art God:** O Sovereign! *Rotherham* . . . O Sovereign Lord, *TCNT* . . . O Master, *Williams C.K.* . . . absolute in power, *Wuest.*

**which hast made heaven, and earth, and the sea, and all that in them is:** . . . you are the Maker of, *Williams* . . . thou that didst make, *ASV* . . . it is thou who hast made the sky...and everything that is in them, *TCNT.*

**4:24.** The warnings and threats of the Jewish leaders did not frighten the believers. Neither did they ignore them. They took them to God. The word "voice" is in the singular here, which means they all joined together and prayed in unison. They prayed also in one accord, that is, with one purpose. Probably, however, the prayer which the Bible records here was given by one of them who became the spokesman for them all.

Much can be learned from this prayer. First, as in the case of most of the prayers in the Bible, they recognized who God is. They addressed Him as Lord (a different word from that used elsewhere in the Bible, this one meaning Master, Owner, Sovereign) and thus presented themselves before Him as His servants, even as His slaves. They were not making demands on Him. They were throwing themselves on His mercy, looking for His grace, His unmerited favor.

Then they recognized that He alone is God, the God of all power, for He is the Creator of the universe and all that is in every part of it. He is Sovereign over the universe, the true King of the universe, by right of creation.

**25. Who by the mouth of thy servant David hast said:** . . . and who by the lips of our ancestor, thy servant David, speaking under the influence of the holy Spirit, hast said, *TCNT* . . . and didst say through the Holy Spirit by the lips of our forefather David, Thy servant, *Weymouth* . . . who was inspired by the Holy Spirit, *Noli.*

**Why did the heathen rage:** Gentiles, *ASV* . . . Unto what end did nations rage, *Rotherham* . . . Why are the nations so angry? *Everyday* . . . heathen roar, *Williams C.K.* . . . rage haughtily, *Darby.*

**and the people imagine vain things?:** And peoples busy themselves with empty things, *Rotherham* . . . And the nations form vain designs, *TCNT* . . . and the peoples form futile plans, *Montgomery* . . . the peoples plan in vain? *Williams C.K.* . . . Why are the people making useless plans? *Everyday* . . . and the nations plot in vain? *Noli* . . . empty stratagems? *Adams* . . . study emptiness? *Klingensmith.*

**4:25.** Second, they based their petition on the inspired Word of God, spoken by the Holy Spirit through the mouth of King David. Again, most of the prayers of the Bible are based on the Word of God already given. Psalm 2:1,2 was a word from the Lord that fitted their situation and made them feel God knew in advance what their situation was and how to deal with it.

Psalm 2 speaks of an opposition like that of the Jewish leaders. It asks why the heathen (the nations, the Gentiles) were raging (with a general hostility against God). It emphasizes the question by repeating it in a little different way and asking why the peoples (plural) imagined (planned, were devising) a vain (empty, foolish, ineffective) thing.

This psalm was, of course, speaking first of all of the Gentiles, the nations who were enemies of God and His people. It tells believers that all the plans men try to devise, hoping to hinder or stop the plan of God, are doomed to failure. God is still in control, but He is also patient.

**26. The kings of the earth stood up:** . . . set themselves in array, *ASV* . . . took their stand, *Williams* . . . took a belligerent stand, *Adams* . . . prepare to fight, *Everyday.*

**4:26.** David further identified this raging, foolish planning as the kings of the earth standing by each other, trying to support each other against God. This idea is repeated for emphasis by saying that the rulers "were gathered together against the Lord (that is,

| **1087.2** noun gen sing fem | **2504.1** conj | **3450.7** art nom pl masc | **752.5** noun nom pl masc | **4714.20** verb 3pl indic aor pass | **1894.3** prep |
|---|---|---|---|---|---|
| γῆς, | καὶ | οἱ | ἄρχοντες | συνήχθησαν | ἐπὶ |
| *gēs* | *kai* | *hoi* | *archontes* | *sunēchthēsan* | *epi* |
| earth, | and | the | rulers | were gathered | on |

| **3450.16** art sing neu | **840.15** prs-pron sing neu | **2567.3** prep | **3450.2** art gen sing | **2935.2** noun gen sing masc | **2504.1** conj | **2567.3** prep |
|---|---|---|---|---|---|---|
| τὸ | αὐτὸ | κατὰ | τοῦ | κυρίου | καὶ | κατὰ |
| *to* | *auto* | *kata* | *tou* | *kuriou* | *kai* | *kata* |
| the | same | against | the | Lord | and | against |

| **3450.2** art gen sing | **5382.2** name gen masc | **840.3** prs-pron gen sing | **4714.20** verb 3pl indic aor pass | **1056.1** conj | **1894.2** prep |
|---|---|---|---|---|---|
| τοῦ | Χριστοῦ | αὐτοῦ. | **27.** Συνήχθησαν | γὰρ | ἐπ' |
| *tou* | *Christou* | *autou* | *Sunēchthēsan* | *gar* | *ep'* |
| the | Christ | his. | Were gathered together | for | on |

27.a.**Var:** 01ℵ,02A,03B 05D,08E,sa.bo.Gries Lach,Treg,Alf,Word Tisc,We/Ho,Weis,Sod UBS/☆

| **223.2** noun gen sing fem | **1706.1** prep | **3450.11** art dat sing fem | **4032.3** noun dat sing fem | **3642.11** dem-pron dat sing fem | **1894.3** prep |
|---|---|---|---|---|---|
| ἀληθείας | [a☆+ ἐν | τῇ | πόλει | ταύτῃ ] | ἐπὶ |
| *alētheias* | *en* | *tē* | *polei* | *tautē* | *epi* |
| a truth | [ in | the | city | this ] | against |

| **3450.6** art acc sing masc | **39.1** adj sing | **3679.1** noun acc sing | **4622.2** prs-pron gen 2sing | **2400.3** name acc masc | **3614.6** rel-pron acc sing masc |
|---|---|---|---|---|---|
| τὸν | ἅγιον | παῖδά | σου | Ἰησοῦν, | ὃν |
| *ton* | *hagion* | *paida* | *sou* | *Iēsoun* | *hon* |
| the | holy | servant | your | Jesus, | whom |

| **5383.1** verb 2sing indic aor act | **2243.1** name nom masc | **4885.1** conj | **2504.1** conj | **4053.1** name nom masc | **3952.1** name nom masc |
|---|---|---|---|---|---|
| ἔχρισας, | Ἡρῴδης | τε | καὶ | Πόντιος | Πιλᾶτος, |
| *echrisas* | *Hērōdēs* | *te* | *kai* | *Pontios* | *Pilatos* |
| you did anoint, | Herod | both | and | Pontius | Pilate, |

| **4713.1** prep | **1477.6** noun dat pl neu | **2504.1** conj | **2967.7** noun dat pl masc | **2447.1** name masc | **4020.41** verb inf aor act |
|---|---|---|---|---|---|
| σὺν | ἔθνεσιν | καὶ | λαοῖς | Ἰσραήλ, | **28.** ποιῆσαι |
| *sun* | *ethnesin* | *kai* | *laois* | *Israēl* | *poiēsai* |
| with | Gentiles | and | peoples | of Israel, | to do |

| **3607.8** rel-pron pl neu | **3450.9** art nom sing fem | **5331.1** noun nom sing fem | **4622.2** prs-pron gen 2sing | **2504.1** conj | **3450.9** art nom sing fem |
|---|---|---|---|---|---|
| ὅσα | ἡ | χείρ | σου | καὶ | ἡ |
| *hosa* | *hē* | *cheir* | *sou* | *kai* | *hē* |
| whatever | the | hand | your | and | the |

28.a.**Txt:** 01ℵ,02A-corr 05D,08E,025P,byz.sa.bo. Gries,Word,Tisc,Sod **Var:** 02A-org,03B,Lach We/Ho,Weis,UBS/☆

| **1005.1** noun nom sing fem | **4622.2** prs-pron gen 2sing | **4168.1** verb 3sing indic aor act | **1090.63** verb inf aor mid | **2504.1** conj |
|---|---|---|---|---|
| βουλή | ⸀a σου ⸁ | προώρισεν | γενέσθαι. | **29.** καὶ |
| *boulē* | *sou* | *proōrisen* | *genesthai* | *kai* |
| purpose | your | predetermined | to come to pass. | And |

| **3450.17** art pl neu | **3431.1** adv | **2935.5** noun voc sing masc | **1881.2** verb 2sing impr aor act | **1894.3** prep | **3450.15** art acc pl fem | **543.4** noun acc pl fem |
|---|---|---|---|---|---|---|
| τὰ | νῦν, | κύριε, | ἔπιδε | ἐπὶ | τὰς | ἀπειλὰς |
| *ta* | *nun* | *kurie* | *epide* | *epi* | *tas* | *apeilas* |
| the | now, | Lord, | look | upon | the | threatenings |

| **840.1** prs-pron gen pl | **2504.1** conj | **1319.25** verb 2sing impr aor act | **3450.4** art dat pl | **1395.8** noun dat pl masc | **4622.2** prs-pron gen 2sing | **3196.3** prep |
|---|---|---|---|---|---|---|
| αὐτῶν, | καὶ | δὸς | τοῖς | δούλοις | σου | μετὰ |
| *autōn* | *kai* | *dos* | *tois* | *doulois* | *sou* | *meta* |
| their, | and | give | to the | servants | your | with |

against the divine Lord, 'Lord' standing for the personal name of God, the Hebrew *YHWH*), and against his Christ," that is, against His Messiah, His Anointed One, God's anointed Prophet, Priest, and King.

This prayer, inspired by the Spirit, recognized that the Jewish leaders were in the same class as the outside nations who were always conspiring against God and His Anointed, in this case, against Jesus. There is precedent for this in that the Old Testament prophets sometimes used the word *gôyim* (usually translated "Gentiles") for Israel because Israel had turned from God.

**4:27.** This prayer then specifically identifies Psalm 2 with those who were gathered together (with hostile purpose) against God's holy child Jesus. Herod here is Herod Antipas, the tetrarch of Galilee and Peraea, the same ruler who put John the Baptist to death. In his Gospel, Luke records how Herod and his soldiers mocked Jesus, threw a brightly colored robe around Him, and sent Him back to Pilate (Luke 23:11). The same day Herod and Pilate were made friends. Their treatment of Jesus caused them to be among those who were gathered together against God and His Son, Jesus.

These enemies of God and Christ also included the Gentiles, in this case the Roman soldiers and the peoples of Israel. *People* is a word ordinarily used of Israel as God's chosen people. The Greek is in the plural here, possibly because the 12 tribes were all represented in Israel, but more probably because the Israelites were divided into various sects, such as the Pharisees and Sadducees. It may also be a recognition that they were in the same category as the Gentiles (literally, *nations*, also in the plural).

As before, Luke used the word "child" (Greek, *paida*) in the sense of "servant." "Holy child" thus means the dedicated, consecrated Servant of the Lord, the same Suffering Servant prophesied in Isaiah 52:13 to 53:12.

**4:28.** Yet they could do only what God's hand (that is, God's power) and God's will had determined before (decided beforehand) to be done. They were, however, responsible for their deeds, for they chose freely to do them.

The believers based their petition on what God did through Jesus. God's hand was in control when He permitted the death of Jesus; Jesus was indeed God's Servant who accomplished God's will in their behalf. They could come to God on the basis of what was fully accomplished through the death and resurrection of Jesus (1 Corinthians 1:23,24; 3:11; 2 Corinthians 1:20).

**4:29.** Their petition was that the Lord would now look on the threatenings of the Sanhedrin and give His servants (slaves) opportunities to keep on speaking the Word with all boldness (and freedom of speech). Perhaps they felt less confident after they left

**and the rulers were gathered together against the Lord:** . . . assembled together, *HBIE* . . . conspired together against, *Noli* . . . mustered themselves against, *MLNT* . . . were united against the Lord, *Norlie*.

**and against his Christ:** . . . his Anointed, *ASV*.

**27. For of a truth against thy holy child Jesus:** . . . conspired against Jesus, your holy servant, *Noli*.

**whom thou hast anointed:** . . . whom thou hast consecrated the Christ, *TCNT* . . . whom thou didst appoint, *Williams C.K.*

**both Herod, and Pontius Pilate, with the Gentiles, and the people of Israel:** . . . not Herod and Pontius Pilate only, but the nations and the people of Israel besides, *TCNT*.

**were gathered together:** They did...assemble, *Weymouth* . . . they have actually gathered in this city, *MLNT*.

**28. For to do whatsoever thy hand and thy counsel determined before to be done:** . . . but only to do all that thy providence and thy will had already determined should be done, *TCNT* . . . to carry out what your hand and will had destined should happen, *Goodspeed* . . . made your plan happen, *NCV* . . . your plan had beforehand decreed to be done, *Kleist* . . . to do all that thy power and thy will had predetermined should be done, *Montgomery* . . . to do what thy hand and thy purpose had determined, *Williams C.K.* . . . marked out beforehand, *Rotherham* . . . and Thy purpose preordained to take place, *MLNT*.

**29. And now, Lord, behold their threatenings:** . . . look upon their threats, *RSV* . . . give heed to their threats, *TCNT* . . . give attention to their threats, *Williams* . . . listen to their threats, *PNT* . . . listen to what they are saying, *Everyday* . . . consider, *Kleist* . . . notice, *MLNT*.

**and grant unto thy servants:** . . . and enable thy servants, *TCNT* . . . Thou endowing Thy slaves, *Concordant* . . . endow Thy servants with fearlessness to speak Thy word, *Berkeley* . . . Your bond servants, *AmpB*.

## Acts 4:30

| 3816.2 noun gen sing fem | 3820.10 adj gen sing fem | 2953.24 verb inf pres act | 3450.6 art acc sing masc | 3030.4 noun acc sing masc | 4622.2 prs-pron gen 2sing |
|---|---|---|---|---|---|
| παῤῥησίας | πάσης | λαλεῖν | τὸν | λόγον | σου, |
| *parrhēsias* | *pasēs* | *lalein* | *ton* | *logon* | *sou* |
| boldness | all | to speak | the | word | your, |

30.a.**Txt:** p45,01א,05D 08E,025P,etc.byz.Tisc Sod
**Var:** p74,02A,03B,Lach Treg,We/Ho,Weis UBS/☆

| 1706.1 prep | 3450.3 art dat sing | 3450.12 art acc sing fem | 5331.4 noun acc sing fem | 4622.2 prs-pron gen 2sing | 1601.1 verb inf pres act |
|---|---|---|---|---|---|
| **30.** ἐν | τῷ | τὴν | χεῖρά | ⸀a σου⸌ | ἐκτείνειν |
| *en* | *tō* | *tēn* | *cheira* | *sou* | *ekteinein* |
| in | the | the | hand | your | to stretch out |

| 4622.4 prs-pron acc 2sing | 1519.1 prep | 2369.2 noun acc sing fem | 2504.1 conj | 4447.2 noun pl neu | 2504.1 conj | 4907.1 noun pl neu |
|---|---|---|---|---|---|---|
| σε | εἰς | ἴασιν, | καὶ | σημεῖα | καὶ | τέρατα |
| *se* | *eis* | *iasin* | *kai* | *sēmeia* | *kai* | *terata* |
| you | for | healing, | and | signs | and | wonders |

| 1090.28 verb inf pres mid | 1217.2 prep | 3450.2 art gen sing | 3549.3 noun gen sing neu | 3450.2 art gen sing | 39.2 adj gen sing |
|---|---|---|---|---|---|
| γίνεσθαι | διὰ | τοῦ | ὀνόματος | τοῦ | ἁγίου |
| *ginesthai* | *dia* | *tou* | *onomatos* | *tou* | *hagiou* |
| to take place | through | the | name | of the | holy |

| 3679.4 noun gen sing fem | 4622.2 prs-pron gen 2sing | 2400.2 name masc | 2504.1 conj | 1183.9 verb gen pl masc part aor pass |
|---|---|---|---|---|
| παιδός | σου | Ἰησοῦ. | **31.** καὶ | δεηθέντων |
| *paidos* | *sou* | *Iēsou* | *kai* | *deēthentōn* |
| servant | your | Jesus. | And | having prayed |

| 840.1 prs-pron gen pl | 4388.7 verb 3sing indic aor pass | 3450.5 art nom sing masc | 4964.1 noun nom sing masc | 1706.1 prep | 3614.3 rel-pron dat sing |
|---|---|---|---|---|---|
| αὐτῶν | ἐσαλεύθη | ὁ | τόπος | ἐν | ᾧ |
| *autōn* | *esaleuthē* | *ho* | *topos* | *en* | *hō* |
| they | was shaken | the | place | in | which |

| 1498.37 verb 3pl indic imperf act | 4714.24 verb nom pl masc part perf mid | 2504.1 conj | 3990.5 verb 3pl indic aor pass |
|---|---|---|---|
| ἦσαν | συνηγμένοι, | καὶ | ἐπλήσθησαν |
| *ēsan* | *sunēgmenoi* | *kai* | *eplēsthēsan* |
| they were | having been assembled, | and | they were filled |

31.a.**Txt:** 08E,025P,byz.
**Var:** 01א,02A,03B,05D Lach,Treg,Alf,Word Tisc,We/Ho,Weis,Sod UBS/☆

| 533.4 adj nom pl masc | 4011.2 noun gen sing neu | 39.2 adj gen sing | 2504.1 conj | 3450.2 art gen sing | 39.2 adj gen sing |
|---|---|---|---|---|---|
| ἅπαντες | ⸂ πνεύματος | ἁγίου, | καὶ | [a☆ τοῦ | ἁγίου |
| *hapantes* | *pneumatos* | *hagiou* | *kai* | *tou* | *hagiou* |
| all | with Spirit | Holy | and | [the | Holy |

| 4011.2 noun gen sing neu | 2953.44 verb indic imperf act | 3450.6 art acc sing masc | 3030.4 noun acc sing masc | 3450.2 art gen sing |
|---|---|---|---|---|
| πνεύματος, ] | ἐλάλουν | τὸν | λόγον | τοῦ |
| *pneumatos* | *elaloun* | *ton* | *logon* | *tou* |
| Spirit, ] | were speaking | the | word | |

| 2296.2 noun gen sing masc | 3196.3 prep | 3816.2 noun gen sing fem | 3450.2 art gen sing | 1156.2 conj | 3988.2 noun gen sing neu |
|---|---|---|---|---|---|
| θεοῦ | μετὰ | παῤῥησίας. | **32.** Τοῦ | δὲ | πλήθους |
| *theou* | *meta* | *parrhēsias* | *Tou* | *de* | *plēthous* |
| of God | with | boldness. | Of the | and | multitude |

32.a.**Txt:** 08E,025P,byz. Sod
**Var:** 01א,02A,03B,Lach Treg,Alf,Tisc,We/Ho Weis,UBS/☆

| 3450.1 art gen pl | 3961.32 verb gen pl masc part aor act | 1498.34 verb sing indic imperf act | 3450.9 art nom sing fem | 2559.2 noun nom sing fem | 2504.1 conj |
|---|---|---|---|---|---|
| τῶν | πιστευσάντων | ἦν | ⸀a ἡ⸌ | καρδία | καὶ |
| *tōn* | *pisteusantōn* | *ēn* | *hē* | *kardia* | *kai* |
| of the | having believed | were | the | heart | and |

the courtroom than while they were in it. Even after a spiritual victory Satan may suggest that believers have acted foolishly, so they must pray for continued boldness. Abraham also became afraid after boldly testifying before the king of Sodom, but God reassured him (Genesis 15:1).

**4:30.** What would provide new opportunities for the apostles to speak boldly and freely for their Lord? They knew how the Lord had used the healing of the lame man to spread the gospel and add new believers to the Church. But the healing of the lame man was just a beginning. There would be more such opportunities provided by God's stretching out His hand (extending through them His power) for healing and for signs and wonders to be done through the name of His holy child (Servant) Jesus. Here the word "holy" means separated to God and His service and emphasizes the consecration and dedication of Jesus to the work His Heavenly Father gave Him to do. Jesus made it clear He was sanctified (made holy, set apart, consecrated, dedicated) by the Father and sent by the Father into the world (John 10:36). He finished the work His Father gave Him to do (John 17:4).

The entire company of believers joined in with this prayer for boldness to keep on doing the same thing that had brought the arrest of Peter and John and the threats of the Sanhedrin. They did not want miracles for miracles' sake, however. Rather, they were opportunities to preach the gospel and signs to help the people recognize that Jesus was indeed risen from the dead and is truly the Christ, the Son of God.

**4:31.** After they prayed, the place where they were gathered was shaken, not by an earthquake but by the Spirit, indicating a mighty move of God. It is probably true that the people were shaken as well. As they felt this shaking, the whole company of believers were all filled with the Holy Spirit; and in His power they all continued speaking the Word of God with boldness (and freedom of speech). This was as great a work of the Spirit as the miracles.

The Greek indicates again a new, fresh filling of the Spirit. Some writers contend that only the new people (the 5,000 mentioned in 4:4) were filled at this time. But the Greek does not uphold this. All the believers, including the apostles, received the fresh filling to meet the continued need and to withstand the pressures upon them. New, fresh fillings of the Holy Spirit are part of God's wonderful provision for all believers.

**4:32.** The increasing number of believers continued in one heart and one soul. They formed a community of believers who were in one accord, with a unity of mind, purpose, and desire. None of

**that with all boldness they may speak thy word:** . . . with all freedom of utterance to speaking, *Rotherham* . . . with all fearlessness, to tell thy Message, *TCNT* . . . to proclaim Thy word with fearless courage, *Weymouth* . . . with perfect courage to continue to speak your message, *Williams* . . . fearlessly, *Phillips.*

**30. By stretching forth thine hand to heal:** . . . while thou stretchest, *ASV* . . . stretchest forth thy hand to heal, *Montgomery.*

**and that signs and wonders may be done:** . . . and to give signs and marvels, *Weymouth.*

**by the name of thy holy child Jesus:** . . . through the name of thy holy servant Jesus, *RSV* . . . Through the power of thy holy Servant Jesus, *TCNT* . . . by the authority of your holy Servant Jesus, *Williams.*

**31. And when they had prayed:** And when they had made supplication, *Rotherham* . . . at their beseeching, *Concordant.*

**the place was shaken where they were assembled together:** . . . their meeting-place shook, *Berkeley* . . . the place where they were was violently moved, *BB.*

**and they were all filled with the Holy Ghost:** . . . and one and all were filled, *Rotherham.*

**and they spake the word of God with boldness:** . . . and began speaking...with freedom of utterance, *Rotherham* . . . and continued to tell God's Message fearlessly, *TCNT* . . . and continued courageously to speak God's Message, *Williams* . . . fearlessly they gave utterance to God's message, *Berkeley* . . . spoke out the message of God with freedom, *Fenton* . . . with confidence, *Douay* . . . without fear, *BB.*

**32. And the multitude of them that believed were of one heart and of one soul:** . . . of the throng, *Rotherham* . . . The whole body of those who had become believers in Christ were animated by one spirit, *TCNT* . . . Now the multitude of the believers, *Montgomery* . . . in the vast number of those who had become believers, *Williams* . . . The host of believers were one in heart and soul, *Berkeley* . . . united in spirit, *SEB.*

## Acts 4:33

32.b.**Txt:** 08E,025P,byz. Sod
**Var:** 01ℵ,02A,03B,Lach Treg,Alf,Tisc,We/Ho Weis,UBS/☆

| 3450.9 art nom sing fem | 5425.1 noun nom sing fem | 1518.5 num card nom fem | 2504.1 conj | 3624.1 conj | 1518.3 num card nom masc | 4948.10 indef-pron sing neu |
|---|---|---|---|---|---|---|
| ˹b ἡ ˺ | ψυχὴ | μία· | καὶ | οὐδὲ | εἷς | τι |
| *hē* | *psuchē* | *mia* | *kai* | *oude* | *heis* | *ti* |
| the | soul | one, | and | not | one | anything |

| 3450.1 art gen pl | 5062.10 verb gen pl neu part pres act | 840.4 prs-pron dat sing | 2978.26 verb 3sing indic imperf act | 2375.4 adj sing | 1498.32 verb inf pres act |
|---|---|---|---|---|---|
| τῶν | ὑπαρχόντων | αὐτῷ | ἔλεγεν | ἴδιον | εἶναι, |
| *tōn* | *huparchontōn* | *autō* | *elegen* | *idion* | *einai* |
| of the | possessing | him | was saying | his own | to be, |

32.c.**Txt:** 01ℵ,02A,08E 025P,byz.Tisc,Sod
**Var:** 03B,05D,Lach We/Ho,Weis,UBS/☆

| 233.1 conj | 1498.34 verb sing indic imperf act | 840.2 prs-pron dat pl | 533.1 adj | 3820.1 adj | 2812.5 adj pl neu |
|---|---|---|---|---|---|
| ἀλλ' | ἦν | αὐτοῖς | ˹ ἅπαντα | [c☆ πάντα ] | κοινά. |
| *all'* | *ēn* | *autois* | *hapanta* | *panta* | *koina* |
| but | were | to them | all things | [ idem ] | common. |

| 2504.1 conj | 3144.11 adj dat sing fem | 1405.3 noun dat sing fem | 1405.3 noun dat sing fem | 3144.11 adj dat sing fem |
|---|---|---|---|---|
| **33.** καὶ | ˹ μεγάλῃ | δυνάμει | [☆ δυνάμει | μεγάλῃ ] |
| *kai* | *megalē* | *dunamei* | *dunamei* | *megalē* |
| And | with great | power | [ power | with great ] |

| 586.20 verb 3pl indic imperf act | 3450.16 art sing neu | 3115.1 noun sing neu | 3450.7 art nom pl masc | 646.4 noun nom pl masc |
|---|---|---|---|---|
| ἀπεδίδουν | τὸ | μαρτύριον | οἱ | ἀπόστολοι |
| *apedidoun* | *to* | *marturion* | *hoi* | *apostoloi* |
| were giving | the | testimony | the | apostles |

| 3450.10 art gen sing fem | 384.2 noun gen sing fem | 3450.2 art gen sing | 2935.2 noun gen sing masc | 2400.2 name masc | 3450.2 art gen sing |
|---|---|---|---|---|---|
| ˹ τῆς | ἀναστάσεως | τοῦ | κυρίου | Ἰησοῦ, | [ τοῦ |
| *tēs* | *anastaseōs* | *tou* | *kuriou* | *Iēsou* | *tou* |
| of the | resurrection | of the | Lord | Jesus, | [ of the |

| 2935.2 noun gen sing masc | 2400.2 name masc | 3450.10 art gen sing fem | 384.2 noun gen sing fem | 5322.1 noun nom sing fem | 4885.1 conj |
|---|---|---|---|---|---|
| κυρίου | Ἰησοῦ | τῆς | ἀναστάσεως, ] | χάρις | τε |
| *kuriou* | *Iēsou* | *tēs* | *anastaseōs* | *charis* | *te* |
| Lord | Jesus | of the | resurrection, ] | grace | and |

| 3144.9 adj nom sing fem | 1498.34 verb sing indic imperf act | 1894.3 prep | 3820.8 adj acc pl masc | 840.8 prs-pron acc pl masc | 3624.1 conj |
|---|---|---|---|---|---|
| μεγάλη | ἦν | ἐπὶ | πάντας | αὐτούς. | **34.** οὐδὲ |
| *megalē* | *ēn* | *epi* | *pantas* | *autous* | *oude* |
| great | was | upon | all | them. | Neither |

34.a.**Txt:** 05D,08E,025P byz.
**Var:** 01ℵ,02A,03B,Lach Treg,Tisc,We/Ho,Weis Sod,UBS/☆

| 1056.1 conj | 1713.1 adj nom sing masc | 4948.3 indef-pron nom sing | 5062.12 verb 3sing indic imperf act | 1498.34 verb sing indic imperf act | 1706.1 prep |
|---|---|---|---|---|---|
| γάρ | ἐνδεής | τις | ˹ ὑπῆρχεν | [a☆ ἦν ] | ἐν |
| *gar* | *endeēs* | *tis* | *hupērchen* | *ēn* | *en* |
| for | in want | anyone | was | [ idem ] | among |

| 840.2 prs-pron dat pl | 3607.2 rel-pron nom pl masc | 1056.1 conj | 2907.1 noun nom pl masc | 5399.4 noun gen pl neu | 2211.1 conj |
|---|---|---|---|---|---|
| αὐτοῖς· | ὅσοι | γὰρ | κτήτορες | χωρίων | ἢ |
| *autois* | *hosoi* | *gar* | *ktētores* | *chōriōn* | *ē* |
| them; | as many as | for | owners | of estates | or |

| 3477.5 noun gen pl fem | 5062.13 verb 3pl indic imperf act | 4310.2 verb nom pl masc part pres act | 5179.22 verb 3pl indic imperf act | 3450.15 art acc pl fem |
|---|---|---|---|---|
| οἰκιῶν | ὑπῆρχον, | πωλοῦντες | ἔφερον | τὰς |
| *oikiōn* | *hupērchon* | *pōlountes* | *epheron* | *tas* |
| houses | were, | selling | were bringing | the |

them said, "What I have is mine and I am afraid I might need it all myself." Instead, they felt a love and responsibility for each other. They recognized they were all partners in the work of God, so all things were shared. God was supplying their needs, and they believed He would continue to provide. The same attitude that sprang up after they were first filled on the Day of Pentecost still prevailed (2:4,5). Again, there was no compulsion. Their sharing was simply an expression of their love and their unity of mind and heart.

This does not mean they turned away from unbelievers who were in need. The Bible urges Christians to be considerate of the poor and to do good to all men, "especially unto them who are of the household of faith," that is, the believers who are in the family of God (Galatians 6:10). Christians have a special responsibility to help fellow believers who are in need.

**neither said any of them that ought of the things which he possessed was his own:** Not one of them claimed any of his goods as his own, *TCNT* . . . no one claimed his belongings just for himself, *Berkeley* . . . And nobody called anything he had his own, *Beck*.

**but they had all things common:** . . . but everything was held for the common use, *TCNT* . . . but everything they had was common property, *Weymouth* . . . but they shared everything that they had, *Williams* . . . was for the use of all, *Fenton*.

**4:33.** In answer to their prayer, the apostles were able to keep on giving witness to the resurrection of the Lord Jesus with great power, that is, with mighty deeds of supernatural power. At this point the apostles were still the chief channels of the miraculous power of God, just as they were the primary witnesses to the resurrection of Jesus. Apparently, this continued to be so for some time. Much later, the apostle Paul declared that through him the signs of an apostle were truly done among the Corinthians in all patient endurance with all kinds of miraculous signs, wonders, and deeds of supernatural power (2 Corinthians 12:12).

This implies also that the thousands of believers were still looking to the apostles, not only to give them teaching but to be the primary ones who were doing the work of God. Later, God did begin to use others. Even at this point, however, the work of the Spirit was not limited to the apostles, for the Word says "great grace was upon them all" (the believers). That is, free grace, the wonderful unmerited favor of God, was mightily upon them all. Grace is also manifested through the gracious gifts of the Spirit, the *charismata*, and these Spirit-filled believers were open to the distribution of His gifts by the Holy Spirit as He willed. (Compare 1 Corinthians 12:11.)

**33. And with great power gave the apostles witness of the resurrection of the Lord Jesus:** The Apostles continued with great power to bear their testimony to the resurrection of Jesus, their Master, *TCNT* . . . propagated the evidence, *Fenton* . . . rendered testimony, *Concordant* . . . told the truth, *Beck* . . . with great effect, *Weymouth*.

**and great grace was upon them all:** . . . great favour, *Rotherham* . . . and divine help was given to them all abundantly, *TCNT* . . . and much good will rested, *Beck* . . . grace rested liberally on all of them, *Berkeley* . . . all held in high esteem, *NEB* . . . God's favour rested richly on them all, *Williams* . . . a wonderful spirit of generosity, *Phillips* . . . goodwill, *Fenton*.

**4:34.** This verse shows a special way in which the grace and graciousness of God were expressed through the believers. There was a gracious gift of giving of help. No one lacked, that is, no one was in need or a needy person, for as many as were owners of fields or houses were selling them and kept bringing the price of the things that were sold.

The Greek here does not mean that everyone sold his property at once. Rather, from time to time someone would sell a piece of property, then later another would sell another piece as the Lord brought the need to their attention.

**34. Neither was there any among them that lacked:** There was not a needy person among them, *RSV* . . . Indeed, there was no poverty among them, *TCNT* . . . And, in fact, there was not a needy man among them, *Weymouth* . . . Not one among them suffered need, *Berkeley* . . . Neither was there one indigent person, *Campbell* . . . no one among them was needy, *Sawyer* . . . was ever in want, *JB*.

**for as many as were possessors of lands or houses sold them:** . . . for all who were owners of, *TCNT* . . . proceeded to sell them, one by one, *Williams*.

**and brought the prices of the things that were sold:** . . . and continued to bring the money received for the things sold, *Williams* . . . and bring the proceeds of the sales, *Beck*.

| **4940.6** noun acc pl fem | **3450.1** art gen pl | **3958.3** verb gen pl neu part pres mid | **2504.1** conj | **4935.25** verb 3pl indic imperf act | **3706.2** prep |
|---|---|---|---|---|---|
| τιμὰς | τῶν | πιπρασκομένων | **35.** καὶ | ἐτίθουν | παρὰ |
| *timas* | *tōn* | *pipraskomenōn* | *kai* | *etithoun* | *para* |
| moneys | the | having been sold, | and | were laying | at |

| **3450.8** art acc pl masc | **4087.7** noun acc pl masc | **3450.1** art gen pl | **646.5** noun gen pl masc | **1233.5** verb 3sing indic imperf mid |
|---|---|---|---|---|
| τοὺς | πόδας | τῶν | ἀποστόλων· | ˊ διεδίδοτο |
| *tous* | *podas* | *tōn* | *apostolōn* | *diedidoto* |
| the | feet | of the | apostles; | distribution was being made |

35.a.**Var:** 01ℵ,02A 03B-org,05D,08E,Lach Treg,Alf,Tisc,We/Ho Weis,Sod

| **1233.6** verb 3sing indic imperf pass | **1156.2** conj | **1524.4** adj dat sing masc | **2502.1** conj | **300.1** partic |
|---|---|---|---|---|
| [a☆ διεδίδετο ] | δὲ | ἑκάστῳ | καθότι | ἄν |
| *diedideto* | *de* | *hekastō* | *kathoti* | *an* |
| [ it was being distributed ] | and | to each | according as | |

36.a.**Txt:** 025P,044,33 byz.sa. **Var:** 01ℵ,02A,03B,05D 08E,bo.Lach,Treg,Alf Word,Tisc,We/Ho,Weis Sod,UBS/☆

| **4948.3** indef-pron nom sing | **5367.3** noun acc sing fem | **2174.44** verb 3sing indic imperf act | **2472.1** name nom masc | **2473.1** name masc |
|---|---|---|---|---|
| τις | χρείαν | εἶχεν. | **36.** ˊ Ἰωσῆς | [a☆ Ἰωσὴφ ] |
| *tis* | *chreian* | *eichen* | *Iōsēs* | *Iōsēph* |
| anyone | need | was having. | Joses | [ Joseph ] |

| **1156.2** conj | **3450.5** art nom sing masc | **1926.13** verb nom sing masc part aor pass | **915.1** name nom masc | **5097.3** prep |
|---|---|---|---|---|
| δὲ | ὁ | ἐπικληθεὶς | Βαρναβᾶς | ˊ ὑπὸ |
| *de* | *ho* | *epiklētheis* | *Barnabas* | *hupo* |
| and | the | having been called | Barnabas | by |

36.b.**Txt:** 05D,byz. **Var:** 01ℵ,02A,03B,08E 025P,Lach,Treg,Alf Word,Tisc,We/Ho,Weis Sod,UBS/☆

| **570.3** prep | **3450.1** art gen pl | **646.5** noun gen pl masc | **3614.16** rel-pron sing neu | **1498.4** verb 3sing indic pres act |
|---|---|---|---|---|
| [b☆ ἀπὸ ] | τῶν | ἀποστόλων, | ὅ | ἐστιν |
| *apo* | *tōn* | *apostolōn* | *ho* | *estin* |
| [ from ] | the | apostles | which | is, |

| **3148.2** verb sing neu part pres mid | **5048.1** noun nom sing masc | **3735.2** noun gen sing fem | **2993.1** name nom sing masc |
|---|---|---|---|
| μεθερμηνευόμενον, | υἱὸς | παρακλήσεως, | Λευίτης, |
| *methermēneuomenon* | *huios* | *paraklēseōs* | *Leuitēs* |
| being interpreted, | Son | of consolation, | a Levite, |

| **2926.1** name-adj nom sing masc | **3450.3** art dat sing | **1079.3** noun dat sing neu | **5062.5** verb gen sing part pres act | **840.4** prs-pron dat sing |
|---|---|---|---|---|
| Κύπριος | τῷ | γένει, | **37.** ὑπάρχοντος | αὐτῷ |
| *Kuprios* | *tō* | *genei* | *huparchontos* | *autō* |
| a Cypriot | by the | birth, | having | to him |

| **67.2** noun gen sing masc | **4310.10** verb nom sing masc part aor act | **5179.14** verb 3sing indic aor act | **3450.16** art sing neu | **5371.1** noun sing neu | **2504.1** conj |
|---|---|---|---|---|---|
| ἀγροῦ | πωλήσας | ἤνεγκεν | τὸ | χρῆμα | καὶ |
| *agrou* | *pōlēsas* | *ēnenken* | *to* | *chrēma* | *kai* |
| land, | having sold | brought | the | money | and |

37.a.**Txt:** p57,p74,02A 03B,05D,025P,byz. We/Ho,Sod **Var:** 01ℵ,08E,Tisc,Weis UBS/☆

| **4935.10** verb 3sing indic aor act | **3706.2** prep | **4242.1** prep | **3450.8** art acc pl masc | **4087.7** noun acc pl masc | **3450.1** art gen pl |
|---|---|---|---|---|---|
| ἔθηκεν | ˊ παρὰ | [a πρὸς ] | τοὺς | πόδας | τῶν |
| *ethēken* | *para* | *pros* | *tous* | *podas* | *tōn* |
| laid | at | [ before ] | the | feet | of the |

| **646.5** noun gen pl masc | **433.1** noun nom sing masc | **1156.2** conj | **4948.3** indef-pron nom sing | **366.3** name masc | **3549.4** noun dat sing neu |
|---|---|---|---|---|---|
| ἀποστόλων. | **5:1.** Ἀνὴρ | δέ | τις | Ἀνανίας | ὀνόματι, |
| *apostolōn* | *Anēr* | *de* | *tis* | *Ananias* | *onomati* |
| apostles. | Man | but | a certain, | Ananias | by name, |

**4:35.** Those who sold the property brought the money and laid it at the apostles' feet. They gave it over to the apostles and gave the apostles full authority to use it as they saw fit. The apostles were faithful to this responsibility, and they distributed the money here and there to each needy person in proportion to the need.

This was an added responsibility put upon the apostles. At first they undoubtedly shared what they had, as did all the rest. But now with the additional 5,000, plus others who were being added to their number daily, the number of needy ones seems to have increased. Thus the distribution to meet their needs was a growing task. But the indication is that the apostles, as leaders and fellow believers, accepted the additional work without complaint.

The distribution of the money was a continuing ministry. As long as there was a need, and as new needs arose, the apostles were made aware of the need and help was given in proportion to the need. They did not help a person once and then forget him or her. On the other hand, there is evidence from later passages that as time went on fewer people needed this monetary help. The Bible always encourages those who are able to work to find employment, so they can be able to give to others and to the work of God. (Compare Ephesians 4:28.)

**4:36.** After making the general statement that those who had land sold it, Luke gave a specific example. This particular example is important because it provides a background for the events of the next chapter.

"Joses" is from a Greek form of *Joseph,* a very common name among the Jews. The apostles gave him special recognition by giving him a very distinctive surname or additional name of "Barnabas."

It is not clear whether the apostles gave him this name at this time or whether they had already done so because of his previous actions. From what is recorded about Barnabas later, he had a character which fitted the meaning of the name *Barnabas,* "son of consolation," which also means "son of exhortation or encouragement." *Son of* was often used in Hebrew and Aramaic to indicate a person's character or nature.

**4:37.** When Barnabas saw the need, his spirit was stirred. He sold a field, brought the money, and laid it at the feet of the apostles. The Greek indicates it was agricultural land, and it was probably of good quality and brought a good price. But the amount of money is not important. From what the Bible says about Barnabas, it seems certain it was the spirit in which he gave that impressed the apostles. He was a good example of those who were concerned about the needy believers.

**5:1.** With the example of Barnabas before them, two individuals who had joined the believing community conspired to get the same

**35. And laid them down at the apostles' feet:** . . . and gave it to the Apostles, *Weymouth* . . . They used to lay them, *NAB* . . . They put the proceeds at the disposal of, *Noli* . . . They gave it to the missionaries, *NLT.*

**and distribution was made unto every man according as he had need:** . . . then they were shared with everyone, *Goodspeed* . . . and then everyone received a share in proportion to his needs, *TCNT* . . . it was then divided up according to every man's need, *Williams C.K.* . . . then distribution was continuously made to everyone in proportion to his need, *Williams* . . . It was divided to each one, *NLT* . . . Then each person was given what he needed, *NCV* . . . as anyone might have necessity, *Wilson.*

**36. And Joses, who by the apostles was surnamed Barnabas:** And Joseph, *ASV* . . . for example, *Beck* . . . who had received from the Apostles the additional name of Barnabas, *TCNT* . . . was called Barnabas by the apostles, *MLNT.*

**(which is, being interpreted, The son of consolation,):** . . . when translated, *Rotherham* . . . Son of exhortation, *ASV* . . . which means The Preacher, *TCNT* . . . signifying Son of Encouragement, *Weymouth* . . . One who encourages, *TNT.*

**a Levite, and of the country of Cyprus:** . . . a native of Cyprus, *Weymouth* . . . a Cyprian Levite, *Berkeley* . . . a Cyprian by birth, *Swann* . . . a Cypriot by race, *TNT.*

**37. Having land, sold it:** . . . having a field, *ASV* . . . sold a farm that belonged to him, *TCNT* . . . sold land which he owned, *Williams C.K.*

**and brought the money, and laid it at the apostles' feet:** . . . and brought the proceeds which he deposited, *Berkeley* . . . brought the payment, *Swann* . . . put it at the disposal of the apostles, *Williams* . . . and made a donation of the money, *NAB.*

**1. But a certain man named Ananias:** There was, however, a man named Ananias, *TCNT* . . . Another man named, *NAB.*

| 4713.1 prep | 4408.1 name dat fem | 4408.2 name dat fem | 3450.11 art dat sing fem | 1129.3 noun dat sing fem | 840.3 prs-pron gen sing |
|---|---|---|---|---|---|
| σὺν | ⸀ Σαπφείρῃ | [ Σαπφίρῃ ] | τῇ | γυναικὶ | αὐτοῦ, |
| sun | Sappheirē | Sapphirē | tē | gunaiki | autou |
| with | Sapphira | [ idem ] | the | wife | his, |

| 4310.6 verb 3sing indic aor act | 2905.1 noun sing neu | 2504.1 conj | 3420.2 verb 3sing indic aor mid | 570.3 prep | 3450.10 art gen sing fem |
|---|---|---|---|---|---|
| ἐπώλησεν | κτῆμα, | 2. καὶ | ἐνοσφίσατο | ἀπὸ | τῆς |
| epōlēsen | ktēma | kai | enosphisato | apo | tēs |
| sold | property, | and | kept back | from | the |

2.a.**Txt:** 05D,025P,byz. Sod
**Var:** 01ℵ,02A,03B,08E Lach,Treg,Alf,Tisc We/Ho,Weis,UBS/☆

| 4940.2 noun gen sing fem | 4774.2 verb gen sing fem part perf act | 4774.3 verb gen sing fem part perf act | 2504.1 conj | 3450.10 art gen sing fem |
|---|---|---|---|---|
| τιμῆς, | ⸀ συνειδυίας | [a☆ συνειδυίης ] | καὶ | τῆς |
| timēs | suneiduias | suneiduiēs | kai | tēs |
| money, | having been aware of | [ idem ] | also | the |

2.b.**Txt:** 08E,025P,byz.sa. bo.
**Var:** 01ℵ,02A,03B,05D Lach,Treg,Alf,Tisc We/Ho,Weis,Sod UBS/☆

| 1129.2 noun gen sing fem | 840.3 prs-pron gen sing | 2504.1 conj | 5179.17 verb nom sing masc part aor act | 3183.1 noun sing neu | 4948.10 indef-pron sing neu |
|---|---|---|---|---|---|
| γυναικός | ⸂b αὐτοῦ, ⸃ | καὶ | ἐνέγκας | μέρος | τι |
| gunaikos | autou | kai | enenkas | meros | ti |
| wife | his, | and | having brought | a part | certain |

| 3706.2 prep | 3450.8 art acc pl masc | 4087.7 noun acc pl masc | 3450.1 art gen pl | 646.5 noun gen pl masc | 4935.10 verb 3sing indic aor act |
|---|---|---|---|---|---|
| παρὰ | τοὺς | πόδας | τῶν | ἀποστόλων | ἔθηκεν. |
| para | tous | podas | tōn | apostolōn | ethēken |
| at | the | feet | of the | apostles | laid, |

3.a.**Var:** 01ℵ,02A,03B 08E,Lach,Treg,Alf,Tisc We/Ho,Weis,Sod UBS/☆

| 1500.5 verb 3sing indic aor act | 1156.2 conj | 3450.5 art nom sing masc | 3935.1 name nom masc | 366.2 name voc masc | 1296.1 adv |
|---|---|---|---|---|---|
| 3. εἶπεν | δὲ | [a☆+ ὁ ] | Πέτρος, | Ἀνανία, | ⸀ διατί |
| eipen | de | ho | Petros | Anania | diati |
| Said | and | | Peter, | Ananias, | why |

| 1217.2 prep | 4949.9 intr-pron sing neu | 3997.3 verb 3sing indic aor act | 3450.5 art nom sing masc | 4423.1 noun nom sing masc |
|---|---|---|---|---|
| [☆ διὰ | τί ] | ἐπλήρωσεν | ὁ | Σατανᾶς |
| dia | ti | eplērōsen | ho | Satanas |
| [ because | why ] | did fill | | Satan |

| 3450.12 art acc sing fem | 2559.4 noun acc sing fem | 4622.2 prs-pron gen 2sing | 5409.7 verb inf aor mid | 4622.4 prs-pron acc 2sing | 3450.16 art sing neu |
|---|---|---|---|---|---|
| τὴν | καρδίαν | σου, | ψεύσασθαί | σε | τὸ |
| tēn | kardian | sou | pseusasthai | se | to |
| the | heart | your, | to lie | you | the |

3.b.**Var:** 05D,025P,sa. Alf

| 4011.1 noun sing neu | 3450.16 art sing neu | 39.1 adj sing | 2504.1 conj | 3420.3 verb inf aor mid | 4622.4 prs-pron acc 2sing |
|---|---|---|---|---|---|
| πνεῦμα | τὸ | ἅγιον, | καὶ | νοσφίσασθαι | [b+ σε ] |
| pneuma | to | hagion | kai | nosphisasthai | se |
| Spirit | the | Holy, | and | to keep back | [ you ] |

| 570.3 prep | 3450.10 art gen sing fem | 4940.2 noun gen sing fem | 3450.2 art gen sing | 5399.1 noun gen sing neu | 3644.1 adv |
|---|---|---|---|---|---|
| ἀπὸ | τῆς | τιμῆς | τοῦ | χωρίου; | 4. οὐχὶ |
| apo | tēs | timēs | tou | chōriou | ouchi |
| from | the | price | of the | estate? | Not |

| 3176.14 verb sing neu part pres act | 4622.3 prs-pron dat 2sing | 3176.29 verb 3sing indic imperf act | 2504.1 conj | 3958.5 verb sing neu part aor pass |
|---|---|---|---|---|
| μένον | σοὶ | ἔμενεν; | καὶ | πραθὲν |
| menon | soi | emenen | kai | prathen |
| remaining | to you | was it remaining? | and | having been sold, |

kind of attention given to him without experiencing the pain of sacrifice. So they, as Barnabas did, sold a field, a piece of farm property. But in every other way what they did was in strong contrast to Barnabas' actions.

Although they listened to the teaching of the disciples and saw the miracles, whether Ananias and Sapphira were really Christians like Barnabas is not specifically stated. But verse 13 says that the divine judgment upon the couple had the following effect: "Of the rest durst no man join himself to them." This could be an indication that Ananias and Sapphira were just such "joiners."

"Ananias" is used in the Greek Septuagint version for both the Hebrew *Hananiah* ("the Lord is gracious") and *Ananiah* ("the Lord protects"). "Sapphira" may mean a sapphire stone, which was considered very precious, or it may be an Aramaic word meaning "fair" or "beautiful." Someone has suggested that their names were not appropriate.

**5:2.** Unfortunately, sometimes those who claim to be believers become liars and deceivers. Ananias made up his mind to keep back part of the price. "Kept back" (*enosphisato*) is from the same verb translated "purloining" (Titus 2:10) in the sense of stealing or embezzling. The Septuagint version of Joshua 7:1 uses it of Achan's sin when he took from Jericho things that were to be dedicated to God. The idea is that Ananias appropriated part of the money for his own benefit and set it aside. Sapphira shared the knowledge of this and was equally guilty since she was in full accord with her husband's actions. Ananias brought a certain part of the money and laid it at the apostles' feet, giving the impression that, like Barnabas, he had done a noble deed.

**5:3.** Peter, acting as representative and spokesman for the 12 apostles, knew immediately what was done. He did not have spies out to report to him, but he had the Holy Spirit. Perhaps this was revealed to him through one of the Holy Spirit's gifts of revelation.

Peter then asked Ananias why Satan (the Satan, the Adversary—compare Revelation 12:9,10) had filled his heart to lie to the Holy Spirit and keep back for himself part of the price of the field. The question "why?" draws attention to the fact that their action was voluntary. There was no excuse for what they did.

**5:4.** Peter made it very clear that no one had asked them to sell their field; they were under no compulsion to sell it. Before they sold it, it remained theirs and could still have remained theirs. After they sold it, the money was still in their power, that is, they had the authority over what they should do with it. There was nothing compelling them to give it all. What they had conceived in their hearts was a lie, not to men but to God.

**with Sapphira his wife:** . . . in partnership with his wife Sapphira, *Williams.*
**sold a possession:** . . . sold some property, *TCNT* . . . sells an acquisition, *Concordant* . . . sold some real estate, *Berkeley* . . . an estate, *Fenton.*

**2. And kept back part of the price:** . . . retained, *Berkeley* . . . deducted part of the price, *Fenton* . . . some of the proceeds, *TCNT* . . . but...dishonestly kept back part of the price received for it, *Weymouth* . . . embezzles from the price, *Concordant* . . . and carried away (part) of the price and concealed it, *Murdock* . . . kept back for themselves a part of the money, *Williams* . . . appropriated a part, *Wilson* . . . reserved part of the price for himself, *Phillips* . . . by fraud, *Douay.*
**his wife also being privy to it:** . . . his wife also being aware of it, *HBIE* . . . with her connivance, *TCNT* . . . with her full knowledge and consent, *Weymouth* . . . with her knowledge and agreement, *Klingensmith.*
**and brought a certain part:** . . . though he brought the rest, *Weymouth.*
**and laid it at the apostles' feet:** . . . and gave it to the Apostles, *Weymouth.*

**3. But Peter said, Ananias, why hath Satan filled thine heart to lie to the Holy Ghost:** . . . how is it that Satan has so taken possession of your heart, that you have defrauded the holy Spirit, *TCNT* . . . the Adversary, *Young* . . . so possessed your mind, *NEB* . . . to falsify, *Concordant* . . . so that you would cheat, *Berkeley* . . . that you should try to deceive the Holy Spirit, *Weymouth* . . . thou shouldest be false, *Rotherham.*
**and to keep back part of the price of the land?:** . . . and dishonestly keep back part of the price paid you for this land, *Weymouth* . . . and covertly withdraw some of the field's price, *Berkeley* . . . keep a part of the receipts from the sale, *Adams.*

**4. Whiles it remained, was it not thine own?:** While it was unsold, was it not your own? *TCNT* . . . you could have kept it, couldn't you? *Adams.*

**Acts 5:5**

| 1706.1 prep | 3450.11 art dat sing fem | 4528.6 adj dat 2sing fem | 1833.3 noun dat sing fem | 5062.12 verb 3sing indic imperf act | 4949.9 intr-pron sing neu |
|---|---|---|---|---|---|
| ἐν | τῇ | σῇ | ἐξουσίᾳ | ὑπῆρχεν; | τί |
| *en* | *tē* | *sē* | *exousia* | *huperchen* | *ti* |
| in | the | your | authority | was it? | why |

| 3617.1 conj | 4935.28 verb 2sing indic aor mid | 1706.1 prep | 3450.11 art dat sing fem | 2559.3 noun dat sing fem | 4622.2 prs-pron gen 2sing |
|---|---|---|---|---|---|
| ὅτι | ἔθου | ἐν | τῇ | καρδίᾳ | σου |
| *hoti* | *ethou* | *en* | *tē* | *kardia* | *sou* |
| that | did you purpose | in | the | heart | your |

| 3450.16 art sing neu | 4088.1 noun sing neu | 3642.17 dem-pron sing neu | 3620.2 partic | 5409.6 verb 2sing indic aor mid | 442.8 noun dat pl masc |
|---|---|---|---|---|---|
| τὸ | πρᾶγμα | τοῦτο; | οὐκ | ἐψεύσω | ἀνθρώποις, |
| *to* | *pragma* | *touto* | *ouk* | *epseusō* | *anthrōpois* |
| the | deed | this? | Not | you did lie | to men, |

5.a.**Var:** 01ℵ,02A,03B 08E,025P,Gries,Lach Treg,Alf,Word,Tisc We/Ho,Weis,Sod UBS/☆

| 233.2 conj | 3450.3 art dat sing | 2296.3 noun dat sing masc | 189.11 verb nom sing masc part pres act | 1156.2 conj | 3450.5 art nom sing masc |
|---|---|---|---|---|---|
| ἀλλὰ | τῷ | θεῷ. | **5.** Ἀκούων | δὲ | [a☆+ ὁ ] |
| *alla* | *tō* | *theō* | *Akouōn* | *de* | *ho* |
| but | | to God. | Hearing | and | |

| 366.3 name masc | 3450.8 art acc pl masc | 3030.8 noun acc pl masc | 3642.8 dem-pron acc pl masc | 3959.11 verb nom sing masc part aor act |
|---|---|---|---|---|
| Ἀνανίας | τοὺς | λόγους | τούτους, | πεσὼν |
| *Ananias* | *tous* | *logous* | *toutous* | *pesōn* |
| Ananias | the | words | these, | having fallen down |

| 1621.1 verb 3sing indic aor act | 2504.1 conj | 1090.33 verb 3sing indic aor mid | 5238.1 noun nom sing masc | 3144.2 adj nom sing masc | 1894.3 prep |
|---|---|---|---|---|---|
| ἐξέψυξεν· | καὶ | ἐγένετο | φόβος | μέγας | ἐπὶ |
| *exepsuxen* | *kai* | *egeneto* | *phobos* | *megas* | *epi* |
| he expired. | And | came | fear | great | upon |

5.b.**Txt:** 08E,025P,byz. **Var:** 01ℵ-org,02A,03B 05D,sa.bo.Lach,Treg Alf,Tisc,We/Ho,Weis Sod,UBS/☆

| 3820.8 adj acc pl masc | 3450.8 art acc pl masc | 189.16 verb acc pl masc part pres act | 3642.18 dem-pron pl neu | 448.11 verb nom pl masc part aor act |
|---|---|---|---|---|
| πάντας | τοὺς | ἀκούοντας | ⸂b ταῦτα. ⸃ | **6.** ἀναστάντες |
| *pantas* | *tous* | *akouontas* | *tauta* | *anastantes* |
| all | the | hearing | these things. | Having risen |

| 1156.2 conj | 3450.7 art nom pl masc | 3365.5 adj comp nom pl masc | 4810.1 verb 3pl indic aor act | 840.6 prs-pron acc sing masc |
|---|---|---|---|---|
| δὲ | οἱ | νεώτεροι | συνέστειλαν | αὐτὸν, |
| *de* | *hoi* | *neōteroi* | *sunesteilan* | *auton* |
| and | the | younger men | wrapped in a shroud | him, |

| 2504.1 conj | 1613.4 verb nom pl masc part aor act | 2267.1 verb 3pl indic aor act | 1090.33 verb 3sing indic aor mid | 1156.2 conj | 5453.1 conj |
|---|---|---|---|---|---|
| καὶ | ἐξενέγκαντες | ἔθαψαν. | **7.** Ἐγένετο | δὲ | ὡς |
| *kai* | *exenenkantes* | *ethapsan* | *Egeneto* | *de* | *hōs* |
| and | having carried out | buried. | It came to pass | and | about |

| 5443.6 noun gen pl fem | 4980.2 num card gen | 1286.1 noun sing neu | 2504.1 conj | 3450.9 art nom sing fem | 1129.1 noun nom sing fem | 840.3 prs-pron gen sing |
|---|---|---|---|---|---|---|
| ὡρῶν | τριῶν | διάστημα | καὶ | ἡ | γυνὴ | αὐτοῦ |
| *hōrōn* | *triōn* | *diastēma* | *kai* | *hē* | *gunē* | *autou* |
| hours | three | afterwards | also | the | wife | his, |

| 3231.1 partic | 3471.23 verb nom sing fem part perf act | 3450.16 art sing neu | 1090.11 verb sing neu part perf act | 1511.3 verb 3sing indic aor act |
|---|---|---|---|---|
| μὴ | εἰδυῖα | τὸ | γεγονὸς | εἰσῆλθεν. |
| *mē* | *eiduia* | *to* | *gegonos* | *eisēlthen* |
| not | having known | what | having come to pass, | came in. |

Satan was behind what Ananias and Sapphira did. They were guilty of jealousy, unbelief, and love of money. This grieved the Spirit of the Lord. These things had not happened overnight. By the time they conspired together, Satan had filled their hearts (their whole inner beings), and they followed a pathway of deceit.

They could have resisted Satan (James 4:7). But they let pride, self, and the love of money possess them. The love of money is the root of all (kinds of) evil (1 Timothy 6:10). Once the love of money takes possession of a person, there is no evil that he cannot or will not do. With the love of money in control, a person will do things he never would do otherwise, including murder and every other sin. It is clear also that if a person is filled with the love of money he cannot love God (Matthew 6:24).

In lying to the Holy Spirit who was guiding the Church, the believers, and the apostles, Ananias and Sapphira were also lying to God. This comparison in verses 3 and 4 makes it clear that the Holy Spirit is a divine Person.

**5:5.** Judgment was immediate. While Ananias was still listening to Peter, he fell down and breathed out his last breath. This sudden death may seem severe punishment. It was indeed. But God brought this judgment near the beginning of the Church's history to let them know what He thinks of unbelief, greed, and self-seeking hypocrisy that lies to the Holy Spirit, lying not just to men but to God. As Peter later reminded believers in 1 Peter 4:17, "The time is come that judgment must begin at the house of God: and if it first begin at us, what shall the end be of them that obey not the gospel of God?"

It should be emphasized also that Ananias' lie was premeditated. When he died "great fear (including terror and awe) came on all" who heard about it. They knew now that the Holy Spirit is a mighty power. He is indeed holy, and it does not pay to lie to Him.

**5:6.** They did not wait long to bury people in those days. Peter and the apostles called in some younger men. Some consider these a class of younger men who assisted the elders of the church. More probably, they were just some of the younger believers who were present. These young men quickly wrapped Ananias in a linen winding sheet, took him out of the city, and buried him. Because of the seriousness of his sin, there was no funeral service or procession, and none of the weeping and mourning that was usually expected among the Jews.

**5:7.** About 3 hours later Sapphira came in, not knowing what had happened to her husband. She obviously was looking for commendation and praise because of what she hoped had been accepted as a generous gift.

**and after it was sold, was it not in thine own power?:** . . . was not the money at your own disposal, *TCNT* . . . you could have used the money any way you wanted, *Everyday, SEB* . . . the money was under your control, *Noli.*

**why hast thou conceived this thing in thine heart?:** How is it that you have cherished this design in your heart, *Weymouth* . . . How could you have the heart to do such a thing, *Williams* . . . How could you think of committing such a sin? *Noli* . . . Why did you think of doing this? *Everyday* . . . How have you let this thing find a place in your heart? *Williams C.K.*

**thou hast not lied unto men, but unto God:** You have not defrauded men, but God, *TCNT* . . . You did not cheat men but God, *Berkeley.*

**5. And Ananias hearing these words fell down, and gave up the ghost:** And as Ananias heard these words he fell and expired, *Rotherham* . . . fell down dead, *Weymouth* . . . breathed his last, *Alford* . . . he collapsed and died, *Phillips.*

**and great fear came on all them that heard these things:** This made a profound impression, *JB* . . . and all who heard the words were awestruck, *Weymouth* . . . a strange awe seized everybody who heard it, *Williams* . . . And all who heard of it were terrified, *Beck* . . . Those who witnessed the event were appalled, *Noli.*

**6. And the young men arose:** But the younger men got up, *TCNT* . . . came forward, *NAB.*

**wound him up:** . . . and after winding the body in a sheet, *TCNT* . . . covered his body, *NLT* . . . enshroud him, *Concordant* . . . wrapped up the body, *NAB.*

**and carried him out, and buried him:**

**7. And it was about the space of three hours after:** And it came to pass, after about three hours interval, *Rotherham* . . . About three hours later, *Everyday.*

**when his wife, not knowing what was done, came in:** . . . still not knowing, *Klingensmith* . . . not knowing what had happened, *RSV* . . . ignorant of what had occurred, *Berkeley.*

# Acts 5:8

8.a.**Txt:** 025P,byz. **Var:** 01ℵ,02A,03B,05D 08E,Lach,Treg,Alf,Tisc We/Ho,Weis,Sod UBS/☆

| 552.6 verb 3sing indic aor pass | 1156.2 conj | 840.11 prs-pron dat sing fem | 4242.1 prep | 840.12 prs-pron acc sing fem |
|---|---|---|---|---|
| **8.** ἀπεκρίθη | δὲ | ⸂ αὐτῇ | [a☆ πρὸς | αὐτὴν ] |
| *apekrithē* | *de* | *autē* | *pros* | *autēn* |
| Answered | and | her | [ to | her ] |

8.b.**Txt:** 05D,08E,025P byz.Sod **Var:** 01ℵ,02A,03B,Lach Treg,Alf,Tisc,We/Ho Weis,UBS/☆

| 3450.5 art nom sing masc | 3935.1 name nom masc | 1500.12 verb 2sing impr aor act | 1466.4 prs-pron dat 1sing | 1479.1 conj | 4965.7 dem-pron gen sing neu |
|---|---|---|---|---|---|
| ⸂b ὁ ⸃ | Πέτρος, | Εἰπέ | μοι | εἰ | τοσούτου |
| *ho* | *Petros* | *Eipe* | *moi* | *ei* | *tosoutou* |
| | Peter, | Tell | me | if | for so much |

| 3450.16 art sing neu | 5399.2 noun sing neu | 586.22 verb 2pl indic aor mid | 3450.9 art nom sing fem | 1156.2 conj | 1500.5 verb 3sing indic aor act |
|---|---|---|---|---|---|
| τὸ | χωρίον | ἀπέδοσθε; | Ἡ | δὲ | εἶπεν, |
| *to* | *chōrion* | *apedosthe* | *Hē* | *de* | *eipen* |
| the | estate | you sold? | The | and | said, |

9.a.**Txt:** 02A,byz.sa.bo. **Var:** 01ℵ,03B,05D,Lach Treg,Alf,Tisc,We/Ho Weis,Sod,UBS/☆

| 3346.1 intrj | 4965.7 dem-pron gen sing neu | 3450.5 art nom sing masc | 1156.2 conj | 3935.1 name nom masc | 1500.5 verb 3sing indic aor act |
|---|---|---|---|---|---|
| Ναί, | τοσούτου. | **9.** Ὁ | δὲ | Πέτρος | ⸂a εἶπεν ⸃ |
| *Nai* | *tosoutou* | *Ho* | *de* | *Petros* | *eipen* |
| Yes, | for so much. | | And | Peter | said |

| 4242.1 prep | 840.12 prs-pron acc sing fem | 4949.9 intr-pron sing neu | 3617.1 conj | 4707.6 verb 3sing indic aor pass | 5050.3 prs-pron dat 2pl |
|---|---|---|---|---|---|
| πρὸς | αὐτήν, | Τί | ὅτι | συνεφωνήθη | ὑμῖν |
| *pros* | *autēn* | *Ti* | *hoti* | *sunephōnēthē* | *humin* |
| to | her, | Why | that | agreed together | you |

| 3847.8 verb inf aor act | 3450.16 art sing neu | 4011.1 noun sing neu | 2935.2 noun gen sing masc | 1481.20 verb 2sing impr aor mid | 3450.7 art nom pl masc |
|---|---|---|---|---|---|
| πειράσαι | τὸ | πνεῦμα | κυρίου; | ἰδοὺ, | οἱ |
| *peirasai* | *to* | *pneuma* | *kuriou* | *idou* | *hoi* |
| to tempt | the | Spirit | of Lord? | Look! | the |

| 4087.4 noun nom pl masc | 3450.1 art gen pl | 2267.2 verb gen pl masc part aor act | 3450.6 art acc sing masc | 433.4 noun acc sing masc | 4622.2 prs-pron gen 2sing |
|---|---|---|---|---|---|
| πόδες | τῶν | θαψάντων | τὸν | ἄνδρα | σου |
| *podes* | *tōn* | *thapsantōn* | *ton* | *andra* | *sou* |
| feet | of the | having buried | the | husband | your |

| 1894.3 prep | 3450.11 art dat sing fem | 2351.3 noun dat sing fem | 2504.1 conj | 1613.6 verb 3pl indic fut act | 4622.4 prs-pron acc 2sing |
|---|---|---|---|---|---|
| ἐπὶ | τῇ | θύρᾳ, | καὶ | ἐξοίσουσίν | σε. |
| *epi* | *tē* | *thura* | *kai* | *exoisousin* | *se* |
| at | the | door, | and | they shall carry out | you. |

10.a.**Txt:** 08E,025P,byz. **Var:** 01ℵ,02A,03B,05D Lach,Treg,Alf,Tisc We/Ho,Weis,Sod UBS/☆

| 3959.5 verb 3sing indic aor act | 1156.2 conj | 3777.1 adv | 3706.2 prep | 4242.1 prep |
|---|---|---|---|---|
| **10.** Ἔπεσεν | δὲ | παραχρῆμα | ⸂ παρὰ | [a☆ πρὸς ] |
| *Epesen* | *de* | *parachrēma* | *para* | *pros* |
| She fell down | and | immediately | at | [ before ] |

| 3450.8 art acc pl masc | 4087.7 noun acc pl masc | 840.3 prs-pron gen sing | 2504.1 conj | 1621.1 verb 3sing indic aor act | 1511.16 verb nom pl masc part aor act |
|---|---|---|---|---|---|
| τοὺς | πόδας | αὐτοῦ | καὶ | ἐξέψυξεν· | εἰσελθόντες |
| *tous* | *podas* | *autou* | *kai* | *exepsuxen* | *eiselthontes* |
| the | feet | his | and | expired. | Having come in |

10.b.**Var:** 02A,Treg

| 1156.2 conj | 3450.7 art nom pl masc | 3358.4 noun nom pl masc | 2128.6 verb indic aor act | 2128.45 verb 3pl indic aor act | 840.12 prs-pron acc sing fem |
|---|---|---|---|---|---|
| δὲ | οἱ | νεανίσκοι | ⸂ εὗρον | [b εὗραν ] | αὐτὴν |
| *de* | *hoi* | *neaniskoi* | *heuron* | *heuran* | *autēn* |
| and | the | young | found | [ idem ] | her |

**5:8.** She did not see her husband, nor did she sense any of what she expected. Peter answered her inquiring look by asking her if she and her husband had sold the land for the amount he brought in. Peter thus gave her an opportunity to confess the truth. But she too lied.

Like her husband, Sapphira was not sensitive to the Holy Spirit. She too had allowed Satan to fill her heart. There's a lesson here for believers. If they remain sensitive to the Spirit, He is faithful to check, convict, and help them. They do not need to allow Satan to take control. The Bible says, "Submit yourselves therefore to God. Resist the devil, and he will flee from you" (James 4:7). Satan is not yet bound, He still goes about like a roaring lion seeking whom he may devour. Believers need to be vigilant, but they also need to keep calm and claim the victory over him (1 Peter 5:8,9).

**5:9.** Peter was just as severe with Sapphira as he had been with Ananias. His question clearly indicated he knew she and her husband had agreed together to tempt (test) the Holy Spirit. They were deliberately trying to see how far they could go in their disobedience without provoking God's wrath. They were also testing the Holy Spirit's knowledge, for they conspired secretly and acted as if they thought even the Holy Spirit would not know what they were doing. This was, in a sense, a denial of His deity.

Like the Israelites who complained to Moses, they acted as if they were just dealing with a man, but they were really putting God to the test (Exodus 17:2). They were acting presumptuously, what the Hebrew calls "with a high hand," and that was casting reproach on the Lord. Under the Law it deserved death (Numbers 15:30). Jesus recognized that it is the devil who tries to get believers to put God to the test in this way, and He reminded Satan of God's warning against this (Luke 4:12; Deuteronomy 6:16).

After his question, Peter directed Sapphira's attention to the young men at the door who had now returned from burying her husband. They would carry her out too. As in the case of his words to Ananias, Peter was not saying this as a result of his own thinking or his own reasoning. He was moved by the Holy Spirit to give this judgment.

**5:10.** Thus, by the same kind of miracle of divine judgment, Sapphira fell down immediately at Peter's feet and breathed out her last breath. The same young men then came in, found her dead, proceeded to carry her out, and then buried her beside Ananias.

Some people wrestle with the severity of God's judgment of Ananias and Sapphira. However, this was the advent of a new era. The Holy Spirit had just recently been poured out and the Church was in its infancy. In light of this, such harsh judgment created a reverent fear of the Lord which protected the Early Church. Believers learned that though God is a God of mercy, He also will send judgment on sin.

**8. And Peter answered unto her:** Peter at once questioned her, *Weymouth* . . . Peter said to her, *Williams C.K.* . . . asked her, *MLNT, Noli.*

**Tell me whether ye sold the land for so much?:** Tell me! was it for so much ye gave up the field, *Rotherham* . . . Is it true...that you sold the land for such and such a sum, *TCNT* . . . Tell me how much money you got for your field. Was it this much? *Everyday, NCV* . . . was this the price for which you sold the field? *TNT* . . . did you sell that piece of property, *NAB* . . . such a price? *Noli* . . . for this amount of money? *NLT.*

**And she said, Yea, for so much:** Yes, she said, that is right, *TNT* . . . Yes, that was the price, *NCV* . . . Yes, for so much, *MLNT* . . . Yes, that was the sum, *NAB* . . . the full amount, *TEV.*

**9. Then Peter said unto her:** Peter then came back at her, *Berkeley* . . . then asked her, *MLNT.*

**How is it that ye have agreed together:** . . . conspired together, *Campbell* . . . How could you two scheme, *NAB* . . . How could you two have talked together, *NLT.*

**to tempt the Spirit of the Lord?:** . . . to try, *ASV* . . . to put to the proof, *Rotherham* . . . to provoke, *TCNT* . . . about lying to, *NLT* . . . to put the Spirit of the Lord to the test, *Weymouth* . . . to defy the Holy Spirit? *Noli.*

**behold, the feet of them which have buried thy husband are at the door, and shall carry thee out:** Listen! The footsteps of those who, *TCNT* . . . are standing at the door, *NLT* . . . can be heard at the door. They stand ready to carry you out too, *NAB.*

**10. Then fell she down straightway at his feet, and yielded up the ghost:** At that, *NAB* . . . And she fell down immediately at his feet, *ASV* . . . Instantly she fell down dead at his feet, *Weymouth* . . . And she fell instantly at his feet, and expired, *Rotherham* . . . At once she collapsed at his feet and died, *TNT* . . . At that moment Sapphira fell down by his feet, *NCV.*

**and the young men came in, and found her dead:** When the young men entered, *Noli.*

| 3361.9 adj acc sing fem | 2504.1 conj | 1613.4 verb nom pl masc part aor act | 2267.1 verb 3pl indic aor act | 4242.1 prep | 3450.6 art acc sing masc |
|---|---|---|---|---|---|
| νεκράν, | καὶ | ἐξενέγκαντες | ἔθαψαν | πρὸς | τὸν |
| *nekran* | *kai* | *exenenkantes* | *ethapsan* | *pros* | *ton* |
| dead; | and | having carried out | they buried | by | the |

| 433.4 noun acc sing masc | 840.10 prs-pron gen sing fem | 2504.1 conj | 1090.33 verb 3sing indic aor mid | 5238.1 noun nom sing masc | 3144.2 adj nom sing masc |
|---|---|---|---|---|---|
| ἄνδρα | αὐτῆς. | **11.** καὶ | ἐγένετο | φόβος | μέγας |
| *andra* | *autēs* | *kai* | *egeneto* | *phobos* | *megas* |
| husband | her. | And | came | fear | great |

| 1894.1 prep | 3513.9 adj acc sing fem | 3450.12 art acc sing fem | 1564.4 noun acc sing fem | 2504.1 conj | 1894.3 prep | 3820.8 adj acc pl masc |
|---|---|---|---|---|---|---|
| ἐφ' | ὅλην | τὴν | ἐκκλησίαν, | καὶ | ἐπὶ | πάντας |
| *eph'* | *holēn* | *tēn* | *ekklēsian* | *kai* | *epi* | *pantas* |
| upon | whole | the | assembly, | and | upon | all |

| 3450.8 art acc pl masc | 189.16 verb acc pl masc part pres act | 3642.18 dem-pron pl neu | 1217.2 prep | 1156.2 conj | 3450.1 art gen pl |
|---|---|---|---|---|---|
| τοὺς | ἀκούοντας | ταῦτα. | **12.** Διὰ | δὲ | τῶν |
| *tous* | *akouontas* | *tauta* | *Dia* | *de* | *tōn* |
| the | hearing | these things. | By | and | the |

12.a.**Txt:** Steph
**Var:** 01ℵ,02A,03B,05D 08E,025P,byz.sa.bo. Elzev,Gries,Lach,Treg Alf,Tisc,We/Ho,Weis Sod,UBS/☆

| 5331.6 noun gen pl fem | 3450.1 art gen pl | 646.5 noun gen pl masc | 1090.33 verb 3sing indic aor mid | 1090.72 verb 3sing indic imperf mid |
|---|---|---|---|---|
| χειρῶν | τῶν | ἀποστόλων | ʿ ἐγένετο | [a☆ ἐγίνετο ] |
| *cheirōn* | *tōn* | *apostolōn* | *egeneto* | *egineto* |
| hands | of the | apostles | came to pass | [ were occurring ] |

| 4447.2 noun pl neu | 2504.1 conj | 4907.1 noun pl neu | 1706.1 prep | 3450.3 art dat sing | 2967.3 noun dat sing masc | 4044.17 adj pl neu |
|---|---|---|---|---|---|---|
| σημεῖα | καὶ | τέρατα | ʿ ἐν | τῷ | λαῷ | πολλὰ· |
| *sēmeia* | *kai* | *terata* | *en* | *tō* | *laō* | *polla* |
| signs | and | wonders | among | the | people | many |

| 4044.17 adj pl neu | 1706.1 prep | 3450.3 art dat sing | 2967.3 noun dat sing masc | 2504.1 conj | 1498.37 verb 3pl indic imperf act |
|---|---|---|---|---|---|
| [☆ πολλὰ | ἐν | τῷ | λαῷ· ] | καὶ | ἦσαν |
| *polla* | *en* | *tō* | *laō* | *kai* | *ēsan* |
| [ many | among | the | people; ] | and | they were |

12.b.**Txt:** 01ℵ,05D,025P etc.byz.Tisc,Sod
**Var:** 02A,03B,08E,Lach Treg,We/Ho,Weis UBS/☆

| 3524.1 adv | 533.4 adj nom pl masc | 3820.7 adj nom pl masc | 1706.1 prep | 3450.11 art dat sing fem |
|---|---|---|---|---|
| ὁμοθυμαδὸν | ʿ ἅπαντες | [b πάντες ] | ἐν | τῇ |
| *homothumadon* | *hapantes* | *pantes* | *en* | *tē* |
| with one accord | all | [ idem ] | on | the |

| 4596.1 noun dat sing fem | 4526.2 name gen masc | 3450.1 art gen pl | 1156.2 conj | 3036.1 adj gen pl | 3625.2 num card nom masc |
|---|---|---|---|---|---|
| Στοᾷ | Σολομῶντος· | **13.** τῶν | δὲ | λοιπῶν | οὐδεὶς |
| *Stoa* | *Solomōntos* | *tōn* | *de* | *loipōn* | *oudeis* |
| porch | of Solomon, | Of the | but | rest | no one |

| 4958.9 verb 3sing indic imperf act | 2827.3 verb inf pres mid | 840.2 prs-pron dat pl | 233.1 conj | 3141.4 verb 3sing indic act |
|---|---|---|---|---|
| ἐτόλμα | κολλᾶσθαι | αὐτοῖς, | ἀλλ' | ἐμεγάλυνεν |
| *etolma* | *kollasthai* | *autois* | *all'* | *emegalunen* |
| was daring | to join | them, | but | were magnifying |

| 840.8 prs-pron acc pl masc | 3450.5 art nom sing masc | 2967.1 noun nom sing masc | 3095.1 adv comp | 1156.2 conj |
|---|---|---|---|---|
| αὐτοὺς | ὁ | λαός· | **14.** μᾶλλον | δὲ |
| *autous* | *ho* | *laos* | *mallon* | *de* |
| them | the | people; | the more | and |

In addition, the property this couple gave was no longer theirs—it was devoted to God. Others in the Old Testament were judged in exactly the same way when they did not show proper respect for the holy things of the Lord, e.g., Nadab and Abihu (Leviticus 10:2), Achan (Joshua 7:25), Uzzah (2 Samuel 6:7).

**and, carrying her forth, buried her by her husband:** They took her out, *NLT* . . . carried her out, *Goodspeed* . . . entomb her, *Concordant* . . . by her husband's side, *TCNT.*

**5:11.** Once more the Bible emphasizes that great fear came upon the whole Church or Assembly. The Greek word *ekklesia* was used for the "congregation" of Israel. It was also used in everyday Greek for any assembly of free citizens. Here the word is used of the whole body of believers in Jerusalem and the surrounding area. It shows that the believers already considered themselves a distinct Body, though they still thought of themselves as Jews.

This great fear also came upon all those outside the Church who heard of these things. But the fear was a holy fear that stirred a reverence for God and a respect for His holiness. It did not split up the Church, nor did it hinder the work of God. But it made them all very careful to walk softly before the Lord.

**11. And great fear came upon all the church, and upon as many as heard these things:** And there came...upon the whole of the assembly, *Rotherham* . . . and all who heard of these events were appalled, *TCNT* . . . great awe fell upon the whole church, *MLNT* . . . was awestruck, and so were all who heard of this incident, *Weymouth* . . . All the members of the church...were terrified, *Noli* . . . were struck with awe, *Williams C.K.*

**5:12.** Luke now gave another summary statement. The apostles continued to be full of the Holy Spirit and power, that is, they were full of power because they were full of the Holy Spirit. They kept right on doing many miraculous signs and supernatural wonders that were impossible to do apart from the mighty power of God.

The Church also remained in one accord, meeting daily at the hours of prayer in Solomon's portico (and probably overflowing into the Court of the Women beside it). This, of course, was the very place where Peter and John had addressed the crowd after the healing of the lame man, where they had been arrested and thrown in jail overnight.

**12. And by the hands of the apostles were many signs and wonders wrought among the people:** The missionaries did many powerful works, *NLT* . . . numerous startling evidences, *Fenton* . . . performed many wonders, *Noli* . . . continued to occur...through the instrumentality of the Apostles, *TCNT.*

**(and they were all with one accord in Solomon's porch:** They gathered on, *NLT* . . . they all met unitedly, *MLNT* . . . and by common consent they all met in Solomon's portico, *Weymouth* . . . met together in Solomon's colonnade, *Noli.*

**5:13.** The fear that resulted from the death of Ananias and Sapphira also affected the unbelievers so that none of them dared to join in with the crowd of believers in the temple.

Some have suggested that the believers also did not dare to join with or come into the company of the apostles lest they be judged as Ananias and Sapphira were. But the evidence is that all the believers continued in just as great a fellowship with the apostles as before, so this interpretation is unlikely.

It is clear that no unbeliever dared to mix in with the crowd of believers. Perhaps out of curiosity some had been pretending to be Christians; or perhaps they hoped to receive part of the overflow of the blessing of the Lord, so evidently upon the believers.

This did not mean, however, that the Church's growth was slowed down. When the people saw how God dealt with sin among the believers, they realized that the Church as a whole was pleasing God and held high standards of honesty and righteousness. Therefore they "magnified them," that is, they held the believers in high esteem.

**13. And of the rest durst no man join himself to them:** No one from outside their own group came in with them, *NLT* . . . but none of the rest ventured to stand by them, *TCNT* . . . None of the outsiders, *MLNT* . . . But none of the others dared to attach themselves, *Weymouth* . . . None of the leaders dared to associate with them, *Noli* . . . no one of the rest dared join them, *Kleist.*

**but the people magnified them:** On the other hand, the people were full of their praise, *TCNT* . . . But those outside the church had respect for the followers, *NLT* . . . And although the common people made much of them, *Kleist* . . . Yet the people held them in high honour, *Weymouth* . . . continued to hold them in high regard, *Williams* . . . spoke highly of them, *Adams* . . . thought very highly of them, *Beck.*

| **4227.11** verb 3pl indic imperf pass | **3961.13** verb nom pl masc part pres act | **3450.3** art dat sing | **2935.3** noun dat sing masc | **3988.4** noun pl neu |
|---|---|---|---|---|
| προσετίθεντο | πιστεύοντες | τῷ | κυρίῳ, | πλήθη |
| *prosetithento* | *pisteuontes* | *tō* | *kuriō* | *plēthē* |
| were being added | believing | to the | Lord, | multitudes |

| **433.7** noun gen pl masc | **4885.1** conj | **2504.1** conj | **1129.7** noun gen pl fem | **5452.1** conj | **2567.3** prep |
|---|---|---|---|---|---|
| ἀνδρῶν | τε | καὶ | γυναικῶν· | **15.** ὥστε | ‹ κατὰ |
| *andrōn* | *te* | *kai* | *gunaikōn* | *hōste* | *kata* |
| of men | both | and | women; | so that | in |

15.a.**Txt:** 05D-org,025P byz.
**Var:** 01ℵ,02A,03B 05D-corr,Lach,Treg Tisc,We/Ho,Weis,Sod UBS/☆

15.b.**Txt:** 08E,025P,byz.
**Var:** 01ℵ,02A,03B,05D Lach,Treg,Alf,Tisc We/Ho,Weis,Sod UBS/☆

| **2504.1** conj | **1519.1** prep | **3450.15** art acc pl fem | **3976.1** adj fem | **1613.2** verb inf pres act | **3450.8** art acc pl masc |
|---|---|---|---|---|---|
| [a☆ καὶ | εἰς ] | τὰς | πλατείας | ἐκφέρειν | τοὺς |
| *kai* | *eis* | *tas* | *plateias* | *ekpherein* | *tous* |
| [ even | into ] | the | streets | to bring out | the |

| **766.4** adj pl masc | **2504.1** conj | **4935.7** verb inf pres act | **1894.3** prep | **2798.3** noun gen pl fem | **2797.1** noun gen sing neu |
|---|---|---|---|---|---|
| ἀσθενεῖς | καὶ | τιθέναι | ἐπὶ | ‹ κλινῶν | [b☆ κλιναρίων ] |
| *astheneis* | *kai* | *tithenai* | *epi* | *klinōn* | *klinariōn* |
| sick, | and | to put | on | beds | [ idem ] |

| **2504.1** conj | **2868.3** noun gen pl masc | **2868.8** noun gen pl masc | **2419.1** conj | **2048.45** verb gen sing masc part pres mid |
|---|---|---|---|---|
| καὶ | ‹ κραββάτων, | [☆ κραβάττων, ] | ἵνα | ἐρχομένου |
| *kai* | *krabbatōn* | *krabattōn* | *hina* | *erchomenou* |
| and | couches | [ idem ] | that | coming |

| **3935.2** name gen masc | **2550.1** conj | **3450.9** art nom sing fem | **4494.1** noun nom sing fem | **1966.3** verb 3sing subj aor act |
|---|---|---|---|---|
| Πέτρου | κἂν | ἡ | σκιὰ | ἐπισκιάσῃ |
| *Petrou* | *kan* | *hē* | *skia* | *episkiasē* |
| of Peter | at least | the | shadow | might overshadow |

| **4948.2** indef-pron dat sing | **840.1** prs-pron gen pl | **4755.20** verb 3sing indic imperf mid | **1156.2** conj | **2504.1** conj |
|---|---|---|---|---|
| τινὶ | αὐτῶν. | **16.** συνήρχετο | δὲ | καὶ |
| *tini* | *autōn* | *sunērcheto* | *de* | *kai* |
| some one | of them. | Were coming together | and | also |

16.a.**Txt:** 05D,08E,025P 044,byz.Sod
**Var:** p74,01ℵ,02A,03B Lach,Treg,Alf,Tisc We/Ho,Weis,UBS/☆

| **3450.16** art sing neu | **3988.1** noun sing neu | **3450.1** art gen pl | **3901.1** adv | **4032.6** noun gen pl fem | **1519.1** prep |
|---|---|---|---|---|---|
| τὸ | πλῆθος | τῶν | πέριξ | πόλεων | ‹a εἰς › |
| *to* | *plēthos* | *tōn* | *perix* | *poleōn* | *eis* |
| the | multitude | of the | round about | cities | to |

| **2395.1** name fem | **5179.8** verb nom pl masc part pres act | **766.4** adj pl masc | **2504.1** conj | **3655.2** verb acc pl masc part pres mid |
|---|---|---|---|---|
| Ἱερουσαλήμ, | φέροντες | ἀσθενεῖς | καὶ | ὀχλουμένους |
| *Hierousalēm* | *pherontes* | *astheneis* | *kai* | *ochloumenous* |
| Jerusalem, | bringing | sick ones | and | being beset |

| **5097.3** prep | **4011.5** noun gen pl neu | **167.6** adj gen pl neu | **3610.2** rel-pron nom pl masc | **2300.20** verb 3pl indic imperf pass |
|---|---|---|---|---|
| ὑπὸ | πνευμάτων | ἀκαθάρτων, | οἵτινες | ἐθεραπεύοντο |
| *hupo* | *pneumatōn* | *akathartōn* | *hoitines* | *etherapeuonto* |
| by | spirits | unclean, | who | were being healed |

| **533.4** adj nom pl masc | **448.9** verb nom sing masc part aor act | **1156.2** conj | **3450.5** art nom sing masc | **744.1** noun nom sing masc | **2504.1** conj |
|---|---|---|---|---|---|
| ἅπαντες. | **17.** Ἀναστὰς | δὲ | ὁ | ἀρχιερεὺς | καὶ |
| *hapantes* | *Anastas* | *de* | *ho* | *archiereus* | *kai* |
| all. | Having risen up | and | the | high priest | and |

**5:14.** The actual result was that more and more believers were "added to the Lord," that is, to the Lord Jesus, not just to the Church as an external body. This amounted to "multitudes (crowds) both of men and of women." It has been suggested the number of believers was over 10,000 by this time.

**5:15.** Because the believers had such confidence in the Lord to meet all their needs, they brought the sick (including the lame, the crippled, the diseased, and the infirm) out "into the streets," that is, into wide streets or into public squares, and "laid them on beds and couches," litters and mattresses or mats, so that when Peter passed by, even his shadow might overshadow them. They believed the Lord would honor Peter's faith and theirs even if Peter was not able to stop and lay hands on each one of them. This undoubtedly also stimulated the faith of those who were sick. It is not always easy for those who are sick to express faith.

Although some claim the Bible never says people actually were healed as the shadow of Peter went over them, the clear implication of the context is that people were healed. God used similar methods to restore health to individuals through supernatural means. For example, the woman with an issue of blood was made whole when she touched the hem of Jesus' garment (Matthew 9:20 and parallels). Also, Acts 19:11,12 says God performed "extraordinary miracles" (NIV) through the apostle Paul. When handkerchiefs and aprons touched by Paul were taken to the sick, diseases were cured and evil spirits departed those who had been demonized.

**5:16.** The word of what God was doing soon spread into the surrounding cities (including towns and villages) of Judea. Soon, because of their newfound faith, crowds of believers began to come and kept on coming, bringing the sick (again, including the diseased, the weak, the lame, and the crippled) and those who were vexed (tormented, troubled) by unclean spirits, that is, by demons.

As in the Gospels, the Bible makes a clear distinction between the sick and the people who were tormented or possessed by demons. There is nothing in the Bible to teach that all who are sick are demon possessed. The Bible indicates that sickness is in the world because of the activity of Satan and because of man's sin. But the Bible again and again makes it clear that in individual cases the sickness may not be caused by either sin or Satan. (Compare John 9:1-3.)

All of the sick and those tormented by unclean spirits were healed. This undoubtedly includes the sick mentioned in verse 15 as well. This was a critical point in the history of the Early Church, and God was doing special things.

**5:17.** Once again the local Sadducees in Jerusalem, including the high priest with his family and his close friends, were upset. In

**14. And believers were the more added to the Lord, multitudes both of men and women.):** . . . and, more than ever, *Williams C.K.* . . . and the more were being added when they believed in the Lord, throngs, *Rotherham* . . . while large numbers, both men and women, kept joining them more readily than ever as they became believers in the Master, *TCNT* . . . However, throngs of men and women who believed in the Lord were increasingly added, *Berkeley* . . . in increasing numbers believed in the Lord, *Noli.*

**15. Insomuch that they brought forth the sick into the streets:** In consequence people, *Montgomery* . . . They went so far as to bring out their sick, *MLNT* . . . They actually brought the sick, *Adams* . . . even into the broadways, *Rotherham.*

**and laid them on beds and couches:** . . . mattresses and mats, *TCNT* . . . beds and pallets, *HBIE* . . . to lay them on rugs and mats, *MLNT* . . . light couches or mats, *Weymouth.*

**that at the least the shadow of Peter passing by might overshadow some of them:** . . . in the hope that, as Peter came, at least his shadow, *TCNT* . . . even the shadow, *Campbell.*

**16. There came also a multitude out of the cities round about unto Jerusalem:** Even from towns outside Jerusalem the crowd came streaming in, *Berkeley, MLNT* . . . the inhabitants of the neighbouring towns flocked, *TNT* . . . Crowds flocked together to, *Noli.*

**bringing sick folks:** They took with them their sick people, *NLT.*

**and them which were vexed with unclean spirits:** . . . those molested, *Concordant* . . . and such as were harassed by impure spirits, *Rotherham* . . . those afflicted by, *Noli* . . . and those who were bothered by evil spirits, *Everyday* . . . troubled with demons, *NLT.*

**and they were healed every one:** . . . all alike cured, *TCNT* . . . all of whom were, *Norlie.*

**17. Then the high priest rose up, and all they that were with him:** On this the High Priest and

| 3820.7 adj nom pl masc | 3450.7 art nom pl masc | 4713.1 prep | 840.4 prs-pron dat sing | 3450.9 art nom sing fem | 1498.26 verb nom sing fem part pres act |
|---|---|---|---|---|---|
| πάντες | οἱ | σὺν | αὐτῷ, | ἡ | οὖσα |
| *pantes* | *hoi* | *sun* | *autō* | *hē* | *ousa* |
| all | the | with | him, | the | being |

| 138.1 noun nom sing fem | 3450.1 art gen pl | 4380.2 name gen pl masc | 3990.5 verb 3pl indic aor pass | 2188.2 noun gen sing |
|---|---|---|---|---|
| αἵρεσις | τῶν | Σαδδουκαίων, | ἐπλήσθησαν | ζήλου, |
| *hairesis* | *tōn* | *Saddoukaiōn* | *eplēsthēsan* | *zēlou* |
| a sect | of the | Sadducees, | were filled | with anger, |

18.a.**Txt:** 08E,025P,byz. sa.bo.Sod
**Var:** 01ℵ,02A,03B,05D Lach,Treg,Alf,Word Tisc,We/Ho,Weis UBS/⋆

| 2504.1 conj | 1896.4 verb 3pl indic aor act | 3450.15 art acc pl fem | 5331.8 noun acc pl fem | 840.1 prs-pron gen pl | 1894.3 prep |
|---|---|---|---|---|---|
| **18.** καὶ | ἐπέβαλον | τὰς | χεῖρας | ⸂a αὐτῶν⸃ | ἐπὶ |
| *kai* | *epebalon* | *tas* | *cheiras* | *autōn* | *epi* |
| and | laid | the | hands | their | on |

| 3450.8 art acc pl masc | 646.7 noun acc pl masc | 2504.1 conj | 4935.33 verb 3pl indic aor mid | 840.8 prs-pron acc pl masc | 1706.1 prep |
|---|---|---|---|---|---|
| τοὺς | ἀποστόλους | καὶ | ἔθεντο | αὐτοὺς | ἐν |
| *tous* | *apostolous* | *kai* | *ethento* | *autous* | *en* |
| the | apostles | and | put | them | in |

19.a.**Txt:** 01ℵ-corr,08E 025P,byz.
**Var:** 01ℵ-org,02A,03B 05D,Lach,Treg,Alf,Tisc We/Ho,Weis,Sod UBS/⋆

19.b.**Var:** 01ℵ,02A,Tisc Sod

| 4932.2 noun dat sing fem | 1212.1 adj dat sing fem | 32.1 noun nom sing masc | 1156.2 conj | 2935.2 noun gen sing masc | 1217.2 prep |
|---|---|---|---|---|---|
| τηρήσει | δημοσίᾳ. | **19.** ἄγγελος | δὲ | κυρίου | διὰ |
| *tērēsei* | *dēmosia* | *angelos* | *de* | *kuriou* | *dia* |
| hold | public. | An angel | but | of Lord | during |

| 3450.10 art gen sing fem | 3433.2 noun gen sing fem | 453.4 verb 3sing indic aor act | 453.9 verb nom sing masc part aor act | 3450.15 art acc pl fem |
|---|---|---|---|---|
| ⸂a τῆς⸃ | νυκτὸς | ⸂ ἤνοιξεν | [b ἀνοίξας ] | τὰς |
| *tēs* | *nuktos* | *ēnoixen* | *anoixas* | *tas* |
| the | night | opened | [ having opened ] | the |

| 2351.1 noun fem | 3450.10 art gen sing fem | 5274.2 noun gen sing fem | 1790.5 verb nom sing masc part aor act | 4885.1 conj | 840.8 prs-pron acc pl masc |
|---|---|---|---|---|---|
| θύρας | τῆς | φυλακῆς, | ἐξαγαγών | τε | αὐτοὺς |
| *thuras* | *tēs* | *phulakēs* | *exagagōn* | *te* | *autous* |
| doors | of the | prison, | having brought out | and | them |

| 1500.5 verb 3sing indic aor act | 4057.5 verb 2pl impr pres mid | 2504.1 conj | 2449.45 verb nom pl masc part aor pass | 2953.10 verb 2pl impr pres act |
|---|---|---|---|---|
| εἶπεν, | **20.** Πορεύεσθε, | καὶ | σταθέντες | λαλεῖτε |
| *eipen* | *Poreuesthe* | *kai* | *stathentes* | *laleite* |
| said, | Go | and | having stood | speak |

| 1706.1 prep | 3450.3 art dat sing | 2387.2 adj dat sing neu | 3450.3 art dat sing | 2967.3 noun dat sing masc | 3820.1 adj | 3450.17 art pl neu |
|---|---|---|---|---|---|---|
| ἐν | τῷ | ἱερῷ | τῷ | λαῷ | πάντα | τὰ |
| *en* | *tō* | *hierō* | *tō* | *laō* | *panta* | *ta* |
| in | the | temple | to the | people | all | the |

| 4343.4 noun pl neu | 3450.10 art gen sing fem | 2205.2 noun gen sing fem | 3642.10 dem-pron gen sing fem | 189.32 verb nom pl masc part aor act |
|---|---|---|---|---|
| ῥήματα | τῆς | ζωῆς | ταύτης. | **21.** Ἀκούσαντες |
| *rhēmata* | *tēs* | *zōēs* | *tautēs* | *Akousantes* |
| words | the | of life | this. | Having heard |

| 1156.2 conj | 1511.1 verb indic aor act | 5097.3 prep | 3450.6 art acc sing masc | 3585.2 noun acc sing masc | 1519.1 prep | 3450.16 art sing neu |
|---|---|---|---|---|---|---|
| δὲ | εἰσῆλθον | ὑπὸ | τὸν | ὄρθρον | εἰς | τὸ |
| *de* | *eisēlthon* | *hupo* | *ton* | *orthron* | *eis* | *to* |
| and | they entered | at | the | dawn | into | the |

fact, they were very upset. This time they were "filled with indignation." The Greek word *zēloō* can mean zeal, enthusiasm, or eagerness in a good sense, or it can mean the worst kind of jealousy, the sense of the word as it is used here. It also implies a party spirit and a zeal for their Sadducean teachings against the resurrection of the dead.

**5:18.** Jealous indignation, then, caused these Sadducees to rise up, go into action, arrest the apostles, and throw them into the common prison. The Greek also indicates they did this publicly. "Common" here is actually an adverb which means "publicly." They made the arrest with the whole crowd looking on. Apparently the priests and Sadducees had become desperate. Many times they had been afraid to arrest Jesus publicly because they were afraid of the reaction of the crowds. When they finally did arrest Him, it was at night when the crowds were not around. But now they were more afraid that if they did not show their authority, the crowds would lose their respect for and fear of the Sanhedrin altogether.

**5:19.** During the night an angel of the Lord came to the prison. (The Greek does not have the article "the," but simply means one of the host of angels who are available as ministering spirits to be sent out to minister to or serve those who are and shall be heirs of salvation; see Hebrews 1:14.) "Angel" means "messenger," and this angel was a messenger sent from the Lord with the power to open the doors of the prison, which he proceeded to do. The prison had guards, but the account does not say what happened to them.

From what the Bible says in other places, it is probable that the Lord caused a deep sleep to come upon these guards so they were totally unaware of the opening of the gates and the departure of the Twelve.

**5:20.** After bringing the apostles out, the angel commanded them to go and take their stand and keep on speaking "in the temple to the people all the words of this life," that is, the words that were giving life to those who believed. Similar phraseology was used by Peter and the Twelve when they recognized that Jesus had the words of eternal life (John 6:68). Later Peter identified this as the Word of the Lord which endures forever, the Word which by the gospel is preached (1 Peter 1:25). In all these instances a form of the Greek *rhēma* is used. *Rhēma* is often a spoken word or utterance, the concrete expression of the Word (*logos*) of God.

**5:21.** Because of the angel's command, the 12 apostles rose up very early in the morning and went into the temple. By dawn they were already proceeding to teach publicly. This must have aston-

all his supporters...were aroused, *TCNT* . . . Now the high priest took a stand, and all his friends, *Williams* . . . and all his party, *Weymouth.*

**(which is the sect of the Sadducees,):** . . . the Sadducee party, *Berkeley* . . . the party of the Liberals, *Klingensmith* . . . who believe no one will be raised from the dead, *NLT.*

**and were filled with indignation:** . . . they were insufferably jealous, *Berkeley* . . . in a fit of jealousy, *TCNT* . . . made them furious, *Norlie* . . . became very jealous, *Everyday, NLT.*

**18. And laid their hands on the apostles:** . . . arrested, the Apostles, *TCNT* . . . So they seized, *Berkeley* . . . took hold, *NLT* . . . they apprehended the apostles, *Montgomery* . . . grabbed the apostles, *SEB.*

**and put them in the common prison:** . . . and had them placed in custody, *TCNT*. . . official custody, *NEB* . . . the public prison, *HBIE* . . . public ward, *ASV* . . . the public jail, *Noli.*

**19. But the angel of the Lord by night:** . . . during the night, *Weymouth* . . . a messenger of the Lord, *Campbell.*

**opened the prison doors, and brought them forth, and said:** . . . threw open the jail doors, *Williams* . . . conducted them out, *Berkeley* . . . and leading them out said, *Rotherham* . . . led the apostles outside, *Everyday.*

**20. Go, stand and speak in the temple to the people all the words of this life:** Go...and take your stand in the Temple Courts, and tell the people all you have to say about the new Life, *TCNT* . . . stand where you have been standing, *NLT* . . . keep on telling the people, *Beck* . . . the full message, *NIV* . . . and continue proclaiming, *Weymouth* . . . proclaim all the doctrines of the Gospel, *Noli* . . . the declarations of this life, *Concordant* . . . all about this life, *Williams C.K.* . . . everything about this new life, *Everyday.*

**21. And when they heard that, they entered into the temple early in the morning, and taught:** Following this instruction, *Norlie*

## Acts 5:22

| 2387.3 adj sing neu | 2504.1 conj | 1315.21 verb 3pl indic imperf act | 3716.7 verb nom sing masc part aor mid | 1156.2 conj | 3450.5 art nom sing masc |
|---|---|---|---|---|---|
| ἱερὸν, | καὶ | ἐδίδασκον. | Παραγενόμενος | δὲ | ὁ |
| *hieron* | *kai* | *edidaskon* | *Paragenomenos* | *de* | *ho* |
| temple, | and | were teaching. | Having come | but | the |

| 744.1 noun nom sing masc | 2504.1 conj | 3450.7 art nom pl masc | 4713.1 prep | 840.4 prs-pron dat sing | 4630.3 verb 3pl indic aor act |
|---|---|---|---|---|---|
| ἀρχιερεὺς | καὶ | οἱ | σὺν | αὐτῷ, | συνεκάλεσαν |
| *archiereus* | *kai* | *hoi* | *sun* | *autō* | *sunekalesan* |
| high priest | and | the | with | him, | they called together |

| 3450.16 art sing neu | 4742.1 noun sing neu | 2504.1 conj | 3820.12 adj acc sing fem | 3450.12 art acc sing fem | 1081.1 noun acc sing fem |
|---|---|---|---|---|---|
| τὸ | συνέδριον | καὶ | πᾶσαν | τὴν | γερουσίαν |
| *to* | *sunedrion* | *kai* | *pasan* | *tēn* | *gerousian* |
| the | Sanhedrin | and | all | the | elderhood |

| 3450.1 art gen pl | 5048.7 noun gen pl masc | 2447.1 name masc | 2504.1 conj | 643.9 verb 3pl indic aor act | 1519.1 prep |
|---|---|---|---|---|---|
| τῶν | υἱῶν | Ἰσραήλ, | καὶ | ἀπέστειλαν | εἰς |
| *tōn* | *huiōn* | *Israēl* | *kai* | *apesteilan* | *eis* |
| of the | sons | of Israel, | and | sent | to |

| 3450.16 art sing neu | 1195.3 noun sing neu | 70.26 verb inf aor pass | 840.8 prs-pron acc pl masc | 3450.7 art nom pl masc |
|---|---|---|---|---|
| τὸ | δεσμωτήριον | ἀχθῆναι | αὐτούς. | **22.** οἱ |
| *to* | *desmōtērion* | *achthēnai* | *autous* | *hoi* |
| the | prison | to have brought | them. | The |

| 1156.2 conj | 5095.3 noun nom pl masc | 3716.10 verb nom pl masc part aor mid | 3716.10 verb nom pl masc part aor mid |
|---|---|---|---|
| δὲ | ⸂ ὑπηρέται | παραγενόμενοι | [☆ παραγενόμενοι |
| *de* | *hupēretai* | *paragenomenoi* | *paragenomenoi* |
| but | officers | having come | [ having come |

| 5095.3 noun nom pl masc | 3620.1 partic | 2128.6 verb indic aor act | 840.8 prs-pron acc pl masc | 1706.1 prep | 3450.11 art dat sing fem | 5274.3 noun dat sing fem |
|---|---|---|---|---|---|---|
| ὑπηρέται ] | οὐχ | εὗρον | αὐτοὺς | ἐν | τῇ | φυλακῇ |
| *hupēretai* | *ouch* | *heuron* | *autous* | *en* | *tē* | *phulakē* |
| officers ] | not | did find | them | in | the | prison; |

| 388.2 verb nom pl masc part aor act | 1156.2 conj | 514.8 verb 3pl indic aor act | 2978.16 verb nom pl masc part pres act | 3617.1 conj |
|---|---|---|---|---|
| ἀναστρέψαντες | δὲ | ἀπήγγειλαν, | **23.** λέγοντες, | Ὅτι |
| *anastrepsantes* | *de* | *apēngeilan* | *legontes* | *Hoti* |
| having returned | and | they reported, | saying, | |

| 3450.16 art sing neu | 3173.1 conj | 1195.3 noun sing neu | 2128.9 verb 1pl indic aor act | 2781.12 verb sing neu part perf mid |
|---|---|---|---|---|
| Τὸ | ⸂a μὲν ⸃ | δεσμωτήριον | εὕρομεν | κεκλεισμένον |
| *To* | *men* | *desmōtērion* | *heuromen* | *kekleismenon* |
| The | truly | prison | we found | having been shut |

| 1706.1 prep | 3820.11 adj dat sing fem | 797.2 noun dat sing fem | 2504.1 conj | 3450.8 art acc pl masc | 5277.2 noun acc pl masc |
|---|---|---|---|---|---|
| ἐν | πάσῃ | ἀσφαλείᾳ, | καὶ | τοὺς | φύλακας |
| *en* | *pasē* | *asphaleia* | *kai* | *tous* | *phulakas* |
| with | all | security, | and | the | keepers |

| 1838.1 adv | 2449.33 verb acc pl masc part perf act | 4112.1 prep | 1894.3 prep | 3450.1 art gen pl | 2351.6 noun gen pl fem |
|---|---|---|---|---|---|
| ⸂b ἔξω ⸃ | ἑστῶτας | ⸂ πρὸ | [c☆ ἐπὶ ] | τῶν | θυρῶν· |
| *exō* | *hestōtas* | *pro* | *epi* | *tōn* | *thurōn* |
| outside | standing | before | [ at ] | the | doors; |

23.a.**Txt:** 08E,025P,byz.sa.bo.Sod
**Var:** 01ℵ,02A,03B,05D Lach,Treg,Alf,Word Tisc,We/Ho,Weis UBS/☆

23.b.**Txt:** Steph
**Var:** 01ℵ,02A,03B,05D 08E,025P,byz.sa.bo. Gries,Lach,Treg,Alf Tisc,We/Ho,Weis,Sod UBS/☆

23.c.**Txt:** 08E,025P,byz.bo.
**Var:** 01ℵ,02A,03B,05D sa.Lach,Treg,Alf,Tisc We/Ho,Weis,Sod UBS/☆

ished the people who had seen them arrested and thrown into the prison the night before. It must also have encouraged the believers and helped all the people to see that God was still with the apostles. It was also further confirmation that their message was true and God was standing behind both them and His Word which they were proclaiming with such boldness.

Sometime later that morning, the high priest and his associates called the Council (the Sanhedrin) together. This Council is further identified as the whole Senate of the people of Israel. (*And* in Greek sometimes means "even." This is the meaning here. The Council and the Senate were the same body.) This seems to mean that all 71 members were present. In the Greek the words "and all the senate of the children (sons) of Israel" are nearly a word-for-word quote of Exodus 12:21 taken from the Septuagint. The Old Testament passage is a reference to the elders whom Moses called prior to the Exodus.

It also implies that on the previous occasion when Peter and John were arrested (as well as on some other occasions such as the trial of Jesus) only those who were Sadducees under the domination of the high priest were called. The Sadducees did make up the major portion of the Sanhedrin and constituted a quorum, so the high priest was able to carry on business this way if he wished. But this time, because they knew they were going against the feeling and desires of most of the people in Jerusalem and Judea, they brought in the full body, expecting them to concur in their decision and uphold the punishment of the apostles. Then they sent to the prison to have the apostles brought in.

**5:22.** The officers who were sent to bring the apostles were not high officers. The word indicates they were servants or attendants of the high priest or of the temple. Imagine their surprise when they came to the prison and found the apostles were not there. This was something unprecedented. When Jesus was arrested, He submitted and made no attempt to escape, though He could have had 12 legions of angels to help Him. When Peter and John were arrested after the healing of the lame man, they were still in the jail the next morning, and when they were sent for there was nothing to hinder their being brought before the Council. But God does not always work in the same way. He has His surprises.

**5:23.** Apparently these temple servants or attendants did not waste any time. There were no hidden corners for the apostles to hide in. So all these attendants could do was go back quickly to the Sanhedrin and tell them what they found. They explained that the prison doors were still "shut with all safety," that is, with full security, which means the doors were all locked. The keepers (the guards) were still standing outside in front of the doors. The Sanhedrin had been careful to be sure that no one could come in and try to rescue the apostles. There was no evidence that anyone had

... they went into the house of God, *NLT* ... just before daybreak, and began to teach, *Weymouth* ... Then they did as they were told, *Williams C.K.*

**But the high priest came, and they that were with him:** Meanwhile the chief priest and his party came, *Kleist* ... When the head religious leader, *NLT* ... and his supporters arrived, *NAB.*

**and called the council together:** ... they summoned the Sanhedrin, *Montgomery* ... They called a meeting of, *NCV* ... they gathered the men of the court, *NLT* ... they convoked the Sanhedrin, *NAB* ... the Supreme Council, *TNT.*

**and all the senate of the children of Israel:** ... even the whole Senate of the sons of Israel, *Berkeley* ... the full council of the elders of Israel, *NAB* ... and the leaders of the Jews together, *NLT.*

**and sent to the prison to have them brought:** They sent word to the jail that the prisoners were to be brought in, *NAB* ... the prison house, *ASV.*

**22. But when the officers came, and found them not in the prison:** But when the attendants came, *Swann* ... But when the temple guard got to the jail, *NAB* ... when the officers arrived, *Williams C.K.* ... they couldn't find them in the jail, *Adams* ... they failed to find them, *MLNT.*

**they returned, and told:** ... and hurried back with the report, *NAB* ... and reported, *RSV* ... told the court, *NLT.*

**23. Saying, The prison truly found we shut with all safety:** The jail was closed and locked, *Everyday* ... we found closed in all safety, *Swann* ... we found locked with all security, *Concordant* ... very securely locked, *Berkeley* ... carefully closed, *Murdock* ... quite securely shut, *TCNT.*

**and the keepers standing without before the doors:** ... with the guards stationed at the doors, *Montgomery* ... and the guards on duty at the doors, *Williams C.K.* ... the sentries standing at the doors, *Noli* ... the guards at their posts outside the gates, *NAB* ... and the soldiers watching the doors, *NLT* ... standing outside in front of the doors, *KJII.*

| 453.10 verb nom pl masc part aor act | 1156.2 conj | 2059.1 adv | 3625.3 num card acc masc | 2128.9 verb 1pl indic aor act | 5453.1 conj |
|---|---|---|---|---|---|
| ἀνοίξαντες | δὲ, | ἔσω | οὐδένα | εὕρομεν. | **24.** Ὡς |
| *anoixantes* | *de* | *esō* | *oudena* | *heuromen* | *Hōs* |
| having opened | but, | inside | no one | we found. | When |

| 1156.2 conj | 189.24 verb 3pl indic aor act | 3450.8 art acc pl masc | 3030.8 noun acc pl masc | 3642.8 dem-pron acc pl masc | 3614.16 rel-pron sing neu | 4885.1 conj |
|---|---|---|---|---|---|---|
| δὲ | ἤκουσαν | τοὺς | λόγους | τούτους | ὅ | τε |
| *de* | *ēkousan* | *tous* | *logous* | *toutous* | *ho* | *te* |
| and | they heard | the | words | these | which | both |

24.a.**Txt:** 025P,byz.
**Var:** 01ℵ,02A,03B,05D 33,sa.bo.Lach,Treg,Alf Tisc,We/Ho,Weis,Sod UBS/*

| 2385.1 noun nom sing masc | 2504.1 conj | 3450.5 art nom sing masc | 4606.1 noun nom sing masc | 3450.2 art gen sing | 2387.1 adj gen sing neu |
|---|---|---|---|---|---|
| ⸂a ἱερεὺς | καὶ | ὁ ⸃ | στρατηγὸς | τοῦ | ἱεροῦ |
| *hiereus* | *kai* | *ho* | *stratēgos* | *tou* | *hierou* |
| priest | and | the | captain | of the | temple |

| 2504.1 conj | 3450.7 art nom pl masc | 744.5 noun pl masc | 1274.2 verb 3pl indic imperf act | 3875.1 prep | 840.1 prs-pron gen pl |
|---|---|---|---|---|---|
| καὶ | οἱ | ἀρχιερεῖς | διηπόρουν | περὶ | αὐτῶν, |
| *kai* | *hoi* | *archiereis* | *diēporoun* | *peri* | *autōn* |
| and | the | chief priests | were perplexed | concerning | them, |

| 4949.9 intr-pron sing neu | 300.1 partic | 1090.44 verb 3sing opt aor mid | 3642.17 dem-pron sing neu | 3716.7 verb nom sing masc part aor mid |
|---|---|---|---|---|
| τί | ἂν | γένοιτο | τοῦτο. | **25.** παραγενόμενος |
| *ti* | *an* | *genoito* | *touto* | *paragenomenos* |
| what | | might be | this. | Having come |

25.a.**Txt:** Steph
**Var:** 01ℵ,02A,03B,05D 08E,025P,byz.sa.bo. Gries,Lach,Treg,Alf Word,Tisc,We/Ho,Weis Sod,UBS/*

| 1156.2 conj | 4948.3 indef-pron nom sing | 514.7 verb 3sing indic aor act | 840.2 prs-pron dat pl | 2978.15 verb nom sing masc part pres act |
|---|---|---|---|---|
| δέ | τις | ἀπήγγειλεν | αὐτοῖς | ⸂a λέγων, ⸃ |
| *de* | *tis* | *apēngeilen* | *autois* | *legōn* |
| but | a certain one | reported | to them, | saying, |

| 3617.1 conj | 1481.20 verb 2sing impr aor mid | 3450.7 art nom pl masc | 433.6 noun nom pl masc | 3614.8 rel-pron acc pl masc | 4935.31 verb 2pl indic aor mid |
|---|---|---|---|---|---|
| Ὅτι | Ἰδοὺ | οἱ | ἄνδρες | οὓς | ἔθεσθε |
| *Hoti* | *Idou* | *hoi* | *andres* | *hous* | *ethesthe* |
| | Look! | the | men | whom | you put |

| 1706.1 prep | 3450.11 art dat sing fem | 5274.3 noun dat sing fem | 1498.7 verb 3pl indic pres act | 1706.1 prep | 3450.3 art dat sing | 2387.2 adj dat sing neu |
|---|---|---|---|---|---|---|
| ἐν | τῇ | φυλακῇ | εἰσὶν | ἐν | τῷ | ἱερῷ |
| *en* | *tē* | *phulakē* | *eisin* | *en* | *tō* | *hierō* |
| in | the | prison | are | in | the | temple |

| 2449.30 verb nom pl masc part perf act | 2504.1 conj | 1315.9 verb nom pl masc part pres act | 3450.6 art acc sing masc | 2967.4 noun acc sing masc |
|---|---|---|---|---|
| ἑστῶτες | καὶ | διδάσκοντες | τὸν | λαόν. |
| *hestōtes* | *kai* | *didaskontes* | *ton* | *laon* |
| standing | and | teaching | the | people. |

| 4966.1 adv | 562.6 verb nom sing masc part aor act | 3450.5 art nom sing masc | 4606.1 noun nom sing masc | 4713.1 prep | 3450.4 art dat pl |
|---|---|---|---|---|---|
| **26.** Τότε | ἀπελθὼν | ὁ | στρατηγὸς | σὺν | τοῖς |
| *Tote* | *apelthōn* | *ho* | *stratēgos* | *sun* | *tois* |
| Then | having gone | the | captain | with | the |

26.a.**Txt:** 02A,08E,025P byz.Gries,Lach,Treg,Alf Sod
**Var:** 01ℵ,03B,05D-corr Tisc,We/Ho,Weis UBS/*

| 5095.5 noun dat pl masc | 70.8 verb 3sing indic aor act | 70.32 verb 3sing indic imperf act | 840.8 prs-pron acc pl masc | 3620.3 partic | 3196.3 prep |
|---|---|---|---|---|---|
| ὑπηρέταις | ⸀ ἤγαγεν | [a* ἦγεν ] | αὐτούς, | οὐ | μετὰ |
| *hupēretais* | *ēgagen* | *ēgen* | *autous* | *ou* | *meta* |
| officers | brought | [were bringing] | them, | not | with |

been careless. But when they opened the doors, they found there was no one inside the prison.

**but when we had opened, we found no man within:** . . . when we went in, *Noli* . . . no one inside, *Swann* . . . the jail was empty! *NCV.*

**5:24.** This report of the attendants caused the high priest and his associates, including the captain of the temple guard, to be in doubt (troubled and at a loss concerning the apostles, wondering what would come of this). "Grow" here translates a form of the Greek word for *become* or *happen.* This also implies they wondered and were very worried about what would happen next.

What a contrast there was between these religious leaders and the common people of Israel. The people were giving respect to the apostles and the believers. They were rejoicing and giving God the praise for the miracles. But these leaders cared nothing for the common people or their needs. They did not want to see revival. They did not want to see God move. All they wanted was to preserve the status quo and to keep their own power structure which they had set up. They did not really want to serve the people or the temple. They wanted the people and the temple to serve them. The question that really filled their minds was how they were going to stop this and keep anything else from happening that would disturb them.

**24. Now when the high priest and the captain of the temple and the chief priests heard these things:** . . . both the magistrate of the temple, *Hanson* . . . When the religious leaders and the leader of the house of God heard this, *NLT* . . . and the leading priests, *NCV* . . . heard this report, *Noli.*

**they doubted of them whereunto this would grow:** . . . were confused, *Everyday* . . . utterly at a loss concerning them, *Rotherham* . . . were perplexed about the apostles, wondering what could have happened, *TNT* . . . they were utterly at a loss to know how this might turn out, *Williams* . . . wondering what would happen next, *Weymouth* . . . they were completely at a loss how to account for it, *Berkeley* . . . they wondered what had become of them, *Noli* . . . wondered anxiously what it could mean, *Williams C.K.* . . . they were much perplexed about it as to how this thing could have happened, *Kleist* . . . they were much troubled as to what might happen, *NLT* . . . what might result from this, *Swann.*

**5:25.** While the Sanhedrin members were still sitting there wondering and upset, someone arrived and reported that the men who were supposed to be in the prison were in the temple, standing there openly and publicly teaching the people. They were doing again the very thing that had brought their arrest the day before.

These Jewish leaders should have learned from this that though they could throw the preachers or proclaimers of the gospel into prison, there is no way God would let them stop the gospel from being preached.

**25. Then came one and told them, saying:** . . . but a man came up and reported, *Williams C.K.* . . . Then someone, coming, announced to them, *Swann.*

**Behold, the men whom ye put in prison are standing in the temple, and teaching the people:** At this very moment, *JB* . . . are actually in the temple, *TNT* . . . are standing right here in the temple square, *Williams* . . . preaching to the people, *Noli.*

**5:26.** The captain (commander of the temple guard) then went with the officers (servants, attendants of the temple) and brought the apostles without violence, that is, without the use of force. This probably means they came up to them in the temple very quietly, gathered around them, and talked to them very politely. These temple officers were very careful because they were afraid the people would turn on them and stone them. They had dealt with mobs before. They knew what a mob spirit and mob violence could do when it was stirred up.

Actually, of course, they did not need to use force. The apostles went willingly even though they also knew they had but to say the word and the mob would have stoned these officers as blasphemers of God's servants and enemies of God. Stoning in Old Testament times had been the punishment of willful, high-handed sin and rebellion.

**26. Then went the captain with the officers:** . . . military commander, *Williams* . . . The leader of the house of God took his men, *NLT.*

**and brought them without violence:** . . . and got them. They did not hurt the missionaries, *NLT* . . . but without using violence, *Weymouth* . . . not, however, by force, *Montgomery* . . . the soldiers did not use force, *Everyday, NCV.*

26.b.**Txt:** 02A,025P,byz.
Tisc
**Var:** 01א,03B,05D,08E
Lach,Treg,We/Ho,Weis
Sod,UBS/☆

| **963.1** noun gen sing fem | **5236.25** verb 3pl indic imperf mid | **1056.1** conj | **3450.6** art acc sing masc | **2967.4** noun acc sing masc | **2419.1** conj |
|---|---|---|---|---|---|
| βίας, | ἐφοβοῦντο | γὰρ | τὸν | λαόν, | ⌜[b] ἵνα ⌝ |
| *bias* | *ephobounto* | *gar* | *ton* | *laon* | *hina* |
| violence, | they were fearing | for | the | people, | that |

| **3231.1** partic | **3008.8** verb 3pl subj aor pass | **70.14** verb nom pl masc part aor act | **1156.2** conj | **840.8** prs-pron acc pl masc |
|---|---|---|---|---|
| μὴ | λιθασθῶσιν. | **27.** Ἀγαγόντες | δὲ | αὐτοὺς |
| *mē* | *lithasthōsin* | *Agagontes* | *de* | *autous* |
| not | they might be stoned. | Having brought | and | them |

| **2449.5** verb 3pl indic aor act | **1706.1** prep | **3450.3** art dat sing | **4742.3** noun dat sing neu | **2504.1** conj | **1890.6** verb 3sing indic aor act |
|---|---|---|---|---|---|
| ἔστησαν | ἐν | τῷ | συνεδρίῳ· | καὶ | ἐπηρώτησεν |
| *estēsan* | *en* | *tō* | *sunedriō* | *kai* | *epērōtēsen* |
| they set | in | the | Sanhedrin. | And | asked |

28.a.**Txt:** 01א-corr,05D
08E,025P,1241,byz.sa.
Sod
**Var:** p74,01א-org,02A
03B,bo.Lach,Treg,Alf
Tisc,We/Ho,Weis
UBS/☆

| **840.8** prs-pron acc pl masc | **3450.5** art nom sing masc | **744.1** noun nom sing masc | **2978.15** verb nom sing masc part pres act | **3620.3** partic |
|---|---|---|---|---|
| αὐτοὺς | ὁ | ἀρχιερεὺς, | **28.** λέγων, | ⌜[a] Οὐ ⌝ |
| *autous* | *ho* | *archiereus* | *legōn* | *Ou* |
| them | the | high priest, | saying, | Not |

| **3714.2** noun dat sing fem | **3715.8** verb 1pl indic aor act | **5050.3** prs-pron dat 2pl | **3231.1** partic | **1315.10** verb inf pres act |
|---|---|---|---|---|
| Παραγγελίᾳ | παρηγγείλαμεν | ὑμῖν | μὴ | διδάσκειν |
| *Parangelia* | *parēngeilamen* | *humin* | *mē* | *didaskein* |
| by a command | did we charge | you | not | to teach |

| **1894.3** prep | **3450.3** art dat sing | **3549.4** noun dat sing neu | **3642.5** dem-pron dat sing masc | **2504.1** conj | **1481.20** verb 2sing impr aor mid |
|---|---|---|---|---|---|
| ἐπὶ | τῷ | ὀνόματι | τούτῳ, | καὶ | ἰδοὺ |
| *epi* | *tō* | *onomati* | *toutō* | *kai* | *idou* |
| in | the | name | this? | and | behold, |

| **3997.11** verb 2pl indic perf act | **3450.12** art acc sing fem | **2395.1** name fem | **3450.10** art gen sing fem | **1316.2** noun gen sing fem |
|---|---|---|---|---|
| πεπληρώκατε | τὴν | Ἱερουσαλὴμ | τῆς | διδαχῆς |
| *peplērōkate* | *tēn* | *Hierousalēm* | *tēs* | *didachēs* |
| you have filled | | Jerusalem | with the | teaching |

| **5050.2** prs-pron gen 2pl | **2504.1** conj | **1007.5** verb 2pl indic pres mid | **1848.3** verb inf aor act | **1894.1** prep | **2231.4** prs-pron acc 1pl | **3450.16** art sing neu |
|---|---|---|---|---|---|---|
| ὑμῶν, | καὶ | βούλεσθε | ἐπαγαγεῖν | ἐφ' | ἡμᾶς | τὸ |
| *humōn* | *kai* | *boulesthe* | *epagagein* | *eph'* | *hēmas* | *to* |
| your, | and | you intend | to bring | upon | us | the |

| **129.1** noun sing neu | **3450.2** art gen sing | **442.2** noun gen sing masc | **3642.1** dem-pron gen sing | **552.12** verb nom sing masc part aor pass |
|---|---|---|---|---|
| αἷμα | τοῦ | ἀνθρώπου | τούτου. | **29.** Ἀποκριθεὶς |
| *haima* | *tou* | *anthrōpou* | *toutou* | *Apokritheis* |
| blood | of the | man | this. | Answering |

29.a.**Txt:** 05D,byz.
**Var:** 01א,02A,03B,08E
025P,Lach,Treg,Alf
Tisc,We/Ho,Weis,Sod
UBS/☆

| **1156.2** conj | **3450.5** art nom sing masc | **3935.1** name nom masc | **2504.1** conj | **3450.7** art nom pl masc | **646.4** noun nom pl masc |
|---|---|---|---|---|---|
| δὲ | ⌜[a] ὁ ⌝ | Πέτρος | καὶ | οἱ | ἀπόστολοι |
| *de* | *ho* | *Petros* | *kai* | *hoi* | *apostoloi* |
| but | | Peter | and | the | apostles |

29.b.**Txt:** 025P,etc.byz.
Sod
**Var:** 01א,02A,03B,08E
Lach,Treg,Alf,Tisc
We/Ho,Weis,UBS/☆

| **1500.3** verb indic aor act | **1500.28** verb 3pl indic aor act | **3842.2** verb inf pres act | **1158.1** verb 3sing indic pres act | **2296.3** noun dat sing masc |
|---|---|---|---|---|
| ⌜ εἶπον, | [[b]☆ εἶπαν, ] | Πειθαρχεῖν | δεῖ | θεῷ |
| *eipon* | *eipan* | *Peitharchein* | *dei* | *theō* |
| said, | [ idem ] | To obey | it is necessary | God |

The apostles did not resist, however, because they had the words of Jesus that they would appear before councils and kings, and the Holy Spirit would give them the words to say (Matthew 10:17-20). They undoubtedly hoped this arrest would become another opportunity to witness for their Messiah and Saviour.

**5:27.** When they brought the apostles into the room where the Sanhedrin was meeting, they made them stand before the Council, that is, before its 71 members. It should be noted that when the high priest began speaking, he avoided asking the apostles how they got out of the prison. It was obviously something supernatural, and it may very well be that he did not want to hear about angels he did not believe in. He probably did not want to hear praise to God for this deliverance either.

**5:28.** The high priest began by asking the apostles if the Sanhedrin had not given them strict orders not to teach in this name. Other versions (NIV, RSV) translate these words as a statement rather than a question. Since the Greek term *parangellia* has the meaning of "injunction," in essence the Sanhedrin was saying, "We gave you an injunction not to teach in this name!" The word "this" was used by him in a belittling sense and was intended to be a derogatory reference to the name of Jesus.

The high priest accused the apostles of filling Jerusalem with their doctrine (teaching), desiring to bring on the Jewish leaders "this man's blood"; that is, they accused the disciples of wanting the people to believe they were guilty of murder in the death of Jesus, hoping the crowd would avenge His death. He evidently forgot the declaration of the crowd recorded in Matthew 27:25, "His blood be on us, and on our children."

The statement that they had filled Jerusalem with their teaching was a great admission of the effectiveness of the apostles' witness. Yet the high priest totally misunderstood their purpose, probably because, in spite of himself, he felt guilty for what had been done to Jesus. The statement that the apostles wanted to bring vengeance on them for the death of Jesus was nothing but pure slander and was completely false.

**5:29.** Peter and the apostles did not apologize. Without hesitation they answered (with Peter as the spokesman), "It is necessary to obey God rather than human beings" (author's translation). "Obey" is a word used of obedience to one in authority as in Titus 3:1. With a consciousness of Christ's authority, the apostles said the equivalent of "We must obey." Before, in 4:19, they said, "You judge." But the Sanhedrin did not judge that the apostles were under divinely appointed necessity to spread the gospel. Therefore, the apostles had to declare themselves very strongly here.

**for they feared the people, lest they should have been stoned:** . . . afraid of being pelted with stones, *Williams* . . . would kill them with stones, *Everyday* . . . afraid the people would throw stones at them, *NLT.*

**27. And when they had brought them, they set them before the council:** . . . and made them stand before, *NCV* . . . the Sanhedrin, *Weymouth* . . . stand in front of the court, *NLT.*

**and the high priest asked them:** The High Priest demanded an explanation from them, *TCNT* . . . examined them, *Berkeley* . . . questioned them carefully, *Klingensmith.*

**28. Saying, Did not we straitly command you that ye should not teach in this name?:** Did we not give you strict orders...to not teach in this name, *Norlie* . . . Did we not positively forbid you, *Williams* . . . We absolutely prohibited you, *Fenton* . . . We gave you a formal warning, *JB* . . . We strictly enjoined you, *Darby* . . . We told you and told you, *Klingensmith* . . . We gave you very clear orders, *BB* . . . We gave you strict orders not to go on teaching, *Everyday.*

**and, behold, ye have filled Jerusalem with your doctrine:** . . . you have actually flooded Jerusalem, *TCNT* . . . You are spreading this teaching over, *NLT* . . . with your teaching, *RSV.*

**and intend to bring this man's blood upon us:** . . . and are wishing to make us responsible for the death of this man, *TCNT* . . . accuse us as responsible for this man's death, *Noli* . . . and now want to bring on us the people's vengeance for this man's death, *Williams* . . . And you want to get us punished for killing this Man, *Beck* . . . you wish to bring upon us the blood of this man, *Klingensmith* . . . Now you are making it look as if we are guilty of killing this Man, *NLT* . . . You are determined to make us responsible for, *Kleist.*

**29. Then Peter and the other apostles answered and said:** . . . and the missionaries said, *NLT.*

**We ought to obey God rather than men:** We must obey, *RSV*

**Acts 5:30**

| 3095.1 adv comp | 2211.1 conj | 442.8 noun dat pl masc | 3450.5 art nom sing masc | 2296.1 noun nom sing masc | 3450.1 art gen pl |
|---|---|---|---|---|---|
| μᾶλλον | ἤ | ἀνθρώποις. | **30.** ὁ | θεὸς | τῶν |
| *mallon* | *ē* | *anthrōpois* | *ho* | *theos* | *tōn* |
| rather | than | men. | The | God | of the |

| 3824.7 noun gen pl masc | 2231.2 prs-pron gen 1pl | 1446.5 verb 3sing indic aor act | 2400.3 name acc masc | 3614.6 rel-pron acc sing masc | 5050.1 prs-pron nom 2pl |
|---|---|---|---|---|---|
| πατέρων | ἡμῶν | ἤγειρεν | Ἰησοῦν, | ὃν | ὑμεῖς |
| *paterōn* | *hēmōn* | *ēgeiren* | *Iēsoun* | *hon* | *humeis* |
| fathers | our | raised up | Jesus, | whom | you |

| 1309.1 verb 2pl indic aor mid | 2883.1 verb nom pl masc part aor act | 1894.3 prep | 3448.2 noun gen sing neu | 3642.6 dem-pron acc sing masc |
|---|---|---|---|---|
| διεχειρίσασθε | κρεμάσαντες | ἐπὶ | ξύλου· | **31.** τοῦτον |
| *diecheirisasthe* | *kremasantes* | *epi* | *xulou* | *touton* |
| killed, | having hanged | on | a tree. | This |

| 3450.5 art nom sing masc | 2296.1 noun nom sing masc | 742.1 noun acc sing masc | 2504.1 conj | 4842.4 noun acc sing masc | 5150.2 verb 3sing indic aor act |
|---|---|---|---|---|---|
| ὁ | θεὸς | ἀρχηγὸν | καὶ | σωτῆρα | ὕψωσεν |
| *ho* | *theos* | *archēgon* | *kai* | *sōtēra* | *hupsōsen* |
| | God | a chief | and | Saviour | exalted |

31.a.**Var:** 01ℵ-org,03B Tisc,We/Ho,Weis UBS/⋆

| 3450.11 art dat sing fem | 1182.5 adj dat sing fem | 840.3 prs-pron gen sing | 3450.2 art gen sing | 1319.31 verb inf aor act | 3211.2 noun acc sing fem |
|---|---|---|---|---|---|
| τῇ | δεξιᾷ | αὐτοῦ, | [a+ τοῦ ] | δοῦναι | μετάνοιαν |
| *tē* | *dexia* | *autou* | *tou* | *dounai* | *metanoian* |
| by the | right hand | of him, | [ the ] | to give | repentance |

| 3450.3 art dat sing | 2447.1 name masc | 2504.1 conj | 852.3 noun acc sing fem | 264.6 noun gen pl fem | 2504.1 conj |
|---|---|---|---|---|---|
| τῷ | Ἰσραὴλ | καὶ | ἄφεσιν | ἁμαρτιῶν. | **32.** καὶ |
| *tō* | *Israēl* | *kai* | *aphesin* | *hamartiōn* | *kai* |
| | to Israel | and | forgiveness | of sins. | And |

32.a.**Txt:** 05D-corr,08E 025P,byz.
**Var:** p74,01ℵ,02A 05D-org,sa.bo.Treg,Tisc We/Ho,Sod,UBS/⋆

| 2231.1 prs-pron nom 1pl | 1498.5 verb 1pl indic pres act | 840.3 prs-pron gen sing | 3116.4 noun nom pl masc | 3450.1 art gen pl | 4343.5 noun gen pl neu |
|---|---|---|---|---|---|
| ἡμεῖς | ἐσμεν | ⸂a αὐτοῦ⸃ | μάρτυρες | τῶν | ῥημάτων |
| *hēmeis* | *esmen* | *autou* | *martures* | *tōn* | *rhēmatōn* |
| we | are | of him | witnesses | of the | things |

32.b.**Txt:** 05D-corr,08E 025P,byz.
**Var:** 01ℵ,02A,03B 05D-org,Lach,Treg,Tisc We/Ho,Weis,Sod UBS/⋆

| 3642.2 dem-pron gen pl | 2504.1 conj | 3450.16 art sing neu | 4011.1 noun sing neu | 1156.2 conj | 3450.16 art sing neu |
|---|---|---|---|---|---|
| τούτων, | καὶ | τὸ | πνεῦμα | ⸂b δὲ⸃ | τὸ |
| *toutōn* | *kai* | *to* | *pneuma* | *de* | *to* |
| these, | also | the | Spirit | and | the |

| 39.1 adj sing | 3614.16 rel-pron sing neu | 1319.14 verb 3sing indic aor act | 3450.5 art nom sing masc | 2296.1 noun nom sing masc | 3450.4 art dat pl |
|---|---|---|---|---|---|
| ἅγιον, | ὃ | ἔδωκεν | ὁ | θεὸς | τοῖς |
| *hagion* | *ho* | *edōken* | *ho* | *theos* | *tois* |
| Holy, | which | gave | | God | to the |

| 3842.1 verb dat pl masc part pres act | 840.4 prs-pron dat sing | 3450.7 art nom pl masc | 1156.2 conj | 189.32 verb nom pl masc part aor act |
|---|---|---|---|---|
| πειθαρχοῦσιν | αὐτῷ. | **33.** Οἱ | δὲ | ἀκούσαντες |
| *peitharchousin* | *autō* | *Hoi* | *de* | *akousantes* |
| obeying | him. | The | but | having heard |

33.a.**Txt:** 01ℵ,05D,025P 1739,byz.it.Gries,Alf Word,Tisc,Sod
**Var:** p74,02A,03B,08E sa.bo.Lach,Treg,We/Ho Weis,UBS/⋆

| 1276.1 verb 3pl indic imperf pass | 2504.1 conj | 1003.6 verb 3pl indic imperf mid | 1007.17 verb 3pl indic imperf mid |
|---|---|---|---|
| διεπρίοντο | καὶ | ⸀ ἐβουλεύοντο | [a ἐβούλοντο ] |
| *dieprionto* | *kai* | *ebouleuonto* | *eboulonto* |
| were infuriated, | and | took counsel | [ idem ] |

**5:30.** The high priest had not mentioned God or His will. Neither did he mention the name of Jesus. But Peter did not hesitate to point them to the God of their fathers, who had raised up Jesus. Then, once again, he contrasted the way God treated Jesus in raising and exalting Him with the way the Jewish leaders treated Him, hanging Him on a tree. (Both the Hebrew and Greek words for *tree* also mean wood or anything made of wood, and so "tree" here includes the cross. The cross was made of rough-hewn wood.)

**5:31.** Contrary to their fears, it was not the apostles' desire, nor was it God's purpose, to punish the Jewish leaders for crucifying Jesus. Rather, God had exalted Jesus, the very One they crucified, with (and also "to") His right hand, to be a Prince (author, founder) and a Saviour, in order to give repentance to Israel and the forgiveness of sins. God's purpose was to offer the opportunity for repentance and forgiveness of sins to Israel.

Peter, of course, did not mean to restrict this offer of repentance and forgiveness to the people of Israel. God's purpose has always been to bring blessing to all the families of the earth by offering forgiveness and salvation to all sinners. Their guilt will be canceled if they repent, whoever they are. By exalting Jesus, God put Him in a position where it should be easy for sinners to repent.

**5:32.** As before, the apostles emphasized they were Christ's witnesses to "these things," that is, to these words (*rhematōn*, used of the "*words* of this life" in 5:20 and therefore of the gospel message the apostles were teaching and preaching). Peter added that the Holy Spirit whom God has given is also a witness. Peter made it clear that God gave, and still gives, the Holy Spirit to those who obey Him. This corresponds to Galatians 3:2 where Paul reminded the Galatians that they received the Spirit by the hearing of faith, and both the hearing and the faith imply obedience. This also points back to Luke 11:13 which says God as a good Father gives the Holy Spirit to them that ask Him, assuming they have right motives (see James 4:3). So asking is normally a part of obedience. He is the Giver (John 15:26). It is also quite clear that the giving of the Spirit was not to be limited to the apostles or to their time.

**5:33.** Apparently the majority of the Sanhedrin took Peter's words to mean the apostles not only considered them guilty of Christ's death but also guilty of a refusal to accept God's authority and obey Him. The apostles had linked their witness to the Spirit's witness. But instead of accepting the offer of repentance, the members of the Sanhedrin were cut to the heart (sawn through, cut through, cut to the quick with anger, indignation, and jealousy). Immediately they started proceedings to kill the apostles. The same word for *kill* is used of killing (murdering) Jesus in 2:23.

. . . Better for us, *NAB* . . . the orders of God, *Phillips*.

**30. The God of our fathers raised up Jesus:** . . . of our early fathers, *NLT* . . . ancestors has raised Jesus from the grave, *TCNT* . . . raised Jesus to life, *Weymouth*.

**whom ye slew and hanged on a tree:** . . . whom you crucified and put to death, *Weymouth* . . . whom you yourselves put to death, by hanging him on a cross, *TCNT* . . . whom you murdered by crucifying him, *Noli* . . . you killed and nailed to a cross, *NLT*.

**31. Him hath God exalted with his right hand to be a Prince and a Saviour:** It is this Jesus, whom God has exalted to his right hand, to be a Guide, *TCNT* . . . to his right side, *TEV* . . . with his right hand to be captain and saviour, *Williams C.K.* . . . as a Ruler, *Adams* . . . our Pioneer, *Klingensmith* . . . our Leader, *Everyday*.

**for to give repentance to Israel, and forgiveness of sins:** . . . so that the people of Israel would have opportunity for repentance, *LivB* . . . Who saves from the penalty of sin, *NLT* . . . so that all Jews could change their hearts and lives and have their sins forgiven, *Everyday*.

**32. And we are his witnesses of these things:** We saw all these things happen, *Everyday* . . . We have seen these things and are telling about them, *NLT*.

**and so is also the Holy Ghost:** The Holy Spirit makes these things known also, *NLT*.

**whom God hath given to them that obey him:** . . . who submit to his government, *Campbell* . . . who obey his commands, *Phillips*.

**33. When they heard that, They were cut to the heart:** The members of the Council grew furious on hearing this, *TCNT* . . . And hearing it, they were convulsed with rage, *HBIE* . . . Infuriated at getting this answer, *Weymouth* . . . they were enraged, *Campbell* . . . burned with indignation, *Murdock* . . . they were stung to madness, *Williams C.K.*

**and took counsel to slay them:** . . . and determined to destroy them, *Berkeley* . . . and made up

| 335.9 verb inf aor act | 840.8 prs-pron acc pl masc | 448.9 verb nom sing masc part aor act | 1156.2 conj | 4948.3 indef-pron nom sing |
|---|---|---|---|---|
| ἀνελεῖν | αὐτούς. | 34. ἀναστὰς | δέ | τις |
| *anelein* | *autous* | *anastas* | *de* | *tis* |
| to put to death | them. | Having risen up | but | a certain one |

| 1706.1 prep | 3450.3 art dat sing | 4742.3 noun dat sing neu | 5168.1 name nom sing masc | 3549.4 noun dat sing neu |
|---|---|---|---|---|
| ἐν | τῷ | συνεδρίῳ | Φαρισαῖος, | ὀνόματι |
| *en* | *tō* | *sunedriō* | *Pharisaios* | *onomati* |
| in | the | Sanhedrin | a Pharisee, | by name |

| 1052.1 name masc | 3410.1 noun nom sing masc | 4941.2 adj nom sing masc | 3820.3 adj dat sing | 3450.3 art dat sing |
|---|---|---|---|---|
| Γαμαλιήλ, | νομοδιδάσκαλος, | τίμιος | παντὶ | τῷ |
| *Gamaliēl* | *nomodidaskalos* | *timios* | *panti* | *tō* |
| Gamaliel, | a teacher of the law, | honored | by all | the |

34.a.**Txt:** 025P,byz.
**Var:** 01ℵ,02A,03B,05D
08E,Lach,Treg,Alf
Word,Tisc,We/Ho,Weis
Sod,UBS/⋆

| 2967.3 noun dat sing masc | 2724.3 verb 3sing indic aor act | 1838.1 adv | 1017.2 adj sing neu | 4948.10 indef-pron sing neu | 3450.8 art acc pl masc |
|---|---|---|---|---|---|
| λαῷ, | ἐκέλευσεν | ἔξω | βραχὺ | ⸂ᵃ τι ⸃ | τοὺς |
| *laō* | *ekeleusen* | *exō* | *brachu* | *ti* | *tous* |
| people, | commanded | out | for a short while | some | the |

34.b.**Txt:** 05D,08E,025P
byz.sa.Sod
**Var:** 01ℵ,02A,03B,bo.
Lach,Treg,Alf,Tisc
We/Ho,Weis,UBS/⋆

| 646.7 noun acc pl masc | 442.9 noun acc pl masc | 4020.41 verb inf aor act | 1500.5 verb 3sing indic aor act |
|---|---|---|---|
| ⸀ ἀποστόλους | [ᵇ⋆ ἀνθρώπους ] | ποιῆσαι, | 35. εἶπέν |
| *apostolous* | *anthrōpous* | *poiēsai* | *eipen* |
| apostles | [ men ] | to put, | Said |

| 4885.1 conj | 4242.1 prep | 840.8 prs-pron acc pl masc | 433.6 noun nom pl masc | 2448.2 name nom pl masc | 4196.2 verb 2pl impr pres act |
|---|---|---|---|---|---|
| τε | πρὸς | αὐτούς, | Ἄνδρες | Ἰσραηλῖται, | προσέχετε |
| *te* | *pros* | *autous* | *Andres* | *Israēlitai* | *prosechete* |
| and | to | them, | Men | Israelites, | be careful |

| 1431.7 prs-pron dat pl masc | 1894.3 prep | 3450.4 art dat pl | 442.8 noun dat pl masc | 3642.3 dem-pron dat pl | 4949.9 intr-pron sing neu |
|---|---|---|---|---|---|
| ἑαυτοῖς | ἐπὶ | τοῖς | ἀνθρώποις | τούτοις | τί |
| *heautois* | *epi* | *tois* | *anthrōpois* | *toutois* | *ti* |
| to yourselves | about | the | men | these | what |

| 3165.5 verb 2pl indic pres act | 4097.13 verb inf pres act | 4112.1 prep | 1056.1 conj | 3642.2 dem-pron gen pl | 3450.1 art gen pl |
|---|---|---|---|---|---|
| μέλλετε | πράσσειν. | 36. πρὸ | γὰρ | τούτων | τῶν |
| *mellete* | *prassein* | *pro* | *gar* | *toutōn* | *tōn* |
| you are about | to do; | before | for | these | the |

| 2232.6 noun gen pl fem | 448.2 verb 3sing indic aor act | 2310.1 name nom masc | 2978.15 verb nom sing masc part pres act | 1498.32 verb inf pres act |
|---|---|---|---|---|
| ἡμερῶν | ἀνέστη | Θευδᾶς, | λέγων | εἶναί |
| *hēmerōn* | *anestē* | *Theudas* | *legōn* | *einai* |
| days | rose up | Theudas, | claiming | to be |

| 4948.5 indef-pron | 1431.6 prs-pron acc sing masc | 3614.3 rel-pron dat sing | 4205.1 verb 3sing indic aor pass | 700.1 noun nom sing masc |
|---|---|---|---|---|
| τινα | ἑαυτόν, | ᾧ | ⸀ προσεκολλήθη | ἀριθμὸς |
| *tina* | *heauton* | *hō* | *prosekollēthē* | *arithmos* |
| somebody | himself, | to whom | were joined | a number |

36.a.**Txt:** byz.
**Var:** 01ℵ,02A,03B,04C
Lach,Treg,Alf,Word
Tisc,We/Ho,Weis,Sod
UBS/⋆

| 433.7 noun gen pl masc | 5448.1 adv | 4203.1 verb 3sing indic aor pass | 433.7 noun gen pl masc | 700.1 noun nom sing masc | 5453.1 conj |
|---|---|---|---|---|---|
| ἀνδρῶν, | ὡσεὶ | [ᵃ⋆ προσεκλίθη | ἀνδρῶν | ἀριθμὸς | ὡς ] |
| *andrōn* | *hōsei* | *proseklithē* | *andrōn* | *arithmos* | *hōs* |
| of men, | about | [ were joined | men | a number | about ] |

**5:34.** This time the entire Sanhedrin was meeting together, and it included some prominent Pharisees. *Pharisees* probably means "separated ones," possibly referring to their emphasis on washings and ceremonial purity. The Sadducees dominated the temple and the priesthood at this time, but the Pharisees had the most influence in the synagogues and among the majority of the Jews. Pharisees were generally careful not to exceed the demands of justice in the administration of the Mosaic law.

Among the Pharisees was Gamaliel, a doctor (authoritative teacher) of the Law, a person valued highly by all the people. In the Jewish Talmud Gamaliel is said to be the grandson of the famous rabbi Hillel. Hillel was the most influential teacher of the Pharisees, a man who continued to be held in high esteem by all later orthodox Jews. The apostle Paul was trained by Gamaliel and became one of his most prominent students. Possibly, Paul, then known as Saul of Tarsus, was already a member of the Sanhedrin at this time.

At this point Gamaliel stood up, took charge of the situation, and ordered the apostles to be taken outside for a little while. Again, it is probable that Paul later told Luke what Gamaliel said and what went on while the apostles were outside.

**5:35.** Gamaliel gave a stern warning to the Sanhedrin. That the Sanhedrin received such advice from him is a strong indication of the great respect afforded to this rabbi. F.F. Bruce quotes the following statement recorded in the Mishnah: "When the Rabban Gamaliel died . . . the glory of the Torah ceased, and purity and 'separateness' died" (*New International Commentary on the New Testament, Acts*, p.115). Bruce goes on to explain that "Rabban" (Aramaic for "our teacher") was a title of great honor bestowed only upon the most distinguished teachers. This title set them apart from others who were called "rabbi," which means "my teacher" (ibid.).

Gamaliel warned the Council that they must be cautious about (and give careful attention to) what they were intending to do (or, were about to do) to these men. Obviously Gamaliel sensed the anger and indignation rising up in the hearts of the members of the Sanhedrin. This kind of anger can become irrational. It can turn thinking men into an unthinking mob, just as it did at the trial of Jesus when the priest-dominated crowd cried out, "Crucify Him!" (Just a few days earlier the crowd had cried out, "Hosanna! Blessed is he who comes in the name of the Lord.")

Again it must be remembered that the high priest gathered only part of the Sanhedrin at night for the trial of Jesus. It is evident that men like Gamaliel were not present on that night. Neither was the crowd that had cried "hosanna" present. Most of them were staying outside the city in the villages around about. Jesus was already being led out by the Roman soldiers to be crucified when the crowds began coming into Jerusalem the following morning. But in the providence of God, the high priest and the Sadducees were not alone this time. Gamaliel and others were present. Perhaps

their minds, *Williams C.K.* . . . and planned to kill them, *Norlie* . . . consulted to put them to death, *Campbell* . . . they talked of killing them, *Klingensmith.*

**34. Then stood there up one in the council:** But there stood up one in the Sanhedrin, *HBIE* . . . a man of the religious leaders' court, *NLT.*

**a Pharisee, named Gamaliel, a doctor of the law:** . . . a Teacher of the Law, *TCNT* . . . a professor of law, *Berkeley* . . . He was a proud religious law-keeper, *NLT.*

**had in reputation among all the people:** . . . honoured by all the people, *Rotherham* . . . held in universal respect, *TCNT* . . . who was highly respected by, *Noli.*

**and commanded to put the apostles forth a little space:** . . . ordered the apostles to leave the meeting for a little while, *Everyday* . . . gave orders to put the men outside for a little time, *Rotherham* . . . the men to be removed for a short time, *Williams C.K.* . . . said that the missionaries should be sent outside, *NLT.*

**35. And said unto them, Ye men of Israel:** Then Gamaliel said...Jewish men, *NLT.*

**take heed to yourselves what ye intend to do as touching these men:** . . . consider carefully, *NIV* . . . be careful what you are about to do in dealing with these men, *Weymouth* . . . beware what you are going to do, *TNT* . . . think well before you take any action against these men, *Noli* . . . be careful how you intend to treat these men, *Berkeley.*

**36. For before these days rose up Theudas:** Years ago, *Montgomery* . . . Remember that some time ago, *Noli* . . . For it is not long ago that Theudas appeared, *TCNT* . . . who became notorious, *JB* . . . made himself conspicuous, *Phillips.*

**boasting himself to be somebody:** . . . affirming himself to be, *Rotherham* . . . claiming to be, *TCNT* . . . professing to be a person of importance, *Weymouth* . . . He said that he was a great man, *Everyday* . . . claimed to be a divine messenger, *Noli.*

**to whom a number of men, about four hundred, joined themselves:** . . . espoused his

| **4919.1** num card gen | **3614.5** rel-pron nom sing masc | **335.12** verb 3sing indic aor pass | **2504.1** conj | **3820.7** adj nom pl masc |
|---|---|---|---|---|
| τετρακοσίων· | ὃς | ἀνῃρέθη, | καὶ | πάντες |
| *tetrakosiōn* | *hos* | *anērethē* | *kai* | *pantes* |
| four hundred; | who | was put to death, | and | all |

| **3607.2** rel-pron nom pl masc | **3844.33** verb 3pl indic imperf pass | **840.4** prs-pron dat sing | **1256.1** verb 3pl indic aor pass | **2504.1** conj |
|---|---|---|---|---|
| ὅσοι | ἐπείθοντο | αὐτῷ | διελύθησαν | καὶ |
| *hosoi* | *epeithonto* | *autō* | *dieluthēsan* | *kai* |
| as many as | were being persuaded | by him | were dispersed | and |

| **1090.38** verb 3pl indic aor mid | **1519.1** prep | **3625.6** num card neu | | **3196.3** prep | **3642.6** dem-pron acc sing masc | **448.2** verb 3sing indic aor act |
|---|---|---|---|---|---|---|
| ἐγένοντο | εἰς | οὐδέν. | **37.** | μετὰ | τοῦτον | ἀνέστη |
| *egenonto* | *eis* | *ouden* | | *meta* | *touton* | *anestē* |
| came | to | nothing. | | After | this one | rose up |

| **2430.1** name nom masc | **3450.5** art nom sing masc | **1050.1** name-adj nom sing masc | **1706.1** prep | **3450.14** art dat pl fem | **2232.7** noun dat pl fem |
|---|---|---|---|---|---|
| Ἰούδας | ὁ | Γαλιλαῖος | ἐν | ταῖς | ἡμέραις |
| *Ioudas* | *ho* | *Galilaios* | *en* | *tais* | *hēmerais* |
| Judas | the | Galilean | in | the | days |

37.a.**Txt:** 02A-corr,08E 025P,044,33,byz.
**Var:** p74,01ℵ,02A-org 03B,1241,sa.Lach,Treg Alf,Tisc,We/Ho,Weis Sod,UBS/⋆

| **3450.10** art gen sing fem | **577.2** noun gen sing fem | **2504.1** conj | **861.1** verb 3sing indic aor act | **2967.4** noun acc sing masc | **2401.2** adj sing |
|---|---|---|---|---|---|
| τῆς | ἀπογραφῆς, | καὶ | ἀπέστησεν | λαὸν | ⸂a ἱκανὸν⸃ |
| *tēs* | *apographēs* | *kai* | *apestēsen* | *laon* | *hikanon* |
| of the | registration, | and | drew away | people | much |

| **3557.1** adv | **840.3** prs-pron gen sing | **2519.6** dem-pron nom sing masc | **616.22** verb 3sing indic aor mid | **2504.1** conj | **3820.7** adj nom pl masc |
|---|---|---|---|---|---|
| ὀπίσω | αὐτοῦ· | κἀκεῖνος | ἀπώλετο, | καὶ | πάντες |
| *opisō* | *autou* | *kakeinos* | *apōleto* | *kai* | *pantes* |
| after | his; | and that | perished, | and | all |

| **3607.2** rel-pron nom pl masc | **3844.33** verb 3pl indic imperf pass | **840.4** prs-pron dat sing | **1281.5** verb 3pl indic aor pass |
|---|---|---|---|
| ὅσοι | ἐπείθοντο | αὐτῷ | διεσκορπίσθησαν. |
| *hosoi* | *epeithonto* | *autō* | *dieskorpisthēsan* |
| as many as | were being persuaded | by him | were scattered abroad. |

| | **2504.1** conj | **3450.17** art pl neu | **3431.1** adv | **2978.1** verb 1sing pres act | **5050.3** prs-pron dat 2pl | **861.6** verb 2pl impr aor act | **570.3** prep |
|---|---|---|---|---|---|---|---|
| **38.** | καὶ | τὰ | νῦν | λέγω | ὑμῖν, | ἀπόστητε | ἀπὸ |
| | *kai* | *ta* | *nun* | *legō* | *humin* | *apostēte* | *apo* |
| | And | the | now | I say | to you, | Withdraw | from |

38.a.**Txt:** 05D,08E,025P byz.Sod
**Var:** 01ℵ,02A,03B,04C Lach,Treg,Alf,Tisc We/Ho,Weis,UBS/⋆

| **3450.1** art gen pl | **442.7** noun gen pl masc | **3642.2** dem-pron gen pl | **2504.1** conj | **1432.6** verb 2pl impr aor act | **856.18** verb 2pl impr aor act |
|---|---|---|---|---|---|
| τῶν | ἀνθρώπων | τούτων, | καὶ | ⸀ἐάσατε | [a⋆ ἄφετε ] |
| *tōn* | *anthrōpōn* | *toutōn* | *kai* | *easate* | *aphete* |
| the | men | these, | and | permit | [ leave ] |

| **840.8** prs-pron acc pl masc | **3617.1** conj | **1430.1** partic | **1498.10** verb 3sing subj pres act | **1523.1** prep gen | **442.7** noun gen pl masc |
|---|---|---|---|---|---|
| αὐτούς· | ὅτι | ἐὰν | ᾖ | ἐξ | ἀνθρώπων |
| *autous* | *hoti* | *ean* | *ē* | *ex* | *anthrōpōn* |
| them, | for | | it may be | from | men |

| **3450.9** art nom sing fem | **1005.1** noun nom sing fem | **3642.9** dem-pron nom sing fem | **2211.1** conj | **3450.16** art sing neu | **2024.1** noun sing neu | **3642.17** dem-pron sing neu |
|---|---|---|---|---|---|---|
| ἡ | βουλὴ | αὕτη | ἢ | τὸ | ἔργον | τοῦτο, |
| *hē* | *boulē* | *hautē* | *ē* | *to* | *ergon* | *touto* |
| the | counsel | this | or | the | work | this, |

also Gamaliel did not feel the same anger and indignation; he was a highly respected, rational, and well-educated man.

**5:36.** By two examples Gamaliel reminded the Sanhedrin that individuals in the past had gathered a following, but came to nothing.

The first example was Theudas, who said of himself that he was something, that is, something great. He was probably a man of the same order as Simon the sorcerer who deceived the Samaritans by his trickery and pretended to be the great power of God.

*Theudas* was a common name, and he was probably one of the rebels who arose after Herod the Great died in 4 B.C. Some have confused this Theudas with a later Theudas of whom Josephus, the Jewish historian, speaks. Josephus referred to this latter individual as a "magician" who persuaded a great many people to gather all their possessions and follow him to the Jordan River. This self-proclaimed prophet boasted that he would command the Jordan to part, as did Elijah and Elisha (*Antiquities* 20.5.1). His grandiose plans were short-lived: Fadus, the procurator who succeeded Agrippa I in A.D. 44, beheaded him (Carter and Earle, *Acts*, p.83). To this Theudas about 400 men attached themselves. He was murdered, and all who obeyed him (and believed in him) were dispersed and came to nothing.

**5:37.** After Theudas, Judas the Galilean rose up in the days of the taxing, that is, of the census which was taken for the purpose of taxing.

The Romans ordered the first census of the people and their property in 10–9 B.C. It reached Palestine about 6 B.C., at the time Jesus was born in Bethlehem (Luke 2:2). There was another similar census every 14 years after that. The second census reached Palestine, however, in A.D. 6 when this Judas arose and, according to Josephus, taught the people not to pay tribute to Caesar.

This Judas of Galilee succeeded in drawing away a considerable number of the Jewish people after him. But he also perished, and all who obeyed him (and believed in him) were scattered.

**5:38.** Gamaliel's conclusion was that they should refrain from "these men" (the apostles), that is, withdraw from them and leave them alone. In other words, they should let them go, for if "this counsel or this work" was from (out from) men (it had a mere human source from human ideas, human thinking, or human plotting) it would come to nought, it would be overthrown or destroyed.

**5:39.** On the other hand, Gamaliel continued, if it was from God they would not be able to overthrow it (or them, that is, the apostles

cause, *Williams* . . . adhered to him, *Berkeley*.

**who was slain:** He himself was killed, *TCNT* . . . who was assassinated, *Concordant*.

**and all, as many as obeyed him, were scattered:** . . . all his supporters, *Berkeley* . . . all his followers were dispersed, *Weymouth* . . . were divided, *NLT*.

**And brought to nought:** . . . and came to nothing, *RSV* . . . and as a party annihilated, *Williams* . . . They were able to do nothing, *Everyday, NCV* . . . and that was the end of them, *TNT* . . . and their movement was suppressed, *Noli* . . . and nothing came of his teaching, *NLT*.

**37. After this man rose up Judas of Galilee:** . . . came into prominence, *Adams*.

**in the days of the taxing:** . . . at the time of the census, *TCNT* . . . of the enrollment for the Roman tax, *Williams* . . . at the time of the registration, *Everyday*.

**and drew away much people after him:** . . . and drew a people into a revolt after him, *Rotherham* . . . and got people to follow him, *TCNT* . . . and was the leader in a revolt, *Weymouth*.

**he also perished:** . . . but he too was destroyed, *Williams C.K.*

**and all, even as many as obeyed him, were dispersed:** . . . were scattered abroad, *ASV* . . . to the winds, *Norlie*.

**38. And now I say unto you:** And in this present case, my advice to you is, *TCNT* . . . What I suggest, therefore, *JB* . . . And so not I tell you, *Everyday*.

**Refrain from these men, and let them alone:** Stand aloof from these men, *Rotherham* . . . leave them alone, *Norlie* . . . keep away from these men, *Beck* . . . keep your hands off these men, let them alone, *Williams C.K.* . . . Stay away from these men, *Everyday* . . . let them go, *NIV*.

**for if this counsel or this work be of men:** If this teaching and work is from, *NLT* . . . for if this scheme or work, *Weymouth* . . . if their movement is of, *Noli* . . . are only of human origin, *TCNT* . . . For, if this program or movement has its origin in man, *Williams* . . . For if what they are planning or doing is man's work, *Williams C.K.*

| 2617.9 verb 3sing indic fut pass | 1479.1 conj | 1156.2 conj | 1523.2 prep gen | 2296.2 noun gen sing masc | 1498.4 verb 3sing indic pres act |
|---|---|---|---|---|---|
| καταλυθήσεται· | 39. εἰ | δὲ | ἐκ | θεοῦ | ἐστιν, |
| *kataluthēsetai* | *ei* | *de* | *ek* | *theou* | *estin* |
| it will be put down; | if | but | from | God | it be, |

39.a.**Txt:** 02A,025P,byz.bo.
**Var:** 01ℵ,03B,04C,05D 087,sa.Lach,Treg,Tisc We/Ho,Weis,Sod UBS/☆

| 3620.3 partic | 1404.6 verb 2pl indic pres mid | 1404.32 verb 2pl indic fut mid | 2617.5 verb inf aor act | 840.15 prs-pron sing neu |
|---|---|---|---|---|
| οὐ | ⸀ δύνασθε | [a☆ δυνήσεσθε] | καταλῦσαι | ⸀ αὐτό, |
| *ou* | *dunasthe* | *dunēsesthe* | *katalusai* | *auto* |
| not | you are able | [ you will be able ] | to suppress | it |

39.b.**Txt:** 04C-org,025P 044,33,byz.sa.bo.
**Var:** 01ℵ,02A,03B 04C-corr,05D,08E,Gries Lach,Treg,Alf,Tisc We/Ho,Weis,Sod UBS/☆

| 840.8 prs-pron acc pl masc | 3246.1 partic | 2504.1 conj | 2291.1 adj nom pl masc | 2128.37 verb 2pl subj aor pass |
|---|---|---|---|---|
| [b☆ αὐτούς ] | μήποτε | καὶ | θεομάχοι | εὑρεθῆτε. |
| *autous* | *mēpote* | *kai* | *theomachoi* | *heurethēte* |
| [ them, ] | lest | also | fighters against God | you be found. |

| 3844.25 verb 3pl indic aor pass | 1156.2 conj | 840.4 prs-pron dat sing | 2504.1 conj | 4200.5 verb nom pl masc part aor mid |
|---|---|---|---|---|
| 40. Ἐπείσθησαν | δὲ | αὐτῷ· | καὶ | προσκαλεσάμενοι |
| *Epeisthēsan* | *de* | *autō* | *kai* | *proskalesamenoi* |
| They were persuaded | and | by him; | and | having called |

| 3450.8 art acc pl masc | 646.7 noun acc pl masc | 1188.6 verb nom pl masc part aor act | 3715.9 verb 3pl indic aor act | 3231.1 partic |
|---|---|---|---|---|
| τοὺς | ἀποστόλους, | δείραντες | παρήγγειλαν | μὴ |
| *tous* | *apostolous* | *deirantes* | *parēngeilan* | *mē* |
| the | apostles, | having beaten | they commanded | not |

| 2953.24 verb inf pres act | 1894.3 prep | 3450.3 art dat sing | 3549.4 noun dat sing neu | 3450.2 art gen sing | 2400.2 name masc | 2504.1 conj |
|---|---|---|---|---|---|---|
| λαλεῖν | ἐπὶ | τῷ | ὀνόματι | τοῦ | Ἰησοῦ, | καὶ |
| *lalein* | *epi* | *tō* | *onomati* | *tou* | *Iēsou* | *kai* |
| to speak | in | the | name | | of Jesus, | and |

40.a.**Txt:** 05D,08E,025P byz.Lach,Sod
**Var:** 01ℵ,02A,03B,04C sa.bo.Treg,Alf,Tisc We/Ho,Weis,UBS/☆

| 624.7 verb 3pl indic aor act | 840.8 prs-pron acc pl masc | 3450.7 art nom pl masc | 3173.1 conj | 3631.1 partic |
|---|---|---|---|---|
| ἀπέλυσαν | ⸂a αὐτούς·⸃ | 41. Οἱ | μὲν | οὖν |
| *apelusan* | *autous* | *Hoi* | *men* | *oun* |
| released | them. | The | | therefore |

| 4057.38 verb 3pl indic imperf mid | 5299.9 verb nom pl masc part pres act | 570.3 prep | 4241.2 noun gen sing neu | 3450.2 art gen sing |
|---|---|---|---|---|
| ἐπορεύοντο | χαίροντες | ἀπὸ | προσώπου | τοῦ |
| *eporeuonto* | *chairontes* | *apo* | *prosōpou* | *tou* |
| were departing | rejoicing | from | presence | of the |

| 4742.2 noun gen sing neu | 3617.1 conj | 5065.1 prep | 3450.2 art gen sing | 3549.3 noun gen sing neu | 840.3 prs-pron gen sing |
|---|---|---|---|---|---|
| συνεδρίου | ὅτι | ⸀ ὑπὲρ | τοῦ | ὀνόματος | αὐτοῦ |
| *sunedriou* | *hoti* | *huper* | *tou* | *onomatos* | *autou* |
| Sanhedrin | that | for | the | name | his |

41.a.**Txt:** byz.
**Var:** 01ℵ,02A,03B,04C Lach,Treg,Alf,Tisc We/Ho,Weis,Sod UBS/☆

| 2631.1 verb 3pl indic aor pass | 2631.1 verb 3pl indic aor pass | 5065.1 prep |
|---|---|---|
| κατηξιώθησαν | [a☆ κατηξιώθησαν | ὑπὲρ |
| *katēxiōthēsan* | *katēxiōthēsan* | *huper* |
| they were accounted worthy | [ they were accounted worthy | for |

| 3450.2 art gen sing | 3549.3 noun gen sing neu | 812.6 verb inf aor pass | 3820.12 adj acc sing fem | 4885.1 conj |
|---|---|---|---|---|
| τοῦ | ὀνόματος ] | ἀτιμασθῆναι· | 42. πᾶσάν | τε |
| *tou* | *onomatos* | *atimasthēnai* | *pasan* | *te* |
| the | name ] | to be dishonored. | Every | and |

and the movement they were leading). They must therefore let these men go, lest perhaps they also would be found to be "ones fighting against God" (one word in the Greek).

It is important to keep in mind here that this was the Pharisee Gamaliel speaking. The Bible here gives us the inspired record which makes it clear that Gamaliel really did say this. But no one must jump to the conclusion that what Gamaliel himself said was inspired. His recorded words were the conclusions of his own thinking, his own human reasoning.

There is a measure of truth in what Gamaliel said. Gamaliel did know the Old Testament Scriptures, and they make it very clear that what is from God cannot be overthrown. It is true also that it is foolish to try to use physical means to overthrow spiritual forces. But it is not true that everything from men will always be quickly overthrown; not every movement or political system of mere human origin has been short-lived.

**5:40.** The whole body of the Sanhedrin was persuaded by the words of Gamaliel. Therefore, they called the 12 apostles back into their council chamber and had them severely flogged with whips. The Greek word for "beaten" actually means "skinned," and is the same word used of flaying, that is, skinning the animals who were sacrificed under the Law. Thus the Sanhedrin still took out their spite and indignation on the apostles. Undoubtedly they followed the law of Deuteronomy 25:2,3 which indicated the persons to be beaten had to lie face down and that the limit was 40 stripes.

Jesus had anticipated this and had warned His disciples they would be beaten (Mark 13:9). Jesus never promised that His followers would always be prosperous in a material sense or that they would always be free from persecution. He told them they would have tribulation (persecution, affliction, distress, pressure), but He promised, "Be of good cheer (take courage); I have overcome (conquered, and am still conqueror over) the world" (John 16:33).

After beating the apostles, the Sanhedrin again commanded (ordered) them not to speak in the name of Jesus (that is, with a view to promoting the authority of Jesus). Then the Council let them go (set them free).

**5:41.** The apostles went away from the presence of the Sanhedrin rejoicing and continuing to rejoice because they were counted worthy to suffer shame (suffer disgrace, be treated disgracefully, dishonored, insulted, and despised) for the sake of the Name. They rejoiced to be disgraced (beaten with the punishment the Law commanded for evil men and criminals) for the sake of all that the name of Jesus includes. They understood the Name to include His character and nature, especially His messiahship, deity, saviourhood, and lordship.

**it will come to nought:** . . . come to nothing, *Weymouth* . . . go to pieces, *Williams* . . . fail, *RSV* . . . break down, *Beck* . . . it will collapse, *Moffatt* . . . it will be wrecked inevitably, *Noli.*

**39. But if it be of God, ye cannot overthrow it:** . . . you will be powerless to put them down, *Weymouth* . . . If it is of divine origin, you cannot put it down, *Noli* . . . it is not in your power to frustrate it, *Murdock* . . . you won't be able to stop them, *Adams.*

**lest haply ye be found even to fight against God:** . . . lest perhaps you find yourselves to be actually fighting against God, *Weymouth* . . . find yourselves to be God resisters, *Berkeley* . . . opposing God, *Norlie.*

**40. and to him they agreed:** And they were persuaded by him, *Rotherham* . . . And to him they assented, *HBIE* . . . His advice carried conviction, *Weymouth* . . . Gamaliel's advice prevailed, *Norlie* . . . They gave in to him, *Montgomery* . . . They were convinced by him, *Williams* . . . They listened to his advice, *Klingensmith.*

**and when they had called the apostles and beaten them:** . . . had them flogged, *TCNT* . . . lashing them, *Concordant* . . . they beat them, *Darby.*

**they commanded that they should not speak in the name of Jesus, and let them go:** . . . they charged them to stop speaking on the authority of Jesus, and then turned them loose, *Williams* . . . released them, *Norlie.*

**41. And they departed from the presence of the council:** But the Apostles left the Council, *TCNT* . . . They, therefore, left the Sanhedrin, *Weymouth.*

**rejoicing that they were counted worthy to suffer shame for his name:** . . . they were fit to suffer, *Klingensmith* . . . the honor of suffering dishonor, *SEB* . . . to suffer disgrace on behalf of the Name, *Weymouth* . . . deemed worthy to be dishonored, *Concordant* . . . suffer abuse, *Murdock* . . . of suffering humiliation, *JB* . . . suffer indignity, *NEB* . . . to suffer shame for Jesus, *Beck.*

| **2232.4** noun acc sing fem | **1706.1** prep | **3450.3** art dat sing | **2387.2** adj dat sing neu | **2504.1** conj | **2567.1** prep | **3486.4** noun acc sing masc | **3620.2** partic |
|---|---|---|---|---|---|---|---|
| ἡμέραν | ἐν | τῷ | ἱερῷ | καὶ | κατ' | οἶκον | οὐκ |
| *hēmeran* | *en* | *tō* | *hierō* | *kai* | *kat'* | *oikon* | *ouk* |
| day | in | the | temple | and | by | house | not |

| **3835.12** verb 3pl indic imperf mid | **1315.9** verb nom pl masc part pres act | **2504.1** conj | **2076.12** verb nom pl masc part pres mid |
|---|---|---|---|
| ἐπαύοντο | διδάσκοντες | καὶ | εὐαγγελιζόμενοι |
| *epauonto* | *didaskontes* | *kai* | *euangelizomenoi* |
| they were ceasing | teaching | and | announcing the glad tidings |

| **2400.3** name acc masc | **3450.6** art acc sing masc | **5382.4** name acc masc | **3450.6** art acc sing masc | **5382.4** name acc masc |
|---|---|---|---|---|
| ⸀ Ἰησοῦν | τὸν | Χριστόν. | [☆ τὸν | Χριστόν, |
| *Iēsoun* | *ton* | *Christon* | *ton* | *Christon* |
| Jesus | the | Christ. | [the | Christ |

| **2400.3** name acc masc | **1706.1** prep | **1156.2** conj | **3450.14** art dat pl fem | **2232.7** noun dat pl fem | **3642.14** dem-pron dat pl fem |
|---|---|---|---|---|---|
| Ἰησοῦν. ] | **6:1.** Ἐν | δὲ | ταῖς | ἡμέραις | ταύταις |
| *Iēsoun* | *En* | *de* | *tais* | *hēmerais* | *tautais* |
| Jesus. ] | In | but | the | days | those |

| **3989.2** verb gen pl masc part pres act | **3450.1** art gen pl | **3073.6** noun gen pl masc | **1090.33** verb 3sing indic aor mid | **1106.1** noun nom sing masc |
|---|---|---|---|---|
| πληθυνόντων | τῶν | μαθητῶν | ἐγένετο | γογγυσμὸς |
| *plēthunontōn* | *tōn* | *mathētōn* | *egeneto* | *gongusmos* |
| multiplying | the | disciples | there arose | a grumbling |

| **3450.1** art gen pl | **1661.1** name gen pl masc | **4242.1** prep | **3450.8** art acc pl masc | **1439.4** name acc pl masc | **3617.1** conj |
|---|---|---|---|---|---|
| τῶν | Ἑλληνιστῶν | πρὸς | τοὺς | Ἑβραίους, | ὅτι |
| *tōn* | *Hellēnistōn* | *pros* | *tous* | *Hebraious* | *hoti* |
| of the | Hellenists | against | the | Hebrews, | because |

| **3779.1** verb 3pl indic imperf pass | **1706.1** prep | **3450.11** art dat sing fem | **1242.3** noun dat sing fem | **3450.11** art dat sing fem |
|---|---|---|---|---|
| παρεθεωροῦντο | ἐν | τῇ | διακονίᾳ | τῇ |
| *paretheōrounto* | *en* | *tē* | *diakonia* | *tē* |
| were overlooking | in | the | distribution | the |

| **2494.1** adj dat sing fem | **3450.13** art nom pl fem | **5339.3** noun nom pl fem | **840.1** prs-pron gen pl | **4200.5** verb nom pl masc part aor mid |
|---|---|---|---|---|
| καθημερινῇ | αἱ | χῆραι | αὐτῶν. | **2.** προσκαλεσάμενοι |
| *kathēmerinē* | *hai* | *chērai* | *autōn* | *proskalesamenoi* |
| daily | the | widows | their. | Having called to |

| **1156.2** conj | **3450.7** art nom pl masc | **1420.1** num card | **3450.16** art sing neu | **3988.1** noun sing neu | **3450.1** art gen pl |
|---|---|---|---|---|---|
| δὲ | οἱ | δώδεκα | τὸ | πλῆθος | τῶν |
| *de* | *hoi* | *dōdeka* | *to* | *plēthos* | *tōn* |
| and | the | twelve | the | multitude | of the |

2.a.**Txt:** 01ℵ,05D,08E 025P,etc.byz.Sod
**Var:** 02A,03B,04C,Lach Treg,Alf,Tisc,We/Ho Weis,UBS/☆

| **3073.6** noun gen pl masc | **1500.3** verb indic aor act | **1500.28** verb 3pl indic aor act | **3620.2** partic | **695.1** adj sing neu |
|---|---|---|---|---|
| μαθητῶν, | ⸀ εἶπον, | [a☆ εἶπαν, ] | Οὐκ | ἀρεστόν |
| *mathētōn* | *eipon* | *eipan* | *Ouk* | *areston* |
| disciples, | said, | [idem] | Not | pleasing |

| **1498.4** verb 3sing indic pres act | **2231.4** prs-pron acc 1pl | **2611.7** verb acc pl masc part aor act | **3450.6** art acc sing masc | **3030.4** noun acc sing masc |
|---|---|---|---|---|
| ἐστιν | ἡμᾶς, | καταλείψαντας | τὸν | λόγον |
| *estin* | *hēmas* | *kataleipsantas* | *ton* | *logon* |
| it is | us, | having left | the | word |

**5:42.** It seems that this beating satisfied the anger of the Jewish priests and leaders for the time being, and their opposition subsided for a considerable period. But the apostles still knew they must obey God rather than men, so they refused to obey the command of the Sanhedrin, and they kept right on preaching and teaching the gospel and honoring the name of Jesus.

Every day in the temple and also going from house to house they never ceased teaching and preaching the good news (the gospel) of Jesus the Christ (the Messiah Jesus). They boldly defied the orders of the Sanhedrin and paid no attention to their threats. They did not even wait for their backs to heal. Instead they engaged in a regular program of teaching and evangelism.

**6:1.** As a result of this regular program of teaching and evangelizing, the number of disciples (learners, believers desiring to learn more about Jesus and the gospel) kept multiplying.

All these newcomers crowding in caused problems. In this case the growing Church was a cross section of society as it was in Jerusalem and Judea. Some of the believers were born there and spoke Hebrew in their homes. (Jerusalem Jews kept alive the Biblical Hebrew.) They knew Greek as a second language, for Greek was the language of trade, commerce, and government since the time of Alexander the Great. But the Jews born outside of Palestine did not know Hebrew well and normally spoke Greek.

In the previous chapters Luke recorded that believers contributed to a common fund for the needy. As time went on, most believers found work and no longer needed this help. Widows, however, could not go out and get a job, and soon they were the only ones left who still needed help from this fund. As the Early Church developed, concern for these widows became more evident. The Epistle of James, for example, considers caring for widows (and orphans) one aspect of the kind of a pure and faultless religion God accepts (James 1:27). Later, Paul specified how congregations were to provide for their widows (1 Timothy 5:3-10).

It seems that the Greek-speaking widows who did not understand Hebrew held back, so they were easily overlooked. The result was that tension built up between the Greek-speaking and Hebrew-speaking believers. Finally a murmuring (a grumbling half under their breath) arose among the Greek-speaking believers against the Hebrew-speaking believers because their widows were being neglected (overlooked) in the daily ministration (service).

**6:2.** When the 12 apostles (including Matthias) realized how serious this division was becoming, they called the multitude (the whole mass) of the disciples together. They told them it was not reasonable (pleasing, satisfactory, or acceptable) for them to leave or abandon the teaching and preaching of God's Word to serve tables (in this case, to take care of money tables). They would have to quit preaching and teaching and give all their time to this ministry if they were to personally see that no widow was neglected.

**42. And daily in the temple, and in every house:** . . . or in private houses, *TCNT.*

**they ceased not to teach and preach Jesus Christ:** . . . they did not for a single day cease, *Confraternity* . . . to teach unceasingly, *Phillips* . . . the Gospel of Jesus, the Messiah, *Montgomery* . . . Jesus is the promised Saviour, *Beck* . . . announcing the glad tidings, *Darby* . . . they kept right on teaching, *NASB* . . . evangelizing, *Alford.*

**1. And in those days:** About this time, *TCNT.*

**when the number of the disciples was multiplied:** . . . was constantly increasing, *TCNT* . . . kept growing, *Berkeley* . . . the number of the students was increased, *Klingensmith.*

**there arose a murmuring of the Grecians against the Hebrews:** . . . protests were made, *BB* . . . the Greeks in the group began to complain, *Norlie* . . . low, undertone murmuring...secretly complaining against, *Wuest* . . . complaints were made by the Greek-speaking Jews against the native Jews, *TCNT* . . . a complaint was brought against those who spoke Aramaic by those who spoke Greek, *Beck.*

**because their widows were neglected in the daily ministration:** . . . were being overlooked in the daily distribution, *TCNT* . . . were habitually overlooked in the distribution of alms, *Montgomery* . . . daily provision of food, *Wuest* . . . daily serving of food, *Adams* . . . daily rationing, *Klingensmith* . . . distribution of relief, *Fenton* . . . when the food was handed out, *Beck.*

**2. Then the twelve called the multitude of the disciples unto them, and said:** The Twelve, therefore, summoned the general body of the disciples and said to them, *TCNT* . . . then convened, *Fenton* . . . the main body, *Moffatt* . . . addressed them, *Rieu.*

**It is not reason that we should leave the word of God:** It will not do for us to neglect God's message, *TCNT* . . . it would be a grave mistake, *NEB* . . . neglect the teaching of God's word, *Berkeley* . . . forsaking, *Rotherham* . . . drop preaching, *Moffatt.*

## Acts 6:3

| 3450.2 art gen sing | 2296.2 noun gen sing masc | 1241.8 verb inf pres act | 4971.4 noun dat pl fem | 1964.6 verb 2pl impr aor mid |
|---|---|---|---|---|
| τοῦ | θεοῦ, | διακονεῖν | τραπέζαις. | 3. ἐπισκέψασθε |
| *tou* | *theou* | *diakonein* | *trapezais* | *episkepsasthe* |
| | of God, | to serve | tables. | Look out |

3.a.**Txt:** 04C,08E,025P 044,33,byz.it.bo.Gries Treg,Word,Sod **Var:** 01ℵ,03B,sa.Tisc We/Ho,Weis,UBS/☆

| 3631.1 partic | 1156.2 conj | 79.6 noun nom pl masc | 433.9 noun acc pl masc | 1523.1 prep gen | 5050.2 prs-pron gen 2pl |
|---|---|---|---|---|---|
| ʼ οὖν, | [a☆ δέ, ] | ἀδελφοί, | ἄνδρας | ἐξ | ὑμῶν |
| *oun* | *de* | *adelphoi* | *andras* | *ex* | *humōn* |
| therefore, | [ and, ] | brothers, | men | from among | yourselves, |

3.b.**Txt:** 02A,04C,08E 025P,byz.sa. **Var:** p8,p74,01ℵ,03B 04C-corr,05D,Gries Lach,Treg,Alf,Tisc We/Ho,Weis,Sod UBS/☆

| 3113.34 verb acc pl masc part pres mid | 2017.1 num card | 3994.2 adj pl | 4011.2 noun gen sing neu | 39.2 adj gen sing |
|---|---|---|---|---|
| μαρτυρουμένους | ἑπτά, | πλήρεις | πνεύματος | ʼb ἁγίου ʽ |
| *marturoumenous* | *hepta* | *plēreis* | *pneumatos* | *hagiou* |
| being borne witness to | seven, | full | of Spirit | Holy |

| 2504.1 conj | 4531.2 noun gen sing fem | 3614.8 rel-pron acc pl masc | 2497.8 verb 1pl indic fut act | 1894.3 prep | 3450.10 art gen sing fem |
|---|---|---|---|---|---|
| καὶ | σοφίας, | οὓς | καταστήσομεν | ἐπὶ | τῆς |
| *kai* | *sophias* | *hous* | *katastēsomen* | *epi* | *tēs* |
| and | wisdom, | whom | we will appoint | over | the |

| 5367.1 noun fem | 3642.10 dem-pron gen sing fem | 2231.1 prs-pron nom 1pl | 1156.2 conj | 3450.11 art dat sing fem | 4194.3 noun dat sing fem | 2504.1 conj |
|---|---|---|---|---|---|---|
| χρείας | ταύτης· | 4. ἡμεῖς | δὲ | τῇ | προσευχῇ | καὶ |
| *chreias* | *tautēs* | *hēmeis* | *de* | *tē* | *proseuchē* | *kai* |
| need | this; | We | but | to the | prayer | and |

| 3450.11 art dat sing fem | 1242.3 noun dat sing fem | 3450.2 art gen sing | 3030.2 noun gen sing masc | 4201.6 verb 1pl indic fut act |
|---|---|---|---|---|
| τῇ | διακονίᾳ | τοῦ | λόγου | προσκαρτερήσομεν. |
| *tē* | *diakonia* | *tou* | *logou* | *proskarterēsomen* |
| the | ministry | of the | word | will steadfastly continue. |

| 2504.1 conj | 694.6 verb 3sing indic aor act | 3450.5 art nom sing masc | 3030.1 noun nom sing masc | 1783.1 prep | 3820.2 adj gen sing |
|---|---|---|---|---|---|
| 5. Καὶ | ἤρεσεν | ὁ | λόγος | ἐνώπιον | παντὸς |
| *Kai* | *ēresen* | *ho* | *logos* | *enōpion* | *pantos* |
| And | pleased | the | saying | before | all |

| 3450.2 art gen sing | 3988.2 noun gen sing neu | 2504.1 conj | 1573.5 verb 3pl indic aor mid | 4587.4 name acc masc | 433.4 noun acc sing masc |
|---|---|---|---|---|---|
| τοῦ | πλήθους· | καὶ | ἐξελέξαντο | Στέφανον, | ἄνδρα |
| *tou* | *plēthous* | *kai* | *exelexanto* | *Stephanon* | *andra* |
| the | multitude; | and | they chose | Stephen, | a man |

5.a.**Var:** 01ℵ,02A 04C-org,05D,08E,025P Lach,Sod

| 3994.3 adj acc sing masc | 3994.1 adj nom sing | 3963.2 noun gen sing fem | 2504.1 conj | 4011.2 noun gen sing neu | 39.2 adj gen sing |
|---|---|---|---|---|---|
| ʼ πλήρη | [a πλήρης ] | πίστεως | καὶ | πνεύματος | ἁγίου, |
| *plērē* | *plērēs* | *pisteōs* | *kai* | *pneumatos* | *hagiou* |
| full | [ idem ] | of faith | and | Spirit | Holy, |

| 2504.1 conj | 5213.4 name acc masc | 2504.1 conj | 4260.1 name acc masc | 2504.1 conj | 3389.1 name acc masc |
|---|---|---|---|---|---|
| καὶ | Φίλιππον, | καὶ | Πρόχορον, | καὶ | Νικάνορα, |
| *kai* | *Philippon* | *kai* | *Prochoron* | *kai* | *Nikanora* |
| and | Philip, | and | Prochorus, | and | Nicanor, |

| 2504.1 conj | 4944.1 name acc masc | 2504.1 conj | 3799.1 name acc masc | 2504.1 conj | 3394.1 name acc masc |
|---|---|---|---|---|---|
| καὶ | Τίμωνα, | καὶ | Παρμενᾶν, | καὶ | Νικόλαον |
| *kai* | *Timōna* | *kai* | *Parmenan* | *kai* | *Nikolaon* |
| and | Timon, | and | Parmenas, | and | Nicolas |

**6:3.** The apostles told the believers to choose from among themselves seven men full of the Holy Spirit and practical wisdom. These the apostles would appoint (set) "over this business" (need). In other words, the apostles laid down the qualifications and the people looked over the congregation to see who had these qualifications to a high degree. Then the people chose the seven through some kind of election. The apostles did not arbitrarily put seven men in charge. The congregation did the choosing, not the apostles.

The seven are not called deacons here, though the verb is related to *diakoneō*, from which *deacon* is derived. Most probably, this election gave a precedent for the office of deacon mentioned later. (See 1 Timothy 3:8-12; Romans 16:1, where Phoebe is called a *diakonon*, the word which is elsewhere translated "deacon, servant," or "minister.")

Some see a special significance in the number seven here as a number of completeness. More likely the only reason for having seven deacons was that seven were needed to keep the accounts and give out the money from the money tables (as the Greek word indicates) to the widows. Notice too that there were no deacons until deacons were needed.

**6:4.** Choosing the 7 would enable the 12 apostles to give themselves to prayer and the ministry (*ministration*; Greek *diakonia*, the same word used in verse 1 for the daily ministration to the widows) of the Word. The apostles would serve the Word, while the seven served tables.

**6:5.** There was no dissent to this direction given by the apostles, for the saying (*word*, Greek, *logos*) pleased the whole crowd of the believers (implying also, that they were all willing to do their part even if it meant serving in this capacity).

They then proceeded to choose Stephen (Greek for *victor's crown* or *wreath*), a man full of faith and the Holy Spirit; Philip (Greek for *lover of horses*), Prochorus, Nicanor, Timon, Parmenas, and Nicolas, a proselyte (a Gentile convert to Judaism) from Antioch of Syria. (Later traditions tried to connect this Nicolas with the Nicolaitans of Revelation 2:6,15, but there is no real evidence of this.)

All of the seven who were chosen had Greek names and were undoubtedly from the Greek-speaking believers. Surely this shows the grace of God and the work of the Holy Spirit in the hearts of the Hebrew-speaking believers. They were in the majority, but they chose all the "deacons" out of the minority group. These seven would have charge of the administration of the fund for the needy of both groups. Thus, no possible complaint could now be lodged by the Greek-speaking believers. This was wisdom and it shows how the Holy Spirit broke down this first barrier that rose up in the Church. Language is still a barrier in the world. But the Holy Spirit

**and serve tables:** . . . to attend, *TCNT* . . . to wait on, *Williams* . . . to attend to mere money matters, *Fenton* . . . to look after the accounts, *Phillips* . . . to hand out food, *NLT.*

**3. Wherefore, brethren, look ye out among you:** . . . choose, *NLT* . . . pick out from among yourselves, *Weymouth* . . . from your number, *Noli.*

**seven men of honest report:** . . . who can be well-attested, *Rotherham* . . . of an attested character, *Campbell* . . . reputable, *Concordant* . . . good testimony, *Murdock* . . . of good standing, *Noli* . . . who are respected, *NLT.*

**full of the Holy Ghost and wisdom:** . . . full of the Spirit, and of good practical sense, *Williams* . . . who are both practical and spiritually-minded, *Phillips.*

**whom we may appoint over this business:** . . . and we will appoint them to undertake this duty, *Weymouth* . . . We will turn this responsibility over to them, *NIV* . . . We will have them take care of this work, *NLT* . . . We will put them in charge of this service, *Noli.*

**4. But we will give ourselves continually to prayer:** But, as for us, we will devote ourselves to prayer, *Weymouth.*

**and to the ministry of the word:** . . . and to the delivery of the Message, *TCNT* . . . and to preaching, *Noli.*

**5. And the saying pleased the whole multitude:** . . . the whole group was pleased with the apostles' proposal, *TEV* . . . was pleasing in the sight of all the throng, *Rotherham* . . . This proposal was unanimously agreed to, *TCNT* . . . This recommendation met with the approval of, *Noli* . . . The suggestion met with general approval, *Weymouth* . . . The whole group liked the idea, *Beck* . . . This plan commended itself to the whole body, *Montgomery.*

**and they chose Stephen:** . . . and they selected Stephen, *Rotherham* . . . they elected Stephen, *Sawyer.*

**a man full of faith and of the Holy Ghost, and Philip, and Prochorus, and Nicanor, and Timon, and Parmenas:**

| 4198.1 noun acc sing masc | 488.1 name acc sing masc | 3614.8 rel-pron acc pl masc | 2449.5 verb 3pl indic aor act | 1783.1 prep |
|---|---|---|---|---|
| προσήλυτον | Ἀντιοχέα, | 6. οὓς | ἔστησαν | ἐνώπιον |
| *prosēluton* | *Antiochea* | *hous* | *estēsan* | *enōpion* |
| a proselyte | of Antioch, | whom | they set | before |

| 3450.1 art gen pl | 646.5 noun gen pl masc | 2504.1 conj | 4195.25 verb nom pl masc part aor mid | 1991.7 verb 3pl indic aor act |
|---|---|---|---|---|
| τῶν | ἀποστόλων· | καὶ | προσευξάμενοι | ἐπέθηκαν |
| *tōn* | *apostolōn* | *kai* | *proseuxamenoi* | *epethēkan* |
| the | apostles; | and | having prayed | they laid |

| 840.2 prs-pron dat pl | 3450.15 art acc pl fem | 5331.8 noun acc pl fem | 2504.1 conj | 3450.5 art nom sing masc | 3030.1 noun nom sing masc |
|---|---|---|---|---|---|
| αὐτοῖς | τὰς | χεῖρας. | 7. Καὶ | ὁ | λόγος |
| *autois* | *tas* | *cheiras* | *Kai* | *ho* | *logos* |
| on them | the | hands. | And | the | word |

| 3450.2 art gen sing | 2296.2 noun gen sing masc | 831.10 verb 3sing indic imperf act | 2504.1 conj | 3989.8 verb 3sing indic imperf pass |
|---|---|---|---|---|
| τοῦ | θεοῦ | ηὔξανεν, | καὶ | ἐπληθύνετο |
| *tou* | *theou* | *ēuxanen* | *kai* | *eplēthuneto* |
| | of God | was increasing, | and | was being multiplied |

| 3450.5 art nom sing masc | 700.1 noun nom sing masc | 3450.1 art gen pl | 3073.6 noun gen pl masc | 1706.1 prep | 2395.1 name fem |
|---|---|---|---|---|---|
| ὁ | ἀριθμὸς | τῶν | μαθητῶν | ἐν | Ἱερουσαλὴμ |
| *ho* | *arithmos* | *tōn* | *mathētōn* | *en* | *Hierousalēm* |
| the | number | of the | disciples | in | Jerusalem |

| 4822.1 adv | 4044.5 adj nom sing masc | 4885.1 conj | 3657.1 noun nom sing masc | 3450.1 art gen pl | 2385.5 noun gen pl masc |
|---|---|---|---|---|---|
| σφόδρα, | πολύς | τε | ὄχλος | τῶν | ἱερέων |
| *sphodra* | *polus* | *te* | *ochlos* | *tōn* | *hiereōn* |
| exceedingly, | a great | and | multitude | of the | priests |

| 5057.9 verb 3pl indic imperf act | 3450.11 art dat sing fem | 3963.3 noun dat sing fem | 4587.1 name nom masc | 1156.2 conj | 3994.1 adj nom sing |
|---|---|---|---|---|---|
| ὑπήκουον | τῇ | πίστει. | 8. Στέφανος | δὲ | πλήρης |
| *hupēkouon* | *tē* | *pistei* | *Stephanos* | *de* | *plērēs* |
| were obedient | to the | faith. | Stephen, | and | full |

8.a.**Txt:** 025P,byz.
**Var:** p74,01ℵ,02A,03B
05D,sa.bo.Gries,Lach
Treg,Alf,Word,Tisc
We/Ho,Weis,Sod
UBS/⋆

| 3963.2 noun gen sing fem | 5322.2 noun gen sing fem | 2504.1 conj | 1405.2 noun gen sing fem | 4020.57 verb 3sing indic imperf act |
|---|---|---|---|---|
| ‘ πίστεως | [a⋆ χάριτος ] | καὶ | δυνάμεως | ἐποίει |
| *pisteōs* | *charitos* | *kai* | *dunameōs* | *epoiei* |
| of faith | [ of grace ] | and | power, | was performing |

| 4907.1 noun pl neu | 2504.1 conj | 4447.2 noun pl neu | 3144.17 adj pl neu | 1706.1 prep | 3450.3 art dat sing | 2967.3 noun dat sing masc |
|---|---|---|---|---|---|---|
| τέρατα | καὶ | σημεῖα | μεγάλα | ἐν | τῷ | λαῷ. |
| *terata* | *kai* | *sēmeia* | *megala* | *en* | *tō* | *laō* |
| wonders | and | signs | great | among | the | people. |

| 448.4 verb 3pl indic aor act | 1156.2 conj | 4948.7 indef-pron nom pl masc | 3450.1 art gen pl | 1523.2 prep gen | 3450.10 art gen sing fem |
|---|---|---|---|---|---|
| 9. ἀνέστησαν | δέ | τινες | τῶν | ἐκ | τῆς |
| *anestēsan* | *de* | *tines* | *tōn* | *ek* | *tēs* |
| Arose | and | certain | of the | of | the |

9.a.**Var:** 01ℵ,02A,33,sa.
bo.Tisc

| 4715.2 noun gen sing fem | 3450.10 art gen sing fem | 2978.34 verb gen sing fem part pres mid | 3450.1 art gen pl | 2978.41 verb gen pl fem part pres mid |
|---|---|---|---|---|
| συναγωγῆς | ‘ τῆς | λεγομένης | [a τῶν | λεγομένων ] |
| *sunagōgēs* | *tēs* | *legomenēs* | *tōn* | *legomenōn* |
| synagogue | the | being called | [ the | being called ] |

can help people of different languages to love and serve one another.

**6:6.** The people brought the seven before the apostles, who laid their hands on them. This laying on of hands was probably like the public recognition of Joshua in Numbers 27:18,19. Stephen and the others were all full of the Spirit before this. The laying on of hands symbolized prayer for God's blessing on them. The apostles probably prayed also that the Spirit would give these men whatever gift and graces would be necessary for this ministry.

**6:7.** Luke concluded this incident with another summary statement: "The Word of God increased" (kept on growing). This implies that not only the apostles were involved in spreading the Word. All the believers were involved in proclaiming the Word. As a result the number of disciples kept on multiplying (increasing) in Jerusalem. Among these new disciples were a large crowd of priests, and they too became obedient to the Faith, the body of truth proclaimed and taught by the apostles. Josephus said there were 20,000 priests at this time. That a large number of them accepted the gospel probably means that many of them were Sadducees. Since they did not believe in the Resurrection, this was a major breakthrough. (Some writers say the priests who were converted were humble priests, like the father of John the Baptist, who were obviously not Sadducees. But most of the priests were Sadducees, so this large number would include at least some of that party.)

**6:8.** The fact that the seven (deacons) were chosen to carry out a rather routine service with the wisdom and grace of the Spirit did not limit their ministry in other areas. Stephen was full of faith (or *grace*, as many Greek manuscripts read). He was both the recipient and the channel of God's grace, God's unmerited favor. He was also full of mighty power, and he began to do (and kept on doing) wonders and great signs among the people. The people were not merely spectators. They also experienced the mighty miracles as God's gifts (or gifts of the Holy Spirit) to meet their needs.

This is the first time the Book of Acts indicates miracles were done by those who were not apostles. The important thing, however, is that the Holy Spirit was working through Stephen.

**6:9.** Soon opposition arose. This time it came from Greek-speaking Jews who, like Stephen, had returned from the Dispersion to live in Jerusalem. They had their own synagogue or synagogues. ("Synagogue," literally, "gathering together place," was a combi-

**and Nicolas a proselyte of Antioch:** . . . and Nicholas of Antioch, a former convert to Judaism, *TCNT.*

**6. Whom they set before the apostles:** These men were taken to the missionaries, *NLT.*

**and when they had prayed they laid their hands on them:** . . . who then prayed and placed their hands on them, *TCNT* . . . and, after prayer, they, *Weymouth* . . . After praying, the missionaries laid their hands on them, *NLT.*

**7. And the word of God increased:** So God's Message spread, *TCNT* . . . Meanwhile God's word continued to spread, *Weymouth* . . . In the meantime, the message of God continued to spread, *Noli* . . . message of God extended, *Fenton* . . . God's Word kept on spreading, *Beck* . . . word of God went on growing, *PNT* . . . spread further, *NLT.*

**and the number of the disciples multiplied in Jerusalem greatly:** . . . exceedingly, *ASV* . . . rapidly, *TCNT* . . . multiplied tremendously, *Concordant* . . . continued to grow, *Williams* . . . greatly increased, *Fenton* . . . became much larger, *NLT.*

**and a great company of the priests were obedient to the faith:** . . . a vast throng, *Concordant* . . . and a large body of the priests accepted the Faith, *TCNT* . . . and a great multitude...were obeying the faith, *HBIE* . . . a large number even of priests continued to surrender to the faith, *Williams* . . . subdued to the faith, *Fenton* . . . Many of the religious leaders believed in the faith of the Christians, *NLT.*

**8. And Stephen, full of faith and power:** . . . full of grace and power, *ASV* . . . full of God's gifts and power, *Beck* . . . active benevolence, *Fenton.*

**did great wonders and miracles among the people:** . . . wrought great wonders and signs, *ASV* . . . wrought notable wonders, *Berkeley.*

**9. Then there arose certain of the synagogue, which is called the synagogue of the Libertines, and Cyrenians, and Alexandrians, and of them of Cilicia and of Asia:** . . . the Freedmen, *Noyes*

| 3006.1 name gen pl masc | 2504.1 conj | 2929.5 name-adj gen pl masc | 2504.1 conj | 219.2 name gen pl masc |
|---|---|---|---|---|
| Λιβερτίνων, | καὶ | Κυρηναίων, | καὶ | Ἀλεξανδρέων, |
| *Libertinōn* | *kai* | *Kurēnaiōn* | *kai* | *Alexandreōn* |
| Libertines, | and | of Cyrenians, | and | of Alexandrians, |

| 2504.1 conj | 3450.1 art gen pl | 570.3 prep | 2763.1 name gen fem | 2504.1 conj | 767.2 name gen fem | 4653.2 verb nom pl masc part pres act |
|---|---|---|---|---|---|---|
| καὶ | τῶν | ἀπὸ | Κιλικίας | καὶ | Ἀσίας, | συζητοῦντες |
| *kai* | *tōn* | *apo* | *Kilikias* | *kai* | *Asias* | *suzētountes* |
| and | of the | from | Cilicia | and | Asia, | disputing |

| 3450.3 art dat sing | 4587.3 name dat masc | | 2504.1 conj | 3620.2 partic | 2453.13 verb 3pl indic imperf act |
|---|---|---|---|---|---|
| τῷ | Στεφάνῳ· | **10.** | καὶ | οὐκ | ἴσχυον |
| *tō* | *Stephanō* | | *kai* | *ouk* | *ischuon* |
| | with Stephen. | | And | not | they were able |

| 434.4 verb inf aor act | 3450.11 art dat sing fem | 4531.3 noun dat sing fem | 2504.1 conj | 3450.3 art dat sing | 4011.3 noun dat sing neu |
|---|---|---|---|---|---|
| ἀντιστῆναι | τῇ | σοφίᾳ | καὶ | τῷ | πνεύματι |
| *antistēnai* | *tē* | *sophia* | *kai* | *tō* | *pneumati* |
| to stand up against | the | wisdom | and | the | spirit |

| 3614.3 rel-pron dat sing | 2953.45 verb 3sing indic imperf act | | 4966.1 adv | 5098.1 verb 3pl indic aor act | 433.9 noun acc pl masc |
|---|---|---|---|---|---|
| ᾧ | ἐλάλει. | **11.** | τότε | ὑπέβαλον | ἄνδρας, |
| *hō* | *elalei* | | *tote* | *hupebalon* | *andras* |
| by which | he was speaking. | | Then | they produced | men, |

| 2978.18 verb acc pl masc part pres act | 3617.1 conj | 189.38 verb 1pl indic perf act | 840.3 prs-pron gen sing | 2953.13 verb gen sing masc part pres act |
|---|---|---|---|---|
| λέγοντας, | Ὅτι | Ἀκηκόαμεν | αὐτοῦ | λαλοῦντος |
| *legontas* | *Hoti* | *Akēkoamen* | *autou* | *lalountos* |
| saying, | | We have heard | him | speaking |

| 4343.4 noun pl neu | 982.3 adj pl neu | 1519.1 prep | 3337.6 name acc masc | 3338.4 name acc masc |
|---|---|---|---|---|
| ῥήματα | βλάσφημα | εἰς | ‘ Μωσῆν | [☆ Μωϋσῆν ] |
| *rhēmata* | *blasphēma* | *eis* | *Mōsēn* | *Mousēn* |
| words | blasphemous | against | Moses | [ idem ] |

| 2504.1 conj | 3450.6 art acc sing masc | 2296.4 noun acc sing masc | | 4638.1 verb 3pl indic aor act | 4885.1 conj | 3450.6 art acc sing masc |
|---|---|---|---|---|---|---|
| καὶ | τὸν | θεόν. | **12.** | Συνεκίνησάν | τε | τὸν |
| *kai* | *ton* | *theon* | | *Sunekinēsan* | *te* | *ton* |
| and | | God. | | They stirred up | and | the |

| 2967.4 noun acc sing masc | 2504.1 conj | 3450.8 art acc pl masc | 4104.2 adj comp acc pl masc | 2504.1 conj | 3450.8 art acc pl masc |
|---|---|---|---|---|---|
| λαὸν | καὶ | τοὺς | πρεσβυτέρους | καὶ | τοὺς |
| *laon* | *kai* | *tous* | *presbuterous* | *kai* | *tous* |
| people | and | the | elders | and | the |

| 1116.2 noun pl masc | 2504.1 conj | 2168.6 verb nom pl masc part aor act | 4780.1 verb 3pl indic aor act | 840.6 prs-pron acc sing masc |
|---|---|---|---|---|
| γραμματεῖς, | καὶ | ἐπιστάντες | συνήρπασαν | αὐτὸν, |
| *grammateis* | *kai* | *epistantes* | *sunērpasan* | *auton* |
| scribes, | and | having come upon | they seized | him, |

| 2504.1 conj | 70.10 verb 3pl indic aor act | 1519.1 prep | 3450.16 art sing neu | 4742.1 noun sing neu | | 2449.5 verb 3pl indic aor act |
|---|---|---|---|---|---|---|
| καὶ | ἤγαγον | εἰς | τὸ | συνέδριον, | **13.** | ἔστησάν |
| *kai* | *ēgagon* | *eis* | *to* | *sunedrion* | | *estēsan* |
| and | brought | to | the | Sanhedrin, | | They set |

nation community center, school, a place for reading and commenting on the Scriptures on the Sabbath. The word here is singular, but many take it as a distributive word and apply it to each group, for Jewish tradition says there were a great many synagogues in Jerusalem at this time.)

The opposition included Jews who were Libertines, former slaves who had been set free by their Roman masters. When the Romans conquered a city they usually took the doctors, lawyers, teachers, and skilled workers and gave them as gifts to their friends. But the Romans also considered it a religious thing to set slaves free, so there was a large class of these freedmen in Rome. Also included in the opposition were Cyrenians from Cyrene, west of Egypt on the Mediterranean coast, and Alexandrians from Alexandria in Egypt where there was a very large Jewish quarter. Others were from Cilicia (Paul's home province in southeastern Asia Minor) and from the province of Asia (in western Asia Minor) where Ephesus was the chief city.

Most of these Jews in the Dispersion had to face many threats to their teaching, living as they did, surrounded by Gentiles. As a result they were quicker to defend themselves against anything different from what their rabbis taught them. So they engaged Stephen in debate and kept trying to dispute the truth of his teachings about Jesus.

**6:10.** Stephen had a distinct advantage. He was not depending on his own wisdom to proclaim the truth, but on the anointing and gifts of the Holy Spirit. So all their arguments fell flat. They did not have the strength or power to stand against the wisdom and the Spirit by which Stephen was speaking.

**6:11.** Though they did not have the Scriptures or reason on their side, these Greek-speaking Jews still refused to believe and only became more and more determined to get rid of Stephen. They suborned men (obtained them in some unfair way) who said they had heard Stephen speaking blasphemous (abusive, scurrilous) words against Moses and against God.

**6:12.** In order to carry out their plan to stop Stephen, these Greek-speaking Jews stirred up the (Jewish) people (violently) and also the elders (who were members of the Sanhedrin) and the scribes (who not only copied the law of Moses, but who claimed to be experts in its interpretation).

With all these groups supporting them, they came upon Stephen suddenly and unexpectedly, caught him (took hold of him violently and kept a firm grip on him), and brought him to the Council.

. . . But some members from the Synagogue known as that of the Freed Slaves and...as well as visitors from Cilicia and Roman Asia, *TCNT.*

**disputing with Stephen:** They all came and argued with, *Everyday.*

**10. And they were not able to resist the wisdom and the spirit by which he spake:** But the Spirit was helping him to speak with wisdom, *Everyday* . . . they could not match, *Norlie* . . . to withstand the wisdom, *ASV* . . . and inspiration, *TCNT* . . . but they could not cope with his good practical sense and the spiritual power, *Williams* . . . to be unable to stand up against his wisdom, *Wuest* . . . They were not able to say anything against what he said, *NLT* . . . the intelligence, *Fenton* . . . either his practical wisdom or the spiritual force, *Phillips.*

**11. Then they suborned men, which said:** In desperation, *Phillips* . . . So they paid some men to say, *Everyday* . . . they secretly instigated men, who said, *RSV* . . . they induced some men to say, *TCNT* . . . they bribed men to say, *Williams C.K.* . . . Then they privately put forward men who declared, *Weymouth* . . . men who alleged, *NEB.*

**We have heard him speak blasphemous words against Moses, and against God:** We heard him slander Moses and God, *Beck.*

**12. And they stirred up the people:** In this way they excited the people, *Weymouth* . . . Thus they got the people wrought up, *Berkeley* . . . And they roused the people, *Darby.*

**and the elders, and the scribes:** . . . and the presbyters, *Hanson* . . . as well as the Councillors and Rabbis, *TCNT* . . . and the men of the Law, *Beck.*

**and came upon him, and caught him:** . . . coming suddenly, *Wilson* . . . and arrested, *TCNT* . . . seized him with violence, *Weymouth* . . . they attacked and grabbed him, *Berkeley* . . . took him by force, *Klingensmith* . . . set upon him, arrested him, *Noli.*

**and brought him to the council:** Sanhedrin, *HBIE* . . . before the court, *Beck.*

## Acts 6:14

| 4885.1 conj | 3116.7 noun acc pl masc | 5406.2 adj acc pl masc | 2978.18 verb acc pl masc part pres act | 3450.5 art nom sing masc | 442.1 noun nom sing masc |
|---|---|---|---|---|---|
| τε | μάρτυρας | ψευδεῖς, | λέγοντας, | Ὁ | ἄνθρωπος |
| *te* | *marturas* | *pseudeis* | *legontas* | *Ho* | *anthrōpos* |
| and | witnesses | false, | saying, | The | man |

| 3642.4 dem-pron nom sing masc | 3620.3 partic | 3835.3 verb 3sing indic pres mid | 4343.4 noun pl neu | 982.3 adj pl neu |
|---|---|---|---|---|
| οὗτος | οὐ | παύεται | ⸂ ῥήματα | βλάσφημα |
| *houtos* | *ou* | *pauetai* | *rhēmata* | *blasphēma* |
| this | not | does cease | words | blasphemous |

13.a.**Txt:** 08E,025P,byz.
**Var:** 01ℵ,03B,04C,sa.bo.
Treg,Tisc,We/Ho,Weis
Sod,UBS/☆

| 2953.12 verb nom sing masc part pres act | 2953.12 verb nom sing masc part pres act | 4343.4 noun pl neu | 2567.3 prep | 3450.2 art gen sing |
|---|---|---|---|---|
| λαλῶν | [a☆ λαλῶν | ῥήματα ] | κατὰ | τοῦ |
| *lalōn* | *lalōn* | *rhēmata* | *kata* | *tou* |
| speaking | [ speaking | words ] | against | the |

13.b.**Txt:** 03B,04C,33
byz.sa.bo.We/Ho,Weis
Sod,UBS/☆
**Var:** p74,01ℵ,02A,05D
08E,025P,0175,Gries
Lach,Treg,Alf,Word
Tisc

| 4964.2 noun gen sing masc | 3450.2 art gen sing | 39.2 adj gen sing | 3642.1 dem-pron gen sing | 2504.1 conj | 3450.2 art gen sing |
|---|---|---|---|---|---|
| τόπου | τοῦ | ἁγίου | ⸂b τούτου ⸃ | καὶ | τοῦ |
| *topou* | *tou* | *hagiou* | *toutou* | *kai* | *tou* |
| place | the | holy | this | and | the |

| 3414.2 noun gen sing masc | 189.38 verb 1pl indic perf act | 1056.1 conj | 840.3 prs-pron gen sing | 2978.14 verb gen sing part pres act | 3617.1 conj |
|---|---|---|---|---|---|
| νόμου. | **14.** ἀκηκόαμεν | γὰρ | αὐτοῦ | λέγοντος, | ὅτι |
| *nomou* | *akēkoamen* | *gar* | *autou* | *legontos* | *hoti* |
| law; | We have heard | for | him | saying, | That |

| 2400.1 name nom masc | 3450.5 art nom sing masc | 3343.1 name nom sing masc | 3642.4 dem-pron nom sing masc | 2617.7 verb 3sing indic fut act |
|---|---|---|---|---|
| Ἰησοῦς | ὁ | Ναζωραῖος | οὗτος | καταλύσει |
| *Iēsous* | *ho* | *Nazōraios* | *houtos* | *katalusei* |
| Jesus | the | Nazarene | this | will destroy |

| 3450.6 art acc sing masc | 4964.4 noun acc sing masc | 3642.6 dem-pron acc sing masc | 2504.1 conj | 234.3 verb 3sing indic fut act | 3450.17 art pl neu |
|---|---|---|---|---|---|
| τὸν | τόπον | τοῦτον, | καὶ | ἀλλάξει | τὰ |
| *ton* | *topon* | *touton* | *kai* | *allaxei* | *ta* |
| the | place | this, | and | will change | the |

| 1478.5 noun pl neu | 3614.17 rel-pron pl neu | 3722.10 verb 3sing indic aor act | 2231.3 prs-pron dat 1pl | 3338.1 name nom masc | 2504.1 conj |
|---|---|---|---|---|---|
| ἔθη | ἃ | παρέδωκεν | ἡμῖν | Μωϋσῆς. | **15.** Καὶ |
| *ethē* | *ha* | *paredōken* | *hēmin* | *Mōusēs* | *Kai* |
| customs | which | delivered | to us | Moses. | And |

15.a.**Txt:** 05D-corr,025P
byz.
**Var:** 01ℵ,02A,03B,04C
05D-org,08E,Lach,Treg
Tisc,We/Ho,Weis,Sod
UBS/☆

| 810.4 verb nom pl masc part aor act | 1519.1 prep | 840.6 prs-pron acc sing masc | 533.4 adj nom pl masc | 3820.7 adj nom pl masc |
|---|---|---|---|---|
| ἀτενίσαντες | εἰς | αὐτὸν | ⸂ ἅπαντες | [a☆ πάντες ] |
| *atenisantes* | *eis* | *auton* | *hapantes* | *pantes* |
| having looked intently | on | him | all | [ idem ] |

| 3450.7 art nom pl masc | 2488.2 verb nom pl masc part pres mid | 1706.1 prep | 3450.3 art dat sing | 4742.3 noun dat sing neu | 1481.1 verb indic aor act |
|---|---|---|---|---|---|
| οἱ | καθεζόμενοι | ἐν | τῷ | συνεδρίῳ | ⸂ εἶδον |
| *hoi* | *kathezomenoi* | *en* | *tō* | *sunedriō* | *eidon* |
| the | sitting | in | the | Sanhedrin | saw |

15.b.**Var:** 02A,Treg
We/Ho

| 1481.7 verb 3pl indic aor act | 3450.16 art sing neu | 4241.1 noun sing neu | 840.3 prs-pron gen sing | 5448.1 adv | 4241.1 noun sing neu |
|---|---|---|---|---|---|
| [b εἶδαν ] | τὸ | πρόσωπον | αὐτοῦ | ὡσεὶ | πρόσωπον |
| *eidan* | *to* | *prosōpon* | *autou* | *hōsei* | *prosōpon* |
| [ idem ] | the | face | his | as | face |

**6:13.** Then those who were trying to stop Stephen set up false witnesses, witnesses who misrepresented the words of Stephen in a false and misleading way, putting him in as bad a light as possible. They took the stand and said this man continued to speak words against this holy place (the temple) and against the Law (of Moses).

It is probable that all Stephen had done was tell how Jesus had overthrown the tables of the money changers in the temple and said they had made the temple a den of thieves (Matthew 21:13). He must have also told of the many times Jesus corrected the misinterpretations of the law of Moses, misinterpretations that the scribes and Pharisees promoted, who, for example, criticized Jesus for doing good on the Sabbath Day (John 5:16; Luke 13:11-17).

**6:14.** These false witnesses also claimed they had heard Stephen say that this Jesus the Nazarene would destroy this place (the temple) and change the customs (including the ceremonies, rites, and institutions) which Moses had delivered (handed down) to them.

On two occasions Jesus did speak of destroying the temple. The first time Jesus chased the money changers (John 2:15), the Jews asked Him, "What sign showest thou unto us, seeing that thou doest these things?" and Jesus answered, "Destroy this temple, and in three days I will raise it up." As so often in the Gospel of John, the Jews misunderstood Jesus, took His words literally, and gave a mocking reply, "Forty-six years was this temple in building and wilt thou rear it up in three days?" But, as the Bible goes on to state, Jesus was speaking of the temple of His body (John 2:18-21).

Jesus also told His disciples that not one stone of the temple would be left upon another (Matthew 24:2). This was something that normally did not happen. All over Palestine and the Middle East are ruins where conquerors destroyed cities, palaces, temples, but left the lower course or at least the foundation stones intact. But the words of Jesus were fulfilled when the armies of the Roman Titus destroyed Jerusalem in A.D. 70.

Actually, there is a sequence of worship in the Bible. First, were the altars of the patriarchs before Moses; second, the tabernacle in the wilderness; third, the temple built by Solomon, rebuilt by Zerrubabbel, and rebuilt again by Herod the Great; fourth, the Church as the temple (Greek, *naos*, the inner sanctuary where the presence of God is manifest). (See 1 Corinthians 3:16 where the word "you" is plural and refers to the local assembly as a body.)

**6:15.** At this point all those who were seated in the Sanhedrin fixed their eyes on Stephen and saw his face as if it were the face of an angel. This probably means there was a glow or a brightness that was more than human and came from heaven. Possibly this was similar to the glory on the face of Moses when he came down from the presence of God on Mount Sinai (Exodus 34:29-35).

**13. And set up false witnesses, which said:** Then they produced, *Williams C.K.* . . . Here they brought forward false witnesses who declared, *Weymouth* . . . There they had witnesses stand up and lie, *Beck* . . . The people were told to lie and say, *NLT* . . . They brought in some men to tell lies about Stephen, *Everyday.*

**This man ceaseth not to speak blasphemous words against this holy place, and the law:** . . . this man never quits uttering statements against, *Berkeley* . . . constantly saying things against, *Goodspeed* . . . speaks incessantly against, *Sawyer* . . . is constantly uttering, *Noli* . . . contrary to the law, *Murdock* . . . incessantly saying things, *TCNT* . . . never ceases speaking words against, *Kleist.*

**14. For we have heard him say:** . . . indeed, we have heard him declare, *TCNT.*

**that this Jesus of Nazareth shall destroy this place:** . . . that Jesus, the Nazarene, *Weymouth* . . . will demolish this place, *Berkeley* . . . will tear this sanctuary down, *Noli* . . . pull down this place, *NLT.*

**and shall change the customs which Moses delivered us:** . . . change the rites, *Murdock* . . . change the constitutions which has been transmitted, *Fenton* . . . will change the things that Moses told us to do, *Everyday* . . . handed down to us, *Williams C.K.* . . . change what Moses taught us, *NLT.*

**15. And all that sat in the council, looked stedfastly on him:** At once the eyes of all who were sitting in the Sanhedrin were fastened on him, *Weymouth* . . . And giving undivided attention to him, *Swann* . . . The men sitting in the religious leader's court, *NLT* . . . As all those seated in the Sanhedrin gazed at him, *Berkeley* . . . The men seated in the council were all staring at Stephen, *Norlie* . . . The eyes of all the members of the council were riveted upon Stephen, *TCNT* . . . were watching Stephen closely, *Everyday* . . . looked intently at him, *TNT.*

**saw his face as it had been the face of an angel:** . . . and they saw his face looking like, *TCNT.*

| 32.2 noun gen sing masc | 1500.5 verb 3sing indic aor act | 1156.2 conj | 3450.5 art nom sing masc | 744.1 noun nom sing masc | 1479.1 conj |
|---|---|---|---|---|---|
| ἀγγέλου. | 7:1. Εἶπεν | δὲ | ὁ | ἀρχιερεύς, | Εἰ |
| *angelou* | *Eipen* | *de* | *ho* | *archiereus* | *Ei* |
| of an angel. | Said | and | the | high priest, | If |

1.a.**Txt:** 05D,08E,025P byz.
**Var:** 01ℵ,02A,03B,04C Lach,Treg,Tisc,We/Ho Weis,Sod,UBS/☆

| 679.1 partic | 3642.18 dem-pron pl neu | 3643.1 adv | 2174.4 verb 3sing indic pres act | 3450.5 art nom sing masc | 1156.2 conj |
|---|---|---|---|---|---|
| ⸂a ἄρα ⸃ | ταῦτα | οὕτως | ἔχει; | 2. ὁ | δὲ |
| *ara* | *tauta* | *houtōs* | *echei* | *ho* | *de* |
| then | these things | so | have? | The | and |

| 5183.4 verb 3sing indic act | 433.6 noun nom pl masc | 79.6 noun nom pl masc | 2504.1 conj | 3824.6 noun nom pl masc | 189.29 verb 2pl impr aor act |
|---|---|---|---|---|---|
| ἔφη, | Ἄνδρες | ἀδελφοὶ | καὶ | πατέρες, | ἀκούσατε. |
| *ephē* | *Andres* | *adelphoi* | *kai* | *pateres* | *akousate* |
| he said, | Men | brothers | and | fathers, | listen. |

| 3450.5 art nom sing masc | 2296.1 noun nom sing masc | 3450.10 art gen sing fem | 1385.2 noun gen sing fem | 3571.21 verb 3sing indic aor pass | 3450.3 art dat sing |
|---|---|---|---|---|---|
| Ὁ | θεὸς | τῆς | δόξης | ὤφθη | τῷ |
| *Ho* | *theos* | *tēs* | *doxēs* | *ōphthē* | *tō* |
| The | God | of the | glory | appeared | to the |

| 3824.3 noun dat sing masc | 2231.2 prs-pron gen 1pl | 11.1 name masc | 1498.22 verb dat sing masc part pres act | 1706.1 prep | 3450.11 art dat sing fem |
|---|---|---|---|---|---|
| πατρὶ | ἡμῶν | Ἀβραὰμ | ὄντι | ἐν | τῇ |
| *patri* | *hēmōn* | *Abraam* | *onti* | *en* | *tē* |
| father | our | Abraham | being | in | |

| 3188.1 name dat fem | 4109.1 adv | 2211.1 conj | 2700.13 verb inf aor act | 840.6 prs-pron acc sing masc | 1706.1 prep |
|---|---|---|---|---|---|
| Μεσοποταμίᾳ | πρὶν | ἢ | κατοικῆσαι | αὐτὸν | ἐν |
| *Mesopotamia* | *prin* | *ē* | *katoikēsai* | *auton* | *en* |
| Mesopotamia, | before | | to dwell | him | in |

| 5324.1 name fem | 2504.1 conj | 1500.5 verb 3sing indic aor act | 4242.1 prep | 840.6 prs-pron acc sing masc | 1814.9 verb 2sing impr aor act |
|---|---|---|---|---|---|
| Χαῤῥάν, | 3. καὶ | εἶπεν | πρὸς | αὐτόν, | Ἔξελθε |
| *Charrhan* | *kai* | *eipen* | *pros* | *auton* | *Exelthe* |
| Haran, | and | said | to | him, | Go out |

3.a.**Txt:** 01ℵ,02A,04C 08E,025P,byz.bo.Tisc Sod
**Var:** 03B,05D,sa.Treg We/Ho,Weis,UBS/☆

| 1523.2 prep gen | 3450.10 art gen sing fem | 1087.2 noun gen sing fem | 4622.2 prs-pron gen 2sing | 2504.1 conj | 1523.2 prep gen | 3450.10 art gen sing fem |
|---|---|---|---|---|---|---|
| ἐκ | τῆς | γῆς | σου | καὶ | ⸂a ἐκ ⸃ | τῆς |
| *ek* | *tēs* | *gēs* | *sou* | *kai* | *ek* | *tēs* |
| from | the | land | your | and | from | the |

3.b.**Var:** 01ℵ,02A,03B 04C-org,05D,08E,Lach Treg,Alf,Word,Tisc We/Ho,Weis,Sod UBS/☆

| 4623.1 noun gen sing fem | 4622.2 prs-pron gen 2sing | 2504.1 conj | 1198.1 adv | 1519.1 prep | 3450.12 art acc sing fem |
|---|---|---|---|---|---|
| συγγενείας | σου, | καὶ | δεῦρο | εἰς | [b☆+ τὴν ] |
| *sungeneias* | *sou* | *kai* | *deuro* | *eis* | *tēn* |
| relatives | your | and | come | into | [ the ] |

| 1087.4 noun acc sing fem | 3614.12 rel-pron acc sing fem | 300.1 partic | 4622.3 prs-pron dat 2sing | 1161.6 verb 1sing act | 4966.1 adv |
|---|---|---|---|---|---|
| γῆν | ἣν | ἂν | σοι | δείξω. | 4. Τότε |
| *gēn* | *hēn* | *an* | *soi* | *deixō* | *Tote* |
| land | which | | to you | I will show. | Then |

| 1814.13 verb nom sing masc part aor act | 1523.2 prep gen | 1087.2 noun gen sing fem | 5302.1 name gen pl masc | 2700.11 verb 3sing indic aor act |
|---|---|---|---|---|
| ἐξελθὼν | ἐκ | γῆς | Χαλδαίων, | κατῴκησεν |
| *exelthōn* | *ek* | *gēs* | *Chaldaiōn* | *katōkēsen* |
| having gone out | from | land | of Chaldeans, | he dwelt |

**7:1.** The high priest (probably Caiaphas) gave Stephen an opportunity to respond to the charges by asking him if these things were so. At least the high priest was going through the proper form of a trial, though he probably did not expect Stephen to take such full advantage of it as he proceeded to do. Stephen did not attempt to refute the charges made against him—he was not primarily interested in clearing himself. Instead, he reiterated the truths which were creating such an uproar among the Jewish leaders (Harrison, p.111).

**7:2.** Stephen politely addressed the Sanhedrin as "Men, brethren, and fathers." By calling them men who were brothers, he wanted them to know he still considered himself an Israelite, a descendant of Abraham, a member of the chosen nation. He had done nothing to cut himself off from his heritage. By calling them fathers, he wanted them to know he still respected the institutions of Israel and was willing to subject himself to any decision they might make that would be in line with God's purpose for Israel which promised blessing to all the families of the earth (Genesis 12:3).

**7:3.** Then Stephen began a review of the history of Israel, a history they all knew well. His purpose was to defend the gospel against false charges and to show a parallel between the way Old Testament Israelites had treated their prophets and the way the Jewish leaders had treated Jesus.

First, Stephen reminded them how the God of glory (the God who reveals himself in glory and who is glorious in all that He is and does) appeared to Abraham while he was in Mesopotamia, that is, in Ur of the Chaldees. (Some archaeologists, such as Cyrus Gordon, believe this was a northern Ur rather than the Ur on the Euphrates east of Babylon [p.132]. There is some evidence that the Chaldeans came from the north and that they did not come into Babylonia until long after Abraham's time.)

The Book of Genesis does not mention this revelation to Abraham in Ur, but it must have been recorded in other ancient records. Nehemiah 9:7 refers to it and shows that it was God who brought Abram out of Ur and later gave him the name Abraham.

**7:4.** After Abraham left Ur of the Chaldees, he settled in Haran and lived there until Terah, his father, died. The Greek indicates a rather permanent establishment of a home there. The Book of Genesis confirms that Haran remained the permanent residence of Abraham's relatives even in the days of Jacob (Genesis 29:4,5). Ancient Jewish tradition says Terah was a maker of idols, especially idols of the moon god, and that he settled in Haran because it was the center of worship for the moon god in western Mesopotamia.

It is not clear from the Hebrew of Genesis 12:1 whether God again spoke to Abraham at the time of his father's death, or whether

**1. Then said the high priest, Are these things so?:** Then the High Priest asked him, Are these statements true, *Weymouth* . . . The head religious leader asked, *NLT* . . . are these statements correct? *Berkeley* . . . These charges are true, are they not? *Norlie* . . . Is this true? *Williams C.K.* . . . Is this accusation true? *Noli* . . . this statement true? *Goodspeed* . . . Is this so? *TNT.*

**2. And he said, Men, brethren, and fathers, hearken:** To this Stephen replied, *NAB* . . . And he said, Brethren and fathers, hearken, *ASV* . . . Brothers and Fathers, listen, *TCNT* . . . Fellow Jews, *Beck* . . . listen to me, *NLT.*

**The God of glory appeared unto our father Abraham:** The Glorious God appeared to our ancestor, *TCNT* . . . Our glorious God, *Everyday* . . . The great God showed Himself to our early father, *NLT* . . . our forefather, *Weymouth.*

**when he was in Mesopotamia:** . . . while, *Rotherham* . . . he was living in, *Weymouth* . . . in the country of, *NLT.*

**before he dwelt in Charran:** This was before he moved to, *NLT* . . . before he settled in Haran, *NAB, TCNT* . . . previous to his settling, *Berkeley* . . . before he ever made him home in Haran, *Williams* . . . before he resided in Haran, *Wilson.*

**3. And said unto him:** . . . and told him, *Berkeley.*

**Get thee out of thy country, and from thy kindred:** Leave your country and your kindred, *TCNT* . . . Get away from, *MLNT* . . . Go forth from, *Kleist* . . . Depart from, *Fenton* . . . your relationship, *Concordant* . . . and your relatives, *Everyday, Noli* . . . your kinsfolk, *NAB* . . . leave your family and this land where you were born, *NLT.*

**and come unto the land which I shall shew thee:** . . . and go into whatever land I point out to you, *Weymouth.*

**4. Then came he out of the land of the Chaldaeans:** Thereupon he left Chaldaea, *Weymouth* . . . So he left the country, *Noli* . . . He went from the land of, *NLT.*

**and dwelt in Charran and from thence, when his father was dead:**

| **1706.1** prep | **5324.1** name fem | **2518.1** conj | **3196.3** prep | **3450.16** art sing neu | **594.20** verb inf aor act |
|---|---|---|---|---|---|
| ἐν | Χαῤῥάν, | κἀκεῖθεν | μετὰ | τὸ | ἀποθανεῖν |
| *en* | *Charrhan* | *kakeithen* | *meta* | *to* | *apothanein* |
| in | Haran, | and from there | after | the | to die |

| **3450.6** art acc sing masc | **3824.4** noun acc sing masc | **840.3** prs-pron gen sing | **3221.1** verb 3sing indic aor act | **840.6** prs-pron acc sing masc | **1519.1** prep |
|---|---|---|---|---|---|
| τὸν | πατέρα | αὐτοῦ, | μετῴκισεν | αὐτὸν | εἰς |
| *ton* | *patera* | *autou* | *metōkisen* | *auton* | *eis* |
| the | father | his, | he removed | him | into |

| **3450.12** art acc sing fem | **1087.4** noun acc sing fem | **3642.12** dem-pron acc sing fem | **1519.1** prep | **3614.12** rel-pron acc sing fem | **5050.1** prs-pron nom 2pl |
|---|---|---|---|---|---|
| τὴν | γῆν | ταύτην | εἰς | ἣν | ὑμεῖς |
| *tēn* | *gēn* | *tautēn* | *eis* | *hēn* | *humeis* |
| the | land | this | in | which | you |

| **3431.1** adv | **2700.3** verb 2pl indic pres act | **2504.1** conj | **3620.2** partic | **1319.14** verb 3sing indic aor act | **840.4** prs-pron dat sing |
|---|---|---|---|---|---|
| νῦν | κατοικεῖτε· | **5.** καὶ | οὐκ | ἔδωκεν | αὐτῷ |
| *nun* | *katoikeite* | *kai* | *ouk* | *edōken* | *autō* |
| now | dwell. | And | not | he did give | to him |

| **2790.3** noun acc sing fem | **1706.1** prep | **840.11** prs-pron dat sing fem | **3624.1** conj | **961.3** noun sing neu | **4087.2** noun gen sing masc |
|---|---|---|---|---|---|
| κληρονομίαν | ἐν | αὐτῇ, | οὐδὲ | βῆμα | ποδός· |
| *klēronomian* | *en* | *autē* | *oude* | *bēma* | *podos* |
| an inheritance | in | it, | not even | tread | of a foot; |

| **2504.1** conj | **1846.3** verb 3sing indic aor mid | **840.4** prs-pron dat sing | **1319.31** verb inf aor act | **1319.31** verb inf aor act | **840.4** prs-pron dat sing |
|---|---|---|---|---|---|
| καὶ | ἐπηγγείλατο | ʻ αὐτῷ | δοῦναι | [☆ δοῦναι | αὐτῷ ] |
| *kai* | *epēngeilato* | *autō* | *dounai* | *dounai* | *autō* |
| and | promised | to him | to give | [ to give | to him ] |

| **1519.1** prep | **2666.2** noun acc sing fem | **840.12** prs-pron acc sing fem | **2504.1** conj | **3450.3** art dat sing | **4543.3** noun dat sing neu |
|---|---|---|---|---|---|
| εἰς | κατάσχεσιν | αὐτὴν, | καὶ | τῷ | σπέρματι |
| *eis* | *kataschesin* | *autēn* | *kai* | *tō* | *spermati* |
| for | a possession | it, | and | to the | seed |

| **840.3** prs-pron gen sing | **3196.2** prep | **840.6** prs-pron acc sing masc | **3620.2** partic | **1498.19** verb gen sing part pres act | **840.4** prs-pron dat sing |
|---|---|---|---|---|---|
| αὐτοῦ | μετ' | αὐτόν, | οὐκ | ὄντος | αὐτῷ |
| *autou* | *met'* | *auton* | *ouk* | *ontos* | *autō* |
| his | after | him, | not | being | to him |

| **4891.2** noun gen sing neu | **2953.27** verb 3sing indic aor act | **1156.2** conj | **3643.1** adv | **3450.5** art nom sing masc | **2296.1** noun nom sing masc |
|---|---|---|---|---|---|
| τέκνου. | **6.** ἐλάλησεν | δὲ | οὕτως | ὁ | θεὸς, |
| *teknou* | *elalēsen* | *de* | *houtōs* | *ho* | *theos* |
| a child. | Spoke | and | thus | | God: |

| **3617.1** conj | **1498.40** verb 3sing indic fut mid | **3450.16** art sing neu | **4543.1** noun sing neu | **840.3** prs-pron gen sing | **3803.4** adj sing neu |
|---|---|---|---|---|---|
| Ὅτι | ἔσται | τὸ | σπέρμα | αὐτοῦ | πάροικον |
| *Hoti* | *estai* | *to* | *sperma* | *autou* | *paroikon* |
| That | shall be | the | seed | his | a stranger |

| **1706.1** prep | **1087.3** noun dat sing fem | **243.5** adj dat sing fem | **2504.1** conj | **1396.2** verb 3pl indic fut act | **840.15** prs-pron sing neu |
|---|---|---|---|---|---|
| ἐν | γῇ | ἀλλοτρίᾳ, | καὶ | δουλώσουσιν | αὐτὸ |
| *en* | *gē* | *allotria* | *kai* | *doulōsousin* | *auto* |
| in | a land | strange, | and | they will enslave | it |

he simply remembered what God had said in Ur of the Chaldees and now he was free to obey by leaving not only his land but also his relatives.

**7:5.** Though Abraham came into the land because of the obedience of faith, God gave him no inheritance in it, not even the space which could be covered by a footstep. Genesis 12:6 shows that Abraham traveled through the land when he first came and found everywhere that "the Canaanite was then in the land." The land was already occupied.

Yet God, while Abraham still had no child, had promised to give the land to him and to his descendants for a (permanent) possession. After Abraham allowed Lot to choose the garden land of the Jordan Valley before Sodom and Gomorrah were destroyed, Abraham was left with the dry hillsides and the unoccupied land between the cities of Palestine where no one else wanted to live. But God saw Abraham's faith and told him to look in every direction, including the direction Lot had taken, and He promised to give it all to him and to his descendants forever. Then God told him to stand up and start walking through the length and breadth of the land, for God was going to give it all to him. Actually it was Abraham's to enjoy, even though he personally did not receive it as an inheritance.

Archaeological discoveries show there were further reasons why it really took faith for Abraham to claim the land. Abraham was not only a shepherd; he was also a merchant prince who dealt in gold, silver, and spices. The Canaanites had laws which allowed such merchant princes to travel in their territory but which made it illegal for them to acquire any land.

**7:6.** God also spoke of Abraham's descendants living temporarily as resident aliens in a land belonging to others who would make them slaves and treat them badly 400 years. "Four hundred" is a round number both here and in Genesis 15:13. In Exodus 12:40,41 the exact number of 430 years is given. Paul, however, seemed to understand (Galatians 3:17) that the 430 years included all the time from Abraham to Moses.

The reference in Genesis 15:13 is part of a passage where God confirmed His promise of the land to Abraham and his descendants by making a covenant (Genesis 15:18-21). This was after Abraham met Melchizedek and refused to take anything for himself from the king of Sodom. That night God's word came to Abraham in a vision telling him to stop being afraid, for God was his Shield and would protect him. God was also his exceeding great reward; that is, God himself would be Abraham's portion. This was God's way also of telling Abraham, "Be concerned with Me!" Then God renewed the promise of a son by taking him out and showing him the stars and saying his descendants would be just as numerous. Because Abraham believed God, his faith was accounted for righteousness.



. . . and from there, after his father's death, *TCNT.*

**he removed him into this land, wherein ye now dwell:** God removed him into this land, *ASV* . . . to migrate, *NEB* . . . he was led to this land, *Norlie* . . . moved him from there, *Adams.*

**5. And he gave him none inheritance in it:** God did not give him any property in it, *TCNT* . . . no possession in it, *Weymouth* . . . no allotment to enjoy in it, *Concordant* . . . He gave him no heritable property in it, *Berkeley* . . . Yet God did not give him any ownership in the land, *Norlie* . . . But He gave him no estate in it, *Fenton* . . . He gave him nothing to call his own, *Beck.*

**no, not so much as to set his foot on:** . . . not even a foot...not even for the sole of his foot, *Klingensmith.*

**yet he promised that he would give it to him for a possession:** And yet He promised to bestow the land as a permanent possession on him, *Weymouth* . . . promised to give it to him, *Wuest* . . . the land should be his, *Norlie* . . . that it should eventually belong, *Phillips* . . . as a tenure, *Concordant.*

**and to his seed after him:** . . . and for his descendants after him, *TCNT* . . . on him, *Montgomery* . . . and his posterity, *Weymouth* . . . it should belong to his children and children's children after him, *Norlie.*

**when as yet he had no child:** . . . and promised this at a time when Abraham was childless, *Weymouth* . . . though up to that time he had no children, *TCNT* . . . even before he had children, *Klingensmith.*

**6. And God spake on this wise:** What God said was this, *TCNT* . . . conversed with him, *Murdock.*

**That his seed should sojourn in a strange land:** Abraham's descendants will live in a foreign country, *TCNT* . . . will be aliens in a foreign land, *Adams* . . . should lodge, *Fenton* . . . in an alien land, *Concordant* . . . foreign land, *Rotherham.*

**and that they should bring them into bondage:** . . . where they will be enslaved, *TCNT* . . . into servitude, *Rotherham.*

# Acts 7:7

| **2504.1** conj | **2530.4** verb 3pl indic fut act | **2073.3** noun pl neu | **4919.3** num card neu | **2504.1** conj | **3450.16** art sing neu |
|---|---|---|---|---|---|
| καὶ | κακώσουσιν | ἔτη | τετρακόσια· | 7. καὶ | τὸ |
| *kai* | *kakōsousin* | *etē* | *tetrakosia* | *kai* | *to* |
| and | will ill treat | years | four hundred; | and | the |

7.a.**Var:** 03B,05D,Lach Treg,We/Ho

| **1477.1** noun sing neu | **3614.3** rel-pron dat sing | **1430.1** partic | **300.1** partic | **1392.11** verb 3pl subj aor act |
|---|---|---|---|---|
| ἔθνος | ᾧ | ⸂ ἐὰν | [a ἂν ] | ⸃ δουλεύσωσιν, |
| *ethnos* | *hō* | *ean* | *an* | *douleusōsin* |
| nation | to which | | | they may be enslaved |

7.b.**Txt:** 01ℵ,03B,08E 025P,byz.Weis
**Var:** 02A,04C,05D,Treg Alf,Tisc,We/Ho,Sod UBS/☆

| **1392.15** verb 3pl indic fut act | **2892.24** verb 1sing indic fut act | **1466.1** prs-pron nom 1sing | **1500.5** verb 3sing indic aor act |
|---|---|---|---|
| [b☆ δουλεύσουσιν ] | κρινῶ | ἐγώ, | ⸂ εἶπεν |
| *douleusousin* | *krinō* | *egō* | *eipen* |
| [ they will serve ] | will judge | I, | said |

| **3450.5** art nom sing masc | **2296.1** noun nom sing masc | **3450.5** art nom sing masc | **2296.1** noun nom sing masc | **1500.5** verb 3sing indic aor act | **2504.1** conj |
|---|---|---|---|---|---|
| ὁ | θεός· | [☆ ὁ | θεὸς | εἶπεν, ] | καὶ |
| *ho* | *theos* | *ho* | *theos* | *eipen* | *kai* |
| | God | | [ God | said; ] | and |

| **3196.3** prep | **3642.18** dem-pron pl neu | **1814.37** verb 3pl indic fut mid | **2504.1** conj | **2973.12** verb 3pl indic fut act |
|---|---|---|---|---|
| μετὰ | ταῦτα | ἐξελεύσονται | καὶ | λατρεύσουσίν |
| *meta* | *tauta* | *exeleusontai* | *kai* | *latreusousin* |
| after | these things | they shall come forth | and | will serve |

| **1466.4** prs-pron dat 1sing | **1706.1** prep | **3450.3** art dat sing | **4964.3** noun dat sing masc | **3642.5** dem-pron dat sing masc | **2504.1** conj |
|---|---|---|---|---|---|
| μοι | ἐν | τῷ | τόπῳ | τούτῳ. | 8. Καὶ |
| *moi* | *en* | *tō* | *topō* | *toutō* | *Kai* |
| me | in | the | place | this. | And |

| **1319.14** verb 3sing indic aor act | **840.4** prs-pron dat sing | **1236.4** noun acc sing fem | **3921.2** noun gen sing fem | **2504.1** conj |
|---|---|---|---|---|
| ἔδωκεν | αὐτῷ | διαθήκην | περιτομῆς· | καὶ |
| *edōken* | *autō* | *diathēkēn* | *peritomēs* | *kai* |
| he gave | to him | a covenant | of circumcision; | and |

| **3643.1** adv | **1074.4** verb 3sing indic aor act | **3450.6** art acc sing masc | **2439.1** name masc | **2504.1** conj | **3919.3** verb 3sing indic aor act |
|---|---|---|---|---|---|
| οὕτως | ἐγέννησεν | τὸν | Ἰσαάκ, | καὶ | περιέτεμεν |
| *houtōs* | *egennēsen* | *ton* | *Isaak* | *kai* | *perietemen* |
| thus | he bore | | Isaac, | and | circumcised |

8.a.**Txt:** 05D-corr,025P byz.
**Var:** 01ℵ,02A,03B,04C 08E,Lach,Treg,Alf,Tisc We/Ho,Weis,Sod UBS/☆

| **840.6** prs-pron acc sing masc | **3450.11** art dat sing fem | **2232.3** noun dat sing fem | **3450.11** art dat sing fem | **3453.3** num ord dat sing fem | **2504.1** conj | **3450.5** art nom sing masc |
|---|---|---|---|---|---|---|
| αὐτὸν | τῇ | ἡμέρᾳ | τῇ | ὀγδόῃ· | καὶ | ⸂a ὁ ⸃ |
| *auton* | *tē* | *hēmera* | *tē* | *ogdoē* | *kai* | *ho* |
| him | the | day | the | eighth; | and | |

8.b.**Txt:** 05D-corr,025P byz.
**Var:** 01ℵ,02A,03B,04C 08E,Lach,Treg,Alf,Tisc We/Ho,Weis,Sod UBS/☆

| **2439.1** name masc | **3450.6** art acc sing masc | **2361.1** name masc | **2504.1** conj | **3450.5** art nom sing masc | **2361.1** name masc | **3450.8** art acc pl masc |
|---|---|---|---|---|---|---|
| Ἰσαὰκ | τὸν | Ἰακώβ, | καὶ | ⸂b ὁ ⸃ | Ἰακὼβ | τοὺς |
| *Isaak* | *ton* | *Iakōb* | *kai* | *ho* | *Iakōb* | *tous* |
| Isaac | | Jacob, | and | | Jacob | the |

| **1420.1** num card | **3828.4** noun acc pl masc | **2504.1** conj | **3450.7** art nom pl masc | **3828.3** noun nom pl masc |
|---|---|---|---|---|
| δώδεκα | πατριάρχας. | 9. Καὶ | οἱ | πατριάρχαι |
| *dōdeka* | *patriarchas* | *Kai* | *hoi* | *patriarchai* |
| twelve | patriarchs. | And | the | patriarchs, |

God gave Abraham further assurance He would fulfill His promise of the land. Abraham was asked to lay out a sacrifice before the Lord. God moved through the midst of the sacrifice from one end to the other in the symbol of a warming oven with a flame coming out of it. By this action God was indicating that He would begin the work of fulfilling His promise and He would finish it.

**7:7.** God also promised to judge the nation that would make Israel slaves (Genesis 15:14). This, of course, was fulfilled by the 10 plagues which climaxed in the death of the firstborn of Egypt, and in the destruction of Pharaoh's cavalry and chariots in the Red Sea.

Then God promised Abraham that after that his descendants would come out of Egypt and serve God "in this place," the Promised Land. "Serve" here is not the word for serving as a slave or even as a servant. It is especially used of the service of worship rendered to God. God wanted a people who would worship Him and Him alone.

**7:8.** God also gave Abraham the covenant of circumcision, so that Isaac was circumcised the eighth day after his birth. Actually, God gave the covenant of circumcision before Isaac was born and assured Abraham by it that Sarah his wife would bear a son and he should call his name Isaac. Then God would establish His covenant with Isaac.

Abraham, then at the age of 99, circumcised himself as a sign of the covenant. He also circumcised Ishmael who was then 13. But the pattern would be to circumcise 8 days after birth (Genesis 17:12). Thus it was Isaac, who was born and circumcised a year later, who set the pattern and began the line of descent that then continued through Jacob and the 12 patriarchs (tribal heads or tribal rulers). This emphasizes that they were all born under the covenant of circumcision. This was a change from the situation before Abraham.

For Abraham and his descendants, circumcision was both the outward sign that one had entered into a covenant relationship with God and also the seal. Paul showed that God imputed righteousness to Abraham solely on the basis of faith (Romans 4), and the sign of circumcision was added later "as a seal of the righteousness of faith which he had yet being uncircumcised" (Romans 4:11). Stephen did not address the legalism that developed around the subject (cf. Acts 15:1).

**7:9.** The patriarchs, actually the 10 sons of Jacob by Leah and his concubines, were moved and filled with envy and jealousy, so they sold Joseph into Egypt. But God was with him.

Stephen was preparing to make a strong contrast between the way Joseph's brothers treated him and the way God treated him. The envy and jealousy arose partly because Joseph was a younger



**and entreat them evil four hundred years:** . . . and treat them ill, four hundred years, *ASV* . . . illtreated, *TCNT* . . . ill-use, *Rotherham* . . . mistreat them, *Beck* . . . they will do cruel things to them, *Everyday* . . . and be cruelly treated, *Williams C.K.* . . . and oppressed, *NAB.*

**7. And the nation to whom they shall be in bondage will I judge, said God:** But I will myself judge the nation, to which they shall be enslaved, *TCNT* . . . I will pass sentence, *Williams* . . . But I will punish the nation where they are slaves, *Everyday* . . . the nation that has enslaved them, *Noli* . . . that nation which they serve, *NAB.*

**and after that shall they come forth:** . . . and after that they will leave the country, *TCNT* . . . they will be freed, *Norlie* . . . Then they will be liberated, *Noli.*

**and serve me in this place:** . . . and render divine service unto me, *Rotherham* . . . and worship me in this very place, *TCNT.*

**8. And he gave him the covenant of circumcision:** And with Abraham He made the sacred compact of, *Williams* . . . the sign for this...was, *NCV* . . . made a covenant, *NAB* . . . agreement, *Everyday, Phillips* . . . gave him the bond of circumcision, *Williams C.K.* . . . circumcision being its seal and sign, *Wuest.*

**and so Abraham begat Isaac, and circumcised him the eighth day:** . . . and it was under these circumstances that Abraham became the father of Isaac, *TCNT* . . . and under this covenant he became the father of, *Weymouth.*

**and Isaac begat Jacob; and Jacob begat the twelve patriarchs:** . . . and Isaac became the father of Jacob, *TCNT* . . . Isaac circumcised his son Jacob, *TEV* . . . and Jacob did the same for his sons, *NCV.*

**9. And the patriarchs, moved with envy:** . . . famous ancestors, *TEV* . . . Now our forefathers were jealous of Joseph, *Williams C.K.* . . . moved with jealousy, *ASV* . . . out of jealousy, *TCNT* . . . burning up with envy of Joseph, *Wuest* . . . envious of Joseph, *Noli.*

## Acts 7:10

| **2189.6** verb nom pl masc part aor act | **3450.6** art acc sing masc | **2473.1** name masc | **586.23** verb 3pl indic aor mid | **1519.1** prep |
|---|---|---|---|---|
| ζηλώσαντες | τὸν | Ἰωσὴφ | ἀπέδοντο | εἰς |
| *zēlōsantes* | *ton* | *Iōsēph* | *apedonto* | *eis* |
| having become jealous | | Joseph, | sold | into |

| **125.4** name acc fem | **2504.1** conj | **1498.34** verb sing indic imperf act | **3450.5** art nom sing masc | **2296.1** noun nom sing masc | **3196.2** prep |
|---|---|---|---|---|---|
| Αἴγυπτον· | καὶ | ἦν | ὁ | θεὸς | μετ' |
| *Aigupton* | *kai* | *ēn* | *ho* | *theos* | *met'* |
| Egypt. | And | was | | God | with |

10.a.**Txt:** byz.
**Var:** 01ℵ,02A,03B,04C 05D,08E,025P,Gries Lach,Treg,Alf,Word Tisc,We/Ho,Weis,Sod UBS/☆

| **840.3** prs-pron gen sing | **2504.1** conj | **1791.4** verb 3sing indic aor mid | **1791.8** verb 3sing indic aor mid | **840.6** prs-pron acc sing masc |
|---|---|---|---|---|
| αὐτοῦ, | 10. καὶ | ʼ ἐξείλετο | [a☆ ἐξείλατο ] | αὐτὸν |
| *autou* | *kai* | *exeileto* | *exeilato* | *auton* |
| him, | and | delivered | [ idem ] | him |

| **1523.2** prep gen | **3820.14** adj gen pl fem | **3450.1** art gen pl | **2324.6** noun gen pl fem | **840.3** prs-pron gen sing | **2504.1** conj | **1319.14** verb 3sing indic aor act |
|---|---|---|---|---|---|---|
| ἐκ | πασῶν | τῶν | θλίψεων | αὐτοῦ, | καὶ | ἔδωκεν |
| *ek* | *pasōn* | *tōn* | *thlipseōn* | *autou* | *kai* | *edōken* |
| out of | all | the | tribulations | his, | and | gave |

| **840.4** prs-pron dat sing | **5322.4** noun acc sing fem | **2504.1** conj | **4531.4** noun acc sing fem | **1710.1** prep | **5166.1** name masc |
|---|---|---|---|---|---|
| αὐτῷ | χάριν | καὶ | σοφίαν | ἐναντίον | Φαραὼ |
| *autō* | *charin* | *kai* | *sophian* | *enantion* | *Pharaō* |
| him | favor | and | wisdom | before | Pharaoh |

| **928.2** noun gen sing masc | **125.2** name gen fem | **2504.1** conj | **2497.4** verb 3sing indic aor act | **840.6** prs-pron acc sing masc |
|---|---|---|---|---|
| βασιλέως | Αἰγύπτου, | καὶ | κατέστησεν | αὐτὸν |
| *basileōs* | *Aiguptou* | *kai* | *katestēsen* | *auton* |
| king | of Egypt, | and | he appointed | him |

10.b.**Txt:** 03B,05D,044 byz.
**Var:** p74,01ℵ,02A,04C 08E,104,323,945,1175 1739,vul.sa.bo.Tisc,Sod

| **2216.6** verb acc sing masc part pres mid | **1894.2** prep | **125.4** name acc fem | **2504.1** conj | **1894.1** prep | **3513.1** adj sing |
|---|---|---|---|---|---|
| ἡγούμενον | ἐπ' | Αἴγυπτον | καὶ | [b+ ἐφ' ] | ὅλον |
| *hēgoumenon* | *ep'* | *Aigupton* | *kai* | *eph'* | *holon* |
| ruling | over | Egypt | and | [ over ] | whole |

| **3450.6** art acc sing masc | **3486.4** noun acc sing masc | **840.3** prs-pron gen sing | **2048.3** verb 3sing indic aor act | **1156.2** conj | **3016.1** noun nom sing masc | **1894.1** prep |
|---|---|---|---|---|---|---|
| τὸν | οἶκον | αὐτοῦ. | 11. ἦλθεν | δὲ | λιμὸς | ἐφ' |
| *ton* | *oikon* | *autou* | *ēlthen* | *de* | *limos* | *eph'* |
| the | house | his. | Came | but | a famine | upon |

11.a.**Txt:** 08E,025P,byz. Sod
**Var:** 01ℵ,02A,03B,04C sa.bo.Lach,Treg,Alf,Tisc We/Ho,Weis,UBS/☆

| **3513.9** adj acc sing fem | **3450.12** art acc sing fem | **1087.4** noun acc sing fem | **125.2** name gen fem | **125.4** name acc fem | **2504.1** conj |
|---|---|---|---|---|---|
| ὅλην | τὴν | ʼ γῆν | Αἰγύπτου | [a☆ Αἴγυπτον ] | καὶ |
| *holēn* | *tēn* | *gēn* | *Aiguptou* | *Aigupton* | *kai* |
| whole | the | land | of Egypt | [ idem ] | and |

| **5313.1** name fem | **2504.1** conj | **2324.1** noun nom sing fem | **3144.9** adj nom sing fem | **2504.1** conj | **3620.1** partic | **2128.1** verb 3indic act |
|---|---|---|---|---|---|---|
| Χανάαν, | καὶ | θλῖψις | μεγάλη· | καὶ | οὐχ | ʼ εὕρισκον |
| *Chanaan* | *kai* | *thlipsis* | *megalē* | *kai* | *ouch* | *heuriskon* |
| Canaan, | and | tribulation | great, | and | not | did find |

11.b.**Txt:** 01ℵ,02A,04C 05D,byz.Tisc,Sod
**Var:** 03B,08E,025P Treg,Alf,We/Ho,Weis UBS/☆

| **2128.47** verb indic imperf act | **5362.1** noun pl neu | **3450.7** art nom pl masc | **3824.6** noun nom pl masc | **2231.2** prs-pron gen 1pl |
|---|---|---|---|---|
| [b☆ ηὕρισκον ] | χορτάσματα | οἱ | πατέρες | ἡμῶν. |
| *hēuriskon* | *chortasmata* | *hoi* | *pateres* | *hēmōn* |
| [ was finding ] | sustenance | the | fathers | our. |

son but was given the tunic of a priest or king, indicating Jacob had chosen him to receive the birthright, and partly because of his dreams where he had seen his brothers and even his father and Leah bowing down to him. That a father and mother would bow down to a son (Leah was now the mother of the family since Rachel had died), or even that older sons would bow down to a younger son, was something unheard of in their culture.

Stephen recognized also that God was with Joseph all along. Joseph reported to his father the misdeeds of his half brothers, the sons of Bilhah and Zilpah (possibly idolatry; Genesis 37:2). The dreams of Joseph showed God was with him. God was with him even when he was sold into Egypt. He could have been sold to a farmer somewhere up the Nile. But he was sold to an officer of the king and put in a position where he could learn to become a business manager and then where he could learn how to handle men.

**7:10.** God delivered Joseph out of all his afflictions and distressing circumstances. He became the best business manager Potiphar ever had. When he was falsely accused and thrown in prison, he was put, not in an ordinary prison, but one where the king's prisoners were kept, which showed Potiphar still had a high regard for him. This high regard was further shown when he was asked to take care of special prisoners, the king's butler and baker. This led to the opportunity to interpret Pharaoh's dream, which gave him favor before Pharaoh and made Pharaoh and his advisers realize the Spirit of God was in Joseph.

Pharaoh recognized his wisdom and made him governor (leader, leading man) over Egypt and over all Pharaoh's household, including all his business affairs. Actually, Joseph was both the business manager for Pharaoh and the prime minister over the whole land. Though his brothers mistreated Joseph, God used it all to bring him to a place of high position, power, and great honor. Truly God was taking care of Joseph.

**7:11.** When the famine came over the land of Egypt, it also spread to Canaan. The patriarchs, now identified as "our fathers," found no food.

Stephen here skipped over the 7 good years in Egypt and the provision Joseph made for the 7 years of famine that followed. Some have wondered why Joseph did not contact his brothers after he was elevated to this high position in Egypt. But Joseph had no desire to tell his brothers, "I told you so." He knew too that if they were jealous of his tunic they might be even more jealous and vindictive if they saw the robes he now wore. More important, he recognized God was with him and he believed God was working it all out for good, so he was leaving it all in God's hand. But while Joseph was still prospering, his brothers were getting into a desperate situation through lack of food. They were used to having plenty, now the famine put them into a state of distress.

**sold Joseph into Egypt:** . . . sold Joseph into slavery in Egypt, *TCNT* . . . and sold him as a slave into Egypt, *Williams* . . . They sold him to be a slave in Egypt, *Everyday* . . . as a slave to the Egyptians, *Noli.*

**but God was with him:** But God helped him, *Noli.*

**10. And delivered him out of all his afflictions:** Joseph had many troubles there, *Everyday* . . . God rescued him from them all, *SEB* . . . from all his trials, *Kleist* . . . extricates him out of all his afflictions, *Concordant* . . . and took him out of all his tribulations, *Rotherham* . . . rescued him from all his afflictions, *Noli* . . . his troubles, *TCNT.*

**and gave him favour and wisdom in the sight of Pharaoh, king of Egypt:** . . . and gave him grace, *Williams C.K.* . . . caused Pharaoh...to approve him for his wisdom, *TNT* . . . and enabled him to win favour and a reputation for wisdom with Pharaoh, *TCNT* . . . respected him, *SEB.*

**and he made him governor over Egypt and all his house:** . . . who appointed him Governor of Egypt and of his whole household, *TCNT* . . . and all the royal household, *Weymouth* . . . appointed him prime minister, *Fenton* . . . chief, *Murdock* . . . in charge of all the people in his palace, *Everyday.*

**11. Now there came a dearth over all the land of Egypt and Canaan:** . . . a famine over all Egypt and Canaan, *ASV* . . . Then a famine spread over the whole of Egypt and Canaan, *TCNT* . . . became so dry that nothing would grow there, *Everyday.*

**and great affliction:** . . . causing great distress, *TCNT* . . . alot of hardship, *Adams* . . . and no little suffering, *Kleist.*

**and our fathers found no sustenance:** . . . since our fathers, *Kleist* . . . and our ancestors could find no food, *TCNT* . . . and our forefathers could not find the simplest food, *Williams* . . . so that our fathers failed to find nourishment, *Berkeley* . . . were not finding sustenance, *Young* . . . not finding pasture, *Rotherham* . . . found no Provisions, *Hanson, Wilson* . . . lacked food, *Murdock.*

| 189.31 verb nom sing masc part aor act | 1156.2 conj | 2361.1 name masc | 1498.18 verb part pres act | 4476.3 noun pl neu | 1706.1 prep |
|---|---|---|---|---|---|
| 12. ἀκούσας | δὲ | Ἰακὼβ | ὄντα | ⸀ σῖτα | ἐν |
| *akousas* | *de* | *Iakōb* | *onta* | *sita* | *en* |
| Having heard | but | Jacob | being | grain | in |

12.a.**Txt:** 025P,byz.
**Var:** 01ℵ,02A,03B,04C
08E,Lach,Treg,Alf
Word,Tisc,We/Ho,Weis
Sod,UBS/☆

| 125.3 name dat fem | 4473.1 noun pl neu | 1519.1 prep | 125.4 name acc fem | 1805.1 verb 3sing indic aor act |
|---|---|---|---|---|
| Αἰγύπτῳ, | [a☆ σιτία | εἰς | Αἴγυπτον ] | ἐξαπέστειλεν |
| *Aiguptō* | *sitia* | *eis* | *Aigupton* | *exapesteilen* |
| Egypt, | [ grain | in | Egypt ] | sent forth |

| 3450.8 art acc pl masc | 3824.9 noun acc pl masc | 2231.2 prs-pron gen 1pl | 4270.1 adv | 2504.1 conj | 1706.1 prep | 3450.3 art dat sing |
|---|---|---|---|---|---|---|
| τοὺς | πατέρας | ἡμῶν | πρῶτον˙ | 13. καὶ | ἐν | τῷ |
| *tous* | *pateras* | *hēmōn* | *prōton* | *kai* | *en* | *tō* |
| the | fathers | our | first; | and | at | the |

13.a.**Txt:** p74,01ℵ,04C
05D,08E,025P,etc.byz.
Tisc,Sod,UBS/☆
**Var:** 02A,03B,Treg
We/Ho,Weis

| 1202.3 num ord dat sing masc | 317.1 verb 3sing indic aor pass | 1101.14 verb 3sing indic aor pass | 2473.1 name masc | 3450.4 art dat pl |
|---|---|---|---|---|
| δευτέρῳ | ⸀ ἀνεγνωρίσθη | [a ἐγνωρίσθη ] | Ἰωσὴφ | τοῖς |
| *deuterō* | *anegnōristhē* | *egnōristhē* | *Iōsēph* | *tois* |
| second time | was made known | [ idem ] | Joseph | to the |

13.b.**Txt:** 05D,025P,byz.
Sod
**Var:** 01ℵ,02A,03B,04C
08E,Lach,Treg,Alf,Tisc
We/Ho,Weis,UBS/☆

| 79.8 noun dat pl masc | 840.3 prs-pron gen sing | 2504.1 conj | 5156.1 adj sing | 1090.33 verb 3sing indic aor mid | 3450.3 art dat sing |
|---|---|---|---|---|---|
| ἀδελφοῖς | αὐτοῦ, | καὶ | φανερὸν | ἐγένετο | τῷ |
| *adelphois* | *autou* | *kai* | *phaneron* | *egeneto* | *tō* |
| brothers | his, | and | known | became | |

13.c.**Var:** 01ℵ,02A,08E
Tisc

| 5166.1 name masc | 3450.16 art sing neu | 1079.1 noun sing neu | 3450.2 art gen sing | 2473.1 name masc | 840.3 prs-pron gen sing |
|---|---|---|---|---|---|
| Φαραὼ | τὸ | γένος | ⸂b τοῦ ⸃ | ⸀ Ἰωσήφ. | [c αὐτοῦ. ] |
| *Pharaō* | *to* | *genos* | *tou* | *Iōsēph* | *autou* |
| to Pharaoh | the | family | | of Joseph. | [ his. ] |

| 643.12 verb nom sing masc part aor act | 1156.2 conj | 2473.1 name masc | 3203.1 verb 3sing indic aor mid | 3450.6 art acc sing masc |
|---|---|---|---|---|
| 14. ἀποστείλας | δὲ | Ἰωσὴφ | μετεκαλέσατο | ⸀ τὸν |
| *aposteilas* | *de* | *Iōsēph* | *metekalesato* | *ton* |
| Having sent | and | Joseph | he called for | the |

| 3824.4 noun acc sing masc | 840.3 prs-pron gen sing | 2361.1 name masc | 2361.1 name masc | 3450.6 art acc sing masc | 3824.4 noun acc sing masc |
|---|---|---|---|---|---|
| πατέρα | αὐτοῦ | Ἰακὼβ, | [☆ Ἰακὼβ | τὸν | πατέρα |
| *patera* | *autou* | *Iakōb* | *Iakōb* | *ton* | *patera* |
| father | his | Jacob, | [ Jacob | the | father |

14.a.**Txt:** 05D,08E,byz.
sa.bo.
**Var:** 01ℵ,02A,03B,04C
025P,Gries,Lach,Treg
Alf,Tisc,We/Ho,Weis
Sod,UBS/☆

| 840.3 prs-pron gen sing | 2504.1 conj | 3820.12 adj acc sing fem | 3450.12 art acc sing fem | 4623.3 noun acc sing fem | 840.3 prs-pron gen sing |
|---|---|---|---|---|---|
| αὐτοῦ ] | καὶ | πᾶσαν | τὴν | συγγένειαν | ⸂a αὐτοῦ, ⸃ |
| *autou* | *kai* | *pasan* | *tēn* | *sungeneian* | *autou* |
| his ] | and | all | the | relatives | his, |

| 1706.1 prep | 5425.7 noun dat pl fem | 1433.1 num card | 3864.1 num card | 2568.14 verb 3sing indic aor act | 1156.2 conj |
|---|---|---|---|---|---|
| ἐν | ψυχαῖς | ἑβδομήκοντα | πέντε, | 15. ⸀ κατέβη | δὲ |
| *en* | *psuchais* | *hebdomēkonta* | *pente* | *katebē* | *de* |
| in | souls | seventy | five. | Went down | and |

15.a.**Txt:** 03B,byz.sa.bo.
We/Ho
**Var:** 01ℵ,02A,04C,08E
025P,Lach,Treg,Alf
Word,Tisc,Weis,Sod
UBS/☆

| 2504.1 conj | 2568.14 verb 3sing indic aor act | 2361.1 name masc | 1519.1 prep | 125.4 name acc fem | 2504.1 conj |
|---|---|---|---|---|---|
| [a☆ καὶ | κατέβη ] | Ἰακὼβ | εἰς | Αἴγυπτον. | καὶ |
| *kai* | *katebē* | *Iakōb* | *eis* | *Aigupton* | *kai* |
| [ and | went down ] | Jacob | into | Egypt | and |

**7:12.** When Jacob heard there was wheat (or bread) in Egypt, he sent the 10 "fathers" of Israel's tribes to Egypt. (The word "corn" in the King James Version is Old English for grain. The Hebrew word means both wheat and the bread made from wheat.)

Joseph immediately knew his brothers. They were mature men when he left them and they had not changed much. But they bowed down to Joseph without knowing who he was. To them he was Zaphnath-paaneah, the Prime Minister of Egypt. His Egyptian name was given as a way of conferring Egyptian citizenship so he could hold his high office. He was dressed like an Egyptian and at 39 looked much different from the 17-year-old boy the brothers had sold into Egypt.

Joseph made sure they would return to Egypt by making his brother Simeon a prisoner and by demanding that they not come back without bringing Benjamin with them. He wanted to be sure they had changed and that they had not shown the same kind of envy to Benjamin they had shown to him. He wanted to help them, but he knew he could not help them very much if they still had the same old attitudes.

**7:13.** As the famine continued, Jacob sent the brothers down to Egypt the second time to buy more grain. He hesitated for a time because he did not want to send Benjamin. But again the lack of food caused such distress that he finally was willing to let him go. This time Joseph had a dinner prepared where the seating arrangement for the 11 brothers was according to their age, and where Benjamin's portion was five times as large as any of the others. This would make it perfectly obvious that the arrangement was not accidental and that somehow Benjamin was the favored one. If they were still full of the old jealousy, this would have spoiled the dinner for the 10 brothers. After one further testing (cf. Genesis 44), Joseph could hold back no longer and revealed himself to his brothers. At first they were afraid of revenge, but Joseph told them not to fear. He saw that God had made all they had done turn out for good.

**7:14.** Then Joseph sent for Jacob and all his relatives who were in Canaan, 75 souls. (The word "souls" here means persons, a very common meaning of the Hebrew word.) Stephen used the number found in the Greek Septuagint version of Genesis 46:27; Exodus 1:5; and in some copies of Deuteronomy 10:22. The Masoretic Hebrew text has the round number 70.

**7:15.** Jacob at first refused to believe Joseph was still alive. He had believed Joseph was killed by a wild animal and may have inferred that perhaps he and Joseph were both under God's judgment. But when he saw the wagons Joseph sent to bring them, he believed. For the first time since he thought Joseph was killed, he was comforted and received encouragement from God to go to

**12. But when Jacob heard that there was corn in Egypt:** . . . when Jacob learned, *MLNT* . . . there was food, *NLT* . . . grain, *ASV* . . . wheat, *Berkeley.*

**he sent out our fathers first:** . . . sent our early fathers, *NLT* . . . he sent forth our fathers the first time, *ASV* . . . our forefathers on their first visit there, *Goodspeed* . . . Jacob sent our ancestors on their first visit to that country, *Moffatt* . . . This was their first trip to Egypt, *Everyday, NCV* . . . sent...there on a first trip, *MLNT* . . . there on a first mission, *NAB.*

**13. And at the second time Joseph was made known to his brethren:** On their second visit, *Goodspeed* . . . Then they went there a second time. This time, Joseph told his brothers, *NCV* . . . The second time they went to the country, *NLT* . . . In the course of their second visit, *TCNT* . . . told...who he was, *Beck.*

**and Joseph's kindred was made known unto Pharaoh:** . . . and Pharaoh learnt the parentage of Joseph, *TCNT* . . . Joseph's kin, *KJII* . . . and his family ties became known, *NAB* . . . Joseph's origin became known, *TNT* . . . and thus Joseph's race was revealed to Pharaoh, *Williams* . . . Pharaoh came to hear of Joseph's parentage, *Williams C.K.* . . . learned about Joseph's family, *NCV.*

**14. Then sent Joseph, and called his father Jacob to him:** Then Joseph sent an invitation to his father, *TCNT* . . . Joseph sent some men, *NCV* . . . asked his father, *NLT* . . . sent for, *NAB* . . . to invite Jacob, his father, to come to Egypt, *Everyday.*

**and all his kindred, threescore and fifteen souls:** He also invited all his relatives, *NCV* . . . all his relations, seventy-five persons in all, *TCNT* . . . all his kinsfolk, *NAB* . . . the whole family, *MLNT* . . . and all his family, numbering seventy-five persons, *Weymouth* . . . There were seventy-five people in the family, *NLT* . . . lives, *Hanson* . . . souls, *Swann.*

**15. So Jacob went down into Egypt:** And Jacob moved down to Egypt, *Norlie* . . . came down, *Goodspeed, MLNT.*

## Acts 7:16

| 4901.5 verb 3sing indic aor act | 840.5 prs-pron nom sing masc | 2504.1 conj | 3450.7 art nom pl masc | 3824.6 noun nom pl masc | 2231.2 prs-pron gen 1pl |
|---|---|---|---|---|---|
| ἐτελεύτησεν | αὐτὸς | καὶ | οἱ | πατέρες | ἡμῶν· |
| *eteleutēsen* | *autos* | *kai* | *hoi* | *pateres* | *hēmōn* |
| died, | he | and | the | fathers | our, |

| 2504.1 conj | 3216.6 verb 3pl indic aor pass | 1519.1 prep | 4818.1 name fem | 2504.1 conj | 4935.32 verb 3pl indic aor pass |
|---|---|---|---|---|---|
| **16.** καὶ | μετετέθησαν | εἰς | Συχὲμ, | καὶ | ἐτέθησαν |
| *kai* | *metetethēsan* | *eis* | *Suchem* | *kai* | *etethēsan* |
| and | were carried over | to | Shechem, | and | were placed |

16.a.**Txt:** 025P,byz.
**Var:** 01ℵ,02A,03B,04C 05D,08E,Gries,Lach Treg,Alf,Word,Tisc We/Ho,Weis,Sod UBS/⋆

| 1706.1 prep | 3450.3 art dat sing | 3282.2 noun dat sing neu | 3450.5 art nom sing masc | 3614.3 rel-pron dat sing | 5441.1 verb 3sing indic aor mid |
|---|---|---|---|---|---|
| ἐν | τῷ | μνήματι | ʻ ὃ | [a⋆ ᾧ ] | ὠνήσατο |
| *en* | *tō* | *mnēmati* | *ho* | *hō* | *ōnēsato* |
| in | the | tomb | the | [ which ] | bought |

| 11.1 name masc | 4940.2 noun gen sing fem | 688.2 noun gen sing neu | 3706.2 prep | 3450.1 art gen pl | 5048.7 noun gen pl masc |
|---|---|---|---|---|---|
| Ἀβραὰμ | τιμῆς | ἀργυρίου | παρὰ | τῶν | υἱῶν |
| *Abraam* | *timēs* | *arguriou* | *para* | *tōn* | *huiōn* |
| Abraham | for a price | of money | from | the | sons |

16.b.**Txt:** p74,05D,025P 044,byz.
**Var:** 01ℵ-org,03B,04C sa.bo.Treg,Tisc,We/Ho Weis,Sod,UBS/⋆

| 1683.1 name masc | 1683.2 name masc | 3450.2 art gen sing | 1706.1 prep |
|---|---|---|---|
| ʻ Ἐμμὸρ | [⋆ Ἑμμὼρ ] | ʻ τοῦ | [b⋆ ἐν ] |
| *Emmor* | *Hemmōr* | *tou* | *en* |
| of Hamor | [ idem ] | | [ in ] |

| 4818.1 name fem | 2503.1 conj | 1156.2 conj | 1443.18 verb 3sing indic imperf act | 3450.5 art nom sing masc |
|---|---|---|---|---|
| Συχέμ. | **17.** Καθὼς | δὲ | ἤγγιζεν | ὁ |
| *Suchem* | *Kathōs* | *de* | *ēngizen* | *ho* |
| of Shechem. | As | but | was drawing near | the |

| 5385.1 noun nom sing masc | 3450.10 art gen sing fem | 1845.1 noun fem | 3614.10 rel-pron gen sing fem | 3523.6 verb 3sing indic aor act |
|---|---|---|---|---|
| χρόνος | τῆς | ἐπαγγελίας | ἧς | ʻ ὤμοσεν |
| *chronos* | *tēs* | *epangelias* | *hēs* | *ōmosen* |
| time | of the | promise | which | swore |

17.a.**Txt:** 025P,044,byz. bo.
**Var:** p74,01ℵ,02A,03B 04C,sa.Lach,Treg,Alf Word,Tisc,We/Ho,Weis Sod,UBS/⋆

| 3533.8 verb 3sing indic aor act | 3450.5 art nom sing masc | 2296.1 noun nom sing masc | 3450.3 art dat sing | 11.1 name masc |
|---|---|---|---|---|
| [a⋆ ὡμολόγησεν ] | ὁ | θεὸς | τῷ | Ἀβραάμ, |
| *hōmologēsen* | *ho* | *theos* | *tō* | *Abraam* |
| [ declared ] | | God | | to Abraham, |

| 831.7 verb 3sing indic aor act | 3450.5 art nom sing masc | 2967.1 noun nom sing masc | 2504.1 conj | 3989.5 verb 3sing indic aor pass | 1706.1 prep |
|---|---|---|---|---|---|
| ηὔξησεν | ὁ | λαὸς | καὶ | ἐπληθύνθη | ἐν |
| *ēuxēsen* | *ho* | *laos* | *kai* | *eplēthunthē* | *en* |
| increased | the | people | and | were multiplied | in |

| 125.3 name dat fem | 884.1 conj | 884.2 conj | 3614.2 rel-pron gen sing | 448.2 verb 3sing indic aor act |
|---|---|---|---|---|
| Αἰγύπτῳ, | **18.** ʻ ἄχρις | [⋆ ἄχρι ] | οὗ | ἀνέστη |
| *Aiguptō* | *achris* | *achri* | *hou* | *anestē* |
| Egypt, | until | [ idem ] | which | arose |

18.a.**Var:** p74,01ℵ,02A 03B,04C,sa.bo.Lach Treg,Tisc,We/Ho,Weis Sod,UBS/⋆

| 928.1 noun nom sing masc | 2066.5 adj nom sing masc | 1894.2 prep | 125.4 name acc fem | 3614.5 rel-pron nom sing masc |
|---|---|---|---|---|
| βασιλεὺς | ἕτερος, | [a⋆+ ἐπ' | Αἴγυπτον ] | ὃς |
| *basileus* | *heteros* | *ep'* | *Aigupton* | *hos* |
| king | another, | [ over | Egypt ] | who |

Egypt, where he was satisfied to die now that he had seen Joseph. Later, all the brothers died there, that is, "our fathers" from whom the 12 tribes of Israel received their names.

**7:16.** After their deaths, the fathers (Jacob's sons) were transferred to Shechem and placed in the tomb bought for a price of silver from the sons of Emmor (the Greek form of *Hamor*), the father of Shechem (Genesis 33:19).

The reference here is to the burial of the 12 patriarchs. Jacob was buried in the cave of Machpelah near Hebron where Abraham and Sarah were buried (Genesis 23:17,19; 50:13). Joseph also was buried in Shechem (Joshua 24:32). Genesis 33:19 and Joshua 24:32 indicate Jacob did the actual buying of the plot in Shechem. However, Abraham was still alive, and it was undoubtedly done in the name of Abraham as the head of the clan.

In all this there is a subtle emphasis on the way Joseph was sold by his jealous brothers, yet was used by God to save their lives. There is also an emphasis on the faith of Abraham who believed God's promise even when he saw absolutely no evidence that it would be fulfilled.

These members of the Sanhedrin were refusing to believe God even though He had provided evidence of the fulfillment of His promise through the resurrection of Jesus. The treatment of Joseph by his brothers and the contrast to the way God treated him was a parallel to the way the Jewish leaders had treated Jesus.

**7:17.** Stephen next recounted the way the Israelites grew and multiplied in Egypt as the time came for the fulfillment of the promise God had sworn to Abraham, the promise that Abraham's descendants would possess the land of Canaan.

Joseph had secured for them the land of Goshen in the well-watered eastern part of the Nile delta. There they would be separated from the people of Egypt and yet be close to Joseph. They would also be able to retain their own customs and language. Through Joseph's provision they prospered and kept increasing in number until the land (Goshen) was filled with them (Exodus 1:7). Later, Moses was able to say that their fathers had gone down into Egypt 70 persons, but by Moses' time the Lord their God had made them "as the stars of heaven for multitude" (Deuteronomy 1:10; 10:22). Truly God had been fulfilling the promise given to Abraham in Genesis 15:5!

**7:18.** This increase of prosperity and numbers continued until a king arose who did not know Joseph. Joseph lived to see his great-grandchildren and died at the age of 110. He was obviously still in favor and was able to help his brothers and their children, grandchildren, and great-grandchildren during this time.

It is not known exactly how long this prosperity continued, for the exact time of the rise of the Pharaoh who knew not Joseph is

**and died, he, and our fathers:** . . . where he and our fathers finished their course, *Berkeley* . . . There he died and our ancestors too, *TCNT* . . . There he died, and so did our forefathers, *Weymouth.*

**16. And were carried over into Sychem:** Later their bodies were moved, *NCV* . . . and their bodies were removed to Shechem, *TCNT* . . . their bodies were brought back, *JB.*

**and laid in the sepulchre that Abraham bought for a sum of money of the sons of Emmor the father of Sychem:** . . . and laid in the tomb, *ASV* . . . and put in a grave there, *Everyday* . . . which Abraham had bought for silver, *Williams C.K.* . . . for its value in silver, *Swann.*

**17. But when the time of the promise drew nigh:** Now just as the time of the promise was drawing near, *TCNT* . . . But as the time drew near for the fulfilment, *Weymouth* . . . that God set in His promise, *Beck* . . . The promise...was soon to come true, *Everyday* . . . But as the promised time approached, *Berkeley* . . . for realizing the promise, *Williams* . . . The time approached for the fulfillment of the promise, *Noli* . . . drew near, *Kleist* . . . was about to happen, *NLT.*

**which God had sworn to Abraham:** . . . that God made to Abraham, *Everyday* . . . which God vouchsafed, *ASV* . . . had made, *Noli, TCNT* . . . promised, *HBIV* . . . ratified, *Alford* . . . The promise...was soon to come true, *NCV.*

**the people grew and multiplied in Egypt:** . . . the people increased largely in numbers in Egypt, *TCNT* . . . the people grew greatly in numbers, *TNT* . . . The number of people in Egypt grew large, *Everyday* . . . increased and grew in number, *Williams C.K.* . . . the people became many times more numerous, *Weymouth.*

**18. Till another king arose, which knew not Joseph:** . . . till a new king, who knew nothing of Joseph, came to the throne, *TCNT* . . . a different king, *Beck* . . . a foreign king, *PNT* . . . became ruler of Egypt, *Noli* . . . Then a new king began to rule

## Acts 7:19

| 3620.2 partic | 3471.11 verb 3sing indic plperf act | 3450.6 art acc sing masc | 2473.1 name masc | 3642.4 dem-pron nom sing masc |
|---|---|---|---|---|
| οὐκ | ᾔδει | τὸν | Ἰωσήφ. | 19. οὗτος |
| *ouk* | *ēdei* | *ton* | *Iōsēph* | *houtos* |
| not | had known | | Joseph. | This |

| 2656.1 verb nom sing masc part aor mid | 3450.16 art sing neu | 1079.1 noun sing neu | 2231.2 prs-pron gen 1pl | 2530.1 verb 3sing indic aor act |
|---|---|---|---|---|
| κατασοφισάμενος | τὸ | γένος | ἡμῶν, | ἐκάκωσεν |
| *katasophisamenos* | *to* | *genos* | *hēmōn* | *ekakōsen* |
| having dealt deceitfully | with the | race | our, | ill treated |

19.a.**Txt:** 02A,04C,08E 025P,044,byz.syr.it.sa. bo.Sod
**Var:** p74,01ℵ,03B,05D Lach,Treg,Alf,Tisc We/Ho,Weis,UBS/⋆

| 3450.8 art acc pl masc | 3824.9 noun acc pl masc | 2231.2 prs-pron gen 1pl | 3450.2 art gen sing | 4020.20 verb inf pres act | 1557.1 adj pl neu |
|---|---|---|---|---|---|
| τοὺς | πατέρας | ⸂[a] ἡμῶν, ⸃ | τοῦ | ποιεῖν | ⸂ ἔκθετα |
| *tous* | *pateras* | *hēmōn* | *tou* | *poiein* | *ektheta* |
| the | fathers | our, | the | to make | exposed |

| 3450.17 art pl neu | 1018.3 noun pl neu | 3450.17 art pl neu | 1018.3 noun pl neu | 1557.1 adj pl neu | 840.1 prs-pron gen pl | 1519.1 prep |
|---|---|---|---|---|---|---|
| τὰ | βρέφη | [⋆ τὰ | βρέφη | ἔκθετα ] | αὐτῶν | εἰς |
| *ta* | *brephē* | *ta* | *brephē* | *ektheta* | *autōn* | *eis* |
| the | infants | [ the | infants | exposed ] | their | to |

| 3450.16 art sing neu | 3231.1 partic | 2208.2 verb inf pres mid | 1706.1 prep | 3614.3 rel-pron dat sing | 2511.3 noun dat sing masc |
|---|---|---|---|---|---|
| τὸ | μὴ | ζῳογονεῖσθαι. | 20. Ἐν | ᾧ | καιρῷ |
| *to* | *mē* | *zōogoneisthai* | *En* | *hō* | *kairō* |
| the | not | to be preserved. | In | which | time |

| 1074.13 verb 3sing indic aor pass | 3337.1 name nom masc | 3338.1 name nom masc | 2504.1 conj | 1498.34 verb sing indic imperf act |
|---|---|---|---|---|
| ἐγεννήθη | ⸂ Μωσῆς, | [⋆ Μωϋσῆς, ] | καὶ | ἦν |
| *egennēthē* | *Mōsēs* | *Mōusēs* | *kai* | *ēn* |
| was born | Moses, | [ idem ] | and | was |

| 785.1 adj nom sing masc | 3450.3 art dat sing | 2296.3 noun dat sing masc | 3614.5 rel-pron nom sing masc | 395.1 verb 3sing indic aor pass | 3243.4 noun acc pl masc |
|---|---|---|---|---|---|
| ἀστεῖος | τῷ | θεῷ· | ὃς | ἀνετράφη | μῆνας |
| *asteios* | *tō* | *theō* | *hos* | *anetraphē* | *mēnas* |
| beautiful | | to God; | who | was brought up | months |

20.a.**Txt:** 05D,08E,byz.
**Var:** 01ℵ,02A,03B,04C 025P,Gries,Lach,Treg Alf,Word,Tisc,We/Ho Weis,Sod,UBS/⋆

| 4980.1 num card nom | 1706.1 prep | 3450.3 art dat sing | 3486.3 noun dat sing masc | 3450.2 art gen sing | 3824.2 noun gen sing masc | 840.3 prs-pron gen sing |
|---|---|---|---|---|---|---|
| τρεῖς | ἐν | τῷ | οἴκῳ | τοῦ | πατρός | ⸂[a] αὐτοῦ. ⸃ |
| *treis* | *en* | *tō* | *oikō* | *tou* | *patros* | *autou* |
| three | in | the | house | of the | father | his. |

21.a.**Txt:** 08E,025P,byz.
**Var:** 01ℵ,02A,03B,04C 05D,Lach,Treg,Alf,Tisc We/Ho,Weis,Sod UBS/⋆

| 1606.2 verb acc sing masc part aor pass | 1156.2 conj | 840.6 prs-pron acc sing masc | 1606.4 verb gen sing masc part aor pass |
|---|---|---|---|
| 21. ⸂ ἐκτεθέντα | δὲ | αὐτόν, | [[a]⋆ ἐκτεθέντος |
| *ektethenta* | *de* | *auton* | *ektethentos* |
| having been exposed | and | he, | [ having been exposed |

21.b.**Txt:** 025P,byz.
**Var:** 01ℵ,02A,03B,04C 05D,08E,Gries,Lach Treg,Alf,Word,Tisc We/Ho,Weis,Sod UBS/⋆

| 1156.2 conj | 840.3 prs-pron gen sing | 335.13 verb 3sing indic aor mid | 335.18 verb 3sing indic aor mid | 840.6 prs-pron acc sing masc |
|---|---|---|---|---|
| δὲ | αὐτοῦ ] | ⸂ ἀνείλετο | [[b]⋆ ἀνείλατο ] | αὐτὸν |
| *de* | *autou* | *aneileto* | *aneilato* | *auton* |
| and | of him ] | took up | [ idem ] | him |

| 3450.9 art nom sing fem | 2341.1 noun nom sing fem | 5166.1 name masc | 2504.1 conj | 395.2 verb 3sing indic aor mid | 840.6 prs-pron acc sing masc |
|---|---|---|---|---|---|
| ἡ | θυγάτηρ | Φαραὼ, | καὶ | ἀνεθρέψατο | αὐτὸν |
| *hē* | *thugatēr* | *Pharaō* | *kai* | *anethrepsato* | *auton* |
| the | daughter | of Pharaoh, | and | brought up | him |

unknown. First Kings 6:1 indicates that Solomon began to build the temple in the fourth year of his full reign (that is, the fourth year after David died). This would put the Exodus from Egypt at 1440 B.C., and the birth of Moses 80 years before that. Some believe Hatshepsut, Egypt's well-known individualistic queen, was the Pharaoh's daughter who rescued Moses. Arguments for a later date are all very weak and can be easily refuted.

This king was undoubtedly of a different dynasty or ruling family from the one under whom Joseph served. He would thus have no regard for the previous kings of Egypt, to say nothing of their prime ministers.

**7:19.** This king of Egypt victimized Israel by trickery and underhanded methods. The reference here is probably first of all to the way he set slave drivers over them and made them work harder and harder. Second, it probably refers to the way the king gave a command, possibly secret, to the midwives to kill the boy babies and let only the girls live.

When the midwives managed to avoid doing what the king commanded, the king told all the Egyptians to throw every son born to the Israelites into the river. Stephen says they cast out their infants so they would not live. "Cast out" is a term used for exposing babies in some place where the elements or wild animals would cause them to die. The later Romans used it of putting unwanted babies out where wild animals would come at night and take them. Here it refers to exposing them in the river to be eaten by crocodiles.

**7:20.** During this time Moses was born and was *asteios* (Hebrew *tôv*, "goodly, fair, beautiful," cf. Exodus 2:2), literally, *fair* (lovely, fine) *to God*. This may mean he was made so by God or considered so by God.

The Bible shows God is always with those He plans to give opportunities for unusual service and God prepares them even from birth. God told Jeremiah, "Before I formed you in (your mother's) body, I knew you, and before you came out of (her) womb I sanctified you (set you apart for my service) and ordained you as a prophet to the nations" (Jeremiah 1:5, author's translation). John the Baptist was filled with the Holy Spirit even from his mother's womb (Luke 1:15).

The parents of Moses were sensitive to God's will and carefully nourished him, keeping him hidden for 3 months.

**7:21.** God's care was shown when Moses was exposed by the water's edge. Of course, his mother's faith and confidence in God made her take an active part in expressing that faith. She made an ark (a vessel for floating, the same word that is used of Noah's ark) in the form of a waterproofed woven basket and put it among the bulrushes growing near a place where Pharaoh's daughter came to



Egypt, *Everyday* . . . who had not been acquainted with Joseph, *Concordant.*

**19. The same dealt subtilly with our kindred:** This king acted deceitfully towards our race, *TCNT* . . . By taking a cunning advantage of our race, *Williams* . . . He defrauded our race, *Berkeley* . . . He exploited our race, *Norlie* . . . He took advantage of our race, *Adams* . . . This man's policy was to exterminate our race, *Fenton* . . . shrewd in scheming, *Beck* . . . adopted a crafty policy, *PNT* . . . He worked some tricks, *Klingensmith* . . . outwitted our race, *Wilson* . . . victimized our race, *Phillips* . . . He oppressed our people, *Noli.*

**And evil entreated our fathers:** . . . ill-treated, *ASV* . . . oppressed our forefathers, *Weymouth* . . . abused, *Berkeley* . . . mistreated, *Adams* . . . He outraged, *Fenton* . . . afflicted, *Confraternity.*

**so that they cast our their young children:** . . . compelled them to expose their infants, *Noli* . . . so as to cause their babies to be exposed, *Rotherham* . . . making them abandon their own infants, *TCNT* . . . with the object that our race might not be reproduced, *Fenton.*

**20. In which time Moses was born:** At which season, *ASV* . . . At this juncture, *AmpB* . . . At this period, *Noli.*

**and was exceeding fair:** . . . beautiful in God's sight, *Berkeley* . . . lovely to God, *Murdock* . . . delightful, *Adams* . . . a divinely beautiful child, *Montgomery* . . . he was no ordinary child, *NIV* . . . child of remarkable beauty, *Phillips.*

**and nourished up in his father's house three months:** . . . reared, *TCNT* . . . cared for, *Weymouth* . . . nurtured in his parental home, *Berkeley.*

**21. And when he was cast out:** At length he was cast out, *Weymouth* . . . but when he was exposed, *Rotherham* . . . and, when he was abandoned, *TCNT.*

**Pharaoh's daughter took him up:** . . . rescued him, *Rotherham* . . . adopted him, *Weymouth* . . . lifts him up, *Concordant.*

# Acts 7:22

| 1431.10 prs-pron dat sing fem | 1519.1 prep | 5048.4 noun acc sing masc | 2504.1 conj | 3674.9 verb 3sing indic aor pass | 3337.1 name nom masc |
|---|---|---|---|---|---|
| ἑαυτῇ | εἰς | υἱόν. | 22. καὶ | ἐπαιδεύθη | ⸀ Μωσῆς |
| *heautē* | *eis* | *huion* | *kai* | *epaideuthē* | *Mōsēs* |
| for herself | for | a son. | And | was instructed | Moses |

22.a.**Var:** 01ℵ,02A,04C 08E,sa.bo.Treg,Alf Word,Tisc

| 3338.1 name nom masc | 1706.1 prep | 3820.11 adj dat sing fem | 4531.3 noun dat sing fem | 124.4 name-adj gen pl masc |
|---|---|---|---|---|
| [☆ Μωϋσῆς ] | [a+ ἐν ] | πάσῃ | σοφίᾳ | Αἰγυπτίων· |
| *Mōusēs* | *en* | *pasē* | *sophia* | *Aiguptiōn* |
| [ idem ] | [ in ] | in all | wisdom | of Egyptians, |

22.b.**Txt:** 08E,025P,byz. **Var:** 01ℵ,02A,03B,04C 05D,Lach,Treg,Alf,Tisc We/Ho,Weis,Sod UBS/☆

| 1498.34 verb sing indic imperf act | 1156.2 conj | 1409.1 adj nom sing masc | 1706.1 prep | 3030.7 noun dat pl masc | 2504.1 conj | 1706.1 prep |
|---|---|---|---|---|---|---|
| ἦν | δὲ | δυνατὸς | ἐν | λόγοις | καὶ | ⸂b ἐν ⸃ |
| *ēn* | *de* | *dunatos* | *en* | *logois* | *kai* | *en* |
| he was | and | mighty | in | words | and | in |

22.c.**Var:** 01ℵ,02A,03B 04C,05D,08E,sa.bo. Gries,Lach,Treg,Alf Word,Tisc,We/Ho,Weis Sod,UBS/☆

| 2024.6 noun dat pl neu | 840.3 prs-pron gen sing | 5453.1 conj | 1156.2 conj | 3997.38 verb 3sing indic imperf pass |
|---|---|---|---|---|
| ἔργοις. | [c☆+ αὐτοῦ. ] | 23. Ὡς | δὲ | ἐπληροῦτο |
| *ergois* | *autou* | *Hōs* | *de* | *eplērouto* |
| deeds | [ his. ] | When | and | was being fulfilled |

| 840.4 prs-pron dat sing | 4911.1 adj nom sing masc | 4911.3 adj nom sing masc | 5385.1 noun nom sing masc |
|---|---|---|---|
| αὐτῷ | ⸀ τεσσαρακονταετὴς | [ τεσσερακονταετὴς ] | χρόνος, |
| *autō* | *tessarakontaetēs* | *tesserakontaetēs* | *chronos* |
| to him | of forty years | [ idem ] | a period, |

| 303.13 verb 3sing indic aor act | 1894.3 prep | 3450.12 art acc sing fem | 2559.4 noun acc sing fem | 840.3 prs-pron gen sing | 1964.7 verb inf aor mid |
|---|---|---|---|---|---|
| ἀνέβη | ἐπὶ | τὴν | καρδίαν | αὐτοῦ | ἐπισκέψασθαι |
| *anebē* | *epi* | *tēn* | *kardian* | *autou* | *episkepsasthai* |
| it came | into | the | heart | his | to look upon |

| 3450.8 art acc pl masc | 79.9 noun acc pl masc | 840.3 prs-pron gen sing | 3450.8 art acc pl masc | 5048.9 noun acc pl masc | 2447.1 name masc |
|---|---|---|---|---|---|
| τοὺς | ἀδελφοὺς | αὐτοῦ | τοὺς | υἱοὺς | Ἰσραήλ. |
| *tous* | *adelphous* | *autou* | *tous* | *huious* | *Israēl* |
| the | brothers | his | the | sons | of Israel; |

| 2504.1 conj | 1481.16 verb nom sing masc part aor act | 4948.5 indef-pron | 90.17 verb acc sing masc part pres mid | 290.1 verb 3sing indic aor mid |
|---|---|---|---|---|
| 24. καὶ | ἰδών | τινα | ἀδικούμενον | ἠμύνατο |
| *kai* | *idōn* | *tina* | *adikoumenon* | *ēmunato* |
| and | having seen | a certain one | being wronged, | he defended |

| 2504.1 conj | 4020.24 verb 3sing indic aor act | 1544.3 noun acc sing fem | 3450.3 art dat sing | 2639.1 verb dat sing masc part pres mid |
|---|---|---|---|---|
| καὶ | ἐποίησεν | ἐκδίκησιν | τῷ | καταπονουμένῳ, |
| *kai* | *epoiēsen* | *ekdikēsin* | *tō* | *kataponoumenō* |
| and | wrought | vengeance | for the | being oppressed, |

| 3822.3 verb nom sing masc part aor act | 3450.6 art acc sing masc | 124.2 name-adj acc sing masc | 3406.10 verb 3sing indic imperf act |
|---|---|---|---|
| πατάξας | τὸν | Αἰγύπτιον. | 25. ἐνόμιζεν |
| *pataxas* | *ton* | *Aiguption* | *enomizen* |
| having struck down | the | Egyptian. | He was supposing |

25.a.**Txt:** 02A,05D,08E 025P,byz.sa.bo.Sod **Var:** 01ℵ,03B,04C,Treg Tisc,We/Ho,Weis UBS/☆

| 1156.2 conj | 4770.7 verb inf pres act | 3450.8 art acc pl masc | 79.9 noun acc pl masc | 840.3 prs-pron gen sing | 3617.1 conj |
|---|---|---|---|---|---|
| δὲ | συνιέναι | τοὺς | ἀδελφοὺς | ⸂a αὐτοῦ ⸃ | ὅτι |
| *de* | *sunienai* | *tous* | *adelphous* | *autou* | *hoti* |
| for | to understand | the | brothers | his | that |

bathe. She also had Miriam, Moses' sister, keep a lookout.

Stephen was drawing attention to God's care through Pharaoh's daughter who took the baby up out of the water and reared him as her own son.

**7:22.** As a prince then, Moses was trained or educated in all the wisdom of Egypt and was mighty (powerful) in his words and deeds. This is significant, for the Egyptians had already made great advances in science, engineering, mathematics, astronomy, and medicine.

**7:23.** The first 40 years of Moses' life were spent as an Egyptian prince. Jewish tradition says he took part in some of Egypt's military campaigns, going up the Nile into Cush (the ancient Ethiopia, now called the Sudan). The same traditions indicate that Moses married a Cushite woman (of the Caucasoid race, not Negroid), who was left behind when he fled Egypt and did not rejoin him until after he had successfully brought Israel out of Egypt.

But Moses never forgot he was an Israelite. In the providence of God, the princess hired his mother to nurse him, and she had him long enough to instill in his heart the promises God gave to Abraham, Isaac, and Jacob, for it is clear that at the burning bush Moses knew what kind of God they served.

At the age of 40, the desire came into Moses' heart to visit his Israelite brothers. "Visit" here is a word that means to look after, take care of, relieve, or protect. It means Moses left his duties at Egypt's capital and went into Goshen with a deep desire to do something to help his people.

**7:24.** When Moses saw one of the Israelites being injured unjustly, he defended him, avenged the ill-treated one, and struck down the Egyptian. "Avenged" here does not speak of revenge. Rather, it means that Moses was concerned to bring justice, and as a prince of Egypt he felt he had the right to bring that justice.

**7:25.** Stephen explained why Moses was seeking to help the Israelites and why he tried to bring justice to this mistreated Israelite. Actually, also, this is the point Stephen was leading up to. Moses did this because he supposed his Israelite brothers (his fellow Israelites) would understand that God, by his hand, would give them deliverance. "Deliverance" here is the Greek *sotērian*, a word usually translated "salvation," though it is also used of deliverance, health, and well-being.

Moses not only must have had faith in God's promise to Abraham, Isaac, and Jacob, but he was sensitive to those promises, and probably remembered the way God had prepared Joseph to bring a great deliverance from the famine. He saw that God's hand had been guiding and preparing him to deliver his people. But though

**and nourished him for her own son:** . . . for herself as a son, *Rotherham* . . . and reared him as her own son, *TCNT* . . . and brought him up as her own son, *Weymouth* . . . raised him, *Beck.*

**22. And Moses was learned in all the wisdom of the Egyptians:** . . . instructed, *ASV* . . . trained, *Rotherham* . . . educated in, *Williams* . . . the science, *Berkeley* . . . the philosophy, *Fenton.*

**and was mighty in words and deeds:** . . . and showed ability in both speech and action, *TCNT* . . . in discourse and in deeds, *Berkeley.*

**23. And when he was full forty years old:** . . . in his fortieth year, *TCNT* . . . As he was rounding out his fortieth year, *Williams.*

**it came into his heart to visit his brethren the children of Israel:** . . . the thought came into his mind that he would visit his brother Israelites, *TCNT* . . . it occurred to him to visit his brethren the descendants of Israel, *Weymouth* . . . visit his own people, *Beck* . . . for the purpose of acquainting himself with thier needs, *Wuest.*

**24. And seeing one of them suffer wrong:** . . . and seeing one being wronged, *Rotherham* . . . and seeing an Israelite ill-treated, *TCNT* . . . being imposed upon, *Weymouth* . . . being mistreated, *Williams* . . . treated unfairly, *Berkeley* . . . suffer injustice, *Young.*

**he defended him:** . . . he took his part, *Weymouth* . . . defended the oppressed man, *Norlie* . . . he wrought redress, *Montgomery* . . . took the part of the wronged man, *Klingensmith.*

**and avenged him that was oppressed:** . . . and secured justice for the ill-treated man, *Weymouth* . . . avenges the one being harried, *Concordant.*

**and smote the Egyptian:** . . . by striking down, *TCNT* . . . by slaying, *Berkeley.*

**25. For he supposed his brethren would have understood:** . . . he concluded, *Fenton* . . . He supposed his brethren to be aware, *Weymouth* . . . he inferred that his brethren understood, *Concordant.*

| 3450.5 art nom sing masc | 2296.1 noun nom sing masc | 1217.2 prep | 5331.2 noun gen sing fem | 840.3 prs-pron gen sing | 1319.2 verb 3sing indic pres act |
|---|---|---|---|---|---|
| ὁ | θεὸς | διὰ | χειρὸς | αὐτοῦ | δίδωσιν |
| *ho* | *theos* | *dia* | *cheiros* | *autou* | *didōsin* |
| | God | by | hand | his | is giving |

| 840.2 prs-pron dat pl | 4843.3 noun acc sing fem | 4843.3 noun acc sing fem | 840.2 prs-pron dat pl | 3450.7 art nom pl masc |
|---|---|---|---|---|
| ʻ αὐτοῖς | σωτηρίαν. | [☆ σωτηρίαν | αὐτοῖς, ] | οἱ |
| *autois* | *sōtērian* | *sōtērian* | *autois* | *hoi* |
| them | salvation. | [ salvation | to them, ] | The |

| 1156.2 conj | 3620.3 partic | 4770.9 verb 3pl indic aor act | 3450.11 art dat sing fem | 4885.1 conj | 1951.1 noun dat sing fem | 2232.3 noun dat sing fem |
|---|---|---|---|---|---|---|
| δὲ | οὐ | συνῆκαν. | 26. τῇ | τε | ἐπιούσῃ | ἡμέρᾳ |
| *de* | *ou* | *sunēkan* | *tē* | *te* | *epiousē* | *hēmera* |
| but | not | understood. | On the | and | following | day |

| 3571.21 verb 3sing indic aor pass | 840.2 prs-pron dat pl | 3136.2 verb dat pl masc part pres mid | 2504.1 conj | 4750.1 verb 3sing indic aor act |
|---|---|---|---|---|
| ὤφθη | αὐτοῖς | μαχομένοις, | καὶ | ʻ συνήλασεν |
| *ōphthē* | *autois* | *machomenois* | *kai* | *sunēlasen* |
| he appeared | to them | fighting, | and | urged |

26.a.**Txt:** 02A,08E,025P byz.bo.
**Var:** 01ℵ,03B,04C,05D sa.Lach,Treg,Word,Tisc We/Ho,Weis,Sod UBS/☆

| 4722.1 verb 3sing indic imperf act | 840.8 prs-pron acc pl masc | 1519.1 prep | 1503.4 noun acc sing fem | 1500.15 verb nom sing masc part aor act |
|---|---|---|---|---|
| [a☆ συνήλλασσεν ] | αὐτοὺς | εἰς | εἰρήνην, | εἰπών, |
| *sunēllassen* | *autous* | *eis* | *eirēnēn* | *eipōn* |
| [ was urging ] | them | to | peace, | having said, |

26.b.**Txt:** 025P,byz.bo.
**Var:** 01ℵ,02A,03B,04C 08E,sa.Lach,Treg,Word Tisc,We/Ho,Weis,Sod UBS/☆

| 433.6 noun nom pl masc | 79.6 noun nom pl masc | 1498.6 verb 2pl indic pres act | 5050.1 prs-pron nom 2pl | 2420.1 adv | 90.2 verb 2pl indic pres act |
|---|---|---|---|---|---|
| Ἄνδρες | ἀδελφοί | ἐστε | ʻb ὑμεῖς˙ ˎ | ἱνατί | ἀδικεῖτε |
| *Andres* | *adelphoi* | *este* | *humeis* | *hinati* | *adikeite* |
| Men | brothers | are | you, | why | wrong you |

| 238.3 prs-pron acc pl masc | 3450.5 art nom sing masc | 1156.2 conj | 90.4 verb nom sing masc part pres act | 3450.6 art acc sing masc | 3999.1 adv |
|---|---|---|---|---|---|
| ἀλλήλους; | 27. Ὁ | δὲ | ἀδικῶν | τὸν | πλησίον |
| *allēlous* | *Ho* | *de* | *adikōn* | *ton* | *plēsion* |
| one another? | The | but | wronging | the | neighbor |

| 676.2 verb 3sing indic aor mid | 840.6 prs-pron acc sing masc | 1500.15 verb nom sing masc part aor act | 4949.3 intr-pron nom sing | 4622.4 prs-pron acc 2sing |
|---|---|---|---|---|
| ἀπώσατο | αὐτὸν, | εἰπών, | Τίς | σε |
| *apōsato* | *auton* | *eipōn* | *Tis* | *se* |
| pushed away | him, | having said, | Who | you |

| 2497.4 verb 3sing indic aor act | 752.4 noun acc sing masc | 2504.1 conj | 1342.1 noun acc sing masc | 1894.1 prep | 2231.4 prs-pron acc 1pl |
|---|---|---|---|---|---|
| κατέστησεν | ἄρχοντα | καὶ | δικαστὴν | ἐφ' | ʻ ἡμᾶς; |
| *katestēsen* | *archonta* | *kai* | *dikastēn* | *eph'* | *hēmas* |
| appointed | ruler | and | judge | over | us? |

27.a.**Txt:** 05D,08E,byz.
**Var:** 01ℵ,02A,03B,04C 025P,Lach,Treg,Word Tisc,We/Ho,Weis,Sod UBS/☆

| 2231.2 prs-pron gen 1pl | 3231.1 partic | 335.9 verb inf aor act | 1466.6 prs-pron acc 1sing | 4622.1 prs-pron nom 2sing | 2286.2 verb 2sing indic pres act |
|---|---|---|---|---|---|
| [a☆ ἡμῶν; ] | 28. μὴ | ἀνελεῖν | με | σὺ | θέλεις, |
| *hēmōn* | *mē* | *anelein* | *me* | *su* | *theleis* |
| [ us? ] | Not | to kill | me | you | wish, |

28.a.**Txt:** 02A,08E,025P byz.Sod
**Var:** 01ℵ,03B-org,04C 05D,Lach,Treg,Alf,Tisc We/Ho,Weis,UBS/☆

| 3614.6 rel-pron acc sing masc | 4999.3 noun acc sing masc | 335.4 verb 2sing indic aor act | 5340.1 adv | 2170.1 adv |
|---|---|---|---|---|
| ὃν | τρόπον | ἀνεῖλες | ʻ χθὲς | [a☆ ἐχθὲς ] |
| *hon* | *tropon* | *aneiles* | *chthes* | *echthes* |
| which | way | you killed | yesterday | [ idem ] |

Moses understood this and thought his people would see it too, they did not.

Stephen's emphasis here shows he was making a clear parallel to the way the Jewish leaders failed to understand what God had done through Jesus to provide salvation. Their rejection of Jesus was no reason to despise Jesus, for their fathers for a time rejected Moses.

This should have brought back to the memory of these Jewish leaders the way Jesus pronounced woes on the scribes and Pharisees who were building the tombs of the prophets as great memorials to them and were decorating the sepulchers of the righteous men of God who had been martyred in earlier times. By this they were saying that if they had lived in the days of their fathers they would not have been partakers with them in the murder of those prophets. But Jesus recognized that all this was for show. Their attitudes were no different from their ancestors, and they would do as they had done.

**how that God by his hand would deliver them:** . . . that God through his hand would give them deliverance, *Rotherham* . . . that God through his instrumentality, *Williams* . . . that he was foreordained by God to liberate them, *Noli* . . . was using him to save them, *Everyday* . . . that God would give them freedom by his help, *Norlie* . . . he was the one by whom God was freeing them, *Beck.*

**but they understood not:** . . . but they failed to understand, *Berkeley* . . . his brethren failed to understand his mission, *Noli.*

**7:26.** Continuing the history, Stephen reminded the Sanhedrin how Moses went out the next day and found two Israelites fighting with each other. This shocked him. He was troubled when he saw how the Egyptians were mistreating the Israelites. He was even more disturbed when he saw his own people mistreating each other. In the midst of all this mistreatment from the Egyptians, they should have been upholding and encouraging one another. So Moses' first thought was to try to reconcile them and have them at peace. So he said, "Men, you are brothers, why do you harm each other?" that is, "Why do you injure each other unfairly?"

**26. And the next day he shewed himself unto them as they strove:** . . . the ensuing day, *Concordant* . . . he came and found two of them fighting, *Weymouth* . . . he came across two of them quarreling, *Noli.*

**and would have set them at one again:** . . . and would have reconciled them in peace, *Rotherham* . . . and tried to make peace between them, *TCNT.*

**saying, Sirs, ye are brethren:** Men! ye are brothers! *Rotherham.*

**why do ye wrong one to another?:** . . . how is it that you are ill treating one another, *TCNT* . . . why should you harm each other, *Williams* . . . why abuse each other, *Berkeley* . . . Why do you injure one another? *Noli.*

**7:27.** But the one harming his neighbor repelled Moses, saying, "Who made you a ruler and a judge over us?" In other words, these Israelites were resisting and rejecting God's purpose. Exodus 2:19 indicates that when Moses came to Midian he was still dressed as an Egyptian and was thought by the Midianites to be an Egyptian. So these Israelites, even if they knew Moses was born of Israelite parents, did not think of him as one of themselves. Nevertheless, Stephen's point was that they did not see God's purpose and for that reason resisted Moses.

**27. But he that did his neighbour wrong thrust him away, saying:** . . . was wronging his neighbour, *Rotherham* . . . But the aggressor thrust him aside, *Noli* . . . The man who was ill treating his fellow workman pushed Moses aside with the words, *TCNT* . . . But the man who was doing the wrong resented his interference, *Weymouth* . . . the aggressor of his neighbour retorted, *Fenton.*

**Who made thee a ruler and a judge over us?:** Who hath appointed, *Rotherham* . . . a chief and a justice, *Concordant.*

**7:28.** The Israelite who was in the wrong then said, "Do you want to kill me the way you killed the Egyptian yesterday?" He was looking at Moses as if he were self-righteous in what he was doing and was not really wanting to help the Israelites. Part of the reason for what he said was undoubtedly a sense of guilt on his part. He knew he was in the wrong, but was trying to put the condemnation and the guilt on Moses instead of admitting his own wrongdoing.

**28. Wilt thou kill me, as thou didst the Egyptian yesterday?:** Dost thou seek to kill me, *Murdock* . . . like you killed that enemy Egyptian? *Klingensmith* . . . Do you mean to murder me, *Noli* . . . the other day? *Fenton.*

| **3450.6** art acc sing masc | **124.2** name-adj acc sing masc | **5180.5** verb 3sing indic aor act | **1156.2** conj | **3337.1** name nom masc |
|---|---|---|---|---|
| τὸν | Αἰγύπτιον; | **29.** Ἔφυγεν | δὲ | ʻ Μωσῆς |
| *ton* | *Aiguption* | *Ephugen* | *de* | *Mōsēs* |
| the | Egyptian? | Fled | and | Moses |

| **3338.1** name nom masc | **1706.1** prep | **3450.3** art dat sing | **3030.3** noun dat sing masc | **3642.5** dem-pron dat sing masc | **2504.1** conj |
|---|---|---|---|---|---|
| [☆ Μωϋσῆς ] | ἐν | τῷ | λόγῳ | τούτῳ, | καὶ |
| *Mōusēs* | *en* | *tō* | *logō* | *toutō* | *kai* |
| [ idem ] | at | the | saying | this, | and |

| **1090.33** verb 3sing indic aor mid | **3803.1** adj nom sing masc | **1706.1** prep | **1087.3** noun dat sing fem | **3071.1** name masc | **3619.1** adv |
|---|---|---|---|---|---|
| ἐγένετο | πάροικος | ἐν | γῇ | Μαδιάμ, | οὗ |
| *egeneto* | *paroikos* | *en* | *gē* | *Madiam* | *hou* |
| became | a stranger | in | land | of Midian, | where |

| **1074.4** verb 3sing indic aor act | **5048.9** noun acc pl masc | **1411.3** num card | **2504.1** conj | **3997.26** verb gen pl neu part aor pass | **2073.4** noun gen pl neu |
|---|---|---|---|---|---|
| ἐγέννησεν | υἱοὺς | δύο. | **30.** Καὶ | πληρωθέντων | ἐτῶν |
| *egennēsen* | *huious* | *duo* | *Kai* | *plērōthentōn* | *etōn* |
| he bore | sons | two. | And | having been fulfilled | years |

| **4910.2** num card | **4910.1** num card | **3571.21** verb 3sing indic aor pass | **840.4** prs-pron dat sing |
|---|---|---|---|
| ʻ τεσσαράκοντα | [ τεσσεράκοντα ] | ὤφθη | αὐτῷ |
| *tessarakonta* | *tesserakonta* | *ōphthē* | *autō* |
| forty | [ idem ] | appeared | to him |

| **1706.1** prep | **3450.11** art dat sing fem | **2031.2** noun dat sing fem | **3450.2** art gen sing | **3598.2** noun gen sing neu | **4469.1** name neu | **32.1** noun nom sing masc |
|---|---|---|---|---|---|---|
| ἐν | τῇ | ἐρήμῳ | τοῦ | ὄρους | Σινᾶ | ἄγγελος |
| *en* | *tē* | *erēmō* | *tou* | *orous* | *Sina* | *angelos* |
| in | the | desert | of the | Mount | Sinai | an angel |

30.a.**Txt:** 05D,08E,025P byz.Sod
**Var:** 01ℵ,02A,03B,04C sa.bo.Lach,Treg,Alf,Tisc We/Ho,Weis,UBS/☆

| **2935.2** noun gen sing masc | **1706.1** prep | **5232.3** noun dat sing fem | **4300.2** noun gen sing neu | **935.1** noun gen sing fem | **3450.5** art nom sing masc |
|---|---|---|---|---|---|
| ʻa κυρίου ˎ | ἐν | φλογὶ | πυρὸς | βάτου. | **31.** ὁ |
| *kuriou* | *en* | *phlogi* | *puros* | *batou* | *ho* |
| of Lord | in | a flame | of fire | of a bush. | |

| **1156.2** conj | **3337.1** name nom masc | **3338.1** name nom masc | **1481.16** verb nom sing masc part aor act | **2273.10** verb 3sing indic aor act |
|---|---|---|---|---|
| δὲ | ʻ Μωσῆς | [☆ Μωϋσῆς ] | ἰδὼν | ʻ ἐθαύμασεν |
| *de* | *Mōsēs* | *Mōusēs* | *idōn* | *ethaumasen* |
| And | Moses | [ idem ] | having seen | marveled at |

31.a.**Txt:** 02A,03B,04C byz.We/Ho,Sod
**Var:** 01ℵ,05D,08E,025P Gries,Alf,Word,Tisc Weis,UBS/☆

| **2273.16** verb 3sing indic imperf act | **3450.16** art sing neu | **3568.1** noun sing neu | **4193.13** verb gen sing masc part pres mid | **1156.2** conj |
|---|---|---|---|---|
| [a☆ ἐθαύμαζεν ] | τὸ | ὅραμα· | προσερχομένου | δὲ |
| *ethaumazen* | *to* | *horama* | *proserchomenou* | *de* |
| [ was marveling ] | the | vision; | coming near | and |

| **840.3** prs-pron gen sing | **2627.7** verb inf aor act | **1090.33** verb 3sing indic aor mid | **5292.1** noun nom sing fem | **2935.2** noun gen sing masc |
|---|---|---|---|---|
| αὐτοῦ | κατανοῆσαι, | ἐγένετο | φωνὴ | κυρίου |
| *autou* | *katanoēsai* | *egeneto* | *phōnē* | *kuriou* |
| he | to consider, | there was | a voice | of Lord |

31.b.**Txt:** 04C,08E,025P byz.sa.
**Var:** 01ℵ,02A,03B,bo. Lach,Treg,Alf,Tisc We/Ho,Weis,Sod UBS/☆

| **4242.1** prep | **840.6** prs-pron acc sing masc | **1466.1** prs-pron nom 1sing | **3450.5** art nom sing masc | **2296.1** noun nom sing masc | **3450.1** art gen pl |
|---|---|---|---|---|---|
| ʻb πρὸς | αὐτόν, ˎ | **32.** Ἐγὼ | ὁ | θεὸς | τῶν |
| *pros* | *auton* | *Egō* | *ho* | *theos* | *tōn* |
| to | him, | I | the | God | of the |

**7:29.** Fearing for his life, Moses fled to the land of Midian where he lived as a resident alien and where two sons were born.

Hebrews 11:24-28 skips over this part of Moses' life. It records only that by faith Moses, when he grew up, repudiated his position where he was called the son of Pharaoh's daughter. He chose rather to be ill-treated along with (to take his share of suffering along with) the people of God, rather than to enjoy the pleasures of sin for a season. He esteemed the reproach of the Messiah (God's anointed) "greater riches than the treasures of Egypt," for he turned his attention to the reward. By faith Moses left Egypt, not fearing the wrath of the king. But at this point Hebrews 11 is talking about how Moses led Israel out of Egypt in connection with the 10th plague and the keeping of the Passover.

Stephen skipped over the second 40 years of Moses' life, telling nothing of his marriage to Zipporah (*little bird*), the daughter of the priest of Midian, telling only of the fact that he had two sons. These 40 years were important in Moses' preparation, however.

**7:30.** When 40 years had passed, an angel of the Lord appeared to Moses in the desert of Mount Sinai in the flame of fire in a thorn bush. Exodus 3:1 calls this the "back side of the desert" and calls the mountain Horeb, the mountain of God.

The angel here was no ordinary angel, but the Angel of the Lord, a manifestation of God himself, or rather of the preincarnate Son. In this passage He is distinguished as a separate person, and yet is identified with God. Jesus is, and has always been, the one Mediator between God the Father and man. He was in Creation (John 1:3). He was and is in redemption (1 Timothy 2:5,6; Hebrews 8:6; 9:15; 12:24). He will be in the coming judgments (John 5:22,27). Thus, it is evident He was the one Mediator in Old Testament times as well.

**7:31.** As Moses continued to look, he saw the bush did not burn up, and he was filled with wonder and amazement at this surprising phenomenon. Curiosity caused him to go near to get a closer look. This was something that deserved careful observation.

As he did so, the voice of the Lord (God) came to him. After 40 years in the desert, it took something unusual to get Moses' attention before he would be sensitive to the voice of God. This voice was the same as that of the Angel mentioned in the preceding verse. "The sight" (Greek, *to horama*) is often translated "the vision," but it is used of objective visions, real appearances that can be seen by the eyes. In other words, this was not a figment of Moses' imagination. He really heard the voice of God.

**7:32.** God then declared himself to be the God of his fathers, the God of Abraham, Isaac, and Jacob. When the Sadducees confronted Jesus with their refusal to believe in the Resurrection and

**29. Then fled Moses at this saying:** Alarmed at this question, Moses fled from the country, *Weymouth* . . . On hearing this, *NAB* . . . At that, *Williams C.K.* . . . At these words Moses fled, *Noli* . . . took to flight, *Fenton.*

**and was a stranger in the land of Madian:** . . . lived as, *Williams C.K.* . . . took up his residence as an alien, *NAB* . . . and became an exile, *TCNT* . . . and lived...in exile, *Noli* . . . became a temporary resident, *Wuest* . . . and became a sojourner in the land of Midian, *ASV, Hanson.*

**where he begat two sons:** There he became the father of two sons, *Weymouth.*

**30. And when forty years were expired:** . . . were fulfilled, *ASV* . . . At the end of forty years, *TCNT* . . . When forty years had passed, *Williams* . . . Forty years later, *NAB, Noli.*

**there appeared to him in the wilderness of mount Sina an angel of the Lord:** . . . in the uninhabited region, *Wuest* . . . in the wilds of, *Williams C.K.* . . . in the Desert of Mount Sinai, *TCNT.*

**in a flame of fire in a bush:** . . . in the flame of a burning thornbush, *Berkeley, NAB* . . . in a flame of fire of brambles, *Klingensmith.*

**31. When Moses saw it, He wondered at the sight:** . . . marvelled, *Rotherham* . . . was astonished, *TCNT* . . . marvels at the vision, *Concordant* . . . at the sight, *Montgomery* . . . wondered at the spectacle, *Noli.*

**and as he drew near to behold it:** . . . and as he was going near to observe, *Rotherham* . . . but, on his going nearer to look at it more closely, *TCNT* . . . and as he drew near to consider it, *HBIE* . . . and as he approached to investigate, *Berkeley* . . . He went near to look closer at it, *Everyday* . . . to examine it, *Noli.*

**the voice of the Lord came unto him:** . . . there came a voice of the Lord, *ASV* . . . the Lord said to him audibly, *Murdock.*

**32. Saying, I am the God of thy fathers:** I am the God of your ancestors, *TCNT* . . . I am the same God your fathers had, *NCV* . . . forefathers, *Weymouth.*

32.a.**Txt:** 05D,08E,025P 33,byz.bo.
**Var:** p74,01ℵ,02A,03B 04C,044,sa.Lach,Treg Alf,Tisc,We/Ho,Weis Sod,UBS/☆

32.b.**Txt:** 05D,08E,025P 33,byz.bo.
**Var:** p74,01ℵ,02A,03B 04C,044,sa.Lach,Treg Alf,Tisc,We/Ho,Weis Sod,UBS/☆

| **3824.7** noun gen pl masc | **4622.2** prs-pron gen 2sing | **3450.5** art nom sing masc | **2296.1** noun nom sing masc | **11.1** name masc | **2504.1** conj |
|---|---|---|---|---|---|
| πατέρων | σου, | ⸂a ὁ | θεὸς ⸃ | Ἀβραὰμ | καὶ |
| *paterōn* | *sou* | *ho* | *theos* | *Abraam* | *kai* |
| fathers | your, | the | God | of Abraham | and |

| **3450.5** art nom sing masc | **2296.1** noun nom sing masc | **2439.1** name masc | **2504.1** conj | **3450.5** art nom sing masc | **2296.1** noun nom sing masc | **2361.1** name masc |
|---|---|---|---|---|---|---|
| ⸂b ὁ | θεὸς ⸃ | Ἰσαὰκ | καὶ | ὁ | θεὸς | Ἰακώβ. |
| *ho* | *theos* | *Isaak* | *kai* | *ho* | *theos* | *Iakōb* |
| the | God | of Isaac | and | the | God | of Jacob. |

| **1774.1** adj nom sing masc | **1156.2** conj | **1090.53** verb nom sing masc part aor mid | **3337.1** name nom masc | **3338.1** name nom masc |
|---|---|---|---|---|
| Ἔντρομος | δὲ | γενόμενος | ⸀ Μωσῆς | [☆ Μωϋσῆς ] |
| *Entromos* | *de* | *genomenos* | *Mōsēs* | *Mousēs* |
| Trembling | and | having become | Moses | [ idem ] |

| **3620.2** partic | **4958.9** verb 3sing indic imperf act | **2627.7** verb inf aor act | **1500.5** verb 3sing indic aor act | **1156.2** conj |
|---|---|---|---|---|
| οὐκ | ἐτόλμα | κατανοῆσαι. | **33.** εἶπεν | δὲ |
| *ouk* | *etolma* | *katanoēsai* | *eipen* | *de* |
| not | he was daring | to consider. | Said | and |

| **840.4** prs-pron dat sing | **3450.5** art nom sing masc | **2935.1** noun nom sing masc | **3061.11** verb 2sing impr aor act | **3450.16** art sing neu | **5104.2** noun sing neu |
|---|---|---|---|---|---|
| αὐτῷ | ὁ | κύριος, | Λῦσον | τὸ | ὑπόδημα |
| *autō* | *ho* | *kurios* | *Luson* | *to* | *hupodēma* |
| to him | the | Lord, | Loose | the | sandal |

| **3450.1** art gen pl | **4087.5** noun gen pl masc | **4622.2** prs-pron gen 2sing | **3450.5** art nom sing masc | **1056.1** conj | **4964.1** noun nom sing masc |
|---|---|---|---|---|---|
| τῶν | ποδῶν | σου· | ὁ | γὰρ | τόπος |
| *tōn* | *podōn* | *sou* | *ho* | *gar* | *topos* |
| of the | feet | your, | the | for | place |

33.a.**Txt:** 08E,025P,byz.
**Var:** 01ℵ,02A,03B,04C 05D,Lach,Treg,Alf,Tisc We/Ho,Weis,Sod UBS/☆

| **1706.1** prep | **1894.1** prep | **3614.3** rel-pron dat sing | **2449.17** verb 2sing indic perf act | **1087.1** noun nom sing fem | **39.10** adj nom sing fem |
|---|---|---|---|---|---|
| ⸀ ἐν | [a☆ ἐφ' ] | ᾧ | ἕστηκας, | γῆ | ἁγία |
| *en* | *eph'* | *hō* | *hestēkas* | *gē* | *hagia* |
| on | [ upon ] | which | you stand, | ground | holy |

| **1498.4** verb 3sing indic pres act | **1481.16** verb nom sing masc part aor act | **1481.1** verb indic aor act | **3450.12** art acc sing fem | **2531.1** noun acc sing fem |
|---|---|---|---|---|
| ἐστίν. | **34.** ἰδὼν | εἶδον | τὴν | κάκωσιν |
| *estin* | *idōn* | *eidon* | *tēn* | *kakōsin* |
| is. | Having seen, | I saw | the | mistreatment |

| **3450.2** art gen sing | **2967.2** noun gen sing masc | **1466.2** prs-pron gen 1sing | **3450.2** art gen sing | **1706.1** prep | **125.3** name dat fem | **2504.1** conj |
|---|---|---|---|---|---|---|
| τοῦ | λαοῦ | μου | τοῦ | ἐν | Αἰγύπτῳ, | καὶ |
| *tou* | *laou* | *mou* | *tou* | *en* | *Aiguptō* | *kai* |
| of the | people | my | | in | Egypt, | and |

34.a.**Txt:** p74,01ℵ,02A 04C,08E,025P,byz.sa.bo. Tisc,Sod
**Var:** 03B,05D,Lach Treg,We/Ho,Weis UBS/☆

| **3450.2** art gen sing | **4577.1** noun gen sing masc | **840.1** prs-pron gen pl | **840.3** prs-pron gen sing | **189.19** verb 1sing indic aor act |
|---|---|---|---|---|
| τοῦ | στεναγμοῦ | ⸀ αὐτῶν | [a αὐτοῦ ] | ἤκουσα· |
| *tou* | *stenagmou* | *autōn* | *autou* | *ēkousa* |
| the | groaning | their | [ idem ] | heard, |

| **2504.1** conj | **2568.13** verb 1sing indic aor act | **1791.6** verb inf aor mid | **840.8** prs-pron acc pl masc | **2504.1** conj | **3431.1** adv |
|---|---|---|---|---|---|
| καὶ | κατέβην | ἐξελέσθαι | αὐτούς· | καὶ | νῦν |
| *kai* | *katebēn* | *exelesthai* | *autous* | *kai* | *nun* |
| and | came down | to take out | them; | and | now |

the future life, Jesus referred to this passage and pointed out that God made it clear here that He *is* (not He *was*) the God of Abraham, Isaac, and Jacob. Thus, they have continued existence after death, for God is not the God of the dead, but of the living (Matthew 22:32; Mark 12:26,27; Luke 20:37).

When Moses heard God thus identify himself, he trembled and did not dare to look. Exodus 3:6 says he hid his face for he did not dare to look on God.

This indicates that Moses knew the kind of God which Abraham, Isaac, and Jacob served. It is not likely there were any written records of the history of these patriarchs. (Some archaeologists would dispute this, for people did keep extensive business records and detailed accounts of government relationships long before Abraham's time, as the Ebla records show.) Nevertheless, Moses' mother trained him and must have passed on to him the stories of these patriarchs.

**7:33.** God commanded Moses to take off his sandal, a leather sole fastened to the foot by leather straps. (The singular is used here in a collective or distributive sense, so in English it is best translated "sandals.") The ground all around the burning bush was holy ground because of the presence of God manifested there. Joshua had a similar experience when he was out looking over the situation with regard to the conquest of Jericho. There the Captain (prince, head, king) of the Lord's host appeared to him, and Joshua worshiped Him. This shows this also was a preincarnate manifestation of Christ, not an ordinary angel. An ordinary angel would have forbidden Joshua's prostration before him. The command for Joshua to remove his sandals also confirms the divine nature of the Captain or Prince. The Law also describes the clothing of Aaron and his sons, but says nothing about sandals or shoes, so it is evident the priests were barefoot as they served at the altar. It should be noted also that the presence of the Lord made it holy ground even though it was far from the Promised Land. It was always important that men be reverent and tread softly in the presence of the Lord.

**7:34.** The repetition of "I have seen" is a Hebrew way of giving strong emphasis to the fact that God had definitely seen the ill treatment of His people in Egypt and had heard their groaning. The repetition also draws attention to the faithfulness of God. Though God has His timing, believers can depend on Him to show himself to be the kind of God He is. He will always be true to His own nature. He will always keep His promises.

In response to Israel's need, God had "come down," that is, He had come down into the earthly scene to go into action, for His purpose was to deliver Israel, to take them out for himself. He wanted them for His people. He wanted to bring them into a new relationship to himself. To bring about this deliverance God called Moses saying, "Come!" (This is the same word used by Jesus when

**the God of Abraham, and the God of Isaac, and the God of Jacob:**

**Then Moses trembled, and durst not behold:** Moses trembled all over, and did not dare to look, *TCNT*... began to tremble and dared look no more, *NAB* ... Moses began to shake with fear and was afraid to look, *Everyday* ... Quaking with fear Moses did not dare to gaze, *Weymouth* ... Moses shook! He was so afraid he did not look at the bush, *NLT* ... Moses felt so shaken, he did not dare to investigate, *Berkeley* ... becoming terrified, *Rotherham*... was so frightened, *MLNT* ... was so terrified, *Williams* ... dared not look, *Hanson* ... and turned away his face, *Noli* ... dared not examine it, *HBIE.*

**33. Then said the Lord to him, Put off thy shoes from thy feet:** Loose the shoes from thy feet, *ASV*... Loose the sandals of thy feet, *Rotherham, Swann* ... Untie the sandals from your feet, *Berkeley*... Remove the sandals from, *NAB* ... Take off your shoes, *Noli*... off your feet! *NLT.*

**for the place where thou standest is holy ground:** ... for the spot, *Weymouth.*

**34. I have seen, I have seen the affliction of my people which is in Egypt:** I have surely seen, *ASV* ... I have certainly observed, *MLNT*... I have attentively seen, *Murdock* ... I have witnessed, *NAB* ... I have indeed seen the ill-treatment, *Rotherham* ... the evil treatment of, *Hanson* ... the evil condition, *Williams C.K.*... I have indeed seen the oppression of my people, who are in Egypt, *TCNT*... seen the evil against my people, *Swann* ... seen the troubles my people have suffered, *Everyday*... seen My people suffer in the country of, *NLT.*

**and I have heard their groaning:** ... their groans, *TCNT* ... heard My people moaning, *SEB* ... have heard their cries, *Williams C.K., NLT.*

**and am come down to deliver them:** ... and I have come down, *RSV* ... to rescue them, *NAB, Rotherham*... to let them go free, *NLT* ... to save them, *Goodspeed.*

**And now come, I will send thee into Egypt:** So get ready! I am

## Acts 7:35

34.b.**Txt:** 025P,byz.
**Var:** 01ℵ,02A,03B,04C 05D,08E,Lach,Treg,Alf Word,Tisc,We/Ho,Weis Sod,UBS/☆

| **1198.1** adv | **643.21** verb 1sing indic fut act | **643.33** verb 1sing subj aor act | **4622.4** prs-pron acc 2sing | **1519.1** prep |
|---|---|---|---|---|
| δεῦρο, | ʻ ἀποστελῶ | [b☆ ἀποστείλω ] | σε | εἰς |
| *deuro* | *apostelō* | *aposteilō* | *se* | *eis* |
| come, | I will send | [ idem ] | you | to |

| **125.4** name acc fem | **3642.6** dem-pron acc sing masc | **3450.6** art acc sing masc | **3338.4** name acc masc | **3614.6** rel-pron acc sing masc |
|---|---|---|---|---|
| Αἴγυπτον. | **35.** Τοῦτον | τὸν | Μωϋσῆν | ὃν |
| *Aigupton* | *Touton* | *ton* | *Mōusēn* | *hon* |
| Egypt. | This | | Moses, | whom |

| **714.9** verb 3pl indic aor mid | **1500.19** verb nom pl masc part aor act | **4949.3** intr-pron nom sing | **4622.4** prs-pron acc 2sing | **2497.4** verb 3sing indic aor act |
|---|---|---|---|---|
| ἠρνήσαντο | εἰπόντες, | Τίς | σε | κατέστησεν |
| *ērnēsanto* | *eipontes* | *Tis* | *se* | *katestēsen* |
| they refused, | having said, | Who | you | appointed |

35.a.**Txt:** p45,p74,02A 03B,024P,6,104,614 1241,byz.vul.
**Var:** 01ℵ,04C,05D,044 36,81,453,1175,cop.

| **752.4** noun acc sing masc | **2504.1** conj | **1342.1** noun acc sing masc | **1894.1** prep | **2231.2** prs-pron gen 1pl | **3642.6** dem-pron acc sing masc |
|---|---|---|---|---|---|
| ἄρχοντα | καὶ | δικαστὴν; | [a+ ἐφ' | ἡμῶν ] | τοῦτον |
| *archonta* | *kai* | *dikastēn* | *eph'* | *hēmōn* | *touton* |
| ruler | and | judge? | [ over | us ] | him |

35.b.**Var:** 01ℵ-corr,02A 03B,05D,08E,Lach Treg,Alf,Tisc,We/Ho Weis,Sod,UBS/☆

| **3450.5** art nom sing masc | **2296.1** noun nom sing masc | **2504.1** conj | **752.4** noun acc sing masc | **2504.1** conj | **3058.1** noun acc sing masc |
|---|---|---|---|---|---|
| ὁ | θεὸς | [b☆+ καὶ ] | ἄρχοντα | καὶ | λυτρωτὴν |
| *ho* | *theos* | *kai* | *archonta* | *kai* | *lutrōtēn* |
| | God | [ and ] | ruler | and | deliverer |

35.c.**Txt:** 025P,byz.
**Var:** 02A,03B,05D,08E Lach,Treg,Alf,Word Tisc,We/Ho,Weis,Sod UBS/☆

| **643.8** verb 3sing indic aor act | **1706.1** prep | **643.17** verb 3sing indic perf act | **4713.1** prep | **5331.3** noun dat sing fem |
|---|---|---|---|---|
| ʻ ἀπέστειλεν | ἐν | [c☆ ἀπέσταλκεν | σὺν ] | χειρὶ |
| *apesteilen* | *en* | *apestalken* | *sun* | *cheiri* |
| sent | by | [ has sent | with ] | hand |

| **32.2** noun gen sing masc | **3450.2** art gen sing | **3571.25** verb gen sing masc part aor pass | **840.4** prs-pron dat sing | **1706.1** prep | **3450.11** art dat sing fem |
|---|---|---|---|---|---|
| ἀγγέλου | τοῦ | ὀφθέντος | αὐτῷ | ἐν | τῇ |
| *angelou* | *tou* | *ophthentos* | *autō* | *en* | *tē* |
| of angel | the | appeared | to him | in | the |

| **935.2** noun dat sing fem | **3642.4** dem-pron nom sing masc | **1790.3** verb 3sing indic aor act | **840.8** prs-pron acc pl masc | **4020.37** verb nom sing masc part aor act |
|---|---|---|---|---|
| βάτῳ. | **36.** οὗτος | ἐξήγαγεν | αὐτοὺς, | ποιήσας |
| *batō* | *houtos* | *exēgagen* | *autous* | *poiēsas* |
| bush. | This one | led out | them, | having wrought |

36.a.**Var:** 03B,04C,sa. Lach,Treg,We/Ho

| **4907.1** noun pl neu | **2504.1** conj | **4447.2** noun pl neu | **1706.1** prep | **1087.3** noun dat sing fem | **3450.11** art dat sing fem | **125.2** name gen fem |
|---|---|---|---|---|---|---|
| τέρατα | καὶ | σημεῖα | ἐν | ʻ γῇ | [a τῇ ] | ʻ Αἰγύπτου |
| *terata* | *kai* | *sēmeia* | *en* | *gē* | *tē* | *Aiguptou* |
| wonders | and | signs | in | land | [ the ] | of Egypt |

36.b.**Txt:** p74,05D,1739 byz.
**Var:** 01ℵ,02A,03B,04C 08E,025P,Gries,Lach Treg,Alf,Tisc,We/Ho Weis,Sod,UBS/☆

| **125.3** name dat fem | **2504.1** conj | **1706.1** prep | **2047.1** name dat fem | **2504.1** conj |
|---|---|---|---|---|
| [b☆ Αἰγύπτῳ ] | καὶ | ἐν | Ἐρυθρᾷ Θαλάσσῃ, | καὶ |
| *Aiguptō* | *kai* | *en* | *Eruthra Thalassē* | *kai* |
| [ in Egypt ] | and | in | Red Sea, | and |

| **1706.1** prep | **3450.11** art dat sing fem | **2031.2** noun dat sing fem | **2073.3** noun pl neu | **4910.2** num card |
|---|---|---|---|---|
| ἐν | τῇ | ἐρήμῳ | ἔτη | ʻ τεσσαράκοντα˙ |
| *en* | *tē* | *erēmō* | *etē* | *tessarakonta* |
| in | the | wilderness | years | forty. |

He called His disciples to come after Him and follow Him.) But then God added the request (Greek, subjunctive, not a command), "Let me send you into Egypt."

**7:35.** Stephen now emphasized his main point in this part of the history. This Moses, whom they had refused (denied, rejected), God sent with the hand (that is, the power) of the Angel who appeared to him in the thorn bush, to be a ruler and a deliverer (a ransomer, a liberator). "Deliverer" here is a word originally used of those who paid a ransom to liberate slaves or set prisoners free.

Thus, the answer to those who first said to Moses, "Who made thee a ruler and a judge?" is "God made him that and more." Once again Stephen had in mind the saying that the stone the builders refused was made the head of the corner (Psalm 118:22). The same God who gave honor and power to Moses gave honor and power to Jesus.

It was because of this that Stephen dared to stand and talk in this manner to the Sanhedrin. Jesus had said, "The disciple (the student) is not above his master (his teacher), nor the servant (the slave) above his lord (his master)." He had also warned them that they would be brought before governors and kings "for my sake, for a testimony against them and the Gentiles" (Matthew 10:18,24). Although Stephen was an unknown, he had the courage to face the Council.

Stephen was in no way demeaning Moses; instead, his speech held him in the highest esteem possible. His high regard for the person and the work of Moses further developed the analogy Stephen was drawing between their actions toward Christ and the actions of their "fathers" toward the prophets who foretold His coming.

**7:36.** Moses, this very person whom the Israelites had earlier rejected, brought them out of Egypt. They had been ready to deliver him up to Pharaoh and to his death. But Moses forgot all this and became their deliverer. Not only so, God used him to do mighty wonders and supernatural signs in Egypt, and then in bringing them through the Red Sea, and caring for them in the wilderness for 40 years.

In all those miraculous events God was revealing himself. For example, Moses let Pharaoh have the advantage by allowing him to set the time for the removal of the plague of the frogs so he might know "that there is none like unto the Lord our God" (Exodus 8:9,10). With the plague of flies, there were no flies in Goshen that Pharaoh might know that God is the Lord "in the midst of the earth" (Exodus 8:22); in other words, God is immanent, not a far-off God. The deliverance at the Red Sea (sea of reeds or weeds) caused Moses and Israel to sing to the Lord and give Him glory. The manna for food and water from the rock provided for their needs. In all of this Moses was God's agent, even though he had once been refused and rejected.



going to send you, *Noli* . . . So come! I will make you, *Goodspeed* . . . I should dispatch you, *Concordant* . . . I will send you back to Egypt as my messenger, *Williams* . . . I will give you a mission to Egypt, *Kleist.*

**35. This Moses whom they refused, saying:** This same Moses, whom they had disowned with the words, *TCNT* . . . This Moses was the same man, *NCV* . . . The people had put Moses aside, *NLT* . . . the Jews said they did not want, *Everyday* . . . whom they denied, *HBIE, Swann* . . . whom they rejected, *Weymouth* . . . whom they renounced, *Wilson* . . . whom they disavowed, *Hanson* . . . when they said, *Montgomery* . . . with the words, *NAB.*

**Who made thee a ruler and a judge?:** Who has appointed you, *NAB* . . . referee? *Williams* . . . a ruler and adjudicator? *Rotherham* . . . Who made you a leader over us? Who said you are the one to say what is right or wrong? *NLT.*

**The same did God send to be a ruler and a deliverer:** . . . a saviour, *BB* . . . this one has God commissioned to be a chief as well as a redeemer, *Concordant* . . . God sent both to rule and to deliver them, *Goodspeed* . . . But God made this man a leader...who brought them out of the country, *NLT* . . . a liberator, *Norlie.*

**by the hand of the angel which appeared to him in the bush:** . . . with the help of the angel, *NCV, TCNT* . . . with the assistance of the angel, *Adams.*

**36. He brought them out:** This man led them forth, *ASV* . . . He it was who led them out, *TCNT.*

**after that he had shewed wonders and signs in the land of Egypt:** . . . having wrought wonders, *ASV* . . . He did powerful works, *NLT* . . . after performing marvels and signs, *Weymouth* . . . by performing wonders and signs, *Williams* . . . having produced terrors and evidences, *Fenton.*

**and in the Red sea, and in the wilderness forty years:** . . . and at the Red Sea, *Weymouth* . . . he led them in the place where no people live, *NLT* . . . in the desert, *Rotherham.*

| 4910.1 num card | 3642.4 dem-pron nom sing masc | 1498.4 verb 3sing indic pres act | 3450.5 art nom sing masc |
|---|---|---|---|
| [ τεσσεράκοντα. ] | 37. Οὗτός | ἐστιν | ὁ |
| *tesserakonta* | *Houtos* | *estin* | *ho* |
| [ idem ] | This | is | the |

37.a.**Txt:** 08E,025P,byz. Sod
**Var:** 01ℵ,02A,03B,04C 05D,Lach,Treg,Alf,Tisc We/Ho,Weis,UBS/☆

| 3338.1 name nom masc | 3450.5 art nom sing masc | 1500.15 verb nom sing masc part aor act | 1500.30 verb nom sing masc part aor act | 3450.4 art dat pl |
|---|---|---|---|---|
| Μωϋσῆς | ὁ | ⸀ εἰπὼν | [a☆ εἴπας ] | τοῖς |
| *Mōusēs* | *ho* | *eipōn* | *eipas* | *tois* |
| Moses | the | having said | [ idem ] | to the |

37.b.**Txt:** 04C,08E,025P byz.
**Var:** p74,01ℵ,02A,03B 05D,sa.bo.Lach,Treg Alf,Tisc,We/Ho,Weis Sod,UBS/☆

| 5048.8 noun dat pl masc | 2447.1 name masc | 4254.3 noun acc sing masc | 5050.3 prs-pron dat 2pl | 448.15 verb 3sing indic fut act |
|---|---|---|---|---|
| υἱοῖς | Ἰσραήλ, | Προφήτην | ὑμῖν | ἀναστήσει |
| *huiois* | *Israēl* | *Prophētēn* | *humin* | *anastēsei* |
| sons | of Israel, | A prophet | to you | will raise up |

37.c.**Txt:** 08E,025P,byz.
**Var:** 01ℵ,02A,03B,04C 05D,sa.bo.Gries,Lach Treg,Alf,Tisc,We/Ho Weis,Sod,UBS/☆

| 2935.1 noun nom sing masc | 3450.5 art nom sing masc | 2296.1 noun nom sing masc | 5050.2 prs-pron gen 2pl | 1523.2 prep gen |
|---|---|---|---|---|
| ⸂b κύριος ⸃ | ὁ | θεὸς | ⸂c ὑμῶν ⸃ | ἐκ |
| *kurios* | *ho* | *theos* | *humōn* | *ek* |
| Lord | | God | your | from among |

37.d.**Txt:** 04C,05D,08E byz.bo.
**Var:** 01ℵ,02A,03B,025P sa.Lach,Treg,Alf,Tisc We/Ho,Weis,Sod UBS/☆

| 3450.1 art gen pl | 79.7 noun gen pl masc | 5050.2 prs-pron gen 2pl | 5453.1 conj | 1466.7 prs-pron acc 1sing | 840.3 prs-pron gen sing |
|---|---|---|---|---|---|
| τῶν | ἀδελφῶν | ὑμῶν | ὡς | ἐμέ. | ⸂d αὐτοῦ |
| *tōn* | *adelphōn* | *humōn* | *hōs* | *eme* | *autou* |
| the | brothers | your | like | me, | him |

| 189.53 verb 2pl indic fut mid | 3642.4 dem-pron nom sing masc | 1498.4 verb 3sing indic pres act | 3450.5 art nom sing masc | 1090.53 verb nom sing masc part aor mid |
|---|---|---|---|---|
| ἀκούσεσθε. ⸃ | 38. Οὗτός | ἐστιν | ὁ | γενόμενος |
| *akousesthe* | *Houtos* | *estin* | *ho* | *genomenos* |
| you shall hear. | This | is | the | having been |

| 1706.1 prep | 3450.11 art dat sing fem | 1564.3 noun dat sing fem | 1706.1 prep | 3450.11 art dat sing fem | 2031.2 noun dat sing fem | 3196.3 prep |
|---|---|---|---|---|---|---|
| ἐν | τῇ | ἐκκλησίᾳ | ἐν | τῇ | ἐρήμῳ | μετὰ |
| *en* | *tē* | *ekklēsia* | *en* | *tē* | *erēmō* | *meta* |
| in | the | assembly | in | the | wilderness | with |

| 3450.2 art gen sing | 32.2 noun gen sing masc | 3450.2 art gen sing | 2953.13 verb gen sing masc part pres act | 840.4 prs-pron dat sing | 1706.1 prep | 3450.3 art dat sing |
|---|---|---|---|---|---|---|
| τοῦ | ἀγγέλου | τοῦ | λαλοῦντος | αὐτῷ | ἐν | τῷ |
| *tou* | *angelou* | *tou* | *lalountos* | *autō* | *en* | *tō* |
| the | angel | of the | speaking | to him | in | the |

| 3598.3 noun dat sing neu | 4469.1 name neu | 2504.1 conj | 3450.1 art gen pl | 3824.7 noun gen pl masc | 2231.2 prs-pron gen 1pl | 3614.5 rel-pron nom sing masc |
|---|---|---|---|---|---|---|
| ὄρει | Σινᾶ, | καὶ | τῶν | πατέρων | ἡμῶν, | ὃς |
| *orei* | *Sina* | *kai* | *tōn* | *paterōn* | *hēmōn* | *hos* |
| mount | Sinai, | and | with the | fathers | our; | who |

38.a.**Txt:** 02A,04C,05D 08E,025P,044,byz.it. Tisc,Sod
**Var:** p74,01ℵ,03B,sa.bo. We/Ho,Weis,UBS/☆

| 1203.5 verb 3sing indic aor mid | 3025.2 noun pl neu | 2180.9 verb part pres act | 1319.31 verb inf aor act | 2231.3 prs-pron dat 1pl | 5050.3 prs-pron dat 2pl |
|---|---|---|---|---|---|
| ἐδέξατο | λόγια | ζῶντα | δοῦναι | ⸀ ἡμῖν, | [a ὑμῖν, ] |
| *edexato* | *logia* | *zōnta* | *dounai* | *hēmin* | *humin* |
| received | oracles | living | to give | to us: | [ to you: ] |

| 3614.3 rel-pron dat sing | 3620.2 partic | 2286.25 verb 3pl indic aor act | 5093.2 adj nom pl masc | 1090.63 verb inf aor mid | 3450.7 art nom pl masc |
|---|---|---|---|---|---|
| 39. ᾧ | οὐκ | ἠθέλησαν | ὑπήκοοι | γενέσθαι | οἱ |
| *hō* | *ouk* | *ēthelēsan* | *hupēkooi* | *genesthai* | *hoi* |
| to whom | not | would | subject | to be | the |

**7:37.** As a climax to this section of his defense, Stephen reminded the Sanhedrin that this was the same Moses (the Moses whom they had rejected and God used to save them out of Egypt) who told the Israelites God would raise up a prophet for them like himself. Him they should hear (listen to and obey).

The Jewish leaders knew how the apostles applied this passage about the prophet like unto Moses. In fact, all the believing Jews applied it to Jesus. They knew Stephen was saying that by not listening to Jesus they were disobeying God and treating not only Jesus, but Moses, with contempt. Jesus himself had told them He would not accuse them to the Father (in heaven), Moses, the very one they put their trust in, was the one accusing them. "For had ye believed Moses, ye would have believed me: for he wrote of me. But if ye believe not his writings, how shall ye believe my words?" (John 5:45-47). Instead of Jesus dishonoring Moses, it was the Jewish leaders who were doing so.

In some ways, Stephen was also building a case for the superiority of Jesus, similar to the writer of Hebrews who said, "This man (Jesus) was counted worthy of more glory than Moses, inasmuch as he who hath builded the house hath more honor than the house" (Hebrews 3:3).

**7:38.** In this section (verses 38-43) Stephen referred to an even worse rejection, a rejection of God himself. Again Stephen spoke of Moses. Moses was in the church in the wilderness. "Church" (Greek, *ekklēsia*, assembly) here refers to the congregation of the people of Israel in the wilderness. (The word *church* in the Bible always refers to an assembly of people, never to a building or an organization or hierarchy.) This Moses was with the angel that spoke to him on Mount Sinai. He was also with all the fathers; that is, with the fathers of Israel (in this case, the 12 tribes of Israel in the wilderness). Keep in mind this mention of the fathers. It prepared for the conclusion Stephen gave in verse 51.

Moses received the living oracles to give to Israel. "Received" also means "welcomed." Moses was happy to receive these words, the Ten Commandments, from God. "Oracles" means "sayings" and is generally used of revelations of God, sayings of Jesus, and of the Scriptures in general. Here the Ten Commandments are called "living" because they provide guidance for the conduct of life, and because they had their source and authorship in the living God.

**7:39.** The fathers, that is, the entire body of the 12 tribes of Israel, had no such longing after the words of God. So instead of waiting patiently for Moses to come down from Mount Sinai, they refused to become obedient to him, rejected him, and in their hearts turned back to Egypt. This, actually, was an attitude that became habitual among the Israelites. Again and again they remembered the spicy food, the leeks, the garlic, and also the fish they had back in Egypt. But they forgot the whip of the slave

**37. This is that Moses, which said unto the children of Israel:** . . . unto the sons of Israel, *Rotherham* . . . to the people of Israel, *TCNT* . . . to the descendants of Israel, *Weymouth* . . . to the Israelites, *NAB.*

**A prophet shall the Lord your God raise up:** God will raise up for you, from among your brothers, a Prophet, as he raised me up, *TCNT* . . . one who speaks for Him like me, *NLT* . . . just as he appointed me, *Norlie.*

**unto you of your brethren, like unto me; him shall ye hear:** He will be one of your own people, *Everyday* . . . He will come from among, *NCV.*

**38. This is he, that was in the church in the wilderness with the angel that spake to him in the mount Sina, and with our fathers:** He was the ambassador, *Fenton* . . . was the go-between between the angel, *Norlie* . . . he that was in the assembly in the wilds, *Williams C.K.* . . . who appeared at the assembly in the Desert, *TCNT* . . . who took part in the assembly of our forefathers, *Noli* . . . with the gathering of the Jews in the desert, *Everyday* . . . church in the waste, *BB.*

**who received the lively oracles to give unto us:** . . . living oracles, *ASV* . . . ever-living utterances to hand on to us, *Weymouth* . . . who was entrusted with words of life, *JB* . . . living Word of God, *Norlie* . . . living truths, *Beck* . . . living words to give them, *Williams C.K.* . . . [the] living sayings, *Hanson* . . . received life-giving oracles to pass on to you, *Kleist* . . . He received commands from God that give life, *Everyday* . . . to be handed down to you, utterances that still live, *Williams* . . . received living messages to give to us, *TNT* . . . the eternal commandments and delivered them to us, *Noli.*

**39. To whom our fathers would not obey:** . . . our fathers would not become obedient, *Hanson* . . . were not willing to become obedient, *HBIE* . . . Our forefathers, however, would not submit to him, *Weymouth* . . . our fathers refused to obey him, *Beck* . . . did not want to obey Moses, *Everyday* . . . would not listen to him, *NLT.*

## Acts 7:40

| 3824.6 noun nom pl masc | 2231.2 prs-pron gen 1pl | 233.1 conj | 233.2 conj | 676.3 verb 3pl indic aor mid | 2504.1 conj |
|---|---|---|---|---|---|
| πατέρες | ἡμῶν, | ‘ ἀλλ’ | [☆ ἀλλὰ ] | ἀπώσαντο, | καὶ |
| *pateres* | *hēmōn* | *all'* | *alla* | *apōsanto* | *kai* |
| fathers | our, | but | [ idem ] | pushed away, | and |

39.a.**Var:** 01ℵ,02A,03B 04C,Lach,Treg,Alf,Tisc We/Ho,Weis,Sod UBS/☆

| 4613.6 verb 3pl indic aor pass | 1706.1 prep | 3450.14 art dat pl fem | 2559.7 noun dat pl fem | 840.1 prs-pron gen pl | 1519.1 prep |
|---|---|---|---|---|---|
| ἐστράφησαν | [a☆+ ἐν ] | ταῖς | καρδίαις | αὐτῶν | εἰς |
| *estraphēsan* | *en* | *tais* | *kardiais* | *autōn* | *eis* |
| were turned back | [ in ] | the | hearts | their | to |

| 125.4 name acc fem | 1500.19 verb nom pl masc part aor act | 3450.3 art dat sing | 2.1 name masc | 4020.34 verb 2sing impr aor act |
|---|---|---|---|---|
| Αἴγυπτον, | **40.** εἰπόντες | τῷ | Ἀαρών, | Ποίησον |
| *Aigupton* | *eipontes* | *tō* | *Aarōn* | *Poiēson* |
| Egypt, | having said | | to Aaron, | Make |

| 2231.3 prs-pron dat 1pl | 2296.8 noun acc pl masc | 3614.7 rel-pron nom pl masc | 4172.2 verb 3pl indic fut mid | 2231.2 prs-pron gen 1pl |
|---|---|---|---|---|
| ἡμῖν | θεοὺς | οἳ | προπορεύσονται | ἡμῶν· |
| *hēmin* | *theous* | *hoi* | *proporeusontai* | *hēmōn* |
| us | gods | who | shall go before | us, |

| 3450.5 art nom sing masc | 1056.1 conj | 3337.1 name nom masc | 3338.1 name nom masc | 3642.4 dem-pron nom sing masc |
|---|---|---|---|---|
| ὁ | γὰρ | ‘ Μωσῆς | [☆ Μωϋσῆς ] | οὗτος |
| *ho* | *gar* | *Mōsēs* | *Mōusēs* | *houtos* |
| | for | Moses | [ idem ] | this |

| 3614.5 rel-pron nom sing masc | 1790.3 verb 3sing indic aor act | 2231.4 prs-pron acc 1pl | 1523.2 prep gen | 1087.2 noun gen sing fem | 125.2 name gen fem |
|---|---|---|---|---|---|
| ὃς | ἐξήγαγεν | ἡμᾶς | ἐκ | γῆς | Αἰγύπτου, |
| *hos* | *exēgagen* | *hēmas* | *ek* | *gēs* | *Aiguptou* |
| who | brought out | us | from | land | of Egypt, |

40.a.**Txt:** 05D,08E,025P byz.
**Var:** 01ℵ,02A,03B,04C Lach,Treg,Alf,Tisc We/Ho,Weis,Sod UBS/☆

| 3620.2 partic | 3471.5 verb 1pl indic perf act | 4949.9 intr-pron sing neu | 1090.3 verb 3sing indic perf act | 1090.33 verb 3sing indic aor mid |
|---|---|---|---|---|
| οὐκ | οἴδαμεν | τί | ‘ γέγονεν | [a☆ ἐγένετο ] |
| *ouk* | *oidamen* | *ti* | *gegonen* | *egeneto* |
| not | we know | what | has happened | [ happened ] |

| 840.4 prs-pron dat sing | 2504.1 conj | 3310.1 verb 3pl indic aor act | 1706.1 prep | 3450.14 art dat pl fem | 2232.7 noun dat pl fem |
|---|---|---|---|---|---|
| αὐτῷ. | **41.** Καὶ | ἐμοσχοποίησαν | ἐν | ταῖς | ἡμέραις |
| *autō* | *Kai* | *emoschopoiēsan* | *en* | *tais* | *hēmerais* |
| to him. | And | they made a calf | in | the | days |

| 1552.14 dem-pron dat pl fem | 2504.1 conj | 319.1 verb 3pl indic aor act | 2355.4 noun acc sing fem | 3450.3 art dat sing | 1487.3 noun dat sing neu |
|---|---|---|---|---|---|
| ἐκείναις, | καὶ | ἀνήγαγον | θυσίαν | τῷ | εἰδώλῳ, |
| *ekeinais* | *kai* | *anēgagon* | *thusian* | *tō* | *eidōlō* |
| those, | and | offered | sacrifice | to the | idol, |

| 2504.1 conj | 2146.13 verb 3pl indic imperf pass | 1706.1 prep | 3450.4 art dat pl | 2024.6 noun dat pl neu | 3450.1 art gen pl | 5331.6 noun gen pl fem |
|---|---|---|---|---|---|---|
| καὶ | εὐφραίνοντο | ἐν | τοῖς | ἔργοις | τῶν | χειρῶν |
| *kai* | *euphrainonto* | *en* | *tois* | *ergois* | *tōn* | *cheirōn* |
| and | were rejoicing | in | the | works | of the | hands |

| 840.1 prs-pron gen pl | 4613.2 verb 3sing indic aor act | 1156.2 conj | 3450.5 art nom sing masc | 2296.1 noun nom sing masc | 2504.1 conj |
|---|---|---|---|---|---|
| αὐτῶν. | **42.** Ἔστρεψεν | δὲ | ὁ | θεὸς | καὶ |
| *autōn* | *Estrepsen* | *de* | *ho* | *theos* | *kai* |
| their. | Turned | but | | God | and |

drivers. They forgot the bondage, the misery, the oppression that caused their boy babies to be thrown to the crocodiles in the Nile River. It is so easy for people even today to remember the so-called pleasures of the world and to forget the hangovers, the spiritual darkness, the satanic oppression.

**7:40.** In addition to their rejection of Moses, the Fathers showed the desires of their hearts by asking Aaron to make gods to go before them. "Gods" here is in the plural, but used this way because the fathers' hearts were not toward Moses and therefore were not in right relation to the one true God. Actually, the fathers had only one God in mind. Joshua at this time called them to a feast to the Lord (YHWH, the divine name of the one true God in Exodus 32:5).

They also showed the attitude of their hearts by despising Moses, for they said in a derogatory way, "As for *this* Moses who brought us out of Egypt, we do not know what has become of him." (See Exodus 32:1.)

**7:41.** Then they made an image of a calf and sacrificed to this image and rejoiced (made merry, reveled) in the works of their own hands.

Many believe this image of a calf was of a small golden bull but was called a calf because of its small size. Aaron made it from the earrings of the people. Since slaves in ancient times did not wear earrings, these were part of the gifts the Egyptians gave them before they left. God gave them favor so they were able to leave, not as slaves fleeing for their lives, but as a triumphant army carrying the spoils of victory, as free people, signified by the earrings in their ears. But now they were going into a different kind of slavery, a slavery to false concepts of religion and of God.

Actually, it was not just Moses they despised. By rejecting their God-given leader they had taken God off the throne of their hearts and put self in His place.

Exodus 32:6 says the people sat down to eat and drink and then rose up to play. "Play" is a word used of joking and amusing themselves. The dancing that Moses saw (Exodus 32:19) was not part of spiritual worship. They were delighting in the work of their hands, so self and the flesh were dominant.

Whether this golden calf was supposed to be a representation of the Lord or simply an idol (cf. Exodus 32:1-6), their attitude toward it was the same as the attitude of the heathen. Thus, even before Moses came down from Mount Sinai with the Decalogue, the people had violated the second commandment, "Thou shalt not make unto thee any graven image" (Exodus 20:4).

**7:42.** Because Israel's worship of the golden calf was a rejection, not merely of Moses but of God, "God turned." This may mean

**but thrust him from them:** . . . thrust him aside, *NAB* . . . thrust him off, *Goodspeed* . . . more than that, they rejected him, *TCNT* . . . but spurned his authority, *Weymouth* . . . on the contrary, they revolted, *Fenton* . . . they ignored him, *Norlie* . . . disregarded him, *Phillips* . . . they repudiated him, *Noli.*

**and in their hearts turned back again into Egypt:** . . . while their hearts longed for Egypt, *Norlie* . . . in their hearts they hankered after Egypt, *Williams* . . . turned back to Egypt in their hearts, *Klingensmith* . . . They wanted to go back to Egypt again, *Everyday.*

**40. Saying unto Aaron, Make us gods to go before us:** Make gods for us, to march in front of us, *Weymouth* . . . Make gods for us, who will lead us, *Beck* . . . who shall go before us, *Darby.*

**for as for this Moses, which brought us out of the land of Egypt:** . . . who led us forth, *ASV.*

**we wot not what is become of him:** . . . we do not know what has, *TCNT* . . . what had happened to him, *Everyday.*

**41. And they made a calf in those days:** Moreover they made a calf at that time, *Weymouth.*

**and offered sacrifice unto the idol:** . . . and brought sacrifice to the image, *Berkeley.*

**and rejoiced in the works of their own hands:** . . . and held festivities in honour of their own handiwork, *TCNT* . . . held a celebration, *Williams* . . . and kept rejoicing in the gods which their own hands had made, *Weymouth* . . . applauded the work of their hands! *Adams* . . . and they celebrated a holiday in honor of their own handiwork, *Noli* . . . were proud of what they had made with their own hands! *Everyday* . . . they rejoiced over their own handiwork, *Fenton* . . . in great glee, *Norlie* . . . delighted, *Beck* . . . over what their own hands had manufactured, *Moffatt.*

**42. Then God turned:** So God turned away, *TCNT* . . . So God turned from them, *Weymouth* . . . God abandoned them, *Norlie* . . . So God turned his back on them, *Noli.*

**Acts 7:43**

| 3722.10 verb 3sing indic aor act | 840.8 prs-pron acc pl masc | 2973.9 verb inf pres act | 3450.11 art dat sing fem | 4607.2 noun dat sing fem | 3450.2 art gen sing |
|---|---|---|---|---|---|
| παρέδωκεν | αὐτοὺς | λατρεύειν | τῇ | στρατιᾷ | τοῦ |
| paredōken | autous | latreuein | tē | stratia | tou |
| delivered up | them | to serve | the | host | of the |

| 3636.2 noun gen sing masc | 2503.1 conj | 1119.22 verb 3sing indic perf mid | 1706.1 prep | 969.3 noun dat sing fem | 3450.1 art gen pl |
|---|---|---|---|---|---|
| οὐρανοῦ· | καθὼς | γέγραπται | ἐν | βίβλῳ | τῶν |
| ouranou | kathōs | gegraptai | en | biblō | tōn |
| heaven; | as | it has been written | in | book | of the |

| 4254.5 noun gen pl masc | 3231.1 partic | 4820.1 noun pl neu | 2504.1 conj | 2355.1 noun fem | 4232.13 verb 2pl indic aor act |
|---|---|---|---|---|---|
| προφητῶν, | Μὴ | σφάγια | καὶ | θυσίας | προσηνέγκατέ |
| prophētōn | Mē | sphagia | kai | thusias | prosēnenkate |
| prophets, | Not | slain beasts | and | sacrifices | did you offer |

| 1466.4 prs-pron dat 1sing | 2073.3 noun pl neu | 4910.2 num card | 4910.1 num card |
|---|---|---|---|
| μοι | ἔτη | ⸀ τεσσαράκοντα | [☆ τεσσεράκοντα ] |
| moi | etē | tessarakonta | tesserakonta |
| to me | years | forty | [ idem ] |

| 1706.1 prep | 3450.11 art dat sing fem | 2031.2 noun dat sing fem | 3486.1 noun nom sing masc | 2447.1 name masc | 2504.1 conj |
|---|---|---|---|---|---|
| ἐν | τῇ | ἐρήμῳ, | οἶκος | Ἰσραήλ; | 43. καὶ |
| en | tē | erēmō | oikos | Israēl | kai |
| in | the | wilderness, | house | of Israel? | And |

| 351.2 verb 2pl indic aor act | 3450.12 art acc sing fem | 4488.4 noun acc sing fem | 3450.2 art gen sing | 3297.1 name masc | 2504.1 conj |
|---|---|---|---|---|---|
| ἀνελάβετε | τὴν | σκηνὴν | τοῦ | Μολὸχ, | καὶ |
| anelabete | tēn | skēnēn | tou | Moloch | kai |
| you took up | the | tabernacle | | of Moloch, | and |

43.a.**Txt:** 01ℵ,02A,04C 08E,025P,byz.bo.Sod **Var:** 03B,05D,sa.Lach Treg,Alf,Tisc,We/Ho Weis,UBS/☆

| 3450.16 art sing neu | 792.1 noun sing neu | 3450.2 art gen sing | 2296.2 noun gen sing masc | 5050.2 prs-pron gen 2pl | 4338.1 name masc |
|---|---|---|---|---|---|
| τὸ | ἄστρον | τοῦ | θεοῦ | ⸂a ὑμῶν ⸃ | ⸀ Ῥεμφάν, |
| to | astron | tou | theou | humōn | Rhemphan |
| the | star | of the | god | your | Remphan, |

43.b.**Txt:** 05D,1739,byz. Steph **Var:** 03B,We/Ho,Weis UBS/☆

| 4338.2 name masc | 3450.8 art acc pl masc | 5020.4 noun acc pl masc | 3614.8 rel-pron acc pl masc | 4020.26 verb 2pl indic aor act |
|---|---|---|---|---|
| [b☆ Ῥαιφάν, ] | τοὺς | τύπους | οὓς | ἐποιήσατε |
| Rhaiphan | tous | tupous | hous | epoiēsate |
| [ Rhompha, ] | the | models | which | you made |

| 4210.8 verb inf pres act | 840.2 prs-pron dat pl | 2504.1 conj | 3221.2 verb 1sing indic fut act | 5050.4 prs-pron acc 2pl | 1885.1 prep |
|---|---|---|---|---|---|
| προσκυνεῖν | αὐτοῖς· | καὶ | μετοικιῶ | ὑμᾶς | ἐπέκεινα |
| proskunein | autois | kai | metoikiō | humas | epekeina |
| to worship | them; | and | I will remove | you | beyond |

| 891.2 name gen fem | 3450.9 art nom sing fem | 4488.1 noun nom sing fem | 3450.2 art gen sing | 3115.2 noun gen sing neu |
|---|---|---|---|---|
| Βαβυλῶνος. | 44. Ἡ | σκηνὴ | τοῦ | μαρτυρίου |
| Babulōnos | Hē | skēnē | tou | marturiou |
| Babylon. | The | tabernacle | of the | testimony |

44.a.**Txt:** 05D-org,08E byz. **Var:** 01ℵ,02A,03B,04C 05D-corr,025P,bo.Lach Treg,Alf,Tisc,We/Ho Weis,Sod,UBS/☆

| 1498.34 verb sing indic imperf act | 1706.1 prep | 3450.4 art dat pl | 3824.8 noun dat pl masc | 2231.2 prs-pron gen 1pl | 1706.1 prep | 3450.11 art dat sing fem |
|---|---|---|---|---|---|---|
| ἦν | ⸂a ἐν ⸃ | τοῖς | πατράσιν | ἡμῶν | ἐν | τῇ |
| ēn | en | tois | patrasin | hēmōn | en | tē |
| was | among | the | fathers | our | in | the |

God turned away from the Israelites as no longer giving them the fullness of His blessing while they were in the wilderness. Or it may mean God turned the Israelites toward the worship of the heavenly bodies. Stephen said God gave them up; that is, handed them over to worship and serve the host of heaven. Thus they received the consequences they deserved because of their action.

Stephen saw this confirmed in the Book of the Prophets, the 12 Minor Prophets which were written on one scroll in his day and called the Book of the Twelve, or the Book of the Prophets. The quotation is from Amos 5:25-27. Stephen quoted the question of Amos in a way that called for a negative answer. It might be paraphrased, "You didn't offer sacrifices and offerings to Me 40 years in the desert, did you?" They had not offered sacrifices to God alone, nor did they offer them with the love and faith they should have.

It is also true that they had neglected the covenant they had accepted, for none of the males who were born in the wilderness were circumcised, and thus they were not brought under the covenant until after they entered the Promised Land at Gilgal (Joshua 5:5). It seems also they may have neglected to keep the Passover during this 40-year period (at least, after the second year). They apparently did go through the forms, but the idolatry that began with the golden calf continued to tempt Israel and did so until they went into exile in Babylonia.

**7:43.** Even in the wilderness after seeing God's glory, the fathers took up the tabernacle (tent) of Moloch (a Venus god worshiped by the Ammonites and several other Semitic peoples). What a contrast this was to the "tabernacle of witness" set up by Moses according to the pattern given in Mount Sinai and decorated by men who were filled with the Spirit of God (Exodus 35:30-35).

They also worshiped the star of the god Remphan (probably the Assyrian name for the planet Saturn, called *Chiun* in Amos 5:26). Both were figures (images) they made for themselves to worship, thus breaking the First Commandment. (These images were probably small images or figurines carried secretly by these Israelites.) As a result, God told Israel He would transport them beyond Babylon. (Stephen was quoting from the Septuagint, and the KJV and other English versions are primarily based on the Masoretic Text [written in Hebrew]. This, in part, accounts for the different wording one finds.)

Stephen was saying it was their fathers who had rejected Moses and the Law, thereby rebelling against the God who gave the Law. Though Stephen did not say so, his audience knew Jesus was not like that.

**7:44.** Stephen continued by answering their accusation concerning what Jesus said about the temple. He did not try to explain what Jesus really meant by "destroy this temple." Instead, he re-

**and gave them up to worship the host of heaven:** He did not try to stop them from worshiping, *Everyday* . . . and abandoned them, *Berkeley* . . . to serve, *ASV* . . . the Starry Host, *TCNT* . . . the army of the sky, *Fenton* . . . the sun, the moon, and the stars, *Beck* . . . the demons of the sky, *Noli.*

**as it is written in the book of the prophets:** This is written in the book of the early preachers, *NLT.*

**O ye house of Israel, have ye offered to me slain beasts and sacrifices by the space of forty years in the wilderness?:** Nation of Jews, was it to Me you gave gifts of sheep and cattle on the altar, *NLT* . . . all those forty years in the Desert, *TCNT* . . . offered me victims and sacrifices, *Darby.*

**43. Yea, ye took up the tabernacle of Moloch:** Nay, you lifted up Moloch's tent, *Weymouth* . . . No, you offered me the tent of Moloch, *Williams* . . . You took with you the tabernacle of Moloch, *TCNT* . . . No, it was Moloch's tent that you took along, *TNT* . . . the false god Molech, *Everyday.*

**and the star of your god Remphan:** And the star of the god Rephan, *TCNT* . . . the constellation of your god Raiphan, *Concordant* . . . and of your god, the star Remphan, *Fenton* . . . star symbol of the god Rampha, *Montgomery.*

**figures which ye made to worship them:** The forms which ye made to bow down unto them, *Rotherham* . . . The images which you had made to worship, *TCNT* . . . to bow down to them, *TNT.*

**and I will carry you away beyond Babylon:** So I will exile you, *TCNT* . . . and I will remove you, *RSV* . . . Therefore I will deport you, *Noli* . . . I will relocate you beyond Babylon! *Berkeley.*

**44. Our fathers had the tabernacle of witness in the wilderness:** The tent of witness was with our fathers in the desert, *Rotherham* . . . The Holy Tent where God spoke to our fathers, *Everyday* . . . the tabernacle of the testimony, *ASV* . . . the tabernacle of Revelation, *TCNT* . . . the tent in which God spake to His people, *Beck* . . . Covenant Tent, *TEV.*

| 2031.2 noun dat sing fem | 2503.1 conj | 1293.7 verb 3sing indic aor mid | 3450.5 art nom sing masc | 2953.12 verb nom sing masc part pres act | 3450.3 art dat sing |
|---|---|---|---|---|---|
| ἐρήμῳ, | καθὼς | διετάξατο | ὁ | λαλῶν | τῷ |
| erēmō | kathōs | dietaxato | ho | lalōn | tō |
| wilderness, | as | commanded | the | speaking | to |

| 3337.4 name dat masc | 3338.5 name dat masc | 4020.41 verb inf aor act | 840.12 prs-pron acc sing fem | 2567.3 prep |
|---|---|---|---|---|
| ʻ Μωσῆ, | [☆ Μωϋσῆ ] | ποιῆσαι | αὐτὴν | κατὰ |
| Mōsē | Mōusē | poiēsai | autēn | kata |
| to Moses, | [ idem ] | to make | it | according to |

| 3450.6 art acc sing masc | 5020.2 noun acc sing masc | 3614.6 rel-pron acc sing masc | 3571.15 verb 3sing indic plperf act | 3614.12 rel-pron acc sing fem | 2504.1 conj |
|---|---|---|---|---|---|
| τὸν | τύπον | ὃν | ἑωράκει· | 45. ἣν | καὶ |
| ton | tupon | hon | heōrakei | hēn | kai |
| the | model | which | he had seen; | which | also |

| 1507.2 verb 3pl indic aor act | 1231.1 verb nom pl masc part aor mid | 3450.7 art nom pl masc | 3824.6 noun nom pl masc |
|---|---|---|---|
| εἰσήγαγον | διαδεξάμενοι | οἱ | πατέρες |
| eisēgagon | diadexamenoi | hoi | pateres |
| brought in | having received by succession | the | fathers |

| 2231.2 prs-pron gen 1pl | 3196.3 prep | 2400.2 name masc | 1706.1 prep | 3450.11 art dat sing fem | 2666.1 noun dat sing fem |
|---|---|---|---|---|---|
| ἡμῶν | μετὰ | Ἰησοῦ | ἐν | τῇ | κατασχέσει |
| hēmōn | meta | Iēsou | en | tē | kataschesei |
| our | with | Joshua | in | the | possession |

| 3450.1 art gen pl | 1477.5 noun gen pl neu | 3614.1 rel-pron gen pl | 1840.1 verb 3sing indic aor act | 3450.5 art nom sing masc | 2296.1 noun nom sing masc |
|---|---|---|---|---|---|
| τῶν | ἐθνῶν, | ὧν | ἐξῶσεν | ὁ | θεὸς |
| tōn | ethnōn | hōn | exōsen | ho | theos |
| of the | nations, | whom | drove out | | God |

| 570.3 prep | 4241.2 noun gen sing neu | 3450.1 art gen pl | 3824.7 noun gen pl masc | 2231.2 prs-pron gen 1pl | 2175.1 conj | 3450.1 art gen pl |
|---|---|---|---|---|---|---|
| ἀπὸ | προσώπου | τῶν | πατέρων | ἡμῶν, | ἕως | τῶν |
| apo | prosōpou | tōn | paterōn | hēmōn | heōs | tōn |
| from | face | of the | fathers | our, | until | the |

| 2232.6 noun gen pl fem | 1132.1 name masc | 3614.5 rel-pron nom sing masc | 2128.8 verb 3sing indic aor act | 5322.4 noun acc sing fem | 1783.1 prep |
|---|---|---|---|---|---|
| ἡμερῶν | Δαβίδ, | 46. ὃς | εὗρεν | χάριν | ἐνώπιον |
| hēmerōn | Dabid | hos | heuren | charin | enōpion |
| days | of David; | who | found | favor | before |

| 3450.2 art gen sing | 2296.2 noun gen sing masc | 2504.1 conj | 153.28 verb 3sing indic aor mid | 2128.21 verb inf aor act | 4493.3 noun sing neu |
|---|---|---|---|---|---|
| τοῦ | θεοῦ, | καὶ | ᾐτήσατο | εὑρεῖν | σκήνωμα |
| tou | theou | kai | ētēsato | heurein | skēnōma |
| | God, | and | asked | to find | a tabernacle |

| 3450.3 art dat sing | 2296.3 noun dat sing masc | 3486.3 noun dat sing masc | 2361.1 name masc | 4526.1 name nom masc |
|---|---|---|---|---|
| τῷ | ʻ θεῷ | [[a]☆ οἴκῳ ] | Ἰακώβ. | 47. Σολομῶν |
| tō | theō | oikō | Iakōb | Solomōn |
| for the | God | [ house ] | of Jacob; | Solomon |

| 1156.2 conj | 3481.8 verb 3sing indic aor act | 3481.21 verb 3sing indic aor act | 840.4 prs-pron dat sing | 3486.4 noun acc sing masc |
|---|---|---|---|---|
| δὲ | ʻ ᾠκοδόμησεν | [☆ οἰκοδόμησεν ] | αὐτῷ | οἶκον. |
| de | ōkodomēsen | oikodomēsen | autō | oikon |
| but | built | [ idem ] | him | a house. |

46.a.**Txt:** 01א-corr,02A 04C,08E,025P,33,byz.it. sa.bo.We/Ho,Sod
**Var:** p74,01א-org,03B 05D,Lach,Tisc,Weis UBS/☆

minded them that the fathers had the tent of the testimony which contained the tablets of stone which were a witness to the covenant between God and His people.

**7:45.** The next generation of the fathers received the tabernacle (the tent) in their turn. They brought it in with Joshua (Greek, *Iēsou*, English *Jesus*, which is derived from the Greek form of Joshua, as in Hebrews 4:8), into what was previously the possession of the Gentiles (the nations) whom God drove out before the fathers until the days of David. This indicates the driving out was not completed until the days of David. Actually, the Book of Joshua indicates the land was subdued in his day, but there was much land yet to be possessed (Joshua 13:1). The Book of Judges shows also that in the days after Joshua the people did not drive out the Canaanites, but instead fell into Canaanite idolatry. They did so again and again, even though God was faithful to raise up judges to deliver them. Not until David's time was Israel fully united and in control of its territory.

Stephen's attention, however, was focused on the tabernacle, and he showed it lasted until the time of David. After the capture of the ark of the covenant by the Philistines the tabernacle was pitched at Nob, a short distance north of Jerusalem, possibly on Mount Scopus. Later, it was at the high place at Gibeon (1 Samuel 21:1; 1 Chronicles 16:39). Finally, Solomon brought to the temple what was left of the nearly 500-year-old tent (1 Kings 8:4; 2 Chronicles 5:5).

**7:46.** David found favor before God. This was shown, of course, by his victories and by the fact that God used him to establish the kingdom of Israel, something King Saul had failed to do.

After David brought back the ark to Jerusalem, he placed it in a temporary tent shelter. But he personally desired to find a tabernacle for the God of Jacob. (Several ancient manuscripts have "for the house of Jacob.") "Tabernacle" here is used as a general word for a dwelling, even more permanent dwellings, and Stephen was thinking of David's desire to build a temple as a dwelling place for God. David expressed this in Psalm 132:4,5 by saying "I will not give sleep to mine eyes or slumber to mine eyelids, until I find out a place for the Lord, a habitation for the mighty God of Jacob."

**7:47.** God did not allow David to build the temple. David served his generation as a warrior, which was necessary for the nation to be established. But God wanted a man of peace to build the temple, so that was designated as Solomon's prime task. (His name means "Peaceful," in Hebrew, *Sh^e^lōmōh*, from *shālôm*, "peace.") Nevertheless, it was David's vision for building a temple that was passed down to his son. It was also David who made preparations and gathered the materials for its construction (see 1 Chronicles 22).

**as he had appointed, speaking unto Moses:** . . . according as he who was speaking...gave instructions, *Rotherham* . . . even as he directed, *HBIE* . . . as He prescribes, *Concordant* . . . as he had arranged, *Klingensmith.*

**that he should make it according to the fashion that he had seen:** . . . according to the figure, *ASV* . . . according to the model, *Rotherham* . . . in imitation of the model, *Weymouth* . . . pattern, *Wuest* . . . like the model Moses had seen, *Williams.*

**45. Which also our fathers that came after:** This Tabernacle, which was handed on to them, *TCNT* . . . which also our fathers in turn received, *HBIE* . . . That Tent was bequeathed to the next generation of our forefathers, *Weymouth* . . . received it by succession, *Wilson.*

**brought in with Jesus:** . . . with Joshua, *RSV.*

**into the possession of the Gentiles:** When the Gentiles had been dispossessed by God, *Noli* . . . actually brought into the land, *Murdock* . . . entered on the possession of the nations, *ASV* . . . at the conquest of the nations, *TCNT* . . . when they were taking possession of the land of the Gentile nations, *Weymouth* . . . into the land of the Pagans, *Klingensmith.*

**whom God drove out before the face of our fathers:** . . . that God thrust out, *ASV* . . . that God drove out, *Klingensmith.*

**unto the days of David:** . . . and remained here down to the time of David, *TCNT* . . . So it continued till David's time, *Weymouth.*

**46. Who found favour before God:** David won favour with God, *TCNT* . . . who found grace before God, *Berkeley.*

**and desired to find tabernacle for the God of Jacob:** . . . and asked to find a habitation, *ASV* . . . and asked permission to find a dwelling, *TCNT* . . . he might find a residence, *Murdock* . . . begged to design a dwelling, *Williams.*

**47. But Solomon built him an house:** But it was Solomon who built a House for God, *TCNT* . . . who actually built it, *SEB.*

| 233.1 conj | 3620.1 partic | 3450.5 art nom sing masc | 5148.1 adj sup nom sing masc | 1706.1 prep | 5335.2 adj dat pl masc |
|---|---|---|---|---|---|
| **48.** Ἀλλ' | οὐχ | ὁ | ὕψιστος | ἐν | χειροποιήτοις |
| *All'* | *ouch* | *ho* | *hupsistos* | *en* | *cheiropoiētois* |
| But | not | the | Most High | in | hand made |

48.a.**Txt:** 025P,byz.
**Var:** 01א,02A,03B,04C
05D,08E,sa.bo.Gries
Lach,Treg,Alf,Word
Tisc,We/Ho,Weis,Sod
UBS/☆

| 3348.5 noun dat pl masc | 2700.2 verb 3sing indic pres act | 2503.1 conj | 3450.5 art nom sing masc | 4254.1 noun nom sing masc | 2978.5 verb 3sing indic pres act |
|---|---|---|---|---|---|
| ʼ[a] ναοῖς ˎ | κατοικεῖ, | καθὼς | ὁ | προφήτης | λέγει, |
| *naois* | *katoikei* | *kathōs* | *ho* | *prophētēs* | *legei* |
| temples | dwells; | as | the | prophet | says, |

| 3450.5 art nom sing masc | 3636.1 noun nom sing masc | 1466.4 prs-pron dat 1sing | 2339.1 noun nom sing masc | 3450.9 art nom sing fem | 1156.2 conj |
|---|---|---|---|---|---|
| **49.** Ὁ | οὐρανός | μοι | θρόνος | ἡ | δὲ |
| *Ho* | *ouranos* | *moi* | *thronos* | *hē* | *de* |
| The | heaven | to me | a throne | the | and |

| 1087.1 noun nom sing fem | 5124.1 noun sing neu | 3450.1 art gen pl | 4087.5 noun gen pl masc | 1466.2 prs-pron gen 1sing | 4029.1 intr-pron sing |
|---|---|---|---|---|---|
| γῆ | ὑποπόδιον | τῶν | ποδῶν | μου· | ποῖον |
| *gē* | *hupopodion* | *tōn* | *podōn* | *mou* | *poion* |
| earth | a footstool | of the | feet | my: | what |

| 3486.4 noun acc sing masc | 3481.12 verb 2pl indic fut act | 1466.4 prs-pron dat 1sing | 2978.5 verb 3sing indic pres act | 2935.1 noun nom sing masc |
|---|---|---|---|---|
| οἶκον | οἰκοδομήσετέ | μοι, | λέγει | κύριος· |
| *oikon* | *oikodomēsete* | *moi* | *legei* | *kurios* |
| house | will you build | me? | says | Lord, |

| 2211.1 conj | 4949.3 intr-pron nom sing | 4964.1 noun nom sing masc | 3450.10 art gen sing fem | 2633.1 noun gen sing fem | 1466.2 prs-pron gen 1sing |
|---|---|---|---|---|---|
| ἢ | τίς | τόπος | τῆς | καταπαύσεώς | μου; |
| *ē* | *tis* | *topos* | *tēs* | *katapauseōs* | *mou* |
| or | what | place | of the | rest | my? |

| 3644.1 adv | 3450.9 art nom sing fem | 5331.1 noun nom sing fem | 1466.2 prs-pron gen 1sing | 4020.24 verb 3sing indic aor act | 3642.18 dem-pron pl neu |
|---|---|---|---|---|---|
| **50.** οὐχὶ | ἡ | χείρ | μου | ἐποίησεν | ταῦτα |
| *ouchi* | *hē* | *cheir* | *mou* | *epoiēsen* | *tauta* |
| not | the | hand | my | made | these things |

| 3820.1 adj | 4499.1 adj nom pl masc | 2504.1 conj | 561.1 adj nom pl masc | 3450.11 art dat sing fem |
|---|---|---|---|---|
| πάντα; | **51.** Σκληροτράχηλοι | καὶ | ἀπερίτμητοι | ʼ τῇ |
| *panta* | *Sklērotrachēloi* | *kai* | *aperitmētoi* | *tē* |
| all? | O stiff-necked | and | uncircumcised | in the |

51.a.**Txt:** 08E,025P,byz.
sa.bo.Gries,Alf
**Var:** 01א,02A,04C,05D
Lach,Treg,Tisc,We/Ho
Weis,Sod,UBS/☆

| 2559.3 noun dat sing fem | 2559.7 noun dat pl fem | 2504.1 conj | 3450.4 art dat pl | 3640.3 noun dat pl neu | 5050.1 prs-pron nom 2pl |
|---|---|---|---|---|---|
| καρδίᾳ | [a☆ καρδίαις ] | καὶ | τοῖς | ὠσίν, | ὑμεῖς |
| *kardia* | *kardiais* | *kai* | *tois* | *ōsin* | *humeis* |
| heart | [ hearts ] | and | in the | ears, | you |

| 103.1 adv | 3450.3 art dat sing | 4011.3 noun dat sing neu | 3450.3 art dat sing | 39.3 adj dat sing | 493.1 verb 2pl indic pres act |
|---|---|---|---|---|---|
| ἀεὶ | τῷ | πνεύματι | τῷ | ἁγίῳ | ἀντιπίπτετε, |
| *aei* | *tō* | *pneumati* | *tō* | *hagiō* | *antipiptete* |
| always | the | Spirit | the | Holy | resist; |

| 5453.1 conj | 3450.7 art nom pl masc | 3824.6 noun nom pl masc | 5050.2 prs-pron gen 2pl | 2504.1 conj | 5050.1 prs-pron nom 2pl | 4949.1 intr-pron |
|---|---|---|---|---|---|---|
| ὡς | οἱ | πατέρες | ὑμῶν, | καὶ | ὑμεῖς. | **52.** τίνα |
| *hōs* | *hoi* | *pateres* | *humōn* | *kai* | *humeis* | *tina* |
| as | the | fathers | your, | also | you. | Which |

**7:48.** Solomon's Temple, however, was not God's permanent dwelling place, and Stephen declared that the Most High (God) does not dwell (or settle down to stay permanently) in what is made by hands.

Solomon himself recognized this. At the dedication of the temple in his prayer before God, he said, "But will God indeed dwell on the earth? behold the heaven and heaven of heavens cannot contain thee; how much less this house that I have builded?" (1 Kings 8:27).

**7:49.** To prove that God did not dwell permanently in the temple, Stephen quoted Isaiah 66:1 and part of verse 2. There, God told Isaiah that heaven is His throne and the earth His footstool (the place where He will show that He is Conqueror). In view of that, what house could they build for Him, or what was the place of His rest? In other words, in what place could God settle down and make His permanent abode (on earth)?

Rest also suggests the ceasing of activity. Where would God do this? As Isaiah 40:28 tells us, God is never weary. He never gets tired. He never ceases His divine activity.

**7:50.** The unreasonableness of limiting God's presence to a temple built by human hands is further seen by the fact that God made the heavens and the earth and everything in them. How could anything made by man match what He has made?

Stephen was not denying that God had manifested His presence in the temple. God did manifest His glory there in the Holy of Holies from the time of Solomon to the time of the destruction of the temple by the Babylonians. Isaiah 57:15 also recognizes that God is the high and lofty One who inhabits the eternity of time and space (who fills the universe) and whose name (and character) is Holy. He dwells in the high and holy place, that is, He has His chief manifestation of His glory in heaven, but He dwells also with the one who has a contrite and humble spirit.

**7:51.** Stephen apparently saw that his message was not being accepted. Possibly there was angry whispering among his hearers. He therefore rebuked them sharply. They were stiffnecked, they were stubborn and uncircumcised in heart and ears. Their attitude and their refusal to listen to the gospel put them in the same class as the Gentiles who were outside God's covenant and were rejecting Him. They were hearing, thinking, and planning in the way unbelieving Gentiles did. Their fathers were actually warned against this. Deuteronomy 10:16 and 30:6 calls for a circumcision of the heart lest they become rebellious and be cut off from God's promises. (See also Jeremiah 6:10; 9:26; Ezekiel 44:7.) In fact, these Jewish leaders were actively resisting the Holy Spirit just as their fathers had.

**48. Howbeit the most High dwelleth not in temples made with hands:** . . . the Highest One, *SEB* . . . does not live in houses, *Everyday* . . . does not dwell in anything handmade, *Berkeley* . . . Yet it is not in buildings made by hands that the Most High dwells, *TCNT* . . . dwells not in hand-made structures, *Fenton* . . . made by human hands, *Beck*.

**49. Heaven is my throne:** The sky is a throne for me, *TCNT* . . . the place where I sit, *NLT*.

**and earth is my footstool:** . . . a rest for my feet, *Fenton* . . . where I rest my feet, *NLT*.

**what house will ye build me? saith the Lord:** What manner of house, *ASV* . . . What kind of a house, *HBIE*.

**or what is the place of my rest?:** Or what place is there where I may rest, *TCNT* . . . Or what resting-place shall I have, *Weymouth* . . . no place where I need to rest! *Everyday, SEB* . . . On what spot could I settle? *Moffatt*.

**50. Hath not my hand made all these things?:** Was it not my hand that made, *TCNT* . . . Did not my hand make this universe, *Montgomery* . . . Remember, I made all these things! *Everyday*.

**51. Ye stiffnecked and uncircumcised in heart and ears:** You obstinate race, heathen in heart and ears, *TCNT* . . . uncircumcised heathen, *Fenton* . . . pagan at heart and deaf to the truth, *Beck* . . . stubborn in will, heathenish in hearts and ears, *Williams* . . . Stubborn people with pagan hearts and ears! *Noli* . . . You have hard hearts and ears that will not listen to me! *NLT*.

**ye do always resist the Holy Ghost:** . . . you are continually at strife with the Holy Spirit, *Weymouth* . . . you are forever resisting the Holy Spirit, *TCNT* . . . ever clashing with, *Concordant* . . . set yourselves against, *Murdock* . . . you are always in opposition, *Fenton* . . . continually fighting, *Klingensmith* . . . working against, *NLT*.

**as your fathers did, so do ye:** Your early fathers did. You do too, *NLT* . . . your ancestors did it, and you are doing it still, *TCNT* . . . just as your forefathers did, *Goodspeed, Noli*.

# Acts 7:53

| 3450.1 art gen pl | 4254.5 noun gen pl masc | 3620.2 partic | 1371.14 verb 3pl indic aor act | 3450.7 art nom pl masc | 3824.6 noun nom pl masc |
|---|---|---|---|---|---|
| τῶν | προφητῶν | οὐκ | ἐδίωξαν | οἱ | πατέρες |
| *tōn* | *prophētōn* | *ouk* | *ediōxan* | *hoi* | *pateres* |
| of the | prophets | not | did persecute | the | fathers |

| 5050.2 prs-pron gen 2pl | 2504.1 conj | 609.7 verb 3pl indic aor act | 3450.8 art acc pl masc | 4152.3 verb acc pl masc part aor act |
|---|---|---|---|---|
| ὑμῶν; | καὶ | ἀπέκτειναν | τοὺς | προκαταγγείλαντας |
| *humōn* | *kai* | *apekteinan* | *tous* | *prokatangeilantas* |
| your? | and | they killed | the | having before announced |

| 3875.1 prep | 3450.10 art gen sing fem | 1647.1 noun gen sing fem | 3450.2 art gen sing | 1337.2 adj gen sing | 3614.2 rel-pron gen sing |
|---|---|---|---|---|---|
| περὶ | τῆς | ἐλεύσεως | τοῦ | δικαίου, | οὗ |
| *peri* | *tēs* | *eleuseōs* | *tou* | *dikaiou* | *hou* |
| concerning | the | coming | of the | Just One, | of whom |

| 3431.1 adv | 5050.1 prs-pron nom 2pl | 4132.2 noun nom pl masc | 2504.1 conj | 5243.3 noun pl masc | 1090.64 verb 2pl indic perf mid |
|---|---|---|---|---|---|
| νῦν | ὑμεῖς | προδόται | καὶ | φονεῖς | ⸂ γεγένησθε˙ |
| *nun* | *humeis* | *prodotai* | *kai* | *phoneis* | *gegenēsthe* |
| now | you | betrayers | and | murderers | have become! |

52.a.**Txt:** 025P,byz. **Var:** 01ℵ,02A,03B,04C 05D,08E,Lach,Treg,Alf Word,Tisc,We/Ho,Weis Sod,UBS/☆

| 1090.36 verb 2pl indic aor mid | 3610.2 rel-pron nom pl masc | 2956.16 verb 2pl indic aor act | 3450.6 art acc sing masc | 3414.4 noun acc sing masc |
|---|---|---|---|---|
| [a☆ ἐγένεσθε, ] | 53. οἵτινες | ἐλάβετε | τὸν | νόμον |
| *egenesthe* | *hoitines* | *elabete* | *ton* | *nomon* |
| [ became, ] | who | received | the | law |

| 1519.1 prep | 1290.2 noun acc pl fem | 32.6 noun gen pl masc | 2504.1 conj | 3620.2 partic | 5278.9 verb 2pl indic aor act |
|---|---|---|---|---|---|
| εἰς | διαταγὰς | ἀγγέλων, | καὶ | οὐκ | ἐφυλάξατε. |
| *eis* | *diatagas* | *angelōn* | *kai* | *ouk* | *ephulaxate* |
| by | order | of angels, | and | not | kept. |

| 189.14 verb nom pl masc part pres act | 1156.2 conj | 3642.18 dem-pron pl neu | 1276.1 verb 3pl indic imperf pass |
|---|---|---|---|
| 54. Ἀκούοντες | δὲ | ταῦτα | διεπρίοντο |
| *Akouontes* | *de* | *tauta* | *dieprionto* |
| Hearing | and | these things | they were being enraged |

| 3450.14 art dat pl fem | 2559.7 noun dat pl fem | 840.1 prs-pron gen pl | 2504.1 conj | 1024.1 verb 3pl indic imperf act | 3450.8 art acc pl masc |
|---|---|---|---|---|---|
| ταῖς | καρδίαις | αὐτῶν, | καὶ | ἔβρυχον | τοὺς |
| *tais* | *kardiais* | *autōn* | *kai* | *ebruchon* | *tous* |
| in the | hearts | their, | and | were gnashing | the |

| 3462.5 noun acc pl masc | 1894.2 prep | 840.6 prs-pron acc sing masc | 5062.6 verb nom sing masc part pres act | 1156.2 conj | 3994.1 adj nom sing |
|---|---|---|---|---|---|
| ὀδόντας | ἐπ' | αὐτόν. | 55. Ὑπάρχων | δὲ | πλήρης |
| *odontas* | *ep'* | *auton* | *Huparchōn* | *de* | *plērēs* |
| teeth | at | him. | Being | but | full |

| 4011.2 noun gen sing neu | 39.2 adj gen sing | 810.3 verb nom sing masc part aor act | 1519.1 prep | 3450.6 art acc sing masc |
|---|---|---|---|---|
| πνεύματος | ἁγίου, | ἀτενίσας | εἰς | τὸν |
| *pneumatos* | *hagiou* | *atenisas* | *eis* | *ton* |
| of Spirit | Holy, | having looked intently | into | the |

| 3636.4 noun acc sing masc | 1481.3 verb 3sing indic aor act | 1385.4 noun acc sing fem | 2296.2 noun gen sing masc | 2504.1 conj | 2400.3 name acc masc |
|---|---|---|---|---|---|
| οὐρανὸν, | εἶδεν | δόξαν | θεοῦ, | καὶ | Ἰησοῦν |
| *ouranon* | *eiden* | *doxan* | *theou* | *kai* | *Iēsoun* |
| heaven, | he saw | glory | of God, | and | Jesus |

**7:52.** None of the prophets escaped persecution by the fathers. (See Matthew 5:11,12; 23:30,31). They killed those who announced beforehand the coming of the Just One (the Righteous One). It was He these Jewish leaders had now betrayed and murdered.

Stephen threw the guilt of Judas back on the ones who commanded that information be given them in order that they might arrest Jesus (which they did some time before Judas came to them; John 11:57).

**7:53.** These Jewish leaders would have acknowledged the guilt of those who killed the prophets was great. But their guilt was even greater. They had received the Law which was given by the disposition (the ordaining, the ordinance) of angels, but they did not keep or observe it.

The mention of angels here comes from Jewish traditions and also from the Septuagint translation which interpreted Deuteronomy 33:2,3 to mean that angels were active in the giving or expounding of the Law. This was part of Moses' blessing given shortly before his death. There he spoke of the Lord's coming from Sinai and His glory shining forth from Seir and Paran (that is, from the direction of Edom). He came with "ten thousands of saints" (holy ones), and at the same time "from his right hand went a fiery law." The saints or holy ones were taken to be angels.

Since the Jewish leaders did not keep the Law, they were the guilty ones. That is, they, not Jesus, nor His followers, had disregarded the Law in killing Jesus, the very One the Law as well as the prophets had prophesied would come.

**7:54.** This severe rebuke cut (sawed through) to the heart of these Sanhedrin members who heard Stephen and brought a vicious reaction. These dignified "senators" of the Jewish people gnashed (crunched) their teeth over Stephen. By this expression of rage and exasperation they only proved they really were resisting the Holy Spirit as Stephen said they were.

**7:55.** In contrast to them, Stephen, being still full of the Holy Spirit, fixed his gaze into heaven and saw the glory of God and Jesus standing at the right hand of God (that is, in the place of honor, power, and authority). Other passages speak of Jesus seated at the right hand of God where He is now interceding for believers (Mark 14:62; Luke 22:69). This seems to indicate that Jesus rose to welcome the first martyr who gave a witness for Him at the cost of His life. (The word *martyr* comes from the Greek *martus* which has a genitive form *marturos* and means "a witness." During the later persecutions of the Early Church so many bore witness to Jesus as they were being killed for their faith that the word came to have its present meaning of martyr as one who dies for his faith.)

**52. Which of the prophets have not your fathers persecuted?:** Was there ever a prophet your fathers didn't persecute, *Beck* . . . every prophet who ever lived, *SEB* . . . Can you name a single prophet whom your fathers did not persecute? *Phillips.*

**and they have slain them which shewed before of the coming of the Just One:** . . . they killed the men who foretold, *Weymouth* . . . they murdered those who foretold the coming, *Fenton.*

**of whom ye have been now the betrayers and murderers:** . . . whose betrayers and murderers you have now become, *Weymouth* . . . now you yourselves have become His betrayers and murderers, *Norlie* . . . you have now handed over, *Klingensmith* . . . and now you betrayed and murdered him, *Beck.*

**53. Who have received the law by the disposition of angels:** Angels were ordered, *Beck* . . . ordination of angels, *Murdock* . . . by arrangement of messengers, *Young* . . . injunction, *Alford* . . . as ordained by the ministry of angels, *Darby* . . . that angels transmitted, *Moffatt.*

**and have not kept it:** . . . and have not guarded it, *Swann* . . . but you did not obey them, *Noli.*

**54. When they heard these things:** As they continued to listen to this address, *Williams.*

**they were cut to the heart:** . . . grew frantic with rage, *TCNT* . . . they were becoming infuriated, *Williams* . . . enraged, *Wilson.*

**and they gnashed on him with their teeth:** . . . grind their teeth at him, *Williams* . . . clinched their teeth, *ET.*

**55. But he, being full of the Holy Ghost:** . . . but possessing fulness of Holy Spirit, *Fenton* . . . But since he was full, *Williams* . . . filled through all his being with the Holy Spirit, *Phillips.*

**looked up stedfastly into heaven, and saw the glory of God:** . . . looking intently into heaven, *Concordant* . . . he looked right into heaven and saw the glory of God, *Williams* . . . he saw a Divine Majesty, *Fenton.*

| **2449.25** verb part perf act | **1523.2** prep gen | **1182.7** adj gen pl neu | **3450.2** art gen sing | **2296.2** noun gen sing masc | **2504.1** conj |
|---|---|---|---|---|---|
| ἑστῶτα | ἐκ | δεξιῶν | τοῦ | θεοῦ, | **56.** καὶ |
| *hestōta* | *ek* | *dexiōn* | *tou* | *theou* | *kai* |
| standing | at | the right hand | | of God, | and |

| **1500.5** verb 3sing indic aor act | **1481.20** verb 2sing impr aor mid | **2311.2** verb 1sing indic pres act | **3450.8** art acc pl masc | **3636.9** noun acc pl masc |
|---|---|---|---|---|
| εἶπεν, | Ἰδοὺ, | θεωρῶ | τοὺς | οὐρανοὺς |
| *eipen* | *Idou* | *theōrō* | *tous* | *ouranous* |
| said, | Look! | I see | the | heavens |

56.a.**Txt:** 05D-corr,08E 025P,byz.
**Var:** 01ℵ,02A,03B,04C Lach,Treg,Alf,Word Tisc,We/Ho,Weis,Sod UBS/☆

| **453.27** verb acc pl masc part perf mid | **1266.7** verb acc pl masc part perf mid | **2504.1** conj | **3450.6** art acc sing masc |
|---|---|---|---|
| ‘ ἀνεῳγμένους, | [a☆ διηνοιγμένους ] | καὶ | τὸν |
| *aneōgmenous* | *diēnoigmenous* | *kai* | *ton* |
| having been opened, | [ idem ] | and | the |

| **5048.4** noun acc sing masc | **3450.2** art gen sing | **442.2** noun gen sing masc | **1523.2** prep gen | **1182.7** adj gen pl neu | **2449.25** verb part perf act |
|---|---|---|---|---|---|
| υἱὸν | τοῦ | ἀνθρώπου | ἐκ | δεξιῶν | ἑστῶτα |
| *huion* | *tou* | *anthrōpou* | *ek* | *dexiōn* | *hestōta* |
| Son | | of man | at | the right | standing |

| **3450.2** art gen sing | **2296.2** noun gen sing masc | **2869.14** verb nom pl masc part aor act | **1156.2** conj | **5292.3** noun dat sing fem | **3144.11** adj dat sing fem |
|---|---|---|---|---|---|
| τοῦ | θεοῦ. | **57.** Κράξαντες | δὲ | φωνῇ | μεγάλῃ |
| *tou* | *theou* | *Kraxantes* | *de* | *phōnē* | *megalē* |
| | of God. | Having cried out | and | with a voice | great |

| **4762.4** verb 3pl indic aor act | **3450.17** art pl neu | **3640.2** noun pl neu | **840.1** prs-pron gen pl | **2504.1** conj | **3592.2** verb 3pl indic aor act |
|---|---|---|---|---|---|
| συνέσχον | τὰ | ὦτα | αὐτῶν | καὶ | ὥρμησαν |
| *suneschon* | *ta* | *ōta* | *autōn* | *kai* | *hōrmēsan* |
| they held | the | ears | their | and | rushed |

| **3524.1** adv | **1894.2** prep | **840.6** prs-pron acc sing masc | **2504.1** conj | **1531.20** verb nom pl masc part aor act | **1838.1** adv |
|---|---|---|---|---|---|
| ὁμοθυμαδὸν | ἐπ' | αὐτόν, | **58.** καὶ | ἐκβαλόντες | ἔξω |
| *homothumadon* | *ep'* | *auton* | *kai* | *ekbalontes* | *exō* |
| with one accord | upon | him. | and | having cast | out of |

| **3450.10** art gen sing fem | **4032.2** noun gen sing fem | **3010.5** verb 3pl indic imperf act | **2504.1** conj | **3450.7** art nom pl masc | **3116.4** noun nom pl masc |
|---|---|---|---|---|---|
| τῆς | πόλεως | ἐλιθοβόλουν. | καὶ | οἱ | μάρτυρες |
| *tēs* | *poleōs* | *elithoboloun* | *kai* | *hoi* | *martures* |
| the | city | they were stoning. | And | the | witnesses |

| **653.1** verb 3pl indic aor mid | **3450.17** art pl neu | **2416.4** noun pl neu | **840.1** prs-pron gen pl | **3706.2** prep | **3450.8** art acc pl masc |
|---|---|---|---|---|---|
| ἀπέθεντο | τὰ | ἱμάτια | αὐτῶν | παρὰ | τοὺς |
| *apethento* | *ta* | *himatia* | *autōn* | *para* | *tous* |
| laid aside | the | garments | their | at | the |

| **4087.7** noun acc pl masc | **3357.2** noun gen sing masc | **2535.28** verb gen sing part pres mid | **4425.2** name gen masc | **2504.1** conj |
|---|---|---|---|---|
| πόδας | νεανίου | καλουμένου | Σαύλου. | **59.** καὶ |
| *podas* | *neaniou* | *kaloumenou* | *Saulou* | *kai* |
| feet | of a young man | being called | Saul. | And |

| **3010.5** verb 3pl indic imperf act | **3450.6** art acc sing masc | **4587.4** name acc masc | **1926.6** verb acc sing masc part pres mid | **2504.1** conj |
|---|---|---|---|---|
| ἐλιθοβόλουν | τὸν | Στέφανον, | ἐπικαλούμενον | καὶ |
| *elithoboloun* | *ton* | *Stephanon* | *epikaloumenon* | *kai* |
| they were stoning | | Stephen, | calling upon | and |

**7:56.** Stephen immediately told what he saw. But this time he did not use the name of Jesus. Instead, he called Him "the Son of man." This was a term the Jewish leaders in the Sanhedrin had often heard Jesus use of himself. During His ministry He used it because of His identification with mankind whom He came to redeem. The term *son of* was also used to indicate nature or character. So Jesus was declaring himself to be truly human as well as truly divine. But it was not a term His enemies could use against Him. Jesus did not want to be arrested and killed before He had opportunity to teach and train His disciples. However, at His trial, Jesus declared He was the Son of Man prophesied by Daniel 7:13, the Son of Man who would come in clouds to receive the kingdom promised to Israel.

**7:57.** The words of Stephen caused the Sanhedrin to start crying out, yelling and shrieking with a loud voice. At the same time they put their hands over their ears to shut out anything further that Stephen might say. Then "with one accord" (that is, with one spontaneous impulse and purpose) they rushed upon him. (The same word is used of the swine rushing down into the sea when the legion of demons took possession of them, Matthew 8:32; Mark 5:13; Luke 8:33. It was also used of the mob rushing into the theater when they were upset because the sale of images was falling off; Acts 19:29.)

**7:58.** Then they dragged Stephen out of the city and stoned him. This time they were still following the letter of the law of Moses where a willful, high-handed unrepentant sinner was to be stoned "outside the camp" (Numbers 15:35).

By stoning him, however, they were defying Roman law which did not allow the Jews to carry out the death penalty (John 18:31). They had bowed to Roman law in seeking to get the death penalty for Jesus, and this led to His being crucified instead of being stoned. It should be noted, however, that this took place probably near the close of Pilate's governorship when he had fallen into disfavor with the Roman government, and these Jews were taking advantage of his weakness.

The Sanhedrin also followed the externals of Jewish legal procedure with the witnesses casting the first stone (Deuteronomy 17:7). They, in fact, took off their outer garments in order to be more free to throw the stones and laid the garments at the feet of a young man named Saul. ("Young man" here means a man in his prime, up to the age of 40. Saul [Paul] was old enough to be a member of the Sanhedrin. Acts 26:10 indicates he cast his vote, and he had to be a member to do that.) Saul was an eyewitness to Stephen's death and probably to his preaching in the synagogue. This is the first mention of Saul, a preparation for what comes later.

**and Jesus standing on the right hand of God:** . . . at his right hand, *Noli.*

**56. And said, Behold, I see the heavens opened:** Look, *Noli* . . . I see an opening in the sky, *NAB.*

**and the Son of man standing on the right hand of God:** . . . the Messiah, *Noli* . . . at God's right side, *NCV.*

**57. Then they cried out with a loud voice:** At this, they shouted with all their might, *Norlie* . . . they uttered a great shout, *Goodspeed* . . . The onlookers were shouting aloud, *NAB* . . . yelled at the top of their voices, *Beck* . . . With a loud outcry, *Montgomery* . . . With a loud shriek, *Moffatt.*

**and stopped their ears:** . . . holding their hands over their ears as they did so, *NAB* . . . holding their hands to, *MLNT.*

**and ran upon him with one accord:** . . . did rush, *Young* . . . and they all pushed on him, *NLT* . . . with one thought in mind, *Adams* . . . and rushed with one accord upon him, *Swann* . . . rushed...in a body, *MLNT* . . . as one man, *NAB.*

**58. And cast him out of the city, and stoned him:** . . . dragged him outside the city, *Montgomery* . . . drove him, *TNT* . . . threw him, *MLNT* . . . Then they took him...and threw stones at him, *NLT* . . . they pelted him, *Concordant.*

**and the witnesses laid down their clothes at a young man's feet, whose name was Saul:** Meanwhile, the witnesses, *NIV* . . . The men who told lies against Stephen, *Everyday* . . . The men who were throwing the stones laid their coats down in front of a young man, *NLT* . . . deposited their clothes, *Fenton* . . . throwing down their clothes, *Goodspeed* . . . meanwhile were piling their cloaks, *NAB.*

**59. And they stoned Stephen, calling upon God, and saying:** While they threw stones at Stephen, he prayed, *NLT* . . . While they were throwing rocks, *NCV* . . . while he is invoking and saying, *Concordant* . . . as he called upon the Lord, *MLNT* . . . called out again and again, *Williams C.K.*

| 2978.13 verb part pres act | 2935.5 noun voc sing masc | 2400.2 name masc | 1203.11 verb 2sing impr aor mid | 3450.16 art sing neu | 4011.1 noun sing neu |
|---|---|---|---|---|---|
| λέγοντα, | Κύριε | Ἰησοῦ, | δέξαι | τὸ | πνεῦμά |
| *legonta* | *Kurie* | *Iēsou* | *dexai* | *to* | *pneuma* |
| saying, | Lord | Jesus, | receive | the | spirit |

| 1466.2 prs-pron gen 1sing | 4935.14 verb nom sing masc part aor act | 1156.2 conj | 3450.17 art pl neu | 1113.3 noun pl neu | 2869.11 verb 3sing indic aor act |
|---|---|---|---|---|---|
| μου. | **60.** θεὶς | δὲ | τὰ | γόνατα | ἔκραξεν |
| *mou* | *theis* | *de* | *ta* | *gonata* | *ekraxen* |
| my. | Having fallen | and | the | knees | he cried |

| 5292.3 noun dat sing fem | 3144.11 adj dat sing fem | 2935.5 noun voc sing masc | 3231.1 partic | 2449.7 verb 2sing subj aor act | 840.2 prs-pron dat pl |
|---|---|---|---|---|---|
| φωνῇ | μεγάλῃ, | Κύριε, | μὴ | στήσῃς | αὐτοῖς |
| *phōnē* | *megalē* | *Kurie* | *mē* | *stēsēs* | *autois* |
| with a voice | loud, | Lord, | not | lay | to them |

| 3450.12 art acc sing fem | 264.4 noun acc sing fem | 3642.12 dem-pron acc sing fem | 3642.12 dem-pron acc sing fem | 3450.12 art acc sing fem |
|---|---|---|---|---|
| ʽ τὴν | ἁμαρτίαν | ταύτην. | [☆ ταύτην | τὴν |
| *tēn* | *hamartian* | *tautēn* | *tautēn* | *tēn* |
| the | sin | this | [ this | the |

| 264.4 noun acc sing fem | 2504.1 conj | 3642.17 dem-pron sing neu | 1500.15 verb nom sing masc part aor act | 2810.5 verb 3sing indic aor pass |
|---|---|---|---|---|
| ἁμαρτίαν. ] | Καὶ | τοῦτο | εἰπὼν | ἐκοιμήθη. |
| *hamartian* | *Kai* | *touto* | *eipōn* | *ekoimēthē* |
| sin. ] | And | this | having said | he fell asleep. |

| 4425.1 name nom masc | 1156.2 conj | 1498.34 verb sing indic imperf act | 4759.4 verb nom sing masc part pres act | 3450.11 art dat sing fem |
|---|---|---|---|---|
| **8:1.** Σαῦλος | δὲ | ἦν | συνευδοκῶν | τῇ |
| *Saulos* | *de* | *ēn* | *suneudokōn* | *tē* |
| Saul | and | was | consenting | to the |

| 334.1 noun dat sing fem | 840.3 prs-pron gen sing | 1090.33 verb 3sing indic aor mid | 1156.2 conj | 1706.1 prep | 1552.11 dem-pron dat sing fem |
|---|---|---|---|---|---|
| ἀναιρέσει | αὐτοῦ. | Ἐγένετο | δὲ | ἐν | ἐκείνῃ |
| *anairesei* | *autou* | *Egeneto* | *de* | *en* | *ekeinē* |
| killing | of him. | Took place | and | on | that |

| 3450.11 art dat sing fem | 2232.3 noun dat sing fem | 1369.1 noun nom sing masc | 3144.2 adj nom sing masc | 1894.3 prep | 3450.12 art acc sing fem |
|---|---|---|---|---|---|
| τῇ | ἡμέρᾳ | διωγμὸς | μέγας | ἐπὶ | τὴν |
| *tē* | *hēmera* | *diōgmos* | *megas* | *epi* | *tēn* |
| the | day | a persecution | great | against | the |

| 1564.4 noun acc sing fem | 3450.12 art acc sing fem | 1706.1 prep | 2389.3 name dat pl neu | 3820.7 adj nom pl masc | 4885.1 conj |
|---|---|---|---|---|---|
| ἐκκλησίαν | τὴν | ἐν | Ἱεροσολύμοις· | πάντες | ʽ τε |
| *ekklēsian* | *tēn* | *en* | *Hierosolumois* | *pantes* | *te* |
| assembly | the | in | Jerusalem, | all | and |

1.a.**Txt:** 02A,byz.
**Var:** 03B,04C,05D,08E 025P,sa.bo.Lach,Treg Alf,We/Ho,Weis,Sod UBS/☆

| 1156.2 conj | 1283.1 verb 3pl indic aor pass | 2567.3 prep | 3450.15 art acc pl fem | 5396.1 noun fem |
|---|---|---|---|---|
| [a☆ δὲ ] | διεσπάρησαν | κατὰ | τὰς | χώρας |
| *de* | *diesparēsan* | *kata* | *tas* | *chōras* |
| [ idem ] | were scattered | throughout | the | countries |

| 3450.10 art gen sing fem | 2424.2 name gen fem | 2504.1 conj | 4397.2 name gen fem | 3993.1 adv | 3450.1 art gen pl |
|---|---|---|---|---|---|
| τῆς | Ἰουδαίας | καὶ | Σαμαρείας | πλὴν | τῶν |
| *tēs* | *Ioudaias* | *kai* | *Samareias* | *plēn* | *tōn* |
| | of Judea | and | Samaria | except | the |

**7:59.** While they were stoning Stephen he was calling on God saying, "Lord Jesus, receive (welcome) my spirit." He knew that to be absent from the body is to be present with the Lord (2 Corinthians 5:8). Although there is a great similarity between Stephen's confession and Jesus' (see verse 60), there is one striking contrast: Jesus "commended" His spirit to the Father but Stephen, to the Lord Jesus. This is one of the earliest and clearest testimonies to Jesus' deity by His followers.

**7:60.** Then Stephen knelt down and cried out with a loud voice "Lord, do not let this sin stand against them." ("Lay not this sin to their charge" is a paraphrase which gives the meaning.) How like Jesus this was! It reminds us of His cry, "Father, forgive them; for they know not what they do" (Luke 23:34).

Having said this, Stephen fell asleep. There was something peaceful about his death in spite of its violent nature. Stephen went to be with Jesus and became the first martyr of the Early Church, the first of a long line of believers who gave their lives for Jesus and the gospel.

**8:1.** The first sentence of this verse really belongs with the end of chapter 7. The Greek is a strong statement. Saul was not only consenting to Stephen's death, he wholly and completely approved of Stephen's murder and continued to act accordingly. He did not share the feelings of his former teacher, Gamaliel, as they were expressed in 5:38. Instead, he considered Stephen's ideas dangerous and felt they should be rooted out. (It seems possible that due to Stephen's strong defense, even Gamaliel may have changed his mind and joined in with the stoning of Stephen.) But they were all going to learn that neither Saul nor the rest of the Sanhedrin could root out the work of the Holy Spirit.

Saul was undoubtedly one of the chief instigators of the great persecution that arose against the Church in Jerusalem at that time (on the very day Stephen was murdered). So intense was this persecution that the believers were scattered in various directions throughout Judea and Samaria.

Some commentators believe the persecution was primarily, or even entirely, against the Hellenistic or Greek-speaking Jewish believers and that only these fled. But the Bible specifically says they all fled except the apostles. Some modern writers also suppose that the Jerusalem church contained no Hellenist believers after this. But the presence of Barnabas, a Hellenist, in 11:22, and his being sent as a representative of the Jerusalem Church, refutes this idea.

The 12 apostles remained undoubtedly because they were constrained to believe that God would still have a church in Jerusalem and that the city still needed to be a center for the further spread of the gospel.

**Lord Jesus, receive my spirit:** . . . take my spirit, *Klingensmith.*

**60. And he kneeled down, and cried with a loud voice:** He fell on his knees, *Everyday* . . . Falling on his knees, he called out loudly, *MLNT.*

**Lord, lay not this sin to their charge:** . . . mayest thou not lay to them this sin, *Young* . . . do not hold this sin against them! *Everyday* . . . do not count this sin against them, *Noli* . . . weigh not, *Fenton* . . . to their account, *Williams C.K.*

**And when he had said this, he fell asleep:** . . . and with these words, *Berkeley* . . . he fell into the sleep of death, *Phillips* . . . slept the sleep of death, *Moffatt* . . . he died, *TNT* . . . fell asleep in death, *MLNT.*

**1. And Saul was consenting unto his death:** Saul agreed that the killing of Stephen was a good thing, *Everyday* . . . Saul, for his part, concurred in the act of killing, *NAB* . . . was taking pleasure with them in his death, *Rotherham* . . . fully approved of his murder, *Weymouth* . . . entirely approved, *Goodspeed* . . . was altogether agreed to his murder, *Berkeley* . . . endorsing his assassination, *Concordant* . . . heartily approved, *Williams* . . . and participating, *Murdock* . . . was well pleased with his slaughter, *Campbell, Swann* . . . applauding it, *Wuest* . . . in hearty agreement with, *NASB.*

**And at that time there was a great persecution against the church which was at Jerusalem:** And there arose on that day, *ASV* . . . On that very day a great storm of persecution burst upon the Church in Jerusalem, *Phillips* . . . That day a great persecution...began, *Williams C.K.* . . . Just then a violent persecution broke out, *Fenton* . . . That very day...began to suffer cruel persecution, *TEV* . . . started that day against the church, *Klingensmith* . . . a fierce attack on the congregation, *SEB.*

**and they were all scattered abroad throughout the regions of Judaea and Samaria, except the apostles:** All Church Members, *Phillips* . . . were all dispersed, *Murdock* . . . among the districts, *Concordant.*

| 646.5 noun gen pl masc | 4643.1 verb 3pl indic aor act | 1156.2 conj | 3450.6 art acc sing masc | 4587.4 name acc masc |
|---|---|---|---|---|
| ἀποστόλων. | 2. συνεκόμισαν | δὲ | τὸν | Στέφανον |
| *apostolōn* | *sunekomisan* | *de* | *ton* | *Stephanon* |
| apostles. | Buried | and | | Stephen |

2.a.**Txt:** 08E,025P,byz. **Var:** 01ℵ,02A,03B,04C 05D,Lach,Treg,Alf Word,Tisc,We/Ho,Weis Sod,UBS/☆

| 433.6 noun nom pl masc | 2107.2 adj nom pl masc | 2504.1 conj | 4020.68 verb 3pl indic aor mid | 4020.27 verb 3pl indic aor act |
|---|---|---|---|---|
| ἄνδρες | εὐλαβεῖς, | καὶ | ʻ ἐποιήσαντο | [a☆ ἐποίησαν ] |
| *andres* | *eulabeis* | *kai* | *epoiēsanto* | *epoiēsan* |
| men | pious, | and | made | [ idem ] |

| 2842.1 noun acc sing masc | 3144.4 adj acc sing masc | 1894.2 prep | 840.4 prs-pron dat sing | 4425.1 name nom masc | 1156.2 conj |
|---|---|---|---|---|---|
| κοπετὸν | μέγαν | ἐπ' | αὐτῷ. | 3. Σαῦλος | δὲ |
| *kopeton* | *megan* | *ep'* | *autō* | *Saulos* | *de* |
| lamentation | great | over | him. | Saul | but |

| 3047.1 verb 3sing indic imperf mid | 3450.12 art acc sing fem | 1564.4 noun acc sing fem | 2567.3 prep | 3450.8 art acc pl masc |
|---|---|---|---|---|
| ἐλυμαίνετο | τὴν | ἐκκλησίαν, | κατὰ | τοὺς |
| *elumaineto* | *tēn* | *ekklēsian* | *kata* | *tous* |
| was ravaging | the | assembly, | according to | the |

| 3486.7 noun acc pl masc | 1515.3 verb nom sing masc part pres mid | 4803.2 verb nom sing masc part pres act | 4885.1 conj | 433.9 noun acc pl masc |
|---|---|---|---|---|
| οἴκους | εἰσπορευόμενος, | σύρων | τε | ἄνδρας |
| *oikous* | *eisporeuomenos* | *surōn* | *te* | *andras* |
| houses | entering, | dragging | and | men |

| 2504.1 conj | 1129.9 noun acc pl fem | 3722.26 verb 3sing indic imperf act | 1519.1 prep | 5274.4 noun acc sing fem | 3450.7 art nom pl masc |
|---|---|---|---|---|---|
| καὶ | γυναῖκας | παρεδίδου | εἰς | φυλακήν. | 4. Οἱ |
| *kai* | *gunaikas* | *paredidou* | *eis* | *phulakēn* | *Hoi* |
| and | women | was delivering up | to | prison. | The |

| 3173.1 conj | 3631.1 partic | 1283.2 verb nom pl masc part aor pass | 1324.1 verb indic aor act |
|---|---|---|---|
| μὲν | οὖν | διασπαρέντες | διῆλθον, |
| *men* | *oun* | *diasparentes* | *diēlthon* |
| indeed | therefore | having been scattered | passed through, |

| 2076.12 verb nom pl masc part pres mid | 3450.6 art acc sing masc | 3030.4 noun acc sing masc | 5213.1 name nom masc |
|---|---|---|---|
| εὐαγγελιζόμενοι | τὸν | λόγον. | 5. Φίλιππος |
| *euangelizomenoi* | *ton* | *logon* | *Philippos* |
| announcing the good news | the | word. | Philip |

5.a.**Var:** p74,01ℵ,02A 03B,Lach,Tisc,We/Ho Weis,UBS/☆

| 1156.2 conj | 2687.4 verb nom sing masc part aor act | 1519.1 prep | 3450.12 art acc sing fem | 4032.4 noun acc sing fem | 3450.10 art gen sing fem |
|---|---|---|---|---|---|
| δὲ | κατελθὼν | εἰς | [a☆+ τὴν ] | πόλιν | τῆς |
| *de* | *katelthōn* | *eis* | *tēn* | *polin* | *tēs* |
| and, | having gone down | to | [ the ] | a city | |

| 4397.2 name gen fem | 2756.20 verb 3sing indic imperf act | 840.2 prs-pron dat pl | 3450.6 art acc sing masc | 5382.4 name acc masc |
|---|---|---|---|---|
| Σαμαρείας | ἐκήρυσσεν | αὐτοῖς | τὸν | Χριστόν. |
| *Samareias* | *ekērussen* | *autois* | *ton* | *Christon* |
| of Samaria, | was proclaiming | to them | the | Christ; |

6.a.**Txt:** 08E,025P,byz. **Var:** 01ℵ,02A,03B,04C 05D-corr,sa.bo.Lach Treg,Alf,Word,Tisc We/Ho,Weis,Sod UBS/☆

| 4196.7 verb 3pl indic imperf act | 4885.1 conj | 1156.2 conj | 3450.7 art nom pl masc | 3657.5 noun nom pl masc |
|---|---|---|---|---|
| 6. προσεῖχον | ʻ τὲ | [a☆ δὲ ] | οἱ | ὄχλοι |
| *proseichon* | *te* | *de* | *hoi* | *ochloi* |
| were paying attention | and | [ idem ] | the | crowds |

**8:2.** This verse indicates that many of the Jerusalem Jews were sympathetic to the believers. Devout men carried Stephen out, buried him, and made a great lamentation, weeping and beating their breasts over him. This was unusual, for Jewish tradition was against showing this kind of respect or sorrow for an executed person.

"Devout men" refers to men like those of 2:5 where the same title is used. They were sincere, godly Jews who had not yet accepted Christ as their Messiah and Saviour, but who respected Stephen and rejected the decision of the Sanhedrin as wrong and unjust. Through them the Church in Jerusalem would grow again.

**8:3.** In contrast to the devout men who lamented over Stephen, Saul became more and more furious, more energetic in his persecution. "He made havoc" of the Church. Literally, he ravaged and devastated it. (The Septuagint version uses the same word of a wild boar tearing up vineyards.) Entering into house after house, he dragged out men and women and handed them over to be put into prison.

**8:4.** If Saul thought persecution would stop the spread of the gospel he was wrong. In fact, it had exactly the opposite effect. Prior to this persecution the believers were receiving teaching and training from the apostles. Now they were ready to move out. It took the persecution to make them do it but move out they did.

Those who were scattered did not go into hiding. Neither did they settle down. Instead, they kept traveling from place to place, spreading the good news, the gospel.

**8:5.** Many preached or proclaimed the gospel publicly, however. After the general statement in verse 4, Luke gave an example of what must have happened all over. Philip the deacon was chosen as this example, not because what happened in Samaria was greater than what happened elsewhere but because of the lessons learned there and because Samaria was next in line in the commission given in 1:8.

Jews avoided going through Samaria if at all possible, so it took courage for Philip to go there. But, like the others, he was led by the Spirit. (The city was rebuilt by Herod the Great and renamed Sebaste, which is Greek for Augustus and thus honored the Emperor, Caesar Augustus, but the Jews still called it Samaria. It was about 10 miles north of where Jesus talked to the woman at the well.) As soon as he arrived, Philip began to preach Christ, proclaiming the truth about Him as the Messiah and Saviour. The ministry of Jesus in Samaria (John 4) was not forgotten. These things were not done in a corner.

**2. And devout men carried Stephen to his burial:** And God fearing men, *BB* . . . While reverent men, *Phillips* . . . religious men, *Everyday* . . . buried Stephen, *ASV* . . . took charge of Stephen's funeral, *Berkeley.*

**and made great lamentation over him:** . . . making a great weeping, *BB* . . . sorrowed much, *Norlie* . . . cried very loudly for him, *Everyday.*

**3. As for Saul, he made havoc of the church:** But Saul laid waste the church, *ASV* . . . But Saul began ravaging the church, *NASB* . . . Now Saul devastated the Ecclesia, *Concordant* . . . On that day the Jews began trying to hurt the church in Jerusalem, *Everyday* . . . continued, *Williams* . . . to harass, *TCNT* . . . shamefully treated, *LivB* . . . worked for the total destruction, *JB.*

**entering into every house:** . . . entering house after house, *TCNT* . . . forcing himself into homes, *Berkeley.*

**and haling men and women committed them to prison:** . . . and dragging off, *Weymouth* . . . both men and women by their feet along the street, *Wuest.*

**4. Therefore they that were scattered abroad:** Nevertheless, *Campbell* . . . As a result, *Adams* . . . Now those who were scattered in different directions, *TCNT* . . . were dispersed, *ABUV* . . . had taken flight, *BB* . . . All the believers...went to different places, *Everyday.*

**went every where preaching the word:** . . . went from place to place, with the good News of the Message, *TCNT* . . . spreading the gospel of God's Word, *Weymouth* . . . proclaiming good news—the word, *Young.*

**5. Then Philip went down to the city of Samaria: and preached Christ unto them:** . . . and proclaimed unto them the Christ, *ASV* . . . and there began proclaiming the Messiah, *Rieu.*

**6. And the people with one accord gave heed unto those things which Philip spake:** Crowds of people with one accord gave attention, *Weymouth* . . . The crowds unanimously attended to the teachings of Philip, *Berkeley*

| 3450.4 art dat pl | 2978.36 verb dat pl neu part pres mid | 5097.3 prep | 3450.2 art gen sing | 5213.2 name gen masc | 3524.1 adv |
|---|---|---|---|---|---|
| τοῖς | λεγομένοις | ὑπὸ | τοῦ | Φιλίππου | ὁμοθυμαδὸν, |
| *tois* | *legomenois* | *hupo* | *tou* | *Philippou* | *homothumadon* |
| to the | being spoken | by | | Philip | with one accord, |

| 1706.1 prep | 3450.3 art dat sing | 189.17 verb inf pres act | 840.8 prs-pron acc pl masc | 2504.1 conj | 984.17 verb inf pres act | 3450.17 art pl neu |
|---|---|---|---|---|---|---|
| ἐν | τῷ | ἀκούειν | αὐτοὺς | καὶ | βλέπειν | τὰ |
| *en* | *tō* | *akouein* | *autous* | *kai* | *blepein* | *ta* |
| in | the | to hear | them | and | to see | the |

7.a.**Txt:** 025P,byz.bo.
**Var:** p74,01ℵ,02A,03B
04C,08E,sa.Lach,Treg
Alf,Tisc,We/Ho,Weis
Sod,UBS/☆

| 4447.2 noun pl neu | 3614.17 rel-pron pl neu | 4020.57 verb 3sing indic imperf act | | 4044.1 adj gen pl | 4044.7 adj nom pl masc |
|---|---|---|---|---|---|
| σημεῖα | ἃ | ἐποίει. | **7.** | ʽ πολλῶν | [a☆ πολλοὶ ] |
| *sēmeia* | *ha* | *epoiei* | | *pollōn* | *polloi* |
| signs | which | he was doing. | | Of many | [ many ] |

| 1056.1 conj | 3450.1 art gen pl | 2174.20 verb gen pl masc part pres act | 4011.4 noun pl neu | 167.5 adj pl neu | 987.4 verb pl neu part pres act |
|---|---|---|---|---|---|
| γὰρ | τῶν | ἐχόντων | πνεύματα | ἀκάθαρτα, | βοῶντα |
| *gar* | *tōn* | *echontōn* | *pneumata* | *akatharta* | *boōnta* |
| for | of the | having | spirits | unclean, | crying |

7.b.**Txt:** byz.
**Var:** 01ℵ,02A,03B,04C
05D,Lach,Treg,Alf
Word,Tisc,We/Ho,Weis
Sod,UBS/☆

| 3144.11 adj dat sing fem | 5292.3 noun dat sing fem | 1814.38 verb 3sing indic imperf mid | 5292.3 noun dat sing fem | 3144.11 adj dat sing fem |
|---|---|---|---|---|
| ʽ μεγάλῃ | φωνῇ | ἐξήρχετο· | [b☆ φωνῇ | μεγάλῃ |
| *megalē* | *phōnē* | *exērcheto* | *phōnē* | *megalē* |
| with a loud | voice | they were going out; | [ voice | with a loud |

| 1814.39 verb 3pl indic imperf mid | 4044.7 adj nom pl masc | 1156.2 conj | 3747.3 verb nom pl masc part perf mid | 2504.1 conj |
|---|---|---|---|---|
| ἐξήρχοντο, ] | πολλοὶ | δὲ | παραλελυμένοι | καὶ |
| *exērchonto* | *polloi* | *de* | *paralelumenoi* | *kai* |
| they were going out, ] | many | and | having been paralyzed | and |

| 5395.4 adj nom pl masc | 2300.15 verb 3pl indic aor pass | | 2504.1 conj | 1090.33 verb 3sing indic aor mid | 5315.1 noun nom sing fem |
|---|---|---|---|---|---|
| χωλοὶ | ἐθεραπεύθησαν. | **8.** | ʽ καὶ | ἐγένετο | χαρὰ |
| *chōloi* | *etherapeuthēsan* | | *kai* | *egeneto* | *chara* |
| lame | were healed. | | And | was | joy |

8.a.**Txt:** 08E,025P,byz.
**Var:** 01ℵ,02A,03B,04C
Lach,Treg,Alf,Tisc
We/Ho,Weis,Sod
UBS/☆

| 3144.9 adj nom sing fem | 1090.33 verb 3sing indic aor mid | 1156.2 conj | 4044.9 adj nom sing fem | 5315.1 noun nom sing fem | 1706.1 prep |
|---|---|---|---|---|---|
| μεγάλη | [a☆ ἐγένετο | δὲ | πολλὴ | χαρὰ ] | ἐν |
| *megalē* | *egeneto* | *de* | *pollē* | *chara* | *en* |
| great | [ was | and | much | joy ] | in |

| 3450.11 art dat sing fem | 4032.3 noun dat sing fem | 1552.11 dem-pron dat sing fem | | 433.1 noun nom sing masc | 1156.2 conj | 4948.3 indef-pron nom sing |
|---|---|---|---|---|---|---|
| τῇ | πόλει | ἐκείνῃ. | **9.** | Ἀνὴρ | δέ | τις |
| *tē* | *polei* | *ekeinē* | | *Anēr* | *de* | *tis* |
| the | city | that. | | A man | but | certain, |

| 3549.4 noun dat sing neu | 4468.1 name nom masc | 4249.1 verb 3sing indic imperf act | 1706.1 prep | 3450.11 art dat sing fem | 4032.3 noun dat sing fem |
|---|---|---|---|---|---|
| ὀνόματι | Σίμων | προϋπῆρχεν | ἐν | τῇ | πόλει |
| *onomati* | *Simōn* | *proupērchen* | *en* | *tē* | *polei* |
| by name | Simon, | was formerly | in | the | city |

9.a.**Txt:** 05D-corr,08E
025P,byz.Sod
**Var:** 01ℵ,02A,03B,04C
Lach,Treg,Alf,Tisc
We/Ho,Weis,UBS/☆

| 3068.1 verb nom sing masc part pres act | 2504.1 conj | 1822.1 verb nom sing masc part pres act | 1822.9 verb nom sing masc part pres act | 3450.16 art sing neu |
|---|---|---|---|---|
| μαγεύων | καὶ | ʽ ἐξιστῶν | [a☆ ἐξιστάνων ] | τὸ |
| *mageuōn* | *kai* | *existōn* | *existanōn* | *to* |
| using magic arts | and | amazing | [ idem ] | the |

**8:6.** The crowds (including all classes of people) with one accord paid attention to Philip's message, listening to him, both hearing and seeing the miracles (signs) he kept doing. The Lord's promise to confirm the Word with signs following was not limited to the apostles (Mark 16:20).

**8:7.** The people heard those having unclean spirits shouting with a loud voice as they came out. They saw those who were paralyzed and who were lame healed. (Palsy here means paralysis.) Here the Bible clearly distinguishes between afflictions that were due to the direct activity of demons and those which were simply "diseases." In both cases, the miraculous healings and deliverances functioned as "signs" which confirmed the message Philip was preaching.

**8:8.** In contrast to the rejection and persecution going on in Jerusalem, the people of Samaria were open to the gospel. There was no opposition, no criticism. Instead, there was great joy and rejoicing. This was the joy of health and salvation.

**8:9.** The success of the gospel in Samaria was an even greater miracle than it first appeared, for these people previously had been filled with astonishment and amazement by a man named Simon. He practiced sorcery (Greek, *mageuōn*, a plural, meaning magic arts or magic tricks). "Bewitched" in the King James Version is the same Greek word which is rendered "wondered" in verse 13. It does not imply any supernatural power on the part of Simon. He depended on trickery, though he may also have dabbled in the occult. He did not claim to be in touch with evil spirits or demon powers as so many heathen magicians did. Instead, he claimed he was someone great (or some great being).

Apparently, he did not say he was a divine being or a messiah, but he talked enough about his greatness and about his powers that he was obviously trying to give the impression that he was more than human.

Simon, also referred to as Simon Magus, is the subject behind a great deal of legend popularized in the Early Church. Irenaeus, for example, reports that Simon was the father of gnosticism. Furthermore, in an apocryphal work by Hippolytus entitled *The Acts of Peter*, Simon is said to have boasted against Peter and claimed that he would rise on the third day if buried alive. He did not (Bruce, *New International Commentary on the New Testament, Acts*, pp.178f.). At this point it is not possible to verify for certain if the Simon of these legends and traditions is in fact the Simon of Acts chapter 8. Nevertheless, the people of the area revered him.

. . . listened very carefully, *SEB* . . . one and all, listened attentively, *TCNT* . . . acquiesced, *Murdock* . . . unitedly paid attention, *Adams.*

**hearing and seeing the miracles which he did:** . . . when they heard of, and saw, the signs, *TCNT* . . . especially when they saw, *Beck* . . . they watched him do powerful works, *NLT.*

**7. For unclean spirits, crying with loud voice:** For there were many cases of people with wicked spirits, *TCNT*. . . came shrieking out of many, *JB* . . . For many of those under the power of foul spirits, *Williams* . . . screaming with a loud voice, *MLNT.*

**came out of many that were possessed with them:** . . . where the spirits, with loud screams, came out of them, *TCNT* . . . those who were plagued, *Beck.*

**and many taken with palsies, and that were lame, were healed:** . . . and many who were paralyzed and lame were cured, *TCNT* . . . and many paralytics and lame persons were restored to health, *Weymouth* . . . Many weak and crippled people were also, *NCV* . . . people could not move their bodies or arms and legs, *NLT.*

**8. And there was great joy in that city:** . . . much joy, *ASV* . . . so that there was great rejoicing throughout that city, *TCNT* . . . much rejoicing in that city, *Berkeley* . . . The rejoicing in that town rose to fever pitch, *NAB* . . . So the people in that city were very happy, *Everyday.*

**9. But there was a certain man, called Simon:** Simon by name, *ASV.*

**which beforetime in the same city used sorcery:** . . . had been using, *KJII* . . . magical arts, *Rotherham* . . . who had been practising magic there, *TCNT* . . . practicing witchcraft, *Beck* . . . did magic tricks, *SEB* . . . and who made great pretensions, *Goodspeed.*

**and bewitched the people of Samaria:** . . . and amazing the nation of Samaria, *HBIE* . . . amazed all the people, *Everyday* . . . and astonishing the Samaritans, *Weymouth* . . . who had kept the Samaritan people thrilled, *Williams*

**Acts 8:10**

| 1477.1 noun sing neu | 3450.10 art gen sing fem | 4397.2 name gen fem | 2978.15 verb nom sing masc part pres act | 1498.32 verb inf pres act | 4948.5 indef-pron |
|---|---|---|---|---|---|
| ἔθνος | τῆς | Σαμαρείας, | λέγων | εἶναί | τινα |
| *ethnos* | *tēs* | *Samareias* | *legōn* | *einai* | *tina* |
| nation | | of Samaria, | saying | to be | some |

| 1431.6 prs-pron acc sing masc | 3144.4 adj acc sing masc | 3614.3 rel-pron dat sing | 4196.7 verb 3pl indic imperf act | 3820.7 adj nom pl masc |
|---|---|---|---|---|
| ἑαυτὸν | μέγαν˙ | **10.** ᾧ | προσεῖχον | πάντες |
| *heauton* | *megan* | *hō* | *proseichon* | *pantes* |
| himself | great one. | To whom | were paying attention | all |

| 570.3 prep | 3262.4 adj gen sing masc | 2175.1 conj | 3144.3 adj gen sing masc | 2978.16 verb nom pl masc part pres act | 3642.4 dem-pron nom sing masc |
|---|---|---|---|---|---|
| ἀπὸ | μικροῦ | ἕως | μεγάλου, | λέγοντες, | Οὗτός |
| *apo* | *mikrou* | *heōs* | *megalou* | *legontes* | *Houtos* |
| from | small | to | great, | saying, | This one |

| 1498.4 verb 3sing indic pres act | 3450.9 art nom sing fem | 1405.1 noun nom sing fem | 3450.2 art gen sing | 2296.2 noun gen sing masc | 3450.9 art nom sing fem |
|---|---|---|---|---|---|
| ἐστιν | ἡ | δύναμις | τοῦ | θεοῦ | ἡ |
| *estin* | *hē* | *dunamis* | *tou* | *theou* | *hē* |
| is | the | power | | of God | the |

10.a.**Var:** p74,01ℵ,02A 03B,04C,05D,08E,33,it. bo.Gries,Lach,Treg,Alf Word,Tisc,We/Ho,Weis Sod,UBS/⋆

| 2535.31 verb nom sing fem part pres mid | 3144.9 adj nom sing fem | 4196.7 verb 3pl indic imperf act | 1156.2 conj |
|---|---|---|---|
| [a⋆+ καλουμένη ] | μεγάλη. | **11.** προσεῖχον | δὲ |
| *kaloumenē* | *megalē* | *proseichon* | *de* |
| [ being called ] | great. | They were paying attention | and |

| 840.4 prs-pron dat sing | 1217.2 prep | 3450.16 art sing neu | 2401.5 adj dat sing masc | 5385.3 noun dat sing masc | 3450.14 art dat pl fem | 3067.1 noun dat pl fem |
|---|---|---|---|---|---|---|
| αὐτῷ, | διὰ | τὸ | ἱκανῷ | χρόνῳ | ταῖς | μαγείαις |
| *autō* | *dia* | *to* | *hikanō* | *chronō* | *tais* | *mageiais* |
| to him, | because | the | for a long | time | with the | magic arts |

| 1822.5 verb inf perf act | 840.8 prs-pron acc pl masc | 3616.1 conj | 1156.2 conj | 3961.23 verb 3pl indic aor act | 3450.3 art dat sing |
|---|---|---|---|---|---|
| ἐξεστακέναι | αὐτούς. | **12.** Ὅτε | δὲ | ἐπίστευσαν | τῷ |
| *exestakenai* | *autous* | *Hote* | *de* | *episteusan* | *tō* |
| to amaze | them. | When | but | they believed | |

12.a.**Txt:** 020L,025P,byz. **Var:** 01ℵ,02A,03B,04C 05D,08E,sa.bo.Lach Treg,Alf,Word,Tisc We/Ho,Weis,Sod UBS/⋆

| 5213.3 name dat masc | 2076.11 verb dat sing masc part pres mid | 3450.17 art pl neu | 3875.1 prep | 3450.10 art gen sing fem |
|---|---|---|---|---|
| Φιλίππῳ | εὐαγγελιζομένῳ | ⸂a τὰ ⸃ | περὶ | τῆς |
| *Philippō* | *euangelizomenō* | *ta* | *peri* | *tēs* |
| Philip | announcing good news | the things | concerning | the |

| 926.1 noun fem | 3450.2 art gen sing | 2296.2 noun gen sing masc | 2504.1 conj | 3450.2 art gen sing | 3549.3 noun gen sing neu |
|---|---|---|---|---|---|
| βασιλείας | τοῦ | θεοῦ | καὶ | τοῦ | ὀνόματος |
| *basileias* | *tou* | *theou* | *kai* | *tou* | *onomatos* |
| kingdom | | of God | and | the | name |

12.b.**Txt:** byz. **Var:** 01ℵ,02A,03B,04C 05D,08E,020L,025P Gries,Lach,Treg,Alf Word,Tisc,We/Ho,Weis Sod,UBS/⋆

| 3450.2 art gen sing | 2400.2 name masc | 5382.2 name gen masc | 901.28 verb 3pl indic imperf pass | 433.6 noun nom pl masc |
|---|---|---|---|---|
| ⸂b τοῦ ⸃ | Ἰησοῦ | Χριστοῦ, | ἐβαπτίζοντο | ἄνδρες |
| *tou* | *Iēsou* | *Christou* | *ebaptizonto* | *andres* |
| | of Jesus | Christ, | they were being baptized | men |

| 4885.1 conj | 2504.1 conj | 1129.6 noun nom pl fem | 3450.5 art nom sing masc | 1156.2 conj | 4468.1 name nom masc | 2504.1 conj |
|---|---|---|---|---|---|---|
| τε | καὶ | γυναῖκες. | **13.** ὁ | δὲ | Σίμων | καὶ |
| *te* | *kai* | *gunaikes* | *ho* | *de* | *Simōn* | *kai* |
| both | and | women. | | And | Simon | also |

**8:10.** To Simon, all (from the least to the greatest in Samaria) gave attention, giving heed to him, even considering themselves to be his followers, for they said, "This man is the power of God which is called great." (Or, as many ancient manuscripts have it, "This man is the great power of God.")

The people were thus deceived by one who drew attention to himself. Like most who dealt with the occult, he encouraged the people to follow their own pride and fleshly inclinations.

Actually, such magicians were quite common in the Roman Empire in New Testament times. The emperor Tiberius, especially in the latter part of his reign, kept a large number of magicians as advisers in his court. The apostle Paul later came in contact with another of them, Elymas, on the island of Cyprus (13:8).

**8:11.** The people of Samaria had given heed, paid attention, and considered themselves followers of Simon for some time, because he amazed them with his magic tricks. The Greek word *mageiais*, "magic tricks," is sometimes translated "sorcery." Actually, sorcery, divination, astrology, witchcraft, fortune-telling, demon worship, and various kinds of magic were all part of the heathen religions of ancient times and are all condemned in the Bible.

This was all the devil's territory, and anything that seemed supernatural had to come from Satan's power or from magic tricks. Archaeologists have found speaking tubes, trap doors, and other such things in ancient temples and shrines. These were used to fool the people and make them think something supernatural was happening. Hypnotism and drugs were also used by ancient magicians to produce special effects. How much of this Simon used is not known, but he probably used a combination of the occult and trickery to amaze the people. The Greek indicates this had a continuing effect on them. They were astounded, astonished, and almost afraid of him.

**8:12.** When Philip came, the people saw something far more wonderful in his miracles. The tricks and false miracles of Simon faded into insignificance in the presence of the genuine power of God. Furthermore, Philip did not draw attention to himself or exalt himself. He brought the good news of the kingdom of God, that is, of God's divine power, rule, and authority that was and is the assurance that God is carrying out His great plan of redemption. He also brought good news of the Name, that is, the authority, nature, and character of Jesus. Philip told the people the facts of the gospel that are found not only in the preaching in the Book of Acts but also in the Gospels. He showed them from the Old Testament Scriptures that the rule and power of God is and will be manifest through Christ in His character and nature.

The people believed, not just Philip but also the truth he proclaimed. They accepted what Philip told them about Christ's work as the crucified and risen Saviour and Lord and were all baptized, both men and women.

. . . and holding the Samaritans spellbound, *NAB* . . . he fooled them with his witchcraft, *NLT*.

**giving out that himself was some great one:** He boasted, *NIV* . . . pretending that he was more than human, *Weymouth* . . . bragged and called himself a great man, *Everyday* . . . some extraordinary person, *Campbell* . . . a man of note, *Norlie* . . . that he was a remarkable person, *MLNT* . . . someone momentous, *JB*.

**10. To whom they all gave heed, from the least to the greatest, saying:** Every one, high and low, listened attentively to him, *TCNT* . . . all sorts and conditions of people attached themselves, *Moffatt* . . . inclined towards him, *Murdock* . . . To him people of all classes paid attention, *Weymouth* . . . Everybody, high and low, kept running after him, *Williams* . . . all paid regard, *Campbell* . . . was fascinated by him, *Phillips*.

**This man is the great power of God:** He must be what they call, *Williams C.K.* . . . This man, they used to say, must be that Power of God which men call The Great Power, *TCNT* . . . the Power of God, known as the Great Power, *Weymouth*.

**11. And to him they had regard:** And they gave heed to him, *ASV* . . . They paid attention to him because, *TNT* . . . the people became his followers, *Everyday*.

**because that of long time he had bewitched them with sorceries:** . . . he had for long astonished them, *Williams C.K.* . . . thrilled them with his magical performances, *Williams* . . . he had astounded them, *Adams* . . . deeds of magic, *Young* . . . his enchantments, *Campbell* . . . his skill in magic, *Norlie*.

**12. But when they believed Philip preaching the things concerning the kingdom of God, and the name of Jesus Christ:** But now they believed, *LivB* . . . Philip's good news, *Williams C.K.* . . . message of the good news of the kingdom, *Weymouth* . . . and the authority of Jesus, *SEB*.

**they were baptized, both men and women:** . . . were constantly baptized, *Williams*.

| **840.5** prs-pron nom sing masc | **3961.20** verb 3sing indic aor act | **2504.1** conj | **901.22** verb nom sing masc part aor pass | **1498.34** verb sing indic imperf act |
|---|---|---|---|---|
| αὐτὸς | ἐπίστευσεν, | καὶ | βαπτισθεὶς | ἦν |
| *autos* | *episteusen* | *kai* | *baptistheis* | *ēn* |
| himself | believed, | and | having been baptized | was |

| **4201.3** verb nom sing masc part pres act | **3450.3** art dat sing | **5213.3** name dat masc | **2311.9** verb nom sing masc part pres act | **4885.1** conj |
|---|---|---|---|---|
| προσκαρτερῶν | τῷ | Φιλίππῳ· | θεωρῶν | τε |
| *proskarterōn* | *tō* | *Philippō* | *theōrōn* | *te* |
| steadfastly continuing | | with Philip; | beholding | and |

| **4447.2** noun pl neu | **2504.1** conj | **1405.5** noun pl fem | **3144.15** adj acc pl fem | **1090.24** verb acc pl fem part pres mid |
|---|---|---|---|---|
| σημεῖα | καὶ | δυνάμεις | μεγάλας | γινομένας, |
| *sēmeia* | *kai* | *dunameis* | *megalas* | *ginomenas* |
| signs | and | works of power | great | being done, |

| **1822.7** verb 3sing indic imperf mid | **189.32** verb nom pl masc part aor act | **1156.2** conj | **3450.7** art nom pl masc | **1706.1** prep |
|---|---|---|---|---|
| ἐξίστατο. | **14.** Ἀκούσαντες | δὲ | οἱ | ἐν |
| *existato* | *Akousantes* | *de* | *hoi* | *en* |
| was being amazed. | Having heard | and | the | in |

| **2389.3** name dat pl neu | **646.4** noun nom pl masc | **3617.1** conj | **1203.17** verb 3sing indic perf mid | **3450.9** art nom sing fem |
|---|---|---|---|---|
| Ἱεροσολύμοις | ἀπόστολοι | ὅτι | δέδεκται | ἡ |
| *Hierosolumois* | *apostoloi* | *hoti* | *dedektai* | *hē* |
| Jerusalem | apostles | that | had received | |

| **4397.1** name nom fem | **3450.6** art acc sing masc | **3030.4** noun acc sing masc | **3450.2** art gen sing | **2296.2** noun gen sing masc | **643.9** verb 3pl indic aor act |
|---|---|---|---|---|---|
| Σαμάρεια | τὸν | λόγον | τοῦ | θεοῦ, | ἀπέστειλαν |
| *Samareia* | *ton* | *logon* | *tou* | *theou* | *apesteilan* |
| Samaria | the | word | | of God, | they sent |

14.a.**Txt:** 020L,025P,byz. **Var:** 01ℵ,02A,03B,04C 05D,08E,Lach,Treg,Alf Word,Tisc,We/Ho,Weis Sod,UBS/☆

| **4242.1** prep | **840.8** prs-pron acc pl masc | **3450.6** art acc sing masc | **3935.4** name acc masc | **2504.1** conj | **2464.4** name acc masc |
|---|---|---|---|---|---|
| πρὸς | αὐτοὺς | ⌜a τὸν⌝ | Πέτρον | καὶ | Ἰωάννην, |
| *pros* | *autous* | *ton* | *Petron* | *kai* | *Iōannēn* |
| to | them | | Peter | and | John; |

| **3610.2** rel-pron nom pl masc | **2568.22** verb nom pl masc part aor act | **4195.18** verb 3pl indic aor mid | **3875.1** prep | **840.1** prs-pron gen pl |
|---|---|---|---|---|
| **15.** οἵτινες | καταβάντες | προσηύξαντο | περὶ | αὐτῶν, |
| *hoitines* | *katabantes* | *prosēuxanto* | *peri* | *autōn* |
| who | having come down | prayed | for | them, |

| **3567.1** conj | **2956.21** verb 3pl subj aor act | **4011.1** noun sing neu | **39.1** adj sing | **3632.1** adv |
|---|---|---|---|---|
| ὅπως | λάβωσιν | πνεῦμα | ἅγιον. | **16.** ⌜ οὔπω |
| *hopōs* | *labōsin* | *pneuma* | *hagion* | *oupō* |
| that | they might receive | Spirit | Holy; | not yet |

16.a.**Txt:** 020L,025P,byz. **Var:** 01ℵ,02A,03B,04C 05D,08E,Lach,Treg,Alf Word,Tisc,We/Ho,Weis Sod,UBS/☆

| **3627.1** adv | **1056.1** conj | **1498.34** verb sing indic imperf act | **1894.2** prep | **3625.7** num card dat neu | **840.1** prs-pron gen pl |
|---|---|---|---|---|---|
| [a☆ οὐδέπω ] | γὰρ | ἦν | ἐπ’ | οὐδενὶ | αὐτῶν |
| *oudepō* | *gar* | *ēn* | *ep'* | *oudeni* | *autōn* |
| [ idem ] | for | was he | upon | not any | of them |

| **1953.6** verb sing neu part perf act | **3303.1** adv | **1156.2** conj | **901.26** verb nom pl masc part perf pass | **5062.13** verb 3pl indic imperf act |
|---|---|---|---|---|
| ἐπιπεπτωκός, | μόνον | δὲ | βεβαπτισμένοι | ὑπῆρχον |
| *epipeptōkos* | *monon* | *de* | *bebaptismenoi* | *hupērchon* |
| having fallen, | only | but | having been baptized | they were |

**8:13.** Finally, even Simon himself believed and was baptized. Then he attached himself persistently and constantly to Philip, following him around, not letting him out of his sight. Simon was accustomed to deceiving people by his magic tricks and knew astonishing things can be done by trickery. He had watched Philip with the professional eye of a magician and had come to the conclusion that the miracles done by Philip were real. Clearly, these signs and great deeds of power were supernatural. So he too "wondered," that is, he was filled with wonder and amazement. He had to admit these miracles were quite unlike the magic tricks and occult practices by which he had gained attention.

Some have questioned whether Simon truly believed. This verse indicates he did. It uses the same form of the verb as is used of the others in Samaria and does not qualify the statement in any way. Moreover, it is likely that Philip, a man led by the Holy Spirit, would not have baptized Simon if he had not given evidence of being a true believer. (Even John the Baptist had enough spiritual discernment not to baptize the Pharisees and Sadducees who came to him but had not genuinely repented. See Matthew 3:7.)

**8:14.** The news that Samaria had "received (welcomed and was continuing to welcome) the Word of God" soon reached the apostles in Jerusalem. They sent Peter and John to Samaria. As a body the apostles commissioned Peter and John as their representatives and sent them with a message and a purpose to encourage the new believers. There is no indication, however, that they wanted to take control of what was going on. Neither is there any indication that they thought Philip's ministry was in any way deficient, inferior, or lacking in any way. They just wanted to help him and encourage and strengthen the new believers. Neither is there any thought that Peter and John were the chief apostles or that Peter was some sort of a pope.

**8:15,16.** When Peter and John arrived, the first thing they did was to pray for the Samaritan believers to receive the Holy Spirit. Elsewhere in Acts, the Holy Spirit was received both at the time of being baptized in the name of Jesus (cf. 2:38,41) and even before water baptism (10:44-48). Several explanations have been given to explain the present situation. Some believe the Spirit was given only when an apostle (or some official delegate of God) laid his hands on an individual. Others say the faith of the Samaritans was somehow defective, that is, they were not truly converted through the preaching (and baptism) of Philip. Another view states that God withheld the Holy Spirit until delegates from the Jerusalem (Jewish Christians) church arrived. He did this in order to emphasize that Samaritans were not to be excluded fellowship in the body of Christ. This "Samaritan Pentecost" was to serve as evidence that God accepts the Gentile as well as the Jew.

One final explanation is that although the Samaritans had become Christians, they had not received the "promise of the Father"

**13. Then Simon himself believed also:** Indeed Simon himself believed, *TCNT* . . . became a believer, *Williams C.K.*

**and when he was baptized:** . . . after his baptism, *Kleist* . . . baptized like the rest, *NAB.*

**he continued with Philip:** . . . devoted himself to Philip, *Goodspeed* . . . and attached himself closely to Philip, *TNT* . . . kept close to, *MLNT, Williams C.K.* . . . and became a devoted follower of, *NAB* . . . He went along with Philip everywhere, *NLT.*

**and wondered, beholding the miracles and signs which were done:** . . . and was full of amazement at seeing such signs and such great miracles performed, *Weymouth* . . . he was always thrilled, *Williams* . . . As he saw the signs and remarkable demonstrations of power which took place, he lived in a state of constant wonder, *Phillips* . . . was amazed at the sight of the signs and exceedingly great miracles being effected, *Kleist* . . . was astonished, *Williams C.K.* . . . he was continually performing, *Norlie.*

**14. Now when the apostles which were at Jerusalem: heard that Samaria had received the word of God:** The apostles were still in Jerusalem, *NCV* . . . heard that the Samaritans had welcomed God's Message, *TCNT* . . . welcomed the message of God, *MLNT* . . . accepted God's message, *Williams.*

**they sent unto them Peter and John:** . . . sent on a mission to them, *Wuest* . . . they despatched, *Moffatt.*

**15. Who, when they were come down, prayed for them, that they might receive the Holy Ghost:** On their arrival, they prayed that the Samaritans might receive the Holy Spirit, *TCNT* . . . prayed for the believers to receive the Holy Spirit, *Berkeley* . . . in order that, *Wuest* . . . prayed that the new followers, *NLT.*

**16. (For as yet he was fallen upon none of them:** . . . so far, *Adams* . . . For He had not as yet fallen upon any of them, *Weymouth* . . . alighted upon, *Fenton* . . . thus far, *Berkeley* . . . had not yet come down on any of them, *SEB.*

| 1519.1 | 3450.16 art | 3549.2 noun | 3450.2 art | 2935.2 noun | 2400.2 |
|---|---|---|---|---|---|
| prep | sing neu | sing neu | gen sing | gen sing masc | name masc |
| εἰς | τὸ | ὄνομα | τοῦ | κυρίου | Ἰησοῦ. |
| *eis* | *to* | *onoma* | *tou* | *kuriou* | *Iēsou* |
| to | the | name | of the | Lord | Jesus. |

17.a.**Txt:** 05D-org,08E 020L,025P,byz.
**Var:** 01ℵ,02A,05D-corr Lach,Treg,Alf,Tisc We/Ho,Weis,Sod UBS/☆

| 4966.1 | 1991.2 verb 3pl | 1991.25 verb 3pl | 3450.15 art | 5331.8 noun |
|---|---|---|---|---|
| adv | indic imperf act | indic imperf act | acc pl fem | acc pl fem |
| **17.** τότε | ‹ ἐπετίθουν | [a ἐπετίθεσαν ] | τὰς | χεῖρας |
| *tote* | *epetithoun* | *epetithesan* | *tas* | *cheiras* |
| Then | they laid | [ were laying ] | the | hands |

| 1894.2 | 840.8 prs-pron | 2504.1 | 2956.36 verb 3pl | 4011.1 noun | 39.1 |
|---|---|---|---|---|---|
| prep | acc pl masc | conj | indic imperf act | sing neu | adj sing |
| ἐπ' | αὐτούς, | καὶ | ἐλάμβανον | πνεῦμα | ἅγιον. |
| *ep'* | *autous* | *kai* | *elambanon* | *pneuma* | *hagion* |
| upon | them, | and | they were receiving | Spirit | Holy. |

18.a.**Txt:** 020L,025P,byz.
**Var:** 01ℵ,02A,03B,04C 05D,08E,Lach,Treg,Alf Word,Tisc,We/Ho,Weis Sod,UBS/☆

| 2277.7 verb nom sing | 1481.16 verb nom | 1156.2 | 3450.5 art | 4468.1 name |
|---|---|---|---|---|
| masc part aor mid | sing masc part aor act | conj | nom sing masc | nom masc |
| **18.** ‹ Θεασάμενος | [a☆ ἰδὼν ] | δὲ | ὁ | Σίμων |
| *Theasamenos* | *idōn* | *de* | *ho* | *Simōn* |
| Having seen | [ idem ] | but | | Simon |

| 3617.1 | 1217.2 | 3450.10 art | 1921.1 noun | 3450.1 | 5331.6 noun | 3450.1 |
|---|---|---|---|---|---|---|
| conj | prep | gen sing fem | gen sing fem | art gen pl | gen pl fem | art gen pl |
| ὅτι | διὰ | τῆς | ἐπιθέσεως | τῶν | χειρῶν | τῶν |
| *hoti* | *dia* | *tēs* | *epitheseōs* | *tōn* | *cheirōn* | *tōn* |
| that | by | the | laying on | of the | hands | of the |

18.b.**Txt:** p45,p74,02A 04C,05D,08E,020L 025P,33,etc.byz.syr.it.bo. Sod
**Var:** 01ℵ,03B,sa.Alf Tisc,We/Ho,Weis UBS/☆

| 646.5 noun | 1319.42 verb 3sing | 3450.16 art | 4011.1 noun | 3450.16 art |
|---|---|---|---|---|
| gen pl masc | indic pres mid | sing neu | sing neu | sing neu |
| ἀποστόλων | δίδοται | τὸ | πνεῦμα | ‹b τὸ |
| *apostolōn* | *didotai* | *to* | *pneuma* | *to* |
| apostles | was given | the | Spirit | the |

| 39.1 | 4232.12 verb 3sing | 840.2 prs- | 5371.2 | 2978.15 verb nom sing |
|---|---|---|---|---|
| adj sing | indic aor act | pron dat pl | noun pl neu | masc part pres act |
| ἅγιον, › | προσήνεγκεν | αὐτοῖς | χρήματα, | **19.** λέγων, |
| *hagion* | *prosēnenken* | *autois* | *chrēmata* | *legōn* |
| Holy, | he offered | to them | riches, | saying, |

| 1319.27 verb | 2476.1 prs- | 3450.12 art | 1833.4 noun | 3642.12 dem- | 2419.1 |
|---|---|---|---|---|---|
| 2pl impr aor act | pron dat | acc sing fem | acc sing fem | pron acc sing fem | conj |
| Δότε | κἀμοὶ | τὴν | ἐξουσίαν | ταύτην, | ἵνα |
| *Dote* | *kamoi* | *tēn* | *exousian* | *tautēn* | *hina* |
| Give | also to me | the | authority | this, | that |

19.a.**Txt:** 05D,Steph
**Var:** 01ℵ,02A,03B,04C 08E,020L,025P,byz. Elzev,Gries,Lach,Treg Alf,Word,Tisc,We/Ho Weis,Sod,UBS/☆

| 3614.3 rel- | 300.1 | 1430.1 | 1991.8 verb 1sing | 3450.15 art |
|---|---|---|---|---|
| pron dat sing | partic | partic | subj aor act | acc pl fem |
| ᾧ | ‹ ἂν | [a☆ ἐὰν ] | ἐπιθῶ | τὰς |
| *hō* | *an* | *ean* | *epithō* | *tas* |
| on whomsoever | | | I may lay | the |

| 5331.8 noun | 2956.7 verb 3sing | 4011.1 noun | 39.1 | 3935.1 name | 1156.2 |
|---|---|---|---|---|---|
| acc pl fem | subj pres act | sing neu | adj sing | nom masc | conj |
| χεῖρας, | λαμβάνῃ | πνεῦμα | ἅγιον. | **20.** Πέτρος | δὲ |
| *cheiras* | *lambanē* | *pneuma* | *hagion* | *Petros* | *de* |
| hands, | he may receive | Spirit | Holy. | Peter | but |

| 1500.5 verb 3sing | 4242.1 | 840.6 prs-pron | 3450.16 art | 688.1 noun | 4622.2 prs- |
|---|---|---|---|---|---|
| indic aor act | prep | acc sing masc | sing neu | sing neu | pron gen 2sing |
| εἶπεν | πρὸς | αὐτόν, | Τὸ | ἀργύριόν | σου |
| *eipen* | *pros* | *auton* | *To* | *argurion* | *sou* |
| said | to | him, | The | money | your |

which Jesus told His disciples to tarry for (1:4,5). It is presumed, from what follows in verse 19, that the supernatural signs recorded in 2:4-8 also accompanied this outpouring of the Holy Spirit. This text, then, serves as evidence for a second work of grace following conversion and is referred to as the baptism of (in) the Holy Spirit, using the wording of 1:5 (see also 2:4ff.).

**8:17.** Not until after they prayed for the Samaritan believers did the apostles lay hands on them. Then God confirmed the faith of the believers, and they received the Holy Spirit, and they kept receiving the Spirit publicly as the apostles laid hands on them.

**8:18.** Whether or not the apostles laid hands on Simon is not explicitly stated in the text. What is stated, however, is that Simon was very interested in possessing the power he observed in Peter and John. He was prepared to pay for the power of imparting the Holy Spirit through the laying on of hands. (Note that the word "simony" refers to buying or selling a position in the church.)

Verse 13 indicates that Simon, after believing and being baptized, observed the miracles which followed Philip's ministry. Nevertheless, he was more impressed by the signs which accompanied the receiving of the Spirit. Many insist that these believers spoke in tongues just as on the Day of Pentecost. This may have been the power Simon sought to purchase: power to impart the gift of speaking in tongues.

**8:19.** Simon's offering was conditional. He would give them the money if they would give him the power (the authority) to lay his hands on people and have them receive the Holy Spirit.

In saying this he jumped to the wrong conclusion. The Bible does not indicate that the apostles could lay hands on whomever they wanted to and have them receive the Spirit. As we have seen, they prayed first. Then they laid hands on the believers.

Simon was wrong too in thinking that the laying on of hands was necessary for receiving the Spirit. There was no laying on of hands on the Day of Pentecost or at the house of Cornelius. Nor was the laying on of hands limited to the apostles or to those delegated by them. Ananias, a layman of Damascus, laid his hands on Saul (who became Paul) for both healing and the receiving of the Holy Spirit. The laying on of hands here was a means of welcoming them as fellow believers and of encouraging their faith to receive (actively) the gift of the Spirit.

**8:20.** Peter rebuked Simon severely. Literally, he said, "Let your money (silver) together with you go into destruction (probably the



**only they were baptized in the name of the Lord Jesus.):** . . . they had simply been baptized, *Montgomery* . . . they had received nothing so far except, *Knox* . . . into the Faith of Jesus, *TCNT* . . . having been baptized, they belonged to the name of the Lord Jesus, *Concordant.*

**17. Then laid they their hands on them:** Then they put their hands on them, *BB* . . . Then, when the two apostles began laying their hands on the people, *Everyday* . . . placed their hands on them, *Berkeley* . . . The pair upon arriving imposed hands on them, *NAB* . . . one after another, *Wuest.*

**and they received the Holy Ghost:** . . . so that the Holy Spirit was given them, *Knox.*

**18. And when Simon saw that through laying on of the apostles' hands the Holy Ghost was given:** . . . perceiving that, *Concordant* . . . was conferred, *Williams* . . . was imparted through, *Goodspeed, Kleist* . . . by the imposition of a hand, *Murdock* . . . was given to people, *Everyday* . . . was granted through the imposition of the apostles' hands, *Knox.*

**he offered them money:** . . . he brought them a sum of money, *TCNT.*

**19. Saying, Give me also this power:** Give this power to me too, *Everyday* . . . Let me too...have such powers, *Knox* . . . this authority, *Rotherham* . . . this prerogative, *Murdock.*

**that on whomsoever I lay hands, he may receive the Holy Ghost:** . . . to communicate the holy Spirit, *Goodspeed* . . . Then I can give the Holy Spirit to anyone, *NLT* . . . when I lay my hands on a person, *Everyday.*

**20. But Peter said unto him, Thy money perish with thee:** Thy silver with thee go to destruction! *Rotherham* . . . May your money go to, *MLNT* . . . Take thy wealth with thee, *Knox* . . . Take your money to perdition with you! *TCNT* . . . May you and your money rot, *NAB* . . . Death to you and your money, *Moffatt* . . . To hell with you and your money! *Phillips* . . . A curse on you and

| **4713.1** prep | **4622.3** prs-pron dat 2sing | **1498.14** verb 3sing opt pres act | **1519.1** prep | **677.3** noun acc sing fem | **3617.1** conj | **3450.12** art acc sing fem |
|---|---|---|---|---|---|---|
| σὺν | σοὶ | εἴη | εἰς | ἀπώλειαν· | ὅτι | τὴν |
| *sun* | *soi* | *eiē* | *eis* | *apōleian* | *hoti* | *tēn* |
| with | you | may it be | to | destruction, | because | the |

| **1424.4** noun acc sing fem | **3450.2** art gen sing | **2296.2** noun gen sing masc | **3406.6** verb 2sing indic aor act | **1217.2** prep | **5371.3** noun gen pl neu |
|---|---|---|---|---|---|
| δωρεὰν | τοῦ | θεοῦ | ἐνόμισας | διὰ | χρημάτων |
| *dōrean* | *tou* | *theou* | *enomisas* | *dia* | *chrēmatōn* |
| gift | | of God | you did think | by | riches |

| **2904.2** verb inf pres mid | **3620.2** partic | **1498.4** verb 3sing indic pres act | **4622.3** prs-pron dat 2sing | **3182.1** noun nom sing fem | **3624.1** conj |
|---|---|---|---|---|---|
| κτᾶσθαι. | **21.** οὐκ | ἔστιν | σοι | μερὶς | οὐδὲ |
| *ktasthai* | *ouk* | *estin* | *soi* | *meris* | *oude* |
| to be obtained. | Not | there is | to you | part | nor |

| **2792.1** noun nom sing masc | **1706.1** prep | **3450.3** art dat sing | **3030.3** noun dat sing masc | **3642.5** dem-pron dat sing masc | **3450.9** art nom sing fem | **1056.1** conj |
|---|---|---|---|---|---|---|
| κλῆρος | ἐν | τῷ | λόγῳ | τούτῳ· | ἡ | γὰρ |
| *klēros* | *en* | *tō* | *logō* | *toutō* | *hē* | *gar* |
| lot | in | the | matter | this; | the | for |

| **2559.2** noun nom sing fem | **4622.2** prs-pron gen 2sing | **3620.2** partic | **1498.4** verb 3sing indic pres act | **2097.1** adj nom sing fem | **1783.1** prep |
|---|---|---|---|---|---|
| καρδία | σου | οὐκ | ἔστιν | εὐθεῖα | ʻ ἐνώπιον |
| *kardia* | *sou* | *ouk* | *estin* | *eutheia* | *enōpion* |
| heart | of you | not | is | right | before |

21.a.**Txt:** 08E,020L 025P,byz.
**Var:** 01ℵ,02A,03B,04C 05D,Gries,Lach,Treg Alf,Word,Tisc,We/Ho Weis,Sod,UBS/☆

| **1709.1** prep | **3450.2** art gen sing | **2296.2** noun gen sing masc | **3210.11** verb 2sing impr aor act | **3631.1** partic |
|---|---|---|---|---|
| [a☆ ἔναντι ] | τοῦ | θεοῦ. | **22.** μετανόησον | οὖν |
| *enanti* | *tou* | *theou* | *metanoēson* | *oun* |
| [ idem ] | | God. | Repent | therefore |

| **570.3** prep | **3450.10** art gen sing fem | **2520.2** noun gen sing fem | **4622.2** prs-pron gen 2sing | **3642.10** dem-pron gen sing fem | **2504.1** conj |
|---|---|---|---|---|---|
| ἀπὸ | τῆς | κακίας | σου | ταύτης, | καὶ |
| *apo* | *tēs* | *kakias* | *sou* | *tautēs* | *kai* |
| from | the | wickedness | your | this, | and |

22.a.**Txt:** 020L,025P,byz.
**Var:** 01ℵ,02A,03B,04C 05D,08E,sa.bo.Lach Treg,Alf,Word,Tisc We/Ho,Weis,Sod UBS/☆

| **1183.7** verb 2sing impr aor pass | **3450.2** art gen sing | **2296.2** noun gen sing masc | **2935.2** noun gen sing masc | **1479.1** conj | **679.1** partic |
|---|---|---|---|---|---|
| δεήθητι | τοῦ | ʻ θεοῦ, | [a☆ κυρίου ] | εἰ | ἄρα |
| *deēthēti* | *tou* | *theou* | *kuriou* | *ei* | *ara* |
| ask | | God, | [ Lord ] | if | indeed |

| **856.30** verb 3sing indic fut pass | **4622.3** prs-pron dat 2sing | **3450.9** art nom sing fem | **1948.1** noun nom sing fem | **3450.10** art gen sing fem |
|---|---|---|---|---|
| ἀφεθήσεταί | σοι | ἡ | ἐπίνοια | τῆς |
| *aphethēsetai* | *soi* | *hē* | *epinoia* | *tēs* |
| may be forgiven | to you | the | thought | the |

| **2559.1** noun fem | **4622.2** prs-pron gen 2sing | **1519.1** prep | **1056.1** conj | **5357.2** noun acc sing fem | **3949.2** noun gen sing fem |
|---|---|---|---|---|---|
| καρδίας | σου· | **23.** εἰς | γὰρ | χολὴν | πικρίας |
| *kardias* | *sou* | *eis* | *gar* | *cholēn* | *pikrias* |
| of heart | your; | in | for | a gall | of bitterness |

| **2504.1** conj | **4736.3** noun acc sing masc | **92.2** noun gen sing fem | **3571.2** verb 1sing indic pres act | **4622.4** prs-pron acc 2sing |
|---|---|---|---|---|
| καὶ | σύνδεσμον | ἀδικίας | ὁρῶ | σε |
| *kai* | *sundesmon* | *adikias* | *horō* | *se* |
| and | a bond | of unrighteousness | I see | you |

destruction of the lake of fire) because you thought the gift of God (that is, God's gift of the Holy Spirit, as in 2:38; 10:45) could be purchased with money (earthly riches)."

**8:21.** Peter further stated that Simon had neither part (share) nor lot (portion) in this matter. "Part" and "lot" are synonyms here. The repetition is for emphasis. The very fact that he tried to buy this power ruled out the possibility of his having any part in it whatsoever.

This further suggests that Simon could have had part or lot in this matter if he had come in faith and received the gift of the Spirit himself instead of offering money.

Peter also, by the insight given him by the Spirit, saw into the heart of Simon. Behind the money he offered, apparently as a generous gift, was a heart which was not right, that is, not upright or straight before God.

**8:22.** Peter then showed that Simon's case was not entirely hopeless by exhorting him to repent from his wickedness and pray to God (request of the Lord) if perhaps the thought (including the purpose) of his heart might be forgiven. There is no question here about God's willingness to forgive. God always freely forgives those who come to Him confessing their sin (1 John 1:9). Peter added the "if perhaps" because of Simon's heart condition. Simon must turn from the pride and greed that caused him to sin in this way.

**8:23.** Peter further perceived and recognized that Simon had an embittered, resentful spirit, because the people ceased to give him prominence. (Compare how the "gall of bitterness" is used in the Old Testament, as in Deuteronomy 29:18.) This may even imply some jealousy because of the attention now given to the gospel and to those who proclaimed it. Such a spirit of bitterness often rejects reconciliation and certainly grieves the Holy Spirit (Ephesians 4:30,31). It is an evil root that can defile everyone around the person who has it (Hebrews 12:15).

Simon was also in the "bond (that is, in the grip) of iniquity" (including injustice and unrighteousness). He was unjust in wanting to receive this power or authority for himself. Also, his wrong attitude had such a grip on him that it would be difficult for him to break loose from its grasp.

However, the Greek could mean Simon was in danger of being in the "gall of bitterness" and the "bond of iniquity." This would mean he was not yet bound by bitterness and unrighteousness, and therefore there was still hope for him if he would repent immediately.

your money, *Williams C.K.* . . . should both be destroyed! *Everyday, SEB.*

**because thou hast thought that the gift of God may be purchased with money:** . . . because you have imagined that you can obtain God's free gift with money, *Weymouth* . . . because you have supposed, *Montgomery* . . . to acquire, *HBIE* . . . How dare you think you could buy the gift of God? *Phillips* . . . the gratuity of God, *Concordant* . . . by a worldly substance, *Murdock.*

**21. Thou hast neither part nor lot:** You have no share or part, *TCNT.*

**in this matter:** . . . in our Message, *TCNT* . . . in the proclamation of this message, *Adams.*

**for thy heart is not right in the sight of God:** . . . not sincere, *Williams* . . . not straight, *Berkeley* . . . not honest, *Phillips.*

**22. Repent therefore of this thy wickedness:** Let your heart be changed, *BB* . . . So, repent of this crookedness of yours, *Berkeley* . . . Change your heart! *SEB* . . . of this evil plan of yours, *TEV* . . . Turn your mind, *Sawyer.*

**and pray God:** . . . pray the Lord, *ASV* . . . beseech the Lord, *Montgomery* . . . plead with the Lord, *Berkeley.*

**if perhaps the thought of thine heart may be forgiven thee:** . . . to forgive you for what you had in mind, *Berkeley.*

**23. For I perceive that thou art in the gall of bitterness:** . . . for I see that you have fallen into bitter jealousy, *TCNT* . . . you are a bitter weed, *Williams* . . . For I can see inside you, and I see a man bitter with jealousy, *Phillips* . . . I see you're turning to bitter poison, *Beck* . . . poisoned with envy, *Norlie* . . . you are trapped, *TEV.*

**and in the bond of iniquity:** . . . and the fetters of sin, *TCNT* . . . and a pack of evil, *Moffatt* . . . and a bundle of crookedness, *Williams* . . . and being chained by wickedness, *Beck* . . . fetter of injustice, *Concordant* . . . slave of wrong-doing, *Norlie* . . . the bond of unrighteousness, *HBIE* . . . a prisoner of sin, *TEV* . . . the chains of sin, *JB* . . . captive to sin, *NIV.*

| 1498.18 verb part pres act | 552.12 verb nom sing masc part aor pass | 1156.2 conj | 3450.5 art nom sing masc | 4468.1 name nom masc |
|---|---|---|---|---|
| ὄντα. | 24. Ἀποκριθεὶς | δὲ | ὁ | Σίμων |
| *onta* | *Apokritheis* | *de* | *ho* | *Simōn* |
| being. | Having answered | and | | Simon |

| 1500.5 verb 3sing indic aor act | 1183.8 verb 2pl impr aor pass | 5050.1 prs-pron nom 2pl | 5065.1 prep | 1466.3 prs-pron gen 1sing | 4242.1 prep |
|---|---|---|---|---|---|
| εἶπεν, | Δεήθητε | ὑμεῖς | ὑπὲρ | ἐμοῦ | πρὸς |
| *eipen* | *Deēthēte* | *humeis* | *huper* | *emou* | *pros* |
| said, | Ask | you | on behalf | of me | to |

| 3450.6 art acc sing masc | 2935.4 noun acc sing masc | 3567.1 conj | 3235.6 num card neu | 1889.2 verb 3sing subj aor act | 1894.2 prep |
|---|---|---|---|---|---|
| τὸν | κύριον, | ὅπως | μηδὲν | ἐπέλθῃ | ἐπ' |
| *ton* | *kurion* | *hopōs* | *mēden* | *epelthē* | *ep'* |
| the | Lord, | so that | nothing | may come | upon |

| 1466.7 prs-pron acc 1sing | 3614.1 rel-pron gen pl | 2029.4 verb 2pl indic perf act | 3450.7 art nom pl masc | 3173.1 conj | 3631.1 partic |
|---|---|---|---|---|---|
| ἐμὲ | ὧν | εἰρήκατε. | 25. Οἱ | μὲν | οὖν |
| *eme* | *hōn* | *eirēkate* | *Hoi* | *men* | *oun* |
| me | of which | you have spoken. | The | indeed | therefore |

25.a.**Txt:** 01ℵ,03B,04C 05D,08E,byz.
**Var:** p74,02A,044,326 bo.

| 1257.8 verb nom pl masc part aor mid | 2504.1 conj | 2953.36 verb nom pl masc part aor act | 3450.6 art acc sing masc | 3030.4 noun acc sing masc |
|---|---|---|---|---|
| διαμαρτυράμενοι | καὶ | λαλήσαντες | τὸν | λόγον |
| *diamarturamenoi* | *kai* | *lalēsantes* | *ton* | *logon* |
| having earnestly testified | and | having spoken | the | word |

25.b.**Txt:** 04C,08E,020L 025P,byz.sa.bo.
**Var:** 01ℵ,02A,03B,05D Lach,Treg,Alf,Word Tisc,We/Ho,Weis,Sod UBS/☆

| 3450.2 art gen sing | 2935.2 noun gen sing masc | 2296.2 noun gen sing masc | 5128.7 verb 3pl indic aor act | 5128.14 verb 3pl indic imperf act |
|---|---|---|---|---|
| τοῦ | ʼ κυρίου, | [ª Θεοῦ ] | ʼ ὑπέστρεψαν | [ᵇ☆ ὑπέστρεφον ] |
| *tou* | *kuriou* | *Theou* | *hupestrepsan* | *hupestrephon* |
| of the | Lord, | [ God ] | returned | [ were returning ] |

25.c.**Txt:** 020L,025P,byz.
**Var:** 01ℵ,02A,03B,04C 05D,08E,Lach,Treg,Alf Tisc,We/Ho,Weis,Sod UBS/☆

| 1519.1 prep | 2395.1 name fem | 2389.1 name | 4044.15 adj acc pl fem | 4885.1 conj |
|---|---|---|---|---|
| εἰς | ʼ Ἱερουσαλήμ, | [ᶜ☆ Ἱεροσόλυμα, ] | πολλάς | τε |
| *eis* | *Hierousalēm* | *Hierosoluma* | *pollas* | *te* |
| to | Jerusalem | [ idem, ] | many | and |

| 2941.4 noun acc pl fem | 3450.1 art gen pl | 4398.3 name gen pl masc | 2076.19 verb 3pl indic aor mid |
|---|---|---|---|
| κώμας | τῶν | Σαμαρειτῶν | ʼ εὐηγγελίσαντο. |
| *kōmas* | *tōn* | *Samareitōn* | *euēngelisanto* |
| villages | of the | Samaritans | announced the good news. |

25.d.**Txt:** 020L,025P,byz. bo.
**Var:** 01ℵ,02A,03B,04C 05D,08E,sa.Lach,Treg Alf,Word,Tisc,We/Ho Weis,Sod,UBS/☆

| 2076.30 verb 3pl indic imperf mid | 32.1 noun nom sing masc | 1156.2 conj | 2935.2 noun gen sing masc |
|---|---|---|---|
| [ᵈ☆ εὐηγγελίζοντο. ] | 26. Ἄγγελος | δὲ | κυρίου |
| *euēngelizonto* | *Angelos* | *de* | *kuriou* |
| [ were announcing the good news. ] | An angel | but | of Lord |

| 2953.27 verb 3sing indic aor act | 4242.1 prep | 5213.4 name acc masc | 2978.15 verb nom sing masc part pres act | 448.8 verb 2sing impr aor act |
|---|---|---|---|---|
| ἐλάλησεν | πρὸς | Φίλιππον, | λέγων, | Ἀνάστηθι |
| *elalēsen* | *pros* | *Philippon* | *legōn* | *Anastēthi* |
| spoke | to | Philip, | saying, | Rise up |

| 2504.1 conj | 4057.4 verb 2sing impr pres mid | 2567.3 prep | 3184.1 noun acc sing fem | 1894.3 prep | 3450.12 art acc sing fem |
|---|---|---|---|---|---|
| καὶ | πορεύου | κατὰ | μεσημβρίαν, | ἐπὶ | τὴν |
| *kai* | *poreuou* | *kata* | *mesēmbrian* | *epi* | *tēn* |
| and | go | towards | south, | on | the |

**8:24.** Simon responded by begging Peter and John to pray for him so none of these things Peter had spoken would come upon him. This is emphatic. Some believe this implies Simon was praying.

There is considerable controversy about what happened to Simon. Some suggest he only wanted prayer because he was afraid of judgment. But the fact that he wanted the apostles to pray for him possibly shows a change of attitude, a change of heart, and therefore may indicate Simon did repent. The Bible says no more about him.

Later writers use the term *simony* for the buying or selling of church office or for the attempt to use a position in a church organization to increase personal gain. By the middle of the Second Century A.D., legends about Simon began to be circulated. Some say he introduced a gnostic sect or that he defended one gnostic sect against another and denied the deity of Christ, making Him just one of the Jewish prophets. Other traditions try to connect him with an Italian deity and say he went to Rome and made himself a god there. In these stories they have Simon constantly opposing Peter, saying that he also died in Rome. But these traditions have no Biblical basis.

**8:25.** Peter and John continued in Samaria for a time, giving strong witness (strong Biblical evidence) and speaking the Word of the Lord. Probably they included more of the life, ministry, and teachings of Jesus. They would certainly be concerned that these believers should receive the same body of teaching that they taught in Jerusalem, the body of teaching recorded in the Gospels.

They preached the same good news in many Samaritan villages on their way back to Jerusalem.

**8:26.** At this point the angel (Greek, an angel) of the Lord spoke to Philip telling him to rise and go toward the south to the road going down from Jerusalem to Gaza, which is desert. "Desert" also means deserted, abandoned, desolate. Here the emphasis is that the area was largely uninhabited. Gaza was the most southern of the five cities of the Philistines in Old Testament times. It was about 60 miles southwest of Jerusalem, and this road was the old road which was seldom used anymore.

The New Testament tells of angels appearing to people comparatively seldom. For example, they appeared to Elisabeth, Zechariah, and Mary (Luke 1:11-38); Joseph (Matthew 1:20-23); Jesus (Mark 1:13; Luke 22:43); and Peter (Acts 12:7); cf. Matthew 28:3; Acts 1:10. Yet they are often present and function as "ministering spirits, sent forth to minister for them who shall be heirs of salvation" (Hebrews 1:14).

Jesus himself referred to their number and activity. When they came to arrest Jesus He said He could have had more than 12 legions of angels to defend Him if He were to ask His Father for them (Matthew 26:53). Hebrews 12:22 speaks of an innumerable

**24. Then answered Simon, and said: Pray ye to the Lord for me:** Simon responded, I need the prayers of all of you, *NAB*... You plead, *Berkeley* ... Both of you pray for me, *NCV*... Plead with the Lord for me yourselves, *MLNT.*

**that none of these things which ye have spoken come upon me:** ... that none of this harm you have spoken of may fall upon me, *Knox* ... so that what you have just said may never happen to me, *NAB* ... that nothing you have said will come to me, *NLT*... may happen to me, *Montgomery.*

**25. And they, when they had testified and preached the word of the Lord:**... having fully borne witness and spoken, *Rotherham* ... So the Apostles, after giving a solemn charge and delivering the Lord's Word, *Weymouth* ... Then after they had thoroughly testified and talked over the Lord's teachings, *Berkeley* ... after having given earnest personal testimony, *Norlie* ... after telling what they had seen and heard, *NLT.*

**returned to Jerusalem:** ... began their return, *Rotherham* ... began their journey back, *Knox*... made their way back to Jerusalem, *TCNT.*

**and preached the gospel in many villages of the Samaritans:** ... carrying the gospel into, *Knox* ... telling the Good News, as they went, in many Samaritan villages, *TCNT*... evangelizing many Samaritan villages as they went, *Montgomery*... to many Samaritan communities, *MLNT.*

**26. And the angel of the Lord spake unto Philip, saying:** Meanwhile an angel, *TCNT* ... then addressed himself to, *NAB* ... was commanded by an angel of the Lord, *Knox.*

**Arise, and go toward the south unto the way that goeth down from Jerusalem unto Gaza:** Rise and proceed south to the road that runs down from Jerusalem to Gaza, *Weymouth* ... about midday go down the road, *MLNT* ... Get ready and go south, *NCV* ... Get up and go south, along the road from, *Moffatt* ... Rise up and go south. Take the road, *Norlie* ... go south to meet the road which leads from, *Knox.*

| **3461.4** noun acc sing fem | **3450.12** art acc sing fem | **2568.9** verb acc sing fem part pres act | **570.3** prep | **2395.1** name fem |
|---|---|---|---|---|
| ὁδὸν | τὴν | καταβαίνουσαν | ἀπὸ | Ἱερουσαλὴμ |
| *hodon* | *tēn* | *katabainousan* | *apo* | *Hierousalēm* |
| way | the | going down | from | Jerusalem |

| **1519.1** prep | **1041.1** name acc fem | **3642.9** dem-pron nom sing fem | **1498.4** verb 3sing indic pres act | **2032.1** adj nom sing | **2504.1** conj |
|---|---|---|---|---|---|
| εἰς | Γάζαν· | αὕτη | ἐστὶν | ἔρημος. | **27.** καὶ |
| *eis* | *Gazan* | *hautē* | *estin* | *erēmos* | *kai* |
| to | Gaza: | the same | is | desert. | And |

| **448.9** verb nom sing masc part aor act | **4057.16** verb 3sing indic aor pass | **2504.1** conj | **1481.20** verb 2sing impr aor mid | **433.1** noun nom sing masc |
|---|---|---|---|---|
| ἀναστὰς | ἐπορεύθη· | καὶ | ἰδοὺ | ἀνὴρ |
| *anastas* | *eporeuthē* | *kai* | *idou* | *anēr* |
| having risen up | he went. | And | behold, | a man |

27.a.**Txt:** 020L,025P,byz.
**Var:** 01א,02A,03B,04C 05D,08E,Lach,Treg,Alf Word,Tisc,We/Ho,Weis Sod,UBS/⋆

| **128.1** name nom sing masc | **2116.1** noun nom sing masc | **1407.1** noun nom sing masc | **2553.1** name gen fem | **3450.10** art gen sing fem |
|---|---|---|---|---|
| Αἰθίοψ | εὐνοῦχος | δυνάστης | Κανδάκης | ⌜a τῆς ⌝ |
| *Aithiops* | *eunouchos* | *dunastēs* | *Kandakēs* | *tēs* |
| an Ethiopian, | a eunuch, | one in power | under Candace | the |

| **931.2** noun gen sing fem | **128.2** name gen pl masc | **3614.5** rel-pron nom sing masc | **1498.34** verb sing indic imperf act | **1894.3** prep |
|---|---|---|---|---|
| βασιλίσσης | Αἰθιόπων, | ὃς | ἦν | ἐπὶ |
| *basilissēs* | *Aithiopōn* | *hos* | *ēn* | *epi* |
| queen | of Ethiopians, | who | was | over |

27.b.**Txt:** 01א-corr,03B 04C-corr,05D-corr,08E 020L,025P,byz.We/Ho Weis,Sod,UBS/⋆
**Var:** 01א-org,02A 04C-org,05D-org,sa. Lach,Tisc

| **3820.10** adj gen sing fem | **3450.10** art gen sing fem | **1040.1** noun gen sing fem | **840.10** prs-pron gen sing fem | **3614.5** rel-pron nom sing masc | **2048.27** verb 3sing indic plperf act |
|---|---|---|---|---|---|
| πάσης | τῆς | γάζης | αὐτῆς, | ⌜b ὃς ⌝ | ἐληλύθει |
| *pasēs* | *tēs* | *gazēs* | *autēs* | *hos* | *elēluthei* |
| all | the | treasure | her, | who | had come |

| **4210.23** verb nom sing masc part fut act | **1519.1** prep | **2395.1** name fem | **1498.34** verb sing indic imperf act | **4885.1** conj |
|---|---|---|---|---|
| προσκυνήσων | εἰς | Ἱερουσαλήμ, | **28.** ἦν | ⌜ τε |
| *proskunēsōn* | *eis* | *Hierousalēm* | *ēn* | *te* |
| worshiping | to | Jerusalem, | was | and |

28.a.**Txt:** 01א,02A,05D 08E,020L,025P,byz.Tisc Sod
**Var:** 03B,04C,sa.bo. We/Ho,Weis,UBS/⋆

| **1156.2** conj | **5128.2** verb nom sing masc part pres act | **2504.1** conj | **2493.6** verb nom sing masc part pres mid | **1894.3** prep | **3450.2** art gen sing |
|---|---|---|---|---|---|
| [a δὲ ] | ὑποστρέφων | καὶ | καθήμενος | ἐπὶ | τοῦ |
| *de* | *hupostrephōn* | *kai* | *kathēmenos* | *epi* | *tou* |
| [ idem ] | returning | and | sitting | in | the |

| **710.1** noun gen sing neu | **840.3** prs-pron gen sing | **2504.1** conj | **312.12** verb 3sing indic imperf act | **3450.6** art acc sing masc | **4254.3** noun acc sing masc |
|---|---|---|---|---|---|
| ἅρματος | αὐτοῦ, | καὶ | ἀνεγίνωσκεν | τὸν | προφήτην |
| *harmatos* | *autou* | *kai* | *aneginōsken* | *ton* | *prophētēn* |
| chariot | his, | and | he was reading | the | prophet |

| **2246.8** name acc masc | **1500.5** verb 3sing indic aor act | **1156.2** conj | **3450.16** art sing neu | **4011.1** noun sing neu | **3450.3** art dat sing |
|---|---|---|---|---|---|
| Ἠσαΐαν. | **29.** εἶπεν | δὲ | τὸ | πνεῦμα | τῷ |
| *Esaian* | *eipen* | *de* | *to* | *pneuma* | *tō* |
| Isaiah. | Said | and | the | Spirit | |

29.a.**Txt:** p50,01א-corr 03B,04C-corr2,05D-corr 08E,byz.
**Var:** p74,01א-org,02A 33,323,945,1175,1739 2495

| **5213.3** name dat masc | **4193.3** verb 2sing impr aor act | **2504.1** conj | **2827.5** verb 2sing impr aor pass | **3450.3** art dat sing |
|---|---|---|---|---|
| Φιλίππῳ, | Πρόσελθε | ⌜a καὶ ⌝ | κολλήθητι | τῷ |
| *Philippō* | *Proselthe* | *kai* | *kollēthēti* | *tō* |
| to Philip, | Go near | and | join yourself | to the |

company of angels. Revelation 5:11 also speaks of great numbers of them. But they must be sent forth by God.

There may have been a special reason for sending an angel to Philip. He was in the midst of a great revival in Samaria. It probably took something unusual to get him to leave the crowds and go down to a deserted back road. Some take "which is desert" to refer to Old Testament Gaza which was destroyed in 93 B.C. In 57 B.C. a new city was built nearer the Mediterranean Sea. The road to old Gaza might be called the road to desert (deserted) Gaza.

**8:27,28.** When the angel spoke, Philip did not hesitate or demur. He arose and went in obedience and with faith and expectation.

At the very time he reached the Gaza road, the chariot of an Ethiopian eunuch was approaching. "Behold" indicates something unexpected or surprising. Philip was surprised, but God's timing was exactly right.

Most officers in palaces were eunuchs in ancient times. This man was a highly placed officer (a potentate), a member of the court of the Ethiopian queen Candace, in charge of all her treasures, with full responsibility for the care and disbursement of funds.

Candace was the hereditary title of the queens of Ethiopia, whose seat of government was on the island of Meroe in the Nile River. Ethiopia here corresponds to what is today called the Sudan, though it probably included part of modern Ethiopia.

This eunuch had come a long distance to worship in Jerusalem. Though he was probably a proselyte to Judaism, because of his being a eunuch, he could only go as far as the Court of the Gentiles. (Some believe he could not have been a full proselyte either, and this would cause him to be classed as a God-fearing Gentile, which would also limit him to the court of the Gentiles.)

Even so, he had purchased scrolls of the Old Testament to take back with him. These were hand-copied and extremely expensive in those days. Usually a whole community of the Jews would join together to buy a set for their synagogue and would keep it locked up for use in worship and teaching.

Now the eunuch was returning home, sitting in his chariot reading the Book (roll, scroll) of Isaiah.

**8:29.** Then the Holy Spirit spoke to Philip. It took an angel to get Philip to leave Samaria, but now that he was aroused to do God's will, he did not need another angel to prompt him. All he needed was the inner voice of the Spirit. Guidance by the Spirit is a prominent theme in the Book of Acts and is worthy of special study. All the early believers learned to be sensitive to the moving and checks of the Spirit. Philip was undoubtedly looking to the Lord, praying as he went along, expecting the Lord to show him what to do.

The Holy Spirit's command was clear and simple. Philip was to go and join himself closely to this chariot. He was to cling to it. He must not let this opportunity pass him by.

**which is desert:** (The town is now deserted), *Goodspeed* . . . (It is now deserted.), *TCNT* . . . crossing the desert, *Weymouth* . . . this is the desert road, *Williams* . . . a lonely road, *Berkeley, MLNT* . . . the desert route, *NAB* . . . It goes through the place where no people live, *NLT* . . . out in the desert, *Knox.*

**27. And he arose and went:** So he got busy and departed, *Kleist* . . . he rose up, *Knox* . . . So he set out on his journey, *TCNT* . . . So Philip got ready and went, *Everyday, NCV.*

**and, behold, a man of Ethiopia, a eunuch of great authority under Candace queen of the Ethiopians:** On the road he saw a man...an important officer, *Everyday* . . . and found there...a courtier, *Knox* . . . an Ethiopian official, *Williams* . . . He had been made so he could not have children, *NLT* . . . and on his way he came upon an official of high rank, in the service of Candace, Queen of the Abyssinians, *TCNT* . . . a high officer, *Noyes* . . . had come from Cush, *Murdock.*

**who had the charge of all her treasure:** He was her Treasurer, *TCNT* . . . He was responsible for taking care of all her money, *NCV* . . . as her treasurer, *Weymouth* . . . of all her finances, *MLNT* . . . in charge of the entire treasury, *NAB* . . . her chief treasurer, *Goodspeed* . . . He cared for all the riches that belonged to Candace, *NLT.*

**and had come to Jerusalem for to worship:** . . . had gone to, *Everyday, NCV.*

**28. Was returning, and sitting in his chariot read Esaias the prophet:** . . . was now on his way home, sitting in his carriage and reading, *TCNT* . . . As he was going back home, he was sitting in his wagon, *NLT* . . . reading aloud, *LivB.*

**29. Then the Spirit said unto Philip, Go near, and join thyself to this chariot:** Go up and keep close to the carriage, *TCNT* . . . walk by the side of, *TNT* . . . contact that chariot, *Berkeley* . . . Go over to that wagon and get on it, *NLT* . . . and stay near it, *Everyday, NCV* . . . and stay by that car, *Goodspeed.*

| **710.2** noun dat sing neu | **3642.5** dem-pron dat sing masc | **4228.2** verb nom sing masc part aor act | **1156.2** conj | **3450.5** art nom sing masc |
|---|---|---|---|---|
| ἅρματι | τούτῳ. | **30.** Προσδραμὼν | δὲ | ὁ |
| *harmati* | *toutō* | *Prosdramōn* | *de* | *ho* |
| chariot | this. | Having run up | and | |

| **5213.1** name nom masc | **189.21** verb 3sing indic aor act | **840.3** prs-pron gen sing | **312.4** verb gen sing masc part pres act | **3450.6** art acc sing masc |
|---|---|---|---|---|
| Φίλιππος | ἤκουσεν | αὐτοῦ | ἀναγινώσκοντος | ʻ τὸν |
| *Philippos* | *ēkousen* | *autou* | *anaginōskontos* | *ton* |
| Philip | heard | him | reading | the |

| **4254.3** noun acc sing masc | **2246.8** name acc masc | **2246.8** name acc masc | **3450.6** art acc sing masc | **4254.3** noun acc sing masc |
|---|---|---|---|---|
| προφήτην | Ἠσαΐαν, | [☆ Ἠσαΐαν | τὸν | προφήτην, ] |
| *prophētēn* | *Esaian* | *Esaian* | *ton* | *prophētēn* |
| prophet | Isaiah, | [ Isaiah | the | prophet, ] |

| **2504.1** conj | **1500.5** verb 3sing indic aor act | **680.1** partic | **1058.1** partic | **1091.2** verb 2sing indic pres act | **3614.17** rel-pron pl neu |
|---|---|---|---|---|---|
| καὶ | εἶπεν, | Ἆρά | γε | γινώσκεις | ἃ |
| *kai* | *eipen* | *Ara* | *ge* | *ginōskeis* | *ha* |
| and | said, | Then | | do you know | what |

| **312.1** verb 2sing indic pres act | **3450.5** art nom sing masc | **1156.2** conj | **1500.5** verb 3sing indic aor act | **4316.1** adv | **1056.1** conj |
|---|---|---|---|---|---|
| ἀναγινώσκεις; | **31.** Ὁ | δὲ | εἶπεν, | Πῶς | γὰρ |
| *anaginōskeis* | *Ho* | *de* | *eipen* | *Pōs* | *gar* |
| you are reading? | The | but | said, | How | for |

| **300.1** partic | **1404.10** verb 1sing opt pres mid | **1430.1** partic | **3231.1** partic | **4948.3** indef-pron nom sing | **3457.3** verb 3sing subj aor act |
|---|---|---|---|---|---|
| ἂν | δυναίμην | ἐὰν | μή | τις | ʻ ὁδηγήσῃ |
| *an* | *dunaimēn* | *ean* | *mē* | *tis* | *hodēgēsē* |
| | should I be able | if | not | someone | should guide |

31.a.**Txt:** 02A,03B-corr 020L,025P,byz.Gries Lach,Weis
**Var:** 01ℵ,03B-org,04C 08E,Treg,Tisc,We/Ho Sod,UBS/☆

| **3457.4** verb 3sing indic fut act | **1466.6** prs-pron acc 1sing | **3731.13** verb 3sing indic aor act | **4885.1** conj | **3450.6** art acc sing masc |
|---|---|---|---|---|
| [a☆ ὁδηγήσει ] | με; | Παρεκάλεσέν | τε | τὸν |
| *hodēgēsei* | *me* | *Parekalesen* | *te* | *ton* |
| [ will guide ] | me? | He encouraged | and | |

| **5213.4** name acc masc | **303.18** verb acc sing masc part aor act | **2495.12** verb inf aor act | **4713.1** prep | **840.4** prs-pron dat sing | **3450.9** art nom sing fem |
|---|---|---|---|---|---|
| Φίλιππον | ἀναβάντα | καθίσαι | σὺν | αὐτῷ. | **32.** ἡ |
| *Philippon* | *anabanta* | *kathisai* | *sun* | *autō* | *hē* |
| Philip | having come up | to sit | with | him. | The |

| **1156.2** conj | **3905.1** noun nom sing fem | **3450.10** art gen sing fem | **1118.2** noun gen sing fem | **3614.12** rel-pron acc sing fem | **312.12** verb 3sing indic imperf act |
|---|---|---|---|---|---|
| δὲ | περιοχὴ | τῆς | γραφῆς | ἣν | ἀνεγίνωσκεν |
| *de* | *periochē* | *tēs* | *graphēs* | *hēn* | *aneginōsken* |
| and | passage | of the | Scripture | which | he was reading |

| **1498.34** verb sing indic imperf act | **3642.9** dem-pron nom sing fem | **5453.1** conj | **4122.1** noun sing neu | **1894.3** prep | **4819.2** noun acc sing fem |
|---|---|---|---|---|---|
| ἦν | αὕτη, | Ὡς | πρόβατον | ἐπὶ | σφαγὴν |
| *ēn* | *hautē* | *Hōs* | *probaton* | *epi* | *sphagēn* |
| was | this, | As | a sheep | to | slaughter |

| **70.25** verb 3sing indic aor pass | **2504.1** conj | **5453.1** conj | **284.1** noun nom sing masc | **1710.1** prep | **3450.2** art gen sing |
|---|---|---|---|---|---|
| ἤχθη, | καὶ | ὡς | ἀμνὸς | ἐναντίον | τοῦ |
| *ēchthē* | *kai* | *hōs* | *amnos* | *enantion* | *tou* |
| he was led, | and | as | a lamb | before | the |

**8:30.** Philip did not need any further exhortation. In obedience he ran to the chariot and began to run alongside it. As he did so he heard the eunuch reading aloud from the prophet Isaiah. (Reading was almost always done aloud in those days.) Philip probably listened for a few moments and then interrupted the eunuch and asked if he understood what he was reading; did he really know and comprehend what Isaiah was writing about?

**8:31.** The eunuch's question shows he did not feel capable of understanding what he was reading. The message of the Book was a mystery to him. The quotation which follows shows he was reading from the Septuagint version, translated in Alexandria, Egypt, beginning about 250 years before Christ. The educated Ethiopians would know Greek, and a person in government service would need to know it very well, for most government business was carried on in Greek in those days. Thus, it was not the language that was causing him difficulty.

Perhaps his difficulty came from his heathen background. The Ethiopians, like the Egyptians, were still pagans at this time, worshiping idols. There were Jewish communities among them, and it may be that the eunuch first heard the Old Testament Scriptures read as he sat with other Gentiles in the back seat of some synagogue. This must have stirred him to go to Jerusalem and learn more. Now he was returning, still with a desire to learn. But he could not grasp what he was reading. He needed someone to guide him, someone to show him the way into an understanding of God's truth. So he welcomed Philip's question and gave Philip a sincere and urgent invitation to come up into the chariot and sit with him.

**8:32.** In the providence of God the eunuch was reading Isaiah 53:7,8. Chapter 53 of Isaiah has been called the Mount Everest of messianic prophecy. There is no other chapter in the Old Testament that more clearly or more specifically tells of the redemptive work of Christ. There is little or no evidence to suppose that the eunuch, or the Jews, would have understood Isaiah 53 as a reference to the Messiah. Jesus was the first to interpret these passages describing the Suffering Servant in messianic terms. For example, Jesus said that He came to give His life as a "ransom for many" (Mark 10:45). While elsewhere in the chapters surrounding Isaiah 53, the "servant" of the Lord may refer to the nation of Israel, the vicarious and propitiatory nature of Isaiah 53:4-6 cannot be applied to anyone but the Lord Jesus Christ.

The discussion of Christ's redemptive work actually begins with Isaiah 52:13 where God refers to the coming Messiah as "my servant." As the Lord's Suffering Servant, the Messiah would be the One to carry out God's work. He would be the Lamb of God who would take away the sin of the world. Like a sheep led to be slaughtered for sacrifice, so He would give His life for sinners. Like a lamb, He would come patiently, and without any word against His

**30. And Philip ran thither to him:** And running near to him, *KJII* . . . ran toward the chariot, *Everyday.*

**and heard him read the prophet Esaias, and said:** . . . and overheard the Etheopian reading, *Kleist* . . . reading aloud, *LivB* . . . from the writings of the early preacher Isaiah, *NLT* . . . He inquired, *Kleist.*

**Understandest thou what thou readest?:** Do you really understand what you are reading, *TCNT, TNT* . . . Do you really grasp, *NAB.*

**31. And he said, how can I, except some man should guide me?:** How in the world could I...teaches me, *Williams* . . . unless someone will explain it to me, *TCNT* . . . should no one be guiding me? *Concordant* . . . someone interprets it, *Kleist* . . . I need someone to explain it to me! *Everyday* . . . unless some one instruct me? *Murdock* . . . show me the way? *Montgomery* . . . unless someone teaches me? *NLT.*

**And he desired Philip that he would come up and sit with him:** And he earnestly invited Philip to come up, *Weymouth* . . . to get in, *Kleist* . . . begged him to get up and sit with him, *Williams* . . . to climb in and to be seated with him, *Berkeley.*

**32. The place of the scripture which he read was this:** . . . the portion of Scripture, *Montgomery* . . . the contents of the Writing, *Young* . . . This was the passage of Scripture, *Goodspeed* . . . the verse of Scripture, *Everyday.*

**He was led as a sheep to the slaughter:** . . . when it is taken, *NCV* . . . being led to be killed, *Everyday* . . . taken away to be killed, *SEB* . . . to be put to death, *NLT.*

**and like a lamb dumb before his shearer:** And as a lamb is mute in the hands of its shearer, *TCNT* . . . He was quiet, as a sheep is quiet, *Everyday* . . . is not bleating, *Concordant* . . . is silent, *Murdock* . . . voiceless, *Berkeley, MLNT* . . . a lamb that makes no sound when someone cuts off its wool, *NCV* . . . does not make a sound while its wool is cut, *NLT* . . . before the man who cut off her wool, *Beck.*

## Acts 8:33

32.a.**Txt:** 03B,byz.
**Var:** p50,p74,01ℵ,02A
04C,08E,36,614,2495

| 2721.1 verb gen sing masc part pres act | 2721.5 verb gen sing masc part aor act | 840.6 prs-pron acc sing masc | 873.1 adj nom sing masc | 3643.1 adv |
|---|---|---|---|---|
| ⸂ κείροντος | [a☆ κείραντος ] | αὐτὸν | ἄφωνος, | οὕτως |
| *keirontos* | *keirantos* | *auton* | *aphōnos* | *houtōs* |
| shearing | [ having sheared ] | him | dumb, | thus |

| 3620.2 partic | 453.1 verb 3sing indic pres act | 3450.16 art sing neu | 4601.1 noun sing neu | 840.3 prs-pron gen sing | 1706.1 prep |
|---|---|---|---|---|---|
| οὐκ | ἀνοίγει | τὸ | στόμα | αὐτοῦ. | 33. Ἐν |
| *ouk* | *anoigei* | *to* | *stoma* | *autou* | *En* |
| not | he opens | the | mouth | his. | In |

33.a.**Txt:** 04C,08E,020L
025P,byz.sa.bo.Sod
**Var:** p74,01ℵ,02A,03B
Lach,Treg,Tisc,We/Ho
Weis,UBS/☆

| 3450.11 art dat sing fem | 4865.2 noun dat sing fem | 840.3 prs-pron gen sing | 3450.9 art nom sing fem | 2893.1 noun nom sing fem |
|---|---|---|---|---|
| τῇ | ταπεινώσει | ⸂a αὐτοῦ ⸃ | ἡ | κρίσις |
| *tē* | *tapeinōsei* | *autou* | *hē* | *krisis* |
| the | humiliation | his | the | judgment |

33.b.**Txt:** 08E,020L
025P,byz.bo.Sod
**Var:** 01ℵ,02A,03B,04C
sa.Lach,Treg,Tisc
We/Ho,Weis,UBS/☆

| 840.3 prs-pron gen sing | 142.24 verb 3sing indic aor pass | 3450.12 art acc sing fem | 1156.2 conj | 1067.4 noun acc sing fem | 840.3 prs-pron gen sing |
|---|---|---|---|---|---|
| αὐτοῦ | ἤρθη, | τὴν | ⸂b δὲ ⸃ | γενεὰν | αὐτοῦ |
| *autou* | *ērthē* | *tēn* | *de* | *genean* | *autou* |
| his | was taken away, | the | and | generation | of him |

| 4949.3 intr-pron nom sing | 1328.6 verb 3sing indic fut mid | 3617.1 conj | 142.22 verb 3sing indic pres mid | 570.3 prep | 3450.10 art gen sing fem |
|---|---|---|---|---|---|
| τίς | διηγήσεται; | ὅτι | αἴρεται | ἀπὸ | τῆς |
| *tis* | *diēgēsetai* | *hoti* | *airetai* | *apo* | *tēs* |
| who | shall declare? | for | is taken | from | the |

| 1087.2 noun gen sing fem | 3450.9 art nom sing fem | 2205.1 noun nom sing fem | 840.3 prs-pron gen sing | 552.12 verb nom sing masc part aor pass |
|---|---|---|---|---|
| γῆς | ἡ | ζωὴ | αὐτοῦ. | 34. Ἀποκριθεὶς |
| *gēs* | *hē* | *zōē* | *autou* | *Apokritheis* |
| earth | the | life | his. | Having answered |

| 1156.2 conj | 3450.5 art nom sing masc | 2116.1 noun nom sing masc | 3450.3 art dat sing | 5213.3 name dat masc | 1500.5 verb 3sing indic aor act |
|---|---|---|---|---|---|
| δὲ | ὁ | εὐνοῦχος | τῷ | Φιλίππῳ | εἶπεν, |
| *de* | *ho* | *eunouchos* | *tō* | *Philippō* | *eipen* |
| and | the | eunuch | | to Philip | said, |

| 1183.1 verb 1sing indic pres mid | 4622.2 prs-pron gen 2sing | 3875.1 prep | 4949.4 intr-pron gen sing | 3450.5 art nom sing masc |
|---|---|---|---|---|
| Δέομαί | σου, | περὶ | τίνος | ὁ |
| *Deomai* | *sou* | *peri* | *tinos* | *ho* |
| I beg | you, | concerning | whom | the |

| 4254.1 noun nom sing masc | 2978.5 verb 3sing indic pres act | 3642.17 dem-pron sing neu | 3875.1 prep | 1431.4 prs-pron gen sing | 2211.1 conj |
|---|---|---|---|---|---|
| προφήτης | λέγει | τοῦτο; | περὶ | ἑαυτοῦ, | ἢ |
| *prophētēs* | *legei* | *touto* | *peri* | *heautou* | *ē* |
| prophet | says | this? | concerning | himself, | or |

| 3875.1 prep | 2066.6 adj gen sing masc | 4948.1 indef-pron gen sing | 453.9 verb nom sing masc part aor act | 1156.2 conj | 3450.5 art nom sing masc |
|---|---|---|---|---|---|
| περὶ | ἑτέρου | τινός; | 35. Ἀνοίξας | δὲ | ὁ |
| *peri* | *heterou* | *tinos* | *Anoixas* | *de* | *ho* |
| concerning | other | some? | Having opened | and | |

| 5213.1 name nom masc | 3450.16 art sing neu | 4601.1 noun sing neu | 840.3 prs-pron gen sing | 2504.1 conj | 751.10 verb nom sing masc part aor mid |
|---|---|---|---|---|---|
| Φίλιππος | τὸ | στόμα | αὐτοῦ, | καὶ | ἀρξάμενος |
| *Philippos* | *to* | *stoma* | *autou* | *kai* | *arxamenos* |
| Philip | the | mouth | his, | and | having begun |

captors He would give himself. Surely it must have been exciting to Philip as he saw how wonderful and how exact God's timing was.

**8:33.** The Hebrew text used by the later Masoretes (Jewish scholars of tradition) reads "from oppression and from judgment he was taken." One scholar, C.R. North, has translated the Hebrew text from which this quote is derived as follows: "After arrest and sentence he was taken off, And on his fate who reflected? For he was cut off from the land of the living" (see Bruce, *New International Commentary on the the New Testament, Acts,* note 49, p.188). Certainly this passage would have been quite an enigma to anyone not familiar with the life of Jesus and His death on the cross.

The Greek text of this verse reads, "In the humiliation his judgment (that is, his punishment) was taken away." He humbled himself to take the place of a servant. Then He humbled himself even further to die the most humiliating kind of death known at that time. But death could not hold Him, and through the Resurrection the punishment He received on our behalf was taken away. (Compare Philippians 2:7-11.) "Who shall declare his generation?" may mean "Who can describe his origin?" (Compare 1 Corinthians 2:8, "Had they known it, they would not have crucified the Lord of glory.") The Masoretic text also reads "for he is cut off from the land of the living." The Greek for "taken" implies killing, thus there is no essential difference between the readings.

**8:34.** The eunuch then requested Philip to tell him about whom the prophet Isaiah was speaking—of himself or of some other person. Isaiah 53 speaks of the One who was to suffer wholly for the sins of others and not for any of His own. The eunuch knew no one who could do that, and he was puzzled.

Some writers speculate that the eunuch could not have been in Jerusalem any length of time without hearing at least something about Jesus, His miracles, His sufferings, death, and resurrection. But it is not known how long he was there. He may have simply come to worship among the thousands who thronged the temple and then gone on his way without coming into contact with any of the believers. If he had heard of Jesus he did not make any connection between Him and Isaiah 53.

**8:35.** This was Philip's great opportunity. Beginning at that very Scripture passage, he preached Jesus; he told the eunuch the good news, the gospel about Jesus. Jesus had never sinned and had never done anything to deserve suffering or death. No passage in the Prophets more clearly pictures the vicarious suffering, death, resurrection, and triumph of Jesus.

Philip undoubtedly pointed out the many ways in which Isaiah 53 speaks of Jesus. But that was only the beginning. He went on



**so opened he not his mouth:** So he refrains from opening his lips, *TCNT* . . . So he made no sound, *BB, NLT* . . . He says nothing, *NCV* . . . in his humility, *Murdock.*

**33. In his humiliation his judgement was taken away:** In his lowly condition justice was denied him, *TCNT* . . . In his humiliation he was deprived of his trial, *Berkeley* . . . He was humiliated and deprived of justice, *TNT* . . . He was shamed; and all his rights were taken away, *NCV* . . . was refused him, *Noyes* . . . deprived of the justice due Him, *Norlie* . . . No one listened to Him because of His shame, *NLT.*

**and who shall declare his generation?:** Who will tell the story of his age, *TCNT* . . . who shall describe, *Campbell* . . . his offspring? *Berkeley* . . . Who will make known His posterity, *Weymouth* . . . Who can tell, *Williams* . . . Who will tell the story to His generation, *Norlie* . . . There will be no story about his descendants, *SEB* . . . without children to continue, *Everyday* . . . Who will describe his descendants? *TNT* . . . his family, *Klingensmith.*

**for his life is taken from the earth:** For He is destroyed from among men, *Weymouth* . . . His life is removed, *Williams* . . . For His life on this earth was taken away, *Norlie* . . . he is deprived of his life on earth? *NAB* . . . his life on earth has ended, *Everyday, NCV.*

**34. And the eunuch answered Philip, and said: I pray thee, of whom speaketh the prophet this?:** I beg of you, *KJII* . . . Will you tell me whom the Prophet is speaking about, *TCNT.*

**of himself, or of some other man?:** . . . himself, or someone else, *TCNT.*

**35. Then Philip opened his mouth:** Then Philip began, *TCNT* . . . began to speak, *Everyday.*

**and began at the same scripture:** . . . and taking this passage as his text, *TCNT* . . . launched out with this Scripture passage as his starting point, *NAB* . . . and starting from this passage, *Good-*

| 570.3 prep | 3450.10 art gen sing fem | 1118.2 noun gen sing fem | 3642.10 dem-pron gen sing fem | 2076.17 verb 3sing indic aor mid |
|---|---|---|---|---|
| ἀπὸ | τῆς | γραφῆς | ταύτης, | εὐηγγελίσατο |
| *apo* | *tēs* | *graphēs* | *tautēs* | *euēngelisato* |
| from | the | Scripture | this, | announced the good news |

| 840.4 prs-pron dat sing | 3450.6 art acc sing masc | 2400.3 name acc masc | | 5453.1 conj | 1156.2 conj | 4057.38 verb 3pl indic imperf mid |
|---|---|---|---|---|---|---|
| αὐτῷ | τὸν | Ἰησοῦν. | **36.** | ὡς | δὲ | ἐπορεύοντο |
| *autō* | *ton* | *Iēsoun* | | *hōs* | *de* | *eporeuonto* |
| to him | | Jesus. | | As | and | they were going |

| 2567.3 prep | 3450.12 art acc sing fem | 3461.4 noun acc sing fem | 2048.1 verb indic aor act | 1894.3 prep | 4948.10 indef-pron sing neu | 5045.1 noun sing neu |
|---|---|---|---|---|---|---|
| κατὰ | τὴν | ὁδόν, | ἦλθον | ἐπί | τι | ὕδωρ· |
| *kata* | *tēn* | *hodon* | *ēlthon* | *epi* | *ti* | *hudōr* |
| along | the | way, | they came | upon | some | water, |

| 2504.1 conj | 5183.2 verb 3sing indic pres act | 3450.5 art nom sing masc | 2116.1 noun nom sing masc | 1481.20 verb 2sing impr aor mid | 5045.1 noun sing neu |
|---|---|---|---|---|---|
| καί | φησιν | ὁ | εὐνοῦχος, | Ἰδοὺ | ὕδωρ· |
| *kai* | *phēsin* | *ho* | *eunouchos* | *Idou* | *hudōr* |
| and | says | the | eunuch, | Behold | water; |

37.a.**Txt:** 08E,Steph
**Var:** p45,p74,01ℵ,02A
03B,04C,020L,025P
044,33,byz.sa.bo.Gries
Lach,Treg,Alf,Tisc
We/Ho,Weis,Sod
UBS/☆

| 4949.9 intr-pron sing neu | 2940.1 verb 3sing indic pres act | 1466.6 prs-pron acc 1sing | 901.25 verb inf aor pass | | 1500.5 verb 3sing indic aor act |
|---|---|---|---|---|---|
| τί | κωλύει | με | βαπτισθῆναι; | **37.** ⸂[a] | Εἶπεν |
| *ti* | *kōluei* | *me* | *baptisthēnai* | | *Eipen* |
| what | prevents | me | to be baptized? | | Said |

| 1156.2 conj | 3450.5 art nom sing masc | 5213.1 name nom masc | 1479.1 conj | 3961.5 verb 2sing indic pres act | 1523.1 prep gen | 3513.7 adj gen sing fem |
|---|---|---|---|---|---|---|
| δὲ | ὁ | Φίλιππος, | Εἰ | Πιστεύεις | ἐξ | ὅλης |
| *de* | *ho* | *Philippos* | *Ei* | *Pisteueis* | *ex* | *holēs* |
| and | | Philip, | If | you believe | from | whole |

| 3450.10 art gen sing fem | 2559.1 noun fem | 1815.1 verb 3sing indic pres act | 552.12 verb nom sing masc part aor pass | 1156.2 conj | 1500.5 verb 3sing indic aor act |
|---|---|---|---|---|---|
| τῆς | καρδίας, | ἔξεστιν. | Ἀποκριθεὶς | δὲ | εἶπεν, |
| *tēs* | *kardias* | *exestin* | *Apokritheis* | *de* | *eipen* |
| the | heart, | it is lawful. | Having answered | and | he said, |

| 3961.4 verb 1sing indic pres act | 3450.6 art acc sing masc | 5048.4 noun acc sing masc | 3450.2 art gen sing | 2296.2 noun gen sing masc | 1498.32 verb inf pres act | 3450.6 art acc sing masc |
|---|---|---|---|---|---|---|
| Πιστεύω | τὸν | υἱὸν | τοῦ | θεοῦ | εἶναι | τὸν |
| *Pisteuō* | *ton* | *huion* | *tou* | *theou* | *einai* | *ton* |
| I believe | the | Son | | of God | to be | |

| 2400.3 name acc masc | 5382.4 name acc masc | | 2504.1 conj | 2724.3 verb 3sing indic aor act | 2449.14 verb inf aor act |
|---|---|---|---|---|---|
| Ἰησοῦν | χριστόν. ⸃ | **38.** | καὶ | ἐκέλευσεν | στῆναι |
| *Iēsoun* | *christon* | | *kai* | *ekeleusen* | *stēnai* |
| Jesus | Christ. | | And | he commanded | to stand still |

| 3450.16 art sing neu | 710.3 noun sing neu | 2504.1 conj | 2568.15 verb 3pl indic aor act | 295.1 adj nom pl masc | 1519.1 prep |
|---|---|---|---|---|---|
| τὸ | ἅρμα, | καὶ | κατέβησαν | ἀμφότεροι | εἰς |
| *to* | *harma* | *kai* | *katebēsan* | *amphoteroi* | *eis* |
| the | chariot. | And | they went down | both | to |

| 3450.16 art sing neu | 5045.1 noun sing neu | 3614.16 rel-pron sing neu | 4885.1 conj | 5213.1 name nom masc | 2504.1 conj | 3450.5 art nom sing masc |
|---|---|---|---|---|---|---|
| τὸ | ὕδωρ, | ὅ | τε | Φίλιππος | καὶ | ὁ |
| *to* | *hudōr* | *ho* | *te* | *Philippos* | *kai* | *ho* |
| the | water, | which | both | Philip | and | the |

to explain the gospel further with its commands, promises, call to repentance, its assurance of salvation, and other aspects of the kingdom of God.

**8:36.** As Philip and the eunuch continued on down the road they came to some water ("certain water"). "Certain water" here can refer to a spring, a pool, or a stream. The eunuch immediately called attention to it. "See" is the same word translated "behold" in verse 27 and indicates something unexpected, even surprising. Most of southern Palestine is rather dry. Not only was this pool or stream unexpected, it might be a long time before they would come to another one. The eunuch did not want to pass it by without being baptized.

The eunuch put his request in the form of a question, "What hinders me from being baptized?" or, "What is there to prevent me from being baptized?" Probably, he was afraid his being a Gentile and a eunuch might bar him from this ordinance of the Church, just as it barred him from most of the Jewish worship.

**8:37.** Philip then asked for a confession of faith coming from the heart of the eunuch. To believe with the whole heart would mean that he really understood now and that he was willing to commit his whole being to Christ to follow and obey Him.

The eunuch's response shows that he accepted Jesus as the Messiah, God's anointed Prophet, Priest, and King, and that he understood who Jesus is, the Son of God, and therefore the believer's Saviour and Lord.

This verse is omitted by some ancient manuscripts and by many modern scholars, but it fits the context and reflects the practice of the Early Church. Several of the ideas represented here are clearly stated elsewhere in the Bible (e.g., Romans 10:8-10,13). It is also quoted by Early Church fathers such as Cyprian and Irenaeus. The Early Church did not hesitate to baptize new believers immediately if they had sufficient background in the Scriptures.

**8:38.** With the assurance that his faith was accepted, the eunuch commanded the driver of the chariot to stop. Then both the eunuch and Philip left the chariot and went down into the water. In fact, Luke drew attention to the fact that both went down (*katabainō*), not merely to the edge of the water, but into the water. Then Philip baptized him and they came up out of the water.

In this context the word "baptized" appears to have its usual meaning of "immerse, submerge, dip under." Archaeologists have also discovered baptistries in the ruins of second-century church buildings, showing that baptism by immersion was practiced quite early in the Church. Nevertheless, many scholars are not willing to be too dogmatic on the issue of whether baptism must only be by immersion.

*speed* . . . started with this same Scripture, *Everyday* . . . started with this part of the Holy Writings, *NLT.*

**and preached unto him Jesus:** . . . told him the Good News about Jesus, *TCNT* . . . proclaimed good news to him—Jesus, *Young* . . . he preached to him the gospel of Jesus, *KJII* . . . he announced to him, *Williams C.K.* . . . gave him the good news, *BB.*

**36. And as they went on their way:** Presently, as they were going along the road, *TCNT* . . . As they continued down the road, *Williams* . . . As they journeyed along, *Kleist* . . . Proceeding on the road, *MLNT* . . . While they were traveling down the road, *Everyday, NCV* . . . as they were going along the way, *KJII* . . . As they moved along the road, *NAB* . . . going on their way, *BB* . . . Now as they went on their journey, *Williams C.K.*

**they came unto a certain water:** . . . came to some water, *Everyday, Kleist, TNT* . . . a brook, *Fenton.*

**and the eunuch said, See, here is water; what doth hinder me to be baptized?:** The officer said...What is stopping me from, *Everyday* . . . what is to prevent my being baptized, *TCNT* . . . why may I not have baptism? *BB* . . . What is there to keep me from being baptized, *Williams* . . . what forbids my being immersed, *HBIE* . . . is there any reason why I should not be baptized now? *Phillips.*

**37. And Philip said, If thou believest with all thine heart, thou mayest:** Philip answered, *Everyday* . . . If you heartily believe, *Berkeley* . . . from the whole heart, it is lawful, *KJII* . . . it is allowable, *Murdock* . . . it can be done, *TNT* . . . it is permitted, *MLNT.*

**And he answered and said, I believe that Jesus Christ is the Son of God:**

**38. And he commanded the chariot to stand still:** Then the officer, *Everyday* . . . So he ordered the carriage to stop, *TCNT.*

**and they went down both into the water, both Philip and the eunuch and he baptized him:** . . . the two descended into, *Wuest*

| 2116.1 noun nom sing masc | 2504.1 conj | 901.8 verb 3sing indic aor act | 840.6 prs-pron acc sing masc | 3616.1 conj | 1156.2 conj |
|---|---|---|---|---|---|
| εὐνοῦχος· | καὶ | ἐβάπτισεν | αὐτόν. | 39. ὅτε | δὲ |
| *eunouchos* | *kai* | *ebaptisen* | *auton* | *hote* | *de* |
| eunuch, | and | he baptized | him. | When | but |

| 303.14 verb 3pl indic aor act | 1523.2 prep gen | 3450.2 art gen sing | 5045.2 noun gen sing neu | 4011.1 noun sing neu | 2935.2 noun gen sing masc |
|---|---|---|---|---|---|
| ἀνέβησαν | ἐκ | τοῦ | ὕδατος | πνεῦμα | κυρίου |
| *anebēsan* | *ek* | *tou* | *hudatos* | *pneuma* | *kuriou* |
| they came up | out of | the | water | Spirit | of Lord |

| 720.5 verb 3sing indic aor act | 3450.6 art acc sing masc | 5213.4 name acc masc | 2504.1 conj | 3620.2 partic | 1481.3 verb 3sing indic aor act |
|---|---|---|---|---|---|
| ἥρπασεν | τὸν | Φίλιππον· | καὶ | οὐκ | εἶδεν |
| *hērpasen* | *ton* | *Philippon* | *kai* | *ouk* | *eiden* |
| caught away | | Philip, | and | not | saw |

| 840.6 prs-pron acc sing masc | 3629.1 adv | 3450.5 art nom sing masc | 2116.1 noun nom sing masc | 4057.36 verb 3sing indic imperf mid | 1056.1 conj |
|---|---|---|---|---|---|
| αὐτὸν | οὐκέτι | ὁ | εὐνοῦχος, | ἐπορεύετο | γὰρ |
| *auton* | *ouketi* | *ho* | *eunouchos* | *eporeueto* | *gar* |
| him | no longer | the | eunuch, | he was going | for |

| 3450.12 art acc sing fem | 3461.4 noun acc sing fem | 840.3 prs-pron gen sing | 5299.8 verb nom sing masc part pres act | 5213.1 name nom masc |
|---|---|---|---|---|
| τὴν | ὁδὸν | αὐτοῦ | χαίρων. | 40. Φίλιππος |
| *tēn* | *hodon* | *autou* | *chairōn* | *Philippos* |
| the | way | his | rejoicing. | Philip |

| 1156.2 conj | 2128.32 verb 3sing indic aor pass | 1519.1 prep | 107.1 name acc fem | 2504.1 conj | 1324.12 verb nom sing masc part pres mid |
|---|---|---|---|---|---|
| δὲ | εὑρέθη | εἰς | Ἄζωτον· | καὶ | διερχόμενος |
| *de* | *heurethē* | *eis* | *Azōton* | *kai* | *dierchomenos* |
| but | was found | at | Azotus, | and | passing through |

| 2076.27 verb 3sing indic imperf mid | 3450.15 art acc pl fem | 4032.5 noun pl fem | 3820.16 adj acc pl fem | 2175.1 conj |
|---|---|---|---|---|
| εὐηγγελίζετο | τὰς | πόλεις | πάσας, | ἕως |
| *euēngelizeto* | *tas* | *poleis* | *pasas* | *heōs* |
| he was announcing the good news | the | cities | all, | till |

| 3450.2 art gen sing | 2048.23 verb inf aor act | 840.6 prs-pron acc sing masc | 1519.1 prep | 2513.3 name acc fem | 3450.5 art nom sing masc |
|---|---|---|---|---|---|
| τοῦ | ἐλθεῖν | αὐτὸν | εἰς | Καισάρειαν. | 9:1. Ὁ |
| *tou* | *elthein* | *auton* | *eis* | *Kaisareian* | *Ho* |
| the | to come | him | to | Caesarea. | |

| 1156.2 conj | 4425.1 name nom masc | 2068.1 adv | 1693.1 verb nom sing masc part pres act | 543.1 noun gen sing fem | 2504.1 conj | 5245.1 noun gen sing masc |
|---|---|---|---|---|---|---|
| δὲ | Σαῦλος, | ἔτι | ἐμπνέων | ἀπειλῆς | καὶ | φόνου |
| *de* | *Saulos* | *eti* | *empneōn* | *apeilēs* | *kai* | *phonou* |
| But | Saul, | still | breathing out | threats | and | murder |

| 1519.1 prep | 3450.8 art acc pl masc | 3073.8 noun acc pl masc | 3450.2 art gen sing | 2935.2 noun gen sing masc | 4193.4 verb nom sing masc part aor act |
|---|---|---|---|---|---|
| εἰς | τοὺς | μαθητὰς | τοῦ | κυρίου, | προσελθὼν |
| *eis* | *tous* | *mathētas* | *tou* | *kuriou* | *proselthōn* |
| toward | the | disciples | of the | Lord, | having come |

| 3450.3 art dat sing | 744.3 noun dat sing masc | 153.28 verb 3sing indic aor mid | 3706.1 prep | 840.3 prs-pron gen sing | 1976.8 noun acc pl fem |
|---|---|---|---|---|---|
| τῷ | ἀρχιερεῖ | 2. ᾐτήσατο | παρ' | αὐτοῦ | ἐπιστολὰς |
| *tō* | *archierei* | *ētēsato* | *par'* | *autou* | *epistolas* |
| to the | high priest | asked | from | him | letters |

The important thing, however, is that the eunuch wanted to obey the command of Jesus and become His disciple and follower. His baptism was the testimony of a good conscience that had been cleansed by his faith in Jesus and His shed blood.

**8:39.** Again Luke had said two men both went down into the water. Now they came up out of the water. Then the Spirit of the Lord suddenly snatched Philip away, and the eunuch never saw him again. A few ancient manuscripts and versions add that the Holy Spirit fell on the eunuch before Philip was snatched away.

**8:40.** Apparently, the Spirit of the Lord gave Philip a miracle ride over to the coast of the Mediterranean Sea at Azotus (near the site of the ancient Ashdod, about 20 miles north of Gaza).

From there Philip proceeded northward along the coast, preaching the gospel (evangelizing, telling the good news, the same good news he told the eunuch) in all the cities along the way until he came to Caesarea. This Caesarea, built by Herod the Great, was the capital of the Roman province of Judea. Philip was still there years later. Evidently he made it his headquarters from this time on. But he still traveled around telling the good news and became known as Philip the evangelist (21:8).

**9:1.** Now the Book of Acts returns to Saul. Some of the Sanhedrin and others who joined in the persecution of 8:1 may have lost their zeal against the Christians, but not Saul. He was still "breathing out threatenings" (the Greek is singular, not plural) and "slaughter" (murder) against those who were disciples (learners, students, and followers) of the Lord Jesus. Later, when he was speaking before King Agrippa, he told how he put many of the saints (the dedicated believers) in prison and how he voted for their death.

"Breathing out" here is literally "breathing in." It is a Greek participle (*empneōn*) indicating this had become characteristic and continuous. Saul created an atmosphere around him of threat and murder so that he was constantly breathing it in. As oxygen enables an athlete to keep going, so this atmosphere kept Saul going.

As a result of this persistent persecution, most of the believers left Jerusalem. What happened in Samaria did not concern Saul. But Philip was only one of those who were scattered in all directions. Saul must have heard rumors that these believers were having success in preaching the gospel. So he determined to do something about it and went to the high priest for permission to do so. This led to an event so important that the Book of Acts records it three times.

**9:2.** Some of those who were scattered went north and on to Damascus. Damascus was the oldest and most important city in

. . . and the official, *Kleist* . . . and he immersed him, *ABUV* . . . Philip gave him baptism, *BB.*

**39. And when they were come up out of the water:** But no sooner had they come up, *Weymouth* . . . from the water, *MLNT.*

**the Spirit of the Lord caught away Philip:** . . . snatched Philip away, *Montgomery, NAB* . . . suddenly took Philip away, *Williams* . . . hurriedly transported Philip, *Berkeley* . . . was carried off by the spirit, *Knox* . . . hurried Philip away, *Goodspeed* . . . seized Philip, *Williams C.K.*

**that the eunuch saw him no more:** . . . the eunuch lost sight of him, *Moffatt* . . . the officer never saw him again, *NCV* . . . saw nothing more of him, *Goodspeed.*

**and he went on his way rejoicing:** . . . but continued, *Montgomery* . . . With a glad heart he resumed his journey, *Weymouth* . . . so he went joyfully on his way, *Berkeley* . . . full of joy, *BB.*

**40. but Philip was found at Azotus: and passing through he preached in all the cities, till he came to Caesarea:** As for Philip, he was next heard of...and from there, *Knox* . . . appeared in a city called, *NCV* . . . found himself at Ashdod and passing through the country he announced the good news to all the towns, *Williams C.K.* . . . he preached the gospel to all the cities, *ASV* . . . and went on telling the good news, *Goodspeed.*

**1. And Saul, yet breathing out threatenings and slaughter against the disciples of the Lord:** In the meantime, *TEV* . . . still uttering murderous threats against, *TCNT* . . . still breathing threats of death, *Kleist* . . . was still trying to frighten the followers...by saying he would kill them, *Everyday* . . . and murder against, *KJII* . . . was still talking much about how he would like to kill the followers of the Lord, *NLT.*

**went unto the high priest:** . . . called on, *Berkeley.*

**2. And desired of him letters to Damascus to the synagogues:** . . . asked him to write letters to, *NCV* . . . and requested of him

| 1519.1 prep | 1149.2 name acc fem | 4242.1 prep | 3450.15 art acc pl fem | 4715.7 noun acc pl fem | 3567.1 conj |
|---|---|---|---|---|---|
| εἰς | Δαμασκὸν | πρὸς | τὰς | συναγωγάς, | ὅπως |
| *eis* | *Damaskon* | *pros* | *tas* | *sunagōgas* | *hopōs* |
| to | Damascus, | to | the | synagogues, | so that |

| 1430.1 partic | 4948.9 indef-pron acc pl masc | 2128.12 verb 3sing subj aor act | 3450.10 art gen sing fem | 3461.2 noun gen sing fem | 1498.25 verb acc pl masc part pres act |
|---|---|---|---|---|---|
| ἐάν | τινας | εὕρῃ | τῆς | ὁδοῦ | ὄντας |
| *ean* | *tinas* | *heurē* | *tēs* | *hodou* | *ontas* |
| if | any | he found | of the | way | being |

| 433.9 noun acc pl masc | 4885.1 conj | 2504.1 conj | 1129.9 noun acc pl fem | 1204.18 verb acc pl masc part perf mid | 70.11 verb 3sing subj aor act |
|---|---|---|---|---|---|
| ἄνδρας | τε | καὶ | γυναῖκας, | δεδεμένους | ἀγάγῃ |
| *andras* | *te* | *kai* | *gunaikas* | *dedemenous* | *agagē* |
| men | both | and | women, | having been bound | he might bring |

| 1519.1 prep | 2395.1 name fem | 1706.1 prep | 1156.2 conj | 3450.3 art dat sing | 4057.15 verb inf pres mid |
|---|---|---|---|---|---|
| εἰς | Ἱερουσαλήμ. | 3. ἐν | δὲ | τῷ | πορεύεσθαι |
| *eis* | *Hierousalēm* | *en* | *de* | *tō* | *poreuesthai* |
| to | Jerusalem. | In | but | the | to go |

| 1090.33 verb 3sing indic aor mid | 840.6 prs-pron acc sing masc | 1443.8 verb inf pres act | 3450.11 art dat sing fem | 1149.1 name dat fem |
|---|---|---|---|---|
| ἐγένετο | αὐτὸν | ἐγγίζειν | τῇ | Δαμασκῷ, |
| *egeneto* | *auton* | *engizein* | *tē* | *Damaskō* |
| it came to pass | him | to draw near | | to Damascus, |

3.a.**Txt:** 08E,020L,025P byz.
**Var:** 01ℵ,02A,03B,04C Lach,Treg,Alf,Word Tisc,Weis,Sod,UBS/☆

| 2504.1 conj | 1794.1 adv | 1794.1 adv | 4885.1 conj | 3878.1 verb 3sing indic aor act |
|---|---|---|---|---|
| ˹ καὶ | ἐξαίφνης | [[a]☆ ἐξαίφνης | τε ] | ˹ περιήστραψεν |
| *kai* | *exaiphnēs* | *exaiphnēs* | *te* | *periēstrapsen* |
| and | suddenly | [ suddenly | and ] | shone round about |

| 840.6 prs-pron acc sing masc | 840.6 prs-pron acc sing masc | 3878.1 verb 3sing indic aor act | 5295.1 noun sing neu | 570.3 prep |
|---|---|---|---|---|
| αὐτὸν | [☆ αὐτὸν | περιήστραψεν ] | φῶς | ˹ ἀπὸ |
| *auton* | *auton* | *periēstrapsen* | *phōs* | *apo* |
| him | [ him | shone round about ] | a light | from |

3.b.**Txt:** 08E,025P,byz.
**Var:** 01ℵ,02A,03B,04C 020L,Lach,Treg,Word Tisc,We/Ho,Weis,Sod UBS/☆

| 1523.2 prep gen | 3450.2 art gen sing | 3636.2 noun gen sing masc | 2504.1 conj | 3959.11 verb nom sing masc part aor act | 1894.3 prep |
|---|---|---|---|---|---|
| [[b]☆ ἐκ ] | τοῦ | οὐρανοῦ, | 4. καὶ | πεσὼν | ἐπὶ |
| *ek* | *tou* | *ouranou* | *kai* | *pesōn* | *epi* |
| [ out of ] | the | heaven, | and | having fallen | on |

| 3450.12 art acc sing fem | 1087.4 noun acc sing fem | 189.21 verb 3sing indic aor act | 5292.4 noun acc sing fem | 2978.21 verb acc sing fem part pres act | 840.4 prs-pron dat sing |
|---|---|---|---|---|---|
| τὴν | γῆν | ἤκουσεν | φωνὴν | λέγουσαν | αὐτῷ, |
| *tēn* | *gēn* | *ēkousen* | *phōnēn* | *legousan* | *autō* |
| the | earth | he heard | a voice | saying | to him, |

| 4406.1 name masc | 4406.1 name masc | 4949.9 intr-pron sing neu | 1466.6 prs-pron acc 1sing | 1371.2 verb 2sing indic pres act |
|---|---|---|---|---|
| Σαοὺλ | Σαούλ, | τί | με | διώκεις; |
| *Saoul* | *Saoul* | *ti* | *me* | *diōkeis* |
| Saul, | Saul, | why | me | are you persecuting? |

| 1500.5 verb 3sing indic aor act | 1156.2 conj | 4949.3 intr-pron nom sing | 1498.3 verb 2sing indic pres act | 2935.5 noun voc sing masc | 3450.5 art nom sing masc |
|---|---|---|---|---|---|
| 5. Εἶπεν | δέ, | Τίς | εἶ, | κύριε; | Ὁ |
| *Eipen* | *de* | *Tis* | *ei* | *kurie* | *Ho* |
| He said | and, | Who | are you, | Lord? | The |

Syria. At this time it was probably outside the Roman Empire and under King Aretas who made it part of Arabia. Aretas was anti-Roman as were the Jews. It seems Aretas allowed Jews freedom and gave the Jerusalem leaders authority over the Jews in Damascus. Saul went to the high priest and asked for official letters giving him authority to arrest any of "this way." He would then bring them bound to Jerusalem (26:11,12). This would mean a trial before the Sanhedrin and probably the death sentence.

Since there was more than one synagogue in Damascus it indicates the city must have had a large Jewish population. Quite a number of them must have responded to the gospel. *The Way* is an interesting title for the believers, one they could accept. Christ is the way of salvation, the way of life. (See 19:9,23; 22:4; 24:14,22.) But it was a way of life Saul was determined to destroy.

**9:3.** Damascus was about 140 miles northeast of Jerusalem, probably nearly 200 miles by road at that time. Near the end of the journey, a light from heaven suddenly shined (like lightning) around Saul.

*Light* in the Bible is often associated with manifestations of the presence of the Lord. In John 17:5, Jesus prayed to His Father, saying, "Glorify thou me with thine own self with the glory I had with thee before the world was." When Jesus rose from the dead, His resurrection body was transformed—it was immortal and incorruptible, no longer subject to aging or decay. Now He appeared to Saul as the risen and glorified Christ. Later on, in 1 Corinthians 15:8, Saul (Paul) referred to this: "Last of all (after the other resurrection appearances of Jesus) he was seen of me also, as of one born out of due time (as a miscarriage, an untimely birth)."

**9:4.** As this brilliant light shone around him, Saul fell to the ground overwhelmed. Then he heard a voice, "Saul, Saul, why do you keep persecuting me?" "Persecuting" also includes pursuing and driving out, the very thing Saul was intent on doing to the believers in Damascus, just as he had done to them in Jerusalem.

In referring to Saul, Luke always used the Greek form of his name (*Saulos*, as in 9:1). But here Luke quoted Jesus using the Hebrew form of his name (*Saoul*), which the Book of Acts is careful to preserve here. Saul later confirmed that Jesus was speaking in the Hebrew language (26:14). *Saul,* in Hebrew, means "asked for," that is, asked of God. Now the Lord was asking for him. He wanted this zealous persecutor for himself.

**9:5.** This appearance of Jesus was something special, something extraordinary, something beyond the normal. Saul did not know who it was at first, but he knew his Hebrew Bible very well and

letters to, *MLNT* . . . addressed to the Jewish congregations at, *TCNT* . . . wanted the high priest to give him the authority, *NCV* . . . to the Jewish places of worship, *NLT* . . . to the synagogues, *Everyday* . . . to the meeting-houses at, *Williams C.K.*

**that if he found any of this way, whether they were men or women:** . . . which would empower him to arrest...living according to the new way, *NAB* . . . to find people, *NCV* . . . If he found any there...people in Damascus who were followers of Christ's Way, *Everyday* . . . giving him authority, *TNT* . . . that were of the Way, *ASV* . . . any men or women there who belonged, *Goodspeed* . . . belonging to The Way, *Williams* . . . to this religion, *Williams C.K.*

**he might bring them bound unto Jerusalem:** . . . bring them in chains, and taken to, *TCNT* . . . convey them shackled to, *Berkeley* . . . he would arrest them and bring them back to Jerusalem, *Everyday* . . . he might bring them in bonds to, *Kleist* . . . as prisoners, to Jerusalem, *BB, MLNT.*

**3. And as he journeyed, he came near Damascus:** On his trip, *Adams* . . . was drawing near, *TNT* . . . it came to pass that he drew nigh unto, *ASV* . . . He was on his way there, *Williams C.K.* . . . as he was getting near, *TCNT* . . . As he traveled on he finally approached, *Williams* . . . as he came near the city, *Everyday* . . . During his journey, it happened, *Kleist.*

**and suddenly there shined round about him a light from heaven:** . . . suddenly a light from the sky flashed all round him, *TCNT* . . . a light out of heaven flashes about him, *Concordant* . . . suddenly beamed all around him, *Berkeley.*

**4. And he fell to the earth:** He fell to the ground, *NAB, TCNT* . . . and falling to the ground, *Kleist.*

**and heard a voice saying unto him, Saul, Saul, why persecutest thou me?:** . . . why are you persecuting me, *TCNT* . . . why are you working so hard against Me? *NLT* . . . Why are you doing things against me? *Everyday.*

## Acts 9:6

5.a.**Txt:** 020L,025P,byz. sa.
**Var:** 02A,03B,04C,Lach Treg,Alf,Word,Tisc We/Ho,Weis,Sod UBS/☆

5.b.**Txt:** it.Steph
**Var:** p74,01ℵ,02A,03B 04C,08E,025P,044,33 byz.sa.bo.Gries,Lach Treg,Alf,Word,Tisc We/Ho,Weis,Sod UBS/☆

| **1156.2** conj | **2935.1** noun nom sing masc | **1500.5** verb 3sing indic aor act | **1466.1** prs-pron nom 1sing | **1498.2** verb 1sing indic pres act |
|---|---|---|---|---|
| δέ | ⸀a κύριος | εἶπεν, ⸌ | Ἐγώ | εἰμι |
| *de* | *kurios* | *eipen* | *Egō* | *eimi* |
| and | Lord | said, | I | am |

| **2400.1** name nom masc | **3614.6** rel-pron acc sing masc | **4622.1** prs-pron nom 2sing | **1371.2** verb 2sing indic pres act | **4497.3** adj sing neu |
|---|---|---|---|---|
| Ἰησοῦς | ὃν | σὺ | διώκεις· | ⸀b σκληρόν |
| *Iēsous* | *hon* | *su* | *diōkeis* | *sklēron* |
| Jesus | whom | you | persecute. | Hard |

| **4622.3** prs-pron dat 2sing | **4242.1** prep | **2730.2** noun pl neu | **2952.1** verb inf pres act | **4981.2** verb nom sing masc part pres act | **4885.1** conj |
|---|---|---|---|---|---|
| σοι | πρὸς | κέντρα | λακτίζειν. | **6.** Τρέμων | τε |
| *soi* | *pros* | *kentra* | *laktizein* | *Tremōn* | *te* |
| for you | against | goads | to kick. | Trembling | and |

| **2504.1** conj | **2261.1** verb nom sing masc part pres act | **1500.5** verb 3sing indic aor act | **2935.5** noun voc sing masc | **4949.9** intr-pron sing neu | **1466.6** prs-pron acc 1sing |
|---|---|---|---|---|---|
| καὶ | θαμβῶν | εἶπεν, | Κύριε, | τί | με |
| *kai* | *thambōn* | *eipen* | *Kurie* | *ti* | *me* |
| and | wondering | he said, | Lord, | What | me |

| **2286.2** verb 2sing indic pres act | **4020.41** verb inf aor act | **2504.1** conj | **3450.5** art nom sing masc | **2935.1** noun nom sing masc | **4242.1** prep |
|---|---|---|---|---|---|
| θέλεις | ποιῆσαι; | Καὶ | ὁ | κύριος | πρὸς |
| *theleis* | *poiēsai* | *Kai* | *ho* | *kurios* | *pros* |
| desire you | to do? | And | the | Lord | to |

6.a.**Var:** p74,01ℵ,02A 03B,04C,08E,025P,044 33,byz.sa.bo.Gries,Lach Treg,Alf,Word,Tisc We/Ho,Weis,Sod UBS/☆

| **840.6** prs-pron acc sing masc | **233.2** conj | **448.8** verb 2sing impr aor act | **2504.1** conj | **1511.11** verb 2sing impr aor act |
|---|---|---|---|---|
| αὐτόν, ⸌ | [a☆+ ἀλλὰ ] | Ἀνάστηθι | καὶ | εἴσελθε |
| *auton* | *alla* | *Anastēthi* | *kai* | *eiselthe* |
| him, | [ But ] | Rise up | and | enter |

| **1519.1** prep | **3450.12** art acc sing fem | **4032.4** noun acc sing fem | **2504.1** conj | **2953.60** verb 3sing indic fut pass | **4622.3** prs-pron dat 2sing |
|---|---|---|---|---|---|
| εἰς | τὴν | πόλιν, | καὶ | λαληθήσεταί | σοι |
| *eis* | *tēn* | *polin* | *kai* | *lalēthēsetai* | *soi* |
| into | the | city, | and | it shall be told | you |

6.b.**Txt:** 08E,020L,025P byz.
**Var:** 01ℵ,02A,03B,04C Lach,Treg,Alf,Tisc Weis,Sod,UBS/☆

| **4949.9** intr-pron sing neu | **3614.16** rel-pron sing neu | **4949.9** intr-pron sing neu | **4622.4** prs-pron acc 2sing | **1158.1** verb 3sing indic pres act |
|---|---|---|---|---|
| ⸀ τί | [b☆ ὅ | τί ] | σε | δεῖ |
| *ti* | *ho* | *ti* | *se* | *dei* |
| what | [ what | something ] | you | it is necessary |

| **4020.20** verb inf pres act | **3450.7** art nom pl masc | **1156.2** conj | **433.6** noun nom pl masc | **3450.7** art nom pl masc | **4772.1** verb nom pl masc part pres act |
|---|---|---|---|---|---|
| ποιεῖν. | 7. Οἱ | δὲ | ἄνδρες | οἱ | συνοδεύοντες |
| *poiein* | *Hoi* | *de* | *andres* | *hoi* | *sunodeuontes* |
| to do. | The | but | men | the | traveling with |

| **840.4** prs-pron dat sing | **2449.24** verb 3pl indic plperf act | **1753.1** adj nom pl masc | **1753.2** adj nom pl masc | **189.14** verb nom pl masc part pres act |
|---|---|---|---|---|
| αὐτῷ | εἱστήκεισαν | ⸀ ἐννεοί, | [☆ ἐνεοί, ] | ἀκούοντες |
| *autō* | *heistēkeisan* | *enneoi* | *eneoi* | *akouontes* |
| him | had stood | speechless, | [ idem ] | hearing |

| **3173.1** conj | **3450.10** art gen sing fem | **5292.2** noun gen sing fem | **3235.4** num card acc masc | **1156.2** conj | **2311.11** verb nom pl masc part pres act |
|---|---|---|---|---|---|
| μὲν | τῆς | φωνῆς | μηδένα | δὲ | θεωροῦντες. |
| *men* | *tēs* | *phōnēs* | *mēdena* | *de* | *theōrountes* |
| indeed | the | voice | no one | but | seeing. |

recognized that this light from heaven had to be a divine manifestation. But the question confused him. Who was he persecuting other than the Christians? So he asked, "Who are you, Lord?" Some take this to mean, "Who are you, sir?" using the word *lord* merely as a term of polite address. But in response to this obviously supernatural manifestation, the word can only mean divine Lord.

The answer came at once, "I (emphatic) am Jesus whom you (emphatic) keep persecuting." In persecuting the Church, Saul was persecuting, driving out, pursuing the body of Christ whose individual members are in Christ. (See Matthew 25:40,45; Ephesians 1:23; 2:6.) Then Jesus added, "It is hard (rough, dangerous) for you to kick against the pricks (against the ox goads)."

By this Jesus recognized that much of Saul's persecution of the Christians was because he knew he had no answer for their arguments. It was a reaction by which he was trying to resist the conviction of the Holy Spirit.

This does not mean Saul was conscious that these were goads, or that he even realized he had no good arguments against the believers. He was so full of fury that he could think of nothing but how he could punish the believers and stop the spread of the gospel. He was zealous for the Jewish religion.

**9:6.** Now that Saul was faced with Jesus, not just a man, but the divine Lord, his whole attitude changed and he answered simply, "What shall I do, Lord?" (This response of Saul was omitted here, probably by an early copyist's mistake, and it is not found in any of the Greek manuscripts now extant. It is found in 22:10, however, and in the Latin Vulgate version it is found in 9:6.)

In response to this evidence of genuine repentance, Jesus told Saul to rise and go into the city of Damascus. There he would be told what would be necessary for him to do. Jesus actually told Saul more at this time, but Luke left the rest for Saul (as the apostle Paul) to tell in his defense before King Agrippa (26:16-18). In Galatians 1:1,11,12, and 16, Saul also made it clear that he was commissioned directly by Jesus himself, not by any man. In other words, Saul was a genuine apostle or "sent one," sent out and commissioned by Jesus himself.

**9:7.** Meanwhile, the men who were traveling with Saul stood speechless (from fright), hearing the voice (the sound, not the words) but seeing no one. When Paul later repeated this incident, the details he emphasized are slightly different. For example, 22:9 says those who were with Saul saw the light but did not hear the voice of the One speaking (cf. 26:13f.). Apparently, the men saw a light but not Christ himself; they heard the sound of a voice but not the words. Only Saul was able to hear both the voice and the words Jesus spoke. As 26:14 says, they all fell to the ground but the men with Saul were able to get up before he did.

**5. And he said, Who art thou, Lord?: And the Lord said, I am Jesus whom thou persecutest:** Saul said...The voice answered...I am the One you are trying to hurt, *Everyday* . . . he asked. Jesus replied, *Kleist* . . . Who are you, sir? *Goodspeed* . . . I am Jehoshua, *Wuest* . . . I am Jesus, whom you are persecuting, *RSV* . . . whom you have been, *MLNT* . . . Whom you are working against, *NLT* . . . and you are persecuting me, *Williams C.K.* . . . whom you are attacking, *BB* . . . was the response, *Fenton*.

**it is hard for thee to kick against the pricks:** This is a thankless task of thine, kicking against, *Knox* . . . the goads, *MLNT, Murdock* . . . to resist and rebel, *Norlie*.

**6. And he trembling and astonished said: Lord, what wilt thou have me to do:** . . . dazed and trembling, *Knox* . . . thou wish me to do? *Young* . . . what do you want me to do? *KJII* . . . was shaken and surprised, *NLT*.

**And the Lord said unto him: Arise, and go into the city:** Get up now, *Everyday* . . . and go into the town, *Williams C.K.*

**and it shall be told thee what thou must do:** Someone there will tell you, *NCV* . . . you will be told what you ought to do, *Goodspeed* . . . it will be made clear to you what you have to do, *BB* . . . what thy work is, *Knox*.

**7. And the men which journeyed with him stood speechless:** Meanwhile his traveling companions remained speechless, *Kleist* . . . His companions stood in bewilderment, *Knox* . . . standing dumb with amazement, *Weymouth* . . . His fellow-travellers stood, *Moffatt* . . . the men who were with him stood speechless, *Williams C.K.* . . . stood there but they said nothing, *Everyday, NCV* . . . were not able to say anything, *BB, NLT* . . . The men accompanying him, however, were stunned, *Fenton*.

**hearing a voice but seeing no man:** . . . hearing the sound of the voice, *TCNT* . . . they heard the voice well enough, *Berkeley, MLNT* . . . hearing indeed the voice, *Noyes* . . . no one was visible to them, *Murdock* . . . but saw no one, *Kliest* . . . but seeing no one, *BB, Fenton, Williams C.K.*

## Acts 9:8

8.a.**Txt:** 020L,025P,byz.
**Var:** 01ℵ,02A,03B,04C 08E,Lach,Treg,Alf Word,Tisc,We/Ho,Weis Sod,UBS/☆

| **1446.20** verb 3sing indic aor pass | **1156.2** conj | **3450.5** art nom sing masc | **4425.1** name nom masc | **570.3** prep | **3450.10** art gen sing fem |
|---|---|---|---|---|---|
| **8.** ἠγέρθη | δὲ | ⸂a ὁ ⸃ | Σαῦλος | ἀπὸ | τῆς |
| *ēgerthē* | *de* | *ho* | *Saulos* | *apo* | *tēs* |
| Rose up | and | | Saul | from | the |

| **1087.2** noun gen sing fem | **453.26** verb gen pl masc part perf mid | **1156.2** conj | **3450.1** art gen pl | **3652.6** noun gen pl masc | **840.3** prs-pron gen sing |
|---|---|---|---|---|---|
| γῆς· | ἀνεῳγμένων | δὲ | τῶν | ὀφθαλμῶν | αὐτοῦ |
| *gēs* | *aneōgmenōn* | *de* | *tōn* | *ophthalmōn* | *autou* |
| ground, | having been opened | and | the | eyes | his |

8.b.**Txt:** 02A-corr,04C 08E,020L,025P,byz.bo.
**Var:** p74,01ℵ,02A-org 03B,sa.Lach,Treg,Word Tisc,We/Ho,Weis,Sod UBS/☆

| **3625.3** num card acc masc | **3625.6** num card neu | **984.22** verb 3sing indic imperf act | **5332.1** verb nom pl masc part pres act | **1156.2** conj |
|---|---|---|---|---|
| ⸀ οὐδένα | [b☆ οὐδὲν ] | ἔβλεπεν. | χειραγωγοῦντες | δὲ |
| *oudena* | *ouden* | *eblepen* | *cheiragōgountes* | *de* |
| no one | [ idem ] | he was seeing. | Leading by the hand | but |

| **840.6** prs-pron acc sing masc | **1507.2** verb 3pl indic aor act | **1519.1** prep | **1149.2** name acc fem | **2504.1** conj | **1498.34** verb sing indic imperf act |
|---|---|---|---|---|---|
| αὐτὸν | εἰσήγαγον | εἰς | Δαμασκόν. | **9.** καὶ | ἦν |
| *auton* | *eisēgagon* | *eis* | *Damaskon* | *kai* | *ēn* |
| him | they brought | to | Damascus. | And | he was |

| **2232.1** noun fem | **4980.1** num card nom | **3231.1** partic | **984.12** verb nom sing masc part pres act | **2504.1** conj | **3620.2** partic | **2052.28** verb 3sing indic aor act |
|---|---|---|---|---|---|---|
| ἡμέρας | τρεῖς | μὴ | βλέπων, | καὶ | οὐκ | ἔφαγεν |
| *hēmeras* | *treis* | *mē* | *blepōn* | *kai* | *ouk* | *ephagen* |
| days | three | not | seeing, | and | not | did eat |

| **3624.1** conj | **3956.11** verb 3sing indic aor act | **1498.34** verb sing indic imperf act | **1156.2** conj | **4948.3** indef-pron nom sing | **3073.1** noun nom sing masc |
|---|---|---|---|---|---|
| οὐδὲ | ἔπιεν. | **10.** Ἦν | δέ | τις | μαθητὴς |
| *oude* | *epien* | *En* | *de* | *tis* | *mathētēs* |
| nor | drink. | There was | and | a certain | disciple |

| **1706.1** prep | **1149.1** name dat fem | **3549.4** noun dat sing neu | **366.4** name nom masc | **2504.1** conj | **1500.5** verb 3sing indic aor act |
|---|---|---|---|---|---|
| ἐν | Δαμασκῷ | ὀνόματι | Ἁνανίας· | καὶ | εἶπεν |
| *en* | *Damaskō* | *onomati* | *Hananias* | *kai* | *eipen* |
| in | Damascus | by name | Ananias. | And | said |

| **4242.1** prep | **840.6** prs-pron acc sing masc | **3450.5** art nom sing masc | **2935.1** noun nom sing masc | **1706.1** prep | **3568.3** noun dat sing neu | **1706.1** prep |
|---|---|---|---|---|---|---|
| πρὸς | αὐτὸν | ⸀ ὁ | κύριος | ἐν | ὁράματι, | [☆ ἐν |
| *pros* | *auton* | *ho* | *kurios* | *en* | *horamati* | *en* |
| to | him | the | Lord | in | a vision, | [in |

| **3568.3** noun dat sing neu | **3450.5** art nom sing masc | **2935.1** noun nom sing masc | **366.6** name voc masc | **3450.5** art nom sing masc | **1156.2** conj |
|---|---|---|---|---|---|
| ὁράματι | ὁ | κύριος, ] | Ἁνανία. | Ὁ | δὲ |
| *horamati* | *ho* | *kurios* | *Hanania* | *Ho* | *de* |
| a vision | the | Lord, ] | Ananias. | The | and |

| **1500.5** verb 3sing indic aor act | **1481.20** verb 2sing impr aor mid | **1466.1** prs-pron nom 1sing | **2935.5** noun voc sing masc | **3450.5** art nom sing masc | **1156.2** conj |
|---|---|---|---|---|---|
| εἶπεν, | Ἰδοὺ | ἐγώ, | κύριε. | **11.** Ὁ | δὲ |
| *eipen* | *Idou* | *egō* | *kurie* | *Ho* | *de* |
| said, | Behold | I, | Lord. | The | and |

| **2935.1** noun nom sing masc | **4242.1** prep | **840.6** prs-pron acc sing masc | **448.9** verb nom sing masc part aor act | **4057.23** verb 2sing impr aor pass | **1894.3** prep |
|---|---|---|---|---|---|
| κύριος | πρὸς | αὐτόν, | Ἀναστὰς | πορεύθητι | ἐπὶ |
| *kurios* | *pros* | *auton* | *Anastas* | *poreuthēti* | *epi* |
| Lord | to | him, | Having risen up | go | into |

**9:8.** Saul, it seems, shut his eyes because of the continuing brightness of the glory, but not until after he saw Jesus. He made it very clear in all his testimony that he was as much an eyewitness to the resurrection of Christ as the other apostles. (See especially 1 Corinthians 9:1; 15:8.)

When Saul got up off the ground, he was blind. His traveling companions led him into Damascus. What a contrast this was with the way he had begun the journey. Once leading, now he was being led. Intending to arrest the believers, he had been arrested by Christ. Having the authority of the high priest, he had come under the authority of the great High Priest. Expecting to put chains on helpless believers, now he was the helpless one.

**9:9.** Saul remained 3 days in the house where he was taken. Unable to see, he neither ate nor drank anything. The Jewish way of counting made the first day the day he entered Damascus, and the third day the day Ananias came. This gave Saul a day to think things over and to pray. Probably, he was so absorbed in prayer and meditation that he had no desire to eat or drink. It also gave the Holy Spirit opportunity to reveal Christ to his heart, mind, and soul.

Now that Saul knew he was wrong about Jesus and the believers, he could not help but realize he had been wrong about his interpretation of the Old Testament and its prophecies.

He had been depending on who he was and what he could do (see Philippians 3:5,6). His zeal was a jealous eagerness to uphold what he thought was God's honor, but that zeal was not according to knowledge (Romans 10:2). It was misdirected. Paul now realized that what he had said and done against Christ and the Church was blasphemy. Surely Saul began to realize all this during these important 3 days. He was in darkness, but the light and love of Christ was being shed abroad in his heart.

**9:10.** On the third day the Lord appeared in a vision to a disciple named Ananias. This was supernatural, not a dream, not a figment of the imagination. Ananias was not asleep, but fully awake and able to respond. He knew it was the Lord, and by saying, "Here I am, Lord," he expressed his availability and willingness to obey the Lord and to do whatever the Lord wanted him to do. Later (22:12) Paul pointed out that Ananias was a devout Jew (converted to the Lord) who still had a good reputation among all the Jews in Damascus.

**9:11.** Jesus told Ananias to arise (that is, get ready) and go to the street (the narrow street) called Straight. In ancient times this street went straight from one end of the city to the other, and it is still an important street in Damascus today. There he was to

**8. And Saul arose from the earth:** Saul got up from the ground, *Moffatt.*

**and when his eyes were opened, he saw no man:** . . . he saw nothing, *ASV* . . . though his eyes were open, he could see nothing, *MLNT* . . . his eyes were wide open, *Williams* . . . He opened his eyes, *Everyday* . . . but on opening his eyes, *Fenton* . . . he could not see, *TNT* . . . unable to see, *NAB* . . . saw no one, *Kleist.*

**but they led him by the hand, and brought him into Damascus:** They had to take him by the hand, *Goodspeed, NAB* . . . They accordingly, leading him, entered into, *Fenton* . . . So the men with Saul took his hand and led him, *Everyday* . . . and he was guided by the hand, *BB* . . . took him by, *Williams C.K.*

**9. And he was three days without sight:** For three whole days, *Kleist* . . . and for three days he was unable to see, *TCNT* . . . and for three days he remained blind, *Berkeley* . . . Saul could not see, *Everyday* . . . he continued blind, *NAB* . . . Here...he remained without sight, *Knox.*

**and neither did eat nor drink:** . . . and he took no food, *BB* . . . and neither ate nor drank, *RSV, Williams C.K.*

**10. And there was a certain disciple at Damascus, named Ananias:** . . . a follower of Jesus, *NCV* . . . a student, *Klingensmith.*

**and to him said the Lord in a vision, Ananias:** The Lord spake to this man in a dream, *Phillips* . . . to whom the Lord said in, *Kleist* . . . to him the Lord called in a vision, *Knox* . . . showed him in a dream what He wanted him to see, *NLT.*

**And he said, Behold, I am here, Lord:** Yes, Master, *TCNT* . . . Yes, Lord, *Goodspeed* . . . I am here, Lord, *Phillips* . . . Behold me, Lord, *Young* . . . Here I am, Lord, *Kleist* . . . came the answer, *NAB* . . . was his reply, *Fenton.*

**11. And the Lord said unto him, Arise, and go into the street which is called Straight:** Get up! *Everyday, NLT* . . . and go to Straight Street, *Weymouth* . . . Go at once, *NAB* . . . go to the road, *Knox.*

| 3450.12 art acc sing fem | 4362.1 noun acc sing fem | 3450.12 art acc sing fem | 2535.34 verb acc sing fem part pres mid | 2097.2 adj acc sing fem | 2504.1 conj |
|---|---|---|---|---|---|
| τὴν | ῥύμην | τὴν | καλουμένην | Εὐθεῖαν, | καὶ |
| *tēn* | *rhumēn* | *tēn* | *kaloumenēn* | *Eutheian* | *kai* |
| the | street | the | being called | Straight, | and |

| 2195.18 verb 2sing impr aor act | 1706.1 prep | 3477.3 noun dat sing fem | 2430.2 name masc | 4425.4 name acc masc | 3549.4 noun dat sing neu | 4869.2 name-adj acc sing masc |
|---|---|---|---|---|---|---|
| ζήτησον | ἐν | οἰκίᾳ | Ἰούδα | Σαῦλον | ὀνόματι, | Ταρσέα. |
| *zētēson* | *en* | *oikia* | *Iouda* | *Saulon* | *onomati* | *Tarsea* |
| seek | in | house | of Judas | Saul | by name, | of Tarsus: |

| 1481.20 verb 2sing impr aor mid | 1056.1 conj | 4195.3 verb 3sing indic pres mid | | 2504.1 conj | 1481.3 verb 3sing indic aor act | 1706.1 prep |
|---|---|---|---|---|---|---|
| ἰδοὺ | γὰρ | προσεύχεται, | **12.** | καὶ | εἶδεν | ‘ ἐν |
| *idou* | *gar* | *proseuchetai* | | *kai* | *eiden* | *en* |
| behold | for | he prays, | | and | he saw | in |

| 3568.3 noun dat sing neu | 433.4 noun acc sing masc | 433.4 noun acc sing masc | 1706.1 prep | 3568.3 noun dat sing neu | 3549.4 noun dat sing neu |
|---|---|---|---|---|---|
| ὁράματι | ἄνδρα | [☆ ἄνδρα | ἐν | ὁράματι ] | ‘ ὀνόματι |
| *horamati* | *andra* | *andra* | *en* | *horamati* | *onomati* |
| a vision | a man | [ a man | in | a vision ] | by name |

| 366.5 name acc masc | 366.5 name acc masc | 3549.4 noun dat sing neu | 1511.12 verb part aor act | 2504.1 conj |
|---|---|---|---|---|
| Ἁνανίαν | [☆ Ἁνανίαν | ὀνόματι ] | εἰσελθόντα | καὶ |
| *Hananian* | *Hananian* | *onomati* | *eiselthonta* | *kai* |
| Ananias | [ Ananias | by name ] | having come | and |

12.a.**Txt:** 020L,025P,byz. sa.
**Var1:** 02A,03B,05D,bo. Treg,Tisc,We/Ho,Weis Sod,UBS/☆
**Var2:** p74,01ℵ-org,04C 81,945,1739

| 1991.14 verb acc sing masc part aor act | 840.4 prs-pron dat sing | 5331.4 noun acc sing fem | 5331.8 noun acc pl fem | 3450.15 art acc pl fem |
|---|---|---|---|---|
| ἐπιθέντα | αὐτῷ | ‘ χεῖρα, | [1a χεῖρας | 2☆ τὰς |
| *epithenta* | *autō* | *cheira* | *cheiras* | *tas* |
| having placed | on him | a hand, | [ hands | the |

13.a.**Txt:** byz.
**Var:** 01ℵ,02A,03B,04C 08E,020L,025P,Gries Lach,Treg,Alf,Word Tisc,We/Ho,Weis,Sod UBS/☆

| 5331.8 noun acc pl fem | 3567.1 conj | 306.7 verb 3sing subj aor act | | 552.6 verb 3sing indic aor pass | 1156.2 conj |
|---|---|---|---|---|---|
| χεῖρας ] | ὅπως | ἀναβλέψῃ. | **13.** | Ἀπεκρίθη | δὲ |
| *cheiras* | *hopōs* | *anablepsē* | | *Apekrithē* | *de* |
| hands ] | so that | he should receive sight. | | Answered | and |

13.b.**Txt:** 020L,025P,byz. Sod
**Var:** 01ℵ,02A,03B,04C 08E,Lach,Treg,Alf,Tisc We/Ho,Weis,UBS/☆

| 3450.5 art nom sing masc | 366.3 name masc | 2935.5 noun voc sing masc | 189.37 verb 1sing indic perf act | 189.19 verb 1sing indic aor act |
|---|---|---|---|---|
| ‘a ὁ ’ | Ἀνανίας, | Κύριε, | ‘ ἀκήκοα | [b☆ ἤκουσα ] |
| *ho* | *Ananias* | *Kurie* | *akēkoa* | *ēkousa* |
| | Ananias, | Lord, | I have heard | [ I heard ] |

| 570.3 prep | 4044.1 adj gen pl | 3875.1 prep | 3450.2 art gen sing | 433.2 noun gen sing masc | 3642.1 dem-pron gen sing |
|---|---|---|---|---|---|
| ἀπὸ | πολλῶν | περὶ | τοῦ | ἀνδρὸς | τούτου, |
| *apo* | *pollōn* | *peri* | *tou* | *andros* | *toutou* |
| from | many | concerning | the | man | this, |

| 3607.8 rel-pron pl neu | 2527.9 adj pl neu | 4020.24 verb 3sing indic aor act | 3450.4 art dat pl | 39.8 adj dat pl masc | 4622.2 prs-pron gen 2sing |
|---|---|---|---|---|---|
| ὅσα | κακὰ | ‘ ἐποίησεν | τοῖς | ἁγίοις | σου |
| *hosa* | *kaka* | *epoiēsen* | *tois* | *hagiois* | *sou* |
| how many | evils | he did | to the | saints | your |

| 3450.4 art dat pl | 39.8 adj dat pl masc | 4622.2 prs-pron gen 2sing | 4020.24 verb 3sing indic aor act | 1706.1 prep | 2395.1 name fem |
|---|---|---|---|---|---|
| [☆ τοῖς | ἁγίοις | σου | ἐποίησεν ] | ἐν | Ἱερουσαλήμ· |
| *tois* | *hagiois* | *sou* | *epoiēsen* | *en* | *Hierousalēm* |
| [ the | saints | your | he did ] | in | Jerusalem; |

inquire (that is, seek, search) in the house of Judas for Saul of Tarsus. The directions are detailed. Ananias was well-known in the Jewish community of Damascus and he would know which Judas lived on Straight Street. Saul was a common name also, so he is identified as being from Tarsus. Tarsus was a city of about a half million people, in Cilicia about 10 miles from the Mediterranean coast.

The reason Ananias was to go was that Saul was praying. The word "behold" (Greek, *idou*) is used to draw attention to something surprising and unexpected. It also gives strong contrast to the atmosphere of threatening and murder Saul had previously created around himself. Notice too that he was not just saying prayers, as he might have done as a Pharisee, but he was really praying. He was humbly waiting before God.

**9:12.** Another reason Ananias was told to go to Saul was that Saul, while he was praying, had already seen a vision (a supernatural, God-given vision) of a man named Ananias coming in and laying his hands on him in order that he might regain his sight. God was preparing Saul even before he began to deal with Ananias to prepare him to go to Saul. This vision given to Saul was in answer to his prayer. It was also intended to raise his faith and help him anticipate further answers to prayer when Ananias came.

Notice too that God did not send for Peter and John, nor was it necessary for any apostle to lay hands on Saul. Ananias was a godly man, but not an apostle. The Book of Acts shows God can and does use ordinary believers to do His will and bring His healing. It also shows Paul did not get his commission through another apostle. He was commissioned directly by Jesus himself and then given further help and direction by another humble believer.

**9:13.** Though Ananias had at first expressed his willingness to obey the Lord, he began to object to the Lord's command as soon as he heard what it was. He knew about this Saul of Tarsus. Many people had told him about the many terrible things Saul had done to the Lord's saints at Jerusalem.

Ananias thus distinguished himself from the believers in Jerusalem. He was either born in Damascus or had lived there a long time. Obviously many of the believers who fled from the persecution after Stephen's death had come there and brought news of Saul's fury.

By the Lord's saints, Ananias meant all the believers. They were saints (holy, dedicated people who were separated and consecrated to the Lord and to His service) because they had turned their backs on the world and sin to follow Jesus. The word *saint* does not imply perfection. Rather, it simply means they were headed in the right direction. In the preaching and writings of the apostle Paul believers are called saints about 40 times.



**and enquire in the house of Judas for one called Saul, of Tarsus: for, behold, he prayeth:** Ask for a man named, *NCV* . . . ask for a certain Saul, *NAB* . . . Find the house of, *Everyday* . . . and make search at the house of Judas for one...for he is at prayer, *BB* . . . inquire at the house of Judah for...a Tarsian, *Fenton* . . . enquire...for a man of Tarsus...Even now he is at his prayers, *Knox* . . . for he is even now praying, *Weymouth*.

**12. And hath seen in a vision a man named Ananias coming in:** . . . and he has seen a man named, *Williams C.K.* . . . he has had a vision of a man called, *Knox* . . . in a dream, *NLT* . . . comes to him, *Everyday* . . . enter, *Kleist*.

**and putting his hand on him, that he might receive his sight:** . . . entering and laying hands, *MLNT* . . . laying his hands on him in order that he may recover his sight, *TNT* . . . to bring back his sight, *Moffatt* . . . so that he might see, *KJII* . . . Then he sees again, *NCV* . . . to restore his sight, *Goodspeed* . . . that he may get his sight back, *Williams C.K.* . . . so that he may be able to see, *BB* . . . to cure him of blindness, *Knox*.

**13. Then Ananias answered, Lord, I have heard by many of this man:** Ananias, however, objected...I have heard from many a person, *Kleist* . . . At this, Ananias answered, *Knox* . . . heard from many sources about this man, *NAB* . . . many people have told me, *Everyday* . . . I have had accounts of this man from a number of people, *BB*.

**how much evil he hath done to thy saints at Jerusalem:** . . . about all the harm, *Klingensmith* . . . all the hurt, *Knox* . . . especially the great suffering he has brought on your people, *Williams* . . . and the terrible things he did to your saints, *NCV* . . . he hath perpetrated towards, *Murdock* . . . how much wrong, *Beck* . . . how much injury he has done to Your holy ones at, *Fenton* . . . how many hardships, *Norlie* . . . He is the reason many of Your followers...had to suffer much, *NLT* . . . your holy people in Jerusalem, *Phillips*.

| 2504.1 conj | 5436.1 adv | 2174.4 verb 3sing indic pres act | 1833.4 noun acc sing fem | 3706.2 prep | 3450.1 art gen pl |
|---|---|---|---|---|---|
| 14. καὶ | ὧδε | ἔχει | ἐξουσίαν | παρὰ | τῶν |
| *kai* | *hōde* | *echei* | *exousian* | *para* | *tōn* |
| and | here | he has | authority | from | the |

| 744.6 noun gen pl masc | 1204.9 verb inf aor act | 3820.8 adj acc pl masc | 3450.8 art acc pl masc | 1926.9 verb acc pl masc part pres mid |
|---|---|---|---|---|
| ἀρχιερέων | δῆσαι | πάντας | τοὺς | ἐπικαλουμένους |
| *archiereōn* | *dēsai* | *pantas* | *tous* | *epikaloumenous* |
| chief priests | to bind | all | the | calling on |

| 3450.16 art sing neu | 3549.2 noun sing neu | 4622.2 prs-pron gen 2sing | 1500.5 verb 3sing indic aor act | 1156.2 conj | 4242.1 prep |
|---|---|---|---|---|---|
| τὸ | ὄνομά | σου. | 15. Εἶπεν | δὲ | πρὸς |
| *to* | *onoma* | *sou* | *Eipen* | *de* | *pros* |
| the | name | your. | Said | and | to |

| 840.6 prs-pron acc sing masc | 3450.5 art nom sing masc | 2935.1 noun nom sing masc | 4057.4 verb 2sing impr pres mid | 3617.1 conj | 4487.1 noun sing neu |
|---|---|---|---|---|---|
| αὐτὸν | ὁ | κύριος, | Πορεύου, | ὅτι | σκεῦος |
| *auton* | *ho* | *kurios* | *Poreuou* | *hoti* | *skeuos* |
| him | the | Lord, | Go, | for | a vessel |

| 1576.2 noun gen sing fem | 1466.4 prs-pron dat 1sing | 1498.4 verb 3sing indic pres act | 1498.4 verb 3sing indic pres act | 1466.4 prs-pron dat 1sing |
|---|---|---|---|---|
| ἐκλογῆς | ⸀ μοι | ἐστίν | [☆ ἐστίν | μοι ] |
| *eklogēs* | *moi* | *estin* | *estin* | *moi* |
| of choice | to me | is | [ is | to me ] |

15.a.**Var:** 03B,04C-org Lach,We/Ho,Weis UBS/☆

15.b.**Var:** 01א,02A,03B 04C,08E,Lach,Treg,Alf Word,Tisc,We/Ho,Weis Sod,UBS/☆

| 3642.4 dem-pron nom sing masc | 3450.2 art gen sing | 934.14 verb inf aor act | 3450.16 art sing neu | 3549.2 noun sing neu | 1466.2 prs-pron gen 1sing |
|---|---|---|---|---|---|
| οὗτος; | τοῦ | βαστάσαι | τὸ | ὄνομά | μου |
| *houtos* | *tou* | *bastasai* | *to* | *onoma* | *mou* |
| this, | the | to bear | the | name | my |

| 1783.1 prep | 3450.1 art gen pl | 1477.5 noun gen pl neu | 4885.1 conj | 2504.1 conj | 928.7 noun gen pl masc |
|---|---|---|---|---|---|
| ἐνώπιον | [a+ τῶν ] | ἐθνῶν | [b☆+ τε ] | καὶ | βασιλέων, |
| *enōpion* | *tōn* | *ethnōn* | *te* | *kai* | *basileōn* |
| before | [ the ] | Gentiles | [ both ] | and | kings, |

| 5048.7 noun gen pl masc | 4885.1 conj | 2447.1 name masc | 1466.1 prs-pron nom 1sing | 1056.1 conj | 5101.3 verb 1sing indic fut act |
|---|---|---|---|---|---|
| υἱῶν | τε | Ἰσραήλ. | 16. ἐγὼ | γὰρ | ὑποδείξω |
| *huiōn* | *te* | *Israēl* | *egō* | *gar* | *hupodeixō* |
| sons | and | of Israel: | I | for | will show |

| 840.4 prs-pron dat sing | 3607.8 rel-pron pl neu | 1158.1 verb 3sing indic pres act | 840.6 prs-pron acc sing masc | 5065.1 prep | 3450.2 art gen sing |
|---|---|---|---|---|---|
| αὐτῷ | ὅσα | δεῖ | αὐτὸν | ὑπὲρ | τοῦ |
| *autō* | *hosa* | *dei* | *auton* | *huper* | *tou* |
| to him | how much | it is necessary | him | for | the |

| 3549.3 noun gen sing neu | 1466.2 prs-pron gen 1sing | 3819.18 verb inf aor act | 562.2 verb 3sing indic aor act | 1156.2 conj |
|---|---|---|---|---|
| ὀνόματός | μου | παθεῖν. | 17. Ἀπῆλθεν | δὲ |
| *onomatos* | *mou* | *pathein* | *Apēlthen* | *de* |
| name | my | to suffer. | Went away | and |

| 366.4 name nom masc | 2504.1 conj | 1511.3 verb 3sing indic aor act | 1519.1 prep | 3450.12 art acc sing fem | 3477.4 noun acc sing fem | 2504.1 conj |
|---|---|---|---|---|---|---|
| Ἁνανίας | καὶ | εἰσῆλθεν | εἰς | τὴν | οἰκίαν, | καὶ |
| *Hananias* | *kai* | *eisēlthen* | *eis* | *tēn* | *oikian* | *kai* |
| Ananias | and | entered | into | the | house; | and |

**9:14.** The news had already come that Saul had authority from the chief priests to bind (with chains and thus make prisoners of) all who called on the name of Jesus. This can mean all who made a practice of calling on the name of Jesus, appealing to Him in prayer. Or, it could mean all who called themselves by the name of Jesus, admitting that they belonged to Him.

It seems probable from this that the Church in Damascus not only knew Saul was coming, but they were getting ready to face the same sort of scattering that had occurred because of the persecution in Jerusalem. All that Ananias had heard made him want to avoid Saul. It seemed it would not be safe for a believer to go near him. Yet Jesus was asking Ananias to go to him. Ananias' first thought must have been that the Lord wanted him to become another martyr like Stephen, and he was not anxious to suffer that way.

**9:15.** The Lord was patient with Ananias. He did not rebuke him for this expressed unwillingness to go. He understood how Ananias felt. So He again commanded Ananias to go and reassured him that he did not need to worry about any trouble or persecution from Saul. Not only was he praying, Saul was Christ's own chosen vessel to carry His name (including His character, nature, and authority) before the Gentiles (that is, before all the nations outside of Israel) and also before kings and the children (sons, descendants, people) of Israel.

"Vessel" is a general word used of anything or any equipment that is useful. "Chosen" also has the idea of choice, excellent, outstanding, well-adapted. Thus, Jesus was saying He considered Saul a choice instrument who would be eminently suited and useful to carry out His purpose in spreading the gospel to the Gentiles. His background, his education, his knowledge of the Old Testament Scriptures, his knowledge of the Greek writers, and his energy and zeal, were all things the Holy Spirit could use once he was brought into right relationship with Jesus, and once he was taught the facts of the gospel. (He was taught many of these facts and even some of the sayings of Jesus by Jesus himself. See Galatians 1:11,12,16.) Thus, the apostle Paul did become the outstanding apostle to the Gentiles.

**9:16.** Moreover, Ananias did not need to fear Saul, for it was Saul who would have to suffer. In fact, Jesus himself would show Saul (warn him, point out to him) how much it would be necessary for him to suffer for the sake of His name.

The necessity of Saul's suffering is emphatic here. But he would not suffer as punishment for his persecution of the Church. He would not suffer because of any failures or lack of faith on his part.

**9:17.** Ananias did not hesitate any longer. He obeyed the Lord's command, went to the house of Judas, entered it, and immediately

**14. And here he hath authority from the chief priests to bind all that call on thy name:** . . . to put in chains all those who invoke your name, *TCNT* . . . and here he is authorized by the High Priests, *Weymouth* . . . with authorization from, *NAB* . . . He came here with the right and the power from the head religious leaders, *NLT* . . . given him the power to arrest everyone who believes in you, *NCV* . . . to put in chains, *TNT* . . . to arrest all who invoke your name, *Kleist* . . . to chain all who call on Your name, *KJII* . . . who worships you, *Everyday.*

**15. But the lord said unto him, Go thy way:** Go, *Weymouth* . . . Still, you must go, *TCNT* . . . You must go! *NAB* . . . the Lord commanded him, *Kleist.*

**for he is a chosen vessel unto me:** . . . my chosen instrument, *TCNT* . . . My choice instrument, *Berkeley* . . . an elect vessel, *Darby* . . . a chosen tool, *Klingensmith* . . . I have chosen Saul for an important work, *NCV* . . . This man is the means I have chosen, *Goodspeed.*

**to bear my name before the Gentiles, and kings, and the children of Israel:** . . . to bring my name, *Williams C.K.* . . . He must tell about me to non-Jews...and to the people of Israel, *Everyday* . . . to carry my name among nations, *Kleist* . . . before the heathen and their kings, *TCNT* . . . among the people who are not Jews, *NLT* . . . as well as before the sons of Israel, *Moffatt.*

**16. For I will shew him how great things he must suffer for my name's sake:** Indeed, I myself will show him, *Phillips* . . . I shall make clear to him, *Norlie* . . . I myself shall indicate to him, *NAB* . . . I will show him how much suffering he must bear, *Williams C.K.* . . . how great are the sufferings, *Williams* . . . he will have to endure for my sake, *Goodspeed* . . . on behalf of, *MLNT.*

**17. And Ananias went his way, and entered into the house:** And Ananias departed, *ASV* . . . With that Ananias left, *NAB* . . . left and went into, *TNT* . . . set out and went to, *Goodspeed* . . . entered the house, *Kleist* . . . went out and came to, *Williams C.K.*

| 1991.12 verb nom sing masc part aor act | 1894.2 prep | 840.6 prs-pron acc sing masc | 3450.15 art acc pl fem | 5331.8 noun acc pl fem | 1500.5 verb 3sing indic aor act |
|---|---|---|---|---|---|
| ἐπιθεὶς | ἐπ' | αὐτὸν | τὰς | χεῖρας | εἶπεν, |
| *epitheis* | *ep'* | *auton* | *tas* | *cheiras* | *eipen* |
| having laid | upon | him | the | hands | he said, |

| 4406.1 name masc | 79.5 noun voc sing masc | 3450.5 art nom sing masc | 2935.1 noun nom sing masc | 643.17 verb 3sing indic perf act |
|---|---|---|---|---|
| Σαοὺλ | ἀδελφέ, | ὁ | κύριος | ἀπέσταλκέν |
| *Saoul* | *adelphe* | *ho* | *kurios* | *apestalken* |
| Saul | brother, | the | Lord | has sent |

| 1466.6 prs-pron acc 1sing | 2400.1 name nom masc | 3450.5 art nom sing masc | 3571.24 verb nom sing masc part aor pass | 4622.3 prs-pron dat 2sing |
|---|---|---|---|---|
| με, | Ἰησοῦς | ὁ | ὀφθείς | σοι |
| *me* | *Iēsous* | *ho* | *ophtheis* | *soi* |
| me, | Jesus | the | having appeared | to you |

| 1706.1 prep | 3450.11 art dat sing fem | 3461.3 noun dat sing fem | 3614.11 rel-pron dat sing fem | 2048.58 verb 2sing indic imperf mid | 3567.1 conj |
|---|---|---|---|---|---|
| ἐν | τῇ | ὁδῷ | ᾗ | ἤρχου, | ὅπως |
| *en* | *tē* | *hodō* | *hē* | *ērchou* | *hopōs* |
| in | the | way | in which | you were coming, | that |

| 306.6 verb 2sing subj aor act | 2504.1 conj | 3990.6 verb 2sing subj aor pass | 4011.2 noun gen sing neu | 39.2 adj gen sing |
|---|---|---|---|---|
| ἀναβλέψῃς | καὶ | πλησθῇς | πνεύματος | ἁγίου. |
| *anablepsēs* | *kai* | *plēsthēs* | *pneumatos* | *hagiou* |
| you might receive sight | and | be filled | with Spirit | Holy. |

18.a.**Txt:** 020L,025P,byz.
**Var:** 01ℵ,02A,03B,04C
08E,Lach,Treg,Alf,Tisc
We/Ho,Weis,Sod
UBS/⋆

| | 2504.1 conj | 2091.1 adv | 628.1 verb 3pl indic aor act | 628.2 verb 3pl indic aor act | 570.3 prep |
|---|---|---|---|---|---|
| **18.** | Καὶ | εὐθέως | ʻ ἀπέπεσον | [ᵃ☆ ἀπέπεσαν ] | ʻ ἀπὸ |
| | *Kai* | *eutheōs* | *apepeson* | *apepesan* | *apo* |
| | And | immediately | fell | [ idem ] | from |

| 3450.1 art gen pl | 3652.6 noun gen pl masc | 840.3 prs-pron gen sing | 840.3 prs-pron gen sing | 570.3 prep | 3450.1 art gen pl |
|---|---|---|---|---|---|
| τῶν | ὀφθαλμῶν | αὐτοῦ | [☆ αὐτοῦ | ἀπὸ | τῶν |
| *tōn* | *ophthalmōn* | *autou* | *autou* | *apo* | *tōn* |
| the | eyes | his | [ his | from | the |

| 3652.6 noun gen pl masc | 5448.1 adv | 5453.1 conj | 2987.1 noun nom pl fem | 306.3 verb 3sing indic aor act |
|---|---|---|---|---|
| ὀφθαλμῶν ] | ʻ ὡσεὶ | [☆ ὡς ] | λεπίδες, | ἀνέβλεψέν |
| *ophthalmōn* | *hōsei* | *hōs* | *lepides* | *aneblepsen* |
| eyes ] | as it were | [ idem ] | scales, | he received sight |

18.b.**Txt:** 04C-corr,08E
020L,byz.sa.
**Var:** 01ℵ,02A,03B
04C-org,025P,bo.Gries
Lach,Treg,Alf,Tisc
We/Ho,Weis,Sod
UBS/⋆

| 4885.1 conj | 3777.1 adv | 2504.1 conj | 448.9 verb nom sing masc part aor act | 901.14 verb 3sing indic aor pass |
|---|---|---|---|---|
| τε | ʻᵇ παραχρῆμα, ˎ | καὶ | ἀναστὰς | ἐβαπτίσθη, |
| *te* | *parachrēma* | *kai* | *anastas* | *ebaptisthē* |
| and | instantly, | and | having risen up | was baptized; |

| | 2504.1 conj | 2956.25 verb nom sing masc part aor act | 5001.3 noun acc sing fem | 1749.2 verb 3sing indic aor act | 1090.33 verb 3sing indic aor mid |
|---|---|---|---|---|---|
| **19.** | καὶ | λαβὼν | τροφὴν | ἐνίσχυσεν˙ | Ἐγένετο |
| | *kai* | *labōn* | *trophēn* | *enischusen* | *Egeneto* |
| | and | having taken | food | he was strengthened. | Was |

19.a.**Txt:** 020L,025P,byz.
**Var:** 01ℵ,02A,03B,04C
08E,sa.bo.Gries,Lach
Treg,Alf,Word,Tisc
We/Ho,Weis,Sod
UBS/⋆

| 1156.2 conj | 3450.5 art nom sing masc | 4425.1 name nom masc | 3196.3 prep | 3450.1 art gen pl | 1706.1 prep | 1149.1 name dat fem |
|---|---|---|---|---|---|---|
| δὲ | ʻᵃ ὁ | Σαῦλος ˎ | μετὰ | τῶν | ἐν | Δαμασκῷ |
| *de* | *ho* | *Saulos* | *meta* | *tōn* | *en* | *Damaskō* |
| and | | Saul | with | the | in | Damascus |

laid his hands on the sightless Saul, calling him "Brother Saul." By this he recognized that Saul was now a believer, and that by faith Saul had been accepted into the family of God with Christ as his elder Brother. Calling each other brother and sister was not just a form in the Early Church. It was something very precious, a wonderful expression of their new relationship to each other in Jesus Christ.

Then Ananias explained that the Lord had sent him, and he identified the Lord as Jesus who had appeared to Saul on the road. This explanation probably seemed necessary to Ananias, for the Jews normally used the term *Lord* to mean Jehovah or Yahweh (the proper pronunciation of this divine Name of the one true God is not known for certain). But it really was not necessary, for Saul had already recognized Jesus as the divine Lord and therefore the divine Son of God.

Ananias added that the Lord had sent him for two reasons. First, that Saul might recover his sight; second, that he might be filled with the Holy Spirit (that is, empowered for the ministry to which the Lord was calling him).

Notice that though Ananias was a "layman," God did not limit this ministry of healing and encouraging believers to the apostles or to officers of the Church. Also, since Ananias was a native of Damascus and the apostles had not left Jerusalem, no apostle had laid hands on him to receive the Spirit, yet he had obviously been filled. Now he was laying hands on Saul because he was acting in simple faith and obedience to the command of Jesus.

**9:18.** Immediately, without any long prayers or any great effort on the part of Ananias, the Lord accomplished His purpose in sending Ananias. Something like scales (fish scales) fell from Saul's eyes and he could see again. A similar incident is recorded in Tobit, an apocryphal work written in the Second Century B.C. (cf. 3:17; 11:13). Then he rose up (probably from his knees) and was baptized in water, thus bearing witness publicly to his newfound faith.

This verse does not tell how Saul received the Spirit; however, Jesus sent Ananias to lay hands on Saul for the recovery of his sight *and* for the filling with the Holy Spirit. It is possible that both happened at the same time. Verse 12 does not say Jesus commanded Ananias to lay hands on Saul so that he might be filled with the Spirit. The testimony he shared with Saul shows that verse 12 does not report everything Jesus said to him in the vision. (Titus 3:5-7 confirms that the Holy Spirit was poured out on Paul abundantly though it does not specify when this occurred.)

**9:19.** Then Saul ended his fast, took food, and became strong. After that he stayed some days with the disciples in Damascus. Nothing more is said about Ananias. He undoubtedly continued to serve the Lord in humble obedience.

**and putting his hands on him said:** . . . and laying, *ASV* . . . He laid his hands on Saul, *NCV.*

**Brother Saul, the Lord, even Jesus, that appeared unto thee in the way as thou camest, hath sent me:** . . . who appeared to you on your journey, *Goodspeed* . . . on the road you traveled, *MLNT* . . . has commissioned me, *Concordant* . . . He is the one you saw on the road on your way here, *Everyday.*

**that thou mightest receive thy sight:** He sent me so that you can see again, *NCV* . . . to help you recover, *NAB* . . . so that you may recover your sight, *TCNT* . . . regain your sight, *Moffatt.*

**and be filled with the Holy Ghost:**

**18. And immediately there fell from his eyes as it had been scales:** Instantly something like scales fell from Saul's eyes, *TCNT* . . . something that looked like, *NCV* . . . And all at once, *Williams* . . . what seemed to be scales, *Weymouth* . . . something like a scab, *Murdock* . . . the appearance of incrustations, *Wuest* . . . as if a scaly substance fell from, *TNT* . . . like fish scales, *Everyday.*

**and he received sight forthwith:** . . . and his sight was restored, *Goodspeed, TCNT* . . . and he could see once more, *Weymouth* . . . he regained his sight, *Moffatt* . . . he instantly saw again, *KJII* . . . He was able to see again! *Everyday, NCV.*

**and arose, and was baptized:** Then he got up, *TCNT* . . . and was immersed, *ABUV* . . . Upon this he rose and received baptism, *Weymouth.*

**19. And when he had received meat, he was strengthened:** . . . he took food, *ASV* . . . After eating some food, his strength returned, *Everyday, NCV* . . . felt his strength return, *TCNT* . . . his strength returned to him after he had taken food, *NAB* . . . and regained his strength, *Weymouth* . . . was invigorated, *Murdock.*

**Then was Saul certain days with the disciples which were at Damascus:** Then he remained some little time, *Weymouth* . . . For several days, *Moffatt* . . . For some time Saul remained with, *MLNT* . . . stayed with the followers of Jesus, *Everyday.*

| 3073.6 noun gen pl masc | 2232.1 noun fem | 4948.9 indef-pron acc pl masc | | 2504.1 conj | 2091.1 adv | 1706.1 prep |
|---|---|---|---|---|---|---|
| μαθητῶν | ἡμέρας | τινάς˙ | 20. | καὶ | εὐθέως | ἐν |
| *mathētōn* | *hēmeras* | *tinas* | | *kai* | *eutheōs* | *en* |
| disciples | days | certain. | | And | immediately | in |

| 3450.14 art dat pl fem | 4715.6 noun dat pl fem | 2756.20 verb 3sing indic imperf act | 3450.6 art acc sing masc | 5382.4 name acc masc |
|---|---|---|---|---|
| ταῖς | συναγωγαῖς | ἐκήρυσσεν | τὸν | ⸀ Χριστόν, |
| *tais* | *sunagōgais* | *ekērussen* | *ton* | *Christon* |
| the | synagogues | he was proclaiming | the | Christ, |

20.a.**Txt:** 020L,025P,byz.
**Var:** p45,p74,01ℵ,02A
03B,04C,08E,sa.bo.
Gries,Lach,Treg,Alf
Word,Tisc,We/Ho,Weis
Sod,UBS/☆

| 2400.3 name acc masc | 3617.1 conj | 3642.4 dem-pron nom sing masc | 1498.4 verb 3sing indic pres act | 3450.5 art nom sing masc |
|---|---|---|---|---|
| [a☆ Ἰησοῦν ] | ὅτι | οὗτός | ἐστιν | ὁ |
| *Iēsoun* | *hoti* | *houtos* | *estin* | *ho* |
| [ Jesus ] | that | this | is | the |

| 5048.1 noun nom sing masc | 3450.2 art gen sing | 2296.2 noun gen sing masc | | 1822.8 verb 3pl indic imperf mid | 1156.2 conj | 3820.7 adj nom pl masc |
|---|---|---|---|---|---|---|
| υἱὸς | τοῦ | θεοῦ. | 21. | ἐξίσταντο | δὲ | πάντες |
| *huios* | *tou* | *theou* | | *existanto* | *de* | *pantes* |
| Son | | of God. | | Were being amazed | and | all |

| 3450.7 art nom pl masc | 189.14 verb nom pl masc part pres act | 2504.1 conj | 2978.25 verb indic imperf act | 3620.1 partic | 3642.4 dem-pron nom sing masc |
|---|---|---|---|---|---|
| οἱ | ἀκούοντες, | καὶ | ἔλεγον, | Οὐχ | οὗτός |
| *hoi* | *akouontes* | *kai* | *elegon* | *Ouch* | *houtos* |
| the | hearing, | and | were saying, | Not | this |

21.a.**Txt:** 03B,04C,08E
020L,025P,etc.byz.
We/Ho
**Var:** 01ℵ,02A,Tisc,Weis
Sod,UBS/☆

| 1498.4 verb 3sing indic pres act | 3450.5 art nom sing masc | 4058.1 verb nom sing masc part aor act | 1706.1 prep | 1519.1 prep |
|---|---|---|---|---|
| ἐστιν | ὁ | πορθήσας | ⸀ ἐν | [a εἰς ] |
| *estin* | *ho* | *porthēsas* | *en* | *eis* |
| is | the | having destroyed | in | [ idem ] |

| 2395.1 name fem | 3450.8 art acc pl masc | 1926.9 verb acc pl masc part pres mid | 3450.16 art sing neu | 3549.2 noun sing neu |
|---|---|---|---|---|
| Ἱερουσαλὴμ | τοὺς | ἐπικαλουμένους | τὸ | ὄνομα |
| *Hierousalēm* | *tous* | *epikaloumenous* | *to* | *onoma* |
| Jerusalem | the | calling on | the | name |

| 3642.17 dem-pron sing neu | 2504.1 conj | 5436.1 adv | 1519.1 prep | 3642.17 dem-pron sing neu | 2048.27 verb 3sing indic plperf act | 2419.1 conj |
|---|---|---|---|---|---|---|
| τοῦτο, | καὶ | ὧδε | εἰς | τοῦτο | ἐληλύθει | ἵνα |
| *touto* | *kai* | *hōde* | *eis* | *touto* | *elēluthei* | *hina* |
| this, | and | here | for | this | had come | so that |

| 1204.18 verb acc pl masc part perf mid | 840.8 prs-pron acc pl masc | 70.11 verb 3sing subj aor act | 1894.3 prep | 3450.8 art acc pl masc |
|---|---|---|---|---|
| δεδεμένους | αὐτοὺς | ἀγάγῃ | ἐπὶ | τοὺς |
| *dedemenous* | *autous* | *agagē* | *epi* | *tous* |
| having been bound | them | he might bring | to | the |

| 744.5 noun pl masc | | 4425.1 name nom masc | 1156.2 conj | 3095.1 adv comp | 1727.8 verb 3sing indic imperf pass |
|---|---|---|---|---|---|
| ἀρχιερεῖς; | 22. | Σαῦλος | δὲ | μᾶλλον | ἐνεδυναμοῦτο, |
| *archiereis* | | *Saulos* | *de* | *mallon* | *enedunamouto* |
| chief priests? | | Saul | but | more | was increasing in power, |

22.a.**Txt:** 01ℵ-corr,02A
04C,08E,020L,025P,etc.
byz.Sod
**Var:** 01ℵ-org,03B,Tisc
We/Ho,Weis,UBS/☆

| 2504.1 conj | 4648.1 verb 3sing indic imperf act | 4648.6 verb 3sing indic imperf act | 3450.8 art acc pl masc | 2428.5 name-adj acc pl masc |
|---|---|---|---|---|
| καὶ | ⸀ συνέχυνεν | [☆ συνέχυννεν ] | ⸂a τοὺς ⸃ | Ἰουδαίους |
| *kai* | *sunechunen* | *sunechunnen* | *tous* | *Ioudaious* |
| and | was confounding | [ idem ] | the | Jews |

**9:20.** Saul immediately became part of the body of disciples in Damascus. No doubt Ananias brought him to the meetings of the local assembly and explained to them what the Lord had done and how He had commissioned Saul to preach the gospel.

Because Saul accepted the Lord's commission, he did not wait to start preaching Christ. Immediately he went to the very synagogues where he had intended to search out the believers and send them bound to Jerusalem. Boldly he preached Christ (that is, that Jesus is the promised Messiah and Saviour) and declared that He is the Son of God. (This is the first time in Acts that the title "Son of God" is used of Jesus.) From what is seen later, it is clear that Saul's preaching included proofs from the Old Testament Scriptures that Jesus died "according to the Scriptures," and that He rose again, "according to the Scriptures," and that He is God's promised Anointed One, God's anointed Prophet, Priest, and King. His proofs that Jesus is the Son of God were also taken from the Scriptures as well as from the fact that God raised Jesus from the dead (Romans 1:4).

**9:21.** Saul's proclamation of the gospel brought amazement to the people in the synagogues who heard him. They were totally astonished, almost knocked out of their senses. They could hardly believe this was really the same person who had brought destruction on those in Jerusalem who called on the name of Jesus (those who called themselves by the name of Jesus, the followers of Jesus). The Jews in Damascus had all heard about Saul's zeal in persecuting the believers. They had also heard the news that Saul's purpose in coming to Damascus was to bring the believers bound to the chief priests in Jerusalem for trial before the Sanhedrin (bad news traveled fast even in those days). Now he was worshiping the One he had hated.

**9:22.** Saul, however, was more and more filled with mighty, supernatural power. He confounded the Jews living in Damascus, proving (deducing from the Scriptures) that this One (Jesus) is the Christ, the promised Messiah, God's Anointed One. He used Old Testament prophecies and showed how they were fulfilled in Jesus.

The fact that he "confounded the Jews" means he not only amazed and surprised them, he also agitated them and threw them into confusion and consternation. Many were upset by what he said, even distraught. The word also implies that some of them looked on him as one stirring up trouble. They knew Saul was not the only one involved in the death of Stephen and in the persecution that followed. If the chief priests had given permission for Saul to come and bind believers, there might soon be others who would come with the same purpose. Saul was ready to suffer for the sake of Christ's name now, but many of these Jews were not. Apparently, Saul's proofs from the Scriptures only angered them and roused

**20. And straightway he preached Christ in the synagogues:** . . . he began right away, *Adams* . . . And immediately he preached Jesus, *Noyes* . . . and began at once to declare, *Goodspeed* . . . he proclaimed Jesus, *ASV* . . . in the Jewish places of worship, *NLT.*

**that he is the Son of God:**

**21. But all that heard him were amazed, and said:** All his hearers were staggered and kept saying, *Phillips* . . . Any who heard it were greatly taken aback, *NAB* . . . was excited, *Klingensmith.*

**Is not this he that destroyed them which called on this name in Jerusalem:** He was trying to destroy those who trust in this name! *NCV* . . . who went about ravaging those, *MLNT* . . . made havoc of them, *ASV* . . . harassed, *Williams* . . . ravages those who are invoking this Name? *Concordant* . . . who beat and killed, *NLT* . . . spread desolation among them, *Campbell.*

**and came hither for that intent:** . . . with the sole object of, *Phillips* . . . Did he not come here purposely to apprehend such people, *NAB* . . . and who came here especially for the purpose, *Goodspeed.*

**that he might bring them bound unto the chief priests?:** . . . put in chains, *TCNT* . . . for the purpose of taking them, *TNT* . . . of arresting such persons and taking them before the high priests? *Goodspeed* . . . all such people as prisoners, *Phillips* . . . to take them as prisoners shackled, *MLNT.*

**22. But Saul increased the more in strength:** Saul's power...kept steadily increasing, *TCNT* . . . gained power more and more, *Weymouth* . . . went on from strength to strength, *Phillips* . . . grew steadily more powerful, *NAB* . . . were so strong, *NCV* . . . being endued with power, *Wuest* . . . gained more and more influence, *Montgomery.*

**and confounded the Jews which dwelt at Damascus:** . . . was confounding, *Rotherham* . . . continued to put to utter confusion, *Williams* . . . reduced the Jewish community of Damascus to silence, *NAB* . . . put to confusion the Jews, *TNT* . . . couldn't withstand his proofs, *LivB*

## Acts 9:23

| **3450.8** art acc pl masc | **2700.9** verb acc pl masc part pres act | **1706.1** prep | **1149.1** name dat fem | **4673.1** verb nom sing masc part pres act |
|---|---|---|---|---|
| τοὺς | κατοικοῦντας | ἐν | Δαμασκῷ, | συμβιβάζων |
| *tous* | *katoikountas* | *en* | *Damaskō* | *sumbibazōn* |
| the | dwelling | in | Damascus | proving |

| **3617.1** conj | **3642.4** dem-pron nom sing masc | **1498.4** verb 3sing indic pres act | **3450.5** art nom sing masc | **5382.1** name nom masc | **5453.1** conj |
|---|---|---|---|---|---|
| ὅτι | οὗτός | ἐστιν | ὁ | Χριστός. | **23.** Ὡς |
| *hoti* | *houtos* | *estin* | *ho* | *Christos* | *Hōs* |
| that | this | is | the | Christ. | When |

| **1156.2** conj | **3997.39** verb 3pl indic imperf pass | **2232.5** noun nom pl fem | **2401.9** adj nom pl fem | **4674.3** verb 3pl indic aor mid |
|---|---|---|---|---|
| δὲ | ἐπληροῦντο | ἡμέραι | ἱκαναί, | συνεβουλεύσαντο |
| *de* | *eplērounto* | *hēmerai* | *hikanai* | *suneboulеusanto* |
| but | were fulfilled | days | many, | consulted together |

| **3450.7** art nom pl masc | **2428.2** name-adj nom pl masc | **335.9** verb inf aor act | **840.6** prs-pron acc sing masc | **1091.43** verb 3sing indic aor pass |
|---|---|---|---|---|
| οἱ | Ἰουδαῖοι | ἀνελεῖν | αὐτόν· | **24.** ἐγνώσθη |
| *hoi* | *Ioudaioi* | *anelein* | *auton* | *egnōsthē* |
| the | Jews | to put to death | him. | Became known |

24.a.**Txt:** 020L,025P,byz.
**Var:** 01א,02A,03B,04C 08E,Lach,Treg,Alf Word,Tisc,We/Ho,Weis Sod,UBS/☆

24.b.**Txt:** 025P,byz.
**Var:** 01א,02A,03B,04C 08E,Lach,Treg,Alf,Tisc We/Ho,Weis,Sod UBS/☆

| **1156.2** conj | **3450.3** art dat sing | **4425.3** name dat masc | **3450.9** art nom sing fem | **1902.1** noun nom sing fem | **840.1** prs-pron gen pl |
|---|---|---|---|---|---|
| δὲ | τῷ | Σαύλῳ | ἡ | ἐπιβουλὴ | αὐτῶν. |
| *de* | *tō* | *Saulō* | *hē* | *epiboulē* | *autōn* |
| but | | to Saul | the | plot | their. |

| **3767.2** verb 3pl indic imperf act | **3767.5** verb 3pl indic imperf mid | **4885.1** conj | **1156.2** conj |
|---|---|---|---|
| ʻ παρετήρουν | [a☆ παρετηροῦντο ] | ʻ τε | [b☆ δὲ |
| *paretēroun* | *paretērounto* | *te* | *de* |
| They were watching | [ idem ] | and | [ and |

| **2504.1** conj | **3450.15** art acc pl fem | **4297.6** noun acc pl fem | **2232.1** noun fem | **4885.1** conj | **2504.1** conj | **3433.2** noun gen sing fem |
|---|---|---|---|---|---|---|
| καὶ ] | τὰς | πύλας | ἡμέρας | τε | καὶ | νυκτὸς, |
| *kai* | *tas* | *pulas* | *hēmeras* | *te* | *kai* | *nuktos* |
| both ] | the | gates | day | both | and | night, |

| **3567.1** conj | **840.6** prs-pron acc sing masc | **335.8** verb 3pl subj aor act | **2956.27** verb nom pl masc part aor act |
|---|---|---|---|
| ὅπως | αὐτὸν | ἀνέλωσιν· | **25.** λαβόντες |
| *hopōs* | *auton* | *anelōsin* | *labontes* |
| so that | him | they might put to death; | having taken |

25.a.**Txt:** 08E,020L 025P,byz.sa.bo.
**Var:** p74,01א,02A,03B 04C,Lach,Treg,Alf,Tisc We/Ho,Weis,Sod UBS/☆

| **1156.2** conj | **840.6** prs-pron acc sing masc | **3450.7** art nom pl masc | **3073.5** noun nom pl masc | **3450.7** art nom pl masc | **3073.5** noun nom pl masc |
|---|---|---|---|---|---|
| δὲ | ʻ αὐτὸν | οἱ | μαθηταὶ | [a☆ οἱ | μαθηταὶ |
| *de* | *auton* | *hoi* | *mathētai* | *hoi* | *mathētai* |
| but | him | the | disciples | [ the | disciples |

| **840.3** prs-pron gen sing | **3433.2** noun gen sing fem | **2496.1** verb 3pl indic aor act | **1217.2** prep | **3450.2** art gen sing | **4886.2** noun gen sing neu |
|---|---|---|---|---|---|
| αὐτοῦ ] | νυκτὸς | ʻ καθῆκαν | διὰ | τοῦ | τείχους, |
| *autou* | *nuktos* | *kathēkan* | *dia* | *tou* | *teichous* |
| his ] | by night | let down | through | the | wall, |

25.b.**Var:** 01א,02A,03B 04C,33,Lach,Treg,Alf Tisc,We/Ho,Weis,Sod UBS/☆

| **1217.2** prep | **3450.2** art gen sing | **4886.2** noun gen sing neu | **2496.1** verb 3pl indic aor act | **840.6** prs-pron acc sing masc |
|---|---|---|---|---|
| [☆ διὰ | τοῦ | τείχους | καθῆκαν ] | [b☆+ αὐτὸν ] |
| *dia* | *tou* | *teichous* | *kathēkan* | *auton* |
| [ through | the | wall | let down ] | [ him, ] |

further opposition just as Stephen's arguments had done earlier in Jerusalem. But now Saul was on the other side, and their opposition only caused him to look to the Lord and the Holy Spirit for even more of His mighty power.

The objections of some were overcome and at least some did accept Jesus as their Messiah and Saviour. The believers also must have been encouraged and strengthened by Saul's conversion and the tremendous change they saw in him. What a proof this is of the power of the gospel!

**9:23.** After a considerable time, the unbelieving Jews who were rejecting the gospel and who were separating themselves from the Jews who had become followers of Christ counseled with one another and came up with a plot to kill Saul.

Acts does not record how long the "many days" were. But Paul told the Galatians that he received the gospel he preached by revelation directly from Jesus himself, not from the other apostles, not from any man (Galatians 1:11,12,16). Even some of the sayings of Jesus may have been given him by Jesus himself. In 20:35 Paul quoted a saying of Jesus that is not recorded in the Gospels: "It is more blessed to give than to receive." In 1 Corinthians 11:23 he said he received the account of the Lord's Supper from Jesus himself. In other places he said he had a word from the Lord, by which he meant he had a saying of Jesus to back up what he was writing in his epistles. He had a commission from Christ himself.

Paul also told the Galatians that he left Damascus for a time during this period and went into Arabia and returned again to Damascus before going to Jerusalem.

Galatians 1:18 also says that it was not until after 3 years that the "many days" were fulfilled. Jesus may have given Saul some of His revelation of the gospel during the time he was blind, but probably most of it was given during the time he was in Arabia.

**9:24.** The plot of the Jews to kill Saul became known to him. Undoubtedly there were some who secretly admired Saul and let the details slip to one of the believers.

The Jews kept watching the gates of Damascus very carefully day and night. Second Corinthians 11:32 indicates that the governor (literally, the ethnarch) under King Aretas IV of Arabia (who reigned from 9 B.C. to A.D. 40) cooperated in this plot, or perhaps was paid by the Jews to give them help in seizing Saul. Saul's life was in danger, but this was only the first of many times when he would risk his life for the sake of the gospel.

**9:25.** The disciples (those converts who had become true students of the gospel and followers of Christ) foiled the plot of the Jews. They let Saul down "by the wall" in a large, flexible basket made of rushes, or something similar, woven together. Second Corin-

. . . could not argue with him, *NCV.*

**proving that this is very Christ:** . . . proving that Jesus was the Christ, *RSV* . . . he demonstrated that this, *Murdock* . . . shewing, by comparison, *Rotherham* . . . with his proofs, *Weymouth* . . . His proofs that Jesus is the Christ, *NCV* . . . proving beyond doubt, *Phillips* . . . His proofs ...were so strong, *Everyday* . . . by which he made it clear that Jesus was, *BB* . . . is the promised Savior, *Beck* . . . to be the Messiah, *TNT.*

**23. And after that many days were fulfilled:** After some time had gone by, *TCNT* . . . after a number of days had elapsed, *Moffatt* . . . After considerable time, *Berkeley* . . . had elapsed, *Fenton.*

**the Jews took counsel to kill him:** . . . the Jews laid a plot to kill Saul, *TCNT* . . . the Jews consulted together, *ABUV* . . . but they were seeking to kill him, *ASV* . . . But they kept trying to murder him, *Williams* . . . made an agreement together, *BB* . . . conspired to destroy him, *MLNT.*

**24. But their laying wait was known of Saul:** . . . but their plot became known, *RSV* . . . but information of their intention was given to him, *Weymouth* . . . but Saul got wind of their plot, *Berkeley* . . . but Saul discovered their plot, *Adams*. . . But their plan became known, *KJII* . . . but Saul learned about their plan, *NCV* . . . their plot came to his attention, *NAB.*

**And they watched the gates day and night to kill him:** . . . and they were even narrowly watching the gates, both day and night, that they might kill him, *Rotherham* . . . They went so far as to keep close watch on the city gates, *NAB* . . . Day and night they kept guarding the city gates, to murder him, *Williams* . . . plan to assassinate him, *Concordant.*

**25. Then the disciples took him by night:** . . . some of his converts, *LivB* . . . managed one night, *Moffatt* . . . conveying him by night, *Fenton* . . . contrived, *Knox.*

**and let him down by the wall in a basket:** . . . lowering him in a

| 5301.3 verb nom pl masc part aor act | 1706.1 prep | 4562.1 noun dat sing fem | 3716.7 verb nom sing masc part aor mid | 1156.2 conj |
|---|---|---|---|---|
| χαλάσαντες | ἐν | σπυρίδι. | 26. Παραγενόμενος | δὲ |
| *chalasantes* | *en* | *spuridi* | *Paragenomenos* | *de* |
| having lowered | in | a basket. | Having arrived | and |

26.a.**Txt:** 020L,025P,byz.
**Var:** 01ℵ,02A,03B,04C sa.bo.Gries,Lach,Treg Alf,Word,Tisc,We/Ho Weis,Sod,UBS/☆

26.b.**Txt:** 08E,020L 025P,byz.
**Var:** p74,01ℵ,02A,03B 04C,Lach,Treg,Tisc We/Ho,Weis,Sod UBS/☆

| 3450.5 art nom sing masc | 4425.1 name nom masc | 1519.1 prep | 2395.1 name fem | 3849.1 verb 3sing indic imperf mid |
|---|---|---|---|---|
| (a ὁ | Σαῦλος ⸃ | εἰς | Ἱερουσαλὴμ, | ( ἐπείρατο |
| *ho* | *Saulos* | *eis* | *Hierousalēm* | *epeirato* |
| | Saul | at | Jerusalem, | he was attempting |

| 3847.22 verb 3sing indic imperf act | 2827.3 verb inf pres mid | 3450.4 art dat pl | 3073.7 noun dat pl masc | 2504.1 conj |
|---|---|---|---|---|
| [b☆ ἐπείραζεν ] | κολλᾶσθαι | τοῖς | μαθηταῖς· | καὶ |
| *epeirazen* | *kollasthai* | *tois* | *mathētais* | *kai* |
| [ idem ] | to join himself | to the | disciples, | and |

| 3820.7 adj nom pl masc | 5236.25 verb 3pl indic imperf mid | 840.6 prs-pron acc sing masc | 3231.1 partic | 3961.13 verb nom pl masc part pres act | 3617.1 conj |
|---|---|---|---|---|---|
| πάντες | ἐφοβοῦντο | αὐτόν, | μὴ | πιστεύοντες | ὅτι |
| *pantes* | *ephobounto* | *auton* | *mē* | *pisteuontes* | *hoti* |
| all | were fearing | him, | not | believing | that |

| 1498.4 verb 3sing indic pres act | 3073.1 noun nom sing masc | 915.1 name nom masc | 1156.2 conj | 1934.5 verb nom sing masc part aor mid |
|---|---|---|---|---|
| ἐστὶν | μαθητής. | 27. Βαρναβᾶς | δὲ | ἐπιλαβόμενος |
| *estin* | *mathētēs* | *Barnabas* | *de* | *epilabomenos* |
| he is | a disciple. | Barnabas | but | having taken |

| 840.6 prs-pron acc sing masc | 70.8 verb 3sing indic aor act | 4242.1 prep | 3450.8 art acc pl masc | 646.7 noun acc pl masc | 2504.1 conj |
|---|---|---|---|---|---|
| αὐτὸν, | ἤγαγεν | πρὸς | τοὺς | ἀποστόλους, | καὶ |
| *auton* | *ēgagen* | *pros* | *tous* | *apostolous* | *kai* |
| him, | brought | to | the | apostles, | and |

| 1328.3 verb 3sing indic aor mid | 840.2 prs-pron dat pl | 4316.1 adv | 1706.1 prep | 3450.11 art dat sing fem | 3461.3 noun dat sing fem | 1481.3 verb 3sing indic aor act |
|---|---|---|---|---|---|---|
| διηγήσατο | αὐτοῖς | πῶς | ἐν | τῇ | ὁδῷ | εἶδεν |
| *diēgēsato* | *autois* | *pōs* | *en* | *tē* | *hodō* | *eiden* |
| related | to them | how | in | the | road | he saw |

| 3450.6 art acc sing masc | 2935.4 noun acc sing masc | 2504.1 conj | 3617.1 conj | 2953.27 verb 3sing indic aor act | 840.4 prs-pron dat sing | 2504.1 conj |
|---|---|---|---|---|---|---|
| τὸν | κύριον, | καὶ | ὅτι | ἐλάλησεν | αὐτῷ, | καὶ |
| *ton* | *kurion* | *kai* | *hoti* | *elalēsen* | *autō* | *kai* |
| the | Lord, | and | that | he spoke | to him, | and |

| 4316.1 adv | 1706.1 prep | 1149.1 name dat fem | 3817.4 verb 3sing indic aor mid | 1706.1 prep | 3450.3 art dat sing |
|---|---|---|---|---|---|
| πῶς | ἐν | Δαμασκῷ | ἐπαῤῥησιάσατο | ἐν | τῷ |
| *pōs* | *en* | *Damaskō* | *eparrhēsiasato* | *en* | *tō* |
| how | in | Damascus | he spoke boldly | in | the |

27.a.**Txt:** 01ℵ,08E,020L 025P,byz.Sod
**Var:** 03B,04C,Lach Treg,Alf,Tisc,We/Ho Weis,UBS/☆

| 3549.4 noun dat sing neu | 3450.2 art gen sing | 2400.2 name masc | 2504.1 conj | 1498.34 verb sing indic imperf act | 3196.2 prep | 840.1 prs-pron gen pl |
|---|---|---|---|---|---|---|
| ὀνόματι | (a τοῦ ⸃ | Ἰησοῦ. | 28. καὶ | ἦν | μετ' | αὐτῶν |
| *onomati* | *tou* | *Iēsou* | *kai* | *ēn* | *met'* | *autōn* |
| name | | of Jesus. | And | he was | with | them |

28.a.**Txt:** byz.
**Var:** 01ℵ,02A,03B,04C 08E,020L,025P,Lach Treg,Alf,Word,Tisc We/Ho,Weis,Sod UBS/☆

| 1515.3 verb nom sing masc part pres mid | 2504.1 conj | 1594.6 verb nom sing masc part pres mid | 1706.1 prep | 1519.1 prep |
|---|---|---|---|---|
| εἰσπορευόμενος | καὶ | ἐκπορευόμενος | ( ἐν | [a☆ εἰς ] |
| *eisporeuomenos* | *kai* | *ekporeuomenos* | *en* | *eis* |
| coming in | and | going out | in | [ into ] |

thians 11:33 adds that he was let down through a window. It was common in those days to build houses directly against the city wall. Then some would add an upper story with a section built over the top of the wall. The exact date of this escape is not certain, but it probably took place in A.D. 38. It was certainly a daring escape.

basket, *Rotherham* . . . let him down over the wall, *RSV* . . . by lowering him in a hamper-basket, *Williams* . . . conveying him, *Fenton* . . . through an opening in the city wall, *Everyday.*

**9:26.** After escaping from Damascus, Saul went south to Jerusalem. The road was familiar, but he was an entirely different person from the one who had traveled that road over 3 years before on the way to Damascus. Arriving in Jerusalem he kept trying to join with the disciples (in the worship and service of the Church), but they were all afraid of him and continued to fear him.

They had not forgotten what Saul had done to the believers, persecuting them, having them put in prison or killed. Perhaps their first thought was that this was surely some sort of trick or deception to find out who they were in order to destroy them.

The news of what had happened in Damascus apparently had not reached them. They had seen the persecution and heard the threats of Saul. After Saul left Jerusalem everything had quieted down. The apostles continued their witness, so many more Jews were converted to Christ, and the Church was reestablished and continued to grow.

No doubt, the believers felt it was wise to be cautious. They knew God does not expect us to believe everyone who comes along. It was hard to believe that the one who was most furious was now a true follower of Christ. But they were soon to learn that the gospel has power to save and deliver even the worst enemies of Christ.

**26. And when Saul was come to Jerusalem:** On his arrival at Jerusalem, *TCNT* . . . On reaching Jerusalem, *MLNT.*

**he assayed to join himself to the disciples:** . . . and made several attempts to associate with the disciples, *Weymouth* . . . and tried to join the disciples, *Moffatt* . . . made efforts to associate, *Berkeley, MLNT* . . . endeavoured, *LivB* . . . the group of followers, *Everyday.*

**but they were all afraid of him, and believed not that he was a disciple:** . . . not believing that he was, *ASV* . . . They even refused to believe, *NAB* . . . unable to believe that he was really, *Moffatt* . . . that he was really a disciple, *Williams* . . . finding it impossible to believe, *Phillips* . . . thought he was faking! *LivB* . . . and all avoided his company, *Knox* . . . that he was really a follower, *Everyday.*

**9:27.** Barnabas, however, was sympathetic, living up to the meaning of his name as the "son of encouragement." Some writers suggest that as a Hellenistic (Greek-speaking) Jew he had come from Cyprus to Jerusalem about the same time as Saul (also a Hellenistic Jew) came from Tarsus to study under Gamaliel, and that they might have known each other in earlier days.

Now Barnabas took an interest in Saul and apparently did some investigation. Then he "brought him to the apostles," that is, to some of the apostles. Galatians 1:18-24 shows that Saul (Paul) met only Peter and James the brother of Jesus at this time, and that he only stayed in Jerusalem 15 days on this visit. Though not one of the Twelve, James was considered an apostle because of Jesus' special appearance to him after the Resurrection (1 Corinthians 15:7). Barnabas explained how Saul had seen the Lord and how he continued to speak boldly, freely, and openly in the name of Jesus in Damascus.

**27. But Barnabas took him, and brought him to the apostles:** Barnabas, however, introduced him to the apostles, *TCNT* . . . took him up and presented him, *Williams* . . . accepted Saul, *Everyday.*

**and declared unto them how he had seen the Lord in the way, and that he had spoken to him:**

**and how he had preached boldly at Damascus in the name of Jesus:** . . . he had spoken out fearlessly, *TCNT* . . . he had fearlessly taught, *Weymouth* . . . and how courageously he had spoken, *Williams* . . . he had discoursed openly, *Murdock* . . . with the utmost boldness, *Phillips.*

**9:28.** For a time Saul was associated with the believers, for they now accepted him. But he did not spend all of his time with them. He went in and out among them, which means he visited other

**28. And he was with them coming in and going out at Jerusalem:** After that, Saul remained at Jerusalem, on familiar terms with the Apostles, *TCNT* . . . he associated with them freely in, *Goodspeed* . . . Henceforth Saul was one of them, *Weymouth* . . . So Saul moved freely among them in Jerusalem, *Kleist* . . . And he went about in the company, *Fenton.*

28.b.**Txt:** 08E,020L 025P,byz.bo.
**Var:** 01ℵ,02A,03B,04C Lach,Treg,Alf,Tisc We/Ho,Weis,Sod UBS/☆

28.c.**Txt:** 01ℵ-corr,020L 025P,byz.
**Var:** 01ℵ-org,02A,03B 08E,sa.bo.Lach,Treg,Alf Word,Tisc,We/Ho,Weis Sod,UBS/☆

| **2395.1** name fem | **2504.1** conj | **3817.1** verb nom sing masc part pres mid | **1706.1** prep | **3450.3** art dat sing |
|---|---|---|---|---|
| Ἱερουσαλήμ. | ⸂[b] καὶ ⸃ | παῤῥησιαζόμενος | ἐν | τῷ |
| *Hierousalēm* | *kai* | *parrhēsiazomenos* | *en* | *tō* |
| Jerusalem, | and | speaking boldly | in | the |

| **3549.4** noun dat sing neu | **3450.2** art gen sing | **2935.2** noun gen sing masc | **2400.2** name masc | **2953.45** verb 3sing indic imperf act |
|---|---|---|---|---|
| ὀνόματι | τοῦ | κυρίου | ⸂[c] Ἰησοῦ˙ ⸃ | **29.** ἐλάλει |
| *onomati* | *tou* | *kuriou* | *Iēsou* | *elalei* |
| name | of the | Lord | Jesus. | He was speaking |

| **4885.1** conj | **2504.1** conj | **4653.6** verb 3sing indic imperf act | **4242.1** prep | **3450.8** art acc pl masc | **1661.2** name acc pl masc |
|---|---|---|---|---|---|
| τε | καὶ | συνεζήτει | πρὸς | τοὺς | Ἑλληνιστάς˙ |
| *te* | *kai* | *sunezētei* | *pros* | *tous* | *Hellēnistas* |
| both | and | was discussing | with | the | Hellenists; |

| **3450.7** art nom pl masc | **1156.2** conj | **2005.2** verb 3pl indic imperf act | **840.6** prs-pron acc sing masc | **335.9** verb inf aor act |
|---|---|---|---|---|
| οἱ | δὲ | ἐπεχείρουν | ⸂ αὐτόν | ἀνελεῖν. |
| *hoi* | *de* | *epecheiroun* | *auton* | *anelein* |
| the | but | were taking in hand | him | to put to death. |

| **335.9** verb inf aor act | **840.6** prs-pron acc sing masc | **1906.10** verb nom pl masc part aor act | **1156.2** conj | **3450.7** art nom pl masc |
|---|---|---|---|---|
| [ ἀνελεῖν | αὐτόν. ] | **30.** ἐπιγνόντες | δὲ | οἱ |
| *anelein* | *auton* | *epignontes* | *de* | *hoi* |
| [ to put to death | him. ] | Having known | but | the |

| **79.6** noun nom pl masc | **2580.1** verb indic aor act | **840.6** prs-pron acc sing masc | **1519.1** prep | **2513.3** name acc fem |
|---|---|---|---|---|
| ἀδελφοὶ | κατήγαγον | αὐτὸν | εἰς | Καισάρειαν, |
| *adelphoi* | *katēgagon* | *auton* | *eis* | *Kaisareian* |
| brothers | brought down | him | to | Caesarea, |

31.a.**Txt:** 08E,020L 025P,1241,byz.
**Var:** p74,01ℵ,02A,03B 04C,1739,sa.Lach,Treg Alf,Word,Tisc,We/Ho Weis,Sod,UBS/☆

31.b.**Txt:** 08E,020L 025P,1241,byz.
**Var:** p74,01ℵ,02A,03B 04C,1739,sa.Lach,Treg Alf,Word,Tisc,We/Ho Weis,Sod,UBS/☆

| **2504.1** conj | **1805.2** verb 3pl indic aor act | **840.6** prs-pron acc sing masc | **1519.1** prep | **4870.2** name acc fem | **3450.13** art nom pl fem |
|---|---|---|---|---|---|
| καὶ | ἐξαπέστειλαν | αὐτὸν | εἰς | Ταρσόν. | **31.** ⸂ Αἱ |
| *kai* | *exapesteilan* | *auton* | *eis* | *Tarson* | *Hai* |
| and | sent away | him | to | Tarsus. | The |

| **3450.9** art nom sing fem | **3173.1** conj | **3631.1** partic | **1564.5** noun nom pl fem | **1564.2** noun nom sing fem |
|---|---|---|---|---|
| [a☆ Ἡ ] | μὲν | οὖν | ⸂ ἐκκλησίαι | [b☆ ἐκκλησία ] |
| *Hē* | *men* | *oun* | *ekklēsiai* | *ekklēsia* |
| [ idem ] | indeed | then | assemblies | [ church ] |

| **2567.2** prep | **3513.7** adj gen sing fem | **3450.10** art gen sing fem | **2424.2** name gen fem | **2504.1** conj | **1049.2** name gen sing fem |
|---|---|---|---|---|---|
| καθ' | ὅλης | τῆς | Ἰουδαίας | καὶ | Γαλιλαίας |
| *kath'* | *holēs* | *tēs* | *Ioudaias* | *kai* | *Galilaias* |
| throughout | whole | the | of Judea | and | Galilee |

31.c.**Txt:** 08E,020L,025P 1241,byz.
**Var:** p74,01ℵ,02A,03B 04C,1739,sa.Lach,Treg Alf,Word,Tisc,We/Ho Weis,Sod,UBS/☆

31.d.**Txt:** 08E,020L 025P,1241,byz.
**Var:** p74,01ℵ,02A,03B 04C,1739,sa.Lach,Treg Alf,Word,Tisc,We/Ho Weis,Sod,UBS/☆

| **2504.1** conj | **4397.2** name gen fem | **2174.42** verb indic imperf act | **2174.44** verb 3sing indic imperf act | **1503.4** noun acc sing fem |
|---|---|---|---|---|
| καὶ | Σαμαρείας | ⸂ εἶχον | [c☆ εἶχεν ] | εἰρήνην, |
| *kai* | *Samareias* | *eichon* | *eichen* | *eirēnēn* |
| and | Samaria | were having | [ idem ] | peace, |

| **3481.16** verb nom pl fem part pres mid | **2504.1** conj | **4057.14** verb nom pl fem part pres mid | **3481.22** verb nom sing fem part pres mid |
|---|---|---|---|
| ⸂ οἰκοδομουμέναι | καὶ | πορευομέναι | [d☆ οἰκοδομουμένη |
| *oikodomoumenai* | *kai* | *poreuomenai* | *oikodomoumenē* |
| being built up | and | going on | [ being built up |

synagogues and probably visited synagogues in the surrounding towns and villages.

**9:29.** During this time Saul continued to speak boldly and freely in the name (and with the authority) of the Lord Jesus. But, because of his own heritage, he was especially attracted to the "Grecians," that is, the Hellenistic or Greek-speaking Jews. He spent much of his time talking to them and disputing (discussing, debating) with them. Thus, he went to the Hellenistic synagogues, including the same ones that had debated with Stephen. He did not visit the churches of Judea (outside Jerusalem) however, for he said later that he was "unknown by face" to them at this time (Galatians 1:22).

The Hellenistic Jews were undoubtedly offended because Saul had once been one of them. His message of the gospel and his proofs from the Scriptures roused their anger. It is strange how many people become angry when they realize they do not have a good case for their own beliefs.

Because of their anger they kept trying to kill Saul. Probably they considered him a traitor who did not need a trial. It is clear however that these attempts failed. God surely protected him.

**9:30.** As soon as the Jerusalem believers found out about these attempts on Saul's life they decided they did not need another martyr and another siege of persecution. So they took Saul and brought him down to Caesarea and sent him away to Tarsus. Jesus also appeared to him and told him to leave Jerusalem (22:17-21).

The believers did not send him away simply to save him from being a martyr, however. The Greek *exapesteilan* means they sent him out as a representative and with a commission. They recognized he was a person qualified to take the gospel to Tarsus, his birthplace. Tarsus, about 300 miles to the north, was the most important city of Cilicia. It was a free city and a well-known university city (which means there were a number of outstanding teachers located there). Its educational opportunities were exceeded only by Athens and Alexandria. Saul was needed there. It was a place where he could freely work and develop his ministry.

**9:31.** With Saul gone, everything quieted down again. This verse is another brief summary, showing that the Church throughout the whole of Judea, Galilee, and Samaria had rest (peace and blessing), was edified (built up both spiritually and in numbers), walked (lived, conducted themselves) in the fear (reverential awe) of the Lord and in the encouragement of the Holy Spirit, and was multiplied.

Up to this point there is not much in Acts to indicate churches were being established in Galilee. But it is clear from this verse that both Galilee and Samaria had been well-evangelized by this time.

**29. And he spake boldly in the name of the Lord Jesus:** . . . speaking courageously, *Kleist* . . . preaching boldly, *ASV, Williams C.K.* . . . spoke eloquently, *Fenton* . . . conversed boldly, *Berkeley.*

**and disputed against the Grecians:** . . . also spoke and argued, *Kleist* . . . and especially talked and argued with, *MLNT* . . . talking and arguing with the Greek-speaking Jews, *TCNT* . . . And he often talked with the Hellenists and had discussions with them, *Weymouth* . . . he also held conversations and debates with the Hellenists, *Moffatt* . . . And he...reasoned with, *KJII* . . . Jews who understood Greek, *Murdock* . . . Grecian Jews, *Montgomery.*

**but they went about to slay him:** . . . were endeavoring, *Noyes* . . . these set themselves to kill him, *Williams C.K.* . . . They for their part responded by trying to kill him, *NAB* . . . but they conspired, *Fenton* . . . But they kept trying to murder him, *Williams* . . . but they undertook to murder him, *MLNT* . . . but they were working for his death, *BB.*

**30. Which when the brethren knew:** But when the Brethren found this out, *TCNT* . . . When the brothers learned about this, *Everyday* . . . heard of this attempt, *Kleist* . . . had knowledge of it, *BB* . . . became aware of it, *Fenton.*

**they brought him down to Caesarea, and sent him forth to Tarsus:** . . . took him down...and sent him off, *Fenton* . . . and then sent him by sea to Tarsus, *Weymouth* . . . sent him on his way to, *Williams C.K.*

**31. Then had the churches rest throughout all Judaea and Galilee and Samaria, and were edified:** . . . the assemblies, *Noyes* . . . So the church...had peace, *ASV* . . . The church everywhere...had a time of peace, *Everyday* . . . being built up, *ABUV* . . . and became well-established, *TCNT* . . . continued to be built up spiritually, *Williams* . . . The church was made strong, *NLT* . . . it was consolidated, *Moffatt* . . . to make progress, and it went on increasing, *TNT* . . . accordingly had rest, *Fenton.*

| 2504.1 conj | 4057.39 verb nom sing fem part pres mid | 3450.3 art dat sing | 5238.3 noun dat sing masc | 3450.2 art gen sing | 2935.2 noun gen sing masc |
|---|---|---|---|---|---|
| καὶ | πορευομένη ] | τῷ | φόβῳ | τοῦ | κυρίου, |
| *kai* | *poreuomenē* | *tō* | *phobō* | *tou* | *kuriou* |
| and | going on ] | in the | fear | of the | Lord, |

| 2504.1 conj | 3450.11 art dat sing fem | 3735.3 noun dat sing fem | 3450.2 art gen sing | 39.2 adj gen sing | 4011.2 noun gen sing neu |
|---|---|---|---|---|---|
| καὶ | τῇ | παρακλήσει | τοῦ | ἁγίου | πνεύματος |
| *kai* | *tē* | *paraklēsei* | *tou* | *hagiou* | *pneumatos* |
| and | in the | encouragement | of the | Holy | Spirit |

31.e.**Txt:** 08E,020L 025P,1241,byz.
**Var:** p74,01ℵ,02A,03B 04C,1739,sa.Lach,Treg Alf,Word,Tisc,We/Ho Weis,Sod,UBS/☆

| 3989.9 verb 3pl indic imperf pass | 3989.8 verb 3sing indic imperf pass | 1090.33 verb 3sing indic aor mid |
|---|---|---|
| ⸀ ἐπληθύνοντο. | [ᵉ☆ ἐπληθύνετο. ] | 32. Ἐγένετο |
| *eplēthunonto* | *eplēthuneto* | *Egeneto* |
| were being increased. | [ was being increased. ] | It came to pass |

| 1156.2 conj | 3935.4 name acc masc | 1324.13 verb acc sing masc part pres mid | 1217.2 prep | 3820.4 adj gen pl | 2687.7 verb inf aor act |
|---|---|---|---|---|---|
| δὲ | Πέτρον | διερχόμενον | διὰ | πάντων, | κατελθεῖν |
| *de* | *Petron* | *dierchomenon* | *dia* | *pantōn* | *katelthein* |
| but | Peter, | passing | through | all | to go down |

| 2504.1 conj | 4242.1 prep | 3450.8 art acc pl masc | 39.9 adj acc pl masc | 3450.8 art acc pl masc | 2700.9 verb acc pl masc part pres act |
|---|---|---|---|---|---|
| καὶ | πρὸς | τοὺς | ἁγίους | τοὺς | κατοικοῦντας |
| *kai* | *pros* | *tous* | *hagious* | *tous* | *katoikountas* |
| also | to | the | saints | the | inhabiting |

32.a.**Txt:** 04C,08E,020L 025P,byz.Sod
**Var:** 01ℵ,02A,03B,33 Lach,Treg,Alf,Tisc We/Ho,Weis,UBS/☆

| 3041.2 name acc fem | 3041.4 name acc fem | 2128.8 verb 3sing indic aor act | 1156.2 conj | 1550.1 adv |
|---|---|---|---|---|
| ⸀ Λύδδαν. | [ᵃ☆ Λύδδα. ] | 33. εὗρεν | δὲ | ἐκεῖ |
| *Luddan* | *Ludda* | *heuren* | *de* | *ekei* |
| Lydda, | [ idem ] | He found | and | there |

| 442.4 noun acc sing masc | 4948.5 indef-pron | 132.1 name acc masc | 3549.4 noun dat sing neu | 3549.4 noun dat sing neu |
|---|---|---|---|---|
| ἄνθρωπόν | τινα | ⸀ Αἰνέαν | ὀνόματι, | [☆ ὀνόματι |
| *anthrōpon* | *tina* | *Ainean* | *onomati* | *onomati* |
| a man | certain, | Aeneas | by name, | [ by name |

| 132.1 name acc masc | 1523.1 prep gen | 2073.4 noun gen pl neu | 3501.1 num card | 2591.2 verb acc sing masc part pres mid | 1894.3 prep |
|---|---|---|---|---|---|
| Αἰνέαν ] | ἐξ | ἐτῶν | ὀκτὼ | κατακείμενον | ἐπὶ |
| *Ainean* | *ex* | *etōn* | *oktō* | *katakeimenon* | *epi* |
| Aeneas ] | for | years | eight | lying | on |

33.a.**Txt:** 08E,020L 025P,byz.
**Var:** 01ℵ,02A,03B UBS/☆

| 2868.1 noun dat sing masc | 2868.5 noun gen sing masc | 3614.5 rel-pron nom sing masc | 1498.34 verb sing indic imperf act |
|---|---|---|---|
| ⸀ κραββάτῳ, | [ᵃ☆ κραβάττου, ] | ὃς | ἦν |
| *krabbatō* | *krabattou* | *hos* | *ēn* |
| a couch, | [ idem ] | who | was |

| 3747.1 verb nom sing masc part perf mid | 2504.1 conj | 1500.5 verb 3sing indic aor act | 840.4 prs-pron dat sing | 3450.5 art nom sing masc |
|---|---|---|---|---|
| παραλελυμένος. | 34. καὶ | εἶπεν | αὐτῷ | ὁ |
| *paralelumenos* | *kai* | *eipen* | *autō* | *ho* |
| having been paralyzed. | And | said | to him | |

34.a.**Txt:** 02A,03B-corr 08E,020L,025P,byz.Sod
**Var:** p74,01ℵ,03B-org 04C,044,33,Lach,Treg Word,Tisc,We/Ho,Weis UBS/☆

| 3935.1 name nom masc | 132.2 name voc masc | 2367.1 verb 3sing indic pres mid | 4622.4 prs-pron acc 2sing | 2400.1 name nom masc | 3450.5 art nom sing masc |
|---|---|---|---|---|---|
| Πέτρος, | Αἰνέα, | ἰᾶταί | σε | Ἰησοῦς | ⸂ᵃ ὁ ⸃ |
| *Petros* | *Ainea* | *iatai* | *se* | *Iēsous* | *ho* |
| Peter, | Aeneas, | heals | you | Jesus | the |

Notice that the word *church* is in the singular. The various assemblies in these regions were in fellowship with each other and constituted one body (Church) under the headship of Christ (Ephesians 1:22,23).

**9:32.** Acts says no more about Saul until 11:30. After the summary statement of verse 31, Luke began a sequence which led to Peter's bringing the gospel to the Gentiles in Caesarea. This was a key turning point in the spread of the gospel. Without this experience of Peter it would have been much more difficult for the Church to approve Saul's ministry as it did at the Jerusalem Council (see chapter 15).

Since the conditions in Jerusalem were now peaceful, Peter was able to leave the city. His purpose was to visit the various congregations which had sprung up as the result of the scattering after the death of Stephen and to build the believers up in the Faith. Like Jesus, he went about doing good, strengthening and edifying the believers, and bringing blessing and healing wherever he went.

As he journeyed about he eventually came to visit the believers at Lydda, called saints because they were dedicated believers who had separated themselves from the ways of the world and to the worship and service of the Lord Jesus.

Lydda was an ancient city on the road to Joppa about 23 miles northwest of Jerusalem and 10 miles southeast of Joppa. It was rebuilt after the Jews returned from Babylon, then taken over by the governor of Samaria. In 145 B.C. it was made part of Judea.

**9:33.** At Lydda Peter found a certain man named Aeneas (Greek, *Aineas,* a Greek name popularized because it was the name of a Trojan hero. It seems to be derived from the Greek word for *praise.*)

Paralyzed, this man had been confined to his bed for 8 years. ("Palsy" here is not the shaking palsy with its uncontrollable tremors. Rather, it is an old word meaning "paralysis.") Since Aeneas had been in this helpless condition for 8 years, his family and friends had long ago given up any hope he would ever get better.

Jesus did not avoid such cases when He was on earth. Peter and John had already experienced what Jesus could do with hopeless cases when they received a gift of healing for the lame man at the Gate Beautiful (chapter 3). They knew that nothing is impossible with the Lord. They had seen Jesus heal people who were paralyzed on more than one occasion. (See Matthew 4:24; 8:6; 9:2-6.)

**9:34.** Peter spoke to this man with the assurance that surely came from the Holy Spirit: "Aeneas, Jesus Christ is healing you. Rise and make your bed." This was a command calling for immediate action. Aeneas must get up off his mattress immediately, and make

**and walking in the fear of the Lord:** . . . lived in reverence for, *Goodspeed* . . . ordering its life by reverence for the Lord, *TCNT* . . . It showed that it feared the Lord by the way it lived, *NCV* . . . and, progressing in the reverence of, *Fenton* . . . showed that they respected the Lord by the way they lived, *Everyday.*

**and in the comfort of the Holy Ghost:** . . . and help, *TCNT* . . . and it was given comfort by, *NLT* . . . the encouragement of the Holy Spirit, *Weymouth* . . . in the strengthening presence of the Holy Spirit, *Phillips* . . . and, stimulated by the holy Spirit, *Goodspeed* . . . the consolation, *Concordant* . . . the encouragement that the Holy Spirit gave, *Williams* . . . by the advocacy of the Holy Spirit, *Rotherham.*

**were multiplied:** Because of this, the group of believers grew, *Everyday* . . . they were being increased through, *Fenton* . . . increased greatly, *BB* . . . More people were added to the church, *NLT.*

**32. And it came to pass, as Peter passed throughout all quarters:** While travelling about in all directions, Peter, *TCNT* . . . Now Peter, as he went to town after town, *Weymouth* . . . It now occurred that Peter, journeying, *Fenton* . . . was traveling through all the area, *Everyday.*

**he came down also to the saints which dwelt at Lydda:** . . . went down to visit the People of Christ living at, *TCNT* . . . the holy people living in Lydda, *Beck* . . . God's people, *Everyday.*

**33. And there he found a certain man named Aeneas:**

**which had kept his bed for eight years, and was sick of the palsy:** . . . who had been bed-ridden for eight years with paralysis, *TCNT* . . . lain on a pallet, *HBIE* . . . being completely paralyzed, *Wuest* . . . could not move his body, *NLT* . . . without power of moving, *BB.*

**34. And Peter said unto him, Aeneas, Jesus Christ maketh thee whole:** Jesus Christ healeth thee, *ASV* . . . Peter, addressing him, said...the Messiah, *Fenton* . . . cures you, *Goodspeed, TCNT* . . . makes you well, *BB.*

| **5382.1** name nom masc | **448.8** verb 2sing impr aor act | **2504.1** conj | **4617.2** verb 2sing impr aor act | **4427.2** prs-pron dat sing masc | **2504.1** conj |
|---|---|---|---|---|---|
| Χριστός· | ἀνάστηθι | καὶ | στρῶσον | σεαυτῷ. | Καὶ |
| *Christos* | *anastēthi* | *kai* | *strōson* | *seautō* | *Kai* |
| Christ; | rise up, | and | spread a bed | for yourself. | And |

| **2091.1** adv | **448.2** verb 3sing indic aor act | **2504.1** conj | **1481.1** verb indic aor act | **1481.7** verb 3pl indic aor act |
|---|---|---|---|---|
| εὐθέως | ἀνέστη· | **35.** καὶ | ʽ εἶδον | [a☆ εἶδαν ] |
| *eutheōs* | *anestē* | *kai* | *eidon* | *eidan* |
| immediately | he rose up. | And | saw | [ idem ] |

| **840.6** prs-pron acc sing masc | **3820.7** adj nom pl masc | **3450.7** art nom pl masc | **2700.6** verb nom pl masc part pres act | **3041.2** name acc fem |
|---|---|---|---|---|
| αὐτὸν | πάντες | οἱ | κατοικοῦντες | ʽ Λύδδαν |
| *auton* | *pantes* | *hoi* | *katoikountes* | *Luddan* |
| him | all | the | inhabiting | Lydda |

| **3041.4** name acc fem | **2504.1** conj | **3450.6** art acc sing masc | **4422.2** name acc masc | **4422.1** name acc masc |
|---|---|---|---|---|
| [b☆ Λύδδα ] | καὶ | τὸν | ʽ Σαρωνᾶν, | [c☆ Σαρῶνα, ] |
| *Ludda* | *kai* | *ton* | *Sarōnan* | *Sarōna* |
| [ idem ] | and | | Sharon, | [ idem ] |

| **3610.2** rel-pron nom pl masc | **1978.6** verb 3pl indic aor act | **1894.3** prep | **3450.6** art acc sing masc | **2935.4** noun acc sing masc | **1706.1** prep |
|---|---|---|---|---|---|
| οἵτινες | ἐπέστρεψαν | ἐπὶ | τὸν | κύριον. | **36.** Ἐν |
| *hoitines* | *epestrepsan* | *epi* | *ton* | *kurion* | *En* |
| who | turned | to | the | Lord. | In |

| **2421.2** name dat fem | **1156.2** conj | **4948.3** indef-pron nom sing | **1498.34** verb sing indic imperf act | **3074.1** noun nom sing fem | **3549.4** noun dat sing neu |
|---|---|---|---|---|---|
| Ἰόππῃ | δέ | τις | ἦν | μαθήτρια | ὀνόματι |
| *Ioppē* | *de* | *tis* | *ēn* | *mathētria* | *onomati* |
| Joppa | and | a certain | was | disciple, | by name |

| **4851.1** name fem | **3614.9** rel-pron nom sing fem | **1323.5** verb nom sing fem part pres mid | **2978.28** verb 3sing indic pres mid | **1387.1** name nom fem |
|---|---|---|---|---|
| Ταβιθά, | ἣ | διερμηνευομένη | λέγεται | Δορκάς· |
| *Tabitha* | *hē* | *diermēneuomenē* | *legetai* | *Dorkas* |
| Tabitha, | which | being interpreted | is being called | Dorcas. |

| **3642.9** dem-pron nom sing fem | **1498.34** verb sing indic imperf act | **3994.1** adj nom sing | **18.1** adj gen pl | **2024.5** noun gen pl neu | **2024.5** noun gen pl neu |
|---|---|---|---|---|---|
| αὕτη | ἦν | πλήρης | ʽ ἀγαθῶν | ἔργων | [☆ ἔργων |
| *hautē* | *ēn* | *plērēs* | *agathōn* | *ergōn* | *ergōn* |
| She | was | full | of good | works | [ works |

| **18.1** adj gen pl | **2504.1** conj | **1641.4** noun gen pl fem | **3614.1** rel-pron gen pl | **4020.57** verb 3sing indic imperf act |
|---|---|---|---|---|
| ἀγαθῶν ] | καὶ | ἐλεημοσυνῶν | ὧν | ἐποίει· |
| *agathōn* | *kai* | *eleēmosunōn* | *hōn* | *epoiei* |
| of good ] | and | of alms | which | she was doing. |

| **1090.33** verb 3sing indic aor mid | **1156.2** conj | **1706.1** prep | **3450.14** art dat pl fem | **2232.7** noun dat pl fem | **1552.14** dem-pron dat pl fem |
|---|---|---|---|---|---|
| **37.** ἐγένετο | δὲ | ἐν | ταῖς | ἡμέραις | ἐκείναις |
| *egeneto* | *de* | *en* | *tais* | *hēmerais* | *ekeinais* |
| It came to pass | and | in | the | days | those |

| **764.15** verb acc sing fem part aor act | **840.12** prs-pron acc sing fem | **594.20** verb inf aor act | **3040.3** verb nom pl masc part aor act | **1156.2** conj |
|---|---|---|---|---|
| ἀσθενήσασαν | αὐτὴν | ἀποθανεῖν· | λούσαντες | δὲ |
| *asthenēsasan* | *autēn* | *apothanein* | *lousantes* | *de* |
| having sickened | her | to die; | having washed | and |

35.a.**Txt:** p53,01א,08E 020L,025P,byz.Weis Sod
**Var:** 02A,03B,04C,Lach Treg,Alf,Tisc,We/Ho UBS/☆

35.b.**Txt:** p53,04C,08E 020L,025P,byz.Gries Word,Sod
**Var:** 01א,02A,03B,33 Lach,Treg,Alf,Tisc We/Ho,Weis,UBS/☆

35.c.**Txt:** p45,byz.
**Var:** p53,p74,01א,02A 03B,04C,08E,Elzev Gries,Lach,Treg,Alf Word,Tisc,We/Ho,Weis Sod,UBS/☆

his own bed, which probably meant he should roll it up and put it away. ("Make your own bed" is a phrase that in Greek can be used of either making a bed or preparing a meal. In Mark 14:15 and Luke 22:12 it is used of preparing the Passover meal in the Upper Room. Thus, another possible meaning here is that Aeneas should immediately prepare himself some food to be strengthened.)

His healing was instantaneous. The fact that he arose immediately showed that Peter was speaking with the authority of Jesus when he used the present tense and said, "Jesus Christ is (now, at this moment) healing you." Notice too that Peter made it very clear that Jesus was the One who was doing the healing. He is the Great Physician, and all the credit, all the glory belongs to Him.

**9:35.** The result of this healing was a great spread of the gospel. All the inhabitants of Lydda and Sharon "saw him, and turned to the Lord." This implies Aeneas was well-known in that area. "Sharon" here means the whole Sharon coastal plain west and northwest of Lydda, stretching toward Mount Carmel and extending east to the hills of Samaria. It was a fertile region, famous for its flowers, especially lilies and anemones. The fact that the people in this region saw him indicates that Aeneas, now that he was healed, was restored to such vigor and such excellent health that he walked all through that region giving his testimony and telling of the wonderful works of the Lord.

**9:36.** Joppa (called Japho in Joshua 19:46) was the only seaport between Haifa and the borders of Egypt. It was important in ancient times, though today it has been reduced to a suburb of Tel Aviv which is on its northern border. From it Jonah fled as he tried to avoid the Lord's command to go to Nineveh.

At Joppa lived Tabitha (her Aramaic name). She was also known by her corresponding Greek name, *Dorcas,* which means "gazelle." The gazelle was a small antelope, a swift runner, and so graceful that it became a symbol for gracefulness. The fact that Dorcas was so well-known by her Greek name shows she was one of the Hellenistic Jews and was probably wealthy and well-educated. But her real riches were her good deeds. She was full of them and constantly enriched the lives of others through them. She was especially active in "almsdeeds," that is, in kind deeds and charitable giving to the poor.

**9:37.** While Peter was at Lydda, Dorcas became sick and died. The Bible does not state the cause of her illness, and there is no indication that she was lacking in faith. Her godly life and good works did not prevent either her sickness or her death. It seems she rapidly became worse and her death was an unexpected shock to her friends and to the entire Christian community. Her friends

**arise, and make thy bed:** Get up, and make your bed, *TCNT* . . . smooth thy bed for thyself, *Rotherham* . . . Stand up, *Everyday* . . . make yourself a meal, *TNT.*

**And he arose immediately:** Aeneas got up instantly, *TCNT* . . . He at once rose to his feet, *Weymouth* . . . At once he rose to his feet, *Montgomery* . . . stood up immediately, *Everyday.*

**35. And all that dwelt at Lydda and Saron saw him:** All the inhabitants of Lydda...were converted to the Lord, *NAB* . . . all who inhabited, *Darby* . . . who were living, *Williams C.K.*

**and turned to the Lord:** . . . came over to the Lord's side, *TCNT* . . . and were converted to, *Kleist* . . . and so they turned to the Lord, *Williams.*

**36. Now there was at Joppa a certain disciple named Tabitha:** . . . a certain female disciple, *Rotherham* . . . Among the disciples at Joppa was a woman called Tabitha, *Weymouth* . . . a follower, *Everyday.*

**which by interpretation is called Dorcas:** . . . or, as the name may be translated, Dorcas, *Weymouth* . . . that is, Gazelle, *Williams* . . . means "a deer," *Everyday.*

**this woman was full of good works and almsdeeds which she did:** Her life was full of the good and charitable actions which she was constantly doing, *Weymouth* . . . Her life was marked by constant good deeds, *NAB* . . . a woman bubbling over with helpful activities and practice of charities, *Berkeley* . . . She was always busy doing good and helping the poor, *Norlie* . . . she was conspicuous, *Fenton* . . . full of good and kindly actions, *Phillips* . . . loving acts which she was always doing, *Klingensmith* . . . charitable practices, *Moffatt* . . . good deeds and acts of charity, *AmpB* . . . and of kind-hearted acts, *KJII* . . . and acts of mercy, *Williams C.K.*

**37. And it came to pass in those days, that she was sick, and died:** It happened that at that time she fell ill, *Williams C.K.* . . . that she fell sick, *ASV* . . . became sick, *Everyday.*

## Acts 9:38

37.a.**Txt:** p53,01ℵ-corr 04C,08E,020L,025P,byz. Sod
**Var:** 03B,We/Ho,Weis UBS/☆

38.a.**Txt:** 03B-corr,08E 020L,025P,byz.Gries Lach,Word,Sod
**Var:** 01ℵ-org,03B-org 04C,Treg,Alf,Tisc We/Ho,Weis,UBS/☆

38.b.**Txt:** p45,p74,01ℵ 02A,03B,04C,05D,36 1175,Steph
**Var:** p29,p38,p53,05D 048,057,0189

38.c.**Txt:** 04C-corr,020L 025P,byz.
**Var:** 01ℵ,02A,03B 04C-org,08E,sa.bo.Lach Treg,Alf,Word,Tisc We/Ho,Weis,Sod UBS/☆

38.d.**Txt:** 04C-corr,020L 025P,byz.
**Var:** 01ℵ,02A,03B 04C-org,08E,sa.bo.Lach Treg,Alf,Word,Tisc We/Ho,Weis,Sod UBS/☆

| **840.12** prs-pron acc sing fem | **4935.11** verb 3pl indic aor act | **1706.1** prep | **5091.1** noun dat sing neu | **1445.1** adv | **1156.2** conj |
|---|---|---|---|---|---|
| ⸂[a] αὐτὴν ⸃ | ἔθηκαν | ἐν | ὑπερῴῳ. | **38.** ἐγγὺς | δὲ |
| *autēn* | *ethēkan* | *en* | *huperōō* | *engus* | *de* |
| her | they put | in | an upper room. | Near | and |

| **1498.27** verb gen sing fem part pres act | **3041.1** name gen fem | **3041.3** name gen fem | **3450.11** art dat sing fem | **2421.2** name dat fem |
|---|---|---|---|---|
| οὔσης | ⸂ Λύδδης | [[a]☆ Λύδδας ] | τῇ | Ἰόππῃ, |
| *ousēs* | *Luddēs* | *Luddas* | *tē* | *Ioppē* |
| being | Lydda | [ idem ] | | to Joppa, |

| **3450.7** art nom pl masc | **3073.5** noun nom pl masc | **189.32** verb nom pl masc part aor act | **3617.1** conj | **3935.1** name nom masc | **1498.4** verb 3sing indic pres act |
|---|---|---|---|---|---|
| οἱ | μαθηταὶ | ἀκούσαντες | ὅτι | Πέτρος | ἐστὶν |
| *hoi* | *mathētai* | *akousantes* | *hoti* | *Petros* | *estin* |
| the | disciples | having heard | that | Peter | is |

| **1706.1** prep | **840.11** prs-pron dat sing fem | **643.9** verb 3pl indic aor act | **1411.3** num card | **433.9** noun acc pl masc | **4242.1** prep |
|---|---|---|---|---|---|
| ἐν | αὐτῇ | ἀπέστειλαν | ⸂[b] δύο | ἄνδρας ⸃ | πρὸς |
| *en* | *autē* | *apesteilan* | *duo* | *andras* | *pros* |
| in | it | sent | two | men | to |

| **840.6** prs-pron acc sing masc | **3731.9** verb nom pl masc part pres act | **3231.1** partic | **3498.1** verb inf aor act | **3231.1** partic |
|---|---|---|---|---|
| αὐτὸν, | παρακαλοῦντες | ⸂ μὴ | ὀκνῆσαι | [[c]☆ Μὴ |
| *auton* | *parakalountes* | *mē* | *oknēsai* | *Mē* |
| him, | urging | not | to delay | [ not |

| **3498.2** verb 2sing subj aor act | **1324.8** verb inf aor act | **2175.1** conj | **840.1** prs-pron gen pl | **2231.2** prs-pron gen 1pl |
|---|---|---|---|---|
| ὀκνήσῃς ] | διελθεῖν | ἕως | ⸂ αὐτῶν. | [[d]☆ ἡμῶν. ] |
| *oknēsēs* | *dielthein* | *heōs* | *autōn* | *hēmōn* |
| may you delay ] | to come | to | them. | [ us. ] |

| **448.9** verb nom sing masc part aor act | **1156.2** conj | **3935.1** name nom masc | **4755.1** verb 3sing indic aor act | **840.2** prs-pron dat pl |
|---|---|---|---|---|
| **39.** ἀναστὰς | δὲ | Πέτρος | συνῆλθεν | αὐτοῖς· |
| *anastas* | *de* | *Petros* | *sunēlthen* | *autois* |
| Having risen up | and | Peter | went with | them, |

| **3614.6** rel-pron acc sing masc | **3716.9** verb acc sing masc part aor mid | **319.1** verb 3pl indic aor act | **1519.1** prep | **3450.16** art sing neu |
|---|---|---|---|---|
| ὃν | παραγενόμενον | ἀνήγαγον | εἰς | τὸ |
| *hon* | *paragenomenon* | *anēgagon* | *eis* | *to* |
| whom, | having arrived | they brought | into | the |

| **5091.2** noun sing neu | **2504.1** conj | **3798.6** verb 3pl indic aor act | **840.4** prs-pron dat sing | **3820.13** adj nom pl fem | **3450.13** art nom pl fem |
|---|---|---|---|---|---|
| ὑπερῷον, | καὶ | παρέστησαν | αὐτῷ | πᾶσαι | αἱ |
| *huperōon* | *kai* | *parestēsan* | *autō* | *pasai* | *hai* |
| upper room, | and | stood by | him | all | the |

| **5339.3** noun nom pl fem | **2772.11** verb nom pl fem part pres act | **2504.1** conj | **1910.5** verb nom pl fem part pres mid | **5345.3** noun acc pl masc | **2504.1** conj |
|---|---|---|---|---|---|
| χῆραι | κλαίουσαι | καὶ | ἐπιδεικνύμεναι | χιτῶνας | καὶ |
| *chērai* | *klaiousai* | *kai* | *epideiknumenai* | *chitōnas* | *kai* |
| widows | weeping | and | showing | tunics | and |

| **2416.4** noun pl neu | **3607.8** rel-pron pl neu | **4020.57** verb 3sing indic imperf act | **3196.2** prep | **840.1** prs-pron gen pl | **1498.26** verb nom sing fem part pres act |
|---|---|---|---|---|---|
| ἱμάτια | ὅσα | ἐποίει | μετ' | αὐτῶν | οὖσα |
| *himatia* | *hosa* | *epoiei* | *met'* | *autōn* | *ousa* |
| garments | which | was making | with | them | being |

washed her body as was the custom, but instead of wrapping it in linen with spices for burial, they took her body and placed it in an upstairs room. (This was a large upstairs room in her own house, another indication that she was a fairly wealthy woman. Most of the poor in those days lived in one-room homes and would not have an upper room large enough for people to gather.)

**whom when they had washed, they laid her in an upper chamber:** . . . and when they had washed her, they, *ASV* . . . After washing her body they laid it out in a room upstairs, *Weymouth* . . . in a room on the second floor, *NLT* . . . in a room which was high up, *BB*.

**9:38.** Lydda was near Joppa (only about 10 miles away). Most probably, the news about the healing of Aeneas had reached the believers in Joppa. Now the believers in Joppa learned that Peter was in Lydda. The believers, here called "disciples" (learners, students and followers of Christ), were not only concerned about Dorcas, but as believers must have spent time asking guidance of their Master Teacher, so they sent two men from their number to Peter. Some writers have wondered why they sent for Peter since there is no previous record in the Book of Acts of the apostles raising the dead. But Jesus raised the dead, and when He first sent out the Twelve He gave them authority to raise the dead (Matthew 10:8). The news that Peter had brought Christ's healing to a man paralyzed for 8 years must also have raised their faith.

The two men were sent with an urgent message, literally, "Do not delay to come to us." The custom in those days was to bury people the same day they died. Their request to Peter "to come" was very emphatic.

**38. And forasmuch as Lydda was nigh to Joppa:** Lydda, however, being near Jaffa, *Weymouth* . . . Then because, *Williams C.K.*

**and the disciples had heard that Peter was there:** The followers in Joppa, *Everyday* . . . the disciples, learning that, *Berkeley* . . . having knowledge, *BB*.

**they sent unto him two men, desiring him that he would not delay to come to them:** . . . with the urgent request, *NAB* . . . Please come to us without delay, *RSV* . . . and begged him, hurry, please come to us! *NCV* . . . to ask him to come at once, *NLT* . . . begging him to be good enough to come to them, *Williams C.K.*

**9:39.** Peter immediately got up and went with the two men from Joppa. As soon as he arrived at the house of Dorcas, they took him upstairs and brought him into the room where she was lying. The room was full of weeping widows who immediately presented themselves to Peter. They were self-appointed mourners and were undoubtedly following the custom of weeping, wailing, and beating their breasts. But they were not like the professional mourners so often hired in those days. Their sorrow was genuine. They could not understand why Dorcas had been cut off in the midst of such a godly and useful life. They were also weeping because they loved and appreciated her for all she had done for them.

While they still wept, they kept showing Peter the tunics (long garments like T-shirts worn next to the skin) and the outer garments (cloaks, robes) that Dorcas was in the habit of making "while she was with them." The Greek indicates the women were wearing the garments they were showing Peter and they were commending her, not only for her charity, but for her constant hard work in their behalf and on behalf of others who were needy.

In some ways Dorcas reminds us of the ideal wife of Proverbs 31 who was industrious and stretched out her hands constantly to help the poor and needy (Proverbs 31:19,20). But she was either not married or her husband was already dead. (The latter is most probable.)

**39. Then Peter arose and went with them:** Peter started with them at once, *TCNT* . . . Peter set out with them, *NAB* . . . So Peter at once got up, *Williams* . . . got ready and went, *Everyday*.

**When he was come, they brought him into the upper chamber:** On his arrival they took him upstairs, *Weymouth* . . . they conducted him to the upper room, *Berkeley*.

**and all the widows stood by him weeping:** All the women whose husbands had died, *NLT* . . . came round him in tears, *TCNT* . . . stood by his side, *TNT* . . . weeping audibly, *Wuest* . . . crying, *Everyday* . . . and with tears, *Kleist*.

**and shewing the coats and garments which Dorcas made, while she was with them:** . . . and showing him all the clothing and cloaks that Dorcas used to make, *Weymouth* . . . the undergarments and coats, *Berkeley* . . . all the shirts, *Williams C.K.* . . . the tunics ...which Dorcas used to make, *Kleist* . . . the various garments, *NAB* . . . the dresses and cloaks, *Phillips* . . . inner and outer garments, *Beck* . . . when she was still alive, *NCV*.

| 3450.9 art nom sing fem | 1387.1 name nom fem | 1531.19 verb nom sing masc part aor act | 1156.2 conj | 1838.1 adv | 3820.8 adj acc pl masc |
|---|---|---|---|---|---|
| ἡ | Δορκάς. | **40.** ἐκβαλὼν | δὲ | ἔξω | πάντας |
| *hē* | *Dorkas* | *ekbalōn* | *de* | *exō* | *pantas* |
|  | Dorcas. | Having put | but | outside | all |

40.a.**Var:** 01ℵ,02A,03B 04C,08E,Lach,Treg,Alf Word,Tisc,We/Ho,Weis Sod,UBS/☆

| 3450.5 art nom sing masc | 3935.1 name nom masc | 2504.1 conj | 4935.14 verb nom sing masc part aor act | 3450.17 art pl neu | 1113.3 noun pl neu |
|---|---|---|---|---|---|
| ὁ | Πέτρος, | [a☆+ καὶ ] | θεὶς | τὰ | γόνατα |
| *ho* | *Petros* | *kai* | *theis* | *ta* | *gonata* |
|  | Peter, | [ and ] | having bowed | the | knees |

| 4195.16 verb 3sing indic aor mid | 2504.1 conj | 1978.11 verb nom sing masc part aor act | 4242.1 prep | 3450.16 art sing neu | 4835.1 noun sing neu |
|---|---|---|---|---|---|
| προσηύξατο· | καὶ | ἐπιστρέψας | πρὸς | τὸ | σῶμα |
| *prosēuxato* | *kai* | *epistrepsas* | *pros* | *to* | *sōma* |
| he prayed. | And | having turned | to | the | body |

| 1500.5 verb 3sing indic aor act | 4851.1 name fem | 448.8 verb 2sing impr aor act | 3450.9 art nom sing fem | 1156.2 conj | 453.4 verb 3sing indic aor act |
|---|---|---|---|---|---|
| εἶπεν, | Ταβιθά, | ἀνάστηθι. | Ἡ | δὲ | ἤνοιξεν |
| *eipen* | *Tabitha* | *anastēthi* | *Hē* | *de* | *ēnoixen* |
| he said, | Tabitha, | Arise. | The | and | opened |

| 3450.8 art acc pl masc | 3652.8 noun acc pl masc | 840.10 prs-pron gen sing fem | 2504.1 conj | 1481.18 verb nom sing fem part aor act | 3450.6 art acc sing masc |
|---|---|---|---|---|---|
| τοὺς | ὀφθαλμοὺς | αὐτῆς· | καὶ | ἰδοῦσα | τὸν |
| *tous* | *ophthalmous* | *autēs* | *kai* | *idousa* | *ton* |
| the | eyes | her, | and | having seen |  |

| 3935.4 name acc masc | 337.1 verb 3sing indic aor act | 1319.28 verb nom sing masc part aor act | 1156.2 conj | 840.11 prs-pron dat sing fem | 5331.4 noun acc sing fem |
|---|---|---|---|---|---|
| Πέτρον | ἀνεκάθισεν. | **41.** δοὺς | δὲ | αὐτῇ | χεῖρα |
| *Petron* | *anekathisen* | *dous* | *de* | *autē* | *cheira* |
| Peter | she sat up. | Having given | and | her | a hand |

| 448.3 verb 3sing indic aor act | 840.12 prs-pron acc sing fem | 5291.9 verb nom sing masc part aor act | 1156.2 conj | 3450.8 art acc pl masc | 39.9 adj acc pl masc |
|---|---|---|---|---|---|
| ἀνέστησεν | αὐτήν, | φωνήσας | δὲ | τοὺς | ἁγίους |
| *anestēsen* | *autēn* | *phōnēsas* | *de* | *tous* | *hagious* |
| he raised up | her, | having called | and | the | saints |

| 2504.1 conj | 3450.15 art acc pl fem | 5339.6 noun acc pl fem | 3798.4 verb 3sing indic aor act | 840.12 prs-pron acc sing fem | 2180.17 verb acc sing fem part pres act |
|---|---|---|---|---|---|
| καὶ | τὰς | χήρας | παρέστησεν | αὐτὴν | ζῶσαν. |
| *kai* | *tas* | *chēras* | *parestēsen* | *autēn* | *zōsan* |
| and | the | widows | he presented | her | living. |

| 1104.4 adj sing neu | 1156.2 conj | 1090.33 verb 3sing indic aor mid | 2567.2 prep | 3513.7 adj gen sing fem | 3450.10 art gen sing fem |
|---|---|---|---|---|---|
| **42.** γνωστὸν | δὲ | ἐγένετο | καθ' | ὅλης | τῆς |
| *gnōston* | *de* | *egeneto* | *kath'* | *holēs* | *tēs* |
| Known | and | it became | throughout | whole | the |

| 2421.1 name gen fem | 2504.1 conj | 4044.7 adj nom pl masc | 3961.23 verb 3pl indic aor act | 3961.23 verb 3pl indic aor act |
|---|---|---|---|---|
| Ἰόππης, | καὶ | ʼ πολλοὶ | ἐπίστευσαν | [☆ ἐπίστευσαν |
| *Ioppēs* | *kai* | *polloi* | *episteusan* | *episteusan* |
| of Joppa, | and | many | believed | [ believed |

| 4044.7 adj nom pl masc | 1894.3 prep | 3450.6 art acc sing masc | 2935.4 noun acc sing masc | 1090.33 verb 3sing indic aor mid | 1156.2 conj |
|---|---|---|---|---|---|
| πολλοὶ ] | ἐπὶ | τὸν | κύριον· | **43.** Ἐγένετο | δὲ |
| *polloi* | *epi* | *ton* | *kurion* | *Egeneto* | *de* |
| many ] | on | the | Lord. | It came to pass | and |

**9:40.** The widows' words about Dorcas shows they thought of her as dead and her work ended. They obviously had no expectation that Peter would be able to do more than give them sympathy and comfort.

Peter made them all leave. An atmosphere of eastern mourning with its hubbub and commotion was not conducive to prayer or faith. The Greek implies that Peter had to force them to leave. Peter knew he had to get alone with God. So after they were gone, he went to his knees in humble prayer. He knew also that the power to raise the dead was inherent in Jesus. In himself he was nothing, so he put himself at the disposal of the risen Christ.

After prayer, Peter turned to the body and said in faith, "Tabitha, arise!" Many see here a parallel to what Jesus did when He raised the daughter of Jairus (Mark 5:41) where He said, "Talitha cumi," because the Aramaic for what Peter said is "Tabitha cumi."

At these words Dorcas opened her eyes. Life had returned and it was as if she had been wakened out of a sleep. Her health had returned as well, so when she saw Peter, she sat up.

**9:41.** Peter gave her his hand and helped her to her feet. Then, calling the saints and the widows, he "presented her alive."

The saints surely included all the believers in the Christian community. Dorcas apparently did not limit her acts of love to believers but reached out to all who were in need. Her name Tabitha, the Aramaic name for the gazelle, also has a meaning that includes beauty, splendor, and honor. Her faith, hope, and love expressed in a godly life gave her a charm and a loveliness that made the people love her and rejoice as Peter presented her to them alive again.

What an evidence it was to these saints and widows that the living Christ was in their midst! Peter took no credit for this. Christ alone had done the work. He alone deserved all the credit, all the glory. Peter's faith-filled and faithful ministry was needed. But God did not give this ministry or this miracle because Peter or Dorcas deserved it. All His healings, all His gifts, flow out of the exceeding riches of His mercy and grace. Believers dare not look to man or put their trust in man's abilities.

**9:42.** Unlike Aeneas, Dorcas did not travel around after her restoration to life. God does not ask everyone to witness in the same way. Apparently, Dorcas just went back to her work among the widows and among the poor where her gracious smile and deeds of love and compassion continued to spread comfort and cheer as they had before. But that was enough. The news spread quickly throughout all the city of Joppa, and many believed on Jesus as Lord.

It is worth noting that the city of Lydda was burned by the Roman Cestius during the time of Nero, and Joppa was destroyed a few years later in A.D. 68. Many souls must be in heaven because of Peter's miracle ministry and the faithfulness of Aeneas and Dorcas.

**40. But Peter put them all forth:** But Peter sent everybody out of the room, *TCNT* . . . first made everyone go outside, *NAB* . . . Peter made them all leave the room, *NLT, Norlie* . . . made them all go, *BB* . . . ejecting them all, *Concordant* . . . put them out of the room, *Williams C.K.* . . . sending them all out, *Kleist.*

**and kneeled, and prayed:** . . . went down on his knees in prayer, *BB* . . . then he knelt down and prayed, *Moffatt* . . . and having knelt, he prayed, *Fenton* . . . went on his knees to pray, *Knox.*

**and turning him to the body said, Tabitha, arise:** . . . and turning to the body, *ASV* . . . Tabitha, stand up, *Everyday, NAB* . . . get up, *BB, Williams C.K.* . . . rise up! *Fenton.*

**And she opened her eyes: and when she saw Peter, she sat up:** . . . seeing Peter, *Kleist* . . . she fell backwards, *Fenton* . . . and got up, *BB* . . . sat up on the bed, *Knox.*

**41. And he gave her his hand, and lifted her up:** But giving her a hand, he assisted her up, *Fenton* . . . took her hand, lifting her up, *BB* . . . Peter raised her up, *TCNT* . . . he raised her to her feet, *Weymouth* . . . helped her to her feet, *NAB, Phillips* . . . helped her up, *Everyday* . . . helped her rise, *Kleist.*

**and when he had called the saints and widows, presented her alive:** Then he called the members of the congregation, *TNT* . . . calling the holy ones, *Fenton* . . . into the room, *Everyday* . . . and, sending for the saints and widows, he gave her to them, living, *BB* . . . he gave her back to them alive, *Goodspeed, Weymouth* . . . he showed her alive, *KJII* . . . a living person, *NLT.*

**42. And it was known throughout all Joppa:** And it became known, *ASV* . . . news of it went all through, *BB* . . . all over Joppa, *Moffatt* . . . through the whole of, *Fenton* . . . learned about this, *Everyday.*

**and many believed in the Lord:** . . . and a number of people had faith in the Lord, *BB* . . . many became believers, *Williams C.K.* . . . put their trust in, *NLT* . . . believed on, *Fenton.*

## Acts 10:1

43.a.**Txt:** 04C,020L 025P,byz. **Var:** p53,01ℵ-org,03B Tisc,We/Ho,Weis UBS/☆

| **2232.1** noun fem | **2401.11** adj acc pl fem | **3176.25** verb inf aor act | **840.6** prs-pron acc sing masc | **1706.1** prep | **2421.2** name dat fem |
|---|---|---|---|---|---|
| ἡμέρας | ἱκανὰς | μεῖναι | ⸂[a] αὐτὸν⸃ | ἐν | Ἰόππῃ |
| *hēmeras* | *hikanas* | *meinai* | *auton* | *en* | *Ioppē* |
| days | many | to abide | him | in | Joppa |

| **3706.2** prep | **4948.2** indef-pron dat sing | **4468.3** name dat masc | **1031.2** noun dat sing masc | **433.1** noun nom sing masc | **1156.2** conj |
|---|---|---|---|---|---|
| παρά | τινι | Σίμωνι | βυρσεῖ. | **10:1.** Ἀνὴρ | δέ |
| *para* | *tini* | *Simōni* | *bursei* | *Anēr* | *de* |
| with | a certain | Simon | a tanner. | A man | but |

1.a.**Txt:** 025P,byz. **Var:** 01ℵ,02A,03B,04C 08E,020L,Gries,Lach Treg,Alf,Word,Tisc We/Ho,Weis,Sod UBS/☆

| **4948.3** indef-pron nom sing | **1498.34** verb sing indic imperf act | **1706.1** prep | **2513.2** name dat fem | **3549.4** noun dat sing neu |
|---|---|---|---|---|
| τις | ⸂[a] ἦν⸃ | ἐν | Καισαρείᾳ | ὀνόματι |
| *tis* | *ēn* | *en* | *Kaisareia* | *onomati* |
| certain | was | in | Caesarea | by name |

| **2856.1** name nom masc | **1529.1** noun nom sing masc | **1523.2** prep gen | **4539.2** noun gen sing fem | **3450.10** art gen sing fem |
|---|---|---|---|---|
| Κορνήλιος, | ἑκατοντάρχης | ἐκ | σπείρης | τῆς |
| *Kornēlios* | *hekatontarchēs* | *ek* | *speirēs* | *tēs* |
| Cornelius, | a centurion | of | a band | the |

| **2535.32** verb gen sing fem part pres mid | **2456.1** name-adj gen fem | **2133.1** adj nom sing masc | **2504.1** conj | **5236.7** verb nom sing masc part pres mid |
|---|---|---|---|---|
| καλουμένης | Ἰταλικῆς, | **2.** εὐσεβὴς | καὶ | φοβούμενος |
| *kaloumenēs* | *Italikēs* | *eusebēs* | *kai* | *phoboumenos* |
| being called | Italian, | godly | and | fearing |

| **3450.6** art acc sing masc | **2296.4** noun acc sing masc | **4713.1** prep | **3820.3** adj dat sing | **3450.3** art dat sing | **3486.3** noun dat sing masc | **840.3** prs-pron gen sing |
|---|---|---|---|---|---|---|
| τὸν | θεὸν | σὺν | παντὶ | τῷ | οἴκῳ | αὐτοῦ, |
| *ton* | *theon* | *sun* | *panti* | *tō* | *oikō* | *autou* |
| | God | with | all | the | house | his, |

2.a.**Txt:** 020L,025P,byz. **Var:** 01ℵ,02A,03B,04C 08E,sa.bo.Lach,Treg,Alf Word,Tisc,We/Ho,Weis Sod,UBS/☆

| **4020.15** verb nom sing masc part pres act | **4885.1** conj | **1641.5** noun acc pl fem | **4044.15** adj acc pl fem | **3450.3** art dat sing |
|---|---|---|---|---|
| ποιῶν | ⸂[a] τε⸃ | ἐλεημοσύνας | πολλὰς | τῷ |
| *poiōn* | *te* | *eleēmosunas* | *pollas* | *tō* |
| doing | both | alms | much | to the |

| **2967.3** noun dat sing masc | **2504.1** conj | **1183.3** verb nom sing masc part pres mid | **3450.2** art gen sing | **2296.2** noun gen sing masc | **1269.1** adv |
|---|---|---|---|---|---|
| λαῷ, | καὶ | δεόμενος | τοῦ | θεοῦ | ⸀ διαπαντός, |
| *laō* | *kai* | *deomenos* | *tou* | *theou* | *diapantos* |
| people, | and | entreating | | God | continually. |

| **1217.2** prep | **3820.2** adj gen sing | **1481.3** verb 3sing indic aor act | **1706.1** prep | **3568.3** noun dat sing neu | **5159.1** adv |
|---|---|---|---|---|---|
| [☆ διὰ | παντός, ] | **3.** εἶδεν | ἐν | ὁράματι | φανερῶς, |
| *dia* | *pantos* | *eiden* | *en* | *horamati* | *phanerōs* |
| [ through | all, ] | He saw | in | a vision | plainly, |

3.a.**Var:** p74,01ℵ,02A 03B,04C,08E,bo.Lach Treg,Alf,Word,Tisc We/Ho,Weis,Sod UBS/☆

| **5448.1** adv | **3875.1** prep | **5443.4** noun acc sing fem | **1750.4** num ord acc sing fem | **1712.3** num ord acc sing fem |
|---|---|---|---|---|
| ὡσεὶ | [[a]☆+ περὶ ] | ὥραν | ⸀ ἐννάτην | [☆ ἐνάτην ] |
| *hōsei* | *peri* | *hōran* | *ennatēn* | *enatēn* |
| about | [ idem ] | hour | the ninth | [ idem ] |

| **3450.10** art gen sing fem | **2232.1** noun fem | **32.4** noun acc sing masc | **3450.2** art gen sing | **2296.2** noun gen sing masc | **1511.12** verb part aor act |
|---|---|---|---|---|---|
| τῆς | ἡμέρας, | ἄγγελον | τοῦ | θεοῦ | εἰσελθόντα |
| *tēs* | *hēmeras* | *angelon* | *tou* | *theou* | *eiselthonta* |
| of the | day, | an angel | | of God | having come |

**9:43.** Because of the open door for ministry, Peter stayed in Joppa for a considerable time with a certain Simon, a tanner. This shows the Holy Spirit was still working to break down the barriers which separate people from each other. The occupation of a tanner was considered unclean. Because of the bad odor, the craft was usually carried on outside a town or city. Usually, the workers would remove the hairs from a hide by lime and then treat it with an infusion of bark (usually oak) to make it firm and pliable. The fact that Peter stayed with a tanner shows he had overcome some of the Jewish scruples, for he recognized God's grace in Simon.

**10:1.** Acts now begins a sequence leading to an important turning point for the gospel. Though Jesus commissioned the apostles to make disciples of all nations (Matthew 28:19), those who were scattered by the persecution after Stephen's death at first preached the gospel to Jews only (11:19). But God was already working in the hearts of Gentiles at Caesarea.

Caesarea, about 30 miles north of Joppa, was built by Herod the Great from 25 to 13 B.C. It became the capital of Judea. Stationed there was a special band, or cohort, of soldiers known as the Italian cohort. (Usually a cohort had 600 foot soldiers under a tribune, but there is evidence that this was an auxiliary cohort of 1,000 men.) One of them, Cornelius, was a centurion commanding 100 infantry.

**10:2.** Like all the centurions mentioned in the New Testament, Cornelius was a good man, and like the one Jesus commended in Matthew 8:10,11, he was also a man of faith.

Some Gentiles in those days were tired of the foolishness and immorality of the religions of Rome and Greece. Many, including Cornelius, found something better in the teaching of the synagogues and accepted the truth of the one true God who is holy, righteous, and good.

Luke called Cornelius "devout." In other words, he was right in his attitudes toward both God and man and by grace was living a godly life. He also feared (that is, reverenced and worshiped) God, as did his entire household (including both his family and his servants). But they had not become full proselytes or converts to Judaism.

Cornelius, however, was generous in charitable giving and prayed to God always (literally, "through all", that is, daily, and in every circumstance of his life and work). In other words, he really trusted the Lord to guide him in all things. From 10:37 it is also quite evident that Cornelius knew the gospel. He had not only heard about Jesus, he knew about His resurrection and the promise of the Holy Spirit.

**10:3.** Without a doubt God saw the desire of Cornelius' heart. About 3 o'clock in the afternoon, the Jewish hour of evening prayer,

**43. And it came to pass, that he tarried many days in Joppa with one Simon a tanner:** Meanwhile Peter stayed some days in Jaffa, *TCNT* . . . It happened that he continued to stay for some time, *Kleist* . . . He afterwards remained in, *Fenton* . . . he was living...for some time with, *BB* . . . stayed many days in, *Williams C.K.* . . . remained for a considerable time, *Weymouth* . . . who was a leatherworker, *NCV*.

**1. There was a certain man in Caesarea called Cornelius:** There was then in Caesarea a man named Cornelius, *TCNT*.

**A centurion of the band called the Italian band:** . . . a Captain in the regiment known as the Italian Regiment, *TCNT* . . . a centurion of a cohort, *ABUV* . . . a captain in an Italian company of the Roman army, *Norlie* . . . a centurion, of the squadron, *Concordant* . . . a colonel, *Williams* . . . of the detachment, *Fenton* . . . of an Italian group of the army, *NLT*.

**2. A devout man, and one that feared God with all his house:** . . . a religious man and one who reverenced God, as also did all his household, *TCNT* . . . who venerated, *AmpB* . . . He was religious and God-fearing, and so was every member of his household, *Weymouth*.

**which gave much alms to the people:** He was liberal in his charities to the people, *TCNT* . . . He practiced liberal benevolences among, *Berkeley* . . . He was generous in giving alms to the people of Israel, *Rieu* . . . He gave much money to the people, *NLT* . . . gave liberally, *Adams*.

**and prayed to God always:** . . . constantly, *TCNT* . . . and was a real man of prayer, *Phillips*.

**3. He saw in a vision evidently about the ninth hour of the day:** He saw in a vision openly, *ASV* . . . One afternoon, about three o'clock, he distinctly saw in a vision, *TCNT* . . . in a vision manifestly, *Young* . . . saw in a vision plainly, *Noyes* . . . clearly and distinctly, *Wuest* . . . he saw in a dream what God wanted him to see, *NLT*.

**an angel of God coming in to him, and saying unto him, Cornelius:** . . . an angel of God enter

| 4242.1 prep | 840.6 prs-pron acc sing masc | 2504.1 conj | 1500.18 verb acc sing masc part aor act | 840.4 prs-pron dat sing | 2856.4 name voc masc |
|---|---|---|---|---|---|
| πρὸς | αὐτὸν, | καὶ | εἰπόντα | αὐτῷ, | Κορνήλιε. |
| *pros* | *auton* | *kai* | *eiponta* | *autō* | *Kornēlie* |
| to | him, | and | having said | to him, | Cornelius. |

| 3450.5 art nom sing masc | 1156.2 conj | 810.3 verb nom sing masc part aor act | 840.4 prs-pron dat sing | 2504.1 conj | 1703.1 adj nom sing masc |
|---|---|---|---|---|---|
| **4.** Ὁ | δὲ | ἀτενίσας | αὐτῷ | καὶ | ἔμφοβος |
| *Ho* | *de* | *atenisas* | *autō* | *kai* | *emphobos* |
| The | but | having looked intently | on him | and | afraid |

| 1090.53 verb nom sing masc part aor mid | 1500.5 verb 3sing indic aor act | 4949.9 intr-pron sing neu | 1498.4 verb 3sing indic pres act | 2935.5 noun voc sing masc |
|---|---|---|---|---|
| γενόμενος | εἶπεν, | Τί | ἐστιν, | κύριε; |
| *genomenos* | *eipen* | *Ti* | *estin* | *kurie* |
| having become | said, | What | is it, | Lord? |

| 1500.5 verb 3sing indic aor act | 1156.2 conj | 840.4 prs-pron dat sing | 3450.13 art nom pl fem | 4194.5 noun nom pl fem | 4622.2 prs-pron gen 2sing |
|---|---|---|---|---|---|
| εἶπεν | δὲ | αὐτῷ, | Αἱ | προσευχαί | σου |
| *eipen* | *de* | *autō* | *Hai* | *proseuchai* | *sou* |
| He said | and | to him, | The | prayers | your |

| 2504.1 conj | 3450.13 art nom pl fem | 1641.3 noun nom pl fem | 4622.2 prs-pron gen 2sing | 303.14 verb 3pl indic aor act | 1519.1 prep |
|---|---|---|---|---|---|
| καὶ | αἱ | ἐλεημοσύναι | σου | ἀνέβησαν | εἰς |
| *kai* | *hai* | *eleēmosunai* | *sou* | *anebēsan* | *eis* |
| and | the | alms | your | are gone up | for |

4.a.**Txt:** 04C,08E,020L 025P,byz.
**Var:** 01ℵ,02A,03B,Lach Treg,Alf,Tisc,We/Ho Weis,Sod,UBS/☆

| 3286.1 noun sing neu | 1783.1 prep | 1699.1 prep | 3450.2 art gen sing | 2296.2 noun gen sing masc |
|---|---|---|---|---|
| μνημόσυνον | ⸂ἐνώπιον | [a☆ ἔμπροσθεν ] | τοῦ | θεοῦ. |
| *mnēmosunon* | *enōpion* | *emprosthen* | *tou* | *theou* |
| a memorial | before | [ idem ] | | God. |

| 2504.1 conj | 3431.1 adv | 3854.10 verb 2sing impr aor act | 1519.1 prep | 2421.3 name acc fem | 433.9 noun acc pl masc |
|---|---|---|---|---|---|
| **5.** καὶ | νῦν | πέμψον | ⸂εἰς | Ἰόππην | ἄνδρας, |
| *kai* | *nun* | *pempson* | *eis* | *Ioppēn* | *andras* |
| And | now | send | to | Joppa | men, |

| 433.9 noun acc pl masc | 1519.1 prep | 2421.3 name acc fem | 2504.1 conj | 3213.5 verb 2sing impr aor mid | 4468.4 name acc masc |
|---|---|---|---|---|---|
| [☆ ἄνδρας | εἰς | Ἰόππην ] | καὶ | μετάπεμψαι | Σίμωνά |
| *andras* | *eis* | *Ioppēn* | *kai* | *metapempsai* | *Simōna* |
| [ men | to | Joppa ] | and | send for | Simon |

5.a.**Var:** p74,02A,03B 04C,1739,bo.Lach,Treg Alf,Tisc,We/Ho,Weis Sod,UBS/☆

| 4948.5 indef-pron | 3614.5 rel-pron nom sing masc | 1926.2 verb 3sing indic pres mid | 3935.1 name nom masc | 3642.4 dem-pron nom sing masc |
|---|---|---|---|---|
| [a☆+ τινα ] | ὃς | ἐπικαλεῖται | Πέτρος· | **6.** οὗτος |
| *tina* | *hos* | *epikaleitai* | *Petros* | *houtos* |
| [ a certain one ] | who | is being called | Peter. | This one |

| 3441.4 verb 3sing indic pres mid | 3706.2 prep | 4948.2 indef-pron dat sing | 4468.3 name dat masc | 1031.2 noun dat sing masc | 3614.3 rel-pron dat sing |
|---|---|---|---|---|---|
| ξενίζεται | παρά | τινι | Σίμωνι | βυρσεῖ, | ᾧ |
| *xenizetai* | *para* | *tini* | *Simōni* | *bursei* | *hō* |
| is being lodged | with | a certain | Simon | a tanner, | whose |

6.a.**Txt:** Steph
**Var:** 01ℵ,02A,03B,04C 08E,020L,025P,Gries Lach,Treg,Alf,Word Tisc,We/Ho,Weis,Sod UBS/☆

| 1498.4 verb 3sing indic pres act | 3477.2 noun nom sing fem | 3706.2 prep | 2258.4 noun acc sing fem | 3642.4 dem-pron nom sing masc |
|---|---|---|---|---|
| ἐστιν | οἰκία | παρὰ | θάλασσαν· | ⸂a οὗτος |
| *estin* | *oikia* | *para* | *thalassan* | *houtos* |
| is | house | by | sea; | this one |

he was fasting and praying. In the temple at Jerusalem, the evening sacrifice was being offered by the priest at about this same time each day. Therefore, praying at this very hour was quite significant; it was almost a way of participating in the priest's offering. (Cf. Psalm 141:2, "Let my prayer be set forth before thee as incense; and the lifting up of my hands as the evening sacrifice.") (See 10:30.) Suddenly an angel appeared to him in a vision ("something seen"), that is, in an actual appearance or revelation, openly in full daylight.

**10:4.** As Cornelius directed his gaze on the angel, he became afraid (full of awe, fear, or even something akin to terror). This was a natural reaction to the supernatural by a man who had never before experienced anything supernatural. But in spite of his fear, he asked, "What is it, Lord?" thus taking the angel to be a divine manifestation. The angel, however, directed his attention to God. Cornelius' prayers and charitable giving had gone up (ascended) as a memorial (reminder, or better, a remembrance offering, which is the meaning in the Old Testament) to God.

**10:5.** The angel did not give any further explanation to Cornelius. He did not tell him what God had in store for him. Neither did he give him any additional teaching to help him. God has not given angels the responsibility to spread the gospel or teach and train the believers. He has given that responsibility to the members of His Body, the Church. Actually, the Church needed to learn some lessons here, and so did the apostles. What Peter was about to learn would help him as much as it would help Cornelius.

The angel directed Cornelius to send men (of his own choosing) to Joppa to summon Simon who was given the (additional) name of Peter. *Simon* (the Hebrew Simeon or Symeon) means "hearing" in the sense of being obedient, and he was obedient to the call to follow Jesus. But Jesus gave him the additional name of Cephas (Aramaic, *Kepha'*, "a stone, a piece of rock"), which corresponds to the Greek *petros*, also meaning a stone or a piece of rock (John 1:35-42). Peter had not been much like a rock in his earlier days, but by the grace of God he had been changed into the strong leader he had now become. Peter would be the one to help Cornelius.

**10:6.** The angel then gave further directions. The messengers of Cornelius would find Peter being entertained as a guest by a certain Simon who was a tanner and whose house was by the shore of the (Mediterranean) Sea, that is, outside of the city of Joppa itself. This is now modern Jaffa.

The statement "This one will tell you what it is necessary to do," is found in the margin of one of the late manuscripts of the Greek New Testament (cursive or minuscule #69) and in the A.D. 1592 edition of the Latin Vulgate of the Roman Catholic Church, but it

his house, *Kleist* . . . coming into his room, and calling him by name, *TCNT*.

**4. And when he looked on him, he was afraid:** Looking steadily at him, and being much alarmed, *Weymouth* . . . Gazing at the angel in awe he said, *Kliest* . . . when he looked intently at him, *KJII* . . . overcome with awe, *TNT* . . . Gazing at him earnestly, and becoming terrified, *Fenton* . . . looking on him in fear, *BB* . . . He stared at the sight, *NAB* . . . He fixed his eyes on him in fear, *Williams C.K.* . . . stared at him in terror, *Goodspeed* . . . being seized with fear, *Douay*.

**and said, What is it, Lord?: And he said unto him, Thy prayers and thine alms are come up for a memorial before God:** . . . and said in fear...and your generosity have risen in God's sight, *NAB* . . . What do you want, Lord? *Everyday* . . . Sir, *Fenton* . . . replied the angel, *Kleist* . . . and your gifts of money, *NLT* . . . and your offerings have come up...and he has kept them in mind, *BB* . . . He has seen what you give to the poor, *Everyday* . . . as a sacrifice to be remembered, *Moffatt* . . . and your gifts to the poor, *Williams C.K.* . . . have ascended as worthy to be remembered, *Berkeley* . . . your charitable acts, *TNT* . . . come to the notice, *Klingensmith*.

**5. And now send men to Joppa, and call for one Simon, whose surname is Peter:** . . . invite over a man named Simon, *Williams* . . . and summon, *NAB* . . . and get one Simon, *BB* . . . and fetch, *Kleist* . . . and bring back a man named, *Everyday* . . . who is called, *Williams C.K.*

**6. He lodgeth with one Simon a tanner:** Who is living with Simon, *BB* . . . the same is a guest, *Rotherham* . . . He is being entertained at the house of, *Goodspeed* . . . is staying with a man, also named Simon, *Everyday* . . . the man who works with leather, *NLT* . . . a leather-worker, *Williams C.K.*

**whose house is by the sea side:** . . . who has a house close to the sea, *Weymouth* . . . whose house stands by the sea, *Moffatt* . . . is by the seaside, *Kleist*.

| **2953.40** verb 3sing indic fut act | **4622.3** prs-pron dat 2sing | **4949.9** intr-pron sing neu | **4622.4** prs-pron acc 2sing | **1158.1** verb 3sing indic pres act |
|---|---|---|---|---|
| λαλήσει | σοι | τί | σε | δεῖ |
| *lalēsei* | *soi* | *ti* | *se* | *dei* |
| will tell | you | what | you | is necessary |

| **4020.20** verb inf pres act | **5453.1** conj | **1156.2** conj | **562.2** verb 3sing indic aor act | **3450.5** art nom sing masc | **32.1** noun nom sing masc |
|---|---|---|---|---|---|
| ποιεῖν. ˋ | **7.** Ὡς | δὲ | ἀπῆλθεν | ὁ | ἄγγελος |
| *poiein* | *Hōs* | *de* | *apēlthen* | *ho* | *angelos* |
| to do. | When | and | departed | the | angel |

7.a.**Txt:** 020L,025P,byz.
**Var:** 01ℵ,02A,03B,04C 08E,sa.Gries,Lach,Treg Alf,Word,Tisc,We/Ho Weis,Sod,UBS/☆

| **3450.5** art nom sing masc | **2953.12** verb nom sing masc part pres act | **3450.3** art dat sing | **2856.3** name dat masc | **840.4** prs-pron dat sing |
|---|---|---|---|---|
| ὁ | λαλῶν | ˊ τῷ | Κορνηλίῳ, | [a☆ αὐτῷ, ] |
| *ho* | *lalōn* | *tō* | *Kornēliō* | *autō* |
| the | speaking | | to Cornelius, | [ to him ] |

7.b.**Txt:** 020L,025P,byz. sa.bo.
**Var:** 01ℵ,02A,03B,04C 08E,Lach,Treg,Alf Word,Tisc,We/Ho,Weis Sod,UBS/☆

| **5291.9** verb nom sing masc part aor act | **1411.3** num card | **3450.1** art gen pl | **3473.4** noun gen pl masc | **840.3** prs-pron gen sing | **2504.1** conj |
|---|---|---|---|---|---|
| φωνήσας | δύο | τῶν | οἰκετῶν | ˊb αὐτοῦ, ˋ | καὶ |
| *phōnēsas* | *duo* | *tōn* | *oiketōn* | *autou* | *kai* |
| having called | two | of the | servants | his, | and |

| **4608.3** noun acc sing masc | **2133.2** adj acc sing masc | **3450.1** art gen pl | **4201.5** verb gen pl masc part pres act | **840.4** prs-pron dat sing |
|---|---|---|---|---|
| στρατιώτην | εὐσεβῆ | τῶν | προσκαρτερούντων | αὐτῷ, |
| *stratiōtēn* | *eusebē* | *tōn* | *proskarterountōn* | *autō* |
| a soldier | godly | of the | continually waiting | on him, |

| **2504.1** conj | **1817.3** verb nom sing masc part aor mid | **840.2** prs-pron dat pl | **533.1** adj | **533.1** adj |
|---|---|---|---|---|
| **8.** καὶ | ἐξηγησάμενος | ˊ αὐτοῖς | ἅπαντα | [☆ ἅπαντα |
| *kai* | *exēgēsamenos* | *autois* | *hapanta* | *hapanta* |
| and | having related | to them | all things | [ all things |

| **840.2** prs-pron dat pl | **643.8** verb 3sing indic aor act | **840.8** prs-pron acc pl masc | **1519.1** prep | **3450.12** art acc sing fem | **2421.3** name acc fem |
|---|---|---|---|---|---|
| αὐτοῖς ] | ἀπέστειλεν | αὐτοὺς | εἰς | τὴν | Ἰόππην. |
| *autois* | *apesteilen* | *autous* | *eis* | *tēn* | *Ioppēn* |
| to them ] | he sent | them | to | | Joppa. |

| **3450.11** art dat sing fem | **1156.2** conj | **1872.1** adv | **3459.1** verb gen pl masc part pres act | **1552.1** dem-pron gen pl | **2504.1** conj |
|---|---|---|---|---|---|
| **9.** Τῇ | δὲ | ἐπαύριον | ὁδοιπορούντων | ἐκείνων | καὶ |
| *Tē* | *de* | *epaurion* | *hodoiporountōn* | *ekeinōn* | *kai* |
| On the | and | next day | journeying | these | and |

| **3450.11** art dat sing fem | **4032.3** noun dat sing fem | **1443.6** verb gen pl masc part pres act | **303.13** verb 3sing indic aor act | **3935.1** name nom masc | **1894.3** prep |
|---|---|---|---|---|---|
| τῇ | πόλει | ἐγγιζόντων, | ἀνέβη | Πέτρος | ἐπὶ |
| *tē* | *polei* | *engizontōn* | *anebē* | *Petros* | *epi* |
| to the | city | drawing near, | went up | Peter | on |

| **3450.16** art sing neu | **1423.2** noun sing neu | **4195.26** verb inf aor mid | **3875.1** prep | **5443.4** noun acc sing fem | **1608.5** num ord acc sing fem |
|---|---|---|---|---|---|
| τὸ | δῶμα | προσεύξασθαι, | περὶ | ὥραν | ἕκτην. |
| *to* | *dōma* | *proseuxasthai* | *peri* | *hōran* | *hektēn* |
| the | housetop | to pray, | about | hour | the sixth. |

| **1090.33** verb 3sing indic aor mid | **1156.2** conj | **4219.1** adj nom sing masc | **2504.1** conj | **2286.32** verb 3sing indic imperf act |
|---|---|---|---|---|
| **10.** ἐγένετο | δὲ | πρόσπεινος | καὶ | ἤθελεν |
| *egeneto* | *de* | *prospeinos* | *kai* | *ēthelen* |
| He became | and | very hungry, | and | was wishing |

is not found in any other ancient manuscripts of any importance. However, it does fit the context and explains why Cornelius should send for Peter.

**he shall tell thee what thou oughtest to do:** . . . thou wilt learn from him what thou hast to do, *Knox.*

**10:7.** As soon as the angel left, Cornelius called two of his household slaves to himself. As verse 2 indicates, these were Godfearers who had accepted the truth about the one true God and were worshiping Him. Cornelius also summoned a devout, loyal soldier.

*Devout* means godly, God-fearing, and reverent. So this soldier must have listened to God's Word in the synagogue and joined in the prayers. He too must have heard about Jesus, His teachings, His ministry, His miracles, His death, and His resurrection. This soldier was also closely attached to Cornelius and must have talked and prayed with him, so Cornelius knew him very well and felt he could trust him to go along with this mission to summon Peter and bring him to Caesarea.

These men were in the military service of Rome as a career. They were part of the Empire's attempt to maintain what was called the "Roman peace," a peace that enabled the gospel to spread more rapidly than it otherwise could have in those days. But the believers were seeking a better peace than Rome could give.

**7. And when the angel which spake unto Cornelius was departed:** . . . who spoke to him had left, *Moffatt* . . . had disappeared, *NAB* . . . had gone away, *Williams.*

**he called two of his household servants:** . . . calling two of the domestics, *Rotherham* . . . his houseboys, *Klingensmith.*

**and a devout soldier of them that waited on him continually:** . . . and a religious soldier who was one of his constant attendants, *TCNT* . . . and a God-fearing soldier, *Weymouth* . . . and a godly soldier, *Williams C.K.* . . . who belonged to his personal retinue, *Moffatt* . . . one of his orderlies, *TNT* . . . in continual attendance, *Wuest.*

**10:8.** Cornelius did more than give a command to his servants and this soldier. He, in fact, did not treat them as servants, but as friends, and explained in detail what the angel had said. Cornelius had received an assurance from God that He had heard his prayers, and he wanted all God had for him. He was also sure that what God had for him was good, so these servants and his soldier would want what God had to offer as well. Then Cornelius sent the three men to Joppa.

**8. And when he had declared all these things unto them:** . . . and having rehearsed, *ASV* . . . after telling them the whole story, *TCNT* . . . told them everything, *Williams C.K.*

**he sent them to Joppa:** . . . dispatches them, *Concordant.*

**10:9.** The next day about the sixth hour (about noon) the three men sent by Cornelius were nearing Joppa. But at this point the Bible's attention shifts to Peter. God is always faithful to work on "both ends of the line," and it was time now to prepare Peter to go with these men to Caesarea to the house of Cornelius.

At that very time Peter went up to the flat roof of Simon's house by an outside stairway with the purpose of spending some time alone in prayer.

Most Jews considered noon one of the hours of prayer. As the psalmist David said, "Evening, and morning, and at noon, will I pray, and cry aloud: and he shall hear my voice" (Psalm 55:17).

**9. On the morrow, as they went on their journey:** . . . as those men were journeying, *Rotherham* . . . The next day, while they were still on their journey, *Weymouth.*

**and drew nigh unto the city:** . . . and just as they were getting near the town, *TCNT* . . . not far from the town, *Williams* . . . approaching the town, *Berkeley.*

**Peter went up upon the house top to pray about the sixth hour:** . . . ascended the balcony, *Fenton* . . . about mid-day, *TCNT* . . . about noon, *Weymouth.*

**10:10.** Apparently Peter prayed for a time, then he became very hungry and wanted to eat. His heart was open to the Lord, and undoubtedly it was the Lord who put this unusual hunger upon

**10. And he became very hungry, and would have eaten:** . . . and desired to eat, *ASV* . . . and wished to eat, *Rotherham* . . . wanted something to eat, *TCNT* . . . wished for some food, *Weymouth* . . . he became ravenous, *Concordant* . . . would have taken a little refreshment, *Campbell* . . . craved something to eat, *Norlie* . . . longed for something, *Phillips* . . . And he was in need of food, *BB* . . . longed to taste something, *Fenton.*

| 1083.8 verb inf aor mid | 3764.1 verb gen pl masc part pres act | 1156.2 conj | 1552.1 dem-pron gen pl |
|---|---|---|---|
| γεύσασθαι˙ | παρασκευαζόντων | δὲ | ⸀ ἐκείνων |
| geusasthai | paraskeuazontōn | de | ekeinōn |
| to eat. | Making ready | but | those |

10.a.**Txt:** 020L,025P,byz.
**Var:** 01ℵ,02A,03B,04C 08E,Lach,Treg,Alf Word,Tisc,We/Ho,Weis Sod,UBS/☆

10.b.**Txt:** 08E,020L 025P,byz.sa.
**Var:** 01ℵ,02A,03B,04C bo.Lach,Treg,Alf,Word Tisc,We/Ho,Weis,Sod UBS/☆

| 840.1 prs-pron gen pl | 1953.2 verb 3sing indic aor act | 1090.33 verb 3sing indic aor mid | 1894.2 prep | 840.6 prs-pron acc sing masc |
|---|---|---|---|---|
| [a☆ αὐτῶν ] | ⸀ ἐπέπεσεν | [b☆ ἐγένετο ] | ἐπ' | αὐτὸν |
| autōn | epepesen | egeneto | ep' | auton |
| [ they ] | fell | [ came ] | upon | him |

| 1598.1 noun nom sing fem | 2504.1 conj | 2311.4 verb 3sing indic pres act | 3450.6 art acc sing masc | 3636.4 noun acc sing masc |
|---|---|---|---|---|
| ἔκστασις, | **11.** καὶ | θεωρεῖ | τὸν | οὐρανὸν |
| ekstasis | kai | theōrei | ton | ouranon |
| a trance, | and | he sees | the | heaven |

11.a.**Txt:** 020L,025P 1241,byz.
**Var:** p74,01ℵ,02A,03B 04C-corr,08E,Gries Lach,Treg,Alf,Word Tisc,We/Ho,Weis,Sod UBS/☆

| 453.23 verb sing part perf mid | 2504.1 conj | 2568.10 verb sing neu part pres act | 1894.2 prep | 840.6 prs-pron acc sing masc |
|---|---|---|---|---|
| ἀνεῳγμένον, | καὶ | καταβαῖνον | ⸂a ἐπ' | αὐτὸν ⸃ |
| aneōgmenon | kai | katabainon | ep' | auton |
| having been opened, | and | descending | upon | him |

| 4487.1 noun sing neu | 4948.10 indef-pron sing neu | 5453.1 conj | 3469.1 noun acc sing fem | 3144.12 adj acc sing fem | 4913.2 num card dat |
|---|---|---|---|---|---|
| σκεῦός | τι | ὡς | ὀθόνην | μεγάλην, | τέσσαρσιν |
| skeuos | ti | hōs | othonēn | megalēn | tessarsin |
| a vessel | certain, | as | a sheet | great, | by four |

11.b.**Txt:** 04C-org,020L 025P,1241,byz.Sod
**Var:** p74,01ℵ,02A,03B 04C-corr,08E,Lach,Treg Tisc,We/Ho,Weis UBS/☆

| 741.6 noun dat pl fem | 1204.16 verb sing part perf mid | 2504.1 conj | 2496.3 verb sing neu part pres mid | 1894.3 prep |
|---|---|---|---|---|
| ἀρχαῖς | ⸂b δεδεμένον, | καὶ ⸃ | καθιέμενον | ἐπὶ |
| archais | dedemenon | kai | kathiemenon | epi |
| corners | having been bound, | and | being let down | upon |

| 3450.10 art gen sing fem | 1087.2 noun gen sing fem | 1706.1 prep | 3614.3 rel-pron dat sing | 5062.12 verb 3sing indic imperf act | 3820.1 adj |
|---|---|---|---|---|---|
| τῆς | γῆς˙ | **12.** ἐν | ᾧ | ὑπῆρχεν | πάντα |
| tēs | gēs | en | hō | hupērchen | panta |
| the | earth; | in | which | were | all |

| 3450.17 art pl neu | 4922.1 adj pl neu | 3450.10 art gen sing fem | 1087.2 noun gen sing fem | 2504.1 conj | 3450.17 art pl neu |
|---|---|---|---|---|---|
| τὰ | τετράποδα | ⸀ τῆς | γῆς | καὶ | τὰ |
| ta | tetrapoda | tēs | gēs | kai | ta |
| the | four footed creatures | of the | earth | and | the |

12.a.**Txt:** 020L,025P,044 1241,byz.
**Var:** p74,01ℵ,02A,03B 04C-corr,Lach,Treg,Alf Tisc,We/Ho,Weis,Sod UBS/☆

12.b.**Txt:** 04C-org,08E 020L,025P,byz.
**Var:** 01ℵ,02A,03B 04C-corr,Lach,Treg,Alf Tisc,We/Ho,Weis,Sod UBS/☆

| 2319.4 noun pl neu | 2504.1 conj | 3450.17 art pl neu | 2046.1 noun pl neu | 2504.1 conj |
|---|---|---|---|---|
| θηρία | καὶ | τὰ | ἑρπετὰ | [a☆ καὶ |
| thēria | kai | ta | herpeta | kai |
| wild beasts | and | the | creeping things | [ and |

| 2046.1 noun pl neu | 3450.10 art gen sing fem | 1087.2 noun gen sing fem | 2504.1 conj | 3450.17 art pl neu | 3932.1 adj pl neu |
|---|---|---|---|---|---|
| ἑρπετὰ | τῆς | γῆς ] | καὶ | ⸂b τὰ ⸃ | πετεινὰ |
| herpeta | tēs | gēs | kai | ta | peteina |
| creeping things | of the | ground ] | and | the | birds |

| 3450.2 art gen sing | 3636.2 noun gen sing masc | 2504.1 conj | 1090.33 verb 3sing indic aor mid | 5292.1 noun nom sing fem | 4242.1 prep |
|---|---|---|---|---|---|
| τοῦ | οὐρανοῦ. | **13.** καὶ | ἐγένετο | φωνὴ | πρὸς |
| tou | ouranou | kai | egeneto | phōnē | pros |
| of the | heaven. | And | came | a voice | to |

him to prepare him for the revelation God was about to give him.

While Peter remained on the roof enjoying the cool breezes off the Mediterranean and waiting for them to prepare the food, he "fell into a trance." This does not mean a trance in the modern sense of the word, however, nor does it imply a hypnotic or unconscious state. The Greek says an *ekstasis* came over him. This simply means his mind was distracted from whatever he was thinking about as he sensed something important was about to happen. It was a consciousness of the presence of the supernatural, a feeling akin to astonishment or amazement. God was about to do something special.

**10:11.** Then Peter saw a sight that must have really filled him with amazement. He saw heaven opening, and a kind of vessel, or container like an enormous sheet or sailcloth tied at the corners, was descending to him as it was let down to the earth.

Seeing the heavens opened is a reminder of Jacob's dream at Bethel where he saw the heavens opened, and the Lord appeared to him (Genesis 28:12-16). It meant God was accessible and He had a message for Jacob. God had a message for Peter, but He gave it in a way quite different from when He sent the angel to Cornelius. The angel was an objective, real appearance. But this experience of Peter was a vision dealing with symbolic things, a dream-type vision, though Peter was fully awake and saw it with his eyes.

**10:12.** The sheet, or sailcloth, was filled with all kinds of quadrupeds, wild animals, reptiles of the earth, and birds of the air. The implication is that they did not include the domesticated animals that were considered clean by the law of Moses and therefore suitable for sacrifice and for eating. Furthermore, all these animals and birds were mixed together. They did not have any of the separation required by the Law.

Many of the prohibitions of the Mosaic law were included by God so that there might be a distinction between and even a separation of the Jews from the heathen around them. As one reads Leviticus 11 and Deuteronomy 14, several if not most of the dietary restrictions seem to be included for just this reason; there seems to be nothing intrinsically harmful about consuming the various foods that were prohibited. In fact, Genesis 9:3 states that God gave Noah "every moving thing that liveth" for food. However, he commanded Noah not to eat meat with the blood still in it (verse 4). This vision was telling Peter that the distinction between Jew and Gentile was abolished at the Cross.

**10:13.** While Peter was observing the contents of the sheet, a voice came to him and commanded him to rise up, kill (these animals and birds), and eat them.

**but while they made ready:** . . . and while they were making ready, *Rotherham* . . . but, while they were preparing it, *Weymouth* . . . But as they were getting the meal ready, *Moffatt* . . . While they were fixing a meal, *Klingensmith* . . . But while the food was being prepared, *Everyday, NCV.*

**he fell into a trance:** . . . he fell into an ecstatic reverie, *Fenton* . . . there came upon him a trance, *Rotherham* . . . he fell into a deep sleep, *Williams C.K.* . . . he saw in a dream things God wanted him to see, *NLT* . . . he fell into an ecstasy, *Kleist* . . . he had a vision, *Everyday* . . . a deep sleep came on him, *BB.*

**11. And saw heaven opened:** . . . opening, *Knox* . . . and saw that the sky was open, *TCNT* . . . He saw a rift in the sky, *NEB.*

**and a certain vessel descending unto him, as it had been a great sheet:** . . . and a bundle, *Knox* . . . something like a great sail was descending, *TCNT* . . . what seemed to be an enormous sheet was, *Weymouth* . . . and an object come down that looked like a big canvas, *NAB* . . . resembling a large sheet, *Fenton* . . . and a receptacle descending like, *Kleist* . . . a container coming down like a wide sheet, *Berkeley* . . . a great linen sheet, *Douay* . . . an enormous sail, *Montgomery* . . . a big piece of canvas, *Klingensmith* . . . like a great sail, *TNT* . . . like a giant sheet, *KJII* . . . like a large linen cloth, *NLT* . . . a great cloth, *BB.*

**knit at the four corners, and let down to the earth:** . . . let down by four corners, *ASV* . . . let down by its four corners towards the earth, *TCNT* . . . supported at the four corners, *Fenton* . . . by ropes at the four corners and lowered to the ground, *Weymouth.*

**12. Wherein were all manner of four footed beasts of the earth, and wild beasts, and creeping things, and fowls of the air:** In which were all sorts of, *BB* . . . In it were all kinds of quadrupeds, reptiles, and birds, *TCNT* . . . animals, *Everyday* . . . and snakes of the earth, *NLT* . . . things that creep on the earth, *Knox* . . . and wild birds, *Williams C.K.* . . . and birds of the sky, *Fenton.*

| 840.6 prs-pron acc sing masc | 448.9 verb nom sing masc part aor act | 3935.5 name voc masc | 2357.6 verb 2sing impr aor act | 2504.1 conj |
|---|---|---|---|---|
| αὐτόν, | Ἀναστάς, | Πέτρε, | θῦσον | καὶ |
| *auton* | *Anastas* | *Petre* | *thuson* | *kai* |
| him, | Having risen up, | Peter, | sacrifice | and |

| 2052.22 verb 2sing impr aor act | 3450.5 art nom sing masc | 1156.2 conj | 3935.1 name nom masc | 1500.5 verb 3sing indic aor act | 3233.1 adv |
|---|---|---|---|---|---|
| φάγε. | **14.** Ὁ | δὲ | Πέτρος | εἶπεν, | Μηδαμῶς, |
| *phage* | *Ho* | *de* | *Petros* | *eipen* | *Mēdamōs* |
| eat. | | But | Peter | said, | Suerly not, |

| 2935.5 noun voc sing masc | 3617.1 conj | 3626.1 adv | 2052.27 verb indic aor act | 3820.17 adj sing neu | 2812.1 adj sing |
|---|---|---|---|---|---|
| κύριε· | ὅτι | οὐδέποτε | ἔφαγον | πᾶν | κοινὸν |
| *kurie* | *hoti* | *oudepote* | *ephagon* | *pan* | *koinon* |
| Lord; | for | never | did I eat | anything | common |

14.a.**Txt:** 04C,05D,08E 020L,025P,byz.bo.
**Var:** 01ℵ,02A,03B,sa. Lach,Treg,Alf,Tisc We/Ho,Weis,Sod UBS/☆

| 2211.1 conj | 2504.1 conj | 167.1 adj sing | 2504.1 conj | 5292.1 noun nom sing fem | 3687.1 adv |
|---|---|---|---|---|---|
| ⸀ἢ | [a☆ καὶ ] | ἀκάθαρτον. | **15.** Καὶ | φωνὴ | πάλιν |
| *ē* | *kai* | *akatharton* | *Kai* | *phōnē* | *palin* |
| or | [ and ] | unclean. | And | a voice | again |

| 1523.2 prep gen | 1202.1 num ord gen sing | 4242.1 prep | 840.6 prs-pron acc sing masc | 3614.17 rel-pron pl neu | 3450.5 art nom sing masc |
|---|---|---|---|---|---|
| ἐκ | δευτέρου | πρὸς | αὐτόν, | Ἃ | ὁ |
| *ek* | *deuterou* | *pros* | *auton* | *Ha* | *ho* |
| from | the second time | to | him, | What | |

| 2296.1 noun nom sing masc | 2483.4 verb 3sing indic aor act | 4622.1 prs-pron nom 2sing | 3231.1 partic | 2813.2 verb 2sing impr pres act |
|---|---|---|---|---|
| θεὸς | ἐκαθάρισεν, | σὺ | μὴ | κοίνου. |
| *theos* | *ekatharisen* | *su* | *mē* | *koinou* |
| God | cleansed, | you | not | make common. |

| 3642.17 dem-pron sing neu | 1156.2 conj | 1090.33 verb 3sing indic aor mid | 1894.3 prep | 4994.1 adv | 2504.1 conj |
|---|---|---|---|---|---|
| **16.** Τοῦτο | δὲ | ἐγένετο | ἐπὶ | τρίς· | καὶ |
| *Touto* | *de* | *egeneto* | *epi* | *tris* | *kai* |
| This | and | took place | upon | three times | and |

16.a.**Txt:** 05D,020L 025P,044,1241,byz.
**Var:** p74,01ℵ,02A,03B 04C,08E,bo.Lach,Treg Alf,Word,Tisc,We/Ho Weis,Sod,UBS/☆

| 3687.1 adv | 2098.1 adv | 351.6 verb 3sing indic aor pass | 351.8 verb 3sing indic aor pass | 3450.16 art sing neu |
|---|---|---|---|---|
| ⸀πάλιν | [a☆ εὐθὺς ] | ⸀ἀνελήφθη | [☆ ἀνελήμφθη ] | τὸ |
| *palin* | *euthus* | *anelēphthē* | *anelēmphthē* | *to* |
| again | [ immediately ] | was taken up | [ idem ] | the |

| 4487.1 noun sing neu | 1519.1 prep | 3450.6 art acc sing masc | 3636.4 noun acc sing masc | 5453.1 conj | 1156.2 conj | 1706.1 prep |
|---|---|---|---|---|---|---|
| σκεῦος | εἰς | τὸν | οὐρανόν. | **17.** Ὡς | δὲ | ἐν |
| *skeuos* | *eis* | *ton* | *ouranon* | *Hōs* | *de* | *en* |
| vessel | into | the | heaven. | As | and | in |

| 1431.5 prs-pron dat sing masc | 1274.1 verb 3sing indic imperf act | 3450.5 art nom sing masc | 3935.1 name nom masc | 4949.9 intr-pron sing neu | 300.1 partic |
|---|---|---|---|---|---|
| ἑαυτῷ | διηπόρει | ὁ | Πέτρος | τί | ἂν |
| *heautō* | *diēporei* | *ho* | *Petros* | *ti* | *an* |
| himself | was perplexed | | Peter | what | |

17.a.**Txt:** 04C,05D,08E 020L,025P,byz.
**Var:** p45,p74,01ℵ,02A 03B,Lach,Treg,Tisc We/Ho,Weis,Sod UBS/☆

| 1498.14 verb 3sing opt pres act | 3450.16 art sing neu | 3568.1 noun sing neu | 3614.16 rel-pron sing neu | 1481.3 verb 3sing indic aor act | 2504.1 conj |
|---|---|---|---|---|---|
| εἴη | τὸ | ὅραμα | ὃ | εἶδεν, | ⸂a καὶ ⸃ |
| *eiē* | *to* | *horama* | *ho* | *eiden* | *kai* |
| might be | the | vision | which | he saw, | also |

**10:14.** Peter's response shows he was spiritually sensitive enough to know this was the voice of the Lord. But his life-style of strict obedience to the Law overcame his normal desire to obey the Lord. So he replied very emphatically, "Not so (not at all, certainly not, never), Lord." He had never eaten anything common (unsanctified, dirty) or unclean (nonkosher). Peter had made some progress. He had accepted the Lord's work in saving the Samaritans. But they were circumcised and kept the forms of the Law about as well as many of the Jews did.

Peter had not faced the biggest barrier, however. Many laws and customs separated the Jews from the Gentiles, especially the dietary laws. They realized these laws were for their good. Actually, Jesus had already prepared His disciples for the abolishing of these food laws by His discussion of what really defiles a man. He made it clear that the true source of spiritual defilement is from within. External washings cannot get rid of the unclean thoughts, greed, malice, pride, and spiritual ignorance that can fill the heart and become the root of all sorts of evil (Mark 7:15-23).

**10:15.** Peter's reply was a contradiction. He called Jesus "Lord," yet refused to do what Jesus asked him to do. It was a human reaction, the same kind that still keeps many people from making a forward move with God. Therefore the voice (of the Lord Jesus) gave an even more emphatic reply, "What God has cleansed, don't you regard as common (unclean)." The negative used here by Jesus is indeed very emphatic.

It is best to be generally conservative, for not every proposed change is of God. On the other hand, a hidebound conservatism can be harmful, if it hinders bringing a wider dissemination of the gospel.

**10:16.** For further emphasis, the command to kill and eat was given three times. A lifetime of careful obedience to the Law is not easy to set aside. But the Lord made the command so emphatic that Peter had to give attention to it.

**10:17.** Peter had enough discernment to understand this vision was symbolic. The fact that he "doubted" means that it was difficult to understand what the vision meant.

Peter's reaction was not unusual. Visions are sometimes open to more than one interpretation. Peter wanted to be sure he discovered the right one. But he did not find the meaning of this vision by weighing the possibilities in his mind. Rather, he was going to be asked to take a step of faith and obedience in response to the guidance of the Holy Spirit.

God did not let Peter speculate for long. The men sent by Cornelius had already asked the way to Simon's house and were stand-

**13. And there came a voice to him, Rise, Peter; kill, and eat:** Sacrifice! *Concordant*... Up, Peter, *Williams C.K.* ... Slaughter, then eat, *NAB.*

**14. But Peter said, Not so, Lord:** On no account, lord, he replied, *Weymouth* ... By no means, Lord, *Berkeley*... No, Sir, I cannot, *TCNT* ... Far be it, *Murdock* ... Sir, it is unthinkable, *NAB.*

**for I have never eaten any thing that is common or unclean:** ... for I have never eaten anything defiled and impure, *TCNT* ... unhallowed and unclean, *Weymouth* ... undedicated and unclean, *Berkeley* ... prohibited or unclean, *Norlie* ... polluted, *Murdock* ... vile, *Fenton.*

**15. And the voice spake unto him again the second time:** Once more the voice came to him, *Berkeley.*

**What God hath cleansed, that call not thou common:** What God has pronounced pure...you must not call defiled, *TCNT* ... you must not regard as unhallowed, *Weymouth*... stop declaring unhallowed, *Wuest* ... never treat as defiled! *Fenton.*

**16. This was done thrice:** This happened, in all, three times, *TCNT*... This took place three times, *Weymouth.*

**and the vessel was received up again into heaven:** ... and then suddenly it was all taken up into the sky, *TCNT*... then the thing was at once taken up into heaven, *Williams C.K.* ... and immediately the sheet was drawn up out of sight, *Weymouth.*

**17. Now while Peter doubted in himself what this vision which he had seen should mean:** ... was still worrying over the meaning, *JB* ... was much perplexed in himself, *ASV*... While Peter was still puzzling over the meaning of the vision he had seen, *TCNT* ... wondering as to the meaning, *Weymouth* ... quite at a loss to know the meaning, *Moffatt* ... was mulling over in his mind, *Berkeley* ... was bewildered in himself, *Concordant*... was still at a loss to know, *Williams*... was reflecting on the vision, *Campbell.*

## Acts 10:18

| 1481.20 verb 2sing impr aor mid | 3450.7 art nom pl masc | 433.6 noun nom pl masc | 3450.7 art nom pl masc | 643.30 verb nom pl masc part perf mid |
|---|---|---|---|---|
| ἰδοὺ, | οἱ | ἄνδρες | οἱ | ἀπεσταλμένοι |
| *idou* | *hoi* | *andres* | *hoi* | *apestalmenoi* |
| behold, | the | men | the | having been sent |

17.b.**Txt:** 02A,04C,05D 020L,025P,byz.
**Var:** p74,01ℵ,03B,08E Tisc,We/Ho,Weis,Sod UBS/☆

| 570.3 prep | 5097.3 prep | 3450.2 art gen sing | 2856.2 name gen masc | 1325.1 verb nom pl masc part aor act |
|---|---|---|---|---|
| ʻ ἀπὸ | [b☆ ὑπὸ ] | τοῦ | Κορνηλίου, | διερωτήσαντες |
| *apo* | *hupo* | *tou* | *Kornēliou* | *dierōtēsantes* |
| from | [ by ] | | Cornelius, | having inquired for |

17.c.**Var:** 01ℵ,02A,03B 04C,05D,Lach,Treg,Alf Word,Tisc,We/Ho,Weis Sod,UBS/☆

| 3450.12 art acc sing fem | 3477.4 noun acc sing fem | 3450.2 art gen sing | 4468.2 name gen masc | 2168.2 verb 3pl indic aor act | 1894.3 prep |
|---|---|---|---|---|---|
| τὴν | οἰκίαν | [c☆+ τοῦ ] | Σίμωνος, | ἐπέστησαν | ἐπὶ |
| *tēn* | *oikian* | *tou* | *Simōnos* | *epestēsan* | *epi* |
| the | house | | of Simon, | stood | at |

| 3450.6 art acc sing masc | 4298.2 noun acc sing masc | 2504.1 conj | 5291.10 verb nom pl masc part aor act | 4299.7 verb 3pl indic imperf mid |
|---|---|---|---|---|
| τὸν | πυλῶνα· | **18.** καὶ | φωνήσαντες | ἐπυνθάνοντο |
| *ton* | *pulōna* | *kai* | *phōnēsantes* | *epunthanonto* |
| the | porch; | and | having called out | they were asking |

| 1479.1 conj | 4468.1 name nom masc | 3450.5 art nom sing masc | 1926.4 verb nom sing masc part pres mid | 3935.1 name nom masc | 1743.1 adv |
|---|---|---|---|---|---|
| εἰ | Σίμων | ὁ | ἐπικαλούμενος | Πέτρος | ἐνθάδε |
| *ei* | *Simōn* | *ho* | *epikaloumenos* | *Petros* | *enthade* |
| if | Simon | the | being called | Peter | here |

| 3441.4 verb 3sing indic pres mid | 3450.2 art gen sing | 1156.2 conj | 3935.2 name gen masc | 1744.2 verb gen sing masc part pres mid |
|---|---|---|---|---|
| ξενίζεται. | **19.** Τοῦ | δὲ | Πέτρου | ʻ ἐνθυμουμένου |
| *xenizetai* | *Tou* | *de* | *Petrou* | *enthumoumenou* |
| is being lodged. | | But | Peter | thinking |

19.a.**Txt:** Steph
**Var:** 01ℵ,02A,03B,04C 05D,08E,020L,025P,byz. Gries,Lach,Treg,Alf Word,Tisc,We/Ho,Weis Sod,UBS/☆

| 1320.1 verb gen sing masc part pres mid | 3875.1 prep | 3450.2 art gen sing | 3568.2 noun gen sing neu | 1500.5 verb 3sing indic aor act |
|---|---|---|---|---|
| [a☆ διενθυμουμένου ] | περὶ | τοῦ | ὁράματος, | εἶπεν |
| *dienthumoumenou* | *peri* | *tou* | *horamatos* | *eipen* |
| [ reflecting ] | about | the | vision, | said |

19.b.**Txt:** p45,05D,08E 020L,025P,byz.
**Var:** 03B,bo.We/Ho Weis,Sod,UBS/☆

19.c.**Txt:** p74,01ℵ,02A 04C,08E,33,1739,sa.bo. Sod
**Var:** 03B,We/Ho,Weis UBS/☆

| 840.4 prs-pron dat sing | 3450.16 art sing neu | 4011.1 noun sing neu | 1481.20 verb 2sing impr aor mid | 433.6 noun nom pl masc | 4980.1 num card nom |
|---|---|---|---|---|---|
| ʻb αὐτῷ ˋ | τὸ | πνεῦμα, | Ἰδοὺ, | ἄνδρες | ʻ τρεῖς |
| *autō* | *to* | *pneuma* | *Idou* | *andres* | *treis* |
| to him | the | Spirit, | Behold, | men | three |

19.d.**Txt:** 02A,04C,05D 08E,020L,025P,byz.Sod
**Var:** p74,01ℵ,03B,Alf Tisc,We/Ho,Weis UBS/☆

| 1411.3 num card | 2195.2 verb 3pl indic pres act | 2195.10 verb nom pl masc part pres act | 4622.4 prs-pron acc 2sing | 233.2 conj |
|---|---|---|---|---|
| [c☆ δύο ] | ʻ ζητοῦσίν | [d ζητοῦντές ] | σε· | **20.** ἀλλὰ |
| *duo* | *zētousin* | *zētountes* | *se* | *alla* |
| [ two ] | are seeking | [ seeking ] | you; | but |

| 448.9 verb nom sing masc part aor act | 2568.17 verb 2sing impr aor act | 2504.1 conj | 4057.4 verb 2sing impr pres mid | 4713.1 prep | 840.2 prs-pron dat pl |
|---|---|---|---|---|---|
| ἀναστὰς | κατάβηθι, | καὶ | πορεύου | σὺν | αὐτοῖς, |
| *anastas* | *katabēthi* | *kai* | *poreuou* | *sun* | *autois* |
| having risen | go down, | and | go | with | them, |

20.a.**Txt:** 020L,025P,byz.
**Var:** 01ℵ,02A,03B,04C 05D,08E,Gries,Lach Treg,Alf,Word,Tisc We/Ho,Weis,Sod UBS/☆

| 3235.6 num card neu | 1246.8 verb nom sing masc part pres mid | 1354.1 conj | 3617.1 conj | 1466.1 prs-pron nom 1sing |
|---|---|---|---|---|
| μηδὲν | διακρινόμενος· | ʻ διότι | [a☆ ὅτι ] | ἐγὼ |
| *mēden* | *diakrinomenos* | *dioti* | *hoti* | *egō* |
| nothing | doubting, | because | [ that ] | I |

ing at the gate. Once again, it is clear how exact God's timing is in all of His dealings. This was a very critical time in the history of the Church, but God was in control.

**10:18.** The three men at Simon's gate were inquiring if Simon who was also called Peter was staying as a guest there. The people in the house were busy preparing the meal, and Peter was lost in his thoughts about what the vision might mean. Fortunately, the men were persistent and did not give up or go away.

**10:19.** Peter was still thinking about the vision, pondering over it, weighing this and that possible interpretation in his mind. He was still trying to understand it by his own reasonings, probably not willing to admit to himself that the unclean animals and birds might represent people who needed the gospel.

So the Holy Spirit interrupted his thoughts and told him to pay attention, for three men were looking for him. Thus, in spite of his background in Judaism, Peter was sensitive enough to the Holy Spirit to recognize His voice (His inner voice) and be open to His leading.

**10:20.** The Holy Spirit then commanded Peter to get up, go down (the outside stairway) from the flat roof, and go with these men. (Outside stairways made of stone may be seen in the ruins of Biblical cities excavated by archaeologists in Palestine.)

The Holy Spirit further commanded that Peter must go with the three men doubting nothing, that is, without any hesitation. (*Doubt* in this verse translates a different Greek word *diakrinomenos* from the one used in verse 17 *diēporei*. The word used in verse 20 implies being at odds with oneself, wavering, and therefore hesitating to obey, in fact, hesitating to do anything at all. The verb in verse 17 emphasizes perplexity about meaning. In verse 20 the perplexity is about whether to take action.) It was important for Peter to meet these men and go with them. Peter must act and act immediately.

It was also important for Peter to meet them and to realize the Holy Spirit had sent them. When the angel gave directions to Cornelius, the Holy Spirit also moved Cornelius to summon and send these three men. The Holy Spirit moved also on their hearts to encourage them to obey with all diligence. Thus, the Holy Spirit was the One who really sent them.

**10:21.** This was enough for Peter. Casting all doubts, perplexities, and indecision aside, he rose up in obedience to the voice of

**behold, the men which were sent from Cornelius had made enquiry for Simon's house:** . . . having just asked the way to Simon's house, *TCNT* . . . having made search for simon's house, *BB* . . . just then, *Kleist* . . . having asked for the house of, *KJII* . . . and on the next day, *Moffatt* . . . having made diligent inquiry regarding, *Wuest* . . . having found out the house of Simon, *Fenton.*

**and stood before the gate:** . . . came up to the entrance, *TNT* . . . came to the door, *BB, Weymouth* . . . They were in fact standing at the very doorway, *Phillips.*

**18. And called, and asked whether Simon, which was surnamed Peter, were lodged there:** . . . inquiring for Simon's house, *Kleist* . . . calling out to ascertain whether Simon...was a guest there, *Berkeley* . . . Is Simon Peter staying here? *NCV* . . . was living there, *BB* . . . lodged there, *Fenton.*

**19. While Peter thought on the vision:** . . . as Peter was pondering, *Rotherham* . . . was earnestly considering the vision, *ABUV* . . . was meditating on the vision, *Williams* . . . was reflecting about, *Fenton* . . . was turning over the vision in his mind, *BB* . . . thinking deeply about the vision, *Phillips* . . . was musing, *LivB* . . . is engrossed, *Concordant.*

**the Spirit said unto him, Behold, three men seek thee:** See, *BB* . . . three men are looking for you, *RSV* . . . looking for you at this moment, *TCNT* . . . are now inquiring for you, *Fenton.*

**20. Arise therefore, and get thee down:** So get up and go down, *TCNT* . . . but rise up, descend, and accompany them, *Fenton.*

**and go with them, doubting nothing:** . . . and do not hesitate to go with them, *TCNT* . . . and go with them without any misgivings, *Weymouth* . . . and depart with them, *Kleist* . . . set out with them unhesitatingly, *NAB* . . . Don't treat them as different people, *Beck* . . . let not thy mind hesitate, *Murdock* . . . without hesitation, *TNT* . . . without scruple, *Noyes.*

| 643.16 verb 1sing indic perf act | 840.8 prs-pron acc pl masc | 2568.20 verb nom sing masc part aor act | 1156.2 conj | 3935.1 name nom masc |
|---|---|---|---|---|
| ἀπέσταλκα | αὐτούς. | 21. Καταβὰς | δὲ | Πέτρος |
| *apestalka* | *autous* | *Katabas* | *de* | *Petros* |
| have sent | them. | Having gone down | and | Peter |

21.a.**Txt:** byz.
**Var:** 01ℵ,02A,03B,04C 05D,08E,020L,025P Gries,Lach,Treg,Alf Word,Tisc,We/Ho,Weis Sod,UBS/*

| 4242.1 prep | 3450.8 art acc pl masc | 433.9 noun acc pl masc | 3450.8 art acc pl masc | 643.31 verb acc pl masc part perf mid | 570.3 prep |
|---|---|---|---|---|---|
| πρὸς | τοὺς | ἄνδρας | ʽa τοὺς | ἀπεσταλμένους | ἀπὸ |
| *pros* | *tous* | *andras* | *tous* | *apestalmenous* | *apo* |
| to | the | men | the | having been sent | from |

| 3450.2 art gen sing | 2856.2 name gen masc | 4242.1 prep | 840.6 prs-pron acc sing masc | 1500.5 verb 3sing indic aor act | 1481.20 verb 2sing impr aor mid |
|---|---|---|---|---|---|
| τοῦ | Κορνηλίου | πρὸς | αὐτόν, ˋ | εἶπεν, | Ἰδοὺ, |
| *tou* | *Kornēliou* | *pros* | *auton* | *eipen* | *Idou* |
| Cornelius | Cornelius | to | him, | said, | Behold, |

| 1466.1 prs-pron nom 1sing | 1498.2 verb 1sing indic pres act | 3614.6 rel-pron acc sing masc | 2195.1 verb 2pl pres act | 4949.3 intr-pron nom sing |
|---|---|---|---|---|
| ἐγώ | εἰμι | ὃν | ζητεῖτε· | τίς |
| *egō* | *eimi* | *hon* | *zēteite* | *tis* |
| I | am | whom | you seek; | what |

| 3450.9 art nom sing fem | 155.2 noun nom sing fem | 1217.1 prep | 3614.12 rel-pron acc sing fem | 3780.4 verb 2pl indic pres act | 3450.7 art nom pl masc |
|---|---|---|---|---|---|
| ἡ | αἰτία | δι' | ἣν | πάρεστε; | 22. οἱ |
| *hē* | *aitia* | *di'* | *hēn* | *pareste* | *hoi* |
| the | cause | for | which | you are come? | The |

22.a.**Txt:** 05D,020L 025P,byz.Sod
**Var:** 01ℵ,02A,03B,04C 08E,Lach,Treg,Alf,Tisc We/Ho,Weis,UBS/*

| 1156.2 conj | 1500.3 verb indic aor act | 1500.28 verb 3pl indic aor act | 2856.1 name nom masc | 1529.1 noun nom sing masc |
|---|---|---|---|---|
| δὲ | ʽ εἶπον, | [a* εἶπαν, ] | Κορνήλιος | ἑκατοντάρχης, |
| *de* | *eipon* | *eipan* | *Kornēlios* | *hekatontarchēs* |
| and | said, | [ idem ] | Cornelius | a centurion, |

| 433.1 noun nom sing masc | 1337.3 adj nom sing masc | 2504.1 conj | 5236.7 verb nom sing masc part pres mid | 3450.6 art acc sing masc | 2296.4 noun acc sing masc |
|---|---|---|---|---|---|
| ἀνὴρ | δίκαιος | καὶ | φοβούμενος | τὸν | θεὸν, |
| *anēr* | *dikaios* | *kai* | *phoboumenos* | *ton* | *theon* |
| a man | righteous | and | fearing | | God, |

| 3113.32 verb nom sing masc part pres mid | 4885.1 conj | 5097.3 prep | 3513.2 adj gen sing | 3450.2 art gen sing | 1477.2 noun gen sing neu |
|---|---|---|---|---|---|
| μαρτυρούμενός | τε | ὑπὸ | ὅλου | τοῦ | ἔθνους |
| *marturoumenos* | *te* | *hupo* | *holou* | *tou* | *ethnous* |
| having borne witness to | and | by | whole | the | nation |

| 3450.1 art gen pl | 2428.3 name-adj gen pl masc | 5372.4 verb 3sing indic aor pass | 5097.3 prep | 32.2 noun gen sing masc |
|---|---|---|---|---|
| τῶν | Ἰουδαίων, | ἐχρηματίσθη | ὑπὸ | ἀγγέλου |
| *tōn* | *Ioudaiōn* | *echrēmatisthē* | *hupo* | *angelou* |
| of the | Jews, | was divinely instructed | by | angel |

| 39.2 adj gen sing | 3213.7 verb inf aor mid | 4622.4 prs-pron acc 2sing | 1519.1 prep | 3450.6 art acc sing masc | 3486.4 noun acc sing masc |
|---|---|---|---|---|---|
| ἁγίου, | μεταπέμψασθαί | σε | εἰς | τὸν | οἶκον |
| *hagiou* | *metapempsasthai* | *se* | *eis* | *ton* | *oikon* |
| holy, | to send for | you | to | the | house |

| 840.3 prs-pron gen sing | 2504.1 conj | 189.36 verb inf aor act | 4343.4 noun pl neu | 3706.2 prep | 4622.2 prs-pron gen 2sing |
|---|---|---|---|---|---|
| αὐτοῦ | καὶ | ἀκοῦσαι | ῥήματα | παρὰ | σοῦ. |
| *autou* | *kai* | *akousai* | *rhēmata* | *para* | *sou* |
| his, | and | to hear | words | from | you. |

the Holy Spirit and went down to the men who were sent to him from Cornelius. He told them he was the person they were looking for, and he politely asked the reason for their coming. Courtesy is an important aspect of the love of Christ.

Even though Peter already had the Spirit's command to go with these men, he did not thrust himself upon them, nor did he immediately reveal to them what the Holy Spirit had told him. Instead, he gave them opportunity to explain their mission. It would be good for their spiritual experience for them to give their testimony of what God had done.

**10:22.** The men then explained, first by drawing attention to the character of Cornelius, the centurion who had sent them. Their first emphasis was on the fact that he was a just man. That is, he was upright, righteous, law-abiding, not only conforming to the laws of the land, but also recognizing the sovereignty of God and keeping a right relationship to Him by trying to live a life that would be pleasing to Him. It also implies honesty, goodness, and even mercy. Cornelius must have been a wonderful person to work for and a wonderful officer to serve under.

His uprightness was the result of his being a fearer of (the one true) God. He had turned his back on all the whole pantheon of Roman gods, goddesses, and semi-divine heroes of their mythology. All those things which were part of his religious background and upbringing in heathenism were now behind him. He no longer believed any of that mythology or followed any of the forms and ceremonies of Roman worship. He had committed himself to worship the true God who had revealed himself in the sacred writings of the Law, the Prophets, and the Psalms, inspired by the Spirit. As a God-fearer, he continually showed reverence and respect for God, and faithfully worshiped Him.

As a result of this, he had a good testimony borne to him by the whole of "the nation of the Jews." He was not only a man of good reputation among them, he was a man whose merit was well-attested and well-known so they approved of and spoke well of him. This implies he had been a member of Rome's occupation force in Palestine for a long time, probably for many years. Though he was now stationed in Caesarea, he may have been assigned previously to other places in Judea and Galilee as well. It is evident also that he had given generously to the needs of the poor among the Jews wherever he went. He had become well-known among the Jewish people.

The men then explained how Cornelius had been given a divine revelation through a holy angel to summon Peter to his house. The "angel of God" of verse 3 is here called a "holy angel," which shows he must have radiated some of the glory of God, just as the seraphim did in Isaiah chapter 6. This made Cornelius conscious that this angel was indeed a messenger from heaven. The angel further directed that they should hear words (Greek, *rhēmata*) from Peter, implying that they should also listen and obey these words of Christian teaching.



**for I have sent them:** . . . for I have sent them myself, *TCNT.*

**21. Then Peter went down to the men:** So Peter went down and said to the men, *Weymouth* . . . accordingly, *Fenton.*

**which were sent unto him from Cornelius; and said:** So Peter went down and said to the men, *Weymouth.*

**Behold, I am he whom you seek:** I am the man you are looking for, *TCNT* . . . I am the man you want, *Fenton.*

**what is the cause wherefore ye are come?:** What is your object in coming, *TCNT* . . . What is the purpose, *Williams* . . . What brings you here, *Beck* . . . Why have you come? *NLT.*

**22. And they said, Cornelius the centurion:** Cornelius, a colonel in the army, *Williams* . . . an army officer, *NCV* . . . a captain, *Fenton.*

**a just man, and one that feareth God:** . . . a pious officer who reverences God, *TCNT* . . . an upright and God-fearing man, *Weymouth* . . . righteous, *Fenton* . . . and he honors God, *NLT.*

**and of good report among all the nation of the Jews:** . . . and is well spoken of by the whole Jewish nation, *TCNT* . . . who enjoys a good reputation, *Kleist* . . . of good reputation among all, *MLNT* . . . and a man of high reputation with, *Williams* . . . whose character can be vouched for by, *Phillips* . . . is attested by the whole of, *Fenton* . . . All the Jewish people respect him, *NCV.*

**was warned from God by an holy angel to send for thee into his house:** . . . had word from God, *BB* . . . has been divinely instructed, *Weymouth* . . . divinely warned, *Young* . . . to summon you to his house, *NAB* . . . to bring you into, *Fenton.*

**and to hear words of thee:** . . . and listen to what you have to say, *TCNT* . . . He wants to hear what you have to say, *NLT* . . . and to listen to your message, *Montgomery* . . . to hear your suggestions, *Berkeley* . . . to listen to instructions from you, *Fenton* . . . to give hearing to your words, *BB* . . . so that he can hear what you have to say, *Everyday.*

## Acts 10:23

| **1512.1** verb nom sing masc part aor mid | **3631.1** partic | **840.8** prs-pron acc pl masc | **3441.2** verb 3sing indic aor act | **3450.11** art dat sing fem |
|---|---|---|---|---|
| 23. Εἰσκαλεσάμενος | οὖν | αὐτοὺς | ἐξένισεν. | Τῇ |
| *Eiskalesamenos* | *oun* | *autous* | *exenisen* | *Tē* |
| Having called in | therefore | them | he lodged, | On the |

23.a.**Txt:** 020L,025P,byz.
**Var:** 01ℵ,02A,03B,05D sa.bo.Gries,Lach,Treg Alf,Word,Tisc,We/Ho Weis,Sod,UBS/☆

| **1156.2** conj | **1872.1** adv | **3450.5** art nom sing masc | **3935.1** name nom masc | **448.9** verb nom sing masc part aor act |
|---|---|---|---|---|
| δὲ | ἐπαύριον | ʻ ὁ | Πέτρος | [[a]☆ ἀναστὰς ] |
| *de* | *epaurion* | *ho* | *Petros* | *anastas* |
| and | next day | | Peter | [ having stood ] |

| **1814.3** verb 3sing indic aor act | **4713.1** prep | **840.2** prs-pron dat pl | **2504.1** conj | **4948.7** indef-pron nom pl masc | **3450.1** art gen pl |
|---|---|---|---|---|---|
| ἐξῆλθεν | σὺν | αὐτοῖς, | καί | τινες | τῶν |
| *exēlthen* | *sun* | *autois* | *kai* | *tines* | *tōn* |
| went forth | with | them, | and | certain | of the |

23.b.**Txt:** byz.
**Var:** 01ℵ,02A,03B,04C 05D,08E,020L,025P Gries,Lach,Treg,Alf Word,Tisc,We/Ho,Weis Sod,UBS/☆

| **79.7** noun gen pl masc | **3450.1** art gen pl | **570.3** prep | **3450.10** art gen sing fem | **2421.1** name gen fem | **4755.3** verb 3pl indic aor act |
|---|---|---|---|---|---|
| ἀδελφῶν | τῶν | ἀπὸ | ʻ[b] τῆς ˋ | Ἰόππης | συνῆλθον |
| *adelphōn* | *tōn* | *apo* | *tēs* | *Ioppēs* | *sunēlthon* |
| brothers | of the | from | | Joppa | went with |

24.a.**Txt:** 020L,025P,byz.
**Var:** 01ℵ,02A,03B,04C 05D,08E,sa.bo.Lach Treg,Alf,Word,Tisc We/Ho,Weis,Sod UBS/☆

| **840.4** prs-pron dat sing | **2504.1** conj | **3450.11** art dat sing fem | **3450.11** art dat sing fem | **1156.2** conj | **1872.1** adv |
|---|---|---|---|---|---|
| αὐτῷ. | 24. ʻ καὶ | τῇ | [[a]☆ τῇ | δὲ ] | ἐπαύριον |
| *autō* | *kai* | *tē* | *tē* | *de* | *epaurion* |
| him. | And | the | [ the | and ] | next day |

24.b.**Txt:** p74,02A,08E 020L,025P,byz.sa.bo. Sod
**Var:** 03B,05D,Lach Treg,We/Ho,Weis UBS/☆

| **1511.1** verb indic aor act | **1511.3** verb 3sing indic aor act | **1519.1** prep | **3450.12** art acc sing fem | **2513.3** name acc fem |
|---|---|---|---|---|
| ʻ εἰσῆλθον | [[b]☆ εἰσῆλθεν ] | εἰς | τὴν | Καισάρειαν· |
| *eisēlthon* | *eisēlthen* | *eis* | *tēn* | *Kaisareian* |
| they entered | [ he entered ] | into | | Caesarea. |

| **3450.5** art nom sing masc | **1156.2** conj | **2856.1** name nom masc | **1498.34** verb sing indic imperf act | **4186.3** verb nom sing masc part pres act |
|---|---|---|---|---|
| ὁ | δὲ | Κορνήλιος | ἦν | προσδοκῶν |
| *ho* | *de* | *Kornēlios* | *ēn* | *prosdokōn* |
| | And | Cornelius | was | expecting |

| **840.8** prs-pron acc pl masc | **4630.5** verb nom sing masc part aor mid | **3450.8** art acc pl masc | **4624.3** adj pl masc | **840.3** prs-pron gen sing |
|---|---|---|---|---|
| αὐτούς, | συγκαλεσάμενος | τοὺς | συγγενεῖς | αὐτοῦ |
| *autous* | *sunkalesamenos* | *tous* | *sungeneis* | *autou* |
| them, | having called together | the | relatives | his |

| **2504.1** conj | **3450.8** art acc pl masc | **314.1** adj acc pl masc | **5224.7** adj acc pl masc | **5453.1** conj | **1156.2** conj |
|---|---|---|---|---|---|
| καὶ | τοὺς | ἀναγκαίους | φίλους. | 25. ʻΩς | δὲ |
| *kai* | *tous* | *anankaious* | *philous* | *Hōs* | *de* |
| and | the | intimate | friends. | As | and |

25.a.**Var:** 01ℵ,02A,03B 04C,08E,020L,025P Gries,Lach,Treg,Alf Word,Tisc,We/Ho,Weis Sod,UBS/☆

| **1090.33** verb 3sing indic aor mid | **3450.2** art gen sing | **1511.21** verb inf aor act | **3450.6** art acc sing masc | **3935.4** name acc masc |
|---|---|---|---|---|
| ἐγένετο | [[a]☆+ τοῦ ] | εἰσελθεῖν | τὸν | Πέτρον, |
| *egeneto* | *tou* | *eiselthein* | *ton* | *Petron* |
| was | [ the ] | to enter | | Peter, |

| **4727.2** verb nom sing masc part aor act | **840.4** prs-pron dat sing | **3450.5** art nom sing masc | **2856.1** name nom masc | **3959.11** verb nom sing masc part aor act |
|---|---|---|---|---|
| συναντήσας | αὐτῷ | ὁ | Κορνήλιος, | πεσὼν |
| *sunantēsas* | *autō* | *ho* | *Kornēlios* | *pesōn* |
| having met | him | | Cornelius, | having fallen |

**10:23.** Though it was only a little after noon, they did not insist on starting back at once. Peter invited the three men into Simon the tanner's house, and Simon, at Peter's request, probably provided them hospitality for the night. Whatever reservations Peter initially had concerning the distinctions between clean and unclean foods were set aside. His encounter with the Lord had an immediate impact on his behavior, and likely, his attitudes and beliefs. As a Jew who had spent a lifetime trying to fulfill the requirements of the Law and the traditions of Judaism, Peter could have understandably been uncomfortable eating with and boarding these three Gentiles. Even though eating with Gentiles would have been strictly forbidden to him according to the customs of current Judaism, the text gives no indication that he was reluctant to receive these visitors. Apparently he quickly grasped the deeper truth portrayed in the vision.

The next day Peter went along with them. But he was careful to take six good, believing Jewish brothers from Joppa with him. (See 11:12.) He knew he would be called into question by other believers for entering a Gentile house, so he wanted witnesses he could depend on. Just to be sure, he took double the two or three required by the Law (Deuteronomy 19:15; compare Matthew 18:16).

**10:24.** The next day this company of 10 men arrived in Caesarea. They found Cornelius waiting for them with a house full of people. He not only believed the Lord was looking with favor on him, as the angel had said, he also believed this meant God wanted to bless him, for he had learned to know God as a good God. He had shared his material wealth with others. So he could not think of keeping to himself all of the blessing he expected God would bring him through Peter. He felt this too should be shared.

He was sure Peter would come. God would see to that as well. Therefore, he estimated the time of Peter's arrival and took it upon himself to call together all his relatives and close friends. He must have explained to them also about the angel's visit. He undoubtedly had already led them to a belief in the one true God and told them what he already knew about Jesus and the gospel. So they were all waiting with great expectation.

**10:25.** As Peter was coming into the house, Cornelius was very conscious that God had sent him. Therefore, as soon as he met Peter, he fell down at Peter's feet and worshiped. That is, he went down on his hands and knees before Peter, prostrating himself, and possibly even kissing his feet. This was the way the Persians bowed before their kings (whom they considered gods). The Greeks and Romans also did it before their gods. It was considered the way to show the highest reverence to them.

Some scholars believe Cornelius only meant to do this as a means of giving Peter a respectful welcome. But it is probably more likely

**23. Then called he them in, and lodged them:** Upon this Peter invited them in and entertained them, *TCNT*... So he took them in for the night, *BB* ... and housed them, *KJII* ... He accordingly invited them in, *Fenton* ... asked the men to come in and spend the night, *Everyday, NCV* ... and treated them as guests, *NAB* ... and asked them to stay with him, *Williams C.K.*

**And on the morrow Peter went away with them:** The next day he set out with them, *Weymouth* ... But next day he got up and traveled with them, *Berkeley* ... the day after, *BB* ... on the following morning, arising, he went with them, *Fenton* ... got ready and went, *Everyday* ... he set off with them, *TNT* ... he went off with them, *NAB* ... started off with them, *Goodspeed.*

**and certain brethren from Joppa accompanied him:** ... taking some of the brothers, *BB* ... and some of the brothers in Joppa went along with him, *Williams* ... by some of the disciples from, *Fenton* ... joined him, *Everyday.*

**24. And the morrow after they entered into Caesarea:** ... and the following day, *TCNT* ... and on the next day, *Moffatt* ... The day after, *Adams* ... day after that, *BB* ... they came to, *Everyday* ... he reached, *Kleist* ... they arrived at, *Fenton.*

**And Cornelius waited for them:** ... was expecting them, *Rotherham* ... was awaiting their arrival, *Weymouth* ... was looking for them, *NLT.*

**and had called together his kinsmen and near friends:** ... his kinsfolk and intimate friends, *Rotherham* ... relatives, *Everyday* ... had collected his...more intimate friends, *Fenton* ... and close friends, *RSV* ... gathered all his family, *NLT* ... having got together his relations and his near friends, *BB* ... all the kindred, *Murdock* ... whom he had invited, *Kleist.*

**25. And as Peter was coming in, Cornelius met him:** So when Peter entered the city, *TCNT* ... When Peter entered the house, *Weymouth* ... came in, Cornelius came to him, *BB.*

**Acts 10:26**

| 1894.3 prep | 3450.8 art acc pl masc | 4087.7 noun acc pl masc | 4210.9 verb 3sing indic aor act | 3450.5 art nom sing masc | 1156.2 conj |
|---|---|---|---|---|---|
| ἐπὶ | τοὺς | πόδας | προσεκύνησεν. | 26. ὁ | δὲ |
| *epi* | *tous* | *podas* | *prosekunēsen* | *ho* | *de* |
| at | the | feet | did homage. | | But |

| 3935.1 name nom masc | 840.6 prs-pron acc sing masc | 1446.5 verb 3sing indic aor act | 1446.5 verb 3sing indic aor act | 840.6 prs-pron acc sing masc |
|---|---|---|---|---|
| Πέτρος | ' αὐτὸν | ἤγειρεν, | [☆ ἤγειρεν | αὐτὸν ] |
| *Petros* | *auton* | *ēgeiren* | *ēgeiren* | *auton* |
| Peter | him | raised, | [ raised | him ] |

| 2978.15 verb nom sing masc part pres act | 448.8 verb 2sing impr aor act | 2476.3 prs-pron nom | 2504.1 conj | 1466.1 prs-pron nom 1sing |
|---|---|---|---|---|
| λέγων, | 'Ανάστηθι· | ' κἀγὼ | [☆ καὶ | ἐγὼ ] |
| *legōn* | *Anastēthi* | *kagō* | *kai* | *egō* |
| saying, | Rise up: | I also | [ also | I ] |

| 840.5 prs-pron nom sing masc | 442.1 noun nom sing masc | 1498.2 verb 1sing indic pres act | 2504.1 conj | 4777.1 verb nom sing masc part pres act |
|---|---|---|---|---|
| αὐτὸς | ἄνθρωπός | εἰμι. | 27. Καὶ | συνομιλῶν |
| *autos* | *anthrōpos* | *eimi* | *Kai* | *sunomilōn* |
| myself | a man | am. | And | talking with |

| 840.4 prs-pron dat sing | 1511.3 verb 3sing indic aor act | 2504.1 conj | 2128.3 verb 3sing indic pres act | 4755.12 verb acc pl masc part perf act |
|---|---|---|---|---|
| αὐτῷ | εἰσῆλθεν, | καὶ | εὑρίσκει | συνεληλυθότας |
| *autō* | *eisēlthen* | *kai* | *heuriskei* | *sunelēluthotas* |
| him | he went in, | and | finds | having gathered together |

| 4044.8 adj acc pl masc | 5183.4 verb 3sing indic act | 4885.1 conj | 4242.1 prep | 840.8 prs-pron acc pl masc | 5050.1 prs-pron nom 2pl |
|---|---|---|---|---|---|
| πολλούς. | 28. ἔφη | τε | πρὸς | αὐτούς, | Ὑμεῖς |
| *pollous* | *ephē* | *te* | *pros* | *autous* | *Humeis* |
| many. | He said | and | to | them, | You |

| 1971.3 verb 2pl indic pres mid | 5453.1 conj | 111.2 adj sing neu | 1498.4 verb 3sing indic pres act | 433.3 noun dat sing masc | 2428.1 name-adj dat sing masc |
|---|---|---|---|---|---|
| ἐπίστασθε | ὡς | ἀθέμιτόν | ἐστιν | ἀνδρὶ | Ἰουδαίῳ |
| *epistasthe* | *hōs* | *athemiton* | *estin* | *andri* | *Ioudaiō* |
| know | how | unlawful | it is | for a man | a Jew |

| 2827.3 verb inf pres mid | 2211.1 conj | 4193.17 verb inf pres mid | 244.1 adj dat sing masc |
|---|---|---|---|
| κολλᾶσθαι | ἢ | προσέρχεσθαι | ἀλλοφύλῳ· |
| *kollasthai* | *ē* | *proserchesthai* | *allophulō* |
| to unite himself | or | to come near to | one of another race. |

| 2504.1 conj | 1466.5 prs-pron dat 1sing | 2476.1 prs-pron dat | 3450.5 art nom sing masc | 2296.1 noun nom sing masc | 1161.8 verb 3sing indic aor act |
|---|---|---|---|---|---|
| ' καὶ | ἐμοὶ | [☆ κἀμοὶ ] | ὁ | θεὸς | ἔδειξεν |
| *kai* | *emoi* | *kamoi* | *ho* | *theos* | *edeixen* |
| And | to me | [ and to me ] | | God | showed |

| 3235.4 num card acc masc | 2812.1 adj sing | 2211.1 conj | 167.1 adj sing | 2978.24 verb inf pres act | 442.4 noun acc sing masc |
|---|---|---|---|---|---|
| μηδένα | κοινὸν | ἢ | ἀκάθαρτον | λέγειν | ἄνθρωπον· |
| *mēdena* | *koinon* | *ē* | *akatharton* | *legein* | *anthrōpon* |
| no | common | or | unclean | to call | man. |

| 1346.1 conj | 2504.1 conj | 368.1 adv | 2048.1 verb indic aor act | 3213.6 verb nom sing masc part aor pass |
|---|---|---|---|---|
| 29. διὸ | καὶ | ἀναντιῤῥήτως | ἦλθον | μεταπεμφθείς. |
| *dio* | *kai* | *anantirrhētōs* | *ēlthon* | *metapemphtheis* |
| Wherefore | also | without arguing | I came, | having been sent for. |

that the excitement of actually seeing this man, whom the angel told him to summon, brought an emotional feeling in his heart and mind that caused him to react the way he was taught to react in his childhood and youth in Rome.

**10:26.** Peter was probably shocked to see Cornelius bowing before him. He knew the commandment that the Jews were not to bow down or worship any other god (Exodus 20:5). He knew that by the time of the Book of Esther, the Jews had learned the further lesson that they were not to bow down to any man either (see Esther 3:2-4).

Therefore, Peter took hold of Cornelius quickly and raised him up, telling him to stand up, and saying to him very emphatically, "I myself also am a man." The Greek here is *anthrōpos*, not a man in the sense of being a male, but man or mankind in the sense of being a human being. Thus he reproved Cornelius very gently, yet firmly. At the same time he did not belittle Cornelius. Peter did not want any exaltation for being used of God. Neither did he want anyone to give any human personality preeminence in the Church.

**10:27.** Peter then began to converse with Cornelius, and while doing so came into the room where all the relatives and close friends of Cornelius were gathered. The text implies Peter was surprised to see so many people.

**10:28.** Peter reminded the assembled crowd that it was unlawful for a Jew to keep company with or come to a foreigner (for fellowship or association). By saying it was unlawful, he was not referring primarily to the law of Moses. "Unlawful" here could be used of any act that showed a lawless spirit or an undisciplined desire or purpose to break the rules accepted by a particular group or society. A better way to put it might be that to a Jew it was not merely illegal but something abominable to join in closely with a foreigner. (The same word is used of Paul's attempting to join in with the disciples and become part of their fellowship at Jerusalem in 9:26.) Coming to these Gentiles also implies more than simply entering the house. It indicates an agreeing with them, acceding to or even giving consent to their heathen ways and desires.

But Peter was there, not because he was turning his back on Jewish ways and customs, but because God had showed him not to call any man (any human being) common (ordinary, profane, ceremonially impure) or unclean (defiled or defiling, and therefore cut off from coming into the presence of God).

**10:29.** Peter did not explain about his vision or how the Lord brought him to the conclusion that he must not call any person common or unclean. It was enough to remind them of the tremendous barrier of prejudice that the Jews had placed between

**and fell down at his feet, and worshipped him:** . . . and throwing himself at Peter's feet, bowed to the ground, *TCNT* . . . did homage, *Rotherham* . . . and did reverence to him, *Berkeley* . . . showed him respect by bowing at his feet, *Fenton*.

**26. But Peter took him up, saying:** . . . raised him up, *ASV* . . . made him stand up, *Beck* . . . lifted him up, *Williams C.K.*

**Stand up; I myself also am a man:** I am only a man like you, *TCNT* . . . Rise, I am a human being, too, *Berkeley* . . . Stand up! I'm not a god! *Taylor*.

**27. And as he talked with him, he went in:** And conversing with him, *Rotherham* . . . Talking with him as he went, *TCNT*.

**and found many that were come together:** . . . where he found a large gathering of people, *TCNT* . . . a large company assembled, *Weymouth* . . . a great crowd had gathered, *Williams* . . . a large number gathered together, *Williams C.K.* . . . a great many gathered, *Norlie* . . . a considerable assemblage, *Fenton*.

**28. And he said unto them, Ye know how that it is an unlawful thing for a man that is a Jew to keep company, or come unto one of another nation:** . . . it is a violation of established order, *Wuest* . . . You are aware...that it is forbidden for a Jew to be on intimate, or even visiting, terms with a foreigner, *TCNT* . . . a Jew is strictly forbidden to associate with a Gentile of visit him, *Weymouth* . . . how wrong it is, *Beck* . . . how abominable it is, *Douay* . . . to be uniting with, *Rotherham* . . . an alien, *Murdock* . . . a person of any other nationality, *Klingensmith*.

**but God hath shewed me that I should not call any man common or unclean:** . . . unhallowed, *Berkeley*.

**29. Therefore came I unto you without gainsaying:** I came readily, *Murdock* . . . So I came immediately, *Klingensmith* . . . without raising any objection, *TCNT* . . . without any demur, *Moffatt* . . . I didn't object to coming here, *Beck* . . . came without debate, *Campbell* . . . without any hesitation, *Norlie*.

# Acts 10:30

| **4299.1** verb 1sing indic pres mid | **3631.1** partic | **4949.2** intr-pron dat sing | **3030.3** noun dat sing masc | **3213.3** verb 2pl indic aor mid |
|---|---|---|---|---|
| πυνθάνομαι | οὖν, | τίνι | λόγῳ | μετεπέμψασθέ |
| *punthanomai* | *oun* | *tini* | *logō* | *metepempsasthe* |
| I inquire | therefore, | for what | reason | did you send for |

| **1466.6** prs-pron acc 1sing | **2504.1** conj | **3450.5** art nom sing masc | **2856.1** name nom masc | **5183.4** verb 3sing indic act | **570.3** prep |
|---|---|---|---|---|---|
| με; | **30.** Καὶ | ὁ | Κορνήλιος | ἔφη, | Ἀπὸ |
| *me* | *Kai* | *ho* | *Kornēlios* | *ephē* | *Apo* |
| me? | And | | Cornelius | said, | From |

| **4915.4** num ord gen sing fem | **2232.1** noun fem | **3230.1** prep | **3642.10** dem-pron gen sing fem | **3450.10** art gen sing fem | **5443.1** noun fem |
|---|---|---|---|---|---|
| τετάρτης | ἡμέρας | μέχρι | ταύτης | τῆς | ὥρας |
| *tetartēs* | *hēmeras* | *mechri* | *tautēs* | *tēs* | *hōras* |
| four | days | until | this | the | hour |

30.a.**Txt:** p50,02A-corr 05D,08E,020L,025P 044,1241,byz.sa.
**Var:** p74,01ℵ,02A-org 03B,04C,bo.Lach,Treg Tisc,We/Ho,Weis,Sod UBS/☆

30.b.**Txt:** 025P,byz.
**Var:** 01ℵ,02A,03B,04C 05D,Lach,Treg,Alf,Tisc We/Ho,Weis,Sod UBS/☆

| **1498.46** verb 1sing indic imperf mid | **3384.5** verb nom sing masc part pres act | **2504.1** conj | **3450.12** art acc sing fem | **1750.4** num ord acc sing fem |
|---|---|---|---|---|
| ἤμην | ⸂[a] νηστεύων, | καὶ⸃ | τὴν | ⸂ἐννάτην |
| *ēmēn* | *nēsteuōn* | *kai* | *tēn* | *ennatēn* |
| I was | fasting, | and | the | ninth |

| **1712.3** num ord acc sing fem | **5443.4** noun acc sing fem | **4195.11** verb nom sing masc part pres mid | **1706.1** prep | **3450.3** art dat sing |
|---|---|---|---|---|
| [☆ ἐνάτην ] | ⸂[b] ὥραν⸃ | προσευχόμενος | ἐν | τῷ |
| *enatēn* | *hōran* | *proseuchomenos* | *en* | *tō* |
| [ idem ] | hour | praying | in | the |

| **3486.3** noun dat sing masc | **1466.2** prs-pron gen 1sing | **2504.1** conj | **1481.20** verb 2sing impr aor mid | **433.1** noun nom sing masc | **2449.3** verb 3sing indic aor act |
|---|---|---|---|---|---|
| οἴκῳ | μου· | καὶ | ἰδοὺ, | ἀνὴρ | ἔστη |
| *oikō* | *mou* | *kai* | *idou* | *anēr* | *estē* |
| house | my; | and | behold, | a man | stood |

| **1783.1** prep | **1466.2** prs-pron gen 1sing | **1706.1** prep | **2051.1** noun dat sing fem | **2959.3** adj dat sing fem | **2504.1** conj |
|---|---|---|---|---|---|
| ἐνώπιόν | μου | ἐν | ἐσθῆτι | λαμπρᾷ, | **31.** καὶ |
| *enōpion* | *mou* | *en* | *esthēti* | *lampra* | *kai* |
| before | me | in | clothing | bright, | and |

| **5183.2** verb 3sing indic pres act | **2856.4** name voc masc | **1508.1** verb 3sing indic aor pass | **4622.2** prs-pron gen 2sing | **3450.9** art nom sing fem |
|---|---|---|---|---|
| φησίν, | Κορνήλιε, | εἰσηκούσθη | σου | ἡ |
| *phēsin* | *Kornēlie* | *eisēkousthē* | *sou* | *hē* |
| said, | Cornelius, | was heard | your | the |

| **4194.1** noun nom sing fem | **2504.1** conj | **3450.13** art nom pl fem | **1641.3** noun nom pl fem | **4622.2** prs-pron gen 2sing |
|---|---|---|---|---|
| προσευχὴ | καὶ | αἱ | ἐλεημοσύναι | σου |
| *proseuchē* | *kai* | *hai* | *eleēmosunai* | *sou* |
| prayer | and | the | alms | your |

| **3279.4** verb 3pl indic aor pass | **1783.1** prep | **3450.2** art gen sing | **2296.2** noun gen sing masc | **3854.10** verb 2sing impr aor act |
|---|---|---|---|---|
| ἐμνήσθησαν | ἐνώπιον | τοῦ | θεοῦ. | **32.** πέμψον |
| *emnēsthēsan* | *enōpion* | *tou* | *theou* | *pempson* |
| were remembered | before | | God. | Send |

| **3631.1** partic | **1519.1** prep | **2421.3** name acc fem | **2504.1** conj | **3203.2** verb 2sing impr aor mid | **4468.4** name acc masc |
|---|---|---|---|---|---|
| οὖν | εἰς | Ἰόππην, | καὶ | μετακάλεσαι | Σίμωνα |
| *oun* | *eis* | *Ioppēn* | *kai* | *metakalesai* | *Simōna* |
| therefore | to | Joppa, | and | call for | Simon |

themselves and the Gentiles. From this Cornelius and his friends would have to understand that it would have to be a revelation from God himself if that barrier was to be broken down. The fact that it was indeed broken down in Peter's experience was shown by his making no objections to their request, and by his coming to them immediately. He wanted their attention to be on what God was doing, not on himself.

Then Peter politely inquired about their reason for sending for him. He had heard this from the two slaves and the soldier Cornelius had sent. But he wanted to hear it from Cornelius himself. Thus he gave Cornelius an opportunity to express what God had told him and in this way to express his faith.

**10:30.** In answer, Cornelius recounted how 4 days before (2 days before yesterday in their method of counting days) he was fasting and praying in his house until about 3 o'clock in the afternoon, and suddenly he looked and a man in bright (shining) clothes stood before him.

Though the Bible called this one an angel (verse 3), Cornelius is giving his first impressions here. It is uncertain if the angel appeared to him in the form of a man, or if God opened his eyes in order that he might perceive a being which was spiritual, not physical by nature. (Cf. 2 Kings 6:16f., where Elisha asked God to open his servant's eyes so that he could see the spiritual forces which surrounded them.)

**10:31.** *Angel* means "messenger," and this young "man" in shining clothes bright with the glory of God had a message. Cornelius now recounted how his prayer had been heard (had been really and truly heard). His charitable giving had also been called to remembrance by God.

This does not mean God had ever forgotten or failed to take notice of either the prayers or the generosity of Cornelius. When the Bible talks about God remembering something or someone, it means God had that person or thing in mind all along, but now the time had come for God to do something specific about it.

God had been taking note of Cornelius and his godliness and his giving to the poor of God's people. In response God was about to bring the proper answer to his prayer.

The prayer here is speaking of one particular prayer, a prayer which must have been on the heart of Cornelius in the midst of all his praying. It undoubtedly involved a desire to have closer fellowship with God and with His people.

**10:32.** Cornelius next repeated the command to send for Simon Peter, drawing attention again to the specific details given by the

**as soon as I was sent for: I ask therefore for what intent ye have sent for me?:** . . . when you sent for me, *Williams C.K.* . . . when I was summoned, *Kleist* . . . when I was asked to come here, *Everyday* . . . I may now be allowed to ask for what reason you have brought me, *Fenton* . . . I therefore ask why you sent for me, *Weymouth* . . . Now I want to know what made you send for me, *Phillips* . . . I should, of course, like to know why you summoned me, *NAB*.

**30. And Cornelius said, Four days ago I was fasting until this hour:** Just three days ago this very hour, *TCNT* . . . about this time, *Williams C.K.* . . . at this very hour, *Kleist*.

**and at the ninth hour I prayed in my house:** I was keeping the ninth hour of prayer, *ASV*. . . observing the time of the three o'clock prayer, *TCNT* . . . I was home for my three o'clock worship, *Berkeley* . . . in my house saying the afternoon prayers, *Williams C.K.* . . . It was at this same time, *Everyday*.

**and, behold, a man stood before me in bright clothing:** All at once, I saw, *NLT* . . . when suddenly, *Williams C.K.* . . . in bright apparel, *ASV* . . . in dazzling clothing, *Goodspeed, TCNT* . . . in shining raiment, *Weymouth* . . . dazzling robes, *NAB* . . . shining garments, *Kleist* . . . wearing shining clothes, *Everyday*.

**31. And said, Cornelius, thy prayer is heard:** . . . and your acts of charity have been remembered by God, *Weymouth* . . . your charitable gifts, *Phillips* . . . God has heard your prayer, *Beck, Everyday*.

**and thine alms are had in remembrance in the sight of God:** He has seen what you give to the poor, and he remembers you, *NCV* . . . your generosity remembered, *NAB* . . . are remembered before, *LivB* . . . have been recalled to mind by God, *Goodspeed* . . . has remembered your gifts of love, *NLT*.

**32. Send therefore to Joppa, and call hither Simon, whose surname is Peter:** . . . and invite Simon, *Weymouth* . . . and sum-

| 3614.5 rel-pron nom sing masc | 1926.2 verb 3sing indic pres mid | 3935.1 name nom masc | 3642.4 dem-pron nom sing masc | 3441.4 verb 3sing indic pres mid |
|---|---|---|---|---|
| ὃς | ἐπικαλεῖται | Πέτρος· | οὗτος | ξενίζεται |
| *hos* | *epikaleitai* | *Petros* | *houtos* | *xenizetai* |
| who | is being called | Peter; | this one | is being lodged |

| 1706.1 prep | 3477.3 noun dat sing fem | 4468.2 name gen masc | 1031.1 noun gen sing masc | 3706.2 prep | 2258.4 noun acc sing fem |
|---|---|---|---|---|---|
| ἐν | οἰκίᾳ | Σίμωνος | βυρσέως | παρὰ | θάλασσαν· |
| *en* | *oikia* | *Simōnos* | *burseōs* | *para* | *thalassan* |
| in | house | of Simon | a tanner | by | sea; |

32.a.**Txt:** 04C,05D,08E 020L,025P,044,byz.it.sa. Sod
**Var:** p45,p74,01ℵ,02A 03B,bo.Lach,Treg,Tisc We/Ho,Weis,UBS/☆

| 3614.5 rel-pron nom sing masc | 3716.7 verb nom sing masc part aor mid | 2953.40 verb 3sing indic fut act | 4622.3 prs-pron dat 2sing |
|---|---|---|---|
| ⸂a ὃς | παραγενόμενος | λαλήσει | σοι. ⸃ |
| *hos* | *paragenomenos* | *lalēsei* | *soi* |
| who | having come | will speak | to you. |

| 1808.1 adv | 3631.1 partic | 3854.5 verb 1sing indic aor act | 4242.1 prep | 4622.4 prs-pron acc 2sing |
|---|---|---|---|---|
| 33. Ἐξαυτῆς | οὖν | ἔπεμψα | πρὸς | σέ· |
| *Exautēs* | *oun* | *epempsa* | *pros* | *se* |
| At once | therefore | I sent | to | you; |

| 4622.1 prs-pron nom 2sing | 4885.1 conj | 2544.1 adv | 4020.23 verb 2sing indic aor act | 3716.7 verb nom sing masc part aor mid | 3431.1 adv |
|---|---|---|---|---|---|
| σύ | τε | καλῶς | ἐποίησας | παραγενόμενος. | νῦν |
| *su* | *te* | *kalōs* | *epoiēsas* | *paragenomenos* | *nun* |
| you | and | well | did | having come. | Now |

| 3631.1 partic | 3820.7 adj nom pl masc | 2231.1 prs-pron nom 1pl | 1783.1 prep | 3450.2 art gen sing | 2296.2 noun gen sing masc |
|---|---|---|---|---|---|
| οὖν | πάντες | ἡμεῖς | ἐνώπιον | τοῦ | θεοῦ |
| *oun* | *pantes* | *hēmeis* | *enōpion* | *tou* | *theou* |
| therefore | all | we | before | | God |

33.a.**Txt:** 01ℵ-org,03B 044,byz.
**Var:** p45,p47,01ℵ-corr3 02A,04C,05D

| 3780.3 verb 1pl indic pres act | 189.36 verb inf aor act | 3820.1 adj | 3450.17 art pl neu | 4225.2 verb pl neu part perf mid |
|---|---|---|---|---|
| πάρεσμεν | ἀκοῦσαι | πάντα | τὰ | προστεταγμένα |
| *paresmen* | *akousai* | *panta* | *ta* | *prostetagmena* |
| are present | to hear | all things | the | having been ordered |

33.b.**Txt:** p74,05D,020L 025P,byz.sa.
**Var:** p45,01ℵ,02A,03B 04C,08E,044,bo.Lach Treg,Tisc,We/Ho,Weis Sod,UBS/☆

| 4622.3 prs-pron dat 2sing | 5097.3 prep | 570.3 prep | 3450.2 art gen sing | 2296.2 noun gen sing masc | 2935.2 noun gen sing masc |
|---|---|---|---|---|---|
| σοι | ⸂a ὑπὸ | [ ἀπὸ ] | ⸂ τοῦ | θεοῦ. | [b☆ κυρίου. ] |
| *soi* | *hupo* | *apo* | *tou* | *theou* | *kuriou* |
| you | by | [ from ] | | God. | [ Lord. ] |

| 453.9 verb nom sing masc part aor act | 1156.2 conj | 3935.1 name nom masc | 3450.16 art sing neu | 4601.1 noun sing neu |
|---|---|---|---|---|
| 34. Ἀνοίξας | δὲ | Πέτρος | τὸ | στόμα |
| *Anoixas* | *de* | *Petros* | *to* | *stoma* |
| Having opened | and | Peter | the | mouth |

| 1500.5 verb 3sing indic aor act | 1894.2 prep | 223.2 noun gen sing fem | 2608.6 verb 1sing indic pres mid | 3617.1 conj |
|---|---|---|---|---|
| εἶπεν, | Ἐπ’ | ἀληθείας | καταλαμβάνομαι | ὅτι |
| *eipen* | *Ep'* | *alētheias* | *katalambanomai* | *hoti* |
| said, | On | a truth | I perceive | that |

| 3620.2 partic | 1498.4 verb 3sing indic pres act | 4239.1 noun nom sing masc | 4239.2 noun nom sing masc |
|---|---|---|---|
| οὐκ | ἔστιν | ⸂ προσωπολήπτης | [☆ προσωπολήμπτης ] |
| *ouk* | *estin* | *prosōpolēptēs* | *prosōpolēmptēs* |
| not | is | a respecter of persons | [ idem ] |

angel of where to find him at the house of Simon the tanner (outside of Joppa) by the seaside.

At this point the majority of the Greek manuscripts have the phrase "who, coming (when he comes), will speak to you." Some of the oldest manuscripts leave it out, but it does fit the context, and it seems obvious that the reason for summoning Peter was to give him opportunity to tell them God's message.

The fact that the Book of Acts takes valuable space to repeat the details of the visit of the angel and the directions to send for Peter shows that God wanted to emphasize the fact that the gospel preached by Peter and the other apostles was and is from God.

This also shows that God prepares hearts to receive the gospel. From time to time there have been unusual revivals in the history of the Church that cannot be explained apart from a sovereign move of God. God has not changed His purpose that He revealed to Abraham so long ago. He still wants all the nations of the world to be blessed.

**10:33.** Cornelius then let Peter know he had not hesitated to obey the angel's command. Immediately (within the same hour), he sent for Peter. Now Peter had "done well" to come. However, Cornelius did not mean here that Peter had done a good thing by coming. The language used by Cornelius is idiomatic and really means they were pleased that Peter had come. Now all of them were gathered there in the presence of God, to hear from Peter everything God had instructed him to tell them. The Greek implies Peter would tell them truths established by God, and therefore fixed, unchangeable, dependable.

**10:34.** The phrase "opened his mouth," was used in New Testament times to introduce an important discourse. In fact, this sermon at the house of Cornelius was a landmark in the history of the Early Church for more than one reason. A number of scholars have drawn attention to the fact that there are important similarities between Peter's preaching here and the Gospel of Mark. Irenaeus, the pastor of the church at Lyons in Gaul wrote in the Second Century A.D. (as did Papias and others before him) that Mark was Peter's disciple and reported Peter's preaching about Christ in his Gospel. In other words, the Gospel of Mark embodies the essence of the teaching that Peter gave wherever he went, with Peter commissioned by Christ and Mark inspired by the Holy Spirit to write.

This sermon is important also because from the start Peter showed that he understood fully the meaning of his vision that was repeated three times on the rooftop. He saw that God truly is no respecter of persons; He does not show favoritism or partiality.

Actually, this was not a new truth. The Old Testament recognized this truth (2 Samuel 14:14, for example). But up to this time Peter had been able to apply it only to the Jews, not to Gentiles.

mon Simon, *Kleist, Moffatt* . . . and ask Simon Peter to come, *Everyday.*

**he is lodged in the house of one Simon a tanner by the sea side: who, when he cometh, shall speak unto thee:** . . . is staying in the house, *Everyday* . . . the man who works with leather, *NLT.*

**33. Immediately therefore I sent to thee:** So, I sent to you at once, *RSV* . . . Accordingly at once I sent for, *Kleist.*

**and thou hast well done that thou art come:** . . . and I thank you heartily for having come, *Weymouth* . . . it was very good of you to come, *Everyday* . . . and you have been kind enough to come, *NAB* . . . you were good enough to come, *Williams C.K.* . . . and you acted nobly, *Berkeley* . . . and you have been most kind in coming, *Phillips.*

**Now therefore are we all here present before God:** That is why all of us are now assembled here in God's presence, *Weymouth* . . . at this moment, *NAB.*

**to hear all things that are commanded thee of God:** . . . to listen to what the Lord has commanded you to say, *Weymouth* . . . to hear everything the Lord has commanded you to tell us, *NCV* . . . to hear whatever directives, *NAB* . . . in which the Lord has instructed you, *MLNT* . . . whatever the Lord has told you to say, *NLT.*

**34. Then Peter opened his mouth, and said:** Then Peter began to speak, *Everyday, Weymouth* . . . began to address them, *Kleist.*

**Of a truth I perceive that God is no respecter of persons:** I discover, *Murdock* . . . to show partiality, *TCNT* . . . I conclude, *Rotherham* . . . Now I truly see that God cares nothing for outward appearances, *Williams C.K.* . . . God makes no distinction between one man and another, *Weymouth* . . . God has no favourites, *Moffatt, TNT* . . . I really understand now that to God every person is the same, *Everyday, NCV* . . . thoroughly understand the truth, *MLNT* . . . I now thoroughly grasp the truth that God is not partial, *Berkeley* . . . doesn't prefer one person to another, *Beck.*

## Acts 10:35

| 3450.5 art nom sing masc | 2296.1 noun nom sing masc | 233.1 conj | 1706.1 prep | 3820.3 adj dat sing | 1477.3 noun dat sing neu |
|---|---|---|---|---|---|
| ὁ | θεός, | 35. ἀλλ' | ἐν | παντὶ | ἔθνει |
| *ho* | *theos* | *all'* | *en* | *panti* | *ethnei* |
| | God, | but | in | every | nation |

| 3450.5 art nom sing masc | 5236.7 verb nom sing masc part pres mid | 840.6 prs-pron acc sing masc | 2504.1 conj | 2021.8 verb nom sing masc part pres mid |
|---|---|---|---|---|
| ὁ | φοβούμενος | αὐτὸν | καὶ | ἐργαζόμενος |
| *ho* | *phoboumenos* | *auton* | *kai* | *ergazomenos* |
| the | fearing | him | and | working |

| 1336.4 noun acc sing fem | 1178.1 adj nom sing masc | 840.4 prs-pron dat sing | 1498.4 verb 3sing indic pres act | 3450.6 art acc sing masc |
|---|---|---|---|---|
| δικαιοσύνην, | δεκτὸς | αὐτῷ | ἐστιν. | 36. τὸν |
| *dikaiosunēn* | *dektos* | *autō* | *estin* | *ton* |
| righteousness, | acceptable | to him | is. | The |

| 3030.4 noun acc sing masc | 3614.6 rel-pron acc sing masc | 643.8 verb 3sing indic aor act | 3450.4 art dat pl | 5048.8 noun dat pl masc | 2447.1 name masc |
|---|---|---|---|---|---|
| λόγον | ὃν | ἀπέστειλεν | τοῖς | υἱοῖς | Ἰσραὴλ, |
| *logon* | *hon* | *apesteilen* | *tois* | *huiois* | *Israēl* |
| word | which | he sent | to the | sons | of Israel, |

| 2076.9 verb nom sing masc part pres mid | 1503.4 noun acc sing fem | 1217.2 prep | 2400.2 name masc | 5382.2 name gen masc |
|---|---|---|---|---|
| εὐαγγελιζόμενος | εἰρήνην | διὰ | Ἰησοῦ | Χριστοῦ, |
| *euangelizomenos* | *eirēnēn* | *dia* | *Iēsou* | *Christou* |
| announcing the good news | peace | through | Jesus | Christ, |

| 3642.4 dem-pron nom sing masc | 1498.4 verb 3sing indic pres act | 3820.4 adj gen pl | 2935.1 noun nom sing masc | 5050.1 prs-pron nom 2pl |
|---|---|---|---|---|
| οὗτός | ἐστιν | πάντων | κύριος, | 37. ὑμεῖς |
| *houtos* | *estin* | *pantōn* | *kurios* | *humeis* |
| this | is | of all | Lord, | you |

| 3471.6 verb 2pl indic perf act | 3450.16 art sing neu | 1090.51 verb sing part aor mid | 4343.1 noun sing neu | 2567.2 prep | 3513.7 adj gen sing fem |
|---|---|---|---|---|---|
| οἴδατε· | τὸ | γενόμενον | ῥῆμα | καθ' | ὅλης |
| *oidate* | *to* | *genomenon* | *rhēma* | *kath'* | *holēs* |
| know; | the | having come | report | through | whole |

37.a.**Txt:** p45,020L,025P byz.Weis,Sod
**Var:** p74,01ℵ,02A,03B 04C,05D,08E,1739 Treg,Alf,Tisc,We/Ho UBS/⋆

| 3450.10 art gen sing fem | 2424.2 name gen fem | 751.13 verb sing neu part aor mid | 751.10 verb nom sing masc part aor mid | 570.3 prep |
|---|---|---|---|---|
| τῆς | Ἰουδαίας, | ᶜ ἀρξάμενον | [a⋆ ἀρξάμενος ] | ἀπὸ |
| *tēs* | *Ioudaias* | *arxamenon* | *arxamenos* | *apo* |
| the | of Judea, | having begun | [ idem ] | from |

| 3450.10 art gen sing fem | 1049.2 name gen sing fem | 3196.3 prep | 3450.16 art sing neu | 902.1 noun sing neu | 3614.16 rel-pron sing neu |
|---|---|---|---|---|---|
| τῆς | Γαλιλαίας, | μετὰ | τὸ | βάπτισμα | ὃ |
| *tēs* | *Galilaias* | *meta* | *to* | *baptisma* | *ho* |
| | Galilee, | after | the | baptism | which |

| 2756.11 verb 3sing indic aor act | 2464.1 name nom masc | 2400.3 name acc masc | 3450.6 art acc sing masc | 570.3 prep |
|---|---|---|---|---|
| ἐκήρυξεν | Ἰωάννης· | 38. Ἰησοῦν | τὸν | ἀπὸ |
| *ekēruxen* | *Iōannēs* | *Iēsoun* | *ton* | *apo* |
| proclaimed | John: | Jesus | the | from |

| 3341.1 name fem | 3341.3 name fem | 5453.1 conj | 5383.2 verb 3sing indic aor act | 840.6 prs-pron acc sing masc |
|---|---|---|---|---|
| ᶜ Ναζαρέτ, | [⋆ Ναζαρέθ, ] | ὡς | ἔχρισεν | αὐτὸν |
| *Nazaret* | *Nazareth* | *hōs* | *echrisen* | *auton* |
| Nazareth, | [ idem ] | how | anointed | him |

**10:35.** Now Peter understood that the barrier that had kept people away from the Lord was broken down by Christ. So Peter emphasized that the way to God is open to all. Anyone who fears (worships and gives reverence to) God and works righteousness (proving he has received divine grace by faith) is acceptable to Him.

God's impartiality was also taught in such passages as Deuteronomy 10:17 and 2 Chronicles 19:7. (See also Amos 9:7.) The New Testament emphasizes it even more in such passages as Romans 2:11, and 1 Peter 1:17. This does not mean God cannot make a choice, but rather that He does not base His choice on, or limit it to national, racial, social, or any other type of external differences. Therefore, these Gentiles, if they fulfilled the qualifications of worship, faith, and faithfulness, were just as acceptable to God as any Jew who worshiped God in spirit and in truth.

Peter now realized this in a new way. So did this houseful of Gentiles. Jewish exclusivism had kept them away from full fellowship. They had undoubtedly heard the Gentiles called dogs. But they probably had never heard any emphasis on the promise that in Abraham and his seed all the families (of all the nations) of the earth would be blessed, a promise that is repeated five times in the Book of Genesis (12:3; 18:18; 22:18; 26:4; 28:14).

**10:36.** Peter next reminded Cornelius and his friends of the word (the message, Greek, *logon*) God sent to Israel preaching (literally, telling) the good news (the gospel) of peace by (through) Jesus Christ. The content of the gospel, the central truth of the good news, is that God has made full provision for the believer's peace through Jesus Christ. That peace includes not only peace with God through the cleansing and forgiveness that comes through Christ's death on the cross, but also all of God's provisions and promises for the believer's entire well-being. Christ has put the "yes" and the "amen" ("truly") on them all (2 Corinthians 1:20).

**10:37.** Peter continued, reminding them of the "word" (the message [Greek, *rhēma*], used here as a synonym interchangeable with *logos*) they already knew. In fact, "you know" is emphatic in the Greek here. This means they already knew the facts about Jesus, about His life, death, and resurrection. Someone had given them the message.

It is one thing, however, to hear the facts of the gospel. It is quite another thing to receive the message as it is given by a Spirit-filled messenger of God. Peter repeated the well-known gospel story so the Spirit could apply it to the hearts and minds of the hearers. Peter made Christ the central part of his message and trusted the Holy Spirit to do the work.

**10:38.** Actually, the message is always Jesus himself. It is Jesus from Nazareth whom God anointed with the Holy Spirit and mighty supernatural power. This anointing was in fulfillment of the proph-

**35. But in every nation he that feareth him, and worketh righteousness:** God accepts anyone who worships him and does what is right...It is not important what country a person comes from, *NCV*. . . . he who reverences him, *TCNT* . . . and practices doing right, *Williams.*

**is accepted with him:** God makes no distinction between one man and another, *Weymouth* . . . He is pleased with any man, *NLT* . . . God has no favourites, *Moffatt* . . . I now thoroughly grasp the truth that God is not partial, *Berkeley* . . . welcomes the man, *Goodspeed* . . . is welcomed by him, *Williams C.K.*

**36. The word which God sent unto the children of Israel:** This is the message he has sent to the sons, *NAB* . . . God has sent his Message to the Israelite people, *TCNT* . . . to the sons of Israel, *ABUV.*

**preaching peace by Jesus Christ: (he is Lord of all:):** . . . announcing the glad tidings of peace through, *Rotherham* . . . spreading, *Williams C.K.* . . . by telling them the good news of peace through, *Williams* . . . He is Lord of all, *Concordant* . . . of everything, *Adams* . . . of all people! *NCV.*

**37. That word, I say, ye know, which was published throughout all Judaea:** . . . you yourselves know what happened throughout, *Williams C.K.* . . . you know how the message spread, *Montgomery* . . . I take it you know what has been reported, *NAB* . . . You know the things that occurred up and down Judaea, *Berkeley* . . . been published, *Douay* . . . which came throughout, *KJII.*

**and began from Galilee, after the baptism which John preached:** . . . beginning in Galilee, *Weymouth.*

**38. How God anointed Jesus of Nazareth with the Holy Ghost and with power:** . . . how God consecrated him his Christ by enduing him with the Holy Spirit and with power, *TCNT* . . . how God appointed, *Williams C.K.* . . . when God had endowed Him, *Fenton* . . . with the power of the Holy Spirit, *Phillips.*

| **3450.5** art nom sing masc | **2296.1** noun nom sing masc | **4011.3** noun dat sing neu | **39.3** adj dat sing | **2504.1** conj | **1405.3** noun dat sing fem |
|---|---|---|---|---|---|
| ὁ | θεὸς | πνεύματι | ἁγίῳ | καὶ | δυνάμει, |
| *ho* | *theos* | *pneumati* | *hagiō* | *kai* | *dunamei* |
| | God | with Spirit | Holy | and | with power, |

| **3614.5** rel-pron nom sing masc | **1324.2** verb 3sing indic aor act | **2088.1** verb nom sing masc part pres act | **2504.1** conj | **2367.2** verb nom sing masc part pres mid |
|---|---|---|---|---|
| ὃς | διῆλθεν | εὐεργετῶν | καὶ | ἰώμενος |
| *hos* | *diēlthen* | *euergetōn* | *kai* | *iōmenos* |
| who | went through, | doing good | and | healing |

| **3820.8** adj acc pl masc | **3450.8** art acc pl masc | **2586.2** verb acc pl masc part pres mid | **5097.3** prep | **3450.2** art gen sing |
|---|---|---|---|---|
| πάντας | τοὺς | καταδυναστευομένους | ὑπὸ | τοῦ |
| *pantas* | *tous* | *katadunasteuomenous* | *hupo* | *tou* |
| all | the | being oppressed | by | the |

| **1222.2** adj gen sing masc | **3617.1** conj | **3450.5** art nom sing masc | **2296.1** noun nom sing masc | **1498.34** verb sing indic imperf act | **3196.2** prep |
|---|---|---|---|---|---|
| διαβόλου, | ὅτι | ὁ | θεὸς | ἦν | μετ' |
| *diabolou* | *hoti* | *ho* | *theos* | *ēn* | *met'* |
| devil, | because | | God | was | with |

39.a.**Txt:** 020L,025P,byz.
**Var:** 01ℵ,02A,03B,04C
05D,08E,Gries,Lach
Treg,Alf,Word,Tisc
We/Ho,Weis,Sod
UBS/☆

| **840.3** prs-pron gen sing | **2504.1** conj | **2231.1** prs-pron nom 1pl | **1498.5** verb 1pl indic pres act | **3116.4** noun nom pl masc | **3820.4** adj gen pl |
|---|---|---|---|---|---|
| αὐτοῦ. | **39.** καὶ | ἡμεῖς | ⸂a ἐσμεν⸃ | μάρτυρες | πάντων |
| *autou* | *kai* | *hēmeis* | *esmen* | *martures* | *pantōn* |
| him. | And | we | are | witnesses | of all |

| **3614.1** rel-pron gen pl | **4020.24** verb 3sing indic aor act | **1706.1** prep | **4885.1** conj | **3450.11** art dat sing fem | **5396.3** noun dat sing fem | **3450.1** art gen pl |
|---|---|---|---|---|---|---|
| ὧν | ἐποίησεν | ἔν | τε | τῇ | χώρᾳ | τῶν |
| *hōn* | *epoiēsen* | *en* | *te* | *tē* | *chōra* | *tōn* |
| which | he did | in | both | the | country | of the |

39.b.**Txt:** 01ℵ,02A,04C
08E,020L,025P,byz.Tisc
Sod
**Var:** 03B,05D,Treg
We/Ho,Weis,UBS/☆

39.c.**Var:** 01ℵ,02A,03B
04C,05D,08E,020L
025P

39.d.**Txt:** 020L,025P,byz.
Sod
**Var:** 01ℵ,02A,03B,04C
05D,08E,Lach,Treg,Alf
Tisc,We/Ho,Weis
UBS/☆

| **2428.3** name-adj gen pl masc | **2504.1** conj | **1706.1** prep | **2395.1** name fem | **3614.6** rel-pron acc sing masc |
|---|---|---|---|---|
| Ἰουδαίων | καὶ | ⸂b ἐν⸃ | Ἰερουσαλήμ· | ὃν |
| *Ioudaiōn* | *kai* | *en* | *Hierousalēm* | *hon* |
| Jews | and | in | Jerusalem; | whom |

| **2504.1** conj | **335.7** verb 3pl indic aor act | **335.16** verb 3pl indic aor act | **2883.1** verb nom pl masc part aor act |
|---|---|---|---|
| [c☆+ καὶ ] | ⸀ ἀνεῖλον | [d☆ ἀνεῖλαν ] | κρεμάσαντες |
| *kai* | *aneilon* | *aneilan* | *kremasantes* |
| [ also ] | they put to death | [ idem ] | having hung |

| **1894.3** prep | **3448.2** noun gen sing neu | **3642.6** dem-pron acc sing masc | **3450.5** art nom sing masc | **2296.1** noun nom sing masc | **1446.5** verb 3sing indic aor act |
|---|---|---|---|---|---|
| ἐπὶ | ξύλου. | **40.** τοῦτον | ὁ | θεὸς | ἤγειρεν |
| *epi* | *xulou* | *touton* | *ho* | *theos* | *ēgeiren* |
| on | a tree. | This one | | God | raised |

40.a.**Var:** 01ℵ-org,04C
Tisc,Weis,UBS/☆

| **1706.1** prep | **3450.11** art dat sing fem | **4995.6** num ord dat sing fem | **2232.3** noun dat sing fem | **2504.1** conj | **1319.14** verb 3sing indic aor act |
|---|---|---|---|---|---|
| [a+ ἐν ] | τῇ | τρίτῃ | ἡμέρᾳ, | καὶ | ἔδωκεν |
| *en* | *tē* | *tritē* | *hēmera* | *kai* | *edōken* |
| [ up ] | on the | third | day, | and | gave |

| **840.6** prs-pron acc sing masc | **1701.2** adj acc sing masc | **1090.63** verb inf aor mid | **3620.3** partic | **3820.3** adj dat sing | **3450.3** art dat sing |
|---|---|---|---|---|---|
| αὐτὸν | ἐμφανῆ | γενέσθαι, | **41.** οὐ | παντὶ | τῷ |
| *auton* | *emphanē* | *genesthai* | *ou* | *panti* | *tō* |
| him | manifest | to become, | not | to all | the |

ecies of Isaiah 11:2 which speak of the sevenfold Spirit of the Lord resting upon Him: (1) the Spirit of the Lord, (2) of wisdom, (3) of understanding, (4) of counsel, (5) of might, (6) of knowledge, and (7) of the fear of the Lord. It also fulfilled Isaiah 61:1,2, "The Spirit of the Lord God is upon me," which Jesus declared was spoken of Him (Luke 4:18,19).

This Jesus, said Peter, went about doing good (kind) deeds and healing all who were oppressed (overpowered or treated harshly) by the devil ("the slanderer," the chief slanderer of all), for God was with Him. God not only sent Jesus, He continued to be with Him in all His ministry so His miracles showed the goodness and kindness of God as well as God's power in every realm, thus giving proof that Jesus was and is indeed God's "Anointed One."

**10:39.** Next, Peter added, "We (meaning the apostles rather than the six believers from Joppa) are witnesses of all things which He did in the land of the Jews (Judea), and in Jerusalem." This emphasis on the apostolic witness is important. Jesus chose the Twelve to be the primary witnesses to the facts of the gospel.

Peter continued his message by pointing out this One who did nothing but good, the One who brought such blessing, healing and deliverance, the Jews killed and hung on a tree.

*Hung* here means crucified. It seems Peter used this word here rather than the ordinary word for "crucify" in order to emphasize the shamefulness of Christ's death. "Tree" basically means "wood," and the word was used to mean any object made of wood. It is translated "wood" in 1 Corinthians 3:12 and Revelation 18:12. It also translates the Hebrew word ʿets, as, for example, when Galatians 3:13 refers to Deuteronomy 21:23. But ʿets is a general word and is translated "wood" over 100 times in the Old Testament. Thus the "tree" here means the cross. The Romans sometimes crucified on an X-shaped cross, but the fact that the inscription was placed over Jesus' head shows that the usual form of the cross was used.

**10:40.** In contrast to what men did to Jesus, God raised (resurrected) Him on the third day. (Some see in this statement a reference to Hosea 6:2 since the apostle Paul spoke of Christ rising on the third day "according to the Scriptures." See 1 Corinthians 15:4,20,23.)

Then God permitted the risen Jesus to be manifest, to be visible, to be revealed. What God did was not something hidden, something mystical, or something merely spiritual.

The Gentiles who were listening to Peter had heard of Christ's resurrection, but they may also have heard the stories circulated by the Jewish leaders who said the disciples stole away the body of Jesus (Matthew 28:13). So Peter emphasized the reality of the bodily resurrection of Jesus and the reality of His appearances.

**who went about doing good:** . . . went everywhere, *Everyday* . . . who traversed the land doing good, *Berkeley.*

**and healing all that were oppressed of the devil:** . . . and making well, *BB* . . . and curing all who were under the power of, *TCNT* . . . and curing all who were harassed by, *Moffatt* . . . and curing all who were overpowered by, *Fenton, Williams* . . . all those who are tyrannized over by the Slanderer, *Concordant* . . . that were suffering from evil, *Murdock* . . . all who were troubled by, *NLT* . . . all who suffered from the devil's power, *Phillips* . . . all that were pressed down by, *KJII* . . . those who were ruled by, *Everyday, NCV* . . . all who were in the grip of, *NAB.*

**for God was with him:** . . . with God at his side, *Knox* . . . because God was, *Rotherham* . . . since, *Williams C.K.* . . . was with Jesus, *Everyday.*

**39. And we are witnesses of all things which he did both in the land of the Jews, and in Jerusalem, whom they slew and hanged on a tree:** We have seen and heard everything He did, *NLT* . . . all that he did in the country of, *Kleist* . . . both in the villages of, *Fenton* . . . whom they put to death, *BB* . . . they hung him up on a tree and killed him, *Williams C.K.* . . . hanging him on, *Kleist* . . . and they murdered Him, *MLNT* . . . They killed him, finally, *NAB* . . . by nailing him to a cross, *Everyday.*

**40. Him God raised up the third day:** This Jesus God raised from the grave, *TCNT* . . . only to have God raise him up, *NAB* . . . raised Jesus to life, *Everyday* . . . God gave him back to life, *BB.*

**and shewed him openly:** . . . permitted him to appear, *Weymouth* . . . allowed him to be seen, *BB, Moffatt* . . . and caused him to be, *Everyday, Kleist* . . . let him be seen clearly, *Klingensmith* . . . with naked eyes, *Murdock* . . . and caused Him to be seen, *KJII* . . . and grant that he be seen, *NAB* . . . to be plainly seen, *Goodspeed, Williams* . . . and granted Him to become visible, *Fenton* . . . granted the clear sight of him, *Knox.*

| 2967.3 noun dat sing masc<br>λαῷ,<br>*laō*<br>people, | 233.2 conj<br>ἀλλὰ<br>*alla*<br>but | 3116.6 noun dat pl masc<br>μάρτυσιν<br>*martusin*<br>to witnesses | 3450.4 art dat pl<br>τοῖς<br>*tois*<br>the | 4259.1 verb dat pl masc part perf mid<br>προκεχειροτονημένοις<br>*prokecheirotonēmenois*<br>having been chosen before |
|---|---|---|---|---|

| 5097.3 prep<br>ὑπὸ<br>*hupo*<br>by | 3450.2 art gen sing<br>τοῦ<br>*tou* | 2296.2 noun gen sing masc<br>θεοῦ,<br>*theou*<br>God, | 2231.3 prs-pron dat 1pl<br>ἡμῖν,<br>*hēmin*<br>to us, | 3610.2 rel-pron nom pl masc<br>οἵτινες<br>*hoitines*<br>who | 4756.4 verb 1pl indic aor act<br>συνεφάγομεν<br>*sunephagomen*<br>ate with |
|---|---|---|---|---|---|

| 2504.1 conj<br>καὶ<br>*kai*<br>and | 4695.1 verb 1pl indic aor act<br>συνεπίομεν<br>*sunepiomen*<br>drank with | 840.4 prs-pron dat sing<br>αὐτῷ<br>*autō*<br>him | 3196.3 prep<br>μετὰ<br>*meta*<br>after | 3450.16 art sing neu<br>τὸ<br>*to*<br>the | 448.14 verb inf aor act<br>ἀναστῆναι<br>*anastēnai*<br>to rise |
|---|---|---|---|---|---|

| 840.6 prs-pron acc sing masc<br>αὐτὸν<br>*auton*<br>him | 1523.2 prep gen<br>ἐκ<br>*ek*<br>from among | 3361.2 adj gen pl<br>νεκρῶν·<br>*nekrōn*<br>dead. | 2504.1 conj<br>**42.** καὶ<br>*kai*<br>And | 3715.7 verb 3sing indic aor act<br>παρήγγειλεν<br>*parēngeilen*<br>he charged |
|---|---|---|---|---|

| 2231.3 prs-pron dat 1pl<br>ἡμῖν<br>*hēmin*<br>us | 2756.18 verb inf aor act<br>κηρύξαι<br>*kēruxai*<br>to proclaim | 3450.3 art dat sing<br>τῷ<br>*tō*<br>to the | 2967.3 noun dat sing masc<br>λαῷ,<br>*laō*<br>people, | 2504.1 conj<br>καὶ<br>*kai*<br>and | 1257.9 verb inf aor mid<br>διαμαρτύρασθαι<br>*diamarturasthai*<br>to testify fully |
|---|---|---|---|---|---|

42.a.**Txt:** p74,01ℵ,02A 025P,byz.Gries,Word Tisc
**Var:** 03B,04C,05D,08E

| 3617.1 conj<br>ὅτι<br>*hoti*<br>that | 840.5 prs-pron nom sing masc<br>ʻ αὐτός<br>*autos*<br>he | 3642.4 dem-pron nom sing masc<br>[a☆ οὗτός ]<br>*houtos*<br>[ this ] | 1498.4 verb 3sing indic pres act<br>ἐστιν<br>*estin*<br>is | 3450.5 art nom sing masc<br>ὁ<br>*ho*<br>the |
|---|---|---|---|---|

| 3587.6 verb nom sing masc part perf mid<br>ὡρισμένος<br>*hōrismenos*<br>having been appointed | 5097.3 prep<br>ὑπὸ<br>*hupo*<br>by | 3450.2 art gen sing<br>τοῦ<br>*tou* | 2296.2 noun gen sing masc<br>θεοῦ<br>*theou*<br>God | 2896.1 noun nom sing masc<br>κριτὴς<br>*kritēs*<br>judge |
|---|---|---|---|---|

| 2180.14 verb gen pl masc part pres act<br>ζώντων<br>*zōntōn*<br>of living | 2504.1 conj<br>καὶ<br>*kai*<br>and | 3361.2 adj gen pl<br>νεκρῶν.<br>*nekrōn*<br>dead. | 3642.5 dem-pron dat sing masc<br>**43.** τούτῳ<br>*toutō*<br>To him | 3820.7 adj nom pl masc<br>πάντες<br>*pantes*<br>all | 3450.7 art nom pl masc<br>οἱ<br>*hoi*<br>the |
|---|---|---|---|---|---|

| 4254.4 noun nom pl masc<br>προφῆται<br>*prophētai*<br>prophets | 3113.6 verb 3pl indic pres act<br>μαρτυροῦσιν,<br>*marturousin*<br>bear witness, | 852.3 noun acc sing fem<br>ἄφεσιν<br>*aphesin*<br>forgiveness | 264.6 noun gen pl fem<br>ἁμαρτιῶν<br>*hamartiōn*<br>of sins | 2956.31 verb inf aor act<br>λαβεῖν<br>*labein*<br>to receive |
|---|---|---|---|---|

| 1217.2 prep<br>διὰ<br>*dia*<br>through | 3450.2 art gen sing<br>τοῦ<br>*tou*<br>the | 3549.3 noun gen sing neu<br>ὀνόματος<br>*onomatos*<br>name | 840.3 prs-pron gen sing<br>αὐτοῦ<br>*autou*<br>his | 3820.1 adj<br>πάντα<br>*panta*<br>everyone | 3450.6 art acc sing masc<br>τὸν<br>*ton*<br>the |
|---|---|---|---|---|---|

| 3961.12 verb acc sing masc part pres act<br>πιστεύοντα<br>*pisteuonta*<br>believing | 1519.1 prep<br>εἰς<br>*eis*<br>on | 840.6 prs-pron acc sing masc<br>αὐτόν.<br>*auton*<br>him. | 2068.1 adv<br>**44.** Ἔτι<br>*Eti*<br>Yet | 2953.13 verb gen sing masc part pres act<br>λαλοῦντος<br>*lalountos*<br>speaking | 3450.2 art gen sing<br>τοῦ<br>*tou* |
|---|---|---|---|---|---|

**10:41.** Peter added that these appearances were not made to all the people, but to witnesses chosen by God beforehand, namely to Peter and the others who ate and drank with Jesus (and thus enjoyed fellowship with Him around the table) after He arose from (out from among) the dead. This was concrete proof of the reality of Christ's resurrection body. He was not a spirit, not a ghost, not a figment of their imagination, but a very real Person who could give them genuine fellowship in this way.

It is also evident that Jesus did not intend to stay on the earth and teach the general public anymore. He gave His time after the Resurrection to opening the minds of His chosen witnesses to the Scriptures so they would be able to understand and proclaim the gospel after He ascended to His place at the Father's throne. (See Luke 24:25-27,32,44-49, noting that He caused the truth to burn in their hearts.)

Actually, 1 Corinthians 15:5-8 reports there was a sufficient number of witnesses. The resurrected Christ was seen by more than 500 believers at once (probably in Galilee), and most of them were still alive at the time Paul wrote to the Corinthians. He was seen also by His half-brother, James, and by all who were apostles, including Paul.

**10:42.** Peter then drew attention to the need for forgiveness in view of the coming judgment day.

Because of Christ's command, these chosen witnesses were proclaiming the good news to the people. (The Great Commission is found in all four Gospels as well as in Acts 1:8.) But Peter did not stop with speaking of the good news. He continued by showing the importance of accepting the good news. As witnesses to Christ's resurrection, the apostles were also under obligation to testify solemnly that Jesus was ordained (designated, appointed) as Judge of the living and the dead.

Peter did not mean the spiritually living and the spiritually dead. Rather, Jesus is and will be the Judge of all who have lived or whoever will live on earth. This bears out what Jesus said in John 5:22, "The Father judges no one, but has given (and continues and will continue to give) all judgment to the Son" (RSV).

**10:43.** The coming judgment need not frighten them, however. For Peter emphasized again the fact that the way is open to all, so no one need be excluded from the benefits of Christ's death and resurrection. But this time Peter drew attention, not to his own vision, but to the command of the Lord and the witness of the prophets to the written Word.

**10:44.** While Peter was still speaking these words (Greek, *rhēmata*, the plural of *rhēma*), there came a sudden unexpected in-

**41. Not to all the people:** But he was not seen by all the people, *Everyday* . . . not to the general public, *Taylor* . . . not of all the people, *Darby*.

**but unto witnesses chosen before of God, even to us:** . . . but to us witnesses previously selected of God, *Berkeley* . . . Only the witnesses that God had already chosen saw him, and we are those witnesses, *Everyday* . . . whom God had designated beforehand, *Goodspeed*.

**who did eat and drink with him:** . . . and we ate and drank with Him, *Norlie*.

**after he rose from the dead:** . . . after his resurrection from the dead, *TCNT* . . . after he was raised from death, *Everyday*.

**42. And he commanded us to preach unto the people:** And he charged us, *ASV* . . . And to us He gave orders, *MLNT* . . . to proclain, *Rotherham* . . . to herald, *Berkeley* . . . to announce to the people, *Goodspeed*.

**and to testify:** . . . and solemnly declare, *Weymouth, TNT* . . . to testify fully, *Norlie* . . . and to tell them, *Everyday*.

**that it is he which was ordained of God to be the Judge of quick and dead:** . . . that He is the One, *Norlie* . . . appointed by God, *TCNT* . . . the Judge of the living and the dead, *ASV* . . . God-ordained Judge, *AmpB*.

**43. To him give all the prophets witness:** To Him all the prophets bear witness, *Weymouth* . . . All the early preachers spoke of this, *NLT* . . . All the prophets say this is true, *Everyday*.

**that through his name whosoever believeth in him shall receive remission of sins:** . . . forgiveness of sins, *TCNT* . . . that remission of sins is to be received through his name by every one that believeth on him, *Rotherham* . . . remission of the penalty of sins, *Wuest* . . . God will forgive his sins through Jesus, *Everyday*.

**44. While Peter yet spake these words:** Before Peter had finished saying these words, *TCNT* . . . Even while Peter was preaching this sermon, *Norlie* . . . Peter had not finished these words

## Acts 10:45

| 3935.2 name gen masc | 3450.17 art pl neu | 4343.4 noun pl neu | 3642.18 dem-pron pl neu | 1953.2 verb 3sing indic aor act | 3450.16 art sing neu |
|---|---|---|---|---|---|
| Πέτρου | τὰ | ῥήματα | ταῦτα, | ἐπέπεσεν | τὸ |
| *Petrou* | *ta* | *rhēmata* | *tauta* | *epepesen* | *to* |
| Peter | the | words | these | fell | the |

| 4011.1 noun sing neu | 3450.16 art sing neu | 39.1 adj sing | 1894.3 prep | 3820.8 adj acc pl masc | 3450.8 art acc pl masc | 189.16 verb acc pl masc part pres act |
|---|---|---|---|---|---|---|
| πνεῦμα | τὸ | ἅγιον | ἐπὶ | πάντας | τοὺς | ἀκούοντας |
| *pneuma* | *to* | *hagion* | *epi* | *pantas* | *tous* | *akouontas* |
| Spirit | the | Holy | upon | all | the | hearing |

| 3450.6 art acc sing masc | 3030.4 noun acc sing masc | 2504.1 conj | 1822.4 verb 3pl indic aor act | 3450.7 art nom pl masc | 1523.2 prep gen |
|---|---|---|---|---|---|
| τὸν | λόγον. | **45.** καὶ | ἐξέστησαν | οἱ | ἐκ |
| *ton* | *logon* | *kai* | *exestēsan* | *hoi* | *ek* |
| the | word. | And | were amazed | the | of the |

45.a.**Var:** 03B,sa.bo. Lach,We/Ho

| 3921.2 noun gen sing fem | 3964.6 adj nom pl masc | 3607.2 rel-pron nom pl masc | 3614.7 rel-pron nom pl masc | 4755.3 verb 3pl indic aor act |
|---|---|---|---|---|
| περιτομῆς | πιστοὶ | ʼ ὅσοι | [a οἳ ] | ʼ συνῆλθον |
| *peritomēs* | *pistoi* | *hosoi* | *hoi* | *sunēlthon* |
| circumcision | believers | as many | [ who ] | came with |

45.b.**Txt:** 02A,05D,08E 020L,025P,etc.byz.Weis Sod
**Var:** 01ℵ,03B,Treg,Tisc We/Ho,UBS/☆

| 4755.2 verb 3pl indic aor act | 3450.3 art dat sing | 3935.3 name dat masc | 3617.1 conj | 2504.1 conj | 1894.3 prep | 3450.17 art pl neu |
|---|---|---|---|---|---|---|
| [b☆ συνῆλθαν ] | τῷ | Πέτρῳ, | ὅτι | καὶ | ἐπὶ | τὰ |
| *sunēlthan* | *tō* | *Petrō* | *hoti* | *kai* | *epi* | *ta* |
| [ idem ] | | Peter, | that | also | upon | the |

| 1477.4 noun pl neu | 3450.9 art nom sing fem | 1424.1 noun nom sing fem | 3450.2 art gen sing | 39.2 adj gen sing | 4011.2 noun gen sing neu |
|---|---|---|---|---|---|
| ἔθνη | ἡ | δωρεὰ | τοῦ | ʼ ἁγίου | πνεύματος |
| *ethnē* | *hē* | *dōrea* | *tou* | *hagiou* | *pneumatos* |
| Gentiles | the | gift | of the | Holy | Spirit |

45.c.**Var:** 03B,05D-corr Lach,We/Ho

| 4011.2 noun gen sing neu | 3450.2 art gen sing | 39.2 adj gen sing | 1619.4 verb 3sing indic perf mid |
|---|---|---|---|
| πνεύματος | [c τοῦ | ἁγίου ] | ἐκκέχυται· |
| *pneumatos* | *tou* | *hagiou* | *ekkechutai* |
| Spirit | [ the | Holy ] | had been poured out; |

| 189.46 verb 3pl indic imperf act | 1056.1 conj | 840.1 prs-pron gen pl | 2953.17 verb gen pl masc part pres act | 1094.7 noun dat pl fem |
|---|---|---|---|---|
| **46.** ἤκουον | γὰρ | αὐτῶν | λαλούντων | γλώσσαις |
| *ēkouon* | *gar* | *autōn* | *lalountōn* | *glōssais* |
| they were hearing | for | them | speaking | with tongues |

| 2504.1 conj | 3141.3 verb gen pl masc part pres act | 3450.6 art acc sing masc | 2296.4 noun acc sing masc | 4966.1 adv | 552.6 verb 3sing indic aor pass |
|---|---|---|---|---|---|
| καὶ | μεγαλυνόντων | τὸν | θεόν. | τότε | ἀπεκρίθη |
| *kai* | *megalunontōn* | *ton* | *theon* | *tote* | *apekrithē* |
| and | magnifying | | God. | Then | answered |

46.a.**Txt:** 05D,08E,020L 025P,byz.
**Var:** 01ℵ,02A,03B,Lach Treg,Alf,Tisc,We/Ho Weis,Sod,UBS/☆

| 3450.5 art nom sing masc | 3935.1 name nom masc | 3252.1 partic | 3450.16 art sing neu | 5045.1 noun sing neu | 2940.10 verb inf aor act |
|---|---|---|---|---|---|
| ʼa ὁ ˋ | Πέτρος, | **47.** Μήτι | τὸ | ὕδωρ | ʼ κωλῦσαί |
| *ho* | *Petros* | *Mēti* | *to* | *hudōr* | *kōlusai* |
| | Peter, | Neither | the | water | to refuse |

| 1404.4 verb 3sing indic pres mid | 1404.4 verb 3sing indic pres mid | 2940.10 verb inf aor act | 4948.3 indef-pron nom sing | 3450.2 art gen sing | 3231.1 partic |
|---|---|---|---|---|---|
| δύναται | [☆ δύναται | κωλῦσαί ] | τις | τοῦ | μὴ |
| *dunatai* | *dunatai* | *kōlusai* | *tis* | *tou* | *mē* |
| can | [ can | to refuse ] | anyone | the | not |

terruption from heaven. The Holy Spirit fell on all those who were listening to the Word (Greek, *logon*). Notice here that what Peter spoke was referred to as *rhēma*, but what they heard, *logos*. Again it is clear that the two Greek words are used interchangeably.

The Holy Spirit is spoken of here as falling on them, using the same word found in 8:16 which says the Holy Spirit had not yet fallen upon those in Samaria who were saved under the preaching of Philip and were baptized in water by him. Thus, in the present context, "falling upon" speaks of receiving the Holy Spirit in a "baptism" for power (cf. 1:5,8).

**10:45.** This outpouring of the Holy Spirit totally amazed the six Jewish believers who had come with Peter. In fact, they could hardly believe they were observing the Holy Spirit poured out on these Gentile Romans.

Luke referred to these six men as "they of the circumcision." Peter, of course, was circumcised, but his mind had been opened. But the Bible draws attention to the fact that these six men, even though believers in Christ, were still very conscious of who they were as heirs of the promise given to Abraham, a promise confirmed by a covenant whose outward sign was circumcision. They did not feel the importance of the part of the promise that spoke of blessing to all the nations of the earth, nor did they see themselves as opening the way for that promise to come to non-Jews. Even Peter's experience had not convinced them their prejudices were wrong, and the truth that God is no respecter of persons had not become as clear in their minds as it had in the mind of Peter. Thus, they did not really expect God to save these Gentiles and fill them with the Holy Spirit in the same way He had done for the Jewish believers.

"Poured out" is used to mean the same thing as "fell upon," and it shows that Peter and the six Jewish believers saw in this experience the same thing that happened on the Day of Pentecost (2:17,33).

**10:46.** The fact that this whole crowd of Romans spoke with tongues (languages they had never learned) and magnified God also relates this outpouring to the outpouring on the Day of Pentecost (2:4). They magnified God as they kept on speaking in other tongues. (The Greek indicates continuous action for both the speaking in tongues and the magnifying or praising, extolling, exalting, and glorifying God.) Since there were not the people of various languages present as there were on the Day of Pentecost, this seems to mean their praise was addressed to God.

Peter apparently observed this for a time, and then he gave a response that was surely inspired by the Holy Spirit.

**10:47.** Peter saw that this kind of evidence was sufficient for the Church to accept these believers, so no one could forbid baptism in water. Peter recognized that these Gentiles were not only ac-



when, *NAB* . . . was still saying this, *Everyday*.

**the Holy Ghost fell on all them which heard the word:** . . . came down on all those who were listenening, *Everyday* . . . listening to his message, *Norlie* . . . overshadowed all them, *Murdock* . . . who hearkened to the message, *Fenton*.

**45. And they of the circumcision which believed were astonished, as many as came with Peter:** And all the Jewish believers who had come with Peter were astonished, *Weymouth* . . . The Jewish faithful, Peter's companions, *Kleist* . . . And the circumcised believers, *Berkeley* . . . were surprised, *Beck* . . . were absolutely amazed, *Phillips*.

**because that on the Gentiles also was poured out the gift of the Holy Ghost:** . . . the holy Spirit had actually been poured out on the Gentiles, *Moffatt* . . . bestowed even upon the heathen, *TCNT* . . . the free-gift, *Rotherham* . . . the grace of the Holy Ghost, *Douay* . . . that the gift of the Holy Spirit had been given even to the non-Jewish people, *Everyday* . . . had been showered upon the heathen too, *Williams* . . . had also been poured forth on, *Kleist* . . . on the Pagans, *Klingensmith*.

**46. For they heard them speak with tongues, and magnify God:** These Jewish believers, *Everyday* . . . for they could hear them speaking with tongues and extolling God, *TCNT* . . . and declaring, *Goodspeed* . . . speaking in other languages and praising God, *Beck* . . . exalting God, *NASB* . . . with diverse tongues, *Murdock* . . . in various languages, *Adams*.

**Then answered Peter:** At this Peter asked, *TCNT* . . . Peter said, *Everyday* . . . Then Peter made the decision, *Kleist*.

**47. Can any man forbid water, that these should not be baptized:** Can any one refuse the water for the baptism of these people, *TCNT* . . . Can anyone keep these people from being baptized with water? *Everyday* . . . Can anyone refuse the baptism of water to these people, *Kleist*.

# Acts 10:48

47.a.**Txt:** 08E,020L 025P,byz.
**Var:** 01ℵ,02A,03B,Lach Treg,Alf,Tisc,We/Ho Weis,Sod,UBS/☆

| **901.25** verb inf aor pass | **3642.8** dem-pron acc pl masc | **3610.2** rel-pron nom pl masc | **3450.16** art sing neu | **4011.1** noun sing neu |
|---|---|---|---|---|
| βαπτισθῆναι | τούτους, | οἵτινες | τὸ | πνεῦμα |
| *baptisthēnai* | *toutous* | *hoitines* | *to* | *pneuma* |
| to be baptized | these, | who | the | Spirit |

48.a.**Txt:** 02A,020L 025P,byz.
**Var:** 01ℵ,03B,08E,33,sa. bo.Treg,Tisc,We/Ho Weis,Sod,UBS/☆

| **3450.16** art sing neu | **39.1** adj sing | **2956.12** verb indic aor act | **2503.1** conj | **5453.1** conj | **2504.1** conj | **2231.1** prs-pron nom 1pl |
|---|---|---|---|---|---|---|
| τὸ | ἅγιον | ἔλαβον | ʽ καθὼς | [a☆ ὡς ] | καὶ | ἡμεῖς; |
| *to* | *hagion* | *elabon* | *kathōs* | *hōs* | *kai* | *hēmeis* |
| the | Holy | received | just as | [ as ] | also | we? |

48.b.**Var:** p74,01ℵ,02A 33,Tisc

| **4225.1** verb 3sing indic aor act | **4885.1** conj | **1156.2** conj | **840.8** prs-pron acc pl masc | **840.2** prs-pron dat pl |
|---|---|---|---|---|
| **48.** προσέταξεν | ʽ τε | [a☆ δὲ ] | ʽ αὐτοὺς | [b αὐτοῖς ] |
| *prosetaxen* | *te* | *de* | *autous* | *autois* |
| He ordered | and | [ idem ] | them | [ idem ] |

| **901.25** verb inf aor pass | **1706.1** prep | **3450.3** art dat sing | **3549.4** noun dat sing neu | **3450.2** art gen sing | **2935.2** noun gen sing masc |
|---|---|---|---|---|---|
| ʽ βαπτισθῆναι | ἐν | τῷ | ὀνόματι | τοῦ | κυρίου. |
| *baptisthēnai* | *en* | *tō* | *onomati* | *tou* | *kuriou* |
| to be baptized | in | the | name | of the | Lord. |

48.c.**Txt:** 020L,025P,byz. Steph
**Var:** 01ℵ,02A,03B,Lach Treg,Tisc,We/Ho,Weis Sod,UBS/☆

| **1706.1** prep | **3450.3** art dat sing | **3549.4** noun dat sing neu | **2400.2** name masc | **5382.2** name gen masc |
|---|---|---|---|---|
| [c☆ ἐν | τῷ | ὀνόματι | Ἰησοῦ | Χριστοῦ |
| *en* | *tō* | *onomati* | *Iēsou* | *Christou* |
| [ in | the | name | of Jesus | Christ |

| **901.25** verb inf aor pass | **4966.1** adv | **2049.10** verb 3pl indic aor act | **840.6** prs-pron acc sing masc | **1946.9** verb inf aor act |
|---|---|---|---|---|
| βαπτισθῆναι. ] | τότε | ἠρώτησαν | αὐτὸν | ἐπιμεῖναι |
| *baptisthēnai* | *tote* | *ērōtēsan* | *auton* | *epimeinai* |
| to be baptized. ] | Then | they asked | him | to remain |

| **2232.1** noun fem | **4948.9** indef-pron acc pl masc | **189.24** verb 3pl indic aor act | **1156.2** conj | **3450.7** art nom pl masc |
|---|---|---|---|---|
| ἡμέρας | τινάς. | **11:1.** Ἤκουσαν | δὲ | οἱ |
| *hēmeras* | *tinas* | *Ēkousan* | *de* | *hoi* |
| days | some. | Heard | and | the |

| **646.4** noun nom pl masc | **2504.1** conj | **3450.7** art nom pl masc | **79.6** noun nom pl masc | **3450.7** art nom pl masc | **1498.23** verb nom pl masc part pres act |
|---|---|---|---|---|---|
| ἀπόστολοι | καὶ | οἱ | ἀδελφοὶ | οἱ | ὄντες |
| *apostoloi* | *kai* | *hoi* | *adelphoi* | *hoi* | *ontes* |
| apostles | and | the | brothers | the | being |

| **2567.3** prep | **3450.12** art acc sing fem | **2424.4** name acc fem | **3617.1** conj | **2504.1** conj | **3450.17** art pl neu | **1477.4** noun pl neu |
|---|---|---|---|---|---|---|
| κατὰ | τὴν | Ἰουδαίαν, | ὅτι | καὶ | τὰ | ἔθνη |
| *kata* | *tēn* | *Ioudaian* | *hoti* | *kai* | *ta* | *ethnē* |
| in | | Judea, | that | also | the | Gentiles |

| **1203.8** verb 3pl indic aor mid | **3450.6** art acc sing masc | **3030.4** noun acc sing masc | **3450.2** art gen sing | **2296.2** noun gen sing masc | **2504.1** conj |
|---|---|---|---|---|---|
| ἐδέξαντο | τὸν | λόγον | τοῦ | θεοῦ. | **2.** ʽ καὶ |
| *edexanto* | *ton* | *logon* | *tou* | *theou* | *kai* |
| received | the | word | | of God; | and |

2.a.**Txt:** 020L,025P,byz.
**Var:** 01ℵ,02A,03B,08E sa.bo.Lach,Treg,Alf,Tisc We/Ho,Weis,Sod UBS/☆

| **3616.1** conj | **3616.1** conj | **1156.2** conj | **303.13** verb 3sing indic aor act | **3935.1** name nom masc | **1519.1** prep |
|---|---|---|---|---|---|
| ὅτε | [a☆ ὅτε | δὲ ] | ἀνέβη | Πέτρος | εἰς |
| *hote* | *hote* | *de* | *anebē* | *Petros* | *eis* |
| when | [ when | and ] | went up | Peter | to |

cepted by God but were also a part of the Church. The Holy Spirit was poured out on believers who were already identified as the Church and as the temple of the Holy Spirit in chapter 2. Thus, their experience was the same as that of the Jewish believers at Pentecost.

**which have received the Holy Ghost as well as we?:** ... since they have received the Holy Spirit, *Williams* ... who the Holy Spirit did receive, *Young* ... have been given, *BB* ... as well as ourselves? *Fenton* ... as we ourselves did, *MLNT* ... even as we also did? *KJII* ... just like ourselves? *Williams C.K.* ... as we did, *Kleist* ... just as we have, *Lamsa.*

**10:48.** Peter did not hesitate any longer. He saw that these Gentile Romans had believed the Word while he was preaching, and were saved, born again from above. Then, while he was still preaching, the Holy Spirit had been poured out upon them. Later, in 15:8, Peter said, "God, which knoweth the hearts, bare them witness, giving them the Holy Ghost, even as he did unto us."

So Peter gave instructions, and they were all baptized in the name (that is, by the authority) of the Lord (Jesus Christ, as is stated in many ancient manuscripts). The authority of Jesus, of course, points back to the command in Matthew 28:19.

This baptism was a public declaration of their faith, a witness to the faith they already had, a witness to the faith that had already brought cleansing to their hearts (15:9).

After being baptized in water, the people asked Peter to remain with them a few days. Undoubtedly, they wanted more instruction in the truths of the gospel and desired to share spiritual fellowship with him, just as the 3,000 who were saved, baptized in water, and filled with the Spirit on the Day of Pentecost wanted to continue in the teaching and fellowship of the apostles (2:42).

**48. And he commanded them to be baptized in the name of the Lord:** And he ordered, *Moffatt* ... So he directed, *MLNT, TCNT* ... And he gave instructions, *TNT* ... So he commanded his companions, *Noli* ... gave orders for them to be baptized in the name of Jesus Christ, *Phillips, Williams C.K.* ... to have baptism, *BB* ... of our Lord, *Lamsa.*

**Then prayed they him to tarry certain days:** ... after this, they asked him to stay on some days, *Knox* ... Afterwards they asked him to stay with them for some days, *Phillips* ... after which they asked him to stay there a few days longer, *TCNT* ... Then they begged him to remain with them for a time, *Weymouth* ... they besought him to stay on there, *Kleist* ... Then they kept him with them, *BB* ... for some days, *Williams C.K.* ... to stay certain days, *KJII* ... they urged him to remain, *Lamsa* ... to remain for some days with them, *Noli.*

**11:1.** Peter was right in believing he would need witnesses with him when he returned to Jerusalem. He also found it necessary to explain everything that happened in Caesarea. The fact that Luke records this, repeating much of what was said in chapter 10, shows how important these events were. From them the Church learned that God would accept the Gentiles without circumcision and without their keeping the forms of the Law, that is, without their becoming Jews. Christianity was not something added to or tacked on to Judaism. Gentiles could come to God directly under the new covenant without coming first under the old covenant.

It was striking news that the Gentiles at the house of Cornelius had received (welcomed) the Word of God willingly, acknowledged its truth, and accepted its full message of repentance, forgiveness, and salvation. But to some of the Jewish believers in Jerusalem this was not good news. Such news, especially when it is considered bad news, travels fast. It reached the apostles and the rest of the believers in Jerusalem before Peter returned.

**1. And the apostles and brethren that were in Judaea heard that the Gentiles had also received the Word of God:** ... brothers who lived in, *MLNT* ... who were resident in Judea, *Fenton* ... that even the heathen had welcomed God's Message, *TCNT* ... The non-Jewish people, too, have accepted God's Word, *Beck* ... and brothers all over, *Kleist* ... had news that, *BB* ... heard that the heathen had also accepted, *Goodspeed* ... also had received the Gospel, *Noli* ... were told how the word of God had been given to the Gentiles, *Knox.*

**2. And when Peter was come up to Jerusalem:** ... went up, *TCNT* ... returned to, *Goodspeed, Weymouth* ... came up, *Knox, TNT* ... had come up to, *Lamsa* ... So when Peter next visited Jerusalem, *Phillips.*

**11:2.** When Peter arrived, "they of the circumcision" (which included all the believers in Jerusalem, for they were all Jews or

## Acts 11:3

2.b.**Txt:** 05D,08E,020L 025P,byz.Sod
**Var:** 01ℵ,02A,03B,Lach Treg,Alf,Tisc,We/Ho Weis,UBS/☆

3.a.**Var:** p74,01ℵ,02A 05D,sa.bo.Lach,Treg Alf,Word,Tisc,Weis UBS/☆

3.b.**Txt:** 08E,025P,byz.
**Var:** p74,01ℵ,02A,05D sa.bo.Lach,Treg,Alf Word,Tisc,We/Ho,Weis Sod,UBS/☆

4.a.**Txt:** 020L,025P,byz.
**Var:** 01ℵ,02A,03B,05D 08E,Lach,Treg,Alf Word,Tisc,We/Ho,Weis Sod,UBS/☆

| **2389.1** name | **2395.2** name fem | **1246.15** verb 3pl indic imperf mid | **4242.1** prep |
|---|---|---|---|
| ⸀ Ἱεροσόλυμα, | [b☆ Ἰερουσαλήμ, ] | διεκρίνοντο | πρὸς |
| *Hierosoluma* | *Ierousalēm* | *diekrinonto* | *pros* |
| Jerusalem, | [ idem ] | were contending | with |

| **840.6** prs-pron acc sing masc | **3450.7** art nom pl masc | **1523.2** prep gen | **3921.2** noun gen sing fem | **2978.16** verb nom pl masc part pres act |
|---|---|---|---|---|
| αὐτὸν | οἱ | ἐκ | περιτομῆς, | 3. λέγοντες, |
| *auton* | *hoi* | *ek* | *peritomēs* | *legontes* |
| him | the | of | circumcision, | saying, |

| **3617.1** conj | **1511.2** verb 2sing indic aor act | **4242.1** prep | **433.9** noun acc pl masc | **201.4** noun acc sing fem |
|---|---|---|---|---|
| "Ὅτι | [a☆+ Εἰσῆλθες ] | πρὸς | ἄνδρας | ἀκροβυστίαν |
| *Hoti* | *Eisēlthes* | *pros* | *andras* | *akrobustian* |
| that | [ You went in ] | to | men | uncircumcised |

| **2174.21** verb acc pl masc part pres act | **1511.2** verb 2sing indic aor act | **2504.1** conj | **4756.3** verb 2sing indic aor act | **840.2** prs-pron dat pl |
|---|---|---|---|---|
| ἔχοντας | ⸂b εἰσῆλθες, ⸃ | καὶ | συνέφαγες | αὐτοῖς. |
| *echontas* | *eisēlthes* | *kai* | *sunephages* | *autois* |
| having | you went in, | and | ate | with them. |

| **751.10** verb nom sing masc part aor mid | **1156.2** conj | **3450.5** art nom sing masc | **3935.1** name nom masc | **1606.3** verb 3sing indic imperf mid |
|---|---|---|---|---|
| 4. Ἀρξάμενος | δὲ | ⸂a ὁ ⸃ | Πέτρος | ἐξετίθετο |
| *Arxamenos* | *de* | *ho* | *Petros* | *exetitheto* |
| Having begun | but | | Peter | was setting |

| **840.2** prs-pron dat pl | **2489.1** adv | **2978.15** verb nom sing masc part pres act | **1466.1** prs-pron nom 1sing | **1498.46** verb 1sing indic imperf mid |
|---|---|---|---|---|
| αὐτοῖς | καθεξῆς | λέγων, | 5. Ἐγὼ | ἤμην |
| *autois* | *kathexēs* | *legōn* | *Egō* | *ēmēn* |
| to them | in order | saying, | I | was |

| **1706.1** prep | **4032.3** noun dat sing fem | **2421.2** name dat fem | **4195.11** verb nom sing masc part pres mid | **2504.1** conj | **1481.1** verb indic aor act |
|---|---|---|---|---|---|
| ἐν | πόλει | Ἰόππῃ | προσευχόμενος, | καὶ | εἶδον |
| *en* | *polei* | *Ioppē* | *proseuchomenos* | *kai* | *eidon* |
| in | city | of Joppa | praying, | and | I saw |

| **1706.1** prep | **1598.3** noun dat sing fem | **3568.1** noun sing neu | **2568.10** verb sing neu part pres act | **4487.1** noun sing neu | **4948.10** indef-pron sing neu |
|---|---|---|---|---|---|
| ἐν | ἐκστάσει | ὅραμα, | καταβαῖνον | σκεῦός | τι |
| *en* | *ekstasei* | *horama* | *katabainon* | *skeuos* | *ti* |
| in | a trance | a vision, | descending | a vessel | certain |

| **5453.1** conj | **3469.1** noun acc sing fem | **3144.12** adj acc sing fem | **4913.2** num card dat | **741.6** noun dat pl fem | **2496.2** verb acc sing fem part pres mid |
|---|---|---|---|---|---|
| ὡς | ὀθόνην | μεγάλην, | τέσσαρσιν | ἀρχαῖς | καθιεμένην |
| *hōs* | *othonēn* | *megalēn* | *tessarsin* | *archais* | *kathiemenēn* |
| like | a sheet | great, | by four | corners | being let down |

| **1523.2** prep gen | **3450.2** art gen sing | **3636.2** noun gen sing masc | **2504.1** conj | **2048.3** verb 3sing indic aor act | **884.1** conj |
|---|---|---|---|---|---|
| ἐκ | τοῦ | οὐρανοῦ. | καὶ | ἦλθεν | ⸀ ἄχρις |
| *ek* | *tou* | *ouranou* | *kai* | *ēlthen* | *achris* |
| out | of the | heaven, | and | it came | as far as |

| **884.2** conj | **1466.3** prs-pron gen 1sing | **1519.1** prep | **3614.12** rel-pron acc sing fem | **810.3** verb nom sing masc part aor act |
|---|---|---|---|---|
| [☆ ἄχρι ] | ἐμοῦ. | 6. εἰς | ἣν | ἀτενίσας |
| *achri* | *emou* | *eis* | *hēn* | *atenisas* |
| [ idem ] | me: | on | which | having looked intently |

proselytes) were ready for him. Immediately they "contended with him," criticizing him severely.

**11:3.** The believers in Jerusalem were quick to take issue with Peter for entering the house of uncircumcised men (which they considered defiling). Even worse, Peter had gone so far as to eat nonkosher food with them.

These believers were so greatly upset that they did not use the usual word for "uncircumcised." Instead, they used a slang word for *foreskin* that was a scornful expression and very derogatory toward the Gentiles.

It is quite probable also that another reason they were upset was because they were afraid Peter's action in bringing Gentiles into the Church might turn the unconverted Jews against them. This would bring an end to the period of peace and quiet they had been enjoying since Saul had ceased his persecution.

**11:4.** Peter understood how they felt, for he had felt the same way. So he did not rebuke them or pass judgment on them the way they were passing judgment on him. Neither did he take a superior attitude. Even as an apostle, he was a member of the Body, subject to submitting himself to their judgment if that judgment came from the guidance of the Spirit and the Word.

**11:5.** Beginning then with Joppa, Peter told the believers how he was praying. Then he had seen, not in a trance in the modern sense of the word but in astonishment, a vision of a certain object coming down out of heaven. It was like a very large sheet. Chapter 10 states the sheet was let down to the earth. Peter here said it came "to where I was." Thus Peter recognized the vision was specifically for him, and since it came down from heaven, God had a lesson in it for him. Even though the vision was symbolic, there was something very personal in the way it was presented to Peter. The Jerusalem Jews were concerned over Peter because they thought what he had done was wrong. Peter wanted them to see that God was concerned over him for a different reason.

In all of this Peter was asking the believers to identify with him, to try to understand why he had done this thing that had caused them to censure him. Believers would not be so critical if they could see things as others see them, especially when God has been dealing with them.

**11:6.** Peter added that the sheet not only came down to him, but came so close he was able to fasten his eyes on it, looking closely

**they that were of the circumcision:** . . . those converts who held to circumcision, *TCNT* . . . the party of circumcision, *Weymouth* . . . those insisting on circumcision, *Berkeley* . . . those who still held to the need of circumcision, *Norlie* . . . in favor of circumcising Gentiles, *TEV.*

**contended with him:** . . . began to find fault with him, *Rotherham* . . . began attacking him, *TCNT* . . . disputed with him, *Montgomery* . . . began to bring charges against him, *Williams* . . . criticized him, *RSV* . . . were full of criticism, *Phillips.*

**3. Saying, Thou wentest in to men uncircumcised, and didst eat with them:** You went into the houses...and you ate with them, *Weymouth.*

**4. But Peter rehearsed the matter from the beginning, and expounded it by order unto them, saying:** But Peter expounded the matter by order unto them from the beginning, saying, *Alford* . . . So Peter began, and explained the facts to them as they had occurred, *TCNT* . . . and gave them an orderly account, *ABUV* . . . Peter, however, explained the whole matter to them from the beginning, *Weymouth* . . . gave them the details, *JB* . . . in consecutive order, *Norlie* . . . to them point by point, *Beck* . . . to explain how the situation had actually arisen, *Phillips* . . . precisely as it had happened, *NIV.*

**5. I was in the city of Joppa praying:** . . . as I was praying, *JB* . . . I was praying in the town of Joppa, *Goodspeed* . . . in prayer, *Williams.*

**and in a trance I saw a vision:** . . . and while in a trance, *TCNT* . . . and while completely unconscious of my surroundings, *Phillips.*

**A certain vessel descend, as it had been a great sheet, let down from heaven by four corners:** . . . something like a big sheet being let down, *JB* . . . something coming down...from heaven, *TEV.*

**and it came even to me:** . . . a sort of vessel, *Noyes* . . . and it came right down to me, *TCNT* . . . and it came close to me, *Weymouth.*

| **2627.8** verb indic imperf act | **2504.1** conj | **1481.1** verb indic aor act | **3450.17** art pl neu | **4922.1** adj pl neu |
|---|---|---|---|---|
| κατενόουν, | καὶ | εἶδον | τὰ | τετράποδα |
| *katenooun* | *kai* | *eidon* | *ta* | *tetrapoda* |
| I was considering, | and | saw | the | four footed creatures |

| **3450.10** art gen sing fem | **1087.2** noun gen sing fem | **2504.1** conj | **3450.17** art pl neu | **2319.4** noun pl neu | **2504.1** conj | **3450.17** art pl neu |
|---|---|---|---|---|---|---|
| τῆς | γῆς | καὶ | τὰ | θηρία | καὶ | τὰ |
| *tēs* | *gēs* | *kai* | *ta* | *thēria* | *kai* | *ta* |
| of the | earth | and | the | wild beasts | and | the |

| **2046.1** noun pl neu | **2504.1** conj | **3450.17** art pl neu | **3932.1** adj pl neu | **3450.2** art gen sing | **3636.2** noun gen sing masc |
|---|---|---|---|---|---|
| ἑρπετὰ | καὶ | τὰ | πετεινὰ | τοῦ | οὐρανοῦ. |
| *herpeta* | *kai* | *ta* | *peteina* | *tou* | *ouranou* |
| creeping things | and | the | birds | of the | heaven. |

7.a.**Var:** 01ℵ,02A,03B 08E,sa.bo.Lach,Treg,Alf Tisc,We/Ho,Weis,Sod UBS/☆

| **189.19** verb 1sing indic aor act | **1156.2** conj | **2504.1** conj | **5292.2** noun gen sing fem | **2978.20** verb gen sing fem part pres act |
|---|---|---|---|---|
| **7.** ἤκουσα | δὲ | [a☆+ καὶ ] | φωνῆς | λεγούσης |
| *ēkousa* | *de* | *kai* | *phōnēs* | *legousēs* |
| I heard | and | [ idem ] | a voice | saying |

| **1466.4** prs-pron dat 1sing | **448.9** verb nom sing masc part aor act | **3935.5** name voc masc | **2357.6** verb 2sing impr aor act | **2504.1** conj | **2052.22** verb 2sing impr aor act |
|---|---|---|---|---|---|
| μοι, | Ἀναστάς, | Πέτρε, | θῦσον | καὶ | φάγε. |
| *moi* | *Anastas* | *Petre* | *thuson* | *kai* | *phage* |
| to me, | Having risen up, | Peter, | sacrifice | and | eat. |

8.a.**Txt:** 020L,025P,byz. **Var:** 01ℵ,02A,03B,05D 08E,sa.Gries,Lach,Treg Alf,Word,Tisc,We/Ho Weis,Sod,UBS/☆

| **1500.3** verb indic aor act | **1156.2** conj | **3233.1** adv | **2935.5** noun voc sing masc | **3617.1** conj | **3820.17** adj sing neu |
|---|---|---|---|---|---|
| **8.** εἶπον | δέ, | Μηδαμῶς, | κύριε, | ὅτι | ⸂a πᾶν ⸃ |
| *eipon* | *de* | *Mēdamōs* | *kurie* | *hoti* | *pan* |
| I said, | but | Surely not, | Lord, | for | anything |

| **2812.1** adj sing | **2211.1** conj | **167.1** adj sing | **3626.1** adv | **1511.3** verb 3sing indic aor act | **1519.1** prep |
|---|---|---|---|---|---|
| κοινὸν | ἢ | ἀκάθαρτον | οὐδέποτε | εἰσῆλθεν | εἰς |
| *koinon* | *ē* | *akatharton* | *oudepote* | *eisēlthen* | *eis* |
| common | or | unclean | never | entered | into |

9.a.**Txt:** 08E,020L,025P 044,33,byz. **Var:** p45,p74,01ℵ,02A 03B,sa.bo.Lach,Treg,Alf Tisc,We/Ho,Weis,Sod UBS/☆

| **3450.16** art sing neu | **4601.1** noun sing neu | **1466.2** prs-pron gen 1sing | **552.6** verb 3sing indic aor pass | **1156.2** conj | **1466.4** prs-pron dat 1sing |
|---|---|---|---|---|---|
| τὸ | στόμα | μου. | **9.** ἀπεκρίθη | δὲ | ⸂a μοι ⸃ |
| *to* | *stoma* | *mou* | *apekrithē* | *de* | *moi* |
| the | mouth | my. | Having answered | but | me |

| **5292.1** noun nom sing fem | **1523.2** prep gen | **1202.1** num ord gen sing | **1523.2** prep gen | **1202.1** num ord gen sing | **5292.1** noun nom sing fem | **1523.2** prep gen |
|---|---|---|---|---|---|---|
| ⸉ φωνὴ | ἐκ | δευτέρου | [ ἐκ | δευτέρου | φωνὴ ] | ἐκ |
| *phōnē* | *ek* | *deuterou* | *ek* | *deuterou* | *phōnē* | *ek* |
| a voice | of | second time | [ of | second time | a voice ] | out |

| **3450.2** art gen sing | **3636.2** noun gen sing masc | **3614.17** rel-pron pl neu | **3450.5** art nom sing masc | **2296.1** noun nom sing masc | **2483.4** verb 3sing indic aor act |
|---|---|---|---|---|---|
| τοῦ | οὐρανοῦ, | Ἃ | ὁ | θεὸς | ἐκαθάρισεν, |
| *tou* | *ouranou* | *Ha* | *ho* | *theos* | *ekatharisen* |
| of the | heaven, | What | | God | cleansed, |

| **4622.1** prs-pron nom 2sing | **3231.1** partic | **2813.2** verb 2sing impr pres act | **3642.17** dem-pron sing neu | **1156.2** conj | **1090.33** verb 3sing indic aor mid |
|---|---|---|---|---|---|
| σὺ | μὴ | κοίνου. | **10.** τοῦτο | δὲ | ἐγένετο |
| *su* | *mē* | *koinou* | *touto* | *de* | *egeneto* |
| you | not | make common. | This | and | took place |

and inspecting the contents without any possibility of being mistaken. What he had observed so carefully and contemplated were quadrupeds of the earth, wild animals, reptiles (specially snakes), and birds of the air. As before, the implication is that none of these were domestic animals or clean animals the Law allowed to be used for food or sacrifice. Some of them, it is also implied, were dangerous animals. It was not something any of these believers or any ordinary Jew would like to confront.

**11:7.** Peter then told how he heard a voice telling him to get up (implying going into action), kill, and eat. This was not a mere suggestion. The words were imperative commands, commands given with his name attached. There was no way he could avoid them or shift the responsibility to someone else. The commands left him no alternative.

**11:8.** Then Peter told of his refusal to obey, using in his reply a strong word meaning "certainly not!" or, as modern language might put it, he gave the Lord a flat "No!" Never would he do such a thing, for nothing common (profane, unsanctified, dirty) or unclean (ceremonially unclean, nonkosher) had ever entered his mouth. Peter wanted these Jerusalem saints to know he had reacted as strongly as any of them would have.

**11:9.** The same voice came to Peter again and gave him the answer that what God had cleansed he was not to call common or unclean.

Most of the commands in the Old Testament that have reference to cleansing are commands for the people to cleanse various things or to cleanse themselves. But David in Psalm 19:12 cried to God to cleanse him from secret faults (things hidden from him, things David was not conscious of). God also prophesied in Joel 3:20,21 concerning Judah and Jerusalem that He would cleanse their blood that He had not (previously) cleansed. But none of this applied to Gentiles. The idea that God would cleanse Gentiles without making them Jews had not occurred to these Jewish believers.

They did know that Gentiles could be saved and enjoy the blessings of God. All through the Old Testament the door was always open. Moses invited his brother-in-law, a Gentile (a Midianite) to come with Israel, indicating he could share the good things God had promised for Israel if he would become one of them (Numbers 10:29). Rahab the Canaanitess, and Ruth the Moabitess, also put their faith in God, and each found an important place in Israel and even became ancestresses of David and of Christ. But all these Gentiles became Jews in their faith.

**6. Upon the which when I had fastened mine eyes:** . . . into which steadfastly looking, *Rotherham* . . . Looking closely at it, *TCNT* . . . On which looking intently, *ABUV* . . . I examined it carefully, *Montgomery.*

**I considered, and saw:** I began to observe, and saw, *Rotherham* . . . I examined it closely, and saw, *Weymouth* . . . and when I looked at it closely, *Phillips* . . . considered it attentively, *Wuest* . . . Looking in, I fixed my eyes, *KJII* . . . I saw there were in it, *Lamsa.*

**fourfooted beasts of the earth, and wild beasts, and creeping things, and fowls of the air:** . . . all sorts of, *BB* . . . quadrupeds, wild beasts, reptiles, and birds, *TCNT* . . . animals and beasts of prey, *RSV* . . . and the wild birds, *Moffatt* . . . of the sky, *KJII.*

**7. And I heard a voice saying unto me:** And I heard also a voice, *ASV.*

**Arise, Peter; slay and eat:** Simon, arise, *Lamsa* . . . Get up, Peter! Kill something and eat it! *Goodspeed* . . . sacrifice and eat! *Fenton* . . . take them for food, *BB.*

**8. But I said, Not so, Lord:** On no account, Lord, I replied, *Weymouth* . . . It cannot be, Lord, *Knox* . . . By no means, Sir, *Fenton* . . . Never, Sir! *Goodspeed* . . . No, Lord, *KJII.*

**for nothing common or unclean hath at any time entered into my mouth:** . . . because that which is unhallowed or unclean, never yet did it enter my mouth, *Wuest* . . . I have never eaten anything that is unholy, *Everyday* . . . for never has anything defiled, *Lamsa* . . . nothing that was not ceremonially cleansed, *Goodspeed* . . . has ever passed my lips, *Phillips.*

**9. But the voice answered me again from heaven, What God hath cleansed, that call not thou common:** And a second utterance came from, *Knox* . . . spoke a second time, *Phillips* . . . the voice from heaven answered again, *Everyday* . . . hath purified, *LivB* . . . has made clean do not you make, *Williams C.K.* . . . you do not make common, *KJII* . . . do not call unclean, *Lamsa.*

## Acts 11:11

| 1894.3 prep | 4994.1 adv | 2504.1 conj | 3687.1 adv | 383.2 verb 3sing indic aor pass | 383.2 verb 3sing indic aor pass |
|---|---|---|---|---|---|
| ἐπὶ | τρίς, | καὶ | ˊ πάλιν | ἀνεσπάσθη | [☆ ἀνεσπάσθη |
| *epi* | *tris* | *kai* | *palin* | *anespasthē* | *anespasthē* |
| upon | three | and | again | was drawn up | [was drawn up |

| 3687.1 adv | 533.1 adj | 1519.1 prep | 3450.6 art acc sing masc | 3636.4 noun acc sing masc | 2504.1 conj |
|---|---|---|---|---|---|
| πάλιν ] | ἅπαντα | εἰς | τὸν | οὐρανόν. | **11.** καὶ |
| *palin* | *hapanta* | *eis* | *ton* | *ouranon* | *kai* |
| again] | all | into | the | heaven. | And |

| 1481.20 verb 2sing impr aor mid | 1808.1 adv | 4980.1 num card nom | 433.6 noun nom pl masc | 2168.2 verb 3pl indic aor act |
|---|---|---|---|---|
| ἰδοὺ, | ἐξαυτῆς | τρεῖς | ἄνδρες | ἐπέστησαν |
| *idou* | *exautēs* | *treis* | *andres* | *epestēsan* |
| behold, | at once | three | men | stood |

| 1894.3 prep | 3450.12 art acc sing fem | 3477.4 noun acc sing fem | 1706.1 prep | 3614.11 rel-pron dat sing fem | 1498.46 verb 1sing indic imperf mid |
|---|---|---|---|---|---|
| ἐπὶ | τὴν | οἰκίαν | ἐν | ᾗ | ˊ ἤμην, |
| *epi* | *tēn* | *oikian* | *en* | *hē* | *ēmēn* |
| at | the | house | in | which | I was, |

11.a.**Txt:** p45,08E,020L 025P,044,33,byz.sa.bo. Sod
**Var:** p74,01ℵ,02A,03B 05D,Lach,Treg,Tisc We/Ho,Weis,UBS/☆

| 1498.36 verb 1pl indic imperf act | 643.30 verb nom pl masc part perf mid | 570.3 prep | 2513.1 name gen fem | 4242.1 prep |
|---|---|---|---|---|
| [a ἦμεν, ] | ἀπεσταλμένοι | ἀπὸ | Καισαρείας | πρός |
| *ēmen* | *apestalmenoi* | *apo* | *Kaisareias* | *pros* |
| [we were, ] | having been sent | from | Caesarea | to |

| 1466.6 prs-pron acc 1sing | 1500.5 verb 3sing indic aor act | 1156.2 conj | 1466.4 prs-pron dat 1sing | 3450.16 art sing neu | 4011.1 noun sing neu |
|---|---|---|---|---|---|
| με. | **12.** εἶπεν | δὲ | ˊ μοι | τὸ | πνεῦμά, |
| *me* | *eipen* | *de* | *moi* | *to* | *pneuma* |
| me. | Said | and | to me | the | Spirit, |

| 3450.16 art sing neu | 4011.1 noun sing neu | 1466.4 prs-pron dat 1sing | 4755.10 verb inf aor act | 840.2 prs-pron dat pl | 3235.6 num card neu |
|---|---|---|---|---|---|
| [☆ τὸ | πνεῦμά | μοι ] | συνελθεῖν | αὐτοῖς, | μηδὲν |
| *to* | *pneuma* | *moi* | *sunelthein* | *autois* | *mēden* |
| [the | Spirit | to me] | to go with | them, | nothing |

12.a.**Txt:** 020L,025P,byz.
**Var:** 01ℵ-corr,02A,03B 33,Lach,Treg,Tisc We/Ho,Weis,Sod UBS/☆

| 1246.9 verb acc sing masc part pres mid | 1246.16 verb part pres mid | 2048.1 verb indic aor act | 1156.2 conj | 4713.1 prep |
|---|---|---|---|---|
| ˊ διακρινόμενον· | [a☆ διακρίναντα. ] | ἦλθον | δὲ | σὺν |
| *diakrinomenon* | *diakrinanta* | *ēlthon* | *de* | *sun* |
| doubting. | [idem] | Went | and | with |

| 1466.5 prs-pron dat 1sing | 2504.1 conj | 3450.7 art nom pl masc | 1787.1 num card | 79.6 noun nom pl masc | 3642.7 dem-pron nom pl masc | 2504.1 conj |
|---|---|---|---|---|---|---|
| ἐμοὶ | καὶ | οἱ | ἕξ | ἀδελφοὶ | οὗτοι, | καὶ |
| *emoi* | *kai* | *hoi* | *hex* | *adelphoi* | *houtoi* | *kai* |
| me | also | the | six | brothers | these, | and |

| 1511.4 verb 1pl indic aor act | 1519.1 prep | 3450.6 art acc sing masc | 3486.4 noun acc sing masc | 3450.2 art gen sing | 433.2 noun gen sing masc |
|---|---|---|---|---|---|
| εἰσήλθομεν | εἰς | τὸν | οἶκον | τοῦ | ἀνδρός. |
| *eisēlthomen* | *eis* | *ton* | *oikon* | *tou* | *andros* |
| we entered | into | the | house | of the | man, |

13.a.**Txt:** 08E,020L 025P,byz.
**Var:** 01ℵ,02A,03B,05D 33,bo.Lach,Treg,Tisc We/Ho,Weis,Sod UBS/☆

| 514.7 verb 3sing indic aor act | 4885.1 conj | 1156.2 conj | 2231.3 prs-pron dat 1pl | 4316.1 adv | 1481.3 verb 3sing indic aor act |
|---|---|---|---|---|---|
| **13.** ἀπήγγειλεν | ˊ τε | [a☆ δὲ ] | ἡμῖν | πῶς | εἶδεν |
| *apēngeilen* | *te* | *de* | *hēmin* | *pōs* | *eiden* |
| he related | and | [idem] | to us | how | he saw |

**11:10.** Peter told his listeners the vision was repeated three times so they would know he had not been carried away by a vision or interpretation that could have been his own imagination. The threefold repetition shows that the vision was not to be ignored. Peter had not arbitrarily changed his mind about the Gentiles. God had changed it for him. God had also made it clear that He was able to cleanse Gentiles. These wild animals and birds still looked outwardly like the same animals and birds they were. But God had cleansed them. So these Gentiles still dressed as Romans and ate the same nonkosher food they were in the habit of eating. But God was not only able to cleanse them, He had done so.

**11:11.** Peter next told how God had not left him in doubt about the interpretation of the vision. To his surprise, immediately three men were standing by the house where Peter was (or, approaching the house), men sent from Caesarea to Peter (sent with a message, sent with a purpose or a commission). The choice of the verb for "sent" is significant here. It is the same verb used of God's sending Jesus and of Jesus' sending out the apostles. They did not just happen to be there. They were there because of God's divine purpose and because of God's perfect timing.

**11:12.** The Holy Spirit then told Peter to go along with these men, that is, they were to go together. Peter was not to go alone, he was not to follow them at a distance, but he was to accompany them, giving them his fellowship as they traveled along. Again, he was to go with them without doubting, without wavering, without hesitation, without being at odds with himself. The Greek may also indicate he was not to take issue or dispute with them, neither was he to pass judgment on them, or separate himself from them as if he were superior in any way. He was to go along simply as a humble servant of the Lord, identifying with them.

Peter was also careful to refer to the six brethren (that is, believers) whom he took along as witnesses and who went in with him when he came to the house of this (uncircumcised) man.

Peter did not tell anything about who Cornelius was or his high position as an officer in the Roman army. He said nothing about all of Cornelius' good works and charitable deeds. He drew no attention to his good reputation or the way he was highly regarded all through the land by the Jews. In fact, he did not even mention the name of Cornelius. Peter knew that none of this would outweigh the fact that Cornelius was uncircumcised, a Gentile, an alien excluded from the commonwealth (citizenship) of Israel. He was a foreigner separated from the covenants of promise, and in their eyes outside of Christ, without hope unless he became a Jew, and therefore without God in the world. (See Ephesians 2:12.)

**11:13.** As a further proof of God's leading, Peter told how Cornelius reported to Peter and the six witnesses that he had seen an

**10. And this was done three times:** This happened, in all, three times, *TCNT* . . . This occurred, *Fenton.*

**and all were drawn up again into heaven:** . . . when everything was drawn up again into the sky, *TCNT* . . . Then the whole thing was taken back, *Everyday* . . . then everything was lifted up into heaven, *Lamsa* . . . it was all drawn back again into the sky, *Goodspeed.*

**11. And, behold, immediately there were three men already come unto the house where I was, sent from Caesarea unto me:** The extraordinary thing is...sent to me personally, *Phillips* . . . And at that minute, *BB* . . . just at that moment, *Goodspeed* . . . And in that very hour...sent to me by Cornelius from Caesarea, *Lamsa* . . . And at that very moment, *Williams C.K.* . . . three men stood before the house in which we were, having been sent, *ASV* . . . three men, who had been sent from Caesarea to find me, *Goodspeed* . . . appeared at the door, *Knox* . . . approached the house where we were, *Fenton* . . . stood at the house...having been sent, *KJII.*

**12. And the spirit bade me go with them:** The Spirit told me to go with them, *TCNT* . . . then instructed me, *Fenton* . . . gave me orders to go, *BB* . . . said for me to go, *KJII* . . . to accompany them, *Kleist.*

**nothing doubting:** . . . making no distinction, *RSV* . . . without hesitation, *TCNT, Williams C.K.* . . . without the least hesitation, *Fenton* . . . without any misgivings, *Weymouth* . . . without any scruple, *Campbell* . . . doubting nothing, *Lamsa.*

**Moreover these six brethren accompanied me:** . . . these six brethren who are now present, *Weymouth* . . . These...brothers here, *Goodspeed* . . . six of these brothers went with me, *KJII.*

**and we entered into the man's house:** . . . and together we entered, *Knox* . . . the house of the man, *KJII.*

**13. And he shewed us how he had seen an angel in his house, which stood and said unto him:** . . . and he related to us, *Lamsa,*

| 3450.6 art acc sing masc | 32.4 noun acc sing masc | 1706.1 prep | 3450.3 art dat sing | 3486.3 noun dat sing masc | 840.3 prs-pron gen sing |
|---|---|---|---|---|---|
| τὸν | ἄγγελον | ἐν | τῷ | οἴκῳ | αὐτοῦ |
| *ton* | *angelon* | *en* | *tō* | *oikō* | *autou* |
| the | angel | in | the | house | his |

13.b.**Txt:** 05D,08E,020L 025P,byz.sa.Sod
**Var:** 01ℵ,02A,03B,bo. Lach,Treg,Tisc,We/Ho Weis,UBS/☆

| 2449.44 verb acc sing masc part aor pass | 2504.1 conj | 1500.18 verb acc sing masc part aor act | 840.4 prs-pron dat sing | 643.11 verb 2sing impr aor act |
|---|---|---|---|---|
| σταθέντα | καὶ | εἰπόντα | (b αὐτῷ, ) | Ἀπόστειλον |
| *stathenta* | *kai* | *eiponta* | *autō* | *Aposteilon* |
| having stood | and | having said | to him, | Send |

13.c.**Txt:** 08E,020L,025P byz.
**Var:** 01ℵ,02A,03B,05D sa.bo.Gries,Lach,Treg Alf,Word,Tisc,We/Ho Weis,Sod,UBS/☆

| 1519.1 prep | 2421.3 name acc fem | 433.9 noun acc pl masc | 2504.1 conj | 3213.5 verb 2sing impr aor mid | 4468.4 name acc masc |
|---|---|---|---|---|---|
| εἰς | Ἰόππην | (c ἄνδρας, ) | καὶ | μετάπεμψαι | Σίμωνα |
| *eis* | *Ioppēn* | *andras* | *kai* | *metapempsai* | *Simōna* |
| to | Joppa | men, | and | send for | Simon |

| 3450.6 art acc sing masc | 1926.6 verb acc sing masc part pres mid | 3935.4 name acc masc | 3614.5 rel-pron nom sing masc | 2953.40 verb 3sing indic fut act |
|---|---|---|---|---|
| τὸν | ἐπικαλούμενον | Πέτρον, | **14.** ὃς | λαλήσει |
| *ton* | *epikaloumenon* | *Petron* | *hos* | *lalēsei* |
| the | being called | Peter, | who | shall speak |

| 4343.4 noun pl neu | 4242.1 prep | 4622.4 prs-pron acc 2sing | 1706.1 prep | 3614.4 rel-pron dat pl | 4834.32 verb 2sing indic fut pass | 4622.1 prs-pron nom 2sing |
|---|---|---|---|---|---|---|
| ῥήματα | πρὸς | σὲ | ἐν | οἷς | σωθήσῃ | σὺ |
| *rhēmata* | *pros* | *se* | *en* | *hois* | *sōthēsē* | *su* |
| words | to | you | by | which | shall be saved | you |

| 2504.1 conj | 3820.6 adj nom sing masc | 3450.5 art nom sing masc | 3486.1 noun nom sing masc | 4622.2 prs-pron gen 2sing | 1706.1 prep | 1156.2 conj |
|---|---|---|---|---|---|---|
| καὶ | πᾶς | ὁ | οἶκός | σου. | **15.** ἐν | δὲ |
| *kai* | *pas* | *ho* | *oikos* | *sou* | *en* | *de* |
| and | all | the | house | your. | In | and |

| 3450.3 art dat sing | 751.14 verb inf aor mid | 1466.6 prs-pron acc 1sing | 2953.24 verb inf pres act | 1953.2 verb 3sing indic aor act | 3450.16 art sing neu |
|---|---|---|---|---|---|
| τῷ | ἄρξασθαί | με | λαλεῖν | ἐπέπεσεν | τὸ |
| *tō* | *arxasthai* | *me* | *lalein* | *epepesen* | *to* |
| the | to begin | me | to speak | fell | the |

| 4011.1 noun sing neu | 3450.16 art sing neu | 39.1 adj sing | 1894.2 prep | 840.8 prs-pron acc pl masc | 5450.1 conj | 2504.1 conj |
|---|---|---|---|---|---|---|
| πνεῦμα | τὸ | ἅγιον | ἐπ' | αὐτούς, | ὥσπερ | καὶ |
| *pneuma* | *to* | *hagion* | *ep'* | *autous* | *hōsper* | *kai* |
| Spirit | the | Holy | upon | them, | even as | also |

| 1894.1 prep | 2231.4 prs-pron acc 1pl | 1706.1 prep | 741.3 noun dat sing fem | 3279.1 verb 1sing indic aor pass | 1156.2 conj |
|---|---|---|---|---|---|
| ἐφ' | ἡμᾶς | ἐν | ἀρχῇ. | **16.** ἐμνήσθην | δὲ |
| *eph'* | *hēmas* | *en* | *archē* | *emnēsthēn* | *de* |
| upon | us | in | beginning. | I remembered | and |

16.a.**Var:** 01ℵ,02A,03B 05D,08E,Gries,Lach Treg,Alf,Word,Tisc We/Ho,Weis,Sod UBS/☆

| 3450.2 art gen sing | 4343.2 noun gen sing neu | 3450.2 art gen sing | 2935.2 noun gen sing masc | 5453.1 conj | 2978.26 verb 3sing indic imperf act |
|---|---|---|---|---|---|
| τοῦ | ῥήματος | [a☆+ τοῦ ] | κυρίου, | ὡς | ἔλεγεν, |
| *tou* | *rhēmatos* | *tou* | *kuriou* | *hōs* | *elegen* |
| the | word | [ the ] | of Lord, | how | was saying, |

| 2464.1 name nom masc | 3173.1 conj | 901.8 verb 3sing indic aor act | 5045.3 noun dat sing neu | 5050.1 prs-pron nom 2pl | 1156.2 conj |
|---|---|---|---|---|---|
| Ἰωάννης | μὲν | ἐβάπτισεν | ὕδατι, | ὑμεῖς | δὲ |
| *Iōannēs* | *men* | *ebaptisen* | *hudati* | *humeis* | *de* |
| John | indeed | baptized | with water, | you | but |

angel in his house who appeared and took his stand firmly so that there could be no question about the objective reality of his presence there. The call to send for Peter thus came from an angelic messenger from heaven, a messenger from God, who gave specific directions. Cornelius did not get the idea to send for Peter from his own reasoning or imagination.

*Rotherham* . . . Then he described to us, *Weymouth* . . . he gave us an account of how, *BB* . . . he saw the angel standing in his house, *KJII.*

**Send men to Joppa, and call for Simon, whose surname is Peter:** Send to the city of Joppa and bring, *Lamsa* . . . and bring, *MLNT* . . . and bid Simon, *Knox* . . . and fetch, *Fenton* . . . whose last name is, *KJII.*

**11:14.** The angel further stated that Peter would speak words (Greek, *rhēmata*) to Cornelius by which Cornelius and all his house would be saved. "House" here means household and normally included the family plus the extended family and the servants or slaves. Peter gave further details which show the angel encouraged Cornelius to bring in his family and friends to hear Peter, for his words were to be the means by which the entire household would be saved.

The expression "words whereby thou and all thy house shall be saved" shows the gospel, the good news about Jesus Christ and His atoning work, is the only message whereby men must be saved (cf. 4:12). This message must never be changed or corrupted (cf. Galatians 1:6-9). It is now the written Word of God.

**14. Who shall tell thee words, whereby thou and all thy house shall be saved:** He will teach you truths by which you and all your household will be saved, *Weymouth* . . . will speak words to you, *KJII* . . . he shall speak to you words by which you and all of your household, *Lamsa* . . . He will tell you how you can be saved; yes, you and your whole household, *Norlie* . . . who will explain to you the means by which you, as well as all your family may be saved! *Fenton* . . . The things he will say will save you, *Everyday.*

**11:15.** Peter knew he could have gone on for hours explaining the gospel and telling more about Jesus. So he told the Jerusalem believers that it was at the beginning of his speaking that the Holy Spirit fell on Cornelius and his household.

Actually, these believers in Jerusalem did not need to hear a summary of Peter's sermon, for they knew the facts of the gospel very well. Nor did Peter want to draw attention to what he preached or how well he preached. The thing that counted, the thing that was important, was what the Holy Spirit did. The fact that the Holy Spirit fell on Cornelius and the other Gentiles gathered in his home was enough to let the Jerusalem believers know that these Gentiles had heard and believed the gospel and that their faith was in Jesus.

By the words "the beginning" Peter meant the Day of Pentecost when the Holy Spirit was first given. Now the Spirit had been poured out upon the Gentile believers just as He was on Jewish believers. This was important not only as a personal experience for Cornelius and his friends, but it also served as a manifestation and divine testimony that the whole New Testament Church, Gentiles as well as Jews, were baptized by one Spirit into one Body. (Cf. 1 Corinthians 12:12f.)

**15. And as I began to speak:** I had just begun to speak, *TCNT* . . . No sooner had I begun to speak than, *Weymouth* . . . But in the beginning of my speech, *Berkeley* . . . at the beginning of my message, *MLNT* . . . when I had set about speaking to them, *Knox* . . . When I began my speech, *Everyday* . . . While I was beginning to tell them, *Phillips.*

**the Holy Ghost fell on them, as on us at the beginning:** . . . descended upon them, *Kleist* . . . just as He fell upon us at the first, *Weymouth* . . . in the same way as upon us, *Fenton* . . . fell on them, exactly as it did on us, *TCNT* . . . even as on us, *KJII* . . . as He originally came on us, *Beck* . . . on them as also on us, *Sawyer* . . . just as upon us also originally, *Rotherham.*

**11:16.** Peter next added something that had gone on in his own mind. He remembered the word of the Lord (Jesus) given in 1:5, that John baptized in water but they would be baptized in the Holy Spirit. ("In water" and "in the Holy Spirit" are the proper translations here.)

**16. Then remembered I the word of the Lord, how that he said:** Then I remembered the Lord's words, *Weymouth* . . . Then I was reminded of what, *Knox* . . . the declaration of, *Fenton* . . . the saying of the Lord, *Goodspeed, Moffatt* . . . came into my mind, *BB* . . . so I was mindful of the Lord's message, *MLNT* . . . the words of our Lord, *Phillips.*

| 901.27 verb 2pl indic fut pass | 1706.1 prep | 4011.3 noun dat sing neu | 39.3 adj dat sing | 1479.1 conj | 3631.1 partic |
|---|---|---|---|---|---|
| βαπτισθήσεσθε | ἐν | πνεύματι | ἁγίῳ. | **17.** Εἰ | οὖν |
| *baptisthēsesthe* | *en* | *pneumati* | *hagiō* | *Ei* | *oun* |
| shall be baptized | with | Spirit | Holy. | If | then |

| 3450.12 art acc sing fem | 2443.4 adj acc sing fem | 1424.4 noun acc sing fem | 1319.14 verb 3sing indic aor act | 840.2 prs-pron dat pl | 3450.5 art nom sing masc |
|---|---|---|---|---|---|
| τὴν | ἴσην | δωρεὰν | ἔδωκεν | αὐτοῖς | ὁ |
| *tēn* | *isēn* | *dōrean* | *edōken* | *autois* | *ho* |
| the | equal | gift | gave | to them | |

| 2296.1 noun nom sing masc | 5453.1 conj | 2504.1 conj | 2231.3 prs-pron dat 1pl | 3961.33 verb dat pl masc part aor act | 1894.3 prep |
|---|---|---|---|---|---|
| θεὸς | ὡς | καὶ | ἡμῖν, | πιστεύσασιν | ἐπὶ |
| *theos* | *hōs* | *kai* | *hēmin* | *pisteusasin* | *epi* |
| God | as | also | to us, | having believed | on |

17.a.**Txt:** 08E,020L 025P,byz.sa.
**Var:** 01ℵ,02A,03B,05D bo.Lach,Treg,Tisc We/Ho,Weis,Sod UBS/☆

| 3450.6 art acc sing masc | 2935.4 noun acc sing masc | 2400.3 name acc masc | 5382.4 name acc masc | 1466.1 prs-pron nom 1sing | 1156.2 conj |
|---|---|---|---|---|---|
| τὸν | κύριον | Ἰησοῦν | Χριστόν, | ἐγὼ | ⸂a δὲ ⸃ |
| *ton* | *kurion* | *Iēsoun* | *Christon* | *egō* | *de* |
| the | Lord | Jesus | Christ, | I | and, |

| 4949.3 intr-pron nom sing | 1498.46 verb 1sing indic imperf mid | 1409.1 adj nom sing masc | 2940.10 verb inf aor act | 3450.6 art acc sing masc |
|---|---|---|---|---|
| τίς | ἤμην | δυνατὸς | κωλῦσαι | τὸν |
| *tis* | *ēmēn* | *dunatos* | *kōlusai* | *ton* |
| who | was I, | able | to hinder | |

| 2296.4 noun acc sing masc | 189.32 verb nom pl masc part aor act | 1156.2 conj | 3642.18 dem-pron pl neu | 2248.3 verb 3pl indic aor act |
|---|---|---|---|---|
| θεόν; | **18.** Ἀκούσαντες | δὲ | ταῦτα | ἡσύχασαν, |
| *theon* | *Akousantes* | *de* | *tauta* | *hēsuchasan* |
| God? | Having heard | and | these things | they were silent, |

18.a.**Txt:** 02A,08E,020L 025P,byz.Weis
**Var:** 01ℵ,03B,05D-corr sa.bo.Lach,Treg,Tisc We/Ho,Sod,UBS/☆

| 2504.1 conj | 1386.18 verb 3pl indic imperf act | 1386.10 verb 3pl indic aor act | 3450.6 art acc sing masc | 2296.4 noun acc sing masc |
|---|---|---|---|---|
| καὶ | ⸀ ἐδόξαζον | [a☆ ἐδόξασαν ] | τὸν | θεὸν, |
| *kai* | *edoxazon* | *edoxasan* | *ton* | *theon* |
| and | were glorifying | [ glorified ] | | God, |

18.b.**Txt:** 08E,020L 025P,byz.
**Var:** 01ℵ,02A,03B,05D Lach,Treg,Tisc,We/Ho Weis,Sod,UBS/☆

| 2978.16 verb nom pl masc part pres act | 682.1 partic | 679.1 partic | 2504.1 conj | 3450.4 art dat pl | 1477.6 noun dat pl neu |
|---|---|---|---|---|---|
| λέγοντες, | ⸀ Ἄραγε | [b☆ Ἄρα ] | καὶ | τοῖς | ἔθνεσιν |
| *legontes* | *Arage* | *Ara* | *kai* | *tois* | *ethnesin* |
| saying, | Then | [ indeed ] | also | to the | Gentiles |

| 3450.5 art nom sing masc | 2296.1 noun nom sing masc | 3450.12 art acc sing fem | 3211.2 noun acc sing fem | 1319.14 verb 3sing indic aor act | 1519.1 prep |
|---|---|---|---|---|---|
| ὁ | θεὸς | τὴν | μετάνοιαν | ⸀ ἔδωκεν | εἰς |
| *ho* | *theos* | *tēn* | *metanoian* | *edōken* | *eis* |
| | God | the | repentance | gave | unto |

| 2205.4 noun acc sing fem | 1519.1 prep | 2205.4 noun acc sing fem | 1319.14 verb 3sing indic aor act | 3450.7 art nom pl masc | 3173.1 conj |
|---|---|---|---|---|---|
| ζωήν. | [☆ εἰς | ζωὴν | ἔδωκεν. ] | **19.** Οἱ | μὲν |
| *zōēn* | *eis* | *zōēn* | *edōken* | *Hoi* | *men* |
| life. | [ unto | life | gave. ] | The | |

| 3631.1 partic | 1283.2 verb nom pl masc part aor pass | 570.3 prep | 3450.10 art gen sing fem | 2324.2 noun gen sing fem |
|---|---|---|---|---|
| οὖν | διασπαρέντες | ἀπὸ | τῆς | θλίψεως |
| *oun* | *diasparentes* | *apo* | *tēs* | *thlipseōs* |
| therefore | having been scattered | by | the | tribulation |

Peter recognized that the gift of the Spirit had been given. The new dispensation, the age of the Spirit prophesied in the Old Testament and promised by Christ, was for all people regardless of race or national origin. Peter had seen it happen to the Jews on the Day of Pentecost (chapter 2), to the Samaritans (chapter 8), and now to the Gentiles in the house of Cornelius (chapter 11).

**11:17.** Peter then went on to say that God had given these Gentiles the like gift as He had given to the Jewish believers. *Like* in the Greek means "equal" or "identical." (The masculine form of the same word is *isos,* and is found in the word *isosceles,* a triangle where two sides are equal, that is, identical.)

The barriers which had been established in the Law were now, and for all time, being broken down. In the plan of God, these "barriers" had served their purpose. Initially they were designed in order to set apart God's people from the idolatrous nations surrounding them. They were to protect Israel from the corrupting elements of heathen religions practiced by their neighbors. But now, God was doing a new thing. His Spirit was being poured out upon the Gentiles. Not even the Jewish converts who still held to a great many of their fathers' traditions (traditions that went beyond the Law and created a barrier God had never intended) doubted that God was at work here.

For Peter to refuse to accept these Gentiles to whom God had given this gift of the Spirit would have been to withstand God, and who was he—who is any man—to do that!

**11:18.** The same thing that convinced Peter convinced the believers in Jerusalem. They could not withstand God either. The facts of the the case silenced all their previous objections. They were responsive enough to the Holy Spirit and to the Word of God to glorify God and to recognize that God had given the Gentiles repentance unto life. God had accepted their repentance and given them spiritual life.

**11:19.** Though the Jerusalem apostles and believers accepted the fact that Gentiles in Caesarea were saved and had become part of the Church, it did not excite them very much. There was no rush to go out and win more Gentiles to the Lord. Even Peter continued to consider his ministry as primarily to the "circumcision" (to the Jews) and kept ministering on most occasions to Jews only (Galatians 2:7-9). Thus, Luke turned his attention at this point to a new center for the spread of the gospel, Antioch of Syria, located on the Orontes River, over 300 miles north of Jerusalem. It was a great trade center, the largest city in Asia Minor, and the capital of the Roman province of Syria.

This verse makes a connection with 8:1,4. (See also 9:31.) Up to this point the examples of what happened in the spread of the gospel were taken from Judea and Samaria. But the wave of itin-

**John indeed baptized with water; but ye shall be baptized with the Holy Ghost:** John's baptism was with water, *Knox.*

**17. Forasmuch then as God gave them the like gift as he did unto us:** If then, *RSV* . . . God had given them the very same gift, *TCNT* . . . exactly the same gift, *Moffatt* . . . gives them the equal gratuity, *Concordant* . . . the identical thing, *JB* . . . equally to them, *Sawyer.*

**who believed on the Lord Jesus Christ:** . . . after believing, *Noyes.*

**what was I, that I could withstand God?:** . . . who was I that I should be able to thwart God, *TCNT* . . . could I stop God? *Beck* . . . to obstruct God? *Campbell* . . . I could hinder God? *HBIE* . . . to stand in God's way? *JB* . . . be able to interfere, *Confraternity.*

**18. When they heard these things:** On hearing this statement, *TCNT* . . . On hearing this, *Weymouth.*

**they held their peace:** . . . they ceased to object, *TCNT* . . . they were silenced, *RSV* . . . they quieted down, *Berkeley* . . . they were satisfied, *Norlie* . . . they stopped arguing, *SEB* . . . This account satisfied them, *JB* . . . they had no further objections, *NIV.*

**and glorified God, saying:** . . . and broke out into praise of God, *TCNT* . . . and they extolled the goodness of God, *Weymouth* . . . but gave God the glory, *Williams.*

**Then hath God also to the Gentiles granted repentance unto life:** So even to the heathen...the repentance which leads to Life! *TCNT* . . . also to the non-Jewish people so that they will live, *Beck* . . . the opportunity to repent and live! *TEV* . . . resulting in life, *Wuest* . . . God gives life...through repentance! *Norlie* . . . conversion into life, *Fenton* . . . has actually allowed the Gentiles to repent and live! *Moffatt.*

**19. Now they which were scattered abroad upon the persecution that arose about Stephen:** . . . the fugitives, *Williams* . . . by reason of the tribulation that took place on account of Stephen, *Rotherham* . . . dispersed by the distress, *Fenton.*

| **3450.10** art gen sing fem | **1090.57** verb gen sing fem part aor mid | **1894.3** prep | **4587.3** name dat masc | **1324.1** verb indic aor act |
|---|---|---|---|---|
| τῆς | γενομένης | ἐπὶ | Στεφάνῳ | διῆλθον |
| *tēs* | *genomenēs* | *epi* | *Stephanō* | *diēlthon* |
| the | having happened | upon | Stephen, | passed through |

| **2175.1** conj | **5240.1** name gen fem | **2504.1** conj | **2927.1** name gen fem | **2504.1** conj | **487.1** name gen fem |
|---|---|---|---|---|---|
| ἕως | Φοινίκης | καὶ | Κύπρου | καὶ | Ἀντιοχείας, |
| *heōs* | *Phoinikēs* | *kai* | *Kuprou* | *kai* | *Antiocheias* |
| to | Phoenicia | and | Cyprus | and | Antioch, |

| **3235.2** num card dat | **2953.16** verb nom pl masc part pres act | **3450.6** art acc sing masc | **3030.4** noun acc sing masc | **1479.1** conj | **3231.1** partic |
|---|---|---|---|---|---|
| μηδενὶ | λαλοῦντες | τὸν | λόγον | εἰ | μὴ |
| *mēdeni* | *lalountes* | *ton* | *logon* | *ei* | *mē* |
| to no one | speaking | the | word | if | not |

| **3303.1** adv | **2428.4** name-adj dat pl masc | **1498.37** verb 3pl indic imperf act | **1156.2** conj | **4948.7** indef-pron nom pl masc | **1523.1** prep gen |
|---|---|---|---|---|---|
| μόνον | Ἰουδαίοις. | **20.** ἦσαν | δέ | τινες | ἐξ |
| *monon* | *Ioudaiois* | *ēsan* | *de* | *tines* | *ex* |
| only | to Jews. | Were | but | certain | of |

| **840.1** prs-pron gen pl | **433.6** noun nom pl masc | **2926.3** name-adj nom pl masc | **2504.1** conj | **2929.4** name-adj nom pl masc | **3610.2** rel-pron nom pl masc |
|---|---|---|---|---|---|
| αὐτῶν | ἄνδρες | Κύπριοι | καὶ | Κυρηναῖοι, | οἵτινες |
| *autōn* | *andres* | *Kuprioi* | *kai* | *Kurēnaioi* | *hoitines* |
| them | men | Cypriots | and | Cyrenians, | who |

20.a.**Txt:** 025P,byz.
**Var:** 01ℵ,02A,03B,05D
08E,020L,sa.bo.Gries
Lach,Treg,Alf,Word
Tisc,We/Ho,Weis,Sod
UBS/⋆

| **1511.16** verb nom pl masc part aor act | **2048.16** verb nom pl masc part aor act | **1519.1** prep | **487.3** name acc fem |
|---|---|---|---|
| ʻ εἰσελθόντες | [a⋆ ἐλθόντες ] | εἰς | Ἀντιόχειαν, |
| *eiselthontes* | *elthontes* | *eis* | *Antiocheian* |
| having entered | [ having come ] | into | Antioch, |

20.b.**Var:** 01ℵ-org,02A
03B,Lach,Treg,Alf,Tisc
We/Ho,Weis,Sod
UBS/⋆

| **2953.44** verb indic imperf act | **2504.1** conj | **4242.1** prep | **3450.8** art acc pl masc | **1661.2** name acc pl masc |
|---|---|---|---|---|
| ἐλάλουν | [b⋆+ καὶ ] | πρὸς | τοὺς | ʻ Ἑλληνιστὰς |
| *elaloun* | *kai* | *pros* | *tous* | *Hellēnistas* |
| were speaking | [ also ] | to | the | Hellenists, |

20.c.**Txt:** 03B,05D-corr
08E,020L,025P,044,byz.
We/Ho,Sod
**Var:** p74,01ℵ-corr,02A
05D-org,Gries,Lach
Treg,Alf,Tisc,Weis

| **1659.7** name acc pl masc | **2076.12** verb nom pl masc part pres mid | **3450.6** art acc sing masc | **2935.4** noun acc sing masc |
|---|---|---|---|
| [c⋆ Ἕλληνας, ] | εὐαγγελιζόμενοι | τὸν | κύριον |
| *Hellēnas* | *euangelizomenoi* | *ton* | *kurion* |
| [ Greeks, ] | announcing the good news | the | Lord |

| **2400.3** name acc masc | **2504.1** conj | **1498.34** verb sing indic imperf act | **5331.1** noun nom sing fem | **2935.2** noun gen sing masc | **3196.2** prep |
|---|---|---|---|---|---|
| Ἰησοῦν. | **21.** καὶ | ἦν | χεὶρ | κυρίου | μετ' |
| *Iēsoun* | *kai* | *ēn* | *cheir* | *kuriou* | *met'* |
| Jesus. | And | was | hand | of Lord | with |

21.a.**Var:** 01ℵ,02A,03B
Lach,Treg,Alf,Tisc
We/Ho,Weis,Sod
UBS/⋆

| **840.1** prs-pron gen pl | **4044.5** adj nom sing masc | **4885.1** conj | **700.1** noun nom sing masc | **3450.5** art nom sing masc | **3961.30** verb nom sing masc part aor act |
|---|---|---|---|---|---|
| αὐτῶν· | πολύς | τε | ἀριθμὸς | [a⋆+ ὁ ] | πιστεύσας |
| *autōn* | *polus* | *te* | *arithmos* | *ho* | *pisteusas* |
| them, | a great | and | number | [ the ] | having believed |

| **1978.4** verb 3sing indic aor act | **1894.3** prep | **3450.6** art acc sing masc | **2935.4** noun acc sing masc | **189.48** verb 3sing indic aor pass |
|---|---|---|---|---|
| ἐπέστρεψεν | ἐπὶ | τὸν | κύριον. | **22.** Ἠκούσθη |
| *epestrepsen* | *epi* | *ton* | *kurion* | *Ēkousthē* |
| turned | to | the | Lord. | Was heard |

erant evangelism did not stop there. Luke did not try to cover everything that was happening everywhere. Instead, following the inspiration of the Holy Spirit, he selected one direction this evangelism took and presented it as an example of what was going on in many different localities. There was a special reason for choosing the direction toward Antioch, however, because it formed a link with the apostle Paul and was a preparation for the account of his journeys.

Even outside of Palestine, however, those who spread the gospel preached the Word only to Jews. This may not have been entirely due to prejudice. The Jews had the Old Testament Scriptures and knew the prophecies, which was a great advantage in dealing with them (Romans 3:1,2). These traveling evangelists based their message on the fact that God, through Jesus as the Messiah, had fulfilled prophecy. Most Gentiles had no background to understand this. But these evangelists were overlooking the fact that many Gentiles had lost their confidence in their idols and were looking for something better.

The Book of Acts mentions certain evangelizers who traveled up the coast of Asia Minor as far as Phenice (Phoenicia) where churches were established in Tyre and Sidon (as 21:3,4 and 27:3 show). From there some went to the island of Cyprus and then to Antioch of Syria.

**11:20.** Some of those who went on to Antioch were men of Cyprus, an island off the coast of Asia Minor over 200 miles northwest of Jerusalem. With them were men of Cyrene, a beautiful city founded by Greek colonists in North Africa nearly 800 miles west of Jerusalem.

These men may have been among the 3,000 who were saved and filled with the Spirit on the Day of Pentecost. Now, at Antioch, they began to speak to Greek-speaking Gentiles, telling them the good news (the gospel) of the Lord Jesus.

**11:21.** When these men of Cyprus and Cyrene took the first step to tell Gentiles about Jesus, the hand of the Lord was with them. This expression, "the hand of the Lord," was used frequently in the Old Testament of the mighty manifestations of the power of God in behalf of His people. Now God was showing the same mighty hand to bring Gentiles out of the bondage of sin.

The same expression was also used in parallel to the Spirit of the Lord (as in Ezekiel 1:3; 3:14,22,24; 8:1; 11:1). It is likely therefore that the miracle-working power of the Lord was manifest, confirming the Word just as was the case with Philip in Samaria (8:5-8). As a result a great number believed and turned to the Lord. They turned away from their heathen customs and worldly ways to follow Jesus and joined the company of those whom the Bible calls saints. As Peter declared, God is not a respecter of persons, He does not show partiality but makes His good gifts available to all.

**travelled as far as Phenice, and Cyprus, and Antioch:** . . . made their way to Phoenicia, *Weymouth* . . . went all the way to, *Goodspeed* . . . even to the land of, *Lamsa* . . . traversed as far as, *Fenton.*

**preaching the word to none but unto the Jews only:** . . . telling the Message—but only to Jews, *TCNT* . . . they told the message to none but, *Goodspeed* . . . giving the message as they went, *Phillips* . . . speaking the message to nobody but, *Kleist* . . . to none except, *MLNT* . . . except to Jews only, *KJII.*

**20. And some of them were men of Cyprus and Cyrene:** But there were some of them, *Fenton* . . . However, among their number were natives of, *Phillips* . . . certain ones of them were men of, *KJII* . . . there were some men among them, *Lamsa.*

**which, when they were come to Antioch:** . . . and these men, on their arrival at, *Phillips* . . . who, on coming to Antioch, *Weymouth* . . . who on reaching Antioch, *Moffatt* . . . who arrived at, *MLNT* . . . these men entered into, *Lamsa.*

**spake unto the Grecians:** . . . proclaimed their message to, *Phillips* . . . began to speak to the Greeks too, *Williams* . . . spoke to heathen men as well, *Williams C.K.* . . . to the Gentiles also, *TNT* . . . to the Greek-speaking Jews, *KJII.*

**preaching the Lord Jesus:** . . . announcing the glad-tidings as to the Lord Jesus, *Rotherham* . . . publishing the good news of the Lord, Jesus, *ABUV* . . . and preached concerning our, *Lamsa* . . . the gospel of, *KJII* . . . good news about, *MLNT.*

**21. And the hand of the Lord was with them:** The Lord's power was with them, *TCNT, TNT* . . . The Lord's hand, *Goodspeed* . . . went with them, *Knox* . . . The Lord blessed their efforts, *Kleist.*

**and a great number believed, and turned unto the Lord:** . . . and there were a vast number who believed, *Weymouth* . . . and a great number had faith, *BB* . . . and there were a great many, *Goodspeed* . . . and very many turned to the Lord, believing, *KJII* . . . became believers, *TNT.*

| 1156.2 conj | 3450.5 art nom sing masc | 3030.1 noun nom sing masc | 1519.1 prep | 3450.17 art pl neu | 3640.2 noun pl neu | 3450.10 art gen sing fem |
|---|---|---|---|---|---|---|
| δὲ | ὁ | λόγος | εἰς | τὰ | ὦτα | τῆς |
| *de* | *ho* | *logos* | *eis* | *ta* | *ōta* | *tēs* |
| and | the | report | in | the | ears | of the |

22.a.**Var:** p74,01ℵ,03B 08E,33,Treg,Tisc We/Ho,Weis,Sod UBS/☆

| 1564.1 noun fem | 3450.10 art gen sing fem | 1498.27 verb gen sing fem part pres act | 1706.1 prep | 2389.3 name dat pl neu |
|---|---|---|---|---|
| ἐκκλησίας | τῆς | [a☆+ οὔσης ] | ἐν | ⸂ Ἱεροσολύμοις |
| *ekklēsias* | *tēs* | *ousēs* | *en* | *Hierosolumois* |
| assembly | the | [ being ] | in | Jerusalem |

22.b.**Txt:** 08E,020L 025P,byz.
**Var:** 01ℵ,02A,03B,05D Lach,Treg,Alf,Word Tisc,We/Ho,Weis,Sod UBS/☆

| 2395.2 name fem | 3875.1 prep | 840.1 prs-pron gen pl | 2504.1 conj | 1805.2 verb 3pl indic aor act |
|---|---|---|---|---|
| [b☆ Ἰερουσαλὴμ ] | περὶ | αὐτῶν· | καὶ | ἐξαπέστειλαν |
| *Ierousalēm* | *peri* | *autōn* | *kai* | *exapesteilan* |
| [ idem ] | concerning | them; | and | they sent out |

22.c.**Txt:** 05D,08E,020L 025P,044,byz.Sod
**Var:** p74,01ℵ,02A,03B 1739,bo.Lach,Treg,Tisc We/Ho,Weis,UBS/☆

| 915.4 name acc masc | 1324.8 verb inf aor act | 2175.1 conj | 487.1 name gen fem | 3614.5 rel-pron nom sing masc |
|---|---|---|---|---|
| Βαρναβᾶν | ⸂c διελθεῖν ⸃ | ἕως | Ἀντιοχείας. | 23. ὃς |
| *Barnaban* | *dielthein* | *heōs* | *Antiocheias* | *hos* |
| Barnabas | to go through | as far as | Antioch: | who |

| 3716.7 verb nom sing masc part aor mid | 2504.1 conj | 1481.16 verb nom sing masc part aor act | 3450.12 art acc sing fem | 5322.4 noun acc sing fem |
|---|---|---|---|---|
| παραγενόμενος | καὶ | ἰδὼν | τὴν | χάριν |
| *paragenomenos* | *kai* | *idōn* | *tēn* | *charin* |
| having come | and | having seen | the | grace |

23.a.**Var:** 01ℵ,02A,03B Lach,Treg,Alf,Tisc We/Ho,Weis,Sod UBS/☆

| 3450.12 art acc sing fem | 3450.2 art gen sing | 2296.2 noun gen sing masc | 5299.16 verb 3sing indic aor pass | 2504.1 conj | 3731.18 verb 3sing indic imperf act |
|---|---|---|---|---|---|
| [a☆+ τὴν ] | τοῦ | θεοῦ | ἐχάρη, | καὶ | παρεκάλει |
| *tēn* | *tou* | *theou* | *echarē* | *kai* | *parekalei* |
| [ the ] | | of God | rejoiced, | and | were exhorting |

| 3820.8 adj acc pl masc | 3450.11 art dat sing fem | 4145.3 noun dat sing fem | 3450.10 art gen sing fem | 2559.1 noun fem | 4215.3 verb inf pres act |
|---|---|---|---|---|---|
| πάντας | τῇ | προθέσει | τῆς | καρδίας | προσμένειν |
| *pantas* | *tē* | *prothesei* | *tēs* | *kardias* | *prosmenein* |
| all | the | purpose | of the | heart | to continue |

| 3450.3 art dat sing | 2935.3 noun dat sing masc | 3617.1 conj | 1498.34 verb sing indic imperf act | 433.1 noun nom sing masc | 18.6 adj nom sing masc |
|---|---|---|---|---|---|
| τῷ | κυρίῳ· | 24. ὅτι | ἦν | ἀνὴρ | ἀγαθὸς |
| *tō* | *kuriō* | *hoti* | *ēn* | *anēr* | *agathos* |
| with the | Lord; | for | he was | a man | good |

| 2504.1 conj | 3994.1 adj nom sing | 4011.2 noun gen sing neu | 39.2 adj gen sing | 2504.1 conj | 3963.2 noun gen sing fem |
|---|---|---|---|---|---|
| καὶ | πλήρης | πνεύματος | ἁγίου | καὶ | πίστεως. |
| *kai* | *plērēs* | *pneumatos* | *hagiou* | *kai* | *pisteōs* |
| and | full | of Spirit | Holy | and | of faith. |

| 2504.1 conj | 4227.6 verb 3sing indic aor pass | 3657.1 noun nom sing masc | 2401.3 adj nom sing masc | 3450.3 art dat sing | 2935.3 noun dat sing masc |
|---|---|---|---|---|---|
| καὶ | προσετέθη | ὄχλος | ἱκανὸς | τῷ | κυρίῳ. |
| *kai* | *prosetethē* | *ochlos* | *hikanos* | *tō* | *kuriō* |
| And | was added | a crowd | large | to the | Lord. |

25.a.**Txt:** 08E,020L 025P,byz.
**Var:** 01ℵ,02A,03B,sa.bo. Lach,Treg,Alf,Tisc We/Ho,Weis,Sod UBS/☆

| 1814.3 verb 3sing indic aor act | 1156.2 conj | 1519.1 prep | 4870.2 name acc fem | 3450.5 art nom sing masc | 915.1 name nom masc |
|---|---|---|---|---|---|
| 25. Ἐξῆλθεν | δὲ | εἰς | Ταρσὸν | ⸂a ὁ | Βαρνάβας ⸃ |
| *Exēlthen* | *de* | *eis* | *Tarson* | *ho* | *Barnabas* |
| Went forth | and | to | Tarsus | | Barnabas |

**11:22.** When news of the conversion of these Gentiles in Antioch reached the Jerusalem church, they recognized that this great spread of the gospel among Gentiles was an important new development. Antioch itself was significant, since it was the third most important city in the entire Roman Empire, exceeded only by Rome and Alexandria. So they sent Barnabas to go as far as Antioch (probably ministering along the way).

The choice of Barnabas is important. It shows that the Jerusalem church (not just the apostles) was concerned about this new assembly in Antioch and sent out their best encourager to help the believers.

Some writers have assumed that sending Barnabas meant the Church in Jerusalem wanted to maintain control over this new development. However, there is no evidence of this. It was brotherly love and concern, the same loving spirit that sent Peter and John to Samaria to help the people there moved the Jerusalem believers also. Barnabas did not have to report back to Jerusualem, nor did he have to seek their advice about further steps in ministry that might be necessary. (See verse 25.)

**11:23.** At Antioch the sight of the manifest grace (unmerited favor) of God made Barnabas rejoice. He accepted these Gentiles just as Peter had accepted the believers at the house of Cornelius. He then lived up to his name by exhorting (and encouraging) them all to purpose openly from their hearts to abide in (or continue with) the Lord. Barnabas knew that difficulties, persecutions, and temptations lay ahead. Persistence in a close walk with the Lord would be needed.

**11:24.** Because Barnabas was a good man and full of the Holy Spirit and faith, a considerable crowd of people were added to the Lord, that is, to the body of Christ, the Church, by entering into a personal relationship and walk with the Lord. His life, not simply his preaching and teaching, proved to be a most effective witness. No doubt his "goodness" meant he was entirely free from Pharisaic judgment. (See Luke 18:11.)

**11:25.** The growth in numbers made Barnabas realize he needed help. He did not, however, seek assistance from those in Jerusalem; he did not ask them to send someone. Instead he went to Tarsus to search for Saul. Since he was the one who took the time and effort to find out about Saul and introduce him to the apostles in Jerusalem earlier (9:27), he obviously knew what God had said about sending Saul to the Gentiles. (See 22:21.) Now it was God's time for Saul to begin this ministry. (Some suggest that Saul had been disinherited by friends and family because of his faith in Christ [cf. Philippians 3:8], and that he had already begun his work of evangelizing Gentiles in his native province of Cilicia.)

**22. Then tidings of these things came unto the ears of the church which was in Jerusalem:** And the report concerning them, *ASV* . . . The news about them reached, *TCNT* . . . When word of it came to the attention of, *Berkeley.*

**and they sent forth Barnabas, that he should go as far as Antioch:** . . . and they despatched Barnabas to Antioch, *Moffatt* . . . And they commissioned Barnabas, *Fenton.*

**23. Who, when he came, and had seen the grace of God, was glad:** On arriving he was delighted to see the grace of God, *Weymouth* . . . the favor God had shown them, he was delighted, *Goodspeed* . . . how gracious God had been to them, he rejoiced, *Norlie* . . . and saw the effects of God's grace, *Kleist* . . . he was delighted to see what God's love had done, *Beck.*

**and exhorted them all, that with purpose of heart they would cleave unto the Lord:** . . . and encouraged them all to make up their minds to be faithful to the Master, *TCNT* . . . and he encouraged them all to remain, with fixed resolve, faithful to the Lord, *Weymouth* . . . to continue to be devoted to the Lord, *Williams* . . . and he made clear to them the need of keeping near the Lord with all the strength of their hearts, *BB* . . . with a firm purpose, *Klingensmith* . . . He urged them all to be resolute, *Phillips.*

**24. For he was a good man, and full of the Holy Ghost and of faith:** . . . for he was a genial man, *Fenton* . . . a splendid man, *Berkeley.*

**and much people was added unto the Lord:** . . . and the number of believers in the Lord greatly increased, *Weymouth* . . . Considerable numbers of people were brought in for the Lord, *Moffatt* . . . So a large number of people were united to the Lord, *Williams* . . . A great multitude was won over to the Lord, *Kleist.*

**25. Then departed Barnabas to Tarsus, for to seek Saul:** Afterwards Barnabas left for Tarsus to look for Saul, *TCNT* . . . He then proceeded to Tarsus, to search for, *Fenton.*

26.a.**Txt:** 020L,025P,byz. sa.bo.
**Var:** 01ℵ,02A,03B,08E Lach,Treg,Alf,Tisc We/Ho,Weis,Sod UBS/☆

26.b.**Txt:** 08E,020L 025P,byz.sa.bo.
**Var:** 01ℵ,02A,03B,Lach Treg,Alf,Tisc,We/Ho Weis,Sod,UBS/☆

26.c.**Txt:** 020L,025P,byz.
**Var:** p74,01ℵ,02A,03B 33,Lach,Treg,Alf,Tisc We/Ho,Weis,Sod UBS/☆

| **325.1** verb inf aor act | **4425.4** name acc masc | **2504.1** conj | **2128.17** verb nom sing masc part aor act | **840.6** prs-pron acc sing masc |
|---|---|---|---|---|
| ἀναζητῆσαι | Σαῦλον, | **26.** καὶ | εὑρὼν | ⸂a αὐτὸν ⸃ |
| *anazētēsai* | *Saulon* | *kai* | *heurōn* | *auton* |
| to seek | Saul; | and | having found | him |

| **70.8** verb 3sing indic aor act | **840.6** prs-pron acc sing masc | **1519.1** prep | **487.3** name acc fem | **1090.33** verb 3sing indic aor mid |
|---|---|---|---|---|
| ἤγαγεν | ⸂b αὐτὸν ⸃ | εἰς | Ἀντιόχειαν. | ἐγένετο |
| *ēgagen* | *auton* | *eis* | *Antiocheian* | *egeneto* |
| he brought | him | to | Antioch. | It came to pass |

| **1156.2** conj | **840.8** prs-pron acc pl masc | **840.2** prs-pron dat pl | **2504.1** conj | **1747.2** noun acc sing masc | **3513.1** adj sing |
|---|---|---|---|---|---|
| δὲ | ⸀ αὐτοὺς | [c☆ αὐτοῖς | καὶ ] | ἐνιαυτὸν | ὅλον |
| *de* | *autous* | *autois* | *kai* | *eniauton* | *holon* |
| and | them | [ them | and ] | a year | whole |

| **4714.23** verb inf aor pass | **1706.1** prep | **3450.11** art dat sing fem | **1564.3** noun dat sing fem | **2504.1** conj |
|---|---|---|---|---|
| συναχθῆναι | ἐν | τῇ | ἐκκλησίᾳ, | καὶ |
| *sunachthēnai* | *en* | *tē* | *ekklēsia* | *kai* |
| to be gathered together | in | the | assembly, | and |

| **1315.18** verb inf aor act | **3657.4** noun acc sing masc | **2401.2** adj sing | **5372.2** verb inf aor act | **4885.1** conj | **4270.1** adv |
|---|---|---|---|---|---|
| διδάξαι | ὄχλον | ἱκανόν, | χρηματίσαι | τε | ⸀ πρῶτον |
| *didaxai* | *ochlon* | *hikanon* | *chrēmatisai* | *te* | *prōton* |
| to teach | a crowd | large; | to be called | and | first |

26.d.**Txt:** 02A,05D-org 08E,020L,025P,byz. Gries,Lach,Word
**Var:** 01ℵ,03B,05D-corr Treg,Alf,Tisc,We/Ho Weis,Sod,UBS/☆

| **4274.1** adv | **1706.1** prep | **487.2** name dat fem | **3450.8** art acc pl masc | **3073.8** noun acc pl masc |
|---|---|---|---|---|
| [d☆ πρώτως ] | ἐν | Ἀντιοχείᾳ | τοὺς | μαθητὰς |
| *prōtōs* | *en* | *Antiocheia* | *tous* | *mathētas* |
| [ idem ] | in | Antioch | the | disciples |

| **5381.3** name acc pl masc | **1706.1** prep | **3642.14** dem-pron dat pl fem | **1156.2** conj | **3450.14** art dat pl fem | **2232.7** noun dat pl fem |
|---|---|---|---|---|---|
| Χριστιανούς. | **27.** Ἐν | ταύταις | δὲ | ταῖς | ἡμέραις |
| *Christianous* | *En* | *tautais* | *de* | *tais* | *hēmerais* |
| Christians. | In | these | and | the | days |

| **2687.3** verb 3pl indic aor act | **570.3** prep | **2389.2** name gen pl neu | **4254.4** noun nom pl masc | **1519.1** prep |
|---|---|---|---|---|
| κατῆλθον | ἀπὸ | Ἱεροσολύμων | προφῆται | εἰς |
| *katēlthon* | *apo* | *Hierosolumōn* | *prophētai* | *eis* |
| came down | from | Jerusalem | prophets | to |

| **487.3** name acc fem | **448.9** verb nom sing masc part aor act | **1156.2** conj | **1518.3** num card nom masc | **1523.1** prep gen |
|---|---|---|---|---|
| Ἀντιόχειαν· | **28.** ἀναστὰς | δὲ | εἷς | ἐξ |
| *Antiocheian* | *anastas* | *de* | *heis* | *ex* |
| Antioch; | having risen up | and | one | from among |

28.a.**Txt:** 01ℵ,02A,08E 020L,025P,etc.byz.sa.bo. Tisc,Sod
**Var:** 03B,Lach,We/Ho Weis,UBS/☆

| **840.1** prs-pron gen pl | **3549.4** noun dat sing neu | **13.2** name nom masc | **4446.2** verb 3sing indic aor act | **4446.4** verb 3sing indic imperf act |
|---|---|---|---|---|
| αὐτῶν | ὀνόματι | Ἅγαβος, | ⸀ ἐσήμανεν | [a ἐσήμαινεν ] |
| *autōn* | *onomati* | *Hagabos* | *esēmanen* | *esēmainen* |
| them, | by name | Agabus, | he signified | [ was signifying ] |

28.b.**Txt:** 05D-org,08E 020L,025P,byz.
**Var:** 01ℵ,02A,03B 05D-corr,Lach,Treg,Alf Word,Tisc,We/Ho,Weis Sod,UBS/☆

| **1217.2** prep | **3450.2** art gen sing | **4011.2** noun gen sing neu | **3016.3** noun acc sing masc | **3144.4** adj acc sing masc | **3144.12** adj acc sing fem |
|---|---|---|---|---|---|
| διὰ | τοῦ | πνεύματος, | Λιμὸν | ⸀ μέγαν | [b☆ μεγάλην ] |
| *dia* | *tou* | *pneumatos* | *Limon* | *megan* | *megalēn* |
| by | the | Spirit, | A famine | great | [ very great ] |

**11:26.** The search for Saul probably took some time. When Barnabas found him, he brought him back to Antioch. The two of them then became the chief teachers of the Church, gathering the believers together and teaching a considerable crowd.

Obviously, these Gentile believers could not be given a Jewish name, nor could they any longer be considered a sect of the Jews. They needed a new name. Soldiers under particular generals in the Roman army often took the name of their general and added "ian" (Latin, *iani*; Greek, *ianos*) to indicate they were soldiers and followers of that general. For example, Caesar's soldiers were called *Caesariani*, and Pompey's soldiers were called *Pompeiani*. Political parties were also designated by the same sort of suffix.

So the people of Antioch began to call the believers *Christiani* or *Christians*, soldiers, followers, partisans of Christ. Some believe the name was first given in derision, but there is no great evidence of this. The believers did not reject the name. They were indeed in the Lord's army, clothed with the full armor of God. (See Ephesians 6:11-18.)

**11:27.** The various assemblies of believers in different places continued to keep in touch with each other. After Barnabas, others came from Jerusalem to help and encourage the believers in Antioch. About the time Saul's first year in Antioch was up, several prophets from Jerusalem came. These men were regularly used by the Holy Spirit in the ministry of the gift of prophecy for edification (to build up spiritually and confirm faith), exhortation (to awaken, encourage, and challenge every believer to move ahead in faithfulness and love), and comfort (to cheer, revive, and encourage faith and expectation), as in 1 Corinthians 14:3. Thus they met the spiritual needs of the believers.

**11:28.** Sometimes the Holy Spirit used these New Testament prophets to reinforce their exhortations with a foretelling of the future. This was the exception rather than the rule, however. Prophecy in the Bible is always primarily "forthtelling" (speaking for God whatever His message may be) rather than foretelling the future. God has always been more interested in helping people to walk with Him in the now than He ever is in giving all the details some would like to know about the future (though He has revealed in His Word that He has a glorious future waiting for believers).

On this occasion Agabus, one of the prophets, stood up and indicated by a word from the Spirit that a great famine was about to come over the whole world (Greek, *oikoumenēn*, "inhabited earth"). To them this meant the Roman Empire, for they used the Greek word in those days to mean the Roman world. The Romans did not think anything outside their empire was worth noticing. The famine did take place in the days of Claudius Caesar who reigned from A.D. 41–54. Two Roman historians, Tacitus and Suetonius, have recorded that during this period there were several localized famines or "dearths." This serves as further evidence that

**26. And when he had found him, he brought him unto Antioch:** . . . and when he had come across him, *BB*.

**And it came to pass, that a whole year they assembled themselves with the church:** . . . it came about that they were working together in that assembly, *Fenton* . . . they were gathered together with the church, *ASV* . . . For a whole year after this they were made welcome, *Knox* . . . where for an entire year they conducted church meetings, *Berkeley* . . . they took part in the meetings of the congregation, *Kleist*.

**and taught much people:** . . . and taught a large number of people, *TCNT* . . . and teach a considerable throng, *Concordant* . . . a great multitude, *Kleist*.

**And the disciples were called Christians first in Antioch:** . . . the disciples, too, at Antioch first called themselves, *Fenton* . . . and it was in Antioch that the disciples first got the name of 'Christians,' *TCNT* . . . the followers were called...for the first time, *Everyday* . . . are styled, *Concordant* . . . also were divinely called first, *Young* . . . called themselves, *Fenton*.

**27. And in those days came prophets from Jerusalem unto Antioch:** . . . some preachers came down, *Fenton*.

**28. And there stood up one of them named Agabus:** . . . came forward, *TCNT* . . . rising, *Concordant* . . . having stood up, *Young* . . . said publicly, *BB*.

**and signified by the Spirit that there should be great dearth throughout all the world:** . . . explained by the Spirit, *Klingensmith* . . . and spoke with the help of...A very hard time is coming, *Everyday* . . . announced, through the influence...that a severe famine would come over all the empire, *Fenton* . . . and revealed through the Spirit, *Kleist* . . . and, under the influence of the Spirit foretold, *TCNT* . . . publicly predicted by the Spirit the speedy coming of a great famine, *Weymouth* . . . under inspiration of the Spirit, *Norlie* . . . being instructed, *Montgomery* . . . there would be serious need of food all over the earth, *BB* . . . over all the inhabited earth, *HBIE*.

## Acts 11:29

28.c.**Txt:** 020L,025P,byz. **Var:** 01ℵ,02A,03B,05D 08E,Lach,Treg,Alf Word,Tisc,We/Ho,Weis Sod,UBS/⋆

28.d.**Txt:** 08E,020L 025P,byz. **Var:** 01ℵ,02A,03B,05D 33,sa.bo.Lach,Treg,Tisc We/Ho,Weis,Sod UBS/⋆

28.e.**Txt:** 08E,020L 025P,byz. **Var:** 01ℵ,02A,03B,05D sa.bo.Gries,Lach,Treg Alf,Word,Tisc,We/Ho Weis,Sod,UBS/⋆

29.a.**Txt:** 025P-corr,byz. **Var:** 01ℵ,02A,03B,05D 08E,025P-org,Lach Treg,Alf,Tisc,We/Ho Weis,Sod,UBS/⋆

| **3165.18** verb inf pres act | **1498.45** verb inf fut mid | **1894.1** prep | **3513.9** adj acc sing fem | **3450.12** art acc sing fem | **3487.4** noun acc sing fem |
|---|---|---|---|---|---|
| μέλλειν | ἔσεσθαι | ἐφ' | ὅλην | τὴν | οἰκουμένην· |
| *mellein* | *esesthai* | *eph'* | *holēn* | *tēn* | *oikoumenēn* |
| to be about | to be | over | whole | the | habitable world; |

| **3610.1** rel-pron nom sing masc | **3610.3** rel-pron nom sing fem | **2504.1** conj | **1090.33** verb 3sing indic aor mid | **1894.3** prep |
|---|---|---|---|---|
| ⸂ ὅστις | [c⋆ ἥτις ] | ⸂d καὶ ⸃ | ἐγένετο | ἐπὶ |
| *hostis* | *hētis* | *kai* | *egeneto* | *epi* |
| whichever | [ idem ] | also | came to pass | under |

| **2777.2** name gen masc | **2512.1** name gen masc | **3450.1** art gen pl | **1156.2** conj | **3073.6** noun gen pl masc |
|---|---|---|---|---|
| Κλαυδίου | ⸂e Καίσαρος. ⸃ | 29. τῶν | δὲ | μαθητῶν |
| *Klaudiou* | *Kaisaros* | *tōn* | *de* | *mathētōn* |
| Claudius | Caesar. | The | and | disciples |

| **2503.1** conj | **2121.1** verb 3sing indic imperf mid | **2121.2** verb 3sing indic imperf mid | **4948.3** indef-pron nom sing |
|---|---|---|---|
| καθὼς | ⸂ ηὐπορεῖτό | [a⋆ εὐπορεῖτό ] | τις, |
| *kathōs* | *ēuporeito* | *euporeito* | *tis* |
| according as | was prospered | [ idem ] | anyone, |

| **3587.3** verb 3pl indic aor act | **1524.3** adj nom sing masc | **840.1** prs-pron gen pl | **1519.1** prep | **1242.4** noun acc sing fem | **3854.17** verb inf aor act |
|---|---|---|---|---|---|
| ὥρισαν | ἕκαστος | αὐτῶν | εἰς | διακονίαν | πέμψαι |
| *hōrisan* | *hekastos* | *autōn* | *eis* | *diakonian* | *pempsai* |
| determined, | each | of them, | for | ministration | to send |

| **3450.4** art dat pl | **2700.8** verb dat pl masc part pres act | **1706.1** prep | **3450.11** art dat sing fem | **2424.3** name dat fem | **79.8** noun dat pl masc |
|---|---|---|---|---|---|
| τοῖς | κατοικοῦσιν | ἐν | τῇ | Ἰουδαίᾳ | ἀδελφοῖς· |
| *tois* | *katoikousin* | *en* | *tē* | *Ioudaia* | *adelphois* |
| to the | dwelling | in | | Judea | brethren; |

| **3614.16** rel-pron sing neu | **2504.1** conj | **4020.27** verb 3pl indic aor act | **643.14** verb nom pl masc part aor act | **4242.1** prep | **3450.8** art acc pl masc |
|---|---|---|---|---|---|
| 30. ὃ | καὶ | ἐποίησαν, | ἀποστείλαντες | πρὸς | τοὺς |
| *ho* | *kai* | *epoiēsan* | *aposteilantes* | *pros* | *tous* |
| which | also | they did, | having sent | to | the |

| **4104.2** adj comp acc pl masc | **1217.2** prep | **5331.2** noun gen sing fem | **915.2** name masc | **2504.1** conj | **4425.2** name gen masc |
|---|---|---|---|---|---|
| πρεσβυτέρους | διὰ | χειρὸς | Βαρναβᾶ | καὶ | Σαύλου. |
| *presbuterous* | *dia* | *cheiros* | *Barnaba* | *kai* | *Saulou* |
| elders | by | hand | of Barnabas | and | Saul. |

| **2567.1** prep | **1552.5** dem-pron acc sing masc | **1156.2** conj | **3450.6** art acc sing masc | **2511.4** noun acc sing masc | **1896.3** verb 3sing indic aor act |
|---|---|---|---|---|---|
| 12:1. Κατ' | ἐκεῖνον | δὲ | τὸν | καιρὸν | ἐπέβαλεν |
| *Kat'* | *ekeinon* | *de* | *ton* | *kairon* | *epebalen* |
| About | that | and | the | time | put forth |

| **2243.1** name nom masc | **3450.5** art nom sing masc | **928.1** noun nom sing masc | **3450.15** art acc pl fem | **5331.8** noun acc pl fem | **2530.3** verb inf aor act |
|---|---|---|---|---|---|
| Ἡρῴδης | ὁ | βασιλεὺς | τὰς | χεῖρας | κακῶσαί |
| *Hērōdēs* | *ho* | *basileus* | *tas* | *cheiras* | *kakōsai* |
| Herod | the | king | the | hands | to harm |

| **4948.9** indef-pron acc pl masc | **3450.1** art gen pl | **570.3** prep | **3450.10** art gen sing fem | **1564.1** noun fem | **335.5** verb 3sing indic aor act |
|---|---|---|---|---|---|
| τινας | τῶν | ἀπὸ | τῆς | ἐκκλησίας. | 2. ἀνεῖλεν |
| *tinas* | *tōn* | *apo* | *tēs* | *ekklēsias* | *aneilen* |
| some | of the | from | the | assembly; | he put to death |

Luke was quite a careful historian himself. Even the small details of his accounts are accurate and verifiable through secular sources. This helps to support the reliability of the Bible. (The date of the arrival of Barnabas in Antioch was about A.D. 41, so Claudius was already on the throne.)

**11:29.** It is wonderful to see the quick response of God's people to a need presented by the moving of the Spirit. Their faith was not dead. (See James 2:14-17.) Furthermore, the disciples in Antioch felt genuine gratitude for the blessings and teaching brought them from Judea.

Church history shows that Gentiles pronounced *Christiani* the same as *Chrestiani,* "followers of Chrestos," which means good, kind, lovingly benevolent, useful, and generous. But it was more than this that made the Gentiles view believers like these as good followers of the Good. They showed their love in practical ways.

They were not illogical in their giving, however. They did not give beyond their means. Each one gave what he could, based on the financial ability the Lord had given him. The believers in Antioch were going to suffer from the famine too. But they knew the Jerusalem believers had already sacrificed their property and possessions for the benefit of the poor and the widows.

**11:30.** When the believers in Antioch had gathered their offering together, they sent it to Jerusalem by Barnabas and Saul. The two men were sent to insure proper accounting of the funds, and the funds were turned over to the elders, the administrative officers of the Jerusalem assembly.

**12:1.** From A.D. 6 to 41 Judea was governed by procurators sent by the Roman emperor. These men were never popular. In A.D. 41 the emperor added Judea to the realm of King Herod Agrippa I, who is the King Herod of this chapter. He was a grandson of Herod the Great. Because Herod Agrippa I was a friend of the Roman emperors, Gaius made him king of part of Syria in A.D. 37. Then, in A.D. 39, he added Galilee and Peraea after exiling Herod Antipas, the Herod who killed John the Baptist.

When Herod Agrippa I became king over Judea and Jerusalem, he did everything he could to gain and hold the favor of the Jews. Unlike most of the other Herods, he practiced the forms of the Jewish religion faithfully. Apparently, he also saw and heard enough from the Jewish leaders to know of their fears and frustration with respect to the apostles and with respect to the continued spread of the Church. He undoubtedly heard also how the Sanhedrin had threatened the apostles and how the apostles continued to preach Jesus.

Somewhere in the early part of his reign over Jerusalem he took steps to show his authority. He seized some from the Church with the intention of treating them badly.

**which came to pass in the days of Claudius Caesar:** This actually happened, *Phillips* . . . which, indeed, did occur under, *Fenton* . . . This happened in the time of, *TNT* . . . a famine which actually occurred in the reign of Claudius, *TCNT* . . . as it did in the reign of, *Knox.*

**29. Then the disciples, every man according to his ability:** So the disciples, without exception...in proportion to their means, *TCNT* . . . The disciples resolved, each according to his means, *TNT* . . . put aside money, every one in proportion to his means, *Weymouth* . . . to their individual ability, *Fenton* . . . as each of them was able to afford it, *Moffatt* . . . as much as he could, *Everyday* . . . what each man could afford, *Williams C.K.*

**determined to send relief unto the brethren which dwelt in Judaea:** . . . planned to send them, *Everyday* . . . to send something to help the Brethren living in Judaea, *TCNT* . . . made a decision to send help to, *BB* . . . for the relief of the brethren living in Judaea, *Weymouth.*

**30. Which also they did, and sent it to the elders by the hands of Barnabas and Saul:** . . . sent it to the Officers of the Church, *TCNT* . . . sending the money officially to the elders by the hand of, *Williams C.K.* . . . forwarding their contribution, *Weymouth* . . . the rulers of the church, *BB* . . . and in sending it to the presbyters they entrusted it to the hands of, *Knox* . . . personally through Barnabas, *Phillips.*

**1. Now about that time Herod the king:** It was at that time, *TCNT* . . . surnamed Agrippa, *Lamsa.*

**stretched forth his hands to vex certain of the church:** . . . exerted his authority to persecute some of those who belonged to the Church, *Knox* . . . put forth his hands to afflict, *ASV* . . . laid his hands upon certain, *Alford* . . . to do them violence, *Weymouth* . . . arrested some, *Williams* . . . made cruel attacks on, *BB* . . . laid violent hands on some members of, *Williams C.K.* . . . those connected with the assembly, *Fenton.*

## Acts 12:3

2.a.**Txt:** 03B-corr 05D-org,08E,020L,025P byz.Sod
**Var:** 01ℵ,02A,03B-org 05D-corr,Treg,Alf,Tisc We/Ho,Weis,UBS/☆

3.a.**Txt:** 05D,020L,025P byz.
**Var:** 01ℵ,02A,03B,08E sa.bo.Lach,Treg,Alf,Tisc We/Ho,Weis,Sod UBS/☆

| **1156.2** conj | **2362.4** name acc masc | **3450.6** art acc sing masc | **79.4** noun acc sing masc | **2464.2** name gen masc | **3134.3** noun dat sing fem |
|---|---|---|---|---|---|
| δὲ | Ἰάκωβον | τὸν | ἀδελφὸν | Ἰωάννου | ˊ μαχαίρᾳ. |
| *de* | *Iakōbon* | *ton* | *adelphon* | *Iōannou* | *machaira* |
| and | James | the | brother | of John | with a sword. |

| **3134.8** noun dat sing fem | | **2504.1** conj | **1481.16** verb nom sing masc part aor act | **1481.16** verb nom sing masc part aor act | **1156.2** conj |
|---|---|---|---|---|---|
| [a μαχαίρῃ. ] | 3. | ˊ καὶ | ἰδὼν | [a☆ ἰδὼν | δὲ ] |
| *machairē* | | *kai* | *idōn* | *idōn* | *de* |
| [ idem ] | | And | having seen | [ having seen | and ] |

| **3617.1** conj | **695.1** adj sing neu | **1498.4** verb 3sing indic pres act | **3450.4** art dat pl | **2428.4** name-adj dat pl masc | **4227.7** verb 3sing indic aor mid |
|---|---|---|---|---|---|
| ὅτι | ἀρεστόν | ἐστιν | τοῖς | Ἰουδαίοις | προσέθετο |
| *hoti* | *areston* | *estin* | *tois* | *Ioudaiois* | *prosetheto* |
| that | pleasing | it is | to the | Jews | he added |

| **4666.6** verb inf aor act | **2504.1** conj | **3935.4** name acc masc | **1498.37** verb 3pl indic imperf act | **1156.2** conj | **2232.5** noun nom pl fem | **3450.1** art gen pl |
|---|---|---|---|---|---|---|
| συλλαβεῖν | καὶ | Πέτρον. | ἦσαν | δὲ | ἡμέραι | τῶν |
| *sullabein* | *kai* | *Petron* | *ēsan* | *de* | *hēmerai* | *tōn* |
| to arrest | also | Peter: | They were | and | days | of the |

| **105.3** adj gen pl neu | **3614.6** rel-pron acc sing masc | **2504.1** conj | **3945.5** verb nom sing masc part aor act | **4935.30** verb 3sing indic aor mid |
|---|---|---|---|---|
| ἀζύμων· | 4. ὃν | καὶ | πιάσας | ἔθετο |
| *azumōn* | *hon* | *kai* | *piasas* | *etheto* |
| unleavened bread: | whom | also | having seized | he put |

| **1519.1** prep | **5274.4** noun acc sing fem | **3722.17** verb nom sing masc part aor act | **4913.2** num card dat | **4917.1** noun dat pl neu |
|---|---|---|---|---|
| εἰς | φυλακήν, | παραδοὺς | τέσσαρσιν | τετραδίοις |
| *eis* | *phulakēn* | *paradous* | *tessarsin* | *tetradiois* |
| in | prison, | having delivered | to four | sets of four |

| **4608.5** noun gen pl masc | **5278.6** verb inf pres act | **840.6** prs-pron acc sing masc | **1007.8** verb nom sing masc part pres mid | **3196.3** prep |
|---|---|---|---|---|
| στρατιωτῶν | φυλάσσειν | αὐτόν, | βουλόμενος | μετὰ |
| *stratiōtōn* | *phulassein* | *auton* | *boulomenos* | *meta* |
| soldiers | to guard | him, | purposing | after |

| **3450.16** art sing neu | **3818.1** noun sing neu | **319.3** verb inf aor act | **840.6** prs-pron acc sing masc | **3450.3** art dat sing | **2967.3** noun dat sing masc |
|---|---|---|---|---|---|
| τὸ | πάσχα | ἀναγαγεῖν | αὐτὸν | τῷ | λαῷ. |
| *to* | *pascha* | *anagagein* | *auton* | *tō* | *laō* |
| the | passover | to bring out | him | to the | people. |

| **3450.5** art nom sing masc | **3173.1** conj | **3631.1** partic | **3935.1** name nom masc | **4931.38** verb 3sing indic imperf pass | **1706.1** prep |
|---|---|---|---|---|---|
| 5. ὁ | μὲν | οὖν | Πέτρος | ἐτηρεῖτο | ἐν |
| *ho* | *men* | *oun* | *Petros* | *etēreito* | *en* |
| | | Therefore | Peter | was being kept | in |

| **3450.11** art dat sing fem | **5274.3** noun dat sing fem | **4194.1** noun nom sing fem | **1156.2** conj | **1498.34** verb sing indic imperf act | **1604.1** adj nom sing fem |
|---|---|---|---|---|---|
| τῇ | φυλακῇ· | προσευχὴ | δὲ | ἦν | ˊ ἐκτενὴς |
| *tē* | *phulakē* | *proseuchē* | *de* | *ēn* | *ektenēs* |
| the | prison; | prayer | but | was | fervent |

5.a.**Txt:** 02A-corr,08E 020L,025P,byz.Sod
**Var:** p74,01ℵ,02A-org 03B,33,Lach,Treg,Alf Tisc,We/Ho,Weis UBS/☆

| **1605.1** adv | **1090.22** verb nom sing fem part pres mid | **5097.3** prep | **3450.10** art gen sing fem | **1564.1** noun fem |
|---|---|---|---|---|
| [a☆ ἐκτενῶς ] | γινομένη | ὑπὸ | τῆς | ἐκκλησίας |
| *ektenōs* | *ginomenē* | *hupo* | *tēs* | *ekklēsias* |
| [ idem ] | being made | by | the | assembly |

**12:2.** Among those arrested was the apostle James, the son of Zebedee. The apostle James, his brother John, and Peter constituted the inner circle of Jesus' disciples while He ministered on earth. Luke did not give any details, but there does not seem to have been a trial. James was given no opportunity even to witness to his faith. Herod simply had him killed (murdered) with a sword (that is, decapitated).

**12:3.** The murder of James pleased (was very acceptable to) the Jewish leaders and their friends. They had never forgotten how the apostles defied them. Moreover, since most of these leaders were Sadducees, they did not like the teachings of the Christians.

When Herod saw how pleased they were, he proceeded to arrest Peter, who was the most outspoken of the apostles. But this arrest took place during the 7 days of the Feast of Unleavened Bread, which was combined with Passover at this time, so that all 8 days beginning with the 14th of Nisan (March–April) were usually called Passover.

**12:4.** For some reason Herod decided to wait until after Passover before bringing Peter out before the people so they would be able to witness his execution.

*Passover* here means the whole Passover season. The King James Version translates *Passover* (Aramaic, *Pascha*) as "Easter." (The Romance languages still use derivatives of *Pascha* as a name for Easter.) But Passover is clearly meant here.

Herod probably wanted to show how strict he was in keeping the Passover season. He may also have wanted to wait until he could get the whole attention of the people for the display he intended to put on. Whatever the reason, Herod put Peter in prison with a heavy guard of four squads of four soldiers each. Herod had heard how apostles had escaped from prison before.

**12:5.** The prison where Peter was kept was probably in the Tower of Antonia at the northwest corner of the temple area. The soldiers probably guarded him in 6-hour shifts. He would be chained to two of them, and the other two would guard the door.

In the meantime, prayer was being made to God continuously and very earnestly on Peter's behalf. The believers must have been overwhelmed by the suddenness and vigor of this new persecution. There was no way they could free Peter, and in the natural the situation seemed hopeless. But they did not give up. They went to God in prayer. The Greek indicates they threw themselves into the work of intercession. This was no silent, sleepy prayer meeting. They loved Peter, and they did not spare themselves. At any hour of the day or night for the next 7 days many were crying out to

**2. And he killed James the brother of John with the sword:** . . . he beheaded, *Weymouth* . . . murdered with a sword, *Williams.*

**3. And because he saw it pleased the Jews:** And when he saw, *ASV* . . . Finding that this gratified the Jews, *Weymouth* . . . was agreeable to the Jews, *Williams* . . . was a pleasing thing to the Jews, *Wuest.*

**he proceeded further to take Peter also:** . . . he went further and arrested Peter as well, *TCNT* . . . he took a next step, *Norlie* . . . to apprehend Peter also, *Noyes* . . . he also set about the apprehension of Peter, *Fenton.*

**(Then were the days of unleavened bread.):** And those were the days of, *ASV* . . . That was during the Passover days, *Berkeley* . . . the time of unfermented bread, *Fenton.*

**4. And when he had apprehended him:** And when he had taken him, *ASV* . . . After seizing Peter, *TCNT* . . . He had him arrested, *Weymouth.*

**he put him in prison:** . . . and put in jail, *Goodspeed* . . . was kept in jail, *SEB.*

**and delivered him to four quaternions of soldiers to keep him:** . . . and entrusted him to the keeping of four Guards of four soldiers each, *TCNT* . . . handing him over to the care of sixteen soldiers, *Weymouth* . . . four detachments, with four in each detachment, *Norlie* . . . four files of soldiers to be kept, *Douay* . . . to guard him constantly, *Wuest.*

**intending after Easter to bring him forth to the people:** . . . to put him on trial in public, *TEV.*

**5. Peter therefore was kept in prison:** So Peter was closely guarded in prison, *Moffatt* . . . confined in prison, *Fenton* . . . and well guarded, *Norlie.*

**but prayer was made without ceasing of the church unto God for him:** . . . were being earnestly offered to God on his behalf, *TCNT* . . . fervent prayer was offered, *Weymouth* . . . was persistently made by the church, *Williams* . . . the congregation was constantly praying, *SEB* . . . for him unremittingly, *JB* . . . all the time, *Klingensmith.*

5.b.**Txt:** 08E,020L,025P byz.
**Var:** 01ℵ,02A-corr,03B 05D,Lach,Treg,Tisc We/Ho,Weis,Sod UBS/☆

6.a.**Txt:** 02A,05D,byz.
**Var:** 01ℵ,03B,08E,020L 025P,Treg,Alf,Tisc We/Ho,Weis,Sod UBS/☆

6.b.**Txt:** 020L,025P,byz.
**Var:** p74,02A,Lach,Alf Tisc,Weis,UBS/☆

| **4242.1** prep | **3450.6** art acc sing masc | **2296.4** noun acc sing masc | **5065.1** prep | **3875.1** prep | **840.3** prs-pron gen sing |
|---|---|---|---|---|---|
| πρὸς | τὸν | θεὸν | ‘ ὑπὲρ | [b☆ περὶ ] | αὐτοῦ. |
| *pros* | *ton* | *theon* | *huper* | *peri* | *autou* |
| to | | God | concerning | [ idem ] | him. |

| **3616.1** conj | **1156.2** conj | **3165.22** verb 3sing indic imperf act | **3165.21** verb 3sing indic imperf act | **840.6** prs-pron acc sing masc |
|---|---|---|---|---|
| 6. ῞Οτε | δὲ | ‘ ἔμελλεν | [a☆ ἤμελλεν ] | ‘ αὐτὸν |
| *Hote* | *de* | *emellen* | *ēmellen* | *auton* |
| When | but | was about | [ idem ] | him |

| **4113.8** verb inf pres act | **4113.13** verb inf aor act | **840.6** prs-pron acc sing masc | **3450.5** art nom sing masc | **2243.1** name nom masc |
|---|---|---|---|---|
| προάγειν | [b☆ προαγαγεῖν | αὐτὸν ] | ὁ | Ἡρῴδης, |
| *proagein* | *proagagein* | *auton* | *ho* | *Hērōdēs* |
| to bring forth | [ to bring forth | him ] | | Herod, |

| **3450.11** art dat sing fem | **3433.3** noun dat sing fem | **1552.11** dem-pron dat sing fem | **1498.34** verb sing indic imperf act | **3450.5** art nom sing masc |
|---|---|---|---|---|
| τῇ | νυκτὶ | ἐκείνῃ | ἦν | ὁ |
| *tē* | *nukti* | *ekeinē* | *ēn* | *ho* |
| in | night | that | was | |

| **3935.1** name nom masc | **2810.2** verb nom sing masc part pres mid | **3212.1** adv | **1411.3** num card | **4608.5** noun gen pl masc |
|---|---|---|---|---|
| Πέτρος | κοιμώμενος | μεταξὺ | δύο | στρατιωτῶν, |
| *Petros* | *koimōmenos* | *metaxu* | *duo* | *stratiōtōn* |
| Peter | sleeping | between | two | soldiers, |

| **1204.17** verb nom sing masc part perf mid | **252.4** noun dat pl fem | **1411.1** num card dat | **5277.1** noun nom pl masc | **4885.1** conj | **4112.1** prep |
|---|---|---|---|---|---|
| δεδεμένος | ἁλύσεσιν | δυσίν, | φύλακές | τε | πρὸ |
| *dedemenos* | *halusesin* | *dusin* | *phulakes* | *te* | *pro* |
| having been bound | with chains | two, | guards | also | before |

| **3450.10** art gen sing fem | **2351.1** noun fem | **4931.29** verb indic imperf act | **3450.12** art acc sing fem | **5274.4** noun acc sing fem | **2504.1** conj |
|---|---|---|---|---|---|
| τῆς | θύρας | ἐτήρουν | τὴν | φυλακήν. | 7. καὶ |
| *tēs* | *thuras* | *etēroun* | *tēn* | *phulakēn* | *kai* |
| the | door | were keeping | the | prison. | And |

| **1481.20** verb 2sing impr aor mid | **32.1** noun nom sing masc | **2935.2** noun gen sing masc | **2168.1** verb 3sing indic aor act | **2504.1** conj | **5295.1** noun sing neu |
|---|---|---|---|---|---|
| ἰδοὺ | ἄγγελος | κυρίου | ἐπέστη, | καὶ | φῶς |
| *idou* | *angelos* | *kuriou* | *epestē* | *kai* | *phōs* |
| behold, | an angel | of the Lord | stood by, | and | a light |

| **2962.2** verb 3sing indic aor act | **1706.1** prep | **3450.3** art dat sing | **3475.1** noun dat sing neu | **3822.3** verb nom sing masc part aor act | **1156.2** conj |
|---|---|---|---|---|---|
| ἔλαμψεν | ἐν | τῷ | οἰκήματι. | πατάξας | δὲ |
| *elampsen* | *en* | *tō* | *oikēmati* | *pataxas* | *de* |
| shone | in | the | building. | Having struck | and |

| **3450.12** art acc sing fem | **3985.1** noun acc sing fem | **3450.2** art gen sing | **3935.2** name gen masc | **1446.5** verb 3sing indic aor act | **840.6** prs-pron acc sing masc |
|---|---|---|---|---|---|
| τὴν | πλευρὰν | τοῦ | Πέτρου | ἤγειρεν | αὐτὸν |
| *tēn* | *pleuran* | *tou* | *Petrou* | *ēgeiren* | *auton* |
| the | side | | of Peter | he woke | him, |

| **2978.15** verb nom sing masc part pres act | **448.7** verb 2sing impr aor act | **1706.1** prep | **4882.1** noun dat sing neu | **2504.1** conj | **1588.5** verb 3pl indic aor act |
|---|---|---|---|---|---|
| λέγων, | ᾿Ανάστα | ἐν | τάχει. | Καὶ | ‘ ἐξέπεσον |
| *legōn* | *Anasta* | *en* | *tachei* | *Kai* | *exepeson* |
| saying, | Rise up | in | haste. | And | fell off |

God earnestly, fervently, strenuously, and continuously. They knew they were in a spiritual battle against the powers of the enemy. Unseen forces of the world, the flesh, and the devil were moving King Herod to try to put a stop to the Church. Herod, of course, was deceived. He could not alter the fact that Jesus had risen from the dead by putting a few church leaders to death.

**12:6.** When the Passover season was finally over, Herod was ready to bring Peter out. He was sure the execution of Peter would please the strict Jews, for Peter was the one who had taken the gospel to the Gentiles at Caesarea and who was known to fraternize with them. It is implied that Herod had also given out the word that the Jews were not to rush away from Jerusalem after the Passover season. He wanted them to remain for the grand spectacle he intended to put on for them.

The night before Herod intended to bring Peter out for trial, sentencing, and execution, Peter was sleeping soundly. The Greek here is like that used in 25:26 of the apostle Paul being brought before King Agrippa. Thus it seems clear that Herod did intend to conduct a trial this time, and Peter knew it. Nevertheless, Peter did not let that trouble him. He must have been able to sleep soundly because he had committed his case to the Lord, even though he expected to face execution the next day. He was at peace. He had Christ with him and the Holy Spirit dwelling within. Death could not separate him from Christ. In fact, if he died it would only mean more of Christ. Like Paul, for him to live was Christ and to die would be gain in Christ, more of Christ (Philippians 1:21). The early believers were so full of Christ they did not fear death. Like Peter, they could face it without any signs of worry and dismay.

**12:7.** Seven days had gone by without any answer or any sign of deliverance. Yet, though God often delays His answers in order to test and develop our faith and patience, He does not delay more than is necessary. Someone has said, "The trains of divine promises arrive in the depot of history always on time."

Peter's faith, however, was in God, not merely in the idea of deliverance. He had committed his way to God (Psalm 37:5). In humility he felt he was no better than Stephen, James, and others who had died for the Lord's sake. Furthermore, he knew from the lips of Jesus himself that he would die a martyr's death (John 21:18,19).

Thus, the sudden appearance of an angel in the middle of the night was unexpected. At the same time as the angel appeared standing by Peter, a bright light shined in the prison, possibly from the angel, or possibly as a separate manifestation so Peter could see what to do. The angel then struck him sharply on the side, aroused him, and told him to get up quickly. (The Greek verb does

**6. And when Herod would have brought him forth, the same night Peter was sleeping between two soldiers:** The very night before, *Moffatt* . . . on the very night...he was to be delivered up, *Lamsa* . . . before Herod was going to bring him up for trial, *Kleist* . . . Herod was-on-the-point, *Rotherham* . . . was about ready, *Klingensmith* . . . was to try him, *JB* . . . was about to produce him to the people, *Fenton* . . . bring him into court, *TNT.*

**bound with two chains:** . . . chained with double chains, *Phillips* . . . securely bound by two chains, *Wuest.*

**and the keepers before the door kept the prison:** . . . and sentries, *RSV* . . . guarding the prison, *TCNT* . . . others were guarding the door, *Lamsa* . . . and there were warders at the door, *Knox* . . . and guards were on duty outside the door, *Weymouth* . . . in front of, *KJII* . . . while guards maintained a strict watch on the doorway of the prison, *Phillips.*

**7. And, behold, the angel of the Lord came upon him:** . . . stood by him, *ASV* . . . stood over, *TNT* . . . All at once an angel, *TCNT* . . . Suddenly an angel, *Weymouth* . . . stood by, *KJII.*

**and a light shined in the prison:** . . . shined in the cell, *ASV* . . . a light shone in his cell, *Williams* . . . a light illumined the building, *Norlie* . . . shone in all the prison, *Lamsa.*

**and he smote Peter on the side, and raised him up:** . . . hitting Peter...he awakened him, *KJII* . . . and by striking Peter on the side the angel woke him, *Williams* . . . then touching Peter in the side, he roused him, *Berkeley* . . . He tapped Peter on the side and woke him up, *Phillips* . . . he pricked his side, *Murdock* . . . slapped Peter on the side, *Norlie* . . . He poked Peter's side, *Adams* . . . so that he came out of his sleep, *BB.*

**saying, Arise up quickly:** . . . and said to him, *Lamsa* . . . saying as he did so: Get up quickly, *TCNT* . . . Get up! Quick! *Beck* . . . Rise quickly! *Concordant* . . . Arise, instantly, *Murdock* . . . Rise in haste, *Young* . . . Hurry and get up! *Norlie* . . . Get up in a hurry, *Klingensmith.*

# Acts 12:8

7.a.**Txt:** 020L,025P,byz.
**Var:** 01ℵ,02A,03B,05D
08E,Lach,Treg,Alf,Tisc
We/Ho,Weis,Sod
UBS/☆

| 1588.12 verb 3pl indic aor act | 840.3 prs-pron gen sing | 3450.13 art nom pl fem | 252.3 noun pl fem | 1523.2 prep gen | 3450.1 art gen pl |
|---|---|---|---|---|---|
| [a☆ ἐξέπεσαν ] | αὐτοῦ | αἱ | ἁλύσεις | ἐκ | τῶν |
| *exepesan* | *autou* | *hai* | *haluseis* | *ek* | *tōn* |
| [ idem ] | his | the | chains | from | the |

8.a.**Txt:** 01ℵ,02A,020L
025P,byz.Tisc,Sod
**Var:** 03B,05D,08E,sa.
Lach,Treg,We/Ho,Weis
UBS/☆

| 5331.6 noun gen pl fem | 1500.5 verb 3sing indic aor act | 4885.1 conj | 1156.2 conj | 3450.5 art nom sing masc | 32.1 noun nom sing masc |
|---|---|---|---|---|---|
| χειρῶν. | **8.** εἶπεν | ‹ τε | [a☆ δὲ ] | ὁ | ἄγγελος |
| *cheirōn* | *eipen* | *te* | *de* | *ho* | *angelos* |
| hands. | Said | and | [ idem ] | the | angel |

8.b.**Txt:** 08E,020L,025P
byz.
**Var:** 01ℵ,02A,03B,05D
Lach,Treg,Alf,Tisc
We/Ho,Weis,Sod
UBS/☆

| 4242.1 prep | 840.6 prs-pron acc sing masc | 3887.3 verb 2sing impr aor mid | 2207.3 verb 2sing impr aor mid | 2504.1 conj |
|---|---|---|---|---|
| πρὸς | αὐτόν, | ‹ Περίζωσαι, | [b☆ Ζῶσαι ] | καὶ |
| *pros* | *auton* | *Perizōsai* | *Zōsai* | *kai* |
| to | him, | Gird yourself about, | [ Gird yourself ] | and |

| 5102.1 verb 2sing impr aor mid | 3450.17 art pl neu | 4404.1 noun pl neu | 4622.2 prs-pron gen 2sing | 4020.24 verb 3sing indic aor act | 1156.2 conj |
|---|---|---|---|---|---|
| ὑπόδησαι | τὰ | σανδάλιά | σου. | Ἐποίησεν | δὲ |
| *hupodēsai* | *ta* | *sandalia* | *sou* | *Epoiēsen* | *de* |
| bind on | the | sandals | your. | He did | and |

| 3643.1 adv | 2504.1 conj | 2978.5 verb 3sing indic pres act | 840.4 prs-pron dat sing | 3879.10 verb 2sing impr aor mid | 3450.16 art sing neu |
|---|---|---|---|---|---|
| οὕτως. | καὶ | λέγει | αὐτῷ, | Περιβαλοῦ | τὸ |
| *houtōs* | *kai* | *legei* | *autō* | *Peribalou* | *to* |
| so. | And | he says | to him, | Cast about | the |

| 2416.1 noun sing neu | 4622.2 prs-pron gen 2sing | 2504.1 conj | 188.3 verb 2sing impr pres act | 1466.4 prs-pron dat 1sing | 2504.1 conj |
|---|---|---|---|---|---|
| ἱμάτιόν | σου, | καὶ | ἀκολούθει | μοι. | **9.** Καὶ |
| *himation* | *sou* | *kai* | *akolouthei* | *moi* | *Kai* |
| garment | your, | and | follow | me. | And |

9.a.**Txt:** 01ℵ-corr,08E
020L,025P,byz.sa.bo.
**Var:** 01ℵ-org,02A,03B
05D,Lach,Treg,Alf,Tisc
We/Ho,Weis,Sod
UBS/☆

| 1814.13 verb nom sing masc part aor act | 188.21 verb 3sing indic imperf act | 840.4 prs-pron dat sing | 2504.1 conj | 3620.2 partic |
|---|---|---|---|---|
| ἐξελθὼν | ἠκολούθει | ‹a αὐτῷ › | καὶ | οὐκ |
| *exelthōn* | *ēkolouthei* | *autō* | *kai* | *ouk* |
| having gone forth | he was following | him, | and | not |

| 3471.11 verb 3sing indic plperf act | 3617.1 conj | 225.5 adj sing neu | 1498.4 verb 3sing indic pres act | 3450.16 art sing neu | 1090.20 verb sing part pres mid |
|---|---|---|---|---|---|
| ᾔδει | ὅτι | ἀληθές | ἐστιν | τὸ | γινόμενον |
| *ēdei* | *hoti* | *alēthes* | *estin* | *to* | *ginomenon* |
| had known | that | real | it is | the | happening |

| 1217.2 prep | 3450.2 art gen sing | 32.2 noun gen sing masc | 1374.22 verb 3sing indic imperf act | 1156.2 conj | 3568.1 noun sing neu | 984.17 verb inf pres act |
|---|---|---|---|---|---|---|
| διὰ | τοῦ | ἀγγέλου, | ἐδόκει | δὲ | ὅραμα | βλέπειν. |
| *dia* | *tou* | *angelou* | *edokei* | *de* | *horama* | *blepein* |
| by | the | angel | was thinking | but | a vision | to see. |

| 1324.7 verb nom pl masc part aor act | 1156.2 conj | 4272.12 num ord acc sing fem | 5274.4 noun acc sing fem | 2504.1 conj |
|---|---|---|---|---|
| **10.** διελθόντες | δὲ | πρώτην | φυλακὴν | καὶ |
| *dielthontes* | *de* | *prōtēn* | *phulakēn* | *kai* |
| Having passed through | and | a first | guard | and |

10.a.**Txt:** 05D,08E,020L
025P,byz.Weis,Sod
**Var:** 01ℵ,02A,03B,Lach
Treg,Alf,Tisc,We/Ho
UBS/☆

| 1202.7 num ord acc sing fem | 2048.1 verb indic aor act | 2048.64 verb 3pl indic aor act | 1894.3 prep | 3450.12 art acc sing fem | 4297.4 noun acc sing fem |
|---|---|---|---|---|---|
| δευτέραν, | ‹ ἦλθον | [a☆ ἦλθαν ] | ἐπὶ | τὴν | πύλην |
| *deuteran* | *ēlthon* | *ēlthan* | *epi* | *tēn* | *pulēn* |
| a second, | they came | [ idem ] | to | the | gate |

not necessarily mean that the angel raised him or lifted him up, but simply that he woke him up.) At the same time, the chains fell off his hands without waking up the soldiers who were guarding him.

Though Peter was willing to die for his Lord, it was not God's time, and Peter's work was not yet done. After this, Peter went to Babylon to the large Jewish community there and, some think, to Rome. The Church would not have his two epistles were it not for this deliverance, and perhaps not even the Gospel of Mark, for Mark, according to early tradition, recorded the preaching of Peter in his Gospel.

**12:8.** After the chains fell off from Peter's hands (or from his wrists, which were considered part of the hands), the angel continued to give Peter directions. It was as if Peter was still half asleep and was slow to respond. So the angel told him to gird himself, that is, tighten his belt around his tunic. Then the angel told him to put on his sandals, throw his long outer garment around him, and follow him.

All this was done very quickly, once the angel finally got Peter to respond. The angel knew what he was doing even if Peter did not. Yet the angel must have kept anyone else in the prison from hearing what was going on. Neither did anyone see the bright light that shone in the prison. Truly God was in control!

**12:9.** Peter obeyed the angel and followed him out of the prison cell. But all the time he did not know what was happening to him was real. He thought he was seeing a dream-type vision. He knew the angel was real, but he did not think what was happening was true. He was probably expecting all this to vanish away and find himself back in his cell still chained to the two soldiers.

This was not due to any lack of faith on Peter's part. By faith he had committed himself into the hands of the Lord for whatever God might allow.

Neither did Peter fear death. He knew that to be absent from the body was to be present with the Lord (2 Corinthians 5:8). Like Paul, he knew that to be with Christ is far better than anything believers can experience here on this earth. He had heard Jesus tell how the angels came and carried the poor beggar Lazarus into Abraham's bosom, and this gave Peter assurance that the angels would carry the humblest believer into the presence of Jesus in paradise. He was once afraid of death, but Jesus had long ago set him free from slavery to that fear. (Compare Hebrews 2:14,15.)

**12:10.** Still following the angel, Peter passed one gate with its guards, then another gate with its guards. This shows that Herod had taken the further precaution of putting Peter in the innermost



**And his chains fell off from his hands:** The chains dropped from his wrists, *TCNT* . . . The fetters dropped, *Moffatt* . . . fell away from, *Phillips.*

**8. And the angel said unto him:** Then the angel said, *BB.*

**Gird thyself, and bind on thy sandals:** Put on your belt and your sandals, *TCNT* . . . Tighten your belt and put on your shoes, *Williams* . . . Hurry! Get up...get dressed, *Everyday* . . . Dress yourself and put on your sandals, *RSV* . . . Put on your clothes, *NIV.*

**And so he did, And he saith unto him:** When Peter had done so, the angel added, *TCNT.*

**Cast thy garment about thee, and follow me:** Throw your cloak round you, *TCNT* . . . Wrap your mantle around you and follow me, *RSV.*

**9. And he went out, and followed him:** Peter went out and followed the angel, *TCNT* . . . And he followed him out, *Moffatt.*

**and wist not that it was true which was done by the angel:** . . . without knowing that what was happening under the angel's guidance was real, *TCNT* . . . yet could not believe that what the angel was doing was real, *Weymouth* . . . having no idea that the angel's activity was real, *Berkeley* . . . not realizing the angel was actually doing this, *Beck* . . . but he was not conscious that what was being done by the angel was real, *Williams.*

**but thought he saw a vision:** . . . but supposed that, *Weymouth* . . . but imagining that, *Moffatt* . . . he thought he was dreaming it, *Williams* . . . he thought it was just a vision, *NEB* . . . thought it was a dream, *Klingensmith* . . . he felt he must be taking part in a vision, *Phillips.*

**10. When they were past the first and the second ward:** After passing the first Guard, and then a second, *TCNT* . . . the first and second watchmen, *BB* . . . guard-points, *Phillips.*

**they came unto the iron gate that leadeth unto the city:** . . . and at last came to the iron gate which led into the city, *Williams* . . . that separated them from the city, *Everyday.*

| 3450.12 art acc sing fem | 4458.3 adj acc sing fem | 3450.12 art acc sing fem | 5179.9 verb acc sing fem part pres act | 1519.1 prep | 3450.12 art acc sing fem |
|---|---|---|---|---|---|
| τὴν | σιδηρᾶν | τὴν | φέρουσαν | εἰς | τὴν |
| *tēn* | *sidēran* | *tēn* | *pherousan* | *eis* | *tēn* |
| the | iron | the | leading | into | the |

10.b.**Txt:** 08E,020L 025P,byz.
**Var:** 01ℵ,02A,03B,05D 33,Lach,Treg,Alf,Tisc We/Ho,Weis,Sod UBS/☆

| 4032.4 noun acc sing fem | 3610.3 rel-pron nom sing fem | 838.1 adj nom sing fem | 453.17 verb 3sing indic aor pass | 453.15 verb 3sing indic aor pass |
|---|---|---|---|---|
| πόλιν, | ἥτις | αὐτομάτη | ʽ ἠνοίχθη | [b☆ ἠνοίγη ] |
| *polin* | *hētis* | *automatē* | *ēnoichthē* | *ēnoigē* |
| city, | which | of itself | was opened | [ idem ] |

| 840.2 prs-pron dat pl | 2504.1 conj | 1814.15 verb nom pl masc part aor act | 4140.1 verb 3pl indic aor act | 4362.1 noun acc sing fem |
|---|---|---|---|---|
| αὐτοῖς· | καὶ | ἐξελθόντες | προῆλθον | ῥύμην |
| *autois* | *kai* | *exelthontes* | *proēlthon* | *rhumēn* |
| to them; | and | having gone out | they went on through | street |

| 1518.8 num card acc fem | 2504.1 conj | 2091.1 adv | 861.2 verb 3sing indic aor act | 3450.5 art nom sing masc | 32.1 noun nom sing masc |
|---|---|---|---|---|---|
| μίαν, | καὶ | εὐθέως | ἀπέστη | ὁ | ἄγγελος |
| *mian* | *kai* | *eutheōs* | *apestē* | *ho* | *angelos* |
| one, | and | immediately | departed | the | angel |

| 570.2 prep | 840.3 prs-pron gen sing | 2504.1 conj | 3450.5 art nom sing masc | 3935.1 name nom masc | 1090.53 verb nom sing masc part aor mid |
|---|---|---|---|---|---|
| ἀπ' | αὐτοῦ. | **11.** καὶ | ὁ | Πέτρος | ʽ γενόμενος |
| *ap'* | *autou* | *kai* | *ho* | *Petros* | *genomenos* |
| from | him. | And | | Peter | having come |

| 1706.1 prep | 1431.5 prs-pron dat sing masc | 1706.1 prep | 1431.5 prs-pron dat sing masc | 1090.53 verb nom sing masc part aor mid | 1500.5 verb 3sing indic aor act |
|---|---|---|---|---|---|
| ἐν | ἑαυτῷ | [☆ ἐν | ἑαυτῷ | γενόμενος ] | εἶπεν, |
| *en* | *heautō* | *en* | *heautō* | *genomenos* | *eipen* |
| to | himself | [ to | himself | having come ] | said, |

11.a.**Var:** 03B,We/Ho Weis,UBS/☆

| 3431.1 adv | 3471.2 verb 1sing indic perf act | 228.1 adv | 3617.1 conj | 1805.1 verb 3sing indic aor act | 3450.5 art nom sing masc |
|---|---|---|---|---|---|
| Νῦν | οἶδα | ἀληθῶς | ὅτι | ἐξαπέστειλεν | [a☆+ ὁ ] |
| *Nun* | *oida* | *alēthōs* | *hoti* | *exapesteilen* | *ho* |
| Now | I know | truly | that | sent forth | |

| 2935.1 noun nom sing masc | 3450.6 art acc sing masc | 32.4 noun acc sing masc | 840.3 prs-pron gen sing | 2504.1 conj | 1791.4 verb 3sing indic aor mid |
|---|---|---|---|---|---|
| κύριος | τὸν | ἄγγελον | αὐτοῦ, | καὶ | ʽ ἐξείλετό |
| *kurios* | *ton* | *angelon* | *autou* | *kai* | *exeileto* |
| Lord | the | angel | his, | and | delivered |

11.b.**Txt:** 025P,byz.
**Var:** 01ℵ,02A,03B,05D 08E,020L,Gries,Lach Treg,Alf,Word,Tisc We/Ho,Weis,Sod UBS/☆

| 1791.8 verb 3sing indic aor mid | 1466.6 prs-pron acc 1sing | 1523.2 prep gen | 5331.2 noun gen sing fem | 2243.2 name gen masc | 2504.1 conj |
|---|---|---|---|---|---|
| [b☆ ἐξείλατό ] | με | ἐκ | χειρὸς | Ἡρῴδου | καὶ |
| *exeilato* | *me* | *ek* | *cheiros* | *Hērōdou* | *kai* |
| [ idem ] | me | out of | hand | of Herod | and |

| 3820.10 adj gen sing fem | 3450.10 art gen sing fem | 4187.1 noun gen sing fem | 3450.2 art gen sing | 2967.2 noun gen sing masc | 3450.1 art gen pl |
|---|---|---|---|---|---|
| πάσης | τῆς | προσδοκίας | τοῦ | λαοῦ | τῶν |
| *pasēs* | *tēs* | *prosdokias* | *tou* | *laou* | *tōn* |
| all | the | expectation | of the | people | of the |

| 2428.3 name-adj gen pl masc | 4744.1 verb nom sing masc part aor act | 4885.1 conj | 2048.3 verb 3sing indic aor act | 1894.3 prep | 3450.12 art acc sing fem |
|---|---|---|---|---|---|
| Ἰουδαίων. | **12.** συνιδών | τε | ἦλθεν | ἐπὶ | τὴν |
| *Ioudaiōn* | *sunidōn* | *te* | *ēlthen* | *epi* | *tēn* |
| Jews. | Having considered | and | he came | to | the |

prison. (Some believe Peter was held prisoner in Herod's palace. Most, however, say the prison was in the fortress of Antonia which was built by Herod the Great in honor of Mark Antony.) Then they came to the great iron gate that opened into the street outside the prison. That gate opened of its own accord (Greek, *automatē*, automatically). Early western manuscripts (represented by Codex Bezae [D]) add that they went down seven steps to the street. This fact was probably added in the margin of the manuscript by an early copyist who was familiar with Jerusalem and who knew about the steps leading down to the street.

The angel led Peter down the narrow street, possibly to the end of the street, or possibly to the first cross street. Then the angel suddenly left him and disappeared.

The angel stayed with Peter as long as Peter needed him. But now Peter was out of danger. The great gate of the prison had undoubtedly closed behind him, also of its own accord. The guards were still completely unaware of what had happened, so Peter would have time to get away before morning. Peter could see where he was, and now it was up to him to act. God's miracles do not relieve believers of responsibility for action. God had done His part, now it was up to Peter to take the next step. He did not need another miracle at this point.

**12:11.** Not until the angel disappeared and Peter found himself alone out in the street of the city did he come to himself and realize that the Lord had actually sent His angel to rescue him from Herod's power and from the expectation of the Jewish people, that is, from the expectation that Herod would do to Peter what he had done to the apostle James.

Peter's first thought was to recognize that God had done this, and thus he gave God the glory. The angel was God's messenger. The hand of Herod was powerful, a heavy hand of persecution and oppression. But the hand of God, that is, the power of God was greater. The victory was God's victory, and undoubtedly Peter's heart was overflowing with praise to Him. Peter did not have any questions anymore. He really knew it was God.

**12:12.** When Peter "considered" this (realized this), he did not waste any time. Though it was the middle of the night, he knew he could count on Christians being in prayer. So he went to the house of Mary, John Mark's mother. (*Mark*, or *Marcus*, was an added Latin name.)

Many believe this was the house of the Upper Room and that Mark's father was now dead. The house was on the higher southwestern hill (wrongly called Zion by the Crusaders, who, as someone has well said, were long on zeal but short on knowledge). Many of the finest homes in Jerusalem were located there.

**which opened to them of his own accord:** . . . of itself, *TCNT* . . . and it automatically opened for them, *Berkeley* . . . opened to them automatically, *Wuest.*

**and they went out, and passed on through one street:** . . . and they passed out and proceeded one block, *Williams* . . . and they went outside and up the street, *Beck.*

**and forthwith the angel departed from him:** . . . and immediately, *RSV* . . . and straightway, *ASV* . . . all at once the angel left him, *TCNT* . . . and then suddenly the angel left him, *Weymouth.*

**11. And when Peter was come to himself, he said:** Peter coming to himself said, *Weymouth* . . . Then Peter came to his senses and said, *Moffatt* . . . said Peter to himself, *Norlie* . . . finally realized what had happened! *LivB.*

**Now I know of a surety:** Now I know of a truth, *ASV* . . . Now I know for certain, *TCNT* . . . I really know, *Williams* . . . I am sure, *RSV.*

**that the Lord hath sent his angel:** . . . hath sent forth his angel, *ASV* . . . sent forth his messenger, *Rotherham.*

**and hath delivered me out of the hand of Herod:** . . . rescued me from Herod's hands, *TCNT.*

**and from all the expectation of the people of the Jews:** . . . the Jewish people were anticipating, *Weymouth* . . . were expecting to do to me, *Williams* . . . what the Jews were devising against me, *Murdock* . . . and from all the things the Jewish people thought would happen, *Everyday* . . . expected to see, *Norlie.*

**12. And when he had considered the thing:** And when he was aware of it, *Alford* . . . As soon as he understood what had happened, *TCNT* . . . So, on reflection, *Weymouth* . . . As the truth broke upon him, *Phillips* . . . having taken in his situation clearly, *Wuest* . . . Then, after thinking it over, *Norlie* . . . Aware of his situation, *TEV* . . . after he had thought things over, *Montgomery* . . . When this had dawned on him, *NIV* . . . When he realized his situation, *Confraternity* . . . And when he became clear about this, *BB.*

## Acts 12:13

12.a.**Var:** 01ℵ,02A,03B 05D,Lach,Treg,Alf Word,Tisc,We/Ho,Weis Sod,UBS/☆

| **3477.4** noun acc sing fem | **3450.10** art gen sing fem | **3109.2** name gen fem | **3450.10** art gen sing fem | **3251.2** noun gen sing fem | **2464.2** name gen masc |
|---|---|---|---|---|---|
| οἰκίαν | [a☆+ τῆς ] | Μαρίας | τῆς | μητρὸς | Ἰωάννου |
| *oikian* | *tēs* | *Marias* | *tēs* | *mētros* | *Iōannou* |
| house | | of Mary | the | mother | of John |

| **3450.2** art gen sing | **1926.5** verb gen sing masc part pres mid | **3111.2** name gen masc | **3619.1** adv | **1498.37** verb 3pl indic imperf act | **2401.6** adj nom pl masc |
|---|---|---|---|---|---|
| τοῦ | ἐπικαλουμένου | Μάρκου, | οὗ | ἦσαν | ἱκανοὶ |
| *tou* | *epikaloumenou* | *Markou* | *hou* | *ēsan* | *hikanoi* |
| the | being called | Mark, | where | were | many |

| **4718.2** verb nom pl masc part perf mid | **2504.1** conj | **4195.13** verb nom pl masc part pres mid | **2898.6** verb gen sing masc part aor act |
|---|---|---|---|
| συνηθροισμένοι | καὶ | προσευχόμενοι. | **13.** Κρούσαντος |
| *sunēthroismenoi* | *kai* | *proseuchomenoi* | *Krousantos* |
| gathered together | and | praying. | Having knocked |

13.a.**Txt:** 08E,byz. **Var:** 01ℵ,02A,03B,05D 020L,025P,sa.bo.Gries Lach,Treg,Alf,Word Tisc,We/Ho,Weis,Sod UBS/☆

| **1156.2** conj | **3450.2** art gen sing | **3935.2** name gen masc | **840.3** prs-pron gen sing | **3450.12** art acc sing fem | **2351.4** noun acc sing fem |
|---|---|---|---|---|---|
| δὲ | ʼ τοῦ | Πέτρου | [a☆ αὐτοῦ ] | τὴν | θύραν |
| *de* | *tou* | *Petrou* | *autou* | *tēn* | *thuran* |
| and | | Peter | [ his ] | the | door |

| **3450.2** art gen sing | **4298.1** noun gen sing masc | **4193.1** verb 3sing indic aor act | **3677.1** noun nom sing fem | **5057.8** verb inf aor act |
|---|---|---|---|---|
| τοῦ | πυλῶνος, | προσῆλθεν | παιδίσκη | ὑπακοῦσαι, |
| *tou* | *pulōnos* | *prosēlthen* | *paidiskē* | *hupakousai* |
| of the | porch, | came | a servant girl | to listen, |

| **3549.4** noun dat sing neu | **4355.1** name nom fem | **2504.1** conj | **1906.13** verb nom sing fem part aor act | **3450.12** art acc sing fem | **5292.4** noun acc sing fem |
|---|---|---|---|---|---|
| ὀνόματι | Ῥόδη· | **14.** καὶ | ἐπιγνοῦσα | τὴν | φωνὴν |
| *onomati* | *Rhodē* | *kai* | *epignousa* | *tēn* | *phōnēn* |
| by name | Rhoda; | and | having recognized | the | voice |

| **3450.2** art gen sing | **3935.2** name gen masc | **570.3** prep | **3450.10** art gen sing fem | **5315.2** noun gen sing fem | **3620.2** partic | **453.4** verb 3sing indic aor act |
|---|---|---|---|---|---|---|
| τοῦ | Πέτρου, | ἀπὸ | τῆς | χαρᾶς | οὐκ | ἤνοιξεν |
| *tou* | *Petrou* | *apo* | *tēs* | *charas* | *ouk* | *ēnoixen* |
| of | Peter, | from | the | joy | not | she opened |

| **3450.6** art acc sing masc | **4298.2** noun acc sing masc | **1516.1** verb nom sing fem part aor act | **1156.2** conj | **514.7** verb 3sing indic aor act |
|---|---|---|---|---|
| τὸν | πυλῶνα, | εἰσδραμοῦσα | δὲ | ἀπήγγειλεν |
| *ton* | *pulōna* | *eisdramousa* | *de* | *apēngeilen* |
| the | porch, | having run in | but | she reported |

| **2449.38** verb inf perf act | **3450.6** art acc sing masc | **3935.4** name acc masc | **4112.1** prep | **3450.2** art gen sing | **4298.1** noun gen sing masc |
|---|---|---|---|---|---|
| ἑστάναι | τὸν | Πέτρον | πρὸ | τοῦ | πυλῶνος. |
| *hestanai* | *ton* | *Petron* | *pro* | *tou* | *pulōnos* |
| to be standing | | Peter | before | the | porch. |

15.a.**Txt:** 08E,020L 025P,byz.Sod **Var:** 01ℵ,02A,03B,Lach Treg,Alf,Tisc,We/Ho Weis,UBS/☆

| **3450.7** art nom pl masc | **1156.2** conj | **4242.1** prep | **840.12** prs-pron acc sing fem | **1500.3** verb indic aor act | **1500.28** verb 3pl indic aor act |
|---|---|---|---|---|---|
| **15.** οἱ | δὲ | πρὸς | αὐτὴν | ʼ εἶπον, | [a☆ εἶπαν, ] |
| *hoi* | *de* | *pros* | *autēn* | *eipon* | *eipan* |
| The | but | to | her | said, | [ idem ] |

| **3077.2** verb 2sing indic pres mid | **3450.9** art nom sing fem | **1156.2** conj | **1334.1** verb 3sing indic imperf mid | **3643.1** adv |
|---|---|---|---|---|
| Μαίνῃ. | Ἡ | δὲ | διϊσχυρίζετο | οὕτως |
| *Mainē* | *Hē* | *de* | *diischurizeto* | *houtōs* |
| You are mad. | The | but | was strongly affirming | thus |

As Peter expected, a considerable number of believers were gathered together in a prayer meeting. After several days, people were still praying day and night for Peter. Faithful prayer marked the Early Church.

**12:13.** Mark's mother's house was a large one. The gate here was more than an ordinary gate. It was actually an entrance passageway which led through the front part of the house to the inner courtyard around which the main rooms of the house were built. The believers were probably assembled in this inner court.

The fact that a slave girl, Rhoda (Greek, *Rodē,* "rose bush"), answered the door shows it was a wealthy home as well. It was obviously the meeting place for a large group of believers. Peter knew he would find people there. He felt a special kinship with the group because Mark was his convert and one to whom he had given special training. (See 1 Peter 5:13 where Peter refers to Mark as "my son" in the sense of "my student.")

Mark (Latin for "a large hammer") was also the cousin of Barnabas (Colossians 4:10 where the Greek *anepsios* means "cousin"). He later accompanied Paul and Barnabas on Paul's first missionary journey, but left them in the lurch just when he was needed. Many speculate that he decided he could not take the hardships of missionary life and deserted them to go back to the comfort of his mother's beautiful home in Jerusalem where he would have servants to wait on him. Barnabas, however, gave Mark another chance, and he matured under Barnabas' leadership and probably with further training from Peter. Thus, Paul later considered Mark profitable for the ministry (2 Timothy 4:11).

Rhoda is called a *paidiskē* in Greek, meaning she was a slave girl employed as a household servant. But she had accepted Jesus as her true Lord and Master. Many slaves in those days became Christians.

**12:14.** The sound of Peter's familiar voice so filled Rhoda with joy that in her excitement she did not open the door to the gateway (the passageway to the inner court). Instead, she ran back into the courtyard and announced Peter's presence to the assembled believers. The logical thing would have been to open the door as soon as she recognized Peter's voice. Her joy and delight should have made her want to welcome him. But when something unexpected takes place, a person does not always do the most logical thing. In her simplicity, the first thing that occurred to her was that she must tell the others that Peter was standing outside the door and their prayers had been answered.

**12:15.** The believers told Rhoda she was raving mad, absolutely crazy, out of her mind completely. But she kept asserting emphatically that it was so; Peter was really there. Then they began to say that it was his angel. Some of the Jews had a tradition that

**he came to the house of Mary the mother of John:** . . . he went, *TCNT.*

**whose surname was Mark:** . . . whose other name was Mark, *RSV* . . . the one called Mark, *Beck.*

**where many were gathered together praying:** . . . a considerable number, *Rotherham* . . . a large number, *Weymouth* . . . many thronged together, *Young* . . . in prayer, *Phillips.*

**13. And as Peter knocked at the door of the gate:** . . . the door of the porch, *Rotherham* . . . When he knocked, *Goodspeed* . . . the door of the gateway, *RSV* . . . the entrance gate, *Beck* . . . at the vestibule door, *Noyes.*

**a damsel came to hearken, named Rhoda:** . . . a maid came to answer, *ASV* . . . a servant-girl, *Williams* . . . a young maid called Rhoda came to answer it, *Phillips* . . . by the name of Rose, *Beck.*

**14. And when she knew Peter's voice:** . . . and recognizing the voice of Peter, *Rotherham.*

**she opened not the gate for gladness, but ran in:** . . . but in her joy, left the gate unopened, and ran in, *TCNT* . . . so overjoyed, *LivB* . . . failed to open the door from sheer joy. Instead she ran inside, *Phillips* . . . for very joy she did not open the door, but ran in, *Weymouth* . . . did not open the entry, *Darby* . . . instead of opening the door, *Moffatt.*

**and told how Peter stood before the gate:** . . . and told them that Peter was standing there, *Weymouth* . . . and reported that Peter was standing on the doorstep, *Phillips* . . . and announced, Peter is standing at the gate, *Beck.*

**15. And they said unto her, Thou art mad:** Thou art raving, *Rotherham* . . . Thou art delirious, *Murdock* . . . You are distracted, *Campbell* . . . You are crazy! *Norlie* . . . You're out of your mind, *NIV* . . . You must be mad! *Phillips.*

**But she constantly affirmed that it was even so:** But she stoutly maintained that it was true, *Weymouth* . . . But she insisted up and down that it was so, *Berkeley* . . . confidently affirmed, *Campbell* . . . asserted strongly, *Sawyer.*

## Acts 12:16

15.b.**Txt:** Steph
**Var1:** 03B,Lach
**Var2:** 01ℵ,02A,05D 08E,020L,025P,byz. Gries,Treg,Alf,Word Tisc,We/Ho,Weis,Sod UBS/☆

| 2174.29 verb inf pres act | 3450.7 art nom pl masc | 1156.1 conj | 2978.25 verb indic imperf act | 1156.2 conj | 1500.28 verb 3pl indic aor act |
|---|---|---|---|---|---|
| ἔχειν. | οἱ | ⸂ δ' | ἔλεγον, | [1b δὲ | εἶπαν, |
| *echein* | *hoi* | *d'* | *elegon* | *de* | *eipan* |
| to be. | The | and | were saying, | [ and | said, |

| 1156.2 conj | 2978.25 verb indic imperf act | 3450.5 art nom sing masc | 32.1 noun nom sing masc | 840.3 prs-pron gen sing |
|---|---|---|---|---|
| 2☆ δὲ | ἔλεγον, ] | Ὁ | ἄγγελός | ⸂ αὐτοῦ |
| *de* | *elegon* | *Ho* | *angelos* | *autou* |
| and | were saying, ] | The | angel | his |

| 1498.4 verb 3sing indic pres act | 1498.4 verb 3sing indic pres act | 840.3 prs-pron gen sing | 3450.5 art nom sing masc | 1156.2 conj | 3935.1 name nom masc |
|---|---|---|---|---|---|
| ἐστιν. | [☆ ἐστιν | αὐτοῦ. ] | 16. Ὁ | δὲ | Πέτρος |
| *estin* | *estin* | *autou* | *Ho* | *de* | *Petros* |
| it is. | [ it is | his. ] | | But | Peter |

| 1946.12 verb 3sing indic imperf act | 2898.3 verb nom sing masc part pres act | 453.10 verb nom pl masc part aor act | 1156.2 conj | 1481.1 verb indic aor act |
|---|---|---|---|---|
| ἐπέμενεν | κρούων· | ἀνοίξαντες | δὲ | ⸂ εἶδον |
| *epemenen* | *krouōn* | *anoixantes* | *de* | *eidon* |
| was continuing | knocking: | having opened | and | they saw |

16.a.**Txt:** 01ℵ,08E,020L 025P,etc.byz.Weis,Sod
**Var:** 02A,03B,Lach Treg,Alf,Tisc,We/Ho UBS/☆

| 1481.7 verb 3pl indic aor act | 840.6 prs-pron acc sing masc | 2504.1 conj | 1822.4 verb 3pl indic aor act | 2648.2 verb nom sing masc part aor act |
|---|---|---|---|---|
| [a☆ εἶδαν ] | αὐτόν, | καὶ | ἐξέστησαν. | 17. κατασείσας |
| *eidan* | *auton* | *kai* | *exestēsan* | *kataseisas* |
| [ idem ] | him, | and | were amazed. | Having made a sign |

| 1156.2 conj | 840.2 prs-pron dat pl | 3450.11 art dat sing fem | 5331.3 noun dat sing fem | 4456.3 verb inf pres act | 1328.3 verb 3sing indic aor mid |
|---|---|---|---|---|---|
| δὲ | αὐτοῖς | τῇ | χειρὶ | σιγᾶν | διηγήσατο |
| *de* | *autois* | *tē* | *cheiri* | *sigan* | *diēgēsato* |
| and | to them | with the | hand | to be silent | he related |

17.a.**Txt:** 03B,05D,08E 044,byz.
**Var:** p74,01ℵ,02A,33 81,1739,vul.

| 840.2 prs-pron dat pl | 4316.1 adv | 3450.5 art nom sing masc | 2935.1 noun nom sing masc | 840.6 prs-pron acc sing masc | 1790.3 verb 3sing indic aor act |
|---|---|---|---|---|---|
| ⸂a αὐτοῖς ⸃ | πῶς | ὁ | κύριος | αὐτὸν | ἐξήγαγεν |
| *autois* | *pōs* | *ho* | *kurios* | *auton* | *exēgagen* |
| to them | how | the | Lord | him | brought |

17.b.**Txt:** 05D,020L 025P,byz.bo.
**Var:** 01ℵ,02A,03B,08E sa.Lach,Treg,Alf,Tisc We/Ho,Weis,Sod UBS/☆

| 1523.2 prep gen | 3450.10 art gen sing fem | 5274.2 noun gen sing fem | 1500.5 verb 3sing indic aor act | 1156.2 conj | 4885.1 conj |
|---|---|---|---|---|---|
| ἐκ | τῆς | φυλακῆς. | εἶπέν | ⸂ δέ, | [b☆ τε, ] |
| *ek* | *tēs* | *phulakēs* | *eipen* | *de* | *te* |
| out of | the | prison. | He said | and, | [ and ] |

| 514.9 verb 2pl impr aor act | 2362.3 name dat masc | 2504.1 conj | 3450.4 art dat pl | 79.8 noun dat pl masc | 3642.18 dem-pron pl neu |
|---|---|---|---|---|---|
| Ἀπαγγείλατε | Ἰακώβῳ | καὶ | τοῖς | ἀδελφοῖς | ταῦτα. |
| *Apangeilate* | *Iakōbō* | *kai* | *tois* | *adelphois* | *tauta* |
| Report | to James | and | to the | brothers | these things. |

| 2504.1 conj | 1814.13 verb nom sing masc part aor act | 4057.16 verb 3sing indic aor pass | 1519.1 prep | 2066.1 adj sing | 4964.4 noun acc sing masc |
|---|---|---|---|---|---|
| καὶ | ἐξελθὼν | ἐπορεύθη | εἰς | ἕτερον | τόπον. |
| *kai* | *exelthōn* | *eporeuthē* | *eis* | *heteron* | *topon* |
| And | having gone out | he went | to | another | place. |

| 1090.57 verb gen sing fem part aor mid | 1156.2 conj | 2232.1 noun fem | 1498.34 verb sing indic imperf act | 4868.1 noun nom sing masc |
|---|---|---|---|---|
| 18. Γενομένης | δὲ | ἡμέρας | ἦν | τάραχος |
| *Genomenēs* | *de* | *hēmeras* | *ēn* | *tarachos* |
| Having come | and | day | there was | disturbance |

a guardian angel could take a person's form. There is absolutely no Biblical ground for such a teaching, but Luke records what they said here to show they thought Peter was already dead, that somehow he had died in prison.

It had been several years since the apostles were delivered from prison, but it was not the passage of time alone that made them lose hope for Peter's deliverance. The shock of James' death made them wonder if perhaps the Lord might allow Peter to be killed too.

Actually, the Bible makes no explanation of why God let James be killed at this time and rescued Peter. But in His divine wisdom He knew James' work was done, and Peter was still needed on earth. God does all things well!

**12:16.** While all this discussion was going on in the prayer group, Peter was still standing out in the street knocking on the door. (The front wall of the houses in old Jerusalem was at the edge of the street.) But finally they opened the door and the sight of Peter astonished them. These believers knew there was no natural explanation for Peter's presence.

**12:17.** Apparently the assembled believers started to cry out excitedly. But Peter waved his hand to silence them and told them how the Lord brought him out of the prison. Then he asked them to take the report of this to James the brother of Jesus and other leaders.

Knowing that by dawn Herod's men would be searching for him, Peter left and went to another place (other than Jerusalem). He did not tell anyone where he was going so they could say honestly that they did not know where he was. Some writers speculate that Peter went to Rome at this time, but there is no evidence for this. In fact, there is no real evidence that Peter ever visited Rome before his martyrdom. Peter was back in Jerusalem for the Jerusalem Conference of chapter 15. He also visited Babylon later, for it was the greatest center of orthodox Judaism outside Palestine. (See 1 Peter 5:13, which must mean actual Babylon, since there was no reason to disguise Rome by calling it Babylon at that time.)

From what Peter says here, it is clear the increasing place of leadership given to James. This may be partly due to the fact that he was Jesus' brother. But Jesus had other brothers, and there is no evidence that any of them drew attention to their relationship to Jesus or that they tried to capitalize on it in any way. Both James and Jude in their epistles simply refer to themselves as servants (slaves) of the Lord Jesus. James continued to be a leading elder in the church at Jerusalem until he was stoned to death in A.D. 61 just after Festus died.

It does seem that after Jesus appeared to James (1 Corinthians 15:7), James won his other brothers to the Lord, and then they all received teaching from the apostles. From that point they gave themselves to prayer and to the service of others. James especially

**Then said they, It is his angel:** It is his guardian angel, *Weymouth.*

**16. But Peter continued knocking:** Meanwhile Peter went on knocking, *TCNT* . . . persisted in knocking, *Concordant* . . . to stand there knocking on the door, *Phillips.*

**and when they had opened the door:** . . . until at last they opened the door, *Weymouth* . . . when they opened up, *KJII.*

**and saw him, they were astonished:** . . . and saw that it was really he, and were filled with amazement, *Weymouth* . . . and recognized him they were simply amazed, *Phillips* . . . they saw to their astonishment that it was he, *MLNT.*

**17. But he, beckoning unto them with the hand to hold their peace:** Peter made signs to them to be quiet, *TCNT* . . . But he motioned with his hand for silence, *Weymouth* . . . He waved his hand to quiet them down, *Beck* . . . made a gesture to them to stop talking, *Phillips* . . . waving to them, *KJII* . . . motioned to them to be quiet, *Goodspeed* . . . to hush, *Concordant* . . . to be silent, *Young.*

**declared unto them how the Lord had brought him out of the prison:** . . . and then related to them, *Goodspeed* . . . while he explained to them, *Phillips* . . . and then described to them, *Weymouth* . . . and explained how the Lord had conducted him out of the prison, *Berkeley.*

**And he said, Go shew these unto James, and to the brethren:** Tell these things, *ASV* . . . Go report these things, *Alford* . . . Give the news, *BB* . . . Let James and the brothers know all this, *MLNT* . . . what has happened, *Phillips.*

**And he departed, and went into another place:** And going out he went his way unto some other place, *Rotherham* . . . Then he left the house, *TCNT* . . . After this he left them, *Phillips.*

**18. Now as soon as it was day:** And when it became day, *Rotherham* . . . In the morning, *TCNT* . . . At daybreak, *Norlie* . . . when morning came, *Goodspeed* . . . With the break of day, *Phillips.*

| **3620.2** partic<br>οὐκ<br>*ouk*<br>no | **3504.3** adj nom sing masc<br>ὀλίγος<br>*oligos*<br>small | **1706.1** prep<br>ἐν<br>*en*<br>among | **3450.4** art dat pl<br>τοῖς<br>*tois*<br>the | **4608.6** noun dat pl masc<br>στρατιώταις,<br>*stratiōtais*<br>soldiers, | **4949.9** intr-pron sing neu<br>τί<br>*ti*<br>what |
|---|---|---|---|---|---|

| **679.1** partic<br>ἄρα<br>*ara*<br>then | **3450.5** art nom sing masc<br>ὁ<br>*ho* | **3935.1** name nom masc<br>Πέτρος<br>*Petros*<br>Peter | **1090.33** verb 3sing indic aor mid<br>ἐγένετο.<br>*egeneto*<br>was become. | **2243.1** name nom masc<br>**19.** Ἡρῴδης<br>*Hērōdēs*<br>Herod | **1156.2** conj<br>δὲ<br>*de*<br>and |
|---|---|---|---|---|---|

| **1919.7** verb nom sing masc part aor act<br>ἐπιζητήσας<br>*epizētēsas*<br>having sought after | **840.6** prs-pron acc sing masc<br>αὐτὸν<br>*auton*<br>him | **2504.1** conj<br>καὶ<br>*kai*<br>and | **3231.1** partic<br>μὴ<br>*mē*<br>not | **2128.17** verb nom sing masc part aor act<br>εὑρών,<br>*heurōn*<br>having found, |
|---|---|---|---|---|

| **348.6** verb nom sing masc part aor act<br>ἀνακρίνας<br>*anakrinas*<br>having examined | **3450.8** art acc pl masc<br>τοὺς<br>*tous*<br>the | **5277.2** noun acc pl masc<br>φύλακας<br>*phulakas*<br>guards | **2724.3** verb 3sing indic aor act<br>ἐκέλευσεν<br>*ekeleusen*<br>he commanded | **516.8** verb inf aor pass<br>ἀπαχθῆναι·<br>*apachthēnai*<br>to be led away. |
|---|---|---|---|---|

| **2504.1** conj<br>καὶ<br>*kai*<br>And | **2687.4** verb nom sing masc part aor act<br>κατελθὼν<br>*katelthōn*<br>having gone down | **570.3** prep<br>ἀπὸ<br>*apo*<br>from | **3450.10** art gen sing fem<br>τῆς<br>*tēs* | **2424.2** name gen fem<br>Ἰουδαίας<br>*Ioudaias*<br>Judea | **1519.1** prep<br>εἰς<br>*eis*<br>to |
|---|---|---|---|---|---|

19.a.**Txt:** 020L,025P,byz. Tisc
**Var:** 01ℵ,02A,03B,05D 08E,Lach,Treg,Alf Word,We/Ho,Weis,Sod UBS/*

| **3450.12** art acc sing fem<br>⸂[a] τὴν⸃<br>*tēn* | **2513.3** name acc fem<br>Καισάρειαν<br>*Kaisareian*<br>Caesarea | **1298.5** verb 3sing indic imperf act<br>διέτριβεν.<br>*dietriben*<br>he was staying. | **1498.34** verb sing indic imperf act<br>**20.** [a]Ἦν<br>*En*<br>Was | **1156.2** conj<br>δὲ<br>*de*<br>and |
|---|---|---|---|---|

20.a.**Txt:** 08E,020L 025P,byz.
**Var:** 01ℵ,02A,03B,05D 33,sa.bo.Gries,Lach Treg,Alf,Word,Tisc We/Ho,Weis,Sod UBS/*

| **3450.5** art nom sing masc<br>⸂[a] ὁ<br>*ho* | **2243.1** name nom masc<br>Ἡρῴδης⸃<br>*Hērōdēs*<br>Herod | **2348.1** verb nom sing masc part pres act<br>θυμομαχῶν<br>*thumomachōn*<br>being in bitter hostility with | **5024.1** name dat pl masc<br>Τυρίοις<br>*Turiois*<br>Tyrians |
|---|---|---|---|

| **2504.1** conj<br>καὶ<br>*kai*<br>and | **4461.1** name-adj dat pl masc<br>Σιδωνίοις·<br>*Sidōniois*<br>Sidonians | **3524.1** adv<br>ὁμοθυμαδὸν<br>*homothumadon*<br>with one accord | **1156.2** conj<br>δὲ<br>*de*<br>but | **3780.13** verb 3pl indic imperf act<br>παρῆσαν<br>*parēsan*<br>they were coming |
|---|---|---|---|---|

| **4242.1** prep<br>πρὸς<br>*pros*<br>to | **840.6** prs-pron acc sing masc<br>αὐτόν,<br>*auton*<br>him, | **2504.1** conj<br>καὶ<br>*kai*<br>and | **3844.7** verb nom pl masc part aor act<br>πείσαντες<br>*peisantes*<br>having gained | **979.1** name acc masc<br>Βλάστον<br>*Blaston*<br>Blastus | **3450.6** art acc sing masc<br>τὸν<br>*ton*<br>the |
|---|---|---|---|---|---|

| **1894.3** prep<br>ἐπὶ<br>*epi*<br>over | **3450.2** art gen sing<br>τοῦ<br>*tou*<br>the | **2819.1** noun gen sing masc<br>κοιτῶνος<br>*koitōnos*<br>bedroom | **3450.2** art gen sing<br>τοῦ<br>*tou*<br>of the | **928.2** noun gen sing masc<br>βασιλέως,<br>*basileōs*<br>king, | **153.35** verb 3pl indic imperf mid<br>ᾐτοῦντο<br>*ētounto*<br>were seeking |
|---|---|---|---|---|---|

| **1503.4** noun acc sing fem<br>εἰρήνην,<br>*eirēnēn*<br>peace | **1217.2** prep<br>διὰ<br>*dia*<br>because of | **3450.16** art sing neu<br>τὸ<br>*to*<br>the | **4982.6** verb inf pres mid<br>τρέφεσθαι<br>*trephesthai*<br>to be fed | **840.1** prs-pron gen pl<br>αὐτῶν<br>*autōn*<br>their | **3450.12** art acc sing fem<br>τὴν<br>*tēn*<br>the |
|---|---|---|---|---|---|

seems to have quickly grown spiritually. A later tradition says he had calluses like those of a camel on his knees from praying. All agree that the anointing of the Spirit made him a spiritual leader.

**12:18.** At dawn there was more than a little disturbance among the soldiers as they tried to find out what had become of Peter.

**12:19.** Though Herod had a thorough search made for Peter, he was not found. Then Herod brought the guards in for a preliminary examination, but did not give them a formal trial. Although the Greek simply says the guards were led away, it is nearly certain that they were led away to be executed. According to Roman law (*Code of Justinian*), which Agrippa may not have been bound to in this case, a guard who permitted someone to escape was subject to the same punishment the prisoner would have suffered. In light of James' execution (verse 2), it can be assumed that Peter, and now the guards, faced certain death (Bruce, *New International Commentary of the New Testament, Acts*, p.253). After that, Herod left Judea and went to the provincial capital on the seacoast (Caesarea) and stayed there. He perhaps felt disgraced by Peter's escape, so he never returned.

**12:20.** At this time, and probably for some time previously, Herod was furiously angry with Tyre and Sidon. He was practically at the point of waging war with them, though war would not have been allowed between two Roman provinces or dependencies. To try to quiet him, the leaders of Tyre and Sidon got together in one accord (with a unity of purpose) and came to Herod. But first they made friends of Blastus, the king's chamberlain, who was one of Herod's confidential advisers. Using his influence, they asked for peace for themselves. They had good reason. Tyre and Sidon are on a narrow strip of land between the Lebanon Mountains and the Mediterranean Sea. That strip varied from a few yards to about 5 miles. Thus they had very little land suitable for agriculture and they were dependent on Palestine for their food supply. (See 1 Kings 5:10,11 where Solomon exchanged food for cedar and fir trees from Lebanon; see also Ezra 3:7; Ezekiel 27:17.)

It is indicated that Barnabas and Saul were in Jerusalem at this time bringing an offering for famine relief. This famine would have affected Tyre and Sidon too, so they must have been desperate for a share of the food Palestine produced. Peace for them was a real necessity.

**12:21.** Herod responded favorably, and the leaders of Tyre and Sidon, and undoubtedly many of the people of Lebanon gathered in Caesarea on an appointed day. The crowd probably gathered

**there was no small stir among the soldiers:** . . . no small commotion, *Rotherham* . . . no little consternation, *Berkeley* . . . no little commotion, *Williams.*
**what was become of Peter:** . . . as to what could possibly have become of Peter, *TCNT* . . . as to what could have happened to Peter, *Phillips.*

**19. And when Herod had sought for him:** . . . had search made for Peter, *TCNT.*
**and found him not:** . . . and had failed to find him, *TCNT* . . . and could not find him, *Weymouth.*
**he examined the keepers:** . . . he cross-questioned the Guard, *TCNT* . . . arraigned, *Murdock* . . . he cross-examined, *NIV.*
**and commanded that they should be put to death:** . . . ordered them to be led away to death, *Rotherham* . . . and ordered them away to execution, *TCNT* . . . he gave orders to have them put to death, *Norlie.*
**And he went down from Judaea to Caesarea, and there abode:** . . . stayed there, *Rotherham* . . . and remained there, *Weymouth.*

**20. And Herod was highly displeased with them of Tyre and Sidon:** Now he was bitterly hostile to, *Rotherham* . . . had incurred Herod's violent displeasure, *Weymouth* . . . Now Herod cherished a bitter grudge against, *Williams* . . . bitter animosity, *AmpB.*
**but they came with one accord to him:** So they sent a large deputation to wait on him, *Weymouth.*
**and, having made Blastus the king's chamberlain their friend:** . . . and having won over Blastus, *TCNT* . . . and having secured the good will of Blastus, his treasurer, *Weymouth* . . . the king's household steward, *Norlie* . . . the king's chief valet, *Wuest.*
**desired peace:** . . . they were suing for peace, *Rotherham* . . . they begged Herod for a peaceful arrangement, *TCNT.*
**because their country was nourished by the king's country:** . . . because their country was dependent on the King's for its food supply, *TCNT* . . . their country depended for its food-supply upon the king's country, *Williams.*

| 5396.4 noun acc sing fem | 570.3 prep | 3450.10 art gen sing fem | 930.3 adj gen sing fem | 4853.1 adj dat sing fem | 1156.2 conj |
|---|---|---|---|---|---|
| χώραν | ἀπὸ | τῆς | βασιλικῆς. | 21. Τακτῇ | δὲ |
| *chōran* | *apo* | *tēs* | *basilikēs* | *Taktē* | *de* |
| country | by | the | king. | On an appointed | and |

| 2232.3 noun dat sing fem | 3450.5 art nom sing masc | 2243.1 name nom masc | 1730.9 verb nom sing masc part aor mid | 2051.2 noun acc sing fem |
|---|---|---|---|---|
| ἡμέρᾳ | ὁ | Ἡρῴδης | ἐνδυσάμενος | ἐσθῆτα |
| *hēmera* | *ho* | *Hērōdēs* | *endusamenos* | *esthēta* |
| day | | Herod | having put on clothing | clothing |

21.a.**Txt:** 02A,05D,08E 020L,025P,etc.byz.sa.bo. Gries,Weis,Sod
**Var:** 01ℵ,03B,Tisc We/Ho,UBS/⋆

| 930.4 adj acc sing fem | 2504.1 conj | 2495.9 verb nom sing masc part aor act | 1894.3 prep | 3450.2 art gen sing | 961.1 noun gen sing neu |
|---|---|---|---|---|---|
| βασιλικὴν, | ⸂[a] καὶ ⸃ | καθίσας | ἐπὶ | τοῦ | βήματος, |
| *basilikēn* | *kai* | *kathisas* | *epi* | *tou* | *bēmatos* |
| royal | and | having sat | on | the | podium, |

| 1209.1 verb 3sing indic imperf act | 4242.1 prep | 840.8 prs-pron acc pl masc | 3450.5 art nom sing masc | 1156.2 conj |
|---|---|---|---|---|
| ἐδημηγόρει | πρὸς | αὐτούς. | 22. ὁ | δὲ |
| *edēmēgorei* | *pros* | *autous* | *ho* | *de* |
| was making an oration | to | them. | The | and |

| 1213.1 noun nom sing masc | 2003.1 verb 3sing indic imperf act | 2296.2 noun gen sing masc | 5292.1 noun nom sing fem | 2504.1 conj | 3620.2 partic |
|---|---|---|---|---|---|
| δῆμος | ἐπεφώνει, | Θεοῦ | φωνὴ | καὶ | οὐκ |
| *dēmos* | *epephōnei* | *Theou* | *phōnē* | *kai* | *ouk* |
| people | were crying out, | Of a god | voice | and | not |

| 442.2 noun gen sing masc | 3777.1 adv | 1156.2 conj | 3822.2 verb 3sing indic aor act | 840.6 prs-pron acc sing masc |
|---|---|---|---|---|
| ἀνθρώπου. | 23. παραχρῆμα | δὲ | ἐπάταξεν | αὐτὸν |
| *anthrōpou* | *parachrēma* | *de* | *epataxen* | *auton* |
| of a man! | Immediately | and | struck | him |

| 32.1 noun nom sing masc | 2935.2 noun gen sing masc | 470.1 prep | 3614.1 rel-pron gen pl | 3620.2 partic | 1319.14 verb 3sing indic aor act |
|---|---|---|---|---|---|
| ἄγγελος | κυρίου, | ἀνθ' | ὧν | οὐκ | ἔδωκεν |
| *angelos* | *kuriou* | *anth'* | *hōn* | *ouk* | *edōken* |
| an angel | of the Lord, | because of | which | not | he gave |

| 3450.12 art acc sing fem | 1385.4 noun acc sing fem | 3450.3 art dat sing | 2296.3 noun dat sing masc | 2504.1 conj | 1090.53 verb nom sing masc part aor mid |
|---|---|---|---|---|---|
| τὴν | δόξαν | τῷ | θεῷ· | καὶ | γενόμενος |
| *tēn* | *doxan* | *tō* | *theō* | *kai* | *genomenos* |
| the | glory | | to God, | and | having been |

| 4517.1 adj nom sing masc | 1621.1 verb 3sing indic aor act | 3450.5 art nom sing masc | 1156.2 conj | 3030.1 noun nom sing masc |
|---|---|---|---|---|
| σκωληκόβρωτος | ἐξέψυξεν. | 24. Ὁ | δὲ | λόγος |
| *skōlēkobrōtos* | *exepsuxen* | *Ho* | *de* | *logos* |
| eaten of worms | he expired. | The | but | word |

24.a.**Txt:** 01ℵ,02A,05D 08E,020L,025P,etc.byz. sa.bo.Tisc,Sod
**Var:** 03B,We/Ho,Weis UBS/⋆

| 3450.2 art gen sing | 2296.2 noun gen sing masc | 2935.2 noun gen sing masc | 831.10 verb 3sing indic imperf act | 2504.1 conj |
|---|---|---|---|---|
| τοῦ | ⸂ θεοῦ | [[a] κυρίου ] | ηὔξανεν | καὶ |
| *tou* | *theou* | *kuriou* | *ēuxanen* | *kai* |
| | of God | [ of the Lord ] | was growing | and |

| 3989.8 verb 3sing indic imperf pass | 915.1 name nom masc | 1156.2 conj | 2504.1 conj | 4425.1 name nom masc |
|---|---|---|---|---|
| ἐπληθύνετο. | 25. Βαρναβᾶς | δὲ | καὶ | Σαῦλος |
| *eplēthuneto* | *Barnabas* | *de* | *kai* | *Saulos* |
| was multiplying. | Barnabas | and | and | Saul |

in the Greek-style stadium or amphitheater beside the Mediterranean Sea, built by Herod the Great. It is still there and its structure is in better condition than most ancient ruins.

With a great deal of pomp and ceremony, King Herod appeared in his royal robes. According to the Jewish historian Josephus, the outer robe was of silver (either adorned with silver or actually woven of silver threads), and the sun's rays were reflected brilliantly from Herod's silver robe.

After taking his seat on an elevated throne especially prepared for him, Herod began a speech using proper oratory in the best Greek or Roman style.

**12:22.** The people of Tyre and Sidon had not only adopted the Greek language, they had adopted the full spectrum of Greek culture including Greek idolatry. It is quite evident that Herod did not say anything about the strict Judaism he practiced to please the Jews. His speech obviously was intended to please the people of Tyre and Sidon, which it did. In fact, it pleased them so much that they began to shout out, "A god's voice, not a man's!" The inference is that when they did so Herod did not rebuke them or try to stop them in any way. Instead, he let them keep on shouting, repeating the same phrase. Thus he accepted their flattery.

Apparently Herod's pride, so deflated by Peter's escape, was greatly puffed up again by the flattering cries of these people who called him a god. Instead of humbling himself, he became quite willing for others to treat him as a little god.

**12:23.** The Bible emphasizes that Herod did not make any objection to the cries of the people of Tyre and Sidon, and he did not give the true God any glory whatsoever. This called for the righteous judgment of God. Immediately an angel of the Lord struck him down. He was eaten by worms and died (expired). He had brought his own doom on himself. Josephus adds that Herod lingered 5 days with agonizing pains in his belly. This agrees with the Bible text which only says he was struck down immediately, not that he died on the spot. Luke the physician said more than Josephus, however, for Luke gave the cause of Herod's death.

This took place in A.D. 44. After that the Roman emperors again appointed procurators over Judea.

**12:24.** None of these events hindered the continued growth of the Church or the spread of the gospel in Palestine. In spite of James' death, Peter's arrest, Herod's attitude, and Herod's death, "The word of God grew and multiplied."

This is a beautiful way of expressing the secret of the growth of the Church. The growth was not due to the leadership of any man. It was not due to better methods or clever new ways men thought up for propagating the gospel. It was due to the power of the Word of God to bring life and growth.

**21. And upon a set day:** And on an appointed day, *Rotherham.*

**Herod, arrayed in royal apparel:** . . . putting on royal apparel, *Rotherham* . . . put on his state-robes, *TCNT* . . . having arrayed himself in royal robes, *Weymouth.*

**sat upon his throne:** . . . took his seat on the tribunal, *Weymouth* . . . sat in the judgment seat, *Douay.*

**and made an oration unto them:** . . . and addressed the assembly, *Lamsa* . . . began to make them a speech, *TCNT* . . . a public address, *NIV.*

**22. And the people gave a shout, saying:** . . . and the assembled people raised the shout, *Weymouth* . . . The mob shouted, *Berkeley* . . . started to applaud, *Norlie* . . . were crying out, *KJII.*

**It is the voice of a god, and not of a man:** This sounds like the voice of, *Lamsa* . . . There is a god speaking, *Phillips.*

**23. And immediately the angel of the Lord smote him:** Instantly an angel of the Lord struck him, *Weymouth* . . . in that very hour, *Lamsa* . . . But the angel of the Lord struck him down immediately, *Goodspeed* . . . struck him down with a deadly disease, *Norlie* . . . afflicted him with a disease, *Wuest.*

**because he gave not God the glory:** . . . because he had usurped the honour due to God, *NEB.*

**and he was eaten of worms:** . . . and being eaten up by worms, *Weymouth* . . . and his flesh was wasted away by worms, *BB* . . . and he was eaten by disease, *Lamsa.*

**and gave up the ghost:** . . . and died, *RSV.*

**24. But the word of God grew and multiplied:** Meanwhile the Lord's Message kept extending, and spreading far and wide, *TCNT* . . . But the word of the Lord continued to gain ground and increase its influence, *Phillips* . . . made progress, *Murdock* . . . extended and increased, *Fenton* . . . continued to increase and spread, *NIV* . . . went on spreading and increasing, *TNT* . . . continued to be preached and to reach many, *Lamsa.*

**Acts 13:1**

25.a.**Txt:** p74,02A,33 949,1739,Steph
**Var:** p45,p48,01ℵ,02A byz.

| 5128.7 verb 3pl indic aor act | 1523.1 prep gen | 1519.1 prep | 2395.2 name fem | 3997.8 verb nom pl masc part aor act |
|---|---|---|---|---|
| ὑπέστρεψαν | ʼ ἐξ | [a εἰς ] | Ἰερουσαλὴμ, | πληρώσαντες |
| *hupestrepsan* | *ex* | *eis* | *Ierousalēm* | *plērōsantes* |
| returned | from | [ to ] | Jerusalem, | having fulfilled |

25.b.**Txt:** 05D-corr,08E 020L,025P,byz.bo.
**Var:** 01ℵ,02A,03B 05D-org,sa.Lach,Treg Tisc,We/Ho,Weis,Sod UBS/*

| 3450.12 art acc sing fem | 1242.4 noun acc sing fem | 4689.2 verb nom pl masc part aor act | 2504.1 conj | 2464.4 name acc masc |
|---|---|---|---|---|
| τὴν | διακονίαν, | συμπαραλαβόντες | ʼb καὶ ˋ | Ἰωάννην |
| *tēn* | *diakonian* | *sumparalabontes* | *kai* | *Iōannēn* |
| the | ministry, | having taken with | also | John |

25.c.**Txt:** 03B,05D,08E 044,byz.UBS/*
**Var:** p74,01ℵ,02A,33 81,1175

| 3450.6 art acc sing masc | 1926.16 verb acc sing masc part aor pass | 1926.6 verb acc sing masc part pres mid | 3111.3 name acc masc |
|---|---|---|---|
| τὸν | ʼ ἐπικληθέντα | [c ἐπικαλούμενον ] | Μᾶρκον. |
| *ton* | *epiklēthenta* | *epikaloumenon* | *Markon* |
| the | having been named | [ being named ] | Mark. |

1.a.**Txt:** 08E,020L,025P byz.
**Var:** 01ℵ,02A,03B,05D sa.bo.Lach,Treg,Alf,Tisc We/Ho,Weis,Sod UBS/*

| | 1498.37 verb 3pl indic imperf act | 1156.2 conj | 4948.7 indef-pron nom pl masc | 1706.1 prep | 487.2 name dat fem |
|---|---|---|---|---|---|
| 13:1. | Ἦσαν | δὲ | ʼa τινες ˋ | ἐν | Ἀντιοχείᾳ |
| | *Esan* | *de* | *tines* | *en* | *Antiocheia* |
| | There were | and | certain | in | Antioch |

| 2567.3 prep | 3450.12 art acc sing fem | 1498.29 verb acc sing fem part pres act | 1564.4 noun acc sing fem | 4254.4 noun nom pl masc |
|---|---|---|---|---|
| κατὰ | τὴν | οὖσαν | ἐκκλησίαν | προφῆται |
| *kata* | *tēn* | *ousan* | *ekklēsian* | *prophētai* |
| in | the | being | assembly | prophets |

| 2504.1 conj | 1314.4 noun nom pl masc | 3614.16 rel-pron sing neu | 4885.1 conj | 915.1 name nom masc | 2504.1 conj |
|---|---|---|---|---|---|
| καὶ | διδάσκαλοι, | ὅ | τε | Βαρναβᾶς | καὶ |
| *kai* | *didaskaloi* | *ho* | *te* | *Barnabas* | *kai* |
| and | teachers, | who | both | Barnabas | and |

| 4677.1 name masc | 3450.5 art nom sing masc | 2535.30 verb nom sing masc part pres mid | 3388.1 name masc | 2504.1 conj | 3038.1 name nom masc |
|---|---|---|---|---|---|
| Συμεὼν | ὁ | καλούμενος | Νίγερ, | καὶ | Λούκιος |
| *Sumeōn* | *ho* | *kaloumenos* | *Niger* | *kai* | *Loukios* |
| Simeon | the | being called | Niger, | and | Lucius |

| 3450.5 art nom sing masc | 2929.1 name-adj nom sing masc | 3099.1 name masc | 4885.1 conj | 2243.2 name gen masc | 3450.2 art gen sing |
|---|---|---|---|---|---|
| ὁ | Κυρηναῖος, | Μαναήν | τε | Ἡρῴδου | τοῦ |
| *ho* | *Kurēnaios* | *Manaēn* | *te* | *Hērōdou* | *tou* |
| the | Cyrenian, | Manaen, | and | of Herod | the |

| 4924.2 noun gen sing masc | 4924.4 noun gen sing masc | 4791.1 adj nom sing masc | 2504.1 conj | 4425.1 name nom masc |
|---|---|---|---|---|
| ʼ τετράρχου | [* τετραάρχου ] | σύντροφος, | καὶ | Σαῦλος. |
| *tetrarchou* | *tetraarchou* | *suntrophos* | *kai* | *Saulos* |
| tetrarch | [ idem ] | a foster brother, | and | Saul. |

| | 2982.2 verb gen pl masc part pres act | 1156.2 conj | 840.1 prs-pron gen pl | 3450.3 art dat sing | 2935.3 noun dat sing masc | 2504.1 conj |
|---|---|---|---|---|---|---|
| 2. | λειτουργούντων | δὲ | αὐτῶν | τῷ | κυρίῳ | καὶ |
| | *leitourgountōn* | *de* | *autōn* | *tō* | *kuriō* | *kai* |
| | Worshiping | and | they | to the | Lord | and |

| 3384.7 verb gen pl masc part pres act | 1500.5 verb 3sing indic aor act | 3450.16 art sing neu | 4011.1 noun sing neu | 3450.16 art sing neu |
|---|---|---|---|---|
| νηστευόντων, | εἶπεν | τὸ | πνεῦμα | τὸ |
| *nēsteuontōn* | *eipen* | *to* | *pneuma* | *to* |
| fasting, | said | the | Spirit | the |

**12:25.** It seems possible that Barnabas and Paul were in Jerusalem, at least during the Passover season, when these events took place. Because Josephus indicates the famine took place in A.D. 46, 2 years after Herod's death, others suggest the visit of Paul and Barnabas did not take place until then.

Though the date is not certain, it is clear that Saul and Barnabas fulfilled their ministry and delivered the famine relief to the Jerusalem elders. (It is possible that because the famine was prophesied in advance by Agabus, Saul and Barnabas brought the money well in advance so it would be available as soon as it was needed.)

The choice of Mark shows they saw in him a desire for ministry and calling they wanted to nurture and develop. There were no schools for the training of Christian workers and Christian ministers. But Jesus had set a precedent by selecting the Twelve to be with Him and to be trained by Him. Now that the Church was beginning to spread out in so many different directions, more workers would be needed to help teach and train the believers.

**13:1.** In time, as the church at Antioch grew, God raised up others besides Barnabas and Saul to aid in ministering to the believers. They are called prophets and teachers here. This may mean they were all prophets and teachers, or it may mean the first three named were prophets and the last two were teachers (as the Greek could be interpreted). As prophets they were used by the Spirit to bring edification, exhortation, and comfort or encouragement. As teachers they received gifts from the Holy Spirit which would enable them to teach the Word of God effectively.

These included Simeon (Simon) called Niger. *Simeon* (Simon) was a common Hebrew name; *Niger* means "black." Some writers believe he was the child of a Jew who had married a Negro. Others speculate he may have been Simon the Cyrenian who carried Christ's cross (Mark 15:21; Luke 23:26).

The next prophet or teacher, Lucius, is definitely said to be from Cyrene in North Africa (west of Egypt). Possibly he was one of those who first brought the gospel to Antioch (11:20).

Manaen (a Greek form of *Menahem*, "comforter"), the other prophet or teacher, was brought up with Herod the Tetrarch (Herod Antipas, who killed John the Baptist). He was literally called a foster brother and was about the same age as Herod. He grew up in the palace, and some believe he also became a courtier or officer of this Herod. John the Baptist must have influenced him. Later Manaen was saved. It is also possible that he was among those present on the Day of Pentecost when the Holy Spirit was first outpoured.

**13:2.** These, along with the congregation, were ministering to the Lord in a public service (as the Greek indicates here). They were also fasting.

During the service, the Holy Spirit spoke and commanded them (the whole church) to separate "to me" (set apart for me) Barnabas and Saul for the work to which He had (already) called them. The

**25. And Barnabas and Saul returned from Jerusalem, when they had fulfilled their ministry:** . . . after visiting Jerusalem in the discharge of their commission, *TCNT* . . . When Barnabas and Saul had finished their helpful service, *Williams* . . . having performed their service, *Noyes* . . . when they had finished their ministry there, *MLNT* . . . their relief work, *Norlie* . . . having fulfilled their service, *LivB* . . . after carrying out, *TNT* . . . had performed their mission to Jerusalem, they went back, *Goodspeed* . . . from Jerusalem to Antioch, *Lamsa.*

**and took with them John, whose surname was Mark:** . . . also bringing with them, *KJII* . . . taking John...with them, *Goodspeed* . . . and brought along, *MLNT* . . . and took along with them John who was called Mark, *Williams.*

**1. Now there were in the church that was at Antioch:** . . . among the members of the Church there, *TCNT* . . . In the congregation at, *SEB* . . . In the local church, *TNT.*

**certain prophets and teachers:** . . . both prophets and, *Phillips* . . . some Prophets and Teachers, *TCNT* . . . doctors, *Douay.*

**as Barnabas, and Simeon that was called Niger:** . . . namely, *Swann* . . . Simeon who went by the name of Black, *TCNT* . . . called Black, *Beck.*

**and Lucius of Cyrene:** . . . from the city of, *SEB.*

**and Manaen, which had been brought up with Herod the tetrarch, and Saul:** Manael, who was the son of the man who brought up, *Lamsa* . . . foster-brother of Prince Herod, *TCNT* . . . who was an intimate friend of the governor, *Williams* . . . a childhood companion of Herod, *Berkeley* . . . the foster-brother, *Noyes* . . . a member of the court of Herod, *AmpB, Noli* . . . who had grown up with, *Everyday.*

**2. As they ministered to the Lord, and fasted:** While they were worshipping the Lord, *TCNT* . . . While the Christians were worshipping, *Beck* . . . making supplication, *Murdock* . . . all serving, *SEB* . . . as they were serving the Lord, *KJII.*

## Acts 13:3

2.a.**Txt:** Steph
**Var:** 01ℵ,02A,03B,04C 05D,08E,020L,025P,byz. Gries,Lach,Treg,Alf Word,Tisc,We/Ho,Weis Sod,UBS/☆

2.b.**Txt:** 01ℵ-org,020L 025P,byz.
**Var:** 01ℵ-corr,02A,03B 04C,05D,08E,Lach Treg,Alf,Word,Tisc We/Ho,Weis,Sod UBS/☆

| **39.1** adj sing | **866.4** verb 2pl impr aor act | **1205.1** partic | **1466.4** prs-pron dat 1sing | **3450.6** art acc sing masc | **4885.1** conj |
|---|---|---|---|---|---|
| ἅγιον, | Ἀφορίσατε | δή | μοι | τὸν | (a τε ) |
| *hagion* | *Aphorisate* | *dē* | *moi* | *ton* | *te* |
| Holy, | Separate | indeed | to me | | both |

| **915.4** name acc masc | **2504.1** conj | **3450.6** art acc sing masc | **4425.4** name acc masc | **1519.1** prep | **3450.16** art sing neu | **2024.1** noun sing neu |
|---|---|---|---|---|---|---|
| Βαρναβᾶν | καὶ | (b τόν ) | Σαῦλον | εἰς | τὸ | ἔργον |
| *Barnaban* | *kai* | *ton* | *Saulon* | *eis* | *to* | *ergon* |
| Barnabas | and | | Saul | for | the | work |

| **3614.16** rel-pron sing neu | **4200.6** verb 1sing indic perf mid | **840.8** prs-pron acc pl masc | **4966.1** adv | **3384.10** verb nom pl masc part aor act |
|---|---|---|---|---|
| ὃ | προσκέκλημαι | αὐτούς. | 3. Τότε | νηστεύσαντες |
| *ho* | *proskeklēmai* | *autous* | *Tote* | *nēsteusantes* |
| to which | I have called | them. | Then | having fasted |

| **2504.1** conj | **4195.25** verb nom pl masc part aor mid | **2504.1** conj | **1991.15** verb nom pl masc part aor act | **3450.15** art acc pl fem | **5331.8** noun acc pl fem |
|---|---|---|---|---|---|
| καὶ | προσευξάμενοι, | καὶ | ἐπιθέντες | τὰς | χεῖρας |
| *kai* | *proseuxamenoi* | *kai* | *epithentes* | *tas* | *cheiras* |
| and | having prayed, | and | having laid | the | hands |

4.a.**Txt:** 08E,020L,025P byz.bo.
**Var:** 01ℵ,02A,03B,Lach Treg,Alf,Tisc,We/Ho Weis,Sod,UBS/☆

| **840.2** prs-pron dat pl | **624.7** verb 3pl indic aor act | **3642.7** dem-pron nom pl masc | **840.7** prs-pron nom pl masc | **3173.1** conj |
|---|---|---|---|---|
| αὐτοῖς, | ἀπέλυσαν. | 4. ( Οὗτοι | [a☆ Αὐτοὶ ] | μὲν |
| *autois* | *apelusan* | *Houtoi* | *Autoi* | *men* |
| on them, | they let go. | These | [They] | indeed |

| **3631.1** partic | **1586.2** verb nom pl masc part aor pass | **5097.3** prep | **3450.2** art gen sing | **4011.2** noun gen sing neu |
|---|---|---|---|---|
| οὖν | ἐκπεμφθέντες | ὑπὸ | τοῦ | ( πνεύματος |
| *oun* | *ekpemphthentes* | *hupo* | *tou* | *pneumatos* |
| therefore | having been sent forth | by | the | Spirit |

4.b.**Txt:** 08E,020L,025P byz.
**Var:** 01ℵ,02A,03B 04C-corr,05D-corr,Lach Treg,Alf,Tisc,We/Ho Weis,Sod,UBS/☆

4.c.**Txt:** 08E,020L,025P byz.
**Var:** 01ℵ,02A,03B 04C-corr,05D,Lach,Treg Alf,Tisc,We/Ho,Weis Sod,UBS/☆

4.d.**Txt:** 08E,020L,025P byz.
**Var:** 01ℵ,02A,03B,04C 05D,Lach,Treg,Alf,Tisc We/Ho,Weis,Sod UBS/☆

| **3450.2** art gen sing | **39.2** adj gen sing | **39.2** adj gen sing | **4011.2** noun gen sing neu | **2687.3** verb 3pl indic aor act |
|---|---|---|---|---|
| τοῦ | ἁγίου, | [b☆ ἁγίου | πνεύματος ] | κατῆλθον |
| *tou* | *hagiou* | *hagiou* | *pneumatos* | *katēlthon* |
| the | Holy, | [Holy | Spirit] | they went down |

| **1519.1** prep | **3450.12** art acc sing fem | **4436.1** name acc fem | **1551.1** adv | **4885.1** conj | **630.2** verb 3pl indic aor act |
|---|---|---|---|---|---|
| εἰς | (c τὴν ) | Σελεύκειαν, | ἐκεῖθέν | τε | ἀπέπλευσαν |
| *eis* | *tēn* | *Seleukeian* | *ekeithen* | *te* | *apepleusan* |
| to | | Seleucia, | from there | and | sailed away |

| **1519.1** prep | **3450.12** art acc sing fem | **2927.2** name acc fem | **2504.1** conj | **1090.55** verb nom pl masc part aor mid | **1706.1** prep |
|---|---|---|---|---|---|
| εἰς | (d τὴν ) | Κύπρον, | 5. καὶ | γενόμενοι | ἐν |
| *eis* | *tēn* | *Kupron* | *kai* | *genomenoi* | *en* |
| to | | Cyprus. | And | having come | into |

| **4386.1** name dat fem | **2576.8** verb 3pl indic imperf act | **3450.6** art acc sing masc | **3030.4** noun acc sing masc | **3450.2** art gen sing |
|---|---|---|---|---|
| Σαλαμῖνι | κατήγγελλον | τὸν | λόγον | τοῦ |
| *Salamini* | *katēngellon* | *ton* | *logon* | *tou* |
| Salamis | they were announcing | the | word | of |

| **2296.2** noun gen sing masc | **1706.1** prep | **3450.14** art dat pl fem | **4715.6** noun dat pl fem | **3450.1** art gen pl | **2428.3** name-adj gen pl masc |
|---|---|---|---|---|---|
| θεοῦ | ἐν | ταῖς | συναγωγαῖς | τῶν | Ἰουδαίων· |
| *theou* | *en* | *tais* | *sunagōgais* | *tōn* | *Ioudaiōn* |
| God | in | the | synagogues | of the | Jews. |

Greek is imperative here and includes a particle expressing a strong command.

How the Holy Spirit gave this message is not indicated. Likely it was a message in prophecy given by one of the other prophets and teachers named in verse 1. This does not give grounds for so-called "directive prophecy," however. It was not meant to give direction for Barnabas and Saul. The Greek perfect tense used here means an action in the past with present results. This shows that the Holy Spirit had already dealt with both Barnabas and Saul personally. But they had responsibilities in ministry to the local church, and the church must be willing to let them go. So the Spirit's message was directed to the whole assembly.

**13:3.** The whole assembly then fasted and prayed further. Later, Paul wrote to the Corinthians (1 Corinthians 14:29) that prophecies should be judged by other members of the Body. It is always wise to hold steady until it is certain prophetic messages are from the Lord.

The assembly also must have prayed for God's blessing on this new ministry. Then they sent Barnabas and Saul away (literally, set them free, released them, from their obligations at Antioch and permitted them to depart).

This was another important step in the progress of the gospel. Up to this point the gospel was carried to new places by those who were scattered abroad by persecution. But there were none who gave themselves specifically to the work of going to new places to start and organize new churches.

**13:4.** The Bible next emphasizes that Barnabas and Saul were sent out by the Holy Spirit. The believers gave them their blessing and let them go. Both the Holy Spirit and the church were involved.

Their first missionary journey took them to the island of Cyprus, over 100 miles to the southwest, then to the mainland cities in the southern part of the Roman province of Galatia, and finally back to Antioch where they reported to the home church (14:26,27).

Seleucia was a city on the Syrian coast of the Mediterranean Sea, 5 miles north of the mouth of the Orontes River and about 16 miles from Antioch.

At Seleucia, Antioch's harbor, they took a sailing ship to Cyprus. There was wisdom in the Holy Spirit's taking them first to the island where Barnabas was born and grew up (4:36).

**13:5.** At Salamis on the eastern end of the island of Cyprus, they took advantage of the opportunities given by the synagogues for visiting rabbis to preach and teach. It was always Saul's practice to go to the Jews first, for they had the Scriptures and the background to understand the gospel. (See Romans 1:16; 3:2; 9:4,5.)

The Bible draws attention to the fact that they took John Mark along as their minister, their attendant. Some believe that like Elisha

**the Holy Ghost said:** . . . said to them, *Lamsa.*

**Separate me Barnabas and Saul for the work whereunto I have called them:** Set apart for me, *ABUV* . . . Appoint for me, *Lamsa* . . . Separate me forthwith, *Alford* . . . have allotted them, *Fenton* . . . Give...to me to do a special work, *Everyday* . . . a special job, *LivB* . . . for a task to which, *Phillips* . . . I have chosen them to do a special work, *SEB.*

**3. And when they had fasted and prayed:** At this, *Phillips* . . . So, the congregation, *SEB* . . . after further fasting and prayer, *Phillips* . . . they gave up eating and prayed, *Everyday.*

**and laid their hands on them:** . . . put their hands on, *SEB* . . . and the laying on of hands, *Weymouth.*

**they sent them away:** . . . and sent them on their way, *TCNT* . . . and set them free for this work, *Phillips* . . . let them go, *Beck* . . . dismissed them, *Campbell* . . . and sent them off, *Noli* . . . sent them out, *Everyday, SEB.*

**4. So they, being sent forth by the Holy Ghost:** . . . sent on this mission, *TCNT* . . . So these two, sent at the Holy Spirit's command, *Phillips* . . . Being sent out in this way, *Goodspeed* . . . Thus, designated by the, *Noli* . . . Indeed, it was really the Holy Spirit who had sent them out, *Norlie* . . . Under the guidance, *Fenton.*

**departed unto Seleucia:** . . . went down to Seleucia, *ASV.*

**and from thence they sailed to Cyprus:** . . . they sailed away, *Alford* . . . to the Island of, *SEB.*

**5. And when they were at Salamis:** And arriving at Salamis, *ABUV* . . . On reaching Salamis, *TCNT* . . . when they had entered the city of, *Lamsa* . . . When they came to, *Everyday.*

**they preached the word of God in the synagogues of the Jews:** . . . they proclaimed, *ASV* . . . they declared, *Rotherham* . . . they began to tell God's message in the Jewish Synagogues, *TCNT* . . . they began to announce, *Weymouth* . . . they announced, *Darby* . . . they preached the divine Gospel, *Noli* . . . they were preaching God's message in, *SEB.*

**Acts 13:6**

| 2174.42 verb indic imperf act | 1156.2 conj | 2504.1 conj | 2464.4 name acc masc | 5095.2 noun acc sing masc |
|---|---|---|---|---|
| εἶχον | δὲ | καὶ | Ἰωάννην | ὑπηρέτην. |
| *eichon* | *de* | *kai* | *Iōannēn* | *hupēretēn* |
| They were having | and | also | John | an attendant. |

6.a.**Var:** 01ℵ,02A,03B 04C,05D,08E,bo.Gries Lach,Treg,Alf,Word Tisc,We/Ho,Weis,Sod UBS/⋆

6.b.**Var:** 01ℵ,02A,03B 04C,05D,Lach,Treg,Alf Word,Tisc,We/Ho,Weis Sod,UBS/⋆

| 1324.7 verb nom pl masc part aor act | 1156.2 conj | 3513.9 adj acc sing fem | 3450.12 art acc sing fem | 3382.4 noun acc sing fem |
|---|---|---|---|---|
| **6.** διελθόντες | δὲ | [a⋆+ ὅλην ] | τὴν | νῆσον |
| *dielthontes* | *de* | *holēn* | *tēn* | *nēson* |
| Having passed through | and | [ whole ] | the | island |

| 884.2 conj | 3836.1 name gen fem | 2128.6 verb indic aor act | 433.4 noun acc sing masc | 4948.5 indef-pron |
|---|---|---|---|---|
| ἄχρι | Πάφου | εὗρον | [b⋆+ ἄνδρα ] | τινὰ |
| *achri* | *Paphou* | *heuron* | *andra* | *tina* |
| as far as | Paphos | they found | [ a man ] | certain, |

| 3069.2 noun acc sing masc | 5413.3 noun acc sing masc | 2428.8 name-adj acc sing masc | 3614.3 rel-pron dat sing | 3549.2 noun sing neu |
|---|---|---|---|---|
| μάγον | ψευδοπροφήτην | Ἰουδαῖον, | ᾧ | ὄνομα |
| *magon* | *pseudoprophētēn* | *Ioudaion* | *hō* | *onoma* |
| a sorcerer | a false prophet | a Jew, | whose | name |

| 914.1 name nom masc | 3614.5 rel-pron nom sing masc | 1498.34 verb sing indic imperf act | 4713.1 prep | 3450.3 art dat sing |
|---|---|---|---|---|
| Βαριησοῦς, | **7.** ὃς | ἦν | σὺν | τῷ |
| *Bariēsous* | *hos* | *ēn* | *sun* | *tō* |
| Barjesus, | who | was | with | the |

| 444.2 noun dat sing masc | 4443.1 name dat masc | 3834.3 name dat masc | 433.3 noun dat sing masc | 4758.1 adj dat sing masc |
|---|---|---|---|---|
| ἀνθυπάτῳ | Σεργίῳ | Παύλῳ, | ἀνδρὶ | συνετῷ. |
| *anthupatō* | *Sergiō* | *Paulō* | *andri* | *sunetō* |
| proconsul | Sergius | Paulus, | man | an intelligent. |

| 3642.4 dem-pron nom sing masc | 4200.4 verb nom sing masc part aor mid | 915.4 name acc masc | 2504.1 conj | 4425.4 name acc masc |
|---|---|---|---|---|
| οὗτος | προσκαλεσάμενος | Βαρναβᾶν | καὶ | Σαῦλον |
| *houtos* | *proskalesamenos* | *Barnaban* | *kai* | *Saulon* |
| This one | having called to | Barnabas | and | Saul |

| 1919.6 verb 3sing indic aor act | 189.36 verb inf aor act | 3450.6 art acc sing masc | 3030.4 noun acc sing masc | 3450.2 art gen sing | 2296.2 noun gen sing masc |
|---|---|---|---|---|---|
| ἐπεζήτησεν | ἀκοῦσαι | τὸν | λόγον | τοῦ | θεοῦ· |
| *epezētēsen* | *akousai* | *ton* | *logon* | *tou* | *theou* |
| desired | to hear | the | word | | of God. |

| 434.8 verb 3sing indic imperf mid | 1156.2 conj | 840.2 prs-pron dat pl | 1668.1 name nom masc | 3450.5 art nom sing masc |
|---|---|---|---|---|
| **8.** ἀνθίστατο | δὲ | αὐτοῖς | Ἐλύμας | ὁ |
| *anthistato* | *de* | *autois* | *Elumas* | *ho* |
| There was standing against | but | them | Elymas | the |

| 3069.1 noun nom sing masc | 3643.1 adv | 1056.1 conj | 3148.1 verb 3sing indic pres mid | 3450.16 art sing neu | 3549.2 noun sing neu |
|---|---|---|---|---|---|
| μάγος· | οὕτως | γὰρ | μεθερμηνεύεται | τὸ | ὄνομα |
| *magos* | *houtōs* | *gar* | *methermēneuetai* | *to* | *onoma* |
| magician, | so | for | is being interpreted | the | name |

| 840.3 prs-pron gen sing | 2195.8 verb nom sing masc part pres act | 1288.3 verb inf aor act | 3450.6 art acc sing masc | 444.3 noun acc sing masc |
|---|---|---|---|---|
| αὐτοῦ, | ζητῶν | διαστρέψαι | τὸν | ἀνθύπατον |
| *autou* | *zētōn* | *diastrepsai* | *ton* | *anthupaton* |
| his, | seeking | to divert | the | proconsul |

who waited on Elijah, Mark helped them as a personal servant while he trained for the ministry. Luke 1:2 uses the same word for "ministers of the Word," however. Others believe they took Mark because he was an eyewitness of the arrest, death, and resurrection of Jesus, probably being the young man mentioned in Mark 14:51,52.

**13:6.** After proclaiming the gospel at Salamis, they traveled throughout the island. The Greek indicates they covered it rather thoroughly stopping at all or most of the towns and cities until they came to Paphos on the western end of Cyprus.

Saul (Paul) changed this method after they left Cyprus. After this, instead of trying to cover the whole territory of a region or province, they went to key cities to establish churches. These local assemblies then became centers where the local body could spread the gospel into the surrounding area.

Paphos here is probably New Paphos. Old Paphos was a city founded by the ancient Phoenicians. New Paphos was a harbor city which became important after the Romans annexed the island in 58 B.C.

At Paphos they came in contact with a Jew named Bar-Jesus ("son of Joshua" or "son of Jesus"). He may have claimed to be a new Joshua sent to lead people into a new promised land of spiritual power. Or he may have claimed to be a follower of Jesus, but only to try to get a following for himself by his trickery.

The Bible identifies him as a sorcerer who falsely claimed to be a prophet. Like Simon the sorcerer in Samaria, he practiced magic to fool the people and gain power over them.

**13:7.** Saul and Barnabas found this sorcerer with the deputy (literally, the *proconsul,* the governor appointed by the Roman Senate; Luke used the correct title). This man, Sergius Paulus, was prudent; he was sensible, intelligent, and well-educated. As governor, he apparently was careful to keep himself informed about what was going on in the island and heard good reports of the ministry of Saul and Barnabas and its effects. So he called in Barnabas and Saul, earnestly seeking to hear the Word of God.

**13:8.** Then the sorcerer, now called by an interpretation of his name, Elymas, took a stand against Saul and Barnabas, actively seeking to turn away (pervert, twist away) the proconsul from the Faith.

This implies Saul and Barnabas presented "the faith," the complete content of the gospel with its full message of the life, death, and resurrection of Jesus, the outpouring of the Holy Spirit, and the hope of His future return. It also means the proconsul was not only listening to the message, he was accepting it.

**and they had also John to their minister:** . . . as their attendant, *ASV* . . . as their assistant, *Weymouth* . . . as their helper, *Norlie.*

**6. And when they had gone through the isle unto Paphos:** . . . the whole island, *RSV* . . . They covered the whole island as far as Paphos, *Moffatt* . . . Traversing the entire island, *Berkeley.*

**they found a certain sorcerer, a false prophet, a Jew:** . . . they there met with a Jewish magician and false prophet, *Weymouth* . . . a Jewish false prophet, *Noyes* . . . wizard, *AmpB.*

**whose surname was Bar-jesus:** . . . whose real name was Barjoshua, *TCNT* . . . Bar-Jesus by name, *Weymouth.*

**7. Which was with the deputy of the country:** He was at the court of the Governor, *TCNT* . . . who was a friend of the Proconsul, *Weymouth* . . . an intimate friend, *Williams* . . . an attendant, *NIV.*

**Sergius Paulus, a prudent man:** . . . a man of understanding, *ASV* . . . an intelligent man, *Rotherham* . . . a man of considerable intelligence, *TCNT.*

**who called for Barnabas and Saul:** . . . who sent for, *TCNT* . . . He summoned, *Montgomery* . . . who urgently invited, *Berkeley.*

**and desired to hear the word of God:** . . . and sought to hear, *RSV* . . . and asked to be told God's Message, *TCNT.*

**8. But Elymas the sorcerer:** . . . the magician, *Alford* . . . the fortune teller, *Klingensmith.*

**(for so is his name by interpretation):** . . . for so, when translated, is his name, *Rotherham* . . . for that is the meaning of the name, *TCNT* . . . for that is the sense of his name, *BB* . . . for this was his nickname, *Klingensmith.*

**withstood them:** . . . opposed them, *TCNT* . . . put himself against them, *BB.*

**seeking to turn away the deputy from the faith:** . . . seeking to turn away the proconsul from the faith, *ASV* . . . and tried to prevent the Proconsul from accepting the faith, *Weymouth* . . . to divert, *Murdock* . . . to dissuade the proconsul from accepting the faith, *Phillips.*

| 570.3 prep | 3450.10 art gen sing fem | 3963.2 noun gen sing fem | | 4425.1 name nom masc | 1156.2 conj | 3450.5 art nom sing masc | 2504.1 conj |
|---|---|---|---|---|---|---|---|
| ἀπὸ | τῆς | πίστεως. | 9. | Σαῦλος | δέ, | ὁ | καὶ |
| *apo* | *tēs* | *pisteōs* | | *Saulos* | *de* | *ho* | *kai* |
| from | the | faith. | | Saul, | but | | also |

9.a.**Txt:** 05D,08E,025P byz.
**Var:** 01ℵ,02A,03B,04C 020L,33,sa.Lach,Treg Alf,Word,Tisc,We/Ho Weis,Sod,UBS/*

| 3834.1 name nom masc | 3990.7 verb nom sing masc part aor pass | 4011.2 noun gen sing neu | 39.2 adj gen sing | 2504.1 conj |
|---|---|---|---|---|
| Παῦλος, | πλησθεὶς | πνεύματος | ἁγίου, | (a καὶ ) |
| *Paulos* | *plēstheis* | *pneumatos* | *hagiou* | *kai* |
| Paul, | having been filled with | Spirit | Holy, | and |

| 810.3 verb nom sing masc part aor act | 1519.1 prep | 840.6 prs-pron acc sing masc | | 1500.5 verb 3sing indic aor act | 5434.1 intrj |
|---|---|---|---|---|---|
| ἀτενίσας | εἰς | αὐτὸν | 10. | εἶπεν, | Ὦ |
| *atenisas* | *eis* | *auton* | | *eipen* | *ō* |
| having looked steadfastly | upon | him | | said, | O |

| 3994.1 adj nom sing | 3820.2 adj gen sing | 1382.2 noun gen sing masc | 2504.1 conj | 3820.10 adj gen sing fem | 4325.1 noun gen sing fem |
|---|---|---|---|---|---|
| πλήρης | παντὸς | δόλου | καὶ | πάσης | ῥᾳδιουργίας, |
| *plērēs* | *pantos* | *dolou* | *kai* | *pasēs* | *rhadiourgias* |
| full of | all | deceit | and | all | craft, |

| 5048.5 noun voc sing masc | 1222.2 adj gen sing masc | 2172.4 adj voc sing masc | 3820.10 adj gen sing fem | 1336.2 noun gen sing fem | 3620.3 partic |
|---|---|---|---|---|---|
| υἱὲ | διαβόλου, | ἐχθρὲ | πάσης | δικαιοσύνης, | οὐ |
| *huie* | *diabolou* | *echthre* | *pasēs* | *dikaiosunēs* | *ou* |
| son | of devil, | enemy | of all | righteousness, | not |

10.a.**Var:** 01ℵ-org,03B We/Ho,Weis,UBS/*

| 3835.10 verb 2sing indic fut mid | 1288.1 verb nom sing masc part pres act | 3450.15 art acc pl fem | 3461.8 noun acc pl fem | 3450.2 art gen sing |
|---|---|---|---|---|
| παύσῃ | διαστρέφων | τὰς | ὁδοὺς | [a*+ τοῦ ] |
| *pausē* | *diastrephōn* | *tas* | *hodous* | *tou* |
| will you cease | perverting | the | ways | [ of the ] |

| 2935.2 noun gen sing masc | 3450.15 art acc pl fem | 2097.3 adj acc pl fem | | 2504.1 conj | 3431.1 adv | 1481.20 verb 2sing impr aor mid |
|---|---|---|---|---|---|---|
| κυρίου | τὰς | εὐθείας; | 11. | καὶ | νῦν | ἰδοὺ, |
| *kuriou* | *tas* | *eutheias* | | *kai* | *nun* | *idou* |
| Lord | the | straight? | | And | now | look, |

11.a.**Txt:** Steph
**Var:** 01ℵ,02A,03B,04C 05D,08E,020L,025P,byz. Gries,Lach,Treg,Alf Word,Tisc,We/Ho,Weis Sod,UBS/*

| 5331.1 noun nom sing fem | 3450.2 art gen sing | 2935.2 noun gen sing masc | 1894.3 prep | 4622.4 prs-pron acc 2sing | 2504.1 conj |
|---|---|---|---|---|---|
| χεὶρ | (a τοῦ ) | κυρίου | ἐπὶ | σέ, | καὶ |
| *cheir* | *tou* | *kuriou* | *epi* | *se* | *kai* |
| hand | of the | Lord | upon | you, | and |

| 1498.39 verb 2sing indic fut mid | 5026.1 adj nom sing masc | 3231.1 partic | 984.12 verb nom sing masc part pres act | 3450.6 art acc sing masc | 2229.4 noun acc sing masc |
|---|---|---|---|---|---|
| ἔσῃ | τυφλὸς, | μὴ | βλέπων | τὸν | ἥλιον |
| *esē* | *tuphlos* | *mē* | *blepōn* | *ton* | *hēlion* |
| you shall be | blind, | not | seeing | the | sun |

11.b.**Var:** p45,01ℵ,04C bo.Tisc

| 884.2 conj | 2511.2 noun gen sing masc | 3777.1 adv | 1156.2 conj | 4885.1 conj | 1953.2 verb 3sing indic aor act |
|---|---|---|---|---|---|
| ἄχρι | καιροῦ. | Παραχρῆμά | ( δὲ | [b τε ] | ( ἐπέπεσεν |
| *achri* | *kairou* | *Parachrēma* | *de* | *te* | *epepesen* |
| for | a time. | Immediately | and | [ idem ] | fell |

11.c.**Txt:** 04C,08E,020L 025P,byz.Weis
**Var:** 01ℵ,02A,03B,05D Lach,Treg,Tisc,We/Ho Sod,UBS/*

| 3959.5 verb 3sing indic aor act | 1894.2 prep | 840.6 prs-pron acc sing masc | 880.1 noun nom sing fem | 2504.1 conj | 4510.1 noun sing | 2504.1 conj |
|---|---|---|---|---|---|---|
| [c* ἔπεσεν ] | ἐπ' | αὐτὸν | ἀχλὺς | καὶ | σκότος, | καὶ |
| *epesen* | *ep'* | *auton* | *achlus* | *kai* | *skotos* | *kai* |
| [ idem ] | upon | him | a mist | and | darkness, | and |

**13:9.** This was a crisis time for the spread of the gospel in Cyprus. But the Holy Spirit knew how to deal with the situation. He gave Saul the power and authority to confront Elymas. The Greek expression here is like that used when Peter received a new special filling of the Holy Spirit when he faced the Sanhedrin (4:8).

Acts notes at this point also that Saul had another name, a Roman name, Paul (from the Latin, *Paulus*, "little"). This is significant because in the rest of the Book of Acts he is always called Paul. In his epistles also he always calls himself Paul.

Also by this filling of the Spirit, the Lord gave Paul the leadership in the missionary journey. Looking ahead to verse 13, instead of Barnabas and Saul, it is "Paul and his company." This is in line also with the prophecy given to Ananias in Damascus after Paul was converted. (See 9:15.)

What Paul did next was not his own idea. It was a prompting given directly by the Holy Spirit who had just filled him anew. This new filling gave him a holy boldness that caused him to fix his eyes on Elymas, looking at him intently, straight in the eye.

**13:10.** The Holy Spirit gave Paul a message that exposed Elymas for what he was. (Some believe this is one way the gift of the discerning of spirits may be manifested; see 1 Corinthians 12:10.)

Paul addressed Elymas as a person full of all kinds of subtlety (deceit, guile, treachery) and mischief (wickedness, unscrupulousness, reckless facility for doing evil, fraud), a son of the devil, an enemy of all righteousness. *Son of* can mean "having the character of," or a disciple of. (See Genesis 3:15, the seed of the serpent, and John 8:44, "your father the devil." The "devil" means the slanderer, and thus, the "false accuser," as the plural form is translated in 2 Timothy 3:3.)

Then Paul asked a rhetorical question which was really an affirmation that Elymas was determined not to cease perverting (twisting, distorting) the right (upright, straight) ways of the Lord (including the way of salvation and God's purposes for the believer).

**13:11.** Because Elymas was so determined to oppose and pervert the ways of the Lord, Paul declared God's judgment upon him. The hand (power) of the Lord would be (at last) upon him to bring the judgment he deserved. Elymas would be totally blind until a fitting season when God would enable him to see again. Probably, this meant God would be merciful and give even Elymas an opportunity to repent.

Mist and darkness immediately fell on Elymas, and he went around searching for someone to lead him by the hand. Apparently the people all withdrew from him, and he had a hard time finding anyone to lead him.

This was God's righteous judgment. Paul did not do this sort of thing very often. Very few can exercise such supernatural disci-

**9. Then Saul, (who also is called Paul,):** . . . however, Saul (who is the same as Paul), *TCNT* . . . Saul—hereafter called Paul, *Norlie.*

**filled with the Holy Ghost:** . . . because he was full of the Holy Spirit, *Williams.*

**set his eyes on him:** . . . fastened his eyes on him, *ASV* . . . fixed his eyes on him, *Alford* . . . looked steadily at him, *Moffatt* . . . looked him straight in the eye, *Williams.*

**10. And said, O full of all subtilty and all mischief:** O full of all guile and all villany, *ASV* . . . You incarnation of deceit and fraud! *TCNT* . . . You who are full of every kind of craftiness and unscrupulous cunning, *Weymouth* . . . You expert in every form of deception and sleight-of-hand, *Williams* . . . O you, who are full of false tricks and evil ways, *BB* . . . all knavery, *Concordant* . . . full of every deceit and villainy, *Berkeley* . . . You professional deceiver, *Norlie* . . . you monster of trickery and evil, *Phillips* . . . You master in every form of deception, *AmpB.*

**thou child of the devil:** . . . thou son of the devil, *ASV.*

**thou enemy of all righteousness:** . . . and foe to all that is right, *Weymouth* . . . hating all righteousness, *BB.*

**wilt thou not cease to pervert the right ways of the Lord?:** Will you never cease diverting the straight paths of the Lord, *TCNT* . . . plotting against the saving purposes of God, *Berkeley* . . . Won't you stop twisting the Lord's right ways? *Beck* . . . always keep trying to turn the Lord's truths into lies! *TEV.*

**11. And now, behold, the hand of the Lord is upon thee:** Listen! The hand...is upon you even now, *TCNT* . . . Right now the hand, *Williams* . . . Now listen, the Lord Himself will touch you, *Phillips.*

**and thou shalt be blind, not seeing the sun for a season:** . . . and you shall be blind for a time and unable to see the sun, *TCNT* . . . for a time, *Noyes.*

**And immediately there fell on him a mist and a darkness:** . . . and instantly, *Rotherham* . . . a mist and then an utter blackness came over his eyes, *Phillips.*

| **3876.2** verb nom sing masc part pres act | **2195.23** verb 3sing indic imperf act | **5333.1** noun acc pl masc | **4966.1** adv |
|---|---|---|---|
| περιάγων | ἐζήτει | χειραγωγούς. | **12.** τότε |
| *periagōn* | *ezētei* | *cheiragōgous* | *tote* |
| going about | he was seeking | ones who lead by the hand. | Then |

| **1481.16** verb nom sing masc part aor act | **3450.5** art nom sing masc | **444.1** noun nom sing masc | **3450.16** art sing neu | **1090.11** verb sing neu part perf act |
|---|---|---|---|---|
| ἰδὼν | ὁ | ἀνθύπατος | τὸ | γεγονὸς |
| *idōn* | *ho* | *anthupatos* | *to* | *gegonos* |
| having seen | the | proconsul | the | having happened |

12.a.**Var:** 03B,Treg We/Ho

| **3961.20** verb 3sing indic aor act | **1592.1** verb nom sing masc part pres mid | **1592.8** verb nom sing masc part pres mid | **1894.3** prep |
|---|---|---|---|
| ἐπίστευσεν, | ⸀ ἐκπλησσόμενος | [a ἐκπληττόμενος ] | ἐπὶ |
| *episteusen* | *ekplēssomenos* | *ekplēttomenos* | *epi* |
| believed, | being astonished | [ idem ] | at |

| **3450.11** art dat sing fem | **1316.3** noun dat sing fem | **3450.2** art gen sing | **2935.2** noun gen sing masc | **319.9** verb nom pl masc part aor pass | **1156.2** conj |
|---|---|---|---|---|---|
| τῇ | διδαχῇ | τοῦ | κυρίου. | **13.** Ἀναχθέντες | δὲ |
| *tē* | *didachē* | *tou* | *kuriou* | *Anachthentes* | *de* |
| the | teaching | of the | Lord. | Having sailed | and |

13.a.**Txt:** 020L,025P,byz. **Var:** 01ℵ,02A,03B,04C 05D,08E,Lach,Treg,Alf Word,Tisc,We/Ho,Weis Sod,UBS/⋆

| **570.3** prep | **3450.10** art gen sing fem | **3836.1** name gen fem | **3450.7** art nom pl masc | **3875.1** prep | **3450.6** art acc sing masc | **3834.4** name acc masc |
|---|---|---|---|---|---|---|
| ἀπὸ | τῆς | Πάφου | οἱ | περὶ | ⸂a τὸν ⸃ | Παῦλον |
| *apo* | *tēs* | *Paphou* | *hoi* | *peri* | *ton* | *Paulon* |
| from | | Paphos | the | about | | Paul |

| **2048.1** verb indic aor act | **1519.1** prep | **3874.3** name acc fem | **3450.10** art gen sing fem | **3690.1** name gen fem | **2464.1** name nom masc |
|---|---|---|---|---|---|
| ἦλθον | εἰς | Πέργην | τῆς | Παμφυλίας· | Ἰωάννης |
| *ēlthon* | *eis* | *Pergēn* | *tēs* | *Pamphulias* | *Iōannēs* |
| came | to | Perga | | of Pamphylia. | John |

| **1156.2** conj | **666.3** verb nom sing masc part aor act | **570.2** prep | **840.1** prs-pron gen pl | **5128.6** verb 3sing indic aor act | **1519.1** prep |
|---|---|---|---|---|---|
| δὲ | ἀποχωρήσας | ἀπ' | αὐτῶν | ὑπέστρεψεν | εἰς |
| *de* | *apochōrēsas* | *ap'* | *autōn* | *hupestrepsen* | *eis* |
| and | having departed | from | them | returned | to |

| **2389.1** name | **840.7** prs-pron nom pl masc | **1156.2** conj | **1324.7** verb nom pl masc part aor act | **570.3** prep |
|---|---|---|---|---|
| Ἱεροσόλυμα. | **14.** αὐτοὶ | δὲ | διελθόντες | ἀπὸ |
| *Hierosoluma* | *autoi* | *de* | *dielthontes* | *apo* |
| Jerusalem. | They | but | having passed through | from |

14.a.**Txt:** 05D,08E,020L 025P,044,33,byz.it.sa.bo. Sod **Var:** p45,p74,01ℵ,02A 03B,04C,Lach,Treg,Alf Tisc,We/Ho,Weis UBS/⋆

| **3450.10** art gen sing fem | **3874.1** name gen fem | **3716.4** verb 3pl indic aor mid | **1519.1** prep | **487.3** name acc fem | **3450.10** art gen sing fem |
|---|---|---|---|---|---|
| τῆς | Πέργης | παρεγένοντο | εἰς | Ἀντιόχειαν | ⸀ τῆς |
| *tēs* | *Pergēs* | *paregenonto* | *eis* | *Antiocheian* | *tēs* |
| | Perga, | came | to | Antioch | |

14.b.**Txt:** 01ℵ-corr,05D 08E,020L,025P,byz.sa. Sod **Var:** 01ℵ-org,03B,04C bo.Treg,Tisc,We/Ho Weis,UBS/⋆

| **3960.1** name gen fem | **3450.12** art acc sing fem | **3960.2** name acc fem | **2504.1** conj | **1511.16** verb nom pl masc part aor act |
|---|---|---|---|---|
| Πισιδίας, | [a⋆ τὴν | Πισιδίαν, ] | καὶ | ⸀ εἰσελθόντες |
| *Pisidias* | *tēn* | *Pisidian* | *kai* | *eiselthontes* |
| of Pisidia, | | [ Pisidia, ] | and | having gone into |

| **2048.16** verb nom pl masc part aor act | **1519.1** prep | **3450.12** art acc sing fem | **4715.4** noun acc sing fem | **3450.11** art dat sing fem | **2232.3** noun dat sing fem |
|---|---|---|---|---|---|
| [b ἐλθόντες ] | εἰς | τὴν | συναγωγὴν | τῇ | ἡμέρᾳ |
| *elthontes* | *eis* | *tēn* | *sunagōgēn* | *tē* | *hēmera* |
| [ having gone ] | into | the | synagogue | on the | day |

pline. The words must come from the Holy Spirit and not from the mind or the emotions. Those who attempt to act in such a way in the power of the flesh could be like the mockers mentioned in Jude 14,15,18, and 19, people characterized as "not having the Spirit."

**13:12.** As soon as the proconsul saw what happened, he believed. But too much emphasis should not be put on the effect of the miracle here. The proconsul was not astonished (astounded, thunderstruck) so much by the judgment on Elymas as by the doctrine (teaching) of the Lord. This event drove home the truth about Jesus, the Cross, the Resurrection, and the rest of the gospel that had been presented to him. The Holy Spirit used the truth to bring him to the place of faith and salvation. (See Romans 10:9,10; Ephesians 2:8; Hebrews 11:6.)

The Bible does not tell anything further about the experience of Sergius Paulus. Archaeologists have found evidence that this proconsul's daughter and her son were baptized believers. This should be taken as further evidence that the proconsul was a true believer. The gospel was reaching into every stratum of society.

**13:13.** From Paphos, Paul and his company set sail for Perga in Pamphylia (a district on the south coast of Asia Minor). Barnabas was still with Paul, of course.

At Perga, John Mark left (deserted) them and returned to Jerusalem. Later (15:38) it is implied that Mark did so when they really needed him. Possibly, the work became more difficult as they encountered unfamiliar territory on the mainland. Since Mark was from a wealthy home where there were servants, perhaps he decided to go home where life would be easier. Paul may have been suffering from some sort of physical sickness. In any case, Paul looked at this as an almost inexcusable failure on the part of Mark. Nor did Mark have any grounds for resenting Paul. Even though Paul had been promised a position of missionary leadership about 15 years before this, Paul had taken the place of humble service through long years of training and preparation, and he had done it willingly. (Notice that Paul was mentioned last in verse 1.) In God's time, the Spirit put Paul in the place God had for him. Paul knew God would do the same for Mark in due time if he would be faithful. Later, Mark was reinstated in Paul's favor (2 Timothy 4:11).

**13:14.** From Perga they went to Antioch in (of) Pisidia; so called to distinguish it from other cities named Antioch and because it was near the border of Pisidia (not actually in Pisidia but in Phrygia) in the southern part of Galatia.

**and he went about seeking some to lead him by the hand:** . . . and he went feeling about for someone to guide him, *TCNT* . . . and he groped about for someone to take him, *Moffatt* . . . going about, he sought someone to lead him, *Swann* . . . walked around lost, trying to find someone to lead him, *SEB* . . . seeking people to lead him, *Noli* . . . begging people to lead him by the hand, *Williams.*

**12. Then the deputy, when he saw what was done, believed:** When the Governor saw what had happened, he became a believer in Christ, *TCNT* . . . the Proconsul, *Swann* . . . he believed, *SEB* . . . saw what had come to pass, *Noyes* . . . for he had witnessed what had happened, *Norlie.*

**being astonished at the doctrine of the Lord:** . . . being greatly struck with the teaching about the Master, *TCNT* . . . was thunderstruck, *Williams* . . . for he was shaken to the core at the Lord's teaching, *Phillips* . . . being gladly amazed at, *KJII* . . . was overcome with awe at the Gospel, *Noli* . . . the teaching about the Lord, *MLNT.*

**13. Now when Paul and his company loosed from Paphos:** . . . his companions, *Phillips* . . . and those with him sailed away from, *NCV* . . . set sail, *ASV* . . . put to sea, *Alford* . . . put out to sea, *Weymouth* . . . leaving Paphos, *Swann.*

**they came to Perga in Pamphylia:** Paul's company came to, *Worrell* . . . They continued their trip from, *NCV.*

**and John departing from them returned to Jerusalem:** Here John quit them, *Williams* . . . withdrawing from them, *Rotherham, Worrell* . . . left them, *TCNT* . . . separated himself from them, *Berkeley* . . . deserted them, *LivB* . . . he went back home to, *SEB.*

**14. But when they departed from Perga:** They continued their trip from, *SEB* . . . But they themselves, passing through, *Weymouth.*

**they came to Antioch in Pisidia:** . . . a city near, *NCV.*

**and went into the synagogue on the sabbath day:** On Saturday they went into the synagog, *Beck.*

| 3450.1 art gen pl | 4378.4 noun gen pl neu | 2495.4 verb 3pl indic aor act | 3196.3 prep | 1156.2 conj | 3450.12 art acc sing fem |
|---|---|---|---|---|---|
| τῶν | σαββάτων | ἐκάθισαν. | **15.** Μετὰ | δὲ | τὴν |
| *tōn* | *sabbatōn* | *ekathisan* | *Meta* | *de* | *tēn* |
| the | sabbath | they sat down. | After | and | the |

| 318.2 noun acc sing fem | 3450.2 art gen sing | 3414.2 noun gen sing masc | 2504.1 conj | 3450.1 art gen pl | 4254.5 noun gen pl masc |
|---|---|---|---|---|---|
| ἀνάγνωσιν | τοῦ | νόμου | καὶ | τῶν | προφητῶν |
| *anagnōsin* | *tou* | *nomou* | *kai* | *tōn* | *prophētōn* |
| reading | of the | law | and | of the | prophets |

| 643.9 verb 3pl indic aor act | 3450.7 art nom pl masc | 747.5 noun nom pl masc | 4242.1 prep | 840.8 prs-pron acc pl masc |
|---|---|---|---|---|
| ἀπέστειλαν | οἱ | ἀρχισυνάγωγοι | πρὸς | αὐτοὺς, |
| *apesteilan* | *hoi* | *archisunagōgoi* | *pros* | *autous* |
| they sent | the | rulers of the synagogue | to | them, |

15.a.**Var:** 01ℵ,02A,03B 04C,05D-org,bo.Lach Treg,Alf,Word,Tisc We/Ho,Weis,Sod UBS/⋆

| 2978.16 verb nom pl masc part pres act | 433.6 noun nom pl masc | 79.6 noun nom pl masc | 1479.1 conj | 4949.3 intr-pron nom sing |
|---|---|---|---|---|
| λέγοντες, | Ἄνδρες | ἀδελφοί, | εἴ | [a⋆+ τίς ] |
| *legontes* | *Andres* | *adelphoi* | *ei* | *tis* |
| saying, | Men | brothers, | if | [ which ] |

| 1498.4 verb 3sing indic pres act | 3030.1 noun nom sing masc | 1706.1 prep | 5050.3 prs-pron dat 2pl | 1706.1 prep | 5050.3 prs-pron dat 2pl |
|---|---|---|---|---|---|
| ἐστιν | ‘ λόγος | ἐν | ὑμῖν | [⋆ ἐν | ὑμῖν |
| *estin* | *logos* | *en* | *humin* | *en* | *humin* |
| there is | a word | among | you | [ among | you |

| 3030.1 noun nom sing masc | 3735.2 noun gen sing fem | 4242.1 prep | 3450.6 art acc sing masc | 2967.4 noun acc sing masc | 2978.2 verb 2pl pres act |
|---|---|---|---|---|---|
| λόγος ] | παρακλήσεως | πρὸς | τὸν | λαόν, | λέγετε. |
| *logos* | *paraklēseōs* | *pros* | *ton* | *laon* | *legete* |
| a word ] | of exhortation | to | the | people, | speak. |

| 448.9 verb nom sing masc part aor act | 1156.2 conj | 3834.1 name nom masc | 2504.1 conj | 2648.2 verb nom sing masc part aor act |
|---|---|---|---|---|
| **16.** Ἀναστὰς | δὲ | Παῦλος, | καὶ | κατασείσας |
| *Anastas* | *de* | *Paulos* | *kai* | *kataseisas* |
| Having risen up | and | Paul, | and | having made a sign |

| 3450.11 art dat sing fem | 5331.3 noun dat sing fem | 1500.5 verb 3sing indic aor act | 433.6 noun nom pl masc | 2448.2 name nom pl masc |
|---|---|---|---|---|
| τῇ | χειρὶ, | εἶπεν, | Ἄνδρες | Ἰσραηλῖται, |
| *tē* | *cheiri* | *eipen* | *Andres* | *Israēlitai* |
| with the | hand, | said, | Men | Israelites, |

| 2504.1 conj | 3450.7 art nom pl masc | 5236.8 verb nom pl masc part pres mid | 3450.6 art acc sing masc | 2296.4 noun acc sing masc | 189.29 verb 2pl impr aor act |
|---|---|---|---|---|---|
| καὶ | οἱ | φοβούμενοι | τὸν | θεόν, | ἀκούσατε. |
| *kai* | *hoi* | *phoboumenoi* | *ton* | *theon* | *akousate* |
| and | the | fearing | | God, | listen. |

| 3450.5 art nom sing masc | 2296.1 noun nom sing masc | 3450.2 art gen sing | 2967.2 noun gen sing masc | 3642.1 dem-pron gen sing | 2447.1 name masc |
|---|---|---|---|---|---|
| **17.** ὁ | θεὸς | τοῦ | λαοῦ | τούτου | Ἰσραὴλ |
| *ho* | *theos* | *tou* | *laou* | *toutou* | *Israēl* |
| The | God | of the | people | this | Israel |

| 1573.3 verb 3sing indic aor mid | 3450.8 art acc pl masc | 3824.9 noun acc pl masc | 2231.2 prs-pron gen 1pl | 2504.1 conj | 3450.6 art acc sing masc |
|---|---|---|---|---|---|
| ἐξελέξατο | τοὺς | πατέρας | ἡμῶν· | καὶ | τὸν |
| *exelexato* | *tous* | *pateras* | *hēmōn* | *kai* | *ton* |
| chose | the | fathers | our, | and | the |

**13:15.** In the synagogue on the Sabbath Day, they listened as usual to someone reading the selections from the Law (the Pentateuch) and from (one of) the Prophets (which in the Hebrew Bible consist of Joshua, Judges, Samuel, Kings, Isaiah, Jeremiah, Ezekiel, and the Book of the Twelve, the Minor Prophets).

Then the rulers (the leaders, the elders) of the synagogue sent to them (for Paul and Barnabas were sitting in the back of the synagogue) and courteously asked them to give a word of exhortation, a word of encouragement or challenge.

**13:16.** Paul then stood, waved his hand for silence, and asked the Israelites and the God-fearers to listen. This implies there were interested Gentiles in the synagogue audience, Gentiles who recognized the Lord as the one true God.

As mentioned previously, many Gentiles were tired of the immorality and idolatry of heathen religion. They were hungry for something better and were attracted to the synagogues and to the worship of the holy, righteous, loving God revealed in the Old Testament, the God so unlike their heathen gods. Yet many of them did not become full proselytes or converts to Judaism because they hesitated to accept circumcision, self-baptism, and the other Jewish rites and ceremonies. Some rabbis did not give them much encouragement to do so, for they would not promise them salvation if they did become Jews. They would only say their children would be counted as Jews and be under the covenant blessings. But these Gentiles still came every Sabbath to hear the Word of God and to learn more about the Holy One of Israel.

Paul's sermon here at Pisidian Antioch is given in considerable detail. Luke recorded it as an example of the kind of preaching Paul did in the Jewish synagogues. It is probable Paul used essentially the same approach the first time he spoke in a synagogue in a new town. The Book of Acts does not go into such detail in the record of later sermons.

As Paul began, he courteously addressed both the Jews and Gentiles in the audience and recognized both groups as "brethren," keeping both in mind throughout the sermon.

**13:17.** The first part of Paul's sermon (verses 17-25) reviewed the history of Israel, beginning with God's choice of Israel and their deliverance from Egypt, and leading up to God's choice of David. All this was very familiar to the Jews in the audience and showed them Paul knew the Scriptures.

Unlike Stephen, Paul did not emphasize Israel's failures. Rather, he spoke of God's choosing (for His own purpose and service) and God's exalting of the Israelites during their sojourn as foreigners (resident aliens) in Egypt. The Israelites who were made subject to oppression and slavery in Egypt saw God set them apart as His special people even during the plagues. When the terrible plague of flies covered Egypt there was not a fly in Goshen. When the

**and sat down:** . . . and took their seats, *Phillips, TCNT.*

**15. And after the reading of the law and the prophets:** After the lessons, *JB* . . . After the lesson from, *Noli* . . . After the rulers had read from, *Norlie.*

**the rulers of the synagogue sent unto them, saying:** . . . the synagogue-rulers sent unto them, *Rotherham* . . . officers of, *TNT* . . . the leaders of the synagogue worship, *Williams* . . . the Presidents of the Synagogue sent them this message, *TCNT* . . . sent a message to, *NCV.*

**Ye men and brethren:** Brethren, *RSV* . . . Fellow Jews, *Beck.*

**if ye have any word of exhortation for the people, say on:** . . . if you have any helpful words to address to the people, now is your opportunity, *TCNT* . . . any message of encouragement for...you may speak, *Williams* . . . any comforting message, *Fenton* . . . if you have any message that will encourage the people, please speak! *NCV* . . . if there is among you any word of exhortation for the people, *Worrell* . . . any word of counsel, *Moffatt* . . . by all means speak, *Phillips* . . . proceed, *Noli.*

**16. Then Paul stood up, and beckoning with his hand said:** So Paul rose, and motioning...for silence, *Weymouth* . . . standing up, and beckoning with his hand, *Worrell* . . . and suggesting silence by a wave, *Berkeley* . . . He raised his hand and said, *NCV.*

**Men of Israel:** Israelites, *Weymouth.*

**and ye that fear God:** . . . and such as revere God! *Rotherham* . . . and all here who reverence God, *TCNT* . . . and you God-fearing people, *Norlie* . . . and God-fearing brothers, *Noli.*

**give audience:** . . . hearken, *ASV, Worrell* . . . listen to me, *TCNT* . . . pay attention to me, *Weymouth* . . . hear my words, *Lamsa.*

**17. The God of this people of Israel:** . . . of this people Israel, *RSV* . . . of the people of Israel, *NIV* . . . The God of our nation, *JB.*

**chose our fathers:** . . . selected our fathers, *Berkeley* . . . chose out, *KJII* . . . chose our ancestors, *TCNT.*

| 2967.4 noun acc sing masc | 5150.2 verb 3sing indic aor act | 1706.1 prep | 3450.11 art dat sing fem | 3802.2 noun dat sing fem | 1706.1 prep | 1087.3 noun dat sing fem |
|---|---|---|---|---|---|---|
| λαὸν | ὕψωσεν | ἐν | τῇ | παροικίᾳ | ἐν | γῇ |
| *laon* | *hupsōsen* | *en* | *tē* | *paroikia* | *en* | *gē* |
| people | exalted | in | the | sojourning | in | land |

17.a.**Txt:** 04C,05D,08E 020L,025P,byz.Tisc
**Var:** 01ℵ,02A,03B,Lach Treg,We/Ho,Weis,Sod UBS/☆

| 125.3 name dat fem | 125.2 name gen fem | 2504.1 conj | 3196.3 prep | 1016.2 noun gen sing masc |
|---|---|---|---|---|
| ⸂ Αἰγύπτῳ, | [a☆ Αἰγύπτου, ] | καὶ | μετὰ | βραχίονος |
| *Aiguptō* | *Aiguptou* | *kai* | *meta* | *brachionos* |
| of Egypt, | [ idem ] | and | with | arm |

| 5146.1 adj gen sing masc | 1790.3 verb 3sing indic aor act | 840.8 prs-pron acc pl masc | 1523.1 prep gen | 840.10 prs-pron gen sing fem | 2504.1 conj |
|---|---|---|---|---|---|
| ὑψηλοῦ | ἐξήγαγεν | αὐτοὺς | ἐξ | αὐτῆς· | **18.** καὶ |
| *hupsēlou* | *exēgagen* | *autous* | *ex* | *autēs* | *kai* |
| high | brought | them | out of | it, | and |

| 5453.1 conj | 4913.1 adj acc sing masc | 4911.2 adj acc sing masc | 5385.4 noun acc sing masc |
|---|---|---|---|
| ὡς | ⸂ τεσσερακονταετῆ | [☆ τεσσαρακονταετῆ ] | χρόνον |
| *hōs* | *tesserakontaetē* | *tessarakontaetē* | *chronon* |
| about | forty years | [ idem ] | time |

18.a.**Txt:** 01ℵ,02A-org 03B,04C-corr2,05D,byz.
**Var:** p74,02A-corr3 04C-org,044,1175

| 5000.1 verb 3sing indic aor act | 5003.1 verb 3sing indic aor act | 840.8 prs-pron acc pl masc | 1706.1 prep |
|---|---|---|---|
| ⸂ ἐτροποφόρησεν | [a ἐτροφοφόρησεν ] | αὐτοὺς | ἐν |
| *etropophorēsen* | *etrophophorēsen* | *autous* | *en* |
| he tolerated | [ cared for as a nurse ] | them | in |

| 3450.11 art dat sing fem | 2031.2 noun dat sing fem | 2504.1 conj | 2479.3 verb nom sing masc part aor act | 1477.4 noun pl neu |
|---|---|---|---|---|
| τῇ | ἐρήμῳ, | **19.** καὶ | καθελὼν | ἔθνη |
| *tē* | *erēmō* | *kai* | *kathelōn* | *ethnē* |
| the | desert. | And | having destroyed | nations |

19.a.**Txt:** byz.
**Var:** 01ℵ,02A,03B,04C 05D,08E,020L,025P Gries,Lach,Treg,Alf Word,Tisc,We/Ho,Weis Sod,UBS/☆

| 2017.1 num card | 1706.1 prep | 1087.3 noun dat sing fem | 5313.1 name fem | 2594.1 verb 3sing indic aor act |
|---|---|---|---|---|
| ἑπτὰ | ἐν | γῇ | Χανάαν, | ⸂ κατεκληροδότησεν |
| *hepta* | *en* | *gē* | *Chanaan* | *kateklērodotēsen* |
| seven | in | land | of Canaan, | he gave by lot |

19.b.**Txt:** 02A,04C 05D-corr,08E,020L 025P,byz.it.sa.
**Var:** p74,01ℵ,03B 05D-org,044,33,Treg Tisc,We/Ho,Weis,Sod UBS/☆

| 2594.1 verb 3sing indic aor act | 840.2 prs-pron dat pl | 3450.12 art acc sing fem | 1087.4 noun acc sing fem |
|---|---|---|---|
| [a☆ κατεκληρονόμησεν ] | ⸂b αὐτοῖς ⸃ | τὴν | γῆν |
| *kateklēronomēsen* | *autois* | *tēn* | *gēn* |
| [ he gave by inheritance ] | to them | the | land |

20.a.**Txt:** 05D-corr,08E 020L,025P,044,byz.
**Var:** p74,01ℵ,02A,03B 04C,33,sa.bo.Lach,Treg Tisc,We/Ho,Weis,Sod UBS/☆

| 840.1 prs-pron gen pl | 2504.1 conj | 3196.3 prep | 3642.18 dem-pron pl neu | 5453.1 conj | 2073.5 noun dat pl neu |
|---|---|---|---|---|---|
| αὐτῶν. | **20.** ⸂a καὶ | μετὰ | ταῦτα, ⸃ | ὡς | ἔτεσιν |
| *autōn* | *kai* | *meta* | *tauta* | *hōs* | *etesin* |
| their. | And | after | these things | about | years |

20.b.**Var:** p74,01ℵ,02A 03B,04C,33,bo.Lach Treg,Tisc,We/Ho,Weis Sod,UBS/☆

| 4919.2 num card dat | 2504.1 conj | 3866.1 num card | 2504.1 conj | 3196.3 prep |
|---|---|---|---|---|
| τετρακοσίοις | καὶ | πεντήκοντα. | [b☆+ καὶ | μετὰ |
| *tetrakosiois* | *kai* | *pentēkonta* | *kai* | *meta* |
| four hundred | and | fifty | [ and | with |

20.c.**Txt:** 04C,05D,08E 020L,025P,byz.Sod
**Var:** 01ℵ,02A,03B,Treg Tisc,We/Ho,Weis UBS/☆

| 3642.18 dem-pron pl neu | 1319.14 verb 3sing indic aor act | 2896.5 noun acc pl masc | 2175.1 conj | 4402.1 name masc | 3450.2 art gen sing |
|---|---|---|---|---|---|
| ταῦτα ] | ἔδωκεν | κριτὰς | ἕως | Σαμουὴλ | ⸂c τοῦ ⸃ |
| *tauta* | *edōken* | *kritas* | *heōs* | *Samouēl* | *tou* |
| these things ] | he gave | judges | until | Samuel | the |

plague of darkness affected Egypt, the sun was shining brightly in Goshen.

Then God confirmed His choice of Israel by leading them out of Egypt with a high arm (corresponding to a lifted-up arm in the Hebrew, that is, by mighty manifestations of His supernatural power; see Exodus 6:1-6; 19:4; Psalm 136:11,12).

**13:18.** Next Paul mentioned how God endured the manners (ways) of the people during the wilderness journey. (Several ancient Greek manuscripts read a word with only one letter different, a word which means God "carried them" as a nurse would a child. Deuteronomy 1:31 in the Septuagint version has the same variant.)

Paul was reminding his listeners of the patience of God with the Israelites during all those times of murmuring, criticizing, and complaining throughout the 40 years. The Book of Numbers shows how God had to deal with human nature in the raw. In Numbers 11, their problem was appetite; Numbers 12, jealousy; Numbers 13, unbelief; Numbers 14, presumption; Numbers 15, rebellion; Numbers 16, mutiny.

**13:19.** Next, Paul quickly summarized Joshua's conquest. The seven nations were the tribes of the Canaanites and others that were in Palestine. (See Deuteronomy 7:1 which names them.)

Then Paul reminded his listeners that God divided or parceled out the land among the tribes of Israel by lot. This refers to Joshua 14:1 which says Joshua distributed the land "for inheritance to them."

**13:20.** Paul summarized the period of the judges. The 450 years (a round number) refers not merely to the period covered by the Book of Judges, but to the whole time after they entered the land up to the beginning of David's reign (with Samuel the prophet being the last judge). (Some manuscripts apply the 450 years to the 400 years in Egypt, plus the time of the conquest up to the time of the dividing of the land in chapter 14 of Joshua; that is, they say that after the 450 years, God gave them judges up to the time of Samuel.)

It should be noted that the periods during which the judges ruled overlapped in many cases. For example, the 40 years of Philistine oppression mentioned in Judges 13:1 began with Judges 10:7 and ended with 1 Samuel 7:10. A careful comparison of the Bible passages concerned shows that the Ammonites oppressed Israel from the east while Philistines oppressed them from the west.

Again, Paul did not emphasize the negative side of the period of the judges. He reminded his listeners only that it was God who gave them the judges, and he named Samuel, the judge who was more than a judge, the only judge who was able to unite all 12 tribes and through his ministry bring a spiritual revival (1 Samuel 7:3-9).



**and exalted the people when they dwelt as strangers in the land of Egypt:** . . . and made the people great during their stay in Egypt, *Weymouth* . . . during the time they lived in Egypt, *NCV* . . . exalted and multiplied them, *Lamsa* . . . lifted up the people in their stay, *KJII* . . . he uplifted by the sojourn in Egypt's land, *Rotherham* . . . prospered the people even while they were exiles, *Phillips* . . . when they were living as strangers in, *TNT* . . . during their residence, *Noli.*

**and with an high arm brought he them out of it:** . . . until with wondrous power He brought, *Weymouth* . . . with an uplifted arm, *Swann* . . . With mighty power, *NIV* . . . He led them forth out of it, *Worrell.*

**18. And about the time of forty years:** For about forty years, *TCNT.*

**suffered he their manners in the wilderness:** . . . he bore with them in the Desert, *TCNT* . . . He fed them like a nurse in the desert, *Weymouth* . . . he put up with their ways, *BB* . . . He endured their behavior, *Berkeley* . . . he was patient with them, *NCV* . . . after he had taken care of them, *Goodspeed* . . . he nourished them, *Noyes* . . . tenderly cared for them, *Wuest.*

**19. And when he had destroyed seven nations in the land of Chanaan:** Then, after overthrowing...Canaan, *Weymouth.*

**he divided their land to them by lot:** . . . he gave them their land for an inheritance, *ASV* . . . he allotted their land to the people, *TCNT* . . . He divided that country among them as their inheritance, *Weymouth* . . . gave their land to Israel to possess, *TNT* . . . giving their land to His people, *SEB* . . . gave the land to his people, *NCV* . . . distributed the land, *Klingensmith* . . . distributed by lot, *Worrell.*

**20. And after that he gave unto them judges about the space of four hundred and fifty years, until Samuel the prophet:** Later on he gave them Judges, of whom the Prophet Samuel was the last, *TCNT* . . . all of which took about, *MLNT* . . . All this happened in about 450 years, *NCV.*

| **4254.2** noun gen sing masc | **2518.1** conj | **153.30** verb 3pl indic aor mid | **928.4** noun acc sing masc | **2504.1** conj |
|---|---|---|---|---|
| προφήτου· | 21. κἀκεῖθεν | ἠτήσαντο | βασιλέα, | καὶ |
| *prophētou* | *kakeithen* | *ētēsanto* | *basilea* | *kai* |
| prophet | and then | they asked for | a king, | and |

| **1319.14** verb 3sing indic aor act | **840.2** prs-pron dat pl | **3450.5** art nom sing masc | **2296.1** noun nom sing masc | **3450.6** art acc sing masc | **4406.1** name masc |
|---|---|---|---|---|---|
| ἔδωκεν | αὐτοῖς | ὁ | θεὸς | τὸν | Σαοὺλ |
| *edōken* | *autois* | *ho* | *theos* | *ton* | *Saoul* |
| he gave | to them | | God | | Saul |

| **5048.4** noun acc sing masc | **2769.1** name masc | **433.4** noun acc sing masc | **1523.2** prep gen | **5279.1** noun gen sing fem | **951.1** name masc |
|---|---|---|---|---|---|
| υἱὸν | Κίς, | ἄνδρα | ἐκ | φυλῆς | Βενιαμίν, |
| *huion* | *Kis* | *andra* | *ek* | *phulēs* | *Beniamin* |
| son | of Kish, | a man | of | tribe | of Benjamin, |

| **2073.3** noun pl neu | **4910.2** num card | **4910.1** num card | **2504.1** conj |
|---|---|---|---|
| ἔτη | ‘ τεσσαράκοντα. | [ τεσσεράκοντα. ] | 22. καὶ |
| *etē* | *tessarakonta* | *tesserakonta* | *kai* |
| years | forty. | [ idem ] | And |

| **3150.3** verb nom sing masc part aor act | **840.6** prs-pron acc sing masc | **1446.5** verb 3sing indic aor act | **840.2** prs-pron dat pl | **3450.6** art acc sing masc |
|---|---|---|---|---|
| μεταστήσας | αὐτὸν | ἤγειρεν | ‘ αὐτοῖς | τὸν |
| *metastēsas* | *auton* | *ēgeiren* | *autois* | *ton* |
| having removed | him | he raised up | to them | |

| **1132.1** name masc | **3450.6** art acc sing masc | **1132.2** name masc | **840.2** prs-pron dat pl | **1519.1** prep | **928.4** noun acc sing masc |
|---|---|---|---|---|---|
| Δαβὶδ | [☆ τὸν | Δαυὶδ | αὐτοῖς ] | εἰς | βασιλέα, |
| *Dabid* | *ton* | *Dauid* | *autois* | *eis* | *basilea* |
| David | | [ David | to them ] | for | king, |

| **3614.3** rel-pron dat sing | **2504.1** conj | **1500.5** verb 3sing indic aor act | **3113.22** verb nom sing masc part aor act | **2128.6** verb indic aor act | **1132.1** name masc |
|---|---|---|---|---|---|
| ᾧ | καὶ | εἶπεν | μαρτυρήσας, | Εὗρον | Δαβὶδ |
| *hō* | *kai* | *eipen* | *marturēsas* | *Heuron* | *Dabid* |
| who | also | he said | having borne witness, | I found | David |

| **3450.6** art acc sing masc | **3450.2** art gen sing | **2397.1** name masc | **433.4** noun acc sing masc | **2567.3** prep | **3450.12** art acc sing fem |
|---|---|---|---|---|---|
| τὸν | τοῦ | Ἰεσσαί, | ἄνδρα | κατὰ | τὴν |
| *ton* | *tou* | *Iessai* | *andra* | *kata* | *tēn* |
| the | of | Jesse, | a man | according to | the |

| **2559.4** noun acc sing fem | **1466.2** prs-pron gen 1sing | **3614.5** rel-pron nom sing masc | **4020.52** verb 3sing indic fut act | **3820.1** adj | **3450.17** art pl neu |
|---|---|---|---|---|---|
| καρδίαν | μου, | ὅς | ποιήσει | πάντα | τὰ |
| *kardian* | *mou* | *hos* | *poiēsei* | *panta* | *ta* |
| heart | my, | who | will do | all | the |

| **2284.4** noun pl neu | **1466.2** prs-pron gen 1sing | **3642.1** dem-pron gen sing | **3450.5** art nom sing masc | **2296.1** noun nom sing masc | **570.3** prep |
|---|---|---|---|---|---|
| θελήματά | μου. | 23. Τούτου | ὁ | θεὸς | ἀπὸ |
| *thelēmata* | *mou* | *Toutou* | *ho* | *theos* | *apo* |
| will | my. | Of this | | God | of |

| **3450.2** art gen sing | **4543.2** noun gen sing neu | **2567.1** prep | **1845.4** noun acc sing fem | **1446.5** verb 3sing indic aor act |
|---|---|---|---|---|
| τοῦ | σπέρματος | κατ’ | ἐπαγγελίαν | ‘ ἤγειρεν |
| *tou* | *spermatos* | *kat’* | *epangelian* | *ēgeiren* |
| the | seed | according to | promise | raised up |

**13:21.** Next Paul reminded them of how the people asked for a king and God gave them Saul (which means "asked for"). The fact that the people asked for a king reminded Paul's listeners of the whole story of how the people wanted a king to be like the other nations. But what Paul was emphasizing is that God was guiding the history of Israel, and He was the One who gave Saul to the people. Saul was also identified as "of the tribe of Benjamin," the same tribe to which the apostle Paul belonged.

The 40 years of King Saul's reign are confirmed by the Jewish historian, Josephus, but they are not given in the Old Testament. (Actually, Josephus seems to mean that Saul reigned 20 years and Samuel judged 20 years, together making the 40.)

First Samuel 13:1 reads literally, "Saul was a son of year in his reigning (when he began to reign), and he reigned two years over Israel." This follows the usual formula for giving the length of a king's reign, like that found in 2 Kings 14:2; 16:2; 18:2. Many believe this means that early in the process of copying the Books of Samuel, the scribe accidentally left out the age of Saul and the length of his reign. Many Bible scholars conjecture that Saul was 40 years old when he began to reign and that he reigned 32 years. This would mean Paul was including in Saul's reign the 7½ years when David reigned in Hebron and Saul's son continued Saul's reign and kingdom. Jews in those days usually rounded off the last half year or part year of a reign and added it as a year to the total, thus giving 40 years here. Other writers conjecture that King Saul reigned 42 years and that Paul rounded it off here to 40 years.

**13:22.** The climax of this historical part of Paul's sermon came when he pointed out that God removed Saul from his throne and gave them (raised up for them) David as their king. One thing was really important about David. God bore witness to him that he was a man after God's own heart, one who would do all God's will. Saul became a self-willed king. In contrast to him, David, deep in his heart, really wanted to do all of God's will. This is what made him a man after God's own heart. God wanted a person who would do all His will whether he felt like it or not.

Outwardly, David was not an obvious choice, a young boy who was relegated to keeping the sheep. But the radiance of his personality and the brightness of his eyes (1 Samuel 16:12) showed that his inner life was clean and pure. He was a young man who looked out over the hills and into the sky, not to dream, but to see the glory of God (Psalm 19:1).

**13:23.** The people in Paul's audience knew of God's promise to David. After David brought back the ark to Jerusalem, he wanted to build a temple. It was not God's time nor God's will for David. But God did not let David go away in disappointment. Because David submitted to God's will, God gave him a new promise, a

**21. And afterward they desired a king:** And when, after a while, they demanded a king, *TCNT* . . . Next they asked for a king, *Weymouth* . . . Then when they begged for, *Phillips.*

**and God gave unto them Saul the son of Cis:** . . . the son of Kish, *ASV.*

**a man of the tribe of Benjamin:** . . . a Benjamite, *Weymouth* . . . from the family group of, *NCV.*

**by the space of forty years:** He was king for, *SEB* . . . who reigned for forty years, *TCNT.*

**22. And when he had removed him:** After removing him, *TCNT* . . . And taking him away, *KJII* . . . After deposing him, *Moffatt* . . . But God took the throne away from him again, *Beck* . . . And when in time God took Saul away, *Lamsa* . . . deposing him, *Berkeley.*

**he raised up unto them David to be their king:** . . . he raised David to the throne, *TCNT* . . . He raised up David for their king, *Berkeley.*

**to whom also he gave testimony, and said:** . . . and he bore also this testimony to him, *TCNT* . . . a man of whom God Himself bore witness in the words, *Phillips* . . . This is what God said about him, *NCV.*

**I have found David the son of Jesse:**

**a man after mine own heart:** . . . a man I love, *Weymouth* . . . a man dear to my heart, *BB* . . . a man agreeable to my mind, *Berkeley* . . . is the man I like, *SEB* . . . the kind of man I want, *NCV.*

**which shall fulfil all my will:** . . . who will carry out all my purposes, *TCNT* . . . obey all My commands, *Weymouth* . . . do all that my will requires, *Williams* . . . carry out My whole program, *Berkeley* . . . who does all my will, *Klingensmith* . . . He will do all the things I want him to do, *SEB.*

**23. Of this man's seed hath God:** It was from this man's descendants that God, *TCNT* . . . Of this man's posterity, *RSV* . . . this man's offspring, *Lamsa* . . . God has brought one of David's descendants, *SEB.*

**according to his promise:** . . . in fulfillment of His promise, *Weymouth.*

23.a.**Txt:** 04C,05D,33 1241,sa.Steph
**Var:** p74,01ℵ,02A,03B 08E,020L,025P,044,byz. bo.Gries,Lach,Treg,Alf Tisc,We/Ho,Weis,Sod UBS/☆

| **70.8** verb 3sing indic aor act | **3450.3** art dat sing | **2447.1** name masc | **4842.4** noun acc sing masc | **2400.3** name acc masc |
|---|---|---|---|---|
| [a☆ ἤγαγεν ] | τῷ | Ἰσραὴλ | σωτῆρα | Ἰησοῦν, |
| *ēgagen* | *tō* | *Israēl* | *sōtēra* | *Iēsoun* |
| [ brought ] | | for Israel | a Saviour | Jesus, |

| | **4155.1** verb gen sing masc part aor act | **2464.2** name gen masc | **4112.1** prep | **4241.2** noun gen sing neu | **3450.10** art gen sing fem |
|---|---|---|---|---|---|
| 24. | προκηρύξαντος | Ἰωάννου | πρὸ | προσώπου | τῆς |
| | *prokēruxantos* | *Iōannou* | *pro* | *prosōpou* | *tēs* |
| | having proclaimed | John | before | face | of the |

| **1513.2** noun gen sing fem | **840.3** prs-pron gen sing | **902.1** noun sing neu | **3211.1** noun gen sing fem | **3820.3** adj dat sing | **3450.3** art dat sing |
|---|---|---|---|---|---|
| εἰσόδου | αὐτοῦ | βάπτισμα | μετανοίας | παντὶ | τῷ |
| *eisodou* | *autou* | *baptisma* | *metanoias* | *panti* | *tō* |
| entrance | his | baptism | of repentance | all | to the |

25.a.**Txt:** 020L,025P,byz. Tisc,Weis
**Var:** 01ℵ,02A,03B,04C 05D,08E,Lach,Treg,Alf We/Ho,Sod,UBS/☆

| **2967.3** noun dat sing masc | **2447.1** name masc | | **5453.1** conj | **1156.2** conj | **3997.15** verb 3sing indic imperf act | **3450.5** art nom sing masc |
|---|---|---|---|---|---|---|
| λαῷ | Ἰσραήλ. | 25. | ὡς | δὲ | ἐπλήρου | ⸂a ὁ ⸃ |
| *laō* | *Israēl* | | *hōs* | *de* | *eplērou* | *ho* |
| people | of Israel. | | As | and | was fulfilling | |

| **2464.1** name nom masc | **3450.6** art acc sing masc | **1402.1** noun acc sing masc | **2978.26** verb 3sing indic imperf act | **4949.1** intr-pron |
|---|---|---|---|---|
| Ἰωάννης | τὸν | δρόμον, | ἔλεγεν, | ⸀ Τίνα |
| *Iōannēs* | *ton* | *dromon* | *elegen* | *Tina* |
| John | the | course, | he was saying, | Who |

25.b.**Txt:** p45,04C,05D 08E,020L,025P,044,byz. bo.
**Var:** p74,01ℵ,02A,03B sa.Lach,Treg,Alf,Tisc We/Ho,Weis,Sod UBS/☆

| **1466.6** prs-pron acc 1sing | **4949.9** intr-pron sing neu | **1466.7** prs-pron acc 1sing | **5120.1** verb 2pl indic pres act | **1498.32** verb inf pres act |
|---|---|---|---|---|
| με | [b☆ Τί | ἐμὲ ] | ὑπονοεῖτε | εἶναι; |
| *me* | *Ti* | *eme* | *huponoeite* | *einai* |
| me | [ Who | me ] | do you suppose | to be? |

| **3620.2** partic | **1498.2** verb 1sing indic pres act | **1466.1** prs-pron nom 1sing | **233.1** conj | **1481.20** verb 2sing impr aor mid | **2048.34** verb 3sing indic pres mid |
|---|---|---|---|---|---|
| οὐκ | εἰμὶ | ἐγώ· | ἀλλ' | ἰδοὺ, | ἔρχεται |
| *ouk* | *eimi* | *egō* | *all'* | *idou* | *erchetai* |
| Not | am | I, | but | lo, | he comes |

| **3196.2** prep | **1466.7** prs-pron acc 1sing | **3614.2** rel-pron gen sing | **3620.2** partic | **1498.2** verb 1sing indic pres act | **510.2** adj nom sing masc |
|---|---|---|---|---|---|
| μετ' | ἐμὲ, | οὗ | οὐκ | εἰμὶ | ἄξιος |
| *met'* | *eme* | *hou* | *ouk* | *eimi* | *axios* |
| after | me, | of whom | not | I am | worthy |

| **3450.16** art sing neu | **5104.2** noun sing neu | **3450.1** art gen pl | **4087.5** noun gen pl masc | **3061.15** verb inf aor act | | **433.6** noun nom pl masc |
|---|---|---|---|---|---|---|
| τὸ | ὑπόδημα | τῶν | ποδῶν | λῦσαι. | 26. | Ἄνδρες |
| *to* | *hupodēma* | *tōn* | *podōn* | *lusai* | | *Andres* |
| the | sandal | of the | feet | to loose. | | Men |

| **79.6** noun nom pl masc | **5048.6** noun nom pl masc | **1079.2** noun gen sing neu | **11.1** name masc | **2504.1** conj | **3450.7** art nom pl masc |
|---|---|---|---|---|---|
| ἀδελφοί, | υἱοὶ | γένους | Ἀβραάμ, | καὶ | οἱ |
| *adelphoi* | *huioi* | *genous* | *Abraam* | *kai* | *hoi* |
| brothers, | sons | of race | of Abraham, | and | the |

| **1706.1** prep | **5050.3** prs-pron dat 2pl | **5236.8** verb nom pl masc part pres mid | **3450.6** art acc sing masc | **2296.4** noun acc sing masc | **5050.3** prs-pron dat 2pl |
|---|---|---|---|---|---|
| ἐν | ὑμῖν | φοβούμενοι | τὸν | θεόν, | ⸀ ὑμῖν |
| *en* | *humin* | *phoboumenoi* | *ton* | *theon* | *humin* |
| among | you | fearing | | God, | to you |

promise beyond David's expectations. This promise, known as the Davidic Covenant, is one of the great covenants of the Bible. It included the promise that David's son would succeed him on the throne and build a temple as a place where God's name could be mentioned in prayer with assurance that God keeps His promises. The covenant also revealed God's purpose to make David's throne eternal (2 Samuel 7:11-16; Psalm 89:29-34). Individual kings of David's line would still be punished for sin, but God would not let David's line be replaced as Saul's had been.

Paul's audience also knew the prophecies that God would raise up a greater seed to David (Isaiah 9:6,7; 11:1-5), as well as the prophecy that He would give David's throne to the One whose right it is (Ezekiel 21:27). Paul declared that God had fulfilled His promise, and from the seed (descendants) of David raised up a Saviour, Jesus (Matthew 1:21).

**13:24.** Paul further identified Jesus as the One John the Baptist recognized as the One who was to come. John the Baptist's ministry was well known everywhere. He had awakened the nation of Israel to their need of repentance as preparation for the coming of the Messiah. Many were sincerely waiting for the consolation (or the Consoler) of Israel and for redemption to come (Luke 2:25,38). John's baptism was a baptism because of repentance, a baptism that symbolized a repentance which had already taken place.

**13:25.** John the Baptist's denial that he was the One to come was also well-known. John's testimony to Jesus was therefore important. John was not trying to start a new sect or religion. He did not seek to build an organization around himself. He was preparing men to meet the Mighty One who held their eternal destiny in His hands. John gained many disciples who became very loyal to him. Yet he kept pointing them ahead to the coming One, the One who would take a position ahead of John in importance and dignity.

John therefore was willing to take the humble place. He confessed he was not worthy to loose (unloose, take off) the shoes (the sandals) of that One. He felt he was not worthy to do the most menial task, a task usually done by a slave.

**13:26.** The second part of this sermon in Antioch (verses 26-37) deals with the death and resurrection of Jesus and with the witness of the apostles as well as the witness of the Old Testament Scriptures.

Paul addressed the Jews in his audience as men, brothers, descendants of the family of Abraham. By this he drew attention to their common heritage of the promises and blessings given to Abraham, a heritage that was intended to bring blessing to all the families (nations) of the earth (Genesis 12:3). He also addressed the Gentiles as those who were "fearers of," that is, those who continually rev-



**raised unto Israel a Saviour, Jesus:** . . . brought Israel a Saviour, *TCNT* . . . given Israel a Saviour, *Norlie* . . . to be their Savior, *SEB.*

**24. When John had first preached before his coming:** John had proclaimed, before Jesus came among them, *TCNT* . . . John's pre-proclamation, *Concordant* . . . Before whose coming, *Lamsa.*

**the baptism of repentance to all the people of Israel:** . . . baptism as an expression of repentance, *Williams* . . . the baptism which goes with a change of heart, *BB* . . . of changed hearts and lives, *NCV* . . . to change their hearts and to be immersed, *SEB.*

**25. And as John fulfilled his course:** As John was drawing towards the end of his career, *TCNT* . . . was finishing his course, *RSV* . . . he was finishing his race, *Montgomery* . . . was completing his work, *BB* . . . finishing the course of his office, *Wuest* . . . was about finished with his work, *Norlie* . . . completing his mission, *Fenton* . . . reached the end of his time, *Phillips* . . . was nearing the end of his life-work, *TNT.*

**he said:** . . . he used to say, *TCNT* . . . repeatedly asked the people, *Montgomery.*

**Whom think ye that I am? I am not he:** What do you think I am? I am not the Christ, *TCNT.*

**But, behold, there cometh one after me:** No, but after me one is coming, *RSV* . . . no, he is coming after me, *Moffatt* . . . He is coming later, *NCV.*

**whose shoes of his feet I am not worthy to loose:** He is so superior to me that I am not worthy, *Noli* . . . whose shoe, even, I am not worthy to untie, *TCNT* . . . whose sandal...to unfasten, *Weymouth* . . . to untie his shoestrings, *Murdock.*

**26. Men and brethren, children of the stock of Abraham:** Brethren! sons of the race of Abraham, *Rotherham* . . . descendants of the family of Abraham, *Weymouth.*

**and whosoever among you feareth God:** . . . all among you who fear God, *Phillips* . . . and you non-Jews who worship God, *NCV.*

## Acts 13:27

26.a.**Txt:** p45,04C,08E 020L,025P,044,byz.it.bo. **Var:** p74,01ℵ,02A,03B 05D,33,sa.Alf,Tisc We/Ho,Weis,Sod UBS/⋆

26.b.**Txt:** 08E,020L 025P,byz. **Var:** 01ℵ,02A,03B,04C 05D,Lach,Treg,Alf Word,Tisc,We/Ho,Weis Sod,UBS/⋆

29.a.**Txt:** Steph **Var:** 01ℵ,02A,03B,04C 05D,08E,020L,025P,byz. Gries,Lach,Treg,Alf Word,Tisc,We/Ho,Weis Sod,UBS/⋆

| **2231.3** prs-pron dat 1pl | **3450.5** art nom sing masc | **3030.1** noun nom sing masc | **3450.10** art gen sing fem | **4843.2** noun gen sing fem |
|---|---|---|---|---|
| [a⋆ ἡμῖν ] | ὁ | λόγος | τῆς | σωτηρίας |
| *hēmin* | *ho* | *logos* | *tēs* | *sōtērias* |
| [ to us ] | the | word | of the | salvation |

| **3642.10** dem-pron gen sing fem | **643.25** verb 3sing indic aor pass | **1805.5** verb 3sing indic aor pass | **3450.7** art nom pl masc |
|---|---|---|---|
| ταύτης | ‘ ἀπεστάλη· | [b⋆ ἐξαπεστάλη. ] | **27.** οἱ |
| *tautēs* | *apestalē* | *exapestalē* | *hoi* |
| this | was sent: | [ was sent out. ] | the |

| **1056.1** conj | **2700.6** verb nom pl masc part pres act | **1706.1** prep | **2395.1** name fem | **2504.1** conj | **3450.7** art nom pl masc |
|---|---|---|---|---|---|
| γὰρ | κατοικοῦντες | ἐν | Ἱερουσαλὴμ | καὶ | οἱ |
| *gar* | *katoikountes* | *en* | *Hierousalēm* | *kai* | *hoi* |
| for | dwelling | in | Jerusalem | and | the |

| **752.5** noun nom pl masc | **840.1** prs-pron gen pl | **3642.6** dem-pron acc sing masc | **49.10** verb nom pl masc part aor act | **2504.1** conj |
|---|---|---|---|---|
| ἄρχοντες | αὐτῶν, | τοῦτον | ἀγνοήσαντες | καὶ |
| *archontes* | *autōn* | *touton* | *agnoēsantes* | *kai* |
| rulers | their, | this one | not having known | and |

| **3450.15** art acc pl fem | **5292.8** noun acc pl fem | **3450.1** art gen pl | **4254.5** noun gen pl masc | **3450.15** art acc pl fem | **2567.3** prep | **3820.17** adj sing neu |
|---|---|---|---|---|---|---|
| τὰς | φωνὰς | τῶν | προφητῶν | τὰς | κατὰ | πᾶν |
| *tas* | *phōnas* | *tōn* | *prophētōn* | *tas* | *kata* | *pan* |
| the | voices | of the | prophets | the | on | every |

| **4378.1** noun sing neu | **312.16** verb acc pl fem part pres mid | **2892.18** verb nom pl masc part aor act | **3997.4** verb 3pl indic aor act |
|---|---|---|---|
| σάββατον | ἀναγινωσκομένας, | κρίναντες | ἐπλήρωσαν· |
| *sabbaton* | *anaginōskomenas* | *krinantes* | *eplērōsan* |
| sabbath | being read, | having judged | they fulfilled. |

| **2504.1** conj | **3235.5** num card acc fem | **155.3** noun acc sing fem | **2265.2** noun gen sing masc | **2128.18** verb nom pl masc part aor act |
|---|---|---|---|---|
| **28.** καὶ | μηδεμίαν | αἰτίαν | θανάτου | εὑρόντες |
| *kai* | *mēdemian* | *aitian* | *thanatou* | *heurontes* |
| And | no one | cause | of death | having found |

| **153.30** verb 3pl indic aor mid | **3952.4** name acc masc | **335.14** verb inf aor pass | **840.6** prs-pron acc sing masc | **5453.1** conj |
|---|---|---|---|---|
| ᾐτήσαντο | Πιλᾶτον | ἀναιρεθῆναι | αὐτόν. | **29.** ὡς |
| *ētēsanto* | *Pilaton* | *anairethēnai* | *auton* | *hōs* |
| they begged | Pilate | to put to death | him. | When |

| **1156.2** conj | **4903.5** verb 3pl indic aor act | **533.1** adj | **3820.1** adj | **3450.17** art pl neu | **3875.1** prep |
|---|---|---|---|---|---|
| δὲ | ἐτέλεσαν | ‘ ἅπαντα | [a⋆ πάντα ] | τὰ | περὶ |
| *de* | *etelesan* | *hapanta* | *panta* | *ta* | *peri* |
| and | they finished | all things | [ idem ] | the | concerning |

| **840.3** prs-pron gen sing | **1119.31** verb pl neu part perf mid | **2479.4** verb nom pl masc part aor act | **570.3** prep | **3450.2** art gen sing |
|---|---|---|---|---|
| αὐτοῦ | γεγραμμένα, | καθελόντες | ἀπὸ | τοῦ |
| *autou* | *gegrammena* | *kathelontes* | *apo* | *tou* |
| him | having been written, | having taken down | from | the |

| **3448.2** noun gen sing neu | **4935.11** verb 3pl indic aor act | **1519.1** prep | **3283.1** noun sing neu | **3450.5** art nom sing masc | **1156.2** conj | **2296.1** noun nom sing masc |
|---|---|---|---|---|---|---|
| ξύλου, | ἔθηκαν | εἰς | μνημεῖον· | **30.** ὁ | δὲ | θεὸς |
| *xulou* | *ethēkan* | *eis* | *mnēmeion* | *ho* | *de* | *theos* |
| tree, | they put | in | a tomb; | | but | God |

erenced (the one, true) God. "To you (both Jew and Gentile) is the word (*logos*, message) of this salvation sent." The message of salvation through faith in Christ was sent to them personally through those commissioned by the Lord Jesus.

**13:27.** Paul next showed that the death of Jesus was the fulfillment of God's prophetic Word and that it was carried out by the Jews living in Jerusalem and their rulers.

It is important to notice here that Paul did not blame the death of Jesus on all the Jews or even on the Jews in general. He put the blame only on those Jews and their rulers in Jerusalem who were actually involved. He also recognized that they did it because they were ignorant of Jesus and of the voices of the prophets whose books were read every Sabbath in their synagogues. The Greek word used here sometimes implies willful ignorance or a deliberate ignoring of the truth. Since they did know these prophecies and had often heard them read, willful ignorance is indeed meant here.

The result was that these Jerusalem Jews and their rulers (which might include the Romans) fulfilled those prophecies by condemning Jesus and handing Him over for sentencing.

**13:28.** Paul also said the Jerusalem Jews found no cause, no real grounds for a death sentence, yet they asked Pilate to have Him killed (done away with, destroyed, put to death in a violent manner). The Jerusalem leaders did seek to find some grounds for condemning Jesus to death but they were never successful.

**13:29.** The Jerusalem dwellers fulfilled all the prophecies concerning the death of the Messiah, the Christ. In their preliminary scourging they fulfilled Isaiah 50:6 and 53:5. In their mockery as they bowed the knee, they portrayed the fact that Jesus is the King of kings and Lord of lords and before Him every knee shall someday bow (Revelation 19:16; cf. Isaiah 45:23; Philippians 2:10,11). The further mocking and beating of their helpless victim and His silent acceptance of it brought a further fulfillment of Isaiah 53:7. Taking Jesus to a place outside the city walls fulfilled the typology of the sin offering on the Day of Atonement (Leviticus 16:27; Hebrew 13:11). Even in casting lots over His clothes, the calloused executioners unconsciously were fulfilling the great prophecy of Psalm 22:16-18.

These prophecies having been fulfilled, Jesus was taken down from the "tree" (the rough wooden cross; compare Deuteronomy 21:23 and Galatians 3:13) and laid in a tomb. "Tree" is a general term here for anything made of wood. Paul did not name Nicodemus and Joseph of Arimathea as the ones who actually took Jesus down from the cross and put Him in Joseph's new tomb (John 19:38,39). Probably they were unknown to the people in the synagogue at Antioch.

**to you is the word of this salvation sent:** . . . it was to us that the Message of this Salvation was sent, *TCNT.*

**27. For they that dwell at Jerusalem, and their rulers:** . . . for the inhabitants of, *TNT.*

**because they knew him not:** . . . not recognizing him, *Rotherham* . . . failing to recognize Jesus, *TCNT* . . . refused to recognize him, *Phillips* . . . because they were ignorant of Him, *Weymouth* . . . did not realize it, *SEB.*

**nor yet the voices of the prophets which are read every sabbath day:** . . . did not understand the predictions of, *Noli* . . . and not understanding the utterances of, *TCNT* . . . and to understand the voice of the prophets, *Phillips.*

**they have fulfilled them in condemning him:** Yet they made the prophets' words come true by condemning Jesus, *TEV* . . . have actually fulfilled the predictions, *Weymouth* . . . the utterances of, *TNT.*

**28. And though they found no cause of death in him:** They found no ground at all for condemning him to death, *TCNT* . . . Without having found Him guilty of any capital offence, *Weymouth* . . . For though they found no cause, *Phillips* . . . couldn't find any real reason why he should die, *SEB* . . . they did not find any reason for the death sentence, *TNT* . . . found nothing to justify his death, *JB.*

**yet desired they Pilate that he should be slain:** . . . and yet demanded his execution from Pilate, *TCNT* . . . they urged Pilate to have Him put to death, *Weymouth* . . . begged Pilate to have him executed, *Phillips* . . . asked Pilate to kill him, *SEB.*

**29. And when they had fulfilled all that was written of him:** After carrying out everything written about him, *TCNT* . . . And when they had completed, *Phillips* . . . had accomplished all that, *TNT* . . . when they finished all things, *KJII.*

**they took him down from the tree:** . . . they took Jesus down from the cross, *TCNT.*

**and laid him in a sepulchre:** . . . and laid him in a tomb, *RSV.*

| 1446.5 verb 3sing indic aor act | 840.6 prs-pron acc sing masc | 1523.2 prep gen | 3361.2 adj gen pl | 3614.5 rel-pron nom sing masc | 3571.21 verb 3sing indic aor pass |
|---|---|---|---|---|---|
| ἤγειρεν | αὐτὸν | ἐκ | νεκρῶν, | 31. ὃς | ὤφθη |
| *ēgeiren* | *auton* | *ek* | *nekrōn* | *hos* | *ōphthē* |
| raised | him | from | dead, | who | appeared |

| 1894.3 prep | 2232.1 noun fem | 3979.3 adj comp pl | 3450.4 art dat pl | 4723.1 verb dat pl masc part aor act | 840.4 prs-pron dat sing |
|---|---|---|---|---|---|
| ἐπὶ | ἡμέρας | πλείους | τοῖς | συναναβᾶσιν | αὐτῷ |
| *epi* | *hēmeras* | *pleious* | *tois* | *sunanabasin* | *autō* |
| for | days | many | the | having come up with | him |

| 570.3 prep | 3450.10 art gen sing fem | 1049.2 name gen sing fem | 1519.1 prep | 2395.2 name fem | 3610.2 rel-pron nom pl masc |
|---|---|---|---|---|---|
| ἀπὸ | τῆς | Γαλιλαίας | εἰς | Ἰερουσαλήμ, | οἵτινες |
| *apo* | *tēs* | *Galilaias* | *eis* | *Ierousalēm* | *hoitines* |
| from | | Galilee | to | Jerusalem, | who |

31.a.**Var:** 01א,02A,04C sa.bo.Lach,Treg,Alf Word,Tisc,We/Ho,Sod UBS/☆

| 3431.1 adv | 1498.7 verb 3pl indic pres act | 3116.4 noun nom pl masc | 840.3 prs-pron gen sing | 4242.1 prep | 3450.6 art acc sing masc |
|---|---|---|---|---|---|
| [a☆+ νῦν ] | εἰσιν | μάρτυρες | αὐτοῦ | πρὸς | τὸν |
| *nun* | *eisin* | *martures* | *autou* | *pros* | *ton* |
| [ now ] | are | witnesses | his | to | the |

| 2967.4 noun acc sing masc | 2504.1 conj | 2231.1 prs-pron nom 1pl | 5050.4 prs-pron acc 2pl | 2076.5 verb 1pl indic pres mid |
|---|---|---|---|---|
| λαόν. | 32. καὶ | ἡμεῖς | ὑμᾶς | εὐαγγελιζόμεθα |
| *laon* | *kai* | *hēmeis* | *humas* | *euangelizometha* |
| people. | And | we | to you | announce the good news |

| 3450.12 art acc sing fem | 4242.1 prep | 3450.8 art acc pl masc | 3824.9 noun acc pl masc | 1845.4 noun acc sing fem | 1090.58 verb acc sing fem part aor mid |
|---|---|---|---|---|---|
| τὴν | πρὸς | τοὺς | πατέρας | ἐπαγγελίαν | γενομένην, |
| *tēn* | *pros* | *tous* | *pateras* | *epangelian* | *genomenēn* |
| the | to | the | fathers | promise | made, |

| 3617.1 conj | 3642.12 dem-pron acc sing fem | 3450.5 art nom sing masc | 2296.1 noun nom sing masc | 1590.1 verb 3sing indic perf act |
|---|---|---|---|---|
| 33. ὅτι | ταύτην | ὁ | θεὸς | ἐκπεπλήρωκεν |
| *hoti* | *tautēn* | *ho* | *theos* | *ekpeplērōken* |
| that | this | | God | has fulfilled |

33.a.**Txt:** 04C-corr,08E 020L,025P,33,1241,byz. Weis,Sod
**Var1:** p74,01א,02A,03B 04C-org,05D,044,Lach Treg,Tisc,We/Ho
**Var2:** UBS/☆

| 3450.4 art dat pl | 4891.6 noun dat pl neu | 840.1 prs-pron gen pl | 2231.3 prs-pron dat 1pl | 2231.2 prs-pron gen 1pl | 2231.3 prs-pron dat 1pl |
|---|---|---|---|---|---|
| τοῖς | τέκνοις | ⸂ αὐτῶν | ἡμῖν, | [1a ἡμῶν | 2☆ ἡμῖν ] |
| *tois* | *teknois* | *autōn* | *hēmin* | *hēmōn* | *hēmin* |
| to the | children | their | to us, | [ our | to us ] |

| 448.10 verb nom sing masc part aor act | 2400.3 name acc masc | 5453.1 conj | 2504.1 conj | 1706.1 prep | 3450.3 art dat sing | 5403.1 noun dat sing masc |
|---|---|---|---|---|---|---|
| ἀναστήσας | Ἰησοῦν· | ὡς | καὶ | ἐν | ⸂ τῷ | ψαλμῷ |
| *anastēsas* | *Iēsoun* | *hōs* | *kai* | *en* | *tō* | *psalmō* |
| having raised up | Jesus; | as | also | in | the | psalm |

| 3450.3 art dat sing | 1202.3 num ord dat sing masc | 1119.22 verb 3sing indic perf mid | 3450.3 art dat sing | 5403.1 noun dat sing masc |
|---|---|---|---|---|
| τῷ | δευτέρῳ | γέγραπται, | [☆ τῷ | ψαλμῷ |
| *tō* | *deuterō* | *gegraptai* | *tō* | *psalmō* |
| the | second | it has been written, | [ the | psalm |

| 1119.22 verb 3sing indic perf mid | 3450.3 art dat sing | 1202.3 num ord dat sing masc | 5048.1 noun nom sing masc | 1466.2 prs-pron gen 1sing |
|---|---|---|---|---|
| γέγραπται | τῷ | δευτέρῳ, ] | Υἱός | μου |
| *gegraptai* | *tō* | *deuterō* | *Huios* | *mou* |
| has been written, | the | second one, ] | Son | my |

**13:30.** In contrast to what man did to Jesus, God raised Him from the dead (out from among those who had died). This was in contrast also to the expectations of those who had Him crucified. God did what to men seemed impossible. The tomb could not hold Him.

**13:31.** After His resurrection Jesus was seen over a period of many days by those who came up with Him to Jerusalem from Galilee. These were not only the 11 apostles who were all from Galilee, but also included the 120 who were present on the Day of Pentecost, and probably others as well. Paul said these were (now, at that time) witnesses to the people. ("The people" here could mean the people of Israel or it could be used in a universal sense meaning "all the people.")

**13:32.** Paul then said this was the glad tidings, the good news, the gospel that he and his company were proclaiming (preaching) to them. This good news concerned the promise given to the fathers (the Old Testament fathers, especially the patriarchs, Abraham, Isaac, and Jacob).

Paul was not speaking of the nearly 100 prophecies which were fulfilled in connection with the death and resurrection of Jesus. Rather, he was speaking of one particular promise, the promise given to Abraham and confirmed to Abraham, Isaac, and Jacob. This promise had its beginning in Genesis 3:15 that a future Seed of the woman would crush the head of the same old serpent who tempted Eve. It was a promise of blessing through the greater Seed of Abraham who is also the greater David, and who, as the Suffering Servant of Isaiah 53 would accomplish our redemption. It was good news too that this promise was not only for the Jews, but for all people of every language and of every nation, family, or group.

**13:33.** The promise made to their fathers was now fulfilled (completely fulfilled) to their children by God's raising Jesus from the dead.

Paul confirmed this by quoting from Psalm 2:7 where God declares the Messianic King to be His Son, and says, "This day have I begotten thee." "Begotten thee" means "I have become your Father (and still am)." It translates a Hebrew phrase that means literally, "I have brought you out." It could be used of a woman who brings a child out into the world at birth. But when this phrase was used by a king, it was a technical formula declared by a king to one who was already his son and was now brought out to the people and declared to be king to share the throne with his father as his associate and as his equal. This was the kind of thing David did when he had Solomon brought out and declared to be king when Adonijah was trying to take over the throne. (See 1 Kings 1:33,34,48.)

**30. But God raised him from the dead:** . . . from among the dead, *Rotherham* . . . out from among the dead, *Wuest* . . . raised him up from death! *SEB.*

**31. And he was seen many days of them which came up with him from Galilee to Jerusalem:** Who appeared during many days unto them who, *Rotherham* . . . After this, for many days, Jesus was seen by the people who had gone with him, *SEB* . . . those who had gone with Jesus...saw him, *NCV.*

**who are his witnesses unto the people:** They are now telling the people the truth about Him, *Beck* . . . these men are his witnesses before, *Noli* . . . These are the ones who tell the people about him, *NLT.*

**32. And we declare unto you glad tidings:** We, too, have the good News to tell you, *TCNT* . . . So we are bringing you the joyful tidings, *Berkeley* . . . We also proclaim to you, *Noli* . . . preach to you, *Lamsa* . . . We are telling you the Good news, *SEB.*

**how that the promise which was made unto the fathers:** What God promised our fathers, *NIV* . . . about the promise made to our ancestors, *TCNT* . . . God has fulfilled for us the promises which he made to, *Noli* . . . about the promise made to our forefathers, *Weymouth* . . . to our early fathers, *NLT.*

**33. God hath fulfilled the same unto us their children:** We are their children, *NCV* . . . that our children have had the promise fulfilled to them by God to the very letter, *TCNT* . . . God has amply fulfilled it to our children, *Weymouth* . . . has fulfilled the promise made to the fathers, *TNT* . . . God has made this promise come true for us, *SEB* . . . God has finished this for us who are their children, *NLT.*

**in that he hath raised up Jesus again:** . . . by his raising Jesus from the grave, *TCNT* . . . from death, *SEB.*

**as it is also written in the second psalm:** This is endorsed, *Phillips* . . . This is just what is said in the second Psalm, *TCNT* . . . We also read about this in Psalm 2, *SEB.*

| 1498.3 verb 2sing indic pres act | 4622.1 prs-pron nom 2sing | 1466.1 prs-pron nom 1sing | 4449.1 adv | 1074.8 verb 1sing indic perf act |
|---|---|---|---|---|
| εἶ | σύ, | ἐγὼ | σήμερον | γεγέννηκά |
| *ei* | *su* | *egō* | *sēmeron* | *gegennēka* |
| are | you | I | today | have begotten |

| 4622.4 prs-pron acc 2sing | 3617.1 conj | 1156.2 conj | 448.3 verb 3sing indic aor act | 840.6 prs-pron acc sing masc |
|---|---|---|---|---|
| σε. | **34.** Ὅτι | δὲ | ἀνέστησεν | αὐτὸν |
| *se* | *Hoti* | *de* | *anestēsen* | *auton* |
| you. | That | and | he raised | him |

| 1523.2 prep gen | 3361.2 adj gen pl | 3239.1 adv | 3165.8 verb part pres act | 5128.4 verb inf pres act |
|---|---|---|---|---|
| ἐκ | νεκρῶν, | μηκέτι | μέλλοντα | ὑποστρέφειν |
| *ek* | *nekrōn* | *mēketi* | *mellonta* | *hupostrephein* |
| from among | dead, | no more | being about | to return |

| 1519.1 prep | 1306.1 noun acc sing fem | 3643.1 adv | 2029.3 verb 3sing indic perf act | 3617.1 conj | 1319.36 verb 1sing indic fut act |
|---|---|---|---|---|---|
| εἰς | διαφθοράν, | οὕτως | εἴρηκεν, | Ὅτι | Δώσω |
| *eis* | *diaphthoran* | *houtōs* | *eirēken* | *Hoti* | *Dōsō* |
| to | corruption | thus | he has spoken: | That | I will give |

| 5050.3 prs-pron dat 2pl | 3450.17 art pl neu | 3603.4 adj pl neu | 1132.1 name masc | 3450.17 art pl neu | 3964.14 adj pl neu |
|---|---|---|---|---|---|
| ὑμῖν | τὰ | ὅσια | Δαβὶδ | τὰ | πιστά. |
| *humin* | *ta* | *hosia* | *Dabid* | *ta* | *pista* |
| to you | the | mercies | of David | the | faithful. |

35.a.**Txt:** 04C,08E,020L 025P,byz.Sod
**Var:** 01ℵ,02A,03B,Lach Treg,Alf,Tisc,We/Ho Weis,UBS/*

| 1346.1 conj | 1354.1 conj | 2504.1 conj | 1706.1 prep | 2066.2 adj dat sing | 2978.5 verb 3sing indic pres act |
|---|---|---|---|---|---|
| **35.** ʻ διό | [a☆ διότι ] | καὶ | ἐν | ἑτέρῳ | λέγει, |
| *dio* | *dioti* | *kai* | *en* | *heterō* | *legei* |
| Wherefore | [ idem ] | also | in | another | he says, |

| 3620.3 partic | 1319.37 verb 2sing indic fut act | 3450.6 art acc sing masc | 3603.2 adj acc sing masc | 4622.2 prs-pron gen 2sing | 1481.19 verb inf aor act |
|---|---|---|---|---|---|
| Οὐ | δώσεις | τὸν | ὅσιόν | σου | ἰδεῖν |
| *Ou* | *dōseis* | *ton* | *hosion* | *sou* | *idein* |
| Not | you will suffer | the | Holy One | your | to see |

| 1306.1 noun acc sing fem | 1132.1 name masc | 3173.1 conj | 1056.1 conj | 2375.10 adj dat sing fem | 1067.3 noun dat sing fem |
|---|---|---|---|---|---|
| διαφθοράν. | **36.** Δαβὶδ | μὲν | γὰρ | ἰδίᾳ | γενεᾷ |
| *diaphthoran* | *Dabid* | *men* | *gar* | *idia* | *genea* |
| corruption. | David | indeed | for | to his own | generation |

| 5094.3 verb nom sing masc part aor act | 3450.11 art dat sing fem | 3450.2 art gen sing | 2296.2 noun gen sing masc | 1005.3 noun dat sing fem |
|---|---|---|---|---|
| ὑπηρετήσας | τῇ | τοῦ | θεοῦ | βουλῇ |
| *hupēretēsas* | *tē* | *tou* | *theou* | *boulē* |
| having ministered | the | | of God | counsel |

| 2810.5 verb 3sing indic aor pass | 2504.1 conj | 4227.6 verb 3sing indic aor pass | 4242.1 prep | 3450.8 art acc pl masc | 3824.9 noun acc pl masc |
|---|---|---|---|---|---|
| ἐκοιμήθη, | καὶ | προσετέθη | πρὸς | τοὺς | πατέρας |
| *ekoimēthē* | *kai* | *prosetethē* | *pros* | *tous* | *pateras* |
| fell asleep, | and | was added | to | the | fathers |

| 840.3 prs-pron gen sing | 2504.1 conj | 1481.3 verb 3sing indic aor act | 1306.1 noun acc sing fem | 3614.6 rel-pron acc sing masc | 1156.2 conj |
|---|---|---|---|---|---|
| αὐτοῦ, | καὶ | εἶδεν | διαφθοράν. | **37.** ὃν | δὲ |
| *autou* | *kai* | *eiden* | *diaphthoran* | *hon* | *de* |
| his | and | saw | corruption. | Whom | but |

Psalm 2 refers to Jesus being declared by God publicly to be His Son. God did this first when Jesus began His ministry and God sent His Spirit upon Him (Luke 3:22). He did it even more unmistakably when He raised Jesus from the dead. As Romans 1:3,4 says, Jesus, who was "made of the seed of David according to the flesh" was "declared to be the Son of God with power, according to the Spirit of holiness (or, by means of the Holy Spirit), by the resurrection from the dead." Since Luke was condensing a sermon that took a considerable time to preach, it is probable that Paul explained these things more fully to his audience.

**13:34.** Since God raised Jesus from the dead He will never again be on the point of returning to corruption (decay); He will never again return to the grave or the place of the dead. Paul meant that Christ's resurrection body is not subject to death or decay.

Paul continued by mentioning Isaiah 55:3 which refers to the sure mercies of David in a passage that speaks of pardon and salvation. By "mercies" he meant the divine decrees which are sure, trustworthy, dependable. The point is that the promises to David were not for David himself, nor for the people of his day, but for "you," that is, for a generation still future to Isaiah. The implication is that this refers to those who will be living after the sacrificial death of the Suffering Servant of Isaiah 53.

**13:35.** Paul then pointed out that those mercies, those promises given to David, include Psalm 16:10 which says God will not permit (give) His Holy One to see corruption (decay or destruction or dissolution of the body). "Holy One" (Greek, *hosion*) is the singular of the same word used of the "mercies" or divine decrees pertaining to David (Greek, *hosia*). When it is used of a person it means consecrated, devout, pleasing to God, and therefore, holy. This fits with the words of Jesus' Heavenly Father who said, "You are my Son, whom I love; with you I am well pleased" (Luke 3:22, NIV). (The ordinary Greek word for holy is *hagios*. *Hosios* is used here to draw attention to the fact that the sure decrees relating to David point to the Messiah, David's greater Son or descendant.)

**13:36.** Psalm 16:10 cannot apply to David for two reasons. First, David did not serve the future generation to whom Isaiah promised the sure decrees pertaining to David. He served his own generation, not the "you" of Isaiah 55:3. David served his own generation in the will of God, but the promise does not apply to him.

Second, after he had finished the work God gave him to do, David fell asleep (in the sleep of death) and was gathered to his forefathers, and his body did see corruption. Thus, the words of Psalm 16:10 cannot possibly apply to David.



**Thou art my Son, this day have I begotten thee:** My son art thou: I this day have begotten thee, *Rotherham* . . . Today I am Your Father, *Beck* . . . I have given you life today, *NLT*.

**34. And as concerning that he raised him up from the dead:** And in that he raised him from among the dead, *Rotherham* . . . And as a proof that he has raised, *Moffatt* . . . he confirmed his Resurrection and his immortality, *Noli* . . . God proved that Jesus was His Son by raising Him, *NLT*.

**now no more to return to corruption:** . . . never again to be in the position of one soon to return to decay, *Weymouth* . . . never to turn to dust, *Berkeley* . . . never again to return to decay, *Norlie* . . . to death's decay, *TNT* . . . He will never die again, *NLT*.

**he said on this wise:** He speaks thus, *Weymouth* . . . He expressed this way, *Berkeley*.

**I will give you the sure mercies of David:** I will give you the sacred promises made to, *TCNT* . . . the holy and trustworthy promises made to, *Weymouth* . . . the sure grace, *Murdock* . . . will finish the promises made, *NLT* . . . sacred blessings, *Berkeley*.

**35. Wherefore he saith also in another psalm:** . . . in another Psalm, it is said, *TCNT*.

**Thou shalt not suffer thine Holy One to see corruption:** Thou wilt not give up...to undergo corruption, *TCNT* . . . You will not let your Loved One experience decay, *Beck* . . . go back to dust! *NLT*.

**36. For David, after he had served his own generation by the will of God:** David, of course, after obediently doing God's will in his own time, *TCNT* . . . after serving his divine missions, *Noli*.

**fell on sleep:** . . . fell asleep, *RSV*.

**and was laid unto his fathers:** . . . was gathered to his forefathers, *Weymouth* . . . and was buried with his fathers, *Berkeley* . . . was put into a grave close to his Father's grave, *NLT*.

**and saw corruption:** . . . his body rotted, *TEV* . . . He did in fact see corruption, *Phillips* . . . He did suffer decay, *TNT*.

| **3450.5** art nom sing masc | **2296.1** noun nom sing masc | **1446.5** verb 3sing indic aor act | **3620.2** partic | **1481.3** verb 3sing indic aor act |
|---|---|---|---|---|
| ὁ | θεὸς | ἤγειρεν | οὐκ | εἶδεν |
| *ho* | *theos* | *ēgeiren* | *ouk* | *eiden* |
| | God | raised up | not | did see |

| **1306.1** noun acc sing fem | **1104.4** adj sing neu | **3631.1** partic | **1498.17** verb 3sing impr pres act | **5050.3** prs-pron dat 2pl |
|---|---|---|---|---|
| διαφθοράν. | **38.** Γνωστὸν | οὖν | ἔστω | ὑμῖν, |
| *diaphthoran* | *Gnōston* | *oun* | *estō* | *humin* |
| corruption. | Known | therefore | let it be | to you, |

| **433.6** noun nom pl masc | **79.6** noun nom pl masc | **3617.1** conj | **1217.2** prep | **3642.1** dem-pron gen sing | **5050.3** prs-pron dat 2pl |
|---|---|---|---|---|---|
| ἄνδρες | ἀδελφοί, | ὅτι | διὰ | τούτου | ὑμῖν |
| *andres* | *adelphoi* | *hoti* | *dia* | *toutou* | *humin* |
| men | brothers, | that | through | this | to you |

39.a.**Txt:** 03B,04C-corr2 08E,044,byz.
**Var:** p74,01ℵ,02A 04C-org,05D

| **852.1** noun nom sing fem | **264.6** noun gen pl fem | **2576.9** verb 3sing indic pres mid | **2504.1** conj |
|---|---|---|---|
| ἄφεσις | ἁμαρτιῶν | καταγγέλλεται· | **39.** ⸂a καὶ ⸃ |
| *aphesis* | *hamartiōn* | *katangelletai* | *kai* |
| forgiveness | of sins | is being announced, | and |

39.b.**Txt:** 08E,020L 025P,byz.
**Var:** 01ℵ,02A,03B,04C 05D,Lach,Treg,Alf,Tisc We/Ho,Weis,Sod UBS/☆

| **570.3** prep | **3820.4** adj gen pl | **3614.1** rel-pron gen pl | **3620.2** partic | **1404.26** verb 2pl indic aor pass | **1706.1** prep | **3450.3** art dat sing |
|---|---|---|---|---|---|---|
| ἀπὸ | πάντων | ὧν | οὐκ | ἠδυνήθητε | ἐν | ⸂b τῷ ⸃ |
| *apo* | *pantōn* | *hōn* | *ouk* | *ēdunēthēte* | *en* | *tō* |
| from | all things | which | not | you could | in | the |

| **3414.3** noun dat sing masc | **3337.2** name gen masc | **3338.2** name gen masc | **1338.18** verb inf aor pass | **1706.1** prep |
|---|---|---|---|---|
| νόμῳ | ⸀ Μωσέως | [☆ Μωϋσέως ] | δικαιωθῆναι, | ἐν |
| *nomō* | *Mōseōs* | *Mōuseōs* | *dikaiōthēnai* | *en* |
| law | of Moses | [ idem ] | to be justified, | in |

| **3642.5** dem-pron dat sing masc | **3820.6** adj nom sing masc | **3450.5** art nom sing masc | **3961.10** verb nom sing masc part pres act | **1338.9** verb 3sing indic pres mid |
|---|---|---|---|---|
| τούτῳ | πᾶς | ὁ | πιστεύων | δικαιοῦται. |
| *toutō* | *pas* | *ho* | *pisteuōn* | *dikaioutai* |
| this | everyone | the | believing | is being justified. |

40.a.**Txt:** 02A,04C,08E 020L,025P,044,byz.it.sa. bo.Sod
**Var:** p74,01ℵ,03B,05D 33,Lach,Treg,Tisc We/Ho,Weis,UBS/☆

| **984.1** verb 2pl pres act | **3631.1** partic | **3231.1** partic | **1889.2** verb 3sing subj aor act | **1894.1** prep |
|---|---|---|---|---|
| **40.** βλέπετε | οὖν | μὴ | ἐπέλθῃ | ⸂a ἐφ’ |
| *blepete* | *oun* | *mē* | *epelthē* | *eph’* |
| Watch out | therefore | not | it may come | upon |

| **5050.4** prs-pron acc 2pl | **3450.16** art sing neu | **2029.16** verb sing neu part perf mid | **1706.1** prep | **3450.4** art dat pl | **4254.6** noun dat pl masc |
|---|---|---|---|---|---|
| ὑμᾶς ⸃ | τὸ | εἰρημένον | ἐν | τοῖς | προφήταις, |
| *humas* | *to* | *eirēmenon* | *en* | *tois* | *prophētais* |
| you | the | having been said | in | the | prophets, |

| **1481.15** verb 2pl impr aor act | **3450.7** art nom pl masc | **2676.1** noun nom pl masc | **2504.1** conj | **2273.13** verb 2pl impr aor act |
|---|---|---|---|---|
| **41.** Ἴδετε, | οἱ | καταφρονηταί, | καὶ | θαυμάσατε |
| *Idete* | *hoi* | *kataphronētai* | *kai* | *thaumasate* |
| Behold, | the | despisers, | and | wonder |

| **2504.1** conj | **846.4** verb 2pl impr aor pass | **3617.1** conj | **2024.1** noun sing neu | **1466.1** prs-pron nom 1sing | **2021.2** verb 1sing indic pres mid |
|---|---|---|---|---|---|
| καὶ | ἀφανίσθητε· | ὅτι | ἔργον | ⸀ ἐγὼ | ἐργάζομαι |
| *kai* | *aphanisthēte* | *hoti* | *ergon* | *egō* | *ergazomai* |
| and | perish; | for | a work | I | am working |

**13:37.** In contrast to what happened to David, the One God raised up from the dead (Jesus) did not see corruption.

Though Paul presented this truth in a little different way than Peter did in 2:29, it is still the same truth. Clearly, the apostle Paul preached the same gospel the other apostles did. This is important, for some unbelievers have tried to put Paul in opposition to the other apostles. But as Galatians 1:8,9; 2:2-8 show, Paul declared there is only one gospel, the one he preached. He presented that gospel to the apostles and elders in Jerusalem. They did not feel they had to add anything to it, but gave Paul full approval, not only to his gospel but to his ministry among the Gentiles.

**13:38.** Now comes the final part of Paul's sermon in Pisidian Antioch (verses 38-41). Its purpose is exhortation.

Again addressing his audience as brothers, Paul said that therefore (because of Christ's death and resurrection) "through this man is preached (proclaimed, announced) unto you forgiveness of sins." This is the good news, not only that Jesus died and rose again, but that He did so on the sinner's behalf so that through Him there can be pardon that includes forgiveness of sins and the cancellation of guilt, so those sins will never be remembered or brought up against any believer in the coming judgment.

**13:39.** By this One (Jesus) also, all believers are justified; they are made righteous in God's eyes, acquitted, and treated as if they had never sinned. This further emphasizes that all who are believing and trusting Jesus are therefore forever freed from the guilt and punishment of their sins. Believers are forgiven of all those things for which the law of Moses was not able to provide justification.

The Greek word order here is, "even from all which you were not able to be justified by the law of Moses, in this One every one believing is justified." Some take this to mean the Law provided justification for some things, and the gospel provides justification for the rest. But the meaning is rather that the Law could not really provide justification at all: only through faith in Jesus Christ is a person justified.

**13:40.** Paul concluded his sermon with a warning. Let his audience, Jews and Gentiles, beware lest the things spoken by the prophets come upon them. They knew the prophets not only spoke of good news, not only prophesied future blessings through the Messiah, but they also gave many warnings, severe warnings. In fact, the major portion of the prophetical books is full of warnings.

**13:41.** The warning Paul emphasized uses language taken from Habakkuk 1:5 in the Septuagint (LXX) version. (Notice the slightly different wording: the Septuagint reads, "Behold, ye *despisers*,"

**37. But he, whom God raised again, saw no corruption:** . . . this man, *Phillips* . . . did not suffer decay, *Moffatt.*

**38. Be it known unto you therefore:** I would, therefore, have you know, *TCNT* . . . Understand therefore, *Weymouth* . . . And so, let it be clear to you, *BB* . . . It should be clear then to you, *Berkeley* . . . It is therefore imperative, *Phillips.*

**men and brethren, that through this man is preached unto you the forgiveness of sins:** . . . that our announcement is, that there is forgiveness of sins for you through Jesus, *TCNT* . . . the putting away of sins, *Klingensmith.*

**39. And by him all that believe are justified from all things:** . . . and that, in union with him, all who believe in him are cleared from every charge, *TCNT* . . . and in Him every believer is absolved from all offences, *Weymouth* . . . through union with Him...is given right standing with God and freed from every charge, *Williams* . . . righteous and free, *Beck* . . . acquitted, *Confraternity.*

**from which ye could not be justified by the law of Moses:** . . . cleared under the Law of Moses, *TCNT* . . . from which you could not be absolved under, *Weymouth* . . . from which you could not be freed by, *Williams* . . . even those from which the law of Moses cannot set you free, *Norlie* . . . not able to be acquitted, *Fenton* . . . could never set him free, *Phillips.*

**40. Beware therefore, lest that come upon you, which is spoken of in the prophets:** Take care, *TCNT* . . . So be careful the prophetic utterance does not become your experience, *Berkeley* . . . Now be careful, or what the prophets said will happen to you, *Beck.*

**41. Behold, ye despisers, and wonder, and perish:** Listen, *Norlie* . . . See, ye despisers, and marvel and disappear, *Rotherham* . . . you scorners, *Klingensmith* . . . and hide your heads, *TCNT* . . . Look, you scoffers! Then wonder and vanish away, *Williams.*

41.a.**Txt:** p74,01א,02A 03B,044,81,945,1739 Steph
**Var:** 05D,08E,byz.

| **2021.2** verb 1sing indic pres mid | **1466.1** prs-pron nom 1sing | **1706.1** prep | **3450.14** art dat pl fem | **2232.7** noun dat pl fem | **5050.2** prs-pron gen 2pl |
|---|---|---|---|---|---|
| [☆ ἐργάζομαι | ἐγὼ ] | ἐν | ταῖς | ἡμέραις | ὑμῶν, |
| *ergazomai* | *egō* | *en* | *tais* | *hēmerais* | *humōn* |
| [ am working | I ] | in | the | days | your, |

41.b.**Txt:** byz.
**Var:** 01א,02A,03B,04C 05D,08E,020L,025P Lach,Treg,Alf,Word Tisc,We/Ho,Weis,Sod UBS/☆

| **2024.1** noun sing neu | **3614.3** rel-pron dat sing | **3614.16** rel-pron sing neu | **3620.3** partic | **3231.1** partic | **3961.1** verb 2pl subj aor act |
|---|---|---|---|---|---|
| ⸂a ἔργον ⸃ | ⸀ ᾧ | [b☆ ὃ ] | οὐ | μὴ | πιστεύσητε |
| *ergon* | *hō* | *ho* | *ou* | *mē* | *pisteusēte* |
| work | which | [ idem ] | not | not | you would believe |

| **1430.1** partic | **4948.3** indef-pron nom sing | **1542.1** verb 3sing subj pres mid | **5050.3** prs-pron dat 2pl | **1821.1** verb gen pl masc part pres act |
|---|---|---|---|---|
| ἐάν | τις | ἐκδιηγῆται | ὑμῖν. | **42.** Ἐξιόντων |
| *ean* | *tis* | *ekdiēgētai* | *humin* | *Exiontōn* |
| if | someone | should declare it | to you. | Departing |

42.a.**Txt:** 025P,byz. Steph
**Var:** p74,01א,02A,03B 04C,05D,08E,044,it.sa. bo.Gries,Lach,Treg,Alf Tisc,We/Ho,Weis,Sod UBS/☆

| **1156.2** conj | **1523.2** prep gen | **3450.10** art gen sing fem | **4715.2** noun gen sing fem | **3450.1** art gen pl | **2428.3** name-adj gen pl masc |
|---|---|---|---|---|---|
| δὲ | ⸀ ἐκ | τῆς | συναγωγῆς | τῶν | Ἰουδαίων, |
| *de* | *ek* | *tēs* | *sunagōgēs* | *tōn* | *Ioudaiōn* |
| and | from | the | synagogue | the | Jews, |

42.b.**Txt:** 020L,025P 1241,byz.
**Var:** p74,01א,02A,03B 04C,05D,08E,sa.bo. Gries,Lach,Treg,Alf Word,Tisc,We/Ho,Weis Sod,UBS/☆

| **840.1** prs-pron gen pl | **3731.20** verb 3pl indic imperf act | **3450.17** art pl neu | **1477.4** noun pl neu | **1519.1** prep | **3450.16** art sing neu |
|---|---|---|---|---|---|
| [a☆ αὐτῶν ] | παρεκάλουν | ⸂b τὰ | ἔθνη ⸃ | εἰς | τὸ |
| *autōn* | *parekaloun* | *ta* | *ethnē* | *eis* | *to* |
| [ their ] | were urging | the | Gentiles | on | the |

| **3212.1** adv | **4378.1** noun sing neu | **2953.57** verb inf aor pass | **840.2** prs-pron dat pl | **3450.17** art pl neu | **4343.4** noun pl neu |
|---|---|---|---|---|---|
| μεταξὺ | σάββατον | λαληθῆναι | αὐτοῖς | τὰ | ῥήματα |
| *metaxu* | *sabbaton* | *lalēthēnai* | *autois* | *ta* | *rhēmata* |
| next | sabbath | to be spoken | to them | the | words |

| **3642.18** dem-pron pl neu | **3061.21** verb gen sing fem part aor pass | **1156.2** conj | **3450.10** art gen sing fem | **4715.2** noun gen sing fem |
|---|---|---|---|---|
| ταῦτα. | **43.** λυθείσης | δὲ | τῆς | συναγωγῆς, |
| *tauta* | *lutheisēs* | *de* | *tēs* | *sunagōgēs* |
| these. | Having broken up | and | the | synagogue, |

| **188.13** verb 3pl indic aor act | **4044.7** adj nom pl masc | **3450.1** art gen pl | **2428.3** name-adj gen pl masc | **2504.1** conj | **3450.1** art gen pl |
|---|---|---|---|---|---|
| ἠκολούθησαν | πολλοὶ | τῶν | Ἰουδαίων | καὶ | τῶν |
| *ēkolouthēsan* | *polloi* | *tōn* | *Ioudaiōn* | *kai* | *tōn* |
| followed | many | of the | Jews | and | of the |

| **4431.4** verb gen pl masc part pres mid | **4198.3** noun gen pl masc | **3450.3** art dat sing | **3834.3** name dat masc | **2504.1** conj |
|---|---|---|---|---|
| σεβομένων | προσηλύτων | τῷ | Παύλῳ | καὶ |
| *sebomenōn* | *prosēlutōn* | *tō* | *Paulō* | *kai* |
| worshiping | proselytes | | Paul | and |

| **3450.3** art dat sing | **915.3** name dat masc | **3610.2** rel-pron nom pl masc | **4212.1** verb nom pl masc part pres act | **840.2** prs-pron dat pl |
|---|---|---|---|---|
| τῷ | Βαρναβᾷ· | οἵτινες | προσλαλοῦντες | αὐτοῖς |
| *tō* | *Barnaba* | *hoitines* | *proslalountes* | *autois* |
| | Barnabas, | who | speaking | to them |

43.a.**Txt:** 020L,025P,byz.
**Var:** 01א,02A,03B,04C 05D,08E,Gries,Lach Treg,Alf,Word,Tisc We/Ho,Weis,Sod UBS/☆

| **3844.19** verb 3pl indic imperf act | **840.8** prs-pron acc pl masc | **1946.4** verb inf pres act | **4215.3** verb inf pres act |
|---|---|---|---|
| ἔπειθον | αὐτοὺς | ⸀ ἐπιμένειν | [a☆ προσμένειν ] |
| *epeithon* | *autous* | *epimenein* | *prosmenein* |
| were persuading | them | to continue | [ to continue in ] |

while the Hebrew [Masoretic text] reads, "Behold ye *among the heathen* [or *nations*]"; cf. Isaiah 28:22.) In Romans 2:4 Paul warned the Jews against despising the riches of God's kindness. Here he warned his audience lest they become despisers of the message of Christ and of the forgiveness of sins Christ offers. Those who do so will be surprised and filled with fear when they face the coming judgment, for they will perish or be removed to destruction. Paul wanted his audience to be on their guard lest an even greater judgment would come on them than that which came on the rebels to whom Habakkuk spoke.

The work of God Habakkuk was talking about was the judgment He was bringing through the Chaldeans (Babylonians) who took the Jews captive and destroyed Jerusalem and Solomon's temple. They did not believe judgment would come, but it did. Many today do not believe the end of this age and the judgments are coming, but they will. The only hope for any person is the salvation and forgiveness of sins that Christ offers. Apart from Him all shall perish. (See John 3:16 where the word "perish" speaks of destruction, ruin, and eternal loss.) The word used to translate *Habakkuk* means to disappear into destruction or ruin. Those who reject Christ will not be present to enjoy the blessings salvation through Christ provides.

**13:42.** As the people were leaving the synagogue, they asked that these words (this message) would continue to be spoken to them the next Sabbath. A large number of ancient manuscripts leave out the words "Jews" and "Gentiles" in this verse. It does seem likely that at this point both Jews and Gentiles wanted Paul to continue giving them these words (Greek, *rhēmata*) from God's Word, a fact which is confirmed by the following verse.

**13:43.** When the meeting of the synagogue ended, many of the Jews and the worshiping (God-fearing) proselytes (converts to Judaism) followed Paul and Barnabas. Normally, they would have gone home to enjoy the Sabbath feast. (Compare Mark 1:29-31 where "she ministered" means she served a meal.) But these who followed Paul and Barnabas were concerned about spiritual food. The apostles had stirred a deeper hunger in their hearts.

Paul and Barnabas did not turn them away, but spent some time with them, speaking to them and effectually persuading them to remain in the grace of God.

This means they took time to explain the gospel more in detail and to show that salvation is indeed by grace through faith apart from the Law. They accepted that grace by believing the message. What joy must have filled the hearts of Paul and Barnabas as they encouraged those who believed to remain or continue in this grace. The same phraseology is used in 11:23 where Barnabas exhorted the new Gentile converts in Syrian Antioch to remain true to the Lord. These serious exhortations are repeated throughout the New Testament.

**for I work a work in your days:** For I am about to do a great work myself, *TCNT* . . . Because I am carrying on a work in your time, *Weymouth.*

**a work which ye shall in no wise believe:** A work which you will never believe, *TCNT* . . . in your times a deed, *Noli* . . . utterly refuse to believe, *Weymouth.*

**though a man declare it unto you:** Though one relate it in full unto you, *Rotherham* . . . even if it is made clear to you, *BB* . . . though one may tell you in detail, *Williams* . . . even if someone were to explain it to you! *SEB* . . . someone tells you about it, *NLT.*

**42. And when the Jews were gone out of the synagogue:** And as they were going out, *Phillips, Rotherham* . . . out of the Jewish place of worship, *NLT.*

**the Gentiles besought that these words might be preached to them the next sabbath:** . . . they kept on beseeching, *Rotherham* . . . they were implored by the people, *Noli* . . . the people begged for a repetition of this teaching, *TCNT* . . . the Gentiles asked that these words, *KJII* . . . this repeated to them, *Moffatt* . . . on the same subjects the next Sabbath, *TNT* . . . the people asked them to talk about these things on the next Day of Rest, *NLT.*

**43. Now when the congregation was broken up:** Now when the meeting was ended, *BB* . . . and when the synagogue was dismissed, *Berkeley* . . . had dispersed, *TNT* . . . went from the place of worship, *NLT.*

**many of the Jews and religious proselytes:** . . . devout converts from heathenism, *Weymouth* . . . God-fearing Gentiles who had become Jews, *BB.*

**followed Paul and Barnabas:** . . . allied themselves with, *Williams.*

**who, speaking to them:** . . . in conversation with them, *TCNT* . . . who spoke personally to them, *Phillips* . . . They preached to them again, *Noli.*

**persuaded them to continue in the grace of God:** . . . urged them to continue to rely on the mercy of God, *TCNT* . . . on the unmerited favor, *Williams.*

## Acts 13:44

| 3450.11 art dat sing fem | 5322.3 noun dat sing fem | 3450.2 art gen sing | 2296.2 noun gen sing masc | 3450.3 art dat sing | 1156.2 conj |
|---|---|---|---|---|---|
| τῇ | χάριτι | τοῦ | θεοῦ. | 44. Τῷ | ⸂ δὲ |
| tē | chariti | tou | theou | Tō | de |
| the | grace | | of God. | The | and |

44.a.**Txt:** p74,01ℵ,02A 04C,05D,044,81,945 1739,Steph
**Var:** 03B,08E,byz.

| 4885.1 conj | 2048.43 verb dat sing part pres mid | 4378.3 noun dat sing neu | 4827.1 adv | 3820.9 adj nom sing fem | 3450.9 art nom sing fem |
|---|---|---|---|---|---|
| [a τε ] | ἐρχομένῳ | σαββάτῳ | σχεδὸν | πᾶσα | ἡ |
| te | erchomenō | sabbatō | schedon | pasa | hē |
| [ idem ] | coming | sabbath | almost | all | the |

| 4032.1 noun nom sing fem | 4714.19 verb 3sing indic aor pass | 189.36 verb inf aor act | 3450.6 art acc sing masc | 3030.4 noun acc sing masc |
|---|---|---|---|---|
| πόλις | συνήχθη | ἀκοῦσαι | τὸν | λόγον |
| polis | sunēchthē | akousai | ton | logon |
| city | was gathered together | to hear | the | word |

44.b.**Var:** p74,01ℵ,02A 03B-corr,1739,sa.Lach Treg,Tisc,Sod

| 3450.2 art gen sing | 2296.2 noun gen sing masc | 2935.2 noun gen sing masc | 1481.17 verb nom pl masc part aor act | 1156.2 conj | 3450.7 art nom pl masc |
|---|---|---|---|---|---|
| τοῦ | ⸂ θεοῦ. | [b κυρίου. ] | 45. ἰδόντες | δὲ | οἱ |
| tou | theou | kuriou | idontes | de | hoi |
| | of God. | [ of Lord. ] | Having seen | but | the |

45.a.**Txt:** 04C,05D,08E 020L,025P,byz.Sod
**Var:** 01ℵ,02A,03B,Lach Treg,Tisc,We/Ho,Weis UBS/☆

| 2428.2 name-adj nom pl masc | 3450.8 art acc pl masc | 3657.8 noun acc pl masc | 3990.5 verb 3pl indic aor pass | 2188.2 noun gen sing |
|---|---|---|---|---|
| Ἰουδαῖοι | τοὺς | ὄχλους, | ἐπλήσθησαν | ζήλου |
| Ioudaioi | tous | ochlous | eplēsthēsan | zēlou |
| Jews | the | crowds, | were filled | with envy, |

45.b.**Txt:** 04C,05D,020L 025P,byz.
**Var:** 01ℵ,02A,03B,08E 33,Lach,Treg,Tisc We/Ho,Weis,Sod UBS/☆

| 2504.1 conj | 480.6 verb 3pl indic imperf act | 3450.4 art dat pl | 5097.3 prep | 3450.2 art gen sing | 3834.2 name gen masc |
|---|---|---|---|---|---|
| καὶ | ἀντέλεγον | τοῖς | ὑπὸ | ⸂a τοῦ ⸃ | Παύλου |
| kai | antelegon | tois | hupo | tou | Paulou |
| and | were contradicting | the things | by | | Paul |

45.c.**Txt:** 05D,025P,1241 byz.Tisc
**Var:** p74,01ℵ,02A,03B 04C,020L,044,33,sa.bo. Lach,Treg,We/Ho,Weis Sod,UBS/☆

| 2978.36 verb dat pl neu part pres mid | 2953.50 verb dat pl neu part pres mid | 480.3 verb nom pl masc part pres act | 2504.1 conj |
|---|---|---|---|
| ⸂ λεγομένοις, | [b☆ λαλουμένοις ] | ⸂c ἀντιλέγοντες | καὶ ⸃ |
| legomenois | laloumenois | antilegontes | kai |
| being spoken, | [ idem ] | contradicting | and |

46.a.**Txt:** 08E,20,025P byz.bo.
**Var:** 01ℵ,02A,03B,04C 05D,33,Lach,Treg,Alf Tisc,We/Ho,Weis,Sod UBS/☆

| 980.4 verb nom pl masc part pres act | 3817.7 verb nom pl masc part aor mid | 1156.2 conj | 4885.1 conj |
|---|---|---|---|
| βλασφημοῦντες. | 46. παρρησιασάμενοί | ⸂ δὲ | [a☆ τε ] |
| blasphēmountes | parrhēsiasamenoi | de | te |
| blaspheming. | Having spoken boldly | and | [ idem ] |

| 3450.5 art nom sing masc | 3834.1 name nom masc | 2504.1 conj | 3450.5 art nom sing masc | 915.1 name nom masc | 1500.3 verb indic aor act |
|---|---|---|---|---|---|
| ὁ | Παῦλος | καὶ | ὁ | Βαρναβᾶς | ⸂ εἶπον, |
| ho | Paulos | kai | ho | Barnabas | eipon |
| | Paul | and | | Barnabas | said, |

46.b.**Txt:** 08E,020L 025P,byz.Sod
**Var:** 01ℵ,02A,03B,05D Lach,Treg,Alf,Tisc We/Ho,Weis,UBS/☆

| 1500.28 verb 3pl indic aor act | 5050.3 prs-pron dat 2pl | 1498.34 verb sing indic imperf act | 314.3 adj sing neu | 4270.1 adv |
|---|---|---|---|---|
| [b☆ εἶπαν, ] | ⸃Ὑμῖν | ἦν | ἀναγκαῖον | πρῶτον |
| eipan | Humin | ēn | anankaion | prōton |
| [ idem ] | To you | was | necessary | first |

| 2953.57 verb inf aor pass | 3450.6 art acc sing masc | 3030.4 noun acc sing masc | 3450.2 art gen sing | 2296.2 noun gen sing masc | 1879.1 conj |
|---|---|---|---|---|---|
| λαληθῆναι | τὸν | λόγον | τοῦ | θεοῦ· | ἐπειδὴ |
| lalēthēnai | ton | logon | tou | theou | epeidē |
| to be spoken | the | word | | of God; | since |

**13:44.** The message, the exhortation, and the further teaching given by Barnabas and Paul must have stirred the new believers to a high pitch of enthusiasm. The God-fearing Gentiles must have been especially excited by this assurance of forgiveness and salvation through Christ. They spread the word about this good news so effectively that the next Sabbath nearly the whole city assembled to hear the words concerning the Lord Jesus. Pisidian Antioch was a center of Greek culture and a prosperous commercial center. It also had a large number of Roman colonists among its chief citizens. Jewish colonists had also settled there for over 200 years, primarily for business and commercial reasons. Since the synagogue had been there so long, the people of the city apparently knew at least something of their teachings, and quite a number of Gentiles had become proselytes or converts to Judaism.

**13:45.** The sight of the crowds thronging to hear Paul filled the Jews with jealousy. Like the Pharisees and Sadducees who became jealous of Jesus, they could not bear to think they were losing their influence and their religious leadership. They undoubtedly interpreted their jealousy, however, as a zeal for God and for the law of Moses. As Paul later said, the Christ-rejecting Jews did have a zeal for God, but not according to knowledge. Actually, the Greek word *zēlos* has the good meaning of zeal and the bad meaning of jealousy or envy. Romans 10:2 indicates that the zeal of the unconverted Jews was a jealous eagerness to uphold what they thought was God's honor.

Because of this jealousy and misplaced zeal, the unconverted Jews in Pisidian Antioch began to speak against what Paul was teaching. They even blasphemed the gospel.

This is a further indication they were afraid of losing their influence over these Gentiles who had been looking to them for teaching. It probably implies also that they had a zeal for a Judaism that had no room for blessings on Gentiles who did not first become Jews.

**13:46.** The opposition of these unconverted Jews did not frighten Paul and Barnabas. Instead, they grew bold and responded with a great deal of fearless freedom of speech. Very openly they told these Jews it was necessary for them to go to the Jew first in order to fulfill God's plan. (Compare Romans 1:16.) Romans 3:2 indicates that the chief reason was because "unto them were committed the oracles (Greek, *logia*, 'sayings, utterances,' including the promises) of God." Romans 9:4,5 adds that they had the adoption (the place of sons; see Exodus 4:22; Isaiah 1:2), the glory, the covenants, the giving of the Law, the service or worship of God, and the promises. It was God's plan that the gospel be announced to them first, but with the intention of using them to spread the gospel to all the nations of the world (as God promised Abraham, Genesis 12:3).

**44. And the next sabbath day came almost the whole city together to hear the word of God:** . . . on the coming Sabbath, *KJII* . . . almost the whole population of the city, *Weymouth* . . . almost all the city, *Young* . . . almost the whole town, *Beck* . . . almost the entire city, *Wuest* . . . almost all the inhabitants of the city had assembled, *Noli* . . . all the people of the town came to hear, *NLT* . . . gathered to hear God's message, *TCNT.*

**45. But when the Jews saw the multitudes:** . . . the crowds of people, *TCNT* . . . immense crowd, *Norlie* . . . when they saw so many people, *NLT.*

**they were filled with envy:** . . . were filled with jealousy, *Rotherham* . . . they became exceedingly jealous, *TCNT* . . . with angry jealousy, *Weymouth* . . . completely overcome by their jealousy, *Williams* . . . terribly jealous, *Berkeley.*

**and spake against those things which were spoken by Paul:** . . . and contradicted the things, *ASV* . . . they interrupted Paul's address, *Norlie* . . . they bitterly opposed the words, *Lamsa* . . . and denied the things spoken by Paul, *KJII* . . . They used abusive language, *TNT* . . . argued against what Paul said, *Everyday.*

**contradicting and blaspheming:** . . . in abusive language, *TCNT* . . . and abused him, *Weymouth* . . . covering him with abuse, *Phillips* . . . even to abuse him, *Williams* . . . talked abusively, *Berkeley* . . . saying slanderous and evil things, *Wuest* . . . said insulting things, *Everyday* . . . by saying he was wrong, *NLT.*

**46. Then Paul and Barnabas waxed bold, and said:** . . . speaking boldly said, *Rotherham* . . . spoke out fearlessly, *TCNT* . . . courageously spoke out, *Williams* . . . did not mince their words but said, *Phillips* . . . said to the people in plain words, *NLT.*

**It was necessary that the word of God should first have been spoken to you:** We were bound to proclaim, *Weymouth* . . . We felt it our duty to speak the message, *Phillips* . . . bound to preach the Gospel to you first, *Noli* . . . to you Jews first, *Williams.*

## Acts 13:47

46.c.**Txt:** 01ℵ-corr,02A 04C,05D-corr,08E,020L 025P,byz.Weis,Sod **Var:** 01ℵ-org,03B 05D-org,sa.bo.Lach Treg,Tisc,We/Ho UBS/*

| **1156.2** conj | **676.1** verb 2pl indic pres mid | **840.6** prs-pron acc sing masc | **2504.1** conj | **3620.2** partic | **510.4** adj acc pl masc |
|---|---|---|---|---|---|
| ([c] δὲ ) | ἀπωθεῖσθε | αὐτὸν, | καὶ | οὐκ | ἀξίους |
| *de* | *apōtheisthe* | *auton* | *kai* | *ouk* | *axious* |
| but | you reject | it, | and | not | worthy |

| **2892.3** verb 2pl pres act | **1431.8** prs-pron acc pl masc | **3450.10** art gen sing fem | **164.2** adj gen sing | **2205.2** noun gen sing fem | **1481.20** verb 2sing impr aor mid |
|---|---|---|---|---|---|
| κρίνετε | ἑαυτοὺς | τῆς | αἰωνίου | ζωῆς, | ἰδοὺ |
| *krinete* | *heautous* | *tēs* | *aiōniou* | *zōēs* | *idou* |
| you judge | yourselves | the | of eternal | life, | behold |

| **4613.4** verb 1pl indic pres mid | **1519.1** prep | **3450.17** art pl neu | **1477.4** noun pl neu | **3643.1** adv | **1056.1** conj |
|---|---|---|---|---|---|
| στρεφόμεθα | εἰς | τὰ | ἔθνη· | **47.** οὕτως | γὰρ |
| *strephometha* | *eis* | *ta* | *ethnē* | *houtōs* | *gar* |
| we turn | to | the | Gentiles; | thus | for |

| **1765.5** verb 3sing indic perf mid | **2231.3** prs-pron dat 1pl | **3450.5** art nom sing masc | **2935.1** noun nom sing masc | **4935.18** verb 1sing indic perf act |
|---|---|---|---|---|
| ἐντέταλται | ἡμῖν | ὁ | κύριος, | Τέθεικά |
| *entetaltai* | *hēmin* | *ho* | *kurios* | *Tetheika* |
| has commanded | us | the | Lord, | I have set |

| **4622.4** prs-pron acc 2sing | **1519.1** prep | **5295.1** noun sing neu | **1477.5** noun gen pl neu | **3450.2** art gen sing | **1498.32** verb inf pres act |
|---|---|---|---|---|---|
| σε | εἰς | φῶς | ἐθνῶν. | τοῦ | εἶναί |
| *se* | *eis* | *phōs* | *ethnōn* | *tou* | *einai* |
| you | for | a light | of Gentiles, | the | to be |

| **4622.4** prs-pron acc 2sing | **1519.1** prep | **4843.3** noun acc sing fem | **2175.1** conj | **2057.2** adj gen sing | **3450.10** art gen sing fem | **1087.2** noun gen sing fem |
|---|---|---|---|---|---|---|
| σε | εἰς | σωτηρίαν | ἕως | ἐσχάτου | τῆς | γῆς. |
| *se* | *eis* | *sōtērian* | *heōs* | *eschatou* | *tēs* | *gēs* |
| you | for | salvation | to | end | of the | earth. |

| **189.10** verb part pres act | **1156.2** conj | **3450.17** art pl neu | **1477.4** noun pl neu | **5299.14** verb 3pl indic imperf act | **2504.1** conj |
|---|---|---|---|---|---|
| **48.** Ἀκούοντα | δὲ | τὰ | ἔθνη | ἔχαιρον, | καὶ |
| *Akouonta* | *de* | *ta* | *ethnē* | *echairon* | *kai* |
| Hearing | and | the | Gentiles | were rejoicing, | and |

| **1386.18** verb 3pl indic imperf act | **3450.6** art acc sing masc | **3030.4** noun acc sing masc | **3450.2** art gen sing | **2935.2** noun gen sing masc | **2504.1** conj |
|---|---|---|---|---|---|
| ἐδόξαζον | τὸν | λόγον | τοῦ | κυρίου, | καὶ |
| *edoxazon* | *ton* | *logon* | *tou* | *kuriou* | *kai* |
| were glorifying | the | word | of the | Lord, | and |

| **3961.23** verb 3pl indic aor act | **3607.2** rel-pron nom pl masc | **1498.37** verb 3pl indic imperf act | **4872.6** verb nom pl masc part perf mid |
|---|---|---|---|
| ἐπίστευσαν | ὅσοι | ἦσαν | τεταγμένοι |
| *episteusan* | *hosoi* | *ēsan* | *tetagmenoi* |
| believed | as many as | were | having been appointed |

| **1519.1** prep | **2205.4** noun acc sing fem | **164.1** adj sing | **1302.6** verb 3sing indic imperf pass | **1156.2** conj | **3450.5** art nom sing masc |
|---|---|---|---|---|---|
| εἰς | ζωὴν | αἰώνιον. | **49.** διεφέρετο | δὲ | ὁ |
| *eis* | *zōēn* | *aiōnion* | *diephereto* | *de* | *ho* |
| to | life | eternal. | Was being carried | and | the |

49.a.**Var:** 01ℵ,02A,33 Tisc

| **3030.1** noun nom sing masc | **3450.2** art gen sing | **2935.2** noun gen sing masc | **1217.1** prep | **2567.2** prep | **3513.7** adj gen sing fem | **3450.10** art gen sing fem |
|---|---|---|---|---|---|---|
| λόγος | τοῦ | κυρίου | ( δι' | [[a] καθ' ] | ὅλης | τῆς |
| *logos* | *tou* | *kuriou* | *di'* | *kath'* | *holēs* | *tēs* |
| word | of the | Lord | through | [ idem ] | whole | the |

But since the Jews had scornfully thrust away and rejected the gospel, they thus judged themselves by their conduct to be unworthy of eternal life. (As John 5:26 and 15:1-6 show, eternal life is Christ's life in the believer, flowing as from the vine to the branches.)

Then the apostles declared that as a result of the Jews' rejecting the gospel, they were turning (at that moment) to the Gentiles. ("Behold" indicates this turning to the Gentiles was something unexpected and surprising to the Jews.)

**but seeing ye put it from you:** . . . but since you reject it, *TCNT* . . . But since you spurn it, *Phillips, Weymouth* . . . you refuse to listen, *Everyday.*

**and judge yourselves unworthy of everlasting life:** . . . and declare yourselves unworthy of, *Noli* . . . to be unworthy, *Weymouth.*

**lo, we turn to the Gentiles:** . . . why, we turn to the heathen! *TCNT* . . . we are now turning to the non-Jews, *Beck* . . . So we will now go to the people of other nations! *Everyday.*

**13:47.** Turning to the Gentiles was not really the apostles' own idea. Rather, it was obedience to the prophetic Word given in Isaiah 49:6 concerning the Messiah, God's Servant. In this context God is saying it was not enough for the tribes of Israel to be regathered and restored. His purpose was to make the Messiah light and salvation for all the nations of the world (which shows how the blessing promised through the Seed of Abraham would be fulfilled). Isaiah 42:6 also speaks of the Messiah as a light to the nations (the Gentiles). When Jesus was brought to the temple as a baby, the godly, Spirit-led Simeon also recognized Him as "a light to lighten the Gentiles, and the glory of thy people Israel" (Luke 2:32). Paul recognized they had the responsibility of bringing the light of Christ to the Gentiles.

**47. For so hath the Lord commanded us, saying:** For this is the Lord's order to us, *TCNT* . . . The Lord gave us a commission. It is this, *Norlie* . . . This is what the Lord told us to do, *Everyday.*

**I have set thee to be a light of the Gentiles:** I have destined thee for a light to the heathen, *TCNT* . . . I have appointed you to enlighten, *Noli* . . . for the non-Jewish nations, *Everyday.*

**that thou shouldest be for salvation unto the ends of the earth:** To be the means of salvation to, *TCNT* . . . to bring salvation to, *Moffatt* . . . to save people all over the earth, *Beck.*

**13:48.** Hearing this, the Gentiles rejoiced and glorified the Word of the Lord. That is, they kept glorifying, giving honor to, and magnifying the Truth, the gospel preached by Paul and Barnabas. While the Jews were trying to contradict the Word concerning Jesus, the Gentiles were telling everyone how wonderful it was and giving God thanks for it.

There is some controversy over the word translated "ordained," (*tassō*). Elsewhere in the New Testament, the word means "to determine" (cf. 22:10, Jesus told Paul that certain things were "appointed," i.e., determined, assigned, for him to do). It can also mean to appoint (cf. 15:2, where Paul, Barnabas, and others were appointed by the church in Antioch to go to Jerusalem). (See also Matthew 28:16; Luke 7:8; Romans 13:1; 1 Corinthians 16:15.) While there is a strong indication of predestination, the text may simply be trying to distinguish between those who were converts (*hosoi*) and those who were not.

**48. And when the Gentiles heard this, they were glad:** On hearing this, the heathen were delighted, *TCNT* . . . The Gentiles listened with delight, *Weymouth* . . . The Gentiles were overjoyed when they heard this, *Norlie.*

**and glorified the word of the Lord:** . . . and extolled God's message, *TCNT* . . . and praised God's message, *Goodspeed* . . . and thanked God for His Message, *Phillips.*

**and as many as were ordained to eternal life believed:** . . . and all who were predestined to eternal Life, *Weymouth* . . . and those marked out by God for, *BB* . . . as many as are disposed, *Alford* . . . many...believed the message, *Everyday.*

**13:49.** The result of the enthusiastic witness by the Gentile believers was that the Word of the Lord (the Word; Greek, *logos*) concerning the Lord Jesus was carried or spread continually by them throughout the whole region.

**49. And the word of the Lord was published throughout all the region:** . . . was spread abroad, *ASV* . . . was disseminated all over that region, *Noli* . . . the message of the Lord was spreading through the whole country, *Everyday.*

| 5396.1 noun fem | 3450.7 art nom pl masc | 1156.2 conj | 2428.2 name-adj nom pl masc | 3813.1 verb 3pl indic aor act | 3450.15 art acc pl fem |
|---|---|---|---|---|---|
| χώρας. | **50.** οἱ | δὲ | Ἰουδαῖοι | παρώτρυναν | τὰς |
| *chōras* | *hoi* | *de* | *Ioudaioi* | *parōtrunan* | *tas* |
| country. | The | but | Jews | excited | the |

50.a.**Txt:** 01ℵ-org,08E 020L,025P,byz.
**Var:** 01ℵ-corr,02A,03B 04C,05D,33,sa.bo.Gries Lach,Treg,Alf,Word Tisc,We/Ho,Weis,Sod UBS/*

| 4431.7 verb acc pl fem part pres mid | 1129.9 noun acc pl fem | 2504.1 conj | 3450.15 art acc pl fem | 2139.3 adj acc pl fem |
|---|---|---|---|---|
| σεβομένας | γυναῖκας | (a καὶ ) | τὰς | εὐσχήμονας, |
| *sebomenas* | *gunaikas* | *kai* | *tas* | *euschēmonas* |
| worshiping | women | and | the | honorable |

| 2504.1 conj | 3450.8 art acc pl masc | 4272.8 num ord acc pl masc | 3450.10 art gen sing fem | 4032.2 noun gen sing fem | 2504.1 conj |
|---|---|---|---|---|---|
| καὶ | τοὺς | πρώτους | τῆς | πόλεως, | καὶ |
| *kai* | *tous* | *prōtous* | *tēs* | *poleōs* | *kai* |
| and | the | principals | of the | city, | and |

| 1877.1 verb 3pl indic aor act | 1369.3 noun acc sing masc | 1894.3 prep | 3450.6 art acc sing masc | 3834.4 name acc masc | 2504.1 conj |
|---|---|---|---|---|---|
| ἐπήγειραν | διωγμὸν | ἐπὶ | τὸν | Παῦλον | καὶ |
| *epēgeiran* | *diōgmon* | *epi* | *ton* | *Paulon* | *kai* |
| stirred up | a persecution | against | | Paul | and |

50.b.**Txt:** 025P,byz.
**Var:** 01ℵ,02A,03B,04C 05D,08E,020L,Lach Treg,Alf,Tisc,We/Ho Weis,Sod,UBS/*

| 3450.6 art acc sing masc | 915.4 name acc masc | 2504.1 conj | 1531.13 verb 3pl indic aor act | 840.8 prs-pron acc pl masc | 570.3 prep |
|---|---|---|---|---|---|
| (b τὸν ) | Βαρναβᾶν, | καὶ | ἐξέβαλον | αὐτοὺς | ἀπὸ |
| *ton* | *Barnaban* | *kai* | *exebalon* | *autous* | *apo* |
| | Barnabas, | and | cast out | them | from |

| 3450.1 art gen pl | 3588.1 noun gen pl neu | 840.1 prs-pron gen pl | 3450.7 art nom pl masc | 1156.2 conj | 1607.3 verb nom pl masc part aor mid |
|---|---|---|---|---|---|
| τῶν | ὁρίων | αὐτῶν. | **51.** οἱ | δὲ | ἐκτιναξάμενοι |
| *tōn* | *horiōn* | *autōn* | *hoi* | *de* | *ektinaxamenoi* |
| the | borders | their. | The | but | having shaken off |

51.a.**Txt:** 05D,08E,020L 025P,byz.sa.bo.
**Var:** 01ℵ,02A,03B,04C Lach,Treg,Alf,Tisc We/Ho,Weis,Sod UBS/*

| 3450.6 art acc sing masc | 2840.1 noun acc sing masc | 3450.1 art gen pl | 4087.5 noun gen pl masc | 840.1 prs-pron gen pl |
|---|---|---|---|---|
| τὸν | κονιορτὸν | τῶν | ποδῶν | (a αὐτῶν ) |
| *ton* | *koniorton* | *tōn* | *podōn* | *autōn* |
| the | dust | of the | feet | their |

| 1894.2 prep | 840.8 prs-pron acc pl masc | 2048.1 verb indic aor act | 1519.1 prep | 2406.3 name neu | 3614.7 rel-pron nom pl masc |
|---|---|---|---|---|---|
| ἐπ' | αὐτούς, | ἦλθον | εἰς | Ἰκόνιον, | **52.** οἵ |
| *ep'* | *autous* | *ēlthon* | *eis* | *Ikonion* | *hoi* |
| against | them, | came | to | Iconium. | Who |

52.a.**Txt:** 01ℵ,04C,05D 08E,020L,025P,byz.sa. bo.Tisc
**Var:** 02A,03B,33,Lach Treg,Alf,We/Ho,Weis Sod,UBS/*

| 1156.2 conj | 4885.1 conj | 3073.5 noun nom pl masc | 3997.39 verb 3pl indic imperf pass | 5315.2 noun gen sing fem | 2504.1 conj |
|---|---|---|---|---|---|
| ( δὲ | [a☆ τε ] | μαθηταὶ | ἐπληροῦντο | χαρᾶς | καὶ |
| *de* | *te* | *mathētai* | *eplērounto* | *charas* | *kai* |
| and | [ idem ] | disciples | were being filled | with joy | and |

| 4011.2 noun gen sing neu | 39.2 adj gen sing | 1090.33 verb 3sing indic aor mid | 1156.2 conj | 1706.1 prep | 2406.2 name dat neu |
|---|---|---|---|---|---|
| πνεύματος | ἁγίου. | **14:1.** Ἐγένετο | δὲ | ἐν | Ἰκονίῳ, |
| *pneumatos* | *hagiou* | *Egeneto* | *de* | *en* | *Ikoniō* |
| Spirit | Holy. | It came to pass | and | in | Iconium |

| 2567.3 prep | 3450.16 art sing neu | 840.15 prs-pron sing neu | 1511.21 verb inf aor act | 840.8 prs-pron acc pl masc | 1519.1 prep |
|---|---|---|---|---|---|
| κατὰ | τὸ | αὐτὸ | εἰσελθεῖν | αὐτοὺς | εἰς |
| *kata* | *to* | *auto* | *eiselthein* | *autous* | *eis* |
| according to | the | same | to enter | them | into |

**13:50.** The unbelieving Jews then got the attention of devout, worshiping, God-fearing women of honorable positions in society, convinced them that Paul and Barnabas were wrong, and urged them to do something. With their help the unbelieving Jews also persuaded the chief men of the city government to try to stop Paul and his company. By this means the unconverted Jews aroused persecution to the point that Paul and Barnabas were forced out of the district. "Their coasts" means the region or district under the control of these city officials. Paul made it clear in 1 Thessalonians 2:15,16 that it was their speaking to the Gentiles that aroused the Jews to this kind of persecution.

**13:51.** Paul and Barnabas did not try to confront the city officials. They knew there were faithful believers who would carry on the work of the Lord. So they simply shook the dust off their feet as a testimony against those who had forced them out of the city. This was something Jesus commanded His disciples to do (Matthew 10:14; Mark 6:11; Luke 9:5; 10:11). It was a sharp rebuke. By rejecting Paul and Barnabas, the Jews were rejecting Christ. By shaking the dust off their feet Paul and Barnabas were indicating the deadly effects of their rejection. It meant these people had broken every bond with God and His true people.

Paul and Barnabas went on to Iconium, a Phrygian city in the southern part of the Roman province of Galatia. It was about 60 miles east and a little south of Pisidian Antioch on a plateau of 3,370 feet elevation. It was a key city on the border between Phrygia near Lycaonia. It was also a center from which five Roman roads radiated. The Book of Acts makes it clear the Holy Spirit was directing Paul and Barnabas and thus it was God's purpose to make this important city the next new gospel center.

**13:52.** The persecutors did not destroy the Church in Pisidian Antioch. The believers continued to be true disciples and followers of Jesus as their Lord and Saviour and were filled with joy and with the Holy Spirit. The Greek tense here indicates they continued to be filled. They obeyed the injunction of Ephesians 5:18 to be "being filled," to keep on being filled with the Holy Spirit. (Though the Epistle to the Ephesians was not yet written, it was surely already part of Paul's teaching.) Notice too how often being filled with joy and being filled with the Spirit go together in the Scriptures!

**14:1.** The preaching at Pisidian Antioch, the great response of the Gentiles, and the persecution that followed set a pattern. Much or all of this was repeated in practically all of the cities Paul visited on his missionary journeys. Iconium was no exception. Arriving there, Paul and Barnabas went first to the synagogue, identified as "the synagogue of the Jews" as a reminder that even though they

**50. But the Jews stirred up the devout and honourable women:** . . . the Jews instigated, *Noyes* . . . worked upon the feelings of religions and respectable, *Phillips* . . . influenced the gentlewomen of rank who worshipped with them, *Weymouth* . . . the devout women of wealth, *Berkeley* . . . the most religious and respected women, *Norlie* . . . incited the women worshippers of high standing, *TNT* . . . the pious ladies, *Noli.*

**and the chief men of the city;** . . . and the leading men of the town, *TCNT* . . . and the leading citizens, *Montgomery* . . . the outstanding men, *Berkeley* . . . the foremost men of, *TNT.*

**and raised persecution against Paul and Barnabas:** . . . and so started a persecution, *Williams* . . . and instigated persecution, *Berkeley.*

**and expelled them out of their coasts:** . . . and drove them out of their neighbourhood, *TCNT* . . . out of the district, *Weymouth* . . . they ejected them from their boundaries, *Concordant* . . . out of their boundaries, *Wuest* . . . expelled them, *Phillips* . . . from their region, *NIV.*

**51. But they shook off the dust of their feet against them:** They, however, shook the dust off, *TCNT* . . . as a protest against them, *Williams.*

**and came unto Iconium:** . . . and went to Iconium, *RSV.*

**52. And the disciples were filled with joy:** . . . leaving the disciples full of joy, *TCNT* . . . and as for the disciples, they were more and more filled with joy, *Weymouth* . . . continued to be full, *Phillips.*

**and with the Holy Ghost:** . . . controlled by the Holy Spirit, *Wuest.*

**1. And it came to pass in Iconium:** Their Iconium experience was similar, *Berkeley* . . . Much the same thing happened, *Phillips.*

**that they went both together into the synagogue of the Jews:** . . . that they entered together, *ASV* . . . went as usual to the Jewish synagogue, *Everyday* . . . went into the Jewish place of worship, *NLT.*

| 3450.12 art acc sing fem | 4715.4 noun acc sing fem | 3450.1 art gen pl | 2428.3 name-adj gen pl masc | 2504.1 conj | 2953.37 verb inf aor act |
|---|---|---|---|---|---|
| τὴν | συναγωγὴν | τῶν | Ἰουδαίων | καὶ | λαλῆσαι |
| tēn | sunagōgēn | tōn | Ioudaiōn | kai | lalēsai |
| the | synagogue | of the | Jews, | and | to speak |

| 3643.1 adv | 5452.1 conj | 3961.36 verb inf aor act | 2428.3 name-adj gen pl masc | 4885.1 conj | 2504.1 conj |
|---|---|---|---|---|---|
| οὕτως | ὥστε | πιστεῦσαι | Ἰουδαίων | τε | καὶ |
| houtōs | hōste | pisteusai | Ioudaiōn | te | kai |
| so | that | to believe | of Jews | both | and |

| 1659.5 name gen pl masc | 4044.16 adj sing neu | 3988.1 noun sing neu | 3450.7 art nom pl masc | 1156.2 conj | 540.4 verb nom pl masc part pres act |
|---|---|---|---|---|---|
| Ἑλλήνων | πολὺ | πλῆθος. | 2. οἱ | δὲ | ⸀ ἀπειθοῦντες |
| Hellēnōn | polu | plēthos | hoi | de | apeithountes |
| Hellenists | a great | number. | The | but | being unpersuaded |

2.a.**Txt:** 08E,020L,025P byz.
**Var:** 01ℵ,02A,03B,04C Lach,Treg,Alf,Tisc We/Ho,Weis,Sod UBS/☆

| 540.11 verb nom pl masc part aor act | 2428.2 name-adj nom pl masc | 1877.1 verb 3pl indic aor act | 2504.1 conj |
|---|---|---|---|
| [a☆ ἀπειθήσαντες ] | Ἰουδαῖοι | ἐπήγειραν | καὶ |
| apeithēsantes | Ioudaioi | epēgeiran | kai |
| [ having been unpersuaded ] | Jews | stirred up | and |

| 2530.2 verb 3pl indic aor act | 3450.15 art acc pl fem | 5425.8 noun acc pl fem | 3450.1 art gen pl | 1477.5 noun gen pl neu | 2567.3 prep |
|---|---|---|---|---|---|
| ἐκάκωσαν | τὰς | ψυχὰς | τῶν | ἐθνῶν | κατὰ |
| ekakōsan | tas | psuchas | tōn | ethnōn | kata |
| harmed | the | souls | of the | Gentiles | against |

| 3450.1 art gen pl | 79.7 noun gen pl masc | 2401.2 adj sing | 3173.1 conj | 3631.1 partic | 5385.4 noun acc sing masc |
|---|---|---|---|---|---|
| τῶν | ἀδελφῶν. | 3. ἱκανὸν | μὲν | οὖν | χρόνον |
| tōn | adelphōn | hikanon | men | oun | chronon |
| the | brothers. | A long | indeed | therefore | time |

| 1298.3 verb 3pl indic aor act | 3817.2 verb nom pl masc part pres mid | 1894.3 prep | 3450.3 art dat sing | 2935.3 noun dat sing masc |
|---|---|---|---|---|
| διέτριψαν | παρρησιαζόμενοι | ἐπὶ | τῷ | κυρίῳ, |
| dietripsan | parrhēsiazomenoi | epi | tō | kuriō |
| they stayed, | speaking boldly, | in | the | Lord, |

3.a.**Var:** 01ℵ-org,02A,bo. Tisc,Weis,UBS/☆

| 3450.3 art dat sing | 3113.9 verb dat sing masc part pres act | 1894.3 prep | 3450.3 art dat sing | 3030.3 noun dat sing masc | 3450.10 art gen sing fem |
|---|---|---|---|---|---|
| τῷ | μαρτυροῦντι | [a+ ἐπὶ ] | τῷ | λόγῳ | τῆς |
| tō | marturounti | epi | tō | logō | tēs |
| the | bearing witness | [ to ] | to the | word | of the |

3.b.**Txt:** 04C,020L,byz.
**Var:** 01ℵ,02A,03B,05D 08E,025P,sa.bo.Gries Lach,Treg,Alf,Word Tisc,We/Ho,Weis,Sod UBS/☆

| 5322.2 noun gen sing fem | 840.3 prs-pron gen sing | 2504.1 conj | 1319.7 verb dat sing masc part pres act | 4447.2 noun pl neu | 2504.1 conj | 4907.1 noun pl neu |
|---|---|---|---|---|---|---|
| χάριτος | αὐτοῦ, | ⸂b καὶ ⸃ | διδόντι | σημεῖα | καὶ | τέρατα |
| charitos | autou | kai | didonti | sēmeia | kai | terata |
| grace | his | and | giving | signs | and | wonders |

| 1090.28 verb inf pres mid | 1217.2 prep | 3450.1 art gen pl | 5331.6 noun gen pl fem | 840.1 prs-pron gen pl | 4829.4 verb 3sing indic aor pass |
|---|---|---|---|---|---|
| γίνεσθαι | διὰ | τῶν | χειρῶν | αὐτῶν. | 4. ἐσχίσθη |
| ginesthai | dia | tōn | cheirōn | autōn | eschisthē |
| to be done | through | the | hands | their. | Was divided |

| 1156.2 conj | 3450.16 art sing neu | 3988.1 noun sing neu | 3450.10 art gen sing fem | 4032.2 noun gen sing fem | 2504.1 conj | 3450.7 art nom pl masc |
|---|---|---|---|---|---|---|
| δὲ | τὸ | πλῆθος | τῆς | πόλεως· | καὶ | οἱ |
| de | to | plēthos | tēs | poleōs | kai | hoi |
| and | the | multitude | of the | city, | and | the |

had turned to the Gentiles in Pisidian Antioch, they still felt it was God's will to go to the Jew first.

As usual, they were given opportunity to speak. Luke did not record the sermon. He simply indicated that they spoke in their usual manner. Paul preached essentially the same message concerning Christ and the forgiveness of sins as he had in Pisidian Antioch and gave the same warning and exhortation as well.

The results were similar. A very large number of both Jews and Greeks (Greek-speaking Gentiles) believed. This would mean they too would then be baptized. They too would be filled with joy and would become excited about spreading the good news to their friends in the city and in the surrounding area.

**14:2.** Then, as before in Pisidian Antioch, unbelieving Jews rose up opposing them. "Unbelieving" here includes the idea of disobedience and rebellion. In fact, the King James Version translates the verb as "disobedient" in Romans 10:21 and 1 Peter 2:7,8; 3:20. Belief brings obedience, unbelief brings rebellion.

These Jews in their mistaken zeal and jealousy aroused the Gentiles and turned them "against the brethren," not only against Paul and his company but also against the new believers.

The Jews in this case, however, were not able initially to get as much support from the Gentiles and city officials as the Jews in Pisidian Antioch had, so Paul and Barnabas were not immediately forced out of the city. Therefore, they dared to stay in Iconium a considerable length of time.

**14:3.** With boldness and freedom of speech they spoke for (or, in) the Lord Jesus (relying on Him and centering all their preaching and teaching in Him). As they did so, the Lord bore witness to the Word (Greek, *logō*, the message) of His grace (His unmerited favor in sending Jesus to save sinners) by giving signs (miraculous signs, supernatural signs) and wonders to be done by their hands.

By these miracles also, the apostles were recognized as Christ's agents doing His work by His authority. (Compare Galatians 3:5 where Paul later showed these Galatians that the miracles which were still being done in their midst were an evidence of God's grace and did not come as a result of the works of the Law.) Luke did not give any details of these miracles, but they surely included a variety as before.

**14:4.** In time the city crowd, that is, the whole population of the city Iconium became sharply divided. Some were with the (unbelieving) Jews. Some held with the apostles.

Notice here that both Paul and Barnabas are called apostles. Barnabas was evidently a witness of the resurrection of Jesus and

**and so spake:** . . . and preached, *Weymouth* . . . and spoke with such conviction, *Phillips* . . . and spoke with such effect, *TNT* . . . spoke...in such a way, *SEB.*

**that a great multitude both of the Jews and also of the Greeks believed:** . . . that a large number of both Jews...believed them, *TCNT* . . . joined the company of believers, *Noli* . . . believed what they said, *SEB.*

**2. But the unbelieving Jews:** But the Jews who refused to believe, *TCNT* . . . the unpersuaded Jews, *Rotherham.*

**stirred up the Gentiles, and made their minds evil affected against the brethren:** . . . stirred up the heathen, and poisoned their minds, *TCNT* . . . rendered them antagonistic, *Wuest* . . . and embittered the minds, *Alford* . . . against the disciples, *Norlie* . . . making them evil-hearted against the brothers, *KJII* . . . to oppress the brethren, *Lamsa* . . . made them persecute the brothers, *SEB.*

**3. Long time therefore abode they:** . . . they tarried there, *ASV* . . . remained there, *Weymouth.*

**speaking boldly in the Lord:** . . . speaking out fearlessly in dependence on the Lord, *TCNT* . . . and continued to speak with courage from the Lord, *Williams.*

**which gave testimony unto the word of his grace:** . . . who bare witness, *ASV* . . . who supported the Message of his mercy, *TCNT* . . . confirmed the message of his grace, *TNT* . . . who confirmed their gracious message, *Noli* . . . proved what they said was true, *SEB.*

**and granted signs and wonders to be done by their hands:** He helped them do miracles, *SEB* . . . by permitting...to take place at their hands, *TCNT* . . . by allowing, *Moffatt* . . . allowing them to perform, *Phillips* . . . to be effected, *Fenton.*

**4. But the multitude of the city was divided:** But the townspeople were divided, *TCNT* . . . the great mass of the people of the city were divided in their opinions, *Phillips* . . . the city split into parties, *Weymouth* . . . The inhabitants of the city, *Noli* . . . became divided, *TNT.*

| 3173.1 conj | 1498.37 verb 3pl indic imperf act | 4713.1 prep | 3450.4 art dat pl | 2428.4 name-adj dat pl masc | 3450.7 art nom pl masc | 1156.2 conj |
|---|---|---|---|---|---|---|
| μὲν | ἦσαν | σὺν | τοῖς | Ἰουδαίοις | οἱ | δὲ |
| *men* | *ēsan* | *sun* | *tois* | *Ioudaiois* | *hoi* | *de* |
| | were | with | the | Jews | the | and |

| 4713.1 prep | 3450.4 art dat pl | 646.6 noun dat pl masc | 5453.1 conj | 1156.2 conj | 1090.33 verb 3sing indic aor mid |
|---|---|---|---|---|---|
| σὺν | τοῖς | ἀποστόλοις. | 5. Ὡς | δὲ | ἐγένετο |
| *sun* | *tois* | *apostolois* | *Hōs* | *de* | *egeneto* |
| with | the | apostles. | When | and | there was |

| 3593.1 noun nom sing fem | 3450.1 art gen pl | 1477.5 noun gen pl neu | 4885.1 conj | 2504.1 conj | 2428.3 name-adj gen pl masc | 4713.1 prep |
|---|---|---|---|---|---|---|
| ὁρμὴ | τῶν | ἐθνῶν | τε | καὶ | Ἰουδαίων | σὺν |
| *hormē* | *tōn* | *ethnōn* | *te* | *kai* | *Ioudaiōn* | *sun* |
| a rush | of the | Gentiles | both | and | Jews | with |

| 3450.4 art dat pl | 752.7 noun dat pl masc | 840.1 prs-pron gen pl | 5036.3 verb inf aor act | 2504.1 conj | 3010.4 verb inf aor act |
|---|---|---|---|---|---|
| τοῖς | ἄρχουσιν | αὐτῶν, | ὑβρίσαι | καὶ | λιθοβολῆσαι |
| *tois* | *archousin* | *autōn* | *hubrisai* | *kai* | *lithobolēsai* |
| the | rulers | their, | to insult | and | to stone |

| 840.8 prs-pron acc pl masc | 4744.2 verb nom pl masc part aor act | 2672.1 verb 3pl indic aor act | 1519.1 prep | 3450.15 art acc pl fem |
|---|---|---|---|---|
| αὐτούς, | 6. συνιδόντες | κατέφυγον | εἰς | τὰς |
| *autous* | *sunidontes* | *katephugon* | *eis* | *tas* |
| them, | having been aware | they fled | to | the |

| 4032.5 noun pl fem | 3450.10 art gen sing fem | 3043.1 name gen fem | 3054.1 name acc sing fem | 2504.1 conj | 1185.1 name acc fem |
|---|---|---|---|---|---|
| πόλεις | τῆς | Λυκαονίας, | Λύστραν, | καὶ | Δέρβην, |
| *poleis* | *tēs* | *Lukaonias* | *Lustran* | *kai* | *Derbēn* |
| cities | | of Lycaonia, | Lystra, | and | Derbe, |

| 2504.1 conj | 3450.12 art acc sing fem | 3926.4 adj acc sing fem | 2517.1 conj | 1498.37 verb 3pl indic imperf act |
|---|---|---|---|---|
| καὶ | τὴν | περίχωρον, | 7. κἀκεῖ | ʻ ἦσαν |
| *kai* | *tēn* | *perichōron* | *kakei* | *ēsan* |
| and | the | country around, | and there | they were |

| 2076.12 verb nom pl masc part pres mid | 2076.12 verb nom pl masc part pres mid | 1498.37 verb 3pl indic imperf act |
|---|---|---|
| εὐαγγελιζόμενοι. | [ εὐαγγελιζόμενοι | ἦσαν. ] |
| *euangelizomenoi* | *euangelizomenoi* | *ēsan* |
| announcing the good news. | [ announcing the good news | they were. ] |

| 2504.1 conj | 4948.3 indef-pron nom sing | 433.1 noun nom sing masc | 1706.1 prep | 3054.2 name dat pl neu | 101.1 adj nom sing masc |
|---|---|---|---|---|---|
| 8. Καί | τις | ἀνὴρ | ʻ ἐν | Λύστροις | ἀδύνατος |
| *Kai* | *tis* | *anēr* | *en* | *Lustrois* | *adunatos* |
| And | a certain | man | in | Lystra, | powerless |

| 101.1 adj nom sing masc | 1706.1 prep | 3054.2 name dat pl neu | 3450.4 art dat pl | 4087.6 noun dat pl masc |
|---|---|---|---|---|
| [☆ ἀδύνατος | ἐν | Λύστροις ] | τοῖς | ποσὶν |
| *adunatos* | *en* | *Lustrois* | *tois* | *posin* |
| [ powerless | in | Lystra ] | in the | feet, |

| 2493.17 verb 3sing indic imperf mid | 5395.2 adj nom sing masc | 1523.2 prep gen | 2809.2 noun gen sing fem | 3251.2 noun gen sing fem | 840.3 prs-pron gen sing |
|---|---|---|---|---|---|
| ἐκάθητο, | χωλὸς | ἐκ | κοιλίας | μητρὸς | αὐτοῦ |
| *ekathēto* | *chōlos* | *ek* | *koilias* | *mētros* | *autou* |
| was sitting, | lame | from | womb | of mother | his |

of His teachings. Possibly he was part of the 70 sent out (Luke 10:1), or possibly he was part of the 120 in the Upper Room. Paul, in defending his apostleship in 1 Corinthians 9:1-6, also included Barnabas with him, as he did in Galatians 2:9,10.

**14:5.** Both unbelieving Gentiles and unbelieving Jews joined together with hostile intent. They purposed to treat the apostles outrageously and stone them to death. The Greek, however, does not mean there was any actual assault, but only the intent and instigation of one. This time, though, they had the support of their rulers including the city officials. Stoning, of course, shows that the Jews were justifying their action by the law of Moses against blasphemy. But they, by despising the gospel message, were blaspheming Christ and God.

**14:6.** The apostles became aware of the plot, however, and fled. Paul showed he was always willing to risk his life for the sake of spreading the gospel. But he did not seek to be a martyr. He fled because there were other places that needed the ministry of the gospel. So he and Barnabas went on eastward to Lystra and Derbe, cities of Lycaonia in the southern part of the Roman province of Galatia. Lystra was about 18 miles south-southwest of Iconium. Like Iconium, it was a Roman military colony.

Derbe was farther east. Recent discoveries have shown it was about 65 miles south-southeast of Lystra and was over the border of the Roman province of Galatia in the realm of King Antiochus of Commagene.

**14:7.** In this whole region round about Lystra and Derbe, the apostles proceeded to preach the gospel and kept on doing so for some time.

Since they were well on the road back to their home base, and since there were no Jewish synagogues in the area, it would have been easy for Barnabas and Paul to remember how they had shaken the dust off their feet against the cities that had rejected them and decide to keep on going back to a place where they knew they would be appreciated. But they felt the pressure of their call and commission to which the Holy Spirit had separated them. So they stayed.

**14:8.** What follows at Lystra gives an example of how Paul preached to Gentiles who had not come in contact with Jews and who had no knowledge of the Old Testament Scriptures.

At Lystra Paul did not go to a synagogue as was his usual custom, because there was none. Instead, it seems he went to the market-

**and part held with the Jews, and part with the apostles:** . . . some siding with the Jews, some with the Apostles, *TCNT* . . . agreed with, *SEB.*

**5. And when there was an assault made:** There was a plot afoot, *NIV.*

**both of the Gentiles, and also of the Jews:** . . . on the part of both heathen and Jews, *TCNT.*

**with their rulers:** . . . with their leading men, *TCNT* . . . with the sanction of their magistrates, *Weymouth* . . . in collaboration with the authorities, *Phillips.*

**to use them despitefully, and to stone them:** . . . to treat them shamefully, *ASV* . . . to illtreat and stone them, *TCNT* . . . to insult, *Moffatt* . . . in order to abuse, *KJII* . . . wanted to stone them to death, *SEB.*

**6. They were ware of it:** . . . they were warned, *KJII* . . . they became aware of it, *ASV* . . . the Apostles heard of it, *TCNT* . . . the apostles got wind of it, *Montgomery* . . . When they became aware of this danger, *Norlie* . . . they found out about it, *Beck* . . . aware of the situation, *AmpB.*

**and fled unto Lystra and Derbe, cities of Lycaonia:** . . . made their escape into the Lycaonian towns of, *Weymouth* . . . they left that town, *SEB.*

**and unto the region that lieth round about:** . . . and the neighbouring country, *Weymouth.*

**7. And there they preached the gospel:** . . . where they continued to tell the Good News, *TCNT.*

**8. And there sat a certain man at Lystra:** There used to sit in the streets of Lystra a man, *TCNT.*

**impotent in his feet:** . . . who had no power in his feet, *TCNT* . . . lame in his feet, *Montgomery* . . . who had not strength in his feet, *Williams* . . . who could not use his feet, *RSV* . . . whose feet were paralyzed, *SEB.*

**being a cripple from his mother's womb:** . . . he had been lame from his birth, *TCNT* . . . a cripple from birth, *Montgomery* . . . who had never walked in his life, *JB* . . . had been born crippled, *SEB.*

## Acts 14:9

8.a.**Txt:** 020L,025P,byz.
**Var:** 01ℵ,02A,03B,04C 05D,08E,33,Gries,Lach Treg,Alf,Word,Tisc We/Ho,Weis,Sod UBS/☆

8.b.**Txt:** 05D,08E,020L 025P,byz.
**Var:** 01ℵ,02A,03B,04C Lach,Treg,Alf,Tisc We/Ho,Weis,Sod UBS/☆

9.a.**Var:** 01ℵ,02A,05D 08E,020L,bo.Lach,Treg Tisc,Sod

| **5062.6** verb nom sing masc part pres act | **3614.5** rel-pron nom sing masc | **3626.1** adv | **3906.24** verb 3sing indic plperf act |
|---|---|---|---|
| ⸂a ὑπάρχων, ⸃ | ὃς | οὐδέποτε | ⸀ περιπεπατήκει. |
| *huparchōn* | *hos* | *oudepote* | *peripepatēkei* |
| being, | who | never | had walked. |

| **3906.18** verb 3sing indic aor act | **3642.4** dem-pron nom sing masc | **189.45** verb 3sing indic imperf act | **189.21** verb 3sing indic aor act |
|---|---|---|---|
| [b☆ περιεπάτησεν. ] | **9.** οὗτος | ⸀ ἤκουεν | [a ἤκουσεν ] |
| *periepatēsen* | *houtos* | *ēkouen* | *ēkousen* |
| [walked.] | This | was hearing | [heard] |

| **3450.2** art gen sing | **3834.2** name gen masc | **2953.13** verb gen sing masc part pres act | **3614.5** rel-pron nom sing masc | **810.3** verb nom sing masc part aor act |
|---|---|---|---|---|
| τοῦ | Παύλου | λαλοῦντος· | ὃς | ἀτενίσας |
| *tou* | *Paulou* | *lalountos* | *hos* | *atenisas* |
| | Paul | speaking, | who, | having looked intently |

| **840.4** prs-pron dat sing | **2504.1** conj | **1481.16** verb nom sing masc part aor act | **3617.1** conj | **3963.4** noun acc sing fem | **2174.4** verb 3sing indic pres act |
|---|---|---|---|---|---|
| αὐτῷ, | καὶ | ἰδὼν | ὅτι | ⸀ πίστιν | ἔχει |
| *autō* | *kai* | *idōn* | *hoti* | *pistin* | *echei* |
| on him, | and | having seen | that | faith | he has |

10.a.**Txt:** 02A,05D-corr 08E,020L,025P,byz. Weis,Sod
**Var:** 01ℵ,03B,04C 05D-org,Lach,Treg,Tisc We/Ho,UBS/☆

| **2174.4** verb 3sing indic pres act | **3963.4** noun acc sing fem | **3450.2** art gen sing | **4834.28** verb inf aor pass | **1500.5** verb 3sing indic aor act |
|---|---|---|---|---|
| [☆ ἔχει | πίστιν ] | τοῦ | σωθῆναι, | **10.** εἶπεν |
| *echei* | *pistin* | *tou* | *sōthēnai* | *eipen* |
| [he has | faith] | the | to be healed, | said |

10.b.**Var:** 04C,05D,08E Lach

| **3144.11** adj dat sing fem | **3450.11** art dat sing fem | **5292.3** noun dat sing fem | **4622.3** prs-pron dat 2sing | **2978.1** verb 1sing pres act | **1706.1** prep |
|---|---|---|---|---|---|
| μεγάλῃ | ⸂a τῇ ⸃ | φωνῇ, | [b+ Σοὶ | λέγω | ἐν |
| *megalē* | *tē* | *phōnē* | *Soi* | *legō* | *en* |
| with a loud | the | voice, | [To you | I say | in |

| **3450.3** art dat sing | **3549.4** noun dat sing neu | **3450.2** art gen sing | **2935.2** noun gen sing masc | **2400.2** name masc | **5382.2** name gen masc |
|---|---|---|---|---|---|
| τῷ | ὀνόματι | τοῦ | κυρίου | Ἰησοῦ | Χριστοῦ ] |
| *tō* | *onomati* | *tou* | *kuriou* | *Iēsou* | *Christou* |
| the | name | of the | Lord | Jesus | Christ] |

| **448.8** verb 2sing impr aor act | **1894.3** prep | **3450.8** art acc pl masc | **4087.7** noun acc pl masc | **4622.2** prs-pron gen 2sing | **3580.1** adj nom sing masc |
|---|---|---|---|---|---|
| Ἀνάστηθι | ἐπὶ | τοὺς | πόδας | σου | ὀρθός. |
| *Anastēthi* | *epi* | *tous* | *podas* | *sou* | *orthos* |
| Stand up | on | the | feet | your | upright. |

10.c.**Txt:** 020L,025P,byz.
**Var:** 01ℵ,02A,03B,04C Gries,Lach,Treg,Alf Word,Tisc,We/Ho,Weis Sod,UBS/☆

| **2504.1** conj | **240.3** verb 3sing indic imperf mid | **240.4** verb 3sing indic aor mid | **2504.1** conj | **3906.28** verb 3sing indic imperf act |
|---|---|---|---|---|
| Καὶ | ⸀ ἥλλετο | [c☆ ἥλατο ] | καὶ | περιεπάτει. |
| *Kai* | *hēlleto* | *hēlato* | *kai* | *periepatei* |
| And | he was springing up | [sprang up] | and | was walking. |

11.a.**Txt:** 04C,05D,08E 020L,025P,byz.sa.Sod
**Var:** 01ℵ,02A,03B,Lach Alf,Tisc,We/Ho,Weis UBS/☆

| **3614.7** rel-pron nom pl masc | **1156.2** conj | **4885.1** conj | **3657.5** noun nom pl masc | **1481.17** verb nom pl masc part aor act | **3614.16** rel-pron sing neu |
|---|---|---|---|---|---|
| **11.** Οἱ | ⸀ δὲ | [a☆ τε ] | ὄχλοι | ἰδόντες | ὃ |
| *Hoi* | *de* | *te* | *ochloi* | *idontes* | *ho* |
| Who | and | [idem] | crowds | having seen | what |

11.b.**Txt:** 020L,025P,byz.
**Var:** 01ℵ,02A,03B,04C 05D,08E,Lach,Treg,Alf Word,Tisc,We/Ho,Weis Sod,UBS/☆

| **4020.24** verb 3sing indic aor act | **3450.5** art nom sing masc | **3834.1** name nom masc | **1854.3** verb 3pl indic aor act | **3450.12** art acc sing fem |
|---|---|---|---|---|
| ἐποίησεν | ⸂b ὁ ⸃ | Παῦλος, | ἐπῆραν | τὴν |
| *epoiēsen* | *ho* | *Paulos* | *epēran* | *tēn* |
| did | | Paul, | lifted up | the |

place or to an open square just inside the city gates (as 14:13 indicates). There he began to preach. Among those nearby was a cripple. To draw attention to the utter hopelessness of his case, the Bible uses a threefold repetition. He was powerless in his feet, he was crippled from his mother's womb, and he had never walked.

**14:9.** This cripple kept listening intently to Paul. Undoubtedly, Paul had to start at the beginning and give teaching about the one true God, His promises, and His plan of salvation. He must have told about the coming of Jesus, His death, resurrection, and the promise of the Spirit. This began to stir faith in the heart and mind of this cripple.

Paul noticed how the man kept listening, fixed his eyes on him, and that he had faith to be healed. ("Healed," Greek *sothenai,* is from the verb *sozo* which is ordinarily translated "saved," but which also means to rescue from danger or from severe situations and thus be restored, healed, or made whole.) From this incident it is clear Paul did not leave anything out of the gospel he preached.

**14:10.** With his eyes still fixed on the cripple, Paul encouraged the man's faith to action by commanding him in a very loud voice to stand up straight (erect) on his feet. Without hesitation the man immediately leaped up. He not only stood up straight, he found he could walk and proceeded to do so.

He showed even greater faith than the cripple at the Gate Beautiful, for there Peter had to encourage the beggar's faith by taking him by the hand. Here the cripple stood up in response to the Word of God and the command given by the Holy Spirit through Paul.

**14:11.** Undoubtedly Paul was preaching to a crowd that kept gathering as he preached. Some of them may have been idly curious. Some may have just been passing by and stopped for a moment to listen. Few, if any, were giving the kind of attention to the message the cripple did. But the loud command of Paul caught the attention of the whole crowd. When they saw the man jump up and start walking around, they began shouting excitedly. However, though they knew the Greek Paul was using in his preaching, in their excitement they reverted to their native Lycaonian language, which Paul and Barnabas did not understand. This sort of thing is a common occurrence. Usually, when a person is educated to use a second language, he will still fall back into his native language, the language of his childhood, when he is excited or under stress. Even Jesus did that on the cross when he quoted Psalm 22:1 in the Aramaic He grew up with, instead of in the Hebrew in which it was written (Mark 15:34).

**who never had walked:** . . . and had never walked at all, *TCNT* . . . in his life, *NEB* . . . had never been able to walk, *Goodspeed, Phillips.*

**9. The same heard Paul speak:** He listened to Paul speaking, *RSV* . . . was hearing Paul, *Worrell* . . . This man was listening to Paul speaking, *TCNT* . . . This man was sitting there and listening to Paul speak, *SEB* . . . listened as Paul spoke, *NLT* . . . to Paul's sermon, *Noli* . . . to Paul's preaching, *Knox.*

**who stedfastly beholding him:** . . . who, fastening his eyes upon him, *ASV* . . . looking him straight in the eye, *Phillips* . . . looked intently at him, *TNT* . . . looking earnestly upon him, *Swann* . . . Paul watched him, *NLT* . . . gazing at him, *Kleist* . . . looking closely at him, *Knox* . . . looked straight at him, *Everyday.*

**and perceiving that he had faith to be healed:** . . . and seeing that he had faith to be made whole, *ASV* . . . saw that the man believed that God could heal him, *SEB* . . . saw that he had faith in his salvation, *Noli* . . . seeing that there was saving faith in him, *Knox* . . . believed he could be healed, *NLT* . . . to be cured, *Kleist, Weymouth* . . . that there was faith in him, *Lamsa* . . . to be made well, *BB, TNT.*

**10. Said with a loud voice:** Calling to him, *NLT* . . . said loudly, *TCNT* . . . So, Paul shouted, *SEB* . . . he shouted aloud to him, *Williams* . . . So he cried out, *NCV.*

**Stand upright on thy feet:** Stand up on your feet, *Everyday, NCV, TCNT* . . . Stand erect on your feet, *Moffatt* . . . Get on your feet and stand erect! *Williams* . . . Stand up straight on your feet, *Berkeley.*

**And he leaped and walked:** And he sprang up and began to walk about, *Rotherham* . . . The man jumped up, and began walking about, *TCNT* . . . walking around, *SEB* . . . sprang up, stood, *Murdock* . . . he leaped up with a single bound, *Wuest.*

**11. And when the people saw what Paul had done:** And the multitudes, *Worrell* . . . The crowds of people, seeing what,

| 5292.4 noun acc sing fem | 840.1 prs-pron gen pl | 3044.1 name-adv | 2978.16 verb nom pl masc part pres act | 3450.7 art nom pl masc |
|---|---|---|---|---|
| φωνὴν | αὐτῶν | Λυκαονιστὶ | λέγοντες, | Οἱ |
| *phōnēn* | *autōn* | *Lukaonisti* | *legontes* | *Hoi* |
| voice | their | in Lycaonian | saying, | The |

| 2296.6 noun nom pl masc | 3529.6 verb nom pl masc part aor pass | 442.8 noun dat pl masc | 2568.15 verb 3pl indic aor act |
|---|---|---|---|
| θεοὶ | ὁμοιωθέντες | ἀνθρώποις | κατέβησαν |
| *theoi* | *homoiōthentes* | *anthrōpois* | *katebēsan* |
| gods, | having become like | men, | are come down |

12.a.**Txt:** 04C-corr,08E 020L,025P,byz.bo. **Var:** 01ℵ,02A,03B 04C-org,sa.Lach,Treg Alf,Tisc,We/Ho,Weis Sod,UBS/☆

| 4242.1 prep | 2231.4 prs-pron acc 1pl | 2535.25 verb 3pl indic imperf act | 4885.1 conj | 3450.6 art acc sing masc | 3173.1 conj |
|---|---|---|---|---|---|
| πρὸς | ἡμᾶς· | **12.** ἐκάλουν | τε | τὸν | ⸂[a] μὲν ⸃ |
| *pros* | *hēmas* | *ekaloun* | *te* | *ton* | *men* |
| to | us. | They were calling | and | the | one |

| 915.4 name acc masc | 2185.2 name acc masc | 3450.6 art acc sing masc | 1156.2 conj | 3834.4 name acc masc | 2044.1 name acc masc |
|---|---|---|---|---|---|
| Βαρναβᾶν | Δία· | τὸν | δὲ | Παῦλον | Ἑρμῆν, |
| *Barnaban* | *Dia* | *ton* | *de* | *Paulon* | *Hermēn* |
| Barnabas | Zeus; | the | and | Paul | Hermes, |

| 1879.1 conj | 840.5 prs-pron nom sing masc | 1498.34 verb sing indic imperf act | 3450.5 art nom sing masc | 2216.5 verb nom sing masc part pres mid | 3450.2 art gen sing |
|---|---|---|---|---|---|
| ἐπειδὴ | αὐτὸς | ἦν | ὁ | ἡγούμενος | τοῦ |
| *epeidē* | *autos* | *ēn* | *ho* | *hēgoumenos* | *tou* |
| because | he | was | the | leading | the |

13.a.**Txt:** 08E,020L 025P,byz.sa.bo. **Var:** 01ℵ,02A,03B 04C-corr,Lach,Treg,Alf Tisc,We/Ho,Weis,Sod UBS/☆

| 3030.2 noun gen sing masc | 3450.5 art nom sing masc | 1156.2 conj | 3614.16 rel-pron sing neu | 4885.1 conj | 2385.1 noun nom sing masc |
|---|---|---|---|---|---|
| λόγου. | **13.** ⸂ ὁ | δὲ | [[a]☆ ὅ | τε ] | ἱερεὺς |
| *logou* | *ho* | *de* | *ho* | *te* | *hiereus* |
| speaking. | The | and | [Who | and ] | priest |

| 3450.2 art gen sing | 2185.1 name gen masc | 3450.2 art gen sing | 1498.19 verb gen sing part pres act | 4112.1 prep | 3450.10 art gen sing fem |
|---|---|---|---|---|---|
| τοῦ | Διὸς | τοῦ | ὄντος | πρὸ | τῆς |
| *tou* | *Dios* | *tou* | *ontos* | *pro* | *tēs* |
| | of Zeus | the | being | before | the |

13.b.**Txt:** 04C-corr,08E 020L,025P,byz. **Var:** 01ℵ,02A,03B 04C-org,05D,33,sa.bo. Gries,Lach,Treg,Alf Word,Tisc,We/Ho,Weis Sod,UBS/☆

| 4032.2 noun gen sing fem | 840.1 prs-pron gen pl | 4873.3 noun acc pl masc | 2504.1 conj | 4576.1 noun pl neu | 1894.3 prep |
|---|---|---|---|---|---|
| πόλεως | ⸂[b] αὐτῶν, ⸃ | ταύρους | καὶ | στέμματα | ἐπὶ |
| *poleōs* | *autōn* | *taurous* | *kai* | *stemmata* | *epi* |
| city, | their | oxen | and | garlands | to |

| 3450.8 art acc pl masc | 4298.6 noun acc pl masc | 5179.17 verb nom sing masc part aor act | 4713.1 prep | 3450.4 art dat pl | 3657.7 noun dat pl masc |
|---|---|---|---|---|---|
| τοὺς | πυλῶνας | ἐνέγκας, | σὺν | τοῖς | ὄχλοις |
| *tous* | *pulōnas* | *enenkas* | *sun* | *tois* | *ochlois* |
| the | gates | having brought, | with | the | crowds |

| 2286.32 verb 3sing indic imperf act | 2357.2 verb inf pres act | 189.32 verb nom pl masc part aor act | 1156.2 conj | 3450.7 art nom pl masc |
|---|---|---|---|---|
| ἤθελεν | θύειν. | **14.** Ἀκούσαντες | δὲ | οἱ |
| *ēthelen* | *thuein* | *Akousantes* | *de* | *hoi* |
| were wishing | to sacrifice. | Having heard | but | the |

| 646.4 noun nom pl masc | 915.1 name nom masc | 2504.1 conj | 3834.1 name nom masc | 1278.4 verb nom pl masc part aor act |
|---|---|---|---|---|
| ἀπόστολοι | Βαρναβᾶς | καὶ | Παῦλος, | διαρρήξαντες |
| *apostoloi* | *Barnabas* | *kai* | *Paulos* | *diarrhēxantes* |
| apostles | Barnabas | and | Paul, | having torn |

The miracle made the people (who were pagan Gentiles) believe the Greek gods had come down, being made like human beings or taking the form of human beings. This would not have been a new idea to them, for their Greek mythology included many stories of gods coming to earth in human form, and the images of their Greek gods were in human form. Because they had never seen such a miracle, they jumped to the conclusion that the apostles were manifestations of their gods.

**14:12.** The people then began to call Barnabas *Dia* (in verse 13, *Dios*), a form of the Greek sky god Zeus, who was identified by the Romans with their chief god Jupiter and by this people with their chief Lycaonian god. Barnabas was identified with the chief god probably because he was older and a larger man than Paul.

Since Paul was the chief speaker (literally, "the leader [or, the guide] of the Word [the *logos*]"), they called him *Hermēn* (Hermes), the messenger and herald of the gods, especially of *Dios* (Zeus, Jupiter). Hermes was identified by the Romans with their god Mercurius (Mercury) who presided over eloquence and cunning as well as commerce and theft. (The King James Version uses Jupiter and Mercurius due to the influence of the Roman Catholic Latin version.) This also indicates Paul had been doing most of the preaching.

**14:13.** In view of this identification of the apostles with their gods, the people of Lystra took what they thought was appropriate action. They contacted the priest of the god *Dios* whose temple was in front of the city. He brought oxen (actually, bulls, the most costly victims they could offer in sacrifice). These were decorated with garlands (wreaths) as part of the sacrifice and brought to the gates of the city where the crowds were gathered, wanting to sacrifice.

Notice that Barnabas is again named first in verses 12 and 14. As *Dios* (Zeus, Jupiter) he was considered the chief god and the leading one for whom the sacrifices were to be made.

**14:14.** All of this was done with a great deal of excitement and shouting in the Lycaonian language, which Paul and Barnabas did not understand. Perhaps they made inquiries about what was going on. Finally, someone must have explained to them in Greek what was happening. When the apostles heard and understood that the people were about to sacrifice these animals to them and offer the wreaths as well, they tore their clothes as a sign of grief and dismay. (This was usually done by taking two hands at the neck and ripping the clothes open part of the way down the front.) After they did this, they immediately rushed out (sprang out) into the midst of the crowd crying out loudly (shouting, almost screaming).

It is not strange that Paul was upset. He would not court or tolerate the praise and attention of man. He knew that loving God

*TCNT* . . . When the people saw Paul's miracle, *Noli* . . . beholding what Paul had done, *Swann.*

**they lifted up their voices, saying in the speech of Lycaonia:** . . . called out in the Lycaonian language, *TCNT* . . . in the language of the country, *Murdock.*

**The gods are come down to us in the likeness of men:** The gods, made like unto men, have come, *Rotherham* . . . The Gods have made themselves like men and come down to us, *TCNT* . . . in the form of men, *Weymouth* . . . in human form, *Moffatt* . . . disguised as men, *JB.*

**12. And they called Barnabas, Jupiter:** They called Barnabas 'Zeus,' *Weymouth* . . . And they began to call Barnabas "Zeus," *Montgomery* . . . Lord of the Gods, *Murdock.*

**and Paul, Mercurius, because he was the chief speaker:** . . . and Paul, Mercury, *ASV* . . . and Paul Hermes, since he was the chief spokesman, *Moffatt* . . . because he led the conversation, *Berkeley* . . . because he was the principal speaker, *Williams* . . . the main speaker, *Beck.*

**13. Then the priest of Jupiter, which was before their city:** And the priest of Zeus, whose temple was in front of the city, *RSV* . . . The priest of Jupiter-beyond-the-Walls, *TCNT* . . . And the priest of Zeus—the temple of Zeus being just outside the city, *Weymouth* . . . In fact, the city-priest for Zeus, *Berkeley* . . . What is more, the High Priest of Jupiter whose temple was at the gateway of the city, *Phillips.*

**brought oxen and garlands unto the gates:** . . . brought bullocks and garlands to the gates, *TCNT* . . . unto the doors of the house, *Alford.*

**and would gave done sacrifice with the people:** . . . was disposed, *Murdock* . . . with the multitudes, *ASV* . . . with the intention of offering sacrifices, *TCNT* . . . and in company with the crowd was intending to offer sacrifices to them, *Weymouth.*

**14. Which when the apostles, Barnabas and Paul, heard of:** . . . understood what the people were doing, *SEB* . . . of their intention, *Phillips.*

## Acts 14:15

14.a.**Txt:** p74,01ℵ-org 04C,05D,08E,020L 025P,byz.Tisc
**Var:** 01ℵ-corr,02A,03B We/Ho,Weis,Sod UBS/☆

14.b.**Txt:** 04C-corr,020L 025P,byz.
**Var:** 01ℵ,02A,03B 04C-org,05D,08E,Gries Lach,Treg,Alf,Word Tisc,We/Ho,Weis,Sod UBS/☆

| **3450.17** art pl neu | **2416.4** noun pl neu | **840.1** prs-pron gen pl | **1431.2** prs-pron gen pl | **1514.2** verb 3pl indic aor act |
|---|---|---|---|---|
| τὰ | ἱμάτια | ⸂ αὐτῶν | [a ἑαυτῶν ] | ⸂ εἰσεπήδησαν |
| *ta* | *himatia* | *autōn* | *heautōn* | *eisepēdēsan* |
| the | garments, | their | [ themselves ] | rushed in |

| **1587.1** verb 3pl indic aor act | **1519.1** prep | **3450.6** art acc sing masc | **3657.4** noun acc sing masc | **2869.4** verb nom pl masc part pres act |
|---|---|---|---|---|
| [b☆ ἐξεπήδησαν ] | εἰς | τὸν | ὄχλον, | κράζοντες |
| *exepēdēsan* | *eis* | *ton* | *ochlon* | *krazontes* |
| [ rushed out ] | to | the | crowd, | crying |

| **2504.1** conj | **2978.16** verb nom pl masc part pres act | **433.6** noun nom pl masc | **4949.9** intr-pron sing neu | **3642.18** dem-pron pl neu |
|---|---|---|---|---|
| 15. καὶ | λέγοντες, | Ἄνδρες, | τί | ταῦτα |
| *kai* | *legontes* | *Andres* | *ti* | *tauta* |
| and | saying, | Men, | why | these things |

| **4020.2** verb 2pl pres act | **2504.1** conj | **2231.1** prs-pron nom 1pl | **3526.2** adj nom pl masc | **1498.5** verb 1pl indic pres act | **5050.3** prs-pron dat 2pl |
|---|---|---|---|---|---|
| ποιεῖτε; | καὶ | ἡμεῖς | ὁμοιοπαθεῖς | ἐσμεν | ὑμῖν |
| *poieite* | *kai* | *hēmeis* | *homoiopatheis* | *esmen* | *humin* |
| do you? | also | we | of like feelings | are | with you |

| **442.6** noun nom pl masc | **2076.12** verb nom pl masc part pres mid | **5050.4** prs-pron acc 2pl | **570.3** prep |
|---|---|---|---|
| ἄνθρωποι, | εὐαγγελιζόμενοι | ὑμᾶς | ἀπὸ |
| *anthrōpoi* | *euangelizomenoi* | *humas* | *apo* |
| men, | announcing the good news to | you | from |

15.a.**Txt:** 020L,025P,byz.
**Var:** 01ℵ-corr,02A,03B 04C,05D-corr,08E,Lach Treg,Alf,Word,Tisc We/Ho,Weis,Sod UBS/☆

15.b.**Txt:** 020L,025P,byz.
**Var:** 01ℵ-corr,02A,03B 04C,05D-corr,08E,Lach Treg,Alf,Word,Tisc We/Ho,Weis,Sod UBS/☆

| **3642.2** dem-pron gen pl | **3450.1** art gen pl | **3124.5** adj gen pl neu | **1978.14** verb inf aor act | **1894.3** prep | **3450.6** art acc sing masc |
|---|---|---|---|---|---|
| τούτων | τῶν | ματαίων | ἐπιστρέφειν | ἐπὶ | ⸂a τὸν ⸃ |
| *toutōn* | *tōn* | *mataiōn* | *epistrephein* | *epi* | *ton* |
| these | the | useless things | to turn | to | |

| **2296.4** noun acc sing masc | **3450.6** art acc sing masc | **2180.9** verb part pres act | **3614.5** rel-pron nom sing masc | **4020.24** verb 3sing indic aor act | **3450.6** art acc sing masc |
|---|---|---|---|---|---|
| θεὸν | ⸂b τὸν ⸃ | ζῶντα, | ὃς | ἐποίησεν | τὸν |
| *theon* | *ton* | *zōnta* | *hos* | *epoiēsen* | *ton* |
| God | the | living, | who | made | the |

| **3636.4** noun acc sing masc | **2504.1** conj | **3450.12** art acc sing fem | **1087.4** noun acc sing fem | **2504.1** conj | **3450.12** art acc sing fem | **2258.4** noun acc sing fem |
|---|---|---|---|---|---|---|
| οὐρανὸν | καὶ | τὴν | γῆν | καὶ | τὴν | θάλασσαν |
| *ouranon* | *kai* | *tēn* | *gēn* | *kai* | *tēn* | *thalassan* |
| heaven | and | the | earth | and | the | sea |

| **2504.1** conj | **3820.1** adj | **3450.17** art pl neu | **1706.1** prep | **840.2** prs-pron dat pl | **3614.5** rel-pron nom sing masc | **1706.1** prep |
|---|---|---|---|---|---|---|
| καὶ | πάντα | τὰ | ἐν | αὐτοῖς· | 16. ὃς | ἐν |
| *kai* | *panta* | *ta* | *en* | *autois* | *hos* | *en* |
| and | all | the things | in | them; | who | in |

| **3450.14** art dat pl fem | **3806.1** verb dat pl fem part perf mid | **1067.7** noun dat pl fem | **1432.3** verb 3sing indic aor act | **3820.1** adj |
|---|---|---|---|---|
| ταῖς | παρῳχημέναις | γενεαῖς | εἴασεν | πάντα |
| *tais* | *parōchēmenais* | *geneais* | *eiasen* | *panta* |
| the | having past | generations | permitted | all |

| **3450.17** art pl neu | **1477.4** noun pl neu | **4057.15** verb inf pres mid | **3450.14** art dat pl fem | **3461.7** noun dat pl fem | **840.1** prs-pron gen pl |
|---|---|---|---|---|---|
| τὰ | ἔθνη | πορεύεσθαι | ταῖς | ὁδοῖς | αὐτῶν· |
| *ta* | *ethnē* | *poreuesthai* | *tais* | *hodois* | *autōn* |
| the | nations | to go | in the | ways | their, |

completely left no room for taking any part in heathen worship. He knew the foolishness and emptiness of idolatry, so it shocked both him and Barnabas that these people of Lystra would be looking at them as if they were gods and wanting to worship them. So immediately they began to shout out their protests.

What happened here also drives home the importance of the Jewish synagogues to the spread of the gospel in this initial thrust of the Apostolic Church during the First Century. Wherever they were scattered through the Roman Empire and beyond, they prepared the way. They taught one true God and high moral standards. The Gentiles who attended knew the Word; they had heard the prophecies. They knew God worked through men "of like passions," for they heard the stories of Moses and Elijah. The synagogues had enough influence on the community around them so no one would ever have interpreted miracles the way these people at Lystra did. The people at Lystra had no such background. All they could do was interpret the miracle in terms of their own pagan ideas.

**14:15.** Paul and Barnabas tried to stop the sacrifices by declaring they were men, human beings with feelings like theirs (implying a nature like theirs). They had come to preach the gospel (the good news) to turn them from these vain (unreal, useless, unfruitful) things to the living God.

Paul took them back to the time of the Creation. He told them of the living God who made all things. Many modern missionaries have found they had to start where Paul did when dealing with people who have no knowledge of the Bible. There is indeed a revelation of God in nature and history for those who will see it.

**14:16.** In times past (literally, generations gone by) God let all nations (all the Gentiles) go their own way (in contrast to going God's way). They all followed various roads, various ways of life of their own choosing, and God let them do it. But He did not give up His plan of redemption or his purpose to bring blessing to all the nations of the earth.

It is clear in Genesis chapters 1 through 11 that God dealt with the world as a whole and gave them a new start through the Flood. But with chapter 12 God ceased to deal with the world as a whole. He dealt with one man, Abraham, and his descendants through whom would come a blood line that would lead to Christ, the greater Seed of Abraham, the One who makes all God's promises good.

Noah worshiped the true God with a simple faith that pleased the Lord, but by the time of Abraham the whole world was full of idolatry. Abraham's relatives worshiped idols in Haran. (See Joshua 24:15 where the Hebrew means "the gods your fathers served [worshiped] on the other side of the [Euphrates] river.") According to Jewish tradition, Abraham's father Terah was actually an idol maker.

**they rent their clothes:** . . . they tore their clothes, *TCNT* . . . they ripped their own clothes, *SEB.*

**and ran in among the people:** . . . and rushed out among the multitude, *RSV* . . . and rushed out into the crowd, *TCNT* . . . dashed forward among the crowds, *Berkeley.*

**crying out:** . . . exclaiming, *Weymouth* . . . shouting, *Moffatt* . . . crying at the top of their voices, *Phillips.*

**15. And saying, Sirs, why do ye these things?:** Friends, why are you doing this, *TCNT* . . . Why are you doing these things? *Concordant* . . . why are you making all this fuss? *Noli.*

**We also are men of like passions with you:** We are only men like you, *TCNT* . . . We also are but human beings with natures like yours, *Weymouth* . . . We too are mortal, *Kleist* . . . are ordinary human beings, *Lamsa* . . . We are men with the same feelings as you, *BB* . . . We are human, with emotions as yourselves, *Berkeley* . . . frail mortals, *Murdock* . . . with experiences like yours, *Beck* . . . men who possess the same kind of feelings, *Wuest.*

**and preach unto you:** . . . and bring you good tidings, *ASV* . . . and we have come with the Good News, *TCNT.*

**that ye should turn from these vanities:** . . . these follies, *TCNT* . . . these empty things, *Montgomery* . . . these foolish things, *Williams* . . . these meaningless things, *Phillips* . . . such superstitions, *Norlie* . . . these useless things, *Murdock* . . . these worthless things, *SEB* . . . from these vain gods, *Kleist* . . . turn from such futile ways, *Moffatt* . . . from these futile things, *TNT.*

**unto the living God, which made heaven, and earth, and the sea:** . . . who made the sky, the earth, the sea, *TCNT* . . . the Creator of earth and sky and sea, *Weymouth.*

**and all things that are therein:** . . . and everything that is in them, *TCNT.*

**16. Who in times past suffered all nations to walk in their own ways:** In the generations that are passed he let all the nations follow their own ways, *Kleist* . . . to go on in their own ways, *Phillips.*

## Acts 14:17

17.a.**Txt:** 01ℵ-org 04C-corr,020L,025P,byz.
**Var:** 01ℵ-corr,02A,03B 04C-org,Lach,Tisc We/Ho,Weis,Sod UBS/☆

17.b.**Txt:** 01ℵ-corr,04C 05D,020L,025P,byz. Weis,Sod
**Var:** 01ℵ-org,02A,03B 08E,Lach,Treg,Tisc We/Ho,UBS/☆

17.c.**Txt:** 05D,08E,020L 025P,byz.
**Var:** 01ℵ,02A,03B,04C Lach,Treg,Alf,Word Tisc,We/Ho,Weis,Sod UBS/☆

17.d.**Txt:** byz.bo.
**Var:** 01ℵ-org,02A,03B 04C,05D,08E,020L 025P,Gries,Lach,Treg Alf,Tisc,We/Ho,Weis Sod,UBS/☆

17.e.**Txt:** 01ℵ-corr,02A 020L,025P,byz.bo.
**Var:** 01ℵ-org,03B,04C 05D,08E,Gries,Lach Treg,Alf,Tisc,We/Ho Weis,Sod,UBS/☆

19.a.**Txt:** 04C,05D,08E 020L,025P,byz.Weis Sod
**Var:** p74,01ℵ,02A,03B Lach,Treg,Alf,Tisc We/Ho,UBS/☆

| **2514.1** adv | **1058.1** partic | **2514.1** adv | **3620.2** partic | **265.1** adj acc sing masc |
|---|---|---|---|---|
| **17.** ʼ καίτοι | γε | [a☆ καίτοι ] | οὐκ | ἀμάρτυρον |
| *kaitoi* | *ge* | *kaitoi* | *ouk* | *amarturon* |
| though | indeed | [ though ] | not | without witness |

| **1431.6** prs-pron acc sing masc | **1431.15** prs-pron acc sing masc | **856.10** verb 3sing indic aor act | **15.3** verb nom sing masc part pres act |
|---|---|---|---|
| ʼ ἑαυτὸν | [b☆ αὑτὸν ] | ἀφῆκεν | ʼ ἀγαθοποιῶν, |
| *heauton* | *hauton* | *aphēken* | *agathopoiōn* |
| himself | [ him ] | he left, | doing good, |

| **14.2** verb nom sing masc part pres act | **3635.1** adv | **2231.3** prs-pron dat 1pl | **5050.3** prs-pron dat 2pl | **5046.3** noun acc pl masc |
|---|---|---|---|---|
| [c☆ ἀγαθουργῶν, ] | οὐρανόθεν | ʼ ἡμῖν | [d☆ ὑμῖν ] | ὑετοὺς |
| *agathourgōn* | *ouranothen* | *hēmin* | *humin* | *huetous* |
| [ idem ] | from heaven | to us | [ to you ] | rains |

| **1319.5** verb nom sing masc part pres act | **2504.1** conj | **2511.8** noun acc pl masc | **2564.1** adj acc pl masc | **1689.1** verb nom sing masc part pres act |
|---|---|---|---|---|
| διδοὺς | καὶ | καιροὺς | καρποφόρους, | ἐμπιπλῶν |
| *didous* | *kai* | *kairous* | *karpophorous* | *empiplōn* |
| giving | and | seasons | fruitful, | filling |

| **5001.2** noun gen sing fem | **2504.1** conj | **2148.1** noun gen sing fem | **3450.15** art acc pl fem | **2559.1** noun fem | **2231.2** prs-pron gen 1pl |
|---|---|---|---|---|---|
| τροφῆς | καὶ | εὐφροσύνης | τὰς | καρδίας | ʼ ἡμῶν. |
| *trophēs* | *kai* | *euphrosunēs* | *tas* | *kardias* | *hēmōn* |
| with food | and | gladness | the | hearts | our. |

| **5050.2** prs-pron gen 2pl | **2504.1** conj | **3642.18** dem-pron pl neu | **2978.16** verb nom pl masc part pres act | **3296.1** adv |
|---|---|---|---|---|
| [e☆ ὑμῶν. ] | **18.** Καὶ | ταῦτα | λέγοντες | μόλις |
| *humōn* | *Kai* | *tauta* | *legontes* | *molis* |
| [ your. ] | And | these things | saying | hardly |

| **2634.2** verb 3pl indic aor act | **3450.8** art acc pl masc | **3657.8** noun acc pl masc | **3450.2** art gen sing | **3231.1** partic | **2357.2** verb inf pres act |
|---|---|---|---|---|---|
| κατέπαυσαν | τοὺς | ὄχλους | τοῦ | μὴ | θύειν |
| *katepausan* | *tous* | *ochlous* | *tou* | *mē* | *thuein* |
| they stopped | the | crowds | the | not | to sacrifice |

| **840.2** prs-pron dat pl | **1889.1** verb 3pl indic aor act | **1889.9** verb 3pl indic aor act | **1156.2** conj | **570.3** prep |
|---|---|---|---|---|
| αὐτοῖς. | **19.** ʼ Ἐπῆλθον | [a☆ Ἐπῆλθαν ] | δὲ | ἀπὸ |
| *autois* | *Epēlthon* | *Epēlthan* | *de* | *apo* |
| to them. | Arrived | [ idem ] | but | from |

| **487.1** name gen fem | **2504.1** conj | **2406.1** name gen neu | **2428.2** name-adj nom pl masc | **2504.1** conj | **3844.7** verb nom pl masc part aor act |
|---|---|---|---|---|---|
| Ἀντιοχείας | καὶ | Ἰκονίου | Ἰουδαῖοι, | καὶ | πείσαντες |
| *Antiocheias* | *kai* | *Ikoniou* | *Ioudaioi* | *kai* | *peisantes* |
| Antioch | and | Iconium | Jews, | and | having persuaded |

| **3450.8** art acc pl masc | **3657.8** noun acc pl masc | **2504.1** conj | **3008.4** verb nom pl masc part aor act | **3450.6** art acc sing masc | **3834.4** name acc masc |
|---|---|---|---|---|---|
| τοὺς | ὄχλους, | καὶ | λιθάσαντες | τὸν | Παῦλον, |
| *tous* | *ochlous* | *kai* | *lithasantes* | *ton* | *Paulon* |
| the | crowds, | and | having stoned |  | Paul, |

| **4803.4** verb 3pl indic imperf act | **1838.1** adv | **3450.10** art gen sing fem | **4032.2** noun gen sing fem | **3406.9** verb nom pl masc part aor act |
|---|---|---|---|---|
| ἔσυρον | ἔξω | τῆς | πόλεως, | ʼ νομίσαντες |
| *esuron* | *exō* | *tēs* | *poleōs* | *nomisantes* |
| were dragging | outside | the | city, | having supposed |

**14:17.** In spite of all this human self-will and rebellion with its false worship, the one true God did not leave himself without witness. He did good deeds, giving rain from heaven and fruit-bearing seasons, filling people with food and gladness.

By saying this, Paul pointed out that God is the real Source of all the good things the earth provides and that mankind as a whole enjoys. As Jesus declared, He is "our Father" (the Father of those who believe, who are born again), but He sets an example of how to treat unbelievers who oppose believers by making His sun to shine on the evil and on the good and by sending rain on the just and on the unjust (Matthew 5:44-48).

Also, after the Flood God gave the rainbow as a sign of His covenant that there would never be a universal flood again to destroy the earth (Genesis 9:8-17), and that as long as the earth remains, "seedtime and harvest, and cold and heat, and summer and winter, and day and night shall not cease" (Genesis 8:22).

As James 1:17 says, "Every good (useful, beneficial) gift . . . is from above." Beginning with creation, God prepared good gifts for man. He put man into an environment where everything was "very good," perfectly suited to man's needs, provided with every opportunity for man's growth and development. Even after man fell, God continued to provide good things to enjoy.

**17. Nevertheless he left not himself without witness, in that he did good:** Yet he has not omitted to give you, in his kindly acts, evidence about himself, *TCNT* . . . and yet by His beneficence He has not left His existence unattested, *Weymouth* . . . without testimony, *Lamsa* . . . without some proof of what he is, *Noli* . . . bestowing blessings, *Kleist.*

**and gave us rain from heaven, and fruitful seasons:** . . . sending you, as he does, rain from Heaven and harvest, *TCNT* . . . he helped us with his bounties, *Noli* . . . in that He sends you, *Weymouth* . . . in that he bestowed good on them, *Lamsa.*

**filling our hearts with food and gladness:** . . . and satisfying your desires with food and good cheer, *TCNT* . . . filling you with food, and making you happy, *Beck* . . . to your hearts' content, *Phillips* . . . filling your stomachs with food and your hearts with gladness, *Adams* . . . satisfied their hearts, *Lamsa.*

**14:18.** Even with saying these things, Paul and Barnabas had a hard time stopping the crowds from their intent to offer sacrifices to them. At first, some in the crowds may have thought Paul and Barnabas were trying to test the sincerity of their intent to offer these sacrifices. Others may have been intent on carrying it out so they could enjoy the feast and carousing that usually accompanied such sacrifices. Still others may have already worked themselves up into some kind of heathen frenzy that often marked their celebrations. Or it may be that all the noise and excited talking in their native Lycaonian language may have made it hard for some to pick up what Paul and Barnabas were saying in Greek.

**18. And with these sayings scarce restrained they the people, that they had not done sacrifice unto them:** Even with this appeal they could hardly prevent the people from offering, *TCNT* . . . Even with words like these they had difficulty in preventing the thronging crowd from, *Weymouth* . . . they hardly restrained the crowds, *Kleist* . . . with difficulty restrained the crowds, *Wuest* . . . difficulty in stopping the crowds, *TNT* . . . the multitudes from doing sacrifice, *ASV.*

**14:19.** Obviously, at least some in the crowds gathered at the city gate did listen to Paul and Barnabas. In fact, there must have been such a great response with so many saved and discipled by the apostles, that the news reached Pisidian Antioch where the Jews had had Paul and Barnabas thrown out of the city. It also reached Iconium where the Jews had wanted to stone Paul to death. Jews from both cities traveled to Lystra and persuaded the heathen crowds to help them, or at least permit them, to carry out their plot. Stoning was the Jewish method of executing blasphemers. It may be that some of the unbelieving people of Lystra felt they were disgraced when Paul and Barnabas did not let them sacrifice to them. They may also have felt the preaching of Paul was blasphemy against their heathen gods, since Paul left no room for their existence. It probably was not too hard to persuade them to allow the stoning of Paul.

**19. And there came thither certain Jews from Antioch and Iconium:** Presently, however, there came some Jews, *TCNT* . . . But now a party of Jews came, *Weymouth.*

**who persuaded the people:** . . . who, after they had won over the people, *TCNT* . . . and, having won over the crowd, *Weymouth* . . . who influenced the populace, *Berkeley* . . . and after turning the minds of the people against Paul, *Phillips* . . . to their side, *Noli.*

**and, having stoned Paul, drew him out of the city:** . . . they stoned Paul, and dragged him, *ASV* . . . dragged him by his feet outside of the city, *Wuest.*

## Acts 14:20

19.b.**Txt:** 04C,08E,020L 025P,byz.
**Var:** 01ℵ,02A,03B,05D Lach,Treg,Alf,Tisc We/Ho,Weis,Sod UBS/☆

19.c.**Txt:** 05D,08E,020L 025P,byz.
**Var:** 01ℵ,02A,03B,04C Lach,Treg,Alf,Tisc We/Ho,Weis,Sod UBS/☆

| **3406.13** verb nom pl masc part pres act | **840.6** prs-pron acc sing masc | **2325.7** verb inf perf act | **2325.8** verb inf perf act |
|---|---|---|---|
| [b☆ νομίζοντες ] | αὐτὸν | ⸂ τεθνάναι. | [c☆ τεθνηκέναι. ] |
| *nomizontes* | *auton* | *tethnanai* | *tethnēkenai* |
| [ supposing ] | him | to have died. | [ idem ] |

| **2917.2** verb gen pl masc part aor act | **1156.2** conj | **840.6** prs-pron acc sing masc | **3450.1** art gen pl | **3073.6** noun gen pl masc |
|---|---|---|---|---|
| **20.** κυκλωσάντων | δὲ | ⸂ αὐτὸν | τῶν | μαθητῶν, |
| *kuklōsantōn* | *de* | *auton* | *tōn* | *mathētōn* |
| Having surrounded | but | him | the | disciples, |

| **3450.1** art gen pl | **3073.6** noun gen pl masc | **840.6** prs-pron acc sing masc | **448.9** verb nom sing masc part aor act | **1511.3** verb 3sing indic aor act |
|---|---|---|---|---|
| [☆ τῶν | μαθητῶν | αὐτὸν ] | ἀναστὰς | εἰσῆλθεν |
| *tōn* | *mathētōn* | *auton* | *anastas* | *eisēlthen* |
| [ the | disciples | him ] | having risen up | he entered |

| **1519.1** prep | **3450.12** art acc sing fem | **4032.4** noun acc sing fem | **2504.1** conj | **3450.11** art dat sing fem | **1872.1** adv |
|---|---|---|---|---|---|
| εἰς | τὴν | πόλιν· | καὶ | τῇ | ἐπαύριον |
| *eis* | *tēn* | *polin* | *kai* | *tē* | *epaurion* |
| into | the | city. | And | on the | next day |

| **1814.3** verb 3sing indic aor act | **4713.1** prep | **3450.3** art dat sing | **915.3** name dat masc | **1519.1** prep | **1185.1** name acc fem |
|---|---|---|---|---|---|
| ἐξῆλθεν | σὺν | τῷ | Βαρναβᾷ | εἰς | Δέρβην. |
| *exēlthen* | *sun* | *tō* | *Barnaba* | *eis* | *Derbēn* |
| he went away | with | | Barnabas | to | Derbe. |

21.a.**Txt:** 01ℵ-corr,03B 04C,020L,byz.We/Ho Sod
**Var:** 02A,05D,08E,025P Lach,Tisc,Weis,UBS/☆

| **2076.22** verb nom pl masc part aor mid | **2076.12** verb nom pl masc part pres mid |
|---|---|
| **21.** ⸂ Εὐαγγελισάμενοί | [a εὐαγγελιζόμενοί ] |
| *Euangelisamenoi* | *euangelizomenoi* |
| Having announced the good news to | [ announcing the good news to ] |

| **4885.1** conj | **3450.12** art acc sing fem | **4032.4** noun acc sing fem | **1552.12** dem-pron acc sing fem | **2504.1** conj | **3072.3** verb nom pl masc part aor act |
|---|---|---|---|---|---|
| τε | τὴν | πόλιν | ἐκείνην, | καὶ | μαθητεύσαντες |
| *te* | *tēn* | *polin* | *ekeinēn* | *kai* | *mathēteusantes* |
| and | the | city | that, | and | having discipled |

| **2401.8** adj acc pl masc | **5128.7** verb 3pl indic aor act | **1519.1** prep | **3450.12** art acc sing fem | **3054.1** name acc sing fem | **2504.1** conj |
|---|---|---|---|---|---|
| ἱκανοὺς | ὑπέστρεψαν | εἰς | τὴν | Λύστραν | καὶ |
| *hikanous* | *hupestrepsan* | *eis* | *tēn* | *Lustran* | *kai* |
| many | they returned | to | | Lystra | and |

21.b.**Var:** 01ℵ,02A,03B 04C,08E,Lach,Treg,Alf Tisc,We/Ho,Sod,UBS/☆

21.c.**Var:** 01ℵ,02A,03B 04C,08E,Lach,Treg,Alf Tisc,We/Ho,Sod,UBS/☆

| **1519.1** prep | **2406.3** name neu | **2504.1** conj | **1519.1** prep | **487.3** name acc fem |
|---|---|---|---|---|
| [b☆+ εἰς ] | Ἰκόνιον | καὶ | [c☆+ εἰς ] | Ἀντιόχειαν· |
| *eis* | *Ikonion* | *kai* | *eis* | *Antiocheian* |
| [ to ] | Iconium | and | [ to ] | Antioch, |

| **1975.2** verb nom pl masc part pres act | **3450.15** art acc pl fem | **5425.8** noun acc pl fem | **3450.1** art gen pl | **3073.6** noun gen pl masc |
|---|---|---|---|---|
| **22.** ἐπιστηρίζοντες | τὰς | ψυχὰς | τῶν | μαθητῶν, |
| *epistērizontes* | *tas* | *psuchas* | *tōn* | *mathētōn* |
| establishing | the | souls | of the | disciples, |

| **3731.9** verb nom pl masc part pres act | **1682.2** verb inf pres act | **3450.11** art dat sing fem | **3963.3** noun dat sing fem | **2504.1** conj | **3617.1** conj |
|---|---|---|---|---|---|
| παρακαλοῦντες | ἐμμένειν | τῇ | πίστει, | καὶ | ὅτι |
| *parakalountes* | *emmenein* | *tē* | *pistei* | *kai* | *hoti* |
| encouraging | to continue | in the | faith, | and | that |

This time these unbelieving Jews did stone Paul and dragged his body out of the city, thinking he was dead. It is clear that he was not actually dead, though he was unconscious and must have been severely bruised all over his body. Undoubtedly he had broken bones as well.

In 2 Corinthians 11:25 Paul included this stoning between beatings and shipwrecks as calamaties he endured. There is no hint there or in this passage that he died. But the beatings and this stoning left scars. In Galatians 6:17 he calls these scars the marks of the Lord Jesus.

Paul was never surprised when he and other believers suffered for Christ's sake. He knew Jesus expected His disciples to suffer with courage and with rejoicing (Matthew 5:10-12; 10:24,25,28; John 15:18,20). Never did he blame the Lord for the rough treatment he received for his faithful service. Always he spoke of his sufferings as but a "light affliction" working "a far more exceeding and eternal weight of glory" (2 Corinthians 4:17).

**14:20.** As soon as the crowd left, the believing disciples surrounded Paul's prostrate form. Undoubtedly they were looking to God, and God did not disappoint them. Suddenly, in what must have seemed like a resurrection, Paul rose up, obviously completely healed, and went back into the city with them. But knowing the mood of the crowds and how easily they might turn into a mob and bring violence on the new believers, he and Barnabas left the next day for Derbe. Jesus himself said that if people do not receive the message in one city, believers should go to another (Luke 10:10-12). Paul often went back and preached in spite of opposition. But he also was sensitive to the leading of the Holy Spirit.

**14:21.** At Derbe also, there was apparently no synagogue. Thus Paul and Barnabas must have preached the gospel much as they did at Lystra, but without the Jewish opposition, since Paul's enemies thought he was dead.

After they had made a considerable number of disciples, and thus established a growing church, they courageously returned to Lystra, Iconium, and Pisidian Antioch.

**14:22.** This time, however, they did not stir up the Jews. Apparently, they did no evangelistic work, leaving that to the local believers. Instead, they ministered to the Church. In each place, they confirmed (strengthened and established) the souls of the disciples. They also challenged and encouraged them to continue in the Faith. The Greek is very strong here. They told the people they must maintain the Faith (the whole gospel), standing by it, and living by its principles.

**supposing he had been dead:** . . . supposing that he was dead, *RSV* . . . thinking him to be dead, *TCNT* . . . where they left him for dead, *Noli* . . . under impression he was dead, *Berkeley* . . . thinking that he had died, *Wuest.*

**20. Howbeit, as the disciples stood round about him:** But when the disciples had gathered round him, *TCNT* . . . But the disciples formed a circle about him, *Williams* . . . gathered in a circle round him, *Phillips* . . . assembled around him, *Murdock* . . . had surrounded him, *TNT.*

**he rose up, and came into the city:** . . . he got up and went back into the town, *TCNT* . . . to own, *Williams* . . . he arose suddenly, *Wuest* . . . and entered the city, *Berkeley.*

**and the next day he departed with Barnabas to Derbe:** Next day he went off, *Moffatt.*

**21. And when they had preached the gospel to that city:** After telling the Good News throughout that town, *TCNT* . . . After proclaiming the gospel to the people there, *Weymouth.*

**and had taught many:** . . . and making a number of converts, *TCNT* . . . and winning many converts, *Montgomery* . . . and having discipled many, *Young.*

**they returned again to Lystra, and to Iconium, and Antioch:** . . . they retraced their steps to, *Weymouth* . . . they went back to, *Montgomery.*

**22. Confirming the souls of the disciples:** . . . reassuring the minds, *TCNT* . . . Everywhere they strengthened the disciples, *Weymouth* . . . They gave new courage to, *TNT* . . . strengthening the hearts of the disciples, *Williams* . . . Strengthening the souls of the converts, *Lamsa* . . . They fortified the souls of, *Noli* . . . reassuring the disciples spiritually, *Berkeley* . . . had ordained to them priests, *Douay.*

**and exhorting them to continue in the faith:** . . . beseeching them to abide in the faith, *Rotherham* . . . urging them to remain true to the Faith, *TCNT* . . . by encouraging them to hold fast, *Weymouth* . . . urging them to stand firm, *Phillips* . . . persevere, *Murdock.*

| 1217.2 prep | 4044.1 adj gen pl | 2324.6 noun gen pl fem | 1158.1 verb 3sing indic pres act | 2231.4 prs-pron acc 1pl | 1511.21 verb inf aor act |
|---|---|---|---|---|---|
| διὰ | πολλῶν | θλίψεων | δεῖ | ἡμᾶς | εἰσελθεῖν |
| *dia* | *pollōn* | *thlipseōn* | *dei* | *hēmas* | *eiselthein* |
| through | many | tribulations | must | we | to enter |

| 1519.1 prep | 3450.12 art acc sing fem | 926.4 noun acc sing fem | 3450.2 art gen sing | 2296.2 noun gen sing masc | 5336.1 verb nom pl masc part aor act |
|---|---|---|---|---|---|
| εἰς | τὴν | βασιλείαν | τοῦ | θεοῦ. | **23.** χειροτονήσαντες |
| *eis* | *tēn* | *basileian* | *tou* | *theou* | *cheirotonēsantes* |
| into | the | kingdom | | of God. | Having chosen |

| 1156.2 conj | 840.2 prs-pron dat pl | 4104.2 adj comp acc pl masc | 2567.1 prep | 1564.4 noun acc sing fem |
|---|---|---|---|---|
| δὲ | αὐτοῖς | ʻ πρεσβυτέρους | κατ' | ἐκκλησίαν, |
| *de* | *autois* | *presbuterous* | *kat'* | *ekklēsian* |
| and | for them | elders | according to | assembly, |

| 2567.1 prep | 1564.4 noun acc sing fem | 4104.2 adj comp acc pl masc | 4195.25 verb nom pl masc part aor mid |
|---|---|---|---|
| [☆ κατ' | ἐκκλησίαν | πρεσβυτέρους ] | προσευξάμενοι |
| *kat'* | *ekklēsian* | *presbuterous* | *proseuxamenoi* |
| [ according to | assembly | elders ] | having prayed |

| 3196.3 prep | 3383.3 noun gen pl fem | 3769.12 verb 3pl indic aor mid | 840.8 prs-pron acc pl masc | 3450.3 art dat sing |
|---|---|---|---|---|
| μετὰ | νηστειῶν | παρέθεντο | αὐτοὺς | τῷ |
| *meta* | *nēsteiōn* | *parethento* | *autous* | *tō* |
| with | fastings | they committed | them | to the |

| 2935.3 noun dat sing masc | 1519.1 prep | 3614.6 rel-pron acc sing masc | 3961.42 verb 3pl indic plperf act | 2504.1 conj |
|---|---|---|---|---|
| κυρίῳ | εἰς | ὃν | πεπιστεύκεισαν. | **24.** καὶ |
| *kuriō* | *eis* | *hon* | *pepisteukeisan* | *kai* |
| Lord, | on | whom | they had believed. | And |

| 1324.7 verb nom pl masc part aor act | 3450.12 art acc sing fem | 3960.2 name acc fem | 2048.1 verb indic aor act | 1519.1 prep |
|---|---|---|---|---|
| διελθόντες | τὴν | Πισιδίαν | ἦλθον | εἰς |
| *dielthontes* | *tēn* | *Pisidian* | *ēlthon* | *eis* |
| having passed through | | Pisidia | they came | to |

24.a.**Var:** 01ℵ,03B,04C 08E,Treg,Tisc,We/Ho Weis,Sod,UBS/☆

| 3450.12 art acc sing fem | 3690.2 name acc fem | 2504.1 conj | 2953.36 verb nom pl masc part aor act | 1706.1 prep |
|---|---|---|---|---|
| [a☆+ τὴν ] | Παμφυλίαν· | **25.** καὶ | λαλήσαντες | ʻ ἐν |
| *tēn* | *Pamphulian* | *kai* | *lalēsantes* | *en* |
| | Pamphylia, | and | having spoken | in |

25.a.**Txt:** 01ℵ-corr,03B 04C,05D,08E,020L 025P,byz.We/Ho,Sod **Var:** 01ℵ-org,02A,Tisc UBS/☆

| 3874.2 name dat fem | 1519.1 prep | 3450.12 art acc sing fem | 3874.3 name acc fem | 3450.6 art acc sing masc | 3030.4 noun acc sing masc |
|---|---|---|---|---|---|
| Πέργῃ | [a εἰς | τὴν | Πέργην ] | τὸν | λόγον |
| *Pergē* | *eis* | *tēn* | *Pergēn* | *ton* | *logon* |
| Perga | [ to | | Perga ] | the | word |

25.b.**Txt:** 03B,05D,byz. **Var:** 01ℵ,02A,04C,044 33,81,614

| 3450.2 art gen sing | 2935.2 noun gen sing masc | 2568.15 verb 3pl indic aor act | 1519.1 prep | 819.1 name acc fem |
|---|---|---|---|---|
| [b+ τοῦ | κυρίου ] | κατέβησαν | εἰς | Ἀττάλειαν· |
| *tou* | *kuriou* | *katebēsan* | *eis* | *Attaleian* |
| [ of the | Lord ] | they came down | to | Attalia; |

| 2518.1 conj | 630.2 verb 3pl indic aor act | 1519.1 prep | 487.3 name acc fem | 3468.1 adv |
|---|---|---|---|---|
| **26.** κἀκεῖθεν | ἀπέπλευσαν | εἰς | Ἀντιόχειαν, | ὅθεν |
| *kakeithen* | *apepleusan* | *eis* | *Antiocheian* | *hothen* |
| and from there | they sailed | to | Antioch, | where |

They also challenged the believers to share the suffering of the apostles and to accept the fact that through much tribulation (persecution, affliction, distress) it is necessary to enter the kingdom of God.

**14:23.** Because the body of believers needed organization to be able to work together and carry out the work of the Lord, the apostles then "ordained" elders (overseers, superintendents of each congregation or assembly) in each place. This, however, was not an ordination in the modern sense. The Greek word for "ordained" here is *cheiratonēsantes,* where *cheir* means hand, and the whole word means they conducted an election by the show of hands.

At the beginning, these elders were Spirit-filled men chosen from among the members of the local congregation. Not until many years later did the churches begin to feel they needed to bring in pastor-teachers from outside the local assembly who could also be the administrative head of the assembly and who could combine the office of elder (also called bishop and presbyter) with the God-called, Spirit-empowered, and gifted ministry of pastor-teacher. *(Pastor* in the New Testament refers to a spiritual ministry, not an office.)

Before Paul and Barnabas went on to the next city, they always spent time in prayer and fasting with the believers. Then they entrusted them (as precious and valuable) to the care and keeping of the Lord (Jesus) in whom they had believed (and continued to believe).

**14:24.** Pisidian Antioch was situated on a plain at 3,600 feet elevation. The apostles took the road south which wound down through Pisidia and Pamphylia to Perga on the Cestrus River near the Mediterranean coast. Though the Bible does not specifically say they evangelized along the way, the Greek verb *dielthontes* is used in other passages of going from place to place preaching the gospel.

**14:25.** Arriving on the rich coastal plain of Pamphylia, they went to Perga and preached the word there apparently without opposition or mistreatment. Some speculate that because Paul became ill there, they pushed on to the higher ground at Pisidian Antioch.

They stayed long enough at Perga to establish a church there. They undoubtedly organized it by having the believers elect elders. With proper organization people learn to work together for the glory of God.

From Perga they went down to Attalia, Perga's seaport, a city of increasing importance. This was the last stop on Paul's first missionary journey.

**14:26.** From Attalia they sailed away to Syrian Antioch. Now they were back in the place where they had started on this missionary



**and that we must through much tribulation enter into the kingdom of God:** . . . and showing that it is only through many troubles, *TCNT* . . . and warned them saying, It is through many afflictions that we must make our way, *Weymouth* . . . We must suffer many things to enter God's kingdom, *Everyday* . . . that only through much tribulation can we enter, *Lamsa.*

**23. And when they had ordained them elders in every church:** They chose elders for each church, *Everyday* . . . after electing elders for them, *KJII* . . . had appointed elders, *RSV* . . . they selected Elders by show of hands, *Weymouth* . . . helped them select elders, *Williams* . . . having elected for them elders, *Fenton* . . . chose leaders, *NLT.*

**and had prayed with fasting:** . . . and, after prayer and fasting, *TCNT* . . . by praying and giving up eating, *Everyday* . . . They went without food during that time so they could pray better, *NLT.*

**they commended them to the Lord:** . . . entrusted them, *Moffatt* . . . these were dedicated, *Norlie* . . . they gave them to the Lord, *KJII* . . . giving them over to, *NLT* . . . put them in the Lord's care, *Everyday* . . . commended to the favor of God, *Sawyer.*

**on whom they believed:** . . . men who had trusted the Lord, *Everyday* . . . on whom their faith rested, *Weymouth.*

**24. And after they had passed throughout Pisidia, they came to Pamphylia:** Paul and Barnabas then went through, *TCNT* . . . After traveling through, *Berkeley* . . . Then they crossed Pisidia, *Phillips.*

**25. And when they had preached the word in Perga, they went down into Attalia:** They preached the message, *Everyday* . . . having spoken the word in, *Swann* . . . they came down to, *Weymouth.*

**26. And thence sailed to Antioch:** . . . and from there they sailed back to Antioch, *Goodspeed* . . . and from there set sail for Antioch, *NEB.*

## Acts 14:27

| 1498.37 verb 3pl indic imperf act | 3722.40 verb nom pl masc part perf mid | 3450.11 art dat sing fem | 5322.3 noun dat sing fem | 3450.2 art gen sing |
|---|---|---|---|---|
| ἦσαν | παραδεδομένοι | τῇ | χάριτι | τοῦ |
| *ēsan* | *paradedomenoi* | *tē* | *chariti* | *tou* |
| were | having been committed | to the | grace | |

| 2296.2 noun gen sing masc | 1519.1 prep | 3450.16 art sing neu | 2024.1 noun sing neu | 3614.16 rel-pron sing neu | 3997.4 verb 3pl indic aor act |
|---|---|---|---|---|---|
| θεοῦ | εἰς | τὸ | ἔργον | ὃ | ἐπλήρωσαν. |
| *theou* | *eis* | *to* | *ergon* | *ho* | *eplērōsan* |
| of God | for | the | work | which | they fulfilled. |

| 3716.10 verb nom pl masc part aor mid | 1156.2 conj | 2504.1 conj | 4714.12 verb nom pl masc part aor act |
|---|---|---|---|
| **27.** παραγενόμενοι | δὲ | καὶ | συναγαγόντες |
| *paragenomenoi* | *de* | *kai* | *sunagagontes* |
| Having arrived | and | and | having gathered together |

27.a.**Txt:** 020L,025P,byz.
**Var:** 01ℵ,02A,03B,04C 33,bo.Lach,Treg,Alf Tisc,We/Ho,Weis,Sod UBS/⋆

| 3450.12 art acc sing fem | 1564.4 noun acc sing fem | 310.5 verb 3pl indic aor act | 310.11 verb 3pl indic imperf act |
|---|---|---|---|
| τὴν | ἐκκλησίαν | ⸀ ἀνήγγειλαν | [a⋆ ἀνήγγελλον ] |
| *tēn* | *ekklēsian* | *anēngeilan* | *anēngellon* |
| the | assembly | they declared | [ they were declaring ] |

| 3607.8 rel-pron pl neu | 4020.24 verb 3sing indic aor act | 3450.5 art nom sing masc | 2296.1 noun nom sing masc | 3196.2 prep | 840.1 prs-pron gen pl |
|---|---|---|---|---|---|
| ὅσα | ἐποίησεν | ὁ | θεὸς | μετ' | αὐτῶν, |
| *hosa* | *epoiēsen* | *ho* | *theos* | *met'* | *autōn* |
| as much as | did | | God | with | them, |

| 2504.1 conj | 3617.1 conj | 453.4 verb 3sing indic aor act | 3450.4 art dat pl | 1477.6 noun dat pl neu | 2351.4 noun acc sing fem | 3963.2 noun gen sing fem |
|---|---|---|---|---|---|---|
| καὶ | ὅτι | ἤνοιξεν | τοῖς | ἔθνεσιν | θύραν | πίστεως. |
| *kai* | *hoti* | *ēnoixen* | *tois* | *ethnesin* | *thuran* | *pisteōs* |
| and | that | he opened | to the | Gentiles | a door | of faith. |

28.a.**Txt:** 08E,020L 025P,byz.sa.bo.
**Var:** 01ℵ,02A,03B,04C 05D,33,Gries,Lach,Treg Alf,Word,Tisc,We/Ho Weis,Sod,UBS/⋆

| 1298.6 verb 3pl indic imperf act | 1156.2 conj | 1550.1 adv | 5385.4 noun acc sing masc | 3620.2 partic | 3504.1 adj sing |
|---|---|---|---|---|---|
| **28.** διέτριβον | δὲ | ⸂a ἐκεῖ ⸃ | χρόνον | οὐκ | ὀλίγον |
| *dietribon* | *de* | *ekei* | *chronon* | *ouk* | *oligon* |
| They were staying | and | there | time | not | a little |

| 4713.1 prep | 3450.4 art dat pl | 3073.7 noun dat pl masc | 2504.1 conj | 4948.7 indef-pron nom pl masc |
|---|---|---|---|---|
| σὺν | τοῖς | μαθηταῖς. | **15:1.** Καί | τινες |
| *sun* | *tois* | *mathētais* | *Kai* | *tines* |
| with | the | disciples. | And | certain |

| 2687.5 verb nom pl masc part aor act | 570.3 prep | 3450.10 art gen sing fem | 2424.2 name gen fem | 1315.21 verb 3pl indic imperf act |
|---|---|---|---|---|
| κατελθόντες | ἀπὸ | τῆς | Ἰουδαίας | ἐδίδασκον |
| *katelthontes* | *apo* | *tēs* | *Ioudaias* | *edidaskon* |
| having come down | from | | Judea | were teaching |

1.a.**Txt:** 08E,020L,025P byz.
**Var:** 01ℵ,02A,03B,04C 05D,Lach,Treg,Alf,Tisc We/Ho,Weis,Sod UBS/⋆

1.b.**Var:** 01ℵ,02A,03B 04C-org,Lach,Treg,Alf Tisc,We/Ho,Weis,Sod UBS/⋆

| 3450.8 art acc pl masc | 79.9 noun acc pl masc | 3617.1 conj | 1430.1 partic | 3231.1 partic | 3919.5 verb 2pl subj pres mid |
|---|---|---|---|---|---|
| τοὺς | ἀδελφοὺς, | Ὅτι | Ἐὰν | μὴ | ⸀ περιτέμνησθε |
| *tous* | *adelphous* | *Hoti* | *Ean* | *mē* | *peritemnēsthe* |
| the | brothers, | That | if | not | you be circumcised |

| 3919.13 verb 2pl subj aor pass | 3450.3 art dat sing | 1478.2 noun dat sing neu | 3450.3 art dat sing | 3338.2 name gen masc |
|---|---|---|---|---|
| [a⋆ περιτμηθῆτε ] | τῷ | ἔθει | [b⋆+ τῷ ] | Μωϋσέως |
| *peritmēthēte* | *tō* | *ethei* | *tō* | *Mōuseōs* |
| [ you were circumcised ] | the | custom | | Moses |

journey. At Antioch they had been given over to the grace of God to do the work which they had now completed. At this time, Paul and Barnabas felt they had fulfilled the ministry for which the Spirit sent them out (13:2-4).

**14:27.** Since Paul and Barnabas considered Antioch their home base, and since the people had fasted and prayed with them before sending them out, the apostles wanted to report to the believers all that God had done. Therefore, they "gathered the church together" and told what great things God did as they worked as fellow laborers with Him. To the Gentiles, also, God had opened a door of faith. (The Greek has "a door," not "the door" here.) This door was through the preaching of the Word.

It is noticeable that in this report Paul and Barnabas put the emphasis on the positive. During most of the journey they faced persecutions, trouble, and difficult circumstances as their daily lot. Yet none of these experiences had robbed them of their zeal and enthusiasm. They finished this journey just as excited about preaching the gospel as they had been when the Lord sent them out.

**14:28.** After giving their report, the two apostles remained "not a little time" with the disciples at Antioch. They resumed a ministry of teaching and help in the assembly of believers for several months, possibly as much as a year.

**15:1.** The Jerusalem Conference dealt with in this chapter is another important turning point in the history of the Early Church. According to Galatians 2:1-10, Paul visited Jerusalem and presented the gospel he preached among the Gentiles. The Church leaders gave their approval to his message and did not require Titus to be circumcised.

A little later (Galatians 2:11-16) Peter came to Antioch, enjoyed table fellowship and ate nonkosher food with the Gentiles. But when some Jewish believers "came from James" (not sent officially, but simply sent to help and encourage the believers), Peter withdrew from that fellowship. When he saw their critical looks, he forgot the lesson he had learned at the house of Cornelius.

Peter's example affected the other Jewish believers in Antioch. Even Barnabas was carried away with this hypocrisy. Paul therefore took a strong stand against Peter and faced him with a rebuke for the hypocrisy of what he was doing (Galatians 2:14).

Later, either these same Jews from James, or another group of what were probably converted Pharisees, went a step further and took things into their own hands. They began teaching the Gentile believers that unless they were circumcised according to the custom of Moses, they could not be saved.

For these "visitors" from Judea, the question was not whether Gentiles could be saved; the Cornelius incident settled this matter (as did the Old Testament which prophesied that Gentiles would

**from where they had been recommended to the grace of God for the work which they fulfilled:** . . . where they had originally been, *JB* . . . had first received the divine grace for the mission, *Noli* . . . This is where the believers had put them into God's care, *NCV* . . . commended to the help of God, *TCNT* . . . from where they had been delivered up to the grace of God, *KJII* . . . had first been commended to the grace...for the task which they had now completed, *Phillips.*

**27. And when they were come:** And when they had arrived, *Rotherham* . . . Upon their arrival, *Weymouth.*

**and had gathered the church together:** . . . they called the Church together, *Weymouth* . . . they called a church meeting, *Berkeley.*

**they rehearsed all that God had done with them:** . . . and gave an account of...with and through them, *TCNT* . . . and proceeded to report in detail all that God, working with them, had done, *Weymouth* . . . and reported all that God had used them to do, *TNT* . . . of all the work that God had achieved through them, *Noli.*

**and how he had opened the door of faith unto the Gentiles:** . . . especially how he had opened to the heathen a door, *TCNT* . . . and how he had thrown open the gates of faith to the Gentiles, *NEB* . . . so that the non-Jews could believe! *NCV.*

**28. And there they abode long time with the disciples:** . . . they stayed...a long time, *TCNT.*

**1. And certain men which came down from Judaea:** In the meantime, *Campbell* . . . some of those coming down, *Fenton.*

**taught:** . . . tried to convince, *Weymouth* . . . and attempted to teach, *Montgomery.*

**the brethren, and said:** . . . and these were their words, *Wuest.*

**Except ye be circumcised:** Unless you are circumcised, *RSV* . . . that without circumcision, *BB.*

**after the manner of Moses:** . . . the custom, *ASV* . . . enjoined by Moses, *TCNT* . . . with the rite of the law, *Murdock* . . . in accordance with the Mosaic doctrine, *Noli.*

## Acts 15:2

2.a.**Txt:** 02A,08E,025P byz.
**Var:** 01ℵ,03B,04C,05D 020L,33,sa.bo.Treg,Tisc We/Ho,Weis,Sod UBS/☆

2.b.**Txt:** Steph
**Var:** 01ℵ,02A,03B,04C 05D,020L,025P,Gries Lach,Treg,Alf,Word Tisc,We/Ho,Weis,Sod UBS/☆

| **3620.3** partic | **1404.6** verb 2pl indic pres mid | **4834.28** verb inf aor pass | **1090.57** verb gen sing fem part aor mid | **3631.1** partic |
|---|---|---|---|---|
| οὐ | δύνασθε | σωθῆναι. | 2. Γενομένης | ʻ οὖν |
| *ou* | *dunasthe* | *sōthēnai* | *Genomenēs* | *oun* |
| not | are able | to be saved. | Having taken place | therefore |

| **1156.2** conj | **4565.2** noun gen sing fem | **2504.1** conj | **4654.1** noun gen sing fem | **2197.4** noun gen sing fem |
|---|---|---|---|---|
| [a☆ δὲ ] | στάσεως | καὶ | ʻ συζητήσεως | [b☆ ζητήσεως ] |
| *de* | *staseōs* | *kai* | *suzētēseōs* | *zētēseōs* |
| [ and ] | a commotion | and | discussion | [ debate ] |

| **3620.2** partic | **3504.8** adj gen sing fem | **3450.3** art dat sing | **3834.3** name dat masc | **2504.1** conj | **3450.3** art dat sing | **915.3** name dat masc |
|---|---|---|---|---|---|---|
| οὐκ | ὀλίγης | τῷ | Παύλῳ | καὶ | τῷ | Βαρναβᾷ |
| *ouk* | *oligēs* | *tō* | *Paulō* | *kai* | *tō* | *Barnaba* |
| not | a little | | by Paul | and | | Barnabas |

| **4242.1** prep | **840.8** prs-pron acc pl masc | **4872.1** verb 3pl indic aor act | **303.11** verb inf pres act | **3834.4** name acc masc |
|---|---|---|---|---|
| πρὸς | αὐτοὺς, | ἔταξαν | ἀναβαίνειν | Παῦλον |
| *pros* | *autous* | *etaxan* | *anabainein* | *Paulon* |
| with | them, | they appointed | to go up | Paul |

| **2504.1** conj | **915.4** name acc masc | **2504.1** conj | **4948.9** indef-pron acc pl masc | **241.8** adj acc pl masc | **1523.1** prep gen |
|---|---|---|---|---|---|
| καὶ | Βαρναβᾶν | καί | τινας | ἄλλους | ἐξ |
| *kai* | *Barnaban* | *kai* | *tinas* | *allous* | *ex* |
| and | Barnabas | and | certain | others | from among |

| **840.1** prs-pron gen pl | **4242.1** prep | **3450.8** art acc pl masc | **646.7** noun acc pl masc | **2504.1** conj | **4104.2** adj comp acc pl masc |
|---|---|---|---|---|---|
| αὐτῶν | πρὸς | τοὺς | ἀποστόλους | καὶ | πρεσβυτέρους |
| *autōn* | *pros* | *tous* | *apostolous* | *kai* | *presbuterous* |
| them | to | the | apostles | and | elders |

| **1519.1** prep | **2395.1** name fem | **3875.1** prep | **3450.2** art gen sing | **2196.2** noun gen sing neu | **3642.1** dem-pron gen sing |
|---|---|---|---|---|---|
| εἰς | Ἱερουσαλὴμ, | περὶ | τοῦ | ζητήματος | τούτου. |
| *eis* | *Hierousalēm* | *peri* | *tou* | *zētēmatos* | *toutou* |
| to | Jerusalem, | about | the | question | this. |

| **3450.7** art nom pl masc | **3173.1** conj | **3631.1** partic | **4170.7** verb nom pl masc part aor pass | **5097.3** prep |
|---|---|---|---|---|
| 3. Οἱ | μὲν | οὖν | προπεμφθέντες | ὑπὸ |
| *Hoi* | *men* | *oun* | *propemphthentes* | *hupo* |
| The | indeed | therefore | having been sent forward | by |

3.a.**Var:** 01ℵ,03B,04C 05D,Lach,Treg,Alf,Tisc We/Ho,Weis,Sod UBS/☆

| **3450.10** art gen sing fem | **1564.1** noun fem | **1324.17** verb 3pl indic imperf mid | **3450.12** art acc sing fem | **4885.1** conj |
|---|---|---|---|---|
| τῆς | ἐκκλησίας | διήρχοντο | τήν | [a☆+ τε ] |
| *tēs* | *ekklēsias* | *diērchonto* | *tēn* | *te* |
| the | assembly | were passing through | | [ both ] |

| **5240.2** name acc fem | **2504.1** conj | **4397.4** name acc fem | **1542.2** verb nom pl masc part pres mid | **3450.12** art acc sing fem |
|---|---|---|---|---|
| Φοινίκην | καὶ | Σαμάρειαν, | ἐκδιηγούμενοι | τὴν |
| *Phoinikēn* | *kai* | *Samareian* | *ekdiēgoumenoi* | *tēn* |
| Phoenicia | and | Samaria, | relating | the |

| **1979.1** noun acc sing fem | **3450.1** art gen pl | **1477.5** noun gen pl neu | **2504.1** conj | **4020.59** verb 3pl indic imperf act | **5315.4** noun acc sing fem |
|---|---|---|---|---|---|
| ἐπιστροφὴν | τῶν | ἐθνῶν· | καὶ | ἐποίουν | χαρὰν |
| *epistrophēn* | *tōn* | *ethnōn* | *kai* | *epoioun* | *charan* |
| conversion | of the | Gentiles. | And | they were causing | joy |

also trust in the Jewish Messiah [Isaiah 11:10; cf. Psalms 18:49; 117:1; Romans 15:8-12]). Rather, these Jews believed that Gentile conversion represented a transfer into a "Christianized" Judaism. Thus in addition to a demand for circumcision and obedience to the Law, intimate social contact with uncircumcised Gentiles (e.g., at fellowship meals or the Lord's Supper) was strictly forbidden. Apparently, Pharisees who became believers in Jesus supported these views (see verse 5). Although the Scriptures teach that a restored Israel would serve to proselytize the nations (Isaiah 2:3; 60:2f.; Zechariah 8:22f.), they held too closely to their own traditions and did not fully understand that a new age, a new "dispensation" of grace, had arrived. These men were later referred to as "Judaizers" (cf. Galatians 2:11-19).

Some false teachers still say a person will lose his salvation if he does not accept their particular doctrine. Others say a person is not fully saved unless he goes through certain prescribed rites or ceremonies. All these false teachers fail to recognize that salvation is by grace through faith alone, as is clearly taught in Romans 10:9,10 and Ephesians 2:8,9.

**15:2.** This Judaizing teaching brought quite an upheaval with much dissension, disturbance, discord, and disputation (or questioning) between them (that is, between the brethren) and Paul and Barnabas. They (the brethren) then assigned Paul, Barnabas, and some others to go to Jerusalem to confer with the apostles and elders "about this question."

**15:3.** The whole assembly of believers at Antioch turned out to escort Paul, Barnabas, and the others for a short distance on the way. By this the members of the assembly showed they still loved, respected, and had confidence in them in spite of the questions raised by these Judaizing teachers. In all the upheaval, discussion, and questioning, they had not lost their love for the leaders God had given them. But they felt that for the sake of the Church as a whole, the questions needed to be resolved.

Paul took the road south through Phoenicia and the province of Samaria, stopping to visit churches all along the way. Phoenicia at this time extended south to Mount Carmel on the Mediterranean coast, so it was not necessary to go through Galilee. From Mount Carmel they took the inland route through Samaria to Jerusalem. In each place Paul gave a complete account of how the Gentiles were turning to the Lord. By giving a full report, Paul undoubtedly included an account of the persecution as well as the miracles.

Now these churches in Phoenicia were made up of Jewish believers. Those in Samaria were Samaritans. Yet they all rejoiced with great joy when they heard the report of the success of the Word of God among the Gentiles. Apparently the Judaizers had not visited these churches. Since Paul and Barnabas had not founded them, the Judaizers probably thought they would reject the Gentiles

**ye cannot be saved:** . . . there is no salvation, *BB.*

**2. When therefore Paul and Barnabas had no small dissension and disputation with them:** Between these newcomers and Paul and Barnabas there was no little disagreement and controversy, *Weymouth* . . . This gave rise to a serious dispute, and much discussion between Paul and Barnabas and these men, *TCNT* . . . Naturally this caused a serious upset among them, *Phillips* . . . sharp dispute, *NIV* . . . in the discussion and disagreement that arose, *Norlie* . . . got into a fierce argument, *TEV* . . . were very much opposed to this teaching, *SEB.*

**they determined that Paul and Barnabas:** . . . the brethren appointed, *ASV* . . . it was arranged that, *Rotherham* . . . it was therefore settled that, *TCNT* . . . to have Paul, *MLNT.*

**and certain other of them:** . . . and others of their number, *TCNT* . . . and some other brethren, *Weymouth.*

**should go up to Jerusalem unto the apostles and elders about this question:** . . . to consult...the Church about the matter under discussion, *TCNT* . . . and presbyters, *Moffatt* . . . about this dispute, *Berkeley* . . . about the whole question, *Phillips* . . . about this controversy, *Adams.*

**3. And being brought on their way by the church:** So they set out, being accompanied for a short distance by the Church, *Weymouth* . . . So they were endorsed and sent on by the church, *Williams* . . . So then, fitted out for their trip by the church, *Berkeley* . . . It was, in fact, the congregation that was sending them, *Norlie* . . . Having therefore been dispatched, *Adams.*

**they passed through Phenice and Samaria:** . . . and they made their way through, *TCNT.*

**declaring the conversion of the Gentiles:** . . . reporting the conversion, *RSV* . . . telling the story, *TCNT* . . . where they narrated in detail, *Berkeley* . . . fully narrating, *Rotherham* . . . they told the whole story how the non-Jews were turning to God, *Beck* . . . telling the details, *Adams.*

4.a.**Txt:** 01א,04C,05D 08E,020L,025P,byz.Tisc **Var:** 02A,03B,Treg We/Ho,Weis,Sod UBS/☆

4.b.**Txt:** 04C,08E,020L 025P,byz. **Var:** 01א,02A,03B 05D-corr,Lach,Treg,Alf Word,Tisc,We/Ho,Weis Sod,UBS/☆

4.c.**Txt:** p74,01א,02A 05D,08E,020L,025P,byz. Tisc,Sod **Var:** 03B,04C,Treg We/Ho,Weis,UBS/☆

| **3144.12** adj acc sing fem | **3820.5** adj dat pl | **3450.4** art dat pl | **79.8** noun dat pl masc | **3716.10** verb nom pl masc part aor mid |
|---|---|---|---|---|
| μεγάλην | πᾶσιν | τοῖς | ἀδελφοῖς. | **4.** παραγενόμενοι |
| *megalēn* | *pasin* | *tois* | *adelphois* | *paragenomenoi* |
| great | all | to the | brothers. | Having come |

| **1156.2** conj | **1519.1** prep | **2395.1** name fem | **2389.1** name |
|---|---|---|---|
| δὲ | εἰς | ′ Ἱερουσαλὴμ | [a Ἱεροσόλυμα ] |
| *de* | *eis* | *Hierousalēm* | *Hierosoluma* |
| and | to | Jerusalem | [idem] |

| **583.3** verb 3pl indic aor pass | **3720.6** verb 3pl indic aor pass | **5097.3** prep | **570.3** prep |
|---|---|---|---|
| ′ ἀπεδέχθησαν | [b☆ παρεδέχθησαν ] | ′ ὑπὸ | [c☆ ἀπὸ ] |
| *apedechthēsan* | *paredechthēsan* | *hupo* | *apo* |
| they were welcomed | [they were received] | by | [from] |

| **3450.10** art gen sing fem | **1564.1** noun fem | **2504.1** conj | **3450.1** art gen pl | **646.5** noun gen pl masc | **2504.1** conj | **3450.1** art gen pl |
|---|---|---|---|---|---|---|
| τῆς | ἐκκλησίας | καὶ | τῶν | ἀποστόλων | καὶ | τῶν |
| *tēs* | *ekklēsias* | *kai* | *tōn* | *apostolōn* | *kai* | *tōn* |
| the | assembly | and | the | apostles | and | the |

| **4104.6** adj comp gen pl masc | **310.5** verb 3pl indic aor act | **4885.1** conj | **3607.8** rel-pron pl neu | **3450.5** art nom sing masc |
|---|---|---|---|---|
| πρεσβυτέρων, | ἀνήγγειλάν | τε | ὅσα | ὁ |
| *presbuterōn* | *anēngeilan* | *te* | *hosa* | *ho* |
| elders, | they declared | and | which things | |

| **2296.1** noun nom sing masc | **4020.24** verb 3sing indic aor act | **3196.2** prep | **840.1** prs-pron gen pl | **1801.1** verb 3pl indic aor act |
|---|---|---|---|---|
| θεὸς | ἐποίησεν | μετ' | αὐτῶν. | **5.** ἐξανέστησαν |
| *theos* | *epoiēsen* | *met'* | *autōn* | *exanestēsan* |
| God | did | with | them. | Rose up |

| **1156.2** conj | **4948.7** indef-pron nom pl masc | **3450.1** art gen pl | **570.3** prep | **3450.10** art gen sing fem | **138.2** noun gen sing fem | **3450.1** art gen pl |
|---|---|---|---|---|---|---|
| δέ | τινες | τῶν | ἀπὸ | τῆς | αἱρέσεως | τῶν |
| *de* | *tines* | *tōn* | *apo* | *tēs* | *haireseōs* | *tōn* |
| and | certain | of the | from | the | sect | of the |

| **5168.5** name gen pl masc | **3961.45** verb nom pl masc part perf act | **2978.16** verb nom pl masc part pres act | **3617.1** conj | **1158.1** verb 3sing indic pres act |
|---|---|---|---|---|
| Φαρισαίων | πεπιστευκότες, | λέγοντες, | Ὅτι | δεῖ |
| *Pharisaiōn* | *pepisteukotes* | *legontes* | *Hoti* | *dei* |
| Pharisees | having believed, | saying, | | It is necessary |

| **3919.2** verb inf pres act | **840.8** prs-pron acc pl masc | **3715.6** verb inf pres act | **4885.1** conj | **4931.11** verb inf pres act |
|---|---|---|---|---|
| περιτέμνειν | αὐτοὺς, | παραγγέλλειν | τε | τηρεῖν |
| *peritemnein* | *autous* | *parangellein* | *te* | *tērein* |
| to circumcise | them, | to charge | and | to keep |

| **3450.6** art acc sing masc | **3414.4** noun acc sing masc | **3338.2** name gen masc | **4714.20** verb 3pl indic aor pass | **1156.2** conj |
|---|---|---|---|---|
| τὸν | νόμον | Μωϋσέως. | **6.** Συνήχθησαν | ′ δὲ |
| *ton* | *nomon* | *Mōuseōs* | *Sunēchthēsan* | *de* |
| the | law | of Moses. | Were gathered together | and |

6.a.**Txt:** 01א,02A,05D 08E,020L,025P,byz.sa. bo.Tisc **Var:** 03B,04C,Treg,Alf We/Ho,Weis,Sod UBS/☆

| **4885.1** conj | **3450.7** art nom pl masc | **646.4** noun nom pl masc | **2504.1** conj | **3450.7** art nom pl masc | **4104.5** adj comp nom pl masc |
|---|---|---|---|---|---|
| [a τε ] | οἱ | ἀπόστολοι | καὶ | οἱ | πρεσβύτεροι |
| *te* | *hoi* | *apostoloi* | *kai* | *hoi* | *presbuteroi* |
| [idem] | the | apostles | and | the | elders |

unless they became Jews. But because they were open to the Word and the Spirit, they accepted what God had done without question.

**15:4.** Arriving in Jerusalem, the apostles and those with them were received (favorably) by the believers. The apostles and elders also welcomed them. Apparently the Judaizers had been so anxious to move on to spread their doctrines in the churches Paul and Barnabas had founded in South Galatia that they had not sent word back to the church in Jerusalem. So there was no opposition at first.

The apostles probably included the Twelve, with the exception of James, who had been martyred. At this point they were still in Jerusalem building up the church and teaching and training the believers in the surrounding area. The elders were probably the elected leaders of the local groups meeting in the various homes in Jerusalem and the surrounding communities.

They all listened to the report of what God had done with (along with) Paul and Barnabas. Paul and Barnabas were just fellow laborers with the Lord. They gave God all the glory. Not only had He been with them, He was the One who really had done the work.

Paul was always careful to recognize that Christian workers, no matter how wonderfully used of God, are but ministers or servants of God and the Church. Each believer has his part.

**15:5.** This welcome and pleasant atmosphere did not last. It was not long before some converted Pharisees rose up out of the assembly in Jerusalem. They forcefully expressed the view that it was (and continued to be) necessary both to circumcise the Gentiles and to command them to keep (observe) the law of Moses.

These Pharisees were still making Moses and the Law central in their religion. They made the covenant of the Law more important than the promise given to Abraham and actually, more important than Christ's crucifixion and resurrection. But the Cross was no afterthought in God's plan. Jesus was and is the Lamb of God "slain from the foundation of the world" (Revelation 13:8). The first promise looking ahead to Christ is in Genesis 3:15, long before the giving of the Law. The Pharisees thought Christianity should be added to the Law. But the reverse is true. As Galatians 3:19 indicates, the Law was added to the promise, not the other way around.

**15:6.** The apostles and elders then assembled to consider the matter. This was what the assembly in Antioch wanted, and this was the purpose for which Paul and Barnabas had come.

The apostles and elders did not ask for a closed meeting, however. Verse 12 indicates a multitude (a crowd) was present. This matter was very important to the believers in Jerusalem, for they

**and they caused great joy unto all the brethren:** . . . to the great joy of all the Brethren, *TCNT* . . . and brought great rejoicing to all the brothers, *Williams* . . . and thus made all the brothers very happy, *Berkeley* . . . And all the brothers were overjoyed to hear about it, *Phillips* . . . unbounded delight, *Fenton.*

**4. And when they were come to Jerusalem:** On their arrival at Jerusalem, *TCNT* . . . When they reached Jerusalem, *Goodspeed.*

**they were received of the church:** . . . they were welcomed by the Assembly, *Rotherham* . . . they were cordially received, *Weymouth* . . . were welcomed gladly by, *KJII* . . . yhey had a meeting with, *BB* . . . the congregation, *Campbell* . . . the church leaders were glad to see them, *NLT.*

**and of the apostles and elders, and they declared:** . . . and they rehearsed, *ASV* . . . and they recounted, *Rotherham* . . . they revealed all, *KJII.*

**all things that God had done with them:** . . . as many things as God wrought with them, *Worrell* . . . had helped them to do, *TCNT* . . . working with them, *Weymouth* . . . how great things God has wrought with them, *HBIE.*

**5. But there rose up certain of the sect of the Pharisees which believed, saying:** Some of the Pharisees' party, who had become believers in Christ, came forward, *TCNT* . . . there had been proud religious law-keepers, *NLT* . . . who had been converted from the sect of, *Lamsa.*

**That it was needful to circumcise them:** It is necessary to circumcise them, *RSV* . . . it was absolutely essential, *Phillips* . . . Gentiles must be circumcised, *Moffatt* . . . said that such converts ought to be, *Goodspeed.*

**and to command them to keep the law of Moses:** . . . and to charge them, *RSV, Worrell* . . . and to direct them to observe, *TCNT* . . . ordered to observe, *Berkeley.*

**6. And the apostles and elders came together:** . . . were gathered together, *ASV* . . . held a meeting, *Noli, TCNT* . . . were assembled, *KJII, Worrell.*

## Acts 15:7

| 1481.19 verb inf aor act | 3875.1 prep | 3450.2 art gen sing | 3030.2 noun gen sing masc | 3642.1 dem-pron gen sing | 4044.10 adj gen sing fem | 1156.2 conj |
|---|---|---|---|---|---|---|
| ἰδεῖν | περὶ | τοῦ | λόγου | τούτου. | 7. πολλῆς | δὲ |
| *idein* | *peri* | *tou* | *logou* | *toutou* | *pollēs* | *de* |
| to see | about | the | matter | this. | Much | and |

7.a.**Txt:** 04C,05D,08E 020L,025P,byz.
**Var:** 01א,02A,03B,33 Treg,Tisc,We/Ho,Weis Sod,UBS/☆

| 4654.1 noun gen sing fem | 2197.4 noun gen sing fem | 1090.57 verb gen sing fem part aor mid | 448.9 verb nom sing masc part aor act |
|---|---|---|---|
| ⸀ συζητήσεως | [a☆ ζητήσεως ] | γενομένης, | ἀναστὰς |
| *suzētēseōs* | *zētēseōs* | *genomenēs* | *anastas* |
| discussion | [ debate ] | having taken place, | having risen up |

| 3935.1 name nom masc | 1500.5 verb 3sing indic aor act | 4242.1 prep | 840.8 prs-pron acc pl masc | 433.6 noun nom pl masc | 79.6 noun nom pl masc |
|---|---|---|---|---|---|
| Πέτρος | εἶπεν | πρὸς | αὐτούς, | Ἄνδρες | ἀδελφοί, |
| *Petros* | *eipen* | *pros* | *autous* | *Andres* | *adelphoi* |
| Peter | said | to | them, | Men | brothers, |

| 5050.1 prs-pron nom 2pl | 1971.3 verb 2pl indic pres mid | 3617.1 conj | 570.1 prep | 2232.6 noun gen pl fem | 739.1 adj gen pl |
|---|---|---|---|---|---|
| ὑμεῖς | ἐπίστασθε | ὅτι | ἀφ' | ἡμερῶν | ἀρχαίων |
| *humeis* | *epistasthe* | *hoti* | *aph'* | *hēmerōn* | *archaiōn* |
| you | know | that | from | days | early |

7.b.**Txt:** 08E,020L,025P 1241,byz.
**Var:** p74,01א,02A,03B 04C,33,Lach,Treg,Alf Tisc,We/Ho,Weis,Sod UBS/☆

| 3450.5 art nom sing masc | 2296.1 noun nom sing masc | 1706.1 prep | 5050.3 prs-pron dat 2pl | 1573.3 verb 3sing indic aor mid | 1706.1 prep |
|---|---|---|---|---|---|
| ⸀ ὁ | θεὸς | ἐν | ὑμῖν | ἐξελέξατο | [b☆ ἐν |
| *ho* | *theos* | *en* | *humin* | *exelexato* | *en* |
|  | God | among | us | chose | [ among |

| 5050.3 prs-pron dat 2pl | 1573.3 verb 3sing indic aor mid | 3450.5 art nom sing masc | 2296.1 noun nom sing masc | 1217.2 prep | 3450.2 art gen sing |
|---|---|---|---|---|---|
| ὑμῖν | ἐξελέξατο | ὁ | θεὸς ] | διὰ | τοῦ |
| *humin* | *exelexato* | *ho* | *theos* | *dia* | *tou* |
| you | chose |  | God ] | through | the |

| 4601.2 noun gen sing neu | 1466.2 prs-pron gen 1sing | 189.36 verb inf aor act | 3450.17 art pl neu | 1477.4 noun pl neu | 3450.6 art acc sing masc |
|---|---|---|---|---|---|
| στόματός | μου | ἀκοῦσαι | τὰ | ἔθνη | τὸν |
| *stomatos* | *mou* | *akousai* | *ta* | *ethnē* | *ton* |
| mouth | my | to hear | the | Gentiles | the |

| 3030.4 noun acc sing masc | 3450.2 art gen sing | 2077.2 noun gen sing neu | 2504.1 conj | 3961.36 verb inf aor act | 2504.1 conj |
|---|---|---|---|---|---|
| λόγον | τοῦ | εὐαγγελίου, | καὶ | πιστεῦσαι· | 8. καὶ |
| *logon* | *tou* | *euangeliou* | *kai* | *pisteusai* | *kai* |
| word | of the | good news, | and | to believe. | And |

| 3450.5 art nom sing masc | 2560.1 noun nom sing masc | 2296.1 noun nom sing masc | 3113.16 verb 3sing indic aor act | 840.2 prs-pron dat pl |
|---|---|---|---|---|
| ὁ | καρδιογνώστης | θεὸς | ἐμαρτύρησεν | αὐτοῖς, |
| *ho* | *kardiognōstēs* | *theos* | *emarturēsen* | *autois* |
| the | knower of hearts | God | bore witness | to them, |

8.a.**Txt:** 04C,08E,020L 025P,byz.sa.bo.Sod
**Var:** 01א,02A,03B,Treg Alf,Tisc,We/Ho,Weis UBS/☆

| 1319.28 verb nom sing masc part aor act | 840.2 prs-pron dat pl | 3450.16 art sing neu | 4011.1 noun sing neu | 3450.16 art sing neu | 39.1 adj sing |
|---|---|---|---|---|---|
| δοὺς | ⸂a αὐτοῖς ⸃ | τὸ | πνεῦμα | τὸ | ἅγιον, |
| *dous* | *autois* | *to* | *pneuma* | *to* | *hagion* |
| having given | to them | the | Spirit | the | Holy, |

9.a.**Txt:** 01א,02A,04C 05D,08E,byz.Sod
**Var:** 03B,020L,025P Treg,Alf,Tisc,We/Ho Weis,UBS/☆

| 2503.1 conj | 2504.1 conj | 2231.3 prs-pron dat 1pl | 2504.1 conj | 3625.6 num card neu | 3628.1 num card neu |
|---|---|---|---|---|---|
| καθὼς | καὶ | ἡμῖν, | 9. καὶ | ⸀ οὐδὲν | [a☆ οὐθὲν ] |
| *kathōs* | *kai* | *hēmin* | *kai* | *ouden* | *outhen* |
| as | also | to us, | and | nothing | [ idem ] |

all still followed the customs of their fathers with respect to the kosher food laws and other Jewish forms and ceremonies.

**15:7.** At first there was much disputing, not in the sense of arguing, but rather there was a great deal of questioning and discussing as the apostles and elders and others tried to probe into the subject. Some may have favored Paul's view. Others may have favored the converted Pharisees who wanted all the Gentiles circumcised. But the Greek implies both sides were sincerely investigating the question, expecting to find a solution. Wisely, the leaders allowed the people to present various points of view. Apparently, this went on for some time, so no one could say he had not had an opportunity to be heard. Thus, the whole question with all its ramifications was brought into the open.

Finally, after this long period of discussion, Peter stood and reminded them that by God's choice he had taken the gospel to the Gentiles at Caesarea and they believed.

Everyone knew about this. Peter had explained the whole story in detail to the Jerusalem leaders and believers after he came back from Caesarea.

But apparently, during all this discussion no one had referred to what happened at Caesarea. This shows how little that important event had influenced most of the Jerusalem believers. They had accepted the fact that God had saved those Gentiles. They had accepted Peter back into their fellowship. But most of them seem to have treated this as an exception rather than something to be expected or sought after. Some may have thought it was all right for Peter to respond the way he did, but it was not for them. But Peter emphasized it was in their presence that God chose him out. In other words, what God had done for Peter was for the benefit of them all.

**15:8.** Peter further reminded the Jerusalem believers it was not his choice to accept the Gentiles at the house of Cornelius into the Church. It was God's choice, for He knows what is in the hearts (and minds) of all. God saw the faith in their hearts. Then God bore witness to the fact that these Gentiles were believers by giving them the Holy Spirit, just as He had to all the Jewish believers. God saw their hearts, then the outpouring of the Holy Spirit became an outward evidence so Peter and the others could see that God had accepted them. It was a seal of His acceptance.

**15:9.** From this experience Peter learned that God does not distinguish between or make a separation between Gentile believers and Jewish believers in any way. Just as in the case of Jewish be-



**for to consider of this matter:** . . . to investigate this question, *Moffatt* . . . to see about this matter, *KJII* . . . to study this problem, *SEB.*

**7. And when there had been much disputing:** . . . much debate, *RSV* . . . much questioning, *ASV* . . . After much discussion, *TCNT* . . . After an exhaustive inquiry, *Phillips* . . . after there had been much talk, *KJII* . . . After a long time of much talking, *NLT.*

**Peter rose up, and said unto them:** Peter stood up and addressed them, *Phillips.*

**Men and brethren:** Brethren, *RSV* . . . Fellow Christians, *Beck.*

**ye know how that a good while ago:** . . . you are aware that, *TNT* . . . that long ago, *TCNT* . . . You will keep in mind that a good while back, *Berkeley* . . . you know what happened in the early days, *NCV.*

**God made choice among us:** God singled me out, *TCNT* . . . it was God's pleasure, *BB.*

**that the Gentiles by my mouth:** . . . that through my mouth the nations, *Rotherham* . . . that through my lips, *TCNT* . . . the non-Jews, *Beck.*

**should hear the word of the gospel:** . . . the glad tidings, *Rotherham* . . . the Message of the Good News, *TCNT.*

**and believe:** . . . and become believers in Christ, *TCNT.*

**8. And God, which knoweth the hearts:** . . . who knows men's inmost thoughts, *Phillips* . . . who reads all hearts, *TCNT* . . . the searcher of hearts, *BB* . . . and the heart-observing God, *Rotherham* . . . who can read men's minds, *NEB* . . . the heart-knowing God, *Darby.*

**bare them witness:** . . . gave His testimony in their favor, *Weymouth* . . . declared his acceptance of the Gentiles, *TCNT* . . . attested this, *Moffatt* . . . gave this testimony in their behalf, *Montgomery* . . . God bore witness, *Worrell* . . . showed them they were to have His loving favor, *NLT.*

**giving them the Holy Ghost:** . . . by bestowing, *Weymouth.*

**even as he did unto us:** . . . exactly as he did to us, *Phillips* . . . just as he did upon us, *Montgomery* . . . even as to us, *Worrell.*

| 1246.5 verb 3sing indic aor act | 3212.1 adv | 2231.2 prs-pron gen 1pl | 4885.1 conj | 2504.1 conj | 840.1 prs-pron gen pl |
|---|---|---|---|---|---|
| διέκρινεν | μεταξὺ | ἡμῶν | τε | καὶ | αὐτῶν, |
| *diekrinen* | *metaxu* | *hēmōn* | *te* | *kai* | *autōn* |
| distinguished | between | us | both | and | them, |

| 3450.11 art dat sing fem | 3963.3 noun dat sing fem | 2483.9 verb nom sing masc part aor act | 3450.15 art acc pl fem | 2559.1 noun fem | 840.1 prs-pron gen pl |
|---|---|---|---|---|---|
| τῇ | πίστει | καθαρίσας | τὰς | καρδίας | αὐτῶν. |
| *tē* | *pistei* | *katharisas* | *tas* | *kardias* | *autōn* |
| by the | faith | having purified | the | hearts | their. |

| 3431.1 adv | 3631.1 partic | 4949.9 intr-pron sing neu | 3847.1 verb 2pl pres act | 3450.6 art acc sing masc |
|---|---|---|---|---|
| **10.** νῦν | οὖν | τί | πειράζετε | τὸν |
| *nun* | *oun* | *ti* | *peirazete* | *ton* |
| Now | therefore | why | are you tempting | |

| 2296.4 noun acc sing masc | 1991.16 verb inf aor act | 2201.3 noun acc sing masc | 1894.3 prep | 3450.6 art acc sing masc | 4976.1 noun acc sing masc |
|---|---|---|---|---|---|
| θεόν, | ἐπιθεῖναι | ζυγὸν | ἐπὶ | τὸν | τράχηλον |
| *theon* | *epitheinai* | *zugon* | *epi* | *ton* | *trachēlon* |
| God | to put | a yoke | upon | the | neck |

| 3450.1 art gen pl | 3073.6 noun gen pl masc | 3614.6 rel-pron acc sing masc | 3641.1 conj | 3450.7 art nom pl masc | 3824.6 noun nom pl masc |
|---|---|---|---|---|---|
| τῶν | μαθητῶν, | ὃν | οὔτε | οἱ | πατέρες |
| *tōn* | *mathētōn* | *hon* | *oute* | *hoi* | *pateres* |
| of the | disciples, | which | neither | the | fathers |

| 2231.2 prs-pron gen 1pl | 3641.1 conj | 2231.1 prs-pron nom 1pl | 2453.8 verb 1pl indic aor act | 934.14 verb inf aor act | 233.2 conj |
|---|---|---|---|---|---|
| ἡμῶν | οὔτε | ἡμεῖς | ἰσχύσαμεν | βαστάσαι; | **11.** ἀλλὰ |
| *hēmōn* | *oute* | *hēmeis* | *ischusamen* | *bastasai* | *alla* |
| our | nor | we | were able | to bear? | But |

11.a.**Var:** 01ℵ,02A,03B 04C,05D,08E,020L 025P,byz.Gries,Lach Treg,Alf,Word,Tisc We/Ho,Weis,Sod UBS/☆

| 1217.2 prep | 3450.10 art gen sing fem | 5322.2 noun gen sing fem | 3450.2 art gen sing | 2935.2 noun gen sing masc | 2400.2 name masc |
|---|---|---|---|---|---|
| διὰ | τῆς | χάριτος | [ᵃ☆+ τοῦ ] | κυρίου | Ἰησοῦ |
| *dia* | *tēs* | *charitos* | *tou* | *kuriou* | *Iēsou* |
| by | the | grace | [ of the ] | Lord | Jesus |

11.b.**Txt:** 04C,05D,byz. **Var:** 01ℵ,02A,03B,08E 020L,025P,sa.Gries Treg,Alf,Word,Tisc We/Ho,Weis,Sod UBS/☆

| 5382.2 name gen masc | 3961.7 verb 1pl indic pres act | 4834.28 verb inf aor pass | 2567.2 prep | 3614.6 rel-pron acc sing masc |
|---|---|---|---|---|
| ⸂ᵇ Χριστοῦ ⸃ | πιστεύομεν | σωθῆναι, | καθ' | ὃν |
| *Christou* | *pisteuomen* | *sōthēnai* | *kath'* | *hon* |
| Christ | we believe | to be saved, | according to | which |

| 4999.3 noun acc sing masc | 2519.4 dem-pron nom pl masc | 4456.4 verb 3sing indic aor act | 1156.2 conj | 3820.17 adj sing neu | 3450.16 art sing neu |
|---|---|---|---|---|---|
| τρόπον | κἀκεῖνοι. | **12.** Ἐσίγησεν | δὲ | πᾶν | τὸ |
| *tropon* | *kakeinoi* | *Esigēsen* | *de* | *pan* | *to* |
| manner | those also. | Kept silence | and | all | the |

| 3988.1 noun sing neu | 2504.1 conj | 189.46 verb 3pl indic imperf act | 915.2 name masc | 2504.1 conj | 3834.2 name gen masc |
|---|---|---|---|---|---|
| πλῆθος, | καὶ | ἤκουον | Βαρναβᾶ | καὶ | Παύλου |
| *plēthos* | *kai* | *ēkouon* | *Barnaba* | *kai* | *Paulou* |
| multitude, | and | were hearing | Barnabas | and | Paul |

| 1817.1 verb gen pl masc part pres mid | 3607.8 rel-pron pl neu | 4020.24 verb 3sing indic aor act | 3450.5 art nom sing masc | 2296.1 noun nom sing masc |
|---|---|---|---|---|
| ἐξηγουμένων | ὅσα | ἐποίησεν | ὁ | θεὸς |
| *exēgoumenōn* | *hosa* | *epoiēsen* | *ho* | *theos* |
| relating | what things | did | | God |

lievers, God purified (cleansed) their hearts by faith, saving them by grace through faith alone (Ephesians 2:8). That is, God had already purified (cleansed) their hearts by faith before He showed there was no distinction by giving to them the Holy Spirit.

From this experience it is very clear that circumcision was not necessary for God to bear witness to the salvation of these Gentiles. Neither was the keeping of the law of Moses necessary for God to bear witness to that faith by pouring out His Holy Spirit.

**15:10.** Peter then asked why they would tempt God (put God to the test) by disregarding what He had done and made plain at Caesarea.

Tempting God, putting God to the test, is a very serious kind of unbelief. God had clearly made His will known, pouring out the Holy Spirit upon the Gentiles. To doubt Him and make trial of Him to see whether He really meant what He did at Caesarea was to say that God is not consistent.

Furthermore, the yoke of the Law was something that neither these Jewish believers in Jerusalem nor their ancestors had been able to bear (had strength to carry). In their human weakness they had found it too burdensome. Even in the Old Testament, God repeatedly showed mercy and grace to those who were failing or falling short under the burden of the Law. (Compare Romans 4:6-8.)

**15:11.** Peter concluded by declaring what "we" (the Christians who were gathered in Jerusalem) "believe": that through the grace of the Lord Jesus Christ Jewish disciples are saved in exactly the same way as Gentiles. (The Greek term for "believe" [*pisteuomen*] is in the present tense and represents continuous action.)

It is clear then that by grace, apart from the heavy yoke of the Law and apart from the legalistic bondage encouraged by the Pharisees, both Jewish and Gentile believers were to continue in their relationship with Christ. The Pharisees were very strict at this time. Jesus spoke of how "they bind heavy burdens and grievous to be borne, and lay them on men's shoulders; but they themselves will not move them with one of their fingers" (Matthew 23:4). Not only did the Pharisees make the legalistic burden heavy, they refused to help anyone carry it. God's grace has, through Christ, removed those burdens.

**15:12.** Peter's words quieted the crowd and they listened in silence, giving their full attention as Barnabas and Paul related (and explained) how many signs and wonders God had done through them among the Gentiles. (Barnabas is mentioned first again, for he was known and respected by the Jerusalem leaders and believers. Thus, this time he was the spokesman.)

**9. And put no difference between us and them:** . . . and he made no distinction, *RSV* . . . Making no division, *BB* . . . does not discriminate, *Concordant* . . . not the slightest distinction, *Moffatt.*

**purifying their hearts by faith:** . . . because he cleansed, *Williams* . . . when He cleansed their hearts, *Adams* . . . by their faith, *TCNT.*

**10. Now therefore why tempt ye God:** . . . why make ye trial of God, *ASV* . . . why are you proving God, *Rotherham* . . . Why, then, do you now provoke God, *TCNT* . . . Now then, why be a trial to God, *Berkeley* . . . now strain the patience of God, *Phillips* . . . why do you try God, *Fenton* . . . we cannot call into question this act of God, *Noli.*

**to put a yoke upon the neck of the disciples:** . . . by trying to put on the shoulders of these disciples a burden, *Phillips* . . . you are putting a heavy load around the necks of, *NCV* . . . by putting too heavy a load on the back of, *NLT.*

**which neither our fathers nor we were able to bear?:** . . . our ancestors, *TCNT* . . . have the strength to bear? *Concordant* . . . strong enough to bear? *Fenton, Worrell.*

**11. But we believe that through the grace of the Lord Jesus Christ:** On the contrary, *Fenton* . . . Instead, we believe that we are saved, *Berkeley* . . . No, we believe that both we and these people, *SEB* . . . only on the mercy, *TCNT.*

**we shall be saved:** . . . are relying for Salvation, *TCNT* . . . we are to be saved, *Fenton.*

**even as they:** . . . just as they are, *Williams.*

**12. Then all the multitude kept silence:** Then the whole assembly remained silent, *Weymouth* . . . entire assembly kept quiet, *Berkeley* . . . the whole meeting quieted down, *Confraternity* . . . the whole group became quiet, *NCV* . . . All those who were gathered together said nothing, *NLT* . . . assembly kept silence, *Fenton.*

**and gave audience to Barnabas and Paul:** . . . and began to hearken unto, *Rotherham* . . . as they listened to, *TCNT.*

| 4447.2 noun pl neu | 2504.1 conj | 4907.1 noun pl neu | 1706.1 prep | 3450.4 art dat pl | 1477.6 noun dat pl neu | 1217.1 prep |
|---|---|---|---|---|---|---|
| σημεῖα | καὶ | τέρατα | ἐν | τοῖς | ἔθνεσιν | δι’ |
| *sēmeia* | *kai* | *terata* | *en* | *tois* | *ethnesin* | *di’* |
| signs | and | wonders | among | the | Gentiles | through |

| 840.1 prs-pron gen pl | 3196.3 prep | 1156.2 conj | 3450.16 art sing neu | 4456.6 verb inf aor act | 840.8 prs-pron acc pl masc |
|---|---|---|---|---|---|
| αὐτῶν. | 13. Μετὰ | δὲ | τὸ | σιγῆσαι | αὐτοὺς |
| *autōn* | *Meta* | *de* | *to* | *sigēsai* | *autous* |
| them. | After | and | the | to keep silence | them |

| 552.6 verb 3sing indic aor pass | 2362.1 name nom masc | 2978.15 verb nom sing masc part pres act | 433.6 noun nom pl masc | 79.6 noun nom pl masc |
|---|---|---|---|---|
| ἀπεκρίθη | Ἰάκωβος | λέγων, | Ἄνδρες | ἀδελφοί, |
| *apekrithē* | *Iakōbos* | *legōn* | *Andres* | *adelphoi* |
| answered | James, | saying, | Men | brothers, |

| 189.29 verb 2pl impr aor act | 1466.2 prs-pron gen 1sing | 4677.1 name masc | 1817.2 verb 3sing indic aor mid | 2503.1 conj |
|---|---|---|---|---|
| ἀκούσατέ | μου. | 14. Συμεὼν | ἐξηγήσατο | καθὼς |
| *akousate* | *mou* | *Sumeōn* | *exēgēsato* | *kathōs* |
| hear | me. | Simeon | related | just as |

| 4270.1 adv | 3450.5 art nom sing masc | 2296.1 noun nom sing masc | 1964.3 verb 3sing indic aor mid | 2956.31 verb inf aor act |
|---|---|---|---|---|
| πρῶτον | ὁ | θεὸς | ἐπεσκέψατο | λαβεῖν |
| *prōton* | *ho* | *theos* | *epeskepsato* | *labein* |
| first | | God | visited | to take |

14.a.**Txt:** 020L,025P,byz.bo.
**Var:** 01ℵ,02A,03B,04C 05D,08E,sa.Lach,Treg Alf,Word,Tisc,We/Ho Weis,Sod,UBS/⋆

| 1523.1 prep gen | 1477.5 noun gen pl neu | 2967.4 noun acc sing masc | 1894.3 prep | 3450.3 art dat sing | 3549.4 noun dat sing neu |
|---|---|---|---|---|---|
| ἐξ | ἐθνῶν | λαὸν | ⸂a ἐπὶ ⸃ | τῷ | ὀνόματι |
| *ex* | *ethnōn* | *laon* | *epi* | *tō* | *onomati* |
| out of | Gentiles | a people | for | the | name |

| 840.3 prs-pron gen sing | 2504.1 conj | 3642.5 dem-pron dat sing masc | 4707.2 verb 3pl indic pres act | 3450.7 art nom pl masc |
|---|---|---|---|---|
| αὐτοῦ. | 15. καὶ | τούτῳ | συμφωνοῦσιν | οἱ |
| *autou* | *kai* | *toutō* | *sumphōnousin* | *hoi* |
| his. | And | with this | agree | the |

| 3030.5 noun nom pl masc | 3450.1 art gen pl | 4254.5 noun gen pl masc | 2503.1 conj | 1119.22 verb 3sing indic perf mid |
|---|---|---|---|---|
| λόγοι | τῶν | προφητῶν, | καθὼς | γέγραπται, |
| *logoi* | *tōn* | *prophētōn* | *kathōs* | *gegraptai* |
| words | of the | prophets: | as | it has been written, |

| 3196.3 prep | 3642.18 dem-pron pl neu | 388.3 verb 1sing indic fut act | 2504.1 conj | 454.1 verb 1sing indic fut act |
|---|---|---|---|---|
| 16. Μετὰ | ταῦτα | ἀναστρέψω | καὶ | ἀνοικοδομήσω |
| *Meta* | *tauta* | *anastrepsō* | *kai* | *anoikodomēsō* |
| After | these things | I will return | and | will build again |

| 3450.12 art acc sing fem | 4488.4 noun acc sing fem | 1132.1 name masc | 3450.12 art acc sing fem | 3959.18 verb acc sing fem part perf act | 2504.1 conj |
|---|---|---|---|---|---|
| τὴν | σκηνὴν | Δαβὶδ | τὴν | πεπτωκυῖαν· | καὶ |
| *tēn* | *skēnēn* | *Dabid* | *tēn* | *peptōkuian* | *kai* |
| the | tabernacle | of David | the | having fallen; | and |

16.a.**Txt:** 02A,04C,05D 08E,020L,025P,byz.Sod
**Var:** 01ℵ,03B,33,Tisc We/Ho,Weis,UBS/⋆

| 3450.17 art pl neu | 2649.2 verb pl neu part perf mid | 2660.2 verb pl neu part perf mid | 840.10 prs-pron gen sing fem |
|---|---|---|---|
| τὰ | ⸀ κατεσκαμμένα | [a κατεστραμμένα ] | αὐτῆς |
| *ta* | *kateskammena* | *katestrammena* | *autēs* |
| the | having been ruined | [ idem ] | of it |

The emphasis is on what God did and implies that the miracles showed God's concern for winning these Gentiles to Christ and establishing them in the faith. The miracles were witness to the fact that God had accepted the Gentiles. It is obvious He would not keep doing miracles among them if He had not accepted their faith and their response to the simple gospel of salvation by grace through faith.

**15:13.** After Barnabas and Paul finished speaking, the crowd waited until James broke the silence by asking them to listen. But in this request James spoke as a humble brother, not as one who had superior authority. Though he was the brother of Jesus, he was a servant of the Lord who was simply responding to the Holy Spirit.

**15:14.** First, James drew attention to what Peter had said, calling Peter by his Hebrew name, *Sumeōn* (another spelling of Simon; both Simon and Simeon are Greek forms of the Hebrew *shimᵉôn*, "hearing"). Then he summarized what Peter had said by saying that God, at the house of Cornelius (before other Gentiles were saved), first visited the Gentiles (the nations) to take out of the Gentiles a people for His name.

God's visiting the Gentiles meant a gracious divine intervention to bring salvation and blessings. It also expressed God's desire to win a people from among the Gentiles. He wanted a people for His name, a people who would honor His name and be His people.

**15:15.** James then gave grounds for God's concern over the Gentiles by quoting from the Prophets. It was important for the Jewish believers to see that this truth was not based on the experience at the house of Cornelius alone but also was founded on the written Word of God that had already been given. Spiritual truths are learned through experience, but experience must always be checked by the Word of God and not the other way around.

**15:16.** The passage James quoted is Amos 9:11,12 from the Septuagint version. The prophet spoke of a time when God would return to associate himself with His people. His purpose would be to build up again the fallen tabernacle (tent) of David. He would build up its ruins and restore it. All this repetition was to emphasize that God will indeed fulfill His promises to David. Apparently also, James (under the inspiration of the Holy Spirit) took the setting up of the fallen tent of David to be parallel to the prophecy that the Messiah would come as a new shoot, or branch, out of the stump of Jesse and the root of David. Isaiah 11:1 speaks of this and applies it to the Messiah, adding that the Spirit of the Lord would rest upon Him.

**declaring what miracles and wonders:** . . . rehearsing what signs and wonders, *ASV* . . . relating how many, *Rotherham* . . . through...evidences and deep impressions, *Fenton.*

**God had wrought among the Gentiles by them:** God had performed, *Moffatt* . . . what God had produced...among the nations, *Fenton.*

**13. And after they had held their peace:** After they had finished speaking, *TCNT* . . . And when they had come to an end, *BB* . . . After a time of silence, *SEB.*

**James answered, saying:** James addressed the Council, *TCNT* . . . James replied, *RSV.*

**Men and brethren, hearken unto me:** . . . hear what I have to say, *TCNT* . . . listen to me, *BB.*

**14. Simeon hath declared:** . . . hath fully told, *Rotherham* . . . has related, *RSV.*

**how God at the first did visit the Gentiles:** . . . the manner in which God first visited, *TCNT* . . . how God first came to the non-Jews, *Beck.*

**to take out of them a people for his name:** . . . in order to take from among them a people to bear his Name, *TCNT* . . . to gain, *Berkeley* . . . a people for Himself, *Beck.*

**15. And to this agree:** This is in full agreement with, *Phillips* . . . This agrees with, *NLT* . . . this is in harmony, *Montgomery.*

**the words of the prophets:** . . . what the prophets wrote, *Phillips* . . . what the early preachers said, *NLT* . . . the language of the Prophets, *Weymouth.*

**as it is written:** . . . as Scripture has it, *NEB.*

**16. After this I will return:** Afterward, *Goodspeed* . . . After these things, *Phillips* . . . There will come a time when I shall return, *Norlie* . . . I will return later, *SEB.*

**and will build again the tabernacle of David:** . . . re-erect it, *Concordant* . . . the dwelling of David, *RSV* . . . the tent of David, *Rotherham* . . . the House of David, *TCNT.*

**which is fallen down:** . . . that hath fallen, *Rotherham.*

| 454.1 verb 1sing indic fut act | 2504.1 conj | 458.2 verb 1sing indic fut act | 840.12 prs-pron acc sing fem | 3567.1 conj |
|---|---|---|---|---|
| ἀνοικοδομήσω· | καὶ | ἀνορθώσω | αὐτήν, | **17.** ὅπως |
| *anoikodomēsō* | *kai* | *anorthōsō* | *autēn* | *hopōs* |
| I will build again, | and | will set up | it, | so that |

| 300.1 partic | 1554.4 verb 3pl subj aor act | 3450.7 art nom pl masc | 2615.1 adj nom pl masc | 3450.1 art gen pl |
|---|---|---|---|---|
| ἂν | ἐκζητήσωσιν | οἱ | κατάλοιποι | τῶν |
| *an* | *ekzētēsōsin* | *hoi* | *kataloipoi* | *tōn* |
| | may seek out | the | rest | of the |

| 442.7 noun gen pl masc | 3450.6 art acc sing masc | 2935.4 noun acc sing masc | 2504.1 conj | 3820.1 adj | 3450.17 art pl neu |
|---|---|---|---|---|---|
| ἀνθρώπων | τὸν | κύριον, | καὶ | πάντα | τὰ |
| *anthrōpōn* | *ton* | *kurion* | *kai* | *panta* | *ta* |
| men | the | Lord, | and | all | the |

| 1477.4 noun pl neu | 1894.1 prep | 3614.8 rel-pron acc pl masc | 1926.20 verb 3sing indic perf mid | 3450.16 art sing neu | 3549.2 noun sing neu |
|---|---|---|---|---|---|
| ἔθνη | ἐφ' | οὓς | ἐπικέκληται | τὸ | ὄνομά |
| *ethnē* | *eph'* | *hous* | *epikeklētai* | *to* | *onoma* |
| nations | upon | whom | has been called | the | name |

17.a.**Txt:** 01ℵ-corr,02A 04C,05D-corr,08E,020L 025P,etc.byz.Sod
**Var:** 01ℵ-org,03B,Lach Treg,Tisc,We/Ho,Weis UBS/*

| 1466.2 prs-pron gen 1sing | 1894.2 prep | 840.8 prs-pron acc pl masc | 2978.5 verb 3sing indic pres act | 2935.1 noun nom sing masc | 3450.5 art nom sing masc |
|---|---|---|---|---|---|
| μου | ἐπ' | αὐτούς· | λέγει | κύριος | (a ὁ ) |
| *mou* | *ep'* | *autous* | *legei* | *kurios* | *ho* |
| my | upon | them, | says | Lord | the |

17.b.**Txt:** 08E,020L 025P,byz.
**Var:** 01ℵ,02A,03B,04C 05D,bo.Gries,Lach,Treg Alf,Word,Tisc,We/Ho Weis,Sod,UBS/*

| 4020.15 verb nom sing masc part pres act | 3642.18 dem-pron pl neu | 3820.1 adj | 1104.5 adj pl neu | 570.2 prep |
|---|---|---|---|---|
| ποιῶν | ταῦτα | (b πάντα. ) | **18.** Γνωστὰ | ἀπ' |
| *poiōn* | *tauta* | *panta* | *Gnōsta* | *ap'* |
| doing | these things | all. | Known | from |

18.a.**Txt:** p74,02A,05D 08E,020L,025P,1241 byz.
**Var:** 01ℵ,03B,04C,044 33,sa.bo.Gries,Treg,Alf Tisc,We/Ho,Weis,Sod UBS/*

| 163.1 noun gen sing masc | 1498.4 verb 3sing indic pres act | 3450.3 art dat sing | 2296.3 noun dat sing masc | 3820.1 adj | 3450.17 art pl neu |
|---|---|---|---|---|---|
| αἰῶνος | (a ἐστιν | τῷ | θεῷ | πάντα | τὰ |
| *aiōnos* | *estin* | *tō* | *theō* | *panta* | *ta* |
| eternity | are | | to God | all | the |

| 2024.4 noun pl neu | 840.3 prs-pron gen sing | 1346.1 conj | 1466.1 prs-pron nom 1sing | 2892.1 verb 1sing act | 3231.1 partic |
|---|---|---|---|---|---|
| ἔργα | αὐτοῦ. ) | **19.** διὸ | ἐγὼ | κρίνω | μὴ |
| *erga* | *autou* | *dio* | *egō* | *krinō* | *mē* |
| works | his. | Wherefore | I | judge | not |

| 3788.1 verb inf pres act | 3450.4 art dat pl | 570.3 prep | 3450.1 art gen pl | 1477.5 noun gen pl neu | 1978.2 verb dat pl masc part pres act |
|---|---|---|---|---|---|
| παρενοχλεῖν | τοῖς | ἀπὸ | τῶν | ἐθνῶν | ἐπιστρέφουσιν |
| *parenochlein* | *tois* | *apo* | *tōn* | *ethnōn* | *epistrephousin* |
| to trouble | the | from | the | Gentiles | turning |

| 1894.3 prep | 3450.6 art acc sing masc | 2296.4 noun acc sing masc | 233.2 conj | 1973.3 verb inf aor act | 840.2 prs-pron dat pl |
|---|---|---|---|---|---|
| ἐπὶ | τὸν | θεόν· | **20.** ἀλλὰ | ἐπιστεῖλαι | αὐτοῖς |
| *epi* | *ton* | *theon* | *alla* | *episteilai* | *autois* |
| to | | God; | but | to write | to them |

20.a.**Txt:** 02A,04C,08E 020L,025P,byz.Sod
**Var:** 01ℵ,03B,05D,Lach Treg,Tisc,We/Ho,Weis UBS/*

| 3450.2 art gen sing | 563.9 verb inf pres mid | 570.3 prep | 3450.1 art gen pl | 232.1 noun gen pl neu | 3450.1 art gen pl |
|---|---|---|---|---|---|
| τοῦ | ἀπέχεσθαι | (a ἀπὸ ) | τῶν | ἀλισγημάτων | τῶν |
| *tou* | *apechesthai* | *apo* | *tōn* | *alisgēmatōn* | *tōn* |
| the | to abstain | from | the | pollutions | of the |

By picturing the kingdom of David as a stump, Isaiah indicated that David's glory and David's kingdom would be like a fallen tree, leaving nothing but a stump behind. Yet, though David's glory was gone, the prophet said God would raise up the Messiah from David's descendants and restore the hope of Israel and also the Gentiles. Isaiah 11:10 goes on to say, "And in that day there shall be a root of Jesse, which shall stand for an ensign of the people (peoples; the Hebrew is plural); to it (to Him) shall the Gentiles seek: and his rest shall be glorious (glory)."

**15:17.** Amos also spoke of the rest of mankind seeking the Lord. This differs from the ordinary Massoretic Hebrew text in that it substitutes "men" (mankind) for the "Edom" of that text. Actually, the Hebrew could also be read "mankind" (Hebrew, *'ādhām*) instead of "Edom." The difference involves only a slight change in the vowels, which the ancient Hebrew did not write anyway. Note also that "Edom" in Amos is parallel to the heathen (the nations, the Gentiles). At least, Edom is representative of the Gentiles. But some Bible scholars believe the vowels for "Edom" were added by later Jews to change the meaning because they knew the Book of Acts used this verse to uphold the acceptance of uncircumcised Gentiles.

Actually, in the same chapter Amos showed that God was just as much concerned over the Gentiles as He was over the Jews. In Amos 9:7, God said, "Are ye not as the children (people) of the Ethiopians unto me, O children of Israel? saith the Lord. Have not I brought up Israel out of the land of Egypt? and the Philistines from Caphtor (probably, Crete), and the Syrians from Kir?" In other words, God was concerned about the Gentiles even though they did not know it.

**15:18.** This was, as the prophets said, the work of the Lord who has known all these things from the beginning of the world (or age), that is, from the beginning of time.

**15:19.** "My sentence is" is better translated, "I think it good." James was not acting as a judge here, nor as a leading elder of the church. (See verse 28.) In this situation James was simply a Christian brother, a member of the Body, who gave a word of wisdom as the Spirit willed. (See 1 Corinthians 12:8,11.)

The Spirit's word of wisdom was that they should not trouble the Gentile believers further. They should not add any further requirements to the faith and practice of the Gentile believers.

**15:20.** James suggested that a letter be written directing the Gentile believers to abstain (keep away) from the pollutions of idols (everything connected with idol worship), from fornication (the various types of heterosexual and homosexual immoralities habit-



**and I will build again the ruins thereof:** Its very ruins I will rebuild, *TCNT* . . . relay its foundations, *Fenton* . . . its broken parts, *BB*.

**and I will set it up:** . . . and restore it, *Berkeley*.

**17. That the residue of men:** . . . that so the rest of mankind, *TCNT*.

**might seek after the Lord:** . . . may seek out, *Rotherham* . . . may earnestly seek, *TCNT*.

**and all the Gentiles:** Even all the nations, *Weymouth* . . . all the heathen, *Fenton*.

**upon whom my name is called:** . . . which are called by My name, *Weymouth* . . . upon whom my name has been bestowed, *TCNT* . . . over whom my name has been invoked, *Berkeley* . . . may take my name upon them, *Fenton* . . . They can be My people, too, *SEB*.

**saith the Lord:** The Lord says this, *Berkeley*.

**who doeth all these things:** . . . whose work it is, *NEB*.

**18. Known unto God are all his works from the beginning of the world:** From eternity all His doings are known, *Berkeley*.

**19. Wherefore my sentence is:** In my judgement, therefore, *TCNT* . . . Therefore it is my opinion, *AmpB* . . . For this reason my decision is, *BB*.

**that we trouble not:** . . . we should not add to the difficulties of, *TCNT* . . . be not harassed, *Berkeley* . . . we should not harass, *Fenton* . . . are not to be disquieted, *Douay*.

**them, which from among the Gentiles are turned to God:** . . . those Gentiles who are turning to God, *TCNT*.

**20. But that we write unto them:** . . . command them, *Alford* . . . Yet, let us send them written instructions, *Weymouth*.

**that they abstain from pollutions of idols:** . . . keep aloof from the defilement of, *Murdock* . . . Do not be guilty of, *NCV* . . . food that has been polluted by being sacrificed to idols, *TCNT* . . . things polluted by connexion with idolatry, *Weymouth* . . . anything that has been contaminated by idols, *Confraternity*.

## Acts 15:21

20.b.**Txt:** p45,01ℵ,04C 08E,020L,025P,byz.Tisc Sod
**Var:** p74,02A,03B,044 33,Lach,Treg,We/Ho Weis,UBS/☆

| **1487.4** noun gen pl neu | **2504.1** conj | **3450.10** art gen sing fem | **4061.1** noun fem | **2504.1** conj | **3450.2** art gen sing |
|---|---|---|---|---|---|
| εἰδώλων | καὶ | τῆς | πορνείας | καὶ | ([b] τοῦ ) |
| *eidōlōn* | *kai* | *tēs* | *porneias* | *kai* | *tou* |
| idols | and | of the | fornication | and | of the |

| **4016.1** adj gen sing neu | **2504.1** conj | **3450.2** art gen sing | **129.2** noun gen sing neu | **3337.1** name nom masc |
|---|---|---|---|---|
| πνικτοῦ | καὶ | τοῦ | αἵματος. | **21.** ( Μωσῆς |
| *pniktou* | *kai* | *tou* | *haimatos* | *Mōsēs* |
| what is strangled | and | of the | blood. | Moses |

| **3338.1** name nom masc | **1056.1** conj | **1523.2** prep gen | **1067.6** noun gen pl fem | **739.1** adj gen pl | **2567.3** prep |
|---|---|---|---|---|---|
| [☆ Μωϋσῆς ] | γὰρ | ἐκ | γενεῶν | ἀρχαίων | κατὰ |
| *Mōusēs* | *gar* | *ek* | *geneōn* | *archaiōn* | *kata* |
| [ idem ] | for | from | generations | of old | according to |

| **4032.4** noun acc sing fem | **3450.8** art acc pl masc | **2756.9** verb acc pl masc part pres act | **840.6** prs-pron acc sing masc | **2174.4** verb 3sing indic pres act | **1706.1** prep |
|---|---|---|---|---|---|
| πόλιν | τοὺς | κηρύσσοντας | αὐτὸν | ἔχει | ἐν |
| *polin* | *tous* | *kērussontas* | *auton* | *echei* | *en* |
| a city | the | proclaiming | him | has | in |

| **3450.14** art dat pl fem | **4715.6** noun dat pl fem | **2567.3** prep | **3820.17** adj sing neu | **4378.1** noun sing neu |
|---|---|---|---|---|
| ταῖς | συναγωγαῖς | κατὰ | πᾶν | σάββατον |
| *tais* | *sunagōgais* | *kata* | *pan* | *sabbaton* |
| the | synagogues, | according to | every | sabbath |

| **312.14** verb nom sing masc part pres mid | **4966.1** adv | **1374.16** verb 3sing indic aor act | **3450.4** art dat pl |
|---|---|---|---|
| ἀναγινωσκόμενος. | **22.** Τότε | ἔδοξεν | τοῖς |
| *anaginōskomenos* | *Tote* | *edoxen* | *tois* |
| being read. | Then | it seemed | to the |

| **646.6** noun dat pl masc | **2504.1** conj | **3450.4** art dat pl | **4104.7** adj comp dat pl masc | **4713.1** prep | **3513.8** adj dat sing fem |
|---|---|---|---|---|---|
| ἀποστόλοις | καὶ | τοῖς | πρεσβυτέροις | σὺν | ὅλῃ |
| *apostolois* | *kai* | *tois* | *presbuterois* | *sun* | *holē* |
| apostles | and | to the | elders | with | whole |

| **3450.11** art dat sing fem | **1564.3** noun dat sing fem | **1573.7** verb acc pl masc part aor mid | **433.9** noun acc pl masc | **1523.1** prep gen |
|---|---|---|---|---|
| τῇ | ἐκκλησίᾳ, | ἐκλεξαμένους | ἄνδρας | ἐξ |
| *tē* | *ekklēsia* | *eklexamenous* | *andras* | *ex* |
| the | assembly, | having chosen | men | from among |

| **840.1** prs-pron gen pl | **3854.17** verb inf aor act | **1519.1** prep | **487.3** name acc fem | **4713.1** prep | **3450.3** art dat sing | **3834.3** name dat masc |
|---|---|---|---|---|---|---|
| αὐτῶν | πέμψαι | εἰς | Ἀντιόχειαν | σὺν | τῷ | Παύλῳ |
| *autōn* | *pempsai* | *eis* | *Antiocheian* | *sun* | *tō* | *Paulō* |
| them | to send | to | Antioch | with | | Paul |

| **2504.1** conj | **915.3** name dat masc | **2430.4** name acc masc | **3450.6** art acc sing masc | **1926.6** verb acc sing masc part pres mid |
|---|---|---|---|---|
| καὶ | Βαρναβᾷ, | Ἰούδαν | τὸν | ( ἐπικαλούμενον |
| *kai* | *Barnaba* | *Ioudan* | *ton* | *epikaloumenon* |
| and | Barnabas, | Judas | the | being named |

22.a.**Txt:** 025P,byz.
**Var:** 01ℵ,02A,03B,04C 05D,08E,020L,Lach Treg,Alf,Word,Tisc We/Ho,Weis,Sod UBS/☆

| **2535.29** verb sing part pres mid | **917.1** name acc masc | **917.2** name acc masc | **2504.1** conj |
|---|---|---|---|
| [a☆ καλούμενον ] | ( Βαρσαβᾶν, | [ Βαρσαββᾶν ] | καὶ |
| *kaloumenon* | *Barsaban* | *Barsabban* | *kai* |
| [ being called ] | Barsabas, | [ idem ] | and |

ually practiced by so many Gentile heathen), from things strangled (meat from animals killed without draining out the blood), and from blood.

The first two requests to keep away from idolatry and all forms of sexual immorality were to uphold the witness to the one true God and the high moral standards He requires. Gentiles should not keep anything from their former idol worship, even though they now knew these were meaningless and harmless, lest others misinterpret them, and lest Jewish visitors be offended.

The Gentile believers also had to be reminded of the high moral standards God requires. They had come from a background where immorality was accepted and even encouraged in the name of religion. Paul had to deal sternly with these things. (See Romans 6:12,13,19-23; 1 Corinthians 5:1,9-12; 6:13,15-20; 10:8; Ephesians 5:3,5; Colossians 3:5,6; 1 Timothy 1:9,10.) In the Book of Acts the word "fornication" is used in the general sense that includes all forms of sexual immorality both before and after marriage.

The second two requests were for the sake of promoting fellowship between Jewish and Gentile believers. If there was anything that would turn a Jewish believer's stomach, it was to eat meat from which the blood had not been drained, or to eat blood itself. If the Jewish believers were going to give up a great deal by eating nonkosher food in Gentile believers' homes, then the Gentile believers could at least avoid serving and eating those things which no Jew, no matter how long he had been a Christian, could stomach.

There was a precedent for these last two requests because long before Moses' time, God had told Noah not to eat blood, for it represented the life.

**15:21.** James was concerned about the testimony of the synagogues in every city (in city after city) where the Jews had been for generations, going back to ancient times.

**15:22.** The apostles, elders, and "the whole church" accepted the word of wisdom from James. But as they considered the situation, they agreed it would be best to send men chosen from themselves to go with Barnabas and Paul to Antioch to present the decision and the letter. They would be able to confirm the truth of what would be contained in the letter as well as the fact that the whole assembly was unanimous in standing behind it. Those chosen were Judas Barsabas (probably meaning "son of the Sabbath," that is, born on the Sabbath) and Silas (short for Silvanus; 2 Corinthians 1:19). These two were recognized as leading men among the believers in Jerusalem.

Some suppose that Judas Barsabas was the brother of Joseph Barsabas, the one who, along with Matthias, was proposed as a possible substitute for Judas (1:23). This, however, is only conjecture, and nothing more is said about him after this chapter.

**and from fornication:** ... keep away from sex sins, *NLT* ... from impurity, *TCNT* ... from sexual vice, *Moffatt* ... and from unchastity, *Berkeley* ... avoid unlawful sexual intercourse, *Norlie* ... prostitution, *Concordant* ... sexual immorality, *Williams* ... sexual sin, *NCV.*

**and from things strangled:** ... and from what is strangled, *ASV* ... the flesh of strangled animals, *TCNT* ... Do not taste blood, *NCV* ... animals that have been killed in ways against the law, *NLT* ... from meat with the blood in it, *Fenton.*

**and from blood:** ... and from blood-meat, *Noli.*

**21. For Moses of old time hath in every city them that preach him:** ... from the earliest times, *Fenton* ... has from ancient generations, *Swann* ... These prescriptions of the law, *Noli* ... has had his preachers in every town, *Goodspeed* ... that proclaim him, *Rotherham* ... in every city from the early days, *NLT* ... for generations long past, *SEB* ... from preceding generations, *Fenton.*

**being read in the synagogues every sabbath day:** ... for he is read every sabbath, *RSV* ... read as he is in the Synagogue, *TCNT* ... read in the meeting-houses, *Fenton.*

**22. Then pleased it the apostles and elders:** Then it seemed good, *ASV* ... It was then decided by the, *TCNT* ... passed a resolution, *Williams* ... agreed, *Phillips.*

**with the whole church:** ... with the assent of the whole Church, *TCNT* ... with the approval of, *Weymouth* ... The group, *SEB* ... the whole assembly, *Fenton.*

**to send chosen men of their own company to Antioch with Paul and Barnabas:** ... to choose men out of their company, *ASV* ... to choose representatives, *Phillips* ... resolved to select representatives and send them, *Goodspeed* ... to select some of their men, *MLNT* ... to choose some of their own men, *SEB* ... men should be chosen from among themselves, *Fenton.*

**namely, Judas surnamed Barsabas, and Silas:** Those chosen were, *TCNT* ... Judah, called, *Fenton.*

| 4464.3 name acc masc | 433.9 noun acc pl masc | 2216.10 verb acc pl masc part pres mid | 1706.1 prep | 3450.4 art dat pl | 79.8 noun dat pl masc |
|---|---|---|---|---|---|
| Σίλαν, | ἄνδρας | ἡγουμένους | ἐν | τοῖς | ἀδελφοῖς, |
| *Silan* | *andras* | *hēgoumenous* | *en* | *tois* | *adelphois* |
| Silas, | men | leading | among | the | brothers, |

23.a.**Txt:** 01ℵ-corr,08E 020L,025P,byz.Sod **Var:** p74,01ℵ-org,02A 03B,bo.Lach,Treg,Alf Tisc,We/Ho,Weis UBS/*

23.b.**Txt:** 01ℵ-corr,08E 020L,025P,044,byz.bo. Weis,Sod **Var:** p33,p74,01ℵ-org 02A,03B,04C,05D,Lach Treg,Alf,Tisc,We/Ho UBS/*

| 1119.14 verb nom pl masc part aor act | 1217.2 prep | 5331.2 noun gen sing fem | 840.1 prs-pron gen pl | 3455.4 dem-pron acc pl neu | 3450.7 art nom pl masc |
|---|---|---|---|---|---|
| 23. γράψαντες | διὰ | χειρὸς | αὐτῶν | ⸂a τάδε ⸃ | Οἱ |
| *grapsantes* | *dia* | *cheiros* | *autōn* | *tade* | *Hoi* |
| having written | by | hand | their | thus: | The |

| 646.4 noun nom pl masc | 2504.1 conj | 3450.7 art nom pl masc | 4104.5 adj comp nom pl masc | 2504.1 conj | 3450.7 art nom pl masc |
|---|---|---|---|---|---|
| ἀπόστολοι | καὶ | οἱ | πρεσβύτεροι | ⸂b καὶ | οἱ ⸃ |
| *apostoloi* | *kai* | *hoi* | *presbuteroi* | *kai* | *hoi* |
| apostles | and | the | elders | and | the |

| 79.6 noun nom pl masc | 3450.4 art dat pl | 2567.3 prep | 3450.12 art acc sing fem | 487.3 name acc fem | 2504.1 conj | 4799.2 name acc fem |
|---|---|---|---|---|---|---|
| ἀδελφοὶ, | τοῖς | κατὰ | τὴν | Ἀντιόχειαν | καὶ | Συρίαν |
| *adelphoi* | *tois* | *kata* | *tēn* | *Antiocheian* | *kai* | *Surian* |
| brothers, | to the | in | | Antioch | and | Syria |

| 2504.1 conj | 2763.2 name acc fem | 79.8 noun dat pl masc | 3450.4 art dat pl | 1523.1 prep gen | 1477.5 noun gen pl neu |
|---|---|---|---|---|---|
| καὶ | Κιλικίαν | ἀδελφοῖς | τοῖς | ἐξ | ἐθνῶν, |
| *kai* | *Kilikian* | *adelphois* | *tois* | *ex* | *ethnōn* |
| and | Cilicia, | brothers | the | from among | Gentiles, |

| 5299.11 verb inf pres act | 1879.1 conj | 189.22 verb 1pl indic aor act | 3617.1 conj | 4948.7 indef-pron nom pl masc |
|---|---|---|---|---|
| χαίρειν. | 24. Ἐπειδὴ | ἠκούσαμεν | ὅτι | τινὲς |
| *chairein* | *Epeidē* | *ēkousamen* | *hoti* | *tines* |
| to greet. | Since | we heard | that | certain |

24.a.**Txt:** p33,p74 01ℵ-corr,02A,04C,05D 08E,025P,etc.byz.it.sa. bo.Tisc,Sod **Var:** 01ℵ-org,03B We/Ho,Weis,UBS/*

| 1523.1 prep gen | 2231.2 prs-pron gen 1pl | 1814.15 verb nom pl masc part aor act | 4866.4 verb 3pl indic aor act | 5050.4 prs-pron acc 2pl |
|---|---|---|---|---|
| ἐξ | ἡμῶν | ⸂a ἐξελθόντες ⸃ | ἐτάραξαν | ὑμᾶς |
| *ex* | *hēmōn* | *exelthontes* | *etaraxan* | *humas* |
| from among | us | having gone out | troubled | you |

| 3030.7 noun dat pl masc | 382.1 verb nom pl masc part pres act | 3450.15 art acc pl fem | 5425.8 noun acc pl fem | 5050.2 prs-pron gen 2pl |
|---|---|---|---|---|
| λόγοις | ἀνασκευάζοντες | τὰς | ψυχὰς | ὑμῶν, |
| *logois* | *anaskeuazontes* | *tas* | *psuchas* | *humōn* |
| by words, | upsetting | the | souls | your, |

24.b.**Txt:** 04C,08E,020L 025P,044,byz. **Var:** p33,p45,p74,01ℵ 02A,03B,05D,33,sa. Lach,Treg,Alf,Tisc We/Ho,Weis,Sod UBS/*

| 2978.16 verb nom pl masc part pres act | 3919.9 verb inf pres mid | 2504.1 conj | 4931.11 verb inf pres act | 3450.6 art acc sing masc |
|---|---|---|---|---|
| ⸂b λέγοντες | περιτέμνεσθαι | καὶ | τηρεῖν | τὸν |
| *legontes* | *peritemnesthai* | *kai* | *tērein* | *ton* |
| saying | to be circumcised | and | to keep | the |

| 3414.4 noun acc sing masc | 3614.4 rel-pron dat pl | 3620.3 partic | 1285.3 verb 1pl indic aor mid | 1374.16 verb 3sing indic aor act |
|---|---|---|---|---|
| νόμον, ⸃ | οἷς | οὐ | διεστειλάμεθα· | 25. ἔδοξεν |
| *nomon* | *hois* | *ou* | *diesteilametha* | *edoxen* |
| law; | to whom | not | we gave command; | it seemed |

| 2231.3 prs-pron dat 1pl | 1090.52 verb dat pl part aor mid | 3524.1 adv | 1573.7 verb acc pl masc part aor mid |
|---|---|---|---|
| ἡμῖν | γενομένοις | ὁμοθυμαδὸν, | ⸀ ἐκλεξαμένους |
| *hēmin* | *genomenois* | *homothumadon* | *eklexamenous* |
| to us | having come | with one accord, | having chosen |

Silas is better known. He was a Roman citizen (16:37-39), and since Paul always referred to him as Silvanus in his epistles, it may be that Silvanus was his Roman *cognomen* or surname, while Silas (a Greek form of the Aramaic *sheila* or Saul) was chosen because of its similar sound and was preferred by his Jerusalem friends, as well as by Luke. Beginning with Paul's second missionary journey, Silas became an important and highly esteemed fellow worker with Paul in the spread of the gospel. Later he worked with Peter and carried Peter's first epistle to the churches of Asia Minor.

**15:23.** The Jerusalem assembly also used Silas and Judas Barsabas as scribes to write the letter that was to be sent by them. This indicates they were well-educated and knew Greek very well. The letter would undoubtedly be written in Greek, since the Gentiles in Antioch, Syria, and Cilicia were Greek-speaking. The people in the other churches of South Galatia founded on the first missionary journey would also speak Greek, at least as a second language.

The letter began with a polite greeting from the apostles, elders and brothers (in the Jerusalem church) to the Gentiles in the churches in Asia Minor. The word for "greetings" actually means "to be glad" or "to rejoice," but it became a common form of greeting among the Greeks.

The letter was addressed specifically to "brothers, the ones out of the nations." That is, they recognized these Gentiles as brothers who were fellow members of the family of God. They had come out from among the nations. Their origin was Gentile, but they were no longer strangers and foreigners to the promises of God, they were brothers. Paul enlarged on this thought in Ephesians 2:11-22. These Gentiles were once outside of Christ, aliens separated from the commonwealth of Israel, strangers cut off from the covenants of promise, having no hope, and without God in the world. But now, through the blood of Christ, they were no longer foreigners but fellow citizens with the saints.

**15:24.** The letter first drew attention to the fact that they had heard the report that some who went out from the Jerusalem assembly had troubled (disturbed, unsettled, agitated, thrown into confusion) these Gentile believers in Antioch and other places "with words," that is, with their message, implying a multitude of arguments. The result was a tearing down, an upsetting, an unsettling of their souls. This implies their words did not come from the Holy Spirit, no matter what these men from Jerusalem might have said.

**15:25.** In order to make their decision known, it seemed best to the Jerusalem believers and their leaders to send chosen (choice) men to the Gentile believers to accompany Barnabas and Paul. This implies the leaders thought their decision and this letter were extremely important, so they sent choice men, excellent men, chosen

**chief men among the brethren:** . . . who were leading men among the Brethren, *TCNT* . . . prominent members of the brotherhood, *Moffatt* . . . leaders among the Christians, *Berkeley* . . . These men were respected, *SEB.*

**23. And they wrote letters by them after this manner:** . . . with the following letter, *RSV* . . . They were bearers of the following letter, *TCNT* . . . They conveyed, *Moffatt.*

**The apostles and elders and brethren send greeting unto the brethren which are of the Gentiles in Antioch and Syria and Cilicia:** . . . to the brothers from among the heathen, *Williams* . . . to their non-Jewish fellow Christians, *Beck* . . . the Brethren of heathen birth, *TCNT* . . . to the Gentile Brotherhood, *Montgomery.*

**24. Forasmuch as we have heard:** As we have been informed, *Weymouth* . . . Having learned, *Moffatt.*

**that certain which went out from us:** . . . that some of our number, *TCNT* . . . quite unauthorized by us, *Moffatt.*

**have troubled you with words:** . . . they continue to upset you, *Beck* . . . had upset you by their orations, *TCNT* . . . have disturbed you by their teaching, *Weymouth* . . . have caused you trouble by their claims, *Norlie* . . . perplexed and disturbed you, *Wuest.*

**subverting your souls:** . . . dismantling your souls, *Rotherham* . . . and unsettled your minds, *TCNT* . . . continuing to unsettle your minds, *Williams* . . . and they continue to upset you, *Beck.*

**saying, Ye must be circumcised, and keep the law:**

**to whom we gave no such commandment:** . . . although we gave them no instructions, *RSV* . . . without instructions from us, *TCNT.*

**25. It seemed good unto us, being assembled with one accord:** . . . we met and decided, *TCNT* . . . being unanimously assembled, *Rotherham* . . . we have unanimously decided, *Weymouth* . . . we have passed a unanimous resolution, *Williams* . . . being of one opinion, *Wesley.*

25.a.**Var:** p45,02A,03B 020L,044,Lach,Treg Word,We/Ho

| **1573.9** verb dat pl masc part aor mid | **433.9** noun acc pl masc | **3854.17** verb inf aor act | **4242.1** prep | **5050.4** prs-pron acc 2pl | **4713.1** prep |
|---|---|---|---|---|---|
| [a ἐκλεξαμένοις ] | ἄνδρας | πέμψαι | πρὸς | ὑμᾶς, | σὺν |
| *eklexamenois* | *andras* | *pempsai* | *pros* | *humas* | *sun* |
| [ idem ] | men | to send | to | you, | with |

| **3450.4** art dat pl | **27.7** adj dat pl | **2231.2** prs-pron gen 1pl | **915.3** name dat masc | **2504.1** conj | **3834.3** name dat masc |
|---|---|---|---|---|---|
| τοῖς | ἀγαπητοῖς | ἡμῶν | Βαρναβᾷ | καὶ | Παύλῳ, |
| *tois* | *agapētois* | *hēmōn* | *Barnaba* | *kai* | *Paulō* |
| the | beloved | our | Barnabas | and | Paul, |

| **442.8** noun dat pl masc | **3722.21** verb dat pl masc part perf act | **3450.15** art acc pl fem | **5425.8** noun acc pl fem | **840.1** prs-pron gen pl |
|---|---|---|---|---|
| **26.** ἀνθρώποις | παραδεδωκόσιν | τὰς | ψυχὰς | αὐτῶν |
| *anthrōpois* | *paradedōkosin* | *tas* | *psuchas* | *autōn* |
| men | having given up | the | lives | their |

| **5065.1** prep | **3450.2** art gen sing | **3549.3** noun gen sing neu | **3450.2** art gen sing | **2935.2** noun gen sing masc | **2231.2** prs-pron gen 1pl | **2400.2** name masc |
|---|---|---|---|---|---|---|
| ὑπὲρ | τοῦ | ὀνόματος | τοῦ | κυρίου | ἡμῶν | Ἰησοῦ |
| *huper* | *tou* | *onomatos* | *tou* | *kuriou* | *hēmōn* | *Iēsou* |
| for | the | name | of the | Lord | our | Jesus |

| **5382.2** name gen masc | **643.18** verb 1pl indic perf act | **3631.1** partic | **2430.4** name acc masc | **2504.1** conj |
|---|---|---|---|---|
| Χριστοῦ. | **27.** ἀπεστάλκαμεν | οὖν | Ἰούδαν | καὶ |
| *Christou* | *apestalkamen* | *oun* | *Ioudan* | *kai* |
| Christ. | We have sent | therefore | Judas | and |

| **4464.3** name acc masc | **2504.1** conj | **840.8** prs-pron acc pl masc | **1217.2** prep | **3030.2** noun gen sing masc | **514.5** verb acc pl masc part pres act |
|---|---|---|---|---|---|
| Σίλαν, | καὶ | αὐτοὺς | διὰ | λόγου | ἀπαγγέλλοντας |
| *Silan* | *kai* | *autous* | *dia* | *logou* | *apangellontas* |
| Silas, | also | themselves | by | word | telling |

| **3450.17** art pl neu | **840.16** prs-pron pl neu | **1374.16** verb 3sing indic aor act | **1056.1** conj | **3450.3** art dat sing | **39.3** adj dat sing |
|---|---|---|---|---|---|
| τὰ | αὐτά. | **28.** ἔδοξεν | γὰρ | ‛ τῷ | ἁγίῳ |
| *ta* | *auta* | *edoxen* | *gar* | *tō* | *hagiō* |
| the | same things. | It seemed | for | to the | Holy |

28.a.**Txt:** 04C,05D,08E 020L,025P,byz.
**Var:** 01ℵ,02A,03B,33 Treg,Word,Tisc,We/Ho Weis,Sod,UBS/☆

| **4011.3** noun dat sing neu | **3450.3** art dat sing | **4011.3** noun dat sing neu | **3450.3** art dat sing | **39.3** adj dat sing | **2504.1** conj |
|---|---|---|---|---|---|
| πνεύματι | [a☆ τῷ | πνεύματι | τῷ | ἁγίῳ ] | καὶ |
| *pneumati* | *tō* | *pneumati* | *tō* | *hagiō* | *kai* |
| Spirit | [ to the | Spirit | the | Holy ] | and |

| **2231.3** prs-pron dat 1pl | **3235.6** num card neu | **3979.9** adj comp sing neu | **1991.19** verb inf pres mid | **5050.3** prs-pron dat 2pl | **916.2** noun sing neu |
|---|---|---|---|---|---|
| ἡμῖν, | μηδὲν | πλέον | ἐπιτίθεσθαι | ὑμῖν | βάρος |
| *hēmin* | *mēden* | *pleon* | *epititesthai* | *humin* | *baros* |
| to us, | no | further | to be laid | upon you | burden |

| **3993.1** adv | **3450.1** art gen pl | **1861.1** adv | **3642.2** dem-pron gen pl | **3642.2** dem-pron gen pl | **3450.1** art gen pl |
|---|---|---|---|---|---|
| πλὴν | ‛ τῶν | ἐπάναγκες | τούτων, | [☆ τούτων | τῶν |
| *plēn* | *tōn* | *epanankes* | *toutōn* | *toutōn* | *tōn* |
| than | the | necessary | these: | [ these | of the |

| **1861.1** adv | **563.9** verb inf pres mid | **1484.2** adj gen pl neu |
|---|---|---|
| ἐπάναγκες, ] | **29.** ἀπέχεσθαι | εἰδωλοθύτων |
| *epanankes* | *apechesthai* | *eidōlothutōn* |
| necessary, ] | to abstain | from things sacrificed to idols, |

because they were the best fitted to explain the decision and encourage the Gentile believers by it.

They were also sending back Barnabas and Paul with the same message. All four would confirm the fact that the decision was made with the assembled believers and their leaders in one accord, with one mind and one purpose, unanimously.

Their words "our beloved Barnabas and Paul" emphasized that the Jerusalem apostles, elders, and all the believers counted Barnabas and Paul as dear friends, worthy of love.

This was important because Paul's epistles indicate the Judaizers were not satisfied to upset the Gentiles by spreading their legalistic doctrines, they also attacked Paul personally.

**15:26.** The letter further recommended Barnabas and Paul as men who had hazarded their lives for the name of our Lord Jesus Christ. The Greek is literally, "handed over their souls for the sake of the name." This must mean they had risked their lives for His name. They recognized that when individuals believe on the name of Jesus, they enter by faith into all He is to the believers. Thus believers are saved by His name—saved by what He is (4:12). Followers of Jesus have life through His name—through what He is to them and in them (John 20:31).

**15:27.** Judas and Silas would personally confirm the contents of the letter to the churches to whom it was addressed. They would also confirm by word of mouth the love and respect the apostles, elders, and the whole Jerusalem church had for Paul and Barnabas. Thus, Paul and Barnabas would not have to defend themselves or the letter.

**15:28.** Only the necessary things which seemed good to the Holy Spirit and to the Jerusalem believers would be asked of them. This shows that the whole assembly in Jerusalem accepted the words of James as a word of wisdom from the Holy Spirit.

All through the Book of Acts the Holy Spirit is shown breaking down barriers—language barriers, cultural barriers, national barriers. Unfortunately, there are always some people who want to build the barriers back up again, even in the name of religion, using Bible passages and twisting them to suit their prejudices. But the Holy Spirit will cause the love of Christ to constrain believers from prejudice and make them channels of His love.

**15:29.** The letter repeated the four things felt to be necessary for fellowship between Jewish and Gentile believers. Since it was dealing largely with table fellowship, abstinence from the polluted things of idolatry meant abstaining from meats offered to idols.

**to send chosen men unto you:** . . . resolved to select, *Noli* . . . to send you outstanding men, *Berkeley* . . . and send them to you, *Williams C.K.*

**with our beloved Barnabas and Paul:** . . . along with, *Williams C.K.* . . . with our dear brothers, *TCNT* . . . in company with our beloved friends, *Weymouth.*

**26. Men that have hazarded their lives:** . . . endangered, *Weymouth* . . . risked, *Moffatt* . . . who personally have jeopardized their lives, *Berkeley* . . . who have sacrificed themselves, *TCNT* . . . lives have been in danger for, *NLT.*

**for the name of our Lord Jesus Christ:** . . . in behalf of the name of, *Rotherham* . . . for the sake of, *Weymouth, Williams C.K.*

**27. We have sent therefore Judas and Silas:** So we are dispatching, *Berkeley* . . . We therefore send, *Williams C.K.*

**who shall also tell you the same things by mouth:** . . . who also themselves by word of mouth can tell you the same things, *Rotherham* . . . who will personally announce these things, *Berkeley* . . . what we are now writing, *TCNT* . . . by word of mouth, *Goodspeed* . . . who will confirm our message, *Noli.*

**28. For it seemed good to the Holy Ghost, and to us:** We have, therefore, decided, under the guidance of the Holy Spirit, *TCNT* . . . The Holy Spirit and we have decided, *Williams C.K.*

**to lay upon you no greater burden than these necessary things:** . . . thinks you should have no more burdens, *SEB* . . . these necessary conditions, *TCNT* . . . no burden heavier than these necessary requirements, *Weymouth* . . . that you should not have a heavy load to carry, *NCV* . . . not to burden you more than is necessary, *Beck* . . . any additional burden, *Murdock* . . . except these essentials, *Berkeley* . . . to put no further load on you than these necessary things, *Williams C.K.* . . . only the following indispensable burdens, *Noli.*

**29. That ye abstain from meats offered to idols:** You are to avoid, *Norlie* . . . Keep away from, *Beck* . . . from idol-sacrifices, *Worrell.*

## Acts 15:30

29.a.**Txt:** p74,01ℵ-corr 02A-corr,08E,020L 025P,044,33,byz.it. **Var:** 01ℵ-org,02A-org 03B,04C,sa.bo.Lach Treg,Alf,Tisc,We/Ho Weis,Sod,UBS/☆

| **2504.1** conj | **129.2** noun gen sing neu | **2504.1** conj | **4016.1** adj gen sing neu | **4016.3** adj gen pl neu |
|---|---|---|---|---|
| καὶ | αἵματος | καὶ | ‘ πνικτοῦ | [a☆ πνικτῶν ] |
| *kai* | *haimatos* | *kai* | *pniktou* | *pniktōn* |
| and | from blood | and | from what is strangled, | [ idem ] |

| **2504.1** conj | **4061.1** noun fem | **1523.1** prep gen | **3614.1** rel-pron gen pl | **1295.1** verb nom pl masc part pres act |
|---|---|---|---|---|
| καὶ | πορνείας· | ἐξ | ὧν | διατηροῦντες |
| *kai* | *porneias* | *ex* | *hōn* | *diatērountes* |
| and | from fornication; | from | which | keeping |

| **1431.8** prs-pron acc pl masc | **2074.1** adv | **4097.25** verb 2pl indic fut act | **4374.1** verb 2pl impr perf mid | **3450.7** art nom pl masc | **3173.1** conj |
|---|---|---|---|---|---|
| ἑαυτοὺς, | εὖ | πράξετε· | Ἔρρωσθε. | **30.** Οἱ | μὲν |
| *heautous* | *eu* | *praxete* | *Errhōsthe* | *Hoi* | *men* |
| yourselves, | well | you will do. | Farewell. | The | |

30.a.**Txt:** 08E,020L 025P,byz. **Var:** 01ℵ,02A,03B,04C 05D,Lach,Treg,Alf,Tisc We/Ho,Weis,Sod UBS/☆

| **3631.1** partic | **624.17** verb nom pl masc part aor pass | **2048.1** verb indic aor act | **2687.3** verb 3pl indic aor act | **1519.1** prep |
|---|---|---|---|---|
| οὖν | ἀπολυθέντες | ‘ ἦλθον | [a☆ κατῆλθον ] | εἰς |
| *oun* | *apoluthentes* | *ēlthon* | *katēlthon* | *eis* |
| therefore, | having been let go | went | [ went down ] | to |

| **487.3** name acc fem | **2504.1** conj | **4714.12** verb nom pl masc part aor act | **3450.16** art sing neu | **3988.1** noun sing neu |
|---|---|---|---|---|
| Ἀντιόχειαν· | καὶ | συναγαγόντες | τὸ | πλῆθος |
| *Antiocheian* | *kai* | *sunagagontes* | *to* | *plēthos* |
| Antioch, | and | having gathered | the | multitude |

| **1914.1** verb 3pl indic aor act | **3450.12** art acc sing fem | **1976.4** noun acc sing fem | **312.10** verb nom pl masc part aor act | **1156.2** conj |
|---|---|---|---|---|
| ἐπέδωκαν | τὴν | ἐπιστολήν. | **31.** ἀναγνόντες | δὲ |
| *epedōkan* | *tēn* | *epistolēn* | *anagnontes* | *de* |
| delivered | the | epistle. | Having read | and |

| **5299.19** verb 3pl indic aor pass | **1894.3** prep | **3450.11** art dat sing fem | **3735.3** noun dat sing fem | **2430.1** name nom masc | **4885.1** conj |
|---|---|---|---|---|---|
| ἐχάρησαν | ἐπὶ | τῇ | παρακλήσει. | **32.** Ἰούδας | τε |
| *echarēsan* | *epi* | *tē* | *paraklēsei* | *Ioudas* | *te* |
| they rejoiced | at | the | consolation. | Judas | and |

| **2504.1** conj | **4464.1** name nom masc | **2504.1** conj | **840.7** prs-pron nom pl masc | **4254.4** noun nom pl masc | **1498.23** verb nom pl masc part pres act |
|---|---|---|---|---|---|
| καὶ | Σίλας, | καὶ | αὐτοὶ | προφῆται | ὄντες, |
| *kai* | *Silas* | *kai* | *autoi* | *prophētai* | *ontes* |
| also | Silas, | also | themselves | prophets | being, |

| **1217.2** prep | **3030.2** noun gen sing masc | **4044.2** adj gen sing | **3731.14** verb 3pl indic aor act | **3450.8** art acc pl masc |
|---|---|---|---|---|
| διὰ | λόγου | πολλοῦ | παρεκάλεσαν | τοὺς |
| *dia* | *logou* | *pollou* | *parekalesan* | *tous* |
| by | discourse | much | encouraged | the |

| **79.9** noun acc pl masc | **2504.1** conj | **1975.3** verb 3pl indic aor act | **4020.39** verb nom pl masc part aor act | **1156.2** conj |
|---|---|---|---|---|
| ἀδελφοὺς, | καὶ | ἐπεστήριξαν. | **33.** Ποιήσαντες | δὲ |
| *adelphous* | *kai* | *epestērixan* | *Poiēsantes* | *de* |
| brothers, | and | established. | Having continued | and |

| **5385.4** noun acc sing masc | **624.15** verb 3pl indic aor pass | **3196.2** prep | **1503.2** noun gen sing fem | **570.3** prep | **3450.1** art gen pl |
|---|---|---|---|---|---|
| χρόνον | ἀπελύθησαν | μετ' | εἰρήνης | ἀπὸ | τῶν |
| *chronon* | *apeluthēsan* | *met'* | *eirēnēs* | *apo* | *tōn* |
| a time | they were let go | in | peace | from | the |

When animals were sacrificed in heathen temples, part of the meat would be taken to the town market and sold. Paul later recognized that the idols were nothing, so meat offered to them was the same as any other meat. However, he said love would not let him eat such meat if it would offend a weaker brother. In this case, even though the Jewish believers were not weaker, it would still offend them, so love would not allow Gentile believers to serve such meat to them.

"Fare ye well," literally, "Make yourselves strong," had become a common phrase used at the end of a letter to mean farewell or good-bye.

**15:30.** The Jerusalem believers then dismissed (set free, released and sent away) Paul and his company accompanied by much prayer and expressions of their love.

When Paul and Barnabas arrived in Antioch, they gathered the whole crowd of the believers together. Then Paul handed over the letter.

**15:31.** The Bible does not say who read the letter to the assembled crowd, but it was probably given to one of their own elected elders.

When the letter was read, the believers rejoiced over the consolation, or comfort, it gave them. They were also glad because of the exhortation and requests contained in the letter. Now they could forget about all the arguments of the Judaizers. Now it was clear they did not need to follow the externals of the law of Moses. They were free from all that legalistic bondage. In return for this freedom, they were only too glad to accept the provisions for fellowship and the exhortations to high moral standards.

**15:32.** Judas and Silas did more than confirm the facts of the letter. By the Holy Spirit they exhorted the brethren. They confirmed (upheld and supported) them. They gave them solid encouragement to forget the arguments of the Judaizers and to maintain their faith in Christ and in the gospel they had received of salvation by grace through faith alone (apart from the works of the Law).

Prophets are also revival men. Because the church at Antioch was upset and thrown into confusion by the Judaizers, the fires of their zeal and the fires of their worship were burning low. Judas and Silas, as prophets, restored, revived, and brought them back into the place where they could serve the Lord with gladness (Psalm 100:2,5).

**15:33.** After a time the brethren (the believers at Antioch) released Judas and Silas with a farewell blessing of peace and well

**and from blood:** . . . the eating of blood, *Norlie.*

**and from things strangled:** . . . the meat of animals that have been strangled, *Williams.*

**and from fornication:** . . . sex impurity, *Norlie* . . . sexual sin, *Beck.*

**from which if ye keep yourselves:** If you guard yourselves against such things, *TCNT.*

**ye shall do well:** . . . you shall prosper, *Rotherham* . . . you will make good progress, *Phillips* . . . you will do right, *Williams C.K.*

**Fare ye well:** May you be happy, *BB* . . . be strong, *Young* . . . Farewell, *Williams C.K.*

**30. So when they were dismissed:** So when they were sent off, *RSV* . . . So the bearers of this letter were sent on their way, *TCNT* . . . were dispatched, *Moffatt.*

**they came to Antioch:** . . . arrived in Antioch, *Berkeley.*

**and when they had gathered the multitude together:** There they called a meeting of all the Brethren, *TCNT* . . . where they called together the whole assembly, *Weymouth.*

**they delivered the epistle:** . . . they handed them the letter, *Moffatt.*

**31. Which when they had read, they rejoiced for the consolation:** The reading of which caused great rejoicing, *TCNT* . . . were delighted with the comfort it brought them, *Weymouth* . . . When the letter was read it gave them both comfort and joy, *Norlie.*

**32. And Judas and Silas, being prophets also themselves:** . . . they also were prophets, *Murdock.*

**exhorted the brethren with many words, and confirmed them:** . . . with much discourse consoled and confirmed the brethren, *Rotherham* . . . further encouraged the Brethren by many an address, *TCNT* . . . a long and encouraging talk, *Weymouth.*

**33. And after they had tarried there a space:** And having remained a while, *HBIE* . . . And when they had been there for some time, *BB.*

## Acts 15:34

33.a.**Txt:** 08E,020L 025P,byz.
**Var:** 01ℵ,02A,03B,04C 05D,sa.bo.Gries,Lach Treg,Alf,Word,Tisc We/Ho,Weis,Sod UBS/☆

34.a.**Txt:** 04C,05D,33 1739,sa.Steph
**Var:** p74,01ℵ,02A,03B 08E,020L,025P,044 Lach,Treg,Alf,Tisc We/Ho,Weis,Sod UBS/☆

| **79.7** noun gen pl masc | **4242.1** prep | **3450.8** art acc pl masc | **646.7** noun acc pl masc | **3450.8** art acc pl masc |
|---|---|---|---|---|
| ἀδελφῶν | πρὸς | ⸂ τοὺς | ἀποστόλους. | [a☆ τοὺς |
| *adelphōn* | *pros* | *tous* | *apostolous* | *tous* |
| brothers | to | the | apostles; | [the |

| **643.34** verb acc pl masc part aor act | **840.8** prs-pron acc pl masc | | **1374.16** verb 3sing indic aor act | **1156.2** conj | **3450.3** art dat sing |
|---|---|---|---|---|---|
| ἀποστείλαντας | αὐτούς. ] | **34.** ⸂a | ἔδοξεν | δὲ | τῷ |
| *aposteilantas* | *autous* | | *edoxen* | *de* | *tō* |
| having sent | them. ] | | it seemed | but | to |

| **4464.2** name dat masc | **1946.9** verb inf aor act | **841.1** adv | **3834.1** name nom masc | **1156.2** conj | **2504.1** conj |
|---|---|---|---|---|---|
| Σίλᾳ | ἐπιμεῖναι | αὐτοῦ. ⸃ | **35.** Παῦλος | δὲ | καὶ |
| *Sila* | *epimeinai* | *autou* | *Paulos* | *de* | *kai* |
| Silas | to remain | there. | Paul | and | and |

| **915.1** name nom masc | **1298.6** verb 3pl indic imperf act | **1706.1** prep | **487.2** name dat fem | **1315.9** verb nom pl masc part pres act |
|---|---|---|---|---|
| Βαρνάβᾶς | διέτριβον | ἐν | Ἀντιοχείᾳ, | διδάσκοντες |
| *Barnabas* | *dietribon* | *en* | *Antiocheia* | *didaskontes* |
| Barnabas | were staying | in | Antioch, | teaching |

| **2504.1** conj | **2076.12** verb nom pl masc part pres mid | **3196.3** prep | **2504.1** conj | **2066.3** adj gen pl | **4044.1** adj gen pl |
|---|---|---|---|---|---|
| καὶ | εὐαγγελιζόμενοι | μετὰ | καὶ | ἑτέρων | πολλῶν, |
| *kai* | *euangelizomenoi* | *meta* | *kai* | *heterōn* | *pollōn* |
| and | announcing the good news | with | also | others | many |

| **3450.6** art acc sing masc | **3030.4** noun acc sing masc | **3450.2** art gen sing | **2935.2** noun gen sing masc | **3196.3** prep | **1156.2** conj |
|---|---|---|---|---|---|
| τὸν | λόγον | τοῦ | κυρίου. | **36.** Μετὰ | δέ |
| *ton* | *logon* | *tou* | *kuriou* | *Meta* | *de* |
| the | word | of the | Lord. | After | but |

| **4948.9** indef-pron acc pl masc | **2232.1** noun fem | **1500.5** verb 3sing indic aor act | **3834.1** name nom masc | **4242.1** prep | **915.4** name acc masc |
|---|---|---|---|---|---|
| τινας | ἡμέρας | εἶπεν | ⸂ Παῦλος | πρὸς | Βαρνάβᾶν, |
| *tinas* | *hēmeras* | *eipen* | *Paulos* | *pros* | *Barnaban* |
| certain | days | said | Paul | to | Barnabas, |

| **4242.1** prep | **915.4** name acc masc | **3834.1** name nom masc | **1978.12** verb nom pl masc part aor act | **1205.1** partic |
|---|---|---|---|---|
| [☆ πρὸς | Βαρναβᾶν | Παῦλος, ] | Ἐπιστρέψαντες | δὴ |
| *pros* | *Barnaban* | *Paulos* | *Epistrepsantes* | *dē* |
| [to | Barnabas | Paul, ] | Having turned back | indeed |

36.a.**Txt:** 020L,025P,byz.
**Var:** 01ℵ,02A,03B,04C 05D,08E,sa.bo.Gries Lach,Treg,Alf,Word Tisc,We/Ho,Weis,Sod UBS/☆

| **1964.5** verb 1pl subj aor mid | **3450.8** art acc pl masc | **79.9** noun acc pl masc | **2231.2** prs-pron gen 1pl | **2567.3** prep |
|---|---|---|---|---|
| ἐπισκεψώμεθα | τοὺς | ἀδελφοὺς | ⸂a ἡμῶν ⸃ | κατὰ |
| *episkepsōmetha* | *tous* | *adelphous* | *hēmōn* | *kata* |
| let us look after | the | brothers | our | according to |

| **3820.12** adj acc sing fem | **4032.4** noun acc sing fem | **4032.4** noun acc sing fem | **3820.12** adj acc sing fem | **1706.1** prep | **3614.14** rel-pron dat pl fem |
|---|---|---|---|---|---|
| ⸂ πᾶσαν | πόλιν | [☆ πόλιν | πᾶσαν ] | ἐν | αἷς |
| *pasan* | *polin* | *polin* | *pasan* | *en* | *hais* |
| every | city | [city | every ] | in | which |

| **2576.7** verb 1pl indic aor act | **3450.6** art acc sing masc | **3030.4** noun acc sing masc | **3450.2** art gen sing | **2935.2** noun gen sing masc |
|---|---|---|---|---|
| κατηγγείλαμεν | τὸν | λόγον | τοῦ | κυρίου, |
| *katēngeilamen* | *ton* | *logon* | *tou* | *kuriou* |
| we announced | the | word | of the | Lord, |

being to go back, not just to the apostles, but as the Greek shows, to the entire group of believers in Jerusalem.

**15:34.** Judas Barsabas decided to return, but Silas chose to remain. (Many modern versions omit verse 34 and suppose Silas went back to Jerusalem and returned to Antioch later.)

**15:35.** Paul and Barnabas also remained in Antioch to teach and preach the gospel. The church in Antioch was still growing, and God raised up many others (in addition to the prophets and teachers of 13:1) to teach and spread the good news of the word (Greek *logos*) of the Lord. The first teachers and preachers in Antioch were believers who came from outside. Most of these new teachers and evangelists were probably from the local assembly. They too were entering into the work of ministry for the edifying or building up of the body of Christ. God's plan is that the Body should be edified most of all spiritually (Ephesians 4:12,15,16). This is the reason Christ gave apostles, prophets, evangelists, and pastor-teachers to the Church. It was not for them to do the work of ministry, but for them to train believers and bring them to maturity in the work of ministry. The results were that the gospel spread and many came to the Lord.

**15:36.** After certain days (probably a considerable time, even up to a year), Paul suggested to Barnabas that they visit the brethren in the churches established during the first missionary journey in Cyprus and South Galatia to see how they were and what their situation was. All these churches were founded in the midst of all kinds of opposition and persecution. Paul had been stoned at Lystra. He had suffered persecution in every place where he preached the gospel. Now Paul felt it was time to go back and see how these churches were doing.

Throughout his ministry, Paul maintained a love and concern that kept him praying for the churches and believers to whom he had ministered. He visited many of them again and again to give them further teaching and encouragement. He knew how important it is to follow up and disciple new believers. When he could not go to them, he wrote them letters. Even in the midst of his own persecution and perils, he did not forget them. Upon him daily was the care and concern for all the churches (2 Corinthians 11:28,29). So now he wanted to visit every city where they had founded churches.

The word "visit" is the same word used of God's gracious visitations where He brought salvation and blessing to His people. It is also often used of visiting the sick to pray for them and to help them. *Visit* has the connotation of caring and looking after. Paul had the heart of a good undershepherd who felt the responsibility of caring for the Lord's flock.



**they were let go in peace from the brethren unto the apostles:** . . . before the brethren let them go home, *Knox* . . . they were dismissed in peace, *ASV* . . . with kind farewells, *TCNT* . . . they were sent back by the brethren with (the greeting) Peace, *AmpB* . . . sent them back in peace to those who had commissioned them, *Phillips* . . . to those that had sent them, *Williams C.K.*

**34. Notwithstanding it pleased Silas to abide there still:** . . . to remain, *ET* . . . though Silas decided to stay there, *MLNT* . . . But Silas thought he should stay there, *NLT.*

**35. Paul also and Barnabas continued in Antioch:** . . . remained, *RSV* . . . tarried in, *Worrell* . . . kept on, *BB* . . . stayed on in, *Williams C.K.*

**teaching and preaching the word of the Lord:** . . . telling the joyful tidings, *Rotherham* . . . told the Good News of the Lord's Message, *TCNT.*

**with many others also:** . . . and joined with many others, *TNT* . . . with the help of many others, *NLT, TCNT* . . . with a number of others, *BB.*

**36. And some days after:** Some time after this, *TCNT* . . . On a later occasion, *JB* . . . A few days later, *SEB* . . . After some time, *Williams C.K.*

**Paul said unto Barnabas, Let us go again:** Let us return now, *ASV* . . . Let us go back, *TCNT* . . . retracing our steps, *Wuest* . . . We should go back, *Everyday* . . . Let us now pay a return, *Fenton.*

**and visit our brethren:** . . . and look in on the brothers, *Berkeley* . . . and see how the brethren fare in, *Swann.*

**in every city where we have preached the word of the Lord:** . . . to all those towns, *Everyday* . . . in which we proclaimed the message, *TNT* . . . have told the Lord's Message, *TCNT* . . . we proclaimed the word of the Lord, *Williams C.K.* . . . where we have given the word of God, *BB.*

**and see how they do:** . . . and see how they are prospering, *TCNT* . . . see how they are proceeding, *Fenton* . . . to see how they are getting along, *MLNT.*

37.a.**Txt:** 020L,025P,byz.
**Var:** 01א,02A,03B,04C
08E,Lach,Treg,Alf
Word,Tisc,We/Ho,Weis
Sod,UBS/☆

37.b.**Var:** 01א,03B
Gries,Lach,Treg,Alf
Tisc,We/Ho,Weis,Sod
UBS/☆

| 4316.1 adv | 2174.6 verb 3pl indic pres act | 915.1 name nom masc | 1156.2 conj | 1003.4 verb 3sing indic aor mid |
|---|---|---|---|---|
| πῶς | ἔχουσιν. | **37.** Βαρναβᾶς | δὲ | ʼ ἐβουλεύσατο |
| *pōs* | *echousin* | *Barnabas* | *de* | *ebouleusato* |
| how | they are. | Barnabas | and | intended |

| 1007.19 verb 3sing indic imperf mid | 4689.3 verb inf aor act | 2504.1 conj | 3450.6 art acc sing masc |
|---|---|---|---|
| [a☆ ἐβούλετο ] | συμπαραλαβεῖν | [b☆+ καὶ ] | τὸν |
| *ebouleto* | *sumparalabein* | *kai* | *ton* |
| [ was wishing ] | to take with | [ also ] | |

| 2464.4 name acc masc | 3450.6 art acc sing masc | 2535.29 verb sing part pres mid | 3111.3 name acc masc | 3834.1 name nom masc |
|---|---|---|---|---|
| Ἰωάννην | τὸν | καλούμενον | Μάρκον· | **38.** Παῦλος |
| *Iōannēn* | *ton* | *kaloumenon* | *Markon* | *Paulos* |
| John | the | being called | Mark; | Paul |

| 1156.2 conj | 511.4 verb 3sing indic imperf act | 3450.6 art acc sing masc | 861.8 verb acc sing masc part aor act | 570.2 prep |
|---|---|---|---|---|
| δὲ | ἠξίου | τὸν | ἀποστάντα | ἀπ' |
| *de* | *ēxiou* | *ton* | *apostanta* | *ap'* |
| but | was thinking it well | the | having withdrawn | from |

| 840.1 prs-pron gen pl | 570.3 prep | 3690.1 name gen fem | 2504.1 conj | 3231.1 partic | 4755.5 verb acc sing masc part aor act |
|---|---|---|---|---|---|
| αὐτῶν | ἀπὸ | Παμφυλίας, | καὶ | μὴ | συνελθόντα |
| *autōn* | *apo* | *Pamphulias* | *kai* | *mē* | *sunelthonta* |
| them | from | Pamphylia, | and | not | having gone with |

| 840.2 prs-pron dat pl | 1519.1 prep | 3450.16 art sing neu | 2024.1 noun sing neu | 3231.1 partic | 4689.3 verb inf aor act |
|---|---|---|---|---|---|
| αὐτοῖς | εἰς | τὸ | ἔργον, | μὴ | ʼ συμπαραλαβεῖν |
| *autois* | *eis* | *to* | *ergon* | *mē* | *sumparalabein* |
| them | to | the | work, | not | to take with |

38.a.**Txt:** 020L,025P,byz.
**Var:** 03B-corr,Lach,Treg
Sod,UBS/☆

| 4689.4 verb inf pres act | 3642.6 dem-pron acc sing masc | 1090.33 verb 3sing indic aor mid |
|---|---|---|
| [a☆ συμπαραλαμβάνειν ] | τοῦτον. | **39.** ἐγένετο |
| *sumparalambanein* | *touton* | *egeneto* |
| [ idem ] | this one. | There occurred |

39.a.**Txt:** 04C,08E,020L
025P,byz.
**Var:** 01א,02A,03B,05D
33,sa.bo.Lach,Treg,Alf
Tisc,We/Ho,Weis,Sod
UBS/☆

| 3631.1 partic | 1156.2 conj | 3810.1 noun nom sing masc | 5452.1 conj | 667.2 verb inf aor pass |
|---|---|---|---|---|
| ʼ οὖν | [a☆ δὲ ] | παροξυσμὸς, | ὥστε | ἀποχωρισθῆναι |
| *oun* | *de* | *paroxusmos* | *hōste* | *apochōristhēnai* |
| therefore | [ and ] | a sharp contention | so that | to be separated |

| 840.8 prs-pron acc pl masc | 570.2 prep | 238.1 prs-pron gen pl | 3450.6 art acc sing masc | 4885.1 conj | 915.4 name acc masc |
|---|---|---|---|---|---|
| αὐτοὺς | ἀπ' | ἀλλήλων, | τόν | τε | Βαρναβᾶν |
| *autous* | *ap'* | *allēlōn* | *ton* | *te* | *Barnaban* |
| them | from | one another, | | and | Barnabas |

| 3741.10 verb acc sing masc part aor act | 3450.6 art acc sing masc | 3111.3 name acc masc | 1589.2 verb inf aor act | 1519.1 prep |
|---|---|---|---|---|
| παραλαβόντα | τὸν | Μᾶρκον | ἐκπλεῦσαι | εἰς |
| *paralabonta* | *ton* | *Markon* | *ekpleusai* | *eis* |
| having taken | | Mark | to sail | to |

| 2927.2 name acc fem | 3834.1 name nom masc | 1156.2 conj | 1937.2 verb nom sing masc part aor mid | 4464.3 name acc masc |
|---|---|---|---|---|
| Κύπρον· | **40.** Παῦλος | δὲ | ἐπιλεξάμενος | Σίλαν |
| *Kupron* | *Paulos* | *de* | *epilexamenos* | *Silan* |
| Cyprus; | Paul | but | having chosen | Silas |

**15:37.** Barnabas felt the same desire to visit and help these churches. But he saw someone else he wanted to help. His cousin John, the one called Mark, wanted to go along, and Barnabas decided to (willed to, purposed to) take him along with him and Paul. Barnabas, as we have seen, was an encourager. Even though Mark had failed them before, Barnabas encouraged him to come.

**15:38.** Paul, however, did not agree. In fact, he kept insisting that they not take him along. He did not think Mark was worthy, fit, or suitable for this ministry. Mark had left them in the lurch at an important point where they needed him for the task of spreading the gospel in new and more difficult areas.

**15:39.** Barnabas, however, was determined to give his cousin another chance, so he refused to give in to Paul's demands that they leave Mark behind.

Both Paul and Barnabas felt so strongly about this that they felt temporary irritation, perhaps indignation. The Greek indicates sharp feelings between them. But they did not let this hinder the work of the Lord and they came up with a peaceful settlement. They decided it was best to separate and divide up the responsibility of visiting and encouraging the believers. Barnabas, therefore, took his cousin Mark and went to Cyprus to visit the churches founded on the first missionary journey. This was wise because Cyprus was familiar territory to Mark. He had been faithful there. It was better to take him back to the area where he had been a success rather than to the place where he had failed.

That Barnabas was right in wanting to give Mark a second chance is shown by the fact that Paul later asked Timothy to bring Mark with him because he was useful for ministry (2 Timothy 4:11). Mark was also with Peter on his vist to Babylon (1 Peter 5:13). Some writers take "Babylon" here to mean Rome. But Babylon had one of the largest Jewish communities outside Palestine. It should not be considered strange that Peter, the apostle to the circumcision, would go there.

**15:40.** Paul then chose Silas who was a mature believer, a prophet already used by the Spirit to challenge and encourage the churches. Silas would be an excellent helper to Paul in his efforts to encourage the churches in South Galatia which were in a most difficult environment.

Since Silas was also an outstanding member of the Jerusalem church, he would also be helpful in showing the Galatian churches the unity between Paul and the Jerusalem leaders. This would further put to rest the arguments of the Judaizers and would con-

**37. And Barnabas determined to take with them John:** . . . was bent on taking, *Weymouth* . . . But Barnabas persisted in wanting to take along John, *Williams* . . . had a desire to take with them, *BB*.

**whose surname was Mark:** . . . who was called Mark, *ASV* . . . whose other name was Mark, *TCNT* . . . named, *BB*.

**38. But Paul thought not good to take him with them:** . . . did not think it wise, *NIV* . . . didn't think it was such a good idea, *SEB* . . . counted him unworthy, *Concordant* . . . not fit to take along with them, *Williams* . . . was of the opinion that it was not right, *BB* . . . thought it unwise, *Montgomery* . . . it was not right to admit such a man to their company, *Knox*.

**who departed from them from Pamphylia:** . . . who withdrew, *ASV* . . . who had deserted, *TCNT* . . . the one who had quit them, *Berkeley* . . . one who had gone away from them, *BB*.

**and went not with them to the work:** . . . instead of accompanying them on active service, *Moffatt* . . . He had not helped them in the work, *NLT* . . . had not gone on with, *BB* . . . and had not continued with them, *Norlie*.

**39. And the contention was so sharp between them:** And there arose an angry feeling, *Rotherham* . . . So there arose a sharp altercation, *Weymouth* . . . so intense, *ET* . . . The disagreement was so sharp, *Williams* . . . In consequence of this strife, *Murdock* . . . After a violent quarrel, *JB* . . . so stirred, *Geneva* . . . had a serious argument, *NCV* . . . there was a sharp argument, *BB*.

**that they departed asunder one from the other:** . . . which resulted in their parting from one another, *Weymouth* . . . that they went their separate ways, *Phillips* . . . They separated and went different ways, *SEB* . . . so that they were parted from one another, *BB*.

**and so Barnabas took Mark, and sailed unto Cyprus:** . . . and went by ship to, *BB*.

**40. And Paul chose Silas and departed:** . . . chose Silas and went forth, *Swann* . . . set out, *Weymouth*.

## Acts 15:41

| 1814.3 verb 3sing indic aor act | 3722.35 verb nom sing masc part aor pass | 3450.11 art dat sing fem | 5322.3 noun dat sing fem | 3450.2 art gen sing |
|---|---|---|---|---|
| ἐξῆλθεν, | παραδοθεὶς | τῇ | χάριτι | ʻ τοῦ |
| *exēlthen* | *paradotheis* | *tē* | *chariti* | *tou* |
| went forth, | having been commended | to the | grace | |

40.a.**Txt:** 04C,08E,020L 025P,byz.bo.
**Var:** 01ℵ,02A,03B,05D sa.Lach,Treg,Alf,Word Tisc,We/Ho,Weis,Sod UBS/*

| 2296.2 noun gen sing masc | 3450.2 art gen sing | 2935.2 noun gen sing masc | 5097.3 prep | 3450.1 art gen pl | 79.7 noun gen pl masc |
|---|---|---|---|---|---|
| Θεοῦ | [a☆ τοῦ | κυρίου ] | ὑπὸ | τῶν | ἀδελφῶν. |
| *Theou* | *tou* | *kuriou* | *hupo* | *tōn* | *adelphōn* |
| of God | [ of the | Lord ] | by | the | brothers. |

| 1324.16 verb 3sing indic imperf mid | 1156.2 conj | 3450.12 art acc sing fem | 4799.2 name acc fem | 2504.1 conj |
|---|---|---|---|---|
| **41.** διήρχετο | δὲ | τὴν | Συρίαν | καὶ |
| *dierchetο* | *de* | *tēn* | *Surian* | *kai* |
| He was passing through | and | | Syria | and |

41.a.**Txt:** 01ℵ,02A,04C 08E,byz.
**Var:** 03B,05D,044,36 453

| 3450.12 art acc sing fem | 2763.2 name acc fem | 1975.1 verb nom sing masc part pres act | 3450.15 art acc pl fem | 1564.1 noun fem |
|---|---|---|---|---|
| [a+ τὴν ] | Κιλικίαν, | ἐπιστηρίζων | τὰς | ἐκκλησίας. |
| *tēn* | *Kilikian* | *epistērizōn* | *tas* | *ekklēsias* |
| | Cilicia, | establishing | the | assemblies. |

1.a.**Var:** 02A,03B,bo. Lach,Treg,We/Ho,Weis Sod,UBS/*

| 2628.1 verb 3sing indic aor act | 1156.2 conj | 2504.1 conj | 1519.1 prep | 1185.1 name acc fem |
|---|---|---|---|---|
| **16:1.** Κατήντησεν | δὲ | [a+ καὶ ] | εἰς | Δέρβην |
| *Katēntēsen* | *de* | *kai* | *eis* | *Derbēn* |
| He arrived | and | [ idem ] | at | Derbe |

1.b.**Var:** 01ℵ,02A,03B Lach,Treg,Tisc,We/Ho Weis,Sod,UBS/*

| 2504.1 conj | 1519.1 prep | 3054.1 name acc sing fem | 2504.1 conj | 1481.20 verb 2sing impr aor mid | 3073.1 noun nom sing masc |
|---|---|---|---|---|---|
| καὶ | [b☆+ εἰς ] | Λύστραν· | καὶ | ἰδοὺ, | μαθητής |
| *kai* | *eis* | *Lustran* | *kai* | *idou* | *mathētēs* |
| and | [ at ] | Lystra: | and | behold, | a disciple |

| 4948.3 indef-pron nom sing | 1498.34 verb sing indic imperf act | 1550.1 adv | 3549.4 noun dat sing neu | 4943.1 name nom masc | 5048.1 noun nom sing masc |
|---|---|---|---|---|---|
| τις | ἦν | ἐκεῖ, | ὀνόματι | Τιμόθεος, | υἱὸς |
| *tis* | *ēn* | *ekei* | *onomati* | *Timotheos* | *huios* |
| certain | was | there, | by name | Timothy, | son |

1.c.**Txt:** 020L,025P,byz. sa.
**Var:** 01ℵ,02A,03B,04C 05D,08E,bo.Gries,Lach Treg,Alf,Word,Tisc We/Ho,Weis,Sod UBS/*

| 1129.2 noun gen sing fem | 4948.1 indef-pron gen sing | 2424.2 name gen fem | 3964.11 adj gen sing fem | 3824.2 noun gen sing masc | 1156.2 conj |
|---|---|---|---|---|---|
| γυναικὸς | ʻc τινος ʼ | Ἰουδαίας | πιστῆς | πατρὸς | δὲ |
| *gunaikos* | *tinos* | *Ioudaias* | *pistēs* | *patros* | *de* |
| of a woman | certain | Jewish | believing | father | but |

| 1659.2 name gen sing masc | 3614.5 rel-pron nom sing masc | 3113.40 verb 3sing indic imperf pass | 5097.3 prep | 3450.1 art gen pl |
|---|---|---|---|---|
| Ἕλληνος· | **2.** ὃς | ἐμαρτυρεῖτο | ὑπὸ | τῶν |
| *Hellēnos* | *hos* | *emartureito* | *hupo* | *tōn* |
| a Greek, | who | was being borne witness to | by | the |

| 1706.1 prep | 3054.2 name dat pl neu | 2504.1 conj | 2406.2 name dat neu | 79.7 noun gen pl masc | 3642.6 dem-pron acc sing masc |
|---|---|---|---|---|---|
| ἐν | Λύστροις | καὶ | Ἰκονίῳ | ἀδελφῶν. | **3.** τοῦτον |
| *en* | *Lustrois* | *kai* | *Ikoniō* | *adelphōn* | *touton* |
| in | Lystra | and | Iconium | brothers. | This one |

| 2286.22 verb 3sing indic aor act | 3450.5 art nom sing masc | 3834.1 name nom masc | 4713.1 prep | 840.4 prs-pron dat sing | 1814.20 verb inf aor act |
|---|---|---|---|---|---|
| ἠθέλησεν | ὁ | Παῦλος | σὺν | αὐτῷ | ἐξελθεῖν, |
| *ēthelēsen* | *ho* | *Paulos* | *sun* | *autō* | *exelthein* |
| wished | | Paul | with | him | to go forth, |

firm the statements of Paul in Galatians 2:1-10 (where he said those leaders accepted his gospel as the same one they were teaching and gave him the right hand of fellowship). It was important also that Silas was an apostle in the sense that he not only heard Jesus teach and saw Him after His resurrection, but was directly commissioned by Him.

The brethren at Antioch then released Paul and Silas and committed them anew to the grace of God.

**15:41.** So Paul and Silas went on their way through Syria and Cilicia, confirming (strengthening) the churches, including the assembly in Paul's home city of Tarsus.

**16:1.** From Cilicia Paul and Silas went through the Taurus mountains by way of a famous pass called the Cilician Gates. Coming from this direction they would first arrive at Derbe, and then go to Lystra.

At Lystra Paul came across a young disciple named Timothy (short for *Timotheus*, "venerating, worshiping, honoring God"). His mother was a believing Jewess named Eunice. His grandmother Lois was also a godly believer. (See 2 Timothy 1:5; 3:14,15.) His father, however, was a Greek, probably a member of a prominent and wealthy family but apparently still unconverted.

Fortunately, the faith and training given Timothy by his mother and grandmother had more effect upon him than the unbelief of his father; they had trained him in the Scriptures from earliest childhood.

**16:2.** When Timothy accepted Christ, he made great progress in the Christian life. The believing brethren at Lystra and in the next town, Iconium, bore witness to him. This clearly means God had given Timothy a spiritual ministry in both cities, and his life and ministry was a blessing to the assemblies there.

It is probable that he was converted under Paul's ministry during one of Paul's previous visits to Lystra. However, when Paul later called him "my son," he was probably using the term *son* to mean "student," as well as younger fellow worker (1 Timothy 1:2,18; 2 Timothy 1:2). Prophetic utterances confirmed Timothy's mission, and the Holy Spirit gave him gifts as Paul and the elders gathered around and laid hands on him. (See 1 Timothy 1:18; 4:14; 2 Timothy 1:6.)

**16:3.** In view of this, Paul wanted to take Timothy with him for further training as well as to help in the spread of the gospel. But when Paul decided to do this, he did something very unusual. He circumcised Timothy. Paul made quite a point in Galatians 2:3-5

**being recommended by the brethren unto the grace of God:** . . . committed unto the favour of the Lord by the brethren, *Rotherham* . . . to the gracious care of the Lord, *TCNT* . . . his fellow Christians entrusting him to the Lord's love, *Beck* . . . having been entrusted by the brethren to the blessing of the Lord, *Fenton* . . . into the Lord's care, *Everyday* . . . asked for the Lord's favor to be on, *NLT* . . . commended...to the grace of God, *Williams C.K.* . . . with the blessing of the brothers, *BB.*

**41. And he went through Syria and Cilicia:** . . . passed, *Williams C.K.* . . . He accordingly travelled through, *Fenton.*

**confirming the churches:** . . . giving strength to, *NCV* . . . strengthening the Churches in the Faith, *TCNT* . . . where he established congregations, *Norlie* . . . where he strengthened the congregations, *Kleist* . . . helping the congregations grow stronger, *SEB* . . . making the churches stronger in the faith, *BB.*

**1.Then came he to Derbe and Lystra and, behold, a certain disciple was there:** At the latter place they found a disciple, *TCNT* . . . he descended to, *Fenton.*

**named Timotheus the son of a certain woman, which was a Jewess, and believed:** . . . whose mother was a Jewess who had become a believer in Christ, *TCNT* . . . son of a woman, a believing Jewess, *Fenton.*

**but his father was a Greek:** . . . but of a Greek father, *Swann* . . . of a Grecian, *Worrell.*

**2. Which was well reported of by the brethren that were at Lystra and Iconium:** . . . who was well attested, *Rotherham* . . . was well spoken of, *RSV* . . . was well recommended, *Berkeley* . . . They said good things about him, *SEB.*

**3. Him would Paul have to go forth with him:** Wishing to take this man with him on his journey, *TCNT* . . . wanted Timothy to travel with him, *Everyday* . . . resolved to take him as a companion on his journey, *Knox* . . . being anxious that he should accompany him, *Fenton* . . . for travel companion, *Berkeley.*

# Acts 16:4

| 2504.1 conj | 2956.25 verb nom sing masc part aor act | 3919.3 verb 3sing indic aor act | 840.6 prs-pron acc sing masc | 1217.2 prep |
|---|---|---|---|---|
| καὶ | λαβὼν | περιέτεμεν | αὐτὸν | διὰ |
| *kai* | *labōn* | *perietemen* | *auton* | *dia* |
| and | having taken | he circumcised | him | on account of |

| 3450.8 art acc pl masc | 2428.5 name-adj acc pl masc | 3450.8 art acc pl masc | 1498.25 verb acc pl masc part pres act | 1706.1 prep | 3450.4 art dat pl |
|---|---|---|---|---|---|
| τοὺς | Ἰουδαίους | τοὺς | ὄντας | ἐν | τοῖς |
| *tous* | *Ioudaious* | *tous* | *ontas* | *en* | *tois* |
| the | Jews | the | being | in | the |

| 4964.6 noun dat pl masc | 1552.7 dem-pron dat pl masc | 3471.13 verb 3pl indic plperf act | 1056.1 conj | 533.4 adj nom pl masc | 3450.6 art acc sing masc |
|---|---|---|---|---|---|
| τόποις | ἐκείνοις· | ᾔδεισαν | γὰρ | ἅπαντες | ⸀ τὸν |
| *topois* | *ekeinois* | *ēdeisan* | *gar* | *hapantes* | *ton* |
| places | those, | they knew | for | all | the |

3.a.**Txt:** 05D,08E,020L
025P,byz.Tisc
**Var:** 01א,02A,03B,04C
33,Lach,Treg,We/Ho
Weis,Sod,UBS/☆

| 3824.4 noun acc sing masc | 840.3 prs-pron gen sing | 3617.1 conj | 1659.1 name nom sing masc | 3617.1 conj | 1659.1 name nom sing masc |
|---|---|---|---|---|---|
| πατέρα | αὐτοῦ | ὅτι | Ἕλλην | [[a] ὅτι | Ἕλλην |
| *patera* | *autou* | *hoti* | *Hellēn* | *hoti* | *Hellēn* |
| father | his | that | a Greek | [ that | a Greek |

| 3450.5 art nom sing masc | 3824.1 noun nom sing masc | 840.3 prs-pron gen sing | 5062.12 verb 3sing indic imperf act | 5453.1 conj | 1156.2 conj |
|---|---|---|---|---|---|
| ὁ | πατὴρ | αὐτοῦ ] | ὑπῆρχεν. | 4. ὡς | δὲ |
| *ho* | *patēr* | *autou* | *hupērchen* | *hōs* | *de* |
| the | father | his ] | he was. | As | and |

| 1273.5 verb 3pl indic imperf mid | 3450.15 art acc pl fem | 4032.5 noun pl fem | 3722.27 verb 3pl indic imperf act |
|---|---|---|---|
| διεπορεύοντο | τὰς | πόλεις | ⸀ παρεδίδουν |
| *dieporeuonto* | *tas* | *poleis* | *paredidoun* |
| they were passing through | the | cities | they were delivering |

4.a.**Txt:** 020L,025P,byz.
**Var:** 01א,02A,03B,05D
08E,Lach,Treg,Alf
Word,Tisc,We/Ho,Weis
Sod,UBS/☆

| 3722.48 verb 3pl indic imperf act | 840.2 prs-pron dat pl | 5278.6 verb inf pres act | 3450.17 art pl neu | 1372.4 noun pl neu |
|---|---|---|---|---|
| [[a]☆ παρεδίδοσαν ] | αὐτοῖς | φυλάσσειν | τὰ | δόγματα |
| *paredidosan* | *autois* | *phulassein* | *ta* | *dogmata* |
| [ idem ] | to them | to keep | the | decrees |

| 3450.17 art pl neu | 2892.39 verb pl neu part perf mid | 5097.3 prep | 3450.1 art gen pl | 646.5 noun gen pl masc | 2504.1 conj |
|---|---|---|---|---|---|
| τὰ | κεκριμένα | ὑπὸ | τῶν | ἀποστόλων | καὶ |
| *ta* | *kekrimena* | *hupo* | *tōn* | *apostolōn* | *kai* |
| the | having been decided on | by | the | apostles | and |

4.b.**Txt:** 08E,020L,025P
byz.
**Var:** 01א,02A,03B,04C
05D,Lach,Treg,Alf
Word,Tisc,We/Ho,Weis
Sod,UBS/☆

| 3450.1 art gen pl | 4104.6 adj comp gen pl masc | 3450.1 art gen pl | 1706.1 prep | 2395.1 name fem |
|---|---|---|---|---|
| ⸂[b] τῶν ⸃ | πρεσβυτέρων | τῶν | ἐν | ⸀ Ἱερουσαλήμ. |
| *tōn* | *presbuterōn* | *tōn* | *en* | *Hierousalēm* |
| the | elders | the | in | Jerusalem. |

4.c.**Txt:** 08E,020L,025P
byz.
**Var:** 01א,02A,03B,04C
05D,Lach,Treg,Alf
Word,Tisc,We/Ho,Weis
Sod,UBS/☆

| 2389.3 name dat pl neu | 3450.13 art nom pl fem | 3173.1 conj | 3631.1 partic | 1564.5 noun nom pl fem |
|---|---|---|---|---|
| [[c]☆ Ἱεροσολύμοις. ] | 5. αἱ | μὲν | οὖν | ἐκκλησίαι |
| *Hierosolumois* | *hai* | *men* | *oun* | *ekklēsiai* |
| [ idem ] | The | | therefore | assemblies |

| 4583.3 verb 3pl indic imperf pass | 3450.11 art dat sing fem | 3963.3 noun dat sing fem | 2504.1 conj | 3915.19 verb 3pl indic imperf act |
|---|---|---|---|---|
| ἐστερεοῦντο | τῇ | πίστει, | καὶ | ἐπερίσσευον |
| *estereounto* | *tē* | *pistei* | *kai* | *eperisseuon* |
| were being strengthened | in the | faith, | and | were increasing |

that the Jerusalem leaders did not require Titus to be circumcised. But Titus was a Gentile. To circumcise him would have meant yielding to the Judaizers who said Gentiles must become Jews to keep their salvation. Timothy, however, had been brought up in the Jewish traditions by a Jewish mother. Jews even today accept a person as a Jew if his mother is Jewish, even if his father is a Gentile. They rightly understand that the mother has the greatest influence on the values and religious attitudes of a young child.

Paul still went to the Jew first in every new city he visited. For him to take an uncircumcised Jew into a synagogue would be like taking a traitor into an army camp. It would be intolerable to the Jews. None of them would listen to him. Thus, for the sake of giving Timothy opportunity to witness to his fellow Jews, Paul took Timothy and circumcised him. From this it is clear Paul did not ask Jews to give up their Jewish customs, but he recognized that circumcision and uncircumcision in themselves mean nothing. (See Galatians 5:6; 6:15; 1 Corinthians 7:19.)

Perhaps 1 Corinthians 9:20-23 gives further insight into Paul's reasoning. He did not go against the cultural norms of the people to whom he ministered unless they were immoral or idolatrous. Thus he brought everything into line with the promotion of the gospel and the salvation of sinners. Everyone knew Timothy's father was a Greek, so Paul had to confirm Timothy's Jewish heritage before they could go on. The elders of the local assembly accepted this, prayed, and sent Timothy with their blessing (1 Timothy 4:14).

**16:4.** As Paul, Silas, and Timothy went on their way through the rest of the cities of South Galatia, they handed over copies of the decrees, or regulations, from the letter recorded in chapter 15, decrees which the Gentile believers were to keep. These regulations were recognized as "ordained." They were decided by the apostles and elders in Jerusalem who then gave their approval to them and sent out the letter. But Paul and Silas no doubt drew attention to 15:28, "It seemed good to the Holy Ghost and to us."

The result was that the upsetting teachings of the Judaizers were counteracted. What had been a critical issue was no longer a threat or a cause of division. Everyone accepted the decision of the Jerusalem Council. Undoubtedly, the Epistle to the Galatians had helped to prepare the way for this. In it Paul dealt with the problem of the Law and circumcision as critical issues and gave strong arguments against the Judaizers.

**16:5.** The assemblies in the various cities were all strengthened not only in faith, but in "the faith." That is, they grew in their understanding of the truth of the gospel and in their obedience to its teachings and precepts. "The faith" was the whole body of truth that was preached and believed.

As a result of this encouragement and teaching the local assemblies continued to grow, increasing in number daily. This growth

**and took and circumcised him because of the Jews which were in those quarters:** Paul caused him to be circumcised on account of the Jews in that neighbourhood, *TCNT* . . . But he was careful to circumcise him, *Knox* . . . out of consideration for the Jews, *NEB* . . . In deference to the Jews of the area, *Taylor* . . . due to the local Jews, *Berkeley* . . . out of respect to the Jews resident in these places, *Fenton* . . . to please the Jews, *Everyday* . . . on account of the Jews in those places, *Williams C.K.*

**for they knew all that his father was a Greek:** . . . for they one and all knew, *Rotherham* . . . for they all had knowledge, *BB.*

**4. And as they went through the cities:** As they passed from, *Williams C.K.* . . . As they travelled from town to town, *TCNT* . . . on their way through the towns, *BB.*

**they delivered them the decrees for to keep:** . . . unto them for observance the decrees, *Rotherham* . . . they handed over into their keeping the decisions made by, *Williams C.K.* . . . they gave them the rules...so that they might keep them, *BB* . . . they delivered into their custody the decrees, *Fenton* . . . they recommended to their observance the decree laid down by, *Knox* . . . they gave the Brethren the decisions...for them to observe, *TCNT* . . . those injunctions, *Murdock* . . . gave the believers the rules and decisions from, *SEB.*

**that were ordained of the apostles and elders which were at Jerusalem:** . . . which had been decided upon by, *Rotherham* . . . which had been reached by, *TCNT* . . . which had been agreed upon by, *Fenton* . . . which had been made by, *Swann* . . . and the rulers of the church, *BB* . . . had written for the Christians to do, *NLT.*

**5. And so were the churches established in the faith:** . . . were being confirmed, *Rotherham* . . . through faith continued to grow in strength, *Williams* . . . were given stability, *Concordant* . . . firmly established in the faith, *Knox* . . . accordingly strengthened in the faith, *Fenton* . . . were made strong, *BB.*

6.a.**Txt:** 020L,025P,byz.
**Var:** 01ℵ,02A,03B,04C 05D,08E,sa.bo.Lach Treg,Alf,Word,Tisc We/Ho,Weis,Sod UBS/☆

6.b.**Txt:** 08E,020L,025P byz.
**Var:** 01ℵ,02A,03B,04C 05D,Lach,Treg,Alf,Tisc We/Ho,Weis,Sod UBS/☆

| **3450.3** art dat sing | **700.3** noun dat sing masc | **2567.2** prep | **2232.4** noun acc sing fem | **1324.7** verb nom pl masc part aor act |
|---|---|---|---|---|
| τῷ | ἀριθμῷ | καθ' | ἡμέραν. | **6.** ⸀ Διελθόντες |
| *tō* | *arithmō* | *kath'* | *hēmeran* | *Dielthontes* |
| the | number | according to | a day. | Having passed through |

| **1324.1** verb indic aor act | **1156.2** conj | **3450.12** art acc sing fem | **5271.2** name acc fem | **2504.1** conj |
|---|---|---|---|---|
| [a☆ Διῆλθον ] | δὲ | ⸂b τὴν ⸃ | Φρυγίαν | καὶ |
| *Diēlthon* | *de* | *tēn* | *Phrugian* | *kai* |
| [ They passed through ] | and | | Phrygia | and |

| **3450.12** art acc sing fem | **1047.1** name-adj acc sing fem | **5396.4** noun acc sing fem | **2940.13** verb nom pl masc part aor pass | **5097.3** prep |
|---|---|---|---|---|
| τὴν | Γαλατικὴν | χώραν, | κωλυθέντες | ὑπὸ |
| *tēn* | *Galatikēn* | *chōran* | *kōluthentes* | *hupo* |
| the | Galatian | country, | having been forbidden | by |

| **3450.2** art gen sing | **39.2** adj gen sing | **4011.2** noun gen sing neu | **2953.37** verb inf aor act | **3450.6** art acc sing masc | **3030.4** noun acc sing masc |
|---|---|---|---|---|---|
| τοῦ | ἁγίου | πνεύματος | λαλῆσαι | τὸν | λόγον |
| *tou* | *hagiou* | *pneumatos* | *lalēsai* | *ton* | *logon* |
| the | Holy | Spirit | to speak | the | word |

7.a.**Var:** 01ℵ,02A,03B 04C,05D,08E,sa.bo. Lach,Treg,Alf,Word Tisc,We/Ho,Weis,Sod UBS/☆

7.b.**Txt:** 020L,025P,byz.
**Var:** 01ℵ,02A,03B,04C 05D,08E,Gries,Lach Treg,Alf,Word,Tisc We/Ho,Weis,Sod UBS/☆

7.c.**Txt:** 04C,05D,020L 025P,byz.
**Var:** 01ℵ,02A,03B,08E 33,Lach,Treg,Alf,Tisc We/Ho,Weis,Sod UBS/☆

7.d.**Var:** 01ℵ,02A,03B 04C-corr,05D,08E,33,bo. Gries,Lach,Treg,Alf Word,Tisc,We/Ho,Weis Sod,UBS/☆

| **1706.1** prep | **3450.11** art dat sing fem | **767.3** name dat fem | **2048.16** verb nom pl masc part aor act | **1156.2** conj | **2567.3** prep |
|---|---|---|---|---|---|
| ἐν | τῇ | Ἀσίᾳ, | **7.** ἐλθόντες | [a+ δὲ ] | κατὰ |
| *en* | *tē* | *Asia* | *elthontes* | *de* | *kata* |
| in | | Asia, | having come | [ and ] | down to |

| **3450.12** art acc sing fem | **3327.1** name acc fem | **3847.9** verb 3pl indic imperf act | **2567.3** prep | **1519.1** prep |
|---|---|---|---|---|
| τὴν | Μυσίαν | ἐπείραζον | ⸀ κατὰ | [b☆ εἰς ] |
| *tēn* | *Musian* | *epeirazon* | *kata* | *eis* |
| | Mysia | they were attempting | down | [ to ] |

| **3450.12** art acc sing fem | **971.2** name acc fem | **4057.15** verb inf pres mid | **4057.29** verb inf aor pass | **2504.1** conj |
|---|---|---|---|---|
| τὴν | Βιθυνίαν | ⸀ πορεύεσθαι· | [c☆ πορευθῆναι, ] | καὶ |
| *tēn* | *Bithunian* | *poreuesthai* | *poreuthēnai* | *kai* |
| | Bithynia | to go; | [ idem ] | and |

| **3620.2** partic | **1432.3** verb 3sing indic aor act | **840.8** prs-pron acc pl masc | **3450.16** art sing neu | **4011.1** noun sing neu | **2400.2** name masc |
|---|---|---|---|---|---|
| οὐκ | εἴασεν | αὐτοὺς | τὸ | πνεῦμα. | [d☆+ Ἰησοῦ· ] |
| *ouk* | *eiasen* | *autous* | *to* | *pneuma* | *Iēsou* |
| not | did allow | them | the | Spirit; | [ of Jesus. ] |

| **3790.7** verb nom pl masc part aor act | **1156.2** conj | **3450.12** art acc sing fem | **3327.1** name acc fem | **2568.15** verb 3pl indic aor act |
|---|---|---|---|---|
| **8.** παρελθόντες | δὲ | τὴν | Μυσίαν | κατέβησαν |
| *parelthontes* | *de* | *tēn* | *Musian* | *katebēsan* |
| having passed by | and | | Mysia | they came down |

9.a.**Txt:** 01ℵ,04C,08E 020L,025P,byz.Sod
**Var:** 02A-corr,03B,05D Lach,Treg,Word,Tisc We/Ho,Weis,UBS/☆

| **1519.1** prep | **5015.3** name acc fem | **2504.1** conj | **3568.1** noun sing neu | **1217.2** prep | **3450.10** art gen sing fem | **3433.2** noun gen sing fem |
|---|---|---|---|---|---|---|
| εἰς | Τρῳάδα. | **9.** καὶ | ὅραμα | διὰ | ⸂a τῆς ⸃ | νυκτὸς |
| *eis* | *Trōada* | *kai* | *horama* | *dia* | *tēs* | *nuktos* |
| to | Troas. | And | a vision | through | the | night |

| **3571.21** verb 3sing indic aor pass | **3450.3** art dat sing | **3834.3** name dat masc | **3450.3** art dat sing | **3834.3** name dat masc | **3571.21** verb 3sing indic aor pass |
|---|---|---|---|---|---|
| ⸀ ὤφθη | τῷ | Παύλῳ· | [☆ τῷ | Παύλῳ | ὤφθη, ] |
| *ōphthē* | *tō* | *Paulō* | *tō* | *Paulō* | *ōphthē* |
| appeared | | to Paul: | | [to Paul | appeared: ] |

implies that the believers put their faith into action. They all became personal witnesses, spreading the truth about Jesus, telling of His death and resurrection, offering His grace and salvation to all of their friends and neighbors.

**16:6.** After Paul and his company went through the region of Phrygia and Galatia, it would have been logical to go next into the Roman province of Asia. Its great city of Ephesus and many other outstanding cities could have provided great opportunities for the gospel. Though God later gave Paul a great ministry there, it was not yet God's time. The Holy Spirit had already forbidden them to speak the Word in that province. (The Greek means "having been forbidden.")

They did have to go through the province of Asia, however. For days, perhaps weeks, they had to travel without spreading the Word, saying nothing in behalf of their Lord. This must have been very difficult for Paul. He felt constrained, moved by the mighty compulsion of Christ's love. (See 2 Corinthians 5:11,13,14,18,20.) He felt necessity laid on him: "Woe is unto me, if I preach not the gospel!" (1 Corinthians 9:16).

**16:7.** Since they were forbidden to preach in Asia, they moved north along the eastern border of Mysia and made an attempt to enter Bithynia to the northeast. Bithynia was another important Roman province which lay along the Black Sea.

Paul was never one to sit around and do nothing when he did not know where God wanted him to go or to do next. He was always conscious of the missionary burden upon him. So when he was checked by the Spirit from going in one direction, he would take a step in another, trusting the Holy Spirit to confirm or check that direction also. Thus he tried to go into Bithynia, but the Spirit would not let them go in that direction either. (However, 1 Peter 1:1 shows that Bithynia was later evangelized by others.)

**16:8.** Since they were not allowed to go east, there was only one direction left, so they turned west and went to Troas. To do this they had to go through Mysia, another Roman province. The Greek says literally that they bypassed Mysia. This can only mean they were not given permission to preach the gospel in Mysia either. This must have been hard for Paul, but because he was obedient to the Spirit, God brought him to Troas when He wanted him there.

**16:9.** Troas was a harbor city of Mysia. It was some distance south of Homer's Troy, which gave the name to the district. It lay on the Aegean Sea across from Macedonia.



**and increased in number daily:** . . . and grew in number from day to day, *Weymouth* . . . the number daily increased, *Fenton* . . . and daily increased in membership, *Norlie* . . . increased in numbers every day, *Williams C.K.* . . . More people were added each day, *NLT* . . . were abounding in number, *Young* . . . grew larger every day, *Everyday.*

**6. Now when they had gone throughout Phrygia and the region of Galatia:** And they passed through, *Rotherham* . . . And after they had gone through the land of, *BB* . . . went through the provinces of, *NCV* . . . Thus they crossed, *Williams C.K.*

**and were forbidden of the Holy Ghost to preach the word in Asia:** . . . kept them from preaching, *NLT* . . . they were prevented by, *Williams C.K.* . . . did not let them take the word into, *BB* . . . but were restrained by, *TCNT.*

**7. After they were come to Mysia:** When they reached the borders of Mysia, *TCNT* . . . when they got as far as Mysia, *Moffatt* . . . having come to, *BB* . . . reached the frontier, *Weymouth.*

**they assayed to go into Bithynia:** . . . they were attempting to journey into, *Rotherham* . . . they were about to enter Bithynia, *Weymouth* . . . they tried to enter, *Kleist* . . . they made an attempt to go into, *BB* . . . they attempted to proceed to, *Fenton.*

**but the Spirit suffered them not:** . . . but the Spirit of Jesus did not permit them, *TCNT* . . . would not allow them to, *NIV* . . . did not let them, *BB, NCV* . . . permitted them not, *Murdock* . . . would not let them go, *NLT* . . . forbad it, *Williams C.K.*

**8. And they passing by Mysia came down to Troas:** Passing through Mysia, they went down to Troas, *TCNT* . . . passing along the frontier of, *Kleist* . . . going past...they came down to, *BB* . . . having passed by...they went down to, *Fenton.*

**9. And a vision appeared to Paul in the night:** . . . and there one night Paul saw a vision, *TCNT* . . . That night Paul had a dream, *NLT.*

## Acts 16:10

| | | | | |
|---|---|---|---|---|
| **433.1** noun nom sing masc | **4948.3** indef-pron nom sing | **1498.34** verb sing indic imperf act | **3082.1** name nom sing masc | **3082.1** name nom sing masc |
| Ἀνὴρ | ⸀ τις | ἦν | Μακεδὼν | [☆ Μακεδών |
| *Anēr* | *tis* | *ēn* | *Makedōn* | *Makedōn* |
| A man | certain | was | of Macedonia | [ of Macedonia |

9.b.**Var:** 01ℵ,02A,03B 04C,08E,Lach,Treg Tisc,We/Ho,Weis,Sod UBS/☆

| | | | | |
|---|---|---|---|---|
| **4948.3** indef-pron nom sing | **1498.34** verb sing indic imperf act | **2449.26** verb sing part perf act | **2504.1** conj | **3731.7** verb nom sing masc part pres act |
| τις | ἦν ] | ἑστὼς, | [b☆+ καὶ ] | παρακαλῶν |
| *tis* | *ēn* | *hestōs* | *kai* | *parakalōn* |
| certain | was ] | standing, | [ and ] | beseeching |

| | | | | |
|---|---|---|---|---|
| **840.6** prs-pron acc sing masc | **2504.1** conj | **2978.15** verb nom sing masc part pres act | **1218.2** verb nom sing masc part aor act | **1519.1** prep |
| αὐτὸν | καὶ | λέγων, | Διαβὰς | εἰς |
| *auton* | *kai* | *legōn* | *Diabas* | *eis* |
| him | and | saying, | Having passed over | into |

| | | | | |
|---|---|---|---|---|
| **3081.4** name acc fem | **990.5** verb 2sing impr aor act | **2231.3** prs-pron dat 1pl | **5453.1** conj | **1156.2** conj |
| Μακεδονίαν | βοήθησον | ἡμῖν. | **10.** Ὡς | δὲ |
| *Makedonian* | *boēthēson* | *hēmin* | *Hōs* | *de* |
| Macedonia | help | us. | When | and |

| | | | | |
|---|---|---|---|---|
| **3450.16** art sing neu | **3568.1** noun sing neu | **1481.3** verb 3sing indic aor act | **2091.1** adv | **2195.15** verb 1pl indic aor act |
| τὸ | ὅραμα | εἶδεν, | εὐθέως | ἐζητήσαμεν |
| *to* | *horama* | *eiden* | *eutheōs* | *ezētēsamen* |
| the | vision | he saw, | immediately | we sought |

10.a.**Txt:** 05D,byz. **Var:** 01ℵ,02A,03B,04C 08E,020L,025P,Lach Treg,Tisc,We/Ho,Weis Sod,UBS/☆

| | | | | |
|---|---|---|---|---|
| **1814.20** verb inf aor act | **1519.1** prep | **3450.12** art acc sing fem | **3081.4** name acc fem | **4673.2** verb nom pl masc part pres act |
| ἐξελθεῖν | εἰς | ⸂a τὴν ⸃ | Μακεδονίαν, | συμβιβάζοντες |
| *exelthein* | *eis* | *tēn* | *Makedonian* | *sumbibazontes* |
| to go forth | to | | Macedonia, | concluding |

10.b.**Txt:** 05D,020L 025P,byz.sa. **Var:** p74,01ℵ,02A,03B 04C,08E,33,bo.Lach Treg,Alf,Tisc,We/Ho Weis,Sod,UBS/☆

| | | | | |
|---|---|---|---|---|
| **3617.1** conj | **4200.7** verb 3sing indic perf mid | **2231.4** prs-pron acc 1pl | **3450.5** art nom sing masc | **2935.1** noun nom sing masc |
| ὅτι | προσκέκληται | ἡμᾶς | ⸀ ὁ | κύριος |
| *hoti* | *proskeklētai* | *hēmas* | *ho* | *kurios* |
| that | had called | us | the | Lord |

11.a.**Txt:** 03B,04C,020L byz.sa.We/Ho,Sod **Var:** 01ℵ,02A,05D,08E 33,bo.Alf,Tisc,Weis UBS/☆

| | | | |
|---|---|---|---|
| **3450.5** art nom sing masc | **2296.1** noun nom sing masc | **2076.25** verb inf aor mid | **840.8** prs-pron acc pl masc |
| [b☆ ὁ | θεὸς ] | εὐαγγελίσασθαι | αὐτούς. |
| *ho* | *theos* | *euangelisasthai* | *autous* |
| | [ God ] | to announce the good news to | them. |

11.b.**Txt:** 020L,byz. **Var:** 01ℵ,02A,03B,04C 05D,08E,33,Lach,Treg Alf,Tisc,We/Ho,Weis Sod,UBS/☆

| | | | | |
|---|---|---|---|---|
| **319.9** verb nom pl masc part aor pass | **3631.1** partic | **1156.2** conj | **570.3** prep | **3450.10** art gen sing fem |
| **11.** Ἀναχθέντες | ⸀ οὖν | [a☆ δὲ ] | ἀπὸ | ⸂b τῆς ⸃ |
| *Anachthentes* | *oun* | *de* | *apo* | *tēs* |
| Having sailed | therefore | [ and ] | from | |

| | | | |
|---|---|---|---|
| **5015.1** name gen fem | **2092.1** verb 1pl indic aor act | **1519.1** prep | **4400.1** name acc fem |
| Τρῳάδος | εὐθυδρομήσαμεν | εἰς | Σαμοθρᾴκην, |
| *Trōados* | *euthudromēsamen* | *eis* | *Samothrakēn* |
| Troas | we came with a straight course | to | Samothrace, |

11.c.**Txt:** byz.Weis **Var:** 01ℵ,02A,03B,04C 08E,020L,sa.bo.Lach Treg,Alf,Tisc,We/Ho Sod,UBS/☆

| | | | | | |
|---|---|---|---|---|---|
| **3450.11** art dat sing fem | **4885.1** conj | **1156.2** conj | **1951.1** noun dat sing fem | **1519.1** prep | **3359.1** name acc fem |
| τῇ | ⸀ τε | [c☆ δὲ ] | ἐπιούσῃ | εἰς | ⸀ Νέαπολιν, |
| *tē* | *te* | *de* | *epiousē* | *eis* | *Neapolin* |
| on the | and | [ idem ] | following day | to | Neapolis, |

Another important turning point in Paul's ministry and missionary travels came at Troas. Had Paul gone into Bithynia, he might have continued eastward and never gone to Greece or Rome. But God had new centers He wanted to establish in Europe. There were opportunities there which would not only allow the establishing of churches, but would call forth several of Paul's epistles. Not only so, it is clear that it was God's purpose in Paul's ministry to establish new centers for the spread of the gospel. It was appropriate, therefore, that he should eventually end up in Rome. The capital of the Roman Empire became a new center from which the gospel could spread toward the uttermost parts of the earth.

Thus it was left for other apostles and believers to go eastward. There is strong tradition that the apostle Thomas went to South India, had a great ministry, and was martyred there near Madras.

The call westward was made clear in a night vision given to Paul. In the vision Paul saw a Macedonian pagan standing and begging him to come over to Macedonia to help them.

**16:10.** Paul and his company did not hesitate once this positive guidance was given. Immediately they sought to go to Macedonia, concluding that God had called them to preach the gospel there.

Up to this time the Book of Acts, in referring to Paul and his company, uses the word *they*. Here, for the first time, Luke used the word "we." This is the first of the "we" passages which indicate Luke, the beloved physician, was part of Paul's company on certain occasions. The other "we" passages are in 20:5 to 21:18 and 27:1 to 28:16. So Luke joined Paul at Troas and continued on the second missionary journey as far as Philippi. Then, on the third missionary journey, Luke rejoined Paul at Philippi and went with him to Jerusalem. Then, it seems, he stayed in Palestine and sailed with Paul from Caesarea to Rome. Luke was a Gentile (Paul distinguished him from his Jewish companions in Colossians 4:11,14). Many early traditions of the church say Luke was a native of Antioch in Syria, and this is quite probable. If so, Luke was a firsthand witness to many of the events he recorded in the Book of Acts even before he became a fellow laborer with Paul.

**16:11.** A ship took Paul and his company about 125 miles from Troas to Neapolis, the harbor town of Philippi, by way of the mountainous island of Samothrace. The wind must have been favorable, for it took only 2 days. Later, the journey in the other direction took 5 days (20:6).

Samothrace (off the coast of Thrace) is a small island of about 30 square miles. It has a 5,000-foot mountain which, in clear weather, guided them on a straight course to it. They were then able to circle north of the island and swing west to Neapolis, keeping fairly close to the coast. (Most ships in ancient times did not venture too far away from land.)

**There stood a man of Macedonia, and prayed him, saying:** A Macedonian was standing and appealing to him, *TCNT* . . . stood by him in entreaty, *Knox* . . . and beseeching him, *Rotherham, Worrell* . . . entreating him, *Campbell* . . . requesting him, *BB* . . . appealing to him in the words, *Kleist* . . . stood there begging him, *SEB* . . . who stood imploring him, saying, *Fenton.*

**Come over into Macedonia, and help us:** Pass over, *Douay* . . . and bring us succour! *Rotherham.*

**10. And after he had seen the vision immediately we endeavoured to go into Macedonia:** As soon as he had the vision, we forthwith made efforts to set out for, *Kleist* . . . That vision once seen, we were eager to sail for, *Knox* . . . Accordingly, having seen this vision, we at once attempted to proceed to, *Fenton* . . . we were eager to start at once, *TCNT* . . . we immediately prepared to leave for, *Everyday, NCV* . . . we immediately sought to go into, *Swann.*

**assuredly gathering that the Lord had called us:** . . . since we concluded, *Beck* . . . concluding that God had called us, *RSV* . . . We understood that God had called, *Everyday, SEB* . . . convinced that God had called us, *Phillips* . . . concluding that God had summoned us, *Rotherham* . . . inferring, *Campbell* . . . being sure, *Confraternity* . . . being assured, *Douay* . . . we agreed that God told us to go to, *NLT* . . . had called us forward, *Fenton.*

**for to preach the gospel unto them:** . . . to evangelize there, *Berkeley* . . . to bring the Good News to its people, *Kleist* . . . evangelize them, *Fenton.*

**11. Therefore loosing from Troas we came with a straight course to Samothracia:** Setting sail therefore from...we steered straight to, *Fenton* . . . and ran before the wind, *TCNT* . . . and struck a bee line for, *Williams* . . . and sailed to the island of, *SEB.*

**and the next day to Neapolis:** . . . and the day following, *ASV* . . . and on the morrow unto New City, *Rotherham* . . . The next day we arrived in Neapolis, *Montgomery.*

11.d.**Txt:** 04C,05D-org 08E,020L,025P,byz. **Var:** 01ℵ,02A,03B 05D-corr,Treg,Tisc We/Ho,Weis,UBS/☆

| 3359.2 name acc fem | | 1551.1 adv | 4885.1 conj | 2518.1 conj |
|---|---|---|---|---|
| [d☆ Νέαν Πόλιν, ] | 12. | ʽ ἐκεῖθέν | τε | [a☆ κἀκεῖθεν ] |
| Nean Polin | | ekeithen | te | kakeithen |
| [ idem ] | | from there | and | [ then ] |

12.a.**Txt:** 025P,byz. **Var:** 01ℵ,02A,03B,04C 05D,08E,33,Lach,Treg Alf,Word,Tisc,We/Ho Weis,Sod,UBS/☆

| 1519.1 prep | 5212.3 name acc masc | 3610.3 rel-pron nom sing fem | 1498.4 verb 3sing indic pres act | 4272.9 num ord nom sing fem | 3450.10 art gen sing fem |
|---|---|---|---|---|---|
| εἰς | Φιλίππους, | ἥτις | ἐστὶν | πρώτη | τῆς |
| eis | Philippous | hētis | estin | prōtē | tēs |
| to | Philippi, | which | is | first | of the |

12.b.**Txt:** 03B,05D,020L 025P,byz.Weis **Var:** p74,01ℵ,02A,04C 08E,Lach,Treg,Tisc We/Ho,Sod,UBS/☆

| 3182.2 noun gen sing fem | 3450.10 art gen sing fem | 3081.2 name gen fem | 4032.1 noun nom sing fem | 2834.1 noun nom sing fem |
|---|---|---|---|---|
| μερίδος | ʽb τῆς ˎ | Μακεδονίας | πόλις, | κολωνία. |
| meridos | tēs | Makedonias | polis | kolōnia |
| part | of the | Macedonia | city, | a colony. |

| 1498.36 verb 1pl indic imperf act | 1156.2 conj | 1706.1 prep | 3642.11 dem-pron dat sing fem | 3450.11 art dat sing fem | 4032.3 noun dat sing fem |
|---|---|---|---|---|---|
| ³Ἦμεν | δὲ | ἐν | ταύτῃ | τῇ | πόλει |
| Emen | de | en | tautē | tē | polei |
| We were | and | in | this | the | city |

| 1298.1 verb nom pl masc part pres act | 2232.1 noun fem | 4948.9 indef-pron acc pl masc | 3450.11 art dat sing fem | 4885.1 conj | 2232.3 noun dat sing fem |
|---|---|---|---|---|---|
| διατρίβοντες | ἡμέρας | τινάς. | 13. τῇ | τε | ἡμέρᾳ |
| diatribontes | hēmeras | tinas | tē | te | hēmera |
| staying | days | certain. | On the | and | day |

| 3450.1 art gen pl | 4378.4 noun gen pl neu | 1814.4 verb 1pl indic aor act | 1838.1 adv | 3450.10 art gen sing fem | 4032.2 noun gen sing fem |
|---|---|---|---|---|---|
| τῶν | σαββάτων | ἐξήλθομεν | ἔξω | τῆς | ʽ πόλεως |
| tōn | sabbatōn | exēlthomen | exō | tēs | poleōs |
| of the | sabbath | we went | outside | the | city |

13.a.**Txt:** 08E,020L 025P,byz. **Var:** 01ℵ,02A,03B,04C 05D,sa.bo.Lach,Treg Alf,Word,Tisc,We/Ho Weis,Sod,UBS/☆

| 4297.2 noun gen sing fem | 3706.2 prep | 4074.4 noun acc sing masc | 3619.1 adv | 3406.12 verb 3sing indic imperf pass |
|---|---|---|---|---|
| [a☆ πύλης ] | παρὰ | ποταμὸν, | οὗ | ʽ ἐνομίζετο |
| pulēs | para | potamon | hou | enomizeto |
| [ gate ] | by | a river, | where | was supposed |

13.b.**Txt:** 08E,020L 025P,byz.Sod **Var:** 02A-corr,03B,04C 33,sa.bo.Lach,Treg,Tisc We/Ho,Weis,UBS/☆

| 4194.1 noun nom sing fem | 3406.14 verb 1pl indic imperf act | 4194.4 noun acc sing fem | 1498.32 verb inf pres act | 2504.1 conj |
|---|---|---|---|---|
| προσευχὴ | [b☆ ἐνομίζομεν | προσευχὴν ] | εἶναι, | καὶ |
| proseuchē | enomizomen | proseuchēn | einai | kai |
| prayer | [ we were supposing | prayer ] | to be, | and |

| 2495.11 verb nom pl masc part aor act | 2953.46 verb 1pl indic imperf act | 3450.14 art dat pl fem | 4755.9 verb dat pl fem part aor act |
|---|---|---|---|
| καθίσαντες | ἐλαλοῦμεν | ταῖς | συνελθούσαις |
| kathisantes | elaloumen | tais | sunelthousais |
| having sat down | we were speaking | to the | having come together |

| 1129.8 noun dat pl fem | 2504.1 conj | 4948.3 indef-pron nom sing | 1129.1 noun nom sing fem | 3549.4 noun dat sing neu | 3042.1 name nom fem |
|---|---|---|---|---|---|
| γυναιξίν. | 14. Καί | τις | γυνὴ | ὀνόματι | Λυδία, |
| gunaixin | Kai | tis | gunē | onomati | Ludia |
| women. | And | a certain | woman, | by name | Lydia, |

| 4070.1 noun nom sing fem | 4032.2 noun gen sing fem | 2340.2 name gen neu | 2340.6 name gen neu |
|---|---|---|---|
| πορφυρόπωλις | πόλεως | ʽ Θυατείρων, | [☆ Θυατίρων ] |
| porphuropōlis | poleōs | Thuateirōn | Thuatirōn |
| a seller of purple | of city | of Thyatira, | [ idem ] |

**16:12.** They did not stay in Neapolis, but went on about 10 miles to Philippi. Paul did not stop in every little town along the way; led by the Spirit, he went to the most important city in that part of Macedonia. His method was to go to the chief cities and establish churches as gospel centers. His converts would then have the privilege of taking the gospel to the surrounding cities and towns.

Philippi, named after Philip, the father of Alexander the Great, was a great city of what was called the first division of the Roman province of Macedonia, north of Greece. The city was also a Roman "colony." That is, in Philippi the Romans had settled a garrison of Roman soldiers who were citizens of Rome and who followed Roman laws and customs. The constitution of the city was modeled on that of Rome. Other cities were given honorary status as colonies, but the Bible only draws attention to the colonial status of Philippi. Apparently, when Augustus made Philippi a military colony, many Romans made it their home.

Philippi was an important city also because it was located at the eastern end of the famous Roman road, the Egnatian Way. Roman soldiers patrolled the road—another reason for the colonial status. The emperor also had given the citizens of Philippi the "Italic right," which meant they had the same rights as cities on Italian soil.

**12. And from thence to Philippi:** From there we made our way to Philippi, *TCNT* . . . Then we went by land to, *Everyday.*

**which is the chief city of that part of Macedonia, and a colony:** . . . a Roman colony, *ASV* . . . the first Macedonian city of the district, *Alford* . . . the leading town in that part of, *Williams* . . . This was an important city in the country of, *NLT* . . . which is the most important town of, *BB* . . . which is the principal town of its district, *Williams C.K.* . . . which is a capital, *Fenton* . . . It is a city for Romans, *SEB.*

**and we were in that city abiding certain days:** . . . we spent several days, *TCNT* . . . There we stayed for some time, *Montgomery* . . . in this city abiding for some days, *Swann* . . . we remained for some days, conferring together, *Knox* . . . stayed there for a few days, *SEB* . . . And we rested for some days in the town itself, *Fenton* . . . in this town we stayed for some days, *Williams C.K.*

**16:13.** There was no Jewish synagogue at Philippi, which probably means the city lacked the 10 adult Jewish men necessary to have a synagogue. It could also mean there was no organized Jewish community, no school for the Jewish children, and no public witness or systematic reading of the Old Testament Scriptures. Yet Paul did not go directly to the Gentiles as he had at Lystra and Derbe where there were no Jews at all. Paul continued to go to the Jew first (Romans 1:16). They at least had some background in the Scriptures.

Probably by making inquiries, Paul heard there was a place of prayer about a mile outside the city gate on the bank of the Gangues River. When the Sabbath Day came, Paul and his fellow workers went down to the riverside, sat down, and proceeded to talk to a group of women who met there. From what follows it is clear that some of the women were Jewish, and some were interested Gentiles; some were single, while others may have been widows or perhaps married to Gentiles.

**13. And on the sabbath we went out of the city by a river side:** And on the day of rest we went forth outside the gate, *Rotherham* . . . On Saturday we, *Beck* . . . went outside the town, by the river, *BB.*

**where prayer was wont to be made:** . . . where we had an idea that there would be, *BB* . . . There we thought we would find a special place for prayer, *NCV* . . . where we were informed prayer was to be, *Fenton* . . . a place of worship, *Berkeley.*

**and we sat down, and spake unto the women which resorted thither:** . . . and having sat down, we spoke to the women who were assembled, *Fenton* . . . and sitting down we went on to speak unto the women who had come together, *Rotherham* . . . talked to the women who had gathered, *Williams C.K.*

**16:14.** As Paul talked about the Lord and began to explain the gospel, the Lord began to work, and the Spirit began to drive home the truth to the hearts of those who heard.

Strangely enough, the first convert was a Gentile, Lydia. She was a wealthy businesswoman, a seller (that is, an independent dealer) of purple-dyed woolen cloth. In ancient times the word *purple* included various shades of crimson and red. The "royal" purple of those days was actually a deep shade of crimson red, later called

**14. And a certain woman named Lydia:** Among them was a woman, named Lydia, *TCNT.*

**a seller of purple:** Her job was selling, *Everyday* . . . purple fabrics, *Wuest* . . . purple dyes, *TCNT* . . . a dealer, *Fenton* . . . purple goods, *Adams* . . . a trader in purple cloth, *BB.*

## Acts 16:15

| 4431.6 verb nom sing fem part pres mid | 3450.6 art acc sing masc | 2296.4 noun acc sing masc | 189.45 verb 3sing indic imperf act | 3614.10 rel-pron gen sing fem |
|---|---|---|---|---|
| σεβομένη | τὸν | θεόν, | ἤκουεν· | ἧς |
| *sebomenē* | *ton* | *theon* | *ēkouen* | *hēs* |
| worshiping | | God, | was hearing; | of whom |

| 3450.5 art nom sing masc | 2935.1 noun nom sing masc | 1266.3 verb 3sing indic aor act | 3450.12 art acc sing fem | 2559.4 noun acc sing fem | 4196.5 verb inf pres act |
|---|---|---|---|---|---|
| ὁ | κύριος | διήνοιξεν | τὴν | καρδίαν | προσέχειν |
| *ho* | *kurios* | *diēnoixen* | *tēn* | *kardian* | *prosechein* |
| the | Lord | opened | the | heart | to pay attention |

14.a.**Txt:** 01א,02A,04C 08E,020L,025P,etc.byz. Sod
**Var:** 03B,05D,Treg,Tisc We/Ho,Weis,UBS/☆

| 3450.4 art dat pl | 2953.50 verb dat pl neu part pres mid | 5097.3 prep | 3450.2 art gen sing | 3834.2 name gen masc | 5453.1 conj |
|---|---|---|---|---|---|
| τοῖς | λαλουμένοις | ὑπὸ | ⸂[a] τοῦ ⸃ | Παύλου. | **15.** ὡς |
| *tois* | *laloumenois* | *hupo* | *tou* | *Paulou* | *hōs* |
| to the | being spoken | by | | Paul. | When |

| 1156.2 conj | 901.14 verb 3sing indic aor pass | 2504.1 conj | 3450.5 art nom sing masc | 3486.1 noun nom sing masc | 840.10 prs-pron gen sing fem |
|---|---|---|---|---|---|
| δὲ | ἐβαπτίσθη | καὶ | ὁ | οἶκος | αὐτῆς |
| *de* | *ebaptisthē* | *kai* | *ho* | *oikos* | *autēs* |
| and | she was baptized | and | the | house | her |

| 3731.13 verb 3sing indic aor act | 2978.19 verb nom sing fem part pres act | 1479.1 conj | 2892.23 verb 2pl indic perf act | 1466.6 prs-pron acc 1sing |
|---|---|---|---|---|
| παρεκάλεσεν | λέγουσα, | Εἰ | κεκρίκατέ | με |
| *parekalesen* | *legousa* | *Ei* | *kekrikate* | *me* |
| she urged | saying, | If | you have judged | me |

| 3964.12 adj acc sing fem | 3450.3 art dat sing | 2935.3 noun dat sing masc | 1498.32 verb inf pres act | 1511.16 verb nom pl masc part aor act | 1519.1 prep |
|---|---|---|---|---|---|
| πιστὴν | τῷ | κυρίῳ | εἶναι, | εἰσελθόντες | εἰς |
| *pistēn* | *tō* | *kuriō* | *einai* | *eiselthontes* | *eis* |
| faithful | to the | Lord | to be, | having entered | into |

15.a.**Txt:** 04C,020L 025P,byz.Sod
**Var:** 01א,02A,03B,05D 08E,Lach,Treg,Tisc We/Ho,Weis,UBS/☆

| 3450.6 art acc sing masc | 3486.4 noun acc sing masc | 1466.2 prs-pron gen 1sing | 3176.23 verb 2pl impr aor act | 3176.2 verb 2pl pres act | 2504.1 conj |
|---|---|---|---|---|---|
| τὸν | οἶκόν | μου, | ⸂ μείνατε· | [a☆ μένετε·] | καὶ |
| *ton* | *oikon* | *mou* | *meinate* | *menete* | *kai* |
| the | house | my, | stay. | [idem] | And |

16.a.**Var:** 01א,02A,03B 04C,08E,Lach,Treg,Alf Word,Tisc,We/Ho,Weis Sod,UBS/☆

| 3711.1 verb 3sing indic aor mid | 2231.4 prs-pron acc 1pl | 1090.33 verb 3sing indic aor mid | 1156.2 conj | 3450.12 art acc sing fem |
|---|---|---|---|---|
| παρεβιάσατο | ἡμᾶς. | **16.** Ἐγένετο | δὲ | [a☆+ τὴν ] |
| *parebiasato* | *hēmas* | *Egeneto* | *de* | *tēn* |
| she urged | us. | It came to pass | and | [the] |

| 4057.11 verb gen pl masc part pres mid | 2231.2 prs-pron gen 1pl | 1519.1 prep | 4194.4 noun acc sing fem | 3677.3 noun acc sing fem |
|---|---|---|---|---|
| πορευομένων | ἡμῶν | εἰς | προσευχὴν, | παιδίσκην |
| *poreuomenōn* | *hēmōn* | *eis* | *proseuchēn* | *paidiskēn* |
| going | us | to | prayer, | a maid servant |

16.b.**Txt:** 04C-corr 05D-corr,08E,020L 025P,byz.Sod
**Var:** 01א,02A,03B 04C-org,05D-org,33 Lach,Treg,Alf,Tisc We/Ho,Weis,UBS/☆

| 4948.5 indef-pron | 2174.25 verb acc sing fem part pres act | 4011.1 noun sing neu | 4294.1 name gen masc | 4294.2 name acc masc |
|---|---|---|---|---|
| τινὰ | ἔχουσαν | πνεῦμα | ⸂ Πύθωνος | [b☆ πύθωνα ] |
| *tina* | *echousan* | *pneuma* | *Puthōnos* | *puthōna* |
| certain, | having | a spirit | of Python, | [a python,] |

16.c.**Txt:** 02A,05D,020L 025P,byz.Sod
**Var:** 01א,03B,04C,08E 33,Treg,Alf,Tisc,We/Ho Weis,UBS/☆

| 524.3 verb inf aor act | 5059.3 verb inf aor act | 2231.3 prs-pron dat 1pl | 3610.3 rel-pron nom sing fem | 2022.2 noun acc sing fem |
|---|---|---|---|---|
| ⸂ ἀπαντῆσαι | [c☆ ὑπαντῆσαι ] | ἡμῖν, | ἥτις | ἐργασίαν |
| *apantēsai* | *hupantēsai* | *hēmin* | *hētis* | *ergasian* |
| to meet | [idem] | us, | who | business |

Turkey red. It was the product of the shellfish murex and was very expensive.

Lydia was from Thyatira, a city in Lydia north of Sardis (the capital of the Lydian region of the Roman province of Asia). Some believe she was named for her native land, though the name *Lydia* was common. Thyatira was famous for another purple dye made of madder root. Some believe it was the real source of Turkey red. Thyatira contained a Jewish colony. Lydia possibly became interested in the things of God by attending the synagogue there. At Philippi she continued to pray and seek God. Because she did, the Lord was able to open her heart to understand the truth of the gospel as she gave her full attention to the things Paul was preaching and teaching.

**16:15.** The result was that Lydia believed the gospel and was baptized in water with her entire household, that is, with her staff and servants. Through her influence they also believed, and together they became the first body of believers in Europe. (Compare Luke 24:32,45; 1 Corinthians 2:13,14.)

This took place over a period of time. By winning her household to the Lord, Lydia demonstrated her own faithfulness to the Lord. On this basis she besought Paul and his entire company to make her large home their home and headquarters. She wanted her household to be established in the Lord. No doubt also, she had many friends and business acquaintances who might not go down to the riverside but who would come to her house. Thus, it was in her house a church would be established.

Lydia kept urging Paul and his fellow workers to come until they finally did so. The assembly soon began to grow. At the end of chapter 16 there were not only women but "brethren" who were now part of the congregation. (See verse 40.) Thus, even though there were small beginnings, God was faithful.

**16:16.** One day as Paul, Silas, Timothy, and Luke were going down to the place of prayer, a demon-possessed slave girl met them. Her "spirit of divination" in the Greek means a spirit of ventriloquism. A demon spirit used her, in spite of herself, to speak and to practice soothsaying or fortune telling. The Greek also calls her a "pythoness." The python was a monstrous constricting snake that Greek mythology said was killed by the god Apollo. Thus the python became a symbol of the Greek god, Apollo. The masters of this slave girl claimed that her fortune telling was the voice of Apollo. This kind of fortune telling was popular and brought much gain (money) to her masters. It seems to be implied also that they used her to attract people to their other businesses.

Various types of fortune telling, astrology, and spiritism or spiritualism were common in all the ancient heathen religions of the Middle East and Europe. Isaiah 47:12-14 shows how all this was part of the heathenism of ancient Babylon and was of no spiritual profit to them. Isaiah 2:6 shows that one of the reasons God had



**of the city of Thyatira which worshipped God:** . . . of the town...and a God-fearing woman, *BB* . . . devout towards God, *Rotherham* . . . reverenced God, *Moffatt.*

**heard us:** . . . was listening, *Worrell* . . . listened to us, *Montgomery* . . . gave ear to us, *BB.*

**whose heart the Lord opened:** The Lord touched this woman's heart, *TCNT* . . . The Lord opened her mind to pay attention to, *NCV.*

**that she attended unto the things which were spoken of Paul:** . . . that she accepted the message spoken by Paul, *Williams* . . . to give attention to the things which Paul was saying, *BB.*

**15. And when she was baptized, and her household:** And when she was immersed, *Rotherham* . . . when she and her family had had baptism, *BB.*

**she besought us, saying:** . . . she urged us to become her guests, *TCNT* . . . she made a request to us, *BB.*

**If ye have judged me to be faithful to the Lord:** If ye are really persuaded, *Murdock* . . . in your judgement, *Weymouth* . . . If you think I am truly a believer, *NCV* . . . If it seems to you that I am true to, *BB* . . . to be a believer in the Lord, *Rotherham.*

**come into my house, and abide there:** . . . come into my house and be my guests, *BB.*

**And she constrained us:** And she insisted on our going so, *TCNT* . . . she persuaded us to stay with her, *NCV* . . . she would take no refusal, *JB* . . . And she compelled us, *Swann.*

**16. And it came to pass, as we went to prayer:** One day, as we were on our way to the Place of Prayer, *TCNT* . . . But it happened, as we were going to the prayer service, *Berkeley.*

**a certain damsel possessed with a spirit of divination met us:** . . . having a spirit of Python, *Rotherham* . . . we were met by a girl possessed by a divining spirit, *TCNT* . . . a slave girl met us, possessed by a spirit of, *Moffatt* . . . by a fortune-telling demon, *Norlie* . . . a spirit of clairvoyance, *Phillips* . . . the gift of magical fortune-telling, *Williams* . . . She had an evil spirit, *SEB.*

| 4044.12 adj acc sing fem | 3792.10 verb 3sing indic imperf act | 3450.4 art dat pl | 2935.8 noun dat pl masc | 840.10 prs-pron gen sing fem | 3104.1 verb nom sing fem part pres mid |
|---|---|---|---|---|---|
| πολλὴν | παρεῖχεν | τοῖς | κυρίοις | αὐτῆς | μαντευομένη. |
| *pollēn* | *pareichen* | *tois* | *kuriois* | *autēs* | *manteuomenē* |
| much | was bringing | to the | masters | her | telling fortunes. |

17.a.**Txt:** 02A,04C,08E 020L,025P,etc.byz.Sod **Var:** 01ℵ,03B,05D,Treg Tisc,We/Ho,Weis UBS/☆

| 3642.9 dem-pron nom sing fem | 2598.1 verb nom sing fem part aor act | 2598.3 verb nom sing fem part pres act |
|---|---|---|
| 17. αὕτη | ᶠ κατακολουθήσασα | [ᵃ☆ κατακολουθοῦσα ] |
| *hautē* | *katakolouthēsasa* | *katakolouthousa* |
| She | having followed | [ following ] |

| 3450.3 art dat sing | 3834.3 name dat masc | 2504.1 conj | 2231.3 prs-pron dat 1pl | 2869.17 verb 3sing indic imperf act | 2978.19 verb nom sing fem part pres act |
|---|---|---|---|---|---|
| τῷ | Παύλῳ | καὶ | ἡμῖν | ἔκραζεν | λέγουσα, |
| *tō* | *Paulō* | *kai* | *hēmin* | *ekrazen* | *legousa* |
| | Paul | and | us | was crying | saying, |

| 3642.7 dem-pron nom pl masc | 3450.7 art nom pl masc | 442.6 noun nom pl masc | 1395.6 noun nom pl masc | 3450.2 art gen sing | 2296.2 noun gen sing masc |
|---|---|---|---|---|---|
| Οὗτοι | οἱ | ἄνθρωποι | δοῦλοι | τοῦ | θεοῦ |
| *Houtoi* | *hoi* | *anthrōpoi* | *douloi* | *tou* | *theou* |
| These | the | men | servants | | of God |

| 3450.2 art gen sing | 5148.2 adj sup gen sing masc | 1498.7 verb 3pl indic pres act | 3610.2 rel-pron nom pl masc | 2576.1 verb dat pl masc part pres act |
|---|---|---|---|---|
| τοῦ | ὑψίστου | εἰσίν, | οἵτινες | καταγγέλλουσιν |
| *tou* | *hupsistou* | *eisin* | *hoitines* | *katangellousin* |
| the | Most High | are, | who | are announcing |

17.b.**Txt:** 02A,04C,020L 025P,33,byz.lect.sa. Steph **Var:** p74,01ℵ,03B,05D 08E,bo.Elzev,Treg,Tisc We/Ho,Weis,Sod UBS/☆

| 2231.3 prs-pron dat 1pl | 5050.3 prs-pron dat 2pl | 3461.4 noun acc sing fem | 4843.2 noun gen sing fem | 3642.17 dem-pron sing neu | 1156.2 conj |
|---|---|---|---|---|---|
| ᶠ ἡμῖν | [ᵇ☆ ὑμῖν ] | ὁδὸν | σωτηρίας. | 18. Τοῦτο | δὲ |
| *hēmin* | *humin* | *hodon* | *sōtērias* | *Touto* | *de* |
| to us | [ to you ] | way | of salvation. | This | and |

| 4020.57 verb 3sing indic imperf act | 1894.3 prep | 4044.15 adj acc pl fem | 2232.1 noun fem | 1272.2 verb nom sing masc part aor pass |
|---|---|---|---|---|
| ἐποίει | ἐπὶ | πολλὰς | ἡμέρας˙ | διαπονηθεὶς |
| *epoiei* | *epi* | *pollas* | *hēmeras* | *diaponētheis* |
| she was doing | for | many | days. | Having been distressed |

18.a.**Txt:** 04C,05D,08E 020L,025P,etc.byz.Sod **Var:** 01ℵ,02A,03B,Treg Tisc,We/Ho,Weis UBS/☆

| 1156.2 conj | 3450.5 art nom sing masc | 3834.1 name nom masc | 2504.1 conj | 1978.11 verb nom sing masc part aor act | 3450.3 art dat sing |
|---|---|---|---|---|---|
| δὲ | ᶠᵃ ὁ ˋ | Παῦλος, | καὶ | ἐπιστρέψας | τῷ |
| *de* | *ho* | *Paulos* | *kai* | *epistrepsas* | *tō* |
| but | | Paul, | and | having turned | to the |

| 4011.3 noun dat sing neu | 1500.5 verb 3sing indic aor act | 3715.1 verb 1sing indic pres act | 4622.3 prs-pron dat 2sing | 1706.1 prep |
|---|---|---|---|---|
| πνεύματι | εἶπεν, | Παραγγέλλω | σοι | ἐν |
| *pneumati* | *eipen* | *Parangellō* | *soi* | *en* |
| spirit | said, | I charge | you | in |

18.b.**Txt:** 05D,020L 025P,byz. **Var:** 01ℵ,02A,03B,04C 08E,Lach,Treg,Alf,Tisc We/Ho,Weis,Sod UBS/☆

| 3450.3 art dat sing | 3549.4 noun dat sing neu | 2400.2 name masc | 5382.2 name gen masc | 1814.20 verb inf aor act | 570.2 prep |
|---|---|---|---|---|---|
| ᶠᵇ τῷ ˋ | ὀνόματι | Ἰησοῦ | Χριστοῦ | ἐξελθεῖν | ἀπ' |
| *tō* | *onomati* | *Iēsou* | *Christou* | *exelthein* | *ap'* |
| the | name | of Jesus | Christ | to come out | from |

| 840.10 prs-pron gen sing fem | 2504.1 conj | 1814.3 verb 3sing indic aor act | 840.11 prs-pron dat sing fem | 3450.11 art dat sing fem | 5443.3 noun dat sing fem |
|---|---|---|---|---|---|
| αὐτῆς. | Καὶ | ἐξῆλθεν | αὐτῇ | τῇ | ὥρᾳ. |
| *autēs* | *Kai* | *exēlthen* | *autē* | *tē* | *hōra* |
| her. | And | it came out | same | the | hour. |

turned away from His people and would have to judge them was because they were soothsayers like the Philistines. Many places in the Bible show that all these things are defiling. They are really part of the devil's territory. The believer who trusts God will have nothing to do with them. The believer's guidance comes through the Spirit and the Word, not through human, magical, or demonic means. God may use fellow believers to encourage Christians, and He may even use circumstances to check them, but He will never use any form of the occult.

**16:17.** This demon-possessed slave girl followed after Paul and his company, repeatedly shouting out in a shrieking, high-pitched voice, "These men are servants (slaves) of the most high God who are announcing to you a way of salvation." (Many Greek manuscripts have "to us" instead of "to you.")

The girl was right in saying Paul and his companions were committed servants, "slaves," fully subject to the Most High God. Her witness, however, was incomplete. It is a question what "the most high God" might mean to the Greeks and the Romans. They might have supposed she was talking about one of their gods, such as Zeus or Jupiter. The word has no definite article. It reads "a way," rather than "the way." Many even today are willing to call the gospel "a way" of salvation, but they are not at all willing to concede that the gospel is "the way," that is, the *only* way.

When missionaries went to India proclaiming Jesus as Saviour, some of the Hindus said, "Fine, we are glad to accept Him as *a* savior. We have many saviors; we can always use one more." Some would still be willing to treat Jesus as an avatar or incarnation of one of their heathen gods. But their universal being, the Brahman or Atman, is not a personal god. Their philosophers admit they cannot say whether this "great soul" exists or not.

**16:18.** The slave girl kept following Paul and his companions for (during) many days. That is, she did not do it continuously, but during part of every day she would follow close after them, shouting out the same thing.

The slave girl's shrieks and cries must have attracted a great deal of attention. But it was not the kind of witness that brings real glory to God, because it did not proclaim the whole truth. Paul was greatly troubled, disturbed, and annoyed by her unpleasant shrieking. It was not the kind of witness Paul needed.

Finally, Paul felt this shrieking had to be stopped. So he claimed the name and the authority of Jesus. Turning to the woman, he spoke, not to her, but to the evil spirit in her, commanding it in the name (by the authority) of Jesus Christ to come out of her. In this he was following the example of Jesus who also spoke directly to the demons who possessed people. It came out of her "in that hour," which really means immediately. (Codex Bezae [D], along with other ancient "western" manuscripts, adds the word *immediately*.) Truly there is power in the name of Jesus.

**which brought her masters much gain:** . . . who made large profits for her masters, *TCNT* . . . who afforded a vast income, *Concordant* . . . she earned a lot of money for her owners, *NCV* . . . Her owner made much money from her power, *NLT*.

**by soothsaying:** . . . by her power of fortune-telling, *Moffatt* . . . by telling the unknown, *Beck* . . . by her prediction, *Swann* . . . which gave knowledge of the future, *BB*.

**17. The same followed Paul and us:** She used to follow after, *Montgomery* . . . followed Paul and us everywhere, *SEB*.

**and cried, saying:** . . . crying out again and again, *Montgomery* . . . shrieking, *Moffatt*.

**These men are the servants:** . . . bondmen, *Darby* . . . are workmen who are owned by, *NLT*.

**of the most high God:** . . . of the Supreme God, *NEB* . . . of the Highest God, *Norlie*.

**which shew unto us:** . . . who proclaim unto you, *ASV* . . . who indeed are declaring unto you, *Rotherham* . . . and they are bringing you news of, *TCNT*.

**the way of salvation:** . . . how you can be saved! *NCV*.

**18. And this did she many days:** And this she continued to do, *Rotherham* . . . This she persisted in for a considerable time, *Weymouth* . . . She kept this up, *NCV* . . . on a number of days, *BB*.

**But Paul, being grieved, turned and said to the Spirit:** But Paul was annoyed, *RSV* . . . worn out and turning unto, *Rotherham* . . . in a burst of irritation, turned round, *Phillips* . . . This bothered Paul, *SEB* . . . being much displeased, *Noyes* . . . was indignant, *Murdock* . . . being exasperated, *Concordant* . . . until Paul in vexation, *Weymouth* . . . being sore troubled, *ASV*.

**I command thee in the name of Jesus Christ to come out of her:** I order you out of her! *Moffatt*. . . to get out of her! *Berkeley* . . . By the authority of, *SEB* . . . By the power, *Fenton, NCV* . . . I charge thee, *Swann*.

**And he came out the same hour:** That very moment the spirit left her, *TCNT* . . . Immediately, *NCV*.

| 1481.17 verb nom pl masc part aor act | 1156.2 conj | 3450.7 art nom pl masc | 2935.6 noun nom pl masc | 840.10 prs-pron gen sing fem | 3617.1 conj |
|---|---|---|---|---|---|
| **19.** Ἰδόντες | δὲ | οἱ | κύριοι | αὐτῆς | ὅτι |
| *Idontes* | *de* | *hoi* | *kurioi* | *autēs* | *hoti* |
| Having seen | and | the | masters | her | that |

| 1814.3 verb 3sing indic aor act | 3450.9 art nom sing fem | 1667.1 noun nom sing fem | 3450.10 art gen sing fem | 2022.1 noun gen sing fem | 840.1 prs-pron gen pl |
|---|---|---|---|---|---|
| ἐξῆλθεν | ἡ | ἐλπὶς | τῆς | ἐργασίας | αὐτῶν, |
| *exēlthen* | *hē* | *elpis* | *tēs* | *ergasias* | *autōn* |
| was gone | the | hope | of the | profit | their, |

| 1934.7 verb nom pl masc part aor mid | 3450.6 art acc sing masc | 3834.4 name acc masc | 2504.1 conj | 3450.6 art acc sing masc | 4464.3 name acc masc |
|---|---|---|---|---|---|
| ἐπιλαβόμενοι | τὸν | Παῦλον | καὶ | τὸν | Σίλαν |
| *epilabomenoi* | *ton* | *Paulon* | *kai* | *ton* | *Silan* |
| having taken hold of | | Paul | and | | Silas |

| 1657.3 verb 3pl indic aor act | 1519.1 prep | 3450.12 art acc sing fem | 57.3 noun acc sing fem | 1894.3 prep | 3450.8 art acc pl masc |
|---|---|---|---|---|---|
| εἵλκυσαν | εἰς | τὴν | ἀγορὰν | ἐπὶ | τοὺς |
| *heilkusan* | *eis* | *tēn* | *agoran* | *epi* | *tous* |
| they dragged | into | the | marketplace | before | the |

| 752.8 noun acc pl masc | 2504.1 conj | 4175.4 verb nom pl masc part aor act | 840.8 prs-pron acc pl masc | 3450.4 art dat pl |
|---|---|---|---|---|
| ἄρχοντας· | **20.** καὶ | προσαγαγόντες | αὐτοὺς | τοῖς |
| *archontas* | *kai* | *prosagagontes* | *autous* | *tois* |
| authorities; | and | having brought up | them | to the |

20.a.**Txt:** 04C,05D,020L 025P,etc.byz.Sod
**Var:** 01ℵ,02A,03B,08E Lach,Treg,Alf,Tisc We/Ho,Weis,UBS/⋆

| 4606.3 noun dat pl masc | 1500.3 verb indic aor act | 1500.28 verb 3pl indic aor act | 3642.7 dem-pron nom pl masc | 3450.7 art nom pl masc |
|---|---|---|---|---|
| στρατηγοῖς | ᾿ εἶπον, | [a⋆ εἶπαν, ] | Οὗτοι | οἱ |
| *stratēgois* | *eipon* | *eipan* | *Houtoi* | *hoi* |
| magistrates | said, | [ idem ] | These | the |

| 442.6 noun nom pl masc | 1600.1 verb 3pl indic pres act | 2231.2 prs-pron gen 1pl | 3450.12 art acc sing fem | 4032.4 noun acc sing fem |
|---|---|---|---|---|
| ἄνθρωποι | ἐκταράσσουσιν | ἡμῶν | τὴν | πόλιν, |
| *anthrōpoi* | *ektarassousin* | *hēmōn* | *tēn* | *polin* |
| men | exceedingly trouble | our | the | city, |

| 2428.2 name-adj nom pl masc | 5062.7 verb nom pl masc part pres act | 2504.1 conj | 2576.1 verb dat pl masc part pres act |
|---|---|---|---|
| Ἰουδαῖοι | ὑπάρχοντες· | **21.** καὶ | καταγγέλλουσιν |
| *Ioudaioi* | *huparchontes* | *kai* | *katangellousin* |
| Jews | being, | and | are announcing |

| 1478.5 noun pl neu | 3614.17 rel-pron pl neu | 3620.2 partic | 1815.1 verb 3sing indic pres act | 2231.3 prs-pron dat 1pl | 3720.4 verb inf pres mid |
|---|---|---|---|---|---|
| ἔθη | ἃ | οὐκ | ἔξεστιν | ἡμῖν | παραδέχεσθαι |
| *ethē* | *ha* | *ouk* | *exestin* | *hēmin* | *paradechesthai* |
| customs | which | not | it is lawful | for us | to receive |

| 3624.1 conj | 4020.20 verb inf pres act | 4371.5 name-adj dat pl masc | 1498.24 verb dat pl masc part pres act | 2504.1 conj |
|---|---|---|---|---|
| οὐδὲ | ποιεῖν, | Ῥωμαίοις | οὖσιν. | **22.** Καὶ |
| *oude* | *poiein* | *Rhōmaiois* | *ousin* | *Kai* |
| nor | to do, | Romans | being. | And |

| 4761.1 verb 3sing indic aor act | 3450.5 art nom sing masc | 3657.1 noun nom sing masc | 2567.1 prep | 840.1 prs-pron gen pl | 2504.1 conj |
|---|---|---|---|---|---|
| συνεπέστη | ὁ | ὄχλος | κατ᾽ | αὐτῶν, | καὶ |
| *sunepestē* | *ho* | *ochlos* | *kat'* | *autōn* | *kai* |
| rose up together | the | crowd | against | them, | and |

**16:19.** Up to this point in Paul's missionary travels, most of the persecution and opposition to the gospel was stirred up by Jews. It came from jealousy over the success of the apostles and from a desire to retain their own position of religious leadership. But in Philippi there was no synagogue, and for the first time persecution came directly from Gentiles.

Actually, the Gentiles paid no attention to Paul at first. The owners of the slave girl did not object to her following Paul, for that only drew attention to the demon spirit in her, which in turn brought more people to her for fortune telling when her masters had their hours of business. But when Paul cast out the evil spirit, their attitude suddenly changed. To them the evil spirit was their hope of gains (profit). The deliverance of the poor demon-possessed girl meant nothing to them. All they saw was that their hope of profit was gone (literally, "cast out"). Greed for material gain all too often makes men take advantage of others. Money was the real god of these men. They cared nothing for Paul or his message. All they cared about was using this slave girl to make a profit.

Because the girl's masters were very upset at their loss, they seized Paul and Silas and dragged them into the marketplace (Greek, *agora*), the center of public life in Greek cities. There they rather violently brought them before the rulers, the two praetors or chief Roman magistrates of the city.

**16:20.** As soon as they brought Paul and Silas before the Roman magistrates they presented their accusation. But they did not mention the real reason they were upset. Instead, they called Paul and Silas big Jewish troublemakers. The Greek word is emphatic. They claimed the apostles were troubling their city greatly (exceedingly).

**16:21.** They went on to say that Paul and Silas were proclaiming customs that were not lawful for Romans to welcome or practice.

Though Judaism was a legal religion in the Roman Empire, it was only tolerated by the majority of the people and was not looked on with any real favor by the government. The fourth Roman emperor, Claudius, had no love for the Jews and expelled them from Rome.

In most of the Greek-speaking cities of Asia Minor where there were synagogues, the Jews influenced quite a number of Gentiles. Also many Gentiles responded to the gospel and accepted Christ as Lord and Saviour. But since there was no synagogue in Philippi, and since they took pride in being Romans, the owners of this slave girl tried to stir up the city officials to take action against Paul and Silas.

**16:22.** The people were ready to believe that Jews could be troublemakers. It is always easy for people to blame their troubles on a minority group among them. The agora was always crowded with people. It was the civic center as well as the marketplace. People

**19. And when her masters saw that the hope of their gains were gone:** . . . seeing that the hope of their gain was gone, *Swann* . . . no hope of further profit from her, *TCNT* . . . their way of making money for the future was gone, *Adams* . . . all their hopes of profit had vanished, *Knox* . . . knew that now they could not use her to make money, *NCV* . . . could not longer use her, *SEB.*

**they caught Paul and Silas:** . . . they took, *BB* . . . they seized, *TCNT* . . . they grabbed, *Berkeley* . . . arresting, *Fenton.*

**and drew them into the marketplace unto the rulers:** . . . and dragged them...before the rulers, *ASV* . . . pulling them...before the rulers, *BB* . . . dragged them into the public square to the authorities, *TCNT* . . . dragged them by their heels, *Wuest* . . . to the law courts, *JB.*

**20. And brought them:** . . . and took them, *TCNT* . . . And when they had taken them, *BB.*

**to the magistrates, saying:** . . . in front of the leaders, *NLT* . . . before the highest Roman officials, *Beck* . . . before the authorities, *BB.*

**These men, being Jews, do exceedingly trouble our city:** . . . mightily disturb, *Campbell* . . . are perturbing, *Concordant* . . . are making trouble in, *SEB* . . . are greatly troubling our town, *BB.*

**21. And teach customs:** . . . and are declaring customs, *Rotherham* . . . and announcing customs, *Swann* . . . they're teaching religious ways, *Beck* . . . Teaching rules of living, *BB.*

**which are not lawful for us to receive, neither to observe, being Romans:** . . . which it is not allowable for us either to accept or observe, *Rotherham* . . . teaching a religion that we Romans are not allowed to follow, *NLT* . . . which it is not right for us to have or to keep, *BB* . . . aren't allowed, *Beck* . . . to welcome, *Berkeley.*

**22. And the multitude rose up together against them:** On this the mob rose as one man against them, *TCNT* . . . The crowd, too, joined in the outcry against them, *Weymouth* . . . also joined in against them, *Swann.*

| **3450.7** art nom pl masc | **4606.2** noun nom pl masc | **3911.1** verb nom pl masc part aor act | **3911.2** verb nom pl masc part aor act |
|---|---|---|---|
| οἱ | στρατηγοὶ | ʻ περιῤῥήξαντες | [☆ περιρήξαντες ] |
| *hoi* | *stratēgoi* | *perirrhēxantes* | *perirēxantes* |
| the | magistrates | having torn off | [ idem ] |

| **840.1** prs-pron gen pl | **3450.17** art pl neu | **2416.4** noun pl neu | **2724.8** verb 3pl indic imperf act | **4320.1** verb inf pres act |
|---|---|---|---|---|
| αὐτῶν | τὰ | ἱμάτια | ἐκέλευον | ῥαβδίζειν˙ |
| *autōn* | *ta* | *himatia* | *ekeleuon* | *rhabdizein* |
| of them | the | garments | were commanding | to beat with rods. |

| | **4044.15** adj acc pl fem | **4885.1** conj | **1991.15** verb nom pl masc part aor act | **840.2** prs-pron dat pl | **3987.8** noun acc pl fem | **900.11** verb 3pl indic aor act |
|---|---|---|---|---|---|---|
| **23.** | πολλάς | τε | ἐπιθέντες | αὐτοῖς | πληγὰς | ἔβαλον |
| | *pollas* | *te* | *epithentes* | *autois* | *plēgas* | *ebalon* |
| | Many | and | having laid | on them | wounds | they cast |

| **1519.1** prep | **5274.4** noun acc sing fem | **3715.12** verb nom pl masc part aor act | **3450.3** art dat sing | **1194.2** noun dat sing masc |
|---|---|---|---|---|
| εἰς | φυλακήν, | παραγγείλαντες | τῷ | δεσμοφύλακι |
| *eis* | *phulakēn* | *parangeilantes* | *tō* | *desmophulaki* |
| into | prison, | having charged | the | jailor |

| **800.1** adv | **4931.11** verb inf pres act | **840.8** prs-pron acc pl masc | | **3614.5** rel-pron nom sing masc | **3714.3** noun acc sing fem |
|---|---|---|---|---|---|
| ἀσφαλῶς | τηρεῖν | αὐτούς˙ | **24.** | ὃς | παραγγελίαν |
| *asphalōs* | *tērein* | *autous* | | *hos* | *parangelian* |
| safely | to keep | them; | | who | a charge |

24.a.**Txt:** 020L,025P,byz.
**Var:** 01א,02A,03B,04C
05D,08E,Lach,Treg,Alf
Word,Tisc,We/Ho,Weis
Sod,UBS/☆

| **4955.10** dem-pron acc sing fem | **2956.35** verb nom sing masc part perf act | **2956.25** verb nom sing masc part aor act | **900.10** verb 3sing indic aor act | **840.8** prs-pron acc pl masc |
|---|---|---|---|---|
| τοιαύτην | ʻ εἰληφὼς | [a☆ λαβὼν ] | ἔβαλεν | αὐτοὺς |
| *toiautēn* | *eilēphōs* | *labōn* | *ebalen* | *autous* |
| such | having received | [ idem ] | threw | them |

| **1519.1** prep | **3450.12** art acc sing fem | **2061.1** adj comp acc sing fem | **5274.4** noun acc sing fem | **2504.1** conj | **3450.8** art acc pl masc | **4087.7** noun acc pl masc |
|---|---|---|---|---|---|---|
| εἰς | τὴν | ἐσωτέραν | φυλακὴν, | καὶ | τοὺς | πόδας |
| *eis* | *tēn* | *esōteran* | *phulakēn* | *kai* | *tous* | *podas* |
| into | the | inner | prison, | and | the | feet |

| **840.1** prs-pron gen pl | **799.1** verb 3sing indic aor mid | **799.1** verb 3sing indic aor mid | **840.1** prs-pron gen pl | **1519.1** prep |
|---|---|---|---|---|
| ʻ αὐτῶν | ἠσφαλίσατο | [☆ ἠσφαλίσατο | αὐτῶν ] | εἰς |
| *autōn* | *ēsphalisato* | *ēsphalisato* | *autōn* | *eis* |
| their | secured | [ secured | their ] | to |

| **3450.16** art sing neu | **3448.1** noun sing neu | | **2567.3** prep | **1156.2** conj | **3450.16** art sing neu | **3187.2** noun sing neu |
|---|---|---|---|---|---|---|
| τὸ | ξύλον. | **25.** | Κατὰ | δὲ | τὸ | μεσονύκτιον |
| *to* | *xulon* | | *Kata* | *de* | *to* | *mesonuktion* |
| the | stocks. | | According to | and | the | midnight |

| **3834.1** name nom masc | **2504.1** conj | **4464.1** name nom masc | **4195.13** verb nom pl masc part pres mid | **5053.3** verb 3pl indic imperf act |
|---|---|---|---|---|
| Παῦλος | καὶ | Σίλας | προσευχόμενοι | ὕμνουν |
| *Paulos* | *kai* | *Silas* | *proseuchomenoi* | *humnoun* |
| Paul | and | Silas | praying | were singing praises to |

| **3450.6** art acc sing masc | **2296.4** noun acc sing masc | **1859.1** verb 3pl indic imperf mid | **1156.2** conj | **840.1** prs-pron gen pl | **3450.7** art nom pl masc |
|---|---|---|---|---|---|
| τὸν | θεόν˙ | ἐπηκροῶντο | δὲ | αὐτῶν | οἱ |
| *ton* | *theon* | *epēkroōnto* | *de* | *autōn* | *hoi* |
| | God, | were listening to | and | them | the |

gravitated there when they had nothing else to do. The sight of these men dragging Paul and Silas before the magistrates could not help but get their attention. They listened to the accusation which stirred up the crowd and joined together in an outbreak of mob violence.

To satisfy the mob, the chief magistrates tore off the clothes from Paul and Silas and ordered them to be severely beaten (flogged) with a rod—a common Roman punishment. Paul (2 Corinthians 11:25) said he was beaten with rods on three different occasions. But on this occasion he had the additional indignity of having his clothes ripped off of him in public. This kind of punishment was illegal for Roman citizens who had not undergone a legal trial. But in all the confusion, no one paid any attention to anything but that these men were Jews.

**and the magistrates rent off their clothes:** . . . stripped them of their clothing, *TCNT* . . . ordered them to be stripped, *Weymouth* . . . tore off their garments, *HBIE* . . . having torn their garments from them, *Young* . . . took their clothing off them, *BB*.

**and commanded to beat them:** . . . and ordered them to be beaten with rods, *TCNT* . . . to scourge them, *Murdock* . . . were giving orders to beat them with rods, *Worrell* . . . gave orders for them to be whipped, *BB*.

**16:23.** After Paul and Silas had been beaten with many blows (strokes of the rod), the magistrates had them thrown into prison. All this indicates the mob was still jumping around, shouting, and encouraging the officers, and that they followed while Paul and Silas were violently dragged away and thrown into the prison. Then the magistrates ordered the jailer to guard them securely.

**23. And when they had laid many stripes upon them:** After beating them severely, *TCNT* . . . and, after severely flogging them, *Weymouth* . . . when they had inflicted many lashes on them, *Knox* . . . after lashing them severely, *Fenton* . . . After they had hit them many times, *NLT* . . . given them a great number of blows, *BB*.

**they cast them into prison:** . . . the Magistrates put them in prison, *TCNT*.

**charging the jailor to keep them safely:** . . . bade the gaoler keep them in safe custody, *Knox* . . . giving orders to the keeper of the prison, *BB* . . . to guard them securely, *Berkeley* . . . guard them carefully, *Kleist* . . . be sure to keep them from getting away, *NLT*.

**16:24.** To make sure Paul and Silas could not escape, the jailer threw them into the inner prison and fastened their feet in wooden stocks. These stocks had holes for the feet and were constructed so the feet could be forced wide apart, causing much pain and making it impossible for the apostles to move their legs.

The inner prison was probably damp, cold, and insect-infested. After all their rough treatment, Paul and Silas must have found these circumstances to be almost unbearable.

**24. Who, having received such a charge:** On receiving so strict an order, the jailor, *TCNT* . . . heard this special order, *SEB* . . . having such orders, *BB*.

**thrust them into the inner prison:** . . . in the inner dungeon, *Norlie*.

**and made their feet fast in the stocks:** . . . and secured their feet in the stocks, *TCNT* . . . with chains on their feet, *BB*.

**16:25.** But Paul and Silas made no complaint. Instead at midnight they prayed. The Greek means they were praying and probably that they had been praying for some time.

Some folk in the same circumstances might have decided at this point the Macedonian call was a mistake and the vision in Troas a bad dream. But Paul and Silas did not give up hope. In spite of the torture, they could still look up to God. They might not have felt like praying at first; they certainly must not have felt like singing. But the times believers do not feel like praying are the times it is most important to pray. Evidently Paul and Silas must have prayed through to victory, for as they prayed joy flooded their souls and they broke out singing hymns of praise to the Lord. They saw that in spite of their discouraging and painful circumstances, God was still worthy to be praised. They had confidence that whatever happened they were still the Lord's. He would see them through!

Apparently, as Paul and Silas continued to pray and sing God's praises, the Holy Spirit lifted their spirits and they began to sing

**25. And at midnight Paul and Silas prayed:** But about midnight Paul and Silas were praying, *RSV* . . . But about the middle of the night...were making prayers, *BB* . . . were worshipping, *Berkeley*.

**and sang praises unto God:** . . . and singing hymns, *ASV*.

**and the prisoners heard them:** . . . in the hearing of the prisoners, *BB* . . . were listening to them, *Worrell*.

# Acts 16:26

| 1192.3 noun nom pl masc | 862.1 adv | 1156.2 conj | 4433.1 noun nom sing masc | 1090.33 verb 3sing indic aor mid |
|---|---|---|---|---|
| δέσμιοι· | 26. ἄφνω | δὲ | σεισμὸς | ἐγένετο |
| *desmioi* | *aphnō* | *de* | *seismos* | *egeneto* |
| prisoners. | Suddenly | and | an earthquake | there was |

| 3144.2 adj nom sing masc | 5452.1 conj | 4388.9 verb inf aor pass | 3450.17 art pl neu | 2287.7 noun pl neu | 3450.2 art gen sing |
|---|---|---|---|---|---|
| μέγας, | ὥστε | σαλευθῆναι | τὰ | θεμέλια | τοῦ |
| *megas* | *hōste* | *saleuthēnai* | *ta* | *themelia* | *tou* |
| great, | so that | to be shaken | the | foundations | of the |

26.a.**Txt:** 020L,025P,byz.
**Var:** 03B,04C,05D,33
Lach,Treg,Alf,We/Ho
Weis,Sod,UBS/☆

| 1195.1 noun gen sing neu | 453.20 verb 3pl indic aor pass | 453.19 verb 3pl indic aor pass | 4885.1 conj |
|---|---|---|---|
| δεσμωτηρίου· | ʻ ἀνεῴχθησαν | [a☆ ἠνεῴχθησαν ] | ʻ τε |
| *desmōtēriou* | *aneōchthēsan* | *ēneōchthēsan* | *te* |
| prison, | were opened | [ idem ] | and |

26.b.**Txt:** 04C,020L
025P,byz.
**Var:** 01ℵ,02A,03B,05D
08E,sa.bo.Lach,Treg,Alf
Tisc,We/Ho,Weis,Sod
UBS/☆

| 1156.2 conj | 3777.1 adv | 3450.13 art nom pl fem | 2351.5 noun nom pl fem | 3820.13 adj nom pl fem | 2504.1 conj |
|---|---|---|---|---|---|
| [b☆ δὲ ] | παραχρῆμα | αἱ | θύραι | πᾶσαι, | καὶ |
| *de* | *parachrēma* | *hai* | *thurai* | *pasai* | *kai* |
| [ idem ] | immediately | the | doors | all, | and |

| 3820.4 adj gen pl | 3450.17 art pl neu | 1193.3 noun pl | 445.4 verb 3sing indic aor pass | 1837.1 adj nom sing masc |
|---|---|---|---|---|
| πάντων | τὰ | δεσμὰ | ἀνέθη. | 27. ἔξυπνος |
| *pantōn* | *ta* | *desma* | *anethē* | *exupnos* |
| all | the | bonds | were loosed. | Awoke out of sleep |

| 1156.2 conj | 1090.53 verb nom sing masc part aor mid | 3450.5 art nom sing masc | 1194.1 noun nom sing masc | 2504.1 conj |
|---|---|---|---|---|
| δὲ | γενόμενος | ὁ | δεσμοφύλαξ | καὶ |
| *de* | *genomenos* | *ho* | *desmophulax* | *kai* |
| and | having been | the | jailor, | and |

| 1481.16 verb nom sing masc part aor act | 453.31 verb acc pl fem part perf mid | 3450.15 art acc pl fem | 2351.1 noun fem | 3450.10 art gen sing fem |
|---|---|---|---|---|
| ἰδὼν | ἀνεῳγμένας | τὰς | θύρας | τῆς |
| *idōn* | *aneōgmenas* | *tas* | *thuras* | *tēs* |
| having seen | having been opened | the | doors | of the |

27.a.**Var:** 03B,04C,05D
Lach,Treg,Alf,We/Ho
Weis,UBS/☆

| 5274.2 noun gen sing fem | 4538.1 verb nom sing masc part aor mid | 3450.12 art acc sing fem | 3134.4 noun acc sing fem | 3165.22 verb 3sing indic imperf act |
|---|---|---|---|---|
| φυλακῆς, | σπασάμενος | [a☆+ τὴν ] | μάχαιραν | ʻ ἔμελλεν |
| *phulakēs* | *spasamenos* | *tēn* | *machairan* | *emellen* |
| prison, | having drawn | [ the ] | a sword | was about |

27.b.**Txt:** 05D,byz.
**Var:** 01ℵ,02A,03B,04C
08E,020L,025P,Lach
Treg,Alf,Tisc,We/Ho
Weis,Sod,UBS/☆

| 3165.21 verb 3sing indic imperf act | 1431.6 prs-pron acc sing masc | 335.3 verb inf pres act | 3406.3 verb nom sing masc part pres act |
|---|---|---|---|
| [b☆ ἤμελλεν ] | ἑαυτὸν | ἀναιρεῖν, | νομίζων |
| *ēmellen* | *heauton* | *anairein* | *nomizōn* |
| [ idem ] | himself | to put to death, | supposing |

| 1614.4 verb inf perf act | 3450.8 art acc pl masc | 1192.5 noun acc pl masc | 5291.6 verb 3sing indic aor act | 1156.2 conj |
|---|---|---|---|---|
| ἐκπεφευγέναι | τοὺς | δεσμίους. | 28. ἐφώνησεν | δὲ |
| *ekpepheugenai* | *tous* | *desmious* | *ephōnēsen* | *de* |
| to have escaped | the | prisoners. | Called out | but |

28.a.**Txt:** 05D,08E,020L
025P,byz.Sod
**Var:** 03B,bo.We/Ho
Weis,UBS/☆

| 5292.3 noun dat sing fem | 3144.11 adj dat sing fem | 3450.5 art nom sing masc | 3834.1 name nom masc | 3834.1 name nom masc |
|---|---|---|---|---|
| ʻ φωνῇ | μεγάλῃ | ὁ | Παῦλος | [a☆ Παῦλος |
| *phōnē* | *megalē* | *ho* | *Paulos* | *Paulos* |
| with a voice | loud | | Paul | [ Paul |

louder and louder, until the prisoners in the main part of the prison woke up and began to listen to them. Somehow, the songs of praise to God must have awed them, for they did not complain or shout out insults at Paul and Silas. At midnight they were still listening.

**16:26.** Suddenly a great earthquake shook the very foundations of the prison. As the walls shook back and forth, the doors flew open and all the prisoners' chains, which were probably fastened into the wall, were broken loose.

One of the earth's great earthquake zones runs through the Mediterranean region. In both ancient and modern times, violent earthquakes have been fairly common there. Many have been violent enough to destroy entire cities. This one was not strong enough to knock down the prison, but it was enough to loosen the prisoners' chains and break the bars on the doors. It came at just the right time—when Paul and Silas had prayed through and gained the attention of the prisoners.

Earthquakes are caused by the build-up of forces along fault lines in the rocks. But God has often used natural phenomena in connection with His miracles to show His control and His timing. He does all things well. Clearly, this earthquake was no accident. God caused it. He saw Paul and Silas and let them suffer a short time to prepare for an even more important event.

**16:27.** The earthquake awakened the jailer. It seems he immediately rushed to the prison, saw the doors were open, and jumped to the conclusion that all the prisoners had escaped. He knew the penalty he would suffer. Under Roman law, the jailer was personally responsible for the lives of the prisoners and was subject to the death penalty if they escaped. The Book of Acts recorded what Herod Agrippa I did to the guards when the angel brought Peter out of prison (12:19). Rather than face the trial, the shame, and the disgraceful death that was sure to come, the jailer drew his sword, intending to commit suicide.

Suicide was not common among the Jews. Only a very few instances are known. One was the case of Ahithophel. He was one of David's trusted counselors. But when Absalom won over the hearts of many of the Israelites and prepared to declare himself king, he sent for Ahithophel and won him over too. But when Absalom did not follow Ahithophel's advice, Ahithophel knew Absalom's cause would lose. He could not bear to face David who had trusted him and whom he had betrayed. So he went home, put his household affairs in order, and hanged himself.

Suicide was more common among the heathen, however. It is still fairly common among many non-Christian religions where human life does not have the value the Bible places upon it.

**16:28.** From the deep darkness of the prison, Paul could see what the jailer was doing even though the jailer could not see into

**26. And suddenly there was a great earthquake:** . . . an earthquake of such violence, *TCNT* . . . a violent earthquake, *Fenton.*

**so that the foundations of the prison were shaken:** . . . the jail was shaken to its foundations, *TCNT* . . . so that the base of the prison was moved, *BB* . . . of the prison rocked, *Knox.*

**and immediately all the doors were opened:** . . . all the doors flew open, *TCNT* . . . At one stroke all the doors sprang open, *Berkeley* . . . all the doors of the jail broke open, *Everyday* . . . came open, *BB.*

**and every one's bands were loosed:** . . . and all the prisoners' chains were loosened, *TCNT* . . . while every one was freed from his bonds, *Fenton* . . . and the chains fell off every prisoner, *Weymouth* . . . all the chains fell apart, *Adams* . . . and every man's chains were undone, *Knox* . . . every man's chains unfastened, *Williams C.K.* . . . and the bands of all were removed, *Wesley* . . . and the fetters, *Wilson.*

**27. And the keeper of the prison awaking out of his sleep:** When the jailer woke up, *Williams C.K.* . . . The warder being accordingly roused from his sleep, *Fenton* . . . startled out of his sleep, *AmpB.*

**and seeing the prison doors open:** . . . wide open, *Weymouth.*

**he drew out his sword, and would have killed himself:** . . . and was about to kill himself, *RSV* . . . intending to kill himself, *TCNT* . . . and was on the point of killing himself, *Weymouth* . . . intent on committing suicide, *Norlie* . . . was about to put himself to death, *BB.*

**supposing that the prisoners had been fled:** . . . because he thought, *Montgomery* . . . under the impression, *TCNT* . . . feeling sure, *Berkeley* . . . for he imagined that all the prisoners, *Phillips* . . . inferring that the prisoners have escaped, *Concordant* . . . fearing that the prisoners had got away, *BB.*

**28. But Paul cried out with a loud voice, saying:** But Paul at once shouted out to him, *Williams* . . . shouted loudly to him, *Weymouth* . . . at the top of his voice, *Phillips.*

| 3144.11 adj dat sing fem | 5292.3 noun dat sing fem | 2978.15 verb nom sing masc part pres act | 3235.6 num card neu | 4097.19 verb 2sing subj aor act |
|---|---|---|---|---|
| μεγάλῃ | φωνῇ ] | λέγων, | Μηδὲν | πράξῃς |
| *megalē* | *phōnē* | *legōn* | *Mēden* | *praxēs* |
| loud | with a voice ] | saying, | Nothing | do |

| 4427.2 prs-pron dat sing masc | 2527.7 adj sing neu | 533.4 adj nom pl masc | 1056.1 conj | 1498.5 verb 1pl indic pres act | 1743.1 adv |
|---|---|---|---|---|---|
| σεαυτῷ | κακόν· | ἅπαντες | γάρ | ἐσμεν | ἐνθάδε. |
| *seautō* | *kakon* | *hapantes* | *gar* | *esmen* | *enthade* |
| to yourself | injury; | all | for | we are | here. |

| 153.17 verb nom sing masc part aor act | 1156.2 conj | 5295.5 noun pl neu | 1514.1 verb 3sing indic aor act | 2504.1 conj |
|---|---|---|---|---|
| **29.** Αἰτήσας | δὲ | φῶτα | εἰσεπήδησεν, | καὶ |
| *Aitēsas* | *de* | *phōta* | *eisepēdēsen* | *kai* |
| Having requested | and | lights | he rushed in, | and |

| 1774.1 adj nom sing masc | 1090.53 verb nom sing masc part aor mid | 4221.1 verb 3sing indic aor act | 3450.3 art dat sing | 3834.3 name dat masc |
|---|---|---|---|---|
| ἔντρομος | γενόμενος | προσέπεσεν | τῷ | Παύλῳ |
| *entromos* | *genomenos* | *prosepesen* | *tō* | *Paulō* |
| trembling | having become | fell down before | | Paul |

29.a.**Txt:** 01ℵ,02A 04C-corr,08E,020L 025P,byz.Tisc,Sod **Var:** 03B,04C-org,05D Lach,Treg,Alf,We/Ho Weis,UBS/*

| 2504.1 conj | 3450.3 art dat sing | 4464.2 name dat masc | 2504.1 conj | 4113.10 verb nom sing masc part aor act | 840.8 prs-pron acc pl masc |
|---|---|---|---|---|---|
| καὶ | (a τῷ ) | Σίλᾳ, | **30.** καὶ | προαγαγὼν | αὐτοὺς |
| *kai* | *tō* | *Sila* | *kai* | *proagagōn* | *autous* |
| and | | Silas. | And | having brought | them |

| 1838.1 adv | 5183.4 verb 3sing indic act | 2935.6 noun nom pl masc | 4949.9 intr-pron sing neu | 1466.6 prs-pron acc 1sing | 1158.1 verb 3sing indic pres act |
|---|---|---|---|---|---|
| ἔξω | ἔφη, | Κύριοι, | τί | με | δεῖ |
| *exō* | *ephē* | *Kurioi* | *ti* | *me* | *dei* |
| out | he said, | Sirs, | what | for me | is necessary |

| 4020.20 verb inf pres act | 2419.1 conj | 4834.25 verb 1sing subj aor pass | 3450.7 art nom pl masc | 1156.2 conj | 1500.3 verb indic aor act |
|---|---|---|---|---|---|
| ποιεῖν | ἵνα | σωθῶ; | **31.** Οἱ | δὲ | ( εἶπον, |
| *poiein* | *hina* | *sōthō* | *Hoi* | *de* | *eipon* |
| to do | that | I may be saved? | The | and | said, |

31.a.**Txt:** 020L,025P,byz. Sod **Var:** 01ℵ,02A,03B,04C 05D,08E,Lach,Treg,Alf Tisc,We/Ho,Weis UBS/*

| 1500.28 verb 3pl indic aor act | 3961.28 verb 2sing impr aor act | 1894.3 prep | 3450.6 art acc sing masc | 2935.4 noun acc sing masc |
|---|---|---|---|---|
| [a☆ εἶπαν, ] | Πίστευσον | ἐπὶ | τὸν | κύριον |
| *eipan* | *Pisteuson* | *epi* | *ton* | *kurion* |
| [ idem ] | Believe | on | the | Lord |

31.b.**Txt:** 04C,05D,08E 020L,025P,byz.sa.Sod **Var:** 01ℵ,02A,03B,bo. Lach,Treg,Alf,Tisc We/Ho,Weis,UBS/*

| 2400.3 name acc masc | 5382.4 name acc masc | 2504.1 conj | 4834.32 verb 2sing indic fut pass | 4622.1 prs-pron nom 2sing |
|---|---|---|---|---|
| Ἰησοῦν | (b Χριστόν, ) | καὶ | σωθήσῃ, | σὺ |
| *Iēsoun* | *Christon* | *kai* | *sōthēsē* | *su* |
| Jesus | Christ, | and | you shall be saved, | you |

| 2504.1 conj | 3450.5 art nom sing masc | 3486.1 noun nom sing masc | 4622.2 prs-pron gen 2sing | 2504.1 conj | 2953.30 verb 3pl indic aor act |
|---|---|---|---|---|---|
| καὶ | ὁ | οἶκός | σου. | **32.** καὶ | ἐλάλησαν |
| *kai* | *ho* | *oikos* | *sou* | *kai* | *elalēsan* |
| and | the | house | your. | And | they spoke |

32.a.**Txt:** p45,p74 01ℵ-corr,02A,04C,05D 08E,020L,025P,etc.byz. it.sa.bo.Tisc,Sod **Var:** 01ℵ-org,03B We/Ho,Weis,UBS/*

| 840.4 prs-pron dat sing | 3450.6 art acc sing masc | 3030.4 noun acc sing masc | 3450.2 art gen sing | 2935.2 noun gen sing masc | 2296.2 noun gen sing masc |
|---|---|---|---|---|---|
| αὐτῷ | τὸν | λόγον | τοῦ | ( κυρίου, | [a θεοῦ ] |
| *autō* | *ton* | *logon* | *tou* | *kuriou* | *theou* |
| to him | the | word | of the | Lord, | [ God ] |

the darkness of the prison. Immediately Paul shouted out, telling the jailer not to harm himself, for all the prisoners were still there.

This must have come as a shock to the jailer. After the way he had treated Paul, and after the beating Paul had received, the jailer would certainly have expected no mercy from Paul or from any other prisoner. Most prisoners in those days, if they had not yet escaped, would have waited in silence until the jailer killed himself and then made their escape. But Paul was always more concerned about others than he was about himself.

**16:29.** After asking for lights to be brought, the jailer rushed into the prison. Trembling with fear, he fell down beside Paul and Silas. That is, he was completely overcome by fear and awe because of what had happened and because Paul had saved him from suicide.

**16:30.** Then, recovering his composure, he brought them out of the prison. The context indicates he brought them into his own house, which was undoubtedly next door. Codex Bezae (D) adds that he first secured the other prisoners. This was undoubtedly true. Apparently because they were so in awe of the prayers, the songs, and the earthquake, none of them had made any attempt to escape.

The jailer then asked Paul and Silas what he must do to be saved. This might seem a strange question from a pagan Roman, but he knew the accusation against Paul and Silas. He must have remembered the words of the ventriloquist spirit that possessed the slave girl—these men could tell him the way of salvation.

**16:31.** Paul's answer let him know he must "believe" rather than "do" in order to be saved. When the people asked Jesus, "What shall we do, that we might work the works of God?" Jesus replied, "This is the work of God, that ye believe on him whom he hath sent" (John 6:28,29). The jailer also needed to know who Jesus is and what it means to believe in Him.

The words "and thy house" must be connected with the believing. Paul did not mean the jailer's household would be saved simply because the jailer was. Neither did he mean the jailer's salvation would guarantee theirs. Paul wanted the jailer to know the offer of salvation was not limited to him. Some cults, popular among the Romans, were composed of all males; some catered to certain classes. But the salvation Christ brings is for all. If the rest of the jailer's household would believe, they too would be saved. Paul wanted to see them all saved, not just one.

**16:32.** The jailer then gathered his entire household (including the servants) for a midnight evangelistic service and teaching session. Paul proclaimed the Word of God to them, explaining the

**Do thyself no harm, for we are all here:** Don't hurt yourself, *Phillips* . . . Do not begin to do yourself one bit of harm, *Wuest* . . . Do yourself no damage, *BB* . . . we are still here, *NAB.*

**29. Then he called for a light, and sprang in:** Calling for a light, the jailor rushed in, *TCNT* . . . Then he ran inside, *NCV* . . . told someone to bring a light, *SEB* . . . Demanding then a light, *Fenton* . . . called for a lamp, *Williams C.K.* . . . sent for lights, *BB.*

**and came trembling, and fell down before Paul and Silas:** . . . becoming agitated, *Rotherham* . . . trembling for fear, *ASV, Hanson* . . . and fell terror-stricken, *Berkeley* . . . and seized with a tremor, *Fenton* . . . being in fear, *Worrell* . . . and flung himself trembling at the feet, *TCNT* . . . shaking with fear, *BB* . . . and got down in front of Paul...He was shaking with fear, *NLT.*

**30. And brought them out, and said:** After a brief interval he led them out, *NAB* . . . conducting them out, *Fenton* . . . and leading them forth outside, *Rotherham* . . . as he led them out, *Knox.*

**Sirs, what must I do to be saved?:** Masters, *Swann* . . . Men, what is it necessary for me to do that I may be saved, *AmpB* . . . what am I to do, to save myself? *Knox* . . . what have I to do to get salvation? *BB.*

**31. And they said, Believe on the Lord Jesus Christ:** Have faith in the Lord Jesus, *BB, Berkeley* . . . Commit yourself, *SEB* . . . Put your trust in, *NLT.*

**and thou shalt be saved, and thy house:** . . . and you shall be saved, you and your household too, *TCNT* . . . and you and your family will have salvation, *BB* . . . and all the people in your house, *Everyday.*

**32. And they spake unto him the word of the Lord and to all that were in his house:** . . . they delivered the message of the Lord to him, with all those in his family, *Fenton* . . . told the story of the Lord Jesus, *SEB* . . . as well as to all who were in his house, *Weymouth* . . . to him and his family, *NLT.*

32.b.**Txt:** 08E,020L 025P,byz.sa.bo.
**Var:** 01ℵ,02A,03B,04C 05D,33,Gries,Lach,Treg Alf,Word,Tisc,We/Ho Weis,Sod,UBS/☆

| **2504.1** conj | **3820.5** adj dat pl | **4713.1** prep | **3820.5** adj dat pl | **3450.4** art dat pl | **1706.1** prep | **3450.11** art dat sing fem |
|---|---|---|---|---|---|---|
| ʻ καὶ | πᾶσιν | [b☆ σὺν | πᾶσιν ] | τοῖς | ἐν | τῇ |
| *kai* | *pasin* | *sun* | *pasin* | *tois* | *en* | *tē* |
| and | to all | [ with | all ] | the | in | the |

| **3477.3** noun dat sing fem | **840.3** prs-pron gen sing | **2504.1** conj | **3741.9** verb nom sing masc part aor act | **840.8** prs-pron acc pl masc | **1706.1** prep |
|---|---|---|---|---|---|
| οἰκίᾳ | αὐτοῦ. | 33. καὶ | παραλαβὼν | αὐτοὺς | ἐν |
| *oikia* | *autou* | *kai* | *paralabōn* | *autous* | *en* |
| house | his. | And | having taken | them | in |

| **1552.11** dem-pron dat sing fem | **3450.11** art dat sing fem | **5443.3** noun dat sing fem | **3450.10** art gen sing fem | **3433.2** noun gen sing fem | **3040.1** verb 3sing indic aor act |
|---|---|---|---|---|---|
| ἐκείνῃ | τῇ | ὥρᾳ | τῆς | νυκτὸς | ἔλουσεν |
| *ekeinē* | *tē* | *hōra* | *tēs* | *nuktos* | *elousen* |
| that | the | hour | of the | night | he washed |

| **570.3** prep | **3450.1** art gen pl | **3987.6** noun gen pl fem | **2504.1** conj | **901.14** verb 3sing indic aor pass | **840.5** prs-pron nom sing masc | **2504.1** conj |
|---|---|---|---|---|---|---|
| ἀπὸ | τῶν | πληγῶν, | καὶ | ἐβαπτίσθη | αὐτὸς | καὶ |
| *apo* | *tōn* | *plēgōn* | *kai* | *ebaptisthē* | *autos* | *kai* |
| from | the | wounds; | and | was baptized | he | and |

33.a.**Txt:** 02A,04C,05D 08E,020L,025P,etc.byz. Sod
**Var:** 01ℵ,03B,Tisc We/Ho,Weis,UBS/☆

| **3450.7** art nom pl masc | **840.3** prs-pron gen sing | **3820.7** adj nom pl masc | **533.4** adj nom pl masc | **3777.1** adv |
|---|---|---|---|---|
| οἱ | αὐτοῦ | ʻ πάντες | [a ἅπαντες ] | παραχρῆμα, |
| *hoi* | *autou* | *pantes* | *hapantes* | *parachrēma* |
| the | his | all | [ idem ] | immediately. |

| **319.2** verb nom sing masc part aor act | **4885.1** conj | **840.8** prs-pron acc pl masc | **1519.1** prep | **3450.6** art acc sing masc | **3486.4** noun acc sing masc |
|---|---|---|---|---|---|
| 34. ἀναγαγών | τε | αὐτοὺς | εἰς | τὸν | οἶκον |
| *anagagōn* | *te* | *autous* | *eis* | *ton* | *oikon* |
| Having brought | and | them | into | the | house |

34.a.**Txt:** 01ℵ,02A,05D 08E,020L,etc.byz.
**Var:** 03B,04C,025P Lach,Alf,Tisc,We/Ho Weis,Sod,UBS/☆

| **840.3** prs-pron gen sing | **3769.2** verb 3sing indic aor act | **4971.3** noun acc sing fem | **2504.1** conj | **21.6** verb 3sing indic aor mid |
|---|---|---|---|---|
| ʻa αὐτοῦ ʼ | παρέθηκεν | τράπεζαν, | καὶ | ἠγαλλιάσατο |
| *autou* | *parethēken* | *trapezan* | *kai* | *ēgalliasato* |
| his | he laid | a table, | and | rejoiced |

| **3694.1** adv | **3694.2** adv | **3961.44** verb nom sing masc part perf act | **3450.3** art dat sing |
|---|---|---|---|
| ʻ πανοικὶ | [☆ πανοικεὶ ] | πεπιστευκὼς | τῷ |
| *panoiki* | *panoikei* | *pepisteukōs* | *tō* |
| with all house, | [ with all household ] | having believed | |

| **2296.3** noun dat sing masc | **2232.1** noun fem | **1156.2** conj | **1090.57** verb gen sing fem part aor mid | **643.9** verb 3pl indic aor act |
|---|---|---|---|---|
| θεῷ. | 35. Ἡμέρας | δὲ | γενομένης | ἀπέστειλαν |
| *theō* | *Hēmeras* | *de* | *genomenēs* | *apesteilan* |
| in God. | Day | and | having come | sent |

| **3450.7** art nom pl masc | **4606.2** noun nom pl masc | **3450.8** art acc pl masc | **4322.2** noun acc pl masc |
|---|---|---|---|
| οἱ | στρατηγοὶ | τοὺς | ῥαβδούχους |
| *hoi* | *stratēgoi* | *tous* | *rhabdouchous* |
| the | magistrates | the | officers, |

| **2978.16** verb nom pl masc part pres act | **624.11** verb 2sing impr aor act | **3450.8** art acc pl masc | **442.9** noun acc pl masc | **1552.8** dem-pron acc pl masc |
|---|---|---|---|---|
| λέγοντες, | Ἀπόλυσον | τοὺς | ἀνθρώπους | ἐκείνους. |
| *legontes* | *Apoluson* | *tous* | *anthrōpous* | *ekeinous* |
| saying, | Release | the | men | those. |

truth and giving them a solid Biblical foundation for believing in Jesus and for following the Christian way of life.

**16:33.** The jailer first showed he truly believed in Jesus by recognizing Paul and Silas as God's messengers. He believed they did not deserve the stripes (the wounds from the beating with rods given by the Roman officers or lictors), so he washed off the dried blood and dirt to indicate this.

Immediately after that, he and all the members of his household (who had also heard the Word and believed) were baptized in water. This was probably done in a pool in the courtyard of the house. Such pools were not uncommon in the larger Roman-style homes of those days (as archaeology shows).

**16:34.** After being baptized, the jailer took the apostles back inside the house and set before them a table loaded with food. After the jailer and his household came to believe, they began to rejoice. Joy does not always come the moment a person believes on Jesus, but it will come. When it does, it is a joy the world knows nothing about.

This passage (see also 11:14; 16:15; 18:8) describes an entire household that was converted. Modern missionaries report a similar phenomenon (referred to as "people movements") in tribes dominated by one (perhaps a few) male leader. A decision by the designated and respected "household" affects each family member. This was not uncommon, for example, in the case of Greeks who converted to Judaism.

**16:35.** The rejoicing probably continued the rest of the night. It would be hard to sleep after such an experience. In the morning the chief magistrates sent officers, called lictors, who were orderlies or attendants (not sergeants in the modern sense), to tell the jailer to let Paul and Silas go. (These lictors were also "rod bearers" and may have been the very ones who had beaten Paul and Silas.)

The Bible does not say why these Roman magistrates changed their minds after commanding the jailer to be sure to guard the prisoners securely. It may be that after thinking over the charges against Paul and Silas, they realized no evidence had been presented against them; nor had there been any mention of any specific way Paul and Silas had agitated the people or thrown them into confusion. In fact, the confusion had come only after the slave owners had dragged Paul and Silas into the agora (the marketplace and civic center). It may be that the earthquake had seemed to be some sort of sign or omen that they had done wrong.

It is also possible that in some way word had come to them of how Paul stopped the jailer from committing suicide. This would have given them a different view of Paul and Silas and might have caused them to feel they should be rewarded by being released.

**33. And he took them the same hour of the night:** At that very hour, *TCNT* . . . took personal charge of them, *Kleist* . . . he took them then and there in the middle of the night, *Williams C.K.* . . . It was late at night, *NLT* . . . at that hour, *Lamsa* . . . at dead of night, *Knox*.

**and washed their stripes:** . . . and when he had given attention to, *BB* . . . and washed their wounds, *Lamsa, TCNT.*

**and was baptized, he and all his, straightway:** . . . and he and all the members of his household at once were baptized, *Williams* . . . on-the-spot, *Rotherham* . . . was baptized at once, himself and all his family, *Williams C.K.* . . . got baptized instantly, *Moffatt* . . . were immersed right away, *SEB* . . . had baptism straight away, *BB* . . . in that very hour, *Lamsa* . . . without delay, *Swann.*

**34. And when he had brought them into his house he set meat before them:** . . . set food, *ASV* . . . offered them food, *Phillips.*

**and rejoiced, believing in God with all his house:** . . . and exulted, *Rotherham* . . . rejoicing that he, with all his household, had come to believe in God, *TCNT* . . . and was filled with gladness, *Weymouth* . . . transported with joy, *Campbell* . . . was extremely happy, *Berkeley* . . . was full of joy, having faith in God with all his family, *BB* . . . were very happy because they now believed in God, *Everyday* . . . filled with great joy, *Williams C.K.* . . . they now trusted in God, *SEB.*

**35. And when it was day:** In the morning, *TCNT* . . . When day broke, *Moffatt.*

**the magistrates sent the serjeants, saying:** . . . the chiefs of the police court sent policemen with the message, *Williams* . . . the officials sent attendants, *Beck* . . . the praetors sent their lictors with the instructions, *Kleist* . . . sent the police, *BB* . . . sent a soldier to say, *NLT* . . . to tell the prison warden, *Lamsa.*

**Let those men go:** Release those men, *Weymouth* . . . Dismiss those men, *Campbell* . . . Liberate these men, *Fenton* . . . Let these men go free! *Everyday* . . . Those men are to be discharged, *Knox.*

## Acts 16:36

| 514.7 verb 3sing indic aor act | 1156.2 conj | 3450.5 art nom sing masc | 1194.1 noun nom sing masc | 3450.8 art acc pl masc |
|---|---|---|---|---|
| 36. Ἀπήγγειλεν | δὲ | ὁ | δεσμοφύλαξ | τοὺς |
| Apēngeilen | de | ho | desmophulax | tous |
| Reported | and | the | jailor | the |

36.a.**Txt:** p74,01ℵ,02A 08E,044,byz.
**Var:** 03B,04C,05D,36 453,1891

| 3030.8 noun acc pl masc | 3642.8 dem-pron acc pl masc | 4242.1 prep | 3450.6 art acc sing masc | 3834.4 name acc masc | 3617.1 conj |
|---|---|---|---|---|---|
| λόγους | (ᵃ τούτους ) | πρὸς | τὸν | Παῦλον, | Ὅτι |
| logous | toutous | pros | ton | Paulon | Hoti |
| words | these | to | | Paul, | |

36.b.**Txt:** 05D,08E,020L 025P,byz.Sod
**Var:** 01ℵ,02A,03B,Lach Treg,Alf,Tisc,We/Ho Weis,UBS/⋆

| 643.20 verb 3pl indic perf act | 643.35 verb 3pl indic perf act | 3450.7 art nom pl masc | 4606.2 noun nom pl masc |
|---|---|---|---|
| ( ἀπέσταλκασιν | [ᵇ⋆ Ἀπέσταλκαν ] | οἱ | στρατηγοὶ |
| apestalkasin | Apestalkan | hoi | stratēgoi |
| Have sent | [ idem ] | the | magistrates |

| 2419.1 conj | 624.16 verb 2pl subj aor pass | 3431.1 adv | 3631.1 partic | 1814.15 verb nom pl masc part aor act |
|---|---|---|---|---|
| ἵνα | ἀπολυθῆτε· | νῦν | οὖν | ἐξελθόντες |
| hina | apoluthēte | nun | oun | exelthontes |
| that | you may be let go. | Now | therefore | having gone out |

| 4057.5 verb 2pl impr pres mid | 1706.1 prep | 1503.3 noun dat sing fem | 3450.5 art nom sing masc | 1156.2 conj | 3834.1 name nom masc |
|---|---|---|---|---|---|
| πορεύεσθε | ἐν | εἰρήνῃ. | 37. Ὁ | δὲ | Παῦλος |
| poreuesthe | en | eirēnē | Ho | de | Paulos |
| depart | in | peace. | | But | Paul |

| 5183.4 verb 3sing indic act | 4242.1 prep | 840.8 prs-pron acc pl masc | 1188.6 verb nom pl masc part aor act | 2231.4 prs-pron acc 1pl | 1212.1 adj dat sing fem |
|---|---|---|---|---|---|
| ἔφη | πρὸς | αὐτούς, | Δείραντες | ἡμᾶς | δημοσίᾳ |
| ephē | pros | autous | Deirantes | hēmas | dēmosia |
| said | to | them, | Having beaten | us | publicly |

| 176.2 adj acc pl masc | 442.9 noun acc pl masc | 4371.6 name-adj acc pl masc | 5062.8 verb acc pl masc part pres act |
|---|---|---|---|
| ἀκατακρίτους, | ἀνθρώπους | Ῥωμαίους | ὑπάρχοντας, |
| akatakritous | anthrōpous | Rhōmaious | huparchontas |
| uncondemned, | men | Romans | being, |

37.a.**Txt:** 01ℵ,02A,08E 020L,025P,etc.byz.Weis Sod
**Var:** 03B,05D,Lach Treg,Alf,Tisc,We/Ho UBS/⋆

| 900.11 verb 3pl indic aor act | 900.44 verb 3pl indic aor act | 1519.1 prep | 5274.4 noun acc sing fem | 2504.1 conj | 3431.1 adv | 2950.1 adv |
|---|---|---|---|---|---|---|
| ( ἔβαλον | [ᵃ⋆ ἔβαλαν ] | εἰς | φυλακήν, | καὶ | νῦν | λάθρᾳ |
| ebalon | ebalan | eis | phulakēn | kai | nun | lathra |
| they threw | [ idem ] | into | prison, | and | now | secretly |

| 2231.4 prs-pron acc 1pl | 1531.4 verb 3pl indic pres act | 3620.3 partic | 1056.1 conj | 233.2 conj | 2048.16 verb nom pl masc part aor act |
|---|---|---|---|---|---|
| ἡμᾶς | ἐκβάλλουσιν; | οὐ | γάρ· | ἀλλὰ | ἐλθόντες |
| hēmas | ekballousin | ou | gar | alla | elthontes |
| us | are they throwing out? | no | indeed, | but | having come |

| 840.7 prs-pron nom pl masc | 2231.4 prs-pron acc 1pl | 1790.4 verb 3pl impr aor act | 310.5 verb 3pl indic aor act |
|---|---|---|---|
| αὐτοὶ | ἡμᾶς | ἐξαγαγέτωσαν. | 38. ( Ἀνήγγειλαν |
| autoi | hēmas | exagagetōsan | Anēngeilan |
| themselves | us | let them bring out. | Reported |

38.a.**Txt:** 020L,025P,byz.
**Var:** 01ℵ,02A,03B,05D 08E,Lach,Treg,Alf Word,Tisc,We/Ho,Weis Sod,UBS/⋆

| 514.8 verb 3pl indic aor act | 1156.2 conj | 3450.4 art dat pl | 4606.3 noun dat pl masc | 3450.7 art nom pl masc |
|---|---|---|---|---|
| [ᵃ⋆ ἀπήγγειλαν ] | δὲ | τοῖς | στρατηγοῖς | οἱ |
| apēngeilan | de | tois | stratēgois | hoi |
| [ idem ] | and | to the | magistrates | the |

**16:36.** The jailer obediently passed on the word from the chief magistrates that it was their decision to let the apostles go. Then he urged them to accept this, leave the prison area, and to proceed on their way in peace. He was undoubtedly very happy about this decision. His words may reflect a little of the Hebrew salutation of peace and blessing.

**16:37.** Paul now did something he did not do very often—he took advantage of his Roman citizenship. In some situations he did this to forestall unnecessary persecution. This time he did it because he knew the crowds gathered around them in the Philippian agora still had a wrong idea, not only about them, but about both Jews and Christians. Paul therefore refused to sneak away like a beaten criminal. The chief magistrate had caused them to be beaten publicly, without any semblance of a trial, even though Paul and Silas were both Roman citizens. Then they had thrown them publicly into prison with the whole crowd looking on. Were they now going to throw them out of prison secretly? Let them come themselves and lead the apostles out publicly. In this way the city of Philippi would know the charges were false.

Paul probably had in mind the welfare and growth of the new assembly of believers. If the crowd was allowed to think Paul and Silas were the big troublemakers they were accused of being, persecution for the new believers would have resulted and would have hindered others in the city from accepting their witness. Paul could not let this happen.

**16:38.** When the lictors reported the Roman citizenship of Paul and Silas to the chief magistrates of the city, they knew they were in the wrong. They should not have yielded to the mob without questioning Paul and Silas. They were afraid because Roman citizens had rights to trial before punishment, rights that could not be ignored with impunity. They knew also what could happen to them if the apostles were to lodge a complaint with the government in Rome.

Imperial Rome was a symbol of power. (Nebuchadnezzar's dream of Daniel 2 describes it as "iron.") But it did provide for the rights of its own citizens, so Paul's appeal to his Roman citizenship had the effect he hoped for.

One ancient manuscript, Codex Bezae (D), inserts an interesting addition at the end of verse 38 that reads as follows: "And when they were come with many of their friends to the prison, they besought them to go out saying: We were ignorant of your circumstances, that you were righteous men. And leading them out, they besought them saying, Depart from this city, lest they again make an insurrection against you, and clamour against you." More likely, the magistrates were ignorant not of Paul and Silas' righteousness,

**36. And the keeper of the prison told this saying to Paul, The Magistrates have sent to let you go:** The jailer said to Paul, The officials, *NCV* . . . The Magistrates have sent an order for your discharge, *TCNT* . . . sent these soldiers to set you free, *SEB* . . . orders for you to be released, *Weymouth.*

**now therefore depart, and go in peace:** . . . so you had better leave the place at once and go quietly away, *TCNT* . . . and go without any trouble, *NLT.*

**37. But Paul said unto them:** But Paul's answer to them was, *TCNT.*

**They have beaten us openly uncondemned:** They have flogged us in public without trial, *TCNT* . . . a public flogging without trial, *Norlie* . . . Your leaders did not prove that we did anything wrong, *SEB* . . . cruelly beating us in public, *Weymouth* . . . yet they whipped us in public, *TEV* . . . a public whipping, *BB* . . . unoffending men, *Murdock.*

**being Romans:** . . . despite the fact, *Phillips* . . . though we are Roman citizens, *TCNT.*

**and have cast us into prison:** . . . have thrown us, *RSV* . . . and sent us to prison, *Knox.*

**and now do they thrust us out privily?:** . . . they are for sending us out secretly! *TCNT* . . . and are they now going to send us away privately, *Weymouth* . . . to get rid of us in this underhand way, *Phillips* . . . Secretly now they are going to get rid of us, *Kleist* . . . are ejecting us surreptitiously! *Concordant* . . . they want to make us go away quietly, *Everyday* . . . do they think they can send us away without anyone knowing? *NLT.*

**nay verily; but let them come themselves and fetch us out:** Certainly not, *Fenton* . . . No, indeed! Let them come and take us out themselves, *TCNT* . . . come in person and fetch us out, *Weymouth* . . . I should say not! These should come themselves, *Beck* . . . and bring us out! *NCV.*

**38. And the serjeants told these words unto the magistrates:** . . . the attendants announced these words to, *Swann* . . . The officers then went and reported this demand to the magistrates, *Norlie.*

| 4322.1 noun nom pl masc | 3450.17 art pl neu | 4343.4 noun pl neu | 3642.18 dem-pron pl neu | 2504.1 conj | 5236.13 verb 3pl indic aor pass |
|---|---|---|---|---|---|
| ῥαβδοῦχοι | τὰ | ῥήματα | ταῦτα· | ʻ καὶ | ἐφοβήθησαν |
| *rhabdouchoi* | *ta* | *rhēmata* | *tauta* | *kai* | *ephobēthēsan* |
| officers | the | words | these. | And | they were afraid |

38.b.**Txt:** 08E,020L 025P,byz.
**Var:** 01ℵ,02A,03B,bo. Lach,Treg,Alf,Tisc We/Ho,Weis,Sod UBS/⋆

| 5236.13 verb 3pl indic aor pass | 1156.2 conj | 189.32 verb nom pl masc part aor act | 3617.1 conj | 4371.3 name-adj nom pl masc |
|---|---|---|---|---|
| [b⋆ ἐφοβήθησαν | δὲ ] | ἀκούσαντες | ὅτι | Ῥωμαῖοί |
| *ephobēthēsan* | *de* | *akousantes* | *hoti* | *Rhōmaioi* |
| [ they were afraid | and ] | having heard | that | Romans |

| 1498.7 verb 3pl indic pres act | 2504.1 conj | 2048.16 verb nom pl masc part aor act | 3731.14 verb 3pl indic aor act | 840.8 prs-pron acc pl masc |
|---|---|---|---|---|
| εἰσιν, | 39. καὶ | ἐλθόντες | παρεκάλεσαν | αὐτούς, |
| *eisin* | *kai* | *elthontes* | *parekalesan* | *autous* |
| they are. | And | having come | they besought | them, |

| 2504.1 conj | 1790.6 verb nom pl masc part aor act | 2049.17 verb 3pl indic imperf act | 1814.20 verb inf aor act |
|---|---|---|---|
| καὶ | ἐξαγαγόντες | ἠρώτων | ʻ ἐξελθεῖν |
| *kai* | *exagagontes* | *ērōtōn* | *exelthein* |
| and | having brought out | they were asking | to go out |

39.a.**Txt:** 020L,025P,byz.
**Var:** 01ℵ,02A,03B,Lach Treg,Alf,Tisc,We/Ho Weis,Sod,UBS/⋆

| 562.12 verb inf aor act | 570.3 prep | 3450.10 art gen sing fem | 4032.2 noun gen sing fem | 1814.15 verb nom pl masc part aor act |
|---|---|---|---|---|
| [a⋆ ἀπελθεῖν | ἀπὸ ] | τῆς | πόλεως. | 40. ἐξελθόντες |
| *apelthein* | *apo* | *tēs* | *poleōs* | *exelthontes* |
| [ to go away | from ] | of the | city. | Having gone forth |

40.a.**Txt:** 02A,05D,08E 020L,025P,byz.
**Var:** 01ℵ,03B,Tisc We/Ho,Weis,Sod UBS/⋆

| 1156.2 conj | 1523.2 prep gen | 570.3 prep | 3450.10 art gen sing fem | 5274.2 noun gen sing fem | 1511.1 verb indic aor act | 1519.1 prep |
|---|---|---|---|---|---|---|
| δὲ | ʻ ἐκ | [a⋆ ἀπὸ ] | τῆς | φυλακῆς | εἰσῆλθον | ʻ εἰς |
| *de* | *ek* | *apo* | *tēs* | *phulakēs* | *eisēlthon* | *eis* |
| and | out of | [ from ] | the | prison | they came | to |

40.b.**Txt:** Steph
**Var:** 01ℵ,02A,03B,05D 08E,020L,025P,Gries Lach,Treg,Alf,Tisc We/Ho,Weis,Sod UBS/⋆

| 4242.1 prep | 3450.12 art acc sing fem | 3042.2 name acc fem | 2504.1 conj | 1481.17 verb nom pl masc part aor act | 3450.8 art acc pl masc |
|---|---|---|---|---|---|
| [b⋆ πρὸς ] | τὴν | Λυδίαν· | καὶ | ἰδόντες | ʻ τοὺς |
| *pros* | *tēn* | *Ludian* | *kai* | *idontes* | *tous* |
| [ idem ] | | Lydia; | and | having seen | the |

40.c.**Txt:** 08E,020L,025P byz.sa.
**Var:** 01ℵ,02A,03B,bo. Lach,Treg,Alf,Tisc We/Ho,Weis,Sod UBS/⋆

| 79.9 noun acc pl masc | 3731.14 verb 3pl indic aor act | 840.8 prs-pron acc pl masc | 3731.14 verb 3pl indic aor act |
|---|---|---|---|
| ἀδελφοὺς | παρεκάλεσαν | αὐτούς, | [c⋆ παρεκάλεσαν |
| *adelphous* | *parekalesan* | *autous* | *parekalesan* |
| brothers | they encouraged | them, | [ they encouraged |

40.d.**Txt:** 02A,03B,08E 020L,025P,byz.Weis Sod
**Var:** 01ℵ,05D,Treg,Tisc We/Ho,UBS/⋆

| 3450.8 art acc pl masc | 79.9 noun acc pl masc | 2504.1 conj | 1814.1 verb indic aor act | 1814.41 verb 3pl indic aor act |
|---|---|---|---|---|
| τοὺς | ἀδελφοὺς ] | καὶ | ʻ ἐξῆλθον. | [d⋆ ἐξῆλθαν. ] |
| *tous* | *adelphous* | *kai* | *exēlthon* | *exēlthan* |
| the | brothers ] | and | went away. | [ idem ] |

| 1347.1 verb nom pl masc part aor act | 1156.2 conj | 3450.12 art acc sing fem | 293.1 name acc fem | 2504.1 conj |
|---|---|---|---|---|
| 17:1. Διοδεύσαντες | δὲ | τὴν | Ἀμφίπολιν | καὶ |
| *Diodeusantes* | *de* | *tēn* | *Amphipolin* | *kai* |
| Having journeyed through | and | | Amphipolis | and |

1.a.**Var:** 01ℵ,02A,03B 08E,Lach,Treg,Tisc We/Ho,Weis,Sod UBS/⋆

| 3450.12 art acc sing fem | 618.1 name acc fem | 2048.1 verb indic aor act | 1519.1 prep | 2309.3 name acc fem |
|---|---|---|---|---|
| [a⋆+ τὴν ] | Ἀπολλωνίαν | ἦλθον | εἰς | Θεσσαλονίκην, |
| *tēn* | *Apollōnian* | *ēlthon* | *eis* | *Thessalonikēn* |
| | Apollonia | they came | to | Thessalonica, |

but of their Roman citizenship. Not even at this stage did they attempt to discover the true reasons behind the mob's actions.

**16:39.** The chief officials of Philippi then came very humbly and besought Paul and Silas; they begged them not to bring charges against them. This was done in the prison, for Paul and Silas had voluntarily left the jailer's house and gone back into the prison so there would be no reason to question the jailer (who had been commanded to keep them locked up securely). The chief magistrates led the apostles out of the prison compound publicly, as Paul had asked.

The magistrates then asked them to leave the city. This was not because they wanted in any way to stop the preaching of the gospel in Philippi. But they were most probably afraid Paul and Silas might change their minds and bring charges against them. They were probably afraid also that the sympathies of the people would now swing to Paul and Silas and against them, because of the unjust beating. So they asked the apostles to leave for the sake of peace in the city.

**16:40.** Before leaving the city, Paul and Silas went to Lydia's house. There a large courtyard or upper room was full of believers who were gathered together, undoubtedly praying for Paul and Silas. After seeing and exhorting the brethren, the apostles left town.

Notice here that the believers were no longer limited to a few women converted out of the prayer group by the riverside. The brethren now took the leadership, though in Hebrew usage, the word *brethren* included the women (just as the phrase "children of Israel" in Hebrew is literally the "sons of Israel" but included both men and women).

It is evident at this point that Luke did not leave with Paul and Silas. The next chapter (17:14) shows that Timothy did leave with them, but Luke no longer used the word "we." It seems obvious Paul and Silas left Luke in Philippi to give further encouragement and teaching to the assembly there. (Luke was still in Philippi in 20:6.) His teaching and guidance is undoubtedly another reason why there were so few problems in this assembly.

**17:1.** After Paul, Silas, and Timothy left Philippi, they proceeded westward on the Egnatian Road. The next two towns of any size (each about a day's journey apart) apparently had no Jewish synagogue and were probably left for the Philippians to evangelize. So the apostles pushed on 100 miles from Philippi to Thessalonica, the most important city of ancient Macedonia, and still important today. It was founded in 315 B.C., and named by Cassander (its founder) for his wife, who was a stepsister of Alexander the Great.

**and they feared, when they heard that they were Romans:** . . . and they were struck with fear when, *Rotherham* . . . who, on hearing that Paul and Silas were Roman citizens, were alarmed, *TCNT* . . . who were horrified to hear, *JB* . . . they were alarmed by this talk of Roman citizenship, *Knox* . . . became terrified, *Fenton.*

**39. And they came and besought them:** . . . and went to the prison, and did their best to conciliate them, *TCNT* . . . Accordingly they came and apologized to them, *Weymouth* . . . and came and plead with them, *Williams* . . . and came to appeal to them, *Kleist* . . . came to appease them, *NIV* . . . apologizing to them, *Berkeley* . . . came and made prayers to them, *BB* . . . came and begged their pardon, *Williams C.K.* . . . told Paul and Silas they were sorry, *Everyday.*

**and brought them out, and desired them to depart out of the city:** Then they took them out and begged them to leave the city, *TCNT* . . . Then they escorted them out, *NEB* . . . urging them, as they brought them out, to leave the city, *Knox* . . . and conducting them out, requested them to leave the town, *Fenton* . . . kept asking them to leave, *SEB.*

**40. And they went out of the prison:** So they left the prison, *Moffatt* . . . Being thus liberated from custody, *Fenton.*

**and entered into the house of Lydia:** . . . and visited Lydia, *RSV.*

**and when they had seen the brethren:** . . . where they saw the brothers, *Berkeley* . . . They met with the Christians, *NLT* . . . having seen, *Fenton.*

**they comforted them, and departed:** . . . they exhorted them, *Alford* . . . they consoled them, *Fenton* . . . and encouraged them, they left the place, *TCNT* . . . Then they left, *Everyday* . . . then they set out on their journey, *Knox* . . . they left the place, *Williams C.K.*

**1. And when they had passed through Amphipolis and Apollonia:** And travelling through, *Rotherham* . . . Then they passed by the cities of, *Lamsa* . . . Travelling then through, *Fenton.*

## Acts 17:2

1.b.**Txt:** 08E,020L,025P byz.
**Var:** 01ℵ,02A,03B,05D sa.bo.Lach,Treg,Tisc We/Ho,Weis,Sod UBS/⋆

| **3562.1** adv | **1498.34** verb sing indic imperf act | **3450.9** art nom sing fem | **4715.1** noun nom sing fem | **3450.1** art gen pl | **2428.3** name-adj gen pl masc |
|---|---|---|---|---|---|
| ὅπου | ἦν | (b ἡ ) | συναγωγὴ | τῶν | Ἰουδαίων. |
| *hopou* | *ēn* | *hē* | *sunagōgē* | *tōn* | *Ioudaiōn* |
| where | was | the | synagogue | of the | Jews. |

| **2567.3** prep | **1156.2** conj | **3450.16** art sing neu | **1522.2** verb sing neu part perf act | **3450.3** art dat sing | **3834.3** name dat masc |
|---|---|---|---|---|---|
| 2. κατὰ | δὲ | τὸ | εἰωθὸς | τῷ | Παύλῳ |
| *kata* | *de* | *to* | *eiōthos* | *tō* | *Paulō* |
| According to | and | the | custom | | with Paul |

| **1511.3** verb 3sing indic aor act | **4242.1** prep | **840.8** prs-pron acc pl masc | **2504.1** conj | **1894.3** prep | **4378.6** noun pl neu |
|---|---|---|---|---|---|
| εἰσῆλθεν | πρὸς | αὐτοὺς, | καὶ | ἐπὶ | σάββατα |
| *eisēlthen* | *pros* | *autous* | *kai* | *epi* | *sabbata* |
| he went in | to | them, | and | for | sabbaths |

2.a.**Txt:** 020L,025P,byz. sa.
**Var:** 01ℵ,02A,03B,bo. Lach,Treg,Tisc,We/Ho Weis,Sod,UBS/⋆

| **4980.4** num card neu | **1250.7** verb 3sing indic imperf mid | **1250.8** verb 3sing indic aor mid | **840.2** prs-pron dat pl | **570.3** prep |
|---|---|---|---|---|
| τρία | ( διελέγετο | [a⋆ διελέξατο ] | αὐτοῖς | ἀπὸ |
| *tria* | *dielegeto* | *dielexato* | *autois* | *apo* |
| three | he was reasoning | [ he reasoned ] | with them | from |

| **3450.1** art gen pl | **1118.6** noun gen pl fem | **1266.1** verb nom sing masc part pres act | **2504.1** conj | **3769.9** verb nom sing masc part pres mid |
|---|---|---|---|---|
| τῶν | γραφῶν, | 3. διανοίγων | καὶ | παρατιθέμενος |
| *tōn* | *graphōn* | *dianoigōn* | *kai* | *paratithemenos* |
| the | Scriptures, | opening | and | setting forth |

| **3617.1** conj | **3450.6** art acc sing masc | **5382.4** name acc masc | **1158.6** verb 3sing indic imperf act | **3819.18** verb inf aor act | **2504.1** conj |
|---|---|---|---|---|---|
| ὅτι | τὸν | Χριστὸν | ἔδει | παθεῖν | καὶ |
| *hoti* | *ton* | *Christon* | *edei* | *pathein* | *kai* |
| that | the | Christ | it was necessary | to suffer | and |

| **448.14** verb inf aor act | **1523.2** prep gen | **3361.2** adj gen pl | **2504.1** conj | **3617.1** conj | **3642.4** dem-pron nom sing masc |
|---|---|---|---|---|---|
| ἀναστῆναι | ἐκ | νεκρῶν, | καὶ | ὅτι | οὗτός |
| *anastēnai* | *ek* | *nekrōn* | *kai* | *hoti* | *houtos* |
| to rise | from among | dead, | and | that | this |

3.a.**Var:** 03B,Alf,We/Ho Weis,UBS/⋆

| **1498.4** verb 3sing indic pres act | **3450.5** art nom sing masc | **5382.1** name nom masc | **3450.5** art nom sing masc | **2400.1** name nom masc |
|---|---|---|---|---|
| ἐστιν | ὁ | Χριστός | [a⋆+ ὁ ] | Ἰησοῦς, |
| *estin* | *ho* | *Christos* | *ho* | *Iēsous* |
| is | the | Christ | | Jesus, |

| **3614.6** rel-pron acc sing masc | **1466.1** prs-pron nom 1sing | **2576.2** verb 1sing indic pres act | **5050.3** prs-pron dat 2pl | **2504.1** conj | **4948.7** indef-pron nom pl masc |
|---|---|---|---|---|---|
| ὃν | ἐγὼ | καταγγέλλω | ὑμῖν. | 4. Καί | τινες |
| *hon* | *egō* | *katangellō* | *humin* | *Kai* | *tines* |
| whom | I | am announcing | to you. | And | some |

| **1523.1** prep gen | **840.1** prs-pron gen pl | **3844.25** verb 3pl indic aor pass | **2504.1** conj | **4191.1** verb 3pl indic aor pass |
|---|---|---|---|---|
| ἐξ | αὐτῶν | ἐπείσθησαν, | καὶ | προσεκληρώθησαν |
| *ex* | *autōn* | *epeisthēsan* | *kai* | *proseklērōthēsan* |
| of | them | were persuaded, | and | joined themselves |

| **3450.3** art dat sing | **3834.3** name dat masc | **2504.1** conj | **3450.3** art dat sing | **4464.2** name dat masc | **3450.1** art gen pl | **4885.1** conj |
|---|---|---|---|---|---|---|
| τῷ | Παύλῳ | καὶ | τῷ | Σίλᾳ, | τῶν | τε |
| *tō* | *Paulō* | *kai* | *tō* | *Sila* | *tōn* | *te* |
| | to Paul | and | | to Silas, | of the | and |

Again Luke's account draws attention to Paul's custom of going to the Jews first. Paul always took advantage of the Jews' background and of the opportunities given in the synagogue to teach.

**17:2.** Paul followed his usual custom (manner, habit, settled policy), and over the space of three sabbaths (or weeks) he ministered in the synagogue. It is possible this means he ministered daily during the entire time, addressing the people, and preaching to them. Discussion with questions and answers may also be implied.

The Book of Acts does not give any details here. But it does draw attention to one very important feature of Paul's preaching. It was Biblical. Paul did not spend time talking about human theories of ethics, economics, or politics. He did not lecture to them out of philosophy or out of the teachings of his former professor, Gamaliel. He knew God's Word is the Holy Spirit's sword to win victories, His tool to do the work of salvation and to make the power and wisdom of Christ effective. It is probable that in his first sermon Paul followed the same pattern as he had in his first sermon in the synagogue at Pisidian Antioch (13:16-41).

**17:3.** The Jews and the believing Gentiles who attended the synagogue believed in a Messiah, but their ideas about the Messiah were rather vague. To most of them the whole subject seemed controversial and speculative. It was necessary for Paul to show them what the Bible teaches about the Messiah before they could believe that Jesus is the Messiah, or Christ.

Paul would open up the meaning of an Old Testament passage and discuss it with them, explaining it fully. Then he would refer to other passages that supported and proved his interpretation. After he was able to get them to see from the Scriptures that the Messiah or Christ would not only reign, but would suffer, die, and rise again, he could point to Jesus. Jesus fulfilled the prophecies. Jesus is the only One who could possibly be the Christ.

Behind Paul's anointed preaching was much prayer and Spirit-directed study of the Scripture. This careful study made it possible for Paul to become a good agent of the Spirit in driving home the truth to human hearts. It is clear also that Paul presented the proofs from the Word in a logical, connected, and reasonable way. (Compare 1 Peter 3:15.)

**17:4.** This verse condenses what took place over a considerable period of time. Some indications point to at least 6 months.

Some of the Jews were persuaded; they believed in Jesus, obeyed the gospel, and threw in their lot with Paul. Weymouth's translation reads, "They attached themselves to Paul and Silas." The same was true of an even larger number of Gentiles. In fact, many God-fearing Greeks, including many wives of the chief men of the city, supported Paul.

**they came to Thessalonica, where was a synagogue of the Jews:** Here the Jews had a Synagogue, *TCNT* . . . had a place of worship there, *NLT* . . . where there was a Jewish meeting-house, *Williams C.K.*

**2. And Paul, as his manner was, went in unto them:** . . . as his custom was, *ASV* . . . as he always did, *NCV, NLT* . . . paid them a visit there, *Knox.*

**and three sabbath days reasoned with them out of the scriptures:** . . . addressed them, drawing his arguments from the Scriptures, *TCNT* . . . he discoursed to them from, *Swann* . . . he argued with them, *Williams C.K.* . . . on three Saturdays had Bible discussions, *Beck* . . . from the holy Writings, *BB.*

**3. Opening and alleging:** He laid before them and explained, *TCNT* . . . illustrating and proving, *Fenton* . . . expounding these and bringing proofs, *Knox* . . . explaining and quoting passages to prove, *Moffatt* . . . and setting forth, *Worrell* . . . and clearly showed that, *SEB* . . . and showing, *Williams C.K.*

**that Christ must needs have suffered, and risen again from the dead:** . . . that it was necessary for the Christ, *RSV* . . . to suffer and rise again from the dead, *NLT* . . . had to be put to death and come back to life again, *BB* . . . rising from the dead were foreordained, *Knox.*

**and that this Jesus, whom I preach unto you, is Christ:** . . . and (saying) This is the Christ—Jesus whom I am declaring unto you, *Rotherham* . . . This Jesus, whom I announce to you, is the Messiah! *SEB.*

**4. And some of them believed:** Some of the Jews were convinced, *NCV* . . . were persuaded, *RSV* . . . became believers, *Norlie* . . . were won over, *Kleist* . . . put their trust in Christ, *NLT* . . . had faith, *BB.*

**and consorted with Paul and Silas:** . . . and cast in their lot with, *Rotherham* . . . and threw in their lot with, *Knox* . . . and attached themselves to, *Weymouth* . . . and joined themselves to, *HBIE* . . . and associated themselves with, *Fenton.*

## Acts 17:5

| **4431.4** verb gen pl masc part pres mid | **1659.5** name gen pl masc | **4044.16** adj sing neu | **3988.1** noun sing neu | **3988.1** noun sing neu |
|---|---|---|---|---|
| σεβομένων | Ἑλλήνων | ⸂ πολὺ | πλῆθος, | [☆ πλῆθος |
| *sebomenōn* | *Hellēnōn* | *polu* | *plēthos* | *plēthos* |
| worshiping | Greeks | a great | multitude, | [ a multitude |

| **4044.16** adj sing neu | **1129.7** noun gen pl fem | **4885.1** conj | **3450.1** art gen pl | **4272.1** num ord gen pl | **3620.2** partic | **3504.10** adj nom pl fem |
|---|---|---|---|---|---|---|
| πολὺ ] | γυναικῶν | τε | τῶν | πρώτων | οὐκ | ὀλίγαι. |
| *polu* | *gunaikōn* | *te* | *tōn* | *prōtōn* | *ouk* | *oligai* |
| great ] | of women | and | the | chief | not | a few. |

5.a.**Txt:** byz.
**Var:** 01ℵ,02A,03B,08E 33,sa.bo.Lach,Treg,Alf Word,Tisc,We/Ho,Weis Sod,UBS/☆

| **2189.6** verb nom pl masc part aor act | **1156.2** conj | **3450.7** art nom pl masc | **540.4** verb nom pl masc part pres act |
|---|---|---|---|
| **5.** Ζηλώσαντες | δὲ | οἱ | ⸂a ἀπειθοῦντες ⸃ |
| *Zēlōsantes* | *de* | *hoi* | *apeithountes* |
| Having become jealous | but | the | being unconvinced |

| **2428.2** name-adj nom pl masc | **2504.1** conj | **4213.7** verb nom pl masc part aor mid | **3450.1** art gen pl | **59.1** adj gen pl masc |
|---|---|---|---|---|
| Ἰουδαῖοι, | καὶ | προσλαβόμενοι | τῶν | ἀγοραίων |
| *Ioudaioi* | *kai* | *proslabomenoi* | *tōn* | *agoraiōn* |
| Jews, | and | having taken | of the | market loungers |

| **4948.9** indef-pron acc pl masc | **433.9** noun acc pl masc | **433.9** noun acc pl masc | **4948.9** indef-pron acc pl masc | **4050.9** adj acc pl masc | **2504.1** conj |
|---|---|---|---|---|---|
| ⸂ τινὰς | ἄνδρας | [☆ ἄνδρας | τινὰς ] | πονηρούς, | καὶ |
| *tinas* | *andras* | *andras* | *tinas* | *ponērous* | *kai* |
| certain | men | [ men | certain ] | evil, | and |

| **3656.1** verb nom pl masc part aor act | **2327.1** verb 3pl indic imperf act | **3450.12** art acc sing fem | **4032.4** noun acc sing fem |
|---|---|---|---|
| ὀχλοποιήσαντες | ἐθορύβουν | τὴν | πόλιν· |
| *ochlopoiēsantes* | *ethoruboun* | *tēn* | *polin* |
| having collected a crowd | were making an uproar | the | city; |

5.b.**Txt:** 020L,025P,byz.
**Var:** 01ℵ,02A,03B,05D 08E,Lach,Treg,Alf,Tisc We/Ho,Weis,Sod UBS/☆

| **2168.6** verb nom pl masc part aor act | **4885.1** conj | **2504.1** conj | **2168.6** verb nom pl masc part aor act | **3450.11** art dat sing fem |
|---|---|---|---|---|
| ⸂ ἐπιστάντες | τε | [b☆ καὶ | ἐπιστάντες ] | τῇ |
| *epistantes* | *te* | *kai* | *epistantes* | *tē* |
| having assaulted | and | [ and | having assaulted ] | the |

| **3477.3** noun dat sing fem | **2371.2** name gen masc | **2195.26** verb 3pl indic imperf act | **840.8** prs-pron acc pl masc | **70.15** verb inf aor act |
|---|---|---|---|---|
| οἰκίᾳ | Ἰάσονος | ἐζήτουν | αὐτοὺς | ⸂ ἀγαγεῖν |
| *oikia* | *Iasonos* | *ezētoun* | *autous* | *agagein* |
| house | of Jason | they were seeking | them | to bring out |

5.c.**Txt:** 025P,byz.
**Var:** 01ℵ,02A,03B,Lach Treg,Alf,Tisc,We/Ho Weis,Sod,UBS/☆

| **4113.13** verb inf aor act | **1519.1** prep | **3450.6** art acc sing masc | **1213.3** noun acc sing masc | **3231.1** partic | **2128.18** verb nom pl masc part aor act |
|---|---|---|---|---|---|
| [c☆ προαγαγεῖν ] | εἰς | τὸν | δῆμον· | **6.** μὴ | εὑρόντες |
| *proagagein* | *eis* | *ton* | *dēmon* | *mē* | *heurontes* |
| [ idem ] | to | the | people; | not | having found |

6.a.**Txt:** 08E,020L,025P byz.
**Var:** 01ℵ,02A,03B,05D Lach,Treg,Tisc,We/Ho Weis,Sod,UBS/☆

| **1156.2** conj | **840.8** prs-pron acc pl masc | **4803.4** verb 3pl indic imperf act | **3450.6** art acc sing masc | **2371.4** name acc masc |
|---|---|---|---|---|
| δὲ | αὐτοὺς | ἔσυρον | ⸂a τὸν ⸃ | Ἰάσονα |
| *de* | *autous* | *esuron* | *ton* | *Iasona* |
| but | them | they were dragging | | Jason |

| **2504.1** conj | **4948.9** indef-pron acc pl masc | **79.9** noun acc pl masc | **1894.3** prep | **3450.8** art acc pl masc | **4033.1** noun acc pl masc |
|---|---|---|---|---|---|
| καί | τινας | ἀδελφοὺς | ἐπὶ | τοὺς | πολιτάρχας, |
| *kai* | *tinas* | *adelphous* | *epi* | *tous* | *politarchas* |
| and | certain | brothers | before | the | city magistrates, |

First Thessalonians 2:1-13 gives a further description of the ministry of Paul and Silas at this time. Their preaching and ministry was very effective. The outrageous treatment they had received at Philippi did not cause them to be timid or fearful. At Thessalonica they preached in a bold, free, open, fearless manner, with pure motives as servants of Jesus Christ. They were gentle to the new converts, giving them all kinds of tender loving care. Yet they were firm in their stand for righteousness and encouraged each one of the believers to live in a manner worthy of the God who had called them to His own kingdom and glory.

**and of the devout Greeks a great multitude:** . . . as did also a large body of Greeks, *TCNT* . . . including great number of God-fearing Greeks, *Weymouth.*

**and of the chief women not a few:** . . . and a great number of women belonging to the leading families, *TCNT* . . . and by a considerable number of influential women, *Phillips.*

**17:5.** Though some of the Jews rejected Paul's message it did not bother him. Even the most powerful, anointed proofs will not convince some people of the truth. The Bible shows believers can expect people to be saved, but they must not be disappointed if all do not believe. (See 2 Corinthians 2:14-16.) When God works it is not unusual for the devil to stir up opposition.

These Jews who rejected Paul's message soon became frustrated by the increasing numbers of Gentiles who were accepting the gospel. As a result, they rebelled against what God was doing. They even went so far as to forbid (hinder, prevent) Paul and his company from speaking (or even talking) to Gentiles with a view to their salvation (1 Thessalonians 2:14-16).

The Gentiles, however, continued to respond to the gospel and paid no attention to these Jewish rebels. Since the Jews had no arguments (that is, no real or effective arguments against the gospel), they resorted to mob violence and proceeded to stir up a riot. First, they took to themselves a group of marketplace loungers who were ruffians always ready for mischief, always ready to join any agitators for the sake of a little excitement. With their help, these unbelieving Jews gathered a crowd and set up a disturbance that threw the whole city into a panic. The mob acted the way mobs always do. A mob does not think; it blindly follows its leaders or promoters and shouts what they shout. The same mob spirit moved those who shouted "Crucify Him!" when Jesus stood before Pilate's judgment seat.

Then the mob, led by the Jewish unbelievers, went to the house of Jason, taking Jason by surprise, seeking to bring out Paul and Silas to the rabble. But evidently Paul and Silas were able to get out another way, and they escaped to another part of the city.

**5. But the Jews which believed not, moved with envy:** . . . in a fury of jealousy, *Phillips* . . . the Jews became jealous, *Everyday.*

**took unto them certain lewd fellows of the baser sort:** . . . wicked fellows of the rabble, *RSV* . . . found confederates among the riff-raff, *Knox* . . . enlisted the aid of some base loafers, *Kleist* . . . engaged some worthless fellows from the streets, *TCNT* . . . and taking to them, of the idlers in the market-place, some vieious men, *HBIE* . . . got some wicked rowdies to join them, *Norlie* . . . got some evil men from the marketplace, *Everyday* . . . They hired some evil men from the city, *SEB.*

**and gathered a company, and set all the city on an uproar:** . . . formed a great mob...they alarmed the city, *Murdock* . . . and gathered a mob, *Alford* . . . and started a riot, *Everyday.*

**and assaulted the house of Jason:** . . . and besieging, *Rotherham* . . . They attacked Jason's house, *TCNT.*

**and sought to bring them out to the people:** . . . with the intention of bringing Paul and Silas before the Popular Assembly, *TCNT* . . . and searched for Paul and Silas, to bring them out before the assembly of the people, *Weymouth.*

**17:6.** Because Paul and Silas were not there, the mob dragged Jason and some of his fellow believers before the rulers. The Greek calls these rulers *politarchs,* and archaeologists have found inscriptions in Thessalonica referring to them by this title. The word *Politarch* was a special title used by Macedonians for chief magistrates here and in a few other cities. Thessalonica had five or six of them.

**6. And when they found them not:** . . . and, not finding them there, *TCNT* . . . And when they were not able to get them, *BB.*

**they drew Jason and certain brethren:** . . . they proceeded to drag Jason and some of the Brethren, *TCNT.*

**unto the rulers of the city:** . . . before the rulers, *ASV* . . . the City Magistrates, *TCNT* . . . the politarches, *Moffatt* . . . the city fathers, *Berkeley.*

## Acts 17:7

| 987.2 verb nom pl masc part pres act | 3617.1 conj | 3450.7 art nom pl masc | 3450.12 art acc sing fem | 3487.4 noun acc sing fem |
|---|---|---|---|---|
| βοῶντες, | Ὅτι | Οἱ | τὴν | οἰκουμένην |
| *boōntes* | *Hoti* | *Hoi* | *tēn* | *oikoumenēn* |
| crying out, | | The | the | habitable world |

| 385.3 verb nom pl masc part aor act | 3642.7 dem-pron nom pl masc | 2504.1 conj | 1743.1 adv | 3780.5 verb 3pl indic pres act |
|---|---|---|---|---|
| ἀναστατώσαντες | οὗτοι | καὶ | ἐνθάδε | πάρεισιν, |
| *anastatōsantes* | *houtoi* | *kai* | *enthade* | *pareisin* |
| having set in confusion | these | also | here | are come, |

| 3614.8 rel-pron acc pl masc | 5103.3 verb 3sing indic perf mid | 2371.1 name nom masc | 2504.1 conj | 3642.7 dem-pron nom pl masc | 3820.7 adj nom pl masc |
|---|---|---|---|---|---|
| **7.** οὓς | ὑποδέδεκται | Ἰάσων· | καὶ | οὗτοι | πάντες |
| *hous* | *hupodedektai* | *Iasōn* | *kai* | *houtoi* | *pantes* |
| whom | has received | Jason; | and | these | all |

| 558.1 prep | 3450.1 art gen pl | 1372.2 noun gen pl neu | 2512.1 name gen masc | 4097.4 verb 3pl indic pres act |
|---|---|---|---|---|
| ἀπέναντι | τῶν | δογμάτων | Καίσαρος | ʿ πράττουσιν, |
| *apenanti* | *tōn* | *dogmatōn* | *Kaisaros* | *prattousin* |
| contrary to | the | decrees | of Caesar | are doing, |

| 4097.27 verb 3pl indic pres act | 928.4 noun acc sing masc | 2978.16 verb nom pl masc part pres act | 2066.1 adj sing | 2066.1 adj sing |
|---|---|---|---|---|
| [☆ πράσσουσι, ] | βασιλέα | ʿ λέγοντες | ἕτερον | [☆ ἕτερον |
| *prassousi* | *basilea* | *legontes* | *heteron* | *heteron* |
| [ idem ] | king | saying | another | [ another |

| 2978.16 verb nom pl masc part pres act | 1498.32 verb inf pres act | 2400.3 name acc masc | 4866.4 verb 3pl indic aor act | 1156.2 conj |
|---|---|---|---|---|
| λέγοντες ] | εἶναι, | Ἰησοῦν. | **8.** Ἐτάραξαν | δὲ |
| *legontes* | *einai* | *Iēsoun* | *Etaraxan* | *de* |
| saying ] | to be | Jesus. | They troubled | and |

| 3450.6 art acc sing masc | 3657.4 noun acc sing masc | 2504.1 conj | 3450.8 art acc pl masc | 4033.1 noun acc pl masc | 189.16 verb acc pl masc part pres act |
|---|---|---|---|---|---|
| τὸν | ὄχλον | καὶ | τοὺς | πολιτάρχας | ἀκούοντας |
| *ton* | *ochlon* | *kai* | *tous* | *politarchas* | *akouontas* |
| the | crowd | and | the | city magistrates | hearing |

| 3642.18 dem-pron pl neu | 2504.1 conj | 2956.27 verb nom pl masc part aor act | 3450.16 art sing neu | 2401.2 adj sing | 3706.2 prep |
|---|---|---|---|---|---|
| ταῦτα. | **9.** καὶ | λαβόντες | τὸ | ἱκανὸν | παρὰ |
| *tauta* | *kai* | *labontes* | *to* | *hikanon* | *para* |
| these things. | And | having taken | the | sufficient | from |

| 3450.2 art gen sing | 2371.2 name gen masc | 2504.1 conj | 3450.1 art gen pl | 3036.1 adj gen pl | 624.7 verb 3pl indic aor act | 840.8 prs-pron acc pl masc |
|---|---|---|---|---|---|---|
| τοῦ | Ἰάσονος | καὶ | τῶν | λοιπῶν | ἀπέλυσαν | αὐτούς. |
| *tou* | *Iasonos* | *kai* | *tōn* | *loipōn* | *apelusan* | *autous* |
| | Jason | and | the | rest | they released | them. |

10.a.**Txt:** 08E,020L 025P,byz.
**Var:** 01ℵ,03B,05D,Lach Treg,Alf,Tisc,We/Ho Weis,Sod,UBS/☆

| 3450.7 art nom pl masc | 1156.2 conj | 79.6 noun nom pl masc | 2091.1 adv | 1217.2 prep | 3450.10 art gen sing fem |
|---|---|---|---|---|---|
| **10.** Οἱ | δὲ | ἀδελφοὶ | εὐθέως | διὰ | ʿa τῆς ˀ |
| *Hoi* | *de* | *adelphoi* | *eutheōs* | *dia* | *tēs* |
| The | but | brothers | immediately | by | the |

| 3433.2 noun gen sing fem | 1586.1 verb 3pl indic aor act | 3450.6 art acc sing masc | 4885.1 conj | 3834.4 name acc masc | 2504.1 conj | 3450.6 art acc sing masc |
|---|---|---|---|---|---|---|
| νυκτὸς | ἐξέπεμψαν | τόν | τε | Παῦλον | καὶ | τὸν |
| *nuktos* | *exepempsan* | *ton* | *te* | *Paulon* | *kai* | *ton* |
| night | sent away | | both | Paul | and | |

As usual, the accusation made before the magistrates was not the real reason for wanting to get rid of Paul and Silas. The unbelieving Jews and their coconspirators accused the apostles of being agitators who were working against the Roman Empire.

The accusation that Paul and Silas had turned the inhabited world upside down has been a thrill and a challenge to true believers ever since. The world turned upside down is at last right side up. (The Romans used "the world" [the inhabited world] to mean the Roman Empire.)

**17:7.** The accusation then turned against Jason. The Jews accused Jason of joining with Paul and Silas to practice things contrary to the decrees of Caesar, speaking of another king (meaning a rival emperor), Jesus.

This was an accusation of open treason. Paul did declare that Jesus is alive at the right hand of the throne of God, and that He is and will be the true King. These Jews were out of character when they pretended to be concerned over the well-being of the Roman Empire and the honor and authority of Caesar. The Jews were notorious for their turbulence, and everyone knew they had no love for the Roman Empire. All Paul had done was to preach the gospel peacefully.

**17:8.** The crowd and the politarchs were disturbed by these things. Part of their problem may have been that they had not observed any evidence of political activity. It is probable also that the believers who were wives of the chief men included the wife of one or more of the politarchs before whom these charges were being made.

There may have been some good in this. When Paul and his company first came into the city, it may be that few gave them more than a passing glance. The Gentiles who attended the synagogue and their friends were soon influenced. But now everyone in town knew that something was happening.

**17:9.** Apparently the politarchs did not take the charges seriously. To satisfy the crowd they took security (surety) from Jason and the others who had been brought before them. This probably means Jason and his friends provided bail as a guarantee that Paul and Silas would leave the city and not come back lest there be further disturbance.

**17:10.** The Christian brethren saw how bitter and determined the unbelieving Jews were, so they took no chances. By night they sent Paul and Silas to Beroea, about 50 miles to the southwest on the road to Greece. The believers probably thought they would be safe there. It was a safer place than Thessalonica.

**crying:** . . . loudly accusing them, *Weymouth* . . . were yelling, *Everyday* . . . shouting out, *Williams C.K.*

**These that have turned the world upside down:** They who have thrown the inhabited world into confusion, *Rotherham* . . . These upsetters of the whole world, *Moffatt* . . . These fellows, who have turned the world topsy-turvy, *Williams* . . . These world revolutionists, *Berkeley* . . . who are setting the world in an uproar, *Kleist* . . . who have been making trouble over all the world, *NLT* . . . turning the state, *Knox.*

**are come hither also:** . . . have now come here, *TCNT* . . . are here now, *Beck.*

**7. Whom Jason hath received:** . . . unto whom Jason has given welcome, *Rotherham* . . . and have been harboured by Jason! *TCNT* . . . Jason is keeping them in his house, *NCV, SEB* . . . has taken into his house, *BB.*

**and these all do contrary to the decrees of Caesar:** They are all defying the decrees of the Emperor, *TCNT* . . . All these folk defy the edicts of, *Knox* . . . working against Caesar's orders, *Williams C.K.*

**saying that there is another king, one Jesus:** They say that some one else is king—a man called Jesus, *TCNT* . . . claiming that there is another king—Jesus, *Berkeley.*

**8. And they troubled the people and the rulers of the city, when they heard these things:** On hearing this, the people ...were much concerned, *TCNT* . . . Great was the excitement among the crowd...when they heard these charges, *Weymouth.*

**9. And when they had taken security of Jason, and of the other:** . . . they took bail from Jason and the others, *TCNT* . . . Jason and the rest gave a bond to keep the peace, *Williams C.K.*

**they let them go:** . . . they released them, *HBIE* . . . and turned them loose, *Williams* . . . and were then dismissed, *Williams C.K.*

**10. And the brethren immediately sent away Paul and Silas by night unto Berea:** That very night the Brethren sent, *TCNT.*

| **4464.3** name acc masc | **1519.1** prep | **953.2** name acc fem | **3610.2** rel-pron nom pl masc | **3716.10** verb nom pl masc part aor mid |
|---|---|---|---|---|
| Σίλαν | εἰς | Βέροιαν· | οἵτινες | παραγενόμενοι, |
| *Silan* | *eis* | *Beroian* | *hoitines* | *paragenomenoi* |
| Silas | to | Beroea; | who, | having arrived, |

| **1519.1** prep | **3450.12** art acc sing fem | **4715.4** noun acc sing fem | **3450.1** art gen pl | **2428.3** name-adj gen pl masc | **545.1** verb 3pl indic imperf act |
|---|---|---|---|---|---|
| εἰς | τὴν | συναγωγὴν | τῶν | Ἰουδαίων | ἀπῄεσαν. |
| *eis* | *tēn* | *sunagōgēn* | *tōn* | *Ioudaiōn* | *apēesan* |
| into | the | synagogue | of the | Jews | were going. |

| **3642.7** dem-pron nom pl masc | **1156.2** conj | **1498.37** verb 3pl indic imperf act | **2083.3** adj comp nom pl masc | **3450.1** art gen pl | **1706.1** prep |
|---|---|---|---|---|---|
| **11.** οὗτοι | δὲ | ἦσαν | εὐγενέστεροι | τῶν | ἐν |
| *houtoi* | *de* | *ēsan* | *eugenesteroi* | *tōn* | *en* |
| These | and | were | more noble than | the | in |

| **2309.2** name dat fem | **3610.2** rel-pron nom pl masc | **1203.8** verb 3pl indic aor mid | **3450.6** art acc sing masc | **3030.4** noun acc sing masc |
|---|---|---|---|---|
| Θεσσαλονίκῃ, | οἵτινες | ἐδέξαντο | τὸν | λόγον |
| *Thessalonikē* | *hoitines* | *edexanto* | *ton* | *logon* |
| Thessalonica, | who | received | the | word |

11.a.**Txt:** 03B,020L 025P,byz.We/Ho,Weis Sod,UBS/☆ **Var:** 01א,02A,05D,08E 33,Lach,Treg,Tisc

| **3196.3** prep | **3820.10** adj gen sing fem | **4147.2** noun gen sing fem | **3450.16** art sing neu | **2567.2** prep | **2232.4** noun acc sing fem |
|---|---|---|---|---|---|
| μετὰ | πάσης | προθυμίας, | (a τὸ \) | καθ' | ἡμέραν |
| *meta* | *pasēs* | *prothumias* | *to* | *kath'* | *hēmeran* |
| with | all | eagerness, | the | according to | day |

| **348.4** verb nom pl masc part pres act | **3450.15** art acc pl fem | **1118.8** noun acc pl fem | **1479.1** conj | **2174.11** verb 3sing opt pres act | **3642.18** dem-pron pl neu |
|---|---|---|---|---|---|
| ἀνακρίνοντες | τὰς | γραφὰς | εἰ | ἔχοι | ταῦτα |
| *anakrinontes* | *tas* | *graphas* | *ei* | *echoi* | *tauta* |
| examining | the | Scriptures | if | might have | these things |

| **3643.1** adv | **4044.7** adj nom pl masc | **3173.1** conj | **3631.1** partic | **1523.1** prep gen | **840.1** prs-pron gen pl |
|---|---|---|---|---|---|
| οὕτως. | **12.** πολλοὶ | μὲν | οὖν | ἐξ | αὐτῶν |
| *houtōs* | *polloi* | *men* | *oun* | *ex* | *autōn* |
| so. | Many | indeed | therefore | from among | them |

| **3961.23** verb 3pl indic aor act | **2504.1** conj | **3450.1** art gen pl | **1663.2** name gen pl fem | **1129.7** noun gen pl fem | **3450.1** art gen pl |
|---|---|---|---|---|---|
| ἐπίστευσαν, | καὶ | τῶν | Ἑλληνίδων | γυναικῶν | τῶν |
| *episteusan* | *kai* | *tōn* | *Hellēnidōn* | *gunaikōn* | *tōn* |
| believed, | and | of the | Grecian | women | the |

| **2139.2** adj gen pl fem | **2504.1** conj | **433.7** noun gen pl masc | **3620.2** partic | **3504.5** adj nom pl masc | **5453.1** conj |
|---|---|---|---|---|---|
| εὐσχημόνων | καὶ | ἀνδρῶν | οὐκ | ὀλίγοι. | **13.** Ὡς |
| *euschēmonōn* | *kai* | *andrōn* | *ouk* | *oligoi* | *Hōs* |
| honorable | and | men | not | a few. | When |

| **1156.2** conj | **1091.18** verb 3pl indic aor act | **3450.7** art nom pl masc | **570.3** prep | **3450.10** art gen sing fem | **2309.1** name gen fem |
|---|---|---|---|---|---|
| δὲ | ἔγνωσαν | οἱ | ἀπὸ | τῆς | Θεσσαλονίκης |
| *de* | *egnōsan* | *hoi* | *apo* | *tēs* | *Thessalonikēs* |
| but | knew | the | from | | Thessalonica |

| **2428.2** name-adj nom pl masc | **3617.1** conj | **2504.1** conj | **1706.1** prep | **3450.11** art dat sing fem | **953.1** name dat fem | **2576.10** verb 3sing indic aor pass |
|---|---|---|---|---|---|---|
| Ἰουδαῖοι | ὅτι | καὶ | ἐν | τῇ | Βεροίᾳ | κατηγγέλη |
| *Ioudaioi* | *hoti* | *kai* | *en* | *tē* | *Beroia* | *katēngelē* |
| Jews | that | also | in | | Beroea | was announced |

Paul did not let his experiences with the unbelieving Jews in Thessalonica discourage or intimidate him. At Beroea he went at once to the synagogue, still feeling the mandate that he must go to the Jew first, even though Jesus had sent him to the Gentiles.

**who coming thither went into the synagogue of the Jews:** . . . who, as soon as they arrived, went, *Alford* . . . they made their way to the Jewish meeting-house, *Williams C.K.*

**17:11.** At this synagogue Paul's faithfulness was rewarded. Instead of the usual opposition, he found an eager enthusiasm for the Word of God. Instead of opposing Paul's message, they welcomed the Word with eagerness. Even more important, they examined the Scriptures daily, to see whether these things were so. Because of their attitude and their searching of the Scriptures, the Bible says they were more noble than the Jews in Thessalonica.

The word "noble" does not have its usual sense of "aristocratic birth" here. Luke used it of God's men and women who showed their nobility by their high-minded, open, generous spirit. They did not let prejudice close their minds to the truth. They gave attention to the preaching of the Word. How this must have encouraged Paul! An expectant audience that loves God's Word draws out the preacher.

Those who honestly want to know the truth God has for all will subject what they hear and read to the test of the Scriptures. Any pet idea deserves to be thrown out if it will not stand examination in the light of the whole Bible. Believers will be blessed by truths the Holy Spirit drives home as they keep searching the Scriptures. The net result will be a strengthening of their faith.

**11. These were more noble than those in Thessalonica:** These Jews of Berea were better disposed, *TCNT* . . . were better people than the ones in, *SEB* . . . were of a better breed than, *Knox* . . . of a nobler disposition than, *Weymouth* . . . were more broad-minded, *Williams C.K.*

**in that they received the word with all readiness of mind:** . . . for they welcomed the Message with great readiness, *TCNT* . . . accepted the message most eagerly, *Phillips* . . . for they gave serious attention to the word, *BB* . . . were very happy to listen to the things, *SEB* . . . welcomed the word with all eagerness, *Knox* . . . were eager to hear, *Norlie* . . . very eager to get the Word, *Beck* . . . with eagerness, *Williams C.K.*

**and searched the scriptures daily:** . . . examining, *RSV* . . . and made a daily study of the scriptures, *Moffatt.*

**whether those things were so:** . . . to see if what was said was true, *TCNT* . . . to see whether it was as Paul stated, *Weymouth* . . . to find out if these things were true, *NCV.*

**17:12.** In Thessalonica some of the Jews had believed. Others had let their old prejudices guide them, and they reacted against the gospel. In Beroea, however, many of the Jews believed, possibly the majority of them. There was no opposition stirred up among them. This indicates they not only accepted the truth of the gospel, but they opened their hearts and let the Holy Spirit apply it for both salvation and Christian living. The response of faith is always obedience.

Many Gentiles also believed, women who had an honorable position in society, and men as well. Notice also that these noble-minded Jews were not upset or jealous when these Gentiles were saved. In their searching of the Scriptures it seems they were reminded of God's promise that *all* the families of the earth would be blessed.

**12. Therefore many of them believed:** As a consequence many of them became believers in Christ, *TCNT* . . . So, many of them believed, *NCV* . . . became Christians, *NLT.*

**also of honourable women which were Greeks, and of men, not a few:** . . . a number of Greek women of good position, *Williams C.K.* . . . including outstanding Greek women and a goodly number of men, *Berkeley* . . . also many noble Greeks, women as well as men, *Beck* . . . important Greek men and women also believed, *NCV.*

**17:13.** While the Beroean Jews were studying the Old Testament systematically, closely, carefully, and candidly, and as they considered Paul's teachings, in the light of the Scripture, somehow the news of Paul's effective proclamation of the gospel was carried back to Thessalonica. The synagogue at Beroea had caused no trouble.

**13. But when the Jews of Thessalonica:** As soon, however, as the Jews, *Weymouth.*

**had knowledge:** . . . came to know, *Rotherham* . . . found out, *TCNT* . . . heard that, *Williams C.K.* . . . had news, *BB* . . . became aware, *Beck.*

| 5097.3 prep | 3450.2 art gen sing | 3834.2 name gen masc | 3450.5 art nom sing masc | 3030.1 noun nom sing masc | 3450.2 art gen sing | 2296.2 noun gen sing masc |
|---|---|---|---|---|---|---|
| ὑπὸ | τοῦ | Παύλου | ὁ | λόγος | τοῦ | θεοῦ, |
| *hupo* | *tou* | *Paulou* | *ho* | *logos* | *tou* | *theou* |
| by | | Paul | the | word | | of God, |

13.a.**Var:** p74,01ℵ,02A 03B,33,sa.Lach,Treg Alf,Tisc,We/Ho,Weis Sod,UBS/☆

| 2048.1 verb indic aor act | 2517.1 conj | 4388.1 verb nom pl masc part pres act | 2504.1 conj | 4866.2 verb nom pl masc part pres act |
|---|---|---|---|---|
| ἦλθον | κἀκεῖ | σαλεύοντες | [a☆+ καὶ | ταράσσοντες ] |
| *ēlthon* | *kakei* | *saleuontes* | *kai* | *tarassontes* |
| they came | there also | stirring up | [ also | stirring up ] |

| 3450.8 art acc pl masc | 3657.8 noun acc pl masc | 2091.1 adv | 1156.2 conj | 4966.1 adv | 3450.6 art acc sing masc |
|---|---|---|---|---|---|
| τοὺς | ὄχλους. | **14.** εὐθέως | δὲ | τότε | τὸν |
| *tous* | *ochlous* | *eutheōs* | *de* | *tote* | *ton* |
| the | crowds. | Immediately | and | then | |

| 3834.4 name acc masc | 1805.2 verb 3pl indic aor act | 3450.7 art nom pl masc | 79.6 noun nom pl masc | 4057.15 verb inf pres mid |
|---|---|---|---|---|
| Παῦλον | ἐξαπέστειλαν | οἱ | ἀδελφοὶ | πορεύεσθαι |
| *Paulon* | *exapesteilan* | *hoi* | *adelphoi* | *poreuesthai* |
| Paul | sent away | the | brothers | to go |

14.a.**Txt:** 020L,025P,044 byz.
**Var:** p74,01ℵ,02A,03B 08E,33,sa.Lach,Treg Tisc,We/Ho,Weis,Sod UBS/☆

| 5453.1 conj | 2175.1 conj | 1894.3 prep | 3450.12 art acc sing fem | 2258.4 noun acc sing fem | 5116.13 verb 3pl indic aor act |
|---|---|---|---|---|---|
| ′ ὡς | [a☆ ἕως ] | ἐπὶ | τὴν | θάλασσαν· | ′ ὑπέμεινάν |
| *hōs* | *heōs* | *epi* | *tēn* | *thalassan* | *hupemeinan* |
| as | [ until ] | to | the | sea; | remained |

14.b.**Txt:** 020L,025P,byz.
**Var:** 01ℵ,03B,Treg,Tisc We/Ho,Weis,Sod UBS/☆

| 1156.2 conj | 5116.13 verb 3pl indic aor act | 4885.1 conj | 3614.16 rel-pron sing neu | 4885.1 conj | 4464.1 name nom masc | 2504.1 conj |
|---|---|---|---|---|---|---|
| δὲ | [b☆ ὑπέμεινάν | τε ] | ὅ | τε | Σίλας | καὶ |
| *de* | *hupemeinan* | *te* | *ho* | *te* | *Silas* | *kai* |
| but | [ remained | and ] | who | both | Silas | and |

15.a.**Txt:** 01ℵ-corr 05D-corr,08E,020L 025P,byz.Sod
**Var:** 02A,03B,Lach Treg,Alf,Tisc,We/Ho Weis,UBS/☆

| 3450.5 art nom sing masc | 4943.1 name nom masc | 1550.1 adv | 3450.7 art nom pl masc | 1156.2 conj | 2497.2 verb nom pl masc part pres act |
|---|---|---|---|---|---|
| ὁ | Τιμόθεος | ἐκεῖ. | **15.** Οἱ | δὲ | ′ καθιστῶντες |
| *ho* | *Timotheos* | *ekei* | *Hoi* | *de* | *kathistōntes* |
| who | Timothy | there. | The | but | conducting |

15.b.**Txt:** 08E,020L 025P,byz.sa.bo.
**Var:** 01ℵ,02A,03B,05D 33,Lach,Treg,Alf,Tisc We/Ho,Weis,Sod UBS/☆

| 2497.12 verb nom pl masc part pres act | 3450.6 art acc sing masc | 3834.4 name acc masc | 70.10 verb 3pl indic aor act | 840.6 prs-pron acc sing masc |
|---|---|---|---|---|
| [a☆ καθιστάνοντες ] | τὸν | Παῦλον | ἤγαγον | ⸂b αὐτὸν ⸃ |
| *kathistanontes* | *ton* | *Paulon* | *ēgagon* | *auton* |
| [ idem ] | | Paul | brought | him |

| 2175.1 conj | 116.1 name gen fem | 2504.1 conj | 2956.27 verb nom pl masc part aor act | 1769.3 noun acc sing fem | 4242.1 prep |
|---|---|---|---|---|---|
| ἕως | Ἀθηνῶν | καὶ | λαβόντες | ἐντολὴν | πρὸς |
| *heōs* | *Athēnōn* | *kai* | *labontes* | *entolēn* | *pros* |
| as far as | Athens; | and | having received | a command | to |

15.c.**Var:** 01ℵ,03B,08E Treg,Tisc,We/Ho,Weis Sod,UBS/☆

| 3450.6 art acc sing masc | 4464.3 name acc masc | 2504.1 conj | 3450.6 art acc sing masc | 4943.4 name acc masc | 2419.1 conj |
|---|---|---|---|---|---|
| τὸν | Σίλαν | καὶ | [c☆+ τὸν ] | Τιμόθεον, | ἵνα |
| *ton* | *Silan* | *kai* | *ton* | *Timotheon* | *hina* |
| | Silas | and | | Timothy, | that |

| 5453.1 conj | 4881.1 adv sup | 2048.9 verb 3pl subj aor act | 4242.1 prep | 840.6 prs-pron acc sing masc |
|---|---|---|---|---|
| ὡς | τάχιστα | ἔλθωσιν | πρὸς | αὐτὸν, |
| *hōs* | *tachista* | *elthōsin* | *pros* | *auton* |
| as | quickly as possible | they should come | to | him, |

But Satan was determined to find some way to oppose the work of God. When he cannot find troublemakers nearby, he will bring them in from the outside. When the unbelieving Jews at Thessalonica heard the news, they came to Beroea and did the same sort of thing they had done at home. They aroused the crowds, trying to incite them to mob violence against Paul.

**17:14.** Before these unbelieving Jews from Thessalonica could do any damage, the Beroean Christian brethren hurried Paul off in the direction of the Aegean Sea, probably intending to send him away by ship. Silas and Timothy stayed behind, since only Paul was the object of the Thessalonian Jews' wrath and bitterness.

Because the Beroean Christians knew this, they believed that with Paul gone, the Thessalonian Jews would go home, and the opposition they had stirred up would subside. Although they were well on their way toward being established in the faith (because of their searching the Scriptures for the basis of the truths of the gospel), Silas and Timothy stayed behind in order that they might further instruct, train, and encourage the whole assembly of believers. Evangelism must be followed by training in discipleship (cf. Matthew 28:19,20).

**17:15.** Those who were conducting Paul toward the sea suddenly changed directions. Possibly they heard that the Thessalonian Jews had not gone home and were plotting something else. It may be they were sending some of their number on ahead to try to ambush Paul. Whatever the reason, the Beroean Christian brethren, or a part of their group, took Paul to Athens. There Paul saw he needed help and he sent the Beroeans back with the command for Silas and Timothy to come to him there as quickly as possible.

First Thessalonians 3:1,2 indicates they did come, but Paul's concern over the Thessalonian assembly of believers caused him to send Timothy back to them to further establish and encourage them with respect to their faith. He knew the Jews who were disappointed in not catching him in Beroea could very well go back and cause further persecution and trouble for the believers in their own city. While he was with them, Paul had told them they would continue to suffer the affliction of trouble and persecution and he wanted to be sure the tempter had not successfully tempted them.

Timothy did come back to Paul later with a good report of the Thessalonian believers' faith and love and their desire to see Paul again. Paul also assured them he was praying most exceedingly, night and day, that he might see them and bring their faith into proper condition (1 Thessalonians 3:10).

In the meantime, with Timothy gone back to Thessalonica and Silas sent to minister elsewhere, Paul determined to wait in Athens. His stay there is important for it gives us an example of how Paul witnessed to those who had no background in Scripture study.



**that the word of God was preached of Paul at Berea:** . . . had been declared by Paul, *Rotherham* . . . was proclaimed, *ASV.*

**they came thither also:** . . . they came there too, *RSV.*

**and stirred up the people:** . . . exciting and disturbing the minds of the people, *TCNT* . . . to cause trouble and spread alarm among the people, *Phillips* . . . and incited the mob to a riot, *Weymouth* . . . to stir up and excite the crowds, *Kleist* . . . They upset the people and made trouble, *Everyday* . . . worked against the missionaries by talking to the people, *NLT* . . . to upset and disturb the minds of the multitude, *Knox* . . . troubling the people and working them up, *BB* . . . disturbing the common people, *Williams C.K.*

**14. And then immediately the brethren sent away Paul to go as it were to the sea:** . . . promptly sent Paul down to the seacoast, *Weymouth* . . . quickly sent Paul away to the coast, *NCV* . . . sent away Paul to journey as far as to the sea, *Worrell* . . . to continue his journey up to the coast, *Knox* . . . away to the sea, *SEB* . . . Sent Paul away at once, *Williams C.K.*

**but Silas and Timotheus abode there still:** . . . stayed behind there, *Rotherham* . . . remained where they were, *Moffatt.*

**15. And they that conducted Paul:** The men who accompanied Paul, *Phillips* . . . The friends who escorted Paul, *TCNT* . . . The men who acted as Paul's bodyguard, *Williams.*

**brought him unto Athens:** . . . took him to the city of, *SEB* . . . took him as far as, *Kleist* . . . all the way to, *Williams C.K.*

**and receiving a commandment unto Silas and Timotheus for to come to him with all speed, they departed:** . . . then went back with his orders, *Williams C.K.* . . . and returned with instructions from him...to rejoin him as soon as possible, *Kleist* . . . and after receiving a message for Silas and Timothy to join him as quickly as possible, *TCNT* . . . they carried a message from Paul back to, *Everyday* . . . Come to me as soon as you can, *NCV* . . . to come to him quickly, *BB.*

| 1821.3 verb 3pl indic imperf act | | 1706.1 prep | 1156.2 conj | 3450.14 art dat pl fem | 116.2 name dat fem |
|---|---|---|---|---|---|
| ἐξῄεσαν. | 16. | Ἐν | δὲ | ταῖς | Ἀθήναις |
| exēesan | | En | de | tais | Athēnais |
| they were departing. | | In | but | | Athens |

| 1538.5 verb gen sing masc part pres mid | 840.8 prs-pron acc pl masc | 3450.2 art gen sing | 3834.2 name gen masc | 3809.2 verb 3sing indic imperf pass |
|---|---|---|---|---|
| ἐκδεχομένου | αὐτοὺς | τοῦ | Παύλου, | παρωξύνετο |
| ekdechomenou | autous | tou | Paulou | parōxuneto |
| waiting for | them | | Paul, | was being enraged |

| 3450.16 art sing neu | 4011.1 noun sing neu | 840.3 prs-pron gen sing | 1706.1 prep | 840.4 prs-pron dat sing | 2311.10 verb dat sing masc part pres act |
|---|---|---|---|---|---|
| τὸ | πνεῦμα | αὐτοῦ | ἐν | αὐτῷ | ⸀ θεωροῦντι |
| to | pneuma | autou | en | autō | theōrounti |
| the | spirit | his | in | him | seeing |

16.a.**Txt:** 05D,020L 025P,byz.
**Var:** 01ℵ,02A,03B,08E Lach,Treg,Alf,Word Tisc,We/Ho,Weis,Sod UBS/☆

| 2311.22 verb gen sing masc part pres act | 2682.1 adj acc sing fem | 1498.29 verb acc sing fem part pres act | 3450.12 art acc sing fem |
|---|---|---|---|
| [a☆ θεωροῦντος ] | κατείδωλον | οὖσαν | τὴν |
| theōrountos | kateidōlon | ousan | tēn |
| [ idem ] | full of idols | being | the |

| 4032.4 noun acc sing fem | | 1250.7 verb 3sing indic imperf mid | 3173.1 conj | 3631.1 partic | 1706.1 prep | 3450.11 art dat sing fem |
|---|---|---|---|---|---|---|
| πόλιν. | 17. | διελέγετο | μὲν | οὖν | ἐν | τῇ |
| polin | | dielegeto | men | oun | en | tē |
| city. | | He was reasoning | indeed | therefore | in | the |

| 4715.3 noun dat sing fem | 3450.4 art dat pl | 2428.4 name-adj dat pl masc | 2504.1 conj | 3450.4 art dat pl | 4431.5 verb dat pl masc part pres mid |
|---|---|---|---|---|---|
| συναγωγῇ | τοῖς | Ἰουδαίοις | καὶ | τοῖς | σεβομένοις, |
| sunagōgē | tois | Ioudaiois | kai | tois | sebomenois |
| synagogue | with the | Jews | and | the | worshiping, |

| 2504.1 conj | 1706.1 prep | 3450.11 art dat sing fem | 57.2 noun dat sing fem | 2567.3 prep | 3820.12 adj acc sing fem |
|---|---|---|---|---|---|
| καὶ | ἐν | τῇ | ἀγορᾷ | κατὰ | πᾶσαν |
| kai | en | tē | agora | kata | pasan |
| and | in | the | marketplace | according to | every |

18.a.**Var:** 01ℵ,02A,03B 05D,020L,025P,Lach Treg,Alf,Word,Tisc We/Ho,Weis,Sod UBS/☆

18.b.**Txt:** 05D,020L 025P,byz.
**Var:** 01ℵ,02A,03B,08E Lach,Treg,Alf,Tisc We/Ho,Weis,Sod UBS/☆

| 2232.4 noun acc sing fem | 4242.1 prep | 3450.8 art acc pl masc | 3770.1 verb acc pl masc part pres act | | 4948.7 indef-pron nom pl masc |
|---|---|---|---|---|---|
| ἡμέραν | πρὸς | τοὺς | παρατυγχάνοντας. | 18. | τινὲς |
| hēmeran | pros | tous | paratunchanontas | | tines |
| day | with | the | meeting with. | | Some |

| 1156.2 conj | 2504.1 conj | 3450.1 art gen pl | 1931.1 name gen pl masc | 2504.1 conj | 3450.1 art gen pl |
|---|---|---|---|---|---|
| δὲ | [a☆+ καὶ ] | τῶν | Ἐπικουρείων | καὶ | ⸂b τῶν ⸃ |
| de | kai | tōn | Epikoureiōn | kai | tōn |
| but | [ idem ] | of the | Epicureans | and | the |

| 4621.1 name-adj gen pl masc | 5222.1 noun gen pl masc | 4671.5 verb 3pl indic imperf act | 840.4 prs-pron dat sing | 2504.1 conj |
|---|---|---|---|---|
| Στωϊκῶν | φιλοσόφων | συνέβαλλον | αὐτῷ· | καί |
| Stōikōn | philosophōn | suneballon | autō | kai |
| Stoics, | philosophers, | were encountering | him. | And |

| 4948.7 indef-pron nom pl masc | 2978.25 verb indic imperf act | 4949.9 intr-pron sing neu | 300.1 partic | 2286.11 verb 3sing opt pres act | 3450.5 art nom sing masc |
|---|---|---|---|---|---|
| τινες | ἔλεγον, | Τί | ἂν | θέλοι | ὁ |
| tines | elegon | Ti | an | theloi | ho |
| some | were saying, | What | | may desire | the |

**17:16.** Athens was famous for its Acropolis and all its temples. Some 600 years before Paul's time it was a world leader in art and philosophy. By this time, however, it had lost its former glory. It was no longer politically important. Its old leadership in culture and education had been taken over by Alexandria in Egypt. Other new centers such as Ephesus, Antioch, and Tarsus far surpassed it as educational centers. It had lost its drive and creativity. It was filled with curiosity seekers and with philosophical speculation that was without depth. Yet it still nurtured the memory of its past. Its temples were still beautiful examples of the best in Greek architecture. But everywhere Paul looked the city was full of images. Alongside the intellectual snobbery of Athens was the most degrading and immoral idolatry.

Paul did not look at the idols as glorious examples of Greek art. He was disturbed by them. His spirit was provoked (almost "angered") within him. All this idol worship made him realize all the more that "the world by wisdom knew not God" (1 Corinthians 1:21).

**17:17.** As always, Paul first went to the synagogue on the Sabbath Day and preached to the Jews and the godly Gentiles. But he was concerned about the rest of the Gentiles too. Their idolatry aroused him to give himself to the proclamation of the gospel as never before. He took every opportunity to speak to groups and to individuals about Jesus and the Resurrection. Throughout every day he carried on discussions with every person he met, especially in the marketplace (the agora, the civic center).

**17:18.** Among those who met him in the marketplace were some Epicurean and Stoic philosophers, and they engaged him in a discussion.

Epicureans were followers of Epicurus (342–270 B.C.). Epicurus taught that nature is the supreme teacher and provides sensations, feelings, and anticipations for the testing of truth. By feelings he meant pleasure and pain. These he said could be used to distinguish between good and evil. He also taught that the gods were incapable of wrath, indifferent to human weakness, and did not intervene or participate in human affairs. Thus, he denied the possibility of miracles, prophecy, and divine providence. In the beginning Epicurus meant "real happiness" by *pleasure*. At first, his followers merely sought a quiet life free from fear, pain, and anger. Later, some made sensual pleasures the goal of life.

Stoics were followers of Zeno of Citium (335–263 B.C.). Zeno believed in a creative power and made duty, reason (or accordance with divine reason), and self-sufficiency the goal of life. He encouraged his followers to accept the laws of nature and conscience and to be indifferent to pleasure, pain, joy, and grief.

Some of these philosophers were quite contemptuous of Paul's gospel and called him a "babbler," literally, "a seed-picker." This

**16. Now while Paul waited for them at Athens:** . . . was waiting for, *Everyday.*

**his spirit was stirred in him:** . . . his soul was deeply vexed, *Berkeley* . . . his spirit was stirred to its depths, *Williams* . . . was exasperated, *Kleist* . . . his heart was moved within him, *Knox* . . . felt deeply troubled, *SEB* . . . it hurt him deeply, *Williams C.K.* . . . was grieved in his spirit, *Fenton.*

**when he saw the city wholly given to idolatry:** . . . at seeing the whole city full of idols, *TCNT* . . . seeing how the city was given to idols, *Rotherham* . . . to see the city completely steeped in idolatry, *Williams* . . . to see the city full of idols, *Williams C.K.* . . . to see the city devoted to idols, *Fenton.*

**17. Therefore disputed he in the synagogue with the Jews:** So he reasoned, *ASV* . . . argued, *TCNT* . . . had discussions, *Weymouth* . . . in the meeting-house with, *Williams C.K.*

**and with the devout persons:** . . . and with those who joined in their worship, *TCNT* . . . and the devout proselytes, *Moffatt* . . . and the devout adherents, *Berkeley* . . . the God-fearing persons, *Williams C.K.*

**and in the market daily:** . . . and he even argued daily in the open market-place, *Phillips* . . . in the business district of the city, *SEB* . . . in the public square day by day, *Williams C.K.*

**with them that met with him:** . . . with them who happened to be at hand, *Rotherham* . . . with the passers-by, *Phillips* . . . with all he met, *Knox* . . . with those whom he chanced to meet, *Williams C.K.*

**18. Then certain philosophers of the Epicureans, and of the Stoicks:** Some members of the...schools of wisdom, *Williams C.K.*

**encountered him:** . . . also encountered him again and again, *Montgomery* . . . joined issue with him, *TCNT* . . . were disputing with him, *HBIE* . . . began to debate with him, *Williams* . . . argued with him, *Everyday* . . . also opposed him, *Williams C.K.*

**And some said:** Some would ask, *TCNT.*

## Acts 17:19

4544.1 adj nom sing masc σπερμολόγος *spermologos* babbler | 3642.4 dem-pron nom sing masc οὗτος *houtos* this | 2978.24 verb inf pres act λέγειν; *legein* to say? | 3450.7 art nom pl masc Οἱ *Hoi* The | 1156.2 conj δέ, *de* and, | 3443.8 adj gen pl neu Ξένων *Xenōn* Of foreign

1134.4 noun gen pl neu δαιμονίων *daimoniōn* demons | 1374.5 verb 3sing indic pres act δοκεῖ *dokei* he seems | 2575.1 noun nom sing masc καταγγελεὺς *katangeleus* a proclaimer | 1498.32 verb inf pres act εἶναι· *einai* to be, | 3617.1 conj ὅτι *hoti* because

3450.6 art acc sing masc τὸν *ton* | 2400.3 name acc masc Ἰησοῦν *Iēsoun* Jesus | 2504.1 conj καὶ *kai* and | 3450.12 art acc sing fem τὴν *tēn* the | 384.4 noun acc sing fem ἀνάστασιν *anastasin* resurrection | 840.2 prs-pron dat pl ʼ αὐτοῖς *autois* to them

18.c.**Txt:** byz.
**Var2:** 01ℵ-org,03B
020L,025P,sa.Treg,Tisc
We/Ho,Weis,Sod
UBS/☆

2076.27 verb 3sing indic imperf mid εὐηγγελίζετο. *euēngelizeto* he was announcing the good news. | 2076.27 verb 3sing indic imperf mid [1c εὐηγγελίζετο *euēngelizeto* [ he was announcing the good news

840.2 prs-pron dat pl αὐτοῖς. *autois* to them. | 2076.27 verb 3sing indic imperf mid 2☆ εὐηγγελίζετο. ] *euēngelizeto* he was announcing the good news. ] | 1934.7 verb nom pl masc part aor mid **19.** ἐπιλαβόμενοί *epilabomenoi* Having taken hold

19.a.**Txt:** 01ℵ,02A,08E
020L,025P,etc.byz.Tisc
Sod
**Var:** 03B,sa.bo.Treg
We/Ho,Weis,UBS/☆

4885.1 conj ʼ τε *te* and | 1156.2 conj [a δὲ ] *de* [ idem ] | 840.3 prs-pron gen sing αὐτοῦ, *autou* of him, | 1894.3 prep ἐπὶ *epi* to | 3450.6 art acc sing masc τὸν *ton* the | 691.2 name acc masc Ἄρειον Πάγον *Areion Pagon* Areopagus

70.10 verb 3pl indic aor act ἤγαγον *ēgagon* they brought | 2978.16 verb nom pl masc part pres act λέγοντες, *legontes* saying, | 1404.5 verb 1pl indic pres mid Δυνάμεθα *Dunametha* Are we able | 1091.29 verb inf aor act γνῶναι *gnōnai* to know | 4949.3 intr-pron nom sing τίς *tis* what | 3450.9 art nom sing fem ἡ *hē* the

2508.3 adj nom sing fem καινὴ *kainē* new | 3642.9 dem-pron nom sing fem αὕτη *hautē* this | 3450.9 art nom sing fem ἡ *hē* the | 5097.3 prep ὑπὸ *hupo* by | 4622.2 prs-pron gen 2sing σοῦ *sou* you | 2953.49 verb nom sing fem part pres mid λαλουμένη *laloumenē* being spoken

1316.1 noun nom sing fem διδαχή; *didachē* teaching? | 3441.1 verb pl neu part pres act **20.** ξενίζοντα *xenizonta* Being strange | 1056.1 conj γάρ *gar* for | 4948.5 indef-pron τινα *tina* certain | 1517.1 verb 2sing indic pres act εἰσφέρεις *eisphereis* you are bringing

1519.1 prep εἰς *eis* to | 3450.15 art acc pl fem τὰς *tas* the | 187.7 noun acc pl fem ἀκοὰς *akoas* hearings | 2231.2 prs-pron gen 1pl ἡμῶν. *hēmōn* our. | 1007.4 verb 1pl indic pres mid βουλόμεθα *boulometha* We wish | 3631.1 partic οὖν *oun* therefore

20.a.**Txt:** 05D,08E,020L
byz.
**Var:** 01ℵ,02A,03B,Lach
Treg,Tisc,We/Ho,Weis
Sod,UBS/☆

1091.29 verb inf aor act γνῶναι *gnōnai* to know | 4949.9 intr-pron sing neu ʼ τί *ti* what | 300.1 partic ἂν *an* | 2286.11 verb 3sing opt pres act θέλοι *theloi* may mean | 4949.1 intr-pron [a☆ τίνα *tina* [ what | 2286.3 verb 3sing indic pres act θέλει ] *thelei* means ]

term was also used as slang for parasites and ignorant plagiarists who would gather information from a variety of sources and try to market it as their own system of knowledge. Then, because Paul preached the good news of Jesus and the Resurrection, they said he seemed to be proclaiming not merely strange gods, but foreign demons. They sneered at the gospel as a foreign religion contrary to all they believed.

**17:19.** Undoubtedly, there were "seed-pickers" who prowled around the marketplace, picking up scraps of information and bits of philosophical ideas and retailing them secondhand. But as these Stoics and Epicurean philosophers listened to Paul, they apparently decided Paul's teaching was dangerous to their ideas and philosophies. Many of the Athenians may have believed in an afterlife and a vague sort of immortality of the soul. But the teaching concerning Jesus and a literal bodily resurrection was startling and bewildering. It could undermine their teachings and their influence. So they seized Paul and brought him before the Council of the Areopagus, the supreme court of Athens. This court formerly met on the Hill of Ares (Mars' Hill), a rocky outcrop or ridge facing the Acropolis. There is some evidence that it no longer met on Mars' Hill in New Testament times, but instead met in a colonnade or roofed portico in the public marketplace (the agora). In any case, it retained the same name wherever it met. It had jurisdiction, not only over criminal cases, but over all public lectures. Paul was taken before it for a sort of preliminary inquiry to give him opportunity to explain his teachings.

The request of the Council of the Areopagus was polite. They asked literally, "Are we able to ascertain something of that new teaching, the one (continually) spoken by you?" This was not an unusual request.

**17:20.** The Council further defined these new things as "strange," not merely foreign or different, but startling and bewildering. It was their will, therefore, for Paul to explain what these things meant. They felt they had a right to know.

Notice that the Council did not give Paul time to prepare a sermon or a defense. But this did not upset Paul. He had the Holy Spirit with him and dwelling in him, so he had the Helper he needed. Not only so, he had been explaining the gospel to everyone he met, so his mind and heart were filled with the truth.

Furthermore, he knew what Jesus taught in Matthew 10:18-20. Jesus told His disciples they would be brought before councils, governors, and kings for His sake, for a testimony to them and to the Gentiles. But when they were arrested or brought before those who would put them on trial or examine them, they must not be anxious or worried about how or what they would speak. What they should speak would be given them at the very time they needed it.



**What will this babbler say?:** What has this beggarly babbler to say, *Weymouth* . . . Whatever does the fellow mean with his scraps of learning, *Moffatt* . . . this amateur talker, *Berkeley* . . . this cock sparrow, *Phillips* . . . This man doesn't know what he is talking about, *Everyday* . . . This man has lots of little things to talk about, *NLT* . . . What can his drift be, this dabbler? *Knox.*

**other some:** . . . and others, *Alford* . . . while others would say, *TCNT.*

**He seemeth to be a setter forth of strange gods:** . . . announceth foreign deities, *Murdock* . . . a Preacher of foreign Deities, *TCNT* . . . Of foreign demons he seemeth to be a declarer, *Rotherham* . . . He seems to be a herald of, *Kleist.*

**because he preached unto them Jesus, and the resurrection:**

**19. And they took him:** So they laid hold of him, *TCNT* . . . they took him by the sleeve, *Knox.*

**and brought him unto Areopagus, saying:** . . . and took him to the city auditorium and said, *Williams* . . . and led him up, *Knox* . . . to the Court of Areopagus, *TCNT* . . . to Mars' Hill, *NLT* . . . to a meeting of the Areopagus Council, *SEB.*

**May we know what this new doctrine, whereof thou speakest, is?:** May we hear what new teaching this is which you are giving, *TCNT* . . . May we know what is this novel teaching of yours, *Moffatt* . . . Will you make clear to us what is this new teaching of yours, *BB* . . . Please explain to us this new idea that you have been teaching, *Everyday* . . . desire to know the purpose of these things, *Swann* . . . We want to know what these things mean, *NLT.*

**20. For thou bringest certain strange things to our ears:** . . . scatterest in our ears, *Murdock* . . . For the things you are saying sound strange to us, *Weymouth* . . . Thou dost introduce terms which are strange to our ears, *Knox* . . . are so new to us, *SEB.*

**we would know therefore what these things mean:** . . . we should like to know what they mean, *TCNT* . . . we have a desire to get the sense of them, *BB.*

| 3642.18 dem-pron pl neu | 1498.32 verb inf pres act | 117.1 name-adj nom pl masc | 1156.2 conj | 3820.7 adj nom pl masc | 2504.1 conj |
|---|---|---|---|---|---|
| ταῦτα | εἶναι. | 21. Ἀθηναῖοι | δὲ | πάντες | καὶ |
| *tauta* | *einai* | *Athēnaioi* | *de* | *pantes* | *kai* |
| these things | to be. | Athenians | now | all | and |

21.a.**Txt:** 020L,025P,byz.
**Var:** 01ℵ,02A,03B,05D 08E,Lach,Treg,Alf,Tisc We/Ho,Weis,Sod UBS/☆

| 3450.7 art nom pl masc | 1912.1 verb nom pl masc part pres act | 3443.3 adj nom pl masc | 1519.1 prep | 3625.6 num card neu | 2066.1 adj sing |
|---|---|---|---|---|---|
| οἱ | ἐπιδημοῦντες | ξένοι | εἰς | οὐδὲν | ἕτερον |
| *hoi* | *epidēmountes* | *xenoi* | *eis* | *ouden* | *heteron* |
| the | sojourning | strangers | in | nothing | else |

21.b.**Txt:** 08E,020L 025P,byz.bo.
**Var:** 01ℵ,02A,03B,05D sa.Lach,Treg,Alf,Tisc We/Ho,Weis,Sod UBS/☆

21.c.**Var:** 01ℵ,02A,03B Lach,Treg,Tisc,We/Ho Weis,Sod,UBS/☆

| 2100.3 verb 3pl indic imperf act | 2100.2 verb 3pl indic imperf act | 2211.1 conj | 2978.24 verb inf pres act |
|---|---|---|---|
| ʼ εὐκαίρουν | [a☆ ηὐκαίρουν ] | ἢ | λέγειν |
| *eukairoun* | *ēukairoun* | *ē* | *legein* |
| were spending their leisure | [ idem ] | than | to tell |

| 4948.10 indef-pron sing neu | 2504.1 conj | 2211.1 conj | 189.17 verb inf pres act | 4948.10 indef-pron sing neu | 2508.10 adj comp sing neu |
|---|---|---|---|---|---|
| τι | ʼ καὶ | [b☆ ἢ ] | ἀκούειν | [c☆+ τι ] | καινότερον. |
| *ti* | *kai* | *ē* | *akouein* | *ti* | *kainoteron* |
| something | and | [ or ] | to hear | [ something ] | newer. |

22.a.**Txt:** 05D,08E,020L 025P,etc.byz.Sod
**Var:** 01ℵ,02A,03B,Lach Treg,Tisc,We/Ho,Weis UBS/☆

| 2449.43 verb nom sing masc part aor pass | 1156.2 conj | 3450.5 art nom sing masc | 3834.1 name nom masc | 1706.1 prep | 3189.1 adj dat sing |
|---|---|---|---|---|---|
| 22. Σταθεὶς | δὲ | ʼa ὁ ʽ | Παῦλος | ἐν | μέσῳ |
| *Statheis* | *de* | *ho* | *Paulos* | *en* | *mesō* |
| Having stood | and | | Paul | in | midst |

| 3450.2 art gen sing | 691.1 name gen masc | 5183.4 verb 3sing indic act | 433.6 noun nom pl masc | 117.1 name-adj nom pl masc |
|---|---|---|---|---|
| τοῦ | Ἀρείου Πάγου | ἔφη, | Ἄνδρες | Ἀθηναῖοι, |
| *tou* | *Areiou Pagou* | *ephē* | *Andres* | *Athēnaioi* |
| the | Areopagus | said, | Men | Athenians, |

| 2567.3 prep | 3820.1 adj | 5453.1 conj | 1169.1 adj comp acc pl masc | 5050.4 prs-pron acc 2pl |
|---|---|---|---|---|
| κατὰ | πάντα | ὡς | δεισιδαιμονεστέρους | ὑμᾶς |
| *kata* | *panta* | *hōs* | *deisidaimonesterous* | *humas* |
| according to | all things | how | very religious | you |

| 2311.2 verb 1sing indic pres act | 1324.12 verb nom sing masc part pres mid | 1056.1 conj | 2504.1 conj | 331.1 verb nom sing masc part pres act |
|---|---|---|---|---|
| θεωρῶ. | 23. διερχόμενος | γὰρ | καὶ | ἀναθεωρῶν |
| *theōrō* | *dierchomenos* | *gar* | *kai* | *anatheōrōn* |
| I behold; | passing through | for | and | beholding |

| 3450.17 art pl neu | 4429.2 noun pl neu | 5050.2 prs-pron gen 2pl | 2128.6 verb indic aor act | 2504.1 conj | 1034.1 noun acc sing masc | 1706.1 prep |
|---|---|---|---|---|---|---|
| τὰ | σεβάσματα | ὑμῶν, | εὗρον | καὶ | βωμὸν | ἐν |
| *ta* | *sebasmata* | *humōn* | *heuron* | *kai* | *bōmon* | *en* |
| the | objects of worship | your, | I found | also | an altar | on |

| 3614.3 rel-pron dat sing | 1909.2 verb 3sing indic plperf pass | 55.1 adj dat sing masc | 2296.3 noun dat sing masc | 3614.6 rel-pron acc sing masc |
|---|---|---|---|---|
| ᾧ | ἐπεγέγραπτο, | Ἀγνώστῳ | θεῷ. | ʼ ὃν |
| *hō* | *epegegrapto* | *Agnōstō* | *theō* | *hon* |
| which | had been inscribed, | To an unknown | God. | Whom |

23.a.**Txt:** 01ℵ-corr 02A-corr,08E,020L 025P,byz.
**Var:** 01ℵ-org,02A-org 03B,05D,Lach,Treg,Alf Word,Tisc,We/Ho,Weis Sod,UBS/☆

| 3614.16 rel-pron sing neu | 3631.1 partic | 49.8 verb nom pl masc part pres act | 2132.1 verb 2pl indic pres act | 3642.6 dem-pron acc sing masc |
|---|---|---|---|---|
| [a☆ ὃ ] | οὖν | ἀγνοοῦντες | εὐσεβεῖτε, | ʼ τοῦτον |
| *ho* | *oun* | *agnoountes* | *eusebeite* | *touton* |
| [ Which ] | therefore | not knowing | you reverence, | this one |

**17:21.** This verse is a parenthesis explaining why the Council of the Areopagus wanted to know, ascertain, and determine the meaning of Paul's new and bewildering teaching. They were Athenians, and the Athenians as a whole, as well as the resident aliens who had accepted the Athenian culture and way of life, spent their (leisure) time telling and hearing something new. They were not great leaders and thinkers as their ancient forebears had been. Rather, they were curiosity seekers and philosophical hangers-on whose only interest was what was new.

**17:22.** Standing in the midst, not of the hill, but of the Council of the Areopagus, Paul wisely began in a positive way. As at Lystra, he took the people where they were and tried to lead them into spiritual truth.

The translation (KJV) that says they were "too superstitious" sounds as if he was intending to insult them. Though the Greek words can bear that meaning, it is better to translate them here with the meaning of "very religious," in the sense of being very respectful to their gods. This was not a statement they would react against. They might have even considered it a compliment.

**17:23.** Then Paul used an inscription on an altar in Athens to give him an opportunity to speak about the one true God in contrast to their many gods. During his walks around Athens he had come across this inscription, "To the Unknown God." In their desire to be sure they did not slight or overlook some god, the Athenians had erected this altar. This was evidence that Paul was not preaching something contrary to the laws of Athens. He could tell them about the God who was unknown to them.

Paul did not mean by this that their worship was acceptable to God. God seeks those who will worship Him in spirit (and in the Spirit) and in truth, not in ignorance and empty forms. Actually, the Greeks did not feel close to any god. Like those who go to the heathen temples today, they would go from god to god, from altar to altar, hoping that somehow one of them might help them. Thus, in spite of their education and highly developed culture, these Greeks were badly in need of the gospel.

Paul used words here that carry another connotation. The word *worship* can mean serving or worshiping one who has a right to your service and worship. The word *ignorantly* often implies willful ignorance that is, therefore, guilty before God. Romans 1:18-32 shows that the Gentiles are guilty because they once knew God, but they turned from Him, refused to give Him glory and thanks, and became full of empty and unreal imaginings so that their foolish hearts were darkened through moral defect. The implication in Paul's letter to the Romans is that they took God off the throne, put self on the throne, and soon were worshiping gods of their own making, gods they thought they could manipulate to do their will.

**21. (For all the Athenians and strangers which were there:** (Now everybody in Athens, *Beck* . . . and the foreign residents, *Fenton* . . . sojourning foreigners, *Rotherham.*

**spent their time in nothing else:** . . . found no time for anything else, *TCNT* . . . spent the whole of their leisure, *Fenton.*

**but either to tell, or to hear some new thing.):** . . . but telling, or listening to, the last new thing.), *TCNT* . . . to talk about any new idea, *SEB.*

**22. Then Paul stood in the midst of Mars' hill, and said:** . . . taking his stand, *Rotherham* . . . in the centre of the High Court, *Fenton.*

**Ye men of Athens:**

**I perceive that in all things ye are too superstitious:** . . . excessive in the worship of demons, *Murdock* . . . on every hand I see signs of your being very devout, *TCNT* . . . I observe at every turn that you are a most religious people, *Moffatt* . . . my own eyes tell me that you are in all respects an extremely religious people, *Phillips* . . . very much given to the worship of divinities, *HBIE* . . . you stand in greatest awe of the deities, *Swann.*

**23. For as I passed by:** For as I was going about, *TCNT* . . . going here and there, *Williams* . . . made my way here, *Phillips.*

**and beheld your devotions:** . . . and studying, *Fenton* . . . I observed the objects of your worship, *RSV* . . . looking at your sacred shrines, *TCNT.*

**I found an altar:** I came upon an altar, *TCNT* . . . I actually came upon, *Moffatt* . . . I particularly noticed an altar, *Phillips.*

**with this inscription:** . . . on which were inscribed the words, *Phillips* . . . with this writing on it, *BB.*

**TO THE UNKNOWN GOD:** THE HIDDEN GOD, *Murdock* . . . TO GOD THE UNKNOWN, *Phillips.*

**Whom therefore ye ignorantly worship:** What therefore you in your ignorance revere, *Rotherham* . . . what you don't know and yet worship, *Beck* . . . What, therefore, you unknowingly worship, *Fenton.*

23.b.**Txt:** 01ℵ-corr 02A-corr,08E,020L 025P,byz.
**Var:** 01ℵ-org,02A-org 03B,05D,Lach,Treg,Alf Word,Tisc,We/Ho,Weis Sod,UBS/☆

| **3642.17** dem-pron sing neu | **1466.1** prs-pron nom 1sing | **2576.2** verb 1sing indic pres act | **5050.3** prs-pron dat 2pl | **3450.5** art nom sing masc |
|---|---|---|---|---|
| [b☆ τοῦτο ] | ἐγὼ | καταγγέλλω | ὑμῖν. | **24.** ὁ |
| *touto* | *egō* | *katangellō* | *humin* | *ho* |
| [ idem ] | I | am announcing | to you. | The |

| **2296.1** noun nom sing masc | **3450.5** art nom sing masc | **4020.37** verb nom sing masc part aor act | **3450.6** art acc sing masc | **2862.4** noun acc sing masc | **2504.1** conj |
|---|---|---|---|---|---|
| θεὸς | ὁ | ποιήσας | τὸν | κόσμον | καὶ |
| *theos* | *ho* | *poiēsas* | *ton* | *kosmon* | *kai* |
| God | the | having made | the | world | and |

| **3820.1** adj | **3450.17** art pl neu | **1706.1** prep | **840.4** prs-pron dat sing | **3642.4** dem-pron nom sing masc | **3636.2** noun gen sing masc | **2504.1** conj |
|---|---|---|---|---|---|---|
| πάντα | τὰ | ἐν | αὐτῷ, | οὗτος | οὐρανοῦ | καὶ |
| *panta* | *ta* | *en* | *autō* | *houtos* | *ouranou* | *kai* |
| all things | the | in | it, | this one | of heaven | and |

| **1087.2** noun gen sing fem | **2935.1** noun nom sing masc | **5062.6** verb nom sing masc part pres act | **5062.6** verb nom sing masc part pres act | **2935.1** noun nom sing masc |
|---|---|---|---|---|
| γῆς | ⸀ κύριος | ὑπάρχων, | [☆ ὑπάρχων | κύριος ] |
| *gēs* | *kurios* | *huparchōn* | *huparchōn* | *kurios* |
| earth | Lord | being, | [ being | Lord ] |

| **3620.2** partic | **1706.1** prep | **5335.2** adj dat pl masc | **3348.5** noun dat pl masc | **2700.2** verb 3sing indic pres act | **3624.1** conj |
|---|---|---|---|---|---|
| οὐκ | ἐν | χειροποιήτοις | ναοῖς | κατοικεῖ, | **25.** οὐδὲ |
| *ouk* | *en* | *cheiropoiētois* | *naois* | *katoikei* | *oude* |
| not | in | handmade | temples | dwells, | nor |

25.a.**Txt:** 09F,020L 025P,byz.sa.bo.
**Var:** 01ℵ,02A,03B,05D Lach,Treg,Alf,Tisc We/Ho,Weis,Sod UBS/☆

| **5097.3** prep | **5331.6** noun gen pl fem | **442.7** noun gen pl masc | **440.5** adj gen pl fem | **2300.11** verb 3sing indic pres mid |
|---|---|---|---|---|
| ὑπὸ | χειρῶν | ⸀ ἀνθρώπων | [a☆ ἀνθρωπίνων ] | θεραπεύεται |
| *hupo* | *cheirōn* | *anthrōpōn* | *anthrōpinōn* | *therapeuetai* |
| by | hands | of men | [ human ] | is being served |

| **4184.1** verb nom sing masc part pres mid | **4948.1** indef-pron gen sing | **840.5** prs-pron nom sing masc | **1319.5** verb nom sing masc part pres act | **3820.5** adj dat pl |
|---|---|---|---|---|
| προσδεόμενός | τινος, | αὐτὸς | διδοὺς | πᾶσιν |
| *prosdeomenos* | *tinos* | *autos* | *didous* | *pasin* |
| needing | anything, | himself | giving | to all |

25.b.**Txt:** 020L,025P,byz. sa.Steph
**Var:** 01ℵ-corr,02A,03B 05D,bo.Elzev,Gries Lach,Treg,Alf,Word Tisc,We/Ho,Weis,Sod UBS/☆

| **2205.4** noun acc sing fem | **2504.1** conj | **4017.2** noun acc sing fem | **2567.3** prep | **3820.1** adj | **2504.1** conj |
|---|---|---|---|---|---|
| ζωὴν | καὶ | πνοὴν | ⸀ κατὰ | πάντα· | [b☆ καὶ |
| *zōēn* | *kai* | *pnoēn* | *kata* | *panta* | *kai* |
| life | and | breath | according to | everything; | [ and |

| **3450.17** art pl neu | **3820.1** adj | **4020.24** verb 3sing indic aor act | **4885.1** conj | **1523.1** prep gen | **1518.1** num card gen |
|---|---|---|---|---|---|
| τὰ | πάντα· ] | **26.** ἐποίησέν | τε | ἐξ | ἑνὸς |
| *ta* | *panta* | *epoiēsen* | *te* | *ex* | *henos* |
| the | all things; ] | he made | and | of | one |

26.a.**Txt:** 05D,08E,020L 025P,044,byz.lect.it.
**Var:** p74,01ℵ,02A,03B 33,sa.bo.Lach,Treg,Alf Tisc,We/Ho,Weis,Sod UBS/☆

| **129.2** noun gen sing neu | **3820.17** adj sing neu | **1477.1** noun sing neu | **442.7** noun gen pl masc | **2700.10** verb inf pres act | **1894.3** prep |
|---|---|---|---|---|---|
| ⸂a αἵματος ⸃ | πᾶν | ἔθνος | ἀνθρώπων, | κατοικεῖν | ἐπὶ |
| *haimatos* | *pan* | *ethnos* | *anthrōpōn* | *katoikein* | *epi* |
| blood | every | nation | of men, | to dwell | upon |

26.b.**Txt:** 020L,025P,byz. Sod
**Var:** 01ℵ,02A,03B,05D Lach,Treg,Alf,Tisc We/Ho,Weis,UBS/☆

| **3820.17** adj sing neu | **3450.16** art sing neu | **4241.1** noun sing neu | **3820.2** adj gen sing | **4241.2** noun gen sing neu |
|---|---|---|---|---|
| ⸀ πᾶν | τὸ | προσώπον | [b☆ παντὸς | προσώπου ] |
| *pan* | *to* | *prosōpon* | *pantos* | *prosōpou* |
| all | the | face | [ all | face ] |

**17:24.** Among the Jews who claimed the Old Testament as their authority, Paul always went right to the prophecies and promises of Scripture. But Paul never started with these when he was dealing with Gentiles who did not know or believe the Bible. In Athens he was led by the Holy Spirit to declare first some facts about the God who made the promises. It was necessary for the Athenians to understand that He is different from the gods they believed in.

Paul first emphasized that God is the Creator of all things, the world (the *kosmos,* the universe, the sum total of the created order) and everything in it. This was a new idea to the Greeks. In their myths they claimed that various gods created various things, always out of preexisting materials. In fact, they looked on the gods themselves as part of what we might call the created universe. They needed to know the true God is above and beyond the universe and that He created it all. This is basic. All through the Old Testament the Bible draws attention to the fact that God is both Creator and Redeemer. The Athenians had to understand first that He is the Creator before they could understand how He could be the Redeemer.

Then Paul emphasized the truth that God is Lord of heaven and earth. That is, by right of creation, He is Lord, Owner, Master. There is no room for other gods. He alone is worthy of our worship.

Furthermore, since He is the Creator and is above all, He is too great to dwell in sanctuaries made by human hands; that is, He cannot be limited to them. This was a truth well understood by Solomon when he said, "Behold, the heaven and heaven of heavens cannot contain thee; how much less this house that I have builded?" (1 Kings 8:27). The prophets also understood it. In Isaiah 66:1 God says, "The heaven is my throne, and the earth is my footstool: where is the house that ye build unto me? and where is the place of my rest?" What a contrast with the little gods of Athens!

**17:25.** The true God does not need to be worshiped with what human hands can do. He does not need to be cared for as a physician would tend a patient, for He does not need anything. After all, how could He need anything and how could He need any care? He is the true Source of and Giver of all life, breath, and all things.

**17:26.** Paul further emphasized that God is the Creator of all by saying God has made out of one blood (that is, from one blood line, in other words, from Adam) every nation of mankind to dwell on the whole face of the earth.

Some ancient manuscripts omit the word "blood" in this verse. The meaning is still the same, however, for it would mean that out of one (person), Adam, God has made all the nations of the earth. This too is important. Some ancient peoples taught they were created by a separate creation from other nations. But in God's eyes, as well as in the facts of history, all are part of Adam's race. Most scientists today say the facts point to a single origin for the human race.

**him declare I unto you:** . . . that I am now proclaiming to you, *TCNT* . . . announce to you, *Berkeley* . . . he is the One I will tell you about, *NLT* . . . that I am revealing to you, *Knox.*

**24. God that made:**

**the world and all things therein:** . . . the universe and everything in it, *Weymouth* . . . the world and all that it contains, *Williams.*

**seeing that he is Lord of heaven and earth:** . . . he, Lord as he is of Heaven and earth, *TCNT* . . . the Lord of the land and the sky, *Everyday.*

**dwelleth not in temples made with hands:** . . . is not housed in buuildings made with hands, *BB* . . . does not dwell in sanctuaries built by man, *Weymouth* . . . He doesn't live in temples, *SEB.*

**25. Neither is worshipped with men's hands:** . . . is waited upon, *Rotherham* . . . nor yet do human hands minister to his wants, *TCNT* . . . And is not dependent on the work of men's hands, *BB* . . . He doesn't need any help from men, *SEB.*

**as though he needed any thing:** . . . as though in want of anything, *Rotherham* . . . as though he needed anything, *TCNT* . . . as if he had need of anything, *BB* . . . He does not need any help from them, *NCV* . . . as if he stood in need of anything, *Knox.*

**seeing he giveth:** . . . for it is he who giveth, *Moffatt.*

**to all life, and breath, and all things:**

**26. And hath made of one blood all nations of men:** And made all nations of men, (created) of one blood, *Alford* . . . He made all races of men from one stock, *TCNT* . . . He caused to spring from one forefather people of every race, *Weymouth* . . . From one man he has created the whole human race, *Kleist* . . . From him came all the different people, *Everyday* . . . of one single stock, *Knox.*

**for to dwell on all the face of the earth:** . . . and caused them to settle on all parts of the earth's surface, *TCNT* . . . for them to live on the whole surface of the earth, *Weymouth* . . . to dwell all over the earth, *Moffatt.*

| 3450.10 art gen sing fem | 1087.2 noun gen sing fem | 3587.4 verb nom sing masc part aor act | 4243.1 verb acc pl masc part perf mid |
|---|---|---|---|
| τῆς | γῆς, | ὁρίσας | ʼ προτεταγμένους |
| tēs | gēs | horisas | protetagmenous |
| of the | earth, | having determined | having arranged before |

26.c.**Txt:** 05D-org,Steph
**Var:** 01ℵ,02A,03B
05D-corr,08E,020L
025P,Gries,Treg,Alf
Word,Tisc,We/Ho,Weis
Sod,UBS/☆

| 4225.3 verb acc pl masc part perf mid | 2511.8 noun acc pl masc | 2504.1 conj | 3450.15 art acc pl fem | 3597.1 noun acc pl fem |
|---|---|---|---|---|
| [c☆ προστεταγμένους ] | καιροὺς | καὶ | τὰς | ὁροθεσίας |
| prostetagmenous | kairous | kai | tas | horothesias |
| [ having prescribed ] | times | and | the | boundaries |

| 3450.10 art gen sing fem | 2703.1 noun gen sing fem | 840.1 prs-pron gen pl | 2195.13 verb inf pres act | 3450.6 art acc sing masc |
|---|---|---|---|---|
| τῆς | κατοικίας | αὐτῶν˙ | 27. ζητεῖν | ʼ τὸν |
| tēs | katoikias | autōn | zētein | ton |
| of the | dwelling | their; | to seek | the |

27.a.**Txt:** 08E,025P,044
lect.Steph
**Var:** p74,01ℵ,02A,03B
020L,sa.bo.Gries,Lach
Treg,Alf,Tisc,We/Ho
Weis,Sod,UBS/☆

| 2935.4 noun acc sing masc | 3450.6 art acc sing masc | 2296.4 noun acc sing masc | 1479.1 conj | 679.1 partic | 1058.1 partic |
|---|---|---|---|---|---|
| κύριον, | [a☆ τὸν | θεὸν ] | εἰ | ἄρα | γε |
| kurion | ton | theon | ei | ara | ge |
| Lord; | | [God ] | if | therefore | indeed |

27.b.**Txt:** 01ℵ,03B,08E
byz.
**Var:** p74,02A,05D,044
36,453,945,1739,1891

| 5419.2 verb 3pl opt aor act | 840.6 prs-pron acc sing masc | 2504.1 conj | 2211.1 conj | 2128.16 verb 3pl opt aor act |
|---|---|---|---|---|
| ψηλαφήσειαν | αὐτὸν | ʼ καὶ | [b ἢ ] | εὕροιεν, |
| psēlaphēseian | auton | kai | ē | heuroien |
| they might feel after | him | and | [ or ] | might find him, |

27.c.**Txt:** 01ℵ,025P-corr
byz.
**Var:** 03B,05D-corr,020L
025P-org,Lach,Treg,Alf
Tisc,We/Ho,Weis,Sod
UBS/☆

| 2515.1 adv | 2504.1 conj | 1058.1 partic | 3620.3 partic | 3084.1 adv | 570.3 prep | 1518.1 num card gen |
|---|---|---|---|---|---|---|
| ʼ καίτοιγε | [c☆ καί | γε ] | οὐ | μακρὰν | ἀπὸ | ἑνὸς |
| kaitoige | kai | ge | ou | makran | apo | henos |
| though indeed | [ and | yet ] | not | far | from | one |

| 1524.2 adj gen sing | 2231.2 prs-pron gen 1pl | 5062.4 verb part pres act | 1706.1 prep | 840.4 prs-pron dat sing | 1056.1 conj |
|---|---|---|---|---|---|
| ἑκάστου | ἡμῶν | ὑπάρχοντα. | 28. Ἐν | αὐτῷ | γὰρ |
| hekastou | hēmōn | huparchonta | En | autō | gar |
| each | of us | being; | in | him | for |

| 2180.3 verb 1pl pres act | 2504.1 conj | 2767.5 verb 1pl indic pres mid | 2504.1 conj | 1498.5 verb 1pl indic pres act | 5453.1 conj | 2504.1 conj |
|---|---|---|---|---|---|---|
| ζῶμεν | καὶ | κινούμεθα | καὶ | ἐσμέν˙ | ὡς | καί |
| zōmen | kai | kinoumetha | kai | esmen | hōs | kai |
| we live | and | move | and | are; | as | also |

| 4948.7 indef-pron nom pl masc | 3450.1 art gen pl | 2567.2 prep | 5050.4 prs-pron acc 2pl | 4023.3 noun gen pl masc | 2029.5 verb 3pl indic perf act |
|---|---|---|---|---|---|
| τινες | τῶν | καθ' | ὑμᾶς | ποιητῶν | εἰρήκασιν, |
| tines | tōn | kath' | humas | poiētōn | eirēkasin |
| some | of the | among | you | poets | have said, |

| 3450.2 art gen sing | 1056.1 conj | 2504.1 conj | 1079.1 noun sing neu | 1498.5 verb 1pl indic pres act | 1079.1 noun sing neu | 3631.1 partic |
|---|---|---|---|---|---|---|
| Τοῦ | γὰρ | καὶ | γένος | ἐσμέν. | 29. Γένος | οὖν |
| Tou | gar | kai | genos | esmen | Genos | oun |
| Of the | for | also | offspring | we are. | Offspring | therefore |

| 5062.7 verb nom pl masc part pres act | 3450.2 art gen sing | 2296.2 noun gen sing masc | 3620.2 partic | 3648.4 verb 1pl indic pres act | 3406.5 verb inf pres act |
|---|---|---|---|---|---|
| ὑπάρχοντες | τοῦ | θεοῦ, | οὐκ | ὀφείλομεν | νομίζειν |
| huparchontes | tou | theou | ouk | opheilomen | nomizein |
| being | | of God, | not | we ought | to think |

God has also fixed the limit of mankind's appointed seasons (times, occasions, and opportunities) as well as the boundaries of mankind's dwelling. Since this points back to what God has done in creation, it must refer to Genesis 1:9,10 where God separated the dry land from the waters.

Other Old Testament passages show that God as the Creator is also the Guide of the family of nations. God regulates the rise and fall of nations (Daniel 4:34,35; 5:18-21). He also is concerned over them and exercises authority over their location and limits their expansion (Amos 9:7; Deuteronomy 32:8).

**17:27.** By saying God has fixed the boundaries of mankind's dwelling, Paul did not mean mankind could not or should not move from one place to another. All people have done that throughout history to a greater or lesser extent. Rather, Paul meant God brought mankind to the places and times where they would have opportunities to seek God, "if perhaps they might touch Him and find Him," though He is actually not far away, not distant from each one. So it should not be hard to find Him. (Romans 1:20,21 points out that "the invisible things of him are clearly seen, being understood by the things that are made, even his eternal power and Godhead; so that they are without excuse." Just looking at the greatness, the complexity, and the beauty of creation should have let the Athenians understand that it was not some little god in a corner who brought all this into being.)

**17:28.** To emphasize that God should not be hard to find, Paul added, "For in Him we live, and move and are (exist, have our being)." This statement is a quotation from one of the ancient poets, possibly Minos or Epimenedes of Crete. Then Paul quoted another of their own (Gentile, Greek-speaking) poets (Aratus of Cilicia) who said, "For we are His offspring." Paul used these quotations, not because they were inspired, but because they are true. God is indeed the Source of our existence and is near us.

Paul's words emphasize that God as Creator is not only above and beyond us as created beings, He is also everywhere present in His creation and wants to be a Friend to all, even to fallen men and women who have lost their way. The Gentile poets did not, of course, understand the full implication of what they said. But the Holy Spirit brought them to Paul's memory to catch the attention of these Athenians and turn their thoughts toward God. Paul, however, made it clear later (verses 30,31) that having their source in God did not make them ready to meet God. They still needed to repent because a final judgment is coming.

**17:29.** Since human beings are the "offspring" of God (in the sense of being created in the image and after the likeness of God), mankind would be totally unreasonable to think of the Godhead (the divine Trinity) as gold, or silver, or stone, an engraved work

**and hath determined the times before appointed:** . . . marking out fitting opportunities, *Rotherham* . . . definitely appointing the pre-established periods, *Berkeley* . . . fixing a time for their rise and fall, *TCNT* . . . He decided exactly when, *NCV* . . . the cycles it was to pass through, *Knox.*

**and the bounds of their habitation:** . . . limits of their settlements, *TCNT* . . . boundaries of their abodes, *Moffatt* . . . boundaries they live in, *Beck* . . . and where they must live, *NCV* . . . having provided proper methods and guides, *Fenton.*

**27. That they should seek the Lord:** . . . search for God, *TCNT* . . . for their research in seeking God, *Fenton.*

**if haply they might feel after him, and find him:** . . . if by any means they might feel their way to him, *TCNT* . . . if perhaps they could grope for Him, *Weymouth* . . . somehow grope their way towards him? *Knox* . . . on the chance of finding him in their groping for him, *Moffatt.*

**though he be not far from every one of us:** . . . although in truth he is already not far, *Rotherham* . . . Though indeed he is close to each one of us, *Moffatt.*

**28. For in him we live, and move, and have our being:** For in him we have life and motion and existence, *BB* . . . and keep on living, *NLT* . . . and exist, *Fenton* . . . and are, *Worrell.*

**as certain also of your own poets have said:** To use the words of some of your own poets, *TCNT* . . . Some...have endorsed this in the words, *Phillips.*

**For we also are his offspring:** From him is our descent, *Murdock* . . . You see, we are His children, *Beck* . . . originate from Him, *Fenton.*

**29. Forasmuch then as we are the offspring of God:** Now then, since we have our being from God, *Beck* . . . possessing an origin from God, *Fenton.*

**we ought not to think:** . . . to be supposing, *Rotherham* . . . we must not think, *TCNT* . . . we ought not to imagine, *Fenton, Weymouth* . . . it is not right for us to have the idea, *BB.*

| **5392.3** noun dat sing masc | **2211.1** conj | **690.3** noun dat sing masc | **2211.1** conj | **3012.3** noun dat sing masc | **5316.2** noun dat sing neu |
|---|---|---|---|---|---|
| χρυσῷ | ἢ | ἀργύρῳ | ἢ | λίθῳ, | χαράγματι |
| *chrusō* | *ē* | *argurō* | *ē* | *lithō* | *charagmati* |
| gold | or | silver | or | stone, | a graven thing |

| **4926.1** noun gen sing fem | **2504.1** conj | **1745.1** noun gen sing fem | **442.2** noun gen sing masc | **3450.16** art sing neu | **2281.2** adj sing neu |
|---|---|---|---|---|---|
| τέχνης | καὶ | ἐνθυμήσεως | ἀνθρώπου, | τὸ | θεῖον |
| *technēs* | *kai* | *enthumēseōs* | *anthrōpou* | *to* | *theion* |
| of art | and | imagination | of man, | the | divine |

| **1498.32** verb inf pres act | **3527.1** adj sing | **3450.8** art acc pl masc | **3173.1** conj | **3631.1** partic | **5385.7** noun acc pl masc |
|---|---|---|---|---|---|
| εἶναι | ὅμοιον. | **30.** Τοὺς | μὲν | οὖν | χρόνους |
| *einai* | *homoion* | *Tous* | *men* | *oun* | *chronous* |
| to be | like. | The | indeed | therefore | times |

| **3450.10** art gen sing fem | **51.1** noun gen sing fem | **5074.1** verb nom sing masc part aor act | **3450.5** art nom sing masc | **2296.1** noun nom sing masc |
|---|---|---|---|---|
| τῆς | ἀγνοίας | ὑπεριδὼν | ὁ | θεὸς, |
| *tēs* | *agnoias* | *huperidōn* | *ho* | *theos* |
| of the | ignorance | having overlooked | | God, |

30.a.**Txt:** p41,p74 01ℵ-corr,02A,05D,08E 020L,025P,etc.byz.Sod **Var:** 01ℵ-org,03B,it. Tisc,We/Ho,Weis UBS/☆

30.b.**Txt:** 020L,025P,byz. **Var:** 01ℵ,02A,03B 05D-corr,08E,Lach,Treg Alf,Tisc,We/Ho,Weis Sod,UBS/☆

31.a.**Txt:** 020L,025P,byz. **Var:** 01ℵ,02A,03B,05D 08E,Lach,Treg,Alf Word,Tisc,We/Ho,Weis Sod,UBS/☆

| **3450.17** art pl neu | **3431.1** adv | **3715.2** verb 3sing indic pres act | **514.14** verb 3sing indic pres act | **3450.4** art dat pl |
|---|---|---|---|---|
| τὰ | νῦν | ‹ παραγγέλλει | [a ἀπαγγέλλει ] | τοῖς |
| *ta* | *nun* | *parangellei* | *apangellei* | *tois* |
| the | now | commands | [ tells ] | the |

| **442.8** noun dat pl masc | **3820.5** adj dat pl | **3820.8** adj acc pl masc | **3699.1** adv | **3210.5** verb inf pres act |
|---|---|---|---|---|
| ἀνθρώποις | ‹ πᾶσιν | [b☆ πάντας ] | πανταχοῦ | μετανοεῖν· |
| *anthrōpois* | *pasin* | *pantas* | *pantachou* | *metanoein* |
| men | all | [ idem ] | everywhere | to repent, |

| **1354.1** conj | **2502.1** conj | **2449.4** verb 3sing indic aor act | **2232.4** noun acc sing fem | **1706.1** prep |
|---|---|---|---|---|
| **31.** ‹ διότι | [a☆ καθότι ] | ἔστησεν | ἡμέραν | ἐν |
| *dioti* | *kathoti* | *estēsen* | *hēmeran* | *en* |
| because | [ idem ] | he set | a day | in |

| **3614.11** rel-pron dat sing fem | **3165.3** verb 3sing indic pres act | **2892.12** verb inf pres act | **3450.12** art acc sing fem | **3487.4** noun acc sing fem |
|---|---|---|---|---|
| ᾗ | μέλλει | κρίνειν | τὴν | οἰκουμένην |
| *hē* | *mellei* | *krinein* | *tēn* | *oikoumenēn* |
| which | he is about | to judge | the | habitable world |

| **1706.1** prep | **1336.3** noun dat sing fem | **1706.1** prep | **433.3** noun dat sing masc | **3614.3** rel-pron dat sing | **3587.2** verb 3sing indic aor act |
|---|---|---|---|---|---|
| ἐν | δικαιοσύνῃ, | ἐν | ἀνδρὶ | ᾧ | ὥρισεν, |
| *en* | *dikaiosunē* | *en* | *andri* | *hō* | *hōrisen* |
| in | righteousness, | by | a man | whom | he appointed; |

| **3963.4** noun acc sing fem | **3792.8** verb nom sing masc part aor act | **3820.5** adj dat pl | **448.10** verb nom sing masc part aor act | **840.6** prs-pron acc sing masc |
|---|---|---|---|---|
| πίστιν | παρασχὼν | πᾶσιν | ἀναστήσας | αὐτὸν |
| *pistin* | *paraschōn* | *pasin* | *anastēsas* | *auton* |
| an assurance | having given | to all | having raised | him |

| **1523.2** prep gen | **3361.2** adj gen pl | **189.32** verb nom pl masc part aor act | **1156.2** conj | **384.4** noun acc sing fem |
|---|---|---|---|---|
| ἐκ | νεκρῶν. | **32.** Ἀκούσαντες | δὲ | ἀνάστασιν |
| *ek* | *nekrōn* | *Akousantes* | *de* | *anastasin* |
| from among | dead. | Having heard | and | a resurrection |

of the art and meditations or thoughts of a human being.

This is one of the strong points of Old Testament teaching. In Deuteronomy 4:15-19 Moses reminded Israel that they saw a genuine manifestation of God's presence at Sinai. But they saw no physical form of any kind. What they saw was glory. (See also Exodus 33:18,22.) Moses gave this as a reason for not making or worshiping idols. The infinite God does not have the kind of form of which you can make an image. Therefore, when men try to make or fashion images, they are getting further away from what God is really like. When they worship these man-made images they are thus worshiping something other than God.

Psalm 115:4-8 points out the foolishness of idols made with human hands. Idols that cannot see, speak, or hear call attention to the stupidity of those who make them (see also Psalm 135:15-18). Isaiah 40:18-22 also uses irony to contrast the gold-plated gods that need silver chains to keep them from falling over with the true God who founded the earth and who sits above the sphere of the earth (see also Isaiah 41:24; 44:9-17).

The words "ought not" also imply guilt. The heathen are wrong to make idols. Their false worship is sin. It is rebellion against the God who made them. Paul said they should have known better.

**17:30.** All of this idolatry showed their ignorance of what God is really like. The times (time periods) of this ignorance God, in His mercy and longsuffering, overlooked. But now He (through the gospel) was announcing to all human beings everywhere that they should repent. They should change their minds and attitudes toward God by turning to Him through Christ and the gospel.

This does not mean those idolaters of past ages were saved. The Old Testament indicates idolatry came into existence after the Flood, probably by the time of the Tower of Babel (Babylon). At least it seems the Tower of Babel became the model for the temple towers or ziggurats of Babylonia. But, though their idolatry was sin and deserved to be judged, God did not bring the judgment day in the time periods between the Flood and Christ.

**17:31.** Paul said the Gentiles must no longer look to their images as gods, for a judgment day is coming. Repentance is therefore imperative. God has indeed appointed a day in which He will judge the earth in righteousness by a Man whom He has revealed and designated as Judge. (Compare Daniel 7:13; John 5:22,27.)

That the day is actually coming and that there will be no escape from it, God guaranteed to all by the fact that He raised that Man (Jesus) out from among the dead. The fact that God raised Jesus from the dead shows He is deity and His teachings are true. He will be the Judge and will judge in righteousness (Isaiah 9:7; 11:4).

**17:32.** As always, there are only two attitudes toward God: faith-obedience and unbelief-rebellion. So here, some rejected Paul's



**that the Godhead is like unto gold, or silver, or stone:** . . . the Divine Nature to be like, *Fenton* . . . that the Deity has any resemblance to anything made of, *TCNT* . . . that His nature resembles, *Weymouth.*

**graven by art and man's device:** . . . a work of human art and imagination, *TCNT* . . . sculptured by the art and inventive faculty of man, *Weymouth* . . . or anything humanly manufactured or invented, *Berkeley.*

**30. And the times of this ignorance God winked at:** God overlooked, *ASV* . . . True, God looked with indulgence on the days of man's ignorance, *TCNT* . . . However, while God paid no attention to those seasons of ignorance, *Berkeley* . . . Now while it is true that God has overlooked the days of ignorance, *Phillips.*

**but now commandeth all men everywhere to repent:** . . . but now he is announcing to every one everywhere the need for repentance, *TCNT.*

**31. Because he hath appointed a day:** . . . fixed a day, *RSV* . . . set a day, *Williams.*

**in the which he will judge the world in righteousness:** . . . on which he intends to judge the world with justice, *TCNT.*

**by that man whom he hath ordained:** . . . by a man whom he hath pointed out, *Rotherham* . . . in the person of a man whom he has destined for this work, *Weymouth* . . . He will use a man to do this, *Everyday.*

**whereof he hath given assurance unto all men:** . . . has given proof of this to all, *Moffatt* . . . He has made this credible to all, *Williams* . . . of which he has given a sign to all men, *Berkeley* . . . He has given everyone a good reason to believe, *Beck* . . . having given the strongest evidence, *Fenton.*

**in that he hath raised him from the dead:** . . . by raising him from among the dead, *Rotherham* . . . by giving him back, *BB.*

**32. And when they heard of the resurrection of the dead:** On hearing of a, *TCNT* . . . When they heard Paul speak of a resurrection of dead men, *Weymouth* . . . The mention of, *Fenton.*

| 3361.2 adj gen pl | 3450.7 art nom pl masc | 3173.1 conj | 5348.2 verb 3pl indic imperf act | 3450.7 art nom pl masc | 1156.2 conj |
|---|---|---|---|---|---|
| νεκρῶν, | οἱ | μὲν | ἐχλεύαζον· | οἱ | δὲ |
| nekrōn | hoi | men | echleuazon | hoi | de |
| of dead, | the | | were mocking, | the | and |

32.a.**Txt:** 02A,05D,020L 025P,etc.byz.Sod **Var:** 01א,03B,08E,Treg Alf,Tisc,We/Ho,Weis UBS/☆

| 1500.3 verb indic aor act | 1500.28 verb 3pl indic aor act | 189.52 verb 1pl indic fut mid | 4622.2 prs-pron gen 2sing | 3687.1 adv |
|---|---|---|---|---|
| ⸂ εἶπον, | [a☆ εἶπαν, ] | Ἀκουσόμεθά | σου | ⸂ πάλιν |
| eipon | eipan | Akousometha | sou | palin |
| said, | [ idem ] | We will hear | you | again |

32.b.**Txt:** 020L,025P,byz. bo. **Var:** 01א,02A,03B,Lach Treg,Alf,Tisc,We/Ho Weis,Sod,UBS/☆

| 3875.1 prep | 3642.1 dem-pron gen sing | 3875.1 prep | 3642.1 dem-pron gen sing | 2504.1 conj | 3687.1 adv |
|---|---|---|---|---|---|
| περὶ | τούτου. | [b☆ περὶ | τούτου | καὶ | πάλιν. ] |
| peri | toutou | peri | toutou | kai | palin |
| concerning | this. | [ concerning | this | also | again. ] |

33.a.**Txt:** 08E,020L 025P,byz.sa.bo. **Var:** 01א,02A,03B,05D Lach,Treg,Alf,Tisc We/Ho,Weis,Sod UBS/☆

| | 2504.1 conj | 3643.1 adv | 3450.5 art nom sing masc | 3834.1 name nom masc | 1814.3 verb 3sing indic aor act | 1523.2 prep gen |
|---|---|---|---|---|---|---|
| 33. | ⸂a Καὶ ⸃ | οὕτως | ὁ | Παῦλος | ἐξῆλθεν | ἐκ |
| | Kai | houtōs | ho | Paulos | exēlthen | ek |
| | And | thus | | Paul | went out | from |

| 3189.4 adj gen sing neu | 840.1 prs-pron gen pl | | 4948.7 indef-pron nom pl masc | 1156.2 conj | 433.6 noun nom pl masc | 2827.7 verb nom pl masc part aor pass |
|---|---|---|---|---|---|---|
| μέσου | αὐτῶν. | 34. | τινὲς | δὲ | ἄνδρες | κολληθέντες |
| mesou | autōn | | tines | de | andres | kollēthentes |
| midst | of them. | | Some | but | men | joining themselves |

| 840.4 prs-pron dat sing | 3961.23 verb 3pl indic aor act | 1706.1 prep | 3614.4 rel-pron dat pl | 2504.1 conj | 1348.1 name nom masc | 3450.5 art nom sing masc |
|---|---|---|---|---|---|---|
| αὐτῷ | ἐπίστευσαν· | ἐν | οἷς | καὶ | Διονύσιος | ὁ |
| autō | episteusan | en | hois | kai | Dionusios | ho |
| to him | believed; | among | whom | also | Dionysius | the |

| 692.1 name nom sing masc | 2504.1 conj | 1129.1 noun nom sing fem | 3549.4 noun dat sing neu | 1147.1 name nom fem | 2504.1 conj |
|---|---|---|---|---|---|
| Ἀρεοπαγίτης, | καὶ | γυνὴ | ὀνόματι | Δάμαρις | καὶ |
| Areopagitēs | kai | gunē | onomati | Damaris | kai |
| Areopagite, | and | a woman | by name | Damaris, | and |

1.a.**Txt:** 08E,020L,025P byz.sa. **Var:** 01א,02A,03B,bo. Lach,Treg,Tisc,We/Ho Weis,Sod,UBS/☆

| 2066.7 adj nom pl masc | 4713.1 prep | 840.2 prs-pron dat pl | | 3196.3 prep | 1156.2 conj | 3642.18 dem-pron pl neu |
|---|---|---|---|---|---|---|
| ἕτεροι | σὺν | αὐτοῖς. | 18:1. | Μετὰ | ⸂a δὲ ⸃ | ταῦτα |
| heteroi | sun | autois | | Meta | de | tauta |
| others | with | them. | | After | and | these things |

1.b.**Txt:** 02A,08E,020L 025P,byz.Sod **Var:** p41,p74,01א,03B 05D,33,sa.bo.Lach,Treg Alf,Tisc,We/Ho,Weis UBS/☆

| 5398.9 verb nom sing masc part aor pass | 3450.5 art nom sing masc | 3834.1 name nom masc | 1523.2 prep gen | 3450.1 art gen pl | 116.1 name gen fem |
|---|---|---|---|---|---|
| χωρισθεὶς | ⸂b ὁ | Παῦλος ⸃ | ἐκ | τῶν | Ἀθηνῶν |
| chōristheis | ho | Paulos | ek | tōn | Athēnōn |
| having departed | | Paul | from | | Athens, |

| 2048.3 verb 3sing indic aor act | 1519.1 prep | 2855.2 name acc fem | | 2504.1 conj | 2128.17 verb nom sing masc part aor act |
|---|---|---|---|---|---|
| ἦλθεν | εἰς | Κόρινθον· | 2. | καὶ | εὑρών |
| ēlthen | eis | Korinthon | | kai | heurōn |
| came | to | Corinth; | | and | having found |

| 4948.5 indef-pron | 2428.8 name-adj acc sing masc | 3549.4 noun dat sing neu | 205.2 name acc masc | 4052.1 name-adj acc sing masc |
|---|---|---|---|---|
| τινα | Ἰουδαῖον | ὀνόματι | Ἀκύλαν, | Ποντικὸν |
| tina | Ioudaion | onomati | Akulan | Pontikon |
| certain | Jew | by name | Aquila, | of Pontus |

message in unbelief. In fact, the mention of the resurrection from the dead brought immediate mockery from some. Others said, "We shall hear you concerning this matter again." This may mean they were at least willing to give Paul's message another hearing.

**17:33.** The statement that they would hear Paul again was also a way of bringing the discussion to a close and thus dismissing Paul. He was now free to leave the council chamber and go his way.

**17:34.** The sessions of the Council of the Areopagus were open to the public. Some responded and became Paul's followers. Among them was Dionysius, a member of the Council, and a prominent woman named Damaris.

Some writers say that what Paul said to the Corinthians, "I determined not to know any thing among you, save Jesus Christ, and him crucified" (1 Corinthians 2:2), means that Paul was disappointed in the results at Athens and was rejecting the approach he had used there. But Paul's words to the Corinthians do not mean he said nothing about other truths. And those who joined with Paul were a sufficient nucleus for a church.

**18:1.** When Paul left Athens the Holy Spirit led him to Corinth, the capital of the Roman province of Achaia. It was a very prosperous city and a Roman colony. It was also a center of idolatry and licentiousness. No city in the Roman Empire was more corrupt. It was filled with Greek adventurers, Roman merchants, lustful Phoenicians, sharp-eyed Jews, ex-soldiers, near-philosophers, sailors, freedmen, slaves, tradesmen, and agents of every kind of vice.

**18:2.** Paul's first task in this great and corrupt city was to find a place to stay and some way to pay expenses. He was alone and without friends or acquaintances in the city. Yet he was not alone. God was with him, and God was already working.

A short time before this the fourth Roman Emperor, Tiberius Claudius Caesar Augustus Germanicus, who ruled A.D. 41–54, had commanded all the Jews to leave Rome. The date was probably sometime in A.D. 49 or 50. Paul probably arrived in Corinth in A.D. 50.

Among the Jews who were expelled were a husband and wife who were to become Paul's most faithful friends and fellow laborers in the gospel. The husband, Aquila, was a Jew from a family of the Roman province of Pontus. Aquila's wife's name, Priscilla, a diminutive or familiar form of Prisca (2 Timothy 4:19), indicates she was a Roman lady of one of the upper classes of society. It is at least possible she was the daughter of Aquila's former master.

**some mocked:** . . . began to mock, *TCNT* . . . began jeering, *Weymouth* . . . some of them laughed, *Everyday* . . . laughed outright, *Phillips* . . . some treated it as a joke, *Williams C.K.*

**and others said, We will hear thee again of this matter:** . . . that they should hear what he had to say about that another time, *TCNT* . . . Let us go more fully into this another time, *BB* . . . We want to listen to you again about this, *NLT.*

**33. So Paul departed from among them:** And so Paul left the Court, *TCNT* . . . went forth out of their midst, *Worrell* . . . the auditorium, *Williams* . . . left the Council, *Williams C.K.* . . . went away from among them, *BB* . . . left them, *Lamsa.*

**34. Howbeit certain men clave unto him:** But certain persons joining themselves unto him, *Rotherham* . . . associated with him, *Berkeley* . . . gave him their support, *BB* . . . and followed him, *Fenton.*

**and believed:** . . . and became believers in Christ, *TCNT* . . . and were converted, *Lamsa.*

**among the which was:** . . . including, *Moffatt.*

**Dionysius the Areopagite:** . . . the Mars-hill judge, *Rotherham* . . . a member of the Court of Areopagus, *TCNT* . . . a member of the Court of Areopagus, *TCNT* . . . the Judge of the High Court, *Fenton* . . . one of the judges of, *Lamsa.*

**and a woman named Damaris, and others with them:** . . . and several others, *TCNT* . . . There were some others, too, *SEB.*

**1. After these things Paul departed from Athens, and came to Corinth:** Before long Paul left Athens and went on to Corinth, *Phillips* . . . On leaving Athens, Paul next went to Corinth, *TCNT* . . . taking his departure from, *Fenton.*

**2. And found a certain Jew named Aquila:** There he met a Jew, *TCNT* . . . came across, *Moffatt.*

**born in Pontus:** . . . from the region of, *Lamsa* . . . a man of Pontus by birth, *BB* . . . a native of, *Williams C.K.*

## Acts 18:3

| **3450.3** art dat sing | **1079.3** noun dat sing neu | **4231.1** adv | **2048.29** verb acc sing masc part perf act | **570.3** prep | **3450.10** art gen sing fem |
|---|---|---|---|---|---|
| τῷ | γένει, | προσφάτως | ἐληλυθότα | ἀπὸ | τῆς |
| *tō* | *genei* | *prosphatōs* | *elēluthota* | *apo* | *tēs* |
| by the | race, | lately | having come | from | |

| **2455.1** name gen fem | **2504.1** conj | **4111.2** name acc fem | **1129.4** noun acc sing fem | **840.3** prs-pron gen sing | **1217.2** prep |
|---|---|---|---|---|---|
| Ἰταλίας, | καὶ | Πρίσκιλλαν | γυναῖκα | αὐτοῦ, | διὰ |
| *Italias* | *kai* | *Priskillan* | *gunaika* | *autou* | *dia* |
| Italy, | and | Priscilla | wife | his, | because |

| **3450.16** art sing neu | **1293.4** verb inf perf act | **2777.3** name acc masc | **5398.6** verb inf pres mid | **3820.8** adj acc pl masc |
|---|---|---|---|---|
| τὸ | διατεταχέναι | Κλαύδιον | χωρίζεσθαι | πάντας |
| *to* | *diatetachenai* | *Klaudion* | *chōrizesthai* | *pantas* |
| the | to have ordered | Claudius | to depart | all |

2.a.**Txt:** 025P,byz.
**Var:** 01ℵ,02A,03B,05D
08E,020L,Lach,Treg
Alf,Word,Tisc,We/Ho
Weis,Sod,UBS/☆

| **3450.8** art acc pl masc | **2428.5** name-adj acc pl masc | **1523.2** prep gen | **570.3** prep | **3450.10** art gen sing fem | **4373.1** name gen fem |
|---|---|---|---|---|---|
| τοὺς | Ἰουδαίους | ⸀ ἐκ | [a☆ ἀπὸ ] | τῆς | Ῥώμης, |
| *tous* | *Ioudaious* | *ek* | *apo* | *tēs* | *Rhōmēs* |
| the | Jews | out of | [ from ] | | Rome, |

| **4193.1** verb 3sing indic aor act | **840.2** prs-pron dat pl | **2504.1** conj | **1217.2** prep | **3450.16** art sing neu | **3536.1** adj acc sing masc |
|---|---|---|---|---|---|
| προσῆλθεν | αὐτοῖς· | 3. καὶ | διὰ | τὸ | ὁμότεχνον |
| *prosēlthen* | *autois* | *kai* | *dia* | *to* | *homotechnon* |
| he came | to them, | and | because of | the | same trade |

| **1498.32** verb inf pres act | **3176.29** verb 3sing indic imperf act | **3706.1** prep | **840.2** prs-pron dat pl | **2504.1** conj | **2021.18** verb 3sing indic imperf mid |
|---|---|---|---|---|---|
| εἶναι | ἔμενεν | παρ' | αὐτοῖς | καὶ | ⸀ εἰργάζετο· |
| *einai* | *emenen* | *par'* | *autois* | *kai* | *eirgazeto* |
| to be, | he was staying | with | them | and | was working; |

3.a.**Txt:** p74,01ℵ-corr
020L,025P,33,etc.byz.
Sod
**Var:** 01ℵ-org,03B,Tisc
We/Ho,Weis,UBS/☆

| **2021.21** verb 3sing indic imperf mid | **1498.37** verb 3pl indic imperf act | **1056.1** conj | **4490.1** noun nom pl masc | **3450.12** art acc sing fem |
|---|---|---|---|---|
| [a☆ ἠργάζετο· ] | ἦσαν | γὰρ | σκηνοποιοὶ | ⸂ τὴν |
| *ērgazeto* | *ēsan* | *gar* | *skēnopoioi* | *tēn* |
| [ idem ] | they were | for | tentmakers | by the |

3.b.**Txt:** byz.
**Var:** 01ℵ,02A,03B,08E
020L,025P,Lach,Treg
Alf,Word,Tisc,We/Ho
Weis,Sod,UBS/☆

| **4926.2** noun acc sing fem | **3450.11** art dat sing fem | **4926.3** noun dat sing fem | **1250.7** verb 3sing indic imperf mid | **1156.2** conj | **1706.1** prep |
|---|---|---|---|---|---|
| τέχνην. | [b☆ τῇ | τέχνῃ. ] | 4. διελέγετο | δὲ | ἐν |
| *technēn* | *tē* | *technē* | *dielegeto* | *de* | *en* |
| trade. | [ by the | trade. ] | He was reasoning | and | in |

| **3450.11** art dat sing fem | **4715.3** noun dat sing fem | **2567.3** prep | **3820.17** adj sing neu | **4378.1** noun sing neu |
|---|---|---|---|---|
| τῇ | συναγωγῇ | κατὰ | πᾶν | σάββατον, |
| *tē* | *sunagōgē* | *kata* | *pan* | *sabbaton* |
| the | synagogue | according to | every | sabbath, |

| **3844.18** verb 3sing indic imperf act | **4885.1** conj | **2428.5** name-adj acc pl masc | **2504.1** conj | **1659.7** name acc pl masc | **5453.1** conj |
|---|---|---|---|---|---|
| ἔπειθέν | τε | Ἰουδαίους | καὶ | Ἕλληνας. | 5. Ὡς |
| *epeithen* | *te* | *Ioudaious* | *kai* | *Hellēnas* | *Hōs* |
| was persuading | both | Jews | and | Greeks. | When |

| **1156.2** conj | **2687.3** verb 3pl indic aor act | **570.3** prep | **3450.10** art gen sing fem | **3081.2** name gen fem | **3614.16** rel-pron sing neu |
|---|---|---|---|---|---|
| δὲ | κατῆλθον | ἀπὸ | τῆς | Μακεδονίας | ὅ |
| *de* | *katēlthon* | *apo* | *tēs* | *Makedonias* | *ho* |
| and | came down | from | | Macedonia | who |

He may have helped her to believe in the one true God, the God of Israel. Then, when he was set free, he married her.

When Paul found them he went to them, that is, to their home. He was undoubtedly being directed by the Holy Spirit, and he never regretted having found them. It is evident that though the Emperor Claudius had expelled them and they had had to leave their home in Rome, they had no bitterness in their hearts. They were godly people who had committed their lives to Him.

**18:3.** Priscilla and Aquila had set up their tentmaking business in their home, and when Paul came to them, these two lonely hearts were quick to welcome him and open their home to him. This gave him a congenial place to carry on his tentmaking business also.

Some writers believe they were also leather workers and makers of felted cloth for tents. Paul's native province of Cilicia was, however, famous for its goats' hair cloth, most of which was used for tentmaking, and tentmaking would be an obvious trade for him as a future rabbi. (Jewish rabbis were expected to learn a trade. Most did not take money for their teaching, and many also believed hard work would help keep them from sin.) There is nothing to indicate whether or not Priscilla and Aquila were Christians before Paul met them. It is possible they knew at least something about the gospel. If they were not believers already, Paul soon won them to the Lord. They became faithful followers of Christ.

**18:4.** As was his custom, Paul went to the synagogue and preached and taught on the Sabbath. This he continued to do every Sabbath for some time, seeking to persuade both Jews and Greeks. Aquila and Priscilla no doubt accompanied him and were further established in the truth of the gospel. Again, it is probable that Paul began the first Sabbath as he had in Pisidian Antioch. Then, as he continued to persuade his listeners from Sabbath to Sabbath, there must have been many who responded to the truth. It is clear that as in most synagogues there were quite a number of God-fearing Greeks who had turned their backs on idolatry and wanted to know more of God.

**18:5.** When Silas and Timothy finally joined Paul at Corinth they found him wholly absorbed, not in tentmaking but in teaching the Word of God. The Greek indicates he felt a greater pressure than the pressure of making a living, a greater pressure than the desire for this world's pleasures and luxuries. He still did a good job in his tentmaking, but the need to teach the Word of God became the impelling, compelling pressure that bore in upon him from all sides. Like Jeremiah, he felt the Word of God as a fire within his

**lately come from Italy, with his wife Priscilla:** He and his wife Priscilla had recently come from Italy, *Weymouth* . . . had but recently migrated from Italy, *Berkeley* . . . had recently moved to, *NCV.*

**(because that Claudius had commanded:** . . . in consequence of the order which had been issued by, *TCNT* . . . when Claudius decreed, *Knox.*

**all Jews to depart from Rome:):** . . . expelling all the Jews from Rome, *Weymouth* . . . to get out of Rome, *SEB* . . . to leave, *Williams C.K.*

**and came unto them:** Paul paid them a visit, *TCNT* . . . called on them, *Berkeley* . . . went to see them, *Williams C.K.*

**3. And because he was of the same craft:** . . . of the same trade, *RSV* . . . they were brothers of the same craft, *Knox* . . . of the same occupation, *Berkeley* . . . of the same profession, *Fenton.*

**he abode with them:** . . . lodged with them, *Weymouth* . . . stayed with them, *Moffatt.*

**and wrought:** . . . and worked, *Alford* . . . and they all worked together, *Moffatt* . . . employing himself, *Fenton.*

**for by their occupation they were tentmakers:** . . . their trade was tent-making, *TCNT* . . . (They were workers in leather by trade.), *Moffatt* . . . they were landscape painters, *Fenton.*

**4. And he reasoned in the synagogue every sabbath:** . . . began reasoning, *Rotherham* . . . Sabbath after Sabbath, he preached, *Weymouth* . . . gave addresses, *TCNT* . . . had discussions, *BB* . . . argued, *Moffatt* . . . he held a disputation, *Knox* . . . debated with the Jews, *SEB.*

**and persuaded:** . . . and tried to persuade, *Montgomery* . . . trying to convince, *TCNT* . . . and tried to win over, *Weymouth* . . . was engaged in earnest discussion, *Fenton.*

**the Jews and the Greeks:** . . . both Jews and Greeks, *Rotherham.*

**5. And when Silas and Timotheus were come from Macedonia:** Now at the time when Silas and Timothy arrived, *Weymouth.*

## Acts 18:6

| 4885.1 conj | 4464.1 name nom masc | 2504.1 conj | 3450.5 art nom sing masc | 4943.1 name nom masc | 4762.10 verb 3sing indic imperf pass |
|---|---|---|---|---|---|
| τε | Σίλας | καὶ | ὁ | Τιμόθεος | συνείχετο |
| te | Silas | kai | ho | Timotheos | suneicheto |
| both | Silas | and | | Timothy | was being pressed |

5.a.**Txt:** 020L,025P,1241 byz.
**Var:** p74,01ℵ,02A,03B 05D,08E,33,it.sa.bo. Gries,Lach,Treg,Alf Word,Tisc,We/Ho,Weis Sod,UBS/⋆

| 3450.3 art dat sing | 4011.3 noun dat sing neu | 3450.3 art dat sing | 3030.3 noun dat sing masc | 3450.5 art nom sing masc | 3834.1 name nom masc |
|---|---|---|---|---|---|
| ' τῷ | πνεύματι | [a⋆ τῷ | λόγῳ ] | ὁ | Παῦλος |
| tō | pneumati | tō | logō | ho | Paulos |
| in the | Spirit | [ by the | word ] | | Paul |

5.b.**Var:** 01ℵ,02A,03B 05D,Lach,Treg,Tisc We/Ho,Weis,Sod UBS/⋆

| 1257.4 verb nom sing masc part pres mid | 3450.4 art dat pl | 2428.4 name-adj dat pl masc | 1498.32 verb inf pres act | 3450.6 art acc sing masc |
|---|---|---|---|---|
| διαμαρτυρόμενος | τοῖς | Ἰουδαίοις | [b⋆+ εἶναι ] | τὸν |
| diamarturomenos | tois | Ioudaiois | einai | ton |
| earnestly testifying | to the | Jews | [ to be ] | the |

| 5382.4 name acc masc | 2400.3 name acc masc | 495.3 verb gen pl masc part pres mid | 1156.2 conj | 840.1 prs-pron gen pl |
|---|---|---|---|---|
| Χριστόν | Ἰησοῦν. | 6. ἀντιτασσομένων | δὲ | αὐτῶν |
| Christon | Iēsoun | antitassomenōn | de | autōn |
| Christ | Jesus. | Setting themselves in opposition | but | they |

| 2504.1 conj | 980.5 verb gen pl masc part pres act | 1607.2 verb nom sing masc part aor mid | 3450.17 art pl neu | 2416.4 noun pl neu |
|---|---|---|---|---|
| καὶ | βλασφημούντων, | ἐκτιναξάμενος | τὰ | ἱμάτια, |
| kai | blasphēmountōn | ektinaxamenos | ta | himatia |
| and | blaspheming, | having shaken | the | garments, |

| 1500.5 verb 3sing indic aor act | 4242.1 prep | 840.8 prs-pron acc pl masc | 3450.16 art sing neu | 129.1 noun sing neu | 5050.2 prs-pron gen 2pl | 1894.3 prep |
|---|---|---|---|---|---|---|
| εἶπεν | πρὸς | αὐτούς, | Τὸ | αἷμα | ὑμῶν | ἐπὶ |
| eipen | pros | autous | To | haima | humōn | epi |
| he said | to | them, | The | blood | your | upon |

| 3450.12 art acc sing fem | 2747.4 noun acc sing fem | 5050.2 prs-pron gen 2pl | 2485.3 adj nom sing masc | 1466.1 prs-pron nom 1sing | 570.3 prep |
|---|---|---|---|---|---|
| τὴν | κεφαλὴν | ὑμῶν· | καθαρὸς | ἐγώ | ἀπὸ |
| tēn | kephalēn | humōn | katharos | egō | apo |
| the | head | your: | clean | I | from |

| 3450.2 art gen sing | 3431.1 adv | 1519.1 prep | 3450.17 art pl neu | 1477.4 noun pl neu | 4057.31 verb 1sing indic fut mid | 2504.1 conj |
|---|---|---|---|---|---|---|
| τοῦ | νῦν | εἰς | τὰ | ἔθνη | πορεύσομαι. | 7. Καὶ |
| tou | nun | eis | ta | ethnē | poreusomai | Kai |
| the | now | to | the | Gentiles | will go. | And |

7.a.**Txt:** 03B,05D-corr3 08E,044,byz.
**Var:** p74,01ℵ,02A 05D-org,33,945,1739

| 3197.5 verb nom sing masc part aor act | 1551.1 adv | 2048.3 verb 3sing indic aor act | 1511.3 verb 3sing indic aor act | 1519.1 prep |
|---|---|---|---|---|
| μεταβὰς | ἐκεῖθεν | ' ἦλθεν | [a⋆ εἰσῆλθεν ] | εἰς |
| metabas | ekeithen | ēlthen | eisēlthen | eis |
| having departed | from there | he came | [ entered ] | to |

7.b.**Var:** p74,03B-org 05D-corr,Treg,Tisc We/Ho,Weis,UBS/⋆

| 3477.4 noun acc sing fem | 4948.1 indef-pron gen sing | 3549.4 noun dat sing neu | 4949.1 name gen masc | 2434.2 name gen masc |
|---|---|---|---|---|
| οἰκίαν | τινὸς | ὀνόματι | [b⋆+ Τιτίου ] | Ἰούστου, |
| oikian | tinos | onomati | Titiou | Ioustou |
| house | a certain | by name | [ Titus ] | Justus, |

| 4431.3 verb gen sing masc part pres mid | 3450.6 art acc sing masc | 2296.4 noun acc sing masc | 3614.2 rel-pron gen sing | 3450.9 art nom sing fem | 3477.2 noun nom sing fem |
|---|---|---|---|---|---|
| σεβομένου | τὸν | θεόν, | οὗ | ἡ | οἰκία |
| sebomenou | ton | theon | hou | hē | oikia |
| worshiping | the | God, | of whom | the | house |

bones, and he could not stop giving it out (Jeremiah 20:9).

Paul wrote First Thessalonians shortly after Silas and Timothy came to him, for they brought good news. In 1 Thessalonians 3:6-10 Paul spoke of this. Timothy reported concerning the faith and love of the Thessalonian believers. The enemies of the gospel had not been able to turn them away from the Lord or from Paul. This wonderful report of their faith and continuance in the gospel cheered him and relieved the pressure of his passionate concern for them, giving him courage to go on.

But he still felt the pressure of the Word and from the Word to spread the gospel in Corinth. Thus, he gave witness with greater and greater intensity and zeal. Everywhere he declared the fact that Jesus is the Messiah, God's anointed Prophet, Priest, and King.

**18:6.** In the Jewish synagogue this increased intensity on Paul's part caused most of the unbelieving Jews to cease their indifference and line up against the gospel. They even blasphemed. They used abusive, vile, and scurrilous language against Paul, calling him all sorts of bad names to gain support and organize the opposition. This seems to mean they persuaded others to speak evil against Paul and against the gospel.

This was too much for Paul. Jesus had told His disciples earlier that when they encountered this kind of opposition they were to leave. As they left they were to shake the dust off their feet as a witness against them (Matthew 10:14,15; Mark 6:11). There are too many people who are hungry for the truth to waste time on those who prove themselves incorrigible rebels.

So Paul shook off his outer garments (robes) against them in a gesture that was like shaking worthless scraps off a work apron. It was a sign he was rejecting their blasphemy. Then he called down their blood on their own heads. That is, he declared they would be responsible for the judgment God would send on them.

The Jews would understand, of course, that he was referring to the responsibility God put on Ezekiel to warn the people (Ezekiel 3:16-21; 33:8,9). Had Paul not been faithful in giving them warning, their blood would have been upon his hands. But he had been faithful. He had done all he could. Now there was nothing for him to do but to turn to others who had not enjoyed so many opportunities to hear the gospel. From this point on Paul would go to the Gentiles.

**18:7.** Again, God was already working. Just as God saw to it that Aquila and Priscilla were in Corinth in time to provide Paul a home and a place to work, so God had a God-fearing Gentile living right next door to the synagogue who was ready to open his house as a new evangelistic center. His name was Titus (or Titius) Justus. His Roman name indicates he was a Roman citizen. Sir William Ramsay

**Paul was pressed in the spirit:** After this, Paul used all his time, *SEB* . . . completely possessed by the message, *Berkeley* . . . was earnestly occupied in discoursing, *Alford* . . . was hard pressed with teaching the word, *Norlie* . . . was preaching fervently, *Weymouth* . . . After this, Paul used all his time telling people the Good news, *Everyday* . . . devoted himself entirely to delivering the Message, *TCNT* . . . was engaged in earnest discussion, *Fenton.*

**and testified to the Jews:** . . . bearing full witness unto the Jews, *Rotherham* . . . earnestly maintaining before the Jews, *TCNT* . . . solemnly affirming to, *Weymouth* . . . strongly urging upon, *Berkeley* . . . showing the Jews as clearly as he could, *Phillips* . . . demonstrating to the Jews, *Fenton.*

**that Jesus was Christ:** . . . that the Christ was Jesus, *RSV* . . . Jesus is the promised Saviour, *Beck* . . . was the Messiah, *Fenton.*

**6. And when they opposed themselves:** But as they began opposing, *Rotherham* . . . However, as they set themselves against him, *TCNT* . . . However, when they turned against him, *Phillips.*

**and blasphemed:** . . . and abused him, *Moffatt.*

**he shook his raiment:** Paul shook his clothes in protest, *TCNT* . . . shook out his robe, *Fenton.*

**and said unto them, Your blood be upon your own heads:** . . . it will be your own fault! *SEB.*

**I am clean:** Pure am I, *Rotherham* . . . My conscience is clear, *TCNT* . . . I am not responsible, *Weymouth* . . . I am innocent, *Berkeley* . . . guiltless, *Fenton.*

**from henceforth I will go:** From this time forward, *TCNT* . . . From now on, *Montgomery.*

**unto the Gentiles:** . . . to the non-Jews, *Beck* . . . to the heathen, *Fenton.*

**7. And he departed thence:** So he left, *TCNT* . . . He accordingly took his departure, *Fenton.*

**and entered into a certain man's house, named Justus, one that worshipped God:** . . . went to the house of a God-fearing man, *Fenton.*

| 1498.34 verb sing indic imperf act | 4778.1 verb nom sing fem part pres act | 3450.11 art dat sing fem | 4715.3 noun dat sing fem | 2894.1 name nom masc |
|---|---|---|---|---|
| ἦν | συνομοροῦσα | τῇ | συναγωγῇ. | 8. Κρίσπος |
| *ēn* | *sunomorousa* | *tē* | *sunagōgē* | *Krispos* |
| was | adjoining | the | synagogue. | Crispus |

| 1156.2 conj | 3450.5 art nom sing masc | 747.1 noun nom sing masc | 3961.20 verb 3sing indic aor act | 3450.3 art dat sing |
|---|---|---|---|---|
| δὲ | ὁ | ἀρχισυνάγωγος | ἐπίστευσεν | τῷ |
| *de* | *ho* | *archisunagōgos* | *episteusen* | *tō* |
| but | the | ruler of the synagogue | believed | the |

| 2935.3 noun dat sing masc | 4713.1 prep | 3513.3 adj dat sing | 3450.3 art dat sing | 3486.3 noun dat sing masc | 840.3 prs-pron gen sing | 2504.1 conj |
|---|---|---|---|---|---|---|
| κυρίῳ | σὺν | ὅλῳ | τῷ | οἴκῳ | αὐτοῦ˙ | καὶ |
| *kuriō* | *sun* | *holō* | *tō* | *oikō* | *autou* | *kai* |
| Lord | with | whole | the | house | his; | and |

| 4044.7 adj nom pl masc | 3450.1 art gen pl | 2854.1 name gen pl masc | 189.14 verb nom pl masc part pres act | 3961.55 verb 3pl indic imperf act | 2504.1 conj |
|---|---|---|---|---|---|
| πολλοὶ | τῶν | Κορινθίων | ἀκούοντες | ἐπίστευον | καὶ |
| *polloi* | *tōn* | *Korinthiōn* | *akouontes* | *episteuon* | *kai* |
| many | of the | Corinthians | hearing | were believing | and |

| 901.28 verb 3pl indic imperf pass | 1500.5 verb 3sing indic aor act | 1156.2 conj | 3450.5 art nom sing masc | 2935.1 noun nom sing masc |
|---|---|---|---|---|
| ἐβαπτίζοντο. | 9. Εἶπεν | δὲ | ὁ | κύριος |
| *ebaptizonto* | *Eipen* | *de* | *ho* | *kurios* |
| were being baptized. | Said | and | the | Lord |

| 1217.1 prep | 3568.2 noun gen sing neu | 1706.1 prep | 3433.3 noun dat sing fem | 1706.1 prep | 3433.3 noun dat sing fem | 1217.1 prep |
|---|---|---|---|---|---|---|
| ˹ δι' | ὁράματος | ἐν | νυκτὶ | [☆ ἐν | νυκτὶ | δι' |
| *di'* | *horamatos* | *en* | *nukti* | *en* | *nukti* | *di'* |
| by | a vision | in | night | [ in | night | by |

| 3568.2 noun gen sing neu | 3450.3 art dat sing | 3834.3 name dat masc | 3231.1 partic | 5236.5 verb 2sing impr pres mid | 233.2 conj |
|---|---|---|---|---|---|
| ὁράματος ] | τῷ | Παύλῳ, | Μὴ | φοβοῦ, | ἀλλὰ |
| *horamatos* | *tō* | *Paulō* | *Mē* | *phobou* | *alla* |
| a vision ] | | to Paul, | Not | fear, | but |

| 2953.8 verb 2sing impr pres act | 2504.1 conj | 3231.1 partic | 4478.3 verb 2sing subj aor act | 1354.1 conj | 1466.1 prs-pron nom 1sing |
|---|---|---|---|---|---|
| λάλει | καὶ | μὴ | σιωπήσῃς˙ | 10. διότι | ἐγώ |
| *lalei* | *kai* | *mē* | *siōpēsēs* | *dioti* | *egō* |
| speak | and | not | be silent; | because | I |

| 1498.2 verb 1sing indic pres act | 3196.3 prep | 4622.2 prs-pron gen 2sing | 2504.1 conj | 3625.2 num card nom masc | 1991.22 verb 3sing indic fut mid |
|---|---|---|---|---|---|
| εἰμι | μετὰ | σοῦ, | καὶ | οὐδεὶς | ἐπιθήσεταί |
| *eimi* | *meta* | *sou* | *kai* | *oudeis* | *epithēsetai* |
| am | with | you, | and | no one | shall set on |

| 4622.3 prs-pron dat 2sing | 3450.2 art gen sing | 2530.3 verb inf aor act | 4622.4 prs-pron acc 2sing | 1354.1 conj | 2967.1 noun nom sing masc |
|---|---|---|---|---|---|
| σοι | τοῦ | κακῶσαί | σε˙ | διότι | λαός |
| *soi* | *tou* | *kakōsai* | *se* | *dioti* | *laos* |
| you | the | to harm | you; | because | people |

| 1498.4 verb 3sing indic pres act | 1466.4 prs-pron dat 1sing | 4044.5 adj nom sing masc | 1706.1 prep | 3450.11 art dat sing fem | 4032.3 noun dat sing fem |
|---|---|---|---|---|---|
| ἐστίν | μοι | πολὺς | ἐν | τῇ | πόλει |
| *estin* | *moi* | *polus* | *en* | *tē* | *polei* |
| there is | to me | much | in | the | city |

and others have suggested his full name was Gaius Titius Justus and that he was the Gaius mentioned in Romans 16:23 and 1 Corinthians 1:14.

**18:8.** Paul, Silas, and Timothy were not the only ones to leave the synagogue. The ruler, that is, the chief elder of the synagogue, Crispus, had come to believe on the Lord. First Corinthians 1:14 shows that Paul baptized him and his household. This loss of their leader must have been quite a shock to the unbelieving Jews and must have set them back in their plans to bring further opposition against Paul. In fact, the conversion of Crispus must have broken up the organized opposition to Paul for a time.

Then many of the Corinthians, that is, the Greeks who were residents of the city, kept listening (to the gospel), and as they heard, they believed and were baptized.

The Jews did not succeed in stopping the spread of the gospel. The move to the house of the Gentile Justus gave an open door to many Gentiles who would never have been willing to set foot in a Jewish synagogue. Thus, there was a constant stream of people hearing the truth, believing, and being baptized.

**18:9.** The Lord soon confirmed to Paul that he had done the right thing. In a night vision He (Jesus himself) told Paul not to be afraid. The form of the Greek used here really means he must stop being afraid. This indicates Paul was beginning to be afraid he would have to leave Corinth as he had so many other cities when persecution began. But Jesus told him he should keep on spreading the Word in Corinth and not be silent (not even begin to be silent).

Paul needed this assurance. He was human like others. The very success of the mission must have reminded him of what had happened in other cities. Perhaps, too, it may have occurred to him that it might be a good idea to leave while things were still going well. More than that, Paul had caught a vision of the need of the world. He was always ready to push on to new fields as the Spirit led. But how tender Jesus was as He dealt with him. He knows how to give new boldness to His witnesses.

**18:10.** Jesus also assured Paul that He was with him and would not allow anyone to lay hands on him (arrest him and bring him to trial) or harm him. The promise that they would not hurt (harm) him is very emphatic. (They did attack him, but they did not hurt him.)

The reason for this promise of protection was the fact the Lord had "much people" in Corinth. Many would yet come to Jesus and become part of the true people of God.

**whose house joined hard to the synagogue:** . . . was next door to, *RSV, SEB* . . . which adjoined, *Kleist* . . . who lived next door to the synagogue, *Knox* . . . to the meeting-house, *Williams C.K.*

**8. And Crispus, the chief ruler of the synagogue:** . . . the President, *TCNT* . . . warden, *Montgomery* . . . a leading man, *Williams C.K.*

**believed on the Lord with all his house:** . . . came to believe in the Lord, and so did all his household, *TCNT* . . . trusted in the Lord, *SEB* . . . became a believer...and so did all his family, *Williams.*

**and many of the Corinthians:** . . . by now many of, *Knox.*

**hearing believed, and were baptized:** . . . as they listened to Paul, became believers in Christ, *TCNT* . . . hearing the word, had faith and were given baptism, *BB* . . . listened and found faith, *Knox* . . . and were immersed, *SEB.*

**9. Then spake the Lord to Paul:** . . . the Lord said to Paul, *Fenton.*

**in the night by a vision:** . . . by night through means of a vision, *Rotherham* . . . in a vision by night, *Weymouth* . . . in a night vision, *Berkeley.*

**Be not afraid:** Have no fear, *TCNT* . . . Dismiss your fears, *Weymouth* . . . Stop being afraid, *Williams.*

**but speak, and hold not thy peace:** . . . but continue to speak, and refuse to be silenced, *TCNT* . . . go on speaking, *Williams C.K.* . . . Continue talking to people and don't be quiet! *NCV* . . . Do not be silent, *Kleist* . . . Do not close your mouth, *NLT.*

**10. For I am with thee:**

**and no man shall set on thee to hurt thee:** . . . and no one shall attack you to injure you, *Weymouth* . . . shall make an attack upon you, *Swann* . . . shall assault you to your hurt, *Beck* . . . shall lift a finger to harm you, *Phillips* . . . no one shall succeed in harming you, *Williams.*

**for I have much people in this city:** There are many in this city who belong to me, *Phillips* . . . many of my people, *Everyday* . . . in this town, *Williams C.K.*

11.a.**Txt:** 08E,020L 025P,byz.
**Var:** 01ℵ,02A,03B,33 Lach,Treg,Alf,Tisc We/Ho,Weis,Sod UBS/☆

| 3642.11 dem-pron dat sing fem | 2495.3 verb 3sing indic aor act | 4885.1 conj | 1156.2 conj | 1747.2 noun acc sing masc |
|---|---|---|---|---|
| ταύτη. | 11. Ἐκάθισεν | ˊ τε | [a☆ δὲ ] | ἐνιαυτὸν |
| *tautē* | *Ekathisen* | *te* | *de* | *eniauton* |
| this. | He remained | and | [ idem ] | a year |

| 2504.1 conj | 3243.4 noun acc pl masc | 1787.1 num card | 1315.6 verb nom sing masc part pres act | 1706.1 prep | 840.2 prs-pron dat pl |
|---|---|---|---|---|---|
| καὶ | μῆνας | ἓξ | διδάσκων | ἐν | αὐτοῖς |
| *kai* | *mēnas* | *hex* | *didaskōn* | *en* | *autois* |
| and | months | six, | teaching | among | them |

| 3450.6 art acc sing masc | 3030.4 noun acc sing masc | 3450.2 art gen sing | 2296.2 noun gen sing masc | 1051.2 name gen masc | 1156.2 conj |
|---|---|---|---|---|---|
| τὸν | λόγον | τοῦ | θεοῦ. | 12. Γαλλίωνος | δὲ |
| *ton* | *logon* | *tou* | *theou* | *Galliōnos* | *de* |
| the | word | | of God. | Gallio | but |

12.a.**Txt:** 08E,020L 025P,byz.
**Var:** 01ℵ,02A,03B,05D 33,Lach,Treg,Alf,Tisc We/Ho,Weis,Sod UBS/☆

| 443.1 verb gen sing part pres act | 444.5 noun gen sing masc | 1498.19 verb gen sing part pres act | 3450.10 art gen sing fem |
|---|---|---|---|
| ˊ ἀνθυπατεύοντος | [a☆ ἀνθυπάτου | ὄντος ] | τῆς |
| *anthupateuontos* | *anthupatou* | *ontos* | *tēs* |
| being proconsul | [ proconsul | being ] | |

| 875.2 name gen fem | 2691.1 verb 3pl indic aor act | 3524.1 adv | 3450.7 art nom pl masc | 2428.2 name-adj nom pl masc |
|---|---|---|---|---|
| Ἀχαΐας | κατεπέστησαν | ὁμοθυμαδὸν | οἱ | Ἰουδαῖοι |
| *Achaias* | *katepestēsan* | *homothumadon* | *hoi* | *Ioudaioi* |
| of Achaia, | rose against | with one accord | the | Jews |

| 3450.3 art dat sing | 3834.3 name dat masc | 2504.1 conj | 70.10 verb 3pl indic aor act | 840.6 prs-pron acc sing masc | 1894.3 prep | 3450.16 art sing neu |
|---|---|---|---|---|---|---|
| τῷ | Παύλῳ, | καὶ | ἤγαγον | αὐτὸν | ἐπὶ | τὸ |
| *tō* | *Paulō* | *kai* | *ēgagon* | *auton* | *epi* | *to* |
| | Paul, | and | led | him | to | the |

| 961.3 noun sing neu | 2978.16 verb nom pl masc part pres act | 3617.1 conj | 3706.2 prep | 3450.6 art acc sing masc |
|---|---|---|---|---|
| βῆμα, | 13. λέγοντες, | "Οτι | παρὰ | τὸν |
| *bēma* | *legontes* | *Hoti* | *para* | *ton* |
| judgment seat, | saying, | That | contrary to | the |

| 3414.4 noun acc sing masc | 3642.4 dem-pron nom sing masc | 373.1 verb 3sing indic pres act | 373.1 verb 3sing indic pres act | 3642.4 dem-pron nom sing masc |
|---|---|---|---|---|
| νόμον | ˊ οὗτος | ἀναπείθει | [☆ ἀναπείθει | οὗτος ] |
| *nomon* | *houtos* | *anapeithei* | *anapeithei* | *houtos* |
| law | this | persuades | [ persuades | this ] |

| 3450.8 art acc pl masc | 442.9 noun acc pl masc | 4431.8 verb inf pres mid | 3450.6 art acc sing masc | 2296.4 noun acc sing masc |
|---|---|---|---|---|
| τοὺς | ἀνθρώπους | σέβεσθαι | τὸν | θεόν. |
| *tous* | *anthrōpous* | *sebesthai* | *ton* | *theon* |
| the | men | to worship | | God. |

| 3165.9 verb gen sing part pres act | 1156.2 conj | 3450.2 art gen sing | 3834.2 name gen masc | 453.3 verb inf pres act |
|---|---|---|---|---|
| 14. Μέλλοντος | δὲ | τοῦ | Παύλου | ἀνοίγειν |
| *Mellontos* | *de* | *tou* | *Paulou* | *anoigein* |
| Being about | but | | Paul | to open |

| 3450.16 art sing neu | 4601.1 noun sing neu | 1500.5 verb 3sing indic aor act | 3450.5 art nom sing masc | 1051.1 name nom masc | 4242.1 prep |
|---|---|---|---|---|---|
| τὸ | στόμα, | εἶπεν | ὁ | Γαλλίων | πρὸς |
| *to* | *stoma* | *eipen* | *ho* | *Galliōn* | *pros* |
| the | mouth, | said | | Gallio | to |

**18:11.** With this encouragement, Paul remained in Corinth 18 months, teaching the Word of God among them. During all this time there was no violence and no one harmed Paul, just as the Lord had promised. Truly the Lord was with him.

**18:12.** Paul's continued success was a source of constant irritation to the unbelieving Jews. In the spring of A.D. 52, a new proconsul named Gallio was appointed by the Roman Senate to govern the province of Achaia (Greece). He was the brother of the famous Stoic philosopher Seneca and a man of great personal charm, known for his great graciousness. He remained in office until the spring of A.D. 53. Later, the Emperor Nero had him put to death.

The unbelieving Jews apparently thought they could take advantage of the new governor's lack of knowledge of the situation. So they rose up against Paul with one accord and brought him before the governor's judgment seat.

Archaeologists have discovered this judgment seat (Greek, *bēma*) at Corinth. It was built of blue and white marble and must have been very impressive.

Now the opposition Paul anticipated had come. But the Lord was still with Paul. It seems Paul was conscious of this and did not offer any resistance as the Jews led him to the *bēma*. He was still trusting God that they would not be able to hurt or harm him.

**18:13.** To Gallio the Jews accused Paul of urging men (human beings) by evil persuasion to worship God in a way "contrary to the law." Since they were before a Roman court or tribunal, this would be taken by Gallio to mean contrary to Roman law. Roman law at that time distinguished between legal and illegal religions. Judaism under that law was considered a legal religion. Thus, the Jews were really accusing Paul of teaching men to worship God in a way contrary to their own views or interpretations of what the Old Testament taught. They knew, of course, that Paul used the Old Testament Scriptures to preach Christ.

Also, by saying that Christianity was illegal, they were declaring that in their view Christianity was not a sect of Judaism, but was a totally different religion. They were also referring to Paul in a derogatory way by calling him "this one" (this fellow).

Actually, Paul still considered himself a Jew, but a believing Jew. He never looked at Christianity as a brand-new religion. It was the continuation and fulfillment of God's plan and promises revealed in the Old Testament. What God is doing through the Church is not something different from what He revealed in the Old Testament; it is all part of His eternal purpose.

**18:14.** Paul did not have to defend himself. He was about to speak when Gallio answered the Jews. He was not the inexperienced man the unbelieving Jews took him to be. He was born in Cordova,

**11. And he continued there a year and six months:** So he settled there for a year and a half, *TCNT* . . . For he had already been in Corinth a year and six months, *Lamsa* . . . And he dwelt there, *Worrell* . . . he remained settled there, *Williams C.K.* . . . for eighteen months, *Phillips.*

**teaching the word of God among them:** . . . teaching among them, *Williams C.K.*

**12. And when Gallio was the deputy of Achaia:** . . . governor of Greece, *TCNT, Williams C.K.* . . . became proconsul, *Weymouth* . . . was leader of the country of, *NLT.*

**the Jews made insurrection with one accord against Paul:** . . . the Jews made a combined attack on Paul, *TCNT* . . . made a concerted attack, *Kleist* . . . without exception, *Moffatt* . . . unanimously, *Williams* . . . worked against Paul, *NLT* . . . with only one thing in mind—to stop Paul, *SEB.*

**and brought him to the judgment seat:** . . . in front of, *NLT* . . . They took him to court, *SEB* . . . dragged him, *Williams C.K.* . . . took him to the judge's seat, *BB* . . . before the court, *Weymouth* . . . the tribunal, *Moffatt* . . . the Governor's Bench, *TCNT.*

**13. Saying, This fellow persuadeth men:** . . . charging him with persuading people, *TCNT* . . . This man, they said, is inducing people, *Weymouth* . . . declaring, This fellow advises the people, *Berkeley* . . . This man is perverting men's minds, *Phillips.*

**to worship God contrary to the law:** . . . to give worship to God, *BB* . . . in a way forbidden by the Lew, *TCNT* . . . in an unlawful manner, *Weymouth* . . . in ways that violate our laws, *Williams* . . . a way that is against our law! *NCV* . . . against the Jewish Law, *NLT* . . . in a manner the law forbids, *Knox.*

**14. And when Paul was now about to open his mouth:** Just as Paul was on the point of speaking, *TCNT* . . . was about to begin his defense, *Weymouth* . . . as Paul was desirous to open his mouth and speak, *Lamsa* . . . just beginning to speak, *Williams* . . . was about to say something, *BB.*

## Acts 18:15

14.a.**Txt:** 020L,025P,byz.
**Var:** 01ℵ,02A,03B,05D
08E,Lach,Treg,Tisc
We/Ho,Weis,Sod
UBS/☆

| **3450.8** art acc pl masc | **2428.5** name-adj acc pl masc | **1479.1** conj | **3173.1** conj | **3631.1** partic | **1498.34** verb sing indic imperf act |
|---|---|---|---|---|---|
| τοὺς | Ἰουδαίους, | Εἰ | μὲν | (a οὖν ) | ἦν |
| *tous* | *Ioudaious* | *Ei* | *men* | *oun* | *ēn* |
| the | Jews, | If | indeed | therefore | it was |

| **91.1** noun sing neu | **4948.10** indef-pron sing neu | **2211.1** conj | **4324.1** noun sing neu | **4050.1** adj sing |
|---|---|---|---|---|
| ἀδίκημά | τι | ἢ | ῥᾳδιούργημα | πονηρόν, |
| *adikēma* | *ti* | *ē* | *rhadiourgēma* | *ponēron* |
| unrighteousness | some | or | criminality | wicked, |

| **5434.1** intrj | **2428.2** name-adj nom pl masc | **2567.3** prep | **3030.4** noun acc sing masc | **300.1** partic |
|---|---|---|---|---|
| ὦ | Ἰουδαῖοι, | κατὰ | λόγον | ἂν |
| *ō* | *Ioudaioi* | *kata* | *logon* | *an* |
| O | Jews, | according to | reason | |

14.b.**Txt:** 05D,08E,020L
025P,byz.Sod
**Var:** 01ℵ-org,02A,03B
33,Lach,Treg,Tisc
We/Ho,Weis,UBS/☆

| **428.4** verb 1sing indic aor mid | **428.9** verb 1sing indic aor mid | **5050.2** prs-pron gen 2pl | | **1479.1** conj | **1156.2** conj |
|---|---|---|---|---|---|
| ʼ ἠνεσχόμην | [b☆ ἀνεσχόμην ] | ὑμῶν, | **15.** | εἰ | δὲ |
| *ēneschomēn* | *aneschomēn* | *humōn* | | *ei* | *de* |
| I should have borne | [ idem ] | with you, | | if | but |

15.a.**Txt:** 05D-org,020L
025P,byz.
**Var:** 01ℵ,02A,03B
05D-corr,08E,sa.bo.
Lach,Treg,Alf,Tisc
We/Ho,Weis,Sod
UBS/☆

| **2196.1** noun sing neu | **2196.3** noun pl neu | **1498.4** verb 3sing indic pres act | **3875.1** prep | **3030.2** noun gen sing masc |
|---|---|---|---|---|
| ʼ ζήτημά | [a☆ ζητήματά ] | ἐστιν | περὶ | λόγου |
| *zētēma* | *zētēmata* | *estin* | *peri* | *logou* |
| a question | [ questions ] | it is | about | a word |

| **2504.1** conj | **3549.5** noun gen pl neu | **2504.1** conj | **3414.2** noun gen sing masc | **3450.2** art gen sing | **2567.2** prep | **5050.4** prs-pron acc 2pl |
|---|---|---|---|---|---|---|
| καὶ | ὀνομάτων | καὶ | νόμου | τοῦ | καθ' | ὑμᾶς, |
| *kai* | *onomatōn* | *kai* | *nomou* | *tou* | *kath'* | *humas* |
| and | names | and | a law | the | among | you, |

15.b.**Txt:** 08E,020L
025P,byz.sa.Sod
**Var:** 01ℵ,02A,03B,05D
bo.Lach,Treg,Alf,Word
Tisc,We/Ho,Weis
UBS/☆

| **3571.33** verb 2pl indic fut mid | **840.7** prs-pron nom pl masc | **2896.1** noun nom sing masc | **1056.1** conj | **1466.1** prs-pron nom 1sing |
|---|---|---|---|---|
| ὄψεσθε | αὐτοί· | κριτὴς | (b γὰρ ) | ἐγὼ |
| *opsesthe* | *autoi* | *kritēs* | *gar* | *egō* |
| you will see | yourselves; | a judge | for | I |

| **3642.2** dem-pron gen pl | **3620.3** partic | **1007.1** verb 1sing indic pres mid | **1498.32** verb inf pres act | | **2504.1** conj | **553.1** verb 3sing indic aor act |
|---|---|---|---|---|---|---|
| τούτων | οὐ | βούλομαι | εἶναι. | **16.** | καὶ | ἀπήλασεν |
| *toutōn* | *ou* | *boulomai* | *einai* | | *kai* | *apēlasen* |
| of these | not | do wish | to be. | | And | he drove |

| **840.8** prs-pron acc pl masc | **570.3** prep | **3450.2** art gen sing | **961.1** noun gen sing neu | | **1934.7** verb nom pl masc part aor mid |
|---|---|---|---|---|---|
| αὐτοὺς | ἀπὸ | τοῦ | βήματος. | **17.** | ἐπιλαβόμενοι |
| *autous* | *apo* | *tou* | *bēmatos* | | *epilabomenoi* |
| them | from | the | judgment seat. | | Having laid hold on |

17.a.**Txt:** 05D,08E,020L
025P,33,byz.it.sa.Sod
**Var:** p74,01ℵ,02A,03B
bo.Lach,Treg,Alf,Word
Tisc,We/Ho,Weis
UBS/☆

| **1156.2** conj | **3820.7** adj nom pl masc | **3450.7** art nom pl masc | **1659.4** name nom pl masc | **4840.2** name acc fem | **3450.6** art acc sing masc |
|---|---|---|---|---|---|
| δὲ | πάντες | (a οἱ | Ἕλληνες ) | Σωσθένην | τὸν |
| *de* | *pantes* | *hoi* | *Hellēnes* | *Sōsthenēn* | *ton* |
| and | all | the | Greeks | Sosthenes | the |

| **747.4** noun acc sing masc | **5021.5** verb 3pl indic imperf act | **1699.1** prep | **3450.2** art gen sing |
|---|---|---|---|
| ἀρχισυνάγωγον | ἔτυπτον | ἔμπροσθεν | τοῦ |
| *archisunagōgon* | *etupton* | *emprosthen* | *tou* |
| ruler of the synagogue, | they were beating | before | the |

Spain, and grew up in the midst of philosophers, poets, and orators in Rome. A man of intelligence and wit, he had sense enough to realize that no crime against the Roman state or against the Roman law was involved, neither was there any evidence of any wicked (evil, malicious) act against morality. Had there been any legal or moral crime indicated, he would have felt it reasonable to listen patiently.

Actually, Paul was a good citizen. He encouraged people to obey the laws of the land and submit to their rulers. He encouraged believers to pray and give thanks "for all that are in authority; that we may lead a quiet and peaceable life in all godliness and honesty" (1 Timothy 2:1,2; see also Titus 3:1).

There was never anything malicious, evil, or immoral about Paul's life or ministry. Part of the proof of his apostleship was that he considered the gospel as a trust to which he must be true. He always endeavored to please God rather than men and never modified the truth to flatter others or gain something for himself.

A further proof of his apostleship was that he was never hard, harsh, high-handed or dictatorial in dealing with people. Rather, he was gentle, like a nurse or a loving father. He poured out his very life in service to the believers, and he lived the kind of devout, upright, blameless life he implored them to live (1 Thessalonians 2:4-12).

**18:15.** It seemed to Gallio that the case against Paul involved nothing but questions (rather, a contemptible parcel of questions) about words and names and their own Jewish law. Therefore, he told them they could see to that for themselves. He refused to be a judge of such matters.

**18:16.** Thus, Gallio dismissed the case and ordered the lictors to drive them from the court or tribunal, which was probably set up in an open public square.

The historian and archaeologist Sir William Ramsay considered this decision of Gallio the "charter of Christian freedom." It set a precedent in Corinth that would keep the Jews from ever trying to use the Roman government or Roman power against the Christians again.

**18:17.** This pleased the crowd, for the Jews were not popular with them. They then took advantage of Gallio's attitude and seized Sosthenes, the new ruler of the synagogue, striking him down before he could leave the tribunal. Some ancient manuscripts leave out "the Greeks" in this verse. On this basis some commentaries suppose it was Jews who beat the president of their congregation, Sosthenes, because of his failure to gain the success of their cause against Paul. But this is not likely. Good manuscripts uphold the reading "the Greeks." The marketplace crowd would be largely Gentile, and they used this opportunity to express their feelings



**Gallio said unto the Jews:**

**If it were a matter of wrong or wicked lewdness, O ye Jews:** Jews, if this were a case of misdemeanor or some serious crime, *TCNT* . . . If it had been some wrongful act or piece of cunning knavery, *Weymouth* . . . some injustice or villainy, *HBIE* . . . of wrongdoing or vicious crime, *RSV* . . . or a serious fraud, *NAB* . . . or reckless evil, *Swann* . . . some malicious contrivance, *Knox*.

**reason would that I should bear with you:** . . . there would be some reason for my listening patiently to you, *TCNT* . . . I might reasonably have listened to you, *Weymouth* . . . It would be only fair that I listen to you, *Beck* . . . to listen to you Jews with patience, *Knox* . . . I would give you...a patient and reasonable hearing, *NAB*.

**15. But if it be a question of:** But if they are questions about, *ASV* . . . but, since it is a dispute about, *TCNT*.

**words and names:** . . . words and persons, *Moffatt* . . . about terminology and titles, *NAB*.

**and of your law:** . . . arguments about your own law, *NCV* . . . and your own law, *RSV* . . . and your kind of Law, *HBIE*.

**look ye to it:** . . . you will have to see to it yourselves, *Williams* . . . So you must solve this problem yourselves, *NCV* . . . you must see to it yourselves, *NAB* . . . take care of it yourselves, *NLT*.

**for I will be no judge of such matters:** I refuse to be a judge, *Weymouth* . . . I decline to adjudicate upon matters like that, *Moffatt* . . . I am not willing, *Montgomery* . . . I am not disposed to be a judge, *Worrell*.

**16. And he drave them from the judgment seat:** And he had them ejected from the court, *Phillips* . . . made them leave the courtroom, *SEB*.

**17. Then all the Greeks took Sosthenes:** . . . laying hold of, *Rotherham* . . . set upon, *TCNT* . . . they all grabbed, *NCV* . . . they all pounced on, *NAB*.

**the chief ruler of the synagogue, and beat him:** . . . began to strike him, *Rotherham* . . . and kept beating him, *Williams*.

# Acts 18:18

| 961.1 noun gen sing neu | 2504.1 conj | 3625.6 num card neu | 3642.2 dem-pron gen pl | 3450.3 art dat sing | 1051.3 name dat masc |
|---|---|---|---|---|---|
| βήματος· | καὶ | οὐδὲν | τούτων | τῷ | Γαλλίωνι |
| bēmatos | kai | ouden | toutōn | tō | Galliōni |
| judgment seat. | And | nothing | of these | | to Gallio |

| 3169.3 verb 3sing indic imperf act | 3450.5 art nom sing masc | 1156.2 conj | 3834.1 name nom masc | 2068.1 adv | 4215.4 verb nom sing masc part aor act |
|---|---|---|---|---|---|
| ἔμελεν. | **18.** Ὁ | δὲ | Παῦλος | ἔτι | προσμείνας |
| emelen | Ho | de | Paulos | eti | prosmeinas |
| it was mattering. | | But | Paul | yet | having remained |

| 2232.1 noun fem | 2401.11 adj acc pl fem | 3450.4 art dat pl | 79.8 noun dat pl masc | 651.3 verb nom sing masc part aor mid |
|---|---|---|---|---|
| ἡμέρας | ἱκανὰς, | τοῖς | ἀδελφοῖς | ἀποταξάμενος, |
| hēmeras | hikanas | tois | adelphois | apotaxamenos |
| days | many, | the | brothers | having taken leave of |

| 1589.3 verb 3sing indic imperf act | 1519.1 prep | 3450.12 art acc sing fem | 4799.2 name acc fem | 2504.1 conj | 4713.1 prep |
|---|---|---|---|---|---|
| ἐξέπλει | εἰς | τὴν | Συρίαν, | καὶ | σὺν |
| exeplei | eis | tēn | Surian | kai | sun |
| was sailing away | to | | Syria, | and | with |

| 840.4 prs-pron dat sing | 4111.1 name nom fem | 2504.1 conj | 205.1 name nom masc | 2721.3 verb nom sing masc part aor mid | 3450.12 art acc sing fem |
|---|---|---|---|---|---|
| αὐτῷ | Πρίσκιλλα | καὶ | Ἀκύλας, | κειράμενος | ⸀ τὴν |
| autō | Priskilla | kai | Akulas | keiramenos | tēn |
| him | Priscilla | and | Aquila, | having shaved | the |

| 2747.4 noun acc sing fem | 1706.1 prep | 2717.1 name dat fem | 1706.1 prep | 2717.1 name dat fem | 3450.12 art acc sing fem |
|---|---|---|---|---|---|
| κεφαλὴν | ἐν | Κεγχρεαῖς· | [☆ ἐν | Κεγχρεαῖς | τὴν |
| kephalēn | en | Kenchreais | en | Kenchreais | tēn |
| head | in | Cenchreae, | [in | Cenchreae | the |

| 2747.4 noun acc sing fem | 2174.44 verb 3sing indic imperf act | 1056.1 conj | 2152.2 noun acc sing fem | 2628.1 verb 3sing indic aor act |
|---|---|---|---|---|
| κεφαλήν, ] | εἶχεν | γὰρ | εὐχήν. | **19.** ⸀ κατήντησεν |
| kephalēn | eichen | gar | euchēn | katēntēsen |
| head, ] | he had | for | a vow: | he came |

19.a.**Txt:** p74,020L,025P 044,byz.bo.
**Var:** 01ℵ,02A,03B,08E 33,sa.Lach,Treg,Alf Tisc,We/Ho,Weis,Sod UBS/☆

| 2628.3 verb 3pl indic aor act | 1156.2 conj | 1519.1 prep | 2163.3 name acc fem | 2519.3 dem-pron acc pl masc |
|---|---|---|---|---|
| [a☆ κατήντησαν ] | δὲ | εἰς | Ἔφεσον, | κἀκείνους |
| katēntēsan | de | eis | Epheson | kakeinous |
| [ they came ] | and | to | Ephesus, | and those |

19.b.**Txt:** 03B,044,0120 byz.
**Var:** p74,01ℵ,02A,05D 08E,33,326,1241,1739

| 2611.3 verb 3sing indic aor act | 841.1 adv | 1550.1 adv | 840.5 prs-pron nom sing masc | 1156.2 conj | 1511.13 verb nom sing masc part aor act |
|---|---|---|---|---|---|
| κατέλιπεν | ⸀ αὐτοῦ· | [b ἐκεῖ ] | αὐτὸς | δὲ | εἰσελθὼν |
| katelipen | autou | ekei | autos | de | eiselthōn |
| left | there. | [ idem ] | He himself | but | having entered |

19.c.**Txt:** 08E,020L,025P byz.Sod
**Var:** 01ℵ,02A,03B,Lach Treg,Tisc,We/Ho,Weis UBS/☆

| 1519.1 prep | 3450.12 art acc sing fem | 4715.4 noun acc sing fem | 1250.5 verb 3sing indic aor pass | 1250.8 verb 3sing indic aor mid |
|---|---|---|---|---|
| εἰς | τὴν | συναγωγὴν | ⸀ διελέχθη | [c☆ διελέξατο ] |
| eis | tēn | sunagōgēn | dielechthē | dielexato |
| into | the | synagogue | debated | [ discussed ] |

| 3450.4 art dat pl | 2428.4 name-adj dat pl masc | 2049.6 verb gen pl masc part pres act | 1156.2 conj | 840.1 prs-pron gen pl | 1894.3 prep |
|---|---|---|---|---|---|
| τοῖς | Ἰουδαίοις. | **20.** ἐρωτώντων | δὲ | αὐτῶν | ἐπὶ |
| tois | Ioudaiois | erōtōntōn | de | autōn | epi |
| with the | Jews. | Asking | and | them | for |

against these troublemakers and show their approval of the verdict of Gallio.

Gallio, as the people expected, paid no attention. He considered the whole matter outside his jurisdiction. The Jews who hoped to turn the governor against Paul found the tables turned. It had looked at first as if the promise Jesus gave Paul that he would not be harmed in Corinth could not be fulfilled. But Paul's enemies, not Paul, were the ones who were harmed.

This must have had a deep effect on Sosthenes. It seems Sosthenes finally yielded to the truth of the gospel. In 1 Corinthians 1:1 Sosthenes joined Paul in greeting the Corinthians. Apparently this is the same Sosthenes. It is unlikely that there would be another prominent Sosthenes who was well-known to the Corinthian church. Truly the grace of God is marvelous! The leader of the opposition became a brother in the Lord. With this victory before Gallio, and the conversion of Sosthenes, there must have been more freedom than ever for the Christians to witness for Christ in Corinth.

**18:18.** After some time, probably after several months, Paul sailed for Syria in the final part of his second missionary journey. He took Priscilla and Aquila with him. As is usually the case, Priscilla is named first. She seems to have been gifted by the Spirit for ministry, but Aquila was always working with her. They must have been a wonderful team. (Note how Paul commended them in Romans 16:3,4.)

At Cenchrea, the port of Corinth (9 miles east on the Saronic Gulf), Paul had his hair cut, for he had taken a vow, probably a modified Nazirite vow, to express total dedication to God and His will. (A few think Aquila took the vow, not Paul.)

**18:19.** When they came to the great city of Ephesus, Paul left Priscilla and Aquila behind to minister there while he went on to Jerusalem. They stayed several years in Ephesus, the capital of the Roman province of Asia. Its population was over 300,000, and it was a very prosperous center of trade and commerce. Thus, there was a great opportunity for witness.

Paul did stay at Ephesus over the following Sabbath, however. This time the Holy Spirit did not check him from preaching in Asia. So he went to the synagogue and found Jews willing to listen to his reasoned presentation of the gospel (and to discuss it with him). There was an openness among the Jews of Ephesus at this time that was more like the reception Paul had received at Beroea.

Their response to Paul was not because he rose to heights of oratory, however. Neither did he use the high-sounding vocabulary and technical language of the Greek philosophers and Jewish theologians. The apostle had a message from God, and he said it simply and directly under the anointing of the Holy Spirit. He trusted the Holy Spirit to drive home the truth to human hearts. Not human wisdom, but the wisdom and power of God were the secret of Paul's success.



**before the judgment seat:** . . . in front of the courthouse, *Phillips* . . . right before the governor, *Norlie* . . . in full view of the bench, *NAB.*

**And Gallio cared for none of those things:** . . . did not trouble himself about any of these things, *TCNT* . . . did not concern himself in the least about this, *Weymouth* . . . did not let this trouble him, *NLT* . . . this did not bother Gallio, *NCV, SEB* . . . paid no attention to it, *NAB* . . . took no notice, *Moffatt, Williams C.K.*

**18. And Paul after this tarried there yet a good while:** Paul remained there some time after this, *TCNT* . . . quite a while longer, *Norlie* . . . stayed a long time more, *Williams C.K.*

**and then took his leave of the brethren:** . . . but eventually he took leave, *NAB* . . . said goodbye to the brothers, *Moffatt.*

**and sailed thence into Syria:** . . . and went by ship to Syria, *BB.*

**and with him Priscilla and Aquila:** . . . accompanied by Priscilla and Aquilla, *Moffatt.*

**having shorn his head in Cenchrea:** . . . but not before his head had been shaved at Cenchreae, *TCNT* . . . He had cut off his hair at Cenchreae, *Weymouth* . . . At the port of, *NAB.*

**for he had a vow:** . . . because he was under a vow, *TCNT* . . . bound by a vow, *Weymouth* . . . for he had taken an oath, *BB* . . . made a promise to God, *Everyday.*

**19. And he came to Ephesus:** When they landed at, *NAB* . . . arrived at, *Williams C.K.*

**and left them there:** . . . and there Paul left his companions behind, *Weymouth.*

**but he himself entered into the synagogue:** . . . while he went personally in the synagogue, *Berkeley.*

**and reasoned with the Jews:** . . . and debated with the Jews, *Phillips* . . . to hold discussions with, *NAB.*

**20. When they desired him:** . . . requested him, *Rotherham* . . . wanted him, *Norlie* . . . asked him, *Williams C.K.*

20.a.**Txt:** 05D,08E,020L 025P,byz.bo.
**Var:** 01ℵ,02A,03B,Lach Treg,Alf,Tisc,We/Ho Weis,Sod,UBS/☆

21.a.**Txt:** 020L,025P,byz. bo.
**Var:** 01ℵ,02A,03B,05D Lach,Treg,Alf,Tisc Weis,Sod,UBS/☆

21.b.**Txt:** 05D,020L 025P,044,byz.
**Var:** p74,01ℵ,02A,03B 08E,33,sa.bo.Lach,Treg Alf,Tisc,We/Ho,Weis Sod,UBS/☆

21.c.**Txt:** 020L,025P,byz.
**Var:** 01ℵ,02A,03B,08E Lach,Treg,Alf,Tisc We/Ho,Weis,Sod UBS/☆

21.d.**Txt:** 08E,020L 025P,044,byz.
**Var:** p74,01ℵ-corr,02A 03B,05D,sa.bo.Lach Treg,Alf,Tisc,We/Ho Weis,Sod,UBS/☆

| **3979.1** adj comp | **5385.4** noun acc sing masc | **3176.25** verb inf aor act | **3706.1** prep | **840.2** prs-pron dat pl | **3620.2** partic |
|---|---|---|---|---|---|
| πλείονα | χρόνον | μεῖναι | ⸂a παρ' | αὐτοῖς ⸃ | οὐκ |
| *pleiona* | *chronon* | *meinai* | *par'* | *autois* | *ouk* |
| a longer | time | to remain | with | them | not |

| **1947.1** verb 3sing indic aor act | | **233.1** conj | **651.2** verb 3sing indic aor mid | **840.2** prs-pron dat pl | **233.2** conj |
|---|---|---|---|---|---|
| ἐπένευσεν· | 21. ⸂ | ἀλλ' | ἀπετάξατο | αὐτοῖς, | [a☆ ἀλλὰ |
| *epeneusen* | | *all'* | *apetaxato* | *autois* | *alla* |
| he did consent, | | but | took leave of | them, | [ but |

| **651.3** verb nom sing masc part aor mid | **2504.1** conj | **1500.15** verb nom sing masc part aor act | **1158.1** verb 3sing indic pres act | **1466.6** prs-pron acc 1sing |
|---|---|---|---|---|
| ἀποταξάμενος | καὶ ] | εἰπών, | ⸂b Δεῖ | με |
| *apotaxamenos* | *kai* | *eipōn* | *Dei* | *me* |
| having taken leave | and ] | having said, | It is necessary | for me |

| **3705.1** adv | **3450.12** art acc sing fem | **1844.4** noun acc sing fem | **3450.12** art acc sing fem | **2048.51** verb acc sing fem part pres mid | **4020.41** verb inf aor act |
|---|---|---|---|---|---|
| πάντως | τὴν | ἑορτὴν | τὴν | ἐρχομένην | ποιῆσαι |
| *pantōs* | *tēn* | *heortēn* | *tēn* | *erchomenēn* | *poiēsai* |
| always | the | feast | the | coming | to keep |

| **1519.1** prep | **2389.1** name | **3687.1** adv | **1156.2** conj | **342.2** verb 1sing indic fut act | **4242.1** prep |
|---|---|---|---|---|---|
| εἰς | Ἱεροσόλυμα· ⸃ | πάλιν | ⸂c δὲ ⸃ | ἀνακάμψω | πρὸς |
| *eis* | *Hierosoluma* | *palin* | *de* | *anakampsō* | *pros* |
| at | Jerusalem, | again | but | I will return | to |

| **5050.4** prs-pron acc 2pl | **3450.2** art gen sing | **2296.2** noun gen sing masc | **2286.13** verb gen sing masc part pres act | **2504.1** conj | **319.6** verb 3sing indic aor pass |
|---|---|---|---|---|---|
| ὑμᾶς, | τοῦ | θεοῦ | θέλοντος. | ⸂d Καὶ ⸃ | ἀνήχθη |
| *humas* | *tou* | *theou* | *thelontos* | *Kai* | *anēchthē* |
| you, | | God | willing. | And | he sailed |

| **570.3** prep | **3450.10** art gen sing fem | **2163.1** name gen fem | | **2504.1** conj | **2687.4** verb nom sing masc part aor act | **1519.1** prep |
|---|---|---|---|---|---|---|
| ἀπὸ | τῆς | Ἐφέσου· | 22. | καὶ | κατελθὼν | εἰς |
| *apo* | *tēs* | *Ephesou* | | *kai* | *katelthōn* | *eis* |
| from | | Ephesus. | | And | having landed | at |

| **2513.3** name acc fem | **303.17** verb nom sing masc part aor act | **2504.1** conj | **776.10** verb nom sing masc part aor mid | **3450.12** art acc sing fem |
|---|---|---|---|---|
| Καισάρειαν, | ἀναβὰς | καὶ | ἀσπασάμενος | τὴν |
| *Kaisareian* | *anabas* | *kai* | *aspasamenos* | *tēn* |
| Caesarea, | having gone up | and | having greeted | the |

| **1564.4** noun acc sing fem | **2568.14** verb 3sing indic aor act | **1519.1** prep | **487.3** name acc fem | | **2504.1** conj |
|---|---|---|---|---|---|
| ἐκκλησίαν | κατέβη | εἰς | Ἀντιόχειαν. | 23. | καὶ |
| *ekklēsian* | *katebē* | *eis* | *Antiocheian* | | *kai* |
| assembly | he went down | to | Antioch. | | And |

| **4020.37** verb nom sing masc part aor act | **5385.4** noun acc sing masc | **4948.5** indef-pron | **1814.3** verb 3sing indic aor act | **1324.12** verb nom sing masc part pres mid |
|---|---|---|---|---|
| ποιήσας | χρόνον | τινὰ | ἐξῆλθεν, | διερχόμενος |
| *poiēsas* | *chronon* | *tina* | *exēlthen* | *dierchomenos* |
| having stayed | time | some | he went forth, | passing through |

| **2489.1** adv | **3450.12** art acc sing fem | **1047.1** name-adj acc sing fem | **5396.4** noun acc sing fem | **2504.1** conj | **5271.2** name acc fem |
|---|---|---|---|---|---|
| καθεξῆς | τὴν | Γαλατικὴν | χώραν | καὶ | Φρυγίαν, |
| *kathexēs* | *tēn* | *Galatikēn* | *chōran* | *kai* | *Phrugian* |
| in order | the | Galatian | country | and | Phrygian, |

**18:20.** The Jews in the Ephesian synagogue were not only impressed by Paul's teaching, they wanted to hear more. So they requested that he stay with them for a longer period of time, but he did not consent.

**18:21.** As Paul took his leave, he explained why he could not stay longer. He felt it was necessary for him to get to Jerusalem in time for the coming feast. He did not explain which feast he was desiring to keep. Usually, when the feast was not specified it was the Passover, for it was the great feast of the Jews.

In his farewell Paul also promised to return to Ephesus again, "God willing." The word "if" is not in the Greek, though we might consider it to be implied. James 4:15 does use the word "if" and warns that believers ought to say, "If the Lord will (that is, if it is His will), we shall live, and do this, or that." This should always be the Christian's attitude, for no one knows what tomorrow will bring.

**18:22.** The sailing vessel Paul took at Ephesus brought him without incident to Caesarea, which was Jerusalem's seaport. Apparently he did not stay there but immediately made the 65-mile journey southeast to Jerusalem. When the phrase *to go up* is used by itself in the New Testament, it often means to go up to Jerusalem for a feast. (Compare John 7:8,10; 12:20.) Though the feast is not mentioned either, it can be inferred that Paul did reach Jerusalem in time for the feast.

Apparently there were no incidents at the feast. Luke only reported that Paul visited the assembly (the Jerusalem church) and "saluted" (greeted, paid his respects to) them. He probably let them know he had been faithful to carry out the instructions of the Jerusalem Council of chapter 15.

From Jerusalem Paul went down to Antioch of Syria. (Note that he went up to Jerusalem and down to Antioch. Antioch was at a lower elevation, but Luke may have been thinking of the exalted position of the city of Jerusalem.)

Thus, Paul completed the circuit and brought his second missionary journey to a close. As before, he felt a responsibility to go back to the church where the Holy Spirit had given assurance that he was to go out into missionary travels to take the gospel to the Gentiles.

**18:23.** Paul spent some time in Antioch, probably until the fall of A.D. 53, continuing his ministry of encouraging and teaching the believers. The church at Antioch continued to be an outstanding evangelistic center. It was important in the history of the Church in the early centuries. (The ruins of about 20 church buildings dated from the Fourth Century A.D. have been discovered by archaeologists.)

**to tarry longer time with them:** . . . to prolong his stay, *TCNT* . . . to remain a longer time with them, *HBIE* . . . to stay on longer, *NAB* . . . a little longer, *Fenton.*

**he consented not:** . . . he declined, *NAB, RSV* . . . he said, No, *BB* . . . he refused, *Phillips.*

**21. But bade them farewell, saying:** . . . but taking his leave of them, *ASV* . . . As Paul was leaving them, *SEB* . . . As he said goodbye he gave them his promise, *NAB* . . . took leave of them, saying, *Williams C.K.*

**I must by all means keep this feast that cometh in Jerusalem:**

**but I will return again unto you:** I will come back to you again, *NAB.*

**if God will:** . . . please God, *TCNT* . . . if it is the will of God, *Moffatt* . . . if God wants me to, *NLT.*

**And he sailed from Ephesus:** He put to sea from, *Kleist* . . . took ship from Ephesus, *BB* . . . He then left Ephesus, *Williams C.K.*

**22. And when he had landed at Caesarea:** On reaching Caesarea, *TCNT.*

**and gone up, and saluted the church:** . . . he went up to Jerusalem and exchanged greetings with the Church, *TCNT* . . . he went up to the town, *Williams C.K.* . . . to pay his respects to the congregation, *Kleist* . . . to say hello to, *NLT* . . . visited, *Fenton* . . . saluting the assembly, *Worrell.*

**he went down to Antioch:** Then he descended to, *Fenton.*

**23. And after he had spent some time there, he departed:** Paul stayed there for some time, *NLT* . . . set out again, *NAB* . . . Paul set out on a tour, *Weymouth* . . . he proceeded on his way, *Fenton.*

**and went over all the country of Galatia and Phyrgia in order:** . . . traveling systematically through the Galatian country, *NAB* . . . and went through, *ASV* . . . and made his way successively through, *Berkeley* . . . and by a definite schedule travelled all over, *Williams* . . . he set out on a tour through, *TCNT* . . . visiting in a regular manner the districts of, *Fenton* . . . he passed through all the country of, *Williams C.K.*

23.a.**Txt:** 05D,08E,020L 025P,byz.Sod
**Var:** 01ℵ,02A,03B,Lach Treg,Alf,Tisc,We/Ho Weis,UBS/⋆

| **1975.1** verb nom sing masc part pres act | **4592.9** verb nom sing masc part pres act | **3820.8** adj acc pl masc | **3450.8** art acc pl masc | **3073.8** noun acc pl masc |
|---|---|---|---|---|
| ʻ ἐπιστηρίζων | [a στηρίζων ] | πάντας | τοὺς | μαθητάς. |
| *epistērizōn* | *stērizōn* | *pantas* | *tous* | *mathētas* |
| establishing | [ idem ] | all | the | disciples. |

| **2428.6** name-adj nom sing masc | **1156.2** conj | **4948.3** indef-pron nom sing | **619.1** name nom masc | **3549.4** noun dat sing neu |
|---|---|---|---|---|
| 24. Ἰουδαῖος | δέ | τις | Ἀπολλῶς | ὀνόματι, |
| *Ioudaios* | *de* | *tis* | *Apollōs* | *onomati* |
| A Jew | but | certain, | Apollos | by name, |

| **219.1** name nom sing masc | **3450.3** art dat sing | **1079.3** noun dat sing neu | **433.1** noun nom sing masc | **3026.1** adj nom sing masc |
|---|---|---|---|---|
| Ἀλεξανδρεὺς | τῷ | γένει, | ἀνὴρ | λόγιος, |
| *Alexandreus* | *tō* | *genei* | *anēr* | *logios* |
| an Alexandrian | by the | birth, | man | an eloquent, |

| **2628.1** verb 3sing indic aor act | **1519.1** prep | **2163.3** name acc fem | **1409.1** adj nom sing masc | **1498.21** verb nom sing masc part pres act |
|---|---|---|---|---|
| κατήντησεν | εἰς | Ἔφεσον, | δυνατὸς | ὢν |
| *katēntēsen* | *eis* | *Epheson* | *dunatos* | *ōn* |
| came | to | Ephesus, | mighty | being |

| **1706.1** prep | **3450.14** art dat pl fem | **1118.7** noun dat pl fem | **3642.4** dem-pron nom sing masc | **1498.34** verb sing indic imperf act |
|---|---|---|---|---|
| ἐν | ταῖς | γραφαῖς. | 25. οὗτος | ἦν |
| *en* | *tais* | *graphais* | *houtos* | *ēn* |
| in | the | Scriptures. | This one | was |

| **2697.7** verb nom sing masc part perf mid | **3450.12** art acc sing fem | **3461.4** noun acc sing fem | **3450.2** art gen sing | **2935.2** noun gen sing masc |
|---|---|---|---|---|
| κατηχημένος | τὴν | ὁδὸν | τοῦ | κυρίου, |
| *katēchēmenos* | *tēn* | *hodon* | *tou* | *kuriou* |
| having been instructed | the | way | of the | Lord, |

| **2504.1** conj | **2186.1** verb nom sing masc part pres act | **3450.3** art dat sing | **4011.3** noun dat sing neu | **2953.45** verb 3sing indic imperf act |
|---|---|---|---|---|
| καὶ | ζέων | τῷ | πνεύματι, | ἐλάλει |
| *kai* | *zeōn* | *tō* | *pneumati* | *elalei* |
| and | being fervent | in the | spirit, | he was speaking |

| **2504.1** conj | **1315.20** verb 3sing indic imperf act | **197.1** adv | **3450.17** art pl neu | **3875.1** prep | **3450.2** art gen sing |
|---|---|---|---|---|---|
| καὶ | ἐδίδασκεν | ἀκριβῶς | τὰ | περὶ | ʻ τοῦ |
| *kai* | *edidasken* | *akribōs* | *ta* | *peri* | *tou* |
| and | was teaching | accurately | the things | concerning | the |

25.a.**Txt:** 025P,byz.lect.
**Var:** p74,01ℵ,02A,03B 05D,08E,020L,it.sa.bo. Lach,Treg,Alf,Word Tisc,We/Ho,Weis,Sod UBS/⋆

| **2935.2** noun gen sing masc | **3450.2** art gen sing | **2400.2** name masc | **1971.5** verb nom sing masc part pres mid | **3303.1** adv |
|---|---|---|---|---|
| κυρίου, | [a⋆ τοῦ | Ἰησοῦ, ] | ἐπιστάμενος | μόνον |
| *kuriou* | *tou* | *Iēsou* | *epistamenos* | *monon* |
| Lord, | | [ Jesus, ] | knowing | only |

| **3450.16** art sing neu | **902.1** noun sing neu | **2464.2** name gen masc | **3642.4** dem-pron nom sing masc | **4885.1** conj |
|---|---|---|---|---|
| τὸ | βάπτισμα | Ἰωάννου. | 26. οὗτός | τε |
| *to* | *baptisma* | *Iōannou* | *houtos* | *te* |
| the | baptism | of John. | This | and |

| **751.5** verb 3sing indic aor mid | **3817.3** verb inf pres mid | **1706.1** prep | **3450.11** art dat sing fem | **4715.3** noun dat sing fem |
|---|---|---|---|---|
| ἤρξατο | παῤῥησιάζεσθαι | ἐν | τῇ | συναγωγῇ· |
| *ērxato* | *parrhēsiazesthai* | *en* | *tē* | *sunagōgē* |
| began | to speak boldly | in | the | synagogue. |

This was Paul's last visit to Antioch. Finally, he felt the pressure of the Holy Spirit directing him to begin his third missionary journey. From Antioch he went north by land on a 1,500 mile journey into the regions of Galatia and Phrygia. One after another he visited the churches established during his first and second journeys.

Paul never founded churches and then forgot them. He always sought to go back to give further teaching and to establish and strengthen the disciples. He was always as much or more concerned with following up the new believers as he was in getting them saved in the first place. This was also the reason for his epistles.

**18:24.** While Paul was ministering in South Galatia and Phrygia, an eloquent Jew named Apollos (short for Apollonius, "pertaining to [the Greek god] Apollo") came from Alexandria to Ephesus.

Alexandria, located on the north coast of Egypt west of the mouth of the Nile River, was the second largest city of the Roman Empire. It was an important seaport and the empire's greatest cultural and educational center. Its library was world famous.

Not only was Apollos eloquent and a great orator, he was very well educated, a real scholar, and powerful in his use of the Old Testament Scriptures.

**18:25.** Apollos had already been instructed orally in the way of the Lord Jesus, probably in his home city of Alexandria. So enthusiastic was he about Jesus that his spirit (his own spirit) was literally boiling over as he spoke.

His teaching was accurate also. He had all the facts straight about the life and ministry of Jesus, as well as about His death and resurrection. But the only baptism he knew was the baptism of John, a baptism which expressed and declared a person's own repentance.

This suggests he must have heard the facts about Jesus from one of the witnesses of Christ's resurrection who, like many of the over 500 (1 Corinthians 15:6), did not come to Jerusalem and were not present at the outpouring of the Holy Spirit on the Day of Pentecost.

**18:26.** Apollos was excited about what he did know about Jesus, however. So he began to speak boldly and freely in the synagogue, pouring out his heart as he endeavored to show from the Scriptures that Jesus is the Messiah, the Christ.

Priscilla and Aquila were present in the synagogue service and heard him. They did not say anything to him in the synagogue to embarrass him. But they could not let him go on spreading a message that did not tell the fullness of what the gospel provides. So they took him aside to give him further instruction. The Greek also implies that they welcomed him and probably took him home with

**strengthening all the disciples:** . . . establishing, *ASV* . . . imparting new strength to, *Williams* . . . in order to strengthen, *Norlie* . . . strengthening the faith of all the disciples as he went, *TCNT* . . . making all the disciples strong in the faith, *BB* . . . encouraging all, *Fenton* . . . confirming, *Alford.*

**24. And a certain Jew named Apollos, born at Alexandrea:** . . . a native of Alexandria, *Weymouth* . . . an Alexandrian by birth, *BB.*

**an eloquent man:** . . . a learned man, *Rotherham* . . . a gifted speaker, *Phillips* . . . and a man of learning, *BB.*

**and mighty in the scriptures:** . . . well versed in, *RSV* . . . and mighty in the Bible, *Beck* . . . he had a great knowledge of the holy Writings, *BB* . . . an authority on Scripture, *NAB.*

**came to Ephesus:** . . . had arrived at, *Williams C.K.* . . . arrived by ship at, *NAB.*

**25. This man was instructed in:** . . . had been orally taught, *Rotherham* . . . had been trained in, *BB* . . . He had had some teaching in, *Williams C.K.*

**the way of the Lord:** . . . the Cause of the Lord, *TCNT.*

**and being fervent in the spirit:** . . . and with burning zeal, *TCNT* . . . and with spiritual fervor, *Williams* . . . and burning in spirit, *BB* . . . and being an enthusiastic soul, *Norlie* . . . his heart was warmed by, *Williams C.K.*

**he spake and taught:** . . . he used to speak and teach, *Weymouth* . . . he preached and taught, *Moffatt.*

**diligently the things of the Lord:** . . . accurately, *RSV* . . . The things he taught about Jesus were correct, *SEB* . . . carefully the facts about Jesus, *TCNT.*

**knowing only the baptism of John:** . . . though he knew of no baptism but John's, *TCNT.*

**26. And he began to speak boldly in the synagogue:** This man began to speak out fearlessly, *TCNT* . . . He began to speak freely, *Berkeley* . . . speak out with confidence, *Fenton* . . . preaching...without fear, *BB* . . . in the meeting-house, *Williams C.K.*

| 189.32 verb nom pl masc part aor act | 1156.2 conj | 840.3 prs-pron gen sing | 205.1 name nom masc | 2504.1 conj | 4111.1 name nom fem |
|---|---|---|---|---|---|
| ἀκούσαντες | δὲ | αὐτοῦ | ⸀ Ἀκύλας | καὶ | Πρίσκιλλα |
| *akousantes* | *de* | *autou* | *Akulas* | *kai* | *Priskilla* |
| Having heard | and | him | Aquila | and | Priscilla |

| 4111.1 name nom fem | 2504.1 conj | 205.1 name nom masc | 4213.4 verb 3pl indic aor mid | 840.6 prs-pron acc sing masc |
|---|---|---|---|---|
| [☆ Πρίσκιλλα | καὶ | Ἀκύλας ] | προσελάβοντο | αὐτὸν, |
| *Priskilla* | *kai* | *Akulas* | *proselabonto* | *auton* |
| [ Priscilla | and | Aquila ] | they took | him, |

| 2504.1 conj | 194.1 adv comp | 840.4 prs-pron dat sing | 1606.1 verb 3pl indic aor mid | 3450.12 art acc sing fem |
|---|---|---|---|---|
| καὶ | ἀκριβέστερον | αὐτῷ | ἐξέθεντο | τὴν |
| *kai* | *akribesteron* | *autō* | *exethento* | *tēn* |
| and | more accurately | to him | expounded | the |

| 3450.2 art gen sing | 2296.2 noun gen sing masc | 3461.4 noun acc sing fem | 3461.4 noun acc sing fem | 3450.2 art gen sing | 2296.2 noun gen sing masc |
|---|---|---|---|---|---|
| ⸀ τοῦ | θεοῦ | ὁδὸν. | [☆ ὁδὸν | τοῦ | θεοῦ. ] |
| *tou* | *theou* | *hodon* | *hodon* | *tou* | *theou* |
| | of God | way. | [ way | | of God. ] |

| 1007.9 verb gen sing masc part pres mid | 1156.2 conj | 840.3 prs-pron gen sing | 1324.8 verb inf aor act | 1519.1 prep |
|---|---|---|---|---|
| 27. βουλομένου | δὲ | αὐτοῦ | διελθεῖν | εἰς |
| *boulomenou* | *de* | *autou* | *dielthein* | *eis* |
| Being intent | and | he | to pass through | into |

| 3450.12 art acc sing fem | 875.4 name acc fem | 4247.1 verb nom pl masc part aor mid | 3450.7 art nom pl masc | 79.6 noun nom pl masc |
|---|---|---|---|---|
| τὴν | Ἀχαιΐαν, | προτρεψάμενοι | οἱ | ἀδελφοὶ |
| *tēn* | *Achaian* | *protrepsamenoi* | *hoi* | *adelphoi* |
| | Achaia, | having exhorted | the | brothers |

| 1119.10 verb 3pl indic aor act | 3450.4 art dat pl | 3073.7 noun dat pl masc | 583.5 verb inf aor mid | 840.6 prs-pron acc sing masc |
|---|---|---|---|---|
| ἔγραψαν | τοῖς | μαθηταῖς | ἀποδέξασθαι | αὐτόν· |
| *egrapsan* | *tois* | *mathētais* | *apodexasthai* | *auton* |
| wrote | to the | disciples | to welcome | him, |

| 3614.5 rel-pron nom sing masc | 3716.7 verb nom sing masc part aor mid | 4671.6 verb 3sing indic aor mid | 4044.16 adj sing neu | 3450.4 art dat pl |
|---|---|---|---|---|
| ὃς | παραγενόμενος | συνεβάλετο | πολὺ | τοῖς |
| *hos* | *paragenomenos* | *sunebaleto* | *polu* | *tois* |
| who | having arrived | helped | much | the |

| 3961.46 verb dat pl masc part perf act | 1217.2 prep | 3450.10 art gen sing fem | 5322.2 noun gen sing fem | 2140.1 adv |
|---|---|---|---|---|
| πεπιστευκόσιν | διὰ | τῆς | χάριτος· | 28. εὐτόνως |
| *pepisteukosin* | *dia* | *tēs* | *charitos* | *eutonōs* |
| having believed | through | the | grace. | Powerfully |

| 1056.1 conj | 3450.4 art dat pl | 2428.4 name-adj dat pl masc | 1240.1 verb 3sing indic imperf mid | 1212.1 adj dat sing fem |
|---|---|---|---|---|
| γὰρ | τοῖς | Ἰουδαίοις | διακατηλέγχετο | δημοσίᾳ, |
| *gar* | *tois* | *Ioudaiois* | *diakatēlencheto* | *dēmosia* |
| for | the | Jews | he was refuting | publicly, |

| 1910.1 verb nom sing masc part pres act | 1217.2 prep | 3450.1 art gen pl | 1118.6 noun gen pl fem | 1498.32 verb inf pres act | 3450.6 art acc sing masc |
|---|---|---|---|---|---|
| ἐπιδεικνὺς | διὰ | τῶν | γραφῶν, | εἶναι | τὸν |
| *epideiknus* | *dia* | *tōn* | *graphōn* | *einai* | *ton* |
| showing | by | the | Scriptures | to be | the |

them to share the fellowship of the Sabbath feast around their table. Then they explained God's way to him more precisely. Just what they said the Bible does not say here, but the next chapter deals with 12 disciples who were in the same position, with the same need for instruction, and details are given there.

It is interesting to note that John Chrysostom ("John of the golden mouth," so nicknamed because of his oratory), the chief pastor of the church in Constantinople about A.D. 400, recognized that Priscilla took the lead in giving this instruction to Apollos. Apollos was a man of culture and education. Priscilla also must have been well educated and a very gracious woman. Paul's epistles also indicate she was, along with her husband, a fellow-worker and missionary.

**18:27.** That Apollos responded to the instruction he received is shown by the letters of recommendation the Christian brethren in Ephesus wrote for him when he wanted to go over to Achaia (Greece).

This statement shows that a church had been established in Ephesus by this time. Paul had preached in the synagogue only one Sabbath. Priscilla and Aquila must have been effective witnesses and must have been the ones God used to establish and train the church. Apollos probably stayed for a while also and by his powerful presentation of the Scriptures convinced quite a number more to take their stand for Christ.

In Greece the Holy Spirit made the ministry of Apollos effective. He became a channel of grace to help the believers. The words "through grace" may apply either to Apollos or to the Corinthian believers. That is, it may mean he was of great assistance through or because of the grace of God that was manifest in his life and preaching. Or it may mean that he was a great help to those who had already believed through grace. The use of the Greek perfect tense here indicates they had already believed before Apollos came. Actually, nothing in the context prevents the application of the phrase "through grace" to both Apollos and the Grecian believers.

**18:28.** One of the chief ways Apollos helped the believers was by vigorously and powerfully refuting the arguments of the unbelieving Jews, showing by the Scriptures that Jesus is the Messiah, the Christ, God's promised Prophet, Priest, and King. This strengthened the faith of the ones who had already believed.

In most of the churches in Greece it is probable that the believers gave God the glory for this help, recognizing it was indeed God who was giving the increase. But in Corinth some of the believers became enamored with Apollos and began to consider themselves his followers. Others reacted by expressing their loyalty to Paul. Still others declared themselves followers of Cephas (Peter). A fourth group may have decided to follow no man and thought themselves more spiritual, naming themselves the Christ party.

**whom when Aquila and Priscilla had heard:**

**they took him unto them:** . . . took him home, *TCNT* . . . took him aside, *Phillips* . . . made friends with him, *Knox.*

**and expounded unto him the way of God more perfectly:** . . . and explained more accurately to him what the Way of God really meant, *Moffatt* . . . and gave him fuller teaching about, *BB* . . . more correctly, *Swann* . . . more particularly, *Knox.*

**27. And when he was disposed to pass into Achaia:** When he wanted to cross to Greece, *TCNT* . . . Then, as he had made up his mind to, *Weymouth* . . . of Southern Greece, *Everyday.*

**the brethren wrote, exhorting the disciples to receive him:** . . . urgently wrote unto the disciples to welcome him, *Rotherham* . . . to the disciples in Corinth, begging them to give him a kindly welcome, *Weymouth* . . . the Brethren furthered his plans, and wrote to the disciples there to welcome him, *TCNT.*

**who, when he was come, helped them much which had believed through grace:** On his arrival he proved of great assistance to those who had, through the loving-kindness of God, become believers in Christ, *TCNT* . . . On his arrival he proved a source of great strength to those who had believed through grace, *Phillips* . . . was a welcome reinforcement to the believers, *Knox.*

**28. For he mightily convinced the Jews, and that publickly:** . . . vigorously confuted, *TCNT* . . . successfully refuted the Jews in public, *Williams* . . . He was a powerful debater and openly refuted, *Norlie* . . . clearly proved, *Everyday* . . . He argued very convincingly in public, *SEB* . . . powerfully and in public overcame the Jews in argument, *Weymouth* . . . for with great force he came out ahead in his public discussions with the Jews, *Berkeley* . . . Publicly and vigorously he proved the Jews were wrong, *Beck.*

**shewing by the scriptures:** . . . proving by, *TCNT* . . . quoting from the scriptures to prove, *Phillips* . . . as he showed from the Bible, *Beck.*

## Acts 19:1

| 5382.4 name acc masc | 2400.3 name acc masc | 1090.33 verb 3sing indic aor mid | 1156.2 conj | 1706.1 prep | 3450.3 art dat sing |
|---|---|---|---|---|---|
| Χριστὸν | Ἰησοῦν. | 19:1. Ἐγένετο | δὲ | ἐν | τῷ |
| *Christon* | *Iēsoun* | *Egeneto* | *de* | *en* | *tō* |
| Christ | Jesus. | It came to pass | and, | in | the |

| 3450.6 art acc sing masc | 619.2 name acc masc | 1498.32 verb inf pres act | 1706.1 prep | 2855.1 name dat fem | 3834.4 name acc masc |
|---|---|---|---|---|---|
| τὸν | Ἀπολλῶ | εἶναι | ἐν | Κορίνθῳ, | Παῦλον |
| *ton* | *Apollō* | *einai* | *en* | *Korinthō* | *Paulon* |
| | Apollos | to be | in | Corinth, | Paul, |

1.a.**Txt:** 03B,byz.
**Var:** p74,01ℵ,02A,08E
044,33,1739

1.b.**Txt:** 05D,08E,020L
025P,sa.
**Var:** 01ℵ,02A,03B,bo.
Lach,Treg,Alf,Tisc
We/Ho,Weis,Sod
UBS/★

| 1324.6 verb acc sing masc part aor act | 3450.17 art pl neu | 506.1 adj pl neu | 3183.4 noun pl neu | 2048.23 verb inf aor act |
|---|---|---|---|---|
| διελθόντα | τὰ | ἀνωτερικὰ | μέρη, | ˊ ἐλθεῖν |
| *dielthonta* | *ta* | *anōterika* | *merē* | *elthein* |
| having passed through | the | upper | parts, | to come |

| 2687.7 verb inf aor act | 1519.1 prep | 2163.3 name acc fem | 2504.1 conj | 2128.17 verb nom sing masc part aor act |
|---|---|---|---|---|
| [a κατελθεῖν ] | εἰς | Ἔφεσον· | καὶ | ˊ εὑρών |
| *katelthein* | *eis* | *Epheson* | *kai* | *heurōn* |
| [ to come down ] | to | Ephesus, | and | having found |

2.a.**Var:** 01ℵ,02A,03B
Lach,Treg,Alf,Tisc
We/Ho,Weis,Sod
UBS/★

| 2128.21 verb inf aor act | 4948.9 indef-pron acc pl masc | 3073.8 noun acc pl masc | 1500.5 verb 3sing indic aor act | 4885.1 conj |
|---|---|---|---|---|
| [b★ εὑρεῖν ] | τινας | μαθητάς, | 2. εἶπέν | [a★+ τε ] |
| *heurein* | *tinas* | *mathētas* | *eipen* | *te* |
| [ to find ] | certain | disciples | he said | [ and ] |

| 4242.1 prep | 840.8 prs-pron acc pl masc | 1479.1 conj | 4011.1 noun sing neu | 39.1 adj sing | 2956.16 verb 2pl indic aor act |
|---|---|---|---|---|---|
| πρὸς | αὐτούς, | Εἰ | πνεῦμα | ἅγιον | ἐλάβετε |
| *pros* | *autous* | *Ei* | *pneuma* | *hagion* | *elabete* |
| to | them, | If | Spirit | Holy | did you receive, |

2.b.**Txt:** 020L,025P,byz.
sa.bo.
**Var:** 01ℵ,02A,03B,05D
08E,Lach,Treg,Alf
Word,Tisc,We/Ho,Weis
Sod,UBS/★

| 3961.31 verb nom pl masc part aor act | 3450.7 art nom pl masc | 1156.2 conj | 1500.3 verb indic aor act | 4242.1 prep | 840.6 prs-pron acc sing masc |
|---|---|---|---|---|---|
| πιστεύσαντες; | Οἱ | δὲ | ˊb εἶπον ˋ | πρὸς | αὐτόν, |
| *pisteusantes* | *Hoi* | *de* | *eipon* | *pros* | *auton* |
| having believed? | The | and | said | to | him, |

| 233.1 conj | 3624.1 conj | 3624.2 adv | 1479.1 conj | 4011.1 noun sing neu | 39.1 adj sing |
|---|---|---|---|---|---|
| Ἀλλ' | ˊ οὐδὲ | [★ οὐδ' ] | εἰ | πνεῦμα | ἅγιον |
| *All'* | *oude* | *oud'* | *ei* | *pneuma* | *hagion* |
| But | not | [ idem ] | if | Spirit | Holy |

3.a.**Txt:** 020L,025P,byz.
sa.bo.
**Var:** 01ℵ,02A,03B,05D
08E,Lach,Treg,Alf
Word,Tisc,We/Ho,Weis
Sod,UBS/★

| 1498.4 verb 3sing indic pres act | 189.22 verb 1pl indic aor act | 1500.5 verb 3sing indic aor act | 4885.1 conj | 4242.1 prep |
|---|---|---|---|---|
| ἔστιν, | ἠκούσαμεν. | 3. Εἶπεν, | τε | ˊa πρὸς |
| *estin* | *ēkousamen* | *Eipen* | *te* | *pros* |
| is, | did we hear. | He said | and | to |

| 840.8 prs-pron acc pl masc | 1519.1 prep | 4949.9 intr-pron sing neu | 3631.1 partic | 901.16 verb 2pl indic aor pass | 3450.7 art nom pl masc |
|---|---|---|---|---|---|
| αὐτούς, ˋ | Εἰς | τί | οὖν | ἐβαπτίσθητε; | Οἱ |
| *autous* | *Eis* | *ti* | *oun* | *ebaptisthēte* | *Hoi* |
| them, | Into | what | then | were you baptized? | The |

3.b.**Txt:** 020L,025P,byz.
Sod
**Var:** 01ℵ,02A,03B,08E
Lach,Treg,Alf,Tisc
We/Ho,Weis,UBS/★

| 1156.2 conj | 1500.3 verb indic aor act | 1500.28 verb 3pl indic aor act | 1519.1 prep | 3450.16 art sing neu | 2464.2 name gen masc |
|---|---|---|---|---|---|
| δὲ | ˊ εἶπον, | [b★ εἶπαν, ] | Εἰς | τὸ | Ἰωάννου |
| *de* | *eipon* | *eipan* | *Eis* | *to* | *Iōannou* |
| and | said, | [ idem ] | Into | the | of John |

**19:1.** After Paul visited the churches of South Galatia founded on his first missionary journey, he passed through the upper or higher-lying regions on his way to Ephesus instead of taking the main road through the fever-ridden valleys.

At Ephesus he found a group of 12 disciples. There can be no doubt that these disciples were truly godly and pious people, but there is much discussion whether they should be regarded as believers in the New Testament meaning (Christians), or if they still lived in an Old Testament relationship with God. Some writers believe they were disciples of John the Baptist, but one objection to this is that everywhere else in Acts, "disciples" means followers of Jesus. Others think these 12 men were won to Christ by Apollos, before Priscilla and Aquila instructed him (18:25), but then one may wonder why they were not more informed about the Holy Spirit at a later time.

**19:2.** The narrative implies Paul discerned something was missing in their spiritual life. His question, "Have ye received the Holy Ghost since ye believed?" indicates they were missing the New Testament gift of the Holy Spirit. Because the final phrase translates an aorist participle, *pisteusantes*, one possible interpretation is "having believed" or "after you believed did you receive the Holy Spirit?" The tense of the participle normally shows its relation to the main verb. Frequently, the aorist participle indicates action that occurs prior to the action of the main verb. In this case, the implication is that belief (i.e., conversion) came prior to receiving the Holy Spirit. However, there are examples of an aorist participle whose action occurs at the same time as the main verb. The sentence would then read, "Did you receive the Holy Spirit *when* you believed?" The answer to Paul's question was quite surprising: "We have not so much as heard whether there be any Holy Ghost." If these men were followers of John, it is difficult to understand why they would not have heard about the Holy Spirit (cf. Matthew 3:11; Mark 1:8; Luke 3:16; John 1:33; Acts 1:5). It might be they probably knew about this element of John's message, but word had not yet reached them that the Holy Spirit had come as Jesus promised He would (Luke 24:49; Acts 1:8; see also John 7:39).

**19:3.** Paul's second question is interesting. It shows he assumed these disciples had been baptized. But as they told that they had no knowledge about the Holy Spirit, Paul naturally must have wondered what kind of baptism they had received. Since Christian baptism is in the name of the Father and the Son and the Holy Ghost (Matthew 28:19), they would have known of the Holy Spirit if this was the way they were baptized. So Paul asked, "Unto what then were ye baptized?" It hardly came as a surprise to him when they said they were baptized with the baptism of John.

**that Jesus was Christ:** . . . that Jesus is the promised Saviour, *Beck* . . . is the Messiah, *SEB*.

**1. And it came to pass, that, while Apollos was at Corinth:** During the stay of apollos in Corinth, *Weymouth* . . . And it came about that while, *BB*.

**Paul having passed through the upper coasts came to Ephesus:** Paul travelled over the hills to get to Ephesus, *Beck* . . . was visiting some places on the way, *NCV* . . . passed through the interior of, *NAB* . . . finished his journey through the inland country, *Knox* . . . along the northern route to, *SEB* . . . passed through the highland district, *Fenton*.

**and finding certain disciples:** There he found some disciples, *TCNT* . . . found a few followers, *NLT* . . . where he found a few disciples, *Weymouth*.

**2. He said unto them:** He asked them, *Weymouth* . . . to whom he put the question, *NAB*.

**Have ye received the Holy Ghost:** Did you get the Holy Spirit, *BB*.

**since ye believed?:** . . . when you first believed, *Weymouth* . . . on your becoming believers, *Berkeley* . . . when you learned to believe? *Knox* . . . when you put your trust in Christ? *NLT* . . . when you had faith? *BB*.

**And they said unto him, We have not so much as heard whether there be any Holy Ghost:** These followers answered him, *SEB* . . . On the contrary, *Fenton* . . . Nay! not even whether there is Holy Spirit did we hear, *Rotherham* . . . No, they said, we never even heard of its existence, *Moffatt* . . . nobody even mentioned to us the existence of, *Knox* . . . we have had no knowledge of, *BB*.

**3. And he said unto them, Unto what then were ye baptized?:** What then was your baptism? Paul asked, *TCNT* . . . What kind of baptism, *Kleist* . . . How were you baptized? *NLT* . . . Into what, then, were ye immersed? *Worrell* . . . What kind of immersion, *SEB* . . . What sort of baptism, *BB* . . . did you have? *Everyday*.

**And they said, Unto John's baptism:** The way John baptized, *NLT* . . . that John taught, *NCV*.

## Acts 19:4

4.a.**Txt:** 08E,020L,025P byz.bo.
**Var:** 01ℵ,02A,03B,05D sa.Gries,Lach,Treg,Alf Tisc,We/Ho,Weis,Sod UBS/⋆

| **902.1** noun sing neu | **1500.5** verb 3sing indic aor act | **1156.2** conj | **3834.1** name nom masc | **2464.1** name nom masc | **3173.1** conj |
|---|---|---|---|---|---|
| βάπτισμα. | 4. Εἶπεν | δὲ | Παῦλος, | Ἰωάννης | ⸂a μὲν ⸃ |
| *baptisma* | *Eipen* | *de* | *Paulos* | *Iōannēs* | *men* |
| baptism. | Said | and | Paul, | John | indeed |

| **901.8** verb 3sing indic aor act | **902.1** noun sing neu | **3211.1** noun gen sing fem | **3450.3** art dat sing | **2967.3** noun dat sing masc |
|---|---|---|---|---|
| ἐβάπτισεν | βάπτισμα | μετανοίας, | τῷ | λαῷ |
| *ebaptisen* | *baptisma* | *metanoias* | *tō* | *laō* |
| baptized | a baptism | of repentance, | to the | people |

| **2978.15** verb nom sing masc part pres act | **1519.1** prep | **3450.6** art acc sing masc | **2048.42** verb sing part pres mid | **3196.2** prep | **840.6** prs-pron acc sing masc |
|---|---|---|---|---|---|
| λέγων, | εἰς | τὸν | ἐρχόμενον | μετ' | αὐτὸν |
| *legōn* | *eis* | *ton* | *erchomenon* | *met'* | *auton* |
| saying, | On | the | coming | after | him |

| **2419.1** conj | **3961.27** verb 3pl subj aor act | **4969.1** verb | **3642.16** dem-pron sing neu | **1498.4** verb 3sing indic pres act |
|---|---|---|---|---|
| ἵνα | πιστεύσωσιν, | ⸀ τουτέστιν | [⋆ τοῦτ' | ἔστιν ] |
| *hina* | *pisteusōsin* | *toutestin* | *tout'* | *estin* |
| that | they should believe, | that is, | [ that | is ] |

4.b.**Txt:** 020L,025P,byz.
**Var:** 01ℵ,02A,03B,08E bo.Gries,Lach,Treg,Alf Tisc,We/Ho,Weis,Sod UBS/⋆

| **1519.1** prep | **3450.6** art acc sing masc | **5382.4** name acc masc | **2400.3** name acc masc | **189.32** verb nom pl masc part aor act |
|---|---|---|---|---|
| εἰς | τὸν | ⸂b Χριστὸν ⸃ | Ἰησοῦν. | 5. Ἀκούσαντες |
| *eis* | *ton* | *Christon* | *Iēsoun* | *Akousantes* |
| on | the | Christ | Jesus. | Having heard |

| **1156.2** conj | **901.17** verb 3pl indic aor pass | **1519.1** prep | **3450.16** art sing neu | **3549.2** noun sing neu | **3450.2** art gen sing |
|---|---|---|---|---|---|
| δὲ | ἐβαπτίσθησαν | εἰς | τὸ | ὄνομα | τοῦ |
| *de* | *ebaptisthēsan* | *eis* | *to* | *onoma* | *tou* |
| and | they were baptized | into | the | name | of the |

| **2935.2** noun gen sing masc | **2400.2** name masc | **2504.1** conj | **1991.13** verb gen sing masc part aor act | **840.2** prs-pron dat pl | **3450.2** art gen sing |
|---|---|---|---|---|---|
| κυρίου | Ἰησοῦ. | 6. καὶ | ἐπιθέντος | αὐτοῖς | τοῦ |
| *kuriou* | *Iēsou* | *kai* | *epithentos* | *autois* | *tou* |
| Lord | Jesus. | And | having laid | on them | |

6.a.**Txt:** 08E,020L,byz. Sod
**Var:** 01ℵ,02A,03B,025P Lach,Treg,Alf,Tisc We/Ho,Weis,UBS/⋆

| **3834.2** name gen masc | **3450.15** art acc pl fem | **5331.8** noun acc pl fem | **2048.3** verb 3sing indic aor act | **3450.16** art sing neu | **4011.1** noun sing neu |
|---|---|---|---|---|---|
| Παύλου | ⸂a τὰς ⸃ | χεῖρας | ἦλθεν | τὸ | πνεῦμα |
| *Paulou* | *tas* | *cheiras* | *ēlthen* | *to* | *pneuma* |
| Paul | the | hands | came | the | Spirit |

| **3450.16** art sing neu | **39.1** adj sing | **1894.2** prep | **840.8** prs-pron acc pl masc | **2953.44** verb indic imperf act | **4885.1** conj |
|---|---|---|---|---|---|
| τὸ | ἅγιον | ἐπ' | αὐτούς, | ἐλάλουν | τε |
| *to* | *hagion* | *ep'* | *autous* | *elaloun* | *te* |
| the | Holy | upon | them, | they were speaking | and |

6.b.**Txt:** 08E,020L,025P byz.
**Var:** 01ℵ,02A,03B,05D Lach,Treg,Alf,Tisc We/Ho,Weis,Sod UBS/⋆

| **1094.7** noun dat pl fem | **2504.1** conj | **4253.15** verb 3pl indic imperf act | **4253.19** verb indic imperf act |
|---|---|---|---|
| γλώσσαις | καὶ | ⸀ προεφήτευον. | [b⋆ ἐπροφήτευον. ] |
| *glōssais* | *kai* | *proephēteuon* | *eprophēteuon* |
| with tongues | and | were prophesying. | [ idem ] |

| **1498.37** verb 3pl indic imperf act | **1156.2** conj | **3450.7** art nom pl masc | **3820.7** adj nom pl masc | **433.6** noun nom pl masc | **5448.1** adv |
|---|---|---|---|---|---|
| 7. ἦσαν | δὲ | οἱ | πάντες | ἄνδρες | ὡσεὶ |
| *ēsan* | *de* | *hoi* | *pantes* | *andres* | *hōsei* |
| Were | and | the | all | men | about |

**19:4.** Paul explained that John's baptism was only preparatory, a baptism of repentance, that is, a baptism that testified to their repentance (cf. Luke 7:30). John refused to baptize those who did not repent (Matthew 3:7,8). John himself told the people they should believe in the Coming One, Jesus. Apparently, this is what these 12 men did; Paul said they "believed" (verse 2). Paul seems to have no doubt they were genuine disciples. Still he did not accept their baptism as the Christian baptism which Jesus ordained after His death and resurrection.

**19:5.** Then, having heard, "they were baptized in the name of the Lord Jesus." They not only listened, they understood and obeyed. This is the only occasion in the New Testament where it is recorded that people received two baptisms. Paul must have further explained the meaning of Christian baptism, including identification with Jesus in His death and resurrection. (See Romans 6:3,4.)

The phrase "in the name of the Lord Jesus" means they were baptized into the worship and service of Jesus, making Him Lord of their lives. This short designation is used several times for Christian baptism. Because Jesus is the revealer of the Father (John 17:6) and the one who baptizes in the Holy Spirit (Matthew 3:11), the baptism "in Jesus name" should not be understood or interpreted as being opposed to baptism in the name of the Trinity. This expression in no way cancels the baptismal formula given by the Lord himself in Matthew 28:19. To do so would be like asserting that Romans 10:13 is in opposition to Acts 16:31 since the first says those who *call upon* the name of the Lord will be saved, and the latter states salvation is based on *belief* in Christ.

**19:6.** After Paul laid his hands on them, the Holy Spirit came upon them. What happened relates to earlier narratives in Acts which tell of an outpouring of the Spirit, variously referred to as a "baptism in the Spirit" (1:5), a "filling with" the Spirit (2:4), the Spirit "falling upon" believers (8:16; 10:44).

As in Samaria (8:17,18) the Spirit was given through laying on of the apostle's hands. In the house of Cornelius the coming of the Spirit was spontaneous (chapter 10). This shows that laying on of hands was not in itself the cause of the giving of the Spirit. However, one cannot diminish the importance of laying on hands as a means or medium of imparting spiritual power, authority, or gifts (see Numbers 27:15-18; Mark 6:5; 16:18; Acts 8:18; 13:3; 28:8; 1 Timothy 4:14; 2 Timothy 1:6).

**19:7.** The number of these disciples was not large. It came to the sum total of about 12 men. There could have been 11 or 13. The exact number is not important, but their experience of the baptism in the Holy Spirit with the evidence of speaking in tongues

**4. Then said Paul, John verily baptized with the baptism of repentance:** John...administered a baptism of repentance, *Weymouth* . . . John's baptism was a baptism upon repentance, *TCNT* . . . a baptism that was an expression of repentance, *Williams* . . . was a baptism of changed hearts and lives, *Everyday* . . . John baptized those who were sorry for their sins, *Beck* . . . for conversion, *Fenton* . . . which goes with a change of heart, *BB.*

**saying unto the people:** . . . telling the people, *Moffatt* . . . bidding the people, *Weymouth* . . . but he always told the people, *Phillips.*

**that they should believe:** . . . they were to have faith, *BB* . . . they must believe, *Phillips* . . . to put their trust, *NEB.*

**on him which should come after him, that is, on Christ Jesus:** Who followed him, *Fenton* . . . on One who was to come after him; namely, on Jesus, *Weymouth.*

**5. When they heard this:** On hearing this, *RSV.*

**they were baptized:** . . . immersed, *Rotherham.*

**in the name of the Lord Jesus:** . . . by the authority of, *SEB* . . . into the Faith of the Lord Jesus, *TCNT.*

**6. And when Paul had laid his hands upon them:** . . . and, after Paul had placed his hands on them, *TCNT.*

**the Holy Ghost came on them:** . . . the Holy Ghost came on them, *TCNT* . . . came down, *NAB.*

**and they spake with tongues, and prophesied:** . . . began speaking with tongues and prophesying, *Rotherham* . . . began to speak with tongues, *TCNT* . . . in different languages, *Everyday* . . . they had the power of talking...and acting like prophets, *BB* . . . and they started to talk in other languages and to speak God's Word, *Beck* . . . started to talk in special sounds, *NLT* . . . spoke languages and preached, *Fenton* . . . and to utter prophecies, *NAB.*

**7. And all the men were about twelve:** There were about twelve of them in all, *RSV* . . . These men numbered about, *Kleist* . . . In this group there were about, *SEB.*

## Acts 19:8

7.a.**Txt:** 020L,025P,byz.
**Var:** 01ℵ,02A,03B,05D 08E,Lach,Treg,Alf Word,Tisc,We/Ho,Weis Sod,UBS/☆

| **1172.1** num card | **1420.1** num card | **1511.13** verb nom sing masc part aor act | **1156.2** conj | **1519.1** prep |
|---|---|---|---|---|
| ⸂ δεκαδύο. | [a☆ δώδεκα. ] | **8.** Εἰσελθὼν | δὲ | εἰς |
| *dekaduo* | *dōdeka* | *Eiselthōn* | *de* | *eis* |
| twelve. | [ idem ] | Having entered | and | into |

| **3450.12** art acc sing fem | **4715.4** noun acc sing fem | **3817.8** verb 3sing indic imperf mid | **1894.3** prep | **3243.4** noun acc pl masc |
|---|---|---|---|---|
| τὴν | συναγωγὴν | ἐπαῤῥησιάζετο, | ἐπὶ | μῆνας |
| *tēn* | *sunagōgēn* | *eparrhēsiazeto* | *epi* | *mēnas* |
| the | synagogue | he was speaking boldly, | for | months |

8.a.**Txt:** 01ℵ,02A,08E 020L,025P,etc.byz.Tisc Sod
**Var:** 03B,05D,Lach Treg,We/Ho,Weis UBS/☆

| **4980.1** num card nom | **1250.2** verb nom sing masc part pres mid | **2504.1** conj | **3844.4** verb nom sing masc part pres act | **3450.17** art pl neu |
|---|---|---|---|---|
| τρεῖς | διαλεγόμενος | καὶ | πείθων | ⸂a τὰ ⸃ |
| *treis* | *dialegomenos* | *kai* | *peithōn* | *ta* |
| three | reasoning | and | persuading | the things |

| **3875.1** prep | **3450.10** art gen sing fem | **926.1** noun fem | **3450.2** art gen sing | **2296.2** noun gen sing masc | **5453.1** conj |
|---|---|---|---|---|---|
| περὶ | τῆς | βασιλείας | τοῦ | θεοῦ. | **9.** Ὡς |
| *peri* | *tēs* | *basileias* | *tou* | *theou* | *Hōs* |
| concerning | the | kingdom | | of God. | When |

| **1156.2** conj | **4948.7** indef-pron nom pl masc | **4500.4** verb 3pl indic imperf pass | **2504.1** conj | **540.10** verb 3pl indic imperf act |
|---|---|---|---|---|
| δέ | τινες | ἐσκληρύνοντο | καὶ | ἠπείθουν, |
| *de* | *tines* | *esklērunonto* | *kai* | *ēpeithoun* |
| but | some | were being hardened | and | were unpersuaded, |

| **2522.2** verb nom pl masc part pres act | **3450.12** art acc sing fem | **3461.4** noun acc sing fem | **1783.1** prep | **3450.2** art gen sing |
|---|---|---|---|---|
| κακολογοῦντες | τὴν | ὁδὸν | ἐνώπιον | τοῦ |
| *kakologountes* | *tēn* | *hodon* | *enōpion* | *tou* |
| speaking evil of | the | way | before | the |

| **3988.2** noun gen sing neu | **861.7** verb nom sing masc part aor act | **570.2** prep | **840.1** prs-pron gen pl | **866.2** verb 3sing indic aor act |
|---|---|---|---|---|
| πλήθους, | ἀποστὰς | ἀπ' | αὐτῶν | ἀφώρισεν |
| *plēthous* | *apostas* | *ap'* | *autōn* | *aphōrisen* |
| multitude, | having departed | from | them | he separated |

| **3450.8** art acc pl masc | **3073.8** noun acc pl masc | **2567.2** prep | **2232.4** noun acc sing fem | **1250.2** verb nom sing masc part pres mid |
|---|---|---|---|---|
| τοὺς | μαθητάς, | καθ' | ἡμέραν | διαλεγόμενος |
| *tous* | *mathētas* | *kath'* | *hēmeran* | *dialegomenos* |
| the | disciples, | according to | a day | reasoning |

9.a.**Txt:** 05D,08E,020L 025P,byz.Sod
**Var:** p74,01ℵ,02A,03B sa.bo.Lach,Treg,Alf,Tisc We/Ho,Weis,UBS/☆

| **1706.1** prep | **3450.11** art dat sing fem | **4833.1** noun dat sing fem | **5022.1** name gen masc | **4948.1** indef-pron gen sing | **3642.17** dem-pron sing neu |
|---|---|---|---|---|---|
| ἐν | τῇ | σχολῇ | Τυράννου | ⸂a τινός. ⸃ | **10.** Τοῦτο |
| *en* | *tē* | *scholē* | *Turannou* | *tinos* | *Touto* |
| in | the | school | of Tyrannus | a certain. | This |

| **1156.2** conj | **1090.33** verb 3sing indic aor mid | **1894.3** prep | **2073.3** noun pl neu | **1411.3** num card | **5452.1** conj | **3820.8** adj acc pl masc |
|---|---|---|---|---|---|---|
| δὲ | ἐγένετο | ἐπὶ | ἔτη | δύο, | ὥστε | πάντας |
| *de* | *egeneto* | *epi* | *etē* | *duo* | *hōste* | *pantas* |
| and | was | for | years | two, | so that | all |

| **3450.8** art acc pl masc | **2700.9** verb acc pl masc part pres act | **3450.12** art acc sing fem | **767.4** name acc fem | **189.36** verb inf aor act | **3450.6** art acc sing masc |
|---|---|---|---|---|---|
| τοὺς | κατοικοῦντας | τὴν | Ἀσίαν | ἀκοῦσαι | τὸν |
| *tous* | *katoikountas* | *tēn* | *Asian* | *akousai* | *ton* |
| the | inhabiting | | Asia | to hear | the |

is. Women are not mentioned, and since Luke usually mentioned them when they were present, it may be assumed that all were men.

**19:8.** On the following Sabbath Paul went to the synagogue. He was following his usual practice of going to the Jew first. But in this case he was also fulfilling his promise that he would return to the Ephesus synagogue and speak to them further (18:21).

For 3 months he was able to speak to them boldly, freely, fearlessly, and openly. No one stopped him as he "disputed" (preached and conducted discussions), seeking to persuade of the things concerning the kingdom of God. He brought reasonable proofs from the Old Testament Scriptures to show that the kingdom (rule, authority) of God is revealed in Jesus, who was now ascended to the right hand of the Father, seated at the Father's throne (2:30-33). Looking ahead to 20:24,25, it is clear that the kingdom or royal rule and royal authority and reign of God is parallel to the gospel or the good news of the grace of God. Romans 14:17 shows that Paul must have dealt with righteousness (including righteous deeds, and the uprightness or righteousness based on faith and bestowed by God; the righteousness of Christ in which we stand), peace (harmony, order, and the well-being that comes with the salvation brought by Christ), and joy in the Holy Spirit (the joy that believers have as the result of the work of the Spirit in their lives).

**19:9.** It took a little longer than usual in Ephesus, but eventually some (a number, but not the majority) of the unconverted Jews became hardened (obstinate, unyielding) and disobedient (rebellious). They showed their rebellious spirit by publicly speaking evil of the Way, that is, of the Christian faith and way of life, before the crowds who gathered to hear the gospel and packed out the synagogue. (It may be implied also that they spread their insults and vile comments through the whole community at Ephesus.)

"The Way" is significant in that it includes the whole of Christian teaching and comprehends all that Christianity and the gospel means. It is truly the better way, the one and only way of salvation.

The opposition of the unbelievers did not discourage Paul. He had learned to expect it. So he simply withdrew from them, separating the disciples (the ones who had set themselves apart to follow Jesus and learn more of Him) and taking them away (from the unbelieving Jews in the synagogue).

Then Paul found a separate place for the disciples to meet, in the schoolroom or lecture hall of Tyrannus. There, instead of meeting only on the Sabbath, Paul preached and taught the gospel daily, conducting discussions with all who would come.

**19:10.** Paul continued these daily discussions and teaching sessions for a period of 2 years. It was his practice also to take the evenings (after 4 p.m.) as a time to go to various homes to teach

**8. And he went into the synagogue:** Paul went to the synagogue there, *TCNT* . . . Then Paul made his way, *Phillips.*

**and spake boldly for the space of three months:** . . . and for three months spoke out fearlessly, *TCNT* . . . continued to preach fearlessly, *Weymouth* . . . courageously spoke, *Williams* . . . spoke with utmost confidence, *Phillips* . . . debated, *NAB.*

**disputing and persuading:** . . . giving addresses and trying to convince, *TCNT* . . . persuasivey discussing, *Berkeley* . . . arguing and pleading about, *RSV* . . . using both argument and persuasion, *Phillips* . . . with persuasive arguments, *NAB.*

**the things concerning the kingdom of God:**

**9. But when divers were hardened, and believed not:** But when some, *ASV* . . . were hardening themselves and refusing to be persuaded, *Rotherham* . . . When some in their obstinacy would not believe, *NAB* . . . grew obstinate in unbelief, *Weymouth* . . . some obstinately resisted and disbelieved, *Fenton* . . . grew harder and harder, *Williams.*

**but spake evil of that way before the multitude:** . . . denouncing the Cause before the people, *TCNT* . . . what is more, spoke offensively about the way in public, *Phillips* . . . actually criticizing, *Williams* . . . and slandered the Christian religion before the crowd, *Beck* . . . and cursed the way of God, *Lamsa* . . . in the presence of the assembly, *NAB.*

**he departed from them:** . . . he turned from them, *Berkeley* . . . Paul simply left them, *NAB.*

**and separated the disciples:** . . . and withdrew his disciples, *TCNT* . . . and, taking with him those who were disciples, *Weymouth.*

**disputing daily in the school of one Tyrannus:** . . . and gave daily addresses in the lecture-hall of Tyrannus, *TCNT* . . . and went on holding daily discussions, *Berkeley.*

**10. And this continued by the space of two years:** . . . for two years, *Rotherham* . . . This went on, *TCNT* . . . kept up, *Berkeley.*

**so that all they which dwelt in Asia heard the word of the Lord**

10.a.**Txt:** 020L,025P,byz. **Var:** 01ℵ,02A,03B,05D 08E,sa.bo.Gries,Lach Treg,Alf,Word,Tisc We/Ho,Weis,Sod UBS/⋆

| **3030.4** noun acc sing masc | **3450.2** art gen sing | **2935.2** noun gen sing masc | **2400.2** name masc | **2428.5** name-adj acc pl masc | **4885.1** conj |
|---|---|---|---|---|---|
| λόγον | τοῦ | κυρίου | ⌈a Ἰησοῦ, ⌉ | Ἰουδαίους | τε |
| *logon* | *tou* | *kuriou* | *Iēsou* | *Ioudaious* | *te* |
| word | of the | Lord | Jesus, | Jews | both |

| **2504.1** conj | **1659.7** name acc pl masc | **1405.5** noun pl fem | **4885.1** conj | **3620.3** partic | **3450.15** art acc pl fem |
|---|---|---|---|---|---|
| καὶ | Ἕλληνας· | **11.** Δυνάμεις | τε | οὐ | τὰς |
| *kai* | *Hellēnas* | *Dunameis* | *te* | *ou* | *tas* |
| and | Greeks. | Works of power | and | not | the |

| **5018.7** verb acc pl fem part aor act | **4020.57** verb 3sing indic imperf act | **3450.5** art nom sing masc | **2296.1** noun nom sing masc | **3450.5** art nom sing masc |
|---|---|---|---|---|
| τυχούσας | ⌈ ἐποίει | ὁ | θεὸς | [⋆ ὁ |
| *tuchousas* | *epoiei* | *ho* | *theos* | *ho* |
| being common | was working | | God | |

| **2296.1** noun nom sing masc | **4020.57** verb 3sing indic imperf act | **1217.2** prep | **3450.1** art gen pl | **5331.6** noun gen pl fem | **3834.2** name gen masc |
|---|---|---|---|---|---|
| θεὸς | ἐποίει ] | διὰ | τῶν | χειρῶν | Παύλου, |
| *theos* | *epoiei* | *dia* | *tōn* | *cheirōn* | *Paulou* |
| [ God | was working ] | by | the | hands | of Paul, |

| **5452.1** conj | **2504.1** conj | **1894.3** prep | **3450.8** art acc pl masc | **764.9** verb acc pl masc part pres act | **2002.5** verb inf pres mid |
|---|---|---|---|---|---|
| **12.** ὥστε | καὶ | ἐπὶ | τοὺς | ἀσθενοῦντας | ⌈ ἐπιφέρεσθαι |
| *hōste* | *kai* | *epi* | *tous* | *asthenountas* | *epipheresthai* |
| so that | even | to | the | being sick | to be brought |

12.a.**Txt:** 05D,020L 025P,byz. **Var:** 01ℵ,02A,03B,08E Lach,Treg,Alf,Tisc We/Ho,Weis,Sod UBS/⋆

| **661.5** verb inf pres mid | **570.3** prep | **3450.2** art gen sing | **5394.1** noun gen sing masc | **840.3** prs-pron gen sing |
|---|---|---|---|---|
| [a⋆ ἀποφέρεσθαι ] | ἀπὸ | τοῦ | χρωτὸς | αὐτοῦ |
| *apopheresthai* | *apo* | *tou* | *chrōtos* | *autou* |
| [ to be carried from ] | from | the | skin | his |

| **4529.3** noun pl neu | **2211.1** conj | **4467.1** noun pl neu | **2504.1** conj | **521.2** verb inf pres mid | **570.2** prep |
|---|---|---|---|---|---|
| σουδάρια | ἢ | σιμικίνθια, | καὶ | ἀπαλλάσσεσθαι | ἀπ' |
| *soudaria* | *ē* | *simikinthia* | *kai* | *apallassesthai* | *ap'* |
| handkerchiefs | or | aprons, | and | to be departed | from |

| **840.1** prs-pron gen pl | **3450.15** art acc pl fem | **3417.4** noun acc pl fem | **3450.17** art pl neu | **4885.1** conj | **4011.4** noun pl neu | **3450.17** art pl neu |
|---|---|---|---|---|---|---|
| αὐτῶν | τὰς | νόσους, | τά | τε | πνεύματα | τὰ |
| *autōn* | *tas* | *nosous* | *ta* | *te* | *pneumata* | *ta* |
| them | the | diseases, | the | and | spirits | the |

12.b.**Txt:** 020L,025P,byz. **Var:** 01ℵ,02A,03B,05D 08E,Gries,Lach,Treg Alf,Word,Tisc,We/Ho Weis,Sod,UBS/⋆

| **4050.10** adj | **1814.35** verb inf pres mid | **570.2** prep | **840.1** prs-pron gen pl | **1594.14** verb inf pres mid |
|---|---|---|---|---|
| πονηρὰ | ⌈ ἐξέρχεσθαι | ἀπ' | αὐτῶν. | [b⋆ ἐκπορεύεσθαι. ] |
| *ponēra* | *exerchesthai* | *ap'* | *autōn* | *ekporeuesthai* |
| wicked | to go out | from | them. | [ to go out. ] |

| **2005.1** verb 3pl indic aor act | **1156.2** conj | **4948.7** indef-pron nom pl masc | **570.3** prep | **3450.1** art gen pl |
|---|---|---|---|---|
| **13.** Ἐπεχείρησαν | δέ | τινες | ⌈ ἀπὸ | τῶν |
| *Epecheirēsan* | *de* | *tines* | *apo* | *tōn* |
| Took in hand | but | certain | from | the |

13.a.**Txt:** 020L,025P,byz. bo. **Var:** 01ℵ,02A,03B,08E Lach,Treg,Alf,Tisc We/Ho,Weis,Sod UBS/⋆

| **2504.1** conj | **3450.1** art gen pl | **3885.3** verb gen pl masc part pres mid | **2428.3** name-adj gen pl masc | **1829.1** noun gen pl masc |
|---|---|---|---|---|
| [a⋆ καὶ | τῶν ] | περιερχομένων | Ἰουδαίων | ἐξορκιστῶν |
| *kai* | *tōn* | *perierchomenōn* | *Ioudaiōn* | *exorkistōn* |
| [ also | of the ] | wandering | Jews, | exorcists, |

and establish the believers and to help win their friends and neighbors to the Lord. (See 20:20.)

The result was that the whole of the Roman province of Asia was evangelized. Both Jews and Gentiles from all directions came in to the schoolroom and heard the Word.

Many other churches were established. Since Ephesus was a great center, people came from all over the province for business, trade, tourism, and various other reasons. Many of them were converted, filled with the Holy Spirit, and taught by Paul. Then they went back to their home cities and towns where the Spirit filled them with zeal and made them powerful witnesses for Christ, each one a nucleus for a new church which soon grew up in their homes.

**19:11.** An important factor in this spread of the gospel in the Roman province of Asia was that God did special (extraordinary) miracles (powers, manifestations of divine power, deeds which showed God's power) by the hands of Paul. The Greek implies mighty miracles were an everyday occurrence in Paul's ministry here.

Notice that the Bible gives first emphasis to Paul's preaching and teaching of the Word. Paul was always wholly absorbed in the Word. Because he was, God confirmed the Word with these unusual miracles. The city of Ephesus was full of heathen priests and magicians, but these miracles so surpassed heathen trickery, overcoming the power of demons and evil spirits, that all were able to see that it was God who was with Paul.

**19:12.** So powerfully was the Lord working through Paul that people did not want to wait for him to minister to them in the lecture hall of Tyrannus. They would come to his workroom where he was busy at his tentmaking and would carry off handkerchiefs (actually, the sweat cloths he used to wipe away perspiration while he was working) and work aprons that had been used and thus had been in contact with his body (Greek, his skin). These they laid upon the sick who were then freed from their diseases. Even evil spirits (demons) came out of those who were possessed, and they too were released, set free.

It seems to be implied that the people took these sweat cloths and work aprons without asking Paul. He did not send them out. Yet he did not seem to mind when the people took them. He knew there was nothing magic about these items. He knew he was not causing the miracles anyway—God was. Paul was only a channel God was using, so he was happy for whatever means God used to bring His healing to others.

Actually, a sick person may not find it easy to express faith. If a person is helped to touch God by any means, it should be a cause for rejoicing. Such rejoicing brings glory to God.

**19:13.** The success of Paul's ministry and the many complete cures and deliverances God gave caught the attention of a group



**Jesus, both Jews and Greeks:** Thus all the inhabitants...were acquainted with, *Noli* . . . so that the whole population of the province, *MLNT* . . . so that everyone who lived in, *Goodspeed.*

**11. And God wrought special miracles:** God also continued to do such wonderworks, *Williams* . . . God gave most unusual demonstrations of power, *Phillips* . . . special works of power, *BB* . . . miracles of an unusual kind, *NEB* . . . extraordinary miracles, *Noli* . . . worked more than the usual miracles, *Kleist* . . . God kept performing special miracles, *Worrell* . . . did mighty, and unusual deeds, *Swann.*

**by the hands of Paul:** . . . through Paul, *Weymouth* . . . by means of Paul, *Moffatt* . . . used Paul to do, *NCV.*

**12. So that from his body were brought unto the sick handkerchiefs or aprons:** . . . so that people would carry home to the sick handkerchiefs or aprons that had touched his body, *TCNT* . . . Kerchiefs or aprons, for instance, which Paul had handled, would be carried to the sick, *Weymouth* . . . or clothing which had been in contact with his body, *Phillips* . . . or his garments, *Noli* . . . People even carried away towels or aprons he had used, *Moffatt* . . . he had handled, *MLNT* . . . which had touched his skin, *TNT.*

**and the diseases departed from them:** . . . to heal the sick of their diseases, *Noli* . . . and they would recover from their ailments, *Weymouth.*

**and the evil spirits went out of them:** . . . and the wicked spirits were goint out, *Rotherham* . . . were made to go, *Berkeley* . . . also went out, *Swann* . . . left them, *NCV.*

**13. Then certain of the vagabond Jews, exorcists:** . . . some itinerant Jews, who were exorcists, *TCNT* . . . Some Jews who made it their business to go around and drive out evil spirits, *Beck* . . . Some traveling Jewish exorcists, *Noli* . . . Some also of the itinerant Jewish exorcists, *TNT* . . . some also of the wandering Jews, *Worrell* . . . who went from place to place, *Goodspeed.*

## Acts 19:14

| 3550.2 verb inf pres act | 1894.3 prep | 3450.8 art acc pl masc | 2174.21 verb acc pl masc part pres act | 3450.17 art pl neu | 4011.4 noun pl neu |
|---|---|---|---|---|---|
| ὀνομάζειν | ἐπὶ | τοὺς | ἔχοντας | τὰ | πνεύματα |
| *onomazein* | *epi* | *tous* | *echontas* | *ta* | *pneumata* |
| to name | over | the | having | the | spirits |

| 3450.17 art pl neu | 4050.10 adj | 3450.16 art sing neu | 3549.2 noun sing neu | 3450.2 art gen sing | 2935.2 noun gen sing masc |
|---|---|---|---|---|---|
| τὰ | πονηρὰ | τὸ | ὄνομα | τοῦ | κυρίου |
| *ta* | *ponēra* | *to* | *onoma* | *tou* | *kuriou* |
| the | wicked | the | name | of the | Lord |

13.b.**Txt:** 020L,025P,byz.sa.
**Var:** 01ℵ,02A,03B,05D 08E,33,bo.Gries,Lach Treg,Alf,Word,Tisc We/Ho,Weis,Sod UBS/☆

| 2400.2 name masc | 2978.16 verb nom pl masc part pres act | 3589.2 verb 1pl indic pres act | 3589.1 verb 1sing indic pres act |
|---|---|---|---|
| Ἰησοῦ, | λέγοντες, | ⸂ Ὁρκίζομεν | [b☆ Ὁρκίζω ] |
| *Iēsou* | *legontes* | *Horkizomen* | *Horkizō* |
| Jesus, | saying, | We exorcise | [ I exorcise ] |

13.c.**Txt:** 020L,byz.
**Var:** 01ℵ,02A,03B,05D 08E,025P,Lach,Treg Alf,Tisc,We/Ho,Weis Sod,UBS/☆

| 5050.4 prs-pron acc 2pl | 3450.6 art acc sing masc | 2400.3 name acc masc | 3614.6 rel-pron acc sing masc | 3450.5 art nom sing masc | 3834.1 name nom masc |
|---|---|---|---|---|---|
| ὑμᾶς | τὸν | Ἰησοῦν | ὃν | ⸂c ὁ ⸃ | Παῦλος |
| *humas* | *ton* | *Iēsoun* | *hon* | *ho* | *Paulos* |
| you | | Jesus | whom | | Paul |

14.a.**Txt:** 01ℵ,02A,020L 025P,byz.Tisc,Sod
**Var:** 03B,05D,08E,Lach Treg,We/Ho,Weis UBS/☆

| 2756.2 verb 3sing indic pres act | 1498.37 verb 3pl indic imperf act | 1156.2 conj | 4948.7 indef-pron nom pl masc | 4948.1 indef-pron gen sing |
|---|---|---|---|---|
| κηρύσσει. | 14. ³Ἦσαν | δέ | ⸂ τινες | [a☆ τινος ] |
| *kērussei* | *Esan* | *de* | *tines* | *tinos* |
| proclaims. | There were | and | certain | [ idem ] |

14.b.**Txt:** 020L,025P,byz.
**Var:** 01ℵ,02A,03B,08E Lach,Treg,Alf,Tisc We/Ho,Weis,Sod UBS/☆

| 5048.6 noun nom pl masc | 4485.1 name gen masc | 2428.7 name-adj gen sing masc | 744.2 noun gen sing masc | 2017.1 num card | 3450.7 art nom pl masc |
|---|---|---|---|---|---|
| ⸂b υἱοὶ ⸃ | Σκευᾶ | Ἰουδαίου | ἀρχιερέως | ἑπτὰ | ⸂ οἱ |
| *huioi* | *Skeua* | *Ioudaiou* | *archiereōs* | *hepta* | *hoi* |
| sons | of Sceva | a Jew, | a high priest | seven | the |

14.c.**Txt:** 020L,025P,byz.
**Var:** 01ℵ,02A,03B,Lach Treg,Tisc,We/Ho,Weis Sod,UBS/☆

| 5048.6 noun nom pl masc | 3642.17 dem-pron sing neu | 4020.17 verb nom pl masc part pres act | 552.15 verb sing neu part aor pass | 1156.2 conj |
|---|---|---|---|---|
| [c☆ υἱοὶ ] | τοῦτο | ποιοῦντες. | 15. ἀποκριθὲν | δὲ |
| *huioi* | *touto* | *poiountes* | *apokrithen* | *de* |
| [ sons ] | this | doing. | Having answered | but |

| 3450.16 art sing neu | 4011.1 noun sing neu | 3450.16 art sing neu | 4050.1 adj sing | 1500.5 verb 3sing indic aor act |
|---|---|---|---|---|
| τὸ | πνεῦμα | τὸ | πονηρὸν | εἶπεν, |
| *to* | *pneuma* | *to* | *ponēron* | *eipen* |
| the | spirit | the | wicked | said, |

15.a.**Var:** 01ℵ,02A,03B 05D,33,sa.bo.Lach,Treg Alf,Word,Tisc,We/Ho Weis,Sod,UBS/☆

15.b.**Var:** 01ℵ-corr,03B 08E,We/Ho,Weis UBS/☆

| 840.2 prs-pron dat pl | 3450.6 art acc sing masc | 3173.1 conj | 2400.3 name acc masc | 1091.1 verb 1sing indic pres act |
|---|---|---|---|---|
| [a☆+ αὐτοῖς, ] | Τὸν | [b☆+ μὲν ] | Ἰησοῦν | γινώσκω, |
| *autois* | *Ton* | *men* | *Iēsoun* | *ginōskō* |
| [ to them, ] | | [ indeed ] | Jesus | I know, |

| 2504.1 conj | 3450.6 art acc sing masc | 3834.4 name acc masc | 1971.1 verb 1sing indic pres mid | 5050.1 prs-pron nom 2pl |
|---|---|---|---|---|
| καὶ | τὸν | Παῦλον | ἐπίσταμαι· | ὑμεῖς |
| *kai* | *ton* | *Paulon* | *epistamai* | *humeis* |
| and | | Paul | I am acquainted with; | you |

| 1156.2 conj | 4949.6 intr-pron nom pl masc | 1498.6 verb 2pl indic pres act | 2504.1 conj | 2159.1 verb nom sing masc part pres mid |
|---|---|---|---|---|
| δὲ | τίνες | ἐστέ; | 16. Καὶ | ⸂ ἐφαλλόμενος |
| *de* | *tines* | *este* | *Kai* | *ephallomenos* |
| but, | who | are? | And | leaping |

of seven traveling (wandering, itinerant) Jewish exorcists who, for a fee, went about claiming to be able to cast out evil spirits or demons by magical formulas. Possibly following the example of other Jewish exorcists, they took it upon themselves to pronounce the name of the Lord Jesus over those who were demon possessed in an attempt to bring deliverance.

The Bible does not imply they had been successful in their previous attempts to cast out demons by their magical formulas. What it does show is that they tried to make a magical formula out of the name of Jesus.

It seems that when they saw Paul cast out demons and heal the sick in the name of the Lord Jesus, they jumped to the conclusion that he was using a magical formula in the same way the heathen did. They thought they would add the name of Jesus to their list. What they did not realize was that Paul, in using the name of Jesus was recognizing Jesus for who He is. Moreover, Paul was filled with the Holy Spirit and in touch with Jesus, doing the work Jesus had called him to do. He did not minister gifts of healing just for the sake of building a reputation for himself. He was preaching the gospel, the true Word of God, and the Lord was confirming the Word with signs following (Mark 16:20). Thus the Word, not the signs, had the important place.

**19:14.** These seven were sons of Sceva (possibly a form of *shāva'*, "oath") who was designated as a Jewish high priest. The title was used of those belonging to one of the high priestly families, especially if they belonged to the Sanhedrin. It was also used of the treasurer of the temple and the captain of the temple police. It could also be used of the head of one of the 24 orders or courses of priests who took turns ministering in the temple. Some writers suggest, however, that Sceva was the head of a company who made exorcism their business and that he took the title of Jewish high priest in order to impress the heathen who would buy their services.

**19:15.** The attempt to use the name of Jesus as a magic formula failed. The evil spirit answered, "Jesus I know (recognize, know about), and Paul I know (I know of, I understand who he is), but as for you, who are you?" (Two different words for "know" are used here.) Thus, the demon recognized that these sons of Sceva only knew Jesus as the name of someone whom Paul was preaching. They did not know Jesus for themselves. They had never come to a place of faith in Jesus as their own Lord and Saviour. The devil knows when there is faith. He is not deceived by ritual or formulas or mere words. It takes the power of Jesus made manifest by the Holy Spirit for evil spirits to tremble and flee.

Notice here also there is a clear distinction between the man in whom the evil spirit was and the evil spirit itself. The man was no longer in control of his senses. The evil spirit or demon who possessed him had taken charge and was able to use the man's speech organs to answer these sons of Sceva.

**took upon them to call over them which had evil spirits the name of the Lord Jesus:** . . . took it upon themselves to invoke the name of, *Knox* . . . to use the Name of the Lord Jesus over those who had wicked spirits in them, *TCNT* . . . who attempted to invoke the name of the Lord Jesus when dealing with those who had, *Phillips* . . . were also trying to make evil spirits go out of people, *SEB* . . . tried to use the name...in the cases of people who had evil spirits in them, *Goodspeed* . . . force the evil spirits out, *Everyday*.

**saying, We adjure you by Jesus whom Paul preacheth:** I command you by that Jesus, *Weymouth* . . . I conjure you, *Knox* . . . I solemnly charge you, *TNT* . . . I charge you on oath, *Swann* . . . I speak to you, *NLT* . . . By the same Jesus that Paul talks about, *Everyday* . . . I order you to come out, *SEB* . . . whom Paul proclaimeth! *Rotherham*.

**14. And there were seven sons of one Sceva, a Jew, and chief of the priests:** The seven sons of Sceva, a Jewish chief Priest, *TCNT* . . . A Jewish leader of the people by the name of, *NLT* . . . an important Jewish priest, *SEB* . . . was a leading Jewish priest, *NCV*.

**which did so:** . . . who did this, *ASV* . . . who were doing this, *Weymouth* . . . practiced this, *Berkeley, MLNT* . . . pronounced this formula over a sick man, *Noli* . . . were engaged in this practice, *Phillips*.

**15. And the evil spirit answered and said:** But the evil spirit retorted, *Moffatt* . . . But on one occasion the evil spirit answered, *Williams* . . . The demon said, *NLT* . . . replied, *Swann* . . . said to these Jews, *SEB*.

**Jesus I know:** Jesus I acknowledge, *TCNT* . . . Jesus I recognize, *Knox* . . . I have heard about Jesus, *SEB*.

**and Paul I know:** I understand, *HBIE, Swann, Worrell* . . . and I am acquainted with Paul, *Phillips* . . . I know about Paul, *NLT* . . . Paul I know well enough, *Knox*.

**but who are ye?:** . . . but who on earth are you, *Phillips* . . . but I do not know you, *Noli*.

16.a.**Txt:** 01ℵ-corr,08E 020L,025P,byz.Sod
**Var:** 01ℵ-org,02A,03B Lach,Treg,Alf,Tisc We/Ho,Weis,UBS/☆

| **2159.2** verb nom sing masc part aor mid | **1894.2** prep | **840.8** prs-pron acc pl masc | **3450.5** art nom sing masc | **442.1** noun nom sing masc |
|---|---|---|---|---|
| [a☆ ἐφαλόμενος ] | ‘ ἐπ’ | αὐτοὺς | ὁ | ἄνθρωπος |
| *ephalomenos* | *ep'* | *autous* | *ho* | *anthrōpos* |
| [ having leaped ] | on | them | the | man |

| **3450.5** art nom sing masc | **442.1** noun nom sing masc | **1894.2** prep | **840.8** prs-pron acc pl masc | **1706.1** prep | **3614.3** rel-pron dat sing |
|---|---|---|---|---|---|
| [☆ ὁ | ἄνθρωπος | ἐπ’ | αὐτοὺς ] | ἐν | ᾧ |
| *ho* | *anthrōpos* | *ep'* | *autous* | *en* | *hō* |
| [ the | man | on | them ] | in | whom |

16.b.**Txt:** 01ℵ-org,020L 025P,byz.Weis
**Var:** 01ℵ-corr,02A,03B 05D,08E,33,sa.bo.Lach Treg,Alf,Word,Tisc We/Ho,Sod,UBS/☆

| **1498.34** verb sing indic imperf act | **3450.16** art sing neu | **4011.1** noun sing neu | **3450.16** art sing neu | **4050.1** adj sing | **2504.1** conj |
|---|---|---|---|---|---|
| ἦν | τὸ | πνεῦμα | τὸ | πονηρὸν, | ‘b καὶ ’ |
| *ēn* | *to* | *pneuma* | *to* | *ponēron* | *kai* |
| was | the | spirit | the | wicked, | and |

16.c.**Txt:** 020L,025P,byz.
**Var:** 01ℵ,02A,03B,05D bo.Lach,Treg,Alf,Tisc We/Ho,Weis,Sod UBS/☆

| **2604.3** verb nom sing masc part aor act | **840.1** prs-pron gen pl | **295.5** adj gen pl masc | **2453.7** verb 3sing indic aor act |
|---|---|---|---|
| κατακυριεύσας | ‘ αὐτῶν | [c☆ ἀμφοτέρων ] | ἴσχυσεν |
| *katakurieusas* | *autōn* | *amphoterōn* | *ischusen* |
| having mastered | them | [ all together ] | prevailed |

| **2567.1** prep | **840.1** prs-pron gen pl | **5452.1** conj | **1125.4** adj acc pl masc | **2504.1** conj | **4974.2** verb acc pl masc part perf mid |
|---|---|---|---|---|---|
| κατ’ | αὐτῶν, | ὥστε | γυμνοὺς | καὶ | τετραυματισμένους |
| *kat'* | *autōn* | *hōste* | *gumnous* | *kai* | *tetraumatismenous* |
| against | them, | so that | naked | and | having been wounded |

| **1614.3** verb inf aor act | **1523.2** prep gen | **3450.2** art gen sing | **3486.2** noun gen sing masc | **1552.2** dem-pron gen sing | **3642.17** dem-pron sing neu |
|---|---|---|---|---|---|
| ἐκφυγεῖν | ἐκ | τοῦ | οἴκου | ἐκείνου. | **17.** τοῦτο |
| *ekphugein* | *ek* | *tou* | *oikou* | *ekeinou* | *touto* |
| to escape | out of | the | house | that. | This |

| **1156.2** conj | **1090.33** verb 3sing indic aor mid | **1104.4** adj sing neu | **3820.5** adj dat pl | **2428.4** name-adj dat pl masc | **4885.1** conj |
|---|---|---|---|---|---|
| δὲ | ἐγένετο | γνωστὸν | πᾶσιν | Ἰουδαίοις | τε |
| *de* | *egeneto* | *gnōston* | *pasin* | *Ioudaiois* | *te* |
| and | became | known | to all | Jews | both |

| **2504.1** conj | **1659.6** name dat pl masc | **3450.4** art dat pl | **2700.8** verb dat pl masc part pres act | **3450.12** art acc sing fem | **2163.3** name acc fem |
|---|---|---|---|---|---|
| καὶ | Ἕλλησιν | τοῖς | κατοικοῦσιν | τὴν | Ἔφεσον, |
| *kai* | *Hellēsin* | *tois* | *katoikousin* | *tēn* | *Epheson* |
| and | Greeks, | the | inhabiting | | Ephesus, |

| **2504.1** conj | **1953.2** verb 3sing indic aor act | **5238.1** noun nom sing masc | **1894.3** prep | **3820.8** adj acc pl masc | **840.8** prs-pron acc pl masc | **2504.1** conj |
|---|---|---|---|---|---|---|
| καὶ | ἐπέπεσεν | φόβος | ἐπὶ | πάντας | αὐτούς, | καὶ |
| *kai* | *epepesen* | *phobos* | *epi* | *pantas* | *autous* | *kai* |
| and | fell | fear | upon | all | them, | and |

| **3141.7** verb 3sing indic imperf pass | **3450.16** art sing neu | **3549.2** noun sing neu | **3450.2** art gen sing | **2935.2** noun gen sing masc | **2400.2** name masc |
|---|---|---|---|---|---|
| ἐμεγαλύνετο | τὸ | ὄνομα | τοῦ | κυρίου | Ἰησοῦ. |
| *emegaluneto* | *to* | *onoma* | *tou* | *kuriou* | *Iēsou* |
| was being magnified | the | name | of the | Lord | Jesus. |

| **4044.7** adj nom pl masc | **4885.1** conj | **3450.1** art gen pl | **3961.43** verb gen pl part perf act | **2048.60** verb 3pl indic imperf mid |
|---|---|---|---|---|
| **18.** Πολλοί | τε | τῶν | πεπιστευκότων | ἤρχοντο |
| *Polloi* | *te* | *tōn* | *pepisteukotōn* | *ērchonto* |
| Many | and | of the | having believed | were coming |

**19:16.** Then the demon-possessed man leaped upon the sons of Sceva and overpowered them all. Some ancient Greek manuscripts say he leaped on (*amphoterōn,* which in earlier Greek usage, before New Testament times, meant "both"). In view of this, some writers suppose that only two of the seven sons of Sceva were involved in this attempt to cast out the evil spirit. However, in New Testament times *amphoterōn* was used in everyday speech to mean "all." Many ancient Greek papyrus manuscripts from secular literature confirm this. So it is most probable that all seven sons were involved.

The demon-possessed man used his strength so effectively against the seven brothers that they all fled out of the house naked (stripped of their outer garments) and wounded. (The Greek indicates the wounds were severe enough to affect them for a while.)

It is important to notice that this evil spirit had such power over this man that it was able to use the man's strength in a superhuman way. Casting out demons is not something to be undertaken lightly or casually. When Jesus came down from the Mount of Transfiguration, He found His disciples unable to cast an evil spirit out of a boy. After bringing the boy's father to a place of faith, Jesus commanded the demon to come out of the boy. But the demon did not come out without a struggle. It used the boy's speech organs to give a last rebellious scream or shriek, tore him with severe convulsions, then came out leaving the boy to all appearances dead. Jesus then reached down His hand, lifted the boy, and completed the healing. (See Mark 9:25-27.) Quite clearly, evil spirits are not to be faced unless believers are sure they have the power of Christ.

**16. And the man in whom the evil spirit was:** . . . spirit dwelt, *MLNT* . . . in whom the evil spirit resided, *KJII* . . . in whom the evil spirit was living, *Phillips* . . . who had the evil spirit in him, *NCV.*

**leaped on them:** . . . sprang on them, *TCNT* . . . flew at them, *NEB* . . . jumped on these Jews, *NCV.*

**and overcame them:** . . . overpowered them all, *Moffatt* . . . overcoming them both, *Worrell* . . . He was much stronger than all of them, *NCV* . . . He gained the upper hand, *TNT* . . . gained the mastery over them all, *Swann.*

**and prevailed against them:** . . . and so completely overpowered them, *TCNT* . . . and treated them with such violence, *Weymouth* . . . and compelled them to rush out of, *Noli* . . . and overcame them all, *TNT* . . . He beat them, *NCV.*

**so that they fled out of that house naked and wounded:** . . . and tore their clothes off, *NCV* . . . stripped of their clothes, and wounded, *TCNT* . . . wounded, with their clothes torn off their backs, *Phillips* . . . tattered and bruised, *Goodspeed.*

**19:17.** The sight of the seven sons of Sceva running out into the street naked and wounded surely must have caught the attention of bystanders. They must have inquired, learned the facts, and soon the news of what had happened spread throughout Ephesus. The result was that a fear (an awe inspired by the supernatural) fell upon Jews and Greeks (Gentiles) alike. This caused the name of the Lord Jesus to be magnified (glorified, praised, held in high esteem). The "name" means the person and authority of Jesus.

It may seem strange that the people felt this way when the attempt to use the Name failed. But it let the people know that such charlatans as these sons of Sceva could not make the name of Jesus a part of their bag of tricks. They saw a great contrast between the sons of Sceva and the apostle Paul. When Paul prayed in the name of the Lord Jesus things happened. People were set free from sickness, disease, and demons, as the case might be. So they saw that the power of the name of Jesus was a revelation of His holy nature as well as of His divine love and grace. His power was nothing to be trifled with. Moreover, His holy name demanded a holy people.

Believers do need to "try the spirits" putting them to the test of God's Word (1 John 4:1). But genuine outpourings of God's Spirit always bring glory to Jesus no matter how the devil tries to hinder. The Holy Spirit will always make people know that the name of Jesus is a name above every name.

**17. And this was known to all the Jews and Greeks also dwelling at Ephesus:** This incident came to the knowledge of all the Jews and Greeks living at Ephesus, *TCNT* . . . When this incident became known, *Noli* . . . All the people...learned about this, *NCV.*

**and fear fell on them all:** . . . they were all awe-struck, *TCNT* . . . They were all frightened, *Beck* . . . filled with fear, *NCV.*

**and the name of the Lord Jesus was magnified:** . . . and great honor was given to the name of, *NCV* . . . and the Name of the Lord Jesus was held in the highest honour, *TCNT* . . . and they began to hold the name of the Lord Jesus in high honor, *Weymouth* . . . while the name of the Lord Jesus became highly respected, *Phillips* . . . was highly praised, *Berkeley* . . . was extolled, *RSV.*

**18. And many that believed came:** Many of those who had professed their faith, *Phillips* . . . were coming, *Worrell.*

| 1827.4 verb nom pl masc part pres mid | 2504.1 conj | 310.3 verb nom pl masc part pres act | 3450.15 art acc pl fem | 4093.4 noun acc pl fem |
|---|---|---|---|---|
| ἐξομολογούμενοι | καὶ | ἀναγγέλλοντες | τὰς | πράξεις |
| *exomologoumenoi* | *kai* | *anangellontes* | *tas* | *praxeis* |
| confessing | and | declaring | the | deeds |

| 840.1 prs-pron gen pl | | 2401.6 adj nom pl masc | 1156.2 conj | 3450.1 art gen pl | 3450.17 art pl neu | 3884.2 adj pl neu | 4097.21 verb gen pl masc part aor act |
|---|---|---|---|---|---|---|---|
| αὐτῶν. | **19.** | ἱκανοὶ | δὲ | τῶν | τὰ | περίεργα | πραξάντων |
| *autōn* | | *hikanoi* | *de* | *tōn* | *ta* | *perierga* | *praxantōn* |
| their. | | Many | and | of the | the | magical arts | having practiced |

| 4702.4 verb nom pl masc part aor act | 3450.15 art acc pl fem | 969.4 noun acc pl fem | 2588.4 verb 3pl indic imperf act | 1783.1 prep |
|---|---|---|---|---|
| συνενέγκαντες | τὰς | βίβλους | κατέκαιον | ἐνώπιον |
| *sunenenkantes* | *tas* | *biblous* | *katekaion* | *enōpion* |
| having brought | the | books | were burning | before |

| 3820.4 adj gen pl | 2504.1 conj | 4711.1 verb 3pl indic aor act | 3450.15 art acc pl fem | 4940.6 noun acc pl fem | 840.1 prs-pron gen pl |
|---|---|---|---|---|---|
| πάντων· | καὶ | συνεψήφισαν | τὰς | τιμὰς | αὐτῶν, |
| *pantōn* | *kai* | *sunepsēphisan* | *tas* | *timas* | *autōn* |
| all. | And | they reckoned up | the | prices | of them, |

| 2504.1 conj | 2128.6 verb indic aor act | 688.2 noun gen sing neu | 3323.4 noun acc pl fem | 3864.1 num card | | 3643.1 adv |
|---|---|---|---|---|---|---|
| καὶ | εὗρον | ἀργυρίου | μυριάδας | πέντε. | **20.** | Οὕτως |
| *kai* | *heuron* | *arguriou* | *muriadas* | *pente* | | *Houtōs* |
| and | found | of silver | myriads | five. | | Thus |

| 2567.3 prep | 2877.1 noun sing neu | 3450.5 art nom sing masc | 3030.1 noun nom sing masc | 3450.2 art gen sing | 2935.2 noun gen sing masc |
|---|---|---|---|---|---|
| κατὰ | κράτος | ‘ ὁ | λόγος | τοῦ | κυρίου |
| *kata* | *kratos* | *ho* | *logos* | *tou* | *kuriou* |
| according to | might | the | word | of the | Lord |

20.a.**Txt:** p74,01ℵ-corr 020L,025P,33,byz.sa.bo. Sod
**Var:** 01ℵ-org,02A,03B Lach,Treg,Alf,Tisc We/Ho,Weis,UBS/⋆

| 3450.2 art gen sing | 2935.2 noun gen sing masc | 3450.5 art nom sing masc | 3030.1 noun nom sing masc | 831.10 verb 3sing indic imperf act | 2504.1 conj |
|---|---|---|---|---|---|
| [a⋆ τοῦ | κυρίου | ὁ | λόγος ] | ηὔξανεν | καὶ |
| *tou* | *kuriou* | *ho* | *logos* | *ēuxanen* | *kai* |
| [ of the | Lord | the | word ] | was increasing | and |

| 2453.12 verb 3sing indic imperf act | | 5453.1 conj | 1156.2 conj | 3997.20 verb 3sing indic aor pass | 3642.18 dem-pron pl neu |
|---|---|---|---|---|---|
| ἴσχυεν. | **21.** | Ὡς | δὲ | ἐπληρώθη | ταῦτα, |
| *ischuen* | | *Hōs* | *de* | *eplērōthē* | *tauta* |
| was strengthened. | | When | and | were fulfilled | these things |

| 4935.30 verb 3sing indic aor mid | 3450.5 art nom sing masc | 3834.1 name nom masc | 1706.1 prep | 3450.3 art dat sing | 4011.3 noun dat sing neu |
|---|---|---|---|---|---|
| ἔθετο | ὁ | Παῦλος | ἐν | τῷ | πνεύματι, |
| *etheto* | *ho* | *Paulos* | *en* | *tō* | *pneumati* |
| purposed | | Paul | in | the | spirit, |

| 1324.5 verb nom sing masc part aor act | 3450.12 art acc sing fem | 3081.4 name acc fem | 2504.1 conj | 875.4 name acc fem |
|---|---|---|---|---|
| διελθὼν | τὴν | Μακεδονίαν | καὶ | Ἀχαΐαν |
| *dielthōn* | *tēn* | *Makedonian* | *kai* | *Achaian* |
| having passed through | | Macedonia | and | Achaia, |

21.a.**Txt:** 020L,025P,byz.
**Var:** 01ℵ,02A,03B,05D 08E,Lach,Treg,Alf,Tisc We/Ho,Weis,Sod UBS/⋆

| 4057.15 verb inf pres mid | 1519.1 prep | 2395.1 name fem | 2389.1 name |
|---|---|---|---|
| πορεύεσθαι | εἰς | ‘ Ἱερουσαλήμ, | [a⋆ Ἱεροσόλυμα, ] |
| *poreuesthai* | *eis* | *Hierousalēm* | *Hierosoluma* |
| to go | to | Jerusalem, | [ idem ] |

**19:18.** All this had an important effect on the believers also. Many of them came confessing and publicly reporting their deeds. The Greek indicates they now came out and out for the Lord (with a total commitment). They realized their need for holiness and righteousness as well as for salvation.

**19:19.** Another result was the fact that they now realized the true power over evil was only in Jesus. Ephesus was a center for the practice of magical arts, especially the putting of spells on people or things. A considerable number of the new believers had practiced magic, including attempts at foretelling or influencing the future. Most of them still had the books they used hidden away. (Archaeologists have discovered books of this kind.)

Now the believers saw that these books with their formulas, spells, and astrological forecasts, were of no value whatsoever. In fact, they were purely heathen, even demonic, in their origin. So they brought together all their books and burned them publicly. Books were very expensive in those days, and when they reckoned up the total price of the books it came to 50,000 pieces of silver (no specific coin is mentioned, though some believe it was the drachma). This was as much as 200 day laborers or soldiers would earn in a year.

**19:20.** Luke's account of this incident concludes the story of the success of the gospel in Ephesus. But it was the Word of the Lord (the Word concerning Jesus) that grew mightily (with divine might and power) and prevailed (in a healthy, vigorous way). The fact that later (20:17) there was a large number of elders in the church at Ephesus shows there were many house churches and that the whole church there continued to grow in a healthy way.

**19:21.** Paul himself felt these things brought not just an end but a fulfillment to his ministry in Ephesus. "Ended" is literally "fulfilled" and indicates he had carried out the ministry he came to accomplish. The tremendous growth of the church during the previous more than 2 years and the training of the people and their leaders meant he could leave them now with confidence and go on to another place of ministry.

Paul's epistles show there had been problems. He says he fought with the "beasts" at Ephesus (1 Corinthians 15:32). This probably means he risked his life opposing men who acted like beasts. He also says he suffered such affliction in Asia (that is, in Ephesus) that he despaired of life but was delivered by God (2 Corinthians 1:8-10).

Now that everything was going well, Paul purposed in the spirit (or, in the Holy Spirit) to visit Rome (see Romans 1:11,14,15; 15:22-25). But he would first revisit the churches of Macedonia and Greece and take their offering to the Jerusalem church (Acts 24:17; Romans

**and confessed, and shewed their deeds:** . . . made public statement of their sins and all their acts, *BB* . . . began openly to admit their former practices, *Phillips* . . . with a full confession of their practices, *TCNT* . . . began to confess openly and tell the evil deeds they had done, *NCV* . . . giving a full account of them, *Knox.*

**19. Many of them also which used curious arts:** . . . that practiced magical arts, *ASV* . . . while a number of people, who had practiced magic, *TCNT* . . . Numbers also of the professors of magic rites, *Fenton.*

**brought their books together:** . . . collected their books, *TCNT.*

**and burned them before all men:** . . . and burnt them publicly, *TCNT.*

**and they counted the price of them:** The total value was reckoned, *Weymouth* . . . They added up the cost of these books, *Beck* . . . Those books were worth about, *NCV.*

**and found it fifty thousand pieces of silver:** . . . came to about twenty-five thousand dollars, *Norlie* . . . 50,000 silver coins, *NCV.*

**20. So mightily grew the word of God and prevailed:** So irresistibly did the Lord's message spread and prevail, *TCNT* . . . Thus mightily did the Lord's word spread and triumph, *Weymouth* . . . In a way of just such power as this the Lord's message kept on spreading and increasing, *Williams* . . . So in a powerful way the word of the Lord kept spreading and growing, *NCV.*

**21. After these things were ended:** Sometime after these events, *TCNT* . . . When matters had reached this point, *Weymouth* . . . With these aims accomplished, *Berkeley.*

**Paul purposed in the spirit:** . . . resolved in his spirit, *Montgomery* . . . the thought in Paul's heart was to go to, *Knox* . . . set his heart on going, *Phillips.*

**when he had passed through Macedonia:** . . . to go through Macedonia and Greece, *TCNT.*

**to go to Jerusalem:** . . . and then make his way to Jerusalem, *TCNT* . . . en route to Jerusalem, *Kleist.*

| 1500.15 verb nom sing masc part aor act | 3617.1 conj | 3196.3 prep | 3450.16 art sing neu | 1090.63 verb inf aor mid | 1466.6 prs-pron acc 1sing |
|---|---|---|---|---|---|
| εἰπών, | Ὅτι | Μετὰ | τὸ | γενέσθαι | με |
| *eipōn* | *Hoti* | *Meta* | *to* | *genesthai* | *me* |
| having said, | | After | the | to have been | me |

| 1550.1 adv | 1158.1 verb 3sing indic pres act | 1466.6 prs-pron acc 1sing | 2504.1 conj | 4373.3 name acc fem | 1481.19 verb inf aor act |
|---|---|---|---|---|---|
| ἐκεῖ | δεῖ | με | καὶ | Ῥώμην | ἰδεῖν. |
| *ekei* | *dei* | *me* | *kai* | *Rhōmēn* | *idein* |
| there | it is necessary | me | also | Rome | to see. |

22.a.**Txt:** 02A,03B,05D 020L,025P,etc.byz. We/Ho,Sod
**Var:** 01ℵ,08E,Tisc,Weis UBS/☆

| | 643.12 verb nom sing masc part aor act | 1156.2 conj | 1519.1 prep | 3450.12 art acc sing fem | 3081.4 name acc fem |
|---|---|---|---|---|---|
| 22. | Ἀποστείλας | δὲ | εἰς | [a τὴν ] | Μακεδονίαν |
| | *Aposteilas* | *de* | *eis* | *tēn* | *Makedonian* |
| | Having sent | and | into | | Macedonia |

| 1411.3 num card | 3450.1 art gen pl | 1241.6 verb gen pl masc part pres act | 840.4 prs-pron dat sing | 4943.4 name acc masc | 2504.1 conj |
|---|---|---|---|---|---|
| δύο | τῶν | διακονούντων | αὐτῷ, | Τιμόθεον | καὶ |
| *duo* | *tōn* | *diakonountōn* | *autō* | *Timotheon* | *kai* |
| two | of the | ministering | with him, | Timothy | and |

| 2020.2 name acc masc | 840.5 prs-pron nom sing masc | 1892.4 verb 3sing indic aor act | 5385.4 noun acc sing masc | 1519.1 prep | 3450.12 art acc sing fem |
|---|---|---|---|---|---|
| Ἔραστον, | αὐτὸς | ἐπέσχεν | χρόνον | εἰς | τὴν |
| *Eraston* | *autos* | *epeschen* | *chronon* | *eis* | *tēn* |
| Erastus, | he | remained | a time | in | |

| 767.4 name acc fem | | 1090.33 verb 3sing indic aor mid | 1156.2 conj | 2567.3 prep | 3450.6 art acc sing masc |
|---|---|---|---|---|---|
| Ἀσίαν· | 23. | Ἐγένετο | δὲ | κατὰ | τὸν |
| *Asian* | | *Egeneto* | *de* | *kata* | *ton* |
| Asia. | | Came to pass | and | according to | the |

| 2511.4 noun acc sing masc | 1552.5 dem-pron acc sing masc | 4868.1 noun nom sing masc | 3620.2 partic | 3504.3 adj nom sing masc | 3875.1 prep |
|---|---|---|---|---|---|
| καιρὸν | ἐκεῖνον | τάραχος | οὐκ | ὀλίγος | περὶ |
| *kairon* | *ekeinon* | *tarachos* | *ouk* | *oligos* | *peri* |
| time | that | disturbance | not | small | concerning |

| 3450.10 art gen sing fem | 3461.2 noun gen sing fem | | 1210.1 name nom masc | 1056.1 conj | 4948.3 indef-pron nom sing |
|---|---|---|---|---|---|
| τῆς | ὁδοῦ. | 24. | Δημήτριος | γάρ | τις |
| *tēs* | *hodou* | | *Dēmētrios* | *gar* | *tis* |
| the | way. | | Demetrius | for | a certain |

| 3549.4 noun dat sing neu | 689.1 noun nom sing masc | 4020.15 verb nom sing masc part pres act | 3348.6 noun acc pl masc | 687.1 adj acc pl masc |
|---|---|---|---|---|
| ὀνόματι, | ἀργυροκόπος, | ποιῶν | ναοὺς | ἀργυροῦς |
| *onomati* | *argurokopos* | *poiōn* | *naous* | *argurous* |
| by name, | a silversmith, | making | temples | silver |

| 730.2 name gen fem | 3792.14 verb 3sing indic imperf mid | 3450.4 art dat pl | 4927.3 noun dat pl masc | 2022.2 noun acc sing fem |
|---|---|---|---|---|
| Ἀρτέμιδος | παρείχετο | τοῖς | τεχνίταις | ‹ ἐργασίαν |
| *Artemidos* | *pareicheto* | *tois* | *technitais* | *ergasian* |
| of Artemis, | was bringing | to the | craftsmen | gain |

| 3620.2 partic | 3504.9 adj acc sing fem | 3620.2 partic | 3504.9 adj acc sing fem | 2022.2 noun acc sing fem | | 3614.8 rel-pron acc pl masc |
|---|---|---|---|---|---|---|
| οὐκ | ὀλίγην· | [☆ οὐκ | ὀλίγην | ἐργασίαν, ] | 25. | οὓς |
| *ouk* | *oligēn* | *ouk* | *oligēn* | *ergasian* | | *hous* |
| no | little; | [ no | little | gain; ] | | whom |

15:26; 1 Corinthians 16:1-4). That purpose was finally realized but not quite the way Paul expected.

"In the spirit" usually means in the Holy Spirit. (In New Testament times the Greek did not distinguish between capital and lower case letters.) It is likely that Paul's own spirit was in harmony with the Holy Spirit and submissive to Him. His purpose was thus a God-planned purpose. This is further confirmed by the statement "I must see Rome." The Greek indicates a divine necessity laid upon Paul. He did not know yet how God was going to get him to Rome. But from this point Rome was the objective in view.

**19:22.** That Paul's purpose to go to Rome was indeed pleasing to the Lord was confirmed later by Jesus himself (23:11) and by an angel (27:23,24).

To prepare the churches in Macedonia for his visit, Paul sent Timothy and Erastus (Greek, "beloved") on ahead. Erastus was a convert who had probably been a high official in Corinth, possibly the city treasurer. He later joined Paul in sending greetings to the Roman converts (Romans 16:23; see 2 Timothy 4:20).

Paul himself stayed for a time in Ephesus. As he told the Corinthians, a great door and an effectual one was still open to him, but there were many adversaries (1 Corinthians 16:8,9). Perhaps he had in mind some of the "beasts" he had been fighting.

**19:23.** Just how many adversaries there were in Ephesus soon became apparent. Luke spoke of what happened next as no small stir (disturbance, tumult). Actually, it was an uprising that might easily have resulted in Paul's death.

**19:24.** The disturbance started through the efforts of a silversmith named Demetrius. His chief product, like that of most silversmiths in Ephesus, was a small silver shrine of Artemis containing a miniature image of this many-breasted fertility goddess of Ephesus. These were used as amulets and charms. Many of them had tiny silver lions in attendance on the goddess. Others may have been models of the temple of Artemis with its 127 columns, many of which were beautifully carved. There is some evidence also that Demetrius and his fellow silversmiths were part of a guild connected with the temple and its priesthood. Most heathen temples in those days carried on large business enterprises. The temple at Ephesus was one of the seven wonders of the ancient world.

This Ephesian goddess actually had no relation to the other Artemis, the Artemis of Greece known as the maiden huntress and identified by the Romans with their goddess Diana (the daughter of Jupiter and Latona; the twin sister of Apollo; she was the Roman goddess of the moon and of hunting).

**saying, After I have been there, I must also see Rome:** I have a desire to, *BB* . . . After these journeys, I must visit, *Noli* . . . I must see Rome as well, *Phillips.*

**22. So he sent into Macedonia:** So he dispatched, *Moffatt* . . . ahead to, *NCV.*

**two of them that ministered unto him:** . . . two of his assistants, *Swann, Weymouth* . . . two of his helpers, *NCV.*

**Timotheus and Erastus; but he himself stayed in Asia for a season:** . . . remained for a while in Roman Asia, *Weymouth* . . . remained for some time longer in Asia, *MLNT.*

**23. And the same time:** And about that time, *ASV* . . . But in process of time, *Berkeley* . . . During that time, *Beck* . . . Just at that time, *Goodspeed.*

**there arose no small stir:** . . . no small disturbance, *Rotherham* . . . there was some serious trouble, *NCV* . . . no small commotion, *Weymouth* . . . no small tumult, *HBIE* . . . a great riot, *Norlie* . . . the cause of a notable disturbance, *Knox.*

**about that way:** . . . concerning the Christians, *Taylor* . . . about the Road, *Klingensmith* . . . the Way of Jesus, *NCV.*

**24. For a certain man named Demetrius, a silversmith:** A silversmith named Demetrius, *TCNT* . . . a silver-beater, *Darby* . . . who worked with silver, *NCV.*

**which made silver shrines for Diana:** . . . who made models of the shrine of Artemis, *TCNT* . . . silver boxes for the images of Diana, *BB* . . . by manufacturing silver shrines of Artemis, *Williams* . . . made miniature silver shrines, *Weymouth* . . . silver models of, *Knox* . . . that looked like the temple of the goddess, *NCV.*

**brought no small gain unto the craftsmen:** . . . men who did this work made much money, *NCV* . . . a business which brought great profits to the craftsmen in his employ, *Weymouth* . . . was making large profits for his workmen, *Goodspeed* . . . and provided the artisans with no small income, *Berkeley* . . . provided the artisans with a large income, *MLNT* . . . no little gain to, *Swann.*

| 4718.1 verb nom sing masc part aor act | 2504.1 conj | 3450.8 art acc pl masc | 3875.1 prep | 3450.17 art pl neu | 4955.14 dem-pron acc pl neu |
|---|---|---|---|---|---|
| συναθροίσας, | καὶ | τοὺς | περὶ | τὰ | τοιαῦτα |
| *sunathroisas* | *kai* | *tous* | *peri* | *ta* | *toiauta* |
| having brought together, | and | the | in | the | such things |

| 2023.5 noun acc pl masc | 1500.5 verb 3sing indic aor act | 433.6 noun nom pl masc | 1971.3 verb 2pl indic pres mid | 3617.1 conj | 1523.2 prep gen |
|---|---|---|---|---|---|
| ἐργάτας, | εἶπεν, | Ἄνδρες, | ἐπίστασθε | ὅτι | ἐκ |
| *ergatas* | *eipen* | *Andres* | *epistasthe* | *hoti* | *ek* |
| workmen, | he said, | Men, | you know | that | from |

| 3642.10 dem-pron gen sing fem | 3450.10 art gen sing fem | 2022.1 noun gen sing fem | 3450.9 art nom sing fem | 2122.1 noun nom sing fem |
|---|---|---|---|---|
| ταύτης | τῆς | ἐργασίας | ἡ | εὐπορία |
| *tautēs* | *tēs* | *ergasias* | *hē* | *euporia* |
| this | the | business | the | wealth |

25.a.**Txt:** 020L,025P,byz. **Var:** 01א,02A,03B,05D 08E,sa.bo.Lach,Treg,Alf Tisc,We/Ho,Weis,Sod UBS/☆

| 2231.2 prs-pron gen 1pl | 2231.3 prs-pron dat 1pl | 1498.4 verb 3sing indic pres act | | 2504.1 conj | 2311.1 verb 2pl pres act | 2504.1 conj |
|---|---|---|---|---|---|---|
| ʽ ἡμῶν | [a☆ ἡμῖν ] | ἐστιν· | **26.** | καὶ | θεωρεῖτε | καὶ |
| *hēmōn* | *hēmin* | *estin* | | *kai* | *theōreite* | *kai* |
| our | [ to us ] | is; | | and | you see | and |

| 189.2 verb 2pl pres act | 3617.1 conj | 3620.3 partic | 3303.1 adv | 2163.1 name gen fem | 233.2 conj | 4827.1 adv |
|---|---|---|---|---|---|---|
| ἀκούετε | ὅτι | οὐ | μόνον | Ἐφέσου | ἀλλὰ | σχεδὸν |
| *akouete* | *hoti* | *ou* | *monon* | *Ephesou* | *alla* | *schedon* |
| hear | that | not | only | of Ephesus | but | almost |

| 3820.10 adj gen sing fem | 3450.10 art gen sing fem | 767.2 name gen fem | 3450.5 art nom sing masc | 3834.1 name nom masc | 3642.4 dem-pron nom sing masc |
|---|---|---|---|---|---|
| πάσης | τῆς | Ἀσίας | ὁ | Παῦλος | οὗτος |
| *pasēs* | *tēs* | *Asias* | *ho* | *Paulos* | *houtos* |
| of all | | Asia | | Paul | this |

| 3844.6 verb nom sing masc part aor act | 3150.2 verb 3sing indic aor act | 2401.2 adj sing | 3657.4 noun acc sing masc | 2978.15 verb nom sing masc part pres act |
|---|---|---|---|---|
| πείσας | μετέστησεν | ἱκανὸν | ὄχλον, | λέγων |
| *peisas* | *metestēsen* | *hikanon* | *ochlon* | *legōn* |
| having persuaded | turned away | a great | multitude, | saying |

| 3617.1 conj | 3620.2 partic | 1498.7 verb 3pl indic pres act | 2296.6 noun nom pl masc | 3450.7 art nom pl masc | 1217.2 prep | 5331.6 noun gen pl fem |
|---|---|---|---|---|---|---|
| ὅτι | οὐκ | εἰσὶν | θεοὶ | οἱ | διὰ | χειρῶν |
| *hoti* | *ouk* | *eisin* | *theoi* | *hoi* | *dia* | *cheirōn* |
| that | not | they are | gods | the | by | hands |

| 1090.21 verb nom pl masc part pres mid | | 3620.3 partic | 3303.1 adv | 1156.2 conj | 3642.17 dem-pron sing neu | 2765.1 verb 3sing indic pres act |
|---|---|---|---|---|---|---|
| γινόμενοι. | **27.** | οὐ | μόνον | δὲ | τοῦτο | κινδυνεύει |
| *ginomenoi* | | *ou* | *monon* | *de* | *touto* | *kinduneuei* |
| being made. | | Not | only | and | this | is dangerous |

| 2231.3 prs-pron dat 1pl | 3450.16 art sing neu | 3183.1 noun sing neu | 1519.1 prep | 554.1 noun acc sing masc | 2048.23 verb inf aor act | 233.2 conj |
|---|---|---|---|---|---|---|
| ἡμῖν | τὸ | μέρος | εἰς | ἀπελεγμὸν | ἐλθεῖν, | ἀλλὰ |
| *hēmin* | *to* | *meros* | *eis* | *apelegmon* | *elthein* | *alla* |
| to us | the | part | into | disrepute | to come, | but |

| 2504.1 conj | 3450.16 art sing neu | 3450.10 art gen sing fem | 3144.10 adj gen sing fem | 2276.1 noun gen sing fem | 730.2 name gen fem | 2387.3 adj sing neu |
|---|---|---|---|---|---|---|
| καὶ | τὸ | τῆς | μεγάλης | θεᾶς | Ἀρτέμιδος | ἱερὸν |
| *kai* | *to* | *tēs* | *megalēs* | *theas* | *Artemidos* | *hieron* |
| also | the | of the | great | goddess | Artemis | temple |

**19:25.** Because sales of the shrines were falling off, Demetrius gathered all his fellow craftsmen together and made a speech. He began by appealing to their self-interest, "Men, you understand that by this business (trade) we get our prosperity." The Greek also implies they knew this was the way to earn a good living.

The way Demetrius began by stirring up self-interest shows their chief concern was not the worship or the honor of the goddess, but their own prosperity. Their attachment to the goddess was simply to make it a means of gain for themselves.

The apostle Paul warned Timothy that even Christians can fall into this same attitude. He warned against those who suppose "gain is godliness," that is, who suppose that the profession of Christianity is a means of making money or getting prestige. He was speaking of false teachers who make a show of their religion in order to collect large sums of money for themselves (1 Timothy 6:5). Then he called on believers to turn away from such teachers to real godliness, that is, to a godly faith that shows itself in devotion and duty, in service to the Lord and other believers in practical ways. This kind of godliness brings a contentment that comes from an inner sufficiency through the full appropriation of God's provisions for the inner man and which is therefore independent of outward circumstances. This benefits in every way. (See 1 Timothy 4:8.)

**19:26.** The next words of Demetrius are a testimony to the power and effectiveness of the gospel. Paul's message had a great effect not only in the city of Ephesus, it had permeated practically the entire Roman province of Asia.

Getting the people to listen to the Old Testament prophets would be sufficient to persuade many of them that the gods, that is the idols were nothings. Isaiah 40:18-20 shows the true God is not to be compared with idols. With tremendous irony Isaiah pictured a rich man hiring a workman to cast and shape an image and then hiring a goldsmith to overlay it with gold. Then he has silver chains made to hold it up. After all, a rich man would not want his gold-plated god to fall over! The poor man, of course, could not afford a goldplated god, so he goes out and cuts down a tree that would not rot and has a wooden god made with a broad base so it would not fall over. It would be a shame if his wooden god fell over and rotted!

**19:27.** Because of Paul's message, the sales of the shrines were diminishing, and the trade of idol making was in danger of falling into disrepute, as more and more people were rejecting the idols and refuting their value.

Verse 37 indicates Paul may not have openly criticized either the silversmiths, their shrines, or their goddess. He preached Christ and taught the people of the greatness and power of the one true God who is our Creator and Redeemer. Nevertheless, 14:15 shows that he was bold in preaching against idols (cf. 17:22-31).

**25. Whom he called together:** . . . called a general meeting of his own men, *JB.*

**with the workmen of like occupation:** . . . as well as the workmen engaged in similar occupations, *TCNT* . . . and others who did similar work, *Beck.*

**and said Sirs:** Men, *RSV.*

**ye know:** . . . you understand, *Berkeley.*

**that by this craft we have our wealth:** . . . this trade is the source of our prosperity, *TCNT* . . . that by this business we make our money, *Montgomery* . . . we're getting a fine income from this business, *Beck.*

**26. Moreover ye see and hear:** If you use your eyes and ears you also know, *Phillips.*

**that not alone at Ephesus, but almost throughout all Asia:** . . . that not only at Ephesus, but in almost the whole of Roman Asia, *TCNT* . . . the whole province of Asia, *Weymouth* . . . practically throughout Asia, *Phillips* . . . the mass of all Asia, *Murdock.*

**this Paul hath persuaded and turned away much people:** . . . has convinced and won over great numbers of people, *TCNT* . . . this fellow Paul has led away a vast number of people, *Weymouth* . . . has succeeded in changing the minds of a great number of people, *Phillips* . . . and enticed away, *Murdock.*

**saying that they be no gods, which are made with hands:** He declares that handmade gods are not gods at all, *Moffatt* . . . by persuading them that manufactured gods are not real gods, *Berkeley.*

**27. So that not only this our craft is in danger to be set at nought:** So that not only is this business of ours likely to fall into discredit, *TCNT* . . . will lose its reputation, *Williams* . . . will get a bad name, *TEV.*

**but also that the temple of the great goddess Diana should be despised:** . . . but there is further danger that the Tenple of the great goddess Artemis will be thought nothing of, *TCNT* . . . her magnificence destroyed, *Noyes* . . . will fall into utter disrepute, *Weymouth* . . . might come to be lightly regarded, *Phillips.*

## Acts 19:28

27.a.**Txt:** 05D,08E,020L byz.
**Var:** 01ℵ,02A,03B,025P Lach,Treg,Alf,Tisc We/Ho,Weis,Sod UBS/☆

| 1519.1 | 3625.6 | 3628.1 | 3023.16 | 3165.18 | 1156.2 |
|---|---|---|---|---|---|
| prep | num card neu | num card neu | verb inf aor pass | verb inf pres act | conj |
| εἰς | ʽ οὐδὲν | [a☆ οὐθὲν ] | λογισθῆναι, | μέλλειν | ʽ δὲ |
| *eis* | *ouden* | *outhen* | *logisthēnai* | *mellein* | *de* |
| for | nothing | [ idem ] | to be reckoned, | to be about | and |

27.b.**Txt:** 020L,Steph
**Var:** 01ℵ,02A,03B,08E 025P,byz.sa.bo.Elzev Gries,Lach,Treg,Alf Tisc,We/Ho,Weis,Sod UBS/☆

| 4885.1 | 2504.1 | 2479.7 | 3450.12 | 3139.3 |
|---|---|---|---|---|
| conj | conj | verb inf pres mid | art acc sing fem | noun acc sing fem |
| [b☆ τε ] | καὶ | καθαιρεῖσθαι | ʽ τὴν | μεγαλειότητα |
| *te* | *kai* | *kathaireisthai* | *tēn* | *megaleiotēta* |
| [ idem ] | also | to be destroyed | the | majesty |

27.c.**Txt:** 020L,025P,byz.
**Var:** 01ℵ,02A,03B,08E Lach,Treg,Alf,Tisc We/Ho,Weis,Sod UBS/☆

| 3450.10 | 3139.1 | 840.10 | 3614.12 | 3513.6 |
|---|---|---|---|---|
| art gen sing fem | noun gen sing fem | prs-pron gen sing fem | rel-pron acc sing fem | adj nom sing fem |
| [c☆ τῆς | μεγαλειότητος ] | αὐτῆς, | ἣν | ὅλη |
| *tēs* | *megaleiotētos* | *autēs* | *hēn* | *holē* |
| [ of the | majesty ] | her, | whom | whole |

| 3450.9 | 767.1 | 2504.1 | 3450.9 | 3487.1 | 4431.1 |
|---|---|---|---|---|---|
| art nom sing fem | name nom fem | conj | art nom sing fem | noun nom sing fem | verb 3sing indic pres mid |
| ἡ | Ἀσία | καὶ | ἡ | οἰκουμένη | σέβεται. |
| *hē* | *Asia* | *kai* | *hē* | *oikoumenē* | *sebetai* |
|  | Asia | and | the | habitable world | worships. |

| 189.32 | 1156.2 | 2504.1 | 1090.55 | 3994.2 |
|---|---|---|---|---|
| verb nom pl masc part aor act | conj | conj | verb nom pl masc part aor mid | adj pl |
| **28.** Ἀκούσαντες | δὲ | καὶ | γενόμενοι | πλήρεις |
| *Akousantes* | *de* | *kai* | *genomenoi* | *plēreis* |
| Having heard | and, | and | having become | full |

| 2349.2 | 2869.18 | 2978.16 | 3144.9 | 3450.9 |
|---|---|---|---|---|
| noun gen sing masc | verb 3pl indic imperf act | verb nom pl masc part pres act | adj nom sing fem | art nom sing fem |
| θυμοῦ, | ἔκραζον | λέγοντες, | Μεγάλη | ἡ |
| *thumou* | *ekrazon* | *legontes* | *Megalē* | *hē* |
| of fury, | they were crying out | saying, | Great |  |

29.a.**Txt:** 08E,020L 025P,byz.sa.
**Var:** 01ℵ,02A,03B,bo. Lach,Treg,Alf,Tisc We/Ho,Weis,Sod UBS/☆

| 730.1 | 2162.1 | 2504.1 | 3990.4 | 3450.9 |
|---|---|---|---|---|
| name nom fem | name-adj gen pl masc | conj | verb 3sing indic aor pass | art nom sing fem |
| Ἄρτεμις | Ἐφεσίων. | **29.** Καὶ | ἐπλήσθη | ἡ |
| *Artemis* | *Ephesiōn* | *Kai* | *eplēsthē* | *hē* |
| Artemis | of Ephesians. | And | was filled | the |

29.b.**Var:** 01ℵ-org,02A 03B,05D-corr,020L 025P,Gries,Treg,Alf Word,Tisc,We/Ho,Weis Sod,UBS/☆

| 4032.1 | 3513.6 | 3450.10 | 4650.1 | 3592.2 |
|---|---|---|---|---|
| noun nom sing fem | adj nom sing fem | art gen sing fem | noun gen sing fem | verb 3pl indic aor act |
| πόλις | ʽa ὅλη ˒ | [b☆+ τῆς ] | συγχύσεως· | ὥρμησάν |
| *polis* | *holē* | *tēs* | *sunchuseōs* | *hōrmēsan* |
| city | whole | [ the ] | with confusion, | they rushed |

| 4885.1 | 3524.1 | 1519.1 | 3450.16 | 2279.1 | 4780.2 |
|---|---|---|---|---|---|
| conj | adv | prep | art sing neu | noun sing neu | verb nom pl masc part aor act |
| τε | ὁμοθυμαδὸν | εἰς | τὸ | θέατρον, | συναρπάσαντες |
| *te* | *homothumadon* | *eis* | *to* | *theatron* | *sunarpasantes* |
| and | with one accord | to | the | theatre, | having seized with |

29.c.**Txt:** Steph
**Var:** 01ℵ,02A,03B,05D 08E,020L,025P,Gries Lach,Treg,Alf,Word Tisc,We/Ho,Weis,Sod UBS/☆

| 1043.2 | 2504.1 | 702.3 | 3082.5 | 4748.2 |
|---|---|---|---|---|
| name acc masc | conj | name acc masc | name acc pl masc | noun acc pl masc |
| Γάϊον | καὶ | Ἀρίσταρχον | Μακεδόνας, | συνεκδήμους |
| *Gaion* | *kai* | *Aristarchon* | *Makedonas* | *sunekdēmous* |
| Gaius | and | Aristarchus, | Macedonians, | fellow travellers |

30.a.**Txt:** 08E,020L 025P,byz.Sod
**Var:** 01ℵ-org,02A,03B Lach,Treg,Alf,Word Tisc,We/Ho,Weis UBS/☆

| 3450.2 | 3834.2 | 3450.2 | 1156.2 | 3834.2 | 3834.2 |
|---|---|---|---|---|---|
| art gen sing | name gen masc | art gen sing | conj | name gen masc | name gen masc |
| ʽc τοῦ ˒ | Παύλου. | **30.** ʽ τοῦ | δὲ | Παύλου | [a☆ Παύλου |
| *tou* | *Paulou* | *tou* | *de* | *Paulou* | *Paulou* |
|  | of Paul. |  | But | Paul | [ Paul |

Then secondarily, Demetrius said something about their goddess. Again his purpose was still to stir up their self-interest. Thus he claimed that the temple of the goddess Artemis (called "Diana of the Ephesians" in KJV, verse 28) was in danger of being accounted as nothing. The goddess itself was also in danger of having its divine majesty (magnificence) diminished (or, destroyed).

Then Demetrius made the exaggerated claim that not only the whole province of Asia, but all the (inhabited) world worshiped it. It may be that many visitors did come from other parts of the Roman Empire, and while in Ephesus visited the magnificent temple and joined in the worship of the goddess. But there is little evidence that she was worshiped or revered elsewhere.

The heathen gods and goddesses were always considered to be limited in their power and in their sphere of activity. Most were considered to have more power in the area dominated by the temples or in the countries where they were especially worshiped. None were believed to be omnipotent, and certainly not everywhere present.

**19:28.** This speech, as Demetrius hoped, brought an outburst of passionate wrath among the silversmiths. They began crying out (and kept crying out again and again) with great emotion, "Great is Artemis (Diana, KJV) of the Ephesians."

The great wealth and prominence of the city of Ephesus was largely due to its great temple. The image was originally of wood (possibly ebony). Later images were of stone or metal. The image had a headdress representing a fortified city wall. From the headdress hung drapery on each side of her face to her shoulders. Rows of breasts completely covered the upper part of the body designating her as the mother goddess, the source of all life in their tradition.

The temple was also a museum where the finest statuary and the most beautiful paintings were preserved. It also employed a large number of people, including these silversmiths. Their livelihood, and the livelihood of many others, depended on making people believe Artemis of the Ephesians was great.

**19:29.** The Greek indicates the silversmiths kept up their shouting until their chant filled the whole city with confusion and disturbance. The result was that they all rushed into the theater which was a Greek-style amphitheater, stadium, or arena, open to the sky with room to seat 25,000 people.

First, however, they seized Gaius and Aristarchus, Macedonians who were among Paul's traveling companions. Their presence shows Paul's company was considerably larger on this missionary journey than on his earlier travels. These two were seized and dragged into the amphitheater because the crowd's anger was stirred against Paul, and they recognized these men as Paul's associates.

**and her magnificence should be destroyed:** . . . will soon be dethroned from her majestic glory! *Williams* . . . and so she...will have all her grandeur destroyed, *Norlie* . . . and then she...will be robbed of her glory, *Beck* . . . her actual majesty might be degraded, *Phillips* . . . It could end up by taking away all the prestige of a goddess venerated, *JB* . . . will be shorn of her majestic rank, *Kleist* . . . will even be deposed from her greatness, *TNT.*

**whom all Asia and the world worshippeth:** . . . she who is now worshipped by the whole province of Asia; nay, by the whole world, *Weymouth* . . . and all the world reveres, *Knox* . . . the world worship will be a thing of the past! *Goodspeed.*

**28. And when they heard these sayings:** After listening to this harangue, *Weymouth* . . . As they listened, *Berkeley* . . . When the workers heard this speech, *Noli.*

**they were full of wrath:** . . . the men were greatly enraged, *TCNT* . . . they all became furiously angry, *Weymouth* . . . all overcome with rage, *Knox.*

**and cried out, saying:** . . . and began shouting, *TCNT* . . . and cried out again and again, *Montgomery.*

**Great is Diana of the Ephesians:** Great is Artemis of Ephesus! *NCV.*

**29. And the whole city was filled with confusion:** Then the city was agitated from end to end, *Berkeley* . . . Soon the whole city was in an uproar, *Phillips* . . . became confused, *NCV.*

**and having caught Gaius and Aristarchus:** . . . and having seized, *ASV* . . . The people grabbed, *NCV* . . . carrying off with them, *Rotherham* . . . dragging with them, *TCNT.*

**men of Macedonia, Paul's companions in travel:** . . . two Macedonians who were Paul's travelling companions, *TCNT* . . . These two men...were traveling with Paul, *NCV.*

**they rushed with one accord into the theatre:** . . . and the people rushed together into the amphitheatre, *TCNT* . . . they jointly stormed, *Berkeley* . . . ran to, *NCV* . . . and by a common impulse, *Goodspeed.*

| **1156.2** conj | **1007.9** verb gen sing masc part pres mid | **1511.21** verb inf aor act | **1519.1** prep | **3450.6** art acc sing masc | **1213.3** noun acc sing masc |
| --- | --- | --- | --- | --- | --- |
| δὲ ] | βουλομένου | εἰσελθεῖν | εἰς | τὸν | δῆμον, |
| *de* | *boulomenou* | *eiselthein* | *eis* | *ton* | *dēmon* |
| but ] | intending | to go in | to | the | people, |

| **3620.2** partic | **1432.9** verb 3pl indic imperf act | **840.6** prs-pron acc sing masc | **3450.7** art nom pl masc | **3073.5** noun nom pl masc | **4948.7** indef-pron nom pl masc |
| --- | --- | --- | --- | --- | --- |
| οὐκ | εἴων | αὐτὸν | οἱ | μαθηταί· | **31.** τινὲς |
| *ouk* | *eiōn* | *auton* | *hoi* | *mathētai* | *tines* |
| not | were allowing | him | the | disciples, | some |

| **1156.2** conj | **2504.1** conj | **3450.1** art gen pl | **769.1** name gen pl masc | **1498.23** verb nom pl masc part pres act | **840.4** prs-pron dat sing |
| --- | --- | --- | --- | --- | --- |
| δὲ | καὶ | τῶν | Ἀσιαρχῶν | ὄντες | αὐτῷ |
| *de* | *kai* | *tōn* | *Asiarchōn* | *ontes* | *autō* |
| and | also | of the | chiefs of Asia | being | to him |

| **5224.4** adj nom pl masc | **3854.15** verb nom pl masc part aor act | **4242.1** prep | **840.6** prs-pron acc sing masc | **3731.20** verb 3pl indic imperf act | **3231.1** partic |
| --- | --- | --- | --- | --- | --- |
| φίλοι, | πέμψαντες | πρὸς | αὐτὸν, | παρεκάλουν | μὴ |
| *philoi* | *pempsantes* | *pros* | *auton* | *parekaloun* | *mē* |
| friends, | having sent | to | him, | were urging | not |

| **1319.31** verb inf aor act | **1431.6** prs-pron acc sing masc | **1519.1** prep | **3450.16** art sing neu | **2279.1** noun sing neu | **241.6** adj nom pl masc |
| --- | --- | --- | --- | --- | --- |
| δοῦναι | ἑαυτὸν | εἰς | τὸ | θέατρον. | **32.** ἄλλοι |
| *dounai* | *heauton* | *eis* | *to* | *theatron* | *alloi* |
| to venture | himself | into | the | theatre. | Some |

| **3173.1** conj | **3631.1** partic | **241.14** adj sing neu | **4948.10** indef-pron sing neu | **2869.18** verb 3pl indic imperf act | **1498.34** verb sing indic imperf act |
| --- | --- | --- | --- | --- | --- |
| μὲν | οὖν | ἄλλο | τι | ἔκραζον. | ἦν |
| *men* | *oun* | *allo* | *ti* | *ekrazon* | *ēn* |
|  | therefore | another | one thing | were crying out; | was |

| **1056.1** conj | **3450.9** art nom sing fem | **1564.2** noun nom sing fem | **4648.5** verb nom sing fem part perf mid | **2504.1** conj | **3450.7** art nom pl masc |
| --- | --- | --- | --- | --- | --- |
| γὰρ | ἡ | ἐκκλησία | συγκεχυμένη, | καὶ | οἱ |
| *gar* | *hē* | *ekklēsia* | *sunkechumenē* | *kai* | *hoi* |
| for | the | assembly | having been confused, | and | the |

32.a.**Txt:** 05D,08E,020L 025P,byz.
**Var:** 01ℵ,02A,03B,Lach Treg,Alf,Tisc,We/Ho Weis,Sod,UBS/☆

| **3979.3** adj comp pl | **3620.2** partic | **3471.13** verb 3pl indic plperf act | **4949.4** intr-pron gen sing | **1736.2** prep | **1736.3** prep |
| --- | --- | --- | --- | --- | --- |
| πλείους | οὐκ | ᾔδεισαν | τίνος | ˊ ἕνεκεν | [a☆ ἕνεκα ] |
| *pleious* | *ouk* | *ēdeisan* | *tinos* | *heneken* | *heneka* |
| most | not | did know | for what | cause | [ idem ] |

| **4755.11** verb 3pl indic plperf act | **1523.2** prep gen | **1156.2** conj | **3450.2** art gen sing | **3657.2** noun gen sing masc |
| --- | --- | --- | --- | --- |
| συνεληλύθεισαν. | **33.** ἐκ | δὲ | τοῦ | ὄχλου |
| *sunelēlutheisan* | *ek* | *de* | *tou* | *ochlou* |
| they had come together. | From among | but | the | crowd |

33.a.**Txt:** 05D-corr,020L 025P,byz.
**Var:** p74,01ℵ,02A,03B 08E,33,Lach,Treg,Tisc We/Ho,Weis,Sod UBS/☆

| **4123.1** verb 3pl indic aor act | **4673.6** verb 3pl indic aor act | **221.3** name acc masc |
| --- | --- | --- |
| ˊ προεβίβασαν | [a☆ συνεβίβασαν ] | Ἀλέξανδρον, |
| *proebibasan* | *sunebibasan* | *Alexandron* |
| they put forward | [ they brought together ] | Alexander, |

| **4120.2** verb gen pl masc part aor act | **840.6** prs-pron acc sing masc | **3450.1** art gen pl | **2428.3** name-adj gen pl masc | **3450.5** art nom sing masc |
| --- | --- | --- | --- | --- |
| προβαλόντων | αὐτὸν | τῶν | Ἰουδαίων· | ὁ |
| *probalontōn* | *auton* | *tōn* | *Ioudaiōn* | *ho* |
| having thrust forward | him | the | Jews. |  |

**19:30.** When Paul wanted to go in among the tumultuous crowd, the disciples would not let him. Paul probably wanted to make a defense before the crowd. But the disciples (the Christians) were concerned about his safety.

**19:31.** Even some of the non-Christians were concerned for Paul's safety. Some of the Asiarchs (officials connected with Roman worship in the Province of Asia) who were friends sent him a message urging him not to offer himself in the amphitheater. No doubt they thought the crowd might tear him to pieces.

These Asiarchs were chosen from the wealthiest and most prominent citizens for an annual term, to which they might be reelected. They were delegates to the provincial council of cities, and presided over the athletic games and religious rites in the amphitheater. They were held in high honor by the people.

**19:32.** In the amphitheater, the crowd was still in confusion. Some were crying out one thing, some another. The major part of the assembly did not have any idea why they had come together.

The "assembly" here is the Greek *ekklēsia.* The derivation of *ekklēsia* from *ek* ("out of") and *kaleō* ("to call") shows it once had the meaning of a "called-out assembly," called out to transact official business, a sort of "town meeting." But by New Testament times, *ekklēsia* had lost the idea of being "called out." It was used in everyday Greek to mean any assembly of citizens, whether officially called, or whether it was an unruly, confused mob come together such as this one in the amphitheater.

In the New Testament, *ekklēsia* is translated "assembly" three times, all in this chapter (verses 32,39,41). In all other places (about 112 times) it is translated "church." But its proper meaning is still an assembly, not of citizens of Rome, but of citizens of heaven. What a contrast this is with the confused mob that made up this assembly in the amphitheater in Ephesus.

**19:33.** At this point the Jews put forward Alexander out of the crowd with the intention of instructing them. They wanted Alexander to explain that the Jews were not responsible for what the Christians were doing.

Alexander was a very common Greek name and shows he was a Hellenistic Jew, well acquainted with Greek thought and Greek oratory. The Jews recognized that the wrath of the silversmiths was directed against the apostle Paul. But they also knew a riot like this could result in mob violence, and an unthinking mob could turn on them, since Paul was a Jew. The Jews were very anxious to let the mob know the Jews were completely innocent and had done nothing to stir up this riot.

**30. And when Paul would have entered in unto the people:** Paul wished to go into the amphitheatre and face the people, *TCNT* . . . wanted to speak to the people himself, *Noli* . . . and address the people, *Weymouth.*

**the disciples suffered him not:** . . . would not hear of it, *Norlie* . . . restrained him, *Murdock* . . . would not allow him to do so, *Noli* . . . tried to prevent it, *Knox.*

**31. And certain of the chief of Asia:** . . . the principal officers of Asia, *Wesley* . . . Some of the Asiarchs, *Kleist* . . . some of the delegates of Asia, *Knox* . . . Some of the religious authorities also, *Goodspeed* . . . some leaders of Asia, *NCV.*

**which were his friends:** . . . being his friends, *ASV* . . . friends of his, *Goodspeed.*

**sent unto him, desiring him that he would not adventure himself into the theatre:** . . . also sent to beg him, *Moffatt* . . . sent him warning, *Berkeley* . . . not to venture, *Montgomery* . . . imploring him not to risk his life in the theatre, *Knox.*

**32. Some therefore cried one thing, and some another:** Meanwhile some were shouting, *TCNT.*

**for the assembly was confused:** . . . for there was no order in the meeting, *BB* . . . for the mass meeting was just a tumult, *Berkeley* . . . meeting was in confusion, *Goodspeed* . . . completely confused, *NCV.*

**and the more part knew not wherefore they were come together:** . . . and the majority, *Montgomery* . . . and most of them, *Goodspeed* . . . not even knowing why they had met, *TCNT* . . . part had no idea why they had come together, *Weymouth.*

**33. And they drew Alexander out of the multitude:** A man called Alexander...was pushed into the forefront of the crowd, *Phillips* . . . some brought out of the crowd Alexander, *Kleist* . . . called up, *Goodspeed.*

**the Jews putting him forward:** . . . the Jews thrusting him forward, *Rotherham* . . . whom the Jews pushed to the front, *TCNT* . . . Some of them had told him what to do, *NCV.*

| 1156.2 conj | 221.1 name nom masc | 2648.2 verb nom sing masc part aor act | 3450.12 art acc sing fem |
|---|---|---|---|
| δὲ | Ἀλέξανδρος | κατασείσας | τὴν |
| de | Alexandros | kataseisas | tēn |
| And | Alexander, | having made a sign with | the |

| 5331.4 noun acc sing fem | 2286.32 verb 3sing indic imperf act | 620.5 verb inf pres mid | 3450.3 art dat sing | 1213.2 noun dat sing masc |
|---|---|---|---|---|
| χεῖρα, | ἤθελεν | ἀπολογεῖσθαι | τῷ | δήμῳ. |
| cheira | ēthelen | apologeisthai | tō | dēmō |
| hand, | was wishing | to make a defense | to the | people. |

34.a.**Txt:** Steph
**Var:** 01ℵ,02A,03B,05D 08E,020L,025P,byz. Gries,Lach,Treg,Alf Word,Tisc,We/Ho,Weis Sod,UBS/☆

| 1906.11 verb gen pl masc part aor act | 1906.10 verb nom pl masc part aor act | 1156.2 conj | 3617.1 conj |
|---|---|---|---|
| 34. ⸂ ἐπιγνόντων | [a☆ ἐπιγνόντες ] | δὲ | ὅτι |
| epignontōn | epignontes | de | hoti |
| Having recognized | [ idem ] | but | that |

| 2428.6 name-adj nom sing masc | 1498.4 verb 3sing indic pres act | 5292.1 noun nom sing fem | 1090.33 verb 3sing indic aor mid | 1518.5 num card nom fem |
|---|---|---|---|---|
| Ἰουδαῖός | ἐστιν, | φωνὴ | ἐγένετο | μία |
| Ioudaios | estin | phōnē | egeneto | mia |
| a Jew | he is, | cry | there was | one |

| 1523.2 prep gen | 3820.4 adj gen pl | 5453.1 conj | 1894.3 prep | 5443.1 noun fem | 1411.3 num card | 2869.5 verb gen pl masc part pres act |
|---|---|---|---|---|---|---|
| ἐκ | πάντων, | ὡς | ἐπὶ | ὥρας | δύο | ⸂ κραζόντων, |
| ek | pantōn | hōs | epi | hōras | duo | krazontōn |
| from | all, | for | about | hours | two | crying out, |

34.b.**Txt:** 03B,05D,08E 020L,025P,byz.We/Ho Sod
**Var:** 01ℵ,02A,Tisc,Weis UBS/☆

| 2869.4 verb nom pl masc part pres act | 3144.9 adj nom sing fem | 3450.9 art nom sing fem | 730.1 name nom fem | 2162.1 name-adj gen pl masc |
|---|---|---|---|---|
| [b κράζοντες, ] | Μεγάλη | ἡ | Ἄρτεμις | Ἐφεσίων. |
| krazontes | Megalē | hē | Artemis | Ephesiōn |
| [ idem ] | Great | | Artemis | of Ephesians. |

| 2657.1 verb nom sing masc part aor act | 1156.2 conj | 3450.5 art nom sing masc | 1116.1 noun nom sing masc | 3450.6 art acc sing masc |
|---|---|---|---|---|
| 35. καταστείλας | δὲ | ὁ | γραμματεὺς | τὸν |
| katasteilas | de | ho | grammateus | ton |
| Having calmed | and | the | recorder | the |

| 3657.4 noun acc sing masc | 5183.2 verb 3sing indic pres act | 433.6 noun nom pl masc | 2162.3 name-adj nom pl masc | 4949.3 intr-pron nom sing | 1056.1 conj |
|---|---|---|---|---|---|
| ὄχλον | φησίν, | Ἄνδρες | Ἐφέσιοι, | τίς | γάρ |
| ochlon | phēsin | Andres | Ephesioi | tis | gar |
| crowd | says, | Men | Ephesians, | what | for |

35.a.**Txt:** 05D-corr,020L 025P,byz.
**Var:** 01ℵ,02A,03B,08E bo.Lach,Treg,Alf,Tisc We/Ho,Weis,Sod UBS/☆

| 1498.4 verb 3sing indic pres act | 442.1 noun nom sing masc | 442.7 noun gen pl masc | 3614.5 rel-pron nom sing masc | 3620.3 partic |
|---|---|---|---|---|
| ἐστιν | ⸂ ἀνθρώπος | [a☆ ἀνθρώπων ] | ὃς | οὐ |
| estin | anthrōpos | anthrōpōn | hos | ou |
| is | man | [ of men ] | who | not |

| 1091.3 verb 3sing indic pres act | 3450.12 art acc sing fem | 2162.1 name-adj gen pl masc | 4032.4 noun acc sing fem | 3373.1 noun acc sing masc |
|---|---|---|---|---|
| γινώσκει | τὴν | Ἐφεσίων | πόλιν | νεωκόρον |
| ginōskei | tēn | Ephesiōn | polin | neōkoron |
| knows | the | of Ephesians | city | temple keepers |

35.b.**Txt:** 020L,025P,byz.
**Var:** 01ℵ,02A,03B,05D 08E,sa.bo.Gries,Lach Treg,Alf,Word,Tisc We/Ho,Weis,Sod UBS/☆

| 1498.29 verb acc sing fem part pres act | 3450.10 art gen sing fem | 3144.10 adj gen sing fem | 2276.1 noun gen sing fem | 730.2 name gen fem |
|---|---|---|---|---|
| οὖσαν | τῆς | μεγάλης | ⸂b θεᾶς ⸃ | Ἀρτέμιδος |
| ousan | tēs | megalēs | theas | Artemidos |
| being | of the | great | goddess | Artemis, |

Perhaps the Jews thought the name Alexander, with its reference to Alexander the Great, would command some respect from these Greek-speaking Ephesians. At least, his oratory would impress them. Some believe this Alexander was the same as Alexander the coppersmith named by Paul in 2 Timothy 4:14,15. The Greek indicates he was a worker in copper, bronze, iron, and other metals. Secular Greek literature shows these metalsmiths also made idols, though Alexander as a Jew would not have done so. However, if this Alexander was indeed a coppersmith, it may be another reason why the Jews put him forward. As a fellow metal worker, he would be known by the silversmiths who had started this riot and hopefully might be able to influence them.

**19:34.** Alexander did not get an opportunity to use his talents. They immediately recognized he was a Jew. Then the whole crowd went wild. With one voice they kept crying for about 2 hours, "Great is Diana (Artemis) of the Ephesians." This image and temple which was such a great source of civic pride to the Ephesians was being threatened, and they became more and more vociferous in proclaiming its greatness.

Actually, in spite of all their shouting, the greatness of Diana (Artemis) of the Ephesians had already begun its decline through Paul's preaching, and nothing would be able to stop it. In time, the pilgrims to the Temple of Artemis came in ever fewer numbers, while the church in Ephesus continued to flourish. Christian tradition tells us the apostle John spent many years in Ephesus in the latter part of his life and wrote his Gospel and Epistles there.

In A.D. 262 the Temple of Diana (Artemis) was again burned, and this time it was never rebuilt. Its influence was gone. Later, Ephesus was such a prominent Christian city that in A.D. 341 a great Council of the Church was held there.

**19:35.** After 2 hours of shouting, the frenzy of the mob began to wane. Finally the town clerk (the secretary of the city) quieted (subdued) the crowd. The town clerk was a citizen of Ephesus. He was the official contact or liaison with the Roman government officials in Ephesus. Thus, he probably had a responsibility to the Romans to help keep order.

When the crowd was quiet he addressed them as men of Ephesus and asked, "Who is there of mankind who does not know the city of Ephesus is the temple keeper (literally, the temple sweeper) of the great Artemis, even the one fallen from the sky (or, from the sky gods)?"

It is probable that a large stone meteor was used as the pedestal for the image of the goddess, since the image itself was originally of wood. However, some of the earlier Greek writers speak of the images of their gods as fallen from heaven, so this may have been fairly common for heathen to use meteorites as pedestals or as a part of the statue or image of their gods.

**And Alexander beckoned with the hand:** . . . motioning with his hand to get silence, *Weymouth.*

**and would have made his defence unto the people:** . . . wanted to defend himself before the people, *Moffatt* . . . to show that he wanted to speak in their defence to the people, *TCNT* . . . tried to give an account of himself, *Knox* . . . because he wanted to explain things to the people, *NCV.*

**34. But when they knew that he was a Jew:** But when they perceived that he was a Jew, *ASV* . . . But recognizing, *Rotherham* . . . No sooner, however, did they see that he was a Jew, *Weymouth.*

**all with one voice about the space of two hours cried out:** . . . one cry broke from them all, and they continued shouting for two hours, *TCNT* . . . then there arose from them all one roar of shouting, lasting about two hours, *Weymouth* . . . they shouted as one man for about two hours, *Phillips.*

**Great is Diana of the Ephesians:** Glory to Artemis, *Noli* . . . Great Artemis of Ephesus! *Williams.*

**35. And when the townclerk:** . . . the chancellor, *Campbell* . . . The Mayor, *TCNT* . . . the main city official, *SEB* . . . the chief secretary, *BB.*

**had appeased the people, he said:** . . . having calmed the multitude, *Rotherham* . . . brought some order in the crowd, *Berkeley* . . . restored quiet among the crowd, *Knox* . . . succeeded in quieting, *Noli.*

**Ye men of Ephesus:** Ephesians, *Rotherham* . . . Gentlemen of Ephesus, *Phillips.*

**what man is there that knoweth not:** . . . who is there of mankind that doth not acknowledge, *Rotherham* . . . who in the world could be ignorant of the fact, *Phillips.*

**how that the city of the Ephesians is a worshipper of the great goddess Diana:** . . . that this city of Ephesus is the Warden of the temple of the great Artemis, *TCNT* . . . is guardian, *Alford* . . . a devotee, *Young* . . . is the custodian of, *Adams.*

| 2504.1 conj | 3450.2 art gen sing | 1350.1 name-adj gen neu | 367.1 adj gen pl neu | 3631.1 partic |
|---|---|---|---|---|
| καὶ | τοῦ | Διοπετοῦς; | 36. ἀναντιῤῥήτων | οὖν |
| *kai* | *tou* | *Diopetous* | *anantirrhētōn* | *oun* |
| and | of the | fallen from Zeus? | Undeniable | therefore |

| 1498.20 verb gen pl part pres act | 3642.2 dem-pron gen pl | 1158.3 verb sing neu part pres act | 1498.4 verb 3sing indic pres act | 5050.4 prs-pron acc 2pl |
|---|---|---|---|---|
| ὄντων | τούτων | δέον | ἐστὶν | ὑμᾶς |
| *ontōn* | *toutōn* | *deon* | *estin* | *humas* |
| being | these things | being necessary | it is | for you |

| 2657.2 verb acc pl masc part perf mid | 5062.11 verb inf pres act | 2504.1 conj | 3235.6 num card neu | 4171.2 adj sing neu |
|---|---|---|---|---|
| κατεσταλμένους | ὑπάρχειν, | καὶ | μηδὲν | προπετὲς |
| *katestalmenous* | *huparchein* | *kai* | *mēden* | *propetes* |
| having been calmed | to be, | and | nothing | reckless |

| 4097.12 verb inf pres act | 4097.13 verb inf pres act | 70.9 verb 2pl indic aor act | 1056.1 conj | 3450.8 art acc pl masc |
|---|---|---|---|---|
| ʻ πράττειν. | [☆ πράσσειν. ] | 37. ἠγάγετε | γὰρ | τοὺς |
| *prattein* | *prassein* | *ēgagete* | *gar* | *tous* |
| to do. | [ idem ] | You brought | for | the |

| 433.9 noun acc pl masc | 3642.8 dem-pron acc pl masc | 3641.1 conj | 2392.1 adj acc pl masc | 3641.1 conj |
|---|---|---|---|---|
| ἄνδρας | τούτους, | οὔτε | ἱεροσύλους | οὔτε |
| *andras* | *toutous* | *oute* | *hierosulous* | *oute* |
| men | these, | neither | temple plunderers | nor |

| 980.6 verb acc pl masc part pres act | 3450.12 art acc sing fem | 2276.2 noun acc sing fem | 2296.4 noun acc sing masc | 5050.2 prs-pron gen 2pl |
|---|---|---|---|---|
| βλασφημοῦντας | τὴν | ʻ θεὰν | [a☆ θεὸν ] | ʻ ὑμῶν. |
| *blasphēmountas* | *tēn* | *thean* | *theon* | *humōn* |
| blaspheming | the | goddess | [ god ] | your. |

| 2231.2 prs-pron gen 1pl | 1479.1 conj | 3173.1 conj | 3631.1 partic | 1210.1 name nom masc | 2504.1 conj |
|---|---|---|---|---|---|
| [b☆ ἡμῶν. ] | 38. εἰ | μὲν | οὖν | Δημήτριος | καὶ |
| *hēmōn* | *ei* | *men* | *oun* | *Dēmētrios* | *kai* |
| [ our. ] | If | indeed | therefore | Demetrius | and |

| 3450.7 art nom pl masc | 4713.1 prep | 840.4 prs-pron dat sing | 4927.2 noun nom pl masc | 4242.1 prep | 4948.5 indef-pron | 3030.4 noun acc sing masc |
|---|---|---|---|---|---|---|
| οἱ | σὺν | αὐτῷ | τεχνῖται | ʻ πρός | τινα | λόγον |
| *hoi* | *sun* | *autō* | *technitai* | *pros* | *tina* | *logon* |
| the | with | him | craftsmen | against | anyone | a matter |

| 2174.6 verb 3pl indic pres act | 2174.51 verb 3pl indic pres act | 4242.1 prep | 4948.5 indef-pron | 3030.4 noun acc sing masc | 59.2 adj nom pl fem |
|---|---|---|---|---|---|
| ἔχουσιν, | [☆ ἔχουσι | πρός | τινα | λόγον, ] | ἀγοραῖοι |
| *echousin* | *echousi* | *pros* | *tina* | *logon* | *agoraioi* |
| have, | [ have | against | anyone | a matter, ] | courts |

| 70.20 verb 3pl indic pres mid | 2504.1 conj | 444.4 noun nom pl masc | 1498.7 verb 3pl indic pres act | 1451.1 verb 3pl impr pres act |
|---|---|---|---|---|
| ἄγονται, | καὶ | ἀνθύπατοί | εἰσιν· | ἐγκαλείτωσαν |
| *agontai* | *kai* | *anthupatoi* | *eisin* | *enkaleitōsan* |
| are being held, | and | proconsuls | there are: | let them accuse |

| 238.2 prs-pron dat pl | 1479.1 conj | 1156.2 conj | 4948.10 indef-pron sing neu | 3875.1 prep |
|---|---|---|---|---|
| ἀλλήλοις. | 39. εἰ | δέ | τι | ʻ περὶ |
| *allēlois* | *ei* | *de* | *ti* | *peri* |
| one another. | If | but | anything | concerning |

37.a.**Txt:** 05D-corr 08E-corr,025P,Steph **Var:** 01ℵ,02A,03B 05D-corr,08E-org,020L Gries,Lach,Treg,Alf Word,Tisc,We/Ho,Weis Sod,UBS/☆

37.b.**Txt:** 08E-org,020L 025P,1241,byz.bo. **Var:** p74,01ℵ,02A,03B 05D,08E-corr,044,sa. Lach,Treg,Alf,Tisc We/Ho,Weis,Sod UBS/☆

**19:36.** The town clerk then argued there was no reason to be so upset and excited since the greatness and reputation of the image, in his opinion, were undeniable. Therefore, it was their duty to quiet down. It would be wrong to do anything rash (impulsive, reckless, or in thoughtless haste).

**19:37.** The town clerk also pointed out that the men they had brought into the amphitheater were neither temple robbers (or sacrilegious), nor were they blasphemers of their goddess. Although Paul had been nearly 3 years in Ephesus, there was no evidence that either he or the Christians ever said anything bad or scurrilous against the temple or the goddess. They simply kept preaching the good news of Jesus Christ. However, Paul certainly confronted the idolatry and heathen practices he observed on his missionary journeys (see 14:15 and 17:22-31, for example). He was not afraid to preach against sin and false religions.

The KJV translation "robbers of churches" is one word in the Greek, *hierosulos.* It was used literally of those taking the gold vessels, the funds, or the sacred books from a temple (Greek, *hieron*). It was also used for sacrilege in general. Here the town clerk obviously means sacrilege in general. He thus declared that Paul and his associates had not committed any offense against their religion or their goddess.

Temple robbery and sacrilege against a temple were considered very serious offenses by the Greeks and Romans. They put them in the same class as treason and murder. Paul in Romans 2:22 includes it in a list with robbery and adultery.

For the Christian this is significant, for our bodies are temples of the Holy Spirit. Fornication (including adultery and all other types of sexual immorality) is a sin against the temple of the Holy Spirit. (See 1 Corinthians 6:13-20.) When believers meet together they are together the temple of the Holy Spirit. Anyone who brings division or a party spirit into the Body is also committing sacrilege (1 Corinthians 3:3,16,17).

**19:38.** The town clerk then proceeded to call for law and order. The court days were kept regularly in the marketplace. He implied also that the courts were in session at that very time. The proconsuls were available. (The plural is general and does not mean there was more than one at a time.) The proconsul was the governor appointed by the Roman Senate for provinces under their jurisdiction (rather than under the jurisdiction of the emperor). Thus the governor would be there to give judgment. If Demetrius and his fellow craftsmen had a case against anyone, let them bring their charges or accusations against "one another" (in a lawful way).

**19:39.** If anyone wanted to seek anything (of public concern) beyond that, or there was anything further they wanted to know

**and of the image which fell down from Jupiter?:** . . . we also keep her holy stone, *NCV* . . . statue which fell down from Zeus, *TCNT* . . . that descended from heaven? *Murdock* . . . which is Jupiter's offspring! *Knox.*

**36. Seeing then that these things cannot be spoken against:** . . . be contradicted, *RSV* . . . are undeniable facts, *TCNT* . . . is beyond question, *Moffatt* . . . being incontrovertible, *Worrell* . . . No one can say that this is not true, *NCV.*

**ye ought to be quiet:** . . . you ought to keep calm, *TCNT* . . . to maintain your self-control, *Weymouth* . . . compose yourselves, *Berkeley* . . . to be tranquil, *Murdock* . . . you must preserve order, *Noli.*

**and do nothing rashly:** . . . and not act recklessly, *Weymouth* . . . and do nothing unwise, *BB* . . . You must stop and think before you do anything, *NCV.*

**37. For ye have brought hither these men:**

**which are neither robbers of churches:** . . . have not stolen anything from her temple, *NCV* . . . who are neither sacrilegious, *RSV* . . . temple destroyers, *Berkeley.*

**nor yet blasphemers of your goddess:** . . . nor insulters of, *Berkeley* . . . have not said anything evil against, *NCV.*

**38. Wherefore if Demetrius, and the craftsmen which are with him:** . . . the artisans, *TCNT* . . . and his fellow tradesmen, *Moffatt.*

**have a matter against any man:** . . . have a charge to make against anyone, *TCNT* . . . have a ground of complaint, *Fenton.*

**the law is open:** They can press charges, *NIV* . . . the courts are in session, *Adams.*

**and there are deputies:** . . . appointed judges, *Alford* . . . Magistrates, *TCNT.*

**let them implead one another:** . . . let both parties take legal proceedings, *TCNT* . . . let them go to law, *Williams.*

**39. But if ye enquire any thing concerning other matters:** But if you want some other matter cleared up, *Norlie.*

## Acts 19:40

39.a.**Txt:** 01א,02A,05D 020L,025P,byz.sa.bo. Tisc
**Var:** p74,03B,33,Lach Treg,We/Ho,Weis,Sod UBS/☆

| **2066.3** adj gen pl | **3870.1** adv comp | **1919.4** verb 2pl indic pres act | **1706.1** prep | **3450.11** art dat sing fem |
|---|---|---|---|---|
| ἑτέρων | [a☆ περαιτέρω ] | ἐπιζητεῖτε, | ἐν | τῇ |
| *heterōn* | *peraiterō* | *epizēteite* | *en* | *tē* |
| other matters | [ further matters ] | you inquire, | in | the |

| **1756.2** adj dat sing fem | **1564.3** noun dat sing fem | **1941.2** verb 3sing indic fut pass | **2504.1** conj | **1056.1** conj |
|---|---|---|---|---|
| ἐννόμῳ | ἐκκλησίᾳ | ἐπιλυθήσεται. | **40.** καὶ | γὰρ |
| *ennomō* | *ekklēsia* | *epiluthēsetai* | *kai* | *gar* |
| lawful | assembly | it shall be solved. | Also | for |

| **2765.2** verb 1pl indic pres act | **1451.6** verb inf pres mid | **4565.2** noun gen sing fem | **3875.1** prep | **3450.10** art gen sing fem |
|---|---|---|---|---|
| κινδυνεύομεν | ἐγκαλεῖσθαι | στάσεως | περὶ | τῆς |
| *kinduneuomen* | *enkaleisthai* | *staseōs* | *peri* | *tēs* |
| we are in danger | to be accused | of rioting | in regard to | the |

| **4449.1** adv | **3235.1** num card gen | **157.2** adj gen sing neu | **5062.5** verb gen sing part pres act | **3875.1** prep |
|---|---|---|---|---|
| σήμερον, | μηδενὸς | αἰτίου | ὑπάρχοντος | περὶ |
| *sēmeron* | *mēdenos* | *aitiou* | *huparchontos* | *peri* |
| day, | not one | cause | existing | concerning |

40.a.**Var:** 01א,02A,03B 020L,025P,byz.Treg,Alf Tisc,We/Ho,Weis,Sod UBS/☆

| **3614.2** rel-pron gen sing | **3620.3** partic | **1404.31** verb 1pl indic fut mid | **586.14** verb inf aor act | **3030.4** noun acc sing masc |
|---|---|---|---|---|
| οὗ | [a☆+ οὐ ] | δυνησόμεθα | ἀποδοῦναι | λόγον |
| *hou* | *ou* | *dunēsometha* | *apodounai* | *logon* |
| which | [ not ] | we shall be able | to give | a reason |

40.b.**Var:** 01א,02A,03B 08E,33,Lach,Treg We/Ho,Weis,Sod UBS/☆

| **3875.1** prep | **3450.10** art gen sing fem | **4815.1** noun gen sing fem | **3642.10** dem-pron gen sing fem | **2504.1** conj |
|---|---|---|---|---|
| [b☆+ περὶ ] | τῆς | συστροφῆς | ταύτης. | **41.** Καὶ |
| *peri* | *tēs* | *sustrophēs* | *tautēs* | *Kai* |
| [ concerning ] | the | mob | this. | And |

| **3642.18** dem-pron pl neu | **1500.15** verb nom sing masc part aor act | **624.6** verb 3sing indic aor act | **3450.12** art acc sing fem | **1564.4** noun acc sing fem |
|---|---|---|---|---|
| ταῦτα | εἰπών, | ἀπέλυσεν | τὴν | ἐκκλησίαν. |
| *tauta* | *eipōn* | *apelusen* | *tēn* | *ekklēsian* |
| these things | having said, | he dismissed | the | assembly. |

| **3196.3** prep | **1156.2** conj | **3450.16** art sing neu | **3835.8** verb inf aor mid | **3450.6** art acc sing masc | **2328.3** noun acc sing masc |
|---|---|---|---|---|---|
| **20:1.** Μετὰ | δὲ | τὸ | παύσασθαι | τὸν | θόρυβον, |
| *Meta* | *de* | *to* | *pausasthai* | *ton* | *thorubon* |
| After | but | the | to cease | the | tumult, |

1.a.**Txt:** 02A,05D,020L 025P,byz.
**Var:** 01א,03B,08E,sa.bo. Treg,Tisc,We/Ho,Weis Sod,UBS/☆

| **4200.4** verb nom sing masc part aor mid | **3213.8** verb nom sing masc part aor mid | **3450.5** art nom sing masc |
|---|---|---|
| ʽ προσκαλεσάμενος | [a☆ μεταπεμψάμενος ] | ὁ |
| *proskalesamenos* | *metapempsamenos* | *ho* |
| having called to | [ idem ] | |

1.b.**Var:** 01א,02A,03B 08E,33,Lach,Treg,Alf Tisc,We/Ho,Weis,Sod UBS/☆

| **3834.1** name nom masc | **3450.8** art acc pl masc | **3073.8** noun acc pl masc | **2504.1** conj | **3731.17** verb nom sing masc part aor act |
|---|---|---|---|---|
| Παῦλος | τοὺς | μαθητὰς, | καὶ | [b☆+ παρακαλέσας, ] |
| *Paulos* | *tous* | *mathētas* | *kai* | *parakalesas* |
| Paul | the | disciples, | and | [ having encouraged, ] |

1.c.**Txt:** 020L,025P,byz.
**Var:** 01א,02A,03B,08E 33,Lach,Treg,Tisc We/Ho,Weis,Sod UBS/☆

| **776.10** verb nom sing masc part aor mid | **1814.3** verb 3sing indic aor act | **4057.29** verb inf aor pass | **4057.15** verb inf pres mid |
|---|---|---|---|
| ἀσπασάμενος, | ἐξῆλθεν | ʽ πορευθῆναι | [c☆ πορεύεσθαι ] |
| *aspasamenos* | *exēlthen* | *poreuthēnai* | *poreuesthai* |
| having greeted, | went away | to go | [ idem ] |

or discuss, it should be explained in the legal (duly constituted) assembly (Greek, *ekklēsia,* the word usually translated "church"), that is, not in a riotous gathering (*ekklēsia*) like this. In other words, a disorganized, tumultuous assembly was no proper place for deciding anything that affected the public welfare or the city's well-being.

**it shall be determined in a lawful assembly:** . . . it shall be settled in the regular assembly, *ASV* . . . settled in a lawful assembly, *Adams* . . . It can be decided at the regular town meeting of the people, *NCV.*

**19:40.** The clerk was actually upset about this riot for it put the city in danger of having a charge of sedition, rebellion, or revolution brought against it. This kind of uprising would run the very real risk of having the Roman government discipline them. In the Roman ruler's eyes, there would be no reason or excuse for the events of the day. They could give no account for this wild assemblage, which the Romans could take as a seditious meeting or conspiracy.

The Romans at this point in their history were very proud of what they called the *pax romana* or Roman peace. They did not tolerate any kind of uprising, or rebellion, or rioting, whatever the cause. In fact, since most rebellion and mob action was directed against the Roman government, they treated everything of that nature as political and as a breach of the Roman peace. They would not understand that this riot was over a purely religious matter.

**40. For we are in danger to be called in question for this day's uproar:** For in connection with today's proceedings there is danger of our being charged with attempted insurrection, *Weymouth* . . . of being accused of revolt, *Rotherham* . . . we run the risk of being accused of rioting, *Noli* . . . as seditious, *Murdock* . . . to be questioned for sedition concerning this day, *Wesley* . . . of starting a rebellion, *Klingensmith.*

**there being no cause whereby we may give an account of this concourse:** . . . we shall be at a loss to give any reason for this disorderly gathering, *TCNT* . . . there having been no real reason for this riot; nor shall we be able to justify the behaviour of this disorderly mob, *Weymouth* . . . particularly as we have no real excuse to offer for this commotion, *Phillips* . . . we cannot give any justifiable reason, *Norlie* . . . been tumultuous without a cause, *Murdock* . . . this disorderly riot, *Wuest* . . . no culprit whom we can hold liable, *Confraternity.*

**19:41.** After having said these things, the town clerk dismissed the assembly (Greek, *ekklēsia*). Thus, they had to release Paul's companions, Gaius and Aristarchus. Just as Paul's Roman citizenship was useful in giving him further opportunities to spread the gospel, so Roman concern for law and order and for keeping the peace proved helpful to the church.

**41. And when he had thus spoken:** With these words, *TCNT.*

**he dismissed the assembly:** . . . he told the people to go home, *NCV.*

**20:1.** Part of the pressure on Paul in Ephesus was his care or deep concern for all the churches. His letters to the Corinthians show he was especially concerned about those in Macedonia and Greece. (See 2 Corinthians 11:28; 12:20.) He had already sent Timothy and Erastus to Macedonia. Now it was time for Paul himself to go there.

After the riot stirred up by the makers of the silver shrines was over, and all the noise had ceased, Paul sent for the disciples (the Ephesian believers) and exhorted or encouraged them. He wanted them to live holy lives and be faithful to the Lord (as the practical sections of all his epistles show). Then, after saying his farewells, he left and went to Macedonia. This was probably the last time he would see this body of believers. When he passed by Ephesus on the way back to Jerusalem later, he only stopped at the seaport and sent for the elders of the assembly.

**1. And after the uproar was ceased:** When the tumult had been quieted down, *Berkeley* . . . After this disturbance died down, *Phillips* . . . When the riot, *Kleist* . . . had subsided, *Adams* . . . was allayed, *Sawyer.*

**Paul called unto him the disciples:** Paul invited the disciples to see him, *Berkeley.*

**and embraced them:** . . . and, with encouraging words, bade them goodbye, *TCNT* . . . and having exhorted and embraced them, *HBIE* . . . he spoke many heartening words, *Phillips.*

**and departed for to go into Macedonia:** . . . and started on his journey to Macedonia, *TCNT* . . . and left for, *Berkeley.*

## Acts 20:2

1.d.**Txt:** 02A,025P,byz.
**Var:** 01ℵ,03B,05D,08E
020L,Lach,Treg,Tisc
We/Ho,Weis,Sod
UBS/☆

| **1519.1** prep | **3450.12** art acc sing fem | **3081.4** name acc fem | **1324.5** verb nom sing masc part aor act | **1156.2** conj |
|---|---|---|---|---|
| εἰς | ⸂d τὴν ⸃ | Μακεδονίαν. | 2. διελθὼν | δὲ |
| *eis* | *tēn* | *Makedonian* | *dielthōn* | *de* |
| to | | Macedonia. | Having passed through | and |

| **3450.17** art pl neu | **3183.4** noun pl neu | **1552.17** dem-pron pl neu | **2504.1** conj | **3731.17** verb nom sing masc part aor act | **840.8** prs-pron acc pl masc |
|---|---|---|---|---|---|
| τὰ | μέρη | ἐκεῖνα, | καὶ | παρακαλέσας | αὐτοὺς |
| *ta* | *merē* | *ekeina* | *kai* | *parakalesas* | *autous* |
| the | parts | those, | and | having encouraged | them |

| **3030.3** noun dat sing masc | **4044.3** adj dat sing | **2048.3** verb 3sing indic aor act | **1519.1** prep | **3450.12** art acc sing fem | **1658.1** name acc fem |
|---|---|---|---|---|---|
| λόγῳ | πολλῷ, | ἦλθεν | εἰς | τὴν | Ἑλλάδα· |
| *logō* | *pollō* | *elthen* | *eis* | *tēn* | *Hellada* |
| with discourse | much, | he came | to | | Greece. |

| **4020.37** verb nom sing masc part aor act | **4885.1** conj | **3243.4** noun acc pl masc | **4980.1** num card nom | **1090.57** verb gen sing fem part aor mid |
|---|---|---|---|---|
| 3. ποιήσας | τε | μῆνας | τρεῖς | γενομένης |
| *poiēsas* | *te* | *mēnas* | *treis* | *genomenēs* |
| Having continued | and | months | three, | having been made |

| **840.4** prs-pron dat sing | **1902.2** noun gen sing fem | **1902.2** noun gen sing fem | **840.4** prs-pron dat sing | **5097.3** prep | **3450.1** art gen pl |
|---|---|---|---|---|---|
| ⸂ αὐτῷ | ἐπιβουλῆς | [☆ ἐπιβουλῆς | αὐτῷ ] | ὑπὸ | τῶν |
| *autō* | *epiboulēs* | *epiboulēs* | *autō* | *hupo* | *tōn* |
| against him | a plot | [ a plot | against him ] | by | the |

| **2428.3** name-adj gen pl masc | **3165.10** verb dat sing part pres act | **319.5** verb inf pres mid | **1519.1** prep | **3450.12** art acc sing fem | **4799.2** name acc fem |
|---|---|---|---|---|---|
| Ἰουδαίων | μέλλοντι | ἀνάγεσθαι | εἰς | τὴν | Συρίαν, |
| *Ioudaiōn* | *mellonti* | *anagesthai* | *eis* | *tēn* | *Surian* |
| Jews | being about | to sail | into | | Syria, |

3.a.**Txt:** 03B-corr,020L
025P,byz.
**Var:** 01ℵ,02A,03B-org
08E,33,Treg,Alf,Tisc
We/Ho,Weis,Sod
UBS/☆

| **1090.33** verb 3sing indic aor mid | **1100.1** noun nom sing fem | **1100.2** noun gen sing fem | **3450.2** art gen sing | **5128.4** verb inf pres act |
|---|---|---|---|---|
| ἐγένετο | ⸂ γνώμη | [a☆ γνώμης ] | τοῦ | ὑποστρέφειν |
| *egeneto* | *gnōmē* | *gnōmēs* | *tou* | *hupostrephein* |
| arose | a decision | [ idem ] | the | to return |

4.a.**Txt:** 02A,08E,020L
025P,044,byz.Sod
**Var:** p74,01ℵ,03B,33,sa.
bo.Tisc,We/Ho,Weis
UBS/☆

| **1217.2** prep | **3081.2** name gen fem | **4752.1** verb 3sing indic imperf mid | **1156.2** conj | **840.4** prs-pron dat sing |
|---|---|---|---|---|
| διὰ | Μακεδονίας. | 4. συνείπετο | δὲ | αὐτῷ |
| *dia* | *Makedonias* | *suneipeto* | *de* | *autō* |
| through | Macedonia. | Was accompanying | and | him |

4.b.**Var:** p74,01ℵ,02A
03B,05D,08E,it.sa.bo.
Gries,Lach,Treg,Alf
Word,Tisc,We/Ho,Weis
Sod,UBS/☆

| **884.2** conj | **3450.10** art gen sing fem | **767.2** name gen fem | **4838.1** name nom masc | **4308.1** name gen masc |
|---|---|---|---|---|
| ⸂a ἄχρι | τῆς | Ἀσίας ⸃ | Σώπατρος | [b☆+ Πύῤῥου ] |
| *achri* | *tēs* | *Asias* | *Sōpatros* | *Purrhou* |
| as far as | | Asia | Sopater | [ of Pyrrhus ] |

| **954.1** name-adj nom sing masc | **2308.2** name-adj gen pl masc | **1156.2** conj | **702.1** name nom masc | **2504.1** conj |
|---|---|---|---|---|
| Βεροιαῖος· | Θεσσαλονικέων | δὲ | Ἀρίσταρχος | καὶ |
| *Beroiaios* | *Thessalonikeōn* | *de* | *Aristarchos* | *kai* |
| a Berean, | of Thessalonians | and | Aristarchus | and |

| **4435.1** name nom masc | **2504.1** conj | **1043.3** name nom masc | **1184.1** name-adj nom sing masc | **2504.1** conj | **4943.1** name nom masc |
|---|---|---|---|---|---|
| Σεκοῦνδος, | καὶ | Γάϊος | Δερβαῖος | καὶ | Τιμόθεος· |
| *Sekoundos* | *kai* | *Gaios* | *Derbaios* | *kai* | *Timotheos* |
| Secundus, | and | Gaius | of Derbe | and | Timothy, |

**20:2.** It is probable that Paul went to Macedonia by way of Troas where the Lord opened a door for him to minister the Word and where he hoped to find Titus (2 Corinthians 2:13). Titus, however, was not there, and Paul went on to Philippi. He did not have an easy time there. He was hard-pressed (afflicted), distressed on every side with fightings (strife, disputes) on the outside and fears within. But then Titus did come with good news of the concern and prayers of the Corinthians for him (2 Corinthians 7:6,7).

During the summer and fall Paul went through the various churches in Macedonia, giving them much exhortation (and encouragement), or, as the Greek says, he exhorted (encouraged) them with much discourse. Probably he also visited the cities west of those visited on the previous journey, since in Romans 15:19 he wrote he "fully preached the gospel" as far as Illyricum (Dalmatia) on the northwest side of Macedonia. The Acts account gives no details, but it is possible he made a journey into the mountainous region of Illyricum or to its coastal cities that were related to or even technically parts of Macedonia. Then, after a rather thorough tour of Macedonia, he went down to Greece.

**20:3.** Paul spent the 3 winter months of A.D. 56–57 in Greece. Most of this time was probably spent in Corinth. Titus had told him of their "fervent mind" toward him, that is, their ardor on Paul's behalf (2 Corinthians 7:7). Paul's letters to the Corinthians show how concerned he was about them and their problems.

Paul was also concerned about the offering which was to be taken to the poor saints (believers) in Jerusalem. While in Macedonia he had used the generosity of the Corinthians to encourage the churches there to give. But when the Corinthians fell behind in their giving, Paul wrote to them, reminding them of God's law of sowing and reaping (2 Corinthians 9:5,6).

Just as he was about to go to Syria, the unbelieving Jews formed a plot against him. So Paul changed his plans. Instead of taking a ship from Greece, he was counseled to return through Macedonia.

**20:4.** Seven men who were accompanying Paul into the Roman province of Asia apparently took the ship as originally planned. These seven included Sopater (also called Sosipater), the son of Pyrrhus of Beroea and therefore one of those who "searched the Scriptures"; Aristarchus, the Macedonian from Thessalonica who had been with Paul at Ephesus; Secundus, also from Thessalonica; Gaius of Derbe; Timothy, Paul's assistant from Lystra; Tychicus, from the province of Asia; and Trophimus, a Gentile Christian from Ephesus.

Many writers believe at least some of these men took the journey to represent the churches who gave money as an offering for the poor among the Jerusalem Christians (1 Corinthians 16:3; see also Acts 19:29; 27:2; Colossians 4:10; Ephesians 6:21,22; 2 Timothy 4:20). They were to see what was done with the money and report to their home churches.

**2. And when he had gone over those parts:** After going through those districts, *TCNT* . . . As he made his journey through those districts, *Phillips* . . . He traveled through all that region, *Noli* . . . As he went through those parts of the country, *NLT.*

**and had given them much exhortation:** . . . and exhorting them with much discourse, *Rotherham* . . . and speaking many encouraging words to the disciples, *TCNT* . . . and encouraging the brethren with many suggestions, *Berkeley* . . . with his sermons, *Noli* . . . he spoke words of comfort and help, *NLT* . . . He said many things to strengthen the followers, *NCV* . . . in a long speech, *MLNT.*

**he came into Greece:** Then he went on to, *NLT* . . . then he entered, *Knox.*

**3. And there abode three months:** . . . where he stayed three months, *TCNT.*

**And when the Jews laid wait for him:** . . . and a plot was laid against him by the Jews, *ASV* . . . The Jews having planned to waylay him, *Weymouth* . . . were planning something against him, *NCV* . . . had made a plan to take him, *NLT.*

**as he was about to sail into Syria:** Just as he was going to sail for Syria, *Goodspeed* . . . on the point of taking ship for Syria, *Weymouth* . . . As he was about to get on a ship for the country of, *NLT* . . . he was meaning to take ship for, *Knox* . . . of setting sail for, *Phillips.*

**he purposed to return through Macedonia:** . . . he changed his mind, *Williams* . . . changed his plans and went back through, *NLT* . . . so he decided to return by way of Macedonia, *TCNT* . . . So he resolved to return, *Kleist* . . . to make his way back through, *Phillips.*

**4. And there accompanied him into Asia Sopater of Berea:** He was accompanied by, *TCNT* . . . Some men were going along with him, *NLT.*

**and of the Thessalonians, Aristarchus and Secundus:** . . . of the city of, *NLT.*

**and Gaius of Derbe, and Timotheus:**

| 768.1 name nom pl masc | 1156.2 conj | 5031.1 name nom masc | 2504.1 conj | 5002.1 name nom masc | 3642.7 dem-pron nom pl masc |
|---|---|---|---|---|---|
| ᾿Ασιανοὶ | δὲ | Τυχικὸς | καὶ | Τρόφιμος. | 5. οὗτοι |
| *Asianoi* | *de* | *Tuchikos* | *kai* | *Trophimos* | *houtoi* |
| of Asia | and | Tychicus | and | Trophimus. | These |

5.a.**Var:** 01ℵ,02A,03B 08E,33,bo.Lach,Treg Alf,Tisc,We/Ho,Weis Sod,UBS/☆

5.b.**Txt:** p74,03B-corr2 05D,36,104,1891 **Var:** 01ℵ,02A,03B-org 08E,015H,020L,044 1739

| 1156.2 conj | 4140.4 verb nom pl masc part aor act | 4193.5 verb nom pl masc part aor act | 3176.30 verb 3pl indic imperf act |
|---|---|---|---|
| [a☆+ δὲ ] | ‘ προελθόντες | [b προσελθόντες ] | ἔμενον |
| *de* | *proelthontes* | *proselthontes* | *emenon* |
| [ and ] | having gone before | [ having approached ] | were waiting for |

| 2231.4 prs-pron acc 1pl | 1706.1 prep | 5015.2 name dat fem | 2231.1 prs-pron nom 1pl | 1156.2 conj | 1589.1 verb 1pl indic aor act |
|---|---|---|---|---|---|
| ἡμᾶς | ἐν | Τρῳάδι· | 6. ἡμεῖς | δὲ | ἐξεπλεύσαμεν |
| *hēmas* | *en* | *Trōadi* | *hēmeis* | *de* | *exepleusamen* |
| us | in | Troas; | we | but | sailed away |

| 3196.3 prep | 3450.15 art acc pl fem | 2232.1 noun fem | 3450.1 art gen pl | 105.3 adj gen pl neu | 570.3 prep |
|---|---|---|---|---|---|
| μετὰ | τὰς | ἡμέρας | τῶν | ἀζύμων | ἀπὸ |
| *meta* | *tas* | *hēmeras* | *tōn* | *azumōn* | *apo* |
| after | the | days | of the | unleavened bread | from |

| 5212.1 name gen masc | 2504.1 conj | 2048.4 verb 1pl indic aor act | 4242.1 prep | 840.8 prs-pron acc pl masc | 1519.1 prep | 3450.12 art acc sing fem |
|---|---|---|---|---|---|---|
| Φιλίππων, | καὶ | ἤλθομεν | πρὸς | αὐτοὺς | εἰς | τὴν |
| *Philippōn* | *kai* | *ēlthomen* | *pros* | *autous* | *eis* | *tēn* |
| Philippi, | and | came | to | them | in | |

| 5015.3 name acc fem | 884.1 conj | 884.2 conj | 2232.6 noun gen pl fem | 3864.1 num card | 3619.1 adv |
|---|---|---|---|---|---|
| Τρῳάδα | ‘ ἄχρις | [☆ ἄχρι ] | ἡμερῶν | πέντε, | ‘ οὗ |
| *Trōada* | *achris* | *achri* | *hēmerōn* | *pente* | *hou* |
| Troas | as far as | [ idem ] | days | five, | where |

6.a.**Txt:** 03B,020L,025P byz. **Var:** 01ℵ,02A,08E,Tisc We/Ho,Weis,Sod UBS/☆

| 3562.1 adv | 1298.2 verb 1pl indic aor act | 2232.1 noun fem | 2017.1 num card | 1706.1 prep | 1156.2 conj |
|---|---|---|---|---|---|
| [a ὅπου ] | διετρίψαμεν | ἡμέρας | ἑπτά. | 7. Ἐν | δὲ |
| *hopou* | *dietripsamen* | *hēmeras* | *hepta* | *En* | *de* |
| [ idem ] | we stayed | days | seven. | On | and |

| 3450.11 art dat sing fem | 1518.7 num card dat fem | 3450.1 art gen pl | 4378.4 noun gen pl neu | 4714.25 verb gen pl masc part perf mid |
|---|---|---|---|---|
| τῇ | μιᾷ | τῶν | σαββάτων, | συνηγμένων |
| *tē* | *mia* | *tōn* | *sabbatōn* | *sunēgmenōn* |
| the | first | of the | week, | having been assembled |

7.a.**Txt:** 020L,025P,byz. **Var:** 01ℵ,02A,03B,05D 08E,sa.Gries,Lach,Treg Alf,Word,Tisc,We/Ho Weis,Sod,UBS/☆

| 3450.1 art gen pl | 3073.6 noun gen pl masc | 3450.2 art gen sing | 2231.2 prs-pron gen 1pl | 2779.6 verb inf aor act | 735.4 noun acc sing masc |
|---|---|---|---|---|---|
| ‘ τῶν | μαθητῶν | τοῦ | [a☆ ἡμῶν ] | κλάσαι | ἄρτον, |
| *tōn* | *mathētōn* | *tou* | *hēmōn* | *klasai* | *arton* |
| the | disciples | the | [ us ] | to break | bread, |

| 3450.5 art nom sing masc | 3834.1 name nom masc | 1250.7 verb 3sing indic imperf mid | 840.2 prs-pron dat pl | 3165.12 verb nom sing masc part pres act |
|---|---|---|---|---|
| ὁ | Παῦλος | διελέγετο | αὐτοῖς, | μέλλων |
| *ho* | *Paulos* | *dielegeto* | *autois* | *mellōn* |
| | Paul | was speaking | to them, | being about |

| 1821.2 verb inf pres act | 3450.11 art dat sing fem | 1872.1 adv | 3766.1 verb 3sing indic imperf act | 4885.1 conj |
|---|---|---|---|---|
| ἐξιέναι | τῇ | ἐπαύριον, | παρέτεινέν | τε |
| *exienai* | *tē* | *epaurion* | *pareteinen* | *te* |
| to depart | on the | next day; | he was continuing | and |

The Early Church was very careful to keep good financial accounts and just as careful to make them known to the members of the congregation. There is no place where honesty, integrity, and openness are more important than in the distribution of funds given by God's people for the service of the Lord and His people.

**20:5.** These seven men went ahead of Paul by ship from Greece to Troas where they waited for Paul. Since Luke used the word "us" in this verse, it seems clear that he remained with Paul and journeyed back into Macedonia with him.

**20:6.** Paul and Luke arrived in Philippi in time for the Feast of Unleavened Bread in April of A.D. 57. Paul had found it necessary to leave Philippi rather abruptly after the conversion of the Philippian jailer. He probably visited it during the previous summer and fall of A.D. 56. Now he was able to spend some time again with the Philippian believers during this feast. (The Jews called the whole period of Passover and Unleavened Bread *Passover.* Perhaps Luke used the old name because Christ is the believer's Passover.)

Later, toward the end of Paul's first Roman imprisonment, Paul wrote his Epistle to the Philippians. This letter was partly in response to a gift sent by the Philippian church and brought by Epaphroditus (Philippians 4:10).

Paul made it clear that his real trust was in the Lord. He had learned to be content whatever his situation. He knew how to be humbled and have everything swept away without feeling the Lord had deserted him. He knew how to abound with material blessings and not feel he deserved them. Christ was his strength, his real source of supply. Yet this did not mean he appreciated the gifts of the Philippians any less. They did right to share with him in his affliction. But he appreciated their sympathetic interest even more. He saw that as a fruit of the Spirit.

After the 7 days of the feast, which the Jewish Christians undoubtedly still celebrated, Paul sailed from Philippi with Luke accompanying him. At Troas they met the others and remained there for 7 days.

**20:7.** At Troas Paul probably went to the synagogue on the Sabbath Day as was his custom. Then on the day following, that is, on Sunday evening (Luke used the Greek method of reckoning days, not the Jewish), the believers gathered with Paul and his company to break bread. This means they all brought food, shared a fellowship meal, and concluded with an observance of the Lord's Supper.

Paul took the opportunity to preach, that is, to conduct a discussion and converse with the people. Since he was going to leave the next day, he prolonged his discourse until midnight. What a wonderful time of fellowship and learning this must have been! Surely it was a joy to listen to Paul talk about the things of God and Christ. He probably dealt with their problems and answered



**and of Asia, Tychicus and Trophimus:** ... of the countries of, *NLT.*

**5. These going before tarried for us at Troas:** ... having gone before us, *PNT* ... These companions went on ahead, *NAB* ... These men went to Troas and waited for us there, *TCNT* ... The latter proceeded to, *Noli* ... These went on in advance, *TNT* ... went first, ahead of Paul, *Everyday* ... waiting for us in the city of, *SEB* ... This party proceeded to Troas to await us there, *Phillips.*

**6. And we sailed from Philippi after the days of unleavened bread:** ... after the Passover, *TCNT* ... after the Feast, *Everyday* ... after the Jewish Festival, *SEB* ... After the supper of bread without yeast we got on a ship in the city of, *NLT* ... and we sailed away from, *Worrell.*

**and came unto them to Troas in five days:** ... and joined them five days later, *TCNT* ... We met these men...It took five days to get there, *NLT.*

**where we abode seven days:** ... where we spent a week, *Phillips* ... where we stayed for a week, *TCNT* ... where we tarried, *Worrell.*

**7. And upon the first day of the week:** On Sunday, *Beck* ... on the first day of the sabbaths, *Worrell.*

**when the disciples came together to break bread:** ... when we had met for the Breaking of Bread, *TCNT* ... we all met together, *Everyday, NCV* ... were assembled to break bread, *Noli* ... come together for the holy meal, *BB* ... to eat the Lord's supper, *NLT.*

**Paul preached unto them:** Paul addressed them, *Goodspeed* ... Paul was discoursing to them, *TNT* ... talked, *NLT* ... spoke to the group, *NCV.*

**ready to depart on the morrow:** He thought he would leave, *NLT* ... as he was going away the next morning, *Goodspeed* ... Because he was planning to leave, *NCV* ... intending to depart, *ASV* ... since he expected to leave the next day, *Norlie* ... He was ready to leave, *SEB* ... he intended to leave on the following day, *Phillips.*

| **3450.6** art acc sing masc | **3030.4** noun acc sing masc | **3230.1** prep | **3187.1** noun gen sing neu | **1498.37** verb 3pl indic imperf act | **1156.2** conj |
|---|---|---|---|---|---|
| τὸν | λόγον | μέχρι | μεσονυκτίου· | **8.** ἦσαν | δὲ |
| *ton* | *logon* | *mechri* | *mesonuktiou* | *ēsan* | *de* |
| the | discourse | until | midnight. | Were | and |

| **2958.2** noun nom pl fem | **2401.9** adj nom pl fem | **1706.1** prep | **3450.3** art dat sing | **5091.1** noun dat sing neu | **3619.1** adv |
|---|---|---|---|---|---|
| λαμπάδες | ἱκαναὶ | ἐν | τῷ | ὑπερῴῳ | οὗ |
| *lampades* | *hikanai* | *en* | *tō* | *huperōō* | *hou* |
| lamps | many | in | the | upper room | where |

8.a.**Txt:** bo.Steph
**Var:** 01ℵ,02A,03B,05D
08E,020L,025P,byz.sa.
Gries,Lach,Treg,Alf
Word,Tisc,We/Ho,Weis
Sod,UBS/☆

9.a.**Txt:** 020L,025P,byz.
**Var:** 01ℵ,02A,03B,05D
08E,Lach,Treg,Alf
Word,Tisc,We/Ho,Weis
Sod,UBS/☆

| **1498.37** verb 3pl indic imperf act | **1498.36** verb 1pl indic imperf act | **4714.24** verb nom pl masc part perf mid | **2493.6** verb nom sing masc part pres mid |
|---|---|---|---|
| ʻ ἦσαν | [a☆ ἦμεν ] | συνηγμένοι. | **9.** ʻ καθήμενος |
| *ēsan* | *ēmen* | *sunēgmenoi* | *kathēmenos* |
| they were | [ we were ] | having been assembled. | Sitting |

| **2488.6** verb nom sing masc part pres mid | **1156.2** conj | **4948.3** indef-pron nom sing | **3357.1** noun nom sing masc | **3549.4** noun dat sing neu |
|---|---|---|---|---|
| [a☆ καθεζόμενος ] | δέ | τις | νεανίας | ὀνόματι |
| *kathezomenos* | *de* | *tis* | *neanias* | *onomati* |
| [ idem ] | and | a certain | youth, | by name |

| **2142.1** name nom masc | **1894.3** prep | **3450.10** art gen sing fem | **2353.1** noun gen sing fem | **2671.2** verb nom sing masc part pres mid |
|---|---|---|---|---|
| Εὔτυχος | ἐπὶ | τῆς | θυρίδος, | καταφερόμενος |
| *Eutuchos* | *epi* | *tēs* | *thuridos* | *katapheromenos* |
| Eutychus, | by | the | window, | being overpowered |

| **5096.2** noun dat sing masc | **895.2** adj dat sing masc | **1250.3** verb gen sing masc part pres mid | **3450.2** art gen sing | **3834.2** name gen masc | **1894.3** prep |
|---|---|---|---|---|---|
| ὕπνῳ | βαθεῖ, | διαλεγομένου | τοῦ | Παύλου | ἐπὶ |
| *hupnō* | *bathei* | *dialegomenou* | *tou* | *Paulou* | *epi* |
| by sleep | deep, | discoursing | | Paul | for |

| **3979.8** adj comp sing neu | **2671.3** verb nom sing masc part aor pass | **570.3** prep | **3450.2** art gen sing | **5096.1** noun gen sing masc |
|---|---|---|---|---|
| πλεῖον, | κατενεχθεὶς | ἀπὸ | τοῦ | ὕπνου |
| *pleion* | *katenechtheis* | *apo* | *tou* | *hupnou* |
| a longer time, | having been overpowered | by | the | sleep |

| **3959.5** verb 3sing indic aor act | **570.3** prep | **3450.2** art gen sing | **4992.1** noun gen sing neu | **2706.1** adv | **2504.1** conj |
|---|---|---|---|---|---|
| ἔπεσεν | ἀπὸ | τοῦ | τριστέγου | κάτω, | καὶ |
| *epesen* | *apo* | *tou* | *tristegou* | *katō* | *kai* |
| he fell | from | the | third story | down, | and |

| **142.24** verb 3sing indic aor pass | **3361.3** adj nom sing masc | **2568.20** verb nom sing masc part aor act | **1156.2** conj | **3450.5** art nom sing masc |
|---|---|---|---|---|
| ἤρθη | νεκρός. | **10.** καταβὰς | δὲ | ὁ |
| *ērthē* | *nekros* | *katabas* | *de* | *ho* |
| was taken up | dead. | Having descended | but | |

| **3834.1** name nom masc | **1953.2** verb 3sing indic aor act | **840.4** prs-pron dat sing | **2504.1** conj | **4694.1** verb nom sing masc part aor act |
|---|---|---|---|---|
| Παῦλος | ἐπέπεσεν | αὐτῷ, | καὶ | συμπεριλαβὼν |
| *Paulos* | *epepesen* | *autō* | *kai* | *sumperilabōn* |
| Paul | fell upon | him, | and | having embraced |

| **1500.5** verb 3sing indic aor act | **3231.1** partic | **2327.2** verb 2pl pres mid | **3450.9** art nom sing fem | **1056.1** conj | **5425.1** noun nom sing fem |
|---|---|---|---|---|---|
| εἶπεν, | Μὴ | θορυβεῖσθε· | ἡ | γὰρ | ψυχὴ |
| *eipen* | *Mē* | *thorubeisthe* | *hē* | *gar* | *psuchē* |
| said, | Not | be troubled, | the | for | life |

their questions. It was his great desire for them to walk and live in the Spirit and bring glory to Jesus.

**20:8.** Paul could continue, for there were plenty of olive oil lamps in the upper room where they were meeting. Such a room would be reached by an outside stairway and would probably hold 200 or 300 people.

**20:9.** A young man, Eutychus ("fortunate"), was sitting on a window sill listening. About midnight he was "borne down" with sleep. That is, he gradually dropped off and was finally overcome by deep, sound sleep. Everyone's attention was on Paul, so no one noticed. As Paul kept on preaching, Eutychus finally fell from the third story window and was taken up dead. This means he was really dead. Luke, as a physician, would be able to determine this.

This must have been quite a shock to the believers gathered there. Their first thought may have been that this young man whose name meant "fortunate" was not so fortunate after all. It is easy for people to feel a sense of tragedy when they see a young man or a young woman killed. The Bible just tells the story factually. It does not indicate why the young man was sitting in the window sill instead of joining in with the believers who were gathered around Paul.

Some suppose the smoke from the many lamps helped to put Eutychus to sleep. But this would hardly be the case by any open window. Others say the devil caused it in an attempt to disrupt the meeting. Still others say the Bible records it as a warning to all who do not give attention to the Word of God when it is being preached or taught. But there is no indication of any blame being put on Satan here; neither is there any reproach put on the young man for having fallen asleep.

The Bible shows he was not merely injured or dying. He was dead. Some writers suggest he was taken up for dead, or taken up as dead. But where that was the case, as in Matthew 28:4, Mark 9:26, and Revelation 1:17, the Greek clearly indicates this. Here the Greek is the same as is used elsewhere when people were actually dead. He was a lifeless corpse. In the natural there was no hope for him.

**20:10.** Immediately Paul went down the outside stairway and threw himself upon the young man, throwing his arms around him in a tight embrace, surely praying as he did so.

Paul had the example of Elijah in this. In 1 Kings 17:17-21 when the widow's son died, Elijah came and stretched himself over the child three times and prayed. The Hebrew indicates Elijah did not put any of his weight on the child. Rather, he bent over the child as an expression of faith in prayer. The emphasis is clearly on prayer. In answer to prayer, the boy was brought back to life. Elisha had a similar experience when the son of the wealthy Shunammite woman died (2 Kings 4:34,35).

**and continued his speech until midnight:** . . . and prolonged his speech until midnight, *ASV* . . . and he went on talking till after the middle of the night, *BB.*

**8. And there were many lights in the upper chamber:** . . . a good many lamps in the upstairs room, *TCNT.*

**where they were gathered together:** . . . where we had met, *TCNT* . . . were assembled, *HBIE* . . . We were all together, *NCV.*

**9. And there sat in a window a certain young man named Eutychus:** And a youth by the name Eutychus, *Weymouth* . . . on the window sill, *Phillips.*

**being fallen into a deep sleep:** . . . was gradually overcome with great drowsiness, *TCNT.*

**and as Paul was long preaching:** . . . while Paul preached at unusual length, *Weymouth* . . . and as Paul's address went on and on, *Moffatt* . . . As Paul continued talking, *NCV.*

**he sunk down with sleep:** . . . so as he sagged down in, *Berkeley* . . . a profound sleep, *Campbell* . . . he went sound asleep, *Klingensmith.*

**and fell down from the third loft:** . . . and fell to the ground from the third floor, *NCV* . . . from the third story, *ASV.*

**and was taken up dead:** When they picked him up, *NCV* . . . a corpse, *Moffatt* . . . lifeless, *Berkeley.*

**10. And Paul went down:** Paul hastened down, *Norlie.*

**and fell on him:** . . . threw himself upon him, *TCNT* . . . lay on him, *Beck* . . . knelt, *NCV.*

**and embracing him said:** . . . took him in his arms and said, *BB* . . . put his arms around him, *NCV* . . . and holding him gently in his arms, *Phillips.*

**Trouble not yourselves:** Stop being alarmed, *Williams* . . . Have no anxiety, *Berkeley* . . . Cease your wailing, *Weymouth* . . . Do not make an uproar, *HBIE* . . . Make no lamentations, *Noyes* . . . Be not troubled, *Wesley* . . . Do not weep, *Klingensmith* . . . Make no tumult! *Worrell* . . . Do not worry, *Noli.*

**for his life is in him:** . . . he is still alive, *TCNT* . . . He's alive, *Beck.*

# Acts 20:11

| 840.3 prs-pron gen sing | 1706.1 prep | 840.4 prs-pron dat sing | 1498.4 verb 3sing indic pres act | 303.17 verb nom sing masc part aor act | 1156.2 conj |
|---|---|---|---|---|---|
| αὐτοῦ | ἐν | αὐτῷ | ἐστιν. | **11.** Ἀναβὰς | δὲ |
| *autou* | *en* | *autō* | *estin* | *Anabas* | *de* |
| his | in | him | is. | Having gone up | and |

11.a.**Var:** 01ℵ-org,02A 03B,04C,05D-org,Lach Treg,Alf,Word,Tisc We/Ho,Weis,Sod UBS/☆

| 2504.1 conj | 2779.5 verb nom sing masc part aor act | 3450.6 art acc sing masc | 735.4 noun acc sing masc | 2504.1 conj | 1083.6 verb nom sing masc part aor mid |
|---|---|---|---|---|---|
| καὶ | κλάσας | [[a]☆+ τὸν ] | ἄρτον | καὶ | γευσάμενος, |
| *kai* | *klasas* | *ton* | *arton* | *kai* | *geusamenos* |
| and | having broken | [ the ] | bread | and | having eaten, |

| 1894.1 prep | 2401.2 adj sing | 4885.1 conj | 3519.2 verb nom sing masc part aor act | 884.1 conj | 884.2 conj |
|---|---|---|---|---|---|
| ἐφ' | ἱκανόν | τε | ὁμιλήσας | ʻ ἄχρις | [☆ ἄχρι ] |
| *eph'* | *hikanon* | *te* | *homilēsas* | *achris* | *achri* |
| for | a long time | and | having conversed | until | [ idem ] |

| 821.1 noun gen sing fem | 3643.1 adv | 1814.3 verb 3sing indic aor act | 70.10 verb 3pl indic aor act | 1156.2 conj | 3450.6 art acc sing masc |
|---|---|---|---|---|---|
| αὐγῆς, | οὕτως | ἐξῆλθεν. | **12.** ἤγαγον | δὲ | τὸν |
| *augēs* | *houtōs* | *exēlthen* | *ēgagon* | *de* | *ton* |
| daybreak, | so | he departed. | They brought | and | the |

| 3679.1 noun acc sing | 2180.9 verb part pres act | 2504.1 conj | 3731.27 verb 3pl indic aor pass | 3620.3 partic | 3227.1 adv |
|---|---|---|---|---|---|
| παῖδα | ζῶντα, | καὶ | παρεκλήθησαν | οὐ | μετρίως. |
| *paida* | *zōnta* | *kai* | *pareklēthēsan* | *ou* | *metriōs* |
| boy | living, | and | were comforted | not | a little. |

13.a.**Txt:** p41,p74,01ℵ 03B-corr2,04C,044,33 36,1739,Steph **Var:** 02A,03B-org,08E byz.

13.b.**Txt:** 05D,020L 025P,byz. **Var:** 01ℵ,02A,03B,04C 08E,Lach,Treg,Alf,Tisc We/Ho,Weis,Sod UBS/☆

| 2231.1 prs-pron nom 1pl | 1156.2 conj | 4140.4 verb nom pl masc part aor act | 4193.5 verb nom pl masc part aor act | 1894.3 prep |
|---|---|---|---|---|
| **13.** Ἡμεῖς | δὲ | ʻ προελθόντες | [[a] προσελθόντες ] | ἐπὶ |
| *Hēmeis* | *de* | *proelthontes* | *proselthontes* | *epi* |
| We | but | having gone before | [ having approached ] | to |

| 3450.16 art sing neu | 4003.1 noun sing neu | 319.7 verb 1pl indic aor pass | 1519.1 prep | 1894.3 prep | 3450.12 art acc sing fem |
|---|---|---|---|---|---|
| τὸ | πλοῖον | ἀνήχθημεν | ʻ εἰς | [[b]☆ ἐπὶ ] | τὴν |
| *to* | *ploion* | *anēchthēmen* | *eis* | *epi* | *tēn* |
| the | ship | sailed | to | [ idem ] | |

| 782.1 adv comp | 1551.1 adv | 3165.13 verb nom pl masc part pres act | 351.1 verb inf pres act | 3450.6 art acc sing masc |
|---|---|---|---|---|
| Ἄσσον, | ἐκεῖθεν | μέλλοντες | ἀναλαμβάνειν | τὸν |
| *Asson* | *ekeithen* | *mellontes* | *analambanein* | *ton* |
| Assos, | there | being about | to take in | |

| 3834.4 name acc masc | 3643.1 adv | 1056.1 conj | 1498.34 verb sing indic imperf act | 1293.11 verb nom sing masc part perf mid |
|---|---|---|---|---|
| Παῦλον· | οὕτως | γὰρ | ʻ ἦν | διατεταγμένος, |
| *Paulon* | *houtōs* | *gar* | *ēn* | *diatetagmenos* |
| Paul; | so | for | he was | having been arranged, |

| 1293.11 verb nom sing masc part perf mid | 1498.34 verb sing indic imperf act | 3165.12 verb nom sing masc part pres act | 840.5 prs-pron nom sing masc |
|---|---|---|---|
| [☆ διατεταγμένος | ἦν ] | μέλλων | αὐτὸς |
| *diatetagmenos* | *ēn* | *mellōn* | *autos* |
| [ having been arranged | he was, ] | being about | himself |

14.a.**Txt:** 04C,05D,020L byz.Sod **Var:** 01ℵ-corr,02A,03B 08E,025P,Lach,Treg Alf,Tisc,We/Ho,Weis UBS/☆

| 3840.1 verb inf pres act | 5453.1 conj | 1156.2 conj | 4671.2 verb 3sing indic aor act | 4671.8 verb 3sing indic imperf act |
|---|---|---|---|---|
| πεζεύειν. | **14.** ὡς | δὲ | ʻ συνέβαλεν | [[a] συνέβαλλεν ] |
| *pezeuein* | *hōs* | *de* | *sunebalen* | *suneballen* |
| to go on foot. | When | and | he met with | [ he was meeting with ] |

After Paul embraced the young man Eutychus, he said, "Don't panic, for his life is in him." That is, his life had returned to him. ("Life" here is the Greek *psuchē* which also means "soul" or "person," but in this case it means physical life.) Apparently, the people had already started noisy lamentations. Paul therefore told them to stop all this noise which was so traditional, especially among the Jews. God had given a miraculous restoration.

**20:11.** It was now after midnight on Monday morning. But Paul went back up to the upper room and broke bread, that is, had a meal which he ate ("tasted") with enjoyment. Then he kept on talking (conversing) a long time, and the believers stayed right with him until daylight. Again the Bible does not say what Paul talked about. But this surely would have been a wonderful opportunity to tell about how Jesus healed the sick and raised the dead and to say more about Christ's own death and resurrection which is the guarantee of every believer's. Then, at daybreak Paul left.

**20:12.** The young man was also brought before the people alive (and fully recovered), and they were very greatly encouraged. Eutychus is called a boy (*paida*) here, which probably means he was still in his teens. (In verse 9 Eutychus is called a *neanias*, a youth.) However, *paida* is also used of a trusted servant or slave. Many slaves did become Christians in those days. This could be another reason he fell asleep. He may have been working hard all day.

The encouragement of these believers was not merely a feeling of relief because Eutychus was alive. It was also undoubtedly an encouragement to their faith in Christ and to their belief in the truth of the resurrection that will take place when Jesus comes again (1 Thessalonians 4:13-18). Paul used the same verb there when he wrote "comfort (encourage) one another with these words."

**20:13.** Luke and the rest of Paul's company did not stay until daybreak. They went on ahead to the ship and set sail for Assos in Mysia south of Troas where they expected to take Paul on board. He had directed them to do this. The ship would go a longer route around a long peninsula (Cape Lectum). The sea journey was nearly twice as far as by land. Paul thus took the land route and walked to Assos. This was his choice.

Luke did not say why Paul did this. But for some reason he wanted to be alone. A little later he told the Ephesian elders that in every city the Holy Spirit bore witness to him that bonds (chains) and affliction (persecution, distress) awaited him in Jerusalem. Probably Paul felt he needed this time alone in order to settle it with the Lord whether it was truly His will for him to go on to Jerusalem. Paul had written to the Romans to pray to God for him that he might be delivered from the unbelievers in Judea so he might minister to the saints in Jerusalem (Romans 15:30,31). But he needed time now to pray and talk to God.

**11. When he therefore was come up again:** Then he went upstairs, *TCNT.*

**and had broken bread, and eaten:** . . . and, after breaking and partaking of the Bread, *TCNT* . . . broke the bread, and took some food, *Weymouth.*

**and talked a long while, even till break of day:** . . . he talked with them at great length till daybreak, *TCNT* . . . and after much conversation that lasted till the sun rose, *Beck* . . . he conversed long with them, *Wesley* . . . even till daylight, *Williams* . . . until it was early morning, *NCV.*

**so he departed:** . . . and then left, *TCNT* . . . at last he parted from them, *Weymouth* . . . and so finally departed, *Phillips.*

**12. And they brought the young man alive:** Meanwhile they had taken the lad away alive, *TCNT* . . . taken the lad home alive, *Weymouth* . . . took the young man home alive, *NCV.*

**and were not little comforted:** . . . comforted beyond measure, *Rotherham* . . . immeasurably consoled, *Concordant* . . . much to their relief, *Moffatt* . . . were enormously encouraged, *Adams* . . . relieved, *Phillips* . . . greatly comforted, *NCV.*

**13. And we went before to ship:** We started first, went on board ship, *TCNT* . . . Meanwhile we had gone aboard the ship, *Phillips* . . . Embarking, *Fenton.*

**and sailed unto Assos:** . . . and sailed for Assos, *TCNT* . . . and sailed on ahead for Assos, *Phillips.*

**there intending to take in Paul:** . . . intending to take Paul on board there, *TCNT* . . . where we were to take Paul on board, *Williams* . . . intending to pick up Paul there, *Phillips.*

**for so had he appointed:** . . . arranged, *Rotherham* . . . He had planned it that way, *Norlie* . . . for such was his arrangement, *Berkeley.*

**minding himself to go afoot:** . . . intending himself to go by land, *ASV* . . . since he himself had planned to go overland, *Phillips.*

**14. And when he met with us at Assos:** When he met us on our arrival at Assos, *Phillips.*

| 2231.3 prs-pron dat 1pl | 1519.1 prep | 3450.12 art acc sing fem | 782.1 adv comp | 351.5 verb nom pl masc part aor act | 840.6 prs-pron acc sing masc |
|---|---|---|---|---|---|
| ἡμῖν | εἰς | τὴν | ᾿Ασσον, | ἀναλαβόντες | αὐτὸν |
| *hēmin* | *eis* | *tēn* | *Asson* | *analabontes* | *auton* |
| us | at | | Assos, | having taken in | him |

| 2048.4 verb 1pl indic aor act | 1519.1 prep | 3276.1 name acc fem | 2518.1 conj | 630.3 verb nom pl masc part aor act |
|---|---|---|---|---|
| ἤλθομεν | εἰς | Μιτυλήνην· | **15.** κἀκεῖθεν | ἀποπλεύσαντες |
| *ēlthomen* | *eis* | *Mitulēnēn* | *kakeithen* | *apopleusantes* |
| we came | to | Mitylene; | and from there | having sailed away, |

| 3450.11 art dat sing fem | 1951.1 noun dat sing fem | 2628.2 verb 1pl indic aor act | 478.2 prep | 478.1 prep |
|---|---|---|---|---|
| τῇ | ἐπιούσῃ | κατηντήσαμεν | ⸀ ἀντικρὺ | [☆ ἄντικρυς ] |
| *tē* | *epiousē* | *katēntēsamen* | *antikru* | *antikrus* |
| on the | following | arrived | opposite | [ idem ] |

15.a.**Txt:** p41,05D,020L 025P,byz.sa.Weis,Sod
**Var:** p74,01ℵ,02A,03B 04C,08E,33,bo.Lach Treg,Tisc,We/Ho UBS/☆

| 5344.1 name gen fem | 3450.11 art dat sing fem | 1156.2 conj | 2066.11 adj dat sing fem | 3708.1 verb 1pl indic aor act | 1519.1 prep | 4401.1 name acc fem |
|---|---|---|---|---|---|---|
| Χίου· | τῇ | δὲ | ἑτέρᾳ | παρεβάλομεν | εἰς | Σάμον· |
| *Chiou* | *tē* | *de* | *hetera* | *parebalomen* | *eis* | *Samon* |
| Chios, | on the | and | next | we arrived | at | Samos; |

15.b.**Var:** p74,01ℵ,02A 03B,04C,08E,33,Lach Treg,Tisc,We/Ho,Sod UBS/☆

| 2504.1 conj | 3176.24 verb nom pl masc part aor act | 1706.1 prep | 5016.1 name dat neu | 3450.11 art dat sing fem | 1156.2 conj |
|---|---|---|---|---|---|
| ⸂a καὶ | μείναντες | ἐν | Τρωγυλλίῳ, ⸃ | τῇ | [b☆+ δὲ ] |
| *kai* | *meinantes* | *en* | *Trōgulliō* | *tē* | *de* |
| and | having remained | at | Trogyllium, | on the | [ and ] |

| 2174.48 verb dat sing fem part pres mid | 2048.4 verb 1pl indic aor act | 1519.1 prep | 3263.3 name acc fem | 2892.15 verb 3sing indic aor act |
|---|---|---|---|---|
| ἐχομένῃ | ἤλθομεν | εἰς | Μίλητον. | **16.** ⸀ ἔκρινεν |
| *echomenē* | *ēlthomen* | *eis* | *Milēton* | *ekrinen* |
| following | we came | to | Miletus: | decided |

16.a.**Txt:** 04C-corr,020L 025P,byz.
**Var:** 01ℵ,02A,03B 04C-org,05D,08E,Gries Lach,Treg,Alf,Word Tisc,We/Ho,Weis,Sod UBS/☆

| 2892.44 verb 3sing indic plperf act | 1056.1 conj | 3450.5 art nom sing masc | 3834.1 name nom masc | 3757.1 verb inf aor act |
|---|---|---|---|---|
| [a☆ κεκρίκει ] | γὰρ | ὁ | Παῦλος | παραπλεῦσαι |
| *kekrikei* | *gar* | *ho* | *Paulos* | *parapleusai* |
| [ had decided ] | for | | Paul | to sail by |

| 3450.12 art acc sing fem | 2163.3 name acc fem | 3567.1 conj | 3231.1 partic | 1090.40 verb 3sing subj aor mid | 840.4 prs-pron dat sing |
|---|---|---|---|---|---|
| τὴν | Ἔφεσον, | ὅπως | μὴ | γένηται | αὐτῷ |
| *tēn* | *Epheson* | *hopōs* | *mē* | *genētai* | *autō* |
| | Ephesus, | so that | not | it might happen | to him |

| 5386.1 verb inf aor act | 1706.1 prep | 3450.11 art dat sing fem | 767.3 name dat fem | 4545.5 verb 3sing indic imperf act | 1056.1 conj |
|---|---|---|---|---|---|
| χρονοτριβῆσαι | ἐν | τῇ | ᾿Ασίᾳ· | ἔσπευδεν | γὰρ |
| *chronotribēsai* | *en* | *tē* | *Asia* | *espeuden* | *gar* |
| to spend time | in | | Asia; | he was eager | for |

16.b.**Txt:** 020L,025P,byz.
**Var:** 01ℵ,02A,03B,04C 08E,Lach,Treg,Alf,Tisc We/Ho,Weis,Sod UBS/☆

| 1479.1 conj | 1409.3 adj sing neu | 1498.34 verb sing indic imperf act | 1498.14 verb 3sing opt pres act | 840.4 prs-pron dat sing | 3450.12 art acc sing fem |
|---|---|---|---|---|---|
| εἰ | δυνατὸν | ⸀ ἦν | [b☆ εἴη ] | αὐτῷ | τὴν |
| *ei* | *dunaton* | *ēn* | *eiē* | *autō* | *tēn* |
| if | possible | it was | [ it might be ] | for him | the |

| 2232.4 noun acc sing fem | 3450.10 art gen sing fem | 3868.1 noun gen sing fem | 1090.63 verb inf aor mid | 1519.1 prep | 2389.1 name |
|---|---|---|---|---|---|
| ἡμέραν | τῆς | πεντηκοστῆς | γενέσθαι | εἰς | Ἱεροσόλυμα. |
| *hēmeran* | *tēs* | *pentēkostēs* | *genesthai* | *eis* | *Hierosoluma* |
| day | | of Pentecost | to be | in | Jerusalem. |

**20:14.** By the time Paul reached Assos it seems he had no more doubts about it being God's will for him to go on to Jerusalem. So he met the ship and they took him on board and proceeded to sail along the coast of Asia Minor until they came to Mitylene, the capital of the island of Lesbos. There they stopped for a brief time. It was an important state at the crossroads of Europe and Asia. The Romans made it a favorite vacation spot. Its fine harbor faced toward the coast of Asia Minor and thus it was a convenient place for the ship to stop. It is probable that it picked up or dropped off cargo and passengers there.

Paul's journey by foot cannot be observed without developing a great deal of respect for the apostle. It was a difficult journey; so difficult, in fact, that Homer said traveling on foot to Assos was enough to kill a person. The trip attests not only to Paul's zeal for the gospel but also to his physical stamina.

**20:15.** From Mitylene they sailed the next day across from Chios, a large island opposite Smyrna. Chios was a free city-state. The ship anchored in the lee of the island for a night. The next day they came near Samos, another large island southwest of Ephesus which had been made a free state by the Roman Emperor Augustus. The ship sailed between Samos and the mainland. This brought them to a narrow strait between the island of Samos and the promontory of Trogyllium. They remained there until morning since it would have been very difficult to make their way through the strait in the darkness. (Some ancient manuscripts leave out any mention of this waiting at Trogyllium, but the majority of Greek manuscripts recognize there was danger here, and this delay most surely did take place.) This promontory was actually between Ephesus and Miletus. So the next day they came to Miletus.

Miletus was on the seacoast of the Roman province of Asia about 36 miles south of Ephesus. It was located on the south shore of the Bay of Latmus near the mouth of the Maeander River (now called the Menderes). The city was founded by the Ionian Greeks. It was a very prosperous commercial city until it was destroyed by the Persians in 494 B.C. It never regained its past glories. The Maeander River brought down a great deal of silt, and in modern times what is left of its harbor is now a lake, leaving the site of the city of Miletus about 6 miles from the present seacoast.

**20:16.** This trip had taken longer than usual with the ship sailing among the islands off the coast of Asia Minor and apparently sailing only by daylight. Paul had decided to bypass Ephesus. He knew if he went there the large number of local assemblies or house churches would all want him to come and visit them and it would take too much time. He had indeed settled it with God that he should go to Jerusalem. Now he was in a hurry to get there by the Day of Pentecost (in May) if possible. This would be a time when the Jewish believers in Palestine would be together, and the offering sent by the Greek and Macedonian churches would be most helpful.

**we took him in:** . . . we took him on board, *Rotherham* . . . aboard, *NCV* . . . taking him up, *Worrell.*

**and came to Mitylene:** . . . and went on to Mitylene, *TCNT* . . . and sailed on to Mitylene, *Williams.*

**15. And we sailed thence, and came the next day over against Chios:** The day after we had sailed from there, we arrived off Chios, *TCNT* . . . and arrived off the coast of Chios the next day, *Phillips* . . . From there we sailed and arrived off, *Noli* . . . and came to a place near, *NCV* . . . And sailing away from there, *KJII* . . . we reached a point opposite Chios, *Knox* . . . to a point facing, *MLNT.*

**and the next day we arrived at Samos:** . . . put in at Samos, *Alford* . . . we sailed to, *NCV* . . . we touched at, *Worrell* . . . docked at Samos, *Berkeley.*

**and tarried at Trogyllium; and the next day we came to Miletus:** . . . we came on the third day to Miletus, *BB* . . . and, on the following day, *Worrell* . . . A day later, we reached, *NCV.*

**16. For Paul had determined to sail by Ephesus:** Paul's plan was to sail past Ephesus, *Weymouth* . . . had already decided not to stop at, *NCV.*

**because he would not spend the time in Asia:** . . . so that he might not be kept in Asia, *BB* . . . with the idea of spending as little time as possible in Asia, *Phillips* . . . as he did not want to be delayed in the province of, *Noli* . . . in order that he might not have to spend time in, *TNT* . . . he did not want to stay too long in, *NCV* . . . lest he spend much time in, *Kleist* . . . for fear of having to waste time in, *Knox.*

**for he hasted:** . . . since he was very desirous, *Weymouth* . . . he was eager, *Williams* . . . He wanted to hurry on, *Norlie* . . . For he was hastening to be in, *Noli.*

**if it were possible for him:** . . . if possible, *TCNT* . . . if he possibly could, *Kleist* . . . if he found it possible, *Knox.*

**to be at Jerusalem the day of Pentecost:** . . . to arrive in Jerusalem, *Rotherham* . . . reach Jerusalem, *Kleist* . . . by the Festival at the close of the Harvest, *TCNT.*

| 570.3 prep | 1156.2 conj | 3450.10 art gen sing fem | 3263.1 name gen fem | 3854.11 verb nom sing masc part aor act | 1519.1 prep |
|---|---|---|---|---|---|
| **17.** Ἀπὸ | δὲ | τῆς | Μιλήτου | πέμψας | εἰς |
| *Apo* | *de* | *tēs* | *Milētou* | *pempsas* | *eis* |
| From | and | | Miletus | having sent | to |

| 2163.3 name acc fem | 3203.1 verb 3sing indic aor mid | 3450.8 art acc pl masc | 4104.2 adj comp acc pl masc | 3450.10 art gen sing fem |
|---|---|---|---|---|
| Ἔφεσον | μετεκαλέσατο | τοὺς | πρεσβυτέρους | τῆς |
| *Epheson* | *metekalesato* | *tous* | *presbuterous* | *tēs* |
| Ephesus | he called for | the | elders | of the |

| 1564.1 noun fem | 5453.1 conj | 1156.2 conj | 3716.4 verb 3pl indic aor mid | 4242.1 prep |
|---|---|---|---|---|
| ἐκκλησίας. | **18.** ὡς | δὲ | παρεγένοντο | πρὸς |
| *ekklēsias* | *hōs* | *de* | *paregenonto* | *pros* |
| assembly. | When | and | they were come | to |

| 840.6 prs-pron acc sing masc | 1500.5 verb 3sing indic aor act | 840.2 prs-pron dat pl | 5050.1 prs-pron nom 2pl | 1971.3 verb 2pl indic pres mid | 570.3 prep |
|---|---|---|---|---|---|
| αὐτὸν | εἶπεν | αὐτοῖς, | Ὑμεῖς | ἐπίστασθε, | ἀπὸ |
| *auton* | *eipen* | *autois* | *Humeis* | *epistasthe* | *apo* |
| him | he said | to them, | You | know, | from |

| 4272.10 num ord gen sing fem | 2232.1 noun fem | 570.1 prep | 3614.10 rel-pron gen sing fem | 1895.1 verb 1sing indic aor act | 1519.1 prep |
|---|---|---|---|---|---|
| πρώτης | ἡμέρας | ἀφ' | ἧς | ἐπέβην | εἰς |
| *prōtēs* | *hēmeras* | *aph'* | *hēs* | *epebēn* | *eis* |
| first | day | from | which | I arrived | in |

| 3450.12 art acc sing fem | 767.4 name acc fem | 4316.1 adv | 3196.1 prep | 5050.2 prs-pron gen 2pl | 3450.6 art acc sing masc | 3820.1 adj |
|---|---|---|---|---|---|---|
| τὴν | Ἀσίαν, | πῶς | μεθ' | ὑμῶν | τὸν | πάντα |
| *tēn* | *Asian* | *pōs* | *meth'* | *humōn* | *ton* | *panta* |
| | Asia, | how | with | you | the | all |

| 5385.4 noun acc sing masc | 1090.30 verb 1sing indic aor mid | 1392.6 verb nom sing masc part pres act | 3450.3 art dat sing | 2935.3 noun dat sing masc | 3196.3 prep |
|---|---|---|---|---|---|
| χρόνον | ἐγενόμην, | **19.** δουλεύων | τῷ | κυρίῳ | μετὰ |
| *chronon* | *egenomēn* | *douleuōn* | *tō* | *kuriō* | *meta* |
| time | I was, | serving | the | Lord | with |

19.a.**Txt:** 04C,020L 025P,byz.
**Var:** 01ℵ,02A,03B,05D 08E,Gries,Lach,Treg Alf,Word,Tisc,We/Ho Weis,Sod,UBS/*

| 3820.10 adj gen sing fem | 4863.1 noun gen sing fem | 2504.1 conj | 4044.1 adj gen pl | 1139.2 noun gen pl neu |
|---|---|---|---|---|
| πάσης | ταπεινοφροσύνης | καὶ | (a πολλῶν ) | δακρύων |
| *pasēs* | *tapeinophrosunēs* | *kai* | *pollōn* | *dakruōn* |
| all | humility | and | many | tears |

| 2504.1 conj | 3848.5 noun gen pl masc | 3450.1 art gen pl | 4670.4 verb gen pl masc part aor act | 1466.4 prs-pron dat 1sing | 1706.1 prep |
|---|---|---|---|---|---|
| καὶ | πειρασμῶν, | τῶν | συμβάντων | μοι | ἐν |
| *kai* | *peirasmōn* | *tōn* | *sumbantōn* | *moi* | *en* |
| and | temptations, | the | having happened | to me | through |

| 3450.14 art dat pl fem | 1902.3 noun dat pl fem | 3450.1 art gen pl | 2428.3 name-adj gen pl masc | 5453.1 conj | 3625.6 num card neu |
|---|---|---|---|---|---|
| ταῖς | ἐπιβουλαῖς | τῶν | Ἰουδαίων· | **20.** ὡς | οὐδὲν |
| *tais* | *epiboulais* | *tōn* | *Ioudaiōn* | *hōs* | *ouden* |
| the | plots | of the | Jews; | how | nothing |

| 5126.2 verb 1sing indic aor mid | 3450.1 art gen pl | 4702.3 verb gen pl neu part pres act | 3450.2 art gen sing | 3231.1 partic |
|---|---|---|---|---|
| ὑπεστειλάμην | τῶν | συμφερόντων | τοῦ | μὴ |
| *hupesteilamēn* | *tōn* | *sumpherontōn* | *tou* | *mē* |
| I kept back | of the | being profitable | the | not |

**20:17.** Paul did not bypass Ephesus because of any lack of concern for the church there. To show his care for them he sent to Ephesus and called the elders of the church, asking them to come and meet with him at Miletus. This would probably be the last time he would ever see them.

God gave Paul the heart of a true shepherd. His words reveal another side of his ministry. Chapter 13 has a summary of the kind of sermons Paul preached to Jews when he first went to the synagogue in a new town. Chapter 17 has a summary of Paul's preaching to purely Gentile audiences when he first met with them. But this chapter contains the only example in Acts of a sermon Paul preached specifically to Christians. It was a deeply moving farewell address. Now Paul gave his final challenge to the elders or administrative officers who were responsible for the teaching and direction of the believers in the great city of Ephesus.

**20:18.** Paul began by reminding them of the kind of person he had been from the first day he set foot in the province of Asia and how he had conducted himself the whole time he was there.

Paul did not intend to glorify himself. He always wanted all the glory to go to Jesus. But in many cases the work of Judaizers and other enemies of the gospel had degenerated into attempts to destroy Paul's message and divide the churches he founded by making personal attacks on him. Paul now reminded the Ephesians that they knew him.

**20:19.** Paul also reminded the Ephesian elders that all the time he was with them he had served the Lord in all humility. He was a true servant-leader. He was humble-minded, modest, and unassuming. The people knew this was a strong contrast to the boastfulness of the false teachers who were trying to draw a following after themselves.

Paul also served with tears, weeping as he sought to bring sinners to Christ, weeping also over the needs of the believers. When he preached judgment, it was out of a broken heart full of love for the people with whom he was dealing. His tears flowed from the love and compassion of Jesus that flooded his own soul.

Paul also continued to serve the Lord with the same humility and tears in the midst of all the testing brought by the plots of unbelieving Jews.

In the midst of all these tests, Paul forgot his own dignity and desires for the sake of fulfilling his God-given task. He was not trying to build up a reputation or a fortune for himself. He was willing to do the jobs no one else wanted to do. He was willing to do anything, however unpleasant or dangerous, if it meant building up the body of Christ.

**20:20.** At the same time, Paul did not let danger or the plots of his enemies cause him to shrink from telling the Ephesians anything

**17. And from Miletus he sent to Ephesus:** Notwithstanding, *Rotherham* . . . he sent messengers to, *MLNT.*

**and called the elders of the church:** . . . and summoned, *Alford* . . . and invited the Officers of the church to meet him, *TCNT* . . . of the assembly, *Rotherham.*

**18. And when they were come to him:** When they came to him, *Moffatt.*

**he said unto them:** . . . he spoke to them as follows, *TCNT* . . . he told them, *Berkeley* . . . he addressed them in these words, *Phillips.*

**Ye know:** You are well acquainted, *Berkeley* . . . I am sure you know, *Phillips* . . . with my behavior, *MLNT.*

**from the first day that I came into Asia:** . . . ever since I set foot in Asia, *Moffatt.*

**after what manner I have been with you at all seasons:** . . . the life that I always led among you, *TCNT* . . . the kind of life I lived among you the whole time, *Weymouth* . . . what my whole life has been like, *BB.*

**19. Serving the Lord:** . . . and how I continued to serve the Lord, *Williams* . . . Doing the Lord's work, *BB.*

**with all humility of mind:** . . . with all lowliness of mind, *ASV* . . . without pride, *BB* . . . with all modestie, *Geneva.*

**and with many tears, and temptations:** . . . with many a tear and many a trial, *Moffatt* . . . and in trials, *Beck* . . . and what tears I have shed over the trials, *Phillips.*

**which befell me:** . . . which I encountered, *Moffatt* . . . I endured, *Beck* . . . and this troubled me very much, *NCV.*

**by the lying in wait of the Jews:** . . . because of the evil designs of the Jews, *BB* . . . The Jews plotted against me, *NCV.*

**20. And how I kept back nothing that was profitable unto you, but have shewed you:** I never shrank from telling you anything that could be helpful to you, *TCNT* . . . anything that was beneficial to you, *Adams* . . . how I never refrained from telling you, *TNT.*

**Acts 20:21**

| 310.7 verb inf aor act | 5050.3 prs-pron dat 2pl | 2504.1 conj | 1315.18 verb inf aor act | 5050.4 prs-pron acc 2pl | 1212.1 adj dat sing fem |
|---|---|---|---|---|---|
| ἀναγγεῖλαι | ὑμῖν, | καὶ | διδάξαι | ὑμᾶς | δημοσίᾳ |
| anangeilai | humin | kai | didaxai | humas | dēmosia |
| to announce | to you, | and | to teach | you | publicly |

| 2504.1 conj | 2567.1 prep | 3486.7 noun acc pl masc | | 1257.4 verb nom sing masc part pres mid | 2428.4 name-adj dat pl masc |
|---|---|---|---|---|---|
| καὶ | κατ' | οἴκους, | **21.** | διαμαρτυρόμενος | Ἰουδαίοις |
| kai | kat' | oikous | | diamarturomenos | Ioudaiois |
| and | according to | houses, | | earnestly testifying | to Jews |

21.a.**Txt:** 02A,05D,020L 025P,byz.
**Var:** 01ℵ,03B,04C,08E Treg,Alf,Tisc,We/Ho Weis,Sod,UBS/⋆

| 4885.1 conj | 2504.1 conj | 1659.6 name dat pl masc | 3450.12 art acc sing fem | 1519.1 prep | 3450.6 art acc sing masc | 2296.4 noun acc sing masc |
|---|---|---|---|---|---|---|
| τε | καὶ | Ἕλλησιν | τὴν | εἰς | ⸀[a] τὸν ⸌ | θεὸν |
| te | kai | Hellēsin | tēn | eis | ton | theon |
| both | and | Greeks | the | toward | | God |

21.b.**Txt:** 08E,020L 025P,byz.
**Var:** 01ℵ,02A,03B,04C 05D,Lach,Treg,Alf,Tisc We/Ho,Weis,Sod UBS/⋆

| 3211.2 noun acc sing fem | 2504.1 conj | 3963.4 noun acc sing fem | 3450.12 art acc sing fem | 1519.1 prep | 3450.6 art acc sing masc | 2935.4 noun acc sing masc |
|---|---|---|---|---|---|---|
| μετάνοιαν | καὶ | πίστιν | ⸀[b] τὴν ⸌ | εἰς | τὸν | κύριον |
| metanoian | kai | pistin | tēn | eis | ton | kurion |
| repentance | and | faith | the | to | the | Lord |

21.c.**Txt:** p74,01ℵ,02A 04C,08E,33,bo.Tisc,Sod
**Var:** 03B,020L,025P,sa. Lach,Alf,We/Ho,Weis UBS/⋆

| 2231.2 prs-pron gen 1pl | 2400.3 name acc masc | 5382.4 name acc masc | | 2504.1 conj | 3431.1 adv | 1481.20 verb 2sing impr aor mid |
|---|---|---|---|---|---|---|
| ἡμῶν | Ἰησοῦν | ⸀[c] Χριστόν. ⸌ | **22.** | καὶ | νῦν | ἰδοὺ |
| hēmōn | Iēsoun | Christon | | kai | nun | idou |
| our | Jesus | Christ. | | And | now, | see, |

| 1466.1 prs-pron nom 1sing | 1204.17 verb nom sing masc part perf mid | 1204.17 verb nom sing masc part perf mid | 1466.1 prs-pron nom 1sing |
|---|---|---|---|
| ⸀ ἐγὼ | δεδεμένος | [⋆ δεδεμένος | ἐγὼ ] |
| egō | dedemenos | dedemenos | egō |
| I, | having been bound | [ having been bound | I ] |

| 3450.3 art dat sing | 4011.3 noun dat sing neu | 4057.1 verb 1sing indic pres mid | 1519.1 prep | 2395.1 name fem | 3450.17 art pl neu |
|---|---|---|---|---|---|
| τῷ | πνεύματι | πορεύομαι | εἰς | Ἱερουσαλήμ, | τὰ |
| tō | pneumati | poreuomai | eis | Hierousalēm | ta |
| in the | spirit, | am going | to | Jerusalem, | the |

22.a.**Txt:** 01ℵ-corr,02A 04C,05D,020L,025P,byz. Sod
**Var:** 01ℵ-org,03B,Tisc We/Ho,Weis,UBS/⋆

| 1706.1 prep | 840.11 prs-pron dat sing fem | 4727.4 verb pl neu part fut act | 1466.4 prs-pron dat 1sing | 1466.5 prs-pron dat 1sing | 3231.1 partic |
|---|---|---|---|---|---|
| ἐν | αὐτῇ | συναντήσοντά | ⸀ μοι | [a ἐμοὶ ] | μὴ |
| en | autē | sunantēsonta | moi | emoi | mē |
| in | it | happening | to me | [ idem ] | not |

| 3471.18 verb nom sing masc part perf act | | 3993.1 adv | 3617.1 conj | 3450.16 art sing neu | 4011.1 noun sing neu | 3450.16 art sing neu |
|---|---|---|---|---|---|---|
| εἰδώς, | **23.** | πλὴν | ὅτι | τὸ | πνεῦμα | τὸ |
| eidōs | | plēn | hoti | to | pneuma | to |
| knowing; | | except | that | the | Spirit | the |

23.a.**Var:** 01ℵ,02A,03B 04C,05D,08E,sa.bo. Gries,Lach,Treg,Alf Word,Tisc,We/Ho,Weis Sod,UBS/⋆

| 39.1 adj sing | 2567.3 prep | 4032.4 noun acc sing fem | 1257.2 verb 3sing indic pres mid | 1466.4 prs-pron dat 1sing |
|---|---|---|---|---|
| ἅγιον | κατὰ | πόλιν | διαμαρτύρεταί | [a⋆+ μοι ] |
| hagion | kata | polin | diamarturetai | moi |
| Holy | according to | city | fully testifies, | [ to me ] |

| 2978.23 verb sing neu part pres act | 3617.1 conj | 1193.3 noun pl | 1466.6 prs-pron acc 1sing | 2504.1 conj | 2324.5 noun nom pl fem |
|---|---|---|---|---|---|
| λέγον | ὅτι | δεσμὰ | ⸀ με | καὶ | θλίψεις |
| legon | hoti | desma | me | kai | thlipseis |
| saying | that | bonds | me | and | tribulations |

that was beneficial (helpful, profitable, useful, advantageous, for their good).

Paul had the heart of a true shepherd. The chief task of the eastern shepherd in Palestine is to find food and water for the sheep, and to protect them from enemies. So Paul was careful to give thorough teaching from the Word of God, both publicly and in every home that was open to him. Much of Paul's teaching and preaching was more like conversation or discussion. He did not try to impress the people with beautiful oratory.

**20:21.** To both Jews and Greeks, then, Paul bore witness to their need of repentance (a fundamental change of mind and attitudes) toward God and faith in the Lord Jesus. This would include the promises of God and a faith, trust, and acceptance of all Jesus had provided. (See, for example, 1:4,5; 2:4.)

**20:22.** Paul next indicated to the Ephesian elders why he believed it was the last time he would have the opportunity to see and encourage them. He told them he was going to Jerusalem, not only because of his own desire but because he was already bound by the Holy Spirit to go. That is, the Spirit had made it clear to him that divine necessity was still upon him to go to Jerusalem, though he did not know what he would encounter there.

Some believe that "bound in the spirit" means Paul was bound in his own spirit, for the King James Version does not capitalize the word "spirit" here. However, the most ancient copies of the New Testament were written completely in capital letters, so the small letter in our English translation tells us nothing. The original Greek uses the definite article here, however, and this would normally indicate the Holy Spirit. The whole context shows Paul was indeed bound or strongly constrained by the Holy Spirit to go on to Jerusalem, no matter what awaited him there.

**20:23.** The one thing Paul knew was that the Holy Spirit in city after city gave solemn witness (probably through the gift of prophecy) that bonds (chains) and afflictions (persecution, distress) awaited him in Jerusalem. (See also Romans 15:31.)

Clearly, these prophecies were not meant to give personal direction to Paul, nor were they intended to stop him from going to Jerusalem. The Bible indicates that prophecy, like most of the gifts of the Spirit, is intended to edify the church (the local assembly or congregations), not to guide individuals. The churches needed to know what was coming so when these things happened to Paul they would not be taken by surprise or have their faith shaken. Satan might have used Paul's imprisonment to discourage some if they

**and have taught you publickly, and from house to house:** . . . and teaching you publicly and in your homes, *Rotherham* . . . or from teaching you both in public and in private, *TCNT* . . . in meetings and in homes, *Beck.*

**21. Testifying both to the Jews, and also to the Greeks:** . . . bearing full witness both to Jews and to Greeks, *Rotherham* . . . and how I earnestly warned, *Beck* . . . earnestly urged Greeks as well as Jews, *Goodspeed.*

**repentance toward God:** . . . to change their lives and turn to God, *NCV* . . . to turn from sin to God, *Beck.*

**and faith toward our Lord Jesus Christ:** . . . and as to belief on our Lord Jesus, *Rotherham* . . . and trust in our Lord Jesus, *NEB* . . . I told them all to believe in our Lord, *NCV.*

**22. And now, behold, I go bound in the spirit unto Jerusalem:** And now, under spiritual constraint, *TCNT* . . . I am impelled by the Spirit, *Williams* . . . under the binding force of, *Moffatt* . . . a prisoner already, *JB* . . . under spiritual compulsion, *Kleist* . . . a prisoner in spirit, *Knox* . . . now I must obey the Holy Spirit and go, *NCV* . . . on my way to...for the Spirit compels me to go there, *Goodspeed.*

**not knowing the things that shall befall me there:** . . . and I have no idea of, *Norlie* . . . what will happen to me, *TCNT.*

**23. Save that the Holy Ghost witnesseth in every city:** . . . in town after town the Holy Spirit plainly declares to me, *TCNT* . . . makes clear to me, *BB* . . . emphatically assures me, *Williams* . . . the Holy Spirit assures me, *Knox* . . . fully testifies, *KJII* . . . tells me, *NCV* . . . testifieth to me, *Worrell* . . . in every town I visit, the holy Spirit warns me, *Goodspeed.*

**saying that bonds and afflictions abide me:** . . . imprisonment and suffering are awaiting me, *Weymouth* . . . that imprisonment and persecution, *Goodspeed, Kleist* . . . prison and pains, *BB* . . . and tribulations, *Worrell* . . . bondage and affliction await me, *Knox* . . . that troubles and even jail wait for me, *NCV.*

## Acts 20:24

24.a.**Txt:** 01ℵ-corr,02A 05D-org,08E,020L,025P byz.
**Var:** 01ℵ-org,03B,04C 05D-corr,sa.Treg,Alf Tisc,We/Ho,Weis,Sod UBS/*

24.b.**Txt:** 08E,020L 025P,byz.
**Var:** 01ℵ-org,03B,04C 05D-corr,sa.Treg,Alf Tisc,We/Ho,Weis,Sod UBS/*

24.c.**Txt:** 08E,020L,025P byz.
**Var:** 01ℵ-org,03B,04C 05D-corr,sa.Treg,Alf Tisc,We/Ho,Weis,Sod UBS/*

24.d.**Txt:** p41,02A,05D 08E,044,byz.
**Var:** 01ℵ,03B,vul.

24.e.**Txt:** 04C,08E,020L 025P,byz.Sod
**Var:** 01ℵ,02A,03B,05D sa.bo.Lach,Treg,Alf,Tisc We/Ho,Weis,UBS/*

25.a.**Txt:** 08E,020L 025P,byz.
**Var:** 01ℵ,02A,03B,04C Lach,Treg,Alf,Word Tisc,We/Ho,Weis,Sod UBS/*

**2504.1** conj [☆ καὶ *kai* [and
**2324.5** noun nom pl fem θλίψεις *thlipseis* tribulations
**1466.6** prs-pron acc 1sing με ] *me* me]
**3176.6** verb 3pl indic pres act μένουσιν. *menousin* await.
**233.1** conj **24.** ἀλλ' *all'* But

**3625.1** num card gen οὐδενὸς *oudenos* of nothing
**3030.4** noun acc sing masc ʻ λόγον *logon* account
**3030.2** noun gen sing masc [ᵃ☆ λόγου ] *logou* [of account]
**4020.60** verb 1sing indic pres mid ποιοῦμαι, *poioumai* I make,
**3624.1** conj ʻᵇ οὐδὲ *oude* nor

**2174.1** verb 1sing pres act ἔχω ˋ *echō* I hold
**3450.12** art acc sing fem τὴν *tēn* the
**5425.4** noun acc sing fem ψυχὴν *psuchēn* life
**1466.2** prs-pron gen 1sing ʻᶜ μου ˋ *mou* my
**4941.6** adj acc sing fem τιμίαν *timian* dear
**1670.2** prs-pron dat 1sing masc ἐμαυτῷ, *emautō* to myself,

**5453.1** conj ὡς *hōs* as
**4896.5** verb inf aor act ʻ τελειῶσαι *teleiōsai* to finish
**4896.3** verb 1sing subj aor act [ᵈ τελειώσω ] *teleiōsō* [I may finish]
**3450.6** art acc sing masc τὸν *ton* the
**1402.1** noun acc sing masc δρόμον *dromon* course

**1466.2** prs-pron gen 1sing μου *mou* my
**3196.3** prep ʻᵉ μετὰ *meta* with
**5315.2** noun gen sing fem χαρᾶς, ˋ *charas* joy,
**2504.1** conj καὶ *kai* and
**3450.12** art acc sing fem τὴν *tēn* the
**1242.4** noun acc sing fem διακονίαν *diakonian* ministry

**3614.12** rel-pron acc sing fem ἣν *hēn* which
**2956.12** verb indic aor act ἔλαβον *elabon* I received
**3706.2** prep παρὰ *para* from
**3450.2** art gen sing τοῦ *tou* the
**2935.2** noun gen sing masc κυρίου *kuriou* Lord
**2400.2** name masc Ἰησοῦ, *Iēsou* Jesus,

**1257.9** verb inf aor mid διαμαρτύρασθαι *diamarturasthai* to testify fully
**3450.16** art sing neu τὸ *to* the
**2077.1** noun sing neu εὐαγγέλιον *euangelion* good news
**3450.10** art gen sing fem τῆς *tēs* of the
**5322.2** noun gen sing fem χάριτος *charitos* grace

**3450.2** art gen sing τοῦ *tou*
**2296.2** noun gen sing masc θεοῦ. *theou* of God.
**2504.1** conj **25.** Καὶ *Kai* And
**3431.1** adv νῦν *nun* now,
**1481.20** verb 2sing impr aor mid ἰδοὺ *idou* see,
**1466.1** prs-pron nom 1sing ἐγὼ *egō* I

**3471.2** verb 1sing indic perf act οἶδα *oida* know
**3617.1** conj ὅτι *hoti* that
**3629.1** adv οὐκέτι *ouketi* no more
**3571.33** verb 2pl indic fut mid ὄψεσθε *opsesthe* will see
**3450.16** art sing neu τὸ *to* the
**4241.1** noun sing neu πρόσωπόν *prosōpon* face

**1466.2** prs-pron gen 1sing μου *mou* my
**5050.1** prs-pron nom 2pl ὑμεῖς *humeis* you
**3820.7** adj nom pl masc πάντες, *pantes* all,
**1706.1** prep ἐν *en* among
**3614.4** rel-pron dat pl οἷς *hois* whom
**1324.1** verb indic aor act διῆλθον *diēlthon* I have gone about

**2756.6** verb nom sing masc part pres act κηρύσσων *kērussōn* proclaiming
**3450.12** art acc sing fem τὴν *tēn* the
**926.4** noun acc sing fem βασιλείαν *basileian* kingdom
**3450.2** art gen sing ʻᵃ τοῦ *tou*
**2296.2** noun gen sing masc Θεοῦ. ˋ *Theou* of God.

had not been forewarned. Or some might have imagined that some sin brought on Paul's imprisonment.



**24. But none of these things move me:** However, I am not concerned about anything, *Berkeley* . . . I make no account (of these things), *PNT* . . . But I do not attach any importance to, *Noli* . . . I care nothing for all that, *Knox.*

**neither count I my life dear unto myself:** . . . frankly I do not consider my own life valuable to me, *Phillips* . . . as of no value unto myself, *Alford* . . . But even the sacrifice of my life I count as nothing, *Weymouth* . . . worth nothing, *NIV* . . . I set no value, *Moffatt* . . . But I don't care about my own life, *NCV* . . . count my life precious compared with my work, *Knox.*

**so that I might finish my course with joy:** . . . if only I may complete the course marked out for me, *TCNT* . . . The most important thing is, *NCV* . . . I want only to complete the race I am running, *Noli* . . . unless I can finish my race, *Klingensmith* . . . if only I accomplish my course, *Kleist* . . . in order to complete my course and the mission, *TNT.*

**and the ministry:** . . . and be faithful to the duty, *Weymouth* . . . the dispensation, *Concordant* . . . I want to finish the work, *NCV* . . . accomplish the ministry, *Montgomery* . . . to fulfill the mission, *Noli* . . . the commission, *Fenton* . . . and complete the ministry, *Phillips* . . . the task of preaching, *Knox.*

**which I have received of the Lord Jesus:** . . . was allotted, *TCNT* . . . which I accepted from, *MLNT* . . . which the Lord Jesus has entrusted to me, *Weymouth* . . . which the Lord Jesus has given me, *Knox.*

**to testify the gospel of the grace of God:** . . . to bear full witness, *Rotherham* . . . of faithfully telling, *Williams* . . . to proclaim the Gospel of the divine grace, *Noli* . . . to tell people the Good News about God's grace, *NCV* . . . so as to full testify, *KJII.*

**25. And now, behold, I know that ye all:** I tell you, I know that none of you, *TCNT* . . . I am perfectly sure that, *Noli.*

**among whom I have gone preaching the kingdom of God:** All the time I was with you, *NCV.*

**shall see my face no more:** . . . will ever seen my face again, *TCNT.*

**20:24.** Paul was not only bound by the Holy Spirit to go to Jerusalem, he was willing to go. On no account did he make his life valuable (precious) to himself. He greatly desired to finish his run (as in a race) with joy, accomplishing the ministry (the service) which he had received from the Lord, giving serious witness to the good news of the grace of God.

In other words, the threat of danger could not turn Paul back from what he knew was God's will because he had already given up everything and put his life on the altar for the Lord (Philippians 3:8). He was not afraid of persecution or even death.

He had a secret. He had seen "the light of the knowledge of the glory of God in the face of Jesus Christ" (2 Corinthians 4:6). He felt in his body "the excellency of the power . . . of God" (2 Corinthians 4:7). He had received the "earnest" or first installment of what the Spirit will make fully real for every believer when Jesus comes again (2 Corinthians 1:22; 5:5; Ephesians 1:14). Therefore, he was willing "to be absent from the body, and to be present with the Lord" (2 Corinthians 5:8). Above all, the resurrection of Jesus from the dead gave him the assurance of his own resurrection, and made it such a real hope that all fear of death was gone (1 Corinthians 15:20,51,54; 2 Corinthians 4:14-16; Hebrews 2:14,15). Death is not a defeat for the Christian for each believer shall rise in glorious victory. The Christian does not need to fear the consequences of anything the Holy Spirit directs him to do. He cannot lose.

**20:25.** Paul next let the elders know this was a final farewell. They would never see him again.

But he did not simply draw attention to the finality of this visit. The thing that concerned him was that he had gone about among them preaching the kingdom of God. This would be the last time he would be able to reinforce that teaching and remind them of the grace of God. That grace had saved him from the life of a willful, murderous Pharisee and had called him to a worldwide, earth-shaking ministry where he proclaimed the kingdom or rule of God, made manifest in and through Jesus by God's grace.

In the same way, Paul showed that the gospel of the grace of God is the same as the preaching of the kingdom of God, and therefore is the same as the gospel of the Kingdom. It is by God's grace that believers are brought under the rule and authority of God through the Lord Jesus, by His death and resurrection. Believers show they are under His rule by righteousness, peace, and joy in the Holy Spirit (Romans 14:17). There is only one gospel, and it includes the present rule of God as well as the future rule when Jesus will establish His kingdom on earth.

## Acts 20:26

26.a.**Txt:** 04C,05D-corr 020L,byz.
**Var:** 01ℵ,02A,03B,08E 025P,Alf,Tisc,We/Ho Weis,Sod,UBS/☆

| **1346.1** conj | **1354.1** conj | **3113.31** verb 1sing indic pres mid | **5050.3** prs-pron dat 2pl | **1706.1** prep |
|---|---|---|---|---|
| **26.** ⸀ διὸ | [a☆ διότι ] | μαρτύρομαι | ὑμῖν | ἐν |
| *dio* | *dioti* | *marturomai* | *humin* | *en* |
| Wherefore | [ Therefore ] | I am testifying | to you | in |

| **3450.11** art dat sing fem | **4449.1** adv | **2232.3** noun dat sing fem | **3617.1** conj | **2485.3** adj nom sing masc | **1466.1** prs-pron nom 1sing |
|---|---|---|---|---|---|
| τῇ | σήμερον | ἡμέρᾳ, | ὅτι | καθαρός | ⸀ ἐγὼ |
| *tē* | *sēmeron* | *hēmera* | *hoti* | *katharos* | *egō* |
| the | today | day | that | clean | I |

26.b.**Txt:** 02A,020L 025P,byz.bo.
**Var:** 01ℵ,03B,04C,05D 08E,sa.Lach,Treg,Alf Tisc,We/Ho,Weis,Sod UBS/☆

| **1498.2** verb 1sing indic pres act | **570.3** prep | **3450.2** art gen sing | **129.2** noun gen sing neu | **3820.4** adj gen pl | **3620.3** partic |
|---|---|---|---|---|---|
| [b☆ εἰμι ] | ἀπὸ | τοῦ | αἵματος | πάντων· | **27.** οὐ |
| *eimi* | *apo* | *tou* | *haimatos* | *pantōn* | *ou* |
| [ am ] | from | the | blood | of all, | not |

27.a.**Txt:** 01ℵ-corr,02A 08E,020L,025P,byz.sa. bo.
**Var:** 01ℵ-org,03B,04C 05D,Lach,Treg,Alf,Tisc We/Ho,Weis,Sod UBS/☆

| **1056.1** conj | **5126.2** verb 1sing indic aor mid | **3450.2** art gen sing | **3231.1** partic | **310.7** verb inf aor act | **5050.3** prs-pron dat 2pl |
|---|---|---|---|---|---|
| γὰρ | ὑπεστειλάμην | τοῦ | μὴ | ἀναγγεῖλαι | ⸂a ὑμῖν ⸃ |
| *gar* | *hupesteilamēn* | *tou* | *mē* | *anangeilai* | *humin* |
| for | I kept back | the | not | to announce | to you |

27.b.**Var:** 01ℵ-org,03B 04C,05D,Lach,Treg,Alf Tisc,We/Ho,Weis,Sod UBS/☆

| **3820.12** adj acc sing fem | **3450.12** art acc sing fem | **1005.4** noun acc sing fem | **3450.2** art gen sing | **2296.2** noun gen sing masc | **5050.3** prs-pron dat 2pl |
|---|---|---|---|---|---|
| πᾶσαν | τὴν | βουλὴν | τοῦ | θεοῦ. | [b☆+ ὑμῖν. ] |
| *pasan* | *tēn* | *boulēn* | *tou* | *theou* | *humin* |
| all | the | counsel | | of God. | [ to you. ] |

28.a.**Txt:** 04C,08E,020L 025P,byz.
**Var:** 01ℵ,02A,03B,05D bo.Treg,Tisc,We/Ho Weis,Sod,UBS/☆

| **4196.2** verb 2pl impr pres act | **3631.1** partic | **1431.7** prs-pron dat pl masc | **2504.1** conj | **3820.3** adj dat sing |
|---|---|---|---|---|
| **28.** προσέχετε | ⸂a οὖν ⸃ | ἑαυτοῖς | καὶ | παντὶ |
| *prosechete* | *oun* | *heautois* | *kai* | *panti* |
| Pay attention | therefore | to yourselves | and | to all |

| **3450.3** art dat sing | **4028.2** noun dat sing neu | **1706.1** prep | **3614.3** rel-pron dat sing | **5050.4** prs-pron acc 2pl | **3450.16** art sing neu | **4011.1** noun sing neu |
|---|---|---|---|---|---|---|
| τῷ | ποιμνίῳ, | ἐν | ᾧ | ὑμᾶς | τὸ | πνεῦμα |
| *tō* | *poimniō* | *en* | *hō* | *humas* | *to* | *pneuma* |
| the | flock, | in | which | you | the | Spirit |

| **3450.16** art sing neu | **39.1** adj sing | **4935.30** verb 3sing indic aor mid | **1969.3** noun acc pl masc | **4025.5** verb inf pres act |
|---|---|---|---|---|
| τὸ | ἅγιον | ἔθετο | ἐπισκόπους, | ποιμαίνειν |
| *to* | *hagion* | *etheto* | *episkopous* | *poimainein* |
| the | Holy | placed | overseers, | to shepherd |

28.b.**Var:** p74,02A 04C-org,05D,08E,33,sa. bo.Gries,Lach,Treg,Tisc Sod

| **3450.12** art acc sing fem | **1564.4** noun acc sing fem | **3450.2** art gen sing | **2296.2** noun gen sing masc | **3450.2** art gen sing | **2935.2** noun gen sing masc |
|---|---|---|---|---|---|
| τὴν | ἐκκλησίαν | ⸀ τοῦ | θεοῦ, | [b τοῦ | κυρίου, ] |
| *tēn* | *ekklēsian* | *tou* | *theou* | *tou* | *kuriou* |
| the | assembly | | of God, | [ of the | Lord, ] |

| **3614.12** rel-pron acc sing fem | **3909.2** verb 3sing indic aor mid | **1217.2** prep | **3450.2** art gen sing | **2375.2** adj gen sing |
|---|---|---|---|---|
| ἣν | περιεποιήσατο | διὰ | τοῦ | ⸀ ἰδίου |
| *hēn* | *periepoiēsato* | *dia* | *tou* | *idiou* |
| which | he purchased | through | the | his own |

28.c.**Txt:** 020L,025P,byz. lect.
**Var:** p74,01ℵ,02A,03B 04C,05D,08E,044,33 Gries,Lach,Treg,Alf Word,Tisc,We/Ho,Weis Sod,UBS/☆

| **129.2** noun gen sing neu | **129.2** noun gen sing neu | **3450.2** art gen sing | **2375.2** adj gen sing | **1466.1** prs-pron nom 1sing |
|---|---|---|---|---|
| αἵματος. | [c☆ αἵματος | τοῦ | ἰδίου. ] | **29.** ἐγὼ |
| *haimatos* | *haimatos* | *tou* | *idiou* | *egō* |
| blood. | [ blood | the | his own. ] | I |

**20:26.** In this final farewell Paul bore witness that he was pure (clean) from the blood of all. Paul undoubtedly had in mind here the reference to Ezekiel who was appointed a watchman and a warner to the people of Israel who were in exile in Babylon (see Ezekiel 3:16-21). God considered Ezekiel as a lookout or sentry watching for sin. A sentry who neglects his duty and lets the enemy through without sounding a warning is, in wartime, court-martialed and executed. God made it clear that if Ezekiel failed, the blood of those he failed would be on his hands; he would be guilty.

**20:27.** Paul was free from guilt. No one could say he had failed in giving warning. Even more important, he never shrank from proclaiming the whole counsel (all the wise counsel, all the wise plan and purpose) of God. He gave himself in full devotion to the Word and will of God. He also told the people what to expect, both with respect to persecutions and difficulties in the present and the glories to come.

Ephesians 1:3-14 also shows what Paul meant by the wise counsel or purpose of God. There Paul showed it is God's will or choice for Christians to be holy in a positive way through dedication and service to God. It is God's will or choice for believers also to be blameless. He pours out heaven's blessings on them, not so they can waste them on the desires of their own flesh and mind, but so they can be like Jesus.

**20:28.** Paul had warned them before. Now he continued to challenge them with a warning which showed his concern over both the present and future welfare of the church.

First, he warned the elders themselves. Let them attend (give attention) to themselves for the sake of the flock. They must realize the greatness of their responsibility, taking care of their own spiritual well-being. They were also to take the same care and give the same attention to all the flock among whom the Holy Spirit had made them bishops (overseers, superintendents, ruling elders, presidents of the local congregations or house churches), to feed or shepherd the assembly (Greek, *ekklēsia*, as in 19:41) of God.

The "assembly of God" includes all whom He (Jesus) made His own through His own blood, that is, through the shedding of His blood when He died in agony on Calvary (Ephesians 1:7; Titus 2:14; Hebrews 9:12,14; 13:12,13).

It is clear here also that the elder and the bishop were interchangeable terms for the same elected office. They were Spirit-filled people who were led by the Spirit. Thus the Holy Spirit really gave the office. They were also dependent on the Holy Spirit for the gifts of administration (governments) and ruling necessary for the carrying out of their office (Romans 12:8; 1 Corinthians 12:28). In addition they needed Spirit-anointed, Christ-given ministries to be pastors (shepherds) and teachers of the assembly.

**26. Wherefore I take you to record this day:** I take you to witness this day, *Alford* . . . Therefore I declare to you this day, *TCNT* . . . So today I can tell you one thing that I am sure of, *NCV* . . . solemnly affirm, *Weymouth.*

**that I am pure from the blood of all men:** . . . that I am clear from, *Montgomery* . . . that I am guiltless, *Berkeley* . . . that, should any of you perish, the responsibility is not mine, *Weymouth* . . . I am not responsible for the fate of any one of you, *TNT* . . . that my conscience is clear as far as any of you is concerned, *Phillips.*

**27. For I have not shunned to declare unto you:** For I have not fallen short at all of preaching to you, *Berkeley* . . . I have never hesitated to announce to you, *TNT.*

**all the counsel of God:** . . . the whole counsel of God, *RSV* . . . the whole purpose of God concerning you, *TCNT* . . . the complete will of God, *Phillips* . . . God's whole plan, *Weymouth.*

**28. Take heed therefore unto yourselves:** Be watchful over yourselves, *TCNT* . . . Give attention to, *BB* . . . Be on guard for yourselves, *Berkeley.*

**and to all the flock:** . . . and over the whole flock, *TCNT* . . . and for every flock, *Phillips.*

**over the which the Holy Ghost hath made you overseers:** . . . has appointed you as, *TNT* . . . has constituted, *Campbell* . . . you bishops, *ASV* . . . shepherds, *Norlie* . . . has placed you in charge, *TCNT* . . . has given into your care, *BB* . . . has made you guardians, *Phillips* . . . sent you to watch, *Klingensmith* . . . The Holy Spirit chose you to guard this flock, *SEB.*

**to feed the church of God:** . . . to be shepherding the assembly of God, *Rotherham* . . . to feed the congregation, *Campbell* . . . to rule the church of God, *Douay.*

**which he hath purchased with his own blood:** . . . which he has bought, *Weymouth* . . . at the cost of his own life, *TCNT* . . . which he acquired, *Rotherham* . . . which he won for himself, *TNT* . . . with the blood of His own Son, *Fenton.*

29.a.**Txt:** 04C-corr,08E 020L,025P,byz.sa.Sod **Var:** 01ℵ-org,02A 04C-org,05D,Lach,Treg Alf,Word,Tisc,We/Ho Weis,UBS/☆

29.b.**Txt:** 04C-corr,08E 020L,025P,byz.Sod **Var:** 01ℵ,02A,03B 04C-org,05D,sa.bo.Lach Treg,Alf,Word,Tisc We/Ho,Weis,UBS/☆

| **1056.1** conj | **3471.2** verb 1sing indic perf act | **3642.17** dem-pron sing neu | **3617.1** conj | **1511.39** verb 3pl indic fut mid |
|---|---|---|---|---|
| (a γὰρ ) | οἶδα | (b τοῦτο, ) | ὅτι | εἰσελεύσονται |
| *gar* | *oida* | *touto* | *hoti* | *eiseleusontai* |
| for | know | this, | that | will come in |

| **3196.3** prep | **3450.12** art acc sing fem | **860.1** noun acc sing fem | **1466.2** prs-pron gen 1sing | **3046.3** noun nom pl masc | **920.1** adj nom pl masc | **1519.1** prep |
|---|---|---|---|---|---|---|
| μετὰ | τὴν | ἄφιξίν | μου | λύκοι | βαρεῖς | εἰς |
| *meta* | *tēn* | *aphixin* | *mou* | *lukoi* | *bareis* | *eis* |
| after | the | departure | my | wolves | grievous | among |

| **5050.4** prs-pron acc 2pl | **3231.1** partic | **5177.3** verb nom pl masc part pres mid | **3450.2** art gen sing | **4028.1** noun gen sing neu | **2504.1** conj |
|---|---|---|---|---|---|
| ὑμᾶς, | μὴ | φειδόμενοι | τοῦ | ποιμνίου· | **30.** καὶ |
| *humas* | *mē* | *pheidomenoi* | *tou* | *poimniou* | *kai* |
| you, | not | sparing | the | flock; | and |

| **1523.1** prep gen | **5050.2** prs-pron gen 2pl | **840.1** prs-pron gen pl | **448.21** verb 3pl indic fut mid | **433.6** noun nom pl masc |
|---|---|---|---|---|
| ἐξ | ὑμῶν | αὐτῶν | ἀναστήσονται | ἄνδρες |
| *ex* | *humōn* | *autōn* | *anastēsontai* | *andres* |
| from among | your | selves | will rise up | men |

| **2953.16** verb nom pl masc part pres act | **1288.6** verb pl neu part perf mid | **3450.2** art gen sing | **639.1** verb inf pres act |
|---|---|---|---|
| λαλοῦντες | διεστραμμένα, | τοῦ | ἀποσπᾶν |
| *lalountes* | *diestrammena* | *tou* | *apospan* |
| speaking | having been perverted things, | the | to draw away |

30.a.**Txt:** 04C,05D,08E 020L,025P,etc.byz.Sod **Var:** 01ℵ,02A,03B,Treg Alf,Tisc,We/Ho,Weis UBS/☆

| **3450.8** art acc pl masc | **3073.8** noun acc pl masc | **3557.1** adv | **840.1** prs-pron gen pl | **1431.2** prs-pron gen pl |
|---|---|---|---|---|
| τοὺς | μαθητὰς | ὀπίσω | ( αὐτῶν. | [a ἑαυτῶν. ] |
| *tous* | *mathētas* | *opisō* | *autōn* | *heautōn* |
| the | disciples | after | themselves. | [ idem ] |

| **1346.1** conj | **1121.3** verb 2pl impr pres act | **3285.6** verb nom pl masc part pres act | **3617.1** conj | **4989.1** noun acc sing fem |
|---|---|---|---|---|
| **31.** διὸ | γρηγορεῖτε, | μνημονεύοντες | ὅτι | τριετίαν |
| *dio* | *grēgoreite* | *mnēmoneuontes* | *hoti* | *trietian* |
| Wherefore | keep watching, | remembering | that | three years |

| **3433.4** noun acc sing fem | **2504.1** conj | **2232.4** noun acc sing fem | **3620.2** partic | **3835.5** verb 1sing indic aor mid | **3196.3** prep | **1139.2** noun gen pl neu |
|---|---|---|---|---|---|---|
| νύκτα | καὶ | ἡμέραν | οὐκ | ἐπαυσάμην | μετὰ | δακρύων |
| *nukta* | *kai* | *hēmeran* | *ouk* | *epausamēn* | *meta* | *dakruōn* |
| night | and | day | not | I ceased | with | tears |

| **3423.3** verb nom sing masc part pres act | **1518.4** num card acc masc | **1524.1** adj sing | **2504.1** conj | **4860.1** adv | **3450.17** art pl neu |
|---|---|---|---|---|---|
| νουθετῶν | ἕνα | ἕκαστον. | **32.** καὶ | ( τανῦν | [☆ τὰ |
| *nouthetōn* | *hena* | *hekaston* | *kai* | *tanun* | *ta* |
| admonishing | one | each. | And | now | [ the |

32.a.**Txt:** 04C,08E,020L 025P,byz. **Var:** 01ℵ,02A,03B,05D 33,sa.bo.Lach,Treg,Alf Tisc,We/Ho,Weis,Sod UBS/☆

| **3431.1** adv | **3769.7** verb 1sing indic pres mid | **5050.4** prs-pron acc 2pl | **79.6** noun nom pl masc | **3450.3** art dat sing |
|---|---|---|---|---|
| νῦν ] | παρατίθεμαι | ὑμᾶς, | (a ἀδελφοί, ) | τῷ |
| *nun* | *paratithemai* | *humas* | *adelphoi* | *tō* |
| now ] | I commit | you, | brothers, | |

32.b.**Txt:** p74,01ℵ,02A 04C,05D,08E,020L 025P,etc.byz.Tisc,Sod **Var:** 03B,bo.We/Ho Weis,UBS/☆

| **2296.3** noun dat sing masc | **2935.3** noun dat sing masc | **2504.1** conj | **3450.3** art dat sing | **3030.3** noun dat sing masc | **3450.10** art gen sing fem |
|---|---|---|---|---|---|
| ( θεῷ | [b κυρίῳ ] | καὶ | τῷ | λόγῳ | τῆς |
| *theō* | *kuriō* | *kai* | *tō* | *logō* | *tēs* |
| to God | [ to Lord ] | and | to the | word | of the |

**20:29.** Another part of the work of the shepherd was to protect the sheep from enemies. The shepherd's staff guided the sheep. The shepherd's rod protected them from the wolves who came to destroy the sheep. Paul therefore warned these elders that after his departure, grievous (heavy, difficult to handle) wolves would come in among them, not sparing the little flock, but injuring them severely. (See Luke 12:32 where the flock means Jesus' disciples.)

**20:30.** These savage wolves would be false teachers who would bring terrible trouble (Matthew 7:15; 2 Timothy 3:5-8; Jude 4,10,12,13; Revelation 2:2).

Not all of these wolves would come into the church from outside. Sad to say, some would rise up from among the believers, even from among these Spirit-filled, Spirit-anointed elders themselves. By perverting the truth or by twisting the Scriptures, they would seek to draw away a following for themselves from the disciples, even splitting up the local assemblies to do it.

Paul's warning indicated the real purpose of these false teachers would be to build up themselves rather than the assembly. They would attempt to draw away disciples who were already believers. They would have little interest in winning the lost for Christ, nor would they desire to build up the churches (assemblies) that were already established.

That this was a very serious and prevalent problem is shown by the many warnings in Paul's epistles. (See Romans 16:17,18; Colossians 2:8; 1 Timothy 4:1-3; Titus 1:10,11.)

**20:31.** The elders needed to be on their guard, not only against such wolves as these, but against becoming one themselves. (Compare 1 Timothy 1:19,20; 4:1-10; 2 Timothy 1:15; 2:17,18; 3:1-9; Revelation 2:2-4.)

Paul set them an example in this too. For the nearly 3 years he had been with them in Ephesus, he had never ceased warning each one of them with tears night and day. He was instant in season and out of season; he was always moved by tender love for them. Nor did he limit himself to office hours. He was always available to meet any need. Again, from Paul's epistles it is clear that during those years he was opposed by many "wolves" and false brethren.

**20:32.** Paul always did more than warn the believers. He also commended (entrusted) them to God and to His gracious Word which was able to edify them (build them up spiritually) and give them the inheritance among all those who are sanctified, that is, among those who are holy, set apart to follow Jesus.

The inheritance Paul was talking about is the very definite, well-known, promised inheritance. Jesus had sent Paul among the Gentiles "that they may receive forgiveness of sins, and inheritance among them which are sanctified by faith that is in me (in Jesus)"

**29. For I know this, that after my departing:** . . . when I am gone, *Weymouth* . . . I know that after I leave, *NCV.*

**shall grievous wolves enter in among you:** . . . some men will come like wild wolves, *NCV* . . . merciless wolves will get in, *TCNT* . . . violent wolves will break in, *Williams* . . . cruel, *Weymouth* . . . ferocious wolves will enter, *Noli.*

**not sparing the flock:** . . . and try to destroy the flock, *NCV* . . . that have no mercy on, *Berkeley.*

**30. Also of your own selves shall men arise:** And even some of you men will start, *Beck* . . . men among your own number, *Knox* . . . from your own group, *NCV.*

**speaking perverse things:** . . . speaking distorted things, *Rotherham* . . . and will teach perversions of truth, *TCNT* . . . who will give wrong teaching, *BB* . . . and teach false doctrines, *Norlie* . . . will speak contrary things, *Klingensmith* . . . who will pervert the truth, *TNT* . . . and twist the truth, *NCV* . . . with a false message, *Knox.*

**to draw away disciples after them:** . . . in order to, *TNT* . . . make them followers of themselves, *Phillips* . . . The will lead away followers after them, *NCV.*

**31. Therefore watch:** . . . be on your guard, *TCNT* . . . be on the alert, *Weymouth* . . . Keep, therefore, on the lookout, *Berkeley* . . . be-on-the-watch, *Rotherham.*

**and remember, that by the space of three years:** . . . for three years, *ET.*

**I ceased not to warn every one night and day with tears:** I never failed...to warn every one of you, even with tears in my eyes, *Phillips* . . . I did not cease counselling each one of you, *TNT.*

**32. And now, brethren, I commend you to God:** Now I am giving you to God, *SEB* . . . I give you into the care of God, *BB* . . . I give you to the Lord for protection, *Klingensmith* . . . For the present I commend, *Kleist.*

**and to the word of his grace:** . . . and to the Message of his love, *TCNT* . . . and to his gracious Son, *Noli.*

32.c.**Txt:** 020L,025P,byz.
**Var:** 01ℵ,02A,03B,04C
05D,08E,Lach,Treg,Alf
Word,Tisc,We/Ho,Weis
Sod,UBS/☆

| **5322.2** noun gen sing fem | **840.3** prs-pron gen sing | **3450.3** art dat sing | **1404.14** verb dat sing masc part pres mid | **2010.4** verb inf aor act |
|---|---|---|---|---|
| χάριτος | αὐτοῦ, | τῷ | δυναμένῳ | ⸀ ἐποικοδομῆσαι |
| *charitos* | *autou* | *tō* | *dunamenō* | *epoikodomēsai* |
| grace | his, | the | being able | to build up |

32.d.**Txt:** 04C,020L
025P,byz.sa.
**Var:** 01ℵ,02A,03B,05D
08E,bo.Lach,Treg,Alf
Tisc,We/Ho,Weis,Sod
UBS/☆

| **3481.10** verb inf aor act | **2504.1** conj | **1319.31** verb inf aor act | **5050.3** prs-pron dat 2pl | **3450.12** art acc sing fem |
|---|---|---|---|---|
| [c☆ οἰκοδομῆσαι ] | καὶ | δοῦναι | ⸂d ὑμῖν ⸃ | [e☆+ τὴν ] |
| *oikodomēsai* | *kai* | *dounai* | *humin* | *tēn* |
| [ idem ] | and | to give | you | [ the ] |

32.e.**Var:** 01ℵ,02A,03B
04C,08E,Treg,Alf,Tisc
We/Ho,Weis,Sod
UBS/☆

| **2790.3** noun acc sing fem | **1706.1** prep | **3450.4** art dat pl | **37.18** verb dat pl masc part perf mid | **3820.5** adj dat pl |
|---|---|---|---|---|
| κληρονομίαν | ἐν | τοῖς | ἡγιασμένοις | πᾶσιν. |
| *klēronomian* | *en* | *tois* | *hēgiasmenois* | *pasin* |
| an inheritance | among | the | having been sanctified | all. |

| **688.2** noun gen sing neu | **2211.1** conj | **5388.2** noun gen sing neu | **2211.1** conj | **2417.2** noun gen sing masc | **3625.1** num card gen |
|---|---|---|---|---|---|
| 33. ἀργυρίου | ἢ | χρυσίου | ἢ | ἱματισμοῦ | οὐδενὸς |
| *arguriou* | *ē* | *chrusiou* | *ē* | *himatismou* | *oudenos* |
| Silver | or | gold | or | clothing | of no one |

34.a.**Txt:** bo.Steph
**Var:** 01ℵ,02A,03B,04C
05D,08E,020L,025P,sa.
Gries,Lach,Treg,Alf
Word,Tisc,We/Ho,Weis
Sod,UBS/☆

| **1922.6** verb 1sing indic aor act | **840.7** prs-pron nom pl masc | **1156.2** conj | **1091.5** verb 2pl indic pres act | **3617.1** conj | **3450.14** art dat pl fem |
|---|---|---|---|---|---|
| ἐπεθύμησα· | 34. αὐτοὶ | ⸂a δὲ ⸃ | γινώσκετε | ὅτι | ταῖς |
| *epethumēsa* | *autoi* | *de* | *ginōskete* | *hoti* | *tais* |
| I desired. | Yourselves | but | know | that | to the |

| **5367.4** noun dat pl fem | **1466.2** prs-pron gen 1sing | **2504.1** conj | **3450.4** art dat pl | **1498.24** verb dat pl masc part pres act | **3196.2** prep | **1466.3** prs-pron gen 1sing |
|---|---|---|---|---|---|---|
| χρείαις | μου | καὶ | τοῖς | οὖσιν | μετ' | ἐμοῦ |
| *chreiais* | *mou* | *kai* | *tois* | *ousin* | *met'* | *emou* |
| needs | my | and | to the | being | with | me |

| **5094.2** verb 3pl indic aor act | **3450.13** art nom pl fem | **5331.5** noun nom pl fem | **3642.13** dem-pron nom pl fem | **3820.1** adj |
|---|---|---|---|---|
| ὑπηρέτησαν | αἱ | χεῖρες | αὗται. | 35. πάντα |
| *hupēretēsan* | *hai* | *cheires* | *hautai* | *panta* |
| ministered | the | hands | these. | All things |

| **5101.1** verb 1sing indic aor act | **5050.3** prs-pron dat 2pl | **3617.1** conj | **3643.1** adv | **2844.8** verb acc pl masc part pres act | **1158.1** verb 3sing indic pres act |
|---|---|---|---|---|---|
| ὑπέδειξα | ὑμῖν | ὅτι | οὕτως | κοπιῶντας | δεῖ |
| *hupedeixa* | *humin* | *hoti* | *houtōs* | *kopiōntas* | *dei* |
| I showed | you | that | thus | laboring | it is necessary |

| **479.2** verb inf pres mid | **3450.1** art gen pl | **764.8** verb gen pl masc part pres act | **3285.7** verb inf pres act |
|---|---|---|---|
| ἀντιλαμβάνεσθαι | τῶν | ἀσθενούντων, | μνημονεύειν |
| *antilambanesthai* | *tōn* | *asthenountōn* | *mnēmoneuein* |
| to aid | the | being weak, | to remember |

| **4885.1** conj | **3450.1** art gen pl | **3030.6** noun gen pl masc | **3450.2** art gen sing | **2935.2** noun gen sing masc | **2400.2** name masc | **3617.1** conj |
|---|---|---|---|---|---|---|
| τε | τῶν | λόγων | τοῦ | κυρίου | Ἰησοῦ | ὅτι |
| *te* | *tōn* | *logōn* | *tou* | *kuriou* | *Iēsou* | *hoti* |
| and | the | words | of the | Lord | Jesus | that |

| **840.5** prs-pron nom sing masc | **1500.5** verb 3sing indic aor act | **3079.1** adj sing | **1498.4** verb 3sing indic pres act | **1319.10** verb inf pres act |
|---|---|---|---|---|
| αὐτὸς | εἶπεν, | Μακάριόν | ἐστιν | ⸀ διδόναι |
| *autos* | *eipen* | *Makarion* | *estin* | *didonai* |
| himself | said, | Blessed | it is | to give |

(26:18). It includes the blessing of Abraham and the promise of the Spirit through faith (Romans 4:13-16; Galatians 3:9,14,18,26,29).

There is a fullness of this inheritance coming to believers in the future as a reward from the Lord. This hope should cause believers to do whatever they do heartily ("out of soul," that is, with the whole being, putting everything they have into it), remembering that they are servants (loveslaves) of the Lord (Colossians 3:23,24). God will not forget any labor of love or the way Christians serve their fellow believers.

**20:33.** It was in view of this inheritance that Paul could serve the Lord and the Church without coveting, even when other Christians had much more in the way of material things than he did. In all that he did, he set them an example of selfless service. He did not desire anyone's silver, gold, or clothing.

**20:34.** The Ephesian elders well knew that Paul set an example, in that by his own hands he served (ministered to) his own needs and the needs of those who were with him. As Paul told the Thessalonians, he worked night and day that he might not be a burden to any of them (1 Thessalonians 2:9).

Paul did tell Timothy that elders who rule well should be given a double pay or honor, for the laborer is worthy of his hire (1 Timothy 5:17,18). But Timothy would be dealing with well-established, growing churches, well-taught assemblies. When Paul came to a new area he was careful to show that he was not preaching the gospel in order to gain material benefits.

**20:35.** Paul worked with his hands also, to set an example for all. The object of every believer should be to give, not just to receive. Christians should become mature and strong and work hard so they can give to help the weak (including the physically sick or weak, as well as those who are spiritually weak).

In Ephesians 4:17-32 Paul implored the Gentile believers to turn away from the empty, meaningless thinking and from the moral debauchery and greed of other Gentiles. The Greek calls for a decisive act of "putting off" their former way of life and "putting on" the new man, which is a new creation, created in the likeness of God and in righteousness (toward others) and true holiness (the kind of dedication to God the Bible calls for). Above all, they must guard against the sins of the disposition, for those sins give a place for the devil to take hold. Included among these exhortations is a command that those who stole steal no more, but work with their hands in order to be able to give to (share with) those in need. By this kind of hard work and gracious giving to the weak, they would be remembering the words of Jesus, "It is more blessed to give than to receive."

**which is able to build you up:** . . . a Message which has the power to build up your character, *TCNT* . . . to make you strong, *BB* . . . is able to give you strength, *NCV.*

**and to give you an inheritance:** . . . your proper possession, *Williams* . . . your salvation, *Beck* . . . give you your place, *Phillips* . . . it will give you the blesings that God has, *NCV.*

**among all them which are sanctified:** . . . among the saints, *Weymouth* . . . among all God's consecrated people, *Williams* . . . all those made holy, *MLNT* . . . among all those who are consecrated to God, *Phillips* . . . for all his holy people, *NCV.*

**33. I have coveted no man's silver, or gold, or apparel:** I desired no one's, *HBIE* . . . never wanted anyone's money or fine clothes, *NCV.*

**34. Yea, ye yourselves know:** . . . yourselves acknowledge, *Rotherham.*

**that these hands have ministered unto my necessities:** . . . that these hands of mine provided not only for my own wants, *TCNT* . . . that these hands supplied my needs, *Berkeley* . . . these hands worked for what I needed, *Beck* . . . I always worked to take care of my own needs, *NCV.*

**and to them that were with me:** . . . but for my companions also, *TCNT* . . . and for the people with me, *Weymouth.*

**35. I have shewed you all things:** In every way I have shown you, *Weymouth* . . . I have in every way pointed out to you, *Berkeley.*

**how that so labouring:** . . . that, labouring as I laboured, *TCNT* . . . how, by working as I do, *Weymouth.*

**ye ought to support the weak:** . . . succor the needy, *Moffatt* . . . the needy must be assisted, *MLNT* . . . and help, *NCV.*

**and to remember the words of the Lord Jesus, how he said:**

**It is more blessed to give than to receive:** There is more spiritual prosperity, *Wuest* . . . There is a greater blessing in giving than in getting, *BB* . . . It is giving rather than receiving that brings happiness, *TNT.*

| 3095.1 adv comp | 3095.1 adv comp | 1319.10 verb inf pres act | 2211.1 conj | 2956.10 verb inf pres act |
|---|---|---|---|---|
| μᾶλλον | [☆ μᾶλλον | διδόναι ] | ἢ | λαμβάνειν. |
| *mallon* | *mallon* | *didonai* | *ē* | *lambanein* |
| more | [ more | to give ] | than | to receive. |

| 2504.1 conj | 3642.18 dem-pron pl neu | 1500.15 verb nom sing masc part aor act | 4935.14 verb nom sing masc part aor act | 3450.17 art pl neu |
|---|---|---|---|---|
| 36. Καὶ | ταῦτα | εἰπὼν, | θεὶς | τὰ |
| *Kai* | *tauta* | *eipōn* | *theis* | *ta* |
| And | these things | having said | having bowed | the |

| 1113.3 noun pl neu | 840.3 prs-pron gen sing | 4713.1 prep | 3820.5 adj dat pl | 840.2 prs-pron dat pl | 4195.16 verb 3sing indic aor mid |
|---|---|---|---|---|---|
| γόνατα | αὐτοῦ | σὺν | πᾶσιν | αὐτοῖς | προσηύξατο. |
| *gonata* | *autou* | *sun* | *pasin* | *autois* | *proseuxato* |
| knees | his | with | all | them | he prayed. |

| 2401.3 adj nom sing masc | 1156.2 conj | 1090.33 verb 3sing indic aor mid | 2778.1 noun nom sing masc | 2778.1 noun nom sing masc |
|---|---|---|---|---|
| 37. Ἱκανὸς | δὲ | ‘ ἐγένετο | κλαυθμὸς | [☆ κλαυθμὸς |
| *Hikanos* | *de* | *egeneto* | *klauthmos* | *klauthmos* |
| Much | and | there was | weeping | [ weeping |

| 1090.33 verb 3sing indic aor mid | 3820.4 adj gen pl | 2504.1 conj | 1953.5 verb nom pl masc part aor act | 1894.3 prep | 3450.6 art acc sing masc |
|---|---|---|---|---|---|
| ἐγένετο ] | πάντων· | καὶ | ἐπιπεσόντες | ἐπὶ | τὸν |
| *egeneto* | *pantōn* | *kai* | *epipesontes* | *epi* | *ton* |
| there was ] | of all: | and | having fallen | upon | the |

| 4976.1 noun acc sing masc | 3450.2 art gen sing | 3834.2 name gen masc | 2674.4 verb 3pl indic imperf act | 840.6 prs-pron acc sing masc |
|---|---|---|---|---|
| τράχηλον | τοῦ | Παύλου | κατεφίλουν | αὐτόν· |
| *trachēlon* | *tou* | *Paulou* | *katephiloun* | *auton* |
| neck | | of Paul | they were ardently kissing | him, |

| 3463.3 verb nom pl masc part pres mid | 3094.1 adv sup | 1894.3 prep | 3450.3 art dat sing | 3030.3 noun dat sing masc | 3614.3 rel-pron dat sing |
|---|---|---|---|---|---|
| 38. ὀδυνώμενοι | μάλιστα | ἐπὶ | τῷ | λόγῳ | ᾧ |
| *odunōmenoi* | *malista* | *epi* | *tō* | *logō* | *hō* |
| being distressed | most of all | for | the | word | which |

| 2029.7 verb 3sing indic plperf act | 3617.1 conj | 3629.1 adv | 3165.6 verb 3pl indic pres act | 3450.16 art sing neu | 4241.1 noun sing neu |
|---|---|---|---|---|---|
| εἰρήκει, | ὅτι | οὐκέτι | μέλλουσιν | τὸ | πρόσωπον |
| *eirēkei* | *hoti* | *ouketi* | *mellousin* | *to* | *prosōpon* |
| he had said, | that | no more | they are about | the | face |

| 840.3 prs-pron gen sing | 2311.15 verb inf pres act | 4170.6 verb 3pl indic imperf act | 1156.2 conj | 840.6 prs-pron acc sing masc |
|---|---|---|---|---|
| αὐτοῦ | θεωρεῖν. | προέπεμπον | δὲ | αὐτὸν |
| *autou* | *theōrein* | *proepempon* | *de* | *auton* |
| his | to see. | They were accompanying | and | him |

| 1519.1 prep | 3450.16 art sing neu | 4003.1 noun sing neu | 5453.1 conj | 1156.2 conj | 1090.33 verb 3sing indic aor mid |
|---|---|---|---|---|---|
| εἰς | τὸ | πλοῖον. | 21:1. Ὡς | δὲ | ἐγένετο |
| *eis* | *to* | *ploion* | *Hōs* | *de* | *egeneto* |
| to | the | ship. | When | and | it was |

| 319.10 verb inf aor pass | 2231.4 prs-pron acc 1pl | 639.4 verb acc pl masc part aor pass | 570.2 prep |
|---|---|---|---|
| ἀναχθῆναι | ἡμᾶς | ἀποσπασθέντας | ἀπ’ |
| *anachthēnai* | *hēmas* | *apospasthentas* | *ap'* |
| to sail | us, | having drawn away | from |

This saying of Jesus is not recorded in any of the four Gospels. However, as indicated by Galatians 1:11,12 Paul received the central truths of the gospel by direct revelation from Jesus himself. In his epistles as well as here, Paul used sayings of Jesus to confirm the Word.

**20:36.** When Paul had finished speaking, he and the elders of Ephesus went to their knees and prayed together. Praying on the knees was common in the Early Church (9:40; 21:5). But they also prayed standing and sitting.

Paul in his prayer expressed, no doubt, his desire for their spiritual welfare and committed them to God. The many prayers in Paul's epistles show he was moved by the Spirit as he prayed and poured out his heart in supplication and intercession for the people. On this occasion the time of prayer was no short, formal prayer. The Early Church knew how to seek God fervently and pour out their hearts to Him in prayer and supplication with thanksgiving.

**20:37.** After this time of prayer, there was a considerable amount of weeping from them all as they fell on (pressed on) Paul's neck and kissed him (probably on both cheeks). The kiss was a common greeting and farewell in all of Bible times. It was a sign of affection and love and also a sign of homage. Here it shows their friendship and affection. In fact, the Bible uses a stronger form of the word here to show how strong their love and concern for Paul was.

**20:38.** This was not the ordinary pain of parting. These elders were filled with acute pain and sorrow, most of all because Paul said they would see his face no more. Paul's self-sacrificing ministry in their behalf had indeed kindled a great love in their hearts for him. Such mutual love drew them together, as love always does. The real cause of divisions in an assembly is that love has gone, and self seeking lust (especially lust for power) has taken its place (James 4:1-4).

Then, after all the weeping and kissing were over, as a further mark of respect, the Ephesian elders escorted Paul to the ship. No doubt they waited on the shore to see the ship depart and to have a last glimpse of their beloved apostle.

**21:1.** The farewell at Miletus must have been very hard for Paul and for Luke and Paul's other companions as well. This verse indicates they literally had to tear themselves away from the crowd of Ephesian elders who pressed around them to the last. Nor would things get any easier. There would be more sad farewells all along the way to Jerusalem.

**36. And when he had thus spoken:** With these words, *Moffatt* . . . When he had finished his talk, *Norlie.*

**he kneeled down, and prayed with them all:** . . . he fell on his knees with them all and prayed, *Williams.*

**37. And they all wept sore:** There was much weeping among them all, *TNT* . . . much, *Rotherham* . . . freely, *Berkeley* . . . All were in tears, *TCNT* . . . with loud lamentation, *Weymouth* . . . they cried bitterly, *Klingensmith.*

**and fell on Paul's neck, and kissed him:** . . . they embraced Paul, *TNT* . . . and throwing their arms round Paul's neck, they kissed him again and again, *TCNT* . . . ardently kissed, *Darby* . . . kissed him fondly, *Concordant* . . . they kept on kissing him, *Wuest* . . . they kissed him lovingly, *KJII* . . . affectionately, *Phillips.*

**38. Sorrowing most of all for the words which he spake:** They were pained most of all at the statement, *TNT* . . . grieving most of all over what he had said, *TCNT* . . . What saddened...was his saying, *Phillips* . . . They were grieved especially over the remark, *MLNT* . . . being distressed especially on account of the word which he had spoken, *Worrell* . . . they had the most anguish, *Murdock* . . . What made them sad most of all was because, *NLT.*

**that they should see his face no more:** . . . that they would never see his face again, *TCNT* . . . never see him again, *NCV.*

**And they accompanied him unto the ship:** Then they escorted him to the ship, *TNT* . . . And they went with him down to, *Phillips* . . . they were escorting him to, *Worrell.*

**1. And it came to pass, that after we were gotten from them:** And when at last we had parted, *Alford* . . . having torn ourselves, *Rotherham* . . . And when we were torn away, *Wesley* . . . having been torn away, *Worrell* . . . After we left them, *NCV, NLT* . . . having departed from them, *Swann* . . . When the parting was over, *Goodspeed* . . . After we all said good-bye to the elders, *SEB.*

## Acts 21:2

| 840.1 prs-pron gen pl | 2092.2 verb nom pl masc part aor act | 2048.4 verb 1pl indic aor act | 1519.1 prep | 3450.12 art acc sing fem |
|---|---|---|---|---|
| αὐτῶν, | εὐθυδρομήσαντες | ἤλθομεν | εἰς | τὴν |
| *autōn* | *euthudromēsantes* | *ēlthomen* | *eis* | *tēn* |
| them, | having run direct | we came | to | |

1.a.**Txt:** 020L,025P,byz.
**Var:** 01ℵ,02A,03B,04C
05D,08E,Gries,Lach
Treg,Alf,Word,Tisc
We/Ho,Weis,Sod
UBS/☆

| 2946.1 name acc fem | 2946.2 name acc fem | 3450.11 art dat sing fem | 1156.2 conj | 1819.1 adv | 1519.1 prep | 3450.12 art acc sing fem |
|---|---|---|---|---|---|---|
| ˊ Κῶν, | [a☆ Κῶ, ] | τῇ | δὲ | ἑξῆς | εἰς | τὴν |
| *Kōn* | *Kō* | *tē* | *de* | *hexēs* | *eis* | *tēn* |
| Coos, | [ idem ] | on the | and | next | to | |

| 4356.1 name acc fem | 2518.1 conj | 1519.1 prep | 3821.1 name neu | 2504.1 conj | 2128.18 verb nom pl masc part aor act |
|---|---|---|---|---|---|
| Ῥόδον, | κἀκεῖθεν | εἰς | Πάταρα. | 2. καὶ | εὑρόντες |
| *Rhodon* | *kakeithen* | *eis* | *Patara* | *kai* | *heurontes* |
| Rhodes, | from there | to | Patara. | And | having found |

| 4003.1 noun sing neu | 1270.2 verb sing neu part pres act | 1519.1 prep | 5240.2 name acc fem | 1895.4 verb nom pl masc part aor act |
|---|---|---|---|---|
| πλοῖον | διαπερῶν | εἰς | Φοινίκην, | ἐπιβάντες |
| *ploion* | *diaperōn* | *eis* | *Phoinikēn* | *epibantes* |
| a ship | passing over | into | Phoenicia, | having gone on board |

| 319.7 verb 1pl indic aor pass | 396.1 verb nom pl masc part aor act | 1156.2 conj | 3450.12 art acc sing fem | 2927.2 name acc fem |
|---|---|---|---|---|
| ἀνήχθημεν. | 3. ἀναφάναντες | δὲ | τὴν | Κύπρον, |
| *anēchthēmen* | *anaphanantes* | *de* | *tēn* | *Kupron* |
| we sailed; | Having sighted | and | | Cyprus, |

| 2504.1 conj | 2611.6 verb nom pl masc part aor act | 840.12 prs-pron acc sing fem | 2158.1 adj acc sing | 3986.5 verb 1pl indic imperf act |
|---|---|---|---|---|
| καὶ | καταλιπόντες | αὐτὴν | εὐώνυμον | ἐπλέομεν |
| *kai* | *katalipontes* | *autēn* | *euōnumon* | *epleomen* |
| and | having left | it | on the left | we were sailing |

3.a.**Txt:** 04C,020L,025P
byz.
**Var:** 01ℵ,02A,03B,08E
sa.bo.Lach,Treg,Alf,Tisc
We/Ho,Weis,Sod
UBS/☆

| 1519.1 prep | 4799.2 name acc fem | 2504.1 conj | 2580.7 verb 1pl indic aor pass | 2687.2 verb 1pl indic aor act |
|---|---|---|---|---|
| εἰς | Συρίαν, | καὶ | ˊ κατήχθημεν | [a☆ κατήλθομεν ] |
| *eis* | *Surian* | *kai* | *katēchthēmen* | *katēlthomen* |
| to | Syria, | and | arrived | [ landed ] |

| 1519.1 prep | 5025.3 name acc fem | 1553.1 adv | 1056.1 conj | 1498.34 verb sing indic imperf act | 3450.16 art sing neu | 4003.1 noun sing neu |
|---|---|---|---|---|---|---|
| εἰς | Τύρον· | ἐκεῖσε | γὰρ | ˊ ἦν | τὸ | πλοῖον |
| *eis* | *Turon* | *ekeise* | *gar* | *ēn* | *to* | *ploion* |
| at | Tyre, | there | for | was | the | ship |

| 3450.16 art sing neu | 4003.1 noun sing neu | 1498.34 verb sing indic imperf act | 664.1 verb sing neu part pres mid | 3450.6 art acc sing masc |
|---|---|---|---|---|
| [☆ τὸ | πλοῖον | ἦν ] | ἀποφορτιζόμενον | τὸν |
| *to* | *ploion* | *ēn* | *apophortizomenon* | *ton* |
| [ the | ship | was ] | discharging | the |

4.a.**Txt:** 04C-corr,020L
025P,byz.
**Var:** 01ℵ,02A,03B
04C-org,08E,sa.bo.Lach
Treg,Alf,Word,Tisc
We/Ho,Weis,Sod
UBS/☆

| 1111.1 noun acc sing masc | 2504.1 conj | 427.2 verb nom pl masc part aor act | 427.2 verb nom pl masc part aor act |
|---|---|---|---|
| γόμον. | 4. ˊ καὶ | ἀνευρόντες | [a☆ ἀνευρόντες |
| *gomon* | *kai* | *aneurontes* | *aneurontes* |
| cargo. | And | having found out | [ having found out |

| 1156.2 conj | 3450.8 art acc pl masc | 3073.8 noun acc pl masc | 1946.6 verb 1pl indic aor act | 841.1 adv | 2232.1 noun fem |
|---|---|---|---|---|---|
| δὲ ] | τοὺς | μαθητὰς, | ἐπεμείναμεν | αὐτοῦ | ἡμέρας |
| *de* | *tous* | *mathētas* | *epemeinamen* | *autou* | *hēmeras* |
| but ] | the | disciples, | we remained | there | days |

When they finally put out to sea, the first day's travel took them by a straight course to Coos (Cos), a very mountainous island about 21 miles long and 6 miles wide. Dorian Greeks first colonized it. The Romans made it a free state though it was still part of the province of Asia.

The next day they sailed to Rhodes ("rose"). The city was the capital of a large island also called Rhodes. The island is about 45 miles long and 20 miles wide. The city was a commercial center, for it was at a point where great commercial sea routes crossed. The city was a splendid one, and the Colossus, a great lighthouse at its harbor, is said to have been about 105 feet high, one of the seven wonders of the ancient world.

From Rhodes, they sailed to Patara, a seaport on the southwest coast of Lycia, a small district on the south coast of Asia Minor. The Western text (Codex Bezae, D) adds "and Myra." But it is not likely Paul went on to Myra. Because of the prevailing winds, Patara was the best starting point for the next part of the trip which would take them to Phoenicia.

**21:2.** At Patara Paul, Luke, and the rest of Paul's company found a ship scheduled to sail directly across to Phoenicia, so they took passage on it. This would be a nonstop journey of about 600 miles.

**21:3.** About halfway to Phoenicia, they sighted the west end of the large island of Cyprus. They kept Cyprus on the left hand and continued sailing southeast to the Roman province of Syria (which included Phoenicia). The ship landed at Tyre and waited there while its cargo was unloaded. Tyre originally had two harbors, one on the coast and one on an island. But when Alexander the Great conquered the island city, he had to build a causeway, or mole, out to it in order to do so. Thus, the city was turned into a peninsula. Long before Paul's time it had recovered much of its importance and was still a major city and seaport.

**21:4.** Paul had never visited Tyre before, but he knew there were believers there. The city was probably evangelized by some of those who were scattered by the persecution which followed the death of Stephen. Paul did not know where the Christians were, but he sought them out and spent 7 days visiting with them.

While Paul and his company were enjoying fellowship with the believers in Tyre, the Spirit, as in many places before, warned of what was going to happen to Paul in Jerusalem. The Bible does not say how the Spirit did this, but from what happened a little later in Caesarea, the warning no doubt came through a prophecy.

The believers "through the Spirit" said (kept saying) to Paul not to go up to Jerusalem. This did not mean God had changed His mind. God is not fickle. He does not change His mind in that way.

**and had launched:** . . . launched forth, *PNT* . . . we sailed away, *SEB* . . . we put out to sea, *NAB.*

**we came with a straight course unto Coos:** . . . we ran before the wind to Cos, *TCNT* . . . we struck a beeline for Cos, *Williams* . . . straight for Cos Island, *SEB* . . . and sailed straight to, *NAB.*

**and the day following unto Rhodes:** . . . the next day, *RSV* . . . we came to Rhodes, *TCNT.*

**and from thence unto Patara:**

**2. And finding a ship sailing over unto Phenicia:** . . . we found a ship which was going to, *SEB* . . . a ship bound for, *Goodspeed* . . . crossing over to, *Worrell.*

**we went aboard, and set forth:** . . . and put to sea, *Weymouth* . . . we embarked and set sail, *Berkeley* . . . We got on it and went along, *NLT* . . . we boarded it and sailed off, *NAB.*

**3. Now when we had discovered Cyprus:** And sighting Cyprus, *Rotherham* . . . We sailed near the island of, *SEB* . . . We caught sight of, *NAB.*

**we left it on the left hand:** . . . and leaving it behind to the left, *Rotherham* . . . leaving it on our left, *Williams* . . . passed it on our left, *Norlie* . . . We could see it on the north side, but we did not stop, *SEB.*

**and sailed into Syria:** . . . we went on to Syria, *BB* . . . as we continued on toward, *NAB* . . . to the country of, *SEB.*

**and landed at Tyre:** . . . and docked at Tyre, *Berkeley* . . . We stopped at the city of, *SEB* . . . we put in at Tyre, *NAB.*

**for there the ship was to unlade her burden:** . . . since that was where, *Phillips* . . . was to discharge her cargo, *Rotherham* . . . was to unload her cargo, *Goodspeed, HBIE* . . . its freight, *Campbell.*

**4. And finding disciples:** Having searched for the disciples and found them, *Weymouth* . . . we found some followers of Jesus, *SEB* . . . We looked for the Christians, *NLT.*

**we tarried there seven days:** . . . we stayed with them, *SEB* . . . and remained there seven days, *Rotherham* . . . and stayed a week with them, *TCNT.*

# Acts 21:5

| **2017.1** num card | **3610.2** rel-pron nom pl masc | **3450.3** art dat sing | **3834.3** name dat masc | **2978.25** verb indic imperf act | **1217.2** prep |
|---|---|---|---|---|---|
| ἑπτά· | οἵτινες | τῷ | Παύλῳ | ἔλεγον | διὰ |
| *hepta* | *hoitines* | *tō* | *Paulō* | *elegon* | *dia* |
| seven; | who | | to Paul | were saying | by |

4.b.**Txt:** 08E,020L,025P byz.
**Var:** 01ℵ,02A,03B,04C Lach,Treg,Alf,Tisc We/Ho,Weis,Sod UBS/☆

4.c.**Txt:** 020L,025P,byz.
**Var:** 01ℵ,02A,03B,04C 08E,Gries,Lach,Treg Alf,Word,Tisc,We/Ho Weis,Sod,UBS/☆

| **3450.2** art gen sing | **4011.2** noun gen sing neu | **3231.1** partic | **303.11** verb inf pres act | **1895.6** verb inf pres act |
|---|---|---|---|---|
| τοῦ | πνεύματος, | μὴ | ʻ ἀναβαίνειν | [b☆ ἐπιβαίνειν ] |
| *tou* | *pneumatos* | *mē* | *anabainein* | *epibainein* |
| the | Spirit, | not | to go up | [ idem ] |

| **1519.1** prep | **2395.1** name fem | **2389.1** name | **3616.1** conj | **1156.2** conj |
|---|---|---|---|---|
| εἰς | ʻ Ἱερουσαλήμ. | [c☆ Ἱεροσόλυμα. ] | 5. ὅτε | δὲ |
| *eis* | *Hierousalēm* | *Hierosoluma* | *hote* | *de* |
| to | Jerusalem. | [ idem ] | When | but |

| **1090.33** verb 3sing indic aor mid | **2231.4** prs-pron acc 1pl | **1806.1** verb inf aor act | **1806.1** verb inf aor act | **2231.4** prs-pron acc 1pl | **3450.15** art acc pl fem |
|---|---|---|---|---|---|
| ἐγένετο | ʻ ἡμᾶς | ἐξαρτίσαι | [ ἐξαρτίσαι | ἡμᾶς ] | τὰς |
| *egeneto* | *hēmas* | *exartisai* | *exartisai* | *hēmas* | *tas* |
| it was | us | to complete | [ to complete | us ] | the |

| **2232.1** noun fem | **1814.15** verb nom pl masc part aor act | **4057.37** verb 1pl indic imperf mid | **4170.1** verb gen pl masc part pres act |
|---|---|---|---|
| ἡμέρας, | ἐξελθόντες | ἐπορευόμεθα, | προπεμπόντων |
| *hēmeras* | *exelthontes* | *eporeuometha* | *propempontōn* |
| days, | having set out | we were journeying, | accompanying |

| **2231.4** prs-pron acc 1pl | **3820.4** adj gen pl | **4713.1** prep | **1129.8** noun dat pl fem | **2504.1** conj | **4891.6** noun dat pl neu | **2175.1** conj |
|---|---|---|---|---|---|---|
| ἡμᾶς | πάντων | σὺν | γυναιξὶν | καὶ | τέκνοις | ἕως |
| *hēmas* | *pantōn* | *sun* | *gunaixin* | *kai* | *teknois* | *heōs* |
| us | all | with | wives | and | children | as far as |

| **1838.1** adv | **3450.10** art gen sing fem | **4032.2** noun gen sing fem | **2504.1** conj | **4935.16** verb nom pl masc part aor act | **3450.17** art pl neu |
|---|---|---|---|---|---|
| ἔξω | τῆς | πόλεως· | καὶ | θέντες | τὰ |
| *exō* | *tēs* | *poleōs* | *kai* | *thentes* | *ta* |
| outside | the | city. | And | having bowed | the |

| **1113.3** noun pl neu | **1894.3** prep | **3450.6** art acc sing masc | **123.1** noun acc sing masc | **4195.17** verb 1pl indic aor mid |
|---|---|---|---|---|
| γόνατα | ἐπὶ | τὸν | αἰγιαλὸν | ʻ προσηυξάμεθα. |
| *gonata* | *epi* | *ton* | *aigialon* | *prosēuxametha* |
| knees | on | the | shore | we prayed. |

5.a.**Txt:** byz.
**Var:** 01ℵ,02A,03B,04C 08E,Lach,Treg,Alf Word,Tisc,We/Ho,Weis Sod,UBS/☆

6.a.**Txt:** 020L,025P,byz.
**Var:** 01ℵ,02A,03B,04C 08E,Lach,Treg,Alf Word,Tisc,We/Ho,Weis Sod,UBS/☆

6.b.**Var:** 01ℵ,02A,03B 04C,08E,Lach,Treg,Alf Word,Tisc,We/Ho,Weis Sod,UBS/☆

| **4195.25** verb nom pl masc part aor mid | **2504.1** conj | **776.11** verb nom pl masc part aor mid |
|---|---|---|
| [a☆ προσευξάμενοι ] | 6. ʻ καὶ | ἀσπασάμενοι |
| *proseuxamenoi* | *kai* | *aspasamenoi* |
| [ having prayed. ] | And | having greeted |

| **532.1** verb 1pl indic aor mid | **238.3** prs-pron acc pl masc | **2504.1** conj | **1895.2** verb 1pl indic aor act |
|---|---|---|---|
| [a☆ ἀπησπασάμεθα ] | ἀλλήλους | [b☆+ καὶ ] | ʻ ἐπέβημεν |
| *apēspasametha* | *allēlous* | *kai* | *epebēmen* |
| [ said farewell ] | one another | [ and ] | we went up |

6.c.**Txt:** 020L,025P,byz.
**Var:** 01ℵ-corr,03B,08E Lach,Treg,We/Ho,Weis UBS/☆

| **1895.7** verb 1pl indic aor act | **1519.1** prep | **3450.16** art sing neu | **4003.1** noun sing neu | **1552.6** dem-pron nom pl masc | **1156.2** conj |
|---|---|---|---|---|---|
| [c☆ ἐνέβημεν ] | εἰς | τὸ | πλοῖον, | ἐκεῖνοι | δὲ |
| *enebēmen* | *eis* | *to* | *ploion* | *ekeinoi* | *de* |
| [ idem ] | into | the | ship, | they | and |

Moreover, Paul was sensitive to the Holy Spirit. When he was forbidden by the Holy Spirit to preach in the Roman province of Asia, in obedience he bypassed it immediately.

Actually, the Greek does not mean the Spirit did not want Paul to go to Jerusalem. The word "through" (Greek, dia) is not the word used in previous passages for the direct agency of the Holy Spirit. (See 13:4 where the Greek is hupo, a word used for direct or primary agency.) Here the Greek is better translated "in consequence of the Spirit," that is, because of what the Spirit said. The Spirit himself definitely did not forbid Paul to go on to Jerusalem. The Spirit was, in fact, constraining Paul to go (20:22). Paul knew the Holy Spirit does not contradict himself. It was not the Spirit but the believers' love for Paul that made them say he should not go. In other words, because of the prophecy of bonds and imprisonment the people voiced their own feeling that he should not go. But Paul refused to let them force their feelings on him. So he still obeyed what the Holy Spirit directed him personally to do, that is, to go on to Jerusalem.

**21:5.** Paul no doubt ministered in Tyre as he had elsewhere, with a deep love for the Lord and for the people. Since this was already a well-established assembly, they knew the facts of the gospel, and they were filled with the Holy Spirit. Thus, Paul was able to give them further instruction and encouragement.

It is clear that during the 7 days all the believers came to know and love Paul. For when the week was up, all of them, along with their wives and children, escorted Paul out of the city to the level, sandy beach outside Tyre. There beside the beautiful blue Mediterranean Sea they knelt and prayed. What a volume of prayer must have gone up before the Lord as they joined in unison, praying for Paul and his company. It is likely that Paul also led out in prayer for them.

**21:6.** After prayer they gave parting greetings to each other. These were very warm greetings and were probably accompanied by a kiss and probably some tears. Then Paul and his company entered the ship, and the believers and their families returned to their homes. This was apparently the one and only time Paul visited the city of Tyre. On his journey as a prisoner to Rome the ship touched at Sidon but not Tyre (27:2f.).

The assembly at Tyre seems to have shown a unity and maturity that must have blessed Paul. The warning of what awaited Paul in Jerusalem also shows that the gifts and ministries of the Spirit were present in the assembly. The Bible shows God uses many types of ministries to train believers and to bring them to a maturity where they can all do a work of ministry and service. Notice, however, that God used Paul in a special way. God does not use merely ministries, but ministers.

**who said to Paul:** They advised Paul, *Berkeley* . . . they warned Paul, *TCNT* . . . Some of them advised, *Fenton* . . . they tried to tell Paul, *NAB*.

**through the Spirit:** Speaking under the influence of the Spirit, *TCNT* . . . felt led by the Spirit again and again, *Phillips* . . . because of impressions made by the Spirit, *Williams* . . . Instructed by the Spirit, *Goodspeed* . . . taught by the Spirit, *Weymouth* . . . Under the Spirit's prompting, *NAB*.

**that he should not go up to Jerusalem:** . . . he should not set foot, *Montgomery* . . . not to proceed to Jerusalem, *Weymouth*.

**5. And when he had accomplished those days:** When, however, our time was up, *Weymouth* . . . When we finished our visit, *Everyday* . . . When our time was up, *NLT* . . . when the days had passed, *Swann*.

**we departed and went our way:** . . . we left and continued our trip, *Everyday, SEB* . . . went out, *Swann* . . . we started out on our journey again, *Williams C.K.* . . . we were resuming our journey, *Worrell*.

**and they all brought us on our way, with wives and children:** . . . escorting us, *TCNT* . . . All of them—wives and children included, *NAB* . . . escorted by all the believers with their wives and children, *MLNT* . . . They all came out to see us off...accompanying us, *Phillips* . . . being conducted by all, *Swann*.

**till we were out of the city:** . . . as far as outside the city, *Rotherham* . . . went with us out of town, *NLT*.

**and we kneeled down on the shore, and prayed:** . . . kneeling on the beach, *Concordant*.

**6. And when we had taken our leave one of another:** . . . and then said goodbye to one another, *TCNT* . . . and said farewell, *Swann* . . . then we bade one another goodbye, *Goodspeed* . . . then embraced one another, *MLNT*.

**we took ship:** . . . we went on board the ship, *RSV* . . . and embarked in the ship, *Alford* . . . we boarded the ship, *NAB* . . . our ship, *Williams C.K.*

| **5128.7** verb 3pl indic aor act | **1519.1** prep | **3450.17** art pl neu | **2375.13** adj pl neu | **2231.1** prs-pron nom 1pl | **1156.2** conj | **3450.6** art acc sing masc |
|---|---|---|---|---|---|---|
| ὑπέστρεψαν | εἰς | τὰ | ἴδια. | **7.** Ἡμεῖς | δὲ | τὸν |
| *hupestrepsan* | *eis* | *ta* | *idia* | *Hēmeis* | *de* | *ton* |
| returned | to | the | own. | We | and, | the |

| **4006.2** noun acc sing masc | **1268.1** verb nom pl masc part aor act | **570.3** prep | **5025.1** name gen fem | **2628.2** verb 1pl indic aor act |
|---|---|---|---|---|
| πλοῦν | διανύσαντες | ἀπὸ | Τύρου | κατηντήσαμεν |
| *ploun* | *dianusantes* | *apo* | *Turou* | *katēntēsamen* |
| voyage | having completed | from | Tyre, | arrived |

| **1519.1** prep | **4282.1** name acc fem | **2504.1** conj | **776.11** verb nom pl masc part aor mid | **3450.8** art acc pl masc | **79.9** noun acc pl masc |
|---|---|---|---|---|---|
| εἰς | Πτολεμαΐδα, | καὶ | ἀσπασάμενοι | τοὺς | ἀδελφοὺς |
| *eis* | *Ptolemaida* | *kai* | *aspasamenoi* | *tous* | *adelphous* |
| at | Ptolemais, | and | having greeted | the | brothers |

| **3176.17** verb 1pl indic aor act | **2232.4** noun acc sing fem | **1518.8** num card acc fem | **3706.1** prep | **840.2** prs-pron dat pl | **3450.11** art dat sing fem |
|---|---|---|---|---|---|
| ἐμείναμεν | ἡμέραν | μίαν | παρ' | αὐτοῖς. | **8.** τῇ |
| *emeinamen* | *hēmeran* | *mian* | *par'* | *autois* | *tē* |
| we remained | day | one | with | them. | The |

8.a.**Txt:** 020L,025P,byz. lect.
**Var:** p74,01ℵ,02A,03B 04C,08E,33,sa.bo.Gries Lach,Treg,Alf,Word Tisc,We/Ho,Weis,Sod UBS/☆

| **1156.2** conj | **1872.1** adv | **1814.15** verb nom pl masc part aor act | **3450.7** art nom pl masc | **3875.1** prep | **3450.6** art acc sing masc |
|---|---|---|---|---|---|
| δὲ | ἐπαύριον | ἐξελθόντες | ⸂a οἱ | περὶ | τὸν |
| *de* | *epaurion* | *exelthontes* | *hoi* | *peri* | *ton* |
| and | next day | having gone forth | the | about | |

8.b.**Txt:** 020L,025P,byz. lect.Steph
**Var:** p74,01ℵ,02A,04C 08E,33,sa.bo.Elzev Gries,Lach,Alf,Word Tisc,Weis,Sod,UBS/☆

| **3834.4** name acc masc | **2048.1** verb indic aor act | **2048.4** verb 1pl indic aor act | **1519.1** prep | **2513.3** name acc fem |
|---|---|---|---|---|
| Παῦλον ⸃ | ⸂ ἦλθον | [b☆ ἤλθομεν ] | εἰς | Καισάρειαν· |
| *Paulon* | *ēlthon* | *ēlthomen* | *eis* | *Kaisareian* |
| Paul | they came | [ we came ] | to | Caesarea; |

| **2504.1** conj | **1511.16** verb nom pl masc part aor act | **1519.1** prep | **3450.6** art acc sing masc | **3486.4** noun acc sing masc | **5213.2** name gen masc |
|---|---|---|---|---|---|
| καὶ | εἰσελθόντες | εἰς | τὸν | οἶκον | Φιλίππου |
| *kai* | *eiselthontes* | *eis* | *ton* | *oikon* | *Philippou* |
| and | having entered | into | the | house | of Philip |

8.c.**Txt:** Steph
**Var:** 01ℵ,02A,03B,04C 08E,020L,025P,byz. Lach,Treg,Alf,Word Tisc,We/Ho,Weis,Sod UBS/☆

| **3450.2** art gen sing | **2078.1** noun gen sing masc | **3450.2** art gen sing | **1498.19** verb gen sing part pres act | **1523.2** prep gen |
|---|---|---|---|---|
| τοῦ | εὐαγγελιστοῦ, | ⸂c τοῦ ⸃ | ὄντος | ἐκ |
| *tou* | *euangelistou* | *tou* | *ontos* | *ek* |
| the | evangelist, | the | being | from among |

| **3450.1** art gen pl | **2017.1** num card | **3176.17** verb 1pl indic aor act | **3706.1** prep | **840.4** prs-pron dat sing | **3642.5** dem-pron dat sing masc | **1156.2** conj |
|---|---|---|---|---|---|---|
| τῶν | ἑπτὰ, | ἐμείναμεν | παρ' | αὐτῷ. | **9.** τούτῳ | δὲ |
| *tōn* | *hepta* | *emeinamen* | *par'* | *autō* | *toutō* | *de* |
| the | seven, | we stayed | with | him. | To this one | and |

| **1498.37** verb 3pl indic imperf act | **2341.6** noun nom pl fem | **3795.4** noun nom pl fem | **4913.1** num card nom | **4913.1** num card nom |
|---|---|---|---|---|
| ἦσαν | θυγατέρες | ⸂ παρθένοι | τέσσαρες | [☆ τέσσαρες |
| *ēsan* | *thugateres* | *parthenoi* | *tessares* | *tessares* |
| there were | daughters | virgins | four | [ four |

| **3795.4** noun nom pl fem | **4253.6** verb nom pl fem part pres act | **1946.3** verb gen pl masc part pres act | **1156.2** conj |
|---|---|---|---|
| παρθένοι ] | προφητεύουσαι. | **10.** ἐπιμενόντων | δὲ |
| *parthenoi* | *prophēteuousai* | *epimenontōn* | *de* |
| virgins ] | prophesying. | Remaining | and |

**21:7.** After they left Tyre, the ship sailed smoothly to Ptolemais where it stopped for 1 day.

Ptolemais was the Old Testament Accho mentioned in Judges 1:31 and is now called Acre or Akka. The city is on a small promontory about 8 miles north of the headland of Mount Carmel, and about 25 miles south of Tyre. In the division of the land after Joshua's conquest, the city was assigned to the tribe of Asher, but they never took possession of it. It remained under the dominion of Tyre and Sidon until the Assyrians took it in about 70 B.C. About 200 B.C. its name was changed to Ptolemais, probably in honor of Ptolemy Philadelphus (285–246 B.C.). In New Testament times it was an important seaport for trade with Galilee, the Decapolis, and Arabia. Many Jews lived there, and in the Roman period the Emperor Claudius settled a group of ex-soldiers from the Roman army in Ptolemais. By the time of Paul's visit there was a well-established church. Paul and his company greeted the believers and stayed with them for the day.

**21:8.** The next day the ship brought them to Caesarea. There they left the ship for the land journey to Jerusalem. But first they went to the house of Philip the evangelist.

God must have blessed Philip materially, for his home was large enough to entertain Paul and his company. It is probable that his home was the chief Christian center in Caesarea and that an assembly of believers gathered there.

This may mean also that Paul had visited there on previous occasions when he had passed through Caesarea and that he was well-known to Philip. Philip obviously welcomed him and persuaded him and his company to stay with him for a time. Hospitality for fellow believers and for traveling teachers and preachers is very strongly advocated in the New Testament.

**21:9.** The Bible now draws attention to Philip's four virgin daughters who prophesied. This is significant for several reasons. First, it indicates Joel's prophecy that both sons and daughters would prophesy was being fulfilled in the Early Church (Joel 2:28; Acts 2:17). The Greek here does not call them prophetesses, but uses an attributive participle in order to emphasize this fulfillment of Joel's prophecy. They were four prophesying virgin daughters.

The use of the participle also indicates they were regularly used by the Holy Spirit in this ministry of prophesying. That they were virgins further indicates they had given themselves to this ministry. It was unusual in those days for a woman not to be married. These daughters had separated themselves for the service of the Lord.

This shows something about Philip also. Ordinarily the father had the responsibility to make arrangements for his daughters to be married. The fact that Philip did not do so shows he was more concerned that his daughters follow the Lord than that they follow the social customs of the day.

**and they returned home again:** . . . they went home, *Goodspeed* . . . went back to their homes, *MLNT.*

**7. And when we had finished our course from Tyre, we came to Ptolemais:** We continued our sailing, going from Tyre to Ptolemais, *Beck* . . . We continued our trip from, *Everyday* . . . The same ship took us from, *NLT* . . . when we finished the voyage from, *Swann.*

**and saluted the brethren:** . . . and exchanged greetings, *TCNT* . . . There we greeted our fellow Christians, *Beck* . . . Here we inquired after the welfare of, *Weymouth* . . . greeted the believers, *Everyday.*

**and abode with them one day:** . . . spent a day with them, *TCNT* . . . stayed, *Williams C.K.*

**8. And the next day we that were of Paul's company departed:** And on the morrow we, *ASV* . . . The next day we left, *TCNT* . . . The following day we departed, *MLNT.*

**and came unto Caesarea:** . . . and arrived at, *MLNT* . . . and reached Caesarea, *TCNT.*

**and we entered into the house of Philip the evangelist:** . . . where we went to the house of Philip, the Missionary, *TCNT* . . . were guests in the house of Philip, the preacher, *BB* . . . where we called at the home of, *MLNT* . . . He was a preacher who goes from town to town, *NLT.*

**which was one of the seven:** . . . who was one of the Seven, *TCNT* . . . seven servants, *SEB* . . . was one of the seven church leaders, *NLT* . . . of the seven helpers, *NCV.*

**and abode with him:** . . . and stayed with him, *Williams C.K.* . . . by whom we were entertained, *MLNT.*

**9. And the same man had four daughters, virgins:** . . . unmarried daughters, *Beck* . . . four maiden daughters, *Fenton.*

**which did prophesy:** . . . who had the gift of prophecy, *TCNT* . . . who were prophetesses, *Weymouth* . . . all of whom spoke by the Spirit of God, *Phillips* . . . They spoke the Word of God, *NLT.*

## Acts 21:11

10.a.**Txt:** 01א-corr,08E 020L,025P,byz.Sod
**Var:** p74,02A,03B,04C Lach,Treg,Alf,Word We/Ho,Weis,UBS/☆

| **2231.2** prs-pron gen 1pl | **2232.1** noun fem | **3979.3** adj comp pl | **2687.1** verb 3sing indic aor act | **4948.3** indef-pron nom sing | **570.3** prep |
|---|---|---|---|---|---|
| ⌜a ἡμῶν ⌝ | ἡμέρας | πλείους | κατῆλθέν | τις | ἀπὸ |
| *hēmōn* | *hēmeras* | *pleious* | *katēlthen* | *tis* | *apo* |
| we | days | many | came down | a certain | from |

| **3450.10** art gen sing fem | **2424.2** name gen fem | **4254.1** noun nom sing masc | **3549.4** noun dat sing neu | **13.2** name nom masc | **2504.1** conj |
|---|---|---|---|---|---|
| τῆς | Ἰουδαίας | προφήτης | ὀνόματι | Ἅγαβος· | **11.** καὶ |
| *tēs* | *Ioudaias* | *prophētēs* | *onomati* | *Hagabos* | *kai* |
| | Judea, | a prophet, | by name | Agabus; | and |

| **2048.13** verb nom sing masc part aor act | **4242.1** prep | **2231.4** prs-pron acc 1pl | **2504.1** conj | **142.16** verb nom sing masc part aor act | **3450.12** art acc sing fem |
|---|---|---|---|---|---|
| ἐλθὼν | πρὸς | ἡμᾶς, | καὶ | ἄρας | τὴν |
| *elthōn* | *pros* | *hēmas* | *kai* | *aras* | *tēn* |
| having come | to | us, | and | having taken | the |

| **2206.2** noun acc sing fem | **3450.2** art gen sing | **3834.2** name gen masc | **1204.7** verb nom sing masc part aor act | **4885.1** conj | **840.3** prs-pron gen sing |
|---|---|---|---|---|---|
| ζώνην | τοῦ | Παύλου, | δήσας | ⌜ τε | αὐτοῦ |
| *zōnēn* | *tou* | *Paulou* | *dēsas* | *te* | *autou* |
| girdle | | of Paul, | having bound | and | himself |

11.a.**Txt:** 020L,025P,byz.
**Var:** 01א,02A,03B,04C 05D,08E,Lach,Treg,Alf Word,Tisc,We/Ho,Weis Sod,UBS/☆

| **1431.4** prs-pron gen sing | **3450.15** art acc pl fem | **5331.8** noun acc pl fem | **2504.1** conj | **3450.8** art acc pl masc | **4087.7** noun acc pl masc |
|---|---|---|---|---|---|
| [a☆ ἑαυτοῦ ] | ⌜ τὰς | χεῖρας | καὶ | τοὺς | πόδας |
| *heautou* | *tas* | *cheiras* | *kai* | *tous* | *podas* |
| [ idem ] | the | hands | and | the | feet |

| **3450.8** art acc pl masc | **4087.7** noun acc pl masc | **2504.1** conj | **3450.15** art acc pl fem | **5331.8** noun acc pl fem | **1500.5** verb 3sing indic aor act |
|---|---|---|---|---|---|
| [☆ τοὺς | πόδας | καὶ | τὰς | χεῖρας ] | εἶπεν, |
| *tous* | *podas* | *kai* | *tas* | *cheiras* | *eipen* |
| [ the | feet | and | the | hands ] | said, |

| **3455.4** dem-pron acc pl neu | **2978.5** verb 3sing indic pres act | **3450.16** art sing neu | **4011.1** noun sing neu | **3450.16** art sing neu | **39.1** adj sing |
|---|---|---|---|---|---|
| Τάδε | λέγει | τὸ | πνεῦμα | τὸ | ἅγιον, |
| *Tade* | *legei* | *to* | *pneuma* | *to* | *hagion* |
| Thus | says | the | Spirit | the | Holy, |

| **3450.6** art acc sing masc | **433.4** noun acc sing masc | **3614.2** rel-pron gen sing | **1498.4** verb 3sing indic pres act | **3450.9** art nom sing fem | **2206.1** noun nom sing fem |
|---|---|---|---|---|---|
| Τὸν | ἄνδρα | οὗ | ἐστιν | ἡ | ζώνη |
| *Ton* | *andra* | *hou* | *estin* | *hē* | *zōnē* |
| The | man | of whom | is | the | girdle |

| **3642.9** dem-pron nom sing fem | **3643.1** adv | **1204.11** verb 3pl indic fut act | **1706.1** prep | **2395.2** name fem | **3450.7** art nom pl masc |
|---|---|---|---|---|---|
| αὕτη | οὕτως | δήσουσιν | ἐν | Ἰερουσαλὴμ | οἱ |
| *hautē* | *houtōs* | *dēsousin* | *en* | *Ierousalēm* | *hoi* |
| this | thus | shall bind | in | Jerusalem | the |

| **2428.2** name-adj nom pl masc | **2504.1** conj | **3722.24** verb 3pl indic fut act | **1519.1** prep | **5331.8** noun acc pl fem | **1477.5** noun gen pl neu |
|---|---|---|---|---|---|
| Ἰουδαῖοι, | καὶ | παραδώσουσιν | εἰς | χεῖρας | ἐθνῶν. |
| *Ioudaioi* | *kai* | *paradōsousin* | *eis* | *cheiras* | *ethnōn* |
| Jews, | and | deliver up | into | hands | of Gentiles. |

| **5453.1** conj | **1156.2** conj | **189.22** verb 1pl indic aor act | **3642.18** dem-pron pl neu | **3731.19** verb 1pl indic imperf act |
|---|---|---|---|---|
| **12.** Ὡς | δὲ | ἠκούσαμεν | ταῦτα, | παρεκαλοῦμεν |
| *Hōs* | *de* | *ēkousamen* | *tauta* | *parekaloumen* |
| When | and | we heard | these things, | were urging |

The church historian Eusebius (A.D. 260–340) quotes Papias as saying these daughters moved to Asia, lived long lives, and continued to minister and witness to the Early Church. Thus they were used "as the Spirit wills." (In 1 Corinthians 12:11 "every man" is literally "each one," including both men and women.)

**21:10.** At Miletus Paul was anxious to hurry on his way. But here the blessing of the Lord was so rich that he stayed a considerable number of days. It seems obvious that the ministry of Philip's four daughters as they prophesied must have brought encouragement and blessing to Paul and his company. According to 1 Corinthians 14:3, when a person prophesies, he or she speaks for God by the Spirit in a language everyone understands. The speaking is to men (human beings, including both men and women). The words of the prophesying bring edification (that builds up spiritually and develops or confirms faith), exhortation (that encourages and awakens, challenging all to move ahead in faithfulness and love), and comfort (that cheers, revives, and encourages hope and expectation). By prophesying, these daughters were blessing, edifying, and building up spiritually all the believers who heard.

Possibly Philip gave Luke much information concerning the early days of the church at Jerusalem, facts which the Holy Spirit was able to direct Luke to use in writing the Book of Acts.

After a number of days the prophet Agabus, the same one who prophesied in 11:28, came down from Judea. He had probably heard the news that Paul was in Caesarea, though it is also possible the Holy Spirit simply directed him to go.

**21:11.** Agabus took Paul's belt (probably a wide belt made of linen cloth, long enough to be wrapped several times around the waist) and bound his own feet and hands as an object lesson. Then he gave a prophecy from the Holy Spirit that the Jews would bind (or be the cause of binding) Paul and give him over into the custody of the Gentiles (the Romans). In general, Paul knew of the things he would suffer because of the gospel (see 9:16), but in particular, he was fully aware of the problems that faced him in Jerusalem (20:23; 21:4). The Spirit, speaking through Agabus, did not forbid the journey to Jerusalem. The trip was too important to cancel just when the goal was in sight.

**21:12.** Because of the prophecy of Agabus, those who were meeting in Philip's house along with Paul's companions all begged him not to go up to Jerusalem. This was undoubtedly like what happened at Tyre. The people, when they heard the Spirit's message, expressed their own feelings and their own concern for Paul's welfare. The Greek indicates they kept on doing so.

**10. And as we tarried there many days:** During our visit, which lasted several days, *TCNT* . . . Now during our somewhat lengthy stay, *Weymouth* . . . After we had stayed there for many days, *SEB* . . . After we had been there for some time, *Everyday* . . . as we remained, *Fenton* . . . During our few days' stay, *NAB* . . . When we had stayed there, *Williams C.K.* . . . During our stay there, *Phillips* . . . We had stopped there for several days, *MLNT* . . . While we were there a few days, *NLT* . . . We spent a number of days there, and in the course of them, *Goodspeed.*

**there came down from Judaea a certain prophet, named Agabus:** . . . a man who speaks for God, *NLT* . . . by the name of, *Phillips* . . . arrived from, *NAB* . . . a preacher of the name of, *Fenton.*

**11. And when he was come unto us, he took Paul's girdle:** . . . and called on us, *MLNT* . . . He came up to us, and taking Paul's belt, *NAB* . . . When he came to see us, *Phillips* . . . borrowed Paul's belt, *Everyday.*

**and bound his own hands and feet, and said:** . . . and, tying his feet and hands, *Berkeley* . . . and used it to tie, *NLT* . . . and fastened his own hands, *Williams C.K.*

**Thus saith the Holy Ghost:** This is what the Holy Spirit says, *TCNT* . . . Thus speaks, *MLNT* . . . These are the words of the Holy Spirit, *Williams C.K.* . . . tells me, *SEB.*

**So shall the Jews at Jerusalem bind the man that owneth this girdle:** This is how the Jews, *Everyday* . . . In like manner shall, *Fenton* . . . will tie the man this belt belongs to, *Beck* . . . The man whose belt this is will be fastened like this, *Williams C.K.* . . . will be bound like this, *Phillips.*

**and shall deliver him into the hands of the Gentiles:** . . . and will hand him over to, *Weymouth* . . . to the heathen! *Goodspeed* . . . to heathen hands, *Fenton.*

**12. And when we heard these things:** As soon as we heard these words, *Weymouth* . . . On hearing this, *Berkeley, MLNT* . . . heard him say this, *Phillips.*

# Acts 21:13

| 2231.1 prs-pron nom 1pl | 4885.1 conj | 2504.1 conj | 3450.7 art nom pl masc | 1770.1 adj nom pl masc | 3450.2 art gen sing | 3231.1 partic |
|---|---|---|---|---|---|---|
| ἡμεῖς | τε | καὶ | οἱ | ἐντόπιοι | τοῦ | μὴ |
| *hēmeis* | *te* | *kai* | *hoi* | *entopioi* | *tou* | *mē* |
| we | both | and | those | of place | the | not |

13.a.**Var:** p74,01ℵ,02A 03B,04C,08E,sa.bo. Lach,Treg,Alf,Word Tisc,We/Ho,Weis,Sod UBS/☆

| 303.11 verb inf pres act | 840.6 prs-pron acc sing masc | 1519.1 prep | 2395.1 name fem | 4966.1 adv |
|---|---|---|---|---|
| ἀναβαίνειν | αὐτὸν | εἰς | Ἱερουσαλήμ. | **13.** [a☆+ τότε ] |
| *anabainein* | *auton* | *eis* | *Hierousalēm* | *tote* |
| to go up | him | to | Jerusalem. | [Then] |

13.b.**Txt:** 04C-org,044 33,byz. **Var:** p74,01ℵ,02A,03B 04C-corr,08E,sa.bo.Lach Treg,Alf,Word,Tisc We/Ho,Weis,Sod UBS/☆

| 552.6 verb 3sing indic aor pass | 1156.2 conj | 3450.5 art nom sing masc | 3834.1 name nom masc | 4949.9 intr-pron sing neu | 4020.2 verb 2pl pres act |
|---|---|---|---|---|---|
| ἀπεκρίθη | (b δὲ ) | ὁ | Παῦλος, | Τί | ποιεῖτε |
| *apekrithē* | *de* | *ho* | *Paulos* | *Ti* | *poieite* |
| Answered | but | | Paul, | Why | do you |

| 2772.6 verb nom pl masc part pres act | 2504.1 conj | 4769.1 verb nom pl masc part pres act | 1466.2 prs-pron gen 1sing | 3450.12 art acc sing fem |
|---|---|---|---|---|
| κλαίοντες | καὶ | συνθρύπτοντές | μου | τὴν |
| *klaiontes* | *kai* | *sunthruptontes* | *mou* | *tēn* |
| weeping | and | breaking | my | the |

| 2559.4 noun acc sing fem | 1466.1 prs-pron nom 1sing | 1056.1 conj | 3620.3 partic | 3303.1 adv | 1204.12 verb inf aor pass | 233.2 conj |
|---|---|---|---|---|---|---|
| καρδίαν; | ἐγὼ | γὰρ | οὐ | μόνον | δεθῆναι | ἀλλὰ |
| *kardian* | *egō* | *gar* | *ou* | *monon* | *dethēnai* | *alla* |
| heart? | I | for | not | only | to be bound | but |

| 2504.1 conj | 594.20 verb inf aor act | 1519.1 prep | 2395.1 name fem | 2072.1 adv | 2174.1 verb 1sing pres act |
|---|---|---|---|---|---|
| καὶ | ἀποθανεῖν | εἰς | Ἱερουσαλὴμ | ἑτοίμως | ἔχω |
| *kai* | *apothanein* | *eis* | *Hierousalēm* | *hetoimōs* | *echō* |
| also | to die | at | Jerusalem | readily | have |

| 5065.1 prep | 3450.2 art gen sing | 3549.3 noun gen sing neu | 3450.2 art gen sing | 2935.2 noun gen sing masc | 2400.2 name masc | 3231.1 partic |
|---|---|---|---|---|---|---|
| ὑπὲρ | τοῦ | ὀνόματος | τοῦ | κυρίου | Ἰησοῦ. | **14.** Μὴ |
| *huper* | *tou* | *onomatos* | *tou* | *kuriou* | *Iēsou* | *Mē* |
| for | the | name | of the | Lord | Jesus. | Not |

| 3844.22 verb gen sing masc part pres mid | 1156.2 conj | 840.3 prs-pron gen sing | 2248.2 verb 1pl indic aor act | 1500.19 verb nom pl masc part aor act |
|---|---|---|---|---|
| πειθομένου | δὲ | αὐτοῦ | ἡσυχάσαμεν | εἰπόντες, |
| *peithomenou* | *de* | *autou* | *hēsuchasamen* | *eipontes* |
| being persuaded | and | he | we were silent, | having said, |

| 3450.16 art sing neu | 2284.1 noun sing neu | 3450.2 art gen sing | 2935.2 noun gen sing masc | 3450.2 art gen sing | 2935.2 noun gen sing masc |
|---|---|---|---|---|---|
| ( Τὸ | θέλημα | τοῦ | κυρίου | [☆ Τοῦ | κυρίου |
| *To* | *thelēma* | *tou* | *kuriou* | *Tou* | *kuriou* |
| The | will | of the | Lord | [Of the | Lord |

14.a.**Txt:** 020L,025P,byz. **Var:** 01ℵ,02A,03B,04C 05D,08E,Lach,Treg,Alf Word,Tisc,We/Ho,Weis Sod,UBS/☆

| 3450.16 art sing neu | 2284.1 noun sing neu | 1090.46 verb 3sing impr aor mid | 1090.18 verb 3sing impr pres mid | 3196.3 prep |
|---|---|---|---|---|
| τὸ | θέλημα ] | ( γενέσθω. | [a☆ γινέσθω. ] | **15.** Μετὰ |
| *to* | *thelēma* | *genesthō* | *ginesthō* | *Meta* |
| the | will ] | be done. | [being done.] | After |

| 1156.2 conj | 3450.15 art acc pl fem | 2232.1 noun fem | 3642.15 dem-pron acc pl fem | 637.1 verb nom pl masc part aor mid |
|---|---|---|---|---|
| δὲ | τὰς | ἡμέρας | ταύτας | ( ἀποσκευασάμενοι |
| *de* | *tas* | *hēmeras* | *tautas* | *aposkeuasamenoi* |
| and | the | days | these, | having packed |

**21:13.** Not only did they keep begging Paul not to go, they became quite emotionally distraught and began to weep. They could not bear to think of anything happening to Paul, they loved and respected him so.

Paul, however, said, "What are you doing, weeping and making me feel crushed to pieces?" Breaking (crushing to pieces) the heart was a phrase used to mean breaking the will, weakening the purpose, or causing a person to "go to pieces" so that he could accomplish nothing. To get them to stop their weeping and begging, Paul declared he was ready not only to be bound, but to die in Jerusalem for the sake of the name of the Lord Jesus. Actually, he had long ago made this kind of commitment. He had often risked his life for the sake of the gospel and for the sake of winning the lost to Christ. He knew too that death might strip him of this present body, but he would be immediately in the presence of the Lord (2 Corinthians 5:6-8). Later he said he was hard pressed to decide between life and death. He had a desire to go and be with Christ, but for the sake of those who needed him, he was willing to stay and be a help (Philippians 1:20-25).

Thus, Paul in this case did not let his friends hinder him. Through the constraint of the Holy Spirit in his own soul, he had a clearer vision of the will of God than they did. For this reason, the threat of persecution did not bring despair to his heart. He had the assurance that whatever happened, even death, it would bring glory to Jesus' name. Though he now had no hope of escaping chains and imprisonment, he voiced his determination to do God's will.

**21:14.** Finally Paul's friends gave up. They had to recognize that they, not Paul, had been unwilling to submit to the will of God. (Compare Luke 22:42.) It was indeed God's will for Paul to go to Jerusalem.

The events which followed show that Paul was right. If he had not gone to Jerusalem, he would have missed a new vision of Jesus (23:11), plus many miracles and opportunities to witness. He would also have missed God's way of getting him to Rome. God's way is sometimes a hard way, but it is always the best way!

It was important also for the Church to have these warnings from the Spirit. Had Paul gone up to Jerusalem without them, there were Judaizers around who would have been quick to take Paul's arrest as a judgment of God. They would have said, "See, did we not tell you? Paul's preaching is all wrong. You Gentiles must become Jews and be circumcised or you will lose your salvation." This would have brought great confusion into the churches. But through these prophecies the Holy Spirit bore witness to Paul and the gospel he preached. At the same time, the Church itself was protected from forces which could have caused division.

**21:15.** After those days in the house of Philip, Paul and his company made preparations to go up to Jerusalem. This probably means they hired horses and saddled them up. Some writers, how-

**both we, and they of that place:** . . . the residents, *Murdock* . . . the people there, *Everyday.*

**besought him not to go up to Jerusalem:** . . . began to entreat Paul, *TCNT* . . . begged Paul not to go, *Everyday.*

**13. Then Paul answered:** His reply was, *Weymouth.*

**What mean ye to weep and to break mine heart?:** What do you achieve by weeping and discouraging me, *Berkeley* . . . unnerving me with all your tears, *Phillips* . . . and crushing my heart? *Rotherham* . . . making me weak in my purpose, *Beck* . . . disheartening me? *Moffatt* . . . weaken my resolution, *JB* . . . Why are you making me so sad? *SEB* . . . with your grief? *Montgomery.*

**for I am ready not to be bound only:** . . . not only to be a prisoner, *BB* . . . I am prepared not merely to be bound, *Berkeley* . . . I am ready to be tied up, *Everyday* . . . to be put in chains, *NLT.*

**but also to die at Jerusalem:** . . . but even to suffer death, *TCNT.*

**for the name of the Lord Jesus:** . . . in behalf of the name of, *Rotherham* . . . for the sake of the Lord Jesus! *Weymouth.*

**14. And when he would not be persuaded:** So when he was not to be dissuaded, *Weymouth* . . . Paul would not listen to us, *NLT* . . . So as he would not yield, *Goodspeed.*

**we ceased, saying:** . . . we said no more to him, *TCNT* . . . we ceased remonstrating with him, *Weymouth* . . . we stopped begging him, *Williams* . . . we kept quiet, *Adams* . . . we acquiesced, *Confraternity* . . . So, we stopped trying, *SEB* . . . we were silent, *Swann.*

**The will of the Lord be done:** Let the purpose of God be done, *BB* . . . We pray that what the Lord wants will be done, *Everyday.*

**15. And after those days:** At the end of our visit, *TCNT* . . . A few days afterwards, *Weymouth.*

**we took up our carriages:** . . . we packed our baggage, *ASV* . . . we got ready, *Everyday, Williams* . . . we packed up, *TCNT* . . . we made our preparations, *Goodspeed.*

15.a.**Txt:** Steph
**Var:** 01ℵ,02A,03B,08E 020L,025P,Lach,Treg Alf,Word,Tisc,We/Ho Weis,Sod,UBS/☆

| **1964.1** verb nom pl masc part aor mid | **303.23** verb 1pl indic imperf act | **1519.1** prep | **2395.1** name fem |
|---|---|---|---|
| [[a]☆ ἐπισκευασάμενοι ] | ἀνεβαίνομεν | εἰς | ʼ Ἱερουσαλήμ. |
| *episkeuasamenoi* | *anebainomen* | *eis* | *Hierousalēm* |
| [ having prepared ] | we were going up | to | Jerusalem. |

15.b.**Txt:** 020L,025P,byz.
**Var:** 01ℵ,02A,03B,04C 05D,08E,Lach,Treg,Alf Word,Tisc,We/Ho,Weis Sod,UBS/☆

| **2389.1** name | **4755.3** verb 3pl indic aor act | **1156.2** conj | **2504.1** conj | **3450.1** art gen pl |
|---|---|---|---|---|
| [[b]☆ Ἱεροσόλυμα· ] | **16.** συνῆλθον | δὲ | καὶ | τῶν |
| *Hierosoluma* | *sunēlthon* | *de* | *kai* | *tōn* |
| [ idem ] | Went | and | also | of the |

| **3073.6** noun gen pl masc | **570.3** prep | **2513.1** name gen fem | **4713.1** prep | **2231.3** prs-pron dat 1pl | **70.6** verb nom pl masc part pres act |
|---|---|---|---|---|---|
| μαθητῶν | ἀπὸ | Καισαρείας | σὺν | ἡμῖν, | ἄγοντες |
| *mathētōn* | *apo* | *Kaisareias* | *sun* | *hēmin* | *agontes* |
| disciples | from | Caesarea | with | us, | bringing |

| **3706.1** prep | **3614.3** rel-pron dat sing | **3441.7** verb 1pl subj aor pass | **3280.1** name dat masc | **4948.2** indef-pron dat sing |
|---|---|---|---|---|
| παρ' | ᾧ | ξενισθῶμεν, | Μνάσωνί | τινι |
| *par'* | *hō* | *xenisthōmen* | *Mnasōni* | *tini* |
| with | whom | we might stay, | Mnason | a certain, |

| **2926.2** name-adj dat sing masc | **739.4** adj dat sing masc | **3073.3** noun dat sing masc | **1090.49** verb gen pl part aor mid | **1156.2** conj |
|---|---|---|---|---|
| Κυπρίῳ, | ἀρχαίῳ | μαθητῇ. | **17.** Γενομένων | δὲ |
| *Kupriō* | *archaiō* | *mathētē* | *Genomenōn* | *de* |
| a Cypriot, | an old | disciple. | Having arrived | and |

| **2231.2** prs-pron gen 1pl | **1519.1** prep | **2389.1** name | **774.1** adv | **1203.8** verb 3pl indic aor mid |
|---|---|---|---|---|
| ἡμῶν | εἰς | Ἱεροσόλυμα | ἀσμένως | ʼ ἐδέξαντο |
| *hēmōn* | *eis* | *Hierosoluma* | *asmenōs* | *edexanto* |
| us | at | Jerusalem | gladly | received |

17.a.**Txt:** 020L,025P,byz.
**Var:** 01ℵ,02A,03B,04C 08E,Lach,Treg,Alf Word,Tisc,We/Ho,Weis Sod,UBS/☆

| **583.7** verb 3pl indic aor mid | **2231.4** prs-pron acc 1pl | **3450.7** art nom pl masc | **79.6** noun nom pl masc | **3450.11** art dat sing fem |
|---|---|---|---|---|
| [[a]☆ ἀπεδέξαντο ] | ἡμᾶς | οἱ | ἀδελφοί. | **18.** τῇ |
| *apedexanto* | *hēmas* | *hoi* | *adelphoi* | *tē* |
| [ idem ] | us | the | brothers. | The |

| **1156.2** conj | **1951.1** noun dat sing fem | **1510.3** verb 3sing indic imperf act | **3450.5** art nom sing masc | **3834.1** name nom masc | **4713.1** prep |
|---|---|---|---|---|---|
| δὲ | ἐπιούσῃ | εἰσῄει | ὁ | Παῦλος | σὺν |
| *de* | *epiousē* | *eisēei* | *ho* | *Paulos* | *sun* |
| and | following | went in | | Paul | with |

| **2231.3** prs-pron dat 1pl | **4242.1** prep | **2362.4** name acc masc | **3820.7** adj nom pl masc | **4885.1** conj | **3716.4** verb 3pl indic aor mid |
|---|---|---|---|---|---|
| ἡμῖν | πρὸς | Ἰάκωβον, | πάντες | τε | παρεγένοντο |
| *hēmin* | *pros* | *Iakōbon* | *pantes* | *te* | *paregenonto* |
| us | to | James, | all | and | assembled |

| **3450.7** art nom pl masc | **4104.5** adj comp nom pl masc | **2504.1** conj | **776.10** verb nom sing masc part aor mid | **840.8** prs-pron acc pl masc |
|---|---|---|---|---|
| οἱ | πρεσβύτεροι. | **19.** καὶ | ἀσπασάμενος | αὐτοὺς |
| *hoi* | *presbuteroi* | *kai* | *aspasamenos* | *autous* |
| the | elders. | And | having greeted | them |

| **1817.4** verb 3sing indic imperf mid | **2567.2** prep | **1518.9** num card neu | **1524.1** adj sing | **3614.1** rel-pron gen pl |
|---|---|---|---|---|
| ἐξηγεῖτο | καθ' | ἓν | ἕκαστον | ὧν |
| *exēgeito* | *kath'* | *hen* | *hekaston* | *hōn* |
| he was relating | according to | one | each | what things |

ever, believe it means simply that they packed their bags (their luggage).

**21:16.** Some of the disciples from Caesarea went with Paul and his company. These believers from Caesarea knew a believer from Cyprus, Mnason (the M is not pronounced). Mnason, like Barnabas, was one of the "old" (original) disciples, that is, one of the 120. (He was not necessarily "old" in age.) He was known as one who delighted to entertain strangers (foreigners).

Some translations indicate that Mnason was visiting in Caesarea at the time Paul was there and came up with them to Jerusalem. But the Greek text does not need to be interpreted this way. It is more likely that the Caesarean believers simply brought Paul and his company to Mnason's house in Jerusalem. The Western text (Codex Bezae, D), however, takes it to mean that Mnason's house was in a village on the way to Jerusalem. Actually, the journey to Jerusalem was too long for 1 day, so it is possible the Western text is correct here in that Mnason's house was west of Jerusalem and became a convenient headquarters for the Jerusalem visit.

**21:17.** At Jerusalem the brethren (including Mnason) welcomed them joyfully and entertained them hospitably. They were really glad to see Paul and his company, including the Gentile believers.

**21:18.** The next day Paul took Luke and the rest of his company to see James, the brother of Jesus, who was now the chief elder of the church in Jerusalem. The other elders were also present. These were undoubtedly the elders (administrative officers, much like the pastors of today) who were responsible for taking care of the house churches or local assemblies in Jerusalem and its environs. What follows shows there were a large number of them.

At this point it is worth noting also that none of the apostles are mentioned. Seven years before, at the Council of Jerusalem (A.D. 49), they were all present. Now it seems, as much of early church tradition says, they were already scattered, spreading the gospel in many different directions. John, for example, went to Ephesus. Some say Andrew was martyred in Scythia, others say in Greece. Tradition is strong that Thomas was martyred in India.

**21:19.** Paul greeted the Jerusalem elders warmly, undoubtedly with a holy kiss, as was the custom (Romans 16:16; 1 Corinthians 16:20; 2 Corinthians 13:12; 1 Thessalonians 5:26). He probably pronounced blessings on them in the name of the Lord Jesus.

After greeting them, Paul gave a detailed account of what God had done among the Gentiles through his ministry. This must have been a step-by-step rehearsal of his second and third missionary journeys. Specifically, he told them everything that had happened since the last time he was with them at the Council referred to in

**and went up to Jerusalem:** . . . and continued our journey, *Weymouth* . . . and started for, *Moffatt* . . . we ascended to, *Fenton.*

**16. There went with us also certain of the disciples of Caesarea:** Some of the disciples from Caesarea, *TCNT* . . . also joined our party, *Weymouth* . . . also accompanied us, *Fenton.*

**and brought with them one Mnason of Cyprus:** . . . by whom we were introduced to, *Fenton.*

**an old disciple:** . . . a disciple of long standing, *TCNT* . . . an aged disciple, *Worrell* . . . He was one of the first followers, *NLT* . . . a disciple from the first, *Fenton.*

**with whom we should lodge:** . . . we were to stay, *TCNT.*

**17. And when we were come to Jerusalem:** On our arrival at Jerusalem, *TCNT* . . . when we arrived at, *Fenton.*

**the brethren received us gladly:** . . . gladly welcomed us, *Rotherham* . . . gave us a hearty welcome, *Goodspeed, TCNT* . . . a very warm welcome, *Phillips* . . . were pleased to see us, *BB* . . . glad to see us, *NLT.*

**18. And the day following:** And on the next day, *Rotherham* . . . on the following morning, *Fenton.*

**Paul went in with us unto James:** Paul went with us to have an interview with, *TCNT* . . . accompanied us to James, *Fenton* . . . to visit James, *Phillips.*

**and all the elders were present:** . . . and all the Officers of the Church, *TCNT* . . . where all the elders assembled, *Fenton* . . . presbyters, *Moffatt.*

**19. And when he had saluted them:** After greeting them, *Fenton, TCNT* . . . After exchanging greetings, *Weymouth.*

**he declared particularly:** . . . he went on to narrate one by one, *Rotherham* . . . Paul related in detail, *TCNT* . . . described in detail, *Moffatt* . . . he recounted to them step by step, *Berkeley* . . . he carefully explained, *Klingensmith* . . . Then he told them exactly how, *SEB* . . . gave a detailed account of, *Goodspeed* . . . and told them everything, *NCV.*

## Acts 21:20

| 4020.24 verb 3sing indic aor act | 3450.5 art nom sing masc | 2296.1 noun nom sing masc | 1706.1 prep | 3450.4 art dat pl | 1477.6 noun dat pl neu |
|---|---|---|---|---|---|
| ἐποίησεν | ὁ | θεὸς | ἐν | τοῖς | ἔθνεσιν |
| *epoiēsen* | *ho* | *theos* | *en* | *tois* | *ethnesin* |
| did | | God | among | the | Gentiles |

| 1217.2 prep | 3450.10 art gen sing fem | 1242.2 noun gen sing fem | 840.3 prs-pron gen sing | 3450.7 art nom pl masc | 1156.2 conj |
|---|---|---|---|---|---|
| διὰ | τῆς | διακονίας | αὐτοῦ. | **20.** οἱ | δὲ |
| *dia* | *tēs* | *diakonias* | *autou* | *hoi* | *de* |
| through | the | ministry | his. | The | and |

20.a.**Txt:** 05D,025P,byz. sa.
**Var:** 01ℵ,02A,03B,04C 08E,020L,bo.Gries,Lach Treg,Alf,Word,Tisc We/Ho,Weis,Sod UBS/☆

| 189.32 verb nom pl masc part aor act | 1386.18 verb 3pl indic imperf act | 3450.6 art acc sing masc | 2935.4 noun acc sing masc | 3450.6 art acc sing masc |
|---|---|---|---|---|
| ἀκούσαντες | ἐδόξαζον | ʽ τὸν | κύριον˙ | [a☆ τὸν |
| *akousantes* | *edoxazon* | *ton* | *kurion* | *ton* |
| having heard | were glorifying | the | Lord. | |

20.b.**Txt:** 02A,03B,020L 025P,byz.Sod
**Var:** 01ℵ,08E,Treg,Tisc We/Ho,Weis,UBS/☆

| 2296.4 noun acc sing masc | 1500.3 verb indic aor act | 1500.28 verb 3pl indic aor act | 4885.1 conj | 840.4 prs-pron dat sing | 2311.3 verb 2sing indic pres act |
|---|---|---|---|---|---|
| θεόν˙ ] | ʽ εἶπόν | [b☆ εἶπάν ] | τε | αὐτῷ, | Θεωρεῖς, |
| *theon* | *eipon* | *eipan* | *te* | *autō* | *Theōreis* |
| [ God. ] | They said | [ idem ] | and | to him, | You see, |

| 79.5 noun voc sing masc | 4073.5 intr-pron nom pl fem | 3323.1 noun nom pl fem | 1498.7 verb 3pl indic pres act | 2428.3 name-adj gen pl masc |
|---|---|---|---|---|
| ἀδελφέ, | πόσαι | μυριάδες | εἰσὶν | ʽ Ἰουδαίων |
| *adelphe* | *posai* | *muriades* | *eisin* | *Ioudaiōn* |
| brother, | how many | myriads | there are | of Jews |

20.c.**Txt:** 020L,025P,044 byz.
**Var:** 02A,03B,04C,08E bo.Lach,Treg,Alf,Word We/Ho,Weis,Sod UBS/☆
**Var:** 01ℵ,Tisc

| 1706.1 prep | 3450.4 art dat pl | 2428.4 name-adj dat pl masc | 3450.1 art gen pl | 3961.43 verb gen pl part perf act |
|---|---|---|---|---|
| [c☆ ἐν | τοῖς | Ἰουδαίοις ] | τῶν | πεπιστευκότων, |
| *en* | *tois* | *Ioudaiois* | *tōn* | *pepisteukotōn* |
| [ among | the | Jews ] | the | having believed, |

| 2504.1 conj | 3820.7 adj nom pl masc | 2190.3 noun nom pl masc | 3450.2 art gen sing | 3414.2 noun gen sing masc | 5062.1 verb 3pl indic pres act |
|---|---|---|---|---|---|
| καὶ | πάντες | ζηλωταὶ | τοῦ | νόμου | ὑπάρχουσιν. |
| *kai* | *pantes* | *zēlōtai* | *tou* | *nomou* | *huparchousin* |
| and | all | zealous | of the | law | are. |

| 2697.5 verb 3pl indic aor pass | 1156.2 conj | 3875.1 prep | 4622.2 prs-pron gen 2sing | 3617.1 conj |
|---|---|---|---|---|
| **21.** κατηχήθησαν | δὲ | περὶ | σοῦ, | ὅτι |
| *katēchēthēsan* | *de* | *peri* | *sou* | *hoti* |
| They were informed | and | concerning | you, | that |

| 640.2 noun acc sing fem | 1315.2 verb 2sing indic pres act | 570.3 prep | 3337.2 name gen masc | 3338.2 name gen masc |
|---|---|---|---|---|
| ἀποστασίαν | διδάσκεις | ἀπὸ | ʽ Μωσέως | [☆ Μωϋσέως ] |
| *apostasian* | *didaskeis* | *apo* | *Mōseōs* | *Mōuseōs* |
| apostasy | you are teaching | from | Moses | [ idem ] |

| 3450.8 art acc pl masc | 2567.3 prep | 3450.17 art pl neu | 1477.4 noun pl neu | 3820.8 adj acc pl masc | 2428.5 name-adj acc pl masc |
|---|---|---|---|---|---|
| τοὺς | κατὰ | τὰ | ἔθνη | πάντας | Ἰουδαίους, |
| *tous* | *kata* | *ta* | *ethnē* | *pantas* | *Ioudaious* |
| the | according to | the | Gentiles | all | Jews, |

| 2978.15 verb nom sing masc part pres act | 3231.1 partic | 3919.2 verb inf pres act | 840.8 prs-pron acc pl masc | 3450.17 art pl neu | 4891.4 noun pl neu |
|---|---|---|---|---|---|
| λέγων | μὴ | περιτέμνειν | αὐτοὺς | τὰ | τέκνα, |
| *legōn* | *mē* | *peritemnein* | *autous* | *ta* | *tekna* |
| telling | not | to circumcise | them | the | children, |

chapter 15. He must have emphasized the vision that gave him the Macedonian call, the conversion of the Philippian jailer, the success at Beroea, the victories at Corinth, the 2 years he taught in the schoolroom of Tyrannus in Ephesus, the special miracles, the burning of the books of magic, and the establishment of the churches in the various cities of the Roman province of Asia.

The brief account of these journeys in the Book of Acts fills believers' hearts with praise to God and admiration for the men God used. But the Book of Acts does not record all that happened. Think what the whole story must have been! Think too that Paul accomplished all this without a printed Bible, and without the help of newspapers, magazines, radio, or television. He had no monthly check, no guaranteed support. In addition, Jews, heathen, and false brethren opposed him on every hand. Again and again he risked his life for the gospel, but the Lord saw him through it all in triumph. As he was leaving for Jerusalem, he wrote the Romans and was able to say, "I will not dare to speak of any of those things which Christ hath not wrought by me, to make the Gentiles obedient, by word and deed, through mighty signs and wonders, by the power of the Spirit of God; so that from Jerusalem, and round about unto Illyricum (on the coast of the Adriatic Sea opposite Italy), I have fully preached the gospel" (Romans 15:18,19).

**21:20.** James and all the Jerusalem elders glorified God because of what He was doing among the Gentiles. But they had a problem. Another matter of deep concern was affecting the Jerusalem church. Though the elders were rejoicing and were willing to congratulate Paul, he would have to do something more if his good report was to influence the thousands of Jewish believers in Palestine.

"Thousands" here is literally tens of thousands. The Jerusalem church was still growing by leaps and bounds. All of these converts from Judaism had accepted Jesus as their Messiah, Lord, and Saviour. Yet they were still zealous of the Law, eagerly devoted to the law of Moses, ardent observers of the Law. Undoubtedly their newfound faith in Christ stirred them up to serve God with new zeal, so they applied this to obeying the Law as they had been taught all their lives.

**21:21.** False teachers had come among the Jewish believers. These were probably Judaizers who were still teaching that Gentiles must become Jews in faith before they could be genuine Christians and be truly saved. Or they may have been unconverted Jews from Asia Minor, Macedonia, or Greece, who were enemies of Paul. They had followed Paul from place to place before and stirred up trouble. They looked on Paul as a sort of religious anarchist or revolutionary who launched malicious attacks on the law of Moses and who was urging Jews everywhere to forsake the Law.

These false teachers told the Jerusalem believers again and again that Paul was teaching all the Jews who lived among the Gentiles (the nations outside of Palestine) not to circumcise their children.



**what things God had wrought among the Gentiles by his ministry:** . . . each of the things, *Rotherham* . . . that God had done among the Gentiles through his efforts, *TCNT* . . . through his service, *Williams.*

**20. And when they heard it:** . . . and they, on hearing this account, *Phillips.*

**they glorified the Lord:** . . . they began praising God, *TCNT* . . . gave glory to God, *Weymouth* . . . thanked God, *Fenton.*

**and said unto him:** They told him, *Beck* . . . remarked, *Fenton.*

**Thou seest, brother:** You see, *NLT.*

**how many thousands of Jews there are which believe:** . . . how many myriads there are, *Rotherham* . . . that the Jews who have become believers in Christ may be numbered by tens of thousands, *TCNT* . . . of Christians there are among, *NLT.*

**and they are all zealous of the law:** . . . naturally earnest in upholding the Jewish Law, *TCNT* . . . zealots for the law, *HBIE* . . . and every one of them is a staunch upholder of the law, *Phillips* . . . all zealous supporters of the law, *Norlie* . . . they all think it is very important to obey, *SEB* . . . ardent upholders, *Moffatt.*

**21. And they are informed of thee:** Now they have heard it rumoured concerning thee, *Rotherham* . . . again and again, *Montgomery* . . . Now what they have been told about you is, *Weymouth* . . . were informed by report concerning you, *Worrell.*

**that thou teachest all the Jews which are among the Gentiles to forsake Moses:** . . . to discard Moses, *TCNT* . . . to turn their backs on Moses, *Williams* . . . to give up the law of Moses, *BB* . . . to disregard the Law of Moses, *Phillips* . . . apostasy from Moses, *PNT* . . . to abandon the law, *SEB* . . . to break away from, *NLT* . . . to leave the law, *NCV.*

**saying that they ought not to circumcise their children:** . . . advising them not to, *Fenton* . . . you continue to tell them to stop circumcising, *Williams* . . . telling them to not do the religious act of becoming a Jew, *NLT.*

# Acts 21:22

| 3234.1 | 3450.4 | 1478.4 | 3906.17 | 4949.9 | 3631.1 |
|---|---|---|---|---|---|
| adv | art dat pl | noun dat pl neu | verb inf pres act | intr-pron sing neu | partic |
| μηδὲ | τοῖς | ἔθεσιν | περιπατεῖν. | 22. τί | οὖν |
| *mēde* | *tois* | *ethesin* | *peripatein* | *ti* | *oun* |
| nor | in the | customs | to walk. | What | then |

22.a.**Txt:** 01ℵ,02A 05D-corr,020L,025P,byz. **Var:** 03B,04C-org,sa.bo. Treg,We/Ho,Weis UBS/☆

| 1498.4 | 3705.1 | 1158.1 | 3988.1 | 4755.10 |
|---|---|---|---|---|
| verb 3sing indic pres act | adv | verb 3sing indic pres act | noun sing neu | verb inf aor act |
| ἐστιν; | πάντως | ⌜a δεῖ | πλῆθος | συνελθεῖν· ⌝ |
| *estin* | *pantōs* | *dei* | *plēthos* | *sunelthein* |
| is it? | certainly | must | a multitude | to come together; |

22.b.**Txt:** p74,01ℵ-corr 02A,05D,08E,020L 025P,byz.Tisc,Sod **Var:** 01ℵ-org,03B,04C sa.bo.Treg,We/Ho,Weis UBS/☆

| 189.54 | 1056.1 | 3617.1 | 2048.25 | 3642.17 |
|---|---|---|---|---|
| verb 3pl indic fut mid | conj | conj | verb 2sing indic perf act | dem-pron sing neu |
| ἀκούσονται | ⌜b γὰρ ⌝ | ὅτι | ἐλήλυθας. | 23. τοῦτο |
| *akousontai* | *gar* | *hoti* | *elēluthas* | *touto* |
| they will hear | for | that | you have come. | This |

| 3631.1 | 4020.34 | 3614.16 | 4622.3 | 2978.6 | 1498.7 |
|---|---|---|---|---|---|
| partic | verb 2sing impr aor act | rel-pron sing neu | prs-pron dat 2sing | verb 1pl indic pres act | verb 3pl indic pres act |
| οὖν | ποίησον | ὅ | σοι | λέγομεν· | εἰσὶν |
| *oun* | *poiēson* | *ho* | *soi* | *legomen* | *eisin* |
| therefore | do | what | to you | we say: | There are |

| 2231.3 | 433.6 | 4913.1 | 2152.2 | 2174.19 | 1894.1 |
|---|---|---|---|---|---|
| prs-pron dat 1pl | noun nom pl masc | num card nom | noun acc sing fem | verb nom pl masc part pres act | prep |
| ἡμῖν | ἄνδρες | τέσσαρες | εὐχὴν | ἔχοντες | ἐφ' |
| *hēmin* | *andres* | *tessares* | *euchēn* | *echontes* | *eph'* |
| with us | men | four | a vow | having | on |

| 1431.2 | 3642.8 | 3741.9 | 47.5 | 4713.1 |
|---|---|---|---|---|
| prs-pron gen pl | dem-pron acc pl masc | verb nom sing masc part aor act | verb 2sing impr aor pass | prep |
| ἑαυτῶν· | 24. τούτους | παραλαβὼν | ἁγνίσθητι | σὺν |
| *heautōn* | *toutous* | *paralabōn* | *hagnisthēti* | *sun* |
| themselves; | these | having taken | be purified | with |

| 840.2 | 2504.1 | 1154.2 | 1894.2 | 840.2 | 2419.1 |
|---|---|---|---|---|---|
| prs-pron dat pl | conj | verb 2sing impr aor act | prep | prs-pron dat pl | conj |
| αὐτοῖς, | καὶ | δαπάνησον | ἐπ' | αὐτοῖς, | ἵνα |
| *autois* | *kai* | *dapanēson* | *ep'* | *autois* | *hina* |
| them, | and | pay expenses | for | them, | that |

24.a.**Txt:** 02A,03B-corr 04C,020L,byz.Weis,Sod **Var:** 01ℵ,03B-org 05D-corr,08E,025P Treg,Alf,Tisc,We/Ho UBS/☆

| 3449.2 | 3449.4 | 3450.12 | 2747.4 | 2504.1 |
|---|---|---|---|---|
| verb 3pl subj aor mid | verb 3pl indic fut mid | art acc sing fem | noun acc sing fem | conj |
| ⌜ ξυρήσωνται | [a☆ ξυρήσονται ] | τὴν | κεφαλήν, | καὶ |
| *xurēsōntai* | *xurēsontai* | *tēn* | *kephalēn* | *kai* |
| they may shave | [ they will shave ] | the | head; | and |

24.b.**Txt:** 020L,025P,byz. **Var:** 01ℵ,02A,03B,04C 05D,08E,Gries,Lach Treg,Alf,Word,Tisc We/Ho,Weis,Sod UBS/☆

| 1091.23 | 1091.52 | 3820.7 | 3617.1 | 3614.1 |
|---|---|---|---|---|
| verb 3pl subj aor act | verb 3pl indic fut mid | adj nom pl masc | conj | rel-pron gen pl |
| ⌜ γνῶσιν | [b☆ γνώσονται ] | πάντες | ὅτι | ὧν |
| *gnōsin* | *gnōsontai* | *pantes* | *hoti* | *hōn* |
| may know | [ will know ] | all | that | of which |

| 2697.6 | 3875.1 | 4622.2 | 3625.6 | 1498.4 |
|---|---|---|---|---|
| verb 3pl indic perf mid | prep | prs-pron gen 2sing | num card neu | verb 3sing indic pres act |
| κατήχηνται | περὶ | σοῦ | οὐδέν | ἐστιν, |
| *katēchēntai* | *peri* | *sou* | *ouden* | *estin* |
| they have been informed | about | you | nothing | is, |

| 233.2 | 4599.1 | 2504.1 | 840.5 | 3450.6 |
|---|---|---|---|---|
| conj | verb 2sing indic pres act | conj | prs-pron nom sing masc | art acc sing masc |
| ἀλλὰ | στοιχεῖς | καὶ | αὐτὸς | ⌜ τὸν |
| *alla* | *stoicheis* | *kai* | *autos* | *ton* |
| but | you walk orderly | also | yourself | the |

They also said Paul taught these Jewish believers to stop walking (conducting their lives) according to their (Jewish) customs.

This was nothing but slander. Paul never taught the Jews they had to become Gentiles or give up their Jewish manners and customs in order to follow Christ. Paul had even circumcised Timothy. He had also taken a vow recently himself.

**21:22.** These accusations against Paul were false, but everyone in Jerusalem had heard them again and again, and thousands of Christians in Palestine who were faithful to the Law misunderstood Paul's ministry and motivation.

Now since everyone in Jerusalem would surely hear that Paul had come, the crowd would come together; so before they did, something had to be done to prevent trouble or even a riot. What should be done?

**21:23.** James and the elders had a suggestion. They saw a way to stop the rumors and show that the bad report about Paul was false. Four of the Jewish believers had taken a vow upon themselves, obviously a temporary Nazarite vow.

The Nazarite vow was instituted after God set apart the Levites to serve the tabernacle and the family of Aaron as priests. God did not want the people to think the priests and Levites were closer to Him or more dedicated to Him than He wanted the people to be. So God gave the Nazarite vow as an opportunity whereby men or women could declare their total dedication to God and His will.

Usually the vow was taken for a limited period of time. During the time they were observing the vow, they were not to cut or trim any of the hair on the head. By this they declared God's will was more important to them than any human custom. They were not to drink wine or grape juice, nor eat grapes or raisins. The grapevine had become a symbol of human pleasures, so they put everything connected with it aside in order to declare that God was their chief joy. They were not to touch any dead human body. Preparing a body for burial was considered the last act of love. By refraining from this, they were declaring their love for God was greater than any human love. It was a complete consecration.

At the close of the period they had chosen for the vow, they would offer rather expensive sacrifices, including a male and female lamb, a ram, and other offerings. They would then shave their heads as a sign the vow was completed (Numbers 6:14-20).

**21:24.** Paul did not have to take the vow himself. But he was asked by the Jerusalem leaders to go through the ceremonies of purifying himself along with the four who were taking the vow and pay their expenses, especially pay for the sacrifices so they could complete their vow and shave their heads.

Numbers 6:9-12 shows that if someone died suddenly beside a person who was observing a Nazarite vow, this would defile him,

**neither to walk after the customs:** . . . or even to observe Jewish customs, *TCNT* . . . old-established customs, *Weymouth* . . . the cherished customs, *Williams* . . . and not to keep the old rules, *BB*.

**22. What is it therefore?:** What shall we do about it, *Beck* . . . Now, how about it, *Berkeley* . . . What then ought you to do, *Weymouth* . . . What is your duty, then, *Williams*.

**the multitude must needs come together:** Undoubtedly, *Concordant* . . . A crowd of them will surely gather about you, *Norlie*.

**for they will hear that thou art come:** . . . as they are certain to hear of your arrival, *TCNT* . . . for they will learn, *Berkeley* . . . for they are simply bound to hear, *Phillips*.

**23. Do therefore this that we say to thee:** Do what we are going to suggest, *TCNT* . . . why not follow this suggestion of ours, *Phillips*.

**We have four men which have a vow on them:** . . . who of their own accord put themselves under a vow, *TCNT*.

**24. Them take:** Make friends, *TCNT* . . . Associate with these men, *Weymouth* . . . Take them along with you, *Williams*.

**and purify thyself with them:** Join in their abstinence, *TCNT*.

**and be at charges with them:** . . . and bear their expenses, *TCNT* . . . and pay their expenses, *Weymouth* . . . and incur expense for them, *Worrell* . . . and bear the costs for them, *HBIE* . . . Pay their bills, *Klingensmith*.

**that they may shave their heads:** . . . so that they may have their hair cut short, *Phillips* . . . shall shave, *Murdock*.

**and all may know:** . . . and then all will see, *TCNT* . . . Then everyone will realize, *Berkeley*.

**that those things, whereof they were informed concerning thee, are nothing:** . . . that the things which they have heard rumoured, *Rotherham* . . . there is nothing in these stories, *Moffatt* . . . that there is no truth in the things they have been told about you, *TCNT* . . . that there is no basis for the reports, *Berkeley*.

| 3414.4 noun acc sing masc | 5278.3 verb nom sing masc part pres act | 5278.3 verb nom sing masc part pres act | 3450.6 art acc sing masc | 3414.4 noun acc sing masc |
|---|---|---|---|---|
| νόμον | φυλάσσων. | [☆ φυλάσσων | τὸν | νόμον. ] |
| *nomon* | *phulassōn* | *phulassōn* | *ton* | *nomon* |
| law | keeping. | [ keeping | the | law. ] |

| 3875.1 prep | 1156.2 conj | 3450.1 art gen pl | 3961.43 verb gen pl part perf act | 1477.5 noun gen pl neu |
|---|---|---|---|---|
| 25. περὶ | δὲ | τῶν | πεπιστευκότων | ἐθνῶν |
| *peri* | *de* | *tōn* | *pepisteukotōn* | *ethnōn* |
| Concerning | but | the | having believed | of the Gentiles |

25.a.**Txt:** 04C,05D,08E 020L,025P,byz.
**Var:** p74,01ℵ,02A,03B 33,sa.bo.Lach,Treg,Tisc We/Ho,Weis,Sod UBS/☆

| 2231.1 prs-pron nom 1pl | 1973.2 verb 1pl indic aor act | 2892.18 verb nom pl masc part aor act | 3235.6 num card neu | 4955.2 dem-pron sing |
|---|---|---|---|---|
| ἡμεῖς | ἐπεστείλαμεν. | κρίναντες | [a μηδὲν | τοιοῦτον |
| *hēmeis* | *epesteilamen* | *krinantes* | *mēden* | *toiouton* |
| we | wrote, | having judged | no | such thing |

| 4931.11 verb inf pres act | 840.8 prs-pron acc pl masc | 1479.1 conj | 3231.1 partic | 5278.18 verb inf pres mid |
|---|---|---|---|---|
| τηρεῖν | αὐτούς, | εἰ | μὴ ] | φυλάσσεσθαι |
| *tērein* | *autous* | *ei* | *mē* | *phulassesthai* |
| to observe | them, | if | not | to keep |

25.b.**Txt:** 020L,025P,byz.
**Var:** p74,01ℵ,02A,03B 04C,05D,33,Lach,Treg Word,Tisc,We/Ho,Weis Sod,UBS/☆

| 840.8 prs-pron acc pl masc | 3450.16 art sing neu | 4885.1 conj | 1484.1 adj sing neu | 2504.1 conj | 3450.16 art sing neu |
|---|---|---|---|---|---|
| αὐτοὺς | τό | τε | εἰδωλόθυτον | καὶ | [b τὸ ] |
| *autous* | *to* | *te* | *eidōlothuton* | *kai* | *to* |
| themselves | the | both | offered to idols, | and | the |

| 129.1 noun sing neu | 2504.1 conj | 4016.2 adj sing neu | 2504.1 conj | 4061.4 noun acc sing fem | 4966.1 adv |
|---|---|---|---|---|---|
| αἷμα | καὶ | πνικτὸν | καὶ | πορνείαν. | 26. Τότε |
| *haima* | *kai* | *pnikton* | *kai* | *porneian* | *Tote* |
| blood, | and | what is strangled, | and | fornication. | Then |

| 3450.5 art nom sing masc | 3834.1 name nom masc | 3741.9 verb nom sing masc part aor act | 3450.8 art acc pl masc | 433.9 noun acc pl masc | 3450.11 art dat sing fem |
|---|---|---|---|---|---|
| ὁ | Παῦλος | παραλαβὼν | τοὺς | ἄνδρας, | τῇ |
| *ho* | *Paulos* | *paralabōn* | *tous* | *andras* | *tē* |
| | Paul | having taken | the | men, | on the |

| 2174.48 verb dat sing fem part pres mid | 2232.3 noun dat sing fem | 4713.1 prep | 840.2 prs-pron dat pl | 47.6 verb nom sing masc part aor pass |
|---|---|---|---|---|
| ἐχομένῃ | ἡμέρᾳ | σὺν | αὐτοῖς | ἁγνισθεὶς |
| *echomenē* | *hēmera* | *sun* | *autois* | *hagnistheis* |
| following | day | with | them | having been purified |

| 1510.3 verb 3sing indic imperf act | 1519.1 prep | 3450.16 art sing neu | 2387.3 adj sing neu | 1223.2 verb nom sing masc part pres act | 3450.12 art acc sing fem |
|---|---|---|---|---|---|
| εἰσῄει | εἰς | τὸ | ἱερόν, | διαγγέλλων | τὴν |
| *eisēei* | *eis* | *to* | *hieron* | *diangellōn* | *tēn* |
| entered | into | the | temple, | declaring | the |

| 1591.1 noun acc sing fem | 3450.1 art gen pl | 2232.6 noun gen pl fem | 3450.2 art gen sing | 48.1 noun gen sing masc | 2175.1 conj |
|---|---|---|---|---|---|
| ἐκπλήρωσιν | τῶν | ἡμερῶν | τοῦ | ἁγνισμοῦ, | ἕως |
| *ekplērōsin* | *tōn* | *hēmerōn* | *tou* | *hagnismou* | *heōs* |
| fulfilment | of the | days | of the | purification, | until |

| 3614.2 rel-pron gen sing | 4232.24 verb 3sing indic aor pass | 5065.1 prep | 1518.1 num card gen | 1524.2 adj gen sing | 840.1 prs-pron gen pl |
|---|---|---|---|---|---|
| οὗ | προσηνέχθη | ὑπὲρ | ἑνὸς | ἑκάστου | αὐτῶν |
| *hou* | *prosēnechthē* | *huper* | *henos* | *hekastou* | *autōn* |
| which | was offered | for | one | each | of them |

that is, make him ceremonially unclean. Then he would have to go through 7 days of ceremonial purification.

It is possible the Jewish Christians considered Paul ceremonially unclean because of his contact with the Gentiles, for he had lived in Gentile homes and eaten nonkosher food with the Gentiles. Thus, Paul would please them by going through the ceremonies of purification himself. This, along with his paying the expenses of the four Jewish believers, would show the whole assembly of believers and everyone else in Jerusalem that Paul did not teach Jewish believers to go against the customs of their fathers. It would also answer all the false things said about Paul and would demonstrate that Paul himself was still willing to observe the Law.

**21:25.** James and the elders then confirmed the decision of the Council (see chapter 15), a decision Paul had already carried to the Gentile believers. Though they wanted Paul, as a Jewish believer, to show he did not ask Jews to live like Gentiles, they were willing to accept Gentile believers without asking them to become Jews.

The Jewish Christian leaders reminded Paul of the previous decision (15:13-21). The Gentile believers did not need to be circumcised or keep the Law. These things had been written in the letter sent out, and as far as the Jerusalem church leaders were concerned, they still stood. They had not changed their minds.

**21:26.** The next day Paul took the four men and did as he was asked to do, spreading the news of the completing of the days of purification until the sacrifice was brought for each of them.

This was not a compromise on Paul's part. Paul knew these Jewish ceremonies had no value as far as salvation is concerned. But he did recognize that God had instituted them and that they had a value as symbols to teach, illustrate, and implant truth in the hearts and minds of Jewish believers. Thus, the Jewish believers could still carry out these ceremonies, not to gain salvation, not to get in right relation with God, but to express a dedication to God that was already settled in their hearts through Christ and through their acceptance of His work on the cross and the justification that comes through His resurrection.

It was also Paul's practice to meet people halfway as long as no fundamental principle of the gospel was compromised. He said, "Unto the Jews I became as a Jew, that I might gain the Jews; to them that are under the law, as under the law, that I might gain them that are under the law; to them that are without law (outside the Jewish law), as without law, (being not without law to God, but under the law to Christ,) that I might gain them that are without law. To the weak became I as weak, that I might gain the weak: I am made all things to all men, that I might by all means save some. And this I do for the gospel's sake, that I might be partaker thereof with you" (1 Corinthians 9:20-23).

Paul taught that Christ fulfilled all the sacrifices of the Law at the Cross. He taught also that it was not circumcision or uncircum-

**but that thou thyself also walkest orderly, and keepest the law:** . . . on-the-contrary, *Rotherham* . . . you yourself rule your life in obedience to the Jewish Law, *TCNT* . . . living as a constant observer, *Williams* . . . but that you personally order your life in observance, *Berkeley* . . . but you live strictly according, *Beck* . . . guarding the law, *Rotherham* . . . respect the law of Moses in your own life, *SEB.*

**25. As touching the Gentiles which believe:** As to the Gentiles who have become believers in Christ, *TCNT* . . . as for non-Jewish believers, *SEB* . . . As for the people who are not Jews, *NLT.*

**we have written and concluded:** . . . we have sent our decision, *TCNT* . . . we have sent them our resolution, *Williams.*

**that they observe no such thing:** . . . they should keep themselves from things, *ASV.*

**save only that they keep themselves from things offered to idols, and from blood, and from strangled, and from fornication:** . . . that has been given to gods...must keep away from sex sins, *NLT* . . . from whoredom, *Murdock* . . . any kind of sexual sin, *SEB.*

**26. Then Paul took the men:** On this Paul joined the men, *TCNT* . . . So Paul associated with the men, *Weymouth* . . . Then Paul took the men along with him, *Williams.*

**and the next day purifying himself with them:** . . . shared in the washing ceremony, *SEB* . . . went through the religious worship of washing with them, *NLT.*

**entered into the temple:** . . . the house of God, *NLT.*

**to signify the accomplishment of the days of purification:** . . . announcing the completion of the days of the purification, *HBIE* . . . when the days of the cleansing ceremony would be ended, *SEB.*

**until that an offering should be offered for every one of them:** . . . and there he remained until the sacrifice for each one of them was offered, *Weymouth* . . . Then the gift for each one of them would be given as an act of worship, *NLT.*

## Acts 21:27

| 3450.9 art nom sing fem | 4234.1 noun nom sing fem | 5453.1 conj | 1156.2 conj | 3165.20 verb indic imperf act | 3450.13 art nom pl fem |
|---|---|---|---|---|---|
| ἡ | προσφορά. | **27.** Ὡς | δὲ | ἔμελλον | αἱ |
| *hē* | *prosphora* | *Hōs* | *de* | *emellon* | *hai* |
| the | offering. | When | but | were about | the |

| 2017.1 num card | 2232.5 noun nom pl fem | 4783.5 verb inf pres mid | 3450.7 art nom pl masc | 570.3 prep | 3450.10 art gen sing fem |
|---|---|---|---|---|---|
| ἑπτὰ | ἡμέραι | συντελεῖσθαι | οἱ | ἀπὸ | τῆς |
| *hepta* | *hēmerai* | *sunteleisthai* | *hoi* | *apo* | *tēs* |
| seven | days | to be completed | the | from | |

| 767.2 name gen fem | 2428.2 name-adj nom pl masc | 2277.8 verb nom pl masc part aor mid | 840.6 prs-pron acc sing masc | 1706.1 prep | 3450.3 art dat sing |
|---|---|---|---|---|---|
| Ἀσίας | Ἰουδαῖοι | θεασάμενοι | αὐτὸν | ἐν | τῷ |
| *Asias* | *Ioudaioi* | *theasamenoi* | *auton* | *en* | *tō* |
| Asia | Jews | having seen | him | in | the |

| 2387.2 adj dat sing neu | 4648.2 verb 3pl indic imperf act | 3820.1 adj | 3450.6 art acc sing masc | 3657.4 noun acc sing masc | 2504.1 conj |
|---|---|---|---|---|---|
| ἱερῷ, | συνέχεον | πάντα | τὸν | ὄχλον, | καὶ |
| *hierō* | *sunecheon* | *panta* | *ton* | *ochlon* | *kai* |
| temple, | were stirring up | all | the | crowd, | and |

27.a.**Txt:** 01ℵ-corr,03B 04C,08E,020L,025P,etc. byz.Weis,Sod
**Var:** 01ℵ-org,02A,Treg Tisc,We/Ho,UBS/⋆

| 1896.4 verb 3pl indic aor act | 1896.11 verb 3pl indic aor act | 3450.15 art acc pl fem | 5331.8 noun acc pl fem | 1894.2 prep | 840.6 prs-pron acc sing masc |
|---|---|---|---|---|---|
| ⸂ ἐπέβαλον | [a ἐπέβαλαν ] | ⸂ τὰς | χεῖρας | ἐπ' | αὐτὸν, |
| *epebalon* | *epebalan* | *tas* | *cheiras* | *ep'* | *auton* |
| laid | [ idem ] | the | hands | upon | him, |

| 1894.2 prep | 840.6 prs-pron acc sing masc | 3450.15 art acc pl fem | 5331.8 noun acc pl fem | 2869.4 verb nom pl masc part pres act |
|---|---|---|---|---|
| [☆ ἐπ' | αὐτὸν | τὰς | χεῖρας, ] | **28.** κράζοντες, |
| *ep'* | *auton* | *tas* | *cheiras* | *krazontes* |
| [ upon | him | the | hands, ] | crying, |

| 433.6 noun nom pl masc | 2448.2 name nom pl masc | 990.2 verb 2pl impr pres act | 3642.4 dem-pron nom sing masc | 1498.4 verb 3sing indic pres act |
|---|---|---|---|---|
| Ἄνδρες | Ἰσραηλῖται, | βοηθεῖτε. | οὗτός | ἐστιν |
| *Andres* | *Israēlitai* | *boētheite* | *houtos* | *estin* |
| Men | Israelites, | help! | this | is |

| 3450.5 art nom sing masc | 442.1 noun nom sing masc | 3450.5 art nom sing masc | 2567.3 prep | 3450.2 art gen sing | 2967.2 noun gen sing masc |
|---|---|---|---|---|---|
| ὁ | ἄνθρωπος | ὁ | κατὰ | τοῦ | λαοῦ |
| *ho* | *anthrōpos* | *ho* | *kata* | *tou* | *laou* |
| the | man | the | against | the | people |

| 2504.1 conj | 3450.2 art gen sing | 3414.2 noun gen sing masc | 2504.1 conj | 3450.2 art gen sing | 4964.2 noun gen sing masc | 3642.1 dem-pron gen sing |
|---|---|---|---|---|---|---|
| καὶ | τοῦ | νόμου | καὶ | τοῦ | τόπου | τούτου |
| *kai* | *tou* | *nomou* | *kai* | *tou* | *topou* | *toutou* |
| and | the | law | and | the | place | this |

28.a.**Txt:** 020L,025P,byz.
**Var:** 01ℵ,02A,03B,04C 05D,08E,Lach,Treg,Alf Word,Tisc,We/Ho,Weis Sod,UBS/⋆

| 3820.8 adj acc pl masc | 3699.1 adv | 3697.1 adv | 1315.6 verb nom sing masc part pres act | 2068.1 adv |
|---|---|---|---|---|
| πάντας | ⸂ πανταχοῦ | [a☆ πανταχῆ ] | διδάσκων· | ἔτι |
| *pantas* | *pantachou* | *pantachē* | *didaskōn* | *eti* |
| all | everywhere | [ idem ] | teaching, | further |

| 4885.1 conj | 2504.1 conj | 1659.7 name acc pl masc | 1507.1 verb 3sing indic aor act | 1519.1 prep | 3450.16 art sing neu | 2387.3 adj sing neu |
|---|---|---|---|---|---|---|
| τε | καὶ | Ἕλληνας | εἰσήγαγεν | εἰς | τὸ | ἱερὸν, |
| *te* | *kai* | *Hellēnas* | *eisēgagen* | *eis* | *to* | *hieron* |
| and | also | Greeks | he brought | into | the | temple, |

cision that counted but being a new creature (creation) in Christ (2 Corinthians 5:17; Galatians 6:15). He also warned the Gentiles that it was foolish to begin in the Spirit and then seek growth and development through legality and outward fleshly ceremonies (Galations 3:1-5). But neither Gentile liberty nor any of these principles were at stake, so Paul graciously yielded to the request of the Jerusalem elders. Thus he set an example for all believers when they are faced with questions that are a matter of doing or not doing some nonessential thing. If this means giving up or putting aside personal ideas, wishes, preferences, or intentions, the Christian thing to do is to yield.

**21:27.** Paul's charitable action of paying for the sacrifices of these four men worked well as far as the Jewish believers were concerned. But as far as the majority of the people who came to the feast in Jerusalem was concerned, it failed. Instead of satisfying the non-Christian Jews, the opposite happened. When the 7 days of purification were almost ended, Jews from the Roman province of Asia were in Jerusalem for the Feast of Pentecost (a harvest festival to the Jews). These may have been some who had persecuted and beaten Paul in their home synagogues. They saw him in the temple. Immediately they went to work stirring up a riot and laid violent hands on Paul.

This was not the first time they had thrown a crowd into confusion. They looked at Paul as a false prophet and considered the miracles he performed as signs meant to test their loyalty to God and to the law of Moses. Back in their hometowns Paul had escaped them. Now was their opportunity. Now they had him.

**21:28.** As these Asian Jews grabbed Paul they began shouting accusations against him. They addressed the rest of the Jews in the temple court as "Men of Israel," drawing attention to them not just as Jews but as God's covenant people crying out for their help.

They kept shouting that Paul taught everyone everywhere against the people, that is, against the Jews and against the law of Moses. Then they added that he had now defiled the temple by bringing in Greeks, that is, Greek-speaking Gentiles.

This was a serious charge. The temple in New Testament times was surrounded by three courts. The innermost court was the Court of Israel. Here the men could come as Israelites and offer sacrifices required by the Law. But that was as far as the men could go. Only the consecrated priests could enter the temple building itself, and only the high priest could enter the inner sanctuary.

The second court was the Court of the Women, so called because it was as far as the women could go. Actually, the whole family could gather in this court for prayer and worship. Rabbis, including Jesus, taught in this court. Christians gathered in it daily at the hours of prayer. But only Jews were allowed to enter it.

The outer court was called the Court of the Gentiles because it was as far as Gentiles could go. Archaeologists have found two of



**27. And when the seven days were almost ended:** But, just as the seven days were drawing to a close, *TCNT* . . . were-on-the-point of being concluded, *Rotherham* . . . were almost finished, *NLT* . . . almost completed, *Swann* . . . at an end, *Williams C.K.*

**the Jews which were of Asia:** . . . the Jews from the province of Asia, *Weymouth* . . . some of the Asiatic Judeans, *Fenton* . . . from Roman Asia, *Williams C.K.*

**when they saw him in the temple:** . . . caught sight of him, *Goodspeed* . . . caught a glimpse of him in the temple, *Williams* . . . observing him, *Fenton* . . . saw Paul in the house of God, *NLT.*

**stirred up all the people:** . . . and began to stir up all the crowd, *Montgomery* . . . They excited the whole crowd into an uproar, *Norlie* . . . They caused all the people to be upset, *Everyday* . . . They made the people turn against him, *NLT* . . . incited the whole of the rabble, *Fenton* . . . threw the whole crowd into disorder, *Williams C.K.*

**and laid hands on him:** . . . by seizing Paul, *TCNT* . . . and seized him, *Williams* . . . and grabbed hold of him, *Berkeley* . . . they threw their hands upon, *Fenton.*

**28. Crying out:** . . . as they kept shouting, *Williams* . . . yelling, *Beck.*

**Men of Israel, help:** Men! Israelites! *Fenton* . . . help! help! *Williams* . . . come to our help, *BB* . . . to our aid! *Berkeley.*

**This is the man:** . . . here is the fellow, *Williams C.K.*

**that teacheth all men every where against the people:** . . . who by his teaching sets everyone everywhere against our people, *Williams C.K.* . . . who goes everywhere preaching to everybody against the Jewish people, *Weymouth.*

**and the law, and this place:** . . . our law, and this sanctuary, *NEB* . . . and the temple, *Williams C.K.*

**and further brought Greeks also into the temple:** . . . and besides, *Goodspeed* . . . and now he has even brought, *Williams C.K.* . . . and, what is more, he has actually brought Greeks into the Temple, *TCNT* . . . non-Jews, *Beck.*

| 2504.1 conj | 2813.6 verb 3sing indic perf act | 3450.6 art acc sing masc | 39.1 adj sing | 4964.4 noun acc sing masc | 3642.6 dem-pron acc sing masc |
|---|---|---|---|---|---|
| καὶ | κεκοίνωκεν | τὸν | ἅγιον | τόπον | τοῦτον. |
| kai | kekoinōken | ton | hagion | topon | touton |
| and | has defiled | the | holy | place | this. |

| 1498.37 verb 3pl indic imperf act | 1056.1 conj | 4167.1 verb nom pl masc part perf act | 5002.2 name acc masc | 3450.6 art acc sing masc |
|---|---|---|---|---|
| 29. ³Ησαν | γὰρ | προεωρακότες | Τρόφιμον | τὸν |
| Ēsan | gar | proeōrakotes | Trophimon | ton |
| They were | for | having seen previously | Trophimus | the |

| 2162.4 name-adj acc masc | 1706.1 prep | 3450.11 art dat sing fem | 4032.3 noun dat sing fem | 4713.1 prep | 840.4 prs-pron dat sing | 3614.6 rel-pron acc sing masc |
|---|---|---|---|---|---|---|
| Ἐφέσιον | ἐν | τῇ | πόλει | σὺν | αὐτῷ, | ὃν |
| Ephesion | en | tē | polei | sun | autō | hon |
| Ephesian | in | the | city | with | him, | whom |

| 3406.11 verb 3pl indic imperf act | 3617.1 conj | 1519.1 prep | 3450.16 art sing neu | 2387.3 adj sing neu | 1507.1 verb 3sing indic aor act |
|---|---|---|---|---|---|
| ἐνόμιζον | ὅτι | εἰς | τὸ | ἱερὸν | εἰσήγαγεν |
| enomizon | hoti | eis | to | hieron | eisēgagen |
| they were assuming | that | into | the | temple | brought |

| 3450.5 art nom sing masc | 3834.1 name nom masc | 2767.6 verb 3sing indic aor pass | 4885.1 conj | 3450.9 art nom sing fem | 4032.1 noun nom sing fem |
|---|---|---|---|---|---|
| ὁ | Παῦλος. | 30. ἐκινήθη | τε | ἡ | πόλις |
| ho | Paulos | ekinēthē | te | hē | polis |
|  | Paul. | Was moved | and | the | city |

| 3513.6 adj nom sing fem | 2504.1 conj | 1090.33 verb 3sing indic aor mid | 4740.1 noun nom sing fem | 3450.2 art gen sing | 2967.2 noun gen sing masc |
|---|---|---|---|---|---|
| ὅλη, | καὶ | ἐγένετο | συνδρομὴ | τοῦ | λαοῦ˙ |
| holē | kai | egeneto | sundromē | tou | laou |
| whole, | and | there was | a rushing together | of the | people; |

| 2504.1 conj | 1934.7 verb nom pl masc part aor mid | 3450.2 art gen sing | 3834.2 name gen masc | 1657.7 verb 3pl indic imperf act |
|---|---|---|---|---|
| καὶ | ἐπιλαβόμενοι | τοῦ | Παύλου | εἷλκον |
| kai | epilabomenoi | tou | Paulou | heilkon |
| and | having laid hold |  | of Paul, | they were dragging |

| 840.6 prs-pron acc sing masc | 1838.1 adv | 3450.2 art gen sing | 2387.1 adj gen sing neu | 2504.1 conj | 2091.1 adv |
|---|---|---|---|---|---|
| αὐτὸν | ἔξω | τοῦ | ἱεροῦ, | καὶ | εὐθέως |
| auton | exō | tou | hierou | kai | eutheōs |
| him | outside | the | temple, | and | immediately |

| 2781.8 verb 3pl indic aor pass | 3450.13 art nom pl fem | 2351.5 noun nom pl fem | 2195.11 verb gen pl masc part pres act | 1156.2 conj |
|---|---|---|---|---|
| ἐκλείσθησαν | αἱ | θύραι. | 31. ζητούντων | ʻ δὲ |
| ekleisthēsan | hai | thurai | zētountōn | de |
| were shut | the | doors. | Seeking | but |

31.a.**Txt:** 05D-corr,020L 025P,byz.sa.bo. **Var:** 01ℵ,02A,03B,08E Lach,Treg,Alf,Tisc We/Ho,Weis,Sod UBS/⋆

| 4885.1 conj | 840.6 prs-pron acc sing masc | 609.12 verb inf aor act | 303.13 verb 3sing indic aor act | 5172.1 noun nom sing fem | 3450.3 art dat sing |
|---|---|---|---|---|---|
| [a⋆ τε ] | αὐτὸν | ἀποκτεῖναι | ἀνέβη | φάσις | τῷ |
| te | auton | apokteinai | anebē | phasis | tō |
| [ and ] | him | to kill | there came | a report | to the |

| 5341.2 noun dat sing masc | 3450.10 art gen sing fem | 4539.2 noun gen sing fem | 3617.1 conj | 3513.6 adj nom sing fem | 4648.4 verb 3sing indic perf mid |
|---|---|---|---|---|---|
| χιλιάρχῳ | τῆς | σπείρης, | ὅτι | ὅλη | ʻ συγκέχυται |
| chiliarchō | tēs | speirēs | hoti | holē | sunkechutai |
| chief captain | of the | band, | that | whole | had been stirred up |

the inscriptions once placed at the entrances to the Court of the Women. They read (in Greek), "No foreigner may enter within this barricade which surrounds the temple and enclosure (its two inner courts). Anyone caught doing so will have himself to blame for his ensuing death."

**21:29.** These false charges of unpatriotic conduct, blasphemy, and sacrilege were reinforced by the mention of a Gentile because these Asian Jews had seen Paul in the city earlier with Trophimus, a Gentile believer from Ephesus. So they jumped to the false conclusion that Paul had brought him into the temple.

Trophimus was well-known as a companion of Paul's. He traveled with Paul during the latter part of his third missionary journey and was with him from Greece all the way through Macedonia, Asia, and the final journey to Jerusalem. Trophimus was thus the innocent cause of the accusation of these Jews from Asia. The very thought that a Gentile who was not a proselyte or convert to Judaism would enter the temple court and defile it filled them with fury. This fury was directed against Paul because they thought he was the one who had brought Trophimus in, deliberately in defiance of the Law. Tertullus later repeated this charge against Paul.

Second Timothy 4:20 indicates that Trophimus remained loyal to the Lord and to Paul. He traveled with Paul again after Paul was released from his first imprisonment in Rome. Many believe also that Trophimus was the unnamed brother mentioned in 2 Corinthians 8:16-24. Paul speaks very highly of him there.

**21:30.** The cries of these Jews from Asia stirred up the whole city of Jerusalem, for many people were already in the temple courts by this time. The Jews ran together from all directions, seized Paul, and dragged him out of the temple (that is, out of the Court of the Women), beating him as they did so. Immediately the great doors of the temple Court of the Women were shut so that the mob would not desecrate the temple. No one seemed to notice that Paul had no Gentiles with him, however.

The gate they closed was probably the gate of Nicanor, that is, the Beautiful Gate. It was the principal gate and was the gift of a wealthy Alexandrian Jew named Nicanor. It was solid Corinthian bronze, 50 cubits (75 feet) high and 40 cubits (60 feet) wide. It was beautifully carved and glittered like gold. From it steps led down into the Court of the Gentiles.

**21:31.** It is clear the mob actually was intending to kill Paul. But the uproar caught the attention of someone who took the news up the steps to the Roman tribune. He was the officer over a cohort of 600 to 1,000 soldiers stationed in the Tower (castle, fortress) of Antonia on the northwest side of the temple where the guards could overlook the temple area. The messenger told the tribune that all Jerusalem was in an uproar or state of confusion.

**and hath polluted this holy place:** . . . defiled, *RSV* . . . desecrated, *Weymouth* . . . and made this holy place unclean, *BB* . . . contaminated, *Concordant* . . . has profaned this holy place, *Wuest* . . . made this holy place common! *Adams* . . . this holy place dirty, *NLT*.

**29. (For they had seen before with him in the city Trophimus an Ephesian:**

**whom they supposed that Paul had brought into the temple.):** . . . and were under the impression, *TCNT* . . . and surmised that Paul had brought him into the temple, *Berkeley*.

**30. And all the city was moved:** And the whole city, *Rotherham* . . . was stirred, *TCNT* . . . was thrown into turmoil, *Moffatt* . . . was thrown into uproar, *Montgomery* . . . The excitement spread through the whole city, *Weymouth*.

**and the people ran together:** . . . quickly collected, *TCNT* . . . and a mob collected, *Phillips* . . . surged together, *Montgomery*.

**and they took Paul:** . . . and they laid hold on Paul, *ASV* . . . seized Paul, *TCNT*.

**and drew him out of the temple: and forthwith the doors were shut:** . . . the doors were immediately shut, *TCNT* . . . and the Temple gates were immediately closed, *Weymouth* . . . and the doors were slammed behind him, *Phillips* . . . instantly, *Murdock*.

**31. And as they went about to kill him:** They were bent on, *TCNT* . . . But while they were trying, *Weymouth* . . . were endeavoring to kill him, *Noyes*.

**tidings came unto the chief captain of the band:** . . . when it was reported to the officer commanding the garrison, *TCNT* . . . the allegation...captain of the squadron, *Concordant* . . . reached the commandant, *Berkeley*.

**that all Jerusalem was in an uproar:** . . . was in confusion, *ASV* . . . was in a ferment, *Weymouth* . . . was out of control, *BB* . . . that the people were rioting all over Jerusalem, *Norlie* . . . learned that there was trouble in the whole city, *Everyday*.

31.b.**Txt:** 020L,025P,byz.
**Var:** 03B-org,Lach,Treg
Alf,UBS/⋆

| 4648.7 verb 3sing indic pres mid | 2395.1 name fem | 3614.5 rel-pron nom sing masc | 1808.1 adv |
|---|---|---|---|
| [b⋆ συγχύννεται ] | Ἱερουσαλήμ. | 32. ὃς | ἐξαυτῆς |
| *sunchunnetai* | *Hierousalēm* | *hos* | *exautēs* |
| [ is being stirred up ] | Jerusalem; | who | at once |

| 3741.9 verb nom sing masc part aor act | 4608.7 noun acc pl masc | 2504.1 conj | 1530.6 noun acc pl masc |
|---|---|---|---|
| παραλαβὼν | στρατιώτας | καὶ | ‹ ἑκατοντάρχους |
| *paralabōn* | *stratiōtas* | *kai* | *hekatontarchous* |
| having taken with | soldiers | and | centurions |

32.a.**Txt:** 05D-corr,020L
025P,byz.Sod
**Var:** 01ℵ,02A,03B
05D-org,08E,33,Lach
Treg,Alf,Word,Tisc
We/Ho,Weis,UBS/⋆

| 1529.4 noun acc pl masc | 2670.1 verb 3sing indic aor act | 1894.2 prep | 840.8 prs-pron acc pl masc | 3450.7 art nom pl masc |
|---|---|---|---|---|
| [a⋆ ἑκατοντάρχας ] | κατέδραμεν | ἐπ' | αὐτούς. | οἱ |
| *hekatontarchas* | *katedramen* | *ep'* | *autous* | *hoi* |
| [ idem ] | ran down | upon | them. | The |

| 1156.2 conj | 1481.17 verb nom pl masc part aor act | 3450.6 art acc sing masc | 5341.3 noun acc sing masc | 2504.1 conj | 3450.8 art acc pl masc |
|---|---|---|---|---|---|
| δὲ | ἰδόντες | τὸν | χιλίαρχον | καὶ | τοὺς |
| *de* | *idontes* | *ton* | *chiliarchon* | *kai* | *tous* |
| and | having seen | the | chief captain | and | the |

| 4608.7 noun acc pl masc | 3835.7 verb 3pl indic aor mid | 5021.2 verb nom pl masc part pres act | 3450.6 art acc sing masc | 3834.4 name acc masc |
|---|---|---|---|---|
| στρατιώτας | ἐπαύσαντο | τύπτοντες | τὸν | Παῦλον. |
| *stratiōtas* | *epausanto* | *tuptontes* | *ton* | *Paulon* |
| soldiers | ceased | beating | | Paul. |

| 4966.1 adv | 1443.12 verb nom sing masc part aor act | 3450.5 art nom sing masc | 5341.1 noun nom sing masc | 1934.2 verb 3sing indic aor mid |
|---|---|---|---|---|
| 33. τότε | ἐγγίσας | ὁ | χιλίαρχος | ἐπελάβετο |
| *tote* | *engisas* | *ho* | *chiliarchos* | *epelabeto* |
| Then | having drawn near | the | chief captain | laid hold |

| 840.3 prs-pron gen sing | 2504.1 conj | 2724.3 verb 3sing indic aor act | 1204.12 verb inf aor pass | 252.4 noun dat pl fem | 1411.1 num card dat |
|---|---|---|---|---|---|
| αὐτοῦ, | καὶ | ἐκέλευσεν | δεθῆναι | ἁλύσεσιν | δυσίν· |
| *autou* | *kai* | *ekeleusen* | *dethēnai* | *halusesin* | *dusin* |
| of him, | and | commanded | to be bound | with chains | two, |

33.a.**Txt:** 08E,020L
025P,byz.
**Var:** 01ℵ,02A,03B,08E
Lach,Treg,Word,Tisc
We/Ho,Weis,Sod
UBS/⋆

| 2504.1 conj | 4299.6 verb 3sing indic imperf mid | 4949.3 intr-pron nom sing | 300.1 partic | 1498.14 verb 3sing opt pres act | 2504.1 conj |
|---|---|---|---|---|---|
| καὶ | ἐπυνθάνετο | τίς | ‹a ἂν › | εἴη, | καὶ |
| *kai* | *epunthaneto* | *tis* | *an* | *eiē* | *kai* |
| and | was inquiring | who | | he might be, | and |

| 4949.9 intr-pron sing neu | 1498.4 verb 3sing indic pres act | 4020.47 verb nom sing masc part perf act | 241.6 adj nom pl masc | 1156.2 conj |
|---|---|---|---|---|
| τί | ἐστιν | πεποιηκώς. | 34. ἄλλοι | δὲ |
| *ti* | *estin* | *pepoiēkōs* | *alloi* | *de* |
| what | it is | having been done. | Some | but |

34.a.**Txt:** 020L,025P,byz.
**Var:** 01ℵ,02A,03B,05D
08E,Lach,Treg,Alf
Word,Tisc,We/Ho,Weis
Sod,UBS/⋆

| 241.14 adj sing neu | 4948.10 indef-pron sing neu | 987.7 verb 3pl indic imperf act | 2003.2 verb 3pl indic imperf act | 1706.1 prep | 3450.3 art dat sing |
|---|---|---|---|---|---|
| ἄλλο | τι | ‹ ἐβόων | [a⋆ ἐπεφώνουν ] | ἐν | τῷ |
| *allo* | *ti* | *eboōn* | *epephōnoun* | *en* | *tō* |
| another | one thing | were crying | [ idem ] | in | the |

34.b.**Txt:** 020L,025P,byz.
**Var:** 01ℵ,02A,03B,08E
Lach,Treg,Alf,Word
Tisc,We/Ho,Weis,Sod
UBS/⋆

| 3657.3 noun dat sing masc | 3231.1 partic | 1404.13 verb nom sing masc part pres mid | 1156.2 conj | 3231.1 partic | 1404.12 verb gen sing part pres mid |
|---|---|---|---|---|---|
| ὄχλῳ· | ‹ μὴ | δυναμένος | δὲ | [b⋆ μὴ | δυναμένου |
| *ochlō* | *mē* | *dunamenos* | *de* | *mē* | *dunamenou* |
| crowd. | Not | being able | and | [ not | being able |

**21:32.** Immediately the tribune took at least two centurions with the soldiers under their command. Since the centurions were officers over 100 men, this made quite a show of force as they ran down the steps from the Tower of Antonia into the Court of the Gentiles.

The Romans stationed these soldiers at the Tower of Antonia for the specific purpose of keeping order in the temple, especially during the Jewish feast days. The law of Moses made three pilgrimage feasts compulsory. These were Passover, Pentecost, and Tabernacles. During these periods a great crowd of Jews gathered in the temple at the hours of prayer. But, like all dictators and oppressors of subject peoples, the Romans were fearful of what might happen when large crowds came together without having a loyalty to Rome. Furthermore, Jewish mobs had been troublesome before.

The sight of the tribune, the centurions, and all the soldiers made the mob stop beating Paul, thus saving his life. The people, of course, knew the soldiers meant business. They had not forgotten the Galileans whose blood Pilate had mingled with their sacrifices (Luke 13:1). These Galileans were probably Jews who refused to pay tribute to Rome. Pilate's men waylaid them and probably slaughtered them and the animals they were about to sacrifice.

**21:33.** Though the tribune (or as we might say, the colonel) rescued Paul from the violence of the mob, he did not set Paul free. Instead, he jumped to the conclusion that Paul, as the cause of all this confusion, must be some vicious criminal. So he immediately placed him under arrest and chained him with hand chains to two soldiers, one on each side. Chaining a prisoner to a soldier was a common practice among the Romans. Chaining Paul to two soldiers was an extra precaution. This was similar to the custom today of handcuffing a prisoner.

The tribune then asked the Jews who Paul was and what he had done. He was anxious to know what had caused the uproar.

**21:34.** In response, the crowd broke out into a confusion of contradictory statements. Everyone was shouting different things, all at the same time.

Actually, most of the people in the crowd did not know Paul, but had run together and joined in when they heard the noise of the riot. Rumors of the wildest kind arise quickly in such a situation. Once a mob spirit takes over, people are swept along and take part in the violence without thinking. It was God's merciful providence that this Roman officer was there to protect Paul.

Paul in his letters had already recognized that God is the One who authorized civil authority. Without it the world would have nothing but anarchy. The Bible teaches respect for officers of the law because of what they stand for and for the sake of the protection

**32. Who immediately took soldiers and centurions:** He instantly got together some officers and men, *TCNT*... So he at once got together some soldiers and captains, *Williams*... and sergeants, *Williams C.K.*

**and ran down unto them:** ... and charged down upon the crowd, *TCNT*... he ran to the place where the crowd was gathered, *Everyday*... he marched down at once upon them, *Williams C.K.*

**and when they saw the chief captain and the soldiers:** At the sight of, *Weymouth*... But as soon as they saw, *Williams* ... when they saw the colonel, *Goodspeed*... saw the commander, *SEB.*

**they left beating of Paul:** ... they stopped hitting Paul, *Beck.*

**33. Then the chief captain came near:** ... came up, *Williams C.K.* ... went up to Paul, *TCNT* ... making his way to him, *Weymouth.*

**and took him:** ... arrested him, *TCNT*... and seized him, *Moffatt*... took charge of him, *Berkeley.*

**and commanded him to be bound with two chains:** ... told his soldiers to tie up Paul, *NCV* ... to be doubly chained, *TCNT* ... gave orders that he should be fastened up with two chains, *Williams C.K.*

**and demanded who he was, and what he had done:** ... and began to inquire who he might be, *Rotherham*... What has he done wrong? *NCV.*

**34. And some cried one thing, some another, among the multitude:** Some of the crowd shouted one accusation against Paul and some another, *Weymouth.*

**and when he could not know the certainty for the tumult:** ... and, as he could get no definite reply on account of the uproar, *TCNT*... so, unable to get at the facts, *Berkeley*... was not able to find out what had happened, *NLT*... could not learn the truth about what had happened, *SEB*... since he could hear nothing for certain, *Williams C.K.*... not being able to ascertain the truth, *Wilson*... because of the shouting that was

| 1156.2 conj | 840.3 prs-pron gen sing | 1091.29 verb inf aor act | 3450.16 art sing neu | 798.2 adj sing neu | 1217.2 prep |
|---|---|---|---|---|---|
| δὲ | αὐτοῦ ] | γνῶναι | τὸ | ἀσφαλὲς | διὰ |
| *de* | *autou* | *gnōnai* | *to* | *asphales* | *dia* |
| but | of him ] | to know | the | certainty | on account of |

| 3450.6 art acc sing masc | 2328.3 noun acc sing masc | 2724.3 verb 3sing indic aor act | 70.24 verb inf pres mid | 840.6 prs-pron acc sing masc |
|---|---|---|---|---|
| τὸν | θόρυβον, | ἐκέλευσεν | ἄγεσθαι | αὐτὸν |
| *ton* | *thorubon* | *ekeleusen* | *agesthai* | *auton* |
| the | uproar, | he commanded | to be brought | him |

| 1519.1 prep | 3450.12 art acc sing fem | 3787.2 noun acc sing fem | 3616.1 conj | 1156.2 conj | 1090.33 verb 3sing indic aor mid |
|---|---|---|---|---|---|
| εἰς | τὴν | παρεμβολήν. | 35. ὅτε | δὲ | ἐγένετο |
| *eis* | *tēn* | *parembolēn* | *hote* | *de* | *egeneto* |
| into | the | barracks. | When | but | he came |

| 1894.3 prep | 3450.8 art acc pl masc | 302.2 noun acc pl masc | 4670.3 verb 3sing indic aor act | 934.17 verb inf pres mid |
|---|---|---|---|---|
| ἐπὶ | τοὺς | ἀναβαθμούς | συνέβη | βαστάζεσθαι |
| *epi* | *tous* | *anabathmous* | *sunebē* | *bastazesthai* |
| on | the | stairs | it happened | to be carried |

| 840.6 prs-pron acc sing masc | 5097.3 prep | 3450.1 art gen pl | 4608.5 noun gen pl masc | 1217.2 prep | 3450.12 art acc sing fem |
|---|---|---|---|---|---|
| αὐτὸν | ὑπὸ | τῶν | στρατιωτῶν | διὰ | τὴν |
| *auton* | *hupo* | *tōn* | *stratiōtōn* | *dia* | *tēn* |
| him | by | the | soldiers | because of | the |

| 963.2 noun acc sing fem | 3450.2 art gen sing | 3657.2 noun gen sing masc | 188.21 verb 3sing indic imperf act | 1056.1 conj | 3450.16 art sing neu |
|---|---|---|---|---|---|
| βίαν | τοῦ | ὄχλου. | 36. ἠκολούθει | γὰρ | τὸ |
| *bian* | *tou* | *ochlou* | *ēkolouthei* | *gar* | *to* |
| violence | of the | crowd. | Was following | for | the |

36.a.**Txt:** 05D,020L 025P,byz.
**Var:** 01ℵ,02A,03B,08E Lach,Treg,Alf,Word Tisc,We/Ho,Weis,Sod UBS/☆

| 3988.1 noun sing neu | 3450.2 art gen sing | 2967.2 noun gen sing masc | 2869.7 verb sing neu part pres act | 2869.4 verb nom pl masc part pres act |
|---|---|---|---|---|
| πλῆθος | τοῦ | λαοῦ | ʻ κράζον, | [a☆ κράζοντες, ] |
| *plēthos* | *tou* | *laou* | *krazon* | *krazontes* |
| multitude | of the | people, | crying, | [ idem ] |

| 142.4 verb 2sing impr pres act | 840.6 prs-pron acc sing masc | 3165.12 verb nom sing masc part pres act | 4885.1 conj | 1507.6 verb inf pres mid |
|---|---|---|---|---|
| Αἶρε | αὐτόν. | 37. Μέλλων | τε | εἰσάγεσθαι |
| *Aire* | *auton* | *Mellōn* | *te* | *eisagesthai* |
| Away with | him. | Being about | but | to be brought |

| 1519.1 prep | 3450.12 art acc sing fem | 3787.2 noun acc sing fem | 3450.5 art nom sing masc | 3834.1 name nom masc | 2978.5 verb 3sing indic pres act |
|---|---|---|---|---|---|
| εἰς | τὴν | παρεμβολὴν | ὁ | Παῦλος | λέγει |
| *eis* | *tēn* | *parembolēn* | *ho* | *Paulos* | *legei* |
| into | the | barracks | | Paul | says |

| 3450.3 art dat sing | 5341.2 noun dat sing masc | 1479.1 conj | 1815.1 verb 3sing indic pres act | 1466.4 prs-pron dat 1sing | 1500.21 verb inf aor act |
|---|---|---|---|---|---|
| τῷ | χιλιάρχῳ, | Εἰ | ἔξεστίν | μοι | εἰπεῖν |
| *tō* | *chiliarchō* | *Ei* | *exestin* | *moi* | *eipein* |
| to the | chief captain, | If | it is permitted | to me | to say |

| 4948.10 indef-pron sing neu | 4242.1 prep | 4622.4 prs-pron acc 2sing | 3450.5 art nom sing masc | 1156.2 conj | 5183.4 verb 3sing indic act |
|---|---|---|---|---|---|
| τι | πρὸς | σέ; | ʽΟ | δὲ | ἔφη, |
| *ti* | *pros* | *se* | *Ho* | *de* | *ephē* |
| something | to | you? | The | and | said, |

they give. The Bible says further that those who are not lawbreakers really have nothing to fear from them.

Because there was no way the tribune could be sure of what was being said in the midst of all the hubbub, he then ordered the soldiers to take Paul into the castle, that is, into the barracks of the fortress, the Tower of Antonia.

**21:35.** The crowd was so violent the soldiers were having a hard time protecting Paul. As they moved toward the stairs which led from the temple court up to the Tower of Antonia, the crowd surged around them. When they reached the stairs, the pressure was so great the soldiers had to lift Paul up and carry him.

The Jews kept up this pressure because they still thought the temple had been desecrated. They were very proud of the temple building with its courts, porticoes, and great stones. But many of them had become like those in Jeremiah's day who trusted more in the temple than they did in God (Jeremiah 7:4,14). It is always easier to give attention to a religious symbol than it is to seek the Lord and do His will.

The mob was also taking something into their own hands that belonged to the Lord. The Law provided for a just and fair trial. These Jews were moved by a false patriotism, and they were going contrary to the Word of God.

**21:36.** Even on the stairs the crowd kept following the soldiers, trying to pull Paul away from them. They also kept crying out, shrieking again and again, "Away with him!" By this they meant they wanted Paul killed. Possibly some in the crowd had cried out in the same way against Jesus (Luke 23:18; John 19:15). But it seemed the crowd was even more angry here. In fact, they would have torn Paul apart if the soldiers had not protected him.

**21:37.** The crowd dropped behind as the soldiers came to the top of the steps and were about to enter the safety of the Fortress of Antonia. At this point Paul, using the Greek language, politely asked the tribune's permission to speak to him. The fact that Paul spoke Greek surprised the tribune, and he showed his surprise by asking a question that had an obvious answer. It showed he could not believe Paul was really speaking Greek.

This should not have been so surprising. Educated people and business people spoke Greek in those days, for it was the language of trade, commerce, education, and government communication all over the Roman Empire. Even the fishermen of Galilee had to know Greek in order to sell their fish in the Greek-speaking cities and towns of Phoenicia and the Decapolis. The Bible makes a point that the Syrophoenician woman was Greek-speaking, so Jesus must have conversed with her in Greek (Mark 7:26). Peter undoubtedly spoke in Greek to Cornelius and those gathered at his home. Greek was a second language for many of the Jews at that time.

going on, *Phillips* . . . Because of all this confusion, *NCV* . . . on account of the noise, *ET.*

**he commanded him to be carried into the castle:** . . . he ordered Paul to be taken into the barracks, *TCNT* . . . gave orders that he should be taken into the fort, *Williams C.K.* . . . the citadel, *Concordant* . . . to be conveyed to the fortress, *Fenton* . . . to the army building, *Everyday* . . . led away to headquarters, *NAB.*

**35. And when he came upon the stairs:** When Paul reached the steps, *TCNT* . . . got to the steps, *Phillips.*

**so it was, that he was borne of the soldiers:** . . . he had to be carried by, *Weymouth* . . . had to carry him on their shoulders, *Klingensmith.*

**for the violence of the people:** . . . because the people were so wild, *SEB* . . . cried out so loud and pushed so hard, *NLT* . . . of the crowd, *Williams C.K.* . . . of the mob, *Phillips.*

**36. For the multitude of the people followed after, crying:** . . . for the people were following in a mass, shouting out, *TCNT* . . . for a tremendous crowd, *Williams* . . . The mob was right behind them, yelling, *Beck* . . . The whole mob was following them, *NCV* . . . pushing and calling out, *NLT.*

**Away with him:** Kill him! *NLT, TCNT* . . . Down with him, *Williams C.K.*

**37. And as Paul was to be led into the castle:** When Paul was on the point of being taken into the fort, *Williams C.K.* . . . barracks, *PNT* . . . fortress, *Fenton* . . . citadel, *Concordant.*

**he said unto the chief captain:** . . . asked the colonel, *Phillips* . . . to the commander, *Williams C.K.*

**May I speak unto thee?:** Do I have the right to say something to you? *SEB* . . . May I say something, *Williams C.K.*

**Who said, Canst thou speak Greek?:** . . . the commander exclaimed, *NAB* . . . You know Greek! *Moffatt* . . . Can you speak the Greek language? *NLT* . . . So you know Greek, do you? *Phillips.*

| 1662.1 name-adv | 1091.2 verb 2sing indic pres act | | 3620.2 partic | 679.1 partic | 4622.1 prs-pron nom 2sing |
|---|---|---|---|---|---|
| Ἑλληνιστὶ | γινώσκεις; | 38. | οὐκ | ἄρα | σὺ |
| *Hellēnisti* | *ginōskeis* | | *ouk* | *ara* | *su* |
| Greek | do you know? | | Not | then | you |

| 1498.3 verb 2sing indic pres act | 3450.5 art nom sing masc | 124.1 name-adj nom sing masc | 3450.5 art nom sing masc | 4112.1 prep | 3642.2 dem-pron gen pl |
|---|---|---|---|---|---|
| εἶ | ὁ | Αἰγύπτιος | ὁ | πρὸ | τούτων |
| *ei* | *ho* | *Aiguptios* | *ho* | *pro* | *toutōn* |
| are | the | Egyptian | the | before | these |

| 3450.1 art gen pl | 2232.6 noun gen pl fem | 385.2 verb nom sing masc part aor act | 2504.1 conj | 1790.5 verb nom sing masc part aor act |
|---|---|---|---|---|
| τῶν | ἡμερῶν | ἀναστατώσας | καὶ | ἐξαγαγὼν |
| *tōn* | *hēmerōn* | *anastatōsas* | *kai* | *exagagōn* |
| the | days | having caused a revolt | and | having led out |

| 1519.1 prep | 3450.12 art acc sing fem | 2031.3 noun acc sing fem | 3450.8 art acc pl masc | 4918.3 num card acc masc | 433.9 noun acc pl masc |
|---|---|---|---|---|---|
| εἰς | τὴν | ἔρημον | τοὺς | τετρακισχιλίους | ἄνδρας |
| *eis* | *tēn* | *erēmon* | *tous* | *tetrakischilious* | *andras* |
| into | the | desert | the | four thousand | men |

| 3450.1 art gen pl | 4462.1 noun gen pl masc | | 1500.5 verb 3sing indic aor act | 1156.2 conj | 3450.5 art nom sing masc | 3834.1 name nom masc |
|---|---|---|---|---|---|---|
| τῶν | σικαρίων; | 39. | Εἶπεν | δὲ | ὁ | Παῦλος, |
| *tōn* | *sikariōn* | | *Eipen* | *de* | *ho* | *Paulos* |
| of the | assassins? | | Said | but | | Paul, |

| 1466.1 prs-pron nom 1sing | 442.1 noun nom sing masc | 3173.1 conj | 1498.2 verb 1sing indic pres act | 2428.6 name-adj nom sing masc |
|---|---|---|---|---|
| Ἐγὼ | ἄνθρωπος | μέν | εἰμι | Ἰουδαῖος, |
| *Egō* | *anthrōpos* | *men* | *eimi* | *Ioudaios* |
| I | a man | indeed | am | a Jew |

| 4869.1 name-adj nom sing masc | 3450.10 art gen sing fem | 2763.1 name gen fem | 3620.2 partic | 761.1 adj gen sing fem | 4032.2 noun gen sing fem |
|---|---|---|---|---|---|
| Ταρσεὺς, | τῆς | Κιλικίας | οὐκ | ἀσήμου | πόλεως |
| *Tarseus* | *tēs* | *Kilikias* | *ouk* | *asēmou* | *poleōs* |
| of Tarsus, | | of Cilicia | no | of insignificant | city |

| 4037.1 noun nom sing masc | 1183.1 verb 1sing indic pres mid | 1156.2 conj | 4622.2 prs-pron gen 2sing | 1994.5 verb 2sing impr aor act | 1466.4 prs-pron dat 1sing |
|---|---|---|---|---|---|
| πολίτης· | δέομαι | δέ | σου, | ἐπίτρεψόν | μοι |
| *politēs* | *deomai* | *de* | *sou* | *epitrepson* | *moi* |
| a citizen, | I beseech | and | you, | allow | me |

| 2953.37 verb inf aor act | 4242.1 prep | 3450.6 art acc sing masc | 2967.4 noun acc sing masc | | 1994.6 verb gen sing masc part aor act |
|---|---|---|---|---|---|
| λαλῆσαι | πρὸς | τὸν | λαόν. | 40. | Ἐπιτρέψαντος |
| *lalēsai* | *pros* | *ton* | *laon* | | *Epitrepsantos* |
| to speak | to | the | people. | | Having allowed |

| 1156.2 conj | 840.3 prs-pron gen sing | 3450.5 art nom sing masc | 3834.1 name nom masc | 2449.26 verb sing part perf act | 1894.3 prep | 3450.1 art gen pl |
|---|---|---|---|---|---|---|
| δὲ | αὐτοῦ, | ὁ | Παῦλος | ἑστὼς | ἐπὶ | τῶν |
| *de* | *autou* | *ho* | *Paulos* | *hestōs* | *epi* | *tōn* |
| and | him, | | Paul | standing | on | the |

| 302.1 noun gen pl masc | 2648.1 verb 3sing indic aor act | 3450.11 art dat sing fem | 5331.3 noun dat sing fem | 3450.3 art dat sing | 2967.3 noun dat sing masc |
|---|---|---|---|---|---|
| ἀναβαθμῶν | κατέσεισεν | τῇ | χειρὶ | τῷ | λαῷ· |
| *anabathmōn* | *kateseisen* | *tē* | *cheiri* | *tō* | *laō* |
| stairs | made a sign | with the | hand | to the | people; |

**21:38.** The real reason the tribune was so surprised was that he had jumped to a conclusion about Paul's identity. He thought Paul was a certain dangerous, dagger-carrying Egyptian assassin who had turned things upside down as a political revolutionist.

About A.D. 54 this Egyptian came to Jerusalem claiming to be a prophet. He led a great crowd of about 4,000 fanatical Jews to the Mount of Olives and promised that the walls of Jerusalem would fall down at his word. The Roman governor Felix sent soldiers who killed about 400 and captured another 200, but the Egyptian, with some of his fanatical followers, escaped into the desert.

His followers were murderers, literally daggermen (sikariōn). These fanatical Jews were known even before this time to mingle with the crowds in Jerusalem during the festival times and would use their daggers to stab to death pro-Roman Jews.

Josephus also mentions this Egyptian but says he gathered 30,000 Jews under his influence and that they all marched toward the Mount of Olives to see the walls of Jerusalem fall.

**21:39.** Paul answered the tribune by identifying himself as a Jew and a citizen of Tarsus, a city that was neither unimportant nor obscure. In fact, it was the chief city of Cilicia in the eastern part of Asia Minor. It was famous also as a university city, and its schools were in the same class as those of Alexandria and Athens. Anyone born and educated there would certainly be fluent in the Greek language and would certainly not be ashamed of his birthplace.

Then Paul asked permission to speak to the people. What a courageous thing this was for Paul to do. All the confusion, the beatings, and the threats would have shattered some people's nerve. Some might have vowed never again to preach to such unappreciative people. Others might have called down Roman judgment on the people and demanded that the soldiers treat the crowd the way they had treated the crowd that followed the Egyptian. But Paul had no desire for revenge, nor did he think of his own feelings or the chains that still bound him to the two soldiers. Love and compassion gave him courage to want to plead and reason with his people about the gospel.

**21:40.** When the tribune gave his permission, Paul was allowed to stand on the stairs. Signaling his desire to speak, he gained the attention of the crowd, and there was sudden quiet. Paul then began to speak in the Hebrew language.

This is generally taken to be Aramaic, the language the Jews brought back from Babylonia after their exile there in the Sixth Century B.C. Aramaic is closely related to Hebrew and belongs to the same branch of the Semitic family of languages. Abraham's relatives in Haran spoke Aramaic (Genesis 31:47 shows Laban gave the "heap of witness" its Aramaic name). Aramaic was also the language of trade and commerce in the fertile crescent from Babylonia to Egypt from before the time of Abraham until Alexander the Great replaced it with Greek.

**38. Art not thou that Egyptian:** Are you by chance, *BB* . . . Then you are not the man I thought you were, *SEB.*

**which before these days madest an uproar:** . . . who some time ago raised an insurrection, *TCNT* . . . who some years ago excited the riot, *Weymouth* . . . who not long ago raised a riot, *Phillips* . . . who caused the riot some time ago, *NAB* . . . recently stirred up the rebellion, *Berkeley* . . . headed a rising, *Williams C.K.*

**and leddest out into the wilderness four thousand men that were murderers?:** . . . led a band of, *NAB* . . . and led the four thousand Bandits out into the desert, *TCNT* . . . of the 4000 cutthroats and led them out into the Desert, *Weymouth* . . . the four thousand men of the assassins? *Darby* . . . and led those four thousand assassins into the desert, *Phillips* . . . and led out the four thousand armed rebels into the wilds? *Williams C.K.* . . . hoodlums, *Klingensmith.*

**39. But Paul said, I am a man which am a Jew of Tarsus, a city in Cilicia:** No, said Paul, I am, *TCNT* . . . a citizen of, *NAB* . . . a native of Tarsus, *Montgomery.*

**a citizen of no mean city:** . . . of that not insignificant city, *Phillips* . . . no obscure city, *Rotherham* . . . no unimportant city, *Weymouth* . . . a city of some note, *TCNT* . . . of a notable town, *Williams C.K.*

**and, I beseech thee, suffer me to speak:** . . . and I beg you to give me permission to speak, *TCNT* . . . I ask you to let me speak, *Phillips* . . . Please give me leave to speak, *Williams C.K.* . . . Please let me speak, *Williams* . . . let me address, *NAB.*

**unto the people:**

**40. And when he had given him license:** The Commanding Officer gave his permission, *TCNT* . . . He granted the request, *Williams* . . . On being given permission, *Phillips.*

**Paul stood on the stairs:** Paul, from the steps, *BB.*

**and beckoned with the hand unto the people:** . . . and motioned to the people to be quiet, *Weymouth* . . . made a gesture with his hand to the people, *Phillips* . . . to silence, *NAB.*

| **4044.10** adj gen sing fem | **1156.2** conj | **4457.2** noun gen sing fem | **1090.57** verb gen sing fem part aor mid | **4235.3** verb 3sing indic aor act |
|---|---|---|---|---|
| πολλῆς | δὲ | σιγῆς | γενομένης | προσεφώνησεν |
| *pollēs* | *de* | *sigēs* | *genomenēs* | *prosephōnēsen* |
| great | and | silence | having taken place | he spoke |

| **3450.11** art dat sing fem | **1441.1** name-adj dat sing fem | **1252.1** noun dat sing fem | **2978.15** verb nom sing masc part pres act | **433.6** noun nom pl masc |
|---|---|---|---|---|
| τῇ | Ἑβραΐδι | διαλέκτῳ | λέγων, | **22:1.** Ἄνδρες |
| *tē* | *Hebraidi* | *dialektō* | *legōn* | *Andres* |
| in the | Hebrew | language | saying, | Men, |

| **79.6** noun nom pl masc | **2504.1** conj | **3824.6** noun nom pl masc | **189.29** verb 2pl impr aor act | **1466.2** prs-pron gen 1sing | **3450.10** art gen sing fem | **4242.1** prep |
|---|---|---|---|---|---|---|
| ἀδελφοὶ | καὶ | πατέρες, | ἀκούσατέ | μου | τῆς | πρὸς |
| *adelphoi* | *kai* | *pateres* | *akousate* | *mou* | *tēs* | *pros* |
| brothers | and | fathers, | hear | my | the | to |

1.a.**Txt:** byz.
**Var:** 01ℵ,02A,03B,05D 08E,020L,025P,Gries Lach,Treg,Alf,Word Tisc,We/Ho,Weis,Sod UBS/☆

| **5050.4** prs-pron acc 2pl | **3431.1** adv | **3432.1** adv | **621.2** noun gen sing fem | **189.32** verb nom pl masc part aor act |
|---|---|---|---|---|
| ὑμᾶς | ⌐ νῦν | [a☆ νυνὶ ] | ἀπολογίας | **2.** Ἀκούσαντες |
| *humas* | *nun* | *nuni* | *apologias* | *Akousantes* |
| you | now | [ idem ] | defense. | Having heard |

| **1156.2** conj | **3617.1** conj | **3450.11** art dat sing fem | **1441.1** name-adj dat sing fem | **1252.1** noun dat sing fem | **4235.4** verb 3sing indic imperf act |
|---|---|---|---|---|---|
| δὲ | ὅτι | τῇ | Ἑβραΐδι | διαλέκτῳ | προσεφώνει |
| *de* | *hoti* | *tē* | *Hebraidi* | *dialektō* | *prosephōnei* |
| and | that | in the | Hebrew | language | he was speaking |

| **840.2** prs-pron dat pl | **3095.1** adv comp | **3792.7** verb 3pl indic aor act | **2249.3** noun acc sing fem | **2504.1** conj | **5183.2** verb 3sing indic pres act |
|---|---|---|---|---|---|
| αὐτοῖς, | μᾶλλον | παρέσχον | ἡσυχίαν. | καὶ | φησίν, |
| *autois* | *mallon* | *pareschon* | *hēsuchian* | *kai* | *phēsin* |
| to them, | the more | they kept | quiet; | and | he says, |

3.a.**Txt:** 020L,025P,byz. bo.Sod
**Var:** 01ℵ,02A,03B,05D 08E,sa.Lach,Treg,Alf Word,Tisc,We/Ho,Weis UBS/☆

| **1466.1** prs-pron nom 1sing | **3173.1** conj | **1498.2** verb 1sing indic pres act | **433.1** noun nom sing masc | **2428.6** name-adj nom sing masc |
|---|---|---|---|---|
| **3.** Ἐγώ | ⌐a μέν ⌐ | εἰμι | ἀνὴρ | Ἰουδαῖος, |
| *Egō* | *men* | *eimi* | *anēr* | *Ioudaios* |
| I | indeed | am | a man | a Jew, |

| **1074.26** verb nom sing masc part perf mid | **1706.1** prep | **4870.1** name dat fem | **3450.10** art gen sing fem | **2763.1** name gen fem |
|---|---|---|---|---|
| γεγεννημένος | ἐν | Ταρσῷ | τῆς | Κιλικίας, |
| *gegennēmenos* | *en* | *Tarsō* | *tēs* | *Kilikias* |
| having been born | in | Tarsus | | of Cilicia, |

| **395.3** verb nom sing masc part perf mid | **1156.2** conj | **1706.1** prep | **3450.11** art dat sing fem | **4032.3** noun dat sing fem | **3642.11** dem-pron dat sing fem |
|---|---|---|---|---|---|
| ἀνατεθραμμένος | δὲ | ἐν | τῇ | πόλει | ταύτῃ |
| *anatethrammenos* | *de* | *en* | *tē* | *polei* | *tautē* |
| having been brought up | but | in | the | city | this |

| **3706.2** prep | **3450.8** art acc pl masc | **4087.7** noun acc pl masc | **1052.1** name masc | **3674.11** verb nom sing masc part perf mid |
|---|---|---|---|---|
| παρὰ | τοὺς | πόδας | Γαμαλιὴλ, | πεπαιδευμένος |
| *para* | *tous* | *podas* | *Gamaliēl* | *pepaideumenos* |
| at | the | feet | of Gamaliel, | having been instructed |

| **2567.3** prep | **193.1** noun acc sing fem | **3450.2** art gen sing | **3833.1** adj gen sing masc | **3414.2** noun gen sing masc |
|---|---|---|---|---|
| κατὰ | ἀκρίβειαν | τοῦ | πατρῴου | νόμου, |
| *kata* | *akribeian* | *tou* | *patrōou* | *nomou* |
| according to | exactness | of the | ancestral | law, |

However, there is some evidence that Jerusalem Jews took pride in being able to use the old (Biblical) Hebrew. Every week in all the synagogues they read the Scriptures. They were first read in Hebrew and then paraphrased into Aramaic. As a result they would all be familiar with the Old Testament Hebrew. Yet, since they would understand both, it is not clear which is meant here. In some other New Testament passages the word "Hebrew" is used to designate Aramaic. Aramaic was used in the homes of Galilee and probably in most of the homes of Judea.

**22:1.** Paul's defense given on the stairs was the first of five he was permitted to make. In it he emphasized his heritage as a Jew and his encounter with Christ. The verses which follow record Paul's answers to the major charge the Jews were leveling against him: that he was an apostate. Although he never specifically answered the accusation that he had defiled the temple by taking a Gentile, Trophimus, into the inner courts, his defense made it clear he was living in a manner consistent with his orthodox heritage. In truth, Paul had taken great care not to offend the Jews upon his arrival in Jerusalem. In fact, he had joined with four Christian Jews who were completing their Nazarite vows (cf. 21:24-26).

Paul politely addressed the crowd as gentlemen who were his brothers and fathers, using the word father as a respectful title for the older men among them. Then he asked them to listen to his defense.

**22:2.** Though the Roman tribune had been speaking to the crowd in Greek and Paul had spoken to him in Greek, Paul was wise to switch to Hebrew in speaking to the crowd. For when the crowd recognized he was speaking in Hebrew, they became even more quiet and gave him full attention. This was not because Hebrew was a sacred language, but because it made them realize he was a Jew, not a Gentile, for Gentiles carried on all their business with the Jews in the Greek language.

**22:3.** Paul then identified himself as a Jew born in Tarsus but brought up in Jerusalem at the feet of Gamaliel. This probably means Paul came to Jerusalem in his early youth, possibly in his early teens.

Gamaliel, a member of the Sanhedrin, was one of the best known rabbis of the day. All the people in the crowd would know who he was. According to the Jewish Talmud, Gamaliel was the grandson of the famous rabbi Hillel, still considered by many as the most outstanding rabbi in the history of the Pharisees. They would have to agree with Paul that as a student of Gamaliel he would have been educated strictly and accurately according to the law of the fathers. That is, Gamaliel trained him with strict attention to every detail, not only of the law of Moses, but the additional laws contained in the traditions of the Scribes and Pharisees.



**And when there was made a great silence:** . . . great hush came over them, *Moffatt* . . . comparative silence, *TCNT* . . . when they were quite quiet, *Williams C.K.* . . . great silence ensuing, *Fenton* . . . deep hush, *Phillips* . . . become fairly quiet, *Kleist* . . . all of them were quiet, *MLNT.*

**he spake unto them:** . . . he addressed them, *Rotherham* . . . as he began to speak to them, *Phillips.*

**in the Hebrew tongue, saying:** Hebrew dialect, *Campbell* . . . vernacular, *Concordant* . . . Jewish language, *Beck* . . . Aramaic, *SEB* . . . as follows, *Fenton* . . . in these words, *MLNT.*

**1. Men, brethren, and fathers:**
**hear ye my defence which I make now unto you:** . . . listen to the defence which I am about to make, *TCNT* . . . my vindication, *Hanson.*

**2. (And when they heard that he spake in the Hebrew tongue to them:** And on hearing him address them in Hebrew, *Weymouth.*

**they kept the more silence:** . . . they quieted down still more, *Beck* . . . they were still quieter, *Berkeley* . . . they kept more quiet, *Worrell.*

**and he saith,):** . . . and Paul went on, *TCNT* . . . and he continued, *Williams.*

**3. I am verily a man which am a Jew:** I am, without question, a Jew, *Norlie.*

**born in Tarsus, a city in Cilicia:** . . . a native of Tarsus, *TCNT.*

**yet brought up in this city:** . . . but nurtured in this city, *Rotherham* . . . but I had my education in this city, *BB.*

**at the feet of Gamaliel:** . . . under the teaching of Gamaliel, *Weymouth.*

**and taught according to the perfect manner of the law of the fathers:** . . . trained after the strictness of our ancestral law, *Rotherham* . . . trained according to the exactness of the ancestral law, *Worrell* . . . accurately instructed, *Hanson* . . . educated according to, *TCNT* . . . strictness of the law, *Swann* . . . strictest observance of our fathers' law, *Phillips.*

| **2190.1** noun nom sing masc | **5062.6** verb nom sing masc part pres act | **3450.2** art gen sing | **2296.2** noun gen sing masc | **2503.1** conj | **3820.7** adj nom pl masc |
|---|---|---|---|---|---|
| ζηλωτὴς | ὑπάρχων | τοῦ | θεοῦ, | καθὼς | πάντες |
| *zēlōtēs* | *huparchōn* | *tou* | *theou* | *kathōs* | *pantes* |
| a zealous one | being | | of God, | even as | all |

| **5050.1** prs-pron nom 2pl | **1498.6** verb 2pl indic pres act | **4449.1** adv | **3614.5** rel-pron nom sing masc | **3642.12** dem-pron acc sing fem | **3450.12** art acc sing fem |
|---|---|---|---|---|---|
| ὑμεῖς | ἐστε | σήμερον· | **4.** ὃς | ταύτην | τὴν |
| *humeis* | *este* | *sēmeron* | *hos* | *tautēn* | *tēn* |
| you | are | today; | who | this | the |

| **3461.4** noun acc sing fem | **1371.12** verb 1sing indic aor act | **884.2** conj | **2265.2** noun gen sing masc | **1189.2** verb nom sing masc part pres act | **2504.1** conj |
|---|---|---|---|---|---|
| ὁδὸν | ἐδίωξα | ἄχρι | θανάτου, | δεσμεύων | καὶ |
| *hodon* | *ediōxa* | *achri* | *thanatou* | *desmeuōn* | *kai* |
| way | persecuted | unto | death, | binding | and |

| **3722.3** verb nom sing masc part pres act | **1519.1** prep | **5274.6** noun acc pl fem | **433.9** noun acc pl masc | **4885.1** conj | **2504.1** conj | **1129.9** noun acc pl fem |
|---|---|---|---|---|---|---|
| παραδιδοὺς | εἰς | φυλακὰς | ἄνδρας | τε | καὶ | γυναῖκας, |
| *paradidous* | *eis* | *phulakas* | *andras* | *te* | *kai* | *gunaikas* |
| delivering up | to | prisons | men | both | and | women; |

| **5453.1** conj | **2504.1** conj | **3450.5** art nom sing masc | **744.1** noun nom sing masc | **3113.3** verb 3sing indic pres act | **1466.4** prs-pron dat 1sing |
|---|---|---|---|---|---|
| **5.** ὡς | καὶ | ὁ | ἀρχιερεὺς | μαρτυρεῖ | μοι, |
| *hōs* | *kai* | *ho* | *archiereus* | *marturei* | *moi* |
| as | also | the | high priest | bears witness | to me, |

| **2504.1** conj | **3820.17** adj sing neu | **3450.16** art sing neu | **4103.1** noun sing neu | **3706.1** prep | **3614.1** rel-pron gen pl |
|---|---|---|---|---|---|
| καὶ | πᾶν | τὸ | πρεσβυτέριον· | παρ' | ὧν |
| *kai* | *pan* | *to* | *presbuterion* | *par'* | *hōn* |
| and | all | the | elderhood; | from | whom |

| **2504.1** conj | **1976.8** noun acc pl fem | **1203.13** verb nom sing masc part aor mid | **4242.1** prep | **3450.8** art acc pl masc | **79.9** noun acc pl masc |
|---|---|---|---|---|---|
| καὶ | ἐπιστολὰς | δεξάμενος | πρὸς | τοὺς | ἀδελφοὺς, |
| *kai* | *epistolas* | *dexamenos* | *pros* | *tous* | *adelphous* |
| also | letters | having received | to | the | brothers, |

| **1519.1** prep | **1149.2** name acc fem | **4057.35** verb 1sing indic imperf mid | **70.17** verb nom sing masc part fut act | **2504.1** conj | **3450.8** art acc pl masc |
|---|---|---|---|---|---|
| εἰς | Δαμασκὸν | ἐπορευόμην, | ἄξων | καὶ | τοὺς |
| *eis* | *Damaskon* | *eporeuomēn* | *axōn* | *kai* | *tous* |
| to | Damascus | I was going, | bringing | also | the |

| **1553.1** adv | **1498.25** verb acc pl masc part pres act | **1204.18** verb acc pl masc part perf mid | **1519.1** prep | **2395.2** name fem |
|---|---|---|---|---|
| ἐκεῖσε | ὄντας | δεδεμένους | εἰς | Ἰερουσαλὴμ, |
| *ekeise* | *ontas* | *dedemenous* | *eis* | *Ierousalēm* |
| there | being, | having been bound | to | Jerusalem, |

| **2419.1** conj | **4945.2** verb 3pl subj aor pass | **1090.33** verb 3sing indic aor mid | **1156.2** conj |
|---|---|---|---|
| ἵνα | τιμωρηθῶσιν. | **6.** Ἐγένετο | δέ |
| *hina* | *timōrēthōsin* | *Egeneto* | *de* |
| in order that | they might be punished. | It came to pass | and |

| **1466.4** prs-pron dat 1sing | **4057.9** verb dat sing masc part pres mid | **2504.1** conj | **1443.4** verb dat sing masc part pres act | **3450.11** art dat sing fem |
|---|---|---|---|---|
| μοι | πορευομένῳ | καὶ | ἐγγίζοντι | τῇ |
| *moi* | *poreuomenō* | *kai* | *engizonti* | *tē* |
| to me | journeying | and | drawing near | |

Paul also declared he was, as a result of his training, a zealot for God, eagerly devoted to God, just as all in his audience were. Clearly, Paul was not blaming or criticizing the people for beating him and trying to kill him. He let them know he understood how they felt, for he in his former zeal would have done the same thing. In fact, he recognized their zeal as a zeal for God. Paul sometimes had to warn believers in the assemblies he founded that false teachers would come among them who claimed to be Christians but who had wrong motives. Paul always gave credit to the Jewish persecutors that they had a zeal for God, even though it lacked knowledge (Romans 10:2). This attitude was one of the things that helped Paul to win so many Jews to Christ in all of his journeys. (Compare Romans 10:1 and 11:1 for more about Paul's attitude.)

**22:4.** Paul then admitted he had in fact persecuted the Christians, referring to the Church as "this way," that is, the way of life that follows the teachings of Jesus and the gospel. He admitted that he actually pursued the believers up to the point of causing their death, binding both men and women and having them put in prison. As chapters 8 and 9 have already shown, he hounded them, creating around himself an atmosphere of violence and murder.

**22:5.** The high priest was a witness to Paul's zeal, as were all the elders of the Sanhedrin. Though Paul did not mention it, he had been with them when they listened to Stephen's defense and took him out to stone him. Paul never forgot how he had persecuted the Church in those days, and he was humbled by that memory, even though he knew he had done it in ignorance. From the high priest and the elders of the Sanhedrin he received letters to the Jews of Damascus, probably to the leaders or rulers of their synagogues. Then he went there with the determined purpose of bringing the believers bound to Jerusalem to be punished.

The Roman government had given the high priest and the Sanhedrin (Jewish Senate and High Court) considerable authority in matters relating to their religion. Though Damascus at this time was outside the limits of the Roman Empire and was ruled by Nabatean Arabs, apparently the Arab king allowed them the same authority in his territory. The Arabs at that time were idolaters, as were all the nations round about Israel. The Jews were still a little island of monotheism in the midst of a whole world that did not worship the one true God. But their persecution of the Christians only helped to spread the gospel.

**22:6.** The question in the mind of Paul's hearers at this point was undoubtedly, "What changed Saul the persecutor into Paul the apostle?" So Paul told the crowd the story of the journey to Damascus and how, as they approached the city, suddenly a very bright light shone from heaven and surrounded him. Later Paul described it as brighter than the noonday sun (26:13). The angels

**and was zealous toward God:** I was as zealous in God's service, *TCNT* . . . I worked hard for God, *NLT* . . . as jealous for the honour of the law, *Knox* . . . very serious about serving God, *Everyday, SEB* . . . given up to the cause of God with all my heart, *BB*.

**as ye all are this day:** . . . just as are all of you here today, *Everyday*.

**4. And I persecuted this way unto the death:** In my persecution of this Cause I did not stop even at the taking of life, *TCNT* . . . persecuted this religion, *Lamsa* . . . I hurt the people who followed...Some of them were even killed, *Everyday*.

**binding and delivering into prisons both men and women:** I put in chains, and, *TCNT* . . . I arrested...and put them in jail, *Everyday* . . . throwing them into prison, Weymouth.

**5. As also the high priest doth bear me witness, and all the estate of the elders:** . . . the council of the elders, *Alford* . . . The head religious leader, *NLT* . . . and all the Eldership, *Rotherham* . . . and to that the High Priest himself and all the council can testify, *TCNT* . . . are witnesses, *Montgomery* . . . and all the presbytery, *Hanson* . . . can tell you that this is true, *Everyday, SEB*.

**from whom also I received letters unto the brethren:** For I had letters of introduction from them, *TCNT* . . . These leaders gave me letters to, *Everyday*.

**and went to Damascus:** . . . and I was on my way to, *TCNT*.

**to bring them which were there bound unto Jerusalem, for to be punished:** So I was going there to arrest these people, *Everyday* . . . where they would be beaten, *NLT*.

**6. And it came to pass, that, as I made my journey:** But something happened to me, *NCV* . . . While I was still on my way, *TCNT*.

**and was come nigh unto Damascus:** . . . just as I was getting close to Damascus, *TCNT* . . . just before I reached Damascus, *Williams* . . . on my way to, *NCV* . . . and was drawing nigh to, *Worrell* . . . when I came close to the city, *SEB*.

| 1149.1 name dat fem | 3875.1 prep | 3184.1 noun acc sing fem | 1794.1 adv | 1523.2 prep gen | 3450.2 art gen sing |
|---|---|---|---|---|---|
| Δαμασκῷ | περὶ | μεσημβρίαν | ἐξαίφνης | ἐκ | τοῦ |
| *Damaskō* | *peri* | *mesēmbrian* | *exaiphnēs* | *ek* | *tou* |
| to Damascus, | about | midday | suddenly | out of | the |

| 3636.2 noun gen sing masc | 3878.2 verb inf aor act | 5295.1 noun sing neu | 2401.2 adj sing | 3875.1 prep | 1466.7 prs-pron acc 1sing |
|---|---|---|---|---|---|
| οὐρανοῦ | περιαστράψαι | φῶς | ἱκανὸν | περὶ | ἐμέ· |
| *ouranou* | *periastrapsai* | *phōs* | *hikanon* | *peri* | *eme* |
| heaven | to shine | a light | great | about | me. |

7.a.**Txt:** 05D,020L,byz.
**Var:** 01ℵ,02A,03B,08E 025P,Lach,Treg,Alf Tisc,We/Ho,Weis,Sod UBS/☆

| 3959.3 verb indic aor act | 3959.4 verb 1sing indic aor act | 4885.1 conj | 1519.1 prep | 3450.16 art sing neu | 1468.1 noun sing neu |
|---|---|---|---|---|---|
| 7. ⸂ ἔπεσόν | [a☆ ἔπεσά ] | τε | εἰς | τὸ | ἔδαφος, |
| *epeson* | *epesa* | *te* | *eis* | *to* | *edaphos* |
| I fell | [ idem ] | and | to | the | ground, |

| 2504.1 conj | 189.19 verb 1sing indic aor act | 5292.2 noun gen sing fem | 2978.20 verb gen sing fem part pres act | 1466.4 prs-pron dat 1sing | 4406.1 name masc |
|---|---|---|---|---|---|
| καὶ | ἤκουσα | φωνῆς | λεγούσης | μοι, | Σαοὺλ, |
| *kai* | *ēkousa* | *phōnēs* | *legousēs* | *moi* | *Saoul* |
| and | heard | a voice | saying | to me, | Saul, |

| 4406.1 name masc | 4949.9 intr-pron sing neu | 1466.6 prs-pron acc 1sing | 1371.2 verb 2sing indic pres act | 1466.1 prs-pron nom 1sing |
|---|---|---|---|---|
| Σαούλ, | τί | με | διώκεις; | 8. Ἐγὼ |
| *Saoul* | *ti* | *me* | *diōkeis* | *Egō* |
| Saul, | why | me | are you persecuting? | I |

| 1156.2 conj | 552.4 verb 1sing indic aor pass | 4949.3 intr-pron nom sing | 1498.3 verb 2sing indic pres act | 2935.5 noun voc sing masc | 1500.5 verb 3sing indic aor act |
|---|---|---|---|---|---|
| δὲ | ἀπεκρίθην, | Τίς | εἶ, | κύριε; | Εἶπέν |
| *de* | *apekrithēn* | *Tis* | *ei* | *kurie* | *Eipen* |
| and | answered, | Who | are you, | Lord? | He said |

8.a.**Txt:** 01ℵ-corr,05D 08E,020L,025P,etc.byz. Sod
**Var:** 01ℵ-org,02A,03B Lach,Treg,Tisc,We/Ho Weis,UBS/☆

| 4885.1 conj | 4242.1 prep | 1466.6 prs-pron acc 1sing | 1466.7 prs-pron acc 1sing | 1466.1 prs-pron nom 1sing | 1498.2 verb 1sing indic pres act |
|---|---|---|---|---|---|
| τε | πρός | ⸂ με, | [a ἐμέ. ] | Ἐγώ | εἰμι |
| *te* | *pros* | *me* | *eme* | *Egō* | *eimi* |
| and | to | me, | [ idem ] | I | am |

| 2400.1 name nom masc | 3450.5 art nom sing masc | 3343.1 name nom sing masc | 3614.6 rel-pron acc sing masc | 4622.1 prs-pron nom 2sing |
|---|---|---|---|---|
| Ἰησοῦς | ὁ | Ναζωραῖος | ὃν | σὺ |
| *Iēsous* | *ho* | *Nazōraios* | *hon* | *su* |
| Jesus | the | Nazarene, | whom | you |

| 1371.2 verb 2sing indic pres act | 3450.7 art nom pl masc | 1156.2 conj | 4713.1 prep | 1466.5 prs-pron dat 1sing | 1498.23 verb nom pl masc part pres act |
|---|---|---|---|---|---|
| διώκεις. | 9. Οἱ | δὲ | σὺν | ἐμοὶ | ὄντες |
| *diōkeis* | *Hoi* | *de* | *sun* | *emoi* | *ontes* |
| are persecuting. | The | but | with | me | being |

9.a.**Txt:** 05D,08E,020L 025P,byz.sa.
**Var:** p74,01ℵ,02A,03B 33,bo.Lach,Treg,Tisc We/Ho,Weis,Sod UBS/☆

| 3450.16 art sing neu | 3173.1 conj | 5295.1 noun sing neu | 2277.5 verb 3pl indic aor mid | 2504.1 conj | 1703.2 adj nom pl masc |
|---|---|---|---|---|---|
| τὸ | μὲν | φῶς | ἐθεάσαντο, | ⸂a καὶ | ἔμφοβοι |
| *to* | *men* | *phōs* | *etheasanto* | *kai* | *emphoboi* |
| the | indeed | light | saw, | and | alarmed |

| 1090.38 verb 3pl indic aor mid | 3450.12 art acc sing fem | 1156.2 conj | 5292.4 noun acc sing fem | 3620.2 partic | 189.24 verb 3pl indic aor act |
|---|---|---|---|---|---|
| ἐγένοντο·⸃ | τὴν | δὲ | φωνὴν | οὐκ | ἤκουσαν |
| *egenonto* | *tēn* | *de* | *phōnēn* | *ouk* | *ēkousan* |
| were, | the | but | voice | not | they did hear |

who announced the birth of Jesus to the shepherds had the glory of the Lord shining around them (Luke 2:9). But this was an even greater manifestation of the glory of God, the glory which Jesus himself had prayed the Father would restore to Him (John 17:5).

**22:7.** Overwhelmed by the brightness of the heavenly light, Paul fell to the ground. He heard a voice asking, "Why do you keep persecuting me?" The One who spoke addressed him with the Hebrew form of his name, Saoul. This too drew attention to the fact Jesus was addressing him as a Jew. Even though Saul was the name of a king who failed, the name was a good name and meant "asked for," that is, asked of God. Yet on the Damascus Road Paul was acting in a very self-willed manner, just as King Saul had.

**22:8.** Paul then inquired who it was that was speaking to him, addressing Him as "Lord." In doing this, Paul was not just being polite. That light made him realize this incident was something more than could be explained by natural causes. It had to be a divine manifestation, a manifestation of God. So he meant "divine Lord" when he said "Lord."

The reply was instant and plain. The One speaking to him was Jesus of Nazareth, the One Paul kept persecuting. Jesus made this very emphatic, meaning literally, "You, yourself are continuing to persecute me." Most of the other Jews had quit persecuting the Christians in Jerusalem. Paul had been the one to keep it up.

Jesus emphasized the fact that Paul was persecuting Him. He is the Head of the Church, and the Church is His body. So, in a very real sense Paul was persecuting Christ when he persecuted Christians. To put it another way, the Christians were Christ's witnesses, His representatives, His ambassadors. An insult to an ambassador is an insult to the country or the king he represents.

This vision of Jesus was behind the prayer of Paul "that the God of our Lord Jesus Christ, the Father of glory, may give unto you the spirit of wisdom and revelation in the knowledge of him: the eyes of your understanding being enlightened; that ye may know what is the hope of his calling, and what the riches of the glory of his inheritance in the saints, and what is the exceeding greatness of his power to usward who believe, according to the working of his mighty power, which he wrought in Christ, when he raised him from the dead, and set him at his own right hand in the heavenly places, . . . and gave him to be the head over all things to the church" (Ephesians 1:17-20,22).

**22:9.** Paul's companions also saw the light, but its intensity was not focused on them as it was on Paul. They also did not hear the voice of Jesus. But this does not mean they did not hear the sound of His voice. The sense is that they did not hear with understanding.

The brightness of the light was enough to make them afraid, however. In fact, it both startled and terrified them.

**about noon:** . . . suddenly about midday, *TNT.*

**suddenly there shone from heaven a great light round about me:** . . . a bright light from heaven flashed all around me, *Everyday* . . . suddenly out of heaven there flashed a great light all around me, *Rotherham* . . . a sudden blaze of light, *Weymouth* . . . suddenly a dazzling light blazed around me, *Noli* . . . an intense light...beamed, *Berkeley* . . . a great light shone on me, *KJII* . . . shined all around me, *SEB.*

**7. And I fell unto the ground:** I fall flat, *Concordant* . . . And when I went down on the earth, *BB* . . . fell upon the ground, *Goodspeed.*

**and heard a voice saying unto me:** . . . a voice asking me, *Beck.*

**Saul, Saul, why persecutest thou me?:** . . . why do you persecute me, *RSV* . . . why do you work so hard against Me? *NLT* . . . why are you attacking me so cruelly? *BB* . . . why are you doing things against me? *Everyday.*

**8. And I answered, Who art thou, Lord?:** Sir? *Williams.*

**And he said unto me:** The voice answered, *SEB* . . . he answered me, *Montgomery* . . . So he told me, *Berkeley.*

**I am Jesus of Nazareth, whom thou persecutest:** I am Jehoshua, *Wuest* . . . the Nazarene, *TNT* . . . Jesus from Nazareth...the One you are trying to hurt, *Everyday* . . . whom you are attacking, *BB.*

**9. And they that were with me saw indeed the light:** The men with me saw the light, *TCNT* . . . (My companions), *Moffatt* . . . My traveling companons saw, *Noli* . . . The men who were with me...saw the light, *SEB* . . . certainly saw, *Berkeley* . . . naturally saw, *Phillips.*

**and were afraid:** . . . but they did not understand, *Worrell.*

**but they heard not the voice of him that spake to me:** . . . but the voice of him who spoke to me they did not understand, *HBIE* . . . did not distinctly hear, *Campbell* . . . but they understood not the voice, *Wilson* . . . but could not catch the voice of him who spoke to me, *Knox* . . . came not to their ears, *BB.*

| 3450.2 art gen sing | 2953.13 verb gen sing masc part pres act | 1466.4 prs-pron dat 1sing | 1500.3 verb indic aor act | 1156.2 conj | 4949.9 intr-pron sing neu |
|---|---|---|---|---|---|
| τοῦ | λαλοῦντός | μοι. | **10.** εἶπον | δέ, | Τί |
| *tou* | *lalountos* | *moi* | *eipon* | *de* | *Ti* |
| of the | speaking | to me. | I said | and, | What |

| 4020.21 verb 1sing act | 2935.5 noun voc sing masc | 3450.5 art nom sing masc | 1156.2 conj | 2935.1 noun nom sing masc | 1500.5 verb 3sing indic aor act |
|---|---|---|---|---|---|
| ποιήσω | κύριε; | Ὁ | δὲ | κύριος | εἶπεν |
| *poiēsō* | *kurie* | *Ho* | *de* | *kurios* | *eipen* |
| shall I do, | Lord? | The | and | Lord | said |

| 4242.1 prep | 1466.6 prs-pron acc 1sing | 448.9 verb nom sing masc part aor act | 4057.4 verb 2sing impr pres mid | 1519.1 prep | 1149.2 name acc fem |
|---|---|---|---|---|---|
| πρός | με, | Ἀναστὰς | πορεύου | εἰς | Δαμασκόν, |
| *pros* | *me* | *Anastas* | *poreuou* | *eis* | *Damaskon* |
| to | me, | Having risen up | go | to | Damascus, |

| 2517.1 conj | 4622.3 prs-pron dat 2sing | 2953.60 verb 3sing indic fut pass | 3875.1 prep | 3820.4 adj gen pl |
|---|---|---|---|---|
| κἀκεῖ | σοι | λαληθήσεται | περὶ | πάντων |
| *kakei* | *soi* | *lalēthēsetai* | *peri* | *pantōn* |
| and there | to you | it shall be told | concerning | all |

| 3614.1 rel-pron gen pl | 4872.5 verb 3sing indic perf mid | 4622.3 prs-pron dat 2sing | 4020.41 verb inf aor act | 5453.1 conj |
|---|---|---|---|---|
| ὧν | τέτακταί | σοι | ποιῆσαι. | **11.** Ὡς |
| *hōn* | *tetaktai* | *soi* | *poiēsai* | *Hōs* |
| which | it has been appointed | you | to do. | As |

| 1156.2 conj | 3620.2 partic | 1676.6 verb 1sing indic imperf act | 570.3 prep | 3450.10 art gen sing fem | 1385.2 noun gen sing fem | 3450.2 art gen sing |
|---|---|---|---|---|---|---|
| δὲ | οὐκ | ἐνέβλεπον | ἀπὸ | τῆς | δόξης | τοῦ |
| *de* | *ouk* | *eneblepon* | *apo* | *tēs* | *doxēs* | *tou* |
| and | not | I was seeing | from | the | glory | of the |

| 5295.2 noun gen sing neu | 1552.2 dem-pron gen sing | 5332.2 verb nom sing masc part pres mid | 5097.3 prep | 3450.1 art gen pl | 4745.1 verb gen pl masc part pres act |
|---|---|---|---|---|---|
| φωτὸς | ἐκείνου, | χειραγωγούμενος | ὑπὸ | τῶν | συνόντων |
| *phōtos* | *ekeinou* | *cheiragōgoumenos* | *hupo* | *tōn* | *sunontōn* |
| light | that, | being led by the hand | by | the | being with |

| 1466.4 prs-pron dat 1sing | 2048.1 verb indic aor act | 1519.1 prep | 1149.2 name acc fem | 366.4 name nom masc | 1156.2 conj |
|---|---|---|---|---|---|
| μοι, | ἦλθον | εἰς | Δαμασκόν. | **12.** Ἁνανίας | δέ |
| *moi* | *ēlthon* | *eis* | *Damaskon* | *Hananias* | *de* |
| me, | I came | to | Damascus. | Ananias | and |

12.a.**Txt:** 08E,byz.
**Var:** 01ℵ,03B,020L
025P,Lach,Treg,Alf
Tisc,We/Ho,Weis,Sod
UBS/⋆

| 4948.3 indef-pron nom sing | 433.1 noun nom sing masc | 2133.1 adj nom sing masc | 2107.1 adj nom sing masc | 2567.3 prep |
|---|---|---|---|---|
| τις, | ἀνὴρ | ‘ εὐσεβὴς | [a⋆ εὐλαβὴς ] | κατὰ |
| *tis* | *anēr* | *eusebēs* | *eulabēs* | *kata* |
| certain, | a man | devout | [ reverent ] | according to |

| 3450.6 art acc sing masc | 3414.4 noun acc sing masc | 3113.32 verb nom sing masc part pres mid | 5097.3 prep | 3820.4 adj gen pl |
|---|---|---|---|---|
| τὸν | νόμον, | μαρτυρούμενος | ὑπὸ | πάντων |
| *ton* | *nomon* | *marturoumenos* | *hupo* | *pantōn* |
| the | law, | being borne witness to | by | all |

12.b.**Txt:** p74,01ℵ,02A
03B,08E,Steph
**Var:** p41,044,byz.

| 3450.1 art gen pl | 2700.7 verb gen pl masc part pres act | 1706.1 prep | 1149.1 name dat fem | 2428.3 name-adj gen pl masc |
|---|---|---|---|---|
| τῶν | κατοικούντων | [b+ ἐν | Δαμασκῷ ] | Ἰουδαίων, |
| *tōn* | *katoikountōn* | *en* | *Damaskō* | *Ioudaiōn* |
| the | dwelling | [ in | Damascus ] | Jews, |

**22:10.** Then Paul told how he asked the Lord what he should do. Then he added, "And the Lord said." This is important. Paul had just told the crowd the voice speaking out of the midst of the light from heaven was Jesus of Nazareth. Now he called Jesus "Lord" with full knowledge of who He is. This makes it clear Paul had immediately accepted Jesus as the divine Lord and as the Lord of his life. He showed it further by putting himself at his Lord's disposal and asking for His direction concerning what to do. It must be remembered also that Lord was the title the Jews used to refer to God the Father in their reading of the Scriptures and in their worship in the synagogues. This does not mean Paul was identifying Jesus as the same Person as God the Father. He was recognizing Jesus as deity.

Jesus then told Paul to get up and go into Damascus. There he would be told of all the things which were appointed for him to do. The use of the Greek perfect tense here means the things Paul would be told had already been appointed for him in advance and were still being commanded or ordered for him. God had a great plan for Paul's life. Now that he had accepted Jesus as Lord of his life, God was ready to put that plan into effect. All Paul needed to do was follow in faith and obedience. But the first step was to go to Damascus where he had intended to arrest the believers. They needed to see that God could turn around the one who persecuted "the Way" and make him a loyal follower of Jesus in the way God had ordained.

**22:11.** Because of the glory of the light from heaven, Paul could not see. His companions had to take him by the hand and lead him into the city. Paul's mention of the glory of the light again drew attention to the fact that it was more than an ordinary light. The glory identified it clearly with the Shekinah, the divine manifestation of glory and light in the Old Testament. Paul was declaring to the crowd that he was now convinced that Jesus is the supernatural Lord, the Son of God, just as the Christians were saying.

**22:12.** Paul also drew attention to the fact that Ananias of Damascus was a devout (godly, God-fearing) man according to the Law, that is, in the way he was careful to keep the Law. He followed Jewish customs and did not despise his Jewish heritage.

The Bible recognizes here that it was important what non-Christians said about Ananias. A believer's reputation in the community may not seem important, but it is important for his witness. God expects Christians to walk in wisdom toward those who are outside the Church (Colossians 4:5). This is a practical wisdom that shows up in right conduct of life. Also, Christians must walk honestly toward non-Christians (1 Thessalonians 4:12). More literally, this means believers must conduct themselves in a life-style that shows decency, dignity, and good order. A Christian's deportment should be above reproach in all things. This includes good social behavior and little details of courtesy in the home and everywhere.

**10. And I said:** And I asked, *Weymouth.*
**What shall I do, Lord?:**
**And the Lord said unto me:** . . . answered, *Williams.*
**Arise, and go into Damascus:** Get up, *TCNT* . . . and proceed to Damascus, *Noli.*
**and there it shall be told thee:** . . . and it will be made clear to you, *BB.*
**of all things which are appointed for thee to do:** . . . about all you are destined to do, *Moffatt* . . . that has been laid out for you to do, *Berkeley* . . . everything you are ordered to do, *Beck* . . . all that you have been assigned to do, *NIV* . . . everything that has been arranged for you, *Adams* . . . all things which have been arranged, *Worrell* . . . the work you are foreordained to accomplish, *Noli* . . . that is destined for thee, *Knox* . . . which have been appointed to you to do, *KJII.*

**11. And when I could not see for the glory of that light:** In consequence, *TCNT* . . . But as I could not see clearly owing to, *Rotherham* . . . As I did not see on account of the glory of that light, *Swann* . . . Due to the brilliancy of that intense light, *Berkeley* . . . As I was blinded by the dazzling light, *Noli.*
**being led by the hand of them that were with me:** . . . guided by the hands of my companions, *Berkeley.*
**I came into Damascus:** . . . and in this way I reached Damascus, *Williams.*

**12. And one Ananias:** . . . a certain, *KJII.*
**a devout man according to the law:** . . . a man devout in strict observance of the law, *Williams* . . . a pious man who obeyed the Law, *Weymouth* . . . a God-fearing man who kept the law, *BB* . . . devout by the standards of the law, *Adams* . . . for his pious observance of the Law, *Noli* . . . a man devoted according to the Law, *KJII.*
**having a good report of all the Jews which dwelt there:** . . . well spoken of by, *RSV* . . . by all the resident Jews, *Worrell* . . . respected him, *NCV* . . . all the Jews in that place had a high opinion, *BB.*

## Acts 22:13

13.a.**Txt:** 08E,020L 025P,etc.byz.Sod
**Var:** 01ℵ,02A,03B,Lach Treg,Tisc,We/Ho,Weis UBS/☆

| **2048.13** verb nom sing masc part aor act | **4242.1** prep | **1466.6** prs-pron acc 1sing | **1466.7** prs-pron acc 1sing | **2504.1** conj | **2168.5** verb nom sing masc part aor act |
|---|---|---|---|---|---|
| **13.** ἐλθὼν | πρός | ʻ με | [a ἐμὲ ] | καὶ | ἐπιστὰς |
| *elthōn* | *pros* | *me* | *eme* | *kai* | *epistas* |
| having come | to | me | [ idem ] | and | having stood by |

| **1500.5** verb 3sing indic aor act | **1466.4** prs-pron dat 1sing | **4406.1** name masc | **79.5** noun voc sing masc | **306.8** verb 2sing impr aor act | **2476.3** prs-pron nom |
|---|---|---|---|---|---|
| εἶπέν | μοι, | Σαοὺλ | ἀδελφέ, | ἀνάβλεψον. | Κἀγὼ |
| *eipen* | *moi* | *Saoul* | *adelphe* | *anablepson* | *Kagō* |
| said | to me, | Saul | brother, | receive sight. | And I |

| **840.11** prs-pron dat sing fem | **3450.11** art dat sing fem | **5443.3** noun dat sing fem | **306.2** verb 1sing indic aor act | **1519.1** prep | **840.6** prs-pron acc sing masc |
|---|---|---|---|---|---|
| αὐτῇ | τῇ | ὥρᾳ | ἀνέβλεψα | εἰς | αὐτόν. |
| *autē* | *tē* | *hōra* | *aneblepsa* | *eis* | *auton* |
| same | in the | hour | received sight | on | him. |

| **3450.5** art nom sing masc | **1156.2** conj | **1500.5** verb 3sing indic aor act | **3450.5** art nom sing masc | **2296.1** noun nom sing masc | **3450.1** art gen pl |
|---|---|---|---|---|---|
| **14.** ὁ | δὲ | εἶπεν, | Ὁ | θεὸς | τῶν |
| *ho* | *de* | *eipen* | *Ho* | *theos* | *tōn* |
| The | and | said, | The | God | of the |

| **3824.7** noun gen pl masc | **2231.2** prs-pron gen 1pl | **4258.1** verb 3sing indic aor mid | **4622.4** prs-pron acc 2sing | **1091.29** verb inf aor act |
|---|---|---|---|---|
| πατέρων | ἡμῶν | προεχειρίσατό | σε | γνῶναι |
| *paterōn* | *hēmōn* | *proecheirisato* | *se* | *gnōnai* |
| fathers | our | appointed | you | to know |

| **3450.16** art sing neu | **2284.1** noun sing neu | **840.3** prs-pron gen sing | **2504.1** conj | **1481.19** verb inf aor act | **3450.6** art acc sing masc | **1337.1** adj sing |
|---|---|---|---|---|---|---|
| τὸ | θέλημα | αὐτοῦ, | καὶ | ἰδεῖν | τὸν | δίκαιον |
| *to* | *thelēma* | *autou* | *kai* | *idein* | *ton* | *dikaion* |
| the | will | his, | and | to see | the | Just One, |

| **2504.1** conj | **189.36** verb inf aor act | **5292.4** noun acc sing fem | **1523.2** prep gen | **3450.2** art gen sing | **4601.2** noun gen sing neu | **840.3** prs-pron gen sing |
|---|---|---|---|---|---|---|
| καὶ | ἀκοῦσαι | φωνὴν | ἐκ | τοῦ | στόματος | αὐτοῦ· |
| *kai* | *akousai* | *phōnēn* | *ek* | *tou* | *stomatos* | *autou* |
| and | to hear | a voice | out of | the | mouth | his; |

| **3617.1** conj | **1498.39** verb 2sing indic fut mid | **3116.1** noun nom sing masc | **840.4** prs-pron dat sing | **4242.1** prep | **3820.8** adj acc pl masc |
|---|---|---|---|---|---|
| **15.** ὅτι | ἔσῃ | μάρτυς | αὐτῷ | πρὸς | πάντας |
| *hoti* | *esē* | *martus* | *autō* | *pros* | *pantas* |
| for | you shall be | a witness | for him | to | all |

| **442.9** noun acc pl masc | **3614.1** rel-pron gen pl | **3571.10** verb 2sing indic perf act | **2504.1** conj | **189.20** verb 2sing indic aor act | **2504.1** conj |
|---|---|---|---|---|---|
| ἀνθρώπους | ὧν | ἑώρακας | καὶ | ἤκουσας. | **16.** καὶ |
| *anthrōpous* | *hōn* | *heōrakas* | *kai* | *ēkousas* | *kai* |
| men | of what | you have seen | and | heard. | And |

| **3431.1** adv | **4949.9** intr-pron sing neu | **3165.2** verb 2sing indic pres act | **448.9** verb nom sing masc part aor act | **901.20** verb 2sing impr aor mid | **2504.1** conj |
|---|---|---|---|---|---|
| νῦν | τί | μέλλεις; | ἀναστὰς | βάπτισαι | καὶ |
| *nun* | *ti* | *melleis* | *anastas* | *baptisai* | *kai* |
| now | why | are you delaying? | Having arisen | be baptized | and |

| **622.2** verb 2sing impr aor mid | **3450.15** art acc pl fem | **264.1** noun fem | **4622.2** prs-pron gen 2sing | **1926.14** verb nom sing masc part aor mid |
|---|---|---|---|---|
| ἀπόλουσαι | τὰς | ἁμαρτίας | σου, | ἐπικαλεσάμενος |
| *apolousai* | *tas* | *hamartias* | *sou* | *epikalesamenos* |
| wash away | the | sins | your, | having called |

**22:13.** Ananias came to Paul and stood by him. Here Paul just summarized what happened. Chapter 9 provides more details and tells how Ananias laid his hands on Paul and records more of what Ananias said. It was Jesus who appeared to Ananias and told him to go to Paul and pray for him to receive his sight. In his defense Paul merely drew attention to the fact that Ananias called him "brother," and he recovered his sight and was able to see the man the Lord had sent to him.

It seems from this that the terms brother and sister were already becoming meaningful to the Christians. They recognized that whether they were Jews or Gentiles they were in the family of God. Paul had had a great education. He had the right to be called "Rabbi." But it was his own studies that gave him that right. Only the Lord could make him a brother.

**22:14.** Ananias then told Paul that the God of their fathers (the God of Abraham, Isaac, and Jacob) had chosen him, that is, appointed him (selected him, a word used always of appointment to an important duty). God's purpose was that Paul would come to know His will (to realize what His will is), that he would see the Just One (the Righteous One, the Righteous Servant of God, that is, the Messiah), and that he would hear His voice, not from a distance but face-to-face.

By referring to Jesus as the Just or Righteous One, Ananias connected Jesus with Old Testament prophecies of the Messiah. (See Isaiah 9:7; 11:4,5; 53:11; Jeremiah 23:5,6.) The fact that Paul heard the voice of Jesus from His mouth also makes it clear that this was not a dream-type vision or a ghostly manifestation. Jesus was present in bodily form. Jesus came to Paul in a way just as real and literal as the way in which He had come to the other apostles after His resurrection. This made Paul a witness to His resurrection on the same level as those who saw Him alive before His ascension.

**22:15.** Ananias specifically told Paul he was to be Christ's witness to all men concerning what he had seen and heard. This means Paul was to be a firsthand witness, just as the other apostles were. His commission was the same as the Great Commission. It was to all mankind (including both men and women). Behind it was the promise to Abraham that in his Seed all the families of the earth would be blessed. Behind it also was the love of God for the whole world, the same love that caused Him to send His Son (John 3:16).

**22:16.** Then Ananias said, "Now what do you intend? Rise, be baptized, and wash away your sins, calling on the name of the Lord" (editor's translation). This was a call to express faith. Paul's sins would be washed away, however, through calling on the Lord's name, not by the water of baptism. The only other place where this word for "wash" is used is in 1 Corinthians 6:11. There it is the Spirit of God that does the washing.

**13. Came unto me:** . . . called on me, *Berkeley.*

**and stood, and said unto me:** . . . stood by me, *Everyday.*

**Brother Saul, receive thy sight:** Saul, my Brother, recover your sight, *TCNT* . . . you may see again! *Phillips* . . . see again! *Beck,* . . . look up and see, *Knox* . . . let your eyes be open, *BB.*

**And the same hour:** And then and there, *TCNT* . . . And at that instant, *Knox* . . . At that very moment, *Noli* . . . Immediately, *Everyday.*

**I looked up upon him:** I recovered my sight and looked up at him, *TCNT* . . . At that moment, *SEB* . . . I regained my sight, *Noli* . . . I looked up into his face, *Knox* . . . I was able to see him, *BB, Everyday.*

**14. And he said, The God of our fathers hath chosen thee:** Ananias told me, *Everyday* . . . You have been marked out by the God of our fathers, *BB* . . . chose you a long time ago, *SEB.*

**that thou shouldest know his will:** . . . to recognize his will, *Berkeley* . . . to learn what he wants, *Beck* . . . to understand His intention, *Fenton* . . . to have knowledge of his purpose, *BB* . . . to know his plan, *Everyday.*

**and see that Just One:** . . . the Righteous One, *ASV.*

**and shouldest hear the voice of his mouth:** . . . and hear Him speak, *Weymouth* . . . to hear words from him, *Everyday.*

**15. For thou shalt be his witness unto all men:** . . . to all the world, *TCNT* . . . to all mankind, *Concordant.*

**of what thou hast seen and heard:** You will tell them about the things, *Everyday.*

**16. And now why tarriest thou?:** . . . why wait any longer, *TCNT* . . . why lingerest thou? *Darby* . . . Now, don't wait any longer, *SEB* . . . why are you waiting? *BB* . . . why art thou wasting time? *Knox.*

**arise, and be baptized:** Get up, *Everyday* . . . Be baptized at once, *TCNT* . . . and be immersed, *Hanson.*

**and wash away thy sins:** . . . be cleansed of your sins, *Berkeley* . . . and wash your sins away, *Williams.*

16.a.**Txt:** 020L,025P,byz.
**Var:** 01ℵ,02A,03B,08E sa.bo.Gries,Lach,Treg Alf,Word,Tisc,We/Ho Weis,Sod,UBS/☆

| **3450.16** art sing neu | **3549.2** noun sing neu | **3450.2** art gen sing | **2935.2** noun gen sing masc | **840.3** prs-pron gen sing | **1090.33** verb 3sing indic aor mid |
|---|---|---|---|---|---|
| τὸ | ὄνομα | ( τοῦ | κυρίου. | [a☆ αὐτοῦ. ] | **17.** Ἐγένετο |
| *to* | *onoma* | *tou* | *kuriou* | *autou* | *Egeneto* |
| the | name | of the | Lord. | [ his. ] | It came to pass |

| **1156.2** conj | **1466.4** prs-pron dat 1sing | **5128.9** verb dat sing masc part aor act | **1519.1** prep | **2395.1** name fem | **2504.1** conj |
|---|---|---|---|---|---|
| δέ | μοι | ὑποστρέψαντι | εἰς | Ἱερουσαλὴμ, | καὶ |
| *de* | *moi* | *hupostrepsanti* | *eis* | *Hierousalēm* | *kai* |
| and | to me | having returned | to | Jerusalem, | and |

| **4195.12** verb gen sing masc part pres mid | **1466.2** prs-pron gen 1sing | **1706.1** prep | **3450.3** art dat sing | **2387.2** adj dat sing neu | **1090.63** verb inf aor mid |
|---|---|---|---|---|---|
| προσευχομένου | μου | ἐν | τῷ | ἱερῷ, | γενέσθαι |
| *proseuchomenou* | *mou* | *en* | *tō* | *hierō* | *genesthai* |
| praying | me | in | the | temple, | to become |

| **1466.6** prs-pron acc 1sing | **1706.1** prep | **1598.3** noun dat sing fem | **2504.1** conj | **1481.19** verb inf aor act | **840.6** prs-pron acc sing masc |
|---|---|---|---|---|---|
| με | ἐν | ἐκστάσει, | **18.** καὶ | ἰδεῖν | αὐτὸν |
| *me* | *en* | *ekstasei* | *kai* | *idein* | *auton* |
| me | in | a trance, | and | to see | him |

| **2978.13** verb part pres act | **1466.4** prs-pron dat 1sing | **4545.2** verb 2sing impr aor act | **2504.1** conj | **1814.9** verb 2sing impr aor act | **1706.1** prep | **4882.1** noun dat sing neu |
|---|---|---|---|---|---|---|
| λέγοντά | μοι, | Σπεῦσον | καὶ | ἔξελθε | ἐν | τάχει |
| *legonta* | *moi* | *Speuson* | *kai* | *exelthe* | *en* | *tachei* |
| saying | to me, | Hurry | and | go away | with | speed |

| **1523.1** prep gen | **2395.1** name fem | **1354.1** conj | **3620.3** partic | **3720.5** verb 3pl indic fut mid | **4622.2** prs-pron gen 2sing |
|---|---|---|---|---|---|
| ἐξ | Ἱερουσαλήμ, | διότι | οὐ | παραδέξονταί | σου |
| *ex* | *Hierousalēm* | *dioti* | *ou* | *paradexontai* | *sou* |
| out of | Jerusalem, | because | not | they will receive | your |

18.a.**Txt:** 08E,020L 025P,byz.
**Var:** 01ℵ,02A,03B,Lach Treg,Tisc,We/Ho,Weis Sod,UBS/☆

| **3450.12** art acc sing fem | **3114.3** noun acc sing fem | **3875.1** prep | **1466.3** prs-pron gen 1sing | **2476.3** prs-pron nom |
|---|---|---|---|---|
| (a τὴν ) | μαρτυρίαν | περὶ | ἐμοῦ. | **19.** Κἀγὼ |
| *tēn* | *marturian* | *peri* | *emou* | *Kagō* |
| the | testimony | concerning | me. | And I |

| **1500.3** verb indic aor act | **2935.5** noun voc sing masc | **840.7** prs-pron nom pl masc | **1971.4** verb 3pl indic pres mid | **3617.1** conj | **1466.1** prs-pron nom 1sing |
|---|---|---|---|---|---|
| εἶπον, | Κύριε, | αὐτοὶ | ἐπίστανται, | ὅτι | ἐγὼ |
| *eipon* | *Kurie* | *autoi* | *epistantai* | *hoti* | *egō* |
| said, | Lord, | themselves | know | that | I |

| **1498.46** verb 1sing indic imperf mid | **5275.1** verb nom sing masc part pres act | **2504.1** conj | **1188.3** verb nom sing masc part pres act | **2567.3** prep |
|---|---|---|---|---|
| ἤμην | φυλακίζων | καὶ | δέρων | κατὰ |
| *ēmēn* | *phulakizōn* | *kai* | *derōn* | *kata* |
| was | imprisoning | and | beating | according to |

| **3450.15** art acc pl fem | **4715.7** noun acc pl fem | **3450.8** art acc pl masc | **3961.15** verb acc pl masc part pres act | **1894.3** prep | **4622.4** prs-pron acc 2sing |
|---|---|---|---|---|---|
| τὰς | συναγωγὰς | τοὺς | πιστεύοντας | ἐπὶ | σέ· |
| *tas* | *sunagōgas* | *tous* | *pisteuontas* | *epi* | *se* |
| the | synagogues | the | believing | on | you; |

20.a.**Txt:** 020L,025P,byz. Sod
**Var:** 01ℵ,02A,03B-org Lach,Treg,Alf,Tisc We/Ho,Weis,UBS/☆

| **2504.1** conj | **3616.1** conj | **1618.3** verb 3sing indic imperf mid | **1619.8** verb 3sing indic imperf mid | **3450.16** art sing neu |
|---|---|---|---|---|
| **20.** καὶ | ὅτε | ( ἐξεχεῖτο | [a☆ ἐξεχύννετο ] | τὸ |
| *kai* | *hote* | *execheito* | *exechunneto* | *to* |
| and | when | was being poured out | [ idem ] | the |

As Peter pointed out, the waters of baptism in and of themselves do not have the power to wash away sins (1 Peter 3:20,21). However, one must not underestimate the value God places on the act of baptism. Jesus himself said, "He that believeth and is baptized shall be saved" (Mark 16:16; cf. Matthew 28:18ff.). Paul also pointed to its importance when he assumed the disciples in Ephesus had been baptized (19:3). Elsewhere he taught that baptism relates the believer to Christ's redemptive work (Romans 6:3-6). Baptism, then, is intimately connected to calling upon Jesus by faith for forgiveness, that is, for the "washing away" of sin.

**22:17.** Paul skipped over the experiences he had in Damascus and told how he returned to Jerusalem. There, while praying in this very temple, he was in a trance. This was not a trance in the modern or heathen sense, but a state in which he felt an overwhelming astonishment; after all, he was in the very presence of Christ. This also shows Paul was not the polluter or defiler of the temple the Asian Jews were saying he was. He was treating it as God's house of prayer.

**22:18.** While Paul was in this state and as he continued to pray, he saw Jesus speaking to him and telling him to hurry out of Jerusalem, for the people of Jerusalem would not receive his witness to them.

This gives us some additional details beyond those already mentioned in chapter 9 which records how Paul spoke boldly to the Hellenistic Jews, probably in the same synagogues where Stephen had witnessed for Christ. The result was that they were making plans to kill him. So the Christians took him down to Caesarea and put him on a ship to Tarsus.

Now it is clear Paul did not go just because his fellow Christians in Jerusalem were afraid he might become another martyr like Stephen. Paul went with them because he had the command of Jesus. This warning from Jesus himself also drew attention to the fact that He is alive and knows what is going on here on earth.

**22:19.** Paul tried to argue that these Hellenistic Jews knew how he imprisoned and beat believers in every synagogue. That is, he systematically went through synagogue after synagogue, arresting, beating, and imprisoning the believers.

The Jewish believers all went to the synagogues on the Sabbath as their custom had been from childhood. Living in a community, they were part of its synagogue. The synagogue was the center of Jewish community life.

**22:20.** Paul argued further that they knew he was present at the violent death of Stephen. Though Stephen was stoned, Paul spoke of the shedding of his blood in order to emphasize the violence of

**calling on the name of the Lord:** . . . and invoke his name, *TCNT* . . . by calling on His name, *Williams* . . . as you call on his name, *Phillips* . . . having previously called, *Wuest* . . . by praying to him, *TEV* . . . at the invocation of his name, *Knox* . . . Do this, trusting in him to save you, *Everyday.*

**17. And it came to pass, that:** Then it came about that, *Norlie* . . . Later, *Everyday.*

**when I was come again to Jerusalem:** . . . when I had returned, *ASV.*

**even while I prayed in the temple:** I was praying, *Everyday.*

**I was in a trance:** . . . in an ecstasy, *Concordant* . . . I had a dream, *NLT* . . . I saw a vision, *Everyday, NCV.*

**18. And saw him saying unto me:** I saw Him and He said to me, *Weymouth* . . . saw the Lord saying, *Everyday.*

**Make haste:** Hurry, *Berkeley.*

**and get thee quickly out of Jerusalem:** . . . and leave Jerusalem at once, *Noli, TCNT* . . . leave Jerusalem quickly, *Weymouth* . . . leave Jerusalem with all speed, *Knox* . . . Leave...now! *Everyday, NCV.*

**for they will not receive thy testimony concerning me:** The people here will not accept the truth about me, *Everyday* . . . not accept thy witness, *Rotherham* . . . not accept the truth you tell about me, *Beck* . . . your evidence about me, *Moffatt.*

**19. And I said, Lord, they know:** I replied, *Weymouth* . . . it is within their own knowledge, *Knox.*

**that I imprisoned and beat in every synagogue them that believed on thee:** . . . how active I was in imprisoning, and flogging, *Weymouth* . . . I put the believers in jail and beat them, *Everyday* . . . and manhandled, *Berkeley* . . . and scourging, *Campbell* . . . I had them beaten, *NLT* . . . and scourge them, *Knox.*

**20. And when the blood of thy martyr Stephen was shed:** They also know that I was there when...your witness, was killed, *Everyday* . . . that when Stephen

| 129.1 noun sing neu | 4587.2 name gen masc | 3450.2 art gen sing | 3116.2 noun gen sing masc | 4622.2 prs-pron gen 2sing | 2504.1 conj |
|---|---|---|---|---|---|
| αἷμα | Στεφάνου | τοῦ | μάρτυρός | σου, | καὶ |
| *haima* | *Stephanou* | *tou* | *marturos* | *sou* | *kai* |
| blood | of Stephen | the | witness | your, | also |

| 840.5 prs-pron nom sing masc | 1498.46 verb 1sing indic imperf mid | 2168.9 verb nom sing masc part perf act | 2504.1 conj | 4759.4 verb nom sing masc part pres act |
|---|---|---|---|---|
| αὐτὸς | ἤμην | ἐφεστὼς | καὶ | συνευδοκῶν |
| *autos* | *ēmēn* | *ephestōs* | *kai* | *suneudokōn* |
| myself | was | standing by | and | consenting |

20.b.**Txt:** 020L,025P,byz. **Var:** 01ℵ,02A,03B,08E sa.bo.Gries,Lach,Treg Alf,Word,Tisc,We/Ho Weis,Sod,UBS/☆

| 3450.11 art dat sing fem | 334.1 noun dat sing fem | 840.3 prs-pron gen sing | 2504.1 conj | 5278.3 verb nom sing masc part pres act |
|---|---|---|---|---|
| ⸂b τῇ | ἀναιρέσει | αὐτοῦ,⸃ | καὶ | φυλάσσων |
| *tē* | *anairesei* | *autou* | *kai* | *phulassōn* |
| to the | putting to death | of him, | and | keeping |

| 3450.17 art pl neu | 2416.4 noun pl neu | 3450.1 art gen pl | 335.2 verb gen pl masc part pres act | 840.6 prs-pron acc sing masc |
|---|---|---|---|---|
| τὰ | ἱμάτια | τῶν | ἀναιρούντων | αὐτόν. |
| *ta* | *himatia* | *tōn* | *anairountōn* | *auton* |
| the | garments | of the | killing | him. |

| 2504.1 conj | 1500.5 verb 3sing indic aor act | 4242.1 prep | 1466.6 prs-pron acc 1sing | 4057.4 verb 2sing impr pres mid | 3617.1 conj |
|---|---|---|---|---|---|
| **21.** Καὶ | εἶπεν | πρός | με, | Πορεύου, | ὅτι |
| *Kai* | *eipen* | *pros* | *me* | *Poreuou* | *hoti* |
| And | he said | to | me, | Go, | for |

| 1466.1 prs-pron nom 1sing | 1519.1 prep | 1477.4 noun pl neu | 3084.1 adv | 1805.3 verb 1sing indic fut act | 4622.4 prs-pron acc 2sing |
|---|---|---|---|---|---|
| ἐγὼ | εἰς | ἔθνη | μακρὰν | ἐξαποστελῶ | σε. |
| *egō* | *eis* | *ethnē* | *makran* | *exapostelō* | *se* |
| I | to | Gentiles | afar off | will send forth | you. |

| 189.46 verb 3pl indic imperf act | 1156.2 conj | 840.3 prs-pron gen sing | 884.2 conj | 3642.1 dem-pron gen sing | 3450.2 art gen sing |
|---|---|---|---|---|---|
| **22.** Ἤκουον | δὲ | αὐτοῦ | ἄχρι | τούτου | τοῦ |
| *Ēkouon* | *de* | *autou* | *achri* | *toutou* | *tou* |
| They were hearing | and | him | until | this | the |

| 3030.2 noun gen sing masc | 2504.1 conj | 1854.3 verb 3pl indic aor act | 3450.12 art acc sing fem | 5292.4 noun acc sing fem | 840.1 prs-pron gen pl |
|---|---|---|---|---|---|
| λόγου, | καὶ | ἐπῆραν | τὴν | φωνὴν | αὐτῶν |
| *logou* | *kai* | *epēran* | *tēn* | *phōnēn* | *autōn* |
| word, | and | lifted up | the | voice | their, |

| 2978.16 verb nom pl masc part pres act | 142.4 verb 2sing impr pres act | 570.3 prep | 3450.10 art gen sing fem | 1087.2 noun gen sing fem | 3450.6 art acc sing masc |
|---|---|---|---|---|---|
| λέγοντες, | Αἶρε | ἀπὸ | τῆς | γῆς | τὸν |
| *legontes* | *Aire* | *apo* | *tēs* | *gēs* | *ton* |
| saying, | Away with | from | the | earth | the |

22.a.**Txt:** 05D-corr,Steph **Var:** 01ℵ,02A,03B 05D-org,08E,020L,025P byz.Gries,Lach,Treg,Alf Word,Tisc,We/Ho,Weis Sod,UBS/☆

| 4955.2 dem-pron sing | 3620.3 partic | 1056.1 conj | 2492.1 verb sing neu part pres act | 2492.3 verb 3sing indic imperf act | 840.6 prs-pron acc sing masc |
|---|---|---|---|---|---|
| τοιοῦτον· | οὐ | γὰρ | ⸀καθῆκον | [a☆ καθῆκεν ] | αὐτὸν |
| *toiouton* | *ou* | *gar* | *kathēkon* | *kathēken* | *auton* |
| such, | not | for | being fit | [ is fit ] | him |

23.a.**Txt:** 01ℵ,05D,08E 020L,025P,byz.bo.Tisc Sod **Var:** 02A,03B,04C,Lach Treg,Alf,Word,We/Ho Weis,UBS/☆

| 2180.19 verb inf pres act | 2878.1 verb gen pl masc part pres act | 1156.2 conj | 4885.1 conj | 840.1 prs-pron gen pl |
|---|---|---|---|---|
| ζῆν. | **23.** Κραυγαζόντων | ⸀δὲ | [a☆ τε ] | αὐτῶν, |
| *zēn* | *Kraugazontōn* | *de* | *te* | *autōn* |
| to live. | Crying out | and | [ idem ] | they, |

his death. He also spoke of Stephen as Christ's martyr. Marturos is translated "witness" about 29 times in the King James Version. "Witness" is the basic meaning, but in time, because so many died because of their Christian witness the word gained its technical sense of a martyr. But in New Testament times those who witnessed for Christ were risking their lives whether they were actually killed or not.

By telling this also, Paul wanted the audience in the temple court below to see that Jesus was patient with him, yet was still in control and knew what the situation really was.

**22:21.** Jesus knew Paul's reasoning was wrong. So He said again to him, "Depart." Paul was to leave Jerusalem at once.

Jesus made it clear to Paul, however, that He was not through with him just because he was stirring up so much opposition, or because his ministry was not successful in winning the thousands to the Lord as the rest of the apostles had been doing in that area. God had not changed His plan. Jesus would send Paul (as an apostle) far away to the Gentiles (the nations outside of Israel).

The emphasis here is not on Paul's leaving Jerusalem, but on the fact that Jesus was sending him out with a commission to reach the Gentiles with the gospel. Because Jesus was now his Lord, he could not disobey. Furthermore, the fact that Jesus sent him out with His commission made Paul an apostle. He was not one of the special group of 12 apostles Jesus first chose, and he never claimed to be. But he was personally sent out by Jesus and was therefore entitled to be called an apostle.

**22:22.** The Jews listened to Paul until he spoke of the command to go to the Gentiles. That God cares about the Gentiles is clear in the Old Testament. God's purpose in calling Abraham was to bring blessing to all the families of the earth (Genesis 12:3). Every time the promise was repeated to Abraham, Isaac, and Jacob, the same truth was reemphasized (Genesis 18:18; 22:18; 26:4; 28:14). Though two different forms of the verb are used in these passages, the context and the continued revelation of the promise confirm that God was promising blessing through the Seed of Abraham for all the peoples and nations of the earth.

However, Roman oppression had blinded the minds of these Jews who were listening to Paul. In their minds Gentiles were dogs, scavengers, as well as enemies of God. Thus, in their prejudice they went into an emotional tantrum and began crying out again for Paul's death. Referring to him scornfully as "such a fellow," they expressed their feeling that he was not worthy to live.

**22:23.** While the Jews were shouting out their demands for Paul's death, they were also throwing their outer garments around as an expression of their uncontrollable anger. The throwing off of their

your witness was put to death, *BB* . . . was poured out, *Swann.*

**I also was standing by, and consenting unto his death:** . . . even I myself, *Rotherham* . . . and well pleased, *HBIE* . . . I was there, giving approval, *BB* . . . I stood there and agreed, *Everyday* . . . endorsing it, *Concordant* . . . I myself was then Chief Justice, and gave the Decision, *Fenton* . . . agreed that they should kill him, *NCV.*

**and kept the raiment of them that slew him:** . . . and watched over the garments of, *Knox* . . . and took charge of the clothes of those who were murdering him, *TCNT* . . . I even held the coats of the men who were killing him! *Everyday* . . . was in charge of the garments of them who stoned him, *Lamsa* . . . the clothes of those who killed him, *KJII.*

**21. And he said unto me, Depart:** Go, *TCNT* . . . Leave, *Berkeley* . . . But the Lord said to me, *Everyday.*

**for I will send thee far hence unto the Gentiles:** . . . because I am to send you out and far away among the heathen, *Williams* . . . to a people who are not Jews, *Beck* . . . I mean to send thee on a distant errand, *Knox* . . . I will send you as my Apostle to the Gentiles all over the world, *Noli.*

**22. And they gave him audience unto this word:** Until they heard this, *Weymouth* . . . Till he said that, *Moffatt* . . . Up to this point the people had been listening to Paul, *TCNT.*

**and then lifted up their voices, and said:** . . . but now with a roar of disapproval they cried out, *Weymouth* . . . But at that they shouted, *Moffatt.*

**Away with such a fellow from the earth:** Kill him! *TCNT* . . . Down with him! *NEB* . . . Rid the world, *Beck.*

**for it is not fit that he should live:** A fellow like this ought not to have been allowed to live, *TCNT* . . . A scoundrel like that is better dead! *NEB* . . . it is a disgrace that he should live, *Knox.*

**23. And as they cried out:** They were howling, *Noli* . . . And when they continued their furious shouts, *Weymouth* . . . They kept on yelling, *Norlie.*

| 2504.1 conj | 4351.1 verb gen pl masc part pres act | 3450.17 art pl neu | 2416.4 noun pl neu | 2504.1 conj | 2840.1 noun acc sing masc |
|---|---|---|---|---|---|
| καὶ | ῥιπτούντων | τὰ | ἱμάτια, | καὶ | κονιορτὸν |
| *kai* | *rhiptountōn* | *ta* | *himatia* | *kai* | *koniorton* |
| and | casting off | the | garments, | and | dust |

| 900.7 verb gen pl masc part pres act | 1519.1 prep | 3450.6 art acc sing masc | 108.3 noun acc sing masc | 2724.3 verb 3sing indic aor act |
|---|---|---|---|---|
| βαλλόντων | εἰς | τὸν | ἀέρα, | **24.** ἐκέλευσεν |
| *ballontōn* | *eis* | *ton* | *aera* | *ekeleusen* |
| throwing | into | the | air, | commanded |

24.a.**Txt:** 020L,025P,byz.
**Var:** 01א,02A,03B,04C 05D,08E,bo.Gries,Lach Treg,Alf,Word,Tisc We/Ho,Weis,Sod UBS/☆

| 840.6 prs-pron acc sing masc | 3450.5 art nom sing masc | 5341.1 noun nom sing masc | 70.24 verb inf pres mid | 3450.5 art nom sing masc |
|---|---|---|---|---|
| ʻ αὐτὸν | ὁ | χιλίαρχος | ἄγεσθαι | [a☆ ὁ |
| *auton* | *ho* | *chiliarchos* | *agesthai* | *ho* |
| him | the | chief captain | to be brought | [ the |

| 5341.1 noun nom sing masc | 1507.6 verb inf pres mid | 840.6 prs-pron acc sing masc | 1519.1 prep | 3450.12 art acc sing fem |
|---|---|---|---|---|
| χιλίαρχος | εἰσάγεσθαι | αὐτὸν ] | εἰς | τὴν |
| *chiliarchos* | *eisagesthai* | *auton* | *eis* | *tēn* |
| chief captain | to be brought into | him ] | into | the |

24.b.**Txt:** 020L,025P,byz.
**Var:** 01א,02A,03B,04C 05D,08E,Lach,Treg,Alf Word,Tisc,We/Ho,Weis Sod,UBS/☆

| 3787.2 noun acc sing fem | 1500.15 verb nom sing masc part aor act | 1500.30 verb nom sing masc part aor act | 3120.3 noun dat pl fem |
|---|---|---|---|
| παρεμβολήν, | ʻ εἰπὼν | [b☆ εἴπας ] | μάστιξιν |
| *parembolēn* | *eipōn* | *eipas* | *mastixin* |
| barracks, | having said | [ idem ] | by whips |

| 424.2 verb inf pres mid | 840.6 prs-pron acc sing masc | 2419.1 conj | 1906.8 verb 3sing subj aor act | 1217.1 prep |
|---|---|---|---|---|
| ἀνετάζεσθαι | αὐτὸν, | ἵνα | ἐπιγνῷ | δι' |
| *anetazesthai* | *auton* | *hina* | *epignō* | *di'* |
| to be examined | him, | that | he might know | for |

| 3614.12 rel-pron acc sing fem | 155.3 noun acc sing fem | 3643.1 adv | 2003.2 verb 3pl indic imperf act | 840.4 prs-pron dat sing |
|---|---|---|---|---|
| ἣν | αἰτίαν | οὕτως | ἐπεφώνουν | αὐτῷ. |
| *hēn* | *aitian* | *houtōs* | *epephōnoun* | *autō* |
| what | cause | thus | they were crying out | against him. |

25.a.**Txt:** 025P,byz.
**Var:** 01א,03B,020L Gries,Lach,Treg,Alf Word,Tisc,We/Ho,Weis Sod,UBS/☆

| 5453.1 conj | 1156.2 conj | 4244.1 verb 3sing indic imperf act | 4244.2 verb 3pl indic aor act |
|---|---|---|---|
| **25.** ὡς | δὲ | ʻ προέτεινεν | [a☆ προέτειναν ] |
| *hōs* | *de* | *proeteinen* | *proeteinan* |
| As | but | he was stretching forward | [ they stretched forward ] |

| 840.6 prs-pron acc sing masc | 3450.4 art dat pl | 2414.2 noun dat pl masc | 1500.5 verb 3sing indic aor act | 4242.1 prep | 3450.6 art acc sing masc |
|---|---|---|---|---|---|
| αὐτὸν | τοῖς | ἱμᾶσιν | εἶπεν | πρὸς | τὸν |
| *auton* | *tois* | *himasin* | *eipen* | *pros* | *ton* |
| him | with the | thongs | said | to | the |

| 2449.25 verb part perf act | 1530.4 noun acc sing masc | 3450.5 art nom sing masc | 3834.1 name nom masc | 1479.1 conj |
|---|---|---|---|---|
| ἑστῶτα | ἑκατόνταρχον | ὁ | Παῦλος, | Εἰ |
| *hestōta* | *hekatontarchon* | *ho* | *Paulos* | *Ei* |
| standing by | centurion | | Paul, | If |

| 442.4 noun acc sing masc | 4371.2 name-adj acc sing masc | 2504.1 conj | 176.1 adj acc sing masc | 1815.1 verb 3sing indic pres act |
|---|---|---|---|---|
| ἄνθρωπον | Ῥωμαῖον | καὶ | ἀκατάκριτον | ἔξεστιν |
| *anthrōpon* | *Rhōmaion* | *kai* | *akatakriton* | *exestin* |
| a man | a Roman | and | uncondemned | it is lawful |

garments may also have expressed their desire to stone Paul for what they considered blasphemy, just as the elders threw off their garments when they stoned Stephen. At the same time, they threw dust in the air as a symbol of their rejection of Paul and his message. No doubt they would have thrown mud if it had been available. Prejudice continued to dominate them and kept them from searching the Scriptures to see if Paul's message was so, as the more noble Beroeans had done (17:11).

**22:24.** Because the Roman tribune was responsible to stop riots, he quickly brought Paul inside the fortress and undoubtedly barred the door against the mob. Because Paul was speaking in Hebrew and the shouts of the mob were in the same language, the tribune did not understand anything that was being said. Therefore he jumped to the conclusion that Paul must have said something terrible to stir up the mob to such violence again. He did not expect Paul to confess the truth about what he was saying, so he told the soldiers to examine him by scourging. That is, they were to question him while torturing him with a whip made of leather thongs with pieces of bone and metal sewn in them. This was a common type of Roman punishment, one to which Pilate had subjected Jesus (John 19:1).

**22:25.** Paul was no stranger to torture. He had already been whipped by Jews five times and beaten with rods by the Romans three times (2 Corinthians 11:24,25). But the punishment by a Roman scourge was far worse and often crippled or killed its victim. In Paul's condition, after having just been dragged by the Jews and nearly beaten by them, a scourging would have meant his death.

To prepare Paul for the scourging, the soldiers made him bend over and stretch forward. They bound him in that position with thongs, that is, with leather straps, to receive the flogging. (This was the more common way of preparing a victim for scourging. However, some writers believe what was done here was even more severe. They interpret this to mean Paul was hung up by the thongs so that his feet dangled a few inches above the floor of the fortress.)

At this point Paul stopped the proceedings. He had been rushed into the fortress, grabbed by the soldiers, and rushed off to wherever they were going to torture him. In the confusion, no one paid attention to anything he was trying to say. But now he was able to get the attention of the centurion who was standing there supervising the soldiers. Paul asked him if it was legal to scourge (whip, flog) a man who was a Roman citizen and uncondemned, that is, his case not even brought to trial.

Paul, of course, knew what they were doing was illegal. He had used his Roman citizenship to help him before. He was willing to suffer for the gospel's sake, but he never sought suffering when it could be avoided.

**and cast off their clothes:** . . . tearing off their clothes, *TCNT* . . . and tearing their mantles, *Rotherham* . . . and ripping their clothes, *Phillips* . . . throwing their clothes into the air, *Weymouth.*

**and threw dust into the air:** . . . and hurling dust into the air, *Phillips.*

**24. The chief captain commanded him to be brought into the castle:** . . . ordered Paul to be taken into the Fort, *TCNT* . . . into the army building, *BB.*

**and bade that he should be examined by scourging:** . . . and directed that he should be examined under the lash, *TCNT* . . . by flogging, *Williams* . . . to get information from Paul by whipping him, *Beck* . . . wanted to force Paul, *SEB* . . . saying that he would put him to the test by whipping, *BB.*

**that he might know:** . . . to tell him, *SEB* . . . that he might find out, *Rotherham* . . . in order to ascertain, *Weymouth* . . . to learn, *Montgomery.*

**wherefore they cried so against him:** . . . the reason for their outcry against him, *TCNT* . . . the reason for such an uproar, *Phillips* . . . exactly why they were shouting, *Adams* . . . they were thus clamoring him, *Worrell* . . . why the people were shouting against him like this, *SEB.*

**25. And as they bound him with thongs:** But when they had stretched him out with the straps, *Rotherham* . . . with the thongs, *Hanson* . . . But just as they had tied him up to be scourged, *TCNT* . . . with the straps (for the lash'), *Weymouth.*

**Paul said unto the centurion that stood by:** . . . standing near, *TCNT* . . . who was present, *BB.*

**Is it lawful for you to scourge a man that is a Roman:** Is it legal for you to scourge a Roman citizen, *TCNT* . . . Have you the right to scourge a man, when he is, *Knox.*

**and uncondemned?:** . . . and one who is uncondemned at that, *Williams* . . . unconvicted, *TCNT* . . . and that without a trial? *Confraternity* . . . not been proven guilty? *SEB* . . . when no one has said he is guilty? *NLT* . . . and has not been judged? *BB.*

| 5050.3 prs-pron dat 2pl | 3119.1 verb inf pres act | 189.31 verb nom sing masc part aor act | 1156.2 conj | 3450.5 art nom sing masc |
|---|---|---|---|---|
| ὑμῖν | μαστίζειν; | **26.** Ἀκούσας | δὲ | ὁ |
| *humin* | *mastizein* | *Akousas* | *de* | *ho* |
| for you | to whip? | Having heard | and | the |

| 1530.1 noun nom sing masc | 1529.1 noun nom sing masc | 4193.4 verb nom sing masc part aor act |
|---|---|---|
| ⸂ ἑκατοντάρχος, | [☆ ἑκατοντάρχης ] | προσελθὼν |
| *hekatontarchos* | *hekatontarchēs* | *proselthōn* |
| centurion, | [ idem ] | having gone |

| 514.7 verb 3sing indic aor act | 3450.3 art dat sing | 5341.2 noun dat sing masc | 3450.3 art dat sing | 5341.2 noun dat sing masc |
|---|---|---|---|---|
| ⸂ ἀπήγγειλεν | τῷ | χιλιάρχῳ | [☆ τῷ | χιλιάρχῳ |
| *apēngeilen* | *tō* | *chiliarchō* | *tō* | *chiliarchō* |
| he reported | to the | chief captain | [ to the | chief captain |

26.a.**Txt:** 05D,020L 025P,byz.sa. **Var:** p74,01ℵ,02A,03B 04C,08E,044,33,bo. Gries,Lach,Treg,Alf Word,Tisc,We/Ho,Weis Sod,UBS/☆

| 514.7 verb 3sing indic aor act | 2978.15 verb nom sing masc part pres act | 3571.5 verb 2sing impr pres act | 4949.9 intr-pron sing neu | 3165.2 verb 2sing indic pres act |
|---|---|---|---|---|
| ἀπήγγειλεν ] | λέγων, | ⸂a Ὅρα ⸃ | Τί | μέλλεις |
| *apēngeilen* | *legōn* | *Hora* | *Ti* | *melleis* |
| he reported ] | saying, | See | what | are you about |

| 4020.20 verb inf pres act | 3450.5 art nom sing masc | 1056.1 conj | 442.1 noun nom sing masc | 3642.4 dem-pron nom sing masc | 4371.1 name-adj nom sing masc |
|---|---|---|---|---|---|
| ποιεῖν; | ὁ | γὰρ | ἄνθρωπος | οὗτος | Ῥωμαῖός |
| *poiein* | *ho* | *gar* | *anthrōpos* | *houtos* | *Rhōmaios* |
| to do? | The | for | man | this | a Roman |

| 1498.4 verb 3sing indic pres act | 4193.4 verb nom sing masc part aor act | 1156.2 conj | 3450.5 art nom sing masc | 5341.1 noun nom sing masc |
|---|---|---|---|---|
| ἐστιν. | **27.** Προσελθὼν | δὲ | ὁ | χιλίαρχος |
| *estin* | *Proselthōn* | *de* | *ho* | *chiliarchos* |
| is. | Having come up | and | the | chief captain |

27.a.**Txt:** 020L,025P,byz. **Var:** 01ℵ,02A,03B,04C 05D,08E,bo.Gries,Lach Treg,Alf,Word,Tisc We/Ho,Weis,Sod UBS/☆

| 1500.5 verb 3sing indic aor act | 840.4 prs-pron dat sing | 2978.11 verb 2sing impr pres act | 1466.4 prs-pron dat 1sing | 1479.1 conj | 4622.1 prs-pron nom 2sing |
|---|---|---|---|---|---|
| εἶπεν | αὐτῷ, | Λέγε | μοι, | ⸂a εἰ ⸃ | σὺ |
| *eipen* | *autō* | *Lege* | *moi* | *ei* | *su* |
| said | to him, | Tell | me, | whether | you |

| 4371.1 name-adj nom sing masc | 1498.3 verb 2sing indic pres act | 3450.5 art nom sing masc | 1156.2 conj | 5183.4 verb 3sing indic act | 3346.1 intrj |
|---|---|---|---|---|---|
| Ῥωμαῖος | εἶ; | Ὁ | δὲ | ἔφη, | Ναί. |
| *Rhōmaios* | *ei* | *Ho* | *de* | *ephē* | *Nai* |
| a Roman | are? | The | and | said, | Yes. |

28.a.**Txt:** 025P,byz. **Var:** 01ℵ,03B,04C,08E bo.Lach,Treg,Tisc We/Ho,Weis,Sod UBS/☆

| 552.6 verb 3sing indic aor pass | 4885.1 conj | 1156.2 conj | 3450.5 art nom sing masc | 5341.1 noun nom sing masc |
|---|---|---|---|---|
| **28.** Ἀπεκρίθη | ⸂ τε | [a☆ δὲ ] | ὁ | χιλίαρχος, |
| *Apekrithē* | *te* | *de* | *ho* | *chiliarchos* |
| Answered | and | [ idem ] | the | chief captain, |

| 1466.1 prs-pron nom 1sing | 4044.2 adj gen sing | 2745.2 noun gen sing neu | 3450.12 art acc sing fem | 4034.2 noun acc sing fem |
|---|---|---|---|---|
| Ἐγὼ | πολλοῦ | κεφαλαίου | τὴν | πολιτείαν |
| *Egō* | *pollou* | *kephalaiou* | *tēn* | *politeian* |
| I | with a great | sum | the | citizenship |

| 3642.12 dem-pron acc sing fem | 2904.3 verb 1sing indic aor mid | 3450.5 art nom sing masc | 1156.2 conj | 3834.1 name nom masc | 5183.4 verb 3sing indic act |
|---|---|---|---|---|---|
| ταύτην | ἐκτησάμην. | Ὁ | δὲ | Παῦλος | ἔφη, |
| *tautēn* | *ektēsamēn* | *Ho* | *de* | *Paulos* | *ephē* |
| this | bought. | | And | Paul | said, |

**22:26.** As soon as the centurion heard Paul was a Roman citizen, he reported it to the tribune, warning him to be careful about what he was doing. The centurion could not rescind the order of the tribune on his own, for the tribune was his superior officer. But he could remind the tribune what was being done was by his orders and, therefore, he (the tribune) would be responsible.

The tribune (chief captain) in Greek, chiliarchos, means literally "the chief of 1,000 (soldiers)." But the title was used more broadly of the chief officer or commandant of a garrison or fortress, whether there were exactly 1,000 soldiers under him or not. In the same way, the centurion (hekatontarchēs) means "chief of 100 (soldiers)," but was used whether there were exactly 100 or not. Here the centurion stood by the soldiers who were preparing Paul for the scourging, even though it was probably a squad of four men who were doing the work.

Both the centurion and the tribune knew very well the rights of Roman citizens, as well as the penalties that would fall on them if they disregarded those rights. Valerian and Porcian laws provided that no judge or officer had the right to bind, scourge, or kill a Roman citizen without proper trial. At first this was by the decision of the general assembly of the citizens of Rome. Later the power was transferred to the emperor, to whom appeal could be made. All a person had to do to claim his rights was to say the words *I am a Roman citizen.* When Paul claimed his rights as a citizen, it was enough to stop the proceedings.

**22:27.** The tribune immediately went to Paul to ask if he was indeed a Roman citizen. He wanted to hear this for himself before he rescinded the order to scourge Paul. Without hesitation, Paul answered, "Yes!"

**22:28.** The tribune then remarked that he bought his Roman citizenship with a great sum of money. But Paul replied he was born a Roman citizen.

Originally the privileges of Roman citizenship were limited to the free people living in the city of Rome itself. Later, citizenship was extended to a number of Italian tribes and cities, then to most of Italy. Emperors kept adding to the places outside Italy that could have Roman citizenship. Often individuals who had rendered some outstanding service to the empire would also receive citizenship for themselves and their families. Paul's father, or grandfather, most probably was in this category because of some unusual service.

It was also possible to purchase Roman citizenship for money, even in towns and cities that had no special privileges otherwise. This selling of Roman citizenship was especially encouraged in the reign of the Emperor Claudius. His wife and other court favorites were allowed to do this, apparently as a means of lining their own pockets. This explains how the tribune gained his Roman citizenship. He probably bought his citizenship as a means of gaining a higher commission in the Roman army.

**26. When the centurion heard that:** On hearing this question, *Weymouth* . . . And hearing this, *KJII* . . . as soon as he heard this, *Knox* . . . When the officer heard, *SEB.*

**he went and told the chief captain, saying:** . . . went to the commander, *Everyday* . . . reported it, saying, *Worrell* . . . went to the colonel, *Goodspeed* . . . reported this statement to the tribune, *Noli* . . . and told him about it, *NCV* . . . and gave him an account of it, *BB.*

**Take heed what thou doest:** What are you intending to do? *Weymouth* . . . Be careful what you do, *Lamsa* . . . Do you know what you are doing? *NCV, TCNT* . . . Do you realize what you were about to do? *Phillips* . . . Listen! What are you doing? *NLT* . . . What art thou about? *Knox* . . . What are you about to do? *BB* . . . What do you propose to do? *Goodspeed.*

**for this man is a Roman:** This man is a Roman citizen, *TCNT.*

**27. Then the chief captain came, and said unto him:** Then the tribune came, *Noli* . . . commander came, *TNT* . . . going forward, *Worrell* . . . came to Paul and asked him, *Weymouth.*

**Tell me, art thou a Roman?:** Give me an answer, *BB* . . . are you really, *Everyday* . . . a Roman citizen? *TNT.*

**He said, Yea:** Yes, replied Paul, *TCNT* . . . He answered, Yes, *Everyday.*

**28. And the chief captain answered:** Whereupon the colonel replied, *Phillips* . . . The commander said, *Everyday.*

**With a great sum obtained I this freedom:** I had to pay a heavy price for my position as citizen, *TCNT* . . . I paid a large sum for this citizenship, *Weymouth* . . . I, for a great sum, acquired this citizenship, *Worrell* . . . I paid a lot of money to become a Roman, *Everyday* . . . I got Roman rights for myself at a great price, *BB* . . . I purchased this citizenship with, *Hanson* . . . I bought this citizenship at a great price, *Swann* . . . it cost me a heavy sum to win this privilege, *Knox* . . . I bought this citizenship with a great sum, *KJII* . . . a great sum of money to obtain this citizenship, *TNT.*

| 1466.1 prs-pron nom 1sing | 1156.2 conj | 2504.1 conj | 1074.22 verb 1sing indic perf mid | 2091.1 adv |
|---|---|---|---|---|
| Ἐγὼ | δὲ | καὶ | γεγέννημαι. | **29.** Εὐθέως |
| *Egō* | *de* | *kai* | *gegennēmai* | *Eutheōs* |
| I | but | even | have been born. | Immediately |

| 3631.1 partic | 861.3 verb 3pl indic aor act | 570.2 prep | 840.3 prs-pron gen sing | 3450.7 art nom pl masc | 3165.13 verb nom pl masc part pres act |
|---|---|---|---|---|---|
| οὖν | ἀπέστησαν | ἀπ' | αὐτοῦ | οἱ | μέλλοντες |
| *oun* | *apestēsan* | *ap'* | *autou* | *hoi* | *mellontes* |
| therefore | departed | from | him | the | being about |

| 840.6 prs-pron acc sing masc | 424.1 verb inf pres act | 2504.1 conj | 3450.5 art nom sing masc | 5341.1 noun nom sing masc | 1156.2 conj |
|---|---|---|---|---|---|
| αὐτὸν | ἀνετάζειν· | καὶ | ὁ | χιλίαρχος | δὲ |
| *auton* | *anetazein* | *kai* | *ho* | *chiliarchos* | *de* |
| him | to examine, | and | the | chief captain | also |

| 5236.12 verb 3sing indic aor pass | 1906.9 verb nom sing masc part aor act | 3617.1 conj | 4371.1 name-adj nom sing masc | 1498.4 verb 3sing indic pres act |
|---|---|---|---|---|
| ἐφοβήθη, | ἐπιγνοὺς | ὅτι | Ῥωμαῖός | ἐστιν, |
| *ephobēthē* | *epignous* | *hoti* | *Rhōmaios* | *estin* |
| was afraid, | having ascertained | that | a Roman | he is, |

| 2504.1 conj | 3617.1 conj | 1498.34 verb sing indic imperf act | 840.6 prs-pron acc sing masc | 840.6 prs-pron acc sing masc | 1498.34 verb sing indic imperf act |
|---|---|---|---|---|---|
| καὶ | ὅτι | ⸀ ἦν | αὐτὸν | [☆ αὐτὸν | ἦν ] |
| *kai* | *hoti* | *ēn* | *auton* | *auton* | *ēn* |
| and | because | he was | him | [ him | was ] |

| 1204.10 verb nom sing masc part perf act | 3450.11 art dat sing fem | 1156.2 conj | 1872.1 adv | 1007.8 verb nom sing masc part pres mid |
|---|---|---|---|---|
| δεδεκώς. | **30.** Τῇ | δὲ | ἐπαύριον | βουλόμενος |
| *dedekōs* | *Tē* | *de* | *epaurion* | *boulomenos* |
| having been bound. | The | and | next day, | desiring |

30.a.**Txt:** 020L,025P,byz.
**Var:** 01ℵ,02A,03B,04C
08E,Lach,Treg,Alf
Word,Tisc,We/Ho,Weis
Sod,UBS/☆

| 1091.29 verb inf aor act | 3450.16 art sing neu | 798.2 adj sing neu | 3450.16 art sing neu | 4949.9 intr-pron sing neu | 2693.13 verb 3sing indic pres mid |
|---|---|---|---|---|---|
| γνῶναι | τὸ | ἀσφαλὲς | τὸ | τί | κατηγορεῖται |
| *gnōnai* | *to* | *asphales* | *to* | *ti* | *katēgoreitai* |
| to know | the | certainty | the | what | he is being accused |

30.b.**Txt:** 020L,025P,byz.
**Var:** 01ℵ,02A,03B,04C
08E,sa.bo.Gries,Lach
Treg,Alf,Word,Tisc
We/Ho,Weis,Sod
UBS/☆

| 3706.2 prep | 5097.3 prep | 3450.1 art gen pl | 2428.3 name-adj gen pl masc | 3061.6 verb 3sing indic aor act |
|---|---|---|---|---|
| ⸀ παρὰ | [a☆ ὑπὸ ] | τῶν | Ἰουδαίων, | ἔλυσεν |
| *para* | *hupo* | *tōn* | *Ioudaiōn* | *elusen* |
| by | [ idem ] | the | Jews, | he loosed |

30.c.**Txt:** 020L,025P,byz.
bo.
**Var:** 01ℵ,02A,03B,04C
08E,sa.Gries,Lach,Treg
Alf,Word,Tisc,We/Ho
Weis,Sod,UBS/☆

| 840.6 prs-pron acc sing masc | 570.3 prep | 3450.1 art gen pl | 1193.4 noun gen pl | 2504.1 conj | 2724.3 verb 3sing indic aor act |
|---|---|---|---|---|---|
| αὐτόν | ⸂b ἀπὸ | τῶν | δεσμῶν, ⸃ | καὶ | ἐκέλευσεν |
| *auton* | *apo* | *tōn* | *desmōn* | *kai* | *ekeleusen* |
| him | from | the | bonds, | and | commanded |

30.d.**Txt:** 020L,025P,byz.
**Var:** 01ℵ,02A,03B,04C
08E,Gries,Lach,Treg
Alf,Word,Tisc,We/Ho
Weis,Sod,UBS/☆

| 2048.23 verb inf aor act | 4755.10 verb inf aor act | 3450.8 art acc pl masc | 744.5 noun pl masc | 2504.1 conj |
|---|---|---|---|---|
| ⸀ ἐλθεῖν | [c☆ συνελθεῖν ] | τοὺς | ἀρχιερεῖς | καὶ |
| *elthein* | *sunelthein* | *tous* | *archiereis* | *kai* |
| to come | [ to gather together ] | the | chief priests | and |

30.e.**Txt:** 020L,025P,byz.
**Var:** 01ℵ,02A,03B,04C
08E,sa.bo.Gries,Lach
Treg,Alf,Word,Tisc
We/Ho,Weis,Sod
UBS/☆

| 3513.1 adj sing | 3820.17 adj sing neu | 3450.16 art sing neu | 4742.1 noun sing neu | 840.1 prs-pron gen pl | 2504.1 conj |
|---|---|---|---|---|---|
| ⸀ ὅλον | [d☆ πᾶν ] | τὸ | συνέδριον | ⸂e αὐτῶν· ⸃ | καὶ |
| *holon* | *pan* | *to* | *sunedrion* | *autōn* | *kai* |
| whole | [ all ] | the | Sanhedrin | their, | and |

(Some older commentaries say the entire city of Tarsus was given Roman citizenship and that was how Paul's family became citizens, but the historical evidence is against this. Paul's father or grandfather must have gained citizenship as individuals.)

**22:29.** The soldiers who were about to question and torture Paul quickly left. The tribune also was afraid. He knew that Paul, as a Roman citizen, had a right to bring charges against him for even putting him in chains.

Paul seemed to take all this as part of the providence of God. He considered civil government to be ordained by God. He therefore accepted the responsibilities the government put upon him and claimed the rights and privileges that went with them. In this Paul set an example for all, and especially believers, with respect to both civic rights and civic duties.

Paul brought this out further in Romans 13:1-7. There he showed that every person is to subject himself of his own free will to the powers or authorities of the government he lives under. This is not a matter of expediency or of fear of the consequences of disobedience. Rather, it is because God has ordained that there be civil government, and therefore to resist government in a stubborn, obstinate way is to resist the ordinance of God. God is still on the throne of the universe, and He is the One who is in ultimate control, as Nebuchadnezzar found out when he had to live like an animal for seven seasons (Daniel 4:25,32,34-37; 5:18-22). Even where the government is not the best, it must be recognized that civil government is of God. Without it there would be nothing but anarchy, society would disintegrate, and in the confusion life would become more and more miserable for all.

Paul's admonition was given despite the fact that the Roman government could be oppressive and that the emperor at this very time was the infamous Nero.

**22:30.** The tribune kept Paul in custody, however, though probably without all the chains. He could not release Paul simply because Paul was a Roman citizen. As the representative of the Roman government, the tribune had the responsibility to try to keep peace in Jerusalem. He therefore had to give the Jews an opportunity to present their case.

Thus, the next day, because he wanted to know for sure why the Jews were accusing Paul, he brought him out, ordered the chief priests and the Sanhedrin to assemble, and made Paul stand up before them.

Actually, it was the Roman custom at this time to let the Jews settle religious matters among themselves. Authority in these matters was delegated to the Sanhedrin. If it had not been for the riot, the tribune would have turned Paul over to them and let them settle the matter. But because of his responsibility to keep the peace, he made them assemble in his presence.



**And Paul said, But I was free born:** I am one by birth, rejoined Paul, *TCNT* . . . But I was born a citizen, *HBIE* . . . Ah, said Paul, but I am a citizen by birth, *Knox.*

**29. Then straightway they departed from him which should have examined him:** The men who were to have examined Paul immediately drew back, *TCNT* . . . So the men who had been on the point of judicially examining him immediately left him, *Weymouth* . . . Then those who were about to scourge him, *Montgomery* . . . moved away from him, *Weymouth* . . . kept their hands off, *Berkeley* . . . intending to scourge him, fled from him, *Murdock* . . . going to torture him left him, *Confraternity* . . . The men who were preparing to torture Paul, *SEB* . . . immediately departed from him, *Hanson.*

**and the chief captain also was afraid:** . . . was struck with fear, *Rotherham* . . . felt worried, *Berkeley* . . . the captain himself was alarmed, to find out, *Knox* . . . was frightened, *NCV.*

**after he knew that he was a Roman:** . . . when he found out, *Rotherham* . . . finding that Paul was a Roman citizen, *TCNT* . . . on discovering that, *Berkeley.*

**and because he had bound him:** . . . especially since he had him bound, *Norlie* . . . had stretched him (for scourging), *Murdock* . . . strapped him for the lash, *ET* . . . because he had already tied Paul up, *NCV.*

**30. On the morrow:** On the next day, *TCNT.*

**because he would have known the certainty:** . . . wishing to find out the real reason, *TCNT* . . . wishing to know exactly, *Weymouth.*

**wherefore he was accused of the Jews:** . . . as to why he was being accused by the Jews, *Rotherham* . . . why Paul was denounced by the Jews, *TCNT.*

**he loosed him from his bands:** . . . released him, *Rotherham* . . . had his chains taken off, *TCNT.*

**and commanded the chief priests and all their council to appear:** . . . to come together, *ASV* . . . to assemble, *Alford, Hanson* . . . to gather for their court, *NLT.*

| **2580.4** verb nom sing masc part aor act | **3450.6** art acc sing masc | **3834.4** name acc masc | **2449.4** verb 3sing indic aor act | **1519.1** prep |
|---|---|---|---|---|
| καταγαγὼν | τὸν | Παῦλον | ἔστησεν | εἰς |
| *katagagōn* | *ton* | *Paulon* | *estēsen* | *eis* |
| having brought down | | Paul | he placed | among |

| **840.8** prs-pron acc pl masc | **810.3** verb nom sing masc part aor act | **1156.2** conj | **3450.5** art nom sing masc | **3834.1** name nom masc |
|---|---|---|---|---|
| αὐτούς. | **23:1.** Ἀτενίσας | δὲ | ὁ | Παῦλος |
| *autous* | *Atenisas* | *de* | *ho* | *Paulos* |
| them. | Having looked intently | and | | Paul |

| **3450.3** art dat sing | **4742.3** noun dat sing neu | **1500.5** verb 3sing indic aor act | **433.6** noun nom pl masc | **79.6** noun nom pl masc |
|---|---|---|---|---|
| τῷ | συνεδρίῳ | εἶπεν, | Ἄνδρες | ἀδελφοί, |
| *tō* | *sunedriō* | *eipen* | *Andres* | *adelphoi* |
| on the | Sanhedrin | said, | Men | brothers, |

| **1466.1** prs-pron nom 1sing | **3820.11** adj dat sing fem | **4743.3** noun dat sing fem | **18.11** adj dat sing fem | **4036.2** verb 1sing indic perf mid |
|---|---|---|---|---|
| ἐγὼ | πάσῃ | συνειδήσει | ἀγαθῇ | πεπολίτευμαι |
| *egō* | *pasē* | *suneidēsei* | *agathē* | *pepoliteumai* |
| I | in all | conscience | good | have conducted myself |

| **3450.3** art dat sing | **2296.3** noun dat sing masc | **884.2** conj | **3642.10** dem-pron gen sing fem | **3450.10** art gen sing fem | **2232.1** noun fem |
|---|---|---|---|---|---|
| τῷ | θεῷ | ἄχρι | ταύτης | τῆς | ἡμέρας. |
| *tō* | *theō* | *achri* | *tautēs* | *tēs* | *hēmeras* |
| | toward God | unto | this | the | day. |

| **3450.5** art nom sing masc | **1156.2** conj | **744.1** noun nom sing masc | **366.4** name nom masc | **1988.5** verb 3sing indic aor act | **3450.4** art dat pl |
|---|---|---|---|---|---|
| **2.** Ὁ | δὲ | ἀρχιερεὺς | Ἁνανίας | ἐπέταξεν | τοῖς |
| *Ho* | *de* | *archiereus* | *Hananias* | *epetaxen* | *tois* |
| The | but | high priest | Ananias | ordered | the |

| **3798.20** verb dat pl masc part perf act | **840.4** prs-pron dat sing | **5021.3** verb inf pres act | **840.3** prs-pron gen sing | **3450.16** art sing neu | **4601.1** noun sing neu |
|---|---|---|---|---|---|
| παρεστῶσιν | αὐτῷ | τύπτειν | αὐτοῦ | τὸ | στόμα. |
| *parestōsin* | *autō* | *tuptein* | *autou* | *to* | *stoma* |
| standing by | him | to strike | his | the | mouth. |

| **4966.1** adv | **3450.5** art nom sing masc | **3834.1** name nom masc | **4242.1** prep | **840.6** prs-pron acc sing masc | **1500.5** verb 3sing indic aor act |
|---|---|---|---|---|---|
| **3.** τότε | ὁ | Παῦλος | πρὸς | αὐτὸν | εἶπεν, |
| *tote* | *ho* | *Paulos* | *pros* | *auton* | *eipen* |
| Then | | Paul | to | him | said, |

| **5021.3** verb inf pres act | **4622.4** prs-pron acc 2sing | **3165.3** verb 3sing indic pres act | **3450.5** art nom sing masc | **2296.1** noun nom sing masc |
|---|---|---|---|---|
| Τύπτειν | σε | μέλλει | ὁ | θεός, |
| *Tuptein* | *se* | *mellei* | *ho* | *theos* |
| To strike | you | is about | | God, |

| **4956.1** noun voc sing masc | **2839.1** verb voc sing masc part perf mid | **2504.1** conj | **4622.1** prs-pron nom 2sing | **2493.2** verb 2sing indic pres mid |
|---|---|---|---|---|
| τοῖχε | κεκονιαμένε· | καὶ | σὺ | κάθῃ |
| *toiche* | *kekoniamene* | *kai* | *su* | *kathē* |
| wall | having been whitened. | And | you | sit |

| **2892.8** verb nom sing masc part pres act | **1466.6** prs-pron acc 1sing | **2567.3** prep | **3450.6** art acc sing masc | **3414.4** noun acc sing masc | **2504.1** conj |
|---|---|---|---|---|---|
| κρίνων | με | κατὰ | τὸν | νόμον, | καὶ |
| *krinōn* | *me* | *kata* | *ton* | *nomon* | *kai* |
| judging | me | according to | the | law, | and |

The Sanhedrin (*sunedrion*) had a long history behind it. Persians granted the Jews authority over their own affairs. When the Persian Empire fell, a governing body arose which was called the *gerousia* (senate). The Romans around 57 B.C. divided Judea into five districts, each governed by a *sunedrion* (assembly). But in A.D. 47 the emperor gave the *sunedrion* (or as the Jews pronounced it, the Sanhedrin) of Jerusalem authority over all Judea. After A.D. 6, under Roman procurators, the Sanhedrin's powers were increased and extended even beyond Judea. Seventy of its members were elders whose Jewish descent was pure and unquestionable.

Verse 30 actually begins the sequence that continues in chapter 23 and thus really belongs with that chapter.

**23:1.** Paul must have understood what he was facing. Some believe he had once been a member of the Sanhedrin and had cast his vote to stone Stephen. Now he stood before them as an accused prisoner.

Paul, however, showed no fear or hesitation. He knew he was in the will of the Lord, and he had learned to depend on the Holy Spirit to guide him and give him the words to say. Fixing his eyes on the council, he began to speak with deep earnestness and yet with friendliness, addressing them as brethren. He still felt a kinship with his brethren or kinsmen in the flesh.

Now Paul declared he had lived his life (and fulfilled his duties) before God with all good conscience up to that day. (See 1 Corinthians 4:4; Philippians 3:6,9.)

**23:2.** Paul's declaration that he was not guilty of any of the charges brought against him infuriated the high priest Ananias. He ordered his attendants who were standing beside him to strike Paul on the mouth, probably as a rebuke for blasphemy.

Some believe Ananias thought Paul arrogant for calling the Sanhedrin his brothers. Others believe Ananias thought Paul was lying. Most probably, it was his own guilty conscience that made Ananias act as he did. This Ananias was well-known as an unscrupulous, grasping politician. He had been appointed about 9 years earlier through political influence. He ruled like a tyrant and, according to the Jewish Talmud, was also a terrible glutton. Such a man as he could not believe anyone could live with a clear conscience before God.

**23:3.** Paul reacted to this immediately because his sense of justice was aroused. This unwarranted and illegal blow on the mouth caused him to say to the high priest, "God will strike you, you whitewashed wall" (TCNT). Whitewash was used to cover over dirt and filth, so this was a strong rebuke.

The elders who were members of the Sanhedrin were sitting there to judge him according to the Law. The Law treated a man as innocent until he was proven guilty. Nevertheless, some today

**and brought Paul down:** . . . and took, *TCNT* . . . he brought Paul out, *Everyday.*

**and set him before them:** . . . and brought him before them, *TCNT* . . . to face them, *Berkeley* . . . and stood him before their meeting, *Everyday, NCV* . . . and set him among them, *KJII.*

**1. And Paul, earnestly beholding the council, said:** Then Paul, fixing a steady gaze on the Sanhedrin, said, *Weymouth* . . . looking steadfastly, *ASV* . . . looking intently, *HBIE* . . . Paul looked straight at the council members and said, *Norlie* . . . With a stedfast gaze, *Montgomery.*

**Men and brethren:** My brothers, *BB* . . . Fellow Jews, *Beck.*

**I have lived in all good conscience before God until this day:** I in all good conscience have used my citizenship for God, *Rotherham* . . . for my part, I have always ordered my life before God, with a clear conscience, up to this very day, *TCNT* . . . I have lived my life in a good way before God up to this day, *Everyday* . . . in the presence of God with an altogether clear conscience, *Berkeley* . . . my life has been upright before God, *BB* . . . with a heart that has said I am not guilty to this day, *NLT.*

**2. And the high priest Ananias commanded them that stood by him:** At this...ordered the men standing near, *TCNT* . . . On hearing this ordered those who were standing near Paul, *Weymouth* . . . ordered the attendants, *Berkeley.*

**to smite him on the mouth:** . . . to strike him, *RSV* . . . to give him a blow, *BB.*

**3. Then said Paul unto him:** . . . to Ananias, *Everyday.*

**God shall smite thee:** God will strike you, *TCNT* . . . God is about to slap you, *Klingensmith.*

**thou whited wall:** You whited sepulcher, *Montgomery* . . . you whitewashed wall! *TCNT* . . . you painted pigpen, *LivB.*

**for sittest thou to judge me after the law:** How dare you, *Phillips* . . . Are you sitting there to try me in accordance with law, *TCNT* . . . Yet in defiance of the Law, *Noli* . . . Do you sit as a judge to try me, *Williams.*

## Acts 23:4

| 3752.1 verb nom sing masc part pres act | 2724.1 verb 2sing indic pres act | 1466.6 prs-pron acc 1sing | 5021.6 verb inf pres mid | 3450.7 art nom pl masc | 1156.2 conj |
|---|---|---|---|---|---|
| παρανομῶν | κελεύεις | με | τύπτεσθαι; | 4. οἱ | δὲ |
| *paranomōn* | *keleueis* | *me* | *tuptesthai* | *hoi* | *de* |
| contrary to law | command | me | to be struck? | The | but |

4.a.**Txt:** 02A,04C,08E 020L,025P,etc.byz.Sod
**Var:** 01ℵ,03B,Treg,Tisc We/Ho,Weis,UBS/☆

| 3798.17 verb nom pl masc part perf act | 1500.3 verb indic aor act | 1500.28 verb 3pl indic aor act | 3450.6 art acc sing masc | 744.4 noun acc sing masc |
|---|---|---|---|---|
| παρεστῶτες | ʼ εἶπον, | [a☆ εἶπαν, ] | Τὸν | ἀρχιερέα |
| *parestōtes* | *eipon* | *eipan* | *Ton* | *archierea* |
| standing by | said, | [ idem ] | The | high priest |

| 3450.2 art gen sing | 2296.2 noun gen sing masc | 3032.1 verb 2sing indic pres act | 5183.4 verb 3sing indic act | 4885.1 conj | 3450.5 art nom sing masc |
|---|---|---|---|---|---|
| τοῦ | θεοῦ | λοιδορεῖς; | 5. Ἔφη | τε | ὁ |
| *tou* | *theou* | *loidoreis* | *Ephē* | *te* | *ho* |
| | of God | are you insulting? | Said | and | |

| 3834.1 name nom masc | 3620.2 partic | 3471.9 verb 1sing indic plperf act | 79.6 noun nom pl masc | 3617.1 conj | 1498.4 verb 3sing indic pres act |
|---|---|---|---|---|---|
| Παῦλος, | Οὐκ | ᾔδειν, | ἀδελφοί, | ὅτι | ἐστὶν |
| *Paulos* | *Ouk* | *ēdein* | *adelphoi* | *hoti* | *estin* |
| Paul, | Not | I was conscious, | brothers, | that | he is |

5.a.**Var:** 01ℵ,02A,03B Treg,Alf,Tisc,We/Ho Weis,Sod,UBS/☆

| 744.1 noun nom sing masc | 1119.22 verb 3sing indic perf mid | 1056.1 conj | 3617.1 conj | 752.4 noun acc sing masc |
|---|---|---|---|---|
| ἀρχιερεύς· | γέγραπται | γὰρ | [a☆+ ὅτι ] | Ἄρχοντα |
| *archiereus* | *gegraptai* | *gar* | *hoti* | *Archonta* |
| a high priest; | it has been written | for, | [ that ] | A ruler |

| 3450.2 art gen sing | 2967.2 noun gen sing masc | 4622.2 prs-pron gen 2sing | 3620.2 partic | 2029.10 verb 2sing indic fut act | 2532.1 adv |
|---|---|---|---|---|---|
| τοῦ | λαοῦ | σου | οὐκ | ἐρεῖς | κακῶς. |
| *tou* | *laou* | *sou* | *ouk* | *ereis* | *kakōs* |
| of the | people | your | not | you shall speak of | evilly. |

| 1091.26 verb nom sing masc part aor act | 1156.2 conj | 3450.5 art nom sing masc | 3834.1 name nom masc | 3617.1 conj | 3450.16 art sing neu |
|---|---|---|---|---|---|
| 6. Γνοὺς | δὲ | ὁ | Παῦλος | ὅτι | τὸ |
| *Gnous* | *de* | *ho* | *Paulos* | *hoti* | *to* |
| Having known | but | | Paul | that | the |

| 1518.9 num card neu | 3183.1 noun sing neu | 1498.4 verb 3sing indic pres act | 4380.2 name gen pl masc | 3450.16 art sing neu |
|---|---|---|---|---|
| ἓν | μέρος | ἐστὶν | Σαδδουκαίων | τὸ |
| *hen* | *meros* | *estin* | *Saddoukaiōn* | *to* |
| one | part | consists | of Sadducees | the |

6.a.**Txt:** 02A,08E,020L 025P,byz.sa.bo.
**Var:** 01ℵ,03B,04C,Treg Alf,Tisc,We/Ho,Weis Sod,UBS/☆

| 1156.2 conj | 2066.1 adj sing | 5168.5 name gen pl masc | 2869.11 verb 3sing indic aor act | 2869.17 verb 3sing indic imperf act |
|---|---|---|---|---|
| δὲ | ἕτερον | Φαρισαίων | ʼ ἔκραξεν | [a☆ ἔκραζεν ] |
| *de* | *heteron* | *Pharisaiōn* | *ekraxen* | *ekrazen* |
| and | other | of Pharisees | cried out | [ was crying out ] |

| 1706.1 prep | 3450.3 art dat sing | 4742.3 noun dat sing neu | 433.6 noun nom pl masc | 79.6 noun nom pl masc |
|---|---|---|---|---|
| ἐν | τῷ | συνεδρίῳ, | Ἄνδρες | ἀδελφοί, |
| *en* | *tō* | *sunedriō* | *Andres* | *adelphoi* |
| in | the | Sanhedrin, | Men | brothers, |

| 1466.1 prs-pron nom 1sing | 5168.1 name nom sing masc | 1498.2 verb 1sing indic pres act | 5048.1 noun nom sing masc | 5168.2 name gen sing masc |
|---|---|---|---|---|
| ἐγὼ | Φαρισαῖός | εἰμι, | υἱὸς | ʼ Φαρισαίου· |
| *egō* | *Pharisaios* | *eimi* | *huios* | *Pharisaiou* |
| I | a Pharisee | am, | son | of a Pharisee: |

believe Paul's indignation here was a failure in self-control. Others see it as justified anger without sin (Ephesians 4:26).

**23:4.** Those who had struck Paul immediately rebuked him for reviling (abusing, insulting) God's high priest. They felt his office deserved respect since God had instituted the high priesthood.

**23:5.** Paul was quick to take the humble place and apologize, for he too recognized the man's position was given honor by the Scriptures regardless of whether the man himself deserved it or not (Exodus 22:28; Deuteronomy 17:8-13).

It is not clear why Paul did not recognize Ananias as the high priest. Some believe on the basis of Galatians 6:11 that Paul had weak eyesight, but there he was emphasizing his own handwriting so the Galatians could recognize it as genuine and not a forgery.

Actually, Paul had no occasion to see this high priest before this time. Ananias was made high priest in A.D. 47 by Herod of Chalcis. Paul had been in Jerusalem since then only a few times and for short periods, so it is not strange he had never before seen this high priest. It is probable also that since the tribune had assembled the Sanhedrin on this occasion, the high priest was sitting among the other members of the court instead of presiding.

Actually, Paul's prediction was carried out. Ananias was deposed a little over a year later. Then in A.D. 66 Jewish zealots assassinated him as pro-Roman.

**23:6.** At this point Paul realized there was an issue he could declare. As he already knew, but now noticed again, part of the Sanhedrin were Sadducees, part Pharisees. The Sadducees were a party made up mostly of powerful priestly families who were aristocrats and who had been influenced by Greek culture and philosophy. They put emphasis on the written laws of the Pentateuch, ignored the rest of the Old Testament, and rejected the traditions of the Pharisees. They denied the resurrection, the afterlife, and any future rewards or punishments.

The Pharisees were a minority party which arose during the time of the Hasmonaeans (Maccabees) in the Second Century B.C. They believed temple worship was not enough and said the individual must fulfill the Law. By their traditions they often modified the Law to meet conditions not expressly mentioned. They claimed to make religion ethical rather than theological, and they believed God overruled in all acts, even in those which seemed to come from man's free will. They also taught the immortality of the soul and believed the hope of the resurrection was fundamental to the hope of Israel.

Paul therefore took advantage of the situation with courage. It was an opportunity to witness to the truth of the resurrection and to the fact of the resurrection of Jesus. He was not out of order.



**and commandest me to be smitten contrary to the law?:** . . . and yet, in defiance of law, order them to strike me, *TCNT* . . . and you yourself break the Law by ordering me to be struck! *Weymouth* . . . and give orders for me to be struck, which is clean contrary to the Law, *Phillips* . . . to be beaten illegally! *Concordant* . . . yet you are telling them to hit me, *SEB* . . . and that is against the law, *Everyday.*

**4. And they that stood by said:** The bystanders objected, *Norlie* . . . The men standing near Paul said to him, *Everyday.*

**Revilest thou God's high priest?:** Do rail at, *Weymouth* . . . Do you revile, *Worrell* . . . Do you dare to insult, *Phillips* . . . Is that the way to talk to, *LivB* . . . Do you slander, *Klingensmith, KJII* . . . Do you know that you are insulting God's High Priest, *TCNT* . . . Are you reproaching, *Swann* . . . You must not talk like that to, *SEB.*

**5. Then said Paul:** Paul answered, *Williams.*

**I wist not, brethren, that he was the high priest:** I knew not, *ASV* . . . I was not aware, *Rotherham* . . . I had no idea that, *BB.*

**for it is written:** . . . after all, *Adams* . . . for Scripture says, *TCNT* . . . The Bible does say, *Beck.*

**Thou shalt not speak evil of the ruler of thy people:** You must not defame a ruler of the people, *Berkeley.*

**6. But when Paul perceived:** But when Paul saw, *BB* . . . was well aware, *JB* . . . As Paul knew, *Klingensmith.*

**that the one part was Sadducees, and the other Pharisees:** . . . that some of those present were Sadducees and other Pharisees, *TCNT* . . . that the Sanhedrin consisted partly of Sadducees and partly of Pharisees, *Weymouth* . . . were Liberals and part Orthodox, *Klingensmith.*

**he cried out in the council:** . . . shouted, right in the Sanhedrin, *Berkeley* . . . raised his voice and said to them, *Phillips.*

**Men and brethren, I am a Pharisee, the son of a Pharisee:** . . . and my father was a Pharisee! *Everyday.*

# Acts 23:7

6.b.**Txt:** 08E,020L,025P byz.sa.bo.
**Var:** 01ℵ,02A,03B,04C Lach,Treg,Alf,Word Tisc,We/Ho,Weis,Sod UBS/☆

| **5168.5** name gen pl masc | **3875.1** prep | **1667.2** noun gen sing fem | **2504.1** conj | **384.2** noun gen sing fem |
|---|---|---|---|---|
| [[b]☆ Φαρισαίων˙ ] | περὶ | ἐλπίδος | καὶ | ἀναστάσεως |
| *Pharisaiōn* | *peri* | *elpidos* | *kai* | *anastaseōs* |
| [ of Pharisees: ] | concerning | a hope | and | resurrection |

6.c.**Txt:** 01ℵ,02A,04C 08E,020L,025P,etc.byz. Tisc
**Var:** 03B,sa.bo.We/Ho Weis,Sod,UBS/☆

| **3361.2** adj gen pl | **1466.1** prs-pron nom 1sing | **2892.28** verb 1sing indic pres mid | **3642.17** dem-pron sing neu | **1156.2** conj | **840.3** prs-pron gen sing |
|---|---|---|---|---|---|
| νεκρῶν | ⸂[c] ἐγὼ ⸃ | κρίνομαι. | 7. Τοῦτο | δὲ | αὐτοῦ |
| *nekrōn* | *egō* | *krinomai* | *Touto* | *de* | *autou* |
| of dead | I | am judged. | This | and | him |

7.a.**Txt:** 04C,020L,025P 044,byz.Tisc
**Var1:** 03B
**Var2:** p74,01ℵ,02A,08E 323,1739,2464,UBS/☆

| **2953.35** verb gen sing masc part aor act | **2953.13** verb gen sing masc part pres act | **1500.16** verb gen sing masc part aor act | **1090.33** verb 3sing indic aor mid |
|---|---|---|---|
| ⸀ λαλήσαντος | [[1a] λαλοῦντος | [2]☆ εἰπόντος ] | ἐγένετο |
| *lalēsantos* | *lalountos* | *eipontos* | *egeneto* |
| having spoken | [ speaking | having spoken ] | there was |

7.b.**Txt:** 020L,byz.
**Var:** 01ℵ,02A,03B,04C 08E,Lach,Treg,Alf Word,Tisc,We/Ho,Weis Sod,UBS/☆

| **4565.1** noun nom sing fem | **3450.1** art gen pl | **5168.5** name gen pl masc | **2504.1** conj | **3450.1** art gen pl | **4380.2** name gen pl masc |
|---|---|---|---|---|---|
| στάσις | τῶν | Φαρισαίων | καὶ | ⸂[b] τῶν ⸃ | Σαδδουκαίων, |
| *stasis* | *tōn* | *Pharisaiōn* | *kai* | *tōn* | *Saddoukaiōn* |
| a dissension | of the | Pharisees | and | the | Sadducees, |

| **2504.1** conj | **4829.4** verb 3sing indic aor pass | **3450.16** art sing neu | **3988.1** noun sing neu | **4380.1** name nom pl masc |
|---|---|---|---|---|
| καὶ | ἐσχίσθη | τὸ | πλῆθος˙ | 8. Σαδδουκαῖοι |
| *kai* | *eschisthē* | *to* | *plēthos* | *Saddoukaioi* |
| and | was divided | the | multitude. | Sadducees |

8.a.**Txt:** 01ℵ,02A,04C 08E,020L,025P,etc.byz. bo.Tisc,Sod
**Var:** 03B,sa.Lach,We/Ho Weis,UBS/☆

| **3173.1** conj | **1056.1** conj | **2978.3** verb 3pl indic pres act | **3231.1** partic | **1498.32** verb inf pres act | **384.4** noun acc sing fem |
|---|---|---|---|---|---|
| ⸂[a] μὲν ⸃ | γὰρ | λέγουσιν | μὴ | εἶναι | ἀνάστασιν |
| *men* | *gar* | *legousin* | *mē* | *einai* | *anastasin* |
| on the one hand | for | say | not | to be | resurrection |

8.b.**Txt:** 020L,025P,byz.
**Var:** 01ℵ,02A,03B,04C 08E,Lach,Treg,Alf Word,Tisc,We/Ho,Weis Sod,UBS/☆

| **3234.1** adv | **3250.1** conj | **32.4** noun acc sing masc | **3250.1** conj | **4011.1** noun sing neu | **5168.4** name nom pl masc |
|---|---|---|---|---|---|
| ⸀ μηδὲ | [[b]☆ μήτε ] | ἄγγελον | μήτε | πνεῦμα˙ | Φαρισαῖοι |
| *mēde* | *mēte* | *angelon* | *mēte* | *pneuma* | *Pharisaioi* |
| nor | [ idem ] | angel | nor | spirit; | Pharisees |

| **1156.2** conj | **3533.3** verb 3pl indic pres act | **3450.17** art pl neu | **295.4** adj pl neu |
|---|---|---|---|
| δὲ | ὁμολογοῦσιν | τὰ | ἀμφότερα. |
| *de* | *homologousin* | *ta* | *amphotera* |
| but on the other hand | confess | the | both. |

| **1090.33** verb 3sing indic aor mid | **1156.2** conj | **2879.1** noun nom sing fem | **3144.9** adj nom sing fem | **2504.1** conj | **448.11** verb nom pl masc part aor act |
|---|---|---|---|---|---|
| 9. ἐγένετο | δὲ | κραυγὴ | μεγάλη˙ | καὶ | ἀναστάντες |
| *egeneto* | *de* | *kraugē* | *megalē* | *kai* | *anastantes* |
| There was | and | an uproar | great, | and | having risen up |

9.a.**Txt:** byz.
**Var:** 01ℵ,03B,04C,sa. Treg,Alf,Tisc,We/Ho Weis,Sod,UBS/☆

| **3450.7** art nom pl masc | **1116.2** noun pl masc | **4948.7** indef-pron nom pl masc | **3450.1** art gen pl | **1116.3** noun gen pl masc |
|---|---|---|---|---|
| ⸀ οἱ | γραμματεῖς | [[a]☆ τινὲς | τῶν | γραμματέων ] |
| *hoi* | *grammateis* | *tines* | *tōn* | *grammateōn* |
| the | scribes | [ some | of the | scribes ] |

| **3450.2** art gen sing | **3183.2** noun gen sing neu | **3450.1** art gen pl | **5168.5** name gen pl masc | **1258.1** verb 3pl indic imperf mid |
|---|---|---|---|---|
| τοῦ | μέρους | τῶν | Φαρισαίων | διεμάχοντο |
| *tou* | *merous* | *tōn* | *Pharisaiōn* | *diemachonto* |
| of the | part | of the | Pharisees | they were contending, |

Some believe Paul can be criticized for seizing on the controversy between the Pharisees and Sadducees to divert attention from himself. They say it was a mere stratagem, ducking the blow, avoiding the issue. However, Paul saw that the truth, not his own personal safety, was the real issue at stake.

Even before his conversion, as a Pharisee Paul realized how deep and important the doctrine of the future resurrection is. Crying out that he was a Pharisee, the son of Pharisees, he declared it was with respect to the hope and resurrection of the dead that he was being called into question.

**23:7.** Paul's declaration split the Sanhedrin into two camps. As they talked to one another, the discord grew. Ordinarily they avoided this issue when they met together.

**23:8.** Actually, the chief thing the Sadducees denied was personal immortality. Like some of the Greek philosophers, they considered body, soul, and spirit to be a unity, so that one could not exist without the other.

In dealing with the Sadducees, Jesus emphasized that God declares himself the God of Abraham, Isaac, and Jacob, that He is not the God of the dead but of the living, so that Abraham, Isaac, and Jacob are indeed still alive to Him (Matthew 22:23-33; Mark 12:18-27; Luke 20:27-40). Jesus recognized the chief argument of the Sadducees was that souls do not exist apart from their bodies, and it was on this basis they denied the resurrection. By showing that Abraham, Isaac, and Jacob are still alive though their bodies were in their graves, Jesus counteracted the chief argument of the Sadducees and removed their grounds for denying the resurrection.

Actually, the Old Testament gives clear teaching of a future resurrection. Job's testimony is outstanding (see Job 19:23-27). Psalm 16:10 shows the Messiah would be raised from the dead (Acts 2:24-32; 13:34-37). Psalm 17:15 shows a hope, not only of going to be with the Lord, but of a change when believers are raised at Christ's coming (1 Corinthians 15:51,52; 1 John 3:2). Psalm 73:23-26 shows faith in personal immortality to be ever with the Lord and implies the hope of the resurrection. Isaiah 53:8-12 also shows the resurrection of the suffering Messiah, and Daniel 12:2 specifically prophesies two resurrections (John 5:29; Revelation 20:4,5,12,13).

**23:9.** The discussion soon became a great outcry as Pharisees and Sadducees clamored against each other. Some of the scribes (experts in the interpretation of the Mosaic law) who were on the side of the Pharisees stood up and greatly strove in Paul's behalf. They found no evil (nothing bad) in him. They even suggested an

**of the hope and resurrection of the dead:** . . . concerning the hope and, *Alford* . . . It is because of my hope of a resurrection of the dead, *Weymouth.*

**I am called in question:** . . . that I am on my trial, *TCNT* . . . I am here to be questioned, *BB* . . . I am accused, *Berkeley.*

**7. And when he had so said:** As soon as he said this, *TCNT* . . . At these words, *Phillips.*

**there arose a dissension:** . . . a dispute arose, *TCNT* . . . there was an argument, *BB* . . . a quarrel broke out, *Moffatt* . . . a split occurred, *Fenton.*

**between the Pharisees and the Sadducees:**

**and the multitude was divided:** . . . the court, *Williams* . . . and there was a sharp division of opinion among those present, *TCNT* . . . and the assembly took different sides, *Weymouth.*

**8. For the Sadducees say:** . . . claim, *Phillips.*

**that there is no resurrection:** . . . no such thing as a resurrection, *TCNT* . . . no coming back from the dead, *BB.*

**neither angel, nor spirit:** . . . and that there is neither angel, nor spirit, *TCNT* . . . and no such thing as an angel or spirit, *Williams.*

**but the Pharisees confess both:** . . . while the Pharisees believe in them, *TCNT* . . . acknowledge them all, *Weymouth* . . . confess the one as well as the other, *Berkeley.*

**9. And there arose a great cry:** So a great uproar ensued, *TCNT* . . . The meeting became very noisy, *Norlie.*

**and the scribes that were of the Pharisees' part:** . . . and some of the teachers of the Law belonging to the Pharisees' party, *TCNT* . . . and some of the scribes on the side of the Pharisees, *BB.*

**arose, and strove, saying:** . . . stood up and hotly protested, *TCNT* . . . sprang to their feet and fiercely contended, *Weymouth* . . . got up and argued vehemently, *Berkeley* . . . jumped to their feet and protested violently, *Phillips.*

| 2978.16 verb nom pl masc part pres act | 3625.6 num card neu | 2527.7 adj sing neu | 2128.4 verb 1pl indic pres act | 1706.1 prep | 3450.3 art dat sing |
|---|---|---|---|---|---|
| λέγοντες, | Οὐδὲν | κακὸν | εὑρίσκομεν | ἐν | τῷ |
| *legontes* | *Ouden* | *kakon* | *heuriskomen* | *en* | *tō* |
| saying, | Nothing | evil | we find | in | the |

| 442.3 noun dat sing masc | 3642.5 dem-pron dat sing masc | 1479.1 conj | 1156.2 conj | 4011.1 noun sing neu | 2953.27 verb 3sing indic aor act |
|---|---|---|---|---|---|
| ἀνθρώπῳ | τούτῳ· | εἰ | δὲ | πνεῦμα | ἐλάλησεν |
| *anthrōpō* | *toutō* | *ei* | *de* | *pneuma* | *elalēsen* |
| man | this; | if | and | a spirit | spoke |

9.b.**Txt:** 020L,025P,byz. sa.
**Var:** 01ℵ,02A,03B,04C 08E,bo.Gries,Lach,Treg Alf,Word,Tisc,We/Ho Weis,Sod,UBS/☆

| 840.4 prs-pron dat sing | 2211.1 conj | 32.1 noun nom sing masc | 3231.1 partic | 2290.1 verb 1pl subj pres act |
|---|---|---|---|---|
| αὐτῷ | ἢ | ἄγγελος | ⸂b μὴ | θεομαχῶμεν.⸃ |
| *autō* | *ē* | *angelos* | *mē* | *theomachōmen* |
| to him | or | an angel, | not | let us fight against God. |

| | 4044.10 adj gen sing fem | 1156.2 conj | 1090.57 verb gen sing fem part aor mid | 4565.2 noun gen sing fem | 2106.1 verb nom sing masc part aor pass |
|---|---|---|---|---|---|
| **10.** | Πολλῆς | δὲ | ⸀γενομένης | στάσεως, | εὐλαβηθεὶς |
| | *Pollēs* | *de* | *genomenēs* | *staseōs* | *eulabētheis* |
| | A great | and | having arisen | dissension, | having feared |

10.a.**Txt:** 020L,025P,byz.
**Var:** 01ℵ,03B,Tisc We/Ho,Weis,UBS/☆

| 1090.75 verb gen sing fem part pres mid | 4565.2 noun gen sing fem | 5236.19 verb nom sing masc part aor pass | 3450.5 art nom sing masc | 5341.1 noun nom sing masc |
|---|---|---|---|---|
| [a☆ γινομένης | στάσεως | φοβηθεὶς ] | ὁ | χιλίαρχος |
| *ginomenēs* | *staseōs* | *phobētheis* | *ho* | *chiliarchos* |
| [ arising | dissension | having feared ] | the | chief captain |

| 3231.1 partic | 1282.1 verb 3sing subj aor pass | 3450.5 art nom sing masc | 3834.1 name nom masc | 5097.2 prep | 840.1 prs-pron gen pl |
|---|---|---|---|---|---|
| μὴ | διασπασθῇ | ὁ | Παῦλος | ὑπ' | αὐτῶν, |
| *mē* | *diaspasthē* | *ho* | *Paulos* | *hup'* | *autōn* |
| not | should be torn in pieces | | Paul | by | them, |

| 2724.3 verb 3sing indic aor act | 3450.16 art sing neu | 4604.3 noun sing neu | 2568.23 verb sing neu part aor act | 720.6 verb inf aor act |
|---|---|---|---|---|
| ἐκέλευσεν | τὸ | στράτευμα | καταβὰν | ἁρπάσαι |
| *ekeleusen* | *to* | *strateuma* | *kataban* | *harpasai* |
| commanded | the | troop | having gone down | to seize |

| 840.6 prs-pron acc sing masc | 1523.2 prep gen | 3189.4 adj gen sing neu | 840.1 prs-pron gen pl | 70.7 verb inf pres act | 4885.1 conj | 1519.1 prep |
|---|---|---|---|---|---|---|
| αὐτὸν | ἐκ | μέσου | αὐτῶν, | ἄγειν | τε | εἰς |
| *auton* | *ek* | *mesou* | *autōn* | *agein* | *te* | *eis* |
| him | from | midst | their, | to bring | and | into |

| 3450.12 art acc sing fem | 3787.2 noun acc sing fem | | 3450.11 art dat sing fem | 1156.2 conj | 1951.1 noun dat sing fem | 3433.3 noun dat sing fem |
|---|---|---|---|---|---|---|
| τὴν | παρεμβολήν. | **11.** | Τῇ | δὲ | ἐπιούσῃ | νυκτὶ |
| *tēn* | *parembolēn* | | *Tē* | *de* | *epiousē* | *nukti* |
| the | barracks. | | The | but | following | night |

| 2168.5 verb nom sing masc part aor act | 840.4 prs-pron dat sing | 3450.5 art nom sing masc | 2935.1 noun nom sing masc | 1500.5 verb 3sing indic aor act |
|---|---|---|---|---|
| ἐπιστὰς | αὐτῷ | ὁ | κύριος | εἶπεν, |
| *epistas* | *autō* | *ho* | *kurios* | *eipen* |
| having stood by | him | the | Lord | said, |

11.a.**Txt:** 04C-corr,020L 025P,byz.
**Var:** 01ℵ,02A,03B 04C-org,08E,sa.bo.Lach Treg,Alf,Word,Tisc We/Ho,Weis,Sod UBS/☆

| 2270.1 verb 2sing impr pres act | 3834.5 name voc masc | 5453.1 conj | 1056.1 conj | 1257.5 verb 2sing indic aor mid |
|---|---|---|---|---|
| Θάρσει | ⸂a Παῦλε·⸃ | ὡς | γὰρ | διεμαρτύρω |
| *Tharsei* | *Paule* | *hōs* | *gar* | *diemarturō* |
| Be of good courage, | Paul; | as | for | you did fully testify |

angel or spirit may have spoken to him and warned that in condemning Paul they might be fighting against God.

**23:10.** The mention of angel and spirit must have stirred up the Sadducees. Even though Jesus had once silenced them, they refused to give up their interpretations. Paul had been right in taking his stand with the Pharisees on the matter of the resurrection here, and at this point they were inclined to listen to him. Actually, it was easier for a Pharisee to become a Christian than it was for a Sadducee. In fact, many Pharisees had already become Christians (15:5; 21:20). But a Sadducee would have to cease being a Sadducee altogether and give up all his basic presuppositions in order to accept the resurrected Christ as his Messiah and Saviour. (Acts 6:7 tells of the great number of the priests who were obedient to the Faith, however, and at least some of them must have been Sadducees.)

Here the Sadducees created so much upheaval, and the discord became so great the tribune became afraid Paul might be torn apart by the Sanhedrin members. So he ordered the soldiers to go down and snatch him out of their midst and bring him back into the Fortress of Antonia. Once again when Paul's life was in jeopardy, God's providence saw to it that the Romans rescued him.

**23:11.** It had been a hard day for Paul. But during the night following, the Lord Jesus suddenly stood beside him and said, "Be of good cheer" (be of good courage, cheer up and do not be afraid). As Paul had testified (given a clear witness) for Christ in Jerusalem, so must he also witness (testify) in Rome. Paul's desire to go to Rome had seemed impossible when he was arrested. But Jesus now said it was still God's will for him. This encouragement upheld Paul in the sufferings and difficulties that were still to come.

One of the marvelous things in the New Testament is the way the Lord Jesus gave encouragement to His servants, sometimes by angels, sometimes by a vision or dream, and sometimes by a personal appearance of the Lord himself.

Paul was human. He really needed this encouragement. After being beaten by the mob he attempted to witness to them, but his witness brought only more riot and rejection. His witness before the Sanhedrin seemed a better opportunity, but the result was the same. In neither case was anyone converted. In fact, it was obvious Paul's enemies were more determined than ever to destroy him.

That night after the excitement was over, Paul must have felt a sense of his own weakness and must have wondered where it would all end. The very words of Jesus imply Paul was beginning to feel a little discouraged and afraid. But how wonderful it must have been when suddenly in the darkness he saw Jesus standing beside him telling him to stop being afraid (as the Greek most probably means).

There was no condemnation in the words of Jesus, only comfort, cheer, and approval. Even though no one was converted, Paul had

**We find no evil in this man:** Nothing bad find we in this man, *Rotherham* . . . We find nothing whatever wrong in this man, *TCNT* . . . We cannot find any fault in this man, *Knox.*

**but if a spirit or an angel hath spoken to him:** Suppose a spirit did speak to him, or an angel, *TCNT* . . . maybe an angel or a spirit did speak to him, *NCV* . . . what if he has had a revelation from, *BB.*

**let us not fight against God:**

**10. And when there arose a great dissension:** But when the dissension became violent, *Montgomery* . . . The dispute was becoming so violent, *TCNT* . . . And as a great fight began, *KJII* . . . They argued all the more, *NLT* . . . Since the dispute kept getting hotter and hotter, *Williams* . . . But the discord grew so bitter, *Berkeley* . . . As the debate became very heated, *Norlie* . . . The argument was beginning to turn into, *NCV.*

**the chief captain, fearing lest Paul should have been pulled in pieces of them:** . . . would be pulled in two by them, *BB* . . . fearing that they would tear him to pieces, *Noli* . . . was afraid that the Jews would tear Paul to pieces, *Everyday.*

**commanded the soldiers to go down:** . . . ordered the military to, *Rotherham* . . . a detachment to march down, *Berkeley.*

**and to take him by force from among them:** . . . and rescue him from them, *Noli, TCNT* . . . and take him out of their hands, *Williams* . . . and snatch him from their midst, *Berkeley* . . . and take Paul away, *Everyday.*

**and to bring him into the castle:** . . . and take him into the Fort, *TCNT* . . . and lead him into, *Worrell* . . . and bring him safe to the soldiers' quarters, *Knox* . . . and put him in the army building, *Everyday.*

**11. And the night following the Lord stood by him, and said:** That night the Lord came, *TCNT* . . . But that same night, *Williams.*

**Be of good cheer, Paul:** Be of good courage! *Rotherham* . . . Paul, be brave, *Norlie* . . . Take heart! *Berkeley* . . . Be strong, *Lamsa, SEB.*

| 3450.17 art pl neu | 3875.1 prep | 1466.3 prs-pron gen 1sing | 1519.1 prep | 2395.1 name fem | 3643.2 adv |
|---|---|---|---|---|---|
| τὰ | περὶ | ἐμοῦ | εἰς | Ἱερουσαλὴμ, | οὕτω, |
| *ta* | *peri* | *emou* | *eis* | *Hierousalēm* | *houtō* |
| the things | concerning | me | at | Jerusalem, | so |

| 4622.4 prs-pron acc 2sing | 1158.1 verb 3sing indic pres act | 2504.1 conj | 1519.1 prep | 4373.3 name acc fem | 3113.24 verb inf aor act |
|---|---|---|---|---|---|
| σε | δεῖ | καὶ | εἰς | Ῥώμην | μαρτυρῆσαι. |
| *se* | *dei* | *kai* | *eis* | *Rhōmēn* | *marturēsai* |
| you | must | also | at | Rome | to bear witness. |

| | 1090.57 verb gen sing fem part aor mid | 1156.2 conj | 2232.1 noun fem | 4020.39 verb nom pl masc part aor act | 4948.7 indef-pron nom pl masc |
|---|---|---|---|---|---|
| 12. | Γενομένης | δὲ | ἡμέρας, | ποιήσαντές | ʻ τινες |
| | *Genomenēs* | *de* | *hēmeras* | *poiēsantes* | *tines* |
| | Having become | and | day, | having made | some |

12.a.**Txt:** 025P,byz.sa.
**Var:** p74,01ℵ,02A,03B
04C,08E,Gries,Lach
Treg,Alf,Word,Tisc
We/Ho,Weis,Sod
UBS/☆

| 3450.1 art gen pl | 2428.3 name-adj gen pl masc | 4815.2 noun acc sing fem | 4815.2 noun acc sing fem | 3450.7 art nom pl masc |
|---|---|---|---|---|
| τῶν | Ἰουδαίων | συστροφὴν | [a☆ συστροφὴν | οἱ |
| *tōn* | *Ioudaiōn* | *sustrophēn* | *sustrophēn* | *hoi* |
| of the | Jews | a plot | [ a plot | the |

| 2428.2 name-adj nom pl masc | 330.3 verb 3pl indic aor act | 1431.8 prs-pron acc pl masc | 2978.16 verb nom pl masc part pres act |
|---|---|---|---|
| Ἰουδαῖοι ] | ἀνεθεμάτισαν | ἑαυτοὺς, | λέγοντες |
| *Ioudaioi* | *anethematisan* | *heautous* | *legontes* |
| Jews ] | put under a curse | themselves, | declaring |

12.b.**Txt:** 01ℵ,02A
03B-corr,04C,08E,020L
025P,etc.byz.Tisc,Sod
**Var:** 03B-org,We/Ho
Weis,UBS/☆

| 3250.1 conj | 2052.25 verb inf aor act | 3250.1 conj | 3956.23 verb inf aor act | 3956.29 verb inf aor act | 2175.1 conj | 3614.2 rel-pron gen sing |
|---|---|---|---|---|---|---|
| μήτε | φαγεῖν | μήτε | ʻ πίειν | [b πεῖν ] | ἕως | οὗ |
| *mēte* | *phagein* | *mēte* | *piein* | *pein* | *heōs* | *hou* |
| neither | to eat | nor | to drink | [ idem ] | until | which |

| 609.9 verb 3pl subj aor act | 3450.6 art acc sing masc | 3834.4 name acc masc | | 1498.37 verb 3pl indic imperf act | 1156.2 conj | 3979.3 adj comp pl |
|---|---|---|---|---|---|---|
| ἀποκτείνωσιν | τὸν | Παῦλον· | 13. | ἦσαν | δὲ | πλείους |
| *apokteinōsin* | *ton* | *Paulon* | | *ēsan* | *de* | *pleious* |
| they should kill | | Paul. | | They were | and | more than |

| 4910.2 num card | 4910.1 num card | 3450.7 art nom pl masc | 3642.12 dem-pron acc sing fem |
|---|---|---|---|
| ʻ τεσσαράκοντα | [ τεσσεράκοντα ] | οἱ | ταύτην |
| *tessarakonta* | *tesserakonta* | *hoi* | *tautēn* |
| forty | [ idem ] | the | this |

13.a.**Txt:** 025P,byz.
**Var:** 01ℵ,02A,03B,04C
08E,Lach,Treg,Alf
Word,Tisc,We/Ho,Weis
Sod,UBS/☆

| 3450.12 art acc sing fem | 4797.1 noun acc sing fem | 4020.49 verb nom pl masc part perf act | 4020.77 verb nom pl masc part aor mid |
|---|---|---|---|
| τὴν | συνωμοσίαν | ʻ πεποιηκότες· | [a☆ ποιησάμενοι· ] |
| *tēn* | *sunōmosian* | *pepoiēkotes* | *poiēsamenoi* |
| the | plot | having made; | [ idem ] |

| | 3610.2 rel-pron nom pl masc | 4193.5 verb nom pl masc part aor act | 3450.4 art dat pl | 744.7 noun dat pl masc | 2504.1 conj |
|---|---|---|---|---|---|
| 14. | οἵτινες | προσελθόντες | τοῖς | ἀρχιερεῦσιν | καὶ |
| | *hoitines* | *proselthontes* | *tois* | *archiereusin* | *kai* |
| | who | having come | to the | chief priests | and |

14.a.**Txt:** 020L,025P,byz.
Sod
**Var:** 01ℵ,02A,03B,04C
08E,Lach,Treg,Alf,Tisc
We/Ho,Weis,UBS/☆

| 3450.4 art dat pl | 4104.7 adj comp dat pl masc | 1500.3 verb indic aor act | 1500.28 verb 3pl indic aor act | 329.2 noun dat sing neu |
|---|---|---|---|---|
| τοῖς | πρεσβυτέροις | ʻ εἶπον, | [a☆ εἶπαν, ] | Ἀναθέματι |
| *tois* | *presbuterois* | *eipon* | *eipan* | *Anathemati* |
| the | elders | said, | [ idem ] | With a curse |

pleased the Lord with his witness in Jerusalem. Jesus accepted his sincerity and the earnestness and truth of his witness.

**23:12.** Paul slept with new peace and confidence, but as soon as it was day some of the Jews met to plot Paul's death. It seems they saw the Romans were determined to protect Paul and give him a fair trial, and they began to despair of ever putting an end to him by legal means. So these plotters determined they would find some way to murder Paul.

This conspiracy was carried on in the same spirit of violence that had characterized the mob that attacked Paul in the temple court. They went so far as to invoke a curse on themselves, saying they would neither eat nor drink until they had killed Paul.

Binding themselves under a curse means they anathematized themselves or invoked a curse on themselves. That is, they said something like: "May God himself punish us by making us the objects of His wrath to destroy us if we eat or drink until we have killed Paul."

By invoking such a curse upon themselves, they were trying to put God in a position where He would have to do their will. But they were heathenish in their thinking when they felt they could bargain with God or put Him in a corner and force Him to do their will. No one can hold a club over God or demand that He do something contrary to His will or contrary to His nature.

Those who are following the Lord in faith and obedience do not need to bargain with God. Out of pure grace He will pour out His blessings upon those who belong to Him. Even under the Law the people were told that if they obeyed God and did His will, they would not need to run after the blessings. The blessings would literally pursue them and overtake them (Deuteronomy 28:1,2). It does no good to bargain with God, because those who try to do so forget that God is God.

**23:13.** Over 40 Jews joined in this conspiracy. They could not believe God would destroy them or make them anathema for the sake of one little despised man like Paul. Possibly they believed that by Paul's becoming a preacher of Christ to the Gentiles, he had become a false prophet. They believed he was enticing people to turn away from the way in which the Lord their God had commanded them to walk, as Deuteronomy 13:5 warns when it commands the death penalty for all who do this. Actually, Deuteronomy is dealing with false prophets who turn the people to the worship of false gods, but the conspirators included it to mean turning from Jewish traditions.

**23:14.** These 40 conspirators then went to the chief priests and elders and explained their plan, telling them how they had bound themselves under a great curse, or anathema, that they would not eat, not even taste anything until they had killed Paul.

**for as thou hast testified of me in Jerusalem:** You have borne witness for me in Jerusalem, *TCNT*... as you fully testified as to the things concerning Me, *Worrell*... as you have been witnessing for me, *BB* ... testified concerning me at, *Lamsa*... You have told people in Jerusalem about me, *Everyday*... For just as you have given a full account of me in Jerusalem, *Norlie*.

**so must thou bear witness also at Rome:**... testify also at Rome, *HBIE*... just so it is necessary for you to testify at Rome, *Berkeley* ... and now thou must carry the same witness to, *Knox* ... You must also go to Rome to do the same thing there! *SEB* ... You must do the same in Rome also, *Everyday*.

**12. And when it was day:** In the morning, *TCNT*... At daybreak, *Berkeley*.

**certain of the Jews banded together:** ... combined together, *TCNT* ... the Jews conspired, *Hanson* ... came together, *BB* ... held a conclave, *Knox* ... made a plot, *KJII*.

**and bound themselves under a curse:** ... and took an oath, *TCNT* ... and solemnly swore, *Weymouth* ... and pledged themselves under an oath, *Berkeley*... They promised each other, *NLT*... They made a vow, *NCV* ... made a plan, *Everyday*.

**saying that they would neither eat nor drink till they had killed Paul:**... that they would not take food or drink till they had put Paul to death, *BB*.

**13. And they were more than forty which had made this conspiracy:** There were more than forty in the plot, *TCNT*... who swore to carry out this plot, *Beck* ... established this compact by oath, *Murdock* ... those that formed this conspiracy were more than, *Hanson* ... were involved in this plot, *Noli* ... who had made this plot, *KJII*... made this plan, *Everyday*.

**14. And they came to the chief priests and elders, and said:** ... approached, *Phillips*... They went and talked to the leading priests and the older Jewish leaders, *Everyday*... to the most important priests, *SEB*.

| 330.2 verb 1pl indic aor act | 1431.8 prs-pron acc pl masc | 3235.1 num card gen | 1083.8 verb inf aor mid | 2175.1 conj |
|---|---|---|---|---|
| ἀνεθεματίσαμεν | ἑαυτοὺς | μηδενὸς | γεύσασθαι | ἕως |
| *anethematisamen* | *heautous* | *mēdenos* | *geusasthai* | *heōs* |
| we have devoted | ourselves, | nothing | to taste | until |

| 3614.2 rel-pron gen sing | 609.8 verb 1pl subj aor act | 3450.6 art acc sing masc | 3834.4 name acc masc | 3431.1 adv |
|---|---|---|---|---|
| οὗ | ἀποκτείνωμεν | τὸν | Παῦλον. | **15.** νῦν |
| *hou* | *apokteinōmen* | *ton* | *Paulon* | *nun* |
| which | we should kill | | Paul. | Now |

| 3631.1 partic | 5050.1 prs-pron nom 2pl | 1702.5 verb 2pl impr aor act | 3450.3 art dat sing | 5341.2 noun dat sing masc |
|---|---|---|---|---|
| οὖν | ὑμεῖς | ἐμφανίσατε | τῷ | χιλιάρχῳ |
| *oun* | *humeis* | *emphanisate* | *tō* | *chiliarchō* |
| therefore | you | make clear | to the | chief captain |

15.a.**Txt:** 020L,025P,byz.
**Var:** 01ℵ,02A,03B,04C 08E,sa.bo.Gries,Lach Treg,Alf,Word,Tisc We/Ho,Weis,Sod UBS/☆

| 4713.1 prep | 3450.3 art dat sing | 4742.3 noun dat sing neu | 3567.1 conj | 833.1 adv | 840.6 prs-pron acc sing masc |
|---|---|---|---|---|---|
| σὺν | τῷ | συνεδρίῳ, | ὅπως | ⌜a αὔριον ⌝ | ⌜ αὐτὸν |
| *sun* | *tō* | *sunedriō* | *hopōs* | *aurion* | *auton* |
| with | the | Sanhedrin, | so that | tomorrow | him |

15.b.**Txt:** 020L,byz.
**Var:** 01ℵ,02A,03B,08E Lach,Treg,Alf,Word Tisc,We/Ho,Weis UBS/☆

| 2580.3 verb 3sing subj aor act | 4242.1 prep | 2580.3 verb 3sing subj aor act | 840.6 prs-pron acc sing masc | 1519.1 prep |
|---|---|---|---|---|
| καταγάγῃ | πρὸς | [b☆ καταγάγῃ | αὐτὸν | εἰς ] |
| *katagagē* | *pros* | *katagagē* | *auton* | *eis* |
| he may bring down | to | [ he may bring down | him | to ] |

| 5050.4 prs-pron acc 2pl | 5453.1 conj | 3165.14 verb acc pl masc part pres act | 1225.1 verb inf pres act | 194.1 adv comp |
|---|---|---|---|---|
| ὑμᾶς, | ὡς | μέλλοντας | διαγινώσκειν | ἀκριβέστερον |
| *humas* | *hōs* | *mellontas* | *diaginōskein* | *akribesteron* |
| you, | as | being about | to examine | more accurately |

| 3450.17 art pl neu | 3875.1 prep | 840.3 prs-pron gen sing | 2231.1 prs-pron nom 1pl | 1156.2 conj | 4112.1 prep |
|---|---|---|---|---|---|
| τὰ | περὶ | αὐτοῦ· | ἡμεῖς | δὲ, | πρὸ |
| *ta* | *peri* | *autou* | *hēmeis* | *de* | *pro* |
| the things | concerning | him, | we | and, | before |

| 3450.2 art gen sing | 1443.14 verb inf aor act | 840.6 prs-pron acc sing masc | 2071.1 adj nom pl | 1498.5 verb 1pl indic pres act | 3450.2 art gen sing |
|---|---|---|---|---|---|
| τοῦ | ἐγγίσαι | αὐτὸν | ἕτοιμοί | ἐσμεν | τοῦ |
| *tou* | *engisai* | *auton* | *hetoimoi* | *esmen* | *tou* |
| the | to draw near | him | ready | we are | the |

| 335.9 verb inf aor act | 840.6 prs-pron acc sing masc | 189.31 verb nom sing masc part aor act | 1156.2 conj | 3450.5 art nom sing masc |
|---|---|---|---|---|
| ἀνελεῖν | αὐτόν. | **16.** Ἀκούσας | δὲ | ὁ |
| *anelein* | *auton* | *Akousas* | *de* | *ho* |
| to put to death | him. | Having heard | but | the |

| 5048.1 noun nom sing masc | 3450.10 art gen sing fem | 78.2 noun gen sing fem | 3834.2 name gen masc | 3450.16 art sing neu | 1733.1 noun sing neu |
|---|---|---|---|---|---|
| υἱὸς | τῆς | ἀδελφῆς | Παύλου | ⌜ τὸ | ἔνεδρον, |
| *huios* | *tēs* | *adelphēs* | *Paulou* | *to* | *enedron* |
| son | of the | sister | of Paul | the | lying in wait, |

16.a.**Txt:** 020L,025P,byz. Steph
**Var:** 01ℵ,02A,03B,04C 08E,Elzev,Gries,Lach Treg,Alf,Tisc,We/Ho Weis,Sod,UBS/☆

| 3450.12 art acc sing fem | 1731.1 noun acc sing fem | 3716.7 verb nom sing masc part aor mid | 2504.1 conj | 1511.13 verb nom sing masc part aor act |
|---|---|---|---|---|
| [a☆ τὴν | ἐνέδραν ] | παραγενόμενος | καὶ | εἰσελθὼν |
| *tēn* | *enedran* | *paragenomenos* | *kai* | *eiselthōn* |
| [ the | lying in wait ] | having come near | and | having entered |

These plotters were not really depending on God. They probably would not have invoked such a serious curse on themselves if they had not been so sure of their own cleverness. They thought they could put Paul in a position where he could not escape them. They were sure the high priest and his company, along with the Sadducee portion of the Sanhedrin, would go along with them.

**We have bound ourselves under a great curse:** . . . taken a solemn oath, *TCNT* . . . sworn ourselves to liability of a curse, *Berkeley* . . . solemn anathema, *Campbell.*

**that we will eat nothing until we have slain Paul:** . . . to taste nothing until we have killed Paul, *ASV* . . . to let nothing pass our lips, *Phillips.*

**23:15.** They asked these leaders to get the Sanhedrin to make an official request to the tribune to bring Paul down, as if they intended to determine more precisely the facts concerning him. Before he got near, they would be waiting, prepared to kill him. That is, they would ambush him on the way, so the Sanhedrin would not be held responsible for his death. Thus the unsuspecting Romans would become tools in their hands.

It is probable also that they did not tell the Pharisees in the Sanhedrin that they intended to ambush Paul. Some of them, at least, were still fearful they might be fighting against God by condemning Paul. But they would be willing to ask for further questioning, since that seemed reasonable.

Unfortunately for the conspirators, they did not know Jesus had already promised to send Paul to Rome, and their plot was therefore doomed to failure. Yet if they had known, it would probably have made no difference to them. They had already rejected Paul's testimony about the appearance of Jesus on the Damascus Road.

It is not known who these plotters were except that they were not members of the Sanhedrin. Since they went to the priests it is probable they were already under the influence of the priests. It is a fact that any society governed by a corrupt priesthood or clergy spawns wicked men who are quite willing to resort to violence and murder in the name of religion.

Thank God, there was no way Paul's enemies could have thwarted God's plan to get Paul to Rome. With the Lord as their Helper, believers need not fear what man can do to them (Hebrews 13:6). David learned this in the midst of difficult circumstances, and he was able to proclaim that the Lord was his light and his salvation, the strength of his life, so he did not need to be afraid of any enemies that might arise (Psalm 27:1-3). The Levitical singers, the sons of Korah, sang out, "God is our refuge and strength, a very present help in trouble" (Psalm 46:1). (See also Psalms 56:4; 91:1-6; 118:6.)

Actually, there was only one person who could have thwarted God's plan for Paul, and that was Paul himself. He could have done it through unbelief (Hebrews 3:19; 4:1,11).

**15. Now therefore ye with the council:** So we want you now, with the consent of the Council, *TCNT* . . . Now then, you, in cooperation with the Sanhedrin, *Berkeley* . . . We therefore ask you, together with the council, *Norlie.*

**signify to the chief captain:** . . . ask, *Montgomery* . . . must now notify, *Williams* . . . send word to, *Berkeley* . . . must make it plain to, *Phillips* . . . make it appear to the officer, *Swann.*

**that he bring him down unto you to morrow:** . . . that you want him to bring Paul down to you, *Phillips.*

**as though ye would enquire something more perfectly concerning him:** . . . determine his matter more regularly, *Alford* . . . as if you meant to get more exact information about him, *Beck* . . . as though you intended to go more fully into his case, *TCNT* . . . It will look as if you want to ask him some things, *NLT* . . . as if you intended to inquire more minutely about him, *Weymouth* . . . as if you meant to examine his cause more precisely, *Knox* . . . pretending you want more correct information about him, *NCV.*

**and we, or ever he come near:** . . . before he comes near, *ASV* . . . Then we, if he comes anywhere near, *Berkeley.*

**are ready to kill him:** . . . are prepared to assassinate him, *Weymouth* . . . will be waiting to put him to death, *BB.*

**23:16.** While the conspirators were discussing their plot with the chief priests and elders, Paul's sister's son happened to come on the scene in time to hear them. Some writers believe he had come to Jerusalem from Tarsus to be educated, just as Paul had years before. The Bible does not say how he happened to be there, but

**16. And when Paul's sister's son:** But Paul's nephew, *SEB, Weymouth* . . . Paul's sister had a son, *Knox.*

**heard of their lying in wait:** . . . hearing of the plot, *TCNT* . . . heard of the intended attack upon him, *Weymouth* . . . got wind of the ambush, *Berkeley* . . . who heard of this ambush being laid, *Knox.*

| 1519.1 prep | 3450.12 art acc sing fem | 3787.2 noun acc sing fem | 514.7 verb 3sing indic aor act | 3450.3 art dat sing | 3834.3 name dat masc |
|---|---|---|---|---|---|
| εἰς | τὴν | παρεμβολὴν | ἀπήγγειλεν | τῷ | Παύλῳ. |
| eis | tēn | parembolēn | apēngeilen | tō | Paulō |
| into | the | barracks | he reported | | to Paul. |

| 4200.4 verb nom sing masc part aor mid | 1156.2 conj | 3450.5 art nom sing masc | 3834.1 name nom masc | 1518.4 num card acc masc |
|---|---|---|---|---|
| 17. προσκαλεσάμενος | δὲ | ὁ | Παῦλος | ἕνα |
| proskalesamenos | de | ho | Paulos | hena |
| Having called | and | | Paul | one |

| 3450.1 art gen pl | 1529.3 noun gen pl masc | 5183.4 verb 3sing indic act | 3450.6 art acc sing masc | 3357.3 noun acc sing masc |
|---|---|---|---|---|
| τῶν | ἑκατονταρχῶν, | ἔφη, | Τὸν | νεανίαν |
| tōn | hekatontarchōn | ephē | Ton | neanian |
| of the | centurions, | said, | The | young man |

17.a.**Txt:** 02A,04C,08E 020L,025P,byz.Weis
**Var:** 01ℵ,03B,Treg,Tisc We/Ho,Sod,UBS/☆

| 3642.6 dem-pron acc sing masc | 516.4 verb 2sing impr aor act | 516.11 verb 2sing impr pres act | 4242.1 prep | 3450.6 art acc sing masc |
|---|---|---|---|---|
| τοῦτον | ‘ ἀπάγαγε | [a ἄπαγε ] | πρὸς | τὸν |
| touton | apagage | apage | pros | ton |
| this | take | [ idem ] | to | the |

| 5341.3 noun acc sing masc | 2174.4 verb 3sing indic pres act | 1056.1 conj | 4948.10 indef-pron sing neu | 514.10 verb inf aor act |
|---|---|---|---|---|
| χιλίαρχον· | ἔχει | γάρ | ‘ τι | ἀπαγγεῖλαί |
| chiliarchon | echei | gar | ti | apangeilai |
| chief captain, | he has | for | something | to report |

| 514.10 verb inf aor act | 4948.10 indef-pron sing neu | 840.4 prs-pron dat sing | 3450.5 art nom sing masc | 3173.1 conj |
|---|---|---|---|---|
| [☆ ἀπαγγεῖλαί | τι ] | αὐτῷ. | 18. Ὁ | μὲν |
| apangeilai | ti | autō | Ho | men |
| [ to report | something ] | to him. | The | indeed |

| 3631.1 partic | 3741.9 verb nom sing masc part aor act | 840.6 prs-pron acc sing masc | 70.8 verb 3sing indic aor act | 4242.1 prep | 3450.6 art acc sing masc |
|---|---|---|---|---|---|
| οὖν | παραλαβὼν | αὐτὸν | ἤγαγεν | πρὸς | τὸν |
| oun | paralabōn | auton | ēgagen | pros | ton |
| therefore | having taken | him | brought | to | the |

| 5341.3 noun acc sing masc | 2504.1 conj | 5183.2 verb 3sing indic pres act | 3450.5 art nom sing masc | 1192.1 noun nom sing masc | 3834.1 name nom masc |
|---|---|---|---|---|---|
| χιλίαρχον, | καὶ | φησίν, | Ὁ | δέσμιος | Παῦλος |
| chiliarchon | kai | phēsin | Ho | desmios | Paulos |
| chief captain, | and | says, | The | prisoner | Paul |

| 4200.4 verb nom sing masc part aor mid | 1466.6 prs-pron acc 1sing | 2049.9 verb 3sing indic aor act | 3642.6 dem-pron acc sing masc | 3450.6 art acc sing masc |
|---|---|---|---|---|
| προσκαλεσάμενός | με | ἠρώτησεν | τοῦτον | τὸν |
| proskalesamenos | me | ērōtēsen | touton | ton |
| having called to | me | asked | this | the |

18.a.**Txt:** 03B,020L 025P,byz.We/Ho
**Var:** 01ℵ,02A,08E,Lach Treg,Alf,Tisc,Weis,Sod UBS/☆

| 3357.3 noun acc sing masc | 3358.2 noun acc sing masc | 70.15 verb inf aor act | 4242.1 prep | 4622.4 prs-pron acc 2sing |
|---|---|---|---|---|
| ‘ νεανίαν | [a☆ νεανίσκον ] | ἀγαγεῖν | πρὸς | σέ, |
| neanian | neaniskon | agagein | pros | se |
| young man | [ idem ] | to lead | to | you, |

| 2174.15 verb part pres act | 4948.10 indef-pron sing neu | 2953.37 verb inf aor act | 4622.3 prs-pron dat 2sing | 1934.5 verb nom sing masc part aor mid |
|---|---|---|---|---|
| ἔχοντά | τι | λαλῆσαί | σοι. | 19. Ἐπιλαβόμενος |
| echonta | ti | lalēsai | soi | Epilabomenos |
| having | something | to say | to you. | Having taken hold |

God saw to it that he was. Though Paul himself was not aware of the danger, God knew it and provided for it. One of the thrills of eternity will be to learn of the dangers believers did not see, but which God saw and kept them from.

Paul's nephew did not hesitate. He went immediately and told Paul about the plot against him.

From this it is evident Paul's nephew was intelligent. He kept his eyes and ears open, and when he found out about this plot, he understood the danger for Paul. It is clear that he loved his uncle. Whether he was a Christian or not, Luke did not say. Possibly he was not, since Luke in Acts usually identified those who were Christians by calling them disciples. But in this sudden peril, the nephew did not let any religious differences that might have existed keep him from trying to help his uncle. He also was prompt. He did not let excuses or any of his own plans or desires keep him from immediate action. He could have been like so many who know their duty but fail to do it. Paul's nephew could have decided he did not want to get involved. He could have told himself he was just a young man without influence and there was nothing he could do. But, thank God, he resisted any of these excuses or temptations that might have come to his mind. He was willing to do what he could and leave the rest in the hands of God.

**23:17.** Paul then called a centurion and asked him to take the young man to the tribune. It took courage for the young man to go to see Paul. If his visit to Paul became known, it could have caused Paul's enemies to direct their wrath against him. It took even more courage for him to be willing to share what he knew with the Roman authorities. He had no way of knowing how they would react. He might have been afraid the tribune would not believe him and would turn him over to the Jews, for he surely knew the Romans allowed the Sanhedrin authority over Jewish affairs. But he was willing to take the risk in order to save Paul.

**23:18.** The centurion took the young man to the tribune. He explained how Paul had said the young man had something to say to him. Paul wisely had not told the centurion about the plot. Only the tribune would be able to do anything about it, and it was better that not too many people know about it.

Paul is called a prisoner here. Actually, he was under protective custody. It may be also that (as was later the case in Rome) his right hand was chained to the left hand of a soldier. But this did not trouble Paul. Later he made it clear that he considered himself a prisoner, not of Rome, but of the Lord (Ephesians 3:1; 2 Timothy 1:8; Philemon 1,9). He had been brought into the glorious freedom and liberty of the children of God (Romans 8:21). Christ had set him free and the Spirit of the Lord gave continued liberty. Nothing could change that.

**he went and entered into the castle, and told Paul:** He went to the fortress, *SEB* . . . went to the army building, *NCV* . . . went to the Fort, and on being admitted, told Paul about it, *TCNT* . . . and he came and got into the barracks, *Goodspeed* . . . he went and gained entrance to, *TNT* . . . came and found his way into, *Phillips* . . . so he came along and entered the barracks to inform Paul, *Berkeley* . . . went to the soldiers' quarters, *Knox* . . . entering the fortress, he reported to Paul, *KJII* . . . and gave news of it to Paul, *BB* . . . reported it to, *Worrell.*

**17. Then Paul called one of the centurions unto him, and said:** . . . called one of the officers and said, *NCV.*

**Bring this young man unto the chief captain:** . . . to take the lad to, *TCNT* . . . Take this young man to, *Weymouth* . . . Conduct this young man to, *Berkeley* . . . to the officer, *Swann* . . . to the commander, *Everyday.*

**for he hath a certain thing to tell him:** . . . for he has information to give him, *Weymouth* . . . he has something to tell him, *NLT* . . . he has news to give him, *Knox* . . . He has a message for him, *Everyday, NCV* . . . has something to report to him, *Phillips.*

**18. So he took him, and brought him to the chief captain, and said:** So the officer took him to the commander, saying, *Moffatt* . . . brought Paul's nephew to the commander, *Everyday* . . . brought him into the colonel's presence, *Phillips.*

**Paul the prisoner called me unto him:** . . . made a request to me, *BB* . . . had me summoned, *Knox* . . . asked me, *Everyday.*

**and prayed me to bring this young man unto thee:** . . . and asked me, *ASV* . . . made a request to me, *BB* . . . and begged me to bring this youth to you, *Weymouth* . . . bring this young man to you, *Lamsa* . . . and asked me to take this young man into thy presence, *Knox.*

**who hath something to say unto thee:** . . . as having somewhat to tell thee, *Rotherham* . . . as he has something to say, *Goodspeed* . . . He wants to tell you something, *Everyday.*

| 1156.2 conj | 3450.10 art gen sing fem | 5331.2 noun gen sing fem | 840.3 prs-pron gen sing | 3450.5 art nom sing masc | 5341.1 noun nom sing masc |
|---|---|---|---|---|---|
| δὲ | τῆς | χειρὸς | αὐτοῦ | ὁ | χιλίαρχος, |
| de | tēs | cheiros | autou | ho | chiliarchos |
| and | of the | hand | his | the | chief captain, |

| 2504.1 conj | 400.4 verb nom sing masc part aor act | 2567.1 prep | 2375.11 adj acc sing fem | 4299.6 verb 3sing indic imperf mid |
|---|---|---|---|---|
| καὶ | ἀναχωρήσας | κατ’ | ἰδίαν | ἐπυνθάνετο, |
| kai | anachōrēsas | kat' | idian | epunthaneto |
| and | having withdrawn | according to | his own | was inquiring, |

| 4949.9 intr-pron sing neu | 1498.4 verb 3sing indic pres act | 3614.16 rel-pron sing neu | 2174.3 verb 2sing indic pres act | 514.10 verb inf aor act |
|---|---|---|---|---|
| Τί | ἐστιν | ὃ | ἔχεις | ἀπαγγεῖλαί |
| Ti | estin | ho | echeis | apangeilai |
| What | is it | which | you have | to report |

| 1466.4 prs-pron dat 1sing | 1500.5 verb 3sing indic aor act | 1156.2 conj | 3617.1 conj | 3450.7 art nom pl masc | 2428.2 name-adj nom pl masc |
|---|---|---|---|---|---|
| μοι; | 20. Εἶπεν | δὲ | Ὅτι | Οἱ | Ἰουδαῖοι |
| moi | Eipen | de | Hoti | Hoi | Ioudaioi |
| to me? | He said | and, | | The | Jews |

| 4786.1 verb 3pl indic aor mid | 3450.2 art gen sing | 2049.14 verb inf aor act | 4622.4 prs-pron acc 2sing | 3567.1 conj | 833.1 adv |
|---|---|---|---|---|---|
| συνέθεντο | τοῦ | ἐρωτῆσαί | σε, | ὅπως | αὔριον |
| sunethento | tou | erōtēsai | se | hopōs | aurion |
| agreed | the | to request | you, | that | tomorrow |

| 1519.1 prep | 3450.16 art sing neu | 4742.1 noun sing neu | 2580.2 verb 2sing subj aor act | 3450.6 art acc sing masc |
|---|---|---|---|---|
| ‘ εἰς | τὸ | συνέδριον | καταγάγῃς | τὸν |
| eis | to | sunedrion | katagagēs | ton |
| into | the | Sanhedrin | you may bring down | |

| 3834.4 name acc masc | 3450.6 art acc sing masc | 3834.4 name acc masc | 2580.2 verb 2sing subj aor act | 1519.1 prep |
|---|---|---|---|---|
| Παῦλον, | [☆ τὸν | Παῦλον | καταγάγῃς | εἰς |
| Paulon | ton | Paulon | katagagēs | eis |
| Paul, | | [ Paul | you may bring down | into |

20.a.**Txt:** byz.it.sa.Steph
**Var1:** 01ℵ-org,33
UBS/☆
**Var2:** p74,02A,03B,08E
bo.Lach,Treg,Alf,Word
Tisc,We/Ho,Weis,Sod

| 3450.16 art sing neu | 4742.1 noun sing neu | 5453.1 conj | 3165.13 verb nom pl masc part pres act | 3165.17 verb sing neu part pres act |
|---|---|---|---|---|
| τὸ | συνέδριον ] | ὡς | ‘ μέλλοντές | [1a☆ μέλλον |
| to | sunedrion | hōs | mellontes | mellon |
| the | Sanhedrin ] | as | being about | [ idem |

| 3165.12 verb nom sing masc part pres act | 4948.10 indef-pron sing neu | 194.1 adv comp | 4299.2 verb inf pres mid |
|---|---|---|---|
| 2 μέλλων ] | τι | ἀκριβέστερον | πυνθάνεσθαι |
| mellōn | ti | akribesteron | punthanesthai |
| idem ] | something | more accurately | to inquire |

| 3875.1 prep | 840.3 prs-pron gen sing | 4622.1 prs-pron nom 2sing | 3631.1 partic | 3231.1 partic | 3844.26 verb 2sing subj aor pass |
|---|---|---|---|---|---|
| περὶ | αὐτοῦ. | 21. σὺ | οὖν | μὴ | πεισθῇς |
| peri | autou | su | oun | mē | peisthēs |
| concerning | him. | You | therefore | not | be persuaded |

| 840.2 prs-pron dat pl | 1732.1 verb 3pl indic pres act | 1056.1 conj | 840.6 prs-pron acc sing masc | 1523.1 prep gen | 840.1 prs-pron gen pl |
|---|---|---|---|---|---|
| αὐτοῖς· | ἐνεδρεύουσιν | γὰρ | αὐτὸν | ἐξ | αὐτῶν |
| autois | enedreuousin | gar | auton | ex | autōn |
| by them, | lie in wait | for | him | of | them |

**23:19.** The tribune received the young man courteously, took him by the hand, and retired into a place where they could talk privately. Then he asked him what he had to tell him.

There must have been something about the bearing of Paul's nephew that impressed the tribune with the seriousness of what the young man had to say. He was probably impressed too by the fact that the young man had not tried to come directly to him, but had gone first to Paul, and then through the centurion. This young man was quite different from the violent, riotous Jews the tribune had been dealing with in the temple court and even in the Sanhedrin. He showed an attitude of trust toward the tribune.

Actually, though Rome's conquests were often barbaric, Rome ruled its conquered territories with a statesmanship that was humane and very tolerant. Beginning with the Emperor Augustus it became Rome's policy to preserve peace throughout the whole empire. They wanted to spread civilization and what they considered to be just laws. They encouraged the spread of Greek culture. But they were tolerant of Judaism and made it one of the licensed religions of the empire. At times the Roman government even protected the Jews from the enmity that was sometimes stirred up against them by their heathen neighbors.

**23:20.** The young man told the tribune how the Jews had agreed together to make a request of the tribune that he would bring Paul down to the Sanhedrin the next day in order to determine or decide his case by a more thorough and exact investigation. This was something that under ordinary circumstances the tribune would certainly consider a reasonable request.

Paul's nephew meant the Jewish leaders had done so, that is, the Jews with whom the tribune had been dealing in the previous trial. The New Testament often uses the term "the Jews" when it means the Jewish leaders who were the representatives of the Jews before the Roman government. It does not mean that every Jew or even every Jew in Jerusalem was involved in the plots and opposition against the Christians or against Christian leaders like Paul.

It does seem strange that these Jews who were the highest religious leaders of the Jewish people would consent to a plot that was pure deception. But this was not the first or last time that high religious leaders had promoted deception and trickery under the guise of religion. But it is a sad thing when lies and deception are used by those claiming to represent the one true God. However, the Jewish leaders were not the only ones guilty of such things. The history of the church is not blameless either.

**23:21.** Paul's nephew went to warn the tribune not to be persuaded by the Jews who would come in a very convincing manner. The young man was very bold and emphatic here as he put the responsibility on the tribune not to be convinced, not to follow the Jews' advice or yield to their request.

**19. Then the chief captain took him by the hand:** . . . taking him by the arm, *Weymouth* . . . led the young man, *Everyday.*

**and went with him aside privately, and asked him:** . . . began privately to ask, *Rotherham* . . . stepped to one side with him privately and inquired, *Berkeley* . . . and drew him aside (where they could not be overheard), *Phillips* . . . withdrew to a private place, *Swann* . . . to a place where they could be alone, *SEB* . . . drew him off to one side, asking, *KJII.*

**What is that thou hast to tell me?:** What have you to tell me, *Weymouth* . . . What is it which thou hast to report unto me, *Rotherham.*

**20. And he said:** He answered, *Williams*. . . And he replied, *Phillips.*

**The Jews have agreed to desire thee:** . . . have decided to ask, *Everyday* . . . to ask thee, *ASV* . . . to request thee, *Rotherham.*

**that thou wouldest bring down Paul to morrow into the council:** . . . to ask you to bring Paul to the courtroom tomorrow, *NLT* . . . to their council meeting, *Everyday.*

**as though they would enquire somewhat of him more perfectly:** . . . on the plea of your making further inquiry into his case, *TCNT* . . . as though you were going to examine his case more carefully, *Williams* . . . on the pretext of obtaining more precise information about him, *NEB* . . . as if they would inquire somewhat more exactly concerning him, *Worrell* . . . They want you to think that they plan to ask Paul more questions, *SEB* . . . They want you to think that they want more information about him, *NCV.*

**21. But do not thou yield unto them:** . . . but do not you give in to them, *Berkeley*. . . Do not grant them this request, *Noli*. . . But do not let them persuade you, *TCNT* . . . I beg you not to comply, *Weymouth* . . . Do not pay attention to them, *Klingensmith* . . . Do not let them talk you into it, *NLT.*

**for there lie in wait for him of them more than forty men:** . . . have ganged up, *Klingensmith* . . . are waiting in secret, *NLT*. . . who are hiding and waiting to kill, *SEB.*

# Acts 23:22

| 433.6 noun nom pl masc | 3979.3 adj comp pl | 4910.2 num card | 4910.1 num card |
|---|---|---|---|
| ἄνδρες | πλείους | ʻ τεσσαράκοντα, | [ τεσσεράκοντα, ] |
| *andres* | *pleious* | *tessarakonta* | *tesserakonta* |
| men | more than | forty | [ idem ] |

| 3610.2 rel-pron nom pl masc | 330.3 verb 3pl indic aor act | 1431.8 prs-pron acc pl masc | 3250.1 conj | 2052.25 verb inf aor act | 3250.1 conj |
|---|---|---|---|---|---|
| οἵτινες | ἀνεθεμάτισαν | ἑαυτοὺς | μήτε | φαγεῖν | μήτε |
| *hoitines* | *anethematisan* | *heautous* | *mēte* | *phagein* | *mēte* |
| who | put under a curse | themselves | neither | to eat | nor |

21.a.**Txt:** 01ℵ,02A 03B-corr,08E,020L 025P,etc.byz.Tisc,Sod **Var:** 03B-org,We/Ho Weis,UBS/⋆

| 3956.23 verb inf aor act | 3956.29 verb inf aor act | 2175.1 conj | 3614.2 rel-pron gen sing | 335.8 verb 3pl subj aor act | 840.6 prs-pron acc sing masc |
|---|---|---|---|---|---|
| ʻ πιεῖν | [a πεῖν ] | ἕως | οὗ | ἀνέλωσιν | αὐτόν· |
| *piein* | *pein* | *heōs* | *hou* | *anelōsin* | *auton* |
| to drink | [ idem ] | until | which | they put to death | him; |

| 2504.1 conj | 3431.1 adv | 2071.1 adj nom pl | 1498.7 verb 3pl indic pres act | 1498.7 verb 3pl indic pres act | 2071.1 adj nom pl |
|---|---|---|---|---|---|
| καὶ | νῦν | ʻ ἕτοιμοι | εἰσιν | [⋆ εἰσιν | ἕτοιμοι ] |
| *kai* | *nun* | *hetoimoi* | *eisin* | *eisin* | *hetoimoi* |
| and | now | ready | they are | [ they are | ready ] |

| 4185.5 verb nom pl masc part pres mid | 3450.12 art acc sing fem | 570.3 prep | 4622.2 prs-pron gen 2sing | 1845.4 noun acc sing fem |
|---|---|---|---|---|
| προσδεχόμενοι | τὴν | ἀπὸ | σοῦ | ἐπαγγελίαν. |
| *prosdechomenoi* | *tēn* | *apo* | *sou* | *epangelian* |
| waiting for | the | from | you | promise. |

| 3450.5 art nom sing masc | 3173.1 conj | 3631.1 partic | 5341.1 noun nom sing masc | 624.6 verb 3sing indic aor act | 3450.6 art acc sing masc |
|---|---|---|---|---|---|
| 22. ʽΟ | μὲν | οὖν | χιλίαρχος | ἀπέλυσεν | τὸν |
| *Ho* | *men* | *oun* | *chiliarchos* | *apelusen* | *ton* |
| The | indeed | therefore | chief captain | dismissed | the |

22.a.**Txt:** 020L,025P,byz. **Var:** 01ℵ,02A,03B,08E Lach,Treg,Alf,Tisc We/Ho,Weis,Sod UBS/⋆

| 3357.3 noun acc sing masc | 3358.2 noun acc sing masc | 3715.11 verb nom sing masc part aor act | 3235.2 num card dat |
|---|---|---|---|
| ʻ νεανίαν, | [a⋆ νεανίσκον ] | παραγγείλας | μηδενὶ |
| *neanian* | *neaniskon* | *parangeilas* | *mēdeni* |
| young man, | [ idem ] | having charged | to no one |

| 1570.1 verb inf aor act | 3617.1 conj | 3642.18 dem-pron pl neu | 1702.3 verb 2sing indic aor act | 4242.1 prep | 1466.6 prs-pron acc 1sing |
|---|---|---|---|---|---|
| ἐκλαλῆσαι | ὅτι | ταῦτα | ἐνεφάνισας | πρός | ʻ με. |
| *eklalēsai* | *hoti* | *tauta* | *enephanisas* | *pros* | *me* |
| to utter | that | these things | you revealed | to | me. |

22.b.**Txt:** 02A,08E,020L 025P,byz.Sod **Var:** 01ℵ,03B,Treg,Tisc We/Ho,Weis,UBS/⋆

| 1466.7 prs-pron acc 1sing | 2504.1 conj | 4200.4 verb nom sing masc part aor mid | 1411.3 num card | 4948.9 indef-pron acc pl masc |
|---|---|---|---|---|
| [b ἐμέ. ] | 23. Καὶ | προσκαλεσάμενος | ʻ δύο | τινὰς |
| *eme* | *Kai* | *proskalesamenos* | *duo* | *tinas* |
| [ idem ] | And | having called to | two | certain |

| 4948.9 indef-pron acc pl masc | 1411.3 num card | 3450.1 art gen pl | 1529.3 noun gen pl masc | 1500.5 verb 3sing indic aor act |
|---|---|---|---|---|
| [ τινας | δύο ] | τῶν | ἑκατονταρχῶν | εἶπεν, |
| *tinas* | *duo* | *tōn* | *hekatontarchōn* | *eipen* |
| [ certain | two ] | of the | centurions | he said, |

| 2069.9 verb 2pl impr aor act | 4608.7 noun acc pl masc | 1244.2 num card acc masc | 3567.1 conj | 4057.22 verb 3pl subj aor pass |
|---|---|---|---|---|
| ʽΕτοιμάσατε | στρατιώτας | διακοσίους | ὅπως | πορευθῶσιν |
| *Hetoimasate* | *stratiōtas* | *diakosious* | *hopōs* | *poreuthōsin* |
| Prepare | soldiers | two hundred, | that | they may go |

Then he informed the tribune of the reason. Even now the men were prepared to carry out their plot. They were just waiting until they received a promise from the tribune. Then they would take their place in the ambush in order to carry out their terrible plot.

The way the young man presented himself to the tribune shows he was sincere, earnest, and had the facts. He showed no fear of the tribune. He did not waste time with undue politeness, but was straightforward and went right to the point. This also must have appealed to the tribune as a Roman. The Gospel of Mark, which was directed to the Romans, shows the same straightforward manner and direct approach. The Holy Spirit must have given this young man wisdom as well as courage.

Jesus had promised that when His disciples came to trial before governors and kings, the Holy Spirit would give them what to say (Matthew 10:18-20). Now it is evident that the Spirit guides others who are raised up to help His people.

**23:22.** The tribune then dismissed the young man (let him go, sent him away) with a command forbidding him to tell anyone what he had revealed (reported) to him.

The tribune gave this order in such an emphatic manner to impress on the young man the need of secrecy and discretion to insure the safety of Paul. It is certain Paul's nephew obeyed the tribune's order. The young man's manner impressed the tribune and caused the tribune to believe him. But the tribune also recognized the youth of his informant. He knew that youth is not always characterized by discretion. So this was another reason he made the command so emphatic.

God was working in all of this. Jesus had appeared to Paul and given him assurance that He would see him through to Rome. But Paul still did not see how this could or would be done. But God was working things out step by step. The very fact that Paul's nephew came must have given Paul's faith further encouragement. The Bible does not say so, but it is very probable that the young man stopped by to see Paul on the way out of the fortress and told him of the favorable way the tribune had received him. Thus, the Lord was encouraging Paul's faith at every step of the way.

It must not be supposed Paul did not need this repeated encouragement. James 5:17 is a reminder that Elijah was a man with a nature like everyone else. In spite of the great faith he showed and the miracles he saw, he too could become discouraged. But God dealt with him and brought him to renewed faith and courage. He encourages believers today as well.

**23:23.** The tribune knew he would be held accountable for Paul, as a Roman citizen in his custody, if Paul were assassinated. That is, the tribune himself would be punished. Therefore, he did not waste any time. Immediately he had 2 centurions get 200 foot soldiers ready to go to Caesarea, along with 70 cavalry and 200 soldiers of another class. Apparently, these were the usual constit-

**which have bound themselves with an oath, that they will neither eat nor drink:** . . . have taken a solemn oath, *Noli.*

**till they have killed him:** . . . assassinated him, *Weymouth* . . . destroyed him, *Berkeley.*

**and now are they ready:** . . . and they are at this very moment in readiness, *TCNT* . . . and they are all set, *Norlie* . . . even now they are in readiness, *Knox* . . . Now these conspirators are lying in ambush for him, *Noli.*

**looking for a promise from thee:** . . . only waiting for thy consent, *Knox* . . . awaiting your consent, *Moffatt* . . . all they want now is for you to give the order, *Phillips* . . . will receive a favourable reply from you, *Fenton* . . . They are all waiting for you to say the word, *NLT* . . . now they are waiting for you to say yes, *NCV* . . . are waiting for a favorable answer from you, *Noli.*

**22. So the chief captain then let the young man depart:** . . . therefore dismissed the young man, *Rotherham* . . . So the Tribune sent the youth home, *Weymouth* . . . sent the young man away, *NCV.*

**and charged him:** . . . cautioning him, *TCNT* . . . with strict directions, *Williams* . . . with the strict advice, *Norlie* . . . with the injunction, *Montgomery* . . . with the following command, *Noli.*

**See thou tell no man:** Tell nobody, *Moffatt* . . . Do not let anyone know, *Weymouth* . . . Don't let a soul know, *Phillips* . . . not to mention to anyone, *TCNT* . . . not to divulge to anyone, *Confraternity* . . . warning him not to let anyone know, *Knox.*

**that thou hast shewed these things to me:** . . . that he had given him that information, *TCNT* . . . that you have informed me of this, *Moffatt* . . . that he had notified him of this plot, *Williams* . . . that he had revealed this secret to him, *Knox.*

**23. And he called unto him two centurions, saying:** He summoned two of the officers, *Moffatt* . . . and ordered them, *TCNT.*

**Make ready two hundred soldiers to go to Caesarea:** . . . to have two hundred men ready to go to Caesarea, *TCNT.*

# Acts 23:24

| 2175.1 conj | 2513.1 name gen fem | 2504.1 conj | 2435.1 noun acc pl masc | 1433.1 num card |
|---|---|---|---|---|
| ἕως | Καισαρείας, | καὶ | ἱππεῖς | ἑβδομήκοντα, |
| *heōs* | *Kaisareias* | *kai* | *hippeis* | *hebdomēkonta* |
| as far as | Caesarea, | and | horsemen | seventy, |

| 2504.1 conj | 1181.1 noun acc pl masc | 1244.2 num card acc masc | 570.3 prep | 4995.5 num ord gen sing fem | 5443.1 noun fem |
|---|---|---|---|---|---|
| καὶ | δεξιολάβους | διακοσίους, | ἀπὸ | τρίτης | ὥρας |
| *kai* | *dexiolabous* | *diakosious* | *apo* | *tritēs* | *hōras* |
| and | spearmen | two hundred, | from | the third | hour |

| 3450.10 art gen sing fem | 3433.2 noun gen sing fem | 2906.3 noun pl neu | 4885.1 conj | 3798.12 verb inf aor act | 2419.1 conj |
|---|---|---|---|---|---|
| τῆς | νυκτός˙ | **24.** κτήνη | τε | παραστῆσαι, | ἵνα |
| *tēs* | *nuktos* | *ktēnē* | *te* | *parastēsai* | *hina* |
| of the | night. | Beasts | and | to have provided, | that |

| 1898.3 verb nom pl masc part aor act | 3450.6 art acc sing masc | 3834.4 name acc masc | 1289.2 verb 3pl subj aor act |
|---|---|---|---|
| ἐπιβιβάσαντες | τὸν | Παῦλον | διασώσωσιν |
| *epibibasantes* | *ton* | *Paulon* | *diasōsōsin* |
| having set on | | Paul | they may carry safe through |

| 4242.1 prep | 5181.4 name acc masc | 3450.6 art acc sing masc | 2215.4 noun acc sing masc | 1119.13 verb nom sing masc part aor act |
|---|---|---|---|---|
| πρὸς | Φήλικα | τὸν | ἡγεμόνα˙ | **25.** γράψας |
| *pros* | *Phēlika* | *ton* | *hēgemona* | *grapsas* |
| to | Felix | the | governor, | having written |

25.a.**Txt:** 02A,020L 025P,byz.
**Var:** 01ℵ,03B,08E,Lach Treg,Tisc,We/Ho,Weis Sod,UBS/☆

| 1976.4 noun acc sing fem | 3886.2 verb acc sing fem part pres act | 2174.25 verb acc sing fem part pres act | 3450.6 art acc sing masc |
|---|---|---|---|
| ἐπιστολὴν | ʿ περιέχουσαν | [a☆ ἔχουσαν ] | τὸν |
| *epistolēn* | *periechousan* | *echousan* | *ton* |
| a letter | having | [ idem ] | the |

| 5020.2 noun acc sing masc | 3642.6 dem-pron acc sing masc | 2777.1 name nom masc | 3051.1 name nom masc | 3450.3 art dat sing |
|---|---|---|---|---|
| τύπον | τοῦτον˙ | **26.** Κλαύδιος | Λυσίας | τῷ |
| *tupon* | *touton* | *Klaudios* | *Lusias* | *tō* |
| form | this: | Claudius | Lysias | to the |

| 2876.1 adj sup dat sing masc | 2215.3 noun dat sing masc | 5181.3 name dat masc | 5299.11 verb inf pres act | 3450.6 art acc sing masc |
|---|---|---|---|---|
| κρατίστῳ | ἡγεμόνι | Φήλικι | χαίρειν. | **27.** Τὸν |
| *kratistō* | *hēgemoni* | *Phēliki* | *chairein* | *Ton* |
| most excellent | governor, | Felix, | to greet. | The |

| 433.4 noun acc sing masc | 3642.6 dem-pron acc sing masc | 4666.9 verb acc sing masc part aor pass | 4666.15 verb acc sing masc part aor pass |
|---|---|---|---|
| ἄνδρα | τοῦτον | ʿ συλληφθέντα | [☆ συλλημφθέντα ] |
| *andra* | *touton* | *sullēphthenta* | *sullēmphthenta* |
| man | this, | having been seized | [ idem ] |

| 5097.3 prep | 3450.1 art gen pl | 2428.3 name-adj gen pl masc | 2504.1 conj | 3165.8 verb part pres act | 335.11 verb inf pres mid |
|---|---|---|---|---|---|
| ὑπὸ | τῶν | Ἰουδαίων, | καὶ | μέλλοντα | ἀναιρεῖσθαι |
| *hupo* | *tōn* | *Ioudaiōn* | *kai* | *mellonta* | *anaireisthai* |
| by | the | Jews, | and | being about | to be put to death |

| 5097.2 prep | 840.1 prs-pron gen pl | 2168.5 verb nom sing masc part aor act | 4713.1 prep | 3450.3 art dat sing | 4604.2 noun dat sing neu |
|---|---|---|---|---|---|
| ὑπ' | αὐτῶν, | ἐπιστὰς | σὺν | τῷ | στρατεύματι |
| *hup'* | *autōn* | *epistas* | *sun* | *tō* | *strateumati* |
| by | them, | having come up | with | the | troop |

uents of a Roman army corps. By 9 o'clock that night they were to be on their way to the Roman capital of Palestine, about 55 miles northwest of Jerusalem.

Caesarea was built by Herod the Great on the coast about 30 miles north of Joppa. Herod also constructed a 200-foot-wide causeway of huge stones in water 60 feet deep in order to enclose an artificial harbor that was unusually large for that day. The Roman procurators or governors made this city their chief residence. Archaeologists have found the name of Pilate inscribed on one of the stones.

**23:24.** Horses were also to be provided for Paul to ride so he might be brought safely to Felix, the Roman governor of the province.

Marcus Antonius Felix was procurator of Judea from A.D. 52 to 59. He was a freedman (former slave) of the Emperor Claudius or of the emperor's mother. A violent man, he slaughtered many Jews as well as others. Tacitus, the Roman historian, wrote that Claudius reveled in cruelty and lust, and wielded the power of a king with the mind of a slave.

But though Felix was a fierce and violent man, Paul was not afraid to be sent to him, for Jesus had promised to be with him.

In the meantime, the more than 40 Jews who had planned to wait in ambush were left without their victim. Perhaps they just went home feeling thwarted in their plans to do away with Paul.

**23:25.** The tribune, of course, could not send Paul to the governor without some explanation, so he wrote a letter to Felix.

Acts says it was "after this manner" (type, pattern, copy). A possible meaning is that what follows is an actual copy of the letter. There has been conjecture that Paul saw the letter, made a copy, and gave it to Luke. How the Holy Spirit worked in this case is not explained.

**23:26.** In the letter the tribune stated his name, Claudius Lysias. Claudius was a Roman name taken by the tribune, probably at the time he bought his Roman citizenship. Lysias was a Greek name common in Syria, indicating his background in Greek culture.

Next he sent greetings to Felix, addressing him as the most noble or most excellent (imperial) governor (a title used of the procurators).

**23:27.** The tribune explained how Paul was seized by the Jews and was about to be killed violently by them. Then, because he had learned Paul was a Roman citizen, he came and rescued Paul.

It was not true that Lysias learned Paul was a Roman before he went to rescue him. He did not learn of this until after he gave orders for his soldiers to scourge Paul. But Lysias does not mention

**and horsemen threescore and ten:** . . . and seventy horsemen, *Rotherham* . . . as well as seventy troopers, *TCNT.*

**and spearmen two hundred:** . . . and two hundred lancers, *TCNT* . . . men with spears, *Everyday.*

**at the third hour of the night:** . . . and have them ready to start, *Beck* . . . starting...tonight! *Weymouth* . . . Be ready to leave at nine o'clock tonight, *Everyday.*

**24. And provide them beasts, that they may set Paul on:** . . . and to have horses ready for Paul to ride, *TCNT* . . . get some horses for Paul to ride, *Everyday.*

**and bring him safe unto Felix the governor:** . . . and convey him safely, *Hanson* . . . and conduct him safely to governor Felix, *Berkeley* . . . He must be taken to Governor Felix safely, *Everyday.*

**25. And he wrote a letter after this manner:** . . . somewhat as follows, *TCNT* . . . He also wrote a letter of which these were the contents, *Weymouth* . . . after this fashion, *Rotherham* . . . to whom he sent the following letter, *Williams* . . . after this model, *Concordant.*

**26. Claudius Lysias unto the most excellent governor Felix sendeth greeting:** . . . to His Excellency, *Noli.*

**27. This man was taken of the Jews:** This man, having been apprehended, *Rotherham* . . . When this man was set upon, *Berkeley* . . . had been seized by the Jews, *TCNT* . . . The Jews had taken this man, *Everyday.*

**and should have been killed of them:** . . . and was on the point of being killed by them, *TCNT* . . . and was within an inch of being murdered by them, *Berkeley* . . . almost assassinated by them, *Fenton* . . . They were ready to murder him, *Noli* . . . who intended to kill him, *Lamsa.*

**then came I with an army:** . . . but I intervened with Roman soldiers, *Lamsa* . . . came upon them with the force under my command, *TCNT* . . . came upon them suddenly, with the troops, *Hanson* . . . with my regiment, *Norlie* . . . when I arrived with my troops, *Phillips.*

## Acts 23:28

27.a.**Txt:** 020L,025P,byz. **Var:** 01ℵ,02A,03B,08E 33,Lach,Treg,Alf,Word Tisc,We/Ho,Weis,Sod UBS/☆

27.b.**Txt:** 020L,025P,byz. **Var:** 01ℵ,02A,03B,08E Lach,Treg,Word,Tisc We/Ho,Weis,Sod UBS/☆

| **1791.3** verb 1sing indic aor mid | **1791.7** verb 1sing indic aor mid | **840.6** prs-pron acc sing masc | **3101.12** verb nom sing masc part aor act |
|---|---|---|---|
| ⸂ ἐξειλόμην | [a☆ ἐξειλάμην, ] | ⸂b αὐτόν, ⸃ | μαθὼν |
| *exeilomēn* | *exeilamēn* | *auton* | *mathōn* |
| I rescued | [ idem ] | him, | having learned |

| **3617.1** conj | **4371.1** name-adj nom sing masc | **1498.4** verb 3sing indic pres act | **1007.8** verb nom sing masc part pres mid | **1156.2** conj |
|---|---|---|---|---|
| ὅτι | Ῥωμαῖός | ἐστιν. | **28.** βουλόμενός | ⸂ δὲ |
| *hoti* | *Rhōmaios* | *estin* | *boulomenos* | *de* |
| that | a Roman | he is. | Desiring | and |

28.a.**Txt:** 020L,025P,byz. **Var:** 01ℵ,02A,03B,Lach Treg,Alf,Tisc,We/Ho Weis,Sod,UBS/☆

| **1091.29** verb inf aor act | **4885.1** conj | **1906.14** verb inf aor act | **3450.12** art acc sing fem | **155.3** noun acc sing fem | **1217.1** prep |
|---|---|---|---|---|---|
| γνῶναι | [a☆ τε | ἐπιγνῶναι ] | τὴν | αἰτίαν | δι' |
| *gnōnai* | *te* | *epignōnai* | *tēn* | *aitian* | *di'* |
| to know | [ and | to know ] | the | charge | on account of |

| **3614.12** rel-pron acc sing fem | **1451.3** verb 3pl indic imperf act | **840.4** prs-pron dat sing | **2580.1** verb indic aor act |
|---|---|---|---|
| ἣν | ἐνεκάλουν | αὐτῷ | κατήγαγον |
| *hēn* | *enekaloun* | *autō* | *katēgagon* |
| which | they were accusing | him | I brought down |

28.b.**Txt:** p48,03B-corr 08E,020L,025P,byz.sa. bo.Sod **Var:** p74,01ℵ,02A,33 Tisc,We/Ho,Weis UBS/☆

| **840.6** prs-pron acc sing masc | **1519.1** prep | **3450.16** art sing neu | **4742.1** noun sing neu | **840.1** prs-pron gen pl | **3614.6** rel-pron acc sing masc |
|---|---|---|---|---|---|
| ⸂b αὐτόν ⸃ | εἰς | τὸ | συνέδριον | αὐτῶν· | **29.** ὃν |
| *auton* | *eis* | *to* | *sunedrion* | *autōn* | *hon* |
| him | to | the | Sanhedrin | their: | whom |

| **2128.6** verb indic aor act | **1451.5** verb acc sing masc part pres mid | **3875.1** prep | **2196.4** noun gen pl neu | **3450.2** art gen sing |
|---|---|---|---|---|
| εὗρον | ἐγκαλούμενον | περὶ | ζητημάτων | τοῦ |
| *heuron* | *enkaloumenon* | *peri* | *zētēmatōn* | *tou* |
| I found | being accused | concerning | questions | of the |

| **3414.2** noun gen sing masc | **840.1** prs-pron gen pl | **3235.6** num card neu | **1156.2** conj | **510.1** adj sing | **2265.2** noun gen sing masc | **2211.1** conj |
|---|---|---|---|---|---|---|
| νόμου | αὐτῶν, | μηδὲν | δὲ | ἄξιον | θανάτου | ἢ |
| *nomou* | *autōn* | *mēden* | *de* | *axion* | *thanatou* | *ē* |
| law | their, | nothing | but | worthy | of death | or |

| **1193.4** noun gen pl | **1455.2** noun sing neu | **2174.15** verb part pres act | **2174.15** verb part pres act | **1455.2** noun sing neu |
|---|---|---|---|---|
| δεσμῶν | ⸂ ἔγκλημα | ἔχοντα. | [☆ ἔχοντα | ἔγκλημα. ] |
| *desmōn* | *enklēma* | *echonta* | *echonta* | *enklēma* |
| of bonds | accusation | having. | [ having | accusation. ] |

30.a.**Txt:** 020L,025P,byz. sa. **Var:** p74,01ℵ,02A,03B 08E,bo.Lach,Treg,Alf Tisc,We/Ho,Weis,Sod UBS/☆

| **3245.4** verb gen sing fem part aor pass | **1156.2** conj | **1466.4** prs-pron dat 1sing | **1902.2** noun gen sing fem | **1519.1** prep | **3450.6** art acc sing masc |
|---|---|---|---|---|---|
| **30.** μηνυθείσης | δέ | μοι | ἐπιβουλῆς | εἰς | τὸν |
| *mēnutheisēs* | *de* | *moi* | *epiboulēs* | *eis* | *ton* |
| Having been intimated | and | to me | a plot | against | the |

30.b.**Txt:** 020L,025P,byz. sa. **Var:** p74,01ℵ,02A,03B 08E,bo.Lach,Treg,Alf Tisc,We/Ho,Weis,Sod UBS/☆

| **433.4** noun acc sing masc | **3165.18** verb inf pres act | **1498.45** verb inf fut mid | **5097.3** prep | **3450.1** art gen pl | **2428.3** name-adj gen pl masc |
|---|---|---|---|---|---|
| ἄνδρα | ⸂a μέλλειν ⸃ | ἔσεσθαι | ⸂b ὑπὸ | τῶν | Ἰουδαιων ⸃ |
| *andra* | *mellein* | *esesthai* | *hupo* | *tōn* | *Ioudaiōn* |
| man | to be about | about to be | by | the | Jews |

| **1808.1** adv | **3854.5** verb 1sing indic aor act | **4242.1** prep | **4622.4** prs-pron acc 2sing | **3715.11** verb nom sing masc part aor act | **2504.1** conj |
|---|---|---|---|---|---|
| ἐξαυτῆς | ἔπεμψα | πρὸς | σέ, | παραγγείλας | καὶ |
| *exautēs* | *epempsa* | *pros* | *se* | *parangeilas* | *kai* |
| at once | I sent | to | you, | having charged | also |

this mistake on his part. Perhaps he felt that to admit this would get the violent Felix sidetracked on another issue. Also he wanted to put himself in the best light possible.

It is in the tribune's favor, however, that from the start he wanted to give the impression that Paul had been unjustly seized and attacked by the Jews. He seemed really concerned to protect Paul and put Paul in the best light possible. The special emphasis on the fact that Paul was a Roman citizen was also intended to get Felix to receive him favorably.

**23:28.** Lysias further explained he had not jumped to conclusions about Paul. He wanted to learn and ascertain exactly and thoroughly the charge or ground for complaint by which the Jews accused or brought charges against Paul. Therefore he brought Paul down to their Sanhedrin.

This, of course, was true. Even though the tribune had made a mistake in commanding Paul to be scourged, he did want to get at the root cause of all the disturbance that had centered around Paul. The tribune did not give the details of this encounter in his letter, but he was still wanting to put Paul in a good light.

Most of the Roman officers described in the New Testament were well-disposed toward the Jews and later on to the Christians. The centurions especially are shown in a good light. Two centurions are mentioned by name: Cornelius of Caesarea and Julius (chapter 27), who conducted Paul to Rome and treated him with consideration and kindness. Other centurions believed and put their faith in Jesus.

**23:29.** The tribune further explained that when Paul was before the Sanhedrin, he (the tribune) found the accusations all pertained to controversial questions related to their (Jewish) law. He further explained he found nothing in their charges or accusations worthy of putting Paul to death or even of putting him in chains or imprisonment.

This letter, as an official Roman report to the governor, declared Paul was innocent of any crime worthy of punishment. It not only showed Paul in a good light, it gave him an advantage should the Jews bring further accusations against him in the future. Obviously, the tribune wanted to make sure Paul would get justice.

**23:30.** The tribune explained how he was told of the Jews' plot to ambush Paul and how he immediately sent Paul to Felix. Then he added something not mentioned before. He gave commandment to Paul's accusers to bring their charges or accusations to Felix also. In view of the fact that he sent Paul away immediately, the tribune probably meant he was about to send this order to the Sanhedrin.

**and rescued him:** ... and took him out of danger, *Berkeley.*

**having understood that he was a Roman:** ... as I learnt that he was a Roman citizen, *TCNT* ... as I had ascertained that, *Moffatt* ... since I had discovered, *Phillips.*

**28. And when I would have known:** And wishing to know, *HBIE* ... Wishing to ascertain exactly, *TCNT* ... And desiring to get at, *BB* ... In the hope of discovering, *Berkeley.*

**the cause wherefore they accused him:** ... the ground of the charges they made against him, *TCNT* ... the offence of which they were accusing him, *Weymouth* ... the crime for which they were accusing him, *HBIE* ... the reason for their attack, *BB* ... the exact charge, *Williams* ... what complaint it was they had, *Knox.*

**I brought him forth into their council:** I took him down into their High-council, *Rotherham* ... Sanhedrin, *Weymouth.*

**29. Whom I perceived to be accused of questions of their law:** ... where I found he was accused of matters relating to, *Moffatt* ... when I found that their charges were connected with questions of their own Law, *TCNT.*

**but to have nothing laid to his charge worthy of death or of bonds:** ... and that there was nothing alleged involving either death or imprisonment, *TCNT* ... and that nothing was said against him which might be a reason for prison or death, *BB* ... but there was none for which he deserved to die or be in chains, *Beck.*

**30. And when it was told me:** But when I was informed, *Rotherham* ... on its being divulged to me, *Concordant.*

**how that the Jews laid wait for the man:** ... that there would be a plot against the man, *ASV* ... that a plot was being concocted against this man, *Berkeley* ... that a conspiracy was preparing against the man, *Alford.*

**I sent straightway to thee:** I am sending him to you at once, *TCNT* ... without delay, *Phillips.*

30.c.**Txt:** 08E,020L,025P byz.Sod
**Var:** 01ℵ,02A,03B,Lach Treg,Tisc,We/Ho,Weis UBS/☆

| 3450.4 art dat pl | 2695.3 noun dat pl masc | 2978.24 verb inf pres act | 3450.17 art pl neu | 4242.1 prep | 840.6 prs-pron acc sing masc |
|---|---|---|---|---|---|
| τοῖς | κατηγόροις | λέγειν | ⸂c τὰ ⸃ | πρὸς | αὐτὸν |
| *tois* | *katēgorois* | *legein* | *ta* | *pros* | *auton* |
| the | accusers | to say | the things | against | him |

30.d.**Txt:** 01ℵ,08E,044 byz.Sod
**Var:** p74,02A,03B,33,sa. bo.Lach,Treg,Alf,Tisc We/Ho,Weis,UBS/☆

| 1894.3 prep | 4622.2 prs-pron gen 2sing | 4374.2 verb 2pl impr perf mid | 3450.7 art nom pl masc | 3173.1 conj | 3631.1 partic |
|---|---|---|---|---|---|
| ἐπὶ | σοῦ. | ⸂d Ἔρρωσο. ⸃ | 31. Οἱ | μὲν | οὖν |
| *epi* | *sou* | *Errhōso* | *Hoi* | *men* | *oun* |
| before | you. | Farewell. | The | indeed | therefore |

| 4608.4 noun nom pl masc | 2567.3 prep | 3450.16 art sing neu | 1293.12 verb sing neu part perf mid |
|---|---|---|---|
| στρατιῶται, | κατὰ | τὸ | διατεταγμένον |
| *stratiōtai* | *kata* | *to* | *diatetagmenon* |
| soldiers, | according to | the | orders having been given |

| 840.2 prs-pron dat pl | 351.5 verb nom pl masc part aor act | 3450.6 art acc sing masc | 3834.4 name acc masc | 70.10 verb 3pl indic aor act |
|---|---|---|---|---|
| αὐτοῖς, | ἀναλαβόντες | τὸν | Παῦλον | ἤγαγον |
| *autois* | *analabontes* | *ton* | *Paulon* | *ēgagon* |
| to them, | having taken | | Paul | brought |

31.a.**Txt:** 020L,025P,byz.
**Var:** 01ℵ,02A,03B,08E Lach,Treg,Alf,Word Tisc,We/Ho,Weis,Sod UBS/☆

| 1217.2 prep | 3450.10 art gen sing fem | 3433.2 noun gen sing fem | 1519.1 prep | 3450.12 art acc sing fem | 491.1 name acc fem |
|---|---|---|---|---|---|
| διὰ | ⸂a τῆς ⸃ | νυκτὸς | εἰς | τὴν | Ἀντιπατρίδα. |
| *dia* | *tēs* | *nuktos* | *eis* | *tēn* | *Antipatrida* |
| by | the | night | to | | Antipatris, |

| 3450.11 art dat sing fem | 1156.2 conj | 1872.1 adv | 1432.5 verb nom pl masc part aor act | 3450.8 art acc pl masc | 2435.1 noun acc pl masc |
|---|---|---|---|---|---|
| 32. τῇ | δὲ | ἐπαύριον | ἐάσαντες | τοὺς | ἱππεῖς |
| *tē* | *de* | *epaurion* | *easantes* | *tous* | *hippeis* |
| the | and | next day | having left | the | horsemen |

32.a.**Txt:** 020L,025P,byz.
**Var:** 01ℵ,02A,03B,08E Lach,Treg,Alf,Tisc We/Ho,Weis,Sod UBS/☆

| 4057.15 verb inf pres mid | 562.23 verb inf pres mid | 4713.1 prep | 840.4 prs-pron dat sing | 5128.7 verb 3pl indic aor act |
|---|---|---|---|---|
| ⸀ πορεύεσθαι | [a☆ ἀπέρχεσθαι ] | σὺν | αὐτῷ, | ὑπέστρεψαν |
| *poreuesthai* | *aperchesthai* | *sun* | *autō* | *hupestrepsan* |
| to go | [ to go away ] | with | him, | they returned |

| 1519.1 prep | 3450.12 art acc sing fem | 3787.2 noun acc sing fem | 3610.2 rel-pron nom pl masc | 1511.16 verb nom pl masc part aor act |
|---|---|---|---|---|
| εἰς | τὴν | παρεμβολήν· | 33. οἵτινες | εἰσελθόντες |
| *eis* | *tēn* | *parembolēn* | *hoitines* | *eiselthontes* |
| to | the | fortress. | Who | having entered |

| 1519.1 prep | 3450.12 art acc sing fem | 2513.3 name acc fem | 2504.1 conj | 323.1 verb nom pl masc part aor act | 3450.12 art acc sing fem |
|---|---|---|---|---|---|
| εἰς | τὴν | Καισάρειαν, | καὶ | ἀναδόντες | τὴν |
| *eis* | *tēn* | *Kaisareian* | *kai* | *anadontes* | *tēn* |
| into | | Caesarea, | and | having given up | the |

| 1976.4 noun acc sing fem | 3450.3 art dat sing | 2215.3 noun dat sing masc | 3798.6 verb 3pl indic aor act | 2504.1 conj | 3450.6 art acc sing masc |
|---|---|---|---|---|---|
| ἐπιστολὴν | τῷ | ἡγεμόνι, | παρέστησαν | καὶ | τὸν |
| *epistolēn* | *tō* | *hēgemoni* | *parestēsan* | *kai* | *ton* |
| letter | to the | governor, | presented | also | |

34.a.**Txt:** 020L,025P,byz.
**Var:** 01ℵ,02A,03B,08E Gries,Lach,Treg,Alf Word,Tisc,We/Ho,Weis Sod,UBS/☆

| 3834.4 name acc masc | 840.4 prs-pron dat sing | 312.9 verb nom sing masc part aor act | 1156.2 conj | 3450.5 art nom sing masc |
|---|---|---|---|---|
| Παῦλον | αὐτῷ. | 34. ἀναγνοὺς | δὲ | ⸂a ὁ |
| *Paulon* | *autō* | *anagnous* | *de* | *ho* |
| Paul | to him. | Having read | and | the |

It is clear also that the tribune wanted both Felix and the Sanhedrin to know Paul was now out of his jurisdiction. Whatever happened to Paul now would be their affair, not his. He seemed anxious to make sure that if anything did happen to Paul the Roman government would know he had done his part well, and no accusation could be brought against him. This is not to say he was more concerned about himself than he was about Paul. But he probably breathed a sigh of relief when he saw the 400 foot soldiers and 60 horsemen leaving the city of Jerusalem, taking Paul and the letter to Felix.

Such a troop movement, even at night, must have attracted attention. Though it may not have been known Paul was in the midst of them then, it was surely known by the next morning. If the traditions of the Jewish Mishnah were held at this time there was provision for a sacrifice or offering to atone for the failure to keep a vow. Thus, there may have been over 40 extra sacrifices brought to the temple that day.

**and gave commandment to his accusers also:** . . . and I have directed, *TCNT* . . . I also told those Jews, *Everyday* . . . giving orders to these who are against him, *BB* . . . At the same time I have notified his accusers, *Phillips*.

**to say before thee what they had against him:** . . . to prosecute him before you, *TCNT* . . . to state before you the case they have against him, *Weymouth* . . . that they must plead their cause before thee, *Knox* . . . to tell you what they have against him, *NCV* . . . to go and contend with him before you, *Lamsa* . . . to state...whatever accusations they have against him, *Noli*.

**Farewell:**

**23:31.** That night the soldiers brought Paul as far as Antipatris, about 30 miles northwest of Jerusalem (possibly about 38 miles by the old Roman road, and about 24 miles from Caesarea). It was located on a fertile plain near the foothills between Judea and Samaria. Herod the Great built the city and named it after his father, Antipater. The Romans had located a Roman colony there, so it was a convenient and safe place for the Roman soldiers to stop and spend the rest of the night.

**31. Then the soldiers, as it was commanded them, took Paul:** The soldiers, in accordance with their orders, took charge of Paul, *TCNT* . . . did the things they were told, *SEB* . . . acting on their orders, *Phillips* . . . obeying their orders, *Knox* . . . did what they were told, *Everyday*.

**and brought him by night to Antipatris:** . . . and, riding through the night, brought him down to Antipatris, *Phillips* . . . conducted him, travelling all night, *Knox* . . . brought him to the city...that night, *Everyday*.

**23:32.** The next day the 400 foot soldiers returned to their barracks in the Fortress of Antonia in Jerusalem. They probably kept watch along the way to be sure none of the Jews were trying to follow Paul.

Then the 60 cavalry conducted Paul the rest of the way to Caesarea. It was felt that the 60 horsemen would be enough to protect Paul for the remainder of the journey. This undoubtedly gave Paul further opportunity to spread his witness for Christ.

**32. On the morrow they left the horsemen to go with him, and returned to the castle:** On the next day, leaving the troopers to go on with him, they returned to the Fort, *TCNT* . . . dismissed the footmen, *Lamsa* . . . The next day the infantry returned to the barracks, leaving the cavalry to proceed with him, *Weymouth* . . . the horsemen went with Paul to Caesarea, *Everyday*.

**23:33.** When the horsemen arrived in Caesarea it must have been an unusual sight to see such a company escorting a prisoner. Those who saw them probably thought Paul was some hero or notable person being escorted to the governor's palace by an honor guard. God has ways of overruling the intentions of the enemies of His people.

The cavalry first delivered the letter to the Roman governor, or procurator, Felix. Then, after giving the governor the letter (and an opportunity to read it), they presented Paul to him also. (It is probable that a centurion accompanied the cavalry. The centurion may have been the one who actually delivered the letter and presented Paul to Felix.)

**33. Who, when they came to Caesarea:** They went into Caesarea, *Phillips*.

**and delivered the epistle to the governor:** . . . and delivered the letter, *RSV* . . . gave the letter to, *Everyday*.

**presented Paul also before him:** . . . and brought Paul before him, *TCNT* . . . and turned Paul over to him, too, *Williams* . . . Then they gave Paul to him, *SEB*.

| 2215.1 noun nom sing masc | 2504.1 conj | 1890.9 verb nom sing masc part aor act | 1523.2 prep gen | 4029.4 intr-pron fem | 1870.1 noun gen sing fem |
|---|---|---|---|---|---|
| ἡγεμών, ˺ | καὶ | ἐπερωτήσας | ἐκ | ποίας | ˹ ἐπαρχίας |
| *hēgemōn* | *kai* | *eperōtēsas* | *ek* | *poias* | *eparchias* |
| governor, | and | having asked | of | what | province |

| 1870.3 noun gen sing fem | 1498.4 verb 3sing indic pres act | 2504.1 conj | 4299.4 verb nom sing masc part aor mid | 3617.1 conj | 570.3 prep |
|---|---|---|---|---|---|
| [☆ ἐπαρχείας ] | ἐστὶν, | καὶ | πυθόμενος | ὅτι | ἀπὸ |
| *eparcheias* | *estin* | *kai* | *puthomenos* | *hoti* | *apo* |
| [ idem ] | he is, | and | having learned | that | from |

| 2763.1 name gen fem | 1245.1 verb 1sing indic fut mid | 4622.2 prs-pron gen 2sing | 5183.4 verb 3sing indic act | 3615.1 conj |
|---|---|---|---|---|
| Κιλικίας, | 35. Διακούσομαί | σου, | ἔφη, | ὅταν |
| *Kilikias* | *Diakousomai* | *sou* | *ephē* | *hotan* |
| Cilicia, | I will hear fully | you, | he said, | when |

| 2504.1 conj | 3450.7 art nom pl masc | 2695.2 noun nom pl masc | 4622.2 prs-pron gen 2sing | 3716.6 verb 3pl subj aor mid |
|---|---|---|---|---|
| καὶ | οἱ | κατήγοροί | σου | παραγένωνται· |
| *kai* | *hoi* | *katēgoroi* | *sou* | *paragenōntai* |
| also | the | accusers | your | may have arrived. |

35.a.**Txt:** 020L,025P,byz.
**Var:** 01ℵ-corr,02A,03B
08E,Lach,Treg,Alf,Tisc
We/Ho,Weis,Sod
UBS/☆

| 2724.3 verb 3sing indic aor act | 4885.1 conj | 840.6 prs-pron acc sing masc | 2724.5 verb nom sing masc part aor act | 1706.1 prep |
|---|---|---|---|---|
| ˹ Ἐκέλευσέν | τε | αὐτὸν | [a☆ κελεύσας ] | ἐν |
| *Ekeleusen* | *te* | *auton* | *keleusas* | *en* |
| He commanded | and | him | [ having commanded ] | in |

| 3450.3 art dat sing | 4091.2 noun dat sing neu | 3450.2 art gen sing | 2243.2 name gen masc | 5278.18 verb inf pres mid |
|---|---|---|---|---|
| τῷ | πραιτωρίῳ | τοῦ | Ἡρῴδου | φυλάσσεσθαι. |
| *tō* | *praitōriō* | *tou* | *Hērōdou* | *phulassesthai* |
| the | praetorium | | of Herod | to be kept. |

35.b.**Var:** 01ℵ,02A,03B
08E,sa.bo.Lach,Treg,Alf
Tisc,We/Ho,Weis,Sod
UBS/☆

| 840.6 prs-pron acc sing masc | 3196.3 prep | 1156.2 conj | 3864.1 num card | 2232.1 noun fem |
|---|---|---|---|---|
| [b☆+ αὐτόν. ] | 24:1. Μετὰ | δὲ | πέντε | ἡμέρας |
| *auton* | *Meta* | *de* | *pente* | *hēmeras* |
| [ him. ] | After | and | five | days |

| 2568.14 verb 3sing indic aor act | 3450.5 art nom sing masc | 744.1 noun nom sing masc | 366.4 name nom masc | 3196.3 prep | 3450.1 art gen pl |
|---|---|---|---|---|---|
| κατέβη | ὁ | ἀρχιερεὺς | Ἁνανίας | μετὰ | ˹ τῶν |
| *katebē* | *ho* | *archiereus* | *Hananias* | *meta* | *tōn* |
| came down | the | high priest | Ananias | with | the |

1.a.**Txt:** 020L,025P,byz.
bo.
**Var:** 01ℵ,02A,03B,08E
sa.Lach,Treg,Alf,Tisc
We/Ho,Weis,Sod
UBS/☆

| 4104.6 adj comp gen pl masc | 4104.6 adj comp gen pl masc | 4948.4 indef-pron gen pl | 2504.1 conj | 4345.1 noun gen sing masc |
|---|---|---|---|---|
| πρεσβυτέρων | [a☆ πρεσβυτέρων | τινῶν ] | καὶ | ῥήτορος |
| *presbuterōn* | *presbuterōn* | *tinōn* | *kai* | *rhētoros* |
| elders | [ elders | some ] | and | an orator |

| 4909.2 name gen masc | 4948.1 indef-pron gen sing | 3610.2 rel-pron nom pl masc | 1702.4 verb 3pl indic aor act | 3450.3 art dat sing |
|---|---|---|---|---|
| Τερτύλλου | τινός, | οἵτινες | ἐνεφάνισαν | τῷ |
| *Tertullou* | *tinos* | *hoitines* | *enephanisan* | *tō* |
| Tertullus | certain, | who | made a report | to the |

| 2215.3 noun dat sing masc | 2567.3 prep | 3450.2 art gen sing | 3834.2 name gen masc | 2535.43 verb gen sing masc part aor pass | 1156.2 conj |
|---|---|---|---|---|---|
| ἡγεμόνι | κατὰ | τοῦ | Παύλου. | 2. κληθέντος | δὲ |
| *hēgemoni* | *kata* | *tou* | *Paulou* | *klēthentos* | *de* |
| governor | against | | Paul. | Having been called | and |

**23:34.** When Felix read the letter he also understood the reasons for sending Paul to him, as well as the reasons for the extra precautions for the protection of Paul on the journey to Caesarea.

After reading the letter, Felix asked Paul what province he was from. Probably Felix asked the question because he had to know if Paul came from a Roman province. Only if he came from a Roman province could Felix, as a Roman governor, take charge of Paul on his own authority (that is, without getting the emperor's permission).

Cilicia was an important district or province in southeast Asia Minor between the Taurus mountains and the Mediterranean Sea. It was separated from Syria on the east by Mount Amanus and was bound on the west by Pamphylia. The western part of the province is mountainous. The eastern part is a fertile, alluvial plain with Tarsus, the birthplace of Paul, as its chief city. The Romans took control of Cilicia beginning with Pompey's conquest about 66 B.C. Cicero, the famous Roman orator, was its governor for a short time in 51–50 B.C.

The fact that Paul was a Roman citizen from this important province meant Felix could not ignore him. Neither could he ignore the complaints of the Jewish leaders of Jerusalem. As governor or procurator he was the chief one responsible to keep peace and promote Roman justice in Judea.

**23:35.** Upon hearing that Paul was from Cilicia, Felix told him he would give him a hearing whenever his accusers arrived to present their case against him. Then Felix commanded that Paul be guarded in Herod's Praetorium. This was the lavish palace built by Herod the Great. It served as the capitol building as well as the official residence of the Roman procurators. Thus, Paul was in a better situation than in Jerusalem, where he had been kept in the soldiers' barracks.

**24:1.** Only once did the Jews bring formal charges against the apostle Paul. It happened after Paul had been in Caesarea 5 days. Then Ananias the high priest came down from Jerusalem with some of the members of the Sanhedrin. Undoubtedly, these elders were mostly Sadducees who were friends of the high priests.

They had hired an orator, a professional public speaker, to act as an advocate, that is, as the counsel for the prosecution.

Tertullus ("little third"), a common Roman name, was probably a Jew who was a Roman citizen trained in Roman oratory and legal methods. The high priest must have given him a large sum of money to get him to go to Caesarea to try to counteract the effect of Paul's Roman citizenship as well as to impress Felix.

**24:2.** Paul was then called, and Tertullus was given opportunity to present his accusation against him.

**34. And when the governor had read the letter:** As soon as Felix had read the letter, *TCNT*... Felix, after reading the letter, *Weymouth.*

**he asked of what province he was:** ...he inquired, *TCNT* ... What part of the country do you come from? *BB*... What area are you from? *Everyday.*

**And when he understood that he was of Cilicia:** When he learned, *RSV* ... that he came from Cilicia, *TCNT.*

**35. I will hear thee, said he:** ... hear your case, *Montgomery* ... will give you a full hearing, *Norlie*... I will listen to all of this, *NLT.*

**when thine accusers are also come:** ... as soon as your accusers have arrived, *TCNT*... when thy accusers, too, are present, *Knox*... as soon as your accusers make their appearance, *Noli* ... when those who are against you come here too, *Everyday.*

**And he commanded him to be kept:** In the meantime, *Noli* ... and gave orders that...he should be kept under guard, *Rotherham*... that he should be kept safe in, *Knox.*

**in Herod's judgment hall:** ... in the praetorium of Herod, *HBIE, Lamsa* ... in the palace, *Everyday.*

**1. And after five days:** Five days later, *Moffatt.*

**Ananias the high priest descended with the elders:** They went to Caesarea, *SEB* ... came down to Caesarea with a number of Elders, *Weymouth* ... with certain presbyters, *Hanson.*

**and with a certain orator named Tertullus:** ... a barrister named Tertullus, *TCNT*... a prosecuting attorney, *Williams* ... and a certain attorney named, *Noli* ... by an advocate named, *Knox.*

**who informed the governor against Paul:** ... who made a complaint against Paul before Felix, *Norlie*... to present their evidence, *Berkeley* ... to make charges against Paul before the governor, *SEB.*

**2. And when he was called forth:** So Paul was sent for, *Weymouth* ... was summoned, *Moffatt* ... Paul was called into the meeting, *NCV.*

## Acts 24:3

| **840.3** prs-pron gen sing | **751.5** verb 3sing indic aor mid | **2693.8** verb inf pres act | **3450.5** art nom sing masc | **4909.1** name nom masc |
|---|---|---|---|---|
| αὐτοῦ | ἤρξατο | κατηγορεῖν | ὁ | Τέρτυλλος |
| *autou* | *ērxato* | *katēgorein* | *ho* | *Tertullos* |
| he | began | to accuse | | Tertullus, |

| **2978.15** verb nom sing masc part pres act | **4044.10** adj gen sing fem | **1503.2** noun gen sing fem | **5018.2** verb nom pl masc part pres act | **1217.2** prep |
|---|---|---|---|---|
| λέγων, | Πολλῆς | εἰρήνης | τυγχάνοντες | διὰ |
| *legōn* | *Pollēs* | *eirēnēs* | *tunchanontes* | *dia* |
| saying, | Great | peace | obtaining | through |

3.a.**Txt:** 020L,025P,byz.
**Var:** 01ℵ,02A,03B,08E
Lach,Treg,Alf,Tisc
We/Ho,Weis,Sod
UBS/☆

| **4622.2** prs-pron gen 2sing | **2504.1** conj | **2705.1** noun gen pl neu | **1350.1** noun gen pl neu |
|---|---|---|---|
| σοῦ, | καὶ | ʻ κατορθωμάτων | [a☆ διορθωμάτων ] |
| *sou* | *kai* | *katorthōmatōn* | *diorthōmatōn* |
| you, | and | excellent measures | [ improvements ] |

| **1090.25** verb gen pl neu part pres mid | **3450.3** art dat sing | **1477.3** noun dat sing neu | **3642.5** dem-pron dat sing masc | **1217.2** prep | **3450.10** art gen sing fem |
|---|---|---|---|---|---|
| γινομένων | τῷ | ἔθνει | τούτῳ | διὰ | τῆς |
| *ginomenōn* | *tō* | *ethnei* | *toutō* | *dia* | *tēs* |
| being done | for the | nation | this | through | the |

| **4528.5** adj gen 2sing fem | **4166.1** noun gen sing fem | **3701.1** adv | **4885.1** conj | **2504.1** conj | **3699.1** adv |
|---|---|---|---|---|---|
| σῆς | προνοίας, | 3. πάντῃ | τε | καὶ | πανταχοῦ |
| *sēs* | *pronoias* | *pantē* | *te* | *kai* | *pantachou* |
| your | forethought, | in every way | both | and | everywhere |

| **583.1** verb 1pl indic pres mid | **2876.2** adj sup voc sing masc | **5181.1** name nom masc | **3196.3** prep | **3820.10** adj gen sing fem |
|---|---|---|---|---|
| ἀποδεχόμεθα, | κράτιστε | Φῆλιξ, | μετὰ | πάσης |
| *apodechometha* | *kratiste* | *Phēlix* | *meta* | *pasēs* |
| we gladly accept, | most excellent | Felix, | with | all |

| **2150.1** noun fem | **2419.1** conj | **1156.2** conj | **3231.1** partic | **1894.3** prep | **3979.8** adj comp sing neu | **4622.4** prs-pron acc 2sing |
|---|---|---|---|---|---|---|
| εὐχαριστίας. | 4. ἵνα | δὲ | μὴ | ἐπὶ | πλεῖόν | σε |
| *eucharistias* | *hina* | *de* | *mē* | *epi* | *pleion* | *se* |
| thankfulness. | That | but | not | to | longer | you |

| **1458.1** verb 1sing subj pres act | **3731.1** verb 1sing indic pres act | **189.36** verb inf aor act | **4622.4** prs-pron acc 2sing | **2231.2** prs-pron gen 1pl |
|---|---|---|---|---|
| ἐγκόπτω | παρακαλῶ | ἀκοῦσαί | σε | ἡμῶν |
| *enkoptō* | *parakalō* | *akousai* | *se* | *hēmōn* |
| I may be a hindrance | I ask | to hear | you | us |

| **4787.1** adv | **3450.11** art dat sing fem | **4528.6** adj dat 2sing fem | **1917.2** noun dat sing fem | **2128.18** verb nom pl masc part aor act | **1056.1** conj |
|---|---|---|---|---|---|
| συντόμως | τῇ | σῇ | ἐπιεικείᾳ. | 5. εὑρόντες | γὰρ |
| *suntomōs* | *tē* | *sē* | *epieikeia* | *heurontes* | *gar* |
| briefly | in the | your | kindness. | Having found | for |

| **3450.6** art acc sing masc | **433.4** noun acc sing masc | **3642.6** dem-pron acc sing masc | **3035.1** noun acc sing masc | **2504.1** conj | **2767.1** verb acc sing masc part pres act |
|---|---|---|---|---|---|
| τὸν | ἄνδρα | τοῦτον | λοιμὸν, | καὶ | κινοῦντα |
| *ton* | *andra* | *touton* | *loimon* | *kai* | *kinounta* |
| the | man | this | a pest, | and | moving |

5.a.**Txt:** 020L,025P,byz.
sa.
**Var:** 01ℵ,02A,03B,08E
bo.Lach,Treg,Tisc
We/Ho,Weis,Sod
UBS/☆

| **4565.4** noun acc sing fem | **4565.5** noun acc pl fem | **3820.5** adj dat pl | **3450.4** art dat pl | **2428.4** name-adj dat pl masc |
|---|---|---|---|---|
| ʻ στάσιν | [a☆ στάσεις ] | πᾶσιν | τοῖς | Ἰουδαίοις |
| *stasin* | *staseis* | *pasin* | *tois* | *Ioudaiois* |
| insurrection | [ disputes ] | among all | the | Jews |

Tertullus did not immediately prefer charges. Instead, he began by flattering the governor with flowery traditional oratory that sugarcoated the truth. He said that through him the Jews were enjoying great peace. This, Felix must have known, was mere flattery, for he well knew it was contrary to the facts. The facts are that Felix had incited robbers to assassinate the high priest, Jonathan, who had displeased him. Then he had many of the same robbers captured and crucified. When false prophets led crowds into the wilderness, Felix attacked them and had great numbers of them killed. When an Egyptian came and led a mob to the Mount of Olives, Felix sent an army, killed about 400 of them, and took about 200 more prisoners.

Tertullus then said reforms had come to the Jewish nation through the forethought (foresight and care) of Felix.

Some ancient manuscripts have "success" (prosperity, good order) instead of "reforms" (Greek *katorthōmatōn*, instead of *diorthōmatōn*). But Felix had brought neither reforms nor great prosperity and success to the Jews. Instead, there was constant turmoil throughout his governorship. His ineffective rule was an important factor leading to the revolt of the Jews which brought the destruction of Jerusalem in A.D. 70.

**24:3.** Tertullus went on to say these things (peace and reforms or great prosperity) the Jews accepted in all ways and in all places with thankfulness. This also was pure flattery. Actually, the Jews were always complaining about Felix. Even after he was replaced and returned to Rome they sent more complaints.

By calling him "most noble," Tertullus was merely using the traditional title of honor given to officials, a title better translated "most excellent," as in 23:26.

**24:4.** As a further gesture of politeness or deference to Felix, Tertullus suggested he did not want to hinder the governor more. The Syriac Peshitta and the Armenian versions (translations) took this to mean "in order not to weary you any further." But he may have meant "in order not to delay or detain you any further." Tertullus promised to be brief and to the point, and declared that he expected Felix to be fair (even though secular history shows Felix was a violent, unfair man).

**24:5.** By a mixture of lies and cleverly twisted half-truths, Tertullus began to accuse Paul falsely on four points.

First, he said Paul was a pestilent fellow; that is, like a disease he was spreading an epidemic that would destroy the people. There was hardly anything worse they could have said about Paul.

Second, Tertullus said Paul was constantly stirring up sedition (discord, revolution, and riot) among all the Jews who were in all the inhabited world.

**Tertullus began to accuse him, saying:** . . . began to impeach him as follows, *Weymouth* . . . began his charge by saying, *Norlie* . . . began his speech for the prosecution, *TCNT* . . . began the prosecution in these words, *Phillips.*

**Seeing that by thee we enjoy great quietness:** . . . we are enjoying profound peace, *TCNT* . . . we dwell in much tranquility, *Murdock* . . . We owe it to you personally...that we enjoy lasting peace, *Phillips.*

**and that very worthy deeds are done unto this nation by thy providence:** . . . it is due to your foresight that the nation enjoys improved conditions of living, *Phillips* . . . by your prudent administration, *Campbell* . . . your wise care, *Moffatt.*

**3. We accept it always, and in all places, most noble Felix, with all thankfulness:** In all things and in all places we are conscious of our great debt to you, *BB* . . . with profound gratitude, *Williams* . . . At all times, and indeed everywhere, we acknowledge these things with the deepest gratitude, *Phillips.*

**4. Notwithstanding, that I be not further tedious unto thee:** However, not to take more of your precious time, *Berkeley* . . . Not to keep you too long, *Beck* . . . intrude on thy time, *Darby* . . . for I must not detain you too long, *Phillips.*

**I pray thee:** I entreat thee, *ASV* . . . I beseech thee, *Rotherham* . . . I beg you, *TCNT* . . . I make a request to you, *BB* . . . I simply want to ask you, *Norlie.*

**that thou wouldest hear us of thy clemency a few words:** . . . with your accustomed fairness, to listen to a brief statement of our case, *TCNT* . . . to grant us in your courtesy a brief hearing, *Moffatt* . . . to listen to a few words from us, *Montgomery* . . . with your usual candor, *Campbell.*

**5. For we have found this man a pestilent fellow:** . . . a public pest, *TCNT* . . . The fact is, we have found this man is a perfect pest, *Moffatt* . . . a source of mischief, *Weymouth* . . . to be a veritable plague, *Berkeley.*

**Acts 24:6**

| 3450.4 art dat pl | 2567.3 prep | 3450.12 art acc sing fem | 3487.4 noun acc sing fem | 4271.1 noun acc sing masc | 4885.1 conj |
|---|---|---|---|---|---|
| τοῖς | κατὰ | τὴν | οἰκουμένην | πρωτοστάτην | τε |
| tois | kata | tēn | oikoumenēn | prōtostatēn | te |
| the | in | the | habitable world, | a leader | and |

| 3450.10 art gen sing fem | 3450.1 art gen pl | 3343.4 name gen pl masc | 138.2 noun gen sing fem | 3614.5 rel-pron nom sing masc | 2504.1 conj |
|---|---|---|---|---|---|
| τῆς | τῶν | Ναζωραίων | αἱρέσεως· | 6. ὃς | καὶ |
| tēs | tōn | Nazōraiōn | haireseōs | hos | kai |
| of the | of the | Nazarenes | sect; | who | also |

| 3450.16 art sing neu | 2387.3 adj sing neu | 3847.6 verb 3sing indic aor act | 946.2 verb inf aor act | 3614.6 rel-pron acc sing masc | 2504.1 conj |
|---|---|---|---|---|---|
| τὸ | ἱερὸν | ἐπείρασεν | βεβηλῶσαι, | ὃν | καὶ |
| to | hieron | epeirasen | bebēlōsai | hon | kai |
| the | temple | attempted | to profane, | whom | also |

6.a.**Txt:** 08E,044,33 Steph
**Var:** p74,01ℵ,02A,03B 020L,025P,sa.bo.Lach Treg,Tisc,We/Ho,Weis Sod,UBS/*

| 2875.13 verb 1pl indic aor act | | 2504.1 conj | 2567.3 prep | 3450.6 art acc sing masc | 2233.1 adj acc 1sing masc |
|---|---|---|---|---|---|
| ἐκρατήσαμεν | ⸂a | καὶ | κατὰ | τὸν | ἡμέτερον |
| ekratēsamen | | kai | kata | ton | hēmeteron |
| we seized, | | and | according to | the | our |

| 3414.4 noun acc sing masc | 2286.23 verb 1pl indic aor act | 2892.12 verb inf pres act | 3790.6 verb nom sing masc part aor act | 1156.2 conj |
|---|---|---|---|---|
| νόμον | ἠθελήσαμεν | κρίνειν. | 7. παρελθὼν | δὲ |
| nomon | ēthelēsamen | krinein | parelthōn | de |
| law | wished | to judge; | having come up | but |

| 3051.1 name nom masc | 3450.5 art nom sing masc | 5341.1 noun nom sing masc | 3196.3 prep | 4044.10 adj gen sing fem | 963.1 noun gen sing fem |
|---|---|---|---|---|---|
| Λυσίας | ὁ | χιλίαρχος | μετὰ | πολλῆς | βίας |
| Lusias | ho | chiliarchos | meta | pollēs | bias |
| Lysias | the | chief captain | with | great | force |

| 1523.2 prep gen | 3450.1 art gen pl | 5331.6 noun gen pl fem | 2231.2 prs-pron gen 1pl | 516.2 verb 3sing indic aor act | 2724.5 verb nom sing masc part aor act |
|---|---|---|---|---|---|
| ἐκ | τῶν | χειρῶν | ἡμῶν | ἀπήγαγεν, | 8. κελεύσας |
| ek | tōn | cheirōn | hēmōn | apēgagen | keleusas |
| out of | the | hands | our | took away, | having commanded |

| 3450.8 art acc pl masc | 2695.4 noun acc pl masc | 840.3 prs-pron gen sing | 2048.53 verb inf pres mid | 1894.3 prep | 4622.4 prs-pron acc 2sing |
|---|---|---|---|---|---|
| τοὺς | κατηγόρους | αὐτοῦ | ἔρχεσθαι | ἐπὶ | σέ·⸃ |
| tous | katēgorous | autou | erchesthai | epi | se |
| the | accusers | his | to come | to | you, |

| 3706.1 prep | 3614.2 rel-pron gen sing | 1404.29 verb 2sing indic fut mid | 840.5 prs-pron nom sing masc | 348.6 verb nom sing masc part aor act |
|---|---|---|---|---|
| παρ' | οὗ | δυνήσῃ | αὐτὸς | ἀνακρίνας |
| par' | hou | dunēsē | autos | anakrinas |
| from | whom | you will be able | yourself, | having examined |

| 3875.1 prep | 3820.4 adj gen pl | 3642.2 dem-pron gen pl | 1906.14 verb inf aor act | 3614.1 rel-pron gen pl | 2231.1 prs-pron nom 1pl |
|---|---|---|---|---|---|
| περὶ | πάντων | τούτων | ἐπιγνῶναι | ὧν | ἡμεῖς |
| peri | pantōn | toutōn | epignōnai | hōn | hēmeis |
| concerning | all | these things | to know | of which | we |

9.a.**Txt:** Steph
**Var:** 01ℵ,02A,03B,08E 020L,025P,byz.Gries Lach,Treg,Alf,Word Tisc,We/Ho,Weis,Sod UBS/*

| 2693.1 verb 1pl indic pres act | 840.3 prs-pron gen sing | 4786.1 verb 3pl indic aor mid | 4751.1 verb 3pl indic aor mid |
|---|---|---|---|
| κατηγοροῦμεν | αὐτοῦ. | 9. ⸂ Συνέθεντο | [a* συνεπέθεντο ] |
| katēgoroumen | autou | Sunethento | sunepethento |
| are accusing | him. | Agreed | [joined in] |

By the inhabited world, Tertullus meant the Roman Empire (as the phrase was commonly understood in those days). It is as if he was accusing Paul of being the causer or arouser of all the uprisings, riots, and strife among the Jews in those times.

Third, Tertullus implicated all the Christians by calling Paul a ringleader of the sect of the Nazarenes, the party or group of people who followed the teachings of the Man of Nazareth.

By calling the Christians a sect, he did not necessarily mean a heretical sect. The same term was used of the various schools of philosophy among the Greeks, and it was applied to the Pharisees and Sadducees by the Jews. This indicates also that Tertullus was looking on the Jewish believers as a Jewish sect.

**24:6.** Fourth, after these general accusations, Tertullus gave the specific charge. Paul, he said, had tried to profane the temple, that is, he had attempted to desecrate it. But they laid hold on him and arrested him before he could desecrate it.

This, of course, was false. Actually, they seized Paul and tried to lynch him without a trial. But Tertullus did not tell of their violence and how they were in the process of beating Paul to death as an act of mob violence.

**24:7.** As most ancient New Testament manuscripts indicate, Tertullus claimed Paul was being judged properly by their law when the tribune Lysias intervened and took Paul out of their hands.

Tertullus made a serious mistake when he tried to put the Roman tribune in a bad light. His claim that the Jews had arrested Paul and were about to give him a fair trial made it seem wrong for Lysias to intervene violently, using the force of Roman soldiers wrongfully.

Felix, however, knew that Roman officers had a responsibility to keep order in Jerusalem. He knew they would not have interfered unless there were near-riot conditions. Besides, Felix had the letter from Lysias which put an entirely different light on the subject. Lysias had said Paul was seized by the Jews and was about to be killed by them. Lysias had only done his duty in rescuing Paul from the mob.

**24:8.** Tertullus further implied Lysias was wrong in sending Paul to Felix. Tertullus said nothing about the plot to assassinate Paul and the willingness of the Jewish Sanhedrin to be a part of the plot by asking that Paul be sent to them for further investigation. But again the letter the tribune sent to Felix told how they were plotting to ambush and kill Paul, so Felix knew the dealings of the Jews were not as honest and legal as Tertullus was trying to say they were.

Tertullus confidently declared that by examining Paul himself the governor would be able to find out these things (these accusations against Paul) were true.

**and a mover of sedition among all the Jews throughout the world:** . . . he stirs up sedition among the Jews all over the world, *Moffatt* . . . an inciter of insurrection among all the Jews of the empire, *Montgomery* . . . raiser of insurrections, *PNT* . . . a promoter of seditions, *Confraternity* . . . a pestilential disturber of the peace...all over the world, *Phillips.*

**and a ringleader of the sect of the Nazarenes:** . . . and the chief mover in the society of the Nazarenes, *BB* . . . of the party of, *Williams C.K.* . . . the Nazarene heretics, *TCNT* . . . heresy of the Nazarenes, *Montgomery* . . . of the Nazareth sect, *Phillips.*

**6. Who also hath gone about to profane the temple:** . . . who also attempted to desecrate even the temple, *Rotherham* . . . He actually tried to desecrate, *Moffatt* . . . who, in addition, was attempting to make the Temple unclean, *BB* . . . he was on the point of desecrating, *Phillips* . . . even tried to bring unclean things into the temple, *Williams C.K.*

**whom we took:** . . . whom we also seized, *Rotherham* . . . but we caught him, *TCNT* . . . when we overcame him, *Phillips.*

**and would have judged according to our law:** . . . and would have sentenced him by our Law, *Berkeley.*

**7. But the chief captain Lysias came upon us, and with great violence took him away out of our hands:**

**8. Commanding his accusers to come unto thee:**

**by examining of whom thyself:** Examine him for yourself, *Moffatt* . . . on all these points, *TCNT* . . . If you will personally cross-question him, *Berkeley.*

**mayest take knowledge of all these things, whereof we accuse him:** . . . to ascertain the things of which we are accusing him, *Rotherham* . . . to learn the truth as to all this we allege against him, *Weymouth* . . . you will be able to find out from him all the facts of the case that we bring against him, *Williams C.K.* . . . will soon discover from the man himself all the facts about which we are accusing him, *Phillips.*

| **1156.2** conj | **2504.1** conj | **3450.7** art nom pl masc | **2428.2** name-adj nom pl masc | **5173.1** verb nom pl masc part pres act | **3642.18** dem-pron pl neu |
|---|---|---|---|---|---|
| δὲ | καὶ | οἱ | Ἰουδαῖοι, | φάσκοντες | ταῦτα |
| *de* | *kai* | *hoi* | *Ioudaioi* | *phaskontes* | *tauta* |
| and | also | the | Jews, | declaring | these things |

10.a.**Txt:** 020L,025P,byz. sa.bo.
**Var:** 01ℵ,02A,03B,08E Lach,Treg,Alf,Tisc We/Ho,Weis,Sod UBS/☆

| **3643.1** adv | **2174.29** verb inf pres act | **552.6** verb 3sing indic aor pass | **1156.2** conj | **4885.1** conj | **3450.5** art nom sing masc |
|---|---|---|---|---|---|
| οὕτως | ἔχειν. | **10.** Ἀπεκρίθη | ʻ δὲ | [a☆ τε ] | ὁ |
| *houtōs* | *echein* | *Apekrithē* | *de* | *te* | *ho* |
| thus | to be. | Answered | but | [ idem ] | |

| **3834.1** name nom masc | **3368.2** verb gen sing masc part aor act | **840.4** prs-pron dat sing | **3450.2** art gen sing | **2215.2** noun gen sing masc |
|---|---|---|---|---|
| Παῦλος, | νεύσαντος | αὐτῷ | τοῦ | ἡγεμόνος |
| *Paulos* | *neusantos* | *autō* | *tou* | *hēgemonos* |
| Paul, | having made a sign | to him | the | governor |

| **2978.24** verb inf pres act | **1523.2** prep gen | **4044.1** adj gen pl | **2073.4** noun gen pl neu | **1498.18** verb part pres act | **4622.4** prs-pron acc 2sing | **2896.3** noun acc sing masc |
|---|---|---|---|---|---|---|
| λέγειν, | Ἐκ | πολλῶν | ἐτῶν | ὄντα | σε | κριτὴν |
| *legein* | *Ek* | *pollōn* | *etōn* | *onta* | *se* | *kritēn* |
| to speak, | From | many | years | being | you | judge |

| **3450.3** art dat sing | **1477.3** noun dat sing neu | **3642.5** dem-pron dat sing masc | **1971.5** verb nom sing masc part pres mid | **2094.1** adv comp |
|---|---|---|---|---|
| τῷ | ἔθνει | τούτῳ | ἐπιστάμενος, | ʻ εὐθυμότερον |
| *tō* | *ethnei* | *toutō* | *epistamenos* | *euthumoteron* |
| for the | nation | this | knowing, | more cheerfully |

10.b.**Txt:** 020L,025P,byz.
**Var:** 01ℵ,02A,03B,08E Lach,Treg,Alf,Tisc We/Ho,Weis,Sod UBS/☆

| **2095.1** adv | **3450.17** art pl neu | **3875.1** prep | **1670.1** prs-pron gen 1sing masc | **620.1** verb 1sing indic pres mid |
|---|---|---|---|---|
| [b☆ εὐθύμως ] | τὰ | περὶ | ἐμαυτοῦ | ἀπολογοῦμαι, |
| *euthumōs* | *ta* | *peri* | *emautou* | *apologoumai* |
| [ cheerfully ] | the things | concerning | myself | I make defense. |

11.a.**Txt:** 020L,025P,byz.
**Var:** 01ℵ,02A,03B,08E 33,Lach,Treg,Alf,Tisc We/Ho,Weis,Sod UBS/☆

| **1404.12** verb gen sing part pres mid | **4622.2** prs-pron gen 2sing | **1091.29** verb inf aor act | **1906.14** verb inf aor act | **3617.1** conj |
|---|---|---|---|---|
| **11.** δυναμένου | σου | ʻ γνῶναι | [a☆ ἐπιγνῶναι ] | ὅτι |
| *dunamenou* | *sou* | *gnōnai* | *epignōnai* | *hoti* |
| Being able | you | to know | [ idem ] | that |

11.b.**Txt:** byz.
**Var:** 01ℵ,02A,03B,08E 020L,025P,Gries,Lach Treg,Alf,Word,Tisc We/Ho,Weis,Sod UBS/☆

| **3620.3** partic | **3979.3** adj comp pl | **1498.7** verb 3pl indic pres act | **1466.4** prs-pron dat 1sing | **2232.5** noun nom pl fem | **2211.1** conj |
|---|---|---|---|---|---|
| οὐ | πλείους | εἰσίν | μοι | ἡμέραι | ʻb ἢ ʼ |
| *ou* | *pleious* | *eisin* | *moi* | *hēmerai* | *ē* |
| not | more than | there are | to me | days | |

11.c.**Txt:** 020L,025P,byz.
**Var:** 01ℵ,02A,03B,08E Lach,Treg,Alf,Tisc We/Ho,Weis,Sod UBS/☆

| **1172.1** num card | **1420.1** num card | **570.1** prep | **3614.10** rel-pron gen sing fem | **303.12** verb 1sing indic aor act |
|---|---|---|---|---|
| ʻ δεκαδύο | [c☆ δώδεκα ] | ἀφ' | ἧς | ἀνέβην |
| *dekaduo* | *dōdeka* | *aph'* | *hēs* | *anebēn* |
| twelve | [ idem ] | from | which | I went up |

11.d.**Txt:** 020L,025P,byz.
**Var:** 01ℵ,02A,03B,08E Lach,Treg,Alf,Word Tisc,We/Ho,Weis,Sod UBS/☆

| **4210.23** verb nom sing masc part fut act | **1706.1** prep | **1519.1** prep | **2395.1** name fem | **2504.1** conj |
|---|---|---|---|---|
| προσκυνήσων | ʻ ἐν | [d☆ εἰς ] | Ἱερουσαλήμ | **12.** καὶ |
| *proskunēsōn* | *en* | *eis* | *Hierousalēm* | *kai* |
| worshiping | at | [ unto ] | Jerusalem, | and |

| **3641.1** conj | **1706.1** prep | **3450.3** art dat sing | **2387.2** adj dat sing neu | **2128.6** verb indic aor act | **1466.6** prs-pron acc 1sing |
|---|---|---|---|---|---|
| οὔτε | ἐν | τῷ | ἱερῷ | εὗρόν | με |
| *oute* | *en* | *tō* | *hierō* | *heuron* | *me* |
| neither | in | the | temple | did they find | me |

**24:9.** The Jews who had come down to Caesarea with the high priest then joined in, pressing charges against Paul, saying again and again that these things were so.

**24:10.** When the governor indicated to Paul that he might speak, Paul addressed the governor courteously, but without the insincere flattery Tertullus had used. Since Felix had been for many years a judge of the Jews, and therefore understood Jewish customs and laws, Paul felt he could make his defense with good courage.

Paul could say this truthfully, and he did not add empty flattery. Of course, Felix knew how the Jews detested him, and he probably appreciated the sincerity of Paul more than the wordy insincerity of Tertullus.

**24:11.** Paul then made his defense in a way that showed he was more than a match for the padded rhetoric and ineffective conclusion of Tertullus.

Some commentators believe Paul should have ignored the false charges against him instead of defending himself. No doubt, there are times when a Christian should ignore false accusations. But Paul had good reasons not to ignore them, for they had to do with his attitude toward God and the truth.

Paul, in fact, gave a very skilled and wise defense. His presentation would have done justice to the best lawyer in the Roman Empire. Of course, he did have the best Lawyer there is, a better Lawyer than any human lawyer or advocate—one of the meanings of the title Comforter, which is given to the Holy Spirit, is Advocate.

Paul began with the accusation that he stirred up riots and discord. He knew this would be of major concern to the Roman government. This accusation really made him the causer of sedition, rebellion, and revolution. In fact, the Jews put this in because they knew it was the only charge a Roman court was likely to convict him on.

Paul did not have difficulty in showing how foolish this charge was. At this time it was still only 12 days since Paul had come to Jerusalem, and this was already the fifth day he had spent in Caesarea (according to the usual Jewish method of counting days). What time did that leave for him to stir up riots or start a revolution? In addition, it was too short a time for the Jews to have investigated him and found him such a dangerous character as they said he was. Furthermore, Paul came to worship, not to cause strife or defile the temple.

**24:12.** In every instance when the Jews met him in the temple, Paul was quietly doing what he came to do, worshiping the Lord. In no case did they find him disputing. He had not even become involved in an argument, to say nothing of being a pest. Nor had he stirred up a crowd in the temple, in the synagogues, or in the city.

**9. And the Jews also assented:** . . . joined in the charge, *ASV* . . . joined in the attack, *Rotherham* . . . agreed, *HBIE* . . . While Tertullus was speaking the Jews kept joining in, *Phillips* . . . also corroborated the charges, *Fenton.*

**saying that these things were so:** . . . asserting, *Phillips* . . . maintaining that these were the facts, *Weymouth* . . . and declared that all he said was exactly so, *Berkeley* . . . confirming the accuracy of, *TCNT* . . . declaring that these accusations were true, *Norlie* . . . insisting that this is the way it was, *Klingensmith* . . . affirming their accuracy, *Fenton.*

**10. Then Paul, after that the governor had beckoned unto him to speak, answered:** And Paul answered, when the governor had motioned him to be speaking, *Rotherham* . . . On a sign from the Governor, Paul made his reply, *TCNT* . . . at a nod from the governor, *Phillips* . . . made signs to Paul to speak, and he made his reply, *Williams C.K.*

**Forasmuch as I know that thou hast been of many years a judge unto this nation:** I am well aware, *Phillips* . . . Knowing, as I do, for how many years you have acted as Judge to this nation, *TCNT* . . . have administered justice to this nation, *Weymouth.*

**I do the more cheerfully answer for myself:** . . . it is with confidence that I undertake my own defence, *TCNT* . . . I find it easier to defend myself on these charges, *Berkeley* . . . I can therefore make my defense with every confidence, *Phillips* . . . I answer all the more confidently for myself, *Fenton.*

**11. Because that thou mayest understand:** For you can easily ascertain, *TCNT* . . . find out, *Norlie* . . . for you can verify the fact, *Williams.*

**that there are yet but twelve days:** . . . it is not more than twelve days ago, *Phillips* . . . have elapsed, *Fenton.*

**since I went up to Jerusalem for to worship:**

**12. And they neither found me:** . . . and it is not true, *JB* . . . I was never found, *Phillips.*

12.a.**Txt:** 020L,025P,byz.
**Var:** 01ℵ,02A,03B,08E
Lach,Treg,Alf,Tisc
We/Ho,Weis,Sod
UBS/⋆

| **4242.1** prep | **4948.5** indef-pron | **1250.4** verb acc sing masc part pres mid | **2211.1** conj | **1983.2** noun acc sing fem |
|---|---|---|---|---|
| πρός | τινα | διαλεγόμενον | ἢ | ʼ ἐπισύστασιν |
| *pros* | *tina* | *dialegomenon* | *ē* | *episustasin* |
| with | anyone | reasoning, | or | a tumultuous gathering |

13.a.**Txt:** 02A,08E,020L
025P,byz.
**Var:** 01ℵ,03B,Lach,Tisc
We/Ho,Weis,Sod
UBS/⋆

| **1971.2** noun acc sing fem | **4020.13** verb part pres act | **3657.2** noun gen sing masc | **3641.1** conj | **1706.1** prep | **3450.14** art dat pl fem |
|---|---|---|---|---|---|
| [a⋆ ἐπίστασιν ] | ποιοῦντα | ὄχλου | οὔτε | ἐν | ταῖς |
| *epistasin* | *poiounta* | *ochlou* | *oute* | *en* | *tais* |
| [ an attack ] | making | of a crowd | neither | in | the |

13.b.**Txt:** bo.Steph
**Var:** 01ℵ,02A,03B,08E
020L,byz.sa.Gries,Lach
Treg,Alf,Word,Tisc
We/Ho,Weis,Sod
UBS/⋆

| **4715.6** noun dat pl fem | **3641.1** conj | **2567.3** prep | **3450.12** art acc sing fem | **4032.4** noun acc sing fem | **3641.1** conj |
|---|---|---|---|---|---|
| συναγωγαῖς | οὔτε | κατὰ | τὴν | πόλιν, | 13. ʼ οὔτε |
| *sunagōgais* | *oute* | *kata* | *tēn* | *polin* | *oute* |
| synagogues | nor | in | the | city; | neither |

13.c.**Var:** 01ℵ,02A,03B
08E,bo.Lach,Treg,Alf
Word,Tisc,We/Ho,Weis
Sod,UBS/⋆

| **3624.1** conj | **3798.12** verb inf aor act | **1466.6** prs-pron acc 1sing | **1404.7** verb 3pl indic pres mid | **4622.3** prs-pron dat 2sing |
|---|---|---|---|---|
| [a⋆ οὐδὲ ] | παραστῆσαι | ʼb με ˋ | δύνανταί | [c⋆+ σοι ] |
| *oude* | *parastēsai* | *me* | *dunantai* | *soi* |
| [ idem ] | to prove | me | are they able | [ to you ] |

| **3875.1** prep | **3614.1** rel-pron gen pl | **3431.1** adv | **3432.1** adv | **2693.3** verb 3pl indic pres act | **1466.2** prs-pron gen 1sing |
|---|---|---|---|---|---|
| περὶ | ὧν | ʼ νῦν | [⋆ νυνὶ ] | κατηγοροῦσίν | μου. |
| *peri* | *hōn* | *nun* | *nuni* | *katēgorousin* | *mou* |
| concerning | which | now | [ idem ] | they are accusing | me. |

| **3533.1** verb 1sing indic pres act | **1156.2** conj | **3642.17** dem-pron sing neu | **4622.3** prs-pron dat 2sing | **3617.1** conj | **2567.3** prep |
|---|---|---|---|---|---|
| 14. ὁμολογῶ | δὲ | τοῦτό | σοι, | ὅτι | κατὰ |
| *homologō* | *de* | *touto* | *soi* | *hoti* | *kata* |
| I confess | but | this | to you, | that | according to |

| **3450.12** art acc sing fem | **3461.4** noun acc sing fem | **3614.12** rel-pron acc sing fem | **2978.3** verb 3pl indic pres act | **138.3** noun acc sing fem | **3643.1** adv |
|---|---|---|---|---|---|
| τὴν | ὁδὸν | ἣν | λέγουσιν | αἵρεσιν, | οὕτως |
| *tēn* | *hodon* | *hēn* | *legousin* | *hairesin* | *houtōs* |
| the | way | which | they call | a sect, | so |

| **2973.1** verb 1sing indic pres act | **3450.3** art dat sing | **3833.2** adj dat sing masc | **2296.3** noun dat sing masc | **3961.10** verb nom sing masc part pres act | **3820.5** adj dat pl |
|---|---|---|---|---|---|
| λατρεύω | τῷ | πατρῴῳ | θεῷ, | πιστεύων | πᾶσιν |
| *latreuō* | *tō* | *patrōō* | *theō* | *pisteuōn* | *pasin* |
| I serve | the | ancestral | God, | believing | all things |

14.a.**Var:** 01ℵ-org,03B
08E,Gries,Treg,Alf,Tisc
We/Ho,Weis,Sod
UBS/⋆

| **3450.4** art dat pl | **2567.3** prep | **3450.6** art acc sing masc | **3414.4** noun acc sing masc | **2504.1** conj | **3450.4** art dat pl |
|---|---|---|---|---|---|
| τοῖς | κατὰ | τὸν | νόμον | καὶ | [a⋆+ τοῖς |
| *tois* | *kata* | *ton* | *nomon* | *kai* | *tois* |
| the | according to | the | law | and | [ the |

| **1706.1** prep | **3450.4** art dat pl | **4254.6** noun dat pl masc | **1119.30** verb dat pl neu part perf mid | **1667.4** noun acc sing fem |
|---|---|---|---|---|
| ἐν ] | τοῖς | προφήταις | γεγραμμένοις, | 15. ἐλπίδα |
| *en* | *tois* | *prophētais* | *gegrammenois* | *elpida* |
| in ] | the | prophets | having been written, | a hope |

15.a.**Var:** 01ℵ,04C,Tisc

| **2174.17** verb nom sing masc part pres act | **1519.1** prep | **4242.1** prep | **3450.6** art acc sing masc | **2296.4** noun acc sing masc | **3614.12** rel-pron acc sing fem |
|---|---|---|---|---|---|
| ἔχων | ʼ εἰς | [a πρὸς ] | τὸν | θεόν, | ἣν |
| *echōn* | *eis* | *pros* | *ton* | *theon* | *hēn* |
| having | in | [ toward ] | the | God, | which |

Paul was not intending to deny there had been riots and disturbances in other places. Actually, in those cases Paul had simply preached the good news, the gospel. Those who had rejected the gospel were the ones who stirred up the people and caused the riots, not Paul. Furthermore, Paul was not on trial for what had happened in other places, but for what had happened in Jerusalem. He was right in saying he had done absolutely nothing to stir up trouble there.

**24:13.** Paul further challenged his accusers by saying that in no way could they prove any of their accusations. They had no evidence, and Paul knew they could prove nothing. He also implied that Tertullus made the accusations in terms of generalities because he had no proof of any of them. Paul's point was well-taken.

**24:14.** Paul was not satisfied merely to deny the charges made against him by the Jews. He seized the opportunity to make a public declaration or confession of his Christian faith and hope. At the same time he made Felix see that the real charge against him was not political, not civil, but religious. The chief thing the Jews had against him was that he worshiped God in a different way from them. Paul was willing to confess this and give clear testimony to it. But he denied he was preaching a new or false religion.

To confirm this, Paul declared that according to the Way called a sect (which they implied was a self-chosen opinion), he continued to serve the God of his fathers. That is, he worshiped the same God the rest of the Jews did, the God of their ancestors. He was no less loyal to the one true God than they were.

Paul also declared that by the way he worshiped God he showed he was still a believer in everything that was according to the Law and everything written in the Prophets. By "the law and . . . the prophets" Paul probably meant the whole of the Jewish sacred books, the entire Old Testament.

The word *believe* also implies he continued to trust and obey God and His Word. Belief, in both the Old and New Testaments, always implies personal confidence and faithfulness. It shows itself always in action, not just in a mental attitude.

**24:15.** By the Law and the Prophets Paul also had a confident hope in God, a hope that these Jews shared or, at least, the majority of Jews shared. This hope involved a confidence in the plan of God, a plan that would culminate in the resurrection of the dead, both of the just and the unjust. It would demonstrate the justice of God.

Paul, of course, did not give all the details in this brief statement. Daniel 12:2 gave the Jews a specific prophecy that many who sleep in the dust of the earth (actually including all of the dead) will awake (be resurrected in a bodily resurrection), some to everlasting life, and some to shame and everlasting contempt.

**in the temple disputing with any man:** . . . disputing with any opponent, *Weymouth* . . . holding discussions with any one, *TCNT* . . . found either arguing with anyone, *Phillips.*

**neither raising up the people:** . . . the multitude, *Alford* . . . or causing a crowd to collect, *TCNT* . . . or causing a riot, *Moffatt* . . . gathering a crowd, *Phillips* . . . nor collecting any company, *Murdock* . . . nor making any insurrection among the multitude, *Wesley.*

**neither in the synagogues, nor in the city:** . . . or throughout the city, *Rotherham* . . . either in the Temple, *TCNT* . . . or in the open air, *Phillips.*

**13. Neither can they prove the things whereof they now accuse me:** These men are quite unable to prove the charges, *Phillips* . . . they cannot furnish you with any proof of their present charges against me, *Moffatt* . . . to substantiate, *Wuest.* . . . and they are not able to give facts in support of the things they say against me now, *BB* . . . Neither can they produce any evidence to substantiate these present charges, *Berkeley.*

**14. But this I confess unto thee:** This, however, I do acknowledge to you, *TCNT* . . . I certainly admit to you, *Moffatt* . . . I will freely admit to you, however, *Phillips.*

**that after the way which they call heresy:** . . . that it is as a believer of the Cause which they call heretical, *TCNT* . . . according to the way which they call a heresy, *Phillips.*

**so worship I the God of my fathers:** . . . that I worship the God of my ancestors, *TCNT* . . . I continue to worship the God of my forefathers, *Williams.*

**believing all things which are written in the law and in the prophets:** At the same time, I believe everything that is in accordance with, *TCNT* . . . taught in the Law or written, *Weymouth* . . . in the scriptural authority of both the Law and the Prophets, *Phillips.*

**15. And have hope toward God:** . . . and I have a hope that rests in God, *TCNT* . . . and trust God, *Beck.*

## Acts 24:16

| 2504.1 conj | 840.7 prs-pron nom pl masc | 3642.7 dem-pron nom pl masc | 4185.2 verb 3pl indic pres mid | 384.4 noun acc sing fem |
|---|---|---|---|---|
| καὶ | αὐτοὶ | οὗτοι | προσδέχονται, | ἀνάστασιν |
| *kai* | *autoi* | *houtoi* | *prosdechontai* | *anastasin* |
| also | themselves | these | receive, | a resurrection |

15.b.**Txt:** 08E,020L 025P,044,byz.
**Var:** p74,01ℵ,02A,03B 04C,33,sa.bo.Lach,Treg Alf,Tisc,We/Ho,Weis Sod,UBS/☆

| 3165.18 verb inf pres act | 1498.45 verb inf fut mid | 3361.2 adj gen pl | 1337.7 adj gen pl masc | 4885.1 conj | 2504.1 conj |
|---|---|---|---|---|---|
| μέλλειν | ἔσεσθαι | ⸀b νεκρῶν, ⸌ | δικαίων | τε | καὶ |
| *mellein* | *esesthai* | *nekrōn* | *dikaiōn* | *te* | *kai* |
| to be about | to be | of dead, | of just | both | and |

16.a.**Txt:** 025P,byz.bo.
**Var:** 01ℵ,02A,03B,04C 08E,020L,sa.Lach,Treg Alf,Word,Tisc,We/Ho Weis,Sod,UBS/☆

| 93.4 adj gen pl masc | 16. 1706.1 prep | 3642.5 dem-pron dat sing masc | 1156.2 conj | 2504.1 conj | 840.5 prs-pron nom sing masc |
|---|---|---|---|---|---|
| ἀδίκων. | 16. ἐν | τούτῳ | ⸀ δὲ | [a☆ καὶ ] | αὐτὸς |
| *adikōn* | *en* | *toutō* | *de* | *kai* | *autos* |
| of unjust. | In | this | and | [ idem ] | myself |

16.b.**Txt:** 01ℵ,02A,04C 08E,044,81,1175,1739 Steph
**Var:** byz.

| 772.1 verb 1sing indic pres act | 671.1 adj acc sing | 4743.4 noun acc sing fem | 2174.29 verb inf pres act | 2174.17 verb nom sing masc part pres act |
|---|---|---|---|---|
| ἀσκῶ, | ἀπρόσκοπον | συνείδησιν | ⸀ ἔχειν | [b ἔχων ] |
| *askō* | *aproskopon* | *suneidēsin* | *echein* | *echōn* |
| I exercise, | without offence | a conscience | to have | [ having ] |

| 4242.1 prep | 3450.6 art acc sing masc | 2296.4 noun acc sing masc | 2504.1 conj | 3450.8 art acc pl masc | 442.9 noun acc pl masc |
|---|---|---|---|---|---|
| πρὸς | τὸν | θεὸν | καὶ | τοὺς | ἀνθρώπους |
| *pros* | *ton* | *theon* | *kai* | *tous* | *anthrōpous* |
| towards | | God | and | the | men |

| 1269.1 adv | 1217.2 prep | 3820.2 adj gen sing | 17. 1217.1 prep | 2073.4 noun gen pl neu | 1156.2 conj |
|---|---|---|---|---|---|
| ⸀ διαπαντός. | [☆ διὰ | παντός. ] | 17. δι' | ἐτῶν | δὲ |
| *diapantos* | *dia* | *pantos* | *di'* | *etōn* | *de* |
| continually. | [ through | everything. ] | Through | years | and |

17.a.**Txt:** 020L,025P,byz. sa.bo.
**Var:** 01ℵ-org,02A,03B 04C,Lach,Treg,Alf,Tisc We/Ho,Weis,Sod UBS/☆

| 3979.2 adj comp gen pl | 3716.2 verb 1sing indic aor mid | 1641.5 noun acc pl fem | 4020.56 verb nom sing masc part fut act |
|---|---|---|---|
| πλειόνων | ⸀a παρεγενόμην ⸌ | ἐλεημοσύνας | ποιήσων |
| *pleionōn* | *paregenomēn* | *eleēmosunas* | *poiēsōn* |
| many | I arrived | alms | bringing |

17.b.**Var:** 01ℵ-org,03B 04C,Lach,Treg,Alf,Tisc We/Ho,Weis,UBS/☆

| 1519.1 prep | 3450.16 art sing neu | 1477.1 noun sing neu | 1466.2 prs-pron gen 1sing | 3716.2 verb 1sing indic aor mid |
|---|---|---|---|---|
| εἰς | τὸ | ἔθνος | μου | [b☆+ παρεγενόμην ] |
| *eis* | *to* | *ethnos* | *mou* | *paregenomēn* |
| to | the | nation | my | [ I arrived ] |

18.a.**Txt:** 020L,025P,byz.
**Var:** 01ℵ,02A,03B,04C 08E,Lach,Treg,Alf,Tisc We/Ho,Weis,Sod UBS/☆

| 2504.1 conj | 4234.5 noun acc pl fem | 18. 1706.1 prep | 3614.4 rel-pron dat pl | 3614.14 rel-pron dat pl fem | 2128.6 verb indic aor act |
|---|---|---|---|---|---|
| καὶ | προσφοράς· | 18. ἐν | ⸀ οἷς | [a☆ αἷς ] | εὗρόν |
| *kai* | *prosphoras* | *en* | *hois* | *hais* | *heuron* |
| and | offerings. | In | which | [ idem ] | they found |

| 1466.6 prs-pron acc 1sing | 47.7 verb sing part perf mid | 1706.1 prep | 3450.3 art dat sing | 2387.2 adj dat sing neu | 3620.3 partic |
|---|---|---|---|---|---|
| με | ἡγνισμένον | ἐν | τῷ | ἱερῷ, | οὐ |
| *me* | *hēgnismenon* | *en* | *tō* | *hierō* | *ou* |
| me | having been purified | in | the | temple, | not |

| 3196.3 prep | 3657.2 noun gen sing masc | 3624.1 conj | 3196.3 prep | 2328.2 noun gen sing masc | 4948.7 indef-pron nom pl masc |
|---|---|---|---|---|---|
| μετὰ | ὄχλου | οὐδὲ | μετὰ | θορύβου, | τινὲς |
| *meta* | *ochlou* | *oude* | *meta* | *thorubou* | *tines* |
| with | crowd | nor | with | turmoil. | Certain |

Jesus made it clear this includes two distinct resurrections, one a resurrection to life (eternal), and the other a resurrection to damnation or judgment (John 5:29). However, He did not draw attention to the time between the two resurrections. God did not reveal to the Old Testament prophets the time between the first and second comings of Christ. Zechariah 9:9, for example, tells of Christ's triumphal entry into Jerusalem, which took place in connection with His first coming. Zechariah 9:10, the next verse, prophesies that His dominion or rule will be from sea to sea and from the river (the Euphrates) even to the ends of the earth. This applies to His second coming and shows that His kingdom will not be limited to the territory promised to Abraham and his descendants, which was only from the River Euphrates to the River of Egypt (Genesis 15:18). Rather, it will cover the entire earth. In the same way Jesus did not reveal the times and the seasons, but left them under the Father's authority.

**24:16.** Because of his confident hope in the resurrection, Paul exercised himself continually to have a conscience free from causing offense to God and men.

This did not mean he tried to conciliate the different parties or sects in Judaism. Actually, they differed too much in both faith and practice. (Judaism today is just as full of diverse elements, from the Orthodox who are much like the Pharisees to the liberal Reformed Jews who accept all the theories of the antisupernatural, destructive critics of the Bible.) What Paul directed attention to was the spiritual religion actually taught in the Old Testament, the genuine spirituality promoted in the Law, the Prophets, and the Psalms. This was true Old Testament religion and found its completion, fulfillment, and highest expression in and through Christ.

**24:17.** After this discourse on the resurrection, Paul returned to recounting the facts of his case. Now, after many years, he had returned to Jerusalem to bring alms to his people and an offering to God. He had been accused of being an enemy of his people. But bringing charitable gifts and offerings was not enmity.

**24:18.** Paul further showed reasons why his conscience was clear. While presenting these offerings, the Jews found Paul in the temple purified. He had entered the temple as a worshiper and was actively fulfilling the requirements of the Law. He was quietly submitting to what was asked of him and was demonstrating that he did not ask the Jews to cease being Jews when they became Christians. He was honoring the Law and the temple. How could they say he was about to defile the temple?

Furthermore, they found him with no crowd, creating no disturbance. Nothing was going on around him. He was giving his whole attention to the worship of God and was doing nothing to

**which they themselves also allow:** . . . a hope which they also cherish, *TCNT* . . . for the same thing they're looking for, *Beck.*

**that there shall be a resurrection of the dead, both of the just and unjust:** . . . that a resurrection there shall certainly be both of righteous and unrighteous, *Rotherham* . . . that there will one day be a resurrection of good and bad alike, *TCNT* . . . of both good men and bad, *Phillips.*

**16. And herein do I exercise myself:** In this I myself also take pains, *HBIE* . . . And in this I do my best, *BB* . . . I therefore exert myself, *Berkeley* . . . With this hope before me I do my utmost to live my whole life, *Phillips.*

**to have always a conscience void of offence toward God, and toward men:** . . . to keep my conscience clear before both God and man, *TCNT* . . . to have in all respects a clear conscience in my relations with God and with men, *Berkeley* . . . to live my whole life with a clear conscience, *Phillips.*

**17. Now after many years:** Now after several years' absence, *Weymouth.*

**I came to bring alms to my nation, and offerings:** I had come to bring charitable gifts...and to make offerings, *TCNT* . . . to bring a sum of money to my countrymen, and offer sacrifices, *Weymouth* . . . I came to give help and offerings to my nation, *BB* . . . to offer sacrifice and fulfill vows, *Confraternity.*

**18. Whereupon:** . . . while engaged in this, *TCNT* . . . While I was busy about these things, *Weymouth* . . . While I was performing these duties, *Williams* . . . It was in the middle of these duties, *Phillips.*

**certain Jews from Asia found me purified in the temple:** . . . that they found me in the Temple, after completing a period of purification, *TCNT* . . . they found me just as I had completed my rites of purification, *Williams* . . . a man purified, *Phillips.*

**neither with multitude, nor with tumult:** . . . or disorder, *TCNT* . . . with no crowd about me and no uproar, *Weymouth* . . . I was not mixed up in any mob or riot, *Moffatt.*

| **1156.2** conj | **570.3** prep | **3450.10** art gen sing fem | **767.2** name gen fem | **2428.2** name-adj nom pl masc | **3614.8** rel-pron acc pl masc |
|---|---|---|---|---|---|
| δὲ | ἀπὸ | τῆς | ᾿Ασίας | ᾿Ιουδαῖοι, | **19.** οὓς |
| *de* | *apo* | *tēs* | *Asias* | *Ioudaioi* | *hous* |
| but | from | | Asia | Jews, | who |

19.a.**Txt:** 020L,byz.sa. Steph
**Var:** 01ℵ,02A,03B,04C 08E,025P,bo.Elzev Gries,Lach,Treg,Alf Word,Tisc,We/Ho,Weis Sod,UBS/⋆

| **1158.1** verb 3sing indic pres act | **1158.6** verb 3sing indic imperf act | **1894.3** prep | **4622.2** prs-pron gen 2sing | **3780.12** verb inf pres act |
|---|---|---|---|---|
| ʻ δεῖ | [a⋆ ἔδει ] | ἐπὶ | σοῦ | παρεῖναι |
| *dei* | *edei* | *epi* | *sou* | *pareinai* |
| it is necessary | [ it was necessary ] | before | you | to appear |

19.b.**Txt:** 020L,025P,byz. Sod
**Var:** 01ℵ,02A,03B,04C 08E,Lach,Treg,Alf,Tisc We/Ho,Weis,UBS/⋆

| **2504.1** conj | **2693.8** verb inf pres act | **1479.1** conj | **4948.10** indef-pron sing neu | **2174.12** verb 3pl opt pres act | **4242.1** prep |
|---|---|---|---|---|---|
| καὶ | κατηγορεῖν | εἴ | τι | ἔχοιεν | πρὸς |
| *kai* | *katēgorein* | *ei* | *ti* | *echoien* | *pros* |
| and | to accuse | if | anything | they may have | against |

20.a.**Txt:** Steph
**Var:** 01ℵ,02A,03B,04C 08E,020L,025P,bo. Gries,Lach,Treg,Alf Word,Tisc,We/Ho,Weis Sod,UBS/⋆

| **1466.6** prs-pron acc 1sing | **1466.7** prs-pron acc 1sing | **2211.1** conj | **840.7** prs-pron nom pl masc | **3642.7** dem-pron nom pl masc |
|---|---|---|---|---|
| ʻ με. | [b⋆ ἐμέ. ] | **20.** ἢ | αὐτοὶ | οὗτοι |
| *me* | *eme* | *ē* | *autoi* | *houtoi* |
| me; | [ idem ] | or | themselves | these |

20.b.**Txt:** 04C,08E,020L 025P,byz.it.sa.bo.
**Var:** p74,01ℵ,02A,03B 33,Lach,Tisc,We/Ho Weis,Sod,UBS/⋆

| **1500.14** verb 3pl impr aor act | **1479.1** conj | **4949.9** intr-pron sing neu | **2128.6** verb indic aor act | **1706.1** prep | **1466.5** prs-pron dat 1sing |
|---|---|---|---|---|---|
| εἰπάτωσαν, | ʻa εἴ ˋ | τί | εὗρον | ʻb ἐν | ἐμοὶ ˋ |
| *eipatōsan* | *ei* | *ti* | *heuron* | *en* | *emoi* |
| let them say, | if | any | they found | in | me |

| **91.1** noun sing neu | **2449.11** verb gen sing masc part aor act | **1466.2** prs-pron gen 1sing | **1894.3** prep | **3450.2** art gen sing |
|---|---|---|---|---|
| ἀδίκημα, | στάντος | μου | ἐπὶ | τοῦ |
| *adikēma* | *stantos* | *mou* | *epi* | *tou* |
| unrighteousness, | having stood | me | before | the |

| **4742.2** noun gen sing neu | **2211.1** conj | **3875.1** prep | **1518.6** num card gen fem | **3642.10** dem-pron gen sing fem |
|---|---|---|---|---|
| συνεδρίου, | **21.** ἢ | περὶ | μιᾶς | ταύτης |
| *sunedriou* | *ē* | *peri* | *mias* | *tautēs* |
| Sanhedrin, | other than | concerning | one | this |

21.a.**Txt:** 08E,020L 025P,byz.
**Var:** 01ℵ,02A,03B,04C Treg,Alf,Tisc,We/Ho Weis,Sod,UBS/⋆

| **5292.2** noun gen sing fem | **3614.10** rel-pron gen sing fem | **2869.10** verb 1sing indic aor act | **2869.21** verb 1sing indic aor act | **2449.26** verb sing part perf act |
|---|---|---|---|---|
| φωνῆς, | ἧς | ʻ ἔκραξα | [a⋆ ἐκέκραξα ] | ʻ ἑστὼς |
| *phōnēs* | *hēs* | *ekraxa* | *ekekraxa* | *hestōs* |
| voice, | which | I cried out | [ idem ] | standing |

| **1706.1** prep | **840.2** prs-pron dat pl | **1706.1** prep | **840.2** prs-pron dat pl | **2449.26** verb sing part perf act | **3617.1** conj |
|---|---|---|---|---|---|
| ἐν | αὐτοῖς, | [⋆ ἐν | αὐτοῖς | ἑστὼς ] | Ὅτι |
| *en* | *autois* | *en* | *autois* | *hestōs* | *Hoti* |
| among | them: | [ among | them | standing ] | |

| **3875.1** prep | **384.2** noun gen sing fem | **3361.2** adj gen pl | **1466.1** prs-pron nom 1sing | **2892.28** verb 1sing indic pres mid |
|---|---|---|---|---|
| Περὶ | ἀναστάσεως | νεκρῶν | ἐγὼ | κρίνομαι |
| *Peri* | *anastaseōs* | *nekrōn* | *egō* | *krinomai* |
| Concerning | a resurrection | of dead | I | am being judged |

21.b.**Txt:** 01ℵ,08E,020L 025P,byz.bo.
**Var:** 02A,03B,04C,Lach Treg,Alf,Word,Tisc We/Ho,Weis,Sod UBS/⋆

| **4449.1** adv | **5097.1** prep | **1894.1** prep | **5050.2** prs-pron gen 2pl | **189.31** verb nom sing masc part aor act |
|---|---|---|---|---|
| σήμερον | ʻ ὑφ' | [b⋆ ἐφ' ] | ὑμῶν. | **22.** ʻ ᾿Ακούσας |
| *sēmeron* | *huph'* | *eph'* | *humōn* | *Akousas* |
| today | by | [ idem ] | you. | Having heard |

draw the attention of the people to himself. But there were certain Jews from the Roman province of Asia who falsely accused him. (They had jumped to a wrong conclusion because they had seen Paul in the city with a Gentile and they supposed Paul had brought him into the temple. Tertullus had not mentioned this because he wanted to give the impression that the Jews had arrested Paul to keep him from defiling the temple.)

**24:19.** Paul then declared that these Jews from the province of Asia were the real accusers. It was really their duty to be the ones to come before Felix and make their accusation if they really had anything against Paul.

Paul was taking advantage of the Law's demand for witnesses to make the accusation. The Law, in fact, demanded at least two or three witnesses in the case of any accusation of wrong for the matter to be established (Deuteronomy 17:6,7; 19:15). Jewish writings after Old Testament times also stressed the importance of the witnesses being cross-examined to be sure they were not false witnesses. This is also indicated in Deuteronomy 19:18. None of this was being done in this trial or any of the previous times Paul had to face the Jews.

**24:20.** Paul made it clear that none of the priests and elders present were witnesses of anything they were claiming against Paul or of anything that went on in the temple. This again meant they were paying no attention to their own law, for they brought no witnesses with them. The passages in Deuteronomy 17:6 and 19:15 indicate there was to be no trial without witnesses. (The New Testament also upholds this; see 2 Corinthians 13:1.) Roman law also recognized the need for witnesses. But all that Paul's accusers brought with them was a clever lawyer.

**24:21.** There was really only one thing this priest and the elders were witnesses of with respect to Paul. They were present when Paul stood before the Sanhedrin in Jerusalem and cried out that it was with respect to the resurrection of the dead that he was called into question. He would willingly let them accuse him of saying that.

Because Paul was first of all a witness for Christ, he could not rest his case without once more bringing to the attention of both the Jews and Felix that the central and basic issue in the promises of God is the hope of the resurrection.

The high priest and elders failed to say anything in reply at this point. They knew very well the Sanhedrin would have acquitted Paul if the Pharisees had been in the majority. The Sadducees also knew that to bring it up again would expose their own sectarian attitude to Felix and would hurt their case.

**19. Who ought to have been here before thee:** . . . who should in my opinion have come before you, *Phillips* . . . who ought to have appeared, *Williams C.K.*

**and object:** . . . and to accuse me, *Alford* . . . and to have made any charge, *TCNT* . . . and to have been my prosecutors, *Weymouth* . . . to prosecute me, *Fenton* . . . and made their accusation, *Phillips* . . . and charged me, *Williams C.K.*

**if they had ought against me:** . . . if they knew anything tangible against me, *Berkeley.*

**20. Or else let these same here say:** . . . let my opponents, *TCNT* . . . let these now present declare, *Fenton* . . . let these men themselves speak out now and say, *Phillips* . . . Let those who are here declare, *NAB.*

**if they have found any evil doing in me:** . . . what misdemeanor they found me guilty of, *Weymouth* . . . what crime, *HBIE* . . . what fault they found in me, *Fenton* . . . what they found to complain of in me, *Williams C.K.* . . . they found me guilty of, *NAB.*

**while I stood before the council:** . . . when brought up before the senate, *Fenton* . . . the Sanhedrin, *Weymouth.*

**21. Except it be for this one voice:** . . . except as to the one sentence, *TCNT* . . . Unless it was that one expression of which I made use, *Weymouth* . . . Yes, there was one thing they resented, *Norlie* . . . unless it be this one exclamation, *Fenton* . . . unless it was that one sentence, *Phillips.*

**that I cried standing among them:** . . . it was what I called out as I stood in their presence, *NAB* . . . that I shouted out as I stood among them, *TCNT* . . . standing in their midst, *Fenton* . . . All I said was this, *Phillips.*

**Touching the resurrection of the dead:** It is about, *Phillips* . . . Concerning the raising of the dead, *Rotherham.*

**I am called in question by you this day:** . . . am I to be judged this day by you, *Rotherham* . . . that I am on my trial before you today, *TCNT* . . . that I am accused this day before you, *Fenton.*

| 1156.2 conj | 3642.18 dem-pron pl neu | 3450.5 art nom sing masc | 5181.1 name nom masc | 304.1 verb 3sing indic aor mid | 840.8 prs-pron acc pl masc |
|---|---|---|---|---|---|
| δὲ | ταῦτα | ὁ | Φῆλιξ | ἀνεβάλετο | αὐτούς, |
| *de* | *tauta* | *ho* | *Phēlix* | *anebaleto* | *autous* |
| and | these things | | Felix | put off | them, |

22.a.**Txt:** 020L,025P,byz.
**Var:** 01ℵ,02A,03B,04C 08E,bo.Gries,Lach,Treg Alf,Word,Tisc,We/Ho Weis,Sod,UBS/☆

| 304.1 verb 3sing indic aor mid | 1156.2 conj | 840.8 prs-pron acc pl masc | 3450.5 art nom sing masc | 5181.1 name nom masc |
|---|---|---|---|---|
| [a☆ ἀνεβάλετο | δὲ | αὐτοὺς | ὁ | Φῆλιξ, ] |
| *anebaleto* | *de* | *autous* | *ho* | *Phēlix* |
| [ postponed | and | them | | Felix, ] |

| 194.1 adv comp | 3471.18 verb nom sing masc part perf act | 3450.17 art pl neu | 3875.1 prep | 3450.10 art gen sing fem |
|---|---|---|---|---|
| ἀκριβέστερον | εἰδὼς | τὰ | περὶ | τῆς |
| *akribesteron* | *eidōs* | *ta* | *peri* | *tēs* |
| more accurately | knowing | the things | concerning | the |

22.b.**Txt:** 08E,020L 025P,byz.Sod
**Var:** 01ℵ,02A,03B,04C Lach,Treg,Alf,Word Tisc,We/Ho,Weis UBS/☆

| 3461.2 noun gen sing fem | 1500.15 verb nom sing masc part aor act | 1500.30 verb nom sing masc part aor act | 3615.1 conj | 3051.1 name nom masc |
|---|---|---|---|---|
| ὁδοῦ, | ⸂ εἰπών, | [b☆ εἴπας, ] | Ὅταν | Λυσίας |
| *hodou* | *eipōn* | *eipas* | *Hotan* | *Lusias* |
| way, | having said, | [ said, ] | When | Lysias |

| 3450.5 art nom sing masc | 5341.1 noun nom sing masc | 2568.16 verb 3sing subj aor act | 1225.2 verb 1sing indic fut mid | 3450.17 art pl neu |
|---|---|---|---|---|
| ὁ | χιλίαρχος | καταβῇ, | διαγνώσομαι | τὰ |
| *ho* | *chiliarchos* | *katabē* | *diagnōsomai* | *ta* |
| the | chief captain | may come down, | I will examine | the things |

23.a.**Txt:** byz.
**Var:** 01ℵ,02A,03B,04C 08E,025P,bo.Lach,Treg Alf,Word,Tisc,We/Ho Weis,Sod,UBS/☆

| 2567.2 prep | 5050.4 prs-pron acc 2pl | 1293.9 verb nom sing masc part aor mid | 4885.1 conj | 3450.3 art dat sing |
|---|---|---|---|---|
| καθ' | ὑμᾶς· | 23. διαταξάμενος | ⸂a τε ⸃ | τῷ |
| *kath'* | *humas* | *diataxamenos* | *te* | *tō* |
| according to | you; | having ordered | and | the |

23.b.**Txt:** 020L,025P,byz.
**Var:** 01ℵ,02A,03B,04C 08E,bo.Gries,Lach,Treg Alf,Word,Tisc,We/Ho Weis,Sod,UBS/☆

| 1529.2 noun dat sing masc | 4931.31 verb inf pres mid | 3450.6 art acc sing masc | 3834.4 name acc masc | 840.6 prs-pron acc sing masc |
|---|---|---|---|---|
| ἑκατοντάρχῃ | τηρεῖσθαι | ⸂ τὸν | Παῦλον, | [b☆ αὐτὸν ] |
| *hekatontarchē* | *tēreisthai* | *ton* | *Paulon* | *auton* |
| centurion | to keep | | Paul, | [ him ] |

| 2174.29 verb inf pres act | 4885.1 conj | 423.2 noun acc sing fem | 2504.1 conj | 3235.4 num card acc masc | 2940.5 verb inf pres act | 3450.1 art gen pl |
|---|---|---|---|---|---|---|
| ἔχειν | τε | ἄνεσιν, | καὶ | μηδένα | κωλύειν | τῶν |
| *echein* | *te* | *anesin* | *kai* | *mēdena* | *kōluein* | *tōn* |
| to have | and | ease, | and | none | to forbid | of the |

23.c.**Txt:** 020L,025P,byz.
**Var:** 01ℵ,02A,03B,04C 08E,bo.Lach,Treg,Alf Word,Tisc,We/Ho,Weis Sod,UBS/☆

| 2375.1 adj gen pl | 840.3 prs-pron gen sing | 5094.1 verb inf pres act | 2211.1 conj | 4193.17 verb inf pres mid | 840.4 prs-pron dat sing |
|---|---|---|---|---|---|
| ἰδίων | αὐτοῦ | ὑπηρετεῖν | ⸂c ἢ | προσέρχεσθαι ⸃ | αὐτῷ. |
| *idiōn* | *autou* | *hupēretein* | *ē* | *proserchesthai* | *autō* |
| own | his | to minister | or | to come | to him. |

| 3196.3 prep | 1156.2 conj | 2232.1 noun fem | 4948.9 indef-pron acc pl masc | 3716.7 verb nom sing masc part aor mid |
|---|---|---|---|---|
| 24. Μετὰ | δὲ | ἡμέρας | τινὰς | παραγενόμενος |
| *Meta* | *de* | *hēmeras* | *tinas* | *paragenomenos* |
| After | and | days | certain | having arrived |

24.a.**Var:** 03B,04C-corr Lach,Treg,Tisc,We/Ho Weis,Sod,UBS/☆

| 3450.5 art nom sing masc | 5181.1 name nom masc | 4713.1 prep | 1403.1 name dat fem | 3450.11 art dat sing fem | 2375.10 adj dat sing fem |
|---|---|---|---|---|---|
| ὁ | Φῆλιξ | σὺν | Δρουσίλλῃ | τῇ | [a☆+ ἰδίᾳ ] |
| *ho* | *Phēlix* | *sun* | *Drousillē* | *tē* | *idia* |
| | Felix | with | Drusilla | the | [ his own ] |

**24:22.** In view of the lack of evidence, Felix should have set Paul free. But Felix gave in to the same temptation that controlled Pontius Pilate. When Pilate found no fault or crime in Jesus, he did not set Jesus free for fear of the Jews. Felix had already angered the Jews on several occasions, and he shrank from offending them further lest they get a hearing for their complaints against him before the emperor in Rome.

Felix had been governor over Judea long enough to have an accurate knowledge of the teachings and way of life of the thousands of Jewish Christians who lived under his rule. He also knew enough about the Jews to realize that if he turned Paul over to these Jewish leaders he would be condemning an innocent man.

Yet, instead of setting Paul free, he compromised and put the Jews off, saying that when the tribune Lysias came down he would learn the details of the things that concerned them. There is no evidence, however, that he ever sent for Lysias.

Felix probably hoped that time and chance would make things easier for him. So, after giving this empty promise to make further investigation, Felix kept Paul in custody.

**24:23.** To salve his conscience, Felix turned Paul over to a centurion, ordering him to give Paul a considerable amount of freedom. More than that, he must not forbid any of Paul's own people from ministering to him. Paul's many friends among the Christians would be allowed to visit him, bring him food, and give him whatever else he needed. In a sense, Paul was in what might be called "house arrest." His friends were free to minister to him in any way at any time.

These friends would include Luke, the physician, who later stood by him so faithfully on the journey to Rome and in both Paul's Roman imprisonments (2 Timothy 4:11, "only Luke is with me"). Many believe Luke wrote his Gospel while Paul was in custody in Caesarea for the following 2 years. Luke would be free also to travel to Jerusalem and talk to Mary and the apostles to confirm the facts. Luke must also have gathered much material for the Book of Acts at the same time. Philip and many other eyewitnesses lived in Caesarea. Still others were nearby.

The many Christians in Caesarea could be counted on to help make Paul's imprisonment there as comfortable as possible. Also, many of Paul's friends from the churches he had established would enter Palestine on their way to Jerusalem for the Feasts by way of Caesarea.

**24:24.** At first it may have been hard for Paul to see how his continued imprisonment in Caesarea fitted in with God's purpose for him. But part of Paul's mission was to testify before rulers (9:15). After some days he had an opportunity to carry this out. Felix, with his wife Drusilla, summoned Paul and listened to him tell of his faith in Christ Jesus; literally, he told of the "in Christ Jesus" faith, that is, the gospel.

**22. And when Felix heard these things:** At this point Felix, *Weymouth.*

**having more perfect knowledge of that way:** . . . who was fairly well informed about the new faith, *Weymouth* . . . who had a fairly clear conception of the principles involved in the Way, *Williams* . . . who was better acquainted with the Way than most people, *Phillips* . . . who knew the Christian religion rather well, *Beck.*

**he deferred them, and said:** . . . adjourned the case...with the promise, *TCNT* . . . adjourned the trial, saying to the Jews, *Weymouth* . . . postponed the case, saying, *Norlie.*

**When Lysias the chief captain shall come down:** As soon as, *Rotherham* . . . Colonel Lysias arrives, *Phillips.*

**I will know the uttermost of your matter:** I will decide your case, *RSV* . . . adjudge your matter, *Alford* . . . give my decision in your case, *TCNT* . . . go carefully into the matter, *Montgomery* . . . finish the examination of your case, *Norlie.*

**23. And he commanded a centurion to keep Paul:** So he gave orders to the Captain in charge of Paul to keep him in custody, *TCNT.*

**and to let him have liberty:** . . . a measure of liberty, *Rotherham* . . . but to relax the regulations, *TCNT* . . . but to allow him some freedom, *Moffatt* . . . but to grant him reasonable liberty, *Phillips* . . . treated with indulgence, *Montgomery* . . . to allow him out on parole, *Fenton.*

**and that he should forbid none of his acquaintance to minister or come unto him:** . . . and not to prevent any of his personal friends from attending to his wants, *TCNT* . . . and allow any of his personal friends to look after his needs, *Phillips* . . . from showing him kindness, *Weymouth.*

**24. And after certain days:** Some days later, *TCNT* . . . Not long after this, *Weymouth.*

**when Felix came with his wife Drusilla, which was a Jewess:** Felix brought along his wife Drusilla, a Jewess, *Berkeley* . . . Felix came again. His wife Drusilla, who was a Jew, was with him, *Beck.*

## Acts 24:25

24.b.**Txt:** 01ℵ-org,08E byz.
**Var:** 03B,04C,020L 025P,Gries,Lach,Treg Alf,Tisc,We/Ho,Weis Sod,UBS/☆

| **1129.3** noun dat sing fem | **840.3** prs-pron gen sing | **1498.28** verb dat sing fem part pres act | **2424.3** name dat fem | **3213.2** verb 3sing indic aor mid |
|---|---|---|---|---|
| γυναικὶ | (b αὐτοῦ ) | οὔσῃ | Ἰουδαίᾳ, | μετεπέμψατο |
| *gunaiki* | *autou* | *ousē* | *Ioudaia* | *metepempsato* |
| wife | his, | being | a Jewess, | he sent for |

| **3450.6** art acc sing masc | **3834.4** name acc masc | **2504.1** conj | **189.21** verb 3sing indic aor act | **840.3** prs-pron gen sing | **3875.1** prep |
|---|---|---|---|---|---|
| τὸν | Παῦλον, | καὶ | ἤκουσεν | αὐτοῦ | περὶ |
| *ton* | *Paulon* | *kai* | *ēkousen* | *autou* | *peri* |
| | Paul, | and | heard | him | concerning |

24.c.**Var:** p74,01ℵ-org 03B,08E,020L,044,it.bo. Lach,Tisc,We/Ho,Weis Sod,UBS/☆

| **3450.10** art gen sing fem | **1519.1** prep | **5382.4** name acc masc | **2400.3** name acc masc | **3963.2** noun gen sing fem |
|---|---|---|---|---|
| τῆς | εἰς | Χριστὸν | [c☆+ Ἰησοῦν ] | πίστεως. |
| *tēs* | *eis* | *Christon* | *Iēsoun* | *pisteōs* |
| the | in | Christ | [ Jesus ] | faith. |

| **1250.3** verb gen sing masc part pres mid | **1156.2** conj | **840.3** prs-pron gen sing | **3875.1** prep | **1336.2** noun gen sing fem |
|---|---|---|---|---|
| **25.** διαλεγομένου | δὲ | αὐτοῦ | περὶ | δικαιοσύνης |
| *dialegomenou* | *de* | *autou* | *peri* | *dikaiosunēs* |
| Reasoning | and | he | concerning | righteousness |

| **2504.1** conj | **1459.2** noun gen sing fem | **2504.1** conj | **3450.2** art gen sing | **2890.2** noun gen sing neu | **3450.2** art gen sing |
|---|---|---|---|---|---|
| καὶ | ἐγκρατείας | καὶ | τοῦ | κρίματος | τοῦ |
| *kai* | *enkrateias* | *kai* | *tou* | *krimatos* | *tou* |
| and | self-control | and | the | judgment | the |

25.a.**Txt:** 020L,025P,byz.
**Var:** 01ℵ,02A,03B,04C 08E,bo.Gries,Lach,Treg Alf,Word,Tisc,We/Ho Weis,Sod,UBS/☆

| **3165.9** verb gen sing part pres act | **1498.45** verb inf fut mid | **1703.1** adj nom sing masc | **1090.53** verb nom sing masc part aor mid | **3450.5** art nom sing masc |
|---|---|---|---|---|
| μέλλοντος | (a ἔσεσθαι ) | ἔμφοβος | γενόμενος | ὁ |
| *mellontos* | *esesthai* | *emphobos* | *genomenos* | *ho* |
| being about | to be, | afraid | having become | |

| **5181.1** name nom masc | **552.6** verb 3sing indic aor pass | **3450.16** art sing neu | **3431.1** adv | **2174.28** verb sing neu part pres act | **4057.4** verb 2sing impr pres mid |
|---|---|---|---|---|---|
| Φῆλιξ | ἀπεκρίθη, | Τὸ | νῦν | ἔχον | πορεύου· |
| *Phēlix* | *apekrithē* | *To* | *nun* | *echon* | *poreuou* |
| Felix | answered, | The | now | having | go, |

| **2511.4** noun acc sing masc | **1156.2** conj | **3205.3** verb nom sing masc part aor act | **3203.3** verb 1sing indic fut mid | **4622.4** prs-pron acc 2sing |
|---|---|---|---|---|
| καιρὸν | δὲ | μεταλαβὼν | μετακαλέσομαί | σε· |
| *kairon* | *de* | *metalabōn* | *metakalesomai* | *se* |
| an opportunity | and | having found | I will call for | you; |

26.a.**Txt:** bo.Steph
**Var:** 01ℵ,02A,03B,04C 08E,020L,025P,Gries Lach,Treg,Alf,Word Tisc,We/Ho,Weis,Sod UBS/☆

| **258.1** adv | **1156.2** conj | **2504.1** conj | **1666.5** verb nom sing masc part pres act | **3617.1** conj | **5371.2** noun pl neu |
|---|---|---|---|---|---|
| **26.** ἅμα | (a δὲ ) | καὶ | ἐλπίζων | ὅτι | χρήματα |
| *hama* | *de* | *kai* | *elpizōn* | *hoti* | *chrēmata* |
| at the same time | too | also | hoping | that | riches |

26.b.**Txt:** 020L,025P,byz. bo.
**Var:** 01ℵ,02A,03B,04C 08E,Lach,Treg,Alf Word,Tisc,We/Ho,Weis Sod,UBS/☆

| **1319.57** verb 3sing indic fut pass | **840.4** prs-pron dat sing | **5097.3** prep | **3450.2** art gen sing | **3834.2** name gen masc | **3567.1** conj |
|---|---|---|---|---|---|
| δοθήσεται | αὐτῷ | ὑπὸ | τοῦ | Παύλου, | (b ὅπως |
| *dothēsetai* | *autō* | *hupo* | *tou* | *Paulou* | *hopōs* |
| will be given | him | by | | Paul, | that |

| **3061.9** verb 3sing subj aor act | **840.6** prs-pron acc sing masc | **1346.1** conj | **2504.1** conj | **4295.3** adj comp sing neu |
|---|---|---|---|---|
| λύσῃ | αὐτόν· ) | διὸ | καὶ | πυκνότερον |
| *lusē* | *auton* | *dio* | *kai* | *puknoteron* |
| he might loose | him: | wherefore | also | more often |

Drusilla was the young daughter of Herod Agrippa I, the Herod who had arrested James the brother of John and killed him with the sword (12:1,2). She was the sister of Herod Agrippa II and Bernice. Felix had seduced her from her former husband, King Aziz of Emesa in the western part of Syria. She was actually the third wife of Felix. His first wife was a granddaughter of Marc Antony, the Roman orator and general, and Cleopatra, the queen of Egypt. His second wife was a princess. Divorce and remarriage were very common among both Romans and Jews in those days. Felix and Drusilla also had a son who died in the eruption of Mount Vesuvius that buried Pompeii in A.D. 79.

Herod Agrippa I was educated in Rome, but when he became king, he was tactful in his treatment of the Jews and tried to curry their favor. Like all the Herods, he was nominally a Jew through his mother who was descended from the Hasmonean (Maccabean) priests who had temporarily reigned over Jerusalem. Through Drusilla, Felix would have learned a great deal about the history and customs, as well as the religion of the Jews.

**24:25.** To Felix and Drusilla, Paul not only presented the facts and the theology but, as he did in all his epistles, he went on to discuss practical matters of righteousness, self-control, and the coming judgment.

There is no doubt Paul told Felix all about the life and teachings of Jesus, as well as about His death, resurrection, and second coming. Paul had recently written the Epistle to the Romans in which he declared he was not ashamed of the gospel (Romans 1:16). He had gone on to tell how all, both Gentiles and Jews, have sinned and need the gospel. Then Paul had told the Romans the gospel means justification by faith, assurance, freedom from sin, and the ultimate glorification of believers.

But when Paul began to deal with God's requirements with respect to righteousness, self-control, and the coming judgment, Felix became terrified. Now their positions were reversed. This time Felix was on trial. The conviction of the Holy Spirit made him tremble.

Jesus said the Holy Spirit would guide into all truth and convince the world with respect to sin, showing that their real sin was unbelief; with respect to righteousness, not their own righteousness or lack of it, but of what righteousness really is as it is seen in Jesus; and with respect to judgment, for they will share in Satan's judgment (John 16:8-11).

Felix, however, resisted the Spirit's conviction and told Paul to go for now. In his "spare time" he would see him again.

**24:26.** Felix was also motivated by greed. The real reason he promised to see Paul again was he hoped Paul would give him a great deal of money (riches) in order to gain his freedom. It is quite possible that when he saw how loyal Paul's friends were, Felix hoped that many of them would get together and present to him a bribe for Paul's release.

**he sent for Paul, and heard him concerning the faith in Christ:** . . . and sending for Paul, listened to what he had to say about faith in Christ Jesus, *TCNT* . . . and heard what he had to say about, *Phillips* . . . faith toward Christ, *Young* . . . about this Christ Jesus faith, *Klingensmith.*

**25. And as he reasoned of righteousness:** But while Paul was speaking at length about righteousness, *TCNT* . . . about justice, *Weymouth* . . . was talking about goodness, *Phillips* . . . But when he discussed purity of life, *Berkeley.*

**temperance:** . . . self control, *ASV* . . . the mastery of passions, *Berkeley* . . . self-mastery, *Moffatt.*

**and judgment to come:** . . . and the coming judgment, *TCNT* . . . and the future judgment, *Weymouth* . . . the coming Day of Judgment, *TEV.*

**Felix trembled, and answered:** Felix was terrified, *Rotherham* . . . was afraid, *Alford* . . . became alarmed, *Noyes, Phillips* . . . became terrified, and broke in with, *TCNT* . . . being filled with fear, *Darby* . . . grew uneasy, *Moffatt.*

**Go thy way for this time:** For the present, *Rotherham* . . . leave me, *Weymouth.*

**when I have a convenient season:** . . . and when I find an opportunity, *Rotherham* . . . When I can spare the time, *Berkeley* . . . and when the right time comes, *BB* . . . when it will be convenient for me, *Norlie* . . . When I get a chance, *Beck* . . . some future opportunity, *Campbell* . . . a convenient moment, *Phillips.*

**I will call for thee:** I will send for thee, *Rotherham* . . . I will summon you, *RSV.*

**26. He hoped also that money should have been given him of Paul:** At the same time he nursed a secret hope that Paul would pay him money, *Phillips* . . . He was hoping, too, for a bribe from Paul, *TCNT.*

**that he might loose him:**

**wherefore he sent for him the oftener:** . . . and so he used to send for him frequently, *TCNT* . . . and so he kept sending for him, *Williams* . . . which is why Paul was frequently summoned to come, *Phillips.*

| 840.6 prs-pron acc sing masc | 3213.1 verb nom sing masc part pres mid | 3519.3 verb 3sing indic imperf act | 840.4 prs-pron dat sing |
|---|---|---|---|
| αὐτὸν | μεταπεμπόμενος | ὡμίλει | αὐτῷ. |
| *auton* | *metapempomenos* | *hōmilei* | *autō* |
| him | sending for | he was conversing | with him. |

| 1327.1 noun gen sing fem | 1156.2 conj | 3997.25 verb gen sing fem part aor pass | 2956.14 verb 3sing indic aor act | 1234.1 noun acc sing masc |
|---|---|---|---|---|
| 27. Διετίας | δὲ | πληρωθείσης | ἔλαβεν | διάδοχον |
| *Dietias* | *de* | *plērōtheisēs* | *elaben* | *diadochon* |
| Two years | but | having been completed | received | successor |

| 3450.5 art nom sing masc | 5181.1 name nom masc | 4060.1 name acc masc | 5184.4 name acc masc | 2286.12 verb nom sing masc part pres act |
|---|---|---|---|---|
| ὁ | Φῆλιξ | Πόρκιον | Φῆστον· | θέλων |
| *ho* | *Phēlix* | *Porkion* | *Phēston* | *thelōn* |
| | Felix | Porcius | Festus; | wishing |

27.a.**Txt:** 025P,byz.Sod
**Var:** 01ℵ-org,02A,03B 04C,bo.Lach,Treg,Alf Word,Tisc,We/Ho,Weis UBS/⋆

| 4885.1 conj | 5322.5 noun acc pl fem | 5322.6 noun acc sing fem | 2667.2 verb inf aor mid | 3450.4 art dat pl |
|---|---|---|---|---|
| τε | ˊ χάριτας | [a⋆ χάριτα ] | καταθέσθαι | τοῖς |
| *te* | *charitas* | *charita* | *katathesthai* | *tois* |
| and | favors | [ idem ] | to acquire for himself | with the |

| 2428.4 name-adj dat pl masc | 3450.5 art nom sing masc | 5181.1 name nom masc | 2611.3 verb 3sing indic aor act | 3450.6 art acc sing masc |
|---|---|---|---|---|
| Ἰουδαίοις | ὁ | Φῆλιξ | κατέλιπεν | τὸν |
| *Ioudaiois* | *ho* | *Phēlix* | *katelipen* | *ton* |
| Jews | | Felix | left | |

| 3834.4 name acc masc | 1204.16 verb sing part perf mid | 5184.1 name nom masc | 3631.1 partic |
|---|---|---|---|
| Παῦλον | δεδεμένον. | 25:1. Φῆστος | οὖν |
| *Paulon* | *dedemenon* | *Phēstos* | *oun* |
| Paul | having been bound. | Festus | therefore |

1.a.**Txt:** 01ℵ-corr,03B 04C,08E,020L,025P,byz. Sod
**Var:** 01ℵ-org,02A,Tisc Weis,UBS/⋆

| 1895.3 verb nom sing masc part aor act | 3450.11 art dat sing fem | 1870.2 noun dat sing fem | 1870.4 noun dat sing fem | 3196.3 prep |
|---|---|---|---|---|
| ἐπιβὰς | τῇ | ˊ ἐπαρχίᾳ, | [a⋆ ἐπαρχείᾳ ] | μετὰ |
| *epibas* | *tē* | *eparchia* | *eparcheia* | *meta* |
| having come into | the | province, | [ idem ] | after |

| 4980.1 num card nom | 2232.1 noun fem | 303.13 verb 3sing indic aor act | 1519.1 prep | 2389.1 name | 570.3 prep |
|---|---|---|---|---|---|
| τρεῖς | ἡμέρας | ἀνέβη | εἰς | Ἱεροσόλυμα | ἀπὸ |
| *treis* | *hēmeras* | *anebē* | *eis* | *Hierosoluma* | *apo* |
| three | days | went up | to | Jerusalem | from |

2.a.**Txt:** 08E,020L,025P byz.bo.
**Var:** 01ℵ,02A,03B,04C Lach,Treg,Alf,Tisc We/Ho,Weis,Sod UBS/⋆

2.b.**Txt:** 025P,byz.
**Var:** 01ℵ,02A,03B,04C 08E,020L,bo.Lach,Treg Alf,Tisc,We/Ho,Weis Sod,UBS/⋆

| 2513.1 name gen fem | 1702.4 verb 3pl indic aor act | 1156.2 conj | 4885.1 conj | 840.4 prs-pron dat sing |
|---|---|---|---|---|
| Καισαρείας, | 2. ἐνεφάνισάν | ˊ δὲ | [a⋆ τε ] | αὐτῷ |
| *Kaisareias* | *enephanisan* | *de* | *te* | *autō* |
| Caesarea. | Made a report before | and | [ idem ] | him |

| 3450.5 art nom sing masc | 744.1 noun nom sing masc | 3450.7 art nom pl masc | 744.5 noun pl masc | 2504.1 conj |
|---|---|---|---|---|
| ˊ ὁ | ἀρχιερεὺς | [b⋆ οἱ | ἀρχιερεῖς ] | καὶ |
| *ho* | *archiereus* | *hoi* | *archiereis* | *kai* |
| the | high priest | [ the | chief priests ] | and |

| 3450.7 art nom pl masc | 4272.7 num ord nom pl masc | 3450.1 art gen pl | 2428.3 name-adj gen pl masc | 2567.3 prep | 3450.2 art gen sing |
|---|---|---|---|---|---|
| οἱ | πρῶτοι | τῶν | Ἰουδαίων | κατὰ | τοῦ |
| *hoi* | *prōtoi* | *tōn* | *Ioudaiōn* | *kata* | *tou* |
| the | chiefs | of the | Jews | against | |

In any case, Felix was still motivated by the hope for a big bribe when he sent for Paul more often and conversed with him. It seems certain that whatever Felix brought up in these sessions Paul would use as an opportunity to talk about Jesus and the gospel. All of these sessions must have continued to deal with righteousness, self-control, and the coming judgment.

**24:27.** These conversations with Paul continued over a 2-year period. Then Felix was replaced by Porcius Festus, who arrived in A.D. 59 and remained in office until his death in A.D. 61. The date of Paul's arrest was thus A.D. 57.

Because Felix still wanted to seek favor with the Jews, he left Paul bound (imprisoned), that is, he left him behind as a prisoner. Truly, Felix not only let his desire for money cause him to resist the Holy Spirit, he now allowed his own self-interest to cause him to turn his back on justice in this last act of his regime. But this did not help him. After he returned to Rome the Jews sent complaints to the emperor Nero. Nero would have punished him if it had not been for the influence of his brother Pallas, who interceded on his behalf. (Pallas at the time was a favorite of the emperor.)

Possibly Felix was removed because of the trouble that was going on in Judea. The assassins who believed in using force to kill and overthrow Romans, as well as to kill Jews who seemed to be favored by the Romans, were active again, murdering and robbing or plundering the countryside. A little later another false messiah led a great crowd of adherents into the wilderness in rebellion against Rome, and Festus was forced to go out after them and slaughter them. Thus, while it was fairly quiet in Caesarea there was trouble elsewhere in Judea.

**25:1.** The Jews in Jerusalem had not given up. They still considered Paul their archenemy and wanted his death. So they were waiting to take advantage of the new governor Festus, with the intent of seeking an opportunity for carrying out their plots.

Festus knew Felix had done much to antagonize the Jews, so he was anxious to conciliate them. After Festus took office in Caesarea, he rested a day and then the next day (according to the Jewish method of counting), he went up to Jerusalem. Though Caesarea was the capital of the province over which he was now governor, Jerusalem was still the center as far as the Jews were concerned, and they carried on their religious government through the high priest and the Sanhedrin in Jerusalem.

**25:2.** As soon as Festus arrived, the chief priests and chief men of the Jews informed him of their charges against Paul. These chief Jews were members of the Sanhedrin, probably the Sadducees in it who were friends and allies of the high priest.

Clearly, the act of Felix in leaving Paul imprisoned was not enough to satisfy the Jewish leaders. The Greek indicates they began to

**and communed with him:** . . . he used to converse with him, *Rotherham* . . . and talk with him, *TCNT* . . . and talked things over with him, *Berkeley.*

**27. But after two years:** But at the close of two years, *Williams* . . . when two full years had passed, *Phillips.*

**Porcius Festus came into Felix' room:** Felix was succeeded by Porcius Festus, *RSV* . . . Porcius Festus took the place of Felix, *BB* . . . succeeded, *Beck.*

**and Felix, willing to shew the Jews a pleasure:** . . . and desiring to gain favor with the Jews, Felix, *ASV* . . . to gain popularity, *TCNT* . . . and being desirous of gratifying the Jews, Felix, *Weymouth* . . . and because he wished to curry favor with, *Montgomery* . . . willing to ingratiate, *Campbell* . . . as he wanted to remain in favor with, *Phillips.*

**left Paul bound:** . . . he left Paul a prisoner, *TCNT* . . . in custody, *Moffatt* . . . kept Paul in chains, *BB.*

**1. Now when Festus was come into the province:** Festus, having entered on his duties as governor of the province, *Weymouth* . . . having entered into the government of the province, *Fenton* . . . after entering upon his provincial office, *Berkeley* . . . had taken over his province, *Phillips* . . . after he had taken charge of the province, *Williams C.K.*

**after three days he ascended from Caesarea to Jerusalem:** . . . three days later went up from Caesarea to Jerusalem, *Weymouth* . . . Festus went up from Caesarea to Jerusalem, *Berkeley.*

**2. Then the high priest and the chief men of the Jews:** . . . leading men among the Jews, *TCNT* . . . Jewish leaders, *Moffatt* . . . Jewish elders, *Williams* . . . most prominent Jews, *Berkeley.*

**informed him against Paul:** . . . made manifest to him, *Young* . . . laid information before him against Paul, *Rotherham* . . . informed him of the case against Paul, *Phillips* . . . complained about Paul, *Klingensmith* . . . appeared before him against Paul, *Fenton.*

## Acts 25:3

| 3834.2 name gen masc | 2504.1 conj | 3731.20 verb 3pl indic imperf act | 840.6 prs-pron acc sing masc | 153.26 verb nom pl masc part pres mid |
|---|---|---|---|---|
| Παύλου, | καὶ | παρεκάλουν | αὐτὸν, | 3. αἰτούμενοι |
| *Paulou* | *kai* | *parekaloun* | *auton* | *aitoumenoi* |
| Paul, | and | were urging | him, | asking |

| 5322.4 noun acc sing fem | 2567.1 prep | 840.3 prs-pron gen sing | 3567.1 conj | 3213.4 verb 3sing subj aor mid | 840.6 prs-pron acc sing masc |
|---|---|---|---|---|---|
| χάριν | κατ' | αὐτοῦ, | ὅπως | μεταπέμψηται | αὐτὸν |
| *charin* | *kat'* | *autou* | *hopōs* | *metapempsētai* | *auton* |
| a favor | against | him, | that | he would send for | him |

| 1519.1 prep | 2395.1 name fem | 1731.1 noun acc sing fem | 4020.17 verb nom pl masc part pres act | 335.9 verb inf aor act |
|---|---|---|---|---|
| εἰς | Ἱερουσαλήμ, | ἐνέδραν | ποιοῦντες | ἀνελεῖν |
| *eis* | *Hierousalēm* | *enedran* | *poiountes* | *anelein* |
| to | Jerusalem, | an ambush | forming | to put to death |

| 840.6 prs-pron acc sing masc | 2567.3 prep | 3450.12 art acc sing fem | 3461.4 noun acc sing fem | 3450.5 art nom sing masc | 3173.1 conj | 3631.1 partic |
|---|---|---|---|---|---|---|
| αὐτὸν | κατὰ | τὴν | ὁδόν. | 4. ὁ | μὲν | οὖν |
| *auton* | *kata* | *tēn* | *hodon* | *ho* | *men* | *oun* |
| him | on | the | way. | | | Therefore |

| 5184.1 name nom masc | 552.6 verb 3sing indic aor pass | 4931.31 verb inf pres mid | 3450.6 art acc sing masc | 3834.4 name acc masc |
|---|---|---|---|---|
| Φῆστος | ἀπεκρίθη | τηρεῖσθαι | τὸν | Παῦλον |
| *Phēstos* | *apekrithē* | *tēreisthai* | *ton* | *Paulon* |
| Festus | answered, | to be kept | | Paul |

4.a.**Txt:** 020L,025P,byz.
**Var:** 01ℵ,02A,03B,04C 08E,Lach,Treg,Alf Word,We/Ho,Weis,Sod UBS/⋆

| 1706.1 prep | 2513.2 name dat fem | 1519.1 prep | 2513.3 name acc fem | 1431.6 prs-pron acc sing masc |
|---|---|---|---|---|
| ‘ ἐν | Καισαρείᾳ, | [a⋆ εἰς | Καισάρειαν, ] | ἑαυτὸν |
| *en* | *Kaisareia* | *eis* | *Kaisareian* | *heauton* |
| at | Caesarea, | [ in | Caesarea, ] | himself |

| 1156.2 conj | 3165.18 verb inf pres act | 1706.1 prep | 4882.1 noun dat sing neu | 1594.14 verb inf pres mid | 3450.7 art nom pl masc |
|---|---|---|---|---|---|
| δὲ | μέλλειν | ἐν | τάχει | ἐκπορεύεσθαι. | 5. Οἱ |
| *de* | *mellein* | *en* | *tachei* | *ekporeuesthai* | *Hoi* |
| and | to be about | in | swiftness | to set out. | The |

| 3631.1 partic | 1409.2 adj nom pl masc | 1706.1 prep | 5050.3 prs-pron dat 2pl | 5183.2 verb 3sing indic pres act | 1706.1 prep |
|---|---|---|---|---|---|
| οὖν | ‘ δυνατοὶ | ἐν | ὑμῖν, | φησίν, | [⋆ ἐν |
| *oun* | *dunatoi* | *en* | *humin* | *phēsin* | *en* |
| therefore | powerful | among | you, | says he, | [ among |

| 5050.3 prs-pron dat 2pl | 5183.2 verb 3sing indic pres act | 1409.2 adj nom pl masc | 4633.1 verb nom pl masc part aor act | 1479.1 conj |
|---|---|---|---|---|
| ὑμῖν, | φησίν, | δυνατοὶ ] | συγκαταβάντες, | εἴ |
| *humin* | *phēsin* | *dunatoi* | *sunkatabantes* | *ei* |
| you, | says he, | powerful ] | having gone down, | if |

| 4949.9 intr-pron sing neu | 1498.4 verb 3sing indic pres act | 1706.1 prep | 3450.3 art dat sing | 433.3 noun dat sing masc | 3642.5 dem-pron dat sing masc |
|---|---|---|---|---|---|
| τί | ἐστιν | ἐν | τῷ | ἀνδρὶ | ‘ τούτῳ, |
| *ti* | *estin* | *en* | *tō* | *andri* | *toutō* |
| anything | is | in | the | man | this, |

5.a.**Txt:** 020L,025P,byz.
**Var:** 01ℵ,02A,03B,04C 08E,bo.Lach,Treg,Alf Tisc,We/Ho,Weis,Sod UBS/⋆

| 818.2 adj sing neu | 2693.4 verb 3pl impr pres act | 840.3 prs-pron gen sing | 1298.4 verb nom sing masc part aor act |
|---|---|---|---|
| [a⋆ ἄτοπον ] | κατηγορείτωσαν | αὐτοῦ. | 6. Διατρίψας |
| *atopon* | *katēgoreitōsan* | *autou* | *Diatripsas* |
| [ improper ] | let them accuse | him. | Having spent |

besiege Festus with repeated accusations against Paul. Undoubtedly the fact that Paul had escaped the hands of the more than 40 Jews who had plotted to ambush and kill him was still a sore point with them. Then they began to beg Festus.

**25:3.** They were begging Festus, not for justice, but for a favor. They were definitely trying to get him to help them do something against Paul. They urgently requested him to send for Paul and have him brought to Jerusalem. Again there was a plot to ambush him and kill him along the road.

**25:4.** Festus must have been informed of their previous plot, so he replied that Paul was kept (guarded) in Caesarea where he would soon be going.

From this we see that Festus, though he wanted to please the Jews, did have a sense of justice which would not allow him to yield entirely. Thus, God used Festus to protect Paul from the renewed plots.

It seems strange these Jewish leaders could be so emotionally disturbed about Paul that they would be willing to subvert justice and resort to murder. They knew the law of Moses taught justice and included even establishing of the rights of the weak, the poor, and the foreigners, as well as seeing to it that they were given their rights. In fact, the entire Old Testament teaches the justice of God. He is the true King, and He is concerned about establishing and maintaining what is right and righteous according to His holy and righteous nature.

Obviously, these Jewish leaders were supposing the end justifies the means. But they were letting their own ideas guide them rather than the Word of the Lord.

**25:5.** Festus then suggested that those among them of power or authority go down with him to Caesarea. If there was anything wrong (out of place, or improper) in Paul, let them accuse him there.

Festus yielded to the Jews to a degree. Though he had politely refused to bring Paul up to Jerusalem, he did rule for a new official trial. This does not mean Festus had prejudged the case or accepted their accusations against Paul. He simply said they would be permitted to present their accusations if they believed there was anything improper or out of place in Paul. Nevertheless, by the very language he used, Festus showed he considered their accusations up to that point to be rather trivial from the point of view of Roman law. He did not yet see that Paul had committed any serious crime. Perhaps if the Jews could send their most prominent men who had real ability and influence, they might be able to come up with something.

**and besought him:** ... urged and begged, *Beck* ... and appealed to him, *Fenton.*

**3. And desired favour against him:** ... and asked a favour of him, to Paul's injury, *TCNT* ... asking it as a favour, to Paul's prejudice, *Weymouth* ... as a special favour, *Williams C.K.*

**that he would send for him to Jerusalem:** ... to have Paul brought, *TCNT* ... send him back to, *Fenton* ... send for him to come to, *Williams C.K.*

**laying wait in the way to kill him:** ... intending to, *Williams C.K.* ... making an ambush to kill him on the way, *Rotherham* ... They meant to lay in wait for him and kill him on the way, *Montgomery* ... themselves plotting to murder him on the road, *Fenton.*

**4. But Festus answered:** ... to which Festus replied, *Berkeley* ... told them in reply, *Fenton.*

**that Paul should be kept at Caesarea:** ... would be kept in Caesarea, *Beck* ... that Paul was under guard, *Berkeley* ... be detained at, *Fenton.*

**and that he himself would depart shortly thither:** ... meant to leave for Caesarea before long, *Moffatt* ... he himself was soon to leave, *Williams C.K.* ... he was himself about to return there at an early date, *Fenton* ... intended to go there shortly, *RSV.*

**5. Let them therefore, said he, which among you are able:** They therefore among you (saith he) who are in power, *Rotherham* ... He also added, Let those therefore who are in authority among you, *Fenton* ... So let the influential men among you, *TCNT* ... Let those then, he said, who are in authority among you, *Montgomery* ... let the proper officials, *Williams C.K.*

**go down with me:** ... come down, *Williams C.K.*

**and accuse this man, if there be any wickedness in him:** ... charge him formally with it, *TCNT* ... and charge the man with whatever crime he has committed, *Moffatt* ... they can indict him, *Fenton* ... present their charges against the man, if he has done anything wrong, *Williams C.K.*

## Acts 25:7

6.a.**Txt:** 020L,025P,byz. **Var:** 01ℵ,02A,03B,04C Gries,Lach,Treg,Alf Word,Tisc,We/Ho,Weis Sod,UBS/☆

| 1156.2 conj | 1706.1 prep | 840.2 prs-pron dat pl | 2232.1 noun fem | 3979.3 adj comp pl | 2211.1 conj | 3620.3 partic |
|---|---|---|---|---|---|---|
| δὲ | ἐν | αὐτοῖς | ἡμέρας | ʻ πλείους | ἢ | [a☆ οὐ |
| de | en | autois | hēmeras | pleious | ē | ou |
| and | among | them | days | more | than | [ not |

| 3979.3 adj comp pl | 3501.1 num card | 2211.1 conj | 1171.1 num card | 2568.20 verb nom sing masc part aor act | 1519.1 prep |
|---|---|---|---|---|---|
| πλείους | ὀκτὼ | ἢ ] | δέκα, | καταβὰς | εἰς |
| pleious | oktō | ē | deka | katabas | eis |
| more than | eight | or ] | ten, | having gone down | to |

| 2513.3 name acc fem | 3450.11 art dat sing fem | 1872.1 adv | 2495.9 verb nom sing masc part aor act | 1894.3 prep | 3450.2 art gen sing |
|---|---|---|---|---|---|
| Καισάρειαν, | τῇ | ἐπαύριον | καθίσας | ἐπὶ | τοῦ |
| Kaisareian | tē | epaurion | kathisas | epi | tou |
| Caesarea, | on the | next day | having sat | on | the |

| 961.1 noun gen sing neu | 2724.3 verb 3sing indic aor act | 3450.6 art acc sing masc | 3834.4 name acc masc | 70.26 verb inf aor pass |
|---|---|---|---|---|
| βήματος | ἐκέλευσεν | τὸν | Παῦλον | ἀχθῆναι. |
| bēmatos | ekeleusen | ton | Paulon | achthēnai |
| judgment seat | he commanded | | Paul | to be brought. |

7.a.**Var:** 01ℵ,02A,03B 04C,020L,Lach,Treg Alf,Word,Tisc,We/Ho Weis,Sod,UBS/☆

| 3716.8 verb gen sing masc part aor mid | 1156.2 conj | 840.3 prs-pron gen sing | 3889.1 verb 3pl indic aor act | 840.6 prs-pron acc sing masc |
|---|---|---|---|---|
| 7. παραγενομένου | δὲ | αὐτοῦ, | περιέστησαν | [a☆+ αὐτὸν ] |
| paragenomenou | de | autou | periestēsan | auton |
| Having come | and | he, | stood round | [ him ] |

| 3450.7 art nom pl masc | 570.3 prep | 2389.2 name gen pl neu | 2568.26 verb nom pl masc part perf act | 2428.2 name-adj nom pl masc |
|---|---|---|---|---|
| οἱ | ἀπὸ | Ἱεροσολύμων | καταβεβηκότες | Ἰουδαῖοι, |
| hoi | apo | Hierosolumōn | katabebēkotes | Ioudaioi |
| the | from | Jerusalem | having come down | Jews, |

7.b.**Txt:** Steph **Var:** 01ℵ,02A,03B,04C 08E,020L,025P,byz. Gries,Lach,Treg,Alf Word,Tisc,We/Ho,Weis Sod,UBS/☆

| 4044.17 adj pl neu | 2504.1 conj | 920.3 adj pl neu | 156.1 noun pl neu | 157.1 noun pl neu |
|---|---|---|---|---|
| πολλὰ | καὶ | βαρέα | ʻ αἰτιάματα | [b☆ αἰτιώματα ] |
| polla | kai | barea | aitiamata | aitiōmata |
| many | and | weighty | charges | [ accusations ] |

7.c.**Txt:** 025P,byz. **Var:** 01ℵ,02A,03B,04C Lach,Treg,Alf,Tisc We/Ho,Weis,Sod UBS/☆

| 5179.8 verb nom pl masc part pres act | 2567.3 prep | 3450.2 art gen sing | 3834.2 name gen masc | 2671.4 verb nom pl masc part pres act |
|---|---|---|---|---|
| ʻ φέροντες | κατὰ | τοῦ | Παύλου, | [c☆ καταφέροντες ] |
| pherontes | kata | tou | Paulou | katapherontes |
| bringing | against | | Paul, | [ bringing ] |

| 3614.17 rel-pron pl neu | 3620.2 partic | 2453.13 verb 3pl indic imperf act | 579.3 verb inf aor act | 620.3 verb gen sing masc part pres mid |
|---|---|---|---|---|
| ἃ | οὐκ | ἴσχυον | ἀποδεῖξαι, | 8. ʻ ἀπολογουμένου |
| ha | ouk | ischuon | apodeixai | apologoumenou |
| which | not | they were able | to prove: | defending |

8.a.**Txt:** 025P,byz. **Var:** 01ℵ,02A,03B,04C Lach,Treg,Alf,Tisc We/Ho,Weis,Sod UBS/☆

| 840.3 prs-pron gen sing | 3450.2 art gen sing | 3834.2 name gen masc | 620.3 verb gen sing masc part pres mid | 3617.1 conj |
|---|---|---|---|---|
| αὐτοῦ, | [a☆ τοῦ | Παύλου | ἀπολογουμένου ] | Ὅτι |
| autou | tou | Paulou | apologoumenou | Hoti |
| he, | | [ Paul | defending, ] | That |

| 3641.1 conj | 1519.1 prep | 3450.6 art acc sing masc | 3414.4 noun acc sing masc | 3450.1 art gen pl | 2428.3 name-adj gen pl masc | 3641.1 conj |
|---|---|---|---|---|---|---|
| Οὔτε | εἰς | τὸν | νόμον | τῶν | Ἰουδαίων | οὔτε |
| Oute | eis | ton | nomon | tōn | Ioudaiōn | oute |
| neither | against | the | law | of the | Jews | nor |

**25:6.** Festus spent some time in Jerusalem ("more than ten days"), probably just getting acquainted with the city. He may have visited the Fortress of Antonia and acquainted himself with the Roman officers and soldiers stationed there. He probably stayed in the palace built by Herod the Great. This magnificent palace stood on the west side of Jerusalem south of the modern Jaffa gate. It had been the official residence of Pilate whenever he visited Jerusalem.

The next day after returning to Caesarea Festus sat on the judgment seat, that is, on his official judge's throne or tribunal. This meant he was calling for a new official trial. Then he had Paul brought in. The Jews who had come down from Jerusalem were also present.

Festus could do this because Felix had never officially handed down a decision. He had only indicated he would carry out further investigation, which he did not do. So, Festus felt justified in calling this new official trial.

The judgment seat or judicial bench was usually on a raised platform in order to give the judge the prominent place and to give an appearance of power and authority. In this case it was in the palace built by Herod the Great, where Paul was also kept.

The same word used here was used by the rabbis of the judgment seat of God and by the New Testament of the judgment seat of Christ. Actually, although neither Festus nor the Jewish leaders seemed to realize it, they were all standing before the judgment seat of God in a real sense. That is, God knew what was going on. God saw the hearts of the Jews. He knew their plots. He knew their concern for themselves and their position and reputations. He saw that Festus was torn between a desire for justice and a desire to please and conciliate the Jews.

But God also saw the heart of Paul. He knew how Paul was committed to Christ and to the preaching of the truth of the gospel. Moreover, God was working out His plan, and it was about to come to an important turning point, though neither Paul, the Jews, nor Festus knew it.

**25:7.** The Jerusalem Jews stood around Festus, making many weighty charges or accusations against Paul. They made it clear they considered these charges very important, but they could prove none of them. The charges against Paul were undoubtedly similar to those Tertullus had brought before Felix.

What follows implies they did add one new accusation, however. Paul had rights and privileges as a Roman citizen. These Jews hoped to counteract those rights by adding the charge that Paul had committed offenses against Caesar, that is, against the current Roman emperor, Nero. But again they had no proof.

**25:8.** It is clear Paul had no trouble defending himself. Luke merely summarized Paul's defense. Paul contended he had not sinned in any way against the Jewish law, the temple, nor against Caesar (including the whole Roman government).

**6. And when he had tarried among them more than ten days:** After spending among them not more than eight or ten days, *Rotherham.*

**he went down unto Caesarea:** . . . and then went, *Phillips.*

**and the next day:** On the day after his arrival, *Phillips.*

**sitting on the judgment seat:** . . . after taking his seat on the judge's bench, *Williams* . . . he took his place in court, *Williams C.K.*

**commanded Paul to be brought:** . . . ordered, *RSV* . . . and sent for Paul, *BB* . . . gave orders that Paul should be brought in, *Williams C.K.* . . . to be brought before him, *TCNT.*

**7. And when he was come:** As soon as he arrived, *Phillips* . . . When he came in, *Williams C.K.* . . . But when he was produced, *Fenton.*

**the Jews which came down from Jerusalem stood round about:** . . . collected round him, *Berkeley* . . . stood up on all sides of him, *Phillips.*

**and laid many and grievous complaints against Paul:** . . . and presented their charges—numerous and weighty, *Berkeley* . . . and made all sorts of serious statements against him, *BB* . . . charging him with many and serious offenses, *Norlie* . . . bringing many heavy accusations, *Campbell* . . . bringing forward many serious accusations, *Phillips* . . . bringing forward numerous as well as serious charges, *Fenton.*

**which they could not prove:** . . . which they failed to establish, *TCNT* . . . were unable to substantiate, *Weymouth* . . . which they were not able to prove, *Rotherham* . . . which were not supported by the facts, *BB.*

**8. While he answered for himself:** While Paul said in his defense, *ASV* . . . Paul, in his defense, maintained, *Phillips* . . . In reply, Paul said, *Weymouth* . . . Paul's defence was, *Williams C.K.*

**Neither against the law of the Jews, neither against the temple, nor yet against Caesar, have I offended any thing at all:** . . . have not committed any offense against the, *TCNT* . . . have committed no crime against, *Montgomery*

# Acts 25:9

| 1519.1 prep | 3450.16 art sing neu | 2387.3 adj sing neu | 3641.1 conj | 1519.1 prep | 2512.3 name acc masc | 4948.10 indef-pron sing neu |
|---|---|---|---|---|---|---|
| εἰς | τὸ | ἱερὸν | οὔτε | εἰς | Καίσαρά | τι |
| *eis* | *to* | *hieron* | *oute* | *eis* | *Kaisara* | *ti* |
| against | the | temple | nor | against | Caesar | anything |

| 262.11 verb indic aor act | 3450.5 art nom sing masc | 5184.1 name nom masc | 1156.2 conj | 3450.4 art dat pl | 2428.4 name-adj dat pl masc |
|---|---|---|---|---|---|
| ἥμαρτον. | **9.** Ὁ | Φῆστος | δὲ | ⸀ τοῖς | Ἰουδαίοις |
| *hēmarton* | *Ho* | *Phēstos* | *de* | *tois* | *Ioudaiois* |
| I sinned. | | Festus | but, | with the | Jews |

| 2286.12 verb nom sing masc part pres act | 2286.12 verb nom sing masc part pres act | 3450.4 art dat pl | 2428.4 name-adj dat pl masc | 5322.4 noun acc sing fem |
|---|---|---|---|---|
| θέλων | [☆ θέλων | τοῖς | Ἰουδαίοις ] | χάριν |
| *thelōn* | *thelōn* | *tois* | *Ioudaiois* | *charin* |
| wishing | [ wishing | with the | Jews ] | favor |

| 2667.2 verb inf aor mid | 552.12 verb nom sing masc part aor pass | 3450.3 art dat sing | 3834.3 name dat masc |
|---|---|---|---|
| καταθέσθαι | ἀποκριθεὶς | τῷ | Παύλῳ |
| *katathesthai* | *apokritheis* | *tō* | *Paulō* |
| to acquire for himself | having answered | | Paul |

| 1500.5 verb 3sing indic aor act | 2286.2 verb 2sing indic pres act | 1519.1 prep | 2389.1 name | 303.17 verb nom sing masc part aor act |
|---|---|---|---|---|
| εἶπεν, | Θέλεις | εἰς | Ἱεροσόλυμα | ἀναβὰς, |
| *eipen* | *Theleis* | *eis* | *Hierosoluma* | *anabas* |
| said, | Are you willing | to | Jerusalem | having gone up |

9.a.**Txt:** 020L,025P,byz. **Var:** 01ℵ,02A,03B,04C 08E,Lach,Treg,Alf Word,Tisc,We/Ho,Weis Sod,UBS/☆

| 1550.1 adv | 3875.1 prep | 3642.2 dem-pron gen pl | 2892.32 verb inf pres mid | 2892.37 verb inf aor pass |
|---|---|---|---|---|
| ἐκεῖ | περὶ | τούτων | ⸀ κρίνεσθαι | [a☆ κριθῆναι ] |
| *ekei* | *peri* | *toutōn* | *krinesthai* | *krithēnai* |
| there | concerning | these things | to be judged | [ idem ] |

| 1894.2 prep | 1466.3 prs-pron gen 1sing | 1500.5 verb 3sing indic aor act | 1156.2 conj | 3450.5 art nom sing masc | 3834.1 name nom masc |
|---|---|---|---|---|---|
| ἐπ' | ἐμοῦ; | **10.** Εἶπεν | δὲ | ὁ | Παῦλος, |
| *ep'* | *emou* | *Eipen* | *de* | *ho* | *Paulos* |
| before | me? | Said | but | | Paul, |

10.a.**Var:** 01ℵ-org,03B Tisc,We/Ho,Weis UBS/☆

| 2449.26 verb sing part perf act | 1894.3 prep | 3450.2 art gen sing | 961.1 noun gen sing neu | 2512.1 name gen masc |
|---|---|---|---|---|
| [a☆+ Ἑστὼς ] | Ἐπὶ | τοῦ | βήματος | Καίσαρός |
| *Hestōs* | *Epi* | *tou* | *bēmatos* | *Kaisaros* |
| [ Standing ] | Before | the | judgment seat | of Caesar |

10.b.**Txt:** 01ℵ-corr,02A 03B,04C,08E,020L 025P,etc.byz.Sod **Var:** 01ℵ-org,Tisc We/Ho,Weis,UBS/☆

| 2449.26 verb sing part perf act | 1498.2 verb 1sing indic pres act | 3619.1 adv | 1466.6 prs-pron acc 1sing | 1158.1 verb 3sing indic pres act | 2892.32 verb inf pres mid |
|---|---|---|---|---|---|
| ⸂b Ἑστὼς ⸃ | εἰμι, | οὗ | με | δεῖ | κρίνεσθαι. |
| *Hestōs* | *eimi* | *hou* | *me* | *dei* | *krinesthai* |
| standing | I am, | where | me | it is necessary | to be judged. |

10.c.**Txt:** 02A,04C,08E 020L,025P,byz.Sod **Var:** 01ℵ,03B,Treg,Tisc We/Ho,Weis,UBS/☆

| 2428.5 name-adj acc pl masc | 3625.6 num card neu | 90.5 verb 1sing indic aor act | 90.20 verb 1sing indic perf act |
|---|---|---|---|
| Ἰουδαίους | οὐδὲν | ⸀ ἠδίκησα, | [c ἠδίκηκα, ] |
| *Ioudaious* | *ouden* | *ēdikēsa* | *ēdikēka* |
| To Jews | nothing | I did wrong, | [ I have done wrong, ] |

| 5453.1 conj | 2504.1 conj | 4622.1 prs-pron nom 2sing | 2537.1 adj comp sing neu | 1906.2 verb 2sing indic pres act | 1479.1 conj |
|---|---|---|---|---|---|
| ὡς | καὶ | σὺ | κάλλιον | ἐπιγινώσκεις. | **11.** εἰ |
| *hōs* | *kai* | *su* | *kallion* | *epiginōskeis* | *ei* |
| as | also | you | very well | know. | If |

It must have been hard for Paul to listen to the same old accusations again and again. He must have felt like crying out, "Enough is enough!" But he had learned long before that God's grace is sufficient under even the most trying circumstances (2 Corinthians 12:9). He was in a position of weakness now as a prisoner, but God's strength was there to help him answer with a graciousness, wisdom, and maturity that was in strong contrast to the way the Jews were acting in their accusations.

Later, Festus showed that Paul bore witness to Christ's death and resurrection as well. As before, Paul never let an opportunity for witness to go by. (See 25:19.) He was always looking for some way to bring in the good news about Jesus and His salvation. Defending the gospel and presenting Christ was always more important to him than defending himself. Yet he did not do it in an offensive way. He always tried to show the meekness and love of Christ in his own attitude as he proclaimed the truth about Jesus, and the Holy Spirit inspired and helped him as he did so.

**25:9.** Festus, then, desired to do the Jews a favor that would give them pleasure. He wanted to gain favor with them. So he responded to Paul by asking him if he would be willing to go up to Jerusalem for another trial before him. That is, he would do as the tribune Lysias had done. He would bring in the whole Sanhedrin and let them bring their accusations against Paul before him.

Like Lysias and Felix, Porcius Festus was trying to avoid giving a decision. He saw that the Jewish leaders were loud, persistent, and determined. He must have also realized that since they were so persistent in bringing false charges against Paul, they would probably be just as persistent and determined in bringing false charges against him if he did not satisfy them. It was easy for Festus to yield to the crowd against his better judgment, the judgment he had expressed when he had earlier refused to have Paul brought up to Jerusalem.

Once again, it is evident that those who seem to be in the majority at the moment are not always right. Paul was all alone in the courtroom. He had no lawyer to defend him. Obviously, none of his faithful friends were allowed. But the Holy Spirit was with him.

**25:10.** Paul, of course, knew what it would mean if he were to go up to Jerusalem. Friends probably had informed him of the new plot to ambush and kill him on the way. Luke, at least, knew about it, and others must have.

Paul, however, knew he had one recourse to keep out of the clutches of the Jewish leaders. Paul recognized that the authority behind the judgment seat or tribunal where Festus sat was Caesar's (that is, it was the current Roman emperor's). As a Roman citizen he had a right to appeal to Caesar. To the Jews he had done no harm or injury, as Festus well knew. Paul's emphasis was that it was necessary, proper, and fitting for him as a Roman to be judged at Caesar's tribunal.



... I have done nothing wrong, *Williams C.K.* ... have I offended in any way, *Fenton* ... I have committed no offense in any way against, *Phillips.*

**9. But Festus, willing to do the Jews a pleasure:** Festus, as he wished to gain popularity with the Jews, *TCNT* ... Then Festus, in hope of winning the favor of the Jews, *Norlie* ... to conciliate the favor, *Murdock* ... wishing to gratify, *Wilson* ... wishing to do the Jews a favour, *Williams C.K.* ... wishing to gain the goodwill of the Jews, *Phillips* ... anxious to ingratiate himself with the Jews, *Fenton.*

**answered Paul, and said:** ... interrupted Paul with the question, *TCNT* ... spoke direct to Paul, *Phillips.*

**Wilt thou go up to Jerusalem:** Art thou willing, *Rotherham* ... Are you prepared to, *Phillips* ... Do you want to, *Beck* ... Do you desire to go, *Fenton.*

**and there be judged of these things before me?:** ... and be tried on these charges before me there, *TCNT* ... and stand your trial over these matters in my presence there? *Phillips* ... to be tried in respect of these matters before me? *Fenton* ... and take your trial there on these charges before me? *Williams C.K.*

**10. Then said Paul, I stand at Caesar's judgment seat:** But Paul said, I am standing before, *RSV* ... Paul replied, I am standing in Caesar's court, *Phillips* ... the seat of Caesar's authority, *BB* ... at Caesar's tribunal, *Berkeley* ... in the Emperor's court, *Williams C.K.* ... before the tribunal of the Emperor, *Fenton.*

**where I ought to be judged:** ... where alone I ought to be tried, *Weymouth* ... and that is where I should be judged, *Phillips.*

**to the Jews have I done no wrong:** I have not wronged the Jews, *TCNT* ... I have done the Jews no injury of any sort, *Weymouth* ... no harm, *Phillips* ... I have never injured Judeans, *Fenton.*

**as thou very well knowest:** ... as you yourself are well aware, *TCNT* ... you know that perfectly well, *Moffatt* ... as also you have clearly ascertained, *Fenton.*

11.a.**Txt:** 020L,025P,byz.
**Var:** 01ℵ,02A,03B,04C
08E,bo.Lach,Treg,Alf
Word,Tisc,We/Ho,Weis
Sod,UBS/☆

| **3173.1** conj | **1056.1** conj | **3631.1** partic | **90.1** verb 1sing indic pres act | **2504.1** conj | **510.1** adj sing |
|---|---|---|---|---|---|
| μὲν | ʽ γὰρ | [ᵃ☆ οὖν ] | ἀδικῶ | καὶ | ἄξιον |
| *men* | *gar* | *oun* | *adikō* | *kai* | *axion* |
| indeed | for | [ therefore ] | I am doing wrong | and | worthy |

| **2265.2** noun gen sing masc | **4097.23** verb 1sing indic perf act | **4948.10** indef-pron sing neu | **3620.3** partic | **3729.1** verb 1sing indic pres mid | **3450.16** art sing neu |
|---|---|---|---|---|---|
| θανάτου | πέπραχά | τι, | οὐ | παραιτοῦμαι | τὸ |
| *thanatou* | *pepracha* | *ti* | *ou* | *paraitoumai* | *to* |
| of death | have done | anything, | not | I do avoid | the |

| **594.20** verb inf aor act | **1479.1** conj | **1156.2** conj | **3625.6** num card neu | **1498.4** verb 3sing indic pres act | **3614.1** rel-pron gen pl |
|---|---|---|---|---|---|
| ἀποθανεῖν· | εἰ | δὲ | οὐδέν | ἔστιν | ὧν |
| *apothanein* | *ei* | *de* | *ouden* | *estin* | *hōn* |
| to die; | if | but | nothing | there is | of which |

| **3642.7** dem-pron nom pl masc | **2693.3** verb 3pl indic pres act | **1466.2** prs-pron gen 1sing | **3625.2** num card nom masc | **1466.6** prs-pron acc 1sing |
|---|---|---|---|---|
| οὗτοι | κατηγοροῦσίν | μου, | οὐδείς | με |
| *houtoi* | *katēgorousin* | *mou* | *oudeis* | *me* |
| they | accuse | me, | no one | me |

| **1404.4** verb 3sing indic pres mid | **840.2** prs-pron dat pl | **5319.10** verb inf aor mid | **2512.3** name acc masc | **1926.1** verb 1sing indic pres mid |
|---|---|---|---|---|
| δύναται | αὐτοῖς | χαρίσασθαι. | Καίσαρα | ἐπικαλοῦμαι. |
| *dunatai* | *autois* | *charisasthai* | *Kaisara* | *epikaloumai* |
| can | to them | to give up. | Caesar | I appeal. |

| **4966.1** adv | **3450.5** art nom sing masc | **5184.1** name nom masc | **4665.3** verb nom sing masc part aor act | **3196.3** prep | **3450.2** art gen sing |
|---|---|---|---|---|---|
| **12.** Τότε | ὁ | Φῆστος | συλλαλήσας | μετὰ | τοῦ |
| *Tote* | *ho* | *Phēstos* | *sullalēsas* | *meta* | *tou* |
| Then | | Festus, | having conferred | with | the |

| **4675.1** noun gen sing neu | **552.6** verb 3sing indic aor pass | **2512.3** name acc masc | **1926.19** verb 2sing indic perf mid | **1894.3** prep |
|---|---|---|---|---|
| συμβουλίου, | ἀπεκρίθη, | Καίσαρα | ἐπικέκλησαι, | ἐπὶ |
| *sumbouliou* | *apekrithē* | *Kaisara* | *epikeklēsai* | *epi* |
| council, | answered, | Caesar | you have appealed, | to |

| **2512.3** name acc masc | **4057.32** verb 2sing indic fut mid | **2232.6** noun gen pl fem | **1156.2** conj | **1224.2** verb gen pl fem part aor mid |
|---|---|---|---|---|
| Καίσαρα | πορεύσῃ. | **13.** Ἡμερῶν | δὲ | διαγενομένων |
| *Kaisara* | *poreusē* | *Hēmerōn* | *de* | *diagenomenōn* |
| Caesar | you shall go. | Days | and | having passed |

| **4948.4** indef-pron gen pl | **66.1** name nom sing masc | **3450.5** art nom sing masc | **928.1** noun nom sing masc | **2504.1** conj | **952.1** name nom fem |
|---|---|---|---|---|---|
| τινῶν, | Ἀγρίππας | ὁ | βασιλεὺς | καὶ | Βερνίκη |
| *tinōn* | *Agrippas* | *ho* | *basileus* | *kai* | *Bernikē* |
| certain, | Agrippa | the | king | and | Bernice |

| **2628.3** verb 3pl indic aor act | **1519.1** prep | **2513.3** name acc fem | **776.12** verb nom pl masc part fut mid |
|---|---|---|---|
| κατήντησαν | εἰς | Καισάρειαν, | ʽ ἀσπασόμενοι |
| *katēntēsan* | *eis* | *Kaisareian* | *aspasomenoi* |
| came down | to | Caesarea, | greeting |

13.a.**Txt:** 044,1739,byz.it.
sa.
**Var:** p74,01ℵ,02A,03B
08E,020L,025P,bo.Treg
Alf,Tisc,We/Ho,Weis
Sod,UBS/☆

| **776.11** verb nom pl masc part aor mid | **3450.6** art acc sing masc | **5184.4** name acc masc | **5453.1** conj | **1156.2** conj |
|---|---|---|---|---|
| [ᵃ☆ ἀσπασάμενοι ] | τὸν | Φῆστον. | **14.** ὡς | δὲ |
| *aspasamenoi* | *ton* | *Phēston* | *hōs* | *de* |
| [ having greeted ] | | Festus. | When | and |

**25:11.** Paul then stated his case for his appeal to Caesar. If he had done anything worthy of death, he would not object to the death penalty.

Paul had faced death often before. In the great resurrection chapter, 1 Corinthians 15, he told how he stood in jeopardy (danger, peril) every hour and he died daily, that is, he faced death every day. To the unbeliever, life is a dead-end street. If he makes a billion dollars he will still die and lose it all. The believer, on the other hand, makes God's work his work. The believer looks forward to his resurrection and knows God will finish His work.

But since there was nothing true about the acts of which Paul was accused, no one had the power and authority to turn him over to the Jews as a favor to them. Therefore, Paul appealed to Caesar.

Up to this point Nero, the emperor at this time, had good advisers, and Paul had reason to believe he would get a fair trial in Rome. But that was not the only reason he wanted to go to Rome. Jesus had assured him he would witness for Him in Rome (23:11).

**25:12.** Festus may not have been pleased with Paul's demand to be sent to Caesar. Festus knew it would not please the Jews. But he conferred with his advisers on the provincial council. They must have made it clear that Paul was within his rights. There was nothing Festus could do but send him to Caesar.

Citizens of Rome were given the right of appeal as early as 509 B.C. At that time they could appeal to the assembly when a judge pronounced sentence on any serious crime. Later on, in 449 and 299 B.C., further enactments reinforced this right of appeal. Then when Rome became an empire the governors or procurators of the provinces had the duty to grant the privilege of a trial at Rome when any Roman citizen demanded it. At first, the trial might be either before the Roman senate or before the emperor, but at this time it was before the emperor.

**25:13.** Some days later, King Agrippa, with his widowed sister Bernice, came to Caesarea to bring official greetings and pay his respects to the new governor of Judea.

Herod Agrippa II, also known as M. Julius Agrippa II, was the son of Herod Agrippa I, the Herod of 12:1-23. The emperor Claudius made him king of Chalcis between the Lebanon and Anti-Lebanon mountains in A.D. 50. Later (A.D. 53) the emperor made him king of the tetrarchy of Philip, east of the Sea of Galilee, and of Lysanius, west and northwest of Damascus. Then in A.D. 56, Nero added cities around the Sea of Galilee, including parts of the Decapolis and Peraea. Agrippa II died in Rome in A.D. 100, still greatly honored as a "praetor" or high officer of Rome.

Bernice ("Victorious") was married first to her uncle, Herod of Chalcis. After his death she married Polemon, king of Cilicia, but deserted him and came to live with her brother, Herod Agrippa II. She lived a very immoral life. Later she became the mistress of the emperor Vespasian and then of the emperor Titus.

**11. For if I be an offender:** If, however, I am breaking the law, *TCNT.*

**or have committed any thing worthy of death:** . . . any offense deserving death, *TCNT* . . . for which I ought to die, *Montgomery* . . . some crime which deserves the death penalty, *Phillips.*

**I refuse not to die:** I am ready for death, *BB* . . . I do not ask to escape it, *TCNT*. . . I am not begging to keep from dying, *Williams.*

**but if there be none of these things:** But if there is no truth, *Weymouth* . . . But as in fact there is no truth, *Phillips.*

**whereof these accuse me:** . . . in the accusations of these people, *TCNT* . . . in what these men allege against me, *Weymouth* . . . in any of their charges against me, *Moffatt.*

**no man may deliver me unto them:** . . . no man hath power to give me unto them as a favour, *Rotherham* . . . I will let no man turn me over to them, *Norlie* . . . no one may sacrifice me to their pleasure, *Murdock* . . . to surrender me to them, *JB* . . . to dispose of me to gratify them, *Fenton.*

**I appeal unto Caesar:** Let my cause come before Caesar, *BB.*

**12. Then Festus, when he had conferred with the council:** . . . having consulted with his council, *HBIE* . . . after a conference with his advisors, *Phillips.*

**answered:** . . . replied to Paul, *Phillips.*

**Hast thou appealed unto Caesar? unto Caesar shalt thou go:** You have said, Let my case come before Caesar; to Caesar you will go, *BB.*

**13. And after certain days:** Some days later, *TCNT* . . . A short time after this, *Weymouth.*

**king Agrippa and Bernice came unto Caesarea:** King Herod Agrippa II, *SEB* . . . arrived at Caesarea, *ASV.*

**to salute Festus:** . . . and paid a visit of congratulation to Festus, *TCNT* . . . to pay a complimentary visit to, *Weymouth* . . . to pay official respects, *Williams* . . . to bid Festus welcome, *Berkeley* . . . to congratulate Festus, *Fenton.*

## Acts 25:15

| 3979.3 adj comp pl | 2232.1 noun fem | 1298.6 verb 3pl indic imperf act | 1550.1 adv | 3450.5 art nom sing masc | 5184.1 name nom masc |
|---|---|---|---|---|---|
| πλείους | ἡμέρας | διέτριβον | ἐκεῖ | ὁ | Φῆστος |
| *pleious* | *hēmeras* | *dietribon* | *ekei* | *ho* | *Phēstos* |
| many | days | they were staying | there | | Festus |

| 3450.3 art dat sing | 928.3 noun dat sing masc | 392.2 verb 3sing indic aor mid | 3450.17 art pl neu | 2567.3 prep | 3450.6 art acc sing masc |
|---|---|---|---|---|---|
| τῷ | βασιλεῖ | ἀνέθετο | τὰ | κατὰ | τὸν |
| *tō* | *basilei* | *anetheto* | *ta* | *kata* | *ton* |
| the | king | laid before | the things | relating to | |

| 3834.4 name acc masc | 2978.15 verb nom sing masc part pres act | 433.1 noun nom sing masc | 4949.3 intr-pron nom sing | 1498.4 verb 3sing indic pres act |
|---|---|---|---|---|
| Παῦλον | λέγων, | Ἀνήρ | τίς | ἐστιν |
| *Paulon* | *legōn* | *Anēr* | *tis* | *estin* |
| Paul, | saying, | A man | certain | there is |

| 2611.12 verb nom sing masc part perf mid | 5097.3 prep | 5181.2 name gen masc | 1192.1 noun nom sing masc | 3875.1 prep |
|---|---|---|---|---|
| καταλελειμμένος | ὑπὸ | Φήλικος | δέσμιος, | **15.** περὶ |
| *kataleleimmenos* | *hupo* | *Phēlikos* | *desmios* | *peri* |
| having been left | by | Felix | a prisoner, | concerning |

| 3614.2 rel-pron gen sing | 1090.50 verb gen sing part aor mid | 1466.2 prs-pron gen 1sing | 1519.1 prep | 2389.1 name |
|---|---|---|---|---|
| οὗ, | γενομένου | μου | εἰς | Ἱεροσόλυμα, |
| *hou* | *genomenou* | *mou* | *eis* | *Hierosoluma* |
| whom, | having been | my | in | Jerusalem, |

| 1702.4 verb 3pl indic aor act | 3450.7 art nom pl masc | 744.5 noun pl masc | 2504.1 conj | 3450.7 art nom pl masc | 4104.5 adj comp nom pl masc |
|---|---|---|---|---|---|
| ἐνεφάνισαν | οἱ | ἀρχιερεῖς | καὶ | οἱ | πρεσβύτεροι |
| *enephanisan* | *hoi* | *archiereis* | *kai* | *hoi* | *presbuteroi* |
| made a report | the | chief priests | and | the | elders |

| 3450.1 art gen pl | 2428.3 name-adj gen pl masc | 153.26 verb nom pl masc part pres mid | 2567.1 prep | 840.3 prs-pron gen sing | 1343.2 noun acc sing fem |
|---|---|---|---|---|---|
| τῶν | Ἰουδαίων, | αἰτούμενοι | κατ' | αὐτοῦ | ‹ δίκην· |
| *tōn* | *Ioudaiōn* | *aitoumenoi* | *kat'* | *autou* | *dikēn* |
| of the | Jews, | asking | against | him | judgment: |

15.a.**Txt:** 08E,020L 025P,byz. **Var:** 01ℵ,02A,03B,04C Lach,Treg,Alf,Word Tisc,We/Ho,Weis,Sod UBS/☆

| 2584.1 noun acc sing fem | 4242.1 prep | 3614.8 rel-pron acc pl masc | 552.4 verb 1sing indic aor pass | 3617.1 conj |
|---|---|---|---|---|
| [a☆ καταδίκην· ] | **16.** πρὸς | οὓς | ἀπεκρίθην, | ὅτι |
| *katadikēn* | *pros* | *hous* | *apekrithēn* | *hoti* |
| [ condemnation: ] | to | whom | I answered, | That |

| 3620.2 partic | 1498.4 verb 3sing indic pres act | 1478.1 noun sing neu | 4371.5 name-adj dat pl masc | 5319.3 verb inf pres mid | 4948.5 indef-pron |
|---|---|---|---|---|---|
| οὐκ | ἔστιν | ἔθος | Ῥωμαίοις | χαρίζεσθαί | τινα |
| *ouk* | *estin* | *ethos* | *Rhōmaiois* | *charizesthai* | *tina* |
| not | it is | a custom | with Romans | to give up | any |

16.a.**Txt:** 020L,025P,byz. **Var:** 01ℵ,02A,03B,04C 08E,bo.Gries,Lach,Treg Alf,Word,Tisc,We/Ho Weis,Sod,UBS/☆

| 442.4 noun acc sing masc | 1519.1 prep | 677.3 noun acc sing fem | 4109.1 adv | 2211.1 conj | 3450.5 art nom sing masc |
|---|---|---|---|---|---|
| ἄνθρωπον | ‹a εἰς | ἀπώλειαν, › | πρὶν | ἢ | ὁ |
| *anthrōpon* | *eis* | *apōleian* | *prin* | *ē* | *ho* |
| man | to | destruction, | before | | the |

| 2693.14 verb nom sing masc part pres mid | 2567.3 prep | 4241.1 noun sing neu | 2174.11 verb 3sing opt pres act | 3450.8 art acc pl masc |
|---|---|---|---|---|
| κατηγορούμενος | κατὰ | πρόσωπον | ἔχοι | τοὺς |
| *katēgoroumenos* | *kata* | *prosōpon* | *echoi* | *tous* |
| being accused | according to | face | may have | the |

**25:14.** Though Agrippa II was educated in Rome, he was a Jew, and the emperor Claudius had given him (in A.D. 50) the government of the temple in Jerusalem. This caused Festus to look on Agrippa II as an authority in the Jewish religion.

Since they were there many days, Festus decided to lay Paul's case before Agrippa, desiring to consult with him about it. Festus would need to write an opinion to send with Paul when he went as a prisoner to Rome. He felt Agrippa could help him.

King Agrippa's general attitude and friendliness must have encouraged Festus to do this. King Agrippa never showed the sort of cold disdain that some of the other Herods often did with regard to their subjects. He helped the Jews whenever he could. For example, he persuaded the emperor to restore the custody of the high priestly robes to the Jews. The Romans had allowed them to be used only on certain occasions.

**25:15.** After telling how Felix had left Paul imprisoned, Festus related how the chief priests and elders of the Jews in Jerusalem informed him (that is, brought charges or accusations against Paul and asked for a sentence of condemnation).

What Festus indicated is that the Jewish leaders in Jerusalem did not really want another trial for Paul. What they wanted was for Festus to accept their accusations at face value and pronounce the death sentence for Paul without any further trial or investigation.

The Jewish leaders were trying the same tactics they used when they brought Jesus before Pilate. When Pilate asked them what formal charge they were bringing against Jesus, they said if He were not an evildoer or criminal they would not have brought Jesus to him.

Now this was a new generation of Jewish leaders and a new high priest. But they had not learned anything from the way the previous generation treated Jesus. They still thought the Romans ought to accept their decision without investigation. It seems they thought the death penalty would get rid of both Paul and the gospel he preached, just as the previous generation had thought that crucifying Jesus would get rid of Him and His teachings.

**25:16.** Festus answered the Jewish leaders by saying it was not the manner or custom of the Romans to hand over any human being (to the death penalty) before the accused person was brought face to face with his accusers and given opportunity to defend himself with respect to the accusation made against him.

Because of his education in the imperial palace in Rome, King Agrippa would be very familiar with Roman law and custom. Actually, it had developed over several hundred years and had often been modified to meet changing needs of the republic and then of the empire. It was eventually codified, and the Roman law codes have influenced the laws of western Europe and America. But at this time much was in the hands of the governor or the king of the particular part of the Roman Empire.

**14. And when they had been there many days:** And as they were spending more days there, *Rotherham* . . . and, during their rather lengthy stay, *Weymouth* . . . They prolonged their stay for some days, *Phillips* . . . Since they were staying there some time, *Williams C.K.*

**Festus declared Paul's cause unto the king:** Festus acquainted the king with Paul's situation, *Berkeley* . . . put Paul's case before the king, *Williams C.K.* . . . submitted the case of Paul to, *Fenton.*

**saying, There is a certain man:** . . . remarking, *Fenton* . . . I have a man here, he said, *Phillips* . . . There is a man here, *Williams C.K.*

**left in bonds by Felix:** . . . left a prisoner by Felix, *ASV* . . . who was left in prison by Felix, *Williams C.K.*

**15. About whom, when I was at Jerusalem, the chief priests and the elders of the Jews informed me:** . . . respecting whom, on my arrival in Jerusalem...Judean senators, *Fenton* . . . made allegations against him, *Phillips* . . . laid information against him, *Williams C.K.*

**desiring to have judgment against him:** . . . demanding judgement against him, *TCNT* . . . and continued to ask, *Williams* . . . and demanded his condemnation, *Moffatt* . . . and asked me to condemn him, *Beck* . . . asked for sentence to be pronounced against him, *Fenton* . . . pass judgment upon him in their favor, *Murdock.*

**16. To whom I answered:** I replied to them, *Williams C.K.*

**It is not the manner of the Romans:** . . . the practice of Romans, *TCNT* . . . that with Romans it is not customary, *Berkeley* . . . the custom, *Williams C.K.*

**to deliver any man to die:** . . . to give up any man to the accusers, *TCNT* . . . for punishment, *Weymouth* . . . to hand a man over gratuitously, *Berkeley.*

**before that he which is accused have the accusers face to face:** . . . until he has been face to face with those who are attacking him, *BB* . . . until he has met those that charge him face to face, *Williams C.K.*

| **2695.4** noun acc pl masc | **4964.4** noun acc sing masc | **4885.1** conj | **621.2** noun gen sing fem | **2956.22** verb 3sing opt aor act |
|---|---|---|---|---|
| κατηγόρους, | τόπον | τε | ἀπολογίας | λάβοι |
| *katēgorous* | *topon* | *te* | *apologias* | *laboi* |
| accusers, | opportunity | and | of defense | he may get |

| **3875.1** prep | **3450.2** art gen sing | **1455.1** noun gen sing neu | **4755.7** verb gen pl masc part aor act |
|---|---|---|---|
| περὶ | τοῦ | ἐγκλήματος. | **17.** συνελθόντων |
| *peri* | *tou* | *enklēmatos* | *sunelthontōn* |
| concerning | the | accusation. | Having come together |

17.a.**Txt:** p74,01ℵ,02A 08E,020L,025P,etc.byz. Tisc,Sod
**Var:** 03B,We/Ho,Weis UBS/☆

| **3631.1** partic | **840.1** prs-pron gen pl | **1743.1** adv | **309.1** noun acc sing fem | **3235.5** num card acc fem |
|---|---|---|---|---|
| οὖν | ⸂[a] αὐτῶν ⸃ | ἐνθάδε, | ἀναβολὴν | μηδεμίαν |
| *oun* | *autōn* | *enthade* | *anabolēn* | *mēdemian* |
| therefore | they | here, | delay | none |

| **4020.69** verb nom sing masc part aor mid | **3450.11** art dat sing fem | **1819.1** adv | **2495.9** verb nom sing masc part aor act | **1894.3** prep | **3450.2** art gen sing |
|---|---|---|---|---|---|
| ποιησάμενος, | τῇ | ἑξῆς | καθίσας | ἐπὶ | τοῦ |
| *poiēsamenos* | *tē* | *hexēs* | *kathisas* | *epi* | *tou* |
| having made, | the | next | having sat | on | the |

| **961.1** noun gen sing neu | **2724.2** verb 1sing indic aor act | **70.26** verb inf aor pass | **3450.6** art acc sing masc | **433.4** noun acc sing masc |
|---|---|---|---|---|
| βήματος | ἐκέλευσα | ἀχθῆναι | τὸν | ἄνδρα· |
| *bēmatos* | *ekeleusa* | *achthēnai* | *ton* | *andra* |
| judgment seat | I commanded | to be brought | the | man; |

| **3875.1** prep | **3614.2** rel-pron gen sing | **2449.45** verb nom pl masc part aor pass | **3450.7** art nom pl masc | **2695.2** noun nom pl masc |
|---|---|---|---|---|
| **18.** περὶ | οὗ | σταθέντες | οἱ | κατήγοροι |
| *peri* | *hou* | *stathentes* | *hoi* | *katēgoroi* |
| concerning | whom | having stood up | the | accusers |

18.a.**Txt:** 025P,byz.
**Var:** 01ℵ,02A,03B,04C 08E,020L,Lach,Treg Alf,Word,Tisc,We/Ho Weis,Sod,UBS/☆

| **3625.5** num card acc fem | **155.3** noun acc sing fem | **2002.4** verb 3pl indic imperf act | **5179.22** verb 3pl indic imperf act | **3614.1** rel-pron gen pl |
|---|---|---|---|---|
| οὐδεμίαν | αἰτίαν | ⸀ ἐπέφερον | [[a]☆ ἔφερον ] | ὧν |
| *oudemian* | *aitian* | *epepheron* | *epheron* | *hōn* |
| no | charge | were bringing | [ idem ] | of which |

| **5120.2** verb indic imperf act | **1466.1** prs-pron nom 1sing | **1466.1** prs-pron nom 1sing | **5120.2** verb indic imperf act |
|---|---|---|---|
| ⸀ ὑπενόουν | ἐγὼ· | [☆ ἐγὼ | ὑπενόουν ] |
| *hupenooun* | *egō* | *egō* | *hupenooun* |
| was supposing | I; | [ I | was supposing; ] |

18.b.**Var:** 01ℵ-corr,03B 08E,Treg,We/Ho,Weis UBS/☆

| **4050.4** adj gen pl | **2196.3** noun pl neu | **1156.2** conj | **4948.5** indef-pron | **3875.1** prep |
|---|---|---|---|---|
| [[b]☆+ πονηρῶν, ] | **19.** ζητήματα | δέ | τινα | περὶ |
| *ponērōn* | *zētēmata* | *de* | *tina* | *peri* |
| [ evil, ] | questions | but | certain | concerning |

| **3450.10** art gen sing fem | **2375.9** adj fem | **1170.1** noun gen sing fem | **2174.42** verb indic imperf act | **4242.1** prep | **840.6** prs-pron acc sing masc |
|---|---|---|---|---|---|
| τῆς | ἰδίας | δεισιδαιμονίας | εἶχον | πρὸς | αὐτὸν, |
| *tēs* | *idias* | *deisidaimonias* | *eichon* | *pros* | *auton* |
| the | own | system of religion | they had | against | him, |

| **2504.1** conj | **3875.1** prep | **4948.1** indef-pron gen sing | **2400.2** name masc | **2325.5** verb gen sing masc part perf act | **3614.6** rel-pron acc sing masc |
|---|---|---|---|---|---|
| καὶ | περί | τινος | Ἰησοῦ | τεθνηκότος, | ὃν |
| *kai* | *peri* | *tinos* | *Iēsou* | *tethnēkotos* | *hon* |
| and | concerning | a certain | Jesus | having died, | whom |

It was also part of the Roman custom to bring in experts who would help the judge, governor, or king make his decisions. So it was not out of order for Festus to ask Agrippa for his opinion.

Actually, what Festus said about Roman law and custom was part of the Jewish law and custom as well. When the chief priests and Pharisees wanted to arrest Jesus, the officers sent to arrest Him were so impressed by His teaching that they did not do so. This upset the Pharisees and they remarked that the crowds who were following Jesus did not know the Law and were accursed. But Nicodemus responded by asking whether their Law judged anyone before giving a hearing and finding out what he was doing (John 7:44-51). The Pharisees were implying that because they knew the Law they had more sense than to believe in Jesus. But they were wanting to kill Jesus without a trial, something which was contrary to the Law.

**25:17.** Festus then related how, after refusing to give the Jews the favor they desired, and after telling them that Paul, as a Roman, deserved to face his accusers, the Jewish leaders came to Caesarea.

Festus had not delayed or postponed the matter. The next day he had taken his seat at the tribunal and given the command or order that Paul be brought out. Festus thus made it clear to Agrippa there had been no laxity on his part. He had done his duty as a Roman governor as he put Paul on trial.

**25:18.** Then when the accusers stood up (took their stand), Festus, as a Roman, was surprised they did not charge Paul with any of the evil things he supposed they would.

The Roman courts considered criminal cases to include extortion, embezzlement, treason, corrupt practices, murder, fraud, and assault. Since the Jewish leaders were obviously wanting Paul killed, Festus supposed Paul must be guilty of something that would be in the same class as these criminal practices. But Paul was not guilty of anything like any of these, and the Jewish leaders did not try to accuse him of any such matters.

**25:19.** Instead, the Jewish leaders had questions against Paul concerning what Festus, as a Roman pagan, considered to be controversial questions or issues concerning "their superstition." Superstition was a word which could be used in a good sense, for it originally meant simply fear of or reverence for a divine being. But the word came to have a bad sense also. The context must determine which meaning is intended. In this case, since King Agrippa was a Jew, it is not likely that Festus would be using the word in an unfavorable sense. It may be better to translate his words "they had some points of dispute about their religion."

Festus added that the dispute also was concerning a certain Jesus who had died (who was put to death), but whom Paul alleged to live (claimed or asserted to be alive).

**and have license to answer for himself:** . . . and have had opportunity to make his defence, *ASV* . . . and an opportunity afforded him of, *Fenton* . . . been given the opportunity of defending himself, *Phillips.*

**concerning the crime laid against him:** . . . on the charges made against him, *Phillips.*

**17. Therefore, when they were come hither:** So they met here, *TCNT* . . . When, therefore, a number of them came here, *Weymouth* . . . Since these Jews came back here with me, *Phillips.*

**without any delay on the morrow I sat on the judgment seat:** I lost no time to occupy the judgment seat, *Berkeley* . . . I didn't delay matters, *Adams* . . . I did not postpone the case, *Williams C.K.* . . . I wasted no time but on the very next day I took my seat on the bench, *Phillips.*

**and commanded the man to be brought forth:** . . . gave orders for, *Williams C.K.* . . . and ordered the man to be brought before me, *TCNT.*

**18. Against whom when the accusers stood up:** . . . and standing up around him, *HBIE* . . . But when his accusers got up to speak, *Phillips.*

**they brought none accusation of such things:** . . . they did not charge him with misdemeanours, *Weymouth* . . . charged him with none of the crimes, *Williams C.K.* . . . not able to substantiate, *Murdock.*

**as I supposed:** . . . such as I had expected, *TCNT* . . . as I had in mind, *BB* . . . as I had anticipated, *Phillips.*

**19. But had certain questions against him of their own superstition:** . . . in dispute between them, *TCNT* . . . But they quarrelled with him, *Weymouth* . . . in regard to their system of religion, *Norlie* . . . they only had certain differences of opinion, *Williams C.K.* . . . Their differences with him were about their own religion, *Phillips.*

**and of one Jesus, which was dead:** . . . and concerning one Jesus, who had died, *Rotherham* . . . and about some dead man called Jesus, *TCNT* . . . one Jesus deceased, *Douay.*

| 5173.3 verb 3sing indic imperf act | 3450.5 art nom sing masc | 3834.1 name nom masc | 2180.19 verb inf pres act | 633.2 verb nom sing masc part pres mid |
|---|---|---|---|---|
| ἔφασκεν | ὁ | Παῦλος | ζῆν. | 20. ἀπορούμενος |
| ephasken | ho | Paulos | zēn | aporoumenos |
| was affirming | | Paul | to be alive. | Being perplexed |

20.a.**Txt:** 04C,08E,020L byz.
**Var:** 01ℵ,02A,03B,025P 33,Treg,Tisc,We/Ho Weis,Sod,UBS/☆

| 1156.2 conj | 1466.1 prs-pron nom 1sing | 1519.1 prep | 3450.12 art acc sing fem | 3875.1 prep | 3642.1 dem-pron gen sing |
|---|---|---|---|---|---|
| δὲ | ἐγὼ | (a εἰς ) | τὴν | περὶ | ( τούτου |
| de | egō | eis | tēn | peri | toutou |
| and | I | to | the | concerning | this |

20.b.**Txt:** 025P,byz.
**Var:** 01ℵ,02A,03B,04C 08E,020L,Lach,Treg Alf,Word,Tisc,We/Ho Weis,Sod,UBS/☆

| 3642.2 dem-pron gen pl | 2197.2 noun acc sing fem | 2978.25 verb indic imperf act | 1479.1 conj | 1007.7 verb 3sing opt pres mid |
|---|---|---|---|---|
| [b☆ τούτων ] | ζήτησιν | ἔλεγον, | εἰ | βούλοιτο |
| toutōn | zētēsin | elegon | ei | bouloito |
| [ these things ] | inquiry | was saying, | If | he be willing |

20.c.**Txt:** 020L,025P,byz.
**Var:** 01ℵ,02A,03B,04C 08E,Lach,Treg,Alf Word,Tisc,We/Ho,Weis Sod,UBS/☆

| 4057.15 verb inf pres mid | 1519.1 prep | 2395.1 name fem | 2389.1 name |
|---|---|---|---|
| πορεύεσθαι | εἰς | ( Ἱερουσαλήμ, | [c☆ Ἱεροσόλυμα ] |
| poreuesthai | eis | Hierousalēm | Hierosoluma |
| to go | to | Jerusalem, | [ idem ] |

| 2517.1 conj | 2892.32 verb inf pres mid | 3875.1 prep | 3642.2 dem-pron gen pl | 3450.2 art gen sing | 1156.2 conj |
|---|---|---|---|---|---|
| κἀκεῖ | κρίνεσθαι | περὶ | τούτων. | 21. τοῦ | δὲ |
| kakei | krinesthai | peri | toutōn | tou | de |
| and there | to be judged | concerning | these things. | | But |

| 3834.2 name gen masc | 1926.15 verb gen sing masc part aor mid | 4931.33 verb inf aor pass | 840.6 prs-pron acc sing masc | 1519.1 prep | 3450.12 art acc sing fem |
|---|---|---|---|---|---|
| Παύλου | ἐπικαλεσαμένου | τηρηθῆναι | αὐτὸν | εἰς | τὴν |
| Paulou | epikalesamenou | tērēthēnai | auton | eis | tēn |
| Paul | having appealed for | to be kept | himself | for | the |

| 3450.2 art gen sing | 4430.1 name-adj gen sing masc | 1227.1 noun acc sing fem | 2724.2 verb 1sing indic aor act | 4931.31 verb inf pres mid |
|---|---|---|---|---|
| τοῦ | Σεβαστοῦ | διάγνωσιν, | ἐκέλευσα | τηρεῖσθαι |
| tou | Sebastou | diagnōsin | ekeleusa | tēreisthai |
| | of Augustus | cognizance, | I commanded | to be kept |

21.a.**Txt:** 020L,025P,byz.
**Var:** 01ℵ,02A,03B,04C 08E,Lach,Treg,Alf Word,Tisc,We/Ho,Weis Sod,UBS/☆

| 840.6 prs-pron acc sing masc | 2175.1 conj | 3614.2 rel-pron gen sing | 3854.4 verb 1sing act | 374.3 verb 1sing subj aor act |
|---|---|---|---|---|
| αὐτὸν | ἕως | οὗ | ( πέμψω | [a☆ ἀναπέμψω ] |
| auton | heōs | hou | pempsō | anapempsō |
| him | until | which | I might send | [ idem ] |

| 840.6 prs-pron acc sing masc | 4242.1 prep | 2512.3 name acc masc | 66.1 name nom sing masc | 1156.2 conj | 4242.1 prep |
|---|---|---|---|---|---|
| αὐτὸν | πρὸς | Καίσαρα. | 22. Ἀγρίππας | δὲ | πρὸς |
| auton | pros | Kaisara | Agrippas | de | pros |
| him | to | Caesar. | Agrippa | and | to |

22.a.**Txt:** 04C,08E,020L 025P,byz.bo.Sod
**Var:** 01ℵ,02A,03B,Lach Treg,Alf,Tisc,We/Ho Weis,UBS/☆

| 3450.6 art acc sing masc | 5184.4 name acc masc | 5183.4 verb 3sing indic act | 1007.16 verb 1sing indic imperf mid | 2504.1 conj | 840.5 prs-pron nom sing masc |
|---|---|---|---|---|---|
| τὸν | Φῆστον | (a ἔφη, ) | Ἐβουλόμην | καὶ | αὐτὸς |
| ton | Phēston | ephē | Eboulomēn | kai | autos |
| | Festus | said, | I was desiring | also | myself |

22.b.**Txt:** 04C,08E,020L 025P,byz.
**Var:** 01ℵ,02A,03B,bo. Lach,Treg,Alf,Tisc We/Ho,Weis,Sod UBS/☆

| 3450.2 art gen sing | 442.2 noun gen sing masc | 189.36 verb inf aor act | 3450.5 art nom sing masc | 1156.2 conj | 833.1 adv |
|---|---|---|---|---|---|
| τοῦ | ἀνθρώπου | ἀκοῦσαι. | (b Ὁ | δέ, ) | Αὔριον, |
| tou | anthrōpou | akousai | Ho | de | Aurion |
| the | man | to hear. | The | and, | Tomorrow |

The truth of the resurrection of Jesus was, of course, the central point at issue, though Festus seemed almost to hesitate to tell King Agrippa about it and added it as if it were something of an afterthought. To Festus, as to the Greek philosophers in Athens, the idea of the Resurrection was something foreign to their thinking. Festus, however, did not mock or make fun of the idea, although he obviously neither understood nor believed Paul's claim.

**25:20.** Festus, however, did not admit to King Agrippa it was because he wanted to seek favor with the Jews that he had asked Paul to go to Jerusalem for another trial before the Jewish priests and elders of the Sanhedrin. Instead, he told Agrippa he was at a loss as to how to investigate these matters. There was truth in this statement. Probably, this was the first time Festus had ever come up against religious questions in a criminal case. Since the Romans had decreed Judaism to be a legal religion in the Roman Empire and had turned over decisions on Jewish religious matters to the Sanhedrin and the high priest, it is not likely Festus ever thought he would have to face a case like Paul's.

**25:21.** Next Festus reported how Paul had refused to go to Jerusalem and had appealed to be kept for the decision of the Augustus, the emperor.

*Caesar* was the family name of the famous Gaius Julius Caesar who was assassinated in Rome in 44 B.C. His grandnephew Octavius became the first Roman emperor and took the name *Augustus Caesar.* "Augustus" then became a title applied to his successors who were also Caesars. *Augustus* means "worthy to be reverenced." It implied respect and veneration that was usually given to their gods and to sacred things. But the title soon became used to encourage the worship of the emperor.

Because of Paul's appeal, Festus ordered Paul to be kept under guard until he could send him to Caesar, that is, to Nero.

The original name of Nero was Lucius Domitius Ahenobarbus. His mother Agrippina was the sister of the emperor Caligula and niece of the emperor Claudius. His father died when Nero was 3 years old, and by intrigue Agrippina married Claudius and had Nero adopted as his son. Claudius was poisoned, and Nero became emperor in A.D. 54. During the first 5 years of his reign, good advisers helped him initiate many reforms, though Nero himself began to indulge in all kinds of excesses.

**25:22.** Agrippa apparently had heard of Paul and of Jesus and had been wishing for an opportunity to hear Paul. This desire pleased Festus, and he promised to arrange a special hearing.

Agrippa spent his early life in Rome and then reigned to the north and northeast of Palestine. As a Jew he must have made pilgrimages to Jerusalem. The Law required all male Jews to go there for the Feasts of Passover, Pentecost, and Tabernacles.

**whom Paul affirmed to be alive:** . . . whom Paul declared to be alive, *TCNT, Williams C.K.* . . . but, so Paul maintained, is now alive, *Weymouth* . . . but whom Paul affirmed over and over was alive, *Montgomery* . . . whom Paul affirmed to be alive, *Douay* . . . asserted to be alive, *Fenton.*

**20. And because I doubted of such manner of questions:** I was at a loss how to investigate such questions, *Weymouth* . . . As I felt uncertain about the proper investigation of such issues, *Berkeley* . . . I was puzzled, *Beck* . . . I was perplexed, *Montgomery* . . . And being myself at a loss how to deal with such questions, *Fenton* . . . was myself uncertain how to enquire into such matters, *Williams C.K.*

**I asked him whether he would go to Jerusalem:** I asked Paul if he were willing to go, *TCNT* . . . I made the suggestion to him to go, *BB.*

**and there be judged of these matters:** . . . and there stand his trial on these matters, *Weymouth* . . . and be tried there on these charges, *Moffatt.*

**21. But when Paul had appealed:** Paul, however, appealed, *TCNT.*

**to be reserved unto the hearing of Augustus:** . . . that his case be retained for examination by Augustus, *Berkeley* . . . to have his case reviewed for the decision of the Emperor, *Montgomery* . . . for his case to be deferred for the decision of, *Fenton* . . . appealed to be kept under guard, *Williams C.K.* . . . the emperor's decision, *Norlie* . . . for his Majesty's decision, *Williams.*

**I commanded him to be kept:** I ordered him, *Rotherham* . . . to be detained in custody, *TCNT* . . . to be held, *Berkeley.*

**till I might send him to Caesar:** . . . until I could send him up to, *Williams C.K.*

**22. Then Agrippa said unto Festus:** Agrippa remarked to Festus, *Berkeley.*

**I would also hear the man myself:** I have a desire to give the man a hearing myself, *BB.*

**To morrow, said he, thou shalt hear him:** . . . you may give him a hearing, *BB.*

## Acts 25:23

| 5183.2 verb 3sing indic pres act | 189.18 verb sing act | 840.3 prs-pron gen sing | 3450.11 art dat sing fem | 3631.1 partic |
|---|---|---|---|---|
| φησίν, | ἀκούσῃ | αὐτοῦ. | **23.** Τῇ | οὖν |
| *phēsin* | *akousē* | *autou* | *Tē* | *oun* |
| he says, | you shall hear | him. | On the | therefore |

| 1872.1 adv | 2048.14 verb gen sing masc part aor act | 3450.2 art gen sing | 66.2 name sing masc | 2504.1 conj | 3450.10 art gen sing fem |
|---|---|---|---|---|---|
| ἐπαύριον | ἐλθόντος | τοῦ | Ἀγρίππα | καὶ | τῆς |
| *epaurion* | *elthontos* | *tou* | *Agrippa* | *kai* | *tēs* |
| next day | having come | | Agrippa | and | |

| 952.2 name gen fem | 3196.3 prep | 4044.10 adj gen sing fem | 5163.1 noun gen sing fem | 2504.1 conj | 1511.17 verb gen pl masc part aor act |
|---|---|---|---|---|---|
| Βερνίκης | μετὰ | πολλῆς | φαντασίας, | καὶ | εἰσελθόντων |
| *Bernikēs* | *meta* | *pollēs* | *phantasias* | *kai* | *eiselthontōn* |
| Bernice, | with | great | pomp, | and | having entered |

23.a.**Txt:** 020L,025P,byz.
**Var:** 01ℵ,02A,03B,04C
08E,Lach,Treg,Alf,Tisc
We/Ho,Weis,Sod
UBS/⋆

| 1519.1 prep | 3450.16 art sing neu | 199.1 noun sing neu | 4713.1 prep | 4885.1 conj | 3450.4 art dat pl |
|---|---|---|---|---|---|
| εἰς | τὸ | ἀκροατήριον, | σύν | τε | ⸂[a] τοῖς ⸃ |
| *eis* | *to* | *akroatērion* | *sun* | *te* | *tois* |
| into | the | hall of audience, | with | both | the |

| 5341.6 noun dat pl masc | 2504.1 conj | 433.8 noun dat pl masc | 3450.4 art dat pl | 2567.1 prep | 1835.1 noun acc sing fem |
|---|---|---|---|---|---|
| χιλιάρχοις | καὶ | ἀνδράσιν | τοῖς | κατ' | ἐξοχὴν |
| *chiliarchois* | *kai* | *andrasin* | *tois* | *kat'* | *exochēn* |
| chief captains | and | men | the | according to | eminence |

23.b.**Txt:** 08E,020L
025P,byz.
**Var:** 01ℵ,02A,03B,04C
Lach,Treg,Alf,Word
Tisc,We/Ho,Weis,Sod
UBS/⋆

| 1498.24 verb dat pl masc part pres act | 3450.10 art gen sing fem | 4032.2 noun gen sing fem | 2504.1 conj | 2724.6 verb gen sing masc part aor act |
|---|---|---|---|---|
| ⸂[b] οὖσιν ⸃ | τῆς | πόλεως, | καὶ | κελεύσαντος |
| *ousin* | *tēs* | *poleōs* | *kai* | *keleusantos* |
| being | of the | city, | and | having commanded |

| 3450.2 art gen sing | 5184.2 name gen masc | 70.25 verb 3sing indic aor pass | 3450.5 art nom sing masc | 3834.1 name nom masc | 2504.1 conj |
|---|---|---|---|---|---|
| τοῦ | Φήστου | ἤχθη | ὁ | Παῦλος. | **24.** καί |
| *tou* | *Phēstou* | *ēchthē* | *ho* | *Paulos* | *kai* |
| | Festus | was brought | | Paul. | And |

| 5183.2 verb 3sing indic pres act | 3450.5 art nom sing masc | 5184.1 name nom masc | 66.2 name sing masc | 928.5 noun voc sing masc |
|---|---|---|---|---|
| φησιν | ὁ | Φῆστος, | Ἀγρίππα | βασιλεῦ, |
| *phēsin* | *ho* | *Phēstos* | *Agrippa* | *basileu* |
| says | | Festus, | Agrippa | king |

| 2504.1 conj | 3820.7 adj nom pl masc | 3450.7 art nom pl masc | 4691.1 verb nom pl masc part pres act | 2231.3 prs-pron dat 1pl | 433.6 noun nom pl masc |
|---|---|---|---|---|---|
| καὶ | πάντες | οἱ | συμπαρόντες | ἡμῖν | ἄνδρες, |
| *kai* | *pantes* | *hoi* | *sumparontes* | *hēmin* | *andres* |
| and | all | the | being present with | us | men, |

| 2311.1 verb 2pl pres act | 3642.6 dem-pron acc sing masc | 3875.1 prep | 3614.2 rel-pron gen sing | 3820.17 adj sing neu |
|---|---|---|---|---|
| θεωρεῖτε | τοῦτον | περὶ | οὗ | ⸀ πᾶν |
| *theōreite* | *touton* | *peri* | *hou* | *pan* |
| you see | this one | concerning | whom | all |

24.a.**Txt:** 020L,025P,byz.
**Var:** 01ℵ,02A,03B,04C
08E,33,Lach,Treg,Alf
Word,Tisc,We/Ho,Weis
Sod,UBS/⋆

| 533.7 adj sing neu | 3450.16 art sing neu | 3988.1 noun sing neu | 3450.1 art gen pl | 2428.3 name-adj gen pl masc | 1777.3 verb 3pl indic aor act |
|---|---|---|---|---|---|
| [a⋆ ἅπαν ] | τὸ | πλῆθος | τῶν | Ἰουδαίων | ἐνέτυχόν |
| *hapan* | *to* | *plēthos* | *tōn* | *Ioudaiōn* | *enetuchon* |
| [ idem ] | the | multitude | of the | Jews | pleaded |

The multitudes of Jewish believers in Jerusalem and Judea could not have escaped his notice. There were also assemblies of believers in Galilee, Peraea, Samaria, and the Decapolis. No doubt, the believers who were scattered after the death of Stephen had established assemblies in his kingdom as well. Agrippa surely had to know something about Jesus. Since there was a great deal of travel and communication between churches, the news about Paul's travels and the churches he established must have been spread in all directions too. So it is not strange that Agrippa wanted to hear Paul.

**25:23.** The next day King Agrippa and his sister Bernice came with great pomp and display. They took it as an opportunity to let the city of Caesarea and all the Jews and Gentiles there see the glory of a Jewish king. So they made a great parade from wherever they were staying to the palace of Herod where Paul was being kept and where the governor Festus had a large audience hall. They paraded in with all their royal robes and with all their attendants in a great show of magnificent pageantry.

Joining in with them were the tribunes of the Roman army stationed in Caesarea and all the prominent men of the city as well. It must have been an impressive sight.

The population of the city included Jews, Jewish and Gentile believers in Christ, Romans, and a great many Syrians. The city had a theater, an amphitheater, and a Roman temple, all built by Herod the Great. It was a cosmopolitan city with a very mixed population. The Gentiles among them had caused trouble already for the Jews under Felix. One reason for all this display of pomp and ceremony may have been to encourage the Jews and show the Gentiles that a neighboring Jewish king had power. If so, it did not have any permanent effect, for it was only a few years later that the Syrians vented their jealousy in a wholesale massacre of Jews in the city. (This was another thing that helped to bring about the revolt of the Jews that ended with the destruction of Jerusalem in A.D. 70.)

**25:24.** After Paul was brought in, Festus addressed King Agrippa and all the others who were present, calling on them to look at this man about whom the whole multitude of the Jerusalem Jews petitioned, both in Jerusalem and at Caesarea, crying out that he must not live any longer.

Festus was quite dramatic in this and exaggerated the truth for the sake of the effect. Actually, the multitude of the Jews in Jerusalem, and the population of Jerusalem as a whole, had not cried out that Paul must be killed. The mob in the temple had when the Jews from the Roman province of Asia stirred them up. But there were many other Jews, including the thousands of Jewish believers who had no part in this. After that, the Jews who demanded the death penalty were primarily the chief priests and the Sadducean members of the Sanhedrin.

**23. And on the morrow:** So the next day, *TCNT* . . . Accordingly, the following day, *Berkeley* . . . When the next day came, *Phillips.*

**when Agrippa was come, and Bernice:** . . . proceeded, *Williams C.K.* . . . arrived, *MLNT.*

**with great pomp:** . . . in full state, *TCNT* . . . with great pomp and ceremony, *Phillips* . . . with great display, *MLNT, Rotherham* . . . in great state, *Williams C.K.* . . . with stately pomp, *Fenton.*

**and was entered into the place of hearing:** . . . and they had entered the audience-chamber, *Rotherham* . . . to the hall of audience, *Williams C.K.* . . . the audience hall, *MLNT.*

**with the chief captains, and principal men of the city:** . . . in the company of military officers, *NAB* . . . superior officers and the principal people, *TCNT* . . . together with the officers of high rank and the chief men of the town, *Williams C.K.* . . . with an escort of military officers and prominent townsmen, *Phillips* . . . with the Generals and the principal men of the city, *Fenton* . . . accompanied by the chief military men and the prominent citizens of the city, *MLNT.*

**at Festus' commandment Paul was brought forth:** . . . by the order of Festus Paul was brought before them, *TCNT* . . . was also brought in, *Fenton.*

**24. And Festus said, King Agrippa, and all men which are here present with us:** . . . and then he spoke, *Phillips* . . . The governor began to speak, *NAB* . . . and all other men now present with us, *Fenton.*

**ye see this man:** . . . you are looking at the person, *Berkeley* . . . look at this man! *NAB* . . . you see before you, *Williams C.K.*

**about whom all the multitude of the Jews have dealt with me:** . . . about whom the whole mass of the Judeans...have distracted me, *Fenton* . . . on whose account the whole constituency of the Jews have made complaint to me, *Berkeley, MLNT* . . . the whole Jewish nation...have made complaint to me, *Williams C.K.* . . . the whole Jewish people...have petitioned me, *Phillips.*

## Acts 25:25

| 1466.4 prs-pron dat 1sing | 1706.1 prep | 4885.1 conj | 2389.3 name dat pl neu | 2504.1 conj | 1743.1 adv |
|---|---|---|---|---|---|
| μοι | ἐν | τε | Ἱεροσολύμοις | καὶ | ἐνθάδε, |
| *moi* | *en* | *te* | *Hierosolumois* | *kai* | *enthade* |
| with me | in | both | Jerusalem | and | here, |

24.b.**Txt:** 04C,08E,020L 025P,byz.Sod
**Var:** 01ℵ,02A,03B,Lach Treg,Tisc,We/Ho,Weis UBS/☆

| 1901.1 verb nom pl masc part pres act | 987.2 verb nom pl masc part pres act | 3231.1 partic | 1158.5 verb inf pres act | 2180.19 verb inf pres act |
|---|---|---|---|---|
| ⸂ ἐπιβοῶντες | [b☆ βοῶντες ] | μὴ | δεῖν | ⸂ ζῆν |
| *epiboōntes* | *boōntes* | *mē* | *dein* | *zēn* |
| crying out | [ crying ] | not | to be necessary | to live |

| 840.6 prs-pron acc sing masc | 840.6 prs-pron acc sing masc | 2180.19 verb inf pres act | 3239.1 adv | 1466.1 prs-pron nom 1sing | 1156.2 conj |
|---|---|---|---|---|---|
| αὐτὸν | [☆ αὐτὸν | ζῆν ] | μηκέτι | 25. ἐγὼ | δὲ |
| *auton* | *auton* | *zēn* | *mēketi* | *egō* | *de* |
| he | [ him | to live ] | no longer. | I | but |

25.a.**Txt:** 01ℵ-org,020L 025P,byz.
**Var:** 01ℵ-corr,02A,03B 04C,08E,Lach,Treg,Alf Word,Tisc,We/Ho,Weis Sod,UBS/☆

| 2608.9 verb nom sing masc part aor mid | 2608.14 verb 1sing indic aor mid | 3235.6 num card neu | 510.1 adj sing |
|---|---|---|---|
| ⸂ καταλαβόμενος | [a☆ κατελαβόμην ] | μηδὲν | ἄξιον |
| *katalabomenos* | *katelabomēn* | *mēden* | *axion* |
| having perceived | [ perceived ] | nothing | worthy |

| 2265.2 noun gen sing masc | 840.6 prs-pron acc sing masc | 840.6 prs-pron acc sing masc | 2265.2 noun gen sing masc | 4097.24 verb inf perf act |
|---|---|---|---|---|
| ⸂ θανάτου | αὐτὸν | [☆ αὐτὸν | θανάτου ] | πεπραχέναι, |
| *thanatou* | *auton* | *auton* | *thanatou* | *peprachenai* |
| of death | him | [ him | of death ] | to have done, |

25.b.**Txt:** 020L,025P,byz.
**Var:** 01ℵ,02A,03B,04C 08E,bo.Lach,Treg,Alf Word,Tisc,We/Ho,Weis Sod,UBS/☆

25.c.**Txt:** 08E,020L,025P byz.bo.
**Var:** 01ℵ,02A,03B,04C Lach,Treg,Alf,Tisc We/Ho,Weis,Sod UBS/☆

| 2504.1 conj | 840.3 prs-pron gen sing | 1156.2 conj | 3642.1 dem-pron gen sing | 1926.15 verb gen sing masc part aor mid | 3450.6 art acc sing masc |
|---|---|---|---|---|---|
| ⸂b καὶ ⸃ | αὐτοῦ | δὲ | τούτου | ἐπικαλεσαμένου | τὸν |
| *kai* | *autou* | *de* | *toutou* | *epikalesamenou* | *ton* |
| also | himself | and | this one | having appealed to | |

| 4430.2 name-adj acc sing masc | 2892.13 verb 1sing indic aor act | 3854.3 verb inf pres act | 840.6 prs-pron acc sing masc | 3875.1 prep |
|---|---|---|---|---|
| Σεβαστὸν, | ἔκρινα | πέμπειν | ⸂c αὐτόν· ⸃ | 26. περὶ |
| *Sebaston* | *ekrina* | *pempein* | *auton* | *peri* |
| Augustus, | I determined | to send | him, | concerning |

| 3614.2 rel-pron gen sing | 798.2 adj sing neu | 4948.10 indef-pron sing neu | 1119.15 verb inf aor act | 3450.3 art dat sing | 2935.3 noun dat sing masc |
|---|---|---|---|---|---|
| οὗ | ἀσφαλές | τι | γράψαι | τῷ | κυρίῳ |
| *hou* | *asphales* | *ti* | *grapsai* | *tō* | *kuriō* |
| whom | certain | anything | to write | to the | lord |

| 3620.2 partic | 2174.1 verb 1sing pres act | 1346.1 conj | 4113.9 verb 1sing indic aor act | 840.6 prs-pron acc sing masc | 1894.1 prep |
|---|---|---|---|---|---|
| οὐκ | ἔχω· | διὸ | προήγαγον | αὐτὸν | ἐφ' |
| *ouk* | *echō* | *dio* | *proēgagon* | *auton* | *eph'* |
| not | I have. | Wherefore | I brought forth | him | before |

| 5050.2 prs-pron gen 2pl | 2504.1 conj | 3094.1 adv sup | 1894.3 prep | 4622.2 prs-pron gen 2sing | 928.5 noun voc sing masc |
|---|---|---|---|---|---|
| ὑμῶν, | καὶ | μάλιστα | ἐπὶ | σοῦ, | βασιλεῦ |
| *humōn* | *kai* | *malista* | *epi* | *sou* | *basileu* |
| you, | and | especially | before | you, | king |

| 66.2 name sing masc | 3567.1 conj | 3450.10 art gen sing fem | 349.1 noun gen sing fem | 1090.57 verb gen sing fem part aor mid |
|---|---|---|---|---|
| Ἀγρίππα, | ὅπως | τῆς | ἀνακρίσεως | γενομένης |
| *Agrippa* | *hopōs* | *tēs* | *anakriseōs* | *genomenēs* |
| Agrippa, | so that | the | examination | having taken place |

Possibly Festus also called on them to look at Paul because he was not an impressive figure as far as his outward appearance went. On the other hand, Paul bore himself with the dignity of a Roman gentleman as he faced these rulers and prominent people.

Actually, it is not certain what Paul really looked like. The fictional apocryphal book, The Acts of Paul and Thecla pictures him as "a man of small stature, with a bald head and crooked legs, in a good state of body, with eyebrows meeting and a nose somewhat hooked, full of friendliness" (Barnstone, p.447). Some believe this description was based on ancient tradition that had some basis in fact, but it seems Festus wanted the people to wonder how such a man as this could cause so great a disturbance.

**25:25.** Then very emphatically Festus again stated that Paul had not committed any crime worthy of death (or anything at all worthy of death). His words might be translated, "As for me, I have found (and fully understand) that he has done (and still has done) nothing worthy of death."

Festus, like many rulers of the day, was primarily concerned with pleasing those who could affect his political career. Although it is quite probable he knew Paul was innocent right from the beginning, Festus would have gladly submitted him to the Jews in order to win their support. However, when Paul appealed to "Caesar," Festus knew it would be unwise or even dangerous to circumvent the appeals system established by Roman law as a means of protecting Roman citizens. Now, before Agrippa, he tried to present himself in the best possible light.

Unfortunately, though Festus had come to an understanding of the fact that Paul was not guilty of anything worthy of death, he had not come to an understanding of what Paul's message was all about. Martin Luther once said, "The object of his (Paul's) mission is to open their eyes—that is, to open and awaken the mind to the truth, and this in order to their conversion. The change is denoted by a twofold contrast—by that between darkness and light, and by that between the ruling power of Satan and the liberating fellowship of God. Finally, the ultimate design of God in their conversion consisted in the forgiveness of sins, and the bestowal of an inheritance, that is, a share in the glory." Festus was still blinded to these truths.

**25:26.** Festus had a problem when it came to making arrangements to send Paul to Rome. He had nothing reliable, nothing definite, nothing trustworthy to write to his lord, that is, to the emperor Nero.

Paul was not on trial here; he was simply being questioned at what may be called an informal hearing. Because the entire matter had become a political issue, the procurators could not treat the situation lightly or dismiss it all together. However, the "evidence" presented both by Paul and the Jews was theological and may not have been understandable to these Roman rulers.



**both at Jerusalem, and also here:** . . . and in this city, *Phillips.*

**crying that he ought not to live any longer:** They loudly insist he ought not to live any longer, *Moffatt* . . . clamoring that he should live no more, *NAB* . . . shouting that he ought not to live, *MLNT* . . . They din it into my ears, *Phillips.*

**25. But when I found:** But I for my part discovered, *Phillips* . . . I did not find, *NAB.*

**that he had committed nothing worthy of death:** . . . that he had not done anything deserving death, *TCNT* . . . nothing he has done that deserves death, *MLNT* . . . which deserves the death penalty, *Phillips.*

**and that he himself hath appealed to Augustus:** . . . and as he himself has made a request to be judged by Caesar, *BB* . . . Since, however, he himself made the appeal, *Kleist* . . . his Imperial Majesty, *TCNT* . . . His Majesty the Emperor, *NAB.*

**I have determined to send him:** I decided to send him, *RSV* . . . to Rome, *Weymouth* . . . send him on, *NAB.*

**26. Of whom I have no certain thing to write unto my lord:** The trouble is, I have nothing definite to write about him to our sovereign, *NAB* . . . But I have nothing definite to write about him to my Imperial Master, *TCNT* . . . Frankly, I have nothing specific to write to the emperor about him, *Phillips* . . . anything reliable to write, *Beck* . . . nothing substantial to write, *MLNT* . . . our Sovereign, *Williams.*

**Wherefore I have brought him forth before you:** . . . and for that reason, *TCNT* . . . That is why I have brought him before all of you, *NAB* . . . and I have therefore brought him forward before you, *Phillips.*

**and specially before thee, O king Agrippa:** . . . and particularly before you, *Berkeley.*

**that, after examination had:** . . . as the result of your cross-examination, *Moffatt* . . . that from this investigation, *NAB* . . . so that after due examination, *MLNT* . . . after an examination of him has been made, *Kleist.*

26.a.**Txt:** 01א,03B,04C byz.
**Var:** p74,02A,08E,044 81,945,1891,2495

| **2174.33** verb | **2174.1** verb | **4949.9** intr-pron sing neu | **1119.15** verb | **1119.6** verb |
|---|---|---|---|---|
| 1sing subj aor act | 1sing pres act | | inf aor act | 1sing act |
| ʽ σχῶ | [ᵃ ἔχω ] | τί | ʽ γράψαι. | [ᵇ☆ γράψω· ] |
| *schō* | *echō* | *ti* | *grapsai* | *grapsō* |
| I may have | [ I have ] | something | to write; | [ I may write; ] |

26.b.**Txt:** 08E,020L 025P,byz.
**Var:** 01א,02A,03B,04C Lach,Treg,Alf,Word Tisc,We/Ho,Weis,Sod UBS/☆

| | **247.1** adj | **1056.1** | **1466.4** prs- | **1374.5** verb 3sing | **3854.2** verb acc sing | **1192.2** noun |
|---|---|---|---|---|---|---|
| | sing neu | conj | pron dat 1sing | indic pres act | masc part pres act | acc sing masc |
| **27.** | ἄλογον | γάρ | μοι | δοκεῖ | πέμποντα | δέσμιον, |
| | *alogon* | *gar* | *moi* | *dokei* | *pemponta* | *desmion* |
| | irrational | for | to me | it seems | sending | a prisoner, |

| **3231.1** | **2504.1** | **3450.15** art | **2567.1** | **840.3** prs- | **155.1** | **4446.3** verb |
|---|---|---|---|---|---|---|
| partic | conj | acc pl fem | prep | pron gen sing | noun fem | inf aor act |
| μὴ | καὶ | τὰς | κατ' | αὐτοῦ | αἰτίας | σημᾶναι. |
| *mē* | *kai* | *tas* | *kat'* | *autou* | *aitias* | *sēmanai* |
| not | also | the | against | him | charges | to signify. |

| | **66.1** name | **1156.2** | **4242.1** | **3450.6** art | **3834.4** name | **5183.4** verb |
|---|---|---|---|---|---|---|
| | nom sing masc | conj | prep | acc sing masc | acc masc | 3sing indic act |
| **26:1.** | Ἀγρίππας | δὲ | πρὸς | τὸν | Παῦλον | ἔφη, |
| | *Agrippas* | *de* | *pros* | *ton* | *Paulon* | *ephē* |
| | Agrippa | and | to | | Paul | said, |

1.a.**Txt:** 03B,byz.
**Var:** p74,01א,02A,04C 08E,33,36,1739

| **1994.7** verb 3sing | **4622.3** prs- | **5065.1** | **3875.1** | **4427.1** prs-pron |
|---|---|---|---|---|
| indic pres mid | pron dat 2sing | prep | prep | gen sing masc |
| Ἐπιτρέπεταί | σοι | ʽ ὑπὲρ | [ᵃ☆ περὶ ] | σεαυτοῦ |
| *Epitrepetai* | *soi* | *huper* | *peri* | *seautou* |
| It is allowed | you | for | [ concerning ] | yourself |

1.b.**Txt:** 020L,025P,byz.
**Var:** 01א,02A,03B,04C 08E,bo.Lach,Treg,Alf Word,Tisc,We/Ho,Weis Sod,UBS/☆

| **2978.24** verb | **4966.1** | **3450.5** art | **3834.1** name | **620.8** verb 3sing |
|---|---|---|---|---|
| inf pres act | adv | nom sing masc | nom masc | indic imperf mid |
| λέγειν. | Τότε | ὁ | Παῦλος | ʽᵇ ἀπελογεῖτο, ʾ |
| *legein* | *Tote* | *ho* | *Paulos* | *apelogeito* |
| to speak. | Then | | Paul | was making a defense |

1.c.**Var:** 01א,02A,03B 04C,08E,bo.Lach,Treg Alf,Word,Tisc,We/Ho Weis,Sod,UBS/☆

| **1601.5** verb nom sing | **3450.12** art | **5331.4** noun | **620.8** verb 3sing |
|---|---|---|---|
| masc part aor act | acc sing fem | acc sing fem | indic imperf mid |
| ἐκτείνας | τὴν | χεῖρα, | [ᶜ☆+ ἀπελογεῖτο, ] |
| *ekteinas* | *tēn* | *cheira* | *apelogeito* |
| having stretched out | the | hand: | [ was making a defense: ] |

| | **3875.1** | **3820.4** | **3614.1** rel- | **1451.4** verb 1sing | **5097.3** |
|---|---|---|---|---|---|
| | prep | adj gen pl | pron gen pl | indic pres mid | prep |
| **2.** | Περὶ | πάντων | ὧν | ἐγκαλοῦμαι | ὑπὸ |
| | *Peri* | *pantōn* | *hōn* | *enkaloumai* | *hupo* |
| | Concerning | all | of which | I am being accused | by |

| **2428.3** name- | **928.5** noun | **66.2** name | **2216.16** verb 1sing | **1670.3** prs-pron |
|---|---|---|---|---|
| adj gen pl masc | voc sing masc | sing masc | indic perf mid | acc 1sing masc |
| Ἰουδαίων, | βασιλεῦ | Ἀγρίππα, | ἥγημαι | ἐμαυτὸν |
| *Ioudaiōn* | *basileu* | *Agrippa* | *hēgēmai* | *emauton* |
| Jews, | king | Agrippa, | I have esteemed | myself |

| **3079.1** | **3165.12** verb nom sing | **620.5** verb | **1894.3** | **4622.2** prs- |
|---|---|---|---|---|
| adj sing | masc part pres act | inf pres mid | prep | pron gen 2sing |
| μακάριον | ʽ μέλλων | ἀπολογεῖσθαι | ἐπὶ | σοῦ |
| *makarion* | *mellōn* | *apologeisthai* | *epi* | *sou* |
| fortunate | being about | to make defense | before | you |

| **4449.1** | **1894.3** | **4622.2** prs- | **3165.12** verb nom sing | **4449.1** |
|---|---|---|---|---|
| adv | prep | pron gen 2sing | masc part pres act | adv |
| σήμερον· | [☆ ἐπὶ | σοῦ | μέλλων | σήμερον |
| *sēmeron* | *epi* | *sou* | *mellōn* | *sēmeron* |
| today, | [ before | you | being about | today |

"My lord" in the Greek is simply "the lord." The Greek *kurios*, "lord," was often used in a way that was to imply showing respect to anyone and would be translated, "Sir!" Among the Romans, however, it was more often used to mean "master" of servants or slaves. It was also used of high officials, and by this time among the Romans it was used of their gods.

Festus then expressed his hope that after this examination before King Agrippa he would have something to write. He hoped Agrippa would be able to ask the right questions and give him something more definite.

**25:27.** Festus further emphasized that it seemed unreasonable to him to send a prisoner to the emperor without pointing out in a letter the charge against him. It apparently was customary to send such a letter, just as Lysias had sent a letter to Felix concerning Paul (23:25).

Obviously, Paul had successfully defended himself against all the flimsy charges the chief priests and elders of the Jews had brought against him. There was certainly nothing in the various categories of Roman civil or criminal law that would cover Paul's case. Festus undoubtedly knew better than to write the confused charges and generalities the Jewish leaders had included in their accusations.

Such a letter, of course, would not determine the emperor's decision. Paul's accusers would have to send representatives to bring charges against him as well. But a favorable letter from Festus would help a great deal.

**26:1.** This final hearing before Agrippa was not an official trial, since its purpose was to gain additional information for the benefit of Festus. Here the Book of Acts records for the third time, the account of Paul's conversion, giving some details not previously recorded in chapters 9 and 22.

Consider the setting. King Agrippa sat there in all the finery of his royal robes. Beside him sat his beautiful 32-year-old sister Bernice, "blazing in all her jewels." All around were the town notables dressed in their best. Then there were the tribunes in their uniforms with glittering swords at their sides.

King Agrippa turned to Paul and told him he was permitted to speak for himself. Paul did not hesitate. Filled once again with the power of the Holy Spirit, he began his defense.

**26:2.** Paul made no criticism of the king's empty display, nor did he refer to the jewelry of Bernice or her unsavory reputation. He was intent not on defending himself but his Master. The cause of Christ was always more important to him than his own cause. Thus, with all courtesy and deep earnestness he began his defense.

He first let King Agrippa know he counted himself happy to make a defense before him and to give an answer with respect to all things of which the Jews were accusing him.

**I might have somewhat to write:** I may find something which I can put into writing, *Weymouth* . . . there may emerge some charge which I may put in writing, *Phillips.*

**27. For it seemeth to me unreasonable:** For it seems to me absurd, *TCNT* . . . ridiculous, *Phillips* . . . odd, *Berkeley* . . . to me pointless, *JB.*

**to send a prisoner:** . . . to send a prisoner up for trial, *Norlie.*

**and not withal to signify the crimes laid against him:** . . . without at the same time stating the charges made against him, *TCNT* . . . without specifying, *Williams* . . . without reporting what he's accused of, *Beck* . . . without indicating the charges against him, *Phillips* . . . the crimes alleged against him, *Campbell* . . . not to designate his offence, *Murdock.*

**1. Then Agrippa said unto Paul:** Turning to Paul, Agrippa said, *TCNT.*

**Thou art permitted to speak for thyself:** You are at liberty to speak for yourself, *TCNT* . . . You have permission, *Phillips* . . . You may put your case before us, *BB.*

**Then Paul stretched forth the hand:** So Paul, extending his hand, *Norlie* . . . with that characteristic gesture of the hand, *Phillips.*

**and answered for himself:** . . . went on to make his defence, *Rotherham* . . . began his defense, *Phillips.*

**2. I think myself happy, king Agrippa:** I have been congratulating myself, King Agrippa, *TCNT* . . . I think myself fortunate, *Weymouth* . . . I must say how fortunate I consider myself to be, *Phillips.*

**because I shall answer for myself this day before thee:** . . . in being able to defend myself today before you, *Moffatt* . . . in making my defense before thee personally today, *Phillips.*

**touching all the things whereof I am accused of the Jews:** . . . with regard to the charges brought against me by, *TCNT* . . . against all the charges which the Jews have preferred against me, *Williams* . . . in answering all the charges that the Jews have made against me, *Phillips.*

## Acts 26:3

| 620.5 verb inf pres mid | 3094.1 adv sup | 1103.1 noun acc sing masc | 1498.18 verb part pres act | 4622.4 prs-pron acc 2sing |
|---|---|---|---|---|
| ἀπολογεῖσθαι, ] | 3. μάλιστα | γνώστην | ὄντα | σε |
| *apologeisthai* | *malista* | *gnōstēn* | *onta* | *se* |
| to make defense, ] | especially | acquainted | being | you |

| 3820.4 adj gen pl | 3450.1 art gen pl | 2567.3 prep | 2428.5 name-adj acc pl masc | 1478.3 noun gen pl neu | 4885.1 conj |
|---|---|---|---|---|---|
| πάντων | τῶν | κατὰ | Ἰουδαίους | ἐθῶν | τε |
| *pantōn* | *tōn* | *kata* | *Ioudaious* | *ethōn* | *te* |
| of all | the | according to | Jews | customs | and |

3.a.**Txt:** 04C,020L,025P byz.bo.
**Var:** 01ℵ,02A,03B,08E Lach,Treg,Alf,Tisc We/Ho,Weis,Sod UBS/☆

| 2504.1 conj | 2196.4 noun gen pl neu | 1346.1 conj | 1183.1 verb 1sing indic pres mid | 4622.2 prs-pron gen 2sing |
|---|---|---|---|---|
| καὶ | ζητημάτων. | διὸ | δέομαι | (ᵃ σου ) |
| *kai* | *zētēmatōn* | *dio* | *deomai* | *sou* |
| also | questions; | wherefore | I urge | you |

| 3088.1 adv | 189.36 verb inf aor act | 1466.2 prs-pron gen 1sing | 3450.12 art acc sing fem | 3173.1 conj | 3631.1 partic |
|---|---|---|---|---|---|
| μακροθύμως | ἀκοῦσαί | μου. | 4. Τὴν | μὲν | οὖν |
| *makrothumōs* | *akousai* | *mou* | *Tēn* | *men* | *oun* |
| patiently | to hear | me. | The | | then |

4.a.**Txt:** 01ℵ,02A 04C-corr,08E,020L 025P,etc.byz.Tisc,Sod
**Var:** 03B,04C-org,Treg We/Ho,Weis,UBS/☆

| 974.1 noun acc sing fem | 1466.2 prs-pron gen 1sing | 3450.12 art acc sing fem | 1523.2 prep gen | 3366.1 noun gen sing fem | 3450.12 art acc sing fem |
|---|---|---|---|---|---|
| βίωσίν | μου | (ᵃ τὴν ) | ἐκ | νεότητος, | τὴν |
| *biōsin* | *mou* | *tēn* | *ek* | *neotētos* | *tēn* |
| manner of life | my | the | from | youth, | the |

| 570.2 prep | 741.2 noun gen sing fem | 1090.58 verb acc sing fem part aor mid | 1706.1 prep | 3450.3 art dat sing | 1477.3 noun dat sing neu |
|---|---|---|---|---|---|
| ἀπ' | ἀρχῆς | γενομένην | ἐν | τῷ | ἔθνει |
| *ap'* | *archēs* | *genomenēn* | *en* | *tō* | *ethnei* |
| from | beginning | having been | among | the | nation |

4.b.**Var:** 01ℵ,02A,03B 08E,Lach,Treg,Alf Word,Tisc,We/Ho,Weis Sod,UBS/☆

| 1466.2 prs-pron gen 1sing | 1706.1 prep | 4885.1 conj | 2389.3 name dat pl neu | 3471.28 verb 3pl indic perf act |
|---|---|---|---|---|
| μου | ἐν | [ᵇ☆+ τε ] | Ἱεροσολύμοις, | ἴσασιν |
| *mou* | *en* | *te* | *Hierosolumois* | *isasin* |
| my | in | [and] | Jerusalem, | know |

4.c.**Txt:** 01ℵ,02A 04C-corr,020L,025P,byz. Tisc
**Var:** p74,03B,04C-org 08E,33,Lach,Treg,Alf We/Ho,Weis,Sod UBS/☆

| 3820.7 adj nom pl masc | 3450.7 art nom pl masc | 2428.2 name-adj nom pl masc | 4126.1 verb nom pl masc part pres act | 1466.6 prs-pron acc 1sing |
|---|---|---|---|---|
| πάντες | (ᶜ οἱ ) | Ἰουδαῖοι, | 5. προγινώσκοντές | με |
| *pantes* | *hoi* | *Ioudaioi* | *proginōskontes* | *me* |
| all | the | Jews, | knowing | me |

| 505.1 adv | 1430.1 partic | 2286.10 verb 3pl subj pres act | 3113.15 verb inf pres act | 3617.1 conj | 2567.3 prep |
|---|---|---|---|---|---|
| ἄνωθεν, | ἐὰν | θέλωσιν | μαρτυρεῖν, | ὅτι | κατὰ |
| *anōthen* | *ean* | *thelōsin* | *marturein* | *hoti* | *kata* |
| from the first, | if | they would | to bear witness, | that | according to |

| 3450.12 art acc sing fem | 195.1 adj sup acc sing fem | 138.3 noun acc sing fem | 3450.10 art gen sing fem | 2233.5 adj gen 1sing fem |
|---|---|---|---|---|
| τὴν | ἀκριβεστάτην | αἵρεσιν | τῆς | ἡμετέρας |
| *tēn* | *akribestatēn* | *hairesin* | *tēs* | *hēmeteras* |
| the | strictest | sect | of the | our |

| 2333.2 noun gen sing fem | 2180.20 verb 1sing indic aor act | 5168.1 name nom sing masc | 2504.1 conj | 3431.1 adv | 1894.2 prep |
|---|---|---|---|---|---|
| θρησκείας | ἔζησα | Φαρισαῖος· | 6. καὶ | νῦν | ἐπ' |
| *thrēskeias* | *ezēsa* | *Pharisaios* | *kai* | *nun* | *ep'* |
| religion | I lived | a Pharisee. | And | now | for |

**26:3.** Paul felt happy or fortunate that it was Agrippa who was to hear his case because Agrippa was an expert in all the things concerning Jewish customs and questions.

Agrippa's father was zealous for the Jewish law up to almost the end of his life. He was concerned about Jewish customs and the temple. Because Agrippa himself was now the Roman official in charge of the temple, he must have learned a great deal from his own experiences as well as from his father's. He would know too how controversial many of the questions were that arose among the Jews and how the customs varied among the different sects such as the Pharisees, Sadducees, and Essenes.

Therefore, because of this expert knowledge, Paul begged Agrippa to listen patiently to what he was about to say. Paul was implying in this that his words would be helpful to Agrippa also, for Agrippa was a Jew and needed to know the facts, not only of Paul's life, but of Paul's message, the gospel.

**3. Especially because I know thee to be expert:** Especially as thou art well versed, *Rotherham* . . . especially as you are well acquainted with, *Kleist* . . . for you are so thoroughly acquainted, *Berkeley* . . . because you are expert, *BB* . . . you are thoroughly familiar, *Phillips.*

**in all customs and questions which are among the Jews:** . . . in all the Jewish customs and questions, *Rotherham* . . . that prevail among the Jews, *Weymouth* . . . and controversial questions, *Norlie* . . . the controversies, *Murdock* . . . and disputes that exist among, *Phillips.*

**wherefore I beseech thee to hear me patiently:** Pray listen to me then with patience, *Moffatt* . . . with indulgence, *Murdock.*

**26:4.** Paul pointed out first that all the Jews knew his manner of life from the beginning (in Tarsus) and during his youth among his own people in Jerusalem.

Paul did not draw attention to his birth in Tarsus, the chief city of Cilicia. Nor did he mention the wealth and influence of his family in that city or even his Roman citizenship. He emphasized that from his early youth he had lived among the Jews in Jerusalem, and they all knew the kind of life he lived. He was open and aboveboard in all that he did. He took part in the affairs of the Jews in Jerusalem, so that they all came to know him well.

He was sent early to Jerusalem to be educated and taught a trade. His teacher, Gamaliel, was one of the most distinguished rabbis of that time and was a grandson of the famous Hillel who is still revered by orthodox Jews. At his feet the young Paul (then called by his Hebrew name, Saul) learned the Old Testament and all the rabbinical traditions and interpretations.

**4. My manner of life from my youth:** The kind of life I have lived from, *Weymouth* . . . The fact that I lived from my youth upwards, *Phillips.*

**which was at the first among mine own nation at Jerusalem:** . . . as exemplified in my early days among, *Weymouth* . . . the early part of which was spent among, *Kleist* . . . among my own people, *Phillips.*

**know all the Jews:** . . . is known to all the Jews, *Weymouth* . . . all the Jews know, *Kleist.*

**26:5.** If those who knew Paul from the beginning (of his stay in Jerusalem) would testify (bear witness), they would have to say Paul lived as a Pharisee, following the teachings of the strictest of the Jewish sects.

The Pharisees were separatists. They not only separated themselves from Greek culture and idolatry, they took a stand against the Maccabean (Hasmonean) priests about 100 years before Christ. They did not like the fact that they took the title of king even though they were not of the line of David. Alexander Jannaeus, a Hasmonean king, showed his hostility toward the Pharisees by crucifying about 800 of them. But force did not stop them, and they maintained their strict religious convictions.

Clearly, Paul was not some stranger or foreigner coming in trying to start a new religion. He was a Jew, a Pharisee, and he lived up to their customs to the best of his ability.

**5. Which knew me from the beginning:** They are fully aware, *Berkeley* . . . They have known all the time, *Phillips* . . . In fact they have long been acquainted with me, *Kleist.*

**if they would testify:** . . . if only they are willing to give evidence, *Kleist* . . . if they choose to give evidence, *TCNT* . . . if they would but testify to the fact, *Weymouth* . . . if they want to tell the truth, *Beck* . . . and could witness to the fact if they wished, *Phillips.*

**that after the most straitest sect of our religion:** . . . according to, *Darby* . . . the strictest sect, *Norlie* . . . the most rigid Sect, *Wilson* . . . the strictest party of our religion, *Beck.*

**I lived a Pharisee:** I lived a true Pharisee, *TCNT* . . . I spent my life as, *Kleist.*

6.a.**Txt:** 04C,020L,025P byz.
**Var:** 01ℵ,02A,03B,08E Lach,Treg,Alf,Word Tisc,We/Ho,Weis,Sod UBS/☆

6.b.**Var:** 01ℵ,02A,03B 04C,08E,bo.Lach,Treg Alf,Word,Tisc,We/Ho Weis,Sod,UBS/☆

| **1667.3** noun dat sing fem | **3450.10** art gen sing fem | **4242.1** prep | **1519.1** prep | **3450.8** art acc pl masc | **3824.9** noun acc pl masc |
|---|---|---|---|---|---|
| ἐλπίδι | τῆς | ⸂ πρὸς | [a☆ εἰς ] | τοὺς | πατέρας |
| *elpidi* | *tēs* | *pros* | *eis* | *tous* | *pateras* |
| hope | of the | to | [ idem ] | the | fathers |

| **2231.2** prs-pron gen 1pl | **1845.1** noun fem | **1090.57** verb gen sing fem part aor mid | **5097.3** prep | **3450.2** art gen sing |
|---|---|---|---|---|
| [b☆+ ἡμῶν ] | ἐπαγγελίας | γενομένης | ὑπὸ | τοῦ |
| *hēmōn* | *epangelias* | *genomenēs* | *hupo* | *tou* |
| [ our ] | promise | having been made | by | |

| **2296.2** noun gen sing masc | **2449.16** verb 1sing indic perf act | **2892.30** verb nom sing masc part pres mid | **1519.1** prep | **3614.12** rel-pron acc sing fem | **3450.16** art sing neu |
|---|---|---|---|---|---|
| θεοῦ | ἕστηκα | κρινόμενος, | 7. εἰς | ἣν | τὸ |
| *theou* | *hestēka* | *krinomenos* | *eis* | *hēn* | *to* |
| God, | I stand | being judged, | to | which | the |

| **1422.1** noun sing neu | **2231.2** prs-pron gen 1pl | **1706.1** prep | **1603.1** noun dat sing fem | **3433.4** noun acc sing fem | **2504.1** conj |
|---|---|---|---|---|---|
| δωδεκάφυλον | ἡμῶν | ἐν | ἐκτενείᾳ | νύκτα | καὶ |
| *dōdekaphulon* | *hēmōn* | *en* | *ekteneia* | *nukta* | *kai* |
| twelve tribes | our | in | earnestness | night | and |

7.a.**Txt:** 020L,025P,byz.
**Var:** 01ℵ,03B,04C,08E Lach,Treg,Alf,Tisc We/Ho,Weis,Sod UBS/☆

7.b.**Txt:** Steph
**Var:** 01ℵ,02A,03B,04C 08E,020L,025P,byz. Gries,Lach,Treg,Alf Word,Tisc,We/Ho,Weis Sod,UBS/☆

7.c.**Var:** 01ℵ,03B,04C 08E,bo.Lach,Treg,Alf Tisc,We/Ho,Weis,Sod UBS/☆

| **2232.4** noun acc sing fem | **2973.8** verb sing neu part pres act | **1666.2** verb 3sing indic pres act | **2628.7** verb inf aor act | **3875.1** prep |
|---|---|---|---|---|
| ἡμέραν | λατρεῦον | ἐλπίζει | καταντῆσαι· | περὶ |
| *hēmeran* | *latreuon* | *elpizei* | *katantēsai* | *peri* |
| day | serving | hope | to arrive; | concerning |

| **3614.10** rel-pron gen sing fem | **1667.2** noun gen sing fem | **1451.4** verb 1sing indic pres mid | **928.5** noun voc sing masc |
|---|---|---|---|
| ἧς | ἐλπίδος | ἐγκαλοῦμαι, | ⸂a βασιλεῦ |
| *hēs* | *elpidos* | *enkaloumai* | *basileu* |
| which | hope | I am being accused, | O king |

| **66.2** name sing masc | **5097.3** prep | **3450.1** art gen pl | **2428.3** name-adj gen pl masc | **928.5** noun voc sing masc |
|---|---|---|---|---|
| Ἀγριππα, ⸃ | ὑπὸ | ⸂b τῶν ⸃ | Ἰουδαίων. | [c☆+ βασιλεῦ. ] |
| *Agrippa* | *hupo* | *tōn* | *Ioudaiōn* | *basileu* |
| Agrippa, | by | the | Jews. | [ O king. ] |

| **4949.9** intr-pron sing neu | **566.1** adj sing | **2892.29** verb 3sing indic pres mid | **3706.1** prep | **5050.3** prs-pron dat 2pl | **1479.1** conj |
|---|---|---|---|---|---|
| 8. τί | ἄπιστον | κρίνεται | παρ' | ὑμῖν | εἰ |
| *ti* | *apiston* | *krinetai* | *par'* | *humin* | *ei* |
| Why | incredible | is it judged | by | you | if |

| **3450.5** art nom sing masc | **2296.1** noun nom sing masc | **3361.7** adj acc pl masc | **1446.1** verb 3sing indic pres act | **1466.1** prs-pron nom 1sing | **3173.1** conj |
|---|---|---|---|---|---|
| ὁ | θεὸς | νεκροὺς | ἐγείρει; | 9. ἐγὼ | μὲν |
| *ho* | *theos* | *nekrous* | *egeirei* | *egō* | *men* |
| | God | dead | raises? | I | indeed |

| **3631.1** partic | **1374.15** verb 1sing indic aor act | **1670.2** prs-pron dat 1sing masc | **4242.1** prep | **3450.16** art sing neu | **3549.2** noun sing neu |
|---|---|---|---|---|---|
| οὖν | ἔδοξα | ἐμαυτῷ | πρὸς | τὸ | ὄνομα |
| *oun* | *edoxa* | *emautō* | *pros* | *to* | *onoma* |
| therefore | thought | in myself | to | the | name |

| **2400.2** name masc | **3450.2** art gen sing | **3343.2** name gen sing masc | **1158.5** verb inf pres act | **4044.17** adj pl neu |
|---|---|---|---|---|
| Ἰησοῦ | τοῦ | Ναζωραίου | δεῖν | πολλὰ |
| *Iēsou* | *tou* | *Nazōraiou* | *dein* | *polla* |
| of Jesus | the | Nazarene | to be necessary | many things |

**26:6.** Now Paul was being judged, not because he had done anything wrong, not because he had turned against his true heritage, but because of the hope of the promise God made to the patriarchs (Abraham, Isaac, Jacob, and the other ancestors of the Jews who received His promises). These would include the promises of blessing, not only for Israel, but for all the families of the earth (Genesis 12:3).

**26:7.** This promise, Paul said, "our twelve tribes" in earnestness served (worshiped) God day and night hoping to attain it (reach it as their God-given destination).

Paul, of course, recognized that the Jews of his day included all 12 tribes, although Judah comprised the largest group who originally returned from Babylon. He was of the tribe of Benjamin. The Jews at that time knew the tribe to which they belonged. The 10 northern tribes were obviously never lost. (Actually, some had intermarried and became Samaritans. Others purified themselves and joined in the worship of the temple after Cyrus sent the Jews back.)

The Jews' accusations against Paul, then, did not refer to any crime. They really concerned this hope of their fathers.

**26:8.** Paul then gave his full attention to Agrippa and asked a pointed question, "Why does it seem incredible (unbelievable) to you that God should raise the dead?"

Agrippa would know that as a Pharisee Paul always believed in the future resurrection of the body and future judgments. Agrippa must also have known the Christians believed God had raised Jesus from the dead and made His resurrection the guarantee of theirs. Actually, since God is God, and since the Old Testament teaches that nothing is too hard, too wonderful, or too impossible for God, it should not have been hard for Agrippa to believe, especially now that God had raised Jesus from the dead.

**26:9.** Paul did not want to imply that Agrippa was foolish or stupid for thinking it hard to believe in the Resurrection. Paul himself had not had an easy time believing in the resurrection of Jesus either. In fact, he had thought it necessary to do many things against the name of Jesus of Nazareth, that is, against what the Name represented: the character, nature, and authority of the Son of God.

Paul did not elsewhere call Jesus "Jesus of Nazareth." Perhaps he did so here because he was thinking of the words of Jesus on the Damascus Road where He identified himself as "Jesus of Nazareth, whom you keep persecuting." But this was the name by which Jesus was known to the Jews, and Agrippa would have no question about which person this was.

**6. And now I stand and am judged:** Even now...I stand here on my trial, *TCNT.*

**for the hope of the promise made of God unto our fathers:** . . . because of my hope in the promise given by God to our ancestors, *TCNT* . . . because I trust the promise God made, *Beck* . . . which came from God a promise to, *Fenton* . . . because of a hope that I hold in a promise that God made, *Phillips.*

**7. Unto which promise our twelve tribes:** . . . a promise which our Twelve Tribes, *TCNT.*

**instantly serving God day and night, hope to come:** . . . hope to attain, *ASV* . . . by earnest service night and day, hope to see fulfilled, *TCNT* . . . as they worship earnestly night and day, hope to gain, *Williams C.K.* . . . serve God zealously day and night, hoping to see it fulfilled, *Phillips* . . . in confident expectation to secure, *Fenton.*

**For which hope's sake, king Agrippa:** It is for this hope, your Majesty, *TCNT* . . . And I am actually impeached by Jews, *Moffatt.*

**I am accused of the Jews:** . . . that I am accused and by Jews themselves! *TCNT* . . . And I am actually impeached by Jews, *Moffatt* . . . I am charged, *Williams C.K.* . . . I am accused as a criminal by the Judeans! *Fenton.*

**8. Why should it be thought a thing incredible with you:** Why is it deemed with all of you a thing past belief, *Weymouth* . . . do you find it impossible to believe, *Williams C.K.*

**that God should raise the dead?:** . . . if God doth raise the dead, *ASV.*

**9. I verily thought with myself:** Fact is that I was possessed of the idea, *Berkeley.*

**that I ought to do many things contrary to the name of Jesus of Nazareth:** . . . my duty to oppose in every way the Name of, *TCNT* . . . a duty to be active in hostility to the name of Jesus, the Nazarene, *Weymouth* . . . to do everything to oppose the name of, *Williams C.K.* . . . to oppose with the utmost vigor the name of, *Phillips* . . . to take extreme measures in hostility to the name, *Williams.*

## Acts 26:10

| 1711.6 adj pl neu | 4097.22 verb inf aor act | 3614.16 rel-pron sing neu | 2504.1 conj | 4020.22 verb 1sing indic aor act | 1706.1 prep |
|---|---|---|---|---|---|
| ἐναντία | πρᾶξαι· | 10. ὃ | καὶ | ἐποίησα | ἐν |
| *enantia* | *praxai* | *ho* | *kai* | *epoiēsa* | *en* |
| contrary | to do. | Which | also | I did | in |

10.a.**Var:** 01ℵ,02A,04C 08E,Lach,Treg,Alf,Tisc We/Ho,Weis,Sod UBS/☆

| 2389.3 name dat pl neu | 2504.1 conj | 4044.8 adj acc pl masc | 4885.1 conj | 3450.1 art gen pl | 39.4 adj gen pl |
|---|---|---|---|---|---|
| Ἱεροσολύμοις, | καὶ | πολλούς | [a☆+ τε ] | τῶν | ἁγίων |
| *Hierosolumois* | *kai* | *pollous* | *te* | *tōn* | *hagiōn* |
| Jerusalem | and | many | [ and ] | of the | saints |

10.b.**Var:** 01ℵ,02A,03B 04C,08E,020L,Gries Lach,Treg,Alf,Word Tisc,We/Ho,Weis,Sod UBS/☆

| 1466.1 prs-pron nom 1sing | 1706.1 prep | 5274.5 noun dat pl fem | 2593.1 verb 1sing indic aor act | 3450.12 art acc sing fem | 3706.2 prep |
|---|---|---|---|---|---|
| ἐγὼ | [b☆+ ἐν ] | φυλακαῖς | κατέκλεισα, | τὴν | παρὰ |
| *egō* | *en* | *phulakais* | *katekleisa* | *tēn* | *para* |
| I | [ in ] | prisons | shut up, | the | from |

| 3450.1 art gen pl | 744.6 noun gen pl masc | 1833.4 noun acc sing fem | 2956.25 verb nom sing masc part aor act | 335.10 verb gen pl masc part pres mid |
|---|---|---|---|---|
| τῶν | ἀρχιερέων | ἐξουσίαν | λαβών· | ἀναιρουμένων |
| *tōn* | *archiereōn* | *exousian* | *labōn* | *anairoumenōn* |
| the | chief priests | authority | having received; | being put to death |

| 4885.1 conj | 840.1 prs-pron gen pl | 2671.1 verb 1sing indic aor act | 5421.1 noun acc sing fem | 2504.1 conj | 2567.3 prep |
|---|---|---|---|---|---|
| τε | αὐτῶν | κατήνεγκα | ψῆφον, | 11. καὶ | κατὰ |
| *te* | *autōn* | *katēnenka* | *psēphon* | *kai* | *kata* |
| and | them | I cast against | a vote. | And | according to |

| 3820.16 adj acc pl fem | 3450.15 art acc pl fem | 4715.7 noun acc pl fem | 4038.1 adv | 4945.1 verb nom sing masc part pres act |
|---|---|---|---|---|
| πάσας | τὰς | συναγωγὰς | πολλάκις | τιμωρῶν |
| *pasas* | *tas* | *sunagōgas* | *pollakis* | *timōrōn* |
| all | the | synagogues | often | punishing |

| 840.8 prs-pron acc pl masc | 313.6 verb 1sing indic imperf act | 980.7 verb inf pres act | 3917.1 adv | 4885.1 conj |
|---|---|---|---|---|
| αὐτοὺς, | ἠνάγκαζον | βλασφημεῖν· | περισσῶς | τε |
| *autous* | *ēnankazon* | *blasphēmein* | *perissōs* | *te* |
| them, | I was compelling | to blaspheme. | Exceedingly | and |

| 1679.1 verb nom sing masc part pres mid | 840.2 prs-pron dat pl | 1371.20 verb indic imperf act | 2175.1 conj | 2504.1 conj |
|---|---|---|---|---|
| ἐμμαινόμενος | αὐτοῖς | ἐδίωκον | ἕως | καὶ |
| *emmainomenos* | *autois* | *ediōkon* | *heōs* | *kai* |
| being furious | against them | I was persecuting | as far as | even |

| 1519.1 prep | 3450.15 art acc pl fem | 1838.1 adv | 4032.5 noun pl fem | 1706.1 prep | 3614.4 rel-pron dat pl |
|---|---|---|---|---|---|
| εἰς | τὰς | ἔξω | πόλεις. | 12. Ἐν | οἷς |
| *eis* | *tas* | *exō* | *poleis* | *En* | *hois* |
| to | the | outside | cities. | During | which |

12.a.**Txt:** 020L,025P,byz. **Var:** 01ℵ,02A,03B,04C 08E,bo.Lach,Treg,Alf Tisc,We/Ho,Weis,Sod UBS/☆

| 2504.1 conj | 4057.7 verb nom sing masc part pres mid | 1519.1 prep | 3450.12 art acc sing fem | 1149.2 name acc fem | 3196.2 prep |
|---|---|---|---|---|---|
| (a καὶ ) | πορευόμενος | εἰς | τὴν | Δαμασκὸν | μετ' |
| *kai* | *poreuomenos* | *eis* | *tēn* | *Damaskon* | *met'* |
| also | journeying | to | | Damascus, | with |

12.b.**Txt:** 04C,020L 025P,byz. **Var:** 01ℵ,02A,03B,08E Treg,Tisc,We/Ho,Weis Sod,UBS/☆

| 1833.1 noun fem | 2504.1 conj | 1995.1 noun gen sing fem | 3450.10 art gen sing fem | 3706.2 prep | 3450.1 art gen pl |
|---|---|---|---|---|---|
| ἐξουσίας | καὶ | ἐπιτροπῆς | τῆς | (b παρὰ ) | τῶν |
| *exousias* | *kai* | *epitropēs* | *tēs* | *para* | *tōn* |
| authority | and | a commission | the | from | the |

**26:10.** Paul had shown his antagonism to Jesus by putting many of the saints in prison, not on his own authority but on the authority he received from the chief priests.

After his conversion Paul called the Christians saints "holy, dedicated, consecrated ones," that is, dedicated or set apart for God and for the worship and service of God. The same adjective is applied to God, Christ, and the angels. Israel was called to be a holy people, that is to be saints. Christians have the same calling (Romans 1:7). In the New Testament a saint is one who has turned his back on the world to follow Jesus.

Paul did more than hold the clothes of the witnesses who stoned the martyr Stephen. He cast his vote against him and many other Christians, a vote that called for the death penalty.

On the basis of Paul's casting his vote against them some have surmised Paul was a member of the Sanhedrin. However, such a young man would not normally be chosen to become a member. Nevertheless, his zeal for the Law, his great intelligence, and the progress he made in his studies under Gamaliel gave him a reputation that caused him to be sought after.

**26:11.** Paul's zeal against Jesus and against those who believed in Him also caused him to go from synagogue to synagogue. He sought out the believers and punished them. Even worse, he tried to compel them to blaspheme the name of Jesus. However, the Greek may indicate he was not able to make them do it; the imperfect tense implies he repeatedly "compelled" them to blaspheme.

So exceedingly and madly enraged had Paul been against the Christians that he pursued them even to foreign cities. Later, in 1 Timothy 1:13, Paul pointed out that he acted in ignorance of the truth. But he never forgot what he had done. He reminded the Galatians that they had heard of his manner of life when he was engaged in the Jews' religion. He said, "Beyond measure I persecuted the church (assembly) of God, and wasted it (tried to destroy it): and profited (advanced, made progress) in the Jews' religion above many of my equals (those of my own age) in mine own nation, being more exceedingly zealous of the traditions of my fathers" (Galatians 1:13,14). He showed this zeal by the way he never let up in his persecution of believers. His aim was to destroy the Church by getting all the Christians to renounce Christ.

**26:12.** After painting such a word picture of his violence against the Christians, Paul recounted for Agrippa the story of his conversion on the Damascus Road. Again Paul made it clear that he had not hounded the Christians on his own authority. He went to Damascus with authority and the full power of a commission from the chief priests. Likely, his anger and the anticipation of arresting the Jewish believers in Damascus caused him to lead the group as he pressed on toward the city. All this provides a contrast for what followed.

**10. Which thing I also did in Jerusalem:**

**and many of the saints did I shut up in prison:** I myself threw many of the People of Christ into prison, *TCNT* . . . I locked up many of the holy people in prison, *Beck* . . . where I shut up in prison many of the holy, *Fenton.*

**having received authority from the chief priests:** Acting on the authority of the Chief Priests, *TCNT* . . . armed with authority received from, *Weymouth.*

**and when they were put to death:** . . . executed, *Berkeley* . . . condemned to death, *Montgomery* . . . on trial for their lives, *Phillips* . . . and when it was proposed to put them to death, *TCNT.*

**I gave my voice against them:** I voted against, *Moffatt* . . . I gave my decision against them, *BB.*

**11. And I punished them oft in every synagogue:** . . . there was not a synagogue where I did not often punish them, *Moffatt* . . . I tortured them, *Murdock* . . . I frequently forced them, by torturing, *Fenton.*

**and compelled them to blaspheme:** . . . and forced them to blaspheme, *Weymouth* . . . to make them renounce their faith, *NEB.*

**and being exceedingly mad against them:** So frantic was I against them, *TCNT* . . . and in my wild fury, *Weymouth* . . . frantic fury, *Moffatt* . . . mad fury, *Montgomery* . . . furious rage, *Norlie* . . . furiously mad against them, *Fenton.*

**I persecuted them even unto strange cities:** . . . as far as foreign cities, *Berkeley* . . . that I pursued them even to towns beyond our borders, *TCNT* . . . and I hounded them to distant cities, *Phillips* . . . into foreign cities, *Norlie.*

**12. Whereupon as I went to Damascus:** While thus engaged, I was travelling one day to Damascus, *Weymouth.*

**with authority and commission from the chief priests:** . . . entrusted with full powers, *TCNT* . . . with discretionary authority, *Adams* . . . and approval of, *Berkeley* . . . authorized and appointed by, *Beck* . . . based on a commission, *Williams.*

# Acts 26:13

| 744.6 noun gen pl masc | 13. 2232.1 noun fem | 3189.3 adj gen sing fem | 2567.3 prep | 3450.12 art acc sing fem | 3461.4 noun acc sing fem |
|---|---|---|---|---|---|
| ἀρχιερέων, | 13. ἡμέρας | μέσης | κατὰ | τὴν | ὁδὸν |
| *archiereōn* | *hēmeras* | *mesēs* | *kata* | *tēn* | *hodon* |
| chief priests, | at day | middle | in | the | way |

| 1481.1 verb indic aor act | 928.5 noun voc sing masc | 3635.1 adv | 5065.1 prep | 3450.12 art acc sing fem | 2960.1 noun acc sing fem |
|---|---|---|---|---|---|
| εἶδον, | βασιλεῦ, | οὐρανόθεν | ὑπὲρ | τὴν | λαμπρότητα |
| *eidon* | *basileu* | *ouranothen* | *huper* | *tēn* | *lamprotēta* |
| I saw, | O king, | from heaven | above | the | brightness |

| 3450.2 art gen sing | 2229.2 noun gen sing masc | 3897.2 verb sing neu part aor act | 1466.6 prs-pron acc 1sing | 5295.1 noun sing neu |
|---|---|---|---|---|
| τοῦ | ἡλίου | περιλάμψαν | με | φῶς |
| *tou* | *hēliou* | *perilampsan* | *me* | *phōs* |
| of the | sun | having shone round about | me | a light |

| 2504.1 conj | 3450.8 art acc pl masc | 4713.1 prep | 1466.5 prs-pron dat 1sing | 4057.13 verb acc pl masc part pres mid | 14. 3820.4 adj gen pl |
|---|---|---|---|---|---|
| καὶ | τοὺς | σὺν | ἐμοὶ | πορευομένους. | 14. πάντων |
| *kai* | *tous* | *sun* | *emoi* | *poreuomenous* | *pantōn* |
| and | the | with | me | journeying. | All |

14.a.**Txt:** 04C,020L 025P,byz.bo.
**Var:** 01ℵ,02A,03B,08E Lach,Treg,Alf,Word Tisc,We/Ho,Weis,Sod UBS/☆

14.b.**Txt:** 020L,025P,byz. Sod
**Var:** 01ℵ,02A,03B,04C Lach,Treg,Alf,Tisc We/Ho,Weis,UBS/☆

14.c.**Txt:** 020L,025P,byz. Sod
**Var:** 01ℵ,02A,03B,04C Lach,Treg,Alf,Tisc We/Ho,Weis,UBS/☆

| 1156.2 conj | 4885.1 conj | 2637.2 verb gen pl masc part aor act | 2231.2 prs-pron gen 1pl | 1519.1 prep | 3450.12 art acc sing fem |
|---|---|---|---|---|---|
| ⸀ δὲ | [a☆ τε ] | καταπεσόντων | ἡμῶν | εἰς | τὴν |
| *de* | *te* | *katapesontōn* | *hēmōn* | *eis* | *tēn* |
| and | [ idem ] | having fallen down | of us | to | the |

| 1087.4 noun acc sing fem | 189.19 verb 1sing indic aor act | 5292.4 noun acc sing fem | 2953.21 verb acc sing fem part pres act |
|---|---|---|---|
| γῆν | ἤκουσα | φωνὴν | ⸀ λαλοῦσαν |
| *gēn* | *ēkousa* | *phōnēn* | *lalousan* |
| ground | I heard | a voice | speaking |

| 2978.21 verb acc sing fem part pres act | 4242.1 prep | 1466.6 prs-pron acc 1sing | 2504.1 conj | 2978.21 verb acc sing fem part pres act |
|---|---|---|---|---|
| [b☆ λέγουσαν ] | πρός | με | ⸂c καὶ | λέγουσαν ⸃ |
| *legousan* | *pros* | *me* | *kai* | *legousan* |
| [ saying ] | to | me | and | saying |

| 3450.11 art dat sing fem | 1441.1 name-adj dat sing fem | 1252.1 noun dat sing fem | 4406.1 name masc | 4406.1 name masc |
|---|---|---|---|---|
| τῇ | Ἑβραΐδι | διαλέκτῳ, | Σαοὺλ, | Σαούλ, |
| *tē* | *Hebraidi* | *dialektō* | *Saoul* | *Saoul* |
| in the | Hebrew | language, | Saul, | Saul, |

| 4949.9 intr-pron sing neu | 1466.6 prs-pron acc 1sing | 1371.2 verb 2sing indic pres act | 4497.3 adj sing neu | 4622.3 prs-pron dat 2sing |
|---|---|---|---|---|
| τί | με | διώκεις; | σκληρόν | σοι |
| *ti* | *me* | *diōkeis* | *sklēron* | *soi* |
| why | me | are you persecuting? | hard | for you |

| 4242.1 prep | 2730.2 noun pl neu | 2952.1 verb inf pres act | 15. 1466.1 prs-pron nom 1sing | 1156.2 conj | 1500.3 verb indic aor act |
|---|---|---|---|---|---|
| πρὸς | κέντρα | λακτίζειν. | 15. Ἐγὼ | δὲ | ⸀ εἶπον, |
| *pros* | *kentra* | *laktizein* | *Egō* | *de* | *eipon* |
| against | goads | to kick. | I | and | said, |

15.a.**Txt:** 01ℵ,020L 025P,byz.
**Var:** 02A,03B,04C,08E Lach,Treg,Alf,Tisc We/Ho,Weis,Sod UBS/☆

| 1500.4 verb 1sing indic aor act | 4949.3 intr-pron nom sing | 1498.3 verb 2sing indic pres act | 2935.5 noun voc sing masc | 3450.5 art nom sing masc | 1156.2 conj |
|---|---|---|---|---|---|
| [a☆ εἶπα, ] | Τίς | εἶ | κύριε; | Ὁ | δὲ |
| *eipa* | *Tis* | *ei* | *kurie* | *Ho* | *de* |
| [ idem ] | Who | are you, | Lord? | The | and |

**26:13.** Paul again addressed the king and told him how in the middle of the day while he was going along the road he saw a great light coming out of heaven and shining around him. Although the story of Paul's conversion is recorded three times in the Book of Acts, this is the only place where the time of day is recorded. The brilliance of the light was greater than the brightness of the noonday sun, and it enveloped not only Paul but the whole company of men who were traveling with him.

Paul here was drawing attention to the supernatural character of this light. Paul was out on the open road. This was no illusion, no mirage. No trick could produce a light brighter than the sun at midday. Nor was it a mere lightning flash. The light shone around them for quite some time. The New Testament uses the word only here and in Luke 2:9 where the glory of the Lord shone around the shepherds when the angel appeared to announce the birth of Jesus.

To King Agrippa, who knew the Old Testament, this would speak of a divine manifestation like the glory Moses saw, or like the glory of God that was manifest in the Holy of Holies above the mercy seat from the time the glory first appeared as recorded in Exodus chapter 40 until it departed (see Ezekiel chapters 8–11). This had to be a manifestation sent by God.

**26:14.** The light was so bright that none of them could stand it. Probably in trying to shield themselves they all fell to the ground. It is likely this brilliant light terrified both Paul and his companions. (The word used of its brightness is also used of a joyousness such as the believer feels when God is pouring out spiritual blessing on those who worship Him.) The sense of the supernatural prepared Paul for the voice that spoke to him by name in the Hebrew language, asking him why he kept persecuting Him, and adding that it was hard for him to kick against the goad. The picture is that of an ox who kicks against the goad of a driver and gets a more severe wound. The present active infinitive of the Greek verb also shows Paul was continually kicking against the goad and had been doing so undoubtedly ever since he heard the defense of Stephen.

The goad was a pointed stick used in place of a whip to spur animals on. The same word is used of a sting, and normally the goad would simply prick the hide of the ox and sting a little without really injuring him unless he kicked against it. Its use here meant that it was hard for Paul to keep resisting God. Though he did it in ignorance, all this human effort and fleshly anger he was expending against the Christians was hurting him more than he knew.

**26:15.** Paul's response showed he recognized not only the light but the Person who spoke to him was from heaven. When he called Him Lord and asked Him to identify himself, it is evident he knew the Person had the right to be addressed as Lord.

What the Lord said must have been as surprising to King Agrippa as it was to Saul (Paul) on the Damascus Road: "I am Jesus whom

**13. At midday, O king, I saw in the way:** On this journey, *NAB* . . . on the journey, at noon, O King, I saw, *Weymouth* . . . upon the road, *Fenton* . . . when in the middle of the day, your Majesty, *Williams C.K.*

**a light from heaven, above the brightness of the sun:** . . . a light brighter than the glare of the sun, *TCNT* . . . a light from heaven, more dazzling than the sun, *Moffatt* . . . more brilliant than the sun, *Berkeley, MLNT* . . . eclipsing the splendour of the sun, *Fenton* . . . far brighter than, *Phillips* . . . a light from the sky, brighter than sunshine, *Kleist* . . . shining in the sky, *NAB.*

**shining round about me and them which journeyed with me:** It surrounded me, *NAB* . . . flash round me and my fellow-travellers, *Moffatt* . . . blazing about me and my fellow travelers, *Phillips* . . . and those travelling with me, *Fenton* . . . and the men who were traveling, *Everyday.*

**14. And when we were all fallen to the earth:** We all fell to the ground, *TCNT.*

**I heard a voice speaking unto me:** . . . and then I heard a voice, *TCNT* . . . saying to me, *NAB.*

**and saying in the Hebrew tongue:** . . . asking me in the Jewish language, *Beck* . . . in the Hebrew dialect, *Fenton* . . . the Hebrew language, *MLNT.*

**Saul, Saul, why persecutest thou me?:** Saul! Saul! Why do you continue to persecute me, *Williams* . . . why are you attacking me so cruelly, *BB* . . . why are you doing things against me? *Everyday.*

**it is hard for thee to kick against the pricks:** By kicking against the goads you are punishing yourself, *TCNT* . . . It is hurting you to keep on kicking, *Williams* . . . It hurts you to kick against the goad, *Williams C.K.* . . . It is not easy for you to kick against your own conscience, *Phillips* . . . You cannot kick against, *Goodspeed* . . . to rebel and to resist, *Norlie* . . . You are only hurting yourself by fighting me, *Everyday.*

**15. And I said, Who art thou, Lord?:** But I said, *MLNT* . . . I said, at that, *NAB* . . . Who are you, Sir? *Fenton* . . . I inquired, *Kleist* . . . said I, *Goodspeed.*

## Acts 26:16

15.b.**Var:** 01ℵ,02A,03B 04C,08E,020L,bo.Lach Treg,Alf,Word,Tisc We/Ho,Weis,Sod UBS/☆

| **2935.1** noun nom sing masc | **1500.5** verb 3sing indic aor act | **1466.1** prs-pron nom 1sing | **1498.2** verb 1sing indic pres act | **2400.1** name nom masc |
|---|---|---|---|---|
| [b☆+ κύριος ] | εἶπεν, | Ἐγώ | εἰμι | Ἰησοῦς |
| *kurios* | *eipen* | *Egō* | *eimi* | *Iēsous* |
| [ Lord ] | said, | I | am | Jesus |

| **3614.6** rel-pron acc sing masc | **4622.1** prs-pron nom 2sing | **1371.2** verb 2sing indic pres act | **233.2** conj | **448.8** verb 2sing impr aor act |
|---|---|---|---|---|
| ὃν | σὺ | διώκεις. | **16.** ἀλλὰ | ἀνάστηθι, |
| *hon* | *su* | *diōkeis* | *alla* | *anastēthi* |
| whom | you | are persecuting: | but | rise up, |

| **2504.1** conj | **2449.9** verb 2sing impr aor act | **1894.3** prep | **3450.8** art acc pl masc | **4087.7** noun acc pl masc | **4622.2** prs-pron gen 2sing | **1519.1** prep |
|---|---|---|---|---|---|---|
| καὶ | στῆθι | ἐπὶ | τοὺς | πόδας | σου· | εἰς |
| *kai* | *stēthi* | *epi* | *tous* | *podas* | *sou* | *eis* |
| and | stand | on | the | feet | your; | for |

| **3642.17** dem-pron sing neu | **1056.1** conj | **3571.20** verb 1sing indic aor pass | **4622.3** prs-pron dat 2sing | **4258.2** verb inf aor mid |
|---|---|---|---|---|
| τοῦτο | γὰρ | ὤφθην | σοι, | προχειρίσασθαί |
| *touto* | *gar* | *ōphthēn* | *soi* | *procheirisasthai* |
| this | for | I appeared | to you, | to appoint |

| **4622.4** prs-pron acc 2sing | **5095.2** noun acc sing masc | **2504.1** conj | **3116.3** noun acc sing masc | **3614.1** rel-pron gen pl | **4885.1** conj |
|---|---|---|---|---|---|
| σε | ὑπηρέτην | καὶ | μάρτυρα | ὧν | τε |
| *se* | *hupēretēn* | *kai* | *martura* | *hōn* | *te* |
| you | an attendant | and | a witness | of what | both |

16.a.**Var:** 03B,04C-org 1739,sa.We/Ho,Weis UBS/☆

| **1481.2** verb 2sing indic aor act | **1466.6** prs-pron acc 1sing | **3614.1** rel-pron gen pl | **4885.1** conj | **3571.27** verb 1sing indic fut pass | **4622.3** prs-pron dat 2sing |
|---|---|---|---|---|---|
| εἶδές | [a☆+ με ] | ὧν | τε | ὀφθήσομαί | σοι, |
| *eides* | *me* | *hōn* | *te* | *ophthēsomai* | *soi* |
| you saw | [ me ] | of what | and | I shall appear | to you, |

| **1791.2** verb nom sing masc part pres mid | **4622.4** prs-pron acc 2sing | **1523.2** prep gen | **3450.2** art gen sing | **2967.2** noun gen sing masc |
|---|---|---|---|---|
| **17.** ἐξαιρούμενός | σε | ἐκ | τοῦ | λαοῦ |
| *exairoumenos* | *se* | *ek* | *tou* | *laou* |
| taking out | you | from among | the | people |

17.a.**Var:** 01ℵ,02A,03B 08E,Lach,Treg,Alf,Tisc We/Ho,Weis,Sod UBS/☆

| **2504.1** conj | **1523.2** prep gen | **3450.1** art gen pl | **1477.5** noun gen pl neu | **1519.1** prep | **3614.8** rel-pron acc pl masc | **3431.1** adv |
|---|---|---|---|---|---|---|
| καὶ | [a☆+ ἐκ ] | τῶν | ἐθνῶν, | εἰς | οὓς | ʻ νῦν |
| *kai* | *ek* | *tōn* | *ethnōn* | *eis* | *hous* | *nun* |
| and | [ from ] | the | nations, | to | whom | now |

17.b.**Txt:** Steph
**Var:** 01ℵ,02A,03B,08E Lach,Treg,Alf,Tisc We/Ho,Weis,Sod UBS/☆

| **4622.4** prs-pron acc 2sing | **643.1** verb 1sing indic pres act | **1466.1** prs-pron nom 1sing | **643.1** verb 1sing indic pres act | **4622.4** prs-pron acc 2sing |
|---|---|---|---|---|
| σε | ἀποστέλλω, | [b☆ ἐγὼ | ἀποστέλλω | σε ] |
| *se* | *apostellō* | *egō* | *apostellō* | *se* |
| you | I send, | [ I | send | you ] |

| **453.11** verb inf aor act | **3652.8** noun acc pl masc | **840.1** prs-pron gen pl | **3450.2** art gen sing | **1978.13** verb inf aor act |
|---|---|---|---|---|
| **18.** ἀνοῖξαι | ὀφθαλμοὺς | αὐτῶν, | τοῦ | ἐπιστρέψαι |
| *anoixai* | *ophthalmous* | *autōn* | *tou* | *epistrepsai* |
| to open | eyes | their, | the | to turn |

| **570.3** prep | **4510.3** noun gen sing neu | **1519.1** prep | **5295.1** noun sing neu | **2504.1** conj | **3450.10** art gen sing fem | **1833.1** noun fem |
|---|---|---|---|---|---|---|
| ἀπὸ | σκότους | εἰς | φῶς | καὶ | τῆς | ἐξουσίας |
| *apo* | *skotous* | *eis* | *phōs* | *kai* | *tēs* | *exousias* |
| from | darkness | to | light | and | the | authority |

you keep persecuting." All Paul had done in persecuting the believers both in Jerusalem and in other cities, he had really done to Jesus, for He is the Head of the Church and the believers constitute the Body.

**26:16.** Next Paul described the way Christ commissioned him and what was included in his call in greater detail than he had done in his previous trials. Jesus commanded him to get up off the ground and stand on his feet. Jesus wanted his full attention. He told Paul that He had appeared to him to appoint him for the important task of being a minister (a servant) and a witness both of the things he had seen and of future revelations from Christ.

Paul was first of all to be a minister. The Greek words translated "minister" all mean servant. The word used here means a "helpful assistant." The word was often used of a physician's assistant as well as other types of practical service. Paul was thus called to be a faithful workman for the Lord.

Paul was also called to be a witness, not only of what he had seen, but of what Christ would continue to reveal to him. This visit of Jesus made him a firsthand witness to Christ's resurrection. Later Jesus revealed to him many other details and made him a firsthand witness of the gospel message as well (Galatians 1:12,16).

**26:17.** It is possible the verb used here means to select or choose out for oneself; thus Paul would be saying Jesus chose him out for himself from the people and the nations. But in this context the other meaning of the verb, "save, deliver, rescue," seems to fit better. That is, Jesus promised to save him from the people and from the nations to whom He was sending him.

Agrippa would understand that "the people" meant the Jews, while the nations meant the Gentiles, that is, all the other nations. This was the common way the Jews looked at the rest of the world.

The mention of the Gentiles did not evoke the kind of reaction it had in Jerusalem (22:21,22). Agrippa had associated with Gentiles in Rome and in the kingdom he ruled. So he was accustomed to treating them more graciously than the Jerusalem Jews were.

**26:18.** Jesus had then made it clear to Paul what he was to do when He sent him to the Gentiles. The light of Christ and the truth of the gospel would open their eyes. The power of Christ and the Holy Spirit would turn them from darkness to light and from the power of Satan to God, that they might receive the forgiveness of sins.

With their forgiveness they would receive an inheritance among those who are sanctified (treated as holy, set apart to God as His people to do His will) by faith in Christ.

King Agrippa and the other Jews present would recognize that much of the language Jesus used in giving this commission to Paul

**And he said, I am Jesus whom thou persecutest:** The Lord said...I am the One you are trying to hurt, *Everyday* . . . I am that Jesus, *NAB* . . . the Lord replied, *Kleist* . . . and you are persecuting me, *Williams C.K.*

**16. But rise, and stand upon thy feet:** . . . get up and stand upright, *TCNT* . . . Stand up! *Everyday.*

**for I have appeared unto thee for this purpose:** . . . for I have shown myself to you for a reason, *Phillips* . . . I have chosen you, *Everyday.*

**to make thee a minister and a witness:** . . . to ordain you a minister, *Campbell* . . . to appoint thee, *ASV* . . . to designate you as, *NAB* . . . you are chosen to be my, *Phillips* . . . a servant, *TCNT.*

**both of these things which thou hast seen:** . . . you will tell people, *Everyday* . . . of those revelations of me which you have already had, *TCNT* . . . of what you have seen of me today, *Phillips.*

**and of those things in the which I will appear unto thee:** . . . and also of what I will reveal to you, *Norlie* . . . This is why I have come to you today, *Everyday* . . . what you will see of me, *NAB* . . . and of those in which I will still show Myself to you, *MLNT* . . . and to the visions you shall have of me, *Kleist* . . . and of other visions of myself which I will give you, *Phillips* . . . and to what I will make you see of me, *Williams C.K.*

**17. Delivering thee from the people, and from the Gentiles:** Rescuing thee from, *Rotherham* . . . I will keep you safe, *BB* . . . I will not let your own people hurt you, *Everyday* . . . delivered you from this people, *NAB* . . . both from your own people, *Phillips* . . . and from the heathen, *Williams C.K.*

**unto whom now I send thee:** . . . to whom I am going to send you, *Williams.*

**18. To open their eyes:** I sent you to open their eyes, *Phillips* . . . that their eyes may be opened, *Moffatt* . . . for the opening of their eyes, *MLNT.*

**and to turn them from darkness to light:** . . . that they may turn, *Moffatt* . . . and their turning from, *MLNT.*

## Acts 26:19

| 3450.2 art gen sing | 4423.2 noun sing masc | 1894.3 prep | 3450.6 art acc sing masc | 2296.4 noun acc sing masc | 3450.2 art gen sing | 2956.31 verb inf aor act |
|---|---|---|---|---|---|---|
| τοῦ | Σατανᾶ | ἐπὶ | τὸν | θεόν, | τοῦ | λαβεῖν |
| *tou* | *Satana* | *epi* | *ton* | *theon* | *tou* | *labein* |
| | of Satan | to | | God, | the | to receive |

| 840.8 prs-pron acc pl masc | 852.3 noun acc sing fem | 264.6 noun gen pl fem | 2504.1 conj | 2792.3 noun acc sing masc | 1706.1 prep |
|---|---|---|---|---|---|
| αὐτοὺς | ἄφεσιν | ἁμαρτιῶν | καὶ | κλῆρον | ἐν |
| *autous* | *aphesin* | *hamartiōn* | *kai* | *klēron* | *en* |
| them | forgiveness | of sins | and | inheritance | among |

| 3450.4 art dat pl | 37.18 verb dat pl masc part perf mid | 3963.3 noun dat sing fem | 3450.11 art dat sing fem | 1519.1 prep | 1466.7 prs-pron acc 1sing |
|---|---|---|---|---|---|
| τοῖς | ἡγιασμένοις | πίστει | τῇ | εἰς | ἐμέ. |
| *tois* | *hēgiasmenois* | *pistei* | *tē* | *eis* | *eme* |
| the | having been sanctified | by faith | the | in | me. |

| 3468.1 adv | 928.5 noun voc sing masc | 66.2 name sing masc | 3620.2 partic | 1090.30 verb 1sing indic aor mid |
|---|---|---|---|---|
| **19.** Ὅθεν, | βασιλεῦ | Ἀγρίππα, | οὐκ | ἐγενόμην |
| *Hothen* | *basileu* | *Agrippa* | *ouk* | *egenomēn* |
| Then, | king | Agrippa, | not | I was |

| 541.1 adj nom sing masc | 3450.11 art dat sing fem | 3634.3 adj dat sing fem | 3564.1 noun dat sing fem | 233.2 conj |
|---|---|---|---|---|
| ἀπειθὴς | τῇ | οὐρανίῳ | ὀπτασίᾳ, | **20.** ἀλλὰ |
| *apeithēs* | *tē* | *ouraniō* | *optasia* | *alla* |
| disobedient | to the | heavenly | vision; | but |

20.a.**Var:** 01ℵ,02A,03B Lach,Treg,Alf,Tisc We/Ho,Weis,Sod UBS/☆

| 3450.4 art dat pl | 1706.1 prep | 1149.1 name dat fem | 4270.1 adv | 4885.1 conj | 2504.1 conj |
|---|---|---|---|---|---|
| τοῖς | ἐν | Δαμασκῷ | πρῶτόν | [a☆+ τε ] | καὶ |
| *tois* | *en* | *Damaskō* | *prōton* | *te* | *kai* |
| to the | in | Damascus | first | [and] | and |

20.b.**Txt:** 08E,020L 025P,byz.Weis,Sod **Var:** p74,01ℵ,02A,03B Lach,Treg,Tisc,We/Ho UBS/☆

| 2389.3 name dat pl neu | 1519.1 prep | 3820.12 adj acc sing fem | 4885.1 conj | 3450.12 art acc sing fem | 5396.4 noun acc sing fem |
|---|---|---|---|---|---|
| Ἱεροσολύμοις, | ⸂b εἰς ⸃ | πᾶσάν | τε | τὴν | χώραν |
| *Hierosolumois* | *eis* | *pasan* | *te* | *tēn* | *chōran* |
| Jerusalem, | to | all | and | the | region |

| 3450.10 art gen sing fem | 2424.2 name gen fem | 2504.1 conj | 3450.4 art dat pl | 1477.6 noun dat pl neu | 514.3 verb nom sing masc part pres act |
|---|---|---|---|---|---|
| τῆς | Ἰουδαίας | καὶ | τοῖς | ἔθνεσιν, | ⸀ ἀπαγγέλλων |
| *tēs* | *Ioudaias* | *kai* | *tois* | *ethnesin* | *apangellōn* |
| | of Judea | and | to the | Gentiles | declaring |

20.c.**Txt:** 020L,025P Steph **Var:** 01ℵ,02A,03B,08E Elzev,Gries,Lach,Treg Alf,Word,Tisc,We/Ho Weis,Sod,UBS/☆

| 514.16 verb 1sing indic imperf act | 3210.5 verb inf pres act | 2504.1 conj | 1978.14 verb inf aor act | 1894.3 prep |
|---|---|---|---|---|
| [c☆ ἀπήγγελλον ] | μετανοεῖν | καὶ | ἐπιστρέφειν | ἐπὶ |
| *apēngellon* | *metanoein* | *kai* | *epistrephein* | *epi* |
| [was declaring] | to repent | and | to turn | to |

| 3450.6 art acc sing masc | 2296.4 noun acc sing masc | 510.6 adj pl neu | 3450.10 art gen sing fem | 3211.1 noun gen sing fem | 2024.4 noun pl neu |
|---|---|---|---|---|---|
| τὸν | θεόν, | ἄξια | τῆς | μετανοίας | ἔργα |
| *ton* | *theon* | *axia* | *tēs* | *metanoias* | *erga* |
| | God, | worthy | of the | repentance | works |

21.a.**Txt:** 01ℵ-corr,02A 08E,025P,byz. **Var:** 01ℵ-org,03B,020L Treg,Tisc,We/Ho,Weis Sod,UBS/☆

| 4097.11 verb acc pl masc part pres act | 1736.3 prep | 3642.2 dem-pron gen pl | 1466.6 prs-pron acc 1sing | 3450.7 art nom pl masc |
|---|---|---|---|---|
| πράσσοντας. | **21.** ἕνεκα | τούτων | με | ⸂a οἱ ⸃ |
| *prassontas* | *heneka* | *toutōn* | *me* | *hoi* |
| doing. | On account of | these things | me | the |

was drawn from the Old Testament. The phraseology comes especially from Isaiah 42:6,7 and 61:1,2. These are prophecies of God's ministry through His Suffering Servant, the Messiah, and point specifically to Jesus.

Paul, in his epistles, recognized the reason unbelievers need to have their eyes opened is because "the god of this world (Satan) hath blinded the minds of them which believe not, lest the light of the glorious gospel of Christ, who is the image of God, should shine unto them" (2 Corinthians 4:4).

**26:19.** Paul again addressed Agrippa. He declared he was not disobedient to the heavenly vision. The word "vision" here does not mean a dream-type vision but an actual appearance where Jesus spoke to him. This was as real as the appearances of Jesus to the apostles and disciples before His ascension. It made the apostle Paul a firsthand witness to the resurrection of Jesus, and the commission of Jesus made him an apostle, one personally sent out by Jesus himself with the same power and authority He had given to the other apostles.

**26:20.** Paul did not use this declaration of obedience to honor himself. Rather, he used it as a further opportunity to clarify the meaning of the gospel and to show what it means to accept Christ as Lord and Saviour.

He declared that his obedience was shown in the way he proclaimed the gospel to the Jews at Damascus, Jerusalem, and all Judea, and also to the Gentiles, that they should repent, turn to God, and then do works worthy of repentance.

"To repent" means to change the mind, not in a superficial way but a deep change that affects one's fundamental attitudes. Christians once loved darkness, now they love the light of the gospel, the light of Christ (John 3:19). They once loved the world and the things in the world, now their love is given to the Lord and to His people as they reach out in love to the lost (1 John 2:15). They were careless about sin before, but now they realize that all sin is against God and they seek first His kingdom (rule) and His righteousness (Matthew 6:33).

Christians must also turn to God. If they truly repent, they will commit their lives to God and cultivate a trusting relationship with Him. Their repentance, if it is genuine, will be shown by works or deeds worthy of repentance. The Greek verb here also indicates this must be ongoing. Believers must keep on doing works or deeds worthy of the changed minds and attitudes they profess.

**26:21.** Paul then declared it was because of this message, which included blessings for the Gentiles, that the Jews seized him in the temple and attempted to kill him.

**and from the power of Satan unto God:** . . . authority of, *Rotherham* . . . dominion of, *HBIE* . . . the devil's control, *Beck* . . . of the Adversary, *Young* . . . to God himself, *Phillips.*

**that they may receive forgiveness of sins:** . . . so that they may know, *Phillips* . . . remission of sins, *ASV* . . . pardon for their sins, *TCNT* . . . release from sins, *Fenton.*

**and inheritance among them which are sanctified by faith that is in me:** . . . and have a possession among, *Williams* . . . and take their place with all those who are made holy, *Phillips* . . . and get a share of what the people enjoy who are made holy, *Beck* . . . by faith in me, *Darby.*

**19. Whereupon, O king Agrippa:** After that, King Agrippa, *TCNT.*

**I was not disobedient unto the heavenly vision:** I could not disobey, *Williams* . . . I did not go against the vision from heaven, *BB* . . . not apathetic, *Fenton.*

**20. But shewed first unto them of Damascus:** . . . but I proceeded to preach first to the people in Damascus, *Weymouth* . . . but first I told, *Beck.*

**and at Jerusalem, and throughout all the coasts of Judaea:** . . . and Jerusalem, and then through the whole of Judaea, *TCNT.*

**and then to the Gentiles:** . . . and to the Gentiles as well, *TCNT* . . . and I preached even to the Gentiles, *Norlie.*

**that they should repent and turn to God:** . . . to turn from sin to God, *Beck.*

**and do works meet for repentance:** . . . and a life befitting that repentance, *TCNT* . . . and live lives consistent with such repentance, *Weymouth* . . . and live lives to prove their change of heart, *Phillips* . . . live lives consistent, *Norlie* . . . to do things to show that they really had changed, *Everyday.*

**21. for these causes the Jews caught me in the temple:** That is why, *TCNT* . . . It was on this account that, *Weymouth* . . . For these very things the Jews arrested me, *Williams* . . . On account of these facts the Jews

# Acts 26:22

21.b.**Txt:** 02A,03B,048 byz.
**Var:** p74,01ℵ,08E,044 33,81,945,1739,2495

| **2428.2** name-adj nom pl masc | **4666.10** verb nom pl masc part aor mid | **1498.18** verb part pres act | **1706.1** prep | **3450.3** art dat sing |
|---|---|---|---|---|
| Ἰουδαῖοι | συλλαβόμενοι | [b☆+ ὄντα ] | ἐν | τῷ |
| *Ioudaioi* | *sullabomenoi* | *onta* | *en* | *tō* |
| Jews | having seized | [ being ] | in | the |

| **2387.2** adj dat sing neu | **3849.2** verb 3pl indic imperf mid | **1309.2** verb inf aor mid | **1932.1** noun gen sing fem |
|---|---|---|---|
| ἱερῷ, | ἐπειρῶντο | διαχειρίσασθαι. | **22.** ἐπικουρίας |
| *hierō* | *epeirōnto* | *diacheirisasthai* | *epikourias* |
| temple, | were attempting | to kill. | Aid |

22.a.**Txt:** 020L,025P,byz.
**Var:** 01ℵ,02A,03B,08E Lach,Treg,Alf,Word Tisc,We/Ho,Weis,Sod UBS/☆

| **3631.1** partic | **5018.5** verb nom sing masc part aor act | **3450.10** art gen sing fem | **3706.2** prep | **570.3** prep | **3450.2** art gen sing |
|---|---|---|---|---|---|
| οὖν | τυχὼν | τῆς | ʼ παρὰ | [a☆ ἀπὸ ] | τοῦ |
| *oun* | *tuchōn* | *tēs* | *para* | *apo* | *tou* |
| therefore | having obtained | the | from | [ idem ] | |

| **2296.2** noun gen sing masc | **884.2** conj | **3450.10** art gen sing fem | **2232.1** noun fem | **3642.10** dem-pron gen sing fem | **2449.16** verb 1sing indic perf act |
|---|---|---|---|---|---|
| θεοῦ | ἄχρι | τῆς | ἡμέρας | ταύτης | ἕστηκα, |
| *theou* | *achri* | *tēs* | *hēmeras* | *tautēs* | *hestēka* |
| God | unto | the | day | this | I have stood, |

22.b.**Txt:** 08E,byz.
**Var:** 01ℵ,02A,03B,020L 025P,Lach,Treg,Alf Word,Tisc,We/Ho,Weis Sod,UBS/☆

| **3113.32** verb nom sing masc part pres mid | **3113.42** verb nom sing masc part pres mid | **3262.5** adj dat sing masc | **4885.1** conj | **2504.1** conj |
|---|---|---|---|---|
| ʼ μαρτυρούμενος | [b☆ μαρτυρόμενος ] | μικρῷ | τε | καὶ |
| *marturoumenos* | *marturomenos* | *mikrō* | *te* | *kai* |
| bearing witness | [ idem ] | to small | both | and |

| **3144.1** adj dat sing | **3625.6** num card neu | **1609.1** adv | **2978.15** verb nom sing masc part pres act | **3614.1** rel-pron gen pl | **4885.1** conj |
|---|---|---|---|---|---|
| μεγάλῳ, | οὐδὲν | ἐκτὸς | λέγων | ὧν | τε |
| *megalō* | *ouden* | *ektos* | *legōn* | *hōn* | *te* |
| to great, | nothing | else | saying | than what | both |

| **3450.7** art nom pl masc | **4254.4** noun nom pl masc | **2953.30** verb 3pl indic aor act | **3165.11** verb gen pl part pres act | **1090.28** verb inf pres mid | **2504.1** conj |
|---|---|---|---|---|---|
| οἱ | προφῆται | ἐλάλησαν | μελλόντων | γίνεσθαι | καὶ |
| *hoi* | *prophētai* | *elalēsan* | *mellontōn* | *ginesthai* | *kai* |
| the | prophets | said | being about | to happen | and |

| **3337.1** name nom masc | **3338.1** name nom masc | **1479.1** conj | **3668.1** adj nom sing masc | **3450.5** art nom sing masc |
|---|---|---|---|---|
| ʼ Μωσῆς, | [☆ Μωϋσῆς, ] | **23.** εἰ | παθητὸς | ὁ |
| *Mōsēs* | *Mōusēs* | *ei* | *pathētos* | *ho* |
| Moses, | [ idem ] | whether | suffering | |

| **5382.1** name nom masc | **1479.1** conj | **4272.5** num ord nom sing masc | **1523.1** prep gen | **384.2** noun gen sing fem | **3361.2** adj gen pl |
|---|---|---|---|---|---|
| Χριστός, | εἰ | πρῶτος | ἐξ | ἀναστάσεως | νεκρῶν |
| *Christos* | *ei* | *prōtos* | *ex* | *anastaseōs* | *nekrōn* |
| Christ; | whether | first | from | resurrection | of dead |

23.a.**Var:** 01ℵ,02A,03B 08E,Lach,Treg,Alf,Tisc We/Ho,Weis,Sod UBS/☆

| **5295.1** noun sing neu | **3165.3** verb 3sing indic pres act | **2576.6** verb inf pres act | **3450.3** art dat sing | **4885.1** conj |
|---|---|---|---|---|
| φῶς | μέλλει | καταγγέλλειν | τῷ | [a☆+ τε ] |
| *phōs* | *mellei* | *katangellein* | *tō* | *te* |
| light | is about | to announce | to the | [ both ] |

| **2967.3** noun dat sing masc | **2504.1** conj | **3450.4** art dat pl | **1477.6** noun dat pl neu | **3642.18** dem-pron pl neu | **1156.2** conj | **840.3** prs-pron gen sing |
|---|---|---|---|---|---|---|
| λαῷ | καὶ | τοῖς | ἔθνεσιν. | **24.** Ταῦτα | δὲ | αὐτοῦ |
| *laō* | *kai* | *tois* | *ethnesin* | *Tauta* | *de* | *autou* |
| people | and | to the | nations. | These things | and | his |

Paul's words emphasized this was a violent arrest and that the Jews in the temple were really trying to murder him. He wanted Agrippa to know the Jewish leaders were not orderly, nor were the Jews giving him a fair trial as they claimed they were.

**26:22.** God's help was indeed with Paul in all that followed. At every step along the way, Paul was able to witness (give testimony to Christ) to both small and great, that is, to those of little importance in the eyes of the world as well as to those who had great position and power. In this way he had continued (stood firm) to that very day. His witnessing was now being directed to the great ones present at this hearing, especially to King Agrippa.

Paul's witness was not limited to his own experience, however. Again he emphasized that everything he said was only what the prophets and Moses had already said would come. His total message was based on the Old Testament Scriptures. He consistently proclaimed the gospel out of the Old Testament. He was faithful to the same Scriptures the Jews who tried to kill him professed to believe.

Paul encouraged others to be faithful to the same Word of God. He had the Old Testament Scriptures in mind when he told Timothy to "Study (be eager, be zealous, make every effort, do your utmost) to show thyself approved unto God, a workman that needeth not to be ashamed, rightly dividing (cutting a straight path for and refusing to be turned aside from) the word of truth" (2 Timothy 2:15).

**26:23.** Paul showed how the Scriptures declared Christ (the Messiah, God's anointed Prophet, Priest, and King) must suffer. They also showed how He, as the first to be resurrected from the dead, would proclaim light to the people (the Jews) and to the Gentiles (the nations).

With this Paul came back to the heart of the gospel: the resurrection of Jesus is the guarantee that God will raise believers from the dead.

In 1 Corinthians 15:20 Paul called Jesus the firstfruits. That is, he pictured the resurrection of the just, which Jesus called the resurrection to life (John 5:29) and John called the first resurrection (Revelation 20:5), as a harvest. The believers' resurrection, which comes at the time when the dead in Christ will rise first (1 Thessalonians 4:16,17), is part of the same harvest, that is, it is part of the same resurrection. This only recognizes the scriptural order: "Christ the firstfruits; afterward they that are Christ's at his coming." Revelation 20:4 adds the further truth that the tribulation martyrs are also part of the same resurrection. They could be thought of as gleanings after the main part of the harvest, and therefore the final part of that harvest. The rest of the dead do not live again (are not resurrected) until after the Millennium (Revelation 20:5,11,15). This message is part of the light of Christ for Jews and Gentiles alike.

grabbed me, *Berkeley*... the Jews seized me in the Temple, *Phillips*.

**and went about to kill me:** ... and kept on trying, *Williams* ... and made attempts upon my life, *TCNT*.

**22. Having therefore obtained help of God:** To this day I have received help from God himself, *Phillips*... And so, by God's help, *BB* ... But God helped me, *Everyday*.

**I continue unto this day:**... to this very day and so stand here, *TCNT*... I have stood firm until now, *Weymouth* ... and is still helping me today, *Everyday*.

**witnessing both to small and great:** ... and have solemnly exhorted, *Weymouth* ... and bear my testimony to high and low alike, *TCNT*... telling all people what I have seen, *Everyday*.

**saying none other things than those which the prophets and Moses did say should come:** ... saying nothing beyond, *Williams C.K.* ... claiming nothing else than, *Norlie*... without adding a word to what the Prophets, as well as Moses, declared should happen, *TCNT*... But I am saying nothing new...what Moses and the prophets said would happen, *Everyday* ... adding nothing to what the prophets and Moses foretold should take place, *Phillips*... never uttering a single syllable beyond, *Moffatt*.

**23. That Christ should suffer:** ... how that the Christ was to be a suffering Christ, *Weymouth* ... the Suffering Messiah, *Fenton* ... would be a sufferer, *Wilson* ... would die, *Everyday*.

**and that he should be the first that should rise from the dead:** ... and being the first to rise from the dead, *Weymouth* ... from death, *Everyday*.

**and should shew light unto the people, and to the Gentiles:**... he would declare the word of light, *Williams C.K.*... he was destined to be the first to bring news of light, *TCNT* ... he was to proclaim a message of light both to the Jewish people and to the Gentiles, *Weymouth* ... would communicate Light, *Wilson* ... would bring light to the Jewish and non-Jewish people, *Everyday* ... and so proclaim the message of light both to our people, *Phillips*.

# Acts 26:25

| 620.3 verb gen sing masc part pres mid | 3450.5 art nom sing masc | 5184.1 name nom masc | 3144.11 adj dat sing fem | 3450.11 art dat sing fem |
|---|---|---|---|---|
| ἀπολογουμένου, | ὁ | Φῆστος | μεγάλῃ | τῇ |
| *apologoumenou* | *ho* | *Phēstos* | *megalē* | *tē* |
| uttering in defense, | | Festus | with loud | the |

24.a.**Txt:** 020L,025P,byz.
**Var:** 01ℵ,02A,03B,08E
Lach,Treg,Alf,Tisc
We/Ho,Weis,Sod
UBS/⋆

| 5292.3 noun dat sing fem | 5183.4 verb 3sing indic act | 5183.2 verb 3sing indic pres act | 3077.2 verb 2sing indic pres mid | 3834.5 name voc masc | 3450.17 art pl neu |
|---|---|---|---|---|---|
| φωνῇ | ˊ ἔφη, | [a⋆ φησιν, ] | Μαίνῃ | Παῦλε· | τὰ |
| *phōnē* | *ephē* | *phēsin* | *Mainē* | *Paule* | *ta* |
| voice | said, | [ says, ] | You are mad, | Paul; | the |

| 4044.17 adj pl neu | 4622.4 prs-pron acc 2sing | 1115.4 noun pl neu | 1519.1 prep | 3102.1 noun acc sing fem | 3922.1 verb 3sing indic pres act |
|---|---|---|---|---|---|
| πολλά | σε | γράμματα | εἰς | μανίαν | περιτρέπει. |
| *polla* | *se* | *grammata* | *eis* | *manian* | *peritrepei* |
| much | you | learning | to | madness | is turning. |

25.a.**Var:** 01ℵ,02A,03B
08E,bo.Lach,Treg,Word
Tisc,We/Ho,Weis,Sod
UBS/⋆

| 3450.5 art nom sing masc | 1156.2 conj | 3834.1 name nom masc | 3620.3 partic | 3077.1 verb 1sing indic pres mid |
|---|---|---|---|---|
| 25. Ὁ | δὲ, | [a⋆+ Παῦλος, ] | Οὐ | μαίνομαι, |
| *Ho* | *de* | *Paulos* | *Ou* | *mainomai* |
| | But, | [ Paul, ] | not | I am mad, |

| 5183.2 verb 3sing indic pres act | 2876.2 adj sup voc sing masc | 5184.5 name voc masc | 233.1 conj | 233.2 conj |
|---|---|---|---|---|
| φησίν, | κράτιστε | Φῆστε, | ˊ ἀλλ᾽ | [⋆ ἀλλὰ ] |
| *phēsin* | *kratiste* | *Phēste* | *all'* | *alla* |
| says, | most noble | Festus, | but | [ idem ] |

| 223.2 noun gen sing fem | 2504.1 conj | 4849.1 noun gen sing fem | 4343.4 noun pl neu | 663.1 verb 1sing indic pres mid |
|---|---|---|---|---|
| ἀληθείας | καὶ | σωφροσύνης | ῥήματα | ἀποφθέγγομαι· |
| *alētheias* | *kai* | *sōphrosunēs* | *rhēmata* | *apophthengomai* |
| of truth | and | sound mind | words | I utter; |

| 1971.2 verb 3sing indic pres mid | 1056.1 conj | 3875.1 prep | 3642.2 dem-pron gen pl | 3450.5 art nom sing masc |
|---|---|---|---|---|
| 26. ἐπίσταται | γὰρ | περὶ | τούτων | ὁ |
| *epistatai* | *gar* | *peri* | *toutōn* | *ho* |
| is informing | for | concerning | these things | the |

| 928.1 noun nom sing masc | 4242.1 prep | 3614.6 rel-pron acc sing masc | 2504.1 conj | 3817.1 verb nom sing masc part pres mid |
|---|---|---|---|---|
| βασιλεύς, | πρὸς | ὃν | καὶ | παῤῥησιαζόμενος |
| *basileus* | *pros* | *hon* | *kai* | *parrhēsiazomenos* |
| king | to | whom | also | speaking confidently |

26.a.**Txt:** p74,01ℵ,02A
08E,020L,025P,etc.byz.
Tisc,Sod
**Var:** 03B,We/Ho,Weis
UBS/⋆

| 2953.1 verb 1sing pres act | 2963.3 verb inf pres act | 1056.1 conj | 840.6 prs-pron acc sing masc | 4948.10 indef-pron sing neu |
|---|---|---|---|---|
| λαλῶ· | λανθάνειν | γὰρ | αὐτὸν | ˊa τι ˋ |
| *lalō* | *lanthanein* | *gar* | *auton* | *ti* |
| I am speaking. | To be hidden from | for | him | any |

26.b.**Txt:** 020L,025P,byz.
**Var:** 01ℵ,03B,Treg,Alf
Tisc,We/Ho,Weis,Sod
UBS/⋆

| 3642.2 dem-pron gen pl | 3620.3 partic | 3844.20 verb 1sing indic pres mid | 3625.6 num card neu | 3628.1 num card neu |
|---|---|---|---|---|
| τούτων | οὐ | πείθομαι | ˊ οὐδέν· | [b⋆ οὐθέν, ] |
| *toutōn* | *ou* | *peithomai* | *ouden* | *outhen* |
| of these things | not | I am persuaded; | nothing | [ idem ] |

| 3620.3 partic | 1056.1 conj | 1498.4 verb 3sing indic pres act | 1706.1 prep | 1131.2 noun dat sing fem | 4097.26 verb sing neu part perf mid |
|---|---|---|---|---|---|
| οὐ | γάρ | ἐστιν | ἐν | γωνίᾳ | πεπραγμένον |
| *ou* | *gar* | *estin* | *en* | *gōnia* | *pepragmenon* |
| not | for | it is | in | a corner | having been done |

**26:24.** This was powerful preaching. Festus felt its conviction and reacted against it by interrupting Paul. Shouting out loudly, he said, "You are raving mad, Paul. Your much learning is turning you into a raving madman." By "much learning" he meant "many writings." He was referring to the Old Testament Scriptures about which Paul had been speaking. He meant it was Paul's (and the Jews') Bible that was turning Paul into a raving maniac right before his eyes.

For the first time Festus was experiencing what the energizing and anointing of the Holy Spirit can do, and he did not understand it. It astonished him. It also made him uncomfortable.

Many of the Romans and Greeks followed philosophies which taught them to have a contempt for the body. This made the very idea of the resurrection of the body abhorrent to them. None of their mythologies or philosophies had any place for bodily resurrection.

**26:25.** Paul replied in a very courteous manner: "I do not speak as a madman, most excellent Festus, but I utter forth (anointed by the Holy Spirit) words (Greek, *rhēmata*, the plural of *rhēma*) of truth and sound good sense" (literal). "Speak (utter) forth" is a form of the same Greek word used in 2:4 where the 120 spoke in other tongues as the Spirit gave "utterance", and which is used also in 2:14 where Peter proclaimed (uttered forth) a message that was the expression of a prophetic gift given by the Holy Spirit. The word used here shows that Paul, in expressing these ideas, was speaking directly under the inspiration of the Holy Spirit. The prophetic anointing which was on the words of Paul demanded a response of faith, rather than the reaction given by Festus.

**26:26.** The fact that Paul's words were sound good sense, not mad ravings, was something others could verify. King Agrippa knew of these things. He could verify them if he wished to do so.

With this Paul turned his attention again to the king. Paul could speak boldly (and freely) to him, for he was persuaded that none of these things were hidden to him (or had escaped his notice), for this (the facts of Christ's death and resurrection, the events of the gospel) had not been done in a corner. They were done publicly and were well known.

The origin of many cults and heathen religions is shrouded in the mists of fancy and legend, but not the origin of Christianity. Eyewitnesses accurately recorded its beginnings.

Even the Pharisees recognized the tremendous effect of the teaching, ministry, and miracles of Jesus for they said, "Behold (look!), the world is gone after him" (John 12:19). The preaching of the gospel also had a tremendous effect, so much so that the unbelieving Jews and their conspirators accused Paul and Silas of turning the inhabited world upside down (17:6). Truly, these things were "not done in a corner." King Agrippa could not help but know of them.

**24. And as he thus spake for himself:** As he was defending himself in this way, *Beck* . . . And when he made his answer in these words, *BB* . . . At this point in Paul's defence, *Williams C.K.*

**Festus said with a loud voice:** Festus exclaimed in a loud voice, *Weymouth* . . . Festus burst out, *Phillips.*

**Paul, thou art beside thyself:** Paul, you are raving mad, *Montgomery* . . . Paul, you are out of your mind, *BB* . . . Paul, you are insane! *Norlie* . . . You're crazy, Paul! *Beck* . . . You are going crazy, Paul! *Williams* . . . you are distracted, *Campbell.*

**much learning doth make thee mad:** Much scripture, *Concordant* . . . That great learning, *Williams* . . . Your great study, *Klingensmith* . . . is turning your brain, *Weymouth* . . . has made you unbalanced, *BB* . . . All this learning is driving you mad, *Williams C.K.* . . . your excessive study has turned you to frenzy, *Berkeley.*

**25. But he said, I am not mad, most noble Festus:** No, your Excellency, *Williams C.K.* . . . I am not out of my mind, *Berkeley.*

**but speak forth the words of truth and soberness:** . . . on the contrary, the statements that I am making are true and sober, *TCNT* . . . I am speaking words of sober truth, *Weymouth* . . . the straight truth, *Williams* . . . of truth and rectitude, *Murdock* . . . speaking the truth in all soberness, *Williams C.K.*

**26. For the king knoweth of these things:** Why, the king is well aware of this! *Moffatt* . . . The King understands these things, *Williams C.K.*

**before whom also I speak freely:** To the king I can speak without the slightest hesitation, *Moffatt* . . . speak boldly, *Alford.*

**for I am persuaded:** I am sure, *TCNT* . . . I do not believe, *Weymouth.*

**that none of these things are hidden from him:** . . . that any detail of them has escaped his notice, *Weymouth* . . . none of these things escaped him, *Confraternity* . . . that he has failed to notice any of them, *Williams C.K.*

**for this thing was not done in a corner:** . . . some obscure corner, *Norlie.*

| 3642.17 dem-pron sing neu | 3961.5 verb 2sing indic pres act | 928.5 noun voc sing masc | 66.2 name sing masc | 3450.4 art dat pl |
|---|---|---|---|---|
| τοῦτο. | 27. πιστεύεις | βασιλεῦ | Ἀγρίππα | τοῖς |
| *touto* | *pisteueis* | *basileu* | *Agrippa* | *tois* |
| this. | Do you believe, | king | Agrippa, | the |

| 4254.6 noun dat pl masc | 3471.2 verb 1sing indic perf act | 3617.1 conj | 3961.5 verb 2sing indic pres act | 3450.5 art nom sing masc | 1156.2 conj |
|---|---|---|---|---|---|
| προφήταις; | οἶδα | ὅτι | πιστεύεις. | 28. ῾Ο | δὲ |
| *prophētais* | *oida* | *hoti* | *pisteueis* | *Ho* | *de* |
| prophets? | I know | that | you believe. | | And |

28.a.**Txt:** 08E,020L 025P,byz.bo.
**Var:** 01ℵ,02A,03B,Lach Treg,Alf,Word,Tisc We/Ho,Weis,Sod UBS/☆

| 66.1 name nom sing masc | 4242.1 prep | 3450.6 art acc sing masc | 3834.4 name acc masc | 5183.4 verb 3sing indic act | 1706.1 prep |
|---|---|---|---|---|---|
| Ἀγρίππας | πρὸς | τὸν | Παῦλον | ⸂a ἔφη, ⸃ | Ἐν |
| *Agrippas* | *pros* | *ton* | *Paulon* | *ephē* | *En* |
| Agrippa | to | | Paul | said, | In |

28.b.**Txt:** 08E,020L 025P,044,byz.it.
**Var:** p74,01ℵ,02A,03B 33,sa.bo.Lach,Treg,Alf Tisc,We/Ho,Weis,Sod UBS/☆

| 3504.2 adj dat sing | 1466.6 prs-pron acc 1sing | 3844.2 verb 2sing indic pres act | 5381.2 name acc sing masc | 1090.63 verb inf aor mid |
|---|---|---|---|---|
| ὀλίγῳ | με | πείθεις | Χριστιανὸν | ⸀ γενέσθαι. |
| *oligō* | *me* | *peitheis* | *Christianon* | *genesthai* |
| a little | me | you persuade | a Christian | to become. |

29.a.**Txt:** 020L,byz.bo.
**Var:** 01ℵ,02A,03B,Lach Treg,Alf,Tisc,We/Ho Weis,Sod,UBS/☆

| 4020.41 verb inf aor act | 3450.5 art nom sing masc | 1156.2 conj | 3834.1 name nom masc | 1500.5 verb 3sing indic aor act |
|---|---|---|---|---|
| [b☆ ποιῆσαι. ] | 29. ῾Ο | δὲ | Παῦλος | ⸂a εἶπεν, ⸃ |
| *poiēsai* | *Ho* | *de* | *Paulos* | *eipen* |
| [ to make. ] | | And | Paul | said, |

| 2153.4 verb 1sing opt aor mid | 300.1 partic | 3450.3 art dat sing | 2296.3 noun dat sing masc | 2504.1 conj | 1706.1 prep | 3504.2 adj dat sing | 2504.1 conj |
|---|---|---|---|---|---|---|---|
| Εὐξαίμην | ἂν | τῷ | θεῷ, | καὶ | ἐν | ὀλίγῳ | καὶ |
| *Euxaimēn* | *an* | *tō* | *theō* | *kai* | *en* | *oligō* | *kai* |
| I would wish | | | to God, | both | in | a little | and |

29.b.**Txt:** 020L,025P,byz.
**Var:** 01ℵ,02A,03B,Lach Treg,Alf,Tisc,We/Ho Weis,Sod,UBS/☆

| 1706.1 prep | 4044.3 adj dat sing | 3144.1 adj dat sing | 3620.3 partic | 3303.1 adv | 4622.4 prs-pron acc 2sing | 233.2 conj |
|---|---|---|---|---|---|---|
| ἐν | ⸀ πολλῷ | [b☆ μεγάλῳ ] | οὐ | μόνον | σὲ | ἀλλὰ |
| *en* | *pollō* | *megalō* | *ou* | *monon* | *se* | *alla* |
| in | much | [ great ] | not | only | you | but |

| 2504.1 conj | 3820.8 adj acc pl masc | 3450.8 art acc pl masc | 189.16 verb acc pl masc part pres act | 1466.2 prs-pron gen 1sing | 4449.1 adv |
|---|---|---|---|---|---|
| καὶ | πάντας | τοὺς | ἀκούοντάς | μου | σήμερον |
| *kai* | *pantas* | *tous* | *akouontas* | *mou* | *sēmeron* |
| also | all | the | hearing | me | this day |

29.c.**Txt:** 010F,020L 025P,byz.Tisc,Sod
**Var:** 03B,044,We/Ho Weis,UBS/☆

| 1090.63 verb inf aor mid | 4955.8 dem-pron acc pl masc | 3560.1 intr-pron nom sing masc | 2476.3 prs-pron nom | 2504.1 conj |
|---|---|---|---|---|
| γενέσθαι | τοιούτους | ὁποῖος | ⸀ κἀγώ | [c☆ καὶ |
| *genesthai* | *toioutous* | *hopoios* | *kagō* | *kai* |
| to become | such | as | I also | [ also |

| 1466.1 prs-pron nom 1sing | 1498.2 verb 1sing indic pres act | 3786.1 prep | 3450.1 art gen pl | 1193.4 noun gen pl | 3642.2 dem-pron gen pl |
|---|---|---|---|---|---|
| ἐγώ ] | εἰμι, | παρεκτὸς | τῶν | δεσμῶν | τούτων. |
| *egō* | *eimi* | *parektos* | *tōn* | *desmōn* | *toutōn* |
| I ] | am, | except | of the | bonds | these. |

30.a.**Txt:** 020L,025P,byz.
**Var:** 01ℵ,02A,03B,bo. Gries,Lach,Treg,Alf Word,Tisc,We/Ho,Weis Sod,UBS/☆

| 2504.1 conj | 3642.18 dem-pron pl neu | 1500.16 verb gen sing masc part aor act | 840.3 prs-pron gen sing | 448.2 verb 3sing indic aor act |
|---|---|---|---|---|
| 30. ⸂a Καὶ | ταῦτα | εἰπόντος | αὐτοῦ, ⸃ | ἀνέστη |
| *Kai* | *tauta* | *eipontos* | *autou* | *anestē* |
| And | these things | having said | him, | rose up |

**26:27.** Then Paul addressed Agrippa in a very pointed manner, asking him if he believed the prophets. Without waiting for an answer, he added that he knew the king believed.

As a Jew, under other circumstances King Agrippa would not have hesitated to say he believed the prophets. That is, he recognized the prophetic books of the Old Testament as part of the Jewish sacred books. But he might have hesitated at this time. To admit that he believed the prophets would mean, in this context, he approved Paul's message and believed the gospel. Paul did not give him a chance to hesitate.

**26:28.** Suddenly, and with surprise, Agrippa realized Paul was trying to convert him. It overwhelmed him that Paul would be trying to get him to make a commitment to the truth of Christ and to all Paul was saying about Jesus and the resurrection.

Agrippa's reply has been translated and interpreted in a number of ways by Bible-believing scholars. Some ancient manuscripts read literally, "In (by) a little, you seek to persuade me to be a Christian." Some take this to be an admission that King Agrippa was almost persuaded to be a Christian.

Other ancient Greek manuscripts read, "In (by) a little, you seek to persuade me to act a Christian," that is, act the part of a Christian. Many Bible scholars take this as a rejection, that he did not want Paul to use him to corroborate the gospel.

"In (by) a little" could also mean "in brief" or "in a few words." Or it may mean "in a very short time." Thus some Bible scholars say Agrippa meant "in brief, you are seeking to persuade me to become a Christian," and they interpret this simply as an expression of surprise. Others interpret the reply as irony: "In so short a time do you really think you can persuade me to become a Christian (act, live like a Christian)?" Still others take Agrippa's words to be a sharp rejection: "In brief, you are trying to persuade me to act (play the part of) a Christian." Whatever the translation, it is clear Agrippa was rejecting Paul's efforts to convert him and was closing his heart and mind to the conviction of the Holy Spirit.

**26:29.** Paul, however, refused to be discouraged. He replied, "I pray to God that both in brief or at length (or in a great degree), not only you, but all who are listening to me today might become such as I am (that is, a Christian like me), except for these chains" (literal). It is possible that at this point Paul held up his hands to show the chains on his wrists.

**26:30.** Paul's courtesy and dignity in his reply still did not convince Agrippa. But he realized that when Paul said that whether in brief or in great measure (or, in a short or a long time, easily

**27. King Agrippa, believest thou the prophets?:** . . . do you believe the Prophets, *Weymouth* . . . Hast thou faith, *Rotherham.*

**I know that thou believest:** I know you do, *TCNT* . . . I am sure you believe, *Williams C.K.* . . . know you believe that, *Fenton.*

**28. Then Agrippa said unto Paul:** . . . answered, *Weymouth* . . . But Agrippa turned to Paul, *Berkeley* . . . returned Agrippa, *Phillips.*

**Almost thou persuadest me to be a Christian:** You are with a little effort convincing enough to make me a Christian, *Berkeley* . . . Much more of this...and you will be making me a Christian, *Phillips* . . . In brief, you are confident that you can make me a Christian, *Weymouth* . . . you are trying to persuade me and make a Christian of me! *Williams* . . . In short, you are doing your best to persuade me to become a Christian, *Montgomery* . . . you are persuading me, *Klingensmith* . . . Much more of this, Paul...and you will be making me a Christian! *Phillips* . . . You are not taking long to persuade me to become a Christian, *Williams C.K.* . . . almost persuade me to be made, *Fenton.*

**29. And Paul said, I would to God, that not only thou:** Paul replied, *Fenton* . . . I could pray God, *HBIE* . . . Long or not, I wish to God, *Williams C.K.* . . . whether in brief or at length, *Weymouth* . . . whether it means 'much more' or 'only a little,' *Phillips.*

**but also all that hear me this day, were both almost, and altogether:** . . . all who listen to me...might become in every respect, *Fenton.*

**such as I am, except these bonds:** . . . just what I am myself—except for these chains, *TCNT* . . . might stand where I stand—but without these chains, *Phillips* . . . in my condition—not including these shackles, *Berkeley* . . . except for these handcuffs, *Williams C.K.*

**30. And when he had thus spoken, the king rose up, and the governor, and Bernice:** Then the

30.b.**Var:** 01ℵ,02A,03B Gries,Lach,Treg,Alf Word,Tisc,We/Ho,Word UBS/⋆,Sod,UBS/⋆

| **4885.1** conj | **3450.5** art nom sing masc | **928.1** noun nom sing masc | **2504.1** conj | **3450.5** art nom sing masc | **2215.1** noun nom sing masc |
|---|---|---|---|---|---|
| [b☆+ τε ] | ὁ | βασιλεὺς | καὶ | ὁ | ἡγεμὼν |
| *te* | *ho* | *basileus* | *kai* | *ho* | *hēgemōn* |
| [ both ] | the | king | and | the | governor |

| **3614.9** rel-pron nom sing fem | **4885.1** conj | **952.1** name nom fem | **2504.1** conj | **3450.7** art nom pl masc | **4626.2** verb nom pl masc part pres mid |
|---|---|---|---|---|---|
| ἥ | τε | Βερνίκη | καὶ | οἱ | συγκαθήμενοι |
| *hē* | *te* | *Bernikē* | *kai* | *hoi* | *sunkathēmenoi* |
| | also | Bernice | and | the | sitting with |

| **840.2** prs-pron dat pl | **2504.1** conj | **400.5** verb nom pl masc part aor act | **2953.44** verb indic imperf act | **4242.1** prep |
|---|---|---|---|---|
| αὐτοῖς· | 31. καὶ | ἀναχωρήσαντες | ἐλάλουν | πρὸς |
| *autois* | *kai* | *anachōrēsantes* | *elaloun* | *pros* |
| them, | and | having withdrawn | they were speaking | to |

| **238.3** prs-pron acc pl masc | **2978.16** verb nom pl masc part pres act | **3617.1** conj | **3625.6** num card neu | **2265.2** noun gen sing masc | **510.1** adj sing |
|---|---|---|---|---|---|
| ἀλλήλους | λέγοντες, | Ὅτι | Οὐδὲν | θανάτου | ʼ ἄξιον |
| *allēlous* | *legontes* | *Hoti* | *Ouden* | *thanatou* | *axion* |
| one another | saying, | | Nothing | of death | worthy |

31.a.**Txt:** 03B,byz. **Var:** p74,01ℵ,02A,044 33,104,1739

| **2211.1** conj | **1193.4** noun gen pl | **2211.1** conj | **1193.4** noun gen pl | **510.1** adj sing | **4948.10** indef-pron sing neu |
|---|---|---|---|---|---|
| ἢ | δεσμῶν | [☆ ἢ | δεσμῶν | ἄξιον ] | [a+ τι ] |
| *ē* | *desmōn* | *ē* | *desmōn* | *axion* | *ti* |
| or | of bonds | [ or | of bonds | worthy ] | [ anything ] |

| **4097.3** verb 3sing indic pres act | **3450.5** art nom sing masc | **442.1** noun nom sing masc | **3642.4** dem-pron nom sing masc | **66.1** name nom sing masc |
|---|---|---|---|---|
| πράσσει | ὁ | ἄνθρωπος | οὗτος. | 32. Ἀγρίππας |
| *prassei* | *ho* | *anthrōpos* | *houtos* | *Agrippas* |
| does | the | man | this. | Agrippa |

| **1156.2** conj | **3450.3** art dat sing | **5184.3** name dat masc | **5183.4** verb 3sing indic act | **624.21** verb inf perf mid |
|---|---|---|---|---|
| δὲ | τῷ | Φήστῳ | ἔφη, | Ἀπολελύσθαι |
| *de* | *tō* | *Phēstō* | *ephē* | *Apolelusthai* |
| and | | to Festus | said, | To have been let go |

| **1404.35** verb 3sing indic imperf mid | **3450.5** art nom sing masc | **442.1** noun nom sing masc | **3642.4** dem-pron nom sing masc | **1479.1** conj | **3231.1** partic |
|---|---|---|---|---|---|
| ἐδύνατο | ὁ | ἄνθρωπος | οὗτος | εἰ | μὴ |
| *edunato* | *ho* | *anthrōpos* | *houtos* | *ei* | *mē* |
| was able | the | man | this | if | not |

| **1926.21** verb 3sing indic plperf mid | **2512.3** name acc masc | **5453.1** conj | **1156.2** conj | **2892.33** verb 3sing indic aor pass |
|---|---|---|---|---|
| ἐπεκέκλητο | Καίσαρα. | 27:1. Ὡς | δὲ | ἐκρίθη |
| *epekeklēto* | *Kaisara* | *Hōs* | *de* | *ekrithē* |
| he had appealed | to Caesar. | When | but | it was decided |

| **3450.2** art gen sing | **630.1** verb inf pres act | **2231.4** prs-pron acc 1pl | **1519.1** prep | **3450.12** art acc sing fem | **2455.2** name acc fem |
|---|---|---|---|---|---|
| τοῦ | ἀποπλεῖν | ἡμᾶς | εἰς | τὴν | Ἰταλίαν, |
| *tou* | *apoplein* | *hēmas* | *eis* | *tēn* | *Italian* |
| the | to sail | us | to | | Italy |

| **3722.27** verb 3pl indic imperf act | **3450.6** art acc sing masc | **4885.1** conj | **3834.4** name acc masc | **2504.1** conj | **4948.9** indef-pron acc pl masc |
|---|---|---|---|---|---|
| παρεδίδουν | τόν | τε | Παῦλον | καί | τινας |
| *paredidoun* | *ton* | *te* | *Paulon* | *kai* | *tinas* |
| they were delivering up | | both | Paul | and | certain |

or with difficulty), Paul was putting Agrippa on trial, and Agrippa did not like that. He had heard enough. So he stood up, thus indicating the hearing was over.

**26:31.** Then they all went out and discussed the hearing. All agreed Paul had done nothing worthy of death or imprisonment. Nothing in Roman law could hold him guilty.

It is probable too they were all feeling uncomfortable because of the conviction of the Holy Spirit. Though Paul addressed Agrippa directly, Festus was affected, and probably the others also. Paul's testimony had the ring of truth to it. They could not deny that the appearance of Christ in His resurrection glory had made a tremendous change in the apostle Paul. They did not try to deny either that the Old Testament Scriptures prophesied the death and resurrection of Jesus and upheld the truth of the gospel. These truths were in their minds, but they did not discuss them.

**26:32.** Agrippa told Festus that Paul might have been set free if he had not appealed to Caesar. In fact, Agrippa was really saying Paul could and should have been set free. In other words, Festus was wrong in not setting Paul free at once after the hearing.

Agrippa implied also that the emperor would recognize Paul's innocence too and would have to set him free. Though Nero was the emperor in A.D. 59, he had not yet embarked on any campaign against the Christians. Under Roman law at this time it was not a crime to be a Christian. Not until Paul's second imprisonment did it become dangerous under the Romans to be a Christian.

It seems from this also that the appeal to Caesar had already been signed and sealed, or at least officially registered, so it was necessary to go through with it. Some Bible students have wondered if Paul had second thoughts now that he knew his appeal to Caesar was the only thing that kept him from being set free. But Paul must have been convinced it was God's will for him to make that appeal. He always obeyed the voice of the Spirit, so he was confident the Spirit was guiding him and was not disturbed. As he told the Philippians, he had learned in whatever state he was to be content, that is, to be content in the sense of being able to keep on an even keel and being able to maintain his purpose to serve God. He never gave up. He never gave way to discouragement (Philippians 4:11). Christ was his strength in every situation. Christ was his sufficient source of supply.

**27:1.** It was not long before arrangements were made for Paul's journey to Rome to present his appeal to Caesar. This account of Paul's journey to Rome gives one of the most interesting and factual accounts of a sea voyage and a shipwreck to be found anywhere in ancient literature. Luke uses "we" throughout the passage, so it is clear he accompanied Paul and was an eyewitness to it all.

king rose to his feet and so did, *Phillips* . . . as well as the governor, *Fenton.*

**and they that sat with them:** . . . all that were seated, *Williams C.K.* . . . with their retinue, *Kleist* . . . and the rest of the company, *NAB.*

**31. And when they were gone aside:** . . . and stepping to one side, *Berkeley, MLNT* . . . retired from the assembly, *Phillips* . . . and withdrawing, *Fenton* . . . After they had left the chamber, *NAB* . . . when they had left the hall, *Williams C.K.* . . . and left the room, *Everyday.*

**they talked between themselves, saying:** . . . discussed the case among themselves, *TCNT* . . . they discussed the matter among themselves and agreed, *Phillips* . . . they said to one another, *Williams C.K.* . . . They were talking to each other, *Everyday* . . . they kept talking the matter over, saying, *Kleist* . . . they talked matters over among themselves and admitted, *NAB* . . . they talked it over together and concluded, *MLNT.*

**This man doeth nothing worthy of death or of bonds:** There is nothing...deserving death or imprisonment in this man's conduct, *TCNT* . . . There is no reason why this man should die or be put in jail, *Everyday* . . . is engaged in no activity that deserves, *Kleist* . . . punishable by death or even imprisonment, *Norlie* . . . or prison, *MLNT.*

**32. Then said Agrippa unto Festus:** Agrippa remarked to Festus, *Phillips* . . . further remarked, *NAB.*

**This man might have been set at liberty:** He might easily have been discharged, *Phillips* . . . We could let this man go free, *Everyday* . . . This man could have been released, *TNT* . . . set free, *Montgomery.*

**if he had not appealed unto Caesar:** . . . but he has asked Caesar to hear his case, *Everyday* . . . to the Emperor, *Fenton.*

**1. And when it was determined that we should sail into Italy:** As it was decided that, *TCNT* . . . As soon as it was decided that we should sail away to, *Phillips* . . . should sail for, *Kleist.*

## Acts 27:2

| **2066.8** adj acc pl masc | **1196.1** noun acc pl masc | **1529.2** noun dat sing masc | **3549.4** noun dat sing neu | **2432.2** name dat masc |
|---|---|---|---|---|
| ἑτέρους | δεσμώτας | ἑκατοντάρχῃ, | ὀνόματι | Ἰουλίῳ, |
| *heterous* | *desmōtas* | *hekatontarchē* | *onomati* | *Iouliō* |
| other | prisoners | to a centurion, | by name | Julius, |

| **4539.2** noun gen sing fem | **4430.3** name-adj gen sing fem | **1895.4** verb nom pl masc part aor act | **1156.2** conj | **4003.3** noun dat sing neu |
|---|---|---|---|---|
| σπείρης | Σεβαστῆς. | 2. ἐπιβάντες | δὲ | πλοίῳ |
| *speirēs* | *Sebastēs* | *epibantes* | *de* | *ploiō* |
| of the band | of Augustus. | Having gone on board | and | a ship |

2.a.**Txt:** 020L,025P,byz.
**Var:** 01ℵ,02A,03B,bo.
Lach,Treg,Alf,Word
Tisc,We/Ho,Weis,Sod
UBS/☆

| **97.1** name-adj dat sing | **3165.13** verb nom pl masc part pres act | **3165.10** verb dat sing part pres act | **3986.4** verb inf pres act |
|---|---|---|---|
| Ἀδραμυττηνῷ | ʽ μέλλοντες | [a☆ μέλλοντι ] | πλεῖν |
| *Adramuttēnō* | *mellontes* | *mellonti* | *plein* |
| of Adramyttium | being about | [ idem ] | to sail |

2.b.**Var:** 01ℵ,02A,03B
Lach,Treg,Alf,Tisc
We/Ho,Weis,Sod
UBS/☆

| **1519.1** prep | **3450.8** art acc pl masc | **2567.3** prep | **3450.12** art acc sing fem | **767.4** name acc fem | **4964.7** noun acc pl masc |
|---|---|---|---|---|---|
| [b☆+ εἰς ] | τοὺς | κατὰ | τὴν | Ἀσίαν | τόπους |
| *eis* | *tous* | *kata* | *tēn* | *Asian* | *topous* |
| [ to ] | the | along | | Asia | places |

| **319.7** verb 1pl indic aor pass | **1498.19** verb gen sing part pres act | **4713.1** prep | **2231.3** prs-pron dat 1pl | **702.2** name gen masc |
|---|---|---|---|---|
| ἀνήχθημεν, | ὄντος | σὺν | ἡμῖν | Ἀριστάρχου |
| *anēchthēmen* | *ontos* | *sun* | *hēmin* | *Aristarchou* |
| we set sail, | being | with | us | Aristarchus |

| **3082.2** name gen sing masc | **2308.1** name-adj gen sing masc | **3450.11** art dat sing fem | **4885.1** conj | **2066.11** adj dat sing fem |
|---|---|---|---|---|
| Μακεδόνος | Θεσσαλονικέως. | 3. τῇ | τε | ἑτέρᾳ |
| *Makedonos* | *Thessalonikeōs* | *tē* | *te* | *hetera* |
| a Macedonian | of Thessalonica. | The | and | next |

| **2580.7** verb 1pl indic aor pass | **1519.1** prep | **4460.3** name acc fem | **5201.1** adv | **4885.1** conj |
|---|---|---|---|---|
| κατήχθημεν | εἰς | Σιδῶνα· | φιλανθρώπως | τε |
| *katēchthēmen* | *eis* | *Sidōna* | *philanthrōpōs* | *te* |
| we landed | at | Sidon. | Kindly | and |

| **3450.5** art nom sing masc | **2432.1** name nom masc | **3450.3** art dat sing | **3834.3** name dat masc | **5366.9** verb nom sing masc part aor mid |
|---|---|---|---|---|
| ὁ | Ἰούλιος | τῷ | Παύλῳ | χρησάμενος |
| *ho* | *Ioulios* | *tō* | *Paulō* | *chrēsamenos* |
| | Julius | | Paul | having treated |

3.a.**Var:** 01ℵ,02A,03B
020L,025P,Gries,Lach
Treg,Alf,Word,Tisc
We/Ho,Weis,Sod
UBS/☆

| **1994.3** verb 3sing indic aor act | **4242.1** prep | **3450.8** art acc pl masc | **5224.7** adj acc pl masc | **4057.25** verb acc sing masc part aor pass |
|---|---|---|---|---|
| ἐπέτρεψεν | πρὸς | [a☆+ τοὺς ] | φίλους | ʽ πορευθέντα |
| *epetrepsen* | *pros* | *tous* | *philous* | *poreuthenta* |
| allowed | to | [ the ] | friends | having gone |

3.b.**Txt:** 020L,025P,byz.
**Var:** 01ℵ,02A,03B,Lach
Treg,Alf,Tisc,We/Ho
Weis,Sod,UBS/☆

| **4057.40** verb dat sing masc part aor pass | **1943.1** noun gen sing fem | **5018.9** verb inf aor act | **2518.1** conj |
|---|---|---|---|
| [b☆ πορευθέντι ] | ἐπιμελείας | τυχεῖν. | 4. κἀκεῖθεν |
| *poreuthenti* | *epimeleias* | *tuchein* | *kakeithen* |
| [ idem ] | care | to receive. | And from there |

| **319.9** verb nom pl masc part aor pass | **5122.1** verb 1pl indic aor act | **3450.12** art acc sing fem | **2927.2** name acc fem | **1217.2** prep |
|---|---|---|---|---|
| ἀναχθέντες | ὑπεπλεύσαμεν | τὴν | Κύπρον | διὰ |
| *anachthentes* | *hupepleusamen* | *tēn* | *Kupron* | *dia* |
| having set sail | we sailed under | | Cyprus | because |

For the trip from Caesarea to Italy, Paul and other prisoners were turned over to a centurion named Julius who belonged to the cohort of Augustus, a cohort directly responsible to the emperor. "Cohort I Augustus" had its headquarters in Bananaea in northeastern Palestine, east of the southern end of the Sea of Galilee, in the territory of King Agrippa II. From the kindness Julius showed Paul some have speculated he might have been present at Paul's trial before King Agrippa. Others speculate he may have known the Roman centurion Cornelius who was converted and filled with the Spirit when Peter came to Caesarea years before. Or it may be that, like other centurions mentioned in the New Testament, he had visited Jewish synagogues and was impressed by the worship of the one true God. (See Mark 15:39; Luke 7:2-10.) He had soldiers under him who were sent along to guard the prisoners (verse 42).

**27:2.** Paul sailed on three different ships on this journey to Rome. They first took passage on a ship belonging to Adramyttium. It was headed up the coast of Asia Minor.

Luke took passage on this ship to be with Paul. So did Aristarchus, a Macedonian believer from Thessalonica. They went along to help Paul and to serve him in every way possible. It must have been a comfort for Paul to have Christian companions with him on this rather long sea voyage.

**27:3.** The next day the ship docked at the port of Sidon, 67 miles north of the starting point (Caesarea). There, Julius, treating Paul with humanitarian kindness, permitted him to go to his Christian friends to obtain care. He was allowed to stay with them until the ship was ready to sail again. To Paul this must have seemed further evidence of the providence of God. God was with him; God was guiding. It was not by chance that he was on his way to Rome.

This is the only mention of Paul's stopping at Sidon. It seems quite clear Paul had not founded the church there. But it is certain there was a well-established church in the city. The church in Sidon is just another evidence that what happened when Philip visited Samaria (chapter 8) was happening in all directions as others spread the good news after the death of Stephen. The believers in Sidon knew of Paul, and it may be that some of Paul's converts now lived there.

**27:4.** The Bible does not tell us how long the ship stayed at Sidon. It may have taken several days to unload or load cargo and take care of the shipowner's business.

Then from Sidon they put out to sea and sailed under the lee of the island of Cyprus, battling contrary westerly winds. Normally they would have sailed directly northwest from Sidon to Myra, the next port of call for this ship. But the westerly winds forced them

**they delivered Paul and certain other prisoners unto one named Julius:** Paul and some other prisoners were put in charge of, *TCNT* . . . they committed...some other prisoners, *MLNT* . . . they handed over Paul and a few other prisoners into the custody of Julius, an officer of the Augustan battalion, *Weymouth.*

**a centurion of Augustus' band:** . . . from the cohort known as, *NAB* . . . a captain of the Augustan Cohort, *MLNT* . . . who served in the Emperor's army, *Everyday* . . . an imperial regiment, *Norlie.*

**2. And entering into a ship of Adramyttium:** And going on board, *Rotherham* . . . We boarded a ship from, *NAB* . . . We embarked on a ship sailing from Adramyttium, *Phillips.*

**we launched, meaning to sail by the coasts of Asia:** . . . that would make the ports along the coast, *MLNT* . . . bound for ports in the province of, *NAB* . . . about to sail along the coasts of Asia, we put to sea, *HBIE* . . . that was going to sail to the ports on the coast of the province of Asia, and we started out, *Beck.*

**one Aristarchus, a Macedonian of Thessalonica, being with us:** . . . went with us, *TCNT.*

**3. And the next day we touched at Sidon:** And on the next day we put into Zidon, *Rotherham* . . . landed at, *HBIE* . . . docked at, *Berkeley* . . . made a stop at, *Norlie* . . . we put in at, *NAB.*

**And Julius courteously entreated Paul:** . . . in a friendly manner, *TCNT* . . . with thoughtful kindness, *Weymouth* . . . treating Paul kindly, *MLNT* . . . humanely, *HBIE.*

**and gave him liberty to go unto his friends:** . . . and allowed him to go to see his friends, *TCNT* . . . to visit his friends, *Weymouth* . . . and permitted him, *HBIE.*

**to refresh himself:** . . . and receive their hospitality, *TCNT* . . . and enjoy their care, *Weymouth* . . . who cared for his needs, *NAB.*

**4. And when we had launched from thence:** After setting sail from there, *Williams* . . . Putting to sea from there, *MLNT* . . . putting out from, *NAB.*

| 3450.16 art sing neu | 3450.8 art acc pl masc | 415.8 noun acc pl masc | 1498.32 verb inf pres act | 1711.3 adj acc pl masc | 3450.16 art sing neu |
|---|---|---|---|---|---|
| τὸ | τοὺς | ἀνέμους | εἶναι | ἐναντίους. | 5. τό |
| *to* | *tous* | *anemous* | *einai* | *enantious* | *to* |
| the | the | winds | to be | contrary. | The |

| 4885.1 conj | 3851.2 noun sing neu | 3450.16 art sing neu | 2567.3 prep | 3450.12 art acc sing fem | 2763.2 name acc fem | 2504.1 conj |
|---|---|---|---|---|---|---|
| τε | πέλαγος | τὸ | κατὰ | τὴν | Κιλικίαν | καὶ |
| *te* | *pelagos* | *to* | *kata* | *tēn* | *Kilikian* | *kai* |
| and | sea | the | along | | Cilicia | and |

5.a.**Txt:** 03B,020L,025P byz.Weis,Sod **Var:** 01ℵ,02A,Treg,Tisc We/Ho,UBS/⋆

| 3690.2 name acc fem | 1271.1 verb nom pl masc part aor act | 2687.2 verb 1pl indic aor act | 2687.9 verb 1pl indic aor act |
|---|---|---|---|
| Παμφυλίαν | διαπλεύσαντες | ˊ κατήλθομεν | [a κατήλθαμεν ] |
| *Pamphulian* | *diapleusantes* | *katēlthomen* | *katēlthamen* |
| Pamphylia | having sailed over | we came | [ idem ] |

| 1519.1 prep | 3322.1 name pl neu | 3450.10 art gen sing fem | 3045.1 name gen fem | 2517.1 conj | 2128.17 verb nom sing masc part aor act |
|---|---|---|---|---|---|
| εἰς | Μύρα | τῆς | Λυκίας. | 6. Κἀκεῖ | εὑρὼν |
| *eis* | *Mura* | *tēs* | *Lukias* | *Kakei* | *heurōn* |
| to | Myra | | of Lycia. | And there | having found |

| 3450.5 art nom sing masc | 1530.1 noun nom sing masc | 1529.1 noun nom sing masc | 4003.1 noun sing neu |
|---|---|---|---|
| ὁ | ˊ ἑκατόνταρχος | [⋆ ἑκατοντάρχης ] | πλοῖον |
| *ho* | *hekatontarchos* | *hekatontarchēs* | *ploion* |
| the | centurion | [ idem ] | a ship |

| 220.2 name-adj acc sing neu | 3986.3 verb sing neu part pres act | 1519.1 prep | 3450.12 art acc sing fem | 2455.2 name acc fem |
|---|---|---|---|---|
| Ἀλεξανδρῖνον | πλέον | εἰς | τὴν | Ἰταλίαν |
| *Alexandrinon* | *pleon* | *eis* | *tēn* | *Italian* |
| of Alexandria | sailing | to | | Italy |

| 1675.1 verb 3sing indic aor act | 2231.4 prs-pron acc 1pl | 1519.1 prep | 840.15 prs-pron sing neu | 1706.1 prep | 2401.10 adj dat pl fem |
|---|---|---|---|---|---|
| ἐνεβίβασεν | ἡμᾶς | εἰς | αὐτό. | 7. ἐν | ἱκαναῖς |
| *enebibasen* | *hēmas* | *eis* | *auto* | *en* | *hikanais* |
| he caused to enter | us | into | it. | For | many |

| 1156.2 conj | 2232.7 noun dat pl fem | 1013.1 verb nom pl masc part pres act | 2504.1 conj | 3296.1 adv | 1090.55 verb nom pl masc part aor mid |
|---|---|---|---|---|---|
| δὲ | ἡμέραις | βραδυπλοοῦντες | καὶ | μόλις | γενόμενοι |
| *de* | *hēmerais* | *braduploountes* | *kai* | *molis* | *genomenoi* |
| and | days | sailing slowly | and | hardly | having come |

| 2567.3 prep | 3450.12 art acc sing fem | 2807.1 name acc fem | 3231.1 partic | 4188.1 verb gen sing masc part pres act | 2231.4 prs-pron acc 1pl |
|---|---|---|---|---|---|
| κατὰ | τὴν | Κνίδον, | μὴ | προσεῶντος | ἡμᾶς |
| *kata* | *tēn* | *Knidon* | *mē* | *proseōntos* | *hēmas* |
| across from | | Cnidus, | not | allowing | us |

| 3450.2 art gen sing | 415.2 noun gen sing masc | 5122.1 verb 1pl indic aor act | 3450.12 art acc sing fem | 2887.3 name acc fem |
|---|---|---|---|---|
| τοῦ | ἀνέμου, | ὑπεπλεύσαμεν | τὴν | Κρήτην |
| *tou* | *anemou* | *hupepleusamen* | *tēn* | *Krētēn* |
| the | wind, | we sailed under | | Crete |

| 2567.3 prep | 4391.1 name acc fem | 3296.1 adv | 4885.1 conj | 3742.1 verb nom pl masc part pres mid |
|---|---|---|---|---|
| κατὰ | Σαλμώνην· | 8. μόλις | τε | παραλεγόμενοι |
| *kata* | *Salmōnēn* | *molis* | *te* | *paralegomenoi* |
| across from | Salmone; | hardly | and | coasting along |

to take the longer route east and then north of the island. Since Cyprus is about 141 miles long, this took them a considerable distance out of their way.

**27:5.** The north side of Cyprus brought them opposite the coast of Cilicia, Paul's native province. After sailing along the coast of Cilicia and the coast of the next province, Pamphylia, they came to the port of Myra in the next province, Lycia. This was almost directly across the Mediterranean from Alexandria in Egypt. Myra was built on a cliff about 2 miles from the seacoast. Its seaport was an important stopping place for ships from Egypt and Cyprus. Its ruins are better preserved than most of those of the ancient cities of that region. They indicate it was a very prosperous city. From it a gorge leads into the rugged interior. In some parts of the province high mountains come down almost to the sea. It had been a Roman province since A.D. 53. Myra, for a time, was its capital and one of its chief trading centers.

**27:6.** At Myra, the centurion transferred Paul and the other prisoners (as well as Luke and Aristarchus) to a ship from Alexandria that was sailing to Italy with a cargo of wheat. (See verse 38.)

Egypt was the chief source of wheat for the city of Rome, and the ships that carried wheat were considered very important. Most of the wheat grown in Egypt was a bearded wheat with multiple heads on the same stalk, rather than the ordinary wheat with a single head, which was the variety commonly grown in Palestine.

Alexandria (founded in the year 332 B.C.) had an excellent harbor. Normally the grain ships would sail directly from its port to Puteoli on the north shore of the Bay of Naples in Italy. But the same contrary westerly winds that caused the first ship to take the lee side of Cyprus had most probably forced this ship off its course so that it stopped at Myra. Otherwise the centurion might have had to wait some time for a ship going to Italy.

Since ancient peoples ate very little meat, bread was the most important article of their diet. The poor in Palestine would eat the cheaper barley bread. But even the poor in Rome wanted wheat bread. With its increased population as the capital of the empire, Egyptian wheat became very important.

**27:7.** The winds continued to be contrary, so they sailed very slowly westward along the south coast of Asia Minor trying to reach the port of Cnidus on the coast of Caria at the southwest point of Asia Minor. The captain probably hoped to reach it, but contrary winds from the northwest forced them southward until they came under the lee of the island of Crete off the promontory of Salmone at the eastern tip of the island.

**we sailed under Cyprus, because the winds were contrary:** . . . we had to sail under the lee of Cyprus, as the wind was against us, *Moffatt* . . . we sailed along the south coast of Cyprus, *Berkeley* . . . and sailed close to the island of, *Everyday.*

**5. And when we had sailed over the sea of Cilicia and Pamphylia:** . . . and, after crossing the sea of, *TCNT* . . . and, sailing the whole length of the sea that lies off, *Weymouth* . . . the deep sea, *PNT* . . . steering across the open sea, *Fenton* . . . went across the sea, *Everyday.*

**we came to Myra, a city of Lycia:** . . . we reached Myra in Lycia, *TCNT* . . . we landed at, *Berkeley.*

**6. And there the centurion found a ship of Alexandria sailing into Italy:** There the sergeant found a ship, *Williams C.K.* . . . on her way to Italy, *TCNT* . . . bound for Italy, *Weymouth.*

**and he put us therein:** . . . and put us on board of her, *TCNT* . . . transferred us to that, *Berkeley.*

**7. And when we had sailed slowly many days:** For several days our progress was slow, *TCNT* . . . For several days we beat slowly to windward, *Phillips.*

**and scarce were come over against Cnidus:** . . . and it was only with difficulty that we arrived off Cnidus, *TCNT* . . . and only just succeeded, *Phillips* . . . we had a hard time reaching, *Everyday.*

**the wind not suffering us:** As the wind was still unfavorable, *TCNT* . . . Then, since the wind was still blowing against us, *Phillips* . . . checked our progress, *Moffatt.*

**we sailed under Crete, over against Salmone:** . . . we ran under the lee of Crete off Salmone, *Weymouth* . . . we sailed south of Crete off Salmone, *Berkeley* . . . So we sailed by the south side of the island of, *Everyday.*

**8. And, hardly passing it:** And with difficulty, by keeping close in shore, *TCNT* . . . And though hardly making any headway, *Norlie* . . . We sailed along the coast, but the sailing was hard, *Everyday.*

| 840.12 prs-pron acc sing fem | 2048.4 verb 1pl indic aor act | 1519.1 prep | 4964.4 noun acc sing masc | 4948.5 indef-pron | 2535.29 verb sing part pres mid |
|---|---|---|---|---|---|
| αὐτὴν | ἤλθομεν | εἰς | τόπον | τινὰ | καλούμενον |
| *autēn* | *ēlthomen* | *eis* | *topon* | *tina* | *kaloumenon* |
| it | we came | to | a place | certain | being called |

| 2541.5 adj acc pl masc | 3014.3 noun acc pl masc | 3614.3 rel-pron dat sing | 1445.1 adv | 1498.34 verb sing indic imperf act | 4032.1 noun nom sing fem |
|---|---|---|---|---|---|
| Καλοὺς | Λιμένας, | ᾧ | ἐγγὺς | ἦν | πόλις |
| *Kalous* | *Limenas* | *hō* | *engus* | *ēn* | *polis* |
| Fair | Havens, | which | near | was | a city |

| 2969.1 name nom fem | 2401.4 adj gen sing masc | 1156.2 conj | 5385.2 noun gen sing masc | 1224.1 verb gen sing part aor mid | 2504.1 conj |
|---|---|---|---|---|---|
| Λασαία. | 9. Ἱκανοῦ | δὲ | χρόνου | διαγενομένου | καὶ |
| *Lasaia* | *Hikanou* | *de* | *chronou* | *diagenomenou* | *kai* |
| Lasea. | Much | and | time | having passed | and |

| 1498.19 verb gen sing part pres act | 2218.1 adv | 1984.1 adj gen sing masc | 3450.2 art gen sing | 4006.1 noun gen sing masc | 1217.2 prep |
|---|---|---|---|---|---|
| ὄντος | ἤδη | ἐπισφαλοῦς | τοῦ | πλοός, | διὰ |
| *ontos* | *ēdē* | *episphalous* | *tou* | *ploos* | *dia* |
| being | already | dangerous | the | voyage, | because |

| 3450.16 art sing neu | 2504.1 conj | 3450.12 art acc sing fem | 3383.2 noun acc sing fem | 2218.1 adv | 3790.10 verb inf perf act |
|---|---|---|---|---|---|
| τὸ | καὶ | τὴν | νηστείαν | ἤδη | παρεληλυθέναι, |
| *to* | *kai* | *tēn* | *nēsteian* | *ēdē* | *parelēluthenai* |
| the | also | the | fast | already | to have past, |

| 3728.2 verb 3sing indic imperf act | 3450.5 art nom sing masc | 3834.1 name nom masc | 2978.15 verb nom sing masc part pres act | 840.2 prs-pron dat pl |
|---|---|---|---|---|
| παρῄνει | ὁ | Παῦλος | 10. λέγων | αὐτοῖς, |
| *parēnei* | *ho* | *Paulos* | *legōn* | *autois* |
| was exhorting | | Paul | saying | to them, |

| 433.6 noun nom pl masc | 2311.2 verb 1sing indic pres act | 3617.1 conj | 3196.3 prep | 5038.1 noun gen sing fem | 2504.1 conj | 4044.10 adj gen sing fem |
|---|---|---|---|---|---|---|
| Ἄνδρες, | θεωρῶ | ὅτι | μετὰ | ὕβρεως | καὶ | πολλῆς |
| *Andres* | *theōrō* | *hoti* | *meta* | *hubreōs* | *kai* | *pollēs* |
| Men, | I perceive | that | with | damage | and | much |

| 2192.1 noun gen sing fem | 3620.3 partic | 3303.1 adv | 3450.2 art gen sing | 5250.1 noun gen sing masc | 5249.4 noun gen sing neu |
|---|---|---|---|---|---|
| ζημίας | οὐ | μόνον | τοῦ | ‘ φόρτου | [a☆ φορτίου ] |
| *zēmias* | *ou* | *monon* | *tou* | *phortou* | *phortiou* |
| loss | not | only | of the | cargo | [ idem ] |

10.a.**Txt:** Steph
**Var:** 01ℵ,02A,03B,020L 025P,Gries,Lach,Treg Alf,Word,Tisc,We/Ho Weis,Sod,UBS/☆

| 2504.1 conj | 3450.2 art gen sing | 4003.2 noun gen sing neu | 233.2 conj | 2504.1 conj | 3450.1 art gen pl | 5425.6 noun gen pl fem | 2231.2 prs-pron gen 1pl |
|---|---|---|---|---|---|---|---|
| καὶ | τοῦ | πλοίου | ἀλλὰ | καὶ | τῶν | ψυχῶν | ἡμῶν |
| *kai* | *tou* | *ploiou* | *alla* | *kai* | *tōn* | *psuchōn* | *hēmōn* |
| and | of the | ship | but | also | of the | lives | our |

| 3165.18 verb inf pres act | 1498.45 verb inf fut mid | 3450.6 art acc sing masc | 4006.2 noun acc sing masc | 3450.5 art nom sing masc | 1156.2 conj |
|---|---|---|---|---|---|
| μέλλειν | ἔσεσθαι | τὸν | πλοῦν. | 11. Ὁ | δὲ |
| *mellein* | *esesthai* | *ton* | *ploun* | *Ho* | *de* |
| to be about | to be | the | voyage. | The | but |

| 1530.1 noun nom sing masc | 1529.1 noun nom sing masc | 3450.3 art dat sing | 2914.2 noun dat sing masc |
|---|---|---|---|
| ‘ ἑκατόνταρχος | [☆ ἑκατοντάρχης ] | τῷ | κυβερνήτῃ |
| *hekatontarchos* | *hekatontarchēs* | *tō* | *kubernētē* |
| centurion | [ idem ] | by the | steersman |

**27:8.** Crete is a 160-mile-long island southeast of Greece. A mountain chain runs through it from east to west, which may have given some protection from the force of the winds. They sailed about half the length of the island to reach Fair Havens, near the island's most southerly point. Its harbor was a small bay easily entered from the east but with two small islands blocking it on the southwest. Lasea was 5 miles to the east and would be the only source of food and supplies. Some authorities call Fair Havens just a "roadstead," a place where ships could ride at anchor, rather than a real harbor.

**27:9.** Because considerable time had passed due to the strong winds that forced them off their course, "the fast" had gone by. By "the fast" Luke meant the Day of Atonement on the 10th day of the 7th month of the Jewish year. This was the only fast commanded by the law of Moses and it lasted just the 1 day. During the Babylonian exile some of the poor Jews left in Palestine had added other fast days to commemorate the destruction of the temple by Nebuchadnezzar and the assassination of the Jewish governor, Gedaliah. But Zechariah prophesied that it was God's purpose to turn their fasts into joyful feasts (Zechariah 8:19). Thus, in New Testament times, the Day of Atonement remained the only fast.

In A.D. 59 the Day of Atonement was on October 5, and Paul recognized that since this had gone by it would be dangerous to continue their voyage. He was an experienced traveler and had been in three shipwrecks already (2 Corinthians 11:25). He knew how dangerous winter storms could be. In fact, he had spent a night and a day adrift on the open sea after one of those shipwrecks.

Sailing was actually considered dangerous on the Mediterranean Sea after September 14. Storms were more frequent, and the sky was so often overcast they could not see the stars and navigation was difficult. Most ships therefore spent the winter in a safe harbor.

**27:10.** Paul went to those in charge of the ship and advised them of the certainty of injury and great loss to the ship and its cargo, as well as danger to their lives, if they continued on. Paul's perception here undoubtedly came not only from his experience, but also from the leading of the Spirit. He was always sensitive to the Holy Spirit, and here he felt a strong sense of disaster ahead. Thus he dared to go and volunteer his advice.

**27:11.** The centurion seems to be the one really in charge. This gives confirmation to the suggestion that this ship was part of the imperial grain fleet that had as its chief business the carrying of wheat from Alexandria to Italy. Most of these ships were quite large for that day: as much as 180 feet long by 45 feet wide with a capacity of over 1,200 tons.

**came unto a place which is called The fair havens:** . . . we reached a place called, *TCNT* . . . Fair Harbours, *Williams C.K.* . . . Safe Harbors, *Everyday.*

**nigh whereunto was the city of Lasea:** . . . near the town of Lasea, *Weymouth* . . . with the town of Lasea near it, *Williams C.K.*

**9. Now when much time was spent:** And when a considerable time had passed, *Rotherham* . . . After considerable delay there, *Fenton* . . . we had lost much time, *Everyday* . . . It was now far on in the season, *Williams C.K.*

**and when sailing was now dangerous:** . . . and the navigation being now unsafe, *Weymouth* . . . and the journey was now full of danger, *BB* . . . and the voyage had become dangerous, *Williams C.K.* . . . was now hazardous, *Campbell.*

**because the fast was now already past:** . . . it was late in the year, *BB* . . . day of fasting had already gone by, *Beck* . . . Day of Atonement, *TEV* . . . autumn fast was already over, *Williams C.K.* . . . it was already after the Day of Cleansing, *Everyday.*

**Paul admonished them:** Paul began to advise, *Rotherham* . . . and so Paul gave this warning, *TCNT.*

**10. And said unto them:**

**Sirs, I perceive:** My friends, I see, *TCNT.*

**that this voyage will be with hurt and much damage:** . . . with danger and heavy loss, *Weymouth* . . . there will be a lot of trouble on this trip, *Everyday* . . . will involve hardship and considerable damage, *Berkeley* . . . end in disaster and great loss, *Norlie.*

**not only of the lading and ship:** . . . not only of the cargo and of the ship, *Rotherham* . . . The ship and the things in the ship will be lost, *Everyday.*

**but also of our lives:** . . . but to our lives, *Williams C.K.* . . . Even our lives may be lost! *Everyday.*

**11. Nevertheless the centurion believed:** . . . paid more attention to, *RSV* . . . was more persuaded by, *Rotherham* . . . put his faith in, *Norlie* . . . was convinced by, *TEV* . . . But the sergeant had more confidence in, *Williams C.K.*

| 2504.1 conj | 3450.3 art dat sing | 3353.1 noun dat sing masc | 3844.32 verb 3sing indic imperf pass | 3095.1 adv comp |
|---|---|---|---|---|
| καὶ | τῷ | ναυκλήρῳ | ⸀ ἐπείθετο | μᾶλλον |
| *kai* | *tō* | *nauklērō* | *epeitheto* | *mallon* |
| and | the | ship owner | was being persuaded | rather |

| 3095.1 adv comp | 3844.32 verb 3sing indic imperf pass | 2211.1 conj | 3450.4 art dat pl | 5097.3 prep |
|---|---|---|---|---|
| [☆ μᾶλλον | ἐπείθετο ] | ἢ | τοῖς | ὑπὸ |
| *mallon* | *epeitheto* | *ē* | *tois* | *hupo* |
| [ rather | was being persuaded ] | than | by the | by |

11.a.**Txt:** 020L,025P,byz. Sod
**Var:** 01ℵ,02A,03B,Lach Treg,Word,Tisc,We/Ho Weis,UBS/☆

| 3450.2 art gen sing | 3834.2 name gen masc | 2978.36 verb dat pl neu part pres mid | 426.1 adj gen sing masc | 1156.2 conj |
|---|---|---|---|---|
| ⸂a τοῦ ⸃ | Παύλου | λεγομένοις. | 12. ἀνευθέτου | δὲ |
| *tou* | *Paulou* | *legomenois* | *aneuthetou* | *de* |
| | Paul | being spoken. | Unsuitable | and |

| 3450.2 art gen sing | 3014.1 noun gen sing masc | 5062.5 verb gen sing part pres act | 4242.1 prep | 3776.1 noun acc sing fem |
|---|---|---|---|---|
| τοῦ | λιμένος | ὑπάρχοντος | πρὸς | παραχειμασίαν, |
| *tou* | *limenos* | *huparchontos* | *pros* | *paracheimasian* |
| the | port | being | to | winter in, |

12.a.**Txt:** 020L,025P,byz.
**Var:** 01ℵ,02A,03B,Lach Treg,Alf,Tisc,We/Ho Weis,Sod,UBS/☆

| 3450.7 art nom pl masc | 3979.3 adj comp pl | 3979.5 adj comp nom pl masc | 4935.33 verb 3pl indic aor mid | 1005.4 noun acc sing fem |
|---|---|---|---|---|
| οἱ | ⸀ πλείους | [a☆ πλείονες ] | ἔθεντο | βουλὴν |
| *hoi* | *pleious* | *pleiones* | *ethento* | *boulēn* |
| the | most | [ idem ] | placed | a decision |

12.b.**Txt:** 025P,byz.
**Var:** 01ℵ,02A,03B,020L bo.Lach,Treg,Alf,Tisc We/Ho,Weis,Sod UBS/☆

| 319.10 verb inf aor pass | 2518.1 conj | 1551.1 adv | 1501.1 conj |
|---|---|---|---|
| ἀναχθῆναι | ⸀ κἀκεῖθεν, | [b☆ ἐκεῖθεν, ] | ⸀ εἴπως |
| *anachthēnai* | *kakeithen* | *ekeithen* | *eipōs* |
| to set sail | from there also, | [ from there, ] | if by any means |

| 1479.1 conj | 4316.1 adv | 1404.11 verb 3pl opt pres mid | 2628.6 verb nom pl masc part aor act | 1519.1 prep |
|---|---|---|---|---|
| [☆ εἴ | πως ] | δύναιντο | καταντήσαντες | εἰς |
| *ei* | *pōs* | *dunainto* | *katantēsantes* | *eis* |
| [ if | somehow ] | they might be able | having arrived | at |

| 5242.1 name acc masc | 3775.1 verb inf aor act | 3014.2 noun acc sing masc | 3450.10 art gen sing fem | 2887.1 name gen fem |
|---|---|---|---|---|
| Φοίνικα | παραχειμάσαι, | λιμένα | τῆς | Κρήτης |
| *Phoinika* | *paracheimasai* | *limena* | *tēs* | *Krētēs* |
| Phoenix | to winter, | a port | | of Crete |

| 984.13 verb acc sing masc part pres act | 2567.3 prep | 3021.1 noun acc sing masc | 2504.1 conj | 2567.3 prep | 5401.1 noun acc sing masc |
|---|---|---|---|---|---|
| βλέποντα | κατὰ | λίβα | καὶ | κατὰ | χῶρον. |
| *bleponta* | *kata* | *liba* | *kai* | *kata* | *chōron* |
| looking | toward | southwest | and | toward | northwest. |

| 5123.1 verb gen sing masc part aor act | 1156.2 conj | 3421.1 noun gen sing masc | 1374.21 verb nom pl masc part aor act |
|---|---|---|---|
| 13. Ὑποπνευσάντος | δὲ | νότου, | δόξαντες |
| *Hupopneusantos* | *de* | *notou* | *doxantes* |
| Having blown gently | and | a south wind, | having thought |

| 3450.10 art gen sing fem | 4145.2 noun gen sing fem | 2875.21 verb inf perf act | 142.17 verb nom pl masc part aor act | 782.1 adv comp |
|---|---|---|---|---|
| τῆς | προθέσεως | κεκρατηκέναι, | ἄραντες | ἆσσον |
| *tēs* | *protheseōs* | *kekratēkenai* | *arantes* | *asson* |
| the | purpose | to have gained, | having weighed | close by |

The ship had a "master" who was the shipmaster in the sense of directing or steering the ship. Today he would be considered the pilot. It also had a captain. The Greek term could mean the captain was the owner of the ship. But since the ship was in the state service of the empire, the same term was applied to the captain even though he was not the actual owner. Instead of listening to Paul, the centurion Julius was persuaded by the pilot and the captain to keep going.

**27:12.** The chief argument against staying in Fair Havens was simply that the harbor was poor, unfavorably situated, and therefore unsuitable to winter in. Apparently, others joined in the discussion and the majority gave counsel to try to reach Phoenix, a harbor which was better located whether the winds came from the northwest or from the southwest.

Phoenix (Phenice, Phinika, Greek, Phoinix, "palm tree"; also the name of the fabled bird of Egypt) was on the south coast of Crete, west of Lasea, over 50 miles west of Fair Havens.

There has been some question about the identification of Phoenix. However, there was only one safe harbor in that part of Crete which was large enough for the imperial grain ships to winter in, and that is at or beside the village of Loutro, directly north of the small island of Cauda. All of the ancient writers who mention Phoenix agree it was in the area of Loutro. Archaeologists have found an inscription from the reign of the emperor Trajan that shows grain ships from Egypt often wintered there.

The harbor at Loutro is open toward the northeast and toward the southeast. This presents a difficulty because the Greek in this verse normally means "open to the southwest and open to the northwest." However, Luke may have been thinking of how it would look to the sailors coming into the harbor.

Some writers have suggested another reason Paul might have desired to stay in Fair Havens was the fact that the city of Gortyna, not much more than a dozen miles away, had a large Jewish population where he could have done some missionary work. Jews in Gortyna had been protected by the Romans since 141 B.C. It may be also that the officers of the ship wanted to go to Phoenix where other ships would be. But the chief concern seems to have been the finding of a safer harbor.

**27:13.** The ship remained in the bay of Fair Havens as long as the northwest winds continued to blow. After a time the direction of the winds changed and a gentle wind came from the southwest. This persuaded the centurion and the other officers they could fulfill their purpose and make it to Phoenix. So they sailed west, keeping close to the south coast of Crete. Paul was not convinced. He undoubtedly had that spiritual sensitivity that let him know there was danger ahead. But the centurion only looked at the immediate present and thought he could take advantage of the pleasant weather.

**the master and the owner of the ship:** . . . the captain and the owner, *TCNT* . . . the navigator, *Concordant* . . . the skipper, *Wuest.*

**more than those things which were spoken by Paul:** . . . rather than by Paul's arguments, *Weymouth* . . . rather than in Paul's suggestions, *Berkeley.*

**12. And because the haven was not commodious to winter in:** . . . was not fit, *Williams* . . . And that harbor was not a good place for the ship to stay for the winter, *Everyday* . . . Moreover, since the harbor is unsuitable for a ship to winter in, *Phillips* . . . was not well situated, *HBIE* . . . was ill-adapted for, *PNT* . . . was badly placed, *Moffatt.*

**the more part advised to depart thence also:** . . . the majority were in favour of continuing the voyage, *TCNT* . . . So most of the men decided that the ship should leave, *Everyday.*

**if by any means they might attain to Phenice:** The men hoped we could go to Phoenix, *Everyday* . . . in the hope of being able to reach Phoenix, *TCNT* . . . on the chance, *RSV.*

**and there to winter:** . . . for the winter, *BB.*

**which is an haven of Crete:** . . . a harbour of Crete, *TCNT.*

**and lieth toward the south west and north west:** . . . facing, *Weymouth* . . . open to the northeast and southeast, *TCNT.*

**13. And when the south wind blew softly:** So when a light wind sprang up from the south, *TCNT* . . . When a light breeze from the south began to blow, *Williams.*

**supposing that they had obtained their purpose:** . . . so that they supposed they were now sure of their purpose, *Weymouth* . . . thinking their purpose was about to be realized, *Williams* . . . found their opportunity, *TCNT* . . . thinking they had obtained just what they wanted, *Phillips* . . . they felt they could easily make it, *Beck* . . . This is the wind we wanted, *SEB.*

**loosing thence:** . . . they weighed anchor, *RSV* . . . they let the ship go, *BB.*

| 3742.2 verb 3pl indic imperf mid | 3450.12 art acc sing fem | 2887.3 name acc fem | 3196.2 prep |
|---|---|---|---|
| παρελέγοντο | τὴν | Κρήτην. | 14. μετ' |
| *parelegonto* | *tēn* | *Krētēn* | *met'* |
| they were going along the coast | | of Crete. | After |

| 3620.3 partic | 4044.16 adj sing neu | 1156.2 conj | 900.10 verb 3sing indic aor act | 2567.1 prep | 840.10 prs-pron gen sing fem | 415.1 noun nom sing masc |
|---|---|---|---|---|---|---|
| οὐ | πολὺ | δὲ | ἔβαλεν | κατ' | αὐτῆς | ἄνεμος |
| *ou* | *polu* | *de* | *ebalen* | *kat'* | *autēs* | *anemos* |
| not | long | but | there came | against | it | a wind |

| 5030.1 adj nom sing masc | 3450.5 art nom sing masc | 2535.30 verb nom sing masc part pres mid | 2129.1 noun nom sing masc |
|---|---|---|---|
| τυφωνικὸς, | ὁ | καλούμενος | ‹ Εὐροκλύδων. |
| *tuphōnikos* | *ho* | *kaloumenos* | *Eurokludōn* |
| thphoon-like, | the | being called | Euroclydon. |

14.a.**Txt:** 020L,025P,044 byz.Sod
**Var:** p74,01ℵ,02A,03B sa.bo.Lach,Treg,Alf Word,Tisc,We/Ho,Weis Sod,UBS/☆

| 2127.1 noun nom sing masc | 4780.4 verb gen sing neu part aor pass | 1156.2 conj | 3450.2 art gen sing |
|---|---|---|---|
| [a☆ Εὐρακύλων·] | 15. συναρπασθέντος | δὲ | τοῦ |
| *Eurakulōn* | *sunarpasthentos* | *de* | *tou* |
| [Euraculon.] | Having been caught | and | the |

| 4003.2 noun gen sing neu | 2504.1 conj | 3231.1 partic | 1404.12 verb gen sing part pres mid | 500.1 verb inf pres act | 3450.3 art dat sing |
|---|---|---|---|---|---|
| πλοίου, | καὶ | μὴ | δυναμένου | ἀντοφθαλμεῖν | τῷ |
| *ploiou* | *kai* | *mē* | *dunamenou* | *antophthalmein* | *tō* |
| ship, | and | not | being able | to face against | the |

| 415.3 noun dat sing masc | 1914.2 verb nom pl masc part aor act | 5179.32 verb 1pl indic imperf pass | 3381.1 noun sing neu |
|---|---|---|---|
| ἀνέμῳ, | ἐπιδόντες | ἐφερόμεθα. | 16. νησίον |
| *anemō* | *epidontes* | *epherometha* | *nēsion* |
| wind, | having given up | we were being driven along. | Small island |

| 1156.2 conj | 4948.10 indef-pron sing neu | 5133.1 verb nom pl masc part aor act | 2535.29 verb sing part pres mid | 2775.1 name acc fem |
|---|---|---|---|---|
| δέ | τι | ὑποδραμόντες | καλούμενον | ‹ Κλαύδην |
| *de* | *ti* | *hupodramontes* | *kaloumenon* | *Klaudēn* |
| but | a certain | having run under | being called | Clauda |

16.a.**Txt:** 020L,025P 1241,byz.lect.
**Var:** 01ℵ-org,02A,33,sa. bo.Alf,Tisc,Weis,Sod UBS/☆

| 2708.1 name | 3296.1 adv | 2453.8 verb 1pl indic aor act | 2453.8 verb 1pl indic aor act | 3296.1 adv |
|---|---|---|---|---|
| [a☆ Καῦδα ] | ‹ μόλις | ἰσχύσαμεν | [☆ ἰσχύσαμεν | μόλις ] |
| *Kauda* | *molis* | *ischusamen* | *ischusamen* | *molis* |
| [Clauda] | hardly | we were able | [we were able | hardly] |

| 3894.1 adj nom pl masc | 1090.63 verb inf aor mid | 3450.10 art gen sing fem | 4482.1 noun gen sing fem | 3614.12 rel-pron acc sing fem |
|---|---|---|---|---|
| περικρατεῖς | γενέσθαι | τῆς | σκάφης· | 17. ἣν |
| *perikrateis* | *genesthai* | *tēs* | *skaphēs* | *hēn* |
| masters | to become | of the | boat; | which |

| 142.17 verb nom pl masc part aor act | 989.2 noun dat pl fem | 5366.10 verb 3pl indic imperf mid | 5107.1 verb nom pl masc part pres act |
|---|---|---|---|
| ἄραντες | βοηθείαις | ἐχρῶντο, | ὑποζωννύντες |
| *arantes* | *boētheiais* | *echrōnto* | *hupozōnnuntes* |
| having taken up | helps | they were using, | undergirding |

| 3450.16 art sing neu | 4003.1 noun sing neu | 5236.8 verb nom pl masc part pres mid | 4885.1 conj | 3231.1 partic | 1519.1 prep |
|---|---|---|---|---|---|
| τὸ | πλοῖον· | φοβούμενοί | τε | μὴ | εἰς |
| *to* | *ploion* | *phoboumenoi* | *te* | *mē* | *eis* |
| the | ship; | fearing | and | not | into |

**27:14.** It was not long before Paul's prediction came true. A vehement, turbulent wind called Euroclydon rushed against them from the east-northeast.

"Euroclydon" seems to mean "the southeast wind that stirs up waves." Another spelling is *eurukludōn,* "the wind that stirs up broad waves." *Eurakulōn* was a word developed by the sailors of these ships from the Greek *euros* and the Latin *aquilo* as a name for a violent northeast wind.

**27:15.** This violent northeast wind caught the ship in its grip and drove it away from the shores of Crete. The sailors tried to make the ship face into the land, but the wind was too strong.

The Greek indicates the wind caught the ship and literally tore it away from its projected course toward Phoenix. The same word is used of the demoniac who was seized by a violent unclean spirit (Luke 8:29). The ship was completely under the control of this wind, and the sailors were totally unable to do anything about it. They could only give themselves up to the wind and let themselves be driven wildly. Some have compared them to a kite in a windstorm. The ship must have been tossed like a cork on the waves.

The apostle Paul did not say "I told you so!" right away. It was quite obvious now that he was right and that the centurion, pilot, and captain had been wrong. No doubt, by the time the sailors gave up and let the ship be driven by the wind, they were all exhausted and this was no time to say anything.

Paul, however, even with all the danger must have had a deep peace in his heart and mind. He still had the assurance given by Jesus himself that he would bear witness in Rome. No storm, no wind or waves could rob him of that promise from His Lord. He knew Christ was with him, and the Holy Spirit gave him peace in the midst of the storm.

**27:16.** The wind kept driving the ship toward the southwest. After several hours it brought them close along the south side of the small island of Clauda. It was also called Cauda, or Kauda, and in later times was known as Gaudos, Gavdhos, Gozzo, and more recently as Gaudho.

Claudа was about 23 miles from where the storm first hit them. In the lee of the island they found a little temporary relief from the full force of the storm. Even then it was with difficulty that they regained control over the small boat that was being towed behind the ship.

**27:17.** After the sailors hoisted the small boat onto the deck of the ship, they used "helps" to undergird the ship. They fastened strong ropes or cables vertically around the ship to try to keep the timbers from straining too much or giving way because of the violence of the wind and waves.

**they sailed close by Crete:** . . . and kept along the coast of Crete, close in shore, *TCNT* . . . and coasted along, hugging the shores of Crete, *Phillips* . . . very close to the island, *Everyday.*

**14. But not long after:** But shortly afterwards, *TCNT* . . . But before long, *Phillips.*

**there arose against it a tempestuous wind, called Euroclydon:** . . . a hurricane came down on us off the land, *TCNT* . . . a furious northeast wind, coming down from the mountains, burst upon us, *Weymouth* . . . a terrific gale, *Norlie* . . . a typhoon, *Rotherham* . . . a very strong wind named the "Northeaster" came from the island, *Everyday.*

**15. And when the ship was caught:** The ship was snatched along by it, *Williams* . . . This wind took the ship and carried it away, *Everyday.*

**and could not bear up into the wind:** . . . and since she could not be brought up into, *Phillips* . . . so, unable to head against, *Berkeley* . . . couldn't face, *Beck* . . . could not sail against it, *Everyday.*

**we let her drive:** . . . so we had to give way and let her drive before it, *TCNT* . . . so we gave up and let her drift, *Berkeley* . . . we let her go and were borne along, *Rotherham* . . . we surrendered, *Wilson* . . . we stopped trying and let the wind blow us, *Everyday.*

**16. And running under a certain island which is called Clauda:** As we passed under the shelter of, *Norlie* . . . We went below a small island named, *Everyday.*

**we had much work to come by the boat:** . . . we were able, though it was hard work, to make the ship's boat safe, *BB* . . . Then we were able to bring in the lifeboat, but it was very hard to do, *Everyday.*

**17. Which when they had taken up:** . . . and after hoisting it on a board, *TCNT.*

**they used helps, undergirding the ship:** . . . they put cords under and round the ship, *BB* . . . to reinforce it, *Beck* . . . tied ropes around the ship to hold it together, *Everyday.*

| 3450.12 art acc sing fem | 4802.1 noun acc sing fem | 1588.7 verb 3pl subj aor act | 5301.3 verb nom pl masc part aor act | 3450.16 art sing neu |
|---|---|---|---|---|
| τὴν | Σύρτιν | ἐκπέσωσιν, | χαλάσαντες | τὸ |
| *tēn* | *Surtin* | *ekpesōsin* | *chalasantes* | *to* |
| the | quicksand | they should fall, | having lowered | the |

| 4487.1 noun sing neu | 3643.1 adv | 5179.33 verb 3pl indic imperf pass | 4823.1 adv | 1156.2 conj |
|---|---|---|---|---|
| σκεῦος | οὕτως | ἐφέροντο. | **18.** Σφοδρῶς | δὲ |
| *skeuos* | *houtōs* | *epheronto* | *Sphodrōs* | *de* |
| gear | so | they were being driven. | Violently | but |

| 5328.1 verb gen pl masc part pres mid | 2231.2 prs-pron gen 1pl | 3450.11 art dat sing fem | 1819.1 adv | 1533.1 noun acc sing fem |
|---|---|---|---|---|
| χειμαζομένων | ἡμῶν | τῇ | ἑξῆς | ἐκβολὴν |
| *cheimazomenōn* | *hēmōn* | *tē* | *hexēs* | *ekbolēn* |
| being tossed by the storm | us | on the | next | a casting out |

| 4020.72 verb 3pl indic imperf mid | 2504.1 conj | 3450.11 art dat sing fem | 4995.6 num ord dat sing fem | 842.1 adj nom pl masc |
|---|---|---|---|---|
| ἐποιοῦντο· | **19.** καὶ | τῇ | τρίτῃ | αὐτόχειρες |
| *epoiounto* | *kai* | *tē* | *tritē* | *autocheires* |
| they were making, | and | on the | third | with own hands |

| 3450.12 art acc sing fem | 4486.1 noun acc sing fem | 3450.2 art gen sing | 4003.2 noun gen sing neu | 4352.1 verb 1pl indic aor act |
|---|---|---|---|---|
| τὴν | σκευὴν | τοῦ | πλοίου | ʻ ἐρρίψαμεν· |
| *tēn* | *skeuēn* | *tou* | *ploiou* | *errhipsamen* |
| the | equipment | of the | ship | we cast away. |

19.a.**Txt:** 020L,025P,byz.
**Var:** 02A,03B-corr,04C
Gries,Lach,Treg,Alf
Weis,Sod,UBS/☆

| 4352.2 verb 3pl indic aor act | 3250.1 conj | 1156.2 conj | 2229.2 noun gen sing masc | 3250.1 conj | 792.3 noun gen pl neu |
|---|---|---|---|---|---|
| [a☆ ἔρριψαν. ] | **20.** μήτε | δὲ | ἡλίου | μήτε | ἄστρων |
| *errhipsan* | *mēte* | *de* | *hēliou* | *mēte* | *astrōn* |
| [ they cast away. ] | Neither | and | sun | nor | stars |

| 1998.1 verb gen pl neu part pres act | 1894.3 prep | 3979.4 adj comp acc pl | 2232.1 noun fem | 5330.2 noun gen sing masc | 4885.1 conj |
|---|---|---|---|---|---|
| ἐπιφαινόντων | ἐπὶ | πλείονας | ἡμέρας, | χειμῶνός | τε |
| *epiphainontōn* | *epi* | *pleionas* | *hēmeras* | *cheimōnos* | *te* |
| appearing | for | many | days, | storm | and |

| 3620.2 partic | 3504.4 adj gen sing masc | 1930.2 verb gen sing masc part pres mid | 3036.8 adj sing neu | 3877.4 verb 3sing indic imperf pass |
|---|---|---|---|---|
| οὐκ | ὀλίγου | ἐπικειμένου, | λοιπὸν | περιῃρεῖτο |
| *ouk* | *oligou* | *epikeimenou* | *loipon* | *periēreito* |
| no | small | lying on, | henceforth | was being taken away |

| 3820.9 adj nom sing fem | 1667.1 noun nom sing fem | 1667.1 noun nom sing fem | 3820.9 adj nom sing fem | 3450.2 art gen sing | 4834.21 verb inf pres mid |
|---|---|---|---|---|---|
| ʻ πᾶσα | ἐλπὶς | [☆ ἐλπὶς | πᾶσα ] | τοῦ | σῴζεσθαι |
| *pasa* | *elpis* | *elpis* | *pasa* | *tou* | *sōzesthai* |
| all | hope | [ hope | all ] | the | to be saved |

21.a.**Txt:** 020L,025P,byz.
bo.
**Var:** 01ℵ,02A,03B,04C
Lach,Treg,Alf,Word
Tisc,We/Ho,Weis,Sod
UBS/☆

| 2231.4 prs-pron acc 1pl | 4044.10 adj gen sing fem | 1156.2 conj | 4885.1 conj | 770.1 noun gen sing fem |
|---|---|---|---|---|
| ἡμᾶς. | **21.** Πολλῆς | ʻ δὲ | [a☆ τε ] | ἀσιτίας |
| *hēmas* | *Pollēs* | *de* | *te* | *asitias* |
| us. | Much | and | [ idem ] | loss of appetite |

| 5062.9 verb gen sing fem part pres act | 4966.1 adv | 2449.43 verb nom sing masc part aor pass | 3450.5 art nom sing masc | 3834.1 name nom masc | 1706.1 prep |
|---|---|---|---|---|---|
| ὑπαρχούσης, | τότε | σταθεὶς | ὁ | Παῦλος | ἐν |
| *huparchousēs* | *tote* | *statheis* | *ho* | *Paulos* | *en* |
| being, | then | having stood up | | Paul | in |

The slight protection of the lee of the island of Clauda was soon behind them. Then, because there was no sign of the storm letting up, they became afraid they would be driven off their course into Syrtis, a quicksand off the coast of North Africa west of the ancient city of Cyrene. So they slackened their tackle (which may mean they took down the topsail) and were carred along by the continuing force of the northeast wind.

*Quick* is Old English for "living." Thus, the quicksand here refers to sandbanks that seem alive in that they move. The ones mentioned here were a terror to the sailors of ancient times.

**and, fearing lest they should fall into the quicksands:** But, afraid of being driven on to the Syrtis Sands, *TCNT* . . . Fearing they would run on the great sandbank near Africa, *Beck.*

**strake sail:** . . . lowered the sail, *Williams.*

**and so were driven:** . . . and went running before the wind, *BB* . . . drifted under bare poles, *TCNT.*

**27:18.** The next day, because they were still in the grip of the storm, the crew began throwing things overboard to lighten the ship so it would ride higher and not be swamped by the worsening waves. Usually they would begin by throwing part of the cargo overboard. But this ship's cargo of wheat was so important to Rome it was the last thing they would get rid of. They probably began with personal baggage and the cabin furniture.

**18. And we being exceedingly tossed with a tempest:** . . . terribly battered, *Moffatt* . . . because we were so violently beaten, *Williams* . . . And still fighting the storm with all our strength, *BB.*

**the next day they lightened the ship:** . . . began to throw the cargo overboard, *Rotherham* . . . they jettisoned, *Concordant* . . . the freight overboard, *Montgomery.*

**27:19.** The third day (according to their way of counting, the day after they began throwing things overboard), with their own hands, they tossed overboard the ship's tackle (probably including the main yard that supported the mainsail).

**19. And the third day:** . . . while two days later, *Moffatt.*

**we cast out with our own hands the tackling of the ship:** . . . flung out, *PNT* . . . the sailing apparatus go over the side, *BB* . . . the ship's equipment, *Beck* . . . the ship's gear, *Moffatt.*

**27:20.** The storm continued many days. By comparing verse 27, which mentions the 14th night, it is probable the storm had continued 11 days at this point. Without any sighting of the sun, moon, or stars, they had no way of knowing where they were, for they had no other means of navigation.

Finally, as this great storm continued to buffet them and press upon them, all hope of rescue was stripped away. Up to this time those on the ship had maintained some hope or expectation or anticipation that something good would happen. They kept before them the prospect that the storm would come to an end, or at least that the winds would lessen and there would be a break in the clouds. But now, after furling the sails and after the grueling work of throwing overboard everything possible, they were cold, wet, and thoroughly exhausted. It is no wonder the men lost all hope and now thought all would be lost, not only the ship but their own lives as well.

**20. And when neither sun nor stars in many days appeared:** As neither sun nor stars were visible for several days, *TCNT* . . . And as we had not seen the sun or stars for a long time, *BB.*

**and no small tempest lay on us:** . . . and, as the gale still continued severe, *TCNT* . . . and the terrific gale still harassed us, *Weymouth* . . . and a great tempest still beat upon us, *Montgomery* . . . and we were still in the grip of the gale, *Phillips.*

**all hope that we should be saved was then taken away:** . . . all hope of our being saved was at last reluctantly abandoned, *TCNT* . . . and at last we had to give up all hope of being saved, *Moffatt* . . . the last ray of hope was now vanishing, *Weymouth* . . . wholly cut off, *Murdock* . . . being stripped away from us, *Wuest.*

**27:21.** For a long time the 276 people on the ship (see verse 37) had abstained from food. The Greek word could mean they lacked food, and some have speculated the sea water had ruined most of their food. But verses 34 to 36 indicate they still had food in good condition on board. The Greek word can also mean abstinence

**21. But after long abstinence:** It was then, when they had gone a long time without food, *TCNT* . . . Since hardly anybody wanted to eat, *Beck* . . . been long fasting, *Young* . . . upon the verge of starvation, *Fenton.*

## Acts 27:22

| 3189.1 adj dat sing | 840.1 prs-pron gen pl | 1500.5 verb 3sing indic aor act | 1158.6 verb 3sing indic imperf act | 3173.1 conj | 5434.1 intrj |
|---|---|---|---|---|---|
| μέσῳ | αὐτῶν | εἶπεν, | Ἔδει | μέν, | ὦ |
| *mesō* | *autōn* | *eipen* | *Edei* | *men* | *ō* |
| midst | their | said, | It was necessary | indeed, | O |

| 433.6 noun nom pl masc | 3842.3 verb acc pl masc part aor act | 1466.4 prs-pron dat 1sing | 3231.1 partic | 319.5 verb inf pres mid |
|---|---|---|---|---|
| ἄνδρες, | πειθαρχήσαντάς | μοι | μὴ | ἀνάγεσθαι |
| *andres* | *peitharchēsantas* | *moi* | *mē* | *anagesthai* |
| men, | having been obedient | to me | not | to have set sail |

| 570.3 prep | 3450.10 art gen sing fem | 2887.1 name gen fem | 2741.8 verb inf aor act | 4885.1 conj | 3450.12 art acc sing fem | 5038.2 noun acc sing fem |
|---|---|---|---|---|---|---|
| ἀπὸ | τῆς | Κρήτης | κερδῆσαί | τε | τὴν | ὕβριν |
| *apo* | *tēs* | *Krētēs* | *kerdēsai* | *te* | *tēn* | *hubrin* |
| from | | Crete | to gain | and | the | disaster |

| 3642.12 dem-pron acc sing fem | 2504.1 conj | 3450.12 art acc sing fem | 2192.2 noun acc sing fem | 2504.1 conj | 4860.1 adv | 3450.17 art pl neu |
|---|---|---|---|---|---|---|
| ταύτην | καὶ | τὴν | ζημίαν. | 22. καὶ | ʼ τανῦν | [☆ τὰ |
| *tautēn* | *kai* | *tēn* | *zēmian* | *kai* | *tanun* | *ta* |
| this | and | the | loss: | and | now | [the |

| 3431.1 adv | 3728.1 verb 1sing indic pres act | 5050.4 prs-pron acc 2pl | 2093.3 verb inf pres act | 575.1 noun nom sing fem |
|---|---|---|---|---|
| νῦν ] | παραινῶ | ὑμᾶς | εὐθυμεῖν· | ἀποβολὴ |
| *nun* | *parainō* | *humas* | *euthumein* | *apobolē* |
| now ] | I advise | you | to be of good cheer, | loss |

| 1056.1 conj | 5425.2 noun gen sing fem | 3625.4 num card nom fem | 1498.40 verb 3sing indic fut mid | 1523.1 prep gen | 5050.2 prs-pron gen 2pl |
|---|---|---|---|---|---|
| γὰρ | ψυχῆς | οὐδεμία | ἔσται | ἐξ | ὑμῶν, |
| *gar* | *psuchēs* | *oudemia* | *estai* | *ex* | *humōn* |
| for | of life | none | shall be | from among | you, |

| 3993.1 adv | 3450.2 art gen sing | 4003.2 noun gen sing neu | 3798.3 verb 3sing indic aor act | 1056.1 conj | 1466.4 prs-pron dat 1sing |
|---|---|---|---|---|---|
| πλὴν | τοῦ | πλοίου. | 23. παρέστη | γάρ | μοι |
| *plēn* | *tou* | *ploiou* | *parestē* | *gar* | *moi* |
| only | of the | ship. | Stood by | for | me |

23.a.**Txt:** 020L,025P,byz. **Var:** 01א,02A,03B,04C Lach,Treg,Alf,Word Tisc,We/Ho,Weis,Sod UBS/☆

| 3450.11 art dat sing fem | 3433.3 noun dat sing fem | 3642.11 dem-pron dat sing fem | 3642.11 dem-pron dat sing fem | 3450.11 art dat sing fem | 3433.3 noun dat sing fem |
|---|---|---|---|---|---|
| ʼ τῇ | νυκτὶ | ταύτῃ | [☆ ταύτῃ | τῇ | νυκτὶ ] |
| *tē* | *nukti* | *tautē* | *tautē* | *tē* | *nukti* |
| the | night | this | [this | the | night ] |

23.b.**Txt:** 03B,04C-org 044,byz. **Var:** p74,01א,02A 04C-corr2

| 32.1 noun nom sing masc | 3450.2 art gen sing | 2296.2 noun gen sing masc | 3614.2 rel-pron gen sing | 1498.2 verb 1sing indic pres act | 1466.1 prs-pron nom 1sing |
|---|---|---|---|---|---|
| ʼa ἄγγελος ˋ | τοῦ | θεοῦ | οὗ | εἰμι | [b+ ἐγὼ ] |
| *angelos* | *tou* | *theou* | *hou* | *eimi* | *egō* |
| an angel | | of God, | whose | I am | [ I ] |

23.c.**Var:** 01א,02A,03B 04C,Lach,Treg,Alf Word,Tisc,We/Ho,Weis Sod,UBS/☆

| 3614.3 rel-pron dat sing | 2504.1 conj | 2973.1 verb 1sing indic pres act | 32.1 noun nom sing masc | 2978.15 verb nom sing masc part pres act |
|---|---|---|---|---|
| ᾧ | καὶ | λατρεύω, | [c+ ἄγγελος ] | 24. λέγων, |
| *hō* | *kai* | *latreuō* | *angelos* | *legōn* |
| whom | and | I serve, | [ an angel ] | saying, |

| 3231.1 partic | 5236.5 verb 2sing impr pres mid | 3834.5 name voc masc | 2512.2 name dat masc | 4622.4 prs-pron acc 2sing | 1158.1 verb 3sing indic pres act |
|---|---|---|---|---|---|
| Μὴ | φοβοῦ | Παῦλε, | Καίσαρί | σε | δεῖ |
| *Mē* | *phobou* | *Paule* | *Kaisari* | *se* | *dei* |
| Not | fear, | Paul; | Caesar | you | must |

from food because of loss of appetite or from seasickness. Because of the storm, many must have been seasick. Even if a person is not seasick himself, the sight and odor of seasickness in others is enough to cause a well person to lose his appetite.

At this point the apostle Paul stood up in the midst of the people and reminded them of the warnings he had given them before they left Fair Havens in Crete. He was not simply saying, "I told you so." He remembered they had refused to listen to him then. He had something very important to say to them now. He wanted them to be sure to listen this time. So he caught their attention by getting them to admit (in their minds) that he was right.

Paul's manner indicated also that he did not share the despair of the rest. Paul later told Timothy God has not given believers a spirit of cowardly fear, but of power, of love, and of a sound mind, that is, of self-control (2 Timothy 1:7).

**27:22.** If Paul had not reminded the people that his previous words had proved true, they might have turned away in the bitterness of their despair and refused to listen. Now, in the midst of this most hopeless situation, Paul began with words of renewed hope and expectation. He called them to be of good courage. Paul explained why they must keep up their courage because not one among them would lose his life. Only the ship would be lost.

**27:23.** There was good reason for his encouraging words. That very night an angel of God had appeared to Paul and stood beside him. The Greek has the article here, so Paul is not referring to just any god, but to the one true God, the God to whom Paul belonged, the God Paul served.

The word "serve" here is also rendered "worship" in the King James Version. In the temple Anna worshiped God with fastings and prayers night and day (Luke 2:37). Paul worshiped and served God with his own spirit as he spread the gospel (Romans 1:9).

**27:24.** After giving God the glory, Paul continued with the message of the angel who had told Paul to stop being afraid. It was necessary for him to come before Caesar. This, of course, was a necessity not because of Paul's appeal to Caesar, or because of the charges brought against him by the Jews. Rather, it was necessary because of the divine plan.

Up to that time all hope was lost. Paul had cooperated with those who were trying to save the ship. With his own hands he threw many things overboard. But when all seemed hopeless, Paul did not give up and do nothing. He must have found some corner where he could be alone and seek the Lord. Then he learned the truth again that angels are ministering spirits, "sent forth to minister for them who shall be heirs of salvation" (Hebrews 1:14).

**Paul stood forth in the midst of them, and said:** . . . that Paul came forward, and said, *TCNT* . . . stood up before them, *Everyday* . . . among them, *NAB.*

**Sirs, ye should have hearkened unto me:** My friends, you should have listened to me, *TCNT* . . . you should have taken my advice, *Everyday.*

**and not have loosed from Crete:** I told you not to leave, *Everyday* . . . and not set sail from, *NAB.*

**and to have gained this harm and loss:** . . . and so incurred this injury and damage, *TCNT* . . . You would then have escaped this suffering and loss, *Weymouth* . . . you would not have all this trouble, *Everyday* . . . this disastrous loss, *NAB.*

**22. And now I exhort you to be of good cheer:** But now I tell you, *Everyday* . . . And even now I advise you to cheer up, *Berkeley* . . . Yet, even as things are, I urge you not to lose courage, *TCNT* . . . But now take courage, *Weymouth* . . . keep up your courage, *NAB.*

**for there shall be no loss of any man's life among you:** . . . for there will not be a single life lost among you, *TCNT* . . . None of you will die! *Everyday* . . . None among you will be lost, *NAB.*

**but of the ship:** . . . only the ship, *NAB, TCNT* . . . the ship will be lost, *Everyday.*

**23. For there stood by me this night the angel of God:** For this very night, *RSV* . . . Last night...God's angel said, *Everyday* . . . a messenger of, *NAB.*

**whose I am, and whom I serve:** This is the God I worship, and I am his, *Everyday* . . . whose man I am, *NAB* . . . to whom I belong and whom I worship, *RSV.*

**24. Saying, Fear not, Paul:** Have no fear, Paul, *TCNT* . . . Dismiss all fear, Paul, *Weymouth* . . . Stop being afraid, Paul, *Williams* . . . do not be afraid! *Everyday.*

**thou must be brought before Caesar:** You must stand before, *Everyday* . . . You are destined to appear before, *NAB* . . . you must appear before the Emperor, *TCNT.*

| **3798.11** verb inf aor act | **2504.1** conj | **1481.20** verb 2sing impr aor mid | **5319.12** verb 3sing indic perf mid | **4622.3** prs-pron dat 2sing |
|---|---|---|---|---|
| παραστῆναι· | καὶ | ἰδοὺ | κεχάρισταί | σοι |
| *parastēnai* | *kai* | *idou* | *kecharistai* | *soi* |
| to stand before; | and | behold | has granted | to you |

| **3450.5** art nom sing masc | **2296.1** noun nom sing masc | **3820.8** adj acc pl masc | **3450.8** art acc pl masc | **3986.2** verb acc pl masc part pres act | **3196.3** prep |
|---|---|---|---|---|---|
| ὁ | θεὸς | πάντας | τοὺς | πλέοντας | μετὰ |
| *ho* | *theos* | *pantas* | *tous* | *pleontas* | *meta* |
| | God | all | the | sailing | with |

| **4622.2** prs-pron gen 2sing | **1346.1** conj | **2093.2** verb 2pl impr pres act | **433.6** noun nom pl masc | **3961.4** verb 1sing indic pres act |
|---|---|---|---|---|
| σοῦ. | **25.** Διὸ | εὐθυμεῖτε | ἄνδρες· | πιστεύω |
| *sou* | *Dio* | *euthumeite* | *andres* | *pisteuō* |
| you. | Wherefore | be of good cheer, | men, | I believe |

| **1056.1** conj | **3450.3** art dat sing | **2296.3** noun dat sing masc | **3617.1** conj | **3643.1** adv | **1498.40** verb 3sing indic fut mid |
|---|---|---|---|---|---|
| γὰρ | τῷ | θεῷ | ὅτι | οὕτως | ἔσται |
| *gar* | *tō* | *theō* | *hoti* | *houtōs* | *estai* |
| for | | God | that | thus | it shall be |

| **2567.2** prep | **3614.6** rel-pron acc sing masc | **4999.3** noun acc sing masc | **2953.58** verb 3sing indic perf mid | **1466.4** prs-pron dat 1sing |
|---|---|---|---|---|
| καθ' | ὃν | τρόπον | λελάληταί | μοι. |
| *kath'* | *hon* | *tropon* | *lelalētai* | *moi* |
| according to | which | way | it has been said | to me. |

| **1519.1** prep | **3382.4** noun acc sing fem | **1156.2** conj | **4948.5** indef-pron | **1158.1** verb 3sing indic pres act | **2231.4** prs-pron acc 1pl |
|---|---|---|---|---|---|
| **26.** εἰς | νῆσον | δέ | τινα | δεῖ | ἡμᾶς |
| *eis* | *nēson* | *de* | *tina* | *dei* | *hēmas* |
| On | island | but | a certain | it is necessary | us |

| **1588.8** verb inf aor act | **5453.1** conj | **1156.2** conj | **4912.1** num ord nom sing fem | **3433.1** noun nom sing fem |
|---|---|---|---|---|
| ἐκπεσεῖν. | **27.** Ὡς | δὲ | τεσσαρεσκαιδεκάτη | νὺξ |
| *ekpesein* | *Hōs* | *de* | *tessareskaidekatē* | *nux* |
| to fall. | When | and | the fourteenth | night |

| **1090.33** verb 3sing indic aor mid | **1302.5** verb gen pl masc part pres mid | **2231.2** prs-pron gen 1pl | **1706.1** prep | **3450.3** art dat sing | **98.1** name dat sing masc |
|---|---|---|---|---|---|
| ἐγένετο | διαφερομένων | ἡμῶν | ἐν | τῷ | Ἀδρίᾳ, |
| *egeneto* | *diapheromenōn* | *hēmōn* | *en* | *tō* | *Adria* |
| was come | being driven about | us | in | the | Adriatic, |

| **2567.3** prep | **3189.5** adj sing neu | **3450.10** art gen sing fem | **3433.2** noun gen sing fem | **5120.2** verb indic imperf act | **3450.7** art nom pl masc |
|---|---|---|---|---|---|
| κατὰ | μέσον | τῆς | νυκτὸς | ὑπενόουν | οἱ |
| *kata* | *meson* | *tēs* | *nuktos* | *hupenooun* | *hoi* |
| according to | middle | of the | night | supposed | the |

| **3355.1** noun nom pl masc | **4175.1** verb inf pres act | **4948.5** indef-pron | **840.2** prs-pron dat pl | **5396.4** noun acc sing fem | **2504.1** conj |
|---|---|---|---|---|---|
| ναῦται | προσάγειν | τινὰ | αὐτοῖς | χώραν· | **28.** καὶ |
| *nautai* | *prosagein* | *tina* | *autois* | *chōran* | *kai* |
| sailors | to near | some | them | country, | and |

| **994.1** verb nom pl masc part aor act | **2128.6** verb indic aor act | **3575.1** noun acc pl fem | **1489.2** num card | **1017.2** adj sing neu | **1156.2** conj |
|---|---|---|---|---|---|
| βολίσαντες | εὗρον | ὀργυιὰς | εἴκοσι· | βραχὺ | δὲ |
| *bolisantes* | *heuron* | *orguias* | *eikosi* | *brachu* | *de* |
| having sounded | they found | fathoms | twenty, | a little | and |

Furthermore, the centurion, the pilot, and the captain had all given up hope along with the rest of the ship's crew. No one seemed to have the wisdom, knowledge, or power to bring the passengers and crew to safety. The ship would have been doomed if there had not been a man on board who still had a God-given work to do.

Then, by the grace of God, that is, by His unmerited favor, the angel gave assurance that for Paul's sake, all those on board, helpless and unworthy though they were, would be saved.

**27:25.** Paul concluded in the same way he had begun. He challenged them to keep up their spirits, to be courageous. The situation had not changed. The storm was still raging. But now they had grounds for courage, hope, and expectation—Paul's faith in God. He did not condemn them for their fears. He had shared them. But now God had spoken. They must get their eyes off the storm, off the discouraging circumstances, and fix their eyes on God.

**27:26.** Paul then added a further revelation given by the angel. They must drift with the storm until the ship would run aground on a certain island. This word also gave further assurance that God knew the future and that Paul was not just guessing. The crew and passengers did not know where they were, but God knew where they were and where they were going. However, God did not reveal which island it was.

**27:27.** On the 14th night they were still being driven by the wind in whatever direction it blew. As they later found out, they were drifting across the Sea of Adria, which is the part of the Mediterranean Sea southeast of Italy (not the Adriatic Sea).

As far as they knew, this was open sea. But about midnight the sailors supposed (had a suspicion) that they were approaching land. Some ancient manuscripts of the New Testament read that the land was resounding. In other words, the sailors thought they could hear waves breaking on the beach in the distance.

**27:28.** The crew threw out a weighted rope to sound the depth and found it to be 20 fathoms, that is, about 120 feet or 36 meters. The fathom was originally the distance measured by the arms stretched out horizontally and it came to be standardized as 6 feet. It was used as a nautical measure of depth.

After they went a little farther, they threw out the weighted rope to sound the depth again and found it to be 15 fathoms (90 feet;

**and, lo:** . . . and note this, *Weymouth* . . . and listen! *Williams* . . . and be assured, *Berkeley* . . . Therefore, as a favor to you, *NAB* . . . And God has given you this promise, *Everyday.*

**God hath given thee all them that sail with thee:** . . . made a gift to thee, *Murdock* . . . God has granted safety to all who are sailing with you, *NAB* . . . He will save the lives of all those men sailing with you, *Everyday.*

**25. Wherefore, sirs, be of good cheer:** Therefore, courage, my friends! *TCNT* . . . be cheerful! *Everyday.*

**for I believe God:** . . . for I have confidence in my God, *Williams* . . . I trust in God, *NAB.*

**that it shall be even as it was told me:** . . . it will all work out, *NAB* . . . that everything will happen exactly as I have been told, *TCNT.*

**26. Howbeit we must be cast upon a certain island:** But we are to be stranded on a certain island, *Weymouth* . . . But we will crash on an island, *Everyday* . . . though we still have to face shipwreck on some island, *NAB.*

**27. But when the fourteenth night was come:** . . . arrived, *Moffatt* . . . It was now the fourteenth night of the storm, *TCNT.*

**as we were driven up and down in Adria:** . . . we were still being driven across the Ionian Sea, *NAB* . . . we were floating around in the Adriatic Sea, *Everyday.*

**about midnight the shipmen deemed:** . . . when toward midnight, *NAB* . . . the mariners, *Campbell* . . . the sailors suspected, *Rotherham* . . . sensed, *Phillips* . . . began to suspect, *Norlie* . . . thought, *Everyday.*

**that they drew near to some country:** That they were drawing near land, *TCNT* . . . that we were nearing land, *Phillips* . . . we were close to land, *Everyday.*

**28. And sounded:** . . . let down the lead, *BB* . . . They took a sounding, *NAB* . . . threw a rope into the water with a weight on the end, *Everyday.*

**and found it twenty fathoms:** . . . and found a depth of, *NAB* . . . and found the water 120 feet deep, *Beck.*

| 1333.2 verb nom pl masc part aor act | 2504.1 conj | 3687.1 adv | 994.1 verb nom pl masc part aor act | 2128.6 verb indic aor act |
|---|---|---|---|---|
| διαστήσαντες | καὶ | πάλιν | βολίσαντες | εὗρον |
| *diastēsantes* | *kai* | *palin* | *bolisantes* | *heuron* |
| having gone farther | and | again | having sounded | they found |

29.a.**Txt:** 020L,025P,byz. **Var:** 01ℵ,03B,04C,Alf We/Ho,Sod,UBS/☆

| 3575.1 noun acc pl fem | 1173.1 num card | 5236.8 verb nom pl masc part pres mid | 4885.1 conj | 3248.1 conj |
|---|---|---|---|---|
| ὀργυιὰς | δεκαπέντε· | **29.** φοβούμενοί | τε | ʼ μήπως |
| *orguias* | *dekapente* | *phoboumenoi* | *te* | *mēpōs* |
| fathoms | fifteen; | fearing | and | lest |

29.b.**Txt:** 020L,025P,byz. **Var:** 01ℵ,02A,03B,04C Lach,Treg,Alf,Word Tisc,We/Ho,Weis,Sod UBS/☆

| 3231.1 partic | 4084.1 adv | 1519.1 prep | 2567.3 prep | 4977.1 adj acc pl masc | 4964.7 noun acc pl masc |
|---|---|---|---|---|---|
| [a☆ μή | που ] | ʼ εἰς | [b☆ κατὰ ] | τραχεῖς | τόπους |
| *mē* | *pou* | *eis* | *kata* | *tracheis* | *topous* |
| [ not | how ] | on | [ down on ] | rocky | places |

29.c.**Txt:** byz.sa. **Var:** 02A,03B,04C,020L 025P,bo.Gries,Lach Treg,Alf,Word,Tisc We/Ho,Weis,Sod UBS/☆

| 1588.7 verb 3pl subj aor act | 1588.13 verb 1pl subj aor act | 1523.2 prep gen | 4261.2 noun gen sing fem |
|---|---|---|---|
| ʼ ἐκπέσωσιν, | [c☆ ἐκπέσωμεν, ] | ἐκ | πρύμνης |
| *ekpesōsin* | *ekpesōmen* | *ek* | *prumnēs* |
| they should fall, | [ we might fall, ] | out of | stern |

| 4352.4 verb nom pl masc part aor act | 44.2 noun acc pl fem | 4913.3 num card acc | 2153.6 verb 3pl indic imperf mid | 2232.4 noun acc sing fem |
|---|---|---|---|---|
| ῥίψαντες | ἀγκύρας | τέσσαρας | ηὔχοντο | ἡμέραν |
| *rhipsantes* | *ankuras* | *tessaras* | *ēuchonto* | *hēmeran* |
| having cast | anchors | four | they were wanting | day |

| 1090.63 verb inf aor mid | 3450.1 art gen pl | 1156.2 conj | 3355.2 noun gen pl masc | 2195.11 verb gen pl masc part pres act | 5180.8 verb inf aor act |
|---|---|---|---|---|---|
| γενέσθαι. | **30.** τῶν | δὲ | ναυτῶν | ζητούντων | φυγεῖν |
| *genesthai* | *tōn* | *de* | *nautōn* | *zētountōn* | *phugein* |
| to come. | The | but | sailors | seeking | to flee |

| 1523.2 prep gen | 3450.2 art gen sing | 4003.2 noun gen sing neu | 2504.1 conj | 5301.4 verb gen pl masc part aor act | 3450.12 art acc sing fem |
|---|---|---|---|---|---|
| ἐκ | τοῦ | πλοίου, | καὶ | χαλασάντων | τὴν |
| *ek* | *tou* | *ploiou* | *kai* | *chalasantōn* | *tēn* |
| out of | the | ship, | and | having let down | the |

| 4482.2 noun acc sing fem | 1519.1 prep | 3450.12 art acc sing fem | 2258.4 noun acc sing fem | 4250.1 noun dat sing fem | 5453.1 conj |
|---|---|---|---|---|---|
| σκάφην | εἰς | τὴν | θάλασσαν, | προφάσει | ὡς |
| *skaphēn* | *eis* | *tēn* | *thalassan* | *prophasei* | *hōs* |
| boat | into | the | sea, | with pretext | as |

30.a.**Txt:** 03B,04C,020L 025P,etc.byz.Sod **Var:** 01ℵ-corr,02A,Lach Tisc,We/Ho,Weis UBS/☆

| 1523.2 prep gen | 4266.2 noun gen sing fem | 4266.3 noun gen sing fem | 3165.11 verb gen pl part pres act | 44.2 noun acc pl fem |
|---|---|---|---|---|
| ἐκ | ʼ πρῴρας | [a☆ πρῴρης ] | ʼ μελλόντων | ἀγκύρας |
| *ek* | *prōras* | *prōrēs* | *mellontōn* | *ankuras* |
| from | prow | [ idem ] | being about | anchors |

| 44.2 noun acc pl fem | 3165.11 verb gen pl part pres act | 1601.1 verb inf pres act | 1500.5 verb 3sing indic aor act |
|---|---|---|---|
| [☆ ἀγκύρας | μελλόντων ] | ἐκτείνειν, | **31.** εἶπεν |
| *ankuras* | *mellontōn* | *ekteinein* | *eipen* |
| [ anchors | being about ] | to cast out, | said |

| 3450.5 art nom sing masc | 3834.1 name nom masc | 3450.3 art dat sing | 1529.2 noun dat sing masc | 2504.1 conj | 3450.4 art dat pl |
|---|---|---|---|---|---|
| ὁ | Παῦλος | τῷ | ἑκατοντάρχῃ | καὶ | τοῖς |
| *ho* | *Paulos* | *tō* | *hekatontarchē* | *kai* | *tois* |
|  | Paul | to the | centurion | and | to the |

about 28 meters). From this it was obvious they were indeed coming close to land of some sort.

**27:29.** No doubt by now the sailors could indeed hear the waves breaking on the shore. They became afraid the ship would run aground on the rocks and break up before they could escape. So they tossed out four sea anchors from the rear of the ship. These anchors were probably of iron or lead and each had two flukes shaped to catch on the sea bottom.

Since it was not long after midnight, it was still pitch dark, and there was nothing else they could do but hope the anchors would keep them from drifting nearer the rocks. Probably in the excitement no one could sleep so they all "wished for the day."

The Greek word could mean "wish." But it more commonly means they kept praying for the day to come. The King James Version translated it "pray" in 2 Corinthians 13:7 and in James 5:16. In the latter case believers are told to pray one for another. In this situation they were no doubt praying that the ship would hold together until there would be enough light to see where they were and what it might be possible for them to do. Even Paul knew he would have to put his faith into action.

**27:30.** The crew did more than wish and pray, however. They decided it would be dangerous to wait the several hours until the daylight, so they made an attempt to flee from the ship.

When they were discovered, they had lowered the small boat under the pretense of putting out anchors from the prow, that is, from the bow or the front end of the ship. They intended to make it to the shore and at least save themselves. Obviously, they did not share the faith of Paul, nor did they accept his assurance that everyone on board would be saved.

It seems also the captain did not interfere and the centurion did not know what to do. It is obvious too that these sailors and their officers were still fearful, so full of fear, in fact, that they thought only of themselves. They were quite willing to leave the more than 200 other people on the ship to die.

These sailors were wrong too to use deception to gain their ends. Moreover, they had no command to put out anchors from the prow. Thus they were also guilty of disobedience.

**27:31.** Again Paul took command of the situation. With a sense of authority given him by the Holy Spirit, he told the centurion that unless these sailors stayed with the ship none of the crew or passengers could be saved.

As it turned out, these sailors were needed to try to get the ship to go aground in the best place. Though Paul had the promise of God that all those on board would be saved, God was not going to

**and when they had gone a little further:** . . . and a little further on, *Moffatt* . . . after sailing on a short distance, *NAB.*
**they sounded again:** . . . threw the rope in again, *Everyday.*
**and found it fifteen fathoms:** . . . and it was ninety feet, *BB.*

**29. Then fearing lest we should have fallen upon rocks:** . . . being driven upon some rocky coast, *TCNT* . . . So, for fear that we might be hurled on the rocks, *Phillips* . . . lest on rough places, *Young* . . . afraid that we would hit the rocks, *Everyday* . . . we should be dashed against some rock coast, *NAB.*
**they cast four anchors out of the stern:** . . . they let down four hooks from the back of the ship, *BB* . . . threw four anchors into the water, *Everyday.*
**and wished for the day:** . . . and kept wishing for daylight to come, *Williams* . . . and longed for daylight, *TCNT* . . . for break of day, *Berkeley* . . . and began praying, *Rotherham* . . . for morning to come, *Beck* . . . prayed for daylight to come, *Everyday* . . . and earnestly wished, *PNT.*

**30. And as the shipmen were about to flee out of the ship:** . . . as the sailors, *ASV* . . . Some of the sailors wanted to leave the ship, *Everyday* . . . tried to abandon, *Berkeley* . . . the ship, *Norlie.*
**when they had let down the boat into the sea:** . . . and they got as far as letting a boat down, *Phillips* . . . they let the ship's boat down, *NAB* . . . lowered the lifeboat, *Everyday* . . . the skiff, *Concordant.*
**under colour as though they would have cast anchors out of the foreship:** . . . by pretext as though, *Rotherham* . . . on pretence of running out anchors from the bows, *TCNT* . . . These sailors wanted the other men to think that they were throwing more anchors from the front of the ship, *Everyday.*

**31. Paul said to the centurion and to the soldiers:** But Paul, addressing Julius and the soldiers, said, *Weymouth* . . . told the officer and the other soldiers, *Everyday* . . . alerted the centurion and the soldiers to this, *NAB.*

| 4608.6 noun dat pl masc | 1430.1 partic | 3231.1 partic | 3642.7 dem-pron nom pl masc | 3176.21 verb 3pl subj aor act | 1706.1 prep |
|---|---|---|---|---|---|
| στρατιώταις, | Ἐὰν | μὴ | οὗτοι | μείνωσιν | ἐν |
| stratiōtais | Ean | mē | houtoi | meinōsin | en |
| soldiers, | If | not | these | remain | in |

| 3450.3 art dat sing | 4003.3 noun dat sing neu | 5050.1 prs-pron nom 2pl | 4834.28 verb inf aor pass | 3620.3 partic | 1404.6 verb 2pl indic pres mid |
|---|---|---|---|---|---|
| τῷ | πλοίῳ, | ὑμεῖς | σωθῆναι | οὐ | δύνασθε. |
| tō | ploiō | humeis | sōthēnai | ou | dunasthe |
| the | ship | you | to be saved | not | are able. |

| | 4966.1 adv | 3450.7 art nom pl masc | 4608.4 noun nom pl masc | 604.2 verb 3pl indic aor act | 604.2 verb 3pl indic aor act |
|---|---|---|---|---|---|
| 32. | τότε | ʽ οἱ | στρατιῶται | ἀπέκοψαν | [☆ ἀπέκοψαν |
| | tote | hoi | stratiōtai | apekopsan | apekopsan |
| | Then | the | soldiers | cut away | [ cut away |

| 3450.7 art nom pl masc | 4608.4 noun nom pl masc | 3450.17 art pl neu | 4831.2 noun pl neu | 3450.10 art gen sing fem | 4482.1 noun gen sing fem |
|---|---|---|---|---|---|
| οἱ | στρατιῶται ] | τὰ | σχοινία | τῆς | σκάφης |
| hoi | stratiōtai | ta | schoinia | tēs | skaphēs |
| the | soldiers ] | the | ropes | of the | boat |

| 2504.1 conj | 1432.4 verb 3pl indic aor act | 840.12 prs-pron acc sing fem | 1588.8 verb inf aor act | | 884.2 conj | 1156.2 conj |
|---|---|---|---|---|---|---|
| καὶ | εἴασαν | αὐτὴν | ἐκπεσεῖν. | 33. | Ἄχρι | δὲ |
| kai | eiasan | autēn | ekpesein | | Achri | de |
| and | let | it | to fall. | | Until | and |

33.a.**Txt:** byz.
**Var:** 03B,04C,Lach
Treg,Alf,We/Ho,Weis
Sod,UBS/☆

| 3614.2 rel-pron gen sing | 3165.22 verb 3sing indic imperf act | 2232.2 noun nom sing fem | 2232.2 noun nom sing fem | 3165.21 verb 3sing indic imperf act |
|---|---|---|---|---|
| οὗ | ʽ ἔμελλεν | ἡμέρα | [ᵃ☆ ἡμέρα | ἤμελλεν ] |
| hou | emellen | hēmera | hēmera | ēmellen |
| which | was about | day | [ day | was about ] |

| 1090.28 verb inf pres mid | 3731.18 verb 3sing indic imperf act | 3450.5 art nom sing masc | 3834.1 name nom masc | 533.5 adj acc pl masc |
|---|---|---|---|---|
| γίνεσθαι, | παρεκάλει | ὁ | Παῦλος | ἅπαντας |
| ginesthai | parekalei | ho | Paulos | hapantas |
| to come, | was encouraging | | Paul | all |

| 3205.4 verb inf aor act | 5001.2 noun gen sing fem | 2978.15 verb nom sing masc part pres act | 4912.2 num ord acc sing fem |
|---|---|---|---|
| μεταλαβεῖν | τροφῆς, | λέγων, | Τεσσαρεσκαιδεκάτην |
| metalabein | trophēs | legōn | Tessareskaidekatēn |
| to partake | of food, | saying, | Fourteenth |

| 4449.1 adv | 2232.4 noun acc sing fem | 4186.5 verb nom pl masc part pres act | 771.1 adj nom pl masc | 1294.1 verb 2pl indic pres act |
|---|---|---|---|---|
| σήμερον | ἡμέραν | προσδοκῶντες | ἄσιτοι | διατελεῖτε, |
| sēmeron | hēmeran | prosdokōntes | asitoi | diateleite |
| today | day | watching | foodless | you continue, |

33.b.**Txt:** 04C,020L
025P,byz.Sod
**Var:** 01א,02A,03B,Lach
Treg,Alf,Tisc,We/Ho
Weis,UBS/☆

| 3235.6 num card neu | 3238.1 adv | 4213.7 verb nom pl masc part aor mid | | 1346.1 conj | 3731.1 verb 1sing indic pres act |
|---|---|---|---|---|---|
| ʽ μηδὲν | [ᵇ☆ μηθὲν ] | προσλαβόμενοι. | 34. | διὸ | παρακαλῶ |
| mēden | mēthen | proslabomenoi | | dio | parakalō |
| nothing | [ idem ] | having taken. | | Wherefore | I urge |

34.a.**Txt:** 020L,025P,byz.
**Var:** 01א,02A,03B,04C
Gries,Lach,Treg,Alf
Word,Tisc,We/Ho,Weis
Sod,UBS/☆

| 5050.4 prs-pron acc 2pl | 4213.1 verb inf aor act | 3205.4 verb inf aor act | 5001.2 noun gen sing fem | 3642.17 dem-pron sing neu |
|---|---|---|---|---|
| ὑμᾶς | ʽ προσλαβεῖν | [ᵃ☆ μεταλαβεῖν ] | τροφῆς· | τοῦτο |
| humas | proslabein | metalabein | trophēs | touto |
| you | to take | [ to partake of ] | food, | this |

send angels to carry them to safety. Nor could they simply let the boat drift in the storm any longer. They were going to have their part to do. God is sovereign; yet He sometimes uses even the ungodly to help accomplish His will. He used the ungodly Assyrians to bring His judgment on Israel, even though they did not know He was using them (Isaiah 10:5-7). He used the idol-worshiping Cyrus to send the Jews back to rebuild the temple (Isaiah 45:1-4). He used heathen sailors to throw Jonah overboard, and a big fish to get Jonah headed back in the direction He wanted him to go. There is no limit to what God can use to accomplish His purposes. It is obvious Paul was not using his own imagination to decide how he wanted God to act or what miracle he would like performed. Rather, he was sensitive to the Holy Spirit and was acting on the wisdom given him by the Spirit.

**27:32.** The soldiers under the centurion not only accepted Paul's authority, they had common sense enough to know he was right. They did not want to take any further chances that some, under the cover of darkness, might try the same thing again. So they cut the ropes holding the small boat and let it fall into the sea. Now they were all going to have to trust Paul's advice.

**27:33.** As they were nearing daybreak, Paul, still in command of the situation, again took charge and encouraged everyone to take food for their own bodily health and welfare. This was the 14th day they were tarrying or waiting. The Greek implies they were expecting the worst. They really thought the storm was going to destroy the ship and that all would be lost. Thus, during all this time they were continually without food.

In recounting his sufferings, Paul had already told the Corinthians of his three previous shipwrecks and also the many perils he faced. Then he added he was "in weariness (labor, toil) and painfulness (hardship), in watchings (wakefulness, sleepless nights) often, in hunger and thirst, in fastings (because lack of food made fasting necessary) often, in cold and nakedness (not stark naked, but poorly dressed because of the lack of clothing)." (See 2 Corinthians 11:27-29.)

**27:34.** Again Paul urged them to take nourishment for their "health" (since it was going to be for their deliverance, preservation, salvation). They were going to need some energy to be able to get to the shore.

Then Paul gave them further positive assurance that not a hair would be lost from anyone's head. Not only would they be saved from what had seemed to be certain death, there would not be the slightest injury to anyone. Paul was encouraging them, not only to take food, but to believe and trust in the promise God had given through the angel who had appeared to him.

**Except these abide in the ship:** Unless the sailors remain on board, *TCNT* . . . Unless these men remain on the ship, *Montgomery* . . . If these men do not stay with the ship, *NAB.*

**ye cannot be saved:** . . . you will not be safe, *BB* . . . Your lives will be sacrificed, *Weymouth* . . . you can't be rescued, *Beck* . . . you have no chance to survive, *NAB.*

**32. Then the soldiers cut off the ropes of the boat:** . . . the ropes which held the boat, *TCNT.*

**and let her fall off:** . . . and let her drift away, *TCNT* . . . go adrift, *Murdock* . . . and let the lifeboat fall into the water, *Everyday* . . . fall away, *Williams C.K.*

**33. And while the day was coming on:** And as day was dawning, *Weymouth* . . . And when dawn was near, *BB* . . . Just before dawn, *Everyday.*

**Paul besought them all to take meat, saying:** Paul urged all on board, *NAB* . . . Paul gave them all orders to take food, saying, *BB* . . . began persuading all the people to eat something, *Everyday* . . . kept begging them...to eat, *Williams.*

**This day is the fourteenth day that ye have tarried:** For fourteen days now, *Williams C.K.* . . . For the past 14 days you have been waiting and watching, *Everyday* . . . that you have been on the strain, *Weymouth* . . . you have uninterruptedly been on the alert, *Berkeley* . . . you have been constantly waiting, *Williams* . . . your being on watch, *Norlie* . . . you have been in constant suspense, *NAB.*

**and continued fasting, having taken nothing:** . . . and have fasted, eating little or nothing, *Weymouth* . . . you have gone without food, *TCNT* . . . you have gone hungry—eaten nothing, *NAB* . . . not even taking a bit, *Williams* . . . that you have not had time to eat, *Norlie* . . . without a proper meal, *Moffatt* . . . without regular rations, *Fenton.*

**34. Wherefore I pray you to take some meat:** So I urge you to take something to eat, *TCNT* . . . I therefore strongly advise, *Weymouth* . . . Now I beg you, *Everyday* . . . So I implore you to eat something, *Berkeley.*

| 1056.1 conj | 4242.1 prep | 3450.10 art gen sing fem | 5052.5 adj gen 2sing fem | 4843.2 noun gen sing fem | 5062.2 verb 3sing indic pres act |
|---|---|---|---|---|---|
| γὰρ | πρὸς | τῆς | ὑμετέρας | σωτηρίας | ὑπάρχει· |
| *gar* | *pros* | *tēs* | *humeteras* | *sōtērias* | *huparchei* |
| for | to | the | your | salvation | is; |

34.b.**Txt:** 01ℵ,020L 025P,byz.
**Var:** 02A,03B,04C,Lach Treg,Alf,Tisc,We/Ho Weis,Sod,UBS/☆

| 3625.1 num card gen | 1056.1 conj | 5050.2 prs-pron gen 2pl | 2336.1 noun nom sing fem | 1523.2 prep gen | 570.3 prep | 3450.10 art gen sing fem |
|---|---|---|---|---|---|---|
| οὐδενὸς | γὰρ | ὑμῶν | θρὶξ | ‘ ἐκ | [b☆ ἀπὸ ] | τῆς |
| *oudenos* | *gar* | *humōn* | *thrix* | *ek* | *apo* | *tēs* |
| no one | for | of you | a hair | of | [ from ] | the |

34.c.**Txt:** 020L,025P,byz. sa.
**Var:** 01ℵ,02A,03B,04C 33,bo.Gries,Lach,Treg Alf,Word,Tisc,We/Ho Weis,Sod,UBS/☆

| 2747.2 noun gen sing fem | 3959.19 verb 3sing indic fut mid | 616.27 verb 3sing indic fut mid | 1500.15 verb nom sing masc part aor act |
|---|---|---|---|
| κεφαλῆς | ‘ πεσεῖται. | [c☆ ἀπολεῖται. ] | 35. ‘ Εἰπὼν |
| *kephalēs* | *peseitai* | *apoleitai* | *Eipōn* |
| head | shall fall. | [ shall be lost. ] | Having said |

35.a.**Txt:** 020L,025P,byz. Sod
**Var:** 01ℵ,02A,03B,04C Lach,Treg,Alf,Tisc We/Ho,Weis,UBS/☆

| 1500.30 verb nom sing masc part aor act | 1156.2 conj | 3642.18 dem-pron pl neu | 2504.1 conj | 2956.25 verb nom sing masc part aor act | 735.4 noun acc sing masc |
|---|---|---|---|---|---|
| [a☆ εἴπας ] | δὲ | ταῦτα | καὶ | λαβὼν | ἄρτον |
| *eipas* | *de* | *tauta* | *kai* | *labōn* | *arton* |
| [ idem ] | and | these things | and | having taken | a loaf |

| 2149.9 verb 3sing indic aor act | 3450.3 art dat sing | 2296.3 noun dat sing masc | 1783.1 prep | 3820.4 adj gen pl | 2504.1 conj |
|---|---|---|---|---|---|
| εὐχαρίστησεν | τῷ | θεῷ | ἐνώπιον | πάντων, | καὶ |
| *eucharistēsen* | *tō* | *theō* | *enōpion* | *pantōn* | *kai* |
| he gave thanks | | to God | before | all, | and |

| 2779.5 verb nom sing masc part aor act | 751.5 verb 3sing indic aor mid | 2052.14 verb inf pres act | 2094.1 adj nom pl masc | 1156.2 conj |
|---|---|---|---|---|
| κλάσας | ἤρξατο | ἐσθίειν. | 36. εὔθυμοι | δὲ |
| *klasas* | *ērxato* | *esthiein* | *euthumoi* | *de* |
| having broken | began | to eat. | Of good cheer | and |

| 1090.55 verb nom pl masc part aor mid | 3820.7 adj nom pl masc | 2504.1 conj | 840.7 prs-pron nom pl masc | 4213.4 verb 3pl indic aor mid |
|---|---|---|---|---|
| γενόμενοι | πάντες | καὶ | αὐτοὶ | προσελάβοντο |
| *genomenoi* | *pantes* | *kai* | *autoi* | *proselabonto* |
| having become | all | also | themselves | took |

37.a.**Txt:** 04C,020L 025P,byz.Sod
**Var:** 01ℵ,02A,03B,Lach Treg,Alf,Word,Tisc We/Ho,Weis,UBS/☆

| 5001.2 noun gen sing fem | 1498.36 verb 1pl indic imperf act | 1498.50 verb 1pl indic imperf mid | 1156.2 conj | 1706.1 prep | 3450.3 art dat sing |
|---|---|---|---|---|---|
| τροφῆς· | 37. ‘ ἦμεν | [a☆ ἤμεθα ] | δὲ | ‘ ἐν | τῷ |
| *trophēs* | *ēmen* | *ēmetha* | *de* | *en* | *tō* |
| food. | We were | [ idem ] | and | in | the |

| 4003.3 noun dat sing neu | 3450.13 art nom pl fem | 3820.13 adj nom pl fem | 5425.5 noun nom pl fem | 3450.13 art nom pl fem | 3820.13 adj nom pl fem | 5425.5 noun nom pl fem |
|---|---|---|---|---|---|---|
| πλοίῳ | αἱ | πᾶσαι | ψυχαὶ | [☆ αἱ | πᾶσαι | ψυχαὶ |
| *ploiō* | *hai* | *pasai* | *psuchai* | *hai* | *pasai* | *psuchai* |
| ship | the | all | lives | [ the | all | lives |

| 1706.1 prep | 3450.3 art dat sing | 4003.3 noun dat sing neu | 1244.3 num card nom fem | 1434.1 num card |
|---|---|---|---|---|
| ἐν | τῷ | πλοίῳ ] | διακόσιαι | ‘ ἑβδομηκονταέξ. |
| *en* | *tō* | *ploiō* | *diakosiai* | *hebdomēkontaex* |
| in | the | ship ] | two hundred | seventy-six. |

| 1433.1 num card | 1787.1 num card | 2853.1 verb nom pl masc part aor pass | 1156.2 conj | 5001.2 noun gen sing fem |
|---|---|---|---|---|
| [☆ ἑβδομήκοντα | ἕξ. ] | 38. κορεσθέντες | δὲ | τροφῆς |
| *hebdomēkonta* | *hex* | *koresthentes* | *de* | *trophēs* |
| [ seventy | six. ] | Having been satisfied | and | with food |

God gave this promise, of course, to meet this particular situation. He does not promise believers will always be protected from any injury. But He is always with them.

**27:35.** Paul did more than urge the people on the ship to take nourishment. He set the example by taking a loaf of bread. But he did not begin to eat at once. Before the whole crowd he gave thanks to God. This was no mere formal prayer. It came from the depths of Paul's heart. It was an anointed prayer. All the people on the ship must have felt the impact of the Holy Spirit as he prayed. Then Paul broke the bread and began to eat.

**27:36.** Paul's example had the effect he wanted it to have. When they saw Paul's joy in the Lord, they were all encouraged. With cheerfulness and in good spirits they also began to take nourishment for themselves.

Paul's faith and example had inspired them with new hope, real hope for the first time since the storm began. It is likely they sensed Paul's love as well. The combination of faith, hope, and love is unbeatable under all circumstances. Paul wrote to the Corinthians, "For whether we be beside ourselves (that is, if we are out of our senses), it is to God: or whether we be sober (that is, in our right mind), it is for your cause (that is, for you). For the love of Christ constraineth us (that is, impels us, urges us on, at the same time embracing us, controlling us, and keeping us within the boundaries set by God's Word); because we thus judge, that if one died for all, then were all dead; and that he died for all, that they which live should not henceforth live unto themselves, but unto him which died for them, and rose again" (2 Corinthians 5:13-15).

**27:37.** The Bible now draws attention to the fact there were 276 souls on board the ship. "Souls" here means living persons, living human beings. This was not the largest audience the apostle Paul had stood before and influenced, but it was an unusually large number to be on any one ship in those days. It was also probably the first time an entire crowd had followed his advice.

**27:38.** After they had all eaten their fill and were satisfied with food, everyone went to work throwing the cargo of wheat overboard. Up to this time they had thrown overboard everything else they could move. But somehow, even after they had given up all real hope that they would be saved, they still had a vague hope

**for this is for your health:** . . . it is necessary for your safety, *MLNT* . . . your safety depends on it, *TCNT* . . . it will sustain your health, *Berkeley* . . . this is conducive, *Campbell* . . . in order to survive, *TEV* . . . You need it to stay alive, *Everyday, SEB* . . . the beginning of your deliverance, *Worrell.*

**for there shall not an hair fall from the head of any of you:** . . . for not one of you will lose even a hair of his head, *TCNT* . . . not a hair of your head will perish, *MLNT* . . . will be lost, *Williams C.K.*

**35. And when he had thus spoken, he took bread:** With these words he took some bread, *TCNT.*

**and gave thanks to God in presence of them all:** . . . he gave thanks unto God before all, *Rotherham* . . . he gave praise to God, *BB* . . . before them all, *Williams C.K.*

**and when he had broken it, he began to eat:** He broke off a piece and began eating, *Everyday.*

**36. Then were they all of good cheer:** Then they all cheered up, *Moffatt* . . . This raised the spirits of all, *Weymouth* . . . And they all took heart, *Williams C.K.* . . . All the men felt better, *Everyday* . . . This gave them new courage, *NAB* . . . Then they all were encouraged, *MLNT.*

**and they also took some meat:** . . . and had something to eat themselves, *TCNT* . . . and began themselves to eat, *Williams C.K.* . . . and started eating too, *Everyday* . . . and they too had something to eat, *NAB* . . . and partook of nourishment, *MLNT.*

**37. And we were in all in the ship two hundred threescore and sixteen souls:** There were two hundred and seventy-six of us, crew and passengers on board, *Weymouth* . . . all told there were 276 of us on board, *Berkeley* . . . in all in the ship, *Williams C.K.*

**38. And when they had eaten enough:** After satisfying their hunger, *TCNT* . . . After eating a hearty meal, *Weymouth* . . . When they had had enough, *NAB, Williams C.K.* . . . We ate all we wanted, *Everyday.*

| 2866.1 verb 3pl indic imperf act | 3450.16 art sing neu | 4003.1 noun sing neu | 1531.27 verb nom pl masc part pres mid | 3450.6 art acc sing masc |
|---|---|---|---|---|
| ἐκούφιζον | τὸ | πλοῖον, | ἐκβαλλόμενοι | τὸν |
| *ekouphizon* | *to* | *ploion* | *ekballomenoi* | *ton* |
| they were lightening | the | ship, | casting out | the |

| 4476.2 noun acc sing masc | 1519.1 prep | 3450.12 art acc sing fem | 2258.4 noun acc sing fem | 3616.1 conj | 1156.2 conj | 2232.2 noun nom sing fem |
|---|---|---|---|---|---|---|
| σῖτον | εἰς | τὴν | θάλασσαν. | **39.** Ὅτε | δὲ | ἡμέρα |
| *siton* | *eis* | *tēn* | *thalassan* | *Hote* | *de* | *hēmera* |
| wheat | into | the | sea. | When | and | day |

| 1090.33 verb 3sing indic aor mid | 3450.12 art acc sing fem | 1087.4 noun acc sing fem | 3620.2 partic | 1906.17 verb 3pl indic imperf act |
|---|---|---|---|---|
| ἐγένετο, | τὴν | γῆν | οὐκ | ἐπεγίνωσκον· |
| *egeneto* | *tēn* | *gēn* | *ouk* | *epeginōskon* |
| it was | the | land | not | they were recognizing; |

| 2831.2 noun acc sing masc | 1156.2 conj | 4948.5 indef-pron | 2627.8 verb indic imperf act | 2174.15 verb part pres act | 123.1 noun acc sing masc |
|---|---|---|---|---|---|
| κόλπον | δέ | τινα | κατενόουν | ἔχοντα | αἰγιαλὸν, |
| *kolpon* | *de* | *tina* | *katenooun* | *echonta* | *aigialon* |
| a bay | but | certain | they were perceiving | having | a shore, |

| 1519.1 prep | 3614.6 rel-pron acc sing masc | 1003.5 verb 3pl indic aor mid | 1003.6 verb 3pl indic imperf mid | 1479.1 conj |
|---|---|---|---|---|
| εἰς | ὃν | ‘ ἐβουλεύσαντο | [a☆ ἐβουλεύοντο ] | εἰ |
| *eis* | *hon* | *ebouleusanto* | *ebouleuonto* | *ei* |
| on | which | they resolved | [ they were resolving ] | if |

| 1404.11 verb 3pl opt pres mid | 1409.3 adj sing neu | 1840.2 verb inf aor act | 3450.16 art sing neu | 4003.1 noun sing neu |
|---|---|---|---|---|
| ‘ δύναιντο | [b δύνατον ] | ἐξῶσαι | τὸ | πλοῖον. |
| *dunainto* | *dunaton* | *exōsai* | *to* | *ploion* |
| they should be able | [ able ] | to drive | the | ship; |

| 2504.1 conj | 3450.15 art acc pl fem | 44.2 noun acc pl fem | 3877.1 verb nom pl masc part aor act | 1432.9 verb 3pl indic imperf act |
|---|---|---|---|---|
| **40.** καὶ | τὰς | ἀγκύρας | περιελόντες | εἴων |
| *kai* | *tas* | *ankuras* | *perielontes* | *eiōn* |
| and | the | anchors | having cut away | they were leaving |

| 1519.1 prep | 3450.12 art acc sing fem | 2258.4 noun acc sing fem | 258.1 adv | 445.3 verb nom pl masc part aor act |
|---|---|---|---|---|
| εἰς | τὴν | θάλασσαν, | ἅμα | ἀνέντες |
| *eis* | *tēn* | *thalassan* | *hama* | *anentes* |
| in | the | sea, | at the same time | having loosened |

| 3450.15 art acc pl fem | 2184.1 noun acc pl fem | 3450.1 art gen pl | 3940.2 noun gen pl neu | 2504.1 conj | 1854.6 verb nom pl masc part aor act |
|---|---|---|---|---|---|
| τὰς | ζευκτηρίας | τῶν | πηδαλίων· | καὶ | ἐπάραντες |
| *tas* | *zeuktērias* | *tōn* | *pēdaliōn* | *kai* | *eparantes* |
| the | bands | of the | rudders, | and | having hoisted |

| 3450.6 art acc sing masc | 731.1 noun acc sing masc | 731.2 noun acc sing masc | 3450.11 art dat sing fem | 4014.5 verb dat sing fem part pres act |
|---|---|---|---|---|
| τὸν | ‘ ἀρτέμονα | [☆ ἀρτέμωνα ] | τῇ | πνεούσῃ |
| *ton* | *artemona* | *artemōna* | *tē* | *pneousē* |
| the | foresail | [ idem ] | to the | blowing |

| 2692.10 verb 3pl indic imperf act | 1519.1 prep | 3450.6 art acc sing masc | 123.1 noun acc sing masc | 3908.3 verb nom pl masc part aor act |
|---|---|---|---|---|
| κατεῖχον | εἰς | τὸν | αἰγιαλόν. | **41.** περιπεσόντες |
| *kateichon* | *eis* | *ton* | *aigialon* | *peripesontes* |
| they were making | for | the | shore. | Having fallen |

39.a.**Txt:** 020L,025P,byz.
**Var:** 01ℵ,03B,04C,Lach Treg,Alf,Word,Tisc We/Ho,Weis,Sod UBS/☆

39.b.**Txt:** 01ℵ,02A,03B 044,81,945,1739,Steph
**Var:** 04C,byz.

that something would happen to make it possible for them to get the cargo of wheat to Rome so they could collect their money. But now they not only believed Paul's promise that they would be saved, they remembered that he said the ship would be lost. Thus, there was no longer any point in making any attempt to save the cargo of wheat. Furthermore, by throwing the wheat overboard they would lighten the ship so it would ride higher. This would help them get closer to the shore and give them a better chance of reaching land safely.

**27:39.** When daylight came they did not recognize the land. Because they had seen neither sun nor stars, they had no idea of their course. It seems the island of Malta was not a regular stopping place for the grain ships going from Egypt to Rome. Undoubtedly, no one on board had ever been there before. But they noticed a bay and decided that if they were able they would run the ship aground on the beach. This would make it easy for them all to go ashore.

St. Paul's Bay, as it is called today, fits exactly the account recorded in this chapter. There are places near the west side of the bay where the depth is actually 20 fathoms and then a little farther in, 15 fathoms. The bay is about 2 miles northwest of Valetta.

**27:40.** The sailors, now that they could see the bay and the opportunity to reach the beach, went to work. They knew what to do, and they no longer hesitated. First, they released the anchors and left them in the sea, because this also would lighten the ship. At the same time they unfastened the rudder (or steering paddle), so they could head the ship in the right direction. Then they raised the foresail (which was set on the bow of the ship) to catch the wind, and headed for the beach.

The storm had not yet ended. It was still raining and the wind was still blowing. The sailors needed to use all the skills they had in order to get the ship as close to the shore as possible. God's promise was good. But He still allowed adverse conditions to test their faith and obedience. Sometimes believers would like Him to bring them to the desired shore on a magic carpet. But instead He makes sure the right people are there with the right skills to help those who need help. In this case it was sailors who knew how to steer the ship and how to set the sail. But whatever the situation, believers too can count on the Lord's care and concern for them. At the same time, believers should not be afraid to use the means which He has made available. Paul and his companions must have been asking God to help the sailors.

These were tense moments. The sailors were doing their best. Many of the others on board may have been feeling a bit apprehensive again, but the believers were trusting in the Lord.

**they lightened the ship:** . . . they further lightened the ship, *TCNT.*

**and cast out the wheat into the sea:** . . . by throwing the grain, *TCNT* . . . by dumping the wheat into the sea, *Berkeley.*

**39. And when it was day:** And when day came, *Rotherham* . . . In the morning, *Beck* . . . When day arrived, *MLNT.*

**they knew not the land:** . . . they could not recognize the coast, *Weymouth* . . . they could not make out what land it was, *TCNT.*

**but they discovered:** But they noticed, *Weymouth* . . . but gradually could see, *Beck.*

**a certain creek with a shore:** . . . a certain creek in which there was a beach, *TCNT* . . . an inlet with a sandy beach, *Weymouth.*

**into the which they were minded:** . . . they consulted, *TCNT* . . . and they began conferring, *Montgomery* . . . on which they determined, *HBIE* . . . into which they decided, *MLNT.*

**if it were possible, to thrust in the ship:** . . . to run the ship aground, *Alford* . . . as to whether they could run this ship safely into it, *TCNT* . . . to beach the ship if they could, *Phillips.*

**40. And when they had taken up the anchors:** And when they had cut away the anchors, *Alford* . . . clearing away the anchors, *Rotherham* . . . After severing the anchors, *Berkeley* . . . After casting off the anchors, *MLNT.*

**they committed themselves unto the sea:** . . . and dropping them in the sea, *MLNT* . . . and abandoned them to the sea, *NAB.*

**and loosed the rudder bands:** . . . cut the ropes which held the steering oars, *Phillips* . . . unlashed the gear of the steering oars, *TCNT* . . . and meanwhile loosening the ropes that held the rudders, *MLNT.*

**and hoisted up the mainsail to the wind:** . . . spread out the foresail to catch the wind, *Beck* . . . hoisted the foresail to the wind, *MLNT.*

**and made toward shore:** . . . and steered the ship to the shore, *Beck* . . . and made for the beach, *MLNT.*

| **1156.2** conj | **1519.1** prep | **4964.4** noun acc sing masc | **1331.1** adj acc sing masc | **2011.1** verb 3pl indic aor act |
|---|---|---|---|---|
| δὲ | εἰς | τόπον | διθάλασσον | ʻ ἐπώκειλαν |
| *de* | *eis* | *topon* | *dithalasson* | *epōkeilan* |
| and | into | a place | where two seas met | they ran aground |

41.a.**Txt:** 03B-corr,020L 025P,byz. **Var:** 01ℵ,02A,03B-org 04C,Lach,Treg,Alf,Tisc We/Ho,Weis,Sod UBS/☆

| **1930.1** verb 3pl indic aor act | **3450.12** art acc sing fem | **3354.1** noun acc sing fem | **2504.1** conj | **3450.9** art nom sing fem | **3173.1** conj |
|---|---|---|---|---|---|
| [a☆ ἐπέκειλαν ] | τὴν | ναῦν· | καὶ | ἡ | μὲν |
| *epekeilan* | *tēn* | *naun* | *kai* | *hē* | *men* |
| [ idem ] | the | vessel; | and | the | |

| **4266.1** noun nom sing fem | **2026.1** verb nom sing fem part aor act | **3176.16** verb 3sing indic aor act | **755.1** adj nom sing fem | **3450.9** art nom sing fem |
|---|---|---|---|---|
| πρῷρα | ἐρείσασα | ἔμεινεν | ἀσάλευτος, | ἡ |
| *prōra* | *ereisasa* | *emeinen* | *asaleutos* | *hē* |
| prow | having stuck fast | remained | immovable, | the |

| **1156.2** conj | **4261.1** noun nom sing fem | **3061.28** verb 3sing indic imperf pass | **5097.3** prep | **3450.10** art gen sing fem | **963.1** noun gen sing fem |
|---|---|---|---|---|---|
| δὲ | πρύμνα | ἐλύετο | ὑπὸ | τῆς | βίας |
| *de* | *prumna* | *elueto* | *hupo* | *tēs* | *bias* |
| but | stern | was being broken | by | the | violence |

41.b.**Txt:** p74,01ℵ-corr 04C,020L,025P,byz.bo. Weis,Sod **Var:** 01ℵ-org,02A,03B Lach,Tisc,We/Ho UBS/☆

| **3450.1** art gen pl | **2922.2** noun gen pl neu | **3450.1** art gen pl | **1156.2** conj | **4608.5** noun gen pl masc | **1005.1** noun nom sing fem |
|---|---|---|---|---|---|
| ʻb τῶν | κυμάτων. ˎ | **42.** τῶν | δὲ | στρατιωτῶν | βουλὴ |
| *tōn* | *kumatōn* | *tōn* | *de* | *stratiōtōn* | *boulē* |
| of the | waves. | Of the | and | soldiers | counsel |

| **1090.33** verb 3sing indic aor mid | **2419.1** conj | **3450.8** art acc pl masc | **1196.1** noun acc pl masc | **609.9** verb 3pl subj aor act |
|---|---|---|---|---|
| ἐγένετο | ἵνα | τοὺς | δεσμώτας | ἀποκτείνωσιν, |
| *egeneto* | *hina* | *tous* | *desmōtas* | *apokteinōsin* |
| was | that | the | prisoners | they should kill, |

| **3252.2** partic | **3231.1** partic | **4948.3** indef-pron nom sing | **1566.1** verb nom sing masc part aor act | **1303.1** verb 3sing opt aor act |
|---|---|---|---|---|
| ʻ μήτις | [☆ μή | τις ] | ἐκκολυμβήσας | ʻ διαφύγοι· |
| *mētis* | *mē* | *tis* | *ekkolumbēsas* | *diaphugoi* |
| lest anyone | [ not | anyone ] | having swum out | should escape. |

42.a.**Txt:** Steph **Var:** 01ℵ,02A,03B,04C 020L,025P,Gries,Lach Treg,Alf,Word,Tisc We/Ho,Weis,Sod UBS/☆

| **1303.2** verb 3sing subj aor act | **3450.5** art nom sing masc | **1156.2** conj | **1530.1** noun nom sing masc |
|---|---|---|---|
| [a☆ διαφύγῃ· ] | **43.** ὁ | δὲ | ʻ ἑκατόνταρχος |
| *diaphugē* | *ho* | *de* | *hekatontarchos* |
| [ might escape. ] | The | but | centurion |

| **1529.1** noun nom sing masc | **1007.8** verb nom sing masc part pres mid | **1289.3** verb inf aor act | **3450.6** art acc sing masc | **3834.4** name acc masc |
|---|---|---|---|---|
| [☆ ἑκατοντάρχης ] | βουλόμενος | διασῶσαι | τὸν | Παῦλον |
| *hekatontarchēs* | *boulomenos* | *diasōsai* | *ton* | *Paulon* |
| [ idem ] | desiring | to save | | Paul |

| **2940.6** verb 3sing indic aor act | **840.8** prs-pron acc pl masc | **3450.2** art gen sing | **1006.1** noun gen sing neu | **2724.3** verb 3sing indic aor act |
|---|---|---|---|---|
| ἐκώλυσεν | αὐτοὺς | τοῦ | βουλήματος, | ἐκέλευσέν |
| *ekōlusen* | *autous* | *tou* | *boulēmatos* | *ekeleusen* |
| hindered | them | of the | purpose, | commanded |

| **4885.1** conj | **3450.8** art acc pl masc | **1404.18** verb acc pl masc part pres mid | **2832.1** verb inf pres act | **635.1** verb acc pl masc part aor act |
|---|---|---|---|---|
| τε | τοὺς | δυναμένους | κολυμβᾶν, | ʻ ἀποῤῥίψαντας |
| *te* | *tous* | *dunamenous* | *kolumban* | *aporrhipsantas* |
| and | the | being able | to swim, | having cast off |

**27:41.** But even using the best of their skills, the winds were such that the sailors could not control the ship. Instead of reaching the beach, they accidentally came to a place between two seas. This was a narrow channel, too shallow for the ship to make it through. Actually, there is a little island called Salmoneta near the entrance to the bay. The rush of breakers on both sides of the island give the appearance of two seas meeting.

The bow of the ship ran aground in mud and clay and stuck fast. Then the stern of the ship began breaking up because of the force (violence) of the waves. It was immediately obvious that everyone would have to leave the ship at once. The ship had already been battered by the storm for a long time and there was no possibility of it holding together.

**27:42.** The soldiers then conferred with one another and their counsel was to kill the prisoners lest they swim away and escape. Their concern was over what would happen to them if they were not able to produce the prisoners when they finally arrived in Rome. They knew the government would hold them responsible and their own lives would be in jeopardy. The Book of Acts has already provided an example of this after the angel brought Peter out of prison just before King Herod Agrippa I was going to have him killed. Herod conducted a legal examination of the guards who had custody of Peter while he was in the prison and had them put to death because of their failure (12:19). To save themselves the soldiers thought it best to kill the prisoners.

**27:43.** The centurion, however, now exercised his authority as the one in command. He wanted to save Paul, so he stepped in and prevented the soldiers from carrying out their purpose.

The word "save" here is an emphatic one. It seems to imply the soldiers were already intent on carrying out their purpose. They may have already gathered the prisoners together. The centurion actually had to rescue Paul and the other prisoners from them. The same word was used when Lysias provided a guard of 460 men to bring Paul safely to the governor, Felix, in Caesarea, thus preventing the Jews from carrying out their purpose to kill Paul at that time (23:23,24).

This was another time this centurion showed favor to Paul. All the way along the kindness of this Roman army officer has been evident. He knew, of course, that Paul was a Roman citizen, but that does not seem to have been the issue here. Rather, the centurion had a personal desire to see Paul safely through to Rome. He was probably grateful for the way Paul had brought new hope and courage, and even for Paul's encouragement for them to eat and gain strength so they would all be able to make it to shore.

The centurion commanded all who could swim to jump overboard first and get to the land. This shows that even though the

**41. And falling into a place where two seas met:** . . . but the ship hit a sandbar, *NAB* . . . hit a sandbank, *Everyday.*

**they ran the ship aground:** . . . they drove the ship aground, *Moffatt* . . . They struck a bank in the water, *Beck.*

**and the forepart stuck fast:** . . . the stem having bilged, *Fenton* . . . and her prow sticking fast, *HBIE* . . . The front of the ship stuck there, *Everyday* . . . The bow stuck fast, *NAB* . . . was fixed in the sand, *BB.*

**and remained unmoveable:** . . . and could not be moved, *TCNT* . . . and remained fixed, *Montgomery* . . . and could not be budged, *NAB.*

**but the hinder part was broken:** . . . but the stern, *ASV* . . . while the stern was shattered, *NAB* . . . began to go to pieces, *Weymouth* . . . break the back of the ship to pieces, *Everyday.*

**with the violence of the waves:** Then the big waves began to, *Everyday* . . . under the violent pounding of the waves, *Norlie* . . . by the pounding of the sea, *NAB* . . . under the strain, *TCNT* . . . under the heavy hammering of the sea, *Weymouth.*

**42. And the soldiers' counsel was:** Now the soldiers recommended, *Weymouth* . . . And the design, *Sawyer* . . . had in mind, *Norlie* . . . And it was the plan of the soldiers, *HBIE* . . . decided to, *Everyday* . . . thought at first, *NAB.*

**to kill the prisoners:** . . . that they should kill, *HBIE.*

**lest any of them should swim out, and escape:** . . . for fear that any of them should swim away and make their escape, *TCNT.*

**43. But the centurion, willing to save Paul:** . . . desiring to save, *ASV* . . . anxious to save, *TCNT* . . . wanted to let Paul live, *Everyday.*

**kept them from their purpose:** . . . prevented their carrying out their intention, *TCNT* . . . put a stop to their plan, *Confraternity* . . . he opposed their plan, *NAB* . . . He did not allow the soldiers, *Everyday.*

**and commanded that they which could swim:** . . . and ordered that those who could swim, *TCNT.*

# Acts 27:44

| **635.2** verb acc pl masc part aor act | **4272.8** num ord acc pl masc | **1894.3** prep | **3450.12** art acc sing fem | **1087.4** noun acc sing fem |
|---|---|---|---|---|
| [☆ ἀπορίψαντας ] | πρώτους, | ἐπὶ | τὴν | γῆν |
| *aporipsantas* | *prōtous* | *epi* | *tēn* | *gēn* |
| [ idem ] | first, | on | the | land |

| **1821.2** verb inf pres act | **2504.1** conj | **3450.8** art acc pl masc | **3036.4** adj acc pl masc | **3614.8** rel-pron acc pl masc | **3173.1** conj |
|---|---|---|---|---|---|
| ἐξιέναι, | **44.** καὶ | τοὺς | λοιποὺς, | οὓς | μὲν |
| *exienai* | *kai* | *tous* | *loipous* | *hous* | *men* |
| to go out; | and | the | rest, | whom | indeed |

| **1894.3** prep | **4405.1** noun dat pl fem | **3614.8** rel-pron acc pl masc | **1156.2** conj | **1894.3** prep | **4948.4** indef-pron gen pl | **3450.1** art gen pl |
|---|---|---|---|---|---|---|
| ἐπὶ | σανίσιν | οὓς | δὲ | ἐπί | τινων | τῶν |
| *epi* | *sanisin* | *hous* | *de* | *epi* | *tinōn* | *tōn* |
| on | boards | whom | and | on | some | of the |

| **570.3** prep | **3450.2** art gen sing | **4003.2** noun gen sing neu | **2504.1** conj | **3643.1** adv | **1090.33** verb 3sing indic aor mid | **3820.8** adj acc pl masc |
|---|---|---|---|---|---|---|
| ἀπὸ | τοῦ | πλοίου· | καὶ | οὕτως | ἐγένετο | πάντας |
| *apo* | *tou* | *ploiou* | *kai* | *houtōs* | *egeneto* | *pantas* |
| from | the | ship; | and | thus | it came to pass | all |

| **1289.7** verb inf aor pass | **1894.3** prep | **3450.12** art acc sing fem | **1087.4** noun acc sing fem | **2504.1** conj |
|---|---|---|---|---|
| διασωθῆναι | ἐπὶ | τὴν | γῆν. | **28:1.** Καὶ |
| *diasōthēnai* | *epi* | *tēn* | *gēn* | *Kai* |
| to be brought safely | to | the | land. | And |

1.a.**Txt:** 04C-corr,020L 025P,byz.
**Var:** 01ℵ,02A,03B 04C-org,bo.Lach,Treg Alf,Word,Tisc,We/Ho Weis,Sod,UBS/☆

| **1289.6** verb nom pl masc part aor pass | **4966.1** adv | **1906.6** verb 3pl indic aor act | **1906.22** verb 1pl indic aor act |
|---|---|---|---|
| διασωθέντες | τότε | ʹ ἐπέγνωσαν | [a☆ ἐπέγνωμεν ] |
| *diasōthentes* | *tote* | *epegnōsan* | *epegnōmen* |
| having been saved | then | they knew | [ we knew ] |

| **3617.1** conj | **3164.1** name nom fem | **3450.9** art nom sing fem | **3382.1** noun nom sing fem | **2535.26** verb 3sing indic pres mid | **3614.7** rel-pron nom pl masc |
|---|---|---|---|---|---|
| ὅτι | Μελίτη | ἡ | νῆσος | καλεῖται. | **2.** Οἵ |
| *hoti* | *Melitē* | *hē* | *nēsos* | *kaleitai* | *Hoi* |
| that | Melita | the | island | is called. | Which |

2.a.**Txt:** 01ℵ,020L,025P byz.bo.
**Var:** 02A,03B,04C,Lach Treg,Alf,Word,Tisc We/Ho,Weis,Sod UBS/☆

| **1156.2** conj | **4885.1** conj | **910.2** adj nom pl masc | **3792.11** verb 3pl indic imperf act | **3620.3** partic | **3450.12** art acc sing fem |
|---|---|---|---|---|---|
| ʹ δὲ | [a☆ τε ] | βάρβαροι | παρεῖχον | οὐ | τὴν |
| *de* | *te* | *barbaroi* | *pareichon* | *ou* | *tēn* |
| and | [ idem ] | barbarians | were showing | no | the |

| **5018.6** verb acc sing fem part aor act | **5200.2** noun acc sing fem | **2231.3** prs-pron dat 1pl | **379.2** verb nom pl masc part aor act |
|---|---|---|---|
| τυχοῦσαν | φιλανθρωπίαν | ἡμῖν· | ʹ ἀνάψαντες |
| *tuchousan* | *philanthrōpian* | *hēmin* | *anapsantes* |
| having happened | kindness | to us; | having kindled |

2.b.**Txt:** 020L,025P,byz.
**Var:** 01ℵ,02A,03B,04C Lach,Treg,Alf,Word Tisc,We/Ho,Weis,Sod UBS/☆

| **674.17** verb nom pl masc part aor act | **1056.1** conj | **4301.1** noun acc sing fem | **4213.4** verb 3pl indic aor mid | **3820.8** adj acc pl masc |
|---|---|---|---|---|
| [b☆ ἅψαντες ] | γὰρ | πυρὰν | προσελάβοντο | πάντας |
| *hapsantes* | *gar* | *puran* | *proselabonto* | *pantas* |
| [ idem ] | for | a fire, | they received | all |

| **2231.4** prs-pron acc 1pl | **1217.2** prep | **3450.6** art acc sing masc | **5046.2** noun acc sing masc | **3450.6** art acc sing masc | **2168.10** verb acc sing masc part perf act |
|---|---|---|---|---|---|
| ἡμᾶς, | διὰ | τὸν | ὑετὸν | τὸν | ἐφεστῶτα |
| *hēmas* | *dia* | *ton* | *hueton* | *ton* | *ephestōta* |
| us, | because of | the | rain | the | having stood by |

ship did not make it to the beach, it was still close enough for good swimmers to get to shore without any difficulty.

**27:44.** After the swimmers jumped in, the rest followed them, some on planks or whatever boards of the ship they could grab, and others on whatever else they could find that would float. So they were all brought safely through the waves to the land. Paul's words of assurance given him by the angel of the one true God were thus proved true. But as Paul also warned, the ship was a total loss.

All of them must surely have been thankful to be alive. But undoubtedly there was praise and thanksgiving in the hearts of Paul and his friends to God and to the Lord Jesus who loved them, died for them, and was now risen, ascended to the right hand of the Father's throne where He was interceding for them through all this. Truly God had kept His promise, not only for Paul, but also for the 275 others who were on board.

**28:1.** After arriving safely on land they learned the island was called Melita (Phoenician or Canaanite for "refuge"), now called Malta.

Malta is about 174 miles from Italy and about 56 miles from the southern tip of Sicily. The African coast lies about 187 miles to the south. (The African coast then curves north, so it can be reached from Malta by going about the same distance to the west.) The island itself is a little over 17 miles long and a little over 9 miles wide, giving it an area of about 95 square miles. Its capital in modern times is Valetta. Because of its central position in the Mediterranean Sea, the Romans made it an important naval station.

**28:2.** The local people had seen what was happening to the ship and how this crowd of 276 people were coming to shore. They spread the word and gathered to try to help the shipwrecked people.

Throughout this passage, Luke called the local inhabitants of Malta barbarians. But he did not mean they were degraded or uncivilized. To the Greeks any foreigner who could not speak Greek was a barbarian. Later they gave the Romans a little leeway by including among the barbarians those who could not speak Greek or Latin.

Actually the people of Malta were descended from Phoenician colonists who probably spoke a dialect closely related to Hebrew. It had for a time been under the domination of Sicilian Greeks, then of Carthage. But the Romans took it from the Carthaginians in 218 B.C. So it had long been under Roman rule.

It is easy to see that the citizens of Malta were good people even if they could not speak Greek. Their kindness went beyond the ordinary. They lit a fire and welcomed all 276 of these strangers who had escaped from the wrecked ship. Because of the rain and

**should cast themselves first into the sea:** . . . should be the first to jump into the sea, *TCNT* . . . to leap off first, *Berkeley* . . . to jump into the water, *Everyday.*

**and get to land:** . . . and try to reach shore, *TCNT* . . . and make for shore, *Berkeley* . . . and swim to land, *Everyday.*

**44. And the rest:**

**some on boards:** . . . used wooden boards, *Everyday.*

**and some on broken pieces of the ship:** . . . or on other debris from the ship, *NAB.*

**And so it came to pass:** In these various ways, *TCNT* . . . In this way it turned out, *Moffatt* . . . And this is how, *Everyday.*

**that they escaped all safe to land:** . . . everyone managed to get safely ashore, *TCNT* . . . they all got safely to land, *Weymouth* . . . all the people made it safely, *Everyday.*

**1. And when they were escaped:** And when we were safely through, *Rotherham* . . . When we were all safe, *TCNT* . . . After our escape, *Confraternity* . . . Once on shore, *NAB.*

**then they knew that the island was called Melita:** . . . discovered, *Weymouth* . . . ascertained, *Montgomery* . . . we learned, *NAB* . . . we found that the island was called Malta, *TCNT.*

**2. And the barbarous people shewed us:** . . . the barbarians, *Murdock* . . . And the natives shewed us, *Alford.*

**no little kindness:** . . . remarkable friendliness, *Berkeley* . . . unusually kind, *Norlie* . . . extraordinary kindness, *NAB* . . . remarkable kindness, *Williams.*

**for they kindled a fire:** . . . for they lit a fire, *TCNT.*

**and received us every one:** . . . and took us all under shelter, *TCNT* . . . and made us all welcome, *Weymouth* . . . and took us in, *BB* . . . and gathering us all around it, *NAB.*

**because of the present rain:** . . . because it was raining, *BB* . . . the pelting rain, *Weymouth* . . . driving rain, *Phillips* . . . there was a cold, drenching rain, *Norlie* . . . it had begun to rain, *NAB.*

## Acts 28:3

| 2504.1 conj | 1217.2 prep | 3450.16 art sing neu | 5427.1 noun sing neu | 4814.1 verb gen sing masc part aor act | 1156.2 conj |
|---|---|---|---|---|---|
| καὶ | διὰ | τὸ | ψῦχος. | 3. Συστρέψαντος | δὲ |
| kai | dia | to | psuchos | Sustrepsantos | de |
| and | because of | the | cold. | Having gathered | and |

3.a.**Var:** 01ℵ,02A,03B 04C,Lach,Treg,Alf Word,Tisc,We/Ho,Weis Sod,UBS/☆

| 3450.2 art gen sing | 3834.2 name gen masc | 5270.1 noun gen pl neu | 4948.10 indef-pron sing neu | 3988.1 noun sing neu | 2504.1 conj |
|---|---|---|---|---|---|
| τοῦ | Παύλου | φρυγάνων | [a☆+ τι ] | πλῆθος, | καὶ |
| tou | Paulou | phruganōn | ti | plēthos | kai |
| | Paul | of sticks | [ certain ] | a quantity, | and |

| 1991.13 verb gen sing masc part aor act | 1894.3 prep | 3450.12 art acc sing fem | 4301.1 noun acc sing fem | 2173.1 noun nom sing fem | 1523.2 prep gen |
|---|---|---|---|---|---|
| ἐπιθέντος | ἐπὶ | τὴν | πυράν | ἔχιδνα | ˊ ἐκ |
| epithentos | epi | tēn | puran | echidna | ek |
| having laid | on | the | fire | a viper | out of |

3.b.**Txt:** byz.
**Var:** 01ℵ,02A,03B,04C 020L,025P,Lach,Treg Alf,Word,Tisc,We/Ho Weis,Sod,UBS/☆

| 570.3 prep | 3450.10 art gen sing fem | 2306.1 noun gen sing fem | 1814.17 verb nom sing fem part aor act | 2482.1 verb 3sing indic aor act |
|---|---|---|---|---|
| [b☆ ἀπὸ ] | τῆς | θέρμης | ἐξελθοῦσα | καθῆψεν |
| apo | tēs | thermēs | exelthousa | kathēpsen |
| [ from ] | the | heat | having come | wound about |

| 3450.10 art gen sing fem | 5331.2 noun gen sing fem | 840.3 prs-pron gen sing | 5453.1 conj | 1156.2 conj | 1481.1 verb indic aor act | 3450.7 art nom pl masc |
|---|---|---|---|---|---|---|
| τῆς | χειρὸς | αὐτοῦ. | 4. ὡς | δὲ | εἶδον | οἱ |
| tēs | cheiros | autou | hōs | de | eidon | hoi |
| the | hand | his. | When | and | saw | the |

| 910.2 adj nom pl masc | 2883.3 verb sing neu part pres mid | 3450.16 art sing neu | 2319.1 noun sing neu | 1523.2 prep gen | 3450.10 art gen sing fem |
|---|---|---|---|---|---|
| βάρβαροι | κρεμάμενον | τὸ | θηρίον | ἐκ | τῆς |
| barbaroi | kremamenon | to | thērion | ek | tēs |
| barbarians | hanging | the | beast | from | the |

| 5331.2 noun gen sing fem | 840.3 prs-pron gen sing | 2978.25 verb indic imperf act | 4242.1 prep | 238.3 prs-pron acc pl masc |
|---|---|---|---|---|
| χειρὸς | αὐτοῦ | ˊ ἔλεγον | πρὸς | ἀλλήλους, |
| cheiros | autou | elegon | pros | allēlous |
| hand | his | they were saying | to | one another, |

| 4242.1 prep | 238.3 prs-pron acc pl masc | 2978.25 verb indic imperf act | 3705.1 adv | 5243.1 noun nom sing masc |
|---|---|---|---|---|
| [☆ πρὸς | ἀλλήλους | ἔλεγον, ] | Πάντως | φονεύς |
| pros | allēlous | elegon | Pantōs | phoneus |
| [ to | one another | they were saying, ] | By all means | a murderer |

| 1498.4 verb 3sing indic pres act | 3450.5 art nom sing masc | 442.1 noun nom sing masc | 3642.4 dem-pron nom sing masc | 3614.6 rel-pron acc sing masc |
|---|---|---|---|---|
| ἐστιν | ὁ | ἄνθρωπος | οὗτος, | ὃν |
| estin | ho | anthrōpos | houtos | hon |
| is | the | man | this, | whom |

| 1289.5 verb acc sing masc part aor pass | 1523.2 prep gen | 3450.10 art gen sing fem | 2258.2 noun gen sing fem | 3450.9 art nom sing fem |
|---|---|---|---|---|
| διασωθέντα | ἐκ | τῆς | θαλάσσης | ἡ |
| diasōthenta | ek | tēs | thalassēs | hē |
| having been saved | from | the | sea | the |

| 1343.1 noun nom sing fem | 2180.19 verb inf pres act | 3620.2 partic | 1432.3 verb 3sing indic aor act | 3450.5 art nom sing masc | 3173.1 conj |
|---|---|---|---|---|---|
| δίκη | ζῆν | οὐκ | εἴασεν. | 5. Ὁ | μὲν |
| dikē | zēn | ouk | eiasen | Ho | men |
| justice | to live | not | permitted. | The | indeed |

the cold, the fire was an act of great kindness and must have been a welcome sight to all who came from the ship. Later the islanders showed further kindness and continued to prove they were a hospitable people. So it was definitely in the providence of God that Paul and his companions were shipwrecked on this particular island.

**28:3.** A little later, knowing the fire would need more fuel, Paul took the place of a servant and went out to gather brushwood. Paul, great spiritual leader that he was, never asked others to do what he was not willing to do himself. He had worked hard all during his ministry at his tentmaking to support not only himself but the labors of his entire evangelistic party. He was always ready to serve others, and he was never afraid to soil his hands in doing so. What an example he set!

Soon he returned with a large bundle of the brushwood and put it on the fire. The heat brought out a viper that had been picked up with the wood. Before Paul could pull away the viper fastened its fangs on his hand.

The viper is a poisonous snake, and many writers take notice of the fact that there are no vipers on Malta today. Some even try to imply that the Bible must be wrong here. However, Malta is a small island and the people eventually got rid of the vipers after Paul's day. The historical facts in the Bible have been vindicated and confirmed so many times that it has been proven the mistakes are in the critics, not in the Bible. Even when there seems to be no answer to the allegations of the critics, the best thing is to hold steady. Time is the best judge.

**28:4.** When the people of Malta saw the wild creature dart out of the brush and bite Paul (vipers can dart several feet in a single quick motion), they jumped to the conclusion that Paul must be a murderer who, though he escaped safely from the sea, vengeance (literally, "the Justice") had not let him live. Paul, as a prisoner, must have had either a chain still attached to one of his wrists, or else the marks of the chains. (It would hardly seem logical that he would be able to make it to shore if they had not taken the chains off at least for the time.) In any case, the obvious fact that he was a prisoner must have helped the islanders to think he was surely a murderer.

By "the Justice" they may have meant their heathen goddess of justice. Or the reference may be simply to a vague sense of retributive justice which was common even among the heathen.

They were like the friends of Job who thought any trouble or misery was always judgment. But the Bible does not treat accidents as punishment. What Paul said about temptations in 1 Corinthians 10:13 can be applied to accidents as well, for they can become a temptation to unbelief and rebellion, or they can become an opportunity to trust God and learn what He can do. As Paul says, these things are common to mankind.



**and because of the cold:** . . . and the cold, *Weymouth.*

**3. And when Paul had gathered a bundle of sticks:** . . . an armful of dry branches, *Beck* . . . Paul had collected a bundle of faggots, *Knox* . . . having gathered a certain lot of fuel, *Worrell* . . . had gathered some wood, *NLT* . . . had got some sticks together, *BB* . . . picked up a pile of sticks, *SEB.*

**and laid them on the fire:** . . . and had thrown them, *Weymouth* . . . was about to put it on, *Phillips.*

**there came a viper out of the heat:** . . . a poisonous snake, *SEB* . . . a snake came out, *BB* . . . crawled out of the heat, *Norlie* . . . coming out to escape the heat, *Knox* . . . because of the heat, *NLT* . . . driven by the heat, *Lamsa.*

**and fastened on his hand:** It held fast to Paul's hand, *NLT* . . . and gave him a bite on the hand, *BB.*

**4. And when the barbarians saw the venomous beast hang on his hand:** . . . the reptile hanging on his hand, *Montgomery* . . . coiled round his hand, *Knox* . . . saw the reptile hanging from, *Noli.*

**they said among themselves:** . . . one to another, *ASV.*

**No doubt this man is a murderer:** Evidently, *TCNT* . . . Assuredly this man is, *Worrell* . . . It may be that, *Lamsa* . . . Beyond doubt, *Weymouth* . . . This man must be a murderer! *Moffatt* . . . This man is a killer, *NLT* . . . This man is certainly a criminal, *Noli* . . . has put someone to death, *BB.*

**whom, though he hath escaped the sea:** . . . for, though he has been saved from the sea, *TCNT* . . . he has been rescued from, *Lamsa* . . . He didn't die in the ocean, *SEB* . . . did not die in the sea, *NCV* . . . whom, though safely escaping from, *Worrell.*

**yet vengeance suffereth not to live:** Justice has not allowed him to live, *TCNT* . . . will not permit him, *SEB* . . . yet it is not right for him to live, *NLT* . . . divine justice will not let him live, *Noli* . . . God will not let him go on living, *BB* . . . does not want him to live, *NCV* . . . justice permitted not to live, *Worrell.*

| 3631.1 partic | 654.2 verb nom sing masc part aor act | 3450.16 art sing neu | 2319.1 noun sing neu | 1519.1 prep | 3450.16 art sing neu |
|---|---|---|---|---|---|
| οὖν | ἀποτινάξας | τὸ | θηρίον | εἰς | τὸ |
| *oun* | *apotinaxas* | *to* | *thērion* | *eis* | *to* |
| then | having shaken off | the | beast | into | the |

| 4300.1 noun sing neu | 3819.11 verb 3sing indic aor act | 3625.6 num card neu | 2527.7 adj sing neu | 3450.7 art nom pl masc | 1156.2 conj |
|---|---|---|---|---|---|
| πῦρ | ἔπαθεν | οὐδὲν | κακόν. | 6. οἱ | δὲ |
| *pur* | *epathen* | *ouden* | *kakon* | *hoi* | *de* |
| fire | suffered | no | injury. | The | but |

| 4186.8 verb 3pl indic imperf act | 840.6 prs-pron acc sing masc | 3165.18 verb inf pres act | 3953.1 verb inf pres mid | 2211.1 conj |
|---|---|---|---|---|
| προσεδόκων | αὐτὸν | μέλλειν | πίμπρασθαι | ἢ |
| *prosedokōn* | *auton* | *mellein* | *pimprasthai* | *ē* |
| were expecting | him | to be about | to become inflamed | or |

| 2637.1 verb inf pres act | 862.1 adv | 3361.1 adj sing | 1894.3 prep | 4044.16 adj sing neu | 1156.2 conj |
|---|---|---|---|---|---|
| καταπίπτειν | ἄφνω | νεκρόν· | ἐπὶ | πολὺ | δὲ |
| *katapiptein* | *aphnō* | *nekron* | *epi* | *polu* | *de* |
| to fall down | suddenly | dead. | For | a long | but |

| 840.1 prs-pron gen pl | 4186.6 verb gen pl masc part pres act | 2504.1 conj | 2311.12 verb gen pl masc part pres act | 3235.6 num card neu |
|---|---|---|---|---|
| αὐτῶν | προσδοκώντων | καὶ | θεωρούντων | μηδὲν |
| *autōn* | *prosdokōntōn* | *kai* | *theōrountōn* | *mēden* |
| them | expecting | and | seeing | nothing |

| 818.2 adj sing neu | 1519.1 prep | 840.6 prs-pron acc sing masc | 1090.20 verb sing part pres mid | 3198.1 verb nom pl masc part pres mid |
|---|---|---|---|---|
| ἄτοπον | εἰς | αὐτὸν | γινόμενον, | ᶜ μεταβαλλόμενοι |
| *atopon* | *eis* | *auton* | *ginomenon* | *metaballomenoi* |
| amiss | to | him | happening, | changing their opinion |

6.a.**Txt:** 01ℵ,020L,byz. Tisc
**Var:** 02A,03B,025P Treg,Alf,We/Ho,Weis Sod,UBS/☆

| 3198.2 verb nom pl masc part aor mid | 2978.25 verb indic imperf act | 2296.4 noun acc sing masc | 840.6 prs-pron acc sing masc |
|---|---|---|---|
| [ᵃ☆ μεταβαλόμενοι ] | ἔλεγον | ᶜ θεόν | αὐτὸν |
| *metabalomenoi* | *elegon* | *theon* | *auton* |
| [ having changed their opinion ] | were saying | a god | him |

| 1498.32 verb inf pres act | 840.6 prs-pron acc sing masc | 1498.32 verb inf pres act | 2296.4 noun acc sing masc | 1706.1 prep | 1156.2 conj | 3450.4 art dat pl |
|---|---|---|---|---|---|---|
| εἶναι. | [☆ αὐτὸν | εἶναι | θεόν. ] | 7. Ἐν | δὲ | τοῖς |
| *einai* | *auton* | *einai* | *theon* | *En* | *de* | *tois* |
| to be. | [ him | to be | a god. ] | In | and | the |

| 3875.1 prep | 3450.6 art acc sing masc | 4964.4 noun acc sing masc | 1552.5 dem-pron acc sing masc | 5062.12 verb 3sing indic imperf act | 5399.3 noun pl neu |
|---|---|---|---|---|---|
| περὶ | τὸν | τόπον | ἐκεῖνον | ὑπῆρχεν | χωρία |
| *peri* | *ton* | *topon* | *ekeinon* | *huperchen* | *chōria* |
| about | the | place | that | were belonging | lands |

| 3450.3 art dat sing | 4272.6 num ord dat sing masc | 3450.10 art gen sing fem | 3382.2 noun gen sing fem | 3549.4 noun dat sing neu | 4055.2 name dat masc |
|---|---|---|---|---|---|
| τῷ | πρώτῳ | τῆς | νήσου, | ὀνόματι | Ποπλίῳ, |
| *tō* | *prōtō* | *tēs* | *nēsou* | *onomati* | *Popliō* |
| to the | chief | of the | island, | by name | Publius, |

| 3614.5 rel-pron nom sing masc | 322.1 verb nom sing masc part aor mid | 2231.4 prs-pron acc 1pl | 4980.1 num card nom | 2232.1 noun fem |
|---|---|---|---|---|
| ὃς | ἀναδεξάμενος | ἡμᾶς | ᶜ τρεῖς | ἡμέρας |
| *hos* | *anadexamenos* | *hēmas* | *treis* | *hēmeras* |
| who | having received | us | three | days |

**28:5.** Paul did not get excited or worried. He did not even cry out, though he must have felt the pain. Neither did he question God, even though he had picked up the snake while he was working hard because of his faithful concern for others.

Note too that he had not picked up the snake deliberately, nor did he do it as an attempt to show his faith. Unfortunately, some have misinterpreted Mark 16:18 to make it a command. However, the Greek word used there is often used of taking away or removing. Matthew 24:39 uses it of the flood sweeping everyone away. Luke 23:18 uses it of the crowd crying out "Away with him!" Other ancient Greek writings outside the New Testament also use the verb in the sense of removing, taking away, and blotting out. It should be kept in mind also that the serpent was symbolic of evil, and the whole context of Mark 16 indicates victory over the works of the devil. The same is true of Luke 10:19 where Jesus said, "Behold, I give (have given and still give) unto you power (authority) to tread on serpents and scorpions, and over all the power (mighty power) of the enemy; and nothing shall by any means hurt you."

Early Christians certainly did not go around picking up snakes. In fact, in Mark's context, the picking up of snakes is presented as something very unlikely. Thus, when Paul accidentally picked up this viper, he simply shook the wild creature off his hand into the fire and suffered no harm.

**28:6.** The local people who had no doubt seen others bitten by the same kind of viper expected Paul to swell up or drop dead. For a long time they kept waiting and watching, but nothing unusual happened to him. So they changed their minds and said he was a god. Based on these outward circumstances their opinion thus shifted from one extreme to the other.

This must have bothered Paul. He had seen how the people of Lystra had thought he and Barnabas were gods and were preparing to sacrifice to them, then very shortly went to the other extreme and were persuaded to stone Paul (14:13,19). He knew how fickle the opinion of the crowd could be.

**28:7.** Nearby were the fields (lands, properties) belonging to the chief man (the governor) of the island, whose name was Publius (meaning "popular"). There is evidence that he held his office under the governor of Sicily, and as the chief Roman official on the island he would be responsible for any Roman soldiers and their prisoners who might come there.

Publius did far beyond what was necessary, for he welcomed them with kindness, and for 3 days entertained them with friendly thoughtfulness. As his name indicates, he was a Roman citizen and no doubt felt special concern for these Romans. Yet it seems that even this does not account for his unusual kindness. In the providence of God, Paul came in contact here with a good man who would help him.

**5. And he shook off the beast into the fire:** But he simply shook the reptile, *Williams* . . . shook off the creature, *Swann.*

**and felt no harm:** . . . without suffering any ill effect, *Phillips* . . . and was none the worse, *Knox* . . . He was not hurt, *SEB* . . . he got no damage, *BB.*

**6. Howbeit they looked when he should have swollen:** . . . were expecting inflamation to set in, *TCNT* . . . they had the idea that they would see him becoming ill, *BB* . . . The natives kept on looking for him to swell up, *Williams* . . . they thought he soon would become inflamed, *KJII.*

**or fallen down dead suddenly:** . . . or suddenly drop dead, *Williams.*

**but after they had looked a great while:** . . . but after waiting for a long time, *TCNT* . . . in suspense, *Fenton* . . . having waited a considerable time, *Swann.*

**and saw no harm come to him:** . . . observed nothing unusual happening to him, *Rotherham* . . . found that there was nothing amiss with him, *Knox* . . . but nothing bad happened, *SEB* . . . and saw nothing extraordinary occur, *Hanson* . . . seeing that no damage came, *BB.*

**they changed their minds:** . . . their opinion, *BB.*

**and said that he was a god:** . . . and said over and over, *Montgomery.*

**7. In the same quarters were possessions of the chief man of the island, whose name was Publius:** In that neighborhood there was an estate belonging to the Governor of the island, *TCNT* . . . In the same part of the island there were lands, *Weymouth* . . . the property of the chief man of the island, *BB* . . . There were some fields around that same area, *SEB* . . . in the vicinity of that place were, *Hanson* . . . owned by the island chief, *KJII.*

**who received us:** . . . who welcomed us to his house, *Weymouth* . . . took us into his house as his guests, *BB.*

**and lodged us three days courteously:** . . . hospitably entertained us, *Rotherham* . . . We stayed in his house for, *SEB* . . . and gave us everything we needed, *NLT.*

| 2232.1 noun fem | 4980.1 num card nom | 5227.1 adv | 3441.2 verb 3sing indic aor act | 1090.33 verb 3sing indic aor mid |
|---|---|---|---|---|
| [ ἡμέρας | τρεῖς ] | φιλοφρόνως | ἐξένισεν. | 8. ἐγένετο |
| *hēmeras* | *treis* | *philophronōs* | *exenisen* | *egeneto* |
| [ days | three ] | in a friendly way | lodged. | It happened |

| 1156.2 conj | 3450.6 art acc sing masc | 3824.4 noun acc sing masc | 3450.2 art gen sing | 4055.1 name gen masc | 4304.3 noun dat pl masc |
|---|---|---|---|---|---|
| δὲ | τὸν | πατέρα | τοῦ | Ποπλίου | πυρετοῖς |
| *de* | *ton* | *patera* | *tou* | *Popliou* | *puretois* |
| and | the | father | | of Publius | fevers |

8.a.**Txt:** byz.
**Var:** 01ℵ,02A,03B,020L 025P,33,Lach,Treg,Alf Word,Tisc,We/Ho,Weis Sod,UBS/☆

| 2504.1 conj | 1413.1 noun dat sing fem | 1413.1 noun dat sing neu | 4762.7 verb acc sing masc part pres mid |
|---|---|---|---|
| καὶ | ʻ δυσεντερίᾳ | [a☆ δυσεντερίῳ ] | συνεχόμενον |
| *kai* | *dusenteria* | *dusenteriō* | *sunechomenon* |
| and | dysentery | [ idem ] | being oppressed with |

| 2591.4 verb inf pres mid | 4242.1 prep | 3614.6 rel-pron acc sing masc | 3450.5 art nom sing masc | 3834.1 name nom masc |
|---|---|---|---|---|
| κατακεῖσθαι, | πρὸς | ὃν | ὁ | Παῦλος |
| *katakeisthai* | *pros* | *hon* | *ho* | *Paulos* |
| to lay, | to | whom | | Paul |

| 1511.13 verb nom sing masc part aor act | 2504.1 conj | 4195.24 verb nom sing masc part aor mid | 1991.12 verb nom sing masc part aor act | 3450.15 art acc pl fem |
|---|---|---|---|---|
| εἰσελθὼν | καὶ | προσευξάμενος, | ἐπιθεὶς | τὰς |
| *eiselthōn* | *kai* | *proseuxamenos* | *epitheis* | *tas* |
| having entered | and | having prayed, | having laid on | the |

| 5331.8 noun acc pl fem | 840.4 prs-pron dat sing | 2367.5 verb 3sing indic aor mid | 840.6 prs-pron acc sing masc | 3642.1 dem-pron gen sing | 3631.1 partic |
|---|---|---|---|---|---|
| χεῖρας | αὐτῷ | ἰάσατο | αὐτόν. | 9. τούτου | ʻ οὖν |
| *cheiras* | *autō* | *iasato* | *auton* | *toutou* | *oun* |
| hands | him | cured | him. | This | therefore |

9.a.**Txt:** 020L,025P,byz.
**Var:** 01ℵ,02A,03B,bo. Lach,Treg,Alf,Tisc We/Ho,Weis,Sod UBS/☆

| 1156.2 conj | 1090.50 verb gen sing part aor mid | 2504.1 conj | 3450.7 art nom pl masc | 3036.3 adj nom pl masc | 3450.7 art nom pl masc |
|---|---|---|---|---|---|
| [a☆ δὲ ] | γενομένου | καὶ | οἱ | λοιποὶ | οἱ |
| *de* | *genomenou* | *kai* | *hoi* | *loipoi* | *hoi* |
| [ and ] | having taken place | also | the | rest | the |

| 2174.19 verb nom pl masc part pres act | 763.1 noun fem | 1706.1 prep | 3450.11 art dat sing fem | 3382.3 noun dat sing fem | 1706.1 prep |
|---|---|---|---|---|---|
| ʻ ἔχοντες | ἀσθενείας | ἐν | τῇ | νήσῳ | [☆ ἐν |
| *echontes* | *astheneias* | *en* | *tē* | *nēsō* | *en* |
| having | infirmities | in | the | island | [ in |

| 3450.11 art dat sing fem | 3382.3 noun dat sing fem | 2174.19 verb nom pl masc part pres act | 763.1 noun fem | 4193.18 verb 3pl indic imperf mid |
|---|---|---|---|---|
| τῇ | νήσῳ | ἔχοντες | ἀσθενείας ] | προσήρχοντο |
| *tē* | *nēsō* | *echontes* | *astheneias* | *prosērchonto* |
| the | island | having | infirmities ] | were coming |

| 2504.1 conj | 2300.20 verb 3pl indic imperf pass | 3614.7 rel-pron nom pl masc | 2504.1 conj | 4044.14 adj dat pl fem | 4940.5 noun dat pl fem |
|---|---|---|---|---|---|
| καὶ | ἐθεραπεύοντο | 10. οἳ | καὶ | πολλαῖς | τιμαῖς |
| *kai* | *etherapeuonto* | *hoi* | *kai* | *pollais* | *timais* |
| and | were being healed: | who | also | with many | honors |

| 4939.7 verb 3pl indic aor act | 2231.4 prs-pron acc 1pl | 2504.1 conj | 319.4 verb dat pl masc part pres mid | 1991.20 verb 3pl indic aor mid | 3450.17 art pl neu |
|---|---|---|---|---|---|
| ἐτίμησαν | ἡμᾶς | καὶ | ἀναγομένοις | ἐπέθεντο | τὰ |
| *etimēsan* | *hēmas* | *kai* | *anagomenois* | *epethento* | *ta* |
| honored | us, | and | setting sail | they laid on | the things |

**28:8.** There was another reason God in His providence brought Paul to Malta at this time. There was a great need here that would become an opportunity for the ministry of the Holy Spirit and for the spread of the gospel of Christ.

It happened that at this time the father of Publius lay sick, suffering from fevers and dysentery. The Greek indicates these were recurring fevers. He had suffered from them all too often before. Luke, the physician, was careful to make note of this. Yet Luke did not go to work to try to apply the knowledge and skill he had as a physician. He, like Paul, was led of the Holy Spirit. He could have used his skill if the Holy Spirit had directed him to do so. But with even the best of ancient medical practice, the care and recovery of the father of Publius would have been a long drawn-out process. Something more was needed, especially to bring a witness to the power of the gospel. God often uses a miracle as an entering wedge to open a new door for the proclamation of the good news about Jesus.

When Paul heard about this sickness of the father of Publius he went in, prayed for him, laid hands on him, "and healed him." Paul, of course, acted as a fellow laborer with the Lord. God did the actual healing.

**28:9.** The news of this miraculous healing soon spread over the whole of this rather small island. It was like a small town. There were no secrets and news spread quickly. So it was not long before the other people of the island who had illnesses began coming to Paul and were all healed.

Though Luke did not mention it here, Paul surely did more than pray for the sick. Throughout the four Gospels and the Book of Acts the healing ministry was closely tied with the ministry of teaching and the message of the forgiveness of sins.

Luke may not have had a part other than prayer in this ministry, for it is possible he did not know the language and the people did not know Greek. It is probable that people spoke a dialect of Phoenician or Canaanite Hebrew, so Paul may well have been able to communicate with them. At least, it should not have been hard for them to find someone who knew both languages and could interpret for them.

**28:10.** Paul no doubt kept ministering to the people of Malta during the 3 winter months that followed. Many of the people must have come to a knowledge of Jesus Christ as Lord and Saviour. It is clear also that the healings of all these illnesses prepared the way for an effective ministry of evangelism. In spontaneous appreciation the people honored Paul and his friends with many honors. The honors probably included gifts of food, clothing, and money to help them stay alive during those winter months. The people surely must have opened their homes and shared fellowship with them as well.

**8. And it came to pass:** And it so happened, *Rotherham* . . . But, *Lamsa.*

**that the father of Publius lay sick:** . . . was lying prostrate, *Rotherham* . . . was lying ill, *Weymouth* . . . happened to be sick, *Beck* . . . lay in distress, *Swann* . . . lay overcome with, *KJII.*

**of a fever and of a bloody flux:** . . . and dysentery, *ASV* . . . with a stomach sickness, *NLT* . . . with a disease of the stomach, *BB.*

**to whom Paul entered in:** So Paul went to see him, *TCNT* . . . went to him, *NCV* . . . went in to where he was lying, *Lamsa.*

**and prayed, and laid his hands on him, and healed him:**

**9. So when this was done:** And when this happened, *Rotherham* . . . After this, *TCNT* . . . After this miracle, *Noli* . . . occurred, *SEB.*

**others also, which had diseases in the island, came, and were healed:** . . . the rest of the sick folk in the island also came and got cured, *Moffatt* . . . a steady procession, *Wuest* . . . suffering from infirmities, *Knox* . . . sick in the island, *Lamsa* . . . kept coming to him, *Williams.*

**10. Who also honoured us with many honours:** Consequently, *Phillips* . . . They also loaded us with honours, *Weymouth* . . . There also showed us honor in many ways, *Norlie* . . . every kind of respect, *Berkeley* . . . They had great respect, *NLT* . . . They also presented us with many gifts, *TCNT* . . . made us rich presents, *Moffatt, Noli* . . . they bestowed on us many rewards, *Sawyer.*

**and when we departed:** . . . and when at last we sailed, *Weymouth* . . . when we embarked, *Knox* . . . when we put to sea, *Swann* . . . When we were ready to leave, *NCV.*

**they laded us with such things as were necessary:** . . . they supplied all our needs, *Berkeley* . . . what should minister to our wants, *Darby* . . . loaded us with all the supplies we needed, *Knox* . . . they heaped on us, *KJII* . . . whatever we needed, *Beck* . . . whatever things we were in need of, *BB* . . . gave us the things we needed, *NCV.*

10.a.**Txt:** 020L,025P,byz.
**Var:** 01ℵ,02A,03B,Lach
Treg,Alf,Word,Tisc
We/Ho,Weis,Sod
UBS/☆

| **4242.1** prep | **3450.12** art acc sing fem | **5367.3** noun acc sing fem | **3450.15** art acc pl fem | **5367.1** noun fem | **3196.3** prep |
|---|---|---|---|---|---|
| πρὸς | ʻ τὴν | χρείαν. | [a☆ τὰς | χρείας. ] | **11.** Μετὰ |
| *pros* | *tēn* | *chreian* | *tas* | *chreias* | *Meta* |
| for | the | need. | [ the | needs. ] | After |

| **1156.2** conj | **4980.1** num card nom | **3243.4** noun acc pl masc | **319.7** verb 1pl indic aor pass | **1706.1** prep | **4003.3** noun dat sing neu |
|---|---|---|---|---|---|
| δὲ | τρεῖς | μῆνας | ἀνήχθημεν | ἐν | πλοίῳ |
| *de* | *treis* | *mēnas* | *anēchthēmen* | *en* | *ploiō* |
| and | three | months | we sailed | in | a ship |

| **3775.2** verb dat sing neu part perf act | **1706.1** prep | **3450.11** art dat sing fem | **3382.3** noun dat sing fem | **220.1** name-adj dat sing neu |
|---|---|---|---|---|
| παρακεχειμακότι | ἐν | τῇ | νήσῳ, | Ἀλεξανδρίνῳ, |
| *parakecheimakoti* | *en* | *tē* | *nēsō* | *Alexandrinō* |
| having wintered | in | the | island, | an Alexandrian, |

| **3763.1** adj dat sing neu | **1353.1** name dat pl masc | **2504.1** conj | **2580.8** verb nom pl masc part aor pass | **1519.1** prep |
|---|---|---|---|---|
| παρασήμῳ | Διοσκούροις· | **12.** καὶ | καταχθέντες | εἰς |
| *parasēmō* | *Dioskourois* | *kai* | *katachthentes* | *eis* |
| with an ensign | Dioscuri. | And | having been brought | to |

| **4798.1** name acc pl fem | **1946.6** verb 1pl indic aor act | **2232.1** noun fem | **4980.1** num card nom | **3468.1** adv |
|---|---|---|---|---|
| Συρακούσας | ἐπεμείναμεν | ἡμέρας | τρεῖς· | **13.** ὅθεν |
| *Surakousas* | *epemeinamen* | *hēmeras* | *treis* | *hothen* |
| Syracuse | we remained | days | three. | Whence |

13.a.**Txt:** 01ℵ-org,03B
044,Steph
**Var:** p74,01ℵ-corr3,02A
066,byz.

| **3877.1** verb nom pl masc part aor act | **3885.2** verb nom pl masc part aor act | **2628.2** verb 1pl indic aor act | **1519.1** prep |
|---|---|---|---|
| ʻ περιελόντες | [a περιελθόντες ] | κατηντήσαμεν | εἰς |
| *perielontes* | *perielthontes* | *katēntēsamen* | *eis* |
| having gone round | [ idem ] | we arrived | at |

| **4340.1** name neu | **2504.1** conj | **3196.3** prep | **1518.8** num card acc fem | **2232.4** noun acc sing fem | **1905.1** verb gen sing masc part aor mid |
|---|---|---|---|---|---|
| Ῥήγιον, | καὶ | μετὰ | μίαν | ἡμέραν | ἐπιγενομένου |
| *Rhēgion* | *kai* | *meta* | *mian* | *hēmeran* | *epigenomenou* |
| Rhegium; | and | after | one | day, | having come on |

| **3421.1** noun gen sing masc | **1200.1** adj nom pl masc | **2048.4** verb 1pl indic aor act | **1519.1** prep | **4082.1** name acc masc |
|---|---|---|---|---|
| νότου | δευτεραῖοι | ἤλθομεν | εἰς | Ποτιόλους· |
| *notou* | *deuteraioi* | *ēlthomen* | *eis* | *Potiolous* |
| a south wind | on the second day | we came | to | Puteoli; |

| **3619.1** adv | **2128.18** verb nom pl masc part aor act | **79.9** noun acc pl masc | **3731.26** verb 1pl indic aor pass | **1894.2** prep |
|---|---|---|---|---|
| **14.** οὗ | εὑρόντες | ἀδελφοὺς | παρεκλήθημεν | ʻ ἐπ' |
| *hou* | *heurontes* | *adelphous* | *pareklēthēmen* | *ep'* |
| where | having found | brothers | we were encouraged | with |

14.a.**Txt:** 020L,025P,byz.
**Var:** 01ℵ,02A,03B,Lach
Treg,Alf,Tisc,We/Ho
Weis,Sod,UBS/☆

| **3706.1** prep | **840.2** prs-pron dat pl | **1946.9** verb inf aor act | **2232.1** noun fem | **2017.1** num card | **2504.1** conj |
|---|---|---|---|---|---|
| [a☆ παρ' ] | αὐτοῖς | ἐπιμεῖναι | ἡμέρας | ἑπτά· | καὶ |
| *par'* | *autois* | *epimeinai* | *hēmeras* | *hepta* | *kai* |
| [ idem ] | them | to remain | days | seven. | And |

14.b.**Txt:** 025P,byz.Weis
Sod
**Var:** 01ℵ,02A,03B,Treg
Alf,Tisc,We/Ho,UBS/☆

| **3643.1** adv | **1519.1** prep | **3450.12** art acc sing fem | **4373.3** name acc fem | **2048.4** verb 1pl indic aor act | **2048.62** verb 1pl indic aor act |
|---|---|---|---|---|---|
| οὕτως | εἰς | τὴν | Ῥώμην | ʻ ἤλθομεν. | [b☆ ἤλθαμεν. ] |
| *houtōs* | *eis* | *tēn* | *Rhōmēn* | *ēlthomen* | *ēlthamen* |
| thus | to | | Rome | we came. | [ idem ] |

When Paul and the others set sail in the spring, the people placed on board the things they needed for the journey. Apparently, the islanders provided not only for Paul, but for all the other 275 people who had been shipwrecked as well.

**28:11.** The rest of the journey to Italy took place on another ship of Alexandria that had wintered in Malta, probably at the good harbor of Valetta. Its figurehead was the Dioscuri. This was their name for the "sons of (the Greek chief god) Zeus," that is, Castor and Pollux. In some of the Greek mythology these were said to be the sons of Zeus and Leda and were considered patrons of sailors and their protectors when in distress. The constellation Gemini ("the Twins") is named after them, and its two brightest stars are called Castor and Pollux.

**28:12.** The ship took a course that went north-northeast and then north in order to go between Sicily and the toe of Italy's boot. When they came to Syracuse on the east coast of Sicily, they stopped 3 days. Syracuse was a famous and beautiful city about 80 miles north of Malta founded and colonized by the Greeks. The Romans made it the capital of the province.

**28:13.** When the ship left Syracuse the wind was not favorable, so they had to "make a circuit," that is, they had to tack against the wind all the way to Rhegium (the modern Reggio) in the toe of Italy's boot opposite Messina in Sicily.

After another day the wind changed, and it took them only one more day to sail the approximately 180 miles between Rhegium and Puteoli (the modern Pozzuoli), the chief port on the bay of Naples. It stood on the north shore of an indentation in the bay and was protected by a massive breakwater.

Because the coast nearer Rome had no good harbors until an artificial one was made by the emperor Claudius, and because Puteoli was a very safe harbor, the Romans made it their chief seaport. Thus, it became the center of commercial activity and was very prosperous. The grain ships that brought wheat from Egypt made it their home port. Other ships brought goods and spices from the Orient by way of the countries bordering on the eastern Mediterranean. At this time its population was about 100,000.

**28:14.** After Paul and his companions went ashore at Puteoli, they found Christian brethren who successfully urged them to stay with them 7 days. Probably they did so because they wanted and felt they needed the teaching and fellowship of the apostle. This week of rest and fellowship must have meant much to Paul and his companions.

**11. And after three months:** Three months later, *Goodspeed* . . . Three months having elapsed, *Fenton* . . . We stayed there three months, *SEB.*

**we departed in a ship of Alexandria:** . . . we put to sea in, *Berkeley* . . . we left, sailing in, *Lamsa.*

**which had wintered in the isle:** . . . that had stayed there during the winter, *NLT.*

**whose sign was Castor and Pollux:** . . . and which bore the sign of, *Lamsa* . . . whose ensign was—The Twin Brothers, *Rotherham* . . . was the sign for the twin gods, *SEB.*

**12. And landing at Syracuse:** We docked at, *Berkeley* . . . We put in at, *TCNT* . . . going into the harbour at, *BB.*

**we tarried there three days:** . . . we remained there, *Lamsa* . . . and stayed there, *TCNT.*

**13. And from thence we fetched a compass:** . . . whence removing, *Hanson* . . . we made a circuit, *AmpB* . . . From there we circled around, *Lamsa* . . . from there we coasted around, *Swann* . . . going in a circuitous course, *Darby* . . . we sailed around, *Beck* . . . Then tacking round, *Moffatt* . . . from there, going about in a curve, *BB* . . . after going around, *KJII* . . . we went around to, *Klingensmith.*

**and came to Rhegium:** . . . and arrived at, *Lamsa.*

**and after one day:** . . . next day, *Moffatt.*

**the south wind blew:** . . . began to blow, *Williams* . . . blew in our favor, *Lamsa.*

**and we came the next day to Puteoli:** . . . and in two days, *Lamsa.*

**14. Where we found brethren:** . . . found some Christians there, *NLT.*

**and were desired to tarry with them seven days:** . . . and were entreated, *ASV* . . . and were urged to stay, *KJII, TCNT* . . . and they begged us, *Williams* . . . and were invited to remain with them, *Hanson* . . . who invited us to stay, *Lamsa.*

**and so we went toward Rome:** . . . and thus towards Rome we came, *Rotherham* . . . Finally, we came near to Rome, *SEB.*

| **2518.1** conj | **3450.7** art nom pl masc | **79.6** noun nom pl masc | **189.32** verb nom pl masc part aor act | **3450.17** art pl neu |
|---|---|---|---|---|
| **15.** κἀκεῖθεν | οἱ | ἀδελφοὶ | ἀκούσαντες | τὰ |
| *kakeithen* | *hoi* | *adelphoi* | *akousantes* | *ta* |
| And from there | the | brothers | having heard | the |

15.a.**Txt:** 020L,025P,byz. Sod
**Var:** 01א,03B,Treg,Alf Tisc,We/Ho,UBS/☆

| **3875.1** prep | **2231.2** prs-pron gen 1pl | **1814.1** verb indic aor act | **2048.64** verb 3pl indic aor act | **1519.1** prep |
|---|---|---|---|---|
| περὶ | ἡμῶν | ⸀ἐξῆλθον | [a☆ ἦλθαν ] | εἰς |
| *peri* | *hēmōn* | *exēlthon* | *ēlthan* | *eis* |
| concerning | us | came out | [ came ] | to |

| **525.1** noun acc sing fem | **2231.3** prs-pron dat 1pl | **884.1** conj | **884.2** conj | **669.1** name gen neu |
|---|---|---|---|---|
| ἀπάντησιν | ἡμῖν | ⸀ἄχρις | [☆ ἄχρι ] | Ἀππίου Φόρου |
| *apantēsin* | *hēmin* | *achris* | *achri* | *Appiou Phorou* |
| meeting | us | as far as | [ idem ] | Appius marketplace |

| **2504.1** conj | **4980.2** num card gen | **4850.1** noun gen pl fem | **3614.8** rel-pron acc pl masc | **1481.16** verb nom sing masc part aor act | **3450.5** art nom sing masc |
|---|---|---|---|---|---|
| καὶ | Τριῶν | Ταβερνῶν· | οὓς | ἰδὼν | ὁ |
| *kai* | *Triōn* | *Tabernōn* | *hous* | *idōn* | *ho* |
| and | Three | Taverns; | whom | having seen | |

| **3834.1** name nom masc | **2149.11** verb nom sing masc part aor act | **3450.3** art dat sing | **2296.3** noun dat sing masc | **2956.14** verb 3sing indic aor act |
|---|---|---|---|---|
| Παῦλος, | εὐχαριστήσας | τῷ | θεῷ | ἔλαβεν |
| *Paulos* | *eucharistēsas* | *tō* | *theō* | *elaben* |
| Paul, | having given thanks | | to God | he took |

16.a.**Txt:** 020L,025P,byz.
**Var:** 01א,03B,Lach,Alf Tisc,Weis,Sod,UBS/☆

| **2271.1** noun sing neu | **3616.1** conj | **1156.2** conj | **2048.4** verb 1pl indic aor act | **1511.4** verb 1pl indic aor act |
|---|---|---|---|---|
| θάρσος. | **16.** Ὅτε | δὲ | ⸀ἤλθομεν | [a☆ εἰσήλθομεν ] |
| *tharsos* | *Hote* | *de* | *ēlthomen* | *eisēlthomen* |
| courage. | When | and | we came | [ we came into ] |

16.b.**Txt:** 020L,025P,byz. lect.sa.Sod
**Var:** 01א,02A,03B,044 bo.Lach,Treg,Alf,Tisc We/Ho,Weis,UBS/☆

| **1519.1** prep | **4373.3** name acc fem | **3450.5** art nom sing masc | **1530.1** noun nom sing masc | **3722.10** verb 3sing indic aor act |
|---|---|---|---|---|
| εἰς | Ῥώμην | ⸀b ὁ | ἑκατόνταρχος | παρέδωκεν |
| *eis* | *Rhōmēn* | *ho* | *hekatontarchos* | *paredōken* |
| to | Rome | the | centurion | delivered |

| **3450.8** art acc pl masc | **1192.5** noun acc pl masc | **3450.3** art dat sing | **4610.1** noun dat sing masc | **3450.3** art dat sing |
|---|---|---|---|---|
| τοὺς | δεσμίους | τῷ | στρατοπεδάρχῃ·⸃ | ⸀τῷ |
| *tous* | *desmious* | *tō* | *stratopedarchē* | *tō* |
| the | prisoners | to the | commander of the camp, | |

16.c.**Txt:** 020L,025P,byz. lect.
**Var:** 01א,02A,03B,044 bo.Lach,Treg,Alf,Tisc We/Ho,Weis,UBS/☆

| **1156.2** conj | **3834.3** name dat masc | **1994.8** verb 3sing indic aor pass | **1994.8** verb 3sing indic aor pass | **3450.3** art dat sing | **3834.3** name dat masc |
|---|---|---|---|---|---|
| δὲ | Παύλῳ | ἐπετράπη | [c☆ ἐπετράπη | τῷ | Παύλῳ ] |
| *de* | *Paulō* | *epetrapē* | *epetrapē* | *tō* | *Paulō* |
| but | Paul | was allowed | [ was allowed | | Paul ] |

| **3176.15** verb inf pres act | **2567.2** prep | **1431.6** prs-pron acc sing masc | **4713.1** prep | **3450.3** art dat sing | **5278.4** verb dat sing masc part pres act | **840.6** prs-pron acc sing masc |
|---|---|---|---|---|---|---|
| μένειν | καθ' | ἑαυτὸν, | σὺν | τῷ | φυλάσσοντι | αὐτὸν |
| *menein* | *kath'* | *heauton* | *sun* | *tō* | *phulassonti* | *auton* |
| to remain | by | himself, | with | the | guarding | him |

| **4608.2** noun dat sing masc | **1090.33** verb 3sing indic aor mid | **1156.2** conj | **3196.3** prep | **2232.1** noun fem | **4980.1** num card nom |
|---|---|---|---|---|---|
| στρατιώτῃ. | **17.** Ἐγένετο | δὲ | μετὰ | ἡμέρας | τρεῖς |
| *stratiōtē* | *Egeneto* | *de* | *meta* | *hēmeras* | *treis* |
| soldier. | It came to pass | and | after | days | three |

**28:15.** From Puteoli, Paul and his companions proceeded on foot toward Rome, taking the famous Roman road, the Appian Way. Paul knew, of course, the Lord wanted him in Rome (23:11), but he did not know what awaited him or how his trial would turn out. As he trudged along, he may have looked back over the 3 years that had passed since he had written to the Romans, expressing his desire to visit them (Romans 1:10,11,15). What a weary 3 years they had been! There had been persecutions and false accusations. The imprisonment at Caesarea had dragged on and on until he had appealed to Caesar. What further severe ordeal awaited him now?

But God had a pleasant surprise for Paul. When he reached the Appii Forum ("the marketplace of Appius"), about 40 miles south of Rome, a delegation of people met him. They were Christians who had come out in order to give him a royal welcome. It was not honor that brought Paul joy, however. The sight of Christian brothers who would walk and talk with him caused him to thank God and take courage. Even mature, spiritual believers need the inspiration and strength which can be derived from Christian fellowship with other believers.

Again, at the village of Three Taverns (rather, Three Shops), about 30 miles from Rome, another delegation of believers met Paul. This was the regular expression for the official welcome of an official or dignitary. The same phrase is used of the Church going for the meeting with Christ in the air (1 Thessalonians 4:17).

**28:16.** At Rome Paul and the other prisoners were handed over to the commander of Nero's praetorian guard (that is, to the general in charge of the Roman legion stationed at the Roman praetorium to guard the emperor Nero and the palace). The other prisoners were probably thrown into a prison. But Paul was permitted to live by himself, lightly chained by the wrist to a soldier who guarded him. As verse 30 indicates, he was able to rent an apartment in a private house and keep it for the 2 years he was in Rome. Luke and Aristarchus also remained in Rome to help him during this period. Paul mentions them in some of the prison Epistles written during this period. (See Colossians 4:10,14; Philemon 24.) The apartment was large enough for quite a few people to gather, as verses 23-25 indicate.

The guard who was chained to Paul's wrist was probably a member of the emperor's praetorian guard, since Paul was appealing to Caesar. They probably served in shifts, with different ones from time to time. Thus the whole praetorian guard came to hear the gospel. (See Philippians 1:13, where "the palace" is literally the praetorian guard.)

Paul was also permitted to have his friends come and go so he could enjoy their fellowship and hospitality. As a Roman citizen he was given better treatment than the other prisoners. Also the centurion Julius may have put in a good word for him with the commander of the guard.

**15. And from thence, when the brethren heard of us:** When the Christians heard of our coming, *NLT* . . . had heard about our affairs, *Swann* . . . heard of our arrival, *Alford, Lamsa* . . . who heard our story, *Knox.*

**they came to meet us as far as Appii forum, and The three taverns:** . . . to have a meeting with us, *BB* . . . as far as the street which is called Appiiforum, *Lamsa* . . . Appius' Market, *Williams* . . . the Market of Appius, *Fenton* . . . the Three Shops, *Beck* . . . and Three Tabernacles, *Berkeley* . . . and Three Inns, *TEV* . . . the Three Stores, *NLT.*

**whom when Paul saw:** And as soon as Paul caught sight of them, *Williams.*

**he thanked God, and took courage:** . . . and took renewed courage, *Norlie* . . . and felt encouraged, *Beck* . . . and was much cheered, *TCNT* . . . greatly encouraged, *Lamsa, Noli.*

**16. And when we came to Rome:** When at last we reached, *Noli* . . . When we finally entered Rome, *Montgomery* . . . On our reaching Rome, *TCNT* . . . Once we were in Rome, *Knox.*

**the centurion delivered the prisoners to the captain of the guard:** . . . commander of the prison camp, *Norlie.*

**but Paul was suffered to dwell by himself with a soldier that kept him:** Paul was allowed to live by himself except for the soldier who was in charge of him, *TCNT* . . . Paul received permission to live by himself, guarded by a soldier, *Weymouth* . . . to live alone with the soldier who was guarding him, *Phillips* . . . was allowed to have his own residence, *Knox* . . . gave permission to Paul to live wherever he pleased with a soldier to guard him, *Lamsa* . . . reside where he pleased, *Murdock* . . . outside the garrison, *Fenton* . . . allowed to live where he wanted to...a soldier was always by his side to watch him, *NLT* . . . with the soldier who guarded him, *Swann* . . . the armed man who kept watch over him, *BB.*

**17. And it came to pass, that after three days:** Three days after our arrival, *TCNT* . . . And it occurred after, *Hanson* . . . Three days later, *Noli.*

17.a.**Txt:** 020L,025P,byz.
**Var:** 01א,02A,03B
Gries,Lach,Treg,Alf
Word,Tisc,We/Ho,Weis
Sod,UBS/☆

| **4630.6** verb inf aor mid | **3450.6** art acc sing masc | **3834.4** name acc masc | **840.6** prs-pron acc sing masc | **3450.8** art acc pl masc |
|---|---|---|---|---|
| συγκαλέσασθαι | ‛ τὸν | Παῦλον | [a☆ αὐτὸν ] | τοὺς |
| *sunkalesasthai* | *ton* | *Paulon* | *auton* | *tous* |
| to call together | | Paul | [ him ] | the |

| **1498.25** verb acc pl masc part pres act | **3450.1** art gen pl | **2428.3** name-adj gen pl masc | **4272.8** num ord acc pl masc | **4755.7** verb gen pl masc part aor act |
|---|---|---|---|---|
| ὄντας | τῶν | Ἰουδαίων | πρώτους· | συνελθόντων |
| *ontas* | *tōn* | *Ioudaiōn* | *prōtous* | *sunelthontōn* |
| being | of the | Jews | chief ones. | Having come together |

| **1156.2** conj | **840.1** prs-pron gen pl | **2978.26** verb 3sing indic imperf act | **4242.1** prep | **840.8** prs-pron acc pl masc | **433.6** noun nom pl masc | **79.6** noun nom pl masc |
|---|---|---|---|---|---|---|
| δὲ | αὐτῶν | ἔλεγεν | πρὸς | αὐτούς, | ‛ Ἄνδρες | ἀδελφοί, |
| *de* | *autōn* | *elegen* | *pros* | *autous* | *Andres* | *adelphoi* |
| and | them | he was saying | to | them, | Men | brothers, |

| **1466.1** prs-pron nom 1sing | **1466.1** prs-pron nom 1sing | **433.6** noun nom pl masc | **79.6** noun nom pl masc | **3625.6** num card neu | **1710.1** prep |
|---|---|---|---|---|---|
| Ἐγὼ | [☆ Ἐγώ, | ἄνδρες | ἀδελφοί, ] | οὐδὲν | ἐναντίον |
| *Egō* | *Egō* | *andres* | *adelphoi* | *ouden* | *enantion* |
| I | [ I, | men | brothers, ] | nothing | against |

| **4020.37** verb nom sing masc part aor act | **3450.3** art dat sing | **2967.3** noun dat sing masc | **2211.1** conj | **3450.4** art dat pl | **1478.4** noun dat pl neu | **3450.4** art dat pl |
|---|---|---|---|---|---|---|
| ποιήσας | τῷ | λαῷ | ἢ | τοῖς | ἔθεσιν | τοῖς |
| *poiēsas* | *tō* | *laō* | *ē* | *tois* | *ethesin* | *tois* |
| having done | the | people | or | the | customs | the |

| **3833.3** adj dat pl neu | **1192.1** noun nom sing masc | **1523.1** prep gen | **2389.2** name gen pl neu | **3722.31** verb 1sing indic aor pass |
|---|---|---|---|---|
| πατρῴοις | δέσμιος | ἐξ | Ἱεροσολύμων | παρεδόθην |
| *patrōois* | *desmios* | *ex* | *Hierosolumōn* | *paredothēn* |
| ancestral | a prisoner | from | Jerusalem | was delivered |

| **1519.1** prep | **3450.15** art acc pl fem | **5331.8** noun acc pl fem | **3450.1** art gen pl | **4371.4** name-adj gen pl masc | **3610.2** rel-pron nom pl masc |
|---|---|---|---|---|---|
| εἰς | τὰς | χεῖρας | τῶν | Ῥωμαίων· | **18.** οἵτινες |
| *eis* | *tas* | *cheiras* | *tōn* | *Rhōmaiōn* | *hoitines* |
| into | the | hands | of the | Romans, | who |

| **348.7** verb nom pl masc part aor act | **1466.6** prs-pron acc 1sing | **1007.17** verb 3pl indic imperf mid | **624.13** verb inf aor act | **1217.2** prep |
|---|---|---|---|---|
| ἀνακρίναντές | με | ἐβούλοντο | ἀπολῦσαι, | διὰ |
| *anakrinantes* | *me* | *eboulonto* | *apolusai* | *dia* |
| having examined | me | were wishing | to let go, | because |

| **3450.16** art sing neu | **3235.5** num card acc fem | **155.3** noun acc sing fem | **2265.2** noun gen sing masc | **5062.11** verb inf pres act | **1706.1** prep |
|---|---|---|---|---|---|
| τὸ | μηδεμίαν | αἰτίαν | θανάτου | ὑπάρχειν | ἐν |
| *to* | *mēdemian* | *aitian* | *thanatou* | *huparchein* | *en* |
| the | not one | cause | of death | to be | in |

| **1466.5** prs-pron dat 1sing | **480.4** verb gen pl masc part pres act | **1156.2** conj | **3450.1** art gen pl | **2428.3** name-adj gen pl masc |
|---|---|---|---|---|
| ἐμοί. | **19.** ἀντιλεγόντων | δὲ | τῶν | Ἰουδαίων |
| *emoi* | *antilegontōn* | *de* | *tōn* | *Ioudaiōn* |
| me. | Speaking against | but | the | Jews |

| **313.7** verb 1sing indic aor pass | **1926.18** verb inf aor mid | **2512.3** name acc masc | **3620.1** partic | **5453.1** conj | **3450.2** art gen sing |
|---|---|---|---|---|---|
| ἠναγκάσθην | ἐπικαλέσασθαι | Καίσαρα, | οὐχ | ὡς | τοῦ |
| *ēnankasthēn* | *epikalesasthai* | *Kaisara* | *ouch* | *hōs* | *tou* |
| I was compelled | to appeal to | Caesar, | not | as | the |

**28:17.** After 3 days Paul called together (that is, sent out an invitation to) the Jewish leaders in Rome, asking them to come to his apartment. Ancient Roman inscriptions show there were several Jewish synagogues in Rome at this time. In fact, the Roman government at the time did more than tolerate the Jews. They favored them by allowing them the privilege of governing themselves and making laws and ordinances for their own community. They even let them send an annual contribution to the temple in Jerusalem.

During his missionary journeys Paul normally went first to the synagogue on his first visit to any city in order to give the Jews the first opportunity to accept the gospel. When he wrote to the Roman Christians, he reminded them the gospel was given to the Jew first (Romans 1:16). He also declared to them his own deep love and concern for his unsaved Jewish brothers (Romans 9:1-5; 10:1). But now, since he was a prisoner, he could not visit the synagogues, so he did the next best thing and invited their leaders to visit him.

When they came he showed a courteous and conciliatory spirit as he humbly explained how he came to be in Rome as a prisoner. He made it clear that his chain did not mark him as a renegade Israelite. He had, in fact, done nothing at all against the people of Israel or against the customs of their fathers to cause him to be handed over out of Jerusalem as a prisoner to the Romans. This was true. He was actually in the process of showing his willingness to follow those customs when he was attacked and arrested.

**28:18.** Paul then explained his innocence by telling how the Romans had examined him (in an official court hearing) and had wanted to set him free, for they found no legal grounds at all for putting him to death. In other words, the Roman authorities were ready to give him a full pardon.

It seems Paul felt it necessary to begin this way in case the Jews in Rome had already had a report from the Jerusalem Jews, or perhaps in anticipation that such a report would soon come. He had no way of knowing how much they knew about him.

**28:19.** After emphasizing his innocence, Paul explained why he appealed to Caesar, being careful not to put any blame on the Jewish nation (the Jewish people) as a whole.

The Jews in Jerusalem, however, had continued to speak against him, opposing him, refusing to accept the decision of the Roman authorities. Therefore, Paul had felt obliged to appeal to Caesar. But his purpose in doing so was not to make any accusation against his nation (his people, the Jews). Rather, he simply wanted the opportunity to defend himself. Thus, he was in Rome as a prisoner, not because he had done anything wrong, but because circumstances had made it a necessity.

The fact that Paul did not want to bring any charge against his own people shows how loving and forgiving he was toward them. No matter what they did to him, he could not hold a grudge or keep anything in his heart against them.

**Paul called the chief of the Jews together:** Paul invited the leading Jews to meet him, *TCNT* . . . he called a meeting of the leading men among the Jews, *Knox* . . . those that were the principal of the Jews, *Hanson* . . . for some of the most important Jewish leaders, *SEB.*

**and when they were come together:** . . . when they had convened, *Sawyer* . . . when they were assembled, *Hanson.*

**he said unto them:**

**Men and brethren:** Fellow Jews, *Beck.*

**though I have committed nothing against the people:** . . . nothing hostile to the interests of our nation, *TCNT.*

**or customs of our fathers:** . . . or the way our early fathers lived, *NLT* . . . or contrary to the customs of our forefathers, *Weymouth* . . . of our ancestors, *SEB.*

**yet was I delivered prisoner from Jerusalem into the hands of the Romans:** . . . handed over to the Romans, *TCNT* . . . yet I was made a prisoner at Jerusalem, *Norlie* . . . yet I was arrested in, *SEB.*

**18. Who, when they had examined me:** After examining me, *Williams* . . . The Romans asked me many questions, *SEB* . . . sharply questioned me, *Weymouth* . . . when they had put questions to me, *BB.*

**would have let me go:** . . . were minded to, *Rotherham* . . . were willing to, *Weymouth* . . . were prepared to, *Phillips* . . . desired to release me, *Hanson* . . . they wished to let me go, *KJII* . . . were ready to let me go, *BB* . . . go free, *SEB.*

**because there was no cause of death in me:** . . . nothing in my conduct deserving death, *TCNT.*

**19. But when the Jews spake against it:** . . . made protest against it, *BB* . . . But owing to the opposition of the Jews, *Weymouth* . . . But the Jews objected, *Beck* . . . objected, so, *Williams.*

**I was constrained to appeal unto Caesar:** . . . and forced me to appeal, *Beck* . . . I was compelled, *Alford* . . . I had to put my cause into Caesar's hands, *BB* . . . forced to ask to have my trial before, *SEB.*

| **1477.2** noun gen sing neu | **1466.2** prs-pron gen 1sing | **2174.17** verb nom sing masc part pres act | **4948.10** indef-pron sing neu | **2693.10** verb inf aor act |
|---|---|---|---|---|
| ἔθνους | μου | ἔχων | τι | ʿ κατηγορῆσαι. |
| *ethnous* | *mou* | *echōn* | *ti* | *katēgorēsai* |
| nation | my | having | anything | to accuse. |

19.a.**Txt:** 020L,025P,byz.Sod
**Var:** 01ℵ,02A,03B,Lach Treg,Alf,Tisc,We/Ho Weis,UBS/☆

| **2693.8** verb inf pres act | **1217.2** prep | **3642.12** dem-pron acc sing fem | **3631.1** partic | **3450.12** art acc sing fem |
|---|---|---|---|---|
| [a☆ κατηγορεῖν. ] | **20.** διὰ | ταύτην | οὖν | τὴν |
| *katēgorein* | *dia* | *tautēn* | *oun* | *tēn* |
| [idem] | For | this | therefore | the |

| **155.3** noun acc sing fem | **3731.11** verb 1sing indic aor act | **5050.4** prs-pron acc 2pl | **1481.19** verb inf aor act | **2504.1** conj |
|---|---|---|---|---|
| αἰτίαν | παρεκάλεσα | ὑμᾶς | ἰδεῖν | καὶ |
| *aitian* | *parekalesa* | *humas* | *idein* | *kai* |
| cause | I called for | you | to see | and |

| **4212.2** verb inf aor act | **1736.2** prep | **1736.1** prep | **1056.1** conj | **3450.10** art gen sing fem |
|---|---|---|---|---|
| προσλαλῆσαι· | ʿ ἕνεκεν | [ εἵνεκεν ] | γὰρ | τῆς |
| *proslalēsai* | *heneken* | *heineken* | *gar* | *tēs* |
| to speak to; | on account of | [idem] | for | the |

| **1667.2** noun gen sing fem | **3450.2** art gen sing | **2447.1** name masc | **3450.12** art acc sing fem | **252.2** noun acc sing fem | **3642.12** dem-pron acc sing fem |
|---|---|---|---|---|---|
| ἐλπίδος | τοῦ | Ἰσραὴλ | τὴν | ἅλυσιν | ταύτην |
| *elpidos* | *tou* | *Israēl* | *tēn* | *halusin* | *tautēn* |
| hope | | of Israel | the | chain | this |

| **3892.1** verb 1sing indic pres mid | **3450.7** art nom pl masc | **1156.2** conj | **4242.1** prep | **840.6** prs-pron acc sing masc | **1500.3** verb indic aor act |
|---|---|---|---|---|---|
| περίκειμαι. | **21.** Οἱ | δὲ | πρὸς | αὐτὸν | ʿ εἶπον, |
| *perikeimai* | *Hoi* | *de* | *pros* | *auton* | *eipon* |
| I have around. | The | and | to | him | said, |

21.a.**Txt:** 020L,byz.Sod
**Var:** 01ℵ,02A,03B,Lach Treg,Alf,Tisc,We/Ho Weis,UBS/☆

| **1500.28** verb 3pl indic aor act | **2231.1** prs-pron nom 1pl | **3641.1** conj | **1115.4** noun pl neu | **3875.1** prep |
|---|---|---|---|---|
| [a☆ εἶπαν, ] | Ἡμεῖς | οὔτε | γράμματα | περὶ |
| *eipan* | *Hēmeis* | *oute* | *grammata* | *peri* |
| [idem] | We | neither | letters | concerning |

| **4622.2** prs-pron gen 2sing | **1203.6** verb 1pl indic aor mid | **570.3** prep | **3450.10** art gen sing fem | **2424.2** name gen fem | **3641.1** conj |
|---|---|---|---|---|---|
| σοῦ | ἐδεξάμεθα | ἀπὸ | τῆς | Ἰουδαίας | οὔτε |
| *sou* | *edexametha* | *apo* | *tēs* | *Ioudaias* | *oute* |
| you | received | from | | Judea, | nor |

| **3716.7** verb nom sing masc part aor mid | **4948.3** indef-pron nom sing | **3450.1** art gen pl | **79.7** noun gen pl masc | **514.7** verb 3sing indic aor act |
|---|---|---|---|---|
| παραγενόμενός | τις | τῶν | ἀδελφῶν | ἀπήγγειλεν |
| *paragenomenos* | *tis* | *tōn* | *adelphōn* | *apēngeilen* |
| having arrived | anyone | of the | brothers | reported |

| **2211.1** conj | **2953.27** verb 3sing indic aor act | **4948.10** indef-pron sing neu | **3875.1** prep | **4622.2** prs-pron gen 2sing | **4050.1** adj sing |
|---|---|---|---|---|---|
| ἢ | ἐλάλησέν | τι | περὶ | σοῦ | πονηρόν. |
| *ē* | *elalēsen* | *ti* | *peri* | *sou* | *ponēron* |
| or | said | anything | concerning | you | evil. |

| **511.1** verb 1pl indic pres act | **1156.2** conj | **3706.2** prep | **4622.2** prs-pron gen 2sing | **189.36** verb inf aor act | **3614.17** rel-pron pl neu |
|---|---|---|---|---|---|
| **22.** ἀξιοῦμεν | δὲ | παρὰ | σοῦ | ἀκοῦσαι | ἃ |
| *axioumen* | *de* | *para* | *sou* | *akousai* | *ha* |
| We think well | but | from | you | to hear | what |

He told the Romans, "I have great heaviness (pain, grief of mind and spirit) and continual sorrow in my heart (my heart is continually grieved). For I could wish that myself were (would be) accursed (*anathema*, accursed and therefore separated) from Christ for my brethren, my kinsmen according to the flesh: who are Israelites" (Romans 9:2-4). That is, Paul would have been willing to give up his own salvation if that could have guaranteed the salvation of the Jews. He knew that was not possible, but that is how much he loved them!

Paul went on in the Book of Romans to show that the Jews who were rejecting Christ were trying to set the conditions on which God would give His mercy and salvation. They trusted in their own works instead of taking the God-appointed way of faith. They trusted in who they were instead of who Christ is. They stumbled at Christ, took offense at Him, when He was really the Chief Cornerstone. So it was not God's fault the Jews rejected Him.

In all this Paul expressed a tremendous concern over the Jews and a heartfelt desire for their salvation, at the same time recognizing their zeal for God, a zeal that was without right knowledge, just as his had been.

**28:20.** Paul's purpose in calling together the Jewish leaders was, however, more than just to explain why he was in Rome as a prisoner. He wanted to testify to the truth that it was for the hope of Israel he was bound by a chain.

In his prison epistles, Paul never drew attention to the fact that he was a prisoner of Rome. Rather, he called himself a prisoner of his Lord (Ephesians 3:1; 4:1).

In his epistles, Paul also called himself a servant, literally, a slave of Jesus Christ (Romans 1:1). In those days the most common way of becoming a slave was to be taken captive by some conqueror. Paul considered he had been taken captive by the risen Christ who then gave him, still as His slave, as an apostle to the Church (Ephesians 4:11). In other words, when Paul accepted Jesus as Lord on the Damascus Road, he gave himself up to Christ completely as his Lord and Master. From that time on he was Christ's captive and slave to do His will. Thus, his whole life was under his Lord's direction. He was in Rome, then, because of the Hope of Israel, Christ.

**28:21.** The Jewish leaders replied that no letters had come from Judea, nor had anyone brought a report of Paul's trial or spoken anything bad concerning him. There is evidence that Roman law punished unsuccessful prosecutors of Roman citizens. So it is possible the Jewish leaders in Jerusalem simply decided it was the better part of wisdom not to oppose Paul in Rome.

**28:22.** These leaders of the Roman Jews expressed a desire to hear Paul tell what he had in his mind. They were not compli-



**not that I had ought to accuse my nation of:** . . . not that I'm accusing my people of anything, *Beck* . . . I have no charge to bring against my people, *NCV*.

**20. For this cause therefore:** This, then, is my reason, *TCNT* . . . This is the reason why, *Montgomery* . . . on account of, *Noli* . . . But it is because of this accusation of the Jews, *Phillips*.

**have I called for you, to see you, and to speak with you:** . . . for urging you to come to see me, *TCNT* . . . I have invited you here, *Weymouth* . . . I have asked for the opportunity of seeing you, *Knox*.

**because that for the hope of Israel:** . . . for on account of, *Rotherham* . . . because I believe in the hope of Israel, *NCV* . . . the Messianic hope of Israel, *Noli*.

**I am bound with this chain:** . . . that I wear this chain, *Knox* . . . I am branded with, *Fenton*.

**21. And they said unto him:** At this they said to him, *Knox*.

**We neither received letters out of Judaea concerning thee:**

**neither any of the brethren that came:** . . . and not one of our Jewish brother has come, *Williams*.

**shewed or spake any harm of thee:** . . . and reported or said anything bad about you, *TCNT* . . . or told us anything bad about you, *NCV* . . . anything to your disadvantage, *Weymouth* . . . with a bad report or gossip about you, *Berkeley* . . . with any ill report or hard words about thee, *Knox* . . . or say any evil about you, *BB* . . . officially or unofficially, *Phillips*.

**22. But we desire to hear of thee what thou thinkest:** But we shall be glad to hear from you what your views are, *TCNT* . . . We think it only right to let you tell your own story, *Moffatt* . . . But we deem it fitting to hear from you what you think, *Swann* . . . But we are eager to hear from you what it is you believe, *Montgomery* . . . We want to hear your ideas, *NCV* . . . we have a desire to give hearing to your opinion, *BB* . . . We ask nothing better than to hear, *Knox* . . . So we want to hear you state your views, *Noli* . . . what thine opinions are, *Rotherham*.

# Acts 28:23

| 5262.2 verb 2sing indic pres act | 3875.1 prep | 3173.1 conj | 1056.1 conj | 3450.10 art gen sing fem | 138.2 noun gen sing fem |
|---|---|---|---|---|---|
| φρονεῖς· | περὶ | μὲν | γὰρ | τῆς | αἱρέσεως |
| *phroneis* | *peri* | *men* | *gar* | *tēs* | *haireseōs* |
| you think, | concerning | indeed | for | the | sect |

| 3642.10 dem-pron gen sing fem | 1104.4 adj sing neu | 1498.4 verb 3sing indic pres act | 2231.3 prs-pron dat 1pl | 2231.3 prs-pron dat 1pl | 1498.4 verb 3sing indic pres act |
|---|---|---|---|---|---|
| ταύτης | γνωστὸν | ‛ ἐστιν | ἡμῖν | [☆ ἡμῖν | ἐστιν ] |
| *tautēs* | *gnōston* | *estin* | *hēmin* | *hēmin* | *estin* |
| this | known | it is | to us | [ to us | it is ] |

| 3617.1 conj | 3699.1 adv | 480.7 verb 3sing indic pres mid | 4872.4 verb nom pl masc part aor mid | 1156.2 conj |
|---|---|---|---|---|
| ὅτι | πανταχοῦ | ἀντιλέγεται. | 23. Ταξάμενοι | δὲ |
| *hoti* | *pantachou* | *antilegetai* | *Taxamenoi* | *de* |
| that | everywhere | it is spoken against. | Having appointed | and |

23.a.**Txt:** 020L,byz.Sod
**Var:** 01ℵ,02A,03B,Lach
Treg,Alf,Tisc,We/Ho
Weis,UBS/☆

| 840.4 prs-pron dat sing | 2232.4 noun acc sing fem | 2223.9 verb 3pl indic imperf act | 2048.1 verb indic aor act | 4242.1 prep | 840.6 prs-pron acc sing masc |
|---|---|---|---|---|---|
| αὐτῷ | ἡμέραν | ‛ ἧκον | [a☆ ἦλθον ] | πρὸς | αὐτὸν |
| *autō* | *hēmeran* | *hēkon* | *ēlthon* | *pros* | *auton* |
| him | a day | came | [ idem ] | to | him |

| 1519.1 prep | 3450.12 art acc sing fem | 3440.1 noun acc sing fem | 3979.5 adj comp nom pl masc | 3614.4 rel-pron dat pl |
|---|---|---|---|---|
| εἰς | τὴν | ξενίαν | πλείονες· | οἷς |
| *eis* | *tēn* | *xenian* | *pleiones* | *hois* |
| to | the | lodging | many, | to whom |

| 1606.3 verb 3sing indic imperf mid | 1257.4 verb nom sing masc part pres mid | 3450.12 art acc sing fem | 926.4 noun acc sing fem |
|---|---|---|---|
| ἐξετίθετο | διαμαρτυρόμενος | τὴν | βασιλείαν |
| *exetitheto* | *diamarturomenos* | *tēn* | *basileian* |
| he was expounding | fully testifying | the | kingdom |

23.b.**Txt:** 020L,byz.
**Var:** 01ℵ,02A,03B,Lach
Treg,Alf,Tisc,We/Ho
Weis,Sod,UBS/☆

| 3450.2 art gen sing | 2296.2 noun gen sing masc | 3844.4 verb nom sing masc part pres act | 4885.1 conj | 840.8 prs-pron acc pl masc | 3450.17 art pl neu |
|---|---|---|---|---|---|
| τοῦ | θεοῦ, | πείθων | τε | αὐτοὺς | ‛b τὰ ` |
| *tou* | *theou* | *peithōn* | *te* | *autous* | *ta* |
| | of God, | persuading | and | them | the |

| 3875.1 prep | 3450.2 art gen sing | 2400.2 name masc | 570.3 prep | 4885.1 conj | 3450.2 art gen sing | 3414.2 noun gen sing masc |
|---|---|---|---|---|---|---|
| περὶ | τοῦ | Ἰησοῦ, | ἀπό | τε | τοῦ | νόμου |
| *peri* | *tou* | *Iēsou* | *apo* | *te* | *tou* | *nomou* |
| concerning | | Jesus, | from | both | the | law |

| 3337.2 name gen masc | 3338.2 name gen masc | 2504.1 conj | 3450.1 art gen pl | 4254.5 noun gen pl masc |
|---|---|---|---|---|
| ‛ Μωσέως | [☆ Μωϋσέως ] | καὶ | τῶν | προφητῶν, |
| *Mōseōs* | *Mōuseōs* | *kai* | *tōn* | *prophētōn* |
| of Moses | [ idem ] | and | the | prophets, |

| 570.3 prep | 4262.1 adv | 2175.1 conj | 2055.2 noun gen sing fem | 2504.1 conj | 3450.7 art nom pl masc |
|---|---|---|---|---|---|
| ἀπὸ | πρωῒ | ἕως | ἑσπέρας. | 24. καὶ | οἱ |
| *apo* | *prōi* | *heōs* | *hesperas* | *kai* | *hoi* |
| from | morning | to | evening. | And | the |

| 3173.1 conj | 3844.33 verb 3pl indic imperf pass | 3450.4 art dat pl | 2978.36 verb dat pl neu part pres mid | 3450.7 art nom pl masc |
|---|---|---|---|---|
| μὲν | ἐπείθοντο | τοῖς | λεγομένοις, | οἱ |
| *men* | *epeithonto* | *tois* | *legomenois* | *hoi* |
| indeed | were being persuaded of | the | being spoken, | the |

mentary to the Christians, however, for they called Christianity a sect that everywhere was opposed. Up to this time most of these leaders may have been indifferent to Christianity, knowing only that it was unpopular. Now, at least, their curiosity was aroused.

Paul's epistle to the Romans shows that the church in Rome was already well-established by A.D. 57 and probably long before that. It probably spread as a sect or party under the umbrella of Judaism as a protected religion. The word "sect" here does not necessarily mean a heretical sect. The same word is used of the Pharisees and Sadducees. However, the fact that the Jewish leaders referred to it as everywhere opposed, shows that the Jews in Rome were beginning to consider it somewhat heretical. Yet their leaders obviously had never bothered to investigate for themselves.

**28:23.** The Jews set a date among themselves and came in considerable numbers to Paul's apartment to receive his hospitality. To these he gave explanation of what was in his mind by bearing solemn witness to the kingdom (rule, power, authority) of God. This would include God's rule manifest through Jesus and through the Holy Spirit. It would also speak of the coming Kingdom when Jesus will return to this earth, take the throne of David, and make it eternal.

Then, as he always did in all the synagogues he visited, Paul used the books of Moses and the prophets, books accepted as God's Word by these Jews, seeking to persuade them that Jesus is truly the Messiah, God's anointed Prophet, Priest, and King.

Paul kept their attention as he continued this teaching from early morning until evening. This means he must have given them the same kind of teaching he gave the Jews in the synagogue at Pisidian Antioch. (See 13:16-41.) He also had time to explain the body of teaching found in the four Gospels. No doubt, there were many questions which he answered from the Scriptures. Paul would not treat this opportunity as an academic exercise. He must have spent much time in prayer preparing for this special day. Nor would he be casual in presenting the truth. His earnestness must have brought tears to his eyes as he sought to explain the truth and exhort these fellow countrymen to accept the gospel, the wonderful good news about Jesus and about the grace of God that brings salvation.

**28:24.** Some of the Jews who listened to Paul were persuaded. They believed and obeyed Paul's message and exhortation. A faith in Jesus as their Messiah, Lord, and Saviour sprang up in their hearts. They accepted the truth and believed in their hearts that God had raised Jesus from the dead and therefore that Christ's death was effective for the redemption of soul and body (Romans 8:18-23). They also accepted the truth that Christ's resurrection is the believers' guarantee, and that His coming is an encouragement to holy living now as well as an encouragement to have hope for the future. So they became born-again believers, members of the body of Christ, sharers in the blessed hope and the heavenly in-

**for as concerning this sect:** . . . for with regard to this sect, *TCNT* . . . As for this new religion, *NLT* . . . concerning this teaching, *Lamsa* . . . regarding this belief, *KJII.*

**we know:** . . . we are well aware, *TCNT* . . . all we know is, *Weymouth.*

**that every where it is spoken against:** . . . that it is spoken against on all sides, *TCNT* . . . objections to it, *Moffatt* . . . it is condemned everywhere, *Norlie* . . . is not received by any one, *Murdock* . . . it is not acceptable to any one, *Lamsa* . . . it is everywhere denounced, *Williams* . . . it is everywhere decried, *Knox* . . . that in all places it is attacked, *BB* . . . everyone is talking against it, *NLT.*

**23. And when they had appointed him a day:** . . . having arranged with him, *Rotherham* . . . So they set a date with Paul, *TEV* . . . So they made an appointment with him, *Knox* . . . set a day for a meeting, *SEB.*

**there came many to him into his lodging:** . . . came in large numbers, *Williams* . . . in even larger numbers, *Noli* . . . many gathered together and came to him where he was staying, *Lamsa.*

**to whom he expounded and testified the kingdom of God:** . . . earnestly telling, *Beck* . . . bearing full witness, *Rotherham* . . . he solemnly explained, *Weymouth* . . . earnestly testifying the reign of God, *Hanson* . . . preached to them about the holy nation of God, *NLT.*

**persuading them concerning Jesus:** . . . tried to convince, *TCNT* . . . tried to persuade them, *Noli.*

**both out of the law of Moses, and out of the prophets:** . . . by arguments drawn from, *TCNT* . . . by appealing to, *NEB* . . . Using the law of Moses, *SEB* . . . by quoting passages from, *Noli.*

**from morning till evening:** . . . spoke to them all day long, *SEB.*

**24. And some believed the things which were spoken:** Some of them were convinced by what he said, *Noli* . . . were in agreement, *BB* . . . indeed persuaded, *KJII* . . . were convinced by his reasonings, *Berkeley.*

| **1156.2** conj | **564.6** verb 3pl indic imperf act | **794.1** adj nom pl masc | **1156.2** conj | **1498.23** verb nom pl masc part pres act |
|---|---|---|---|---|
| δὲ | ἠπίστουν. | 25. ἀσύμφωνοι | δὲ | ὄντες |
| *de* | *ēpistoun* | *asumphōnoi* | *de* | *ontes* |
| but | were disbelieving. | Disagreements | and | being |

| **4242.1** prep | **238.3** prs-pron acc pl masc | **624.23** verb 3pl indic imperf mid | **1500.16** verb gen sing masc part aor act | **3450.2** art gen sing |
|---|---|---|---|---|
| πρὸς | ἀλλήλους | ἀπελύοντο, | εἰπόντος | τοῦ |
| *pros* | *allēlous* | *apeluonto* | *eipontos* | *tou* |
| with | one another | they were departing; | having spoken | |

| **3834.2** name gen masc | **4343.1** noun sing neu | **1518.9** num card neu | **3617.1** conj | **2544.1** adv | **3450.16** art sing neu | **4011.1** noun sing neu |
|---|---|---|---|---|---|---|
| Παύλου | ῥῆμα | ἕν, | Ὅτι | Καλῶς | τὸ | πνεῦμα |
| *Paulou* | *rhēma* | *hen* | *Hoti* | *Kalōs* | *to* | *pneuma* |
| Paul | word | one, | | Well | the | Spirit |

| **3450.16** art sing neu | **39.1** adj sing | **2953.27** verb 3sing indic aor act | **1217.2** prep | **2246.6** name gen masc | **3450.2** art gen sing |
|---|---|---|---|---|---|
| τὸ | ἅγιον | ἐλάλησεν | διὰ | Ἠσαΐου | τοῦ |
| *to* | *hagion* | *elalēsen* | *dia* | *Esaiou* | *tou* |
| the | Holy | spoke | by | Isaiah | the |

25.a.**Txt:** 020L,025P,byz.
**Var:** p74,01ℵ,02A,03B
044,33,sa.bo.Lach,Treg
Alf,Tisc,We/Ho,Weis
Sod,UBS/☆

| **4254.2** noun gen sing masc | **4242.1** prep | **3450.8** art acc pl masc | **3824.9** noun acc pl masc | **2231.2** prs-pron gen 1pl | **5050.2** prs-pron gen 2pl |
|---|---|---|---|---|---|
| προφήτου | πρὸς | τοὺς | πατέρας | ⸀ ἡμῶν, | [a☆ ὑμῶν ] |
| *prophētou* | *pros* | *tous* | *pateras* | *hēmōn* | *humōn* |
| prophet | to | the | fathers | our, | [ your ] |

26.a.**Txt:** 02A,byz.
**Var:** 01ℵ,03B,020L
025P,33,Treg,Alf,Tisc
We/Ho,Weis,Sod
UBS/☆

| **2978.23** verb sing neu part pres act | **2978.15** verb nom sing masc part pres act | **4057.23** verb 2sing impr aor pass | **4242.1** prep | **3450.6** art acc sing masc |
|---|---|---|---|---|
| 26. ⸀ λέγον, | [a☆ λέγων, ] | Πορεύθητι | πρὸς | τὸν |
| *legon* | *legōn* | *Poreuthēti* | *pros* | *ton* |
| saying, | [ idem ] | Go | to | the |

26.b.**Txt:** byz.
**Var:** 01ℵ,02A,03B,08E
020L,025P,Gries,Lach
Treg,Alf,Word,Tisc
We/Ho,Weis,Sod
UBS/☆

| **2967.4** noun acc sing masc | **3642.6** dem-pron acc sing masc | **2504.1** conj | **1500.5** verb 3sing indic aor act | **1500.29** verb 2sing impr aor act | **187.3** noun dat sing fem |
|---|---|---|---|---|---|
| λαὸν | τοῦτον | καὶ | ⸀ εἶπέν, | [b☆ εἰπόν, ] | Ἀκοῇ |
| *laon* | *touton* | *kai* | *eipen* | *eipon* | *Akoē* |
| people | this, | and | he said, | [ say, ] | Hearing |

| **189.43** verb 2pl indic fut act | **2504.1** conj | **3620.3** partic | **3231.1** partic | **4770.10** verb 2pl subj aor act | **2504.1** conj |
|---|---|---|---|---|---|
| ἀκούσετε | καὶ | οὐ | μὴ | συνῆτε· | καὶ |
| *akousete* | *kai* | *ou* | *mē* | *sunēte* | *kai* |
| you shall hear, | and | not | not | understand, | and |

| **984.14** verb nom pl masc part pres act | **984.20** verb 2pl indic fut act | **2504.1** conj | **3620.3** partic | **3231.1** partic | **1481.12** verb 2pl subj aor act |
|---|---|---|---|---|---|
| βλέποντες | βλέψετε, | καὶ | οὐ | μὴ | ἴδητε· |
| *blepontes* | *blepsete* | *kai* | *ou* | *mē* | *idēte* |
| seeing | you shall see, | and | not | not | perceive. |

| **3837.1** verb 3sing indic aor pass | **1056.1** conj | **3450.9** art nom sing fem | **2559.2** noun nom sing fem | **3450.2** art gen sing | **2967.2** noun gen sing masc |
|---|---|---|---|---|---|
| 27. ἐπαχύνθη | γὰρ | ἡ | καρδία | τοῦ | λαοῦ |
| *epachunthē* | *gar* | *hē* | *kardia* | *tou* | *laou* |
| Has grown fat | for | the | heart | of the | people |

| **3642.1** dem-pron gen sing | **2504.1** conj | **3450.4** art dat pl | **3640.3** noun dat pl neu | **912.1** adv | **189.24** verb 3pl indic aor act |
|---|---|---|---|---|---|
| τούτου, | καὶ | τοῖς | ὠσὶν | βαρέως | ἤκουσαν, |
| *toutou* | *kai* | *tois* | *ōsin* | *bareōs* | *ēkousan* |
| this, | and | with the | ears | heavily | they have heard, |

heritance that Paul proclaimed (Romans 10:9,10). Paul no doubt urged them to join in the worship of Christ as part of one of the local assemblies in Rome.

Others of the Jews disbelieved. In spite of Paul's testimony, in spite of all the proofs he brought from the Old Testament Scriptures, they refused to put their faith in Jesus. Paul did not consider this a failure on his part, however. He always gave thanks to God, "which always causeth us to triumph in Christ, and maketh manifest the savor (fragrance) of his knowledge (the knowledge of God) by us in every place" (2 Corinthians 2:14).

**28:25.** The fact that some believed and were saved while others rejected the truth brought disagreement and a line of separation, just as the truth always does. Jesus himself warned His disciples that when the truth about Him was proclaimed it would bring division (Luke 12:51).

Paul did not let them leave without one final exhortation, however. He quoted for them what the Holy Spirit in Isaiah 6:9,10 said to their ancestors in the year King Uzziah died because of his presumptuous sin. (The quotation here follows the Greek Septuagint version of the Old Testament, a version much used by the Early Church.)

**28:26.** Paul quoted from Isaiah because he wanted those Jews who were rejecting the gospel to realize they were not merely turning away from him and his message. They were closing their hearts and minds to God and His plan, and in doing so they were coming under judgment just as the Israelites did who rejected Isaiah's message when it was first given over 700 years before.

God sent Isaiah to a people who would hear but not understand, who would see but not perceive. That is, they would not consider that there was any truth in the prophet's message. They would have no expectation that God would bring any fulfillment of the prophet's warnings. Later they mocked Isaiah and, though he did see a period of revival after Sennacherib left Jerusalem, they eventually killed him.

**28:27.** The reason for Israel's rejection of Isaiah's message was the fact that their hearts had grown fat (that is, such a thick layer of unbelief had grown around their hearts and minds that the truth had a hard time penetrating). Their ears had become dull, and they had closed their eyes. In other words, they were deliberately unreceptive with an arrogance that willfully disregarded God and His Word. Moreover, this willfullness was keeping them from repenting (turning back to God) so God could heal (and deliver) them. God wanted to give them healing from their sins and deliverance from their enemies, but their unbelief was shutting them off from Him and from the good things He wanted to do for them.

**and some believed not:** . . . others refused to believe, *Weymouth* . . . others, however, rejected it, *TCNT* . . . yet some disbelieved, *Concordant* . . . were skeptical, *JB* . . . Others did not share his views at all, *Noli.*

**25. And when they agreed not among themselves:** Unable to agree, *Weymouth* . . . still at variance among themselves, *Knox* . . . they did not agree with each other, *NLT.*

**they departed:** . . . began to disperse, *TCNT* . . . and they took their leave, *Knox.*

**after that Paul had spoken one word:** . . . but not before Paul had spoken a parting word, *Weymouth* . . . one last word, *Knox* . . . added this last remark, *Noli.*

**Well spake the Holy Ghost:** The Holy spirit spoke the truth, *Beck* . . . It was a true utterance the Holy Spirit made, *Knox* . . . an apt word, *Moffatt* . . . beautifully expressed it, *Williams.*

**by Esaias the prophet unto our fathers:** . . . to your ancestors, *TCNT.*

**26. Saying, Go unto this people, and say:** . . . and tell them, *Knox.*

**Hearing ye shall hear:** You will hear with your ears, *TCNT* . . . You will listen and listen, *Knox.*

**and shall not understand:** . . . without ever understanding, *TCNT* . . . but not catch the meaning, *Berkeley.*

**and seeing ye shall see:** And will look and look, *Weymouth* . . . and never see, *NLT.*

**and not perceive:** . . . and yet will in nowise, *Rotherham* . . . understand, *ET.*

**27. for the heart of this people is waxed gross:** . . . hath become dense, *Rotherham* . . . For the mind of this nation, *TCNT* . . . has grown callous, *Weymouth* . . . For this people's soul, *Williams* . . . For this people's heart is stupefied, *Hanson* . . . this people's mind is dull, *Noli* . . . is grown obtuse, *Montgomery.*

**and their ears are dull of hearing:** . . . scarcely hear, *Williams* . . . hardly hear, *Norlie* . . . their ears are slow to listen, *Knox* . . . they hear with difficulty, *Swann.*

| 2504.1 conj | 3450.8 art acc pl masc | 3652.8 noun acc pl masc | 840.1 prs-pron gen pl | 2547.1 verb 3pl indic aor act | 3246.1 partic |
|---|---|---|---|---|---|
| καὶ | τοὺς | ὀφθαλμοὺς | αὐτῶν | ἐκάμμυσαν· | μήποτε |
| *kai* | *tous* | *ophthalmous* | *autōn* | *ekammusan* | *mēpote* |
| and | the | eyes | their | they have closed, | lest |

| 1481.13 verb 3pl subj aor act | 3450.4 art dat pl | 3652.7 noun dat pl masc | 2504.1 conj | 3450.4 art dat pl | 3640.3 noun dat pl neu |
|---|---|---|---|---|---|
| ἴδωσιν | τοῖς | ὀφθαλμοῖς, | καὶ | τοῖς | ὠσὶν |
| *idōsin* | *tois* | *ophthalmois* | *kai* | *tois* | *ōsin* |
| they should see | with the | eyes, | and | with the | ears |

| 189.27 verb 3pl subj aor act | 2504.1 conj | 3450.11 art dat sing fem | 2559.3 noun dat sing fem | 4770.11 verb 3pl subj aor act |
|---|---|---|---|---|
| ἀκούσωσιν, | καὶ | τῇ | καρδίᾳ | συνῶσιν, |
| *akousōsin* | *kai* | *tē* | *kardia* | *sunōsin* |
| they should hear, | and | with the | heart | they should understand, |

27.a.**Txt:** 08E,byz.
**Var:** 01ℵ,02A,03B,020L 025P,Treg,Alf,Tisc We/Ho,Weis,Sod UBS/⋆

| 2504.1 conj | 1978.8 verb 3pl subj aor act | 2504.1 conj | 2367.7 verb 1sing subj aor mid | 2367.19 verb 1sing indic fut mid |
|---|---|---|---|---|
| καὶ | ἐπιστρέψωσιν, | καὶ | ʿ ἰάσωμαι | [a⋆ ἰάσομαι ] |
| *kai* | *epistrepsōsin* | *kai* | *iasōmai* | *iasomai* |
| and | should turn, | and | I should heal | [ I shall heal ] |

| 840.8 prs-pron acc pl masc | 1104.4 adj sing neu | 3631.1 partic | 1498.17 verb 3sing impr pres act | 5050.3 prs-pron dat 2pl |
|---|---|---|---|---|
| αὐτούς. | **28.** Γνωστὸν | οὖν | ἔστω | ὑμῖν, |
| *autous* | *Gnōston* | *oun* | *estō* | *humin* |
| them. | Known | therefore | be it | to you, |

28.a.**Var:** 01ℵ-org,02A 03B,Lach,Treg,Alf,Tisc We/Ho,Weis,Sod UBS/⋆

| 3617.1 conj | 3450.4 art dat pl | 1477.6 noun dat pl neu | 643.25 verb 3sing indic aor pass | 3642.17 dem-pron sing neu | 3450.16 art sing neu |
|---|---|---|---|---|---|
| ὅτι | τοῖς | ἔθνεσιν | ἀπεστάλη | [a⋆+ τοῦτο ] | τὸ |
| *hoti* | *tois* | *ethnesin* | *apestalē* | *touto* | *to* |
| that | to the | Gentiles | was sent | [ this ] | the |

| 4844.2 adj sing neu | 3450.2 art gen sing | 2296.2 noun gen sing masc | 840.7 prs-pron nom pl masc | 2504.1 conj | 189.54 verb 3pl indic fut mid |
|---|---|---|---|---|---|
| σωτήριον | τοῦ | θεοῦ, | αὐτοὶ | καὶ | ἀκούσονται. |
| *sōtērion* | *tou* | *theou* | *autoi* | *kai* | *akousontai* |
| salvation | | of God; | they | and | will hear. |

29.a.**Txt:** 020L,025P,byz. it.
**Var:** p74,01ℵ,02A,03B 08E,sa.bo.Lach,Treg,Alf Tisc,We/Ho,Weis,Sod UBS/⋆

| 2504.1 conj | 3642.18 dem-pron pl neu | 840.3 prs-pron gen sing | 1500.16 verb gen sing masc part aor act | 562.1 verb indic aor act |
|---|---|---|---|---|
| **29.** ʿa Καὶ | ταῦτα | αὐτοῦ | εἰπόντος | ἀπῆλθον |
| *Kai* | *tauta* | *autou* | *eipontos* | *apēlthon* |
| And | these things | he | having said | went away |

| 3450.7 art nom pl masc | 2428.2 name-adj nom pl masc | 4044.12 adj acc sing fem | 2174.19 verb nom pl masc part pres act | 1706.1 prep |
|---|---|---|---|---|
| οἱ | Ἰουδαῖοι, | πολλὴν | ἔχοντες | ἐν |
| *hoi* | *Ioudaioi* | *pollēn* | *echontes* | *en* |
| the | Jews, | much | having | among |

30.a.**Txt:** 01ℵ-corr,02A 08E,020L,025P,byz.
**Var:** 01ℵ-org,03B,Treg Alf,Tisc,We/Ho,Weis Sod,UBS/⋆

| 1431.7 prs-pron dat pl masc | 4654.2 noun acc sing fem | 3176.16 verb 3sing indic aor act | 1682.4 verb 3sing indic aor act |
|---|---|---|---|
| ἑαυτοῖς, | συζήτησιν. ˎ | **30.** ʿ Ἔμεινεν | [a⋆ Ἐνέμεινεν ] |
| *heautois* | *suzētēsin* | *Emeinen* | *Enemeinen* |
| themselves | discussion. | Abode | [ remained ] |

30.b.**Txt:** 020L,025P,byz.
**Var:** 01ℵ,02A,03B,08E bo.Gries,Lach,Treg,Alf Word,Tisc,We/Ho,Weis Sod,UBS/⋆

| 1156.2 conj | 3450.5 art nom sing masc | 3834.1 name nom masc | 1327.2 noun acc sing fem | 3513.9 adj acc sing fem | 1706.1 prep |
|---|---|---|---|---|---|
| δὲ | ʿb ὁ | Παῦλος ˎ | διετίαν | ὅλην | ἐν |
| *de* | *ho* | *Paulos* | *dietian* | *holēn* | *en* |
| and | | Paul | two years | whole | in |

Isaiah's prophecy did not in any way imply God's plan would fail, however. Isaiah saw a godly remnant among the Jews, as did Amos and many of the other Old Testament prophets.

Paul also recognized there was a godly remnant among the Jews in his day who were accepting the Lord Jesus Christ as their Messiah and Saviour (Romans 9:6; 11:5). The problem was that the unbelieving Jews were trying to dictate to God what the way of salvation should be. They forgot how Israel had lost out back in the days of Isaiah and Hosea, so God said they had become Lo-ammi, "not my people" (Hosea 1:9). Only God's grace and mercy preserved a remnant of the people in that day and kept the nation from complete destruction. The remnant were the ones who realized God made faith a condition on which His mercy and blessing is given. His promises are never a wholesale gift presented to everyone whether they want it or not. They are only for those who accept God's conditions of faith and obedience.

**28:28.** Paul then added that God's salvation was also sent to the Gentiles (a reference to his own call). They (emphatic) would also hear (and obey).

Paul thus declared the door was wide open to the Gentiles. As he told the Romans, they could be grateful for the goodness and severity of God which has resulted in the spread of the gospel to all nations and has made possible the salvation of all who hear.

The believers' attitude toward the Jews, however, should be one of compassion, not pride or superiority. Though they have rejected Christ and have been cut out of what Paul calls the "olive tree" (of God's continuing plan and blessing), God is able to graft them in again; and the Bible implies He will (Romans 11:17-24).

**28:29.** After Paul concluded these exhortations, the Jews left his apartment, but they were still carrying on a great discussion or debate among themselves. No doubt those who believed and obeyed were trying to persuade their friends to accept the truth of the gospel Paul had proclaimed and demonstrated to them from the Scriptures.

**28:30.** This day of presenting the gospel to the Jews was not Paul's last opportunity. For 2 whole years he was able to live in his own rented apartment in a house where all who wished to visit him could come and go freely. Paul was happy to welcome them all.

Some believe Paul was released after those 2 years when he was called before the emperor, and the Jerusalem Jews had sent no accusation and no lawyer to represent them.

Others believe there was no trial and the case was automatically dismissed at the end of the 2 years because no charges were presented. Roman law gave the prosecution a limited time to present

**and their eyes have they closed:** . . . they keep their eyes shut, *Knox* . . . They have shut their eyes, *SEB* . . . shut tight, *Williams* . . . their eyes are blind, *Noli.*

**lest they should see with their eyes:** So they will never see with, *Noli* . . . for fear they might, *Norlie* . . . so that their eyes don't see, *Beck* . . . Otherwise, they would see, *SEB.*

**and hear with their ears:** . . . will never hear with, *Noli.*

**and understand with their heart:** . . . never understand, *Noli* . . . with their minds, *Weymouth* . . . with that heart, *Knox* . . . their minds do not understand, *NLT.*

**and should be converted:** . . . will never turn back to me, *Noli* . . . and turn to me, *Williams.*

**and I should heal them:** . . . let Me heal them, *Norlie* . . . and I cure them, *Swann.*

**28. Be it known therefore unto you:** Understand, then, *TCNT* . . . Let it be plainly understood then, *Phillips* . . . You should know, *Beck* . . . let it be a matter of knowledge to you, *Swann* . . . Take notice, then, *Knox.*

**that the salvation of God is sent unto the Gentiles:** . . . that this salvation, *Alford* . . . God has sent His salvation to non-Jewish people, *SEB* . . . this Gospel of divine salvation will be preached to, *Noli* . . . how to be saved from the penalty of sin has been sent to the people who are not Jews, *NLT.*

**and that they will hear it:** . . . and they will listen, *TCNT* . . . they, at least, will listen to it, *Knox* . . . they...will give heed, *Weymouth* . . . they also will hear, *Hanson.*

**29. And when he had said these words, the Jews departed:**

**and had great reasoning among themselves:** . . . with much dissension among themselves, *Knox* . . . arguing at great length with one another, *Noli.*

**30. And Paul dwelt two whole years in his own hired house:** . . . paid money to live in a house by himself, *NLT* . . . two entire years, *Sawyer* . . . which he rented for himself, *TCNT* . . . in his rented lodging, *Swann* . . . at his own expense, *Noli.*

## Acts 28:31

| 2375.3 adj dat sing | 3274.1 noun dat sing neu | 2504.1 conj | 583.6 verb 3sing indic imperf mid | 3820.8 adj acc pl masc | 3450.8 art acc pl masc |
|---|---|---|---|---|---|
| ἰδίῳ | μισθώματι, | καὶ | ἀπεδέχετο | πάντας | τοὺς |
| *idiō* | *misthōmati* | *kai* | *apedecheto* | *pantas* | *tous* |
| his own | hired house, | and | was welcoming | all | the |

| 1515.6 verb acc pl masc part pres mid | 4242.1 prep | 840.6 prs-pron acc sing masc | | 2756.6 verb nom sing masc part pres act | 3450.12 art acc sing fem |
|---|---|---|---|---|---|
| εἰσπορευομένους | πρὸς | αὐτόν, | **31.** | κηρύσσων | τὴν |
| *eisporeuomenous* | *pros* | *auton* | | *kērussōn* | *tēn* |
| coming in | to | him, | | proclaiming | the |

| 926.4 noun acc sing fem | 3450.2 art gen sing | 2296.2 noun gen sing masc | 2504.1 conj | 1315.6 verb nom sing masc part pres act | 3450.17 art pl neu |
|---|---|---|---|---|---|
| βασιλείαν | τοῦ | θεοῦ, | καὶ | διδάσκων | τὰ |
| *basileian* | *tou* | *theou* | *kai* | *didaskōn* | *ta* |
| kingdom | | of God, | and | teaching | the |

| 3875.1 prep | 3450.2 art gen sing | 2935.2 noun gen sing masc | 2400.2 name masc | 5382.2 name gen masc | 3196.3 prep |
|---|---|---|---|---|---|
| περὶ | τοῦ | κυρίου | Ἰησοῦ | Χριστοῦ, | μετὰ |
| *peri* | *tou* | *kuriou* | *Iēsou* | *Christou* | *meta* |
| concerning | the | Lord | Jesus | Christ, | with |

| 3820.10 adj gen sing fem | 3816.2 noun gen sing fem | 207.1 adv |
|---|---|---|
| πάσης | παῤῥησίας | ἀκωλύτως. |
| *pasēs* | *parrhēsias* | *akōlutōs* |
| all | freedom | unhinderedly. |

its case, depending on the distance they had to come. Philemon 22 shows Paul did expect to be released.

**28:31.** During the 2 years Paul was able to preach and teach boldly and freely, proclaiming the kingdom or rule of God and teaching the things concerning Jesus Christ openly, boldly, and with freedom of speech. This was an answer to his requests for prayer sent to some of the churches he had founded (Ephesians 6:19,20; Colossians 4:3,4). Even some from Caesar's household were converted (Philippians 4:22). This probably came about through the witness the soldiers made to the whole praetorian guard or palace (Philippians 1:13).

First Timothy shows Paul was indeed released and went to the Roman province of Asia. Ancient tradition says he went to Spain also. This was followed by Paul's second imprisonment and death. Second Timothy 4:13 indicates he left his cloak at Troas, possibly because of a sudden arrest. By the time Paul wrote his last epistle, Second Timothy, it had then become a crime to be a Christian.

The Book of Acts breaks off suddenly. It has no formal conclusion. Some believe Luke intended to write another volume. Others believe Luke suffered martyrdom along with Paul. But the important point is that the Book of Acts had no formal ending. It is still going on today.

**and received all that came in unto him:** He welcomed, *Noli* . . . and was wont to welcome, *Worrell* . . . welcoming all, *TCNT* . . . He was happy for all who came to see him, *NLT* . . . to visit him, *Moffatt.*

**31. Preaching the kingdom of God:** He continued to preach, *Montgomery* . . . publishing the reign of God, *Hanson.*

**and teaching those things which concern the Lord Jesus Christ:** . . . teaching openly about, *Lamsa* . . . and boldly taught the truth about, *Beck.*

**with all confidence, no man forbidding him:** . . . with perfect fearlessness, unmolested, *TCNT* . . . He was very bold, *SEB* . . . with utmost freedom and without hindrance from anyone, *Phillips* . . . fearlessly and unhindered, *Norlie* . . . with entire freedom, none forbidding him, *Hanson* . . . with full freedom and without any hindrance, *Noli* . . . without any restraint, *Campbell* . . . unforbidden, *Concordant* . . . and nobody stopped him, *Beck* . . . with unlimited freedom, *Fenton* . . . freedom of speech, *Wesley* . . . with all freedom of speech, *Worrell* . . . openly, *Klingensmith* . . . and unhindered, *Swann* . . . without being hindered, *KJII* . . . and no one tried to stop him from speaking, *NCV.*

# Overview

The *Overview* is a significant section of the *Study Bible.* It offers important background information concerning each book. It usually provides a comprehensive outline of the book, then presents in-depth studies on themes which relate to the subject matter. Since it serves as a background, it does not necessarily cover every chapter or section. It provides material for which there would not be enough space in the *Verse-by-Verse Commentary.*

The Book of Acts forms a natural transition between the Gospels and the Epistles of the New Testament. The Gospels record what "Jesus began both to do and teach" (Acts 1:1); Acts picks up the story of Christ's continued work by His Holy Spirit through the apostles.

Actually Acts is the second part of a two-part work, the first part being the third Gospel. The opening words of Acts show this clearly, for they refer to the "first book" written by the author and dedicated to Theophilus. Although this concerns two distinct pieces of literature, there is a connection between them. The last document picks up the theme where the first ends. It is rather obvious from a comparison of Acts and Paul's letters that it is the physician Luke who has authored both of these writings. The ancient church, likewise, supports this tradition (cf. the opening of Luke's Gospel).

For many years Luke was Paul's coworker. Together they are responsible for over one-half of the New Testament, each writing about one-fourth. This alone indicates what a vital place Luke has among the New Testament writers.

## Sources and Background

One quite natural question arises when examining the Books of Acts: Where did Luke get his material? Concerning his "first book," the Gospel of Luke, Luke directly states that he has utilized sources: "Forasmuch as many have taken in hand to set forth in order a declaration of those things which are most surely believed among us, even as they delivered them unto us, which from the beginning were eyewitnesses, and ministers of the word; it seemed good to me also, having had perfect understanding of all things from the very first, to write unto thee in order" (Luke 1:1-3). He mentions "which from the beginning (were) eyewitnesses and ministers of the word" as among his sources of information (verse 2). Thus we may say that Luke does not record an account solely based upon his own experience; rather, he relies upon oral and written sources.

With regard to the second portion of his two-part work, the Book of Acts, Luke says nothing about using particular sources; nevertheless, it is apparent that he maintains the same thoroughness and accuracy in telling the story. Luke displays very remarkable reliability as a historian. W.M. Ramsay calls him a historian of first quality who should be considered among the greatest.

Throughout the last half of Acts, Luke to a large extent did not depend upon outside sources. He did not have to. As the coworker of Paul he could chiefly draw from his own experiences, as the so-called we-sections indicate. Neither was Luke necessarily dependent upon written sources for the first half, which principally takes place in and around Jerusalem and Israel. Internal evidence of Acts, as well as the letters of Paul, demonstrate that Luke enjoyed personal contact with and knowledge of those who lived in the midst of the events he describes. For example, Mark and Luke were in Rome simultaneously (Colossians 4:10-14); Mark had firsthand knowledge of the Jerusalem church (Acts 21:17,18). Luke contacted Philip the evangelist, one of Stephen's coworkers (Acts 21:28). In addition to this he associated with Paul and his companions. All of this made firsthand information readily accessible. The Book of Acts contains no less than

65 historical facts about Paul, which are referred to in 11 of his letters.

### Time and Location of Composition

Since we know that Luke accompanied Paul during his imprisonment in Rome (Acts chapters 27 and 28; cf. Colossians 4:14), it is reasonable to suppose that Acts was written in Rome during this time. This might explain the rather abrupt ending of Acts. Luke records the history up until the time he is writing and thus closes the book. However, it is not universally accepted that the ending is actually as abrupt as it appears.

Since it states that Paul worked unimpeded for 2 whole years, we can probably conclude that the period in which the opponents had to accuse Paul before the emperor's court had expired. If the legal precepts were enforced, then Paul would have been released at this time.

Additional evidence may further support the view that Acts was written during Paul's imprisonment in Rome: the book gives one the impression of being a defense of Paul and Christianity. Paul's legal battles are covered from the initial confrontation with the Jewish High Court until he reaches the supreme court of the land—the court of the Roman Emperor.

Therefore, much indicates that the Book of Acts was written in Rome, no later than A.D. 64-65 and perhaps earlier. The first volume, the Gospel of Luke, precedes this, probably around A.D. 60.

The hypothesis that Acts intends to justify/defend Paul in his case before the emperor's court is intriguing. Although it may be merely secondary, a slight apologetic intent does seem to appear throughout the document. The matter itself, however, is of primary interest: what is the relationship between Christianity and Roman government?

As long as Christianity was regarded as a sect of Judaism believers could take advantage of the special privileges afforded the Jews by Rome. As an accepted religion, Judaism was tolerated; its adherents were exempt from worshiping the emperor. The Jewish leaders attempted to deprive Christians of that same freedom. If the Roman government believed the Jews, Christianity would be considered a new cult. The effect of that would mean serious consequences to the churches. Early Christians had to emphasize that they were neither revolutionary nor anti-social; Christianity was not a "kingdom of this world." Jesus was not an insurrectionist and neither were His disciples. One theme permeating Acts is that the Roman officials were much kinder to the Christian heralds than were the countrymen of these witnesses.

This leads us to another theme of the book. Evidently Acts intends to demonstrate that it is the Jews' own fault that the promises of the gospel went from the Jews to the Gentiles. In every case the message was preached "to the Jew first"; their status as God's "chosen people" was honored. The first chapters of Acts reveal that many Jews did in fact receive the gospel and did believe in Jesus as Messiah. However, overall, as a nation they rejected the Messiah. Consequently, a tremendous shift occurs with respect to God's design— salvation moves from being exclusively Jewish to being universal.

Although the external impetus for the mission to the Gentiles might be the Jewish rejection of the gospel, the deeper cause lies in God's own design. He fully intended from the outset that through His people Israel "all people should be blessed" (cf. the promise to Abraham, Genesis 12:3). Now the fulfillment of that promise occurs in the gospel. In accordance with its universal character, the offering of the gospel to the Gentiles is a major theme of Acts.

The chief purpose of Acts is to record salvation history. The main point of Acts is not that the writing initiates the history of the Church; rather it forms the climax of salvation's revelation in Jesus Christ. Many have discussed the appropriateness of "Acts" as descriptive of the book's contents. It should be considered in this regard that one of the book's primary goals is to validate the apostle's ministry. Without the authentication of the apostles that one finds in Acts, the New Testament epistles would lack a great deal of their authority. Just as Jesus began both "to do and teach" (Acts 1:1), the apostles of Christ continue to "do" as well as to "teach" by the power of the Holy Spirit. Just as Jesus' mighty miracles confirmed His being Messiah, the works of the apostles confirm their endorsement and authorization by God (e.g., 2 Corinthians 12:12).

Those offering instruction in the faith in the epistles of the New Testament are authorized as men taught by God. This further explains why Paul's activity receives such a large amount of attention. References to Paul are first and foremost because he is the apostle to all peoples, not because he was such an effective missionary.

At this point the intent of Acts is reflected in the opening words of the third Gospel: "That thou mightest know the certainty of those things, wherein thou hast been instructed." Luke desires to affirm the reliability of the Christian faith. Every other recognized motif must be subordinate to this dominant theme.

And this is a matter which must take place within full public view. The book was possibly made available to the public by the chief recipient of the work, Theophilus. Similar to the Gospel of Luke, the Acts of the Apostles is especially directed to the cultured Greco-Roman world. Simultaneously it presents history and proclamation.

## Content and Character

Without any hesitation one can call Acts the first church-and-mission history of its kind. But the work does not provide a complete description of the history and growth of the early Christian faith. For example, Luke tells us nothing of the gospel's spread into the countries east and south of Israel. What Luke shows is the path of the gospel's spread from Jerusalem, the religious center of Judaism, to the center of the world at that time, Rome. Chronologically the book covers approximately 30 years, from around A.D. 30 to A.D. 60.

Acts 1:8 affords a programmatic outline for the whole book: "Ye shall be witnesses unto me both in Jerusalem, and in all Judea, and in Samaria, and unto the uttermost part of the earth." When the Holy Spirit descended upon the disciples they filled Jerusalem with their teaching (Acts 5:28). The second phase, the evangelization of Judea and Samaria, began seriously when persecution broke out and scattered the believers (Acts 8:1). The third phase was initiated with Peter's preaching to the house of Cornelius (Acts 10:34f.). It became fully realized in the missionary journeys of Paul. Their groundbreaking work will continue and extend "unto the uttermost part of the earth" (Acts 1:8) through the body of Christ, His Church. This will be the objective of the Church "unto the end of the world (the time)" (Matthew 28:20).

Acts naturally divides itself into two sections. In chapters 1-12, which especially deal with the early missionary efforts among the Jews, Peter is the principal character. The second part centers on Paul. Here the primary theme is the missionary thrust to the Gentiles. The following outline reflects the structure of Acts:

Section 1: The Focus on Peter (chapters 1-12)

I. Jerusalem (chapters 1-7)
  1. The ascension of Jesus and the selection of Judas' replacement (chapter 1)
  2. The Day of Pentecost:
     a. The outpouring of the Spirit (2:1-13)
     b. Peter's sermon (2:14-40)
     c. The Early Church (2:41-47)
  3. The healing of the lame man and Peter's sermon on the porch of Solomon (3:1-26)
  4. First appearance before the Sanhedrin (4:1-22)
  5. The life in the ancient church (4:23-37)
  6. Ananias and Sapphira (5:1f.)
  7. Stephen
     a. Ministry (6:8-15)
     b. Sermon (7:1-53)
     c. Martyrdom (7:54-60)

II. Judea and Samaria (chapters 8,9)
  1. Philip in Samaria (8:1-25)
  2. The Ethiopian eunuch (8:26-40)
  3. The conversion and first preaching of Paul (9:1-30)
  4. The missionary activity of Peter (9:31-43)

III. The Gentile Mission (chapters 10-12)
  1. Peter in the house of Cornelius (chapter 10)
  2. The church in Jerusalem approves the Gentile mission (11:1-18)
  3. The first Gentile Christian church in Antioch (11:19-30)
  4. The persecution of Herod; Peter's deliverance (chapter 12)

Section 2: The Focus on Paul (chapters 13-28)

I. First Missionary Journey (chapters 13-15)
  1. Cyprus (chapters 13:4-12)
  2. Asia Minor (13:13 to 14:28)
  3. Jerusalem Council (chapter 15)

II. Second Missionary Journey (chapters 16-18)
  1. Journey through Asia Minor (15:40 to 16:8)
  2. Missionary activity in Europe (16:09 to 18:22)

III. Third Missionary Journey (chapters 19,20)
  1. Ministry in Ephesus (chapter 19)
  2. New visit to Europe (20:1-4)
  3. Troas and Miletus; farewell to Ephesian elders (20:5-38)

IV. The Journey to Jerusalem (chapters 21-26)
  1. Tyre and Caesarea (21:1-16)

2. In Jerusalem (21:17 to 23:22)
3. Two years in Caesarea (23:23 to 26:32)

V. The Voyage to Rome (chapters 27,28)
1. Voyage and shipwreck (chapter 27)
2. Stay on Malta (28:1-10)
3. From Malta to Rome (28:11-16)
4. Two years in Rome (28:17-31)

## The Acts of the Apostles: The Title

"The Acts of the Apostles," *praxeis tōn apostolōn* in the Greek or *acta apostolorum* in Latin—hence the name "Acts" in common parlance—is the ancient title of the book. By and large the ancient church knows of no other title. The only variation is that three manuscripts omit the article *tōn*, so the title reads "Acts of Apostles" or "apostles' acts." The question remains: Is this the original designation of the book?

The data against this being the author's choice include that the subject matter to a certain extent does not agree with that title. It is true that all the apostles are mentioned by name (1:13), but the focus does not fall upon each one's activity. As mentioned above, the first twelve chapters are devoted to Peter's activities primarily; John plays only a secondary role, and the only mention of James his brother is that he died.

From chapter 13 on the only "acts" recorded are those of Paul, who for good reason is not one of the apostles in the list of 1:13. Witnesses other than the apostles do receive a lot of attention; for example, Stephen (chapters 6,7) and Philip the Evangelist (chapter 8) are given a lot of space. Above all, it is clear that Luke is not merely writing "biographies" of the apostles. In fact, the source of the "acts" is resurrected, ascended, and glorified Jesus Christ. He, through His Spirit, performs His mighty works through His apostles, who are merely His instruments.

However, strong evidence indicates that the heading is the title selected by the author himself. The book originally was titled. A writing dedicated to a person of such high standing and caliber as Theophilus, as well as probably being "published" by him, almost certainly had the name of the book and the name of the author. "The Acts of Apostles" conveys a somewhat broader meaning than we first imagine. It actually relates the ministry of Jesus Christ through His apostles and His church. The earliest apostles had witnessed the resurrection of our Lord. It is to this group that Paul belongs for he received a special revelation of the Risen Lord and a unique call. Also included among others who continued the ministry of Jesus are the coworkers of the apostles who built upon the "foundation of the apostles and prophets" (Ephesians 2:20). The apostolic witnesses proclaimed the gospel from Jerusalem—the focal point and beginning of the salvation message—to Rome, the heart of the Gentile world.

## The Most Ancient Witnesses to Acts

Polycarp, bishop of Smyrna, writes a letter to the church in Philippi around the year A.D. 107. In it he quotes so freely from Acts of the Apostles that it is obvious the document was generally known to the church at large. Perhaps this insight confirms a close relationship between the author of Acts and the church at Philippi (see below).

## The Author

The author is not mentioned in connection with the title of the work or within the document itself. But at least two facts are clear and are useful for identifying the author's background, his environment, and his purpose.

First, the opening words of the Book of Acts (1:1,2) together with verse 3 form not so much an introduction as they do a "summary" of what preceded. The first-person "I" of the opening verses of Acts is undoubtedly the same "I" in the opening words of the third Gospel. While the third Gospel has a true "introduction," the opening words of Acts are a summary and continuation—a reference to Luke 1:1-4—of Jesus' words and work. This theme is merely resumed.

Since this indeed is the intent of the author of Acts, we can be certain that this is the same individual responsible for the third Gospel. Acts is the second volume of two by the same author. Further supporting this is the fact that the language and style of both works are the same.

Second, we observe from the introduction to the third Gospel that the Book of Acts is written to the same individual—"most excellent Theophilus." The name literally means, "he who loves God." Some interpreters suggest that Theophilus is actually a personification of the (any) person seeking God, a Gentile seeking the truth—all of fallen humanity yearning for their God and Creator, who may be "unknown" but not forgotten (cf. Acts 17:23). Now God has revealed himself to all mankind through the gospel of Jesus Christ.

Others speculate that Theophilus is a pseudonym of an individual whose name must remain anonymous. "Theophilus" characterizes him nonetheless. Both of these opinions could in one sense pick up the intent and purpose of the writing very adequately. Nonetheless, both suppositions are unacceptable. First, the kind of dedication such as the one made to Theophilus—lacking any pseudonymic qualities or personification—were common in Hellenistic literature of that period. Second, the use of the name in the Gospel diminishes the chances of its being merely a literary convention. Whether or not the title "most excellent" refers to the high office of its bearer or whether it is simply a respectful address, we can be sure that Theophilus was a man of high social status and wealth.

Moreover, the dedication of literary work to an individual of significant social status corresponds with the custom of the time. In so doing the work came under the auspices of the person to whom it was dedicated; his name thus became a sort of "recommendation" for the book. The need for such an endorsement of a book is entirely in keeping with the custom of the time, when no commercial marketing of a book was possible. Thus, the use of the adjective *kratistos* to describe Theophilus helped fill a need. *Kratistos* itself means "the most excellent," "the highly esteemed" (formally a superlative form). "Your Excellency" (Today's English Version) thus describes a real person.

Luke's introduction to his Gospel affords no insight into the identity of Theophilus or his whereabouts. Historical records offer no help in that regard, since Theophilus was a relatively common name in both Hellenism and Judaism, being attested by literature and inscription.

Even the title *kratistos* provides little information about the recipient of the work. It corresponds to the Latin *vir egregius*, a title applied to the Roman governors of the emperor or the Roman procurators, such as Felix in Judea (Acts 23:26; 24:3) or Festus (Acts 26:25). Thus it may be describing Theophilus as a man having a high political position; however, it may also simply be a title of respect without any reference to social standing. It often occurs in dedications to a wealthy benefactor who placed money and influence at the disposal of his scribes (slaves), who were responsible for publishing a work.

If one then couples this with the unanimous tradition that Luke the physician (see below) authored Acts, and keeping in mind that physicians were often, though not always, released slaves, the picture emerges that as a physician and a freed slave, Luke was favored by a prosperous man, perhaps in a high political office. Theophilus then would be the "patron" or "benefactor" of the work as well as the recipient.

But the introduction of the third Gospel and its transitional "bridge" in the opening paragraphs of the Book of Acts can teach us much more about the relationship between Luke and Theophilus. This somewhat formal dedication, typical of its historical climate, tells us that the recipient was a cultured Hellenist. A rather late tradition of the Early Church notes that he lived in Antioch in Syria. But this may have been influenced by another tradition that the author was from Antioch (see discussion below).

Of more importance is the last sentence of the Gospel's introduction that informs us that Theophilus had received instructions concerning the Christian faith: "those things, wherein thou hast been instructed" (Luke 1:4). The verb here, *katēcheo* (actively, "to give lessons"; passively, "to be taught"), implies "to inform," such as a teacher "informs" a student (cf. Acts 22:3). In the language of the Church this stood for the "teaching" of the way of Christianity (cf. Acts 18:25). About the middle of the Second Century *katēcheo* became a technical term for catechetical instruction (see e.g., 2 Clement 17:1). A recipient of such instruction was a catechumen. As early as the New Testament this trend is beginning. We read of the "elementary teachings about Christ" (Hebrews 6:1) and "elementary truths of God's word" (Hebrews 5:12). Possibly a form of baptismal catechesis (instruction) was instituted quite early. There may be a trace of it, for example, in 1 John 2:20-27 and Ephesians 4:20.

Naturally, it cannot be determined for certain whether Theophilus was baptized already or he was a catechumen, i.e., a candidate for baptism. If he were a catechumen, it can probably be assumed that the Gospel that was dedicated to him, along with the Book of Acts, are related to his instruction and that of his fellow disciples. Thus, if this is true, Luke would be his *kathēchōn*, "teacher" (cf. Galatians 6:6). A similar teacher in the Church is called a *didaskalos* on another occasion. There were many of them in Antioch (Acts 13:1).

We are uncertain of the spiritual heritage of the "most excellent Theophilus," or why he became a catechumen in the Church. Possibly he was one of the many "devout" men (*sebomenos*) touched by the gospel (e.g., Acts 13:50; 17:4,17), or perhaps a "God-fearer" (*phobumenos*) like Cornelius (10:2). He might have regularly attended synagogue or he might have been a Jewish proselyte (convert), "fruit" of the Jewish mission among the Gentiles (cf. 13:43, a reference to one in Antioch). He could also have been an enlightened Gentile, tired of the emptiness of paganism, such as Sergius Paulus, the proconsul of Cyprus who "desired to hear the word of God" (Acts 13:7). He subsequently became a believer who listened, "being astonished at the doctrine of the Lord" (Acts 13:12).

One purpose of the book, clearly discernible from the final words in the dedication (Luke 1:4), is that both the Gospel and Acts were written in order to give Theophilus spiritual guidance. There is an "in order that" *hina* clause which implies more than simply providing information. This involved Christian proclamation. We encounter the teaching of historical data: the human origins of Jesus; His words and deeds; His death and resurrection. Since God has wrought a saving work in Christ, the message about Jesus Christ is "words by which we become saved." Through personal witness in the first and second parts of this work the author assists the reader in personally experiencing that "faithful saying . . . worthy of all acceptation: that Christ Jesus came into the world to save sinners" (1 Timothy 1:15).

Saving faith involves a knowledge of the events surrounding Christ's salvation. We have all assurance that the message of salvation has been handed down faithfully and unchanged; it is reliable and eternal.

Theophilus is not the only reader. The dedication implies that—in accordance with the custom of the day—the book is for all those in the same situation as Theophilus. The document is particularly relevant to Gentiles inquiring into the Christian faith as well as those Gentile Christians in need of confirmation of the reality of the Christian message. Everyone willing to be led *ad fontes* "to the sources," discovers the dependable, solid, tradition of the Christian church—the apostolic witness.

The writer does not repeat or elaborate upon the first dedication. The most natural explanation is that the two volumes are so closely tied together in terms of time and content that the shortened opening is adequate since there had been a complete statement in the first volume.

### A Historian

With regards to discovering the character of the author of Acts we can extract much more insight from the introduction of the Gospel of Luke and its relationship to the opening words of Acts.

The author is a historian and works historically and methodically. He presents himself to the reader in this way in Luke 1:3: "It seemed good to me also, having had perfect understanding of all things from the very first, to write unto thee in order." The Acts of the Apostles corroborates this purpose in its careful and exact presentation at every turn. The author possesses firsthand knowledge of the world and time in which he recounts the course of the spread of the gospel. He fully grasps the historical situation, realizing from personal experience the impact of the gospel. For example: He makes accurate geographical statements. He knows from experience that Perga lies in Pamphylia (13:13); Antioch in Pisidia (13:14); Lystra and Derbe in Lycaonia (14:6); while Myra can be located in Lycia (27:5). He has a thorough knowledge of the territorial divisions of Macedonia (16:12). He knows that Philippi is a Roman settlement. He is aware of Fair Havens near the city of Lasea. He knows Phoenix, the harbor, faces both the southwest and northwest (27:12). The divine Author, the Holy Spirit was able to use Luke's knowledge and abilities as He inspired him to write this part of the Scriptures.

Luke records many details. It should also be pointed out he knows the names of the apostles and their coworkers, he also knows their addresses. Paul is living in the "street which is called Straight" in Damascus (9:11). Peter lodged with Simon, a tanner, "whose house is by the sea side" (10:6). Lydia, whose house became the base for the first European missionary outreach, was a "seller of purple" from Thyatira (16:14). In Thessalonica Jason and his household suffered because he opened it to "these" (17:5f.). Paul was hosted in Corinth by Titius Justus, "whose house joined hard to the synagogue" (18:7).

The author is able to provide information about the Roman governmental structure without difficulty. He is thoroughly familiar with the historical data. He knows that in the senate of the provinces the proconsul presides (13:7f.; 18:12; 19:38). He is familiar with the "Asiatics" in Ephesus (19:31), and he is aware of the "strategists" in Philippi (16:36f.) and the "politicians" in Thessalonica (17:6f.). Modern historians specializing in the Roman judicial system discover that Luke is accurate in regard to Roman judicial proceedings in his description of Paul's trial before Gallio (18:12f.), Felix (chapter 24), as well as Festus (25:26). He, furthermore, fully understood the implications of what it means to be a Roman citizen (16:37f; 21:39; 22:25f.; 23:27). Indeed, Luke so presents the geographical, political, and judicial circumstances of the First Century A.D. in the regions around the Mediterranean Sea—even in minute details—that we are forced to regard him as a reliable historian. His writing must be considered as a primary source of the first order for the investigation of such matters.

## A Theologian

Nonetheless, the author of Acts is more than a mere historian. He is first and foremost a theologian, a careful and historical theologian; a theologian who believes his message—his heart burns for the gospel of Jesus Christ (cf. Luke 24:32).

This becomes apparent in the introduction to his first volume in the opening sentences of the second: "The former treatise have I made, O Theophilus, of all that Jesus began both to do and teach, until the day in which he was taken up." Not expressed, but implied in this is: "In this second volume I will continue to relate the deeds and words of Jesus from the time He was taken up until today."

The entire two volume work—Luke-Acts—its goal, its unity, as well as its appearing in two volumes, is of a theological nature. The Gospel of Luke and the Acts of the Apostles do not involve two different subjects or themes. Both are concerned with what Jesus "did and taught." In one word the theme of both is the "gospel," the joyous message of God's saving, redeeming work for all of creation and for fallen humanity by Jesus Christ. The first volume presents this gospel, the history of its origins. The second volume recalls the history of the spread of that message. Or, to put it another way: the Gospel tells of the work fulfilled in Jerusalem for the salvation of all the world; the second part, the Book of Acts, involves the preaching of the salvation "unto the uttermost part of the earth!" (Acts 1:8).

The relationship between these two books as a unified whole as well as their uniqueness as two separate works can also be expressed in these terms: The first volume concerns the Son of God, Jesus Christ, who became man, and who, through His life, death, and resurrection, demonstrates in word and deed God's saving power. In the second volume Jesus continues to carry out His mission, but now He does it as the one who has been "taken up," i.e., the "ascended Lord." Now He accomplishes His work through His new body, the Church, by His word and by the Holy Spirit. Thus we see two phases, two epochs of salvation history. But prior to telling the history of the second epoch there are five basic affirmations to be noted:

(1) The "taking up" the Ascension (Acts 1:9-11) brought to a close the first volume and it opens the second. It therefore unites the two epochs. Just as the Son of God "descended" to earth becoming a man among men, He "ascended" when He fulfilled His work; that is, He left the human realm of time and space and moved into the realm of the eternal, into the almighty and divine realm of the omnipresent God. A "cloud," the Shekinah of God—the symbol of His glory and presence—overshadowed Christ, and now He "sits at the right hand of God." Just as the mystery of the Incarnation, Christ's becoming a man, opened the first epoch, the mystery of the Ascension underlies the second epoch.

(2) The Ascension itself is the background for the events of the Book of Acts. Because Jesus ascended the Spirit comes (Acts 2:1-13). Through the Spirit the Risen Lord is present in the world. Now the Third Person of the Trinity continues the ministry of the Ascended Lord.

(3) The Spirit as the one carrying on the work of Jesus is not a vague influence. Rather, He works in and through the Church, the *ekklēsia*, the people of God on earth. This explains why chapter 2 not only relates the arrival of the Spirit, but necessarily the "birth" of the Church

that had been "conceived" (created) when Jesus called His disciples. Therefore, the Church is the new body of Jesus Christ, the sign of His presence and the instrument and dwelling place of His Spirit.

(4) Just as a person needs skills to perform a certain task, or just as a worker needs tools to be efficient, the Church needs a "tool" for carrying out the ministry of the Spirit. That "tool" is the Word of God. Peter in his sermon on the Day of Pentecost emphasizes its role and authority. Later we see the power of the Word revealed in the preaching, in missionary outreaches, in baptism or in the Lord's Supper, and in fellowship and worship, throughout the entire work.

(5) That a new epoch is in effect is confirmed by the reestablishment of the apostles (Acts 1:12-26). The ministry of the true Church is apostolic. The Church and the apostles cannot exist independently of one another.

This is chiefly because the Church is built upon the foundation of the apostles and the prophets, Jesus Christ himself being the chief cornerstone (Ephesians 2:20). This takes place because the apostles are the authentic, original, and principal witnesses of Jesus and they are responsible—according to God's own choice and will (Acts 1:2)—to continue Jesus' words and deeds. They witnessed the Resurrection and Jesus' triumphant victory over death—the announcement of salvation. Thus Acts opens with the fact that the Risen One "showed himself to these men and gave many convincing proofs" (NIV). For 40 days He instructed them about their testimony (cf. Moses on Sinai, Exodus 24:18). He did not appear in "visions"; He was truly seen. He revealed himself to them and confirmed their apostolic calling.

Furthermore, the 12 apostles represent the sum of the people of God, the "12 tribes." Israel awaited the promise of restoration, when the 12 patriarchs, the sons of Jacob, along with the 12 tribes they ruled over, would be reunited. Now the fulfillment of the promises becomes fully realized. The people of God is made up of all peoples, tribes and tongues, to the glory of God. The 12 apostles of Jesus Christ are the firstfruits, the promise of a larger harvest. From them people of God would grow and become great. This would take place in Jerusalem (Luke 24:47).

### An Eyewitness

An important feature of Luke's writing is that in certain sections of the documents there are "we passages." According to the reliable Western text representative, Codex Bezae (D), considered by some to be a "rough draft" or a "first edition," there is a first-person plural ("we") reading as early as 11:28: "when we had gathered together." Generally Codex D is regarded as being relatively accurate historically and it contains many fascinating details not otherwise attested.

Elsewhere, the "we passages" include 16:10-27; 20:5 to 21:18; 27:1 to 28:16. By writing "we," the writer indicates he personally participated in the events and missionary work he describes. The personal nature of these recollections serves to underscore the reliability of what is being told. Here we have the testimony of an eyewitness.

The "we" of the sections mentioned naturally refers back to the "I" in the opening sentences of the work. This, in turn, points back to the "I" in the introduction to the third Gospel. In every instance we meet the careful, accurate hand of a historian and theologian of literary and personal integrity inspired by the Holy Spirit.

Neither can linguistic or stylistic differences be appealed to as indicating a difference in the "we passages" from the remainder of the book. From start to finish Luke-Acts represents a homogeneous authorship. Even a scholar of such critical views as Adolf von Harnack strongly endorses the unity and homogeneity of the various elements of the two books, including the "we sections" of the Book of Acts (Harnack, p. xlii).

In addition to von Harnack others strongly advocate a common authorship and a date for Acts around the end of Paul's first Roman imprisonment. According to the tradition, and as yet most probable chronology, this means about the year A.D. 60. One of the weightiest arguments is that Acts almost certainly was not composed after the Pauline epistles. They all existed, except for the Letters to Titus and 1 and 2 Timothy, when Paul was released (ca. A.D. 60). These should also be regarded as "epistles," in other words, preaching and admonition intended for the churches. At that time the letters undoubtedly were circulating among the churches; nonetheless, the author of Acts would not have had access to any "collection" of these letters, since it was still too early for that.

The chronological relationship between the Pauline epistles and Acts, and their respective recording of Paul's whereabouts is not always clear. This in fact supports the trustworthiness of Acts. Acts is an independent recollection of selected events, many of which come from the hand of an eyewitness. If the date of composition were later one can be sure that the writer would have made his material conform to Paul's own letters. This would be easily discernible, since it would have included "quotes" or allusions to Paul's letters.

## The Lucan Tradition

A unanimous tradition of the ancient church ascribes the authorship of the third Gospel as well as Acts to Luke. The first occurrence of this tradition is the prologue to the Gospel of Luke in the anti-Marcionite canon, around A.D. 150. It is also attested in the Muratorian Canon, named after its discoverer, L.A. Muratori (d. 1750). This fragment is supposedly an official ecclesiastical document issued from Rome around A.D. 170. The Muratorian Canon was written by an ecclesiastical authority, and it deals with which documents the Church accepts and permits to be read in the worship service as a part of its liturgy—Gospels, Epistles and lection (according to a church calendar). The purpose is obvious: The list combats heretics and their false writing. As a result of that struggle the Church is forced to determine standards of faith and practice. *Kanōn,* thus means "rule," "guide."

An Early Church father wrote that the third Gospel was written by Luke, that he wrote about what he had learned from others, because he himself had not seen Jesus in the flesh. He collected all the available information and began his account with the birth of John. The writer also stated that the acts of the apostles were recorded in one book. Luke presented to Theophilus a report of the events he had "firsthand" information of. He was selective in his presentation. For example, he omitted the martyrdom of Peter and Paul's journey from Rome to Spain.

The records of the ancient church mention no name other than Luke in speaking of the authorship of the third Gospel and Acts. In actuality, neither is it rejected by later critics, at least not to the extent that it has gained wide acceptance. Furthermore, it is totally incredible to think that someone in the Second Century could have affixed a name of a First-Century disciple or apostle to a document later accepted into the New Testament canon, especially in a period in which such a practice was so commonly denounced (cf. the apocryphal "acts" of the various apostles written from the second through the fifth centuries).

## Luke in the New Testament

Who, then, is this "Luke"? The name *Loukas* (Greek) is actually a variation of the Roman *Lucanus* (the name of a Roman poet at the time of Nero), just as Silas is the abbreviated form of the Roman name *Silvanus.* Some have speculated that these may be the same person, since Silvanus comes from the Latin *silva,* "wood," and Luke might be connected with *Lucus,* which means a "grove" (of trees?) that is dedicated to the gods. But this is merely fanciful speculation and it does not correspond to Acts, which refers to the apostle/disciple Silas in the third person.

## A Gentile Christian

We learn from Colossians 4 that Luke was apparently a Gentile Christian. Although it is not stated explicitly it is plain from the context. At the close of his letter to the church in Colossae Paul mentions his coprisoners Aristarchus and Mark—Barnabas' nephew—together with Jesus Justus, as the only coworkers of the circumcised group who comforted him. In addition to the founder of the church, Epaphras, Paul mentions Luke and Demas (cf. Colossians 4:10,11, 12-14). Thus these three were not members of the circumcised group, being non-Jewish Gentiles. Therefore, Luke is probably the only New Testament author not of Jewish descent.

## A Greek Physician

From the same text we learn that Luke was a trained physician (Colossians 4:14). With respect to the training and skills of doctors at this time we know that in the Fourth Century B.C. the science of medicine, after the time of Hippocrates (d. ca. 380 B.C.), was studied first in Alexandria, Egypt, and from there it reached Rome.

Physicians in the capital of the empire were

initially Greeks, ordinarily released slaves. During Luke's time the famous writing of Celsus, *De Medicina*, was in circulation. Also at that time there was a "board of health" under the control of the Government. This group, in part, examined and authorized men to practice medicine in the empire. New doctors were closely supervised by their older colleagues; mistakes were severely punished. For example, their right to practice, *just practicandi*, might be suspended.

Thus Luke, as a physician, possessed no small amount of technical and practical experience, and because he came into contact with so many individuals he also had a wealth of knowledge about human nature. As a Greek by birth and as a physician by training and occupation, Luke was understandably more cultured and precise in his use of the Greek language than the other New Testament writers. The Holy Spirit used all these qualites and background as He inspired the writer.

During earlier times of research, importance was often attached to unique medical expressions in both Luke's writings. For instance, in Acts 9:18—the description of Paul regaining his sight—appeal was made in support of the tradition that Luke was the author. However, not as much significance is attached to "medical terminology" in current studies. Although Luke does use medical terminology, at times we find the same expressions used in authors who are not physicians. Thus the words and phrases must be in common use.

### From Antioch?

Much indicates that we are on historical grounds when we investigate the tradition of the ancient church that Luke was from Antioch, or at least that he lived in Antioch in Syria. Antioch was the capital of Syria and the third largest city in the Roman Empire with a half million inhabitants. Eusebius (d. 340) maintains that Luke was from Antioch. (Eusebius, *Histonia Ecclesiastica,* Books 3,4:7,8)He had studied there. Jerome (d. 420) also supports the tradition and he, too, grew up in Antioch as a child. —Jerome, *De viris illustribus, chap. 7)*

The New Testament can lend support to this hypothesis. The thoroughness and personal concern reflected in the accounts of Acts about particular locations or events in and around Antioch indicate such a relationship may indeed be possible. He knows and tells about the establishment of the church in Antioch. He realizes that some of those who lived in Antioch were among Jesus' disciples who had to flee from Jerusalem because of the persecution following Stephen's martyrdom. These Jews from Cyprus and Cyrene, he recounts, in contrast to others, testified to Greeks that Jesus from Nazareth was Lord *kurios* and Christ. With obvious joy he relates the outcome of their preaching: a great number believed (Acts 11:20ff.). Furthermore, he knows that Barnabas, as the first emissary from the Jerusalem church, was responsible for this Gentile outreach. He states that Barnabas himself went to Tarsus, sought out Paul, and asked him to join him in the work of the church in Antioch. They worked together there for an entire year. Luke also remembers that it was in Antioch that believers were first called "Christians" because they confessed Jesus the Christ as Lord (Acts 11:22- 26).

Luke was also aware of the close relationship between the mother church in Jerusalem and the young gathering in Antioch; he knew the liaison between them. He remembers the occasion that Agabus (from Jerusalem) prophesied by the Spirit of a coming famine. As a result the church sent some to minister to those in Judea (Acts 11:27f.).

Luke was moreover familiar with the names of the prophets and teachers in the Antiochean church (Acts 13:1). Why did he mention them specifically by name—besides Barnabas and Paul, Simeon, who was called Niger, Lucius from Cyrene, as well as Manaen, who was brought up with Herod—unless he knew them personally? He perhaps regarded their teaching and preaching very highly.

We find a brief but vivid account of the church service in which the church in Antioch, with the laying on of hands, sends out Barnabas and Paul as missionaries called by the Lord (Acts 13:2). For the most part Antioch is considered by Luke to be the home church of the missionaries. They return there in between missionary journeys and report to all the church what the Lord is doing in the mission fields (Acts 14:26-28; 15:35; 18:22).

Additionally, Luke's familiarity with the local and theological issues in Antioch is impressive. He gives detailed accounts of the choosing and sending of representatives to the Jerusalem Council, a decisive point in the early history of the Church. He recalls the delegates' stop along the way in the churches of Phoenicia and Samaria. In precise detail he describes the proceedings of the Jerusalem Council as well as recalling the recollections of the delegates upon their return. Indeed, he knows the meeting's resolution (Acts 15:1-34).

He must also intimately know the life of the church in Antioch and without hesitation—an indication of the integrity of Luke—he recalls the disputes in the church, even the unfortunate, bitter dispute between Paul and Barnabas that resulted in their breakup. Barnabas and John Mark travel one direction and Paul and Silas another, but both pairs are carrying on the work of the gospel (Acts 15:35-41).

In light of all of this it is not unreasonable to conclude that Luke the physician was an active member of the Gentile church in Antioch.

The enthusiasm with which he remembers the revival that swept over the city may indicate that he himself was one of its "fruits." Barnabas comes to the forefront as the leader of this revival and other missionary pushes (11:22ff.). Even after Paul arrives, Barnabas continues to be mentioned first (e.g., 11:30; 12:25; 13:1, 2,7; 14:14). As the older servant of the Lord, Barnabas would have naturally assumed a position of leadership. But the emphasis placed upon Barnabas could indicate that Barnabas played an important role in the conversion of the Greek physician Luke. If that is the case, Luke's calling Barnabas "a good man and full of the Holy Spirit and of faith" takes on a quality of personal thankfulness and respect.

### The Coworker of Paul

According to the New Testament it was Paul with whom Luke was so closely associated, both as a fellow-worker in the gospel and as a personal friend to the end. During his first imprisonment in Rome, Paul writes of "Luke, the beloved *agapētos* physician" (Colossians 4:14). This could, of course, simply mean "our dear doctor Luke." It might also indicate that he was a believer and a member of the Church, a man who together with Paul knows that he is obligated to show the love *agapē* of God in Jesus Christ. Nevertheless, the words may also connote a special bond of friendship and confidence between Paul and Luke.

Perhaps the phrase "beloved physician, Luke" can be understood to mean all these things, for in Philemon (verse 24) Luke is explicitly called Paul's coworker. In Paul's supposedly last epistle, the farewell letter to Timothy, Luke is portrayed as being special to Paul, "Only Luke is with me" (2 Timothy 4:11). Paul is writing this at a time in which almost everyone else has deserted him. It is immediately prior to his death, apparently: "I am now ready to be offered, and the time of my departure is at hand" (2 Timothy 4:6f.).

What bond united these two men of God? If we can assume that Luke was connected with the church in Antioch (see above), then their original meeting took place during the early 40s. The joining of forces began around the year 50, however, when Paul's missionary focus rested upon Europe.

Paul and Silas set out on foot through Syria and Asia Minor at this time on their second missionary journey. The disciples "increased in number daily" (Acts 16:5). Thus it was necessary to expand the missionary workers. Timothy from Lystra joined their ranks and together these three worked their way through Phrygia, Galatia, and Mysia. In Troas Paul and his coworkers met another great and unexpected challenge: the call to go to Macedonia (16:9) and to preach the gospel in Europe. They could not refuse this call and responded "immediately" (Acts 16:10).

Precisely at this intersection we encounter the "we passage" phenomenon mentioned before. We might conclude that at this juncture, impressed by the tremendous challenge before them, Paul sent to the base church in Antioch for "reinforcements." Here Paul mentions Luke as useful in that capacity. Luke, as quickly as possible—either by ship or over land through Asia Minor—joined the group. The time was around A.D. 50.

Why did Paul choose Luke, or more precisely, why did the Spirit set him apart (cf. 13:2)? As we have noted, there were other possibilities, such as Simeon Niger, Lucius, and Manaen. One answer bringing the gospel to the heart of Greek civilization. What better choice than the Greek-educated Luke?

Some would claim Paul needed Luke's help as a physician. However, Paul's frequent recollections of his gospel-related suffering give no indication that he was sick (1 Corinthians 4:9-13; 2 Corinthians 4:8,9; 6:4-10; 11:23-29). For the same reason 2 Corinthians 12:7, "a thorn in the flesh" cannot be adduced as proof that Paul was so chronically ill as to need the services of a physician on a regular basis.

From the "we passages" and the aforementioned places in the Pauline epistles we may conclude that Luke remained with Paul and his group except on those occasions where the ministry of the gospel demanded he be elsewhere.

### The Sources of Luke

Every author, even the most "original" draws from certain or unconsciously from sources. This is especially true of an historical author.

Of course, this applies to Luke too. He himself describes this in his introduction to his first volume, the Gospel of Luke (Luke 1:1-4). He used many sources, for "many have taken in hand." They wrote "to set forth in order a declaration." These originated from eyewitnesses of the ministry of Jesus and they rest upon a conscientious, reliable, accurate, oral tradition of the Church "delivered unto us," and "which are most surely believed among us."

In Acts the author included himself in the circle of the eyewitnesses and his own testimony. The origin of the "we passages" is interpreted differently. Are they abstracts of a diary kept by Luke? Keeping a journal would not be strange for a physician or unparalleled. Or it might include written testimony at the "lawcourt of the emperor" during Paul's trial in Rome. Perhaps similar notes were kept by the author during the shipwreck at Malta and the events that took place there.

These eyewitness accounts cover the period of Paul's second missionary journey in the years 49-51. According to the "shorter text" this includes the journey from Troas. According to the longer reading of Codex D, it includes the journey from inland Mysia up to and including Philippi. Apparently Luke remained in Philippi to protect the gains made by the gospel into that area. Next the "we" sections span the years 52-55, the third missionary journey from Philippi to Jerusalem, including Paul's arrest and imprisonment. The "we" sections probably include Paul's imprisonment in Caesarea (A.D. 55-57). At least they cover Paul's dramatic voyage to Italy in the winter of A.D. 57-58 and his first two-year imprisonment in Rome (A.D. 58-60). This last point is substantiated by Paul's mentioning Luke in two letters written during this period.

What sources has Luke drawn upon for the rest of his story? Undoubtedly he had access to the same kind of sources he employed in his first volume. This would especially hold true in the accounts immediately after the Resurrection, the Ascension, and the outpouring of the Spirit on the Day of Pentecost, as well as in the earliest history of the church in Jerusalem. Included here too should be the account of the gospel's first being preached to the Gentiles— Peter's visit to Cornelius' house.

In telling of the establishment of the different churches Luke could depend upon traditions and personal conversations he had with those who were present. Luke learned of the traditions on his journeys and he includes them in his second volume. When he tells of the establishment of the church in Antioch, he is certainly relying upon his own recollection.

Involved in the writing of Acts is the personal knowledge and recollection of the author, together with his investigation of the "eyewitnesses and ministers of the word." A glance at Acts with this "source" in mind reveals that the prime sources of information of that day and time were none other than such men as Peter, John, and James the brother of our Lord (cf. 21:17f.)—the early apostles, as well as the evangelists and apostolic coworkers like Barnabas, John Mark, and Silas. Just think what Paul and Luke must have discussed as they traveled on foot across the miles and lived together for 2 years in Rome while Paul was under house arrest.

But to underscore the unity of the document again: Acts is a unified whole in both language and content. It possesses a literary and technical consistency unmatched. It is a unity which at the deepest level comes from the Spirit who inspired its writing.

That is not just a pious remark by a believer oblivious to the critical questions. Of course there are "sources." But the ultimate source is the gospel, the Word and the Spirit, the Church and the apostolate that the author serves.

### The Time of Writing of the Document

Nothing in the first or second volume (Luke-Acts) indicates the year of the composition. In order to estimate the time of composition we must deduce it from the arguments themselves in light of history. Opinions are wide-ranging in this regard. Some have thought that Acts was written around the Second Century with the intention to "harmonize" divergent views between Pauline and Petrine Christianity. Others assert that the book originates in the anti-Marcionite struggle. Still others regard Acts as a defense of Paul designed to declare his apostolic authority as genuine.

In contrast to these opinions is the theory that the document is genuine history drawn from the apostolic period. The earliest time of composition is apparently A.D. 60, the date of the last events it records. There is strong evidence against a late date of composition:

(1) The relationship to the third Gospel, whose themes clearly continue into Acts; the well-attested Lucan tradition.

(2) The similarities between Luke and Acts, on the one hand, compared with the "unique" style and format of later "acts" written during the post-apostolic period, on the other.

(3) The convincing arguments of von Harnack: a late date would be evident in harmonizing tendency between Acts and the Pauline letters. This "harmonizing" is not present.

(4) The accuracy of historical, geographical, and cultural statements about the First Century and the unmistakable sense that it is an eyewitness telling the story.

All of the above demonstrate that the document was written during the First Century. But can we narrow the date of composition any further? The evidence suggests the answer is "yes."

(1) Acts must have been written prior to A.D. 70. The temple in Jerusalem is still standing according to Acts (cf. 2:46; 21:26). If Acts were written after the Jewish War and after the destruction of the temple (A.D. 70), then the writing would have naturally reflected that.

(2) Some interpreters suggest A.D. 64 as the date of composition. This was the year Paul was martyred, during Nero the emperor's persecution of Christians, because of the Rome fire he charged they set.

We learn from 2 Timothy 4:9-11 that Paul, immediately prior to his death, sends for Timothy and asks him to bring along Mark. He requests also that he bring "the books, especially the parchment books." Luke is at this time the only coworker of Paul remaining. Some have interpreted this data as indication of Paul's last literary work. Probably with the help of Luke and Mark—both effective writers—Paul wished to complete this task.

However, nothing can be proven, although it may have a certain degree of possibility. If there had been such a cooperation, what would it have involved? A continuation of Acts would be fitting; that document ends abruptly and it seems as if something was supposed to follow. It is true that Luke-Acts does achieve the goal it sets for itself (cf. Acts 1:8): the spread of the gospel from Jerusalem to Rome, the "end of the earth" symbolically and the capital of the known world. Even if Luke meant the "end of the earth" in a literal sense he would have meant the pillars of Hercules in Spain, because the then-known world ended there. Indeed, Luke could have continued.

Almost without doubt Paul was acquitted in his trial before the emperor in A.D. 60. From that time he began a new ministry. The New Testament may offer credible support of this. Paul was in the province of Asia once more and he returned to Macedonia and Achaia (1 Timothy 1:3). He visited Crete and Nicopolis (Titus 1:5; 3:12). The tradition of the Early Church holds that Paul succeeded in fulfilling his objective of reaching Spain with the gospel before he died (Romans 15:28). The First Epistle of Clement (before A.D. 100) testifies to this.

This letter, up until the Second Century, was placed on the same level as other writings which later became canonical. According to Irenaeus, Clement knew Peter and Paul. Clement says in chapter 5: "Let us set before our eyes the good apostles: Peter, . . . (and) Paul . . . seven times he was in bonds, he was exiled, he was stoned, he was a herald both in the East and in the West,...and when he had reached the limits of the West he gave his testimony before the rulers, and thus passed from the world. . . ." (1 Clement 5:3-7, Loeb Classical Library).

An author like Clement, who himself lived in Rome, could not have meant Rome by "limits of the West." He must have thought of Spain. It would have been difficult to invent a story about Paul traveling to Spain from Rome only 30 years after his death. And from Clement's description of Paul's suffering as a missionary it is apparent that he does not have Paul's letters or Acts in front of him. He relates some generally known information.

All this suggests the unlikelihood that Acts was written during this time. An additional volume to Acts is conceivable, but not the writing of the New Testament Book of Acts.

Given the political and ecclesiastical turmoil of the years around A.D. 64, the positive, irenic messages of Luke and Acts do not belong. That was a time of dangerous conflict. Acts' thoroughly positive portrayal of the empire and Roman government are inconsistent with such an atmosphere as A.D. 64. The Emperor Nero's persecution of the Christian church culminated in mass trials and executions of such proportions that they remained etched on the mind of the world for a long time. Ecclesiastical documents remember it again and again.

(3) On the other hand the picture of Acts corresponds nicely with the political and ecclesiastical climate of the year A.D. 60. That is not to say that there was peace and tranquility. The insanity of the young emperor, who appeared so promising on other respects, was beginning to show, but nothing to the extent it did later! The judicial system was still intact. Paul's trial ends in acquittal, in accordance with due process of law in Jerusalem, Caesarea, and Rome (Philippians 1:7).

Acts closes on a somewhat positive note: Although Paul is a prisoner, he is free to come and go as he pleases (Acts 28:16) and he lives in his own lodgings (Acts 28:30). He has visitors (28:23) and in fact has companions with him. And most importantly, from dawn to late at night he preaches and teaches Jesus Christ is Lord *kurios* without restrictions and in all honesty and boldness (Acts 28:23-31).

Not only this, there are some indications that Paul's preaching of Jesus as Lord became a topic of conversation not only among his own countrymen but among Gentiles, too, even those in high official capacities. "The entire praetorium" ("whole palace guard," NIV) listened to and contemplated Paul's message. Members of the "household of the emperor" were won to Christ and followed Him in baptism, becoming members of the church (Philippians 1:13; 4:22).

This is where Acts fits. As it was mentioned, some parts of Acts may have evolved from the written records of Paul's trial. Indeed, the whole work, Luke-Acts might have formed part of Paul's defense. Of course it is speculation to think that Theophilus could have been Paul's "attorney" in his trial before the emperor and Luke-Acts evidence for Paul's defense; nevertheless, such a bold hypothesis does explain the ending of Acts. If the objection is raised that there is too much irrelevant material in the volumes for this to have been the case, it might be supposed that it was only later expanded for Theophilus' personal use.

Whatever the case, the notion that Luke-Acts is essentially an apologetical (a "defense") work is correct. This is especially true of their political stance. It is hardly an accident that the Roman authorities are consistently spoken of in positive terms.

For example, Pilate does not find Jesus guilty and he wants to release Him (Luke 23). The governor of Cyprus becomes a believer (Acts 13:7-12). The magistrates of Philippi discreetly come to the aid of Paul and Silas after they see they were unjustly treated (Acts 16:37f.). Likewise, Gallio, the governor of Achaia (18:12f.), comes to Paul's defense against the attacks of the Jews. The local "Asians" in Ephesus are accepted by the Roman officials, thus as their friends, Paul and his companions receive fair treatment by the city clerk who comes to their aid (19:31). Felix and Festus, Roman proconsuls, treat Paul in keeping with Roman law (Acts 24:1 to 26:32). And finally, Paul's Roman citizenship is respected everywhere (16:37; 25:10 and elsewhere).

### Later Traditions

An author of the personality and status (apostolic coworker) of Luke naturally evokes the interest of later times. Just out of gratitude for his preservation of the early history of the Church, we have made him the topic of much study. We even desire to know more about his life than the historical sources provide.

Origen of Alexandria, an Early Church father (d. ca. A.D. 251) thought that Luke was one of the 70 disciples sent out by Jesus during His earthly ministry (Luke 10). This, however, can be dismissed, since it fails to correspond with Luke's own description of himself in the preface to the Gospel.

He clearly states he was not among the "eyewitnesses and ministers of the word."

In the same way we must disregard Theophylact's (an Eastern exegete, ca. A.D. 1000) comments upon Luke 24:13f. He concludes on the basis of silence that the unnamed disciple on the Emmaus road was actually Luke the evangelist, who was too modest to mention his own name, choosing only to name his fellow-disciple Cleopas. Since Luke was not an eyewitness of Jesus' earthly ministry, he cannot be among the Greeks wanting to see Jesus during Passover Week (John 12:20).

Nothing absolute is known about Luke's death, but there appears to be a rather firm tradition that he died in Greece. Supposedly he worked there for a number of years following Paul's death. Ancient tradition says he died a martyr's death there. We cannot be certain of his martyrdom, but his two-volume masterpiece of Luke-Acts is one of the tremendous witnesses to the life, death, and resurrection of our Saviour, and of the ancient church.

## Religious Groups

Five different religious groups existed in the First Century which are relevant to the time in which Christianity developed. Before outlining each of these groups, a rough distinction can be made: Jews and Jewish Christians are of Jewish birth; Proselytes, God-fearers, and Gentiles are all Gentile-born.

Proselytes are Gentiles who became Jews. God-fearers had a close affinity for Judaism, but they never fully adopted the Jewish religion (circumcision was often the distinguishing step they did not take). The New Testament indicates that individuals from both of these groups later became Christians. Jewish Christians are those Jews who acknowledge that Jesus is Messiah. They did not see themselves as forsaking Judaism; rather, Jesus was the fulfillment of Jewish expectation. Others did not view them as "ex-Jews" either. Gentile Christians have faith in God through Jesus Christ, but this does not make them Jews.

## Jews

The label *Jew* was used by Jew and non-Jew alike for those people who confessed faith in the God of Abraham, Isaac, and Jacob. It denotes a national and religious affiliation—actually inseparable concepts in Israel's religion. Some writers of that day do use the term in a derogatory manner, but since it is also employed by Jewish authors, *Jew* can be understood in a neutral manner. In the Book of Acts *Jew* at times stands in parallel to the term "Israelite." Jews often made use of this latter term in reference to their position as "the people of God." *Israelite* is only rarely used by Gentile writers to denote the Jewish people.

*Jew* and *Israelite* appear to be used synonymously in Acts. For example, in Acts 2:14 we read the exhortation, "Ye men of Judea!"; but in Acts 2:22; 3:12; 5:35; 13:16 and in similar contexts we hear, "Ye men of Israel!" It is difficult to discern any difference in usage.

Elsewhere in Acts we observe that the term *Jew* often functions neutrally or objectively in reference to the Jewish people or their religion. Paul thus testifies to the Jews that Jesus is the Christ (Acts 18:5). The inhabitants of a city are depicted in two groups: Jews and Greeks (Acts 18:4; 19:10,17). The false prophet Bar-Jesus was Jewish, but there is nothing negative in that fact. Furthermore, Luke presents Christian Jews as Jews, for example, Aquila and Apollos (cf. below, Jewish Christians). Indeed, even following Paul's experience on the Damascus road Paul can introduce himself as "a man which am a Jew of Tarsus" (Acts 21:39).

Jesus ministered in the "land of the Jews" (Acts 10:39). Luke takes it for granted that Jesus from Nazareth is himself a Jew with whom the God of Abraham, Isaac, and Jacob has dealt in a unique way (Acts 3:13).

Although some interpreters attempt to show that the author of Acts intentionally distanced himself from the Jewish people through his use of the term *Jews*, this theory does not hold water. His use of that terminology can be compared with how the Jewish historian Josephus describes his own people when he writes to non-Jewish people. Moreover, all of the speeches in Acts, all the material about Jesus, indeed, all of Acts, has Jewish coloring. It is the God of Israel, the God of the Jews, who sent Jesus, the Messiah and Lord of all who believe.

Clearly Luke shares Paul's opinion that those who are truly "Jews" are those who believe in Jesus. Anyone who rejects Jesus Christ—whatever nationality he or she may be—has only a doubtful claim to that name. But Luke does use the term often when speaking of the Jewish rejection of the gospel. Nonetheless, just as both Jews and Greeks believe (14:1), so too, both Gentiles (Greeks) and Jews want to harm or kill the apostles (14:5).

For example, in Acts 9:23 we read that the Jews plotted to kill Paul. Of course this refers to those Jews living in Damascus and not to the entire Jewish people (cf. 9:22). In Acts 13:48, 50 we are told that the two groups in the synagogue in Iconium split. The "Gentiles" probably are the "God-fearers." When it is said in 17:5 that the Jews were jealous of Paul, this refers to those Jews in Thessalonica. Thus *Jews* refers to a local constituency of Jews, say from a synagogue. It does not refer to Jews in general. Luke clearly distinguishes between those Jews who believe and those who oppose the gospel (cf. the reputation of the Jews in Berea:

"These were more noble than those in Thessalonica" [17:11]).

Some texts reading "Jews" might be interpreted as a reference to Jews in general. In the account of the murder of James, the brother of John, it is said: "And because he saw it pleased the Jews, he proceeded further to take Peter also" (Acts 12:3). A similar understanding may occur in the expression "the Jewish people," a symbol of all of Judaism (Acts 12:11). Such an expression, however, must not be exaggerated or interpreted apart from the larger portrait of Jews in Acts. There was no monolithic response to Christianity by the Jewish people.

With respect to the responsibility for Jesus' death, the Jews are not viewed as solely responsible. Herod and Pilate are both mentioned in that connection; the Gentiles as well as the people of Israel participated: "For of a truth against thy holy child Jesus, whom thou hast anointed, both Herod, and Pontius Pilate, with the Gentiles, and the people of Israel, were gathered together" (Acts 4:27). The same attitude recurs in Acts 2:23, where the mystery of the divine plan is explained: "Him, being delivered by the determinate counsel and foreknowledge of God, ye have taken, and by wicked hands have crucified and slain."

Finally it should be noted that the use of "Jew" in the Book of Acts carries no anti-Semitic overtones. Luke plainly states that the God of the Christians is the God of Jews. Jesus was a Jew; the first Christians were themselves Jews who preached to Jews and Gentiles alike. Some Israelites accepted the gospel message; others rejected it. Those who acknowledged its truth did not cease being Jewish. This is the best evidence that the term *Jew* does not carry negative implications in Acts. But there are differences among the Jews, just as there are differences among the Gentiles (cf. Romans 2:28f.: true Jews are those who believe in Jesus as Messiah and Lord).

### Proselytes

Proselytes and God-fearers are those not of Jewish ethnic descent. Both groups appear in Acts, and in contrast to other Gentiles and Greeks, proselytes and God-fearers were attracted to the Jewish religion, to the one true God, and to the ethical life-style of Judaism. Thus they share a positive relationship to Judaism. Nevertheless, one must distinguish between these two groups. Proselytes became Jews in the fullest sense of the word; God-fearers remained Gentiles.

From the Jewish perspective a proselyte is a Gentile who converts to Jewish religion, who believes in the God of Israel, and who attempts to follow the Mosaic law. For Gentile men proselytes, becoming a proselyte involved three steps: circumcision, a ritual bath (baptism), and offering a sacrifice. For women only the last two were applicable. Following the destruction of the temple (A.D. 70) even sacrificing was no longer allowed.

As a proselyte one was obligated to keep all the commandments of the Mosaic law. Since a proselyte was technically a Jew, it meant both responsibilities and privileges. Rabbinic sources disclose that discussions often concerned the rights of proselytes. For example, it was debated by some that proselytes in private prayer should say: "the God of *the* fathers of Israel," and in their synagogue prayers: "the God of *their* fathers"—instead of the normal "God of *our* fathers."

Furthermore, proselytes were forbidden from holding certain public positions. The female proselyte could not marry a priest. Nevertheless, technically they were Jews and had both the obligations and duties of any other Jew.

The rabbis, however, tried to further distinguish between the righteous and true proselyte, who genuinely desired to follow the God of Israel, and the proselyte, who became such for improper reasons. For example, a man or woman wishing to marry a Jew would become a proselyte in order to be able to do so; however his or her intentions might be unrelated to any desire to serve the God of Israel. Rabbis declared such pretenders "false proselytes." Another reason for becoming a proselyte might be a desire to advance socially and economically. This too was condemned.

Accounts of forcing someone to become a proselyte are rare. One exception is John Hyrcannus, who toward the close of the Second Century B.C. forced the Idumeans to be circumcised. The various schools of rabbinic thought differed in their opinions about whether or not it was even desirable that Gentiles be converted to Judaism. Particular examples of this are the schools of Shammai and Hillel. Shammai tried to make the path to Judaism as difficult as possible for potential proselytes. Hillel, on the other hand, wanted to make the step relatively easy. There is a familiar story about Hillel's teaching of a Gentile:

"What you do not like that anyone do to you, you shall neither do your neighbor. This is the law. The rest is explanation. Go and learn this."

The term "proselyte" occurs only four times in the New Testament. Jesus disparages the eagerness of the scribes and Pharisees to make converts/proselytes (Matthew 23:15). Some have questioned the historicity of His statement. Although present discussion continues about the extent of Jewish missionary efforts, available Jewish sources clearly state that some Jewish groups encouraged Gentiles to adopt the Jewish religion. And most agree that the number of proselytes within Judaism at the time of Jesus was great. This held especially true in the region of the Diaspora, where the faith and practice of Jews often sharply contrasted the corrupt Gentile pattern of life. Nevertheless, many rabbis were skeptical about inviting Gentiles to become Jews. One reason for their hesitancy might be because during periods of intense persecution the proselytes often returned to their former way of life.

The three remaining instances of "proselyte" occur in the Book of Acts. Jews and proselytes are present on the Day of Pentecost (2:5). In the list of those appointed to minister to the needs of the widows, Nicolas, the last one mentioned, is described as a "proselyte" from Antioch (6:5). The other six should probably be considered fully Jewish.

A puzzling usage occurs in Acts 13:43, where the issue concerns "Jews and religious proselytes." The conjunction of the words "religious" and "proselytes" is unique. Some think that "proselyte" is an early "gloss" (explanatory comment) that entered the text at a very early stage. However, there is no textual support for such a view. Thus, it is best to not try and separate the two; it is a unique expression for proselytes. It might be compared with the expression in Acts 2:5, "Jews, devout men."

### God-Fearers

Using different Greek terms Luke describes one group of Gentiles in Acts as "God-fearers." Although this terminology elsewhere does not function this way, the similar idea occurs in his descriptions of the centurion of Luke 7:1-10 as a God-fearing Gentile. He had even given money to build a synagogue. Cornelius is a God-fearer according to Acts 10:2,22, and we observe that in the synagogue in Antioch in Pisidia Paul addresses two groups of listeners: "Men of Israel, and ye that fear God, give audience" (Acts 13:16). This phenomenon is repeated in Thessalonica and Athens (Acts 17:4,17). Lydia, the seller of purple, is described as a worshiper of God (16:14). Later in 18:7 we read that Paul stayed in Corinth in the house of "one that worshipped God," Titus Justus.

This group of individuals are those who did not take the final step of conversion to Judaism. They did not become proselytes; however, Judaism appeals to them. They participate in the synagogue services and abide at least by the Noahic covenantal commands. Regardless of how closely a God-fearer followed Jewish guidelines and laws, this still did not make him or her a Jew. To the Jews, "God-fearers" were called "righteous Gentiles." They were thought to have a share in the Age to Come. Although rabbis differed in their estimate of these God-fearers, most regarded them with much skepticism.

Paul's preaching especially appealed to this group, which continued to be closely associated with other Gentiles (cf. Acts 13:48). When Paul preached in the synagogues these God-fearers were often present. A large crowd of God- fearing Greeks join Paul in Thessalonica (Acts 17:4; cf. 14:1; 17:12; 18:4). In contrast to synagogue custom Paul preached that circumcision was unnecessary for those believing the gospel message and putting their faith in Jesus.

### Jewish Christians

The common denominator between Jewish Christians and Gentile Christians is their faith that Jesus is the Messiah and the Lord. They are united by faith and in baptism without being totally alike. Gentiles did not have to become Jewish before becoming Christian. Christian Jews regarded themselves as fully Jewish.

The Early Christian Church began as a Jewish Christian congregation in Jerusalem. The earliest Jewish Christians did not "change Gods" when they accepted Jesus as Messiah. Neither did they consider themselves "ex-Jews." Rather, they understood their faith as the true religion of the Old Testament. They thought themselves the true people of God in contrast to their countrymen who rejected Jesus.

Just as Jesus was Jewish, with a Jewish mother and reared in Jewish environment, with the Old Testament Scriptures as His Bible, likewise, the first apostles were Jewish. Paul was

Jewish and regarded himself to still be one even after his "conversion." He would have protested if someone had maintained that by believing in Jesus he ceased being Jewish. This holds true despite the fact that later Jewish factions disassociated themselves from Paul because of his missionary efforts among the Gentiles and his contention that Gentile Christians were free from the obligations of the Law.

The mother church in Jerusalem primarily consisted of Jewish Christians. During its early stages, the missionary activity of the Early Church was directed toward Jew and Gentile alike by Jewish Christians. Gentiles considered these Jewish Christians as Jews. One part of the charge against Silas and Paul in Philippi shows this plainly: "These men, being Jews, do exceedingly trouble our city" (Acts 16:20). (Cf. also the comments of Gallio, the Roman proconsul, 18:15.)

A brief examination of the principal characters in Acts reveals the same tendency. Most of the main personages are Jewish Christians. The apostles are Jewish (Acts 1): six of the seven chosen to minister to the needs of the widows are Jewish (Nicolas was a proselyte); and James, the brother of our Lord and one of the leading figures in the Jerusalem church, was also Jewish. Likewise Paul, Barnabas, Silas, and John Mark came from Jewish stock. Timothy's mother was Jewish, although his father was a Greek (Acts 16:1). Paul had him circumcised. Aquila and Priscilla and Apollos were of Jewish lineage (cf. Acts 18:2,24). Although one of Luke's chief objectives is to explain how the Christian message reached from Jerusalem to Rome and how it is welcomed by Gentiles but largely rejected by the Jews, he strongly emphasizes now it is Jewish Christians who carry the gospel message into the world. Neither does he tone down the Jewish character of the message; instead, it is more the opposite.

The Jewish character of the Jerusalem church surfaces in a number of ways. There is no indication that Sabbath-Day observances were dropped, other than its being reinterpreted in terms of what Jesus did on the Sabbath. In addition to continuing the practice of going to the temple to worship, the Early Church members also met in homes or other special spots where they could pray, study the Old Testament Scriptures, sing together, and share the Lord's Supper. Like Jesus, they probably continued to attend the synagogue service as well.

Evidence abounds in support of this: "And they, continuing daily with one accord in the temple" (Acts 2:46); "Peter and John went up together into the temple at the hour of prayer, being the ninth hour" (Acts 3:1); "They were all with one accord in Solomon's porch" (Acts 5:12); and "Go, stand and speak in the temple to the people all the words of this life" (Acts 5:20).

The above examples depict the situation in the first year of the new movement as Luke sees it. A short time later the situation remains largely the same, despite the inclusion of Gentiles. Some interesting material is given about the situation following Paul's third missionary journey (Acts 21:17f.). The above examples do not tell us whether the Jewish Christians continued to participate in the temple sacrifices. However, we cannot ignore the fact that Acts 21:17f. indicates that this is indeed the case. The Jewish Christian believers in Jerusalem tell Paul: "Thou seest, brother, how many thousands of Jews there are which believe; and they are all zealous of the law" (verse 20).

It is of particular interest that Paul, following the advice of James, joins four men of Jerusalem who had taken a vow, and he even pays their expenses. Thus in doing this Paul puts to rest rumors which speculated that he had forsaken the Law. Paul's actions suggest that when he finished his third missionary journey he might have participated in the sacrifice at the temple. At the least he paid for and consented to other believers doing so. The sacrifices offered by these four men (which Paul paid for) were probably eight lambs, four rams, and oil and flour (cf. Numbers 6:13-21).

It would be a likely mistake to assume that Paul was compelled to join them. Jews are Jewish just as Greeks are Greek (1 Corinthians 9:20). Paul clearly taught that circumcision has no spiritual value, but he also taught that not to be circumcised had no spiritual value either (Galatians 6:15). If these four men had hoped to be justified by these sacrifices Paul would never have sponsored them. The issue was the fulfillment of a Nazarite vow. The old covenant was weak and ineffective (Hebrews 7:18), but it was only injurious to someone if he considered such action as means of securing salvation.

Christ abolished the old covenant. The new covenant is in effect, but the old must pass off the scene. The author of the Letter to the Hebrews states that the old "is ready to vanish away" (Hebrews 8:13). When he wrote these words the sacrificial service still existed and it would continue as long as the "first tabernacle was yet standing" (Hebrews 9:8,9). The worship service of the temple continued up until the time the temple was destroyed (A.D. 70). At that time the vestiges of an antiquated sacrificial system were lost.

Since Paul submitted to the ritual purification in the temple, and since he paid the expenses of the sacrifices (burnt, sin, thanksgiving), we can deduce that Paul did not require Jewish Christians to relinquish their unique Jewish heritage, not even when this involved the Jewish system of sacrifice. Apparently one could continue to live like a Jew if one were born a Jew.

The judgment and decision of the Apostolic Council, in light of the preceding evidence, do not disagree with this understanding. The issue of the Apostolic Council involved the life-style and moral conduct of Gentile Christians (Acts 15). After "much discussion" (15:7) everyone agreed that the Gentiles did not have to become Jews or live as Jews in order to be a part of the people of God. This decision rested on the opposite premise that Jews were not required to live as Gentiles in order to be saved.

Paul, as well as the church in Jerusalem, apparently abided by this decision. Nevertheless, not all the issues were resolved. Some from the Pharisaic party who had become believers raised some questions. For one, must Gentiles be circumcised in order to be saved? (cf. 15:1-5). A similar problem occurs in Galatia. Concerning the assertion that Gentiles must be circumcised Paul says just one thing: "If ye be circumcised, Christ shall profit you nothing" (Galatians 5:2).

The Christian freedom of the Jewish Christians thus has its limits, as Galatians 2:11-16 makes clear. Peter ate with Gentile Christians, but when Jewish Christians from James arrived, Peter withdrew from table fellowship with them. Paul sharply rebukes such action. The superior principle of love supersedes any Jewish Christian custom. We cannot investigate this difficult problem any further, but Acts transparently depicts the first Jewish Christians as thoroughly Jewish and as living essentially in keeping with Jewish customs. Not even Paul criticizes them for this.

Several items warrant discussion in order to explain the Jewish element in the faith of the earliest believers.

(1) Early Christian proclamation and missionary preaching is thoroughly saturated with material from the Old Testament. The God of Israel, the God of the covenant, is the Father of those who believe in Messiah (see, e.g., Acts 2:5 and elsewhere in Acts).

(2) A few of the sermons in Acts contain some formulaic, stock phrases, such as the phrase "our fathers." This phrase appears in Stephen's defense about 10 times. Whereas Stephen identifies himself with the transgression of the patriarchs, at the close of his sermon he says "your fathers" instead of "our fathers." He says: "Ye stiffnecked and uncircumcised in heart and ears, ye do always resist the Holy Ghost: as your fathers did, so do ye" (Acts 7:51). The "fathers" here, however, are not Abraham, Isaac, Jacob, Moses, David, etc. These men were revered by Jewish Christians too. The continuity between the Old Testament and its story of salvation history is highlighted. Jewish Christians are the true children of the true fathers.

(3) Another minor stock phrase is "brothers" ("brethren"). This may mean "Christian brethren" (e.g., 1:16), but it is also used of fellow Jews who do not believe in Jesus (e.g., 2:29; 7:2; 28:17). By calling non-believing Jews "brothers," the Jewish Christians reveal that they consider themselves Jews. They do not feel they have broken away from the Jewish people. Jews unreceptive of Jesus are merely Jews who reject the God of their fathers.

(4) A couple of terms descriptive of Jewish Christians prove interesting as well. They may be termed "Jews who believe" or even "Pharisees who believe" (Acts 15:5). Those confronting Peter in Jerusalem, called the "circumcised believers," were Jewish Christians. And, as pointed out earlier, most of the central characters in Acts are Jewish (e.g., Acts 18:1f.).

These observations demonstrate that Jewish Christians continued to regard themselves as Jews. It was also shown that Paul and the Jerusalem church ultimately agreed upon the relationship between Jewish Christians and Gentile believers. Some interpreters have sought to resolve the differences in the Early Church by suggesting that the issues were never resolved and that an ongoing struggle existed between Paul and the Jerusalem church. Acts, however, points to another solution: agreement between the two was most likely.

This is not to say that Paul had no opposition. Some Jewish Christians resisted Paul's missionary efforts among the Gentiles from the outset. It is entirely possible that their allegiance to Judaism proved stronger than their new-found faith in Jesus the Messiah. Despite the lack of the necessary historical data for answering these questions fully, we do know from Second-Century sources that Jewish Christianity existed in many different forms. Such branches—like those which occurred when not all accepted the decision of the Apostolic Council (Acts 15), or like those who disagreed with Paul's outreach to the Gentiles—probably originated very early. Some advocate an early date for such "splits," although evidence only confirms that the separation occurred later. The reason for the Apostolic Council and the attitude of some Jewish Christians there favor an early fragmentation of the new movement.

It would be impossible to isolate each group that formed from the Jewish Christians "stock" of early believers. However, it is beyond question that some of these gradually became more Jewish in their orientation, while others drifted into the currents of Gnosticism. Below we will examine the two basic forms of Jewish Christianity, which were at least present during the Second Century. Their origin, however, is not certain.

(1) One group within Jewish Christianity was essentially the same as the Gentile church; that is, the Gentile church which continued in the apostolic tradition. (Even among Gentile Christianity there were peripheral groups.) Both groups respected the decisions of the Apostolic Council. For the most part Jewish Christians continued to live as Jews, but they did not insist that the Gentiles must follow Jewish customs and practices. With respect to Jesus' identity, these Jewish Christians held the virgin birth of Jesus to be an essential element of their Christology.

(2) Another group within Jewish Christianity insisted that Gentiles must live in accordance with Jewish custom if they were to be truly Christians. Thus they opposed the Gentile church. They refused to accept Paul's apostolic claim, perhaps because before his "conversion" Paul had persecuted the Church. And more importantly, in their eyes Paul continued to destroy the Church because he advocated the inclusion of Gentiles into the new covenant and reinterpreted the old covenant and law in terms unacceptable to many. This group, furthermore, denied the deity of Christ and rejected His virgin birth.

Gentile Christianity, which was theologically oriented around the message of the New Testament and the apostolic tradition, could not, of course, accept the latter group. At the same time, it is regrettable that the former group was not always received with understanding and appreciation for its unique place in salvation history. In Justin's *Dialogue with Trypho* (Trypho was Jewish), written around the middle of the Second Century, we find an example of Justin's conviction that Jewish Christians will be saved if they do not demand that Gentile Christians live as Jews. But in the same breath Justin concedes that there are Gentile Christians who do not agree with him.

That last point of view came to be the dominant one in Christianity. Gradually the Jewish element of the Christian faith diminished; Jewish Christians lost out. After numerous struggles, in which Gentile Christianity should have shown more understanding for the Jewish Christian's search for identity, Jewish Christianity disappeared around the Fourth Century.

Finally to emphasize our findings: The first Jewish Christians did not meet a new God through faith in Jesus Christ; rather, they met God in a new way. Faith in Christ did not mean they relinquished their Jewish identity; instead, they became the people of God that God desired for all peoples.

### Gentile Christians

The preceding pages have indirectly discussed the group of Christianity made up principally of Gentiles. Consequently, summary comments will be sufficient. One of Luke's chief objectives is to demonstrate the spread of the Christian faith among the Gentiles. Faith in Jesus extends to cities in Asia Minor, Macedonia, Greece, and Rome, the capital of the world at that time. Philip the evangelist preaches to the Samaritans, who were not Jewish or Gentile; later he baptizes an Ethiopian eunuch on the road to Gaza (Acts 8). Peter baptizes Cornelius (Acts 10). Those Jewish Christians scattered in connection with the persecution following the stoning of Stephen initially preach to Jews. Later, though, they proclaim the gospel to Greeks in Antioch and Syria (Acts 11:19f.). Antioch became one of the main centers for Christianity outside of Jerusalem. Believers in Christ first received the name "Christians" in Antioch (Acts 11:26).

Elsewhere we can point to Paul's missionary efforts. Normally he enters the synagogues, where he preaches to Jews as well as God-fearing Gentiles. The gospel is most welcomed among the latter. Through faith in Jesus and by following Him in baptism they could become full members of the Christian faith. Jews and Gentiles alike heard the message of "repent, believe, and be baptized." Paul sharply rejected any notion that Gentiles had to become Jewish in order to be Christians. All peoples were to travel the same road to salvation; nonetheless, it is tragic that many in the Church soon forgot that the God of Christianity was the God of Israel who had revealed himself in Jesus Christ. Moreover, Paul's caution in Romans 11:16f. not to be arrogant or unconcerned about the unique problems of Jewish Christianity, was soon forgotten. The relationship between Jewish Christianity, the Jewish people as a whole, and the Gentile element of Christianity is admittedly a dark chapter in the history of the Church. However, it must not be forgotten but confessed.

### The Damascus Event

On more than one occasion in his letters Paul refers to what happened to him on the road to Damascus. He mentions it at least 20 times, 5 times explicitly and 15 whose meaning would be hard to pin down apart from the background of his experience on the road to Damascus. This does not imply that Paul's understanding revolves solely around his "conversion." Even given the impact that the experience had upon Paul's life, that alone does not entitle it to the place of prominence it receives. But, as we will see, Paul's experience involves a final link in the actualization of God's plan. On the road to Damascus Paul was confronted by the Risen Lord; on this basis the founding of the Church begins.

The centrality of the event is also reflected in the fact that Luke includes it three times in his Book of Acts (chapters 9,22,26). The principal elements are as follows:

(1) *The first account (chapter 9).* The account in chapter 9 picks up on the aside-like comments of 7:58 and 8:1-3. There we learn that Saul (Paul) hated the disciples of Jesus. This is particularly "fleshed out" in his probable official role in the stoning of Stephen. He continued to persecute the church in Jerusalem, entering house by house and dragging out men and women alike and casting them into prison. Jerusalem, however, is not enough! He takes it upon himself to expand his persecution of the "people of the Way." He requests that Caiaphas, the high priest (from A.D. 18-36) and leader of the Sanhedrin, give him permission and authority to track down and capture disciples of Jesus in the Syrian city of Damascus. He was to bring them back to Jerusalem for trial.

Evidently a large Jewish population existed in Damascus; there were several synagogues. These synagogues came under the jurisdiction of the authorities in Jerusalem, the spiritual "capital" of all of Judaism. However, Saul's actions were not solely based upon religious motives. The Roman government gave authority to the Sanhedrin to carry out police action among the Jews outside Palestine. Those disciples of Jesus who fled Jerusalem because of the persecution following Stephen's death were Jewish. Consequently they could be tracked down to Jewish synagogues elsewhere.

Saul, together with his traveling companions—probably "policemen" and other persecutors—is traveling towards Damascus when something happens: Suddenly a bright light from above, from heaven (the dwelling place of God), shines forth. The "glory" (Greek *doxa*; Hebrew *kabod*) of flashing light, the eternal and almighty majesty of God which no man can stand to see, surrounds Saul (cf. Exodus 24:16f.; 33:18-23; Ezekiel 1:4f.; Isaiah 6:1f.; 1 Timothy 6:16). Like Ezekiel (Ezekiel 1:28), Saul is forced to the ground. He looks for a human being in the midst of the glorious light (Acts 9:7,17,27), but he does not know who it is. Is it an angel? But out of the glorious light a voice calls out his Jewish name, "Saul, Saul, why do you persecute me?" (Acts 9:4).

Not understanding, Saul asks, "Who are you, Lord?" "I am Jesus, whom you are persecuting," answered the Voice. Now Saul realizes that the divine light is coming from none other than Jesus of Nazareth, who is risen from the dead and is alive and ascended into heaven. There Jesus shares in the glory *doxa* of God. It is none other than the gloried Christ, the Lord *Kurios*, the very one of whom the disciples of Jesus were proclaiming. By persecuting these disciples Saul was persecuting the living and glorified Christ. As Augustine puts it, "The head of the church in heaven has cried out on behalf of his earthly members."

From this moment Saul relinquishes control of his life and person. He is under the command of the Lord: "Arise, and go into the city, and it shall be told thee what thou must do."

No discussion or arguing is possible; Saul is subdued and drafted into the service of his Lord (cf. Ezekiel 2:1f.).

Paul's traveling companions also experienced something on that day. Thus it is clear that this was no "subjective" experience of Paul; rather, it was an external, verifiable event. Those with him stand speechless with fear. They hear the Voice, but they do not see anyone.

Saul rises, but the blinding effects of the light are not just temporary. Blind and helpless he is led by the hand into the city. Once there he lodges with a countryman named Judas, who lives on "the street which is called Straight." Saul's blindness continues for 3 days. This blindness is a sign that the glorified Jesus Christ wants to tell him something. Blinded, Saul is totally dependent and subdued. Neither eating nor drinking Saul fasts, makes atonement, repents, and prays. He thus prepares himself to receive his call, the command of the Lord Jesus. During his fasting and praying Saul receives a vision of a man named Ananias (Hebrew, *Hananya*, the "Lord is compassionate"). Ananias becomes the instrument of the Lord's compassion as he leads Saul into a new life in Christ.

Ananias is himself called to this task, and he answers the call in a prophetic manner (cf. 1 Samuel 3:1f.; Isaiah 6:8; Exodus 3:4). He is an ordinary disciple of Jesus, but he exemplifies the promise of the Day of Pentecost, the fulfillment of Joel's prophecy: "On my servants and on my handmaidens I will pour out in those days of my Spirit, and they shall prophesy" (Acts 2:18). He is instructed by the Lord to visit Paul, but he initially refuses—in typical prophetic character (e.g., Exodus 3:11; Jeremiah 1:6). Ananias has no personal knowledge of Saul, but he has heard rumors about him from many quarters. He heard of his hatred of disciples of Jesus and he knew of his intention in Damascus. But we can probably say that Ananias was not among those disciples scattered from Jerusalem. He was perhaps persuaded by their testimony. The Lord changes Ananias' mind, but it is interesting to note that the Lord does not demand "blind obedience" from His servant; instead, He explains that He chose Saul to be His instrument in the proclamation of His name, the Lord *Kurios* (Philippians 2:11). Saul is thus called to be a witness to the Resurrection to the Gentiles and the Jewish people alike. Part of this call includes the inevitable sufferings preaching Jesus will incur.

Ananias obeys the Lord; he finds Saul and greets him with these words: "Saul, brother!" Next he lays his hands upon him and becomes the Lord's instrument for restoring Paul's sight. Paul is baptized into Christ and is welcomed by the Christians in Damascus. He vividly illustrates that which he writes to the church in Corinth many years later: "If any man be in Christ, he is a new creature: old things are passed away; behold, all things are become new" (2 Corinthians 5:17).

Paul immediately breaks his fast and begins to preach what he is convinced to believe: Jesus from Nazareth is the Messiah, the Son of God. Preaching this throughout the synagogues in Damascus not only creates natural interest among the people, they are amazed that the former persecutor of the Church is now a chief spokesperson. Paul's former association with the Jerusalem church was well known in this Syrian city and so was his previous purpose for going to Damascus.

Those Jews not believing in Jesus responded with their familiar arguments, but Paul was strengthened in spiritual power and wisdom (cf. Stephen, Acts 6:8-10) to prove to them from the Scriptures that the crucified Jesus was indeed the Messiah. The Greek word used to describe Paul's efforts is the term *sumbibazō*, "to demonstrate, prove, instruct." Paul demonstrates that Jesus is Messiah by "uniting" (another meaning of *sumbibazō*) Jesus of Nazareth with the messianic prophecies of Scripture. As a teacher he wins disciples (Acts 9:25).

As time went by the enmity against Paul increased (Acts 9:23). The "Jews" conspire to kill Paul, but the disciples in Damascus thwart their plans and save Paul by letting him down over the wall in a basket. Later editions, such as the United Bible Societies' 3d edition *Greek New Testament* and *Nestle-Aland's 26th edition Novum Testamentum*, read "his disciples" in verse 25. However, the editorial committee's comments upon that verse indicate that it is totally unreasonable to assume the Jewish converts to Christianity would be termed "Paul's disciples." They conclude that in all likelihood the original reading was *auton* instead of *autou*. The transcriptional error, therefore, took place at a very early stage. Later manuscripts, particularly from the Byzantine text type and the so-called Textus Receptus text, read *auton* in an effort to rectify the difficulties. The actual sense in any case is that the disciples took him and let him down over the wall. "The disciples" occurs seven other times absolutely in this chapter (see Metzger, *A Textual Commentary on the Greek New Testament,* 366).

After Paul arrived in Jerusalem, he naturally tried to contact the followers of Jesus there; however, his attempts were understandably met with great suspicion. Barnabas then "took him under his wing" and introduced him to the circle of apostles. At that point he was received into the church. For a period he preached in Jerusalem, especially among the Hellenistic Jews living there. But hatred and plots against his life prompted the church to intervene and to advise Paul to "go underground" in his native city of Tarsus.

(2) *The second account (Acts 22:2-21).* In this version Paul himself recalls what happened to him that caused him to believe that Jesus was Messiah and to be called an apostle. He begins by stating that he is a Jew, not a Gentile who had unlawfully entered the temple. Actually he was born in Tarsus in Cilicia, but he "grew up" in Jerusalem. The verb here, *anatrephō,* can either mean "brought up" (as a child) or "taught" (as a student). This recalls Paul's "sitting at the feet of Gamaliel," the famous rabbi through whom Paul received his instruction in the Law. Under Gamaliel Paul learned the strictness of the Law and he calls himself "zealous" for God.

This "zeal" for God and the Law manifests itself in Paul's persecution of those who declared and followed the only way of salvation, the way of Jesus Christ. A similar account of this occurs also in chapter 9.

Paul's experience on the road to Damascus is described in essentially the same terms as before (chapter 9); here, though, it is noted that the brilliant light flashed around Paul and his companions "about noon," that is, in the middle of the day. Paul describes his companions' experience as seeing the light but not hearing the voice. Furthermore, the Lord's command is more explicit here than in chapter 9. He is instructed to rise and go into Damascus, and "there it shall be told thee of all things which are appointed for thee to do." This involves the divine will for Paul's life, and the use of the verb *tetaktai* (*tassō,* often used in classical Greek for the installing of someone in an office) suggests Paul's impending apostleship.

Ananias' Christian faith is not mentioned in this account, and neither does Paul tell of his dual vision (Acts 9:10,12). Actually Ananias is portrayed as a devout Jew, who was highly respected by his fellow countrymen. His devotion to the Law is also noted. Apparently Paul intends to portray Ananias as first and foremost a reliable witness.

The plan for Paul's life following his "conversion," which according to Acts 9:15 is told to Ananias during his vision, and which presumably Paul learned about at the house of Judas, is relayed to Paul in Acts 22:14. Ananias says, "The God of our fathers hath chosen (cf. Paul's terminology in Galatians 1:15f.) thee (Paul), that thou shouldest know his will (i.e., the counsel of God concerning the salvation of mankind through Jesus Christ; Ephesians 1:9) and see that Just One (i.e., to see Jesus, who is authenticated as God's Messiah by the Resurrection; John 16:10) and shouldest hear the voice of his mouth."

Ananias goes on to say that Paul's experience on the road to Damascus established Paul as a witness to the resurrected Jesus Christ. Thus, what Paul "saw and heard" will be the basis of his testimony to "all men." In other words, Ananias declares by the Spirit that Paul is called to be an apostle. This means an apostolic calling on par with that of the early apostles. He witnessed the Resurrection just as they did, and in the same way he has "seen and heard" Jesus. In every aspect Paul's apostolic calling is identical to those first apostles. Just like them he is called to preach the message "both in Jerusalem, and in all Judea, and in Samaria, and unto the uttermost part of the earth" (cf. 1:8; 4:20). There in the house of Judas, in the street called "Straight," Paul stood on the same foundation and in the same position as the 12 apostles whom Jesus selected from His followers during His earthly ministry (Luke 6:13). One morning, following a night of prayer (Mark 3:13f.; Luke 6:12f.), Jesus chose 12 to be His apostles; now that "morning" came for Paul following 3 days of "darkness" like night.

Since the Risen, exalted Lord summoned Paul, there was no excuse for delay. Ananias makes this plain with his question: "And now why tarriest thou (Paul)? arise, and be baptized, and wash away thy sins, calling on the name of the Lord" (Acts 22:16). The baptismal confession of the most ancient of churches is brief but totally effective: Jesus is Lord *Kurios* (1 Corinthians 12:3; Romans 10:9; 1 John 2:22f.; 4:14f.).

This account offers no other information about what happened in Damascus. Paul's stay with the disciples there, his sermon and teaching in the synagogues, the persecution against him, and his escape are all omitted. Paul begins relating immediately his experience in Jerusalem: in the temple, where in a trance he sees the Risen Lord and hears Him say, "Make haste, and get thee quickly out of Jerusalem; for they will not receive thy testimony concerning me" (Acts 22:18).

At first Paul disagrees with this advice, thinking that he, better than anyone else, had the qualifications to minister in Jerusalem. The Lord interrupts his stalling saying, "Depart: for I will send thee far hence unto the Gentiles" (cf. Ephesians 2:13,17). We should note that Paul's well- intended and logical plans were contradicted by the Lord on other occasions (see, e.g., Acts 16:6f.).

(3) *The third account (Acts 26:1-20).* In the third account of Paul's experience on the Damascus Road we are, for the second time, given Paul's own version. But this second recollection is given in an entirely different context.

Once again Paul recalls his former life. He always lived as a Jew; as a youth he lived in the heart of Judaism, Jerusalem. Everyone should know this. They should also be aware that he was a member of that party in Judaism which emphasized strict obedience to the law of God—the Pharisees. He puts his hope in God's promise to Israel that the Messiah would come and bring salvation, the same hope that many of the "12 tribes" sought to obtain through fulfilling the demands of the Law and through continual temple attendance.

Paul explains that his zeal for this hope and for the temple service caused him to feel obligated to contest the offensive name of Jesus of Nazareth and to battle that power causing divisions in Israel. Paul's descriptions of his actions in this regard do not differ from the earlier accounts.

He explicitly states that he acted under official authority when he arrested, tried, and sentenced to death disciples of Jesus. This does not necessarily mean that Paul was a member of the Sanhedrin. It might suggest that as some kind of "prosecuting attorney" he sentenced those he captured in accordance with the law. Furthermore, he admits that he tortured people in the synagogues. He scourged followers of Jesus with "forty strokes minus one," just as Jesus had predicted (Mark 13:9). He attempted to force believers to blaspheme the name of Jesus, perhaps as some were doing in the Corinthians church later (1 Corinthians 12:3: "Jesus is accursed!"). Paul states that his intense hatred for Christians prompted him to expand his persecution efforts to cities abroad as well as to Damascus.

The heavenly light that surrounded Paul en route to Damascus is said to be brighter than the sun (Acts 26:13). Just like Acts 22:9 it is emphasized that the traveling companions also were illumined by this light. It is also stated that all of them—Paul as well as his fellow travelers—fell to the ground when the light hit them. In contrast only Paul heard the voice of the Risen One. In addition we are told that the voice spoke to him in Hebrew (perhaps Aramaic) and told him, "It is hard for thee to kick against the pricks."

One aspect of this account that stands out is that Ananias' role is omitted. Both chapters 9 and 22, the other accounts, tell that Paul is told to go into Damascus for further instructions. Next they describe how the Lord uses Ananias as his instrument and spokesman. But in chapter 26 Paul, then and there, receives a revelation about his calling from the Lord with these words: "Rise, and stand upon thy feet!" Chapters 9 and 22 indicate more clearly that this involves a prophetic call similar to the call of the Old Testament prophets (see e.g., Ezekiel 2:1; Daniel 10:11).

At this point the Lord chooses Paul to be His servant and witness. He is to testify of what he has seen here—his experience on the road to Damascus. Later he will bear witness to other things that will be revealed to him (cf. the vision in the sanctuary, 22:17-21). Paul's apostolic calling is for the people of Israel as well as the Gentiles (26:17). The prediction that the Lord will deliver him from the hands of "the people" (Israel) and from the Gentiles (cf. Jeremiah 1:8) indicates the opposition and hardship that will be part and parcel of his apostolic call. Ananias was also shown what lay in store for Paul (9:16). Serving the Lord and suffering are inseparably bound together. Suffering is the sign of service (Ephesians 3:13). Just as the prophets of old were persecuted, so too, were the apostles (Luke 11:49f.).

Another indication that the Damascus experience resembles the prophetic vision of call to ministry is that the call of Paul to the Gentiles comes from Isaiah 42:1-7, the first of the servant songs of the Lord. This text indicates that the Servant of the Lord will be a "covenant for the people," i.e., Israel. But it also says he will be a "light unto the Gentiles." Both groups,

Israel and non-Israelites alike, will be made holy and saved by the same grace of God—through faith in the Risen Lord Jesus Christ (cf. Ephesians 2:11-22).

Paul concludes this account of his call by stating to Agrippa the king that he was not disobedient to his divine vision of the glorified Jesus. Such action would have been to resist stubbornly the living God himself. When Paul reflects upon his life he realizes—just like Jeremiah—that he was persuaded and compelled into the Lord's service by God himself (cf. Jeremiah 20:7-12). From the moment of his call to that point, Paul was not his own master; he had a master superior to him—the Lord. As a result of this relationship he was compelled to journey throughout the world preaching the message of the Resurrected Lord—first to Israel, in Damascus as well as Jerusalem and Judea— and then to the "nations."

### Unity and Diversity

As we have seen, there are differences among the three accounts at various points. Some interpreters emphasize these differences so much that one must distinguish between "genuine" and "artificial" elements. As a result the "discrepancies" become "ammunition" in the battle to prove that Acts is a composite of conflicting sources. It is argued that the author did not even know these "discrepancies" existed, but he took them as he received them and joined them carelessly and in haphazard fashion. Finally, some have undertaken to judge the accounts' quality; thus, the account in chapter 26 is considered "the oldest and most valuable." Chapters 9 and 22, on the other hand, are regarded as embellished versions based upon chapter 26 (e.g., Ananias would be considered as "embellishment").

To this assertion it must be immediately responded that none of the differences are of such a magnitude as to pose any serious problem to the integrity of the accounts. All three accounts are essentially the same. Only the manner in which the recollections are given is different. That even eyewitness testimonies of one and the same account seldom, if ever, coincide exactly is widely recognized. One person witnessing an event might perceive something one way, while another might have an entirely different impression. Even one's own recollection of personal experiences may unconsciously differ in terms of vocabulary, length, details, or focus, according to one's audience and the reason for the retelling.

The multiple context and occasion for the giving of the three accounts explain the variation within the telling of Paul's experience on the road to Damascus:

(1) *The context of chapter 9.* In this section Luke recalls the experience as he personally heard it from Paul or as he had received it from a grateful Christian church in Damascus. This has to do with the tradition of the church in Damascus that was carefully received and passed on in accordance with the well-established pattern of tradition. Quite understandably we see the Damascus tradition version contains the information about Ananias (himself from Damascus).

(2) *The context of chapter 22.* This passage centers around Paul's opening defense of himself (he was interrupted before he could continue). From the steps of the Roman army barracks Paul asks permission to speak to the furious shouting crowd that surrounded him. Except for the presence of the Roman officer Paul would have been lynched.

Luke emphasizes twice that the speech was given in Aramaic. Paul stresses his unquestioned Jewish ancestry, his upbringing in Jerusalem, and his studies under Gamaliel, the famous rabbi. This is the context of the speech. The account of Ananias also functions to highlight his close connection with Judaism. Ananias is characterized as a devout man, highly respected among his people.

More importantly for the purpose and audience of this speech, Paul does not mention his stay in Damascus, choosing instead to explain immediately what happened to him upon his return to Jerusalem.

Because of his setting he emphasizes that it was during a worship service in the temple, while he was praying in the sanctuary, that he received his call to undertake a mission to the Gentiles to tell them of the saving grace of Jesus the Messiah. At this time he was also forewarned of the negative reaction his Jerusalem countrymen would have to him and his message. His explicit description of his actions as a persecutor of Christians prior to the Risen One's breaking into his life additionally fits well the context of Jerusalem.

(3) *The context of chapter 26.* An entirely different situation elicits Paul's telling of his Damascus Road experience in chapter 26. On this occasion the setting is the audience room

in the palace of Herod in Caesarea, the residence of Festus the Roman governor; and the language Paul speaks is Greek. The speech has a twofold purpose. In part, Paul appears because Fetus, who has inherited Paul from his predecessor, needs some information in order to carry out his investigation of the matter. But at the same time Paul wants to testify before Herod Agrippa II, the king, who, along with his sister, was welcoming the new governor. The Roman governor perhaps wished to entertain the Jewish King Herod with something he supposes will be of interest to him, since he supervises the temple of the Jews.

Formally the speech is directed to the king. During his opening Paul compliments Agrippa for his intimate knowledge of Jewish affairs, customs, and controversies. Here we note one particular aim of the speech: Paul intends to emphasize his attitude toward the Law. He belongs to the party of the Pharisees and he believes in the messianic promises. In fact, Paul sees his being accused because he takes God's promises seriously. Jesus from Nazareth, the son of a carpenter, was sentenced to death and executed on a Roman cross. That He is the fulfillment of the messianic promises was not just offensive to the Jew; Paul used every means possible to overcome its message in the beginning and he thought he was doing his duty.

Up until the moment the Risen Lord stood alive and glorified before him, Paul kept this attitude. The Lord "stopped him in his tracks" and called him to be His servant and witness. After falling to the ground and believing that Jesus is indeed the Messiah of God, Paul is sent by God throughout the world telling people about Jesus. In time Festus, thinking Paul is insane because of his excitement and ardor, interrupts. It seems natural that Paul's passionate telling of his "conversion" left little room for details about his stay with Ananias. Paul's call is the fulfillment of the expectations of Moses and the prophets: life is proclaimed to the dying: light to those dwelling in darkness; all this is possible only through Jesus Christ, the crucified and Risen Lord.

As we said, the different ways of saying and the different circumstances in which they were told, clearly explain the differences in the accounts. And in regard to this also, one must not overlook the relationship between Paul and Luke. Throughout the years, off and on, Luke worked closely with Paul. This should caution us against perceiving "discrepancies" in the various versions. In the Letter to the Galatians, which was probably not written any later than A.D. 55 at the latest (5 years before Luke wrote Acts), Paul guarantees his truthfulness in telling history (Galatians 1:20). This may suggest the presence of other versions of his experience during his time. But a friend and companion as loyal, dependable, and close to the apostle Paul as Luke would by no means risk inaccuracy. Even less likely is the possibility that he would lie or distort the truth.

None of the variations of the accounts that are called into question by some offer compelling reason for detecting essential disagreement among the accounts.

Often great emphasis is placed upon the fact that in Acts 9:7 Luke writes that companions of Paul "stood" speechless during the experience, while in Acts 26:14 Paul says that "we were all fallen to the earth." Actually everyone was driven to the ground by the awesomeness of the event. Soon, however, Paul's fellow travelers rose to their feet, where they stood confused and ignorant to what took place. Saul, though, continued to lie on the ground, stunned not only by the divine light but by the heavenly Voice that spoke to him as well.

Another point of controversy is that in 9:7 it is recalled that the fellow travelers heard a voice but did not see anyone. Acts 22:9, however, states that they "saw indeed the light, and were afraid; but they heard not the voice of him that spake to me." Both stories tell only that part of the event that the others might have experienced; but the ultimate meaning of the event was only understood by Paul.

From a linguistic standpoint it can be noted that the Greek verb *akouō* ("I hear") can indicate that perception takes place through hearing; thus hearing equals understanding and from that one obeys what is understood. Moreover, the Greek word *phōnē* ("sound") can describe sound in general or an articulate sound, i.e., a voice, speech that is understood. These two meanings may be determined from the context on a grammatical basis. *Phōnē* stands alone 9:7; the fellow travelers heard the *phōnē*, the "sound," but they did not see anyone. They saw no one in the glorious light, although they did hear something, is perhaps the correct understanding.

The other instances of *phōnē* in the account of the Damascus Road are accompanied by an explanatory modifier. Sometimes it is followed by the present participle of *legō* ("I say, I speak"). Thus in 9:4 it is said that Saul "heard a *phōnē* speaking to him"; and in 22:7, "I heard a voice saying unto me" and in 26:14, "I heard a *phōnē* speaking to me in Hebrew." *Phōnē* is often followed by a noun in the genitive case denoting the source of the voice. For example in 22:9: "The companions heard not the *phōnē* of him that spake to me."

A third point of dispute, which we already discussed somewhat, is the three different accounts of Paul's call to be the apostle to the Gentiles. We are told in chapter 9 that Ananias receives a revelation of the Lord's purpose for detaining and manifesting himself to Paul. Chapter 22 concerns Ananias' revelation in Damascus (verses 12-15) as well as Paul's vision in the temple in Jerusalem (verses 17-21). Then in chapter 26 we read that Paul received his call as apostle to the Gentiles on the road to Damascus and that he received it from the Lord himself.

All three accounts unanimously agree that it is the Risen Lord who called Paul into the apostolic outreach to the Gentiles. They also concur that this took place in connection with the experience of Paul on the Damascus Road. The call, however, was confirmed to Paul in various ways. Chapter 9 highlights that Ananias' objections and suspicions about Paul are laid to rest when God declared to Ananias that Saul from Tarsus was a chosen instrument of God to preach the gospel. Chapter 22 reiterates that Ananias confirmed what God had already told Saul about his future work. In that same context we read that Paul, too, received a confirmatory vision of his call in the temple. Chapter 26 informs us that on the road to Damascus Paul was initially called to be an apostle.

As we have seen before, the explanations for this are closely tied to the context in which the events are recounted. That the divine call was put into effect by a human agent like Ananias may have proved of decisive interest for certain Christian readers. Furthermore, that part emerged out of the tradition of the Damascus church, so it fits naturally in this context of chapter 9. This was also important for believers in Jerusalem who may have known Ananias, who was himself Jewish. Naturally Paul would mention this in his speech from the steps of the Roman barracks in Jerusalem (as we read in chapter 22). But to King Agrippa and the governor Festus such information would not be of any interest. Such details would only appear irrelevant and unrelated at the trial in Caesarea.

Some skeptical interpreters reject all three versions. They point to the fact that the historical basis for Paul's call to a mission to the Gentiles is quite obviously Barnabas, who searched him out in order to enlist Paul in the preaching of the gospel to Gentiles in Antioch (11:19-26). They place the three accounts in the category of "anecdotes." Against this reasoning stands Paul's express statement that his call to be the apostle to the Gentiles came through his encounter on the Damascus Road with the Resurrected Lord Jesus Christ.

Nevertheless the call came to Paul in a variety of ways; one might say in stages. This kind of experience is typical of the call of a missionary or a preacher. Many of the Lord's servants can testify that ever since they were children they have known their calling in life. This does not negate the possibility that they can receive additional, personal revelations at a later date. Neither does this prevent their inner call from God from being confirmed by the external call of the church of God. The fact that Ananias told Paul of his call and life's work in no way abolished the call that Paul personally received from the Lord on the Damascus Road—a revelation to which Ananias himself refers (9:17). Neither did Barnabas' invitation to join him in mission work (11:26) or the sending by the church in Antioch (13:2) eliminate the validity of Paul's testimony in Galatians: "I certify you, brethren, that the gospel which was preached of me is not after man. For I neither received it of man, neither was I taught it, but by the revelation of Jesus Christ" (Galatians 1:11f.).

Even though Paul stresses the divine source of his apostolic call as well as his gospel message (he did not consult with "flesh and blood"; Galatians 1:16), this can in no way be interpreted to mean that Paul never incorporated the insights of others' call and "conversion." Just as Peter was sent to Cornelius, Ananias was sent to Saul. Entrance into the fellowship of the Church through baptism always requires a human instrument. Moreover, the fact that Paul received a divine revelation from the Lord did not exclude the possibility that God still spoke to him through the Holy Scriptures, where the Word of the Lord was put into effect by "the holy men of God" (2 Peter 1:20,21). Neither does it remove the possibility that God spoke to Paul through members of His living church.

The Lord indeed sent Ananias to Paul with His message. And more importantly, we know from Paul's own words that the gospel—which Paul strongly perceives as being directly from God—is the holy tradition of the Church. He "passed this on" in his own preaching. Paul summarizes this holy tradition in 1 Corinthians 15:1-11: Christ died for our sins according to the Scriptures; He was buried; He arose; He was seen alive by witnesses. Paul adds to this: "And last of all he was seen of me also"; he assures his readers that his preaching is identical to that of the other apostles: "Therefore whether it were I or they, so we preach and so ye believed."

Paul's use of the terms *receive* and *deliver* is recognized as a use of Jewish technical terminology for sacred tradition. It denotes transmission by word of mouth, which acquired so much significance that the tradition was repeated word for word and in the same form when it was passed on. Furthermore the term *tradition* became equivalent to Christian tradition, such as the gospel tradition, the ritual tradition, the confessional tradition, or the admonition tradition. This applies to ancient Christian tradition since the time of the apostles. Paul did not position himself outside of that tradition. As an apostle and witness to the Resurrected Lord, Paul transmitted the gospel tradition; but the gospel message is first and foremost "from the Lord."

Paul declares emphatically in his letter to the Galatians that his gospel has divine origins. He stresses the "objectivity" of the revelation and apostolic call he received on the road to Damascus. Only the Sovereign Lord is responsible for his call. That did not originate with some internal, psychological, moral, mental, or religious decision on his part. Neither did he acquire his through instruction by others, not even the original apostles. All three versions distinctly testify to this objectivity.

*Psychological Explanations.* The experience on the Damascus Road is interpreted in various ways. Those unwilling to acknowledge any supernatural element in the account often attempt to present a psychological explanation. Paul's encounter with God on the Damascus Road, therefore, is explained as the result or climax of a lengthy process.

With various modifications the account is presented thus:

A young Jewish theologian from Tarsus, during his training in Jerusalem, decides to follow the teachings of the Pharisees. Paul is convinced that righteousness before God can be obtained by fulfilling the Mosaic law and the prescriptions of oral tradition. Such thinking is not merely abstract theory; he takes it seriously, applying it to his religious as well as ordinary existence.

But being honest and having integrity, he has to admit his inability to fulfill this system's obligations. Especially in his struggle to keep the Law's commandments, he recognizes the power of sin. His pangs of conscience increase steadily. The spiritual turmoil intensifies; he recognizes that it is unavoidably true that "cursed is every one that continueth not in all things which are written in the book of the law to do them!" (Galatians 3:10; cf. Deuteronomy 27:26). He feels himself under this curse. The despair implicit in the words of Romans 7:14 and 24: "I am carnal, sold under sin—O wretched man that I am! Who shall deliver me from the body of this death?" echo his own condition that gradually emerged as he tried to adhere to the Pharisaic legalism.

But parallel to this is another thought: From his earliest childhood Paul lived in Jerusalem; indeed, he is "brought up in this city" (Acts 22:3). More precisely we learn from 2 Corinthians 5:16 that Paul actually saw and heard Jesus of Nazareth "after the flesh." This might suggest that Paul knew Jesus from the perspective of his (Paul's) fallen nature. He judged Jesus a blasphemer. Or it might be interpreted to mean according to Jesus' human appearance as a carpenter from Galilee. In either case the person and words of Jesus left an indelible mark on Paul's conscience that he was unable to remove.

In any case, Paul took great offense at the thought that the Man from Galilee might be the Messiah. A poor, homeless Galilean, surrounded by unlearned followers and persons of questionable character such as tax-collectors, prostitutes, and sinners; the One sentenced to death and crucified; the One who died under the curse of the Law; could this man possibly be the promised king for whom Israel had waited throughout its history? To Saul such a thought was utterly absurd and not worth taking seriously.

Moreover, the sect of the Nazarenes, followers of Jesus increased steadily. They believed in Jesus as Messiah, the Son of God, the Lord. They asserted that He had risen from the dead and that He continued to live and act in history. They must have indirectly influenced Paul's thinking.

Soon Saul began to debate with these followers of Jesus the Nazarene. With zeal and because of his formal training, he combats that which he can only interpret as blasphemy. Saul does not come out of the battle unscathed; their application of Scripture and their burning hearts have to make their impression. Stephen's wisdom and spirit could not be resisted. While Saul struggles to stick to his training, the doubt continues to grow. Could those followers of Jesus be correct? Their joy and their openness contrast his own burdensome obligation to the demands of the Law.

Next the doubt drives him from debate to persecution. But as he contests with the Nazarenes it increasingly becomes a wrestling with his own doubt; he does not want to be conquered by their faith. He intensifies his efforts. With the authority of the high priest Paul is present at scourgings, imprisonments, trials, inquiries, and even at the stoning of Stephen, the "blasphemer." In a last effort to conquer his anxiety Paul volunteers to lead an expedition to Damascus, a prominent city containing a large Jewish population, where the members of the Way were gaining more and more adherents. There he hopes to arrest many and bring them to trial. With the authority of the high priest he hurries with other "vigilantes" to carry out the task. Motivated by guilt, doubt, and indecision, Paul tries to get rid of his doubt by planning the tracking, capture, arrest, and trial in Jerusalem of the Nazarenes.

But then, just outside of Damascus, the pressure of his doubts becomes unbearable and a "psychological explosion" devastates him. The disciples of Jesus are correct; Jesus is the Messiah, Kurios! Saul must give in!

Subsequently Paul's thoughts reverse totally. Everything that previously seemed scandalous and offensive to his Pharisaic and scribal character now becomes understandable. It now becomes the foundation to Pauline theology: The Son of God in the form of a servant died on the cross and in so doing He provided salvation which the Law could not afford; He brought righteousness through the forgiveness of sins.

Thus is the "psychological interpretation" of Paul's transformation (with some degree of variation). However, this theory of the spiritual transformation of the apostle Paul, the former Pharisee, has one essential flaw: There is serious lack of any concrete evidence that this is indeed what happened. It is a psychological analysis of a non-existent personage who is more at home in poetry than in Biblical narrative. Such a theory fails to correspond with Luke's portrait of Paul in Acts and with Paul's own story in his letters. In fact, the primary sources give an entirely different portrait!

None of the primary material offers any basis for supposing that such a personality shift took place. Moreover the conjecture that an internal crisis culminated in the Damascus Road experience is a psychological absurdity.

Of course it cannot be ignored that Paul, as a person with deep and sincere feelings, probably did experience internal turmoil in the time prior to his "conversion." Paul knows the Law as "our schoolmaster to bring us unto Christ" (Galatians 3:24), but a passage like Romans 7:7-25 has a depth of understanding that would be foreign to someone not born anew; consequently these are not merely autobiographical confessions of the pre-Christian life. The words reflect that experience, but Paul is evaluating that existence in light of the Spirit's transforming power. It is almost certainly not a picture of normative Christian living, but neither is it strictly the frustration of an unregenerate person living under the Law rather than being born of the Spirit.

It is true that recognition of one's sin comes through the Law (Romans 3:20). But it is also correct that the distorted view of Pharisaic Judaism was not its failure to admit sin; rather, it was their distortion of the Law as a means of attaining righteousness (cf. Luke 18:9). Paul was a Pharisee of the Pharisees. He lived his life in a "clear conscience" not only after becoming a Christian, but during his former life as a Pharisee (Acts 23:1; cf.2 Timothy 1:3). He persecuted the church of God "ignorantly" (1 Timothy 1:13), and he was deeply persuaded in his soul that according to his Jewish obligations he was right and actually doing what God wanted!

According to the standards of Judaism, if anyone could put trust in their "flesh" it was Paul, who considered himself "touching the righteousness which is in the law, blameless" (Philippians 3:4-6). His eagerness and zeal for the tenets and customs of Judaism surpassed many of his peers' (Galatians 1:14). Furthermore, he was pleased with himself. In light of all of this hard evidence it is difficult to endorse the construction of a psychological profile of his conversion. Such an approach lacks any degree of probability. The conversion and apostolic call of Paul was not an internal psychological process. It is a consequence of a divine encounter on the road to Damascus.

*A Visionary Experience?* Another attempt to explain the Damascus Road encounter in psychological terms involves interpreting it as a visionary experience. At this point the question emerges, what precisely constitutes a vision? To some interpreters a "vision" could be a natural experience, explainable as a psychological phenomenon. In this type of experience one hears or sees things in a kind of dream-like state that are not based in reality. This resembles a kind of variation of mental "enlightenment," a change based upon sensation.

Many interpreters quickly adopt such a view of Paul's mental condition. They consider Paul's experience on the Damascus Road a "vision," in the sense that internal factors—not external, or only slightly external—led to the event. This view sees the experience as a fabrication of Paul's conscience; it has no basis in reality. The three accounts recorded by Luke as well as the other Pauline references to his experience on the Damascus Road are likewise catalogued in such terms. Although Paul sees his divine encounter on that day as a starting point of his faith and call, according to this theory Paul should be reckoned among those whom Paul himself condemns: those "intruding into those things which he hath not seen" (Colossians 2:18), those who "make you vain" and speak "a vision of their own heart" (Jeremiah 23:16).

But there is another point of view as to what constitutes a "vision." This might resemble what the prophets term "visions from God" (Ezekiel 1:1), such as the "vision" which foresaw the coming events on the Day of Pentecost (Joel 2:28). This understanding does not deny the supernatural nature. The basis for such genuine, spiritual visions is not the "internal condition of conscience," but the revelation of God.

However, what is perplexing in this case is that this understanding of "vision" does not describe what transpired on the road to Damascus. It is true that Paul was open to the reality of visions. Although he sees nothing inherently advantageous in having visions, he does speak of "visions and revelations of the Lord" (2 Corinthians 12:1). These are particularly associated with a previous experience of being caught up into heaven, where he heard "unspeakable words, which it is not lawful for a man to utter" (2 Corinthians 12:4).

With less hesitation he recalls visions relating to God's guiding him in his ministry. Following his return to Jerusalem after a stay in Damascus, Paul was worshiping in the temple when he saw Jesus in a trance and heard Him speak. Through this vision Paul receives his confirmation as the Apostle to the Gentiles (Acts 22:17-21). He also comes to realize that Gentiles will receive a full share of the inheritance (Ephesians 3:2-7).

A revelation also preceded Paul's visiting the apostles in Jerusalem one final time (Galatians 2:2). Luke also is aware of the "vision in the night"— and who else could have told him of this except the apostle himself?—which summons Paul to Europe (Acts 16:9,10). Later, when Paul almost seems to give up the idea of missionary work in Corinth because of the severe opposition, it was once again a "vision in the night" which the Lord used to tell him to continue without fear, and which prompted him to extend his stay there for 1 ½ years (18:9-11). And at the height of crisis on the voyage to Rome, when everyone had abandoned hope of being saved, Paul encourages them not to be afraid, because that night "the angel of God, whose I am, and whom I serve," stood before him in a vision saying, "fear not" (Acts 27:22-24).

Thus we note that Paul was personally familiar with visions and revelations. Likewise, "vision" forms a part of his experience on the Damascus Road. This type of vision was both visual and audible, i.e., Paul saw somebody as well as he heard the One he saw (Acts 9:4-7,17; 22:14; 26:16). Nonetheless, our primary sources—Luke's Acts and Paul's letters—draw a clear distinction between visionary revelations and the unique encounter Paul had on the way to Damascus. All three accounts make it plain that the "vision" stressed the prophetic nature of the event, as we mentioned before (cf. Exodus 24:16f.; 33:18-23; Isaiah 6:1f.; 42:1-7; Ezekiel 1:4f.; 2:1f.; Jeremiah 1:8; 20:7-12; Daniel 10:11).

A frequently found phrase among many interpreters is "the Damascus experience." Instead, the "Damascus event" might be more appropriate. This distinction would help separate the visionary experiences of Paul from this dramatic event. This would also place his event on the road on a par with the other apostolic witnesses who saw the risen, living Lord Jesus Christ. The entire life of Paul and his attitude before the Damascus event are "separated by a chasm over which no other bridge crosses other than the visible revelation of

Christ" (cf. O. Moe).

Therefore, there is no difference between the revelation of the Risen Saviour to Paul on the road to Damascus and those appearances of Jesus to His disciples in between the Resurrection and the Ascension. Luke introduces his second volume by referring to these appearances as the indication that the beginning of the end has begun. He speaks of chosen apostles to whom Jesus presented himself alive following His death, proving himself alive with many undisputable proofs, being seen by them for 40 days while He spoke to them about the kingdom of God (Acts 1:1-3). By virtue of witnessing these appearances the apostles became "apostles," that is, being a witness to the Resurrection is a requirement for the status of apostle (verse 22). This is precisely what Paul experienced on the road to Damascus.

"Last of all he was seen of me also," says Paul in 1 Corinthians 15:8. By saying this Paul puts himself on a par with Cephas, the Twelve, more than 500 brethren, James, and all the apostles. The reality of the empty tomb, the certainty of the Resurrection confront us here, not just some subjective, internal experience. Here we have assurance that Jesus lives in spite of His death and burial.

As mentioned previously, in 1 Corinthians 15 Paul recalls some of the fundamentals of gospel proclamation. The Word of God has the power to save (verse 2; cf. Acts 11:14: "words, whereby thou and all thy house shall be saved"). The saving Word is the message of the person and work of Christ, His death and resurrection. This announcement of salvation was passed on through the apostolic tradition, by witnesses of the Resurrected Lord. Consequently, any visionary dimension to the Damascus event must be subordinated to the historical reality of Christ's resurrection. Whenever the New Testament speaks of the apostolic tradition that was passed on, it never refers to subjective, internal experience; rather, it always suggests actual historically verifiable facts. The events that took place on the Damascus Road firmly belong to such a historical category.

*The Apostolic Call.* That Paul's apostolic calling is intricately bound to the Damascus event is evident not only from 1 Corinthians 15:1-11, but also from several passages in his letters.

In the salutation of the Epistle to the Romans Paul introduces himself as "called to be an apostle." This call to apostleship is expressly connected with Him, who according to His spiritual origin is "declared to be the Son of God with power, according to the spirit of holiness, by the resurrection from the dead" (Romans 1:4). Through Jesus Christ Paul received grace and his apostleship in order to lead the Gentiles to an obedience of faith (verse 5).

We encounter the same understanding in the first letter to the Corinthian church. With the Damascus event in the background Paul poses the question: "Am I not an apostle? am I not free? have I not seen Jesus Christ our Lord?" (1 Corinthians 9:1).

The resurrection of Christ once again confirms Paul's apostolic calling in Paul's opening words to the Galatians (Galatians 1:1). This theme is picked up again in verse 12, a reference to Paul's reception of the gospel through "the revelation of Jesus Christ." From this basis Paul maintains his equality with Peter as an apostle of Jesus Christ (cf. Galatians 2:8).

Actually, it is only recognizing the background of the Damascus event as the basis for Paul's emphatic conviction of his apostolic call that keeps Paul from sounding arrogant in asserting his authority. Apart from this context Paul's strident assertion of apostleship and its implicit authority would be pointless; or worse yet, a by-product of his own psyche.

## The Missionary Journeys of Paul

*First Missionary Journey (ca. A.D. 45-47) (Acts 13:4 to 14:26).* Paul and Barnabas, along with Mark as their helper, crossed Seleucia and sailed from there to Cyprus, where they preached in the cities of Salamis and Paphos. From there they traveled to the south of Asia Minor. Arriving in Perga in Pamphylia, John Mark departed and returned to Jerusalem. Paul and Barnabas continued to Pisidian Antioch and from there on into Iconium, Lystra, and Derbe. At each stop they began in the Jewish synagogues, but when the Jews rejected their message they also announced the good news to the Gentiles. Paul's missionary strategy was: "to the Jew first and also to the Greek" (Romans 1:16). Their preaching was confirmed by signs and wonders, and in spite of persecution churches were founded.

In many ways the times were "ripe" for the gospel. Already the beginnings of a trend toward monotheism were stirring. This was a direct response to the religious decay of the time. Elsewhere, philosophies—also in response to this decline—developed in the direction of a more religious nature. They stressed high moral ideals in an effort to counter the moral degradation that was sweeping through society at that time (cf. Romans 1). Many saw life as worthless and even despised.

Diaspora Judaism persisted in promoting the Jewish religion during these times, thus it laid much of the groundwork for the early Christian missionary efforts. The well-structured Roman governmental system afforded public peace and security. This, together with a sophisticated public transportation system (some Roman roads are still extant) and a common commercial language throughout the empire, contributed to the "perfect timing" of the early Christian mission. The cities visited by Paul were ordinarily prominent and large, making it possible for Paul to contact a large number of people from a variety of cultures.

*Second Missionary Journey (ca. A.D. 49-52) (Acts 15:36 to 18:22).* This journey began with a sharp conflict between Paul and Barnabas. Barnabas wanted to invite John Mark, while Paul obviously felt hesitant, since John Mark had left them during their first missionary outing (Acts 13:13). Paul opposed having John Mark along and the result was a split in the team. Barnabas and Mark left for Cyprus, while Paul chose Silas (Silvanus) to accompany him. They visited the churches in Syria and Asia Minor. In Lystra Timothy joined them.

Guided by the Holy Spirit, Paul and his coworkers arrived in Troas via Phrygia and Galatia. At this point Luke joins them (cf. the "we" in 16:10f.; perhaps he joined them even earlier). While staying in Troas Paul has a vision in the night instructing him to take his group over to Macedonia. Here they met Philip the evangelist and traveled to Thessalonica and Berea, where they established two new churches in spite of the opposition. Leaving Timothy and Silas behind in Berea, Paul traveled to Athens. There he gave his famous speech on Areopagus (Acts 17:22-31). Although he was interrupted as soon as he mentioned the resurrection of Jesus, some believed in the gospel (verse 34).

Paul spent his longest time in Corinth. Once again he was reunited with his coworkers. At that time Corinth stood as the largest city in Greece as well as being the political capital for that region. Paul's hosts in Corinth were Priscilla and Aquila, who later had a great impact upon the missionary efforts in Ephesus and Rome (Acts 18:24-26; Romans 16:3,4) as "advance men" for Paul. From Corinth Paul wrote his two letters to the church in Thessalonica. First Thessalonians is considered the oldest New Testament document; it is dated with relative certainty around the end of the year A.D. 50 or the first part of A.D. 51. (Some statisticians date the writing of James' Epistle as A.D. 47,48.) These letters express the apostle's deep love for this church (1 Thessalonians 3:6-10; 2 Thessalonians 1:11). Apologizing for having to leave them so quickly (cf. Acts 17:10), Paul now instructs and admonishes them on the basis of Timothy's report (1 Thessalonians 3:6). Next Paul travels to Caesarea via Ephesus; after a visit to Jerusalem he returns to Antioch.

*Third Missionary Journey (ca. A.D. 52-56) (Acts 18:23 to 21:17).* Once again Asia Minor was the primary target of the mission, especially Ephesus, the capital of the province of Asia. It served as a center for Paul's activity for almost 3 years. Prior to his arrival Priscilla and Aquila worked there. In addition to other activity they had guided Apollos, the educated Alexandrian Jew, in the rudiments of the faith. During his efforts in the synagogues Paul came in contact with some disciples of John the Baptist who were perhaps associated with Apollos in some way.

When the opposition forced Paul to vacate the synagogue, he relocated in the school of Tyrannus. In fact, it was so effective that the silversmith of Ephesus, who made shrines for the goddess Diana and sold them, threatened to cause a public riot when they saw their income dwindling as a result of the gospel. The church in Ephesus probably emerged during this period.

Residing in Ephesus Paul composes the Letter to the Galatians. In it he contests the Judaistic tendencies of some. He also writes the first letter to Corinth, where he is faced with both opposition and misconduct by the church. On his journey through Macedonia he sends the second letter to that church, and in it he must defend himself against the false accusations of his opponents. Later, spending the winter in Corinth, he writes the more "theological" Epistle to the Romans. Although he does not know them personally yet, he hopes to meet them at a later time (Romans 15:23,24). From Corinth Paul returns to Jerusalem via the same route as before. He is taking to Jerusalem a "gift" to the mother church (2 Corinthians 8-9).

## The Purpose of Acts

Supposedly the close of Acts provides relatively reliable evidence of when and where the book was written: In Rome during the interval of Paul's waiting for trial before the court of the emperor. It may also be a clue as to the primary intent of the overall writing: to provide a written defense for Paul in his appearance before the Roman high court.

Nevertheless, when a document has the distinction of being a sacred writing and inspired by the Holy Spirit, one must exert caution before jumping to such conclusions. According to God's larger purposes the double volume of Luke-Acts was written in order that the church of God might read it until the end of time. In that case we clearly have something more than a draft of a written legal defense.

On the other side of things, there is not necessarily a contradiction between these tacitly different purposes. Paul sees God's divine purpose at work in his imprisonment and impending trial: that the gospel might be known and that he might defend the gospel (Philippians 1:12f.).

Luke was closely associated with Paul and accompanied him on a number of his journeys, at least on those paths depicted in the so-called "we-passages." If he intended to compose a biography of Paul much more could have been written. From Paul's epistles we learn of other dramatic events not recorded in Acts. Items that a contemporary story might dwell upon are passed over silently.

The question might be raised, what principle of selection did Luke follow when he wrote Acts? A very striking tendency appears to be present here. Throughout his Gospel account Luke emphasizes the Jewish authorities' and the crowd's role in sending Jesus to the cross. But the Roman authorities as well as King Herod do not get blamed. With respect to Acts it is not difficult to see that the book's structure is built around a series of accusations, trials, and vindications by the Roman authorities. This can be detected in the arrest of the apostles in chapters 4 and 5, and had Stephen been tried in accordance with Roman law he would not have been sentenced.

Luke's account of the spread of Christianity from Jerusalem to Judea and Samaria and on into the Greco-Roman world contains much data that would substantiate Paul's case before the Roman court, and that would put the accusations of the Jews in another perspective. The trouble that arose because of Paul's efforts was primarily caused by the Jews themselves. It is the Jews who incited the people against Paul in Antioch in Pisidia (Acts 13), just as it is in Iconium and Lystra (chapter 14). But in Philippi (chapter 16) and Ephesus (chapter 19) the Gentiles assault him. The picture of Jewish enmity reappears in chapter 21: the Jews stir up the crowd against Paul, but the Roman authorities protect him and give him an opportunity to defend himself in a legal court setting. The court does not find Paul guilty, in spite of the accusation of the Jews. Ultimately the court of the Roman emperor will make the final decision in the case.

Acts 17, the account of Paul's appearance on the Areopagus, also contains material that might have proved crucial in his appearance before the emperor's court. Although no judicial proceedings took place on Areopagus, there may have been an official board that monitored the education of youths in Athens.

All of Paul's defenses (speeches) under the different trial circumstances were actually Christian proclamation. The speeches are legal briefs in the form of theology; "testimonies" in the legal as well as the religious sense of that word. Thus Acts focuses much of its attention on these speeches. The larger divine purpose, therefore, is to afford Christians in the generations to come valid testimonies of the origin and message of the Christian faith.

We can regard these speeches as sworn depositions of the authenticity and historicity of Christianity. As a legal document and as Holy Scripture, Acts has one and the same purpose. The reliability of the Christian tradition is presented.

Acts apparently ends very abruptly; however, it may not be as abrupt as it seems. If the book originally served as a draft of Paul's defense before the emperor, then its ending is not as abrupt as it seems. As was mentioned earlier, according to an official edict of the emperor, cases to be heard by the emperor were delayed 1½ years (Eger, 1919, made this conclusion in a study of the Roman legal system). If the accusers failed to appear within the 1½ years, the indictment was dropped. Luke's recalling that Paul preached from his rented quarters for 2 years, and yet not mentioning any appearance before the royal court, suggests that the case was dropped against Paul.

# Manuscripts

## Egyptian Papyri

*Note*: (a) designates the section of the New Testament on which the manuscript is based; (b) designates the century in which it is believed the manuscript was written (using the Roman numerals); (c) provides information on the present location of the manuscript.

p1 (a) Gospels; (b) III; (c) Philadelphia, University of Pennsylvania Museum, no. E2746.

p2 (a) Gospels; (b) VI; (c) Florence, Museo Archeologico, Inv. no. 7134.

p3 (a) Gospels; (b) VI, VII; (c) Vienna, Österreichische Nationalbibliothek, Sammlung Papyrus Erzherzog Rainer, no. G2323.

p4 (a) Gospels; (b) III; (c) Paris, Bibliothèque Nationale, no. Gr. 1120, suppl. 2º.

p5 (a) Gospels; (b) III; (c) London, British Museum, P. 782 and P. 2484.

p6 (a) Gospels; (b) IV; (c) Strasbourg, Bibliothèque de la Université, 351ʳ, 335ᵛ, 379, 381, 383, 384 copt.

p7 (a) Gospels; (b) V; (c) now lost, was in Kiev, library of the Ukrainian Academy of Sciences.

p8 (a) Acts; (b) IV; (c) now lost; was in Berlin, Staatliche Museen, P. 8683.

p9 (a) General Epistles; (b) III; (c) Cambridge, Massachusetts, Harvard University, Semitic Museum, no. 3736.

p10 (a) Paul's Epistles; (b) IV; (c) Cambridge, Massachusetts, Harvard University, Semitic Museum, no. 2218.

p11 (a) Paul's Epistles; (b) VII; (c) Leningrad, State Public Library.

p12 (a) General Epistles; (b) late III; (c) New York, Pierpont Morgan Library, no. G. 3.

p13 (a) General Epistles; (b) III, IV; (c) London, British Museum, P. 1532 (verso), and Florence, Biblioteca Medicea Laurenziana.

p14 (a) Paul's Epistles; (b) V (?); (c) Mount Sinai, St. Catharine's Monastery, no. 14.

p15 (a) Paul's Epistles; (b) III; (c) Cairo, Museum of Antiquities, no. 47423.

p16 (a) Paul's Epistles; (b) III, IV; (c) Cairo, Museum of Antiquities, no. 47424.

p17 (a) General Epistles; (b) IV; (c) Cambridge, England, University Library, gr. theol. f. 13 (P), Add. 5893.

p18 (a) Revelation; (b) III, IV; (c) London, British Museum, P. 2053 (verso).

p19 (a) Gospels; (b) IV, V; (c) Oxford, Bodleian Library, MS. Gr. bibl. d. 6 (P.).

p20 (a) General Epistles; (b) III; (c) Princeton, New Jersey, University Library, Classical Seminary AM 4117 (15).

p21 (a) Gospels; (b) IV, V; (c) Allentown, Pennsylvania, Library of Muhlenberg College, Theol. Pap. 3.

p22 (a) Gospels; (b) III; (c) Glasgow, University Library, MS. 2-x. 1.

p23 (a) General Epistles; (b) early III; (c) Urbana, Illinois, University of Illinois, Classical Archaeological and Art Museum, G. P. 1229.

p24 (a) Revelation; (b) IV; (c) Newton Center, Massachusetts, Library of Andover Newton Theological School.

p25 (a) Gospels; (b) late IV; (c) now lost, was in Berlin, Staatliche Museen, P. 16388.

p26 (a) Paul's Epistles; (b) c. 600; (c) Dallas, Texas, Southern Methodist University, Lane Museum.

p27 (a) Paul's Epistles; (b) III; (c) Cambridge, England, University Library, Add. MS. 7211.

p28 (a) Gospels; (b) III; (c) Berkeley, California, Library of Pacific School of Religion, Pap. 2.

p29 (a) Acts; (b) III; (c) Oxford, Bodleian Library, MS. Gr. bibl. g. 4 (P.).

p30 (a) Paul's Epistles; (b) III; (c) Ghent, University Library, U. Lib. P. 61.

p31 (a) Paul's Epistles; (b) VII; (c) Manchester, England, John Rylands Library, P. Ryl. 4.

p32 (a) Paul's Epistles; (b) c. 200; (c) Manchester England, John Rylands Library, P. Ryl. 5.

p33 (a) Acts; (b) VI; (c) Vienna, Österreichische Nationalbibliothek, no. 190.

p34 (a) Paul's Epistles; (b) VII; (c) Vienna, Österreichische Nationalbibliothek, no. 191.

p35 (a) Gospels; (b) IV (?); (c) Florence, Biblioteca Medicea Laurenziana.

p36 (a) Gospels; (b) VI; (c) Florence, Biblioteca Medicea Laurenziana.

p37 (a) Gospels; (b) III, IV; (c) Ann Arbor, Michigan, University of Michigan Library, Invent. no. 1570.

p38 (a) Acts; (b) c. 300; (c) Ann Arbor, Michigan, University of Michigan Library, Invent. no. 1571.

p39 (a) Gospels; (b) III; (c) Chester, Pennsylvania, Crozer Theological Seminary Library, no. 8864.

p40 (a) Paul's Epistles; (b) III; (c) Heidelberg, Universitätsbibliothek, Inv. Pap. graec. 45.

p41 (a) Acts; (b) VIII; (c) Vienna, Österreichische Nationalbibliothek, Pap. K.7541-8.

p42 (a) Gospels; (b)VII, VIII; (c) Vienna, Österreichische Nationalbibliothek, KG 8706.

p43 (a) Revelation; (b) VI, VII; (c) London, British Museum, Pap. 2241.

p44 (a) Gospels; (b) VI, VII; (c) New York, Metropolitan Museum of Art, Inv. 14-1-527.

p45 (a) Gospels, Acts; (b) III; (c) Dublin, Chester Beatty Museum; and Vienna, Osterreichische Nationalbibliothek, P. Gr. Vind. 31974.

p46 (a) Paul's Epistles; (b) c. 200; (c) Dublin, Chester Beatty Museum, and Ann Arbor, Michigan, University of Michigan Library, Invent. no. 6238.

p47 (a) Revelation; (b) late III; (c) Dublin, Chester Beatty Museum.

p48 (a) Acts; (b) late III; (c) Florence, Museo Medicea Laurenziana.

p49 (a) Paul's Epistles; (b) late III; (c) New Haven, Connecticut, Yale University Library, P. 415.

p50 (a) Acts; (b) IV, V; (c) New Haven, Connecticut, Yale University Library, P. 1543.

p51 (a) Paul's Epistles; (b) c. 400; (c) London British Museum.

p52 (a) Gospels; (b) early II; (c) Manchester, John Rylands Library, P. Ryl. Gr. 457.

p53 (a) Gospels, Acts; (b) III; (c) Ann Arbor, Michigan, University of Michigan Library, Invent. no. 6652.

p54 (a) General Epistles; (b) V, VI; (c) Princeton, New Jersey, Princeton University Library, Garrett Depos. 7742.

p55 (a) Gospels; (b) VI, VII; (c) Vienna, Österreichische Nationalbibliothek, P. Gr. Vind. 26214.

p56 (a) Acts; (b) V, VI; (c) Vienna, Österreichische Nationalbibliothek, P. Gr. Vind. 19918.

p57 (a) Acts; (b) IV, V; (c) Vienna, Österreichische Nationalbibliothek, P. Gr. Vind. 26020.

p58 (a) Acts; (b) VI; (c) Vienna, Österreichische Nationalbibliothek, P. Gr. Vind. 17973, 36133[54], and 35831.

p59 (a) Gospels; (b) VII; (c) New York, New York University, Washington Square College of Arts and Sciences, Department of Classics, P. Colt. 3.

p60 (a) Gospels; (b) VII; (c) New York, New York University, Washington Square College of Arts and Sciences, Department of Classics, P. Colt. 4.

p61 (a) Paul's Epistles; (b) c. 700; (c) New York, New York University, Washington Square College of Arts and Sciences, Department of Classics, P. Colt. 5.

p62 (a) Gospels; (b) IV; (c) Oslo, University Library.

p63 (a) Gospels; (b) c. 500; (c) Berlin, Staatliche Museen.

p64 (a) Gospels; (b) c. 200; (c) Oxford, Magdalen College Library.

p65 (a) Paul's Epistles; (b) III; (c) Florence, Biblioteca Medicea Laurenziana.

p66 (a) Gospels; (b) c. 200; (c) Cologny/Genève, Bibliothèque Bodmer.

p67 (a) Gospels; (b) c. 200; (c) Barcelona, Fundación San Lucas Evangelista, P. Barc. 1.

p68 (a) Paul's Epistles; (b) VII (?); (c) Leningrad, State Public Library, Gr. 258.

p69 (a) Gospels; (b) III; (c) place (?)

p70 (a) Gospels; (b) III; (c) place (?)

p71 (a) Gospels; (b) IV; (c) place (?)

p72 (a) General Epistles; (b) III, IV; (c) Cologny/Genève, Bibliothèque Bodmer.

p73 (a) Gospels; (b)—; (c) Cologny/Genève, Bibliothèque Bodmer.

p74 (a) Acts, General Epistles; (b) VII; (c) Cologny/Genève, Bibliothèque Bodmer.

p75 (a) Gospels; (b) early III; (c) Cologny/Genève, Bibliothèque Bodmer.

p76 (a) Gospels; (b) VI; (c) Vienna, Österreichische Nationalbibliothek, P. Gr. Vind. 36102.

**Major Codices**

| | |
|---|---|
| 01, aleph: | Sinaiticus |
| 02, A: | Alexandrinus |
| 03, B: | Vaticanus |
| 04, C: | Ephraemi Rescriptus |
| 05, D: | Bezae Cantabrigiensis |
| 06, E: | Claromontanus |

## Majuscules

| No. | Contents | Century |
|---|---|---|
| 01, *aleph* | Total New Testament | 4th |
| 02, A | Total New Testament | 5th |
| 03, B | New Testament, Revelation | 4th |
| 04, C | Total New Testament | 5th |
| 05, D | Gospels, Acts | 6th |
| 06, D | Paul's Epistles | 6th |
| 07, E | Gospels | 8th |
| 08, E | Acts | 6th |
| 09, F | Gospels | 9th |
| 010, F | Paul's Epistles | 9th |
| 011, G | Gospels | 9th |
| 012, G | Paul's Epistles | 9th |
| 013, H | Gospels | 9th |
| 015, H | Paul's Epistles | 6th |
| 016, I | Paul's Epistles | 5th |
| 017, K | Gospels | 9th |
| 018, K | Acts, Paul's Epistles | 9th |
| 019, L | Gospels | 8th |
| 020, L | Acts, Paul's Epistles | 9th |
| 021, M | Gospels | 9th |
| 022, N | Gospels | 6th |
| 023, O | Gospels | 6th |
| 024, P | Gospels | 6th |
| 025, P | Acts, Paul's Epistles, Revelation | 9th |
| 026, Q | Gospels | 5th |
| 028, S | Gospels | 10th |
| 029, T | Gospels | 9th |
| 030, U | Gospels | 9th |
| 031, V | Gospels | 9th |
| 032, W | Gospels | 5th |
| 033, X | Gospels | 10th |
| 034, Y | Gospels | 9th |
| 036, | Gospels | 10th |
| 037, | Gospels | 9th |
| 038, | Gospels | 9th |
| 039, | Gospels | 9th |
| 040, | Gospels | 6th-8th |
| 041, | Gospels | 9th |
| 042, | Gospels | 6th |
| 043, | Gospels | 6th |
| 044, | Gospels, Acts, Paul's Epistles | 8th-9th |

In addition to these manuscripts identified by a letter (letter uncials), there are 200 other numbered majuscule manuscripts. Even though most of these manuscripts are very valuable, there is not enough room to list them all. Our apparatus gives the official numbers, 046, 047 etc.

## Minuscules

There are about 2800 of these. A total classification of these is only possible in specialized literature dealing with textual criticism.

## Early Versions

| Abbrev. | Name | Century |
|---|---|---|
| it | Itala, early Latin | II-IV |
| vul | Vulgate, Latin | IV-V |
| old syr | Old Syrian | II-III |
| syr pesh | Peshitta | V |
| got | Gothic | IV |
| arm | Armenian | IV-V |
| geo | Georgian | V |
| cop | Coptic | VI |
| nub | Nubian | VI |
| eth | Ethiopian | VI |

# Early Church Fathers

*Ambrosius,* deacon of Alexandria, and intimate friend of Origen, died 250.

*Athanasius,* was bishop of Alexandria, 326; died in 373.

*Athenagoras,* a Christian philosopher of Athens, flourished in 178.

*Augustine,* 354-430.

*Basil* the Great, bishop of Caesarea, born in Cappadocia, 329; died 379.

*Bede,* the Venerable, born 673.

*Chrysostom,* bishop of Constantinople, born 344; died 407.

*Clemens Alexandrinus,* Clement of Alexandria, the preceptor of Origen, died 212.

*Clemens Romanus,* Clement of Rome, *supposed* to have been fellow laborer with Peter and Paul, and bishop of Rome, 91.

*Cyprian,* bishop of Carthage, in 248; was martyred, 258.

*Cyrillus Alexandrinus,* this Cyril was patriarch of Alexandria 412; died 444.

*Cyrillus Hierosolymitanus,* Cyril, bishop of Jerusalem, was born 315; died 386.

*Ephraim Syrus,* Ephraim the Syrian, was deacon of Edessa; and died 373.

*Eusebius* of Caesarea, c.260-340.

*Gregory* the Great, bishop of Rome, flourished in 590.

*Gregory Thaumaturgus,* was a disciple of Origen, and bishop of Neocaesarea in 240.

*Hippolytus,* a Christian bishop, flourished 230; died 235.

*Ignatius,* bishop of Antioch, was martyred about 110.

*Irenaeus,* disciple of Polycarp; born in Greece about 140; martyred 202.

*Jerome,* also called Hieronymus, one of the most eminent of the Latin fathers; author of the translation of the Scriptures called the Vulgate; born about 342, died in 420.

*Justin Martyr,* a Christian philosopher, martyred 165.

*Origen,* one of the most eminent of the Greek fathers, 185-254.

*Tertullian,* a most eminent Latin father, died about 220.

# Books of the New and Old Testament and the Apocrypha

## New Testament Books

Matthew
Mark
Luke
John
Acts
Romans
1 Corinthians
2 Corinthians
Galatians
Ephesians
Philippians
Colossians
1 Thessalonians
2 Thessalonians
1 Timothy
2 Timothy
Titus
Philemon
Hebrews
James
1 Peter
2 Peter
1 John
2 John
3 John
Jude
Revelation

## Old Testament Books

Genesis
Exodus
Leviticus
Numbers
Deuteronomy
Joshua
Judges
Ruth
1 Samuel
2 Samuel
1 Kings
2 Kings
1 Chronicles
2 Chronicles
Ezra
Nehemiah
Esther
Job
Psalms
Proverbs
Ecclesiates
Song of Solomon
Isaiah
Jeremiah
Lamentations
Ezekiel
Daniel
Hosea
Joel
Amos
Obadiah
Jonah
Micah
Nahum
Habakkuk
Zephaniah
Haggai
Zechariah
Malachi

## Books of the Apocrypha

1 & 2 Esdras
Tobit
Judith
Additions to Esther
Wisdom of Solomon
Ecclesiasticus or the Wisdom of Jesus Son of Sirach
Baruch
Prayer of Azariah and the Song of the Three Holy Children
Susanna
Bel and the Dragon
The Prayer of Manasses
1–4 Maccabees

# Bibliography


## Modern Greek Texts

Aland, K. et al. in cooperation with the Institute for New Testament Textual Research. *The Greek New Testament.* 2nd ed. London: United Bible Societies. 1968.

Aland, K. et al. in cooperation with the Institute for New Testament Textual Research. *The Greek New Testament.* 3rd ed. New York: United Bible Societies. 1975.

Nestle, E. and K. Aland. *Novum Testamentum Graece.* 25th ed. Stuttgart: Deutsche Bibelstiftung. 1963.

Nestle, E. and K. Aland. et al. *Novum Testamentum Graece.* 26th ed. Stuttgart: Deutsche Bibelstiftung. 1979.

## General Reference Sources with Abbreviations

**BAGD**
Bauer, W., W.F. Arndt and F.W. Gingrich. *A Greek-English Lexicon of the New Testament and Other Early Christian Literature.* 2nd ed. Revised and augmented by F.W. Gingrich and F.W. Danker. Chicago: University of Chicago Press. 1958.

**NIDNTT**
Brown, Colin. ed. *The New International Dictionary of New Testament Theology.* 4 vols. Grand Rapids: Zondervan. 1975.

**TDNT**
Kittel, G. and G. Friedrich. *Theological Dictionary of the New Testament.* Trans. by G.W. Bromiley. 10 vols. Grand Rapids: Wm.B. Eerdmans. 1964-72.

**LSJ**
Liddell, H.G. and R. Scott. *A Greek-English Lexicon.* 9th ed., Ed. by H. Stuart Jones and R. McKenzie. Oxford: Clarendon. 1940.

**M-M**
Moulton, J.H. and G. Milligan. *The Vocabulary of the Greek Testament Illustrated from the Papyri and Other Non-Literary Sources.* London: Hodder and Stoughton. 1914-30. Reprint. Grand Rapids: Wm. B. Eerdmans. 1985.

## General Bibliography


Alexander, J. A. *Commentary on the Acts of the Apostles.* 1857. Reprint. London: Banner of Truth Trust. 1979.

Bruce, F. F. *Acts. The New International Commentary on the New Testament.* Ed. by F. F. Bruce. Grand Rapids: William B. Eerdmans Publishing Co. 1974.

Carter, Charles, and Ralph Earle. *The Acts of the Apostles.* Grand Rapids: Zondervan Publishing House. 1959.

DeWitt, Norman W. *St. Paul and Epicurus.* Minneapolis: University of Minnesota Press. 1954.

Earle, Ralph. *The Acts of the Apostles.* Kansas City: Beacon Hill Press. 1965.

Eusebius. *Ecclesiastical History.* Trans. by Kirsopp Lake. Loeb Classical Library. Cambridge: Harvard University Press. 1965.

Gordon, Cyrus H. *The Ancient Near East.* 3d ed. New York: W. W. Norton and Company, Inc. 1965.

Guthrie, Donald. *The Apostles.* Grand Rapids: Zondervan Publishing House. 1975.

Gutzke, Manford G. *Plain Talk on Acts.* Grand Rapids: Zondervan Publishing House. 1966.

Hackett, H. B. *A Commentary on the Acts of the Apostles.* Philadelphia: American Baptist Publication Society. 1882.

Haenchen, Ernst. *The Acts of the Apostles: A Commentary.* Trans. by Bernard Noble and Gerald Shinn. Philadelphia: The Westminster Press. 1971.

Harnack, Adolf. *The Acts of the Apostles.* Trans. by J. R. Wilkinson. London: Williams and Norgate. 1909.

Harrison, E. F. *Acts: The Expanding Church.* Chicago: Moody Press. 1975.

Horton, Stanley M. *What the Bible Says about the Holy Spirit.* Springfield, MO: Gospel Publishing House. 1976.

Lenski, P. C. H. *The Interpretation of the Acts of the Apostles.* Columbus, Ohio: The Wartburg Press. 1940.

Longenecker, R. N. *The Acts of the Apostles.* In *John–Acts.* Vol. 9 of *The Expositor's Bible Commentary.* Ed. by Frank E. Gaebelein. Grand Rapids: Zondervan Publishing House. 1981.

Longenecker, R. N. *Paul, Apostle of Liberty.* Grand Rapids: Baker Book House. 1976.

Metzger, Bruce M. *A Textual Commentary on the Greek New Testament.* 3d ed. New York: United Bible Societies. 1971.

Newman, B. M., and Eugene Nida. *A Translators Handbook on the Acts of the Apostles.* New York: United Bible Societies. 1972.

Pache, Rene. *The Person and Work of the Holy Spirit.* Rev. ed. Chicago: Moody Press. 1966.

Packer, J. W. *Acts of the Apostles.* Cambridge: Cambridge University Press. 1975.

Pink, A. W. *The Holy Spirit.* Grand Rapids: Baker Book House. 1970.

Rackham, Richard B. *The Acts of the Apostles.* Cambridge: Cambridge University Press. 1975.

Ramsay, W. M. *The Cities of Saint Paul.* 1901. Reprint. Grand Rapids: Baker Book House. 1964.

Rutherford, John. "Partition, the Middle Wall of." In *The International Standard Bible Encyclopedia*. Ed. by James Orr. 4 vols. Grand Rapids: William B. Eerdmans Publishing Co. 1943.

Thomas, David. *Acts of the Apostles.* 1870. Reprint. Grand Rapids: Baker Book House. 1956.

Willis, Barnstone, ed. *The Other Bible.* New York: Harper and Row. 1984.

# Various Versions Acknowledgments

Scripture quotations found in Various Versions were taken from the following sources with special permission as indicated. The sources listed may be found in one or all of the volumes of THE COMPLETE BIBLICAL LIBRARY.

**AB**

Fitzmyer, Joseph A., S.J., trans. *The Gospel According to Luke I-IX, (Anchor Bible).* New York: Doubleday & Company, Inc. 1985. Reprinted with permission. © 1981, 1985.

**ADAMS**

Adams, Jay E. *The Christian Counselor's New Testament: a New Translation in Everyday English with Notations, Marginal References, and Supplemental Helps.* Grand Rapids, MI: Baker Book House. 1977. Reprinted with permission. © 1977.

**ALBA**

Condon, Kevin. *The Alba House New Testament.* Staten Island, NY: Alba House, Society of St. Paul copublished with The Mercier Press Ltd. 1972. Reprinted with permission. *The Mercier New Testament.* Cork, Ireland: The Mercier Press Ltd. © 1970.

**ALFORD**

Alford, Henry. *The New Testament of Our Lord and Saviour Jesus Christ: After the Authorized Version.* Newly compared with the original Greek, and revised. London: Daldy, Isbister. 1875.

**AMPB**

*The Amplified Bible.* Grand Rapids, MI: Zondervan Publishing House. 1958. Reprinted with permission from the *Amplified New Testament.* © The Lockman Foundation. 1954, 1958.

**ASV**

*(American Standard Version) The Holy Bible Containing the Old and New Testaments:* Translated out of the original tongues; being the version set forth A.D. 1611, compared with the most ancient authorities and rev. A.D. 1881-1885. New York: Thomas Nelson Inc., Publishers. 1901, 1929.

**BARCLAY**

Barclay, William. *The New Testament: A New Translation.* Vol. 1, *The Gospels and the Acts of the Apostles.* London: William Collins Sons & Co. Ltd. 1968. Reprinted with permission. © 1968.

**BB**

*The Basic Bible: Containing the Old and New Testaments in Basic English.* New York: Dutton. 1950. Reprinted with permission. *The Bible In Basic English.* © Cambridge University Press. 1982.

**BECK**

Beck, William F. *The New Testament in the Language of Today.* St. Louis, MO: Concordia Publishing House. 1963. Reprinted with permission. © Mrs. William Beck, *An American Translation.* Leader Publishing Company: New Haven, MO.

**BERKELEY**

*The Holy Bible: the Berkeley Version in Modern English Containing the Old and New Testaments.* Grand Rapids: Zondervan Publishing House. 1959. Used by permission. © 1945, 1959, 1969.

**BEZA**

*Iesv Christi, D.N. Novum Testamentum.* Geneva: Henricus Stephanus. 1565.

**BLACKWELDER**

Blackwelder, Boyce W. *The Four Gospels: An Exegetical Translation.* Anderson, IN: Warner Press, Inc. 1980.

**BLACKWELL**

Blackwell, Boyce W. *Letters from Paul: An Exegetical Translation.* Anderson, IN: Warner Press, 1971.

**BRUCE**

Bruce, F.F. *The Letters of Paul: An Expanded Paraphrase.* Printed in Parallel with the RV. Grand Rapids: William B. Eerdmans Publishing Co. 1965. Reprinted with permission. F.F. Bruce. *An Expanded Paraphrase of the Epistles of Paul.* The Paternoster Press: Exeter, England. © 1965, 1981.

**CAMPBELL**

Campbell, Alexander. *The Sacred Writings of the Apostles and Evangelists of Jesus Christ commonly styled the New Testament:* Translated from the original Greek by Drs. G. Campbell, J. Macknight & P. Doddridge with prefaces, various emendations and an appendix by A. Campbell. Grand Rapids: Baker Book House. 1951 reprint of the 1826 edition.

**CKJB**

*The Children's 'King James' Bible: New Testament.* Translated by Jay Green. Evansville, IN: Modern Bible Translations, Inc. 1960.

**CLEMENTSON**

Clementson, Edgar Lewis. *The New Testament: a Translation.* Pittsburg, PA: Evangelization Society of Pittsburgh Bible Institute. 1938.

**CONCORDANT**

*Concordant Version: The Sacred Scriptures:* Designed to put the Englished reader in possession of all the vital facts of divine revelation without a former knowledge of Greek by means of a restored Greek text. Los Angeles: Concordant Publishing Concern. 1931. Reprinted with permission. *Concordant Literal New Testament.* Concordant Publishing Concern. 15570 Knochaven Road, Canyon Country, CA 91351. © 1931.

**CONFRATERNITY**

*The New Testament of Our Lord and Savior Jesus Christ:* Translated from the Latin Vulgate, a revision of the Challoner-Rheims Version edited by Catholic scholars under the patronage of the Episcopal Committee of the Confraternity Christian Doctrine. Paterson, NJ: St. Anthony Guild Press. 1941. Reprinted with permission by the Confraternity of Christian Doctrine, Washington, DC. © 1941.

**CONYBEARE**

Conybeare, W.J. and Rev. J.S. Howson D.D. *The Life and Epistles of St. Paul.* Rev. ed. 2 vols. London: Longman, Green, Longman, and Roberts. 1862.

**COVERDALE**

*The New Testament: The Coverdale Version.* N.p. 1535(?), 1557.

**CRANMER**

Cranmer or Great Bible. *The Byble in Englyshe,...* translated after the veryte of the Hebrue and Greke text, by ye dilygent studye of dyverse excellent learned men, expert in the forsayde tonges. Prynted by Richard Grafton & Edward Whitchurch. Cum privilegio ad Imprimendum solum. 1539.

**DARBY**

Darby, J.N. *The Holy Scriptures A New Translation from the Original Languages.* Lansing, Sussex, England: Kingston Bible Trust. 1975 reprint of the 1890 edition.

**DOUAY**

*The Holy Bible containing the Old and New Testaments:* Translated from the Latin Vulgate... and with the other translations diligently compared, with annotations, references and an historical and chronological index. New York: Kennedy & Sons. N.d.

**ET**

Editor's Translation. Gerard J. Flokstra, Jr., D.Min.

**EVERYDAY**

*The Everyday Bible: New Century Version.* Fort Worth: Worthy Publishing. 1987. Reprinted with permission. World Wide Publications. *The Everyday Study Bible: Special New Testament Study Edition.* Minneapolis: World Wide Publications. 1988.

**FENTON**

Fenton, Farrar. *The Holy Bible in Modern English.* London: A. & C. Black. 1944 reprint of the 1910 edition.

**GENEVA**

*The Geneva Bible:* a facsimile of the 1560 edition. Madison, WI: University of Wisconsin Press. 1969.

**GENEVA (1557)**

*The Nevve Testament of Ovr Lord Iesus Christ.* Printed by Conrad Badius. 1557.

**GOODSPEED**

*The Bible: An American Translation.* Translated by Edgar J. Goodspeed. Chicago: The University of Chicago Press. 1935.

**HANSEN**

Hansen, J.W. *The New Covenant.* 2nd. ed. 2 vols. Boston: Universalist Publishing House. 1888.

**HBIE**

*The Holy Bible containing the Old and New Testaments:* an improved edition (based in part on the Bible Union Version). Philadelphia: American Baptist Publication Society. 1913.

**HISTNT**

*The Historical New Testament:* Being the literature of the New Testament arranged in the order of its literary growth and according to the dates of the documents: a new translation by James Moffatt. Edinburgh: T & T Clark. 1901.

**HOERBER**

Hoerber, Robert G. *Saint Paul's Shorter Letters.* Fulton, MO: Robert G. Hoerber. 1954.

**JB**

*TheJerusalem Bible.* Garden City, NY: Darton, Longman & Todd, Ltd. and Doubleday and Co, Inc. 1966. Reprinted by permission of the publisher. © 1966.

**KJII**

*King James II New Testament.* Grand Rapids: Associated Publishers and Authors, Inc. © Jay P. Green. 1970.

**KLEIST**

*The New Testament Rendered from the Original Greek with Explanatory Notes.* Translated by James A. Kleist and Joseph L. Lilly. Milwaukee: The Bruce Publishing Company. 1954.

**KLINGENSMITH**

Klingensmith, Don J. *Today's English New Testament.* New York: Vantage Press. 1972. Reprinted by permission of author. © Don J. Klingensmith, 1972.

**KNOX**

Knox, R.A. *The New Testament of our Lord and Saviour Jesus Christ: A New Translation.* New York: Sheen and Ward. 1946. Reprinted by permission of The Liturgy Commission.

**LAMSA**

Lamsa, George M. *The Holy Bible From Ancient Eastern Text.* Translated from original Aramaic sources. Philadelphia: Holman. 1957. From *The Holy Bible From Ancient Eastern Text* by George Lamsa. © 1933 by Nina Shabaz; renewed 1961 by Nina Shabaz. © 1939 by Nina Shabaz; renewed 1967 by Nina Shabaz. © 1940 by Nina Shabaz; renewed 1968 by Nina Shabaz. © 1957 by Nina Shabaz. Reprinted by permission of Harper & Row, Publishers, Inc.

**LATTIMORE**

Lattimore, Richmond. *Four Gospels and The Revelation:* Newly translated from the Greek. New York: Farrar, Straus, Giroux, Inc. 1979. Reprinted by permission of the publisher. © Richard Lattimore, 1962, 1979.

**LAUBACH**

Laubach, Frank C. *The Inspired Letters in Clearest English.* Nashville: Thomas Nelson Publishers. 1956.

**Lilly**

*The New Testament Rendered from the Original Greek with Explanatory Notes.* Translated by James A. Kleist and Joseph L. Lilly. Milwaukee: The Bruce Publishing Company. 1954.

**LIVB**

*The Living Bible: Paraphrased.* Wheaton, IL: Tyndale House Publishers. 1973. Used by permission of the publisher. © Tyndale House Publishers. 1971.

**LOCKE**

Locke, John. *A Paraphrase and Notes on the Epistles of St. Paul to the Galatians, First and Second Corinthians, Romans, and Ephesians:* To which is prefixed an essay for the understanding of St. Paul's Epistles. Cambridge, England: Brown, Shattuck; Boston: Hilliard, Gray, and Co. 1832.

**MACKNIGHT**

Macknight, James. *New Literal Translation:* From the original Greek, of all the Apostolical Epistles, with a commentary, and notes, philological, critical, explanatory, and practical. Philadelphia: Wardkem. 1841.

**MACKNIGHT**

Macknight, James. *Harmony of the Four Gospels:* 2 vols. in which the natural order of each is preserved, with a paraphrase and notes. London: Longman, Hurst, Rees, Orme and Brown. 1819.

**MJV**

*English Messianic Jewish Version.* May Your Name Be Inscribed in the Book of Life. Introduction and footnotes by The Messianic Vision. Washington, D.C.: © 1981. Bible text by Thomas Nelson, Inc. Nashville: Thomas Nelson Publishing Company. © 1979.

**MLNT**

*The Modern Language New Testament: The New Berkeley Version.* Grand Rapids: Zondervan Publishing House. 1969.

**MOFFATT**

*The New Testament: A New Translation.* New York: Harper and Row Publishers, Inc.; Kent, England: Hodder and Stoughton Ltd. c.1912. Reprinted with permission.

**MONTGOMERY**

Montgomery, Helen Barrett. *The Centenary Translation of the New Testament:* Published to signalize the completion of the first hundred years of work of the American Baptist Publication Society. Philadelphia: American Baptist Publishing Society. 1924. Used by permission of Judson Press. *The New Testament in Modern English* by Helen Barrett Montgomery. Valley Forge: Judson Press. 1924, 1952.

**MURDOCK**

Murdock, James. *The New Testament: The Book of the Holy Gospel of our Lord and Our God, Jesus the Messiah:* A literal translation from the Syriac Peshito version. New York: Stanford and Swords. 1851.

**NAB**

*The New American Bible.* Translated from the original languages with critical use for all the ancient sources by members of the Catholic Biblical Association of America. Encino, California: Benzinger. 1970.

**NASB**

*The New American Standard Bible.* Anaheim, CA: Lockman Foundation. 1960. Reprinted with permission. © The Lockman Foundation 1960, 1962, 1963, 1968, 1971, 1972, 1973, 1975, 1977.

**NCV**

*The Word: New Century Version New Testament.* Fort Worth, TX: Sweet Publishing. 1984.

**NEB**

*The New English Bible: New Testament.* Cambridge, England: Cambridge University Press. 1970. Reprinted by permission. © The Delegates of the Oxford University Press and The Syndics of the Cambridge University Press 1961, 1970.

**NIV**

*The Holy Bible: New International Version.* Grand Rapids: Zondervan Publishing House. 1978. Used by permission of Zondervan Bible Publishers. © 1973, 1978, International Bible Society.

**NKJB**

*The New King James Bible, New Testament.* Nashville, TN: Royal Pub. 1979. Reprinted from *The New King James Bible-New Testament.* © 1979, 1982, Thomas Nelson, Inc., Publishers.

**NLT**

*The New Life Testament.* Translated by Gleason H. Ledyard. Canby, Oregon: Christian Literature Foundation. 1969.

**NOLI**

Noli, S. *The New Testament of Our Lord and Savior Jesus Christ:* Translated into English from the Approved Greek Text of the Church of Constantinople and the Church of Greece. Boston: Albanian Orthodox Church in America. 1961.

**NORLIE**

Norlie, Olaf M. *Simplified New Testament: In plain English for today's reader: A new translation from the Greek.* Grand Rapids: Zondervan Publishing House. 1961. Used by permission. © 1961.

**NORTON**

Norton, Andrews. *A Translation of the Gospels with Notes.* Boston: Little, Brown. 1856.

**NOYES**

Noyes, George R. *The New Testament:* Translated from the Greek text of Tischendorf. Boston: American Unitarian Association. 1873.

**NTPE**

*The New Testament: A New Translation in Plain English.* Translated by Charles Kingsley Williams. Grand Rapids: Wm. B. Eerdmans Publishing Company. 1963.

**PANIN**

Panin, Ivan., ed. *The New Testament from the Greek Text as Established by Bible Numerics.* Toronto, Canada: Clarke, Irwin. 1935.

**PHILLIPS**

Phillips, J.B., trans. *The New Testament in Modern English.* Rev. ed. New York: Macmillan Publishing Company, Inc. 1958. Reprinted with permission. © J.B. Phillips 1958, 1960, 1972.

**PNT**

*A Plain Translation of the New Testament by a Student.* Melbourne, Australia: McCarron, Bird. 1921.

**RHEIMS**

*The Nevv Testament of Iesus Christ.* Translated faithfully into English, out of the authentical Latin, . . . In the English College of Rhemes. Printed at Rhemes by Iohn Fogny. Cum privilegio. 1582.

**RIEU**

Rieu, E.V. *The Four Cospels.* London: Penguin Books Ltd. 1952. Reprinted with permission. © E.V. Rieu, 1952.

**ROTHERHAM**

Rotherham, Joseph B. *The New Testament:* Newly translated (from the Greek text of Tregelles) and critically emphasized, with an introduction and occasional notes. London: Samual Bagster. 1890.

**RPNT**

Johnson, Ben Cambell. *The Heart of Paul: A Relational Paraphrase of the New Testament.* Vol. 1. Waco: Word Books. 1976.

**RSV**

*Revised Standard Version;* The New Covenant commonly called the New Testament of our Lord and Saviour Jesus Christ: Translated from the Greek being the version set forth A.D. 1611, revised A.D. 1881, A.D. 1901. New York: Thomas Nelson Inc. Publishers. 1953. Used by permission. © 1946, 1952, 1971, 1973 by the Division of Christian Education of the National Council of the Churches of Christ in the U.S.A.

**RV**

*The New Testament of our Lord and Savior Jesus Christ:* Translated out of the Greek . . . being the new version revised 1881. St. Louis, MO: Scammell. 1881.

**SAWYER**

Sawyer, Leicester Ambrose. *The New Testament:* Translated from the original Greek, with chronological arrangement of the sacred books, and improved divisions of chapters and verses. Boston: Walker, Wise. 1861.

**SCARLETT**

Scarlett, Nathaniel. *A translation of the New Testament from the original Greek:* humbly attempted. London: T. Gillett. 1798.

**SEB**

*The Simple English™ Bible, New Testament:* American edition. New York: International Bible Translators, Inc. 1981. Used by permission from International Bible Translators, Inc.

**SWANN**

Swann, George. *New Testament of our Lord and Saviour Jesus Christ.* 4th. ed. Robards, KY: George Swann Company. 1947.

**TCNT**

*The Twentieth Century New Testament: a Translation into Modern English Made from the Original Greek:* (Westcott & Hort's text). New York: Revell. 1900.

**TEV**

*The Good News Bible, Today's English Version.* New York: American Bible Society. 1976. Used by permission. © American Bible Society, 1966, 1971, 1976.

**TNT**

*The Translator's New Testament.* London: The British and Foreign Bible Society. 1973.

**TORREY**

Torrey, Charles Cutler. *The Four Gospels: A New Translation.* New York: Harper and Row Publishers Inc. 1933. Reprinted by permission. © 1933.

**TYNDALE**

Tyndale, William. *The Newe Testament dylygently corrected and compared with the Greke.* and fynesshed in the yere of oure Lorde God anno M.D. and XXXIIII in the month of Nouember. London: Reeves and Turner. 1888.

**TYNDALE (1526)**

*The First New Testament in the English Language (1525 or 1526).* Reprint. Bristol. 1862. Or Clevland: Barton. N.d.

**WADE**

Wade, G. W. *The Documents of the New Testament: Translated & Historically Arranged with Critical Introductions.* N.p., n.d.

**WAY**

Way, Arthur S., trans. *Letters of St. Paul: To seven churches and three friends with the letter to the Hebrews.* 8th ed. Chicago: Moody. 1950 reprint of the 1901 edition.

**WESLEY**

Wesley, John. *Explanatory notes upon the New Testament.* London: Wesleyan-Methodist Book-room. N.d.

**WEYMOUTH**

Weymouth, Richard Francis. *The New Testament in Modern Speech:* An idiomatic translation into everyday English from the text of the "Resultant Greek Testament." Revised by J.A. Robertson. London: James Clarke and Co. Ltd. and Harper and Row Publishers Inc. 1908. Reprinted by permission.

**WILLIAMS**

Williams, Charles B. *The New Testament: A Translation in the Language of the People.* Chicago: Moody Bible Institute of Chicago. 1957. Used by permission of Moody Press. Moody Bible Institute of Chicago. © 1937, 1966 by Mrs. Edith S. Williams.

**WILLIAMS C.K.**

Williams, Charles Kingsley. *The New Testament: A New Translation in Plain English.* Grand Rapids: William B. Eerdmans Publishing Co. 1963.

**WILSON**

Wilson, Benjamin. *The Emphatic Diaglott containing the original Greek Text of what is commonly styled the New Testament* (according to the recension of Dr. F.F. Griesback) with interlineary word for word English translation. New York: Fowler & Wells. 1902 reprint edition of the 1864 edition.

**WORRELL**

Worrell, A.S. *The New Testament: Revised and Translated:* With notes and instructions; designed to aid the earnest reader in obtaining a clear understanding of the doctrines, ordinances, and primitive assemblies as revealed. Louisville, KY: A.S. Worrell. 1904.

**WUEST**

Wuest, Kenneth S. *The New Testament: An Expanded Translation.* Grand Rapids: William B. Eerdmans Publishing Co. 1961. Used by permission of the publisher. © 1961.

**WYCLIF**

Wyclif(fe), John. *The Holy Bible containing the Old and New Testaments with the Apocryphal Books:* in the earliest English version made from the Latin Vulgate by John Wycliffe and his followers. London: Reeves and Turner. 1888.

**YOUNG**

Young, Robert. *Young's Literal Translation of the Holy Bible.* Grand Rapids: Baker Book House. 1953 reprint of the 1898 3rd edition.